Dietary Reference Intakes (DRIs): Recommended Intakes for Individuals, Elements
Food and Nutrition Board, Institute of Medicine, National Academies

Life Stage Group	Calcium (mg/d)	Chromium (μg/d)	Copper (μg/d)	Fluoride (mg/d)	Iodine (μg/d)	Iron (mg/d)	Magnesium (mg/d)	Manganese (mg/d)	Molybdenum (μg/d)	Phosphorus (mg/d)	Selenium (μg/d)	Zinc (mg/d)
Infants												
0–6 mo	210*	0.2*	200*	0.01*	110*	0.27*	30*	0.003*	2*	100*	15*	2*
7–12 mo	270*	5.5*	220*	0.5*	130*	**11**	75*	0.6*	3*	275*	20*	**3**
Children												
1–3 y	500*	11*	**340**	0.7*	**90**	**7**	**80**	1.2*	**17**	**460**	**20**	**3**
4–8 y	800*	15*	**440**	1*	**90**	**10**	**130**	1.5*	**22**	**500**	**30**	**5**
Males												
9–13 y	1,300*	25*	**700**	2*	**120**	**8**	**240**	1.9*	**34**	**1,250**	**40**	**8**
14–18 y	1,300*	35*	**890**	3*	**150**	**11**	**410**	2.2*	**43**	**1,250**	**55**	**11**
19–30 y	1,000*	35*	**900**	4*	**150**	**8**	**400**	2.3*	**45**	**700**	**55**	**11**
31–50 y	1,000*	35*	**900**	4*	**150**	**8**	**420**	2.3*	**45**	**700**	**55**	**11**
51–70 y	1,200*	30*	**900**	4*	**150**	**8**	**420**	2.3*	**45**	**700**	**55**	**11**
> 70 y	1,200*	30*	**900**	4*	**150**	**8**	**420**	2.3*	**45**	**700**	**55**	**11**
Females												
9–13 y	1,300*	21*	**700**	2*	**120**	**8**	**240**	1.6*	**34**	**1,250**	**40**	**8**
14–18 y	1,300*	24*	**890**	3*	**150**	**15**	**360**	1.6*	**43**	**1,250**	**55**	**9**
19–30 y	1,000*	25*	**900**	3*	**150**	**18**	**310**	1.8*	**45**	**700**	**55**	**8**
31–50 y	1,000*	25*	**900**	3*	**150**	**18**	**320**	1.8*	**45**	**700**	**55**	**8**
51–70 y	1,200*	20*	**900**	3*	**150**	**8**	**320**	1.8*	**45**	**700**	**55**	**8**
> 70 y	1,200*	20*	**900**	3*	**150**	**8**	**320**	1.8*	**45**	**700**	**55**	**8**
Pregnancy												
≤18 y	1,300*	29*	**1,000**	3*	**220**	**27**	**400**	2.0*	**50**	**1,250**	**60**	**12**
19–30 y	1,000*	30*	**1,000**	3*	**220**	**27**	**350**	2.0*	**50**	**700**	**60**	**11**
31–50 y	1,000*	30*	**1,000**	3*	**220**	**27**	**360**	2.0*	**50**	**700**	**60**	**11**
Lactation												
≤ 18 y	1,300*	44*	**1,300**	3*	**290**	**10**	**360**	2.6*	**50**	**1,250**	**70**	**13**
19–30 y	1,000*	45*	**1,300**	3*	**290**	**9**	**310**	2.6*	**50**	**700**	**70**	[illegible]
31–50 y	1,000*	45*	**1,300**	3*	**290**	**9**	**320**	2.6*	**50**	**700**	**70**	[illegible]

NOTE: This table presents Recommended Dietary Allowances (RDAs) in **bold type** and Adequate Intakes (AIs) in ordinary type followed by an asterisk (*). RDAs and AIs may both be used as goals for individual intake. RDAs are set to meet all (97 to 98 percent) individuals in a group. For healthy breastfed infants, the AI is the mean intake. The AI for other life stage and gender groups is believed to cover needs of all individuals in the group, but lack of data or uncertainty in th ing able to specify with confidence the percentage of individuals covered by this intake.

SOURCES: Dietary Reference Intakes for Calcium, Phosphorus, Magnesium, Vitamin D, and Fluoride (1997); Dietary Reference Intakes for Thiamin, Riboflavin, Niacin, Vitamin B6, Folate, Vitamin B12, Pantothenic Acid, Biotin, and Choline (erence Intakes for Vitamin C, Vitamin E, Selenium, and Carotenoids (2000); and Dietary Reference Intakes for Vitamin A, Vitamin K, Arsenic, Boron, Chromium, Copper, Iodine, Iron, Manganese, Molybdenum, Nickel, Silicon, Vanadium, anc These reports may be accessed via www.nap.edu.

Dietary Reference Intakes (DRIs): Recommended Intakes for Individuals, Macronutrients

Food and Nutrition Board, Institute of Medicine, National Academies

Life Stage Group	Carbohydrate (g/d)	Total Fiber (g/d)	Fat (g/d)	Linoleic Acid (g/d)	α-Linoleic Acid (g/d)	Protein[a] (g/d)
Infants						
0–6 mo	60*	ND	31*	4.4*	0.5*	9.1*
7–12 mo	95*	ND	30*	4.6*	0.5*	**13.5**
Children						
1–3 y	**130**	19*	ND[b]	7*	0.7*	**13**
4–8 y	**130**	25*	ND	10*	0.9*	**19**
Males						
9–13 y	**130**	31*	ND	12*	1.2*	**34**
14–18 y	**130**	38*	ND	16*	1.6*	**52**
19–30 y	**130**	38*	ND	17*	1.6*	**56**
31–50 y	**130**	38*	ND	17*	1.6*	**56**
51–70 y	**130**	30*	ND	14*	1.6*	**56**
> 70 y	**130**	30*	ND	14*	1.6*	**56**
Females						
9–13 y	**130**	26*	ND	10*	1.0*	**34**
14–18 y	**130**	26*	ND	11*	1.1*	**46**
19–30 y	**130**	25*	ND	12*	1.1*	**46**
31–50 y	**130**	25*	ND	12*	1.1*	**46**
51–70 y	**130**	21*	ND	11*	1.1*	**46**
> 70 y	**130**	21*	ND	11*	1.1*	**46**
Pregnancy						
14–18 y	**175**	28*	ND	13*	1.4*	**71**
19–30 y	**175**	28*	ND	13*	1.4*	**71**
31–50 y	**175**	28*	ND	13*	1.4*	**71**
Lactation						
14–18 y	**210**	29*	ND	13*	1.3*	**71**
19–30 y	**210**	29*	ND	13*	1.3*	**71**
31–50 y	**210**	29*	ND	13*	1.3*	**71**

NOTE: This table presents Recommended Dietary Allowances (RDAs) in **bold type** and Adequate Intakes (AIs) in ordinary type followed by an asterisk (*). RDAs and AIs may both be used as goals for individual intake. RDAs are set to meet the needs of almost all (97 to 98 percent) individuals in a group. For healthy breastfed infants, the AI is the mean intake. The AI for other life stage and gender groups is believed to cover needs of all individuals in the group, but lack of data or uncertainty in the data prevent being able to specify with confidence the percentage of individuals covered by this intake.

[a]Based on 0.8g protein/kg body weight for reference body weight.

[b]ND = not determinable at this time

SOURCES: Dietary Reference Intakes for Energy, Carbohydrate, Fiber, Fat, Fatty Acids, Cholesterol, Protein, and Amino Acids (2002). This report may be accessed via www.nap.edu.

IMPORTANT:

HERE IS YOUR REGISTRATION CODE TO ACCESS YOUR PREMIUM McGRAW-HILL ONLINE RESOURCES.

For key premium online resources you need THIS CODE to gain access. Once the code is entered, you will be able to use the Web resources for the length of your course.

If your course is using **WebCT** or **Blackboard**, you'll be able to use this code to access the McGraw-Hill content within your instructor's online course.

Access is provided if you have purchased a new book. If the registration code is missing from this book, the registration screen on our Website, and within your WebCT or Blackboard course, will tell you how to obtain your new code.

Registering for McGraw-Hill Online Resources

To gain access to your McGraw-Hill web resources simply follow the steps below:

1. USE YOUR WEB BROWSER TO GO TO: **www.mhhe.com/wardlawpers6**
2. CLICK ON **FIRST TIME USER**.
3. ENTER THE REGISTRATION CODE* PRINTED ON THE TEAR-OFF BOOKMARK ON THE RIGHT.
4. AFTER YOU HAVE ENTERED YOUR REGISTRATION CODE, CLICK **REGISTER**.
5. FOLLOW THE INSTRUCTIONS TO SET-UP YOUR PERSONAL UserID AND PASSWORD.
6. WRITE YOUR UserID AND PASSWORD DOWN FOR FUTURE REFERENCE. KEEP IT IN A SAFE PLACE.

TO GAIN ACCESS to the McGraw-Hill content in your instructor's **WebCT** or **Blackboard** course simply log in to the course with the UserID and Password provided by your instructor. Enter the registration code exactly as it appears in the box to the right when prompted by the system. You will only need to use the code the first time you click on McGraw-Hill content.

Thank you, and welcome to your McGraw-Hill online resources!

Mc Graw Hill Higher Education

* YOUR REGISTRATION CODE CAN BE USED ONLY ONCE TO ESTABLISH ACCESS. IT IS NOT TRANSFERABLE.

0-07-291877-2 T/A WARDLAW: PERSPECTIVES IN NUTRITION, 6E

MCGRAW-HILL

ONLINE RESOURCES

REGISTRATION CODE

byzantines-35293273

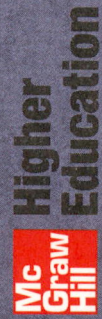

Mc Graw Hill Higher Education

NutritionCalc Plus CD-ROM

Want to learn how your exercise level matches up with your diet? Want to set personalized weight loss or gain goals? It's a snap with NutritionCalc Plus.

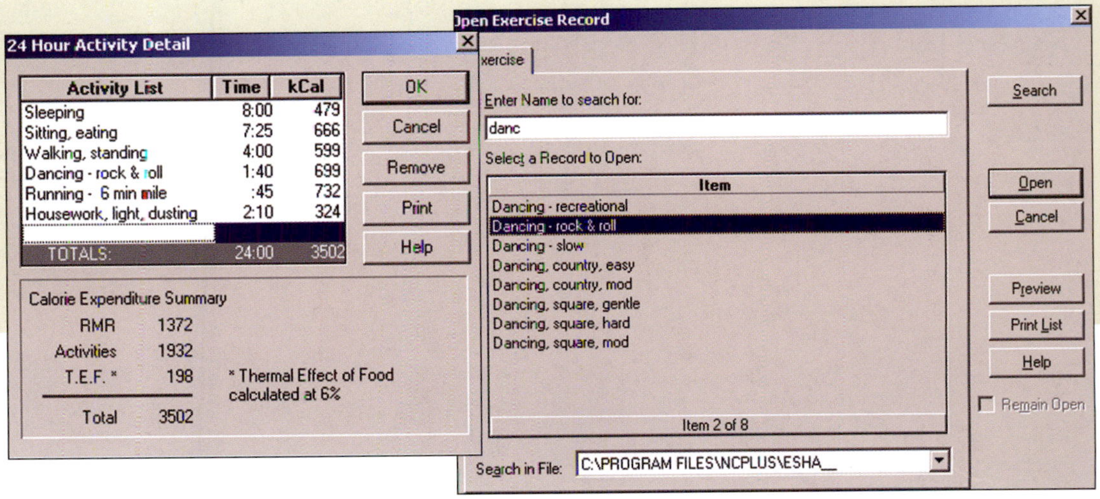

NutritionCalc Plus generates a broad range of reports that supply a thorough analysis of your diet.

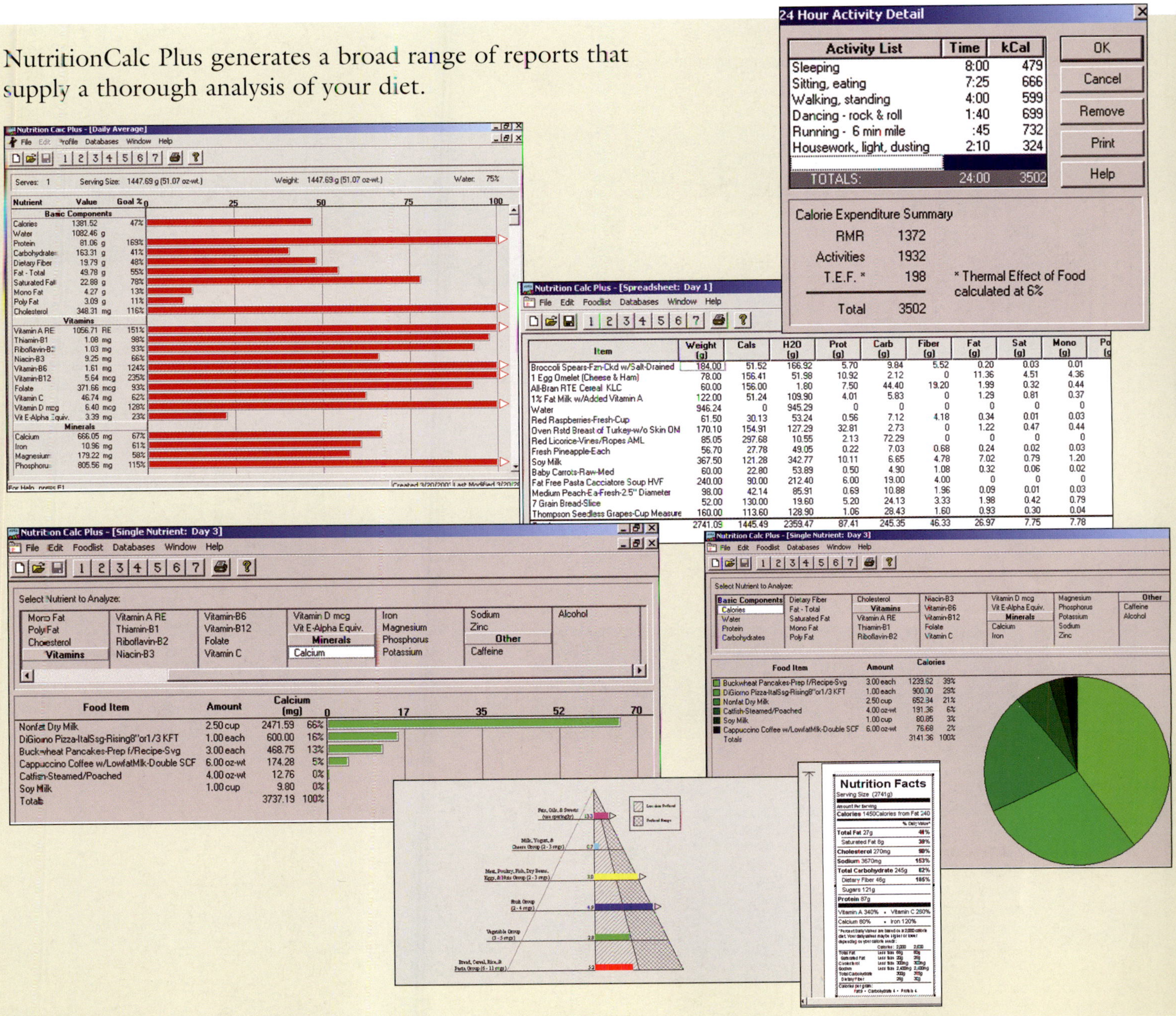

NutritionCalc Plus Online

Now you have a choice in diet analysis software! If you are looking for software that is accurate, reliable, and easy to use, check out **NutritionCalc Plus *CD-ROM*** (front page) and **NutritionCalc Plus *Online*.**

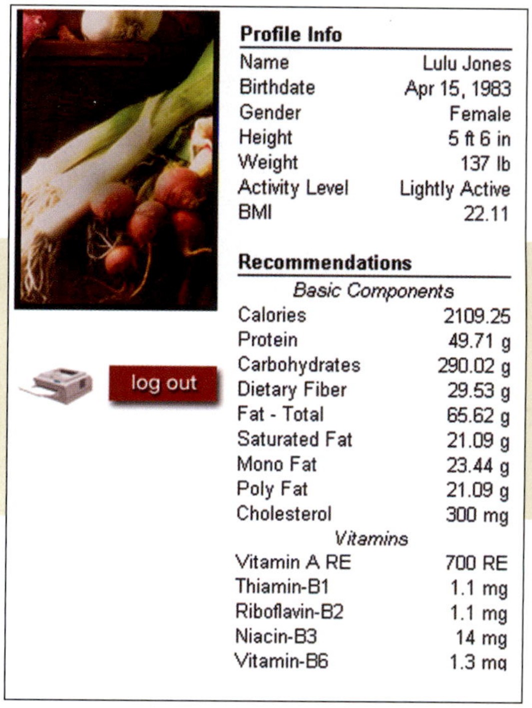

Profile Info
Name Lulu Jones
Birthdate Apr 15, 1983
Gender Female
Height 5 ft 6 in
Weight 137 lb
Activity Level Lightly Active
BMI 22.11
log out
Recommendations
Basic Components
Calories 2109.25
Protein 49.71 g
Carbohydrates 290.02 g
Dietary Fiber 29.53 g
Fat - Total 65.62 g
Saturated Fat 21.09 g
Mono Fat 23.44 g
Poly Fat 21.09 g
Cholesterol 300 mg
Vitamins
Vitamin A RE 700 RE
Thiamin-B1 1.1 mg
Riboflavin-B2 1.1 mg
Niacin-B3 14 mg
Vitamin-B6 1.3 mg

Helpful icons make it easy to create your own personal profile of nutrient needs and goals.

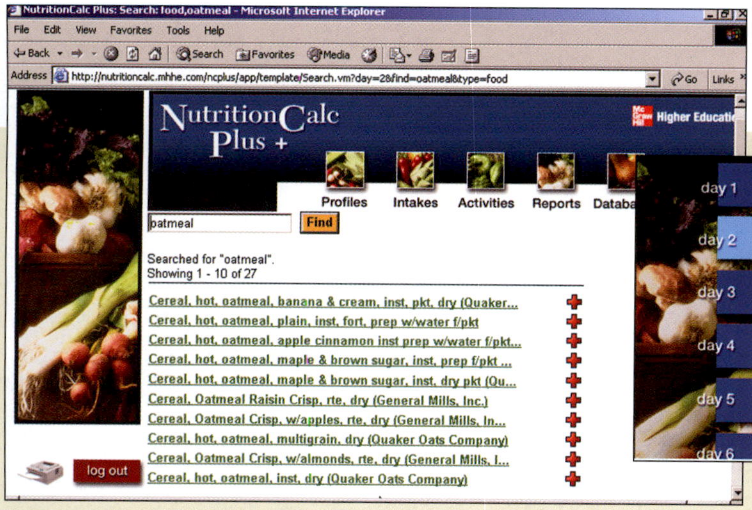

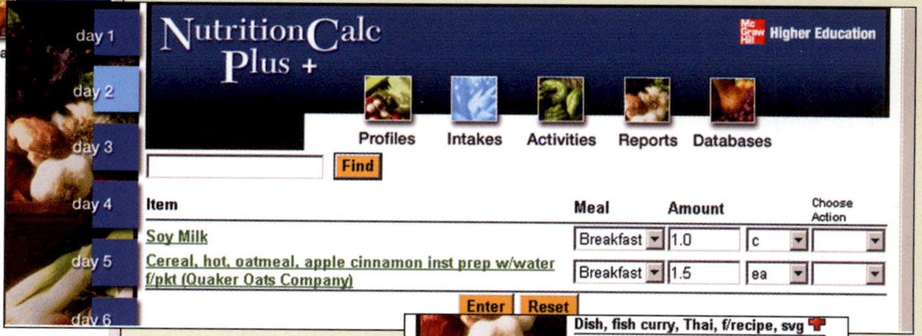

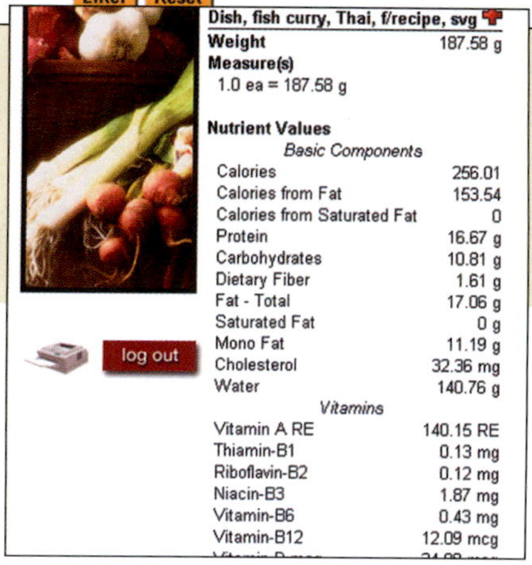

Dish, fish curry, Thai, f/recipe, svg
Weight 187.58 g
Measure(s)
1.0 ea = 187.58 g
Nutrient Values
Basic Components
Calories 256.01
Calories from Fat 153.54
Calories from Saturated Fat 0
Protein 16.67 g
Carbohydrates 10.81 g
Dietary Fiber 1.61 g
Fat - Total 17.06 g
Saturated Fat 0 g
Mono Fat 11.19 g
Cholesterol 32.36 mg
Water 140.76 g
Vitamins
Vitamin A RE 140.15 RE
Thiamin-B1 0.13 mg
Riboflavin-B2 0.12 mg
Niacin-B3 1.87 mg
Vitamin-B6 0.43 mg
Vitamin-B12 12.09 mcg
log out

NutritionCalc Plus Online makes searching and compiling your food list easy. The ESHA database provides an extensive variety of foods with accurate, dependable nutrient data.

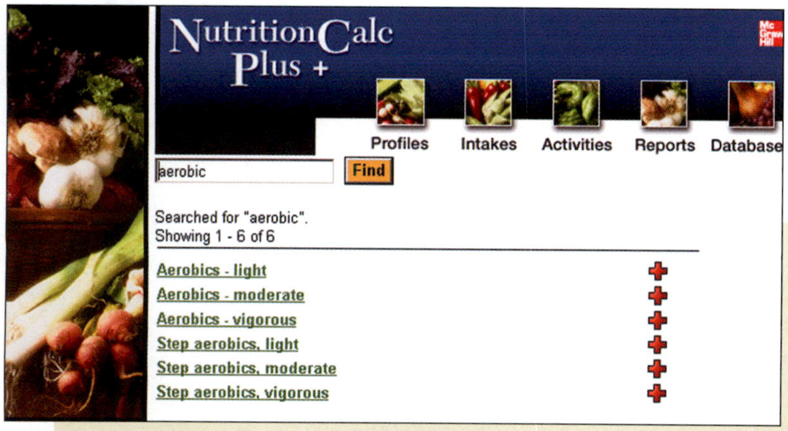

You can compare your energy expenditure with your food intake by compiling a list of your daily activities.

NutritionCalc Plus Online

NutritionCalc Plus generates a broad range of reports that supply a thorough analysis of your diet.

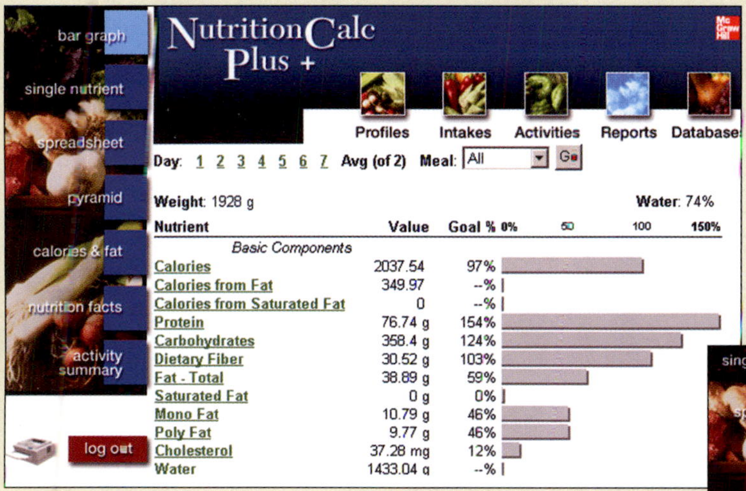

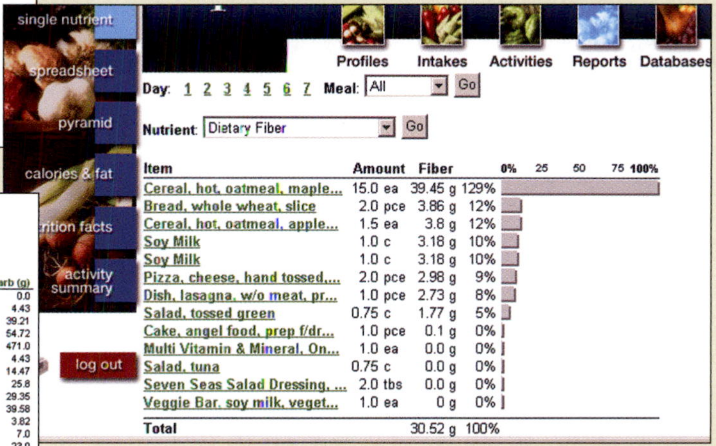

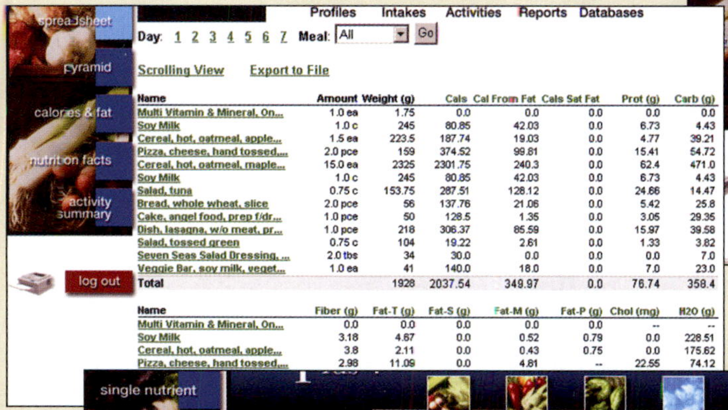

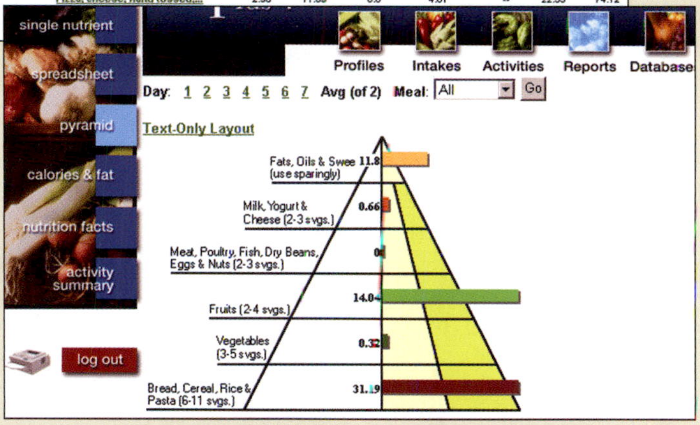

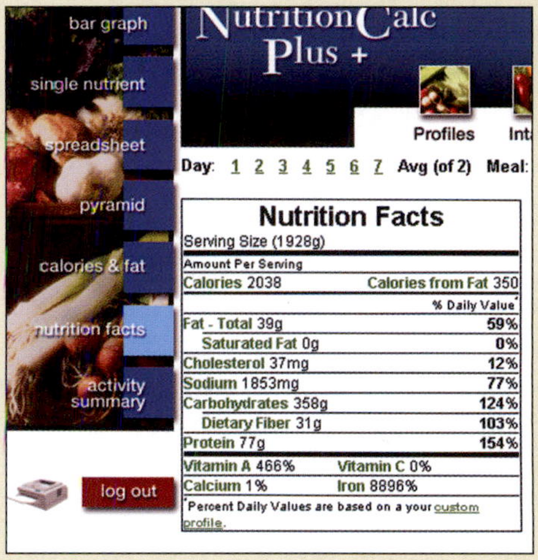

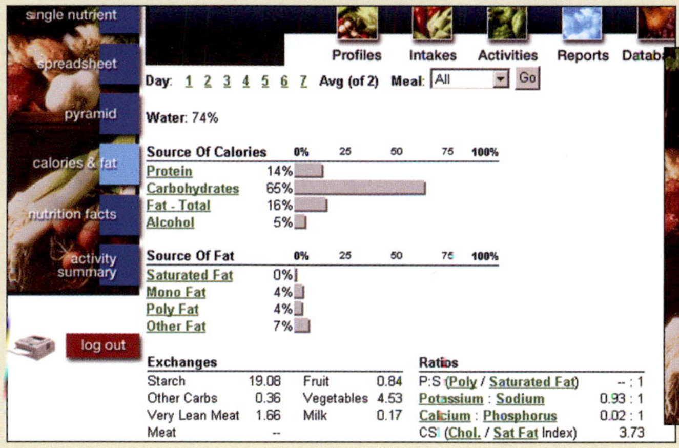

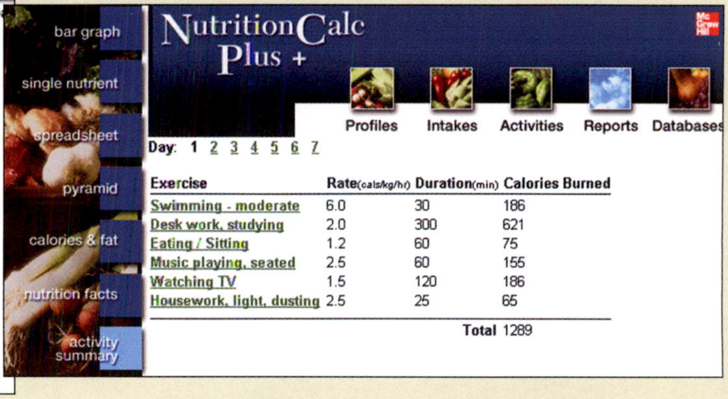

NutritionCalc Plus CD-ROM

Now you have a choice in diet analysis software! If you are looking for software that is accurate, reliable, and easy to use, check out **NutritionCalc Plus** ***CD-ROM*** and **NutritionCalc Plus** ***Online*** (back page).

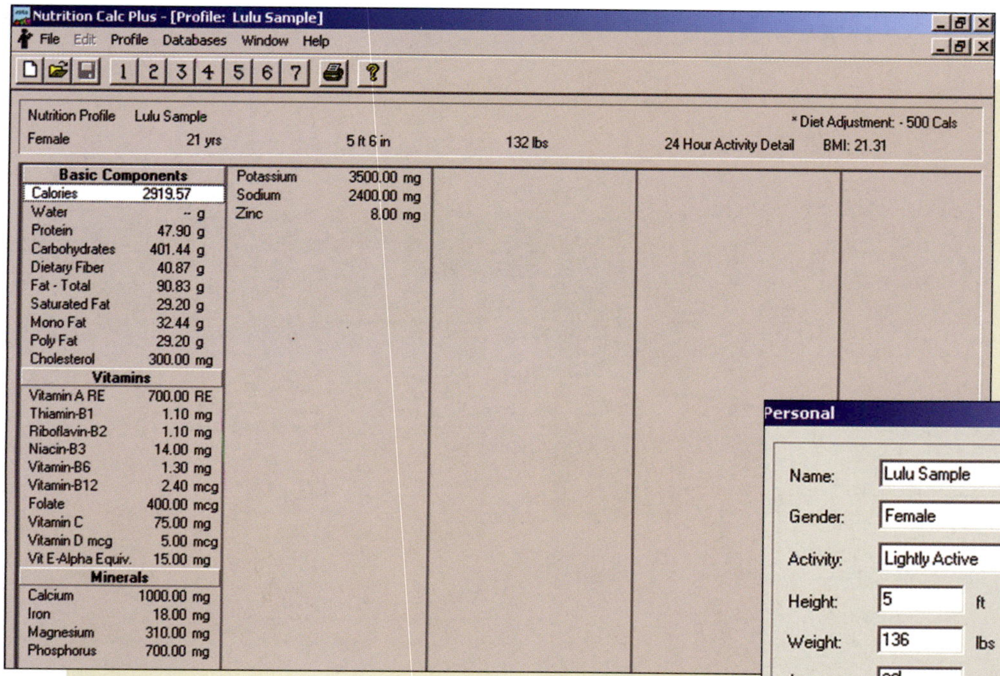

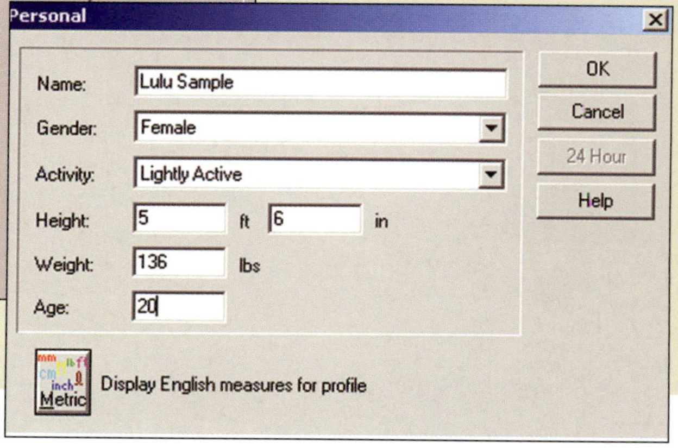

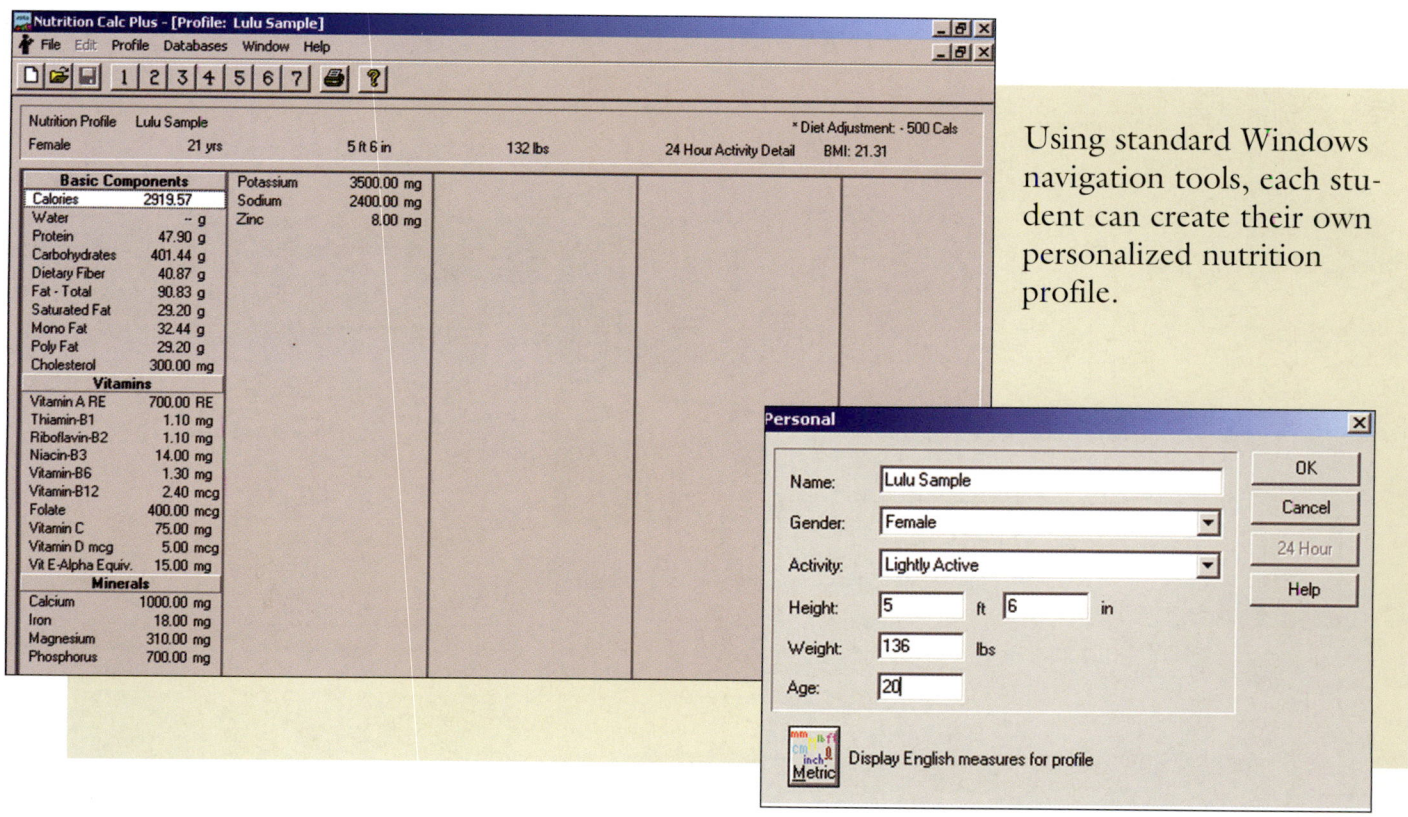

Using standard Windows navigation tools, each student can create their own personalized nutrition profile.

The extensive ESHA database makes analyzing your food intake easy and dependable.

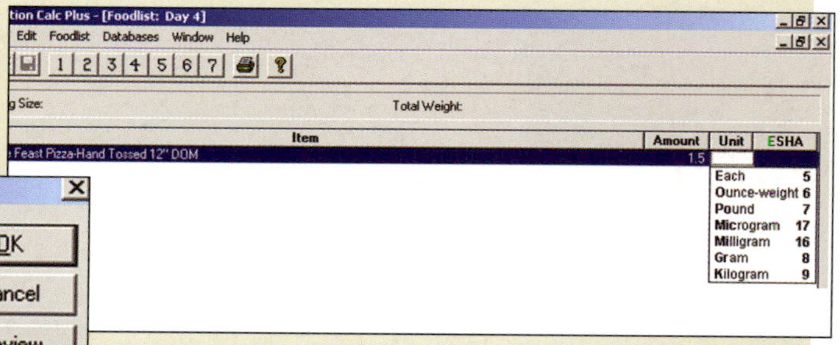

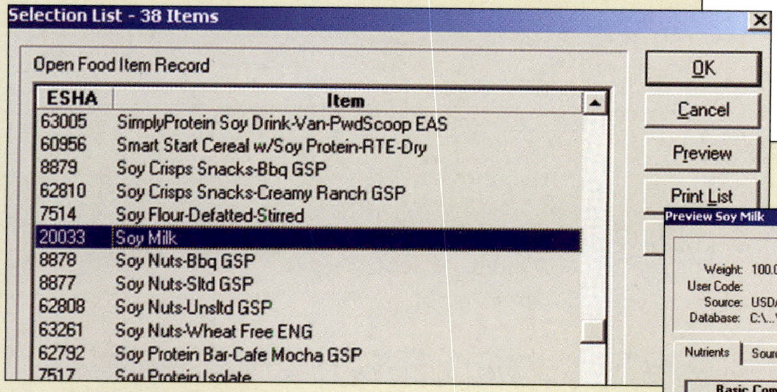

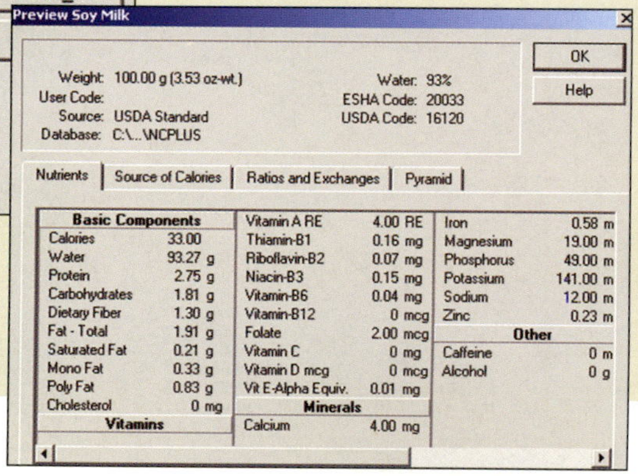

SIXTH EDITION

Perspectives in NUTRITION

Gordon M. Wardlaw
Ph.D., R.D., L.D.
The Ohio State University

Jeffrey S. Hampl
Ph.D., R.D.
Arizona State University

Robert A. DiSilvestro
Ph.D.
The Ohio State University

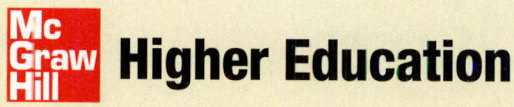

McGraw-Hill Higher Education

Boston Burr Ridge, IL Dubuque, IA Madison, WI New York San Francisco St. Louis
Bangkok Bogotá Caracas Kuala Lumpur Lisbon London Madrid Mexico City
Milan Montreal New Delhi Santiago Seoul Singapore Sydney Taipei Toronto

The McGraw-Hill Companies

Higher Education

PERSPECTIVES IN NUTRITION, SIXTH EDITION

Published by McGraw-Hill, a business unit of The McGraw-Hill Companies, Inc., 1221 Avenue of the Americas, New York, NY 10020.

Some ancillaries, including electronic and print components, may not be available to customers outside the United States.

This book is printed on acid-free paper.

International 1 2 3 4 5 6 7 8 9 0 DOW/DOW 0 9 8 7 6 5 4 3
Domestic 1 2 3 4 5 6 7 8 9 0 DOW/DOW 0 9 8 7 6 5 4 3

ISBN 0-07-244212-3
ISBN 0-07-121518-2 (ISE)

Publisher: *Colin H. Wheatley*
Senior developmental editor: *Lynne M. Meyers*
Marketing manager: *Tami Petsche*
Lead project manager: *Joyce M. Berendes*
Production supervisor: *Kara Kudronowicz*
Senior media project manager: *Tammy Juran*
Senior media technology producer: *Barbara R. Block*
Coordinator of freelance design: *Rick D. Noel*
Cover/interior designer: *Ellen Pettengell*
Cover image: © *EyeWire, image number EPE_004*
Senior photo research coordinator: *John C. Leland*
Photo research: *Mary Reeg*
Supplement producer: *Brenda A. Ernzen*
Compositor: *GAC/Indianapolis*
Typeface: *10/12 Galliard*
Printer: *R.R. Donnelley Willard, OH*

The credits section for this book begins on page C-1 and is considered an extension of the copyright page.

Library of Congress Cataloging-in-Publication Data

Wardlaw, Gordon M.
Perspectives in nutrition / Gordon M. Wardlaw, Jeffrey S. Hampl, Robert A. DiSilvestro.—6th ed.
p. cm.
Includes bibliographical references and index.
ISBN 0-07-244212-3 (hard copy : alk. paper)
1. Nutrition. I. Hampl, Jeffrey S. II. DiSilvestro, Robert A. III. Title.

QP141.W38 2004
613.2—dc21 2003003875
CIP

INTERNATIONAL EDITION ISBN 0-07-121518-2

www.mhhe.com

brief contents

contents

part two The Energy-Yielding Nutrients and Alcohol

part four Energy Production and Energy Balance

part five Nutrition Applications in the Life Cycle

part six Putting Nutrition Knowledge into Practice

About the Authors

Gordon M. Wardlaw, Ph.D., R.D., L.D. teaches introductory nutrition courses to students in the Department of Human Nutrition at The Ohio State University. Dr. Wardlaw is the author of many articles that have appeared in prominent nutrition, biology, physiology, and biochemistry journals and was the 1985 recipient of the American Dietetic Association's Mary P. Huddleson Award. Dr. Wardlaw is a member of the American Society for Nutritional Sciences and is certified as a Specialist in Human Nutrition by the American Board of Nutrition.

Jeffrey S. Hampl, Ph.D., R.D. teaches coursework in public health nutrition in the Department of Nutrition at Arizona State University. Prior to his university appointment, Dr. Hampl worked as a nutritionist with the Special Supplemental Nutrition Program for Women, Infants, and Children (WIC) and as an outpatient dietitian in a major medical center. Dr. Hampl's research, which has been funded by the U.S. Department of Agriculture and the State of Arizona, focuses on the nutritional status of resource-constrained children and their families, and he has published articles in leading nutrition and medical journals. The winner of the 2002 Dannon Award for Excellence in Community Nutrition, Dr. Hampl is a member of the American Dietetic Association, the American Public Health Association, and the American Society for Nutritional Sciences. He is also a spokesperson for the American Dietetic Association and was the lead author for the Association's position paper on disease prevention and health promotion.

Robert A. DiSilvestro, Ph.D. (biochemistry) is a Professor of Human Nutrition at The Ohio State University. He also has appointments with the Ohio Agricultural Research & Development Center and is a research member of The Ohio State University Comprehensive Cancer Center. His teaching responsibilities include two introductory nutrition courses. One is intended to meet general education curriculum requirements and the other is intended for majors in nutrition or other majors with a distinct need for nutrition (e.g., nursing). Dr. DiSilvestro has published numerous peer-reviewed research articles, mostly in the areas of trace minerals and antioxidant actions of vitamins and phytochemicals, especially in relation to exercise. Dr. DiSilvestro is a member of the American Society for Nutritional Sciences and the American College of Sports Medicine.

preface

To the Instructor

Since you teach nutrition, you undoubtedly find it a fascinating and challenging subject. You probably also find that teaching nutrition is a challenge in and of itself. Claims and counterclaims abound regarding the need for certain dietary components. For example, one group of researchers promotes a reduction in salt intake for the general population as a means of preventing hypertension. Other researchers assert that despite excess salt intakes, most North Americans maintain normal blood pressure values. This apparent dichotomy only adds to the challenge of teaching in a rapidly changing field.

As textbook authors, we understand the importance of providing accurate, balanced, and up-to-date coverage of nutrition topics, particularly those that are controversial. To provide students with a sound introduction to the study of nutrition, we draw on as many reliable sources as possible. This sixth edition of *Perspectives in Nutrition* reflects new material from the recently published Dietary Reference Intakes by the Food and Nutrition Board, articles in major nutrition and medical journals and leading nutrition and health newsletters, and chapters in *Present Knowledge in Nutrition,* edited by Bowman and Russell. We constantly scour the literature with the goal of providing clear and balanced perspectives on recent research so that you and your students can better understand and participate in the debates of current nutrition issues.

Personalized Approach to Nutrition

A prominent theme in nutrition today is *individuality.* Nutrition advice is not a one-size-fits-all proposition. For example, not all of us find that saturated fat in our diet raises our blood cholesterol values above recommended standards. Individuals respond differently, often idiosyncratically, to certain nutrients. The goal of understanding how nutrients affect us as individuals is a key objective of this text.

Moreover, even at this introductory level, we do not assume that all nutrition students are alike. We incorporate opportunities, such as the Take Action activities, for students to learn more about their own health and nutrition. In this way, students can apply the knowledge they gain to improve their health. Throughout the chapters, we strive for the same objective as many of our colleagues, to educate students to become judicious consumers of both food and nutrition information. We seek to help students sort through the wealth of nutrition information and misinformation available to them. This text is designed to help them better understand and evaluate the nutrition information they encounter on cereal box labels, articles in popular magazines, nutrition- and diet-related websites, guidelines issued by government agencies, and more.

Once students have achieved a solid working knowledge of nutrition, our goal is to assist them in assessing their personal nutrition needs, rather than strictly adhering to every guideline issued for an entire population. After all, a population by definition includes a scope of varying genetic and cultural backgrounds, along with varying responses to diet.

As a final note, we know that students often come to this course with many preconceptions and questions about nutrition "hot topics." To address students' concerns, we have included coverage of topics that touch their lives: eating disorders, ethnic diets, nutritional supplements, phytochemicals, vegetarianism, diets for athletes, popular (fad) diets, and complementary and alternative medical practices. (See the Chapter Highlights section for examples.) Regardless of the topic, the overall emphasis remains the same—the importance of understanding one's food choices and diet practices to best meet personal needs.

Intended Audience

We have developed this book with nutrition and science majors in mind. The chemistry, biochemistry, and physiology presented in the text assume that students have had at least some college-level science. Because this course often attracts students from a fairly broad range of majors, we have been careful to include examples and explanations that are relevant to nutrition, health education, human ecology, human performance, nursing, and other health-related majors. For students who wish to learn more or need assistance with the science involved in metabolism and body systems, additional information can be found in Appendix A, "Chemistry: A Tool for Understanding Nutrition" and Appendix C, "Human Physiology: A Tool for Understanding Nutrition."

Key Revisions to the Sixth Edition

Creating a textbook is a dynamic process. Rather than simply updating facts and numbers with each new edition, we seek to be responsive to changing instructor and student needs. We challenge ourselves to take a fresh look at each new edition to find ways to refine and improve and make the book a better teaching tool all around. Many of the new features in the sixth edition are a direct result of feedback we have received from instructors. Their advice on the level and presentation of science has been invaluable. We have also learned a great deal from the students in the courses we teach. Their feedback can be seen in improved illustrations and clearer discussions of difficult concepts.

New Author Team

The most significant change in *Perspectives in Nutrition,* sixth edition, is the addition of two new co-authors: Jeffrey Hampl and Robert DiSilvestro. This edition benefits greatly from their professional areas of expertise and their experiences teaching introductory nutrition. Jeff's extensive background in nutrition practice and community nutrition research and Bob's keen interest and research in the micronutrients, have all been helpful in this revision.

Up-to-Date Nutrient Guidelines

A major component of this revision involves the updating of data and discussions related to the latest Dietary Reference Intakes. Also included are the latest guidelines from the National Cholesterol Education Program, American Heart Association, the American Medical Association, and the American Cancer Society, Inc.

Refocused Science Coverage

You will find many examples in this edition where we paid particular attention to addressing the level of science and to making the science more accessible for students. For example, Chapter 3, "Human Digestion and Absorption" now focuses on the gastrointestinal system, with coverage of related body systems included in the fifth edition moved to Appendix C, "Human Physiology: A Tool for Understanding Nutrition." Although an interesting approach, the inclusion of all this material in one chapter made Chapter 3 too overwhelming for many of our reviewers, given the allotted amount of class time. The discussion of micronutrients has been simplified as well. For example, the Estimated Average Requirements for nutrients have been moved to Appendix M, such as for the B vitamins.

Throughout the book, there are many dynamic new illustrations that will help students grasp important scientific concepts with greater clarity. Chapters 3 and 4 contain many new digestion and metabolism diagrams. Complex subjects, such as glycolysis and the citric acid cycle, have been reinterpreted with color and omission of chemical structures to help students comprehend the steps involved in these processes. The more detailed depictions of these pathways are now in Appendix B.

Content Reorganization

Based upon feedback from instructors and our own classroom experiences, we have opted to make some adjustments to content coverage within the chapters. Some key examples include restoring the discussion of nutrition assessment to Chapter 2, "The Basis of a Healthy Diet." In turn, coverage of the Exchange System has been moved from Chapter 2 to Appendix E to keep the chapter to a reasonable length and depth. Also in the micronutrient chapters (Chapters 9–12), each nutrient is now discussed first in terms of its food sources and RDA/AI, which is then followed by the effects of nutrient deficiency.

To better address the needs of students at this level, we have replaced the Food Guide Pyramids in the macronutrient and micronutrient chapters with more complete lists of individual foods and their nutrient content. Each list is conveniently located in the margin next to the text discussion of food sources. If you still want to use the various pyramids in your teaching, these can be found on the Digital Content Manager 2003 CD.

High-Interest Learning Tools

We have also reevaluated the pedagogical aids within this edition. In addition to a beautiful new design layout, we attempt to draw students into the book through thought-provoking devices, such as the Case Scenarios that open each chapter (some are new). Our goal is to heighten student interest with real-life examples that they will revisit with the Case Scenario Follow-Up later in the chapter.

Each chapter also now includes Chapter Objectives that will help students identify the key concepts they should expect to master as they study. We typically start our lectures with specific objectives, and we hope you and your students will find these valuable as well.

Each chapter generally concludes with a list of about 18–20 Annotated References. While this list does not reflect every resource (i.e., most major nutrition and medical journals and popular health and nutrition newsletters) we consulted in writing this text, we have chosen these because they were especially helpful in verifying and updating chapter content. We hope both instructors and students will find the references useful.

Chapter Highlights

The following is a list of some of the key changes, updates, and enhancements that have been incorporated into the sixth edition chapters.

Chapter 1 What Nourishes You?
- CDC's latest data on leading causes of death in the United States
- Basic chemical structures of carbohydrates, proteins, and fats
- Influences on food choices
- Growing use of energy bars
- 1994 Dietary Supplement and Health Education Act
- New "Expert Opinion," *Who Are North America's Nutrition Experts?* by Dr. Anne M. Smith

Chapter 2 The Basis of a Healthy Diet
- A, B, C, D, Es of nutritional assessment
- Food and Nutrition Board's new Estimated Energy Requirements
- Alternative Food Guide Pyramids (e.g., discussion of Dr. Walter Willett's Healthy Eating Pyramid)
- Visual guide to food serving sizes
- Organic food logo

Chapter 3 Human Digestion and Absorption
- New case scenario on gastroesophageal reflux disease (GERD)
- Increased focus on the gastrointestinal system and less coverage of related body systems
- Figure on the pH scale showing pH values of common substances
- More realistic physiologic illustrations (e.g., GI tract sites of absorption)
- Diagram of enterohepatic circulation
- Updated "Expert Opinion," *Probiotics, Prebiotics, and Human Health* by Dr. Steve Hertzler

Chapter 4 Metabolism
- Debate over high-protein versus high-carbohydrate diets added to "Expert Opinion," *Why Is an Understanding of Energy Metabolism Important?* by Dr. Michael Keenan
- New "Nutrition Perspective," *Inborn Errors of Metabolism*
- Easier-to-comprehend illustrations on glycolysis and citric acid cycle

Chapter 5 Carbohydrates
- Clarification of oligosaccharide terminology
- Food and Nutrition Board's current definition of fiber and latest fiber recommendations
- Carbohydrate RDA
- Improved illustrations of carbohydrate digestion and absorption
- Sample 1600-kcal and 2000-kcal diets meeting the new fiber recommendations
- Coverage of Neotame (alternative sweetener)
- Table on glycemic index (GI) and glycemic load (GL) of common foods
- Chemical structures of alternative sweeteners
- Table comparing type 1 and type 2 diabetes

Chapter 6 Lipids
- Latest Food and Nutrition Board guidelines on fat and cholesterol intake
- New "Expert Opinion," *A Closer Look at Omega-3 and Omega-6 Fatty Acids and Related Eicosanoids* by Dr. Kenneth Broughton
- Sample 2400-kcal diet with 40% of energy as fat
- Improved figures on digestion and absorption of fat, and production of trans fatty acids
- Latest National Heart, Lung, and Blood Institute lipid profile guidelines

Chapter 7 Proteins
- Improved protein digestion and absorption figure
- Latest Food and Nutrition Board guidelines for protein intake
- Photos of kwashiorkor and marasmus
- New "Expert Opinion," *A New Appreciation for the* Nut *in* Nut*rition* by Dr. Penny M. Kris-Etherton
- Revised Vegetarian Diet Pyramid

Chapter 8 Alcohol
- Figure relating blood alcohol concentration and number of drinks
- Table summarizing benefits and risks of alcohol use
- New "Expert Opinion," *Alcoholism and Nutrition* by Dr. Charles Halsted
- Table showing the impact of binge drinking on college campuses

Chapter 9 The Fat-Soluble Vitamins
- New case scenario on nutrient supplement use
- Simplified discussions (e.g., absorption, transport, storage, and excretion of vitamin A; functions of vitamins D and E)
- New "Expert Opinion," *Carotenoids and Human Health: Beyond Conversion to Vitamin A* by Drs. Thomas Boileau and John Erdman
- Lists of food sources and RDA/AI values for each vitamin
- Updated discussion on use of multivitamin and mineral supplements
- Improved figures showing how retinoic acid directs cell differentiation and how retinal operates in vision

Chapter 10 The Water-Soluble Vitamins
- Easier-to-comprehend scientific discussions (e.g., functions of vitamin B-6; collagen synthesis)
- Steps within the homocysteine metabolism diagram more clearly displayed
- New "Expert Opinion," *Looking Beyond the Water-Soluble Vitamins: Phytochemicals in Health Promotion and Disease Prevention* by Dr. Clare Hasler
- Latest available cancer death statistics

Chapter 11 Water and the Major Minerals
- Revised water balance diagram better conveys concept of intake and output
- Blood calcium regulation diagram
- New "Expert Opinion," *The Many Benefits of Calcium in Your Diet* by Dr. Gregory Miller

Latest guidance surrounding estrogen replacement therapy and the use of bisphosphonate medications for prevention/treatment of osteoporosis

Chapter 12 Trace Minerals

More comprehensible science discussions (e.g., iron deficiency; functions of zinc)

New "Nutrition Perspective," *Modern Mineral Status Research: Searching for Subtleties*

Chapter 13 Energy Balance and Weight Control

More complete discussion of process of satiety

Photos of BodPod and DEXA scan

Discussion of Lap band procedure for gastric reduction surgery

More individualized approach to reducing energy intake

Chapter 14 Nutrition for Fitness and Sports

Appropriate use of energy bars and their nutrient composition

Updated fluid requirements for athletes

Expanded coverage of ergogenic aids in the "Nutrition Perspective"

Chapter 15 Eating Disorders: Anorexia Nervosa, Bulimia Nervosa, Binge-Eating Disorder, and Other Conditions

Revised figure comparing symptoms of anorexia nervosa and bulimia nervosa

New "Expert Opinion," *A Closer Look at the Female Athlete Triad* by Dr. Jackie Berning

Chapter 16 Pregnancy and Breastfeeding

Improved let-down reflex figure

Latest macronutrient needs for pregnant women issued by the Food and Nutrition Board

New "Expert Opinion," *Supporting Breastfeeding* by Mary Ellen Rivero

Chapter 17 Nutrition from Infancy Through Adolescence

Latest CDC growth charts for children

Latest macronutrient recommendations for infants and children issued by the Food and Nutrition Board

New "Expert Opinion," *Obesity and Type 2 Diabetes in Childhood: Lessons from the Pima Indians* by Dr. Arline Salbe

Chapter 18 Nutrition During Adulthood

Simplified discussion of possible causes of aging

Simplified discussion of Alzheimer's disease

Expanded coverage of complementary and alternative medical practices

Chapter 19 Food Safety

Additional microorganisms added to table on causes of foodborne illnesses

New "Expert Opinion," *Food Safety: Why Should You Care?* by Dr. Lydia Medeiros

USDA's food safety logo

Chapter 20 Undernutrition Throughout the World

Diagram showing downward spiral of poverty and poor nutrition

New "Expert Opinion," *Food Security* by Dr. David Holben

Updated information on worldwide impact of AIDS

Expanded discussion of genetically modified foods

Special Acknowledgments

We would like to thank students Kim Didino, Wendy Wilson, Eric Souers, Becky Tippett, and Shadi Jurdi for their help with this revision. Kim and Wendy assisted in the development of each chapter and read the entire final draft. Eric, Becky, and Shadi helped proofread the manuscript. Our editor, Lynne Meyers, supported and assisted us through every step of the revision and facilitated decisions that arose as we planned and produced the sixth edition. Joyce Berendes diligently monitored the copyediting and production tasks. All these individuals contributed key expertise to the project.

Thank You to Reviewers and Contributors

As with each edition, our goal remains the same, to produce the most accurate, up-to-date, and useful textbook possible. These ambitious goals would not be possible without the meticulous, professional assistance of colleagues who have assisted us in so many ways. Their advice and suggestions have greatly helped refine the content of this edition. We owe our sincere thanks to the following individuals for providing feedback on the fifth edition, responding to the changes made in the sixth edition, contributing their insights on teaching as part of a nutrition education workshop, responding to e-mail surveys, or even sharing their opinions on the cover image. We, along with our editors, would like to recognize these educators whose contributions did so much to guide the direction of *Perspectives in Nutrition,* sixth edition.

Becky Alejandre, *American River College*
Janet B. Anderson, *Utah State University*
Nancy L. Canolty, *University of Georgia*
Tina Crook, *University of Central Arkansas*
Betty J. Forbes, *West Virginia University*
Leonard E. Gerber, *University of Rhode Island*
Jill Golden, *Orange Coast College*
Roschelle Heuberger, *Central Michigan University*
Catherine Jen, *Wayne State University*
Connie Jones, *Northwestern State University of Louisiana*
Younghee Kim, *Bowling Green State University*
Allen Knehans, *University of Oklahoma Health Sciences Center*
Robert D. Lee, *Central Michigan University*
Mary Mead, *University of California Berkeley*
Juliet Mevi-Shiflett, *Diablo Valley College*
Mohey Mowafy, *Northern Michigan University*
Judy Myhand, *Louisiana State University*
Erwina B. Peterson, *Yakima Valley Community College*
William R. Proulx, *State University of New York College at Oneonta*
Brent J. Shriver, *Texas Tech University*
Carole A. Sloan, *Henry Ford Community College*
Mollie Smith, *California State University—Fresno*

Bernice G. Spurlock, *Hinds Community College*
Robin Sytsma, *Solano Community College*
Elsie Takeguchi, *Sacramento City College*
Delores Truesdell, *Florida State University*

A Request to Professors Who Use This Book

As you might imagine, it is difficult to stay abreast of the vast range of nutrition science, following all the various controversies and new developments. We try our best but realize that sometimes we miss an element that deserves attention. If you find content that you question or believe warrants further consideration, feel free to contact us by mail, fax, or e-mail.

We extend our best wishes for success to you and your students.

Gordon Wardlaw Ph.D., R.D., L.D.
Department of Human Nutrition
The Ohio State University
347C Campbell Hall
1787 Neil Avenue
Columbus, OH 43210
Fax: (614) 292-8880
E-mail: wardlaw.1@osu.edu

Jeffrey Hampl Ph.D., R.D.
Department of Nutrition
Arizona State University
7001 E. Williams Field Road
Mesa, Arizona 85212
Fax: (480) 727-1064
E-mail: jeff.hampl@asu.edu

Robert DiSilvestro Ph.D.
Department of Human Nutrition
The Ohio State University
345 Campbell Hall
1787 Neil Avenue
Columbus, OH 43210
Fax: (614) 292-8880
E-mail: rdisilvestro@hec.ohio-state.edu

To the Student

Cholesterol, sports drinks, food labeling, bulimia nervosa, alternative sweeteners, vegetarianism, *Salmonella* foodborne illness, and genetically engineered foods—we suspect you have heard about these topics. Which topics are important enough to be a consideration in your life or in the life of someone you know?

Americans pride themselves on their individuality. Nutritional advice should be given accordingly. For example, not all of us have high blood cholesterol and other significant risk factors for developing premature cardiovascular disease. The need to tailor dietary advice to each person's individual nature is the basic approach of this book. First, you are given a brief introduction to the study of nutrition; then, how to be a knowledgeable consumer is discussed. With so much information available—both accurate and inaccurate—you should know how to make informed decisions about your nutritional well-being. Second, you are encouraged to learn the basic principles of nutrition and to discover how to apply the concepts in this book that pertain specifically to you.

The text discusses some of the most interesting and important elements of nutrition and food consumption to help you understand both how your body works and how your food choices affect your health.

Features

Planning a New Way of Eating

Early in the text, many of the basic guidelines for planning a healthy diet are presented, including a description of the USDA Food Guide Pyramid, in Chapter 2. Later, in Chapter 13, the steps involved in setting nutritional goals and designing a diet plan to attain those goals are reviewed.

Understanding the World Around Us

In a college environment, it is often difficult to envision how real the problem of world hunger is. Chapter 20 examines the tragedy of undernutrition and the conditions that create it. The chapter allows you to explore possible solutions that offer hope for the future of our world.

Pedagogy

The sixth edition of *Perspectives in Nutrition* incorporates some important tools to help you learn the nutrition concepts in this text. Following is a guide to those tools:

1. Each chapter begins with a Refresh Your Memory box reminding you of previous chapter content (or coursework) that will be helpful to know for understanding the current chapter. Following this is a case scenario, which allows you to apply knowledge gained from the chapter in a real-life setting. An answer to each case scenario is provided in the chapter at the point at which the specific content needed to answer the case scenario is covered.
2. **Chapter Objectives** then help you focus your attention on key ideas in the chapter.
3. Throughout each chapter are **boldfaced key terms,** many of which are defined in the margin. All boldfaced terms appear with their definitions and pronunciations in the glossary at the end of the text.
4. Also throughout each chapter are **margin notes,** which further explain ideas, provide references to other chapters. Some URLs to nutrition-related websites are in these margin notes, as well as in the text itself.
5. The numerous **tables** throughout the text present major points.
6. The **Concept Checks,** which follow the major sections within each chapter, summarize key points. If you are having trouble understanding the material in the Concept Check, you should reread the preceding section.
7. Each chapter ends with a **summary,** which conveys the main ideas in the chapter, and **study questions**—both provide a review of chapter material.
8. **Annotated References** are provided to back up material presented in the chapter. If you are preparing a research paper for your class, or would just like more information on specific topics, consult these sources.
9. Also at the end of each chapter are **Take Action** boxes, which make major concepts presented in the chapter relevant to daily life. For example, you may be asked to look more carefully at your own diet, examine your family history, or apply information you've learned to friends or family.
10. **Critical Thinking** questions ask you to apply information as you learn it. This fosters understanding of the material.
11. **Nutrition Perspective** essays at the end of each chapter develop current topics in nutrition, often covered earlier in the chapter, in greater detail.
12. A variety of supplements to this text, including dietary analysis software, are available to you. These instructional aids are designed to help you learn the major concepts developed in the text and prepare for class examinations.
13. The website www.mhhe.com/wardlawpers6 contains an **Online Learning Center,** with quizzes, flash cards, other activities, and web links designed to further help you learn about nutrition. This is organized according to each chapter in the book.

A Request to Students Who Use This Book

We try our best but realize that sometimes we miss a side of an argument that deserves attention or do not make something perfectly clear. If you find content that you question or believe warrants more detail or a clearer explanation, feel free to contact us by mail, fax, or e-mail.

Gordon M. Wardlaw Ph.D., R.D., L.D.
Department of Human Nutrition
The Ohio State University
347C Campbell Hall
1787 Neil Avenue
Columbus, OH 43210
Fax: (614) 292-8880
E-mail: wardlaw.1@osu.edu
Website: hec.osu.edu/people/gwardlaw

Jeffrey S. Hampl Ph.D., R.D.
Department of Nutrition
Arizona State University
7001 E. Williams Field Road
Mesa, Arizona 85212
Fax: (480) 727-1064
E-mail: jeff.hampl@asu.edu

Robert A. DiSilvestro Ph.D.
Department of Human Nutrition
The Ohio State University
345 Campbell Hall
1787 Neil Avenue
Columbus, OH 43210
Fax: (614) 292-8880
E-mail: rdisilvestro@hec.ohio-state.edu

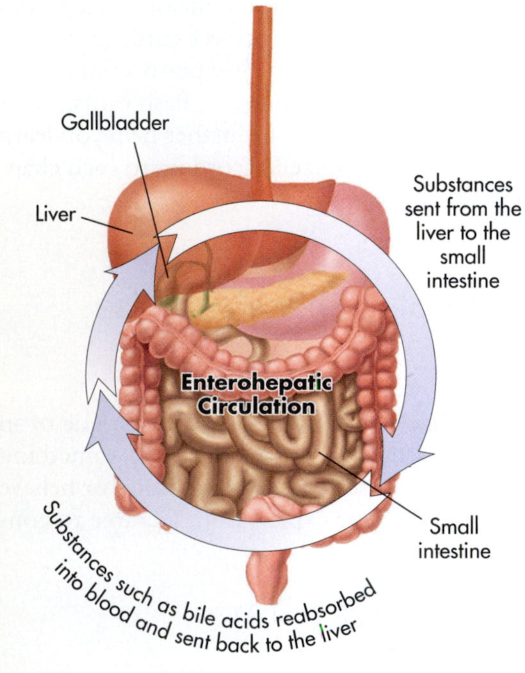

Thoughtfully Crafted New Illustrations

The presentation of scientific concepts has been enhanced by dynamic new illustrations. Realistic renderings and careful color-coding of processes assist students in grasping difficult concepts.

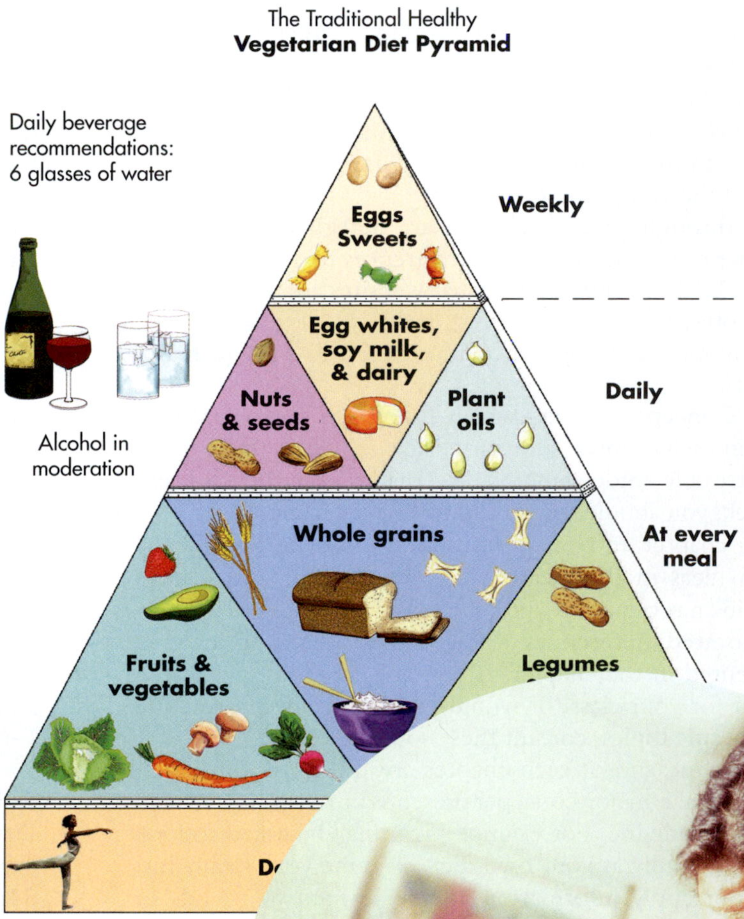

Dynamic Photographs

Over 100 new photographs of people in real-life situations help enliven and bring relevance to the text.

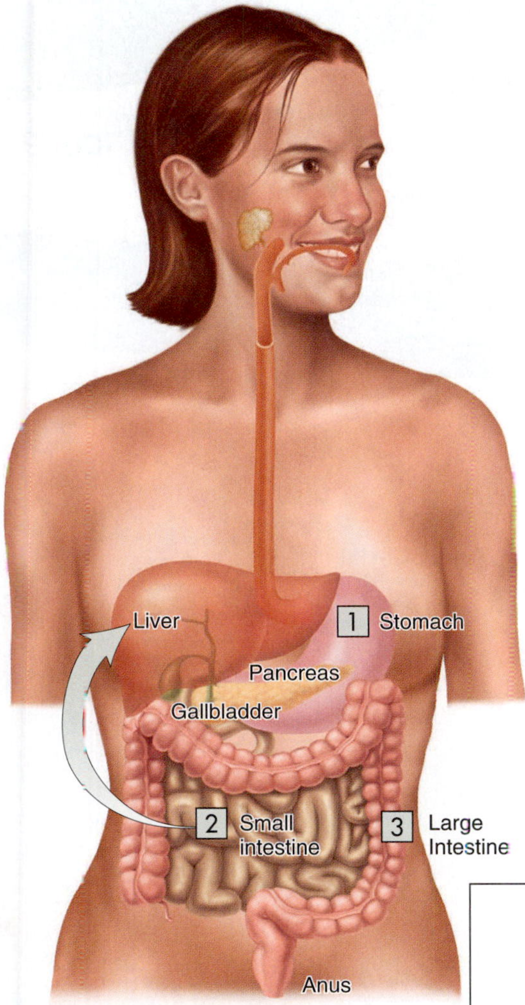

	Organ	Nutrient Absorbed
1	Stomach	Alcohol (20% of total)
2	Small Intestine	Calcium, magnesium, i
		Glucose
		Amino acids
		Fats
		Most vitamins
		Water
		Alcohol (about 80% of
		Bile acids
3	Large Intestine	Sodium
		Potassium
		Some fatty acids
		Gases

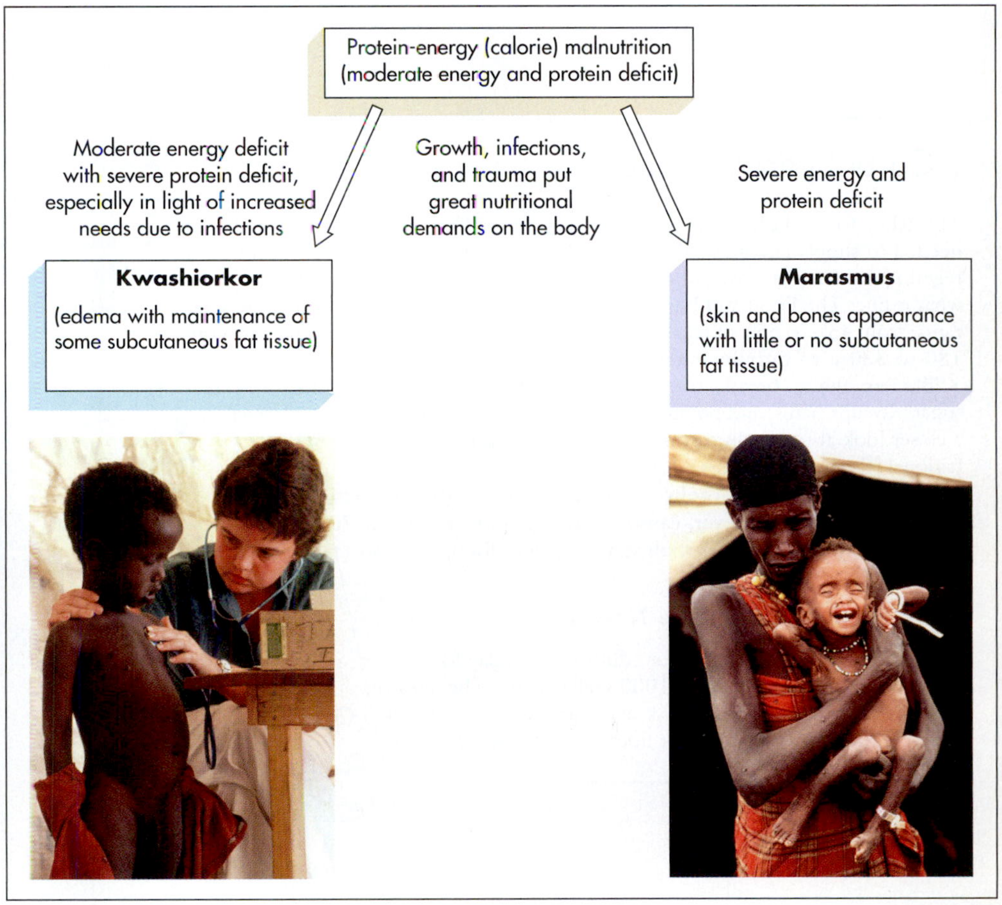

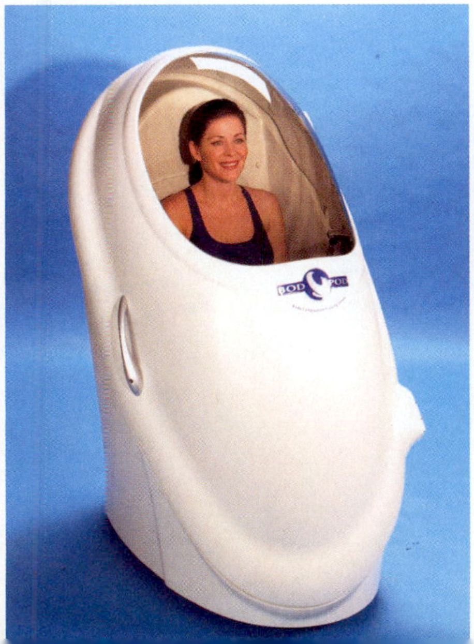

Expert Opinion

Looking Beyond the Water… Phytochemicals in Health P… Disease Prevention

Clare M. Hasler, Ph.D.

In addition to vitamins and other macro- and micronutrients necessary for the growth… nance, and repair of body tissues… fat, carbohydrates, vitamins, and… plant-based diet contains numerou… known as "phytochemicals" (e.g., c… plants), which are not absolutely re… sic body function but nonetheless ma… portant role in health enhancement.

Phytochemicals are secondary p… lites … to protect the plant f… …ught …

tion. Of the various are…

Expert Opinion

Why Is Weight Management so Difficult?

Sachiko T. St. Jeor, Ph.D., R.D.

Currently we are expecting a worldwide epidemic of obesity; approximately 65% of adults in the United States are overweight (body mass index, or BMI, ≥ 85th percentile of 25.0 to 29.9 kg/m²) or obese (BMI in the ≥ 95th percentile or > 30.0 kg/m²). This is a sad commentary on th… history of weight gain over the … North Americans …

Second, little emphasis has been placed on weight maintenance or on the prevention of weight gain. This epidemic of obesity … been partially halted if … weight …

at maintainin… …eir weight. The weig… …ve better health pr… being more physic… …m-solving and self-… …d more "normalize… …port, and self-effica… …fficulty of implemen… …r weight managem…

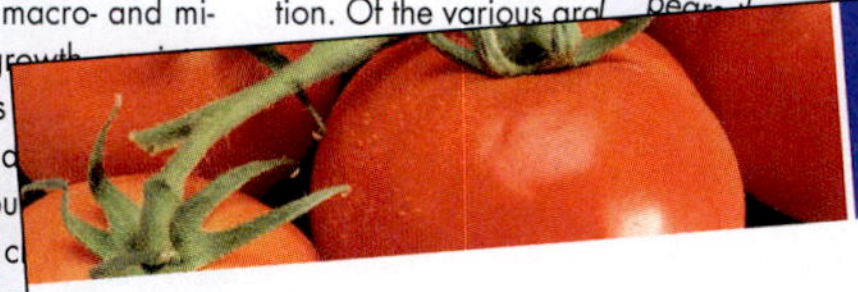

Nutrition | Perspective

Binge Drinking

College students are drinking more heavily and more frequently than ever before. Excessive alcohol consumption is an even bigger problem than illicit drug use on college campuses today (Table 8-5). Many college students consider drinking alcohol to be a "rite of passage" into adulthood. The heaviest drinking population in North America is young, Caucasian college students. Bars near campus typically promote heavy drinking. Alcohol producers frequently target college students with advertising and other marketing efforts. Adding to the overall problem is that typically half of all college students are not of legal drinking age. In … …ual overall cost related to al… … by those under 2…

Current Topics of Note

The latest nutrition issues reported in the media are explained in clear, scientific terms. Students learn how to read beyond the headlines to make sound nutrition judgments.

Carbohydrate Needs

The RDA for carbohydrates is 130 g/day for adults. This is based on the am… needed to supply adequate glucose for the central nervous system, without havin… rely on partial replacement of glucose by ketone bodies. Exceeding this amount sc… what is fine; The Food and Nutrition Board recommends that carbohydrate intake … range from 45% to 65% of total energy intake.[6] The average North American consum… 180 to 330 g of carbohydrates per day. The top five carbohydrate sources for U.S. adults are white bread, soft drinks, cookies and cakes (includ… doughnuts), sugars/syrups/jams, and potatoes. Clearly, many of us (teenagers incl… a closer look at our main carbohydrate sources and strive to improv… tritional standpoint.[12]

In North America, carbohydrates supply about 50% of dietar… adults. Worldwide, however, carbohydrates account for about 70… sumed. In some countries, carbohydrates account for up to 80% of …

How Much Fiber Do We Need?

The Adequate Intake for fiber for adults is 25 g/day for women… This is based on a goal of 14 g/1000 kcal in a diet. The rationale… is the ability of fiber to reduce risk of cardiovascular disease (an… betes). The Daily Value used for fiber on food and supplemen…

Latest Dietary Reference Intakes

Throughout the text, content has been updated to reflect the recently released latest Dietary Reference Intakes. Students will have access to the latest guidelines for protein, carbohydrates, fiber, and fats.

Table 2-6 Comparison of Daily Values with the Latest RDAs and Other Nutrien…

Dietary Constituent	Unit of Measure	Current Daily Values for People Over 4 Years of Age
Total Fat‡	g	<65
Saturated fatty acids‡	"	<20
Protein‡	"	50
Cholesterol§	mg	<300
Carbohydrate‡	g	300
Fiber	"	25
Vitamin A	µg Retinol activity equivalents	
Vitamin D	International u…	
Vitamin E		

A Personalized Approach to Nutrition

The authors provide ample opportunities for students to apply nutrition concepts and guidelines to their own lives. Real-life examples and individualized activities make the material relevant and help students learn to assess the validity of nutrition claims.

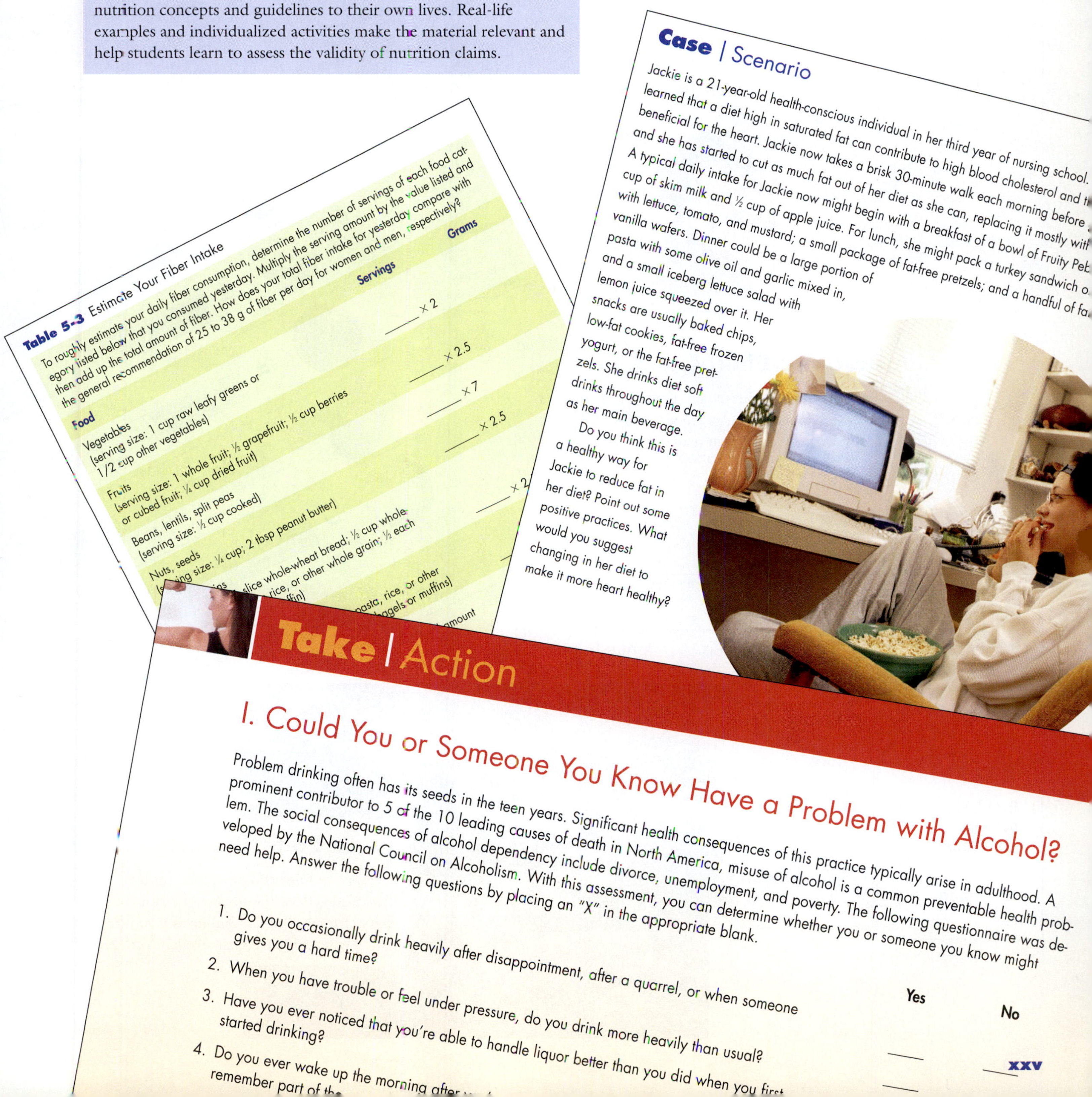

Table 5-3 Estimate Your Fiber Intake

To roughly estimate your daily fiber consumption, determine the number of servings of each food category listed below that you consumed yesterday. Multiply the serving amount by the value listed and then add up the total amount of fiber. How does your total fiber intake for yesterday compare with the general recommendation of 25 to 38 g of fiber per day for women and men, respectively?

Food	Servings	Grams
Vegetables (serving size: 1 cup raw leafy greens or 1/2 cup other vegetables)	____ × 2	
Fruits (serving size: 1 whole fruit; ½ grapefruit; ½ cup berries or cubed fruit; ¼ cup dried fruit)	____ × 2.5	
Beans, lentils, split peas (serving size: ½ cup cooked)	____ × 7	
Nuts, seeds (serving size: ¼ cup; 2 tbsp peanut butter)	____ × 2.5	

Case | Scenario

Jackie is a 21-year-old health-conscious individual in her third year of nursing school. She learned that a diet high in saturated fat can contribute to high blood cholesterol and that fiber is beneficial for the heart. Jackie now takes a brisk 30-minute walk each morning before class, and she has started to cut as much fat out of her diet as she can, replacing it mostly with carbohydrates. A typical daily intake for Jackie now might begin with a breakfast of a bowl of Fruity Pebbles with a cup of skim milk and ½ cup of apple juice. For lunch, she might pack a turkey sandwich on white bread with lettuce, tomato, and mustard; a small package of fat-free pretzels; and a handful of fat-free vanilla wafers. Dinner could be a large portion of pasta with some olive oil and garlic mixed in, and a small iceberg lettuce salad with lemon juice squeezed over it. Her snacks are usually baked chips, low-fat cookies, fat-free frozen yogurt, or the fat-free pretzels. She drinks diet soft drinks throughout the day as her main beverage.

Do you think this is a healthy way for Jackie to reduce fat in her diet? Point out some positive practices. What would you suggest changing in her diet to make it more heart healthy?

Take | Action

I. Could You or Someone You Know Have a Problem with Alcohol?

Problem drinking often has its seeds in the teen years. Significant health consequences of this practice typically arise in adulthood. A prominent contributor to 5 of the 10 leading causes of death in North America, misuse of alcohol is a common preventable health problem. The social consequences of alcohol dependency include divorce, unemployment, and poverty. The following questionnaire was developed by the National Council on Alcoholism. With this assessment, you can determine whether you or someone you know might need help. Answer the following questions by placing an "X" in the appropriate blank.

	Yes	No
1. Do you occasionally drink heavily after disappointment, after a quarrel, or when someone gives you a hard time?	____	____
2. When you have trouble or feel under pressure, do you drink more heavily than usual?	____	____
3. Have you ever noticed that you're able to handle liquor better than you did when you first started drinking?	____	____
4. Do you ever wake up the morning after ... remember part of the ...	____	____

Digital Content Manager CD-ROM

If you're looking for illustrations, photographs, tables, and animations to incorporate into your lecture presentations, handouts, or quizzes, this easy-to-use CD contains hundreds of digital assets from *Perspectives in Nutrition, 6e*. Simply click on the chapter folder, select an image, and you're ready to import the image into the application of your choice. It's that simple!

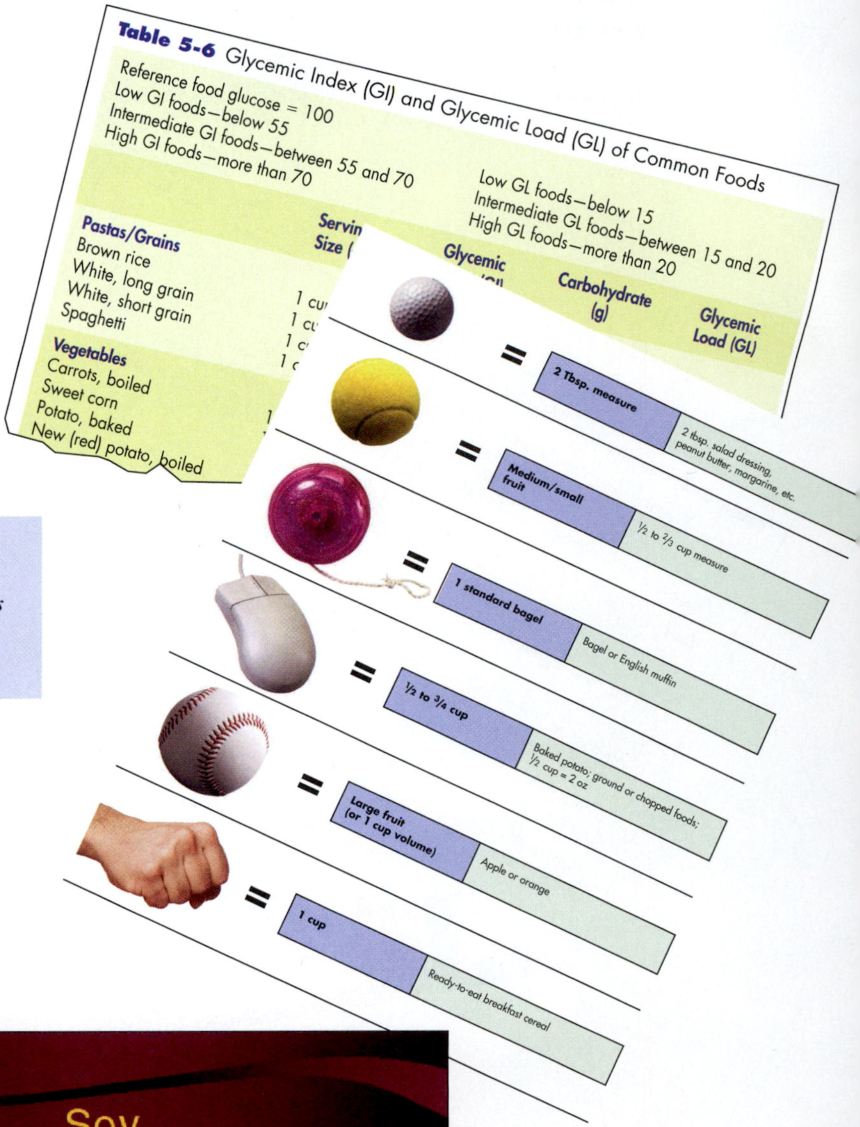
Table 5-6 Glycemic Index (GI) and Glycemic Load (GL) of Common Foods
Reference food glucose = 100
Low GI foods—below 55
Intermediate GI foods—between 55 and 70
High GI foods—more than 70
Low GL foods—below 15
Intermediate GL foods—between 15 and 20
High GL foods—more than 20
Carbohydrate (g)
Glycemic Load (GL)
Pastas/Grains
Brown rice
White, long grain
White, short grain
Spaghetti
Vegetables
Carrots, boiled
Sweet corn
Potato, baked
New (red) potato, boiled
2 Tbsp. measure
2 tbsp. salad dressing, peanut butter, margarine, etc.
Medium/small fruit
½ to ⅔ cup measure
1 standard bagel
Bagel or English muffin
½ to ¾ cup
Baked potato; ground or chopped foods; ½ cup = 2 oz
Large fruit (or 1 cup volume)
Apple or orange
1 cup
Ready-to-eat breakfast cereal

Illustrations, Photos, and Tables

Full-color digital files of the art and tables in *Perspectives in Nutrition* are logically organized and allow you to easily customize your classroom materials.

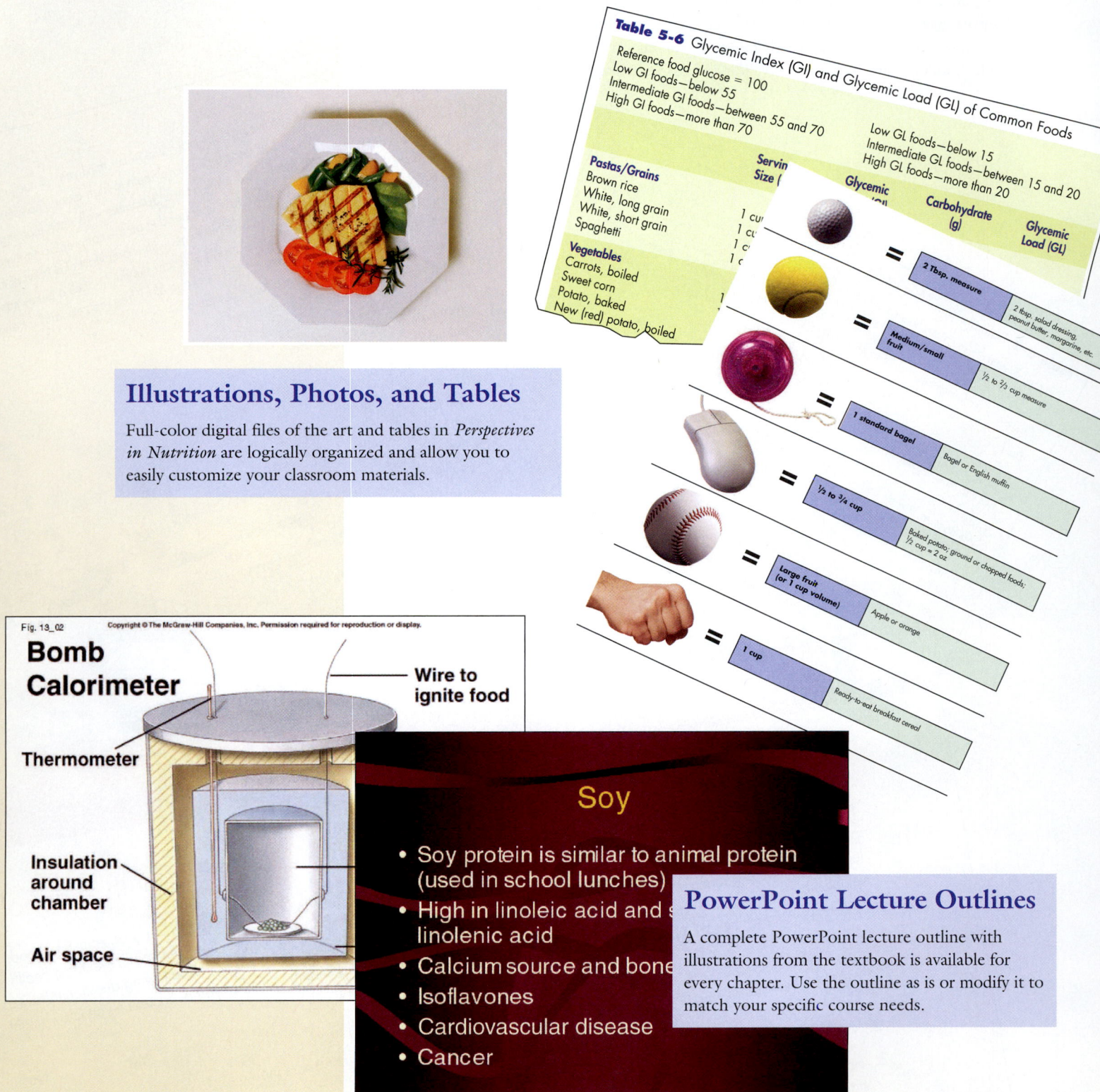

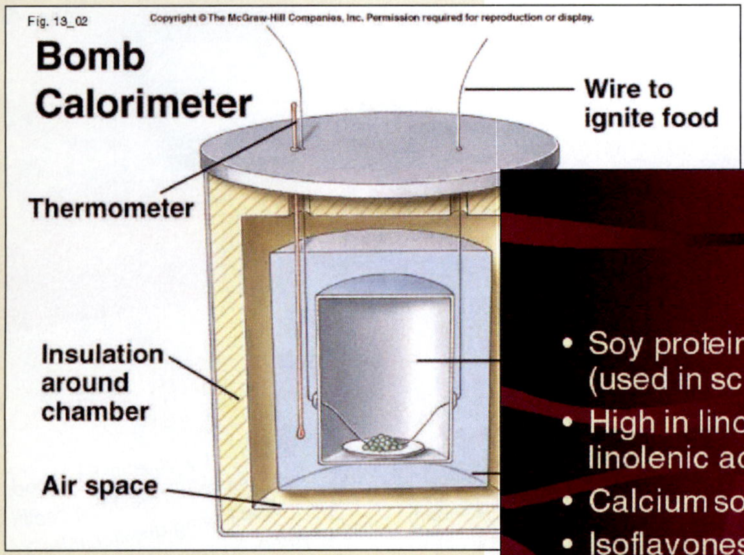
Fig. 13_02
Copyright © The McGraw-Hill Companies, Inc. Permission required for reproduction or display.
Bomb Calorimeter
Wire to ignite food
Thermometer
Insulation around chamber
Air space

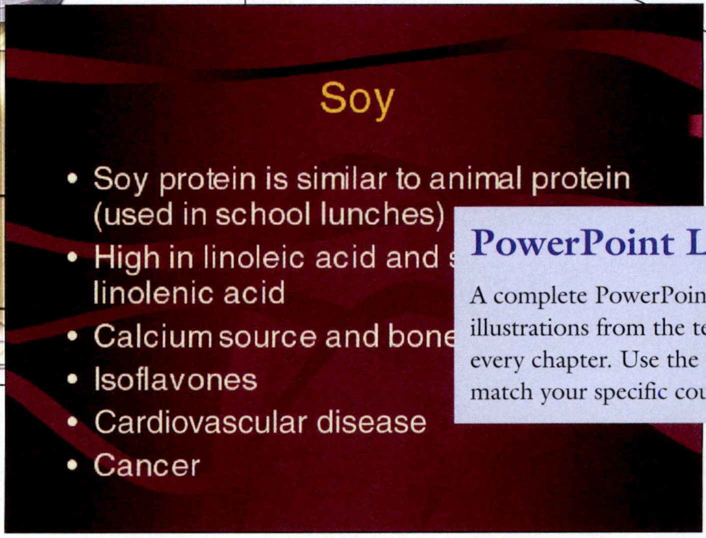
Soy
• Soy protein is similar to animal protein (used in school lunches)
• High in linoleic acid and
linolenic acid
• Calcium source and bone
• Isoflavones
• Cardiovascular disease
• Cancer

PowerPoint Lecture Outlines

A complete PowerPoint lecture outline with illustrations from the textbook is available for every chapter. Use the outline as is or modify it to match your specific course needs.

Animations

Animations found on the Digital Content Manager CD-ROM allow you to harness the visual impact of processes in motion. You can import the animations into presentations or online course materials.

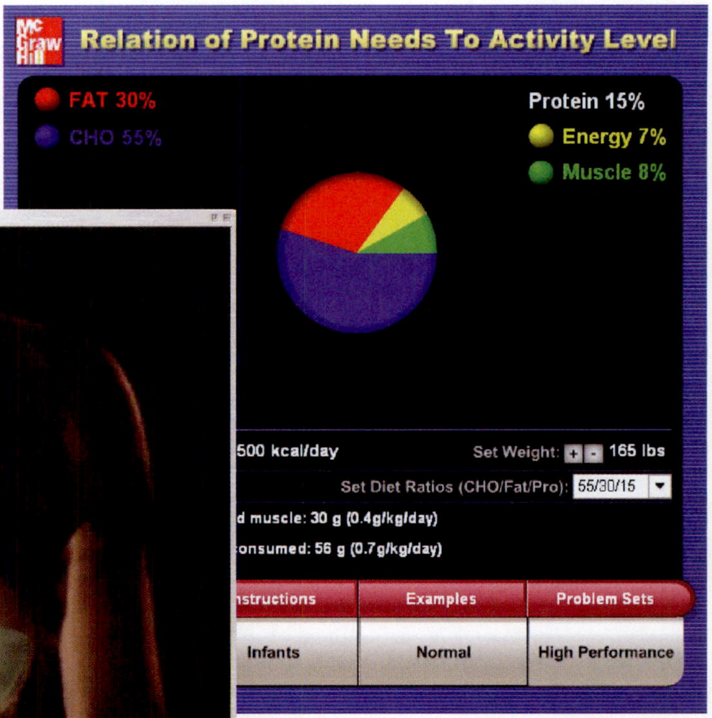

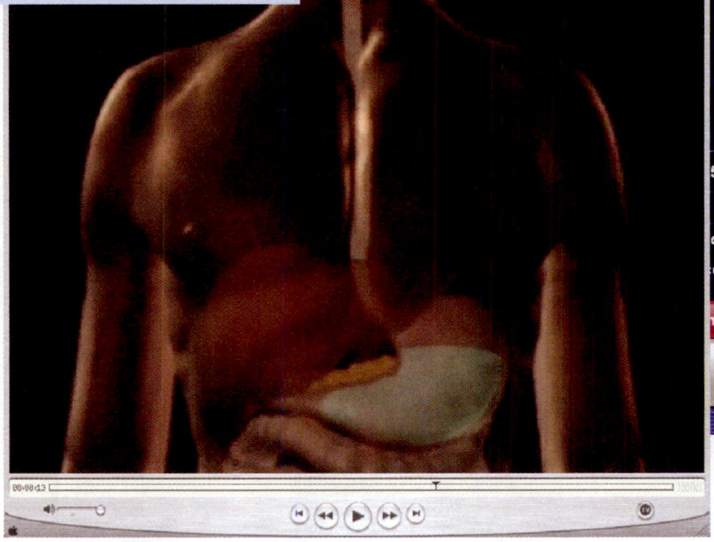

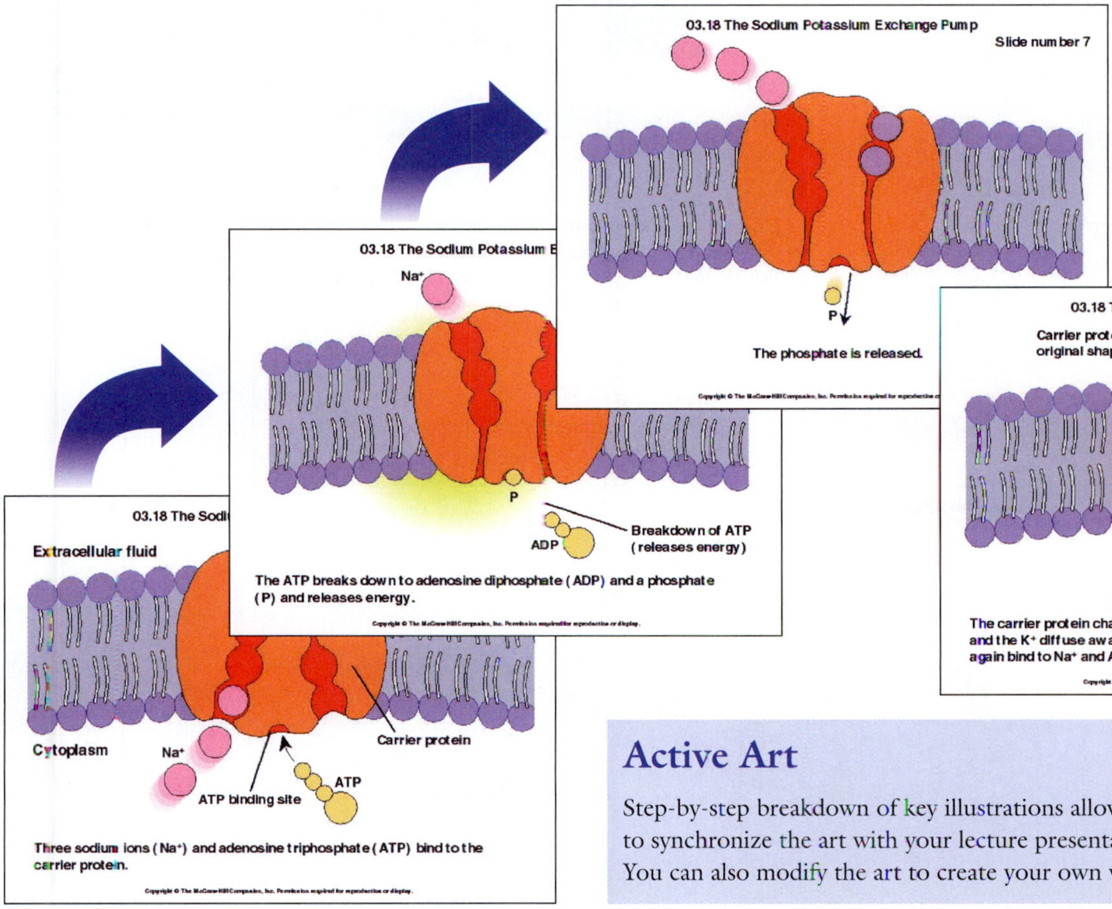

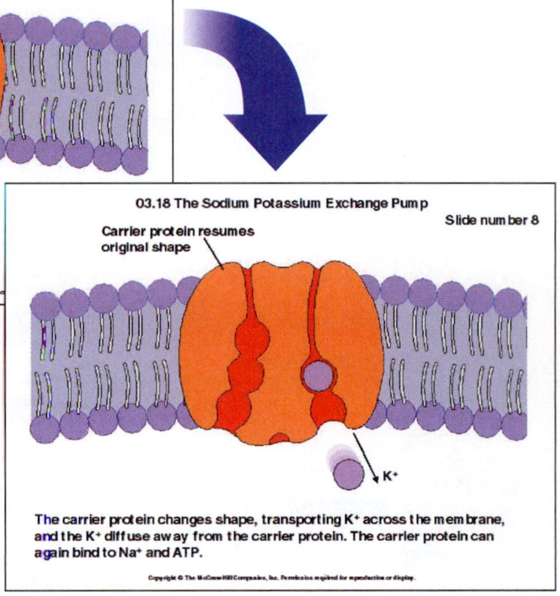

Active Art

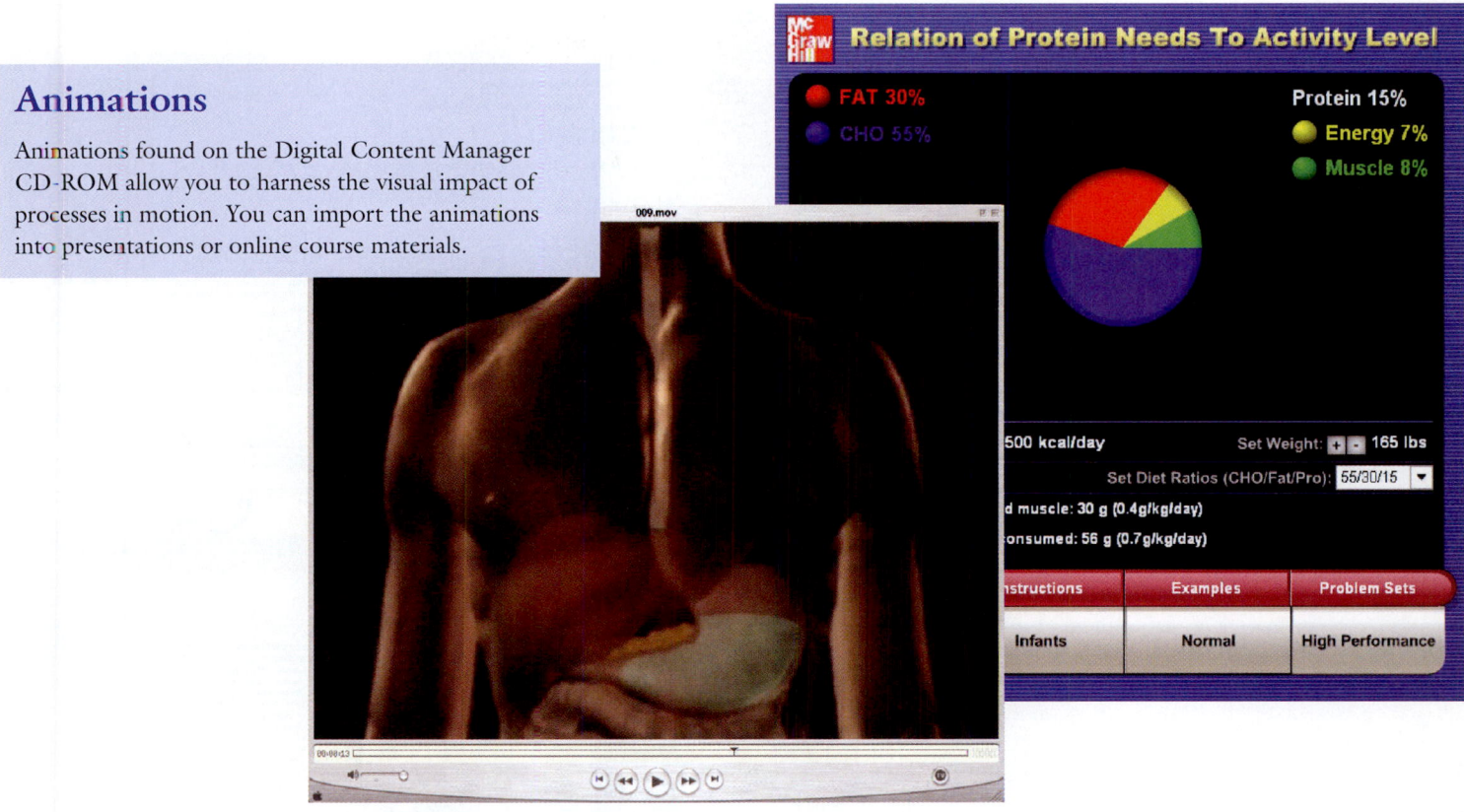

Step-by-step breakdown of key illustrations allows you to synchronize the art with your lecture presentation. You can also modify the art to create your own version.

Online Learning Center (www.mhhe.com/wardlawpers6)

This online resource is home to a wide variety of resources for instructors and students, all coordinated to *Perspectives in Nutrition, 6e*. For students, this site acts as a complete online Study Guide to help them get the most from their study time.

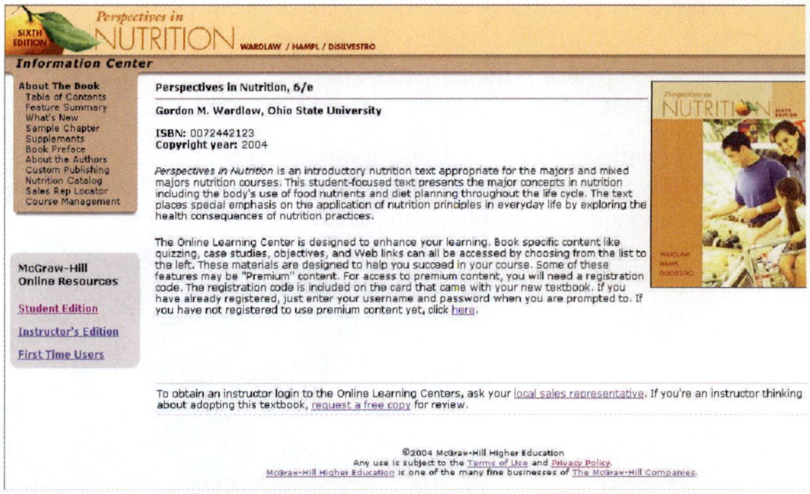

Chapter Quizzes and Activities

Students can test their knowledge by taking chapter quizzes and get immediate feedback on their answers. Crossword puzzles, vocabulary activities, and more boost student confidence in mastering new content.

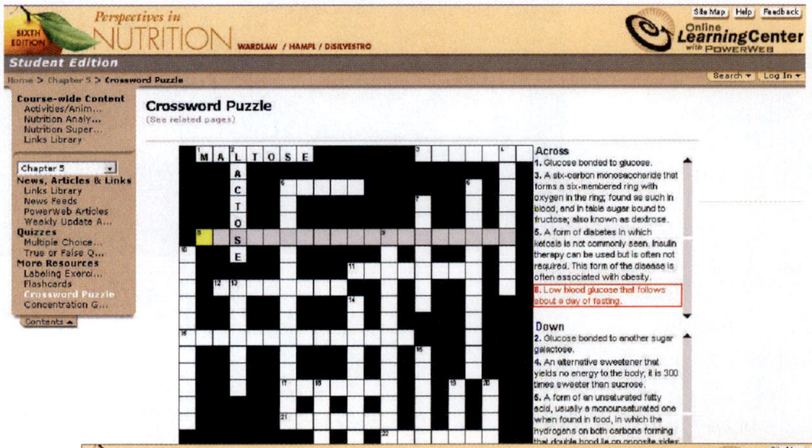

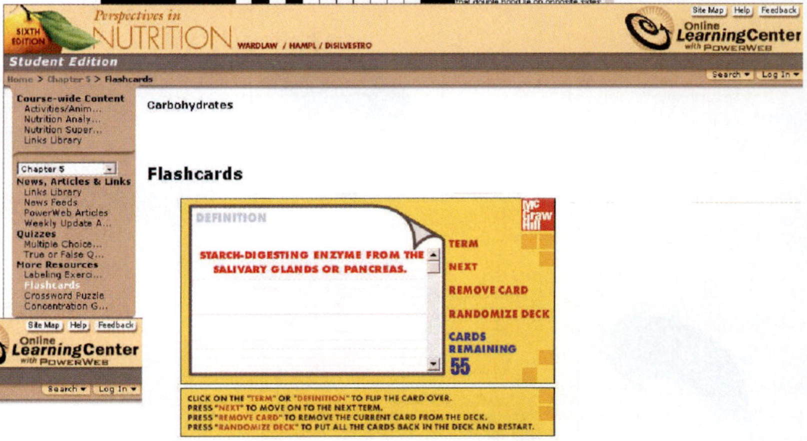

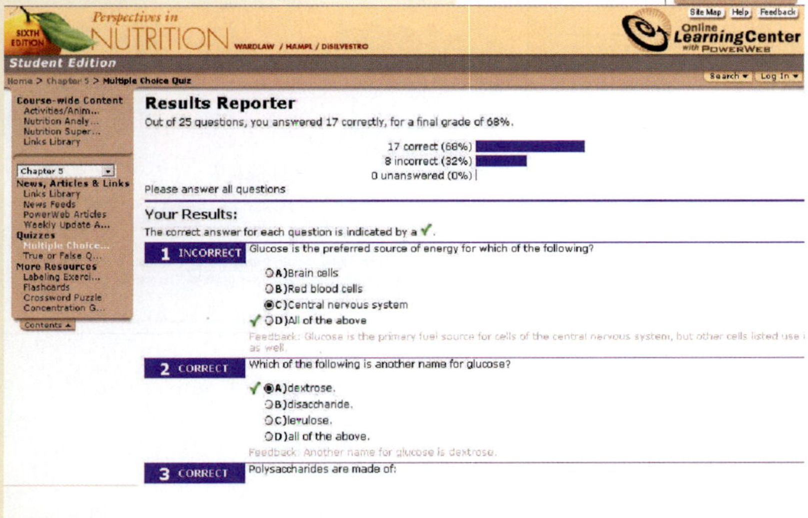

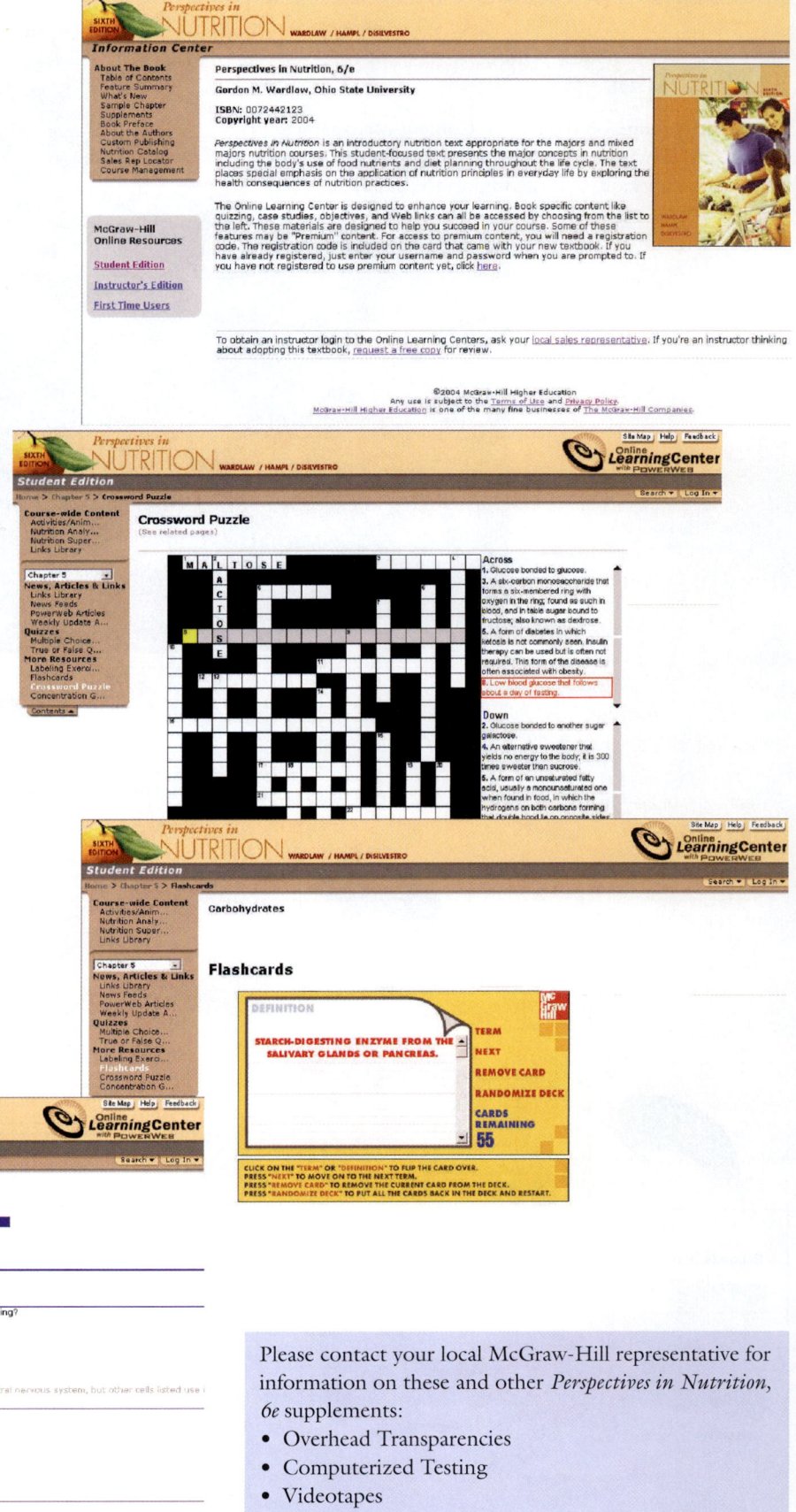

Please contact your local McGraw-Hill representative for information on these and other *Perspectives in Nutrition, 6e* supplements:

- Overhead Transparencies
- Computerized Testing
- Videotapes

www.mhhe.com/rep

chapter 1

What Nourishes You?

Chapter | Outline

Case | Scenario

Brendon listens to talk radio as he commutes to school each morning. He hears numerous advertisements for food supplements. Commentators also warn about the dangers of certain unhealthy behaviors. News briefs discuss the latest breakthroughs, touting new findings regarding both positive and negative health practices. Typical terms he hears are *cardiovascular disease (also called heart disease), diabetes, fiber, cancer, obesity, vitamin E, omega-3 fatty acids, cholesterol,* and *creatine.* These are all topics generally covered in an introductory nutrition class. One advantage of taking such a class is to be able to decipher the health news that one reads in newspapers, hears on the radio, and is exposed to via television.

Start your exploration of nutrition by looking up these terms in the glossary at the back of this book. You will likely find this an interesting task, one that will heighten your awareness of nutrition and, so, help you in your study of nutrition. Also, consider adding a few other words you are curious about and look those up as well in the glossary, or use the index if the glossary does not contain the word.

Refresh | Your Memory

As you begin your study of nutrition in Chapter 1, you may want to review:

- Basic concepts in chemistry in Appendix A.
- The metric system in Appendix L.

Boost | Your Study

Check out the ***Perspectives in Nutrition: Online Learning Center*** www.mhhe.com/wardlawpers6 *for quizzes, flash cards, activities, and web links designed to further help you learn about what nourishes you.*

Chapter | Objectives

Chapter 1 is designed to allow you to:

1. Define the terms *nutrition, carbohydrates, proteins, lipids (fats), alcohol, vitamins, minerals, water, kilocalories (kcal),* and *fiber.*
2. Use the caloric values of energy-yielding nutrients to determine the total energy content (kcal) in a food or diet.
3. List the major characteristics of the North American diet and the food habits that often need to be improved.
4. Describe the various factors that affect our daily food choices.
5. List various attributes of a healthful lifestyle that are consistent with the *Healthy People 2010* goals.
6. Identify diet and lifestyle factors that contribute to the 10 leading causes of death in North America.
7. Understand the basis of the scientific method as it is used in developing hypotheses and theories in the field of nutrition.
8. Identify reliable sources of nutrition information.
9. Understand the role of genetic background in the development of nutrition-related diseases.

Do you need to take vitamin and mineral supplements? Are you eating too much fat and cholesterol? Is much of what you eat unsafe? Are some foods actually *junk foods?* Should you become a vegetarian? If you're confused about what you should eat, you are not alone. This chapter will help you sort out some of these issues as you are introduced to the science of nutrition.

And, as you begin this study of nutrition, keep this in mind. Research over the last 40 years has shown that a healthy diet—especially one rich in fruits and vegetables—coupled with regular prolonged, vigorous exercise and some strength-building exercise can both prevent and treat many age-related diseases. Overall, it is clear that the nutritional lifestyles of some (but not all) North Americans are out of balance with their physiology. And, since we live longer than our ancestors, preventing the age-related diseases that develop later in life is a more important focus today than in the past.

By optimizing dietary choices, we can strive to bring the goal of a long, healthy life within reach.[13, 18] This is the primary theme not just in this chapter but throughout the entire book.

Nutrition and Your Health

In your lifetime, you will eat about 70,000 meals and 60 tons of food. This opening chapter will take a close look at the general classes of nutrients supplied by this food intake, the role research plays in sorting out which food components are essential for the maintenance of health, and the powerful effect of genetic background in determining both nutrition-related and overall health.

What Actually Is Nutrition?

The Council on Food and Nutrition of the American Medical Association defines **nutrition** as "The science of food, the nutrients and the substances therein, their action, interaction, and balance in relation to health and disease, and the process by which the organism ingests, digests, absorbs, transports, utilizes, and excretes food substances."

nutrition The Council on Food and Nutrition of the American Medical Association defines nutrition as "the science of food; the nutrients and the substances therein; their action, interaction, and balance in relation to health and disease; and the process by which the organism (i.e., body) ingests, digests, absorbs, transports, utilizes, and excretes food substances."

glucose A six-carbon carbohydrate found in blood, as well as in table sugar bound to fructose; also known as *dextrose,* it is one of the simple sugars.

Nutrients Come from Food

What is the difference between food and **nutrients?** Food provides both the energy and the nutrients needed to build and maintain all body cells. Many of these nutrients are **essential nutrients,** if the body can't make them (or make enough of them) to meet needs. For a nutrient to be considered essential, three characteristics are needed. First, its omission from the diet must lead to a decline in certain aspects of human health, such as function of the nervous system. Second, if the omitted nutrient is restored to the diet before permanent damage occurs, those aspects of human health hampered by its absence should regain normal function. Third, a specific biological function must be identified.[8]

Some nutrients that perform life-sustaining functions can be produced by the body if they are missing from the diet, such as **glucose.** In addition, the body requires vitamin D, but the skin is capable of synthesizing its own vitamin D upon receiving sunlight. This reduces the need from dietary sources among people who experience regular sun exposure, making its essentiality less clear-cut (see Chapter 9).

Why Study Nutrition?

Nutrition is one key to developing and maintaining a state of health that is optimal for you. A poor diet coupled with a sedentary lifestyle are known to be **risk factors** for life-threatening **chronic** diseases and deaths: **cardiovascular (heart) disease, stroke, hypertension, diabetes,** and some forms of **cancer** (Table 1-1). Together, these disorders account for two-thirds of all deaths in the United States and the rest of North America (Table 1-2). Not consuming enough essential nutrients in younger years also makes us more likely to suffer health consequences in later years, such as bone fractures from the disease **osteoporosis.** Iron-deficiency **anemia** is another possibility. At the same time, taking too much of a nutrient supplement—such as vitamin A, vitamin D, vitamin B-6, calcium, or copper—can be harmful. Another dietary problem, drinking too much alcohol, is associated with **cirrhosis** of the liver, some forms of cancer, accidents, and suicides.

All of these consequences of modern living are partly an "affliction of affluence." Note, however, that these diseases are often preventable.[18] Age fast or age slowly: It is partly your choice. U.S. government scientists have calculated that a poor diet combined with a lack of sufficient physical activity account for 300,000 fatal cases of cardiovascular disease, cancer, and diabetes each year. Thus, the combination of poor diet and too little physical activity is indirectly the second leading cause of death. In addition, **obesity** is considered the second leading cause of preventable death (smoking is the first). Put together, obesity and smoking spell even more trouble healthwise.

As you gain understanding about your nutritional habits and increase your knowledge about nutrition, you have the opportunity to dramatically reduce your risk for many common health problems.[1] To help, the U.S. government provides two websites that can link you to many sites providing health and nutrition information (www.healthfinder.gov and www.nutrition.gov).

The major health problems in North America are largely caused by a poor diet, excessive energy intake, and not enough physical activity.

Table 1-1 Glossary Terms to Aid Your Introduction to Nutrition*

anemia	Generally refers to a decreased oxygen-carrying capacity of the blood. This can be caused by many factors, such as iron deficiency or blood loss.
body mass index (BMI)	Weight (in kilograms) divided by height (in meters) squared. A value of 25 or greater indicates a higher risk for weight-related health disorders if one is also overfat.
cancer	A condition characterized by uncontrolled growth of abnormal cells.
carbohydrate	A compound containing carbon, hydrogen, and oxygen atoms; most are known as *sugars*, *starches*, and *fibers*.
cardiovascular (heart) disease	A disease characterized by the deposition of fatty material in the blood vessels, often called hardening of the arteries. These deposits restrict blood flow, which in turn can lead to heart damage and death. Also termed *coronary heart disease* (CHD), as the vessels of the heart are often the primary site of disease. The term cardiovascular disease (CVD) is typically used, since in addition to the heart, the arteries that serve the rest of the body can experience the same deterioration.
cholesterol	A waxy lipid found in all body cells; it has a structure containing multiple chemical rings (steroid structure). Cholesterol is found only in foods that contain animal products.
chronic	Long-standing, developing over time. When referring to disease, this term indicates that the disease process, once developed, is slow and tends to remain; a good example is cardiovascular disease.
cirrhosis	A loss of functioning liver cells, which are replaced by nonfunctioning connective tissue. Any substance that poisons liver cells can lead to cirrhosis. The most common cause is a chronic, excessive alcohol intake.
diabetes	A disease characterized by high blood glucose, resulting from either insufficient or no release of the hormone insulin by the pancreas or general inability of insulin to act on certain body cells, such as muscle cells. The two major forms are type 1 (requires daily insulin therapy) and type 2 (may or may not require insulin therapy).
essential nutrient	In nutritional terms, a substance that, when left out of a diet, leads to signs of poor health. The body either can't produce this nutrient or can't produce it fast enough to meet its needs. Then, if added back to a diet before permanent damage occurs, the affected aspects of health are restored.
hypertension	A condition in which blood pressure remains persistently elevated. Obesity, inactivity, alcohol intake, and excess salt intake all can contribute to the problem.
kilocalorie (kcal)	The heat energy needed to raise the temperature of 1000 g (1 liter) of water 1° Celsius. Also written as Calorie, with a capital C.
lipid	A compound containing much carbon and hydrogen, little oxygen, and sometimes other atoms. Lipids dissolve in ether or benzene, but not in water, and include fats, oils, and cholesterol.
minerals	Elements used in the body to promote chemical reactions and to form body structures.
nutrients	Chemical substances in food that contribute to health, many of which are essential parts of a diet. Nutrients nourish us by providing energy, materials for building body parts, and factors to regulate necessary chemical processes in the body.
obesity	A condition characterized by excess body fat, typically defined in clinical settings as a body mass index (BMI) of 30 or above.
osteoporosis	Decreased bone mass where no obvious disease can be found. This bone loss is related to the effects of aging, genetic background, poor diet, and hormonal changes occurring in postmenopausal women.
protein	Food and body components made of amino acids; proteins contain carbon, hydrogen, oxygen, nitrogen, and sometimes other atoms, in a specific configuration. Proteins contain the form of nitrogen most easily used by the human body.
risk factor	A term used frequently when discussing diseases and the factors contributing to their development. A risk factor is an aspect of our lives—such as heredity, lifestyle choices (i.e., smoking), or nutritional habits—that may make us more likely to develop a disease.
stroke	The loss of body function that results from a blood clot or other change in arteries in the brain that affects blood flow. This in turn causes the death of brain tissue. Also called a *cerebrovascular accident*.
vitamins	Compounds needed in very small amounts in the diet to help regulate and support chemical reactions in the body.
water	The universal solvent; chemically, H_2O. The body is composed of about 60% water. Water (fluid) needs are about 8 cups per day; needs are greater if one exercises heavily (see Chapter 14).

*Bold terms in the book are defined in a glossary, which follows Chapter 20. Many bold terms are also defined in the chapter margin.

Table 1-2 Ten Leading Causes of Death in the United States

Rank	Cause of Death	Percent of Total Deaths
	All causes	100
1	Diseases of the heart (primarily coronary heart disease)*†‡	29
2	Cancer*†‡	22
3	Cerebrovascular diseases (stroke)*‡#	7
4	Chronic obstructive pulmonary diseases and allied conditions (lung diseases)‡	5
5	Accidents and adverse effects†	4
	Motor vehicle accidents	(2)
	All other accidents and adverse effects	(2)
6	Diabetes*	3
7	Influenza and pneumonia	3
8	Alzheimer's disease*	2
9	Kidney disease*‡	2
10	Blood-borne infections	1

From Centers for Disease Control and Prevention, *National Vital Statistics Report*, accessed October 9, 2002. Canadian statistics are quite similar.

*Causes of death in which diet plays a part

†Causes of death in which excessive alcohol consumption plays a part

‡Causes of death in which tobacco use plays a part

#Diseases of the heart and cerebrovascular disease are included in the more global term "cardiovascular disease."

Increasing vegetable intake, such as a daily salad, is one strategy to combat development of many chronic diseases.

Classes and Sources of Nutrients

To begin the study of nutrition, let's start with an overview of the various classes of nutrients. You are probably already familiar with the terms **carbohydrates, lipids** (fats and oils), **proteins, vitamins,** and **minerals** (Figure 1-1). These, plus **water,** make up the six classes of nutrients found in food.

Nutrients can then be assigned to three functional categories: (1) those that primarily provide us with energy (typically expressed in **kilocalories [kcal]**); (2) those that are important for growth and development (and later maintenance); and (3) those that act to keep body functions running smoothly. Some overlap exists among these groupings. The energy-yielding nutrients make up a major portion of most foods.

Vitamins and minerals are needed in such small amounts in the diet that they are called micronutrients. Because carbohydrates, proteins, lipids, and water are needed in much larger amounts, they are called macronutrients.

Provide Energy	Promote Growth and Development	Regulate Body Processes
Carbohydrates	Proteins	Proteins
Proteins	Lipids	Lipids
Lipids (fats and oils)	Vitamins	Vitamins
	Minerals	Minerals
	Water	Water

Let's now look more closely at these six classes of nutrients.

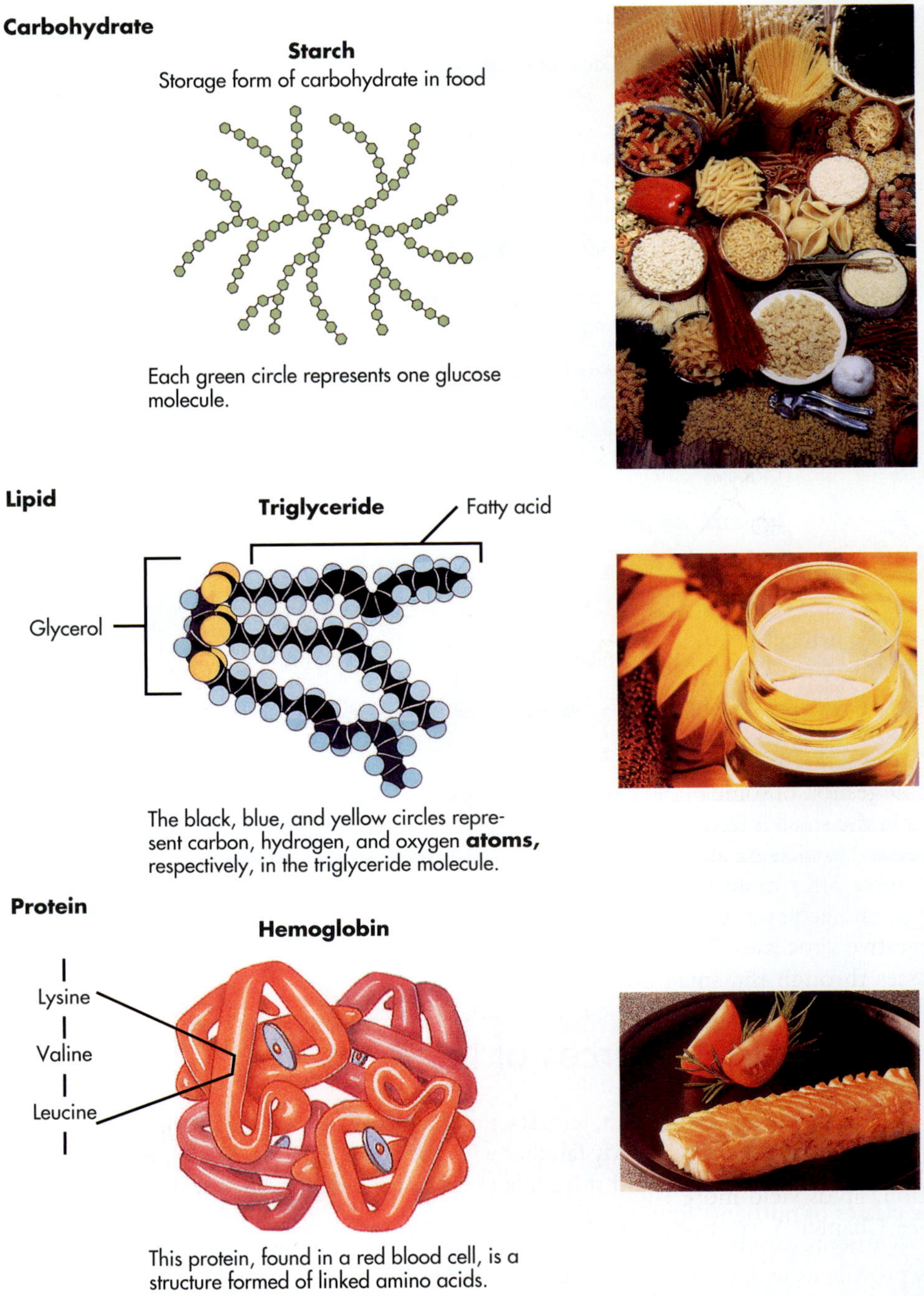

Figure 1-1 Two views of carbohydrates, lipids, and proteins—chemical and dietary perspectives.
Illustrations by William Ober.

atom Smallest combining unit of an element. An atom contains protons, neutrons, and electrons.

Carbohydrates

element A substance that cannot be separated into simpler substances by chemical processes. Common elements in nutrition include carbon, oxygen, hydrogen, nitrogen, calcium, phosphorus, and iron.

Carbohydrates are composed mainly of the **elements** carbon, hydrogen, and oxygen. Carbohydrates provide a major source of fuel for the body, on average 4 kcal per gram (kcal/g). Small carbohydrate structures are called sugars or simple sugars. Table sugar (sucrose) is an example. It is made up of the sugars glucose and fructose. Some simple sugars, such as glucose, can chemically bond to form large storage carbohydrates, called polysaccharides or complex carbohydrates (review Fig. 1-1). An example of this type of carbohydrate is the **starch** in potatoes.

Carbohydrates

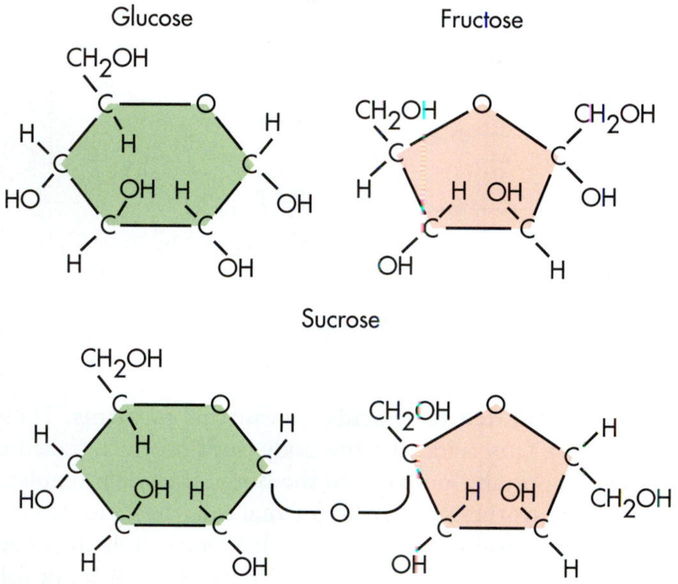

Aside from enjoying their taste, we need sugars and other carbohydrates in our diets primarily to satisfy the energy needs of our body cells. Glucose, which the body can produce from most carbohydrates, is a major source of energy in most cells. When not enough carbohydrate is eaten to supply sufficient glucose, the body is forced to make glucose from proteins.

Digestion of some dietary starch begins in the mouth. The digestive process continues in the small intestine until starches break down into single sugar molecules (such as glucose), which are absorbed into the bloodstream using cells in the small intestine (see Chapter 3 for more on digestion and absorption). However, the bonds between the sugar molecules in certain complex carbohydrates cannot be broken down by human digestive processes. These carbohydrates are part of what is called **fiber.** Such fiber passes through the small intestine undigested to provide bulk for the stool (feces), which is formed in the large intestine (colon). Chapter 5 focuses on carbohydrates.

Lipids

Lipids (mostly fats and oils) are composed of the elements carbon and hydrogen; they contain fewer oxygen atoms than carbohydrates. Because of this difference in composition, lipids yield more energy per gram than carbohydrates—on average, 9 kcal/g. (See Chapter 4 for more details concerning the reason for the high-energy yield of lipids.) Lipids are insoluble in water but can dissolve in certain organic solvents (e.g., ether and benzene).

The basic structure of most lipids is the three-carbon glycerol molecule with a **fatty acid** attached to each of the three carbons (review Fig. 1-1). This form of lipid is generally called a **triglyceride.** Triglycerides are a key energy source for the body and the major form of fat in foods. They are also the major form for energy storage in the body.

In this book, the more familiar term *fats* or *fats and oils* will generally be used, rather than *lipids* or *triglycerides.* Fats are lipids that are solid at room temperature and oils are lipids that are liquid at room temperature.

Most lipids can be separated into two basic types—**saturated** and **unsaturated**—based on the chemical structure of their dominant fatty acids. This property determines whether such a lipid is solid or liquid at room temperature. Saturated fatty acids contain no carbon-carbon double bonds, while unsaturated fatty acids contain one or more. Plant oils tend to contain many unsaturated fatty acids, which makes them liquid. Animal fats are often rich in saturated fatty acids, which makes them solid. Almost all foods contain a variety of saturated and unsaturated fatty acids.

fiber Substances in plant foods that are not digested by the processes that take place in the stomach or small intestine. These add bulk to feces. Fibers naturally found in foods as a class are also called dietary fiber.

fatty acid Major part of most lipids; composed of a chain of carbons flanked by hydrogen with an acid group (—C(=O)—OH) at one end and a methyl group ($—CH_3$) at the other.

triglyceride The major form of lipid in the body and in food. It is composed of three fatty acids bonded to glycerol, an alcohol.

Much attention has been given to saturated fat in the past few years. This is because saturated fat bears a great deal of the responsibility for raising blood cholesterol. High blood cholesterol leads to clogged arteries and, so, can eventually lead to cardiovascular disease. For this reason, it is recommended that people limit the amount of saturated fat in their diet.

Lipids

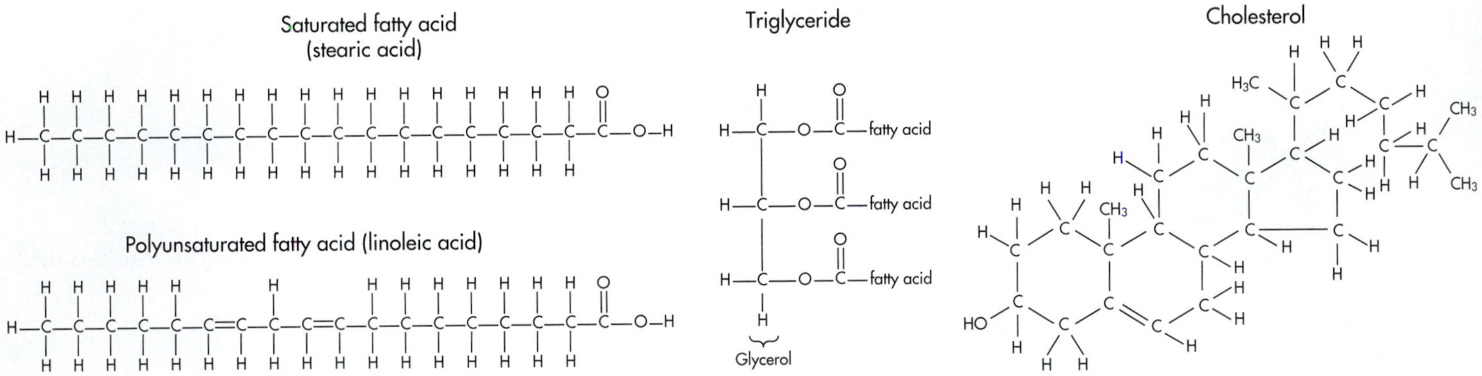

Two specific **polyunsaturated fatty acids** are essential nutrients. These must come from our diets. These key fatty acids that the body can't produce, called essential fatty acids, perform several important functions in the body: they help regulate blood pressure and play a role in the synthesis and repair of vital cell parts. However, we need only a few tablespoons of a common vegetable oil (such as the canola or soybean oil found in supermarkets) each day to supply the essential fatty acids. Adding fish in a diet at least twice a week adds to this benefit derived from the inclusion of vegetable oil. The unique unsaturated fatty acids in fish complement the healthy aspects of vegetable oil. This will be explained in greater detail in Chapter 6, which focuses on lipids.

polyunsaturated fatty acid A fatty acid containing two or more carbon-carbon double bonds.

Many health-food stores market protein powders and shakes for body-builders and other athletes. However, the North American diet contains nearly two times the required amount of protein. Thus, these products are unnecessary; diet can suffice.

Proteins

Like carbohydrates and fats, proteins are composed of the elements carbon, oxygen, and hydrogen. But, unlike the other energy-yielding nutrients, all proteins also contain nitrogen. Proteins are the main structural material in the body (review Fig. 1-1). For example, proteins constitute a major part of bone and muscle; they are also important components in blood, cell membranes, **enzymes,** and immune factors. Furthermore, proteins can also provide energy for the body—on average, 4 kcal/g. Typically, the body uses little protein for the purpose of meeting daily energy needs. Proteins are formed by the bonding together of **amino acids.** Twenty common amino acids are found in food; nine of these are essential nutrients for adults, and one additional amino acid is essential for infants. Chapter 7 focuses on proteins.

enzyme A compound that speeds the rate of a chemical process but is not altered by the process. Almost all enzymes are proteins (some are made of nucleic acids).

amino acid The building block for proteins containing a central carbon atom with a nitrogen atom and other atoms attached.

Amino Acids

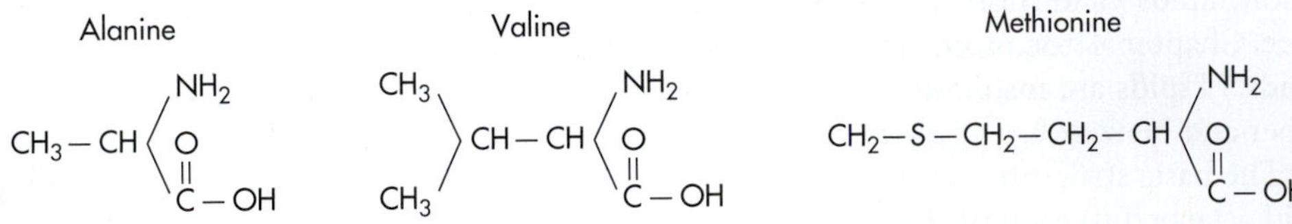

Three other classes of nutrients are vitamins, minerals, and water. Although vitamins and minerals are vital to good health, they are needed only in small amounts in the diet and provide no direct source of energy for the body.

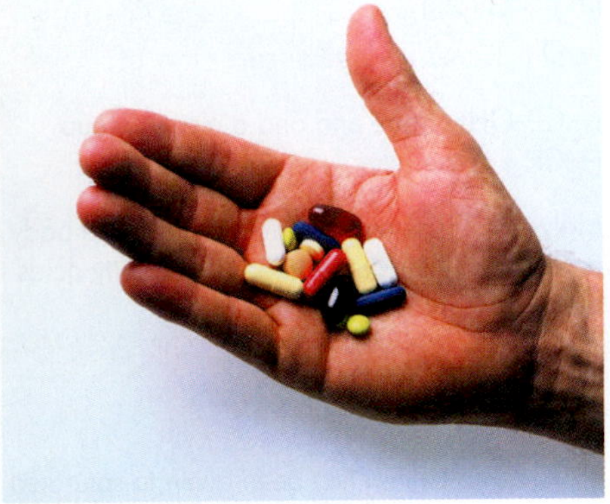

Taking a balanced multivitamin and mineral supplement daily is generally safe. Some nutrition and medical experts even recommend the practice. However, taking numerous nutrient supplements as shown in the photo can lead to health problems. Chapter 9 will explore the appropriate and safe use of supplements in detail.

Vitamins

Vitamins exhibit a wide variety of chemical structures and can contain the elements carbon, hydrogen, nitrogen, oxygen, phosphorus, sulfur, and others. The main function of vitamins is to enable many **chemical reactions** to occur in the body. Some of these reactions help release the energy trapped in carbohydrates, lipids, and proteins. Remember, however, that vitamins themselves provide no usable energy for the body.

The 13 vitamins are divided into two groups: four that are **fat soluble** (vitamins A, D, E, and K) and nine that are **water soluble** (vitamin C and the B vitamins). The two groups of vitamins often act quite differently. For example, cooking destroys water-soluble vitamins much more readily than it does fat-soluble vitamins. Water-soluble vitamins are also excreted from the body much more readily than are fat-soluble vitamins. Thus, the fat-soluble vitamins, especially vitamin A, are much more likely to accumulate in excessive amounts in the body, which then can cause toxicity. The vitamins are the focus of Chapters 9 and 10.

Critical | Thinking

Believing that supplements provide the nutrition her body needs, Janice regularly takes numerous supplements while paying relatively little attention to daily food choices. How would you explain to her that this practice may lead to health problems?

For suggested answers to the Critical Thinking questions in this and every chapter, turn to page NA-1.

Minerals

The nutrients discussed so far are all **organic** compounds, whereas minerals are structurally very simple, **inorganic** substances, which exist as groups of one or more of the same atoms. These terms, *organic* and *inorganic*, have nothing to do with gardening but are based on simple chemistry concepts (see Chapter 2 for use of the term on food labels). Inorganic substances for the most part do not contain carbon atoms.

Minerals typically function as such in the body (Na^+, K^+), or as parts of simple mineral combinations, such as bone mineral [$Ca_{10}(PO_4)_6$ OH_2]. Because of their simple structure, minerals are not destroyed during cooking, but they can still be lost if they leak into the water used for cooking and then discarded if that water is not consumed. Although minerals themselves yield no energy as such for the body, they are critical players in nervous system functioning, other cellular processes, water balance, and structural (e.g., skeletal) systems.

The amounts of the 16 or more essential minerals that are required in the diet for good health vary enormously. Thus, they are divided into two groups: major minerals and trace minerals, based on dietary needs. If daily needs are less than 100 mg, the mineral is put in the trace mineral class. The actual dietary requirement for some trace minerals has yet to be determined. Minerals are the focus of Chapters 11 and 12.

organic Any substance that contains carbon atoms bonded to hydrogen atoms in the chemical structure.

inorganic Any substance lacking carbon atoms bonded to hydrogen atoms in the chemical structure.

Water

Water is the sixth class of nutrients. Although sometimes overlooked as a nutrient, water is the macronutrient needed in the largest quantity. Water (chemically, H_2O) has numerous vital functions in the body. It acts as a **solvent** and lubricant, as a medium for transporting nutrients and waste, and as a medium for temperature regulation and chemical processes. For these reasons, and because the human body is approximately 60% water, we require about 2 liters (L)—equivalent to 2000 g or 8 cups—of water and/or fluids containing water every day.

Water is not only available from the obvious sources, but it is also the major component in some foods, such as many fruits and vegetables (e.g., lettuce, grapes, and melons). The body even makes some water as a by-product of **metabolism.** Water is examined in detail in Chapter 11.

solvent A substance that other substances dissolve in.

metabolism Chemical processes in the body by which energy is provided in useful forms and vital activities are sustained.

Nutrient Composition of Diets and the Human Body

The quantities of the various nutrients that people consume vary widely, and the nutrient amounts present in different foods also vary a great deal. The total daily intake of protein, fat, and carbohydrate amounts to about 500 g. In contrast, the typical daily mineral intake totals about 20 g, and the daily vitamin intake totals less than 300 mg. Although each day we require nearly a gram of some minerals, such as calcium and phosphorus, we need only a few milligrams or less of other minerals. For example, we need about 10 mg of zinc per day, which is just a few specks of the mineral.

Figure 1-2 contrasts the relative concentrations of all the major classes of nutrients in a lean man and a lean woman with the composition of both a cooked steak and french fries. Note how the nutrient composition of the body differs from the nutritional profiles

Alcoholic beverages are rich in energy, but alcohol is not an essential nutrient.

Composition (percent of weight)				
Nutrient	**French fries**	**Steak**	**Healthy man**	**Healthy woman**
Carbohydrate	37%	0%	<1%	<1%
Protein	4%	27%	16%	13%
Fat	17%	18%	16%	25%
Minerals	1%	1%	6%	5%
Water	41%	54%	62%	57%

Figure 1-2 You aren't what you eat. The proportions of nutrients in the human body do not match those found in typical foods—animal or vegetable.

genes The hereditary material on chromosomes that makes up **DNA.** Genes provide the blueprints for the production of cell proteins.

deoxyribonucleic acid (DNA) The site of hereditary information in cells; DNA directs the synthesis of cell proteins.

alcohol Ethyl alcohol (CH_3CH_2OH).

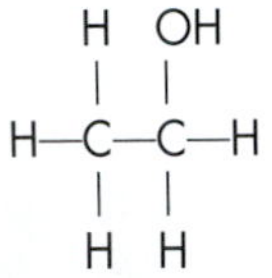

compound A group of different types of atoms bonded together in definite proportion (see also molecule). Not all chemical compounds exist as molecules. Some compounds are made up of ions attracted to each other, such as Na^+CL^- (table salt).

ion An atom with an unequal number of electrons and protons. Negative ions have more electrons than protons; positive ions have more protons than electrons.

In many scientific journals, the kilojoule (kJ), rather than the kilocalorie, is used to express the energy content of food. A mass of 1 gram moving at a velocity of 1 meter/sec possesses the energy of 1 joule (J); 1000J = 1 kJ. Since heat and work are just two forms of energy, measurements expressed in terms of kilocalories (a heat measure) are interchangeable with measurements expressed in terms of kilojoules (a work measure): 1 kcal = 4.18 kJ.

of the foods we eat. This is because growth, development, and later maintenance of the human body are directed by the genetic material inside the cell nucleus. This genetic blueprint determines how each cell uses the essential nutrients to perform body functions. These nutrients can come from a variety of sources. Cells are not concerned whether available amino acids come from animal or plant sources. The carbohydrate glucose can come from sugars or starches. Thus, you really aren't what you eat. Rather, what you eat provides cells with basic materials to function according to the directions supplied by the genetic material **(genes)** housed in the cell (see the Nutrition Perspective at the end of this chapter).

Energy Sources and Uses

Humans obtain the energy needed to perform body functions and do work from carbohydrates, fats, and proteins. Foods generally provide more than one energy source.

Vegetable oil is an exception; it is 100% fat. **Alcohol** is also a source of energy for some of us, supplying about 7 kcal/g. It is not considered an essential nutrient, however, because it has no required function. Still, alcoholic beverages—generally also rich in carbohydrate, such as beer—are a contributor of energy to the diet of some adults.

The body transforms the energy trapped in carbohydrate, protein, and fat (and alcohol) into other forms of energy in order to:

- Build new **compounds**
- Perform muscular movements
- Promote nerve transmissions
- Maintain **ion** balance within cells

Chapter 4 describes how that energy is released from chemical bonds and then used by body cells to support the processes just described.

You have likely noticed on food labels that the energy in food is often expressed in terms of calories. (Chapter 13 has a diagram of the instrument used to measure calories in foods [bomb calorimeter].) Technically, a calorie is the amount of heat energy it takes to raise the temperature of 1 g of water 1 degree **Celsius** (1°C, centigrade scale). Because a calorie is such a tiny measure of heat, food energy is more accurately expressed in terms of the kilocalorie (kcal), which equals 1000 calories. (If the "c" in calories is capitalized, this also signifies kilocalories.) A kcal is the amount of heat energy it takes to raise the temperature of 1000 g (1 L) of water 1°C. The term *kilocalorie* and its abbreviation *kcal* are used throughout this book. In everyday life, the word *calorie* (without a capital "c") is also used loosely to mean *kilocalorie.* Any values given on food labels in calories are actually in kilocalories (Fig. 1-3). A suggested intake of 2000 calories per day on a food label is really 2000 kcal.

Carbohydrates, proteins, lipids, and alcohol provide the body with differing amounts of energy. Use the 4-9-4 estimates for carbohydrate, fat, and protein introduced over

Nutrition Facts

Serving Size 1 slice (36g) Servings Per Container 19

Amount Per Serving			
Calories 80		Calories from Fat 10	
	% Daily Value*		% Daily Value*
Total Fat 1g	2%	**Total Carbohydrate** 15g	5%
Saturated Fat 0g	0%	Dietary Fiber 2g	8%
Cholesterol 0mg	0%	Sugars less than 1g	
Sodium 200mg	8%	**Protein** 3g	

Vitamin A 0% Vitamin C 0% Calcium 0% Iron 4%

*Percent Daily Values (DV) are based on a 2,000 calorie diet. Your daily values may be higher or lower depending on your calorie needs:

		Calories: 2,000	2,500
Total Fat	Less than	65g	80g
Sat Fat	Less than	20g	25g
Cholesterol	Less than	300mg	300mg
Sodium	Less than	2,400mg	2,400mg
Total Carbohydrate		300g	375g
Dietary Fiber		25g	30g

INGREDIENTS: WHOLE WHEAT, WATER, ENRICHED WHEAT FLOUR [FLOUR, MALTED BARLEY, NIACIN, REDUCED IRON, THIAMINE MONONITRATE (VITAMIN B1) AND RIBOFLAVIN (VITAMIN B2)], CORN SYRUP, PARTIALLY HYDROGENATED COTTONSEED, OIL, SALT, YEAST.

HONEY WHEAT BREAD

Figure 1-3 Use the nutrient values on the Nutrition Facts label to calculate energy content of a food. A serving of this food contains about 80 kcal ([15 × 4] + [1 × 9] + [3 × 4] = 81).

the last few pages to determine energy content of a food. Consider a typical deluxe hamburger sandwich:

Carbohydrate	39 grams × 4 =	156 kcal
Fat	32 grams × 9 =	288 kcal
Protein	30 grams × 4 =	120 kcal
Total		564 kcal

Note also that the 4-9-4 estimates have been adjusted for (1) **digestibility** and (2) substances not available for energy use. Such substances include waxes and some fibrous parts of plants. The energy estimates are then rounded to whole numbers.

digestibility Corresponds to the proportion of food substances eaten that can be broken down into individual nutrients in the intestinal tract for absorption into the body.

You can also use the 4-9-4 estimates to determine what portion of total energy intake is contributed by the various energy-yielding nutrients. Assume that one day you consume 290 g of carbohydrates, 60 g of fat, and 70 g of protein. This consumption yields a total of 1980 kcal ([290 × 4] + [60 × 9] + [70 × 4] = 1980). The percentage of your total energy intake derived from each nutrient can then be determined:

$$\text{\% of kcal as carbohydrate} = (290 \times 4) \div 1980 = 0.59 \times 100 = 59\%$$

$$\text{\% of kcal as fat} = (60 \times 9) \div 1980 = 0.27 \times 100 = 27\%$$

$$\text{\% of kcal as protein} = (70 \times 4) \div 1980 = 0.14 \times 100 = 14\%$$

Check your calculations by adding the percentages together. Do they total 100?

Concept | Check

Nutrition is the study of food and nutrients—their digestion, absorption and metabolism, and their effect on health and disease. Food contains vital nutrients that are essential for good health: carbohydrates, lipids (fats and oils), proteins, vitamins, minerals, and water. Nutrients have three general functions in the body: (1) to provide materials for building and maintaining the body; (2) to act as regulators for key metabolic reactions; and (3) to participate in metabolic reactions that provide the energy necessary to sustain life. A common unit of measurement for this energy is the kilocalorie (kcal). On average, carbohydrates and protein provide 4 kcal/g of energy to the body, while lipids provide 9 kcal/g. Alcohol provides about 7 kcal/g. The other classes of nutrients do not supply energy but are essential for proper body functioning.

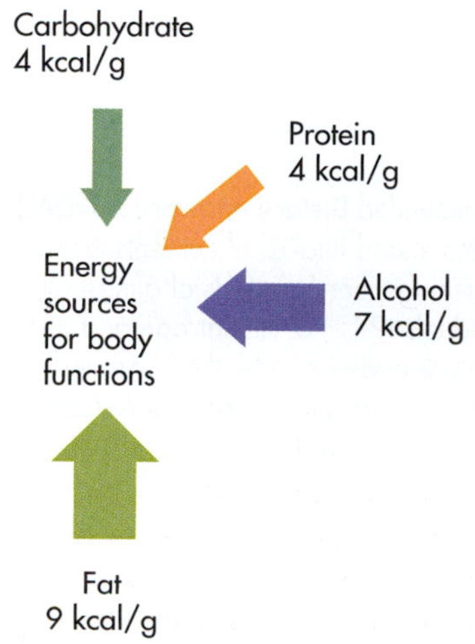

Interest in the Field of Nutrition Has a Long History

In the fifth century BC, Hippocrates said "Let food be your medicine and medicine be your food."

The science of nutrition evolved primarily from the disciplines of physiology, chemistry, and medicine.[8] Our interest in the relationship between food and the maintenance of health has a long history, beginning some 2400 years ago in Greece, during the time of Hippocrates. The Bible even contains references to the importance of certain foods, such as beans, for maintaining health.

The science of nutrition began in the 1600s in Europe. A British physician, Sydenham, in 1674 showed that iron filings in wine can be used to treat anemia. In the 1740s, a British naval surgeon, Lind, found that the consumption of citrus fruits—lemons and limes—cures the disease **scurvy** in sailors. Between 1770 and 1794, Lavoisier and Laplace in France discovered that certain carbon-containing compounds are the source of energy for body functions. Adding to this observation, in 1816 German scientist Magendie showed that dogs fed only carbohydrate and fat lost much body protein and died within a few weeks.

scurvy The deficiency disease that results after a few weeks to months of consuming a diet that lacks vitamin C; pinpoint hemorrhages on the skin are an early sign.

By 1830, it was known that foods contain three major constituents: proteins, carbohydrates, and fats. By 1850, at least six mineral elements—calcium, phosphorous, sodium, potassium, chloride, and iron—had been established as essential for the diets of higher animals. Nutrition as a scientific discipline was now born, as scientists realized that components in foods, some of which are present in very small amounts, contribute to health.

Many foods are rich sources of nutrients.

During the 1880s, a Japanese physician, Takaki, showed that a common disease of sailors, called beriberi, can be treated with evaporated milk and meat. Later research in the Dutch East Indies by both Eijkman and Grijns showed that the same disease is associated with the use of refined rice, whereas use of the whole rice grain prevented the problem. By 1901, it was assumed that refined rice lacks an essential nutrient (later called water-soluble B and then eventually found to be the vitamin thiamin), which was present in the whole-grain product.

In the 1890s, Rubner in Germany and Atwater in the United States established the energy (kcal) content of protein, carbohydrate, and fat. This research also quantified human energy output, showing that, on average, we expend about 2000 to 3000 kcal/day, with some variation at both ends of the range.

In 1906, the amino acid tryptophan was shown to be essential for mice by Willcock and Hopkins in Britain. By 1913, Osborne and Mendel in the United States had shown that food proteins are quite different in terms of their amino acid content.

The year 1912 was a banner year—the term *vitamine* was coined by Polish scientist Funk at this time to describe certain compounds present in very small amounts in foods that promote health. *Vita* came from the Latin for "life," and *amine* came from the term for nitrogen bonded to carbon (technically, called an amine). (The *e* was dropped from *vitamine* to form *vitamin* in the 1920s, when it was shown that some vitamins do not contain nitrogen.)

By 1915, nutrition experts knew that six minerals, four amino acids, and three vitamins—A, B (later shown to be a group of vitamins), and the anti-scurvy factor (later shown to be ascorbic acid, which we also call vitamin C)—were essential nutrients.

Recommended Dietary Allowances (RDAs) Recommended intakes of nutrients that are sufficient to meet the needs of almost all individuals (97%) of similar age and gender. These are established by the Food and Nutrition Board of the National Academy of Sciences.

From the 1920s to today, nutrition research has been a key part of the intense scientific inquiry that characterized the twentieth century. **Recommended Dietary Allowances (RDAs)** for nutrients were first published in the United States in 1943 in response to growing recognition of the poor nutritional health of many Americans. All vitamins we know of today had been characterized by 1949. The research on vitamins such as thiamin, vitamin K, vitamin C, and vitamin B-12 even led to Nobel prizes such as for Eijkman, Dam, Szent-Gyorgyi, and the group of researchers Minot, Murphy, and Whipple. By 1950, some 35 nutrients had been shown to be necessary to maintain human health. Today we know that the minimum diet for humans must contain about 45 essential nutrients in order to maintain health (Table 1-3).

In 1968, Dudrick in the United States was able to support the nutrient needs of dogs using only intravenous feedings of purified nutrients. Soon after, it was shown that

Table 1-3 Essential Nutrients in the Human Diet and Their Classes*

Energy-Yielding Nutrients			
Carbohydrate	**Fat (Lipids)†**	**Protein (Amino Acids)**	**Water**
Glucose‡ (or a carbohydrate that yields glucose)	Linoleic acid (omega-6) a-Linolenic acid (omega-3)	Histidine Isoleucine Leucine Lysine Methionine Phenylalanine Threonine Tryptophan Valine	Water

Vitamins		Minerals		
Water-Soluble	**Fat-Soluble**	**Major**	**Trace**	**Some Questionable Minerals**
Thiamin Riboflavin Niacin Pantothenic acid Biotin B-6 B-12 Folate C	A D§ E K	Calcium Chloride Magnesium Phosphorus Potassium Sodium Sulfur	Chromium Copper Fluoride‖ Iodide Iron Manganese Molybdenum Selenium Zinc	Arsenic Boron Nickel Silicon Vanadium

*This table includes nutrients that the current *Dietary Reference Intakes* and related publications list for humans. Some disagreement exists over the questionable varieties, and certain other minerals not listed. Fiber could be added to the list of essential substances, but it is not a nutrient (see Chapter 5). Alcohol is a source of energy but is not an essential nutrient.

†The lipids listed are needed only in small amounts, about 5% of total energy needs (see Chapter 6).

‡To supply fuel for the brain and other cells, as well as prevent ketosis and the muscle loss that would occur if protein were used to synthesize carbohydrate (see Chapter 5)

§Sunshine on the skin also allows the body to make vitamin D for itself (see Chapter 9).

‖Primarily for dental health (see Chapter 12)

this is also possible for humans. Thus, we had evidence that meeting the needs for nutrients known to be essential at that time sufficed to maintain health.

Over the past 30 years, interest in nutrition has grown. Health-conscious consumers are especially interested in the topic. U.S. government policymakers stepped up their interest after the 1970 White House conference on food, nutrition, and health, and as well increased support of federal feeding programs. Following this, more and more research, much of which was funded by the U.S. federal government, supported the role of nutrition in the maintenance of health, as well as showed a link between poor nutrition (both inadequate and excessive nutrient intakes) and various health problems. To date, we have made much progress in the field of nutrition, but more work needs to be done, and nutrition problems still plague peoples in North America and around the world (see Chapter 20).[16] In fact, the Worldwatch Institute estimates that the number of overweight people now equals the number of undernourished people in the world; each group contains roughly 1 billion people.

The vitamin-like compound choline plays essential roles in the body but is not listed under the vitamin category at this time. Rough estimates of human needs for this compound recently have been set (see the inside cover of the text). Note, however, that body synthesis suffices during many stages of life (see Chapter 10 for details).

Current State of the North American Diet

Humans derive energy mostly from carbohydrates, fats, and proteins. If we ignore alcohol, North American adults consume on average 16% of their energy intake as proteins,

The Food and Nutrition Board also recommends limiting saturated fat and cholesterol intake when putting their diet guidelines into place.

Acceptable Macronutrient Distribution Range (AMDR) Range of intake for a specific macronutrient that is associated with a reduced risk of chronic diseases, while also providing for recommended intakes of essential nutrients. AMDR are set for carbohydrate, protein, and fat (various forms); each is intended to provide guidance in dietary planning.

50% as carbohydrates, and 33% as fats. These percentages are estimates and vary slightly from year to year and to some extent from person to person. This pattern falls within the 10% to 35%, 45% to 60%, and 20% to 35% distribution of energy intake from protein, carbohydrate, and fat, respectively, advocated by the latest advice from the Food and Nutrition Board of the National Academy of Sciences that applies to both the United States and Canada (see Chapter 2). These percentages for each macronutrient AMDR make up what is termed the **Acceptable Macronutrient Distribution Range (AMDR).**[5] Note that recommendations for different distributions of energy intake among protein, carbohydrate, and fat come and go in the popular press.[2] This will be reviewed in Chapters 5, 6, and 7.

Animal sources supply about two-thirds of protein intake for most North Americans; plant sources supply only about one-third. In many other parts of the world, it is just the opposite: plant proteins—from rice, beans, corn, and other vegetables—dominate protein intake. About half the carbohydrate in North American diets comes from simple sugars; the other half comes from starches (such as in pastas, breads, and potatoes). About 60% of dietary fat comes from animal sources and 40% from plant sources.

Assessing the Current North American Diet

Information about the North American diet comes from large surveys designed to find out what and when people eat. The U.S. government uses two primary methods to collect data about food and nutrient consumption: the Continuing Survey of Food Intakes by Individuals (CSFII) conducted by USDA and the National Health and Nutrition Examination Survey (NHANES) administered by the U.S. Department of Health and Human Services. In Canada, this information is gathered by Health Canada in conjunction with Agriculture and Agrifood Canada. Results from these surveys and other studies show that we eat a wide variety of foods. Many people are meeting their nutrient needs; some are not. Chapter 2 will look at this situation in more detail. For now, note that studies show that some of us should choose more foods that are rich in iron, calcium, vitamin A, various B vitamins, vitamin C, vitamin D, vitamin E, zinc, and fiber. Daily intake of a balanced multivitamin and mineral supplement to help meet these nutrient needs is also a strategy, but does not make up for a poor diet in all respects (see Chapter 9).[1]

salt Generally refers to a compound of sodium and chloride in a 40:60 ratio.

Routinely, experts also recommend that we pay more attention to balancing energy intake with need. An excess intake of energy is usually tied to an overindulgence in sugar, fat, and alcoholic beverages.[11] African Americans in particular may need to pay special attention to the amount of **salt** and alcohol in their diets. This is because they have a greater chance of developing hypertension than do other ethnic groups in North America, and these substances are two of the many factors linked to that health problem. Actually, a careful look at salt and alcohol intake—along with saturated fat, cholesterol, and total energy intake—is a useful and recommended task for all adults.[12]

Many North Americans would benefit from a more helpful balance of foods in their diets—greater moderation in the intake of some foods is needed, such as sugared soft drinks and fried foods, while increasing the variety of other foods, such as fruits and vegetables.[5] Few adults currently meet the "five-a-day" minimum recommendation for total servings of vegetables and fruits.

What Influences These Food Choices?

Scientists suspect we are born with a taste for sweets and over time acquire a taste for fat.

We eat primarily for nourishment—we have to eat to survive. But food means far more to us than that. Food symbolizes much of what we think about ourselves. Throughout our lives, we spend 13 to 15 years eating. Important reasons for the specific foods we choose are:[1, 7, 11, 19]

- Flavor, texture, and appearance. These are the most important factors determining our food choices. Creating more flavorful foods that are both healthy and profitable is a major focus of the food industry.

- Early influences. These expose us to various people, places, and situations, and go on to influence our lifelong food choices. Many aspects of ethnic diet patterns (discussed more fully in Chapter 2) begin as we are introduced to foods as children.
- Routines and habits. Most of us eat from a core group of foods: About 100 basic items account for 75% of an individual's total food intake. Overall, food habits and food availability and convenience strongly influence choices.
- Nutrition, or what we think of as "healthy foods." North Americans who tend to make health-related food choices are often well-educated, middle-class professionals. These same people are generally health oriented, have active lifestyles, and focus on weight control.
- Advertising. The food industry in the United States alone spends well over $30 billion annually on advertising. Some of this advertising is helpful, as it promotes the importance of calcium and dietary fiber intake. However, the food industry also advertises highly sweetened cereals, cookies, cakes, and pastries because they often reap high profits.
- Restaurants. Today, about 45% of all food dollars in North America is spent on meals outside of home. This food is often very energy-dense, served in overly-generous portions, and of poorer nutritional quality compared to foods made at home. However, over the past 10 years, restaurants have placed healthier items on their menus.
- Social changes. A general "time famine" exists for many of us. This creates the need for convenience. Supermarkets now supply already-prepared meals, microwave entrees, and various quick-prep frozen products.
- Economics. Food cost is important, but only plays a moderate role in food choices, as North Americans spend only about 12% of after-tax income on food (compared to 50% in India). However, as income increases, so do meals eaten away from home.

A market research firm surveyed the eating habits of people in 2000 North American households. The top meal choice was pizza, followed by ham sandwich, hot dog, peanut butter and jelly sandwich, steak, macaroni and cheese, turkey sandwich, cheese sandwich, hamburger on a bun, and spaghetti.

Daily food intake is a complicated mix of innate and social influences. These factors are depicted in Figure 1-4. Chapters 13 and 15 will look at issues of food choice with specific reference to weight control and eating disorders. The first Take Action activity in this chapter asks you to keep track of what influences your food intake on a daily basis. This assessment is an important part of developing a plan to improve your diet. How are you the same or different from the typical North American?

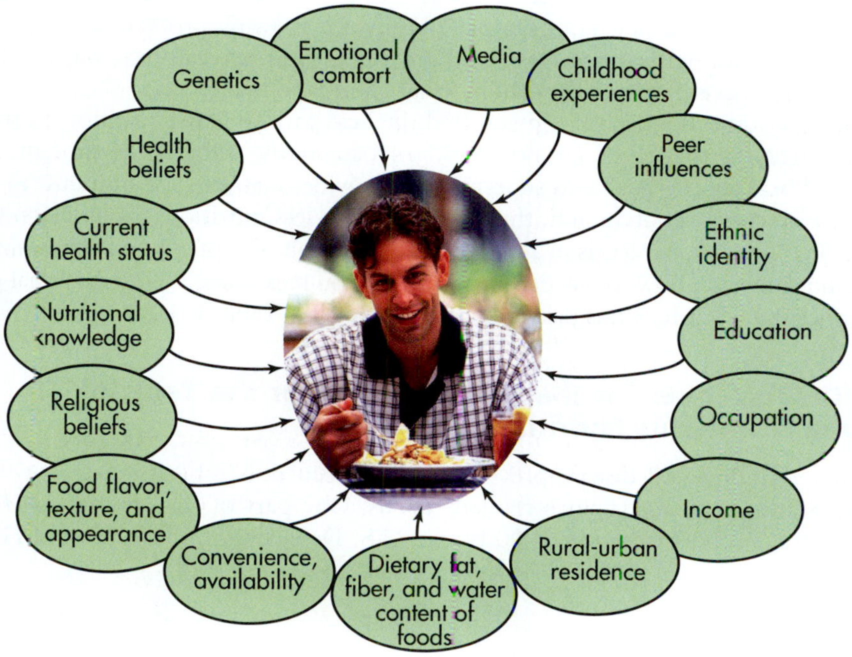

Figure 1-4 Food behavior is influenced by many sources. Which are important in your life?

Improving Our Diets

The fast-paced life for some of us requires eating on the run. What we choose should be as important as how fast it is served.

As discussed, while more efforts by the general public are needed to lower saturated fat and cholesterol intakes and to improve variety in our diets, our cultural diversity, varied cuisines, and generally high nutritional status should be points of pride for North Americans. Today we can choose from a tremendous variety of food products, the result of continual innovation by food manufacturers.

During the past hundred years, North America has led the world in creating new food products. From toaster pastries to microwave popcorn, the variety of food products in a typical supermarket is nearly limitless. Even astronauts in space have their unique food product: a plastic bag containing the nutritional equivalent of an entree, two side dishes, and a beverage, which is kneaded for several minutes and then squeezed into the mouth.

Today we are eating more breakfast cereals, pizza, pasta entrees, stir-fried meat and vegetables served on rice, salads, vitamin- and mineral-fortified juices, tacos, burritos, and fajitas than ever before. Sales of whole milk are down, whereas in the same time period sales of nonfat and 1% low-fat milk have increased. Consumption of frozen vegetables, rather than canned vegetables, is also on the rise. Still, soft drinks are more popular than milk, although not as beneficial to the diet.[12]

One recent trend by food manufacturers has been to promote meal replacement bars (also called "energy" bars). These bars typically contain about 180–250 kcal, with a protein:carbohydrate:fat ratio typical of common diets. However, some bars replace much of the carbohydrate with protein. All of the bars are fortified with vitamins and minerals in amounts ranging from about 25 to 100% of typical human needs. Some people find these bars provide a convenient way to consume a meal (or snack) on the run, while also focusing on certain nutrients they may underconsume, such as the vitamin folate or the mineral calcium. These bars generally cost $1 to $2. Critics suggest these products are really just the nutritional equivalent of a low-fat yogurt and piece of fruit. Typical brands are Ensure® bar, Balance® bar, Gatorade® Energy bar, Slim-Fast® bar, Genisoy® bar, Luna™ bar, Cliff™ bar, PowerBar®, and Centrum® bar. Overall, many of these recent diet changes are advantageous; some are not.

According to Dr. Andrew Weil, the primary danger from food is overindulgence.

North Americans currently are living longer, and many enjoy better general health. Many also have more money, more diverse food and lifestyle choices to consider, and more time to relax and enjoy life. The nutritional consequences of these trends are not fully known. Deaths from cardiovascular disease, for example, have dropped dramatically since the late 1960s, partly because of better medical care and diets. Still, if affluence leads to sedentary lifestyles and high intakes of saturated fat, sodium, and alcohol, health problems can result. For example, obesity is a growing problem in our population.[16] Because of better technology and greater choices, we can have a much better diet today than ever before—if we know what choices to make.

The goal of this book is to help you find the best path to good nutrition. Nutrition experts often say that there are no "junk" or bad foods.[2] Obviously, though, many foods and beverages available in supermarkets provide relatively few nutrients in comparison with energy content and, thus, contribute to less nutritious food habits. One's overall diet is the proper focus in a nutritional evaluation. Chapter 2 will emphasize this point and show you how to balance your diet. As you reexamine your nutritional goals, remember that your health is partly your responsibility (Table 1-4).[18]

Regular physical activity complements a healthy diet; practice both each day. A total of one hour per day is the current recommendation.

Health Objectives for the United States for the Year 2010 Include Numerous Nutrition Objectives

Health promotion and disease prevention have been public health strategies in the United States and Canada since the late 1970s. One part of this strategy is *Healthy People 2010,* a report issued in 2000 by the U.S. Department of Health and Human

Table 1-4 Recommendations for Health Promotion and Disease Prevention: What Can Adults Expect from Adequate Nutrition and Good Health Habits?[2, 3, 10, 18]

Diet

Consuming enough essential nutrients, including fiber, while moderating energy, saturated fat, cholesterol, and alcohol intake can result in:

- Reduced risk for deficiency diseases, such as cretinism (lack of iodide), scurvy (lack of vitamin C), and anemia (lack of iron, folate, or other nutrients)
- Increased bone mass during childhood and adolescence
- Prevention of some adult bone loss and osteoporosis, especially in older adults
- Fewer dental caries
- Prevention of digestive problems, such as constipation
- Decreased susceptibility to some cancers
- Decreased degradation of the retina (intake of green and orange vegetables in particular)
- Lower risk of obesity and related diseases, such as type 2 diabetes
- Lower risk of cardiovascular diseases

Physical Activity

Adequate, regular physical activity (preferably a total of 60 minutes on most or all days) helps prevent:

- Obesity
- Type 2 diabetes
- Cardiovascular disease
- Some adult bone loss and loss of muscle tone
- Premature aging
- Colon and breast cancer

Lifestyle

Minimizing alcohol intake (no more than two drinks per day for men and one drink for both women and all adults age 65 years and older) helps prevent:

- Liver disease
- Accidents

Not smoking cigarettes or cigars helps prevent:

- Lung cancer, other lung disease, kidney disease, cardiovascular disease, and degenerative eye diseases

In addition, minimum use of medication, no illicit drug use, adequate sleep (7–8 hours), adequate water and related fluid intake (about 8 cups per day), and a reduction in stress (practice better time management, relax, listen to music, have a massage, and stay physically active) provide a more complete approach to good nutrition and health. Add to this maintaining close relationships with others and a positive outlook on life. Finally, consultation with health-care professionals on a regular basis is important. This is because early diagnosis is especially useful for controlling the damaging effects of many diseases. Prevention of disease is an important investment of one's time, including during the college years.

Probably the worst food-related trend in North America is super-sized servings of foods, especially in restaurants.[17] Consumers might see these as a bargain, but few need the extra energy supplied by the increased serving sizes. One response could be to share the super-sized portion with someone else.

Today soft drinks are more popular than milk, although not as beneficial to the diet. For example, soft drinks account for on average 10% of the energy intake of teenagers and, in turn, contribute to generally poor calcium intakes in this age group.

Table 1-5 A Sample of Nutrition-Related Objectives from *Healthy People 2010*

	Target	Current Estimate
Increase the proportion of adults who are at a healthy weight (defined as a body mass index between 18.5 and 25).	60%	35%
Reduce the proportion of adults who are obese (body mass index of 30 or more).	15%	23%
Reduce the proportion of children and adolescents who are overweight or obese.	5%	10%
Increase the proportion of persons age 2 years and older who consume at least two daily servings of fruit.	75%	28%
Increase the proportion of persons age 2 years and older who consume at least three daily servings of vegetables, with at least one-third being dark green or deep yellow vegetables.	50%	3%
Increase the proportion of persons age 2 years and older who consume at least six daily servings of grain products, with at least three being whole grains (e.g., whole wheat bread and oatmeal).	50%	7%
Increase the proportion of persons age 2 years and older who consume less than 10% of energy intake from saturated fat.	75%	36%
Increase the proportion of persons age 2 years and older who consume 6 g or less of salt (2400 mg or less of sodium) daily.	65%	21%
Increase the proportion of persons age 2 years and older who meet dietary recommendations for calcium (see inside cover of this book).	75%	46%
Reduce iron deficiency among young children and females of childbearing age.	6%	10%

Note: Related objectives include those addressing osteoporosis, various forms of cancer, diabetes prevention and treatment, food allergies, cardiovascular disease (coronary heart disease and stroke), low birth weight, nutrition during pregnancy, breastfeeding, eating disorders, physical activity, and alcohol use (see later chapters).

Services' Public Health Service. This report consists of health promotion and disease prevention objectives for the year 2010 and assigns each of the objectives to appropriate U.S. federal agencies to address. Many nutrition-related objectives are part of the overall plan (Table 1-5).[9]

The main objectives of *Healthy People 2010* are to promote healthful lifestyles and to reduce preventable death and disability. Minority groups, in particular, are the focus of *Healthy People 2010* programs, as overall health status currently lags in these population groups, especially with respect to hypertension, type 2 diabetes, and obesity.

Concept | Check

Surveys in North America show that we generally have a variety of food available to us. However, some of us could improve our diets by focusing on rich food sources of iron, calcium, vitamin A, various B vitamins, vitamin C, vitamin D, vitamin E, zinc, and fiber. In addition, many of us should reduce our consumption of energy, sugar, saturated fat, salt, and alcoholic beverages. These recommendations are consistent with an overall goal to attain and maintain good health. Our specific food choices depend on taste, texture, appearance, habits and routines, health knowledge and concerns, advertising, and various social trends such as increased use of restaurants.

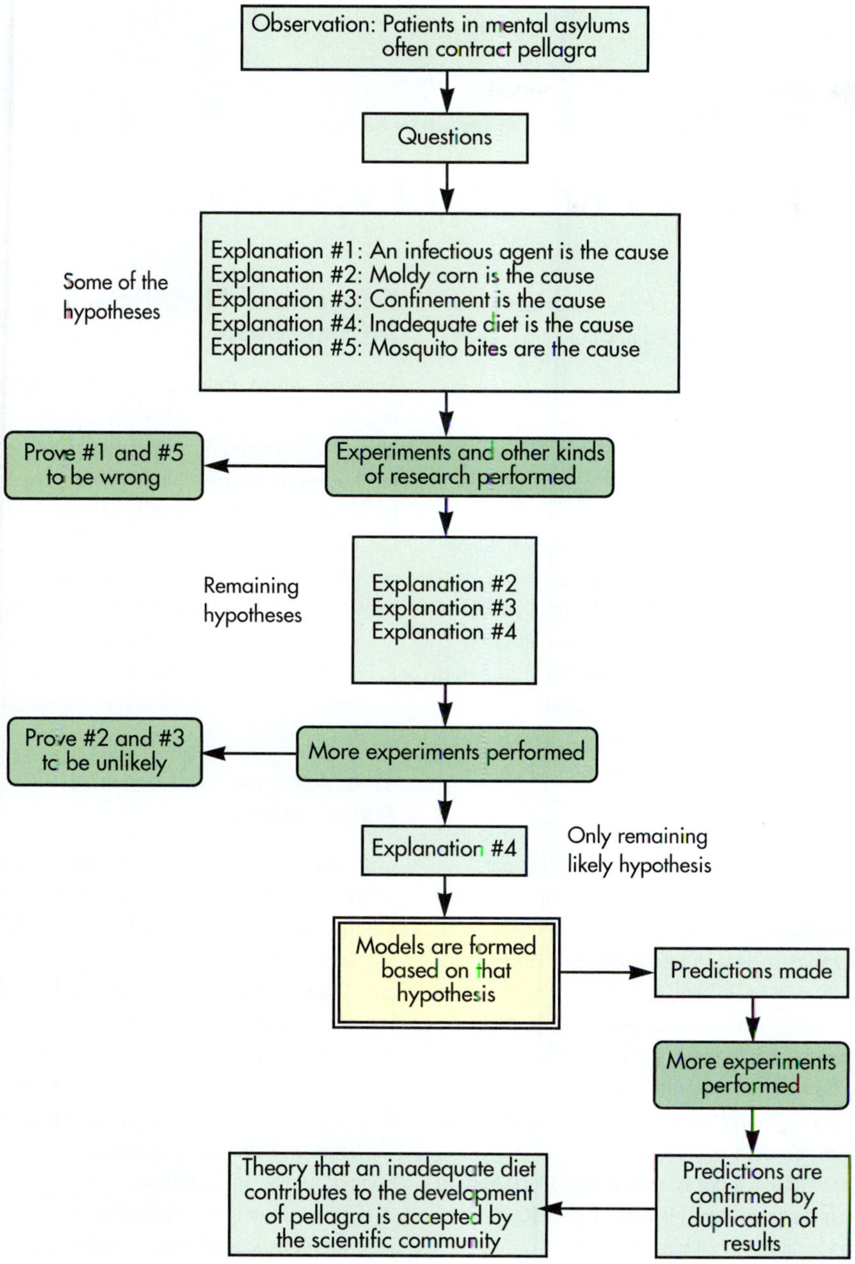

Figure 1-5 From question to theory—the process of science applied to nutrition. Only after careful and thorough analysis and repeated experimentation should a research finding influence our food choices, such as the need to consume the vitamin niacin to prevent the development of pellagra.

Using Scientific Research to Determine Nutrient Needs

People certainly are interested in nutrition (see the Expert Opinion by Dr. Anne M. Smith, p. 20). How do we know what we know about nutrition? How has this knowledge been gained? In a word, research. Like other sciences, the research that sets the foundation for nutrition has developed through the use of the *scientific method*, a procedure for testing designed to detect and eliminate error. The first step is the observation of a natural phenomenon. Scientists then suggest possible explanations, called **hypotheses,** about its cause. Distinguishing a true cause-and-effect relationship from mere coincidence can be difficult.[15] For instance, earlier in the past century, many patients in mental hospitals suffered from the disease **pellagra,** which suggested a possible relationship between mental illness and this disease. In time, it became clear that

hypotheses "Educated guesses" by a scientist to explain a phenomenon.

pellagra A disease characterized by inflammation of the skin, diarrhea, and eventual mental incapacity; results from an insufficient amount of the vitamin niacin in the diet.

Expert Opinion

Who Are North America's Nutrition Experts?

Anne M. Smith, Ph.D., R.D.

Today North Americans are bombarded with information about food and nutrition and its effects on health and well-being. Information on food and nutrition topics is everywhere: in the daily newspaper, magazines and books, on television news and talk shows, on food and dietary supplement labels, and now on the World Wide Web. To no surprise, this explosion of nutrition information has also been accompanied by an increase in North America's hunger for nutrition facts.

North Americans Hunger for Nutrition Information

For over a decade, the American Dietetic Association (ADA) has conducted a public opinion survey every two years in the United States to gauge consumer's attitudes, knowledge, beliefs, and behaviors on important issues in food and nutrition. According to ADA's most recent survey, *Nutrition and You: Trends 2002*, more adults are seeking information on food and nutrition than at any other time in the past decade. Not only are more of us reading about nutrition, we are also listening to healthful-eating messages and, most importantly, acting to improve our nutrition and health.

In ADA's 2002 survey:

- 85% of U.S. consumers said that diet and nutrition are "important to them personally,"
- 75% said that they carefully select foods in order to achieve balanced nutrition and a healthful diet, and
- 58% said they actively seek information about nutrition and healthful eating.

Consumers Are Confused

Although these statistics tell us that North Americans are hungry for nutrition information, consumers are also saying, more than ever, that the vast array of nutrition information is confusing to them. ADA's 2002 survey found that a growing number of consumers (63%) agreed with the statement, "It seems like I am always hearing information about what not to eat rather than what I should eat." This statistic is up from the ADA's 2000 survey, which found that only 37% said that the news "only tells me what I should not eat."

There is such an abundant and continuous flow of nutrition information, but unfortunately its reliability varies widely. A major concern about nutrition information is that certain messages about what to eat or not eat change frequently. Nutrition messages have changed over the years based on new findings from research studies in nutrition science. As with other health and medical sciences, nutrition research is more active today than ever, and new findings are constantly reported. Sorting through the information is difficult and can lead to misconceptions about a healthful diet.

Sources of Nutrition Information

Knowing which sources of nutrition information are most reliable would make decision making about nutrition and healthy lifestyle choices easier for the general public. Since you are reading this textbook, you have already chosen one of the most reliable sources of nutrition facts. Completing a nutrition course at an accredited college or university will provide you with significantly more nutrition knowledge than the average consumer. A list of many reliable sources of nutrition information is available in this text in Appendix K.

The American Dietetic Association

Consumers should know that the best source of reliable nutrition information is literally at their fingertips. Typing www.eatright.org into your web browser takes you to the web page of the American Dietetic Association. The ADA is the top source of reliable food and nutrition facts. The ADA with its nearly 70,000 members is the largest organization of food and nutrition professionals in the nation. The organization is based in Chicago and serves the consumer by promoting optimal health and nutrition.

Online Nutrition Resources for consumers from the American Dietetic Association include:

---

this supposed connection was simply coincidental; the real culprit was the poor diet common in mental institutions at that time.

To test hypotheses and eliminate coincidental explanations, scientists perform controlled scientific **experiments.** The data gathered from these experiments may either support or refute each hypothesis (Figure 1-5). If the results of many experiments support a hypothesis, the hypothesis becomes generally accepted by scientists and can be called a **theory** (such as the theory of gravity). Very often, the results from one experiment suggest a new set of questions to be answered.

experiments Tests made to examine the validity of a hypothesis.

theory An explanation for a phenomenon that has numerous lines of evidence to support it.

The scientific method requires a skeptical attitude. Scientists must not accept proposed hypotheses and theories until they are supported by considerable evidence, and

- Daily Nutrition Tips
- Good Nutrition Reading List
- Health Lifestyle Tips
- Nutrition Feature
- Journal Highlights
- Food Guide Pyramid
- Nutrition Fact Sheets
- Excerpts from *The Complete Food & Nutrition Guide®* and *Dieting for Dummies®*
- Rate Your Plate Quiz
- Frequently Asked Questions

The nutrition topic that has always been surrounded by the most controversy is the area of dieting and weight loss. In 1999 ADA teamed up with the publishers of the "Dummy" books to produce *Dieting for Dummies®*. *Dieting for Dummies®* presents the concept of dieting by focusing on weight management throughout the lifespan. In addition to the wealth of online information from the American Dietetic Association, ADA's Consumer Nutrition Information Line (800) 366-1655 operates 24 hours daily and provides recorded messages that are timely and practical as well as referrals to registered dietitians.

The Registered Dietitian

A registered dietitian (R.D.) is the most reliable source of nutrition information. R.D.'s are an integral part of the healthcare team. Registered dietitians provide objective nutrition information by separating facts from fads and translating the latest scientific findings into practical nutrition information. The registered dietitian's unique ability to translate current research findings into usable information is a result of their extensive education in the sciences, including courses in physiology, anatomy, and biochemistry. The dietitian's credentials, R.D., certify that he/she: (1) has a minimum of a bachelor's degree from an accredited college or university, (2) has completed the rigorous academic curriculum and extensive practical experience requirements established by the Commission on Dietetic Registration, the credentialing agency for ADA, (3) has demonstrated his/her knowledge of food and nutrition by passing the comprehensive national credentialing exam, and (4) continues to keep up-to-date by completing continuing professional development requirements for recertification. Many states in the United States regulate the practice of dietetics through licensing or certification of registered dietitians. The American Dietetic Association's Nationwide Nutrition Network, available online or from the Nutrition Information Line, is a national referral service linking consumers with dietitians in a variety of nutrition areas.

Registered dietitians are a reliable source of nutrition advice.

Dietetics is an exciting and growing field. North America's increased hunger for nutrition information and growing desire to eat right for a healthier lifestyle has increased career opportunities in the field of dietetics. Traditionally, dietetic professionals have worked in healthcare, communities, and food service. Dietetic positions are now common in government, education, research, restaurant management, fitness, and food companies. Registered dietitians frequently work in sales, marketing and public relations and many establish their own private practices. The successful registered dietitian enjoys working with people and has a strong interest in food and nutrition science.

In summary, one of the best sources of food and nutrition information is at your fingertips. The American Dietetic Association and its members, dietetic professionals, have been trained and certified specifically to be our "nutrition experts" and to remain current to promote optimal health and nutrition. For the most current reliable nutrition information visit ADA at www.eatright.org and tell your friends about it.

Anne M. Smith is an Associate Professor of Human Nutrition and Medical Dietetics and director of the Didactic Program in Dietetics at The Ohio State University.

they must reject those that fail to pass critical analyses. Likewise, students should adopt a healthy skepticism and be critical of many current ideas about nutrition.[2]

A recent example of this need for skepticism involves stomach **ulcers.** Not so many years ago, "everyone knew" that stomach ulcers were caused mostly by a stressful lifestyle and a poor diet. Then, in 1983, an Australian physician, Marshall, reported in a respected medical journal that ulcers are usually caused by a common microorganism called *Helicobacter pylori*. Furthermore, he stated that a cure is possible using antibiotics. At first, other physicians were skeptical about this finding and continued to prescribe medications that reduce stomach acid. But, as more studies were published, and patients were cured of ulcers using antibiotics, the medical profession eventually

ulcer Erosion of the tissue lining, usually in the stomach (gastric ulcer) or the upper small intestine (duodenal ulcer). These are generally referred to as peptic ulcers.

accepted the findings, and today, ulcers are managed for the most part by medications that destroy the pathogen. We can expect that scientific discoveries will always be subject to challenge and change.

As you will see, scientific research requires that:

1. Questions are asked.
2. Hypotheses are generated.
3. Research is conducted (experiments).
4. Incorrect explanations are rejected.
5. The most likely explanation is used as the basis for a model.
6. Research results are subjected to review by other scientists and published in a scientific journal.
7. The results are confirmed by more experiments and studies.

Asking Questions and Generating Hypotheses

Historical events have provided clues to important relationships in nutrition science. In the fifteenth and sixteenth centuries, for example, many European sailors on the long voyages to the Americas developed the disease scurvy. The sailors ate few fruits and vegetables, and eventually a British naval surgeon, Lind, as noted earlier, discovered that lime juice prevents or cures the scurvy. After this, sailors were given a ration of lime juice, earning them the nickname "limeys." This simple practice ensured a healthy workforce for the British navy and helped it dominate the seas worldwide. About 200 years later, scientists identified vitamin C, the nutrient present in fruits and vegetables that prevents scurvy.[8]

In a related approach to using historical observation, scientists establish nutritional hypotheses by studying the dietary and disease patterns among various populations in today's world. If one group tends to develop a certain disease but another group does not, scientists can speculate about the role diet plays in this difference. The study of diseases in populations is called **epidemiology** and ultimately forms the bases for many laboratory studies.[14]

epidemiology The study of how disease rates vary among different population groups. For example, the rate of stomach cancer in Japan could be compared with that in Germany.

infectious disease Any disease caused by invasion of the body by microorganisms, such as bacteria, fungi, or viruses.

An example of this approach occurred in the 1920s, in the United States, when Goldberger noticed that residents in mental institutions—but not their caretakers—suffered from pellagra. He reasoned that, if pellagra were an **infectious disease,** both populations would suffer from it. Since this was not the case, he concluded that pellagra is probably caused by a dietary deficiency.

Historical and epidemiological findings can suggest hypotheses about the role of diet in various health problems. To prove the role of particular dietary components, however, requires controlled experiments. For instance, once the high incidence of pellagra in mental institutions during the 1920s was linked to poor diet, various foods were given to patients who had the disease. These experiments showed that yeast and high-protein foods could cure these patients if the disease was not in its final stage, indicating that pellagra results from a deficiency of some nutrient present in these foods. Eventually, this nutrient was found to be the B vitamin called niacin.[8]

Research using laboratory animals contributes to our nutrition knowledge.

Laboratory Animal Experiments

When scientists cannot test their hypotheses by experiments with humans, they often use laboratory animals. Much of what we know about human nutritional needs and functions has been generated from laboratory animal experiments. Still, human experiments are the most convincing to scientists. In the 1930s, scientists showed that a pellagra-like disease seen in dogs, called *blacktongue,* is cured by nicotinic acid. Only when nicotinic acid actually cured the disease in humans were scientists convinced that nicotinic acid (later classified as the vitamin niacin) was the critical dietary factor.

Today, we know that low doses of the mineral fluoride can stimulate growth in rats. However, we still do not know whether this is true for humans, because it is not practical to control the fluoride intake of humans accurately enough to answer the question. Thus, fluoride might stimulate growth in humans, but real proof is lacking.

In addition, the use of humans in certain types of experiments is considered unethical. Although some people argue that laboratory animal experiments are also unethical, most people believe that the careful, humane use of animals is an acceptable alternative to using human subjects. For example, most people would think it is reasonable to feed rats a low-copper diet to study the importance of this mineral in the formation of blood vessels. Almost universally, however, people would object to a similar study in infants.

The use of laboratory animal experiments to study the role of nutrition in certain human diseases depends on the availability of an **animal model**—a disease in such animals that closely mimics a particular human disease. If no animal model is available and human experiments are ruled out, scientific knowledge often cannot advance beyond what can be learned from epidemiological studies.

animal model Study of disease in laboratory animals that duplicates human disease. This can be used to understand more about human disease.

Human Experiments

Various experimental approaches are used to test research hypotheses in humans, including case-control and double-blind studies.[14]

Case-Control Study

In a **case-control study,** individuals who have the condition in question, such as lung cancer, are compared with individuals who do not have the condition. Comparisons are made only between groups that are matched for other major characteristics (e.g., age, race, and gender) not under study. You can think of such a study as a "mini" epidemiological study. This type of study may identify factors other than the disease in question, such as fruit and vegetable intake, that differ between the two groups, thus providing researchers with clues about the cause, progression, and prevention of the disease, but no specific evidence of cause and effect.

case-control study Individuals who have the condition in question, such as lung cancer, are compared with individuals who do not have the condition.

double-blind study An experimental design in which neither the participants nor the researchers are aware of each participant's assignment (test or placebo) or the outcome of the study until it is completed. An independent third party holds the code and the data until the study has been completed.

control group Participants in an experiment who are not given the treatment being tested.

placebo Generally a fake medicine used to disguise the roles of participants in an experiment; if fake surgery is performed, it is called a *sham operation.*

Double-Blind Study

An important approach for more definitive testing of hypotheses is the **double-blind study,** in which a group of participants—the experimental group—follows a specific protocol (e.g., consuming a certain food or nutrient), and participants in a corresponding **control group** conform to their normal habits. People are randomly assigned to each group, such as by the flip of a coin. Scientists then observe the experimental group over time to see if there is any effect that is not found in the control group. Sometimes individuals are used as their own control: First they are observed for a period of time, and then they are treated and their responses noted.

Two features of a double-blind study help reduce the introduction of bias (prejudice), which can easily affect the outcome of an experiment. First, neither the participants nor the researchers know which individuals are in the experimental group and which are in the control group. Second, the expected effects of the experimental protocol are not disclosed to the participants or researchers until after the entire study is completed. This approach reduces the possibility that researchers may see the change they want to see in the participants to prove a certain "pet" hypothesis, even though such a change did not actually occur. This approach also reduces the chance that the persons participating begin to feel better simply because they are involved in a research study or are receiving a new treatment, a phenomenon called the *placebo effect.*

Derived from the Latin word ***placebo,*** meaning "I shall please," the placebo effect cannot be explained by pharmacological or other direct physical action. It may instead be linked to a simple reduction in stress and anxiety. Overall, it is critical to make allowances for the placebo effect in research studies.[15]

In a double-blind experiment, the control group often receives a sugar pill (or other placebo treatment) to camouflage who is in which group and thereby eliminate the bias introduced by the placebo effect. During the course of the experiment, neither the researchers nor the participants know who is getting the real treatment and who is getting a placebo. Sometimes only a single-blind protocol is possible, in which the

Before researchers conduct any research process using humans (or laboratory animals), they must first obtain approval from the Human Use (or Animal Use) Committee at their university or company. The committee determines if the experimental protocol is valid and assesses the risks and benefits of the potential therapy to the subject and, when appropriate, society at large. In human studies, the committee insists that a document depicting the risks and benefits of the study be developed, which the participants must receive and sign. The process is called *informed consent,* meaning the participant knows what he or she is expected to do in the research study and the associated risks.

participants (and possibly some of the researchers) are kept in the dark. Either way, now it is up to the experimental treatment—not just the practice of both groups taking a pill—to show an effect, if one is possible.

Drug studies lend themselves to double-blind protocols because it is often easy to substitute a placebo for the drug. However, food studies often cannot be placebo controlled. For example, disguising a diet high in fruits and vegetables from one low in them is difficult. In such a study, the experimenters should try to ensure that the results from blood assays or other measurements are not revealed until the end of the study. In addition, the results should be kept from the participants until the end of the study. These precautions can eliminate much potential bias. The more bias that is controlled in an experiment, the more confidence we can have in the results.

A recent example illustrates the need to test hypotheses based on epidemiological observations in double-blind studies. Epidemiologists using primarily case-control studies found that smokers who regularly consumed fruits and vegetables had a lower risk for lung cancer than smokers who ate few fruits and vegetables. Some scientists proposed that beta-carotene, a pigment present in many fruits and vegetables, could reduce the damage that tobacco smoke creates in the lungs. This hypothesis helped fuel sales of supplements of beta-carotene.

Two other common types of studies are migrant and cohort. Migrant studies look at changes in health in people who move from one country to another. Cohort studies start with a healthy population and follow them, looking for the development of disease.

However, in double-blind studies involving heavy smokers, the risk of lung cancer was found to be higher for those who took beta-carotene than for those who did not. Some investigators criticized this research, arguing that the beta-carotene was given too late in the smokers' lives to be of much use, but even these critics did not suspect that the substance would increase cancer risk. Soon after these results were reported, the U.S. federal agency supporting two other large ongoing studies that employed beta-carotene supplements called a halt to the research, stating that these supplements are ineffective in preventing both lung cancer and cardiovascular disease.

Overall, health and nutrition advice provided by grandparents, parents, friends, and other well-meaning individuals can't be verified unless it is put to the ultimate scientific test—blinded studies. Until that is done, we can't be sure that the substance or procedure in question is truly effective.[15] One reason for this is the power of the placebo effect. In addition, many common symptoms, such as sneezing, lower back pain, and headache, go away within a month or so without any treatment, reflecting the natural course of the underlying diseases. When people say, "I get fewer colds now that I take vitamin C," they overlook the fact that many cold symptoms disappear quickly with no treatment; the apparent curative effect of vitamin C or any other remedy is often coincidental rather than causal to the natural healing process.

Careful research contributes to nutrition knowledge, more so than personal experience.

All consumers need to become more sophisticated about science, its accepted standards of evidence, and its current limitations. Failure to do so leads many to a frantic pursuit of fraudulent remedies. To ignore science is to follow an inferior path and learn about the dangers of various health practices primarily from the experiences of being harmed by them. Medical science does not ignore novel approaches to disease prevention and cure. Anecdotes and personal experiences are important clues to fruitful experimentation, but they are not credible evidence.[2]

Peer Review of Experimental Results

Once an experiment is complete, scientists summarize the findings and publish the results in scientific journals. At the end of each chapter in this book, many reports are listed describing important experiments that have been published in scientific journals. Generally, before articles are published in scientific journals, they are critically reviewed by other scientists familiar with the subject. The objective of this peer review is to ensure that only high-quality research findings are published. This is an important step because most scientific research in this country is funded by the federal government, nonprofit foundations, drug companies, and other private industries. All these funding sources can have strong expectations about the research outcomes. In theory, the scientists conducting these research studies will be fair in evaluating their results and will not be in-

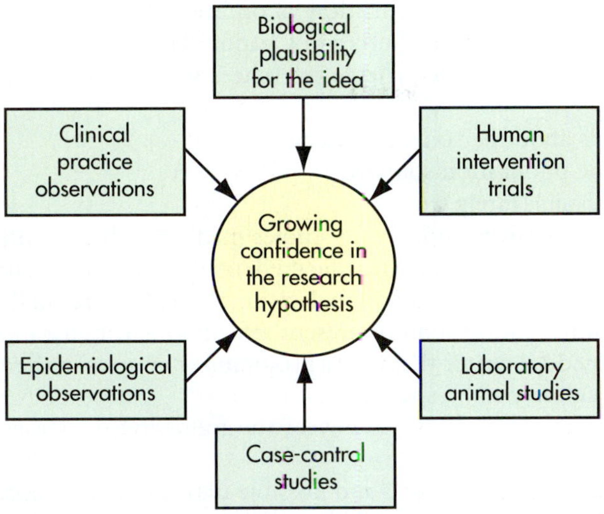

Figure 1-6 Data from a variety of sources can come together to support a research hypothesis. For example, epidemiological studies show that type 2 diabetes is characteristically found in obese populations, compared with leaner populations. Physicians notice in clinical practice that type 2 diabetes is much more likely in their obese patients, compared with their leaner patients. Case-control studies show that obese patients are much more likely to have type 2 diabetes than the leaner comparison group that is matched for other characteristics. Laboratory animal studies show that overfeeding that eventually leads to obesity often leads to the development of type 2 diabetes. Finally, human intervention trials show that weight loss can correct type 2 diabetes in many people. Laboratory researchers also show that the enlarged fat cells associated with obesity are much less responsive to the hormonal signals involved in blood glucose regulation (see Chapter 5). All these lines of data come together with biological plausibility from various laboratory studies to support the research hypothesis that obesity can lead to type 2 diabetes.

Critical | Thinking

For thousands of years, early humans consumed a diet rich in vegetable products and low in animal products. These diets were generally lower in fat and higher in dietary fiber than modern diets. Do the differences in human diets throughout history necessarily tell us which diet is better—that of early humans or of modern humans? If not, what is a more reliable way to pursue this question of potential diet superiority?

fluenced by the funding agency. Peer review helps ensure that the researchers are as objective as possible. This then helps ensure that results published in **peer-reviewed journals**, such as the *American Journal of Clinical Nutrition, The New England Journal of Medicine,* and the *Journal of the American Dietetic Association,* are much more reliable than those found in popular magazines or promoted on television talk shows. Unfortunately, hyped-up press releases from reputable journals and major universities are the main sources for the information presented in the popular media, and claims are seldom scrutinized by journalists themselves for accuracy and scientific validity.[15]

peer-reviewed journal A journal that publishes research only after two or three scientists who were not part of the study agree it was well conducted and the results are fairly represented. Thus, the research has been approved by peers of the research team.

Follow-Up Studies

Even if an acceptable protocol has been followed and the results of a study have been accepted by the scientific community, one experiment is never enough to prove a particular hypothesis or provide a basis for nutritional recommendations. Rather, the results obtained in one laboratory must be confirmed by experiments conducted in other laboratories. Only then can we really trust and use the results. The more lines of evidence available to support an idea, the more likely it is to be true (Figure 1-6). It is important to avoid rushing to accept new ideas as fact or incorporating them into your health habits until they are proved by several lines of evidence.[2]

How to Use This Knowledge to Evaluate Nutrition Claims and Advice

Based on what has been covered so far, the following suggestions should help you make healthful and logical nutrition decisions:

Recently major nutrition organizations put together 10 red flags that they consider signals for poor nutrition advice:

1. Recommendations that promise a quick fix
2. Dire warnings of dangers from a single product or regimen
3. Claims that sound too good to be true
4. Simplistic conclusions drawn from a complex study
5. Recommendations based on a single study
6. Dramatic statements that are refuted by reputable scientific organizations
7. Lists of "good" and "bad" foods
8. Recommendations made to help sell a product
9. Recommendations based on studies published without peer review
10. Recommendations from studies that ignore differences among individuals or groups

megadose Generally an intake of a nutrient in excess of 10 times human need.

1. Apply the basic principles of nutrition as outlined in this chapter (and the Food Guide Pyramid and related resources in Chapter 2) to any nutrition claim. Do you note any inconsistencies? Do reliable references support the claims? Beware of the following:
   - Testimonials about personal experience
   - Disreputable publication sources
   - Dramatic results (rarely true)
   - Lack of evidence from supporting studies made by other scientists
2. Examine the background and scientific credentials of the individual, organizations, or publication making the nutritional claim. Usually, a reputable author is one whose educational background or present affiliation is with a nationally recognized university or medical center that offers programs or courses in the field of nutrition, medicine, or a closely allied specialty.
3. Be wary if the answer is "Yes" to any of the following questions about a health-related nutrition claim:
   - Are only advantages discussed and possible disadvantages ignored?
   - Are claims made about "curing" disease? Do they sound too good to be true?
   - Is extreme bias against the medical community or traditional medical treatments evident? Physicians as a group strive to cure diseases in their patients, using what proven techniques are available. They do not ignore reliable cures.
   - Is the claim touted as a new or secret scientific breakthrough?
4. Note the size and duration of any study cited in support of a nutrition claim. The larger it is and the longer it went on, the more dependable its findings. Also consider the type of study: epidemiology versus case-control versus double-blind. Check out the group studied; a study of men or women in Sweden may be less relevant than one of men or women of Southern European, African, or Hispanic descent, for example. Keep in mind that "contributes to," "is linked to," or "is associated with" does not mean "causes."
5. Beware of press conferences and other hype regarding the latest findings. Much of this will not survive more detailed scientific evaluation.
6. When you meet with a nutrition professional, you should expect that he or she will do the following:
   - Ask questions about your medical history, lifestyle, and current eating habits.
   - Formulate a diet plan tailored to your needs, as opposed to simply tearing a form from a tablet that could apply to almost anyone.
   - Schedule follow-up visits to track your progress, answer any questions, and help keep you motivated.
   - Involve family members in the diet plan, when appropriate.
   - Consult directly with your physician and readily refer you back to your physician for those health problems a nutrition professional is not trained to treat.
7. Be skeptical of practitioners who prescribe **megadoses** of vitamin and mineral supplements for everyone.
8. Examine product labels carefully. Be skeptical of any product promotion not clearly stated on the label. A product is not likely to do something that is not specifically claimed on its label or package insert (legally part of the label).

This cautious approach to nutrition-related advice and products is even more important today because of sweeping changes in federal law in the United States passed in 1994.

The Dietary Supplement Health and Education Act (DSHEA) of 1994 classified vitamins, minerals, amino acids, and herbal remedies as "foods," effectively restraining the U.S. Food and Drug Administration (FDA) from regulating them as heavily as food additives and drugs. According to this act, rather than the manufacturer having to prove a nutritional product is safe, FDA must prove it is unsafe before preventing its sale. In contrast, the safety of food additives and drugs must be demonstrated to FDA's satisfaction before they are marketed.

Currently, a dietary supplement (or herbal product) can be marketed in the United States without FDA approval if (1) there is a history of its use or other evidence that it is expected to be reasonably safe when used under the conditions recommended or suggested in its labeling, and (2) the product is labeled as a dietary supplement. It is permissible for the labels on such products to claim a benefit related to a classic nutrient-deficiency disease, describe how a nutrient affects human body structure or function (called structure/function claims; see the section on nutrition labeling in Chapter 2 for details), and claim that general well-being results from consumption of the ingredient(s). Examples could be "maintains bone health" or "improves blood circulation." However, the label of products bearing such claims also must prominently display in boldface type the following disclaimer: "This statement has not been evaluated by the Food and Drug Administration. This product is not intended to diagnose, treat, cure, or prevent any disease." Despite this warning, when consumers find these products on the shelves of supermarkets, health-food stores, and pharmacies, they may mistakenly assume FDA has carefully evaluated the products. (The effectiveness and safety of many herbal and related products is discussed in more detail in the Nutrition Perspective in Chapter 18.)

The fact remains that many of us are willing to try untested nutrition products and believe in their miraculous actions.[2] Popular products claim to increase muscle growth, enhance sexuality, boost energy, reduce body fat, increase strength, supply missing nutrients, increase longevity, and even improve brain function. Clearly, many nutritional products commonly found in stores are not strictly regulated in terms of effectiveness.[15] The actual amount of product in the package and potency are also often in question. In general, national brands are more reliable with respect to these questions. Finally, few have been thoroughly evaluated by reputable scientists. So if you embark on a self-cure by means of such products, you will probably waste money and possibly risk ill health. A better approach is to consult a physician or **registered dietitian** first. You can find a registered dietitian in North America by visiting www.eatright.org or www.dietitians.ca, consulting the Yellow Pages in the telephone directory, contacting the local dietetic association, or calling the dietary department of a local hospital. Make sure the person has the credentials "R.D." after his/her name ("R.D.N." is also used in Canada). This indicates the person has completed rigorous classroom and clinical training in nutrition and participates in continuing education.[2] Appendix K also lists many reputable sources of nutrition advice for your use. Finally, the following websites can help you evaluate ongoing nutrition and health claims:

www.acsh.org
www.quackwatch.com
www.ncahf.org
dietary-supplements.info.nih.gov
www.fda.gov
navigator.tufts.edu

The sites are maintained by groups or individuals committed to providing reasoned and authoritative nutrition and health advice to consumers. If you would like a daily email on the latest in nutrition research, contact subscribe@NutritionNewsFocus.com and leave a blank message. Nutrition is a rapidly advancing field and there are always new findings.

registered dietitian (R.D.) A person who has completed a baccalaureate degree program approved by the American Dietetic Association, performed at least 900 hours of supervised professional practice, and passed a registration examination.

The American Dietetic Association has a toll-free hotline (800) 366-1655 that provides dietitian referrals through the Nationwide Nutrition Network and nutrition messages in English and Spanish. You can also find out more about nutrition on their website **www.eatright.org**. In Canada, use **www.dietitians.ca**.

Concept | Check

The scientific method is the procedure for testing the validity of possible explanations of a phenomenon, called hypotheses. Experiments are conducted to either support or refute a specific hypothesis. Once we have much experimental information that supports a specific hypothesis, it then can be called a theory. Ideally, experiments are conducted in a blinded fashion, where the subjects and researchers (preferably both) do not find out the results of an experiment until after the experiment is completed. This reduces bias in the results and minimizes the placebo effect. All of us need to be skeptical of new ideas in the nutrition field. We should wait until many lines of experimental evidence support a concept before adopting any suggested dietary practice.

Summary

1. Nutrition is the study of the food substances vital for health and the study of how the body uses these substances to promote and support growth, maintenance, and reproduction of cells. Research in the field has been especially vigorous from the past century to present times.
2. Nutrients in foods fall into six classes: (1) carbohydrates, (2) lipids (mostly fats and oils), (3) proteins, (4) vitamins, (5) minerals, and (6) water. The first three, along with alcohol, provide energy for the body to use.
3. The body transforms the energy contained in carbohydrate, protein, and fat into other forms of energy, which allow the body to function. Fat provides, on average, 9 kcal/g, whereas protein and carbohydrate each provides, on average, 4 kcal/g. Vitamins, minerals, and water do not supply energy to the body but are essential for proper body function.
4. A basic plan for health promotion and disease prevention includes eating a varied diet, performing regular physical activity, not smoking, not abusing nutrient supplements (if used), getting adequate fluid and sleep, limiting alcohol intake (if consumed), and limiting or coping with stress.
5. The focus of nutrition planning should be on food, not primarily on dietary supplements. The focus on foods to supply nutrient needs avoids the possibility of severe nutrient imbalances.
6. Results from large nutrition surveys in the United States and Canada suggest that some of us need to concentrate on consuming foods that supply more of certain vitamins and minerals and fiber.
7. The flavor, texture, and appearance of foods primarily influence our food choices. Several other factors also help determine food habits and choices: our upbringing, various social and cultural factors, the image we want to project to others, convenience, economics, and concerns about health.
8. There are no true "junk" or "bad" foods. The focus should be on balancing a total diet by choosing many nutritious foods.
9. The scientific method is the procedure for testing the validity of possible explanations of a phenomenon, called hypotheses. Experiments are conducted to either support or refute a specific hypothesis. Once we have much experimental information that supports a specific hypothesis, it then can be called a theory. All of us need to be skeptical of new ideas in the nutrition field, waiting until many lines of experimental evidence support a concept before adopting any suggested dietary practice.

Study Questions

1. Name one chronic disease associated with poor nutrition habits. Now list a few corresponding risk factors.
2. Explain the concept of energy as it relates to foods. What are the fuel (energy) values used for a gram of carbohydrate, fat, protein, and alcohol?
3. Identify three ways that water is used in the body.
4. Wendy's Big Bacon Classic contains 44 g carbohydrate, 36 g fat, and 37 g protein. Calculate the percentage of energy derived from fat.
5. Describe two types of fat and explain why the differences are important in terms of overall health.
6. According to national nutrition surveys, which nutrients tend to be underconsumed by many adult North Americans? Why is this the case?
7. List four health objectives for the United States for the year 2010. How would you rate yourself in each area? Why?
8. List one food habit you should work on to improve your health. Indicate why and list three actions to take.
9. What nutrition-related disease is common in your family? What step(s) could you take at this point to minimize your risk?
10. List one nutrition claim you have heard recently that sounds too good to be true. What do you suspect is the motive of the person providing the advice?

Annotated References

1. ADA Reports: Position of the American Dietetic Association: Total diet approach to communicating food and nutrition information. *Journal of the American Dietetic Association* 102:100, 2002.

   The American Dietetic Association states that there are no good or bad foods, only good or bad diets or eating styles. No single food or type of food insures good health, just as no single food or type of food is necessarily detrimental to health. Adults should emphasize adequacy of the total diet over time, the importance of obtaining nutrients from foods, and portion control, coupled with weight control and regular physical activity.

2. ADA Reports: Position of the American Dietetic Association: Food and nutrition misinformation. *Journal of the American Dietetic Association* 102:260, 2002.

   Much food and nutrition misinformation pervades North American society. Individuals should carefully consider the training of those who give such advice, and be assured that registered dietitians are a reliable source.

3. Annual smoking-attributable mortality, years of potential life lost, and economic costs—United States, 1995–1999. *Journal of the American Medical Association* 287:2355, 2002.

Smoking causes approximately 440,000 premature deaths in the United States each year. Even secondhand smoke leads to premature deaths. Both exposures should be avoided.

4. Collins FS, McKusick VA: Implications of the Human Genome Project for medical science. *Journal of the American Medical Association* 285:540, 2001.

In the coming years, genetic tests will be available for many common conditions. This will allow individuals who wish to know this information to learn more about their individual susceptibilities, and to take steps to reduce those risks for which interventions are available. These could include diet and lifestyle modifications and drug therapy. One concern is the potential for discrimination in the workplace once a person's genetic information is known. Ideally, federal legislation will outlaw that practice.

5. Food and Nutrition Board: Dietary reference intakes for energy, carbohydrate, fiber, fat, fatty acids, cholesterol, protein, and amino acids. The National Academy Press, Washington DC 2002.

This report provides the latest guidance for macronutrient intakes. With regard to the amounts of carbohydrate, fat, and protein in a diet, this should be 40%–65%, 20%–35%, and 10%–35%, respectively.

6. Friend SH, Stoughton RB: The magic of microarrays. *Scientific American*, p. 44, February 2002.

DNA microarrays—also called gene chips—are likely to soon revolutionize medical care. Each person will be able to have their own genetic background analyzed; this will help physicians diagnose diseases and tailor health advice. The process of using DNA microarrays is described in detail.

7. Glanz K and others: Why Americans eat what they do: Taste, nutrition, cost, convenience, and weight control concerns as influences on food consumption. *Journal of the American Dietetic Association* 98:1118, 1998.

Nutrition concerns are, unfortunately, less relevant to most people than taste and cost when it comes to food choice. One implication is that nutrition education programs should promote nutritious diets that are tasty and inexpensive.

8. Harper A: Defining the essentiality of nutrients. In Shills ME and others (eds.): *Modern nutrition in health and disease.* 9th ed. Baltimore, MD: Williams & Wilkins, 1999.

A short history of nutrition is provided in the context of the definition of an essential nutrient. Much of the progress in nutrition science has been made in the past 100 years.

9. *Healthy People 2010* targets healthy diet and healthy weight as critical goals. *Journal of the American Dietetic Association* 100:300, 2000.

Many of the nutrition goals included in Healthy People 2010 *are enumerated. Two key goals are to reduce obesity and inactivity in the American population.*

10. Kant AK and others: A prospective study of diet quality and mortality in women. *Journal of the American Medical Association* 283:2109, 2000.

Women whose diets included plenty of fruits, vegetables, whole grains, and low-fat meats and dairy products showed a 30% reduction in death, compared with those who ate the most unhealthy diets.

11. Liebman B: Defensive eating: Staying lean in a fattening world. *Nutrition Action Healthletter*, p. 1, December 2001.

Food in North America is widely available and generally inexpensive, and the number of opportunities to eat has risen dramatically—drugstores, gas stations, and shopping malls to name a few. In response, one strategy for weight control is to fill your plate with salad greens and vegetables and use energy-dense foods as condiments. Also watch portion size—the bigger the portion, the more people eat.

12. Liebman B, Schardt D: Diet and health: Ten megatrends. *Nutrition Action Healthletter*, p. 1, January/February 2001.

Both positive and negative trends in the American diet in the past 30 years are shown in graphic form, demonstrating that improvements have been made in deaths from cardiovascular disease, but obesity is increasingly becoming a problem. Large restaurant serving sizes are one contributor to this problem.

13. Lifestyle and aging. *Mayo Clinic Health Letter*, p. 4, July 1999.

Mayo Clinic physicians provide their advice for a healthy lifestyle, such as getting regular exercise, opting for many whole-grain choices, and drinking alcohol in moderation, if at all.

14. McBean LD: Nutrition research: What can studies tell us? *Dairy Council Digest* 72(6): 31, 2001.

Different types of nutrition research studies vary in their strengths and weaknesses. Rarely can a single study provide evidence of cause and effect between diet and disease. This cause and effect relationship becomes more probable when data from several different types of studies are consistent.

15. McBean LD: Good science: Its role in setting the record straight. *Dairy Council Digest* 72(5):25, 2001.

The public should be skeptical about any nutrition information when the telltale signs of junk science described in the chapter are present. Consumers also should read beyond the headlines and be conscious about those claims that are contrary to current government guidelines and recommendations of reputable health and nutrition organization. It is important to remember there are no simple answers or "magic" bullets.

16. Nelson DE and others: State trends in health risk factors and receipt of clinical preventive services among U.S. adults during the 1990s. *Journal of the American Medical Association* 287:2659, 2002.

Positive health practices enjoying greater acceptance are use of safety belts, mammography for women, and vaccinations. Negative health practices that are currently worsening are smoking, obesity, and binge alcohol use. Physical inactivity is also quite common.

17. Rolls BJ and others: Portion size of food affects energy intake in normal-weight and overweight men and women. *American Journal of Clinical Nutrition* 76: 1207, 2002.

Choosing large portion sizes is an independent measure of total energy intake. This habit should be addressed in connection with the prevention and treatment of obesity.

18. Wellness guide to preventive care. *UC Berkeley Wellness Letter*, p. 4, November 2001.

Important habits that contribute to wellness are: maintaining a healthy weight; performing regular exercise; choosing a diet low in animal fat and sodium and rich in fruits, vegetables, whole grains, and low-fat or nonfat dairy products; eating at least two servings of fish a week; and moderating alcohol consumption if used.

19. Wetter AC and others: How and why do individuals make food and physical activity choices? *Nutrition Reviews* 59(3):S11–S20, 2001.

Health habits are influenced by a number of factors: beliefs, values, life experiences, socioeconomic status, educational attainment, interpersonal relationships, life stage, and social roles. Each decision made regarding health practices depends on input from these and other factors.

20. Wulfsberg DA: The impact of genetic testing on primary care: Where's the beef? *American Family Physician* 61:971, 2000.

Recent genetic research has led to a better understanding of many rare genetic disorders. However, the lack of effective interventions and public resistance suggest genetic technologies will be slow to be introduced into common medical practice. Currently, genetic testing is especially useful for people who have a family history of disorders in which the tests are applicable.

Take | Action

I. Examine Your Eating Habits More Closely.

Choose one day of the week that is typical of your eating pattern. Using the first table found in Appendix G, list all foods and drinks you consumed for 24 hours. In addition, write down the approximate amounts of food you ate in units, such as cups, ounces, teaspoons, and tablespoons. Check the food composition table in Appendix N for examples of appropriate serving units for different types of foods, such as meat and vegetables. After completing this activity, you will use this list of foods for future assignments.

After you record the amount of each food and drink consumed, indicate in the table why you chose to consume the item. Use the following symbols to indicate your reasons. Place the corresponding abbreviation in the space provided to indicate why you picked that food or drink.

FLVR	Flavor/texture	ADV	Advertisement	PEER	Peers
CONV	Convenience	WTCL	Weight control	NUTR	Nutritive value
EMO	Emotions/comfort	HUNG	Hunger	$	Cost
AVA	Availability	FAM	Family/cultural	HLTH	Health

There can be more than one reason for choosing a particular food or drink.

Application

Now ask yourself what your most frequent reason is for eating or drinking. To what degree is health a reason for your food choices? Should you make it a higher priority?

II. Create Your Family Tree for Health-Related Concerns.

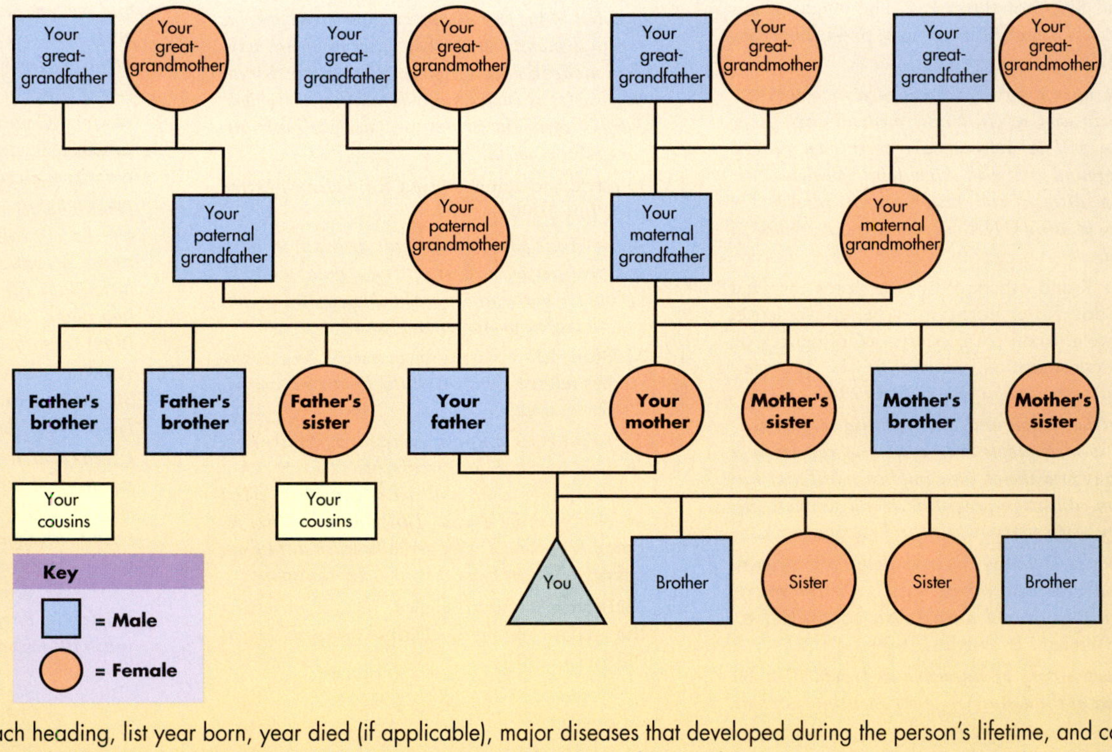

Under each heading, list year born, year died (if applicable), major diseases that developed during the person's lifetime, and cause of death (if applicable). Figure 1-7 in the Nutrition Perspective provides one such example.

Note that you are likely to be at risk for any diseases listed. Creating a plan for preventing such diseases when possible, especially those that developed in your family members before age 50 to 60 years, is advised. Speak with your physician about any concerns arising from this exercise.

Genetics and Nutrition

The growth, development, and maintenance of cells, and ultimately of the entire organism, are directed by genes present in the cells. The genes contain the codes that control the expression of individual traits, such as height, eye color, and susceptibility to many diseases. An individual's genetic risk for a given disease is an important factor, although often not the only factor, in determining whether he or she develops that disease.[4]

Interest in the human genetic code and its relationship to specific diseases has exploded in recent years. The U.S. federal government and a private company have each recently sequenced the more than 35,000 genes present on human chromosomes.[5] These efforts have not actually sequenced the genes of just one person, but compiled a composite genome based on the DNA contributed by a few individuals. Each gene essentially represents a recipe, noting the ingredients (specifically, amino acids) and how those ingredients should be put together. The human genome then would be the cookbook.

It is likely that soon it will be relatively easy to screen a person's DNA for genes that increase the risk for disease. Currently, a woman can pay about $2600 to be tested for a **mutation** in the BRCA1 and BRCA2 genes; these mutations greatly increase the risk for breast cancer (see a later section in this feature). To date, scientists have developed about 600 genetic tests. Many are for very rare diseases and fortunately often are much less expensive than for the BRCA genes. These genetic tests are especially valuable for families plagued by certain illnesses, but more routine testing of now-healthy people to predict future risks of cancer or other diseases is poised to grow rapidly. This is a brand new field and is about to mushroom into a significant part of medical practice, as almost every medical condition has a genetic component. Most, however, are not single gene disorders but, instead, arise from alterations in a number of genes.

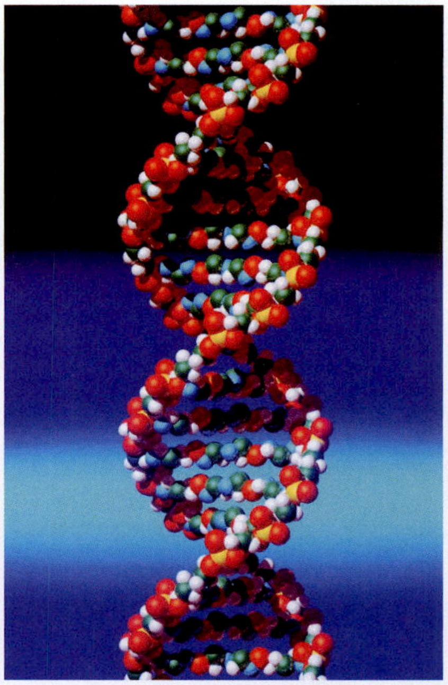

Genes are present on DNA—a double helix. The cell nucleus contains most of the DNA in the body.

Each year new links between specific genes and diseases are reported. It is thought that the decoding of the human genome will ultimately transform the practice of medicine, allowing for the prediction years in advance of what illnesses will likely eventually develop in a person. The hope is then to replace genes that encourage diseases, such as cancer and Alzheimer's, with those that do not.[20]

An exciting application of the Human Genome Project are DNA microarrays, also called gene chips.[6] About 100,000 pieces of DNA can be loaded onto a chip the size of a fingernail. Blood can be processed and then placed on the chip and rapidly tested for altered genes. Genetic material binding to certain areas on the chip can signal a healthy form of a specific gene or alternately a form that is associated with disease. Currently, about 75 laboratories in the United States are using this technology to investigate disease risk. Such information provides opportunities for physicians in the future to diagnose disease more accurately and to prescribe individual medical therapies, instead of treating all patients with the same disease using essentially the same therapy. It is likely that many medications may be more appropriate in certain people given their genetic traits.[4]

mutation A change in the chemistry of a gene that is perpetuated in subsequent divisions of the cell in which it occurred; a change in the sequence of the DNA.

Nutritional Diseases with a Genetic Link

Most chronic diseases in which nutrition plays a role are also influenced by genetics. The risks of developing cardiovascular disease, hypertension, obesity, diabetes, cancer, and osteoporosis are influenced by interactions between genetic and nutritional factors. Studies of families, including those with twins and adoptees, provide strong support for the effect of genetics in these disorders. In fact, family history is considered to be one of the important risk factors in the development of many nutrition-related diseases.

Cardiovascular Disease

About one of every 500 people in the North American population has a defective gene that greatly delays cholesterol removal from the bloodstream. As you will learn in Chapter 6, this and other genetic effects lead to an increased risk of developing cardiovascular disease at a young age. Diet changes can help these people, but medications and possibly surgery may be needed to address these problems.

Hypertension

An estimated 10 to 15% of the North American population is very sensitive to salt intake. When these salt-sensitive individuals consume too much salt, their blood pressure climbs above the desirable range. The fact that more of these people are African American than White suggests a genetic component. At present, the only way to determine whether individuals with hypertension are salt sensitive is to place them on a salt-restricted diet and see if their blood pressure falls. Note also that many cases of hypertension are unrelated to salt sensitivity and are caused by other factors (see Chapter 11).

Obesity

Most obese North Americans have at least one parent who is also obese. Findings from many human studies suggest that a variety of genes (likely 60 or more) are involved in the regulation of body weight (see Chapter 13 for more details). Little is known, however, about the specific nature of these genes in humans or how the actual changes in body metabolism (such as lower energy use in general or fat use in particular) are produced.

Still, although some individuals may be genetically predisposed to store body fat, whether they actually do so depends on how much excess energy—above energy needs—they ultimately consume. A common concept in nutrition is that *nurture*—how people live and the environmental factors that influence them—allows *nature*—each person's genetic potential—to be expressed. Although not everyone with a genetic tendency toward obesity develops this condition, he or she does have a higher lifetime risk than individuals without a genetic predisposition to obesity.

Critical | Thinking

Wesley notices that at family gatherings his parents, uncles, aunts, and older siblings typically drink excessive amounts of alcohol. His father has been arrested for driving while intoxicated, as has one of his aunts. Two of his uncles died before the age of 60 from alcohol abuse. As Wesley approaches the age of legal drinking, he wonders if he is destined to fall into the pattern of alcohol abuse. What advice would you give to Wesley concerning his future use of alcohol?

Diabetes

Both of the two common types of diabetes have genetic links, as revealed by family and twin studies. Only sensitive and expensive testing can determine who is at risk. The form of diabetes involved in about 90% of all cases, type 2 diabetes, also has a strong link to obesity. A genetic tendency for type 2 diabetes is expressed once a person becomes obese but often not before, again illustrating that nurture affects nature (see Chapter 5 for more details).

Cancer

A few types of cancer (e.g., some forms of colon, prostate, and breast cancer) have a strong genetic link, and genetics may play a role in others. Because obesity increases the risk of several forms of cancer, a diet with excess energy is also a risk factor. And one-third of all cancers result from smoking. Again, genetics is often not enough—environment also contributes to the risk profile (see Chapter 10 for more details).

Osteoporosis

bone mass Total mineral substance (such as calcium or phosphorus) in a cross section of bone, generally expressed as grams per centimeter of length.

Bone mass, and in turn bone strength, is similar in twins, as well as in mothers and their daughters. The exact relative importance of genetic versus dietary factors is unknown, but a number of genes have been shown to contribute to a person's overall risk of low bone mass. In any case, children and adolescents need to consume sufficient calcium to build strong, dense bones, thus reducing the risk of osteoporosis in later life. Adults should then continue that practice. The porous bones that are a result of osteoporosis greatly increase the risk of fractures, especially in the wrist, spine, and hip. As discussed in Chapter 11, the risk of osteoporosis in women can be greatly reduced by a combination of medical and nutritional means if therapy is started at least by midlife.

Your Genetic Profile

From this discussion, you can see that a family history of certain diseases raises your risk of developing those diseases. By recognizing your potential for developing a particular disease, you can avoid behavior that contributes to it. For example, women with a family history of breast cancer should avoid becoming obese, should minimize alcohol use, and should obtain mammograms regularly. In general, the

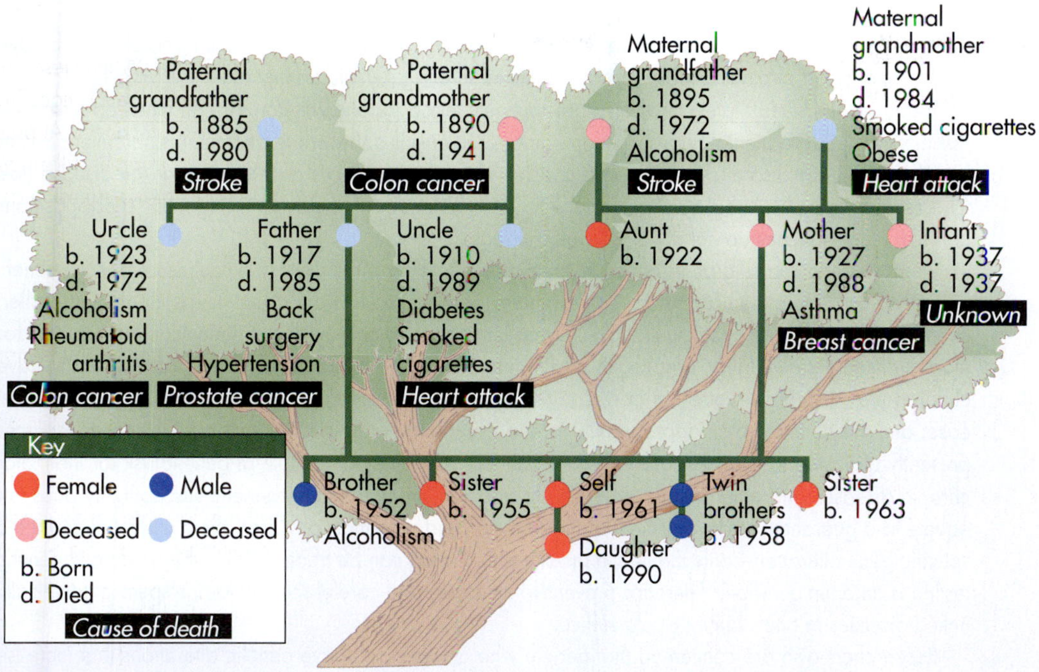

Figure 1-7 Example of a family tree depicting disease presentation in family members.

more of your relatives who had a genetically transmitted disease and the closer they are related to you, the greater your risk. One way to assess your risk is to put together a family tree of illnesses and deaths by compiling a few key facts on your primary relatives: siblings, parents, aunts and uncles, and grandparents, as suggested in the Take Action section.

Figure 1-7 shows an example of a family tree (also called a genogram). High-risk conditions include two or more first-degree relatives in a family with a specific disease (first-degree relatives include one's parents, siblings, and offspring). Another sign of risk of inherited disease is development of the disease in a first-degree relative before age 50 to 60 years. In the family in Figure 1-7, prostate cancer killed the man's father. This means that the son should be tested regularly for prostate cancer. His sisters should consider frequent mammograms and other preventive practices because the mother died of breast cancer. Because heart attack and stroke are also common in the family, all the children should adopt a lifestyle that minimizes the risk of developing these conditions, such as a moderate fat and sodium intake. Colon cancer is also evident in the family, so careful screening throughout life is important.

Gene Therapy

Scientists are currently developing therapies to correct some genetic disorders. Typically, the gene of interest is inserted into a virus, and then this virus is injected into the target tissue. For example, a gene that stimulates blood vessel growth has been inserted into a **virus,** and this combination has been injected into the hearts of people with poor heart circulation. This gene therapy has led to improvement in health. In addition, a number of infants worldwide were treated for a severe immune deficiency disease with genetic therapy by putting new genes in their white blood cells. Many are alive and well today. Scientists hope that one day gene therapy applications such as these can be used to treat many diseases, especially inherited diseases. Still, much more research is needed for that to happen on a routine basis.

virus The smallest known type of infectious agent, many of which cause disease in humans. They do not metabolize, grow, or move by themselves. They reproduce by the aid of a living cellular host. Viruses are essentially a piece of genetic material surrounded by a coat of protein.

Genetic Testing

In recent years, scientists have developed ways of testing a person's genes for the likelihood of developing certain diseases. For cases such as Huntington's disease, a degenerative brain disorder, a positive gene test guarantees the eventual development of the disease. However, with diseases such as cancer and

phenylketonuria (PKU) A disease caused by a defect in the ability of the liver to metabolize the amino acid phenylalanine into the amino acid tyrosine. Toxic by-products of phenylalanine can then build up in the body and lead to mental retardation.

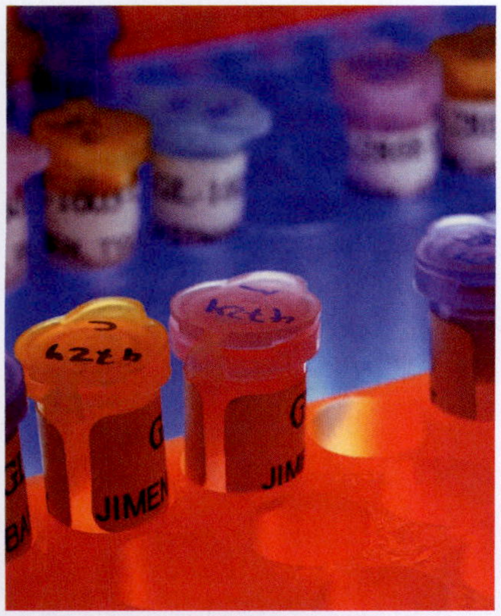

Genetic testing for disease susceptibility will be more common in the future as the genes that increase risk for various diseases are isolated and deciphered.

Alzheimer's disease, a positive gene test simply indicates a greater risk for developing the disease. In addition to the diseases mentioned, risk factors for birth defects, cystic fibrosis, certain forms of muscular dystrophy, and a host of other diseases can be detected through genetic testing.

Today in the United States, newborns are routinely tested for **phenylketonuria,** an inherited metabolic disease that leads to mental retardation and other problems if appropriate treatment is not given. Infants found to have this disorder are put on a special diet, which reduces development of the disease (see Chapter 4 for details). In contrast to infants with phenylketonuria, individuals with genetic predispositions to many other diseases do not always develop disease.

Because genetic background does influence disease risk, certain dietary guidelines are more beneficial for some people than for others. For example, people prone to osteoporosis, as mentioned earlier, need to be more aware of calcium intake. Overall, the benefits of genetic testing include the potential for more individualized nutrition and health advice, more informed decisions by couples attempting to have children (i.e., alternatives such as adoption or therapeutic abortion), increased surveillance for the disease, and the ability to plan appropriately for the future. However, it is not possible, given the resources presently allocated to medical care in North America, to identify all people at genetic risk for the major chronic diseases and other health problems. In addition, in many cases genetic susceptibility does not equate to a guarantee of development of the disease. And, in almost all cases, there is no way to cure a specific gene alteration—only the health problems that result can be treated. Thus, the wisdom of genetic testing is an open question.[20] Perhaps preventive measures and careful scrutiny for the specific genetically linked diseases in one's family would suffice.

Researchers also are concerned that people who are found to have genetic alterations that increase disease risk may face job and insurance discrimination. Testing positive could also lead to unnecessary radical treatment. As well, a seemingly hopeless diagnosis could result in depression or withdrawal from life when a cure is out of reach.[4]

Some experts recommend that anyone considering genetic testing should first undergo genetic counseling.[20] Genetic counselors are trained to analyze family history and evaluate risk of developing or passing along an inherited disease. They can also help determine whether testing is worth the time and trouble, since genetic tests are primarily for people whose family history puts them at especially high risk of having a genetic defect. Genetic counselors can be found by contacting a local hospital or nearby university-affiliated hospital or medical school.

In the final analysis, would you rather know if you were at risk for a specific disease that a genetic test could point out? If so, ask your physician about the possibility and wisdom of testing you for the genetically linked diseases in your family tree. Also, be aware that, throughout this book, discussions will point out how you can personalize nutrition advice based on your genetic background. In this way, you can identify and avoid the "controllable" risk factors that would contribute to the development of genetically linked diseases present in your family.

The following web links will help you gather more information about genetic conditions and testing:

www.geneticalliance.org Alliance of Genetic Support Groups.
www.kumc.edu/gec/support Information on genetic conditions and rare conditions.
cancernet.nci.nih.gov/p_genetics.html Genetics information from the National Cancer Institute.
www.nhgri.nih.gov National Human Genome Research Institute (at the NIH) home page. Describes latest research findings, discusses ethical issues, and provides a talking glossary.
www.faseb.org/genetics Compilation of major genetics societies throughout the world. Information on genetics meetings, society policy statements, etc.
vector.cshl.org Cold Spring Harbor Labs DNA Learning Center home page; includes animation of genetic techniques.
www.ncgr.org National Center for Genomic Resources home page.

chapter 2

The Basis of a Healthy Diet

Chapter | Outline

Case | Scenario

Andy is like many other college students. He grew up on a quick bowl of cereal and milk for breakfast and a hamburger, french fries, and cola for lunch, either in the school cafeteria or at a local fast-food restaurant. At dinner, he generally avoided eating any of his salad or vegetables, and by 9 o'clock he was deep into bags of chips and cookies. Andy has taken most of these habits to college. He prefers coffee for breakfast and possibly a chocolate bar. Lunch is still mainly a hamburger, french fries, and cola, but pizza and tacos now alternate more frequently than when he was in high school. One thing Andy really likes about the restaurants surrounding campus is that, for just about half a dollar more, he can *supersize* his meal. This helps him stretch his food dollar; searching out value meals for lunch and dinner now has become part of a typical day.

Provide some dietary advice for Andy. Start with his positive habits and then provide some constructive criticism, based on what you now know.

Refresh | Your Memory

As you begin your study of diet planning in Chapter 2, you may want to review:

- The terms in the margin in Chapter 1 and Table 1-1.
- The impact of the Dietary Supplement Health and Education Act (DSHEA) on certain label claims in Chapter 1.
- The impact of genetic background on the risk of developing certain chronic diseases in Chapter 1.

Boost | Your Study

Check out the ***Perspectives in Nutrition: Online Learning Center*** www.mhhe.com/wardlawpers6 *for quizzes, flash cards, activities, and web links designed to further help you learn about various tools for diet planning.*

Chapter | Objectives

Chapter 2 is designed to allow you to:

1. Develop an eating plan based on the concepts of variety, balance, moderation, nutrient density, and energy density.
2. Outline the ABCDEs of nutrition assessment: anthropometric, biochemical, clinical, dietary, and economic.
3. Describe what the Recommended Dietary Allowances (RDA) represent and how these relate to the other standards included in the new Dietary Reference Intakes.
4. Learn the food groupings used in the Food Guide Pyramid and list potentially inadequate nutrients in that diet plan.
5. List the Dietary Guidelines for Americans and the diseases these guidelines are designed to prevent or minimize.
6. Describe what a nutrition label currently consists of and which health claims are allowed on a food package.
7. Describe various ethnic influences on the North American diet.

How many times have you heard wild claims about how healthful certain foods are for you? As consumers focus more and more on diet and disease, food manufacturers are asserting that their products have all sorts of health benefits. Supermarket shelves have begun to look like an 1800s medicine show. "Take fish oil capsules to avoid a heart attack." "Eat more olive oil and oat bran to lower blood cholesterol." Hearing these claims, you would think that food manufacturers have solutions to all of our health problems.

Advertising aside, nutrient intakes out of balance with our needs—such as excess energy, saturated fat, salt, alcohol, and sugar intake—are linked to many leading causes of death in North America, including obesity, hypertension, cardiovascular disease, cancer, liver disease, and type 2 diabetes.[19] In Chapter 2, you will explore the components of a healthy diet—a diet that will minimize your risks of developing nutrition-related diseases. The goal is to provide you with a firm understanding of basic diet-planning concepts before you study the nutrients in detail.

A Food Philosophy That Works

You may be surprised to learn that what you should eat to minimize the risk of developing the common nutrition-related diseases seen in North America is exactly what you've heard many times before: *Consume a variety of foods balanced by a moderate intake of each food.* A variety of foods is best because no one food meets all your nutrient needs. Human milk comes close to meeting all of an infant's needs, except that it provides only limited amounts of iron, vitamin D, and fluoride. Cow's milk contains very little iron; neither form of milk provides fiber. Meat provides protein but little calcium. Eggs have no vitamin C and provide little calcium because the calcium is mostly in the shell. Thus, you need variety in your diet because the required nutrients are scattered among many different foods.

Variety—choose different types of foods within each food group.
Balance—choose foods from all five food groups.
Moderation—control portion size so that balance and variety are possible in your diet.

Health professionals have recommended the same basic diet and health plan for the past 30 years: Watch how much you eat, focus on the major food groups, and stay physically active. Whole grains, fruits, and vegetables are among the foods most emphasized for our diet.[3]

A healthful diet requires only some simple planning and doesn't have to mean deprivation and misery. Besides, eliminating favorite foods typically doesn't work for "dieters" in the long run. The best plan consists of learning the basics of a healthful diet—a variety and balance of foods from all food groups and moderate consumption of all foods. Let's now fine-tune this advice—by focusing on variety, balance, moderation, nutrient density, and energy density.

Some people might like to live on pizza alone. What are pizza's nutrient strengths and inadequacies? Check the food composition table in Appendix N for the vitamin C content of cheese pizza. How many slices would you need to eat to yield the vitamin C RDA of 75–95 mg?

(Answer: 30–40 slices)

Variety Contributes to Diet Adequacy

Variety in your diet means choosing a number of different foods within any given food group, rather than eating the "same old thing" day after day. Variety makes meals more interesting and helps ensure that a diet contains sufficient nutrients. For example, carrots may be your favorite vegetable; however, if you choose carrots every day as your only vegetable source, you may miss out on the vitamin folate. Other vegetables, such as broccoli and asparagus, are rich sources of this nutrient. This concept is true of all classes of foods: fruits, vegetables, grains, and so on. Different foods within each class vary somewhat in the nutrients they contain, but they generally provide similar types of nutrients.

phytochemical A chemical found in plants. Some phytochemicals may contribute to a reduced risk of cancer or cardiovascular disease in people who consume them regularly.

An added bonus of variety in the diet, especially within the fruit and vegetable groups, is the inclusion of a rich supply of what scientists call **phytochemicals.** These substances are not absolutely required elements of the diet. Still, many of these substances probably provide significant health benefits. Considerable research attention is focused on various phytochemicals in reducing the risk for certain diseases such as cancer.[5] Because current multivitamin and mineral supplements contain few or none of these potentially beneficial substances, they generally are available only from food.

Numerous epidemiological studies show reduced cancer among people who regularly consume fruits and vegetables.[18] This is true for cancer of the gastrointestinal (GI) tract, breast, lung, and bladder. Researchers surmise that some phytochemicals present in the fruits and vegetables block the cancer process. Phytochemicals are discussed in detail in the Expert Opinion in Chapter 10, and the cancer process also is described in the Nutrition Perspective in that chapter. For now, realize that cancer develops over many years via a multistep process. If an agent such as a phytochemical can block any one of the steps in this process, the chances that cancer will ultimately appear in the body are reduced. Other phytochemicals have been linked to a reduced risk of cardiovascular disease. Could it be that, because humans evolved on a wide variety of plant-based foods, the body developed with a need for these phytochemicals to maintain optimal health?

Focus on nutrient-rich foods as you strive to meet your nutrient needs.

It will likely take many years for scientists to unravel the important effects of the myriad of phytochemicals in foods, and it is unlikely that all will ever be available in

Fruits, vegetables, beans, and whole grains are typically rich in phytochemicals.

Table 2-1 Phytochemical Compounds Under Study [5, 9, 13, 14]

Phytochemical	Food Sources
Allyl sulfides/organosulfurs	Garlic, onions, leeks
Saponins	Garlic, onions, legumes
Phenolic acids	All plants
Protease inhibitors	Soybeans and all other plants
Carotenoids	Orange, red, yellow fruits and vegetables (egg yolks are a source as well)
Monoterpenes	Oranges, lemons, grapefruit
Capsaicin	Chili peppers
Lignans	Flaxseed, berries, whole grains
Triterpenoids	Citrus fruit, mushrooms
Indoles	Cruciferous vegetables (broccoli, cabbage, kale)
Isothiocyanates	Cruciferous vegetables, especially broccoli
Phytosterols	Soybeans, other legumes, cucumbers, other fruits and vegetables
Flavonoids	Citrus fruit, onions, apples, grapes, wine, tea, chocolate
Isoflavones	Soybeans
Ellagic acid	Strawberries, raspberries, grapes, apples, bananas
Anthocyanosides	Red, blue, and purple plants (eggplant, blueberries)
Curcumin	Turmeric
Dithiolthiones	Carrots
Fructooligosaccharides	Onions, bananas, oranges (small amounts)
Resveratrol	Red wine, peanuts, grapes

Some related compounds under study are found in animal products, such as sphingolipids (meat and dairy products) and conjugated linoleic acid (meat and cheese). These are not phytochemicals per se because they are not from plant sources, but they have been shown to have health benefits.

Some research suggests that increasing variety in a diet can lead to overeating. Thus as one incorporates a wide variety of foods in a diet, attention to total energy intake is also important to consider.

supplement form. For this reason, leading cardiovascular disease and cancer researchers suggest that a diet rich in a wide variety of fruits and vegetables is the most reliable way to obtain the potential benefits of phytochemicals.[9] Table 2-1 lists a variety of phytochemicals under study, with their common food sources. Table 2-2 provides a number of suggestions for including more phytochemicals in your diet—essentially more whole grains, fruits, and vegetables—as does the website www.5aday.com.

Balance Means Not Overconsuming Any One Food

One way to balance your diet as you consume a variety of foods is to select foods from the five major food groups every day:

- Bread, cereal, rice, and pasta
- Fruit
- Vegetables
- Milk, yogurt, and cheese
- Meat, poultry, fish, dry beans, eggs, and nuts

Table 2-2 Tips for Including Foods Rich in Phytochemicals in a Diet

• Include vegetables in main and side dishes. Add these to rice, omelets, potato salad, tuna salad, and pastas. Try broccoli or cauliflower florets, mushrooms, peas, carrots, corn, or peppers.
• Choose fruit-filled cookies, such as fig bars. Use fresh or canned fruit as a topping for puddings, hot or cold cereal, pancakes, and frozen desserts.
• Put raisins, grapes, apple chunks, pineapples, grated carrots, zucchini, or cucumber into coleslaw, chicken salad, or tuna salad.
• Be creative at the salad bar: try fresh spinach, leaf lettuce, red cabbage, zucchini, yellow squash, cauliflower, peas, mushrooms, or red or yellow peppers.
• Pack fresh or dried fruit for snacks away from home instead of grabbing a candy bar or going hungry.
• Add slices of cucumber, zucchini, spinach, or carrot slivers to the lettuce and tomato on your sandwiches.
• Try one or two vegetarian meals per week: beans and rice or pasta, Chinese vegetable stir fry, or spaghetti and tomato sauce.
• Look for quick-fixing grain side dishes in the supermarket. Pilafs, couscous, rice mixes, and tabbouleh are just a few that you'll find.
• When daily protein intake more than meets recommended amounts, reduce the meat, fish, or poultry in casseroles, stews, and soups by one-third to one-half and add more vegetables and legumes.
• In the refrigerator, keep a bowl of fresh vegetables handy for snacks.
• Choose 100% fruit or vegetable juices instead of soft drinks.
• Substitute tea for coffee or soft drinks on a regular basis.
• Have a bowl of fruit on hand.
• Switch from crisphead lettuce to leaf lettuce, such as romaine.
• Use salsa as a dip for chips.
• Choose whole-grain breakfast cereals, breads, and crackers.
• Flavor food with plenty of herbs and spices, including ginger, rosemary, basil, thyme, garlic, parsley, and chives.
• Experiment with soy products, such as tofu, soy milk, soy protein isolate, and roasted soybeans (see Chapter 7).

Choosing whole-grain cereals is an excellent way to increase nutrient value of a diet. Ideally, the cereal should have ≥3 g of fiber per serving.

A term has been coined to refer to foods rich in phytochemicals—*functional foods.*[1] This term indicates that the food provides health benefits beyond those supplied by the traditional nutrients it contains. Since a tomato contains the phytochemical lycopene, it can be called a functional food. The food industry especially has begun to use this term.

A lunch consisting of a bean burrito with tomatoes accompanied by a glass of milk and an apple covers all groups. Fats, oils, and sweets can also be added to your diet in moderation to increase its flavor and to help deliver certain nutrients, such as vitamin E and essential fatty acids.

Critical | Thinking

Andy, described in the Case Scenario, would benefit from more variety in his diet. What are some practical tips he can use to increase fruit and vegetable intake?

Moderation Refers Mostly to Portion Size

Eating moderately requires planning your entire day's diet, so that you don't overconsume nutrient sources. For example, if you eat something relatively high in fat, sugar, or energy, such as a bacon cheeseburger with a regular soft drink at a fast-food (also called quick-service) restaurant, you should eat other foods that are less concentrated sources of the same nutrients, such as fruits and salad greens, the same day. If you prefer whole milk to low-fat or nonfat milk, reduce the fat elsewhere in your meals. Try low-fat salad dressings, or use jam rather than butter or margarine on toast. Overall, strive to simply moderate—rather than eliminate—intake of some foods.

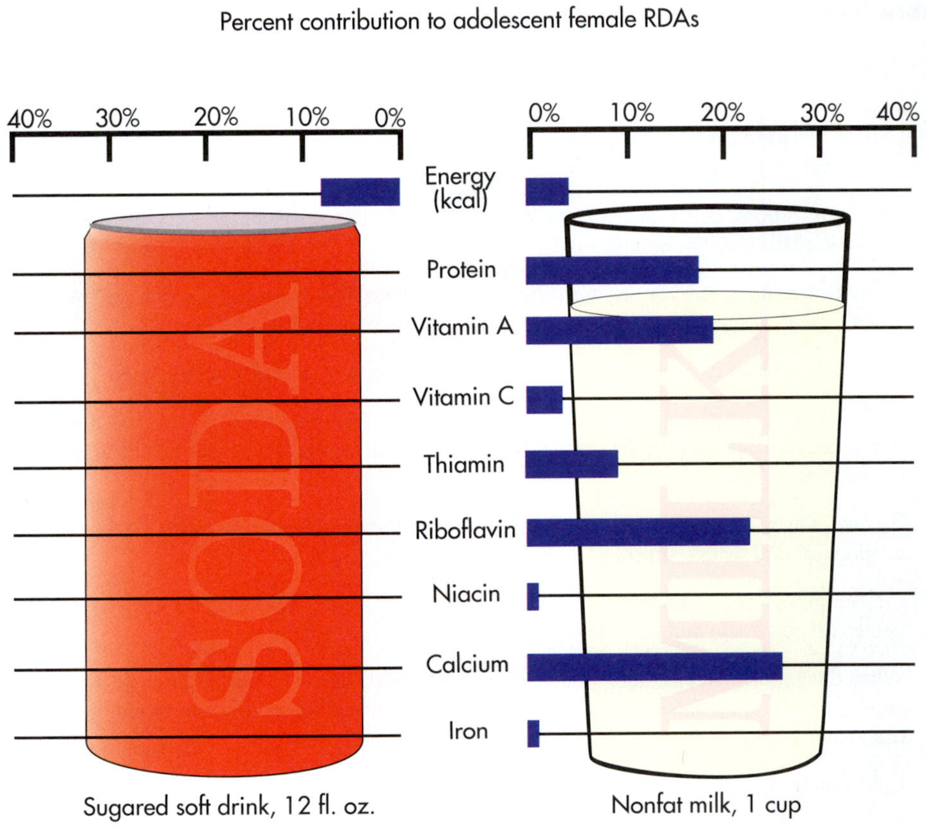

Figure 2-1 Comparison of the nutrient density of a sugared soft drink with that of nonfat milk. Both contribute fluid to the diet. However, choosing a glass of nonfat milk makes a significantly greater contribution to nutrient intake in comparison with a sugared soft drink. An easy way to determine nutrient density is to see how many of the nutrient bars in the graph are longer than the energy (kcal) bar. The soft drink has zero longer nutrient bars. Nonfat milk has longer nutrient bars for protein, vitamin A, thiamin, riboflavin, and calcium. Including many nutrient-dense foods in your diet aids in meeting nutrient needs.

As noted in Chapter 1, nutrition experts often say there are no "good" or "bad" foods. However, many North Americans have diets overloaded with high-fat foods (e.g., whole milk, doughnuts, french fries, hot dogs), white bread and related refined-wheat products, and sugared soft drinks. Such diets lack the foundations of a healthy food plan—variety, balance, and moderation—and pose substantial risks for nutrition-related diseases.[10]

Nutrient Density Can Also Help Guide Food Choice

nutrient density The ratio derived by dividing a food's contribution to nutrient needs by its contribution to energy needs. When the contribution to nutrient needs exceeds the energy contribution, the food is considered to have a favorable nutrient density.

Nutrient density has gained acceptance in recent years for assessing the nutritional quality of an individual food. To determine the nutrient density of a food, simply compare its vitamin or mineral content with the amount of energy it provides. A food is said to be nutrient dense if it provides a large amount of a nutrient for a relatively small amount of kcal (compared with other food sources). The higher a food's nutrient density, the better it is as a nutrient source. Comparing the nutrient density of different foods is an easy way to estimate their relative nutritional quality. Generally, nutrient density is assessed with respect to individual nutrients. For example, many fruits and vegetables have a high content of vitamin C, compared with their modest energy content: That is, they are nutrient-dense foods for vitamin C. Moreover, as Figure 2-1 shows, nonfat milk is much more nutrient dense than sugared soft drinks for many nutrients.

As we have noted before, menu planning focuses mainly on the total diet—not on the selection of one critical food as key to an adequate diet. Nonetheless, nutrient-dense foods—such as nonfat and low-fat milk, lean meats, beans, oranges, carrots, broccoli, whole-wheat bread, and whole-grain breakfast cereals—do help balance less nutrient-dense foods—such as cookies and potato chips—which many people like to

Table 2-3 Energy Density of Common Foods (Listed in Relative Order)

Very Low Energy Density (< 0.6 kcal/g)	Low Energy Density (0.6 to 1.5 kcal/g)
Lettuce	Whole milk
Tomatoes	Oatmeal
Strawberries	Cottage cheese
Broccoli	Beans
Salsa	Bananas
Grapefruit	Broiled fish
Nonfat milk	Fat-free yogurt
Carrots	Breakfast cereals with 1% low-fat milk
Vegetable soup	Plain baked potato
	Cooked rice
	Spaghetti noodles
Medium Energy Density (1.5 to 4 kcal/g)	**High Energy Density (> 4 kcal/g)**
Eggs	Graham crackers
Ham	Fat-free sandwich cookies
Pumpkin pie	Chocolate
Whole-wheat bread	Chocolate chip cookies
Bagels	Tortilla chips
White bread	Bacon
Raisins	Potato chips
Cream cheese	Peanuts
Cake with frosting	Peanut butter
Pretzels	Mayonnaise
Rice cakes	Butter or margarine
	Vegetable oils

Data adapted from Rolls B, Barnett RA: *Volumetrics*. New York: HarperCollins, 2000.

Salads are low in energy density if we limit additional energy content added from salad dressing, and especially if we minimize bacon bits, cheese crumbles or cubes, and croutons.

eat. The latter are often called empty-calorie foods because they tend to supply much energy as sugar and/or fat but few other nutrients.

Searching for nutrient-dense foods is especially important in some cases. For example, this strategy can aid diet planning for people who tend to consume little food energy, including some older people and those following weight-loss diets.

Energy Density Especially Influences Energy Intake

Energy density is a concept that has captured the attention of nutrition scientists in recent years. Energy density of a food is determined by comparing energy (kcal) content with the weight of food. A food that is rich in energy but that weighs relatively very little is considered energy dense. Examples include nuts, cookies, fried foods in general, and fat-free snacks, such as fat-free cookies. Foods with low energy density include fruits, vegetables, and any food that incorporates lots of water during cooking, such as oatmeal (Table 2-3).

energy density A comparison of the energy (kcal) content of a food with the weight of the food. An energy-dense food is high in calories but weighs very little (e.g., many fried foods), whereas a food low in energy density provides little energy but weighs a lot, such as an orange.

Researchers have shown that having low-energy-density foods in a meal contributes to our sense of fullness after a meal without contributing many calories.[16] This is probably because we tend to consume a constant weight of food at a meal, rather than a constant amount of energy. How this constant weight of food is regulated is not known, but careful laboratory studies show that people consume less energy in a meal if the food choices are low in energy density, compared with foods high in energy density. Following (or maintaining) such a diet low in energy density can aid in losing weight.

Overall, foods with lots of water and fiber provide a low-energy-density contribution to a meal and help one feel full, whereas foods with high energy density—especially those high in fat—must be eaten in greater amounts in order to contribute to fullness.

One more dietary strategy to consider is increased meal frequency. Eating smaller, more frequent meals and snacks provides benefits to the body—such as lower blood glucose, cholesterol, and triglycerides—since body metabolism is not as overwhelmed as is seen with large meals. Chapter 6 will discuss this in more detail. For now, know that as long as overall energy intake remains appropriate, spreading food throughout the day is healthy. One idea is to pack a lunch and consume it throughout the day, rather than all at once at noontime.

This is one more reason to support a diet rich in fruits, vegetables, and whole grains, a pattern that also is typical of many ethnic diets throughout the world (see the Nutrition Perspective at the end of this chapter). Still, favorite foods, even if they are high in energy density, can have a place in your dietary pattern if you plan for them. For example, chocolate is a very energy-dense food, but a small portion at the end of a meal can supply a satisfying finale. In addition, foods with high energy density can help people with poor appetites, such as older people, to maintain or gain weight.

Concept | Check

Basic diet-planning concepts include consuming a variety of foods, balancing a diet by consuming foods from each of the five food groups, and moderating portion size with each food choice, so that the diet is not excessive in energy. Choosing nutrient-dense foods, such as nonfat milk, fruits, vegetables, and whole grains, helps supply a diet with many nutrients but not an excessive energy content. Many of these foods are also rich sources of phytochemicals, supplying an even greater health benefit to the diet. Consuming foods of low energy density, such as fruits and vegetables, may also help in weight control, in that these provide a sense of fullness after a meal because of their large volume.

States of Nutritional Health

nutritional status The nutritional health of a person as determined by anthropometric measurements (height, weight, circumferences, and so on), biochemical measurements of nutrients or their by-products in blood and urine, a clinical (physical) examination, a dietary analysis, and economic evaluation; also called nutritional state.

malnutrition Failing health that results from long-standing dietary practices that do not coincide with nutritional needs.

overnutrition A state in which nutritional intake greatly exceeds the body's needs.

undernutrition Failing health that results from a long-standing dietary intake that does not meet nutritional needs.

The body's nutritional health is determined by the sum of its **nutritional status** with respect to each needed nutrient. Three general categories are recognized: desirable nutrition, undernutrition, and overnutrition. Maintaining a state of desirable nutrition is the basis for establishing human nutrient needs and the diet plans to meet those needs that are discussed later in the chapter. The common term **malnutrition** can refer to either **overnutrition** or **undernutrition.** Neither state is conducive to good health.

Desirable Nutrition

The nutritional state for a particular nutrient is desirable when body tissues have enough of the nutrient to support normal metabolic functions as well as surplus stores that can be used in times of increased need. A desirable nutritional state can be achieved by obtaining essential nutrients from a variety of foods.

Undernutrition

Undernutrition occurs when nutrient intake does not meet nutrient needs. Stores are then used up and health declines. Many nutrients are in high demand due to the constant state of cell loss and later regeneration in the body, such as in the gastrointestinal tract. For this reason, certain nutrient stores are exhausted rapidly, such as for many of the B vitamins. In turn, a regular intake is needed. In addition, some women in North America do not consume sufficient iron to meet monthly losses and eventually deplete their iron stores. Reduced biochemical functions and ultimately clinical evidence of an iron deficiency can develop (Table 2-4).

Reduced Biochemical Functions

biochemical lesion An indication of reduced biochemical function (e.g., low concentrations of nutrient by-products or enzyme activities in the blood or urine) resulting from a nutritional deficiency.

Once nutrient stores are depleted, a continuing nutritional deficit drains body tissues further. The body can only compensate to a certain point. When tissue concentrations of an essential nutrient fall sufficiently low, the body's metabolic processes eventually slow down or even stop. This response results from a **biochemical lesion,** which develops in response to the nutrient deficiency. Diminished enzyme function often is the

Table 2-4 Categories of Nutritional Status with Respect to Iron*

General Conditions	Condition with Respect to Iron
Overnutrition: nutrients consumed in excess of body needs (degree of toxicity varies for each nutrient)	Results in toxic damage to liver cells; may contribute to cardiovascular disease
Desirable nutrition: nutrients consumed to support body functions and stores of nutrients for times of increased need	Adequate liver stores of iron, adequate blood values for iron-related compounds
Undernutrition: nutrient intake does not meet nutrient needs; biochemical changes then take place	Many changes in body functions associated with a decline in iron status (e.g., iron-containing proteins and pigments in the blood drop below acceptable amounts [e.g., 12 ng/ml] and oxygen supply to body tissues is reduced)
Clinical signs and symptoms; these effects eventually are seen	Pale complexion; fatigue upon exertion; "spooning" of the nails in a severe deficiency; poor body temperature regulation

*This general scheme can apply to all nutrients. Iron was chosen because you are likely to be familiar with this nutrient. Note that ng refers to nanograms, or 10^{-9} grams.

cause of the slowdown in biochemical function. This type of nutrient deficiency is termed **subclinical** because there are no signs or symptoms. At the subclinical stage for poor iron status, low concentrations of hemoglobin (a red blood cell protein) are found in the blood because the synthesis of hemoglobin requires iron.

A sign is a feature visible on examination, such as flaky skin. A symptom is a change in body function that is not necessarily apparent to an examiner. An example is stomach pain.

Clinical Signs and Symptoms

If a biochemical deficit becomes severe, clinical signs and symptoms eventually develop and become outwardly apparent. It is then possible to note **clinical lesions** in the body, perhaps in the skin, hair, nails, tongue, or eyes. In the case of an iron deficiency, the complexion may become very pale in Caucasians, and fatigue can quickly develop during even moderate activity.

subclinical Disease or disorder that is present but not severe enough to produce signs and symptoms that can be detected or diagnosed.

clinical lesion A sign seen on physical examination or a symptom perceived by the patient resulting from a nutritional deficiency.

Overnutrition

Prolonged consumption of more nutrients than the body needs can lead to overnutrition. In the short run, for instance a week or two, overnutrition may cause only a few symptoms, such as stomach distress from excess fiber or iron intake. But if kept up, some nutrients may increase to toxic amounts, which can lead to serious disease. For example, too much vitamin A can have negative effects, particularly in children, pregnant women, and older adults.

The most common type of overnutrition in industrialized nations—excess intake of energy-yielding nutrients—often leads to obesity. In the long run, obesity can then lead to other serious diseases, such as type 2 diabetes and certain forms of cancer. Use the website shapeup.org to learn more about the importance of avoiding this form of overnutrition.

For most vitamins and minerals, the gap between desirable intake and overnutrition is wide. Therefore, even if people take a typical multivitamin and mineral supplement daily, they probably won't receive a harmful amount of any nutrient. However, the gap between optimal intake and overnutrition is very narrow for vitamin A, calcium, iron, copper, and other minerals. Thus, if you take nutrient supplements, keep a close eye on your total vitamin and mineral intake both from food and from supplements to avoid toxicity. Men in general and older women should be especially cautious of supplements containing iron (see Chapter 9 for further advice on use of nutrient supplements).

Table 2-5 Conducting an Evaluation of Nutritional Health

Component	Example
Background histories	Medical history, including current diseases and past surgeries
	Medications history
	Social history (marital status, cooking facilities)
	Family history
	Economic status
	Education attainment
Nutritional parameters	Anthropometric assessment: height, weight, skinfold thickness, arm muscle circumference, and other parameters
	Biochemical (laboratory) assessment of blood and urine: enzyme activities, concentrations of nutrients or their by-products
	Clinical assessment (physical examination): general appearance of skin, eyes, and tongue; rapid hair loss; sense of touch; ability to walk
	Diet history: usual intake or record of previous days' meals

How Could Your Nutritional State Be Measured?

To find out how nutritionally fit *you* are, a nutritional assessment—either whole or in part—needs to be performed (Table 2-5). Generally, this is performed by a physician, often with the aid of a registered dietitian.

Analyzing Background Factors

Since family history plays an important role in determining nutritional and health status, it must be carefully recorded and critically analyzed as part of a nutritional assessment (review the Nutrition Perspective in Chapter 1). Other related background components include: a medical history, especially for any disease states or treatments such as medications that could impede nutrient absorptive processes or ultimate use; economic history to determine the ability to purchase and prepare appropriate foods needed to maintain health; and educational attainment to determine the degree of complexity that can be used in written materials and oral discussions.

Evaluating the ABCDEs

anthropometric Pertaining to the measurement of body weight and the lengths, circumferences, and thicknesses of parts of the body.

Four additional components further add to the complete nutritional picture. **Anthropometric** measurements of height, weight, body skinfolds, and body circumferences are an excellent first line of attack. They are easy to obtain and are generally reliable. However, an in-depth examination of nutritional health is impossible without the more expensive process of biochemical assessment. This involves the measurement of specific blood enzyme activities and of the concentrations of nutrients and nutrient by-products in the blood, urine, and feces. For example, in Chapter 10 you will learn that the status of the vitamin thiamin in the body is measured in part by determining the activity of an enzyme (specifically, transketolase) used in the breakdown of glucose. It is possible to isolate that enzyme from cells, such as red blood cells, and determine if it can process its starting products quickly enough. To test for this, such cells are broken open and thiamin is added to the preparation to see if this speeds the rate of the transketolase enzyme by more than 25%. If so, we say that the red blood cells lack sufficient thiamin for the enzyme to function at maximal capacity. Presumably, the body would benefit if maximal capacity were possible.

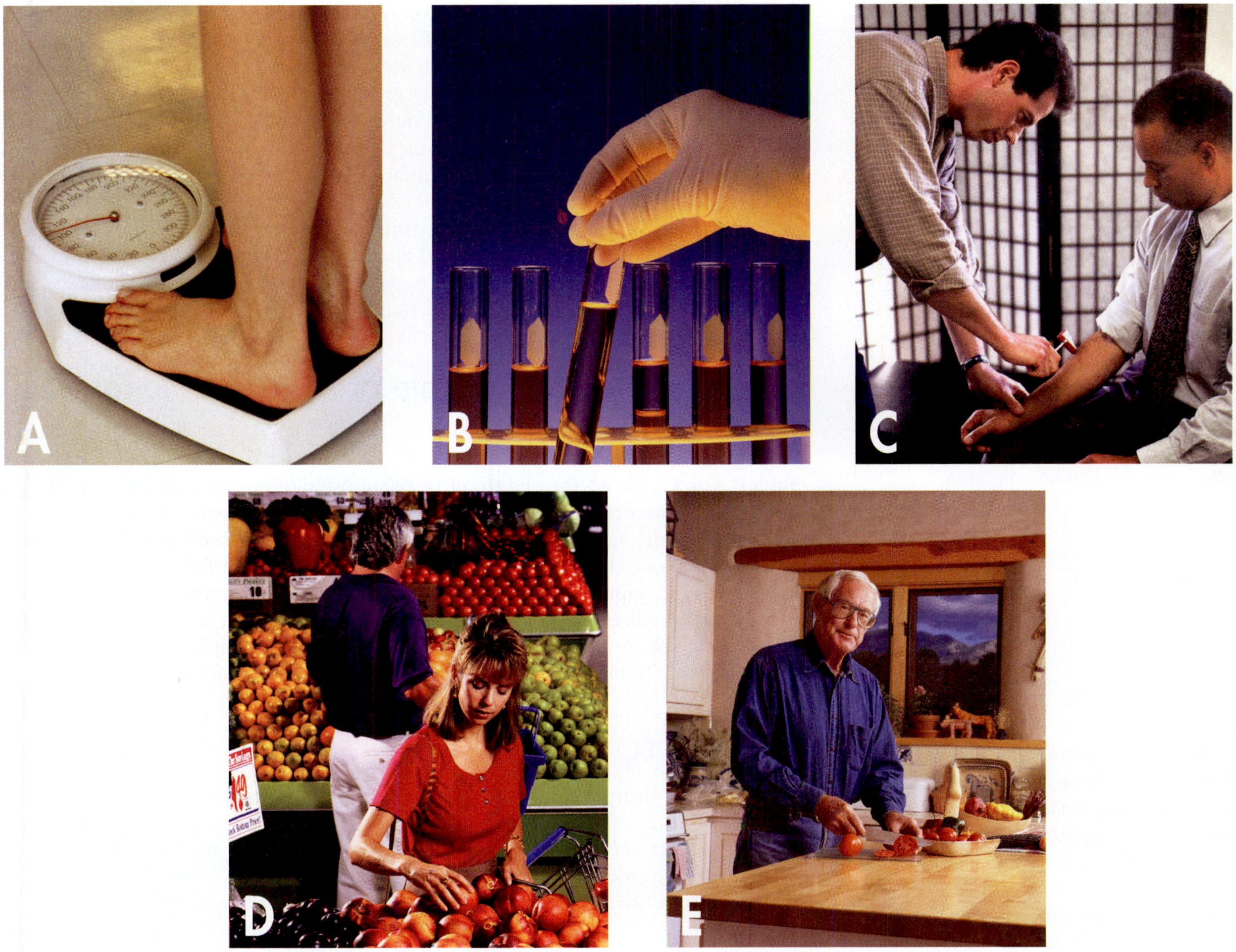

Figure 2-2 (a) **A**nthropometric, (b) **B**iochemical, (c) **C**linical, and (d) **D**ietary information helps determine a person's nutritional state. (e) **E**conomic status adds further information, rounding out the **ABCDEs** of nutritional assessment.

A clinical examination would follow, during which a health professional would search for any physical evidence of diet-related diseases. Then, a diet history, documenting at least the previous few days' intake, would look into possible problem areas. Finally, current economic status, discussed earlier, is added to the picture, such as the ability to purchase and prepare appropriate foods needed to maintain health. Now the true nutritional state of a person emerges (Figure 2-2). Together these activities form the ABCDEs of nutritional assessment: **a**nthropometric measurement, **b**iochemical assessment, **c**linical examination, **d**iet history, and **e**conomic status.

Recognizing the Limitations of Nutritional Assessment

As mentioned, a long time may elapse between the initial development of poor nutritional health and the first clinical evidence of a problem. Recall that a diet high in saturated (typically solid) fat often increases blood cholesterol, but without producing any clinical evidence for years. However, when the blood vessels become sufficiently blocked by cholesterol and other materials, chest pain during physical activity or a heart

A practical example using the ABCDEs for evaluating nutritional state can be illustrated in a person who chronically abuses alcohol. Upon evaluation, the physician notes:

(a) Low weight-for-height, muscle wasting in the upper body
(b) Low amounts of the vitamins thiamin and folate in the blood
(c) Psychological confusion, facial sores, and uncoordinated movement
(d) Dietary intake of little more than alcohol-fortified wine and hamburgers for the last week
(e) Currently residing in a homeless shelter; $35.00 in wallet; unemployed

Evaluation: This person needs professional attention, including nutrient repletion.

attack may occur. Much current nutrition research aims to develop better methods for early detection of nutrition-related problems such as this.

Another example in the delay of evidence that serious consequences are occurring is with a calcium deficiency, a particularly relevant issue for adolescent females. Many young women consume well below the needed amount of calcium but often suffer no ill effects in their younger years. However, women whose bone structures do not reach full potential during the years of growth are likely to face an increased risk for osteoporosis later in life.

Furthermore, clinical evidence of nutritional deficiencies is often not very specific, such as diarrhea, an irregular walk, and facial sores. These may have different causes. Long lag times and vague evidence often make it difficult to establish a link between an individual's current diet and nutritional state.

Concern About the State of Your Nutritional Health Is Important

Table 1-4 in Chapter 1 showed the close relationship of nutrition and health. The good news is that this attention to maintaining nutritional health contributes to the goal of achieving a long, vigorous life. For example, a recent study found that women who ate a varied diet (one that was rich in fiber, that included some fish, and that was low in fried foods and animal fat), avoided overweight, regularly drank a small amount of alcohol daily, exercised on a daily basis for at least 30 minutes, and avoided smoking reduced their risk of cardiovascular disease by over 80%, compared to women without these habits.[17] Should all adults follow this example (alcohol use is optional)?

Critical | Thinking

Tom loves to eat hamburgers, fries, and lots of pizza with double amounts of cheese. He rarely eats any vegetables and fruits but, instead, snacks on cookies and ice cream. He insists that he has no problems with his health, is rarely ill, and doesn't see how his diet could cause him any health risks. How would you explain to Tom that, despite his current good health, his diet could predispose him to future health problems?

Concept | Check

A desirable nutritional status results when the body has enough nutrients to function fully and contains stores to use in times of increased needs. When nutrient intake fails to meet body needs, undernutrition develops. Symptoms of such an inadequate nutrient intake can take months or years to develop. Overloading the body with nutrients, leading to overnutrition, is another potential problem to avoid. Nutritional status can be assessed by using anthropometric measurements, biochemical evidence, clinical evaluation, diet history, and economic status (ABCDEs).

Setting Nutrient Needs—Dietary Reference Intakes (DRIs)

Using the tools of nutrition research and nutrition assessment discussed so far, the amount of each nutrient needed by the human body can be determined. People have actually puzzled over this question for centuries. During World War II, when many men were rejected from military service because of the effects of poor nutrition on their health, the need for official dietary recommendations was recognized. In 1941, a group of 25 scientists formed the first Food and Nutrition Board. They established dietary standards for evaluating the nutritional intakes of large populations and for planning agricultural production, first published in 1943.

The current Food and Nutrition Board was formed in 1993. The framework of the latest recommendations are named **Dietary Reference Intakes (DRIs)** and have been released in stages throughout the last few years.

Dietary Reference Intakes (DRIs) The term used to encompass the latest nutrient recommendations made by the Food and Nutrition Board of the National Academy of Sciences. These include RDAs.

Under the umbrella of the DRIs, four sets of standards have been established: Estimated Average Requirements (EARs), Recommended Dietary Allowances (RDAs),

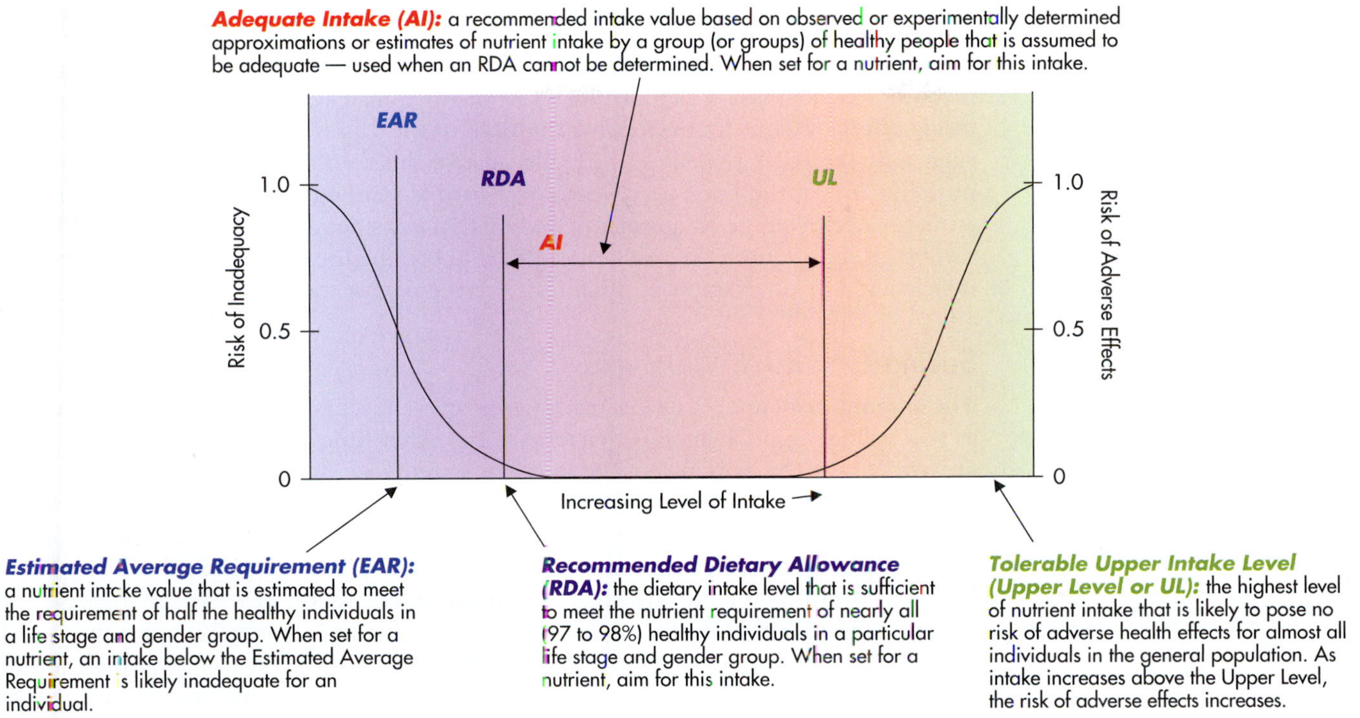

Adequate Intake (AI): a recommended intake value based on observed or experimentally determined approximations or estimates of nutrient intake by a group (or groups) of healthy people that is assumed to be adequate — used when an RDA cannot be determined. When set for a nutrient, aim for this intake.
EAR
RDA
AI
UL
1.0
0.5
0
Risk of Inadequacy
Risk of Adverse Effects
Increasing Level of Intake
Estimated Average Requirement (EAR): a nutrient intake value that is estimated to meet the requirement of half the healthy individuals in a life stage and gender group. When set for a nutrient, an intake below the Estimated Average Requirement is likely inadequate for an individual.
Recommended Dietary Allowance (RDA): the dietary intake level that is sufficient to meet the nutrient requirement of nearly all (97 to 98%) healthy individuals in a particular life stage and gender group. When set for a nutrient, aim for this intake.
Tolerable Upper Intake Level (Upper Level or UL): the highest level of nutrient intake that is likely to pose no risk of adverse health effects for almost all individuals in the general population. As intake increases above the Upper Level, the risk of adverse effects increases.

Figure 2-3 Dietary Reference Intakes (DRIs). This figure shows that 50% of North Americans would have an inadequate intake by consuming the *Estimated Average Requirement (EAR),* whereas 50% would have their needs met. Only about 2 to 3% of such people would have an inadequate intake if each were to meet the *Recommended Dietary Allowance (RDA),* whereas 97 to 98% would have their needs met. At intakes between the RDA and the *Tolerable Upper Intake Level* (*Upper Level* or *UL*), the risk of either an inadequate diet or adverse effects from the nutrient in question is close to 0. The Upper Level is then the highest level of nutrient intake that is likely to pose no risks of adverse health effects to almost all individuals in the general population. At intakes above the Upper Level, the margin of safety to protect against adverse effects is reduced. The *Adequate Intake (AI),* set for some nutrients instead of an RDA, lies somewhere between the Estimated Average Requirement and the Upper Level. In determining the Adequate Intake for a nutrient, it is expected that the amount exceeds the RDA for that nutrient, if an RDA were known. Thus, the Adequate Intake should cover the needs of more than 97 to 98% of individuals. The actual degree to which the Adequate Intake exceeds the RDA is likely to differ among the various nutrients and population groups. The Food and Nutrition Board states that there is no established benefit for healthy individuals if they consume nutrient intakes above the RDA or Adequate Intake.

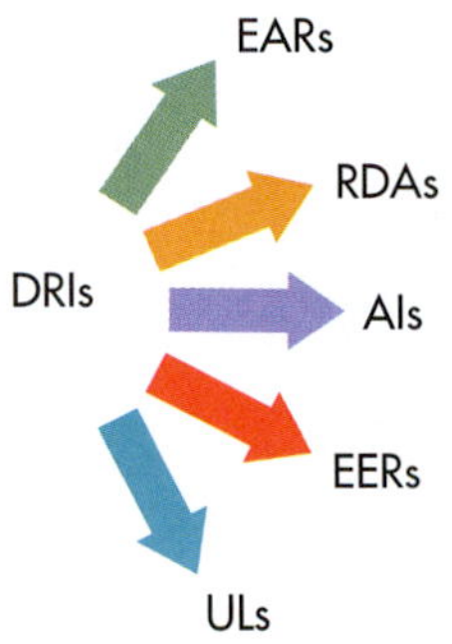

DRIs
EARs
RDAs
AIs
EERs
ULs

Adequate Intakes (AIs), and Tolerable Upper Intake Levels (Upper Levels or ULs) (see the inside cover of this textbook). All refer to intake averaged over a number of days, not a single day.[2] Following is a more detailed discussion of each of these standards.

Estimated Average Requirements (EARs)

Estimated Average Requirements are the nutrient intake that is estimated to meet the needs of 50% of the individuals in a certain age and gender group (Fig. 2-3). To set an Estimated Average Requirement, the Food and Nutrition Board must be able to agree on a specific measurable functional marker to use for establishing nutrient adequacy. Such markers are typically the activity of an enzyme in the body or the ability of a cell to maintain physiological health. (The specific markers used for various nutrients will be discussed in Chapters 9 through 12.) If no measurable functional marker is available, no Estimated Average Requirement can be set. This is the case for the mineral calcium. The Estimated Average Requirement also includes an adjustment for the amount of each nutrient that passes through the digestive tract unabsorbed. At this intake, though, the needs of the other 50% of the population would not be met. Thus, the Estimated Average Requirement can only be used to evaluate the adequacy of diets of a group of people.[2] Specific Estimated Average Requirements are listed in Appendix M.

Estimated Average Requirements (EARs) An amount of nutrient intake that is estimated to meet the needs of 50% of the individuals in a specific age and gender group.

Recommended Dietary Allowances (RDAs)

Recommended Dietary Allowances (RDAs) Recommended intakes of nutrients that meet the needs of nearly all (97 to 98%) healthy individuals of similar age and gender.

Recommended Dietary Allowances represent intake of a nutrient that is sufficient to meet the needs of nearly all individuals (97 to 98%) in an age and gender group (see the inside cover). RDAs are based on a multiple of the Estimated Average Requirements (generally the RDA = EAR × 1.2).[2] Because of this relationship, RDAs can be set for nutrients only if the Food and Nutrition Board has enough information to determine an Estimated Average Requirement. Additional consideration in setting an RDA also can be given to a nutrient's ability to prevent chronic disease, rather than just prevent deficiency. A good example is vitamin C (see the next section).

Setting One RDA: Vitamin C

The amount of vitamin C needed each day to prevent scurvy is about 10 mg. However, as you will learn in Chapter 10, vitamin C has other functions as well, some of which are involved in the workings of the immune system (see Appendix C for details on the immune system). Based on this relationship, the concentration of vitamin C in one component of the immune system—notably, white blood cells (specifically neutrophils)—can be used as a marker for vitamin C adequacy in an individual. The Food and Nutrition Board concluded that near-maximal saturation of white blood cells with vitamin C is, in fact, the best marker for optimal vitamin C status. Research published to date suggests that, for adults 19 to 30 years of age, it takes, on average, a daily intake of 75 mg for men and 60 mg for women for near-saturation of white blood cells. These average amounts then become the Estimated Average Requirement for young adult men and women.

The Estimated Average Requirement for vitamin C is multiplied by 1.2 to yield the RDA; in this case, the RDA becomes 90 mg for men and 75 mg for women. Other age groups have slightly different recommendations; smokers should add 35 mg to the RDA for their age and gender (see Chapter 10 for details).

Putting the RDA for Vitamin C to Use

If you total the amount of vitamin C you eat in 1 week and divide by 7, you will have your average daily vitamin C consumption. If that value is close to the RDA, you are most likely consuming enough vitamin C. Even if you eat less than the RDA, you will not likely suffer ill effects because your needs are most likely less than the RDA, as it is set to include almost all individuals, some of whom probably need more vitamin C than you do. As a general rule, however, the further you stray below the RDA on a regular basis—particularly as you approach the Estimated Average Requirement—the greater your risk of a nutritional deficiency. Symptoms of a vitamin C deficiency may be subtle and develop slowly. It takes a long time to detect problems such as a weakened immune system and even poor wound healing. If you suspect that your diet is not nutritious enough, don't wait for warning signs to develop. Start eating a diet that meets the RDAs set for vitamin C (and all the other nutrients listed for your age and gender), rather than risk the development of health problems from poor nutrition.

Adequate Intakes (AIs)

Adequate Intakes (AIs) Recommendations for nutrient intake when not enough information is available to establish an RDA. AIs are based on observed or experimentally determined estimates of the average nutrient intake that appears to maintain a defined nutritional state (e.g., bone health) in a specific population. Used when no RDA can be set.

Nutrients for which there is not enough information to establish an Estimated Average Requirement are assigned **Adequate Intakes** (see the inside cover). Adequate Intakes are based on observed or experimentally determined estimates of the average nutrient intake that appears to maintain a defined nutritional state (for example, normal circulating nutrient values or bone health) in a certain population. Adequate Intakes have been set for essential fatty acids, fiber, some B-vitamins, the vitamin-like choline, vitamin D, and some minerals such as calcium and fluoride. In addition, Adequate Intakes are being set for all nutrients for infants under 1 year of age.

Estimated Energy Requirements (EERs)

RDAs and Adequate Intakes for nutrients are set high enough to meet the needs of almost all healthy individuals. In contrast, the standard used to express energy needs, called **Estimated Energy Requirements,** refers to the average needs for various age groups and genders (see the inside cover). Unlike most vitamins and minerals, excess energy consumed (above energy needs) is not excreted. Thus, to promote weight maintenance, a more conservative standard was used for energy needs than for nutrient needs. Overall, an Estimated Energy Requirement is only a rough estimate, because energy needs depend on energy use, and in some cases the need for growth or human milk production.[8] For most adults, the ability to obtain and maintain a healthy weight is the best yardstick of energy balance—energy intake matching energy output.

Estimated Energy Requirements (EERs) An estimate of the amount of energy intake that will balance energy needs of an average person within specific gender, age, and other considerations.

Tolerable Upper Intake Levels (Upper Levels or ULs)

The **Tolerable Upper Intake Level** is the maximum level of daily intake of a nutrient that is unlikely to cause adverse health effects in almost all people (97 to 98%) in a population (see the inside cover). The number applies to chronic daily use and is set to protect even very susceptible people in the healthy general population. This Upper Level is not a goal for nutrient intake but, rather, is a ceiling below which nutrient intake should remain. Still, for many of us there is a margin of safety above the UL before any adverse effects are likely to occur. Not enough information is available to set an Upper Level for all nutrients, but this does not mean that toxicity from these nutrients is impossible. Furthermore, there is no clear-cut evidence that intakes above the RDA or Adequate Intake confer any additional health benefits for most of us.

The Upper Level for most nutrients is based on the combined intake of food, water, supplements, and fortified foods. Four exceptions are the vitamin niacin and the minerals magnesium, zinc, and nickel, for which the Upper Level for each refers only to nonfood sources, such as medicines and supplements. This is because toxicity due to dietary intake of niacin, magnesium, zinc, or nickel is unlikely.[2]

Tolerable Upper Intake Levels (ULs) Maximum chronic daily intake of a nutrient that is unlikely to cause adverse health effects in almost all people in a population. This number applies to a chronic daily use.

Energy needs in adulthood are based on an energy intake required to maintain weight.

Appropriate Uses of the DRIs

The DRIs are intended mainly for diet planning. Specifically, a diet plan should aim to meet any RDAs set. If no RDA has been determined, it is reasonable to use the Adequate Intake as a guide for nutrient intake. Finally, the Upper Level for a nutrient should not be exceeded.[2] Keep in mind also that none of these dietary standards are necessarily appropriate amounts for individuals who are already undernourished or for those with diseases that require higher intakes. This concept will be covered in Chapters 9 through 12.

Concept | Check

Dietary Reference Intakes are set for specific nutrients in order to guide food intake. These standards include Recommended Dietary Allowances (RDAs), Adequate Intakes (AIs), and Tolerable Upper Intake Levels (Upper Levels or ULs). Recommended Dietary Allowances represent the nutrient needs for healthy individuals. RDAs are established for specific age and gender categories. No one knows his or her own nutritional requirements; the best general rule is that, the further you stray from nutrient standards set for your age and gender, especially below the Estimated Average Requirement (EAR), the greater your chance of having a nutritional deficiency or toxicity. Adequate Intakes are set when there is not enough information to set a more precise RDA. An Estimated Energy Requirement (EER) has also been set for various ages and genders. Intakes above Upper Levels generally should not be consumed on a regular basis unless a physician prescribes the practice and monitors the person carefully, as toxic effects are possible.

Current U.S. dietary standards apply to Canadians as well, as their establishment was a joint venture of scientists from both countries.

Daily Values (DVs): The Standards Used for Food Labeling

Daily Values Standard nutrient-intake values developed by FDA and used as a reference for expressing nutrient content on nutrition labels. The Daily Values include two types of standards—RDIs and DRVs.

Reference Daily Intakes (RDIs) Nutrient-intake standards set by FDA based on the 1968 RDAs for various vitamins and minerals. RDIs have been set for four categories of people: infants, toddlers, people over 4 years of age, and pregnant or lactating women. Generally the highest RDA value in each category is used as the RDI. The RDIs constitute part of the Daily Values used in food labeling.

Daily Reference Values (DRVs) Nutrient-intake standards established for protein, carbohydrate, and some dietary components lacking an RDA or a related nutrient standard, including total fat, saturated fat, and cholesterol. The DRVs for cholesterol, sodium, and potassium are constant; those for the other nutrients increase as energy intake increases. The DRVs constitute part of the Daily Values used in food labeling.

The DRIs and accompanying nutrient standards are not used in food labeling because they are age and gender specific. We can't have different packages for men and women or for teens and adults. The Food and Drug Administration (FDA) has developed a set of generic standards, called **Daily Values,** which are used to express the nutrient content of foods for the Nutrition Facts panel on food labels. The content of a particular nutrient is listed on labels as a percentage of the Daily Value. These percentages serve as a benchmark for evaluating the nutrient content of foods. They do not, however, represent a set of tailor-made recommendations for an adult. You will see why once the method for setting Daily Values is described.

The Daily Values are based on two sets of dietary standards. The first, **Reference Daily Intakes (RDIs),** are for vitamins and minerals. The second, **Daily Reference Values (DRVs),** are standards for protein and various dietary components that have no RDA or other established nutrient standard (e.g., total fat and cholesterol). These two terms—*Reference Daily Intakes* and *Daily Reference Values*—do not appear on labels. To make reading labels less confusing for consumers, the term *Daily Value* is used to represent the combination of these two sets of dietary standards, since the differences between Reference Daily Intakes and Daily Reference Values for typical consumers are inconsequential. For health professionals and nutrition experts, though, it is important to understand how nutrition label information (Reference Daily Intakes vs. Daily Reference Values) is actually derived:

Daily Values, used on food labels, are a combination of RDI and DRV standards.

For food labels, standards are set for nutrients that have RDAs or other established nutrient standards, called RDIs.	For food labels, standards are set for many nutrients that do not have RDAs or other established nutrient standards, called DRVs.

Reference Daily Intakes (RDIs)

Reference Daily Intakes (RDIs) make up the majority of the Daily Values (DVs). The Reference Daily Intakes have been set by FDA using a compilation of the nutrient standards published in 1968. Essentially, Reference Daily Intakes use the highest RDA values of any age category set in 1968. For example, consider iron: In 1968, the RDA for adult men was 10 mg/day and that for adult women and adolescents was 18 mg/day. The iron Reference Daily Intake for adults is the higher value: 18 mg/day. Table 2-6 lists the Reference Daily Intakes used for various age groups.

The Reference Daily Intake values currently in use, which are based on the 1968 RDAs, are generally slightly higher than current RDAs and related nutrient standards. FDA will likely soon revise the Reference Daily Intakes to reflect the latest nutrient standards.

Canada also has a set of Daily Values for use on food labels in that country (see Appendix D).

Daily Reference Values (DRVs)

The Daily Values for some food constituents are based on Daily Reference Values (DRVs) rather than RDIs. Daily Reference Values cover certain dietary components that have no RDA or related nutrient standard at this time, such as saturated fatty acids and cholesterol. (Protein is the exception, as it has a Daily Value and also an RDA.) The Daily Reference Values are intended to help consumers evaluate their food choices by comparing their actual intakes of these food constituents with desirable (or maximum) intakes. Table 2-7 lists the Daily Reference Values. The amounts for energy-yielding nutrients are based on 30% of total energy intake from fat, 60% from carbohydrate, and 10% from protein, which corresponds to the Dietary Guidelines for Americans (see the section entitled Dietary Guidelines for Americans—Another Tool for Menu Planning).

Table 2-6 Comparison of Daily Values with the Latest RDAs and Other Nutrient Standards*

Dietary Constituent	Unit of Measure	Current Daily Values for People Over 4 Years of Age	RDA or other current dietary standard: Males 19 Years Old	RDA or other current dietary standard: Females 19 Years Old
Total Fat‡	g	<65	–	–
Saturated fatty acids‡	"	<20	–	–
Protein‡	"	50	56	46
Cholesterol§	mg	<300	–	–
Carbohydrate‡	g	300	130	130
Fiber	"	25	38	25
Vitamin A	μg Retinol activity equivalents	1000	900	700
Vitamin D	International units	400	200	200
Vitamin E	"	30	22–33	22–33
Vitamin K	μg	80	120	90
Vitamin C	mg	60	90	75
Folate	μg	400	400	400
Thiamin	mg	1.5	1.20	1.10
Riboflavin	"	1.7	1.30	1.10
Niacin	"	20	16	14
Vitamin B-6	"	2	1.30	1.30
Vitamin B-12	μg	6	2.40	2.40
Biotin	mg	0.3	0.03	0.03
Pantothenic acid	"	10	5	5
Calcium	"	1000	1000	1000
Phosphorus	"	1000	700	700
Iodide	μg	150	150	150
Iron	mg	18	8	18
Magnesium	"	400	400	310
Copper	"	2	0.9	0.9
Zinc	"	15	11	8
Sodium†	"	<2400	500	500
Potassium†	"	3500	2000	2000
Chloride†	"	3400	750	750
Manganese	"	2	2.3	1.8
Selenium	μg	70	55	55
Chromium	"	120	35	25
Molybdenum	"	75	45	45

Abbreviations: g = gram, mg = milligram, μg = microgram

*Daily Values are generally set at the highest nutrient recommendation in a specific age and gender category. Many Daily Values exceed current nutrient standards. This is in part because aspects of the Daily Values were originally developed in the early 1970s using estimates of nutrient needs published in 1968. The Daily Values have yet to be updated to reflect the current state of knowledge.

†The considerably higher Daily Values for sodium and chloride are there to allow for more diet flexibility, but the extra amounts are not needed to maintain health.

‡These Daily Values are based, instead, on a 2000 kcal diet, with a caloric distribution of 30% from fat (and one-third of this total from saturated fat), 60% from carbohydrate, and 10% from protein.

§Based on recommendations of federal agencies

Table 2-7 Daily Reference Values (DRVs)*

Food Component	Unit of Measure	DRV (2000 kcal Intake)	DRV (2500 kcal Intake)	DRV (3200 kcal Intake)
Total Fat	g	<65	<80	<107
Saturated fatty acids	g	<20	<25	<36
Protein	g	50	65	80
Cholesterol	mg	<300	<300	<300
Carbohydrate	g	300	375	480
Fiber	g	25	30	37
Sodium	mg	<2400	<2400	<2400
Potassium	mg	3500	3500	3500

*Daily Reference Values based on an energy intake of 2000 kcal constitute the Daily Values used as reference standards for food labeling. Note that the Daily Reference Values for some nutrients (e.g., total fat) increase as energy intake increases.

Nutrition educators often instruct patients to look only at the total amount of a nutrient (shown on the left side of the Nutrition Facts panel) rather than the % Daily Value when watching a specific nutrient. This is because the % Daily Value is not correct unless that person consumes 2000 kcal/day. For example, if a person is to limit his or her saturated fat intake to 20 g per day, the % Daily Value does not provide adequate information to assess grams of saturated fat consumed in a day.

Note that many of the Daily Reference Values, such as those for saturated fat, total fat, and fiber, are related to total energy intake. By accounting for this, you can evaluate your diet even if your energy intake is more or less than the standard energy intake, 2000 kcal, used on the label. For example, if you consume only 1600 kcal per day, the total percentage of Daily Value for each of these nutrients should add up to no more than 80% because 1600 ÷ 2000 = 0.8, or 80%. If you eat 2800 kcal, your total percentage of Daily Value for each nutrient in all the foods you eat in one day can add up to 140%, because 2800 ÷ 2000 = 1.4, or 140%. However, the % Daily Values for some dietary constituents, such as cholesterol and sodium, are not adjusted for differences in energy intake.

In the same way, you can calculate the amount of a certain nutrient you have left in a day by using the % Daily Value. For example, if you consume 2000 kcal per day, your total fat intake for the day should be 65 g or less. If you consume 10 g of fat at breakfast, you have 55 g, or 85%, of your Daily Value left for the rest of the day.

Daily Values in Perspective

The Nutrition Facts panel on the label of a food product lists various components of the food as a percentage of their Daily Values (see the later section entitled What Do Food Labels Have to Offer in Diet Planning? for details). Use this information on food labels to learn more about your food choices. Unfortunately most adults do not do this. To practice using this information, suppose that one serving of a macaroni and cheese product contains 15% of the Daily Value for iron. Since the Daily Value for iron is 18 mg, this product contains about 3 mg of iron per serving (18 × 0.15 = 2.7 mg).

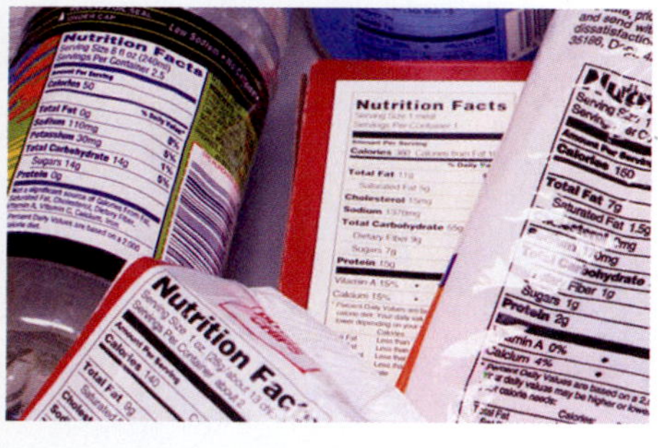

Use the Nutrition Facts label to learn more about the nutrient content of the foods you eat. Nutrient content is expressed as a percentage of the Daily Value.

Concept | Check

Daily Values are currently used as a benchmark for representing the nutrient content of foods on nutrition labels. Nutrient content is expressed as a percentage of the Daily Value for a nutrient, which in turn is based on a Reference Daily Intake (RDI) or Daily Reference Value (DRV). The Reference Daily Intakes for vitamins and minerals constitute the majority of Daily Values and are based on the 1968 RDA standards. The Daily Reference Values have been set for some nutrients that don't have an RDA or Adequate Intake, such as fat and cholesterol. To decrease confusion, the Daily Value is the only term that appears on food labels.

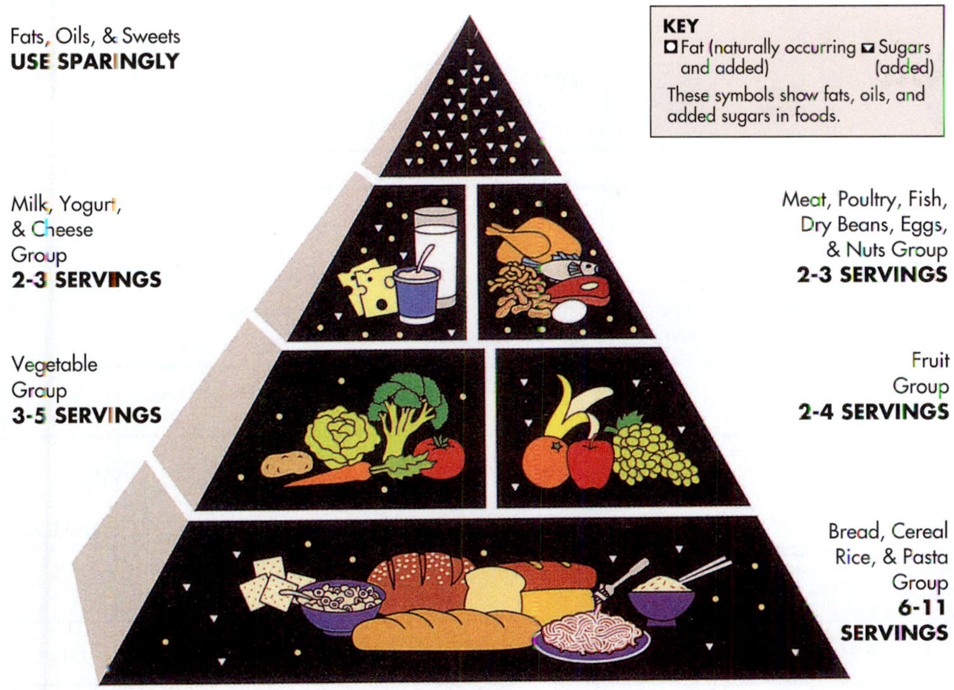

Figure 2-4 USDA's Food Guide Pyramid. The Food Guide Pyramid lists the food groups and the amount to consume from each group. Note that for children, teenagers, and middle-age and older adults, three servings should be chosen from the milk, yogurt, and cheese group. Once you have estimated your energy needs, recommended servings from the other groups with wider ranges are as follows:

Energy Intake	*1600 kcal*	*2200 kcal*	*2800 kcal*
Bread, etc. group	6	9	11
Vegetable group	3	4	5
Fruit group	2	3	4
Milk, etc. group	2–3	2–3	2–3
Meat, etc. group (oz)*	5	6	7
Total fat (g)	53	73	93
Total added sugars (tsp)	6	12	18

*For some foods in this group an ounce measure does not apply (e.g., eggs).

From Nutrient Recommendations to Food Choices

The following sections of the chapter will describe various guidelines for planning healthy diets.

The Food Guide Pyramid—A Menu-Planning Tool

Since the early twentieth century, researchers have worked to clarify the science of nutrition into practical terms, so that people with no special training could estimate whether their nutritional needs were being met. A seven food-group plan, based on foods traditionally eaten by people in the United States, was one of the first formats designed by USDA. Daily food choices had to include items from each group. This plan had been simplified by the mid-1950s to a four food-group plan: a milk group, a meat group, a fruit and vegetable group, and a bread and cereal group. The entire plan was designed to provide a minimum foundation for an adequate diet, and represented about 1200 to 1400 kcal per day. Other food choices were to be added to meet daily energy needs.

The Food Guide Pyramid, first released in 1992, is designed to represent a total diet providing sufficient protein, vitamins, and minerals. It is widely advocated for diet planning (Fig. 2-4).[7] This pyramid goes beyond earlier food guides to suggest a pattern of food choices for the entire day, rather than simply a foundation diet.

Appendix D contains the Canadian Food Guide to Healthy Eating.

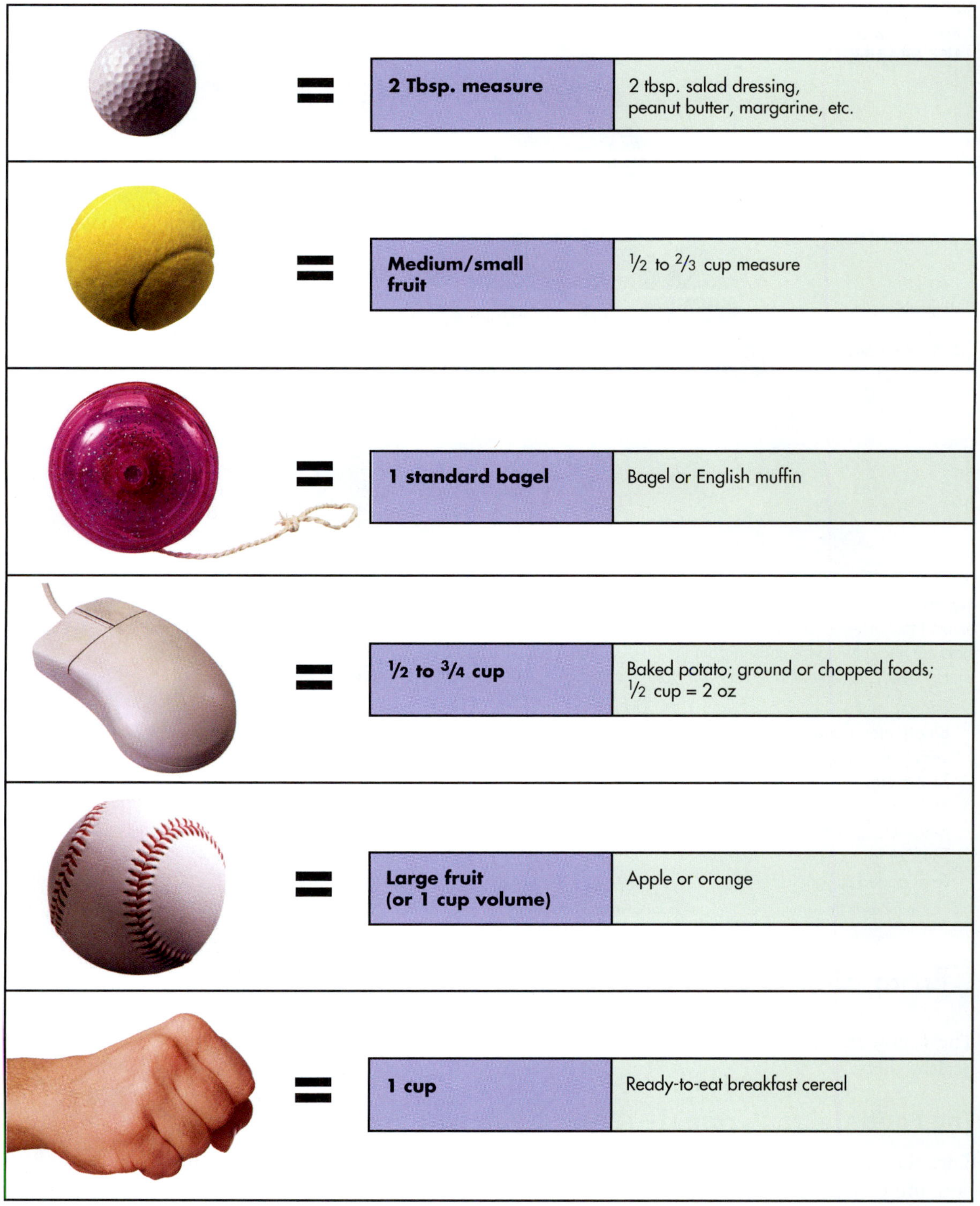
2 Tbsp. measure
2 tbsp. salad dressing, peanut butter, margarine, etc.
Medium/small fruit
½ to ⅔ cup measure
1 standard bagel
Bagel or English muffin
½ to ¾ cup
Baked potato; ground or chopped foods; ½ cup = 2 oz
Large fruit (or 1 cup volume)
Apple or orange
1 cup
Ready-to-eat breakfast cereal

Figure 2-5 A golf ball, tennis ball, large yo-yo, computer mouse, baseball, and fist make convenient guides to judge Food Guide Pyramid serving sizes.

Experts recommend that we pay close attention to the stated serving size for each choice when following the Food Guide Pyramid. This aids in controlling total energy intake. Figure 2-5 above provides a convenient guide to estimating serving size. Note that serving sizes listed for one serving in a Food Guide Pyramid group are often less than typically served in restaurants today.

Components of the Food Guide Pyramid

The number of servings to consume from each food group in the current Food Guide Pyramid depends on a person's age and energy needs. Serving size is also adjusted downward for young children (see Chapter 17). Table 2-8 lists serving sizes and the recommended number of servings to consume per day for adults. The table also lists the major nutrients each food group supplies. Note the similarities and differences among the groups.

Table 2-8 The Food Guide Pyramid—A Summary

Food Category	Major Contributions	Foods and Individual Serving Sizes†
Milk, yogurt, and cheese	Calcium Phosphorus Carbohydrate Protein Riboflavin Vitamin D Magnesium Zinc	1 cup milk (includes low-lactose products) 1½ oz cheese 2 oz processed cheese 1 cup yogurt 2 cups cottage cheese 1 cup soy-based beverage with added calcium
Meat, poultry, fish, dry beans, eggs, and nuts	Protein Thiamin Riboflavin Niacin Vitamin B-6 Folate§ Vitamin B-12‖ Phosphorus Magnesium§ Iron Zinc	2–3 oz cooked meat, poultry, or fish 1–1½ cups cooked dry beans 4 tbsp peanut butter 2 eggs ⅔–1 cup nuts 5 oz soyburger
Fruit	Carbohydrate Vitamin A Vitamin C Folate Magnesium Potassium Fiber	¼ cup dried fruit ½ cup cooked or canned fruit ¾ cup juice 1 whole piece of fruit 1 melon wedge (about ¼) ½ cup berries
Vegetable	Carbohydrate Vitamin A Vitamin C Folate Magnesium Potassium Fiber	½ cup raw or cooked vegetables 1 cup raw leafy vegetables ¾ cup vegetable juice
Bread, cereal, rice, and pasta	Carbohydrate Thiamin Riboflavin¶ Niacin Folate# Magnesium‡ Iron¶# Zinc# Fiber‡	1 slice of bread 1 oz (about ¾ cup) ready-to-eat cereal ½ cup cooked cereal, rice, or pasta ½ hamburger roll, bagel, or English muffin 3–4 plain crackers 1 small roll, biscuit, or muffin 1 6″ tortilla
Fats, oils, and sweets	Food from this category should not replace any from the other groups. Amounts consumed should be determined by individual energy needs.	

†May be reduced for child servings
§Primarily in plant protein sources
‖Only in animal foods
¶If enriched
#Whole grains and some enriched/fortified products
‡Whole grains

To quickly estimate serving sizes, use the following equivalents (some were shown in Figure 2-5):

Thumb = 1 oz of cheese	Palm of a hand = 3 oz	Computer mouse = ½ to ¾ cups
4 stacked dice = 1 oz cheese	1 ice cream scoop = ½ cup	Ping-pong or golf ball = 2 tbsp
Thumb tip to first joint = 1 tsp	Fist or baseball = 1 cup	Large yo-yo or hockey puck = 1 bagel serving
Matchbox = 1 oz meat	Handful = 1 or 2 oz of a snack food	
Bar of soap or deck of cards = 3 oz meat	Tennis ball = 1 medium fruit serving	

The plan for an adult over age 18 essentially consists of the following:

- 6 to 11 servings from the bread, cereals, rice, and pasta group
- 2 to 4 servings from the fruit group
- 3 to 5 servings from the vegetable group
- 2 servings from the milk, yogurt, and cheese group
- 2 to 3 servings from the meat, poultry, fish, dry beans, eggs, and nuts group (5 to 7 ounces total)

Note also that some food choices will contain servings of more than one food group (e.g., lasagna contains pasta, cheese, and tomatoes, and likely ingredients from other food groups as well).

For some population groups—children and teenagers (including teenagers who are pregnant or breastfeeding)—three servings of the milk, yogurt, and cheese group are recommended due to higher calcium needs. The same is also true for middle-age and older adults (51 years or older). Alternately, some of those servings also could be replaced with calcium-fortified foods or a calcium supplement (see Chapter 11).

Foods in a final category at the tip of the pyramid, which is not a group per se, include fats, oils, and sweets. These can be eaten to help meet individual energy needs but should not replace foods from other groups.

Menu Planning with the Food Guide Pyramid

Table 2-9 illustrates a 1-day menu based on the Food Guide Pyramid. Remember the following points when using the Food Guide Pyramid to plan your daily menus:

1. The guide does not apply to infants or children under 2 years of age.
2. No one food is absolutely essential to good nutrition. Each food is deficient in at least one essential nutrient.
3. No one food group provides all essential nutrients in adequate amounts. Each food group makes an important, distinctive contribution to nutritional intake.
4. Variety is the key to success of the guide and is first guaranteed by choosing foods from all the groups. Furthermore, one should consume a variety of foods within each group, except possibly in the milk, yogurt, and cheese group.
5. The foods within a group may vary widely with respect to nutrient and energy content. For example, the energy content of 3 ounces of baked potato is 98 kcal, whereas that of 3 ounces of potato chips is 470 kcal. Compare an orange and an apple with respect to vitamin C using the food composition table in Appendix N.

The Food Guide Pyramid incorporates the foundations of a healthy diet: variety, balance, and moderation. The nutritional adequacy of diets planned using this tool, however, depends on selection of a variety of foods. In addition, to ensure enough vitamin E, vitamin B-6, magnesium, and zinc—nutrients sometimes low in diets based on this plan—consider the following advice:

1. Choose primarily low-fat and nonfat items from the milk, yogurt, and cheese group. By reducing energy intake in this way, you can select more items from other food groups. If milk causes intestinal gas and bloating, emphasize yogurt and cheese. (See Chapter 5 for details on the problem of lactose maldigestion and intolerance. Milk is rich in lactose.)
2. Include plant foods that are good sources of proteins, such as beans and nuts, at least several times a week because many are rich in vitamins (such as vitamin E), minerals (such as magnesium), and fiber.
3. For vegetables and fruits, try to include a dark green vegetable for vitamin A and a vitamin C–rich fruit, such as an orange, every day. Don't focus primarily on potatoes for your vegetable choices. Surveys show that fewer than 5% of adults eat a full serving of a dark green vegetable on any given day. Increased consumption of these foods is important because they contribute vitamins, minerals, fiber, and phytochemicals.

Table 2-9 Putting the Food Guide Pyramid into Practice

Meal	Servings/Food Group*
Breakfast	
1 small, peeled orange	1 fruit
¾ cup Healthy Choice Low-fat Granola	1 bread
with ½ cup nonfat milk	½ milk
½ toasted, small raisin bagel	1 bread
with 1 tsp soft margarine	1 fat/sweet
Optional: coffee or tea	
Lunch	
Ham sandwich	
2 slices whole wheat bread	2 bread
2 oz ham	1 meat
2 tsp mustard	
1 small apple	1 fruit
2 oatmeal-raisin cookies (small)	2 fat/sweet
Optional: diet soft drink	
3 P.M. Study Break	
6 multigrain crackers	2 bread
1 tbsp peanut butter	¼ meat
½ cup nonfat milk	½ milk
Dinner	
Lettuce salad	
1 cup romaine lettuce	1 vegetable
½ cup sliced tomatoes	1 vegetable
1½ tbsp Italian dressing	1½ fat/sweet
½ grated carrot	1 vegetable
3 oz broiled salmon	1 meat
½ cup rice	1 bread
½ cup green beans	1 vegetable
with 1 tsp soft margarine	1 fat/sweet
Optional: coffee or tea	
Late-Night Snack	
1 cup "light" fruit yogurt	1 milk
Nutrient Breakdown	
1800 kcal	
Carbohydrate	56% of energy intake
Protein	18% of energy intake
Fat	26% of energy intake

This menu meets nutrient needs for all vitamins and minerals for an average adult. For adolescents, teenagers, and middle-age and older adults, add one additional serving from the milk, yogurt, and cheese group or seek other calcium-rich sources.

*Names of food groups abbreviated as follows: milk = milk, yogurt, and cheese group; meat = meat, poultry, fish, dry beans, eggs, and nuts group; bread = bread, cereal, rice, and pasta group; fat/sweet = fats, oils, and sweets category.

Tomatoes are a rich source of nutrients and phytochemicals.

4. Choose mostly whole-grain varieties of breads, cereals, rice, and pasta because they contribute vitamin E and fiber. A plate about two-thirds covered by grains, fruits, and vegetables and one-third or less covered by protein-rich foods promotes this diet advice. As well, a daily serving of a whole-grain, ready-to-eat breakfast cereal is an excellent choice because the vitamins (such as vitamin B-6) and minerals (such as zinc) typically added to it, along with fiber, help fill in the potential gaps listed earlier.
5. Include some plant oils on a daily basis, such as those in salad dressing, and eat fish at least twice a week. This supplies you with health-promoting fatty acids.

Following the Food Guide Pyramid makes it possible to create daily diets containing as few as 1600 to 1800 kcal (review Table 2-9), sufficient for a sedentary adult or an older person. Not following this advice can leave a diet 1600 to 1800 kcal short on many essential nutrients. Recall that excessive consumption of any one food—even those considered "healthy"—is also undesirable and possibly risky.

If 1600 to 1800 kcal represents too much food energy for you, you should first consider becoming more physically active rather than eating less. Obtaining enough nutrients from a diet that supplies fewer than 1600 kcal per day is very difficult. If you can't increase your energy output, you can make a special attempt to choose some nutrient-fortified foods regularly (e.g., ready-to-eat breakfast cereals) or take a balanced multivitamin and mineral supplement (see Chapter 9). In addition, for those whose diets do not include meat or other animal products, the Nutrition Perspective on vegetarianism in Chapter 7 provides advice on adapting the Food Guide Pyramid to that dietary practice.

Evaluation of the Current North American Diet Using the Food Guide Pyramid

The average North American diet, based on surveys, fails to meet the serving recommendations in the Food Guide Pyramid for many food groups. For example, the average diet included only 1 to 2 fruit servings (rather than the recommended 2 to 4 servings) and only 2 to 3 vegetable servings (rather than 3 to 5 servings), and much of that comes from potatoes, not a particularly nutrient-dense vegetable choice. Overall, fruits and vegetables are the most underrepresented groups. In contrast, the fats, oils, and sweets are well represented.

How Does Your Current Diet Rate?

Regularly comparing your daily food intake with the Food Guide Pyramid recommendations is a relatively simple way to evaluate your overall diet. Strive to meet the recommendations. If that is not possible, identify the nutrients that are low in your diet based on the nutrients found in each food group (review Table 2-8). For example, if you do not consume enough servings from the milk, yogurt, and cheese group, your calcium intake is most likely too low. After completing the Take Action activity at the end of this chapter, you will be able to determine more accurately which nutrients are too low in your current diet and by how much. Armed with this knowledge, find foods that you enjoy that supply those nutrients, such as calcium-fortified orange juice. To learn more, see the website sponsored by USDA (www.usda.gov/cnpp). At this site, you can view the entire booklet describing the pyramid.

Criticisms of the Food Guide Pyramid

Another criticism of the Food Guide Pyramid is that the advice is not specific enough. For example, most vegetable servings could be potatoes, or none of the bread, cereal, rice, and pasta servings could be whole-grain. In either case, diet quality is compromised.

The Food Guide Pyramid has recently come under criticism on three accounts (excluding the call for the elimination of all animal products issued by some groups).[15] First, as mentioned before, some people have difficulty digesting large amounts of the sugar lactose. A focus on dairy products in the pyramid has been criticized as inappropriate for these people. A second criticism is that refined grains and whole grains are lumped together; it would be healthier to emphasize primarily whole-grain choices because of their fiber content. Third, fat need not necessarily be placed at the top of the pyramid, indicating caution should be used with intake. Fat could be a more central part of the diet if the fat is primarily from plant oils.[20] And, as you will see in the next section, the latest Dietary Guidelines for Americans issued by the U.S. federal government and advice from the Food and Nutrition Board recommend moderation in fat consumption (limitation applies primarily to saturated fat and cholesterol intake).[8] This would again allow for more plant oil use than is suggested by the placement of fat at the top of the pyramid. Whole grains are also emphasized in these Dietary Guidelines (see the next section for details).

In the final analysis, however, the Food Guide Pyramid provides enough latitude that one can make appropriate choices based on personal health concerns and still consume the recommended servings of the five food groups. Some additional fat from plant oils is fine, as long as overall energy balance is maintained. Following a diet that avoids all animal products, which will be covered in Chapter 7, is another matter altogether.

USDA is currently evaluating the Food Guide Pyramid for possible revision. A new version is due in 2004.

Alternative Pyramids and Related Food Plans

During the last few years a number of organizations and experts have proposed alternate pyramids and diet plans to replace the Food Guide Pyramid.

The Mayo Clinic has developed a Healthy Weight Pyramid with physical activity at the center of the pyramid. The plan allows for unlimited amounts of fruits and vegetables in the diet, 4 to 8 servings of carbohydrates (grains), 3 to 7 servings of protein/dairy products, 3 to 5 servings of fats, and very limited amounts of sweets (75 kcal/day)(www.mayo.edu/news/pyramid.jpg).

The Dietary Approaches to Stop Hypertension (DASH) Pyramid helps treat elevated blood pressure. It contains more fruit and vegetable choices (total of 8 to 10) than the Food Guide Pyramid (see the Nutrition Perspective in Chapter 11).

Oldways Preservation Trust has developed Latin American, Asian, and Mediterranean pyramids to reflect traditional diets in these ethnic groups (see the Nutrition Perspective in this chapter). Oldways Preservation Trust has also developed a vegetarian pyramid (see the Nutrition Perspective in Chapter 7).

Dr. Walter Willett, a well-respected nutrition scientist, has created a Healthy Eating Pyramid. The diet plan emphasizes a daily generous intake of whole grains, plant oils, and vegetables; fruits at least two to three times per day, nuts and legumes one to three times per day; fish, poultry, and eggs zero to two times per day; dairy products or calcium supplements one to two times per day; and little use of red meat, butter, white rice, white bread, potatoes, pasta, and sweets. Regular physical activity and weight control is also recommended, as is alcohol intake in moderation (if of legal age) and a multivitamin and mineral supplement for most people. Chapter 6 discusses the rationale and implications of this diet plan. To view the pyramid see www.hsph.harvard.edu/ now/aug24/ or the January 2003 issue of *Scientific American* (p. 64).

The American Institute for Cancer Research is promoting a plate instead of a pyramid for menu planning. The plate should be covered two-thirds or more by vegetables, fruits, and whole grains and one-third or less by meat, fish, poultry, and low-fat dairy products (www.aicr.org).

All of these plans share a common pattern of emphasizing fruits, vegetables, and grains—preferably, mostly whole grains—in a diet.

There is no shortage of pyramids to choose from when planning a diet. To examine various food guides used worldwide, see Painter J and others: Comparison of international food guide pictorial representations. *Journal of the American Dietetic Association* 102:483, 2002. Which pyramid looks best to you?

Concept | Check

The Food Guide Pyramid translates the general needs for carbohydrate, protein, fat, vitamins, and minerals into the recommended number of daily servings from each of five major food groups. It is one of many convenient and valuable tools for planning daily menus.

Dietary Guidelines for Americans—Another Tool for Menu Planning

The Food Guide Pyramid was designed to help meet nutritional needs for carbohydrate, protein, fat, vitamins, and minerals. However, most of the major chronic "killer" diseases in North America, such as cardiovascular disease, cancer, and alcoholism, are not primarily associated with deficiencies of these nutrients. Deficiency diseases such as scurvy (vitamin C deficiency) and pellagra (niacin deficiency) are no longer common. For many North Americans, the primary dietary culprit is an overconsumption of one or more of the following: energy, saturated fat, cholesterol, alcohol, and salt (sodium).

Appendix D contains nutrient guidelines for Canadians.

Underconsumption of calcium, iron, folate and other B-vitamins, vitamin D, vitamin E, zinc, or fiber is also a problem for some people, but easy to fix as the major dietary problems are addressed.

In response to concerns regarding these killer disease patterns, since 1980 the USDA and U.S. Department of Health and Human Services (DHHS) have published **Dietary Guidelines for Americans** to aid diet planning.[11] Nutritional and medical experts outside of government have also contributed their expertise to the process. The latest Dietary Guidelines begin with three overarching messages and then list the following 10 specific guidelines:

Dietary Guidelines for Americans General goals for nutrient intakes and diet composition set by the USDA and the U.S. Department of Health and Human Services.

Aim for Fitness

1. *Aim for a healthy weight*
(body mass index of 18.5 to 24.9 and a waist circumference no more than 35 inches [88 centimeters] in women and 40 inches [102 centimeters] in men; see Chapter 13).
2. *Be physically active each day*
(30 minutes of moderate to vigorous physical activity on most or all days of the week is listed in the Dietary Guidelines pamphlet [60 minutes per day is even better]; see Chapter 14).

Build a Healthy Base

3. *Let the pyramid guide your food choices*
(see the previous section on the Food Guide Pyramid).
4. *Choose a variety of grains daily, especially whole grains*
(see the Food Guide Pyramid and Chapter 5).
5. *Choose a variety of fruits and vegetables daily*
(see the Food Guide Pyramid).
6. *Keep foods safe to eat*
(proper cooking and refrigeration of perishable foods is especially important; see Chapter 19).

Choose Sensibly

7. *Choose a diet that is low in saturated fat and cholesterol and moderate in total fat*
(animal fats and fast food are the chief sources; see Chapter 6).
8. *Choose beverages and foods to moderate your intake of sugars*
(soft drinks, cookies, and candy are the chief sources; see Chapter 5).
9. *Choose and prepare foods with less salt*
(it is easy to adjust to a lower salt intake; see Chapter 11).
10. *If you drink alcoholic beverages, do so in moderation*
(no more than one to two drinks per day for men and one drink for women. The one drink limit also applies to both men and women 65 years or older; see Chapter 8).

Logo for the current Dietary Guidelines for Americans.

These guidelines are intended for healthy children (2 years and older) and adults of any age. You can view the entire Dietary Guidelines booklet at www.usda.gov/cnpp.

Advice from the American Dietetic Association suggests five basic principles with regard to diet and health. Be realistic, making small changes over time. Be adventurous, trying new foods regularly. Be flexible, balancing some sweet and fatty foods with physical activity. Be sensible, including favorite foods in smaller portions. Finally, be active, including physical activity in daily life.

Practical Use of the Dietary Guidelines

The Dietary Guidelines are designed to promote adequate vitamin and mineral intake. The guidelines also emphasize changes that will reduce the risk of obesity, hypertension, cardiovascular disease, type 2 diabetes, alcoholism, and foodborne illness.

The Dietary Guidelines are not difficult to implement (Table 2-10). In addition, this overall diet approach is not especially expensive, as some people suspect. Fruits, vegetables, and low-fat and nonfat milk are no more expensive than the chips, cookies, and sugared soft drinks they should in part replace.

Note also that diet recommendations for adults have been issued by other scientific groups, such as the American Heart Association, U.S. Surgeon General, National Academy of Sciences, American Cancer Society, Canadian Ministries of Health (see Appendix D), and World Health Organization. All are consistent with the spirit of the Dietary

Table 2-10 Advice for Applying the Dietary Guidelines to Practical Situations

If You Usually Eat This	Eat This More Often
White bread	Whole-wheat bread (fewer nutrients lost in refinement/processing and more fiber)
Sugared breakfast cereal	Low-sugar (and high-fiber) cereal (use the calories you save for a side dish of fruit)
Cheeseburger and french fries	Hamburger (hold the mayonnaise) and baked beans (for less fat and cholesterol, and the benefits of plant proteins)
Potato salad at the salad bar	Three-bean salad
Doughnut, chips, salty snack foods	Bran muffin or bagel (little or no cream cheese)
Soft drinks	Diet soft drinks (save the calories for more nutritious foods)
Boiled vegetables	Steamed vegetables (for more nutrient retention)
Canned vegetables	Frozen vegetables (fewer nutrients lost in processing)
Fried meats	Broiled meats (watch the fat drain away)
Fatty meats, such as ribs	Lean meats, such as ground round (also, eat chicken and fish often)
Whole milk and ice cream	Low-fat or nonfat milk and sherbet or frozen yogurt (to reduce saturated fat intake)
Mayonnaise or sour cream salad dressing	Oil and vinegar dressings or diet varieties (to save calories)
Cookies for a snack	Popcorn (air popped with minimal margarine or butter)
Heavily salted foods	Foods flavored primarily with herbs, spices, lemon juice

Guidelines. These groups encourage people to modify their eating behavior in ways that are both healthful and pleasurable.

The Dietary Guidelines and You

When using the Dietary Guidelines, you should consider your own state of health. Make specific changes and see whether they are effective. Note that results are sometimes disappointing, even when you are following a diet change very closely. Some people can eat a lot of saturated fat and still keep blood cholesterol under control. Other people, unfortunately, have high blood cholesterol even if they eat a diet low in saturated fat. Differences in genetic background are a key cause, as discussed in Chapter 1. Thus, we have individual nutritional needs and risks of developing certain diseases. Dr. David M. Klurfeld discusses this in more detail in the Expert Opinion. One's diet should be planned with this individuality in mind when possible, taking into account one's current health status and family history for specific diseases. However, tailoring a unique nutrition program for every North American citizen is currently unrealistic. The Food Guide Pyramid and the Dietary Guidelines provide typical adults with simple advice, which can be actively practiced by anyone willing to take a step toward good health.

Concept | Check

Dietary Guidelines for Americans have been set with input from government and other nutrition and medical experts. These guidelines are designed to reduce the risk of developing obesity, hypertension, type 2 diabetes, cardiovascular disease, alcoholism, and foodborne illness. To do so, they recommend eating a variety of foods, which is fostered by following the Food Guide Pyramid. They also recommend performing regular physical activity, aiming for a healthy weight, and moderating total fat, saturated fat, cholesterol, salt, sugar, and alcohol intake, while focusing more on fruits, vegetables, and grain products in daily menu planning. Safe food preparation and storage are also highlighted.

Expert Opinion

What Should I Eat to Live Longer?

David M. Klurfeld, Ph.D.

The fountain of youth emanates, according to popular culture, from a proper diet. This rosy view stems, in part, from the dietary recommendations made to reduce the risk of several chronic diseases. Implicit in the recommendations is the promise of longer life—but how long and for whom?

Cardiovascular disease and cancer account for almost three-fourths of all deaths in affluent societies. One reason for this is that many causes of premature death—infections, poor sanitation, and accidents—have been dramatically allayed. This change translates into a life expectancy at birth in the United States of 76.9 years. At the same time, more people are overweight, and health-care costs are a greater percentage of the economy than in any other country, so we have lots of room for improvement. In spite of our highly publicized "killer diet," deaths from cardiovascular disease, stroke, and cancer unrelated to tobacco have all declined markedly over the past 35 years.

We don't know for sure why this drop has occurred, but it has been attributed, in part, to less use of tobacco and reductions in hypertension and blood cholesterol, along with better medical care. These changes in risk factors point to the multifaceted causes of both cardiovascular disease and cancer. In addition, since many environmental factors interact with genetic predisposition to a disease, we simply don't know enough to attribute a specific portion of risk for chronic diseases to diet.

Many of the estimates of dietary contribution to the risk of cancer are made by default; that is, cancers that are not traceable to other risk factors are often lumped as being caused by diet. While many health recommendations emphasize a Mediterranean diet, there is no single diet that fits this description (see the Nutrition Perspective at the end of this chapter for one example). In addition, there is no evidence that populations living around the Mediterranean Sea have a longer life expectancy than people in the United States, Japan, or Scandinavia, where diets differ substantially.

The only dietary change effective in reducing many types of cancer and increasing life span in animals is caloric restriction. When energy intake is reduced to about 70% of what would normally be eaten—but all nutrient requirements are met—the result is physiologically younger animals. Long-term studies of monkeys eating such low-calorie diets have found reduced body fat and lower blood glucose, insulin, and lipids when compared with animals given free access to food. These studies have been in progress long enough for some of the monkeys to have died from natural causes; fewer in the low-calorie groups have died. Circumstantial evidence for a calorie effect in people includes the fact that the highest concentration of centenarians is found in Okinawa. The people over 100 years old have been found to eat fewer calories, more fruits, vegetables, and meat than in the rest of Japan; and most of the very elderly in *every* society tend to be slimmer and shorter than average.

Healthful aging is fostered by wise food choices.

Can we reduce cardiovascular disease by dietary means with some degree of certainty? Probably, according to epidemiological and animal data. But epidemiology offers only leads—it cannot prove cause and effect. Today, there's little controversy over increased risk of cardiovascular disease with elevated blood cholesterol. What is debated is at what point dietary or drug treatments should begin. And, although the consensus recommendation is to reduce blood cholesterol below 200 mg/dl (dl stands for 100 ml), some argue that this is too modest a target, whereas others contend that it's an unnecessary one. Still, the slope of cardiovascular disease versus blood cholesterol is quite steep at the upper concentra-

Case Scenario | Follow-up

The most positive aspect of Andy's diet is that it contains adequate protein, zinc, and iron because it is rich in animal protein. On the downside, his diet is low in calcium, some B-vitamins (such as folate), and vitamin C. This is because it is low in dairy products, fruits, and vegetables. It is also low in many of the phytochemical (plant-based) substances discussed at the beginning of this chapter. In addition, fiber intake is low because fast-food restaurants primarily use refined grain products, rather than whole-grain products. And, since most super-sized options apply to foods rich in fat (french fries) and sugar (soft drinks), his diet is likely excessive in those two components.

tions (over 250 mg/dl) but shallow near 210 mg/dl, the average adult concentration. Thus, much less benefit is derived from lowering average cholesterol values.

Several prospective epidemiological studies have reported that a healthy dietary pattern, rather than an intake of individual nutrients predicts longer life expectancy. One study found a strong dose-response relationship evidenced by decreased mortality in subjects who consumed more fruits, vegetables, whole grains, low-fat dairy, and lean meats and poultry. Another large study implicated high consumption of cereal fiber, some fish, the vitamin folate, along with a high polyunsaturated:saturated fat ratio, and low consumption of trans fatty acids (present primarily in stick margarine, shortening, and deep-fat-fried foods; see Chapter 6), simple sugars, and refined carbohydrates as a dietary pattern linked to a reduced risk of cardiovascular disease. However, this dietary pattern strongly correlated with lower body mass index status, more exercise, nonsmoking, moderate alcohol intake, and daily use of a multivitamin and mineral supplements. Although scientists often attempt to sort out these factors to find the most important, it is becoming apparent that a combination of healthy habits achieves the desired benefits.

There's a strong statistical correlation of gross national product, telephones, flush toilets, and other signs of wealth with the incidence of cancer and cardiovascular disease because life expectancy is longer in more affluent countries. The chronic diseases are much more common among older individuals. Populations that can afford to eat a lot of fat, sugar, and salt do so because these three dietary components are what people think make food taste good.

Everyone in the country has been told to follow a low-sodium diet when only a minority of young and middle-aged adults are hypertensive, and only some of those are salt sensitive. There is also substantial evidence implicating protein, calcium, potassium, and magnesium intakes in controlling blood pressure.

A potential explanation for the lack of uniformity in response to dietary factors is that perhaps only some of the population shows elevated blood cholesterol from eating saturated fat, and only some people are genetically predisposed to colon cancer, whereas a fortunate few are destined to live long, healthy lives no matter what rules they violate. This observation does not discount the importance of nutrition in longevity but suggests that recommendations for dietary modification should not be blanket public health policies. Instead, these need to be made on individualized bases—that is, dietary guidelines for those who are at increased risk for specific diseases via family history or the presence of other risk factors may differ. This conclusion should not be taken to mean that a good diet is unimportant. High consumption of fruits, vegetables, and whole grains is associated with a lower incidence of obesity, type 2 diabetes, intestinal disorders, cardiovascular disease, and cancer.

Observational studies have implicated a high intake of vitamin E as a protective factor against cardiovascular disease. However, increased survival has not been found in bottles of antioxidant supplements. All but one of the many intervention studies have failed to find a significant benefit of vitamin E on cardiovascular disease rates or mortality, and even the results of that study have been questioned (see Chapter 6). However, diets low in this vitamin and other antioxidants are associated with excess mortality from both cancer and cardiovascular disease. In addition, none of the many studies performed using laboratory animals has shown benefits on longevity from consuming extra antioxidants.

The explanation that diet modification wouldn't hurt may satisfy some, but it's certainly not scientific. The burden of proof falls on those who suggest specific dietary changes, rather than on those who question the efficacy of those changes. Although what is written today will surely be outdated in the future, there are two nutritional rules that will make sense over time: (1) Eat a variety of foods and (2) consume all foods in moderation. Dietary changes made in isolation may be doomed to failure. Combining these recommendations with adequate physical activity and the avoidance of tobacco and excess alcohol is a lifestyle that promotes good health and extra years. Boring, perhaps, but advice one can take to heart.

Dr. Klurfeld is professor and chairman of the Department of Nutrition and Food Science at Wayne State University.

He could alternate between tacos and bean burritos to gain the benefits of plant proteins in a diet. He could choose a low-fat granola bar instead of the candy bar for breakfast, or he could take the time to eat a bowl of whole-grain breakfast cereal with low-fat or nonfat milk to increase fiber intake (and calcium intake in the latter case). He could also order milk at least half the time at his restaurant visits and substitute diet soft drinks for the regular variety. This would help *moderate* his sugar intake. Overall, his diet is most lacking in a variety of fruit and vegetable choices and dairy products because it lacks *variety* in food choice and *balance* among the five food groups.

Critical | Thinking

Athe has grown up eating the typical North American diet. Having recently read and heard many news items about the relationship between nutrition and health, she is beginning to look critically at her diet and is considering making changes. However, she doesn't know where to begin. What advice would you give her?

What Do Food Labels Have to Offer in Diet Planning?

Today, nearly all foods sold in the grocery store must be labeled with the product name, name and address of the manufacturer, amount of product in the package, and ingredients listed in descending order by weight. This food and beverage labeling is monitored by government agencies such as Food and Drug Administration (FDA). The listing of certain food constituents also is required—specifically, on a Nutrition Facts panel (Fig. 2-6). Use this information to learn more about what you eat. The following components must be listed: total calories, calories from fat, total fat, saturated fat, cholesterol, sodium, total carbohydrate, fiber, sugars, protein, vitamin A, vitamin C, calcium, and iron. In addition to these required components, manufacturers can choose to list polyunsaturated and monounsaturated fat, potassium, and others. Listing

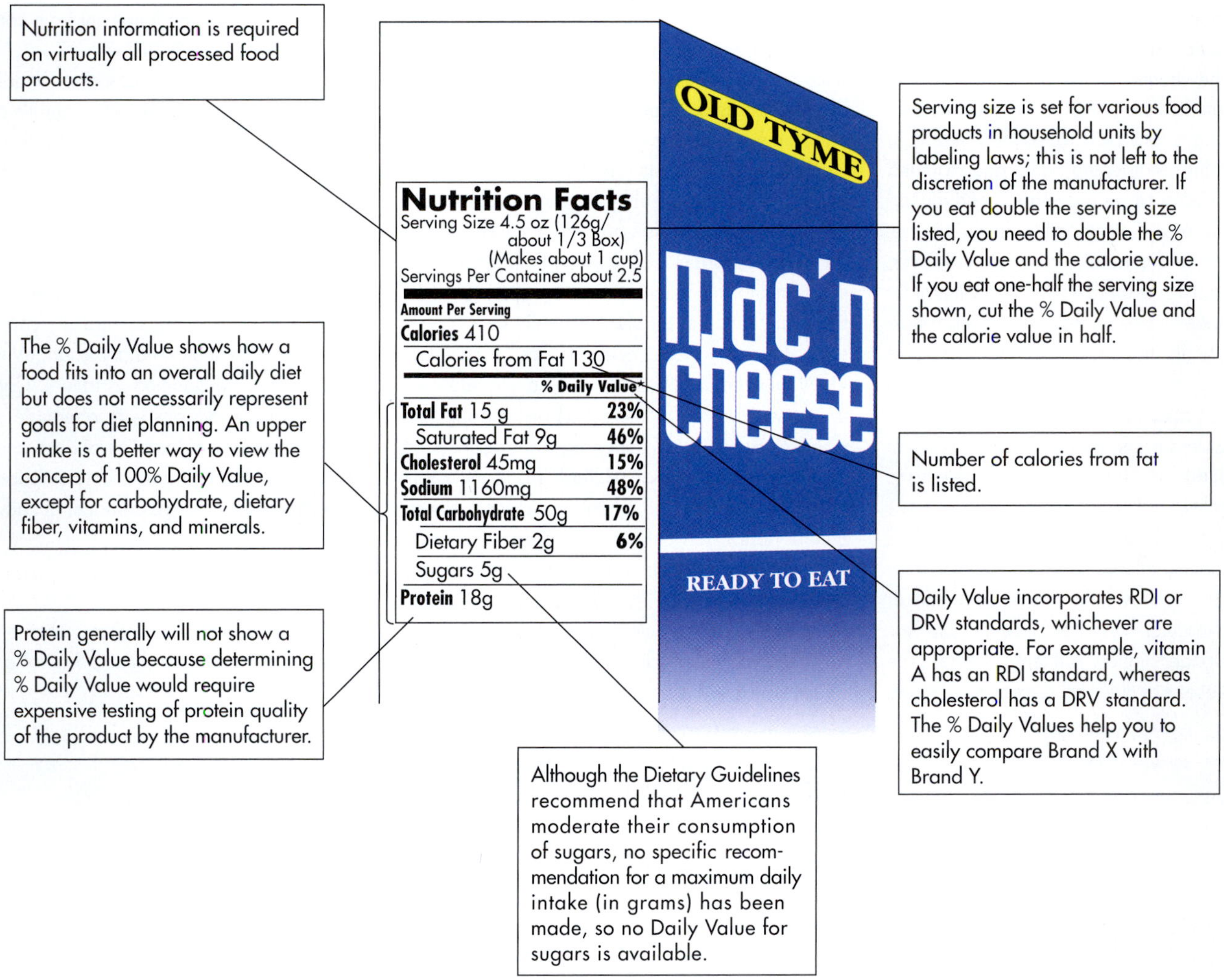
Nutrition information is required on virtually all processed food products.
The % Daily Value shows how a food fits into an overall daily diet but does not necessarily represent goals for diet planning. An upper intake is a better way to view the concept of 100% Daily Value, except for carbohydrate, dietary fiber, vitamins, and minerals.
Protein generally will not show a % Daily Value because determining % Daily Value would require expensive testing of protein quality of the product by the manufacturer.
Nutrition Facts
Serving Size 4.5 oz (126g/ about 1/3 Box)
(Makes about 1 cup)
Servings Per Container about 2.5
Amount Per Serving
Calories 410
Calories from Fat 130
% Daily Value*
Total Fat 15 g 23%
Saturated Fat 9g 46%
Cholesterol 45mg 15%
Sodium 1160mg 48%
Total Carbohydrate 50g 17%
Dietary Fiber 2g 6%
Sugars 5g
Protein 18g
OLD TYME
mac'n cheese
READY TO EAT
Serving size is set for various food products in household units by labeling laws; this is not left to the discretion of the manufacturer. If you eat double the serving size listed, you need to double the % Daily Value and the calorie value. If you eat one-half the serving size shown, cut the % Daily Value and the calorie value in half.
Number of calories from fat is listed.
Daily Value incorporates RDI or DRV standards, whichever are appropriate. For example, vitamin A has an RDI standard, whereas cholesterol has a DRV standard. The % Daily Values help you to easily compare Brand X with Brand Y.
Although the Dietary Guidelines recommend that Americans moderate their consumption of sugars, no specific recommendation for a maximum daily intake (in grams) has been made, so no Daily Value for sugars is available.

Figure 2-6a The Nutrition Facts panel on a current food label. This figure is broken into two parts: (*a*) the top and (*b*) the bottom of a Nutrition Facts label. The % Daily Value listed on the label is the percentage of the generally accepted amount of a nutrient needed daily that is present in one serving of the product. You can use the % Daily Values to compare your diet with current nutrition recommendations for certain diet components. Let's consider fiber (listed as dietary fiber). Assume that you consume 2000 kcal per day, which is the energy intake corresponding to the % Daily Values listed on labels. If the total % Daily Value for fiber in all the foods you eat in one day adds up to 100%, your diet meets the recommendations for fiber. Food labels also contain the name and address of the food manufacturers. This allows consumers to contact the manufacturer if they desire.

Illustration by William Ober.

these components is *required,* however, if a claim is made about the health benefits of the specific nutrient (see the section in this chapter entitled "Health Claims on Food Labels") or if the food is fortified with that nutrient.

The percentage of the Daily Value (% Daily Value) is usually given for each nutrient per serving. It is important to understand that these percentages are based on a 2000 kcal diet. In other words, they are not as applicable to people who require considerably more or less than 2000 kcal per day with respect to fat and carbohydrate intake.

Serving sizes on the Nutrition Facts panel must be consistent among similar foods. This means that all brands of ice cream, for example, must use the same serving size on their labels. In addition, food claims made on packages must follow legal definitions (Table 2-11). For example, if a product claims to be "low sodium," it must have 140 mg of sodium or less per serving.

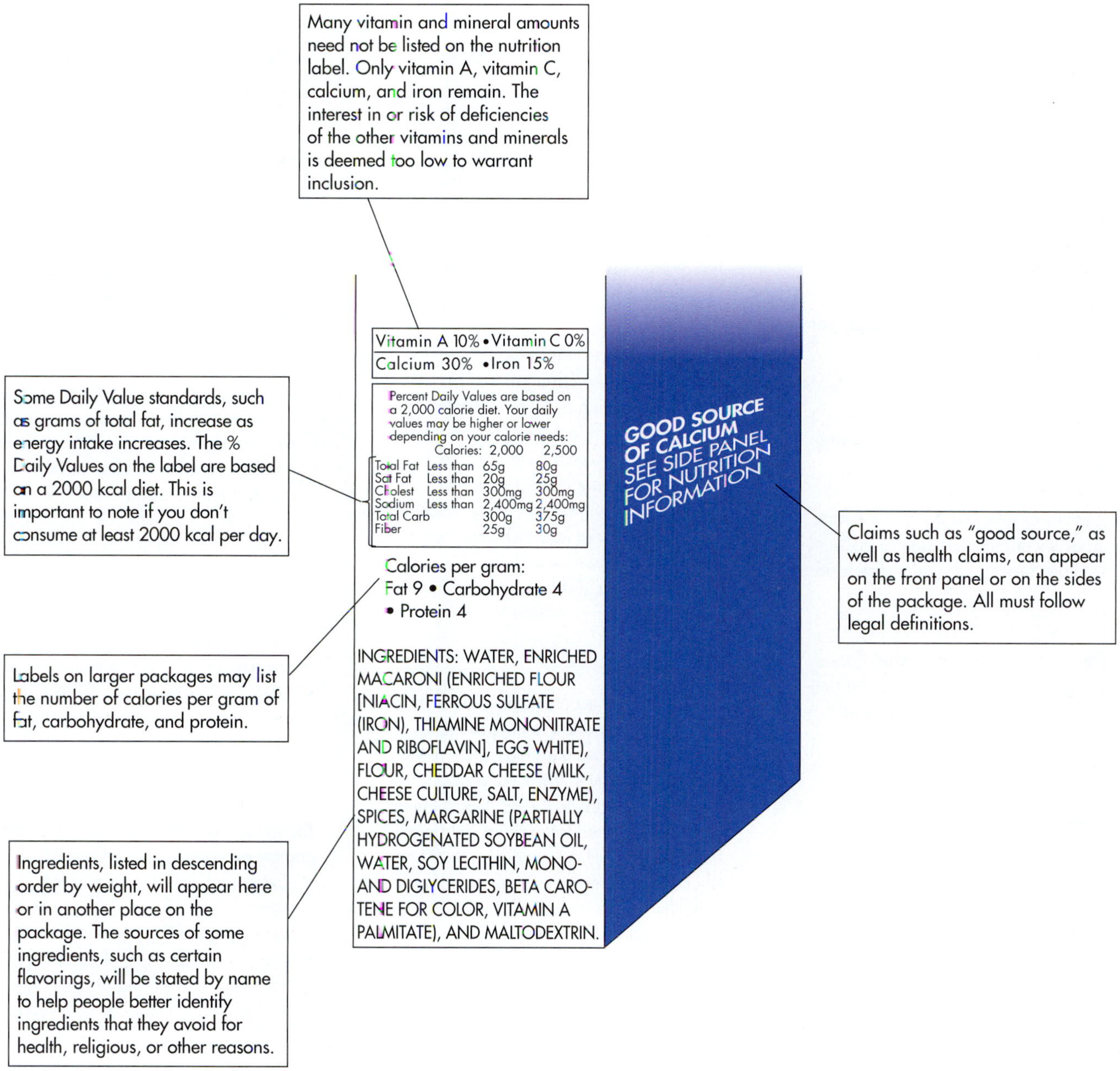
Many vitamin and mineral amounts need not be listed on the nutrition label. Only vitamin A, vitamin C, calcium, and iron remain. The interest in or risk of deficiencies of the other vitamins and minerals is deemed too low to warrant inclusion.
Vitamin A 10% • Vitamin C 0%
Calcium 30% • Iron 15%
Some Daily Value standards, such as grams of total fat, increase as energy intake increases. The % Daily Values on the label are based on a 2000 kcal diet. This is important to note if you don't consume at least 2000 kcal per day.
Percent Daily Values are based on a 2,000 calorie diet. Your daily values may be higher or lower depending on your calorie needs:
Calories: 2,000 2,500
Total Fat Less than 65g 80g
Sat Fat Less than 20g 25g
Cholest Less than 300mg 300mg
Sodium Less than 2,400mg 2,400mg
Total Carb 300g 375g
Fiber 25g 30g
GOOD SOURCE OF CALCIUM
SEE SIDE PANEL FOR NUTRITION INFORMATION
Claims such as "good source," as well as health claims, can appear on the front panel or on the sides of the package. All must follow legal definitions.
Calories per gram:
Fat 9 • Carbohydrate 4 • Protein 4
Labels on larger packages may list the number of calories per gram of fat, carbohydrate, and protein.
INGREDIENTS: WATER, ENRICHED MACARONI (ENRICHED FLOUR [NIACIN, FERROUS SULFATE (IRON), THIAMINE MONONITRATE AND RIBOFLAVIN], EGG WHITE), FLOUR, CHEDDAR CHEESE (MILK, CHEESE CULTURE, SALT, ENZYME), SPICES, MARGARINE (PARTIALLY HYDROGENATED SOYBEAN OIL, WATER, SOY LECITHIN, MONO- AND DIGLYCERIDES, BETA CAROTENE FOR COLOR, VITAMIN A PALMITATE), AND MALTODEXTRIN.
Ingredients, listed in descending order by weight, will appear here or in another place on the package. The sources of some ingredients, such as certain flavorings, will be stated by name to help people better identify ingredients that they avoid for health, religious, or other reasons.

Figure 2-6b For legend see previous page.

Table 2-11 Definitions for Comparative and Absolute Nutrient Claims on Food Labels

Sugar
- *Sugar free:* less than 0.5 grams (g) per serving
- *No added sugar; without added sugar; no sugar added:*
    - No sugars were added during processing or packing, including ingredients that contain sugars (for example, fruit juices, applesauce, or jam).
    - Processing does not increase the sugar content above the amount naturally present in the ingredients. (A functionally insignificant increase in sugars is acceptable for processes used for purposes other than increasing sugar content.)
    - The food that it resembles and for which it substitutes normally contains added sugars.
    - If the food doesn't meet the requirements for a low- or reduced-calorie food, the product bears a statement that the food is not low calorie or calorie reduced and directs consumers' attention to the nutrition panel for further information on sugars and calorie content.
- *Reduced sugar:* at least 25% less sugar per serving than reference food

Calories
- *Calorie free:* fewer than 5 kcal per serving
- *Low calorie:* 40 kcal or less per serving and, if the serving is 30 g or less or 2 tablespoons or less, per 50 g of the food
- *Reduced or fewer calories:* at least 25% fewer kcal per serving than reference food

Fiber
- *High fiber:* 5 g or more per serving (foods making high-fiber claims must meet the definition for low fat, or the level of total fat must appear next to the high-fiber claim)
- *Food source of fiber:* 2.5 to 4.9 g per serving
- *More or added fiber:* at least 2.5 g more per serving than reference food

Fat
- *Fat free:* less than 0.5 g of fat per serving
- *Saturated fat free:* less than 0.5 g per serving, and the level of trans fatty acids does not exceed 0.5 g per serving
- *Low fat:* 3 g or less per serving and, if the serving is 30 g or less or 2 tablespoons or less, per 50 g of the food. 2% milk can no longer be labeled low-fat, as it exceeds 3 g per serving. *Reduced fat* will be the term used instead.
- *Low saturated fat:* 1 g or less per serving and not more than 15% of kcal from saturated fatty acids
- *Reduced or less fat:* at least 25% less per serving than reference food
- *Reduced or less saturated fat:* at least 25% less per serving than reference food

Cholesterol
- *Cholesterol free:* less than 2 mg of cholesterol and 2 g or less of saturated fat per serving
- *Low cholesterol:* 20 mg or less cholesterol and 2 g or less of saturated fat per serving and, if the serving is 30 g or less or 2 tablespoons or less, per 50 g of the food
- *Reduced or less cholesterol:* at least 25% less cholesterol and 2 g or less of saturated fat per serving than reference food

Sodium
- *Sodium free:* less than 5 mg per serving
- *Very low sodium:* 35 mg or less per serving and, if the serving is 30 g or less or 2 tablespoons or less, per 50 g of the food
- *Low sodium:* 140 mg or less per serving and, if the serving is 30 g or less or 2 tablespoons or less, per 50 g of the food
- *Light in sodium:* at least 50% less per serving than reference food
- *Reduced or less sodium:* at least 25% less per serving than reference food

Other Terms
- *Fortified/enriched:* Vitamins and/or minerals have been added to the product in amounts in excess of at least 10% of that normally present in the usual product.
- *Healthy:* An individual food that is low-fat and low saturated fat and has no more than 360 to 480 mg of sodium or 60 mg of cholesterol per serving can be labeled "healthy" if it provides at least 10% of vitamin A, vitamin C, protein, calcium, iron, or fiber.
- *Light or lite:* The descriptor *light* or *lite* can mean two things: first, that a nutritionally altered product contains one-third fewer kcal or half the fat of reference food (if the food derives 50% or more of its kcal from fat, the reduction must be 50% of the fat) and, second, that the sodium content of a low-calorie, low-fat food has been reduced by 50%. In addition, "light in sodium" may be used for foods in which the sodium content has been reduced by at least 50%. The term *light* may still be used to describe such properties as texture and color, as long as the label explains the intent—for example, "light brown sugar" and "light and fluffy."
- *Diet:* A food may be labeled with terms such as *diet, dietetic, artificially sweetened,* or *sweetened with nonnutritive sweetener* only if the claim is not false or misleading. The food can also be labeled *low calorie* or *reduced calorie.*
- *Good source: Good source* means that a serving of the food contains 10 to 19% of the Daily Value for a particular nutrient.
- *High: High* means that a serving of the food contains 20% or more of the Daily Value for a particular nutrient.
- USDA ORGANIC *Organic:* Federal standards for organic foods allow claims when much of the ingredients do not use chemical fertilizers or pesticides, genetic engineering, sewage sludge, antibiotics, or irradiation in their production. At least 95% of ingredients (by weight) must meet these guidelines to be labeled "organic" on the front of the package or use the USDA organic seal. For livestock, the animals need to be allowed to graze outdoors and as well be fed organic feed. They also cannot be exposed to antibiotics or growth hormones. If the front label instead says "made with organic ingredients," only 70% of the ingredients must be organic.
- *Natural:* The food must be free of food colors, synthetic flavors, or any other synthetic substance.

The following terms apply only to meat and poultry products regulated by USDA.
- *Extra lean:* less than 5 g of fat, 2 g of saturated fat, and 95 mg of cholesterol per serving (or 100 g of an individual food)
- *Lean:* less than 10 g of fat, 4.5 g of saturated fat, and 95 mg of cholesterol per serving (or 100 g of an individual food)

Many definitions are from FDA's *Dictionary of Terms,* as established in conjunction with the 1990 NLEA.

Many manufacturers list the Daily Values set for dietary components such as fat, cholesterol, and carbohydrate on the Nutrition Facts panel. This can be useful as a reference point. As noted before, they are based on 2000 kcal; if the label is large enough, amounts based on 2500 kcal are listed as well. Recall also from Chapter 1 that the term *calories* is used to express energy content on the labels; however, scientifically speaking this is an incorrect use of the term unless the first letter of the word is capitalized.

The food labels on these three products can be combined to indicate nutrient intake for a meal—a peanut butter and jelly sandwich. (Note that Canadian food labels have a slightly different format and follow different labeling guidelines (see Appendix D).)

Exceptions to Food Labeling

Foods such as fresh fruits and vegetables, fish, meats, and poultry currently are not required to have Nutrition Facts labels. However, many grocers and some meat packers have voluntarily chosen to provide their customers with information on these products. Nutrition Facts labels on meat products will also likely be required in the coming years. The next time you are at the grocery store, ask where you might find information on the fresh products that do not have a Nutrition Facts panel. You will likely find a poster or pamphlet near the product; often, these pamphlets contain recipes in which to use your favorite fruit, vegetable, or cut of meat. They may even assist you in your endeavor to improve your diet.

Because protein deficiency is not a public health concern in the United States, declaration of the % Daily Value for protein is not mandatory on foods for people over 4 years of age. If the % Daily Value is given on a label, FDA requires that the product be analyzed for protein quality. Because this procedure is expensive and time-consuming, many companies opt not to list a % Daily Value for protein rather than undergo the expense. However, labels on food for infants and children under 4 years of age must include the % Daily Value for protein, as must the labels on any food carrying a claim about protein content (see Chapter 17).

Nutrient and herbal supplements have a different layout with a "Supplement Facts" heading. Chapters 9 and 18 show examples of these labels.

Health Claims on Food Labels

As a marketing tool directed toward the health-conscious consumer, food manufacturers are asserting that their products have all sorts of health benefits. After reviewing hundreds of comments by the food industry, nutrition scientists, and others on the proposed rule allowing health claims, the Food and Drug Administration (FDA), which has legal oversight over most food products, decided to permit certain health claims with specific restrictions.

As covered in Chapter 1, some products make so-called "structure/function" claims, such as "improves blood circulation." These are not approved by FDA because of laws passed by the U.S. Congress in 1994 (see Chapter 1). View any of these non-FDA-approved claims skeptically.

Currently, FDA limits the use of health messages to specific instances in which there is significant scientific agreement concerning the relationship between a nutrient, food, or food constituent and the disease.[8] The claims allowed at this time may show a link between the following:

- A diet with enough calcium and a reduced risk of osteoporosis
- A diet low in total fat and a reduced risk of some cancers
- A diet low in saturated fat and cholesterol and a reduced risk of cardiovascular (heart) disease (typically referred to as heart disease on the label)
- A diet rich in fiber-containing grain products, fruits, and vegetables and a reduced risk of some cancers
- A diet low in sodium and high in potassium and a reduced risk of hypertension and stroke
- A diet rich in fruits and vegetables and a reduced risk of some cancers
- A diet adequate in the synthetic form of the vitamin folate (called folic acid) and a reduced risk of neural tube defects (a type of birth defect)
- Use of sugarless gum and a reduced risk of tooth decay, especially when compared with foods high in sugars and starches
- A diet rich in fruits, vegetables, and grain products that contain fiber and a reduced risk of cardiovascular disease. Oats (oatmeal, oat bran, and oat flour) and psyllium

Canada has established a set of health claims for their nutrition labels (see Appendix D).

Eating fish at least twice a week contributes to overall health.

are two fiber-rich ingredients that can be singled out in reducing the risk of cardiovascular disease, as long as the statement also says the diet should also be low in saturated fat and cholesterol.

- A diet rich in whole-grain foods and other plant foods, as well as low in total fat, saturated fat, and cholesterol, and a reduced risk of cardiovascular disease and certain cancers
- A diet low in saturated fat and cholesterol that also includes 25 g of soy protein and a reduced risk of cardiovascular disease. The statement "one serving of the (name food) provides _____ g of soy protein" must also appear as part of the health claim.
- Omega-3 fatty acids from oils present in fish and a reduced risk of cardiovascular disease
- Margarines containing plant stanols and sterols and a reduced risk of cardiovascular disease (see Chapter 6 for more details on plant stanols and sterols).

A "may" or "might" qualifier must be used in any statement.

In addition, before a health claim can be made for a food product, it must meet two general requirements. First, the food must be a "good source" of dietary fiber, protein, vitamin A, vitamin C, calcium, or iron. The legal definition of "good source" appeared in Table 2-11. Keep in mind that for a food to be labeled as a "good source," those nutrients have to be present *before* the food is fortified. This is known as the "Jelly Bean Rule," and it keeps health claims off fortified soft drinks and bottled waters, chewing gums and lozenges, and other foods of low nutritional value. Second, a single serving of the food product cannot contain more than 13 g of fat, 4 g of saturated fat, 60 mg of cholesterol, or 480 mg of sodium. If a food exceeds any one of these amounts, no health claim can be made for it, despite its other nutritional qualities. For example, even though whole milk is high in calcium, its label can't make the health claim about calcium and osteoporosis because whole milk contains 5 g of saturated fat per serving.

In addition, the product must meet criteria specific to the health claim being made. For example, a health claim regarding fat and cancer can be made only if the product contains 3 g or less of fat per serving, which is the standard for low-fat food.

The bottom line for health claims is honesty. FDA is vigilant in controlling the claims made about foods on supermarket shelves.[8]

The Exchange System is a final menu-planning tool. This tool organizes foods based on energy, protein, carbohydrate, and fat content. The result is a manageable framework for designing diets. For more information on the Exchange System see Appendices E and F.

Concept | Check

The Nutrition Facts panel on a food label provides key information for helping track one's food intake. Nutrient quantities are compared with the Daily Values and expressed on a percentage basis (% Daily Value). This information can be used to either increase or reduce intake of specific nutrients. Health claims on food labels are closely regulated by FDA. Fruits, vegetables, whole grains, soy, and rich sources of calcium are prominent among the foods that can make specific health claims.

Summary

1. *Variety, balance,* and *moderation* are three watchwords of diet planning.
2. Nutrient density is a useful concept. It reflects the nutrient content of a food in relation to its energy (kcal) content. Nutrient-dense foods are relatively rich in nutrients, in comparison with energy content.
3. Energy density of a food is determined by comparing energy content with the weight of food. A food that is rich in energy but weighs relatively very little, such as nuts, cookies, fried foods in general, and fat-free snacks, is considered energy dense. Foods with low energy density include fruits, vegetables, and any food that incorporates lots of water during cooking, such as oatmeal.
4. A person's nutritional state can be categorized as *desirable nutrition,* in which the body has adequate stores for times of increased needs; *undernutrition,* which may be present with or without clinical symptoms; and *overnutrition,* which can lead to vitamin and mineral toxicities and various chronic diseases.
5. Evaluation of nutritional state involves analyzing background factors, anthropometric measurements, biochemical parameters, clinical evidence, diet history, and economic status. It is not always

possible to detect nutritional inadequacies via nutrition assessment since such evidence often does not appear for many years.

6. Recommended Dietary Allowances (RDAs) are set for many nutrients. These amounts yield enough of each nutrient to meet the needs of healthy individuals within specific gender and age categories. Adequate Intakes (AIs) are used when not enough information is available to set an RDA. Estimated Energy Requirements (EERs) provide a benchmark for energy needs. Tolerable Upper Intake Levels (Upper Levels or ULs) for nutrient intake have been set for some vitamins and minerals. All of the many dietary standards fall under the term *Dietary Reference Intakes (DRIs)*. Daily Values are used as a basis for expressing the nutrient content of foods on the Nutrition Facts panel and are based for the most part on the RDAs published in 1968.

7. The Food Guide Pyramid is designed to translate nutrient recommendations into a food plan that exhibits variety, balance, and moderation. The best results are obtained by using low-fat or nonfat dairy products; incorporating some vegetable proteins into the diet in addition to animal-protein foods; including citrus fruits and dark green vegetables; and emphasizing whole-grain breads and cereals.

8. Dietary Guidelines for Americans have been issued to help reduce chronic diseases in our population. The guidelines emphasize eating a variety of foods; performing regular physical activity; maintaining or improving weight; moderating consumption of fat, cholesterol, sugar, salt, and alcohol; eating plenty of grain products, fruits, and vegetables; and safely preparing and storing foods, especially perishable foods.

9. Food labels are a powerful tool to track your nutrient intake and learn more about the nutritional characteristics of the foods you eat. Any health claims listed must follow specific legal criteria set by FDA.

Study Questions

1. Describe the philosophy underlying the creation of the Food Guide Pyramid. What dietary changes would you need to make to meet the Pyramid guidelines on a regular basis?

2. Trace the progression, in terms of physical results, of a person who went from an overnourished to an undernourished state.

3. How could the nutritional state of the person at each state in question 2 be evaluated?

4. Describe the intent of the Dietary Guidelines for Americans. Point out one criticism for its general application to all North American adults.

5. Based on the discussion of the Dietary Guidelines, suggest two key dietary changes the typical North American adult should consider making.

6. How do RDAs and Adequate Intakes differ from Daily Values in intention and application?

7. How would you explain the concepts of nutrient density and energy density to a fourth-grade class?

8. Nutritionists encourage all people to read labels on food packages to learn more about what they eat. What four nutrients could easily be tracked in your diet if you read the Nutrition Facts panels regularly on food products?

9. Explain why consumers can have confidence in FDA-approved health claims on food packages.

10. Relate the importance of variety in a diet, especially with regard to fruit and vegetable choices, to the discovery of various phytochemicals in foods.

Annotated References

1. ADA Reports: Position of the American Dietetic Association: Functional foods. *Journal of the American Dietetic Association,* 99:1278, 1999.

   The philosophy that food can be health promoting beyond its traditional nutritional value (i.e., phytochemical content) is gaining acceptance among scientists and health professionals. Never before have the health benefits of food had so much support.

2. Barr SI and others: Interpreting and using the Dietary Reference Intakes in dietary assessment of individuals in groups. *Journal of the American Dietetic Association* 102:780, 2002.

   This article describes appropriate uses of the Estimated Average Requirements, Recommended Dietary Allowances, Adequate Intakes, and Tolerable Upper Intake Levels. Dietary intakes from a group of individuals is best evaluated with the Estimated Average Requirements, while intakes of individual people are best evaluated using the Recommended Dietary Allowances and Adequate Intakes.

3. Bruce B and others: A diet high in whole and unrefined foods favorably alters lipids, antioxidant defenses and colon function. *Journal of the American College of Nutrition* 19:61, 2000.

   A diet abundant in phytochemical-rich foods beneficially affected blood lipids, the antioxidant defense mechanism in the body, and colon function.

4. Campbell TC, Chen J: Diet and health in rural China: Lessons learned and unlearned. *Nutrition Today* 34:116, 1999.

   Studies of rural Asian subjects show that their traditional, primarily plant-based diet contributes to their low risk for chronic degenerative diseases. These findings are consistent with the observations of Asian migrants; they experience more of these diseases when they switch to a more westernized approach.

5. Clairmont MA: Nutraceuticals, phytochemicals and functional foods: A field of dreams for dietitians. *Today's Dietitian,* p. 36, April 2000.

   Growing evidence supports the role of phytochemicals in disease prevention. Phytochemical-rich foods discussed include broccoli, cabbage, tomatoes, tea, soy, whole grains, oranges, grapes, and onions.

6. Curtis BM and O'Keefe JH: Understanding the Mediterranean diet: Could this be the new "gold standard" for heart disease prevention? *Postgraduate Medicine* 112(2):35, 2002.

   The Mediterranean diet has been around for thousands of years. Traditional diets among some Mediterranean cultures (e.g., Greece, Crete, southern France, parts of Italy) include an abundance of fruits and vegetables, along with olive oil, fish, nuts, and moderate amounts of wine. This diet offers a practical, effective, and enjoyable strategy that is relatively easy to adopt and more likely to be successful over the long term than most other heart-healthy diets. The article specifically reviews the cardioprotective effects of the diet and presents practical ideas for implementation.

7. Davis CA and others: Past, present, and future of the Food Guide Pyramid. *Journal of the American Dietetic Association* 101:881, 2001.

   The historical objective of food guides such as the Food Guide Pyramid has been to translate dietary standards and recommendations into simple nutrition education tools that are useful to consumers. Some researchers have suggested that the current Food Guide Pyramid has limitations such as lack of advice for more healthy types of carbohydrates, essential fatty acids, iron, and calcium. The Food Guide Pyramid is currently being reevaluated for possible improvements.

8. Food and Nutrition Board: Dietary reference intakes for energy, carbohydrate, fiber, fat, fatty acids, cholesterol, protein, and amino acids. The National Academy Press, Washington D.C. 2002.

   This report provides the latest guidance for macronutrient and energy intakes. With regard to energy intake in adulthood, this should generally match energy output so weight maintenance is achieved.

9. Hasler CM: Functional foods: Benefits, concerns, and challenges—A position paper from the American Council on Science and Health. *Journal of Nutrition* 132: 3772, 2002.

   We now know that our diet and its constituents from both plant and animal sources provide more than the essential nutrients such as protein and vitamins, namely a variety of phytochemical and other components that also contribute to health. Foods rich in specific phytochemicals are often termed functional foods. This article lists a variety of phytochemicals under study, as well as current approved health claims for food labels.

10. Kant AK: Consumption of energy-dense, nutrient-poor foods by adult Americans: nutritional and health implications. The third National Health and Nutrition Examination Survey, 1984–1994. *American Journal of Clinical Nutrition* 72:929, 2000.

    Many adults consume diets rich with energy-dense, nutrient-poor foods such as refined grains. This pattern leads to increased risk for following a diet high in energy and marginal in vitamin and mineral content.

11. Keenan DP, Abusabha R: The fifth edition of the Dietary Guidelines for Americans: lessons learned along the way. *Journal of the American Dietetic Association* 101:631, 2001.

    A comparison of the Dietary Guidelines from the first edition, fourth edition, and current fifth edition is presented. The fifth edition is considered a significant improvement over earlier editions, but still could undergo more fine-tuning to be more useful for consumers. One example is that the maximum amount of sugars to be consumed daily is not specified.

12. Laudan R: Birth of the modern diet. *Scientific American*, p. 76, August 2000.

    Advances in knowledge concerning diet and nutrition have had a great effect on our diets over the last 300 years. Recognizing the importance of fruits and vegetables scores high marks for our current diet, while the central rule of fat in our diets because of the importance given to meat and fat-based sauces is blamed for the high amounts of obesity in most developed nations.

13. McKay DL and Blumberg JB: The role of tea and health: an update. *Journal of the American College of Nutrition* 21(1):1, 2002.

    Tea is an important dietary source of phytochemicals such as flavanols and flavonols. Many, but not all, studies of tea consumption suggest that the phytochemicals present reduce the risk of developing a number of chronic diseases, especially cardiovascular disease and cancer.

14. Rao AV, Agarwal S: Role of the antioxidant lycopene in cancer and heart disease. *Journal of the American College of Nutrition* 19:563, 2000.

    Tomatoes and tomato products are a rich source of lycopene. It is a major carotenoid found in the bloodstream and in various body tissues. Regular intake of lycopene has been reported to reduce the risk of developing both cancer and cardiovascular disease.

15. Richards L: Food Pyramid controversies. *Today's Dietitian*, p. 34, June 2002.

    A number of pyramids have been proposed that compete with the Food Guide Pyramid, such as the Dietary Approaches to Stop Hypertension (DASH) Pyramid and the pyramid proposed by Dr. Walter Willett. Health contributions of the Food Guide Pyramid are greatly improved if one emphasizes whole grains instead of mostly refined grains and uses mostly whole fruit instead of mostly fruit juices.

16. Rolls BJ: The role of energy density in the overconsumption of fat. *Journal of Nutrition* 130:2685, 2000.

    Eating foods that have a low energy density is one way to feel full without consuming a lot of energy. If the food is high in fat, even small portions may have a high energy content; energy-dense foods are generally consumed in larger quantities in order to feel full at the end of a meal.

17. Stampfer JM and others: Primary prevention of coronary heart disease in women through diet and lifestyle. *The New England Journal of Medicine* 343:16, 2000.

    Women who consume a varied diet (one rich in fiber, includes some fish, and is low in fried foods and animal fat), avoid overweight, drink small amounts of alcohol, exercise on a daily basis for about 30 minutes, and avoid smoking reduce their risk of heart attack by over 80%, compared with women without these habits.

18. Van Duyn MAS, Pivonka E: Overview of the health benefits of fruit and vegetable consumption for the dietetics professional: Selected literature. *Journal of the American Dietetic Association* 100:1511, 2000.

    Epidemiologic evidence for the protective role for fruits and vegetables in cancer prevention is substantial. Current scientific evidence also suggests a protective role for fruits and vegetables in the prevention of various forms of cardiovascular disease. In addition, fruits and vegetables may protect against cataracts, pulmonary disease, certain intestinal disorders, and possibly hypertension.

19. Weisburger JH: Approaches for chronic disease prevention based on current understanding of underlying mechanisms. *American Journal of Clinical Nutrition* 71(Suppl):1710S, 2000.

    Consuming adequate fruits and vegetables, having a high fiber intake, and having an ample fluid intake reduce the risk for many chronic diseases. We should put these recommendations into practice.

20. Willett WC: *Eat, drink, and be healthy.* New York: Simon & Schuster, 2001 (or Willet WC, Stampfer MJ: Rebuilding the pyramid. *Scientific American* p. 64, January 2003).

    The diet plan proposed emphasizes whole grains, plant oils, vegetables eaten daily; fruits at least 2–3 times per day; nuts and legumes 1–3 times per day; fish, poultry, and eggs eaten 0–2 times per day; dairy products or calcium supplements one to two times per day; and little use of red meat, butter, white rice, white bread, potatoes, pasta, and sweets. Regular physical activity and weight control is also recommended, as is alcohol intake in moderation (if of legal age) and a multivitamin and mineral supplement for most people.

Take | Action

I. Does Your Diet Meet Nutrient Needs, Food Guide Pyramid Recommendations, and the Dietary Guidelines for Americans?

Complete either Part I or Part II. Then complete Parts III, IV, and V. (For help in following the instructions for this activity, see the sample assessment in Appendix G.)

Part I

Manual RDA Analysis

A. Take the information from the 1-day food-intake record you completed in Chapter 1 and record it on the blank form provided in Appendix G or by your instructor. Be sure to record the food or drink ingested and the amount (e.g., weight) consumed. Note: Your instructor may require you to keep the food record for more than 1 day.
B. Review the various nutrient standards on the inside cover of this book and choose the appropriate recommendations for your gender and age. Write the appropriate value for each nutrient on the line on the form labeled "Nutrient Need."
C. Look up the foods and drinks that you listed on the form in the food composition table, Appendix N. Record on the form the amounts of each nutrient and their energy content, based on the serving size and the number of servings you ate. For example, if you drank 2 cups of milk and the serving size listed in Appendix A is 1 cup, double all nutrient values as you record them. If the food is not listed, choose a substitute, such as cola for root beer.
D. For each food and drink, add the amounts in each column and record the results on the line labeled "Totals."
E. Compare the totals to your nutrient needs. Divide the total for each nutrient by the specific amount and multiply that by 100. Record the result on the line labeled "% of Nutrient Needs."
F. Keep this assessment for use in subsequent activities in other chapters.

Part II

Computer Diet Analysis

A. Load the software (shrink-wrapped with this book) into the computer.
B. Choose RDAs and related nutrient standards based on your age and gender.
C. Enter the information from the 1-day food-intake record you kept in Chapter 1. Be sure to enter each food and drink and the specific amount you ate.
D. This software program will give you the following results:
   1. The appropriate RDA (or related standard) for each nutrient
   2. The total amount of each nutrient and the kcal consumed for the day
   3. The percentage intake compared with needs for each nutrient that you consumed
E. Keep this assessment for use in subsequent activities in other chapters.

Part III

Evaluation of Nutrient Intakes as a Percentage of Nutrient Needs

Remember that you don't necessarily need to consume your estimated nutrient needs every day. A general standard is meeting needs averaged over 5 to 8 days. It is best not to exceed the Upper Level (if set) over the long term to avoid potential toxic effects for some nutrients.

A. For which nutrients did your intakes fall below estimated nutrient needs?
B. Did you exceed the sodium needs? To what degree?
C. For which nutrients did you exceed the Upper Level (if set)?
D. What dietary changes could you make to correct or improve your dietary profile? If you're not sure, Chapters 5 through 12 will help guide your decisions.

Part IV

Food Guide Pyramid

Using the same food-intake record used in Part I or II, place each food item in the appropriate group of the Food Guide Pyramid chart in Appendix G. That is, for each food item, indicate how many servings it contributes to each group based on the amount you ate (see

Take | Action

Table 2-8 for serving sizes). Note that many of your food choices may contribute to more than one group. For example, toast with margarine contributes to two categories: (1) the breads, cereals, rice, and pasta group; and (2) fats, oils, and sweets. After entering all the values, add the number of servings consumed in each group. Finally, compare your total in each food group with the recommended number of servings shown in Figure 2-4. Enter a minus sign (−) if your total falls below the recommendation or a plus sign (+) if it equals or exceeds the recommendation.

Part V

Further Diet Evaluation

Do the weaknesses, if any, suggested in your nutrient analysis (see Part III) correspond to missing servings in the Food Guide Pyramid chart? If so, consider changing your food choices based on the Food Guide Pyramid to help improve your nutrient profile. Finally, indicate whether your day's diet did or did not conform to the following items in the Dietary Guidelines for Americans:

	Yes	No
Aim for Fitness		
• Aim for a healthy weight.	______	______
• Be physically active each day.	______	______
Build a Healthy Base		
• Let the pyramid guide your food choices.	______	______
• Choose a variety of grains daily, especially whole grains.	______	______
• Choose a variety of fruits and vegetables daily.	______	______
• Keep foods safe to eat.	______	______
Choose Sensibly		
• Choose a diet that is low in saturated fat and cholesterol and moderate in total fat.	______	______
• Choose beverages and foods to moderate your intake of sugars.	______	______
• Choose and prepare foods with less salt.	______	______
• If you drink alcoholic beverages, do so in moderation.	______	______

If your diet comes up short on any of these evaluations, take appropriate action to improve your eating patterns.

II. Applying the Nutrition Facts Label to Your Daily Food Choices.

Imagine that you are at the supermarket looking for a quick meal before a busy evening. In the frozen food section, you find two brands of frozen cheese manicotti (see labels a and b). Which of the two brands would you choose? What information on the Nutrition Facts label in the figure contributed to this decision?

____

____

____

____

Nutrition Facts
Serving Size 1 Package (260g)
Servings Per Container 1

Amount Per Serving	
Calories 390	Calories from Fat 160
	% Daily Value*
Total Fat 18g	**27%**
Saturated Fat 9g	**45%**
Cholesterol 45mg	**14%**
Sodium 880mg	**36%**
Total Carbohydrate 38g	**13%**
Dietary Fiber 4g	**15%**
Sugars 12g	
Protein 17g	
Vitamin A 10% • Vitamin C 4%	
Calcium 40% • Iron 8%	

*Percent Daily Values are based on a 2,000 calorie diet. Your daily values may be higher or lower depending on your calorie needs:

	Calories:	2,000	2,500
Total Fat	Less than	65g	80g
Sat Fat	Less than	20g	25g
Cholesterol	Less than	300mg	300mg
Sodium	Less than	2,400mg	2,400mg
Total Carbohydrate		300g	375g
Dietary Fiber		25g	30g

(a)

Nutrition Facts
Serving Size 1 Package (260g)
Servings Per Container 1

Amount Per Serving	
Calories 230	Calories from Fat 35
	% Daily Value*
Total Fat 4g	**6%**
Saturated Fat 2g	**10%**
Cholesterol 15mg	**4%**
Sodium 590mg	**24%**
Total Carbohydrate 28g	**9%**
Dietary Fiber 3g	**12%**
Sugars 10g	
Protein 19g	
Vitamin A 10% • Vitamin C 10%	
Calcium 35% • Iron 4%	

*Percent Daily Values are based on a 2,000 calorie diet. Your daily values may be higher or lower depending on your calorie needs:

	Calories:	2,000	2,500
Total Fat	Less than	65g	80g
Sat Fat	Less than	20g	25g
Cholesterol	Less than	300mg	300mg
Sodium	Less than	2,400mg	2,400mg
Potassium		3,500mg	3,500mg
Total Carbohydrate		300g	375g
Dietary Fiber		25g	30g

(b)

Ethnic Influences on the North American Diet

Human societies have developed under widely varying conditions. These conditions affected which foods were available (e.g., rice vs. wheat) and how long each food could be stored (e.g., tropical vs. temperate climates). This, in turn, influenced the dietary patterns of these various cultures. As these various cultures migrated to new locations, the migrants kept some traditional dietary habits, or *foodways,* changed some habits, and abandoned others.[12] As people migrate and mingle with those of other cultures, their cuisines tend to mingle as well. Note that about 25% of all restaurants in the United States have an ethnic theme. Recent changes in affluence and technology also affect dietary habits, some for better and some for worse. This Nutrition Perspective examines how the cuisines of various cultures throughout the world have affected the North American diet.

Native American Influences

The size and varied geography of the North American continent meant that different foods were available to people living in different locations. Some of these people were hunter-gatherers, depending on wild vegetation and wild game for subsistence. Others learned to grow vegetable crops. Depending on where they lived, Native American groups cultivated early forms of such plant foods as tomatoes, sweet potatoes, squash, vanilla, and cocoa. Their diets tended to be low in sodium and fat and high in fiber. In the far north, populations subsisted on fish, sea mammals, other game, and a few plants, such as seaweed, willow leaves, and berries.

Studies have shown that the diseases that affected these societies differed significantly from the diseases common in North American society today. For example, Alaskan natives who still eat the traditional diet have cardiovascular disease rates lower than those in the general North American population. Younger generations of Alaskan natives, however, who usually do not eat the traditional diet, have developed cardiovascular disease at rates similar to North Americans in general. This is also true of the Pima Indian tribe in Arizona. These and other studies indicate that, as societies become more uniform, so, too, do disease patterns.

Hispanic Influences

When Spanish colonists arrived in what is now called Latin America, they brought foods, flavors, and cooking techniques, which they combined with locally available foods. Several cuisines developed from those combinations, influenced also by the arrival of other groups. Thus, the Cuban cuisine combined native foods with those of both Spanish and Chinese immigrants, whereas the Puerto Rican cuisine combined native foods with Spanish and African contributions. In Mexico, the Spanish influence mingled with that of local Native American cuisines.

Our cooking habits often reflect our ethnic heritage.

The Mayans, Aztecs, and other populations in Mexico grew corn, beans, and chili peppers; these were the basis of Mexican cuisine. They also grew such fruits as avocados, papayas, and pineapples. By the end of the fifteenth century, wheat, chickpeas, melons, radishes, grapes, and sugar cane had been brought to the New World. Rice, citrus fruits, and some kinds of nuts came soon afterward. The Spanish also introduced beef, lamb, and chicken. Native inhabitants had previously eaten mostly fish and wild game. Spices such as cinnamon, black pepper, cloves, thyme, marjoram, and bay leaves were introduced and became part of the cuisine.

Mexican cuisine today shows regional variety. In southern Mexico, savory sauces and stews and corn tortillas reflect the native heritage. The Gulf states are renowned for delicious seafood dishes prepared with tomatoes, herbs, and olives, whereas Yucatan cuisine follows Mayan tradition, with such specialties as wild turkey and fish flavored with lime juice. Fresh produce adds color, flavor, and nutrition to authentic Mexican dining. Markets in North America are beginning to offer some of these plant foods, such as chayote, squash, jicama root, plantains, and cactus leaves and fruit. Traditional Mexican cooking is healthful in that it is high in beans, fruits, and vegetables, particularly those rich in vitamins A and C. This

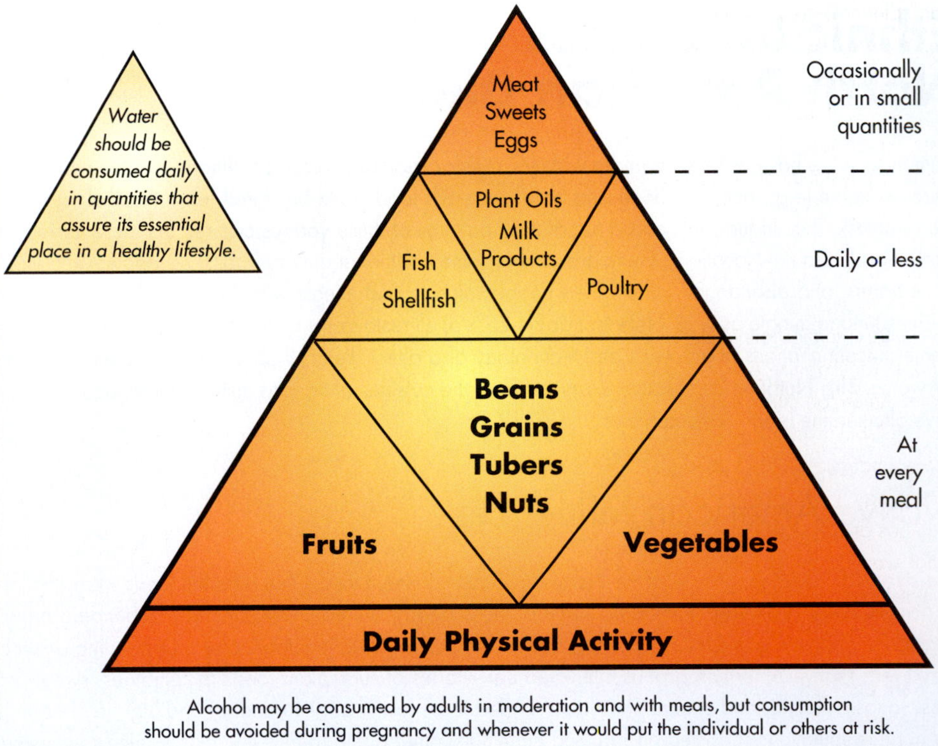
Water should be consumed daily in quantities that assure its essential place in a healthy lifestyle.
Meat
Sweets
Eggs
Occasionally or in small quantities
Plant Oils
Milk
Products
Fish
Shellfish
Poultry
Daily or less
Beans
Grains
Tubers
Nuts
Fruits
Vegetables
At every meal
Daily Physical Activity
Alcohol may be consumed by adults in moderation and with meals, but consumption should be avoided during pregnancy and whenever it would put the individual or others at risk.

Figure 2-7 The traditional healthy Latin American Diet Pyramid. A variety of diet pyramids have been developed by Oldways Preservation & Exchange Trust. These pyramids reflect the typical diets of rural peoples in the region—in this case, Latin America. Text accompanying the Latin American Pyramid, as is true for the other Oldways ethnic pyramids, states that alcohol may be consumed with meals, but consumption should be avoided during pregnancy and whenever it would put the individual or others at risk. As you will notice throughout this Nutrition Perspective, all pyramids developed by governmental or private organizations always have fruits, vegetables, and grains at the base. The Latin American Diet Pyramid then adds nuts and beans to this base; other pyramids also slightly alter the base.

pattern is reflected in the Latin American Diet Pyramid issued by Oldways Preservation & Exchange Trust in 1996 (Fig. 2-7). For more information on this and other ethnic diet pyramids, see the website www.oldwayspf.org. Today, true Mexican cooking bears little resemblance to the dishes usually found in "Mexican" restaurants in North America. Usually it is neither oily nor heavy and is based primarily on rice and beans. Restaurant Mexican food tends to use larger portions of meat, as well as adding portions of high-fat sour cream, guacamole, and cheese to many dishes.

Northern European Influences

Immigrants from Western Europe are responsible for the "meat-and-potatoes" presentation of traditional North American home cooking. The first large group of settlers from Europe—the English, French, and Germans—brought their traditional foodways with them. As all cooks and cultures must do, these immigrants adapted to the foods available in the regions in which they settled. Native Americans shared foods, which are now staples of the North American diet: corn and corn products, such as popcorn and hominy; some kinds of squash; and tomatoes.

However, because the immigrants often settled in regions of the "new land" that most closely resembled their homes in Europe, they were able to grow many familiar foods and retain many of their traditional foodways. One of these foodways involved the way food is presented.

A sizable portion of meat arranged with vegetables and potatoes in separate portions on a plate is the Northern European pattern, compared with other cuisines in which a mixture of starch, vegetables, and a much smaller portion of protein (such as a stir-fry) is more typical. The meat on the "North American" dinner plate may be, for example, sausage or roast beef, the potatoes may be boiled or mashed, and the vegetable may be sauerkraut or green peas. Whatever the choices, the Northern European pattern is still followed by many in North America.

This traditional pattern provides abundant protein and nutrients from dairy and meat products. However, the protein also contains saturated fat, and the large portions of protein and refined starches may mean that insufficient amounts of whole grains, vegetables, and fruits are eaten.

African Influences

Involuntary immigrants to the New World, people from West Africa struggled to survive under harsh conditions. Their ability to adapt familiar foodways to new conditions became a lasting influence on today's North American cuisine.

The "soul food" of African Americans is the basis of the regional cuisines of the southern United States. Many understand "soul food" to consist mainly of barbecued meat, fried chicken, sweet potatoes, and chitterlings. In fact, true soul food includes a wide range of dishes. African Americans used traditional methods and foods brought from their homelands, such as sweet potatoes, okra, and peanuts, as well as what was available in the New World. African American women, cooking for their families, created dishes that they often adapted for the plantation owner's table as well, creating the basis of Southern cuisine. The combination of these foodways with Native American, Spanish, and French traditions produced the Cajun and Creole cuisines enjoyed today in Louisiana and throughout the nation.

Black-eyed peas are one African contribution to the North American diet.

Pork and corn products were the basis of soul food. The plantation owner ate the better parts of the pig. As with other foods, slaves learned to make the less desirable parts of the pig, such as entrails, feet, ears, and head, palatable. Corn was ground for corn bread. Unrefined yellow cornmeal was mixed with water and lard to make "hoecake," baked on a hoe blade by cooks who had neither ovens nor cooking utensils for their own use. The plantation owner probably ate white cornbread made from refined cornmeal.

Among other dishes still considered soul food staples are greens, usually cooked with a small portion of smoked pork. The greens used include collards, mustard, turnip, or dandelion greens, and kale. Black-eyed peas, first brought to the New World by slaves, are also cooked with pork. Sweet potatoes remain a basic soul food; sweet potato pie is the soul food equivalent of pumpkin pie.

Today's traditional African American cuisine has both nutritional benefits and deficits. The variety of fruits, vegetables, and grain products used provides ample vitamins, minerals, and fiber. For instance, African Americans in general consume more cruciferous vegetables and fruits and vegetables containing vitamins A and C than do other ethnic groups in North America. However, cured pork products contribute undesirable levels of salt as well as saturated fat. Traditional reliance on frying, especially with lard, also adds saturated fat to the diet. Boiling vegetables for long periods depletes water-soluble vitamins. Dairy products may not be used enough, especially by older people who follow traditional dietary customs. This avoidance is based in part on the difficulty many African American adults experience in digesting lactose; see Chapter 5 for details.

To help guide African Americans toward a healthy food plan, Hebni Nutrition Consultants has developed a Soul Food Pyramid. It differs from the Food Guide Pyramid primarily by emphasizing lactose-reduced dairy products in the milk, yogurt, and cheese group and placing very-high-fat meats, such as bacon and sausage, in the fats, oils, and sweets category. To obtain a copy of the Soul Food Pyramid, call/fax 407-345-7999.

Critical | Thinking

Two issues addressed by various ethnic diet pyramids developed by Oldways Preservation & Exchange Trust but not specifically included as part of the Food Guide Pyramid diagram are physical activity and alcohol intake. The ethnic diet pyramids recommend daily physical activity. Alcohol may be consumed by adults in moderation with meals, but consumption should be avoided during pregnancy and whenever it would put the individual or others at risk. Would you include these two recommendations in the Food Guide Pyramid? Why or why not?

Asian Influences

Okinawa, an island southwest of Japan, boasts some of the oldest, healthiest people in the world. Their diet of fresh vegetables, minimal amounts of meat (mainly pork and fish), and moderate fat (lower than North American diets but higher than traditional Japanese fare) has influenced the eating habits of Japan and North America alike. Studies show that the Okinawan diet of more fresh versus pickled vegetables, more fish and fiber, less salt, and a little more fat than traditional Japanese cuisine has protected them from premature death from problems such as cardiovascular disease. Since this discovery, the Japanese diet has become more like that of the Okinawans.

Stir-fry is commonly used in Chinese cooking.

This idea of large portions of vegetables and grains, and small portions of meat, is becoming known in North America, but people are having difficulty complying with this more disciplined way of eating. Also influenced by Japanese cuisine is the growing popularity of soy products, such as tofu, soy milk, and miso, as well as use of flavors such as soy sauce, cilantro, and ginger.

More than 200 different vegetables are used in Chinese cuisine; bok choy and other forms of Chinese cabbage are perhaps the most widely eaten vegetables in the world. In the southeastern coastal region of China, home of the Cantonese cuisine, the number of dishes may be as high as 50,000. Rice is the core of the diet in southern China, whereas, in the temperate North, wheat is used to make noodles (China is the original home of pasta), bread, and dumplings. Popular dishes include hot pots (stews containing many ingredients) and stir-fried mixtures of vegetables and small amounts of meat or fish cooked in a lightly oiled, very hot pan. This primarily plant-based diet yields numerous health benefits to the population.[4]

An Asian Diet Pyramid has been proposed to reflect the Asian dietary pattern (Fig. 2-8). Like the Latin American Diet Pyramid, the bulk of the diet consists of grains, fruits, vegetables, and plant sources of protein, such as legumes, nuts, and seeds.

The Asian Pyramid does fall short in calcium but otherwise can form the basis of a healthy diet. Overall, most attention should be paid to the bottom portion of whichever pyramid you choose, and if dairy products are not included on a daily basis, other rich sources of calcium should be sought (see Chapter 11 for options).

Chinese immigration to North America began with the California gold rush in the middle of the nineteenth century. Chinese workers brought with them food-preparation methods that tend to preserve nutrients, as well as a variety of sauces and seasonings, such as gingerroot, garlic, rice wine, scallions, and sesame seeds and oil. Although many of the traditional foodways have been preserved, North American restaurant versions of Chinese cuisine, whether Cantonese, Szechwan, or Mandarin, are usually not authentic. Such food is often prepared with far more fat than in true Chinese cooking, which tends to use flavorful but fat-free sauces and seasoning. The restaurant versions of Chinese dishes also contain much larger portions of protein.

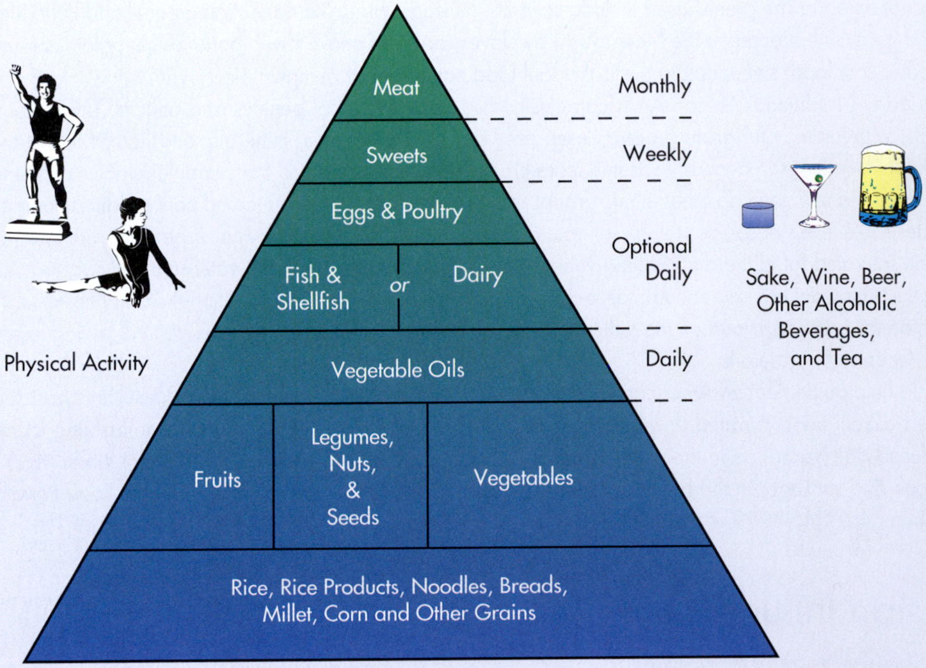

Figure 2-8 The Asian Diet Pyramid. This pyramid was inspired by the cuisines of South and East Asia, including such countries as China, Japan, South Korea, India, Thailand, Vietnam, Cambodia, Indonesia, Malaysia, Philippines, and other related Pacific Rim areas. If meat is consumed more often than monthly, it should be in small amounts. If dairy foods are consumed on a daily basis, they should be used in low to moderate amounts, and preferably low in fat. Grain products chosen should be minimally refined whenever possible.

Italian Influences

Authentic Italian cuisine, like Asian cuisine, is more diverse than most North Americans realize. Foods of different regions reflect Italy's varied geography and climate. Northern Italy, the more affluent part of the country, is the principal producer of meat and dairy products, such as butter and cheese. Rice dishes, such as risotto, are popular there. Fish is more important in regions near the sea and lighter foods, such as fresh vegetables prepared with herbs, garlic, and olive oil, are characteristic. The poorer regions south of Rome, as well as the island of Sicily, have a diet rich in grains, vegetables, dried beans, and fish, with little meat or oil. Compared with northern Italians of the same class, southern Italians eat less beef, veal, chicken, and butter and more bread, pasta, vegetables, fruit, and fish.

Pasta is the heart of the Italian diet. Italians eat six times more of this simple wheat and water product than do North Americans, although we have also learned to enjoy this nutritious dish. Pasta in North America, however, often means spaghetti, with a tomato-based sauce that includes meatballs or sausage. In contrast, Italians eat pasta in a variety of shapes and with a variety of sauces, often excluding meat.

Most of the Italian cuisine found in restaurants offers foods more common to the north of Italy, including veal, cheese, and cream and pesto sauces for pasta. Pizza, a southern Italian dish, is the exception, and it is fast becoming the most frequently consumed food in North America. Purists in Naples, however, insist that classic pizza consists only of a thin crust, tomato, basil, and mozzarella cheese.

Although some components of the Italian diet contain substantial amounts of saturated fat, nutritionists now know that other components, such as pasta, olive oil, fish, nuts, fruits, and vegetables, contribute to healthy diets.[6] One approach to Italian cuisine could be the Mediterranean Diet Pyramid (Figure 2-9). This is a plan based on food choices like those traditionally found in the simple cuisines of Greece and southern Italy. The Mediterranean Diet Pyramid allows up to 35% of total calories as fat in the diet. However, it recommends consuming the type of fat consumed in the Mediterranean region: olive oil. A cheaper version, which has a similar fat profile and health benefit, is canola oil (see Chapter 6 for details).

Olive oil is a principal fat source in the Mediterranean diet. Note that canola oil has a similar fatty acid profile and is much less expensive in North America.

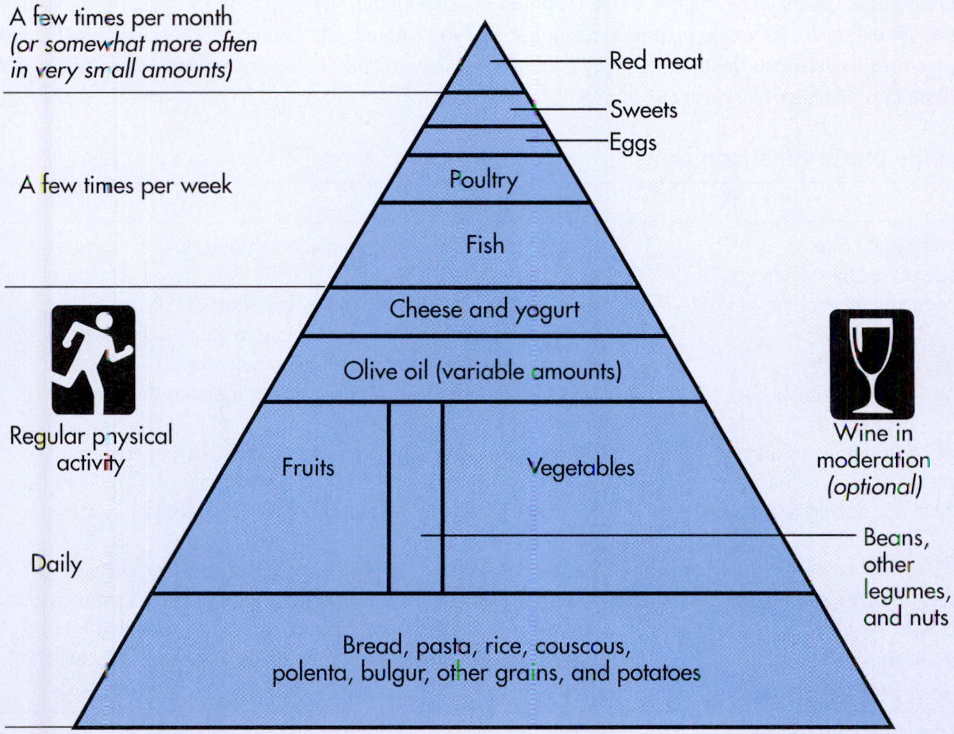

Figure 2-9 The traditional healthy Mediterranean Diet Pyramid. This plan is based on long-standing eating habits in southern Italy, Crete, and Greece. The base of the diet is bread and grains, fruits and vegetables, and beans and potatoes. Red meat is consumed sparingly—moderate amounts of fish and poultry are preferred. Wine may be included with meals. Most of the fat in this plan comes from olive oil. Cheese and yogurt supply some fat and calcium. Other low-fat and nonfat milk products also can be included, if desired.

Jewish Influences

Although Jewish immigrants arrive from all over the world, the two predominant groups are the Ashkenazic Jews, from Eastern European countries such as Russia, Germany, Poland, and Romania and from South Africa; and the Sephardic Jews from Spain, Portugal, and North Africa. Religious laws influence the dietary practices of some Jews. These Jewish laws dictate the separation of meat and milk products in a meal as well as in pots and pans used for cooking. In addition, it is important for meat to be completely drained of blood. To be sure that food laws are followed in processing, foods are labeled "kosher," meaning that a rabbi has approved food handling. Today, however, many discontinue such practices, especially as they become more integrated into North America.

Common foods for Ashkenazic Jews include dark rye bread, borscht, and herring. The Sephardic Jews eat foods that are also common in the Middle East, such as eggplant, humus, tahini, and couscous. Many of these foods have become popular in North American cuisine, including rye bread, bagels with cream cheese, corned beef, and pastrami. In Israel the food practices are similar to that of the Sephardic Jews, who traditionally ate only small amounts of meat due to economic constraints. The Ashkenazic diet is traditionally higher in fat and salt due to the consumption of foods such as high-fat meats, chicken fat, chopped liver, cream cheese, corned beef, smoked fish, sauerkraut, and pickles. Clearly, foodways of each group of Jewish immigrants have been preserved. Some are beneficial to health, while others should be practiced only occasionally.

Ethnic Diets and Present Trends

Like many ethnic foods, Asian foods are highly prized by many North Americans.

Only seven ethnic diets have been described here (Table 2-12). Many other cuisines have also influenced the North American diet, and new arrivals continue to bring their traditions and foodways to this country. For example, social upheavals have increased the immigration of Russians and other Eastern European peoples to North America. On the other side of the world, continuing unrest in Southeast Asia has brought peoples from that area here. Restaurants serving traditional Russian or Thai fare, for instance, are offering new eating patterns to those willing to experiment.

Based on research also begun many years ago, still other scientists suggest that a healthful diet consists of the inexpensive traditional dishes based on grains, fruits, and vegetables that form the backbone of a number of ethnic cuisines. These are precisely the dishes that people abandon as they become affluent and seek convenience. Simple foods prepared in simple ways have fed most of humanity for virtually its entire existence. As we begin a new century, some North Americans are rediscovering the simple foods of their respective pasts, learning to enjoy a variety of cuisines, and finding out how each cuisine can contribute to a healthier North American diet.

Table 2-12 The World's Fare Has Influenced the North American Diet

Diet Influences	Advantages	Shortcomings
Native American	Variety of seafood, lean wild game; early Native Americans ate many types of vegetables, berries, leaves	High fat content of some meat/seafood; low in calcium
Hispanic	Excellent variety of vegetables, legumes, fruits; high in fiber	Traditional Hispanic diet may fall short in calcium; Mexican-American restaurants serve much high-fat fare, rich in sour cream, cheese, and guacamole
Northern European	Abundant sources of protein, iron, calcium from meat and dairy groups	Less variety from vegetables, fruits, legumes; high in fat
African	Good variety of vegetables; high fiber; many variations, including Cajun and Creole dishes	Traditional meals high in fat; may fall short in calcium
Asian	Excellent variety of vegetables, grains; cooking methods retain nutrients in foods	Some sauces high in salt and fat; may fall short in calcium
Italian	Varies regionally—some regions provide excellent variety of seafood; overall high grain intake, good vegetable and fruit variety	Italian-American restaurants often serve many foods made with high-fat cheese, sauces, and meats, likely low in calcium
Jewish	Good variety of whole-grain products, legumes, and some types of seafood. Many traditions regarding food as an important part of Jewish culture have been retained.	Traditional Jewish foods are often high in saturated fat and salt. Limited variety from vegetables and fruits; may fall short on calcium.

This is a brief summary of healthful attributes and shortcomings of the ethnic influences covered in this Nutrition Perspective.

chapter 3

Human Digestion and Absorption

Chapter | Outline

Case | Scenario

Elise is a 20-year-old college sophomore. Over the last few months, she has been experiencing regular bouts of heartburn. This usually happens after a large lunch or dinner. Occasionally she has even bent down after dinner to pick up something and had some stomach contents travel back up her esophagus and into her mouth. This especially frightened Elise, so she visited the University Health Center.

The nurse practitioner at the Center told Elise it was good she came in for a checkup. She suspects she has a disease called gastroesophageal reflux disease (GERD). She tells Elise that this can lead to serious problems if not controlled, such as a rare form of cancer. She provides Elise with a pamphlet describing GERD and schedules an appointment with a physician for further evaluation.

What type of dietary habits likely contribute to Elise's symptoms of GERD? What types of medications have been especially useful for treating this problem? Overall, how will Elise cope with this health problem, and will it ever go away?

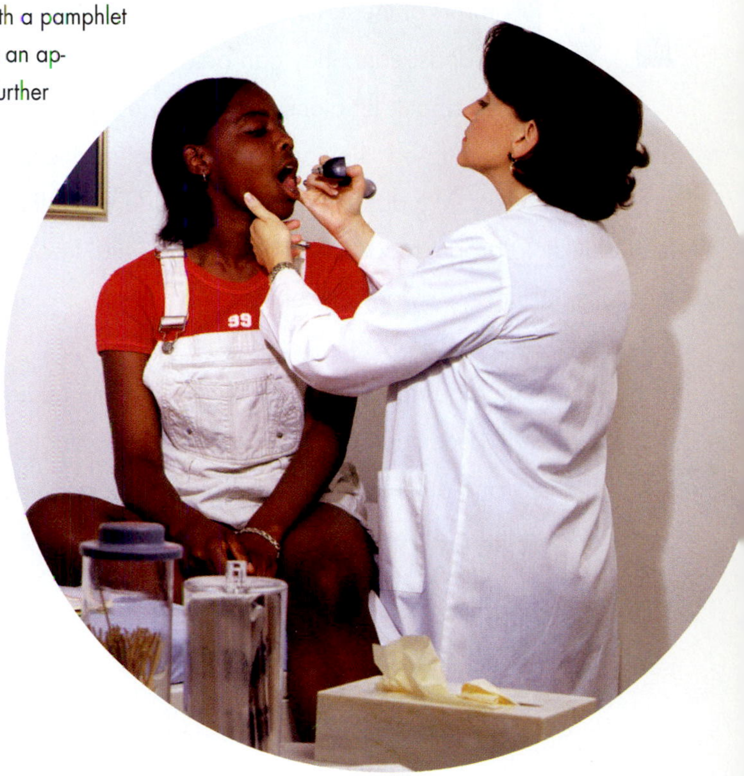

Refresh | Your Memory

As you begin your study of human digestion and absorption in Chapter 3, you may want to review:

- The basic chemical composition of carbohydrates, proteins, and lipids in Chapter 1.
- Cell structure and function in Appendix C.
- Physiology of the major body systems (aside from the digestive system) in Appendix C.

Boost | Your Study

Check out the ***Perspectives in Nutrition: Online Learning Center*** **www.mhhe.com/wardlawpers6** *for quizzes, flash cards, activities, and web links designed to further help you learn about issues surrounding human digestion and absorption.*

Chapter | Objectives

Chapter 3 is designed to allow you to:

1. Define tissue, organ, and organ system.
2. List some characteristics of the 12 organ systems and outline a role for each related to nutrition, especially the cardiovascular system, endocrine system, nervous system, immune system, and urinary system.
3. Outline the overall processes of digestion and absorption, including the roles played by the organs of the gastrointestinal tract and the related accessory organs: liver, gallbladder, and pancreas.
4. Become familiar with some specific enzymes and hormones that act in digestion of the various nutrient groups.
5. Identify the major nutrition-related gastrointestinal health problems and typical approaches to treatment.

Merely eating food won't nourish you. You must first digest the food—in other words, break it down into usable forms of the essential nutrients that can be absorbed into the bloodstream. Once nutrients are taken up by the bloodstream, they can be distributed to body cells.[11]

We rarely think about, let alone control, digesting and absorbing foods. Except for a few voluntary responses—such as deciding what and when to eat, how well to chew food, and when to eliminate the remains—most digestion and absorption processes control themselves. We don't consciously decide when the pancreas will secrete digestive substances into the small intestine or how quickly to propel foodstuffs down the intestinal tract. Various hormones and the nervous system mostly control these functions.[9] Your only awareness of these involuntary responses may be a hunger pang right before lunch or a "full" feeling after eating that last slice of pizza.

Let's examine digestion and absorption and some related aspects of the human physiology that support nutritional health. In the process you will become acquainted with the basic anatomy (structure) and physiology (function) of the circulatory and endocrine systems. These and other body systems control our nutritional status, and the nutrients derived from food contribute to the proper functioning of these systems.

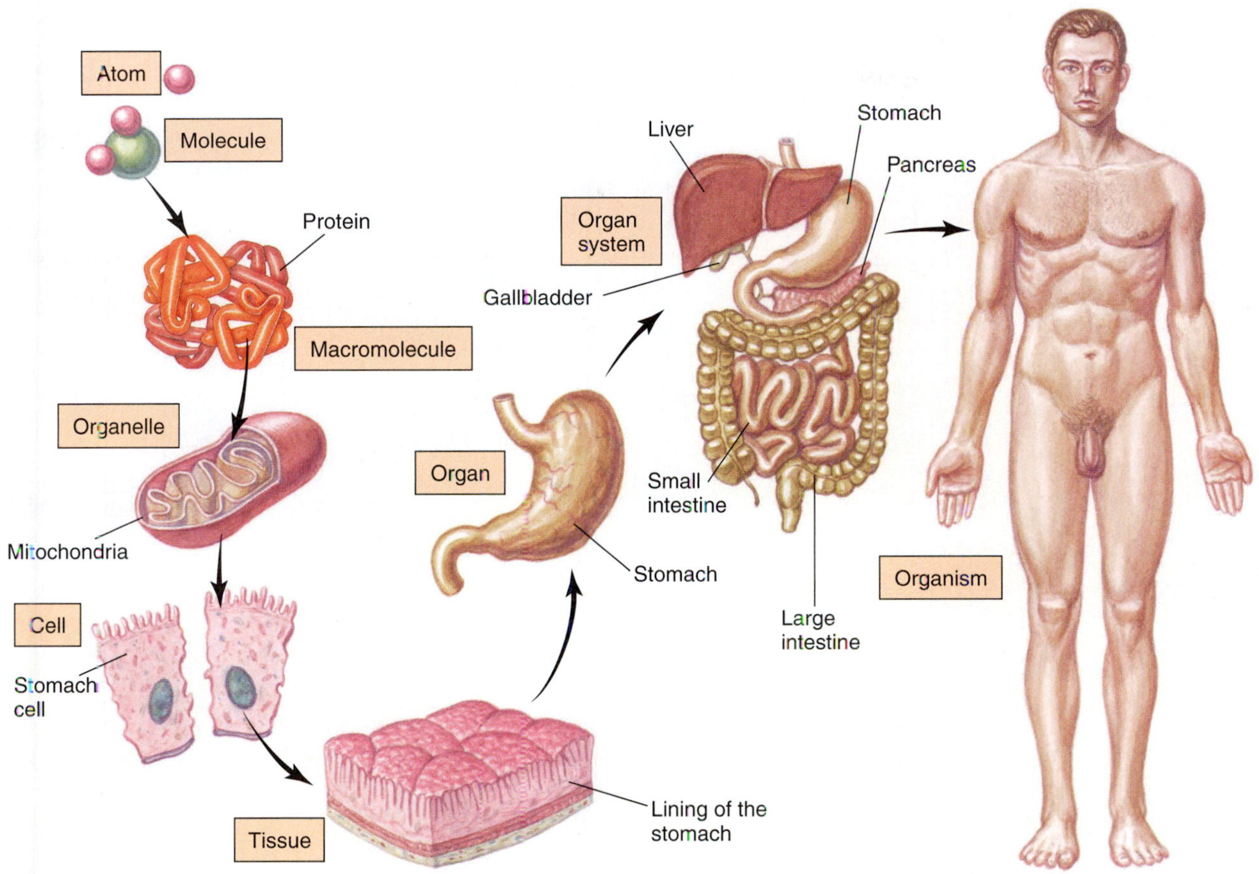

Figure 3-1 Levels of organization of the human body. Each level is more complex than the previous level. The organ system shown is the gastrointestinal (GI) tract. For your review, Appendix C covers cell physiology in detail.

The Cell Is the Basis of Human Physiology

The body is composed of about a trillion cells. Each cell is a self-contained, living entity.[16] Cells of the same type join together, typically using intercellular substances, to form **tissues,** such as muscle tissue. One, two, or more tissues combine in a particular way to form more complex structures, called **organs.** All organs contribute to nutritional health, and a person's overall nutritional state determines how well each organ functions. At a still higher level of coordination, several organs can cooperate for a common purpose to form an **organ system,** such as the digestive system. Overall, the human body is an organism made up of a coordinated unit of many highly structured organ systems (Fig. 3-1).

Chemical reactions occur constantly in every living cell: The production of new substances is balanced by the breaking down of older ones, as exemplified by the constant formation and degradation of bone. For this turnover of substances to occur, cells require a continuous supply of energy in the form of dietary carbohydrate, protein, and/or fat. Almost all cells need oxygen to transform the energy in these nutrients to a form of energy the body can use—**adenosine triphosphate,** or **ATP** (see Chapter 4 for more on ATP). Cells also need water; building supplies, especially amino acids and minerals; and chemical regulators, such as the vitamins. All of these substances enable the tissues, constituted from individual cells, to function properly.

tissues Collections of cells adapted to perform a specific function.

organ A group of tissues designed to perform a specific function—for example, the heart, which contains muscle tissue, nerve tissue, and so on.

organ system A collection of organs that work together to perform an overall function.

adenosine triphosphate (ATP) The main energy currency for cells. ATP energy is used to promote ion pumping, enzyme activity, and muscle contraction.

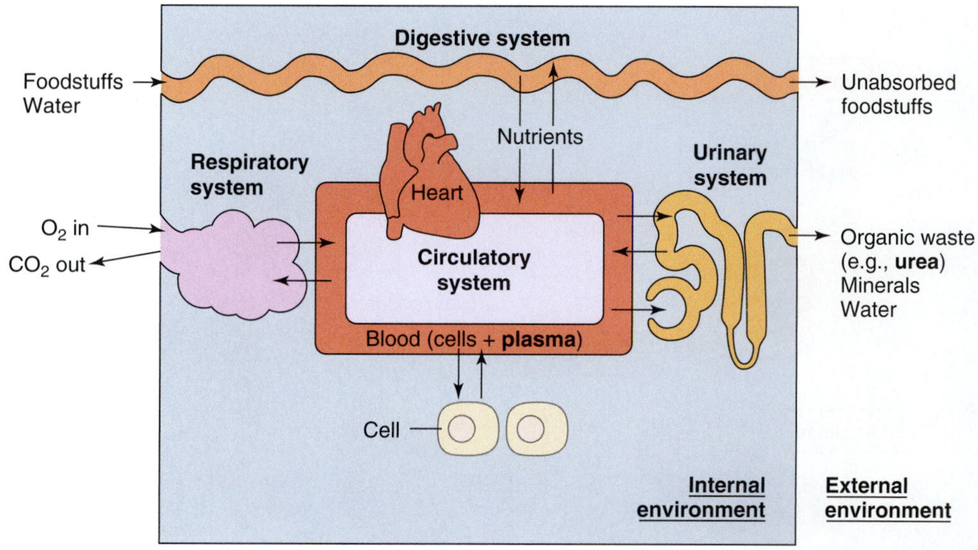

Figure 3-2 Exchanges of nutrients occur between our external environment and the internal environment of the circulatory system via the digestive, respiratory, and urinary systems. Overall, the human body is a combination of 12 systems working together to support cell needs.

Getting an adequate supply of all nutrients to the body's cells begins with a healthful diet. To assure optimal use of nutrients, the body's cells, tissues, organs, and organ systems also must work efficiently.[2]

Organization of the Human Body

As noted earlier, when groups of similar cells work together to accomplish a specialized task, the arrangement is referred to as a tissue. Humans are composed of four primary types of tissue: **epithelial, connective, muscle,** and **nervous.**[17] Epithelial tissue is composed of cells that cover surfaces both outside and inside the body. These cells secrete important substances, absorb nutrients, and excrete waste. Connective tissue supports and protects the body, stores fat, and produces blood cells. Muscle tissue is designed for movement. Nervous tissue found in the brain and spinal cord is designed for communication. These four tissues then go on to form various organs and, ultimately, organ systems (review Fig. 3-1).

We will be particularly concerned in this chapter with the digestive system. The nutrients we consume in food are unavailable until they have been processed by the digestive system. Using chemical and mechanical means to alter food, nutrients can be released and absorbed into the body for distribution to body tissues. Table 3-1 summarizes the components and functions of the various systems.

Sometimes organs within a system can serve another system. For example, the primary function of the digestive system is to convert the food we eat into absorbable nutrients. At the same time, the digestive system serves the immune system by preventing dangerous pathogens from invading the body and causing illness. As you study nutrition, you will note the multiple roles played by many organs (Fig. 3-2). Appendix C contains more details on these various systems.

The overriding theme of human nutrition is to understand the actions of nutrients as they affect different cells, tissues, organs, and organ systems. Each type of organ system is impacted by nutrient intake and simultaneously helps to determine how each nutrient is used.

Our task now is to explore the key systems in the body as they specifically relate to the study of human digestion and absorption.

epithelial tissue The surface cells that line the outside of the body and all external passages within it.

connective tissue Cells and their protein products that hold different structures in the body together. Some structures are made up of connective tissue—notably, **tendons** and **cartilage.** Connective tissue also forms part of bone and the nonmuscular structures of arteries and veins.

muscle tissue A type of tissue adapted to contraction.

nervous tissue Tissue composed of highly branched, elongated cells, which transport nerve impulses from one part of the body to another.

plasma The fluid, noncellular portion of the circulating blood. This includes the blood serum plus all blood-clotting factors. In contrast, serum is the fluid that results after the blood is first allowed to clot before being centrifuged; this does not contain the blood-clotting factors.

urea Nitrogenous waste product of protein metabolism; major source of nitrogen in the urine, chemically

$$H_2N{-}\overset{\overset{\large O}{\|}}{C}{-}NH_2$$

Table 3-1 Organ Systems of the Body[14]

System	Major Components	Functions Related to Nutrition
Cardiovascular	Heart, blood vessels, and blood	Transports nutrients, waste products, gases, and hormones throughout the body and plays a role in the immune response and the regulation of body temperature
Lymphatic	Lymph vessels, lymph nodes, and other lymph organs	Removes foreign substances from the blood and lymph, combats disease, maintains tissue fluid balance, and aids in fat absorption
Nervous	Brain, spinal cord, nerves, and sensory receptors	A major regulatory system: detects sensation, controls movements, and controls physiological and intellectual functions
Endocrine	Endocrine glands, such as the pituitary, thyroid, and adrenal glands	A major regulatory system: participates in the regulation of metabolism, reproduction, and many other functions through the action of hormones
Immune	White blood cells, lymph vessels and nodes, spleen, thymus gland, and other lymph tissues	Provides defense against foreign invaders; formation of white blood cells
Digestive	Mouth, esophagus, stomach, intestines, and accessory structures	Performs the mechanical and chemical processes of digestion, absorption of nutrients, and elimination of wastes
Urinary	Kidneys, urinary bladder, and the ducts that carry urine	Removes waste products from the circulatory system and regulates blood acid-base balance, overall chemical balance, and water balance
Integumentary	Skin, hair, nails, and sweat glands	Protects the other organ systems, regulates temperature, prevents water loss, and produces a substance that converts to vitamin D upon sun exposure
Skeletal	Bones, associated cartilage, and joints	Protects, supports, and allows body movement, produces blood cells, and stores minerals
Muscular	Smooth, cardiac, and skeletal muscle	Produces body movement, maintains posture, and produces body heat
Respiratory	Lungs and respiratory passages	Exchanges gases (oxygen and carbon dioxide) between the blood and the air and regulates blood acid-base (pH) balance
Reproductive	Gonads, accessory structures, and genitals of males and females	Performs the processes of reproduction and influences sexual functions and behaviors

The cardiovascular and lymphatic organ systems together make up the circulatory system, and so contribute to circulatory functions in the body. The endocrine and nervous organ systems contribute to the regulatory functions. The digestive, urinary, integumentary, and respiratory organ systems contribute to the excretory functions, while the muscular and skeletal organ systems contribute to storage functions in the body.

The Physiology of Digestion

The **gastrointestinal (GI) tract** is a long tube stretching from the mouth to the anus (Fig. 3-3). This tube, also known as the *alimentary canal,* is partitioned from the body in such a way that nutrients must pass through its walls to be absorbed into the bloodstream. Just eating a food is not enough—most nutrients must be **digested** and all nutrients must be absorbed to be of use to body cells.[11] Disease may hamper digestion and/or absorption, denying the body use of dietary nutrients.

The GI tract is a complex system that performs a variety of physiological functions: movement **(motility),** secretion, digestion, absorption, elimination, and nutrient production. (*Nutrient production* refers to the synthesis of vitamins by bacteria that live in the intestine.) Most of these processes are under autonomic control; that is, they are involuntary. Almost all functions involved in digestion and absorption are controlled by **hormones,** hormonelike compounds, and the nervous system.

The most important aspects of GI tract physiology from a nutritional viewpoint are discussed in this chapter. A more detailed discussion of all the organs and processes involved can be found in a physiology textbook.[14]

gastrointestinal (GI) tract Comprises the main sites in the body used in digestion and absorption of nutrients. The tract consists of the mouth, esophagus, stomach, small intestine, large intestine, rectum, and anus.

digestion The process by which large ingested molecules are mechanically and chemically broken down to produce smaller molecules that can be absorbed across the wall of the GI tract.

hormone A compound with a specific site of synthesis that, when secreted into the bloodstream, controls the function of cells in its target organ or organs. Hormones can be amino acidlike (epinephrine), proteinlike (insulin), or fatlike (estrogen).

Figure 3-3 Major organs of the gastrointestinal (GI) tract and accessory organs (4, 5, and 6) used in digestion and absorption of nutrients.

GI Tract Flow

Mouth
↓
Esophagus (10 in long)
↓
Stomach—4-cup (1-liter) capacity. Food remains about 2 to 3 hours. Large meals take the longest time to empty.
↓
Small intestine—duodenum (10 in long), jejunum (4 ft long), ileum (5 ft long)—about 10 ft (3.1 meters) in total length. Food remains about 3 to 10 hours.
↓
Large intestine (colon)—cecum, ascending colon, transverse colon, descending colon, sigmoid colon—3½ ft (1.1 meters) in total length. Food can remain up to 72 hours.
↓
Rectum
↓
Anus

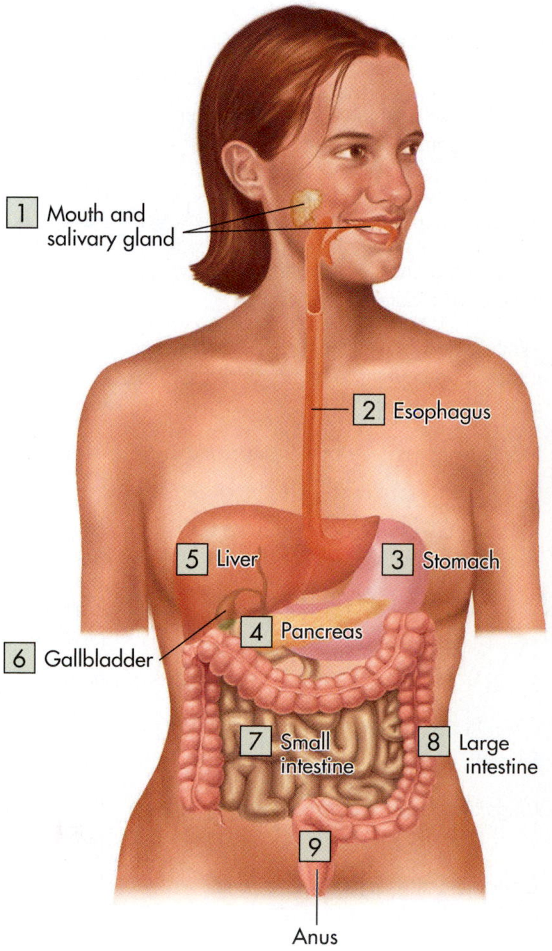

The Flow of Digestion

Before we eat a bite of most foods, the work of digestion—the breakdown of foods into usable forms we can absorb—is already partially accomplished. Cooking or other preparations, such as marinating, pounding, and dicing, generally begin the process. Starch granules in foods swell as they soak up water during cooking, making them much easier to digest. Cooking also softens the tough connective tissues in meats and the fibrous tissue of plants, such as that in broccoli stalks. As a result, the food is easier to chew, swallow, and break down during digestion. As you will see in Chapter 19, cooking also makes many foods, such as eggs, meat, fish, and poultry, much safer to eat.

Now let's begin by reviewing the major parts of the body used in digestion. In the mouth, glands produce **saliva** (Fig. 3-4). Saliva contains enzymes that break down carbohydrates to simple sugars and **mucus** that lubricates the morsel of food (Table 3-2). Chewing divides solid food into smaller, more manageable pieces, which increases the surface area exposed to the digestive action of enzymes. The food is now referred to as a **bolus.** Saliva also contains **lysozyme,** a set of enzymes that kill bacteria by rupturing their cell membranes.

The tongue contains taste receptors for sweet, salt, sour, and bitter tastes.[15] The salty taste is due to Na^+ enhanced by Cl^-. The sour taste is due to the presence of hydrogen ions (H^+). Bitter and sweet tastes are generated by specific components in the food that interact with membrane receptors on the tongue. A fifth taste sensation called umami

saliva A watery fluid, produced by the salivary glands in the mouth, that contains lubricants, enzymes, and other substances.

mucus A thick fluid secreted by glands throughout the body. It contains a compound that has both a carbohydrate and a protein nature. It acts as both a lubricant and a means of protection for cells.

bolus A mass of food that is swallowed.

lysozyme A set of enzyme substances produced by a variety of cells; it can destroy bacteria by rupturing cell membranes.

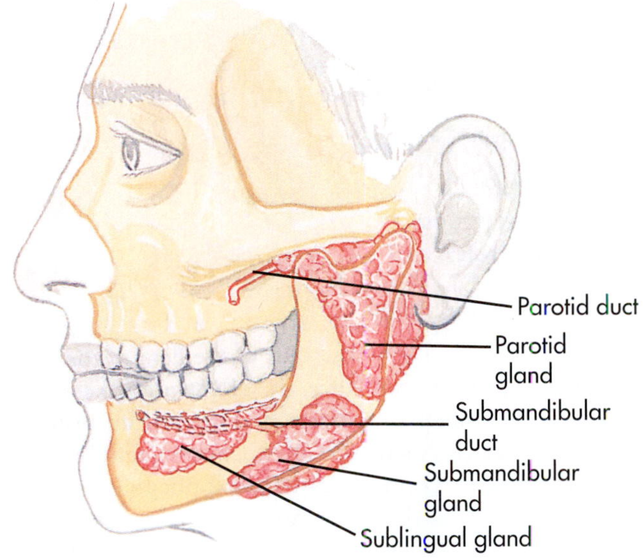

Figure 3-4 Location of the salivary glands. These glands produce saliva to aid in swallowing and digesting food. Incisor and canine (pointed) teeth at the front of the mouth are useful for tearing food, such as from a chicken leg. The molars (flat) at the back of the mouth are used to grind the food into small pieces.

Illustration by William Ober.

Table 3-2 Important Secretions and Products of the Digestive Tract

Secretion	Site of Production	Purpose
Saliva	Mouth	Contributes to starch digestion, lubrication, swallowing
Mucus	Mouth, stomach, small intestine, large intestine	Protects cells, lubricates
Enzymes: **(amylases, lipases, proteases)**	Mouth, stomach, small intestine, pancreas	Promote digestion of foodstuffs into particles small enough for absorption
Acid	Stomach	Promotes digestion of protein among other functions
Bile **(bile acids, cholesterol, and lecithins)**	Liver (stored in gallbladder)	Suspends fat in water to aid fat digestion in the small intestine
Bicarbonate	Pancreas, small intestine	Neutralizes stomach acid when it reaches the small intestine
Hormones **(gastrin, secretin, cholecystokinin, gastric-inhibitory polypeptide)**	Stomach, small intestine	Stimulate production and/or release of acid, enzymes, bile, and bicarbonate; help regulate peristalsis and overall GI tract flow

has been proposed. This taste sensation is elicited by monosodium glutamate, a substance often added to Chinese and Japanese foods to enhance flavor. Brothy, meaty, and savory are examples of umami sensations.[18] Finally, receptors for the taste of both water and fat are likely present.

This sensation of flavor is then augmented by input from approximately 6 million **olfactory** cells in the nose. Flavor is also affected by human genetic variation in both taste and olfactory sensations. The ability to detect bitter substances—such as in broccoli or cabbage—is one example. This is important since some bitter substances are also quite toxic.

olfactory Sense of smell.

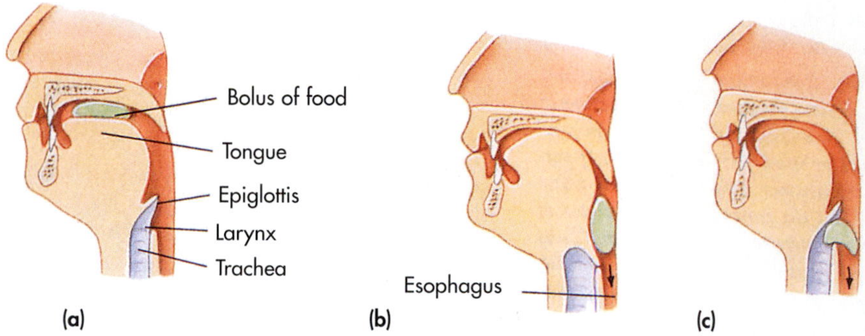

Figure 3-5 The process of swallowing. (*a*) During swallowing, food does not normally enter the trachea because the epiglottis closes over the larynx. (*b*) The arrow shows that the closed epiglottis allows food to proceed down the esophagus. (*c*) When a person chokes, food becomes lodged in the trachea, blocking air flow to the lungs. The food should have moved down the esophagus.
Illustration by William Ober.

A variety of diseases and drugs, as well as the effects of aging, can alter the sense of taste.[3] Overall, flavor is a complex combination of taste, olfaction, physical sensations from certain chemicals in foods (such as in chili peppers), and textural sensations.

The mouth and stomach are connected by the esophagus. At its entrance is a valve-like flap of tissue, the **epiglottis,** that prevents food from being lodged in the trachea (windpipe). When food is swallowed it lands on the epiglottis, which then covers the larynx (the opening of the trachea). Breathing automatically stops. These involuntary responses ensure that swallowed food travels only down the esophagus, aided by muscle contractions of the esophagus and by gravity (Fig. 3-5). As food exits the esophagus, it enters the stomach (another term is gastric). The stomach has a capacity of about 4 cups (1 L). The stomach continues the digestive process by secreting very strong acid (hydrochloric acid [HCl]) from the **parietal cells,** as well as enzymes from the **chief cells** (Figs. 3-6 and 3-7). This acid and enzymes are then slowly mixed into the food.

epiglottis Flap that folds down over the trachea during swallowing.

parietal cell Gastric gland cell that secretes hydrochloric acid and intrinsic factor.

chief cell Gastric gland cell that secrets pepsinogen, precursor of pepsin.

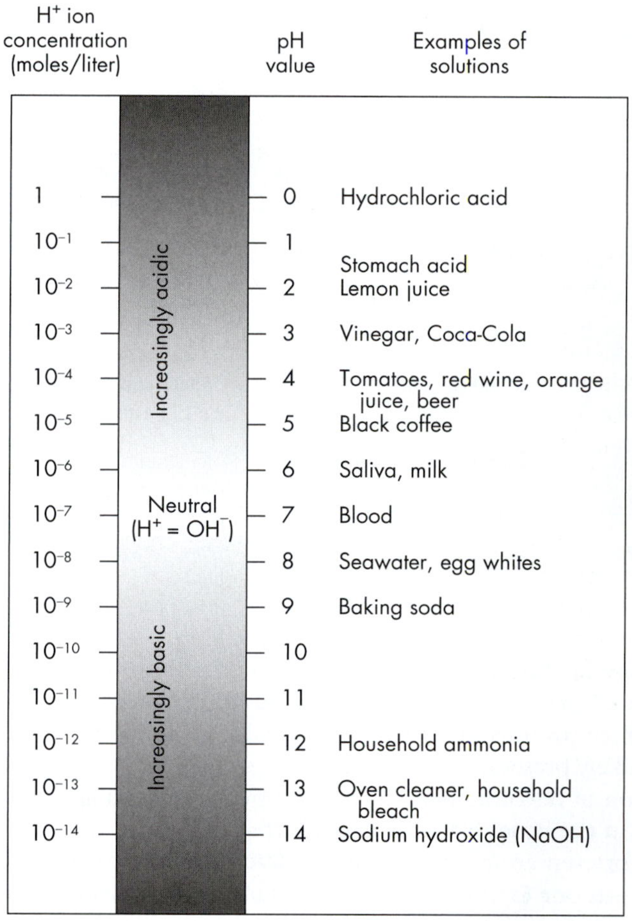

Figure 3-6 The pH values of common substances. Note that tomatoes aren't really that acidic, but stomach acid is.

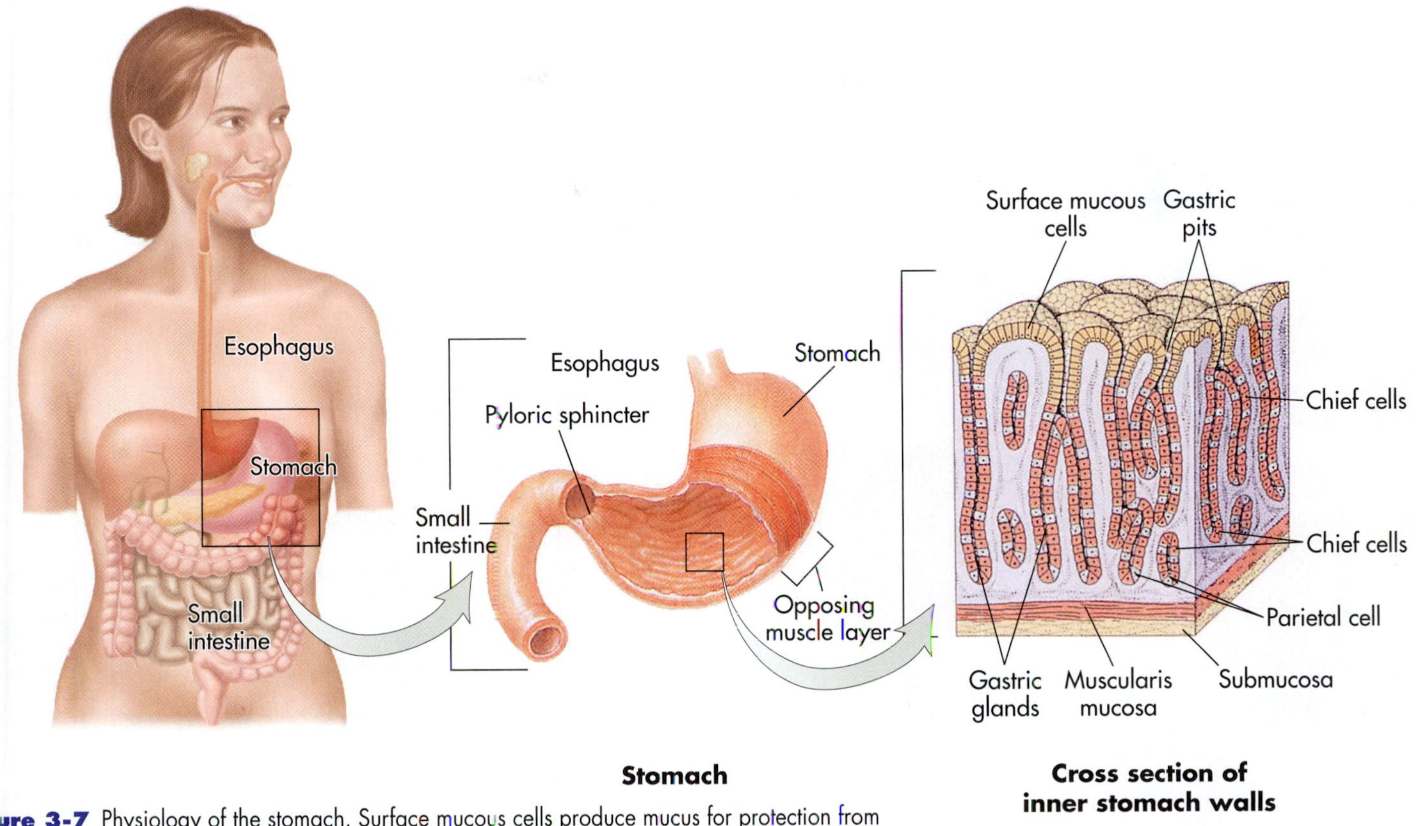

Figure 3-7 Physiology of the stomach. Surface mucous cells produce mucus for protection from stomach acid and enzymes. Parietal cells produce the hydrochloric acid (HCl) and chief cells produce the enzymes. Mucous neck cells (also called goblet cells) scattered among the surface mucous cells in the gastric pits also produce mucus.

The resulting soupy mass of food and secretions is called **chyme.** The chyme is usually ready to leave the stomach within 2 to 4 hours after food is eaten. The more solid the chyme, the longer it takes to leave the stomach.

chyme A mixture of stomach secretions and partially digested food.

The hydrochloric acid produced by the stomach is very important. It destroys the biological activity of ingested proteins. Otherwise protein substances such as certain plant and animal hormones in food could go on to affect human functions. The acid also converts some inactive stomach enzymes into active forms and solubilizes dietary minerals such as calcium so they can be more easily absorbed.

You might wonder how the stomach protects itself from the acid and enzymes it produces. First, the stomach has a thick layer of mucus secreted by goblet cells in the stomach lining. This mucus helps prevent the stomach from "digesting" itself. The production of acid and enzymes is also tied to the release of a specific hormone (gastrin). This release does not occur except when we are thinking about eating or are actually in the process of eating. Lastly, as the concentration of acid in the stomach increases, acid production tapers off, also because of hormonal control.

One other important function of the stomach is the production of a substance called **intrinsic factor.** This vital material is essential for the absorption of one of the B vitamins, vitamin B-12 (see Chapter 10).[11]

intrinsic factor A substance present in stomach secretions that enhances vitamin B-12 absorption.

The stomach empties into the small intestine, which is coiled below it in the abdomen (Fig. 3-8). The small intestine is divided into three sections: the first part, the duodenum, is about 10 in. long (0.3 m); the middle segment, the jejunum, is about 4 ft long (1.3 m); and the last section, the ileum, is about 5 ft long (1.6 m). The small intestine is considered small because of its narrow diameter (1 in. [2.5 cm]), not its length. Most digestion is completed in the duodenum and upper jejunum, with the help of enzymes made by intestinal cells and the pancreas. Muscular contractions in the

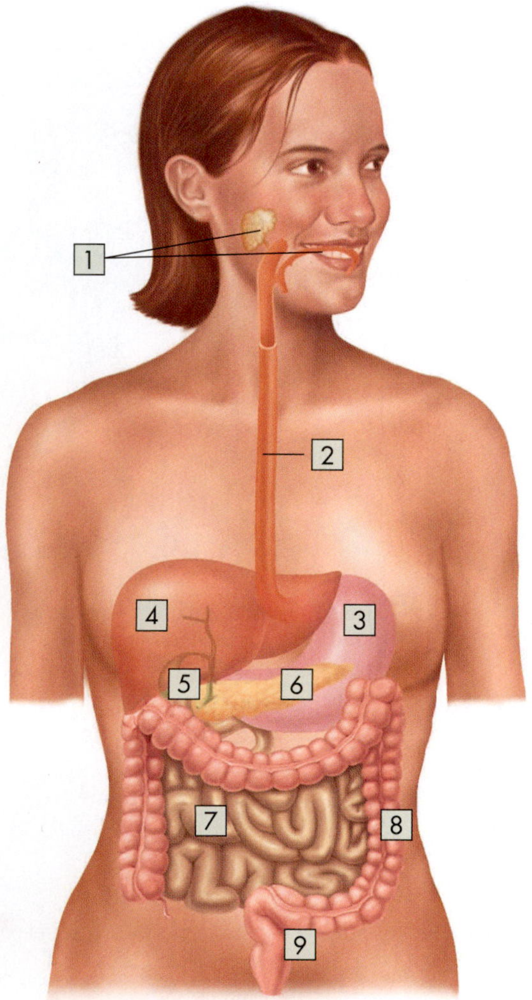

Organ	Secretions	Functions
1 Mouth and salivary glands		Chewing begins; initiation of swallowing reflex
	Salt and water	Moisten food
	Mucus	Lubrication
	Amylase	Starch-digesting enzyme
2 Esophagus		Move food to stomach by peristaltic waves
	Mucus	Lubrication
3 Stomach		Store, mix, dissolve, and continue digestion of food; regulate emptying of dissolved food into small intestine
	Acid (HCl)	Dissolve food particles; kill microbes
	Pepsin	Protein-digesting enzyme
	Mucus	Lubricate and protect stomach surface
4 Liver		Secretion of bile
	Bile acids, lecithin, and cholesterol	Aid in fat digestion and absorption
5 Gallbladder	Bicarbonate	Neutralize stomach acid entering small intestine
6 Pancreas		Secretion of enzymes and sodium bicarbonate
	Enzymes	Digest carbohydrates, fats, and proteins
7 Small intestine		Digestion and absorption of most substances; mixing and propulsion of contents
	Enzymes	Food digestion
	Salt and water	Maintain fluidity of intestinal contents
	Mucus	Lubrication
8 Large intestine		Storage and concentration of undigested matter; absorption of sodium, potassium, and water; mixing and propulsion of contents; elimination of feces from the body
	Mucus	Lubrication
9 Rectum		Store feces and expel via the anus

Figure 3-8 Physiology of the GI tract. Many organs cooperate in a regulated fashion to allow digestion and subsequent absorption of nutrients in foods.

small intestine constantly mix the food with digestive fluids, enhancing digestion. A meal remains in the small intestine about 3 to 10 hours.[11]

The small intestine empties into the large intestine, or colon. This organ is about 3½ ft long (1.1 m) and is separated into five sections: the cecum, ascending colon, transverse colon, descending colon, and sigmoid colon. Little digestion occurs in this organ; however, this is not of concern—about 95% of total digestion has already taken place in the small intestine. Food that reaches the large intestine is mostly indigestible. This residue remains in the large intestine for about 24 to 72 hours before elimination from the body as **feces.**

The terminus of the large intestine is attached to the rectum, which is connected to the anus. These final sections of the GI tract work with the large intestine to prepare the feces for elimination.

The liver, pancreas, and gallbladder work with the GI tract but are not a physical part of it. They are thus called accessory organs. The liver provides **bile,** which aids in fat digestion and absorption and is stored in the gallbladder until needed. The bile duct

feces Substances discharged from the bowel during defecation, including undigested food residue, dead GI tract cells, mucus, bacteria, and other waste material. Another term for feces is *stool.*

bile A liver secretion that is stored in the gallbladder and released through the common bile duct into the duodenum. It is essential for the digestion and absorption of fat.

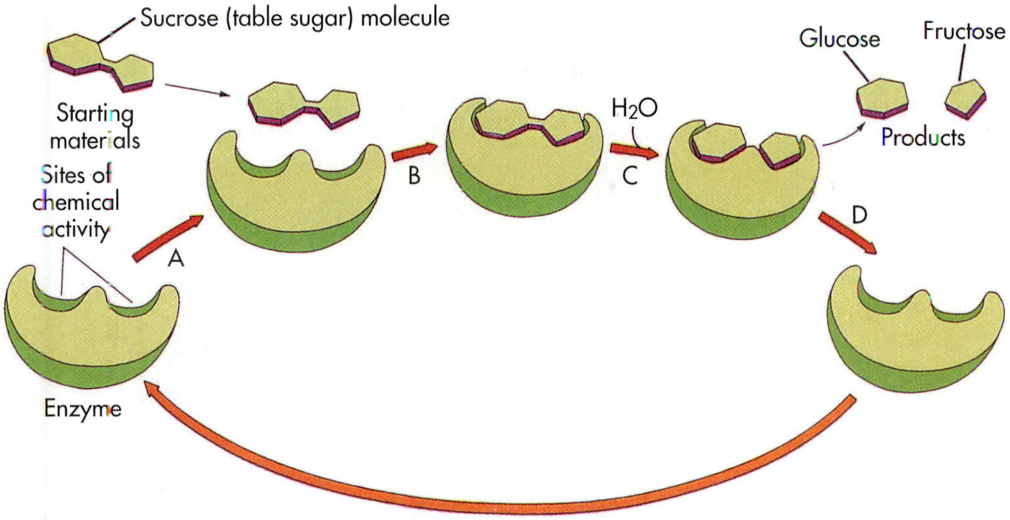

Figure 3-9 A model of enzyme action. Enzymes act as catalysts to speed chemical reactions, including those that contribute to the digestion of foodstuffs. In this example, an enzyme is contributing to the breakdown of sucrose (from *A* to *D*) into the smaller sugar forms glucose and fructose. Only these smaller sugars are absorbed from the small intestine into the bloodstream. Note that with some enzymes the reaction can go both ways. In addition, sometimes energy input is needed to allow the enzyme to push the reaction along.

Illustration by William Ober.

leads from the gallbladder and connects with the pancreatic duct, which allows digestive enzymes and other products from the pancreas, such as sodium bicarbonate ($NaHCO_3$) to be mixed with bile before entering the duodenum for digestion. The later section entitled Gastrointestinal Control Valves: Sphincters discusses the role of bicarbonate in the small intestine.

A Closer Look at Enzymes in Digestion

Enzymes speed up digestion by catalyzing chemical reactions, bringing certain molecules close together, and then creating a favorable environment for the intended reaction. The enzyme lowers the amount of activation energy needed for the action to proceed (Fig. 3-9). (Appendix A provides more detail on enzyme action.) Enzymes usually act only on a specific substance; for example, enzymes that recognize table sugar (sucrose) ignore milk sugar (lactose). It is also possible for some of these enzymes to digest the digestive tract itself. For this reason, enzyme release is controlled by nerve and hormonal mechanisms in the digestive tract. Enzymes are released as needed, but generally not at other times.[11]

The naming system for enzymes is often quite simple. The first part of the enzyme name usually indicates the target; the ending is then *-ase*. For example, lipase is the enzyme that digests certain lipids.

It is important to recognize that digestion is a chemical process known as **hydrolysis,** in which water is used to split large molecules into smaller ones. The process eventually yields basic molecules, which can be absorbed through the intestinal wall.

hydrolysis A chemical reaction in which a compound is broken down by the addition of water. One product receives a hydrogen ion (H^+), while the other product receives a hydroxyl ion (OH^-). Hydrolytic enzymes break down compounds using water in the manner just described.

A few digestive enzymes are made by the mouth and stomach. Most are synthesized by the pancreas and small intestine (Chapters 5, 6, and 7 will review these in detail). The pancreas is capable of responding to changes in nutrient intake with appropriate changes in enzyme production. Increased protein intake leads to increased protein digestive capability. This is likely linked to the ability of the hormone cholecystokinin (CCK) to increase the synthesis of protein-digesting enzymes by the pancreas. Diets high in fat and low in carbohydrate lead to an increase in fat-digesting enzymes.

When either the small intestine or the pancreas is diseased, inadequate quantities of important digestive enzymes may be produced. This scarcity can result in incomplete digestion and very limited absorption. In such cases, nutrients in the undigested food

Table 3-3 Gastrointestinal Tract Hormones

Hormone	Stimulus to Secretion	Secreted by	Action
Gastrin	Food in the stomach, especially proteins, caffeine; spices; alcohol	Pyloric region of the stomach and upper duodenum	Stimulates parietal cells to produce acid, stimulates chief cells to produce enzyme that begins digestion of protein
Secretin	Acid chyme, partially digested protein	Duodenum, jejunum	Stimulates pancreas to produce bicarbonate
Cholecystokinin (CCK)	Food, especially fat and proteins in duodenum	Duodenum, jejunum	Stimulates contraction of gallbladder, secretes pancreatic digestive enzymes, inhibits stomach motility
Gastric inhibitory peptide	Protein and fat in chyme	Small intestine	Inhibits stomach motility, stimulates insulin secretion

travel into the large intestine rather than being absorbed into the bloodstream. In the large intestine the undigested food is metabolized into acids and gases by bacteria. The resultant feces appear foamy and greasy due to trapped gases and the presence of undigested fat. Intestinal malabsorption also often causes a distended abdomen due to intestinal gas.[2]

Gastrointestinal Hormones—A Key to Orchestrating Digestion

People who have pancreatic disease may not produce sufficient enzymes for digestion. In cystic fibrosis, excess production of mucus may block release of enzymes from the pancreas. This results in malabsorption of nutrients and associated discomfort. An affected person can consume replacement enzymes with meals. Some forms are coated to protect against destruction by stomach acid.

Four hormones, part of the endocrine system, regulate the GI tract: gastrin, secretin, cholecystokinin, and gastric inhibitory peptide[5] (Table 3-3). The term *hormone* comes from the Greek "to stir or excite." To be a true hormone, a regulatory compound must have a specific synthesis site from which it enters the bloodstream to reach target cells. Note that hormones are not available to all cells in the body, but only those with the correct receptor protein.[17] These receptors are highly specific for a certain hormone, and are generally found on the cell membrane. The hormone binds to a receptor on the cell membrane. This activates a "second messenger" system within the cell to carry out the assigned task. The hormone insulin acts in such a manner. Many hormones activate a form of ATP as the second messenger. Another common second messenger is calcium.

A few hormones can penetrate the cell membrane and bind to receptors in the cytoplasm. This hormone–receptor complex then travels to the nucleus and binds to DNA (e.g., thyroid hormones). Still other hormones use a third method; they bind directly to DNA (e.g., estrogen). All this binding to DNA eventually goes on to direct protein synthesis (see Chapter 7 for details).

Many hormonelike compounds, such as vasoactive intestinal peptide, bombesin, substance P, and somatostatin, also control important aspects of GI function. These compounds diffuse from cells or nerve endings to nearby cells. Many hormonelike compounds are found in the intestine and the brain. When a person thinks about eating or prepares to eat, the whole GI tract begins to prime itself for action. Hormonelike substances participate in this process. The cells that synthesize these hormones and hormonelike compounds are scattered throughout the GI tract.[5]

Gastrointestinal Control Valves: Sphincters

sphincter A muscular valve that controls flow of foodstuff in the GI tract.

A **sphincter** is a circular muscle arrangement (as in the anus) that acts as a valve to regulate passage or flow of material. The intestinal tract includes several sphincters, which respond to stimuli from nerves, hormones, hormonelike compounds, and pressure that builds up around them.[16]

The flow of food through the esophagus is controlled by the upper and lower esophageal sphincters. The lower esophageal sphincter (also known as the *cardiac sphincter* due to its proximity to the heart) prevents backflow (reflux) of stomach contents into the esophagus. It generally opens only in response to muscle contractions in the esophagus, which propel ingested food down to the stomach. The lower esophageal sphincter should otherwise remain closed, as the stomach contents are highly acidic. If stomach acid comes in contact with the esophagus, it can cause a pain known as **heartburn** (see the Nutrition Perspective, p. 103).

heartburn Pain caused by stomach acid backing up into the esophagus and irritating the tissue in that organ.

The **pyloric sphincter,** located at the junction of the stomach and first part of the small intestine (duodenum), controls the movement of the stomach contents into the small intestine. Under hormonal and nervous system control, the pyloric sphincter allows only a few milliliters (about a teaspoon) of stomach contents at a time to squirt into the small intestine. This rate allows bicarbonate ions released from the pancreas to efficiently neutralize the hydrogen ions coming from the stomach acid. This neutralization is critical to reduce the risk of acid erosion of the small intestine. Such erosion might produce an **ulcer** (see the Nutrition Perspective, p. 103). The pyloric sphincter also prevents backflow of intestinal contents into the stomach, thereby protecting the stomach lining from bile in the intestinal contents.

pyloric sphincter Ring of smooth muscle between the stomach and the duodenum.

ulcer Erosion of the tissue lining in either the stomach (gastric ulcer) or upper small intestine (duodenal ulcer). The general condition in either area is often termed a *peptic ulcer.*

The sphincter of Oddi lies at the end of the common bile duct. When the hormone **cholecystokinin (CCK)** stimulates the gallbladder to contract during digestion, the sphincter of Oddi relaxes and allows the contents of the gallbladder to flow down the common bile duct and enter the duodenum.

cholecystokinin (CCK) A hormone that stimulates enzyme release from the pancreas and bile release from the gallbladder.

The **ileocecal sphincter** is found at the end of the small intestine and opens in response to the presence of intestinal contents in its vicinity. Otherwise the sphincter remains closed to prevent the contents of the large intestine from backing up into the small intestine. In this way bacteria from the large intestine are prevented from invading and colonizing the small intestine. The small intestine must have a relatively low concentration of bacteria because bacteria can compete for nutrients and disrupt absorption, especially for fat.[2]

ileocecal sphincter The ring of smooth muscle between the ileum of the small intestine and the colon.

At the far end of the large intestine are two anal sphincters, one under voluntary control. Once toilet-trained, a child can determine when to relax the sphincter and when to keep it constricted.

Thus sphincters along the intestinal tract perform important functions. Without them we would suffer more heartburn, ulcers, and diarrhea.

Gastrointestinal Muscularity: Mixing and Propulsion

Food is propelled down the GI tract by a process called **peristalsis.** Watching a snake swallow its prey graphically illustrates the process. Most of the GI tract has two layers of muscles—circular and longitudinal. Peristalsis consists of a coordinated squeezing and shortening of these muscles (Fig. 3-10). This begins in the esophagus in the form of two waves of muscle action closely following each other. In the stomach, peristaltic waves create a mixing and grinding action as often as three times per minute during digestion. The stomach wall is composed of three opposing muscle layers (circular, diagonal, and longitudinal), which in combination enable the stomach to contract in enough directions to fully mix food with gastric juices[14] (review Fig. 3-7).

peristalsis A coordinated muscular contraction that propels food down the GI tract.

The most prominent peristalsis occurs in the small intestine, where contractions occur about every 4 to 5 seconds. The large intestine has comparatively sluggish peristalsis, employing occasional **mass movements** to help eliminate the feces.

mass movement A peristaltic wave that simultaneously coordinates contraction over a large area of the large intestine. Mass movements propel material from one portion of the large intestine to another and from the large intestine into the rectum.

Concept | Check

The gastrointestinal (GI) tract includes the mouth, esophagus, stomach, small intestine, large intestine (colon), rectum, and anus. Associated with the GI tract are the salivary glands, liver, gallbladder, and pancreas. Together these organs perform the digestion and absorption needed to extract nutrients from food and deliver them to the bloodstream.

Hormones, such as gastrin and cholecystokinin (CCK), regulate digestion. Sphincters throughout the GI tract control the flow of food by blocking the passage between organs until the proper time.

In the GI tract, a coordinated muscular activity called peristalsis propels food from the esophagus to the anus. Segmentation in the intestines divides and mixes the contents, aiding digestion and absorption. Enzymes produced by cells in the mouth, stomach, pancreas, and small intestine digest the food to forms of nutrients that can be absorbed. The time from ingestion of food to the eventual elimination of the feces from the body is usually about 1 to 3 days.

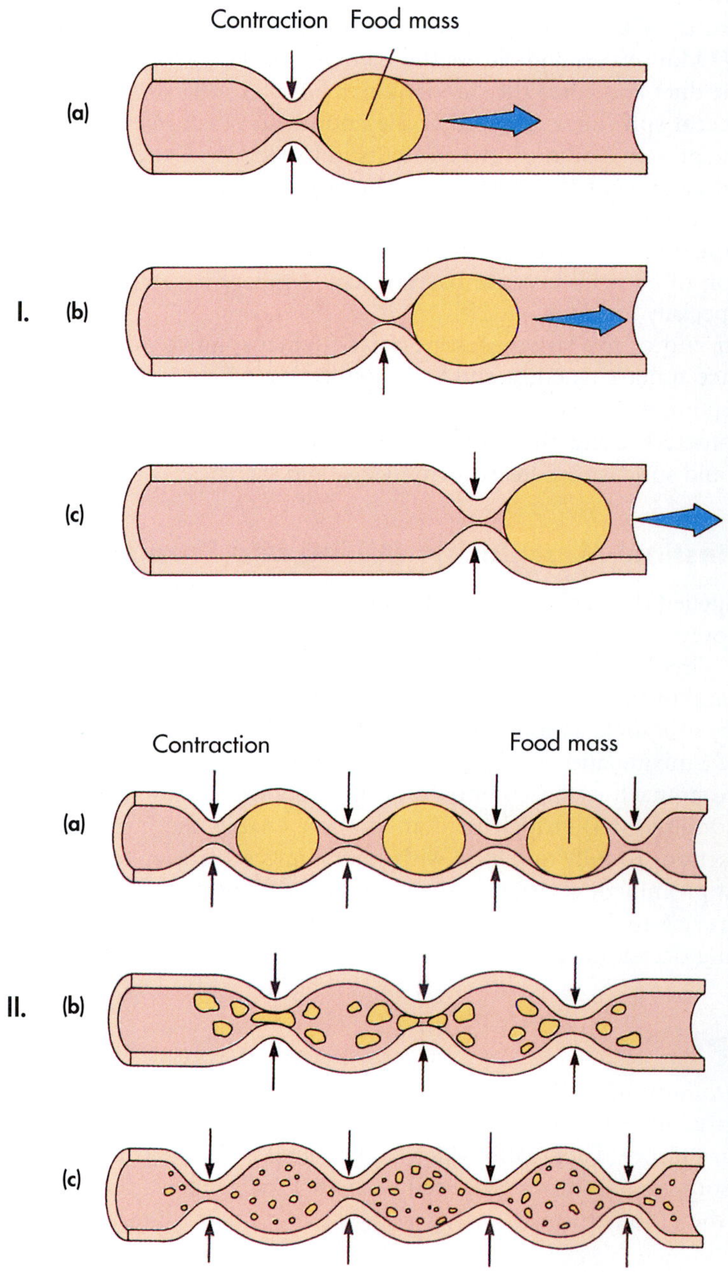

Figure 3-10 Peristalsis and segmentation. *I. Peristalsis.* Peristalsis is a progressive movement, propelling material along the GI tract. (*a*) A ring of contraction occurs where the GI wall is stretched, passing the food mass forward. (*b*) The moving food mass triggers a ring of contraction in the next region, which pushes the food mass even farther along. (*c*) The ring of contraction moves like a wave along the GI tract, pushing the food mass forward.

II. Segmentation. Segmentation is the back-and-forth action that breaks apart chunks of the food mass and mixes in digestive juices. (*a*) Ringlike regions of contraction occur at intervals along the GI tract. (*b*) Previously contracted regions relax and adjacent regions contract, effectively "chopping" the contents of each segment into smaller chunks. (*c*) Contracted regions continue to alternate back and forth, chopping and mixing the contents of the GI tract.

The Physiology of Absorption

Most nutrient **absorption** occurs in the small intestine; the stomach and large intestine participate to a minor extent. The small intestine can ultimately absorb about 95% of the food energy it receives in the form of protein, carbohydrate, fat, and alcohol. In general, only water, a portion of alcohol intake, and certain types of fats are absorbed to a significant extent by the stomach. Some minerals, water, and short-chain fatty acids (produced by bacterial action) are absorbed in the large intestine.[11]

The extent and efficiency of absorption in the small intestine are linked to its incredible surface area. The wall of the small intestine is folded, and within the folds are fingerlike projections called villi (Fig. 3-11). The "fingers" trap nutrients between each other to enhance absorption. Each villus "finger" is made up of numerous **absorptive cells** (enterocytes). Each of these cells has a brush border, made up of microvilli, and covered with glycocalyx. Intestinal enzymes are often found on the glycocalyx. All these folds, fingers, and indentations in the small intestine increase its surface area 600 times beyond that of a simple tube.[4]

absorption The process by which nutrient molecules are absorbed by the GI tract and enter the bloodstream.

absorptive cells A class of cells, also called *enterocytes*, that cover the surface of the villi (fingerlike projections in the small intestine) and participate in nutrient absorption.

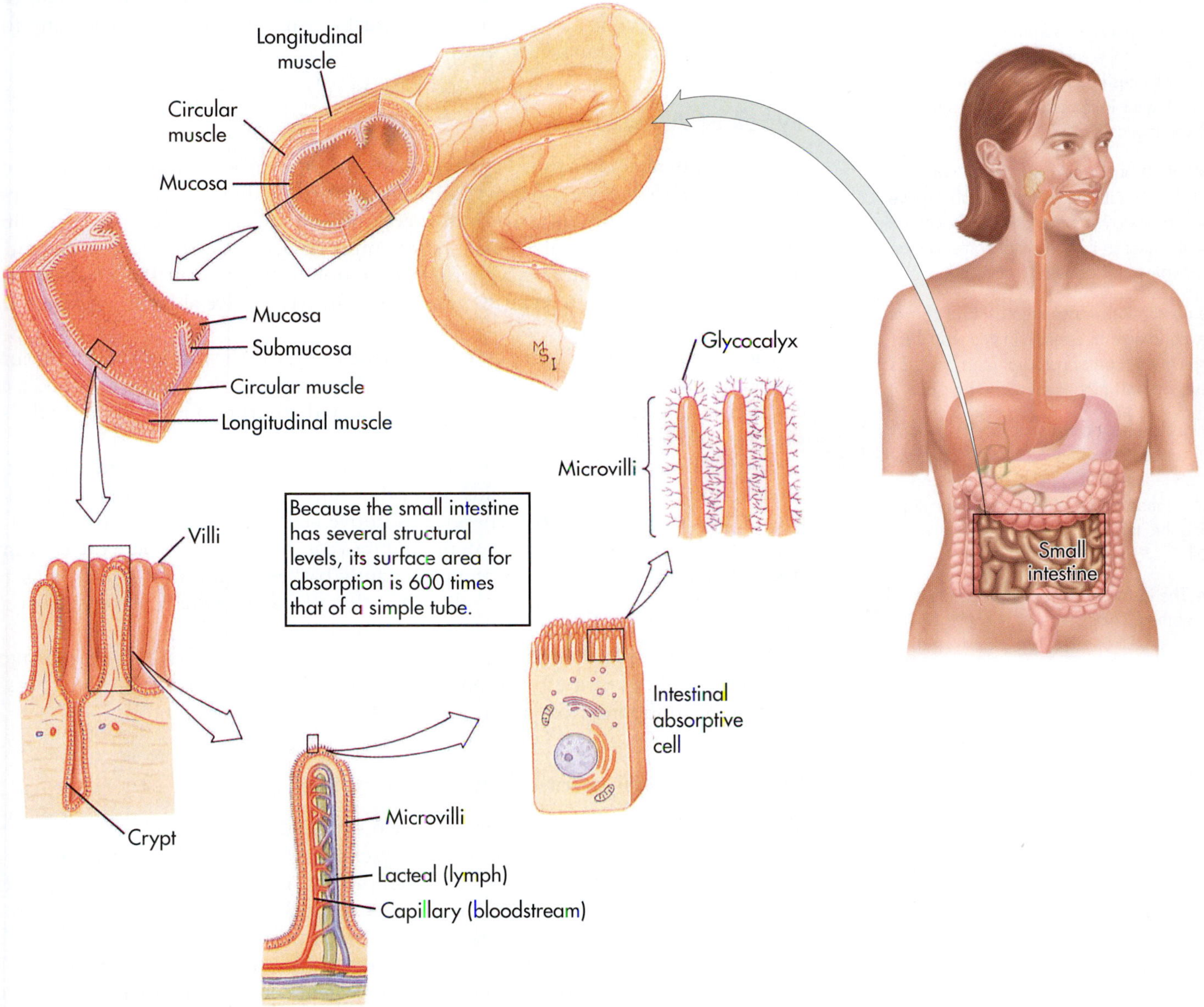

Figure 3-11 Organization of the small intestine. The small intestine has several structural levels, which increase the surface area for absorption up to 600 times that of a simple tube.

Absorptive Cells

mucosa Mucous membrane consisting of cells and supporting connective tissue. In the digestive tract there is also a layer of smooth muscle supporting the mucosa. Mucosa lines cavities that open to the outside of the body, such as the stomach and intestine, and generally contains glands that secrete mucus.

The absorptive cells of the small intestine lie side by side with goblet cells, which produce mucus, and endocrine cells, which produce hormones and hormonelike substances. All these cells form a principal part of the intestinal **mucosa.** The absorptive cells are produced in open-ended pits (called *crypts*) buried deep in the mucosa of the small intestine and migrate from the crypts to the tips of the villi. As the cells migrate, they mature, and their absorptive efficiency increases. By the time they reach the tips of the villi, however, they have been partially degraded by digestive enzymes and are ready to be sloughed off. Newly formed absorptive cells constantly migrate from the crypts to replace dying ones; this takes approximately 2 to 5 days. Since cell production requires a variety of nutrients, groups of cells undergoing constant replacement have a correspondingly enhanced need for nutrients. For this reason, the small intestine rapidly deteriorates during a nutrient deficiency or in semistarvation even though many of the old cells can be broken down and their components reused.[2]

If a disease causes the villi to lie down, the surface area of the small intestine decreases and malabsorption results. This happens in celiac disease (also called *gluten-induced enteropathy*). This disease is caused by an allergic response to a protein called *gluten,* found in wheat, rye, barley, and buckwheat. To prevent attacks, any foods derived from these grains must be avoided.

passive absorption Absorption that requires permeability of the substance through the wall of the small intestine and a concentration gradient higher in the intestinal contents than in the absorptive cell.

facilitated absorption Absorption in which a carrier shuttles substances into the absorptive cell but no energy is expended. A concentration gradient higher in the intestinal contents than in the absorptive cell drives the absorption.

active absorption Absorption using a carrier and expending ATP energy. In this way the absorptive cell can absorb nutrients, such as glucose, against a concentration gradient.

endocytosis (phagocytosis/pinocytosis) Forms of active absorption in which the absorptive cell forms an indentation in its membrane and particles (phagocytosis) or fluids (pinocytosis) entering the indentation are then engulfed by the cell.

lumen The inside of a tube, such as the inside cavity of the GI tract.

Types of Absorption

The small intestine uses four basic types of absorptive processes: **passive, facilitated, active,** and **endocytosis (phagocytosis/pinocytosis)**[17] (Fig. 3-12). Passive absorption occurs when nutrients enter absorptive cells without a carrier or energy expenditure. For this to happen, the wall of the intestine must be permeable to the nutrient and the nutrient must be present in a higher concentration in the intestinal **lumen** than in the absorptive cells. The difference in concentration drives passive absorption. Water, most fats, and some minerals are passively absorbed.

Facilitated absorption uses a carrier molecule to shuttle the nutrients from the lumen of the small intestine into the absorptive cells, but no energy is expended. Again, a concentration difference drives the reaction. Facilitated absorption takes place for the simple sugar fructose.

Active absorption uses a carrier and the process requires energy. The single sugars glucose and galactose, amino acids, and other nutrients are actively absorbed. ATP is the energy source. Using this energy, absorptive cells can take up a substance in low concentration in the intestinal contents and move it into the cell, where the concentration is higher. Since the bloodstream constantly bathes the absorptive cells, their relative concentration of glucose is higher than that of the intestinal contents. Therefore the ability to absorb against a concentration gradient is critical.

A second type of active absorption involves the processes of endocytosis: phagocytosis (literally, "cell eating") and pinocytosis (literally, "cell drinking"). An infant's absorption of antibodies from the mother's milk occurs this way.

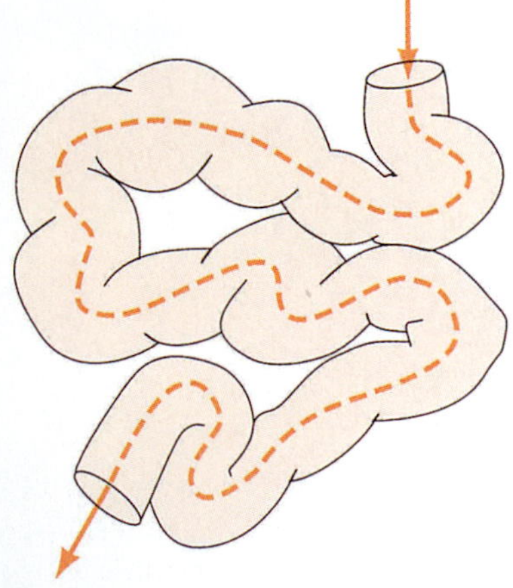

Portal and Lymphatic Circulation in Absorption

portal vein A large vein leaving from the intestine and stomach that connects to the liver.

The villi in the intestine are drained by two different sets of vessels, portal and lymphatic. The nutrients follow one of these systems based on solubility in either (1) water or (2) organic solvents. The nutrients that are soluble in water (proteins, carbohydrates, short- and medium-chain fatty acids, B vitamins, and vitamin C) are absorbed into the blood.[11] Blood leaves the heart via the arteries, travels to the small intestine, and eventually ends up at the capillary beds inside the villi (review Fig. C-5 in Appendix C). The blood exits the capillary beds and collects in a large **portal vein,** which leads directly to the liver. This direct path enables the liver to process absorbed nutrients before they enter the general circulation. Blood flow used for portal absorption accounts for 30% of the heart's total output.

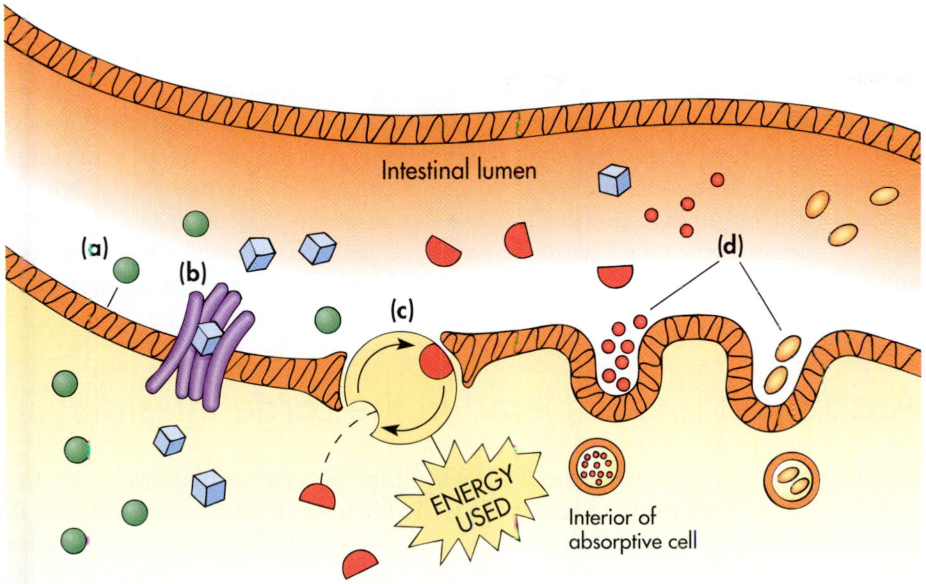

Figure 3-12 Nutrient absorption relies on these major forms of absorptive processes. (*a*) Diffusion involves simple diffusion of substances across the cell membrane of absorptive cells. No energy is expended because the substances follow a favorable concentration gradient (from high to low concentrations). Water and fats are absorbed in this manner. (*b*) Facilitated diffusion uses a carrier protein or other process to aid in the absorption of specific substances, such as fructose. No energy is expended; the process is simply aided by the carrier. (*c*) Active absorption (transport) uses a carrier protein and expends energy in the process. The use of energy allows the absorptive cell to absorb nutrients against their concentration gradient (from low to high concentrations). Glucose undergoes active absorption. (*d*) Phagocytosis—"cell eating"—involves cells taking in substances, including whole particles, by forming an indentation in the cell membrane and then surrounding the particle, with eventual incorporation into the cell. This is an active form of transport of substances. Pinocytosis—"cell drinking"—involves the cellular uptake of liquids in a manner analogous to phagocytosis. Exocytosis (not illustrated) packages products destined for export from the cell. The products are contained within a membrane-enclosed vesicle, which fuses with the plasma membrane so that the products can be discharged into the extracellular fluid.

Critical | Thinking

Cancer treatments often involve the use of medications (chemotherapy) to prevent rapid cell production and growth. Cancer cells are the intended target. Diarrhea is a common side effect of chemotherapy. Why would this happen?

The **lymphatic system** also drains the villi. The lymphatic vessels carry particles that are either fat soluble (long-chain fatty acids and the fat-soluble vitamins A, D, E, and K) or too large to pass through the capillaries into the bloodstream (large proteins that escape from the bloodstream and chylomicrons that form after the absorption of fat).[11] Substances are squeezed through the spongelike vessels of the lymphatic system by muscular activity (again, review Fig. C-5 in Appendix C). The lymphatic vessels from the intestine drain into the thoracic duct, which stretches from the abdomen to the neck. This duct is connected to the bloodstream via a large vein near the neck, the left subclavian vein.

lymphatic system A system of vessels that can accept fluid surrounding cells and large particles, such as products of fat absorption. This lymph fluid eventually passes into the bloodstream via the lymphatic system.

Enterohepatic Circulation

During meals, bile circulates through the liver to the gallbladder, through the small intestine into the portal vein, and then returns to the liver. This recycling is called **enterohepatic circulation.**[11] Approximately 98% of the bile is recycled; only 1 to 2% is removed from the body by elimination in the feces. (See Chapter 6 for a practical application of the knowledge of this process, employed by a class of blood cholesterol–lowering medications and certain brands of margarine and salad dressings.)

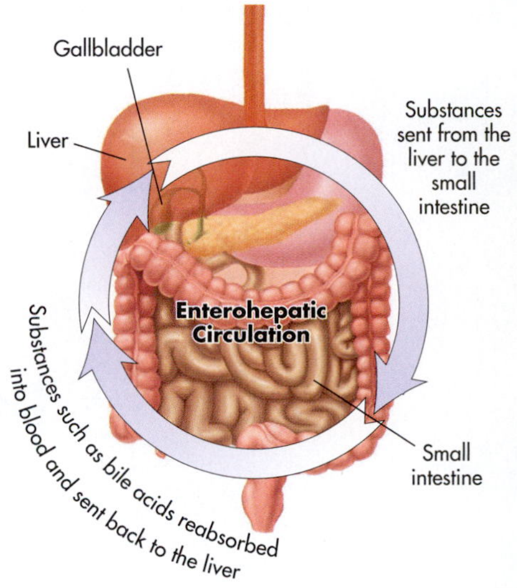

enterohepatic circulation A continual recycling of compounds between the small intestine and the liver; bile acids are one example of a recycled compound.

Concept | Check

The small intestine is the major site for absorption. Numerous folds and fingerlike projections increase the surface area to 600 times that of a simple tube. This provides a large area for nutrient absorption. Absorptive cells have a life span of 2 to 5 days, so the lining of the small intestine is constantly being renewed. These cells perform

Critical | Thinking

The medical history of a young girl who is greatly underweight shows that she had three-quarters of her small intestine removed after she was injured in a car accident. Explain how this accounts for her underweight condition, even though her medical chart shows that she eats well.

passive absorption, promoted by a concentration gradient; facilitated absorption, promoted by a concentration gradient plus a carrier; and active absorption, which uses energy in addition to a carrier to work against a concentration gradient. Absorptive cells also engulf compounds and liquids via endocytosis (phagocytosis/pinocytosis). The products of absorption, if water soluble, pass into the portal vein and enter the liver. The products of fat digestion mostly enter the lymphatic system. Some participants in digestion, such as bile, are reabsorbed after use in the small intestine and returned to the liver, to be sent back again to the small intestine during another round of digestion. This circulation is called *enterohepatic circulation*.

Absorption Is Completed in the Large Intestine

The small intestine is responsible for 85 to 90% of the water absorbed from the GI tract (Fig. 3-13). This absorption reduces the 9 L the GI tract receives (2 L of dietary fluid plus 7 L of GI tract secretions) to about 1.5 L. The remnants of digestion that enter the large intestine are the remaining water, some minerals, and undigested food fibers

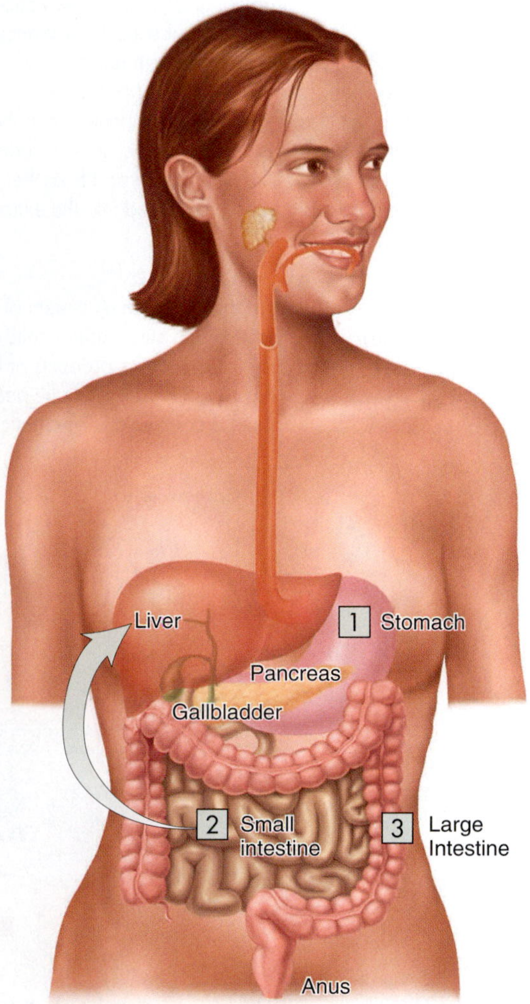

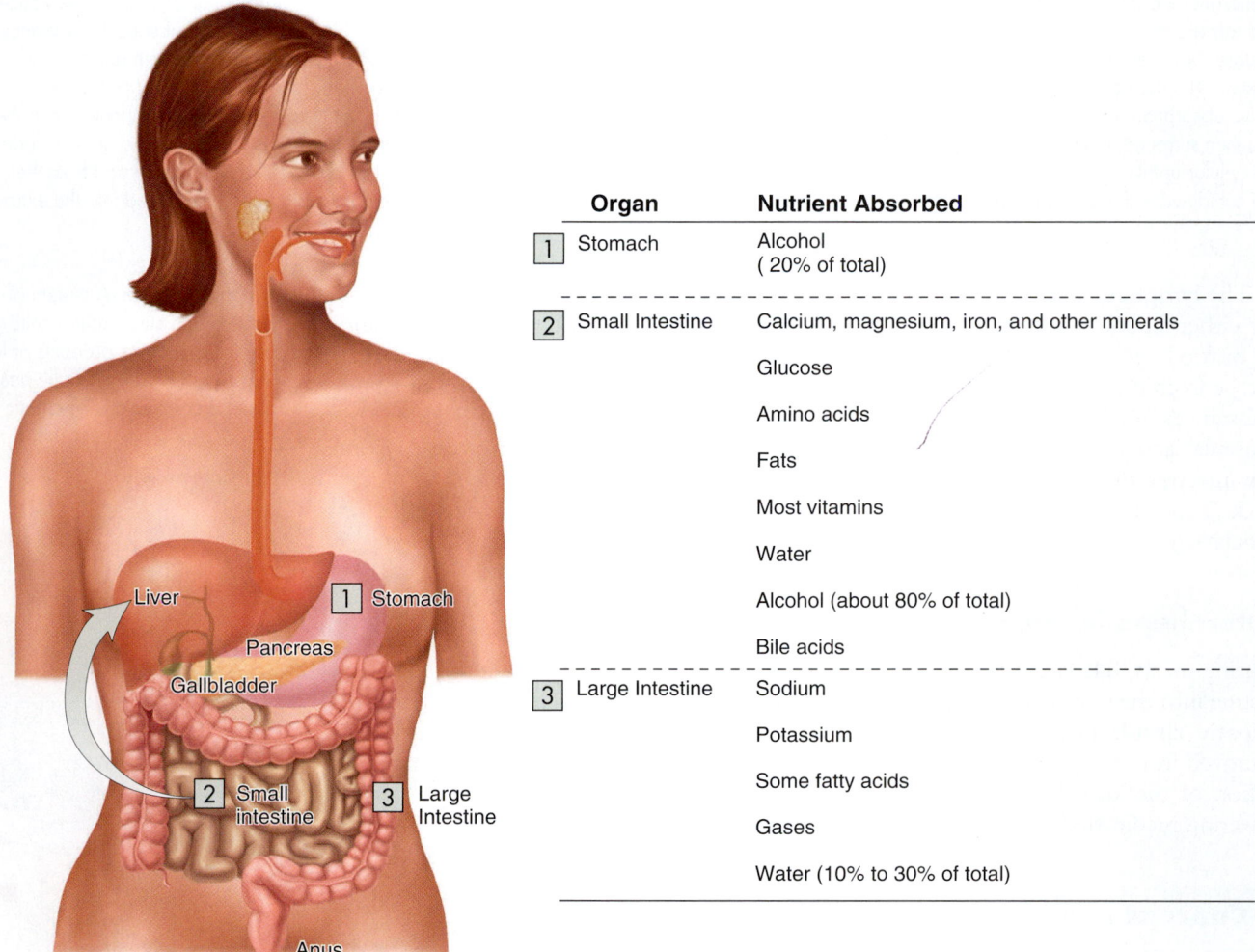

	Organ	Nutrient Absorbed
1	Stomach	Alcohol (20% of total)
2	Small Intestine	Calcium, magnesium, iron, and other minerals
		Glucose
		Amino acids
		Fats
		Most vitamins
		Water
		Alcohol (about 80% of total)
		Bile acids
3	Large Intestine	Sodium
		Potassium
		Some fatty acids
		Gases
		Water (10% to 30% of total)

Figure 3-13 Major sites of absorption along the GI tract. Note that some absorption of vitamin K and biotin takes place in the large intestine. All nutrients except most of those that are fat soluble travel through the portal vein to the liver after their absorption.

and starches. Only a minor amount (5%) of carbohydrate, protein, and fat escapes absorption in the small intestine.[11]

The large intestine absorbs primarily sodium and potassium, along with some water, leaving only about 0.2 L of water unabsorbed. This occurs mostly in the first half of the large intestine. Short-chain fatty acids made from both the bacterial **fermentation** of some plant fibers and undigested starches are also absorbed in the large intestine, along with some vitamins synthesized by bacteria, such as vitamin K and biotin.[10] Dr. Steve Hertzler discusses the latest findings on the effects of this bacterial action in the Expert Opinion on probiotics and prebiotics. By the time the contents of the large intestine pass through the first two-thirds of its length, a semisolid mass is formed. This remains in the large intestine until peristaltic waves (called haustrations) and mass movements push it into the rectum for elimination through the anus (Table 3-4).

fermentation The metabolism, without the use of oxygen, of carbohydrates to alcohols, acids, and carbon dioxide.

The presence of feces in the rectum powerfully stimulates defecation. This process involves muscular reflexes in the sigmoid colon and rectum, as well as relaxation of the anal sphincters. The feces primarily consist of indigestible plant fibers, tough connective tissue from animal foods, and bacteria from the large intestine.[11]

Storage Capabilities of the Body

The human body must maintain reserves of nutrients. Otherwise, we would need to eat continuously. Storage capacity varies for each nutrient. Most fat is stored at sites designed specifically for this—adipose tissue. Short-term storage of carbohydrate occurs in muscle and liver, and the blood maintains a small reserve of glucose and amino acids. Many vitamins and minerals are stored in the liver, while other nutrient stores are found at other sites in the body.[4]

Nutrient intake also directly influences nutrient absorption. For example, vitamin C in a meal increases iron absorption in the same meal because it changes iron into a more absorbable state.

When people do not meet their nutrient needs, some nutrients are obtained by breaking down a tissue that contains high concentrations of the nutrient. Calcium is taken from bone and protein is taken from muscle. These nutrient losses in cases of long-term deficiency harm these tissues.

Many people believe that if too much of a nutrient is obtained—for example, from a vitamin or mineral supplement—only what is needed is stored and the rest is excreted by the body. This is true for many vitamins and minerals. However, large dosages of vitamin A can cause harmful side effects because it is not readily excreted. This is one reason why obtaining your nutrients primarily (or exclusively) from a balanced diet, rather

Table 3-4 A Summary of Digestion Functions, Organ-by-Organ

Organ	Functions
Mouth	Chewing of food Some digestion of starch
Esophagus	Passageway
Stomach	Food storage; acidity kills bacteria Some digestion of protein
Small intestine	Final digestion of all energy-yielding nutrients Absorption of nutrients
Large intestine	Absorption of water and some minerals; storage of nondigestible remains
Anus	Elimination of waste as feces
Liver	Production of bile
Gallbladder	Storage and release of bile
Pancreas	Production and release of enzymes and bicarbonate into the small intestine

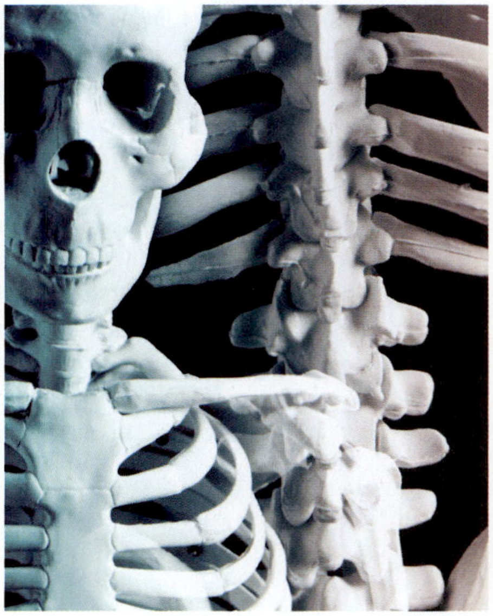

The skeletal system provides a reserve of calcium for day-to-day needs when dietary intake is inadequate. Long-term use of this reserve, however, reduces bone strength.

Expert Opinion

Probiotics, Prebiotics, and Human Health

Steve Hertzler, Ph.D., R.D.

The human body contains over 100 trillion (10^{14}) cells, 90% of which are bacterial!

The Bacteria Down Below

The large intestine (colon) harbors most of these bacteria, containing an amazingly large and diverse population of microorganisms (called microflora) made up of over 400 different species. Within this vast ecosystem reside both beneficial and potentially harmful microorganisms. Health-promoting functions of colonic bacteria include: (1) protecting against invading pathogenic bacteria; (2) synthesizing vitamins such as vitamin K; and (3) producing short-chain fatty acids (e.g., acetate and butyrate) that play important roles as energy sources and for regulating the growth and development of colon cells. In addition, it has been recognized recently that bacterial metabolism is necessary to convert isoflavones (beneficial estrogen-like compounds found in foods such as soy) into a form that can be absorbed from the intestine.

It is important to emphasize that, while many of the functions of the colonic bacteria are positive, there can be negative impacts on health as well. Some colonic bacteria contain high levels of enzymes that can retoxify drugs and other chemicals that were originally detoxified by the liver and shipped into the small intestine for excretion. Similarly, bacterial enzyme activities are involved in the conversion of bile acids and undigested proteins into toxic substances. There is even speculation that certain types of bacteria may be involved in the causation of diseases such as ulcerative colitis. Thus, it is clear we must attempt to shift the activities of the colonic bacteria toward health promotion. The use of probiotics, prebiotics, or synbiotics (the combination of pro- and prebiotics) to accomplish this aim continues to grow. Sales of probiotic supplements in the United States had reached $100 million annually by the year 2000.

Probiotics

Probiotics, which means "for life" in Greek, refers to "living microorganisms, which, upon ingestion in certain numbers, exert health benefits beyond inherent general nutrition." Thus, the probiotic approach involves the ingestion of live bacterial cells, mainly lactic acid-producing bacteria (e.g., the *Lactobacillus* or *Bifidobacterium* genera), in foods or as dietary supplements. Numerous studies have shown that the lactic acid produced by these organisms tends to inhibit the growth of less acid-tolerant organisms such as *E. coli* and the genus *Clostridium* that are generally regarded as harmful.

Key requirements for the successful use of probiotics are the survival of the probiotic organism as it makes its way through the gastrointestinal tract and the subsequent colonization of the organism in the gut. The hurdles that probiotic bacteria face include destruction by stomach acid or bile and competition with other bacteria in the colon. One method for overcoming this problem is the selection of probiotic bacteria that are highly resistant to stomach acid and bile, and that also possess the ability to colonize the GI tract. This approach requires meticulous laboratory testing of many bacterial strains using *in vitro* systems that can only roughly approximate actual conditions inside the body.

Despite the challenges associated with probiotic survival, the evidence for the health benefits of certain probiotics continues to accumulate. Some of the strongest evidence for probiotics relates to the prevention and treatment of several types of diarrhea, including traveler's diarrhea, relapsing *Clostridium difficile*-induced intestinal inflammation and diarrhea, rotavirus diarrhea in infants, antibiotic-associated diarrhea, and diarrhea associated with tube feedings in hospitalized patients. A recent meta-analysis (summary of several studies grouped together) of nine studies showed a 61 to 66% reduction in the risk of antibiotic-associated diarrhea when probiotics were given concurrently. Probiotic organisms used for the prevention and treatment of diarrhea include: *Lactobacillus rhamnosus* GG, *Saccharomyces boulardii, Enterococcus faecium* SF68, *Bifidobacterium bifidum,* and *Streptococcus thermophilus.* In addition to the prevention of diarrhea caused by pathogenic microorganisms, diarrhea caused by lactose malabsorption and intolerance can be reduced as well. Previous studies have clearly shown that fermented dairy foods, such as yogurt, which contain live cultures, can improve lactose digestion in the small intestine. Recently, my laboratory has demonstrated that kefir, a type of fermented milk that is like a drinkable yogurt, improves lactose digestion similarly to yogurt. This improvement in lactose digestion from these products is due to the presence of the enzyme lactase in the bacterial cells of the starter culture that is released when the cells encounter bile in the small intestine.

The active cultures in fermented dairy foods also provide other nutritional advantages, including: (1) short chains of amino acids formed from milk proteins during yogurt fermentation that may lower blood pressure; (2) compounds with stimulating effects on the immune system; and (3) a natural inhibitor of the enzyme that synthesizes

Yogurt is a convenient source of probiotic bacteria to your diet. These bacteria contribute to GI tract health.

cholesterol in the body, resulting in the possible lowering of blood lipids. The optimal amount of yogurt to be eaten each day to derive these benefits has yet to be established. Dosage is often expressed in colony-forming units (CFU) of bacteria and is generally in the range of 10^8 to 10^{12} CFU per day. (Yogurt with active cultures must have at least 10^8 CFU/ml; an 8-ounce serving of yogurt contains 240 ml.) To date, unrealistically high doses of yogurt (>2 liters/day) have been fed in some of the studies that have shown blood cholesterol-lowering effects. Finally, there has been the suggestion that some strains of *Lactobacillus acidophilus* (not to be confused with *Lactobacillus* GG) may help to counter the growth of *Helicobacter pylori*, the organism responsible for most of the cases of ulcers. It is important to note that *L. acidophilus* alone cannot eradicate *H. pylori* infection, but that its use in conjunction with standard medications may improve the eradication rate. A physician's guidance should be sought before taking a probiotic for these purposes.

Many probiotic dietary supplements, including *Lactobacillus* GG (Culturelle®) and *Lactobacillus reuteri* (Probiotica®) have recently become available in North America. *Lactobacillus* GG has been extensively studied and found in animal studies to be safe at doses much higher than the 10^9 to 10^{10} CFU/day that people would normally consume in fermented foods or supplements (Culturelle® has 10^{10}, or 10 billion, CFU per capsule and costs about $20 for a one-month supply). Probiotica® contains 10^8, or 100 million cells of *L. reteuri* per tablet and costs $15 for a two-month supply (one tablet per day).

Prebiotics

Because it is difficult for many probiotic bacteria to survive and colonize the GI tract, a second approach to promoting the growth of healthy bacteria has developed. Prebiotics are "nondigestible food ingredients that beneficially affect the host by selectively stimulating the growth of one or a limited number of bacteria in the colon." The emphasis in prebiotics is on the provision of an energy source, usually a nondigestible carbohydrate, for the beneficial bacteria that already reside in the colon. The key to a good prebiotic is that it must be selectively utilized: beneficial bacteria will be able to use it while harmful bacteria will not.

The most popular prebiotic carbohydrate is fructooligosaccharide (FOS). The chemical structure of FOS consists of a molecule of glucose joined with 2, 3, or 4 fructose units, with the fructose units linked by beta chemical bonds (see Chapter 5 for details on beta chemical bonds in various carbohydrates). Because of its structure, FOS is not digested in the small intestine and becomes available to the colonic bacteria. There it selectively promotes the growth of bifidobacteria in the colon, since bifidobacteria are one of only a few types of bacteria that possess the enzyme necessary to digest FOS. The major brand of FOS in the United States is NutraFlora®. FOS is 30% as sweet as table sugar, contains only 1 to 2 kcal/g, and does not increase blood glucose, which may make it useful in food products for people with diabetes. FOS has been widely used in Japan for its bifidobacteria-stimulating effect. (The recommended dose is 1 to 4 g/day and costs about $14/ month.) It has recently been included in oral meal replacement formulas used for hospitalized patients in the United States.

The potential health benefits of FOS include: (1) increasing bifidobacteria concentrations in the colon; (2) the lowering of harmful enzyme activities of other colonic bacteria; (3) increasing calcium absorption from the intestine; (4) lowering of blood lipids; and (5) inhibiting dental decay (does not promote dental caries). While the ability of FOS to increase bifidobacteria counts has been well documented, additional studies are needed to confirm the results of preliminary work on the other potential health benefits. The use of FOS in North America has been growing at a slow pace, perhaps because of fears that eating FOS-containing products will cause increased intestinal gas or other abdominal symptoms. However, a recent study from my laboratory (not yet published) has shown that prolonged feeding of FOS results in decreased intestinal gas production over time, similar to what is reported anecdotally with high-fiber foods such as beans.

Steve Hertzler, Ph.D., R.D., is currently an Assistant Professor of Medical Dietetics at The Ohio State University. He earned his Ph.D. in Human Nutrition from the University of Minnesota in 1995 and is actively researching FOS as a prebiotic supplement as well as the glycemic response to different carbohydrates.

than relying on supplements, is the safest means to acquire the building blocks you need to maintain good health.

This review of human anatomy and physiology from a digestion and absorption perspective sets the stage for developing a more detailed understanding of the nutrients. Chapters 5, 6, and 7 will build on this information.

Concept | Check

Some water and mineral absorption occurs in the large intestine. The remaining contents form the feces, which consist primarily of indigestible plant fibers, tough connective tissue from animal foods, and bacteria. Nutrients are constantly present in the blood for immediate use and are stored to a greater or lesser extent in body tissues for later use when sufficient amounts from food intake are unavailable. However, when the body suffers a nutrient deficiency caused by an inadequate diet, it breaks down vital tissues for their nutrients, which can lead to ill health. Additionally, too much of any nutrient can be detrimental. It's best to focus primarily (or exclusively) on obtaining all essential nutrients from a balanced diet.

Summary

1. The basic structural unit of the human body is the cell. Cellular structure varies according to the type of job the cell must perform.
2. Cells join together to make up tissues; tissues unite to form organs; and organs work together as an organ system.
3. The gastrointestinal (GI) tract consists of the mouth, esophagus, stomach, small intestine, large intestine (colon), rectum, and anus. Most absorption of nutrients occurs in the small intestine.
4. The salivary glands, liver, gallbladder, and pancreas participate in digestion and absorption. Products from the last three organs enter the small intestine where enzymes and bile play important roles in digesting protein, fat, and carbohydrates.
5. The GI tract contains valves (sphincters) that control the flow of food. Muscular contractions, called *peristalsis,* propel the food down the GI tract. Segmentation contractions mechanically break down and mix the intestinal contents. Nerves, hormones, and hormonelike compounds control the activity of the sphincters and peristaltic and segmentation processes.
6. The mouth chews food to break it into smaller parts, increasing its surface area, which enhances enzyme activity. Some starch digestion occurs in the mouth. Protein digestion begins in the stomach. Carbohydrate and protein digestion are finished in the small intestine, where fat digestion begins in earnest and is completed. Some plant fibers are digested by the bacteria present in the large intestine; undigested plant fibers exit the body in the feces.
7. Digestive enzymes are secreted by the mouth, stomach, pancreas, and cells forming the wall of the small intestine. Bile needed for fat digestion is synthesized by the liver, stored in the gallbladder, and released in digestion.
8. The major absorptive sites are fingerlike projections in the small intestine called *villi*. The absorptive cells that cover the villi are replaced every 2 to 5 days. Thus the intestinal lining continually renews itself. Absorptive cells can perform passive, facilitated, and active absorption, as well as endocytosis (phagocytosis/pinocytosis), a specific type of active absorption.
9. Water-soluble compounds in the absorptive cells, such as glucose and amino acids, enter the portal vein and travel to the liver. Fat-soluble compounds enter the lymphatic system, which eventually connects to the bloodstream. Some substances used in digestion, such as bile, are absorbed by the small intestine, sent back to the liver through the portal vein, and released into the small intestine again to act in further digestion of food. This recycling is called enterohepatic circulation.
10. Final water and mineral absorption, as well as absorption of products from bacterial metabolism of some plant fibers, occurs in the large intestine. Once the feces enter the rectum, the impetus for elimination is strong.
11. Limited stores of nutrients are present in the blood for immediate use and stored to a greater or lesser extent in body tissues for later use when sufficient food is unavailable. When the body suffers a nutrient deficiency it breaks down vital tissues for their nutrients, which can lead to ill health. Additionally, too much of any nutrient can be detrimental.

Study Questions

1. Identify at least one contribution to overall nutrition status provided by each of the 12 organ systems of the body.
2. Contrast active and passive absorption. Indicate the role of ATP in active absorption.
3. Outline the possible results on digestion and absorption of a diseased pancreas.
4. Describe why the small intestine is better suited than the other GI tract organs to carry out the absorptive process.
5. Identify the two organs that empty their contents into the small intestine. How do the digestive substances made by these organs contribute to the digestion of food?

6. Where is hydrochloric acid (HCl) secreted, and how is its production regulated? What are its roles in digestion?
7. Describe the actions of the digestive hormones.
8. Describe the actions of the digestive enzymes and explain how they function in digestion.
9. How is blood routed through the digestive system? Which nutrients enter the bloodstream directly? Which nutrients are first absorbed into the lymph?
10. The body has the ability to recycle some substances. How is this true for the digestive tract?

Annotated References

1. Arce DA and others: Evaluation of constipation. *American Family Physician* 65:2283, 2002.

   Constipation is very common in children and older adults. To determine the underlying cause, it is important for a physician to evaluate the person's general health, psychosocial status, medical illnesses, fiber and fluid intake, and use of constipating medicines.

2. Baum C and others: Gastrointestinal disease. In Bowman BA, Russell RM (eds.): *Present knowledge in nutrition*. 8th ed. Washington, DC: ISLI Press, 2001.

   Disruption in any number of the steps in the digestive process can lead to malabsorption and in turn to protein, energy, and micronutrient deficiencies. Just as the GI tract is essential for nutrient utilization, ingested nutrients also play an active role in maintaining gastrointestinal health and function.

3. Bromley SM: Smell and taste disorders: A primary care approach. *American Family Physician* 61:427, 2000.

   Disorders of smell and taste can result from many reasons, such as use of certain medications. Advancing age especially has been associated with impairments of smell and taste. Enhancing food flavor and appearance can improve nutrient intake in such cases.

4. Ganong WF: *Review of medical physiology.* 25th ed. New York NY: Lange Medical Books/McGraw-Hill Medical Publishing Division, New York NY, 2001.

   This is an excellent resource for learning more about digestion and absorption. Specific chapters refer to the general process of digestion and absorption, as well as regulation of gastrointestinal function.

5. Granner DK: Hormones of the pancreas and gastrointestinal tract. In Murray RK and others (eds.): *Harper's biochemistry.* 25th ed. Stamford, CT: Appleton & Lange, 2000.

   The gastrointestinal tract secretes many hormones, perhaps more than any other organ system. Gastrointestinal hormones assist in all the functions of the GI tract, including the propelling of foodstuffs to sites of digestion, providing the proper environment for digestive processes, and moving digestive products across the intestinal mucosa.

6. *H. pylori:* What's the story? *Health News,* p. 1, December 2001.

   People who should be tested for the presence of H. pylori *include those with active stomach ulcers and those with stomach cancer or a family history of stomach cancer. Therapy generally includes the use of two antibiotics plus a proton pump inhibitor. It is successful in more than 90% of cases.*

7. Horwitz BJ, Fisher RS: Irritable bowel syndrome. *The New England Journal of Medicine* 344:1846, 2001.

   People with irritable bowel syndrome often benefit from a diet adequate in fiber and low in caffeine, alcohol, fatty foods, gas-forming vegetables, and products containing sorbitol, such as sugarless gum and dietetic candy. Certain medications are also helpful in treating such individuals.

8. Kaynard A, Flora K: Gastroesophageal reflux disease (GERD). *Postgraduate Medicine* 110 (3):42, 2001.

   Large surveys show that half of the general adult population experiences monthly heartburn. A trial of high doses of proton pump inhibitors is an accepted therapy for GERD. Complications of long-standing GERD include damage to the esophagus and a form of esophageal cancer.

9. Klein S and others: The alimentary tract in nutrition: A tutorial. In Shils ME and others (eds.): *Health and disease.* 9th ed. Baltimore MD: Williams & Wilkins, 1999.

   This chapter is a review of the GI tract structure, blood supply, nervous system control, GI tract hormones, nutrient absorption, intestinal microorganisms, and immune system. The response of the GI tract to food is also explained.

10. Kopp-Hoolihan L: Prophylactic and therapeutic uses of probiotics: A review. *Journal of the American Dietetic Association* 101:229, 2001.

    Probiotic microbes in foods beneficially affect the human host. These benefits include improving intestinal tract health, enhancing immune function, synthesizing some nutrients, enhancing bioavailability of some nutrients, reducing symptoms of lactose maldigestion and intolerance, decreasing the prevalence of allergies in susceptible individuals, and reducing risk of certain cancers. Certain forms of fluid milk, fermented milk, and yogurt contain probiotic microbes, such as Lactobacillus.

11. Mayes PA: Digestion and absorption. In Murray RK and others (eds.): *Harper's biochemistry.* 25th ed. Stamford, CT: Appleton & Lange, 2000.

    Most foodstuffs ingested are initially unavailable to humans; they cannot be absorbed by the digestive system until broken down into smaller molecules. This chapter provides a clear step-by-step description of this digestion, and subsequent absorption.

12. Meurer LN, Bower DJ: Management of *Helicobactor pylori* infection. *American Family Physician* 65:1327, 2002.

    Helicobactor pylori *is the cause of most peptic ulcer disease and is also a risk factor for gastric cancer. Eradication of this organism is important for ulcer healing and reducing the risk of ulcer reoccurrence. Generally a two-week period of antibiotics and acid suppression is employed. Follow-up testing with analysis of breath or fecal samples is recommended for people who do not respond to therapy.*

13. Olden KW: Diagnosis of irritable bowel syndrome. *Gastroenterology* 122:1701, 2002.

    The classic symptoms of irritable bowel syndrome are lower abdominal pain, bloating, and changes in bowel habits. Still, it is a difficult disease to diagnose. For example, a history of sexual abuse often complicates the diagnosis, as well as later management, of the disease.

14. Seeley RR and others: *Anatomy and physiology.* 6th ed. Boston: McGraw-Hill, 2003.

    This text provides comprehensive coverage of the anatomy and physiology of the gastrointestinal tract, as well as other related body systems.

15. Smith DV, Margolskee RF: Making sense of taste. *Scientific American,* p. 32, March 2001.

    Taste buds are scattered throughout the tongue, rather than in specific regions, as was previously thought. These taste buds sense sweet, salty, bitter, sour, and umami. When the compounds that cause these taste sensations bind to appropriate taste buds, changes in ion balance ultimately take place in the cell. This triggers the message that is sent to the nervous system.

16. Tso P, Crissinger K: Overview of digestion and absorption. In Stepanuk MH (ed.): *Biochemical and physiological aspects of human nutrition.* W. B. Saunders, 2000.

    One chapter in this textbook identifies the major structures and functions of the digestive tract. Control of absorption and related metabolism is explained.

17. Vander A and others: *Human physiology: The mechanisms of body function.* 8th ed. Boston: McGraw-Hill, 2000.

    This text covers the fundamentals of physiology for the undergraduate student. Topics include basic cell functions, biological control mechanisms, actions of the various organ systems, and coordination of body functions.

18. Yamaguchi S, Ninomiya S: Umami and food palatability. *Journal of Nutrition* 130:9321S, 2000.

    Umami is the term used to identify the taste of substances such as glutamate salts and is the main taste in Japanese stock and bouillon.

Take | Action

I. Are You Taking Care of Your Digestive Tract?

People need to think about the health of their digestive tracts. There are symptoms we need to notice, as well as habits we need to practice in order to protect it. The following assessment is designed to help you examine habits and symptoms associated with the health of your digestive tract. The Nutrition Perspective explains why these habits are important to examine. Put a *Y* in the blank to the left of the question to indicate yes and an *N* to indicate no.

_____ 1. Are you currently experiencing greater than normal stress and tension?

_____ 2. Do you have a family history of digestive tract problems (e.g., ulcers, hemorrhoids, diverticulosis, constipation, lactose intolerance)?

_____ 3. Do you experience pain in your stomach region about 2 hours after you eat?

_____ 4. Do you smoke cigarettes?

_____ 5. Do you take aspirin frequently?

_____ 6. Do you have heartburn at least once per week?

_____ 7. Do you commonly lie down after eating a large meal?

_____ 8. Do you drink alcoholic beverages more than two or three times per day?

_____ 9. Do you experience abdominal pain, bloating, and gas about 30 minutes to 2 hours after consuming milk products?

_____ 10. Do you often have to strain while having a bowel movement?

_____ 11. Do you consume less than 8 cups of a combination of water and other fluids per day?

_____ 12. Do you perform physical activity (e.g., jog, swim, walk briskly, row, stair climb) less than 30 to 60 minutes on most or all days of the week?

_____ 13. Do you eat a diet relatively low in dietary fiber (recall that significant dietary fiber is found in whole fruits, vegetables, legumes, nuts and seeds, whole-grain breads, and whole-grain cereals)?

_____ 14. Do you frequently have diarrhea?

_____ 15. Do you frequently use laxatives or antacids?

Interpretation

Add up the number of yes answers you gave and record the total in the blank to the right. _____

If your score is from 8 to 15, your habits and symptoms put you at risk for experiencing future digestive tract problems. Take particular note of the habits to which you answered yes. Consider trying to cooperate more with your digestive tract.

II. Over-the-Counter Medications for Treating Common GI Tract Problems.

After you have read the Nutrition Perspective "When the Digestive Processes Go Awry," visit your local pharmacy and check out the medications on sale for treating indigestion, heartburn, constipation, diarrhea, and hemorrhoids. Select one category and compare four brands for

1. Price/usual daily dose
2. Active ingredients
3. Warning to users
4. Advice as to when to see a physician

Write a critique of your discoveries about these products and summarize what you would say about the safety and efficacy of these products.

When the Digestive Processes Go Awry

The fine-tuned organ system we call the *GI tract* can develop problems. Knowing about these common problems can help you avoid them.

Ulcers

Many adults develop ulcers each year. About 25 million North Americans develop them during their lifetimes. The principal causes are an acid-resistant bacterial infection *(Helicobacter pylori [H. pylori])*, the heavy use of aspirin and related medications, and disorders that cause excessive acid production in the stomach (Fig. 3-14).[12] And, after being out of favor for some years, stress is now regarded as a predisposing factor for ulcers, especially if the person is infected with *H. pylori* or has certain anxiety disorders.

As the stomach lining deteriorates in ulcer development and loses its mucus layer protection, the acid erodes the stomach tissue. Acid can also erode the tissue lining of the first part of the small intestine. *Peptic ulcer* is the general term for both of these conditions. Most ulcers in young people occur in the small intestine; in older people they occur primarily in the stomach.

The typical symptom of an ulcer is pain about 2 hours after eating. Stomach acid acting on a meal irritates the ulcer after most of the meal has moved from the site of the ulcer.

The primary risk associated with an ulcer is the possibility that it will erode entirely through the stomach or intestinal wall. The GI contents could then spill into the body cavities, causing a massive infection. In addition, an ulcer may erode a blood vessel, leading to massive blood loss into the stomach or small intestine. For these reasons, it is important not to ignore the early warning signs of ulcer development.

In the past, milk and cream therapy—the so-called Sippy diet—was used to help cure ulcers. Clinicians now know that milk and cream are two of the worst foods a person with an ulcer could eat. The calcium in these foods stimulates stomach acid secretion and actually inhibits ulcer healing.

Today, a combination of approaches is used for ulcer therapy. People infected with *H. pylori* are given antibiotics with stomach acid-blocking medications called proton pump inhibitors (e.g., omeprazole [Prilosec], esomeprazole [Nexium], and lansoprazole [Prevacid]) to eradicate *H. pylori*.[6] (Recall that proton is another term for the hydrogen ion that creates acidity.) In many cases, there is a 90% cure rate for *H. pylori* in the first week of this treatment. Recurrence is unlikely if the infection is cured, but an incomplete cure almost certainly leads to repeated ulcer formation.

Antacid medications may also be part of ulcer care, as is a class of medicines called **H_2 blockers.** These include cimetidine (Tagamet), ranitidine (Zantac), and famotidine (Pepcid), all of which prevent **histamine**-related acid secretion in the stomach. Some of these medications are now available over the counter in nonprescription doses for cases of indigestion and heartburn (see next section). Medications that coat the ulcer, such as sucralfate (Carafate), are also commonly used.

H_2 blockers Medications such as cimetidine (Tagamet) that block the increase of stomach acid production caused by histamine.

histamine A breakdown product of the amino acid histidine that stimulates acid secretion by the stomach and has other effects on the body, such as contraction of smooth muscles, increased nasal secretions, relaxation of blood vessels, and constriction of airways. It appears to decrease hunger and food intake.

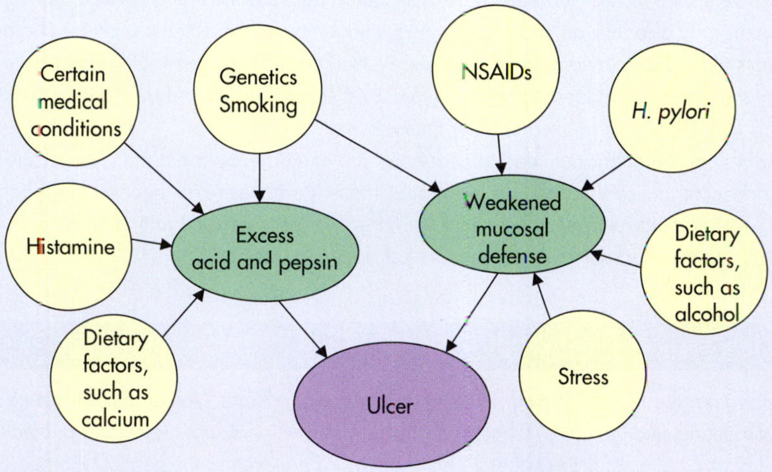

Figure 3-14 Pathogenesis of a peptic ulcer. *H. pylori* bacteria and NSAIDs cause ulcers by impairing mucosal defense. In the same way, smoking, genetics, and stress can impair mucosal defense, as well as cause an increase in the release of pepsin and stomach acid. All of these factors can contribute to development of ulcers.

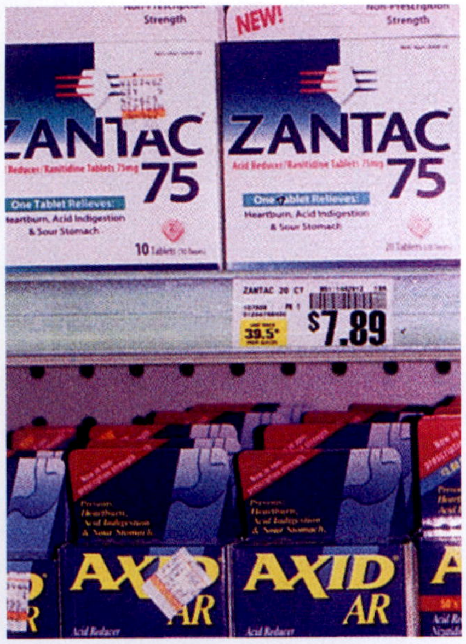

A number of over-the-counter medications are marketed for heartburn. Attention to diet and lifestyle, however, is generally a more important measure to take.

Table 3-5 Recommendations to Prevent Ulcers and Heartburn from Occurring or Recurring

Ulcers

1. Stop smoking if you are now a smoker.
2. Avoid large doses of aspirin, ibuprofen, and other NSAID compounds unless a physician advises otherwise. For people who must use these medications, FDA has approved an NSAID combined with a medication to reduce gastric damage. The medication reduces gastric acid production and enhances mucus secretion.
3. Limit consumption of coffee, tea, and alcohol (especially wine), if this helps.
4. Limit consumption of pepper, chili powder, and other strong spices, if this helps.
5. Eat nutritious meals on a regular schedule; include enough fiber (see Chapter 5 for sources of fiber).
6. Chew foods well.
7. Lose weight if you are currently overweight.

Heartburn

1. Wait about 2 hours after a meal before lying down.
2. Don't overeat at mealtime. Smaller meals that are low in fat are advised.
3. Try elevating the head of the bed (6-inch blocks).
4. Observe the recommendations for ulcer prevention.
5. Stop smoking cigarettes.
6. Lose excess weight.

Aspirin is part of the class of medications called nonsteroidal anti-inflammatory drugs (NSAIDs). Also included are ibuprofen (Motrin or Advil) and naproxen (Aleve).

People with ulcers should also refrain from smoking and minimize the use of aspirin and related NSAIDs. These practices reduce the mucus secreted by the stomach. Medications that are used to treat arthritis pain, called "Cox-2 inhibitors" (e.g., celecoxib [Celebrex]), are less likely to cause stomach ulcers and, so, have been used as a replacement for NSAIDs. They do offer some advantages over NSAIDS, but they may not be totally safe for some people. Overall, this combination of lifestyle therapy and medical treatment has so revolutionized ulcer therapy that dietary changes are of minor importance today. Current diet-therapy approaches recommend simply avoiding foods that increase ulcer symptoms (Table 3-5).

Note also that stomach acid is not a problem for those not prone to or currently experiencing ulcers. As explained earlier in the chapter, this acid performs important functions. This means that, despite their usual presence alongside the breath mints in a convenience store, antacids should not be used excessively. If an antacid contains magnesium (and many do), magnesium toxicity is another possible result of antacid abuse.

Heartburn

gastroesophageal reflux disease (GERD) A disease that results from stomach acid backing up into the esophagus. The acid irritates the lining of the esophagus, causing pain.

About half of North American adults experience occasional heartburn. This gnawing pain in the upper chest is caused by the movement of acid from the stomach into the esophagus and, so, the more serious form of the problem is called **gastroesophageal reflux disease (GERD).**[8] Unlike the stomach, the esophagus produces very little mucus to protect it, so acid quickly erodes the lining of the esophagus, causing pain. Symptoms may also include nausea, gagging, coughing, or hoarseness. GERD is characterized by such symptoms of acid reflux two or more times per week. People who have GERD experience occasional relaxation of the lower esophageal sphincter. Typically it should be relaxed only during swallowing, but in individuals with GERD it is relaxed at other times as well.

Certain physical conditions can lead to heartburn. For example, both pregnancy and obesity result in increased production of estrogen and progesterone. These hormones relax the lower esophageal sphincter, making heartburn more likely. In the latter case, adipose tissue turns certain circulating hormones into estrogen; thus, the more adipose tissue, the more estrogen is produced.

Case Scenario | Follow-up

Elise's GERD can be treated, but currently it is a lifelong condition. Typical dietary advice includes consuming smaller, more frequent meals that are low in fat, not overeating at mealtimes, waiting about 2 hours after meals before lying down, and elevating the head of the bed about

6 inches (review Table 3-5). All of these recommendations reduce the risk of stomach contents forcing their way back up the esophagus. Other helpful advice includes stopping smoking if practiced, losing excess weight if overweight, and limiting intake of chili powder, onions, garlic, peppermint, caffeine, alcohol, and chocolate. All of these factors encourage relaxation of the lower esophageal sphincter and/or irritate the esophagus. If this advice doesn't control Elise's symptoms, the primary medications used to control GERD inhibit acid production in the stomach (see the earlier discussion on the ulcer medication(s) such as omeprazole [Prilosec]). If this and other medical therapy fails to control the problem, surgery to strengthen the lower esophageal sphincter is possible, but generally will not cure the problem. Lifetime diet and lifestyle management, and most likely medications as well, will still be needed to manage the problem. Such management is important since long-standing GERD increases the risk of esophageal cancer.

Constipation and Laxatives

Constipation, which is difficult or infrequent evacuation of the bowels, is commonly reported by adults. Slow movement of fecal material through the large intestine causes constipation. As fluid is increasingly absorbed during the extended time the feces stay in the large intestine, they become dry and hard.

constipation A condition characterized by infrequent bowel movements.

Constipation can result when people regularly inhibit their normal bowel reflexes for long periods. People may ignore normal urges when it is inconvenient to interrupt occupational or social activities. Muscle spasms of an irritated large intestine can also slow the movement of feces and contribute to constipation. Medications such as antacids and calcium and iron supplements can also cause constipation.[1]

Eating foods with plenty of fiber, such as whole-grain breads and cereals, is the best method for treating typical cases of constipation. Fiber stimulates peristalsis by drawing water into the large intestine and helping form a bulky, soft fecal output. People with constipation should also drink more fluids, and eating dried fruits can help stimulate the bowel. In addition, people with constipation may need to develop more regular bowel habits; allowing the same time each day for a bowel movement can help train the large intestine to respond routinely. Finally, relaxation facilitates regular bowel movements, as does regular physical activity.

Laxatives can also lessen constipation. These work by irritating the intestinal nerve junctions to stimulate the peristaltic muscles, or by drawing water into the intestine to enlarge fecal output. The larger output stretches the peristaltic muscles, making them rebound and then constrict. Regular use of laxatives, especially irritating ones, however, can decrease muscle action in the large intestine—in time, causing more constipation. The GI tract can then actually become dependent on laxatives. Thus, it is unwise for anyone to use laxatives routinely, although people in certain circumstances—for example, those who are bedridden or quite elderly—may need periodic help from laxatives to relieve constipation.

laxative A medication or other substance that stimulates evacuation of the intestinal tract.

Hemorrhoids

Hemorrhoids, also called *piles*, are swollen veins of the rectum and anus. The blood vessels in this area are subject to intense pressure, especially during bowel movements. Added stress to the vessels from pregnancy, obesity, prolonged sitting, violent coughing or sneezing, or straining during bowel movements, particularly with constipation, can lead to a hemorrhoid. Hemorrhoids can develop unnoticed until a strained bowel movement precipitates symptoms, which may include pain, itching, and bleeding.

Itching, caused by moisture in the anal canal, swelling, or other irritation, is perhaps the most common symptom. Pain, if present, is usually aching and steady. Bleeding may result from a hemorrhoid and may appear in the toilet as a bright red streak in the feces. The sensation of a mass in the anal canal after a bowel movement is symptomatic of an internal hemorrhoid that protrudes through the anus.

Anyone can develop a hemorrhoid, and about half of adults over age 50 do. Pressure from prolonged sitting or exertion is often enough to bring on symptoms, although diet, lifestyle, and possibly heredity play a role. For example, a low-fiber diet can lead to hemorrhoids as a result of constipation and straining during bowel movements. If you think you have a hemorrhoid, you should consult your physician. Rectal bleeding, although usually caused by hemorrhoids, may also indicate other problems, such as cancer.

A physician may suggest a variety of self-care measures for hemorrhoids. Pain can be lessened by applying warm, soft compresses or sitting in a tub of warm water for 15 to 20 minutes. Dietary

Perhaps you have heard that taking laxatives after overeating prevents deposition of body fat from the excess energy intake. This erroneous and dangerous premise has gained popularity among followers of numerous fad diets. You may temporarily feel less full after using a laxative because laxatives hasten emptying of the large intestine and increase fluid loss. Most laxatives, however, do not speed the passage of food through the small intestine, where digestion and most nutrient absorption take place. As a result, you can't count on laxatives to prevent fat gain from excess energy intake.

recommendations are the same as those for treating constipation, emphasizing the need to consume adequate fiber and fluid. Over-the-counter remedies, such as Preparation H, can also offer relief of symptoms.

Critical | Thinking

Joci is considering going on a new diet that emphasizes eating only fruits before noon, meat at lunchtime, and starch and vegetables at dinner. In addition, the diet recommends "cleansing" the intestines with laxatives and enemas every other week. What reasons would you give Joci to steer clear of this regimen? What are some possible harmful effects that could result?

Irritable Bowel Syndrome

Many adults have irritable bowel syndrome, a combination of cramps, gassiness, bloating, and irregular bowel function (diarrhea, constipation, or alternating episodes of both). It is more common in women than in men. The disease leads to about 3.5 million physician visits each year.

Symptoms associated with irritable bowel syndrome include visible abdominal distension, pain relief after a bowel movement, increased stool frequency with pain onset, looser stools with pain onset, mucus in the feces, and a feeling of incomplete elimination even after a bowel movement.[13]

The cause is thought to be altered intestinal peristalsis, coupled with a decreased pain threshold for abdominal distension—in other words, a minor amount of abdominal bloating causes pain that the average person would not sense. It is also noteworthy that up to 50% of sufferers report a history of verbal or sexual abuse.

Therapy is individualized and can include a trial of high-fiber foods, as well as elimination diets that focus on avoiding dairy products and gas-forming foods, such as legumes and certain vegetables (cabbage, beans, and broccoli) and fruits (grapes, raisins, cherries, and cantaloupe). The patient should have only moderate caffeine intake or eliminate caffeine-containing foods/beverages altogether. Low-fat and more frequent, small meals may help the patient because large meals can trigger contractions of the large intestine. Other strategies include a reduction in stress, psychological counseling, antidepressants, and other medications, such as diphenoxylate (Lomotil), alosetron (Lotronex), and tegaserod (Zelnorm).[7]

Referral to a registered dietitian can be beneficial, as many patients experience improvement with the elimination of specific problem foods. A good patient/physician relationship is also important for the treatment of irritable bowel syndrome. Although irritable bowel syndrome can be uncomfortable and upsetting, it is essentially harmless; it carries no risk for cancer or other serious digestive problems. The website www.ibsgroup.org provides further information.

Diarrhea

Diarrhea, a GI tract disease that generally lasts only a few days, is defined as increased fluidity, frequency, or amount of bowel movements compared to a person's usual pattern. Most cases of diarrhea result from infections in the intestines, with bacteria and viruses the usual offending agents. They produce substances that cause the intestinal cells to primarily secrete fluid rather than absorb fluid. Another form of diarrhea can be caused by consumption of substances that are not readily absorbed, such as the sugar alcohol sorbitol found in sugarless gum (see Chapter 5). When consumed in large amounts such unabsorbed substance(s) draw excess water into the intestine, leading to diarrhea. Treatment of diarrhea generally requires drinking lots of fluid (to compensate for fluid losses); reduced intake of the poorly absorbed substance also is important if that is a cause. Prompt treatment—within 24 to 48 hours—is especially important for infants and older people, as they are more susceptible to the effects of dehydration associated with diarrhea (see Chapters 17 and 18). Diarrhea that lasts more than 7 days in adults should be investigated by a physician as it can be a symptom of more serious intestinal disease, especially if there is also blood in the feces.

A Recap

Overall, typical medical disorders of the GI tract arise from differences in anatomical features and lifestyle habits among individuals. Because of the importance of various nutrition and lifestyle habits, such as adequate fiber and fluid intake, as well as not smoking or abusing NSAID medications, nutrition and lifestyle therapy is often effective in helping treat GI tract disorders.

chapter 4

Metabolism

Chapter | Outline

Case | Scenario

Andrea is a 6-year-old who suffers from epilepsy. Her physicians have tried many combinations of medicines to reduce the number of seizures she experiences. These seizures result from a brief disturbance in brain function due to abnormal nerve cell discharge in the brain. Andrea is not alone in suffering from this disease; it affects approximately 0.5% of the North American population. Because her current seizure medication regimens have not been effective, her physicians recommend that she undergo a trial of a very-low-carbohydrate (ketogenic) diet. The physicians note that it is still not clear why this diet works to control seizures in some people, but research going as far back as the 1920s shows that a rise in ketone bodies in the blood can help.[8]

The main drawback of this ketogenic diet is that it is very low in carbohydrates, amounting to about one-tenth of her usual carbohydrate intake. In place of that carbohydrate, she must consume much more fat than is typical for her. The physicians tell her parents that this will be a very difficult diet to implement, since many of the foods Andrea likes are rich in carbohydrate. However, the physicians feel that, if this diet is effective in reducing her seizures, the restriction in carbohydrate intake will outweigh the inconvenience of following such a plan. In addition, some people find that following this diet for a few years stops the seizures, even when they return to a more normal diet.

What actually are ketone bodies, and why does a very-low-carbohydrate diet produce an increase in ketone bodies in the blood? Can you speculate at this time why this is the case? Ketone bodies is one theme of this chapter. By developing a greater understanding of this and other aspects of metabolism, you will be able to explain to Andrea's parents why a very-low-carbohydrate diet causes a buildup of ketone bodies.

Refresh | Your Memory

As you begin your study of metabolism in Chapter 4, you may want to review:

- Various components of the macronutrient classes—carbohydrates, proteins, and lipids—in Chapter 1.
- Basic chemistry concepts in Appendix A.
- The components of the cell and functions of various organelles in Appendix C.
- Enzyme function and regulation in Chapter 3.
- Hormone function in Chapter 3.

Boost | Your Study

Check out the ***Perspectives in Nutrition: Online Learning Center*** **www.mhhe.com/wardlawpers6** *for quizzes, flash cards, activities, and web links designed to further help you learn about metabolism.*

Chapter | Objectives

Chapter 4 is designed to allow you to:

1. Define the terms energy metabolism, aerobic metabolism, and anaerobic metabolism.
2. Describe aerobic and anaerobic metabolism of glucose, with reference to lactic acid production.
3. Describe why adenosine triphosphate (ATP) is considered the energy source of the cell.
4. Outline how the energy potential of glucose, fatty acids, amino acids, and alcohol is extracted—using metabolic pathways such as glycolysis, the citric acid cycle, and the electron transport chain—and eventually deposited into ATP.
5. Describe the roles vitamins and minerals play in energy metabolism.
6. Explain the origin of CO_2 and H_2O generated by energy metabolism.
7. Describe the central role of acetyl-CoA in cell metabolism.
8. State the source of ketone bodies and their role in energy metabolism.
9. Describe the fate of energy from macronutrients during the fed state.
10. Describe the fate of energy-yielding substances in the body during the fasting state.
11. Briefly explain how metabolism is regulated.

Metabolism refers to the entire network of chemical processes involved in maintaining life. It encompasses all the sequences of chemical reactions that occur in the body. These biochemical reactions enable us to release and use energy from foods, synthesize one substance from another, and prepare waste products for excretion. More than 1000 kinds of chemical reactions take place in a simple single-celled bacterium.[7]

Studying metabolism can help you comprehend a variety of nutrition concepts. Understanding metabolism clarifies how proteins, carbohydrates, fats, and alcohol are interrelated; how the carbons in proteins become the carbons of glucose; and why the carbons of most fatty acids *cannot* become the carbons of glucose.[1]

Studying metabolic pathways in the cell also sets the stage for examining the roles of vitamins and minerals. Most vitamins function as coenzymes. Many minerals function as cofactors. These compounds, coenzymes and cofactors, contribute to enzyme activity and, thus, are important to metabolic reactions in the cell. Overall, the functions of both macronutrients and micronutrients will be easier to understand if you are familiar with the basic metabolic processes in the cell.

Metabolism—Chemical Reactions in the Body

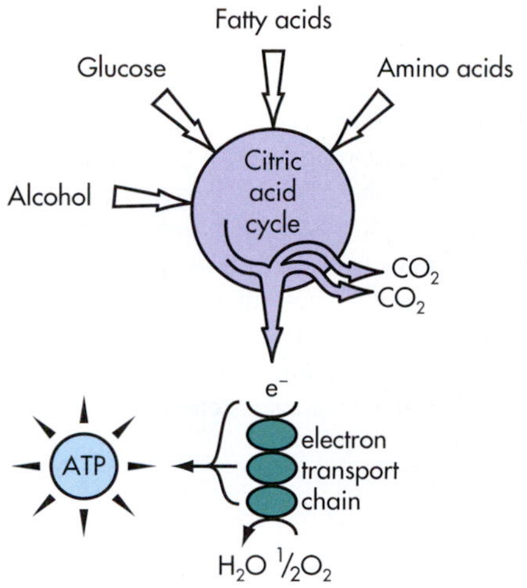

Generation of ATP from fuels during respiration. Dietary carbohydrates are converted mainly to glucose, dietary lipids to fatty acids, and dietary protein to amino acids. The symbol e^- represents electrons.

As noted in the chapter overview, *metabolism* refers to the entire network of chemical processes involved in maintaining life and encompasses all of the sequences of chemical reactions that occur in the body. These chemical reactions enable cells to release and use energy from foods, convert one substance into another, and prepare waste products for excretion.

A progression of metabolic chemical reactions from beginning to end is called a *pathway*. Compounds formed as the pathway proceeds are called **intermediates.** Virtually every step in any pathway depends on an enzyme to initiate the necessary chemical reaction (review Figure 3-8 in Chapter 3 for an example).[7]

Anabolic pathways build compounds. Energy must be expended for anabolic processes to take place. For example, the chemical reactions involving the synthesis of $-C-C-$ bonds (fatty acid synthesis), $-\overset{\overset{\displaystyle O}{\|}}{C}-N-$ bonds (protein synthesis), $-C-N-$ bonds (urea synthesis), and $-C-O-$ bonds (triglyceride synthesis) require such energy input (see Appendix A for details). The chemical elements and compounds used to form the new substances often are called *building blocks.*

Conversely, **catabolic** pathways break down compounds into small units. For example, complete catabolism of glucose results in the release of carbon dioxide (CO_2) and water (H_2O). Energy is released in the process: some is trapped for cell use and the rest is lost as heat.

The production of energy for cell use occurs in three stages. In the first stage, large food molecules, such as proteins, starches, and triglycerides, are broken down during digestion and absorption into smaller units, such as amino acids, **monosaccharides** (simple sugars), and fatty acids. In the second stage, most of these smaller compounds are further degraded to the two-carbon intermediate compound acetic acid $CH_3\overset{\overset{\displaystyle O}{\|}}{C}-OH$, the acid found in vinegar.[3] In the third stage, acetic acid (acetate when a hydrogen ion is missing) is degraded to carbon dioxide and water. The electrons and hydrogen ions released during this metabolic process are donated to oxygen atoms to form water. Some of the energy released in this catabolic process drives the synthesis of adenosine triphosphate (ATP). ATP is energy in a form that cells use (Fig. 4-1). Chapter 3 introduced the first stage, digestion and absorption. Let's now examine the last two stages.

monosaccharide A class of simple sugars, such as glucose, that can be absorbed into the body without further chemical alteration.

Acids commonly lose a hydrogen ion at the pH found in human cells (pH 7.4). When that ion is lost, the name of the acid is changed by dropping the reference to acid and adding an *ate* ending. Thus, *acetic acid* becomes *acetate.*

Energy for the Cell

The energy that human cells use comes from chemical bonds found between the atoms in carbohydrate, fat, protein, and alcohol. This energy is originally produced during **photosynthesis,** when plants use solar energy to make glucose and other organic (carbon-containing) compounds. The chemical reactions in photosynthesis form compounds that contain more energy than carbon dioxide and water, the building blocks used. Virtually all organisms use the sun—either directly or indirectly, as we do—as their source of energy (review Fig. 4-1*a*).

photosynthesis The process by which plants use energy from the sun to produce energy-yielding compounds, such as glucose.

The by-products of eventual human energy metabolism are carbon dioxide, water, and heat. Overall, chemical energy from ingested food that passes through body cells is eventually and irretrievably dissipated to the environment as heat (review Fig. 4-1*a*).

Thus, in human **respiration,** the starting materials are energy-yielding compounds, such as glucose, which, through an elaborate multistep process, are converted to end products, such as carbon dioxide and water. This process results in the transfer of energy from food to cells, which in turn allows energy-requiring pathways in cells to function.

respiration The use of oxygen; in the human organism, the inhalation of oxygen and the exhalation of carbon dioxide; in cells, the oxidation (electron removal) of food molecules, particularly in the citric acid cycle, to obtain energy.

Many chemical reactions in the body could not occur without the addition of outside energy supplied by food. Outside energy permits compounds, such as amino acids, to be transformed into products such as glucose, as mentioned earlier. And although amino

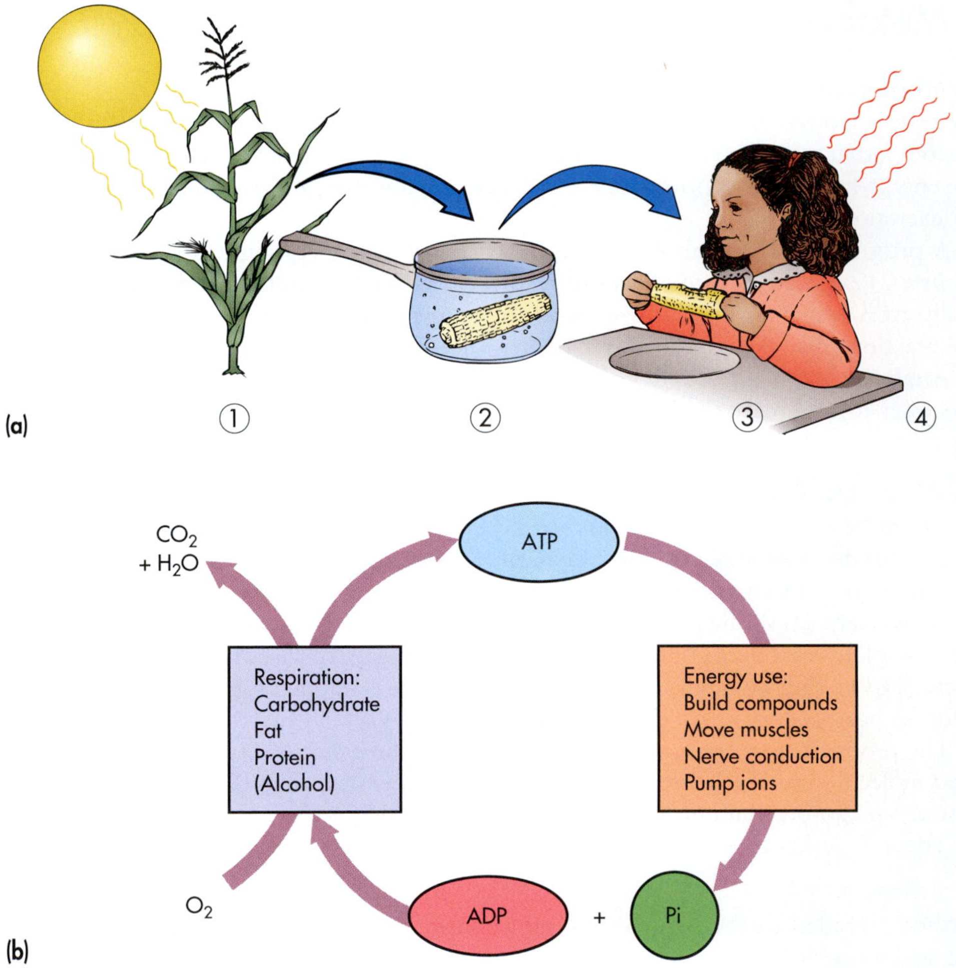

Figure 4-1 (*a*) From solar energy to human energy output. (*1*) The corn plant uses solar energy to synthesize glucose from carbon dioxide and water. (*2*) We cook and eat the corn, (*3*) transferring much of the energy in the glucose from the corn to ATP energy for our cells to use. (*4*) Eventually, this energy leaves our bodies as heat. Some energy may be stored as fat if we overeat, and a small amount is lost in urine and feces. (*b*) ATP synthesis and use. Energy from foods is used to synthesize ATP. The ATP then provides energy for the cell.

Sunflowers capture solar energy and transfer it into chemical energy in the form of protein, carbohydrate, and fat in the sunflower seeds.

acids and glucose molecules themselves contain the energy needed for synthesis of still other compounds, these and other energy-yielding molecules provide neither the right amount of energy for a chemical reaction nor a form of energy that cells can use directly. For example, a glucose molecule contains over 100 times more energy than required to facilitate an individual chemical reaction in a cell. Thus, a cell must have a means of breaking down energy-yielding molecules to release and then convert the chemical energy trapped in them into smaller, usable energy forms.[7]

Cells Use Adenosine Triphosphate (ATP) as an Energy Source

The form of energy that cells generally use for chemical, mechanical, electrical, and osmotic processes is ATP (review Fig. 4-1*b*). To release the energy in ATP, cells split it into adenosine diphosphate (ADP) plus Pi, a free (inorganic) phosphate group (Fig. 4-2). ADP can also be split into adenosine monophosphate (AMP) plus Pi to yield energy, in a reaction muscles are capable of performing during intense exercise when ATP is in short supply (ADP + ADP → ATP + AMP).[2]

Only energy in ATP and its derivatives can be used directly by the cell. Energy released from breaking carbon-hydrogen bonds in a glucose molecule is one of the "fuels" used by body cells to make ATP.

Metabolic pathways exist in every cell that can combine ADP and Pi to form ATP. An enzyme later can break the ATP bond to release energy needed for metabolic reactions.

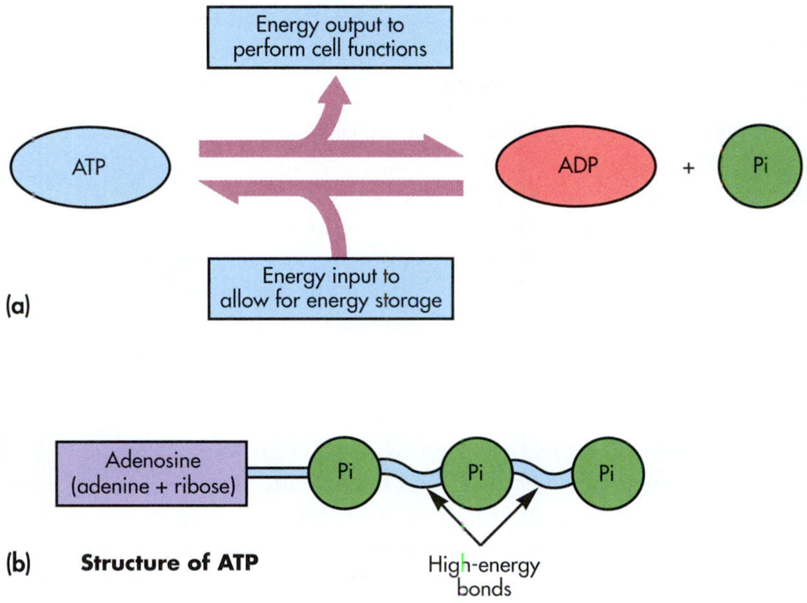

Figure 4-2 ATP stores and yields energy. ATP is the high-energy state; ADP is the lower-energy state. (*a*) When ATP is broken down to ADP plus Pi, energy is released for cell use. (*b*) When energy is trapped by ADP plus Pi, ATP can be formed. Thus, ATP represents a storage form of energy for cell use. Pi is the abbreviation for a phosphate group.

ATP itself is very stable, so it takes an enzyme to unlock the energy that is stored in the molecule.

During metabolism, a cell is constantly breaking down ATP in one organelle while rebuilding it in another. An exhausted muscle cell has a very high concentration of ADP and a very low concentration of ATP. When this happens, muscle cell activity, such as muscle contraction, may slow down or cease altogether. A low ATP concentration then stimulates metabolic processes that produce ATP. Only by resynthesizing needed ATP can the muscle cell ready itself for future action.[1]

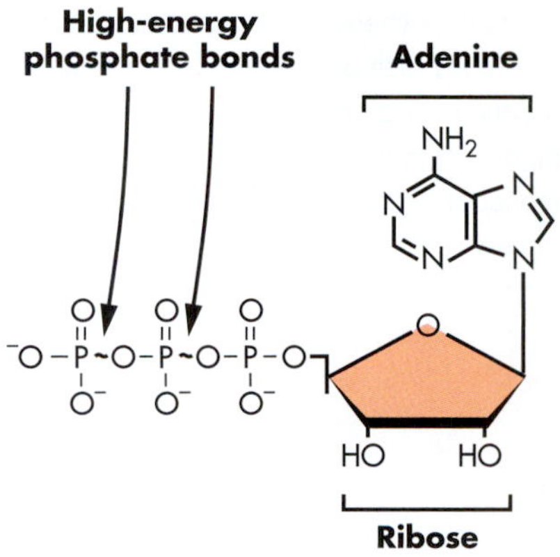

Adenosine triphosphate (ATP).

The energy used to perform physical activity is in the form of ATP.

Oxidation-Reduction Reactions—Key Processes in Energy Metabolism

Oxidation-reduction reactions form a vital link between the energy-yielding nutrients and the formation of ATP. The formal meaning of oxidation and reduction can be summarized as:[7]

A substance is *oxidized* when it loses one or more electrons.

A substance is *reduced* when it gains one or more electrons.

Electron flow governs oxidation-reduction processes. If one substance loses electrons (is oxidized), another substance must gain electrons (is reduced). The two processes go together; one cannot occur without the other.

Consider the oxidation-reduction reaction between zinc and the copper ion Cu^{2+}:

$$Zn + Cu^{2+} \rightarrow Zn^{2+} + Cu$$

Now that you are familiar with oxidation and reduction reactions, we can examine the term **antioxidant.** This term is typically used to describe a compound that can donate electrons to oxidized compounds, putting them into a more reduced (stable) state. Oxidized compounds tend to be highly reactive; they seek electrons from other compounds to stabilize their chemical configuration. Dietary antioxidants such as vitamin E and vitamin C can donate electrons to these highly reactive compounds, in turn, putting these oxidized compounds into a less reactive state (see Chapters 9 and 10 for details).

Here, Zn has lost two electrons (has been oxidized) ($Zn \rightarrow Zn^{2+} + 2e^-$). At the same time, copper has gained two electrons (has been reduced) ($Cu^{2+} + 2e^- \rightarrow Cu$). Another example is the iron in hemoglobin, which can be oxidized from Fe^{2+} to Fe^{3+} and reduced from Fe^{3+} to Fe^{2+}. This occurs during the transport of oxygen to body cells.

Oxidation-reduction reactions involving carbon-containing compounds are somewhat more difficult to visualize. A simple rule has been developed to determine oxidation reduction in these compounds. If the compound gains oxygen or loses hydrogen, it has been oxidized. If it loses oxygen or gains hydrogen, the compound has been reduced. The following process illustrates this definition.

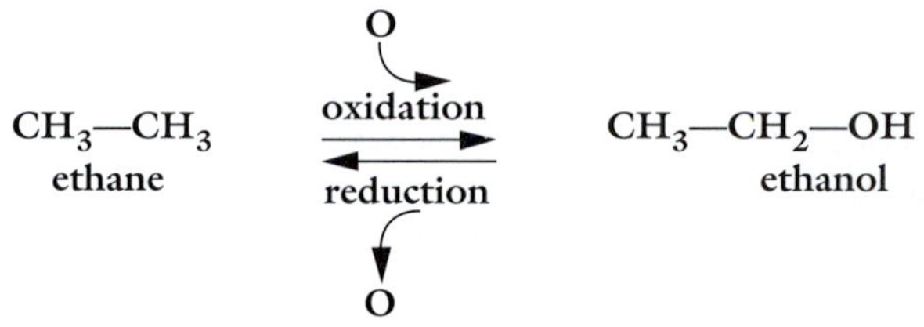

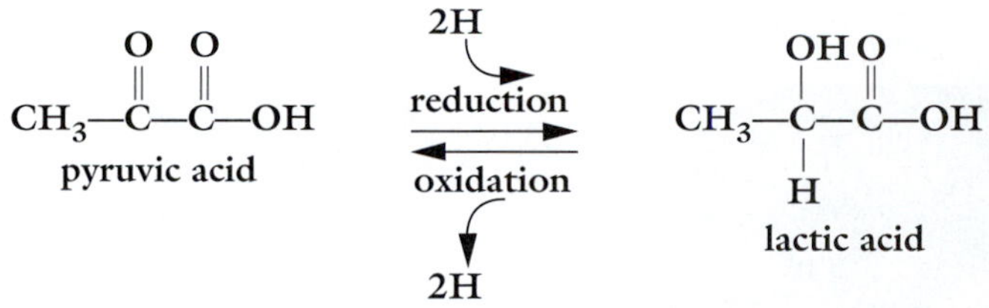

This method of determining oxidation and reduction—determining oxygen and hydrogen exchange—is used extensively in nutrition. For example, in the reaction illustrated, pyruvic acid (made from glucose) is reduced to form lactic acid by gaining two hydrogens. This happens during intense exercise (see Chapter 14). Lactic acid is oxidized back to pyruvic acid by losing two hydrogens.

Scientists generally use the terms *oxidation* and *reduction* as verbs or adjectives. As a verb, pyruvic acid is said to be reduced to lactic acid, and lactic acid is oxidized to pyruvic acid. As an adjective, lactic acid is said to be the reduced form of pyruvic acid, while pyruvic acid is the oxidized form of lactic acid.

Oxidation-reduction reactions in the body are controlled by enzymes. One important class of these enzymes, designated *dehydrogenases,* removes hydrogens from energy-yielding nutrients or their breakdown products. These hydrogens are eventually donated to the final acceptor, oxygen, to form water. In the process, large amounts of energy are transferred to ADP plus Pi to make ATP.[7]

Two B vitamins, niacin and riboflavin, assist dehydrogenase enzymes and, in turn, play a role in transferring the hydrogens from glucose to oxygen in the metabolic pathways of the cell. Niacin functions as the **coenzyme** named **nicotinamide adenine dinucleotide (NAD).** This is the oxidized form, which can accept one hydrogen ion and

coenzyme A compound that combines with an inactive protein, called an apoenzyme, to form a catalytically active protein, called a holoenzyme. In this manner, coenzymes aid in enzyme function.

nicotinamide adenine dinucleotide (NAD) A compound that readily accepts and donates electrons and hydrogen ions; formed from the vitamin niacin.

two electrons to become NADH + H^+. (The extra hydrogen ion remains free in the cell.) In other words, the oxidized form of niacin, NAD^+, is reduced to form NADH + H^+. Note that NAD^+ indicates it has one less electron than in its complete configuration. By accepting two electrons and one hydrogen ion, NAD^+ becomes NADH + H^+, with no net charge on the coenzyme.

Riboflavin plays a similar role. In its oxidized form, the coenzyme form is known as **flavin adenine dinucleotide (FAD).** When it is reduced (gains two hydrogens, equivalent to two hydrogen ions and two electrons), it is known as $FADH_2$.

The reduction of oxygen (O) to form water (H_2O) is the ultimate driving force for life, as it is vital to the way cells synthesize ATP. Thus, oxidation-reduction reactions are a key to life.[1]

flavin adenine dinucleotide (FAD) A compound that readily accepts and donates electrons and hydrogen ions; formed from the vitamin riboflavin.

Concept | Check

Metabolism encompasses all of the sequences of chemical reactions in the body. Anabolic pathways build compounds using energy input, whereas catabolic pathways break down compounds into small units, yielding energy. Adenosine triphosphate (ATP) is the form of energy used by a cell. The synthesis of ATP from ADP and Pi involves the transfer of energy from foodstuffs. This uses oxidation-reduction reactions, where electrons (along with hydrogen ions) are transferred from carbohydrates, proteins, fats, and alcohol eventually to oxygen. This reaction forms water and releases much energy, which can be used to produce ATP.

Carbohydrate Metabolism Begins with Glycolysis

Let's now look at how ATP is generated in a human cell. The easiest place to begin studying ATP synthesis is in the metabolism of carbohydrates (Fig. 4-3). Next we'll look at fat and protein metabolism. All of these fuels can be used to synthesize ATP. (We will wait until Chapter 8 to discuss alcohol metabolism in detail.)

As each of the subsequent pathways is described, a good way to understand them is to diagram each step as you go. Afterward, compare your figures with those provided throughout the chapter. In addition, more detailed pathways than shown in the chapter can be found in Appendix B.

Glycolysis—Glucose to Pyruvate

Glycolysis literally means "breaking down glucose." The glycolysis pathway, found in the cytosol portion of the cytoplasm of all cells, has a dual role: It degrades monosaccharides to generate energy and provides building blocks for synthesizing needed cell compounds, such as **glycerol** for triglyceride synthesis.[7]

Before glycolysis can begin, a cell must obtain glucose. Only a few types of cells, such as liver and kidney cells, can produce their own glucose from amino acids (see section on **gluconeogenesis,** p. 125), and only liver and muscle cells store glucose to a major extent. This glucose is stored as glycogen. Liver and muscle cells break down the glycogen to glucose (or a closely related form). Other body cells must obtain glucose from the bloodstream, so the body needs to maintain a fairly constant concentration of blood glucose to survive (see Chapter 5 for details).

The product of glycolysis is two units of a three-carbon compound called *pyruvic acid (pyruvate)* (Figs. 4-4 and 4-5). Some cells then convert pyruvate to lactic acid (lactate).

To begin glycolysis, a phosphate group is added to glucose, which makes the glucose more reactive. Another phosphate group is added to the newly formed glucose-phosphate compound, which then splits into two three-carbon compounds. These are converted through a series of steps into two molecules of the three-carbon compound pyruvate. Thus, in glycolysis a cell starts with a six-carbon glucose molecule and produces two molecules of the three-carbon compound pyruvate. In the process, four hydrogens (containing a total of four electrons) are removed and four ATP are generated. The electrons and hydrogen ions are picked up by a carrier—in this case, NAD^+. Recall

glycolysis The metabolic pathway that converts glucose into 2 molecules of pyruvic acid, with the net gain of 2 ATP and 2 NADH + H^+.

glycerol A three-carbon alcohol that provides the backbone to form triglycerides.

gluconeogenesis The production of new glucose molecules by metabolic pathways in the cell. Amino acids derived from protein usually provide the carbons for this glucose.

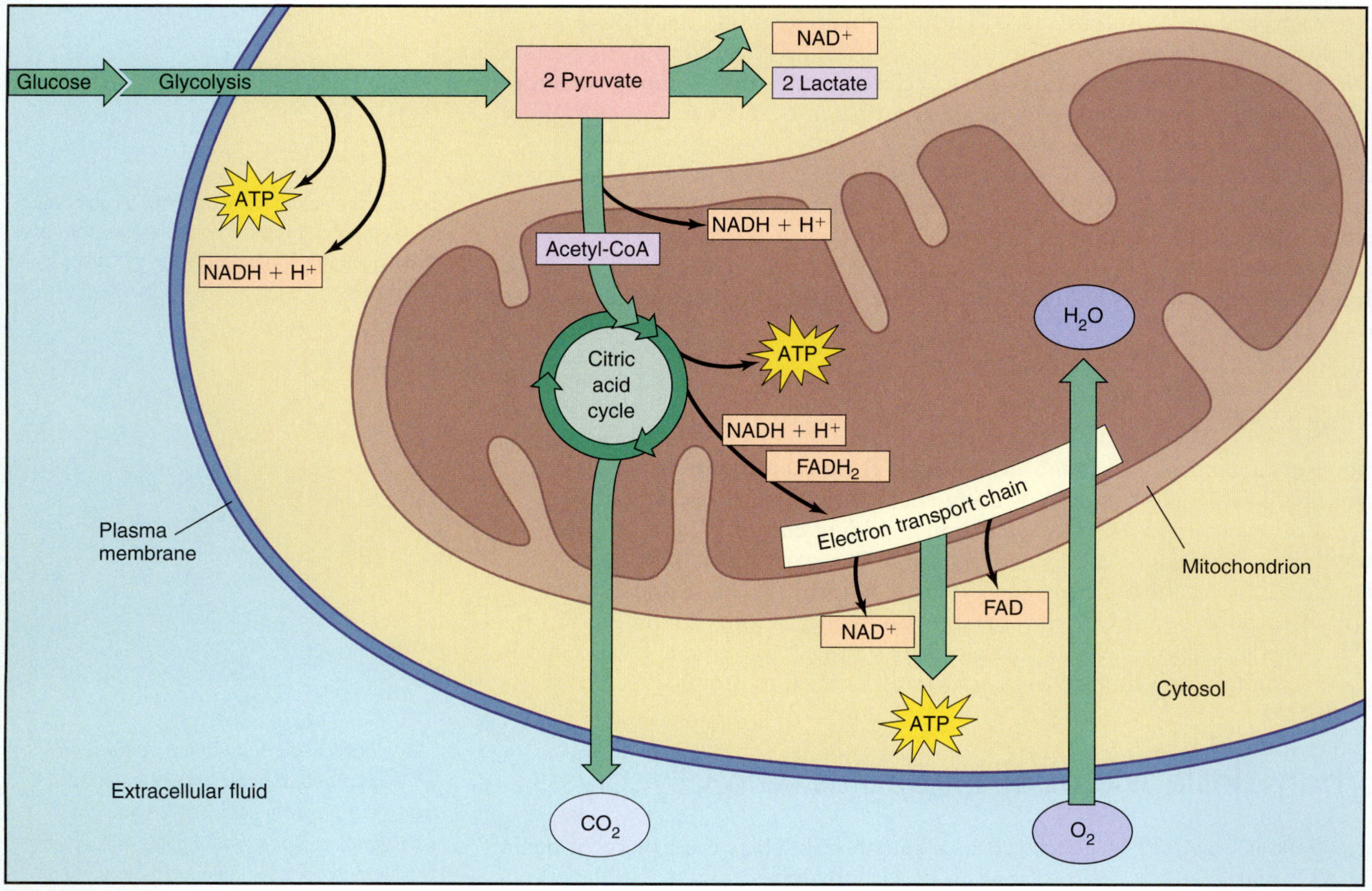

Figure 4-3 An overview of the cellular respiration of glucose.

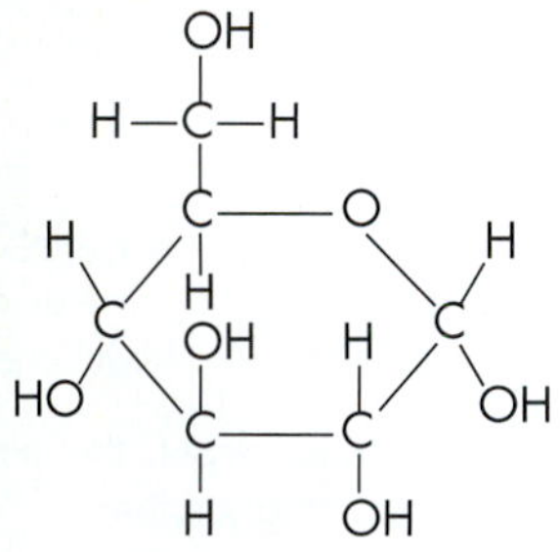

Glucose

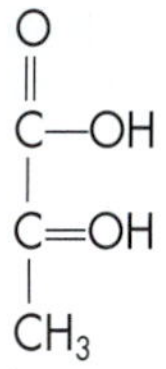

Pyruvic acid

that each NAD^+ (oxidized form) accepts two electrons and one hydrogen ion, yielding $NADH + H^+$(reduced form). Thus, an end result of glycolysis is also the synthesis of two $NADH + H^+$.

Where Is the ATP?

In glycolysis, the first reaction involves one ATP donating a phosphate group to glucose. In the 3rd step, another ATP is used to add a second phosphate group. Thus, to begin the pathway, a cell uses two ATP. As the two three-carbon molecules are converted to pyruvate, each one generates two ATP, for a total of four ATP. The net energy produced thus far from glycolysis is two ATP, as two ATP prime the system and four ATP are produced. There are more ATP to come; this represents only about 5% of the total ATP production possible from one glucose molecule.[7]

Chemical energy stored in the bonds of $NADH + H^+$ can eventually be transferred to ATP. Generally, each $NADH + H^+$ provides enough energy to yield 2.5 ATP.[1] Thus, $NADH + H^+$ is a form of *potential energy for the cell.* A cell eventually uses the energy in $NADH + H^+$ to form ATP. A later discussion describes how this happens in the mitochondria.

The other monosaccharides, fructose and galactose, are converted to intermediate compounds of the glycolytic pathway and follow the same sequence of events as glucose. Pyruvate is eventually formed.

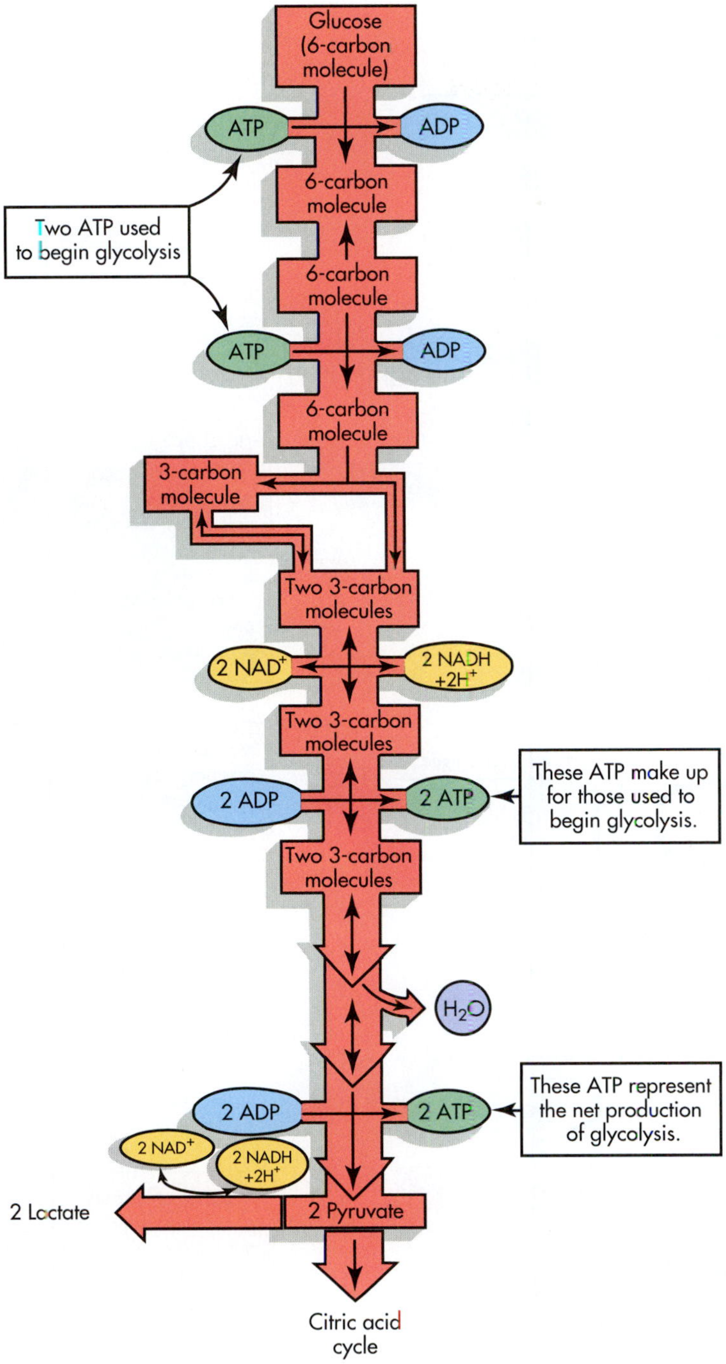

Figure 4-4 Glycolysis simplified. The process begins with one glucose ($C_6H_{12}O_6$) and ends with two pyruvates ($C_3H_4O_3$). Some ATP is produced by the process. The four electrons and two of the hydrogen ions released are captured by two NAD^+. The other two hydrogen ions float free in the cytosol. Pyruvate then can undergo further metabolism in the citric acid cycle or form lactate under anaerobic conditions.

Lactate Production Is the Endpoint of Anaerobic Glycolysis

Some cells lack the oxygen-requiring **(aerobic)** pathway needed for using NADH + H^+ for ATP synthesis, and in turn they lack the ability to use this process to recycle NADH + H^+ back to NAD^+. The red blood cell is an example. Thus, as a red blood cell converts glucose to pyruvate, NADH + H^+ builds up in the cell. Eventually, the NAD^+ concentration falls too low to permit glycolysis to continue, since most of the NAD^+ present is in the form NADH + H^+.[7]

To compensate, a red blood cell reacts pyruvate with an NADH + H^+ and a free hydrogen ion to form lactate (review Figs. 4-3 and 4-4). In the process, NADH + H^+ turns into NAD^+. This process allows the red blood cell to resupply itself with NAD^+ as these cells do not contain mitochondria. Exercising muscles also produce lactate

aerobic Requiring oxygen.

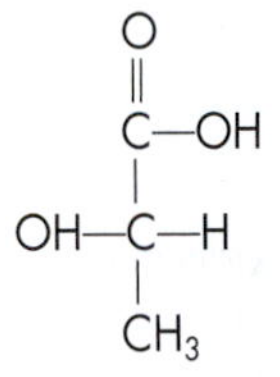

Lactic acid

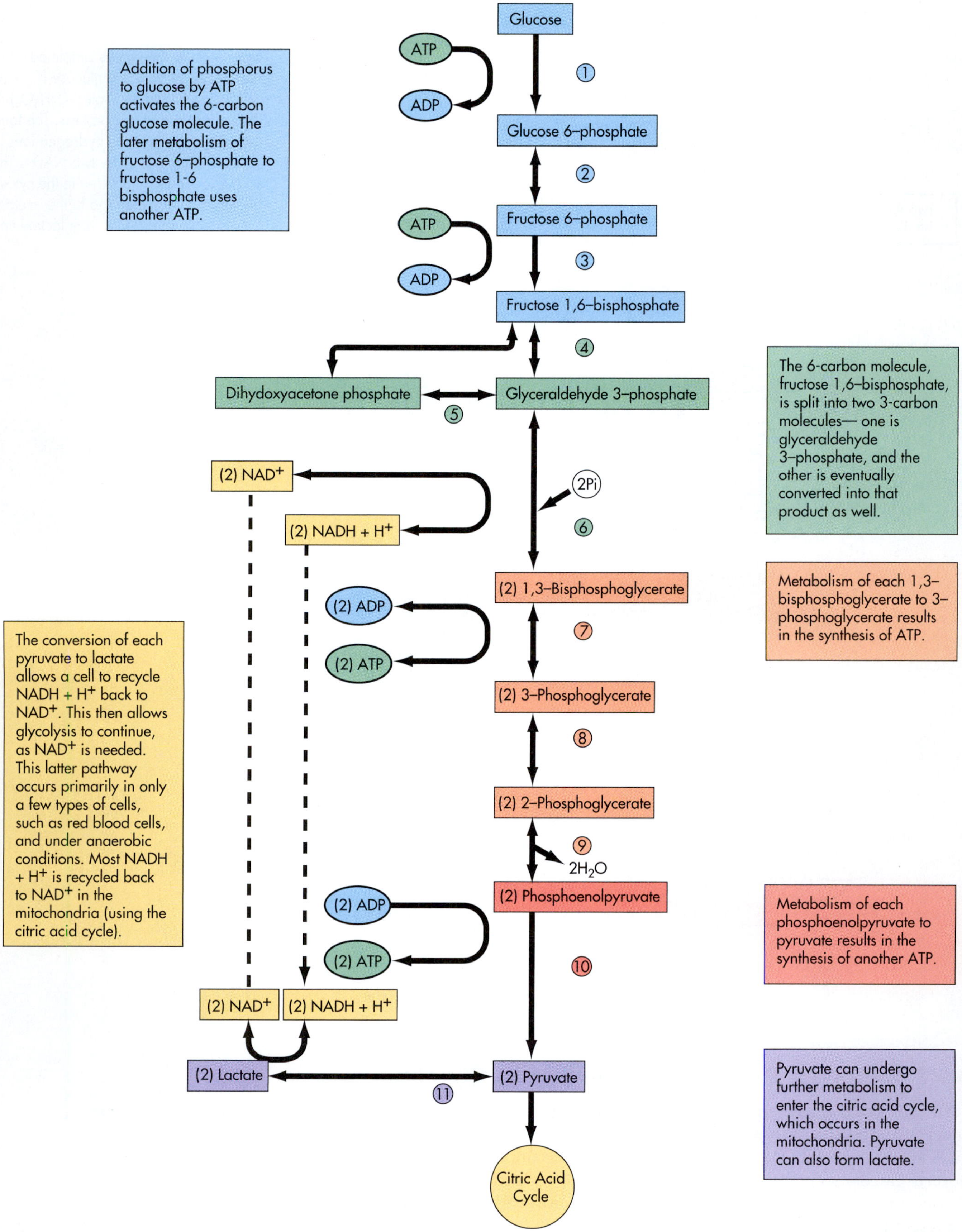

Glucose
ATP
ADP
1
Glucose 6–phosphate
2
ATP
ADP
Fructose 6–phosphate
3
Fructose 1,6–bisphosphate
4
Dihydoxyacetone phosphate
Glyceraldehyde 3–phosphate
5
(2) NAD+
(2) NADH + H+
2Pi
6
(2) 1,3–Bisphosphoglycerate
(2) ADP
(2) ATP
7
(2) 3–Phosphoglycerate
8
(2) 2–Phosphoglycerate
9
2H2O
(2) Phosphoenolpyruvate
(2) ADP
(2) ATP
10
(2) NAD+
(2) NADH + H+
(2) Lactate
(2) Pyruvate
11
Citric Acid Cycle
Addition of phosphorus to glucose by ATP activates the 6-carbon glucose molecule. The later metabolism of fructose 6–phosphate to fructose 1-6 bisphosphate uses another ATP.
The 6-carbon molecule, fructose 1,6–bisphosphate, is split into two 3-carbon molecules— one is glyceraldehyde 3–phosphate, and the other is eventually converted into that product as well.
Metabolism of each 1,3–bisphosphoglycerate to 3–phosphoglycerate results in the synthesis of ATP.
The conversion of each pyruvate to lactate allows a cell to recycle NADH + H+ back to NAD+. This then allows glycolysis to continue, as NAD+ is needed. This latter pathway occurs primarily in only a few types of cells, such as red blood cells, and under anaerobic conditions. Most NADH + H+ is recycled back to NAD+ in the mitochondria (using the citric acid cycle).
Metabolism of each phosphoenolpyruvate to pyruvate results in the synthesis of another ATP.
Pyruvate can undergo further metabolism to enter the citric acid cycle, which occurs in the mitochondria. Pyruvate can also form lactate.

Figure 4-5 The individual chemical reactions that comprise glycolysis—glucose to pyruvate. Glycolysis takes place in the cytosol of the cell. The enzymes in the cytosol that participate at each step are (*1*) hexokinase, (*2*) phosphohexose isomerase, (*3*) phosphofructokinase, (*4*) aldolase, (*5*) phosphotriose isomerase, (*6*) glyceraldehyde-3-phosphate dehydrogenase, (*7*) phosphoglycerate kinase, (*8*) phosphoglycerate mutase, (*9*) enolase, (*10*) pyruvate kinase, and sometimes (*11*) lactate dehydrogenase. Pi represents a phosphate group. See Figure B-1 in Appendix B for a more detailed view.

when they run out of NAD^+. The increase in lactate in turn contributes to muscle fatigue (see Chapter 14).

The production of lactate by a cell allows **anaerobic** glycolysis to continue, as there remains a steady supply of NAD^+. Again, this pathway yields only about 5% of the potential ATP per glucose molecule. But, for some cells, such as red blood cells, which lack mitochondria, anaerobic glycolysis is the only available method for making ATP. The lactate is released into the bloodstream, picked up primarily by the liver, and synthesized into glucose.[1]

Regenerating NAD^+ by using lactate represents a fermentation reaction. Some yeasts produce alcohol (ethanol) instead of lactate to regenerate NAD^+ in anaerobic conditions. This is also a fermentation reaction.

anaerobic Not requiring oxygen.

Concept | Check

To begin glycolysis, 2 phosphate groups from 2 ATP molecules are added to glucose to make the glucose more reactive. This doubly phosphorylated glucose becomes fructose 1, 6 bisphosphate. It eventually splits into 2 molecules of a 3-carbon compound glyceraldehyde 3-phosphate. These molecules go through a series of chemical reactions (steps ⑥ through ⑩) to become the 3-carbon compound pyruvate. Thus in glycolysis, glucose with 6 carbons, 12 hydrogens, and 6 oxygens ($C_6H_{12}O_6$) is converted to 2 molecules of pyruvate containing 3 carbons, 4 hydrogens, and 3 oxygens ($C_3H_4O_3$). In the process, 4 hydrogens (containing 4 protons and 4 electrons) are removed and NAD^+ is reduced to form $NADH + H^+$. Each NAD^+ accepts 2 electrons and 1 proton, producing $NADH + H^+$ (the extra H^+ is an unbound proton). Also produced in this phase of glycolysis is 4 ATP (steps ⑦ and ⑩). Pyruvate is either broken down further or converted to lactate. Red blood cells perform the latter reaction as part of *anaerobic glycolysis*. The conversion of pyruvate to lactate allows the cell to oxidize $NADH + H^+$ into NAD^+. This provides the NAD^+ needed for glycolysis. $NADH + H^+$ can also be oxidized to NAD^+ via oxygen-requiring pathways, found in most cells.

Carbohydrate, protein, fat, and alcohol all contribute chemical energy to the body.

The Citric Acid Cycle Completes Glucose Catabolism

The two pyruvate (or lactate) molecules formed at the end of glycolysis still contain much stored energy. Pyruvate passes from the cell cytosol into the mitochondria. A cell then uses pathways found there to extract the remaining energy from pyruvate to form more ATP. One key pathway is called the *citric acid cycle*.

Pyruvate to Acetyl-CoA Is an Irreversible Step

Before the citric acid cycle can begin, pyruvate must lose a carbon dioxide group and eventually form acetyl-CoA. This overall reaction is irreversible, which has important metabolic consequences, as you will see. As pyruvate is converted to acetyl-CoA, another $NADH + H^+$ is formed from NAD^+, so more potential ATP molecules are produced.[4] The conversion of pyruvate to acetyl-CoA requires the B vitamins thiamin, riboflavin, niacin, and pantothenic acid. For this reason, carbohydrate metabolism depends on the presence of these vitamins.

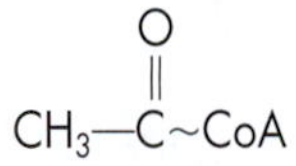

Acetyl-CoA

The Citric Acid Cycle

The citric acid cycle is an elegant sequence of chemical reactions used by cells to convert the carbons of acetate to carbon dioxide and to yield energy. Acetyl-CoA enters the cycle, and the reactions eventually yield two molecules of carbon dioxide. In the process, the cell produces $NADH + H^+$ and other related molecules, which eventually are used to form many ATP.[4]

Other names for the citric acid cycle are the tricarboxylic acid cycle (TCA cycle) and the Krebs cycle, named after Sir Hans Krebs, the scientist who first described it.

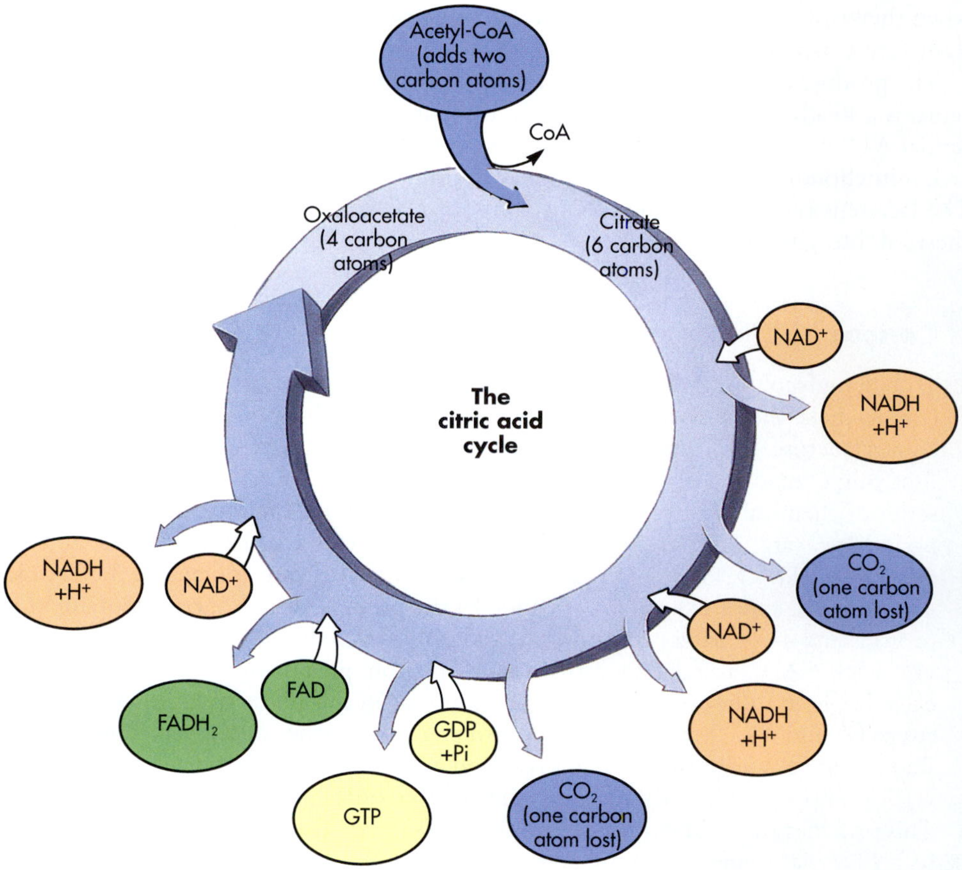

Figure 4-6 The citric acid cycle simplified. The four carbons from oxaloacetate combine with two carbons from acetyl-CoA to form the six-carbon compound *citric acid,* or citrate. The citrate is ultimately re-formed into the original four-carbon oxaloacetate, with a net loss of two carbons as carbon dioxide. The pathway thus begins and ends with the same compound, oxaloacetate, which makes it a cycle. The GTP formed can be used to synthesize ATP. Overall, one turn of the cycle yields 2 CO_2, 3 NADH + H^+, 1 $FADH_2$, and 1 GTP (ATP).
Illustration by William Ober.

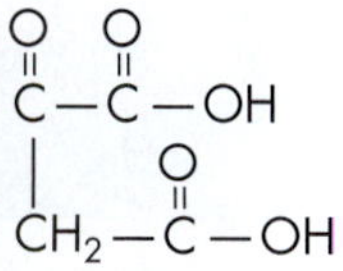

Oxaloacetic acid

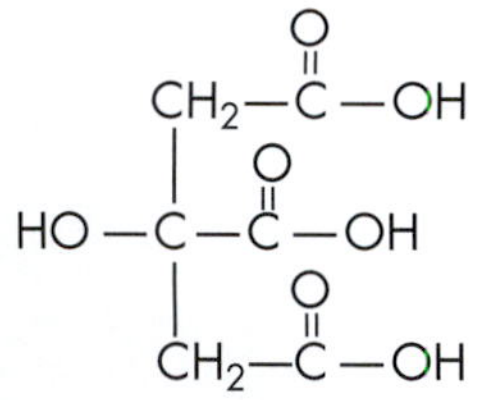

Citric acid

To begin the citric acid cycle, acetyl-CoA combines with a four-carbon compound, oxaloacetic acid (or oxaloacetate) to form the six-carbon compound citric acid (or citrate) (Fig. 4-6). In the process, the CoA molecule is released. During one turn of the citric acid cycle, the six-carbon citrate molecule is metabolized to the four-carbon oxaloacetate molecule (steps ② through ⑨ in Figure 4-7) and two carbon dioxide molecules are released (steps ④ and ⑤). The cycle is ready to begin again with oxaloacetate and another acetyl-CoA. Each turn of the cycle yields potential ATP in the form of guanosine triphosphate (GTP) (step ⑥), NADH + H^+ and $FADH_2$. FAD is another hydrogen carrier. It can pick up a pair of hydrogens at step ⑦. Each $FADH_2$ provides enough energy to synthesize 1.5 ATP, *one less than* NADH + H^+.

To review carbohydrate metabolism so far, the cell started with a six-carbon glucose and eventually produced six carbon dioxide molecules, two at the pyruvate to acetyl CoA step, two each at isocitrate to alpha-ketoglutarate step (step ④), and two each at alpha-ketoglutarate to succinyl-CoA step (step ⑤). Remember, it takes two turns around the citric acid cycle to process one glucose, since the glucose was split into two three-carbon fragments as a result of glycolysis. As a result, all the carbons in glucose are released in the form of carbon dioxide. The carbon dioxide eventually leaves the body by way of the lungs. In the process, ATP is synthesized directly using both the glycolysis and citric acid cycle pathways, and NADH + H^+ and $FADH_2$ are formed from NAD^+ and FAD. The NADH +H^+ and $FADH_2$ molecules can be used to supply the energy needed for ATP synthesis in the electron transport chain (see discussion on p. 120).

In this way, some of the energy in the chemical bonds of glucose is transferred to ATP. Thus, some of the energy in food yields a form of energy that cells can use, rather than just being converted immediately to heat, as would have happened if you had ignited the food with a match. In engineering terms, cells capture about 40% of the chemical energy in glucose and transfer it to a useful form when needed—namely, ATP.

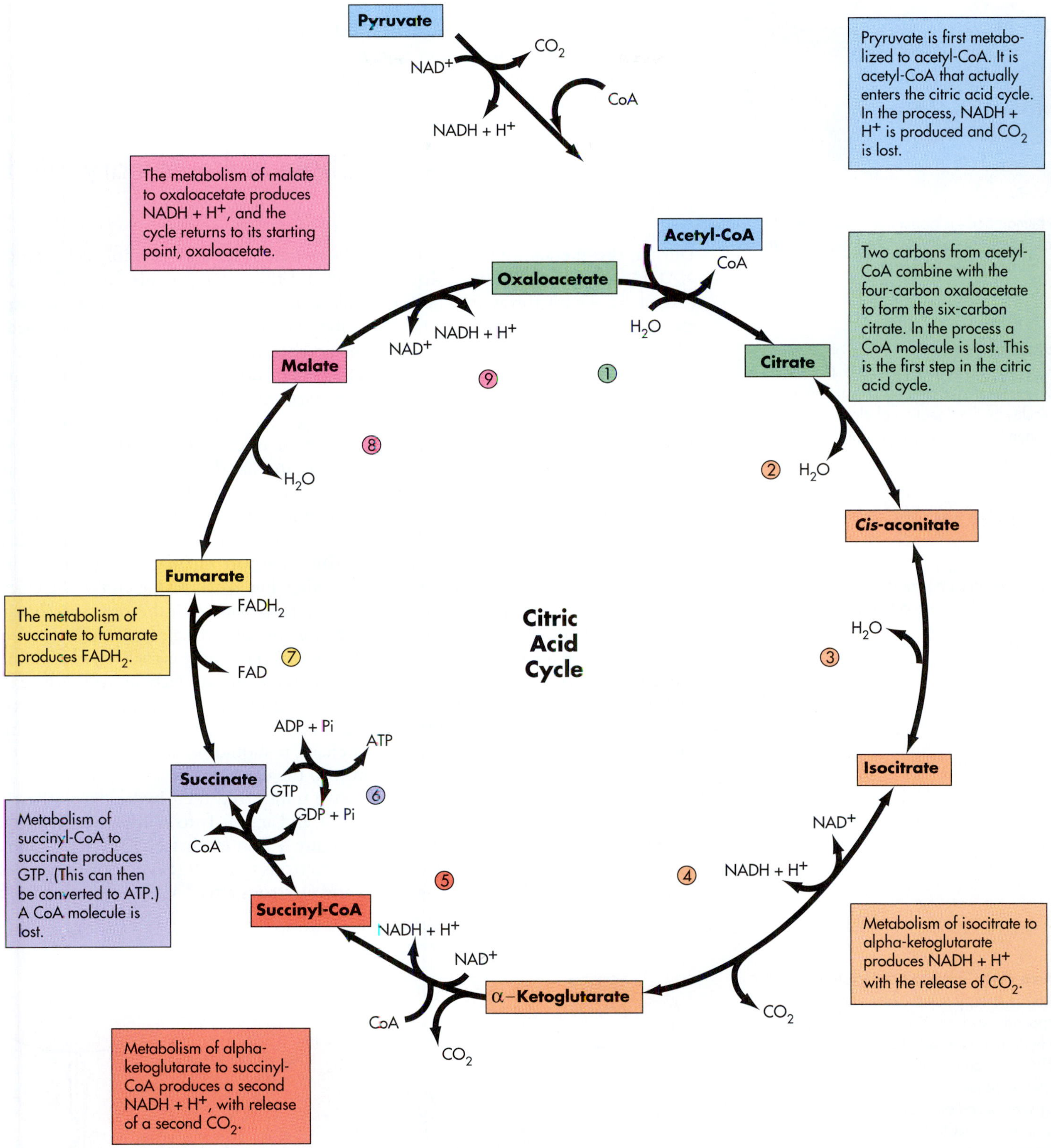

Pyruvate
NAD+
CO2
CoA
NADH + H+
Pryruvate is first metabolized to acetyl-CoA. It is acetyl-CoA that actually enters the citric acid cycle. In the process, NADH + H+ is produced and CO2 is lost.
The metabolism of malate to oxaloacetate produces NADH + H+, and the cycle returns to its starting point, oxaloacetate.
Acetyl-CoA
CoA
Oxaloacetate
H2O
NADH + H+
NAD+
Malate
Citrate
Two carbons from acetyl-CoA combine with the four-carbon oxaloacetate to form the six-carbon citrate. In the process a CoA molecule is lost. This is the first step in the citric acid cycle.
1
9
8
H2O
2
H2O
Cis-aconitate
Fumarate
FADH2
The metabolism of succinate to fumarate produces FADH2.
FAD
7
Citric Acid Cycle
H2O
3
ADP + Pi
ATP
Succinate
GTP
6
GDP + Pi
Isocitrate
NAD+
CoA
Metabolism of succinyl-CoA to succinate produces GTP. (This can then be converted to ATP.) A CoA molecule is lost.
5
4
NADH + H+
Succinyl-CoA
NADH + H+
NAD+
Metabolism of isocitrate to alpha-ketoglutarate produces NADH + H+ with the release of CO2.
α−Ketoglutarate
CoA
CO2
CO2
Metabolism of alpha-ketoglutarate to succinyl-CoA produces a second NADH + H+, with release of a second CO2.

Figure 4-7 Conversion of pyruvate to acetyl-CoA and the individual chemical reactions of the citric acid cycle. Conversion of pyruvate to acetyl-CoA uses an enzyme complex that includes pyruvate dehydrogenase. The enzymes used in the citric acid cycle are (*1*) citrate synthase, (*2*) aconitase, (*3*) aconitase, (*4*) isocitrate dehydrogenase, (*5*) alpha-ketoglutarate dehydrogenase, (*6*) succinate thiokinase, (*7*) succinate dehydrogenase, (*8*) fumarase, and (*9*) malate dehydrogenase. CoA stands for coenzyme A, which is made from the vitamin pantothenic acid (see Chapter 10 for the chemical structure). Note that the CO_2 molecules lost during one turn of the citric acid cycle are not those from the carbons donated by acetyl-CoA. Instead, the carbons are broken off of the portion of the citrate molecule derived from oxaloacetate. See Figure B-2 in Appendix B for a more detailed view.

The human body is about four times more efficient than automobiles in extracting energy from carbon-based compounds.

This is the main goal of energy metabolism. The remaining energy (60%) escapes as heat via all the reactions that take place in which ATP, GTP, NADH + H^+, or $FADH_2$ are not made. The same 40:60 ratio applies for the energy metabolism of fatty acids and amino acids. That's fairly efficient, compared with an automobile engine, which captures only about 10% of the chemical energy in gasoline.[1]

The Electron Transport Chain Is the Primary Site for ATP Synthesis

During the metabolism of protein, carbohydrate, fat, and alcohol, cells generate NADH + H^+ and $FADH_2$. Most cells can use these compounds for ATP synthesis (Fig. 4-8). The pathway that performs this function is called the **electron transport chain.**[1] The process, which occurs in the inner membrane of mitochondria, is called *oxidative phosphorylation*. The minerals iron and copper are needed for this process.

electron transport chain A series of reactions using oxygen to convert NADH + H^+ and $FADH_2$ molecules to free NAD^+ and FAD molecules by the donation of electrons and hydrogen ions to oxygen, yielding water and ATP.

In the electron transport chain, NADH + H^+ donates its chemical energy to an FAD-related compound called *flavin mononucleotide (FMN)*. FMN is followed at a junction by Coenzyme Q (CoQ), which separates the pairs of electrons so they can proceed one electron at a time through the rest of the electron transport chain (Fig. 4-9). Later you will see the hydrogens take another route that does not use the cytochromes. (Note that a product called Coenzyme Q-10 is sold as a nutrient supplement in Health Food Stores. However, when the mitochondria need Coenzyme Q, they make it. Thus it is not needed in the diet or in the form of a supplement to maintain overall health.)

The next structures used in the electron transport chain are a group of iron-containing molecules called **cytochromes** (review Fig. 4-9). At the end of the chain of cytochromes is a special cytochrome whose job is to donate all the electrons that have moved down the chain to oxygen. The action of the cytochromes is like a bucket brigade, picking up an electron and handing it off to the next cytochrome until finally, at the end of the chain, there is oxygen waiting to accept the electron. At this final step, each hydrogen ion reunites with the electrons to form hydrogen, which in turn combines with oxygen to form water. Thus, although NADH + H^+ and $FADH_2$ transfer their hydrogens to the electron transport chain, it should be noted that the hydrogen ions (H^+) are not carried down the chain with the electrons.

cytochromes Electron-transfer compounds that participate in the electron transport chain.

Once the NADH + H^+ and $FADH_2$ have transferred their hydrogen to the chain they are again in the form of NAD^+ and FAD, and are ready to shuttle more hydrogens to the chain from the citric acid cycle. In Figure 4-9, note that NADH + H^+ donates its hydrogen, associated hydrogen ion, and electrons to FMN (flavin mononucleotide). $FADH_2$ donates its pair of hydrogen ions and electrons after FMN to the cytochromes.

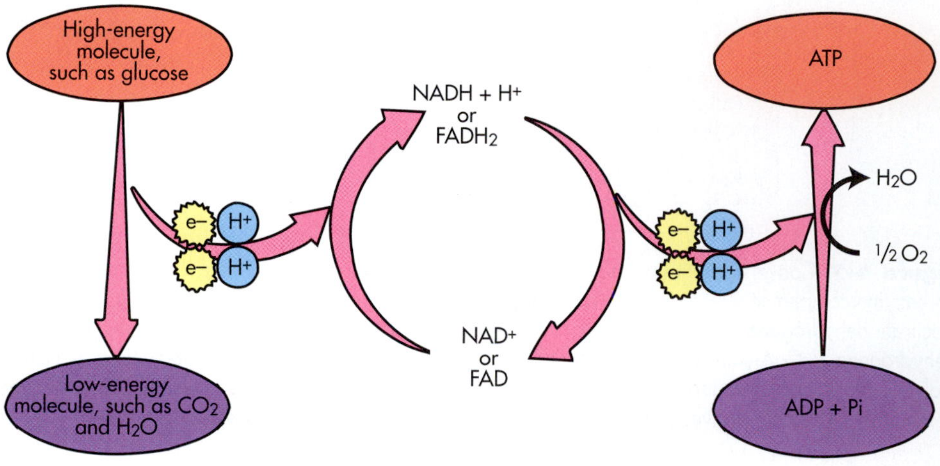

Figure 4-8 Simplified depiction of electron transfer in energy metabolism. High-energy compounds, such as glucose, give up electrons and hydrogen ions to NAD^+ and FAD. The NADH + H^+ and $FADH_2$ that are formed transfer these electrons and hydrogen ions, using specialized electron carriers, to oxygen to form water (H_2O). The energy yielded by the entire process is used to generate ATP from ADP and Pi.
Illustration by William Ober.

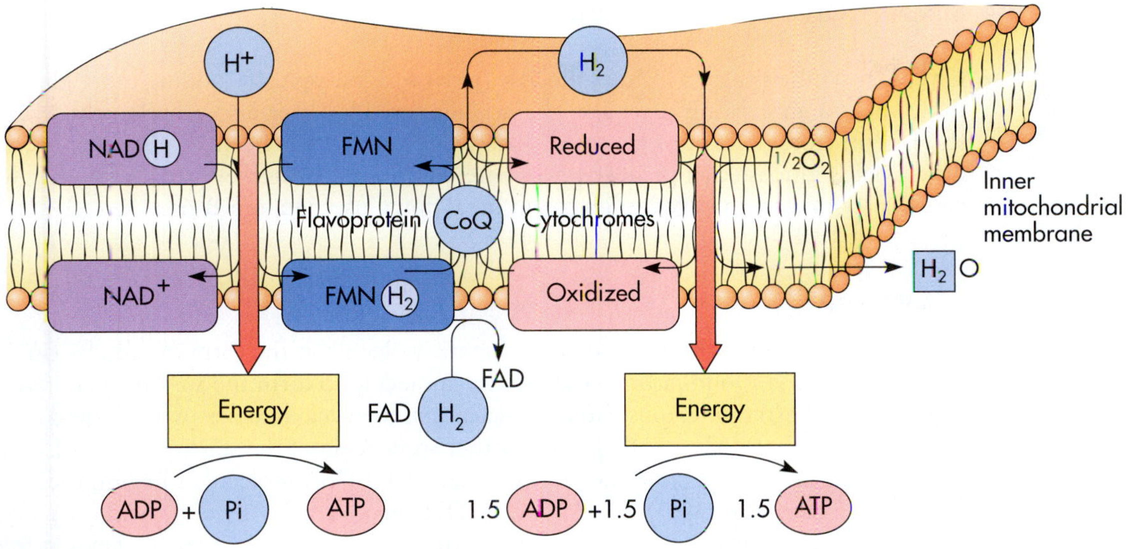

Figure 4-9 More detailed depiction of the electron transport chain. NADH and $FADH_2$ transfer their hydrogen ions and electrons to electron carriers located on the inner mitochondrial membrane. Between FMN and the cytochromes sits Coenzyme Q (CoQ), which separates the pairs of electrons so they can proceed one electron at a time down the electron transport chain. The electrons and hydrogen ions combine with oxygen to form water (H_2O). The energy yielded by the entire process is used to generate ATP. The oxygen atoms attract the electrons down the electron transport chain. Each NADH + H^+ in the mitochondria releases enough energy to form the equivalent of 2.5 ATP, while each $FADH_2$ releases enough energy to form the equivalent of 1.5 ATP. Of the 30 to 32 ATP yielded by the complete oxidation of glucose, almost 90% are synthesized in the electron transport chain. See Figure B-3 in Appendix B for a more detailed view.
Illustration by William Ober.

As the electrons move along the chain they release energy which is used to phosphorylate ADP to ATP. This different placement of FAD and NAD^+ in the chain results in a difference in ATP production. Each NADH + H^+ in the mitochondria releases enough energy to form the equivalent of 2.5 ATP, while each $FADH_2$ (which entered lower down the chain) releases enough energy to form the equivalent of 1.5 ATP.[1]

In the meantime, the hydrogen ions are moved between the inner and outer mitochondrial membrane by pumps that deliver the hydrogen ion to the electrons to form hydrogen. The net result of the electron transport chain is the production of ATP and water.

Since oxygen is essential to these processes, the electron transport chain is part of aerobic metabolism. NADH + H^+ and $FADH_2$ produced during the citric acid cycle can be regenerated into NAD^+ and FAD only by the eventual transfer of their electrons and hydrogen ions to oxygen. The citric acid cycle has no way to re-form NADH + H^+ and $FADH_2$ back to NAD^+ and FAD analogous to the way that anaerobic glycolysis produces lactate. This is ultimately why oxygen is essential to life; a final acceptor of the electrons and hydrogen ions generated from the breakdown of energy-yielding nutrients is needed. Without oxygen, most of our cells are unable to extract enough energy from fuels to sustain life.[7]

This entire description of the metabolism of glucose depicts the essence of metabolism. Cells need to release energy stored in food fuels and then trap as much as possible as ATP. The body cannot afford to lose all energy immediately as heat. Some heat is necessary for warmth, but the body also needs mobilizing energy. Glycolysis, the citric acid cycle, and the electron transport chain accomplish many things. Most important, however, is that they enable cells to capture the chemical energy in food in the form of ATP, which acts as cellular fuel.

Glycogen Metabolism

Critical | Thinking

While looking at electron microscopy slides of muscle cells, you observe various organelles. However, the large number of mitochondria you see is remarkable. Your instructor asks you to explain this observation to your classmates. How would you do so?

Glycogen synthesis uses a form of glucose (glucose 1-phosphate), adding more glucose molecules to an existing glycogen chain. This provides liver and muscle cells with a short-term storage form of glucose.[6] Later, when glucose is needed, glycogen breakdown yields glucose as a glucose-phosphate compound, which eventually begins glycolysis. An enzyme involved in glycogen breakdown uses vitamin B-6.

Concept | Check

In the citric acid cycle, a two-carbon acetate molecule in the form of acetyl-CoA combines with a four-carbon oxaloacetate molecule to form the six-carbon citrate molecule. Through various chemical reactions, the cycle releases two carbon dioxide molecules and eventually yields another oxaloacetate, the starting material. This new oxaloacetate can combine with another acetyl-CoA molecule to begin the process again. The $NADH + H^+$ and $FADH_2$ produced in the citric acid cycle donate their electrons and hydrogen ions to the electron transport chain, yielding free NAD^+ and FAD, water, and ATP.

Lipolysis: Fat Breakdown

lipolysis The breakdown of triglycerides to glycerol and fatty acids.

Lipolysis is part of a process of splitting—breaking down—triglycerides into free fatty acids and glycerol. The further breakdown of the fatty acids for energy production is called *fatty acid oxidation,* since the donation of electrons from fatty acids to oxygen is the net reaction in the energy-yielding process. This takes place in the mitochondria and peroxisomes of the cell, but only mitochondria can use the energy released to form ATP.[7]

carnitine A compound used to shuttle fatty acids from the cytosol of the cell into mitochondria.

Fatty acids are liberated from lipid storage in adipose cells by an enzyme called *hormone-sensitive lipase.* The activity of this enzyme is increased by the hormones glucagon, growth hormone, epinephrine, and others, and is decreased by the hormone insulin. The fatty acids are taken up from the bloodstream by cells and are shuttled from the cell cytosol into the mitochondria using a carrier called **carnitine.** In healthy people, cells produce the carnitine needed for this process. During acute illness in hospitalized patients, carnitine synthesis may not meet their needs. Thus, it may be added to intravenous total parenteral nutrition solutions provided to these patients.

beta oxidation The breakdown of a fatty acid into numerous acetyl-CoA molecules.

Almost all fatty acids in nature are composed of an even number of carbons, ranging from 2 to 26. The first step in transferring the energy in a fatty acid to ATP (fatty acid oxidation) is to cleave the carbons, two at a time, and convert the two-carbon fragments to acetyl-CoA. The process of converting a free fatty acid to multiple acetyl-CoA molecules is called **beta-oxidation,** since the second carbon on a fatty acid (counting after the acid $\left[-\overset{\overset{\displaystyle O}{\|}}{C}-OH\right]$ end) is called the *beta carbon.* This is where the reaction begins. During beta-oxidation, $NADH + H^+$ and $FADH_2$ are produced. So as with glucose, a fatty acid is eventually degraded into the two-carbon compound acetate, in the form of acetyl-CoA. Some of the chemical energy contained in the starting compound is transferred to $NADH + H^+$ and $FADH_2$.[5]

The acetyl-CoA enters the citric acid cycle and two carbon dioxides are released, just as with the acetyl-CoA produced from glucose. Thus, the breakdown product of both glucose and fatty acids, acetyl-CoA, uses a common pathway—the citric acid cycle. One big difference, however, is that a 16-carbon fatty acid yields 108 ATP, whereas the 6-carbon glucose yields only 30 to 32 ATP. That results in a ratio of about 7 ATP per carbon for fatty acids versus about 5 ATP per carbon for glucose.[7] This difference results from the greater number of C–H bonds per carbon in a fatty acid compared to glucose. It is the oxidation of these chemical bonds that provides most of the energy to drive

ATP synthesis. Note that many of the carbons in glucose are also bonded to hydroxyl groups (–OH), rather than only to hydrogen atoms, as was primarily the case in the fatty acid. Thus, as a whole, the carbons of glucose exist in a more oxidized state. This is why fats yield more kcals/g than carbohydrates (9 versus 4)—fats are less oxidized (more reduced) than carbohydrates.

No matter how many carbons a fatty acid contains, it is usually broken down into acetyl-CoA. Occasionally, a fatty acid has an odd number of carbons, so the cell forms many acetyl-CoA, plus one three-carbon compound (propionyl-CoA). This enters the citric acid cycle directly, bypassing acetyl-CoA. It can then go on to yield carbon dioxide and other products, even glucose.

Carbohydrate Aids Fat Metabolism

In addition to its role in energy production, the citric acid cycle provides compounds that leave the cycle and enter biosynthetic pathways, such as those used to make the red blood cell protein hemoglobin. This means that, even though most oxaloacetate is reused in the cycle, a minimum amount of synthesis must still be maintained because this removal from the citric acid cycle for biosynthetic reactions could slow citric acid cycle activity. One potential source of this additional oxaloacetate is pyruvate. Thus, as fatty acids create acetyl-CoA, carbohydrates, such as glucose, are needed to keep the concentration of pyruvate high enough to resupply oxaloacetate to the citric acid cycle. We could say that "fats burn in a fire of carbohydrate," since the entire pathway for fatty acid oxidation works better when carbohydrate is available.[1]

Ketogenesis: Producing Ketone Bodies from Fatty Acids

Ketone bodies are products of incomplete fatty acid oxidation. Hormonal imbalances—chiefly, inadequate insulin production to balance glucagon action in the body—allow some metabolic conditions to develop that lead to significant production of ketone bodies called ***ketosis.***[5]

1. Fatty acids stored in adipose cells are rapidly released into the bloodstream. A fall in blood insulin is the key reason, as insulin inhibits lipolysis and, instead, favors fat storage. The bulk of the increase in fatty acids in the blood is taken up by the liver.
2. Fatty acid oxidation to acetyl-CoA predominates over fatty acid synthesis in the liver.
3. As the liver takes up the fatty acids and degrades them to acetyl-CoA, the capacity of the citric acid cycle to process the resulting acetyl-CoA molecules decreases. This is mostly because the metabolism of fatty acids to acetyl-CoA yields many ATP, and high amounts of ATP slow citric acid cycle activity in liver cells. Essentially, there is no need to use the citric acid cycle—the main role of which is to transfer energy from fuels for use in ATP synthesis—when the cells have plenty of ATP already.

These metabolic changes encourage the liver cells to first form acetyl-CoA and then unite two acetyl-CoA molecules to form a four-carbon compound. This compound is further metabolized and eventually secreted into the bloodstream as the ketone bodies acetoacetic acid and two related compounds, beta-hydroxybutyric acid and acetone.

Most ketone bodies are subsequently converted back into acetyl-CoA in other body cells, which use the ketone bodies for fuel. The acetyl-CoA is then pushed through the citric acid cycle. One of the ketone bodies formed (acetone) leaves the body via the lungs, giving the breath of a person in ketosis a characteristic, fruity smell.

Ketosis in Semistarvation or Fasting

When a person is in a state of semistarvation or fasting, carbohydrate availability falls, and so insulin production falls. This fall in blood insulin then causes fatty acids to flood into the bloodstream and eventually form ketone bodies. The heart, muscles, and some parts of the kidneys then use ketone bodies for fuel. After a few days of ketosis, the brain also begins to metabolize ketone bodies for energy.

ketone bodies Incomplete breakdown products of fat, containing three or four carbons. Most contain a chemical group called a ketone, hence the name. An example is acetoacetic acid.

ketosis The condition of having a high concentration of ketone bodies and related breakdown products in the bloodstream and tissues.

Key steps in ketosis

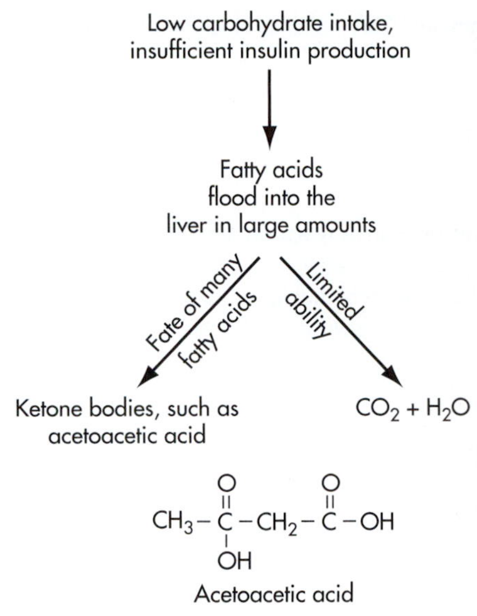

The use of a very-low-carbohydrate diet to induce ketosis for weight loss is covered in Chapters 5 and 13. Note for now that such diets have not been shown to be effective in the long term and can lead to health problems. Careful physician monitoring is needed if this type of diet is followed, especially in children.

This is an important adaptive response to semistarvation or fasting. As more body cells begin to use ketone bodies for fuel, the need for glucose as a body fuel diminishes. This then reduces the need for the liver and kidneys to produce glucose from amino acids (and as well from the glycerol released from lipolysis), sparing much body protein from being used as a fuel source. The maintenance of body protein mass is a key to survival in semistarvation or fasting. Death is seen when about half of the body protein is depleted, usually coming after about 50 to 70 days of total fasting. In prolonged fasting, about half of the energy needs are met by the use of ketone bodies; only 5 percent of energy use comes from glucose that was made from amino acids.[5]

Ketosis in Diabetes Can Be Especially Harmful

In type 1 diabetes, little to no insulin is produced. This lack of insulin does not allow for normal carbohydrate and fat metabolism. Without sufficient insulin and the related inability to readily utilize carbohydrate, excess production of ketone bodies occurs, as just noted. If the concentration of ketone bodies rises too high in the blood, the excess spills into the urine, pulling sodium and potassium ions with it. Eventually, severe ion imbalances occur in the body. The blood also becomes more acidic because two of the three forms of ketone bodies contain acid groups. The resulting condition, known as *diabetic ketoacidosis (DKA),* can induce coma or death if not treated immediately, such as with insulin and fluids (see Chapter 5 for more details). Ketoacidosis usually occurs only in ketosis caused by uncontrolled type 1 diabetes; in fasting, blood concentrations of ketone bodies usually do not rise high enough to cause the problem.[5]

Lipogenesis: Building Fatty Acids

lipogenesis The building of fatty acids using derivatives of acetyl-CoA.

Lipogenesis is the formation of lipid. The majority of the pathways used are found in the cytosol of liver cells. Ingested protein or carbohydrate that the body does not use immediately can be converted into triglycerides and stored as such. Some of the protein can reside in amino acid pools in the body, but the amount is not significant. Most carbohydrate is stored as glycogen, but the total amount rarely exceeds 350 g in the entire body. Thus, when a lot of amino acids and/or glucose are left over in the body after a large meal containing protein and/or carbohydrate, some of the carbons can be used to synthesize fatty acids. This process requires ATP and the B-vitamins biotin, niacin, and pantothenic acid. Since ATP is used, lipogenesis is an energy-losing proposition for a liver cell.

malonyl-CoA Building block in fatty acid synthesis: $HO\text{–}\overset{\overset{O}{\|}}{C}\text{–}CH_2\text{–}\overset{\overset{O}{\|}}{C}\text{–Coenzyme A}$

very-low-density lipoprotein (VLDL) The lipoprotein created in the liver that carries both the cholesterol and lipids taken up, and that are newly synthesized, by the liver.

In lipogenesis, the liver begins with carbons from glucose and the carbons from amino acids that are metabolized to acetyl-CoA. Cells in the liver bond the acetate parts of acetyl-CoA molecules (actually in the form of **malonyl-CoA**) together in a series of steps to form a 16-carbon saturated fatty acid, palmitic acid. Insulin increases activity of a key enzyme used in the pathway (fatty acid synthase).[7] This 16-carbon fatty acid can later be lengthened to an 18- or 20-carbon chain either in the cytosol or mitochondria.[1] Ultimately, the fatty acids are joined to a form of glycerol (produced during glycolysis from glyceraldehyde 3-phosphate) to yield a triglyceride. The triglyceride is later released to the general circulation as a **very-low-density lipoprotein, or VLDL** (see Chapter 6). Cells that take up fat may use it for ATP production, or it may be stored in cells (mostly adipose cells), along with other fats that originate from dietary intake.

Case Scenario | Follow-up

A very-low-carbohydrate diet leads to ketosis because such a diet reduces insulin secretion by the pancreas. This then results in a decrease in the insulin/glucagon ratio, which in turn creates a catabolic state in the body. Triglycerides in the adipose cells break down to yield fatty acids;

these flood out of the adipose cells into the bloodstream and are taken up by the liver. The liver metabolizes the fatty acids to ketone bodies and releases these ketone bodies into the bloodstream. Complete metabolism of the fatty acids to CO_2 and H_2O in the liver is not possible, as this would yield so much ATP that many enzymes that are part of citric acid cycle activity in the cell would be inhibited. Partial metabolism of fatty acids to ketone bodies yields some ATP for the liver cells, but not so much ATP that such problems arise. Eventually, the blood concentration of ketone bodies then begins to rise. In essence, anything that can lead to a long-term reduction in insulin output causes ketosis. This is seen with very-low-carbohydrate diets, as well as in prolonged fasting and uncontrolled type 1 diabetes.

Concept | Check

Fatty acids are degraded into numerous acetyl-CoA molecules. These molecules participate in the citric acid cycle and electron transport chain to yield carbon dioxide, water, and ATP. To synthesize fat, a cell binds numerous acetate molecules together to form a fatty acid. Three fatty acids can then be joined to glycerol to yield a triglyceride. If acetyl-CoA oxidation in liver cells is limited, such as in cases of long-term fasting, the acetyl-CoA resulting from fatty acid oxidation tends to force the production of ketone bodies. These ketone bodies enter the bloodstream and are eventually metabolized to carbon dioxide and water (after being converted back to acetyl-CoA) by various cells.

Protein Metabolism

Protein metabolism begins after proteins are degraded into amino acids. To use an amino acid for fuel, cells must first split off the amino group ($-NH_2$) (see Chapter 7). These pathways often require vitamin B-6 to function. Removal of the amino group produces **carbon skeletons,** which mostly enter the citric acid cycle. Some carbon skeletons also yield acetyl-CoA or pyruvate (Fig. 4-10).[7]

carbon skeleton Amino acid after the amino group ($-NH_2$) has been removed.

Amino acid metabolism mostly takes place in the liver. Only branched-chain amino acids—leucine, isoleucine, and valine—are metabolized primarily at other sites—in this case, the muscles. As you will see in future chapters, this knowledge has applications. Branched-chain amino acids are added to some liquid meal replacement supplements given to hospitalized patients. Some fluid replacement formulas marketed to athletes also contain branched-chain amino acids (see Chapter 14).

It is important to note that some carbon skeletons enter the citric acid cycle as acetyl-CoA, whereas others form intermediates of the citric acid cycle or glycolysis. Any part of the carbon skeleton that can bypass acetyl-CoA and enter the citric acid cycle directly, or form pyruvate, can eventually become part of glucose via gluconeogenesis. Such is true for the amino acids alanine, methionine, arginine, histidine, aspartic acid, and others (review Fig. 4-10).

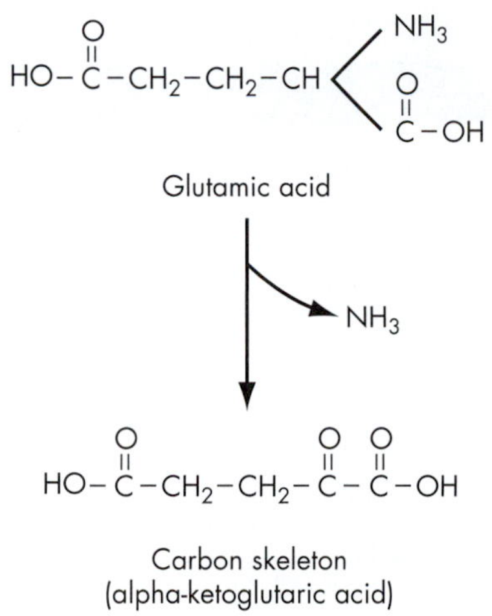

Gluconeogenesis: Producing New Glucose Molecules from Amino Acids and Other Compounds

The entire gluconeogenesis pathway is present only in liver cells and in certain kidney cells. The starting material for gluconeogenesis is oxaloacetate, which is derived primarily from the carbon skeletons of some amino acids, mostly the amino acid alanine. Pyruvate can also be converted to oxaloacetate (review Fig. 4-10).[3]

The four-carbon oxaloacetate loses one carbon dioxide and converts to a three-carbon compound phosphoenolpyruvate, which then reverses the path back through glycolysis

Expert Opinion

Why Is an Understanding of Energy Metabolism Important?

Michael Keenan, Ph.D.

An overall understanding of energy metabolism allows you to see the big picture of what happens in your body without getting lost in the details of a myriad of individual chemical reactions.

Energy Sources for Cells

One of your body's highest priorities is to maintain blood glucose in a normal range so that the central nervous system (including the brain), retina, kidneys, and smooth muscles have adequate energy. Too little blood glucose **(hypoglycemia)** results in not enough of an energy supply for these cells. Too much blood glucose **(hyperglycemia)** for a prolonged period results in too much glucose entering nerve cells and other tissues, which in the long run can lead to cellular damage.

Except for instances of fasting for several days or so, your brain uses only glucose for energy. Most of your other organs and tissues use a combination of glucose, fatty acids, amino acids, lactic acid, and ketone bodies. Glucose and fatty acid use also spares protein from excessive use for energy needs.

Glucose is the predominant energy source of all tissues for a couple of hours after a meal, called the absorptive phase. In contrast, the major energy source for most tissues between meals, called the post-absorptive phase, is fatty acids. Dietary carbohydrate, if not already absorbed in the form of glucose, is converted under most conditions to glucose in the liver (e.g., fructose as part of sucrose and galactose as part of lactose). In the absorptive phase, glucose is either used immediately for energy or is stored as glycogen (the latter predominantly in the liver and muscle). Small amounts of glucose are also converted to fat for storage; this process especially increases as the carbohydrate content increases in the diet.

During the post-absorptive phase, blood glucose is maintained for use by the brain and other cells mainly by the breakdown of liver glycogen. However, some glucose is produced by gluconeogenesis, the predominant source of this glucose being glucogenic amino acids present in body proteins. If the post-absorptive phase lasts too long (about 16 hours, as when skipping breakfast), or if very little carbohydrate is present in the diet, gluconeogenesis becomes excessive. Thus, adequate amounts of dietary carbohydrate and timely consumption of food will spare body protein.

Fatty acids cannot fully spare body protein in fasting because they do not provide carbons that can be used for gluconeogenesis. The reason for this is that fatty acids are catabolized to the two-carbon compound acetate. In mammalian cells, acetate cannot be converted to pyruvate or other intermediates of glycolysis, or to any citric acid cycle intermediates, and it is only compounds that are catabolized to these forms that can contribute carbons for glucose synthesis. A good example to test your understanding of metabolism is to answer the following question: How many glucose molecules could be made from one 57-carbon triglyceride? The answer is none. It would actually take two 57-carbon triglycerides to produce one glucose molecule, since it is only the three-carbon glycerol backbone of a triglyceride that can enter the glycolysis pathway. This glycerol can be used for gluconeogenesis; two glycerols provide the six carbons needed for one glucose molecule.

In contrast, all carbons from the three fatty acids become part of the two-carbon acetate (acetyl-CoA). This acetate attaches to the four-carbon oxaloacetate to become the six-carbon citrate; this is the first step in the citric acid cycle. On its way to becoming the four-carbon succinate, citrate loses two carbons as carbon dioxide.

Another aspect of the big picture of metabolism is that glucose is also used to replace citric acid cycle intermediates when they are removed for the biosynthesis of a variety of compounds in cells. These citric acid cycle intermediates are present in the cell mitochondria only in small (catalytic) amounts.

Keep in mind that the two components of metabolism—catabolism and anabolism—are interwoven. Metabolism could be viewed as a tree. For catabolism, arrows would be drawn down-

to glucose. It takes two of this three-carbon compound to produce the six-carbon glucose. Some steps in gluconeogenesis are simply a reversal or variation of the glycolysis pathway. This entire process requires ATP as well as coenzyme forms of the B-vitamins biotin, riboflavin, niacin, and B-6.

To learn more about gluconeogenesis, let's trace the pathway by converting glutamic acid, an amino acid, to glucose in Figure 4-10. Glutamic acid first loses its amino group to form its carbon skeleton. This enters the citric acid cycle directly and is converted by stages to oxaloacetate. Oxaloacetate loses one carbon as carbon dioxide, and

ward from branches leading to the trunk, and the trunk includes glycolysis and the citric acid cycle. Anabolism would be represented by having the arrows pointing upward out of the trunk and into the branches.

One final thought to consider is the question of which of the two energy sources—glucose or fatty acids—is the primary or major energy source for the body. Often, glucose is given this distinction, but this must always be qualified. Glucose is the primary fuel for the brain and several other organs, as well as for all tissues in the absorptive phase. Fatty acids are the primary fuel for most tissues during the post-absorptive phase, but glucose participates in this use of fatty acids. Glucose is the major overall fuel if you are maintaining your weight and following current dietary recommendations by eating a carbohydrate-rich diet and a physically active lifestyle. However, if you happen to consume a low-carbohydrate diet that is high in fat and you are not in positive energy balance, then dietary fat becomes the major overall fuel for energy. (Note also that if you follow such a diet, such as the Atkin's diet, make sure it is mostly comprised of plant oils, not animal fat.)

Diets high in protein, low in fat, and moderate in carbohydrate also have become popular for weight loss in recent years. These diets appear to be effective because they increase the body's metabolic rate higher than other diets for several hours after a meal. Consumption of high-protein diets results in protein becoming a more significant energy source. High-protein diets probably are safe as long as the protein intake does not exceed either 2 grams per kg body weight per day or 35% of the energy in the diet. However, intakes at/above these extremes are not recommended for long-term use because there is currently insufficient evidence to determine an Upper Level for protein, and so caution is advised when consuming very high amounts of protein in the diet. In addition, the Food and Nutrition Board recently concluded that there may not be a physiological need for protein consumption above 0.8 grams per kilogram of body weight (the RDA), or about 10% of total energy intake. This includes weight-lifting or endurance athletes.

Metabolism is part of everyday life, and such activity increases when we increase physical activity.

In the final analysis, most nutritionists believe that a high-carbohydrate diet is preferable to one high in fat or protein, but it should be primarily in the form of whole grains, fruits, and vegetables that contain fiber and water that dilute the energy content of these foods. These foods also provide numerous phytochemicals that promote health. The recommendation for people to eat high unrefined carbohydrate diets will probably remain unchanged in the future because research studies indicate that diets high in such carbohydrates and moderate in fat promote overall health, and are most effective in both weight loss and in the long-term maintenance of that loss.

Your overall understanding of metabolism now helps you clearly see the roles of the energy macronutrients. Carbohydrate is used for maintaining blood glucose and the efficient use of fat, and fatty acids are an important source of energy for most tissues between meals. However, fatty acids cannot completely replace carbohydrate. Protein can be used for fuel, but its use for energy in most cases is limited by the metabolism of carbohydrate and fat for energy.

Dr. Keenan is an associate professor in the Division of Human Nutrition and Foods at the Louisiana State University in Baton Rouge, Louisiana. His research interests include the area of obesity in post-menopausal women.

the three-carbon phosphoenolpyruvate produced then moves through glycolysis to form glucose. Eventually, two glutamic acid molecules are needed to form one glucose molecule. Dr. Michael Keenan, in the Expert Opinion, discusses why the same synthesis of glucose is not possible using fatty acids.

The only part of a triglyceride that can become glucose is the glycerol portion. Propionyl-CoA formed from the metabolism of odd-chain fatty acids can do the same, as mentioned earlier. Glycerol enters into the glycolysis pathway, and propionyl-CoA can directly enter the citric acid cycle at succinyl-CoA. Propionyl-CoA can then flow

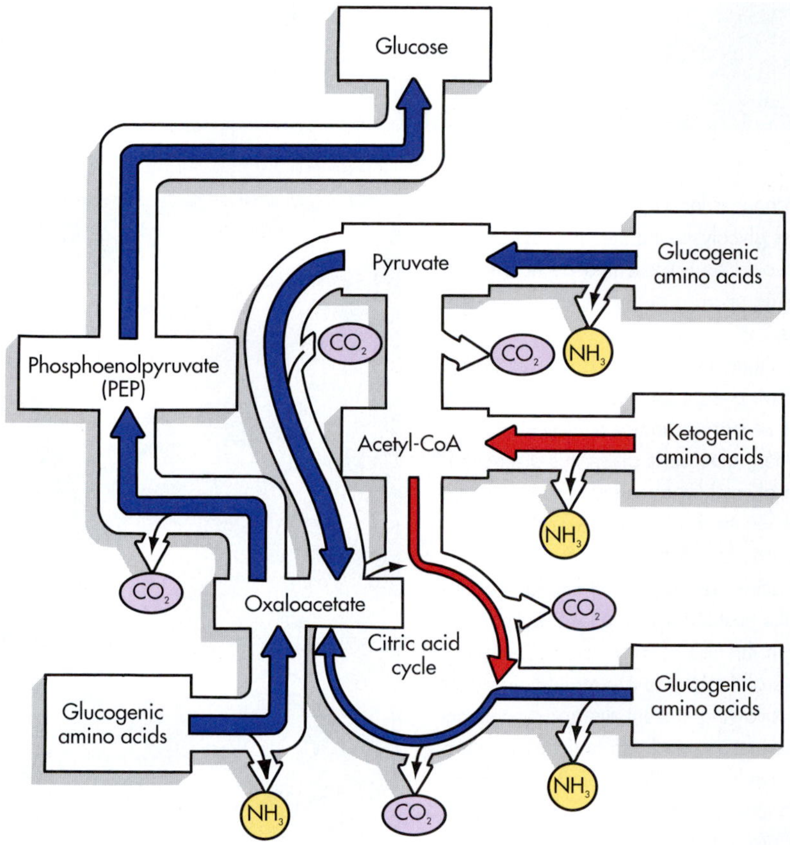

Figure 4-10 Gluconeogenesis. Carbon skeletons of amino acids that enter directly into the citric acid cycle (such amino acids include asparagine, arginine, aspartic acid, histidine, glutamic acid, glutamine, isoleucine, methionine, proline, valine, and phenylalanine) or become pyruvate (such as alanine, glycine, cysteine, serine, and threonine) are called *glucogenic amino acids* because these carbons can become the carbons of glucose. Any parts of carbon skeletons that become acetyl-CoA are called *ketogenic* because these carbons cannot become parts of glucose molecules. These include leucine and lysine, and parts of isoleucine, phenylalanine, tryptophan, and tyrosine. The deciding factor is whether part or all of the carbon skeleton of the amino acid yields a "new" oxaloacetate molecule during metabolism, two of which are needed to form glucose.[1]

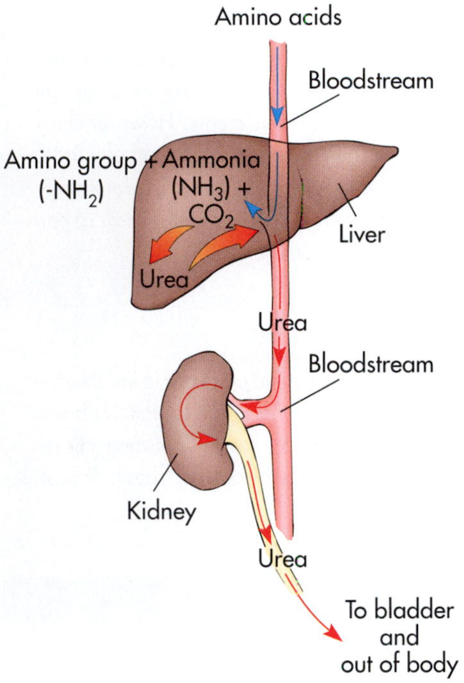

Figure 4-11 Disposal of excess amino groups. The nitrogen groups, one as ammonia and the other as an amino group, form part of urea, which is excreted in urine ($H_2N\overset{\overset{O}{\|}}{C}NH_2$). The nitrogen groups originally came from amino acids that went through transamination reactions and ultimately deamination to yield the free nitrogen groups. Illustration by William Ober.

through the citric acid cycle to oxaloacetate and then through the process of gluconeogenesis to convert to glucose. Glycerol can follow the gluconeogenesis pathway from glyceraldehyde 3-phosphate to glucose. Glucose yield from these compounds is insignificant, however, since the body produces little propionyl-CoA and only about 10% of the molecular weight of a triglyceride is glycerol.[7]

Recall from the earlier discussion on ketosis that, if there is an insufficient amount of carbohydrate in the body to meet ongoing needs, the liver and kidneys are forced to synthesize glucose from body protein to support the energy needs of the brain and red blood cells. Liver and kidney cells primarily begin with carbon skeletons from amino acids that are able to directly enter the citric acid cycle or form pyruvate. These compounds are converted to oxaloacetate, then to a three-carbon intermediate compound, phosphoenolpyruvate, and finally to glucose.

Disposing of Excess Amino Groups from Amino Acid Metabolism

The catabolism of amino acids yields amino groups ($-NH_2$), which then form ammonia (NH_3). The ammonia needs to be excreted because its buildup is toxic to cells. The liver prepares the amino groups for excretion in the urine using the urea cycle. During the urea cycle, two nitrogen groups—one ammonia group and one amino group—react through a series of steps with carbon dioxide molecules to form urea ($H_2N\overset{\overset{O}{\|}}{C}NH_2$) and water.[1] Eventually, urea is excreted in the urine (Fig. 4-11). In liver disease, ammonia can build up to toxic concentrations in the blood, whereas in kidney disease the toxic agent is urea. The form of nitrogen in the blood—ammonia or urea—is a diagnostic tool for detecting liver or kidney disease.

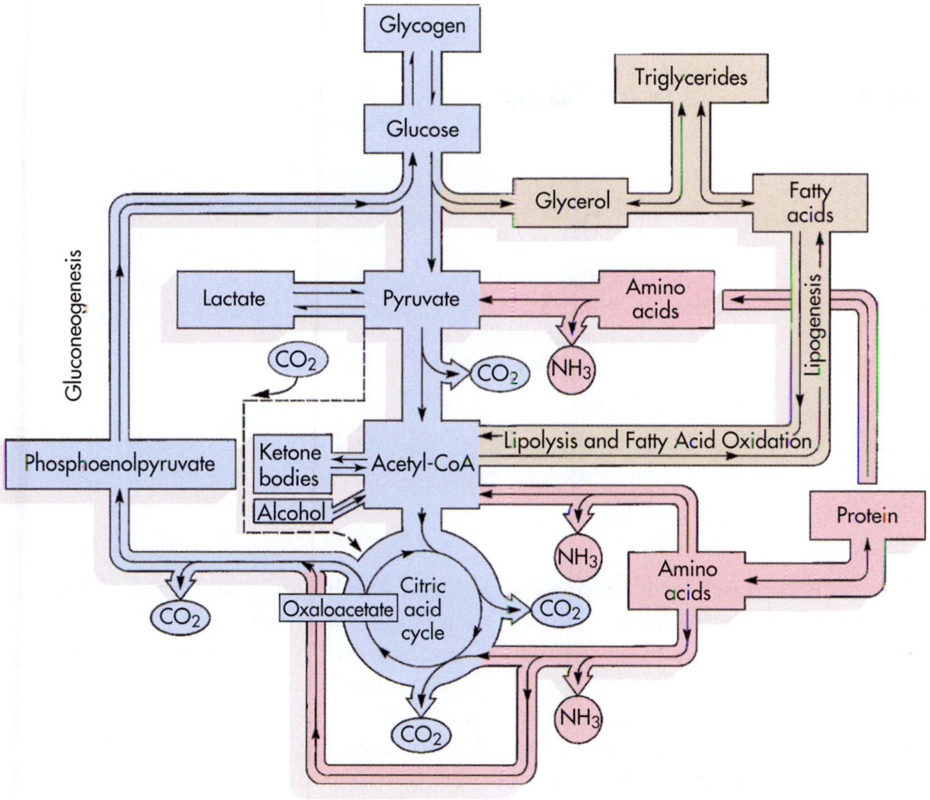

Figure 4-12 A bird's-eye view of cell metabolism. Note that acetyl-CoA forms a crossroads for many pathways and that the citric acid cycle can also be used to help build compounds, such as certain amino acids. Anabolic and catabolic processes may appear to share the same pathways, but generally this is true for only a few steps. Separate enzymes control anabolic and catabolic flow in a pathway. This allows the cell significant control over metabolism, since a specific set of enzymes can be activated to promote either anabolism or catabolism. If the chemical reactions in anabolism and catabolism were catalyzed by the same set of enzymes, the direction of flow of compounds through these pathways would be dictated exclusively by the concentration of the starting materials, rather than by the cell's changing needs for energy or synthesis of needed compounds.
Illustration by William Ober.

Concept | Check

Individual amino acids lose an amino group and become carbon skeletons. Many carbon skeletons can be further metabolized so that they enter either the citric acid cycle or the glycolysis pathway. The carbons can then proceed through gluconeogenesis to form new glucose. If the carbon skeleton forms acetyl-CoA, glucose production is not possible from that part of the amino acid. The amino groups go on to form part of urea, which is excreted from the body in urine.

What Happens Where—A Review

Glycolysis takes place in the cytosol of a cell. The end product of glycolysis, pyruvate, enters the mitochondria, where it is further degraded in the citric acid cycle. The NADH + H^+ made in the cytosol during glycolysis must be shuttled into the mitochondria if the electron transport chain is to be used to convert NADH + H^+ back to NAD^+ and simultaneously produce ATP. The type of shuttle determines how many ATP each NADH + H^+ yields. Generally, 2.5 ATP are formed. One type of shuttle system results in the loss of one potential ATP, so only 1.5 ATP result.[1]

Fatty acid oxidation also occurs in the mitochondria. The product of beta-oxidation, acetyl-CoA, is metabolized by the citric acid cycle in the mitochondria. Fatty acids are synthesized primarily in the cytosol.

Gluconeogenesis begins in the mitochondria with the production of oxaloacetate. Oxaloacetate eventually returns to the cytosol, where new glucose is produced. The same is true for the urea cycle; some stages occur in the cytosol and some in the mitochondria (Fig. 4-12).

Since the electron transport chain yields most of the ATP for the cell, the mitochondria are the cell's major energy-producing organelles. Cells that need to make a lot

Critical | Thinking

An alternative pathway for the metabolism of glucose is the pentose phosphate pathway. This yields ribose and deoxyribose for RNA and DNA synthesis, respectively, as well as a variation of NADH + H^+ (NADPH + H^+) used in synthetic reactions, such as the synthesis of fatty acids. The pentose phosphate pathway is very active in liver cells. Why would this be the case?

Table 4-1 Summary of Energy-Yielding Nutrient Metabolism

Nutrient in Diet	Contributes to Energy Needs	Yields Glucose?	Yields Amino Acids for Body Proteins?	Yields Fat for Adipose Tissue Stores?	Energy Cost of Conversion to Adipose Tissue Stores
Carbohydrate (glucose)	Yes	Yes	Yes, can provide carbons for the carbon skeletons of certain amino acids	Yes, but not readily	High
Lipid (triglycerides)	Yes	Generally not; the glycerol present provides a minimal amount	Indirectly by adding carbons to oxaloacetate that then can form a carbon skeleton for certain amino acids from a citric acid cycle intermediate	Yes	Minimal
Protein (amino acids)	Yes, but generally not much	Yes, excess amino acids can be converted to glucose	Yes	Yes	High

"Feasting" encourages
- Glycogen synthesis
- Protein synthesis
- Fat synthesis
- Urea synthesis

"Fasting" encourages
- Glycogen breakdown
- Fat breakdown
- Gluconeogenesis
- Synthesis of ketone bodies

of ATP, such as muscle cells, have thousands of mitochondria, whereas cells that need very little ATP, such as adipose cells, have fewer mitochondria.[7]

Energy metabolism can take many forms in the body. By stringing together the glycolysis pathway and the citric acid cycle, cells can convert carbohydrates into fatty acids, convert carbohydrates into carbon skeletons for synthesis of certain amino acids, and use the energy in carbohydrates to form ATP (review Fig. 4-12). These pathways can also turn carbon skeletons of some amino acids into carbon skeletons of others. Furthermore, they can convert carbon skeletons from some amino acids to glucose or have them drive ATP synthesis. Finally, fatty acids can provide energy for ATP synthesis or produce ketone bodies. The glycerol part of the triglyceride can either be converted into glucose or contribute to ATP synthesis (Table 4-1).

"Feasting," with the resultant increased insulin production by the pancreas, encourages the synthesis of glycogen, fat, and protein, especially the first two. Urea synthesis also increases in response to using some of the protein for fuel. "Fasting," with the resultant fall in insulin production, encourages gluconeogenesis, protein breakdown, and fat breakdown with subsequent production of ketone bodies. However, this is not the only time that production of ketone bodies can occur.

Acetyl-CoA plays a central role in energy metabolism. As noted before, no matter what type of diet you eat—high-carbohydrate, high-protein, or high-fat—almost all pathways that contribute to ATP synthesis include acetyl-CoA at one point.[3]

"Feasting" especially encourages the synthesis of glycogen, and fat.

Regulating Metabolism

Metabolism is regulated by various means. Enzymes are the key regulators for metabolic pathways; both their presence and their rate of activity are critical to chemical reactions in the body. Enzyme synthesis and rates of activity are controlled by cells and by the products of the reactions in which the enzymes participate.[7] For example, diets rich in protein lead to increased synthesis of enzymes associated with amino acid catabolism and gluconeogenesis. Within hours after a shift to a high-carbohydrate diet, synthesis of these enzymes slows.

Hormones, including insulin, glucagon, and epinephrine, also serve as regulators of metabolic processes. Blood glucose concentration is one parameter under their widespread influence.[1]

ATP concentration in a cell regulates metabolism. High ATP concentrations decrease energy-yielding reactions such as glycolysis and promote synthetic reactions such as lipogenesis, which use ATP. High ADP concentrations, on the other hand, stimulate energy-yielding pathways.[2]

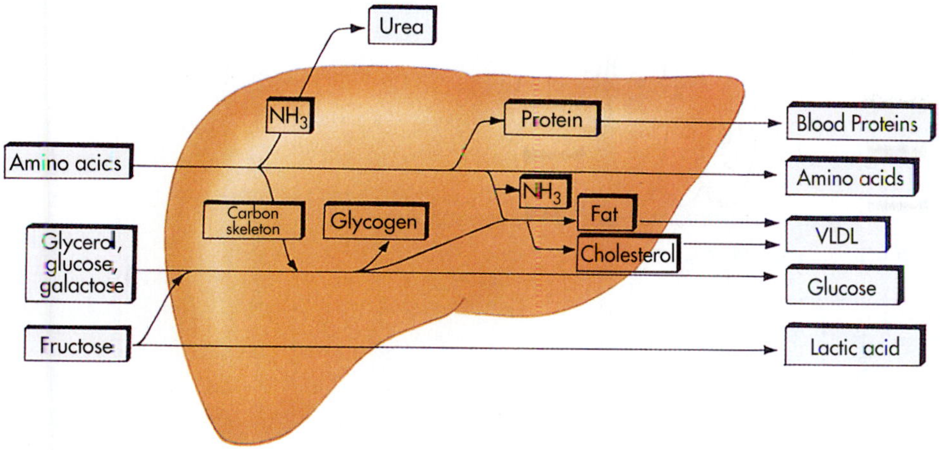

Figure 4-13 The liver is the location of many nutrient interconversions. Most nutrients must pass first through the liver after absorption into the body. What leaves the liver is often different from what entered. Key metabolic functions of the liver include monosaccharide conversion, fat and cholesterol synthesis, production of ketone bodies, amino acid metabolism, urea production, and alcohol metabolism. Nutrient storage is an additional liver function. VLDL stands for very-low-density lipoprotein. Recall that this lipoprotein carries fat from the liver to other body cells (see Chapter 6 for details).
Illustration by William Ober.

A final factor in regulating metabolism is the liver. It contains a variety of enzymes and most nutrients pass through it, providing an opportunity for metabolic control (Fig. 4-13).[1] Many vitamins and minerals also participate in metabolism (Fig. 4-14).

Concept | Check

Glycolysis takes place in the cytosol of the cell; the citric acid cycle and electron transport chain occur in the mitochondria. Fatty acid oxidation occurs in the mitochondria; fatty acids are synthesized mostly in the cytosol. The urea cycle and gluconeogenesis take place in both the mitochondria and the cytosol. Hormone balance, enzyme activity, and the need for ATP all influence the rate at which these metabolic pathways operate. Since many metabolic pathways converge at acetyl-CoA, it is central to energy metabolism.

Critical | Thinking

Stephanie begins a new diet program in which she can eat unlimited amounts of carbohydrate and protein but only very small amounts of fat. Stephanie believes that, if she eats no fat, she can gain no fat. Is this true? How would you explain the body processes that relate to this diet proposition?

Summary

1. ATP is the major form of energy used for cellular metabolism. As ATP breaks down to ADP plus Pi, energy is released from the broken bond. All energy available to humans ultimately comes from the sun as solar energy. Plants capture solar energy by way of photosynthesis. In humans, metabolic pathways make it possible to extract energy from C-H bonds in food and transform it into ATP; in the process, some energy is lost as heat.
2. In glycolysis, glucose is degraded into two pyruvate molecules, yielding NADH + H^+ (a form of potential energy) and ATP. Pyruvate can proceed through aerobic pathways to form carbon dioxide and water. Pyruvate also can react with NADH + H^+ in an anaerobic pathway to form lactate. Both pathways allow NADH + H^+ to eventually be re-formed into NAD^+, which is needed for glycolysis to continue.
3. Prior to entry into the citric acid cycle, pyruvate is formed into acetyl-CoA. A carbon dioxide molecule is released in the process. Acetyl-CoA then undergoes many metabolic conversions in the citric acid cycle, eventually yielding two more carbon dioxide molecules. In this way, the citric acid cycle accepts two carbons from acetyl-CoA and yields two carbons as carbon dioxide. In the process, NADH + H^+, $FADH_2$, and a form of energy that can yield ATP directly (GTP) are formed. The NADH + H^+ and $FADH_2$ then enter the electron transport chain to yield numerous ATP molecules. Water forms as oxygen combines with the electrons and hydrogen ions (released from NADH + H^+ and $FADH_2$) in the electron transport chain.
4. In fatty acid oxidation, two-carbon fragments are cleaved from a fatty acid at a time, producing multiple acetyl-CoA molecules. These enter the citric acid cycle and electron transport chain, as did the acetyl-CoA that arose from carbohydrate breakdown, to yield ATP, carbon dioxide, and water. In fat synthesis, acetate molecules in effect are combined to yield a fatty acid, primarily the 16-carbon palmitic acid. These fatty acids can then react with a form of glycerol to produce a triglyceride.
5. During low carbohydrate intakes and uncontrolled diabetes, more acetyl-CoA is produced in the liver than can be metabolized to carbon dioxide and water. This excess acetyl-CoA is synthesized into ketone bodies, which flood into the bloodstream and are metabolized by other tissues, such as nervous tissue.
6. Amino acids lose their amino group and become carbon skeletons. These can be metabolized to other compounds that enter the citric acid cycle, eventually yielding energy for ATP synthesis. Some carbon skeletons can be formed into oxaloacetate, an intermediate found in the citric acid cycle, which in turn can be used to form glucose. Converting the carbon skeletons of amino acids to glucose is part of a process known as gluconeogenesis. Acetyl-CoA

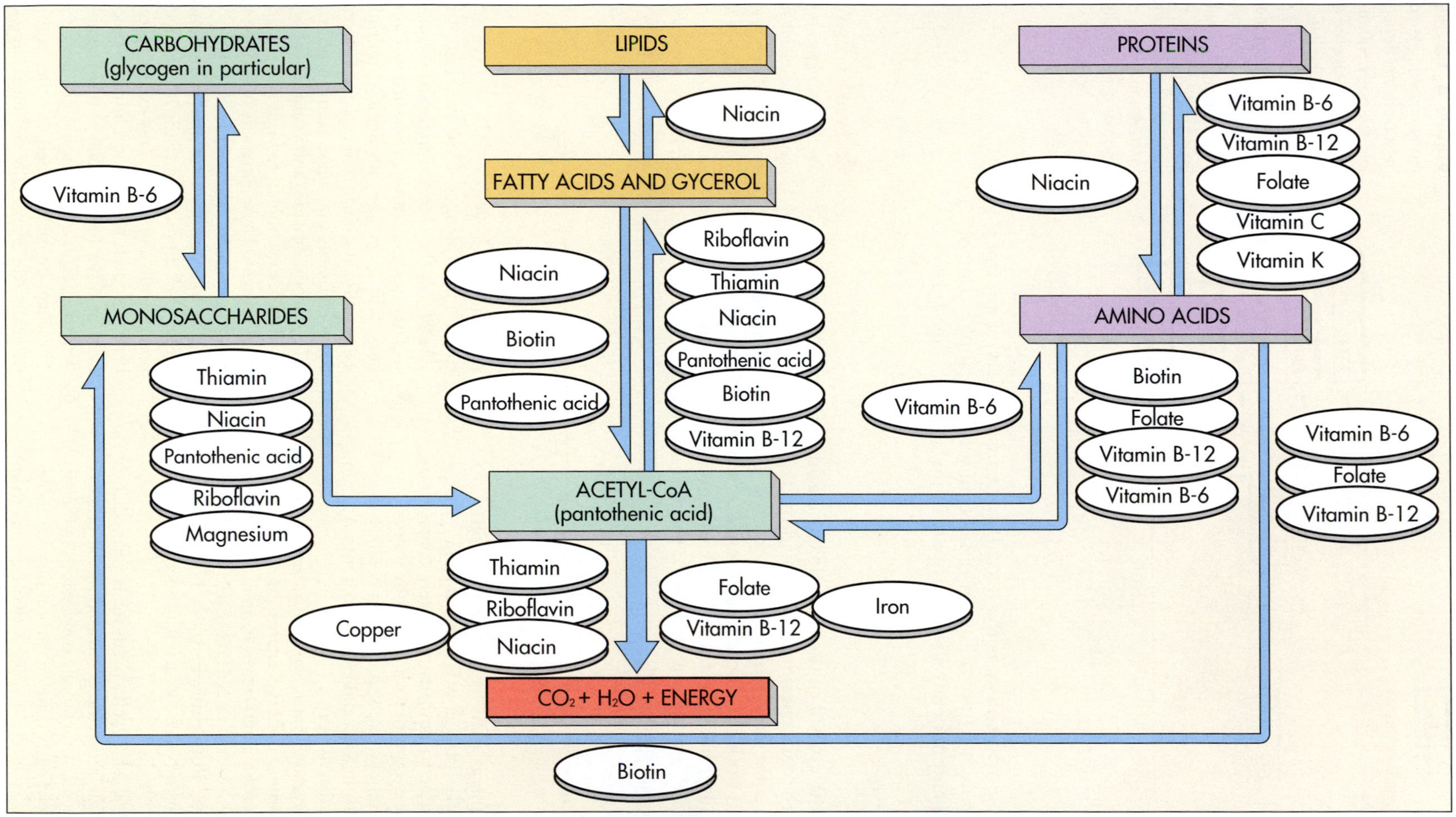

Figure 4-14 Many vitamins and minerals participate in the metabolic pathways. Most notable are the B-vitamins thiamin, riboflavin, niacin, pantothenic acid, biotin, vitamin B-6, folate, and vitamin B-12, as well as the minerals iron and copper. Many health problems can develop from nutrient deficiencies, since so many metabolic pathways depend on nutrient input.

Illustration by William Ober.

molecules, and thus fatty acids in general, cannot participate in gluconeogenesis.

7. Glycolysis takes place in the cytosol of a cell, whereas the citric acid cycle and the electron transport chain take place in the mitochondria. Fatty acid oxidation takes place in the mitochondria, and fatty acids for the most part are synthesized in the cytosol. The synthesis of urea and the pathway for gluconeogenesis both take place partly in the cytosol and partly in the mitochondria. Urea is made in the liver, while glucose is made in the liver and kidneys.

8. Acetyl-CoA is pivotal in cell metabolism because carbohydrates, proteins, amino acids, fatty acids, and alcohol all can yield acetyl-CoA during their metabolism. The coordination of various metabolic pathways for food fuels allows the carbons of glucose to become the carbons of fatty acids and the carbons of some amino acids to become the carbons of glucose.

9. The vitamins thiamin, niacin, riboflavin, biotin, pantothenic acid, and vitamin B-6, and the minerals magnesium, iron, and copper, play important roles in the metabolic pathways.

Study Questions

1. Many vitamins and minerals are used in energy metabolism. Identify three vitamins and/or minerals and describe their roles in ATP synthesis.
2. For what purposes do cells use ATP energy?
3. Explain how the ATP concentration is maintained in a cell. What is the key stimulus to ATP production?
4. What is the "common denominator" compound of the many pathways of energy metabolism (citric acid cycle, glycolysis, beta-oxidation, etc.)? Why is it considered important in the body's chemical processes?
5. What is lactate and how and where is it formed in the cell? Which tissues produce the most lactate? Why?
6. Trace the steps in gluconeogenesis from body protein to the formation of glucose.
7. What is the meaning of the phrase "fats burn in a fire of carbohydrate"?
8. List the metabolic processes discussed throughout this chapter and their location in the cell.
9. Describe the reason why most fatty acids do not turn into glucose in the body.
10. Explain how physicians can use certain aspects of protein metabolism to diagnose kidney or liver disease.

Annotated References

1. Berg JM and others: *Biochemistry.* 5th ed. New York: WH Freeman and Company, 2002.

   Excellent textbook covering the latest findings in metabolism. Details regarding the concepts discussed in this chapter are available. There are also detailed figures showing the various metabolic pathways.

2. Mayes PA: Bioenergetics: The role of ATP. In Murray RK and others (eds.): *Harper's biochemistry.* 25th ed. Stamford, CT: Appleton & Lange, 2000.

   ATP is a high-energy compound due to its chemical structure. The great amount of energy released on breakdown of ATP to ADP and Pi is due to the relief of the repulsion between phosphate groups. ATP acts as the "energy currency" of the cell, transferring energy from substances of higher energy potential to those of lower energy potential.

3. Mayes PA: Overview of intermediary metabolism. In Murray RK and others (eds.): *Harper's biochemistry.* 25th ed. Stamford, CT: Appleton & Lange, 2000.

   In the breakdown of carbohydrate, proteins, and fat for energy needs, all the pathways lead to the production of acetyl-CoA.

4. Mayes PA: The citric acid cycle: The catabolism of acetyl-CoA. In Murray RK and others (eds.): *Harper's biochemistry.* 25th ed. Stamford, CT: Appleton & Lange, 2000.

   The citric acid cycle is a series of reactions in the mitochondria that brings about the catabolism of acetyl-CoA, liberating hydrogen ions. Upon oxidation, these hydrogen ions lead to the release of most of the available energy of tissue fuels and eventual capture as ATP.

5. Mayes PA: Oxidation of fatty acids: Ketogenesis. In Murray RK and others (eds.): *Harper's biochemistry.* 25th ed. Stamford, CT: Appleton & Lange, 2000.

   Ketosis does not occur unless there is an increase in the level of circulating free fatty acids in the bloodstream. These free fatty acids are the precursors of ketone bodies made by the liver.

6. National Institutes of Health Consensus Development Panel: National Institutes of Health Consensus Development Conference Statement: Phenylketonuria: screening and management, October 16–18, 2000. *Pediatrics* 108:972, 2001.

   Genetic testing for phenylketonuria has been in place for almost 40 years, and has been very successful in preventing severe mental retardation in thousands of children and adults. Metabolic control of phenylketonuria is necessary across the lifespan of such individuals.

7. Nelson DL, Cox MM: *Lehninger principles of biochemistry.* 3rd ed., New York, NY: Worth Publishers, 2000.

   Principles of Biochemistry *is a comprehensive look at the subject. Many of the concepts in this chapter are discussed in greater detail in* Principles of Biochemistry. *One new concept is the lower yield of ATP from glucose and fatty acid metabolism compared to what was projected in previous editions of the book. For example, classically the ATP yielded from complete metabolism of glucose was thought to be 36 to 38 ATP. Currently a closer estimate is 30 to 32 ATP.*

8. Nordli DR and others: Experience with the ketogenic diet in infants. *Pediatrics* 108:129, 2001.

   In this study of 32 infants with epilepsy, over half remained seizure-free when treated with a ketogenic diet. This diet also allowed for reduction in the use of anti-seizure medications. The diet was generally tolerated and almost all infants maintained appropriate growth patterns.

9. Saudubray JM and others: Clinical approach to inherited metabolic disorders in neonates: An overview. *Seminars in Neonatology* 7(1):3, 2002.

   There are almost 100 inborn errors of metabolism which can start in infancy; about 20 are amenable to treatment. Typically the infant is born after a normal pregnancy and delivery, but soon deteriorates physically for no apparent reason and does not respond to typical medical therapy. Presenting symptoms are seizures, evidence of liver failure, various heart disorders, and hypoglycemia.

10. Trahms CM: Medical nutrition therapy for metabolic disorders. In *Krause's food, nutrition, & diet therapy.* 10th ed. Mahan LK, Escott-Stump S (eds.). Philadelphia: WB Saunders Company, 2000.

    Excellent chapter on the medical nutrition therapy for inborn errors of metabolism. The chapter provides much detail on the role of nutrition in such disorders.

Take | Action

I. Put Your Knowledge of Metabolism into Practice.

A friend is very overweight and describes to you his method of weight loss. He fasted completely for 1 week and then initiated a strict diet of 400 to 600 kcal/day under a physician's supervision. The food energy comes from a liquid formula, which he drinks for breakfast. He skips lunch and eats a small dinner of 3 ounces of protein, ½ cup of vegetables, 1 cup of fruit, and two starch items (a small potato, a piece of bread, etc.). He has lost approximately 25 pounds in 12 weeks.

Based on your knowledge of energy metabolism, answer the following questions he poses:

1. During the fasting stage, what were the likely sources of energy for the body's cells? What metabolic processes occurred to provide glucose for red blood cells? brain? kidneys?
2. During the restrictive phase, how did the metabolic processes in the body most likely change from the fasting state?

Possible Answers

1. During fasting, gluconeogenesis supplied the glucose needed for the brain, red blood cells, and kidneys. The carbons used came mostly from body protein, leading to a decrease in lean body mass. Eventually, production of ketone bodies from fatty acid breakdown increased, leading to elevated ketone bodies in the blood and, in turn, greater use of ketone bodies by many types of body cells. Insulin output fell, leading to glycogen depletion in the liver. Fatty acids from fat stores were dumped into the bloodstream. Thus, fatty acids became the major energy-yielding fuel for the body.
2. During the restrictive phase, insulin output in the body rose as carbohydrate intake increased. This led to a reduction in production of ketone bodies and spared some body protein from being used as a source of carbons for glucose synthesis. The body switched from using primarily fat as fuel to using more of a mixture of fat and carbohydrate.

II. Reinforce Your Knowledge of Metabolism.

By this stage in your education, you have likely had a number of exposures to the topic of cell metabolism. Review your textbooks or notes from previous courses that discussed metabolism and see how the following topics were presented from the standpoint of that discipline. For example, coverage of glycolysis might have a different emphasis in a biology class than in a nutrition class.

ATP
Glycolysis
Citric acid cycle
Electron transport chain
Hormones that regulate aspects of metabolism:
  Insulin
  Glucagon
Enzyme activity

A general knowledge of metabolism will benefit you throughout a career in the sciences, whether in the health sciences or the biological sciences. Understanding metabolism especially will help you see how new developments in your field relate to cell function.

Inborn Errors of Metabolism

Your knowledge of metabolism has a very practical application: Some of us have inborn errors of metabolism.[9] This means that the person lacks a specific enzyme to perform normal metabolic functions. The metabolic pathway in which this enzyme is supposed to participate now no longer functions properly. Typically this will cause alternative metabolic products to be formed, some of which are toxic to the body.

How does one develop an inborn error of metabolism? The person inherits defective genes coding for a specific enzyme from both parents. Each parent is likely a carrier in that they have one healthy gene and one defective gene for the enzyme in their chromosomes. Each parent then donates the defective form of the gene to the offspring, causing the offspring to have two defective copies of the gene, and therefore little or no activity of the enzyme that the gene normally would produce. Chapter 7 will cover in detail how a gene is used to produce proteins such as enzymes. For now, realize that if one has a defective gene, one will produce a defective protein based on the instructions contained in that defective gene. There is also the possibility that one or both parents may actually have the disease themselves and not simply be carriers. Generally, however, these individuals are counseled against having children, or at the very least should see a genetic counselor to assess the risk of passing the inborn error of metabolism on to their offspring.

The characteristics of inborn errors of metabolism include:

- Appearance soon after birth. Such a disorder is suspected when otherwise physically well children develop loss of appetite, vomiting, dehydration, physical weakness, or developmental delays soon after birth. For some of these conditions, infants are screened for the potential to have a specific inborn error of metabolism, such as phenylketonuria (PKU). (Recall PKU was discussed in Chapter 1.)
- Very specific, involving only one or a few enzymes. These enzymes usually participate in catabolic pathways (in which compounds are degraded), such as for the amino acid phenylalanine.
- No cure is possible, but typically inborn errors of metabolism can be controlled. This control might include reducing intake of the substance that must be catabolized, such as phenylalanine. Other examples of therapies in specific cases include pharmacological doses of vitamins, such as vitamin B-12, and replacement of the blocked product, such as the amino acid tyrosine in PKU (see next section for details).

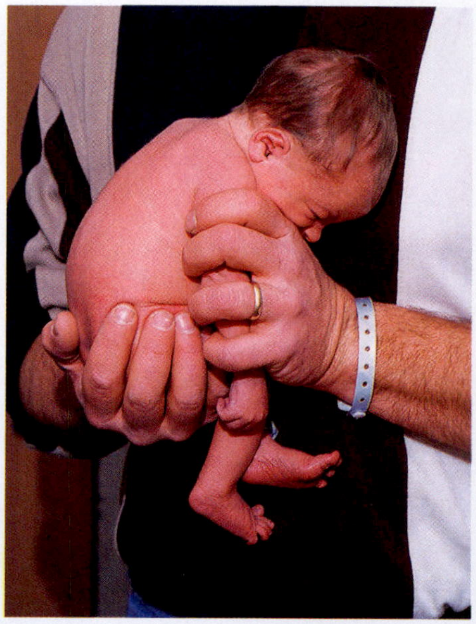

An infant who does not develop properly may have an inborn error of metabolism. A physician needs to investigate this possibility.

Phenylketonuria

The majority of cases of PKU occur because the enzyme phenylalanine hydroxylase does not function efficiently in the liver. Because of this, phenylalanine builds up in the blood of the person with PKU. If not corrected early (within 30 days of birth), this buildup of phenylalanine leads to production of toxic phenylalanine by-products, such as phenylpyruvic acid. This then can lead to severe mental retardation.

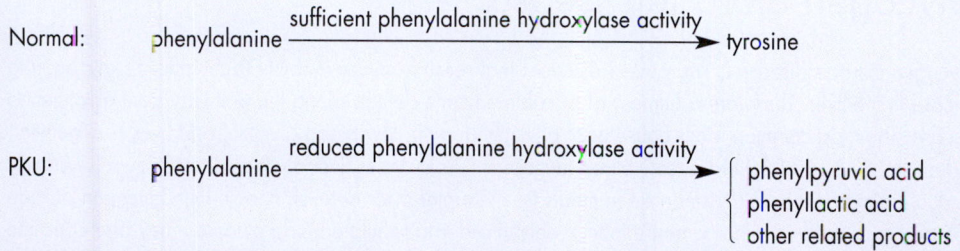

Normal: phenylalanine —(sufficient phenylalanine hydroxylase activity)→ tyrosine

PKU: phenylalanine —(reduced phenylalanine hydroxylase activity)→ { phenylpyruvic acid; phenyllactic acid; other related products }

PKU occurs in about one per 10,000 births. Most carriers can be detected with a simple blood test. People of Irish descent are especially affected. Today, most infants are diagnosed within a few days of life, and started on a phenylalanine-restricted diet.[6] They are placed on a low-phenylalanine infant formula, which is very expensive. During infancy, nutritional needs can change on a weekly basis, so these infants are monitored continually through blood phenylalanine testing.

With regard to nutrient intake, phenylalanine, protein, and energy intakes must be carefully monitored. Phenylalanine is an essential amino acid, which means that even someone with PKU has to obtain

Children with PKU must be careful not to consume diet soft drinks containing aspartame, as this contains phenylalanine.

phenylalanine from his or her diet; however, the amount of phenylalanine consumed needs to be monitored carefully to prevent toxic amounts from building up.

Starting in infancy, special formulas are available to provide nutrients for those with PKU. Because infants have high-protein needs, satisfying protein requirements—without also having high intakes of phenylalanine—is impossible without these specially prepared formulas. Some of these formulas provide no phenylalanine; others provide a small amount. For infants, formulas are designed to provide about 90% of protein needs and 80% of energy needs. Human milk or regular infant formula then can be used to make up the difference.[10]

Later, foods can be used to make up the difference, especially those low in phenylalanine. Fruits and vegetables are naturally low in phenylalanine, and breads and cereals have a moderate amount. Dairy products, eggs, meats, nuts, and cheeses are very high in phenylalanine, and so are not allowed on the diet. Diet soft drinks and other foods and beverages containing the alternative sweetener aspartame are also not allowed as these contain phenylalanine (see Chapter 5 for details). Older children and adults can use a formula that is very low in phenylalanine. This allows the person to consume more foods, but still limits intake of phenylalanine. Overall, the majority of the person's nutrient intake throughout life will come from a special formula. Note that this formula has a very disagreeable smell and taste.

The diet is ideally followed for life. Physicians used to recommend that it was appropriate to end the diet after age 6 since brain development was complete. Later it was found, however, that diet discontinuation led to decreased intelligence and behavior problems, such as aggressiveness, hyperactivity, and inattention.[6]

If a woman with PKU has gone off the diet, she needs to return to the diet at least 6 months before becoming pregnant. Otherwise the fetus—even though it does not have PKU—will be exposed to a high blood phenylalanine and related toxic products from the mother. This could result in miscarriage, or the infant could be born with a low birth weight or heart defects.

Galactosemia

galactosemia A rare genetic disease characterized by the buildup of the single sugar galactose in the bloodstream, resulting from the inability of the liver to metabolize it. If present at birth and left untreated, this disease can cause severe mental retardation and cataracts in the infant.

In **galactosemia,** two principal specific enzyme defects lead to a reduction in the galactose metabolism to glucose (a third form is very rare). Galactose then builds up in the bloodstream; this can lead to very serious bacterial infections, mental retardation, and cataracts in the eye. Such infants typically develop vomiting after a few days of consuming infant formula or breast milk. Both contain much galactose as part of the milk sugar lactose. Such a child will be switched to a soy formula. In addition, all dairy products and other lactose-containing products (butter, milk solids), organ meats, and some fruits and vegetables must be avoided.[10] Strict label reading is also important for controlling the disease as lactose can be found in a variety of products. Note that even in well-controlled cases, slight mental retardation (such as speech delays) and cataracts are seen. Galactosemia occurs in 1 in 65,000 births.

Glycogen Storage Disease

Glycogen storage disease is a group of diseases that result from the inability to metabolize glycogen to glucose in the liver. There are a number of possible enzyme defects along the pathway from glycogen to glucose. The most common forms cause poor physical growth, low blood glucose, and liver enlargement, and occur in 1 in 60,000 births. Low blood glucose results because liver glycogen breakdown is typically used to maintain blood glucose between meals (see Chapter 5 for details). People with glycogen storage disease typically have to consume frequent meals in order to regulate blood glucose. They also consume raw cornstarch between meals; this is slowly digested and so helps maintain steady blood glucose. Careful monitoring of blood glucose is very important in these people in order to know when blood glucose is too low and to treat it accordingly.[10]

There also are a number of other very rare inborn errors of metabolism, such as those involving various amino acids, fatty acids, and the sugars fructose and sucrose.[10] Typically, in large hospitals and in state health departments, there are physicians, nurses, and registered dietitians that can help the affected person and their family with these and other inborn errors of metabolism.

chapter 5

Carbohydrates

Chapter | Outline

Case | Scenario

Myeshia is a 19-year-old African American female who recently read about the health benefits of calcium and decided to increase her intake of dairy products. To start, she drank 1 cup of 1% milk at lunch. Not long afterward, she experienced bloating, cramping, and increased gas production. She suspected that the source of this pain was the milk she consumed, especially since her parents and her sister complain of the same problem. She wanted to try to determine if the milk was, in fact, the cause of her gastrointestinal discomfort. So the next day she substituted a cup of yogurt for the glass of milk at lunch. She had heard that yogurt is easier to tolerate than milk for some people. Subsequently, she did not have any pain. What has Myeshia discovered? What component of milk is likely causing the problem?

Refresh | Your Memory

As you begin your study of carbohydrates in Chapter 5, you may want to review:

- The health claims on food labels for various carbohydrates in Chapter 2.
- The anatomy and physiology of digestion and absorption in Chapter 3.
- The processes of glycolysis, gluconeogenesis, and ketosis in Chapter 4.

Boost | Your Study

Check out the ***Perspectives in Nutrition: Online Learning Center*** **www.mhhe.com/wardlawpers6** *for quizzes, flash cards, activities, and web links designed to further help you learn about carbohydrates.*

Chapter | Objectives

Chapter 5 is designed to allow you to:

1. Identify the basic structures and food sources of the major carbohydrates—monosaccharides, disaccharides, polysaccharides (e.g., starches), and fiber.
2. List the functions of carbohydrate in the body and the problems that result from not eating enough carbohydrate.
3. Outline the beneficial effects of fiber on the body.
4. State the RDA for carbohydrate and various guidelines for carbohydrate intake.
5. Describe food sources of carbohydrate and list some alternate sweeteners.
6. Describe the regulation of blood glucose and the nutrients that can become blood glucose.
7. Identify the consequences of lactose maldigestion and diabetes, and explain appropriate dietary measures to take to reduce these health problems.

What did you eat to obtain the energy you are using right now? The next three chapters will examine this question by focusing on the nutrients the human body uses for fuel. These energy-yielding nutrients are mainly carbohydrates (on average, 4 kcal/g) and fats and oils (on average, 9 kcal/g). Little of the other common fuel—protein (on average, 4 kcal/g)—is used for that purpose by the body. Most people know that potatoes have carbohydrates and steak has fat and protein, but few people, besides scientists and registered dietitians, know what those terms signify.

It is likely that you have recently consumed fruits, vegetables, dairy products, cereal, breads, and pasta. All these foods supply carbohydrates.[4] Unfortunately, the benefits of these foods are often misunderstood. Many people think carbohydrate-rich foods are fattening—they are not. Pound for pound, carbohydrates are much less fattening than fats and oils. Furthermore, carbohydrates, especially fiber-rich foods such as fruits, vegetables, whole grains, and legumes, have been promoted by many experts for the important health benefits these foods supply.[8, 10, 13] Some people think sugars necessarily cause diabetes or hyperactivity—not so, according to well-designed scientific investigations. Almost all carbohydrate-rich foods, except pure sugars, provide essential nutrients and should constitute 45 to 60% of our daily energy intake.[6] Let's take a closer look at carbohydrates.

Carbohydrates—An Introduction

Carbohydrates are a primary fuel source for some cells, such as those in the nervous system and red blood cells. Muscles also rely on a dependable supply of carbohydrate in order to support intense physical activity. Yielding on average 4 kcal/g, carbohydrates are a readily available fuel for all cells in the form of blood glucose and stored in the liver and muscles as glycogen. Carbohydrate stored in the liver can be used to maintain blood glucose availability in times when the diet does not supply enough. Regular intake of carbohydrate is important, because liver glycogen stores are exhausted in about 18 hours if no carbohydrate is consumed. After that point, the body is forced to produce its own carbohydrate from body and food protein; this eventually leads to health problems.[6]

We have sensors on our tongues that recognize sweet carbohydrates. Researchers surmise that this sweetness indicated a safe energy source to early humans, and so carbohydrate became an important energy source. The returning Crusaders brought sugar from the Holy Land to Europe. Columbus introduced sugarcane to the Americas. The French later exploited sugar beets as a source of sugar.

Primarily choosing the healthiest carbohydrate sources, while moderating intake of those that are less healthful, contributes to a well-planned diet. It is difficult to eat so little carbohydrate that body needs are not met, but it is easy to overconsume the carbohydrates that can contribute to health problems.[6] Let's explore this concept further as we look at carbohydrates in detail.

Fruits such as peaches are an excellent source of carbohydrate for a diet.

Structures and Functions of Simple Carbohydrates

Most forms of carbohydrates are composed of carbon, hydrogen, and oxygen in the ratio of 1:2:1, respectively. The general formula is $(CH_2O)n$, where n represents the number of times the ratio is repeated. The chemical formula for glucose is $C_6H_{12}O_6$, or $(CH_2O)_6$. The simpler forms of carbohydrates are called **sugars** and often take the form of single or double sugars, called **monosaccharides** and **disaccharides,** respectively. The more complex forms of carbohydrates are **polysaccharides,** typically either **starches** or **fibers.**[6]

Plants use carbon dioxide, water, and energy (from the sun) to produce the carbohydrates we eat. This complex process is called **photosynthesis.**

$$CO_2 + H_2O \rightarrow (CH_2O)n + O_2$$

Monosaccharides: Glucose, Fructose, and Galactose

The common monosaccharides (*mono* meaning "one" and *saccharide* meaning "sugar") are glucose, fructose, and galactose. Glucose is the principal monosaccharide in the body. Other names for glucose are *dextrose* or *blood sugar.* In Figure 5-1, the chemical structure of glucose is shown in both its linear and ring forms. Glucose exists in the body in the ring form. Because it is a six-carbon monosaccharide, glucose is called a **hexose** (*hex* meaning "six," for six carbons; *ose* is the standard word ending for carbohydrates).[3]

Fructose is related to glucose. It is a hexose and can form either a five- or six-member ring (see Fig. 5-1). Fructose, also called levulose, is found in

- Fruit
- Honey (about half fructose, half glucose)
- **High-fructose corn syrup,** which is used in the production of soft drinks, frozen desserts, and confections. The presence of fructose in these products makes it a major sugar in our diets. In most North American diets, fructose accounts for about 8 to 10% of total energy intake.

sugar A simple carbohydrate with the chemical composition $(CH_2O)n$. Most sugars form ringed structures when in solution. Generally refers to monosaccharides and disaccharides.

monosaccharide A class of simple sugars, such as glucose, which is not broken down further during digestion.

disaccharides A class of sugars formed by the chemical bonding of two monosaccharides.

polysaccharides Carbohydrates containing many glucose units, from 10 to 1000 or more.

starch A carbohydrate made of multiple units of glucose attached together in a form the body can digest; also known as *complex carbohydrate.*

fiber Substances in plant foods that are not digested by the processes that take place in the stomach or small intestine. These add bulk to feces. Fibers naturally found in foods are also called dietary fiber.

hexose A general term describing a carbohydrate containing six carbons.

fructose A monosaccharide with six carbons that form a five-membered or six-membered ring with oxygen in the ring; found in fruits and honey.

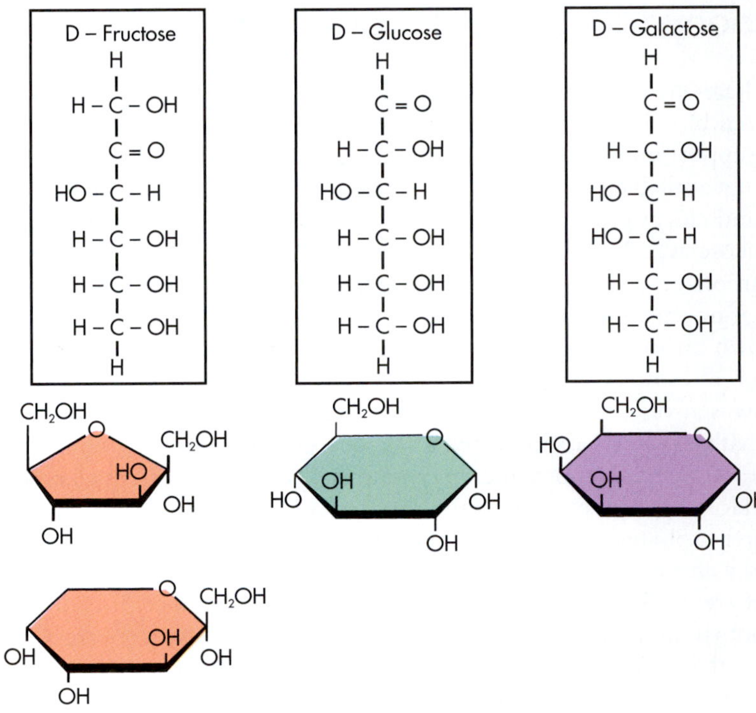

Figure 5-1 Forms of the D-isomer of the six-carbon monosaccharides—fructose, glucose, and galactose—shown in the linear form and in the ring form where each corner represents a carbon atom unless otherwise indicated. Hydrogen atoms are also omitted. (Appendix A reviews this shortcut notation.) This ring structure is the predominant form when in solution. Only the D-isomer forms are metabolized by the body. Appendix A also reviews the concepts of isomers.

Illustration by William Ober.

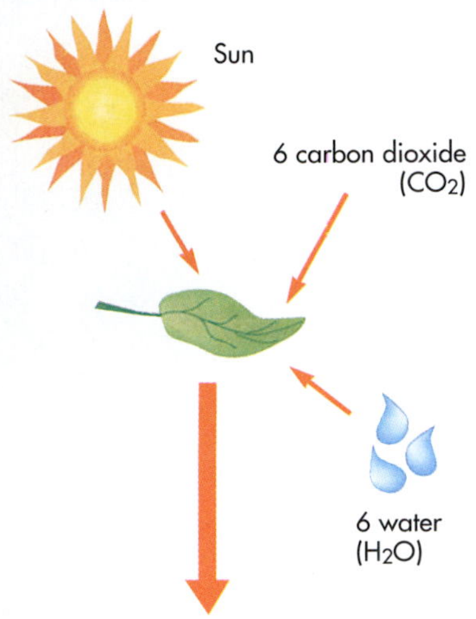

A summary of photosynthesis. Glucose is stored in the leaf but can also undergo further metabolism to form starch and fiber in the plant.

lactic acid A three-carbon acid, also called lactate, that is formed during anaerobic cell metabolism; a partial breakdown product of glucose.

galactose A six-carbon monosaccharide; an isomer of glucose.

sorbitol An alcohol derivative of glucose that yields about 3 kcal/g but is slowly absorbed from the small intestine. It is used in some sugarless gums and dietetic foods.

maltose Glucose bonded to glucose.

sucrose Fructose bonded to glucose; table sugar.

lactose A sugar composed of glucose linked to another sugar called galactose.

alpha (α) bond A type of bond that can be digested by human intestinal enzymes; drawn as C⌞O⌟C.

beta (β) bond A type of bond that cannot be broken by human intestinal enzymes during digestion when it is part of a long chain of glucose molecules (e.g. cellulose) drawn as C⌜O⌟C.

Fructose, after absorption by the small intestine and transport to the liver, is almost all metabolized to glucose or to intermediates in the glycolysis pathway. Some fructose is then converted to glycogen, **lactic acid,** or fat, depending on the amount consumed. Synthesis of lactic acid and fat is stimulated by fructose intakes that are two or more times typical intakes.

Galactose is the third major monosaccharide of nutritional importance. Comparison of the structure of this simple sugar with that of glucose shows that the two structures are almost identical, except that the hydrogen (–H) and the hydroxyl group (–OH) on carbon-4 are reversed (review Fig. 5-1). Galactose is not usually found free in nature in large quantities but, rather, combines with glucose to form a disaccharide called *lactose* (present in milk and other dairy products). Once absorbed into the body, galactose is converted into glucose in the liver, which is used to provide immediate energy or is stored as *glycogen*.

Another monosaccharide found in nature is **ribose,** a five-carbon sugar (or pentose; *penta* means "five"). This is present in a cell's genetic material. Very little ribose is present in our diet; we produce this sugar from other foods we eat.

Finally, a few sugar alcohols are present in foods and will be discussed later in this chapter, in the section on nutritive sweeteners in foods. Currently, the major sugar alcohol used in the manufacture of edible products is **sorbitol.**

Once you are familiar with the chemical forms of the sugars, it is much easier to understand how they are interrelated, combined, digested, metabolized, and synthesized.

Disaccharides: Maltose, Sucrose, and Lactose

Carbohydrates containing two sugar units are called disaccharides (*di* means "two"). These are formed when two monosaccharides combine. The three most common disaccharides found in nature are **maltose, sucrose,** and **lactose.** All contain glucose (Fig. 5-2).[6]

One carbon on each participating monosaccharide is chemically bound together by oxygen. Two forms of this C—O—C bond exist in nature, called **alpha (α) bonds** and **beta (β) bonds,** and are depicted slightly differently. As shown in Figure 5-2, maltose and sucrose contain the alpha form, whereas lactose contains the beta form. Many

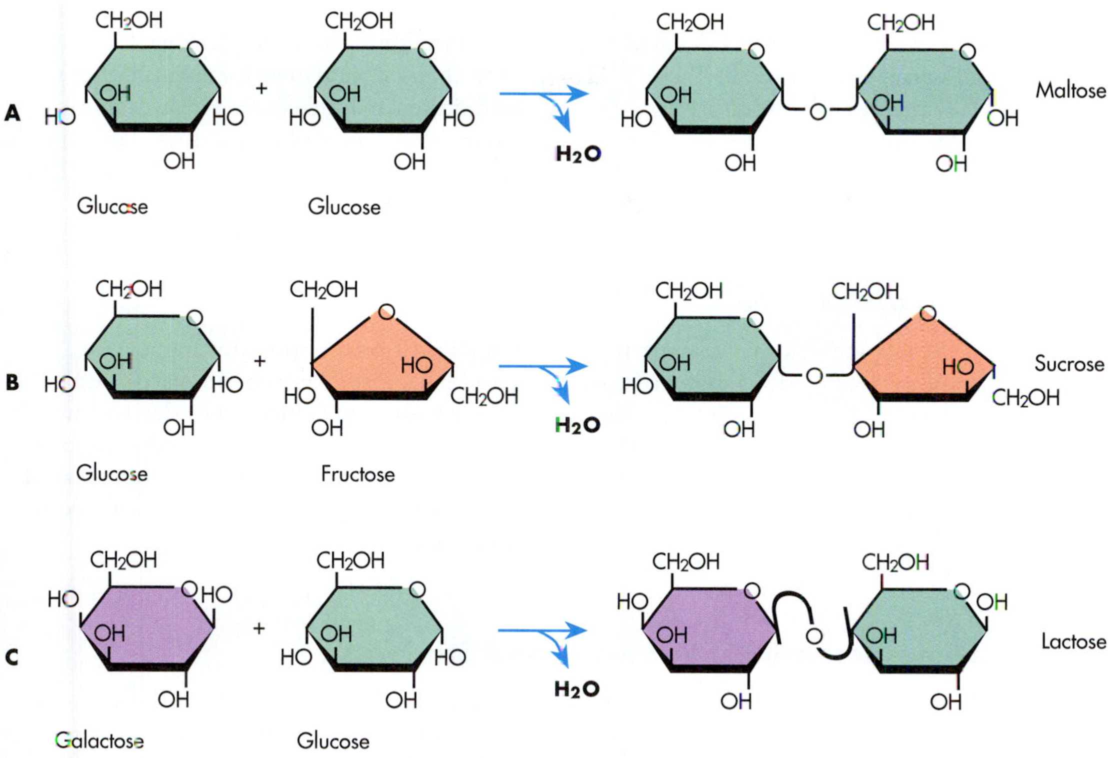

Figure 5-2 Joining of two monosaccharides forms a disaccharide. (*A*) Maltose is made up of two glucose molecules and is formed in germinating grains. (*B*) Sucrose, or common table sugar, is made up of glucose and fructose. (*C*) Lactose, or milk sugar, is made up of glucose and galactose. Note that lactose contains a different type of bond (beta, or β) from that of maltose and sucrose (alpha, or α), a property that makes lactose difficult to digest for individuals who show a low activity of the enzyme lactase.
Illustration by William Ober.

carbohydrates contain glucose polymers with the individual molecules bonded together by either alpha or beta bonds. Humans can digest such carbohydrates only if the glucose molecules are linked by alpha bonds.[3] This topic will be covered later in this chapter, when fiber is discussed.

Maltose consists of two glucose molecules joined by an alpha bond. When seeds sprout, they produce enzymes that break down the polysaccharides (starch) to sugars such as maltose and glucose. It is this sugar that provides the energy for the plant to initiate growth. In a process called malting, the sprouting process is stopped by heat. This is the first step in the production of alcoholic beverages such as beer. Yeast in the absence of oxygen converts most of the carbohydrates to ethanol (alcohol) and carbon dioxide in a process called **fermentation.** There will be more about the production of alcoholic products in Chapter 8. Few other food products and beverages contain maltose. In fact, most maltose that we ultimately digest in the small intestine is produced during the digestion of starch (see a later section on digestion in this chapter).

fermentation The conversion, without the use of oxygen, of carbohydrates to alcohols, acids, and carbon dioxide.

Sucrose, common table sugar, is composed of glucose and fructose linked via an alpha bond. Large amounts of sucrose are found only in plants, such as sugarcane, sugar beets, and maple syrup. The sucrose from these sources may be purified to various degrees. Brown, white, and powdered sugars are common forms of sucrose sold in grocery stores.

Lactose, the primary sugar in milk and milk products, consists of glucose joined to galactose via a beta bond. As discussed in a later section of this chapter, many people are unable to digest large amounts of lactose because they don't produce enough of the enzyme lactase that is capable of breaking its beta bond. This can cause intestinal gas, bloating, cramping, and discomfort as the unabsorbed lactose is metabolized into acids and gases by bacteria in the large intestine.[17]

A common misconception is that honey contains vitamins and minerals. You can prove to yourself that honey is no more nutritious than sucrose by consulting Appendix N. Only the sweetener molasses, a by-product of sucrose production, contains any appreciable amount of minerals. However, our consumption of molasses is very low.

Simple	**Monosaccharides**	
↓	Glucose, fructose, galactose	
	Disaccharides	
	Sucrose, lactose, maltose	
	Oligosaccharides	
	Raffinose, stachyose	
	Polysaccharides	
	Starches (amylose and amylopectin), glycogen	
Complex	Most fibers	

You are likely to encounter many different words referring to the monosaccharides and disaccharides just discussed or products containing these simple sugars. Note that all of the terms listed in Table 5-7 later in the chapter are names for sugars either naturally present in food products or added during their manufacture. These monosaccharides and disaccharides are often referred to as *simple sugars* because they contain only one or two sugar units and, therefore, have a simple chemical structure. Food labels lump all these sugars under one category, listing them as "sugars."

Concept | Check

Monosaccharides are single sugars. From a nutritional standpoint, important monosaccharides are glucose, fructose, and galactose. Disaccharides are double sugars. The major disaccharides in the diet are sucrose (glucose bonded to fructose), maltose (glucose bonded to glucose), and lactose (glucose bonded to galactose). The disaccharides have either alpha or beta bonds. Our bodies are unable to break down most of the beta bonds. Once absorbed into the body, most carbohydrates are ultimately transformed into glucose by the liver.

Oligosaccharides: Raffinose and Stachyose

raffinose An indigestible oligosaccharide made of three monosaccharides (galactose-glucose-fructose).

stachyose An indigestible oligosaccharide made of four monosaccharides (galactose-galactose-glucose-fructose).

From a nutritional standpoint, oligosaccharides contain 3 to about 10 single sugar units (*oligo* means "scant").[6] (Chemists and biochemists, however, often lump disaccharides in the oligosaccharide category as well.[3]) Two oligosaccharides of nutritional importance are **raffinose** and **stachyose,** which are found in beans and other legumes. These are constructed of typical monosaccharides but are bonded together in such a way that digestive enzymes cannot break them apart. Thus, when we consume beans and other legumes, raffinose and stachyose remain undigested on reaching the large intestine. There, bacteria metabolize them, producing gas and other by-products.

Many people have no trouble digesting beans and other legumes, but others experience unpleasant side effects from intestinal gas. An enzyme preparation called Beano®, which prevents these side effects, can help such people if taken right before a meal. Once consumed, the enzyme preparation breaks down many of the indigestible oligosaccharides in legumes and other vegetables in the gastrointestinal tract before they reach the large intestine. Beano® is made from mold, so persons sensitive to molds may react allergically and should avoid it or use with caution. For more information or free samples, contact the manufacturer (800-257-8650).

Beano® can be used to reduce intestinal gas produced by bacterial metabolism of oligosaccharides in the large intestine.

Structures and Functions of the More Complex Carbohydrates

The polysaccharides, often referred to as *complex carbohydrates,* include some that are digestible (e.g., starch) and some that are largely indigestible, such as fiber.

Digestible Polysaccharides: Starch and Glycogen

Polysaccharides are polymers containing many monosaccharide units, up to 1000 or more. Most polysaccharides of nutritional importance are synthesized from glucose, as when vegetables turn glucose into starch during maturation. This makes peas and corn sweetest when they are young. Starch, the major digestible polysaccharide in our diet, is the storage form of energy in plants. There are two types of plant starch—**amylose** and **amylopectin**—both of which are a source of energy for plants and animals.

amylose A straight-chain type of starch composed of glucose units.

amylopectin A branched-chain type of starch composed of glucose units.

Both amylose and amylopectin contain many glucose units linked by alpha (digestible) bonds. The primary difference between the two types of starch is that amylose

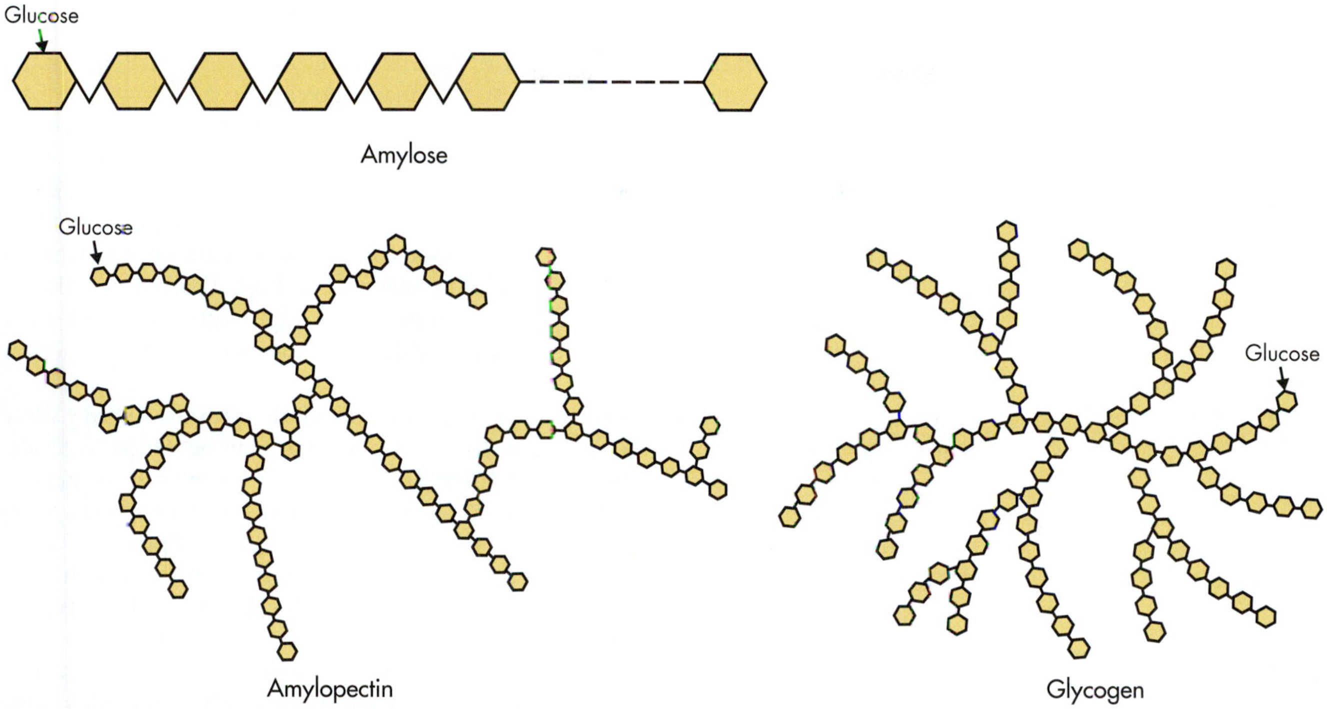

Figure 5-3 Some common starches. We consume essentially no glycogen. All glycogen found in the body is made by our cells, primarily in the liver and muscles.

is a straight-chain polymer, whereas amylopectin is highly branched (Fig. 5-3). Cooking increases the digestibility of these starches by making them more soluble in water and thus more available for attack by digestive enzymes. Amylose and amylopectin are found in potatoes, beans, breads, pasta, rice, and other starchy products, typically in a ratio of about 1:4. Amylopectin raises blood glucose much more readily than amylose, since its numerous branches provide many areas for digestive enzyme activity. The enzymes act only at the ends of the glucose chains. The more numerous the branches of a starch, the more sites (ends) are available for enzyme action (see the discussion of glycemic index in a later section of this chapter).[6]

The branches in amylopectin also allow it to form a very stable starch gel, enabling it to retain water and resist water seepage. Food manufacturers commonly use starches rich in amylopectin in sauces and gravies for frozen foods because they remain stable over a wide temperature range. Manufacturers may also use processes to bond the starch molecules to one another, further increasing their stability. The resulting product, called **modified food starch,** is used in baby foods, salad dressings, and instant puddings.

Glycogen, the storage form of carbohydrate in humans and other animals, is a glucose polymer with alpha bonds and numerous branches. The amount of carbohydrate in a diet greatly influences the glycogen stored. The structure of glycogen is similar to that of amylopectin, but the branching patterns are more complicated (review Fig. 5-3). As with amylopectin, because glycogen is so highly branched, it is quickly broken down by enzymes in body cells in which it is stored.[6] The liver and muscles are the major storage sites for glycogen. Because only about 120 kcal of glucose are available as such in body fluids, muscle and liver storage sites for carbohydrate energy—amounting to about 1800 kcal—are extremely important. As noted in this chapter's introduction, the 400 kcal of liver glycogen can be turned into blood glucose, while the 1400 kcal of muscle glycogen cannot. Still, glycogen in muscles supplies glucose for muscle use, especially during high-intensity and endurance exercise. (See Chapter 14 for a detailed discussion of carbohydrate use during physical activity.)

As some vegetables age, their sugars are converted to starches.

modified food starch A product consisting of chemically linked starch molecules that is more stable than normal, unmodified starches.

dietary fiber Fiber found in food.

functional fiber Fiber added to foods that has shown to provide health benefits.

cellulose A straight-chain polysaccharide of glucose molecules that is undigestible because of the presence of beta bonds; part of insoluble fiber.

hemicellulose A dietary fiber containing xylose, galactose, glucose, and other monosaccharides bonded together.

pectin A dietary fiber containing chains of galacturonic acid and other monosaccharides; characteristically found between plant cell walls.

gums A dietary fiber containing chains of galactose, glucuronic acid, and other monosaccharides; characteristically found in exudates from plant stems.

mucilages A dietary fiber consisting of chains of galactose, mannose, and other monosaccharides; characteristically found in seaweed.

lignins An insoluble fiber made up of a multiringed alcohol (noncarbohydrate) structure.

whole grains Grains containing the entire seed of the plant, including the bran, germ, and endosperm (starchy interior).

insoluble fibers Fibers that mostly do not dissolve in water and are not generally metabolized by bacteria in the large intestine. These include cellulose, some hemicelluloses, and lignins. More formally called poorly fermented fibers.

Indigestible Polysaccharides: Fibers

Folklore surrounding fiber has been a part of American culture since the 1800s. In the 1820s and 1830s, a minister named Sylvester Graham traveled up and down the East Coast extolling the virtues of fiber. He left us a legacy—the graham cracker. However, today's graham cracker bears little resemblance to the whole-grain product he promoted. The next wave of fiber frenzy crested in the mid-1870s with Dr. John Harvey Kellogg and his brother William, of breakfast cereal fame. Dr. Kellogg became the first person to earn a million dollars from "health foods." One of his patients was Charles W. Post, who followed the Kelloggs' lead and started the Post Toasted Cornflakes Company. In 1901 alone, Post netted $1 million from his Grape-Nuts cereal and other products. As you will see, present-day scientific evidence supports this early promotion of fiber as part of a total diet.

The definition of fiber has recently been expanded to include both the **dietary fiber** that is found naturally in foods, and other forms of fiber that may be added to foods. This second category is called **functional fiber;** any of these fibers must show beneficial effects in humans to be included in the category. **Total fiber** (or just the term *fiber*) is then the combination of dietary fiber and functional fiber in the food product.[6] Currently the Nutrition Facts label only includes the category dietary fiber; the label has yet to be updated to reflect the latest definition of fiber by the Food and Nutrition Board.

In terms of their chemical composition, fibers are composed primarily of the nonstarch polysaccharides **cellulose, hemicelluloses, pectins, gums,** and **mucilages.** The only noncarbohydrate components of dietary fibers are **lignins,** which includes complex alcohol derivatives (Table 5-1). Almost all forms of fiber come from plants and, as a group, none are digested in the human stomach or small intestine.[6]

Cellulose is a straight-chain glucose polymer similar to amylose; however, unlike amylose, which contains alpha bonds, the glucose units in cellulose are linked by beta bonds. As noted earlier, glucose molecules joined by beta bonds are not broken down by human digestive enzymes. Thus, cellulose is not digestible by humans and is classified as a dietary fiber, not a starch. Because the long glucose chains of cellulose are linear, they can pack closely together, forming fibrous structures of great strength. Overall, cellulose, hemicelluloses, and lignins form the structural part of the plant. A cotton ball is pure cellulose. Bran fiber is rich in hemicelluloses. Since bran layers form the outer covering of all grains, **whole grains** are good sources of this fiber (Fig. 5-4). The woody fibers in broccoli are partly lignins. As a class, these undigestible dietary fibers generally do not dissolve in water and thus are called **insoluble fibers** (or poorly fermented fibers).

Table 5-1 Classification of Dietary Fibers

Type	Component(s)	Examples	Physiological Effects	Major Food Sources
Insoluble (Poorly Fermented)				
Noncarbohydrate	Lignins	Wheat bran	Increases fecal bulk; estrogen-like effects	Whole grains
Carbohydrate	Cellulose Hemicelluloses	Wheat products Brown rice	Increases fecal bulk Decreases intestinal transit time	All plants Wheat, rye, rice, vegetables
Soluble (Viscous)				
Carbohydrate	Pectins, gums, mucilages, some hemicelluloses	Apples, bananas, oranges, carrots, barley, oats, kidney beans	Delays gastric emptying; slows glucose absorption; can lower blood cholesterol	Citrus fruits, oat products (beta-glucan in particular), beans, thickeners added to foods

Pectins, gums, and mucilages are found inside and around plant cells. They help "glue" plant cells together (review Fig. 5-4). These dietary fibers either dissolve or swell when put into water and thus are called **soluble fibers** (or viscous fibers). Some forms of hemicellulose also fall into this soluble-fiber category. Soluble fibers such as gum arabic, guar gum, locust bean gum, and various pectins are present in numerous food products, especially salad dressings, inexpensive ice creams, jams, and jellies. Other rich sources of soluble fibers include fruits and vegetables in general, soybean fiber, rice bran, and **psyllium** seeds (found in many commercial fiber laxatives).

soluble fibers Fibers that either dissolve or swell in water and are metabolized (fermented) by bacteria in the large intestine. These include pectins, gums, and mucilages. More formally called viscous fibers.

psyllium A mostly soluble type of dietary fiber found in the seeds of the plantain plant.

One workable definition of fiber is the foodstuffs that remain undigested as they enter the large intestine. There is really no common property that characterizes various fibers, except their ability to resist digestion in the small intestine. Since some fibers—especially the soluble fibers—are fermented by bacteria in the large intestine, it is not accurate to say that fiber is simply that found in the feces.

Bacteria in the large intestine ferment soluble fibers into products such as short-chain fatty acids (e.g., acetic acid, butyric acid, and propionic acid) and gases, such as hydrogen (H_2) and methane (CH_4). These acids, especially butyric acid, provide fuel for the cells in the large intestine and enhance their health. All these products can also be absorbed into the bloodstream. As a result of bacterial metabolism, soluble dietary fibers yield about 1.5 to 2.5 kcal/g on average, although the actual value is still in question.[6] Thus, high-fiber foods should not be looked at as calorie-free, though they are often lower in energy content per serving than low-fiber alternatives.

When intake of fiber is high, its breakdown by bacteria can cause methane and hydrogen to increase in the breath. This is not harmful. In addition, the body tends to adapt over time to a high-fiber intake, leading to less gaseous symptoms and adjusting to the increased pressure in the large intestine.

Currently food labels use the term *soluble fiber,* rather than the more formal *viscous fiber.* We will use soluble fiber in this and other chapters since it is still the term found on the Nutrition Facts label. It is likely that the term *soluble* will be phased out in the future and replaced with the term *viscous.*

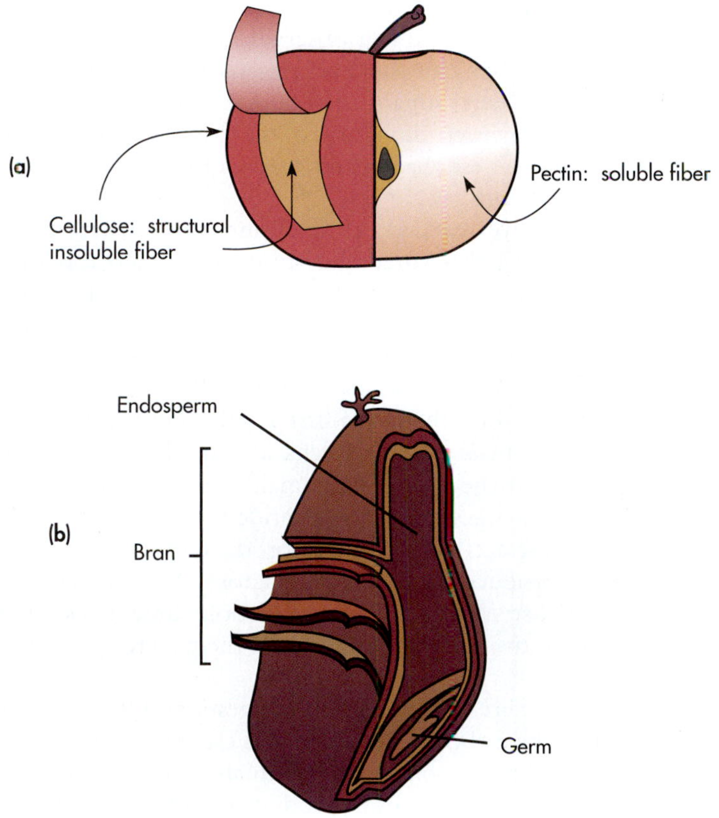

Figure 5-4 Various forms of fiber. (*a*) The skin of an apple consists of the insoluble (also called poorly fermented) fiber cellulose, which provides structure for the fruit. The soluble (also called viscous) fiber pectin "glues" the fruit cells together. (*b*) The outside layer of a wheat kernel is made of layers of bran—insoluble fiber—making this whole grain a good source of fiber. Fruits, vegetables, whole grains, and legumes such as beans are rich in fiber.

Critical | Thinking

Celia decides to go on a diet and buys over-the-counter pills. You look at the ingredients and note that the pills contain psyllium, a word you recognize from the nutrition course you're taking. What advice can you give Celia about the wisdom of using these diet pills?

An outmoded term used for fiber is *crude fiber*. This term arose during the early 1900s to reflect the amount of indigestible foodstuff present in animal feed. The animal feed was boiled for 1 hour in acid and for another hour in an alkaline solution. The remains of that chemical digestion was called crude fiber; it consisted mostly of cellulose and lignins. All other types of fiber were destroyed by the chemical action.

Concept Check

Amylose, amylopectin, and glycogen are all storage forms of glucose, called polysaccharides. Amylose and amylopectin combine in varying proportions to form food starch, such as that found in potatoes and bread. Glycogen is a storage form of glucose in humans. Liver glycogen yields a ready source of blood glucose.

Fiber is essentially the portion of ingested food that remains undigested as it enters the large intestine. Fiber components include cellulose, hemicelluloses, lignins, pectins, gums, and mucilages. There are two general classes of fiber: insoluble and soluble. Insoluble fibers (or poorly fermented fibers) are mostly made up of cellulose, hemicelluloses, and lignins. Soluble fibers (or viscous fibers) are made up mostly of pectins, gums, and mucilages. Both insoluble and soluble fibers are resistant to human digestive enzymes, but bacteria in the large intestine can break down soluble fibers.

In the search for fiber sources, berries are often overlooked. Just ½ cup contains up to 3 g of fiber.

amylase Starch-digesting enzyme from the salivary glands or pancreas.

Carbohydrate Digestion and Absorption

Food preparation can be viewed as the start of carbohydrate digestion because cooking softens the tough fibrous tissue of plants, such as broccoli stalks. When starches are heated, the starch granules swell as they soak up water, making them much easier to digest. All these effects of cooking generally make these foods easier to chew, swallow, and break down during digestion.

Digestion

The enzymatic digestion of starch begins in the mouth, when the saliva, which contains an enzyme called salivary **amylase,** mixes with the starchy products during the chewing of the food. This amylase breaks down starch into many smaller units (e.g., disaccharides, such as maltose) (Fig. 5-5). You can observe this conversion while chewing a saltine cracker. Prolonged chewing of the cracker causes it to taste sweeter as some starch breaks down into the sweeter sugars, such as maltose. Still, food is in the mouth for such a short amount of time that this phase of digestion is negligible. In addition, once the food moves down the esophagus and reaches the stomach, the acidic environment (pH 1-2) inactivates salivary amylase.

After the carbohydrates have reached the small intestine—where the pH of 7 or more is well suited for further carbohydrate digestion—the pancreas releases enzymes, such as pancreatic amylase. The original carbohydrates in a food are present in the small intestine as monosaccharides (mostly any glucose and fructose present as such in food), as well as disaccharides (maltose from starch breakdown, lactose mainly from dairy products, and sucrose from food and that added at the table).

The polysaccharides in the food that were first acted on in the mouth are then digested further by pancreatic amylase. The disaccharides are digested to their monosaccharide units once they reach the wall of the small intestine, where the specialized enzymes on the mucosal cells digest each disaccharide into the monosaccharide components. The enzyme maltase acts on maltose to produce two glucose molecules. Sucrase acts on sucrose to produce glucose and fructose. Lactase acts on lactose to produce glucose and galactose. When considering carbohydrate digestion, you should remember that the key digestive enzymes come from the pancreas and the cells of the intestinal wall.[6]

Intestinal diseases can interfere with the efficient digestion of the sugars maltose, lactose, and sucrose. Some of the carbohydrates therefore escape digestion and are not absorbed. When these unabsorbed carbohydrates eventually reach the large intestine, the bacteria there use the sugars for energy needs, producing acids and gases as by-products

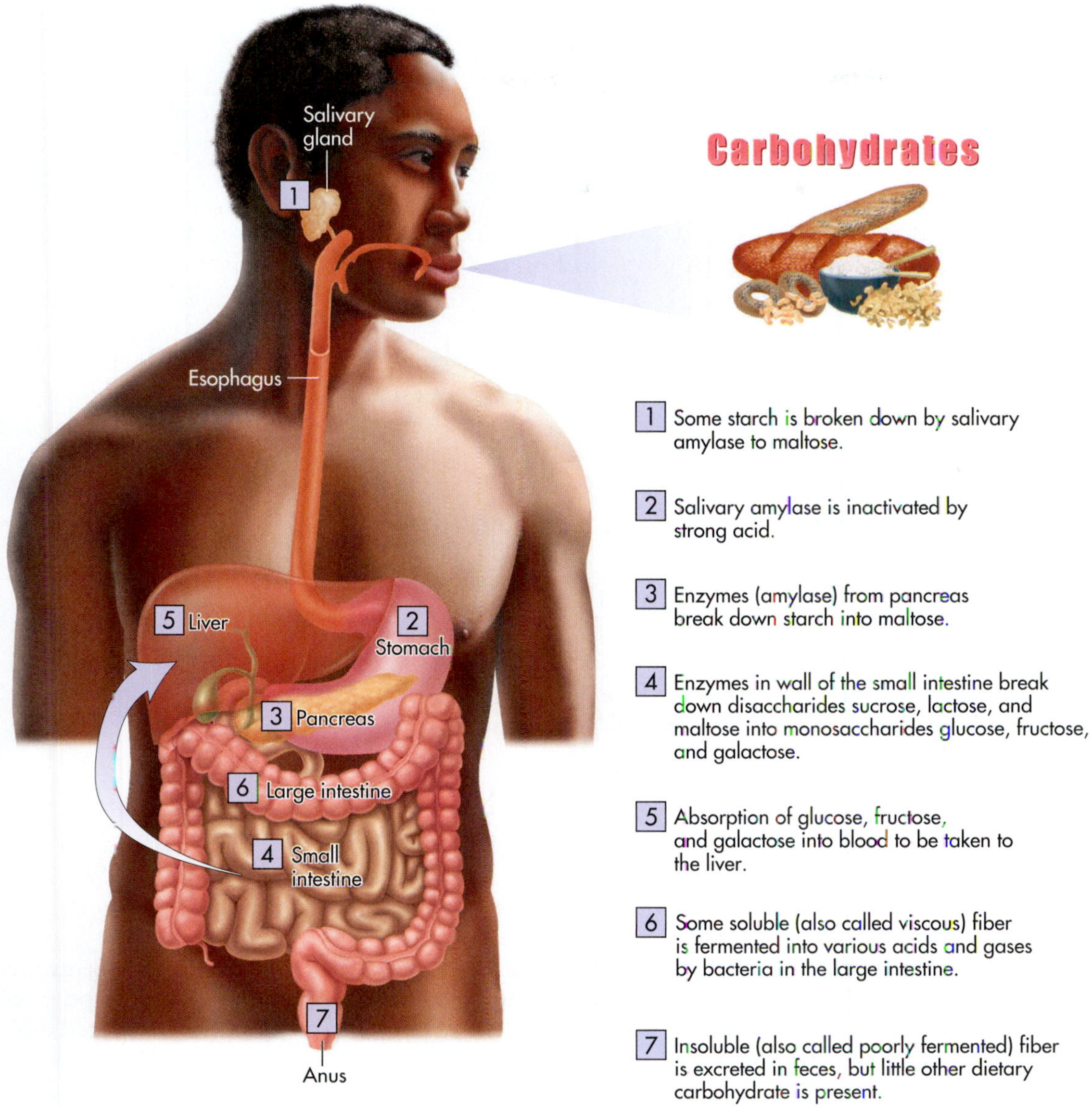
Salivary gland
1
Carbohydrates
Esophagus
1 Some starch is broken down by salivary amylase to maltose.
2 Salivary amylase is inactivated by strong acid.
3 Enzymes (amylase) from pancreas break down starch into maltose.
4 Enzymes in wall of the small intestine break down disaccharides sucrose, lactose, and maltose into monosaccharides glucose, fructose, and galactose.
5 Absorption of glucose, fructose, and galactose into blood to be taken to the liver.
6 Some soluble (also called viscous) fiber is fermented into various acids and gases by bacteria in the large intestine.
7 Insoluble (also called poorly fermented) fiber is excreted in feces, but little other dietary carbohydrate is present.
5 Liver
2 Stomach
3 Pancreas
6 Large intestine
4 Small intestine
7
Anus

Figure 5-5 Carbohydrate digestion and absorption. Enzymes made by the mouth, pancreas, and small intestine participate in the process of digestion. Most carbohydrate digestion and absorption take place in the small intestine. Note that Chapter 3 covered the physiology of digestion and absorption in detail.

(review Fig. 5-5). If produced in large amounts, these gases can cause abdominal discomfort. People recovering from intestinal disorders, such as diarrhea or bacterial infections, may need to avoid lactose for a few weeks if temporary lactose malabsorption is experienced. A few weeks is sufficient time for the small intestine to resume producing enough lactase enzyme to allow for more complete lactose digestion.

Absorption

Simple sugars found naturally in foods and those formed as by-products of earlier starch digestion in the mouth and small intestine follow an active absorption process (except fructose). Recall from Chapter 3 that this is a process that requires a specific carrier and energy input in order for the substance to be taken up by the absorptive cells in the small intestine. Glucose and its close relative, galactose, undergo active absorption. They are

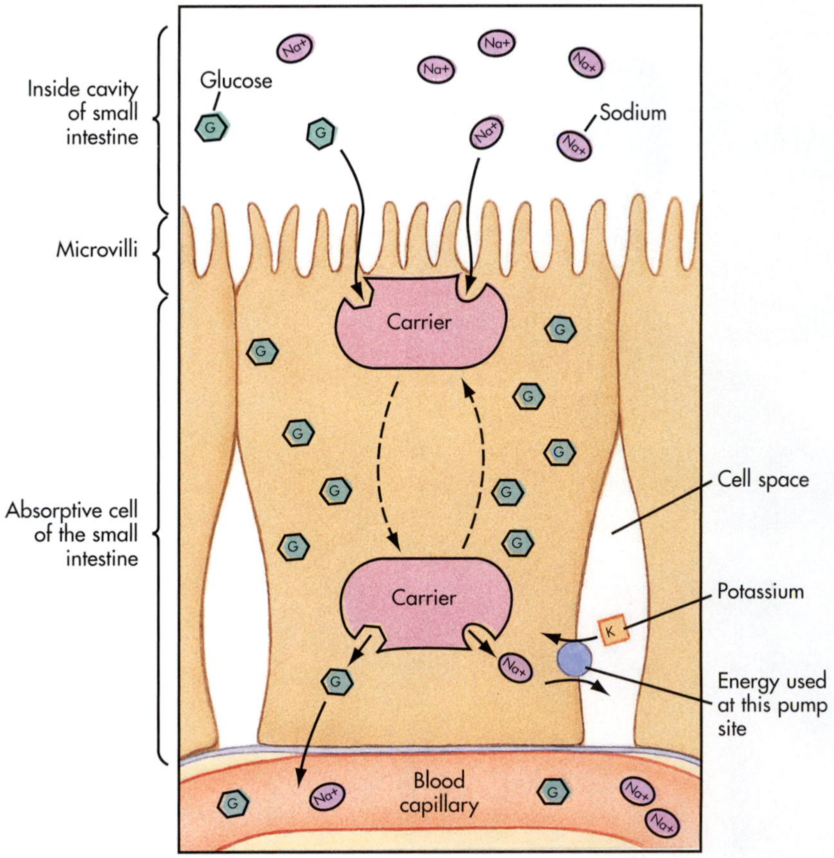

Figure 5-6 Active absorption of glucose. Glucose and sodium pass across the cell membrane of the intestinal absorptive cell in a carrier-dependent, energy-requiring process. The energy is used for maintaining a low concentration of sodium in the cell. Once inside the absorptive cell, glucose can exit by facilitated diffusion down its concentration gradient and enter the bloodstream.

pumped into the absorptive cells along with sodium (Fig. 5-6).[6] The ATP energy used in the process is actually needed to pump the sodium ion back out of the absorptive cell.

Fructose on the other hand is taken up by the absorptive cells via facilitated diffusion. In this case, a carrier is used, but no energy input is needed. This absorptive process is slower than that seen with glucose or galactose. Thus, large doses of fructose are not readily absorbed and can contribute to diarrhea as they remain in the small intestine and attract water via osmosis. (Chapter 11 will discuss osmosis in detail.)

Once glucose, galactose, and fructose enter the intestinal cells, some fructose is metabolized to glucose. The single sugars in the absorptive cells are then transported via the portal vein that goes directly to the liver. The liver then exercises its metabolic options:

- transforming the monosaccharides into glucose and releasing it directly into the bloodstream for transport to organs such as the brain, muscles, kidneys, and adipose tissues
- producing the storage form of carbohydrate: glycogen
- producing fat

Of these three options, producing fat is the least likely.[6]

A small portion of starch (about 10%) escapes digestion. This type of starch is called *resistant starch,* as it resists digestion. The reason for the lack of digestion varies depending on the specific type of resistant starch in a food. This travels down to the large intestine and is fermented there by bacteria. Then some of the starch is absorbed in the form of acids and gases produced by bacterial metabolism, as is true for undigested lactose. As mentioned before, scientists suspect that some of these products actually promote the health of the large intestine by providing a source of energy.

Concept | Check

Carbohydrate digestion is the process of breaking down larger carbohydrates into their absorbable components. The enzymatic digestion of starches begins in the mouth with salivary amylase. Enzymes made by the pancreas and small intestine complete the digestion of carbohydrates to single sugars in the small intestine. Primarily following an active absorption process, the single sugars (glucose and galactose)—either resulting from the digestive process or present in the meal—are taken up by absorptive cells in the intestine. Fructose undergoes facilitated diffusion; once in the absorptive cell most is metabolized to glucose. All the monosaccharides then enter the portal vein and travel to the liver. The liver finally exercises its metabolic options, primarily producing glucose and glycogen from the monosaccharides.

Functions of Glucose and Other Sugars in the Body

Glucose yields energy, but it has many other functions as well. Since the other sugars can generally be converted to glucose, and more complex carbohydrates (e.g., starches) are broken down to yield glucose, the functions described here apply to most carbohydrates.

Glucose is also used to synthesize the ribose and deoxyribose sugars used in RNA and DNA synthesis, respectively.

Yielding Energy

The main function of glucose is to act as a source of energy to body cells. Certain tissues, such as the red blood cells and most parts of the brain, derive almost all of their energy from glucose. In fact, except when the diet contains almost no carbohydrates, the brain and the rest of the **central nervous system** use mostly glucose for fuel. Glucose can also fuel muscle cells and other body cells, but many of these cells usually use fat to meet energy needs.

central nervous system (CNS) The brain and spinal cord portions of the nervous system.

Sparing Protein from Use as an Energy Source

Glucose is protein sparing. That is, dietary protein can be used to make body tissues and to perform other vital processes only when carbohydrate intake provides enough glucose for body needs. Therefore, if you do not consume enough carbohydrate to yield that glucose, your body is forced to make it from other nutrients, such as proteins found in muscle tissue. This process is termed **gluconeogenesis,** which means "production of new glucose" (review Chapter 4 for details). If the process continues for weeks, these organs can become partially weakened. Generally, North Americans consume adequate sources of protein, so sparing protein is not an essential function of carbohydrate in the diet under such conditions. It does become important in some energy-reduced diets and in starvation. (Chapters 7 and 20 discuss specific effects of starvation and famine.)

gluconeogenesis The production of new glucose by metabolic pathways in the cell. Amino acids derived from protein usually provide the carbons for this glucose.

The life-threatening wasting of protein that occurs during long-term fasting (or starvation) has prompted companies that produce products used for rapid weight loss, such as Optifast, to include enough carbohydrate to supply 100 g/day or more. This significantly decreases protein breakdown and thus helps protect vital tissues and organs, including the heart, during rapid weight loss.

Preventing Ketosis

An adequate intake of carbohydrates—glucose, other sugars, or starch—is necessary for the complete metabolism of fats to carbon dioxide (CO_2) and water (H_2O) in the body. A low carbohydrate intake, with the resulting decline in release of the hormone **insulin,**

insulin A hormone produced by beta cells of the pancreas. Insulin increases the synthesis of glycogen in the liver and the movement of glucose from the bloodstream into muscle and adipose cells, among other processes.

Expert Opinion

The Benefits of a High-Carbohydrate Diet

William E. Connor, M.D.

The great civilizations of the world developed and flourished consuming high-carbohydrate diets. The classic examples are the Chinese civilization, based on rice; the Egyptian and Babylonian cultures, which consumed wheat; and, in the Americas, the Maya, Inca, and Aztec peoples, whose staples were corn and beans. Except for the affluent countries of the Western world, the majority of the world's population continues to consume a high-carbohydrate diet derived from cereals, legumes, vegetables, and fruits. Indeed, typical amounts of carbohydrates consumed are large, in the range of 400 to 500 g/day, predominantly as starch or other polysaccharides, and constituting from 75 to 80% of the total energy intake. An example of a culture that my colleagues and I have studied is the Tarahumara Indians of Mexico; they have consumed a high-carbohydrate diet for generations, with the principal foods being corn, beans, and wild plants. Their diet contains ample protein and is nutritionally adequate.

Ecologically, a high-carbohydrate diet makes better use of the world's resources. Cereal crops and legumes require about one-fifth of the resources needed to yield the same energy that beef would require. Thus, the available resources of the world would not be sufficient to produce the high-animal-fat diet of North America for everyone.

Historically (and today) a high-carbohydrate diet has been based largely on plant foods that contain starch as the carbohydrate source. The only plant exception is fruit, in which the carbohydrates are glucose, fructose, and sucrose, as well as pectin, a fiber. Even nuts, which contain about 50% fat in terms of total energy content, also contain a considerable amount of carbohydrate, 20 to 30% of total energy. Foods derived from animals, on the other hand, contain very little or no carbohydrate, instead being composed of protein and fat.

Some hunter-gatherers of the past consumed very little carbohydrate because plant foods were simply not available. The Eskimo of the Arctic are the classic example; most of their calories were derived from seal, fish, whale, caribou, and other land animals. However, for most humans, the only time in life when a high-carbohydrate diet is not consumed is during infancy, when the diet of human milk or infant formulas contains about 50% of the energy from fat and is fairly low in carbohydrate, about 40% of the energy content. Even in the United States, adults consume 45 to 50% of the total energy as carbohydrate. For children and adults, practical high-carbohydrate diets usually contain from 60 to 65% of total energy, an amount suggested by the Coronary Heart Disease Prevention Group at the Oregon Health Sciences University. Such an alternative diet would contain protein as 15% of energy, fat as 20 to 25% of energy, and cholesterol intake of 100 mg/day or less. This high-carbohydrate diet is designed to prevent not only cardiovascular disease but also other diseases associated with an affluent lifestyle, such as cancer.

From the health point of view, a high-carbohydrate diet consisting largely of plant foods is a diet that is rich in fiber, minerals, vitamins, saponins (a phytochemical; see Chapter 2), sitosterol (see Chapter 6 for details), and essential fatty acids. It is thus a diet high in bulk from fiber and, so, weighs considerably more than a low-carbohydrate diet. It is a diet rich in antioxidants, such as vitamin E, ascorbic acid, and carotenoids, especially lutein and zeaxanthin. These are important in preventing cardiovascular disease and cancer, and in delaying the aging process. A high-carbohydrate diet is also rich in folate; this is sometimes in short supply in the highly purified

leads to release of fatty acids from adipose cells and subsequent incomplete breakdown of the fatty acids in the liver. This then results in formation of ketone bodies—acetoacetic acid and its derivatives. Chapter 4 covered this condition in detail, called ketosis.

In starvation, people do not consume enough carbohydrate, so ketone bodies soon appear in the blood. Again, this is the normal metabolic response to a fuel shortage. Over time, part of the brain and other tissues can use these ketone bodies for fuel. In fact, the use of ketone bodies by the brain and other organs, such as the heart, is an important adaptive mechanism for survival during starvation. If part of the brain could not use ketone bodies, the body would be forced to produce much more glucose from protein to support the brain's energy needs. The resulting self-cannibalization would rapidly break down the muscles, heart, and other organs, severely limiting the body's ability to tolerate starvation.

type 1 diabetes A form of diabetes in which the person with the disease is prone to ketosis and requires insulin therapy.

In untreated **type 1 diabetes,** excessive production of ketone bodies can occur, partly because there is not enough insulin to allow for normal glucose metabolism. In

North American diet. Folate helps control abnormal homocysteine levels—an emerging cardiovascular risk factor. Since it comes from plant foods, the high-carbohydrate diet has another advantage in that it is typically low in fat, low in saturated fat, and low in cholesterol content. This means that populations that consume a high-carbohydrate diet have low blood cholesterol and LDL-cholesterol, as well as a low incidence of cardiovascular disease. A lower-fat diet would reduce the amount of fat in the bloodstream after a meal; this fat contains particles that can contribute to atherosclerosis (see Chapter 6 for details).

Fiber includes several carbohydrates that are largely indigestible by the human gut, such as cellulose, hemicellulose, lignin, pectin, and beta-glucans. Fiber is found only in plants and is common in unprocessed cereals, legumes, vegetables, and fruits. In ruminant animals, fiber is completely digested and is used as a source of energy. In humans, fiber contributes little to the energy content of the diet but promotes satiety through its bulk and promotes proper functioning of the colon and rectum. Fiber may help prevent certain diseases of the colon and rectum, such as appendicitis, hemorrhoids, and diverticulitis.

Sugar is a conspicuous component of the North American diet, perhaps now even increasing from the usual amount of about 20% of total energy intake. Sugar, of course, includes sucrose, fructose, and glucose. Fruits are natural sources of sugars but would supply only a small amount of sugars vis-à-vis the total energy intake and would contribute valuable nutrients. The addition of large quantities of sucrose and fructose to processed food, baked goods, and candies would supply only energy, without the other nutritive benefits of fruit consumption. In the high-carbohydrate diet I recommend, most of the carbohydrate would be supplied by starch. The consumption of sugar would even be reduced from the current 20% of energy to 10 to 15% of energy intake. It would be expected that incidence of dental caries then would be reduced as sugar intake declined.

A high-carbohydrate diet should emphasize whole grains within the breads, cereals, rice, and pasta group of the Food Guide Pyramid.

Another advantage of a high-carbohydrate diet based on plant foods is in the prevention of obesity. There is good evidence that North Americans lose weight more easily with a high-carbohydrate diet and are less inclined to gain weight than are those whose carbohydrate intake is lower and fat intake is higher. The energy cost of metabolizing a high-starch source of carbohydrate (e.g., corn or beans) is much higher than the energy expenditure necessary to metabolize a dense nutrient, such as meat, or the fat from french fries or even olive oil. Finally, the advantages of a high-carbohydrate, lower-fat diet apply in the control of hypertension.

Given all these benefits, a reexamination of the relative amount of carbohydrate in one's diet is warranted. Much research supports the recommendation to increase complex carbohydrates from vegetables, whole grains, beans, and fruits.

Dr. Connor is a professor of medicine in the Division of Endocrinology, Diabetes, and Clinical Nutrition at the Oregon Health Sciences University, Portland, Oregon. He is a former president of the American Society for Clinical Nutrition and a former member of the Food and Nutrition Board of the National Academy of Sciences.

such patients, the resulting ketosis can cause numerous complications (see the Nutrition Perspective at the end of this chapter for further discussion of diabetes).

Functions of Fiber

Fiber supplies mass to the feces, making elimination much easier. This is especially true for insoluble fibers. When enough fiber is consumed, the stool is large and soft because many types of plant fibers attract water. The larger size stimulates the intestinal muscles, which aids elimination. Consequently, less pressure is necessary to expel the stool.

When too little fiber is eaten, the opposite can occur: the stool may be small and hard. Constipation may result, which can force one to exert excessive pressure in the large intestine during defecation. This high pressure can force parts of the large intestine (colon) wall out from between the surrounding bands of muscle, forming small

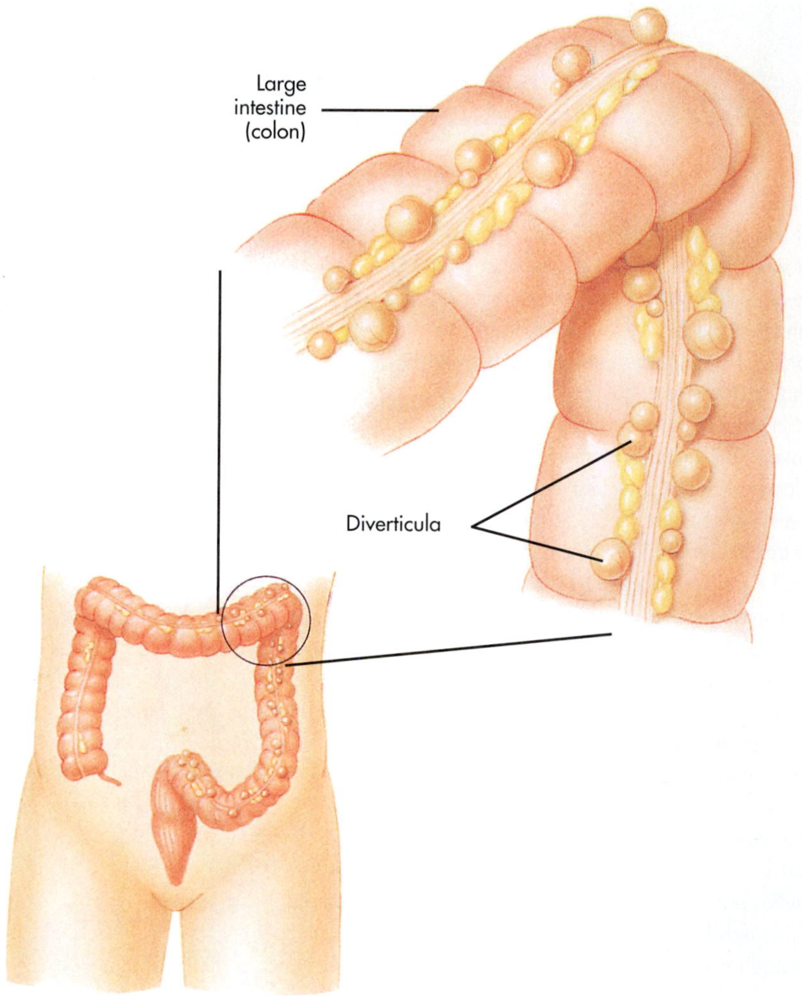

Figure 5-7 Diverticula in the colon. A low-fiber diet increases the risk of developing diverticula. About ⅓ of people over age 45 have the disease, while ⅔ of people over 85 do.

Illustration by William Ober.

diverticula Pouches that protrude through the exterior wall of the large intestine.

hemorrhoid A pronounced swelling of a large vein, particularly veins found in the anal region.

diverticulosis The condition of having many diverticula in the large intestine.

diverticulitis An inflammation of the diverticula caused by acids produced by bacterial metabolism inside the diverticula.

Critical | Thinking

Karla has a family history of colon cancer, and at age 20 she is curious about the lifestyle factors she can employ to prevent developing the disease. What advice would you provide her?

pouches called **diverticula.** Multiple diverticula are normally present (Fig. 5-7). **Hemorrhoids** may also result from excessive straining during defecation (see Chapter 3).

Diverticula are asymptomatic in about 80% of affected people; that is, they are not noticeable. The asymptomatic form of this disease is called **diverticulosis.** If the diverticula become filled with food particles, such as hulls and seeds, they may eventually become inflamed, a condition known as **diverticulitis.** Intake of fiber then should be reduced to limit further bacterial activity. Once the inflammation subsides, a high-fiber diet is resumed to ease stool elimination and reduce the risk of a future attack.

Additional health benefits can accrue from the consumption of fiber. A diet high in fiber likely aids weight control and reduces the risk of developing obesity.[10] The bulky nature of high-fiber foods fills us up without yielding much energy. Increasing intake of foods rich in fiber is one strategy for remaining satisfied after a meal (review the discussion on energy density in Chapter 2).

Over the past 30 years, many population studies have shown a link between increased fiber intake and a decrease in colon cancer development. However, recent research has questioned the relationship between intake of fiber and colon cancer development.[6] Currently, most of the research on colon cancer is focusing on the potential preventive effects of vegetable intake; regular exercise; the use of aspirin and related pain medications; and adequate folate, selenium, and calcium intakes. Smoking, obesity in men, and processed red meat intake are under study as potential causative factors.[15] Overall, the health benefits to the colon that stem from a high-fiber diet are probably due mostly to the nutrients that are commonly part of high-fiber foods, such as vitamins, minerals, phytochemicals, antioxidants, and in some cases essential fatty acids. Thus it is more advisable to increase fiber intake using fiber-rich foods, rather than mostly relying on fiber supplements.

When consumed in large amounts, soluble fibers slow glucose absorption from the small intestine, and so contribute to better blood glucose regulation.[14] This effect can be helpful in the treatment of diabetes. In fact, adults whose main carbohydrate source is low-fiber foods are much more likely to develop diabetes than those who have high-fiber diets (see the Nutrition Perspective at the end of this chapter).[8]

A high intake of soluble fiber also inhibits absorption of cholesterol and bile acid (cholesterol-rich) from the small intestine, thereby reducing blood cholesterol and possibly reducing the risk of cardiovascular disease and gallstones.[6, 13] The short-chain fatty acids resulting from bacterial degradation of soluble fiber (e.g., proprionic acid) also probably reduce cholesterol synthesis in the liver. In addition, the slower glucose absorption that occurs with diets high in soluble fiber is linked to a decrease in insulin release. Since insulin stimulates cholesterol synthesis in the liver, this reduction in insulin may contribute to the ability of soluble fiber to lower blood cholesterol. Overall, a fiber-rich diet containing fruits, vegetables, beans, and whole grains (including whole-grain breakfast cereals) is advocated as part of a strategy to reduce cardiovascular disease (coronary heart disease and stroke) risk.[1, 6]

Oatmeal is a rich source of soluble (also called viscous) fiber, namely beta-glucan. FDA allows a health claim for the benefits of oatmeal to lower blood cholesterol that arise from the effects of this soluble fiber.

Concept | Check

Carbohydrates provide glucose for the energy needs of red blood cells and parts of the brain and central nervous system. Eating little carbohydrates forces the production of glucose (via gluconeogenesis), using carbons from amino acids. These amino acids are derived from the breakdown of proteins in body organs. An inadequate carbohydrate intake also inhibits efficient fat metabolism, which in turn can lead to ketosis.

Fiber forms a vital part of the diet by adding mass to the stool, which eases elimination. It also helps in weight control and reduces the risk of developing obesity and cardiovascular disease. Soluble fiber can also be useful for controlling blood glucose in patients with diabetes and in lowering blood cholesterol. Whole grains, vegetables, beans, and fruits are excellent sources of fiber.

Recall from Chapter 2 that FDA has approved the following claim: "Diets rich in whole-grain foods and other plant foods and low in total fat, saturated fat, and cholesterol may decrease the risk for cardiovascular (heart) disease and certain cancers."

Carbohydrate Needs

The RDA for carbohydrates is 130 g/day for adults. This is based on the amount needed to supply adequate glucose for the central nervous system, without having to rely on partial replacement of glucose by ketone bodies. Exceeding this amount somewhat is fine; the Food and Nutrition Board recommends that carbohydrate intake should range from 45 to 65% of total energy intake.[6] North Americans consume about 180 to 330 g of carbohydrates per day. The top five carbohydrate sources for U.S. adults are white bread, soft drinks, cookies and cakes (including doughnuts), sugars/syrups/jams, and potatoes. Clearly, many of us (teenagers included) should take a closer look at our main carbohydrate sources and strive to improve these from a nutritional standpoint.[12]

In North America, carbohydrates supply about 50% of dietary energy intake for adults. Worldwide, however, carbohydrates account for about 70% of all energy consumed. In some countries, carbohydrates account for up to 80% of the energy consumed.

Advice from the Dietary Guidelines regarding carbohydrates is:

- Choose a variety of grains daily, especially whole grains.
- Choose a variety of fruits and vegetables daily.
- Choose beverages and foods that limit your intake of sugars.

How Much Fiber Do We Need?

The Adequate Intake for fiber for adults is 25 g/day for women and 38 g/day for men. This is based on a goal of 14 g/1000 kcal in a diet. The rationale for the Adequate Intake is the ability of fiber to reduce risk of cardiovascular disease (and likely many cases of diabetes). The Daily Value used for fiber on food and supplement labels is 25 g for a 2000

Figure 5-8 Reading the Nutrition Facts on food labels helps us choose more nutritious foods. Based on the information from these nutrition labels, which cereal is the better choice for breakfast? Consider the amount of fiber in each cereal. Do the ingredient lists give you any clues? (Note: Ingredients are always listed in descending order by weight on a label.) When choosing a breakfast cereal, it is generally wise to focus on those that are rich sources of fiber. Simple sugar content can also be used for evaluation. However, sometimes this number does not reflect added sugar but simply the addition of fruits, such as raisins, complicating the evaluation.

Nutrition Facts

Serving Size 1 cup (55g/2.0 oz.)
Servings Per Container 10

Amount Per Serving	Cereal	Cereal with ½ Cup Vitamins A & D Skim Milk
Calories	170	210
Calories from Fat	10	10
	% Daily Value**	
Total Fat 1.0g*	**2%**	**2%**
Sat. Fat 0g	**0%**	**0%**
Cholesterol 0mg	**0%**	**0%**
Sodium 300mg	**13%**	**15%**
Potassium 340mg	**10%**	**16%**
Total Carbohydrate 43g	**14%**	**16%**
Dietary Fiber 7g	**28%**	**28%**
Sugars 16g		
Other Carbohydrate 20g		
Protein 4g		
Vitamin A	15%	20%
Vitamin C	20%	22%
Calcium	2%	15%
Iron	65%	65%
Vitamin D	10%	25%
Thiamin	25%	30%
Riboflavin	25%	35%
Niacin	25%	25%
Vitamin B_6	25%	25%
Folate	30%	30%
Vitamin B_{12}	25%	35%
Phosphorus	20%	30%
Magnesium	20%	25%
Zinc	25%	25%
Copper	10%	10%

*Amount in cereal. One half cup skim milk contributes an additional 40 calories, 65mg sodium, 6g total carbohydrate (6g sugars), and 4g protein.
**Percent Daily Values are based on a 2,000 calorie diet. Your daily values may be higher or lower depending on your calorie needs:

	Calories:	2,000	2,500
Total Fat	Less than	65g	80g
Sat Fat	Less than	20g	25g
Cholesterol	Less than	300mg	300mg
Sodium	Less than	2,400mg	2,400mg
Potassium		3,500mg	3,500mg
Total Carbohydrate		300g	375g
Dietary Fiber		25g	30g

Calories per gram:
Fat 9 • Carbohydrate 4 • Protein 4

Ingredients: Wheat bran with other parts of wheat, raisins, sugar, corn syrup, salt, malt flavoring, glycerin, iron, niacinamide, zinc oxide, pyridoxine hydrochloride (vitamin B_6), riboflavin (vitamin B_2), vitamin A palmitate, thiamin hydrochloride (vitamin B_1), folic acid, vitamin B_{12}, and vitamin D.

Nutrition Facts

Serving Size: 1 Cup (40g/1.5 oz.)
Servings Per Package: About 14

Amount Per Serving	1 Cup Cereal	Cereal With ½ Cup Skim Milk
Calories	160	200
Calories from Fat	0	5
	%Daily Value**	
Total Fat 0g*	**0%**	**1%**
Saturated Fat 0g	**0%**	**1%**
Cholesterol 0mg	**0%**	**1%**
Sodium 55mg	**2%**	**4%**
Potassium 80mg	**2%**	**8%**
Total Carbohydrate 35g	**9%**	**11%**
Dietary Fiber 1g	**4%**	**4%**
Sugars 20g		
Other Carbohydrate 14g		
Protein 2g		
Vitamin A	25%	30%
Vitamin C	0%	2%
Calcium	0%	15%
Iron	10%	10%
Vitamin D	10%	20%
Thiamin	25%	25%
Riboflavin	25%	35%
Niacin	25%	25%
Vitamin B6	25%	25%
Folate	25%	25%
Vitamin B12	25%	30%
Phosphorus	4%	15%
Magnesium	4%	8%
Zinc	10%	10%
Copper	2%	2%

*Amount in Cereal. One-half cup skim milk contributes an additional 65mg sodium, 6g total carbohydrate (6g sugars), and 4g protein.
**Percent Daily Values are based on a 2000 calorie diet. Your daily values may be higher or lower depending on your calorie needs:

	Calories:	2,000	2,500
Total Fat	Less than	65g	80g
Sat. Fat	Less than	20g	25g
Cholesterol	Less than	300mg	300mg
Sodium	Less than	2,400mg	2,400mg
Potassium		3,500mg	3,500mg
Total Carbohydrate		300g	375g
Dietary Fiber		25g	30g

Calories per gram:
Fat 9 • Carbohydrate 4 • Protein 4

Ingredients: Wheat, Sugar, Corn Syrup, Honey, Caramel Color, Partially Hydrogenated Soybean Oil, Salt, Ferric Phosphate, Niacinamide (Niacin), Zinc Oxide, Vitamin A (Palmitate), Pyridoxine Hydrochloride (Vitamin B6), Riboflavin, Thiamin Mononitrate, Folic Acid (Folate), Vitamin B12 and Vitamin D.

Whole grains are an excellent source of fiber.

Healthy People 2010 has the following goals related to carbohydrate intake:

- Increase the proportion of persons age 2 years and older who consume at least six daily servings of grain products, with at least three being whole grains.
- Increase the proportion of persons age 2 years and older who consume at least two daily servings of fruit.
- Increase the proportion of persons age 2 years and older who consume at least three daily servings of vegetables, with at least one-third being dark green or orange vegetables.

kcal diet. In North America, the average whole-grain intake is less than one serving per day; fiber intake averages 13 g/day for women and 17 g/day for men. This low intake is attributed to the lack of knowledge on the benefits of whole grains, as well as the lack of ability to recognize whole-grain products at the time of purchase. Thus, most of us should increase our fiber intake. At least three servings of whole grains per day is recommended. Eating a high-fiber cereal (≥ 3 g of fiber per serving) for breakfast is one easy

Table 5-2 Sample of Menus Containing 1600 kcal and 25 g of Fiber, and 2000 kcal and 38 g of Fiber*

	25 g Fiber			38 g Fiber		
Menu	**Serving Size**	**Carbohydrate Content (g)**	**Fiber Content (g)**	**Serving Size**	**Carbohydrate Content (g)**	**Fiber Content (g)**
Breakfast						
Orange juice (with pulp)	1 cup	28	0.5	1 cup	28	0.5
Wheaties	¾ cup	17	2	¾ cup	17	2
2% milk	½ cup	6	—	½ cup	6	—
Whole-wheat toast	1 slice	13	2	1 slice	13	2
Margarine	1 tsp	—	—	1 tsp	—	—
Coffee		1	—		1	—
Lunch						
Lean ham	2 oz	—	—	2 oz	—	—
Whole-wheat bread	2 slices	26	4	2 slices	26	4
Mayonnaise	2 tsp	2	—	2 tsp	2	—
Lettuce	¼ cup	—	0.2	¼ cup	—	0.2
Cooked white beans	⅓ cup	15	4	1 cup	45	12
Pear (with skin)	½	12	2	1	25	4
1% milk	½ cup	6	—	½ cup	6	—
Snack						
Carrot (as carrot sticks)	1	8	2	1	8	2
Dinner						
Broiled chicken (no skin)	3 oz	—	—	3 oz	—	—
Baked potato (large, with skin)	½	15	1.5	1	30	3
Margarine	1½ tsp	—	—	1½ tsp	—	—
Cooked green beans	1 cup	10	4	1 cup	10	4
Margarine	½ tsp	—	—	½ tsp	—	—
1% milk	1 cup	12	—	1 cup	12	—
Apple (with peel)	½	16	1.8	1	32	3.7
Snack						
Raisin bagel	1	39	1.2	1	39	1.2
Total		226 g	25 g		300 g	38 g

*The overall diet pattern is based on the Food Guide Pyramid. Breakdown of approximate energy content: carbohydrate, 55%; protein, 20%; fat, 25%.

way to increase fiber intake (Fig. 5-8). As mentioned before, whole-food sources such as cereals, not bran supplements, are preferable because foods provide a broader variety of nutrients. This is especially true for many natural high-fiber foods—whole grains, fruits, vegetables, and beans.

Table 5-2 shows a diet containing 25 and 38 g of fiber within a very moderate energy intake. Diets to meet the fiber recommendations are possible if you like whole-wheat bread, fruits, vegetables, and beans. Use Table 5-3 to estimate the fiber content of your diet. What is *your* fiber score?

Table 5-3 Estimate Your Fiber Intake

To roughly estimate your daily fiber consumption, determine the number of servings of each food category listed below that you consumed yesterday. Multiply the serving amount by the value listed and then add up the total amount of fiber. How does your total fiber intake for yesterday compare with the general recommendation of 25 to 38 g of fiber per day for women and men, respectively?

Food	Servings	Grams
Vegetables (serving size: 1 cup raw leafy greens or 1/2 cup other vegetables)	______ × 2	
Fruits (serving size: 1 whole fruit; ½ grapefruit; ½ cup berries or cubed fruit; ¼ cup dried fruit)	______ × 2.5	
Beans, lentils, split peas (serving size: ½ cup cooked)	______ × 7	
Nuts, seeds (serving size: ¼ cup; 2 tbsp peanut butter)	______ × 2.5	
Whole grains (serving size: 1 slice whole-wheat bread; ½ cup whole-wheat pasta, brown rice, or other whole grain; ½ each bran or whole-grain muffin)	______ × 2.5	
Refined grains (serving size: 1 slice bread, ½ cup pasta, rice, or other processed grains; and ½ each refined bagels or muffins)	______ × 1	
Breakfast cereals (serving size: check package for serving size and amount of fiber per serving)	______ × grams fiber per serving	
Total Grams of Fiber =	____________	

Adapted from Fiber: Strands of protection. *Consumer Reports on Health*, p. 1, August 1999.

Metabolic Syndrome A condition in which the person has insulin resistance, hypertension, increased blood triglycerides, and decreased HDL cholesterol levels. This condition is usually accompanied by obesity, lack of physical activity, and a diet high in refined carbohydrates. Also called Syndrome X.

Currently, recommendations for carbohydrate intake vary widely in the scientific literature and popular press. Aside from the low intakes used to induce ketosis as part of a plan for quick weight loss (note that this diet is not recommended for long term use; see Chapter 13), recommendations vary from 45 to 60% of energy intake by the Food and Nutrition Board to more than 70% in the *Pritikin Program* and *Eat More, Weigh Less* plan. The Nutrition Facts panel on food labels uses 60% of energy intake as the standard for recommended carbohydrate intake. In addition, one recommendation on which almost all experts agree is that one's carbohydrate intake should be base primarily on fruits, vegetables, whole grains, and beans, not mostly on refined grains and sugar.[2] Dr. William Connor discussed this in detail in the Expert Opinion on page 150.

Only when a person's blood triglycerides are high is a carbohydrate-rich diet not recommended. (This will be covered further in Chapter 6 with respect to the **Metabolic Syndrome,** also called Syndrome X. Note that about 25% of North American adults have this condition.[7]) Actually, the chief culprits in this case are not carbohydrates as a class of nutrients but excessively large meals full of foods both rich in simple sugars and refined starches and low in fiber, coupled with little physical activity.[7] These practices should not form the basis of daily habits, but unfortunately, they do for many adults.[12]

Note that manufacturers list enriched white (refined) flour as wheat flour on food labels. Most people think that if "wheat bread" is on the label, they are buying a whole-wheat product. Not so. If the label does not list "whole-wheat flour" first, then the product is not primarily a whole-wheat bread and thus does not contain as much fiber as it could. Careful reading of labels is important in the search for more fiber—look especially for whole grains.

Keep in mind, however, that any nutrient can lead to health problems when consumed in excess, including carbohydrate and fiber. High carbohydrate, high fiber, and low fat does not mean zero calories. Carbohydrates help moderate energy intake in comparison with fats, but the contribution of high-carbohydrate foods to total energy intake still has to be accounted for.

Problems with High-Fiber Diets

Very high intakes of fiber—for example, 60 g/day—can pose some health risks and, so, require close physician supervision if used. A high fiber intake especially requires a high fluid intake. Not consuming enough fluid with the fiber can leave the stool very hard and make it difficult and painful to eliminate. Large amounts of fiber provide certain components that may also bind essential minerals, such as zinc and iron (see Chapter 12).[6]

High-fiber diets often contribute to intestinal gas and occasionally to the production of fiber balls, called **phytobezoars,** in the stomach. These have been found in diabetic patients and in older adults who consume large amounts of fiber. Phytobezoars can lead to blockage of intestinal flow. Fiber may also contribute to blockages in the intestine when intake is high and sufficient fluid is not consumed. Finally, large amounts of fiber may add such an excess of bulk to a child's diet that energy intake is reduced; fiber fills the stomach before food intake meets energy needs.

phytobezoars Pellets of dietary fiber, characteristically found in the stomach.

Moderating Intake of Simple Sugars Is Important for Many of Us

The sweetness of sugars improves the taste of many foods, such as grapefruit (Table 5-4). A small amount of sugars in the diet is fine. In addition, sugars provide certain functional properties to foods, such as texture, body, and browning capacity.[6] Nutrition experts suggest that sugars added to foods should provide no more than about 10% of total energy intake daily, with an upper limit of 25%.[6] Beyond this limit diet quality typically declines, such as with calcium intake. The more moderate intake corresponds to a maximum of about 50 g (or 12 teaspoons) of sugars per day, based on a 2000 kcal diet. On average, North Americans eat about 82 g of added sugars daily, amounting to about 16% of energy intake. Added sugars are defined as sugars and syrups that are added to foods during processing or preparation. Major sources of added sugars include soft drinks, cakes, cookies, fruit punch, and dairy desserts. The specific sugars added include white sugar, brown sugar, corn syrup, fructose, and other sources. Not included are sugars that naturally occur in foods such as lactose in milk and fructose in fruit. Table 5-5 suggests ways to reduce intake of sugars. For many of us, this would be a healthful practice.

In the United States, a *juice* is defined as a fruit or vegetable beverage with no added sugars. Some fruits, such as cranberries and grapefruits, are so tart that sugar is added to make them palatable as a beverage. For example, cranberry juice *cocktail* technically isn't a juice because of the sugar added during manufacturing. Its sugar content is comparable to true juices, though, but is still very nutritious.

Most of the sugars that we eat come from foods and beverages to which sugar has been added during processing and/or manufacture. The major sources are soft drinks, candy, cakes, cookies, pies, fruitades, and dairy desserts, such as ice cream. The rest of the sugar in our diets is present naturally in foods, such as fruits, or comes from the sugar bowl. During food processing, the sugar content is often increased. The more processed the food, generally the higher the simple-sugar content.

Problems with High-Sugar Diets

The main problem with consuming an overabundant amount of sugar is that it provides empty calories; this translates to a decline in the nutritional value of a diet.

There are many forms of sugar on the market. Used in many foods, together they contribute to our daily intake of approximately 82 g (20 tsp) of added sugars in our diets.

Stevia comes from a South American shrub; it is 100 to 300 times sweeter than sucrose and provides zero calories. This is a sweetener that has been used in small amounts by the Japanese since the 1970s. FDA has not approved the use of stevia in foods, but stevia can be purchased at health-food stores as a dietary supplement.

There is a widespread notion that high sugar intake by children causes hyperactivity, typically part of the syndrome called *attention deficit hyperactive disorder (ADHD)*. However, most researchers find that sucrose may actually have the opposite effect.[6] A high-carbohydrate meal, if also low in protein and fat, has a calming effect and induces sleep; this effect may be linked to changes in the synthesis of certain neurotransmitters in the brain, such as serotonin (see Chapter 13). If there is a problem, it is probably the excitement or tension in situations in which high sugar-rich foods are served, such as at birthday parties and on Halloween.

Table 5-4 The Sweetness of Sugars and Alternative Sweeteners

Type of Sweetener	Relative Sweetness* (Sucrose = 1)	Typical Sources
Sugars		
Lactose	0.2	Dairy products
Maltose	0.4	Sprouted seeds
Glucose	0.7	Corn syrup
Sucrose	1.0	Table sugar, most sweets
Invert sugar†	1.3	Some candies, honey
Fructose	1.2–1.8	Fruit, honey, some soft drinks
Sugar Alcohols		
Sorbitol	0.6	Dietetic candies, sugarless gum
Mannitol	0.7	Dietetic candies
Xylitol	0.9	Sugarless gum
Alternative Sweeteners		
Cyclamate	30	Not currently in use in the United States
Aspartame	180	Diet soft drinks, diet fruit drinks, sugarless gum, powdered diet sweetener
Acesulfame-K	200	Sugarless gum, diet drink mixes, powdered diet sweeteners, puddings, gelatin desserts
Saccharin (sodium salt)	300	Diet soft drinks
Sucralose	600	Diet soft drinks, tabletop use, sugarless gums, jams, frozen desserts
Neotame	7000 to 13,000	Tabletop sweetener, baked goods, frozen desserts, jams and jellies

From the American Dietetic Association, 1993, and other sources.

*On a per gram basis

†Sucrose broken down into glucose and fructose

Diet Quality

Overcrowding the diet with sweet treats can leave little room for important, nutrient-dense foods, such as fruits and vegetables. Children and teenagers are at the highest risk for overconsuming empty calories in place of nutrients that are essential for growth. Many children and teenagers are drinking an excess of sugared soft drinks and other sugar-containing beverages and much less milk than ever before. Milk contains calcium and vitamin D, both of which are essential for bone health; therefore, this exchange of soft drinks for milk can compromise bone health.

Supersizing beverages is also a growing problem; for example, in the 1950s a typical serving size of soft drink was a 6½ oz bottle, and now a 20 oz plastic bottle is a typical serving. This one change contributes 170 extra kcal to the diet. Most convenience stores now offer cups that will hold 64 oz of soft drinks. Filling up on sugared soft drinks in place of foods is not a healthy practice, but enjoying an occasional soft drink or limiting intake to one 12 oz serving a day is generally fine. Switching to diet soft drinks would spare the simple sugar calories, but still lacks in nutritional value, except for the fluid.

The sugar found in cakes, cookies, and ice cream supplies many extra calories that promote weight gain, unless an individual is physically active. Today's low-fat and fat-

Table 5-5 Suggestions for Reducing Simple-Sugar Intake

At the Supermarket

- Read ingredient labels. Identify all the added sugars in a product. Select items lower in total sugar when possible.
- Buy fresh fruits or fruits packed in water, juice, or light syrup, rather than those packed in heavy syrup.
- Buy fewer foods that are high in sugar, such as prepared baked goods, candies, sugared cereals, sweet desserts, soft drinks, and fruit-flavored punches. Substitute vanilla wafers, graham crackers, bagels, English muffins, and diet soft drinks, for example.
- Buy reduced-fat microwave popcorn to replace candy for snacks.

In the Kitchen

- Reduce the sugar in foods prepared at home. Try new recipes or adjust your own. Start by reducing the sugar gradually until you've decreased it by one-third or more.
- Experiment with spices such as cinnamon, cardamom, coriander, nutmeg, ginger, and mace to enhance the flavor of foods.
- Use home-prepared items (with less sugar) instead of commercially prepared ones that are higher in sugar.

At the Table

- Use less of all sugars. This includes white and brown sugars, honey, molasses, and syrups.
- Choose fewer foods high in sugar, such as prepared baked goods, candies, and sweet desserts.
- Reach for fresh fruit instead of a sweet for dessert or between-meal snacks.
- Add less sugar to foods—coffee, tea, cereal, and fruit. Get used to using half as much; then see if you can cut back even more.
- Cut back on the number of sugared soft drinks, punches, and fruit juices you drink. Substitute water, diet soft drinks, and whole fruits rather than fruit juice.

Modified from USDA *Home and Garden Bulletin* No. 232-5, 1986.

Many foods we enjoy are sweet. These should be eaten in moderation.

free snack products usually contain lots of added sugar to produce a product with an acceptable taste. The result is to produce a high-calorie food that is equal to or greater in energy content than the high-fat food product it was designed to replace. Following the recommendation of having no more than 10% of added sugars is easier if sweet desserts such as cakes, cookies, and ice cream (full and reduced fat) are consumed sparingly.[12]

Dental Caries

Sugars in the diet (and starches that are readily fermented in the mouth, such as crackers and white bread) also increase the risk of developing **dental caries.**[6] Caries are formed when sugars and other carbohydrates are metabolized into acids by bacteria that live in the mouth (Fig. 5-9). These acids dissolve the tooth enamel and underlying structure. Bacteria also use the sugars to make plaque, a sticky substance that both adheres bacteria to teeth and diminishes the acid-neutralizing effect of saliva.

dental caries Erosion in the surface of a tooth caused by acids made by bacteria as they metabolize sugars.

The worst offenders in terms of dental caries are sticky and gummy foods high in sugars, such as caramel, because they stick to the teeth and supply the bacteria with a long-lived carbohydrate source. These long-lived carbohydrates are termed **cariogenic** (*cario* means "cavity"). Although liquid sugar sources (e.g., fruit juices) are not as potent at causing dental caries as sticky and gummy foods, they still warrant consideration. Some experts caution that sports drinks may also lead to dental caries due to their acid content.

cariogenic Literally, "caries-producing"; a substance, often carbohydrate-rich (such as caramel), that promotes dental caries.

Snacking regularly on sugary foods is also likely to cause caries because it gives the bacteria on the teeth a steady source of carbohydrate from which to continually make

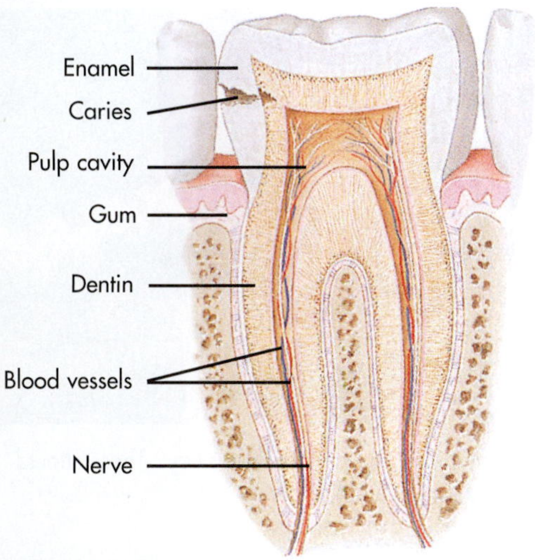

Figure 5-9 Dental caries. Bacteria can collect in various areas on a tooth. Using simple sugars such as sucrose, bacteria then create acids that can dissolve tooth enamel, leading to caries. If the caries process progresses and enters the pulp cavity, damage to the nerve and resulting pain are likely. The bacteria also produce plaque whereby they adhere to the tooth surface.

acid. Sugared gum chewed between meals is a prime example of a poor dental habit. Still, sugar-containing foods are not the only foods that allow acid production by the bacteria in the mouth. As mentioned, if starch-containing foods (e.g., crackers and bread) are held in the mouth for a long time, they can be acted on by enzymes in the mouth that break down the starch to sugars; bacteria can then produce acid from these sugars. Overall, the sugar and starch content of a food and its retentive ability largely determine its cariogenicity.

Fluoridated water and toothpaste have contributed to fewer dental caries in North American children over the past 20 years due to the mineral's tooth-strengthening effect (see Chapter 12). Research has also indicated that certain foods—such as cheese, peanuts, and sugar-free chewing gum—can actually help reduce the amount of acid on teeth. In addition, rinsing the mouth after meals and snacks reduces the acidity in the mouth. Certainly, good nutrition, habits that do not present an overwhelming challenge to oral health (e.g., chewing sugar-free gum), and routine visits to the dentist all contribute to improved dental health.

High Glycemic Index and Glycemic Load

Many foods high in sugar and starch produce a high **glycemic index (GI)** and resulting high **glycemic load (GL)** in the body. Glycemic index is defined as the blood glucose response to a given food, compared to a standard (typically, glucose or white bread) (Table 5-6).[14] Glycemic index is influenced by starch structure, fiber content, food processing, physical structure, and macronutrients in the meal, such as fat. Foods with particularly high glycemic index values are baking potatoes (not seen as much with red potatoes, as these are low in amylopectin), mashed potatoes (due to greater surface area exposed), short grain white rice, honey, and jelly beans.

Another way of looking at how different foods affect blood glucose and insulin levels is the glycemic load. The glycemic load actually better reflects a food's effect on one's blood glucose than either the amount of carbohydrate or glycemic index alone.[20] To calculate the glycemic load of a food, the amount of carbohydrate found in a food is multiplied by the glycemic index of that carbohydrate. For example, vanilla wafers have a glycemic index of 77, which is considered high. On the other hand, when calculating the glycemic load of vanilla wafers by multiplying the glycemic index by 15 grams of carbohydrate (a small serving), the result is a very low glycemic load of only 12 ($0.77 \times 15 = 12$).

glycemic index (GI) The blood glucose response of a given food, compared to a standard (typically, glucose or white bread). Glycemic index is influenced by starch structure, fiber content, food processing, physical structure, and macronutrients in the meal, such as fat.

glycemic load (GL) The amount of carbohydrate in a food multiplied by the glycemic index of that carbohydrate.

low-density lipoprotein (LDL) The lipoprotein in the blood, containing primarily cholesterol; elevated LDL cholesterol is strongly linked to cardiovascular disease risk.

Nutritionists are concerned about the effect of high glycemic load carbohydrates on blood glucose because these foods especially increase insulin output from the pancreas. Chronically high insulin output leads to many deleterious effects on the body: high blood triglycerides; smaller **low-density lipoprotein (LDL)** particles, which are more prone to lead to cardiovascular disease; increased fat deposition in adipose tissue; increased tendency for blood to clot; increased fat synthesis in the liver; and a more rapid return of hunger after a meal (insulin rapidly lowers the macronutients in the blood as it stimulates their storage). Over time, this increase in insulin output may actually cause the muscles to become resistant to the action of insulin, creating a state of insulin resistance and eventually type 2 diabetes in some people.[13]

There are many ways to address this problem of high glycemic load foods. The most important is to not overeat these foods at any one meal. This greatly minimizes their effects on blood glucose and the related increased insulin release. Consider substituting at least once per meal a food which has a low glycemic load for one with a higher value, such as long grain rice or spaghetti for short grain white rice. Combining a low glycemic load food, such as an apple, kidney beans, milk, or salad with dressing, with a high glycemic load food also reduces the effect on blood glucose. In addition, maintaining a healthy body weight and performing regular physical activity further reduces the effects of a high glycemic load diet.

As you will see in the Nutrition Perspective at the end of the chapter, a focus on low glycemic load helps in the treatment of diabetes; Chapter 14 discusses the use of foods with different glycemic load values in planning diets for athletes.

Table 5-6 Glycemic Index (GI) and Glycemic Load (GL) of Common Foods

Reference food glucose = 100
Low GI foods—below 55
Intermediate GI foods—between 55 and 70
High GI foods—more than 70

Low GL foods—below 15
Intermediate GL foods—between 15 and 20
High GL foods—more than 20

	Serving Size (g)	Glycemic Index (GI)	Carbohydrate (g)	Glycemic Load (GL)
Pastas/Grains				
Brown rice	1 cup	55	46	25
White, long grain	1 cup	56	45	25
White, short grain	1 cup	72	53	38
Spaghetti	1 cup	41	40	16
Vegetables				
Carrots, boiled	1 cup	49	16	8
Sweet corn	1 cup	55	39	21
Potato, baked	1 cup	85	57	48
New (red) potato, boiled	1 cup	62	29	18
Dairy Foods				
Milk, whole	1 cup	27	11	3
Milk, skim	1 cup	32	12	4
Yogurt, low-fat	1 cup	33	17	6
Ice cream	1 cup	61	31	19
Legumes				
Baked beans	1 cup	48	54	26
Kidney beans	1 cup	27	38	10
Lentils	1 cup	30	40	12
Navy beans	1 cup	38	54	21
Sugars				
Honey	1 tsp	73	6	4
Sucrose	1 tsp	65	5	3
Fructose	1 tsp	23	5	1
Lactose	1 tsp	46	5	2
Breads and Muffins				
Bagel	1 small	72	30	22
Whole-wheat bread	1 slice	69	13	9
White bread	1 slice	70	10	7
Croissant	1 small	67	26	17
Fruits				
Apple	1 medium	38	22	8
Banana	1 medium	55	29	16
Grapefruit	1 medium	25	32	8
Orange	1 medium	44	15	7
Beverages				
Apple juice	1 cup	40	29	12
Orange juice	1 cup	46	26	13
Gatorade	1 cup	78	15	12
Coca-Cola	1 cup	63	26	16
Snack Foods				
Potato chips	1 oz	54	15	8
Vanilla wafers	5 cookies	77	15	12
Chocolate	1 oz	49	18	9
Jelly beans	1 oz	80	26	21

Source: Foster-Powell K and others: International table of glycemic index and glycemic load. *American Journal of Clinical Nutrition* 76:5, 2002.

Carrots, much maligned in the popular press for having a high glycemic index (which isn't even true), actually contribute a low glycemic load to a diet.

Moderation in Lactose Intake Is Important for Some People

lactose maldigestion (primary and secondary) Primary lactose maldigestion occurs when lactase production declines for no apparent reason. Secondary lactose maldigestion occurs when a specific cause, such as long-standing diarrhea, results in a decline in lactase production. When noticeable symptoms develop after lactose intake, it is then called lactose intolerance.

Lactose maldigestion (when noticeable symptoms develop after lactose intake it is then called lactose intolerance) is a normal pattern of physiology that often begins to develop after early childhood, about ages 3 to 5 years.[17] It can lead to symptoms of abdominal pain, gas, and diarrhea after consuming lactose, generally when eaten in large amounts. This *primary* form of lactose maldigestion is estimated to be present in about 75% of the world's population, although not all of these individuals experience symptoms.

Another form of the problem, *secondary* lactose maldigestion, is a temporary condition in which lactase production is decreased in response to an underlying disease, such as intestinal diarrhea. The bloating and gas in lactose maldigestion are caused by bacterial fermentation of lactose in the large intestine. The diarrhea is caused by undigested lactose in the large intestine as it draws water from the circulatory system into the large intestine (osmotic effect; see Chapter 11 for more on osmosis).

In North America, approximately 25% of adults show signs of decreased lactose digestion in the small intestine, many of whom are Asian Americans, African Americans, and Hispanic Americans, especially as they age. Still, many of these individuals can consume moderate amounts of lactose with minimal or no gastrointestinal discomfort because of eventual lactose breakdown by bacteria in the large intestine, in turn reducing the osmotic effect. Thus, it is unnecessary for these people to greatly restrict their intake of lactose-containing foods. These calcium-rich food products are important for maintaining bone health. Obtaining enough calcium and vitamin D from the diet is much easier if milk and milk products are included.

It is hypothesized that approximately 3000 to 5000 years ago, a genetic mutation occurred in regions that relied on milk and dairy foods as a main food source, allowing those individuals (mostly in northern Europe, pastoral tribes in Africa, and the Middle East) to retain the ability to maintain high lactase output for their entire lifetime. This was not seen in other populations in the world, and so such digestive capability was not retained.

Recent studies have shown that nearly all individuals with decreased lactase production can tolerate ½ to 1 cup of milk with meals, and that most individuals adapt to intestinal gas production resulting from the breakdown of lactose by bacteria in the large intestine.[6] Combining lactose-containing foods with other foods also helps because certain properties of foods can have positive effects on rates of digestion. For example, fat in a meal slows digestion, leaving more time for lactase action. Hard cheese and yogurt also are more easily tolerated than milk. Much of the lactose is lost in the production of cheese, and the active bacteria cultures in yogurt digest the lactose when these bacteria are broken apart in the small intestine and release lactase. In addition, an array of products, such as low-lactose milk and lactase pills, are available to assist lactose maldigesters; still, few people actually need to use these products because their degree of maldigestion is moderate.[17]

Use of yogurt helps people with lactose maldigestion and intolerance meet calcium needs.

Concept | Check

The RDA for carbohydrate is 130 g per day. The typical North American diet provides 180 to 330 g/day. A reasonable goal is to have about half of our energy intake coming from starch and our total carbohydrate intake making up about 60% of our energy intake, with a range of 45 to 65%. This should allow for the recommended intake of 25 to 38 g of fiber/day for men and women, respectively. High-fiber diets must be accompanied by adequate fluid intakes to avoid constipation and phytobezoars and should be followed under a physician's guidance.

North Americans eat about 82 g of sugars added to foods each day. Most of these sugars are added to foods and beverages in processing. To reduce consumption of sugars, one must reduce consumption of items with added sugars, such as some baked goods, sweetened beverages, and presweetened ready-to-eat breakfast cereals. This is one practice that can help reduce the development of dental caries and likely improve diet quality. Lactose maldigestion is a condition that results when cells of the intestine do not make sufficient lactase, the enzyme necessary to digest lactose, resulting in symptoms such as abdominal gas, pain, and diarrhea. Most people with lactose maldigestion can tolerate cheeses and yogurt, as well as moderate amounts of milk.

Case Scenario | Follow-up

In the case scenario, Myeshia suspected she was sensitive to milk because, when she consumed it during one meal, she developed bloating and gas. She tried to reproduce these symptoms by eating yogurt, but was not successful. In this way, she discovered that yogurt in conjunction with milk during the meal did not produce any symptoms. As you just learned, yogurt is tolerated better than milk by people with lactose maldigestion because the bacteria that are present in yogurt digest much of the lactose. Note, however, many people with lactose maldigestion can consume moderate amounts of milk with few or no symptoms from the lactose present.

Rice is a rich source of carbohydrate.

Carbohydrates in Foods: Food Sweeteners

The foods that yield the highest percentage of energy from carbohydrates are table sugar, honey, jam, jelly, fruit, and plain baked potatoes. These foods are rich sources of carbohydrate; carbohydrates deliver much of their food energy. Corn flakes, rice, bread, and noodles all contain at least 75% of energy as carbohydrates. Foods with moderate amounts of carbohydrate energy are peas, broccoli, oatmeal, dry beans and other legumes, cream pies, french fries, and skim milk. In these foods, the carbohydrate content is diluted either by protein, as in the case of skim milk, or by fat, as in the case of a cream pie. Foods with essentially no carbohydrates include beef, eggs, chicken, fish, vegetable oils, butter, and margarine.

In planning a high-carbohydrate diet, you need to emphasize grains, pasta, fruits, and vegetables. On the other hand, you can't create a diet high in carbohydrate energy from chocolate, potato chips, and french fries because these foods contain too much fat. The percentage of energy from carbohydrate is more important than the total amount of carbohydrate in a food when planning a high-carbohydrate diet.

The various substances that impart sweetness to foods fall into two broad classes: nutritive sweeteners, which can be metabolized to yield energy, and alternative sweeteners, which provide no food energy. As was shown in Table 5-4, the alternative sweeteners are much sweeter on a per-gram basis than the nutritive sweeteners.

Food Sources of Carbohydrate

Food Item and Amount	*Carbohydrate (g)*
Baked potato, 1	51
Cola drink, 12 fluid ounces	39
M&M's plain chocolate candies, 1.5 ounces	30
Banana, 1	28
Cooked rice, ½ cup	22
Cooked corn, ½ cup	21
Yogurt with aspartame, 1 cup	19
Kidney beans, ½ cup	19
Spaghetti noodles, ½ cup	19
Orange, 1	16
Seven grain bread, 1 slice	12
Milk, 1 cup	12
Pineapple, ½ cup	10
Cooked carrots, ½ cup	8
Peanuts, 1 oz	6

Nutritive Sweeteners

Both sugars and sugar alcohols provide energy along with sweetness. Sugars are found in many different food products, whereas sugar alcohols have rather limited uses.

Sugars

All of the monosaccharides (glucose, fructose, and galactose) and disaccharides (sucrose, lactose, and maltose) that we discussed earlier are designated *nutritive sweeteners* (Table 5-7). The taste and sweetness of sucrose make it the benchmark against which all other sweeteners are measured.

A sweetener used frequently today is high-fructose corn syrup, which is 40 to 90% fructose. High-fructose corn syrup is made by treating cornstarch with acid and enzymes. This treatment breaks down much of the starch into glucose. Then some of the glucose is converted by enzymes into fructose. The final syrup is usually as sweet as sucrose. Its major advantage is that it is cheaper than sucrose. Also, it doesn't form crystals, and it has better freezing properties. High-fructose corn syrups are used in soft drinks, candies, jam, jelly, other fruit products, and desserts (e.g., packaged cookies).

In addition to sucrose and high-fructose corn syrup, brown sugar, turbinado sugar (sold as raw sugar), honey, maple syrup, and other sugars are also added to foods. Turbinado sugar is a partially refined version of raw sucrose; it has a slight molasses flavor. Brown sugar is essentially sucrose containing some molasses; either the molasses is not totally removed from the sucrose during processing or it is added to the sucrose crystals.

Table 5-7 Names of Sugars Used in Foods

Sugar	Invert sugar	Honey	Maple syrup
Sucrose	Glucose	Corn syrup or sweeteners	Dextrin
Brown sugar	Sorbitol	High-fructose corn syrup	Dextrose
Confectioner's sugar (powdered sugar)	Levulose	Molasses	Fructose
Turbinado sugar	Polydextrose	Date sugar	Maltose
	Lactose		Caramel
	Mannitol		Fruit sugar

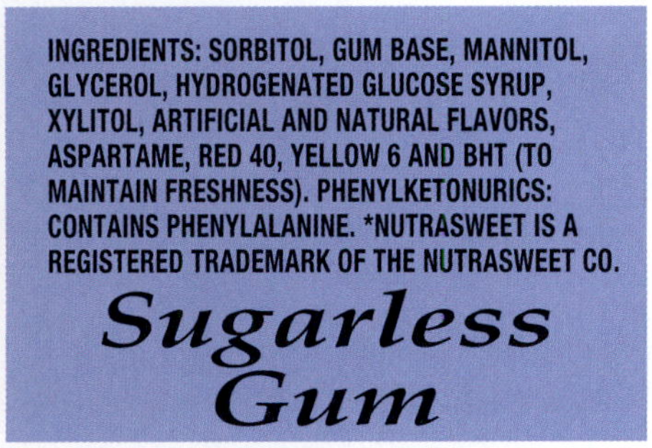

INGREDIENTS: SORBITOL, GUM BASE, MANNITOL, GLYCEROL, HYDROGENATED GLUCOSE SYRUP, XYLITOL, ARTIFICIAL AND NATURAL FLAVORS, ASPARTAME, RED 40, YELLOW 6 AND BHT (TO MAINTAIN FRESHNESS). PHENYLKETONURICS: CONTAINS PHENYLALANINE. *NUTRASWEET IS A REGISTERED TRADEMARK OF THE NUTRASWEET CO.
Sugarless Gum

Sugar alcohols can be found in sugarless gum. Note that the alternate sweetener, aspartame, is also used to sweeten this product.

Maple syrup is made by boiling down and concentrating the sap that runs during the late winter in sugar maple trees. Most pancake syrup sold in supermarkets is not pure maple syrup, which is quite expensive. Instead, it is primarily corn syrup and high-fructose corn syrup with maple flavor added.

Honey is a product of plant nectar that has been altered by bee enzymes. The enzymes break down much of the nectar's sucrose into fructose and glucose. As we noted earlier, honey offers essentially the same nutritional value as other simple sugars—a source of energy and little else. However, honey is not safe to feed to infants because it can contain spores of the bacterium *Clostridium botulinum*. These spores can become the bacteria that cause fatal foodborne illness. Honey does not pose the same threat to adults because the acidic environment of an adult's stomach inhibits the growth of the bacteria. An infant's stomach, however, does not produce much acid, making infants susceptible to the threat that this bacterium poses (see Chapters 17 and 19).

Sugar Alcohols

The sugar alcohols **sorbitol, mannitol,** and **xylitol** are also used as nutritive sweeteners. Although sugar alcohols contribute energy (about 3 kcal/g), they are absorbed and metabolized to glucose more slowly than sugars. In large quantities sugar alcohols can cause diarrhea. In fact, any products whose foreseeable consumption may result in a daily ingestion of 50 g of sorbitol or mannitol must bear this labeling statement: "Excess consumption may have a laxative effect."

Sugar alcohols must be listed on labels, and if only one sugar alcohol is used in a product it must be distinguished; however, if two or more are used in one product they are grouped together under the heading "sugar alcohols." The actual energy value is calculated, taking in account each sugar alcohol, so that, when one reads the total energy content of a product, it includes the sugar alcohols in the overall amount.

Sorbitol and xylitol are used in sugarless gum, breath mints, and candy. These are not readily metabolized by bacteria in the mouth and thus do not promote dental caries nearly so readily as simple sugars such as sucrose. Recall from Chapter 2 that such a health claim can be made on these products.

Alternative Sweeteners

Often called artificial sweeteners, alternative sweeteners include **saccharin, cyclamate, aspartame, neotame, sucralose,** and **acesulfame-K** (Fig. 5-10).[9] Alternative sweeteners yield little or no energy when consumed in amounts typically used in food products. Five are currently available in the United States: saccharin, aspartame, neotame, acesulfame-K, and sucralose. Cyclamate was banned for use in the United States in 1970, although it has never been conclusively proved to cause health problems when used appropriately. Cyclamate is used in Canada as a sweetener in medicines and as a tabletop sweetener.

sorbitol An alcohol derivative of glucose that yields about 3 kcal/g but is slowly absorbed from the small intestine. It is used in some sugarless gums and dietetic foods.

mannitol An alcohol derivative of fructose.

xylitol An alcohol derivative of the five-carbon monosaccharide xylose.

saccharin An alternative sweetener that yields no energy to the body; it is 300 times sweeter than sucrose.

cyclamate An alternative sweetener that yields no energy to the body; it is 30 times sweeter than sucrose.

aspartame An alternative sweetener made from two amino acids and methanol; it is 200 times sweeter than sucrose.

neotame A general-purpose nonnutritive sweetener that is approximately 7000 to 13,000 times sweeter than table sugar. It has a chemical structure similar to aspartame. Neotame is heat stable and can be used as a tabletop sweetener as well as in cooking applications. It is not broken down in the body after consumption to its amino acid components.

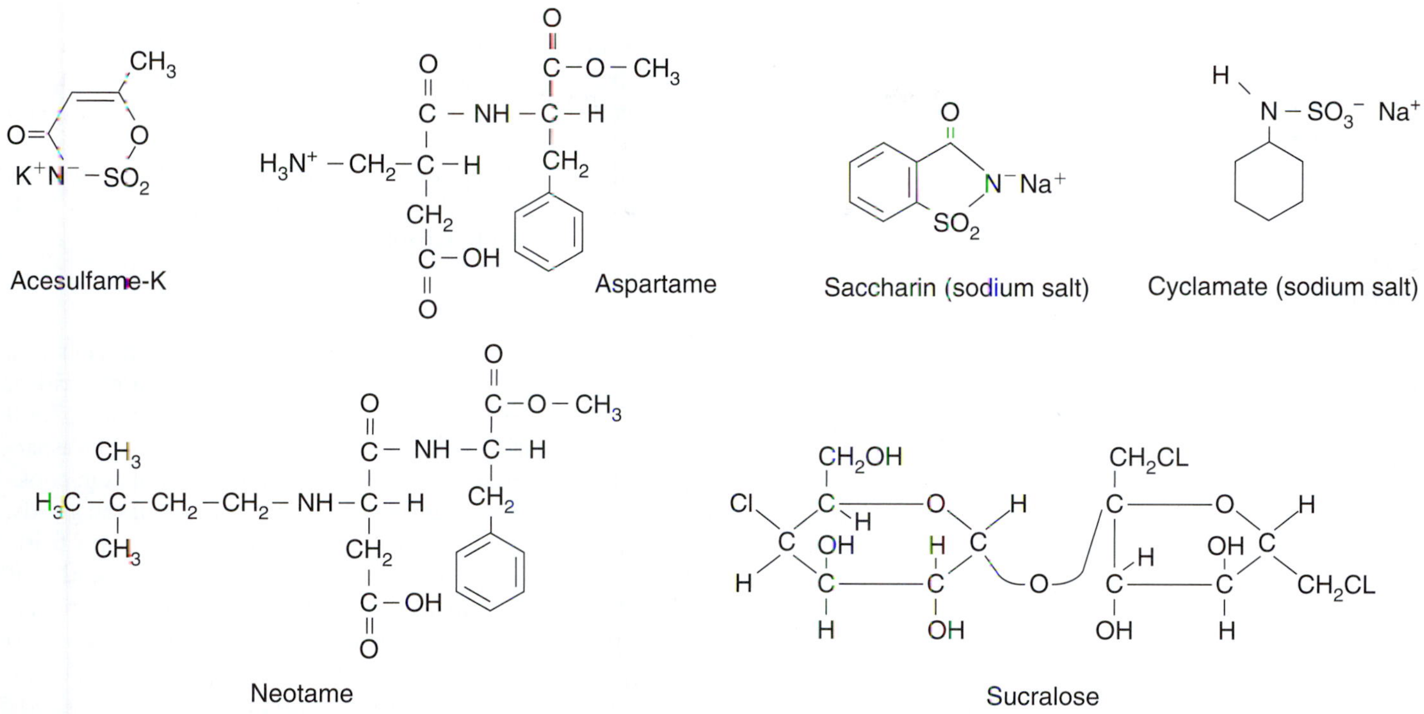

Figure 5-10 Chemical Structures of Alternative Sweeteners*

*Cyclamate is available in Canada, but not in the United States.

Saccharin

The oldest alternative sweetener, saccharin (sodium salt), was first produced in 1879 and is currently approved for use in more than 90 countries. Saccharin was once thought to pose a risk of bladder cancer based on laboratory animal studies, but it is no longer listed as a potential cause of cancer in humans since the earlier research is now considered weak and inconclusive.

Aspartame

In 1981, the alternative sweetener aspartame became available. When the NutraSweet company held the patent on aspartame, it was sold as NutraSweet when added to foods and Equal when sold as a powder. Now, though, other companies manufacture aspartame. Aspartame is in widespread use throughout the world. It has been approved for use by more than 90 countries, and its use has been endorsed by the World Health Organization, the American Medical Association, the American Diabetes Association, and the American Academy of Pediatrics Committee on Nutrition.[9]

The components of aspartame are the amino acids phenylalanine and aspartic acid, along with methanol. Recall that amino acids are the building blocks of proteins, so aspartame is more of a protein than a carbohydrate. Aspartame yields about 4 kcal/g, but it is 180 to 200 times sweeter than sucrose. Thus, only a small amount of aspartame is needed to obtain the desired sweetness, so the amount of energy added is insignificant unless the product is abused. Today aspartame is used in beverages, gelatin desserts, chewing gum, toppings and fillings in precooked bakery goods, and cookies. Aspartame does not cause tooth decay. Like other proteins, however, aspartame is damaged when heated for a long time and thus cannot be widely used in products requiring cooking.

Some complaints have been filed with FDA by people claiming to have had adverse reactions to aspartame: headaches, dizziness, seizures, nausea, and other side effects. It is important for people who are sensitive to aspartame to avoid it, even though the percentage of people being affected is likely to be small. The relatively limited number of complaints about aspartame, considering its wide use in food products, means that most people can use it.

CONTAINS: CARBONATED WATER, ORANGE JUICE, CITRIC ACID, NUTRASWEET* BRAND OF ASPARTAME**, POTASSIUM BENZOATE (A PRESERVATIVE), CITRUS PECTIN, POTASSIUM CITRATE, CAFFEINE, MALTODEXTRIN, GUM ARABIC, NATURAL FLAVORS, BROMINATED VEGETABLE OIL, YELLOW #5 AND ERYTHORBIC ACID (TO PROTECT FLAVOR).
*NUTRASWEET® AND THE NUTRASWEET SYMBOL ARE REGISTERED TRADEMARKS OF THE NUTRASWEET COMPANY.
PHENYLKETONURICS: CONTAINS PHENYLALANINE.

Note the warning above for people with PKU that this diet soft drink with aspartame contains phenylalanine.

Critical | Thinking

John and Mike are identical twins who like the same games, sports, and foods. However, John likes to chew sugar-free gum and Mike doesn't. At their last dental visit, John had no cavities, but Mike had two. Mike wants to know why John, who chews gum after eating, doesn't have cavities and he does. How would you explain this to him?

The acceptable daily intake of aspartame set by FDA is 50 mg/kg of body weight per day. This is equivalent to about 14 cans of diet soft drink for an adult or about 80 packets of Equal. Aspartame appears to be safe for pregnant women and children, but some scientists suggest cautious use by these groups, especially young children, who need ample food energy to grow.

Persons with an uncommon disease called phenylketonuria (PKU), which interferes with the metabolism of phenylalanine, should avoid aspartame because of its high phenylalanine content. (PKU was discussed in Chapter 4.)

Neotame

Neotame was recently approved by FDA for use as a general-purpose sweetener in a wide variety of food products, other than meat and poultry. Neotame is a nonnutritive, high-intensity sweetener that, depending on its food application, is approximately 7000 to 13,000 times sweeter than table sugar. It has a chemical structure similar to aspartame. Neotame is heat stable and can be used as a tabletop sweetener as well as in cooking applications. Examples of uses for which it has been approved include baked goods, nonalcoholic beverages (including soft drinks), chewing gum, confections and frostings, frozen desserts, gelatins and puddings, jams and jellies, processed fruits and fruit juices, toppings and syrups. Neotame is safe for use by the general population, including children, pregnant and lactating women, and people with diabetes. In addition, no special labeling for people with phenylketonuria is needed since after consumption neotame is not broken down in the body to its amino acid components.

Acesulfame-K

acesulfame-K An alternative sweetener that yields no energy to the body; it is 200 times sweeter than sucrose.

sucralose An alternative sweetener that has chlorines in place of some hydroxyl (–OH) groups on sucrose. It is 600 times sweeter than sucrose.

The alternative sweetener acesulfame-K (the K stands for potassium) (Sunette) was approved by FDA in July 1988. It is approved for use in more than 40 countries and has been in use in Europe since 1983. Acesulfame-K is 200 times sweeter than sucrose. It contributes no energy to the diet because it is not digested by the body, and it does not cause dental caries.

Unlike aspartame, acesulfame-K can be used in baking because it does not lose its sweetness when heated. In the United States, it is currently approved for use in chewing gum, powdered drink mixes, gelatins, puddings, baked goods, tabletop sweeteners, candy, throat lozenges, yogurt, and nondairy creamers; additional uses may soon be approved. One recent trend is to combine it with aspartame in soft drinks.

Sucralose

Sucralose (Splenda) is 600 times sweeter than sucrose. It is made by substituting three chlorines (Cl) for three hydroxyl groups (-OH) on sucrose. FDA approved sucralose's use in 1998 as an additive to foods such as soda, gum, baked goods, syrups, gelatins, frozen dairy desserts such as ice cream, jams, and processed fruits and fruit juices and for tabletop use. Sucralose doesn't break down under high heat conditions and can be used in cooking and baking. It is also excreted as such in the feces. The little that is absorbed is excreted in the urine. Canadians had access to sucralose before its U.S. introduction.

Overall, alternative sweeteners enable people with diabetes to enjoy the flavor of sweetness while controlling sugars in their diets; they also provide noncaloric or very-low-calorie sugar substitutes for persons trying to lose (or control) body weight.

Diet soft drinks typically take advantage of the alternative sweeteners such as saccharin, aspartame, and acesulfame-K.

Concept | Check

Foods that are essentially all carbohydrate are sugars, jam, jelly, fruit, and plain baked potatoes. Grains and vegetables are also rich sources of carbohydrate. Five major alternative sweeteners are available in the United States today—saccharin, aspartame, neotame, acesulfame-K, and sucralose. Canadians also have access to cyclamate. These can aid in the goal of reducing sugar intake.

Summary

1. The common monosaccharides are glucose, fructose, and galactose. Once these are absorbed from the small intestine and delivered to the liver, much of the fructose and galactose is converted to glucose.
2. The major disaccharides are sucrose (glucose plus fructose), maltose (glucose plus glucose), and lactose (glucose plus galactose). When digested, these yield their component monosaccharides.
3. One major group of polysaccharides consists of storage forms of glucose: starches in plants and glycogen in humans. In these polymers, the multiple glucose units are linked by alpha bonds, which can be broken by human digestive enzymes, releasing the glucose units. The main plant starches—straight-chain amylose and branched-chain amylopectin—are digested by enzymes in the mouth and small intestine. In humans, glycogen is synthesized in the liver and muscle tissue from glucose. Under the influence of hormones, liver glycogen is readily broken down to glucose, which can enter the bloodstream.
4. Fiber is composed primarily of the polysaccharides cellulose, hemicellulose, pectin, gum, and mucilage, as well as the noncarbohydrate lignins. These substances are not broken down by human digestive enzymes. However, soluble (also called viscous) fiber is fermented by bacteria in the large intestine.
5. Some starch digestion occurs in the mouth. Carbohydrate digestion is completed in the small intestine. Some plant fibers are digested by the bacteria present in the large intestine; undigested plant fibers become part of the feces. Monosaccharides in the intestinal contents mostly follow an active absorption process. They are then transported via the portal vein that leads directly to the liver.
6. Carbohydrates provide energy (on average, 4 kcal/g), protect against wasteful breakdown of food and body protein, and prevent ketosis. The RDA for carbohydrate is 130 g/day to meet the energy needs of the central nervous system. If carbohydrate intake is inadequate to supply the body's needs, protein is metabolized to provide glucose (gluconeogenesis) for energy needs. However, the price is loss of body protein, ketosis, and eventually a general body weakening. For this reason, low-carbohydrate diets are not recommended for extended periods (greater than 4 to 6 weeks).
7. Insoluble (also called poorly fermented) fiber provides mass to the feces, thus easing elimination. In high doses, soluble fiber can help control blood glucose in diabetic people and lower blood cholesterol.
8. Diets high in complex carbohydrates are encouraged as a replacement for high-fat diets. A goal of about half of energy as complex carbohydrates is a good one, with about 60% of total energy coming from carbohydrates in general. Foods to consume are whole-grain cereal products, pasta, legumes, fruits, and vegetables. Many of these foods are rich in fiber.
9. Moderating sugar intake, especially between meals, in turn reduces the risk of dental caries. Other health benefits also occur, such as a reduced glycemic load for a meal or snack. Alternative sweeteners, such as aspartame, aid in reducing intake of sugars.
10. The ability to digest large amounts of lactose often diminishes with age. People in some ethnic groups are especially affected. This condition develops early in childhood and is referred to as *lactose maldigestion*. Undigested lactose travels to the large intestine, resulting in such symptoms as abdominal gas, pain, and diarrhea. Most people with lactose maldigestion can tolerate cheese and yogurt and moderate amounts of milk.

Study Questions

1. Identify the three major disaccharides. Describe how each plays a part in the human diet.
2. How do amylose, amylopectin, and glycogen differ from one another? Why can this be important metabolically and in food processing?
3. What are the possible roles that dietary fiber plays in the diet?
4. Why must we generally limit our fiber intake to no more than 60 g/day? What are the possible effects of a diet too high in fiber (or too low in fluid relative to fiber content)?
5. Briefly describe the chemical structure, sweetness, and food uses of alternative sweeteners.
6. Why do we need carbohydrates in the diet? Briefly describe two reasons.
7. State the RDA for carbohydrate and summarize current carbohydrate intake recommendations.
8. Write a list of suggestions for a patient who has been diagnosed with lactose maldigestion. Design a 1-day sample menu that provides adequate calcium (1000 mg) for this patient.

After reading the Nutrition Perspective, answer the following questions:

9. How does type 1 diabetes differ from type 2 diabetes in cause and treatment?
10. What treatment is recommended for the typical form of hypoglycemia?

Annotated References

1. ADA Reports: Position of the American Dietetic Association: Health implications of dietary fiber. *Journal of the American Dietetic Association* 102:993, 2002.

   It is preferable that this fiber be obtained from foods as opposed to fiber supplements. This paper discusses the possible health benefits of fiber, as well as some of the potential negative effects of excessive fiber intake.
2. American Diabetes Association Position Statement: Evidence-based nutrition principles and recommendations for the treatment and prevention of diabetes and related complications. *Journal of the American Dietetic Association* 102:109, 2002.

   This paper discusses the goals of medical nutrition therapy for both type 1 and type 2 diabetes. Recommendations are given for amount of carbohydrate, sweeteners, alcohol, fat, cholesterol, protein, and total energy contained in the diabetic diet.

3. Berg JM and others: *Biochemistry.* New York: W. H. Freeman and Company, 2002.

   This is a college-level biochemistry textbook that serves as an excellent reference for understanding many biochemistry concepts needed in the study of nutrition, such as that regarding carbohydrate biochemistry and metabolism.

4. Diabetes: A growing public health concern. *FDA Consumer,* p. 26, January–February 2002.

   Between 1958 and 1997, the number of people diagnosed with diabetes has increased more than sixfold. Currently, it is estimated that approximately 16 million people in the United States have diabetes.

5. Diabetes Prevention Program Research Group: Reduction in the incidence of type 2 diabetes with lifestyle intervention or metformin. *The New England Journal of Medicine* 346:393, 2002.

   A lifestyle intervention program (i.e., at least a 7% weight loss and at least 150 minutes of physical activity per week) was compared to the administration of the oral diabetes medication metformin to determine the ability of each approach to lower the incidence of type 2 diabetes in those individuals who exhibit several risk factors for the disease. The authors stated that the lifestyle approach was more effective in preventing type 2 diabetes.

6. Food and Nutrition Board: *Dietary reference intakes for energy, carbohydrate, fiber, fat, fatty acids, cholesterol, protein, and amino acids.* Washington, DC: The National Academy Press, 2002.

   This report provides the latest guidance for macronutrient intakes. With regard to carbohydrate, the RDA has been set at 130 g/day. Carbohydrate intake should range from 45 to 60% of energy intake. Sugars added to foods should constitute no more than 25% of energy intake.

7. Ford E and others: Prevalence of the metabolic syndrome among U.S. Adults: findings from the Third National Health and Nutrition Examination Survey: *Journal of the American Medical Association* 287:356, 2002.

   Approximately 25% of all adults have the metabolic syndrome, with 42% of those adults aged 60 years or older having the metabolic syndrome. The underlying causes of the metabolic syndrome include a lack of physical activity and inappropriate dietary practices.

8. Fung TT and others: Whole-grain intake and the risk of type 2 diabetes: A prospective study in men. *American Journal of Clinical Nutrition* 76:535, 2002.

   In men, a diet high in whole grains is associated with a reduced risk of type 2 diabetes. This is especially seen with regard to cereal fiber intake.

9. Henkel J: Sugar substitutes: Americans opt for sweetness and lite. *FDA Consumer,* p. 12, November/December 1999.

   FDA stands behind its approval of current sugar substitutes.

10. Howarth N and others: Dietary fiber and weight regulation. *Nutrition Reviews* 59:129, 2001.

    While controversial, some researchers believe that high intakes of fiber can lead to improved weight regulation, through fiber's effects on hunger, satiety, and energy intake. In general, a high-fiber diet usually has a low energy density, slows gastric emptying, and may reduce absorption of fat and protein.

11. Inzucchi S: Oral antihyperglycemic therapy for type 2 diabetes. *Journal of the American Medical Association* 287:360, 2002.

    In the past 6 years, there has been an increase in the number of oral antihyperglycemic agents available for treatment of type 2 diabetes. This article provides summary information concerning the use of these various drug classes.

12. Johnson R, Fray C: Choose beverages and foods to moderate your intake of sugars: The 2000 Dietary Guidelines for Americans—what's all the fuss about? *Journal of Nutrition* 131:2766S, 2001.

    The 2000 Dietary Guidelines for Americans suggest that Americans attempt to moderate their intake of sugars by limiting the amount of high-sugar foods and beverages they consume. According to recent U.S. Food Supply data, Americans' per capita consumption of added sugars increased approximately 23% between 1970 and 1996, with the largest source of these added sugars being regular soft drinks.

13. Liu S: Intake of refined carbohydrates and whole-grain foods in relation to risk of type 2 diabetes mellitus and coronary heart disease. *Journal of the American College of Nutrition* 21:298, 2002.

    This review paper provides a summary of the research concerning intake of refined carbohydrate versus whole-grain carbohydrate in the development of type 2 diabetes and coronary heart disease. Epidemiological studies suggest that a higher consumption of whole-grain foods results in a lower risk of both coronary heart disease and type 2 diabetes.

14. Ludwig D: The glycemic index: Physiological mechanisms relating to obesity, diabetes, and cardiovascular disease. *Journal of the American Medical Association* 287:2414, 2002.

    In general, foods can be classified as either high-, moderate-, or low-glycemic index foods. The average glycemic index of the North American diet has increased in recent years, due to increased consumption of refined carbohydrate-containing foods.

15. Pignone M, Levin B: Recent developments in colorectal cancer screening and prevention. *American Family Physician* 66:297, 2002.

    The authors of this article provide a review of recent research concerning the accuracy and precision of screening methods as well as current research regarding the prevention of colorectal cancer, such as an adequate folate, selenium, and calcium intakes, and regular use of nonsteroidal anti-inflammatory drugs, including aspirin and COX-2 inhibitors.

16. Spanheimer R: Reducing cardiovascular risk in diabetes: Which factors to modify first? *Postgraduate Medicine* 109:26, 2001.

    Diabetes can eventually result in both microvascular and macrovascular complications, and diabetes is considered a major cardiovascular risk factor by the American Heart Association. To prevent cardiovascular disease in diabetes, tight glucose control should be maintained, high blood lipids should be managed, hypertension should be controlled, and a healthy weight should be encouraged.

17. Swagerty D and others: Lactose intolerance. *American Family Physician* 65:1845, 2002.

    Lactose maldigestion and intolerance results from a deficiency in the lactose-digesting enzyme, lactase. This is present in up to 15% of Northern Europeans, 22% of American Whites, 70% of Indians, 80% of Blacks and Hispanics, and 100% of American Indians and Asians. Most individuals with lactose maldigestion and intolerance can consume small amounts of dairy products without experiencing symptoms, and yogurts with live cultures tend to be especially well tolerated.

18. Tuomilehto J and others: Prevention of type 2 diabetes mellitus by changes in lifestyle among subjects with impaired glucose tolerance. *New England Journal of Medicine* 344:1343, 2001.

    The onset of type 2 diabetes can be delayed or prevented when high-risk people make lifestyle changes that include weight reduction, increased physical activity, adequate fiber intake, and moderation in total fat and saturated fat intake.

19. van Dam R and others: Dietary patterns and risk for type 2 diabetes mellitus in U.S. men. *Annals of Internal Medicine* 136:201, 2002.

    Using data from the Health Professionals Follow-up Study, researchers were able to classify subject's diets as "prudent," (consisting of generous amounts of fish, fruits, vegetables, poultry, and whole grains) or "western" (consisting of a higher consumption of red meat, processed meats, French fries, refined grains, sweets, and desserts). The "prudent" dietary pattern was associated with a slight decreased risk for developing type 2 diabetes, while the "western" dietary pattern was associated with a greatly increased risk for developing type 2 diabetes.

20. Willet W and others: Glycemic index, glycemic load, and risk of type 2 diabetes. *American Journal of Clinical Nutrition* 76:274S, 2002.

    Research from several recent studies indicates that diets with a high glycemic index and/or a high glycemic load are associated with an increased risk of type 2 diabetes. Replacing high glycemic load carbohydrates with low glycemic load carbohydrates may lead to a decreased risk of diabetes, as well as improved blood glucose control in diabetics.

Take | Action

I. How Does Your Diet Rate for Carbohydrate and Fiber?

Let's reevaluate the nutritional assessment you completed at the end of Chapter 2. Here are your tasks:

1. Look at your analysis and find the total number of grams of carbohydrate you ate.

   TOTAL GRAMS OF CARBOHYDRATE __________

   A. Did you consume at least the RDA of 130 g?

   B. Now calculate the percentage of energy in your diet from carbohydrate. You will need the total grams of carbohydrate from your assessment, as well as the total kcals you ate. Use this formula to calculate it:

   $$\frac{\text{Total grams of carbohydrate} \times 4}{\text{Total kcals consumed}} \times 100 = \text{\% of energy intake from carbohydrate}$$

   ANSWER: __________

   Was about 60% of your total energy intake from carbohydrate? Yes _______ No _______

   If not, list several ways you could increase your carbohydrate intake.

   ____

   ____

   ____

2. Look again at the list of foods you ate, including the amounts, and determine the total amount of fiber you consumed. If you have a computer analysis of your diet, your fiber intake is listed in the printout. Otherwise, look up the fiber content of each food you ate in the food composition table in Appendix N; then calculate your total intake, taking into account the amount of each food you ate.

   TOTAL AMOUNT OF FIBER CONSUMED _______ g

   A. Did you consume the 25 to 38 g suggested for women and men, respectively, in this chapter?

   B. If not, what could you do to increase your fiber intake? What foods could you substitute for some of the foods you ate?

   ____

   ____

   ____

3. Finally, use Table 5-5 as a guide if you need to reduce your intake of added sugars, especially if you need to watch your total energy intake to maintain an appropriate weight. What three foods might you, in fact, limit in the future?

   ____

   ____

   ____

Take | Action

II. Can You Choose the Sandwich with the Most Fiber?

Assume the sandwiches on the blackboard below are available at your local deli and sandwich shop. All of the sandwiches provide about 350 kcal. The fiber content ranges from about 1 g to about 7.5 g. Rank the sandwiches from highest amount of fiber to lowest amount; then check your answers at the bottom of the page.

Deli Specials
Turkey & Swiss on Rye
Served with tomato slices, sliced cucumbers, romaine lettuce, and mustard
Ham & Swiss on Sourdough
Extra-lean ham served with mayonnaise
Tuna Salad on Whole Wheat
Our tuna salad contains tuna, grated carrots, onions, and mayonnaise and is served with celery sticks, romaine lettuce, and cucumber slices
Hot Dog
Served on a white bun with relish, mustard, and catsup
Soyburger
Served on a whole-wheat English muffin with tomato and pickle slices, romaine lettuce, and mayonnaise
PB & J
Soft white bread with strawberry jelly and smooth peanut butter

Answer Key: 1. Soyburger: 7.5 g, 2. Tuna Salad on Whole Wheat: 7 g, 3. Turkey & Swiss on Rye: 4 g, 4. PB&J: 3 g, 5. Ham & Swiss on Sourdough: 1.5 g, 6. Hot Dog: 1g.

When Blood Glucose Regulation Fails

Improper regulation of blood glucose results in either hyperglycemia (high blood glucose) or hypoglycemia (low blood glucose). High blood glucose is most commonly associated with diabetes (technically, *diabetes mellitus*), a disease that affects about 6% of North Americans.[4] The diagnostic criteria is based on a fasting blood glucose of 126 mg/dl or greater (dl represents 100 ml [deciliter]). Of those affected, it is estimated that about ⅓ of these people do not know that they have the disease. In addition, at least another 6% of our population shows evidence of insulin resistance, but not actual diabetes (indicated by a fasting blood glucose of 110–125 mg/dl). Diabetes leads to about 200,000 deaths each year in North America, and the number of new cases is climbing yearly. New recommendations promote testing fasting blood glucose in adults over age 45 every 3 years to help diagnose these missed cases. In contrast, low blood glucose is a much rarer condition.

Previously, a fasting blood glucose of 140 mg/dl was required to diagnose diabetes. Recently, though, amounts in the 120 mg/dl range have been found to cause tissue damage. For this reason, the diagnostic trigger for diabetes using fasting blood glucose has been decreased to 126 mg/dl. The corresponding cut-off value taken 2 hours after a 75 g glucose load is 200 mg/dl.

Regulation of Blood Glucose

Under normal circumstances, blood glucose usually varies between about 70 and 109 mg/dl of blood in the fasting state, which is normally established a few hours after a meal is eaten. If blood glucose rises above 170 mg/dl, glucose begins to spill over into the urine. This leads to hunger and thirst, and eventually to weight loss. If blood glucose falls below 40 to 50 mg/dl, a person begins to feel nervous, irritable, and hungry and may develop a headache. Having high blood glucose is called **hyperglycemia.** Having low blood glucose is called **hypoglycemia.** It is not too surprising that a headache then results, because the brain is fueled almost entirely by glucose.

hyperglycemia High blood glucose, above 125 mg/dl of blood on a fasting basis.

hypoglycemia Low blood glucose, below 40 to 50 mg/dl of blood.

The liver is the main organ for controlling the amount of glucose that is eventually found in the bloodstream. Since it is the first organ to screen the sugars absorbed from the small intestine, the liver serves as a guard, helping control the amount of glucose that enters the bloodstream after a meal (review Fig. 5-5).

The pancreas is another important site of blood glucose control. Small amounts of insulin are released by the pancreas as soon as a person starts to eat. Once much of the dietary glucose enters the bloodstream, the pancreas releases large amounts of insulin. Insulin affects blood glucose in a variety of ways. It promotes increased glycogen synthesis and thus glucose storage in the liver, as well as increased glucose uptake by muscle cells, adipose cells, and some other cells. Both of these actions of insulin lower blood glucose and help return it to the normal fasting range within a few hours after a person eats. In addition, insulin reduces gluconeogenesis by the liver.[3]

Other hormones counteract the effects of insulin. When a person has not eaten carbohydrates for a few hours, the amount of glucose in the blood is maintained by the hormone glucagon, which is also released from the pancreas. This hormone prompts the breakdown of glycogen in the liver, resulting in the release of glucose to the bloodstream. Glucagon also enhances gluconeogenesis. In these ways, glucagon helps restore blood glucose to normal concentrations (Fig. 5-11).

At the same time, the hormones epinephrine (adrenaline) and norepinephrine are released from the adrenal glands and nearby nerve endings. These hormones trigger the breakdown of glycogen in the liver; the resulting glucose is released into the bloodstream. These hormones are responsible for the "fight or flight" reaction. They are released in large amounts in response to a perceived threat, such as a car approaching head-on. The resulting rapid release of glucose into the bloodstream promotes quick mental and physical reactions. Other hormones, such as cortisol and growth hormone, also help regulate blood glucose (Table 5-8).[3]

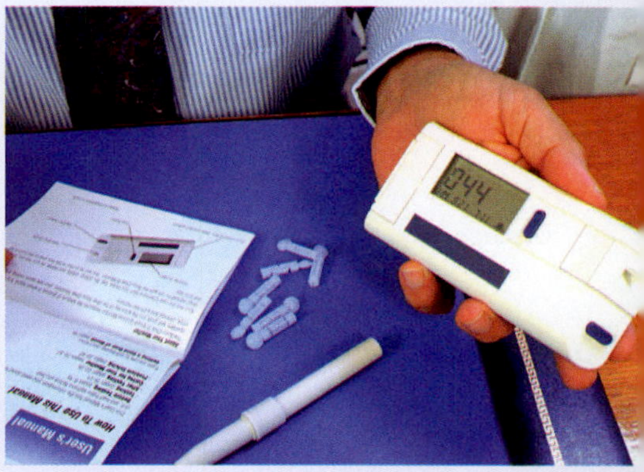

Regularly checking blood glucose is part of diabetes therapy today.

In essence, the actions of insulin on blood glucose are balanced by the actions of glucagon, epinephrine, norepinephrine, cortisol, and other hormones. If hormonal balance is not maintained, such as during overproduction or underproduction of insulin or glucagon, major changes in blood glucose concentrations

Figure 5-11 Regulation of blood glucose. Insulin and glucagon are key factors in controlling blood glucose. Other hormones, such as epinephrine, norepinephrine, cortisol, and growth hormone, also contribute to blood glucose regulation (see Table 5-8 for details).
Illustration by William Ober.

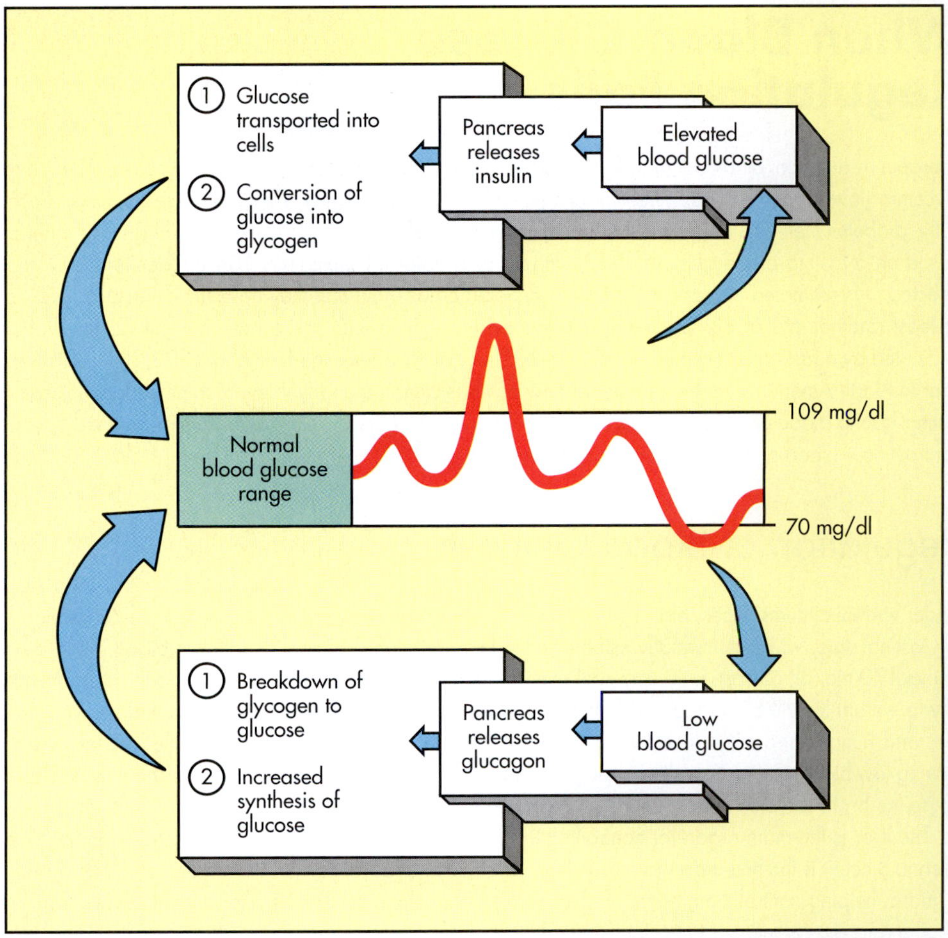

Table 5-8 Role of Various Hormones in the Regulation of Blood Glucose

Hormone	Source	Target Organ or Tissue	Overall Effect on Organ or Tissue	Effect on Blood Glucose
Insulin	Pancreas	Liver, muscle, adipose tissue	Increases glucose uptake by muscles and adipose tissue, increases glycogen synthesis, suppresses gluconeogenesis	Decrease
Glucagon	Pancreas	Liver	Increases glycogen breakdown, with release of glucose by the liver; increases gluconeogenesis	Increase
Epinephrine Norepinephrine	Adrenal glands and nerve endings	Liver, muscle	Increase glycogen breakdown, with release of glucose by the liver; increase gluconeogenesis	Increase
Cortisol	Adrenal glands	Liver, muscle	Increases gluconeogenesis by the liver, decreases glucose use by muscles and other organs	Increase
Growth hormone	Adrenal glands	Liver, muscle, adipose tissue	Decreases glucose uptake by muscles, increases fat mobilization and utilization, increases glucose output by the liver	Increase

Table 5-9 Type 1 vs. Type 2 Diabetes

	Type 1 Diabetes	Type 2 Diabetes
Incidence	5–10% of cases of diabetes	90% of cases of diabetes
Cause	Autoimmune Moderate genetic predisposition	Insulin resistance Strong genetic predisposition
Characteristics	Distinct symptoms (frequent thirst, hunger, and urination) Ketotic	Mild symptoms, especially in early phases of the disease (fatigue and nighttime urination) Generally nonketotic
Treatment	Diet Exercise Insulin	Diet Exercise Oral agents Insulin
Monitor	Blood glucose Urine ketones HbA1c	Blood glucose HbA1c

A common clinical method to determine a person's success in controlling blood glucose is to measure glycated (also termed glycosylated) hemoglobin (hemoglobin A1c). Over time, blood glucose attaches to (glycates) hemoglobin in red blood cells, and more so when blood glucose remains elevated. A hemoglobin A1c value of over 7% indicates poor blood glucose control. An acceptable value is 6% or less. Elevated blood glucose also leads to glycation of various proteins and fats in the body, forming what are called advanced glycation endproducts. These have been shown to be toxic to cells, especially those of immune systems. (Cigarette smoke is also a source.)

occur. This system of checks and balances for blood glucose regulation is typical of how the body maintains blood and other tissue concentrations of its key constituents within fairly narrow ranges.

Diabetes Mellitus

There are two major forms of diabetes: **type 1 diabetes** (formerly called insulin-dependent or juvenile-onset diabetes), and **type 2** (formerly called **non–insulin-dependent** or adult-onset **diabetes**) (Table 5-9).[2] The change in names to type 1 and type 2 diabetes stems from the fact that many "non–insulin-dependent" diabetics eventually have to also rely on insulin injections as a part of their treatment. In addition, many children today have type 2 diabetes. A third form, called gestational diabetes, occurs in pregnant women (see Chapter 16). It is usually treated with an insulin regimen and diet, and resolves after delivery of the baby. However, evidence of this problem suggests that women are at high risk for developing diabetes later in life.

Traditional symptoms of diabetes, known as the three polys, are polyuria (excessive urination), polydipsia (excessive thirst), and polyphagia (excessive hunger). No one symptom is diagnostic of diabetes, and other symptoms—such as unexplained weight loss, exhaustion, blurred vision, tingling in hands and feet, frequent infections, poor wound healing, and impotence—often accompany traditional symptoms.

Type 1 Diabetes

Type 1 diabetes often begins in late childhood, around the age of 8 to 12 years, but can occur at any age. The disease runs in certain families, indicating a clear genetic link. Children usually are admitted to the hospital with abnormally high blood glucose after eating, with ketosis.

The onset of type 1 diabetes is generally associated with decreased release of insulin from the pancreas. As insulin in the blood declines, blood glucose increases, especially after eating. When blood glucose exceeds the kidney's threshold, excess glucose spills over into the urine—hence the term *diabetes mellitus*, which means "flow of much urine" (*diabetes*) that is "sweet" (*mellitus*). Figure 5-12 shows a typical glucose tolerance curve observed in a patient with this form of diabetes, following a test load of 75 g (15 teaspoons) of glucose.

An exciting finding regarding the cause of type 1 diabetes may help physicians treat this disease or even prevent its onset in the future. Most cases of type 1 diabetes begin with an immunological disorder, which causes destruction of the insulin-producing beta cells in the pancreas. Most likely, a virus or protein foreign to the body sets off the **autoimmune** destruction. In response to their destruction, the affected beta cells release other proteins, which stimulate a more furious attack. Eventually, the pancreas loses its ability to synthesize insulin, and the clinical stage of the disease begins. Consequently, early treatment to stop the immune-linked destruction in children may be important. Research on this is continuing.

Before 1921, if a person had type 1 diabetes, a high-fat, low-calorie diet was recommended. This approach was found to be the best way to control blood glucose. It was somewhat effective but resulted in

type 1 diabetes A form of diabetes in which the person with the disease is prone to ketosis and requires insulin therapy.

type 2 (non–insulin-dependent) diabetes A form of diabetes in which ketosis is not commonly seen. Insulin therapy can be used but is often not required. This form of the disease is often associated with obesity.

autoimmune Immune reaction against normal body cells; self against self.

Figure 5-12 Glucose tolerance test. These are typical responses seen after consumption of 75 g (19 teaspoons) of glucose by a healthy person and by a person with uncontrolled diabetes or reactive hypoglycemia. Blood glucose concentration is determined during fasting and then at regular intervals after the person consumes the glucose test load. The depiction of reactive hypoglycemia is theoretical; the actual existence of this syndrome is in question. In any case, true hypoglycemia is rare.
Illustration by William Ober.

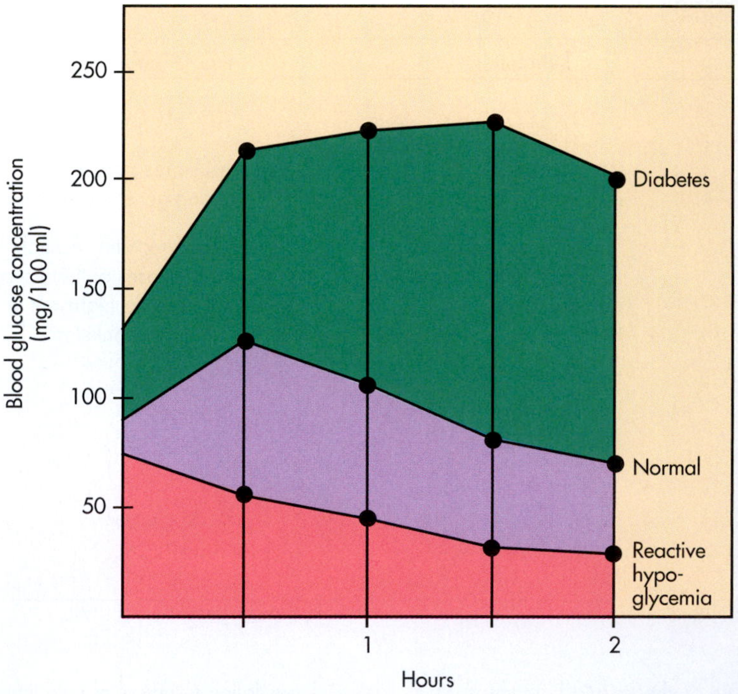

In both type 1 and type 2 diabetes, control of blood pressure and blood lipids and not smoking are keys to long-term health (see Chapters 6 and 11 for strategies).[16]

carbohydrate counting A diet method that assigns a certain number of food exchanges or carbohydrate grams to each meal and snack. Insulin is matched to carbohydrate intake (i.e., 1 unit of insulin per 10 to 15 g of carbohydrates), and carbohydrate grams can come from several combinations of exchanges.

A recent study showed no benefit when people with diabetes took vitamin E supplements.

poor growth in childhood and was difficult to implement. In the early part of the 1900s, a clinician could walk into a diabetes ward in a hospital and see scores of young, emaciated children. The isolation of insulin by Banting and Best in 1921 and the first use of it soon after in children opened a new door in diabetes care.

Today, type 1 diabetes is treated primarily by insulin therapy, either with injections two to six times a day or with an insulin pump. The pump dispenses insulin at a steady rate into the body, with greater amounts delivered after each meal. Dietary measures include three regular meals and one or more snacks (including one at bedtime), having a regulated carbohydrate:protein:fat ratio to maximize insulin action and minimize swings in blood glucose.[1] If one does not eat often enough, the injected insulin can cause severe hypoglycemia, since it acts on whatever little glucose is available. The diet should be rich in low glycemic load carbohydrates, include ample fiber and polyunsaturated fat, supply an amount of energy in balance with energy needs, and be low in both animal and other solid fats (e.g., stick margarine and shortenings), as well as moderate in high glycemic load carbohydrates.[19]

Type 1 patients often make excellent candidates for **carbohydrate counting,** a method that focuses on the amount of carbohydrates in each food choice. Type 1 patients are often very familiar with the exchange system and are motivated enough to learn how to use it to count carbohydrate intake. This method results in improved blood glucose control with a wider selection of foods.

If a high carbohydrate intake raises triglyceride and cholesterol in the blood beyond desired ranges, carbohydrate intake can be reduced and replaced with unsaturated fat. This change tends to reduce blood triglycerides and cholesterol. Chapter 6 discusses how to implement such a diet. Moderate consumption of sugars with meals is fine, as long as blood glucose regulation is preserved and the sugars replace other carbohydrates in the meal, so that undesirable weight gain does not take place.[2]

Because people with diabetes (type 1 as well as type 2) are at a high risk for cardiovascular disease and related heart attacks, they should take an aspirin each day (generally 80 mg/day to 160 mg/day) if their physicians find no reason not to do so. As discussed in Chapter 6, this practice reduces the risk of heart attack. In fact, the latest evidence suggests that diabetes essentially guarantees development of cardiovascular disease. Vitamin E (200 milligrams [about 400 IU] per day) may be prescribed because of this increased risk of cardiovascular disease. However, there is no convincing evidence that this vitamin E use produces such a benefit with regard to prevention of cardiovascular disease in people with diabetes (see Chapters 6 and 9 for details on vitamin E and cardiovascular disease).

The hormone imbalances that occur in people with untreated type 1 diabetes lead to mobilization of body fat, which is released into liver cells. Ketosis is the result because the fat is mostly converted to ketone bodies. These can rise excessively in the blood, eventually forcing ketone bodies into the urine. These pull sodium and potassium ions with them into the urine. This series of events can contribute to a chain reaction, which eventually leads to dehydration, ion imbalance, coma, and even death, especially in patients with poorly controlled type 1 diabetes. Treatment includes insulin and fluids, as well as sodium, potassium, and chloride.

Other complications of diabetes can be degenerative conditions, such as blindness, cardiovascular disease, and kidney disease; all are caused by poor blood glucose regulation. Nerves can also deteriorate, resulting in many changes that decrease proper nerve stimulation. When this occurs in the intestinal tract, intermittent diarrhea and constipation result. Because of nerve deterioration in the extremities, many people with diabetes lose the sensation of pain associated with injuries or infections. Not having as much pain, they often delay treatment of hand or foot problems. This delay, combined with a rich environment for bacterial growth (bacteria thrive on glucose) sets the stage for complications in the extremities, such as the need for amputation of feet and legs. High blood glucose also contributes to a rapid buildup of fats in blood vessel walls, which eventually limits the blood supply to various organs such as the heart. See Chapter 6 for details.

Current research, such as the Diabetes Control and Complications Trail (DCCT), has shown that the development of blood vessel and nerve complications of diabetes can be slowed with aggressive treatment directed at keeping blood glucose within the normal range. The therapy poses some risks of its own, such as hypoglycemia, so it must be implemented under the close supervision of a physician.[16]

A person with diabetes generally must work closely with a physician and dietitian to make the correct alterations in diet and medications and to perform physical activity safely. Physical activity enhances glucose uptake by muscles independent of insulin action, which in turn can lower blood glucose. This outcome is beneficial, but people with diabetes need to be aware of their own blood glucose response to physical activity and compensate appropriately.[2]

Type 2 Diabetes

Regular exercise is a key part of a plan to prevent (and control) type 2 diabetes.

Type 2 diabetes typically begins after age 40. This is the most common type of diabetes, accounting for about 90% of the cases diagnosed in North America. Minority populations such as Latino/Hispanic, African Americans, Asian Americans, Native Americans, and Pacific Islanders are at particular risk. The number of people affected with this form of diabetes is especially on the rise, primarily because of widespread inactivity and obesity in our population. In fact, recently there has been a substantial increase in type 2 diabetes in children, due mostly to an increase in overweight in this population (coupled with limited physical activity).[4] This type of diabetes is also genetically linked, but the initial problem is not with the beta cells of the pancreas. Instead, it arises with the insulin receptors on the cell surfaces of certain body tissues, especially muscle tissue. In this case, blood glucose is not readily transferred into cells, so the patient develops hyperglycemia as a result of the glucose's remaining in the bloodstream. The pancreas attempts to increase insulin output to compensate, but there is a limit to its ability to do this. Thus, rather than insufficient insulin production, there is an abundance of insulin, particularly during the onset of the disease. As the disease develops, pancreatic function can fail, leading to reduced insulin output. Because of the genetic link for type 2 diabetes, those who have a family history should be careful to avoid risk factors such as obesity, a diet rich in animal and other solid fats, and high glycemic load foods, and inactivity. Being tested regularly for hyperglycemia is also important.[19]

Many cases of type 2 diabetes (about 80%) are associated with obesity (especially fat located in the abdominal region), but the hyperglycemia is not directly caused by the obesity. In fact, some lean people also develop this type of diabetes. Obesity associated with oversized fat cells simply increases the risk for insulin resistance by the body, in turn increasing the risk for type 2 diabetes.

Type 2 diabetes linked to obesity often disappears as weight is lost. Achieving a healthy weight should be a primary goal of treatment, but even limited weight loss can lead to better blood glucose regulation.[5, 18] Oral medications can also help. Some examples are medications that reduce glucose production by the liver (metformin [Glucophage]), increase the ability of the pancreas to release insulin (glipizide [Glucotrol]), and increase the body's response to its own insulin (rosiglitazone [Avandia]). Another class of oral agents used works by delaying carbohydrate digestion and glucose absorption (acarbose [Precose]). A tablet is taken with the first bite of each meal and may be combined with other therapy.[11] (Note that pregnant women cannot use these oral medications because they will affect the blood glucose of the developing fetus.)

Recently people with diabetes have been cautioned not to cook foods at high temperatures for prolonged periods of time. This leads to advanced glycation endpoints forming in food. Use of a lower power setting with a microwave oven, lower oven temperatures, and minimal use of prolonged broiling and prolonged frying is advised. Colas and coffee are also sources of these compounds.

For more information on diabetes, consult the following websites: **www.diabetes.org** and **ndep.nih.gov**

reactive hypoglycemia Low blood glucose that follows a meal high in simple sugars, with corresponding symptoms of irritability, headache, nervousness, sweating, and confusion; also called *postprandial hypoglycemia*.

fasting hypoglycemia Low blood glucose that follows about a day of fasting.

Sometimes it may be necessary to provide insulin injections in type 2 diabetes because nothing else is able to control blood glucose. (This eventually becomes the case in about half of all cases of type 2 diabetes.) Regular physical activity also helps the muscles take up more glucose. And regular meal patterns, with an emphasis on control of energy intake, consumption of low glycemic load foods, with ample fiber, is important therapy. Note that nuts fulfill the last two goals. (An almost daily [$\geq 5\times$/week] intake of nuts was even shown to reduce the risk of developing type 2 diabetes in one recent study.) Some intake of sugars is fine with meals, but again these must be substituted for other carbohydrates, not simply added to the meal plan. Distributing carbohydrates throughout the day is also important, as this helps minimize the high and low swings in blood glucose concentrations.[2] Moderate alcohol use is fine (one serving per day). One recent study showed that this practice substantially reduced heart attack risk in people with type 2 diabetes. Still, the person must be warned that alcohol can lead to hypoglycemia and that the person must test him- or herself regularly for this possibility. Supplemental vitamin E may also be prescribed, as was discussed for type 1 diabetes, but again the benefits of such a practice are in doubt.

People with type 2 diabetes who have high blood triglycerides should moderate their carbohydrate intake and increase their intake of unsaturated fat and fiber, as noted earlier for people with type 1 diabetes.

Although many cases of type 2 diabetes can be relieved by reducing excess fat stores, many people are not able to lose weight. They remain affected with diabetes and may experience the degenerative complications seen in the type 1 form of the disease. Ketosis, however, is not usually seen in type 2 diabetes.

Hypoglycemia

As noted earlier, diabetic people who are taking insulin sometimes have hypoglycemia if they don't eat frequently enough. Hypoglycemia can also develop in nondiabetic individuals. The two common forms of nondiabetic hypoglycemia are termed *reactive* and *fasting*.

Reactive hypoglycemia (also called postprandial hypoglycemia) is described as irritability, nervousness, headache, sweating, and confusion 2 to 4 hours after eating a meal, especially a meal high in simple sugars. The cause of reactive hypoglycemia is unclear, but it may be overproduction of insulin by the pancreas in response to rising blood glucose. Some researchers are unwilling even to acknowledge the existence of reactive hypoglycemia, pointing out that the symptoms are more likely tied to recent, intense exercise, psychological stress, medication use, or excess alcohol consumption. **Fasting hypoglycemia** usually is caused by pancreatic cancer, which may lead to excessive insulin secretion. In this case, blood glucose falls to low concentrations after fasting for about 8 hours to 1 day. This form of hypoglycemia is rare.

The diagnosis of hypoglycemia requires the simultaneous presence of low blood glucose and the typical hypoglycemic symptoms. Blood glucose of 40 to 50 mg/100 ml is suggestive, but just having low blood glucose after eating is not enough evidence to make the diagnosis of hypoglycemia. Although many people think they have hypoglycemia, few actually do.

It is normal for healthy people to have some hypoglycemic symptoms, such as irritability, headache, and shakiness, if they have not eaten for a prolonged period of time. Although not diagnostic of hypoglycemia, if you sometimes have symptoms of hypoglycemia, the standard nutrition therapy is one we all could follow. You need to eat regular meals, make sure you have some protein and fat in each meal, and eat low glycemic load carbohydrates with ample soluble fiber. Avoid meals or snacks that contain little more than sugar. If symptoms continue, try small protein-containing snacks between meals or fruits and juice. Fat, protein, and soluble fiber in the diet tend to moderate swings in blood glucose. Last, moderate caffeine and alcohol intake.

chapter 6

Lipids

Chapter | Outline

Case | Scenario

Jackie is a 21-year-old health-conscious individual in her third year of nursing school. She recently learned that a diet high in saturated fat can contribute to high blood cholesterol and that exercise is beneficial for the heart. Jackie now takes a brisk 30-minute walk each morning before going to class, and she has started to cut as much fat out of her diet as she can, replacing it mostly with carbohydrates. A typical daily intake for Jackie now might begin with a breakfast of a bowl of Fruity Pebbles with 1 cup of skim milk and ½ cup of apple juice. For lunch, she might pack a turkey sandwich on white bread with lettuce, tomato, and mustard; a small package of fat-free pretzels; and a handful of fat-reduced vanilla wafers. Dinner could be a large portion of pasta with some olive oil and garlic mixed in, and a small iceberg lettuce salad with lemon juice squeezed over it. Her snacks are usually baked chips, low-fat cookies, fat-free frozen yogurt, or the fat-free pretzels. She drinks diet soft drinks throughout the day as her main beverage.

Do you think this is a healthy way for Jackie to reduce fat in her diet? Point out some positive practices. What would you suggest changing in her diet to make it more heart healthy?

Refresh | Your Memory

As you begin your study of lipids in Chapter 6, you may want to review:

- Legal definitions for various labeled descriptors, such as low-fat and nonfat in Chapter 2.
- The concept of energy density in Chapter 2.
- The Mediterranean Diet Pyramid in Chapter 2.
- The process of digestion and absorption and gastrointestinal hormones in Chapter 3.
- The glycemic load of foods, the relationship between overweight status and insulin resistance, and the Metabolic Syndrome (also called Syndrome X) in Chapter 5.

Boost | Your Study

*Refer to **Perspectives in Nutrition: Online Learning Center** www.mhhe.com/wardlawpers6 for quizzes, flash cards, activities, and web links designed to further help you learn about dietary lipids.*

Chapter | Objectives

Chapter 6 is designed to allow you to:

1. List four classes of lipids (fats) and the role of each in nutritional health.
2. Differentiate between fatty acids and triglycerides.
3. Differentiate among saturated, monounsaturated, and polyunsaturated fatty acids in terms of structure and food sources.
4. Name the two essential fatty acids and explain why they are called "essential."
5. Name the classes of lipoproteins and classify them according to their functions.
6. Discuss the implications of various fats, including omega-3 fatty acids, with respect to cardiovascular disease.
7. Identify available fat replacements.
8. Characterize the symptoms of cardiovascular disease and highlight some known risk factors.

Your doctor informs you that your "triglycerides are too high." Your bill from a medical laboratory reads "Blood lipid profile—$55." A health food advertisement suggests using cholestin, a dietary supplement, to lower blood cholesterol. Advertisers plug foods "lowest in saturated fat." All of these substances—triglycerides, saturated fat, and cholesterol—are lipids, a collective term referring to fats and oils.

Lipids contain more than twice the energy per gram (on average, 9 kcal) as proteins and carbohydrates (on average, 4 kcal each). Consumption of common saturated fatty acids also contributes to the risk of cardiovascular disease (CVD).[18] For this reason, some concern about lipids is warranted, but certain lipids also play vital roles both in the body and in foods. Their presence in the diet is essential to good health and should in general comprise 20 to 35% of our total energy intake.[5]

Let's look at lipids in detail—their forms, functions, metabolism, and food sources. This chapter will then conclude with a look at the link between lipid intake and the major "killer" disease in North America: cardiovascular disease which involves both the coronary arteries (coronary heart disease) and other arteries in the body.

Lipids: Common Properties and Main Types

Humans need very little fat in their diet to maintain health. In fact, daily consumption of 2 to 4 tbsp of plant oil incorporated into foods and at least twice weekly consumption of fatty fish such as salmon or tuna meet the body's need for the essential fatty acids.[5] If fish is not consumed, the essential fatty acids in canola oil and soybean oil contribute some of the same health benefit as those found in fish. Thus, one could follow a purely vegetarian diet containing about 10% of energy from fat and still maintain health. However, as long as saturated fat, cholesterol, and partially hydrogenated fat (technically called *trans fat*) is minimized, fat intake can be considerably higher than that 10% allotment. Recent recommendations from the Food and Nutrition Board suggest that fat intake can be as high as 35% of energy intake.[5] Some experts suggest that an intake as high as 40% of energy intake is appropriate. After learning more about lipids—fats, oils, and related compounds—in this chapter, you can decide for yourself how much fat you want to consume, as well as how to track your daily intake.

Lipids are a diverse group of chemical compounds. They share one main characteristic: They do not readily dissolve in water but do so in organic solvents, such as chloroform, benzene, and ether. Think of an oil and vinegar salad dressing. The oil is not soluble in the water-based vinegar; on standing, the two separate into distinct layers, with oil on top and vinegar on the bottom.

The diversity of lipids is evident when you compare the structures of two common examples: a **fatty acid** versus cholesterol, shown in Figure 6-1. Triglycerides are the most common type of lipid found in the body and in foods. Each triglyceride molecule consists of a **glycerol** with three fatty acids attached to it. **Phospholipids** and **sterols** are also classified as lipids, although their structures can be quite different from the structure of triglycerides (see Fig. 6-1). All these lipid compounds are described in this chapter.

As noted in Chapter 1, lipids that are solid at room temperature are called *fats*, and lipids that are liquid are called *oils*. Most people use the word *fat* to refer to all lipids because they don't realize there is a difference. As already covered, however, *lipid* is a generic term that includes triglycerides and many other substances. To simplify our discussion, this chapter primarily uses the term *fat;* however, as you will see later, not all the substances we call fats truly are fats. When necessary for clarity, the name of a specific lipid, such as cholesterol, will be used. This word usage is consistent with the way many people use these terms in health-care settings.

fatty acid A chain of carbons chemically bonded together and surrounded by hydrogen molecules. These hydrocarbons are found in lipids and contain a carboxyl (acid group) ($-\overset{O}{\overset{\|}{C}}-OH$) at one end and a methyl group ($-CH_3$) at the other.

glycerol A three-carbon alcohol used to form triglycerides.

phospholipid Any of a class of fat-related substances that contain phosphorus, fatty acids, and a nitrogen-containing base. The phospholipids are an essential part of every cell.

sterol A compound containing a multi-ring (steroid) structure and a hydroxyl group (–OH).

Fatty Acids: The Simplest Form of Lipids

The fatty acid is common to most lipids, both those in the body and in foods. It is basically a long chain of carbons linked together and flanked by hydrogens. At one end of the molecule, designated the *alpha end,* is an acid (specifically a carboxyl [$-\overset{O}{\overset{\|}{C}}-OH$]) group. At the other end, called the *omega (ω) end,* is a methyl group ($-CH_3$) (Fig. 6-1*A*). In the Greek alphabet, *alpha* is the first letter and *omega* is the last.

In some cases *n* is used rather than omega (ω). Thus, you may see n-3 or ω-3 fatty acids as the term used.

Fats in foods are not composed of a single type or category of fatty acid. Rather, each dietary fat is a complex mixture of different fatty acids.

If all the chemical bonds between the carbons are single connections and the carbons are filled with hydrogens, a fatty acid is said to be **saturated** (Fig. 6-1*A*). To understand this concept, picture a sponge saturated (full) with water. In this sense, the fatty acid is saturated with hydrogen.

saturated fatty acid A fatty acid with no carbon-carbon double bonds.

As noted earlier, most fats high in saturated fatty acids, such as animal fats, remain solid at room temperature. A good example is the solid fat surrounding a piece of uncooked steak at room temperature. Chicken fat, semisolid at room temperature, contains less saturated fat. In some foods, such as whole milk, saturated fats are suspended in liquid, so the solid nature of these fats at room temperature is less apparent. Milk actually contains a combination of liquid and solid fats, as will be discussed shortly.

Figure 6-1 The families of lipids and some metabolic products (the eicosanoids). For simplicity's sake, the last three structures have most of the carbons and hydrogens deleted. Wherever there is a corner, it represents a carbon with two hydrogens, since a carbon atom must form four bonds for a stable structure (see Appendix A for details). Note also the shorthand notation used to describe fatty acids. The first number indicates the number of carbons; the second number lists the number of double bonds. Thus, stearic acid (structure *A*) is C18:0.

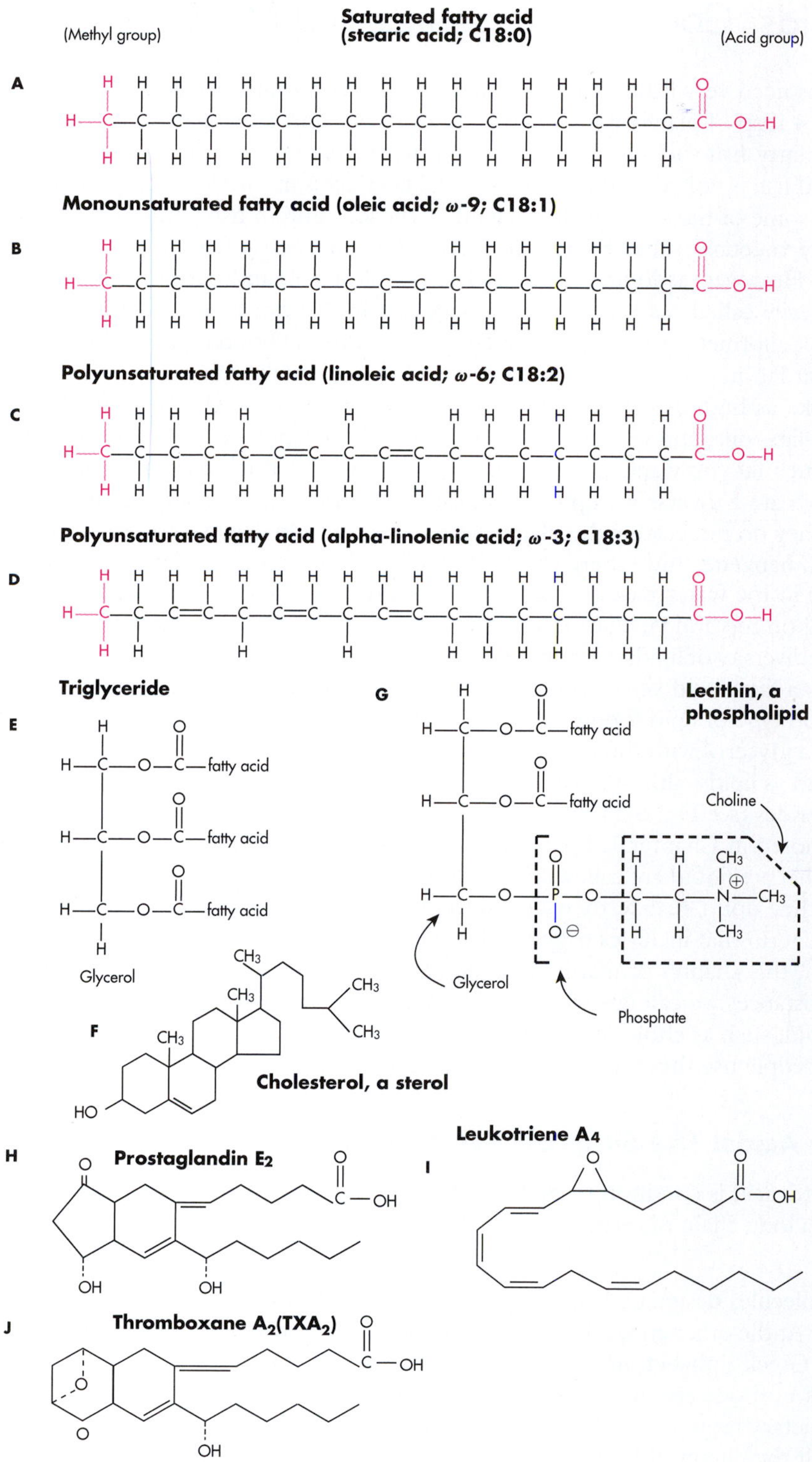

monounsaturated fatty acid A fatty acid containing one carbon-carbon double bond.

polyunsaturated fatty acid A fatty acid containing two or more carbon-carbon double bonds.

If a fatty acid is unsaturated, hydrogens are missing from the carbon chain—specifically, at the area of the carbon-carbon double bonds. If a fatty acid has one double bond between the carbons, it is **monounsaturated** (Fig. 6-1*B*). Canola and olive oils contain a high percentage of monounsaturated fatty acids. If two or more bonds between the carbons are double bonds, the fatty acid is **polyunsaturated** and thus even less saturated with hydrogens (Fig. 6-1*C, D*). Corn, soybean, sunflower, and safflower oils are rich in polyunsaturated fatty acids.

Dietary fat	Cholesterol (mg/tbsp)	Saturated fatty acid	Linoleic acid	Alpha-linolenic acid	Monounsaturated fatty acid
Canola oil	0	6%	22%	10%	62%
Safflower oil	0	10%	77%	Trace –	13%
Sunflower oil	0	11%	69%		20%
Corn oil	0	13%	61%		25%
Olive oil	0	14%	8%	– 1%	77%
Soybean oil	0	15%	54%	7%	24%
Margarine	0	17%	32%	– 2%	49%
Peanut oil	0	18%	33%		49%
Vegetable shortening	0	28%	26%	– 2%	44%
Palm oil	0	45%	12%	– 1%	37%
Palm kernel oil	0	52%	10%	– 1%	11%
Coconut oil	0	92%	2%		6%
Lard	12	41%	11%	– 1%	47%
Beef fat	14	52%	3%	– 1%	44%
Butter fat	33	66%	2%	– 2%	30%

Breakdown of fatty-acid content (normalized to 100%). Polyunsaturated fat: linoleic acid, alpha-linolenic acid.

Figure 6-2 Comparison of dietary fats in terms of saturated fatty acids, the most common unsaturated fatty acids, and cholesterol content.

Olive and canola oils are rich in monounsaturated fat; olive oil has been awarded much attention in recent years. Canola oil, however, is a much less expensive choice for consumers. Safflower oil is rich in polyunsaturated fat.

Saturated fatty acids are linear, allowing them to pack tightly together. In contrast, unsaturated fatty acids have a kinked shape and thus pack together only loosely (this is depicted later in the chapter in Fig. 6-11). The loose organization of unsaturated fats is more easily disrupted by heat than is the more ordered organization of saturated fats. Thus, dietary fats high in unsaturated fatty acids melt at a lower temperature than fats high in saturated fatty acids (especially **long-chain** ones [12 carbons or longer]).

Overall, a fat or an oil is classified as saturated, monounsaturated, or polyunsaturated based on the nature of the fatty acids present in the greatest concentration (Fig. 6-2).

Triglycerides that contain primarily saturated fatty acids are solid at room temperature, especially if the fatty acids have a long chain. **Medium-chain** saturated fatty acids (6 to 10 carbons long), such as those in coconut oil, produce liquid oils at room temperature. This remains true even though coconut oil consists primarily of saturated fatty acids, because the shorter chain length overrides the effect of saturation. **Short-chain** saturated fatty acids (less than 6 carbons long) also form liquid oils at room temperature. Dairy fats are sources of these short-chain fatty acids. Triglycerides containing primarily polyunsaturated or monounsaturated fatty acids are also usually liquid at room temperature. These are not affected by chain length.

long-chain fatty acids Fatty acids that contain 12 or more carbons.

medium-chain fatty acid A fatty acid that contains 6 to 10 carbons.

short-chain fatty acids Fatty acids that contain fewer than six carbon atoms.

omega-3 (ω-3) fatty acid An unsaturated fatty acid with the first double bond on the third carbon from the methyl end ($-CH_3$).

omega-6 (ω-6) fatty acid An unsaturated fatty acid with the first double bond on the sixth carbon from the methyl end ($-CH_3$).

alpha-linolenic acid An essential omega-3 fatty acid with 18 carbons and three double bonds (C18:3, ω-3).

linoleic acid An essential omega-6 fatty acid with 18 carbons and two double bonds (C18:2, ω-6).

oleic acid An omega-9 fatty acid with 18 carbons and one double bond (C18:1, ω-9).

Essential Fatty Acids

The actual location of the carbon-carbon double bonds in the carbon chain of a polyunsaturated fatty acid makes a big difference in how the body metabolizes it. If the first double bond starts at three carbons from the methyl (omega) end of the fatty acid, it is an **omega-3 (ω-3) fatty acid** (see Fig. 6-1*D*). If the first double bond starts at six carbons from the methyl end of the fatty acid, it is an **omega-6 (ω-6) fatty acid** (see Fig. 6-1*C*). Following the same scheme, an omega-9 fatty acid has the first double bond starting nine carbons from the methyl end of the fatty acid. In foods, **alpha-linolenic acid** is the major omega-3 fatty acid; **linoleic acid** is the major omega-6 fatty acid; and **oleic acid** is the major omega-9 fatty acid.[5]

essential fatty acids Fatty acids that must be supplied by the diet to maintain health. Currently, only linoleic acid and alpha-linolenic acid are classified as essential.

eicosanoids Hormonelike compounds synthesized from polyunsaturated fatty acids, such as arachidonic acid. Within this class of compounds are prostaglandins, thromboxanes, and leukotrienes.

Because we must obtain linoleic acid (ω-6) and alpha-linolenic acid (ω-3) from foods in order to maintain health, they are called **essential fatty acids.** These omega-3 and omega-6 fatty acids form parts of vital body structures, perform important roles in immune system function and vision, help form cell membranes, and produce hormonelike compounds called **eicosanoids** (see Fig. 6-1*H, I*).[5] This dietary necessity arises because cells in the human body can produce carbon-carbon double bonds in a fatty acid only starting at the ninth carbon numbered from the methyl end. In other words, human cells do not produce the enzyme to place double bonds between the methyl end and the ninth carbon. On the other hand, omega-9 fatty acids can be synthesized in the body because the double bond falls after the ninth carbon.

Some fish pose a risk for mercury exposure, including swordfish. For these fish infrequent intake is suggested (see Chapter 19 for details). As noted in Chapter 16, this practice is especially important for pregnant and lactating women.

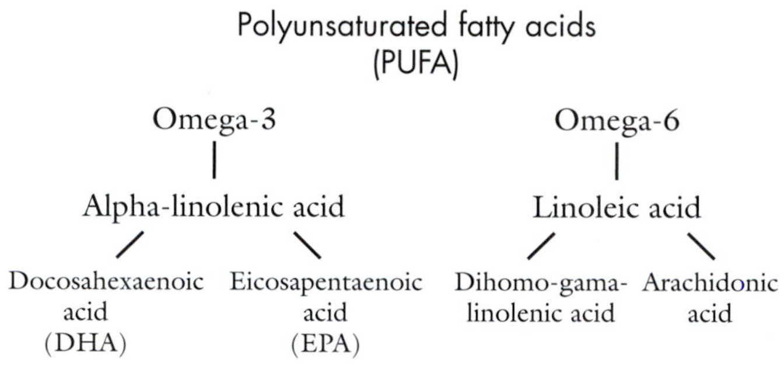

Essential fatty acid (EFA) family. All are available from dietary sources; linoleic acid and alpha-linolenic acid must be consumed as body synthesis does not take place. These are the essential fatty acids. The other fatty acids in this figure can be synthesized to some extent from the essential fatty acids.

Still, we need to consume only about 5% of our total energy intake from essential fatty acids.[5] That corresponds to about 2 to 4 tbsp of plant oil each day. We can easily get that much via mayonnaise, salad dressings, margarine, and other foods. Regular consumption of whole grains and vegetables also help supply essential fatty acids.

eicosapentaenoic acid (EPA) An omega-3 fatty acid with 20 carbons and five carbon-carbon double bonds (C20:5, ω-3). It is present in large amounts in fish oils and is synthesized slowly in the body from alpha-linolenic acid. EPA is metabolized to eicosanoids.

docosahexaenoic acid (DHA) An omega-3 fatty acid with 22 carbons and six carbon-carbon double bonds (C22:6, ω-3). It is present in large amounts in fish oils and is synthesized slowly in the body from alpha-linolenic acid. DHA is especially present in the retina and brain.

We also need to specifically include a regular intake of alpha-linolenic acid or one of its related omega-3 fatty acids, **eicosapentaenoic acid (EPA)** and **docosahexaenoic acid (DHA).** This would almost certainly require at least twice weekly consumption of fatty fish, such as salmon, tuna, sardines, herring, mackerel, whitefish, wild trout, swordfish, and halibut; regular intake of canola or soybean oil; or consumption of walnuts or flax seeds. All are sources of omega-3 fatty acids. In some instances, fish oil capsules can be safely substituted (under a physician's guidance) for fish consumption if a person does not like fish. Generally, about 1 gram of omega-3 fatty acids (about three capsules) from fish oil per day is recommended, especially if a person has evidence of cardiovascular disease.[4] The importance of omega-3 fatty acid intake will be explored further in the Expert Opinion by Dr. Kenneth S. Broughton.

Effects of a Deficiency of Essential Fatty Acids

total parenteral nutrition The intravenous provision of all necessary nutrients, including the most basic forms of protein, carbohydrates, lipids, vitamins, minerals, and electrolytes. This solution is generally infused for 12 to 24 hours a day in a volume of about 2 to 3 L.

If humans fail to consume enough essential fatty acids, their skin becomes flaky and itchy, and diarrhea and other symptoms such as infections often are seen. Growth and wound healing may be restricted, and anemia can develop. These signs of deficiency have been seen in people fed **total parenteral nutrition** solutions containing little or no fat for 2 to 3 weeks (rarely done today), as well as in infants receiving formulas low in fat.[5] However, because our bodies need the equivalent of only about 2 to 4 tbsp of plant oils a day, even a low-fat diet will provide enough essential fatty acids if it follows a balanced plan such as the Food Guide Pyramid and includes a serving of fish at least twice a week.

Concept | Check

Lipids are a group of compounds that dissolve in organic solvents but do not dissolve readily in water. They include fatty acids, triglycerides, phospholipids, and sterols. Fatty acids differ from one another mainly in the number and location of the double bonds between carbons in the carbon chain. Saturated fatty acids contain no carbon-carbon double bonds; that is, they are fully saturated with hydrogens. Monounsaturated fatty acids contain one carbon-carbon double bond, and polyunsaturated fatty acids contain two or more carbon-carbon double bonds.

Length of the carbon chain in fatty acids affects the consistency of triglycerides at room temperature. Specifically, long-chain saturated fatty acids (greater than or equal to 12 carbons) form solid varieties at room temperature, whereas medium-chain (6 to 10 carbons) and short-chain (less than 6 carbons) saturated fatty acids form liquid varieties at room temperature, as do triglycerides composed of monounsaturated polyunsaturated fatty acids.

If a double bond first occurs starting at the third carbon from the methyl ($-CH_3$) end of the carbon chain, the fatty acid is an omega-3 fatty acid. If a double bond first occurs starting at the sixth carbon, it is an omega-6 fatty acid. Because humans can't synthesize some omega-3 and omega-6 fatty acids, which perform vital functions in the body, they are designated *essential fatty acids,* indicating that they must be included in the diet to maintain health.

Critical | Thinking

Advertisements often claim that fats are bad. Your classmate Mike asks, "If fats are so bad for us, why do we need to have any in our diets?" How would you answer him?

Triglycerides

Fats and oils in foods are mostly in the form of triglycerides. The same is true for fats found in body structures. Some fatty acids are found attached to proteins in the bloodstream as they are being transported, but most fatty acids do not exist in the body as such. Instead, they form into triglycerides.

Triglycerides contain a simple three-carbon alcohol, glycerol, which serves as a backbone for the three attached fatty acids. A fatty acid is attached to each of the three hydroxyl groups (–OH) of glycerol. Three water molecules are released in the process of bonding three fatty acids to glycerol (Fig. 6-3). Note that triacylglyceride is the chemical name of the molecule, as *acyl* refers to a fatty acid that has lost its hydroxyl group, and a hydroxyl group is lost when each fatty acid attaches to glycerol.

The bonds between glycerol and each fatty acid are called *ester bonds.* The process of chemically attaching fatty acids to glycerol is called **esterification.** The release of fatty acids from glycerol is called *deesterification.*

By breaking off (deesterifying) one of the fatty acids of a triglyceride molecule, a diglyceride (glycerol with two attached fatty acids) is formed. The deesterification of two of the fatty acids on a triglyceride produces a **monoglyceride** (glycerol with one attached fatty acid). Free fatty acids, monoglycerides, and glycerol—but not triglycerides—can cross cell membranes.

During digestion, enzymes in the small intestine eventually break down the triglycerides in the foods to free fatty acids and monoglycerides; only a small portion of

esterification The process of attaching fatty acids to a glycerol molecule, creating an ester bond and releasing water. Removing a fatty acid is called deesterification; reattaching a fatty acid is called reesterification.

monoglyceride A breakdown product of a triglyceride consisting of one fatty acid bonded to a glycerol backbone.

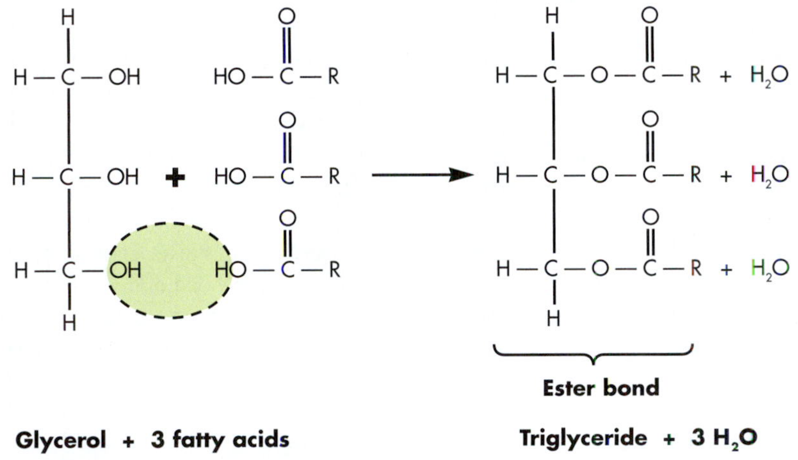

Figure 6-3 Forming a triglyceride via esterification. This process yields water as a byproduct as ester bonds are formed. The *R* represents the fatty acids.
Illustration by William Ober.

Expert Opinion

A Closer Look at Omega-3 and Omega-6 Fatty Acids and Related Eicosanoids

Kenneth S. Broughton, Ph.D.

Linoleic acid and alpha-linolenic acid are the two primary 18-carbon polyunsaturated fatty acids consumed in the North American diet. Through desaturation (loss of hydrogens) and elongation (addition of carbons) pathways, these two fatty acids are converted to **arachidonic acid** and eicosapentaenoic acid, respectively. The desaturation and elongation pathways can take eicosapentaenoic acid beyond this point to docosahexaenoic acid (DHA). DHA is the final fatty acid produced from alpha-linolenic acid and is particularly important in eye and brain function.

For a closer look, linoleic acid can be lengthened to 20 carbons and undergo desaturation to form dihomo-gamma-linolenic acid.

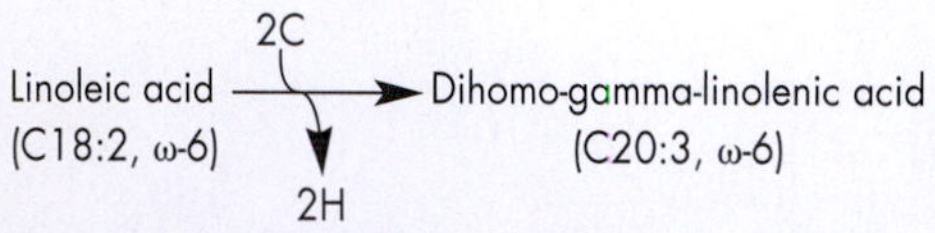

This can be further desaturated to form arachidonic acid.

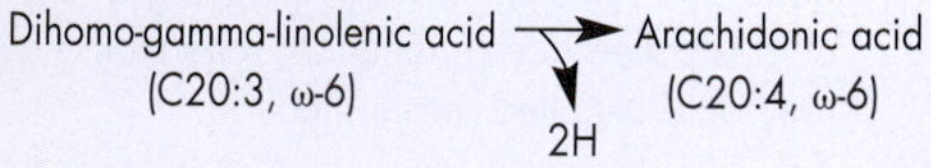

Alpha-linolenic acid can be elongated to 20 carbons and have two more carbon-carbon double bonds added to produce eicosapentaenoic acid.

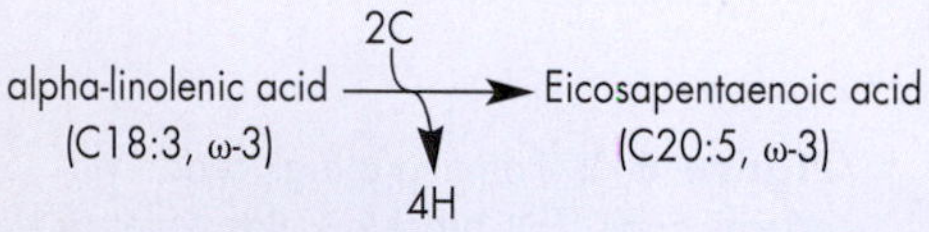

Eicosapentaenoic acid can also be elongated to 22 carbons and have one more carbon-carbon double bond added to produce docosahexaenoic acid.

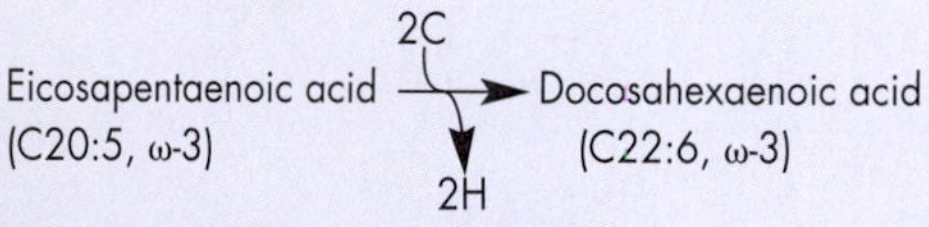

Additionally, arachidonic acid and eicosapentaenoic acid can be consumed directly, with the former found at appreciable levels in beef and poultry, and the latter found in fish. These two fatty acids, in addition to the arachidonic acid precursor, **dihomo-gamma-linolenic acid,** are the precursors for a class of hormonelike compounds known as the eicosanoids. Eicosanoids are 20-carbon molecules with hormone-like properties that act within the immediate vicinity in which they are produced, unlike typical hormones that are carried to distant sites by the circulatory system.

Arachidonic acid, eicosapentaenoic acid, and dihomo-gamma-linolenic acid are bound in the central position on a phospholipid and are liberated through the action of an enzyme called **phospholipase.** Once released from a phospholipid, free arachidonic acid, eicosapentaenoic acid, or dihomo-gamma-linolenic acid can then be metabolized to an eicosanoid. Eicosanoids are separated into three major families. These families are differentiated on the basis of the enzymatic pathway that gives rise to the particular eicosanoid. Once a parent fatty acid is liberated from the phospholipid membrane, it can be acted upon by an **oxygenase** enzyme system to take on oxygen, resulting in the formation of a specific eicosanoid family. One family is made up of the **prostanoids,** consisting of the **prostaglandins (PG), prostacyclins (PGI),** and **thromboxanes (TxA)** (review Fig. 6-1H and Fig. 6-1J). These eicosanoids are products of the **cyclooxygenase** metabolic pathway. Other families of these compounds include the **leukotrienes (LT)** (review Fig. 6-1I). These eicosanoids are products of **lipoxygenase** metabolic pathways.

The use of aspirin or ibuprofen to treat a headache or arthritis is based on the inhibition of the cyclooxygenase enzyme and a subsequent reduction in prostanoid synthesis. This enzyme inhibition may be attempted for numerous reasons which will be elaborated upon momentarily. The new anti-asthma agent known as Zyflo is a lipoxygenase inhibitor. It reduces leukotriene synthesis to levels that will significantly decrease the severity of symptoms for 40 to 50% of asthmatics.

Eicosanoids in the Body

Eicosanoids are involved in numerous physiological processes and are derived from virtually every cell in the body. Without eicosanoid involvement at some critical point, practically every normal physiologic process would come to an abrupt halt (Table 6-1). Looking at tissues in which eicosanoids are involved reads like a Who's Who of the human body, as eicosanoids are involved from the top of the head in the brain to the nerves at the bottom of the feet and everywhere in between. An explanation for the widespread involvement of eicosanoids in many body tissues may lie in part in the diversity of cells from which they are derived. While it was originally believed that eicosanoids were simply products of immune cells, many cells not of immune origin can also give rise to eicosanoids.

Eicosanoid Actions and Interactions

Of the numerous members of the prostanoid family of eicosanoids, thromboxane and prostacyclin are noteworthy as they antagonize the action of one another. This is an important relationship in that while thromboxane promotes vasoconstriction (or closing down) of arteries and blood vessels, as well as platelet aggregation and, so therefore, blood clot formation, prostacyclin induces vasodilation (or opening) of the arteries and prevents blood clotting. Thus, thromboxane is essential in preventing bleeding to death from a simple cut, but when overproduced, it increases the likelihood of stroke. Chronic use of aspirin to reduce the likelihood of a stroke may be thought to act by "thinning the blood," but in reality aspirin actually acts to prevent a stroke by reducing spontaneous blood clot formation. And while prostacyclin would simultaneously be lowered with aspirin ingestion, it may be more critical that thromboxane biosynthesis is altered.

In ovulation, an antagonistic relationship also exists between two prostaglandins known as PGE_2 and $PGF_{2\alpha}$, both made from arachidonic acid. While PGE_2 is necessary for reproduction, evidence from animal studies indicates that when PGE_2 is present at elevated levels it may suppress ovulation, while $PGF_{2\alpha}$ promotes ovulation. Appropriate balance between these two prostaglandins is therefore necessary for the regulation of the ovulatory process, and PGE_2 overproduction has been shown to inhibit ovulation. PGE_2 also has been shown to play an antagonistic role in many processes in the body. Thus, while PGE_2 has many regulatory roles, its overproduction exerts a number of adverse effects.

Chronic overproduction of leukotrienes made from arachidonic acid leads to increased problems with asthma and many chronic obstructive pulmonary diseases. However, these same eicosanoids are necessary for normal function of the gastrointestinal tract and the maintenance of blood pressure. Thus, while it is possible to pharmacologically control the production of these leukotrienes in an effort to alter the severity of asthma, as mentioned earlier, complete inhibition could have an adverse effect on other physiologic processes.

While there are many pharmaceuticals that have been developed to control eicosanoid production, nutritionists are always interested in attempting to accomplish the same end by dietary means. Problems encountered with eicosanoid production are often attributable to uncontrolled overproduction of eicosanoids derived from arachidonic acid. This overproduction may be due to a genetic aberration in which an individual chronically overproduces eicosanoids such as the leukotrienes made from arachidonic acid as is the case in asthma, or may be attributable to supplying too much initial substrate for the metabolic process. The latter scenario can be partially attributed to dietary recommendations to increase polyunsaturated fatty acid intakes. For a large portion of the population, this generally means generous intakes of vegetable oils rich in linoleic acid. By consuming diets high in linoleic acid, there is an increase in arachidonic acid, leading to an increase in the amount of related prostanoids and leukotrienes that can be synthesized. Excess synthesis of these eicosanoids can increase the predisposition to all of the adverse problems noted in Table 6-1. This potential deleterious effect can be negated by the balanced consumption of the other polyunsaturated fatty acid, alpha-linolenic acid.

Table 6-1 Locations of Various Eicosanoids in the Body

Tissues Where Eicosanoids Act	Diseases Eicosanoids Are Involved In (Eicosanoid Involved)
Brain	Arthritis (PGE_2)
Cornea	Asthma (LT)
Esophagus	Cancer (PGE_2)
Kidney	Diabetes (PG)
Large intestine	Hypertension (PG, LT)
Liver	Immunity (PGE_2)
Lung	Osteoporosis (PGE_2)
Skin	Psoriasis (PG, LT)
Stomach	Periodontal disease (PGE_2)

Omega-3 fatty acids in the form of eicosapentaenoic acid also compete with arachidonic acid for incorporation into tissue phospholipids. Further, eicosapentaenoic acid also competes with arachidonic acid at the active site of both the cyclooxygenase and lipoxygenase enzymes. In the cyclooxygenase pathway, eicosapentaenoic acid serves as a poor substrate for the enzyme in most systems, thus, the net effect is an overall reduction in prostanoid biosynthesis when eicosapentaenoic acid is present in tissues. This is especially important when considering that excessive release of compounds such as TxA derived from arachidonic acid could be life threatening when associated with a stroke. However, when eicosapentaenoic acid is used in this same enzyme system, it has been found that many of these same compounds have little to no biological activity. For example, it was noted previously that TxA_2 derived from arachidonic acid promotes vasoconstriction. In contrast, TxA_3 originating from eicosapentaenoic acid has very little comparative biological activity. As also noted, excessive PGE_2 derived from arachidonic acid

Eating fish at least two times a week is a healthy practice, as many are rich in omega-3 fatty acids.

suppresses ovulation. On the other hand, PGE_3 coming from eicosapentaenoic acid is almost pro-ovulatory by virtue of its role in alleviating the suppressive effect of PGE_2.

While eicosapentaenoic acid is a poor substrate for the cyclooxygenase pathway, it serves as a very good substrate for the lipoxygenase pathway giving rise to certain leukotrienes. However, as was mentioned for the prostanoids, the leukotrienes originating from eicosapentaenoic acid are not nearly as biologically active as their arachidonic acid–derived counterparts. While both types of leukotrienes promote constriction of the airways along with increased mucus secretion,

—continued

Expert Opinion (concluded)

the leukotrienes made from eicosapentaenoic acid are not nearly as physiologically active and pose a much smaller health risk for an asthmatic.

Dietary Implications of These Findings

These omega-3 associated research findings, when coupled with the demonstrated ability of these fatty acids to lower blood triglycerides, have led to recent recommendations to increase omega-3 fatty acid intake. The American Heart Association has recommended consuming fish a minimum of two times per week. More recently, it has been recommended that we should increase intake of omega-3 fatty acids in the form of eicosapentaenoic acid and docosahexaenoic acid to 0.65 grams a day, the amount in 2 oz of tuna or 1.5 oz of salmon. Due to differences in biological effectiveness, an individual would require approximately 10 times this amount of alpha-linolenic acid for a similar eicosanoid benefit. Similarly, in the form of encapsulated fish oil (average 28% omega-3), one would have to consume 2.3 g of fish oil. These recommendations are derived from research that indicates that once a dietary omega-6:omega-3 ratio of about 2.3:1 is obtained, there is a beneficial alteration in both prostanoid and leukotriene synthesis, leading to a more balanced combination of eicosanoids. And while intake of a higher amount of omega-3 intake would be beneficial, for most non-fish-consuming populations, it would be unrealistic to achieve these intakes.

Dr. Broughton is an Associate Professor of Nutrition at the University of Wyoming. He specializes in the effect of omega-3 fatty acids and their impact on asthma, ovulation, and inflammatory processes. More recently he has initiated studies examining the role of specific fats and their role in the development of diabetes.

When at rest or during light activity, the body uses mostly fatty acids for fuel.

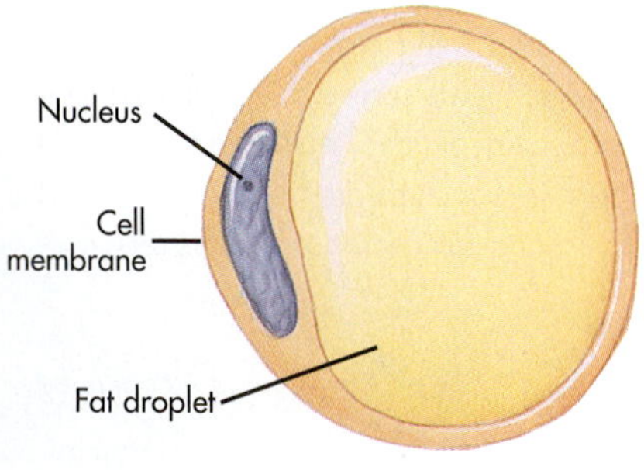

Adipose cell

dietary triglycerides is broken down completely to free fatty acids and glycerol. After the free fatty acids, monoglycerides, and any free glycerol enter the intestinal cells, most of these components are rebuilt into new triglycerides (see later section on fat digestion and absorption). The reattachment of fatty acids to glycerol is called *reesterification.* Every time a triglyceride enters or leaves a cell, it must also be deesterified; after entering a cell, the free fatty acids are reesterified into triglycerides. Thus, the body must continually break down and rebuild triglycerides.

Many key functions of fat in the body use triglycerides. These contribute to energy storage, insulation, and transportation of fat-soluble vitamins.

Providing Energy for the Body

Triglycerides both contained in the diet and stored in adipose tissue are the main fuel for muscles while at rest and during light activity. Only in endurance exercise, such as long-distance running and cycling, or in short bursts of intense activity, such as a 200-meter run, do muscles oxidize a lot of carbohydrate in addition to fatty acids supplied by triglycerides. Other body tissues also use fatty acids for energy. Overall, about half of the energy used by the entire body at rest and during light activity comes from fatty acids. On a whole-body basis, the use of fatty acids by skeletal and cardiac muscle is balanced by the use of glucose by the nervous system and red blood cells.[5] Recall from Chapter 4 that cells also need carbohydrate to efficiently process fatty acids for fuel.

Storing Energy for Later Use

We store energy mainly in the form of triglycerides. The body's ability to store fat is essentially limitless. Its fat storage sites, adipose cells, can increase about 50 times in weight. If the amount of fat to be stored exceeds the ability of the cells to expand, the body can form new adipose cells. (This is discussed further in Chapter 13.)

An important advantage of using triglycerides to store energy in the body is that they are energy dense. Recall that these yield, on average, 9 kcal/g, whereas proteins and carbohydrates yield only about half that much. In addition, triglycerides are chemically very stable, so they are not likely to react with other cell constituents, making them a safe form for storing energy. Finally, when we store triglycerides in adipose cells, we store little else; adipose cells contain about 80% lipid and only 20% water and protein.[14] In contrast, imagine if we were to store energy as muscle tissue, which is about 73% water. Body weight linked to energy storage would increase dramatically.

Insulating and Protecting the Body

The insulating layer of fat just beneath the skin is made mostly of triglycerides. Fat tissue also surrounds and protects some organs—kidneys, for example—from injury. We usually don't notice the important insulating function of fat tissue, because we wear clothes and add more as needed. But a layer of insulating fat is quite apparent in animals, particularly those in cold climates. Polar bears, walruses, and whales all build a thick layer of fat tissue around themselves to insulate against cold-weather environments. The extra fat also provides energy storage for times when food is scarce.

People with **anorexia nervosa** often lose 25% or more of body weight and become about as fat free as is biologically possible. In turn, they lose the insulating property of fat storage. This poses many other health risks, such as bone loss linked to cessation of menstrual periods (see Chapter 15). In place of the layer of fat tissue under the skin, people with anorexia nervosa often develop downy hair, called **lanugo,** all over the body. These hairs insulate the body by standing up and trapping warm air.

Unabsorbed fatty acids also can bind minerals, such as calcium and magnesium, and draw them into the stool for elimination. This can harm mineral status (see Chapter 11).

anorexia nervosa An eating disorder involving a psychological loss or denial of appetite and self-starvation, related in part to a distorted body image and to various social pressures commonly associated with puberty.

lanugo Downlike hair that appears after a person has lost much body fat through semistarvation. The hair stands erect and traps air, acting as insulation for the body to compensate for the relative lack of body fat, which usually functions as insulation.

Transporting Fat-Soluble Vitamins

Triglycerides and other fats in food carry fat-soluble vitamins to the small intestine and aid their absorption.[5] If the small intestine is diseased, however, it may not be able to adequately digest and absorb fat from foods. When this happens, the unabsorbed fat carries the fat-soluble vitamins—A, D, E, and K—into the large intestine. From there, they are eliminated in the feces, and the body loses the benefits of the vitamins. If the disease doesn't resolve quickly, medical attention is necessary.

People who absorb fat poorly, such as those with the disease cystic fibrosis, are also at risk for deficiencies of fat-soluble vitamins. A similar risk accrues from taking mineral oil as a laxative at mealtimes. Because the body cannot digest or absorb mineral oil, the undigested oil carries the fat-soluble vitamins from the meal into the feces, where they are eliminated.

Peanuts are a source of lecithins, as are wheat germ and egg yolks.

Phospholipids

Phospholipids are another class of lipid. Like triglycerides, they are built on a backbone of glycerol. However, at least one fatty acid is replaced with a compound containing phosphorus (and often other elements, such as nitrogen). Many types of phospholipids exist in the body, especially in the brain. They form important parts of cell membranes. The various forms of **lecithins** are common examples of phospholipids (Fig. 6-1*G*). These are found in body cells, where they participate in fat digestion in the intestine. Peanuts contain lecithins in abundance, as do liver, wheat germ, soybeans, and egg yolks. It is not necessary to consume phospholipids, such as lecithins, in the diet because the body can synthesize them and use them when and where they are needed.[5]

Cell membranes are composed primarily of phospholipids. A cell membrane looks much like a sea of phospholipids with protein "islands" (review Fig. C-1 in Appendix C). Among their many roles, the proteins form receptors for hormones, function as enzymes, and act as transporters for nutrients. About 5 to 15% of cell membrane fatty acids is made up of arachidonic acid. This serves as a source for eicosanoid synthesis described earlier in the Expert Opinion. Some cholesterol is also present in the membrane.

lecithins A group of phospholipids containing two fatty acids, a phosphate group, and a choline molecule. Lecithins are a group of compounds, since they can differ based on the types of fatty acids found on each lecithin molecule.

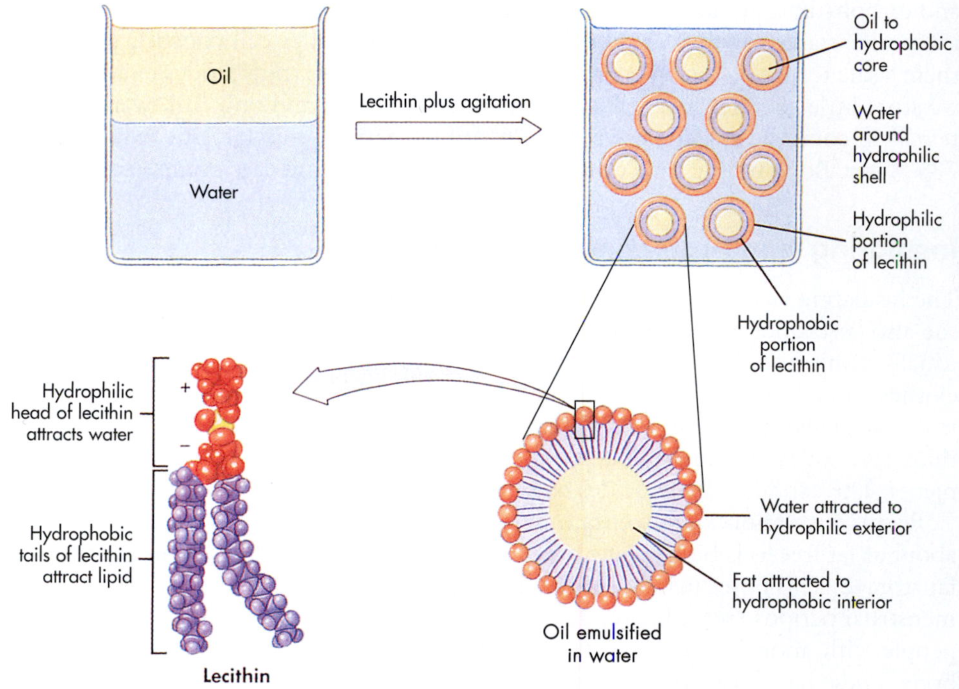

Figure 6-4 Emulsification and emulsifiers. Emulsifiers organize oil and water into droplets of oil surrounded by water. The emulsifier molecules form a bridge between the oil and water molecules, isolating one from the other. In the droplet, oil enters the central core, while water surrounds the core. The emulsifier molecules are sandwiched between the two. Formation of such emulsions is a key step in digestion of dietary fat and is important in the manufacture of certain food products, such as mayonnaise and cakes.

Illustration by William Ober.

Some phospholipids, such as the family of compounds mentioned earlier called *lecithins,* function as **emulsifiers.** These allow fat and water to mix. By breaking fat globules into small droplets, emulsifiers enable a fat to be suspended in water. Here's how the process works: The fatty acid ends of lecithins attract fat. The phosphorus and nitrogen at the other end of lecithins form an area containing positive and negative charges. This area attracts water. Since water is attracted to the charges on lecithin, this part of lecithin is called hydrophilic, which means "loving water." The parts with fatty acids are called hydrophobic, since they don't attract (they "fear") water.

When an emulsifier is mixed with oil and water in the proper proportions, it forms spherical structures, in which the hydrophobic parts of the emulsifier molecules are oriented toward the interior and the hydrophilic parts toward the exterior (Fig. 6-4). In this way, the emulsifier acts as a bridge between the oil and water by forming tiny oil droplets surrounded by thin shells of water.

The body's main emulsifiers are the lecithins and **bile acids,** which are produced by the liver and released into the small intestine via the gallbladder during digestion.[13] By breaking up the fat globules, the emulsifiers create more fat surface for fat-digesting enzymes to act on. These very stable emulsified products are called **micelles** (see later section on fat digestion).

Sterols

Sterols are the last class of lipids this chapter covers. Their characteristic multiringed structure makes them different from the other lipids already discussed. Consider the sterol cholesterol. This waxy substance doesn't look like a triglyceride—it doesn't have a glycerol backbone or any fatty acids. Still, because it doesn't readily dissolve in water, it is a lipid. The main building block for the synthesis of cholesterol in the body is acetyl-CoA, a derivative of **acetic acid,** the smallest fatty acid. (Synthesis of longer fatty acids, triglycerides, and phospholipids also makes use of acetyl-CoA.)[14]

Cholesterol forms part of some important hormones, such as the estrogens, testosterone, and a form of the active vitamin D hormone—namely, 1,25(OH_2) vitamin D. Cholesterol is also the precursor of bile acids, which are needed for fat digestion. Finally, cholesterol is an essential structural component of cell membranes and the particles that

emulsifier A compound that can suspend fat in water by isolating individual fat droplets, using a shell of water molecules or other substances to prevent the fat from coalescing.

bile acids Emulsifiers synthesized by the liver and released by the gallbladder during digestion.

micelles Water-soluble, spherical structures, formed by lecithin and bile acids, in which the hydrophobic parts of the molecules face inward and the hydrophilic parts face outward. Lipids enclosed within micelles do not separate into an oily layer, as they normally do when mixed with water.

acetic acid A two-carbon fatty acid that is used in the synthesis of lipids.

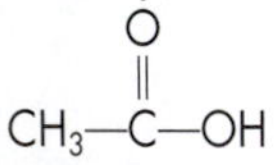

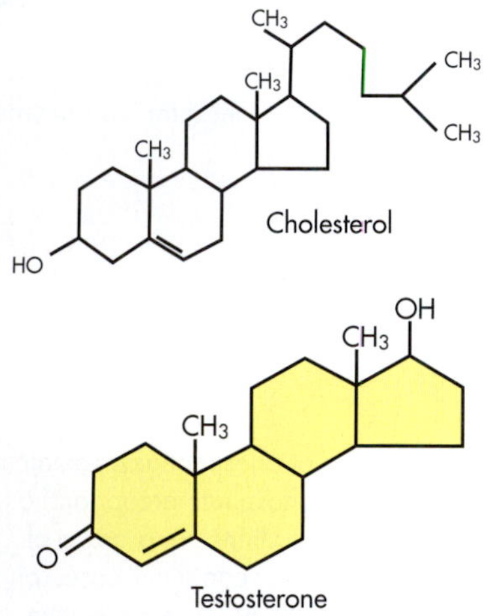

Illustration by William Ober.

Table 6-2 Cholesterol Content of Selected Foods in Ascending Order

Food	Amount	Cholesterol in Milligrams	Food	Amount	Cholesterol in Milligrams
Skim milk	1 cup	4	Oysters, salmon	3 oz	40
Mayonnaise	1 tbsp	10	Clams, halibut, tuna	3 oz	55
Butter	1 pat	11	Chicken, turkey* (white meat)	3 oz	70
Lard	1 tbsp	12	Beef,* pork	3 oz	75
Cottage cheese	½ cup	15	Lamb, crab	3 oz	85
Low-fat milk (2%)	1 cup	22	Shrimp, lobster	3 oz	110
Half-and-half	¼ cup	23	Heart, beef	3 oz	165
Hot dog*	1	29	Egg (egg yolk)*†	1	210
Ice cream, ~10% fat	½ cup	30	Liver, beef	3 oz	410
Cheese, cheddar	1 oz	30	Kidney	3 oz	540
Whole milk*	1 cup	34	Brains	3 oz	2640

*Leading contributors of cholesterol to the North American diet.

†Egg whites are cholesterol-free.

transport lipids in the blood, as discussed in the next section. The cholesterol content of the heart, liver, kidney, and brain is quite high, reflecting its critical role in these organs.

Cholesterol is made by body cells (two-thirds of total daily body exposure) and is consumed in the diet (about one-third of total daily body exposure). Each day, our cells produce approximately 875 mg of cholesterol.[5] Of this, about 400 mg is used to make new bile acids to replenish those lost in the feces, and about 50 mg is used to make steroid hormones. With respect to diet, we consume about 180 to 325 mg of cholesterol per day from animal-derived food products, with men consuming the higher amount compared to women (Table 6-2). Of that, we absorb about 40 to 60%. There is no need to consume cholesterol per se, as body cells can make all that they need.[5]

Some plants have related sterols, such as ergosterol, that can form a type of vitamin D. However, the plant-based foods we eat do not contain cholesterol per se unless animal products have been added.

Eggs are the principal source of cholesterol in the North American diet. The Food and Nutrition Board suggests limiting intake of this and other high-cholesterol foods.[5]

Concept | Check

Triglycerides are the major form of fat in the body and in food. They are used for and stored as energy, they insulate and protect body organs, and they transport fat-soluble vitamins. Phospholipids have both hydrophilic and hydrophobic parts and, so, are effective emulsifiers—compounds that can suspend fat in water. Phospholipids also form parts of cell membranes and various compounds in the body. Cells produce all the phospholipids the body needs. Cholesterol, a sterol, forms part of cell membranes, some hormones, and bile acids; it is essential to the body. Cholesterol is found in animal products and is synthesized by body cells; if sufficient amounts are not ingested, the body makes what it needs.

Fat Digestion and Absorption

Given the right conditions, about 95% of fat consumed is absorbed.

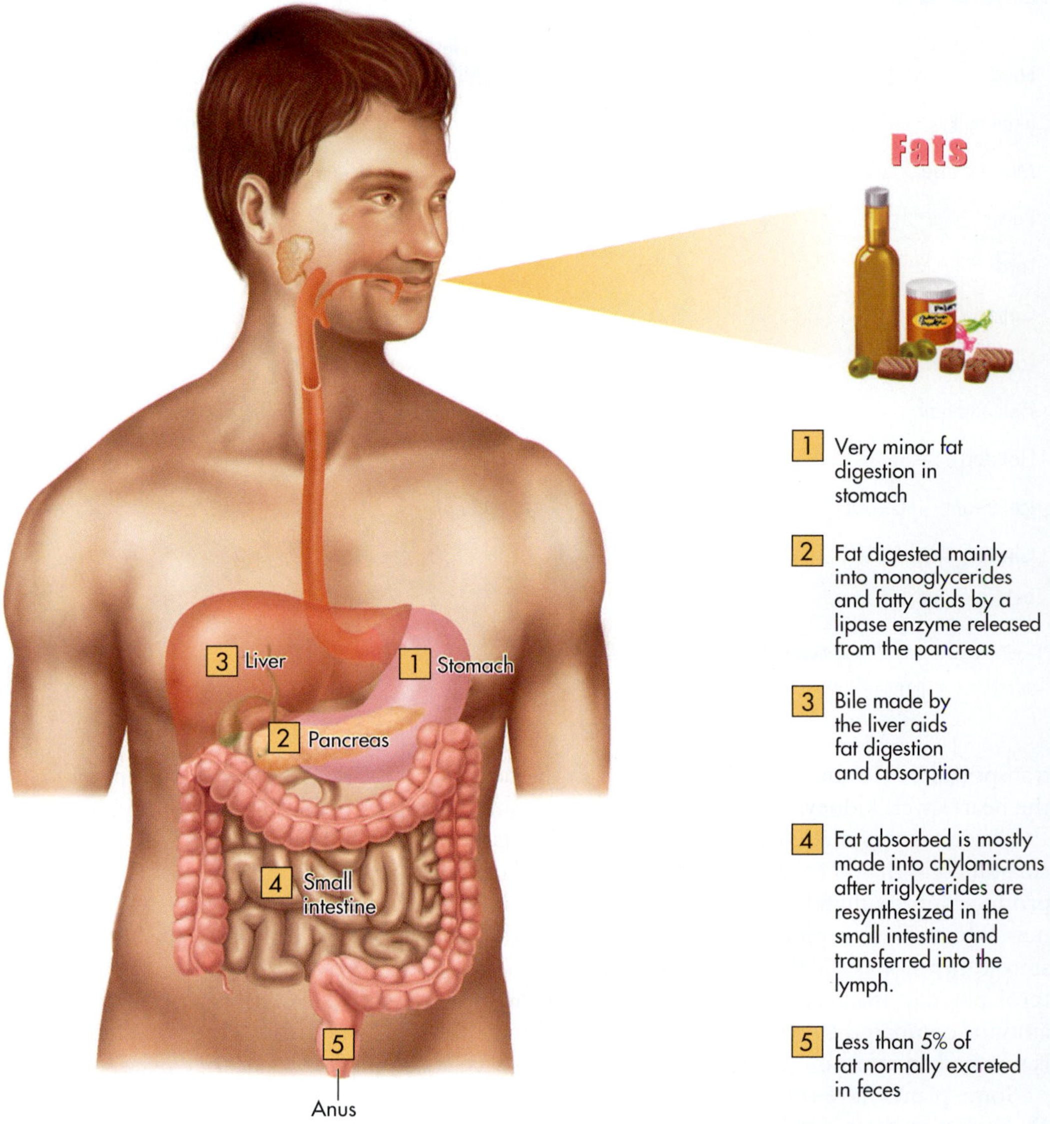

Figure 6-5 A summary of fat digestion and absorption. Chapter 3 covered general aspects of this process.

Digestion

Fat digestion begins in the stomach, using the enzymes lingual (mostly in infancy) and gastric lipase. These enzymes break down triglycerides containing short- and medium-chain fatty acids into free fatty acids and diglycerides, such as found in milk fat. Since fat may remain in the stomach for up to 2 to 4 hours, there is an opportunity to digest some of these triglycerides and to absorb the fatty acids released through the stomach wall. The short- and medium-chain fatty acids then enter the portal vein. In contrast, long-chain fatty acids are not acted on until they reach the small intestine (Fig. 6-5).[13]

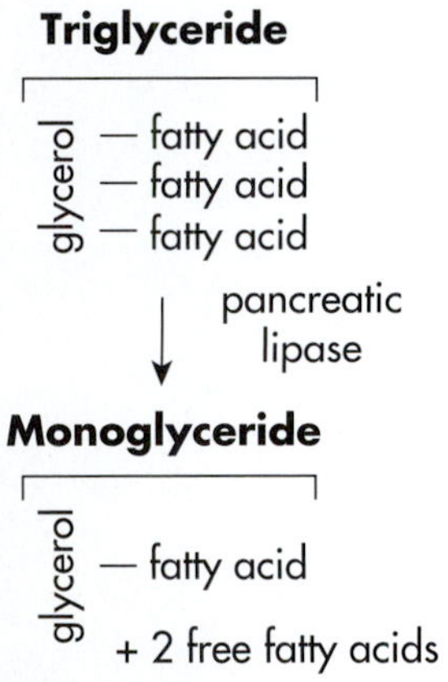

Once the fat reaches the small intestine, the hormone cholecystokinin (CCK) is released from certain intestinal cells. This hormone stimulates the release of bile from the gallbladder and lipase enzyme from the pancreas. The bile contains bile acids, lecithin, and cholesterol. The lipase released travels through the pancreatic duct to be mixed with bile in the common bile duct; finally, both enter together into the small intestine. In the small intestine, pancreatic lipase contributes to fat digestion by digesting (specifically hydrolyzing) the triglycerides into monoglycerides and fatty acids. The amount of pancreatic lipase released is much greater than what is needed in most circumstances to

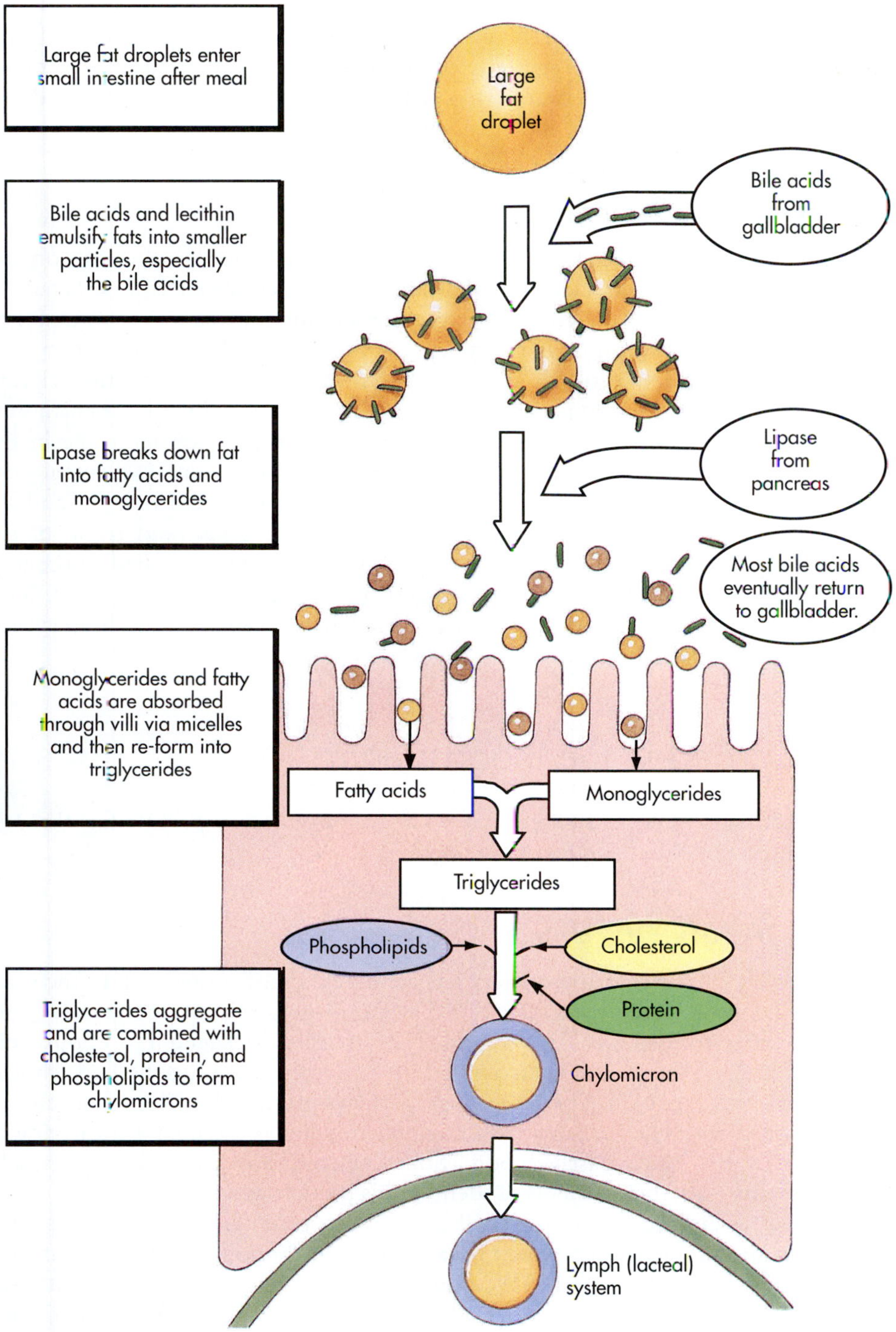
Large fat droplets enter small intestine after meal
Large fat droplet
Bile acids from gallbladder
Bile acids and lecithin emulsify fats into smaller particles, especially the bile acids
Lipase from pancreas
Lipase breaks down fat into fatty acids and monoglycerides
Most bile acids eventually return to gallbladder.
Monoglycerides and fatty acids are absorbed through villi via micelles and then re-form into triglycerides
Fatty acids
Monoglycerides
Triglycerides
Phospholipids
Cholesterol
Protein
Chylomicron
Triglycerides aggregate and are combined with cholesterol, protein, and phospholipids to form chylomicrons
Lymph (lacteal) system

Figure 6-6 A simplified look at absorption of triglycerides made up of long-chain fatty acids. These primarily form monoglycerides and free fatty acids. These are absorbed using bile acids and then re-formed into triglycerides in the absorptive cells. The triglycerides are then formed into chylomicrons and enter the lymphatic system. Note that short- and medium-chain fatty acids for the most part pass directly into the portal circulation (not depicted). Under normal conditions, about 95% of dietary fat is absorbed, primarily as chylomicrons. Only a small portion is found in the feces.

digest the fat in a meal. This "overkill" makes fat digestion very rapid and thorough in the right circumstances, which include the presence of bile acids and lecithin from the gallbladder and a protein called **colipase.** Colipase is found in pancreatic secretions, and it functions by ensuring the attachment of lipase to the lipid droplet.

Since fat is hydrophobic, it needs a medium that will carry it throughout the intestinal tract. Bile acids help do this by emulsifying the fatty substances in the small intestine into micelles, as previously discussed. Emulsification improves digestion and absorption because, as large fat globules are broken down into smaller ones, the total surface area for lipase action increases (Fig. 6-6).

colipase A protein the pancreas secretes that changes the shape of pancreatic lipase, facilitating its action.

With regard to phospholipid and cholesterol digestion, phospholipase enzymes from the pancreas and glandular cells in the wall of the small intestine digest phospholipids. The eventual products are glycerol, fatty acids, phosphoric acid, and remaining constituents such as choline. Cholesterol esters (cholesterol with a fatty acid attached) are broken down to free cholesterol and fatty acids.

Absorption

The lipid content of the micelles is absorbed into the brush border of the absorptive cells lining the duodenum and jejunum. Through this process about 95% of dietary fat is absorbed. The carbon chain length of fatty acids and monoglycerides absorbed then affects their fate after absorption. If a fatty acid is a short- or medium-chain variety (less than 12 carbons), it is water soluble and probably travels out of the absorptive cell (enterocyte) and through the portal vein to the liver. If the fatty acid is a long-chain variety (12 or more carbons), it is first re-formed into a triglyceride molecule in the absorptive cell. After further packaging (described in the next section), it eventually enters circulation via the lymphatic system, carrying with it fat-soluble vitamins and absorbed cholesterol (review Fig. 6-6).[14] The leftover bile acids (and some of the cholesterol released in the bile) are reabsorbed in the ileum and returned to the liver (by the portal vein) to be used again in fat digestion (about 98% of bile acids are recycled, only 1 to 2% are eliminated in the feces). Recall from Chapter 3 that this recycling is termed enterohepatic circulation.

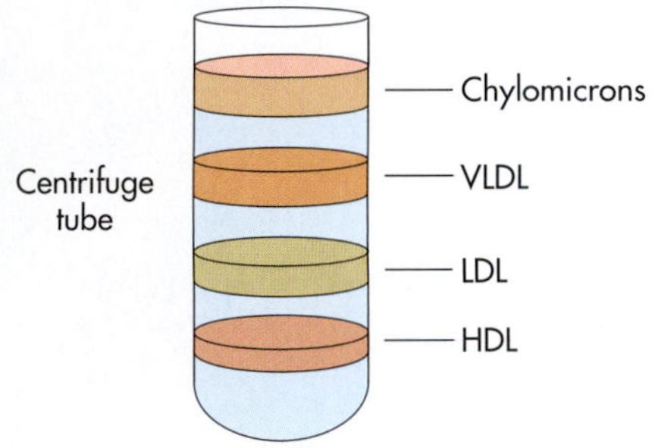

One way to measure the amount of chylomicrons, VLDL, LDL, and HDL particles in the bloodstream is to centrifuge the serum portion of the blood at high speed for about 24 hours in a sucrose-rich solution. The lipoproteins settle out in the centrifuge tube based on their density, with chylomicrons at the top and HDLs at the bottom.

Fats Carried in the Bloodstream

The incompatibility of fat and water presents a challenge in transporting fats through the watery media of blood and lymph systems.

Carrying Dietary Fats Utilizes Chylomicrons

As just reviewed, once the various dietary fats are digested and absorbed into the small intestine cells, most of the byproducts of digestion—glycerol, monoglycerides, and fatty acids—are re-formed into triglycerides. They are then packaged into **lipoprotein** particles—large droplets of lipid surrounded by a thin shell of phospholipid, cholesterol, and protein (Fig. 6-7). The lipoprotein particles produced by intestinal cells are called **chylomicrons.** The shell around a chylomicron allows the lipid it is carrying to float freely in the water-based blood. Some of the proteins present—namely, **apolipoproteins**—also help other cells identify this particle as a chylomicron.[14]

After being assembled in intestinal cells, chylomicrons enter the lymphatic system and travel to the thoracic duct, which is located along the spinal column. This duct opens into a large vein in the neck called the subclavian vein. Chylomicrons enter the general circulation of the bloodstream at that point (see Fig. C-5 in Appendix C for a view of lymphatic circulation).

Once chylomicrons enter the bloodstream, the triglycerides in the chylomicrons are broken down into fatty acids and glycerol by an enzyme on the inside wall of the blood vessel, **lipoprotein lipase.** Muscle cells, adipose cells, and other cells in the vicinity then absorb most of the fatty acids. Cells can immediately use absorbed fatty acids for energy needs, or they can re-form them into triglycerides and store them as such. Muscle cells tend to metabolize fatty acids, whereas adipose cells tend to store them.

After eating a meal, the whole process of clearing chylomicrons from the blood via lipoprotein lipase activity takes about 2 to 10 hours, depending in part on fat content. After 12 to 14 hours of fasting, the chylomicrons should be totally absent from the bloodstream. People should fast for 12 to 14 hours before having certain blood tests to assure that chylomicrons, whose presence could affect the results, have been cleared.

lipoprotein A compound found in the bloodstream containing a core of lipids with a shell composed of protein, phospholipid, and cholesterol.

chylomicron Lipoprotein made of dietary fats surrounded by a shell of cholesterol, phospholipids, and protein. Chylomicrons are formed in the absorptive cells (enterocytes) of the small intestine after fat absorption and travel through the lymphatic system to the bloodstream.

apolipoprotein A protein attached to the surface of a lipoprotein or embedded in its outer shell. Apolipoproteins can help enzymes function, act as a lipid-transfer protein, or assist in the binding of a lipoprotein to a cell-surface receptor.

lipoprotein lipase An enzyme attached to the outside endothelial cells that line the capillaries in the blood vessels; it breaks down triglycerides into free fatty acids and glycerol.

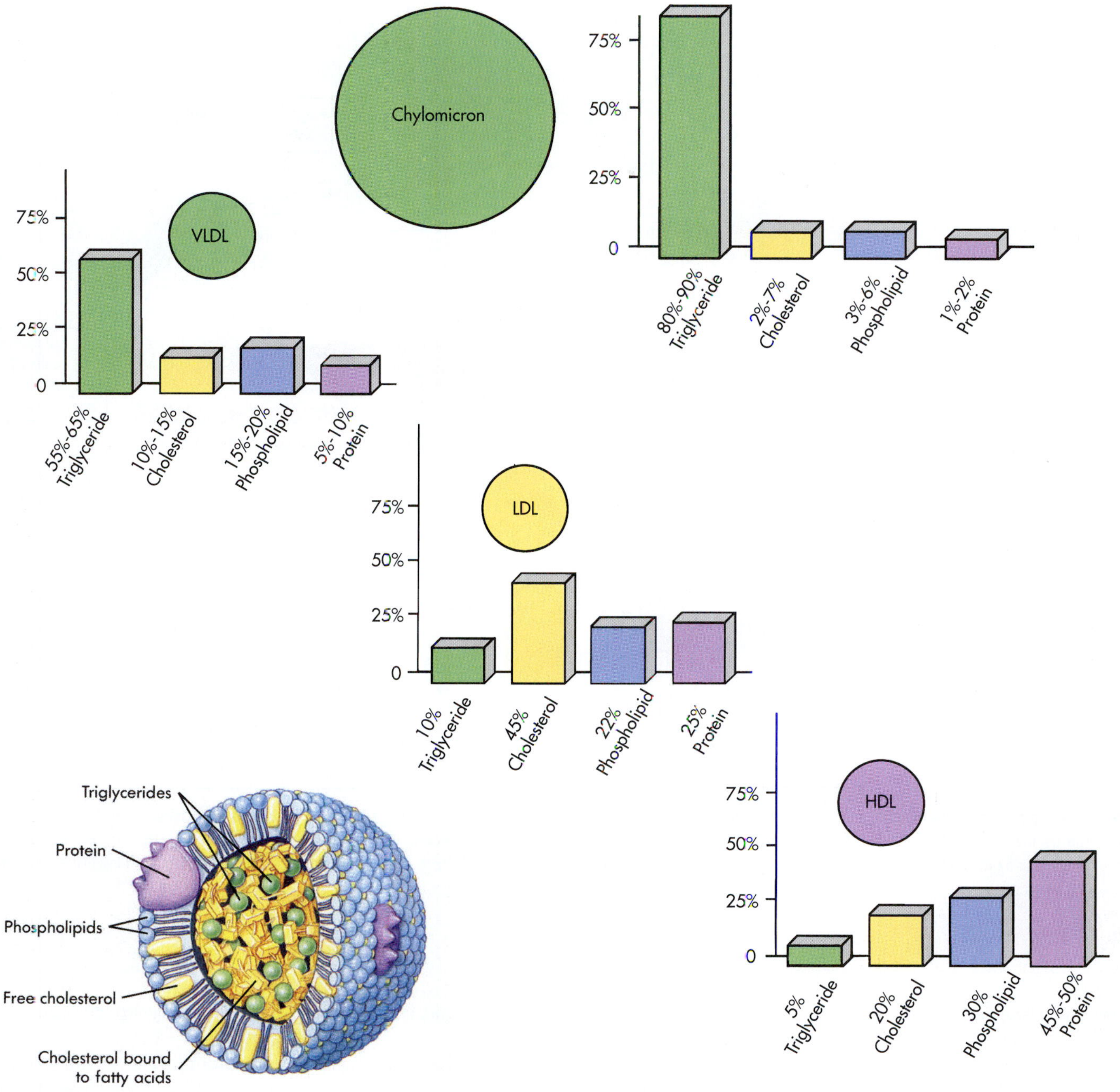

Figure 6-7 Structure and composition of lipoproteins. This lipoprotein structure allows fats to circulate in the bloodstream. Note that, for each class of lipoprotein, there are various subclasses of slightly different composition, including those based upon their different apolipoproteins. For our purposes, we will ignore this observation.

Transporting Lipids Mostly Made by the Body Uses Very-Low-Density Lipoproteins

The liver produces some fat and cholesterol. The source of the needed carbon, hydrogen, and energy to make such substances as glycerol, fatty acids, triglycerides, and cholesterol includes the carbohydrate and protein the liver takes up from the bloodstream. However, free fatty acids taken up from the bloodstream by the liver are the major source for triglyceride synthesis. The liver coats the cholesterol and triglycerides that collect, including some taken up from the bloodstream, with a shell of protein and

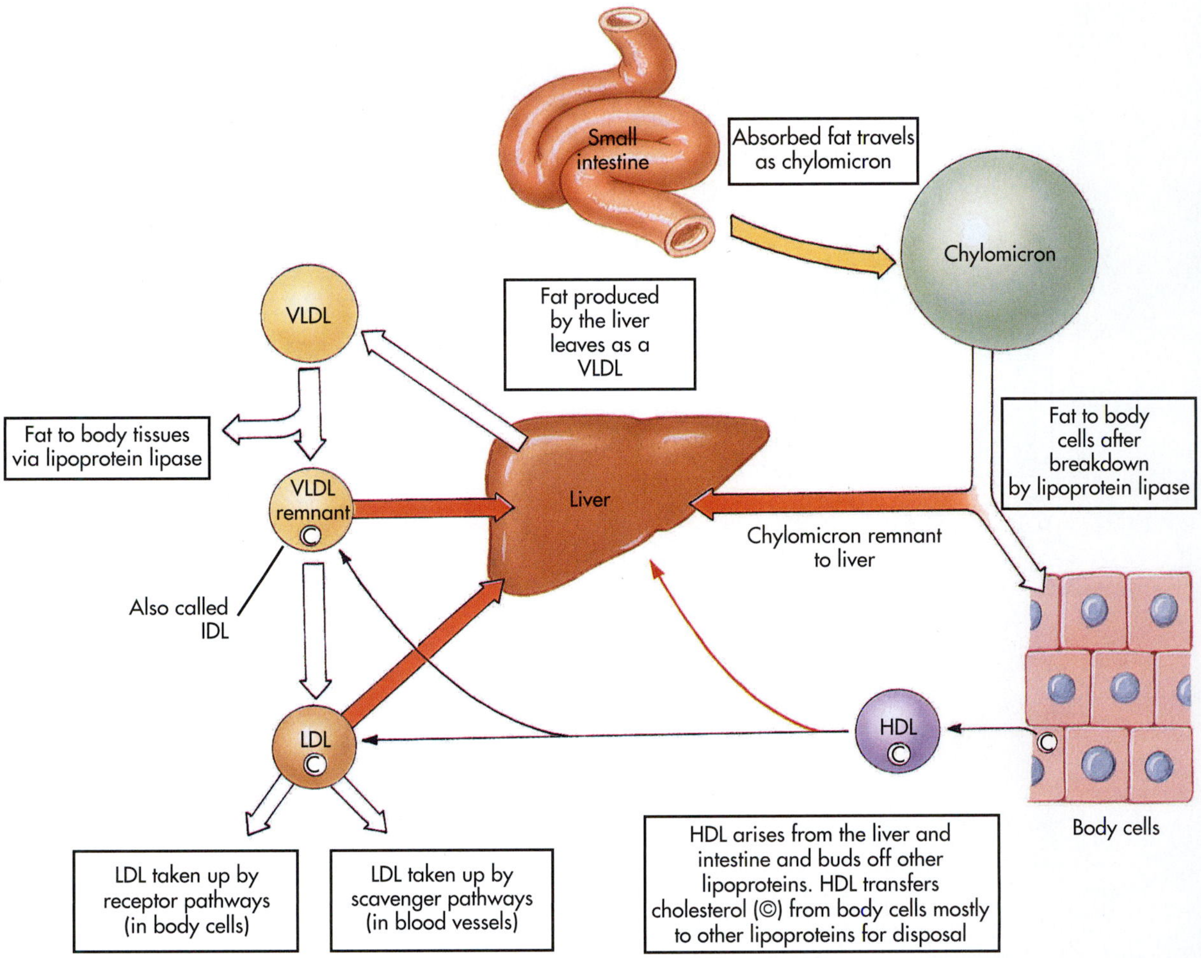

Figure 6-8 Lipoprotein interactions. Chylomicrons carry absorbed fat to body cells. VLDL carries fat taken up from the bloodstream by the liver, as well as any fat made by the liver, to body cells. LDL arises from VLDL and carries mostly cholesterol to cells. HDL arises from body cells, mostly in the liver and intestine, as well as from particles that bud off the other lipoproteins. HDL carries cholesterol from cells to other lipoproteins and to the liver for excretion.
Illustration by William Ober.

very-low-density lipoprotein (VLDL) The lipoprotein created in the liver that carries cholesterol and lipids taken up from the bloodstream, and any lipids newly synthesized by the liver.

receptor pathway for cholesterol uptake A process by which LDL is bound by cell receptors and incorporated into the cell.

scavenger pathway for cholesterol uptake A process by which LDL is taken up by scavenger cells embedded in the blood vessels.

lipids. This process produces what is called a **very-low-density lipoprotein (VLDL)** fraction (Fig. 6-8).

When the VLDL leaves the liver, the enzyme lipoprotein lipase on the blood vessels breaks down the triglyceride in the VLDL into fatty acids and glycerol. Again, fatty acids and glycerol are released into the bloodstream and are taken up by the body cells. Because fats are less dense than water, the VLDL becomes proportionately denser as triglyceride is released. Much of what eventually remains of the VLDL fraction becomes particles called low-density lipoprotein (LDL) fraction. LDL is composed primarily of cholesterol.

LDL particles are absorbed from the bloodstream by receptors on cells, internalized, and broken down. Most LDL is taken up by receptors on liver cells. Diets low in saturated fat and cholesterol encourage this process, whereas diets high in those lipids can reduce LDL uptake by the liver (see the Nutrition Perspective at the end of this chapter). The cholesterol and protein parts absorbed then are transported throughout the cell. By this process, called the **receptor pathway for cholesterol uptake,** cells take up some of the building blocks necessary for cell growth and development (Fig. 6-9).[14]

A second process, called the **scavenger pathway for cholesterol uptake,** can also remove LDL from the circulation. This pathway is carried out by certain "scavenger"

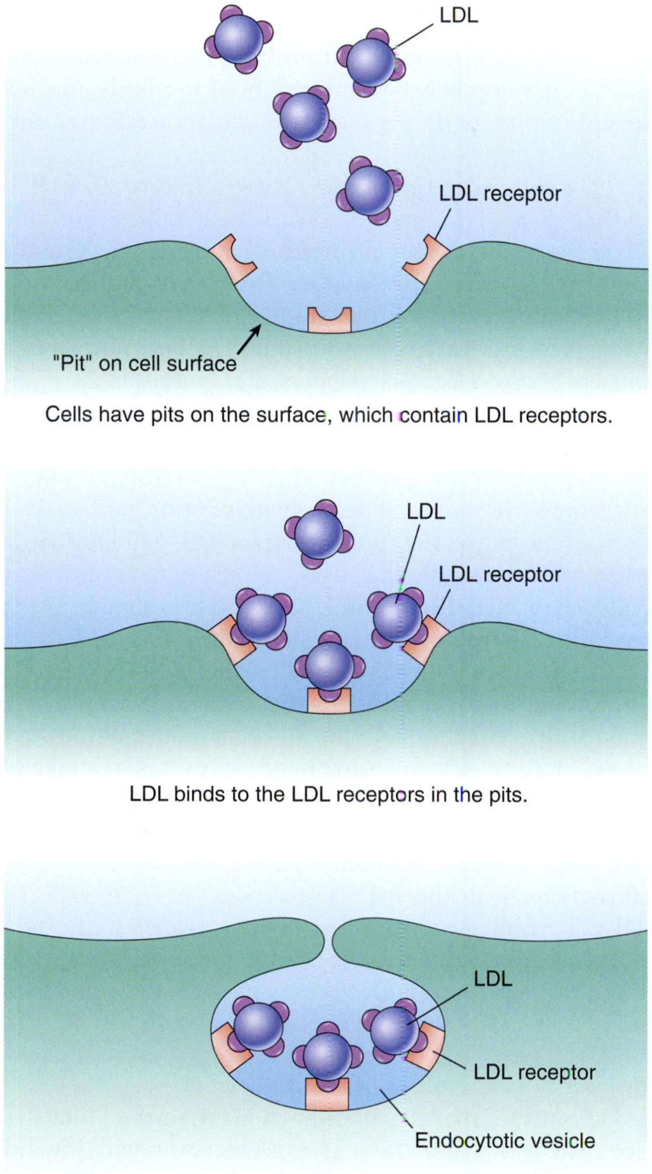
LDL
LDL receptor
"Pit" on cell surface
Cells have pits on the surface, which contain LDL receptors.
LDL
LDL receptor
LDL binds to the LDL receptors in the pits.
LDL
LDL receptor
Endocytotic vesicle

Figure 6-9 Transport of LDL into cells. LDL receptors capture circulating LDL and release it inside the cell to be metabolized. Once free of their load, LDL receptors return to the cell surface to await new LDL.

white blood cells, which leave the bloodstream and bury themselves in blood vessels. These scavenger cells detect, alter (oxidize), engulf, and digest the extra circulating LDL. Once within the scavenger cells, the oxidized LDL is prevented from reentering the bloodstream. Over time, cholesterol builds up in the scavenger cells, especially when the amount of LDL in the bloodstream is excessive.[17]

When scavenger cells have collected and deposited cholesterol for many years at a heavy pace, cholesterol builds up on the inner blood vessel walls—especially in arteries—and **plaque** develops (see Fig. 6-14 in the Nutrition Perspective at the end of this chapter). The plaque eventually mixes with connective tissue (collagen) and is then covered with a cap of smooth muscle cells and calcium. **Atherosclerosis,** also referred to as *hardening of the arteries,* develops as plaque grows in the vessel. This eventually chokes off the blood supply to organs, setting the stage for a heart attack and other problems, or it breaks apart and leads to clot formation in this or another artery. Plaque is probably first deposited to repair damage to the cells lining the arteries (called endothelial cells). The damage that starts plaque formation can be caused by smoking,

plaque A cholesterol-rich substance deposited in the blood vessels; it contains various white blood cells, smooth muscle cells, connective tissue (collagen), cholesterol and other lipids, and eventually calcium.

atherosclerosis Buildup of fatty material (plaque) in the arteries, including those surrounding the heart.

homocysteine An amino acid not used in protein synthesis, but instead arises during metabolism of the amino acid methionine. Homocysteine is likely toxic to many cells, such as those lining the blood vessels.

carotenoids Plant pigments, some of which can yield vitamin A.

A number of large-scale trials testing the hypothesis that megadose vitamin E therapy (e.g., 600 IU every other day) can help prevent cardiovascular disease in otherwise healthy people are underway. Results are due by 2007.

menopause The cessation of menses in women, usually beginning at about age 50.

Two approaches have been shown to cause regression of atherosclerosis in the body. One employs a vegan diet and other lifestyle changes that are part of the Dr. Dean Ornish program. The other employs aggressive LDL-lowering with medications (see the Nutrition Perspective).

diabetes, hypertension, **homocysteine** (likely, but not a major factor), and LDL itself. Viral and bacterial infections are also implicated as well as ongoing blood vessel inflammation.[4, 15, 17, 18] (There is a test for this ongoing inflammation [evidenced by elevated C-reactive protein in the blood], but it is not yet a part of routine medical practice. This topic is discussed further in the Nutrition Perspective in this chapter.) Note also that these plaques can develop in arteries throughout the body, not just the coronary arteries. This explains our use of the term cardiovascular disease to describe the general condition.

Some nutrients have antioxidant properties. These likely reduce LDL oxidation in the bloodstream and thus slow LDL uptake into scavenger cells. Fruits and vegetables are rich in such antioxidants as the various **carotenoids** and vitamins C and E. Eating fruits and vegetables regularly is one positive step we can take to reduce cholesterol buildup and slow the progression of cardiovascular disease. Fruits and vegetables that are rich sources of antioxidants include dried plums (prunes), raisins, various berries, plums, oranges, grapes, spinach, broccoli, red bell peppers, and onions. Consuming megadoses of antioxidant vitamins to do the same thing is controversial. Chapter 9 will discuss this controversy in detail. Currently, the American Heart Association does not support the use of antioxidant supplements, such as vitamin E, in an effort to reduce cardiovascular disease risk.[9] Most large-scale studies of people with existing cardiovascular disease have shown no benefit from megadose vitamin E therapy (200–400 mg/day; about 400–800 IU/day).[6, 19] Other studies are ongoing, using people with cardiovascular disease and those with no evidence of such disease. Still, some experts suggest that megadose vitamin E use (200 mg [about 400 IU] per day) may be helpful for *preventing* cardiovascular disease, but should be taken under a physician's guidance. This caution is because, in some cases, the megadose use of antioxidant supplements can cause harm, especially if one is taking certain anticoagulant medications, which reduce blood clotting, as vitamin E also reduces blood clotting. On the other hand, an excessive intake of iron probably speeds LDL oxidation, making it unwise to take an iron supplement unless a physician prescribes it. People who experience iron storage disease and men in general should pay special attention to this warning (see Chapter 12).

A final critical participant in this extensive process of fat transport is high-density lipoprotein (HDL). Its high proportion of protein makes it the heaviest (densest) lipoprotein. The liver and intestine produce most of the HDL in the blood. It roams the bloodstream, picking up cholesterol from dying cells and other sources. HDL donates the cholesterol primarily to other lipoproteins for transport back to the liver to be excreted. Some HDL travels directly back to the liver. Another beneficial function of HDL is that it may block oxidation of LDL.

Many studies demonstrate that the amount of HDL in the bloodstream can closely predict the risk for cardiovascular disease. The risk increases with low HDL because little blood cholesterol is transported back to the liver and excreted. Women tend to have high amounts of HDL, especially before **menopause,** whereas low amounts are more common in men.

Because high amounts of HDL slow the development of cardiovascular disease, any cholesterol carried by HDL can be considered "good" cholesterol. By convention, then, cholesterol carried by LDL would be "bad" cholesterol because high amounts of LDL speeds the development of cardiovascular disease. Still, LDL is only a problem when it is too high in the bloodstream; lower amounts are needed as part of routine body functions.[14]

Concept | Check

In the stomach, gastric and lingual lipase break down short- and medium-chain triglycerides into smaller components, a minor amount of which is absorbed through the stomach wall. All end up in the portal vein and are transported to the liver. In the small intestine, the enzyme pancreatic lipase digests long-chain triglycerides into monoglycerides and free fatty acids. These breakdown products diffuse into the absorptive cells of the small intestine and are mostly resynthesized into triglycerides. The bloodstream carries absorbed dietary fat as chylomicrons.

Lipid synthesized by the liver is carried in the bloodstream as very-low-density lipoprotein (VLDL). Once a VLDL has most triglycerides removed by lipoprotein lipase, it eventually becomes low-density lipoprotein (LDL), which is rich in cholesterol. LDL is picked up by receptors on body cells, especially liver cells. Scavenger cells in the arteries may do the same, speeding the development of atherosclerosis. High-density lipoprotein (HDL) picks up cholesterol from cells and transports it primarily to other lipoproteins for eventual transport back to the liver. HDL may also decrease LDL oxidation, thereby reducing LDL uptake into atherosclerotic plaque. Elevated amounts of LDL in the bloodstream is one major risk factor associated with cardiovascular disease, as is low amounts of HDL.

Fat is an important component of the flavor and overall appeal of cheese.

Another Dimension of Fat—Properties in Food

Various fats play important roles in foods. Much ingenuity must go into the production of fat-reduced products to preserve flavor and texture. In some cases, "fat-free" also means tasteless.

Fat in Food Provides Some Satiety and Flavor

Fat in foods has generally been considered to be the most **satiating** of all the macronutrients. However, this assumption has been called into question because recent studies show that protein and carbohydrate probably lead to more satiety (gram for gram). High-fat meals do provide satiety, but primarily because one consumes a lot of energy in the process. A high-fat meal is likely to be an energy-rich meal.

satiety A state in which there is no longer a desire to eat; a feeling of satisfaction.

Fat components in foods provide important textures and carry flavors. If you've ever eaten a high-fat yellow cheese or cream cheese, you probably agree that fat melting on the tongue feels good. The fat in reduced-fat and whole milk also gives body, which nonfat milk lacks, and the most tender cuts of meat are high in fat, visible as the marbling of meat. In addition, many flavorings dissolve in fat. Heating spices in oil intensifies the flavors of an Indian curry or a Mexican dish by carrying the flavors to the sensory cells in the mouth that discriminate taste and smell. For these reasons, a person who has been following a typical North American diet will probably need some time to adjust to a lower-fat diet. For example, if one changes from the regular use of whole milk to 1% low-fat milk but then after a few weeks switches back to the whole milk, it will taste more like cream than milk. One has thus adjusted to the flavor of the low-fat milk and will likely now find the whole milk to be not as palatable.

Hydrogenation of Fatty Acids Aids in Food Formulation but Increases Trans Fatty Acid Content

As previously mentioned, fats with long-chain saturated fatty acids are solid at room temperature, and those with unsaturated fatty acids are liquid at room temperature. In some types of food production, solid fats work better than liquid oils. In pie crust, for example, solid fats yield a flaky product, whereas pie crusts made with liquid oils tend to be greasy and more crumbly. If they are used to replace solid fats, oils with unsaturated fatty acids often must be made more saturated (with hydrogen), as this solidifies the vegetable oils into shortenings and margarines. Hydrogen is added by bubbling hydrogen gas under pressure into liquid vegetable oils in a process called **hydrogenation** (Fig. 6-10). The fatty acids aren't fully hydrogenated to the saturated fatty acid form,

hydrogenation The addition of hydrogen to a carbon-carbon double bond, producing a single bond. Because hydrogenation of unsaturated fatty acids in a vegetable oil increases its hardness, this process is used to convert liquid oils into more solid fats, which are used in making margarine and shortening. Trans fatty acids are a by-product of hydrogenation of vegetable oils.

Figure 6-10 How liquid oils become solid fats. (*a*) Unsaturated fatty acids are present in liquid form. (*b*) Hydrogens are added (hydrogenation), changing some carbon-carbon double bonds to single bonds and producing some trans fatty acids. (*c*) The completed partially hydrogenated product is likely to be used in margarine, shortening, or deep-fat frying.

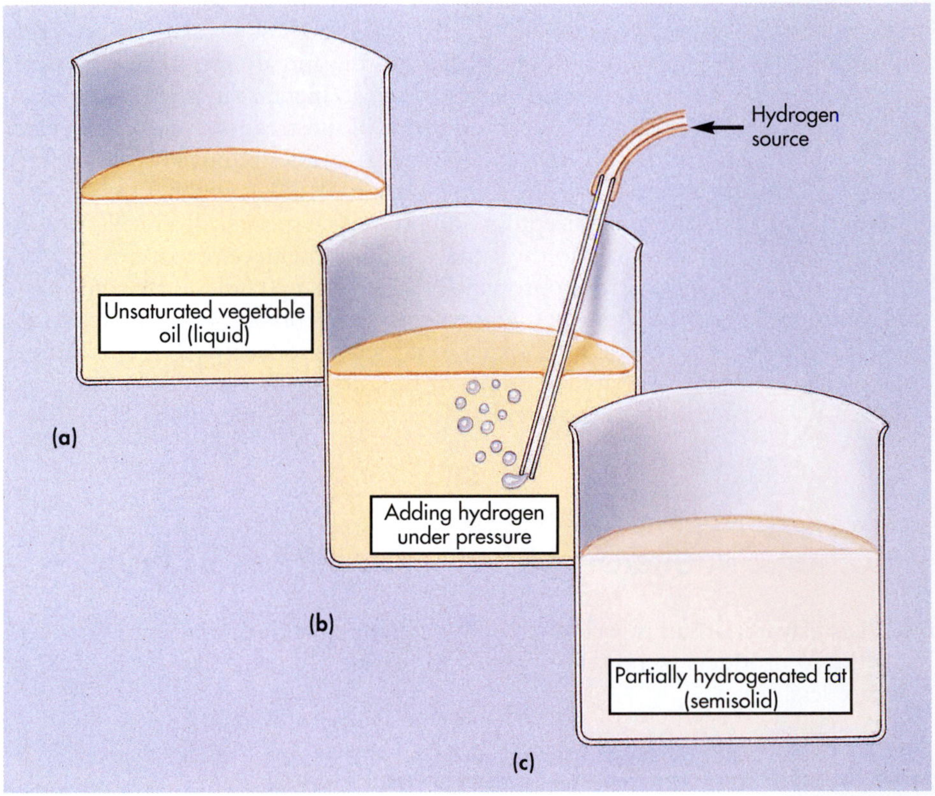

Figure 6-11 *Cis* and *trans* isomers of fatty acids. Cis fatty acids are more common in foods than trans fatty acids. The latter are primarily found in foods containing partially hydrogenated fats—notably, stick margarine, shortening, and deep fat–fried foods. Trans fatty acids raise LDL and lower HDL, so a generous intake is discouraged. The Food and Nutrition Board suggests limiting intake as much as possible.[5]

Illustration by William Ober.

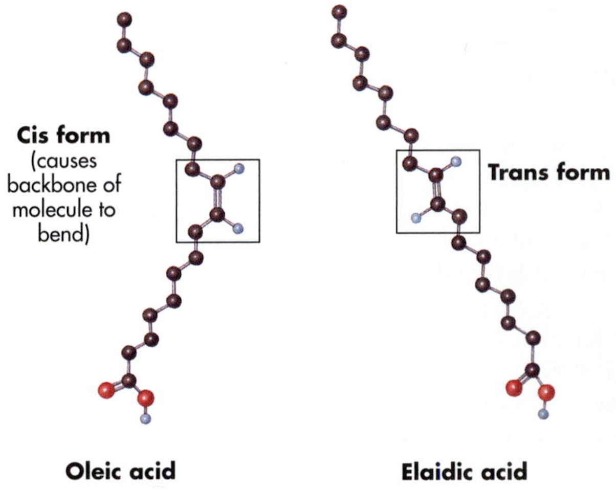

as this would make the product too hard and brittle. Partial hydrogenation—leaving some monounsaturated trans fatty acids—creates a semisolid product.

In their natural form, monounsaturated and polyunsaturated fatty acids usually are in the *cis* form (Fig. 6-11). By definition, the hydrogens are on the same side of the carbon-carbon double bond. During hydrogenation, some hydrogens are transferred to opposite sides of the carbon-carbon double bond, creating the *trans* form, or a **trans fatty acid.** As seen in Figure 6-11, the *cis* bond causes the fatty acid backbone to bend, whereas the *trans* bond allows the backbone to remain straighter. This makes it similar to the shape of a saturated fatty acid. This may be the mechanism whereby trans fatty

trans fatty acid A form of an unsaturated fatty acid, usually a monounsaturated one when found in food, in which the hydrogens on both carbons forming the double bond lie on opposite sides of that bond. A *cis* fatty acid has the hydrogens lying on the same side of the carbon-carbon double bond.

acids raise LDL. Trans fatty acids also lower HDL. Thus, people with elevated LDL should limit intake of partially hydrogenated fat.[18] There is also evidence in the scientific literature indicating the potentially deleterious effects of high trans fatty acid intakes during pregnancy in terms of the growth and development of infants during the neonatal period. It is less clear that this attention to trans fat intake is important for the average person, as long as trans fatty acid intake is not excessive and the diet is adequate in polyunsaturated fat. However, since these fatty acids serve no particular role in maintaining body health, many experts concur with the latest Dietary Guidelines and advice from both the American Heart Association and the Food and Nutrition Board that recommend minimal trans fatty acid intake.[5, 9]

As public pressure has persuaded manufacturers to eliminate the tropical oils rich in saturated fat (palm, palm olein, and coconut) from food processing, partially hydrogenated soybean oil—rich in trans fatty acids—has become the major replacement. Currently, trans fatty acid intake in the United States is estimated to contribute about 3% of total energy intake, amounting to on average about 10 g/day. A recent Canadian assessment indicated the average intake of trans monounsaturated fat to be 8.4 g/person/day, or 3.7% of the total energy intake for Canadian adults, with the highest intakes occurring among the younger population.

FDA is in the process of requiring the labeling of trans fatty acid content in foods. Currently no such labeling is present. The agency hopes to make consumers more aware of trans fatty acid intake, as well as the negative health consequences associated with high intakes of trans fatty acids. Companies are already responding to this issue before labeling is in place by creating products that are lower in or free of trans fatty acids. For example, Promise, Smart Beat, and some Fleischmann's margarines are now trans fatty acid–free products (less than 0.5 g per serving).

The eventual addition of trans fatty acids to food labels will help consumers at the grocery store, but, when dining out, consumers are left in the dark as to which foods contain trans fatty acids. Currently, restaurant foods are rich not only in saturated fatty acids but also in trans fatty acids (Table 6-3). Knowing which foods are low in trans

Tub margarine is much lower in trans fatty acids than stick margarine or shortenings (9%, 14%, and 26% of fatty acids respectively).

Table 6-3 Trans Fatty Acids in Restaurant Foods

Fried Foods	Calories	Total Fat (g)	Trans Fat (g)
Onion Rings (8 rings—6 oz)	650	47	7
Burger King french fries (king-size—6 oz)	540	24	7
McDonald's chicken nuggets (9)	510	29	3
McDonald's french fries (large—5 oz)	470	19	4
Fried mozzarella sticks (4 sticks—4 oz)	370	23	3
Fried fish (6 oz)	350	16	3
Miscellaneous Foods			
Prime rib, untrimmed (6 oz precooked weight)	480	35	3
Hamburger (5 oz)	470	26	2
Chicken pot pie (7 oz)	370	20	3
KFC biscuit (2 oz)	210	12	4
Pastries and Desserts			
Cinnabon Cinnabun (8 oz)	670	34	6
Apple pie (3.5 oz)	236	12	3

Adapted from *Nutrition Action Health Letter,* June 1999.

French fries are a common source of fat and trans fatty acids for many adults. There is currently a trend in the restaurant industry to use fats with lower trans fatty acid compositions compared to that previously used.

fatty acids when ordering at a restaurant is extremely difficult because the information on how these foods are prepared or the precise fat composition is typically not available. You can follow this tip when ordering to limit trans fatty acids: Limit fried (especially deep-fat fried) food items, any pastries or flaky bread products (such as pie crusts, crackers, croissants, and biscuits), and cookies.

We can make educated guesses on the trans fatty acid content of foods that have a Nutrition Facts label. Add up the amount of saturated fat, monounsaturated fat, and polyunsaturated fat and then subtract that number from the total fat grams listed. In most cases, the difference can be attributed to trans fatty acid content.

Looking at the ingredients on a food label is another way to estimate the amount of trans fatty acids in a product. If partially hydrogenated vegetable oil is one of the first three ingredients on the label, you can assume there is a significant amount of trans fatty acids in the product. Unfortunately, partially hydrogenated vegetable oil is a broad term that does not indicate the extent of hydrogenation. Although currently unavailable, this information would be helpful because, the more hydrogenated a product is, the more trans fatty acids it contains.

Limiting trans fatty acids at home is a much easier task. Most important, use little or no stick margarine or shortening; instead, substitute vegetable oils and softer tub margarines (whose labels list vegetable oil or water as the first ingredient). Avoid deep-fat frying any food in shortening. Substitute baking, pan-frying, broiling, steaming, grilling, or deep fat-frying in unhydrogenated vegetable oils. Replace nondairy creamers with reduced-fat or nonfat milk, since most nondairy creamers are rich in hydrogenated vegetable oils.

Fat Rancidity Limits Shelf Life of Foods

Decomposing oils emit a disagreeable odor and taste sour and stale. Stale potato chips and fish that has been in your refrigerator for several days are good examples. As double bonds in fatty acids break down, rancid by-products appear. Ultraviolet rays of light, oxygen, and certain procedures can break double bonds and in turn destroy the structure of polyunsaturated fatty acids. Saturated fats and trans fats can much more readily resist these effects, as they have few or no carbon-carbon double bonds.

Rancidity is not a major problem for consumers because, although eating rancid oils can cause sickness, the odor and taste generally discourage us from eating enough to become sick. However, rancidity is a problem for manufacturers because it reduces a product's shelf life. For this reason, manufacturers often add hydrogenated plant oils to products to increase shelf life. Foods most likely to become rancid are deep-fried foods and foods with a large amount of exposed surface (such as powdered eggs or powdered milk). The fat in fish is very susceptible to rancidity because it is highly polyunsaturated.

Vitamin E helps protect foods against rancidity because it acts as an antioxidant. It guards against the fat breakdown caused by various agents, such as metals found as impurities in vegetable oils. The vitamin E in plant oils reduces the breakdown of double bonds in fatty acids. (In Chapter 9, the role of vitamin E is explained more fully.) When food manufacturers want to prevent rancidity in polyunsaturated fats, they often add **BHA** and **BHT.** (Chapter 19 discusses the safety of these and other food additives.) Look for these food additives in salad dressings, cake mixes, and other products that contain fat. They can even be added to a food's paper packaging. Vitamin C may also be added for the same reason. Manufacturers also tightly seal products and use other methods to reduce oxygen levels inside packages.

BHA, BHT Butylated hydroxyanisol and butylated hydroxytoluene—two common synthetic antioxidants added to foods.

Fats Act as Emulsifiers

Food manufacturers add emulsifiers in the preparation of many food products, primarily to improve texture. For example, lecithins, polysorbate 60, and other emulsifiers are added to salad dressings to keep the vegetable oil suspended in water. Eggs added to cake batters likewise emulsify the fat with the milk. Monoglycerides and related compounds are also good emulsifiers and, for that reason, are sometimes used in cake mixes and salad dressings. Over the next few days, examine the labels of salad dressings and cake mixes, and see how many emulsifiers are listed.

Concept | Check

Fat has a variety of roles in foods, including that of contributing to flavor, texture, and satiety. Fat also provides the pleasurable mouth feel of many of our favorite foods, intensifies the taste of many spices, and tenderizes many popular cuts of meat.

Hydrogenation of unsaturated fatty acids consists of adding hydrogen to carbon-carbon double bonds to produce single bonds. This results in the creation of some trans fatty acids. Hydrogenation changes vegetable oil to solid fat. It is wise to monitor trans fatty acid intake, as this form of fat raises LDL and lowers HDL.

The carbon-carbon double bonds in polyunsaturated fatty acids are easily broken, yielding products responsible for rancidity. The presence of antioxidants, such as vitamin E in oils, naturally protects unsaturated fatty acids against oxidative destruction. Manufacturers can use partially hydrogenated fats and add synthetic antioxidants to reduce the likelihood of rancidity.

Manufacturers of commercial salad dressings find practical use for emulsification. Emulsifiers, such as lecithins, polysorbate 60, and monoglycerides, are added to salad dressings and other fat-rich products to keep the vegetable oils and other fats suspended in the water.

Recommendations for Fat Intake

There is no RDA for total fat intake for adults, although there is an Adequate Intake set for total fat for infants (see Chapter 17).

Regarding essential fatty acids, the Food and Nutrition Board has made recommendations for both omega-6 and omega-3 fatty acids. Specifically, an Adequate Intake for adults for linoleic acid is 17 g/day for men and 12 g/day for women. The respective Adequate Intakes for alpha-linolenic acid are 1.6 and 1.1 g/day. This works out to about 5% of energy intake for the total of both essential fatty acids. Infants and children have lower needs (again, see Chapter 17).[5] Adults should also eat fish at least twice a week.

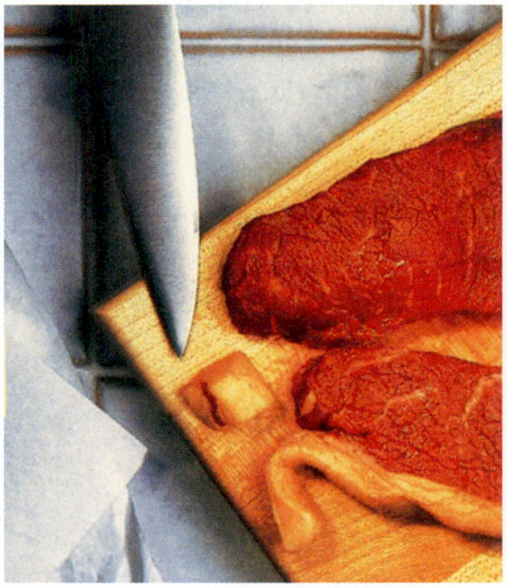

Trim meats before cooking to reduce intake of saturated fat, the major dietary fat that increases blood cholesterol.

The typical North American diet derives about 7% of energy content from polyunsaturated fatty acids, and thus meets needs. An upper limit of 10% of energy intake as polyunsaturated fatty acids is often recommended, in part because the breakdown (oxidation) of those present in lipoproteins is linked to increased cholesterol deposition in the arteries, as previously discussed. Depression of immune function is also suspected to be caused by an excessive intake of polyunsaturated fats.

General consensus among nutrition experts suggests that we should limit saturated fat, cholesterol, and trans fatty acid intake as much as possible, and that the diet needs to contain some omega-3 and omega-6 fatty acids. Furthermore, if fat intake exceeds 30% of calories, the extra fat should come from monounsaturated fat.[5, 8, 10] Meeting fiber needs is also important.[11]

Dietary fat supplies about 33% of the average North American's total energy intake, in which the major sources are animal flesh, whole milk, pastries, cheese, margarine, and mayonnaise. In contrast, the major sources of fat in the Mediterranean Pyramid diet include liberal amounts of olive oil and the fat found in the small amount of animal flesh and dairy products allowed on the diet. The main sources of fat in Dr. Dean Ornish's purely vegetarian **(vegan)** diet plan are a scant amount of vegetable oil used in cooking and the small amounts found in various plant foods.

vegan A person who eats only plant foods.

Because many Americans are at risk for developing cardiovascular disease, the American Heart Association (AHA) promotes dietary and lifestyle goals aimed at reducing this risk. One set of recommendations is made for the general public (Table 6-4). Then a more detailed list of recommendations is made for those at high risk or who currently are at high risk or have cardiovascular disease (Table 6-5). For these latter individuals the AHA recommends that total fat intake should not exceed 20 to 30% of total energy

Table 6-4 Current Dietary Guidance for the General Population (2 Years of Age and Older) from the American Heart Association[9]

Population Goals	Major Guidelines
Overall Healthy Eating Pattern	Include a variety of fruits, vegetables, grains, low-fat or nonfat dairy products, fish, legumes, poultry, lean meats.
Appropriate Body Weight	Match energy intake to overall energy needs, with appropriate changes to achieve weight loss when indicated.
Desirable Blood Cholesterol Profile	Limit foods high in saturated fat and cholesterol; and substitute unsaturated fat from vegetables, fish, legumes, nuts.
Desirable Blood Pressure	Limit salt and alcohol (see Table 6-5); maintain a healthy body weight (see Table 6-5); and a diet with emphasis on vegetables, fruits, and low-fat or nonfat dairy products.

Table 6-5 Specific Dietary Recommendations from American Heart Association, Especially for Those People at High Risk or Currently Have Cardiovascular Disease[9]

Diet	Consume at least:
	5 servings of fruits and vegetables each day. Up to 9 servings per day is advised if the person has hypertension. 6 servings of grains, including some whole grains, each day. At least 2 servings of fish (3-oz portions) per week (or 1 g of a combination of EPA and DHA from fish oil supplements per day). 25 g of fiber each day, including some sources of soluble fiber.†
	Consume no more than: 30% of energy from total fat or 20% if blood lipids are still too high. 10% of energy as saturated fat, or 7% if blood lipids are still too high. As well, limit trans fatty acid intake (combine with saturated fat gram allowance). 300 mg of cholesterol per day (on average), or 200 mg per day if blood lipids are still too high or the person has diabetes or cardiovascular disease. 6 g of salt each day (6 g equals 2400 mg of sodium). 2 alcoholic drinks per day for men and one drink for women.
	Additional advice includes: Specifically meeting vitamin B-6, folate, vitamin B-12, and potassium needs, limiting sugar intake, and possible use of soy protein and stanol/sterol-containing margarines (see the Nutrition Perspective for details). Megadose vitamin E supplements are not recommended at this time, and vitamin C and beta-carotene supplements provide no benefit.
Body weight	Maintain a body mass index between 18.5 and 25. Waist circumference should not exceed 40 inches (102 cm) in men or 35 inches (88 cm) in women (see Chapter 13 for details).
Physical activity	30 to 60 minutes of brisk activity on most if not all days of the week.

These specific recommendations apply to individuals 2 years of age and older. The latest guidelines from the National Cholesterol Education Program in the United States also concur with this advice for high-risk individuals, except that fat could be as high as 35% of energy intake if saturated fat intake is 7% of energy intake or less and cholesterol intake does not exceed 200 mg/day.

†Note that the latest guidance for fiber from the Food and Nutrition Board is that men consume 38 g/day, while 25 g/day is fine for women.

intake, with no more than 7 to 10% of total energy intake from saturated fat (include trans fat in the allowance). The intake of saturated fats currently averages about 13% of energy intake. Cholesterol intake should be no more than 200 to 300 milligrams per day. Recall that we consume 180 to 320 mg/day, with men consuming the greater amount. Table 6-6 shows a diet that follows those guidelines. The latest guidelines

Table 6-6 Daily Menu Examples Containing 2000 kcal and Various Percentages of Fat

30% of Energy as Fat		20% of Energy as Fat	
Food	**Fat (g)**	**Food**	**Fat (g)**
Breakfast			
Orange juice, 1 cup	0.5	Same	0.5
Shredded wheat, ¾ cup	0.5	Shredded wheat, 1 cup	0.7
Toasted bagel	1.1	Same	1.1
Tub margarine, 3 tsp	11.4	Tub margarine, 2 tsp	7.6
1% low-fat milk, 1 cup	2.5	Nonfat skim milk, 1 cup	0.6
Lunch			
Whole-wheat bread, 2 slices	2.4	Same	2.4
Roast beef, 2 oz	4.9	Light turkey roll, 2 oz	0.9
Mayonnaise, 3 tsp	11.0	Mayonnaise, 2 tsp	7.3
Lettuce	—	Same	—
Tomato	—	Same	—
Oatmeal cookie, 1	3.3	Oatmeal cookie, 2	6.6
Snack			
Apple	—	Same	—
Dinner			
Chicken tenders frozen meal	18.0	Fat-free chicken tenders	—
Dinner roll, 1	2.0	Same	2.0
Margarine, 1 tsp	3.8	Same	3.8
Banana	0.6	Same	0.6
1% low-fat milk, 1 cup	2.5	Non-fat skim milk, 1 cup	0.6
Snack			
Raisins, 2 tsp	—	Raisins, ½ cup	—
Air-popped popcorn, 3 cups	1.0	Air-popped popcorn, 6 cups	2.0
Margarine, 2 tsp	7.6	Same	7.6
Totals	73.1		44.3

from the National Cholesterol Education Program in the United States concur with this advice, except fat intake could be as high as 35% of total energy intake as long as saturated fat intake does not exceed 7% of energy intake and cholesterol intake does not exceed 200 mg/day.[4] The Food and Nutrition Board also accepts this recommendation for fat intake, suggesting a range of 20 to 35% of energy intake.[5] Making sure weight gain does not become a problem is also important when switching to a higher-fat diet.

Monitoring by a physician is important when fat is restricted to 20% of calories, as the resulting increase in carbohydrate intake can increase blood triglycerides in some people, which is not a healthful change.[4] Over time, however, this problem of high blood triglycerides on a low-fat diet may self-correct, as has been shown in people following the Dr. Dean Ornish vegan diet for a year or more. Their blood triglycerides increased initially on the diet but, within a year, fell to normal values as long as they emphasized carbohydrate sources high in fiber, controlled (or improved) body weight status, and followed a regular exercise program.

Recently some researchers have begun to question the dietary fat recommendation of 20 to 35% of total energy intake, stating that a diet can be as high as 40% of energy intake from fat as long as saturated fat and trans fat intake is minimal and body weight is maintained (or improved). This change in advice is discussed in the book by Dr. Walter C. Willett, entitled *Eat, Drink, and Be Healthy* (2001). The diet plan in the book emphasizes whole grains, plant oils, vegetables in abundance, fruits at least two to three times per day, nuts and legumes one to three times per day, fish, poultry, and eggs zero

The Food and Nutrition Board set the upper range for fat intake at 35% of energy intake because an intake greater than this likely leads to weight gain.

Table 6-7 A 2400 kcal Diet Containing 40% of the Calories as Fat but Low in Saturated Fat and Trans Fat

Food	Fat (g)	Saturated Fat (g)
Breakfast		
¾ cup fresh orange juice	—	—
1 whole-grain bagel	2.0	—
2 tsp soft trans fat-free margarine	7.6	1.3
Snack		
1 cup raw carrots	—	—
2 celery stalks	—	—
3 tbsp smooth trans fat-free peanut butter	24.5	5.0
Lunch		
¾ cup apple juice	—	—
Sandwich:		
2 slices whole-wheat bread	1.0	—
2 tsp mayonnaise	4.7	0.7
2 oz light meat turkey	4.1	1.2
2 pieces lettuce	—	—
1 slice tomato	—	—
Salad:		
1½ cups tossed green salad	—	—
3 tbsp Italian salad dressing	21.3	3.1
2 tsp dry sunflower seeds	3.0	0.3
1 oz low-fat cheddar cheese	2.0	1.2
¼ cup green pepper slices	—	—
3 baby carrots	—	—
Snack		
1 cup fresh strawberries	0.6	—
½ cup plain skim yogurt	0.2	0.1
Dinner		
1 cup V8 juice	—	—
3.5 oz broiled chicken breast	6.1	1.7
⅛ cup Italian dressing (marinade)	14.2	2.1
⅔ cup brown rice	—	—
2 tsp soft trans fat-free margarine	7.6	1.3
½ cup green beans	—	—
2 tsp soft trans fat-free margarine	7.6	1.3
1 cup grapes	0.7	—
Snack		
3 cups air-popped popcorn	1.0	—
Total	108	19

This diet contains 7% of the energy as saturated fat. Whether monounsaturated fat or polyunsaturated fat would dominate depends on the type of oil used for salad dressings, such as canola oil for monounsaturated fat versus corn oil for polyunsaturated fat. Use of a vegetable oil rich in monounsaturated fat is the preferred choice. The cholesterol content is 180 mg. The trans fat content is less than 1% of the energy content.

to two times per day, dairy products one to two times per day, and little use of red meat, butter, white rice, white bread, potatoes, pasta, and sweets. Overall, this diet especially avoids simple sugars and refined carbohydrates because diets high in these constituents tend to raise blood triglycerides, which is not a healthful result. Diets high in these carbohydrates are discouraged, especially if a person is overweight (and so likely insulin-resistant; see Chapter 5 for details) and performs little physical activity (regular physical activity increases carbohydrate use). Table 6-7 shows a diet that contains 40% of energy as fat and otherwise follows the plan indicated by Dr. Willett. This type of diet is also advocated for people who have Metabolic Syndrome, (also called Syndrome X).[3] Still, neither the American Heart Association nor the Food and Nutrition Board endorses such a high fat intake.

Most people probably have no idea how much of the energy in their diets comes from fat. You've already tracked your food intake for one day. A Take Action exercise at the end of the chapter asks you to compare your fat intake with current guidelines. Using the information on food labels and recording and analyzing daily food intake also allow you to track fat intake.

The advice to consume 20 to 30% of energy as fat from the American Heart Association does not apply to infants and toddlers below the age of 2 years. These youngsters are forming new tissue, especially in the brain, so their intake of fat and cholesterol should not be greatly restricted. After that age, children should gradually adopt a diet that generally follows the American Heart Association guidelines (see Chapter 17 for details).

Fats in Food

Table 6-6 provided an example of the amount of fat in foods in a day's menu. The foods richest in fat are salad oils, butter, margarine, and mayonnaise. All contain close to 100% of energy as fat. In fat-reduced margarines, water replaces some of the fat. Typical margarines are 80% fat by weight (11 g/tbsp). Some fat-reduced margarines are as low as 30% fat by weight (4 g/tbsp). The extra water added to these margarines can cause texture and volume changes when used in recipes. Cookbooks can provide guidance for appropriate use of these products by suggesting alterations in recipes to compensate.

Walnuts, bologna, avocados, and bacon have about 80% of energy as fat. Peanut butter and cheddar cheese have about 75%. Marbled steak and hamburgers (ground chuck) have about 60%, and chocolate bars, ice cream, doughnuts, and whole milk have about 50% of energy as fat. Eggs, pumpkin pie, and cupcakes have 35%, as do lean cuts of meat, such as top round (and ground round) and sirloin. Bread contains about 15%. Cornflakes, sugar, and nonfat milk have essentially no fat. Careful label reading is necessary to determine the true fat content of food—these are only rough guidelines.

Animal fats, which contain about 40 to 60% of total fat as saturated fatty acids, are the chief contributors of saturated fatty acids to the North American diet. Saturated fatty acids with 12, 14, and 16 carbons (lauric acid, myristic acid, and palmitic acid, respectively) are the primary contributors to elevated LDL. Of these, the 14-carbon myristic acid is mainly responsible for elevating LDL.[17] Dairy fats are rich sources of myristic acid. The 16-carbon palmitic acid also increases LDL, primarily when there is more than 200 to 300 mg of cholesterol in the diet and LDL is already elevated. The saturated fatty acids with 12, 14, or 16 carbons generally constitute about 25 to 50% of the total fat in animal foods. In general, dairy fats and meat are rich in the fatty acids that raise LDL. In some plant oils, these saturated fatty acids also make up a notable percentage of the total fat—for example, cottonseed oil (27%) and coconut oil (89%).

Plant oils contain mostly unsaturated fatty acids, ranging from 73 to 94% of total fat. Canola oil, olive oil, and peanut oil contain moderate to high amounts of total fat as monounsaturated fatty acids (49 to 77%). Some animal fats are also good sources of monounsaturated fatty acids (30 to 47%) (review Fig. 6-2). Corn, cottonseed, sunflower, soybean, and safflower oils contain mostly polyunsaturated fatty acids (54 to 77%) in terms of total fat. These plant oils supply the majority of the linoleic acid and alpha-linolenic acid in the North American food supply. Note that plant oils vary in their content of polyunsaturated fatty acids. Oils that are similar in appearance still may vary significantly in fatty acid composition.

Cholesterol is found only in the animal foods we eat (review Table 6-2). An egg yolk contains about 210 mg of cholesterol. This is our main dietary source of cholesterol, along with meats and whole milk. Some plants contain related sterols, but none we typically eat contains cholesterol. Manufacturers who advertise peanut butter, vegetable shortening, margarines, and vegetable oils as containing no cholesterol are taking advantage of uninformed consumers. Peanut butter and margarine never contain cholesterol—it's not naturally present.

Food Sources of Fat

Food Item and Amount	*Fat (g)*
T-Bone steak, 3 oz	17
Mixed nuts, 1 oz	16
Canola oil, 1 tbsp	14
Hamburger with bun, 1 each	12
Margarine, 1 tbsp	12
Avocado, ½ cup	11
Cheddar cheese, 1 oz	10
Whole milk, 1 cup	8
Chicken breast with skin, 3 oz	7
Whole milk yogurt, 8 oz	7
Snack crackers, 1 oz	7
Baked beans, ½ cup	7
M&M chocolate candies, 1 oz	6
Flax seeds, 1 tbsp	3
Fig Newton Cookies, 2 each	3

The North American diet contains many high-fat foods—including typical cookie choices. Portion control with these foods is thus important, especially if one is trying to control energy intake.

Fat Replacement Strategies

Manufacturers offer a variety of low-cholesterol foods. The general recommendation is to consume 200 to 300 mg/day or less of cholesterol.

Currently, five types of fat replacements are available in the United States. Addition of these substances during manufacture yields products that, to varying degrees, satisfy consumers' desire for fat-reduced products that are still tasty.

Water, Starch Derivatives, and Gums

The first and simplest fat replacement is water. The addition of water yields a product, such as diet margarine, with less fat per serving than the normal product. Starch derivatives that bind water form a second type of fat replacement. The resulting gel replaces some of the mouth feel lost by the removal of fat. Z-trim, the newest starch derivative, was recently created by USDA. It is made from the hulls of oats, soybeans, peas, and rice or bran from corn or wheat. Other derivatives commonly used by food manufacturers include cellulose, Maltrin, Stellar, and Oatrim. These substances are used in a variety of foods, including luncheon meats, salad dressings, frozen desserts, table spreads, dips, baked goods, and candies. Most starch derivatives contain some calories, although they have at least less than half the amount that is in fat. Note that these starch derivatives cannot be used in fried foods.

Gums extracted from plants can also be used to replace fat. They thicken a product and replace some of the body that fat provides. Diet salad dressings have gums added for this reason.

Protein-Derived Fat Replacements

One type of fat replacement on the market consists of proteins that have been treated to produce microscopic, mistlike protein globules. Both egg and milk proteins can be used. When these substances replace fat in a food product, they feel like fat in the mouth, although the product does not contain any fatty acids. One example is Dairy-Lo, which is used in milk and other dairy products, baked goods, frostings, salad dressings, and mayonnaise-type products. Such fat replacements yield some energy—but only about 1 to 2 kcal/g, much less than the 9 kcal/g supplied by regular fats. They have this low energy value primarily for two reasons: Proteins contain only 4 kcal/g and the products have a high water content.

Engineered Fats and Related Products

The fifth form of fat replacement is the engineered fat. This type of product is synthesized in the laboratory from various food constituents. Olestra (Olean) is a good example. It is made by chemically linking fatty acids to sucrose (table sugar). The resulting product cannot be digested by either human digestive enzymes or bacteria that live in the intestine. Therefore, olestra yields no energy to the body.

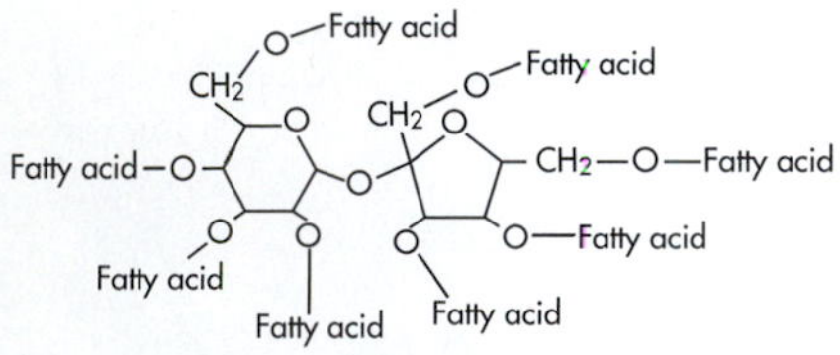

Olestra, a sucrose polyester (with the maximum number of fatty acids attached).

Olestra can replace all of the fat in salad dressings and cakes and is the first fat replacement that can be used in fried foods. After almost 200 animal and human studies over a 25-year period, olestra was approved by FDA in 1996 for use in fried snack foods. It underwent such strict scrutiny because it did not exist as such in nature or arise from typical cooking procedures, as is the case for the other products mentioned.

Some problems are associated with the use of olestra. It binds the fat-soluble vitamins A, D, E, and K, thus reducing absorption. To compensate, the manufacturer adds these vitamins to olestra. Olestra also may cause abdominal cramping and loose stools in some people because, even though it is not absorbed in the small intestine, it still may influence intestinal function. The problem is seen mostly with intakes of 20 g at a meal. In comparison, a 1-ounce bag of chips has about 10 g of olestra and has little effect. Those who experience such symptoms as a result of eating olestra should limit or avoid using products that contain this fat replacement.

The following statement is required on all products made with olestra: "This product contains olestra. Olestra may cause abdominal cramping and loose stools. Olestra inhibits the absorption of some vitamins and other nutrients. Vitamins A, D, E, and K have been added."

Canada has turned down the use of olestra in food products; this decision makes the United States the sole country that permits the use of this fat substitute in foods.

One final problem linked to olestra is its ability to bind carotenoids, the yellow, orange, or red pigments found in many fruits and vegetables. Recall from Chapter 2 the discussion of phytochemicals and their proposed contribution to overall health; one class of phytochemicals is carotenoids. There is no planned attempt to add carotenoids to olestra. This effect of olestra is most important when it is consumed in large amounts with meals rich in carotenoids. Typical projected intakes of 10 to 20 g don't have much of an effect. Nevertheless, this ability to bind carotenoids has caused some experts to recommend that we not consume olestra. At the very least, organizations such as the American Heart Association recommend moderate intake until we know more about its long-term effects.

Food manufacturers are working on still other types of engineered fats, which either wholly or partially escape absorption by the body. One example is salatrim, which is marketed under the name Benefat and yields only about 5 kcal/g. It is generally composed of stearic acid, which the body absorbs poorly, and short-chain fatty acids. This product is currently used in reduced-fat chocolate. Another product is Appetize, which blends animal fats stripped of cholesterol with plant oils. This produces a stable frying fat low in trans fatty acid content, and is found in some margarines.

Hidden Fat

Some fat discussed so far is obvious: butter on bread, mayonnaise in potato salad, and marbling in raw meat. Fat is harder to detect in other foods that also contribute much fat to our diets. Fat is hidden in whole milk, pastries, cookies, cake, cheese, hot dogs, crackers, french fries, and ice cream. When we try to cut down on fat intake, hidden fats need to be exposed and controlled, along with the more obvious sources.

A place to begin searching for hidden fat is on the Nutrition Facts labels of foods you buy in the supermarket. Some signals that can alert you to the presence of fat are chocolate; animal fats, such as bacon, beef, ham, lamb, pork, chicken, and turkey fats; lard; vegetable oils; nuts; dairy fats, such as butter and cream; egg and egg-yolk solids; and hydrogenated shortening or vegetable oil. Conveniently, the label lists ingredients by order of weight in the product. If fat is one of the first ingredients listed, you are probably looking at a high-fat product. Use food labels to learn more about the fat content of the foods you eat (Fig. 6-12). Table 2-11 in Chapter 2 listed the definitions for various fat descriptors on food labels, such as "low-fat," "fat-free," and "reduced-fat." Recall that "low-fat" signifies in most cases that a product contains no more than 3 g of fat per serving. Products claimed to be fat free must have less than ½ g of fat per serving. A claim of "reduced-fat" means the product has at least 25% less fat than is usually found in that food.

Figure 6-12 Reading labels helps locate hidden fat. Who would think that wieners (hot dogs) can contain 85% of food energy as fat? Looking at the hot dog itself does not suggest that almost all of its food energy comes from fat, but the label shows otherwise.

Many manufacturers are trying to devise products that are lower in fat. However, these help reduce energy intake only if energy content is also considered.

When many North Americans think of a low-fat diet, they include reduced-fat versions of pastries, cookies, and cakes. When health professionals refer to a low-fat diet, they often have a very different plan in mind: replacing high-fat snacks with fruits, vegetables, and whole grains. Most North Americans could benefit from this paradigm shift.

Table 6-8 Tips for Avoiding Too Much Fat, Saturated Fat, and Trans Fatty Acids.

1.	Steam, boil, or bake vegetables. For a change, stir-fry in a small amount of vegetable oil. Consider buying an insert for a pot, so you can easily steam your vegetables.
2.	Season vegetables with herbs and spices, rather than with sauces, butter, or margarine.
3.	Try lemon juice on salad or use limited amounts of oil-based salad dressing.
4.	To reduce saturated fat, use vegetable oils and tub margarine instead of butter, stick margarine, or hydrogenated shortenings in baked products.
5.	Limit baked goods made with large amounts of fat, especially croissants, doughnuts, muffins, biscuits, and butter rolls.
6.	Try whole-grain flours to enhance flavors when baking goods with less fat. Use applesauce and other fruit purees in place of fat when possible, such as in quick breads.
7.	Replace whole milk with nonfat or reduced-fat milk in puddings, soups, and baked products and for use as a beverage.
8.	Substitute plain low-fat yogurt, blender-whipped low-fat cottage cheese, or buttermilk in recipes that call for sour cream or mayonnaise.
9.	Choose lean cuts of meat. Limit bacon, ribs, and meat loaf.
10.	Trim fat from meat before and after cooking.
11.	Roast, bake, or broil meat, poultry, and fish, so that fat drains away as the food cooks.
12.	Remove skin from poultry before cooking. This eliminates the temptation to eat it along with the meat.
13.	Use a nonstick pan for cooking, so that added fat will be unnecessary; use a vegetable spray for frying.
14.	Chill meat or poultry broth until the fat solidifies. Spoon off the fat before using the broth.
15.	Eat a vegetarian main dish at least once a week. Include fish (cooked without much added fat) in the diet two times or more a week. Think about this when you make choices in a restaurant.
16.	Choose fat-reduced ice cream, low-fat frozen yogurt, sorbet, and popsicles as substitutes for regular ice cream.
17.	Try angelfood cake, fig bars, and gingersnaps as substitutes for commercially baked goods high in saturated fat.
18.	Limit high-fat cheese intake.
19.	Read labels on commercially prepared foods to find out what type of fat or how much saturated fat they contain.
20.	Use jam, jelly, or marmalade on bread and toast instead of butter or margarine.
21.	Buy whole-grain breads and rolls. They have more flavor and do not need butter or margarine to taste good. The dietary fiber present is an added bonus.
22.	Think about the balance of fats in the menu. If a meal contains whole milk, cheese, ice cream, a higher-fat meat, or poultry with skin, use tub margarine and unsaturated vegetable oils for your spreads and dressings. Small amounts of butter, sour cream, or cream cheese can be included if other menu items are low in saturated fat.

When there is no Nutrition Facts label to inspect, moderating portion size is a good way to control fat intake. Table 6-8 lists many ways to help avoid eating too much total fat and saturated fat. Whether or not to choose a fat-rich food should depend on how you intend to use it: as a staple item, as an occasional treat, or as a garnish for other foods. In addition, if you plan to eat a high-fat food at your evening meal, such as cheesecake, you could reduce your fat intake at a previous meal in order to balance overall fat intake for the day.

Wise Use of Reduced-Fat Foods

In recent years, manufacturers have introduced reduced-fat versions of numerous food products. The fat content of these alternatives ranges from 0% in fat-free Fig Newtons to about 75% of the original fat content in other products. However, the total energy content of most fat-reduced products is not substantially lower than that of their conventional versions. Generally, when fat is removed from a product, something must be added—commonly, sugars—in its place. It is very difficult to reduce both the fat and sugar content of a product at the same time. For this reason, many fat-reduced products (for example, cakes, cookies, and yogurt) are still very energy dense. Similarly, some cookbooks are modifying recipes to make them lower in fat. This is accomplished by replacing the fat with applesauce or other fruit purees. Keep in mind that these carbohydrate replacements still contain calories, but not as much as the fat that is left out. As noted in Chapter 5, don't be fooled into thinking you can eat substantially more of such foods just because some or all of the fat has been removed. "Reduced-fat" is not a license to overeat. Use the Nutrition Facts label to guide the portion size you choose.

Critical | Thinking

Allison has decided to start eating a low-fat diet. Allison has mentioned to you that all she needs to do is add less butter, oil, or margarine to her foods and she will dramatically lower her fat intake. How can you explain to Allison that she needs to be aware of the hidden fats in her diet as well?

Case Scenario | Follow-up

Jackie's approach to lowering blood cholesterol does not incorporate the best choices; she has excluded a great deal of fat in her diet by merely replacing it with refined carbohydrates. To make a shift to a more heart-healthy diet, Jackie would need to include at least two fruit and three vegetable servings a day, along with more whole-grain products (such as whole-wheat bread and a breakfast cereal that has at least 3 g of fiber per serving). Lowering fat as drastically as she has is not really necessary, especially for a 21-year-old female who is physically active. Jackie could allow a more liberal amount of fat in her diet by including more monounsaturated fats (canola oil and olive oil, as well as fats found in nuts and avocados). These do not increase blood cholesterol. In addition to allowing more liberal fat intake from monounsaturated oils and including more fruits, vegetables, and whole grains, Jackie would benefit from including good sources of omega-3 fatty acids (fatty fish, flaxseeds, walnuts, or soybean and canola oil). One option is to use a canola oil-and-vinegar dressing on her salad, rather than lemon juice.

Concept | Check

There is no RDA for total fat intake. We need about 5% of total energy intake from plant oils to meet the Adequate Intakes set for essential fatty acids. Eating fish at least twice a week is also advised to supply omega-3 fatty acids. Many health-related agencies recommend a diet containing no more than 35% of energy intake as fat, with limited amounts of saturated fat, cholesterol, and trans fatty acids. The current North American diet contains about 33% of energy content as fat, with about 13% of energy content as saturated fat and about 3% as trans fatty acids. Fat-dense foods—those with more than 60% of total energy as fat—include plant oils, butter, margarine, mayonnaise, walnuts, bacon, avocados, peanut butter, cheddar cheese, steak, and hamburger. Of the foods we typically eat, cholesterol is found naturally only in those of animal origin, with eggs being a primary source. Fat is often hidden in foods such as whole milk, pastries, cookies, cake, cheese, hot dogs, crackers, french fries, ice cream, and quick-service foods. Fat free doesn't mean calorie free; moderation in the use of fat-reduced products is still important.

Summary

1. Compared with carbohydrates and proteins, lipids are a group of relatively oxygen-poor compounds that dissolve in organic solvents, such as chloroform, benzene, and ether. Saturated fatty acids contain no carbon-carbon double bonds, monounsaturated fatty acids contain one carbon-carbon double bond, and polyunsaturated fatty acids contain two or more carbon-carbon double bonds in the carbon chain. Triglycerides rich in long-chain saturated fatty acids tend to be solid at room temperature, whereas those rich in polyunsaturated fatty acids are liquid at room temperature.
2. In omega-3 polyunsaturated fatty acids, the first of the carbon-carbon double bonds is located three carbons from the methyl end of the carbon chain. In omega-6 polyunsaturated fatty acids, the first carbon-carbon double bond counting from the methyl end occurs at the sixth carbon. Both omega-3 and omega-6 fatty acids are essential fatty acids; these must be included in the diet to maintain health. Body cells can synthesize hormone compounds called eicosanoids from both omega-3 and omega-6 fatty acids.
3. Triglycerides are formed from a glycerol backbone with three fatty acids. Triglyceride is the major form of fat in both food and the body. It allows for efficient energy storage, protects certain organs, transports fat-soluble vitamins, and helps insulate the body. Phospholipids are derivatives of triglycerides. Phospholipids are important parts of cell membranes, and some act as efficient emulsifiers.
4. Cholesterol forms vital biological compounds, such as hormones, components of cell membranes, and bile acids. Cells in the body make cholesterol whether we eat it or not. It is not a necessary part of an adult's diet.
5. Fat digestion takes place primarily in the small intestine. Lipase enzyme released from the pancreas digests the long-chain triglycerides into smaller breakdown products—namely, monoglycerides (glycerol backbones with single fatty acids attached) and fatty acids. The breakdown products are then absorbed by the absorptive cells of the small intestine. These products are mostly resynthesized into triglycerides and combined with cholesterol, protein, and other substances to yield a chylomicron. Chylomicrons enter the lymphatic system, in turn passing into the bloodstream.
6. Lipids are carried in the bloodstream by various lipoproteins, which are particles consisting of a central triglyceride core encased in a shell of protein, cholesterol, and phospholipid. Chylomicrons are released from intestinal cells and carry lipids arising from dietary intake. Very-low-density lipoprotein (VLDL) and low-density lipoprotein (LDL) carry lipids both taken up and synthesized in the liver. High-density lipoprotein (HDL) picks up cholesterol from cells and acts in allowing transport of it back to the liver.
7. In the blood, elevated amounts of LDL and low amounts of HDL are strong predictors of the risk for cardiovascular disease.
8. Fat adds flavor and texture to foods and provides some satiety after meals. Hydrogenation is the process of converting carbon-carbon double bonds into single bonds by adding hydrogen at the point of unsaturation. Hydrogenation of fatty acids in vegetable oils changes the oils to solid fats and helps reduce rancidity, which results from the breakdown of fatty acids. Hydrogenation also increases the trans fatty acid content. High amounts of trans fatty acids in the diet are discouraged, as these increase LDL and reduce HDL. When fatty acids break down, food becomes rancid, emitting a foul odor and flavor. Some phospholipids are used in food as emulsifiers. These suspend fat in water.
9. There is no RDA for total fat intake. We need about 5% of total energy intake from plant oils to obtain the needed essential fatty acids based on the Adequate Intake for these nutrients. Fish is a rich source of omega-3 fatty acids and should be consumed at least twice a week.
10. The typical North American diet contains about 33% of total energy as fat. Many health agencies and scientific groups suggest a fat intake of no more than 35% of energy intake. If fat intake exceeds 30% of total calories, the diet should emphasize monounsaturated fat.
11. Fat-reduced products aid in the goal of reducing fat intake, but they still must be eaten in moderate amounts to maintain control of total energy intake.

Study Questions

1. Describe the chemical structures of saturated and polyunsaturated fatty acids and their different effects in both food and the human body.
2. Relate the need for omega-3 fatty acids in the diet to the recommendation to consume fish twice a week.
3. Describe the structures, origins, and roles of the four major blood lipoproteins.
4. What are the recommendations of health-care professionals regarding fat intake? What does this mean in terms of actual food choices?
5. What are two important attributes of fat in food? How are these different from the general functions of lipids in the human body?
6. What are the significance of and possible uses for reduced-fat foods?
7. Does the total cholesterol concentration in the bloodstream tell the whole story with respect to cardiovascular disease risk?

Read the Nutrition Perspective before answering the following questions:

8. List five risk factors for the development of cardiovascular disease.
9. What lifestyle factors were found to decrease the risk of cardiovascular disease development in the Nurses Health Study?
10. When are medications most effective in cardiovascular disease therapy, and how in general do the various classes of medications operate to reduce risk?

Annotated References

1. Albert C and others: Blood levels of long-chain n-3 fatty acids and the risk of sudden death. *The New England Journal of Medicine* 346:1113, 2002.

   Using data from the Physicians' Health Study, researchers have demonstrated an inverse relationship between the amount of omega-3 fatty acids found in the bloodstream, and risk of sudden death from cardiovascular disease in healthy men. Omega-3 fatty acids are thought to protect against sudden death from cardiovascular disease due to their antiarrhythmic properties.

2. Beckman J and others: Diabetes and atherosclerosis: Epidemiology, pathophysiology, and management. *Journal of the American Medical Association* 287:2570, 2002.

   Cardiovascular disease is the most common cause of death in diabetic individuals. A review of the literature concerning diabetes and cardiovascular disease suggests that the risk of cardiovascular disease can be reduced in a diabetic individual if blood pressure is controlled, high cholesterol is lowered, and certain medications are used. Intensive cardiovascular disease prevention efforts are encouraged for the diabetic population.

3. Coleman E: Monounsaturated fat, metabolic syndrome, and CHD. *Today's Dietitian*, p. 15, February 2002.

   A high-carbohydrate, low-fat diet is often encouraged for individuals at risk for cardiovascular disease. However, a high-carbohydrate diet has been implicated in increasing triglycerides, lowering HDL-cholesterol, and worsening blood glucose control in those individuals with the metabolic syndrome (also called syndrome X). Recent studies have demonstrated that supplementing the traditional high-carbohydrate, low-fat diet with monounsaturated fat results in a smaller decrease in HDL-cholesterol and a smaller increase in triglycerides than the traditional low-fat diet. For individuals with the metabolic syndrome, a high monounsaturated-fat diet can be an appropriate alternative to the traditional low-fat diet in the treatment and prevention of cardiovascular disease.

4. Expert Panel on Detection, Evaluation, and Treatment of High Blood Cholesterol in Adults: Executive summary of the third report of the National Cholesterol Education Program (NCEP) expert panel on detection, evaluation, and treatment of high blood cholesterol in adults (Adult Treatment Panel III). *Journal of the American Medical Association* 285:2486, 2001.

   All adults ages 20 years or older should have a fasting lipoprotein profile (total cholesterol, LDL-cholesterol, HDL-cholesterol, and triglycerides) once every 5 years. Diabetes no longer is considered just a risk factor for cardiovascular disease, but virtually guarantees the disease will develop. Other new recommendations are using a combination of age, total blood cholesterol, HDL-cholesterol, blood pressure, and smoking history in a formula to determine which persons need cholesterol-lowering medications.

5. Food and Nutrition Board: *Dietary reference intakes for energy, carbohydrate, fiber, fat, fatty acids, cholesterol, protein, and amino acids.* Washington DC: The National Academy Press, 2002.

   This report provides the latest guidance for macronutrient intakes. With regard to fat intake, Adequate Intakes were set for omega-6 and omega-3 fatty acids. Intake of total fat can range from 20 to 35% of energy intake. Intake of saturated fat, cholesterol, and trans fat should be minimal as these dietary constituents are not essential nutrients, and are associated with increasing risk for cardiovascular disease.

6. Heart Protection Study Collaborative Group: MRC/BHF Heart protection study of antioxidant vitamin supplementation in 20,536 high-risk individuals: A randomized placebo-controlled trial. *The Lancet* 360:23, 2002.

   Data from observational studies have suggested that supplementation with antioxidant vitamins can lead to a reduced risk of developing cardiovascular disease and cancer. However, a recent placebo-controlled study involving over 20,500 subjects found that while consuming antioxidant supplements was safe, these supplements did not lead to a lower incidence of either cardiovascular disease or cancer. It is recommended that proven strategies to prevent cardiovascular disease (such as aspirin, statin drugs, increased physical activity, decreased consumption of saturated fat, and smoking cessation) be emphasized over antioxidant supplementation.

7. Hu FB, Willett WC: Optimal diets for prevention of coronary heart disease. *Journal of the American Medical Association* 288: 2569, 2002.

   Substantial evidence indicates that diets using nonhydrogenated unsaturated fats as the predominant form of dietary fat, whole grains as the main form of carbohydrates, an abundance of fruits and vegetables, some nuts, and adequate omega-3 fatty acids can offer significant protection against CHD. Together with regular physical activity, avoidance of smoking, maintenance of a healthy body weight, and limited alcohol use (if desired), these practices in combination may prevent the majority of cardiovascular disease in Western populations.

8. Hu FB and others: Types of dietary fat and risk of coronary heart disease: A critical review. *Journal of the American College of Nutrition* 20:5, 2001.

   Replacing saturated fat with unsaturated fat is more effective for lowering the risk of cardiovascular disease than simply reducing total fat consumption. There is strong evidence that a higher intake of omega-3 fatty acids from fish or plant sources lowers cardiovascular disease risk. The belief that fat is bad is widespread but is incorrect; saturated fat and trans fat should get the attention when recommending lower fat intakes.

9. Krauss RM and others: AHA Dietary Guidelines: Revision 2000: A statement for healthcare professionals from the Nutrition Committee of the American Heart Association. *Circulation* 102:2284, 2000.

   This report contains the latest advice for the public regarding diet and cardiovascular disease from the American Heart Association. The revised guidelines place an increased emphasis on the need for weight control and heart-healthy diet.

10. Liebman B: Face the fats. *Nutrition Action Health Letter*, p. 1, July/August 2002.

    The author of this article reviews the current research concerning dietary fat and disease risk, and provides recommendations for consumers about dietary fat intake. It is recommended that both saturated and trans fat intake combined make up no more than 10% of total energy intake, that canola oil be used as the main vegetable oil at home, and consumers aim for an intake of between 500 mg and 1000 mg of omega-3 fatty acids per day, either through fish intake or fish oil supplements.

11. Liu S: Intake of refined carbohydrates and whole grain foods in relation to risk of type 2 diabetes mellitus and coronary heart disease. *Journal of the American College of Nutrition* 21:298, 2002.

    Diets rich in high-fiber whole grains are associated with lower risk of coronary heart disease and type 2 diabetes. Whole grains produce favorable lipid profiles and glycemic control compared to refined grains.

12. MacMahon S: Blood pressure and the risk of cardiovascular disease. *The New England Journal of Medicine* 342:50, 2000.

    Reducing blood pressure is beneficial for people at high risk for major cardiovascular disease events. Aggressive blood pressure reduction in people with diabetes using either an angiotensin-converting enzyme (ACE) inhibitor or a beta-blocker allowed more protection from cardiovascular disease than less aggressive blood pressure reduction therapy.

13. Mayes PA: Digestion and absorption. In Murray RK and others (eds.): *Harper's biochemistry.* 25th ed. Stamford, CT: Appleton & Lange, 2000.

    Fat digestion primarily takes place in the small intestine with the participation of the enzyme lipase, bile acids, and lecithin. Most absorbed fat is in the form of monoglycerides. These reform into triglycerides and exit the absorptive cell as chylomicrons.

14. Mayes PA: Lipid storage and transport. In Murray RK and others (eds.): *Harper's biochemistry.* 25th ed. Stamford, CT: Appleton & Lange, 2000.

    This chapter provides an excellent review of lipoprotein metabolism. The following chapter in the book, on cholesterol synthesis, transport, and excretion, is also very informative. Both document the role of statin drugs in reducing cholesterol synthesis in the liver; the roles of other medications to reduce lipid synthesis in the liver are also discussed. Finally, an additional chapter on eicosanoids by this author (Chapter 25) is quite informative.

15. Nash D: Keeping an eye on cardiovascular risk. *Postgraduate Medicine* 111:107, 2002.

    Risk factors for cardiovascular disease can be classified as either major (including smoking, diabetes, high cholesterol, etc.), conditional (including high homocysteine levels, elevated triglycerides), or predisposing (including obesity, physical inactivity, and insulin resistance). Individuals are generally classified as "low," "medium," or "high risk" for developing cardiovascular disease based on the presence or absence of these risk factors. Despite this current system of determining cardiovascular disease risk, more than half of all heart attacks occur in individuals who are not considered "high risk." Physicians are encouraged to use aggressive cardiovascular disease prevention tactics in populations at risk for the development of cardiovascular disease.

16. Nicolosi RJ and others: Dietary effects on cardiovascular disease risk factors: Beyond saturated fat and cholesterol. *Journal of the American College of Nutrition* 20(5):4215s, 2001.

    Soy protein, soluble fiber, and plant sterols are all helpful in lowering blood cholesterol. Fruits, vegetables, and minimally processed grains are also helpful in lowering cardiovascular disease risk.

17. Schaefer E: Lipoproteins, nutrition, and heart disease. *American Journal of Clinical Nutrition* 75:191, 2002.

    The risk of developing cardiovascular disease can be lowered by controlling blood pressure, lowering LDL and raising HDL, and not smoking. Further recommendations the author makes include decreasing saturated fat intake to less than 7% of energy intake, decreasing total fat intake to between 15 and 30% of energy intake, avoiding trans fat, decreasing dietary cholesterol intake to less than 200 mg/day, consuming between 5 and 10% of energy as omega-6 fatty acids, and consuming at least 1% of energy as omega-3 fatty acids. Lifestyle modifications should be the foundation for cardiovascular disease prevention.

18. Stampfer M and others: Primary prevention of coronary heart disease in women through diet and lifestyle. *The New England Journal of Medicine* 343:16, 2000.

    Following a set of specific lifestyle factors, including a balanced diet with a small amount of wine each day, exercise, and abstinence from smoking, can help protect women from coronary heart disease.

19. Truan TL: Antioxidant supplements to prevent heart disease: Real hope or empty hype? *Postgraduate Medicine* 109(1):109, 2001.

    The notion that antioxidant supplements can prevent cardiovascular disease is not supported by current clinical evidence. Until conclusive evidence is available regarding the efficacy, safety, and appropriate dosage of antioxidants, the more prudent recommendation for the general public is to consume more fruits, vegetables, and whole grains.

20. Wilson PWF: Homocysteine and coronary heart disease. *Journal of the American Medical Association* 288:2042, 2002.

    Homocysteine is not a strong risk factor for cardiovascular disease in the general public. It can however, help explain why people without traditional risk factors still present with evidence of significant cardiovascular disease.

Take | Action

I. Are You Eating a Diet That Includes Many Saturated-Fat and Trans Fatty Acid Sources?

Instructions:

Check the food you would typically select from the two choices given.

1.	_____ Bacon and eggs	_____ Ready-to-eat whole-grain breakfast cereal
2.	_____ Doughnut or sweet roll	_____ Whole-wheat (or white) roll, bagel, or bread, no margarine
3.	_____ Breakfast sausage	_____ Fruit
4.	_____ Whole milk	_____ Reduced-fat, 1%, or nonfat milk
5.	_____ Cheeseburger	_____ Turkey sandwich, no cheese
6.	_____ French fries	_____ Plain baked potato with minimal added fat or salad with low-cal or fat-free dressing
7.	_____ Meal including fried hamburger or fatty beef	_____ Meal including broiled lean hamburger (ground round), chicken, or fish
8.	_____ Creamed soup	_____ Non-creamed soup (could contain some meat or vegetables)
9.	_____ Potato salad	_____ Baked potato, limited added fat
10.	_____ Cream/fruit pie	_____ Graham crackers
11.	_____ Ice cream	_____ Frozen yogurt, sherbet, or fat-reduced ice cream
12.	_____ Butter or stick margarine	_____ Vegetable oils or soft margarine in a tub

Interpretation

The foods listed on the left tend to be high in saturated fat, trans fatty acids, and cholesterol. Those on the right generally are low. If you want to help reduce the risk of cardiovascular disease, choose the foods on the right more often than the foods on the left.

Take | Action

II. What is Your Current Fat and Cholesterol Intake?

How do your food practices compare with general guidelines suggested for fat, saturated fat, and cholesterol intake? Refer to the nutritional assessment you completed at the end of Chapter 2, and compare it with the following guidelines, issued by the American Heart Association and the National Cholesterol Education Program for people at high risk for development of cardiovascular disease.

- Limit or reduce total fat intake to 20 to 35% or less of total energy intake.
- Reduce saturated fat intake to 7 to 10% of energy intake or less.
- Limit cholesterol to 200 to 300 mg/day.

To compare your nutritional assessment with these guidelines, first fill in the values for your intakes of the following:

TOTAL ENERGY: ______ **TOTAL FAT:** ______ **SATURATED FAT:** ______ **CHOLESTEROL:** ______

Now complete the following steps:

1. Multiply your total grams of fat by 9 (kcal/g of fat). Then divide the result by your total energy intake. Next multiply this number by 100. This will give you the percentage of energy you consumed from fat.
   % OF ENERGY FROM FAT ______ IS IT 35% OR LESS OF TOTAL ENERGY? YES ______ NO ______
2. Multiply your grams of saturated fat by 9 (kcal/g of fat). Divide the result by your total energy intake. Now multiply this number by 100. This will give you the percentage of energy you consumed from saturated fat.
   % OF ENERGY FROM SATURATED FAT ______
   IS IT 7 to 10% OF ENERGY OR LESS? YES ______ NO ______
3. Look at your milligrams of cholesterol.
   IS YOUR INTAKE LESS THAN 200 to 300 mg? YES ______ NO ______
4. Look back at the foods you ate and notice the foods that contributed the most fat, saturated fat, and cholesterol. If you didn't meet one or more of the guidelines and had elevated LDL, how could you change what you ate that day to improve your diet?
5. Now take the next step. Do you know your HDL and LDL values? If not, have them checked soon. All adults should know whether these values are in the abnormal ranges.
6. Finally, fill in the following assessment of your risk for developing cardiovascular disease. Decide today how you could modify your diet and lifestyle, if necessary, to reduce your risk.

Do you have	**YES**	**NO**		**YES**	**NO**
A history of smoking?	______	______	Diabetes?	______	______
Hypertension?	______	______	A history of physical inactivity?	______	______
High LDL?	______	______	A family history of premature heart disease (before age 60 years)?	______	______
Low HDL?	______	______	A history of obesity?	______	______
			A diet that lacks sufficient B vitamins, such as vitamin B-6, folate, and vitamin B-12?	______	______

Other factors also could be considered, as discussed in the Nutrition Perspective, but this provides a good start for assessing your risk.

Cardiovascular Disease

A heart attack can strike with the sudden force of a sledgehammer, with pain radiating up the neck or down the arm. It can also sneak up at night, masquerading as indigestion, with slight pain or pressure in the chest. Many times, the symptoms are so subtle in women that it often is too late once she or the health professional realizes that a heart attack is taking place. If there is any suspicion at all that a heart attack is taking place, the person should first chew an aspirin (325 mg) thoroughly and then call 911. Aspirin helps reduce the blood clotting that precipitates a heart attack. Typical warning signs are:

- Intense, prolonged chest pain or pressure, sometimes radiating to other parts of the upper body (men and women)
- Shortness of breath (men and women)
- Sweating (men and women)
- Nausea and vomiting (especially women)
- Dizziness (especially women)
- Weakness (men and women)
- Jaw, neck and shoulder pain (especially women)
- Irregular heartbeat (men and women)

Heart disease typically involves the coronary arteries and thus is frequently termed coronary heart disease (CHD) or coronary artery disease (CAD). Since the buildup of atherosclerosis slows blood flow in the arteries, the disease is also called **ischemic** heart disease (IHD). Ischemia represents an obstruction of blood flow. The general term for this obstruction is **stenosis.**

ischemia Lack of blood flow due to mechanical obstruction of the blood supply, mainly from arterial narrowing.

stenosis Narrowing or stricture of a duct or canal.

Cardiovascular disease (CVD)—is the major killer of North Americans.[4] Each year about 500,000 people die of coronary heart disease in the United States, about 60% more than die of cancer. The figure rises to almost 1 million if strokes and other circulatory diseases are included in the global term *cardiovascular disease.* About 1.5 million people in the United States each year have a heart attack. The overall male-to-female ratio for heart disease is about 2:1. Women generally lag about 10 years behind men in developing the disease. Still, it eventually kills more women than any other disease—twice as many as cancer. And, for each person in North America who dies of cardiovascular disease, 20 more (over 13 million people) have symptoms of the disease.

Worldwide, the highest incidence of cardiovascular disease occurs in the Russian Federation; in contrast, the lowest incidence occurs in Japan. North American numbers are midway between these two countries. This highlights the powerful influence of environment and lifestyle factors on its development.

Healthy People 2010 has set a goal of reducing death from coronary heart disease by 30%, compared with today's incidence.

Development of Cardiovascular Disease

The symptoms of cardiovascular disease develop over many years and often do not become obvious until old age. Nonetheless, autopsies of young adults under 20 years of age have shown that many of them had atherosclerotic plaque in their arteries. This finding indicates that plaque buildup can begin in childhood and continue throughout life, although it usually goes undetected for quite some time.

Preventing premature cardiovascular disease—that which appears before age 60 years—deserves everyone's consideration. Heart attacks at ages 40 through 60 are closely linked to the risk factors discussed later in this feature. Most people at risk can greatly improve their chance to avoid premature cardiovascular disease by making some long-term lifestyle changes.[17] (See Chapter 18 for further discussion of the premature appearance of disease in adulthood and how to work to prevent it.)

Coronary heart disease and strokes are associated with inadequate blood circulation in the heart and brain. Blood supplies the heart muscle and brain—and other body organs—with oxygen and nutrients. When blood flow via the coronary arteries surrounding the heart is interrupted, the heart muscle can be damaged. A heart attack, or **myocardial infarction,** may result (Fig. 6-13). This may cause the heart to beat irregularly or to stop altogether. About 25% of people do not survive their first heart attack. If blood flow to parts of the brain is interrupted long enough, part of the brain dies, causing a **cerebrovascular accident (CVA),** or stroke. When a stroke causes loss of muscle control, death may occur.

myocardial infarction Death of part of the heart muscle.

cerebrovascular accident (CVA) Death of part of the brain tissue due typically to a blood clot. Also termed a stroke.

More than 95% of all heart attacks are caused by blood clots that stop blood flow to the heart or brain. Clots form more readily where atherosclerotic plaque has built up in the arteries that serve the heart (coronary arteries) or brain (carotid arteries) (Fig. 6-14). Actually, the most dangerous lesions aren't the large, advanced ones but the smaller, unstable lesions covered by a thin fibrous cap. In essence, heart attacks generally are caused not by total blockage of the coronary arteries by plaque but by disruption of a partial blockage, leading to eventual clot formation.

Figure 6-13 The road to a heart attack. Injury to an artery wall begins the process. This is followed by a progressive buildup of plaque in the artery walls. The heart attack represents the terminal phase of the process. Blockage of the left coronary artery by a blood clot is evident. The heart muscle that is served by the portion of the coronary artery beyond the point of blockage lacks oxygen and nutrients and is damaged and may die. This can lead to a significant drop in heart function and often total heart failure.
Illustration by William Ober.

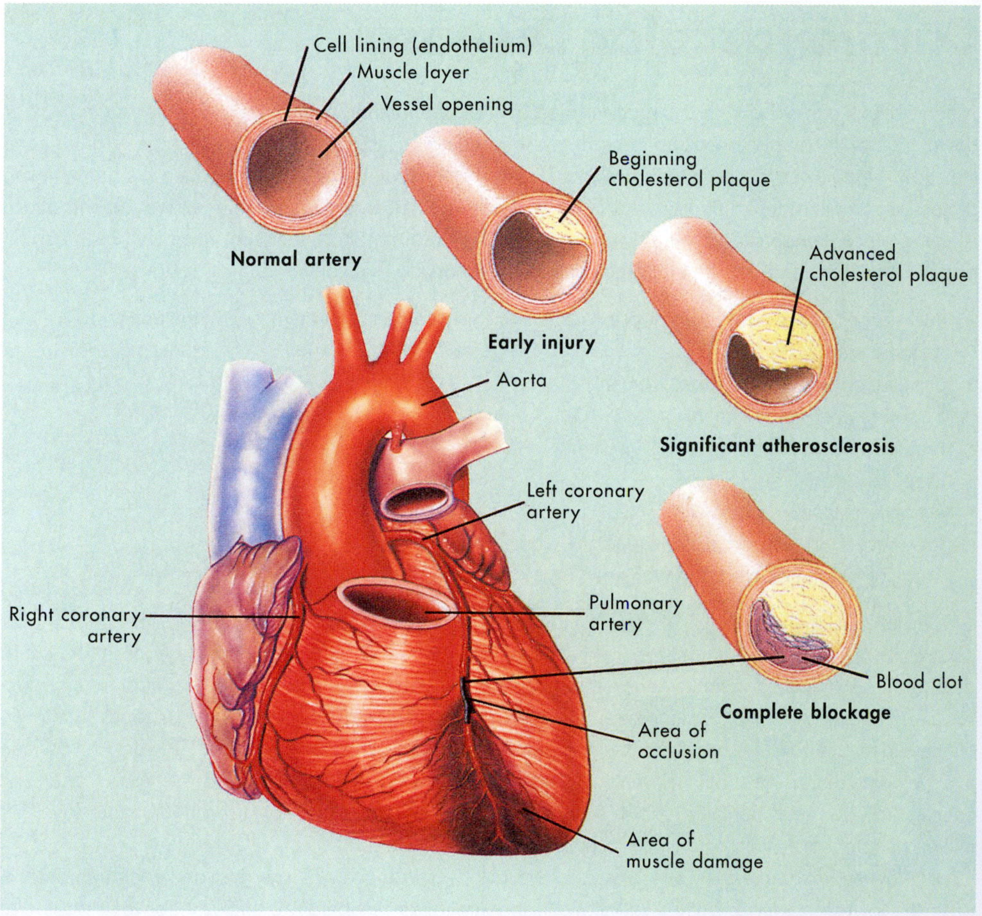

As mentioned earlier in this chapter, plaque is probably first deposited to repair injuries in a vessel lining. It develops especially at points where an artery branches into two arteries. Much stress is placed on an artery at these points from the changes in blood flow that occur at the branch point. The *athero* in *atherosclerosis* comes from the Greek and means "gruel or paste." This process of damage repair is part of the initiation phase of atherosclerosis. The rate of further plaque deposition in the next phase, called the progression phase, partly depends on the amount of LDL in the blood. The plaque thickens as layers of cholesterol (part of LDL), connective tissue (collagen), smooth muscle, and calcium are deposited. Arteries harden and narrow as plaque builds up, making them less elastic. They are thus unable to expand to accommodate alterations in blood pressure.

Affected arteries become further damaged as blood pumps through them and pressure increases. Finally, in the terminal phase, a clot or spasm in a plaque-clogged artery leads to a myocardial infarction.

Factors that typically bring on a heart attack in a person at risk include dehydration, acute emotional stress (such as firing an employee), strenuous physical activity when not otherwise physically fit (shoveling snow, for example), waking during the night or getting up in the morning (linked to an abrupt increase in stress), and consuming high-fat meals (increases blood clotting).

When 28-year-old gold medallist Sergei Grinkov died suddenly of a heart attack while ice skating, researchers investigated the case and discovered a protein abnormality in his blood. This abnormal protein caused Grinkov's blood to clot more easily than normal. Grinkov was otherwise healthy, with an elevated total blood cholesterol, but normal HDL, blood triglycerides, and LDL. The main risk factor he had was that his father died of heart disease at the age of 52. It is thought that up to 25% of North Americans have this same protein abnormality and that the only sign is a family history of heart-related death under age 60. For this reason, it is wise for all adult North Americans to have a careful evaluation of cardiovascular disease risks conducted by a physician.

Risk Factors for Cardiovascular Disease

Many of us are free of the risk factors that contribute to rapid development of atherosclerosis. If so, the advice of health experts is to simply consume a balanced diet, perform regular physical activity, have a complete fasting lipoprotein performed at age 20 or beyond, and reevaluate risk factors every 5 years.[4]

People who face the highest risk for premature cardiovascular disease have a rare genetic defect, which substantially blocks the clearance of chylomicrons and triglycerides from the blood, reduces LDL uptake by the liver, limits synthesis of HDL, or enhances blood clotting. Other medical conditions, such as

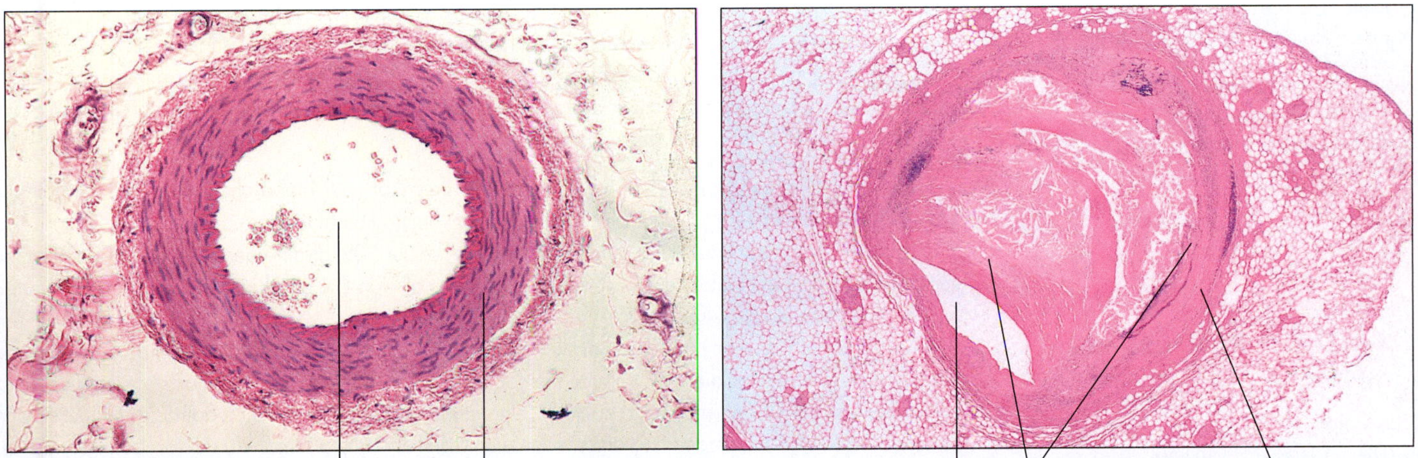

Figure 6-14 Atherosclerosis. (*a*) Cross section of a healthy coronary artery. (*b*) Cross section of a coronary artery with advanced atherosclerosis. The greatly reduced lumen in the diseased artery can easily be blocked by a blood clot or portion of plaque that breaks off another site and lodges in the narrowed portion of the artery. The latest research indicates, however, that these large plaques pose less of a risk than smaller plaques with a thinner fibrous cap, as the smaller plaques rupture very readily. This then leads to blood clots.

certain forms of liver and kidney disease, low concentrations of thyroid hormone, and use of certain medications to treat hypertension, can increase LDL and thus increase the risk for cardiovascular disease.

For most people, however, the most likely risk factors are:[2, 4, 9, 12, 15]

- Total cholesterol over 200 mg/dl of blood especially when it is at or over 240 mg/dl and coupled with LDL-cholesterol at or over 160 mg/dl (130 mg/dl is used for the cutoff if one has two or more other risk factors). We use the term LDL-cholesterol (and HDL-cholesterol) when expressing the serum concentration since it is the cholesterol content of these lipoproteins that is actually measured. The reference standard for expressing blood lipid concentrations also generally refers to the serum concentration. Recall that serum concentration is what remains after blood clots; blood is then centrifuged to remove all red and white blood cells and clotting factors. Although *blood cholesterol* is a common term, the value actually refers to the concentration in the serum portion of the blood.
- HDL-cholesterol under 40 mg/dl, especially when the ratio of total cholesterol to HDL-cholesterol is greater than 4:1. Women often have high values for HDL-cholesterol and therefore it is important for this to be measured in women to establish cardiovascular disease risk. A value ≥60 mg/dl is especially protective.
- Age. Men over 45 years and women over 55 years.
- Family history of premature cardiovascular disease, especially before age 60.
- Smoking. This generally negates the female advantage of later presentation of the disease and is the main cause of about 20% of cardiovascular disease deaths. A combination of smoking and oral contraceptive use worsens matters even more. Smoking greatly increases the ultimate expression of a person's genetically linked risk for cardiovascular disease and even increases risk if one's blood lipids are low. Smoking also makes blood more likely to clot. Even secondhand smoke has been implicated.
- Hypertension. **Systolic blood pressure** over 140 (millimeters of mercury) and **diastolic blood pressure** over 90 indicate hypertension. Ideal blood pressure values are <120 and <80, respectively. (Treatment of hypertension is reviewed in Chapter 11.)
- Diabetes. This disease negates the female advantage. Insulin increases cholesterol synthesis in the liver, in turn increasing LDL release into the bloodstream. Recently, diabetes has even been removed from the list of risk factors, stating its presence virtually guarantees development of cardiovascular disease, and so puts such a person in the high-risk group, even if LDL-cholesterol is not elevated.
- Obesity (especially fat accumulation in the waist). Typical weight gain seen in adults is a chief contributor to the increase in LDL-cholesterol seen with aging. Obesity also leads to insulin resistance in many people, creating a diabetes-like risk, as discussed.

Most commonly, LDL-cholesterol is not actually measured in a serum sample but is calculated using the following equation: LDL-cholesterol = total cholesterol − HDL-cholesterol − (triglycerides/5). This formula cannot be used, however, if blood triglycerides are >400 mg/dl. Recently laboratories have also implemented a test that measures LDL-cholesterol directly (without the use of this formula). Refer to Table 6-9 for typical LDL-cholesterol cut-off values.

Critical | Thinking

As part of his annual health checkup, Juan has a blood sample drawn for the measurement of cholesterol values. The results of the test indicate that his total cholesterol is 210 mg/dl, HDL cholesterol is 65 mg/dl, and triglycerides are 100 mg/dl. Juan has read that total cholesterol should be less than 200 mg/dl to minimize cardiovascular problems. However, he is happy with the results of the blood test. How would Juan explain his satisfaction to his parents?

systolic blood pressure The pressure in the arterial blood vessels associated with the pumping of blood from the heart.

diastolic blood pressure The pressure in the arterial blood vessels when the heart is between beats.

hyperlipidemia The presence of an abnormally large amount of lipids in the circulating blood.

dyslipidemia Generally refers to a state in which various blood lipids are markedly elevated, such as LDL or triglycerides, or in the case of HDL, very low.

Table 6-9 Fasting Blood Cholesterol Profile (mg/dl)

LDL, Cholesterol	
<100	Optimal
100–129	Near optimal/ above optimal
130–159	Borderline high
160–189	High
≥190	Very high
Total Cholesterol	
<200	Desirable
200–239	Borderline high
≥240	High
HDL, Cholesterol	
<40	Low
≥60	High
Triglycerides	
<100	Optimal
100–149	Near optimal
150–199	Borderline high
200–499	High
≥500	Very high

Healthy People 2010 has set a goal of reducing total blood cholesterol among adults from an average of 206 mg/dl to 199 mg/dl, as well as a reduction in the percentage of adults with high blood cholesterol from 21 to 17%.

- Inactivity. Exercise conditions the arteries to adapt to physical stress. Regular exercise also improves insulin action in the body. The corresponding reduction in insulin output leads to a reduction in lipoprotein synthesis in the liver. Both regular aerobic exercise and resistance exercise are recommended. A person with existing cardiovascular disease should seek physician approval before starting such a program, as should older adults (see Chapter 14).

Table 6-9 outlines some blood cholesterol profiles. If any of your blood cholesterol values fall in the column labeled "High," consult your physician because you may be at risk for cardiovascular disease. According to the National Heart, Lung, and Blood Institute, about 50% of all American adults have elevated blood cholesterol. The combined or individual risk factors of high LDL and high triglycerides are referred to as **hyperlipidemia** or **dyslipidemia.**

Researchers are currently trying to unravel and quantify numerous other factors that may be linked to premature cardiovascular disease, such as the connection between inadequate intake of vitamin B-6, folate, and vitamin B-12 and increased homocysteine in the blood. Homocysteine damages the cells lining the blood vessels, in turn promoting atherosclerosis. It is likely only a minor risk factor, but likely causes some cases (see Chapter 10 for a detailed discussion of homocysteine).[20] Ongoing blood vessel inflammation is also gaining much attention, as mentioned in the chapter (Table 6–10).

The term *risk factor* is not intended to mean causality; nevertheless, the more of these risk factors one has, the greater the chances of ultimately developing cardiovascular disease. A good example is the Metabolic Syndrome (also called Syndrome X). Recall from Chapter 5 that such a person would have abdominal obesity, high blood triglycerides, low HDL-cholesterol, hypertension, and evidence of insulin resistance (i.e., high fasting blood glucose) and increased blood clotting. This profile raises the risk for cardiovascular disease considerably. About 25% of North American adults are so affected. On a positive note, premature cardiovascular disease is rare in populations who have low LDL-cholesterol, have normal blood pressure, and do not smoke. By minimizing these three risk factors, along with following the Food Guide Pyramid (or related pyramid) and staying physically active, one will most likely reduce many of the other, less common controllable risk factors as well. In other words, develop and follow a total lifestyle plan. In addition, if a person has a history of premature cardiovascular disease in the family but the usual risk factors aren't present, a rarer defect might be the cause. In this case, it is wise to undergo a detailed physical examination for other potential causes because only about 50% of one's risk for cardiovascular disease can be accounted for by the main risk factors just discussed (review Table 6-10).

Lowering LDL-Cholesterol by Diet Changes

If your LDL-cholesterol is high, the first step should be a detailed examination by a physician. Some diseases (for example, a form of kidney disease) raise LDL-cholesterol, and treating the disease may remedy the LDL problem as well. If no such disease is present, diet change is advised.

Nutrition experts recommend several approaches for lowering LDL-cholesterol. Because changes that work for one person may be ineffective for another, values should be rechecked a month or so after any of the changes discussed here are implemented.

Reducing Dietary Saturated Fat and Cholesterol Intake

Reducing saturated-fat intake can lower elevated LDL-cholesterol. Although high total cholesterol in the blood indicates that an individual is at risk for cardiovascular disease, the most potent dietary factor associated with a high LDL-cholesterol value is overconsumption of saturated fat.[17]

Almost everyone who minimizes saturated-fat intake can lower elevated LDL-cholesterol by about 15 to 20%, especially if the person has been eating lots of foods that are high in saturated fat. About 10% of the population has trouble decreasing LDL-cholesterol by dietary means. Genetic defects are one reason. On the other hand, about 10% can expect an even bigger drop.

Many, but not all, people who eat a diet low in saturated fat find that reducing dietary cholesterol lowers LDL-cholesterol even more.[5] Most authorities encourage limiting cholesterol intake to less than 200 to 300 mg/day, especially for people with diabetes. Reducing cholesterol intake minimizes the cholesterol content of the chylomicrons that arise right after eating. Deposition of cholesterol from circulating chylomicrons probably contributes to atherosclerosis. In addition, as noted in this chapter, the tendency for palmitic acid—one of the main saturated fatty acids in our diets—to raise LDL-cholesterol is especially prominent when dietary cholesterol intake exceeds 200 to 300 mg/day and blood cholesterol is elevated.

Table 6-10 Possible Factors Related to Cardiovascular Disease That Are Currently Under Evaluation by Researchers[4, 7, 9, 15, 16, 17]

Factor	Probable Mechanism
LDL particle size	Small LDL particles appear to enter atherosclerotic lesions more readily than larger LDL particles. Genetics influences the size of LDL made by each of us. High blood triglycerides are associated with these small LDL particles.
Lipoprotein patterns that develop after eating (postprandial)	Remnants of chylomicron and VLDL metabolism appear to contribute to atherosclerosis and blood clotting, especially after a high-fat meal is consumed.
Meal frequency	Studies show that increasing meal frequency (from three to nine meals per day or so) can reduce blood triglycerides, LDL-choleterol, and blood glucose swings. These effects are beneficial for the body in many ways, including heart health.
Certain forms of apolipoproteins	Certain apolipoproteins of the E class (apoprotein E_4) delay lipoprotein clearance from the bloodstream, thus enhancing atherosclerosis. On the other hand, certain apolipoproteins of the A class are associated with a significant reduction in cardiovascular disease risk.
Loneliness and stress	Social isolation and stress have been linked to an increased risk of myocardial infarction, especially if cardiovascular disease is already present. Increased blood clotting is one likely mechanism.
Coffee preparation	Boiled coffee as served in Scandinavia and French-pressed coffee is associated with increased LDL-cholesterol, linked to specific compounds in the coffee bean. These in turn may influence liver metabolism of lipoproteins.
Excess iron absorption	Iron likely speeds oxidation of LDL, which makes LDL more atherogenic. The degree to which this takes place in the body is a subject of debate. The effect is especially prominent in people with elevated LDL-cholesterol.
Nonnutrient substances in plants (see Chapter 2)	Quercetin, found in plants, and related substances found in red wine, tea, and soy may reduce oxidation of LDL and thus reduce atherosclerosis development. Grapefruit and grapefruit juice contain a compound that increases potency of the statin class of blood cholesterol–lowering medications.
Nitric oxide	Nitric oxide is made by cells and causes muscles controlling the arteries to relax. The amino acid arginine is used to produce nitric oxide; plants are rich sources of arginine in comparison with animal products.
Various blood-clotting factors	People with high concentrations of various clotting factors in their blood show higher risks of heart attack.
Dietary calcium intake	Some studies show a fall in LDL-cholesterol when calcium intake increases from about 400 mg/day to 1200 mg/day or more. At the higher intake, calcium is likely binding fatty acids in the intestine, in turn reducing fat absorption.
Tocotrienols	These compounds in the vitamin E class may reduce cholesterol synthesis in the liver, but the evidence is mixed.
Soy compounds	Phytosterols and fiber present in soy products likely reduce cholesterol absorption from the intestine, while the protein present may affect cholesterol metabolism in the body.
Pharmacologic intake of antioxidants	Work is ongoing to see if intake of antioxidants well above that generally available from a diet (e.g., 600 IU every other day) reduces cardiovascular disease. A vitamin E supplement providing 200 mg (about 400 IU) per day is recommended by some experts, but even these experts recognize there are many more studies that refute this advice than support it. Anyone taking anticoagulant or cholesterol-lowering medications should be especially cautious, as vitamin E supplements may interfere with their otherwise beneficial effects.
Lipoprotein(a)	Lipoprotein(a) [Lp(a)] appears to lead to atherosclerosis and increased blood clotting. It consists of LDL with a large protein attached that is related to a blood-clotting factor. Trans fatty acids increase Lp(a).
Metabolic Syndrome	Metabolic Syndrome (also called Syndrome X) includes high insulin values, hypertension, high blood triglycerides, and low HDL-cholesterol. It is linked to increased cardiovascular disease risk. The best way to treat this problem is to lose weight, become physically active, and make a few minor adjustments to the diet, especially concentrating on reducing refined carbohydrates and including more whole-grain products, fruits, and vegetables. Fat intake up to 40% of energy intake, with most of the percentage coming from monounsaturated sources, is also recommended.
Glycemic load	A diet rich in high glycemic load foods (primarily, sugars, refined carbohydrates, and white potatoes) increases risk for cardiovascular disease (see Chapter 5 for a review of glycemic load values for foods). The mechanism is primarily the increase in insulin output caused by these foods, which in turn increases lipoprotein synthesis in the liver.
Blood vessel inflammation	This inflammation may lead to disruption of plaques in the blood vessels, in turn spurring blood clotting and ultimate vessel blockage. A rise in C-reactive protein in the blood suggests such ongoing inflammation. Experts have mixed opinions about testing the general public for elevated C-reactive protein, but the test costs only about $20.00. Elevated C-reactive protein can be treated with aspirin, statin medications (discussed later in this Nutrition Perspective), regular exercise, and weight loss (if needed). Currently there is no evidence that treating elevated C-reactive protein reduces the risk of cardiovascular events, such as myocardial infarction. A large study is currently testing this hypothesis.

High intakes of saturated fat affect the liver's ability to clear LDL from the bloodstream, leading to increased LDL-cholesterol values. It appears that saturated fatty acids promote an increase in the amount of free cholesterol (not attached to fatty acids) in the liver, whereas unsaturated fatty acids do the opposite. As free cholesterol in the liver increases, it causes the liver to reduce cholesterol uptake from the bloodstream, contributing to elevated LDL-cholesterol. (Trans fatty acids are thought to act in the same ways as saturated fatty acids.)

Only animal and fish products contain cholesterol (review Table 6-2). Although egg whites contain no cholesterol, a single egg yolk contains about 210 mg of cholesterol. Thus, to meet the recommendation for cholesterol intake of no more than 300 mg/day, intake of egg yolks must be limited to no more than 1 per day. A reduction to 200 mg/day would essentially mean consuming egg yolks only occasionally. Many egg-containing foods (for example, pancakes, French toast, cookies, and cakes) can be prepared using egg whites rather than whole eggs. Cholesterol-free egg substitutes are also available in the grocery store. Most of these are egg whites colored yellow, to which a small amount of fat has been added to improve the flavor. Trimming the fat before and after cooking a 3- to 4-ounce serving of chicken, beef, or pork leaves roughly one-third to one-half the cholesterol content of an egg. A 10-ounce portion of meat can contain 260 mg of cholesterol, slightly more than the amount of one egg. If meats have a reputation for being high in cholesterol, it is mainly because of an overly generous portion size.

Most fruits and vegetables are low in fat; however, avocados are an exception. Still, most of this fat is monounsaturated and, so, is heart healthy.

Increasing Monounsaturated and Polyunsaturated Fat Intake

Until recently, polyunsaturated fatty acids, but not monounsaturated fatty acids, were recommended as a substitute for saturated fatty acids in the diet to lower LDL-cholesterol. However, recent studies show that both monounsaturated and polyunsaturated fatty acids have this effect. In fact, monounsaturated fatty acids may be more beneficial, since LDLs containing these fatty acids are less likely to be oxidized. Recall that oxidized LDL probably contributes more to plaque formation in the arteries than does LDL itself. The key here is to replace saturated fat with monounsaturated fat, not simply to add it to the diet. This may also be beneficial for both blood triglycerides and HDL, because diets that are very low in fat and very high in carbohydrate tend to raise triglycerides and decrease HDL-cholesterol in some people. This can be avoided by replacing saturated fat in the diet with mostly monounsaturated fat.[3]

However, increasing intake of monounsaturated fat is difficult for the typical North American. Foods and meals rich in monounsaturated fats are not widely available here, nor are they a big part of our cuisine. If you do much of your own cooking, using canola oil, canola oil blended with other vegetable oils, and olive oil on a regular basis will increase your intake of monounsaturated fats. A further emphasis on monounsaturated fat would probably require the counsel of a registered dietitian to design a specific meal pattern. One approach could be the Mediterranean Pyramid discussed in Chapter 2.

Increasing Dietary Fiber Intake

Another dietary means of reducing LDL-cholesterol is increasing intake of soluble (viscous) fibers, as discussed in Chapter 5. These bind bile acids and, so, reduce their reabsorption. The liver must pull cholesterol out of the bloodstream to make new bile acids. This then lowers LDL in the bloodstream. Although large amounts of fiber must be eaten to have a significant effect, any amount helps—and has other health benefits.[11]

The American Heart Association recently suggested that fish oil supplements (providing 2–4 grams of omega-3 fatty acids per day) could be employed to treat elevated blood triglycerides. This must be done under physician supervision since such a practice raises the risk for increased bleeding.

Lowering Blood Triglycerides

Blood triglycerides are the most diet-responsive blood lipid. Not overeating, limiting alcohol, fat, and sugar intake, spreading meals throughout the day (not just one or two), and including some fish in the diet all help. Controlling diabetes, if present, also is important, as are avoiding smoking, losing excess weight, and performing regular physical activity.[4]

Raising HDL-Cholesterol: A Difficult Task

Physical activity is one way to raise HDL-cholesterol. Exercising for at least 45 minutes four times a week can raise it by about 5 mg/dl. Sedentary people, in particular, should focus on increasing physical activity because this has other heart-healthy benefits as well. Losing excess weight (especially around the waist) and avoiding smoking also help maintain or raise HDL-cholesterol.[4]

In addition, eating regularly (three or more balanced meals daily), balancing the amount of energy eaten with that expended, and eating less total fat often raise HDL-cholesterol because these practices lower blood triglycerides. This in turn is associated with higher HDL-cholesterol. The reason for this is not clear. Certain medications, such as high doses of nicotinic acid and the medications gemfibrozil (Lopid) and simvistatin (Zocar), also lower blood triglycerides, thereby indirectly increasing HDL-cholesterol.

Consumption of alcohol is also associated with higher HDL-cholesterol and reduced blood clotting—two factors that reduce the risk of heart attack. However, excessive consumption of alcohol has many negative effects. The Dietary Guidelines indicate that most people can consume one to two drinks daily (no more) without negative health consequences. But, for people at risk for alcoholism, any alcohol may be too much (see Chapter 8).

It is unfortunate that raising HDL-cholesterol is difficult. Lowering LDL-cholesterol is much easier. Sometimes, as LDL-cholesterol falls, so does HDL-cholesterol. This often occurs with very-low-fat diets. However, if LDL-cholesterol drops to about 100 mg/dl, the fall in HDL-cholesterol is not of much concern. Researchers note that the main problem with low HDL-cholesterol is for people who have high LDL-cholesterol. In this case, the HDL fraction has not increased to compensate for the high LDL-cholesterol value.[17] Researchers also note that people in rural Asia who eat low-fat diets generally have low LDL-cholesterol and HDL-cholesterol, but they also show low risk for cardiovascular disease.

Primary Prevention Versus Secondary Prevention of Cardiovascular Disease

The diet and lifestyle strategies discussed so far to reduce cardiovascular disease risk are appropriate for both **primary prevention** (where a heart attack has not yet taken place but the person has risk factors or where clinical symptoms are evident) and **secondary prevention** (after a heart attack has taken place). However, some people need even more aggressive therapy added to their regimen. The clearest indication for this more aggressive approach is in secondary prevention, but its use in primary prevention in cases of very abnormal blood lipoprotein patterns and diabetes also deserves consideration.

primary prevention The attempt to prevent a disease from developing in the first place—for example, following a diet low in saturated fat and cholesterol in an attempt to prevent cardiovascular disease.

secondary prevention Interventions to prevent further development of a disease so as to reduce the risk of further damage to health; for example, smoking cessation for a person who has already suffered a heart attack.

Medications are the cornerstone of this more aggressive therapy. The National Cholesterol Education Program in the United States has developed a formula based on age, total blood cholesterol, HDL-cholesterol, smoking history, and blood pressure to determine who needs such medications. Check out this formula at www.nhlbi.nih.gov/guidelines/cholesterol/index/htm.[4] Currently, medications work to lower LDL-cholesterol in one of two ways. Statins (e.g., fluvastatin [Lescol], lovastatin [Mevacor], simvistatin [Zocor]), and atorvistatin [Lipitor] reduce cholesterol synthesis in the liver by inhibiting the enzyme HMG-CoA reductase. This then reduces the cholesterol content in the liver cells. The cells respond by increasing LDL receptor activity in order to pull cholesterol from the bloodstream to make up for the loss. Recall that LDL is 50% cholesterol. Usually, the first line of defense in secondary prevention, statins can reduce LDL-cholesterol up to as much as 60%, depending on the drug used and the prescribed dosage. The cost of being on one of the statin drugs ranges from $1000–$1800 per year, depending on the dose needed. Use can also lead to side effects, such as muscle damage, and so requires physician supervision.

A second group of medications binds bile acids in the small intestine, as does soluble fiber, and leads to their elimination, forcing the liver to synthesize new bile acids. The liver removes LDL from the blood to do this. For this reason, these drugs are called bile acid sequestrants or resins (e.g., cholestyramine [Questran] and colestipol [Colestid]). These medications taste gritty and therefore are not very popular with patients. Generally, the resins are not used alone in adults because of this unpleasant texture. The use of one or both of these classes of medications should ideally drive LDL-cholesterol down to less than 100 mg/dl—the current therapeutic goal for secondary prevention.

A third group of drugs can be used to lower blood triglycerides by decreasing the triglyceride production of the liver. As mentioned, these include gemfibrozil (Lopid) and megadoses of the vitamin nicotinic acid. The use of nicotinic acid does result in pesky side effects (e.g., flushing); however, but these are typically manageable. Finally, a fourth, and relatively new class of drugs reduces cholesterol absorbtion in the small intestine (ezetimibe [Zetia]).

It is troubling to note that, currently, many North American adults with evidence of cardiovascular disease quit risk-reducing therapy within the first year of diagnosis. Part of this is due to the cost and side effects of some of the medications typically used. Overall, mortality from cardiovascular disease is reduced when treatment to lower elevated LDL-cholesterol in people who are at high risk for such disease or who have had a heart attack is followed for a few years or more by a physician. Furthermore, new research shows that plaque even regresses in arteries when high LDL-cholesterol is treated aggressively. It is suspected that these aggressive therapies to lower LDL-cholesterol stabilize the development of atherosclerotic plaque, thereby lowering the risk of rupture and reducing the chance of myocardial infarction caused by clot formation.

As noted in the chapter, aspirin in small doses reduces blood clotting by reducing Thromboxane A_2 production, it is often used under a physician's guidance to treat people at risk for heart attack or stroke, especially if one has already occurred. Studies show this with 325 mg of aspirin per day. A recent study showed that only 80 to 160 mg/day may be needed for benefits. This lower amount would decrease the side effects of the aspirin, such as risk for ulcers (see Chapter 3). Individuals who may especially benefit from aspirin therapy are men over 40, smokers, postmenopausal women, and people with diabetes, hypertension, or a family history of cardiovascular disease.

Other Medical Therapies for Cardiovascular Disease

Medicare is funding the Dr. Dean Ornish vegan plan for elderly Americans who suffer from severe coronary heart disease to see if that plan can reverse arterial blockage and can be an alternative to surgery.

The two most popular surgical treatments for coronary artery blockage are percutaneous transluminal coronary angioplasty (PTCA) and coronary artery bypass graft (CABG). PTCA involves the insertion of a balloon catheter into an artery in the arm or groin. Once it is advanced to the area of the lesion, the balloon is expanded to crush the lesion. This method works best when only one vessel is blocked, and it may need to be repeated within weeks or months. CABG involves the removal of a saphenous vein or use of a mammary artery. The saphenous vein is sewn to the main heart vessel (aorta) and then used to bypass the blocked artery, as is the mammary artery. The procedure usually remains effective for 5 to 10 years and can be performed on one to five blockages. Related therapy is used to keep LDL-cholesterol to about 100 mg/dl.

For more information on cardiovascular disease, see the website of the American Heart Association at **www.americanheart.org** or the heart disease section of Healthfinder at **www.healthfinder.gov/tours/heart.htm**. This is a site created by the U.S. government for consumers. In addition, visit the website **www.nhlbi.nih.gov**

Cholestin comes from a strain of Chinese red yeast that has been used as a natural flavoring agent and food coloring in Chinese cooking for many years. Cholestin has an active component called lovastatin, which is in the prescription drug Mevacor (a cholesterol-lowering drug approved by FDA). Cholestin has been successful in reducing blood cholesterol in numerous studies. However, currently FDA does not regulate this product based on the limitation put on FDA by Congress with regard to dietary supplements (see the Nutrition Perspective in Chapter 18). Cholestin is labeled as a dietary supplement and can be purchased in many stores. However, to self-prescribe cholestin as a drug in the treatment of high blood cholesterol is not recommended by many physicians, due to lack of regulation by FDA. The lack of FDA oversight means that consumers cannot be sure the dietary supplement contains the active ingredient or the amount specified on the bottle. Cholestin is also very expensive. Overall, high blood cholesterol is a serious disease that requires medical supervision. In addition, if a physician does not follow a person, how will the person know that cholestin is actually lowering blood cholesterol? For this reason, cholestin should be used in conjunction with a physician's supervision.

FDA has approved two margarines that have positive effects on blood cholesterol levels—Benecol and Take Control. These margarines contain plant stanol/sterols, which have been researched since the 1950s for their cholesterol-lowering effects. However, it wasn't until the mid-1990s that researchers modified the plant stanols to be fat-soluble and found a suitable medium for consumption. The plant stanol/sterols work by binding cholesterol in the intestine, thereby decreasing absorption of cholesterol and lowering its return to the liver through enterohepatic circulation. The liver responds by taking up more cholesterol from the blood. The studies done on the cholesterol-lowering effect of these margarines have found that 2 to 5 g of plant stanols/sterols per day reduces total blood cholesterol by 8 to 10% and LDL-cholesterol by 9 to 14% (similar to what is seen with some blood cholesterol-lowering drugs).

Benecol is made from plant stanols called sitostanols, which are extracted from wood pulp. This product is sold as margarine and has been added to salad dressings. Take Control is made from plant sterols called sitosterols, which are isolated from soybeans. The recommended amount for both is about 2 to 3 grams per day as part of at least two meals; this works out to about 2 tbsp of Take Control or 1 tbsp of Benecol per day. Use would cost about $1.00 per day.

In people who have borderline high total blood cholesterol (between 200 and 239 mg/dl), these margarines can be helpful in avoiding future drug therapy. Even though these products exhibit significant results, it is still important to follow a balanced diet low in saturated fat, cholesterol, and trans fatty acids, as well as to exercise on a regular basis. People with high total blood cholesterol (>240 mg/dl) who plan to consume these margarines should inform their physicians because, if they are currently on cholesterol-lowering drug therapy, their physicians may be able to decrease the dosage. For healthy individuals with total blood cholesterol within normal limits, the use of these margarines is unnecessary, especially because their cholesterol-lowering effect is not needed and they are expensive.

General Strategy for Reducing Cardiovascular Disease Risk

This Nutrition Perspective, coupled with Tables 6-4 and 6-5, provide comprehensive strategy for lowering LDL-cholesterol and preventing cardiovascular disease development. Of particular interest with regard to dietary strategies is the results obtained from a Harvard study conducted with nurses.[18] This study revealed that women who used a group of lifestyle factors had a greater than 80% lower risk for cardiovascular disease than those who did not include these advantageous lifestyle factors in their lives. The lifestyle factors that translated into such a drop in risk are a healthy body weight, moderate to vigorous activity (e.g., brisk walking) for at least ½ hour per day, nonsmoking or quitting smoking, an average of ½ drink of alcohol per day, and a score in the highest intakes of the following categories on a food intake questionnaire: cereal fiber, omega-3 fatty acids, and the vitamin folate. In addition, these women had a higher intake of polyunsaturated fatty acid with low-saturated and trans-fatty-acids intake and consumed a low glycemic load. This study shows that combining several lifestyle factors is highly effective in protecting against cardiovascular disease. The bottom line for adults is to combine these lifestyle factors (aside from possibly alcohol intake) as a comprehensive approach to reduce cardiovascular disease risk.[7]

chapter 7

Proteins

Chapter | Outline

Case | Scenario

Shannon is a freshman in college. She lives in a campus dorm and is an aerobics instructor in the afternoon. She eats two or three meals a day at the dorm cafeteria and snacks between meals. Shannon and her roommate both decided to become vegetarians because they recently read a magazine article describing the health benefits of a vegetarian diet.

Yesterday her vegetarian diet consisted of a danish pastry for breakfast and a tomato-pasta dish (no meat) with pretzels and a diet soft drink for lunch. In the afternoon, after her aerobic class, she had a few cookies. At dinnertime, she had a vegetarian sub sandwich with two glasses of fruit punch. In the evening, she had a bowl of popcorn.

What type of vegetarian is she? How could she improve her new diet to meet her nutritional needs?

Refresh | Your Memory

As you begin your study of proteins in Chapter 7, you may want to review:

- The anatomy and physiology of digestion and absorption in Chapter 3.
- Amino acid use in energy metabolism in Chapter 4.
- The processes of gluconeogensis and ketosis in Chapter 4.
- The disease phenylketonuria (PKU) in the Nutrition Perspective in Chapter 4.
- The immune system in Appendix C.

Boost | Your Study

Check out the ***Perspectives in Nutrition: Online Learning Center*** **www.mhhe.com/wardlawpers6** *for quizzes, flash cards, activities, and web links designed to further help you learn about proteins.*

Chapter | Objectives

Chapter 7 is designed to allow you to:

1. Describe how amino acids make up proteins.
2. Distinguish between essential (indispensable) and nonessential (dispensable) amino acids.
3. Explain why adequate amounts of each of the essential amino acids are required for protein synthesis.
4. List the primary functions of protein in the body.
5. List the factors that influence protein needs, and calculate the RDA for protein for an adult when a healthy weight is given.
6. Describe what is represented by positive nitrogen balance, negative nitrogen balance, and nitrogen equilibrium in terms of protein status in the body.
7. Distinguish between high-quality and lower-quality proteins and the sources of each, as well as describe how two lower-quality proteins can be complementary for each other and so provide enough of all of essential amino acids for a diet.
8. Outline two methods used to measure protein quality of foods, including assessment of biological value.
9. Describe how protein-energy malnutrition can eventually lead to disease in the body.
10. Develop vegetarian diet plans that meet the body's nutrient needs.

Consuming enough protein is vital for maintaining health. Proteins form important structures in the body, make up a key part of the blood, help regulate many body functions, and can fuel body cells.[4]

Americans eat a lot of protein—generally more than is needed to maintain health. Our daily protein intake comes mostly from meat, poultry, fish, eggs, milk, and cheese. In contrast, our Stone Age ancestors obtained a greater percentage of their protein from vegetables. They primarily picked and gathered their dietary protein, rather than hunted it. Not until *Homo erectus,* our immediate ancestors, emerged about 1 million years ago did meat displace other foods in a primarily vegetarian diet. Diets that are mostly vegetarian still predominate in much of Asia and areas of Africa.

Few of us wish to exchange our comfortable modern lifestyles with those of our Stone Age ancestors, yet we could benefit from eating more plant sources of proteins. It is possible—and desirable—to incorporate the most nutritious practices of both eras and enjoy the benefits of animal and plant protein.[10] Let's see why this is worth your attention.

Protein—An Introduction

The term *protein* comes from the Greek word *protos,* which means "to come first." In the developing world, such a primary focus on protein in diet planning is important because diets in those areas of the world can be deficient in protein. In contrast, diets in the developed world are generally rich in protein, and therefore a specific focus on eating enough protein for the most part is not needed.[4]

High-protein diets have come and gone over the past 30 years. Recently, these have risen again as weight-loss diets, such as the Atkins Diet, which contains about 35% of energy as protein. This does fall within the latest advice for protein intake from the Food and Nutrition Board: 10 to 35% of energy intake.[4] Still, as discussed in Chapter 13, these types of weight loss diets are hardly a magic bullet for weight loss.

Although proteins were given a primary focus in diet planning in ancient times, most of us today need not focus specifically on protein intake. Protein is available from a wide variety of foods and is ample in North American diets.[4]

Small amounts of animal protein in a meal easily add up to meet daily protein needs.

Proteins—Vital to Life

Thousands of substances in the body are made of proteins. Aside from water, proteins form the major part of lean body tissue, totaling about 17% of body weight. Much of this lean body mass is made up of muscle tissue. Amino acids—the building blocks for proteins—contain a special form of nitrogen: essentially, carbon linked to nitrogen. Plants combine nitrogen from the soil with carbon and other elements to form amino acids. They then bond these amino acids together to make proteins. We get the nitrogen we need by consuming dietary proteins. Proteins are thus very important because they supply nitrogen in a form we can readily use—namely, amino acids. Directly using simpler forms of nitrogen is, for the most part, impossible for humans.[4]

Proteins are crucial to the regulation and maintenance of the body. Body functions such as blood clotting, fluid balance, hormone and enzyme production, visual processes, and cell repair require specific proteins. The body generates proteins in many configurations and sizes, so that they can serve these greatly varied functions.[1] All these proteins use the amino acids in the protein-containing foods we eat, plus some arising from cell synthesis. Proteins also can supply energy for the body—on average, 4 kcal/g.

If you fail to consume an adequate amount of protein for weeks at a time, many metabolic processes slow down. This is because the body does not have enough amino acids available to build the proteins it needs. For example, the immune system no longer functions efficiently when it lacks key proteins, thereby increasing the risk of infections, disease, and eventually death.

Amino acids contain carbon, hydrogen, oxygen, and nitrogen, and some contain sulfur. Body proteins are made using 20 amino acids, each with different metabolic fates in the body (e.g., some can be made into glucose or hormones) and varying composition.[1] Each amino acid is composed of a central carbon bonded to four groups. The first three of these groups are a nitrogen group ($-NH_2$), called an amino group (or amine group), an acid group ($-\overset{O}{\overset{\|}{C}}-OH$), and a hydrogen ($-H$). The fourth group, often signified by *R*, completes the amino acid. In the margin is the basic model of an amino acid and structures of two amino acids, glycine and alanine. The chemical structures of the rest of the amino acids are shown in Appendix A.

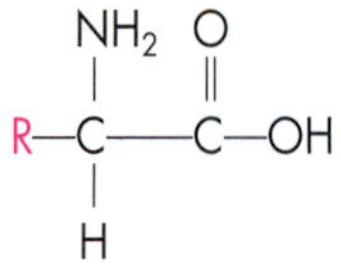

"Generic" amino acid

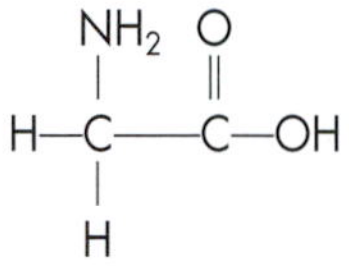

Glycine

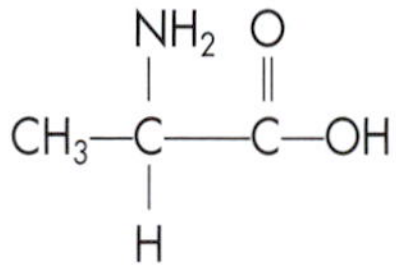

L-alanine

The L isomer is the form of amino acid used by the body for protein synthesis.

Amino Acid Form Determines Function

The form that the R portion of the amino acid assumes determines the type name of the amino acid. If R is a hydrogen, the amino acid is glycine, if R is a methyl group

Because two cysteine molecules can bind to form a new amino acid called cystine, the number of nonessential amino acids is sometimes listed as 12. If this form of cysteine is not counted as a unique form, then there are 11 nonessential amino acids. Our discussion will not count cystine and thus use the figure of 20 amino acids in foods—9 essential and 11 nonessential.

Table 7-1 Classification of Amino Acids

Essential (Indispensable) Amino Acids	Nonessential (Dispensable) Amino Acids
Histidine	Alanine
Isoleucine*	Arginine†
Leucine*	Asparagine
Lysine	Aspartic acid
Methionine	Cysteine†
Phenylalanine	(Cystine)
Threonine	Glutamic acid
Tryptophan	Glutamine†
Valine*	Glycine†
	Proline†
	Serine
	Tyrosine†

*A branched-chain amino acid.

†These amino acids are also classed as semiessential.

($-CH_3$), the amino acid is alanine, and so on. Some amino acids have chemically similar R portions. These related amino acids form special classes, such as acidic amino acids, basic amino acids, or branched-chain amino acids. This distinction with regard to classes of amino acids has important practical implications. For instance, branched-chain amino acids are used for fuel by the muscles, especially during injury and other related forms of trauma. Liquid formulas used to feed hospitalized patients may be enriched in branched-chain amino acids in order to provide ample amounts of these amino acids. The same holds true for some fluid replacement drinks marketed to athletes (see Chapter 14).

The body needs to use 20 different forms of amino acids to function. Although they are all important, 11 of these amino acids are considered **nonessential** (also called dispensable)—it isn't essential to consume them because our bodies make them using other amino acids we consume (Table 7-1). The nine amino acids the body cannot make are known as **essential** (also called indispensable)—they must be obtained from foods.[4] This is because body cells cannot make the needed carbon backbone (also called carbon skeleton) of the amino acid, cannot put a nitrogen group on the needed carbon backbone, or just cannot do the whole process fast enough to meet body needs. The first estimates of these amino acid requirements of humans were made in the 1940s.

nonessential amino acids Amino acids that can be synthesized by a healthy body in sufficient amounts; there are 11 nonessential amino acids. These are also called *dispensable amino acids*.

essential amino acids The amino acids that cannot be synthesized by humans in sufficient amounts and therefore must be included in the diet; there are nine essential amino acids. These are also called *indispensable amino acids*.

Two amino acids—cysteine and tyrosine—are synthesized in the body from methionine and phenylalanine, respectively. Both methionine and phenylalanine are essential amino acids. Cysteine and tyrosine must be made from their essential amino acid counterparts unless they are consumed in the diet. If cysteine and tyrosine are consumed, the body can synthesize protein from them directly. Thus, consumption of cysteine and tyrosine then frees the essential amino acids methionine and phenylalanine to contribute directly to protein synthesis. Therefore, cysteine and tyrosine are classed as semiessential (also called *conditionally dispensable*) amino acids. In some health states, such as infancy or adults with traumatic injury, other amino acids are also considered semiessential (review Table 7-1).[4]

Both nonessential and essential amino acids are present in foods that contain protein. If you don't consume enough food to yield a sufficient supply of essential amino

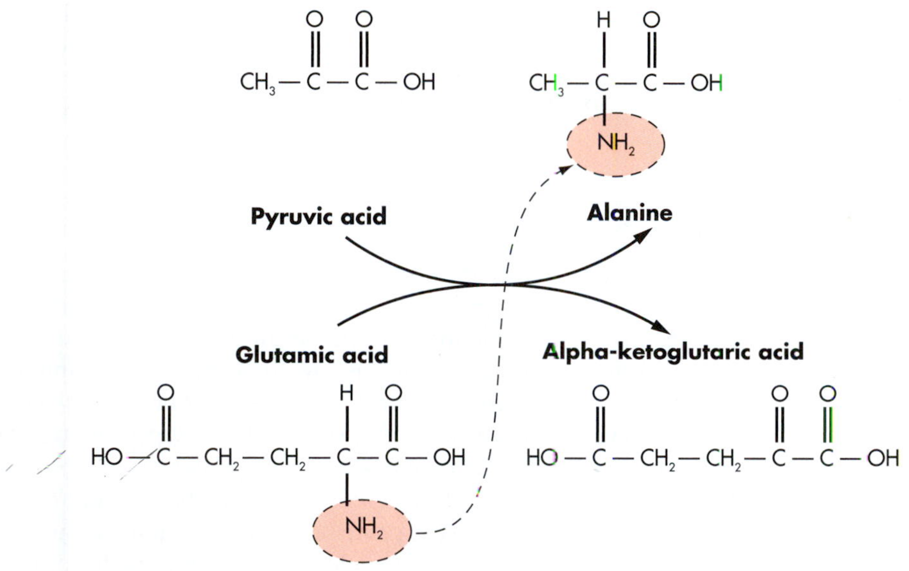

$$CH_3 - \overset{\overset{\textstyle O}{\|}}{C} - \overset{\overset{\textstyle O}{\|}}{C} - OH \qquad CH_3 - \overset{\overset{\textstyle H}{|}}{\underset{\underset{\textstyle NH_2}{|}}{C}} - \overset{\overset{\textstyle O}{\|}}{C} - OH$$

Pyruvic acid   **Alanine**

Glutamic acid   **Alpha-ketoglutaric acid**

$$HO - \overset{\overset{\textstyle O}{\|}}{C} - CH_2 - CH_2 - \overset{\overset{\textstyle H}{|}}{\underset{\underset{\textstyle NH_2}{|}}{C}} - \overset{\overset{\textstyle O}{\|}}{C} - OH \qquad HO - \overset{\overset{\textstyle O}{\|}}{C} - CH_2 - CH_2 - \overset{\overset{\textstyle O}{\|}}{C} - \overset{\overset{\textstyle O}{\|}}{C} - OH$$

Figure 7-1 Transamination. This pathway allows cells to synthesize nonessential amino acids. In this example, pyruvic acid gains an amino group to form the amino acid alanine. By looking only at the bottom half of the reaction, deamination is seen when glutamic acid loses its amino group. The enzymes used in these reactions are called aminotransferases.

acids, your body first struggles to conserve what essential amino acids it can. However, eventually your body progressively slows production of new proteins until at some point you will break down protein faster than you can make it. When this happens, as noted, health deteriorates. Therefore, the two main functions of proteins in our diets are (1) to provide the nine essential amino acids needed by our bodies and (2) to provide either the nonessential amino acids our bodies use or nitrogen from an amino acid, which in turn can be used to make the nonessential amino acids.[4]

Transamination and Deamination

A common metabolic process for synthesizing nonessential amino acids is called **transamination.** This process requires vitamin B-6.[1] Figure 7-1 illustrates transamination: Pyruvic acid (this is not an amino acid) accepts the amino group ($-NH_2$) from the amino acid glutamic acid and becomes the amino acid alanine.

Some amino acids, such as glutamic acid, can simply lose their amino group without transferring it to another carbon skeleton. This process is called **deamination.** The amino group, in the form of ammonia, is incorporated into **urea** in the liver. The urea is then transferred through the bloodstream to the kidneys and is mostly excreted in the urine. Once an amino acid breaks down to its amino-free carbon skeleton, the carbon skeleton can be used for fuel or synthesized into other compounds, such as glucose (see Chapter 4).

Putting Essential and Nonessential Amino Acids into Perspective

Eating a balanced diet can supply us with both the essential and nonessential amino-acid building blocks needed to maintain good health. Let's now take a more detailed look at this concept of essential amino acids, especially in relation to nonessential amino acids.

Physiological Aspects

The disease phenylketonuria (PKU) illustrates the importance of one essential amino acid. Recall from Chapter 4 that a person with PKU has a limited ability to metabolize the essential amino acid phenylalanine. Normally, the body uses an enzyme to convert much of our dietary phenylalanine intake into the nonessential amino acid tyrosine by adding a hydroxyl group ($-OH$).

transamination The transfer of an amino group from an amino acid to a carbon skeleton to form a new amino acid.

deamination The removal of an amino group from an amino acid.

urea Nitrogenous waste product of protein metabolism; The major source of nitrogen in the urine; chemically $NH_2 - \overset{\overset{\textstyle O}{\|}}{C} - NH_2$.

Critical | Thinking
Rina is 7 months pregnant and has read about various tests that her baby will undergo when he or she is born. How can you explain to Rina the purpose and significance of one of those tests, the one that screens for PKU?

In PKU-diagnosed persons, the enzyme activity may be grossly or mildly insufficient in processing phenylalanine to tyrosine. When the enzymes cannot synthesize enough tyrosine, both amino acids must be derived from foods. The key point here is that now tyrosine becomes *essential* in terms of dietary needs because the body can't produce enough of it.

Dietary Considerations

Animal and plant proteins can differ greatly in proportions of essential and nonessential amino acids. Animal proteins contain ample amounts of all nine essential amino acids. (Gelatin—made from the animal protein collagen—is an exception because it loses one essential amino acid during processing and is low in other essential amino acids.) With the exception of soybeans, plant proteins don't match our need for essential amino acids as precisely as animal proteins. Many plant proteins, especially those found in grains, are low in one or more of the nine essential amino acids.[4]

As you might expect, human tissue composition resembles animal tissue more than it does plant tissue. The similarities enable us to use proteins from single animal sources more efficiently to support human growth and maintenance than we do those from single plant sources. For this reason, animal proteins, except gelatin, are considered **high-quality** (also called **complete**) **proteins**—they contain all the nine essential amino acids we need in sufficient amounts. Individual plant sources of proteins, except for soybeans, are considered **lower-quality** (also called **incomplete**) **proteins** because they are either quite low in or missing one or more of the nine essential amino acids. This arises because their amino acid patterns are quite different from ours. A single plant protein, such as corn alone, then cannot support body growth and maintenance. To obtain a sufficient amount of the nine essential amino acids, a variety of plant proteins needs to be consumed.

high-quality (complete) proteins Dietary proteins that contain ample amounts of all nine essential amino acids.

lower-quality (incomplete) proteins Dietary proteins that are low in or lack one or more essential amino acids.

limiting amino acid The essential amino acid in lowest concentration in a food or diet relative to body needs.

complementary proteins Two food protein sources that make up for each other's inadequate supply of specific essential amino acids; together they yield a sufficient amount of all nine and, so, provide high-quality (complete) protein for the diet.

Even when only lower-quality protein foods are consumed, enough of the nine essential amino acids needed for protein synthesis may not be obtained. Therefore, a greater amount of this type of protein is needed to meet the needs of protein synthesis, if that is even possible. Moreover, once any of the nine essential amino acids in the plant protein were used up, further protein synthesis would be impossible. The remaining amino acids would be used for energy or converted to carbohydrate or fat and stored as such. Because the depletion of just one of the essential amino acids prevents protein synthesis, the process illustrates the *all-or-none principle:* Either all nine essential amino acids are available or none can be used. The essential amino acid in smallest supply in a food or diet in relation to body needs becomes the limiting factor (called the **limiting amino acid**) because it limits the amount of protein the body can synthesize.[4]

For example, assume the letters of the alphabet represent the 20 or so different amino acids we consume. If *A* represents an essential amino acid, we need four of these letters to spell the hypothetical protein *ALABAMA*. If the body had an *L,* a *B,* and an *M,* but only three *A*s, the "synthesis" of *ALABAMA* would not be possible. *A* would then be seen as the limiting amino acid.

Amino acids in vegetables are best used when a combination of vegetable protein sources is consumed.

When two or more proteins combine to compensate for deficiencies in essential amino acid content in each protein, the proteins are called **complementary proteins** (Table 7-2).[9] Mixed diets generally provide high-quality protein because a complementary protein pattern results. Therefore, healthy adults should have little concern about balancing foods to yield the proteins needed to obtain enough of all nine essential amino acids. Even on plant-based diets, complementing proteins need not be consumed at the same meal by adults. Meeting amino acid needs over the course of a day is a reasonable goal for adults because there is a ready supply of amino acids from those present in body cells and in the blood (see Figure 7-3 on page 233). In addition, adults need only about 11% of their total protein requirement to be supplied by essential amino acids.[20] Typical diets supply an average of 50% of protein as essential amino acids.

The estimated needs for essential amino acids for infants and preschool children are about 40% of total protein intake.[20] Consequently, diets for young children must be

Table 7-2 Limiting Amino Acids in Plant Foods

Food	Limiting Amino Acids	Good Plant Source of the Limiting Amino Acids*	Traditional Uses in Which the Proteins Complement Each Other in a Meal
Beans (legumes)	Methionine	Grains, nuts, seeds	Red beans and rice
Grains	Lysine, threonine	Legumes	Rice and red beans; lentil curry and rice
Nuts and seeds	Lysine	Legumes	Soybeans and ground sesame seeds (miso); peanuts, rice, and black-eyed peas; green peas and sunflower seeds
Vegetables	Methionine	Grains, nuts, seeds	Green beans and almonds
	Tryptophan, lysine	Legumes	Corn tortillas and beans

Note: As you might suspect from the information in this table, the amino acids most likely to be low in a diet are lysine, methionine, threonine, and tryptophan. If a diet is low in an amino acid, nutrition experts recommend finding a good food source to supply it. Finding the right combinations of amino acids, such as a dish of rice and beans, is recommended. Forget about amino acid supplements—they can lead to problems, such as decreased absorption of other, similar amino acids.[4] Amino acids as such also have a disagreeable odor and flavor, and are much more expensive than food protein.

*Animal products in the diet serve the same purpose, such as when fish is consumed with rice.

When combined with vegetables, high-protein foods, such as meats, also help balance the amino acid content of the diet.

carefully planned to make sure enough proteins are present to yield high-quality protein intake. Including some animal products in the diet, such as human milk or formula for infants, or cow's milk for children helps ensure this. Otherwise, complementary amino acids from plant proteins should be consumed in each meal or within two subsequent meals. A major health risk for children occurs in famine situations in which only one type of cereal grain is available, increasing the probability that one or more of the nine essential amino acids are lacking in the total diet. This is discussed further in a later section in this chapter on protein-energy malnutrition.

Concept | Check

The human body uses 20 different amino acids from protein-containing foods. Because a healthy body can synthesize 11 of the amino acids, it is not necessary to get all amino acids from foods—only 9 of these must be obtained from the diet and are therefore termed *essential (indispensable) amino acids*. Foods that contain all nine essential amino acids in about the proportions we need are considered high-quality (complete) protein foods. Those low in one or more essential amino acids are lower-quality (incomplete) protein foods. When different lower-quality protein foods are eaten together, the total intake of amino acids generally makes up for the individual foods' shortcomings to yield a high-quality protein meal.

Critical | Thinking

Leon, a vegetarian, has heard of the "all-or-none principle" of protein synthesis but doesn't understand how this rule applies to protein synthesis in the body. He asks you, "How important is this nutritional concept for diet planning?" How would you answer his question?

Proteins—Amino Acids Bonded Together

One way of classifying proteins is based on the number of amino acids present. Two amino acids chemically bonded together form a dipeptide, and three amino acids form a tripeptide. An oligopeptide has more than 3 but fewer than 50 amino acids. A **polypeptide** has 50 or more amino acids.[1] Most foods are made up of proteins that contain polypeptide chains of more than 100 amino acids. However, specialized liquid meal replacement supplements used in hospitals often contain various small peptides, as

polypeptide Fifty to 100 amino acids bonded together.

these show enhanced absorption, compared with larger polypeptides (see a later section in this chapter).

peptide bond A chemical bond formed to link amino acids in a protein.

Amino acids are joined by a strong, covalent **peptide bond.** An amino group ($-NH_2$) reacts with a carboxyl group ($-\overset{\overset{\large O}{\|}}{C}-OH$), and a water molecule is split off in an enzyme-catalyzed reaction. The body can synthesize many different proteins by joining the 20 types of amino acids with peptide bonds.

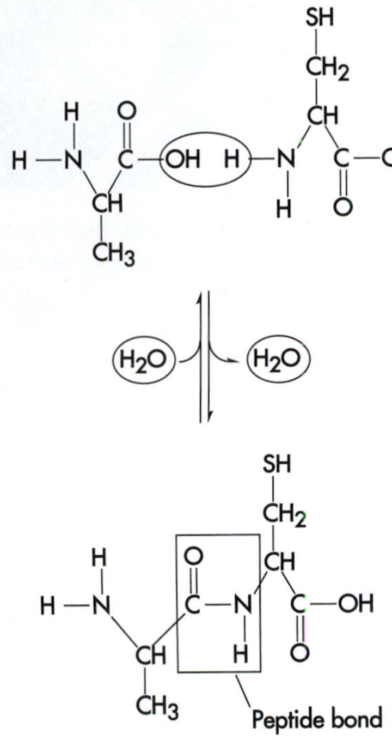

Protein Synthesis

Since the human genome was deciphered in 2000, interest in human genetics and the role it plays in disease has increased. We discussed that in Chapter 1. What wasn't covered in detail in that chapter is how cells use the genome to make body proteins.

We need to begin with the composition of DNA, present in the nucleus of the cell. Recall from Chapter 1 that DNA is a double-stranded molecule in a helical form. Each strand of DNA is composed of four nucleotides: adenine (A), guanine (G), cytosine (C), and thymine (T). Each of the nucleotides is complementary to (binds to) another nucleotide; A and T are complementary, as are C and G. Soon you will see why that is important.

DNA contains coded instructions for protein synthesis consisting of a sequence of three nucleotides per unit of instruction (i.e., which specific amino acid is to be placed in a protein).[5] These nucleotide units (e.g., GAG) are called codons. Each DNA codon represents a specific amino acid. For example, the codon CTC represents the amino acid glutamic acid. Some amino acids have only one possible codon, whereas others have as many as six. The amino acid glutamic acid actually has two codons: CTC and CTT. Having the correct codons in the DNA is critical for producing the correct protein, since the order of the codons in the DNA indicates the order of the specific amino acids needed to synthesize a particular protein. This is important, since mistakes in the order or types of amino acids in a protein can result in profound health consequences (see the discussion of sickle cell disease in a later section of this chapter).

Protein synthesis in a cell takes place in the cytosol, not in the nucleus. Thus, the DNA code used for synthesis of a specific protein must be transferred to the cytosol to allow for such synthesis. That is the job of messenger RNA (mRNA). To produce mRNA, the DNA in the nucleus unwinds from its supercoiled state. Enzymes read the code on the DNA and transcribe that into a complementary single-stranded mRNA, called the primary transcript (Fig. 7-2). This is the transcription phase of protein synthesis. The segment that is read is the gene. In this process, A becomes uracil (U), C becomes G, T becomes A, and G becomes C. You might wonder why A did not become T, as A and T are complementary. It turns out that mRNA uses uracil (U) instead of thymine (T) in its code. Thus, the DNA code ACTGAT yields an mRNA of UGACUA. The actual DNA codons are ACT and GAT:

A	C	T	G	A	T
↓	↓	↓	↓	↓	↓
U	G	A	C	U	A

The primary transcript mRNA undergoes processing in the nucleus to remove any parts of the DNA code that do not code for protein synthesis, called introns (these actually make up much of the DNA). (The portions of the DNA that code for protein synthesis are called exons.) Some additional processing then takes place and the final (mature) mRNA transcript is ready to leave the nucleus.

The mRNA travels to the ribosomes in the cytosol, present on the rough endoplasmic reticulum. The ribosomes read the codons on the mRNA and translate those instructions in order to produce a specific protein. This is the translation phase of protein synthesis. Amino acids are added one at a time to the polypeptide chain as directed by the instructions on the mRNA. Energy input from ATP is needed to add each amino

(a)

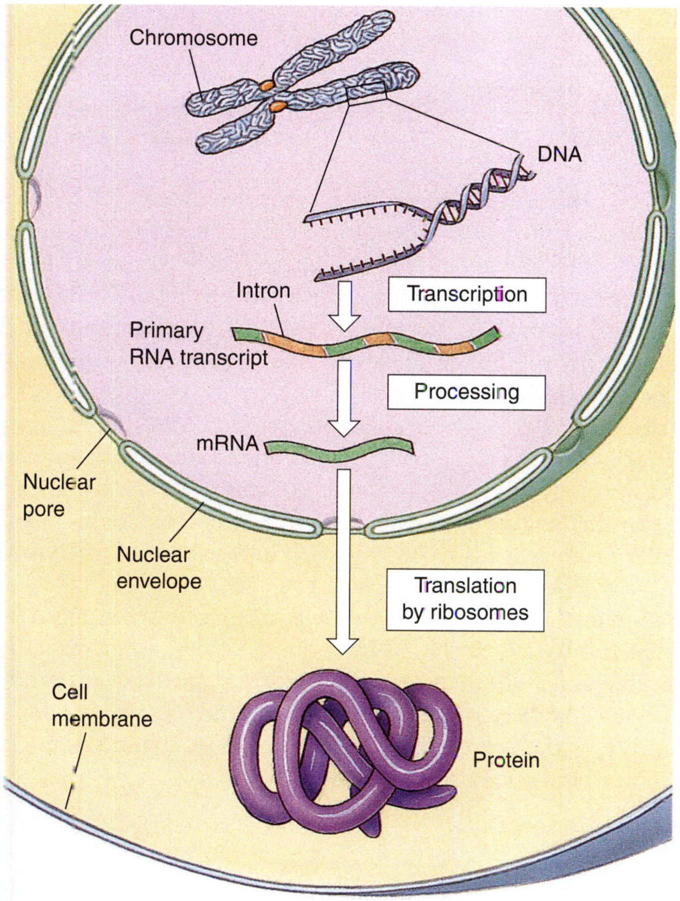

Figure 7-2 Protein synthesis (simplified). (*a*) DNA present in the nucleus of the cell is composed of four nucleotides: adenine (A), guanine (G), cytosine (C), and thymine (T). The DNA code is read, three nucleotides at a time, with each specific unit being called a codon. Each DNA codon represents a specific amino acid. The DNA unwinds from its supercoiled state and the code embedded in the order of the nucleotides is transcribed into a complementary messenger RNA (mRNA; labeled as the primary RNA transcript). The mRNA is processed in the nucleus and then is ready to leave the nucleus. The mRNA travels to the cytosol, where the ribosomes then read the codons on the mRNA and translate those instructions in order to produce a specific protein (see Figure 7-2b). (*b*) Protein synthesis at the ribosomes begins at a specific starting point, indicated by AUG. Protein synthesis then continues by adding one amino acid at a time to the growing polypeptide chain until a specific ending (stop) codon is reached, such as UAA, UAG, or UGA. Transfer RNA (tRNA) units bring amino acids to the ribosomes as needed during protein synthesis. The tRNA carriers have a complementary code to the mRNA—such that, if an arginine were needed during synthesis, the AGA on the mRNA would correspond to UCU on the tRNA. Numerous tRNA carriers are present during protein synthesis to continually supply the ribosomes with needed amino acids. ATP is used to supply the energy needed to activate tRNA in order to form each new peptide bond. The polypeptide is then released from the ribosome when it encounters the ending (stop) codon. Appendix A contains the abbreviations used for the amino acids in this figure, such as "met" for "methionine."

(b)

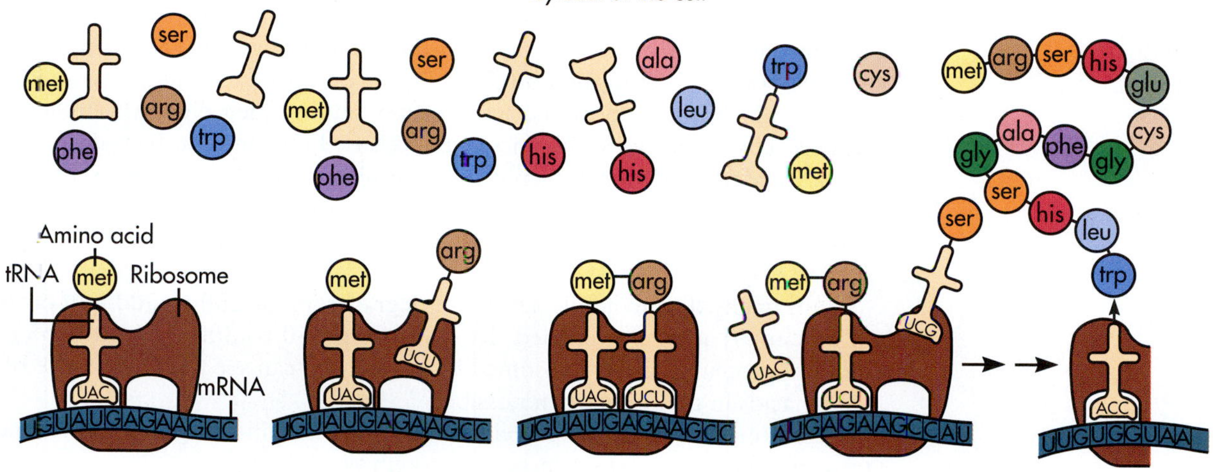

The initiation complex forms when the ribosomal subunits and the first tRNA molecule lock into a strand of mRNA at the start codon (AUG).

A tRNA carrying the amino acid specified second in the mRNA sequence plugs into the complex.

A peptide bond forms between the adjacent amino acids.

As the first tRNA detaches from the mRNA template, the second moves over, trailing its small amino acid chain. A third tRNA sits down at the vacated site, which is now situated over the next codon in the sequence.

Polypeptide released when the ribosome encounters the ending (stop) codon, which in this example is UAA.

A Synopsis of the Steps in Protein Synthesis

Part of DNA code (gene) is transcribed to mRNA in the nucleus.

↓

mRNA leaves the nucleus and travels to cytosol.

↓

Ribosomes in the cytosol and rough endoplasmic reticulum read the mRNA code and translate that into directions for a specific order of amino acids in a polypeptide chain.

↓

To produce the polypeptide, tRNA brings the appropriate amino acid to the ribosome as dictated by the mRNA code. The amino acid is added to the existing amino acid chain, which begins with the amino acid methionine.

↓

When synthesis of the polypeptide is complete, it is released from the ribosome.

↓

Often the polypeptide will undergo further cell metabolism in order to function as a specific body protein once it folds into its active form.

acid to the growing polypeptide chain, making protein synthesis very "costly" to the body in terms of energy use. Many ribosomes can combine to simultaneously translate a large mRNA.

Protein synthesis begins at a specific starting point on the mRNA, indicated by AUG. It then continues until a specific ending (stop) codon is reached, such as UAA, UAG, or UGA.

One key participant in protein synthesis in the cytosol is transfer RNA (tRNA). These units bring amino acids to the ribosomes as needed during protein synthesis (review Fig. 7-2). The tRNA carriers have a complementary code to the mRNA—such that, if an arginine were needed during synthesis, the AGA on the mRNA would correspond to UCU on the transfer RNA. Numerous tRNA carriers are present during protein synthesis to continually supply the ribosomes with needed amino acids.

Once synthesis of the polypeptide is completed, indicated by the ending codon, it is released from the ribosome, as is the mRNA. The polypeptide may then undergo further metabolism in the cell, such as is true for the hormone insulin, or be functional as such, as a specific body protein after it twists and folds into a very complex three-dimensional structure (see the section on protein organization for details).[1] Generally, if synthesis of a particular protein needs to be increased in a cell, more mRNA for that protein is made.

The important message in this discussion is the relationship between DNA and the ultimate proteins produced by a cell. If the DNA contains errors, an incorrect mRNA will be produced. The ribosomes will then read this incorrect message and produce an incorrect polypeptide chain. As discussed in Chapter 1, ultimately we may be able to correct gene defects such that the correct DNA code can be placed in the nucleus, so that the correct protein can be made by the ribosomes.

Protein Turnover

Cell proteins are constantly undergoing degradation (breakdown) and synthesis. This process, called protein turnover, allows cells to adapt to changing circumstances. For example, when we eat more protein, the liver needs to make more enzymes to process the waste product of some the resulting amino acid metabolism—ammonia—into urea. The amino acids needed to make the enzymes can come from the diet and from amino acids released from the breakdown of other proteins in cells. For example, the GI tract lining is constantly **sloughed** off. The digestive tract treats sloughed cells just like food particles and absorbs the amino acids released during their digestion. In fact, most protein breakdown products—amino acids—released throughout the body can be recycled and are added to the pool of amino acids available for future protein synthesis. Overall, protein turnover is a process by which a cell can respond to its changing environment and produce needed proteins while reducing the quantity of proteins not currently needed (Fig. 7-3).

sloughed Shed or cast off.

During any day, an adult makes and degrades about 250 to 300 g of protein; many of the amino acids are recycled. By comparing 250 to 300 g with the 65 to 95 g or more of protein typically consumed by adults, you can see the importance of recycling amino acids in the body when possible.[12]

Hormones that increase protein synthesis are insulin and growth hormone. In contrast, the hormone cortisol increases protein breakdown.

A practical example of the concept of protein turnover occurs in untreated **acquired immunodeficiency syndrome (AIDS),** as seen in the developing world (see Chapter 20). Rates of protein synthesis are similar in healthy people and those with untreated or untreatable cases of AIDS, but the rates of protein degradation are much higher due to the effects of the disease. Over time, this results in much protein wasting in such people with AIDS.[12]

acquired immunodeficiency syndrome (AIDS) A disorder in which a virus (human immunodeficiency virus [HIV]) infects specific types of immune system cells. This leaves the person with reduced immune function and, in turn, defenseless against numerous infectious agents; typically contributes to the person's death.

Protein Organization

The sequential order of the amino acids in the polypeptide chain, called *primary structure,* determines a protein's shape. The key point is that only correctly positioned

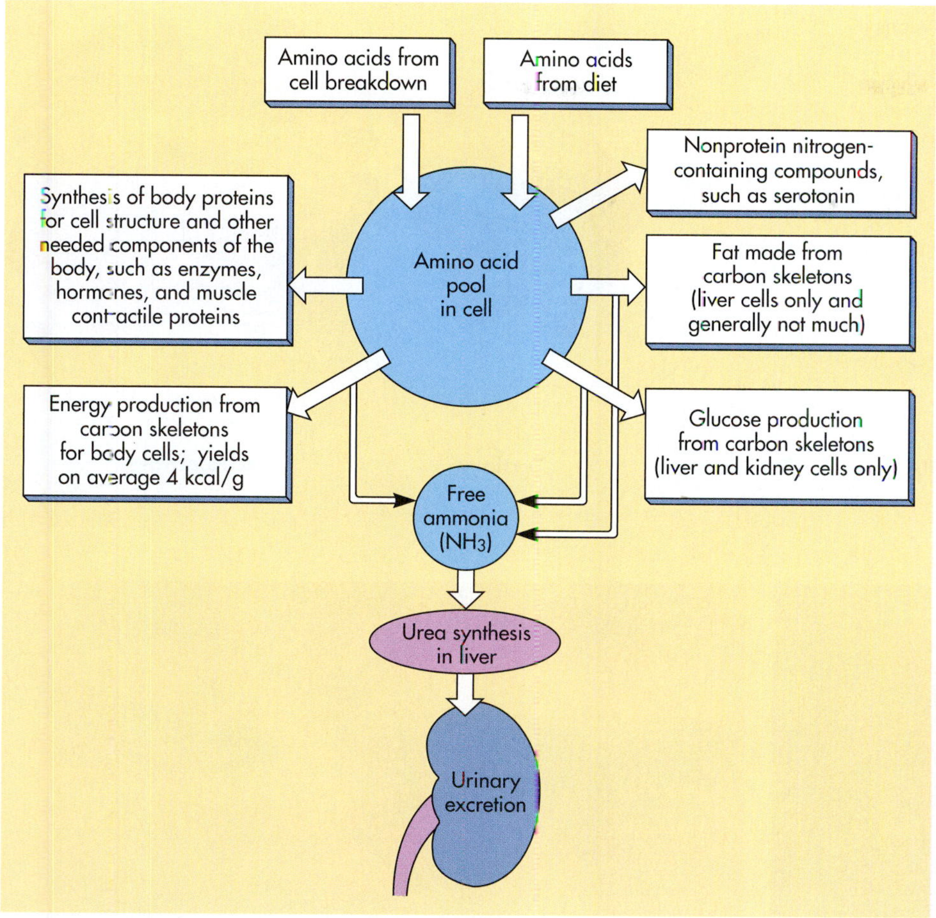

Figure 7-3 Amino acid metabolism. The amino acid **pool** in a cell can be used to yield body proteins, as well as a variety of other possible products—from fat and glucose to urea. The urea is a waste product made from the nitrogen-containing ammonia (NH_3) released during amino acid breakdown.

pool The amount of a nutrient found within the body that can be easily mobilized when needed.

Critical | Thinking

Samantha's mother's blood concentration of urea is high. From a health status point of view, what might this indicate?

amino acids can interact and fold properly to form the intended shape for the protein and, in turn, allow for the chemical attractions to form between amino acids near each other that are needed to stabilize the structure, such as hydrogen bonds (see Appendix A for details). This is part of what is called *secondary structure*. The resulting unique three-dimensional form, called *tertiary structure*, dictates the function of each protein. If a protein lacks the appropriate configuration, it cannot function.[1]

In some cases, two or more separate polypeptide units interact to form an even larger new protein form, termed a *quaternary structure* (Fig. 7-4).[1] This level of organization becomes significant when it is important to have a protein active only at certain times. A protein may be active when the units are joined but inactive when the units are separate.

Sickle cell disease (also called **sickle-cell anemia**) illustrates what happens when amino acids are out of order in the primary structure of a particular protein. African Americans (about 3 cases per 1000 births) are especially prone to this genetic disease.[8] It originates from a mutation in the DNA sequence and results in defective production of the protein chains of hemoglobin, a compound found in red blood cells. In two of its four protein chains, an error in the amino acid order occurs, one on each chain. This small error produces a profound change in hemoglobin structure: It can no longer form the shape needed to carry oxygen efficiently inside the red blood cell. Instead of forming normal biconcave disks, the red blood cells collapse into crescent shapes (Fig. 7-5). Health deteriorates, and eventually episodes of severe bone and joint pain, abdominal pain, headache, convulsions, and paralysis may occur. This is because the sickled cells clump in the capillary beds, hampering blood flow to the target tissue. Treatment for this disease includes blood transfusions and possibly medications (e.g., hydroxyurea) to increase red blood cell synthesis.

Sulfur-containing amino acids stabilize many compounds, such as the hormone insulin. Sulfur atoms can bond together (–S–S–), creating a bridge between two protein strands or two parts of the same strand. This stabilizes the structure of the molecule and is also part of what is called *secondary structure*.

sickle-cell disease (sickle-cell anemia) An anemia that results from a malformation of the red blood cell because of an incorrect primary structure in part of its hemoglobin protein chains. The disease can lead to episodes of severe bone and joint pain, abdominal pain, headache, convulsions, paralysis, and even death.

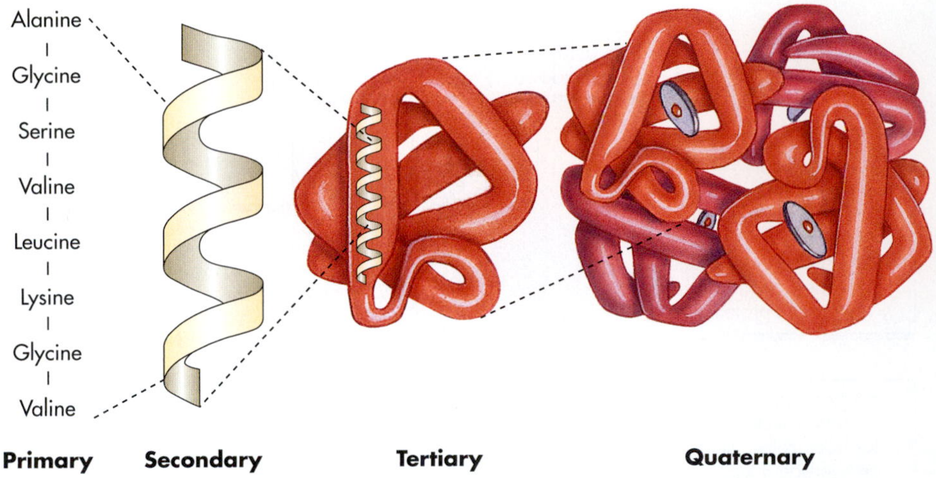

Figure 7-4 Levels of protein structure. Four different levels of structure are found in proteins. The primary structure of a protein is the linear sequence of amino acids in the polypeptide chain. Secondary structure consists of areas in the polypeptide chain that have a specific shape stabilized by hydrogen and other bonds. The total three-dimensional shape of entire proteins is called tertiary structure. Some proteins also show quaternary structure where two or more protein units join together to form a larger protein, such as hemoglobin depicted in the figure.

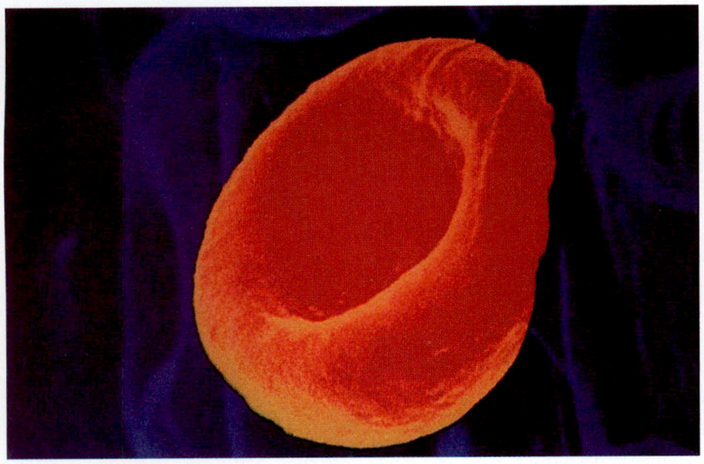

(a)

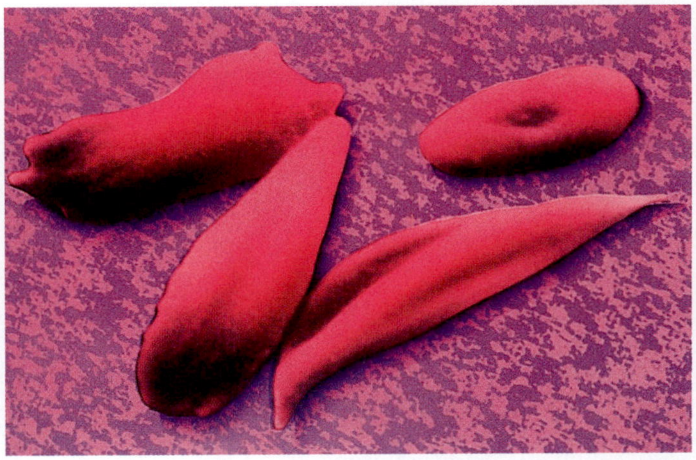

(b)

Figure 7-5 Sickle-cell disease from the perspective of the red blood cell. (*a*) Normal red blood cell, (*b*) blood from a person with sickle-cell disease. Note the abnormal crescent (sicklelike) shape of the red blood cell near the center.

Denaturation of Proteins

denaturation Alteration of a protein's three-dimensional structure, usually because of treatment by heat, enzymes, acid or alkaline solutions, or agitation.

Treatment with acid or alkaline substances, heat, or agitation can alter a protein's structure, leaving it in a **denatured** state. The protein can no longer perform its function.[1] For example, once the bacteria in yogurt have synthesized enough acid and enzymes to precipitate some of the milk protein, the product solidifies irreversibly. Note that denaturation does not affect the primary structure.

Unraveling a protein's shape often destroys its normal functioning, such that it loses its biological activity. That characteristic is useful for some body processes, such as digestion. The secretion of stomach acid denatures some bacteria, plant hormones, many active enzymes, and other forms of proteins in foods. The heat produced during cooking likewise denatures proteins. Both processes make foods safer to eat. Digestion is also enhanced because the unraveling increases exposure of the food to digestive enzymes. Denaturing proteins in some foods can also reduce their tendencies to cause allergic reactions.

Recall that we need proteins in the diet to supply essential amino acids—not the active proteins themselves. We dismantle the dietary proteins and use the amino acid building blocks to assemble proteins we need.[11]

Concept | Check

Amino acids are linked together in specific sequences to form distinct proteins. Proteins in cells are in a constant state of turnover. The degradation of existing proteins and synthesis of new proteins takes place on a minute-by-minute basis, amounting to a turnover about 250 to 300 g a day for the entire human body. DNA provide the directions for synthesizing these new proteins. Specifically, DNA directs the order of the amino acids on the protein. The amino acid order within a protein determines its ultimate shape and function. Destroying the shape of a protein denatures it. Acid conditions present during the body's digestive processes, heat, and other factors can denature proteins, causing them to lose their biological activity.

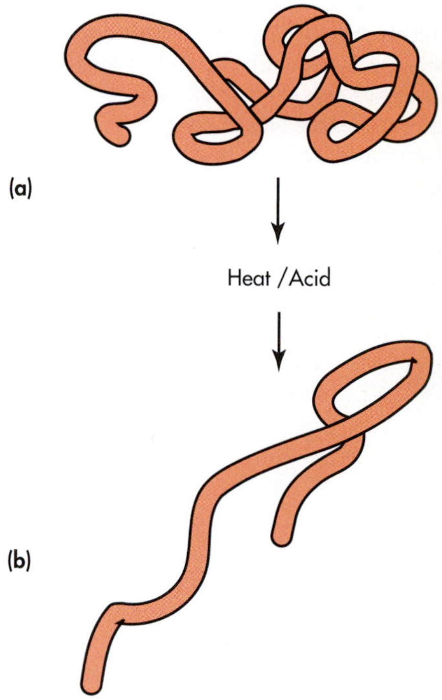

(*a*) Protein showing a typical coiled state. (*b*) Protein is now partly uncoiled, exhibiting a denatured state. This uncoiling typically reduces or eliminates protein function.

Protein Digestion and Absorption

As with carbohydrates, cooking food can be viewed as a first step in protein digestion. Cooking unfolds (denatures) proteins and softens tough connective tissue in meat. Cooking also makes many protein-rich foods easier to chew, swallow, and break down during later digestion and absorption. As you will see in Chapter 19, cooking also makes many protein-rich foods, such as meats, eggs, fish, and poultry, much safer to eat.

Digestion

The enzymatic digestion of protein begins in the stomach.[11] Once proteins are denatured by stomach acid, **pepsin,** a major enzyme for digesting proteins, goes to work (Fig. 7-6). The action of stomach acid is key to beginning the process since it unravels the proteins. Now pepsin can attack the polypeptide chains and break them down into shorter chains of amino acids. Pepsin does not completely separate proteins into amino acids because it can break only a few of the many peptide bonds found in these large molecules. The reaction that takes place is a hydrolysis reaction, since water is used to break down the bond.

pepsin A protein-digesting enzyme produced by the stomach.

Pepsinogen, the inactive form of pepsin (called a **zymogen**), is produced by the chief cells of the stomach. In proximity are acid-forming cells (parietal cells) and mucus-forming cells (e.g., goblet cells) in the stomach (review Fig. 3-6). If pepsin were not stored as an inactive enzyme, it would digest the stomach glands while waiting to be secreted from the pits. Once pepsinogen enters the stomach's acidic environment (pH between 1 and 2), part of the molecule is split off, forming the active enzyme pepsin.

zymogen An inactive form of an enzyme that requires the removal of a minor part of the chemical structure for it to work. The zymogen is converted into an active enzyme at the appropriate time, such as when released into the stomach or small intestine.

The release of pepsin is controlled by the hormone **gastrin** (review Table 3-3). Thinking about food or chewing food stimulates gastrin-producing cells in the terminus of the stomach to release the hormone. Gastrin also strongly stimulates the stomach's parietal cells to produce acid.

gastrin A hormone that stimulates enzyme and acid secretion by the stomach.

The partially digested proteins move with the rest of the nutrients and other substances in a meal (chyme) from the stomach into the duodenum, the first part of the small intestine. Once in the small intestine, the polypeptide units (and any fats accompanying them) trigger the release of the hormone cholecystokinin (CCK) from the walls of the small intestine. CCK, in turn, travels through the bloodstream to its target organs, the pancreas and gallbladder. Its arrival causes the pancreas to release the protein-splitting enzymes **trypsin,** chymotrypsin, and carboxypeptidase, which are released into the small intestine in their zymogen forms and then activated by digestive secretions. Together, these digestive enzymes divide the polypeptides into short peptides and amino acids. Eventually, digestion of all peptides into amino acids occurs, using other enzymes secreted into the intestinal lumen by glands located in the wall of the small intestine, as well as enzymes present inside the absorptive cells of the small intestine.[4]

trypsin A protein-digesting enzyme secreted by the pancreas to act in the small intestine.

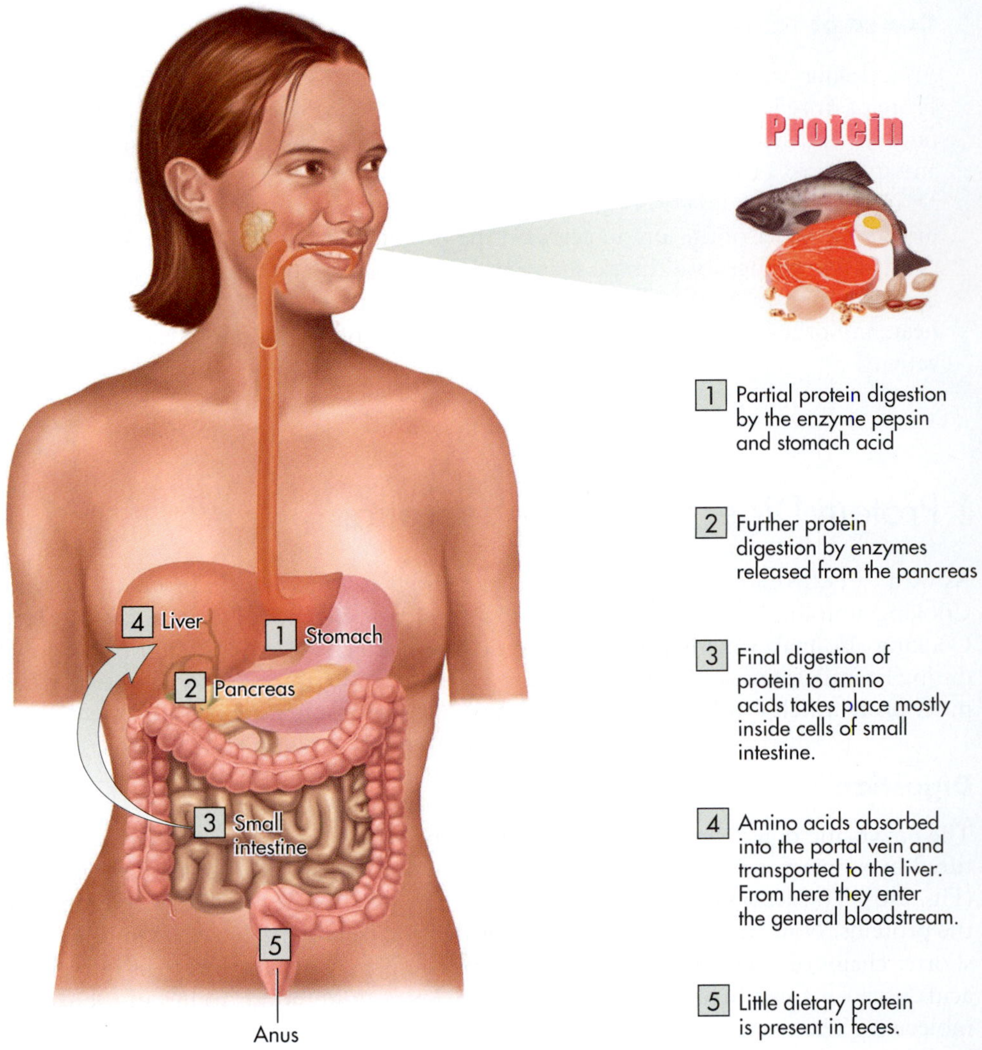

Protein
1 Partial protein digestion by the enzyme pepsin and stomach acid
2 Further protein digestion by enzymes released from the pancreas
3 Final digestion of protein to amino acids takes place mostly inside cells of small intestine.
4 Amino acids absorbed into the portal vein and transported to the liver. From here they enter the general bloodstream.
5 Little dietary protein is present in feces.
4 Liver
1 Stomach
2 Pancreas
3 Small intestine
5
Anus

Figure 7-6 A summary of protein digestion and absorption. Enzymatic protein digestion begins in the stomach and ends in the absorptive cells of the small intestine, where the last peptides are broken down into single amino acids. Stomach acid and enzymes contribute to protein digestion. Absorption from the intestinal lumen into the absorptive cells requires energy input.

Absorption

The small peptides and amino acids in the lumen of the small intestine are actively absorbed into the cells of the small intestine (Fig. 7-7). Eleven or so different amino acid transport mechanisms in the intestinal tract have been described.[11] Few whole proteins are absorbed. The only time that this is not true is during infancy (up to 4 to 5 months of age). During this time, whole proteins can be absorbed by the intestines of infants. This is particularly harmful if infants are fed cow's milk or egg whites, as these may predispose the infant to food allergies (see Chapter 17 for details).

The absorbed small peptides, then, are eventually broken down to individual amino acids inside the intestinal cells. The amino acids travel via the portal vein that drains the intestinal tract and connects to the liver. There the amino acids are combined into protein, converted to glucose or fat, used for energy needs, or released into the bloodstream.

Concept | Check

Enzymatic protein digestion begins in the stomach. In the small intestine, protein breakdown products formed in the stomach separate into dipeptides and tripeptides and finally into amino acids, as these further breakdown products enter the absorptive cells of the small intestine. The amino acids then travel via the portal vein that connects to the liver.

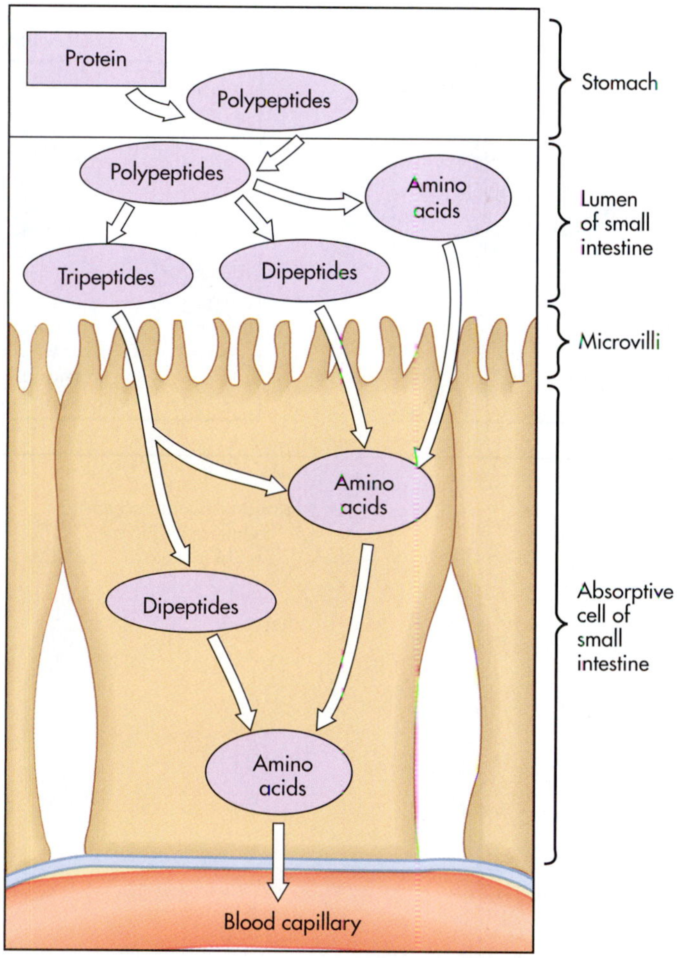

Figure 7-7 Protein digestion and amino acid absorption. This takes place in the stomach, lumen of the small intestine, and the absorptive cells of the small intestine. In a sodium-dependent, energy-requiring process (active absorption) much like glucose absorption, all of the end products of protein digestion are absorbed at the microvilli surface. Any remaining peptides are broken down to amino acids within the absorptive cell. These free amino acids are released into the bloodstream. The enzymes used come from the stomach, pancreas, and absorptive and glandular cells that line the small intestine.
Illustration by William Ober.

Functions of Proteins

As you have learned, proteins function in many crucial ways in human metabolism and in the formation of body structures (review Figure 7-3). We rely on foods to supply the amino acids needed to form these proteins. Note, however, that only when we also eat enough carbohydrate and fat can food proteins be used most efficiently. If we don't consume enough energy to meet energy needs, some amino acids from proteins are broken down to produce needed energy, rather than used to make needed body proteins.

Producing Vital Body Constituents

Every cell contains protein. Muscle tissue, connective tissue, mucus, blood-clotting factors, transport proteins in the bloodstream, lipoproteins, enzymes, immune bodies, some hormones, visual pigments, and the support structure inside bones are mainly made of protein.[1] Half of body protein is made up of the structural proteins collagen, actin, and myosin, as well as the oxygen-transporting protein hemoglobin.[4] This structural role is the primary function of protein in the body. Measurements of the amounts of certain body proteins, particularly some of those in the blood, are used as indicators of health or disease. Excess protein in the diet doesn't necessarily enhance the synthesis of body components, but eating too little can impede it.

As mentioned before, most vital body proteins are in a constant state of breakdown, rebuilding, and repair, especially in the bone marrow and the intestine. If a person

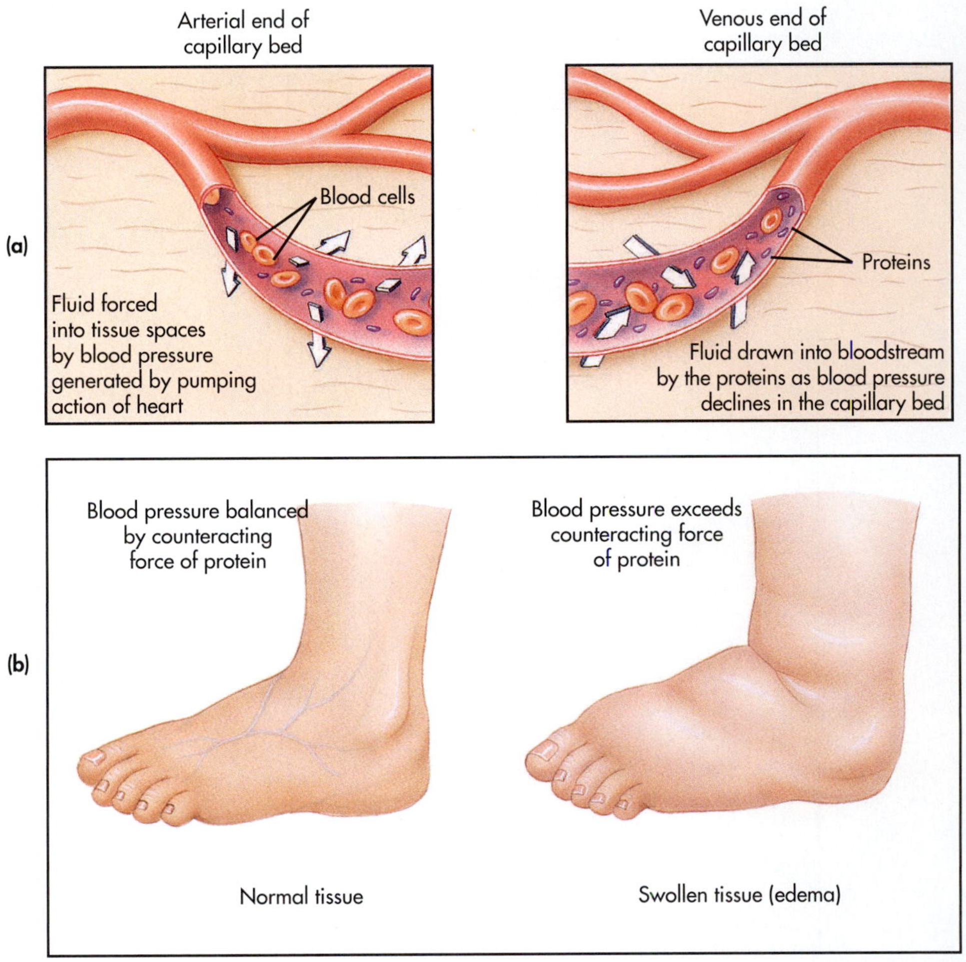

Figure 7-8 Blood proteins in relation to fluid balance. (*a*) Blood proteins are important for maintaining the body's fluid balance, since they draw fluid back into the capillary bed. (*b*) Without sufficient protein in the bloodstream, edema develops because the counteracting force to blood pressure provided by blood proteins declines.

Illustration by William Ober.

habitually doesn't eat enough protein, the rebuilding and repairing process slows. Eventually, skeletal muscles, heart, liver, blood proteins, and other organs decrease in size or volume. Only the brain resists protein breakdown.

Maintaining Fluid Balance

Blood proteins—albumins and globulins—maintain body fluid balance. Blood pressure in the arteries forces blood into capillary beds. The blood fluid then moves from the **capillary beds** into the spaces between nearby cells **(extracellular spaces)** to provide nutrients to those cells (Fig. 7-8). Proteins in the bloodstream such as albumin are too large to move out of the capillary beds into the tissues. The presence of these proteins in the capillary beds attracts the fluid back to the blood, partially counteracting the force of blood pressure. This is especially true in the areas of the capillary beds right next to their venous connections.

Unless enough protein is consumed, the concentration of proteins eventually decreases in the bloodstream. Excessive fluid then builds up in the surrounding tissues because the counteracting force produced by the smaller amount of blood proteins is too weak to pull much of the fluid back from the tissues into the bloodstream. As fluids pool in the tissues, the tissues swell, causing clinical **edema.** Because edema sometimes leads to serious medical problems, the cause must be identified. An important step in diagnosing the cause is to measure the concentration of blood proteins, although many other medical problems cause edema.

capillary bed Minute vessels one cell thick that create a junction between arterial and venous circulation. It is here that gas and nutrient exchange occurs between body cells and the blood.

extracellular space The space outside cells.

edema The buildup of excess fluid in extracellular spaces.

Figure C-5 in Appendix C provides a detailed view of a capillary bed.

Contributing to Acid-Base Balance

Proteins help regulate the acid-base balance in the blood. Proteins located in cell membranes pump chemical ions in and out of cells. The pumping action, among other factors, keeps the blood slightly alkaline. **Buffers**—compounds that maintain acid-base conditions within a narrow range—are another means of regulating acid-base balance in the blood. Some blood proteins are especially good buffers for the body. Hemoglobin is extremely important in maintaining normal blood pH.

buffers Compounds that cause a solution to resist changes in acid-base balance.

Forming Hormones and Enzymes

Amino acids are required for the synthesis of many hormones—our internal body messengers. Some hormones, such as the thyroid hormones, are made from only one amino acid, tyrosine. Insulin, on the other hand, is composed of 51 amino acids. These and other hormones classified as proteins perform important regulatory functions in the body, such as controlling the metabolic rate and amount of glucose taken up from the bloodstream.

Almost all enzymes are proteins or have a protein component. Enzymes are compounds that speed chemical reactions. Occasionally, a cell lacks the correct genetic information to make needed enzymes. For example, as described in Chapter 4, an infant who has the disease galactosemia can't make an enzyme needed to metabolize the single sugar galactose. If the infant is not started on a galactose-free diet soon after birth—which in practical terms means no cow's milk, human milk, liver, and certain other foods—its mental development will be impaired. A special infant formula must be used. The galactose-free diet is then continued, ideally throughout life. This example underscores the crucial roles that enzymes, and thus proteins, play in cell function.

Neurotransmitters, released by nerve endings, are often derivatives of amino acids. This is true for dopamine (synthesized from the amino acid tyrosine), norepinephrine (synthesized from the amino acid tyrosine), and serotonin (synthesized from the amino acid tryptophan). The way in which diet influences the synthesis of some of these neurotransmitters is currently under study. For example, high-carbohydrate meals can induce sleepiness as a result of increased serotonin synthesis in the brain.

Contributing to Immune Function

Proteins compose key parts of the cells used by the immune system. Also, the antibodies produced by one type of immune cell (β-lymphocytes) are proteins. These antibodies can bind to foreign proteins in the body, an important step in removing invaders from the body. Without sufficient dietary protein, the immune system lacks the cells and other tools needed to function properly. Thus, immune incompetence—**anergy**—and a protein-deficient diet often appear together. Anergy can turn measles into a fatal disease for a malnourished child. It also can encourage unusual infections, such as widespread yeast *(Candida)* growth in the mouth and throat of a hospitalized adult.

anergy Lack of an immune response to foreign compounds entering the body.

Forming Glucose

In Chapter 5 you learned that the body must maintain a fairly constant concentration of blood glucose to supply energy for red blood cells and nervous tissue. At rest, the brain uses about 19% of the body's energy requirements, and it gets most of that energy from glucose. If you don't consume enough carbohydrate to supply the glucose, your liver (and kidneys, to a lesser extent) will be forced to make glucose from amino acids present in body tissues (review Fig. 7-3). Recall from Chapter 4 that the process is called gluconeogenesis (review Figure 4-10).

Making some glucose from amino acids is normal. For example, when you skip breakfast and haven't eaten since 7 P.M. the preceding evening, glucose must be manufactured. Taken to an extreme, however, such as occurs in starvation, the conversion of amino acids into glucose wastes much muscle tissue and can produce edema.

The vitamin niacin can be made from the amino acid tryptophan, illustrating another role of proteins.

Providing Energy

Proteins supply very little of the energy to the body, except during prolonged exercise (see Chapter 14 for information about the use of amino acids for energy during exercise).

Under most conditions, cells use primarily fats and carbohydrates for energy. Proteins and carbohydrates contain the same amount of usable energy—on average, 4 kcal/g. However, proteins are a very costly source of energy, considering the amount of metabolism and processing the liver and kidneys must perform to use this energy source. The monetary cost of protein-rich foods is also a consideration.

Concept | Check

Vital body constituents—such as muscle, connective tissue, blood transport proteins, enzymes, hormones, buffers, and immune factors—are mainly proteins. Proteins can also provide fuel for the body and be used for glucose production.

Protein Needs

How much protein (actually, amino acids) do we need to eat each day? People who aren't growing need to eat only enough protein to match daily losses from protein breakdown products in the urine, as well as protein lost as such from feces, skin, hair, nails, and so on. In short, people need to balance protein intake with such losses (Fig. 7-9).[4]

When a body is growing or recovering from an illness, it needs extra protein to supply the raw materials required to build new tissues. To achieve this, a person must eat more protein daily than he or she loses. In addition, the hormones insulin, growth hormone, and testosterone all stimulate this building of new tissue. Merely eating more

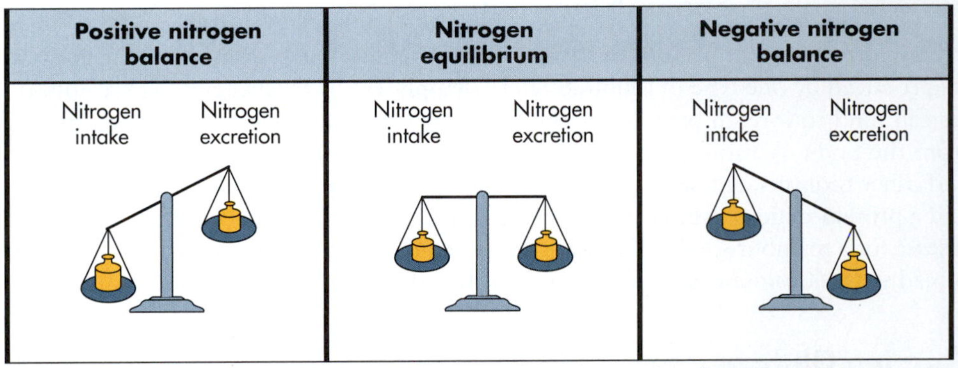

Figure 7-9 Nitrogen balance in practical terms. Determining this balance requires measuring nitrogen intake and loss.

Situations in which nitrogen balance is positive:

Growth
Pregnancy
Recovery stage after illness
Athletic training*
Increased secretion of certain hormones, such as insulin, growth hormone, and testosterone

Situations in which nitrogen balance is negative:

Inadequate intake of protein (fasting, intestinal tract diseases)
Inadequate energy intake
Conditions such as fevers, burns, and infections
Bed rest (for several days)
Deficiency of essential amino acids (e.g., poor quality protein consumed)
Increased protein loss (as in some forms of kidney disease)
Increased secretion of certain hormones, such as thyroid hormone and cortisol

*Only when additional lean body mass is being gained. Nevertheless, the athlete is probably already eating enough protein to support this extra protein synthesis; protein supplements are not needed.

protein does not produce additional body tissue unless the right hormonal condition exists. Resistance exercise (weight training) also enhances protein synthesis.

For healthy people, the amount of dietary protein needed to maintain protein equilibrium (where protein intake compensates for all evidence of protein losses) can be determined by increasing protein intake until it just equals such losses. Energy needs must be met so that amino acids are not diverted for energy use.

To determine this balance between protein gain and loss by the body, researchers actually calculate nitrogen balance (review Fig. 7-9). It is much easier to track nitrogen intake and loss, and as well only a small amount of protein as such is lost from the body. Nitrogen makes up about 16% of the weight of a protein, so nitrogen intake or output divided by 0.16 yields a rough estimate of protein intake or output. One can also multiply by the reciprocal of 0.16, which is 6.25:

$$\text{nitrogen (g)} \times 6.25 = \text{protein (g)}$$

As an example of the measurement of nitrogen balance, first a person's protein intake is monitored: This includes protein that comes in the form of fluids and foods. The grams of protein consumed is divided by 6.25 to yield the approximate grams of nitrogen (N) consumed. This value is then compared with the amount of nitrogen lost from the body. To do this, urine output for the same 24-hour period is collected and analyzed for urea nitrogen content. This value is then put into one of various formulas available to estimate total nitrogen loss from the body. Since most of the nitrogen lost from the body is in the form of urea, this approach is fairly accurate. The other factors in a specific formula account for nitrogen loss in the urine that is not in the form of urea (e.g., 0.2 × urinary urea N), as well as nitrogen loss from all other body sources, such as hair, skin, feces, and other nonurine sources (e.g., 2 g).

$$\text{nitrogen balance} = \frac{\text{protein intake}}{6.25 \text{ g}} - \text{g urinary urea N} - (0.2 \times \text{urinary urea N}) - 2 \text{ g}$$

For example, suppose a person consumes 70 g of proteins in a 24-hour period; during that time he excreted 7 g of nitrogen as urea. His state of nitrogen balance is 0.8, based on the following calculation:

$$\text{nitrogen balance} = \frac{70}{6.25} - 7 - (0.2 \times 7) - 2$$
$$= 0.8$$

Since this is a positive number, the person is in slight positive nitrogen, as so protein, balance. Due to measurement error, he could also simply be in equilibrium.

Today the best estimate for the amount of protein required for nearly all adults to maintain protein equilibrium is 0.8 g of protein per kilogram (kg) of healthy body weight (the concept of healthy weight is discussed in Chapter 13). This 0.8 g/kg is the RDA for protein.[4] Healthy weight is used as a baseline because excess fat storage doesn't contribute much to protein needs. This RDA works out to about 56 g of protein daily for a 70-kg (154-lb) man and about 46 g of protein daily for a 57-kg (125-lb) woman.

Pregnant and lactating women and infants and children under 19 years of age have different RDAs for protein (see Chapters 16 and 17).

Convert weight from pounds to kg:

$$\frac{154 \text{ pounds}}{2.2 \text{ pounds/kg}} = 70 \text{ kg}$$

$$\frac{125 \text{ pounds}}{2.2 \text{ pounds/kg}} = 57 \text{ kg}$$

Calculate RDA:

$$70 \text{ kg} \times \frac{0.8 \text{ g protein}}{\text{kg body weight}} = 56 \text{ g}$$

$$57 \text{ kg} \times \frac{0.8 \text{ g protein}}{\text{kg body weight}} = 46 \text{ g}$$

Table 7-3 The Protein Content of a 1200 kcal Diet and a 2400 kcal Diet*

1200 kcal Diet	Protein (Grams)	2400 kcal Diet	Protein (Grams)
Breakfast			
Nonfat milk, 1 cup	8	2% reduced-fat milk, 1 cup	8
Cheerios, 1 cup	2	Cheerios, 1 cup	2
Orange	1	Eggs, soft cooked, 2	12
		Orange	1
Lunch			
Whole-wheat bread, 2 slices	5	Whole-wheat bread, 2 slices	5
Chicken breast, 2 oz	17	Chicken breast, 2 oz	17
Mayonnaise, 1 tsp	—	Provolone cheese, 2 oz	15
Tomato slices, 2	—	Tomato slices, 2	—
Carrot sticks, 1 cup	1	Mayonnaise, 1 tsp	—
Fig, 1 large	0.5	Oatmeal-raisin cookies, 2	2
Diet soda	—	Figs, 2	1
		Diet soda	—
Dinner			
Mixed green salad, ½ cup	—	Mixed green salad, ½ cup	—
Italian dressing, 2 tsp	—	Italian dressing, 2 tsp	—
Beef tenderloin, 2 oz	14	Beef tenderloin, 4 oz	28
Spinach pasta, 1 cup, with garlic butter, 1 tsp	7	Spinach pasta, 1 cup, with garlic butter, 1 tsp	7
Zucchini, ½ cup, sauteed in oil, 1 tsp	0.5	Zucchini, ½ cup, sauteed in oil, 1 tsp	0.5
Nonfat milk, 1 cup	8	Carrot sticks, ½ cup	0.5
Bagel, toasted, ½ of a 3½" bagel	4		
Jam, 2 tsp	—	Snack	
		2% reduced-fat milk, 1 cup	8
		Bagel, toasted, ½ of 3½" bagel	4
		Jam, 2 tsp	—
		Fruited yogurt, 1 cup	10
TOTAL	70		122

*This table illustrates how little energy need be consumed while still meeting the RDA for protein. It also shows how much protein we eat when we consume typical energy intakes. The amounts work out to be about 25% of energy intake as protein, quite a generous amount.

The RDA for protein translates into about 10% of energy intake. Many experts recommend about 15% of energy intake to provide more flexibility in diet planning, in turn allowing for the variety of protein-rich foods North Americans typically consume.[6]

Approximate protein needs are listed in the inside cover of this textbook. It is easy to consume the amount of protein currently suggested each day to meet body needs (Table 7-3). North American men typically consume about 95 g of protein daily, whereas women typically consume 65 g daily.

Most of us consume much more protein than RDA amounts because we like many high-protein foods and can afford to buy them. Excess protein eaten cannot be stored as such, so its carbon skeletons are turned into glucose or fat and then either stored or metabolized for energy needs (review Fig. 7-3). Note also that mental stress, physical labor, and routine weekend sports activities do not require an increase in the protein RDA.[4]

To support the training needs of endurance and highly trained athletes, protein consumption may need to exceed the RDA. The Food and Nutrition Board does not support an increased need,[4] but some experts suggest that an intake of 1.2–1.5 g/kg of protein per day may be needed (see Chapter 14). Many North Americans already consume that much protein, especially men. Protein intake may even need to be increased to 1.6–1.8 g/kg per day for athletes beginning a strength training regimen. However, studies supporting these high intakes are few. The Food and Nutrition Board also suggests that protein intake not exceed 35% of energy intake;[4] other experts suggest a maximum protein intake of 2 g/kg per day.[14] Athletes can calculate both amounts and use the lesser of these two guidelines as an upper limit for protein intake. In addition, athletes do not need individual amino acid supplements. These are a needless expense. All of us, athletes included, can meet our protein needs using basic foods (see Chapter 14 for details).

Surveys show that only older women as a group fail to eat enough protein to meet the RDA, and the deficiency is very slight. In response, older women should strive to include a rich source of protein at every meal (and snack).

Animal protein foods are typically our favorite sources of amino acids.

Does Eating a High-Protein Diet Harm You?

People frequently ask whether the high-protein intake of adults in North America is harmful. The extra vitamin B-6, iron, and zinc that accompany protein foods are often beneficial. However, high-protein diets typically may be low in plant foods and, so, low in fiber, some vitamins (e.g., folate), some minerals (e.g., magnesium), and phytochemicals. As well, these diets are typically rich in saturated fat and cholesterol, and thus do not follow the recommendations of the Dietary Guidelines for Americans or the Food and Nutrition Board.

Some studies show that high-protein diets can increase calcium loss in urine. Certain types of amino acids—especially some of those rich in animal proteins—cause this effect. Based on the research to date, it is reasonable to assume that individuals who have inadequate calcium intakes are further compromising bone health by consuming excessive amounts of protein. People meeting their calcium needs should not be concerned about this effect of dietary protein.[19] (However, many people have calcium-deficient diets.) The increased calcium loss may also contribute to kidney stone formation in people who have a history of forming such stones. Thus such persons should not consume a high-protein diet.[3]

Too little protein in the diet also contributes to poor bone health.[19] This effect has been shown in older people who do not eat enough protein. For anyone following a balanced diet, this is not a concern.

Excessive intake of red meat, especially processed meats such as ham and salami, is linked to colon cancer in population studies. This link could be attributable to the protein or fat in the food products or to substances that are used during processing (e.g. nitrates/nitrites) or those that form during cooking of red meat at high temperatures (e.g. heterocyclic amines) (see the Nutrition Perspective in Chapter 10 for details).[2, 16] Excessive fat intake associated with diets rich in red meat, or low-fiber intake, may also be a contributing factor. Because of this concern with red meat, some nutrition experts suggest we focus more on poultry, fish, nuts, legumes (beans), and seeds to meet protein needs.[7] In addition, any meat should be trimmed of all visible fat before grilling.

Some researchers have also expressed the concern that a high-protein intake may unduly burden the kidneys by forcing them to excrete the resulting excess nitrogen as urea. Low-protein diets marginally slow the decline in kidney function in humans if begun early in the course of developing kidney disease, and laboratory animal studies show that protein intakes that just meet nutritional needs preserve kidney function over time better than high-protein diets. Preserving kidney function is especially important for people with diabetes, for people who show signs of kidney disease, and for people who have only one functioning kidney. High-protein diets are discouraged in these cases. For people without diabetes or kidney disease, the risk of suffering kidney failure is very low; thus, the risk of a high-protein diet's contributing to kidney disease (aside from kidney stones) in later life is also low.

Infants' diets must be limited in protein because their kidneys have difficulty excreting large amounts of urea and minerals, which remain after protein metabolism. Thus, regular cow's milk must not be used for feeding young infants—it is too high in protein and other nutrients (see Chapter 17 for details).

The amino acids most likely to cause toxicity when consumed in large amounts are methionine and tyrosine. The potential for amino acid imbalances and toxicities is too great to recommend that any be taken individually as supplements. As emphasized earlier, the body is designed to handle whole proteins as a dietary source of amino acids. When individual amino acid supplements are taken, they can overwhelm the absorptive mechanism in the small intestine, triggering amino acid imbalances in the body. These imbalances occur because groups of chemically similar amino acids compete for absorption sites in the absorptive cells. An excess of one can hamper other amino acids from being absorbed. Overall, every amino acid taken in excess can be harmful. We should stick to whole foods as sources for amino acids.[4]

Expert Opinion

A New Appreciation for the *Nut* in *Nut*rition

Penny M. Kris-Etherton, Ph.D., R.D.

There has been a marked shift in our thinking about the role of nuts in a healthy diet. The impetus for this is a substantive and growing body of scientific evidence demonstrating marked health benefits of nut consumption. Data from four large epidemiologic studies have convincingly shown that frequent consumption of nuts (1 oz of nuts consumed 5 times/week) is associated with a decreased risk of cardiovascular disease morbidity and/or mortality in the range of approximately 30 to 50% in many different population groups.

What the Specific Research Studies Show

The Adventist Health Study was a landmark prospective epidemiologic study conducted with 34,198 Seventh Day Adventists in California that was the first to report a protective effect of nuts on cardiovascular disease. Individuals who ate nuts ≥ 5 times/week experienced a 51% reduction in risk of acute myocardial infarction. Those who ate nuts 1 to 4 times/week had a 22% reduced risk compared with a group eating nuts < 1 time/week.

Since this pioneering study, other epidemiologic studies have reported cardioprotective effects of nut consumption. These studies include the Iowa Women's Health Study, Nurses' Health Study, and Physicians' Health Study. In the Iowa Women's Health Study with 34,500 postmenopausal women followed for 5 years, cardiovascular mortality was inversely associated with nut consumption. Women who consumed nuts > 1 time/week had a 40% reduction in cardiovascular disease risk compared with women who ate nuts less frequently. In the Nurses' Health Study with 86,016 women, frequent nut consumption (> 5 oz/week) was associated with a 35% reduction in cardiovascular disease risk. The magnitude of risk reduction was similar for both fatal and nonfatal myocardial infarction. The Physicians' Health Study conducted with 21,454 male participants reported that those who consumed nuts 2 or more times/week had reduced risks of sudden cardiac death (by 47%) and total cardiovascular disease death (by 30%). Collectively, the epidemiologic evidence is compelling and has established a dose-response relationship between nut consumption and reduced cardiovascular disease risk. Moreover, subsequent analyses conducted with these databases have shown that the protective effect of nut consumption is consistent among many different population subgroups including men and women (as noted), younger and older subjects, normotensive and hypertensive individuals, and in subjects varying in weight, smoking status, and physical activity level.

Putting Nuts into Focus

Numerous controlled clinical studies with different nuts as well as peanuts (which are a legume) have been conducted. The studies differed in design and dietary control. Some studies were specifically designed to evaluate the effects of nuts on blood lipids and lipoproteins. Other studies used nuts and other fat sources to achieve a fatty acid profile of an experimental diet that was evaluated. The studies, in general, evaluated diets that were low in saturated fat and cholesterol because nuts were used to replace food sources of saturated fat. Both moderate-fat and low-fat diets were studied. Across dietary fat levels, experimental diets containing nuts reduced total and low-density lipoprotein (LDL)-cholesterol concentrations by about 4 to 16% and 9 to 20%, respectively. In addition, the diets that contained nuts did not reduce high-density lipoprotein (HDL)-cholesterol nor did they increase triglyceride levels as did the comparative low-fat, high-carbohydrate control diets. It is evident that the decrease in total and LDL-cholesterol levels with the nut diets reflects the decrease in saturated fat and increase in unsaturated fat. In

Food Sources of Protein

Food Item and Amount	*Protein (g)*
Canned tuna, 3 oz	21.6
Broiled chicken, 3 oz	21.3
Beef chuck, 3 oz	15.3
Yogurt, 1 cup	10.6
Kidney beans, ½ cup	8.1
Milk, 1 cup	8.0
Peanuts, 1 oz	7.3
Cheddar cheese, 1 oz	7.0
Egg, 1	5.5
Cooked corn, ½ cup	2.7
Seven grain bread, 1 slice	2.6
White rice, ½ cup	2.1
Pasta, 1 oz	1.2
Banana, 1	1.2
Cooked corn, ½ cup	0.9

Protein in Foods

The most nutrient-dense source of protein is water-packed tuna, which has over 80% of its energy as protein. Other good sources are meat, poultry, fish, milk and some milk products, beans, and nuts. Based on the typical foods we eat in North America, about 70% of protein comes from animal sources. Worldwide, 35% of protein comes from animal sources. In Africa and East Asia, about 20% of the protein eaten comes from animal sources.

A relatively new source of protein comes from fermented fungus, and is called quorn. It is mixed with other food products to form various low-fat meat substitutes. Consumers can decide if these products fit into their diets; FDA has approved its use.

addition, the effects of the nut test diets on HDL-cholesterol and triglycerides could be explained by their higher total fat content.

A key question is whether the effects of nuts on blood lipids are solely due to their fat and fatty acid profile, or whether there are other bioactive compounds in nuts (see below for details) that contribute to the lipid and lipoprotein responses noted. Nonetheless, it is clear that when nuts replace food sources of saturated fat, total cholesterol and LDL-cholesterol are reduced, resulting in a decreased risk of cardiovascular disease. The American Heart Association Dietary Guidelines 2000 advise that to attain a desirable cholesterol profile one should limit foods high in saturated fat and cholesterol, and substitute unsaturated fat from vegetables, fish, legumes, and nuts. Thus, this dietary recommendation acknowledges the health benefits of unsaturated fats and recognizes nuts and legumes as important food sources of unsaturated fats.

Plant proteins, like walnuts, can be incorporated into one's diet in numerous ways, such as adding them to banana bread.

Nuts as a Source of Nutrition

Nuts are a powerhouse of nutrients including unsaturated fats (both monounsaturated and polyunsaturated), plant protein, fiber, vitamin E, folate, vitamin B-6, niacin, magnesium, copper, zinc, and potassium, all of which can contribute to cardiovascular health. In addition, a wide range of bioactive compounds such as ellagic acid, flavonoids, phenolic compounds (including the polyphenol, resveratrol), and isoflavones are present in nuts and could play a role in cardiovascular health. Mechanisms of action of these bioactive compounds that could account for the cardioprotective effects of nuts include: decreased LDL oxidative susceptibility; decreased platelet aggregation; increased synthesis of cardioprotective eicosanoids; and enhanced antioxidant status. In addition, the omega-3 fatty acid (alpha-linolenic acid) in nuts may protect against sudden death and secondary cardiovascular events. Nuts also are a source of plant sterols which inhibit cholesterol absorption. Thus, there are multiple mechanisms by which nuts can protect against cardiovascular disease.

One ounce of nuts (an amount that fits in the palm of a hand) provides about 160 to 180 kcal. Thus, as nuts and legumes are incorporated in the diet, it is important to assure that control of energy intake is maintained. This can be done by substituting nuts for other fats. For example, season vegetables with nuts in place of butter/margarine, use nuts on salads in place of some of the salad dressing, and use nut butters rather than dairy butter, margarine, or cream cheese. Eat a sandwich with peanut butter rather than lunch meat. Finally, nuts can be enjoyed as a healthy snack instead of a savory snack such as chips. With a new appreciation for the *nut* in nutrition, enjoy nuts in moderation for good nutrition and cardiovascular health!

Dr. Kris-Etherton is the Distinguished Professor of Nutrition in the Department of Nutrition at the Pennsylvania State University. Over the years her research has focused on numerous interventions to reduce cardiovascular disease risk, which recently has included the use of nuts.

The Value of Plant Protein

Vegetable sources of proteins deserve more attention from North Americans. Many plant foods—in proportion to the amount of energy they supply—provide not only much protein but also ample magnesium and dietary fiber, along with other benefits.[11] The protein is used somewhat less efficiently by the body than are animal proteins (10 to 20% less), but this drop is not significant enough to influence diet planning when a variety of foods is used. The vegetable proteins we eat also contain no cholesterol and little saturated fat, unless these are added during processing. Regular use of plant proteins makes a valuable addition to a diet because these supply a variety of other nutrients.[10,18] Nuts are receiving much attention today. Dr. Penny M. Kris-Etherton discusses why in the Expert Opinion.

Recall from Chapter 5 that consumption of the oligosaccharides in beans can lead to intestinal gas and that a preparation called Beano® can greatly lessen symptoms if taken right before the meal.[10]

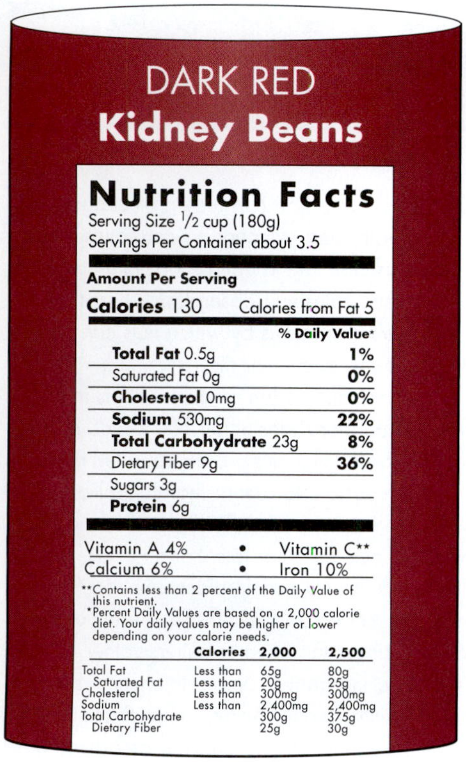
DARK RED
Kidney Beans
Nutrition Facts
Serving Size 1/2 cup (180g)
Servings Per Container about 3.5
Amount Per Serving
Calories 130 Calories from Fat 5
% Daily Value*
Total Fat 0.5g 1%
Saturated Fat 0g 0%
Cholesterol 0mg 0%
Sodium 530mg 22%
Total Carbohydrate 23g 8%
Dietary Fiber 9g 36%
Sugars 3g
Protein 6g
Vitamin A 4% • Vitamin C**
Calcium 6% • Iron 10%
**Contains less than 2 percent of the Daily Value of this nutrient.
*Percent Daily Values are based on a 2,000 calorie diet. Your daily values may be higher or lower depending on your calorie needs.
Calories 2,000 2,500
Total Fat Less than 65g 80g
Saturated Fat Less than 20g 25g
Cholesterol Less than 300mg 300mg
Sodium Less than 2,400mg 2,400mg
Total Carbohydrate 300g 375g
Dietary Fiber 25g 30g

Figure 7-10 Legumes are rich sources of protein. One-half cup meets about 10% of protein needs, and at a cost of only about 5% of energy needs.

Legumes are a plant family with pods that contain a single row of seeds: garden and black-eyed peas; green, black, red, great northern, lima, kidney, pinto, and garbanzo beans; lentils; peanuts; and soybeans. Dried varieties of the mature seeds—what we know as beans—also make an impressive contribution to the protein, vitamin, mineral, and fiber content of a meal (Fig. 7-10). Regularly consuming these legume protein sources can add substantial amounts of nutrients to a diet.[10] Moreover, as discussed in Chapter 5, legumes contain soluble fiber, which can help lower blood cholesterol. In addition, the soluble fiber moderates the swings in blood glucose that occur after eating.

A Closer Look at Soy Protein in Particular

North American farmers harvest soybeans mostly to feed livestock, but lately health researchers are highlighting the health benefits of this plant. Since 1999, soy has had an FDA-approved health claim for lowering blood cholesterol. The effect is modest (about a 6% drop), but can help treat the problem.[17] The claim is limited to foods high in soy protein, and the recommended daily intake is 25 g of such protein to acquire the benefits. As noted in Chapter 2, qualifying for the health claim requires an individual product to have at least 6.25 g of soy protein and less than 3 g of fat, 1 g of saturated fat, and 20 mg of cholesterol per serving.

Soy is one of just a few foods that contain a source of the phytochemical class called *isoflavones.* The two primary isoflavones found in soy are genistein and diadzein. These isoflavones act as plantlike estrogens, especially when the body is deficient in estrogen. Menopause is the common time for women to be deficient in estrogen. The isoflavones may help compensate by acting as weak estrogens. Women have been encouraged to experiment with consuming soy products to relieve menopausal symptoms, but the actual intake of soy protein needed to produce the benefit and the specific magnitude of the effect are still under investigation (about 40 g per day is the typical dose used in studies).[17]

The switch to daily soy consumption may be difficult at first, but as one becomes accustomed to the taste, receives more recipes, and learns the varying preparation methods, it is possible. Common soy protein sources include tofu, soy milk, soy flour, textured soy protein, tempeh, and miso. Soy protein powders are also available. This is certainly worth a try to combat high blood cholesterol, and to possibly treat menopausal symptoms in women. For others, 2 to 4 servings a week of soy-based foods such as tofu and soy milk is a good target, especially as it replaces animal proteins such as red meat in the diet.

There is some interest that regular soy intake may decrease breast cancer risk by blocking estrogen action, but increasing soy in the diet is not recommended for women with breast cancer. This is because the isoflavones can also stimulate the growth of breast cancer cells, especially after menopause when the natural output of estrogen is dwindling. Women diagnosed with breast cancer (or a family history of the disease) should talk to their physicians before consuming soy on a regular basis. People with a history of kidney stones should do the same, as regular use of soy has been linked to that problem. (See the discussion of oxalates in Chapter 11. Soy is a source.)

Evaluation of Protein Quality

A final consideration with regard to proteins in foods is protein quality, which is the ability of a food protein to support body growth and maintenance. Methods exist to both measure and estimate protein quality. Each has its uses and limitations. Keep in mind, also, that the concept of protein quality applies only under conditions in which the amount of protein consumed is equal to or less than the amount of protein required to meet the need for essential amino acids. When protein intake exceeds this amount, efficiency of protein use declines, regardless of the balance of amino acids present. This occurs even with the highest-quality proteins because, after the need for essential amino acids has been met, the remaining essential and nonessential amino acids cannot be stored on a long-term basis and will primarily be degraded and used as a source of energy.

Biological Value

$$BV = \frac{\text{g nitrogen retained}}{\text{g nitrogen absorbed}} \times 100$$

The **biological value (BV)** of a protein is a measure of how efficiently food protein, once absorbed from the GI tract, can be turned into body tissues. If a food possesses enough of all nine essential amino acids, it should allow a person to efficiently incorporate the food protein into body proteins. The biological value of a food, then, depends on how closely its amino acid pattern reflects the amino acid pattern in body tissues. The better the match, the more completely food protein turns into body protein. We actually measure protein retention by measuring nitrogen retention in the body. Both humans and laboratory animals are used to generate data for determining biological value of food proteins.

If the amino acid pattern in a food is quite unlike tissue amino acid patterns, many amino acids in the food will not become body protein. They simply become "leftovers." Their nitrogen groups are removed and excreted in the urine as urea (review Fig. 7-3). Because not much of the nitrogen is retained, the ratio of retained nitrogen to absorbed nitrogen, and the consequent biological value, is low.

Egg-white protein has a biological value of 100, the highest biological value of any single food protein. In other words, essentially all nitrogen that is absorbed from egg protein can be retained. Milk and meat proteins also have high biological values. This makes sense because humans and other animals have similar tissue amino acid compositions. Plant amino acid patterns differ greatly from those of humans. For example, corn has only a moderate biological value of 70; it is high enough to support body maintenance, but not growth. Peanuts consumed as the only source of protein show a low biological value of about 40.

The concept of biological value has clinical importance whenever protein intake must be limited. This is because we want what little protein that is consumed to be used efficiently by the body. For example, protein intake during liver disease and kidney disease may need to be controlled in order to lessen the effects of the disease. In these cases, most of the protein consumed should come from high biological value sources, such as eggs, milk, and meat.

Protein Efficiency Ratio

The **protein efficiency ratio (PER)** is another means of measuring a food's protein quality. FDA uses this method to set standards for labeling of foods intended for infants. The PER compares the amount of weight (in grams) gained by a growing rat after 10 days or more of eating a standard amount of protein (9.09% of its energy intake) from a single protein source to the grams of protein consumed. The PER of a food reflects its biological value, since both basically measure protein retention by body tissues. Plant proteins, because of their incomplete nature, generally yield low PER values, whereas the values for animal proteins are higher, often above 2.0.

$$\text{PER} = \frac{\text{g weight gain}}{\text{g protein consumed}}$$

Chemical Score of Protein

Protein quality of a food can be estimated by its chemical score. To calculate a food's **chemical score,** the amount of each essential amino acid provided by a gram of the food's protein is divided by an "ideal" amount for that essential amino acid per gram of food protein. The "ideal" protein pattern is based on the minimal amount (in milligrams) of each of the nine essential amino acids that is needed per gram of food protein.[4] The lowest amino acid ratio calculated for any essential amino is the chemical score. Scores vary from 0 to 1.0.

$$\text{Chemical score} = \frac{\text{actual mg of each essential amino acid per g of protein}}{\text{Required mg needs of that essential amino acid per g of protein}}$$

Protein Digestibility Corrected Amino Acid Score (PDCAAS)

The most widely used measure of protein quality is the **Protein Digestibility Corrected Amino Acid Score (PDCAAS).** This is used in place of PER evaluations for foods intended for children over 1 year of age and for nonpregnant adults. To calculate the PDCAAS of a protein, its chemical score is determined. For example, wheat has a chemical score of 0.47. The score is then multiplied by the digestibility of the protein (generally, 0.9 to 1.0), in turn yielding the PDCAAS.[4] The PDCAAS for wheat is about 0.47 × 0.90, which equals about 0.40. The maximum value is 1.0, which is the value of milk, eggs, and soy protein. A protein totally lacking any of the nine essential amino acids has a PDCAAS of 0, since its chemical score is 0. For labeling purposes, protein content when listed as % Daily Value is reduced if the PDCAAS is less than 1. For example, if the protein content of ½ cup of spaghetti noodles is 3 g, only 1.2 g will be counted when calculating % Daily Value, since the PDCAAS of wheat is 0.40 (3 g × 0.40 = 1.2). Other PDCAAS values are egg white, 1.0; soy protein, 0.92 to 0.99; beef, 0.92; and black beans, 0.53. Currently the Nutrition Facts panel rarely contains the % Daily Value for protein because the manufacturers do not want to spend the money needed to determine the PDCAAS.

$$\text{PDCAAS} = \text{Chemical score} \times \text{digestibility}$$

Concept | Check

The Recommended Dietary Allowance (RDA) for adults is 0.8 g of protein per kg of healthy body weight. This is approximately 56 g of protein daily for a 70-kg (154-lb) person. The average North American man consumes about 95 g of protein daily, and a woman consumes about 65 g. Thus, typically we eat more than enough protein to meet our needs. Diets high in protein can increase calcium loss in the urine and compromise kidney health in people with diabetes and those with kidney disease. Diets rich in animal protein sources are generally high in saturated fat and cholesterol, and as well likely increase kidney stone and colon cancer risk (red and processed meats for the latter).

Most protein in the North American diet comes from meat. Plant protein sources can play an important role in the diet. *Protein quality* refers to the ability of a protein to contribute to protein needs. Using any of the methods available for testing, individual foods with ample amounts of all nine essential amino acids show high protein quality.

Protein-Energy Malnutrition

Rarely an isolated condition, protein deficiency usually accompanies a deficiency of dietary energy and other nutrients resulting from insufficient food intake. In developing areas of the world, people often have diets low in energy and also in protein. This state of undernutrition stunts the growth of children and makes them more susceptible to disease throughout life.[18] (Note that undernutrition is a main focus of Chapter 20). People who consume too little protein and food energy can go on to develop **protein-energy malnutrition (PEM),** also referred to as *protein-calorie malnutrition (PCM)*. In its milder form, it is difficult to tell if a person with PEM is consuming too little energy or protein, or both. But if the nutrient deficiency—especially for energy—is quite severe, a deficiency disease called **marasmus** can result. When an inadequate intake of nutrients, including protein, is combined with an already existing disease, a form of malnutrition called **kwashiorkor** can develop. Both are seen primarily in children, but can also develop in adults. These two conditions form the tip of the iceberg with respect to states of undernutrition, and symptoms of these two conditions even can be present in the same person (Fig. 7-11).

protein-energy malnutrition (PEM) A condition resulting from regularly consuming insufficient amounts of energy and protein. The deficiency eventually results in body wasting, primarily of lean tissue, and an increased susceptibility to infections.

marasmus A disease that results from consuming a grossly insufficient amount of protein and energy; one of the diseases classed as protein-energy malnutrition. Victims have little or no fat stores, little muscle mass, and poor strength. Death from infections is common.

kwashiorkor A disease occurring primarily in young children who have an existing disease and consume a marginal amount of energy and considerably insufficient protein in relation to needs. The child generally suffers from infections and exhibits edema, poor growth, weakness, and an increased susceptibility to further illness.

As many as 2 million people worldwide die each year from tuberculosis, as this disease reemerges as the world's leading fatal infectious disease. A protein deficiency may lead to susceptibility to tuberculosis, and an improved diet may help delay fatalities. Unfortunately, as covered in Chapter 20, improving the diets for protein-malnourished people around the world remains an overwhelming task and will not likely be solved soon.

Kwashiorkor

Kwashiorkor is a word from Ghana that means "the disease that the first child gets when the new child comes." From birth, an infant is usually breastfed. Often by the time the child reaches 1 to 1.5 years of age, the mother is pregnant or has already given birth again, and breastfeeding is no longer possible for the first child. This child's diet abruptly changes from nutritious human milk to starchy roots and gruels. These foods have low protein densities, compared with total energy. Additionally, the foods are usually full of plant fibers, which are often bulky, making it difficult for the child to consume enough to meet energy needs. The child may also have infections and parasites, which acutely raise energy and protein needs, or be exposed to toxins found in moldy grains. Overall, energy needs of these children are met marginally, at best, and their protein needs are not met, especially when needs are greatly increased by infections and marginal energy intakes. Usually, many vitamin and mineral needs are also far from being fulfilled. Famine victims face similar problems.

The major symptoms of kwashiorkor are apathy, diarrhea, listlessness, failure to grow and gain weight, various infections, and withdrawal from the environment. These symptoms complicate other diseases present. For example, a condition such as measles, a

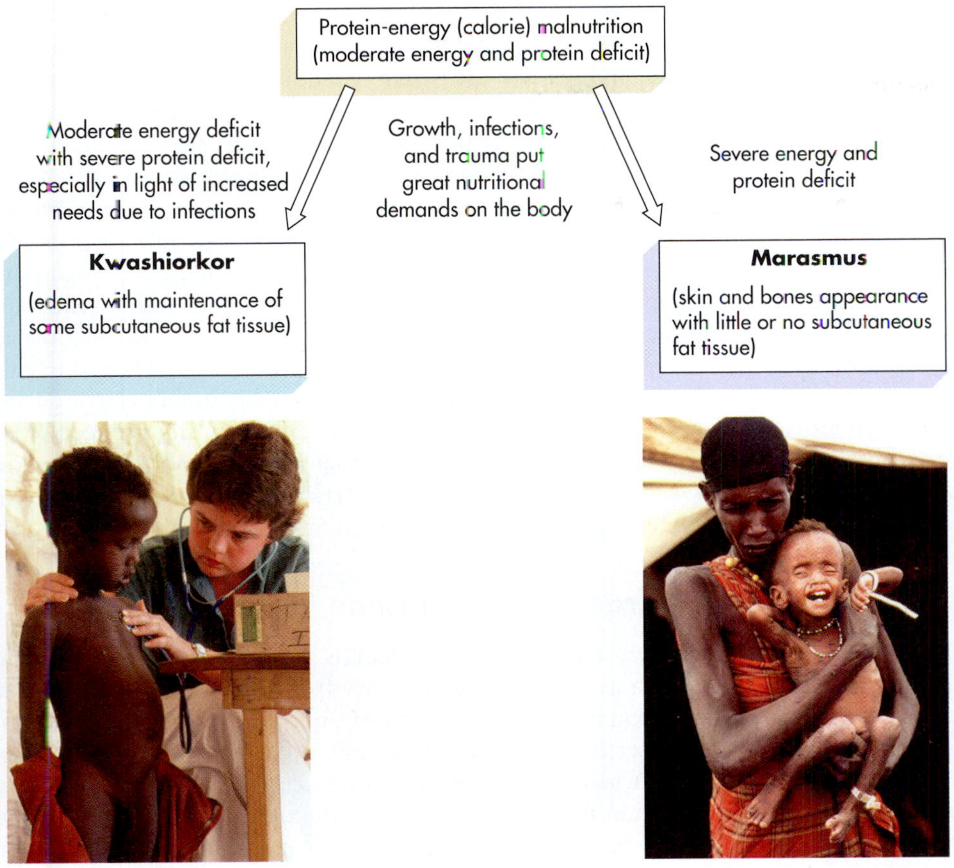

Figure 7-11 Schema for classifying undernutrition in children. The presence of subcutaneous fat (directly underneath the skin) is a diagnostic key for distinguishing kwashiorkor from marasmus.
Illustration by William Ober.

disease that normally makes a healthy child ill for only a week or so, can become severely debilitating and even fatal. Further signs and symptoms of the disease are changes in hair color, potassium deficiency, flaky skin, fatty infiltration in the liver, reduced muscle mass, and massive edema in the abdomen and legs. The presence of edema in a child who has some subcutaneous fat still present is the hallmark of kwashiorkor (review Fig. 7-11). In addition, these children seldom move. If you pick them up, they don't cry. When you hold them, you feel the plumpness of edema, not muscle and fat tissue.

Many symptoms of kwashiorkor can be explained based on what we know about proteins. Proteins play important roles in fluid balance, lipoprotein transport, immune function, and production of tissues, such as skin and hair. We should not expect children with an insufficient protein intake to grow and mature normally. And they don't.

If children with kwashiorkor are helped in time—if infections are treated and a diet ample in protein, energy, and other essential nutrients is provided—the disease process reverses. They begin to grow again and may even show no signs of their previous condition, except perhaps shortness of stature. Unfortunately, by the time many of these children reach a hospital or care center, they already have severe infections. In spite of the best care, they still die. Or, if they survive, they return home only to repeat the cycle.

Marasmus

Marasmus typically occurs as an infant slowly starves to death. It is caused by diets containing minimal amounts of protein, energy, and other nutrients. As previously noted, the condition is also commonly referred to as *protein-energy malnutrition*, especially when experienced by older children and adults. Typically, it occurs in infants who are slowly starving to death. The word *marasmus* means "to waste away." Victims have a "skin and bones" appearance, with little or no subcutaneous fat (see Fig. 7-11).

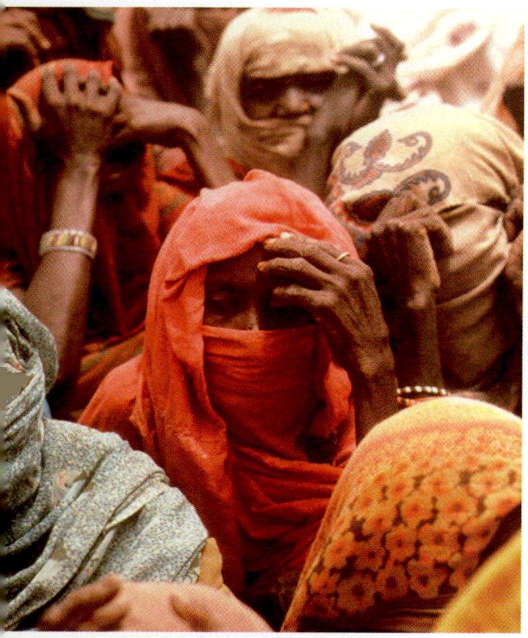

Famine conditions can provoke protein-energy malnutrition in adults as well as infants and children.

Marasmus commonly develops in infants who either are not breastfed or have stopped breastfeeding in the early months. Often the weaning formula used is improperly prepared because of unsafe water and because the parents cannot afford sufficient infant formula for the child's needs. The latter problem may lead the parents to dilute the formula to provide more feedings, not realizing that this provides only more water for the infant.

Marasmus in infants commonly occurs in the large cities of poverty-stricken countries. In the cities, bottle-feeding is often necessary because the infant must be cared for by others when the mother is working or away from home. When people are poor and sanitation is lacking, bottle-feeding often leads to marasmus. An infant with marasmus requires large amounts of energy and protein—like a preterm infant—and, unless the child receives them, full recovery from the disease may never occur. The majority of brain growth occurs between conception and the child's first birthday. In fact, the brain is growing at its highest rate at birth. If the diet does not support brain growth during the first months of life, the brain may not grow to its full adult size. This reduced or retarded brain growth may lead to diminished intellectual function. Both kwashiorkor and marasmus wreak havoc on infants and children; mortality rates in developing countries are often 10 to 20 times higher than in the United States.

Kwashiorkor and Marasmus Malnutrition in the Hospital

Kwashiorkor can result when a hospitalized patient is fed primarily glucose intravenously for many days, such as when a slow recovery from surgery prevents normal food consumption. Or a person may feel too sick to eat, in spite of the increased nutrient needs caused by his or her disease. Intravenous glucose feeding can meet energy needs to some extent but provides no protein. As a result, the person develops edema, and often the immune function is diminished, leaving the patient at great risk for infections. One of the best markers for kwashiorkor is a person's albumin concentration in the blood. When the value falls below the normal range, the person is at a very high risk for infections and disease.

Studies have demonstrated that a hospital patient with low body weight, low albumin, and a low white blood cell (especially lymphocyte) count is at a four to six times greater risk of complications and death than a patient with normal values for those three factors. In response, nutrition support teams have been formed in hospitals. One of their missions is to ensure that patients receive enough oral or balanced intravenous total parenteral nutrition support to meet their needs for energy, protein, carbohydrate, and other nutrients.

Marasmus occurs in a hospitalized patient who simply does not receive enough energy and other nutrients. This can be caused by anorexia nervosa, cancer, HIV/AIDS, and some intestinal disorders. The person either does not eat enough food or does not absorb enough nutrients from the intestinal tract to meet nutritional needs. Muscle, vital organ tissue, and fat stores waste away, and the person eventually looks like "skin and bones." Skinfold measurements of the arm can be used as an indication of marasmus. (Chapter 13 reviews this technique.) However, appearance alone is often enough to indicate the disease. Death from starvation or heart failure can result. A hospitalized person may also have mixed kwashiorkor-marasmus. This is characterized by edema in a person with greatly diminished fat stores.

Concept | Check

Most undernutrition consists of mild deficits in energy, protein, and often other nutrients. If a person needs more nutrients because of disease and infection but does not consume enough energy and protein, a condition known as kwashiorkor can develop. The person suffers from edema and weakness. Children around age 2 are especially susceptible to kwashiorkor, particularly if they already have other diseases. Famine situations in which only starchy root products are available to eat contribute to this problem. Marasmus is a condition wherein people—infants, especially—starve to death. Symptoms include muscle wasting, absence of fat stores, and weakness. Both an adequate diet and the treatment of concurrent diseases must be promoted to maintain nutritional health. This also is true in an adult suffering from anorexia nervosa, cancer, or HIV/AIDS. The symptoms of marasmus, especially, are seen in these situations.

Summary

1. Amino acids, the building blocks of proteins, contain a very usable form of nitrogen for humans. Of the 20 types of amino acids found in food, nine must be consumed as food and the rest can be synthesized by the body.
2. High-quality, also called complete, protein foods contain ample amounts of all nine essential amino acids. Furthermore, foods derived from an animal source provide high biological value protein. Lower-quality, also called incomplete, protein foods lack sufficient amounts of one or more essential amino acids. This is typical of plant foods, especially cereal grains. Different types of plant foods eaten together often complement each other's amino acid deficits, thereby providing high-quality protein in the diet.
3. Individual amino acids are linked together to form proteins. The sequential order of amino acids determines the protein's ultimate shape and function. This order is directed by DNA in the cell nucleus. Diseases such as sickle cell anemia can occur if the amino acids are incorrect on a polypeptide chain. When the three-dimensional shape of the protein is unfolded—denatured—by treatment with heat, acid or alkaline solutions, or other processes, the protein also loses its biological activity.
4. Protein digestion begins in the stomach, dividing the proteins into breakdown products containing shorter chains of amino acids. In the small intestine, these polypeptide chains eventually separate into mostly dipeptides and amino acids. These are absorbed by the enterocytes and broken down into amino acids. The amino acids then travel via the portal vein to the liver.
5. Important body components—such as muscles, connective tissue, transport proteins in the bloodstream, visual pigments, enzymes, some hormones, and immune bodies—are made of proteins. These proteins are in a state of constant turnover. Proteins also provide carbons, which can be used to synthesize glucose when necessary.
6. The protein RDA for adults is 0.8 g per kg of healthy body weight. For a typical 70-kg (154-lb) person, this corresponds to 56 g of protein daily; for a 57-kg (125-lb) person, this corresponds to 46 g/day. The North American diet generally supplies plenty of protein: Men typically consume about 95 g of protein daily, and women consume closer to 65 g. The combined protein intake is also of sufficient quality to support body functions.
7. Almost all animal products are rich sources of protein. The high quality of these proteins means that they can be easily converted into body proteins. Plant foods generally contain less than 20% of their energy content as protein; however, legumes are an excellent source of high-quality protein if eaten with grains or animal products.
8. Protein quality can be measured by determining the extent to which the body can retain the nitrogen contained in the amino acids absorbed; this is called biological value. In addition, the balance of essential amino acids in a food can be compared with an ideal pattern. The comparison with the ideal pattern is referred to as the chemical score. When multiplied by the degree of digestibility, the chemical score yields the Protein Digestibility Corrected Amino Acid Score (PDCAAS).
9. Undernutrition can lead to protein-energy malnutrition in the form of kwashiorkor or marasmus. Kwashiorkor results primarily from an inadequate energy and protein intake in comparison with body needs, which often increase with concurrent disease and infection. Kwashiorkor often occurs when a child is weaned from human milk and fed mostly starchy gruels. Marasmus results primarily from extreme starvation—a negligible intake of both protein and energy. Marasmus commonly occurs during famine, especially in infants. Variations of these diseases appear in some hospitalized North Americans.

Study Questions

1. Discuss the relative importance of essential and nonessential amino acids in the diet. Why is it important for essential amino acids lost from the body to be replaced in the diet?
2. Explain the process for synthesizing nonessential amino acids. When an amino acid loses its amino group without transferring it to another carbon skeleton the chemical reaction is called ________________.
3. What is a limiting amino acid? Explain why this concept is a concern in a vegetarian diet. How can a vegetarian compensate for limiting amino acids in specific foods?
4. Briefly describe the organization of proteins (i.e., primary structure, etc.). How can this organization be altered or damaged? What might be a result of damaged protein organization?
5. Describe four functions of proteins? Provide an example of how the structure of a protein relates to its function.
6. How are DNA and protein synthesis related?
7. What would be one health benefit of preventing protein-energy malnutrition in children?
8. What characteristics of vegetable proteins could improve the North American diet? What foods would you include to provide a diet that has ample protein from both plant and animal sources but is moderate in fat?
9. Outline the major differences between kwashiorkor and marasmus.
10. What are the possible long-term effects of an inadequate intake of dietary protein among children between the ages of 6 months and 4 years?

Annotated References

1. Berg JM and others: *Biochemistry.* 5th ed. New York, NY: W.H. Freeman and Company, 2002.

   This undergraduate biochemistry textbook provides clear explanations of protein biochemistry. Both protein synthesis and functions in the cell are reviewed.

2. Bingham SA and others: Effect of white versus red meat on endogenous N-nitrosation in the human colon and further evidence of a dose response. *Journal of Nutrition* 132:3522S, 2002.

   As red meat intake increases in a diet, so does the ultimate presence of carcinogens in the colon. The same is not seen for white meat.

3. Borghi L and others: Comparison of two diets for the prevention of recurrent stones in idiopathic hypercalciuria. *The New England Journal of Medicine* 346:77, 2002.

   In men with a history of calcium oxalate stones and exhibiting increased calcium in the urine, restricted intakes of animal protein and salt, combined within normal calcium intakes, provided protection against recurrence of such stones.

4. Food and Nutrition Board: *Dietary reference intakes for energy, carbohydrate, fiber, fat, fatty acids, cholesterol, protein, and amino acids.* The National Academy Press (Washington DC) 2002.

   This report provides the latest guidance for macronutrient intakes. With regard to protein intake, the RDA has been set at 0.8 g/day. Protein intake can range from 10 to 35% of energy intake. The 10% allotment approximates the RDA, based on typical energy intakes.

5. Granner DK: Protein synthesis and the genetic code. In Murray RK and others (eds.): *Harper's biochemistry.* 25th ed. Stamford, CT: Appleton & Lange, 2000.

   Protein synthesis is a complex process utilizing numerous cell components. DNA, mRNA, tRNA, amino acids, and ribosomes all participate. The discussion in your textbook only begins to describe the process.

6. How much protein is enough? *Consumer Reports on Health,* p. 8, February 2001.

   It is particularly important for pregnant women, breastfeeding women, young children, and older adults to meet protein needs. A daily intake of about 15% of total calorie intake is adequate to meet the protein needs of most people.

7. Is it time to stop eating meat? *Harvard Health Letter,* p. 6, September 2001.

   It is best to consume red meat on an occasional basis, rather than daily. Chicken, fish, legumes, and nuts are healthier, protein-rich alternatives.

8. JAMA patient page: Facts about sickle-cell anemia. *Journal of the American Medical Association* 281:176, 1999.

   Sickle-cell anemia is particularly common among people whose ancestry is from sub-Saharan Africa, South and Central America, Cuba, Saudi Arabia, India, Greece, and Italy. Early diagnosis of sickle-cell anemia is important, so that children who have the disorder can receive proper treatment. Antibiotics, blood transfusions, and some medications may be helpful during flare-ups of the disease.

9. Johnston TK: Nutritional implications of vegetarian diets. In Shils ME and others (eds.): *Modern nutrition in health and disease.* 9th ed. Baltimore: Williams & Wilkins, 1999.

   Vegetarian diets have a long history. There are many positive aspects of a primarily plant-based diet, including ample consumption of fruits and vegetables. Many typical diseases, such as cardiovascular disease and osteoporosis, are less common in vegetarians than in people consuming animal protein-rich diets. These findings are discussed in detail.

10. Liebman B, Hurley J: Beans: No longer a bore. *Nutrition Action Health Letter,* p. 13, May 1999.

    If one hasn't consumed beans on a regular basis, it is best to start with small portions and increase this gradually over a few weeks, so one's GI tract has a chance to adjust. Use of the product Beano® can also help reduce intestinal gas-related discomfort.

11. Mayes PA: Digestion and absorption. In Murray RK and others (eds.): *Harper's biochemistry.* 25th ed. Stamford, CT: Appleton & Lange, 2000.

    The enzymatic digestion of protein begins in the stomach. Pepsin splits proteins into large polypeptides. Enzymes in the small intestine such as trypsin and aminopeptidases complete the digestion process, yielding amino acids. A multiplicity of carriers are then used to transport the amino acids into the absorptive cells.

12. McNurlan MA, Garlick PJ: Protein synthesis and degradation. In Stipanuk MH (ed.): *Biochemical and physiological aspects of human nutrition.* Philadelphia: W.B. Saunders, 2000.

    Cells are constantly degrading existing proteins and synthesizing new proteins. DNA in the cell is transcribed to mRNA. This mRNA is translated by ribosomes in the cytosol to the new protein. Total protein turnover in the body is about 300 g degraded and 300 g synthesized each day.

13. Messina V, Mangels AR: Considerations in planning vegan diets: Children. *Journal of the American Dietetic Association* 101:661, 2001.

    Vegans must find good sources of vitamin B-12, riboflavin, zinc, calcium, and, if sun exposure is not adequate, vitamin D. This should not be problematic, due to the growing number and availability of fortified vegan foods that can help meet all nutrient needs. With appropriate food choices, vegan diets can be adequate, even for children.

14. Metges CC, Barth CA: Metabolic consequences of a high dietary-protein intake in adulthood: Assessment of the available evidence. *Journal of Nutrition* 130:886, 2000.

    In a healthy population, there is no need to increase protein intake above that habitually consumed by well-nourished populations in technically advanced nations (above 2 g per kg of body weight per day). Physical activity does not increase protein needs significantly because it has a positive effect on nitrogen retention, as long as energy needs are met.

15. Milea D and others: Blindness in a strict vegan. *The New England Journal of Medicine* 342:897, 2000.

    Vitamin B-12 supplementation is essential in persons who are strict vegetarians. Not doing so can result in vitamin B-12 deficiency, leading to severe, irreversible damage to the optic nerve.

16. Norat T, Riboli E: Meat consumption and colorectal cancer: A review of epidemiologic evidence. *Nutrition Reviews* 59(2): 37, 2001.

    The risks of colorectal cancer are somewhat higher in people who consume diets rich in processed meat and red meat compared to individuals who consume small amounts.

17. Schart D: Got soy? *Nutrition Action Healthletter,* p. 8, November 2002.

    The best evidence for regular soy protein intake is the ability to lower blood cholesterol. The ability of soy protein to treat menopausal symptoms (or prevent breast and prostate cancer) have not been conclusively demonstrated.

18. Torun B, Chew F: Protein-energy malnutrition. In Shils ME and others (eds.): *Modern nutrition in health and disease.* 9th ed. Baltimore: Williams & Wilkins, 1999.

    Protein-energy malnutrition can affect all age groups, but is more frequent among infants and young children. This is because ongoing growth increases nutritional requirements. In addition, persons in this age group often cannot obtain food by their own means. Infants who are weaned prematurely from the breast or who are breastfed for a prolonged time without adequate complementary feeding become malnourished from a lack of adequate energy and protein intake. Older children usually have milder forms of protein-energy malnutrition because they can cope better with social and food availability limitations.

19. Whiting SJ and others: Dietary protein, phosphorus, and potassium are beneficial to bone mineral density in adult men consuming adequate dietary calcium. *Journal of the American College of Nutrition* 21:409, 2002.

    It is important to meet calcium needs to offset any potential negative effects of protein intakes in excess of the RDA on bone health. Meeting phosphorus and potassium needs are also important.

20. Young VR: Protein and amino acids. In Bowan BA, RM Russell (eds.): *Present knowledge in nutrition.* Washington, DC: ILSI Press, 2001.

    Adults need about 11% of their amino acid intake in the form of essential amino acids, while infants need 4 times this much.

Take | Action

I. Is Your Protein Intake Sufficient to Meet Your Needs?

1. How much protein do you eat in a typical day? Look at the nutrition assessment you completed at the end of Chapter 2. Review it closely. Find the figure indicating the amount of protein you consumed on that day, and write it in the space below:

   TOTAL PROTEIN ______

   Compare your protein intake with your RDA for protein. Find your healthy weight for height (in pounds) using Table 13-3 in Chapter 13. Choose a midrange value between a Body Mass Index of 18.5 to 24.9. Divide this number by 2.2 to reveal your healthy weight in kilograms. Next, multiply by 0.8 per kilogram of this weight, or your current body weight if the numbers are close. This will indicate the RDA for protein for your weight and gender. Write it in the space below:

   RDA FOR PROTEIN ______

   How does your consumption compare with your RDA?

   If you consumed either more or less than the RDA, what foods could you add, delete, or eat more or less of? (Look at the foods you ate.)

   Was most of your protein from animal or plant sources?

   If your protein intake was primarily from plants, did this come from a wide variety to encourage protein complementarity for the day?

II. Protein and the Vegetarian.

Alana is excited about all the health benefits that might accompany a vegetarian diet. However, she is concerned that she will not consume enough protein to meet her needs. She is also concerned about possible vitamin and mineral deficiencies. Use your nutrition software to see if her concerns are valid.

	Protein (g)
Breakfast	
Calcium fortified orange juice, 1 cup	
Soybean milk, 1 cup	
Fortified bran flakes, 1 cup	
Banana, medium	
Snack	
Calcium-enriched granola bar	
Lunch	
GardenBurger, 4 oz	
Whole-wheat bun	
Mustard, 1 tbsp	
Soy cheese, 1 oz	
Apple, medium	
Green leaf lettuce, 1½ cups	
Peanuts, 1 oz	
Sunflower seeds, ¼ cup	
Tomato slices, 2	
Mushrooms, 3	
Vinaigrette salad dressing, 2 tbsp	
Iced Tea	
Dinner	
Kidney beans, ½ cup	
Brown rice, ¾ cup	
Fortified margarine, 2 tbsp	
Mixed vegetables, ¼ cup	
Hot Tea	
Dessert	
Strawberries, ½ cup	
Angel food cake, 1 small slice	
Soy milk, ½ cup	
TOTAL PROTEIN (g)	______

Alana's diet contained 2150 kcal, with _____ g (you fill in) of protein (plenty for her), 360 g of carbohydrate, 57 g of total dietary fat (only 9 g of which came from saturated fat), and 50 g of fiber. Her vitamin and mineral intake with respect to those of concern to vegetarians—vitamin B-12, vitamin D, calcium, iron, and zinc—met her needs.

Vegetarian Diets

Vegetarianism has evolved over the centuries from a necessity into an option. Historically, vegetarianism was linked with specific philosophies and religions or with science. In the sixth century B.C., Pythagoras advocated a meatless diet for its physical health, ecological, religious, and philosophical benefits.

Today, there are about 12 million vegetarians in the United States alone, about double the number in 1985. Over the past two decades, vegetarian diets have gone from dull to delicious, with the inclusion of such new products as soy-based sloppy joes, chili, tacos, burgers, and more. In addition, cookbooks that feature the use of a variety of fruits, vegetables, and seasonings are enhancing food selection for vegetarians of all degrees.

Vegetarianism is popular among college students. Fifteen percent of college students in one survey said they select vegetarian options at lunch or dinner on any given day. In response, dining services offer vegetarian options at every meal, the most common being pastas with meatless sauce and pizza. Many teenagers are also turning to vegetarianism out of respect for animals. And a survey by the National Restaurant Association found that 20% of its customers want a vegetarian option when they eat out. Many customers cite health and taste as reasons for choosing vegetarian fare.

As nutrition science has grown, new information has enabled the design of adequate vegetarian diets. It is important for vegetarians to take advantage of this information because a diet of only plants can lead to various nutrient deficiencies and a substantial growth retardation in infants and children. People who choose a vegetarian diet can meet their nutritional needs by following a few basic rules and knowledgeably planning their diets (Table 7-4).

Studies show that death rates from some chronic diseases, such as certain forms of cardiovascular disease, cancer, type 2 diabetes, and obesity, are lower for vegetarians than for nonvegetarians. Healthful lifestyles (not smoking, abstaining from alcohol and drugs, and increasing physical activity) and social class bias probably partially account for these findings.[9]

Primarily vegetarian diets are typical among rural peoples throughout the world.

Table 7-4 Food-Group Plan for Lactovegetarians and Vegans§

	Servings		
Group†	**Lactovegetarian‡**	**Vegan§ ||**	**Key Nutrients Supplied**
Grains¶	6–11	8–11	Protein, thiamin, niacin, folate, vitamin E, zinc, magnesium, iron, and dietary fiber
Legumes	1–2	2	Protein, vitamin B-6, zinc, magnesium, and dietary fiber
Nuts, seeds	1–2	2	Protein, vitamin E, and magnesium
Vegetables	3–5 (include one dark green or leafy variety daily)	4–6 (include one dark green or leafy variety daily)	Vitamin A, vitamin C, and folate
Fruits	2–4	4	Vitamin A, vitamin C, and folate
Milk	2–3	—	Protein, riboflavin, vitamin D, vitamin B-12, and calcium

†Base serving size on those listed for the Food Guide Pyramid (see Chapter 2). This plan yields about 1600 to 1800 kcal. Increase the number of servings, or add other foods to meet higher energy needs.

‡Contains about 75 grams of protein in 1650 kcal.

§A calcium-fortified food, such as orange juice or soy milk, is needed unless a calcium supplement is used. In addition, use of a supplement source of vitamin B-12 or foods fortified with vitamin B-12 is a must. Overall, fortified soy milk makes a valuable contribution to a vegan diet.

||Contains about 79 grams of protein in 1800 kcal.

¶One serving of vitamin- and mineral-enriched breakfast cereal is recommended. Alternately, a balanced multivitamin and mineral supplement can be used to meet possible nutrient gaps.

Why Do People Become Vegetarian?

People choose vegetarianism for a variety of reasons. Some believe that killing animals for food is unethical. Hindus and Trappist monks eat vegetarian meals as a practice of their religion. In the United States, many Seventh Day Adventists base their practice of vegetarianism on biblical texts and believe it is a more healthful way to live.

People might choose vegetarianism after realizing that animals are not efficient protein factories. Animals actually use much of the protein they eat just to maintain themselves rather than to synthesize new muscle tissue. Note that 40% of the world's grain production is used to breed meat-producing animals. Animals that humans eat sometimes eat grasses that humans cannot digest. Many, however, also eat grains that humans can eat.

People might also practice vegetarianism because it encourages a high intake of carbohydrates; vitamins A, E, and C; carotenoids; magnesium; and fiber while limiting saturated fat and cholesterol intake. This produces a diet closely resembling that suggested in the Dietary Guidelines for Americans, covered in Chapter 2.

Food Planning for Vegetarians

vegan A person who eats only plant foods.

fruitarian A person who primarily eats fruits, nuts, honey, and vegetable oils.

lactovegetarian A person who consumes plant products and dairy products.

lactoovovegetarian A person who consumes plant products, dairy products, and eggs.

There are a variety of vegetarian styles. **Vegans** eat only plant foods (and as well do not use animal products for other purposes, such as leather shoes or feather pillows). **Fruitarians** primarily eat fruits, nuts, honey, and vegetable oils. This plan is not recommended because it can lead to nutrient deficiencies in people of all ages. **Lactovegetarians** modify vegetarianism a bit—they include dairy products and plant foods. **Lactoovovegetarians** modify the diet even further and eat dairy products and eggs, as well as plant foods. Including these animal products makes food planning easier because they are rich in some nutrients that are missing or present in low amounts in plants. The more variety in the diet, the easier it is to meet nutritional needs. Thus, the practice of eating no animal sources of food significantly separates the vegans and fruitarians from all other semivegetarian styles.

It has been suggested that "almost vegetarians" (those who allow some dairy and regular fish intake) are the healthiest group of all vegetarians. Perhaps this is due to the health benefits of a high fruit and vegetable diet, rather than the complete exclusion of all animal products.

Most people who call themselves vegetarians consume at least some dairy products, if not all dairy products and eggs. A food-group plan has been developed for lactovegetarians and vegans (review Table 7-4). This plan includes servings of nuts, grains, legumes, and seeds to help meet protein needs. There is also a vegetable group, a fruit group, and a milk group. Figure 7-12 shows a pyramid for vegetarians developed by Oldways Preservation & Exchange Trust. The base consists of fruits, vegetables, whole grains, and legumes (at every meal). The middle tier is nuts, seeds, egg whites, soy milks, dairy products, and plant oils (daily). Eggs and sweets form the tip (small quantities). Alcohol intake in moderation is optional and daily physical activity is recommended (see the Oldways Preservation & Exchange Trust website at www.oldwayspt.org for further information).

The Vegan

Table 7-2, earlier in this chapter, lists traditional dishes in which vegetable proteins combine to provide high-quality (complete) protein in the meal.

A vegan diet requires some creative planning. A real effort must be made to use grains and legumes to yield high-quality protein and other key nutrients in meals, especially when used with infants and children. Then, if energy needs are satisfied, protein needs should also be met. Including a wide variety of protein sources should provide all amino acids needed for a high-quality protein diet. The essential amino acids deficient in one food protein are supplied by those of another protein source consumed at the same meal or the next. For example, many legumes do not provide enough of the essential amino acid methionine, and cereals are limited in lysine. When a combination of these two foods is eaten, the body is supplied with adequate amounts of both amino acids, so cereals and legumes complement each other.

Purchasing some vegetarian cookbooks will simplify the task of menu planning. They provide numerous ideas for imaginative and nutritious ways to use plant foods.

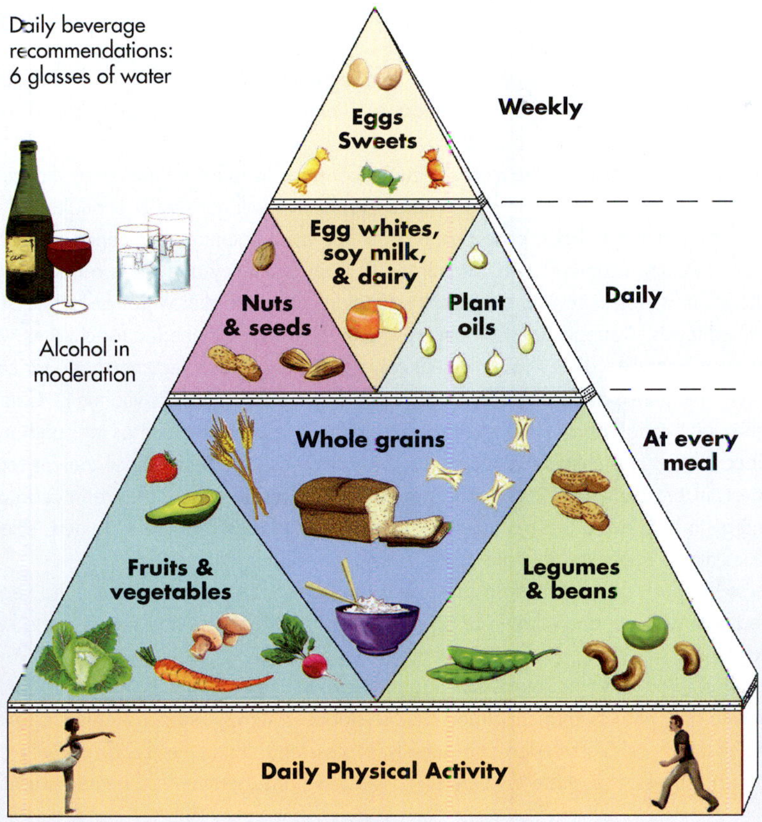

Figure 7-12 The Oldways Preservation & Exchange Trust traditional vegetarian diet. Note that alcohol should only be used by adults of legal age. The organization emphasizes that such a diet has the advantage of being low in saturated fat, high in fiber, and rich in antioxidants. However, it can pose a risk for an inadequate iron, vitamin D (if the person has limited sun exposure), and vitamin B-12 intake. Inclusion of some fortified foods, such as a whole-grain, ready-to-eat breakfast cereal or a balanced vitamin and mineral supplement, is advised.

Chapter 6 noted that a vegan diet coupled with regular exercise and other lifestyle changes can lead to a reversal of atherosclerotic plaque in the coronary arteries.

The vegan diet must also include good sources of riboflavin, vitamins D and B-12, calcium, iron, and zinc. A typical ready-to-eat breakfast cereal provides a good start in meeting those needs. Riboflavin can be obtained from green leafy vegetables, whole grains, yeast, and legumes, part of most vegan diets. A major source of riboflavin in the typical North American diet is milk, which is omitted from the vegan diet. Vitamin D can be obtained through regular sun exposure and fortified margarine. Otherwise, a supplemental source of vitamin D should be considered (see Chapter 9).

The vegan should find a reliable source of vitamin B-12, such as fortified soybean milk or ready-to-eat breakfast cereals and special yeast grown on media rich in vitamin B-12. Use of a balanced vitamin and mineral supplement containing vitamin B-12 is another option. Vitamin B-12 occurs naturally only in animal foods, although plants can contain soil or microbial contamination that provides at most a trace amount of vitamin B-12. Because the body can store enough vitamin B-12 for about 4 years, a deficiency can take a long time to develop after animal foods are removed from the diet. If a deficiency develops, nerves can be damaged irreversibly and brain function can decrease.[15] Evidence of a vitamin B-12 deficiency has been noted in vegetarian mothers and their infants. The milk produced by the vegetarian mothers is low in vitamin B-12. The earliest sign of a vitamin B-12 deficiency is mental dysfunction; a prolonged deficiency can lead to irreversible nerve damage. Excess blood concentration of homocysteine has also been noted in vegans who underconsume vitamin B-12. This can lead to other health problems. Therefore, vegans need to be careful to prevent a vitamin B-12 deficiency.

To obtain calcium, the vegan can drink fortified soy milk or fortified orange juice and consume calcium-rich tofu (check the label) or other calcium-fortified foods, such as certain ready-to-eat breakfast cereals and snacks. Green leafy vegetables and nuts also contain calcium, but the calcium is either not well absorbed or not very plentiful. Calcium supplements are another option (see Chapter 11).

Vegetarian adaptations of traditional foods is a growing trend in our society.

Meeting omega-3 fatty acid needs also becomes an issue. For the vegan, regular use of canola oil, soybean oil, flax seeds, or walnuts is advised to obtain alpha-linolenic acid, the omega-3 fatty acid. Seaweed is also a possible source of omega-3 fatty acids.

For iron, the vegan can consume whole grains, dried fruits and nuts, and legumes. The iron in these foods is not absorbed as well as that found in animal foods, but a good source of vitamin C taken with these foods modestly enhances iron absorption. Thus, a recommended strategy is to consume vitamin C with every meal that contains adequate iron-rich plant foods. Cooking in iron pots and skillets can also add iron to the diet (see Chapter 12).

The vegan can find zinc in whole grains, nuts, and legumes, but phytic acid and other substances in these foods limit zinc absorption. Grains are most nutritious when leavened, as in bread, because this process reduces the influence of phytic acid.

Of all these nutrients, calcium is the most difficult to consume in sufficient quantities. Special diet planning is required, as even a multivitamin and mineral supplement will not supply enough.

Veganism during childhood can pose problems.[13] The most common nutritional concerns are deficiencies of iron, calcium, vitamin D, and vitamin B-12. Iron deficiency anemia is a frequent occurrence during childhood; however, it can be avoided by supplementing the diet with iron-fortified cereal, and other iron-fortified foods. A supplement containing vitamin B-12 may be needed for children who exclude all animal products from their diets. A supplement containing vitamin D is recommended for children who do not get much sunlight exposure and who do not have any dietary source of vitamin D. Calcium can be obtained in the diet through dairy products or calcium-enriched products, such as tofu and orange juice. Finally, the fiber content of a child's diet may need to be decreased with high-fiber sources replaced with some refined grain products, fruit juices, and peeled fruit. Overall, vegan children need concentrated sources of energy to help avoid these problems. Examples include fortified soy milk, nuts, dried fruits, avocados, cookies made with vegetable oils or tub margarine, and fruit juices.

Soy milk, soy yogurt, and soy cheese are excellent choices for vegan children (and vegan adults). When fortified with calcium and vitamin B-12, these substitutes can provide many of the key nutrients found in milk.

Finding excellent iron and zinc sources is important in planning vegan diets, especially for infants and children. Overall, both infancy and childhood are life stages in which vegetarianism is appropriate, but it must be implemented with knowledge and, ideally, professional guidance. Especially informative websites on vegetarianism in general are **www.ivu.org**, **www.vrg.org**, and **www.vegetariannutrition. net/**.

Case Scenario | Follow-up

Shannon is a vegan if she had no cheese on the sub sandwich, and a lactovegetarian if she did have cheese. Her dietary intake for this day is not healthy, as it does not come close to following the recommendations in this Nutrition Perspective. Where are the whole grains, nuts, soy products, beans, two to four fruits, and three to five vegetables, that form the base of such diets? The diet is also low in the many phytochemicals under study. Overall, she is not benefiting as she had hoped to from her vegetarian diet, since so little care has gone into following a healthy pattern.

chapter 8

Alcohol

Chapter | Outline

Case | Scenario

Alyssa, a college student, has a boyfriend named Todd, also a college student. Todd was a very serious student in high school and achieved excellent grades, but as a college student he has begun binge drinking. As a result, his grades have fallen sharply and he is becoming socially isolated. He has been arrested once for drunk driving.

Last night, he had eight beers and three shots of whiskey at an off-campus party he attended with Alyssa. Unfortunately, everyone who knows Todd says he tends to get angry and says things he doesn't mean when he drinks too much. He often becomes cruel and destructive to those he cares for and respects. He also has been involved in several fights.

As the party began to die down, Alyssa tried to get Todd to leave. He responded rudely and forcefully grabbed her arm. She became frightened with his aggressive behavior and left without him.

The next morning, Alyssa awoke early, still thinking about the hurtful events of the previous night. Having known of one student who died from an overdose of alcohol (he drank 23 shots of whiskey on his 21st birthday) Alyssa decided to e-mail Todd, expressing her anxiety about his alcohol abuse. She did not want to see everything he had worked so hard for be ruined by alcohol.

What should Alyssa say in the e-mail about alcohol and how it affects various organs in the body? What long-term problems are associated with such alcohol abuse? Is Alyssa correct in taking the initiative in communicating to Todd her concerns about his drinking problem?

Refresh | Your Memory

As you begin your study of alcohol in Chapter 8, you may want to review:

- The role of the GI tract, liver, and pancreas in digestion and absorption in Chapter 3.
- Oxidation and reduction reactions in Chapter 4.
- Glycolysis, the citric acid cycle, and electron transport chain in Chapter 4.
- Fermentation reactions in Chapter 4.
- Forms of carbohydrates in Chapter 5.
- Protein-energy malnutrition in Chapter 7.

Boost | Your Study

*Check out the **Perspectives in Nutrition: Online Learning Center** www.mhhe.com/wardlawpers6 for quizzes, flash cards, activities, and web links designed to further help you learn about issues surrounding alcohol use and abuse.*

Chapter | Objectives

Chapter 8 is designed to allow you to:

1. Describe the process of alcohol metabolism.
2. Describe some benefits of moderate alcohol consumption and define "moderate drinking."
3. List some nutrients that are most likely to be deficient in the diet of a person who abuses alcohol.
4. Explain how alcohol abuse damages body organs, such as the liver, heart, brain, and kidneys.
5. Identify body organs most likely to develop cancer because of alcohol abuse.
6. Outline the methods used to diagnose alcohol abuse.
7. List the typical strategies used in treating alcoholism, including the typical medications employed.
8. Describe the risks of binge drinking and the corresponding amount of alcohol this represents.

Alcohol use is an issue requiring careful attention by health professionals, law enforcement officials, the courts, elected officials, the entertainment industry, university professors, parents, students, and those engaged in the production and distribution of alcoholic beverages. Although not an essential nutrient, alcohol is a source of energy for about half of all adults, constituting about 5% of total energy intake in the North American diet when averaged across the population.[19] We also know that moderate consumption of alcohol by a person of legal age is an acceptable practice, and has some health benefits. But when it leads to excessive consumption, many unfortunate consequences are almost inevitable. By far the most commonly abused drug, alcohol can destroy families and friendships; spur deadly behaviors such as suicide, rape, and violence; and fill jails and prisons.[8]

Nearly 14 million people in the United States alone are currently classified as having alcoholism, and another 31.9 million engage in binge drinking. Approximately 11 million current drinkers are under the legal age of 21. From teenage through later years in life, excess alcohol intake has damaging effects on one's nutritional status and overall health. Alcohol abuse is also a major problem in Canada.[8]

The American Medical Association defines alcoholism as an illness characterized by significant impairment directly related to persistent and excessive use of alcohol. Impairment can involve physiological and social dysfunction, and for psychological, social, and genetic reasons some people are more vulnerable to this disorder than others.[16] Alcohol abuse touches many of our lives, so let's examine this substance in detail.

Alcohol—An Introduction

Given the wide spectrum of alcohol use and abuse—often starting in teenage and college years—knowledge of alcohol consumption and its relationship to overall health is essential to the study of nutrition. Alcohol, chemically known as ethanol, has played many roles throughout history. Alcohol contributes energy to the diet (about 7 kcal/g) (Table 8-1). It is also a social stimulant because it takes away inhibitions, it is a thirst quencher when used as a safe alternative to polluted water (such as when water is contaminated with certain microorganisms), and it is an analgesic to treat aches and pain.

Alcohol requires no digestion. It is absorbed rapidly from the GI tract by simple diffusion—no specific transport mechanisms are required for alcohol to enter a cell—so it is the most efficiently absorbed of all energy sources. Different parts of the GI tract absorb alcohol at different rates. The upper parts of the small intestine absorb alcohol fastest, depending on how quickly the stomach empties, which in turn depends on the kinds of foods consumed along with the alcohol.[19] Alcohol then goes on to act on various organs as you will see, but has no cellular receptors per se, unlike other compounds that affect the body, such as insulin and some fat-soluble vitamins.

The following servings of each type of alcoholic beverage provide the same amount of alcohol (about 15 g): wine—5 oz, hard liquor—1.5 oz, beer or wine cooler—12 oz. In determining a safe level of intake, it is important to observe these serving sizes.

How Alcoholic Beverages Are Produced

Any number of natural foods can be fermented. Recall from Chapter 4 that this represents the breakdown of carbohydrates without the use of oxygen. Alcohol, carbon dioxide (CO_2), and various acids are by-products. Production temperatures and composition of the food itself determine the characteristics of the final product. High-carbohydrate

Table 8-1 Energy, Carbohydrate, and Alcohol Content of Alcoholic Beverages*

Beverage	Amount (fluid oz)	Alcohol (g)	Carbohydrates (g)	Energy (kcal)
Beer				
Regular	12	13	13	146
Light	12	11	5	99
Distilled Spirits				
Gin, rum, vodka, bourbon, whiskey (80 proof)	1.5	14	—	96
Brandy, cognac	1.5	14	—	96
Wine				
Red	5	14	2	102
White	5	14	1	100
Dessert, sweet	5	23	17	225
Rosé	5	14	2	100
Mixed Drinks				
Manhattan	3	26	3	191
Martini	3	27	—	189
Bourbon and soda	3	11	—	78
Whiskey sour	3	14	13	144

*There is little to no fat or protein contribution to energy content.

Source: USDA.

Beer is a source of alcohol and carbohydrates.

foods especially encourage the growth of yeast, the microorganism responsible for alcohol production. Brewer's yeast is one source of the enzyme that is necessary to make alcohol production possible.

During glycolysis, glucose is first converted to pyruvate. Yeast cells then convert pyruvate to alcohol and carbon dioxide in a simple, two-step process. In the first step, the 3-carbon pyruvate is converted to the 2-carbon acetaldehyde in an irreversible reaction with the release of CO_2. In the second step, another enzyme donates a pair of hydrogens to acetaldehyde to form ethanol. This enzyme uses the B-vitamin niacin in the form of the coenzyme $NADH + H^+$ (review Chapter 4 for details). Ethanol and CO_2 are the end products of the process.[19]

1. $\text{Glucose} \longrightarrow\!\!\!\!\longrightarrow \text{Pyruvate} \longrightarrow \text{Acetaldehyde} + CO_2$

2. $\text{Acetaldehyde} \xrightarrow{NADH + H^+ \;\to\; NAD^+} \text{Ethanol}$

The overall reaction is

$$\underset{\text{Glucose}}{C_6H_{12}O_6} + 2\ ADP + 2\ P_i \longrightarrow \underset{\text{Ethanol}}{2\ C_2H_5OH} + 2\ CO_2 + 2\ ATP + 2\ H_2O$$

Thus, under anaerobic conditions, two glucose molecules are fermented by yeast to two ethanol, two carbon dioxide, and two water molecules. The 2 ATP that result are used by the yeast for energy.

Wine is a historic beverage. It has been produced and consumed for more than 10,000 years.

The carbohydrate must be a simple sugar, such as maltose or glucose, in order for the yeast to use it as food. If the carbohydrate is a starch, such as that found in cereal grains, it must be broken down to these smaller forms, or "malted." During malting, the cereal grain seeds are allowed to sprout to produce the enzymes that break down the starches to simple sugars. The sprouting is then stopped by heating, and the yeast cells and water are added to the malt. The yeast grows using the sugars for energy. When the oxygen in the vat (the mixture of water, yeast, and malt) is used up, the yeast ferments the remaining sugar to produce alcohol and carbon dioxide. After fermentation has ceased, the product is finished in a variety of ways. In some cases, the alcohol itself is recovered from the product.

Beer is made from malted cereal grain, such as barley; it is flavored with hops and brewed by slow fermentation. The carbon dioxide released is collected and used to carbonate the beer, thus producing the desirable fizz associated with a quality beverage.

Wine is the fermented juice of grapes. Climate, geographic region, and variety of grape determine the quality of the wine. After fermentation, wines are aged in oak barrels to decrease the acidity and remove undesirable impurities.

distillation A physical method used to separate liquids based on their boiling points.

Distilled spirits are made from the **distillation** of the alcohol after fermentation. Any number of fruits, vegetables, and grains can be fermented and the resulting mash distilled. The difference between the boiling point of water and the boiling point of alcohol allows these two liquids to be separated by distillation and the alcohol to be recovered. Some distilled spirits are marketed "unaged." Vodka and gin are examples of unaged beverages. Other spirits, such as whiskeys, rums, and brandies, are aged in oak barrels, some more than 20 years.

Alcohol proof represents twice the percentage of alcohol in the product. 80 proof vodka is thus 40% alcohol.

Alcohol Metabolism

After a person drinks an alcoholic beverage, his or her blood concentration of alcohol rises rapidly. Alcohol is readily absorbed into the blood from different segments of the GI tract by simple diffusion. You've probably been warned, with good reason, not to drink alcohol on an empty stomach. Alcohol absorption depends partly on the rate of stomach emptying. Food slows the stomach's emptying rate and stimulates secretions, such as gastric acid, which dilute the alcohol and slow its absorption into the bloodstream. Certain drugs also control stomach-emptying time and, thus, overall absorption.[19]

Alcohol is readily distributed in all the fluid compartments within the body because alcohol is found wherever water is distributed in the body. Alcohol moves easily through the cell membranes; however, as it does, it damages proteins in the membranes. Most of alcohol's damaging effects are concentrated in the liver because this is the first organ that is exposed to alcohol after absorption, and the liver is the chief site for alcohol metabolism. Although it is true that cells of the GI tract are in contact with alcohol, they are constantly being replaced because of their naturally short life span. Thus, they are not subject to the same degree of damage as liver cells, which have a much longer life span.

Metabolism of alcohol is dependent on numerous factors, such as gender, race, size, physical condition, what is eaten, the alcohol content of the beverage, and even how much sleep one has had. The ability to produce the enzyme **alcohol dehydrogenase (ADH)** is the key to alcohol metabolism, as it acts on about 90% of the dose consumed.[19] Women absorb and metabolize alcohol differently than men do. A woman cannot metabolize much alcohol in the cells that line her stomach because of low activity of ADH. Women also have less body water in which to dilute the alcohol than do men (the same is also true for older men and older women). So, when a young man and a woman of similar size drink equal amounts of alcohol, a larger proportion of the alcohol reaches and remains in the woman's bloodstream. Men metabolize about 30% of the alcohol ingested in this manner, but women metabolize only 10%. Overall, women develop alcohol-related ailments, such as **cirrhosis** of the liver, more rapidly than men do with the same alcohol-consumption habits. Also, certain drugs used to treat ulcers and heartburn inhibit ADH activity in the stomach, as does chronic alcohol abuse and aging.

alcohol dehydrogenase (ADH) An enzyme used in alcohol (ethanol) metabolism; the major enzyme used in the liver when alcohol is in low concentration.

cirrhosis A loss of functioning liver cells, which are replaced by nonfunctioning connective tissue. Any substance that poisons liver cells can lead to cirrhosis. The most common cause is a chronic, excessive alcohol intake.

Most of the remaining alcohol consumed is then metabolized in the same way by alcohol dehydrogenase to carbon dioxide and water in the liver. Only a small percentage of alcohol intake is excreted as such through the lungs, urine, and sweat. (Since the alcohol content of expired air exhibits a constant relationship to the blood alcohol concentration in the lungs, it is used as the basis of the breathalyzer test.) As one continues to drink, one's blood alcohol concentration (BAC) continues to rise (Fig. 8-1). A social drinker who weighs 150 pounds and has normal liver function metabolizes about 5 to 7 g of alcohol per hour.[19] This is about one half of a beer or one fourth of an ordinary-sized drink. When the rate of alcohol consumption exceeds the liver's metabolic capacity, blood alcohol rises and symptoms of intoxication appear as the brain begins to be exposed to alcohol (Table 8-2).

Because alcohol cannot be stored in the body, it has absolute priority in metabolism as a fuel source. When needed, the liver also has two other pathways to metabolize alcohol. Each—along with alcohol dehydrogenase—produces acetaldehyde. The other pathways are the **microsomal ethanol oxidizing system (MEOS)** and the enzyme **catalase.** These other two systems are also active in other cells in the body.

microsomal ethanol oxidizing system (MEOS) An alternative pathway for alcohol metabolism when alcohol is in high concentration in the liver; uses rather than yields energy for the body, in contrast to alcohol dehydrogenase activity.

catalase An alternative enzyme pathway to alcohol metabolism; alcohol is broken down in conjunction with the breakdown of hydrogen peroxide (H_2O_2) by this enzyme.

Alcohol Dehydrogenase Pathway

During the first step, alcohol at a low to moderate quantity is converted to acetaldehyde by the action of alcohol dehydrogenase and the coenzyme NAD^+. NAD^+ (oxidized coenzyme form) picks up two hydrogens from the alcohol to form $NADH + H^+$ (reduced form) and produces the intermediate acetaldehyde (Fig. 8-2).

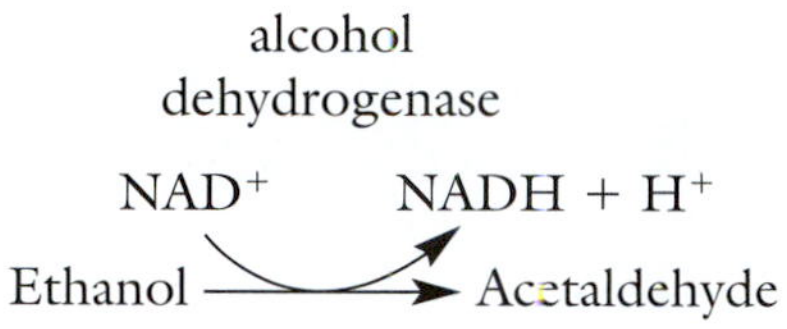

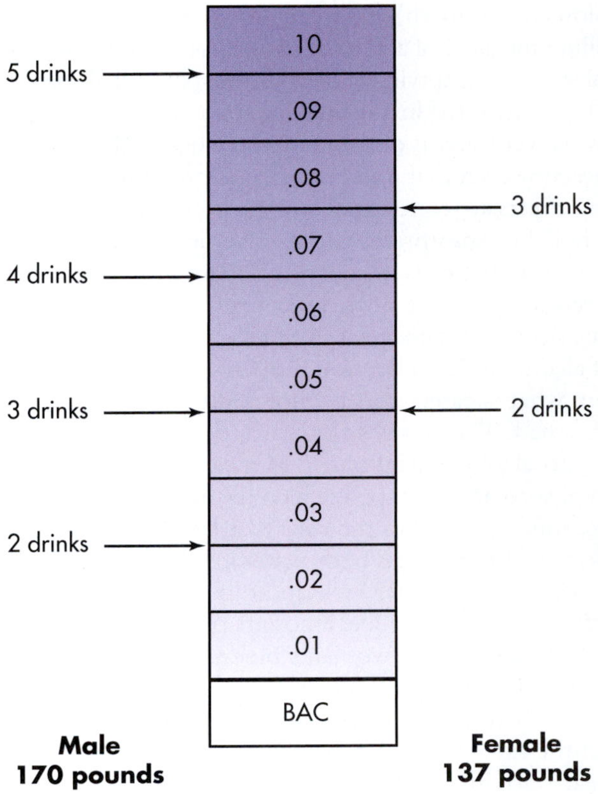

Figure 8-1 Approximate relationship between alcohol consumption and blood alcohol concentration (BAC). Note that effects can vary among people and whether food is also consumed. A BAC of 0.02 begins to impair driving. One is legally intoxicated at a BAC of 0.08 in most states in the United States and throughout Canada. In October 2003, 0.08 will be the U.S. standard.

Table 8-2 Blood Alcohol Concentration and Symptoms

Concentration*	Sporadic Drinker	Chronic Drinker	Hours for Alcohol to Be Metabolized
50 (party high) (0.05%)	Congenial euphoria; decreased tension; noticeable impairment in driving and coordination	No observable effect	2–3
75 (0.075%)	Gregarious	Often no effect	
100 (0.1%)	Uncoordinated; 0.1% would be legally drunk (as in drunk driving) in all states in the United States; note that 0.08% is legal drunkenness in Canada and in most states in the United States	Minimal signs	4–6
125–150 (0.125–0.15%)	Unrestrained behavior; episodic uncontrolled behavior; legally drunk	Pleasurable euphoria or beginning of uncoordination	6–10
200–250 (0.2–0.25%)	Alertness lost; lethargic	Effort is required to maintain emotional and motor control.	10–24
300–350 (0.3–0.35%)	Stupor to coma	Drowsy and slow	
>500 (>0.5%)	Some will die	Coma	>24

*Milligrams of alcohol per 100 milliliters of blood (mg/dl).

Modified from Wyngaarder JB, Smith LH: *Cecil Textbook of Medicine*, fourth edition, Philadelphia, 1988, WB Saunders. Used with permission.

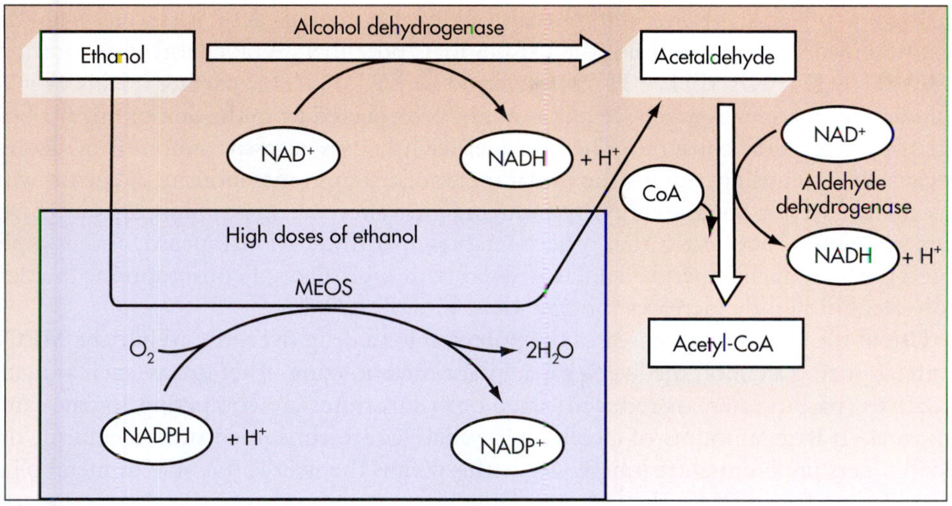

Figure 8-2 Alcohol metabolism. At low alcohol intake, the alcohol dehydrogenase pathway in the cytoplasm is used. At high alcohol intake, the microsomal ethanol oxidizing system (MEOS) in the cytoplasm also is used. The MEOS uses rather than yields energy.

Illustration by William Ober.

Distinctly different forms of alcohol dehydrogenase are found in the liver and the stomach. Each varies in its rate of alcohol metabolism. This enzyme requires the mineral zinc for activity.

The acetaldehyde formed is then converted to acetyl-CoA, again yielding NADH + H^+ with the aid of aldehyde dehydrogenase and coenzyme A.

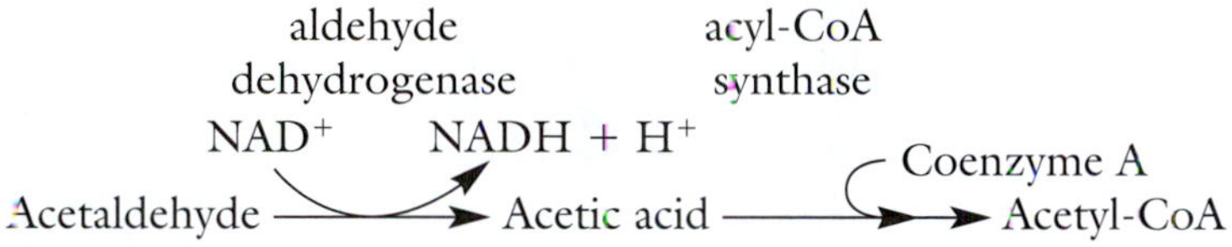

The increase in NADH + H^+ may promote fatty acid synthesis and reduce fatty acid oxidation, with accumulation of body fat.[20] For any acetyl-CoA that enters the citric acid cycle, the NADH + H^+, $FADH_2$, and GTP molecules produced can then be used to synthesize ATP via the electron transport chain (review Chapter 4).

Structurally, ethanol with its hydroxyl group (-OH) resembles a carbohydrate. However, since it is converted directly into acetyl-CoA, alcohol carbons cannot support glucose production. Thus, alcohol is metabolized more like a fatty acid than a carbohydrate and is considered fat in metabolic terms.

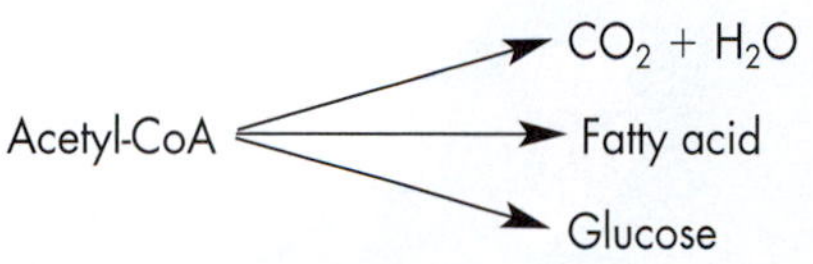

Metabolic fates of acetyl-CoA.

Microsomal Ethanol Oxidizing System (MEOS)

When a person drinks moderate to excessive amounts of alcohol, the enzyme alcohol dehydrogenase cannot keep up with the demand to metabolize all of the alcohol into acetaldehyde. For this and other reasons, another enzyme system exists to metabolize alcohol. This system is called the microsomal ethanol oxidizing system (MEOS).

The liver (and other body cells as well) uses the MEOS to metabolize drugs and other foreign substances. When the liver is overwhelmed with excess amounts of alcohol, it treats the excess as a foreign substance and activates the MEOS. This system uses oxygen—another niacin coenzyme ($NADP^+$)—and produces water and acetaldehyde. Once the MEOS is active, alcohol tolerance increases because the rate of alcohol metabolism increases.[19]

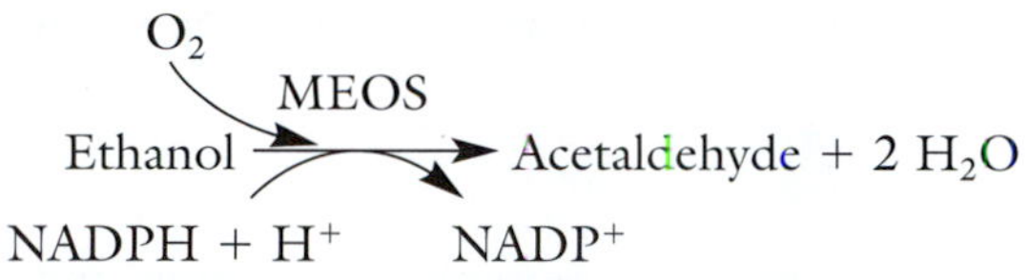

There are two interesting aspects of the body's reliance on MEOS. First, rather than forming the niacin-containing coenzyme, NADH + H^+ as with alcohol dehydrogenase, the MEOS uses the niacin-containing coenzyme NADPH + H^+, a compound

Compared with Caucasians, some Asians and Native Americans make relatively little aldehyde dehydrogenase, and so are more likely to suffer from hangovers.

Of all the alcohol sources, red wine is often singled out as the best choice because of the added bonus of the many phytochemicals (e.g., polyphenols) present.[20] These were leached out from the grape skins as the red wine was fermented. Recent studies also show that beer contains similar phytochemicals, but a lower amount.

analogous to NADH + H^+. Rather than yielding "potential" ATP molecules from the first step in alcohol metabolism, the MEOS *uses* "potential" ATP energy in the form of NADPH + H^+. NADPH + H^+ is converted to $NADP^+$. This partly explains why alcoholics do not gain as much weight as might be expected from the amount of alcohol-derived energy they consume. The liver inefficiently uses excessive amounts of alcohol because it requires energy for the initial metabolic step in metabolism. A person with alcoholism wastes some energy by inducing this alternate metabolic pathway. Liver damage from alcohol, such that other metabolic pathways are hampered, also is implicated in the reduced energy yield associated with high alcohol consumption. In addition, alcohol slightly increases the metabolic rate of the body.[17]

Use of the MEOS also increases the potential for a drug overdose. While the MEOS is metabolizing alcohol, the liver's capacity for metabolizing other drugs, such as many sedatives (barbiturates), is reduced, since both substrates are competing for the same enzymes. If large amounts of alcohol and sedatives are consumed simultaneously, the alcohol gets preferential treatment. Since this means the liver is not able to metabolize the sedatives fast enough, the user may lapse into a coma and even die. This is due to a lack of enzymes to convert the sedatives to harmless substances. Alcohol itself is toxic in high quantities. Mixed with sedatives, it creates an extremely lethal combination.

Catalase

The catalase enzyme found in the liver and other cells contributes to a minor pathway for metabolizing alcohol.[19] It is located in the cell organelle, the peroxisomes.

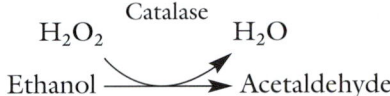

$$\text{Ethanol} + H_2O_2 \xrightarrow{\text{Catalase}} \text{Acetaldehyde} + H_2O$$

Benefits of Moderate Alcohol Use

One attribute of alcohol use is the pleasurable and social aspects experienced.

ischemic stroke A stroke caused by the absence of blood flow to a part of the brain.

The benefits of alcohol use are linked to specific intakes of about one drink a day for men and slightly less than one for women.[8] One standard drink is universally defined as one 12-ounce bottle of beer or wine cooler, one 5-ounce glass of wine, 3 ounces of sherry or liqueur, or 1.5 ounces of 80-proof distilled spirits. Note that beer ranges considerably in its alcohol content, with malt liquor being higher in alcohol than most other forms of beer.

The benefit of moderate alcohol use begins with the many pleasurable and social aspects of its use. People enjoy meeting a friend over a beer or settling down to a glass of wine in the evening with dinner. These behaviors are not considered excessive, as long as they are practiced by people of legal drinking age, remain under control, and cause no obvious harm. Development of cardiovascular disease and especially cardiovascular disease-related deaths, such as from coronary heart disease, are lower in middle-aged and older adults at risk for the disease who consume moderate amounts of alcohol.[10,12] **Ischemic stroke** risk also is decreased in light-to-moderate drinkers as opposed to those who abstain from alcoholic beverages.[5, 10] Still other potential health benefits are listed in Table 8-3.

Many of the benefits of moderate alcohol use are effective only in the short term, such as on an almost daily basis. More intermittent users and previous consumers of alcohol no longer experience the benefits of alcohol when consumption ceases.[12]

Concept | Check

Alcohol is not an essential nutrient. It requires no digestion, and alcohol metabolism takes precedence over metabolism of the other energy-yielding nutrients. Alcohol is metabolized in the liver and other tissues. Metabolism mostly depends on the enzyme alcohol dehydrogenase. A number of individual factors, such as gender,

Table 8-3 A Summary of Benefits and Risks of Alcohol Use[1, 2, 4, 5, 6, 9, 10, 11, 12, 13, 18, 20]

	Moderate Use	Alcohol Abuse
Coronary heart disease	Decreased risk of death in those at high risk for coronary heart disease-related death, primarily by increasing HDL-cholesterol in some people, decreasing blood clotting, and relaxing blood vessels	Heart rhythm disturbances, heart muscle damage, increased blood triglycerides and homocysteine
Hypertension and stroke	Mild decrease in blood pressure; less ischemic strokes in people with normal blood pressure	Increased blood pressure (hypertension); more hemorrhagic strokes
Peripheral vascular disease	Decreased risk due to reduced blood clotting	No benefit
Blood glucose regulation and type 2 diabetes	Some increase in insulin sensitivity and a decreased risk of death from cardiovascular disease	Hypoglycemia, reduced insulin sensitivity, and damage to pancreas (site of insulin production)
Bone and joint health	Some increase in bone mineral content in women, linked to increased estrogen output	Loss of active bone-forming cells and eventual osteoporosis (many nutrient deficiencies also contribute to the problem); increased risk of gout
Brain function	Enhanced brain function and decreased risk of dementia by increasing blood circulation in the brain	Brain tissue damage and decreased memory, especially in the teenage and young adult years
Skeletal muscle health	No benefit	Skeletal muscle damage
Cancer	No benefit	Increased risk of oral, esophageal, stomach, liver, lung, colorectal, and breast cancer, to name a few (especially if the person's diet is deficient in the vitamin folate). Breast cancer risk is elevated even more if a woman is on estrogen replacement therapy (e.g., for menopausal symptoms).
Liver function	No benefit	Fat infiltration and eventual cirrhosis, especially if a person is also infected with hepatitis C; iron toxicity
GI tract disease	Decreased risk of certain bacterial infections in the stomach	Inflammation of the stomach (and pancreas); absorptive cell damage leading to malabsorption of nutrients
Immune system function	No benefit	Reduced function and increased infections
Nervous system function	No benefit	Loss of nerve sensation and nervous system control of muscles
Sleep disturbances	Some relaxation	Fragmented sleep patterns; worsens sleep apnea
Impotence and decreased libido	No benefit	Contributes to the problem in both men and women
Drug overdose	No benefit	Contributes to the problem, especially with sedatives
Obesity	No benefit	Increased abdominal fat distribution, contributes to positive energy balance
Nutrient intake	May supply some B vitamins and iron	Leads to numerous nutrient deficiencies: protein, vitamins, and minerals
Alcoholism	No benefit	Increases risk of developing alcoholism
Fetal health	No benefit	Variety of toxic effects on the fetus when alcohol is consumed by pregnant women (see Chapter 16)
Socialization and relaxation	Provides some benefit to socialization and leads to relaxation by increasing **serotonin** and **dopamine** neurotransmitter activity	Contributes to violent behavior and agitation
Traffic deaths and other violent deaths	No benefit (and likely even an increase in traffic accidents)	Contributes to both traffic death and violent death

The risks from alcohol abuse begin at intake of more than two to three drinks per day for men and one to two drinks per day for both women and adults over age 65. Binge drinking (more than four drinks in a row for women and more than five drinks for men can be especially harmful [see the Nutrition Perspective]). The Swiss chemist Paracelsus (1493–1541) made the observation that "the dose determines the poison." This is especially true for alcohol, as alcohol abuse typically reduces a person's life expectancy by 15 years.[16]

race, and body composition, determine how a person reacts to alcohol. The microsomal ethanol oxidizing system (MEOS) is used whenever the liver detects more alcohol than can be processed by the alcohol dehydrogenase enzymes. Once the MEOS is active, alcohol tolerance increases because alcohol is being metabolized more rapidly.

The benefits of alcohol use are realized with moderate consumption. Under the correct circumstances, alcohol can be pleasurable, add to social occasions, and decrease the risk of coronary heart disease-related deaths and ischemic stroke. Mortality risk is somewhat greater in those who abstain from alcohol, and the risk appears to be decreased in men consuming up to two drinks per day. Furthermore, the protective dose of alcohol is somewhat less in women.

Health Problems from Alcohol Abuse

Alcohol intake encourages fat deposition, especially in the abdominal region.

Despite the benefits of regular, moderate alcohol use, the risks of abuse are more numerous and harmful. Alcoholism, in and of itself, is the third leading cause of preventable death in North America. In fact, excessive consumption of alcohol contributes significantly to 5 of the 10 leading causes of death in North America—heart failure, certain forms of cancer, cirrhosis of the liver, motor vehicle and other accidents, and suicides (review Table 8-3). Tobacco, often used simultaneously, interacts with alcohol in a way that reinforces its effects and causes esophageal and oral cancer. In addition, excessive alcohol drinking increases the risk of heart rhythm disturbances, hypertension and hemorrhagic stroke, osteoporosis, brain damage, colorectal and breast cancer, inflammation of the stomach lining, suppression of the immune system (and, thus, an increased risk of infections), sleep disturbances, impotence, hypoglycemia, and high blood triglycerides.[9,10] Figure 8-3 illustrates many of these risks. As mentioned before, alcohol ingestion also reduces use of fat by body cells and promotes a positive energy balance, thus contributing to risk for obesity, especially abdominal obesity.[17] Finally, by reducing the action of antidiuretic hormone, alcohol increases urination. Death from alcohol abuse usually results from respiratory failure or inhalation of vomit (the latter if the blood alcohol concentration is lower).

As a nutrient source, alcohol has little nutritional value and, thus, nutrient deficiencies are also a common result of alcoholism.[8] The protein and vitamin content is extremely low, except in beer, where it is marginal. Iron content varies from drink to drink, with red wine ranking especially high in iron. Excess use of some alcoholic beverages can even lead to iron toxicity, as well as that from lead or cobalt.

If a person were to use beer as a nutrient source, he or she would need to consume daily:

- 40 to 55 bottles (12-oz) to meet protein needs
- 65 bottles for thiamin needs
- 6 bottles for niacin needs

Many micronutrient deficiencies are seen in alcoholism. These arise mostly due to poor nutrient intakes, but fat malabsorption linked to poor pancreatic function and increased urinary losses are also important in some cases. On the other hand, micronutrient toxicity is also of concern, particularly with vitamin A and iron. In both cases, damage to the GI tract and liver enhance the potential for toxicity from these nutrients. Dr. Charles Halsted discusses these problems in detail in the Expert Opinion. The immediate aim in nutritional treatment of alcoholism is eliminating alcohol intake. Then attention turns to replenishing nutrient stores, generally with nutrient supplements.

A Closer Look at Cirrhosis

Long-term alcohol use causes fatty liver, inflammation of the liver (alcoholic hepatitis), and eventually cirrhosis. Cirrhosis is a chronic and usually relentlessly progressive disease characterized by fatty infiltration of the liver.[15] Fatty liver occurs in response to increased synthesis of fat and decreased utilization for energy by the liver. Eventually, the enlarged fat deposits choke off the blood supply, depriving the liver cells of oxygen and nutrients. Liver cells can accumulate so much fat that they burst and die and are replaced by connective (scar) tissue. This scarring process is called *cirrhosis*. When too many liver

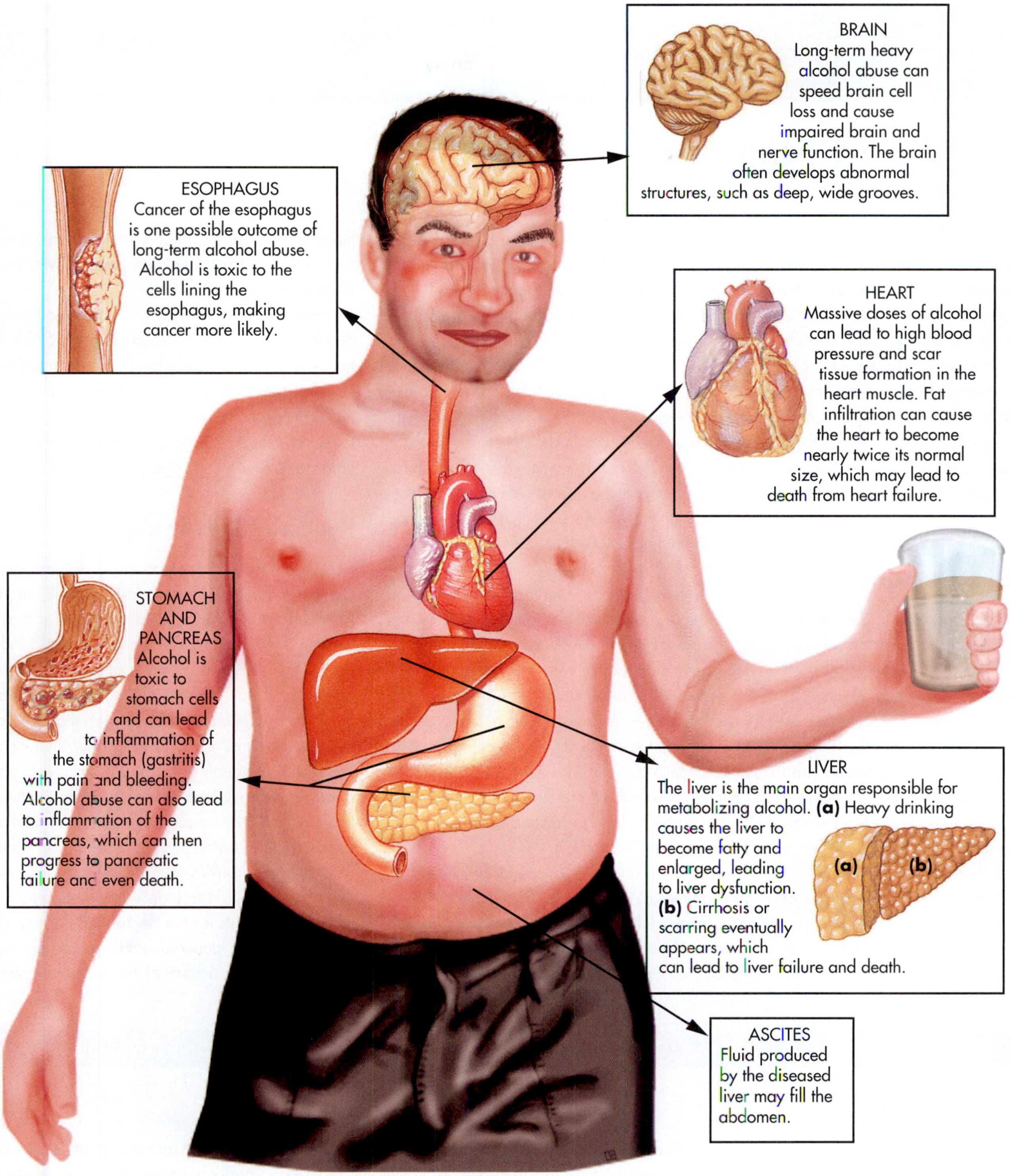
BRAIN
Long-term heavy alcohol abuse can speed brain cell loss and cause impaired brain and nerve function. The brain often develops abnormal structures, such as deep, wide grooves.
ESOPHAGUS
Cancer of the esophagus is one possible outcome of long-term alcohol abuse. Alcohol is toxic to the cells lining the esophagus, making cancer more likely.
HEART
Massive doses of alcohol can lead to high blood pressure and scar tissue formation in the heart muscle. Fat infiltration can cause the heart to become nearly twice its normal size, which may lead to death from heart failure.
STOMACH AND PANCREAS
Alcohol is toxic to stomach cells and can lead to inflammation of the stomach (gastritis) with pain and bleeding. Alcohol abuse can also lead to inflammation of the pancreas, which can then progress to pancreatic failure and even death.
LIVER
The liver is the main organ responsible for metabolizing alcohol. (a) Heavy drinking causes the liver to become fatty and enlarged, leading to liver dysfunction. (b) Cirrhosis or scarring eventually appears, which can lead to liver failure and death.
(a)
(b)
ASCITES
Fluid produced by the diseased liver may fill the abdomen.

Figure 8-3 Some effects of alcohol abuse on the body. The mind-altering effects of alcohol begin soon after it enters the bloodstream. Virtually every organ system is affected by alcohol. Within minutes, alcohol inhibits nerve cells in the brain. The heart muscle strains to cope with alcohol's depressive action. If drinking continues, rising blood alcohol causes impaired speech, vision, balance, and judgment. With an extremely high blood alcohol content, respiratory failure is possible. Over time, alcohol abuse increases the risk of liver and pancreas failure and certain forms of heart damage and cancer, among other disorders. Table 8-3 summarizes all the negative effects of excessive alcohol use on physical health.

Expert Opinion

Alcohol and Nutrition

Charles H. Halsted, M.D.

Nutritional problems are common among alcoholics. Alcohol abuse can interfere with nutrient intake if alcohol replaces some or all of the food in the diet. When an individual relies on alcohol for the majority of his or her energy needs, protein-energy malnutrition can result. The symptoms of this protein-energy malnutrition are similar to those seen in children with marasmus (see Chapter 7). In addition to potential protein and energy deficiencies, deficiencies of a variety of other nutrients are possible, particularly certain vitamins and minerals.

Water-Soluble Vitamins

Excessive alcohol intake can lead to deficiencies in the water-soluble vitamins thiamin, niacin, vitamin B-6, vitamin B-12, folate, and vitamin C (see Chapter 10 for more details on these effects). Thiamin deficiency can be caused by decreased intake or decreased absorption of thiamin. The typical symptoms include **polyneuropathy** and nervous system problems. Often patients with extreme thiamin deficiency are admitted to the hospital, and must be given thiamin injections to recover from this medical emergency, which, if untreated, can result in irreversible paralysis of ocular muscles, neuropathy with loss of sensation in lower extremities, loss of balance with abnormal gait, and memory loss. In patients with decreased thiamin stores, administration of large amounts of intravenous glucose can accelerate the symptoms of thiamin deficiency.

The metabolism of alcohol requires large quantities of niacin as NAD^+ and $NADP^+$, thus limiting the amount of niacin available for other metabolic activities in the body. If alcoholics consume a diet low in niacin and consume insufficient protein, they are at risk for niacin deficiency, and the corresponding classical deficiency disease, pellagra.

Acetaldehyde, the primary metabolite of alcohol, can interfere with vitamin B-6 metabolism. Acetaldehyde displaces B-6 from its binding protein, resulting in increased vitamin B-6 urinary excretion. If the alcoholic consumes a diet with inadequate amounts of vitamin B-6, he or she is at risk for developing **sideroblastic anemia** and peripheral neuropathy.

Excessive alcohol intake can also impair the absorption of vitamin B-12 as a result of decreased release of the digestive enzyme trypsin by the pancreas. Trypsin is needed to release vitamin B-12 from the R-protein, so that it can then be bound by intrinsic factor and be absorbed by the body (see Chapter 10).

Insufficient intake of folate by an individual who abuses alcohol can be especially problematic. Folate deficiency may lead to a decreased number of absorptive cells in the small intestine, which then can result in decreased absorption of many other nutrients. **Megaloblastic anemia** is not uncommon in folate-depleted patients who consume excess alcohol.

Vitamin C deficiency can ultimately lead to the development of scurvy. When more than 30% of total energy intake comes from alcohol, vitamin C intake is usually less than the RDA. Daily supplementation may be required for weeks or months to restore blood and urinary vitamin C concentrations back to normal ranges.

Fat-Soluble Vitamins

Excessive alcohol intake can also result in deficiencies in the fat-soluble vitamins A, D, E, and K (see Chapter 9 for more details on these effects). Vitamin A deficiency may be caused by a deficient diet, increased metabolism and biliary excretion, or by an inability of the liver to produce the vitamin A (retinol)-binding protein that delivers the vitamin to all parts of the body. Vitamin A stores in individuals with alcoholism are diminished regardless of whether dietary vitamin A intake is low, adequate, or high. Vitamin A concentrations are especially low in individuals with alcoholic cirrhosis. Chronic alcohol consumption is thought to induce metabolic systems in the liver that hasten the degradation of vitamin A. In addition, a pancreas damaged by alcohol releases a smaller amount of the enzymes needed

polyneuropathy A disease process involving a number of peripheral nerves.

sideroblastic anemia A form of anemia characterized by red blood cells containing an internal ring of iron granules. This anemia may respond to vitamin B-6 treatment.

megaloblastic anemia A form of anemia characterized by large, nucleated, immature red blood cells that result from the inability of precursor cells to divide normally.

cells die, the liver dies, and the alcoholic patient dies. In North America, most cases of cirrhosis are caused by alcohol consumption. Cirrhosis develops in about 15 to 20% of cases of alcoholism and affects about 2 million people in the United States alone. It is the second leading cause of the need for liver transplants. In addition to the amount and duration of alcohol consumption, genetic factors and individual differences determine one's risk for the disease, such as obesity, exposure to hepatotoxins (e.g., acetaminophen [Tylenol™]), and infections with hepatitis C.[14] Note that about 4 million people in the United States are infected with the virus that causes hepatitis C. Once a person has cirrhosis, there is a 50% chance of death within 4 years, a far worse prognosis than many forms of cancer. Most of the deaths from alcoholic cirrhosis occur in people between the ages of 40 and 65 years. The actual death rate in the United States is 8.8 per 100,000 people.

Alcoholism is a common cause of micronutrient malnutrition in North America.

to digest fat than a healthy pancreas, that, together with decreased bile secretion in alcoholic liver disease, results in decreased capacity to solubilize fat-soluble vitamins and reduced vitamin A absorption. Finally, alcohol can interact with beta-carotene, a precursor of vitamin A, ultimately reducing the amount of beta-carotene converted to vitamin A. Many alcoholics have trouble seeing in the dark (night blindness) due to this alcohol-induced vitamin A deficiency.

Vitamin D deficiency can result from inadequate dietary intake of the vitamin and/or lack of exposure to sunlight. A pancreas damaged by alcohol releases fewer fat-digesting enzymes, resulting in decreased fat absorption and consequently, decreased vitamin D absorption. A liver damaged by alcohol is compromised in its ability to convert vitamin D to the biologically active hormone form. Vitamin D deficiency can also result in reduced calcium absorption and increased parathyroid hormone secretion, both of which can lead to the development of osteoporosis.

Deficiencies in vitamins E and K also occur in individuals who have alcohol-damaged pancreases. Here again, the damaged pancreas is less able to release necessary digestive enzymes, leading to impaired digestion and absorption of fat and fat-soluble nutrients. Individuals with alcoholic liver disease are less able to synthesize vitamin K-dependent clotting factors, while individuals with vitamin E deficiency can develop peripheral neuropathy and tunnel vision.

Minerals

Individuals who abuse alcohol can also develop problems with magnesium, zinc, and iron metabolism (see Chapters 11 and 12 for more details on these effects). Severe alcohol abuse can result in magnesium deficiency by increasing urinary excretion of this mineral. Alcoholics can develop low blood concentrations of magnesium, which can result in **tetany,** characterized by muscle twitches, cramps, carpopedal spasms, and seizures. In addition, impairment of the central nervous system can also result. Magnesium deficiency is partly responsible for the hallucinations experienced by people withdrawing from alcohol intoxication.

Alcoholics can develop zinc deficiency as a result of decreased zinc absorption as well as increased urinary excretion. The consequences of alcoholism combined with zinc deficiency include changes in taste and smell, loss of appetite, trouble seeing at night, and impaired wound healing.

Both iron deficiency and iron overload are possible in alcoholics. Excessive alcohol consumption can damage the gastrointestinal tract and cause GI bleeding. This bleeding can eventually result in an iron deficiency. In contrast, alcohol can also increase the uptake and storage of iron in the liver, which can hasten the development of cirrhosis.

Clinicians need to be aware of the nutrition-related problems that can occur in alcoholism. Nutrient repletion is an important aspect of the treatment plan for alcoholic patients.

Dr. Halsted is professor of Internal Medicine and Nutrition in the division of Endocrinology, Clinical Nutrition and Vascular Metabolism at the University of California–Davis School of Medicine. Dr. Halsted is editor of the American Journal of Clinical Nutrition *and has published widely on the effects of alcohol on nutritional health.*

A number of possible mechanisms underlie the liver damage from alcohol abuse. In chronic alcoholism, acetaldehyde concentration also increases in the liver, and is thought to be the underlying cause of the toxic effects of alcohol.[15] Another cause of liver damage is the production of free radicals from alcohol metabolism. These highly reactive molecules destroy cell membranes and DNA. A by-product of free radical damage, inflammation, can destroy healthy liver tissue.

No specific amount of alcohol consumption guarantees cirrhosis. One perceptible pattern is that cirrhosis commonly results from a 10-year or longer consumption of approximately 80 g of alcohol (the equivalent of seven beers) per day. Some evidence suggests that damage is caused by a dose as low as 40 g/day for men and 20 g/day for women. Early stages of alcoholic liver injury are reversible, but advanced stages usually are not. If a person is terminally ill, a liver transplant is necessary for survival.

tetany A state marked by sharp contraction of muscles with failure to relax afterward; usually caused by abnormal calcium metabolism.

The overt signs of liver failure associated with cirrhosis are jaundice (the whites of the eyes and the skin turn yellow), **ascites** (fluid produced by the liver accumulates in the abdomen), and significant enlargement of the veins in the neck.

A nutritious diet helps prevent some complications associated with alcoholism, but usually alcoholism brings about serious destruction of vital tissues regardless of the quality of the food consumed. Laboratory animal studies show clearly that, even when a nutritious diet is consumed, alcohol abuse can lead to cirrhosis. Still, deficient nutritional status compounds the problem of cirrhosis, as it makes the liver more vulnerable to toxic substances by depleting supplies of antioxidants, such as vitamins E and C. If present in adequate amounts, these two vitamins can reduce free radical damage to the liver. A folate deficiency also compounds the damage. Because of this observation, daily use of a balanced multivitamin and mineral supplement is especially important for people who abuse alcohol.

Other Problems Associated with Alcohol Abuse

Some people even have food-related allergic and asthmatic reactions to alcohol.

Many social problems accompany the medical problems associated with alcohol abuse.

Problem Drinking in the Workplace

Problem drinking can result in decreased job performance, an increased number of sick days, interference with regular sleep at home, and increased sleeping on the job. Accidents, violence, suicide, and workplace problems are often caused in part by the misuse of alcohol.[7] Rather than ignoring the issue, it is important that these alcohol-related problems be addressed. We all know people who dislike their jobs or a specific coworker. Because we spend about one-third of our lives working, the job environment can have a strong effect on quality of life. Workplace alienation can lead to drinking. Some workplace cultures accept and encourage alcohol consumption, whereas others forbid or discourage this behavior. Alcohol availability is strongly linked to consumption in the workplace. Sometimes it is very easy to bring alcohol onto the job site. Employer-sponsored health promotion programs may help reduce employee drinking and increase awareness of these issues.

Drinking and driving should never be combined. The consequences are dangerous and possibly deadly.

Operation of Motor Vehicles and Related Equipment

It is extremely dangerous to mix drinking with activities requiring sound judgment and responsibility. Driving, boating, athletics, and water sports are all activities in which alcohol does not belong. Consuming alcohol prior to or during these and many other activities increases the risk of injury to oneself and others because it reduces coordination and judgment. In 2001 there were 17,500 deaths related to drunk driving in the United States. Most occur in the age group 21–24 years. Note the warning label on alcoholic beverages regarding drinking and driving.

Sexually Transmitted Diseases

sexually transmitted disease (STD) A contagious disease usually acquired by sexual intercourse or genital contact. Common examples include AIDS, gonorrhea, and syphilis. Also called venereal disease.

Due to the inhibition-reducing effect of alcohol, drinking increases the incidence of high-risk sexual activity and infection by a **sexually transmitted disease (STD).** Unplanned and unprotected sexual intercourse often results from overconsumption of alcohol. Multiple sex partners also increase the risk for contracting an STD, as well as hepatitis C and HIV/AIDS.

Unplanned Pregnancy

fetal alcohol syndrome (FAS) A group of irreversible physical and mental abnormalities in the infant that result from the mother's consuming alcohol during pregnancy.

Along with STDs, an unplanned pregnancy can be the result of unprotected sex while under the influence of alcohol. And, if the drinking continues during the first month of pregnancy, the chances of delivering an infant with **fetal alcohol syndrome** increase[8] (see Chapter 16).

Children of Alcoholics

Alcoholism affects the entire family. Children of alcoholics have a hard time developing in a normal way. Living with an alcoholic family member causes stress for everyone, and, for a child, this dysfunction reduces the chances of becoming intellectually, culturally, and socially independent. Almost one in four North American children grow up with an alcoholic in the family, and this environment influences children's perception of alcohol use, especially when it comes to their own decisions about this issue. Children of alcoholics often have long-lasting emotional problems, which carry over into adulthood.

Critical | Thinking

When people consume alcohol, they often do things they would not normally do. Unplanned sexual activity, the damaging of property, and other harmful events can occur. For many people, drinking and smoking go hand-in-hand. What risks and diseases could correlate with the combination of these behaviors with excessive alcohol use?

Concept | Check

Excessive alcohol use can result in an array of medical problems. It increases the risk of developing hypertension, certain forms of strokes and heart damage, birth defects, inflammation of the pancreas, damage to the brain, and malnutrition, to name a few. Furthermore, alcoholism interferes with all aspects of family, professional, and social life.

Guidance Regarding Alcohol Use

The U.S. Surgeon General's office, the National Academy of Science, and the USDA/DHHS do not specifically recommend drinking alcohol. The text of the *2000 Dietary Guidelines for Americans* (discussed in Chapter 2) does mention alcohol intake. It contains this statement: "Drinking in moderation may lower risk for coronary heart disease, mainly among men over age 45 and women over age 55. However, there are other factors that reduce the risk of heart disease, including a healthy diet, physical activity, avoidance of smoking, and maintenance of a healthy weight. Moderate consumption provides little, if any, health benefit for younger people." All groups, however, caution that if adults do consume alcohol, they should (1) drink alcohol only in moderation with meals (no more than two drinks a day for men and one for women or anyone over age 65 years); (2) avoid drinking any alcohol before or while driving, operating machinery, taking medications, or engaging in any other activity requiring sound judgment; and (3) avoid drinking alcohol while pregnant.

Recall from Chapter 2 that one of the *2000 Dietary Guidelines for Americans* is: "If you drink alcoholic beverages, do so in moderation." As our understanding of the relationship between drinking alcohol and health grows, nutritionists and other health professionals can promote healthy lifestyles—not by encouraging indiscriminate drinking—but rather by reassuring the public that light-to-moderate alcohol consumption may have beneficial health outcomes.

There is no recommendation for a nondrinker to start consuming alcohol for health benefits, but people of legal age who have one drink or so each day, and are not prone to abuse, should know there's nothing wrong with moderate drinking (as long as they are not putting others at risk). In fact, as shown earlier, many studies have shown that light-to-moderate alcohol consumption—defined as no more than one drink per day for women and older adults and no more than two drinks per day for men—has a protective effect against death from ischemic stroke, coronary heart disease, and type 2 diabetes.[6]

Currently, about 32% of all North American adults have three drinks or less each week, about 22% have two drinks or less a day, and only about 11% have more than two drinks a day.

Young people benefit most from a healthy diet and exercise to decrease future risk of cardiovascular disease. There is no related benefit at this age for alcohol use.

Healthy People 2010 set an important goal regarding alcohol use: Reduce by 25% the proportion of adults who exceed the guidelines for appropriate alcohol use (currently, 73% of those who consume alcohol).

Alcohol Dependency and Abuse

Many factors determine a person's chances of developing **alcohol dependence.** Studies have shown links tying gender, genetics, ethnicity, parental influence, nurture, and

alcohol dependence The person experiences repeated alcohol-related difficulties, such as inability to control use, spending a great deal of time associated with alcohol use, continued use of alcohol despite physical or psychological consequences, persistent desire or unsuccessful efforts to cut down or control alcohol use, and withdrawal symptoms. Tolerance is also seen.

alcohol abuse The person experiences severe alcohol-related problems, such as an inability to fulfill major obligations, use in hazardous situations (e.g., driving), related legal problems, or use despite social and interpersonal difficulties.

depression to alcohol dependency and abuse.[8] For some people, alcohol can be addictive and dangerous, and can eventually lead to **alcohol abuse.** This is true for about 10 to 15% of men and 5% of women in Western countries who drink alcohol. Such alcohol abuse leads to 100,000 deaths in the United States each year.

Some studies suggest that 40 to 60% of a person's risk for alcoholism comes from genetic factors, although the gene, or genes, have not been identified.[16] The genetic influence on alcohol dependency and abuse has been indicated by a number of studies, including twin and adoption research. Twins and first-degree relatives share a tendency toward alcohol addiction. Children of alcoholics have a fourfold-increased risk of developing alcoholism, even when adopted by a family with no history of alcoholism. This suggests that individuals with a family history of alcoholism need to be especially alert for evidence of the early signs of alcohol dependence.

It is suggested that children with a family history of alcoholism be warned of the dangers of drinking by the age of 10.[3] At this age, they are old enough to understand the consequences of alcoholism but are not yet under the strong influence of their peers. Children as young as 10 may begin experimenting with alcohol to feel grown up, to fit in and belong to a group, to relax and feel good, to take risks and rebel against authority, or simply to satisfy curiosity. When there are alcoholic beverages available in the home, it is easy for a child to sample a variety of drinks and to share them with friends.

Ability to "hold one's liquor" is a strong indicator of genetic risk.

A low threshold of response to alcohol may be genetic. If this is the case, it requires greater amounts of alcohol to produce the desired effect. Other studies question the relative importance of the genetic component. Any one of us can become addicted if we drink long enough and consume ever-increasing quantities of alcohol.

Gender plays a key role in alcohol metabolism, dependency, and, surprisingly, treatment. The male:female ratio of alcohol dependency is 4:1, but there is evidence that women delay seeking treatment for alcohol abuse. As previously noted, the recommended limit for alcohol use is also different for men and women, as women's bodies have more fat and less muscle tissue than do men's. Alcohol can be diluted by water-holding muscle tissue, but not by adipose tissue. As also mentioned before, women cannot metabolize alcohol as quickly as men and, so, it remains in their blood longer. Higher blood alcohol concentrations make women more susceptible to alcoholic liver disease, heart muscle damage, cancer, and brain injury.

Many ethnic distinctions play an important role in the probability of alcohol dependency and abuse. Compared with Caucasians, Asians and Native Americans are very susceptible to the damaging effects of alcohol for reasons discussed earlier. The major cause of death among Native Americans is unintentional injuries related to alcohol use, especially high rates of motor vehicle accidents. Other alcohol-related mortality statistics confronting Native Americans are suicide, homicide, domestic abuse, and fetal alcohol syndrome. African American alcoholics are at greater risk than other racial groups for tuberculosis, hepatitis C, HIV/AIDS, and other infectious diseases. Hispanic Americans are at particular risk for cirrhosis-related death.[15]

Critical | Thinking

Jose is a well-liked 17-year-old. It always seems as if everything is going his way—an A on a test, a scholarship to his dream school, you name it. Lately, however, Jose has experienced some disappointments. His grandfather has just passed away, and he and his girlfriend of 6 months have broken up. When he arrived home late with the smell of alcohol on his breath, his parents started to worry. They talked to his school counselor, who suggested they look for certain signs that could indicate depression and/or alcohol dependence. What might those signs be?

Depression and alcohol abuse often go hand-in-hand. Researchers have discovered that the risk for heavy drinking is higher among women with a history of depression than among women with no such history. This finding holds up even when other factors that increase the risk of heavy drinking, such as age, family history of drinking, and personality disorder, are accounted for. The more symptoms of depression women report, the more likely they are to drink heavily. There may be several reasons for this association. One reason is self-medication to relieve the symptoms of depression. Research has shown that, although alcohol may alleviate depression in the short term, it tends to increase it over time. A second reason is that women who are more depressed may not pay attention to their drinking and may not be concerned about the effects it can have on their health and behavior.

The majority of suicides and interfamily homicides are alcohol-related. Clinicians need to be careful when dealing with depressed alcoholic patients to determine the psychological reasons for their drinking and how these behaviors might cause the death of the alcoholic or a family member. Alcohol consumption appears to be associated with youth suicide. The younger the drinker, the more likely he or she is to commit suicide.[2]

Alcohol dependence is the most common psychiatric disorder, affecting 13% of the North American population. Overall, about $185 billion is spent annually in terms of lost productivity, premature deaths, direct treatment expenses, and legal fees associated with alcoholism in the United States alone. A liver transplant costs about $150,000 and is needed in cases of excessive alcohol use. On the positive side, it costs only about $5000 to treat a person who is abusing alcohol with a typical counseling program. Identifying alcoholism early can be a way to control and decrease health-care costs.

Alcohol addiction is seen frequently among homeless individuals.

Alcoholism Diagnosis

Alcoholism is often considered a two-phase problem. Initially, it begins as problem drinking. This includes the repetitive use of alcohol, often to alleviate anxiety or solve other emotional problems. Alcohol addiction, the second phase, is defined as a true addiction following the repeated use of alcohol.

The diagnosis of alcoholism is based on a list of major criteria. These criteria do not fit every individual but are commonly seen in cases of alcoholism:[7]

- Physiologic dependence on alcohol manifested by evidence of withdrawal symptoms when intake is interrupted
- Tolerance to the effects of alcohol, prompting greater alcohol intake to achieve the desired effect
- Evidence of alcohol-associated illnesses such as alcoholic liver disease or irreversible brain damage exhibited by memory loss, inability to concentrate, and decline in intellectual functions
- Continued drinking in defiance of strong medical and social contraindications and disruptions in normal life
- Depression and blackouts, as well as impairment in social and occupational functioning

Other signs of alcoholism include the basic alcohol stigmas: alcohol odor on the breath, flushed face and reddened skin (the latter due to breakage of small blood vessels, which allows blood to seep under the skin), and nervous system disorders, such as tremors. Unexplained work absences, frequent accidents, and falls or injuries of vague origin may all lead a clinician to consider the possibility of alcoholism. Laboratory tests are also helpful. These tests include measures of liver function, enlarged red blood cell size, and triglyceride and uric acid concentrations in the blood.

Do You Have a Problem with Alcohol?

Asking a person about the quantity and frequency of alcohol consumption is an important means of detecting abuse and dependence. The CAGE questionnaire is commonly used in routine health care.[7]

C: Have you ever felt you ought to *cut* down on drinking?

A: Have people *annoyed* you by criticizing your drinking?

G: Have you ever felt bad or *guilty* about your drinking?

E: Have you ever had a drink first thing in the morning to steady your nerves or get rid of a hangover (*eye-opener*)?

More than one positive response to the CAGE questionnaire suggests an alcohol problem. Another key point to probe is tolerance. Does it take more to make you inebriated than it did in the past?

Alcohol use often begins in young adulthood and is carried into later years.

Other questions to ask along with the CAGE questionnaire are:

1. Have you had memory lapses or blackouts due to drinking?
2. Do you continue to drink even though you have health problems caused by alcohol?
3. Do you get withdrawal symptoms, such as headaches, chills, shakes, and a strong craving for alcohol, and, as a result, drink more to get rid of these symptoms?

4. Do you take part in high-risk behaviors, such as having unsafe sex in a nonmonogamous relationship or driving a boat or car when under the influence of alcohol?
5. Has drinking caused trouble at home, at work, or in relationships with others?
6. Do you have to drink alcohol for any of the following reasons?
   a. To get through the day or unwind at the end of the day
   b. To cope with stressful life events
   c. To escape from ongoing problems

Answering yes to any of these questions should prompt the respondent to consult a family physician or a certified counselor for help.

Treatment of Alcoholism

Once a diagnosis of alcohol abuse or dependence is established, one should seek the guidance of a physician to arrange appropriate treatment and counseling for the person and family.[7] An important goal of counseling is to identify ways to compensate for the loss of pleasure from drinking. This helps the drinker confront the immediate problem of how to stop drinking. Total abstinence must be the ultimate objective. For alcoholics, there is no such thing as controlled drinking. A problem drinker cannot return safely to social drinking.

The person should enter an Alcoholics Anonymous (AA) 12-step program (Al-Anon for the spouse), or another reputable therapy program for people with alcoholism. For more information, one can check with a local mental health treatment center for programs available in the community or call 800-245-4656. Substance Abuse and Mental Health Services can be reached at 800-729-6686 or www.health.org for alcohol and drug information. In addition, one may visit the Alcoholics Anonymous web page at www.alcoholics-anonymous.org or contact AA at:

To learn more about alcoholism, visit these websites:
www.niaaa.nih.gov
www.asam.org
www.mentalhelp.net/selfhelp

AA World Services, Inc.
P.O. Box 459
New York, NY 10163
212-870-3400

According to AA's literature, "AA is a fellowship of men and women who share their experience, strength, and hope with each other that they may solve their common problem and help others recover from alcoholism." As an informal society chartered in 1935, Alcoholics Anonymous includes more than 2 million recovered alcoholics. The only requirement for membership is the desire to stop drinking. There are no rules, regulations, dues, or fees. In addition, the group is not a political or formal organization.

It is helpful for the spouse to join the treatment program as well. AA has two types of meetings—open and closed. Alcoholics and their families and friends are invited to the open meetings, whereas the closed meetings are reserved for alcoholics only.

Current research does not support the generally negative public opinion about the prognosis for alcoholism. In most job-related alcoholism treatment programs, wherein workers are socially stable and—because of the risk to jobs and pensions—well motivated, recovery rates reach 60% or more. This remarkably high cure rate is probably accounted for by early detection. Once a person moves from problem drinking to an advanced stage of alcoholism, success rates seldom exceed 50%. Early identification and intervention remain the most important steps in the treatment of alcoholism. Success is usually proportionate to participation in AA, other social agencies' programs, and religious counseling. About 2 years of treatment should be expected.

Two medications are available to treat alcoholism. The medication naltrexone (ReVia) blocks the craving for alcohol and the pleasure of intoxication (Fig. 8-4). Disulfiram (Antabuse) causes physical reactions, such as vomiting, when drinking alcohol. It does so by blocking acetaldehyde metabolism. Detoxification drugs are also important in treating alcoholism, as is using some form of psychotherapy.[7]

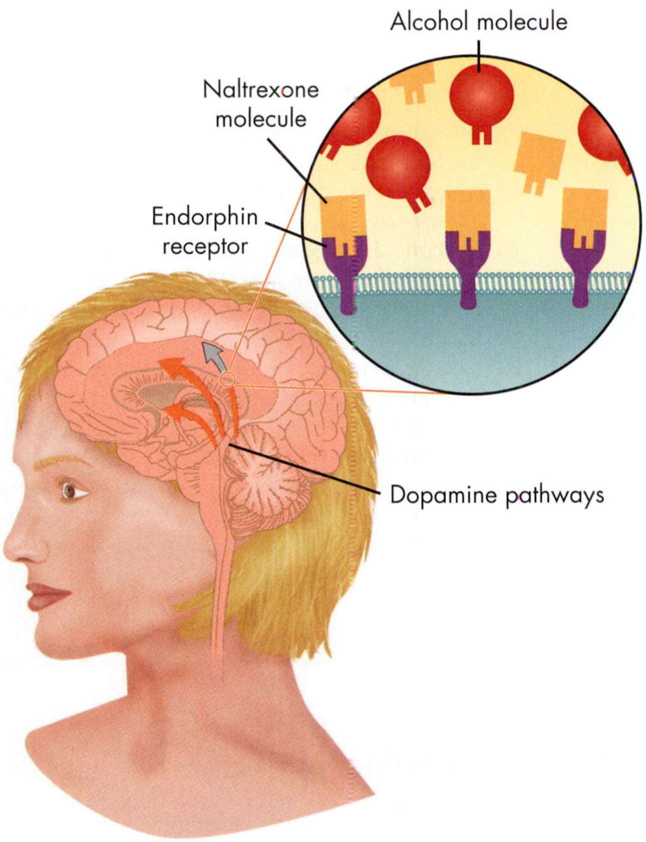

Figure 8-4 The euphoria that arises from alcohol use involves alcohol binding to specific receptors in the brain. It is likely that this binding, in turn, causes a release of the neurotransmitter dopamine. The increase in dopamine in the brain is thought to cause the characteristic high associated with alcohol use. Naltrexone (ReVia) works by blocking alcohol's ability to bind to brain receptors. This, then, reduces dopamine release and blocks the pleasant feelings elicited by alcohol use.

Concept | Check

Treatment of alcoholism often includes the use of medicine, counseling, and social support. The clinicians involved must treat the entire person. Alcoholics Anonymous and other support groups are very helpful. Naltrexone can be prescribed to decrease alcohol cravings. Another option is disulfiram, which produces an ill feeling when the patient consumes both the medicine and alcohol. With all of the treatments for alcoholism, it is important to find the one that works best for the individual with alcoholism.

Case Scenario | Follow-up

Alcohol is a central nervous system depressant that affects both respiration and heart rate. In large quantities, alcohol can depress both systems to the point of terminating respiration and cardiac function. Obviously, this is fatal. Alcohol abuse is a common problem, and continued alcohol abuse can lead to dependence problems, although alcohol abuse and dependence are different.

As a close friend, Alyssa has a responsibility to hold Todd accountable for his actions. Sometimes it is difficult to realize that one has a drinking problem, although it may be obvious to others. Alyssa should talk privately to Todd when he is sober and calm about the most recent incident. It is important to deal with situations such as these very carefully, as the problem drinker will probably respond defensively. She could explain how his drinking is causing problems for both of them, she could tell him about the harmful consequences of his drinking, and she could refuse to go with him to any alcohol-related events, but she must be prepared to carry out the threat. Alyssa could talk with a counselor, who may help her learn ways to approach Todd effectively. Offering to go with Todd to a treatment program or an AA meeting and get help is one idea. There is strength in numbers, so other members of Todd's family or close friends also should be enlisted to help, under the guidance of a therapist trained in treating alcoholics.

There is no such thing as controlled drinking once a person has alcoholism. Total abstinence is mandatory.

Summary

1. Alcohol use is a complex issue because it involves psychological, social, economic, health, legal, and family issues.
2. Alcohol is metabolized in the liver and other tissues. Metabolism depends on the enzyme alcohol dehydrogenase. A number of factors, such as gender, race, and body composition, determine how a person reacts to alcohol.
3. The body uses the microsomal ethanol oxidizing system (MEOS) whenever the liver detects more alcohol than can be processed by the alcohol dehydrogenase enzymes. Once the MEOS is active, alcohol tolerance increases because alcohol is being metabolized more rapidly.
4. The benefits of alcohol use are associated with low-to-moderate alcohol consumption. These benefits include the pleasurable and social aspects of alcohol use, a reduction in various forms of cardiovascular disease-related deaths, increase in insulin sensitivity, and protection against some harmful stomach bacteria.
5. Alcohol use also creates many health risks. Excessive consumption of alcohol contributes significantly to 5 of the 10 leading causes of death in North America. Alcohol increases the risk of developing certain forms of heart damage, inflammation of the pancreas, GI tract damage, vitamin and mineral deficiencies, cirrhosis of the liver, certain forms of cancer, hypertension, and hemorrhagic stroke—to name a few.
6. If alcohol is consumed, it should be consumed in moderation with meals. Women are advised to drink no more than one drink per day, as are adults 65 years and older; men are advised to limit intake to two drinks a day.
7. Gender, genetics, ethnic background, and ongoing depression all determine a person's chances of becoming alcohol dependent.
8. Early detection of alcoholism is key to successful treatment and a reduction of health-care costs. The CAGE questionnaire can help a person determine whether or not he or she has an alcohol problem.
9. Many methods are available to treat alcoholism. Alcoholics Anonymous and the medication ReVia are among the typical approaches.

Study Questions

1. Where in the body does most of the metabolism of alcohol take place? What is a by-product of alcohol metabolism?
2. Why does it take a woman longer than a man to metabolize alcohol?
3. List two potential health benefits of alcohol use.
4. List four problems associated with alcohol abuse.
5. Which two nutrient deficiencies are common in alcoholism? Why?
6. Define the term *one drink*. How much alcohol use is considered to be moderate for men? for women?
7. Why can some ethnic groups hold their liquor better than others can?
8. Name four criteria that might indicate someone has a problem with alcohol. What is this group of criteria checklist called?
9. Describe a method used in treating alcoholism. List a pro and con.
10. After reading the Nutrition Perspective, answer the following: What is binge drinking? Within which segment of the population is this increasing in popularity?

Annotated References

1. Abramson JL and others: Moderate alcohol consumption and risk of heart failure among older persons. *Journal of the American Medical Association* 285:1971, 2001.

   Moderate alcohol consumption was found to reduce the risk of heart failure in older people. The authors of the study caution, however, that heavy consumption can lead to negative cardiovascular outcomes. Thus individuals should continue to be cautioned against drinking excessive amounts of alcohol.

2. Ajani UA and others: Alcohol consumption and risk of type 2 diabetes mellitus among U.S. male physicians. *Archives of Internal Medicine* 160:1025, 2000.

   Healthy men who consumed light-to-moderate amounts of alcohol had a decreased risk of developing type 2 diabetes. The effect is likely due to positive effects on insulin action in the body.

3. American Academy of Pediatrics Committee on Substance Abuse: Alcohol use and abuse: A pediatric concern. *Pediatrics* 108:185, 2001.

   Alcohol use and abuse by children and adolescents continues to be a major health problem. Health professionals who work with children and adolescents should ask questions about alcohol use by himself or herself, within the family, and by friends.

4. Baer DJ and others: Moderate alcohol consumption lowers risk factors for cardiovascular disease in postmenopausal women fed a controlled diet. *American Journal of Clinical Nutrition* 75:593, 2002.

   Consuming one to two drinks per day improved blood lipoprotein profiles in women. This subject showed a decline in LDL-cholesterol and triglycerides, and an increase in HDL-cholesterol.

5. Berger K and others: Light-to-moderate alcohol consumption and the risk of stroke among U.S. male physicians. *The New England Journal of Medicine* 341:1557, 1999.

   One to four drinks per week reduced the risks of total stroke and of ischemic stroke in a group of healthy, predominantly White physicians. The authors suggest, however, that any public health recommendation that emphasizes the positive aspects of alcohol would likely do more harm than good.

6. Davies MJ and others: Effects of moderate alcohol intake on fasting insulin and glucose concentrations and insulin sensitivity in postmenopausal women. *Journal of the American Medical Association* 287:2559, 2002.

   Moderate alcohol use increases insulin sensitivity in women. This may reduce future risk of type 2 diabetes.

7. Enoch MA, Goldman D: Problem drinking and alcoholism: Diagnosis and treatment. *American Family Physician* 65(3):441, 2001.

Excellent review on the diagnosis and treatment of alcoholism. Problem drinking is to be especially discouraged. This is defined as more than seven drinks per week or more than three drinks per occasion for women, and more than 14 drinks per week or more than four drinks per occasion for men.

8. Health risks and benefits of alcohol consumption. *Alcohol Research & Health* 24 (1):5, 2000.

   The lowest observed risk for overall mortality is associated with an average of 10 g of alcohol (<1 drink) per day for men, and slightly less for women. Still, in people at low risk for death from cardiovascular diseases, alcohol provides little or no reduction in overall mortality.

9. Hines LM: Genetic variation in alcohol dehydrogenase and the beneficial effect of moderate alcohol consumption on myocardial infarction. *The New England Journal of Medicine* 344:549, 2001.

   Certain genetic differences influence the effective alcohol on HDL-cholesterol synthesis. The genetic difference in this study specifically was linked to the activity of the enzyme aldehyde dehydrogenase.

10. Klatsky AL: Drink to your health? *Scientific American* p. 75. February 2003.

    Moderate alcohol use provides some health benefits, but alcohol abuse poses many health risks. In light of current knowledge, a person with an established moderate drinking pattern should generally not be advised to abstain from alcohol. However, nondrinkers should not be advised to start drinking for health reasons.

11. Lamon-Fava S: High-density lipoproteins: Effects of alcohol, estrogen, and phytoestrogens. *Nutrition Reviews* 60(1):1, 2002.

    Alcohol increases HDL-cholesterol by increasing the synthesis of the apolipoprotein that makes up this lipoprotein. This may be a major reason why moderate alcohol use reduces cardiovascular disease risk.

12. Mukamal KJ and others: Roles of drinking pattern and type of alcohol consumed in coronary heart disease in men. *The New England Journal of Medicine* 348:109, 2003.

    Men who drank alcohol at least three to four times per week had a reduced risk of myocardial infarction. The association was strongest with beer and liquor, the predominant types of beverage consumed by this population.

13. Rapuri PB and others: Alcohol intake and bone metabolism in elderly women. *American Journal of Clinical Nutrition* 72:1206, 2000.

    Moderate alcohol use in women was associated with an increase in bone mass. This may be due to the ability of alcohol to increase blood estrogen concentrations.

14. Riley TR, Bhatti AM: Preventive strategies in chronic liver disease. Part 1. Alcohol, vaccines, toxic medications and supplements, diet and exercise. *American Family Physician* 64:1555, 2001.

    Alcohol consumption can lead to alcoholic hepatitis, fatty infiltration of the liver, accelerated progression of liver disease, and certain forms of liver cancer. The daily consumption of more than four drinks of alcohol increases the risk of these disorders. People infected with hepatitis C especially should abstain from alcohol, as this worsens the negative effects of alcohol on the liver.

15. Riley TR, Bhatti AM: Preventive strategies in chronic liver disease. Part 2. Cirrhosis. *American Family Physician* 64:1735, 2001.

    Cirrhosis is a relatively frequent cause of death in the United States. Alcohol abuse is a major risk factor for this disease.

16. Schuckit MA: Alcohol and alcoholism in Braunwald E and others (eds.): *Harrison's Principles of Internal Medicine.* 15th ed. New York: McGraw-Hill, 2001.

    This chapter provides support for the content in the chapter, as well as further details regarding alcohol and alcoholism. One disturbing statistic mentioned is that men and women who abuse alcohol decrease their life span by approximately 15 years, even if the people have high levels of education and socioeconomic functioning.

17. Schutz Y: Role of substrate utilization and thermogenesis on body-weight control with particular reference to alcohol. *Proceedings of the Nutrition Society* 59:511, 2000.

    Alcohol metabolism tends to reduce the metabolism of fatty acids in the liver. This could be one reason why alcohol abuse leads to fatty buildup in the liver.

18. Singletary KW, Gapstur SM: Alcohol and breast cancer: Review of epidemiologic and experimental evidence and potential mechanisms. *Journal of the American Medical Association* 286:2143, 2001.

    Consumption of more than one drink per day increases breast cancer risk in women. The effect is especially pronounced with three or more drinks per day.

19. Suter PM: Alcohol: Its role in health and nutrition in Bowman BA, RM Russell (eds.): *Present knowledge in nutrition.* Washington, DC: ILSI Press, 2001.

    Alcohol contributes about 5% of calories to the U.S. diet, but in a heavy drinker, this would rise to 50%. A healthy person can metabolize about 5 to 7 g of alcohol per hour.

20. Wollin SD, Jones PJH: Alcohol, red wine, and cardiovascular disease. *Journal of Nutrition* 131:1401, 2001.

    Moderate alcohol use has a protective effect on cardiovascular disease, especially related deaths. The choice of red wine may provide the greatest effect as it contributes a variety of phytochemical compounds as well as alcohol.

Take | Action

I. Could You or Someone You Know Have a Problem with Alcohol?

Problem drinking often has its seeds in the teen years. Significant health consequences of this practice typically arise in adulthood. A prominent contributor to 5 of the 10 leading causes of death in North America, misuse of alcohol is a common preventable health problem. The social consequences of alcohol dependency include divorce, unemployment, and poverty. The following questionnaire was developed by the National Council on Alcoholism. With this assessment, you can determine whether you or someone you know might need help. Answer the following questions by placing an "X" in the appropriate blank.

	Yes	No
1. Do you occasionally drink heavily after disappointment, after a quarrel, or when someone gives you a hard time?	____	____
2. When you have trouble or feel under pressure, do you drink more heavily than usual?	____	____
3. Have you ever noticed that you're able to handle liquor better than you did when you first started drinking?	____	____
4. Do you ever wake up the morning after you've been drinking and discover that you can't remember part of the evening before, even though your friends tell you that you didn't pass out?	____	____
5. When drinking with other people, do you try to have a few extra drinks when others won't know it?	____	____
6. Are there certain occasions when you feel uncomfortable if alcohol isn't available?	____	____
7. Have you recently noticed that when you begin drinking, you're in more of a hurry to get the first drink than you used to be?	____	____
8. Do you sometimes feel a little guilty about your drinking?	____	____
9. Are you secretly irritated when your family or friends discuss your drinking?	____	____
10. Have you recently noticed an increase in the frequency of memory blackouts?	____	____
11. Do you often find that you wish to continue drinking after your friends say they've had enough?	____	____
12. Do you usually have a reason for the occasions when you drink heavily?	____	____
13. When you're sober, do you often regret things you have done or said while drinking?	____	____
14. Have you tried switching brands or following different plans to control your drinking?	____	____
15. Have you often failed to keep promises you've made to yourself about controlling or stopping your drinking?	____	____
16. Have you ever tried to control your drinking by changing jobs or moving to a new location?	____	____
17. Do you try to avoid family or close friends while you're drinking?	____	____

	Yes	No
18. Are you having an increasing number of financial and work problems?	____	____
19. Do more people seem to be treating you unfairly without good reason?	____	____
20. Do you eat very little or irregularly when you're drinking?	____	____
21. Do you sometimes have the "shakes" in the morning and find that it helps to have a little drink?	____	____
22. Have you recently noticed that you can't drink as much as you once did?	____	____
23. Do you sometimes stay drunk for several days at a time?	____	____
24. Do you sometimes feel very depressed and wonder whether life is worth living?	____	____
25. Sometimes after periods of drinking do you see or hear things that aren't there?	____	____
26. Do you get terribly frightened after you have been drinking heavily?	____	____

Interpretation

These are all symptoms that may indicate alcoholism. "Yes" answers to several of the questions indicate the following stages of alcoholism:

Questions 1–8:	Potential drinking problem
Questions 9–21:	Drinking problem likely
Questions 22–26:	Definite drinking problem

It is vital that people assess themselves honestly. If you or someone you know demonstrates some or a number of these symptoms, it is important that help be sought. If there is even a question in your mind, go talk to a professional about it. Alcohol abuse is one of many problems adults, including older people, face.

II. Investigate Alcohol Use with the CAGE Questionnaire.

Have a few of your friends complete the CAGE questionnaire on page 275. What observations have you made? Alcoholism often has its seeds in young adulthood. Do you see evidence of that in you or your friends?

Binge Drinking

College students are drinking more heavily and more frequently than ever before. Excessive alcohol consumption is an even bigger problem than illicit drug use on college campuses today (Table 8-4). Many college students consider drinking alcohol to be a "rite of passage" into adulthood. The heaviest drinking population in North America is young, Caucasian college students. Bars near campus typically promote heavy drinking. Alcohol producers frequently target college students with advertising and other marketing efforts. Adding to the overall problem is that typically half of all college students are not of legal drinking age. In fact, the annual overall cost related to alcohol use by those under 21 is estimated at more than $58 billion dollars. This estimate includes costs associated with violent crime, traffic accidents, treatment, and alcohol poisonings, among others.

Binge drinking is also common among college students. Young athletes are more likely to abuse alcohol this way than their nonathlete peers. Drunken athletes are more likely to drive while drinking, fight, experience memory loss, and be in academic trouble. This binging is defined as four or more drinks in a row for women and five or more for men. **Acute alcohol intoxication** is a major cause of suicide and

acute alcohol intoxication A temporary deterioration in mental function, accompanied by muscular incoordination and partial paralysis as a result of drinking alcoholic beverages too rapidly.

Healthy People 2010 recommends an important goal regarding binge drinking: Reduce by at least one-half the number of high school and college students engaging in binge drinking (currently estimated at 32% and 40%, respectively).

Table 8-4 Sobering Statistics on the Yearly Impact of Binge Drinking on College Campuses

Death: 1400 college students between the ages of 18 and 24 die each year from alcohol-related unintentional injuries, including motor vehicle crashes.

Injury: 500,000 students between the ages of 18 and 24 are unintentionally injured under the influence of alcohol.

Assault: More than 600,000 students between the ages of 18 and 24 are assaulted by another student who has been drinking.

Sexual abuse: More than 70,000 students between the ages of 18 and 24 are victims of alcohol-related sexual assault or date rape.

Unsafe sex: 400,000 students between the ages of 18 and 24 had unprotected sex and more than 100,000 students between the ages of 18 and 24 having been too intoxicated to know if they consented to having sex.

Academic problems: About 25% of college students report academic consequences of their drinking, including missing class, falling behind, doing poorly on exams or papers, and receiving lower grades overall.

Health problems/Suicide attempts: More than 150,000 students develop an alcohol-related health problem and between 1.2 and 1.5% of students indicate that they tried to commit suicide within the past year due to drinking or drug use.

Drunk driving: 2.1 million students between the ages of 18 and 24 drove under the influence of alcohol last year.

Vandalism: About 11% of college student drinkers report that they have damaged property while under the influence of alcohol.

Property damage: More than 25% of administrators from schools with relatively low drinking levels and over 50% from schools with high drinking levels say their campuses have a "moderate" or "major" problem with alcohol-related property damage.

Police involvement: About 5% of 4-year college students are involved with the police or campus security as a result of their drinking and an estimated 110,000 students between the ages of 18 and 24 are arrested for an alcohol-related violation, such as public drunkenness or driving under the influence.

Alcohol abuse and dependence: 31% of college students met criteria for a diagnosis of alcohol abuse and 6% for a diagnosis of alcohol dependence in the past 12 months, according to questionnaire-based self-reports about their drinking.

The consequences of excessive and underage drinking affect virtually all college campuses, college communities, and college students, whether they choose to drink or not.

Source: www.collegedrinkingprevention.gov/facts/snapshot.aspx

hazing deaths related to binge drinking. Regular binge drinking also often leads to academic failure. About 50% of college students practice binge drinking.

Binge drinking has a variety of contraindications. It can lead to unplanned sexual activity, damaged property, injury to oneself or others, and death. Death due to alcohol misuse can result, for example, from inhalation of vomit. In other cases, the body systems slowly shut down due to alcohol's overpowering depressant effect (Table 8-5). Other injuries can occur, resulting in paralysis or other lifelong medical problems. For example, in 2000, a student at the University of Michigan rapidly drank 20 shots to celebrate his 21st birthday and died shortly after with a blood alcohol concentration of 0.39%. A student at Old Dominion University choked to death on his own vomit during a pledge-week drinking binge. A student at Ohio State University on the diving team became so intoxicated he dove head-first while "mud-diving." He is lucky to be alive but is paralyzed from the neck down. Still other students have drowned while intoxicated, even though they knew how to swim.

Many problems associated with binge drinking can affect all aspects of life. Binge drinkers are more likely to miss class, damage property, and experience impaired academic performance than are students who are light drinkers or abstainers. Students who live around binge drinkers experience more unwanted sexual advances, assaults, and insults/humiliations. Bingers often do not think they have a problem because binge drinking has become so acceptable on college campuses.

According to U.S. law, one must be 21 years old to drink in all 50 states. In Canada, one must be age 18 or 19, depending on the province. However, alcohol use often begins in adolescence. For example, 31% of 12th-graders in the United States reported frequent drinking during 1999, and about 11% of all alcohol consumed is done so by those under 21. Premature alcohol use is often seen in conjunction with athletics, as older, highly visible role models advertise products or are seen consuming alcohol. Peer pressure at school and on sports teams can cause many adolescents to drink. These habits become dangerous when young adults choose to drive drunk or ride with friends who are intoxicated. They are also creating habits that may continue and worsen throughout their lives. Education and prevention strategies should focus on behavioral and psychosocial consequences because athletic performance typically does not suffer initially.[3]

Efforts to curb binge drinking on college campuses are taking a variety of approaches:

- Developing student activities that don't involve alcohol
- Enforcing strict policies against alcohol on campus
- Creating an environment less conducive to drinking; for example, dorms could ban the practice of stacking empty beer cans in rooms
- Informing incoming freshmen through marketing and ad campaigns that they don't have to drink to be part of a group
- Reducing off-campus availability of alcohol

Overall, it is important that binge drinkers be aware that these habits can cause lifelong problems, especially when such drinking becomes habitual. Note also that older adults also contribute to the over 1 billion episodes of binge drinking each year in the United States. Prevention then cuts across most of society.

Table 8-5 Signs and Symptoms of Alcohol Poisoning

Being aware of the warning signs and dangers of alcohol poisoning is important. It could help save the life of someone you love. The warning signs and symptoms include the following:

- Semiconsciousness or unconsciousness
- Slow respiration of eight or fewer breaths per minute or lapses between breaths of more than 8 seconds
- Cold, clammy, pale, or bluish skin
- Strong odor of alcohol, which usually accompanies these symptoms

Note: Although these are obvious warning signs of alcohol poisoning, the list is certainly not all inclusive.

Critical | Thinking

Imagine you are president of your college or university where there is a tradition of the "fourth-year fifth," a long-standing practice of seniors to consume a fifth of liquor during the last quarter/semester prior to graduation. Every weekend between 3 and 10 students arrive in the local emergency room with alcohol poisoning or alcohol-related injuries, and there are several alcohol-related deaths each year. As the head of this institution, how do you and the Board of Trustees tackle this problem?

Know your limit when you party: two drinks for men and one drink for women, and certainly no binge drinking.

chapter 9

The Fat-Soluble Vitamins

Chapter | Outline

Case | Scenario

Kristen works nights at a local package distribution center to make some extra money. The combination of taking a full course load at college and working nights has created a lot of stress for her. Kristen's many commitments also make it important that she not become ill. On a recent coffee break at her job, a co-worker suggested she take *Nutramega* supplements to help prevent colds, flu, and other illnesses. The product's label suggests that *Nutramega* helps prevent such problems, especially those associated with the changing of seasons. The label recommends taking two to three tablets every 3 hours at the first sign of a decline in well-being, and two to three tablets daily for health maintenance. Kristen looks at the Supplement Facts label on the bottle and finds that each tablet contains (as percent of the Daily Value): 33% for vitamin A (three-quarters of which is preformed vitamin A), 700% for vitamin C, 50% for zinc, and 10% for selenium. A month's supply also costs about $50.

Should Kristen use this product? Are there health risks associated with this product, especially considering the dosage recommended on the label?

Refresh | Your Memory

As you study Chapter 9 on fat-soluble vitamins, you may want to review:

- Implications of the Dietary Supplement Health and Education Act (DSHEA) in Chapter 1.
- The gastrointestinal system for the digestion and absorption of fat-soluble nutrients in Chapter 3.
- Oxidation and reduction reactions in Chapter 4.
- The digestion and absorption of dietary lipids and the formation of lipoproteins in Chapter 6.
- Protein synthesis in Chapter 7.

Boost | Your Study

Check out the ***Perspectives in Nutrition: Online Learning Center*** **www.mhhe.com/wardlawpers6** *for quizzes, flash cards, activities, and web links designed to further help you learn about the fat-soluble vitamins.*

Chapter | Objectives

Chapter 9 is designed to allow you to:

1. Define the term *vitamin* and list three characteristics of vitamins as a group.
2. Classify the vitamins according to whether they are fat-soluble or water-soluble.
3. List the major functions and deficiency symptoms for each fat-soluble vitamin.
4. State the conditions in which deficiencies of fat-soluble vitamins are likely to occur.
5. List three important food sources for each fat-soluble vitamin.
6. Describe toxicity symptoms from excess consumption of certain fat-soluble vitamins.
7. Evaluate the use of vitamin and mineral supplements with respect to their potential benefits and hazards to the body.

At one time, nutrition was mainly identified with macronutrients and minerals. Then, in the early twentieth century, tiny amounts of organic molecules were found to prevent or even reverse striking sets of physical symptoms. These compounds were given the name "vitamines," a shorter version of the expression: "vital amines." Eventually, it was realized that these compounds were not all amines (nitrogen-containing compounds), but the name remained, except that the "e" was dropped and the word "vitamin" was created. Some of these compounds are lipids and are known as the fat-soluble vitamins. In some circumstances, severe deficiencies of fat-soluble vitamins still occur, though this is not the only health issue with these vitamins.[5] Researchers are also considering whether intake of certain vitamins in excess of our current estimates of human needs, such as vitamin E, can prevent certain health problems that are not strictly deficiency diseases (e.g., cardiovascular disease). This remains a controversial area.[14] In contrast, there can also be toxicity of vitamins, especially for vitamin A.[6,7]

Recently two companion articles in the *Journal of the American Medical Association* recommend all adults take a multivitamin and mineral supplement daily.[5] The rationale is that for many of us our diets are so unbalanced. Should you jump on this supplement bandwagon?

This chapter begins with concepts on vitamins in general. Then, the bulk of the chapter is given to specific concepts on fat-soluble vitamins including body processing, functions, food sources, and signs and symptoms of a deficiency. The need for vitamin and mineral supplementation is then addressed. Chapter 10 reviews water-soluble vitamins.

Vitamins: Vital Dietary Components

Vegetables are rich sources of many vitamins.

By definition, vitamins are essential organic (carbon-containing) substances needed in small amounts in the diet for the normal function, growth, and maintenance of body tissues. Although vitamins themselves provide no energy to the body, some can facilitate energy-yielding chemical reactions. Vitamins A, D, E, and K dissolve in organic solvents, such as ether and benzene, and are referred to as fat-soluble vitamins. The B-vitamins and vitamin C, in contrast, dissolve in water and are the water-soluble vitamins.

Vitamins are generally indispensable in human diets because they can't be synthesized in sufficient quantities to meet individual need, or synthesis is curtailed by environmental factors, or they can't be synthesized at all. Vitamins such as niacin and vitamin D can be synthesized by the body under certain conditions, and vitamin K and biotin are synthesized to some extent by bacteria in the intestinal tract.

To be designated a vitamin, the substance must be organic, must carry out one or more biochemical or physiological reactions in the body, and must be required in the diet in very small quantities. Also, if the vitamin intake is insufficient to meet needs, a deficiency occurs, accompanied by a measurable decline in health. If the deficiency is not too far advanced, the symptoms disappear when the vitamin is restored to the body.

In addition to their use in correcting deficiency diseases, a few vitamins have also proved useful as pharmacological agents in treating a limited number of nondeficiency diseases. These medical applications often require the administration of **megadoses,** well above the typical human needs for the vitamin. For example, megadoses of a form of niacin are used as part of blood cholesterol-lowering treatment for appropriately selected individuals (see the Nutrition Perspective in Chapter 6). Another example is the use of vitamin D **analogs** for psoriasis. Nevertheless, at this time any claimed benefits for the use of vitamin supplements, especially intakes in excess of the Upper Limit (if set) should be viewed critically because many unproved claims have been, and are continually, made.[7, 8, 9]

megadose Generally an intake of a nutrient in excess of 10 times of human needs.

analog A chemical compound that differs slightly from another naturally occurring compound. Analogs generally contain extra or altered chemical groups and may have similar or opposite metabolic effects, compared with the native compound.

Both plant and animal foods supply vitamins in the human diet. Whether isolated from foods or synthesized in the laboratory, vitamins are the same chemical compounds and generally work equally well in the body. Contrary to claims in the health-food literature, "natural" vitamins isolated from foods are for the most part no more healthful than those synthesized in a laboratory, but there are exceptions. Vitamin E is about twice as potent in its natural form compared to its synthetic form.[8] On the other hand, folic acid, the synthetic form of the vitamin added to grain products, is more potent than the natural form, folate. Some vitamins exist in several related forms that differ in chemical or physical properties. These forms exist both in nature and in synthesized vitamin supplements. It is important to have enough of the specific vitamin forms that the body can use; the various forms will be identified throughout this chapter and Chapter 10.

Historical Perspective on the Vitamins

Long before any vitamins had been identified, certain foods were known to cure illnesses brought on by what we now recognize to be vitamin deficiencies. The ancient Egyptians, for example, treated night blindness with topical applications of juice extracted from liver, a rich source of vitamin A. As you'll see, vitamin A plays a critical role in vision. During the fifteenth and sixteenth centuries, British sailing ships did not carry sufficient amounts of fresh fruits and vegetables with them for long sea voyages. This resulted in a tremendous loss of life. In one expedition, 1000 men set out from England for the Pacific but only 145 returned. The rest had died from the disease known as scurvy. Scientists eventually discovered that lime juice cured scurvy; after lemons and limes were included as a routine part of British sailors' rations, cases of scurvy declined greatly. We now know that this disease, marked by weakness, blood vessel rupture, and poor immune function, results from a deficiency of vitamin C.

As scientists began to identify various vitamins, related deficiencies, such as scurvy, were dramatically cured. For the most part, as the vitamins were discovered, they were named alphabetically: A, B, C, D, and E. Later, some substances originally classified as vitamins were found not to be essential for humans and were dropped from the list, such as vitamin P. Other vitamins thought at first to have a single chemical form turned out to exist in many forms, so "vitamin B" now comprises eight separate entities.

It took some time to uncover the true nature of the various vitamins. For example, when scientists realized that both protein foods and nicotinic acid (a form of the vitamin niacin) can cure pellagra, they eventually went on to discover that the amino acid tryptophan can be synthesized into niacin. Finally, as mentioned, it was determined that some vitamins (such as biotin and vitamins D and K) can be synthesized by the body or bacteria present in the intestinal tract.

We can be relatively confident that all vitamins needed by humans have been discovered. The ability of total parenteral nutrition (TPN) to support human life for years strongly supports this view. With TPN, the patient receives intravenously a carefully formulated preparation containing all necessary nutrients. The gastrointestinal tract is completely bypassed, as no food or beverages are consumed. Those who receive protein, carbohydrate, fat, and all known vitamins and essential minerals in this manner may continue not only to live but also to build body tissue, have a baby, heal wounds, and combat existing diseases. Although a difficult way to meet nutrient needs, it is a lifesaver for those who need it.

Evidence suggests that health declines when choline, a substance the body makes, is not included in a diet during some life stages, such as growth spurts. Thus, one day choline may be added to the list of known vitamins. Currently, an Adequate Intake (AI) has been established. This is discussed later in more detail in Chapter 10.

Storage of Vitamins in the Body

Except for vitamin K, the fat-soluble vitamins are not readily excreted from the body. In contrast, most water-soluble vitamins are generally lost from the body quite rapidly, partly because the water in cells dissolves these vitamins and flushes them out of the body via the kidneys. Two exceptions are vitamin B-12 and vitamin B-6, which are stored much more readily than the other water-soluble vitamins. Because of the limited storage of many vitamins, they should be consumed in the diet daily, although an occasional lapse in the intake of even water-soluble vitamins generally causes no harm. An average person, for example, must consume no thiamin for 10 days or no vitamin C for 20 to 40 days before developing the first signs and symptoms of a related deficiency. The signs and symptoms of a vitamin deficiency occur only when that vitamin is lacking in the diet and body stores are essentially exhausted.

Vitamin Toxicity

Because fat-soluble vitamins are not readily excreted, some can easily accumulate in the body and cause toxic effects. And, although a toxic effect from an excessive intake of any vitamin is theoretically possible, toxicities of the fat-soluble vitamin A and the water-soluble vitamin B-6 are those most likely to occur.[7, 9] Vitamin D can also cause toxic effects, especially in infants.[8] These vitamins are unlikely to cause toxic effects unless taken in supplement (pill) form. However, vitamin A can cause toxicity with long-term intake beginning at just 2 to 4 times human needs, especially in older adults, as they can't readily excrete any excess amounts.[6, 7]

Critical | Thinking

Many vitamin supplements supply nutrients in amounts that exceed the Daily Values listed on the label. Miguel believes that "more is better." How can you explain to him that the supplement he is about to start taking is "worse," since it contains amounts that exceed the Daily Values by 10 times for many nutrients, including vitamin A ?

Because regular use of a "one-a-day" type of multivitamin and mineral supplement usually contains less than 2 times the Daily Values of the components, this practice is unlikely to cause toxic effects in adults. But consuming many vitamin pills can cause problems. See the Nutrition Perspective at the end of this chapter to explore whether you should take a multivitamin and mineral supplement and, if so, how to do it safely.

Malabsorption of Vitamins

Vitamins consumed in foods must be absorbed efficiently from the intestine to meet body needs. If absorption of a vitamin is defective, a person must consume larger amounts of it or he or she is likely to develop deficiency symptoms. As discussed in a following section, fat malabsorption resulting from various diseases is associated with poor absorption of the fat-soluble vitamins.[7, 8, 9] Alcohol abuse and certain intestinal diseases also can lead to malabsorption of some B-vitamins (e.g., thiamin and folate).

Preservation of Vitamins in Foods

Substantial amounts of vitamins in foods can be lost from the time a fruit or vegetable is picked until it is eaten. The water-soluble vitamins—particularly thiamin, vitamin C, and folate—can be destroyed with improper storage and excessive cooking. Heat, light, exposure to the air, cooking in water, and alkalinity are all factors that can destroy vitamins. The sooner a food is eaten after harvest, the less chance of nutrient loss.

In general, if the food is not eaten within a few days, freezing is the best method to retain nutrients. In fact, frozen vegetables and fruits are often as nutrient-rich as supermarket-fresh ones. Frozen foods are often processed immediately after harvesting. As part of the freezing process, vegetables are quickly blanched in boiling water. This destroys the enzymes that would otherwise degrade the vitamins. Table 9-1 provides some tips to aid in preserving the vitamins in food.

The rapid cooking of vegetables in minimal fluids aids in preserving vitamin content. Stir-frying is one possible method.

Absorption of the Fat-Soluble Vitamins

The discussion of the individual fat-soluble vitamins—A, D, E, and K—begins by looking at how they are absorbed (Fig. 9-1). You can see from the chemical structures at the beginning of each vitamin section that these vitamins are lipidlike molecules. Because these vitamins are absorbed along with dietary fat, adequate absorption of the fat-soluble vitamins depends on efficient fat absorption. This, in turn, depends on fat digestion, utilizing bile salts and the enzyme lipase in the small intestine, as well as adequate absorptive capacity from a healthy intestinal wall. Under these conditions, about

Table 9-1 Tips for Preserving the Vitamin Content of Foods

What to Do	Why
Keep fruits and vegetables cool.	Enzymes in food begin to degrade vitamins once the fruit or vegetable is picked. Chilling reduces this process. Refrigerate fresh produce (except for potatoes, tomatoes, bananas, and onions) until they are consumed.
Refrigerate foods in moisture-proof containers.	Nutrients keep best at temperatures near freezing, at high humidity, and away from exposure to air.
Avoid trimming and cutting fruits and vegetables into small pieces as much as possible.	The more surface exposed, the faster oxygen breaks down vitamins. Keep in mind the outer leaves of lettuce and other greens have higher values of vitamins and minerals than the inner, tender leaves or stems. Potato skins and apple skins are higher in vitamins, minerals, and phytochemicals than the inner parts.
To retain the maximum amounts of nutrients in vegetables, microwave cooking, steaming, or using a pan or wok with very small amounts of cooking oil and a tight-fitting lid is best.	The less contact with water and the shorter the cooking time, the more nutrients are retained. Whenever possible, cook fruits or vegetables in their skins.
Minimize reheating food.	Prolonged reheating reduces vitamin content.
Do not add fats to vegetables during cooking if you plan to discard the liquid.	Discarding fat can lead to loss of fat-soluble vitamins in the liquid. Add fats to vegetables after they are fully cooked and drained.
Don't add baking soda to vegetables to enhance the green color.	Alkalinity destroys much vitamin D, thiamin, and other vitamins.
Store canned goods in a cool place.	To get maximal nutritive value from the canned goods, serve any liquid packed with the food whenever possible. Canned foods vary in the amount of nutrients lost, largely because of differences in storage time and temperatures in the canning process.

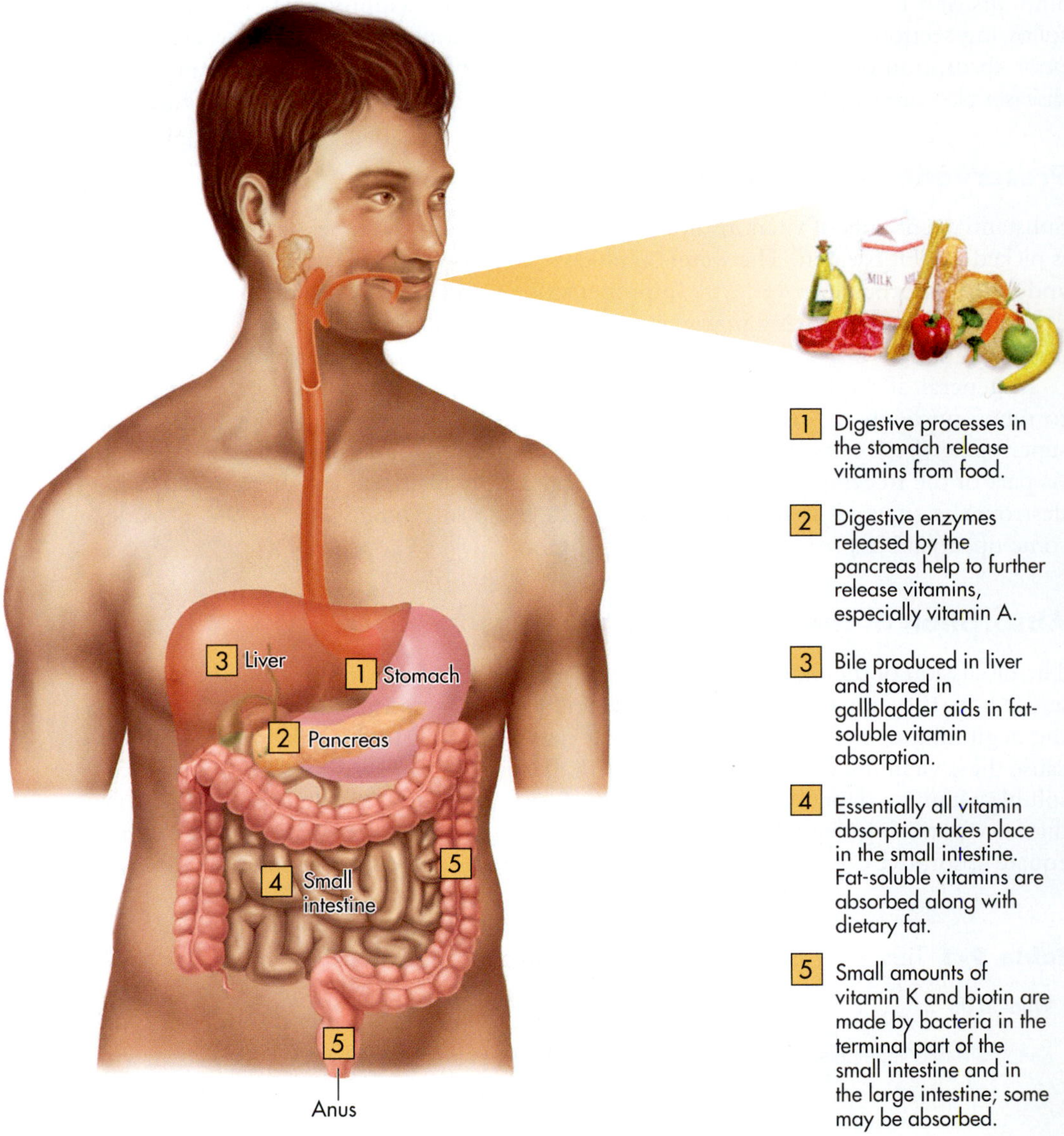
MILK
3 Liver
1 Stomach
2 Pancreas
4 Small intestine
5
5
Anus
1 Digestive processes in the stomach release vitamins from food.
2 Digestive enzymes released by the pancreas help to further release vitamins, especially vitamin A.
3 Bile produced in liver and stored in gallbladder aids in fat-soluble vitamin absorption.
4 Essentially all vitamin absorption takes place in the small intestine. Fat-soluble vitamins are absorbed along with dietary fat.
5 Small amounts of vitamin K and biotin are made by bacteria in the terminal part of the small intestine and in the large intestine; some may be absorbed.

Figure 9-1 An overview of the digestion and absorption of vitamins. Key participants in the process include bile, pancreatic enzymes, intestinal enzymes, and a healthy small intestine absorptive surface. Adequate fat digestion and absorption are critical for the ultimate absorption of fat-soluble vitamins. Carotenoids are absorbed mainly in the small intestine in conjunction with dietary fat.

cystic fibrosis A disease that often leads to overproduction of mucus. Mucus can invade the pancreas, decreasing enzyme output.

celiac disease An immunological or allergic reaction to the protein gluten in certain cereals, such as wheat or rye. The effect is to destroy the intestinal enterocytes, resulting in a much reduced surface area due to flattening of the villi. The elimination of wheat, rye, and certain other grains from the diet restores the intestinal surface.

Crohn's disease An inflammatory disease of the gastrointestinal tract, but generally more pronounced in the terminal ileum. A family history is a major risk factor. The disease limits the absorptive capacity of the small intestine.

40 to 90% of the fat-soluble vitamins consumed are absorbed when they are taken in typical amounts.[7, 8, 9] Absorption efficiency generally falls with intakes greatly in excess of human needs.

Once absorbed, fat-soluble vitamins are packaged and delivered to target cells throughout the body in a manner similar to that used for dietary fats—namely, by way of chylomicrons and other blood lipoproteins. This process is needed because the vitamins are not water-soluble. Recall also from Chapter 6 that, as a chylomicron circulates in the bloodstream, much of its triglyceride content is removed by body cells. What remains—the remnant—is taken up by the liver. This remnant contains the fat-soluble vitamins absorbed from the diet. The liver can "repackage" fat-soluble vitamins with blood proteins for transport in the general circulation, or they can be stored in the liver for future use.

People with **cystic fibrosis, celiac disease, Crohn's disease,** or any other disease that hampers fat absorption absorb fat-soluble vitamins poorly. Some medications, such as the weight-loss drug orlistat (Xenical), also interfere with fat absorption. Unabsorbed fat carries these vitamins to the large intestine, where they are incorporated into the feces and excreted. People with such conditions are especially susceptible to vitamin K deficiency because body stores of vitamin K are lower than those of the other fat-soluble vitamins.[7] A multivitamin and mineral supplement, taken under a physician's guidance, is part of the treatment for preventing the nutrient deficiencies associated with fat malabsorption (Chapter 13 discusses orlistat use in detail).

Concept | Check

In general, the fat-soluble vitamins—A, D, E, and K—are less readily excreted than are the water-soluble B-vitamins and vitamin C. When a person ingests a vitamin-free diet, the first deficiency signs will be due to a lack of thiamin and will appear after about 10 days. This shows that even water-soluble vitamins persist to some extent in the body, so an occasional inadequate daily consumption is of no health concern. It is important, however, to regularly consume foods rich in both water-soluble and fat-soluble vitamins.

Vitamin A

North Americans are at little risk of developing a severe deficiency of vitamin A, since this vitamin is abundant in our food supply.[7] But vitamin A deficiency constitutes one of the major public health problems in developing countries. Worldwide, vitamin A deficiency is the leading cause of nonaccidental blindness. Children from impoverished nations in Africa, Asia, and South America are especially susceptible because their inadequate intake and diminished stores of vitamin A fail to meet the increased needs associated with rapid growth. Among the world's most destitute nations, hundreds of thousands of children become blind each year because they lack vitamin A.[7]

Vitamin A refers to the preformed **retinoids,** plus the provitamin A **carotenoids** that can form retinoids. Vitamin A is a ring structure with a fatty acid tail. As preformed vitamin A, it exists in three forms: retinol (an alcohol), retinal (an aldehyde), and retinoic acid. The tail terminates in one of these three chemical groups.

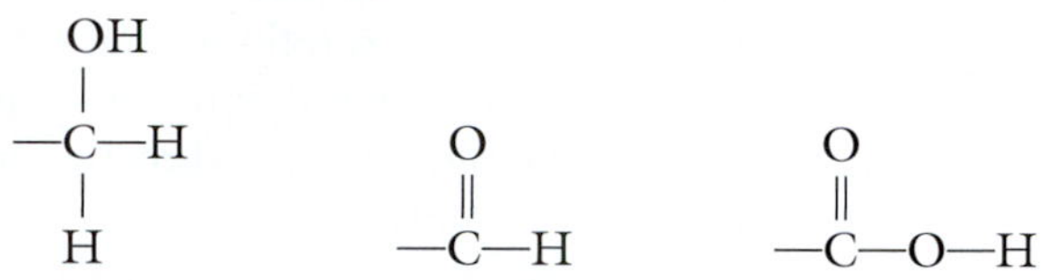

Retinol   Retinal   Retinoic acid

To some extent these forms can be interconverted, but retinoic acid is a "dead end" in metabolic terms.

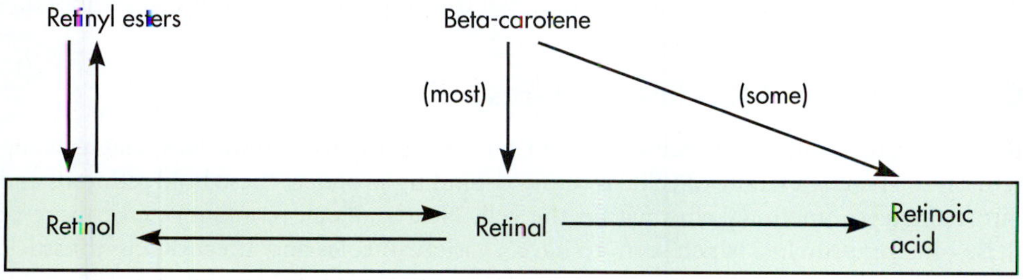

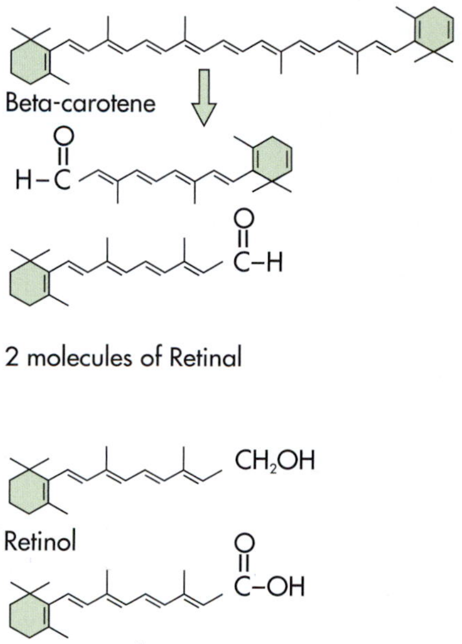

Vitamin A family.

retinoids Collective term for the biologically active forms of vitamin A including retinol, retinal, and retinoic acid.

carotenoids Pigment materials in fruits and vegetables that range in color from yellow to orange to red.

See Appendix A to review *cis* and *trans* isomers

The tail of the vitamin A molecule can vary from *cis* to *trans* configuration. This orientation influences the function of the specific retinoid (see section, Functions of Vitamin A).

Cis *Trans*

Preformed vitamin A is present in animal foods as retinol, the alcohol form, and retinyl ester-compounds that have a fatty acid attached to retinol. The retinyl esters don't exhibit vitamin A activity but are hydrolyzed to retinol in the intestinal tract.

The first fat-soluble vitamin was recognized as *A* in 1916.

Provitamin A carotenoids also can be enzymatically split to form retinal within the intestinal cells or in liver cells within the body. Some is also made into retinoic acid. The provitamin A carotenoids are alpha-carotene, beta-carotene, and beta-cryptoxanthin. (The yellow-orange pigment in fruits and vegetables is due to provitamin A beta-carotene.) Other carotenoids in nature do not appear to have vitamin A activity in humans.[7]

Absorption, Transport, Storage, and Excretion of Vitamin A

In the small intestine, retinyl esters are hydrolyzed so that the fatty acid is cleaved off, leaving free retinol. This hydrolysis reaction requires bile to make the retinyl esters soluble and also to activate the hydrolyzing enzymes, particularly pancreatic lipase and retinyl ester hydrolase.

After hydrolysis, up to 90% of retinol is absorbed into the cells of the small intestine. After absorption, a fatty acid is then attached to retinol to form a new retinyl ester. These retinyl esters are packaged into chylomicrons, along with other lipids, before entering the lymph. The chylomicrons deliver vitamin A to tissues for storage or to be used. Over 90% of the body's vitamin A storage can be found in the liver, but retinoids also are found in adipose tissue cells, kidneys, bone marrow, testicles, and eyes. Normally, the liver stores enough vitamin A to last for several months, so some time will pass before the signs and symptoms of vitamin A deficiency arise.[18]

Carotenoids are absorbed intact; this causes their absorption rate to be much lower than that of retinol. After being absorbed in the small intestine, carotenoids can be cleaved to yield retinal, which is then formed into retinol. This retinol can then have a fatty acid attached to it to become a retinyl ester and enter the lymph as part of a chylomicron. Carotenoids also can enter the bloodstream directly; however, the mechanisms that allow this to happen aren't well understood.

During protein-energy malnutrition, synthesis of retinol-binding protein and transthyretin (prealbumin) is reduced by the lack of amino acids and energy. These proteins are used as clinical indicators of protein synthesis in a person because decreased concentrations in the blood suggest inadequate protein intake.

When vitamin A as a retinoid is released from the liver into general circulation, it is bound to a protein called retinol-binding protein, produced mainly by the liver. In the bloodstream, retinol-binding protein is bound to another protein called transthyretin (more commonly known as prealbumin). In contrast, when carotenoids are released from the liver, they are carried by the lipoprotein VLDL.

Vitamin A is not readily excreted by the body; only some is lost in the urine. Kidney disease increases the risk of vitamin A toxicity if this route of excretion is compromised.[18]

Cellular Retinoid-Binding Proteins

Retinoids are bound to specific retinoid-binding proteins within cells that take up retinoids. There is a family of cellular retinoid-binding proteins; these hold retinoids and direct them to functional sites within the cell. Nearly all cells contain one or more of these binding proteins, which seem to have a variety of roles and affect different tissues. Besides transport, these binding proteins protect retinoids from breakdown.

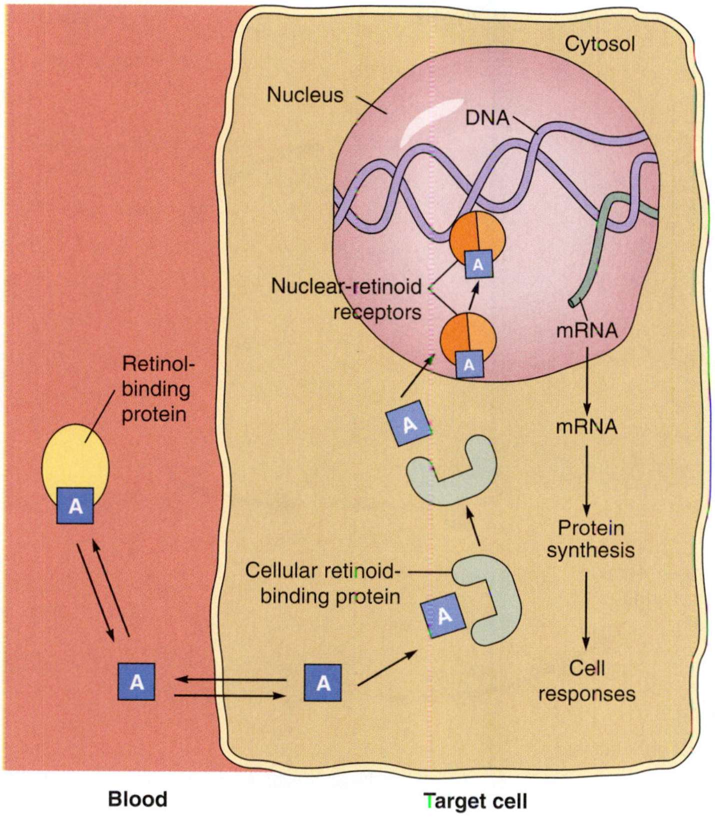

Figure 9-2 The mechanism of the action of vitamin A (as retinoic acid) on the target cell. Vitamin A is carried by retinol-binding protein in the blood. Upon release vitamin A enters the target cell. Vitamin A then enters the nucleus and binds to its nuclear-retinoid receptors (RAR and RXR). This complex then binds to DNA, activating gene transcription. The resulting messenger RNA (mRNA) has the code for the protein that ultimately produces the cellular responses (see Chapter 7 for details on protein synthesis using mRNA). Nearly all cells have at least one member of the RAR and RXR families of nuclear-binding proteins. It is interesting that vitamin D in its active hormone form acts in a similar way. However, the retinoic acid receptor (RAR) portion is replaced by the vitamin D receptor (VDR).

Use of some synthetic retinoids has been shown to lead to a remission in various forms of cancer. The mechanism is probably through the fundamental role of retinoids in cell differentiation.

Nuclear-Retinoid Receptors

One way the retinoids influence health is to bind to two main families of nuclear-retinoid receptors (called **RAR** and **RXR**). Once these receptors within the cell nucleus bind specific retinoids (actually forms of retinoic acid), the complex then binds to DNA. This binding in turn regulates the activity of retinoid-responsive genes on DNA. The binding to the nuclear-retinoid receptors permits the interaction of the vitamin with a specific area of DNA, thus regulating the formation of mRNA and the subsequent production of body proteins (and body processes), known as **gene expression.** This can go on to direct **cell differentiation** (Fig. 9-2).[18]

RXR, RAR The abbreviations for retinoid X receptor and retinoic acid receptor. These two subfamilies of retinoid receptors interact with retinoic acid and bind with specific sites on DNA. This allows for gene expression.

gene expression The activation of a specific site on DNA, which results in either the activation or the inhibition of the gene.

cell differentiation The process of transforming an unspecialized cell into a specialized cell.

Functions of Vitamin A

The active forms of vitamin A—retinol, retinal, and retinoic acid—perform three basic functions. These biochemical or physiologic actions are vision, the growth and development of many types of tissues, and immunity.

Vision

Vitamin A (as retinal) is needed in the retina of the eye to turn visual light into nerve signals to the brain (Fig. 9-3). In addition, vitamin A (as retinoic acid) is needed to maintain normal differentiation of the cells that make up the various structural components of the eye, such as the cornea and rod cells.[18]

The sensory elements of the retina consist of specialized cells known as rods and cones. The rods are responsible for the visual processes that occur in dim light, translating objects into black-and-white images and detecting motion. The cones are responsible for the visual processes occurring under bright light, translating objects into color images.

In the rods, 11-*cis*-retinal binds to a protein called opsin to form the visual pigment called **rhodopsin** (visual purple). The absorption of a **photon** of light catalyzes a change

rhodopsin A photoreceptor in the rod cells composed of 11-*cis*-retinal and opsin.

photon A unit of light intensity at the retina having the brightness of one candle.

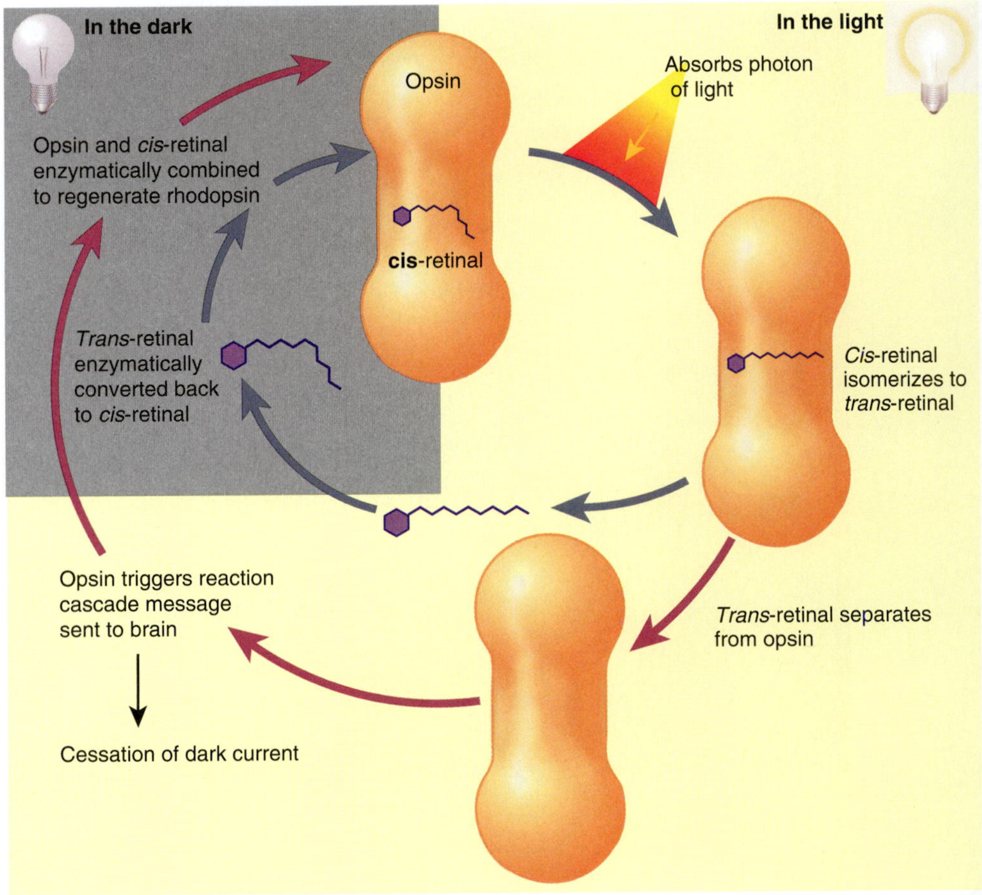
In the dark
In the light
Absorbs photon of light
Opsin
cis-retinal
Opsin and *cis*-retinal enzymatically combined to regenerate rhodopsin
Trans-retinal enzymatically converted back to *cis*-retinal
Cis-retinal isomerizes to *trans*-retinal
Trans-retinal separates from opsin
Opsin triggers reaction cascade message sent to brain
Cessation of dark current

Figure 9-3 The bleaching and regeneration of rhodopsin. The yellow background indicates the bleaching events that occur in the light; the gray background indicates the regenerative events that are independent of light. The latter occur in both light and dark conditions. Note that 11-*cis* retinal has a kink in the molecule, but all-*trans* retinal is a straight chain. As shown in Chapter 6, this change in configuration is typical when lipidlike molecules convert from *cis* to *trans* shapes.

in the shape of 11-*cis*-retinal to all-*trans* retinal, causing opsin to separate from all-*trans* retinal. This isomerization event leads to a cascade of biochemical events, which trigger a change in ion permeability of the photoreceptor cells. This, in turn, initiates a signal to the nerve cells that communicate with the brain's visual center. Actually, thousands of rod cells containing millions of molecules of rhodopsin are triggered simultaneously.

In order to keep the visual processes functioning, the 11-*cis*-retinal in the rod cells must be regenerated in the pigment-containing cells in the eye. All-*trans* retinal is converted to retinol, then to 11-*cis*-retinol, and finally back to 11-*cis*-retinal. This is a slow process, which can take several minutes. The 11-*cis*-retinal then moves back to the photoreceptor site, where it recombines with opsin and is ready for another cycle.

The release of 11-*cis*-retinal from opsin is designated a **bleaching process.** During exposure to bright light, the rods' rhodopsin is completely activated and cannot respond to more light until it returns to its resting state. Enzymes regenerate the initial form of rhodopsin, so that it can respond to light again. If there is a limited amount of rhodopsin in the rod cells, it is difficult to adapt to seeing in dim light (night blindness).[17]

bleaching process The process by which light depletes the rhodopsin concentration in the eye. This fall in rhodopsin concentration allows the eye to become adapted to bright light.

Not all retinal is reused, so there is a pool of retinyl esters in the eye to keep a supply of vitamin A on hand. Should the pool of vitamin A be low, the process of **dark adaptation** is slowed down. Children are more likely to experience a lack of vitamin A because they haven't had time to build up body stores.[2]

dark adaptation The process by which the rhodopsin concentration in the eye increases in dark conditions. This, in turn, allows improved vision in the dark.

Growth and Differentiation of Cells

Besides its function with opsin, vitamin A is important to the eyes in another way. Various cell types in the retina, cornea, and **epithelium** of the eye depend on the presence of retinoic acid for maintaining structural integrity. Vitamin A is delivered to the target sites by tears. In this case, vitamin A is acting in its role in gene expression and ultimate cell differentiation. Two forms of vitamin A, all-*trans* retinoic acid and 9-*cis*-retinoic acid, regu-

epithelium The covering of internal and external surfaces of the body, including the lining of vessels and other small cavities. It consists of epithelial cells joined by a small amount of cementing material.

late finely tuned gene expression through the action of their nuclear receptors, as discussed earlier. Retinoic acid is also necessary for the production, the structure, and the normal function of epithelial cells in the lungs, trachea, skin, gastrointestinal tract, and many other systems. It is also essential in the formation and maintenance of mucus-forming cells in these organs.[18] Because of its effect on skin, forms of retinoic acid (e.g. tretinoin [Retin-A]) are used to treat skin damage, such as wrinkles. It has a modest effect.

Dr. Tom W.-M. Boileau and Dr. John W. Erdman, Jr. discuss the functions of carotenoids that are not specifically linked to conversion to vitamin A in the Expert Opinion.

Immunity

As early as the 1920s, researchers recognized that vitamin A (mostly as retinoic acid) is important for immune system functions, and a vitamin A deficiency is associated with decreased resistance to infections. The severity of some infections, such as measles and diarrhea, is reduced by vitamin A supplementation in people who show a deficiency.[7]

Many vegetables, such as asparagus and broccoli, are rich in provitamin A carotenoids.

Vitamin A in Foods

Retinoids (preformed vitamin A) are found in liver, fish, fish oils, fortified milk, and eggs. Margarine is fortified with vitamin A. Provitamin A carotenoids are mainly found in dark green and yellow-orange vegetables and some fruits. Carrots, spinach and other greens, winter squash, sweet potatoes, broccoli, romaine lettuce, mangoes, cantaloupe, peaches, and apricots are examples of such sources. About 65 to 75% of the vitamin A in the typical North American diet comes from animal (preformed vitamin A) sources, whereas provitamin A predominates in the diet among poor people in other parts of the world.[6]

Beta-carotene accounts for some of the orange color of carrots. In vegetables such as broccoli, this yellow-orange color is masked by dark-green chlorophyll pigments. Still, green vegetables contain provitamin A. Consuming a varied diet rich in green vegetables and carrots will provide enough vitamin A to meet needs.

Food Sources of Vitamin A

Food Item and Amount	*Vitamin A (µg RAE)*
Fried beef liver, 1 oz	3042
Sweet potato, ½ cup	958
Spinach, ⅔ cup	494
Mango, 1	402
Baby carrots, 5	375
Acorn squash, ⅔ cup	244
Cooked kale, ½ cup	206
Skim milk, 1 cup	150
Broccoli, 1 cup	138
Apricot, 3	137
Cheddar cheese, 1 oz	78
Romaine lettuce, 1 cup	72
Margarine, 1 pat	50
Scallions, 1 tbsp	32
Peach, 1	26

RDA adult man, 900 µg RAE
RDA adult woman, 700 µg RAE

Retinol Activity Equivalent (RAE)

At one time, the amounts of most nutrients in foods were expressed in **international units (IUs)**, a crude measure of vitamin activity. Today we can directly measure very small quantities of nutrients more precisely; consequently, milligrams (1/1000 of a gram) and micrograms (1/1,000,000 of a gram) have generally replaced international units as customary units of measure, although vitamin supplements may still display the older IU values.

international unit (IU) A crude measure of vitamin activity, often based on the growth rate of animals. Today these units often have been replaced by precise measurements of actual quantities in milligrams or micrograms.

For vitamin A, the current unit of measurement is the retinol activity equivalent (RAE), which is basically 1 µg of retinol. In this system, it is assumed that 12 µg of beta-carotene yield 1 µg of vitamin A activity and that 24 µg of the other two provitamin A carotenoids (alpha carotene and beta-cryptoxanthin) yield 1 µg of vitamin A activity. The total RAE value for a food is calculated by adding the actual weight of retinol and the adjusted equivalent weights of the provitamin A carotenoids present in the food. For example, a diet that contains 500 µg retinol, 1800 µg beta-carotene and 2,400 µg alpha-carotene supplies 750 µg RAE $(500 + (1800 \div 12) + (2400 \div 24) = 750$ µg RAE).[7]

Table 9-2 is a tool for converting amounts of vitamin A and carotenes expressed in one unit of measure into another unit of measure.

Table 9-2 Conversion Values for Retinol Activity Equivalents

1 retinol activity equivalent (RAE)	1 IU vitamin A activity
= 1 µg of all-*trans*-retinol	= 0.3 µg of all-*trans*-retinol
= 12 µg of dietary all-*trans*-beta-carotene	= 3.6 µg of dietary all-*trans*-beta-carotene
= 24 µg of other dietary provitamin A carotenoids	= 7.2 µg other dietary provitamin A carotenoids

Expert Opinion

Carotenoids and Human Health: Beyond Conversion to Vitamin A

Thomas W.-M. Boileau, Ph.D., and John W. Erdman, Jr., Ph.D.

Of the over 600 carotenoids found in nature, only a handful are found in fruits and vegetables typically consumed. These carotenoids are readily absorbed from foods and deposited in human tissues and blood. Although it's been known since the 1930s that certain dietary carotenoids can be converted to vitamin A within the body, it's only been since the mid-1980s that carotenoid research has focused on functions beyond conversion to vitamin A. Let's look at the most active research areas in non-provitamin A functions of carotenoids.

Beta-Carotene and Lung Cancer

Probably the most familiar carotenoid is beta-carotene which is found in most common fruits and vegetables. It is important to our health since it can be centrally cleaved to two molecules of vitamin A, thus making it the carotenoid with the most vitamin A activity. In humans, beta-carotene can also be absorbed intact, without being converted to vitamin A, and deposited into most tissues. Beta-carotene provides the brilliant orange color of carrots and cantaloupe, and is also found in dark green leafy vegetables. Because of its chemical structure, it has been suggested that beta-carotene may be an antioxidant within tissues protecting them from damage by free radicals. Probably one of the most important lessons that scientists in the area of nutrition have learned has been as a result of the beta-carotene lung cancer trials. Since the consumption of fruits and vegetables rich in beta-carotene was associated with greatly reduced risk of lung cancer, several groups of scientists set up two large prevention trials that investigated the effects of pure beta-carotene on the development of lung cancer in high-risk populations of smokers and asbestos workers. Unfortunately, what they found was that beta-carotene actually increased risk for lung cancer in two separate trials. These studies have demonstrated that beta-carotene alone is not a preventative agent for lung cancer, and that dietary recommendations should focus on increasing consumption of fruits and vegetables to prevent this and other free radical-related diseases.

Xanthophyll Carotenoids and Ocular Health

Lutein and zeaxanthin are the yellow pigments in corn, and also are found in dark green, leafy vegetables (although their color is masked by the greens of chlorophyll). One of the hottest areas in carotenoid research is the role of these two carotenoids in the maintenance of eye health. Interestingly, these two compounds are the primary carotenoids that accumulate in the yellow spot in the back of the eye, the macular pigment, and in the lens. They have been implicated in protecting against the age-related diseases, macular degeneration and cataracts. Studies in humans have documented that (1) people who have macular degeneration have lower lutein and zeaxanthin concentrations in their blood and eyes, (2) dietary supplementation with foods rich in these two xanthophylls can increase their concentrations in the eye, and (3) increased dietary lutein and zeaxanthin is associated with reduced risk of macular degeneration and age-related cataract. However, a direct link between intake of lutein and zeaxanthin and prevention of cataract and macular degeneration has not been tested by randomized clinical trials. Additionally, the mechanisms of action of these carotenoids in ocular tissue is actively being

A diet rich in vegetables is also rich in phytochemicals such as the carotenoids.

The retinal equivalent (RE) is an older unit for vitamin A. This RE assumed that there was a greater contribution to vitamin A needs from carotenoids than we assume today. Food composition tables and nutrient databases generally contain this older RE standard. It will take some time to update these resources.

To compare the older RE (or IU) standards to current RAE recommendations, assume that for any preformed vitamin A in a food or added to food, 1 RE (or 3.3 IU) = 1 RAE. There is no easy way to convert RE or IU units to RAE units for foods that naturally contain provitamin A carotenoids, such as carrots, spinach, and apricots. A general rule of thumb is to divide the older values for foods containing carotenoids by 2, and then do the conversion from RE or IU to RAE as shown in Table 9-2. There is

studied. We will have to wait for these study results to make a firm statement.

Tomatoes, Lycopene, and Prostate Cancer

Lycopene is the red pigment in tomatoes and unlike beta-carotene, it cannot be converted to vitamin A. Much of the recent interest in lycopene has been related to its role in preventing prostate cancer. In 1995, a large study (47,000 men) related a greater dietary intake of tomatoes and tomato products with a reduced risk of developing prostate cancer. Subsequently it was shown that lycopene accumulates in the human prostate at relatively high concentrations and that men with low levels of blood lycopene have greater risk of developing prostate cancer. Taken together, these studies suggest that lycopene from tomatoes protects against prostate cancer. However, tomatoes contain many phytochemicals other than lycopene, and thus it remains possible that lycopene may simply be a marker of tomato intake and that other compounds are actually the protective ones. The hypothesis that tomatoes contain protective phytochemicals other than lycopene was tested by inducing prostate cancer in rats while feeding them either tomato powder or pure lycopene as part of their normal diets. Interestingly, it was found that rats eating the tomato powder had reduced risk of prostate cancer while feeding pure lycopene had a lesser effect. These recent data support a concept that tomatoes contain compounds in addition to lycopene that protect against prostate cancer. Further studies will be needed to more clearly define relationships between tomato phytochemicals, lycopene, and risk for developing prostate cancer.

Carotenoids and UV-induced Skin Damage

In the 1960s it was demonstrated that supplemental beta-carotene could reduce the adverse effects of certain skin disorders that were caused by sensitivity to sunlight. These findings have led to a more recent interest in the ability of carotenoids to protect the skin from ultraviolet radiation-mediated damage and potentially reduce the risk for sunburn, cancer, and other disorders of the skin. Indeed, it has been demonstrated that dietary carotenoids are accumulated in the skin and that carotenoids can increase the antioxidant capacity of skin tissue. Lycopene appears to be a more effective antioxidant in skin than beta-carotene because upon exposure to UV light, lycopene is preferentially oxidized.

Carotenoids and Cardiovascular Disease

Because carotenoids travel in the blood in lipoproteins, their ability to inhibit LDL oxidation has been studied. Indeed several studies have observed that dietary carotenoids can reduce LDL oxidation and, thus, might be able to reduce risk for developing atherosclerosis. In large supplementation trials, beta-carotene alone has not been consistently shown to greatly reduce the risk of cardiovascular disease. There is accumulating evidence, however, that lycopene may reduce risk for cardiovascular disease. In a large human study, men with greater concentrations of adipose tissue lycopene had a significantly reduced risk for myocardial infarction (heart attack). In laboratory (in vitro) studies, lycopene has been shown to reduce LDL oxidation, decrease cholesterol synthesis and increase LDL receptor activity, which may help to explain its protective effects.

Summary

The ability of carotenoids to enhance human health by mechanisms beyond conversion to vitamin A have been of interest to scientists since the mid-1980s. Beta-carotene is the most well-studied carotenoid, but little benefit of supplementation has been shown with lung cancer and cardiovascular disease. The effects of lycopene on prostate cancer and cardiovascular disease, lutein and zeaxanthin in health of the eye, and lycopene and beta-carotene protecting the skin are currently active and promising areas of research. For now, focus on a diet rich in fruits and vegetables.

Dr. Boileau is a post-doctoral fellow in the Department of Human Nutrition at the Ohio State University. Dr. Erdman is Professor of Nutrition in the Department of Food Science and Human Nutrition and the Division of Nutritional Sciences at the University of Illinois Urbana-Champaign. Dr. Erdman is also currently president of the American Society for Nutritional Sciences, as well as a member of the antioxidant panel for Food and Nutrition Board of the National Academy of Sciences, and has been a leader in carotenoid research for nearly 20 years.

also no easy way to do this calculation for food containing a mixture of preformed vitamin A and carotenoids. We will just have to wait for all of the food tables to be updated. Generally speaking, any values listed for such foods provide less vitamin A than the RE or IU values suggest.

Vitamin A Needs

The RDA for vitamin A is 900 μg Retinol Activity Equivalents for adult men and 700 μg Retinol Activity Equivalents for adult women. At this intake, adequate body stores of vitamin A are maintained, which is the basis for setting the RDA. Average intakes for adult men and women in North America meet the RDA. Most adults have liver reserves of vitamin A that are three to five times greater than needed to provide good health. Thus, the use of vitamin A supplements by most people is unnecessary. At present, there is no separate RDA for beta-carotene or any of the other provitamin A carotenoids.[8]

Measuring vitamin A in the blood is one way to assess a person's status. However, this is an insensitive measure, since concentrations do not fall until vitamin A stores in the liver are very low.

Vitamin A Deficiency

Deficient vitamin A status may be seen in preschool children who do not eat enough vegetables.[2] The urban poor, older adults, and people with alcoholism or liver disease (which limits vitamin A storage) can also show diminished vitamin A status, especially with respect to stores. Finally, children and adults with severe fat-malabsorption syndromes, as in cases of celiac disease, chronic diarrhea, pancreatic insufficiency, Crohn's disease, cystic fibrosis, HIV and AIDS, may also experience vitamin A deficiency. Such a deficiency can have widespread effects on the body.

When the retinol in the blood is insufficient to replace the retinal lost during the visual cycle, the rod cells in the eye recover from flashes of light more slowly. The resulting night blindness is a common early symptom of vitamin A deficiency, as discussed earlier. As well, without vitamin A, mucus-forming cells deteriorate and are no longer able to synthesize mucus, the essential lubricant used throughout the body. The eye, especially the cornea, is adversely affected by the loss of mucus, which keeps the eye surface moist and washes away dirt and other particles that settle on the eye. Deterioration of the eye results from bacterial invasion, because vitamin A plays an important role in resistance to infection. Conjunctival xerosis (abnormal dryness of the **conjunctiva** of the eye) and Bitot's spots (drying out of the eye and appearance of hardened epithelial cells) appears as vitamin A deficiency worsens. The corneal ulceration and keratomatacia (softening of the cornea) result in scarring (Fig. 9-4). The ultimate scarring may be barely detectable, or it could lead to loss of sight. This sequence of changes in the eye—collectively known as **xerophthalmia**—causes irreversible blindness in millions of people worldwide.[18]

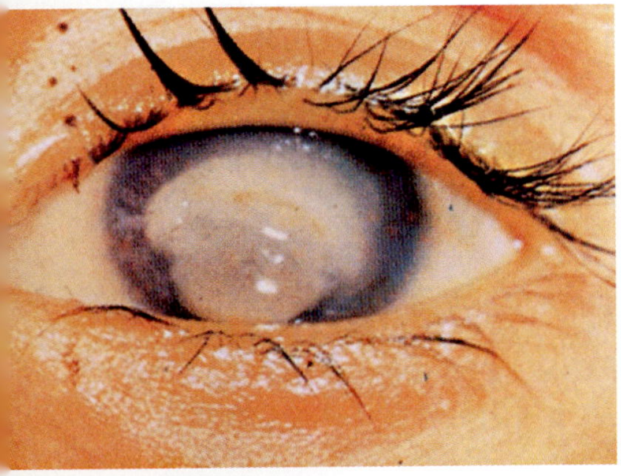

Figure 9-4 Vitamin A deficiency can eventually lead to blindness. Note the severe effects on this eye. This problem is commonly seen today in Southeast Asia. In contrast, the leading cause of blindness in North America is accidents in children and diabetes in adults.

Vitamin A deficiency also produces skin changes referred to as **follicular hyperkeratosis.** Keratin, the normal component of the outer layers of skin, protects the inner layers and reduces water loss through the skin. During severe vitamin A deficiency, keratinized cells normally present only in the outer layers replace the normal epithelial cells in the underlying skin layers. Hair follicles become plugged with keratin, giving a bumpy appearance and rough texture to the skin, and the skin is very dry.

In areas of the world where vitamin A deficiency exists, poor growth follows. If liver vitamin A stores are established after an infant is weaned, they can supply retinol for several months or even longer. Vitamin A deficiency in children occurs most often during the postweaning period. Giving supplements of 15,000 to 60,000 µg to young children at risk may protect them for up to 6 months. Finding a suitable food to improve intake is a must for a long-term solution to vitamin A deficiency. One problem is that most children do not like the vegetables that are the richest source of provitamin A, and insufficient dietary fat inhibits the absorption of what little vitamin A there is in the diet.

conjunctiva The mucous membrane covering the anterior surface of the eyeball and the posterior surface of the eyelids.

xerophthalmia A condition, marked by dryness of the cornea and eye membranes, that results from vitamin A deficiency and can lead to blindness. The specific cause is a lack of mucus production by the eye, which then leaves it more vulnerable to surface dirt and bacterial infections.

follicular hyperkeratosis A condition in which keratin, a protein, accumulates around hair follicles.

teratogenic Tending to produce physical defects in a developing fetus (literally "monster forming").

Vitamin A Toxicity

As noted in the chapter introduction, signs and symptoms of toxicity from excessive vitamin A—called **hypervitaminosis A**—can appear with long-term supplement use at 2 to 4 times the RDA for preformed vitamin A, especially in older adults (Fig. 9-5). Three kinds of vitamin A toxicity exist: acute, chronic, and **teratogenic.** Acute toxicity is caused by the ingestion of one very large dose of vitamin A or several large doses taken over several days (about 100 times the RDA). The effects of acute toxicity are largely gastrointestinal upset, headache, blurred vision, and muscular incoordination.[17] Once the dosing is stopped, these signs disappear. Extraordinarily large doses, about 12 g (13,000 times the RDA), however, can be fatal.

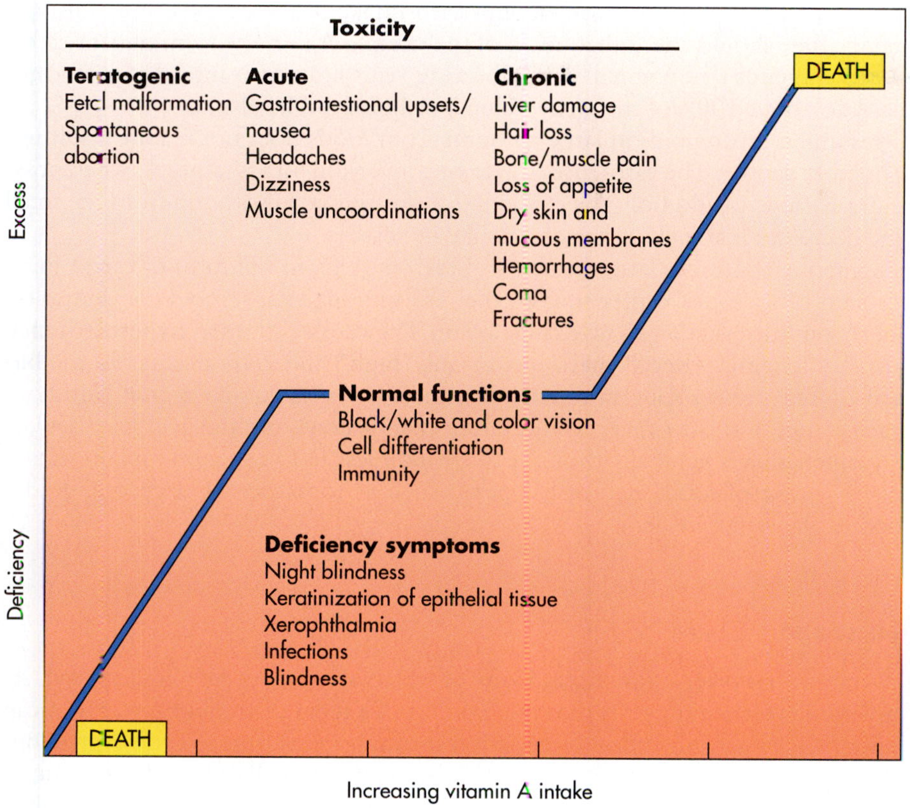

Figure 9-5 Consuming the right amount of vitamin A is critical to overall health. A very low (deficient) or a very high (toxic) vitamin A intake (as retinoids) can produce damaging signs and symptoms and even lead to death. The severity of effects and the intake range vary among individuals.

In chronic toxicity, infants and adults show a wide range of signs and symptoms: bone and muscle pain, loss of appetite, various skin disorders, headache, dry skin, hair loss, liver damage, double vision, hemorrhage, vomiting, hip fractures, and coma.[6,7] Vitamin A also is particularly harmful in early pregnancy, a time when many women do not know that they are pregnant. Hypervitaminosis A may cause a spontaneous abortion or birth defects.

Toxicity of vitamin A probably causes instability in retinoid-sensitive membranes and the inappropriate expression of certain genes. The treatment is simply to discontinue the supplement. Effects then decrease over the next few weeks to a month as blood concentrations fall to within a normal range. Permanent damage to the liver, bones, and eyes, as well as recurrent joint and muscle pain, however, can occur with chronic ingestion of excessive amounts of the vitamin. The Upper Level for vitamin A intake is established at 3000 μg preformed vitamin A for adult men and women. This amount is based on the presence of birth defects occurring during pregnancy and liver toxicity in general with chronic intakes above this amount.

People in developing countries typically pose an exception to the rule that moderately large doses of vitamin A can cause toxicity. Because of their minimal storage of vitamin A, these people can tolerate intermittent large doses of the vitamin.

The most serious and tragic effects of hypervitaminosis A are teratogenic—most notably, the birth defects just mentioned. Vitamin A and its related analog forms, all-*trans*-retinoic acid (topical tretinoin mentioned earlier) and 13-*cis*-retinoic acid (oral isotretinoin, or Accutane), have been subjects of concern for years. These vitamin A analog medications are used to treat various skin disorders, such as acne and psoriasis. Accutane causes spontaneous abortion and birth defects in experimental animals. The risk is significant for pregnant women taking large doses of vitamin A analogs. Their offspring show congenital malformations of the head, probably because neural crest cells, which are important in the development of the head and brain, are known to be very sensitive to excess amounts of vitamin A. Women of childbearing age are advised to take oral contraceptives immediately before, during, and for some time after taking these medications to prevent pregnancies that could result in such fetal malformations.

It is even possible for women to get too much vitamin A from food if they consume high-vitamin A foods, such as liver and fortified breakfast cereals. For this reason, it is

Critical | Thinking

Check out the ready-to-eat breakfast cereals at your local supermarket. Which ones have beta-carotene added? Why do you think the manufacturers are pursuing this kind of fortification?

recommended that pregnant women limit their intake of these foods, and, if using supplements, they should check that much of the vitamin A is in the form of beta-carotene. FDA recommends that women of childbearing years limit their intake of preformed vitamin A to about 100% of the Daily Value listed on food labels.

Consuming carotenoids in large amounts from foods does not readily result in toxicity in most people. The carotenoids' rate of conversion into vitamin A, when possible, is relatively slow. In addition, the efficiency of carotenoid absorption from the small intestine decreases markedly as the oral intake increases.

If someone consumes large amounts of carrots (e.g., in the form of carrot juice) or if an infant eats a lot of winter squash, the resulting high carotenoid concentrations in the body can turn skin a yellow-orange color. The result is termed **hypercarotenemia,** or just carotenemia. (Recall that *hyper* means "high" and *emia* means "in the bloodstream.") The person appears to have jaundice; however, unlike a true jaundice, the sclerae (whites of the eyes) are white (rather than yellow) and the liver is not enlarged. This carotenemia is generally thought to be harmless.[18] Lycopenodermia results from excessive intake of foods rich in lycopene; such as tomatoes. A deep orange discoloration of the skin is evident.

hypercarotenemia Elevated amounts of carotenoids in the bloodstream, usually caused by consuming a diet high in carrots or squash or by taking beta-carotene supplements.

Concept | Check

Vitamin A has diverse functions, many of which are not yet fully understood. Accumulating evidence suggests that the binding of a form of vitamin A to DNA can influence cell growth and differentiation through regulation of gene expression. Vitamin A is important for maintaining vision and epithelial tissues, reproduction, growth, and ensuring proper function of the immune system. Vitamin A in the diet comes in two forms: retinoids (preformed vitamin A) and certain carotenoids (provitamin A). A diet that meets the RDA for vitamin A and contains plenty of carotenoid-containing fruits and vegetables is considered sound nutrition. Major food sources of vitamin A include liver, carrots, eggs, tomatoes, milk, and many vegetables. North Americans most at risk for poor vitamin A status are preschool children and alcoholics. Large doses of preformed vitamin A can be toxic, even at chronic dosages only about 2 to 4 times the RDA, especially during early pregnancy and one's older years.

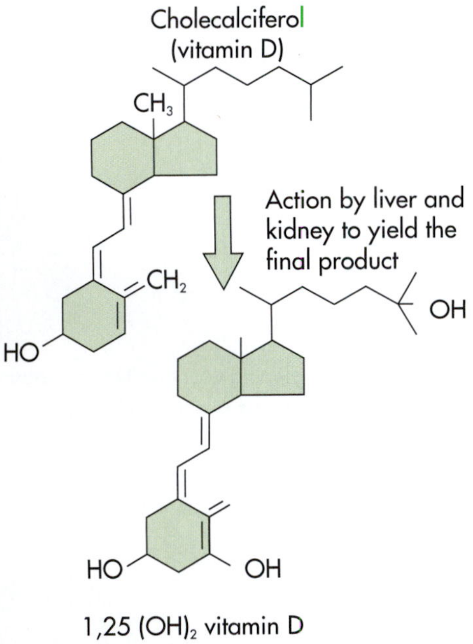

Vitamin D family. The form produced by the body is called vitamin D_3.

Vitamin D

The status of vitamin D as a vitamin is ambiguous because, in the presence of sunlight, skin cells are capable of synthesizing a sufficient supply of the vitamin from a derivative of cholesterol. Since a dietary source is not required in this case, the vitamin is more correctly classified as a "conditional" vitamin or **prohormone** (i.e., a precursor of an active hormone).

The prohormone form of vitamin D, whether synthesized in the body or obtained from the diet, is converted to the active form by enzymes in the liver and kidneys. The active form then is delivered to target organs, where it exerts its biological effects (Fig. 9-6). *Vitamin D* is a generic term for both the provitamin (prohormone) and the active vitamin form. Vitamin D achieves vitamin status because the diseases **rickets** and **osteomalacia** can be prevented and, to some extent, treated by the consumption of vitamin D-rich foods.[9]

For North Americans in general, sun exposure provides about 90% of our vitamin D needs.[13] The amount of sun exposure individuals need to produce vitamin D depends on skin color, age, time of day, season of the year, and geographic location. Experts recommend that people expose their hands, face, and arms 2 to 3 times a week to 25% of the amount of sun needed to cause a sunburn. In other words, for a person who would sunburn in just an hour, 15 minutes of exposure is recommended. Persons with dark

rickets A disease characterized by inadequate mineralization of the bones caused by poor calcium deposition during growth. This deficiency disease arises in infants and children with poor vitamin D status.

osteomalacia The weakening of the bones that occurs in adults as a result of poor bone mineralization linked to inadequate vitamin D status in adults.

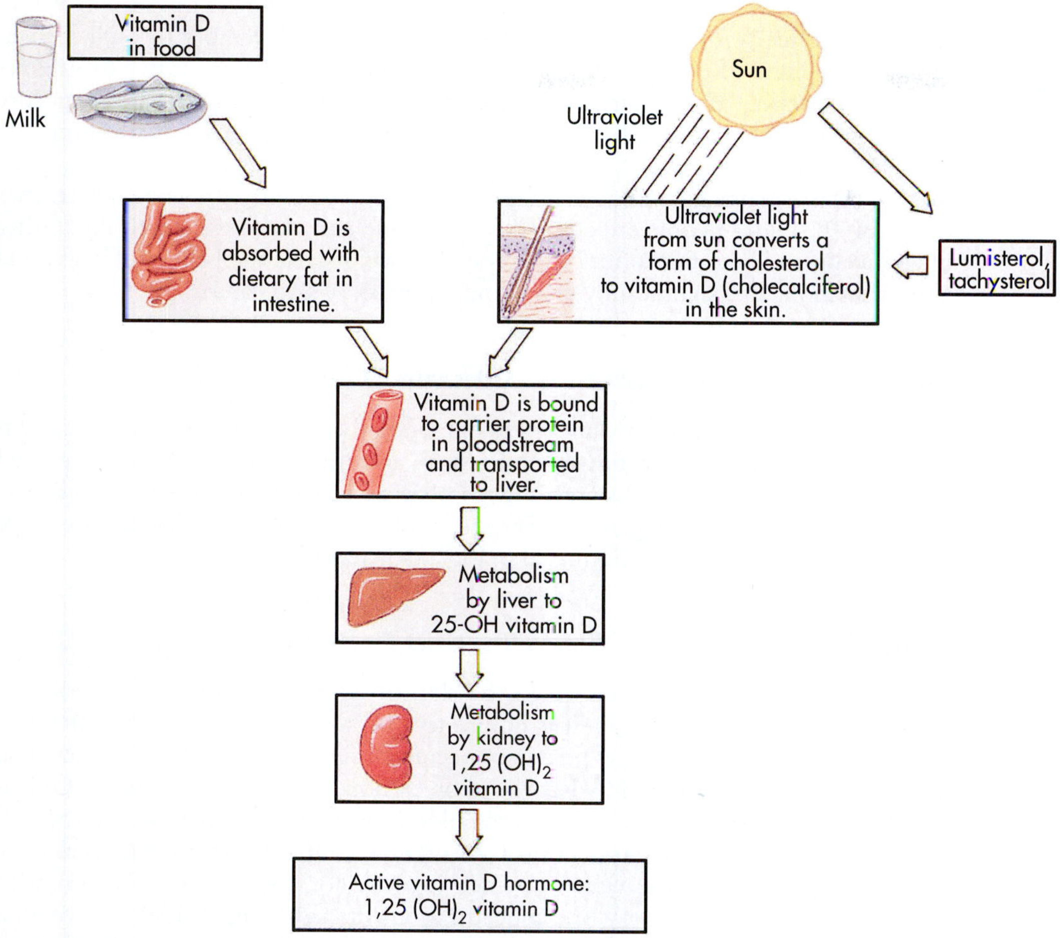

Figure 9-6 The many facets of vitamin D metabolism. Whether synthesized in the body or obtained from foods, vitamin D ultimately functions as a hormone. During exposure to sunlight, some of the epidermal reservoir of 7-dehydrocholesterol is converted to previtamin D. Lumisterol and tachysterol in the skin can also be converted to previtamin D with the action of sunlight.

skin would need additional exposure, about 5 times the amount just recommended. The more pigment in the skin, the less vitamin D is made. Melanin acts as a natural sunscreen. Compared to Caucasians, African Americans are much more likely to have low levels of vitamin D in their blood.[15] This sun exposure is only effective for vitamin D synthesis if sunscreen over SPF 8 is not used and it is done between about 8 A.M. and 4 P.M. Still, it is not effective at all in the winter in northern climates. Some people may be able to use the vitamin D that was stored from summer months in their fat cells, but most people in northern climates should find alternate vitamin D sources in the winter months. Overall, anyone who does not receive enough sunshine to synthesize an adequate amount of vitamin D (the most reliable source) should seek a dietary source of the vitamin, but including some sun exposure is still important.[11]

Vitamin D Formation in the Skin

Synthesis of vitamin D begins with provitamin D (7-dehydrocholesterol), located in the skin. During exposure to sunlight, one ring on the molecule breaks open creating **previtamin D.** Over the next few hours, previtamin D undergoes a transformation aided by body heat to form vitamin D. This change allows vitamin D to enter the bloodstream, bound to a protein. It is now on its way to becoming a hormone.

previtamin D The precursor of one form of vitamin D, produced as a result of sunlight opening a ring on 7-dehydrocholesterol in the skin.

Solar radiation provides on average 90% of the vitamin D humans use. This is also the most reliable way to maintain vitamin D status. Dietary vitamin D is less effective.

In Boston, Massachusetts (42° N), production of previtamin D in the skin is adequate to meet needs from March through October. From November through February, the UV light is too low on the horizon to produce previtamin D. In Los Angeles (34° N), production of previtamin D occurs throughout the year. Prolonged exposure doesn't increase the production of vitamin D beyond needs, since any excess is rapidly degraded.

Aging decreases production of vitamin D in the skin by about 70% when one reaches the age of 70. Older people are advised to get some sun exposure, especially during early morning and late afternoon. In this way they will receive the benefit of vitamin D synthesis without also significantly increasing their risk of skin cancer.

Absorption and Formation of Vitamin D from Food

Following the consumption of vitamin D-containing foods, about 80% of vitamin D is incorporated into micelles in the small intestine and then absorbed and transported to the liver by chylomicrons through the lymphatic system. Patients with chronic fat-malabsorption syndromes (e.g., cystic fibrosis, Crohn's disease, and celiac disease) have trouble absorbing vitamin D and may develop a deficiency.

Metabolism, Transport, Storage, and Excretion of Vitamin D

When vitamin D (either synthesized in the skin or consumed from food or supplements) enters general circulation, it is bound to a protein. The formation of the hormone form of vitamin D from its precursor occurs in the liver and kidneys (review Fig. 9-6). In the liver, the vitamin is hydroxylated on carbon 25, converting it to 25-OH vitamin D. This inactive form circulates in the blood for weeks. The next stop is the kidney, the principal site for the production $1,25(OH)_2$ vitamin D, also known as calcitriol or the hormone form of the vitamin, which is active for about 1 day. Patients with chronic kidney failure have very low concentrations of circulating $1,25(OH)_2$ vitamin D. They are routinely treated with $1,25(OH)_2$ vitamin D. Thus, the kidney is the organ in which activation of vitamin D occurs.[16]

Once vitamin D enters general circulation, it can be stored in fat tissues for later use or converted to 25-OH vitamin D in the liver. When there is a shortage of calcium in the blood, the parathyroid glands increase production of parathyroid hormone (PTH). Parathyroid hormone then increases the production of $1,25(OH)_2$ vitamin D in the kidney. Eventual excretion of vitamin D takes place mostly via the bile, with small amounts leaving via the urine.

Functions of Vitamin D

Vitamin D has hormone functions that affect the body's use of calcium and phosphorus. The effects on calcium are summarized in Figure 9-7. The effects on calcium can have two somewhat opposite impacts on bone. On the one hand, vitamin D hormonal actions (as $1,25(OH)_2$ vitamin D) increase intestinal absorption of calcium from foods (review Fig. 9-2 for the general nuclear mechanism of vitamin D action). This makes calcium available for body cells, as well for incorporation into bone when there is more calcium in the blood than is needed for the other basic life functions of calcium. Note that a form of calcium phosphate comprises the main structural component of bone. On the other hand, vitamin D hormonal actions can release calcium from bone into the blood, working with parathyroid hormone. The latter action occurs to the greatest extent when blood calcium levels start to fall. This fall is reversed by vitamin D hormone-induced release of calcium from the bone. Although this action, if it occurs too much and too long, can weaken the bones, there is a benefit to this action. Calcium is needed for many basic life functions, as just noted, including heartbeat (see Chapter 11). If the bones did not supply calcium for these functions, a person could quickly have serious,

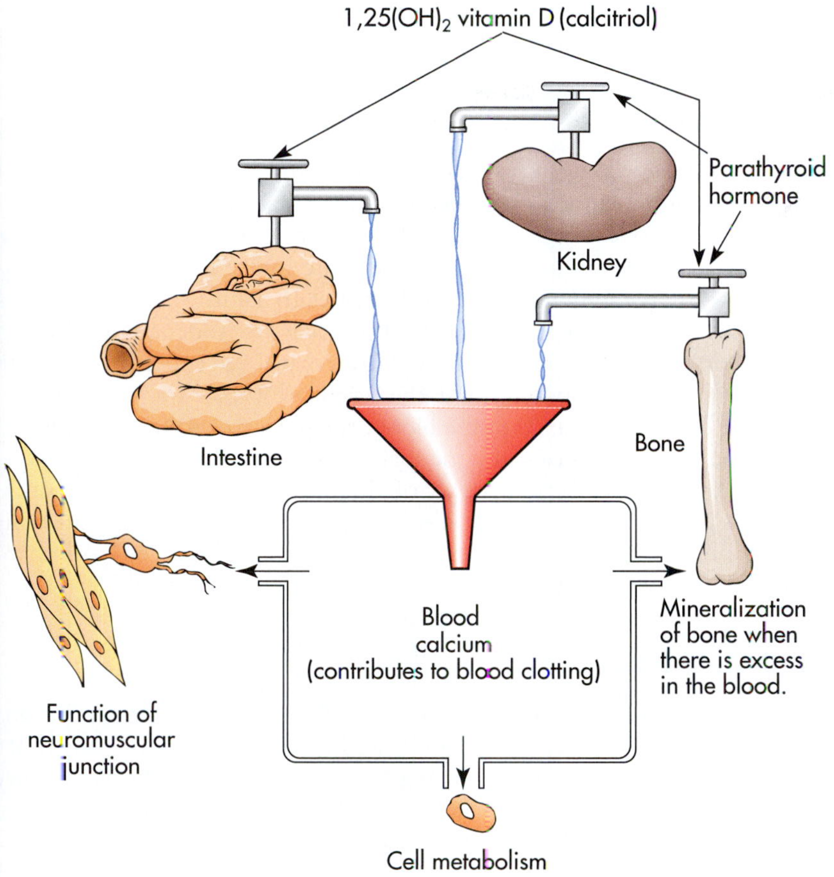

Figure 9-7 The active vitamin D hormone—$1,25(OH)_2$ vitamin D (calcitriol)—and parathyroid hormone interact to control blood calcium concentration. Normal amounts of calcium in the blood are needed to support nerve function, muscle action, bone health, and other functions. Low blood calcium is a trigger for many hormonal responses. Parathyroid hormone and $1,25(OH)_2$ vitamin D mobilize calcium from the bone. $1,25(OH)_2$ vitamin D by itself stimulates intestinal calcium absorption. All these responses raise blood calcium. Conversely, when calcium in the blood becomes too high, the hormone **calcitonin** responds by promoting calcium deposition in the bone (see Fig. 11-8 in Chapter 11).

even fatal, health consequences.[16] Thus, vitamin D preserves these important functions of calcium, even if dietary calcium intakes are not optimal.

Vitamin D hormonal actions also help calcium with some of this mineral's regulatory functions. A prime example is providing enough calcium to maintain the function of the **neuromuscular junction** (see Chapter 11). In addition, vitamin D hormonal actions affect the body's use of phosphorus, which again partners with calcium to form calcium phosphate, the main component of bone structure.

Human epidermal cells have nuclear receptors for $1,25(OH)_2$ vitamin D. Activated receptors then affect the differentiation of skin cells. At present, there are 20 different cell types in the human body that are sensitive to the hormonal effects of vitamin D.[16] Vitamin D is also capable of influencing differentiation in some cancer cells, such as skin, bone, and breast cancer cells. Indeed, adequate vitamin D status has been linked to a reduced risk of developing breast, colon, and prostate cancer.

calcitonin A thyroid gland hormone that inhibits bone resorption.

neuromuscular junction A chemical synapse between a motor neuron and a muscle fiber.

Vitamin D in Foods

Because some people may not receive enough sun exposure to generate sufficient active vitamin D for the body's needs, they need to pay attention to dietary sources. Actually, few foods contain appreciable amounts of vitamin D.

Good sources of vitamin D are fatty fish (e.g., sardines and salmon), fortified milk, and some fortified breakfast cereals. In North America, milk is generally fortified with 10 μg (400 IU) per quart. Although eggs, butter, liver, and a few brands of margarine contain some vitamin D, large servings must be eaten to obtain an appreciable amount of the vitamin; thus, these foods are not considered significant sources.

Foods of animal origin contain vitamin D_3, the same as humans produce, whereas supplements and fortified foods may contain a slightly different provitamin D—called

Food Sources of Vitamin D

Food Item and Amount	*Vitamin D (μg)*	*Vitamin D (IU)*
Baked herring, 3 oz	44.4	1775
Smoked eel, 1 oz	25.5	1020
Cod liver oil, 1 tbsp	11.3	453
Baked salmon, 3 oz	6.0	238
Sardines, 1 oz	3.4	136
Canned tuna, 3 oz	3.4	136
1% milk, 1 cup	2.5	99
Nonfat skim milk, 1 cup	2.5	98
Soft margarine, 1 tsp	1.5	60
Italian pork sausage, 3 oz	1.1	44
Soy milk, 1 cup	1.0	40
Raisin Bran cereal, ¾ cup	1.0	38
Baked bluefish, 3 oz	0.9	34
Special K cereal, ¾ cup	0.8	30
Cooked egg yolk, 1	0.6	25

Adequate Intake, young adults, 5 μg (200 IU)

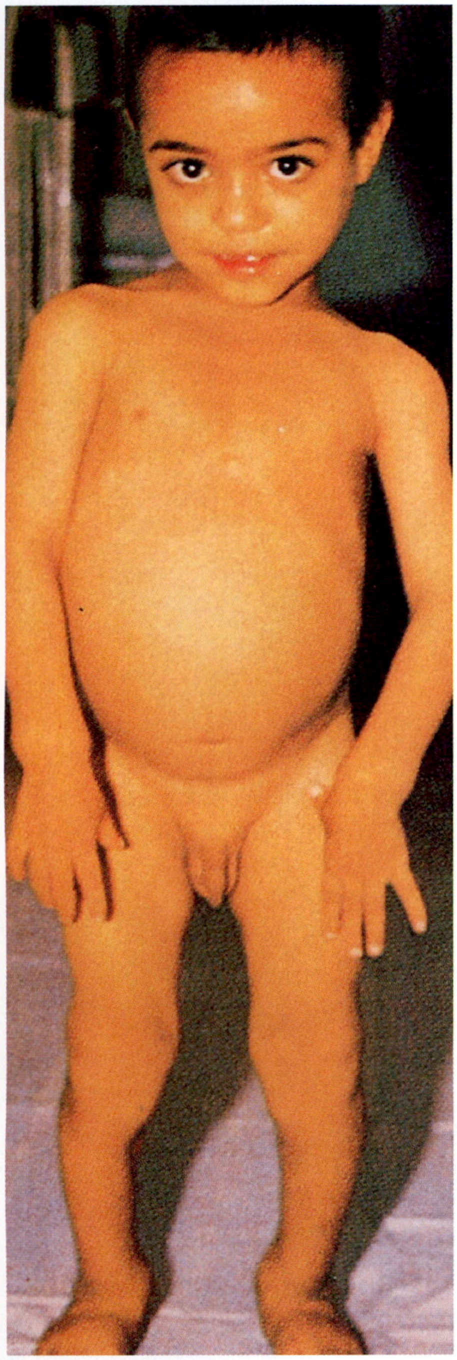

Figure 9-8 The bowed legs of rickets, a vitamin D-deficiency disease.

ergosterol, or vitamin D_2. This compound has vitamin D activity in humans but is not as effective at raising blood levels of 25-OH vitamin D as vitamin D_3.

Vitamin D Needs

The Food and Nutrition Board has set an Adequate Intake for vitamin D (see Chapter 2 for details about Adequate Intakes and how these standards differ from RDAs). A more precise RDA could not be set because the amount of vitamin D produced by sunlight is too variable between individuals. The Adequate Intake for vitamin D is 5 μg/day (200 IU/day) for people under age 51 and increases to 10 μg/day (400 IU/day) for people between 51 and 70 and 15 μg/day (600 IU/day) for older adults. Young, light-skinned people can produce enough vitamin D from casual sun exposure on just the face and hands. The marker used to determine the Adequate Intake for young adults is the concentration of 25-OH vitamin D in the blood, the precursor to the active form of the vitamin. For older persons indicies of bone maintenance are also used.[9]

Infants are born with a sufficient supply of vitamin D to last about 6 months. At or before that time, a breastfed infant should be regularly exposed to some sunlight or treated with a vitamin D supplement under a physician's guidance. Note that infant formulas are fortified with vitamin D.

Vitamin D Deficiency

Without adequate calcium and phosphorus in the blood available for deposition in the bone, the skeleton fails to mineralize properly and bones weaken and bow under pressure. When these effects occur in the growing bones of a child, the disease is called rickets (Fig. 9-8). Signs of rickets include enlarged head, joints, and rib cage; a deformed pelvis; and bowed legs. In North America today, rickets is most commonly associated with fat malabsorption, such as is seen in children with cystic fibrosis, but an increase in cases has been seen related to a decrease in milk consumption and the use of clothing that, for religious or social reasons, limits skin exposure to the sun.[4]

Rickets in adults is called osteomalacia, which means "soft bones." It is characterized by poor calcification of newly synthesized bone. It can cause fractures in the hip, spine, and other bones. (Do not confuse this with the disease osteoporosis, which will be discussed in Chapter 11.) Osteomalacia is most likely to occur in people with kidney, stomach, gallbladder, or intestinal disease (especially when most of the intestine has been removed) and in those with cirrhosis of the liver. These diseases affect both vitamin D metabolism and calcium absorption. Combinations of sun exposure and treatment with vitamin D or $1,25(OH)_2$ vitamin D can be used to treat osteomalacia.

Studies suggest older people and anyone else who stays indoors most of the day and ingests little or no vitamin D are at risk for developing a vitamin D deficiency. This is a particularly important concern for older people who live in northern climates or reside in nursing homes. Not only do these people experience little sun exposure, they also can have defective $1,25(OH)_2$ vitamin D production from kidney resistance, which decreases conversion to the active form of the hormone.[18]

One epidemiological survey of older nursing home residents (free living and hospitalized) who took supplements containing vitamin D or drank two to three glasses of vitamin D-fortified milk per day showed that 80% were still borderline deficient at the end of winter. Thus, it is suggested that the older persons, especially those over age 70, obtain sunlight exposure during spring, summer, and autumn to provide vitamin D for storage in fat tissue for use during winter months, as well as consume 15 μg (600 IU) to 20 μg (800 IU) per day. Little or no sun exposure would raise this dietary recommendation to 25 μg (1000 IU) per day.[4] Providing 1250 mg (50,000 IU) once a month is another strategy.[13]

The best way to assess a person's vitamin D status is to determine the concentration of 25-OH vitamin D in the blood.

If a person has a low circulating concentration of 25-OH vitamin D, he or she should take 20 μg (800 IU) of vitamin D each day until the concentration reaches the midnormal range. People who are likely to fall into this category are dark-skinned people, older people (especially those with osteoporosis), and people with malabsorption syndromes, liver failure, and kidney disease or failure. After blood concentrations are normal, 10 μg (400 IU/day) from a multivitamin and mineral supplement should be sufficient. Some sun exposure would also be helpful.

Vitamin D Resistance

Some humans show resistance to the action of certain vitamins, including vitamin D. Resistance to vitamin D can be caused either by a lack of 1,25$(OH)_2$ vitamin D synthesis in the kidney or by an inability of 1,25$(OH)_2$ vitamin D to bind to its nuclear (VDR) receptors throughout the body. In both cases, the treatment is a large dose of 1,25$(OH)_2$ vitamin D. This treatment works well in the first case but is not as successful in the second.

Pharmacologic Use of Vitamin D

Normal keratinocytes (skin-producing cells) require 28 to 44 days to move from the basal cell layer of the skin to the surface of the epidermis. Among patients with psoriasis, the movement takes only 4 days. This results in a scaly and embarrassing dermatitis. Today, vitamin D analogs applied to the skin are used as a safe, effective treatment of psoriasis.

Milk is usually fortified with vitamin D, as well as vitamin A.

Vitamin D Toxicity

Vitamin D can be a very toxic substance, but some experts suggest that vitamin D is not as toxic to adults as it was once thought to be. The Upper Level set for vitamin D is 50 μg/day (2,000 IU/day), based on development of an excess concentration of calcium in the blood.[9] However, the Upper Level does not imply that exceeding 50 μg/day will necessarily pose a risk to adults. In fact, there is a comfortable margin of safety over 50 μg/day before any sign of vitamin D toxicity would arise. Infants, in contrast, are most susceptible to toxic amounts of vitamin D. Severe vitamin D toxicity causes mental retardation, narrowing of pulmonary arteries and the aorta, and changes in facial characteristics.

Concept | Check

Vitamin D is a vitamin only for people who fail to produce enough from exposure to sunlight. Most people can synthesize adequate vitamin D by the action of sunlight on the skin. Older people and breastfed infants are at risk of a vitamin D deficiency. Vitamin D_3 is later activated by the liver and kidneys to form the active hormone 1,25$(OH)_2$ vitamin D. This hormone increases calcium absorption in the intestine and works with other hormones to maintain proper blood calcium concentrations and calcium metabolism in bones and other organs in the body. The hormone 1,25$(OH)_2$ vitamin D is also an important regulator of cell differentiation in many tissues of the body. Fish oils and fortified milk are significant food sources of vitamin D. An excess of vitamin D can be quite toxic, especially during infancy. Sun exposure poses no risk of vitamin D toxicity.

Vitamin E

North Americans are spending more than $1 billion on vitamin E supplements each year. The following section attempts to sort out fact from fiction in the debate over this high-profile vitamin.

A vitamin E deficiency in laboratory animals can result in muscular dystrophy, inability to produce viable offspring, and impotence. The link between vitamin E deficiency and inability to reproduce in rats, first noted in 1922, gave vitamin E its chemical name

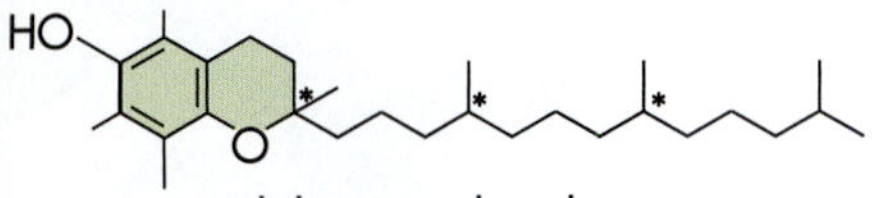

Vitamin E. The carbon chain attached to the ringed structure exists in many possible isomer forms. The specific carbons that have isomer forms (termed R and S) are starred.

tocopherol (*toco* means "related to childbirth"). Overt vitamin E deficiency in humans is not common, though there are a few situations where it does occur. Most of the interest in vitamin E is not from the deficiency standpoint, but more in terms of an optimal intake for promoting health. This area is still controversial; hopefully, ongoing research will provide more insight.[14]

It is important to take a close look at vitamin E chemistry in order to understand the units used to express vitamin E activity and, as well, understand issues regarding potential vitamin E toxicity. As you can see in the margin figure, vitamin E has a long carbon tail. In this tail, the three carbon atoms with a star can exist in two different spatial orientations, designated R and S (see Appendix A to learn more about R and S stereoisomers). If one has two different possibilities at three different sites, this yields eight different isomers ($2^3 = 8$). Only vitamin E isomers that have the R configuration at the first starred site are active in the body, as the S form leads to an unwanted "kink" in the tail of the vitamin E molecule.[8] All the vitamin E found naturally in foods has R at that first starred carbon atom and so is active. (Actually it is R in all 3 positions, and so is RRR vitamin E.) Synthetic vitamin E will only have R on the first starred carbon atom in half of the isomers present, while the others will have the S configuration. Thus, only about half of the vitamin E in synthetic formulations is active in the body.

When you look at food or supplement labels, however, you will not see R and S designations concerning the type of vitamin E in the product. Instead, you will see "d" and "l." This is another way of describing isomers, but it has been inappropriately assigned to vitamin E. The d and l isomers are only appropriate if only one carbon atom in a compound has different orientations, and you know that vitamin E has three carbon atoms that have different orientations. Food and supplement labels, however, still use this older terminology because researchers did not understand much about vitamin E chemistry until recent years, and the label terminology has not been updated. From a practical standpoint, if you see d next to vitamin E on a label, all of that vitamin E will be active in the body. If you see dl on a label, only about half of that vitamin E will be active in the body.

What we call vitamin E is actually a family of eight naturally occurring compounds—four **tocopherols** (alpha, beta, gamma, delta) and four **tocotrienols** (alpha, beta, gamma, delta)—with widely varying degrees of biological activity.[8] The most active form of the vitamin is the so-called "d" isomer of alpha-tocopherol (again, actually RRR).[7] This is the form found in nature, and in varying amounts in vitamin supplements. However, recent research shows that other forms, such as gamma-tocopherol, may also be important to the body.

tocopherols A group of four structurally similar compounds that have vitamin E activity. The RRR ("d") isomer of alpha-tocopherol is the most active form.

tocotrienols A group of four compounds with the same basic chemical structure as the tocopherols but containing slightly altered side chains. They exhibit much less vitamin E activity than the corresponding tocopherols.

Absorption, Transport, Storage, and Excretion of Vitamin E

The degree of absorption of vitamin E depends on the total absorption of dietary fat. Like the other fat-soluble nutrients, vitamin E must be incorporated into micelles within the lumen of the small intestine, which in turn is dependent on bile and pancreatic enzymes. Once taken up by the absorptive cells, vitamin E is incorporated into chylomicrons for transport by the lymph and eventually the bloodstream to tissues and the liver. The precise degree of absorption is not known.

The chylomicron remnants release the vitamin E to the liver, which can then deliver the vitamin to the lipoproteins VLDL and HDL. Vitamin E can be stored in the liver and in adipose tissues and skeletal muscle. Eventually, vitamin E positions itself in cell membranes, where it is associated with phospholipids.

Excretion of vitamin E is via the bile and urine. Because of the limited absorption of vitamin E from the intestinal tract, there is a significant amount in the feces.

Functions of Vitamin E

Vitamin E functions as an antioxidant. Some research has also shown that vitamin E can affect a number of other body processes, such as platelet aggregation, but it is not yet known if these effects are directly related to antioxidant actions. As an antioxidant, vitamin E functions as a chain-breaking molecule that prevents the propagation of chain reactions caused by **free radicals.**

free radical The short-lived form of a compound that has an unpaired electron, causing it to seek an electron from another compound. Free radicals are strong oxidizing agents and can be very destructive to electron-dense cell components, such as the DNA and cell membranes.

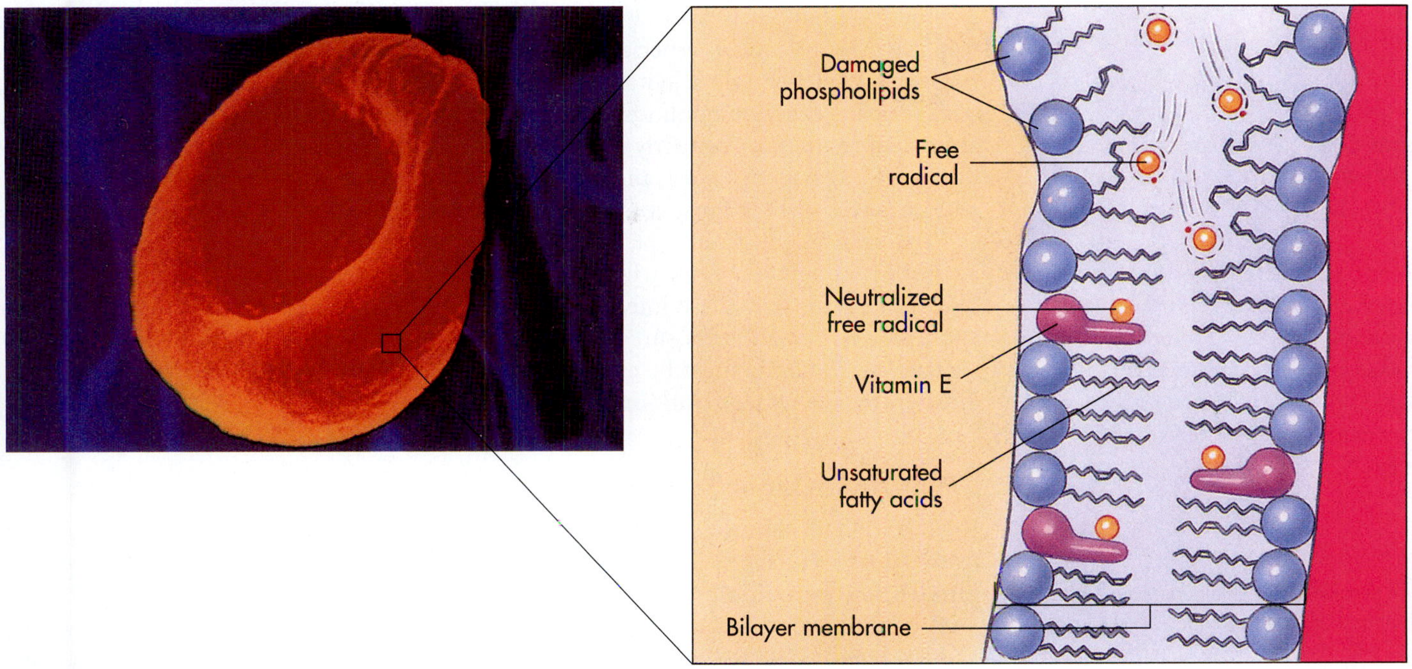

Figure 9-9 Vitamin E protects unsaturated fatty acid components of cell membranes from free-radical attack by itself becoming oxidized. If not interrupted, these free-radical chain reactions cause extensive oxidative damage to cells and premature cell death.

Free radicals are reactive species with unpaired electrons that start oxidant chain reactions that create oxidant stress. Strictly speaking, an oxidant reaction is any reaction where electrons are donated to another molecule. This includes reactions that are part of aerobic respiration. However, when the term "oxidant stress" is used, the reference is to just certain types of oxidant reactions. Specifically, these reactions involve free radicals and produce damage to biological molecules (Fig. 9-9). The health consequences of oxidant stress have been publicized extensively in regard to cardiovascular disease, cancer, skin aging, and arthritis, but oxidant stress also compromises immune function and may have many other less obvious effects.

An antioxidant is any agent that can in some manner work against the damage of oxidant stress. This can happen in a variety of ways. Vitamin E works mainly as a chain-breaking antioxidant in lipid environments.[8] A prime example of how this can work can be described as follows. A free radical reacts with an unsaturated fatty acid in a phospholipid located in a cell membrane or lipoprotein. This can start a series of reactions that includes breaking fatty acids apart and creating one type of free radical, a lipid **peroxyl radical.** The lipid peroxyl radical is symbolized by the term R–O–O$^\cdot$, where R is a carbon-hydrogen chain from a broken fatty acid and the dot is an unpaired electron. This is also termed a **reactive oxygen species (ROS),** as it is a free radical that contains an oxygen radical. This lipid peroxyl radical then reacts with a new unsaturated fatty acid, which creates a new lipid peroxyl radical. This radical continues the chain reaction until two radicals meet and neutralize each other. By that time, however, many fatty acids have been broken apart. Vitamin E reacts with the lipid peroxyl radical and stops the chain reaction. Hence, we use the term chain-breaking antioxidant ($R^\cdot + O_2 \rightarrow$ R–O–O$^\cdot$ and then R–O–O$^\cdot$ + vitamin E-OH $\rightarrow$ R–O–O–H + vitamin E–O$^\cdot$). In effect, the cell traded a very reactive free radical for a much less reactive vitamin E radical. This chain-breaking reaction is important both to protect cells from dying and limit LDL oxidation, a contributor to atherosclerosis.

A vitamin E molecule is "used up" during its chain-breaking action. However, there is some evidence that vitamin C may be able to regenerate some vitamin E to allow it

peroxyl radical A compound containing –O–O– are peroxides. The radical has one unpaired electron, designated R–O–O$^\cdot$.

reactive oxygen species (ROS) Several oxygen derivatives produced during the formation of ATP. Formed constantly in the human body and shown to kill bacteria and inactivate proteins, they are implicated in a number of diseases and inflammatory processes.

to function again. This works well in vitro (in a test tube), but we don't know yet how well it works in real life, especially since vitamin C tends to be located in watery environments while vitamin E tends to stay with lipids. Overall, as just noted, an antioxidant protects other compounds by becoming oxidized itself. Thus, in a chemical sense antioxidants are more properly **redox agents** in that they can readily undergo both oxidation (loss of an electron), and later reduction (regaining an electron). Nevertheless, antioxidant is still the most commonly used term, even in the scientific literature.

redox agents Chemicals that can readily undergo both oxidation (loss of an electron) and reduction (gain of an electron).

Oxidizing agents that cells encounter include highly reactive oxygen species such as singlet oxygen ($^1O_2$), hydrogen peroxide (H_2O_2), hydroxyl radical ($^{\bullet}OH$), superoxide ($O_2^{\bullet -}$), ozone (O_3) and nitrogen-oxygen combinations that are typical of air pollutants ($NO^{\bullet}$).

Free radicals, however, are not all bad. As part of the immune system's arsenal against invading pathogens, white blood cells (leukocytes) generate free radicals to destroy the agents that cause infections. Also, free radicals stimulate normal cell growth and division. Overall, exposure to free radicals is part of life, and for the most part essential, but the body must be able to regulate this exposure and avoid the undesirable effects, a task assigned to antioxidants.

Other Antioxidant Systems in the Body

In addition to vitamin E, the body has various other mechanisms for protecting itself from oxidant damage.[16] The body also contains numerous antioxidant enzymes such as **glutathione peroxidase, superoxide dismutase,** and **catalase.**

glutathione peroxidase A selenium-containing enzyme that can destroy peroxides. It acts in conjunction with vitamin E to reduce free radical damage to cells.

superoxide dismutase Enzymes containing manganese, copper, or zinc that destroy superoxide.

catalase An enzyme that breaks down hydrogen peroxide to water.

Glutathione peroxidase catalyzes the breakdown of hydrogen peroxides (H-O-O-H) and lipid peroxides (R-O-O-H). These compounds are not radicals, but they can easily become radicals. Glutathione peroxidase eliminates peroxides before this happens. Consequently the need for vitamin E decreases because fewer free radicals will be formed. Glutathione peroxidase thus aids vitamin E in reducing oxidative damage to cells. The activity of glutathione peroxidase depends on the mineral selenium, the functional part of this enzyme. (Thioredoxin is another selenium-dependent antioxidant enzyme [see Chapter 12 for details].) An adequate dietary intake of selenium reduces the need for vitamin E, whereas an inadequate intake of selenium increases the need.

The enzyme catalase performs a similar function to that of glutathione peroxidase but has a different cell location (peroxisomes). Another important defense is the family of enzymes known as superoxide dismutase. These three enzymes eliminate one particular free radical called superoxide. Two of the superoxide dismutase enzymes contain copper and zinc. One is located in the cell cytosol and the other is found outside of cells. Intake of the essential nutrient copper can affect the activities of these two superoxide dismutase enzymes, but zinc intake only seems to have major effects on the enzyme that is found outside the cells. The third superoxide dismutase enzyme is found in the mitochondria and requires the mineral manganese for function.

In addition to vitamin E and antioxidant enzymes, there are other antioxidants. Phytochemicals (such as many carotenoids) can neutralize free radicals (see the Expert Opinion in Chapter 10) and possibly prevent certain radicals from forming. Since there are limits as to how much of any one antioxidant compound can accumulate in any one cell, it may be advantageous to consume a variety of antioxidant phytochemicals along with vitamin E and vitamin C. Furthermore, some phytochemicals may be better at protecting against certain radicals or their precursors than others. For example, carotenoids may be especially good at dealing with singlet oxygen, which is not a radical itself but can initiate oxidant stress. Proteins in the blood also bind metals—this limits the ability of metals to catalyze free radical production. The bottom line is that antioxidant protection is a team effort. Systems also exist in cells to repair molecules that have been oxidatively damaged, such as DNA.

This discussion raises the question of the relative role of vitamin E in oxidant protection in the body. It is unknown whether taking vitamin E supplements confers any additional protection against cardiovascular disease and cancer than that achieved by improving one's diet, performing regular physical activity, not smoking, and controlling (or improving) body weight.[12, 14]

Research from Great Britain in the mid-1990s suggested that daily megadose vitamin E therapy (200 to 400 mg; about 400 to 800 IU) reduced the risk of heart attacks in people who already had cardiovascular disease. This study has been criticized, however, because of some problems in experimental design, such as that a significant number of people dropped out of the study before its conclusion. This then makes it difficult to interpret research outcomes.[14] Follow-up trials using megadose vitamin E therapy have routinely failed to show any benefit in reducing heart attacks or cardiovascular disease-related death in people who have the disease. These studies have included thousands of people and had durations of approximately 5 years.[12, 20] This has caused most experts to discount the benefit of megadose vitamin E therapy in high-risk people.[14] Currently, the major hope is that megadose vitamin E therapy (about 200 mg/day [400 IU/day]) in healthy people will *prevent* future development of cardiovascular disease. Two large trials are currently testing this hypothesis, and results will be available by 2007. Doses used in these studies vary from 400 to 600 IU taken every other day. Until we have results from these studies, scientists can't be sure if megadose vitamin E therapy is helpful or not in healthy individuals. As recently as October 2000, the American Heart Association stated that it is premature to recommend vitamin E supplements to the general populations, based on current knowledge (review Chapter 6). This conclusion is in agreement with the latest report on vitamin E by the Food and Nutrition Board.[8] In addition, FDA recently denied the request of the supplement industry to make a health claim that vitamin E supplements reduce the risk of cardiovascular disease.

Plant oils are rich sources of vitamin E.

Vitamin E in Foods

Good food sources of vitamin E are plant oils (e.g., corn, soybean, safflower, sunflower, cottonseed, and wheat germ oil), wheat germ, asparagus, and peanuts. Products made from the plant oils—margarine, shortenings, and salad dressing—are also good sources. Finfish and shellfish add vitamin E to the diet. In addition, grain meals, such as oatmeal; nuts (e.g., almonds); and seeds (e.g., sunflower seeds) are other good sources. In milling whole grains, most of the vitamin E is lost and not restored. Animal fats have practically no vitamin E.

The actual vitamin E content of a food depends on harvesting, processing, storage, and cooking because vitamin E is highly susceptible to destruction by oxygen, metals, light, and deep-fat frying. In any case, a varied diet supplies the vitamin E needed for good health. Synthetic antioxidants, such as BHA and BHT, also add to the cellular protection provided by vitamin E (see Chapter 19 for more on BHA and BHT).

Food Sources of Vitamin E

Food Item and Amount	*Vitamin E (mg)*	*Vitamin E (IU)*
Total Raisin Bran cereal, ¾ cup	22.5	33.5
Sunflower oil, 2 tbsp	16.3	24.3
Dry-roasted sunflower seeds, 1 oz	14.3	21.2
Dry-roasted almonds, 1 oz	7.5	11.1
Safflower oil, 1 tbsp	5.9	8.7
Canola oil, 2 tbsp	5.7	8.5
Wheat germ, ¼ cup	5.2	7.7
Almonds, 1 oz	4.5	6.8
Oil-roasted sunflower seeds, 1 tbsp	3.4	5.0
Italian dressing, 2 tbsp	3.1	4.5
Mayonnaise, 1 tbsp	3.0	4.5
Avocado, 1	2.7	4.0
Chunky peanut butter, 2 tbsp	2.4	3.6
Mango, 1	2.3	3.5
Peanuts, 1 oz	2.1	3.1

RDA adults, 15 mg

Vitamin E Needs

The RDA for vitamin E is 15 mg/day of alpha-tocopherol for both men and women.[8] The RDA is based on the amount of vitamin E needed to prevent breakdown of red blood cell membranes, a process called **hemolysis.** The 15 mg allotment is equivalent to 22 IU of a natural source and 33 IU of a synthetic source. The RDA established for vitamin E will certainly prevent deficiency and fulfill a number of functions. Some experts contend that this intake level is, however, not optimal for protecting against developing health problems that are not specifically vitamin E deficiency diseases (such as cardiovascular disease, arthritis, cancer, etc.), but this has yet to be proven.

Adults consume on average about two-thirds of the RDA for vitamin E each day. Daily intake of nuts and seeds, or a ready-to-eat breakfast cereal containing vitamin E, or use of a multivitamin and mineral supplement would close this gap.

To convert from the older IU system, 10 IU equals about 4.5 mg, based on the synthetic (dl isomer) form of vitamin E found in most supplements. If vitamin E is from a natural source (d isomer), 10 IU equals 6.7 mg, as the natural form of vitamin E is more potent than the synthetic form. Thus the 200 mg recommendation made earlier actually represents 300 IU (d isomer) to 450 IU (dl isomer). Incidentally, 200 mg/day is thought to supply the maximum amount of vitamin E that can be retained by the body over time.[8] The Daily Value used on food and supplement labels for vitamin E is 30 IU.

hemolysis The destruction of red blood cells, caused by the breakdown of the red blood cell membrane. This allows the cell contents to leak into the fluid portion (plasma) of the blood.

One way to assess the vitamin E status of a person is to incubate a sample of his or her red blood cells with peroxide for 3 hours and then measure the extent of red blood cell destruction. A newer method uses the same procedure but measures the amount of a breakdown product of polyunsaturated fatty acids. These tests can be used in addition to measuring vitamin E in the blood.

preterm An infant born before 37 weeks of gestation; also referred to as premature.

Vitamin E Deficiency

Smokers are especially likely to develop a vitamin E deficiency and related oxidant damage in the body.[10] (Smoking readily destroys vitamin E in the lungs, but there is no easy way to test for this in clinical practice.) But studies have shown that even using megadoses of vitamin E is ineffective in preventing this damage. Others at considerable risk of a vitamin E deficiency include adults on very low-fat diets or those with fat malabsorption. **Preterm** infants are particularly susceptible to the hemolysis of red blood cells, since they are born with limited tissue stores of vitamin E and are inefficient in absorbing vitamin E from the intestinal tract. Second, the rapid growth of preterm infants exhausts what little vitamin E stores exist. To prevent hemolytic anemia, special formulas and supplements for preterm infants are prescribed to prevent vitamin E-related disorders of preterm births.

Deficiency occurs also as a result of a genetic abnormality in lipoprotein synthesis. In these cases, the primary vitamin E deficiency symptom is nervous system damage. Immune function is also reduced.

Vitamin E Toxicity

The Upper Level for vitamin E is based on hemorrhagic effects in adults. It applies to all eight isomers of alpha-tocopherol. For adults the Upper Level is 1000 mg/day of any form of supplementary alpha-tocopherol. In international units, the Upper Level is 1500 IU for vitamin E isolated from natural sources and 1100 IU for synthetic vitamin E. The lower IU value for the synthetic form reflects the greater number of isomers present in the synthetic product, some of which do not contribute to vitamin E activity in cells but are still absorbed.[8] This Upper Level also is confined to a healthy population. Individuals who are vitamin K-deficient or who are taking anticoagulants are especially at risk for hemorrhaging from megadose vitamin E use. People taking "statin" medications may also not get all the benefits of this therapy if on megadose vitamin E therapy.[14] The Food and Nutrition Board confined their discussion of adverse effects to supplements, food fortification, and pharmacological agents. The synthetic forms of vitamin E are used almost exclusively in these cases.

Concept | Check

Enzymes and other body mechanisms scavenge and minimize the formation of free radicals and other oxidative compounds, but they are not 100% effective. Hence, diet-derived antioxidants may be critical in diminishing cumulative oxidative damage and helping us to stay healthy. Vitamin E is one such nutrient that functions primarily as an antioxidant. By providing electrons to free radicals, vitamin E helps prevent oxidative damage, especially of cell membranes. The best sources of vitamin E are plant oils. When more plant oils are consumed, more vitamin E is needed to protect the double bonds found in plant oils from oxidation. However, the vitamin E content in plant oils is usually high. Because of their poor vitamin E status, preterm infants are particularly susceptible to oxidative breakdown of their red blood cell membranes (hemolysis). Among adults, people who smoke or experience long-term fat malabsorption run the biggest risk of vitamin E deficiency. At present, there is controversy about whether taking large amounts of vitamin E in supplement form over a long period of time provides any special health benefits; research is ongoing.

Vitamin K

Vitamin K is essential for blood clotting. A Danish researcher first noted the relationship between vitamin K and blood clotting and named the fat-soluble vitamin "K" after *koagulation*, the Danish spelling for *coagulation*.

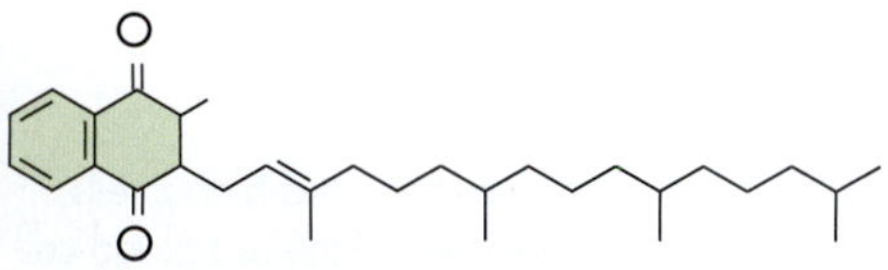
Phylloquinone (K_1)

Vitamin K

The family of compounds known as vitamin K includes **phylloquinone** (vitamin K_1) from plants and the menaquinones (vitamin K_2) found in fish oils and meats. The menaquinones are also synthesized by bacteria in the human intestine.

phylloquinone A form of vitamin K that comes from plants; also called vitamin K_1.

Absorption, Transport, Storage, and Excretion of Vitamin K

It appears that up to 80% of dietary vitamin K as phylloquinone and menaquinone is taken up by cells that line the small intestine and incorporated into chylomicrons. The process requires bile and pancreatic juice. The menaquinones synthesized by bacteria in the colon are absorbed, but the amount absorbed likely provides only 10% of the vitamin K we need. Some vitamin K is stored in the liver and some is incorporated in the lipoproteins VLDL, LDL, and HDL for transport throughout the body. Mineral oil and other nonabsorbable lipids interfere with vitamin K absorption, so their use close to meals should be discouraged. Most vitamin K excretion occurs via the bile, with a small amount of excretion via the urine.[7]

Functions of Vitamin K

Vitamin K contributes to the synthesis by the liver of seven blood-clotting factors (Fig. 9-10). Vitamin K is required for the conversion of some precursor proteins to the active clotting factors. In this reaction, carbon dioxide (CO_2) is added to a glutamic acid in the precursor protein, yielding the active factor containing the unique amino acid gamma-carboxyglutamic acid. Proteins that have undergone this conversion are called "Gla proteins," where Gla stands for gamma-carboxyglutamic acid.[7] One example of this process is the conversion of a precursor protein to **prothrombin,** one of the participants in the blood-clotting cascade. All these vitamin K-dependent clotting proteins depend on calcium interaction with gamma-carboxyglutamic acid in order to participate in the clotting reaction.[6]

In the body, vitamin K is converted to an inactive form once it has acted. This must be reactivated for its biological action to persist. The body does this readily. However, drugs such as warfarin, which strongly inhibit this reactivation process, act as powerful anticoagulants. People taking oral anticoagulants, such as warfarin, to lessen blood clotting should not consume vitamin K supplements and have a consistent vitamin K intake.

Vitamin K also participates in the conversion of protein-bound glutamate residues to gamma-carboxyglutamate residues and the synthesis of two bone "Gla" proteins. The first protein is **osteocalcin,** secreted by bone-building cells. The second bone protein, called "matrix Gla protein," is found in the protein matrix of bone. Both these proteins depend on vitamin K for the gamma-carboxylation reaction involving glutamic acid. Low concentrations of circulating vitamin K have been associated with low bone mineral density. It may be that inadequate intake of vitamin K increases the risk of hip fracture in women.[3] Finally, vitamin K may also participate in various blood vessel functions.

prothrombin One of the numerous proteins that participate in the formation of blood clots. Conversion of its precursor protein to the active blood-clotting factor in the liver requires vitamin K.

osteocalcin A protein produced in bone that is thought to bind calcium; the synthesis of osteocalcin is aided by vitamin K.

Dietary Sources of Vitamin K

Good food sources of vitamin K are liver, green leafy vegetables (e.g., kale, turnip greens, salad greens, cabbage, and spinach), broccoli, peas, and green beans. One reason to consume a diet rich in green vegetables is to obtain sufficient vitamin K. Other sources are vegetable oils, such as soy and canola. Vitamin K also is quite resistant to cooking losses.

Food Sources of Vitamin K

Food Item and Amount	*Vitamin K (μg)*
Brussels sprouts, ½ cup	483
Raw kale, ½ cup	274
Cooked broccoli, ½ cup	211
Raw turnips, 1 cup	138
Raw spinach, 1 cup	120
Raw cauliflower, 3 florets	120
Looseleaf lettuce, 1 cup	118
Raw cabbage, 1 cup	101
Cooked green beans, ½ cup	49
Asparagus spears, 5	38
Boiled egg, 1	31
Sauerkraut, ½ cup	30
Green peas, ½ cup	26
Soybean oil, 1 tbsp	25
Canola oil, 1 tbsp	17

Adequate Intake adult men, 120 μg
Adequate Intake adult women, 90 μg

Vitamin K Needs

For adult women the Adequate Intake for vitamin K is 90 μg/day and for adult men the amount is 120 μg/day. This is based on the amount adults usually consume.[7] The Daily Value used on food and supplement labels for vitamin K is 80 μg. Average

The most reliable clinical evidence of vitamin K deficiency is an increase in clotting time, which is a measure of how quickly prothrombin in the blood can form a clot. The actual vitamin K and prothrombin concentration in the blood can also be measured.

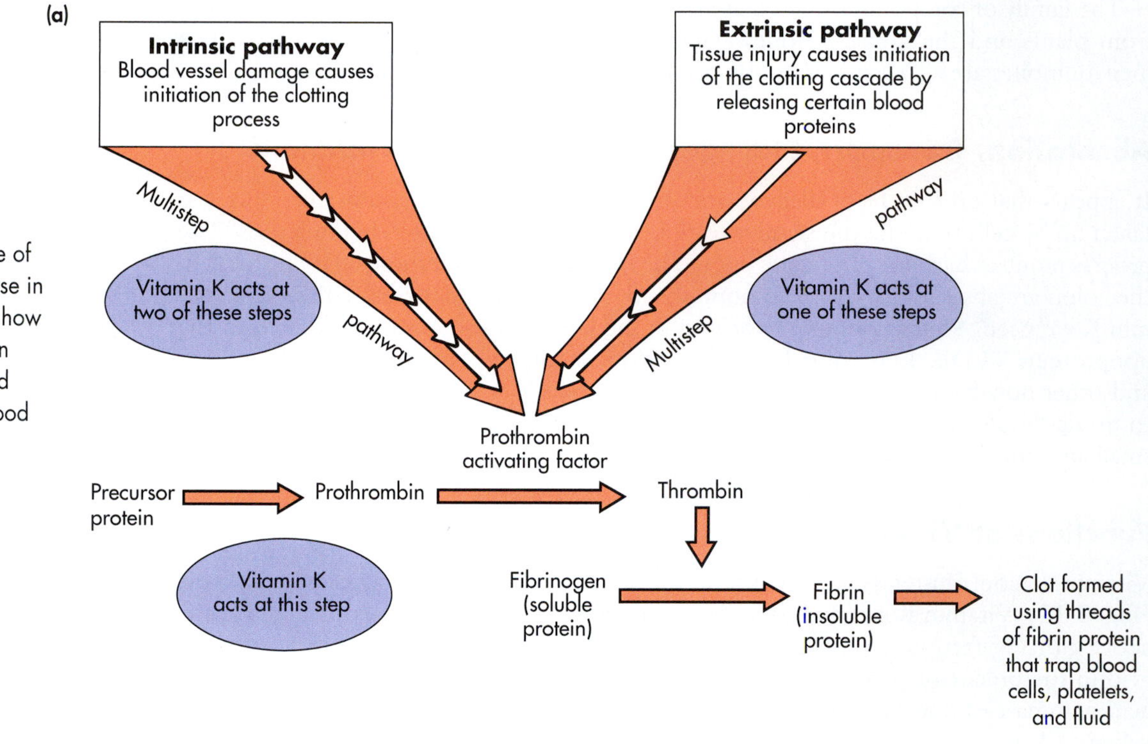
(a)
Intrinsic pathway
Blood vessel damage causes initiation of the clotting process
Extrinsic pathway
Tissue injury causes initiation of the clotting cascade by releasing certain blood proteins
Multistep pathway
Vitamin K acts at two of these steps
Multistep pathway
Vitamin K acts at one of these steps
Prothrombin activating factor
Precursor protein
Prothrombin
Thrombin
Vitamin K acts at this step
Fibrinogen (soluble protein)
Fibrin (insoluble protein)
Clot formed using threads of fibrin protein that trap blood cells, platelets, and fluid

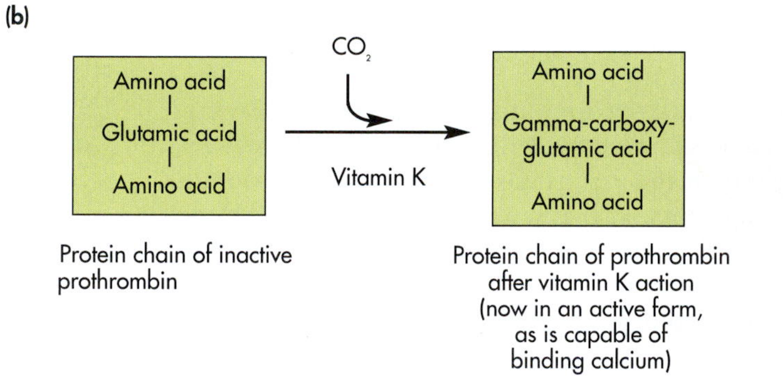
(b)
Amino acid
Glutamic acid
Amino acid
CO2
Vitamin K
Amino acid
Gamma-carboxy-glutamic acid
Amino acid
Protein chain of inactive prothrombin
Protein chain of prothrombin after vitamin K action (now in an active form, as is capable of binding calcium)

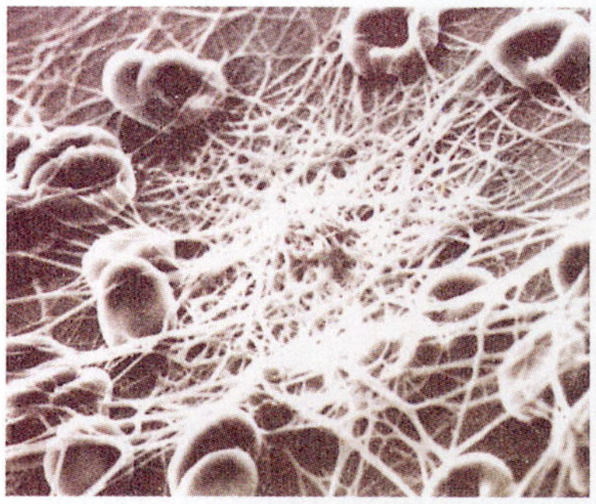

Figure 9-10 Vitamin K metabolism. (*a*) Forming a blood clot requires the participation of vitamin K in both the intrinsic and extrinsic blood-clotting pathways. Note that, although the two pathways are activated by different events, there is some overlap in the pathways, but for simplicity we have not shown that. (*b*) Vitamin K specifically adds a carbon dioxide to glutamic acid in a precursor protein to yield gamma-carboxyglutamic acid in that protein. This change imparts calcium-binding capacity to the protein, as in the conversion of a precursor protein to prothrombin, an active clotting factor.

A salad containing dark greens (or other green vegetables) each day provides abundant vitamin K for a diet.

consumption is 60 to 200 μg/day, with men showing higher intakes. Most vitamin K consumed in a day disappears from the body in the next few days. Thus, no Upper Level for vitamin K has been set. Nevertheless, vitamin K is abundant in the diet, and a deficiency from diet alone is not common. Laboratory animal studies have shown that excessive amounts of vitamin A and vitamin E are known to antagonize the actions of vitamin K. Vitamin A is thought to interfere with the absorption of vitamin K from the intestine. Large doses of vitamin E can lead to a decrease in vitamin K-dependent clotting factors and increased bleeding tendency. In either case, megadose supplements of these vitamins may pose a risk to vitamin K status.

Vitamin K Deficiency

A deficiency of vitamin K most likely occurs when a person takes certain types of antibiotics that disrupt vitamin K metabolism or has impaired fat absorption.

Vitamin K deficiency also can occur in newborns. Their vitamin K stores are typically low at birth. Infants run the risk of defective blood clotting and eventual hemorrhage because of a lack of vitamin K. To prevent this possible vitamin K deficiency, physicians in North America routinely provide vitamin K by injections within 6 hours of delivery. Finally, some older people may be at risk of deficiency due to scant green vegetable intake.

The fat-soluble vitamins are reviewed in Table 9-2.

Critical | Thinking

Tim was diagnosed as having blood clots in his leg and has been using anticoagulant medications for 2 months. On examination, the doctor is surprised to find that the clots he expected to have dissolved are still there. What is a possible nutritional explanation for this finding?

Table 9-2 Summary of the Fat-Soluble Vitamins: Their Functions, Deficiency Conditions, and Food Sources

Major Vitamin	Functions	Deficiency Symptoms	People at Risk	Sources	RDA or Adequate Intake	Toxicity Symptoms*
Vitamin A Preformed retinoids and provitamin A carotenoids	Vision in dim light and color vision, cell differentiation and growth, immunity	Poor growth, night blindness, blindness, dry skin, xerophthalmia	Rare in United States but common in preschool children living in poverty in developing countries, alcoholics	**Preformed vitamin A:** liver, fortified milk, fish liver oils **Provitamin A:** red, orange, dark green, and yellow vegetables; orange fruits	700-900 μg RAE	Headache, vomiting, double vision, hair loss, dry mucous membranes, bone and joint pain, fractures, liver damage, hemorrhage, coma, teratogenic effects: spontaneous abortions, birth defects. Upper Level is 3000 μg of preformed vitamin A (10,000 IU), based on the risk of birth defects and liver toxicity.
Vitamin D Cholecalciferol Ergocalciferol	Maintenance of intracellular and extracellular calcium concentrations	Rickets in children, osteomalacia in older adults	Dark-skinned individuals, older adults, breastfed infants from vitamin D-deficient mother	Vitamin D-fortified milk, fish oils	5–10 μg (200–400 IU) 15 μg > 70 yrs (600 IU)	Calcification of soft tissues, growth restriction, excess calcium excretion via the kidney. Upper Level is 50 μg (2000 IU), based on the risk of elevated blood calcium.
Vitamin E Tocopherols Tocotrienols	Antioxidant, prevention of propagation of free radicals	Hemolysis of red blood cells, degeneration of sensory neurons	Patients with fat-malabsorption syndromes, smokers (overt deficiency is rare)	Plant oils, seeds, nuts, products made from oils	15 mg alpha-tocopherol for men and women (22 IU natural form, 33 IU synthetic form)	Inhibition of vitamin K metabolism. Upper Level is 1000 mg (1100 IU synthetic form, 1500 IU natural form), based on the risk of hemorrhage.
Vitamin K Phylloquinone Menaquinone	Synthesis of blood-clotting factors and bone proteins	Hemorrhage, fractures	Those taking antibiotics for a long period of time; older adults with scant green vegetable intake	Green vegetables, liver synthesis by intestinal microorganisms	90-120 μg	No Upper Level has been set.

*For vitamins D, E, and K, toxicity is seen only with supplement use; foods pose no threat.

Concept | Check

Vitamin K is important for blood clotting because it stimulates the conversion of precursor proteins to active clotting factors, such as prothrombin. This conversion involves the addition of carbon dioxide to glutamic acid in the precursor protein, yielding gamma-carboxyglutamic acid, which in turn can bind calcium. About 10% of the vitamin K we absorb every day comes from bacterial synthesis in the intestines, but most comes from the diet. The amount in the diet alone generally meets our needs. Thus, except for newborns and possibly some older people, a deficiency of vitamin K is unlikely, even though it is readily excreted from the body.

Summary

1. Vitamins are essential organic (carbon-containing) compounds needed for important metabolic reactions in the body. They are not a source of energy. Instead, they promote many energy-yielding and other reactions in the body, thereby aiding in the growth, development, and maintenance of various body tissues. Vitamins A, D, E, and K are fat soluble, whereas the B-vitamins and vitamin C are water soluble. Fat-soluble vitamins are excreted less readily from the body and are less susceptible to cooking loss than are water-soluble vitamins.
2. Some fat-soluble vitamins pose a potential threat for toxicity. Vitamins A and D can readily accumulate in the body to toxic concentrations. The water-soluble vitamins niacin, vitamin B-6, and vitamin C can also induce toxic signs and symptoms, but only at doses much higher than their RDAs.
3. Fat-soluble vitamins are absorbed along with dietary fat. They travel by way of the lymphatic system into general circulation, carried by chylomicrons, one type of lipoprotein. In disease states in which fat digestion is limited, fat-soluble vitamin status may be compromised, especially with vitamins A, E, and K.
4. Vitamin A consists of a family of retinoid compounds: retinal, retinol, and retinoic acid. A plant derivative known as beta-carotene, along with two other carotenoids, yields vitamin A after metabolism by the intestine or liver. Vitamin A contributes to the maintenance of vision, the proper development of cells (especially mucus-forming cells), and immune function. Vitamin A is found in foods of animal origin, such as liver, fish oils, and fortified milk. Carotenoids are obtained from plants and are especially plentiful in dark green and orange vegetables and in some fruits.
5. North Americans at risk for poor vitamin A status are people exhibiting limited fat absorption and alcoholics. Vitamin A can be quite toxic when taken at doses 2 to 4 times or more the RDA, but only with preformed vitamin A. Use is especially dangerous during pregnancy because it can lead to fetal malformations.
6. For most people, vitamin D is more correctly viewed as a hormone rather than a vitamin because sufficient amounts of it can be produced by the body. Provitamin D is synthesized in the skin from a derivative of cholesterol in a process that depends on ultraviolet light. With adequate sun exposure, no dietary intake of vitamin D is needed. The provitamin, whether produced in the skin or obtained from the diet, is metabolized in the liver and kidneys to yield $1,25(OH)_2$ vitamin D (or calcitriol), the active hormonal form of vitamin D. $1,25(OH)_2$ vitamin D is important for calcium absorption from the intestine and, with other hormones, it helps regulate bone metabolism. Vitamin D is found in fish oils and fortified milk.
7. Vitamin E functions as a chain-breaking antioxidant. By donating electrons to electron-seeking compounds (oxidizing agents), it neutralizes their action. One group of electron-seeking compounds, known as free radicals, can cause widespread destruction, both to cell membranes and to DNA. Vitamin E is one of several components in the body's defense system against such oxidizing agents. Vitamin E is plentiful in plant oils and food products that contain these oils. Overt vitamin E deficiency is rare; marginal status is usually associated with problems in fat absorption and smoking. To date, the use of megadose supplements of vitamin E by healthy adults to limit cardiovascular disease risk (and certain other health problems) is still a research question. Use in high-risk people has been proven ineffective in major clinical trials.
8. Vitamin K contributes to the body's blood-clotting ability by facilitating the conversion of precursor proteins to active clotting factors, such as prothrombin, which promotes blood coagulation. Vitamin K also plays a role in bone metabolism. About 10% of the vitamin K absorbed each day likely comes from bacterial synthesis in the intestine; most comes from foods, primarily green leafy vegetables and vegetable oils. Vitamin K is readily excreted from the body, but the usual daily intake from diet alone meets one's needs.

Study Questions

1. Describe two forms of vitamin A that are available in common foods.
2. Explain how retinal functions in black-and-white and color vision.
3. Describe how retinoic acid participates in protein synthesis.
4. What factors determine whether a person needs a dietary source of vitamin D or can rely on self-synthesis?
5. Describe how vitamin D, parathyroid hormone, and calcitonin regulate the concentration of calcium and phosphorus in the blood.

6. Define a free radical and explain how vitamin E controls free radical damage.
7. List several important dietary sources for each of the fat-soluble vitamins. Identify the Adequate Intake or RDA and the Upper Level for each of the fat-soluble vitamins.
8. Identify the two primary functions of vitamin K in the body.
9. What properties of the fat-soluble vitamins make them a greater risk for toxicity than the water-soluble vitamins?
10. Identify the North Americans most at risk for fat-soluble vitamin deficiencies.

Annotated References

1. ADA Reports: Position of the American Dietetic Association: Food fortification and dietary supplements. *Journal of the American Dietetic Association* 101:115, 2001.

   The best nutritional strategy for promoting optimal health and reducing the risk of chronic disease is to wisely choose a wide variety of foods. Additional vitamins and minerals from fortified foods and/or a multivitamin and mineral supplement can help some people meet their nutritional needs.

2. Ballew C and others: Serum retinol distributions in residents of the United States: Third National Health and Nutrition Examination Survey, 1988–1994. *American Journal of Clinical Nutrition* 73:594, 2001.

   Data from a survey of nutrition status in the United States indicate that while vitamin A status in children has improved since the 1970s, some children (especially minorities) continue to be at risk for suboptimal vitamin A intake. Children with higher body mass index, of greater age, and who use vitamin A containing supplements had higher blood retinol concentrations as compared to other children without these characteristics.

3. Booth S and others: Dietary vitamin K intakes are associated with hip fracture but not with bone mineral density in elderly men and women. *American Journal of Clinical Nutrition* 71:1201, 2000.

   Data from a recent study show a relationship between dietary vitamin K intake and risk of hip fractures. Individuals with the highest intakes of vitamin K had a lower incidence of hip fractures as compared to individuals with the lowest intakes of vitamin K.

4. Do you need more vitamin D? *Consumer Reports on Health,* p. 1, November 2002.

   Younger and middle-aged adults should consume 10 μg (400 IU) vitamin D daily if sun exposure is infrequent. Older adults with little sun exposure need 15 to 20 μg (600 to 800 IU) daily. Anyone who rarely gets sun exposure needs 25 μg (1000 IU) daily.

5. Fairfield K, Fletcher R: Vitamins for chronic disease prevention in adults: Scientific review and clinical applications. *Journal of the American Medical Association* 287:3116, 2002 and 287:3127, 2002.

   While vitamin deficiency diseases are no longer common in North America, many physicians are suggesting that marginal intakes of many vitamins and minerals consumed by some North Americans may increase the risk of developing some chronic diseases, including cancer and cardiovascular disease. To help ensure optimal intakes of most of the vitamins and minerals, the authors recommended that adult North Americans consume a daily multivitamin and mineral supplement.

6. Feskanich D and others: Vitamin A intake and hip fractures among postmenopausal women. *Journal of the American Medical Association* 287:47, 2002.

   Intakes of preformed vitamin A at just 2 times the RDA may increase the risk of hip fracture in older women. This is in part because preformed vitamin A in high doses inhibits the activity of bone-forming cells. Any supplement use should carefully consider preformed vitamin A intake and not exceed about 2 times the RDA.

7. Food and Nutrition Board, Institute of Medicine: *Dietary reference intakes for vitamin A, vitamin K, arsenic, boron, chromium, copper, iodine, iron, manganese, molybdenum, nickel, silicon, vanadium, and zinc.* Washington, DC: National Academy Press, 2001.

   Recommendations for vitamin A and vitamin K intake are listed. The rationale used to set the RDA or Adequate Intake and Upper Level for these nutrients is discussed in detail.

8. Food and Nutrition Board, Institute of Medicine: *Dietary Reference Intakes for vitamin C, vitamin E, selenium, and carotenoids.* Washington, DC: National Academy Press, 2000.

   The functions of antioxidant nutrients, how RDA and related standards were determined, and deficiency and toxicity symptoms are explained. This is the definitive report by the panel of experts on nutrient needs for dietary antioxidants.

9. Food and Nutrition Board, Institute of Medicine: *Dietary Reference Intakes for calcium, phosphorus, magnesium, vitamin D, and fluoride.* Washington, DC: National Academy Press, 1997.

   The RDAs and related standards for vitamin D and some minerals are discussed in detail. A major change in setting these new (and all other) estimates of human needs is the use of a specific biological marker or estimate of current intakes that shows adequacy.

10. Fuller CJ and others: The effect of vitamin E and vitamin C supplementation on LDL oxidizability and neutrophil respiratory burst in young smokers. *Journal of the American College of Nutrition* 19(3):361, 2000.

    Smoking cessation is the only means by which smokers can reduce oxidative damage in their bodies. Supplements of vitamin E or C provide no reliable benefit in reducing oxidant stress in smokers.

11. Heany RP and others: Human serum 25-hydroxycholecalciferol response to extended oral dosing with cholecalciferol. *American Journal of Clinical Nutrition* 11:204, 2003.

    Regular sunlight exposure is important for maintaining vitamin D status. Vitamin D intake is only partially effective.

12. Heart Protection Study Collaborative Group: MRC/BHF Heart protection study of antioxidant vitamin supplementation in 20,536 high-risk individuals: A randomized placebo-controlled trial. *The Lancet* 360:23, 2002.

    This placebo-controlled study involving over 20,500 subjects found that while consuming megadoses of vitamin E was safe (600 mg/day), such use did not lead to a lower incidence of cardiovascular disease (or cancer). It is recommended that proven strategies to prevent cardiovascular disease (such as aspirin, statin drugs, increased physical activity, decreased consumption of saturated fat and cholesterol, and smoking cessation) be emphasized over antioxidant supplementation.

13. Holick MF: Meeting vitamin D needs of the elderly. *Nutrition & the M.D.,* p. 1, May 2001.

    Older adults are likely to be deficient in vitamin D if they do not receive regular sun exposure or consume enough vitamin D-fortified foods, such as milk. Needs for vitamin D can usually be met by exposure to sunlight 2 to 3 times per week. Exposure time should be about 25% of that required to cause a sunburn. This may not provide vitamin D for older people, however, as aging decreases the ability of the skin to produce vitamin D. Thus, a yearly determination of vitamin D status, using 25-OH vitamin D as a measure of this, should be a part of the health evaluation by a physician for all older adults, and low status corrected with vitamin D supplements.

14. Liebman B: Antioxidants: No magic bullet. *Nutrition Action Healthletter,* p. 1, April 2002.

    Epidemiological studies have suggested that increased intakes of antioxidants such as vitamin C, vitamin E, and beta-carotene may prevent or slow the development of a variety of chronic diseases. However, when more rigorous clinical trials were conducted, antioxidants were not found to be as beneficial as previously believed at preventing further disease or death in people with existing cardiovascular disease. The possibility that megadose vitamin E might prevent cardiovascular disease development in otherwise healthy individuals is still a research question.

15. Nesby-O'Dell S and others: Hypovitaminosis D prevalence and determinants among African American and White women of reproductive age. *American Journal of Clinical Nutrition* 76:187, 2002.

    African Americans are at considerable risk for a vitamin D deficiency. Regular assessment of vitamin D status is particularly important in this ethnic group.

16. Norman A: Vitamin D. In Bowman BA, RM Russel (eds.): *Present knowledge in nutrition.* Washington, DC: ILSI Press, 2001.

    This chapter is a valuable reference for understanding vitamin D: mechanism of action, biological properties, nutritional considerations such as food sources, needs, and consequences of a deficiency.

17. Russell RM: The vitamin A spectrum: From deficiency to toxicity. *American Journal of Clinical Nutrition* 71:878, 2000.

    Vitamin A toxicity is more common among older adults than young adults. The longer a person overdoses on the vitamin, the greater the potential for toxicity.

18. Solomons N: Vitamin A and carotenoids. In Bowman BA, RM Russel (eds.): *Present knowledge in nutrition.* Washington, DC: ILSI Press, 2001.

    This chapter provides an excellent overview of the bioavailability, absorption, metabolism, functions, and dietary sources of both vitamin A and the carotenoids.

19. Willet WC, Stampfer MJ: What vitamin should I be taking, doctor? *The New England Journal of Medicine* 345:1819, 2001.

    Use of a daily multivitamin and mineral supplement is a reasonable dietary practice, but it does not substitute for avoiding smoking, weight control, and regular physical activity. These supplements also do not contain needed fiber or essential fatty acids. Use of up to 400 IU of vitamin E may be considered, but evidence supporting specific health benefits is still a research question.

20. Yusuf S: Vitamin E supplementation and cardiovascular events in high-risk patients. *The New England Journal of Medicine* 342:254, 2000.

    In patients at high risk for cardiovascular events, treatment with 400 IU vitamin E per day for 4.5 years had no apparent effect on cardiovascular disease-related outcomes.

Take | Action

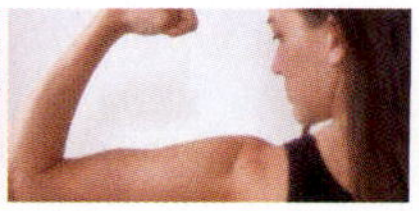

I. Measuring Your Vitamin Intake Against the RDAs.

This activity requires you to reexamine the nutritional assessment you did for Chapters 1 and 2. You recorded all the foods and drinks you consumed for 1 day and their quantities. Then you assessed your intake by recording the total amounts of nutrients you consumed. You were then asked to compare your nutrient intake with established standards. Take your completed assessment and look at your intakes of vitamins A, E, C, B-6, and B-12, and thiamin, riboflavin, niacin, and folate. Record these numbers in the following table. Next, record the RDA for each of these nutrients from your assessment. Then, record the percentage of the RDA you consumed for each vitamin. Lastly, place +, −, or = in the space provided, reflecting an intake higher than, lower than, or equal to the RDA.

Vitamin	Intake	RDA	% of RDA	+, −, =
A				
E				
C				
Thiamin				
Riboflavin				
Niacin				
Vitamin B-6				
Folate				
Vitamin B-12				

Analysis

1. Which of your vitamin intakes equaled or exceeded the RDA?

2. Which of your vitamin intakes were below the RDA?

3. What foods could you eat to improve your dietary intake of vitamins in low amounts in your diet? (Review sources of certain vitamins in this chapter and the next.)

Take | Action

II. A Closer Look at Supplement Use.

With the current popularity of vitamin and mineral supplements, it is more important than ever to understand how to evaluate a supplement. Study the label of a supplement you use, or one readily available from a friend or the supermarket. Then answer the following questions.

1. What is the recommended dosage of this supplement?

2. Based on the recommended dosage, are there any individual vitamins for which the intake would be greater than 100% of the Daily Value? List these vitamins.

3. Are any suggested intakes above the Upper Level for the nutrient?

4. Are there any superfluous ingredients, such as herbs or flavors, in the supplement? You can often tell this because these ingredients do not have a percent of Daily Value.

5. Does at least 50% of the vitamin A in the product come from beta-carotene or other provitamin A carotenoids (to reduce risk of preformed vitamin A toxicity)?

6. Are there any warnings on the label as to populations who should not consume this product?

7. Are there any other signs that tip you off that this may not be a safe product?

Nutrient Supplements: Who Needs Them?

Today, supplements are marketed as good for anything that ails you. This cure-all approach is promoted by the supplement industry and countless health-food stores, pharmacies, and supermarkets.[1]

According to the Dietary Supplement Health and Education Act of 1994 (discussed in Chapter 1), a supplement in the United States is a product intended to supplement the diet that bears or contains one or more of the following dietary ingredients:

- A vitamin
- A mineral
- An herb or another botanical
- An amino acid
- A dietary substance to supplement the diet, which could be an extract or a combination of the first four ingredients in this list

The definition is very broad and covers a wide variety of nutritional substances. The use of supplements to the diet is a common practice among North Americans and generates about $14 billion annually for the industry in the United States alone.[1] Recall also from the Nutrition Issue in Chapter 1 that unless FDA has evidence that a supplement is inherently dangerous or marketed with an illegal claim, it will not regulate such products closely. (The vitamin folate is an exception.) Currently, FDA has limited resources to police supplement manufacturers, and has to act against these manufacturers one at a time. Thus, we cannot rely on FDA to protect us from vitamin and mineral supplement overuse and misuse. We bear that responsibility ourselves, coupled with professional advice from a physician or registered dietitian.

Currently, the supplement makers can make broad claims about their products under the "structure or function" provision of the law, allowing the product onto the market without testing for safety or efficacy. The products, however, cannot claim to prevent, treat, or cure a disease. Since menopause and aging are not diseases per se, products alleging to treat these conditions can be marketed without FDA approval. For example, a product that claims to treat hot flashes can be sold without any definitive testing to prove that the product actually works, but a product that claims to decrease the risk of cardiovascular disease by reducing blood cholesterol must have scientific studies that justify the claim.

Why do people take supplements? Reasons that are frequently given include the following:

- To reduce susceptibility to health problems (e.g., colds)
- To prevent heart attacks
- To prevent cancer
- To reduce stress
- To increase "energy"

Focus first on foods that meet nutrient needs.

Because recent research on a variety of nutrient supplements has revealed a lack of product quality, the USP (United States Pharmacopeia) designation is being extended to an increasing number of nutrient supplements. The USP standards designate strength, quality, purity, packaging, labeling, speed of dissolution, and acceptable length of storage of ingredients for drugs. The purpose of applying them to vitamin and mineral supplements is to establish professionally accepted standards for these products. Consumers who buy nutrient supplements should look for a USP label when comparing similar products, such as calcium supplements. If no USP label is present, the next best approach is to purchase nationally advertised brands. Most brand name nutrient supplements aren't labeled USP because the manufacturers prefer to guarantee the products via their brand names.

Long-term intake of just 2 to 4 or more times the Daily Value for some fat-soluble vitamins—particularly vitamin A (as retinoids)—can cause toxic effects. Know what you are taking if you use supplements.

Should you take a supplement? This is up to you. Currently, opinions vary about the wisdom and safety of supplement use even among knowledgeable scientists. Typically, nutrition scientists have recommended that supplement use is needed only by a few groups of our population at large. However, over the last few years many reputable nutrition and medical scientists have recommended supplementation of specific nutrients for most (or all) adults.[5, 19]

This change in philosophy has arisen primarily because many North Americans have been unwilling to change their food habits, such as including ample fruits and vegetables. This gap can leave diets low in the vitamin folate. Adequate folate status when a woman becomes pregnant helps reduce the risk of certain birth defects in her offspring (400 μg per day of synthetic folic acid is recommended). Folate also limits homocysteine in the blood, a likely risk factor for cardiovascular disease that can affect all of us. In addition, the committee appointed by the Food and Nutrition Board that set current nutrient standards for vitamin B-12 suggested that adults over age 50 consume vitamin B-12 in a synthetic form, such as that added to ready-to-eat breakfast cereals or present in supplements. Synthetic vitamin B-12 is more easily absorbed than that found in food; this helps compensate for the fall in vitamin B-12 absorption typically seen as we age into our later years. This latter observation has caused nutrition experts at Tufts University to add a recommendation for vitamin B-12 supplements to the Food Guide Pyramid they developed for older persons. The Tufts scientists also include calcium and vitamin D supplements, as these nutrients can be deficient in the diets of older persons (see Chapter 18).

Nutrition expert Dr. Walter Willett also recommends in his book *Eat, Drink, and Be Healthy* (discussed in Chapter 2), that most people take a multivitamin and mineral supplement, citing that this is one inexpensive way to decrease the risk of developing a number of chronic diseases. A further example of this change in philosophy is a recent article in *The New England Journal of Medicine* entitled "What supplement should I be taking, doctor?" The authors recommended a multivitamin and mineral supplement and possibly some extra vitamin E.[19] Recently two companion articles in the *Journal of the American Medical Association* supported the first recommendation.[5] Still, all these experts note that many of the health-promoting effects of foods cannot be found in a bottle; recall the discussions of phytochemicals in Chapter 2 and the benefits of fiber in Chapter 5. Few or no phytochemicals and no fiber are present in supplements. Multivitamin and mineral supplements also contain little calcium in order to keep the pill size small, and the form of zinc and copper used in many supplements (oxides) are not as well absorbed as forms found in foods.

Overall, supplement use cannot fix a poor diet in all respects. Uninformed megadose supplement use also can lead to harm.[7, 8, 9] Currently, most nutrient toxicity is a result of supplement use. Thus, we are advised to first take a good look at our dietary habits and then improve them, as outlined in Chapter 2. Finally, find out which nutrient gaps remain, and identify food sources that can help. Examples could be ready-to-eat breakfast cereals to increase vitamin E, folic acid, and vitamin B-6 intake and provide highly absorbable forms of vitamin B-12 (many currently contain up to RDA amounts [or more] per serving). One needs to be careful, however, as these products may provide the appropriate amount of nutrients in 1 serving, but the typical consumer may eat more than 1 serving. This can lead to an excessive intake of some nutrients, such as vitamin A, iron, and synthetic folic acid. Calcium-fortified orange juice could be used to increase calcium intake, or milk and yogurt to increase vitamin D and calcium intake.

If supplement use is desired, one should discuss this practice with a physician or registered dietitian, as some supplements can interfere with certain medicines. For example, vitamin B-6 can offset the action of L-dopa (used in treating Parkinson's disease), high intakes of vitamin K or vitamin E alter the action of oral anticoagulants, large doses of vitamin C can interfere with certain cancer therapy regimens, excessive zinc intake can inhibit copper absorption, and large amounts of folate can mask signs and symptoms of a vitamin B-12 deficiency (see the section on toxicity of folate in the next chapter). Remember, you can get too much of a good thing.

People Most Likely to Need Supplements

Various medical and health-related organizations suggest that the following vitamin and mineral supplementation can be important for certain groups of healthy people:

- Women in their childbearing years may need extra synthetic folic acid if their dietary patterns do not supply enough (again, 400 μg).
- Women with excessive bleeding during menstruation may need extra iron.

- Women who are pregnant or breastfeeding may need extra iron, folate, and calcium.
- People with very low energy intakes (less than about 1200 kcal per day) may need a range of vitamins and minerals. This is true of some women and many older people.
- Strict vegans may need extra calcium, iron, zinc, and vitamin B-12.
- Newborns, under the direction of a physician, need a single dose of vitamin K.
- Some infants may need fluoride supplements, as directed by a dentist.
- People with limited milk intake and sunlight exposure may need extra vitamin D. This includes many breastfed infants, especially those who are dark skinned (this reduces vitamin D synthesis by the skin), and many older people.
- People with lactose maldigestion or intolerance, and those with allergies to dairy products, may need extra calcium.
- Adults over age 50 may need a synthetic source of vitamin B-12.
- People on very low-fat diets or diets low in plant oils and nuts may need some extra vitamin E.

Individuals with certain medical conditions (e.g., vitamin-resistance diseases or long-standing fat malabsorption) and those who use certain medications also may require supplementation with specific vitamins and minerals. Children who are "picky eaters" may do so as well (see Chapter 17). Finally, smokers and alcohol abusers may benefit from supplementation, but cessation of these two activities is far more beneficial than any supplementation.

Case Scenario | Follow-up

Use of *Nutramega* poses some health risks for Kristen. Taking 2 to 3 tablets every 3 hours would mean taking at least 16 tablets per day. This alone would provide an intake of vitamin A, vitamin C, and zinc well in excess of the Upper Levels for these nutrients. Intake of preformed vitamin A would be 1.3 times the Upper Level, intake of vitamin C would be 3.4 times the Upper Level, and intake of zinc would be 3 times the Upper Level. Intake of selenium, however, falls well below the Upper Level set for that nutrient. This is how the math works out.

Vitamin A

33% (0.33) times the Daily Value of 1000 μg RAE equals 330 μg RAE per tablet. Sixteen tablets would yield 5280 μg RAE. The Upper Level is 3000 μg RAE for preformed vitamin A. Since 75% of the vitamin A is preformed vitamin A, this yields 3960 μg RAE of preformed vitamin A ($5280 \times 0.75 = 3960$), or 1.3 times the Upper Level ($3960/3000 = 1.3$).

Vitamin C

700% (7) times the Daily Value of 60 mg equals 420 mg per tablet. 16 tablets would yield 6720 mg. The Upper Level is 2000 mg. This would then yield 3.4 times the Upper Level ($6720/2000 = 3.4$).

Zinc

50% (0.5) times the Daily Value of 15 milligrams equals 7.5 mg per tablet. 16 tablets would yield 120 mg. The Upper Level is 40 mg. This would then yield 3 times the Upper Level ($120/40 = 3$).

Selenium

10% (0.1) times the Daily Value of 70 μg equals 7 μg per tablet. 16 tablets would yield 112 μg. This is less than the Upper Level of 400 μg.

The maintenance dose of two to three tablets per day poses no risk per se, but *Nutramega* is very expensive compared to the cost of the typical multivitamin and mineral supplement (a 1-month supply would cost about $2 compared to about $15 for *Nutramega*). Overall, Kristen is smart to be concerned about meeting her nutrient needs, but the stress she is under does not increase nutrient needs. A healthy diet, as shown in Table 2-9 in Chapter 2, should be her primary focus. Taking a balanced multivitamin and mineral supplement is also a reasonable practice. Actually, however, it is most important for Kristen to get adequate sleep; this is the main health habit that will help her through her current schedule.

Which Supplement Should You Choose?

If you decide to take a multivitamin and mineral supplement, which one should you choose? As a start, choose a national brand (from a supermarket or pharmacy) that contains about 100% of the Daily Values for the nutrients present. A multivitamin and mineral supplement should also generally be taken with or just after meals to maximize absorption. Make sure also that intake from the total of this supplement, any other supplements used, and highly fortified foods such as ready-to-eat breakfast cereals provide no more than the Upper Level for each vitamin and mineral. (See the inside cover of this textbook for Upper Levels.) This is especially important with regard to vitamin A intake by women in their child-bearing years. Two exceptions are that both men and older women should make sure any product used is low in iron or iron-free to avoid possible iron overload (see Chapters 12 and 18 for details), and exceeding the Upper Level for vitamin D somewhat by adults is likely a safe practice. One should read the labels carefully to be sure of what is being taken (Fig. 9-11).

Another consideration in choosing a supplement is avoiding superfluous ingredients, such as para-aminobenzoic acid (PABA), hesperidin complex, inositol, bee pollen, and lecithins. These are not needed in our diets. They are especially common in expensive supplements sold in health-food stores and by mail. In addition, use of l-tryptophan and high doses of beta-carotene or fish oils are discouraged.

Five websites to help you evaluate ongoing claims and evaluate safety of supplements are:

www.acsh.org
www.quackwatch.com
www.ncahf.org
dietary-supplements.info.nih.gov
www.eatright.org

The sites are maintained by groups or individuals committed to providing reasoned and authoritative nutrition and health advice to consumers.

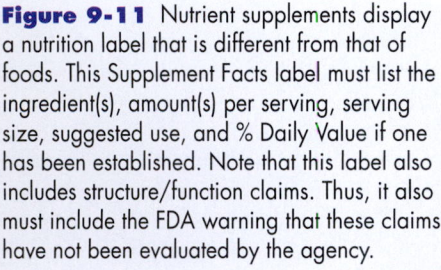

Figure 9-11 Nutrient supplements display a nutrition label that is different from that of foods. This Supplement Facts label must list the ingredient(s), amount(s) per serving, serving size, suggested use, and % Daily Value if one has been established. Note that this label also includes structure/function claims. Thus, it also must include the FDA warning that these claims have not been evaluated by the agency.

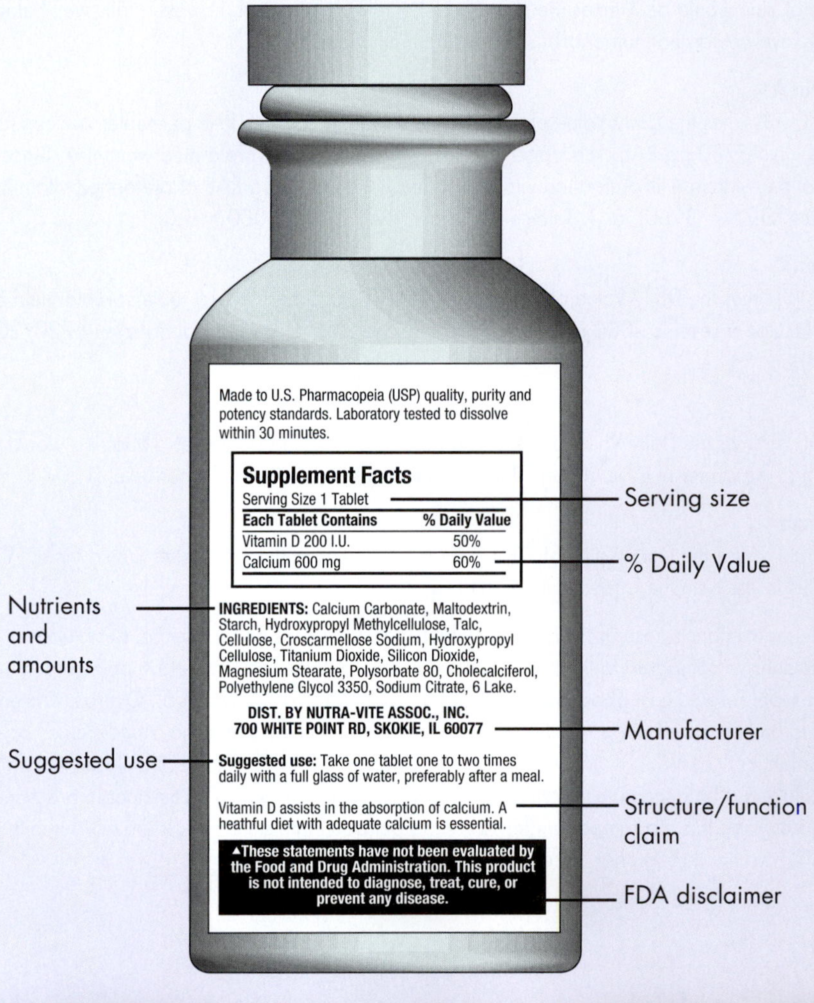

Made to U.S. Pharmacopeia (USP) quality, purity and potency standards. Laboratory tested to dissolve within 30 minutes.
Supplement Facts
Serving Size 1 Tablet
Each Tablet Contains
% Daily Value
Vitamin D 200 I.U.
50%
Calcium 600 mg
60%
INGREDIENTS: Calcium Carbonate, Maltodextrin, Starch, Hydroxypropyl Methylcellulose, Talc, Cellulose, Croscarmellose Sodium, Hydroxypropyl Cellulose, Titanium Dioxide, Silicon Dioxide, Magnesium Stearate, Polysorbate 80, Cholecalciferol, Polyethylene Glycol 3350, Sodium Citrate, 6 Lake.
DIST. BY NUTRA-VITE ASSOC., INC.
700 WHITE POINT RD, SKOKIE, IL 60077
Suggested use: Take one tablet one to two times daily with a full glass of water, preferably after a meal.
Vitamin D assists in the absorption of calcium. A healthful diet with adequate calcium is essential.
▲These statements have not been evaluated by the Food and Drug Administration. This product is not intended to diagnose, treat, cure, or prevent any disease.
Serving size
% Daily Value
Nutrients and amounts
Manufacturer
Suggested use
Structure/function claim
FDA disclaimer

chapter 10

The Water-Soluble Vitamins

Chapter | Outline

Case | Scenario

Suzanne and Ted are expecting their first child. Prior to conception, Ted (who completed one university-level nutrition course) had been trying to persuade Suzanne to eat a folic acid-rich breakfast cereal or take a multivitamin-mineral supplement every morning. Ted is concerned because Suzanne's sister gave birth to a child with spina bifida last year. Suzanne doesn't like to be hassled about her eating habits but admits her diet is "awful." Breakfast is usually a sweet pastry and coffee, lunch is whatever snack is available from a vending machine, and dinner is frequently eaten at a fast-food restaurant. She consumes no more than one or two servings of fruits and vegetables per day.

Her first visit to the obstetrician has her worried about the health of her fetus. How concerned should she be, especially given her current diet?

Refresh | Your Memory

As you begin your study of the water-soluble vitamins, you will want to review:

- The gastrointestinal system for the digestion and absorption of nutrients in Chapter 3.
- Energy metabolism, especially glycolysis, the citric acid cycle, and the electron transport chain in Chapter 4.
- Oxidation-reduction reactions in Chapter 4.
- The metabolism of carbohydrates in Chapter 4.
- Amino acid metabolism and the link between DNA and protein synthesis in Chapter 7.

Boost | Your Study

Check out the ***Perspectives in Nutrition: Online Learning Center*** www.mhhe.com/wardlawpers6 *for quizzes, flash cards, activities, and web links designed to further help you learn about the water-soluble vitamins.*

Chapter | Objectives

Chapter 10 is designed to allow you to:

1. Identify the water-soluble vitamins.
2. List the major functions and deficiency symptoms for each water-soluble vitamin.
3. List three important food sources for each water-soluble vitamin.
4. Describe toxicity symptoms from excess consumption of certain water-soluble vitamins.
5. Distinguish between vitamins and nonvitamins, such as inositol and taurine.
6. Describe some cancer-causing mechanisms, and describe how diet and nutrition are related to their minimization.

As defined in Chapter 9, vitamins are essential organic substances needed in very small amounts to support the metabolism, growth, and maintenance of cells. The water-soluble vitamins discussed in this chapter include eight B-vitamins, vitamin C, and a newcomer to the list of important nutrients, a dietary component called choline.[7, 8] The B-vitamins form coenzymes—organic compounds that enable certain enzymes to function. As a group, the B-vitamins are necessary for energy metabolism, transforming nutrients into characteristic cell structures, and creating various proteins, lipids, and carbohydrates. Vitamin C participates in a wide variety of metabolic processes, although not in the form of a coenzyme. Choline is needed to form lecithin and other compounds.

The end of the chapter briefly describes some "vitamin-like" compounds, which some people may require in their diets under atypical circumstances. These compounds currently are not classified as true vitamins because a healthy person does not require a dietary source of them and no specific deficiency disease results when they are absent from the diet. The chapter then finishes with a look at how diet and other factors influence cancer risk.

General Properties of the Water-Soluble Vitamins

For most of human history, diseases such as scurvy and pellagra caused enormous suffering and death. Early in the twentieth century, scientists began to recognize that these illnesses were caused by the absence of certain vital substances from the diet—now called the B-vitamins and vitamin C. The scientists discovered that restoring these vitamins to the diet dramatically reversed these deficiency diseases if done before significant deterioration of the body took place.

The second vitamin to be discovered was designated vitamin B, according to the letter convention discussed in Chapter 9. This water-soluble substance, which can cure **beriberi,** was initially thought to be a single chemical compound. When subsequent research showed that this substance actually consists of several compounds, they were named the B-vitamins, and numbers were added to the letter B to distinguish them. Of the eight B-vitamins, only two are still commonly referred to by letter and number: vitamin B-6 and vitamin B-12. The others now are usually referred to by the following names: thiamin (previously B-1), riboflavin (previously B-2), niacin (previously B-3), pantothenic acid, biotin, and folate. The older designations, however, are sometimes used on vitamin supplement labels.

All B-vitamins function as **coenzymes.** This classification falls under the general term **cofactor,** which also includes inorganic ions.[1] Cofactors as a class are necessary for certain enzymatic reactions to take place. Coenzymes specifically are molecules consisting of a vitamin, such as a B-vitamin, plus other chemical units. The body can make the other units and put the coenzyme together, but cannot make the B-vitamin. Since coenzymes fall under the cofactor designation, they also work with some of the body's enzymes to allow chemical reactions in a cell to proceed (Fig. 10-1). All the eight B-vitamins participate in energy metabolism; some also have other roles in the chemical reactions that take place within cells. Although vitamin C does not function as a coenzyme, it plays a role in the synthesis of several important compounds.

The B-vitamins are present in foods in their coenzyme forms bound to specific proteins. After ingestion, the bound vitamin coenzymes are released in the stomach and small intestine. The free vitamins are then absorbed in the small intestine.

Typically, about 50 to 90% of the B-vitamins in the diet are absorbed. (100% of synthetic folic acid is absorbed when taken on an empty stomach.) Once inside cells, the coenzyme forms of the vitamins are resynthesized. Health-food stores sell the coenzyme forms of some vitamins, although they have no specific benefits to the consumer, since vitamins are not absorbed in this form.

Because they are water soluble, most of the B-vitamins and vitamin C are more easily excreted from the body than the fat-soluble vitamins. Moreover, some of the water-soluble vitamins are rather easily destroyed during cooking due to heat or alkalinity; all are subject to leaching into the cooking water. Retention of the B-vitamins and vitamin C is greatest in foods that are prepared by steaming, stir-frying, microwaving, or simmering in minimal moisture (review Table 9-1 in Chapter 9).

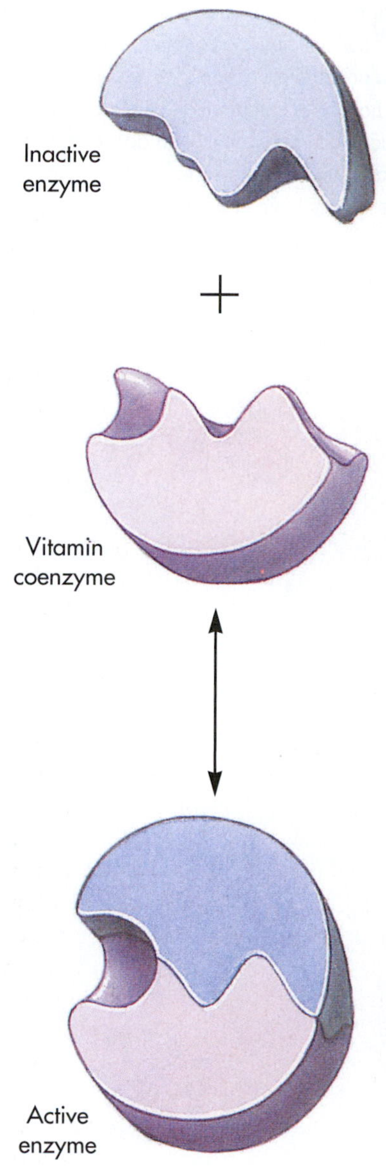

Figure 10-1 The enzyme-coenzyme interaction. The B-vitamins form coenzymes, which are compounds that enable specific enzymes to function.
Illustration by William Ober.

beriberi The thiamin-deficiency disorder characterized by muscle weakness, loss of appetite, nerve degeneration, and sometimes edema.

coenzyme An organic compound that combines with an inactive protein called an apoenzyme to form a catalytically active protein called a holoenzyme. In this manner, coenzymes aid in enzyme function.

cofactor An organic or inorganic substance that binds to a specific region on an enzyme and is necessary for the enzyme's activity.

B-Vitamin and Vitamin C Status of North Americans

The nutritional status of most North Americans with respect to the B-vitamins and vitamin C is generally good. Our typical diets contain ample and varied natural sources of these vitamins (Table 10-1).[7,8] In addition, many common foods are fortified with one or more of the water-soluble vitamins. In some developing countries, however, deficiencies of the water-soluble vitamins are more common, and the resulting deficiency diseases pose significant public health problems. (A detailed discussion of nutritional deficiencies worldwide is presented in Chapter 20.)

Despite the generally good B-vitamin and vitamin C status of North Americans, marginal deficiencies of the water-soluble vitamins may occur among some North

One group that is susceptible to B-vitamin deficiencies is alcoholics. The extremely unbalanced diets of some people with alcoholism, in combination with alcohol-induced alteration of vitamin absorption and metabolism, create a significant risk. Chapter 8 covered this topic in detail.

Table 10-1 Sample Meal Plan That Meets B-Vitamin and Vitamin C Needs

Breakfast		**Dinner**
Hard-cooked egg, 1	Nonfat milk, ¾ cup	Hamburger: Hamburger bun; Ground beef patty, 3 oz; Ketchup, 2 tsp; Mustard, 2 tsp — French fries, 3 oz
Low-fat toasted oat cereal, 1 cup	Orange juice, 1 cup	Salad: Lettuce, 1 cup; Shredded carrots, 2 tbsp; Cauliflower, ¼ cup; Broccoli, ¼ cup; Low-calorie Italian dressing, 2 tbsp
Snack		
Granola bar, 1		
Lunch		
Bagel sandwich	Celery, 3 stalks	
Whole-wheat bagel, 1	Peanut butter, 3 tbsp	
Ham, 2 slices	Pretzels, ½ oz	
Lettuce, 1 leaf	Apple, 1	
Mustard, 2 tsp	Nonfat milk, 1 cup	
Snack		**Snack**
Hard Cheese, 2 oz and crackers, 6		Fat-free pudding snack, 1
Low-fat yogurt, ½ cup		

This sample plan provides approximately 2200 kcal, roughly the minimum amount of energy needed for an active college student.

Americans and others in the Western world, especially older adults. The long-term effects of such marginal deficiencies are as yet unknown, but increased risk of cardiovascular disease, cancer, and cataracts of the eye is suspected.[16, 17, 20] However, in the short run, in most people such a marginal deficiency likely leads only to fatigue or other bothersome and unspecific signs and symptoms.

Enrichment and Fortification of Foods with B-Vitamins

In the milling of grains, the seeds are crushed and the germ, bran, and husk layers are removed. This process leaves just the starch-containing endosperm, which is used to make flour, bread, and cereal products. Since the discarded fractions are rich in many nutrients, the time-honored milling process leads to loss of vitamins and minerals.

To counteract this nutrient loss, bread and cereal products made from milled grains are enriched with four B-vitamins—thiamin, riboflavin, niacin, and folic acid—and with the mineral iron. This enrichment program, which began in the 1940s in the United States with all the nutrients listed except folic acid, has helped protect North Americans from the common deficiency diseases associated with a dietary lack of the added nutrients. (Folic acid fortification began in 1998.) This fortification, however, still leaves the products with less vitamin B-6, vitamin E, magnesium, and zinc (and fiber) than that present in the whole grains. This is one reason nutrition experts advocate the regular consumption of whole-grain products, such as whole-wheat bread, rather than consuming mostly enriched grain products.

Another reason not to depend too much on enriched foods for vitamins is that whole grains, as well as fruits and vegetables, contain many phytochemicals. Phytochemicals are not vitamins, nor even absolutely essential nutrients. However, they may still be helpful to good health (i.e., they may decrease the risk of certain diseases). Phytochemicals were briefly mentioned in Chapter 2, where a list of examples of phytochemical compounds was given. The possible health benefits of some of these phytochemicals are discussed further in this chapter's Expert Opinion by Dr. Clare Hasler.

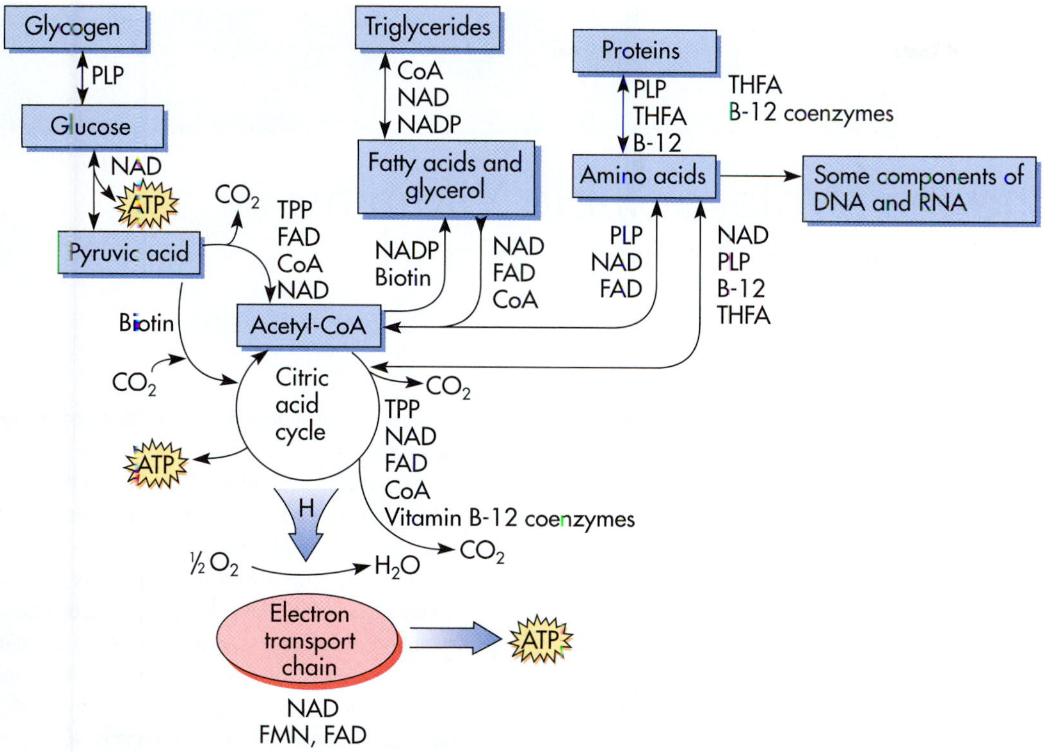

Figure 10-2 Many metabolic pathways, including those involved in energy metabolism, use coenzyme forms of the B-vitamins: thiamin as thiamin pyrophosphate TPP; riboflavin as flavin adenine dinucleotide (FAD) and flavin mononucleotide (FMN); niacin as nicotinamide adenine dinucleotide (NAD) and nicotinamide adenine dinucleotide phosphate (NADP); pantothenic acid as coenzyme A; vitamin B-6 as pyridoxal phosphate (PLP); and folate as tetrahydrofolic acid (THFA). Vitamin B-12 exists in two coenzyme forms. Biotin exists as a cofactor. Other, minor pathways associated with energy metabolism also exist but are not depicted in this figure.

Thiamin

Thiamin consists of a central carbon, to which is attached a six-member nitrogen-containing ring and a five-member sulfur-containing ring. The name comes from *thio,* meaning "sulfur," and *amine,* referring to the nitrogen groups in the molecule. In modern spelling, the *e* is dropped from the word.

The chemical bond between each ring and the central carbon in thiamin is easily broken by prolonged exposure to heat (overcooked foods), thus destroying the functions of the vitamin. This is also true if food is cooked in alkaline solutions (pH > 8.0). Sometimes baking soda is added to the water in which fresh green beans are cooked to retain their bright green color; this practice is not recommended.

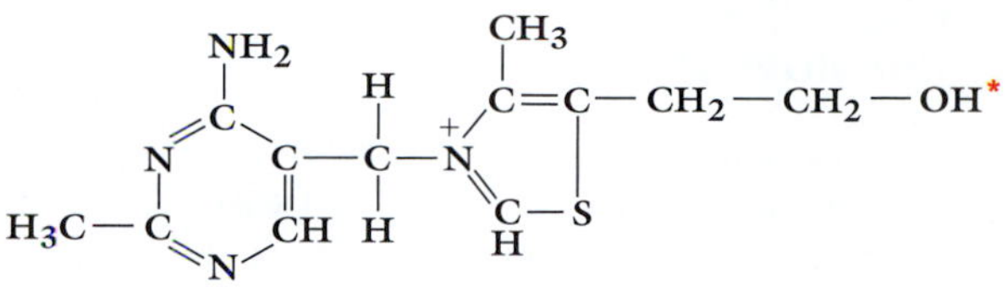

Thiamin

Thiamin has two phosphate groups added here (red asterisk) to form the coenzyme thiamin pyrophosphate (TPP).

Absorption, Transport, Metabolism, and Excretion of Thiamin

Thiamin is absorbed mainly in the small intestine by a carrier-mediated system. It is transported in the blood as such or in its coenzyme form by red blood cells. Since storage is poor, any excess is promptly excreted in the urine.[7]

Functions of Thiamin

Thiamin functions as the coenzyme thiamin pyrophosphate (TPP) in the metabolism of carbohydrates and branched-chain amino acids (leucine, isoleucine, and valine) (Fig. 10-2).[1] It specifically participates in **decarboxylation** of **alpha keto acids** and in the action

decarboxylation The action of removing one molecule of carbon dioxide from a carboxylic acid.

alpha keto acids The breakdown product of several amino acids.

Expert Opinion

Looking Beyond the Water-Soluble Vitamins: Phytochemicals in Health Promotion and Disease Prevention

Clare M. Hasler, Ph.D.

In addition to vitamins and other macro- and micronutrients necessary for the growth, maintenance, and repair of body tissues (e.g., protein, fat, carbohydrates, vitamins, and minerals), a plant-based diet contains numerous components known as "phytochemicals" (e.g., chemicals from plants), which are not absolutely required for basic body function but nonetheless may play an important role in health enhancement.

Phytochemicals are secondary plant metabolites which serve to protect the plant from external stressors such as heat, drought, excessive sunlight, and attack by insects and animals. Thus, phytochemicals may be viewed as analogous to the human immune system. Such compounds are also present in foods of animal origin and are referred to as "zoochemicals." This Expert Opinion will provide a very brief overview of the role of some of the major food phytochemicals in health promotion and disease prevention.

Phytochemicals and Cardiovascular Health

Numerous plant foods have been shown to reduce the risk of cardiovascular disease, the leading cause of death in the United States, by lowering total cholesterol, lowering low-density lipoprotein cholesterol (LDL-C), increasing high-density lipoprotein cholesterol (HDL-C), or reducing triglycerides. These include oats, garlic, nuts, and soybeans.

Increasing intake of certain kinds of dietary fiber has also been recommended as a safe and practical approach for blood cholesterol reduction. Of the various grain products that have been clinically studied, oat products have the highest amount of soluble fiber (beta-glucan). In 1997, FDA approved a health claim on food labels relating consumption of 3 g/day of oat soluble fiber with reduced risk of coronary heart disease. In 1998, FDA extended the soluble fiber health claim to include psyllium fiber.

The health benefits of garlic are primarily due to the presence of a number of biologically active water- and lipid-soluble organosulfur components including allicin, alliin, diallyl disulfide and S-allylcysteine. A comprehensive analysis of 13 placebo-controlled double blind trials indicated that 600 to 900 mg standardized garlic powder or 10 mg steam-distilled oil significantly reduced blood cholesterol in comparison to placebo by 4 to 6%. Similarly, a review of nearly three dozen randomized, controlled trials also concluded that short-term garlic supplementation could reduce blood cholesterol approximately 5%.

Evidence is accumulating on the cardiovascular benefits of certain nuts when they are consumed in moderate amounts (1–2 oz/day). This is likely due in part to their high content of monounsaturated fat and vitamin E, but phytochemicals could also play a role. Clinical trials have found that a variety of tree nuts, such as walnuts and almonds, significantly reduced total blood cholesterol and LDL when eaten as part of a diet that is low in saturated fat and cholesterol. In March of 2002, the California Walnut Commission petitioned FDA to approve health claims for use in the labeling of foods comprising whole and chopped walnuts, communicating that diets including walnuts can reduce the risk of coronary heart disease.

Numerous clinical trials have shown that substitution of soy protein for animal sources of protein can lower total blood cholesterol and LDL-C. In 1999, FDA approved a health claim for this diet-disease relationship based on a daily consumption value 25 g/day. Soybeans contain many physiologically active phytochemicals, including sterols, saponins, omega-3 fatty acids, and isoflavones, which may contribute to the blood lipid–lowering effect of this legume. The isoflavones in soybeans, which are referred to as "phytoestrogens" due to their weak estrogenic activity, are one of the soy phytochemicals thought to be responsible for the cancer chemoprevention activity of this legume.

Phytochemicals and Cancer Risk Reduction

Overwhelming evidence supports the observation that a plant-based diet may reduce the risk of a wide variety of cancers. A comprehensive report of over 4500 laboratory, animal, and human studies from the American Institute for Cancer Research and the World Cancer Research Fund confirmed that cancer is a largely preventable disease. These groups recommend consumption of a variety of fruits and vegetables year-round (400–800 g/day) as well as a variety of starchy or protein-rich foods of plant origin to reduce cancer risk. In addition to the soybean mentioned above, some of the foods which have been inversely related to cancer incidence include tea and tomatoes.

A daily salad is one way to include a number of phytochemicals in your diet.

The effect of green or black tea consumption on cancer risk has been the focus of numerous studies. More than 100 epidemiological studies have examined the effect of tea consumption on cancer risk and research in animals. These studies consistently show that consumption of green tea reduces the risk of various types of cancers. Green tea is abundant in specific polyphenolic flavonoid components known as catechins. The major catechins in green tea are (−)−epicatechin, (−)−epicatechin-3-gallate, (−)−epigallocatechin, and (−)−epigallocatechin-3-gallate (EGCG). One cup (240 mL) of brewed green tea contains up to 200 mg.

Tomatoes and tomato products are also being investigated for their role in cancer chemoprevention and are unique because they are the most significant dietary source of lycopene, a non-provitamin A carotenoid that is also a potent antioxidant. A comprehensive review of 72 epidemiological studies found an inverse association between tomato intake or blood lycopene concentration and the risk of cancer at a defined anatomical site in 57 of the 72 studies reviewed. Cancers of the prostate, lung, and stomach showed the strongest inverse association. However, most ongoing clinical trials involving lycopene and cancer prevention are focused on prostate cancer, in large part because of a 1995 study, which involved more than 47,000 men followed from 1986 to 1992, and which found that more than 10 servings per week of tomato sauce, tomatoes, tomato juice, or pizza could reduce risk of prostate cancer by 35%; advanced prostate cancer was reduced by 53%. Of the 46 fruits and vegetables evaluated, tomato products were the only foods that were associated with reduced risk of prostate cancer. The protective effect of tomato products is likely due to the fact that lycopene selectively accumulates in the prostate gland, perhaps exerting an antioxidant action in that organ. This hypothesis was strengthened by a recent study that found that men with localized prostate adenocarcinoma had significantly reduced prostate DNA oxidative damage following a 3-week consumption of tomato sauce–based meals containing 30 mg lycopene.

Phytochemicals and Other Health Outcomes

The cranberry has been recognized since the 1920s for its efficacy in treating urinary tract infections (UTIs). A landmark clinical trial published in 1994 involving 153 elderly women confirmed this therapeutic effect. More recent research has confirmed that condensed tannins (proanthocyanidins) in cranberry are the biologically active component and prevent *E. coli* from adhering to the epithelial cells lining the urinary tract. New preliminary research suggests that the antiadhesion properties of the cranberry may also provide other health benefits, including some in the oral cavity.

Another carotenoid that has received recent attention for its role in disease risk reduction is lutein. More specifically, research is focusing on the role of lutein in eye health due to its ability to neutralize free radicals that can damage the eye and its ability to prevent photooxidation. Thus, individuals who have a diet high in lutein may be less likely to develop age-related macular degeneration or cataracts, the two most common causes of vision loss in adults. Good sources of lutein include green, leafy vegetables such as spinach (7.4 mg/100g) and cooked cabbage (14.4 mg/100g).

In summary, the role of phytochemicals in health promotion and disease prevention is a very active area of research across the globe. Numerous physiologically active compounds from plants have been shown to reduce the risk of cancer and cardiovascular disease or otherwise promote health. The consumption of a plant-based diet rich in fruits and vegetables (5 to 9 servings per day) is one of the soundest dietary practices we can adopt to enhance our health.

Dr. Clare M. Hasler earned a dual Ph.D. in Environmental Toxicology and Human Nutrition from Michigan State University. She is currently an Assistant Professor of Nutrition at the University of Illinois and Executive Director of the Functional Foods for Health (FFH) Program, a joint effort between the Chicago and Urbana-Champaign campuses of the University of Illinois. Dr. Hasler writes extensively on phytochemicals and functional foods, and is a widely requested speaker on the topic by industry, academia, and the media.

transketolase An enzyme whose functional component is TPP (thiamin pyrophosphate); it converts glucose to pentose sugars.

In November 1996, the United States began to experience a shortage of multivitamins for total parenteral nutrition feedings. Patients who did not receive adequate thiamin for more than 7 days developed lactic acidosis, as pyruvate could not be converted to acetyl-CoA. Instead, the pyruvate was turned into lactate.

Food Sources of Thiamin

Food Item and Amount	*Thiamin (mg)*
Brewer's yeast, 2 tbsp	2.4
Canned lean ham, 3 oz	0.9
Pork chops, 4 ounces	0.6
Wheat germ, ¼ cup	0.5
Canadian bacon, 2 oz	0.5
Acorn squash, 1 cup	0.4
Soy milk, 1 cup	0.4
Flour tortilla, 1	0.4
Ham lunch meat, 2 pieces	0.3
Watermelon, 1 slice	0.2
Fresh orange juice, 1 cup	0.2
Cooked green peas, ½ cup	0.2
Baked beans, ½ cup	0.2
Navy beans, ½ cup	0.2
Corn, ½ cup	0.2

RDA adult men, 1.2 mg; adult women, 1.1 mg

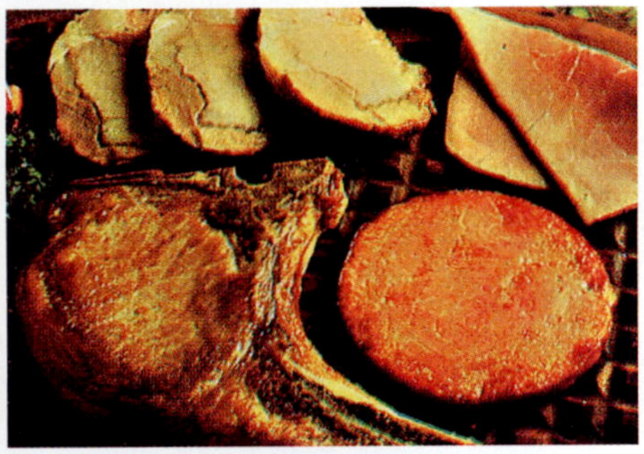

Pork is a good source of thiamin.

of the enzyme **transketolase.** The decarboxylation reaction removes a carboxyl group

O
||
(—C—OH) from a substrate and releases it as carbon dioxide. Several amino acids can undergo decarboxylation with the aid of TPP. The conversion of pyruvate to acetyl-CoA is also an example; this is a critical step in the aerobic metabolism of glucose.

Thiamin as TPP

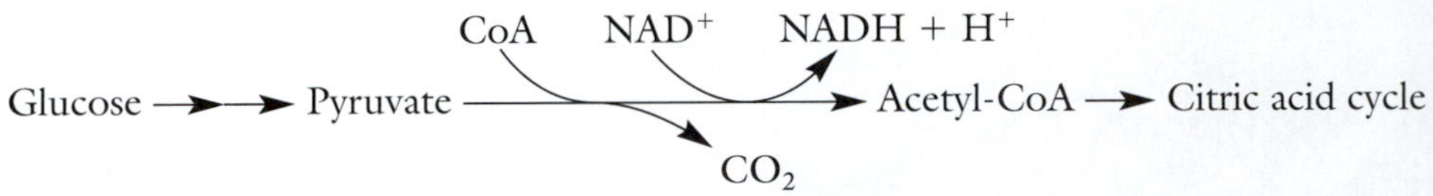

In the citric acid cycle, TPP converts the intermediate compound, alpha-ketoglutarate, to succinyl CoA in a second decarboxylation step.

Thiamin as TPP

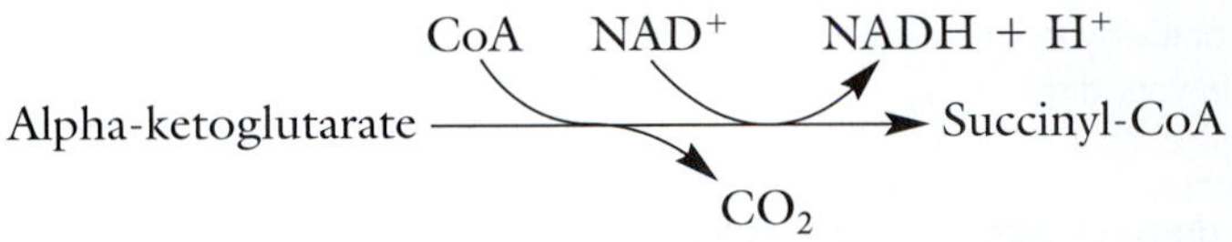

Transketolase is the TPP-dependent enzyme responsible for the formation of the five-carbon sugar components of RNA and DNA from the six-carbon glucose using a series of reactions called the pentose phosphate pathway. TPP also plays a role in nerve function. It may aid in the synthesis of neurotransmitters and participate in the conduction of nerve impulses.[7]

Thiamin in Foods

Thiamin is found in a wide variety of foods, although generally in a small amount. Major individual contributors of thiamin to our diets are white bread and rolls, crackers, pork, hot dogs, luncheon meats, ready-to-eat cereals, and orange juice. White bread, bakery products, and cereals are usually enriched with thiamin.

Foods rich in thiamin are pork products, sunflower seeds, legumes, wheat germ, and watermelon. Whole grains and enriched grains, green beans, asparagus, organ meats (such as liver), peanuts and other seeds, and mushrooms also are good sources. Eating a variety of foods in line with the Food Guide Pyramid (or related pyramid) is a reliable way to obtain sufficient thiamin.

Thiamin Needs

The RDA for thiamin for adult men and women is approximately 1.2 mg/day and 1.1 mg/day, respectively (refer to the inside cover of this text for vitamin recommendations for other age groups).[7] The Daily Value for thiamin used on food and supplement labels is 1.5 mg. The activity of transketolase in red blood cells is used to set the RDA. To measure this, the blood cells are broken open, and the thiamin coenzyme is added to a portion of the broken cells. The enzyme activity with and without the added coenzyme is then compared. Someone in good thiamin status would show little difference in the two measurements.

Recent national surveys indicate that the average daily intake for thiamin in the United States for young men is close to 2 mg per day. For young women, it is approximately 1.2 mg/day. Canadian studies show a slightly lower intake. Thiamin needs rise in physically active people, but not to as great an extent as once thought. If active people increase their total food intake to meet higher energy needs, they will usually meet their thiamin needs.

There appear to be no adverse effects with excess intake of thiamin from food or supplements. Thus, there is no Upper Level for this nutrient.

Thiamin-Deficiency Diseases

The classic thiamin-deficiency disease, beriberi, has afflicted polished rice-eating populations for centuries. If little besides polished rice is eaten for weeks at a time, the disease develops. Since thiamin is so important to energy metabolism, and since all cells need energy, it might seem that a thiamin deficiency should affect every organ and organ system. However, three parts of the body are especially vulnerable to a deficiency of thiamin, as well as other B-vitamins involved in energy metabolism. One part is the nervous system because nerve cells use a lot of chemical energy compared to most cells. In addition, the skin and GI tract are very sensitive to deficiencies of thiamin or other B-vitamins involved in energy metabolism.[7] The reason is that skin and GI tract cells are replaced frequently, which requires much energy input. As symptoms are listed for B-vitamin deficiencies, notice how many can involve the nervous system, GI tract, or skin.

When physicians see a person suffering from unexplained delirium in the emergency room, they must consider whether it may be caused by a thiamin deficiency related to alcoholism. The treatment is an injection of thiamin. Dietary supplementation will not suffice because thiamin is absorbed slowly, especially in a person with alcoholism.

Beriberi

In Sinhalese, the language spoken by the inhabitants of Sri Lanka, the word *beriberi* means "I can't, I can't." This is because thiamin-deficient individuals are very weak and poorly coordinated due to impaired function of the cardiovascular, muscular, nervous, and gastrointestinal systems.

The clinical signs of thiamin deficiency include anorexia, weight loss, apathy, loss of short-term memory, confusion, GI tract distress, irritability, **peripheral neuropathy** and muscle weakness. There are two distinct types of beriberi: wet and dry. In wet beriberi, in addition to peripheral neuropathy, edema occurs along with an enlarged heart and congestive heart failure. In dry beriberi extreme muscle wasting occurs in addition to peripheral neuropathy. Some of the clinical signs of beriberi can be observed after only 7 days on a thiamin-free diet.

peripheral neuropathy Impaired sensory, motor, and reflex functions, affecting arms and legs and causing calf muscle tenderness and difficulty in rising from a squatting position.

Wernicke-Korsakoff Syndrome

The thiamin-deficiency disease found primarily in North America is among people with heavy alcohol consumption and is called Wernicke-Korsakoff syndrome. Alcoholics have a triple problem related to thiamin. Alcohol diminishes thiamin absorption, alcohol increases thiamin excretion, and alcoholics consume such a poor quality diet that there may be few, if any, vitamins in the foods and beverages consumed. Since the vitamin is not readily stored, the symptoms can occur rapidly. Ocular motor signs; **ataxia,** a staggering gait; and deranged mental functions characterize it. The ocular signs include double vision, cross eyes, and rapid eye movements. The disorientation, listlessness, memory loss, and other symptoms, including alcohol withdrawal, are due to lesions in the brain. Not all alcoholics experience Wernicke-Korsakoff syndrome, so it is assumed that there must be a genetic predisposition to the disease.

ataxia An inability to coordinate muscle activity during voluntary movement; incoordination.

Riboflavin

Riboflavin contains three linked six-membered rings, with a sugar alcohol attached to the middle ring. The name comes from its yellow color (*flavin* means "yellow" in Latin). Riboflavin is a component of two coenzymes: flavin mononucleotide (FMN) and flavin adenine dinucleotide (FAD).[1]

Critical | Thinking

Gary suffers from alcoholism and pays no attention to his diet. In addition to the detrimental effects on the liver, excess alcohol consumption can cause deficiencies in certain B-vitamins. Explain why this can occur.

Absorption, Transport, Metabolism, and Excretion of Riboflavin

In the stomach, HCl releases riboflavin from its bound forms. Absorption is primarily via active or facilitated transport in the small intestine. In the blood, riboflavin is transported by protein carriers. Riboflavin is converted to its coenzyme forms, FMN and FAD, in most tissues, but mainly in the small intestine, liver, heart, and kidney. A small amount of riboflavin is stored in the liver; any excess is excreted in the urine. For people who take excessive amounts in supplement form, riboflavin imparts a bright yellow color to the urine.

Functions of Riboflavin

Riboflavin coenzymes have redox reaction functions. This means that these coenzymes either take electrons from a substrate or give electrons to a substrate. In the first case, the riboflavin coenzyme undergoes reduction (gains electrons) and the substrate undergoes oxidation (loses electrons). In other cases, the sequence is reversed (the riboflavin is oxidized and the substrate is reduced). Unlike some redox reactions, riboflavin does not exchange isolated electrons, but rather moves hydrogen atoms.

Riboflavin coenzymes are involved in many enzyme reactions, a number of which are critical to energy metabolism. For example, the enzyme succinate dehydrogenase is an FAD-containing enzyme that accepts hydrogens from succinate to form fumarate during the citric acid cycle. The hydrogens are then passed on to the electron transport chain.

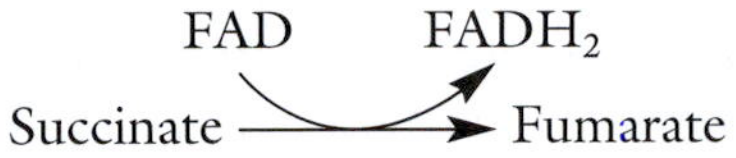

Another FAD-containing enzyme participates in the breakdown of fatty acids (beta oxidation) to acetyl-CoA, the entry compound for the citric acid cycle. And another riboflavin-containing coenzyme, FMN, shuttles hydrogen atoms into the electron transport chain. Still other FAD-containing enzymes help form the vitamin B-6 coenzyme, convert the amino acid tryptophan to the B-vitamin niacin, and participate in folate metabolism (and in this way indirectly in homocysteine metabolism). Metabolism of the oxidized form of glutathione (abbreviated GS; this binds to another GS to form GS-SG) to the reduced form (2 GSH) is dependent on the FAD-requiring enzyme glutathione reductase. Recall from Chapter 9 that this enzyme is part of the cell's antioxidant defense system.

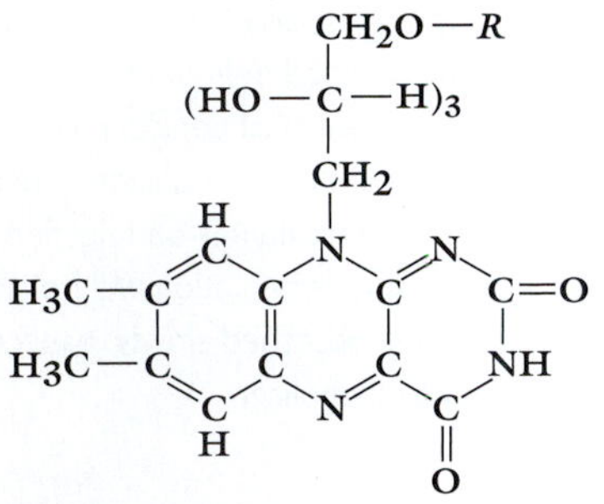

Riboflavin (oxidized)

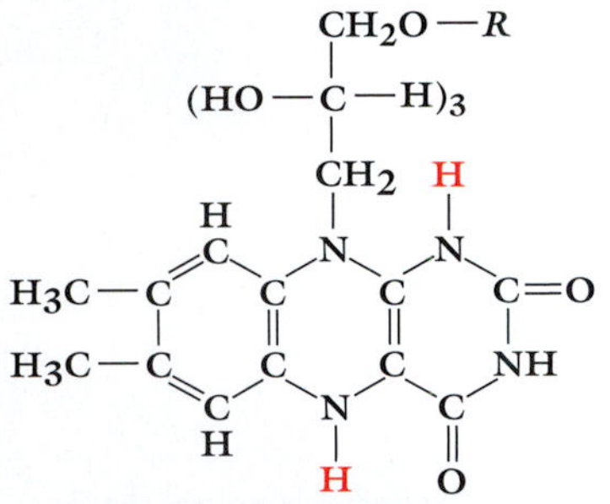

Riboflavin (reduced)

For riboflavin, the italicized *R* denotes H in the free vitamin; phosphate in FMN; and an adenine dinucleotide in FAD. In the reduced form of riboflavin, the hydrogens are shown in red in this figure.

Riboflavin in Foods

One-quarter of the riboflavin in our diets comes from milk products. The rest of our riboflavin intake typically comes from enriched white bread, rolls, and crackers, as well as eggs and meat. Foods rich in riboflavin are liver, mushrooms, spinach and other green leafy vegetables, broccoli, asparagus, low-fat and nonfat milk, and cottage cheese.

Exposure to light (ultraviolet radiation) causes riboflavin to break down rapidly. To prevent this light-induced breakdown, paper and plastic cartons—not glass—should be used in packaging riboflavin-rich foods, such as milk, milk products, and cereals.

Food Sources of Riboflavin

Food Item and Amount	*Riboflavin (mg)*
Multigrain Cheerios, ¾ cup	1.3
Fried beef liver, 1 ounce	1.2
Steamed oysters, 10	1.1
Plain yogurt, 1 cup	0.5
Brewer's yeast, 2 tablespoons	0.5
Raw mushrooms, 5	0.5
Braunschweiger sausage, 1	0.4
Cooked spinach, 1 cup	0.4
1% milk, 1 cup	0.4
Buttermilk, 1 cup	0.4
Boiled egg, 1	0.3
Sirloin steak, 3 ounces	0.3
Feta cheese, 1 ounce	0.2
Tortilla, 1	0.2
Lean ham, 3 ounces	0.2

RDA adult men, 1.3 mg; adult women, 1.1 mg

Riboflavin Needs

The RDA for riboflavin is 1.1 to 1.3 mg/day for adults. The most commonly used method for assessing riboflavin status involves the determination of erythrocyte (red blood cell) glutathione reductase activity and urinary riboflavin excretion. These data were used to establish the RDA.[7] The Daily Value for riboflavin used on food and supplement labels is 1.7 mg. Based on recent survey data, North Americans have an intake of approximately 2.1 mg/day for men and 1.5 mg/day for women.

There appear to be no adverse effects from consuming large amounts of riboflavin due to limited absorption and rapid excretion via the urine and, so, there is no Upper Level.

Riboflavin Deficiency

ariboflavinosis A condition resulting from a lack of riboflavin. The *a* means "without," and the *osis* stands for "a condition of."

The signs and symptoms associated with a pure riboflavin deficiency (technically, called **ariboflavinosis**) include inflammation of the tongue (glossitis), cracking of tissue around the corners of the mouth (cheilosis), seborrheic dermatitis (a disease of the sebaceous glands of the skin), inflammation of the mouth (stomatitis) and throat, various eye and nervous system disorders, and confusion (Fig. 10-3). At present, little is known about the possible consequences of a marginal riboflavin deficiency. One possibility is that people may become tired more quickly during physical activity, although evidence for this is not conclusive. The first evidence of a severe deficiency is inflammation of the mouth and tongue. The complete picture of a deficiency develops after approximately 2 months on a riboflavin-deficient diet (consuming one-fourth of the RDA). Diseases such as cancer, certain forms of cardiovascular disease, and diabetes also are known to precipitate or worsen a riboflavin deficiency. However, a deficiency disease associated with an isolated lack of dietary riboflavin is rarely seen in otherwise healthy people. Because riboflavin functions along with other B-vitamins (e.g., vitamin B-6, niacin, thiamin, and folate) in numerous metabolic pathways, some symptoms ascribed to riboflavin deficiency are actually caused by the failure of metabolic pathways associated with a lack of other nutrients. And, as already noted, this assortment of B-vitamins, such as riboflavin, thiamin, and niacin, is often found in the same foods.

Alcoholics risk a riboflavin deficiency because they often eat a very nutrient-deficient diet. Long-term use of phenobarbital may also compromise riboflavin status, as this drug produces metabolic changes in the liver that increase the breakdown of the vitamin. Marginal intakes may also be seen in those who do not consume milk or milk products. Such people would be wise to search for another plentiful dietary source of riboflavin, such as enriched breads or ready-to-eat breakfast cereals.

Milk is a good source of many vitamins, including riboflavin.

Niacin

The B-vitamin niacin actually exists in two forms—nicotinic acid (niacin) and nicotinamide (niacinamide). In the body, both forms of the vitamin perform the functions associated with niacin. The two coenzyme forms of niacin are nicotinamide adenine dinucleotide (NAD^+) and nicotinamide adenine dinucleotide phosphate ($NADP^+$).[1]

Absorption, Transport, Storage, and Excretion of Niacin

Nicotinic acid and nicotinamide are readily absorbed from the stomach and the intestine by active transport and passive diffusion, so that almost all niacin consumed is absorbed. Niacin is transported from the liver to all tissues, where it is converted to its coenzyme forms, NAD^+ and $NADP^+$, which function in either oxidized or reduced forms. Niacin coenzymes are stored in the liver. Any excess niacin is excreted as a variety of metabolic products in the urine.

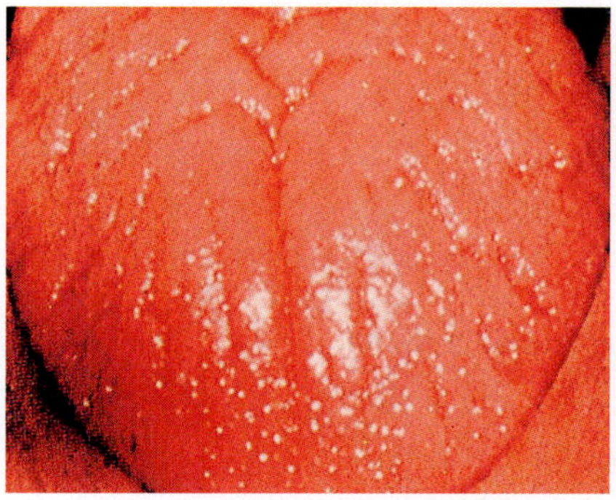

Figure 10-3 A painful, inflamed tongue (glossitis) can signal a deficiency of riboflavin, niacin, vitamin B-6, folate, or vitamin B-12. Often more than one deficiency is the cause. Since other medical conditions can also cause glossitis, further evaluation is needed before a nutrient deficiency can be diagnosed.

Functions of Niacin

Like the coenzyme forms of riboflavin, the coenzyme forms of niacin, NAD^+ and $NADP^+$, are active participants in oxidation-reduction reactions. The niacin coenzymes function in at least 200 reactions in cellular metabolic pathways, especially those used to produce ATP.[1] NAD^+ participates in catabolic reactions, acting as an electron and hydrogen ion acceptor in glycolysis (i.e., the conversion of glucose to pyruvate) and the citric acid cycle. Under anaerobic conditions, the resulting reduced form, $NADH + H^+$, is used in converting pyruvate to lactate, thereby regenerating NAD^+.

Glucose to Pyruvate

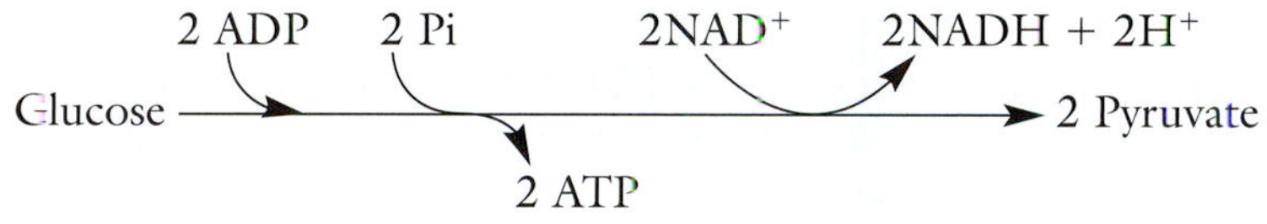

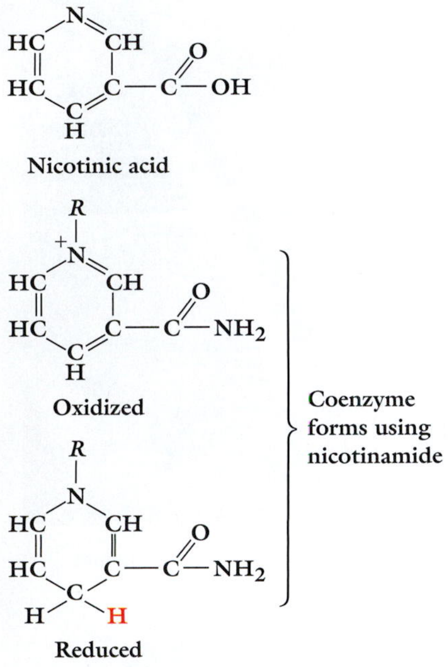

The two coenzyme forms of niacin, NAD and NADP, contain nicotinamide linked to adenine dinucleotide or adenine dinucleotide phosphate, indicated by the italicized *R*. Both coenzymes undergo oxidation and reduction by loss or addition of an electron and a hydrogen (red) in this figure.

The Citric Acid Cycle

$$\text{Isocitrate} \xrightarrow{\text{NAD}^+ \rightarrow \text{NADH} + \text{H}^+} \text{Alpha-ketoglutarate}$$

$$\text{Alpha-ketoglutarate} \xrightarrow{\text{NAD}^+ \rightarrow \text{NADH} + \text{H}^+} \text{Succinyl} - \text{CoA}$$

$$\text{Malate} \xrightarrow{\text{NAD}^+ \rightarrow \text{NADH} + \text{H}^+} \text{Oxaloacetate}$$

Pyruvate to Lactate

$$\text{Pyruvate} \xrightarrow{\text{NAD}^+ \rightarrow \text{NADH} + \text{H}^+} \text{Lactate}$$

Under aerobic conditions, NADH + H^+ also donates an electron and hydrogen to other acceptor molecules in the electron-transport chain.

In the Electron Transport Chain

$$\xrightarrow{\text{NADH} + \text{H}^+ \rightarrow \text{NAD}^+} 2\,\text{H}^+ + 2e^- + \tfrac{1}{2}\,\text{O}_2 \longrightarrow \text{H}_2\text{O}$$

Alcohol dehydrogenase also uses NAD to convert alcohol to acetaldehyde (review Chapter 8).

Each of the reactions shown above starts with an oxidized form of a niacin coenzyme. However, synthetic pathways in the cell—those that make new compounds—use a reduced form of the niacin coenzyme, specifically NADPH + H^+. This coenzyme is important in the biochemical pathway for fatty-acid synthesis. Cells that synthesize a lot of fatty acids (e.g., those in the liver and female mammary glands) have higher concentrations of NADPH + H^+ than cells not involved in fatty-acid synthesis (e.g., muscle cells).

Niacin in Foods

Niacin can be found in foods as the vitamin itself, or as the amino acid tryptophan, which can be converted to niacin by the body.[7] About 25% of the preformed niacin in North American diets comes from poultry and mixed dishes that include meat, fish, and poultry. Another 11% comes from bread and bread products. In the United States, milled grain products have been fortified with niacin in a form that is much more bioavailable than the natural form. If on a high-tryptophan intake, much of the tryptophan is available for conversion to niacin, since needs for protein synthesis are met (each 60 mg yields 1 mg of niacin). The overall number of milligrams of niacin supplied by dietary protein can be estimated by dividing dietary protein intake (in grams) by 6. For example, if one consumes 90 g of protein, the body will synthesize about 15 mg of niacin. In this way we synthesize much of our need for niacin. Coffee and tea contribute a little niacin to the diet. Unlike some other water-soluble vitamins, niacin is very heat stable, and little is lost in cooking. Rich sources of niacin are mushrooms, wheat bran, tuna (as well as other fish), chicken, turkey, asparagus, and peanuts. Animal proteins (except gelatin) are especially rich in tryptophan.

Since food composition tables list only preformed niacin, they can underestimate the total niacin supplied by protein foods. For example, although eggs and milk lack niacin, they contain abundant tryptophan and thus indirectly contribute substantial amounts of niacin.

Populations that eat corn as a staple food are prone to a niacin deficiency, called pellagra. In light of this, you might be surprised to learn that the niacin content of corn is similar to that of rice and considerably higher than that of most other vegetables. However,

Food Sources of Niacin

Food Item and Amount	*Niacin (mg)*
Tuna, 3 oz	11.3
Roasted chicken, 3 oz	10.1
Peanuts, ½ cup	9.9
Baked salmon, 3 oz	8.6
Turkey lunch meat, 3 oz	5.4
Ground beef, 3 oz	5.0
Raw mushrooms, 5	4.7
Lean steak, 4 oz	4.5
Chunky peanut butter, 2 tbsp	4.4
Fried beef liver, 1 oz	4.1
Raisin Nut Bran cereal, ¾ cup	3.8
Tortilla, 1	2.6
Baked cod, 3 oz	2.1
Potato, 1	2.1
Broiled halibut, 3 oz	1.6

RDA adult men, 16 mg NE; adult women, 14 mg NE

the niacin in corn is marginally absorbed because it is tightly bound by a protein. Soaking corn in an alkaline solution, such as lime water (calcium hydroxide dissolved in water), releases bound niacin, rendering it more usable by the body. Look for evidence of this form of processing on the label when you buy corn-meal products, such as tortillas. Because this practice was common among native peoples of Mexico and Central and South America, they did not suffer from a niacin deficiency. Early Spanish explorers of the New World took corn—a crop native to the Americas—back to Europe, but they were unaware of the importance of soaking corn in lime water. Thus, as the use of corn as a staple spread in Europe, pellagra became widespread during the 1700s. In contrast, Spanish settlers in Latin America learned from the native populations to soak corn meal in lime water before using it in cooking. The Hispanic populations descended from these settlers continued this practice and rarely suffered from pellagra, whereas other North Americans who used untreated corn as a staple food often did (see below).

Chicken is a good source of niacin. The tryptophan present can also be metabolized to niacin.

Niacin Needs

For adult men the RDA for niacin is 16 mg/day, and for adult women it is 14 mg/day. The RDA for niacin is expressed as niacin equivalents (NE) to account for niacin received preformed from the diet, as well as that synthesized from tryptophan. The primary criterion used to establish the RDA for niacin is the urinary excretion of N-methyl nicotinamide, a niacin metabolite. The Daily Value for niacin used on food and supplement labels is 20 mg.

About the only population groups to exhibit a niacin deficiency in North America today are people with rare disorders of tryptophan metabolism (e.g., Hartnup's disease), alcoholics, and those with diseases that greatly impair food intake.

Niacin Deficiency

The first official record of the niacin-deficiency disease, pellagra, was made by Spanish physician Casal in 1735. It was named *mal de la rosa,* or "red sickness." The typical red rash appears in areas exposed to sunlight, especially around the neck, which is today called "Casal's necklace." Later the disease was renamed *pellagra* (from Italian *pelle,* meaning "skin," and *agra,* meaning "rough").

Since almost every metabolic pathway uses either NAD^+ or $NADP^+$, it is not surprising that a niacin deficiency causes widespread damage in the body. The effects of pellagra are known as the three *Ds*—dementia, diarrhea, and dermatitis (Fig. 10-4). If the disease is not successfully treated, death (the fourth D) follows. Clinical evidence of pellagra develops 50 to 60 days after instituting a niacin-deficient diet. Early symptoms include diminished appetite, weight loss, and weakness.

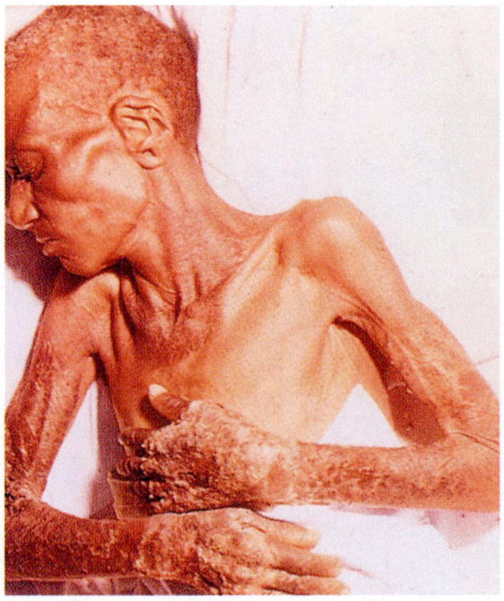

Figure 10-4 The dermatitis of pellagra. Dermatitis on both sides of the body (bilateral) is a typical symptom of pellagra. Sun exposure worsens the condition.

Pellagra is the only dietary deficiency disease ever to reach epidemic proportions in the United States. During the early 1900s, cases of pellagra increased dramatically in the southeastern region of the country, where corn—a poor source of naturally available niacin and the amino acid tryptophan—was being increasingly used as a primary component of the diet. More than 10,000 Americans died of pellagra in 1915. From the end of World War I until the end of World War II, an estimated 200,000 Americans suffered from the disease. So many had such severe dementia that they were forced to live out their lives in mental institutions. One reason why pellagra remained a problem in the southeastern United States for so long was the misimpression that this was an infectious disease. This was disproved by a public health specialist Dr. Joseph Goldberger. He and some colleagues exposed themselves in a variety of ways to biological samples from pellagra patents to demonstrate that the disease was not infectious in nature. Goldberger also induced and cured pellagra in a prison population using dietary interventions.

The introduction of niacin-enriched grains in 1941 and improved intake of dietary protein resulting from post-wartime prosperity finally led to the rapid disappearance of pellagra in the United States. Pellagra is still found today throughout Southeast Asia and Africa among populations whose diets lack sufficient protein and niacin.

A niacin deficiency also can result from deficiencies of other nutrients involved in the synthesis of niacin from tryptophan, such as riboflavin and vitamin B-6.

Pharmacologic Use and Toxicity of Niacin

Consuming 1.5 to 2 g of nicotinic acid per day—about 75 to 100 times the RDA—can decrease LDL-cholesterol and increase HDL-cholesterol. When combined with diet, exercise, and other cholesterol-lowering drugs, megadoses of niacin can slow and even reverse the progression of atherosclerosis. Niacin prescribed for high LDL-cholesterol must have a time-release coating. Otherwise, such megadose therapy may have adverse effects, including flushing of the skin (the initial adverse effect), itching, gastrointestinal upsets (such as nausea and vomiting), and liver damage. These effects (gastrointestinal disturbances and liver damage) have been observed at 1.5 g nicotinic acid per day. Some people experience symptoms at dosages as low as 50 mg/day. Even with the time-release coating, megadose use must be supervised by a physician because of the potential for side effects. The use of various other medications can lessen the side effects. For example, premedication with aspirin reduces the flushing reactions.

Flushing from excess niacin intake was considered the most appropriate effect on which to base the Upper Level. For adults, this is 35 mg/day of supplemental niacin and/or that from fortified foods, the point at which this symptom may begin. Niacin naturally found in food is not counted.

Critical | Thinking

Both the vitamin niacin and protein-rich foods can cure pellagra. Why are both effective?

Concept | Check

The B-vitamins thiamin, niacin, and riboflavin function in various biochemical pathways used for the metabolism of glucose, amino acids, and fatty acids. Enriched grains are adequate sources of all three vitamins. Otherwise, pork is an excellent source of thiamin; milk is an excellent source of riboflavin; and protein foods in general are excellent sources of niacin. Deficiencies of all three vitamins can occur with alcoholism; of the three, a thiamin deficiency is the most likely. Only niacin leads to toxic effects when consumed in high doses.

Pantothenic Acid

Pantothenic acid is part of coenzyme A (CoA).[1] This coenzyme is formed when the vitamin combines with a derivative ADP and part of the amino acid cysteine. Cysteine provides the sulfur atom, which is the functional end of the coenzyme.

Functions of Pantothenic Acid

Glucose
↓
Fatty acids → Acetyl-CoA ← Amino acids
↑
Alcohol

Coenzyme A is essential for the formation of ATP from the breakdown of carbohydrate, protein, alcohol, and fat. The formation of acetyl-CoA from the two-carbon acetate that arises from their metabolism allows the acetate to enter the citric acid cycle. In another series of reactions, acetyl-CoA condenses with carbon dioxide to begin the synthesis of fatty acids:[1]

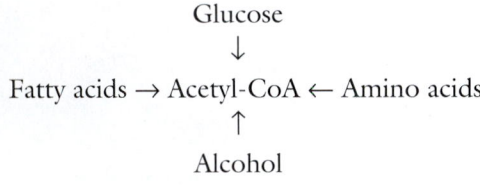

$$\underset{\text{2 carbons}}{\text{Acetyl-CoA}} \xrightarrow{CO_2} \underset{\text{3 carbons}}{\text{Malonyl-CoA}} \dashrightarrow \text{Fatty acid}$$

Pantothenic acid also forms part of a compound called the *acyl carrier protein*. This protein attaches to fatty acids and shuttles them through the metabolic pathway designed to increase their chain length. Finally, pantothenic acid as coenzyme A also donates fatty acids to proteins in a process that can determine their location and function within a cell.

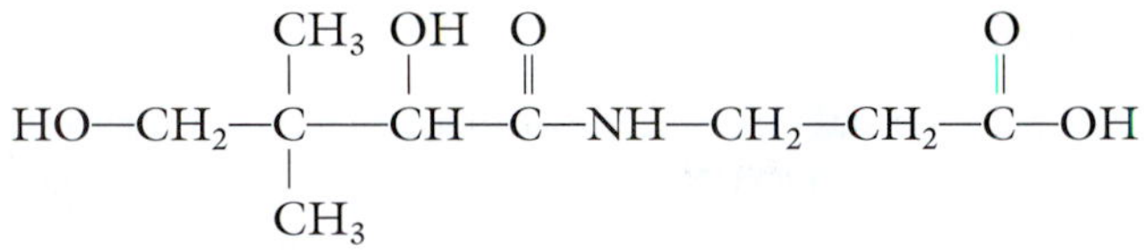

$$HO-CH_2-\underset{\underset{CH_3}{|}}{\overset{\overset{CH_3}{|}}{C}}-\overset{\overset{OH}{|}}{CH}-\overset{\overset{O}{\|}}{C}-NH-CH_2-CH_2-\overset{\overset{O}{\|}}{C}-OH$$

Pantothenic acid

$$RO-CH_2-\underset{\underset{CH_3}{|}}{\overset{\overset{CH_3}{|}}{C}}-\overset{\overset{OH}{|}}{CH}-\overset{\overset{O}{\|}}{C}-NH-CH_2-CH_2-\overset{\overset{O}{\|}}{C}-\boxed{NH-CH_2-CH_2-SH}$$

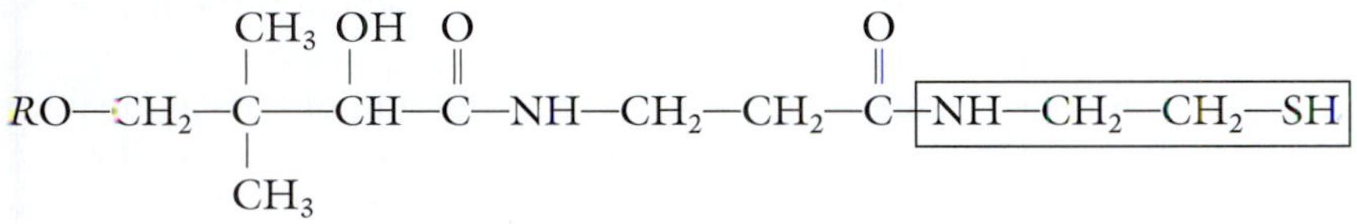

Coenzyme A (CoA)

Pantothenic acid is converted to coenzyme A by combining with a part of the amino acid cysteine (box) and with a derivative of adenosine diphosphate (ADP), represented by the italicized *R*.

Pantothenic Acid in Foods

The Greek word *pantothen,* meaning "from every side," reflects the ample supply of pantothenic acid in foods. Common sources include meat, milk, and many vegetables. Rich sources of pantothenic acid are mushrooms, liver, peanuts, eggs, yeast, broccoli, and milk.

Pantothenic Acid Needs

For adults, the Adequate Intake set for pantothenic acid is 5 mg/day.[7] (Recall that an Adequate Intake is an acceptable intake established by the Food and Nutrition Board for some nutrients for which insufficient data are available to set RDAs.) North American adults generally consume that much and more. The primary criterion used to estimate an Adequate Intake for pantothenic acid is the amount needed to replace urinary excretion. The Daily Value for pantothenic acid used on food and supplement labels is 10 mg.

A deficiency of pantothenic acid might occur in cases of alcoholism in which a very-nutrient-deficient diet is consumed. However, the effects would probably be hidden among deficiencies of thiamin, riboflavin, vitamin B-6, and folate, so the pantothenic acid deficiency might go unrecognized. When a deficiency was experimentally induced in humans, symptoms of headache, fatigue, impaired muscle coordination, and GI tract disturbances were seen. There is no known toxicity for pantothenic acid, and so there is no Upper Limit.

Biotin

Biotin is commonly found in two forms in foods: the free vitamin and the protein-bound coenzyme form, called biocytin. In the formation of biocytin, biotin forms a bond with the amino acid lysine in a protein. Biotin is absorbed from the small intestine, whereas the biocytin form is not absorbed until the enzyme biotinidase, which is present in the small intestine, cleaves the bond linking biotin to a protein, releasing the free vitamin.

About 1 in 60,000 infants is born with a genetic defect that leaves the infant with very low amounts of the enzyme biotinidase. Because the infant cannot break down biocytin to the absorbable free form, a biotin deficiency is likely to develop. If a deficiency is suspected, the infant is treated with 100 μg of biotin, which is about three times typical biotin needs.

Dietary Sources of Pantothenic Acid

Food Item and Amount	Pantothenic Acid (mg)
Total corn flakes cereal, ¾ cup	11.8
Power bar, 1	10.0
Luna bar, 1	9.9
Sunflower seeds, ¼ cup	2.3
Fried beef liver, 1 oz	1.7
Raw mushrooms, 5	1.7
Plain yogurt, 1 cup	1.5
Acorn squash, 1 cup	1.2
Peanuts, ½ cup	1.0
1% milk, 1 cup	0.9
Roasted chicken breast, 3 oz	0.8
Broccoli, 1 cup	0.8
Baked potato, 1	0.7
Legumes, ½ cup	0.7
Cooked egg yolk, 1	0.6

Adequate Intake adults, 5 mg

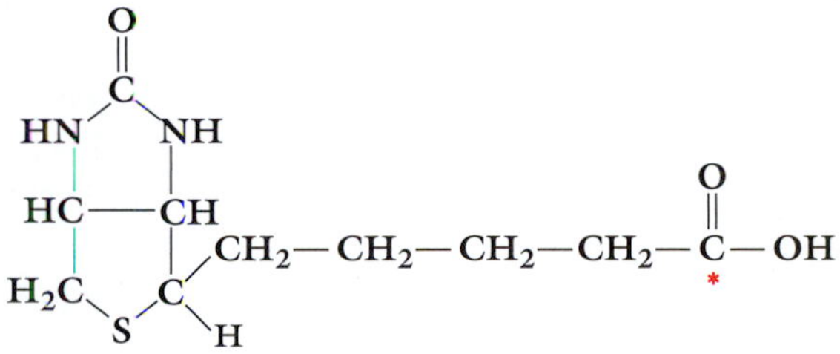

Mushrooms are a good source of pantothenic acid.

Biotin

The vitamin biotin attaches to a protein by formation of a bond between its carboxyl group (red asterisk) and lysine in a protein, yielding the bound cofactor form called biocytin.

Functions of Biotin

Biotin functions as an essential cofactor for four carboxylase enzymes, which bind to biotin.[1] Carboxylases add carbon dioxide to a substance. Three of the four carboxylase enzymes are involved in energy and amino acid metabolism, while the other is involved in making certain fatty acids. The specific function related to fatty acid synthesis is for a biotin carboxylase to catalyze the carboxylation of acetyl-CoA to form malonyl-CoA (see the section on pantothenic acid for reaction). This reaction is the first step in the elongation of the carbon chain to form a fatty acid.

A second biotin carboxylase reaction involves the addition of carbon dioxide to the 3-carbon pyruvate to yield the 4-carbon oxaloacetate, an intermediate in the citric acid cycle. This reaction replenishes lost oxaloacetate and, so, helps keep the citric acid cycle functioning. In the liver and kidney, oxaloacetate also can be converted to glucose when glucose supplies are running low; this is an initial step in gluconeogenesis.

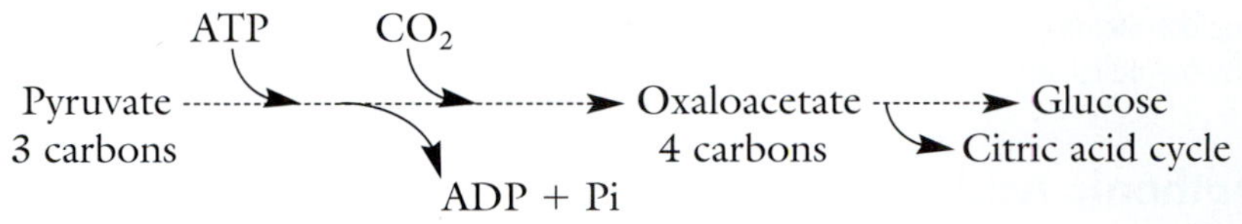

If biotin were missing, the citric acid cycle could not run effectively, resulting in a buildup of lactate, the anaerobic by-product of glycolysis. This condition would be accompanied by a decrease in aerobic metabolism.

A third biotin-dependent carboxylase contributes to the breakdown of the amino acid leucine for energy needs, while a fourth does the same for the amino acids threonine, methionine, and isoleucine. Clearly, biotin is required for the metabolism of carbohydrates, amino acids, and fatty acids.

Food Sources of Biotin

Food Item and Amount	*Biotin (μg)*
Smooth peanut butter, 2 tbsp	30.1
Cooked lamb liver, 1 oz	11.6
Boiled egg, 1	9.3
Cooked egg yolk, 1	8.1
Low-fat yogurt, 1 cup	7.4
Wheat germ, ¼ cup	7.2
Roasted peanuts, 5	6.5
Wheat bran, ¼ cup	6.4
Skim milk, 1 cup	4.9
Salmon, 3 oz	4.3
Egg noodles, 1 cup	4.0
Swiss cheese, 2 oz	2.2
Cheddar cheese, 2 oz	1.7
Raw cauliflower, 1 cup	1.5
American cheese, 2 oz	1.4

Adequate Intake adults, 30 μg

Sources of Biotin: Food and Microbial Synthesis

Biotin content of food has been determined for only a small number of foods, so foods containing biotin are not included in most food composition tables. Biotin is widely distributed in food but concentration varies considerably. Sources include whole grains, eggs, nuts, and legumes.

It is likely that the intestinal synthesis of biotin by bacteria supplies at least part of our needs, as evidenced by the rather rare incidence of biotin deficiency. In fact, we excrete more biotin than we consume. However, questions remain about the actual bioavailability of the biotin synthesized by the intestinal bacteria, since this production takes place mostly in the large intestine, whereas biotin is most efficiently absorbed from the small intestine.

A protein called **avidin** in raw egg whites binds biotin and inhibits its absorption. Feeding many raw egg whites to animals leads to the classic "egg-white injury" deficiency disease. An occasional raw egg would not cause this problem because it would take a regular daily consumption of 12 to 24 raw eggs to produce a biotin deficiency. Biotin deficiency resulting from consuming raw eggs has been reported, however, in people with alcoholism who eat as few as three raw eggs a day. These people probably exist on very deficient diets.

avidin A protein found in raw egg whites that can bind biotin and inhibit absorption; cooking destroys avidin.

Biotin Needs

The Adequate Intake for biotin for adults of 30 μg/day is extrapolated from the intake seen in exclusively breastfed infants.[7] The results of such an extrapolation likely overestimates the amount needed for adults because adults require biotin only for maintenance, not for growth. One U.S. study of biotin intake estimated average intake in young women at 39 μg/day. A similar Canadian study showed an estimated dietary intake of 62 μg/day. The Daily Value for biotin used on food and supplement labels is 300 μg, 10 times our current estimate of needs.

There is no Upper Level for biotin.

Biotin Deficiency

If undetected, a lack of biotinidase activity leads to a severe biotin deficiency in infants. Signs and symptoms may appear within a few months of life, beginning with a skin rash and hair loss. Other signs and symptoms include convulsions, other neurological disorders, and impaired growth. Most other well-documented cases of biotin deficiency have occurred with total parental nutrition, when the biotin was omitted from the formula. Overall, a biotin deficiency is rare.

Vitamin B-6

Vitamin B-6 is actually a family of three compounds: pyridoxal, pyridoxine, and pyridoxamine.[1] All three forms can be phosphorylated to the active vitamin B-6 coenzymes, the primary one being pyridoxal phosphate (PLP). The generic name for the vitamin is B-6.

Absorption, Metabolism, Excretion, and Storage of Vitamin B-6

Both the coenzyme and free forms of vitamin B-6 can be absorbed by passive means. Vitamin B-6 as such is transported to the liver via the portal blood, where ultimately the three forms of the vitamin are phosphorylated. From the liver the phosphorylated forms (mainly PLP) are released to general circulation bound to a blood protein (albumin) for transport. The main storehouse of vitamin B-6 in the body is muscle tissue. At very high intakes, much of the vitamin B-6 is excreted in the urine.

Vitamin B-6
(represented by pyridoxal)

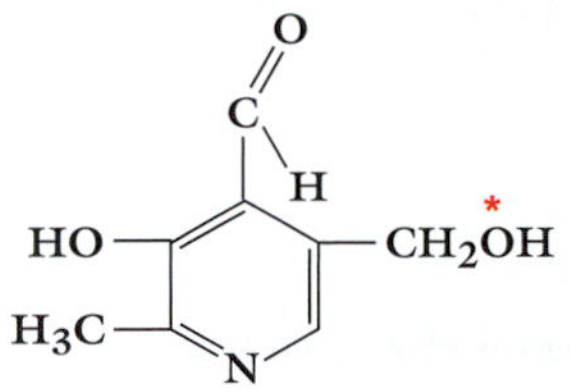

Pyridoxal, one form of vitamin B-6, is converted to an active coenzyme—pyridoxal phosphate (PLP)—by the addition of a phosphate group to the hydroxyl group, indicated in this figure by the red asterisk.

Functions of Vitamin B-6

Vitamin B-6 as PLP plays a coenzyme role in more than 100 enzymatic reactions, almost all of which involve nitrogen-containing compounds.[1]

Amino Acid Metabolism

A major role of PLP is to participate in amino acid metabolism. For example, PLP participates in reactions to form nonessential amino acids. (If we didn't have the services of PLP, every amino acid would be essential as it would have to be supplied by the diet.) PLP is responsible for the interconversion of D- and L-amino acids—it acts as a **racemase.** Recall from Chapter 7 that humans only use the L form of amino acids for protein synthesis. PLP can also be involved in the conversion of homocysteine to cysteine, which occurs during methionine (an amino acid) metabolism.

racemase A group of enzymes that catalyzes reactions involving structural rearrangement of a molecule (e.g., conversion of D-alanine isomer to L-alanine isomer).

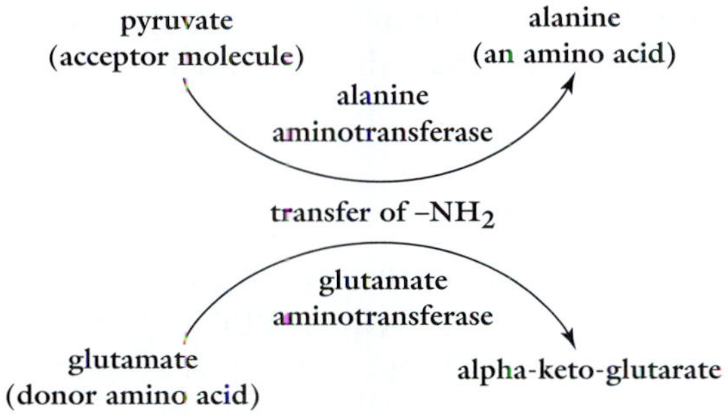

An example of a transaminase enzyme that utilizes vitamin B-6.

Heme Synthesis

In the red blood cell, PLP catalyzes a step in the synthesis of heme. Heme is a nitrogen-containing ring. It is inserted into certain proteins to hold iron in place. The best known of these proteins is hemoglobin, which uses the iron to transport oxygen in the blood.

Carbohydrate Metabolism

PLP is part of the enzyme that releases glucose from glycogen during glycogen breakdown. Therefore, vitamin B-6 helps maintain blood glucose concentrations. This is an exception to the rule that vitamin B-6 works with nitrogen-containing compounds. The chemistry of PLP with this glycogen breakdown enzyme differs from the typical chemistry of PLP with enzymes.

Neurotransmitter Synthesis

Amino acids are not only used to build proteins, but they are also used to make nonprotein nitrogen compounds. Many of these compounds are neurotransmitters, which are important for brain function. PLP plays in the synthesis of the neurotransmitters serotonin from tryptophan, dopamine (DOPA) and norepinephrine from tyrosine, histamine from histadine, and gama-aminobutyric acid (GABA) from glutamic acid. These biochemical actions have led many physicians to prescribe megadoses of vitamin B-6 to patients with various "psychological problems." At this time, it is unclear whether this therapy is effective.

In the early 1950s, some infants were accidentally fed a commercial formula in which vitamin B-6 had been destroyed by oversterilization. The infants developed abnormal electroencephalogram (EEG) readings and experienced convulsions. The reason was probably associated with a lack of neurotransmitter synthesis in the brain. The situation was successfully treated with vitamin B-6.

Vitamin Formation

PLP participates in the conversion of the amino acid tryptophan to the B-vitamin niacin.

Immune Function and Lipid Metabolism

PLP affects immune function and lipid metabolism, probably via its roles in amino acid metabolism, hormone production, and possibly other functions.

Food Sources of Vitamin B-6

Food Item and Amount	*Vitamin B-6 (mg)*
Baked salmon, 3 oz	0.8
Baked potato, 1 medium	0.7
Banana, 1	0.7
Avocado, 1	0.6
Brewer's yeast, 2 tbsp	0.5
Roasted chicken breast, 3 oz	0.5
Acorn squash, 1 cup	0.5
Special K cereal, ¾ cup	0.5
Whole wheat bread, 1 slice	0.5
Fried beef liver, 1 oz	0.4
Roasted turkey lunch meat, 3 oz	0.4
Sirloin steak, 3 oz	0.4
Lean ham, 3 oz	0.4
Watermelon, 1 slice	0.3
Sunflower seeds, ¼ cup	0.3
Cooked spinach, ½ cup	0.2

RDA adults, 1.3 mg

Vitamin B-6 in Foods

Vitamin B-6 is stored in the muscle tissues of animals, and thus meat, fish, and poultry are some of the best sources of this vitamin. Although vitamin B-6 in animal foods is often more readily absorbed than that in plant foods, whole grains also are good sources of vitamin B-6. However, vitamin B-6 is lost during the refining of grains, and this is not one of the vitamins added during enrichment. Most fruits and vegetables are not good vitamin B-6 sources, but there are some exceptions: carrots, potatoes, spinach, bananas, and avocados. Other sources of vitamin B-6 include peanut butter, garbanzo beans, and ready-to-eat breakfast cereals.

Vitamin B-6 is not stable under heat or alkaline conditions. Heat processing and other destructive processing technologies can reduce the vitamin B-6 content of a food by 10 to 50%.

Vitamin B-6 Needs

The adult RDA for vitamin B-6 is 1.3 to 1.7 mg/day. The RDA is based on the amount needed to maintain adequate PLP in the blood. The Daily Value used on food and supplement labels is 2 mg. Average daily consumption of vitamin B-6 for adult men and women is somewhat above the RDA.

microcytic hypochromic anemia An anemia characterized by small, pale red blood cells that lack sufficient hemoglobin and thus have reduced oxygen-carrying ability. It often also is caused by an iron deficiency.

Vitamin B-6 Deficiency

The symptoms of vitamin B-6 deficiency include seborrheic dermatitis, **microcytic hypochromic anemia** (and occasionally a sideroblastic anemia, as described in Chapter

8), convulsions, depression, and confusion. The anemia reflects a decline in heme synthesis due to an inadequate amount of PLP; the accumulation of abnormal metabolites of tryptophan in the brain or a lack of neurotransmitters may cause the convulsions. Because vitamin B-6 is essential for the formation of a type of white blood cell, a deficiency is associated with diminished immune function. These deficiencies are rare, but there are some documented occurrences, sometimes due to alcoholism, or to a genetic condition that causes an anemia that can often be reversed by increased vitamin B-6 intake. When alcohol is metabolized in the body, an intermediate, acetaldehyde, is produced. Acetaldehyde decreases the formation of PLP by cells and perhaps competes with PLP for protein-binding sites.

A number of medications—especially L-DOPA, used to treat Parkinson's disease, and isoniazid, a common antituberculosis medication—reduce blood concentrations of PLP. Patients should be advised to obtain extra vitamin B-6 when taking these medications, under a physician's guidance. Finally, some older people have been found to exhibit signs of a mild deficiency, such as reduced immune function and a high concentration of homocysteine in the blood.

Bananas are a good plant source of vitamin B-6.

Pharmacologic Use of Vitamin B-6 and Toxicity

Carpal tunnel syndrome, a nerve disorder in the wrist, has been treated with large daily doses of vitamin B-6. However, because of defects in the design of trials, and conflicting data on its effectiveness, vitamin B-6 is currently not recommended for this condition.

Studies of vitamin B-6 and **premenstrual syndrome (PMS)** indicate that the evidence is so shaky that it is unwise to make a definitive recommendation for taking vitamin B-6. Since there are no laboratory tests for PMS, and the cause of symptoms has not yet been elucidated, well-controlled trials are needed to clarify the possible benefits and side effects of vitamin B-6 in the treatment of PMS. Some physicians, however, advise doses of 50 to 100 mg/day as a possible part of therapy.

premenstrual syndrome (PMS) A disorder found in some women a few days before a menstrual period begins. It is characterized by depression, anxiety, headache, bloating, and mood swings. Severe cases are currently termed premenstrual dysphoric disorder (PDD).

Intakes of 2 to 6 g of vitamin B-6 per day for 2 or more months can lead to irreversible nerve damage, as can long-term intakes of greater than 200 mg/day. Body builders and women attempting to treat themselves for PMS have sustained symptoms such as walking difficulties and hand and foot numbness. Some nerve damage in individual sensory neurons is probably reversible, but damage to ganglia (where many nerve fibers converge) is probably permanent. The Upper Level for adults is set at 100 mg of vitamin B-6 per day, based on development of such nerve damage.[7]

Concept | Check

Pantothenic acid and biotin both participate in metabolism of carbohydrate, protein, and fat. A deficiency of either vitamin is unlikely because pantothenic acid is found in a wide variety of foods and our need for biotin is partially met by synthesis from intestinal bacteria. Vitamin B-6 is important for protein metabolism, neurotransmitter synthesis, and other key metabolic functions. Headache, anemia, nausea, and vomiting can result from a vitamin B-6 deficiency. Animal protein sources and plant foods such as potatoes, spinach, and bananas are good sources of vitamin B-6. Doses of vitamin B-6 in excess of approximately 1500 times the RDA for a few months or 150 times the RDA for long-term use can cause nerve destruction.

Folate

Spinach is a good source of folate.

The word folate derives from the Latin word for leaf (folium) because dark green, leafy vegetables are among the best sources of this vitamin. It was once thought that a folate-deficient diet was virtually impossible to produce, unless the diet was grossly deficient

Folic acid, also called folate monoglutamate, is the form absorbed in the intestine. This is the form found in fortified foods and supplements. Most of the folate naturally found in foods, however, contains additional glutamate molecules linked to the carboxyl group, indicated in this figure by the red asterisk. These additional glutamates decrease folate bioavailability.

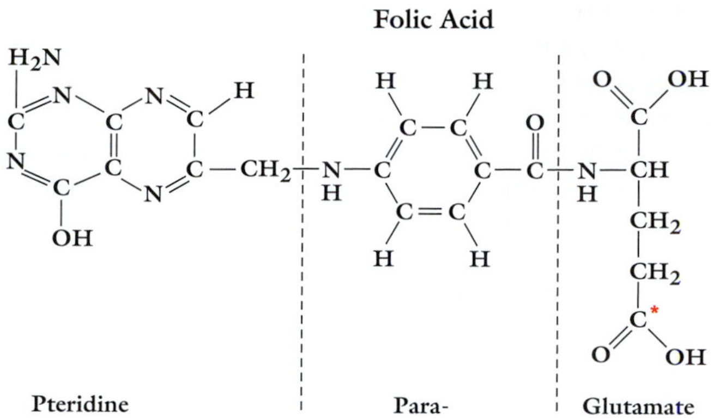

in many nutrients. Nowadays, this attitude has changed as dietary folate intake has become a major issue of interest.

Folate and vitamin B-12 produce a number of identical deficiency signs and symptoms when omitted from the diet.[7] These two water-soluble vitamins share a close relationship because a vitamin B-12 coenzyme is needed to recycle a folate coenzyme for repeated function.

What we call folate today was known earlier as either folic acid or folacin. Today, the term *folate* is a generic name for the vitamin and also refers to the various forms of the vitamin found naturally in foods. Folic acid refers specifically to the form of the vitamin found in supplements and fortified foods.

Folate consists of three parts: pteridine, para-aminobenzoic acid (PABA), and one or more molecules of the amino acid glutamic acid (glutamate). If only one glutamate molecule is present, it is designated folic acid (folate monoglutamate). In food, about 90% of the folate molecules have three or more glutamates attached and are known as polyglutamates. PABA by itself is sometimes added to supplements, but there is no current scientific rationale for this.

Metabolism, Absorption, Storage, and Excretion of Folate

conjugase Enzyme systems in the intestine that enhance folate absorption; they remove glutamate molecules from polyglutamate forms of folate.

To be absorbed, folate polyglutamates must be broken down (hydrolyzed) to the monoglutamate form in the gastrointestinal tract.[7] Enzymes, folate **conjugases,** located in the absorptive cells accomplish the removal of the excess glutamates. The monoglutamate form is then actively transported across the intestinal wall. Very large doses of folic acid from supplements are also absorbed by passive diffusion. When synthetic folic acid is consumed as a supplement and without food, it is nearly 100% bioavailable. Consumed with food, as in fortified cereal grains, absorption is slightly reduced.

The portal blood draining the small intestine delivers the monoglutamate form of folate to the liver, where it is changed back to the polyglutamate form. This is either stored in the liver or released into the blood or bile. Most of the urinary excretion of folate exits as metabolic products. Biologically active folate is also excreted into the bile and is reabsorbed by enterohepatic circulation. Alcohol interferes with this process, which is one reason alcoholics often become folate deficient.

Intestinal bacteria synthesize folate, but probably nearly all of this is excreted in the feces. Therefore, it has been difficult to determine how much excreted folate comes from the diet and how much is from microbial synthesis.

Functions of Folate

THFA transfers the following single-carbon groups: methyl ($—CH_3$), formyl ($—CH{=}O$), methylene ($—CH_2—$), and metheynyl ($—CH{=}$).

In cells, all forms of folate are readily converted to the basic coenzyme form, called tetrahydrofolic acid (THFA). There are actually five active coenzyme forms of THFA.

These participate in metabolic reactions by accepting and donating single-carbon groups.[1]

Metabolic Reactions

Transfer of these single-carbon units is needed for the synthesis of DNA and the metabolism of various amino acids and their derivatives. A crucial reaction requiring THFA is the transfer of a one-carbon methylene group (—CH_2—) to uridylate, forming thymidylate, an essential component of DNA and thus cell replication:

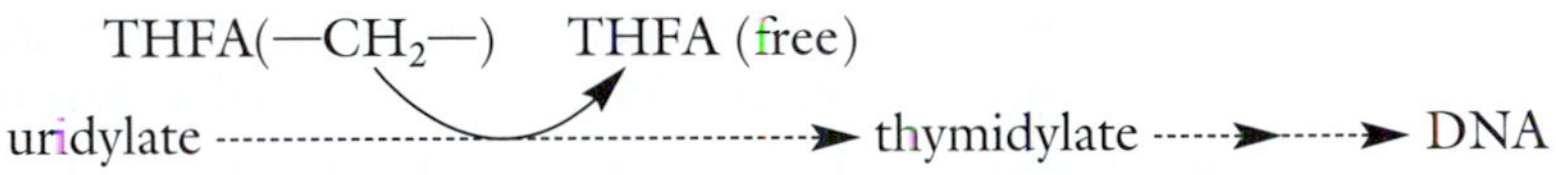

THFA is also needed for the synthesis of adenine and guanine, so DNA synthesis and repair may decline as a result of a folate shortage.

Because THFA is needed for DNA synthesis, folate deficiency may be induced during a common form of cancer therapy. One example is the cancer drug methotrexate. It inhibits a key aspect of folate metabolism. When methotrexate is taken in high doses, it reduces DNA synthesis throughout the body by interfering with folate metabolism. This reduction in DNA synthesis can halt the growth of cancer cells, but it also affects other rapidly proliferating cells, such as intestinal cells and red blood cells. Therefore, the typical side effects of methotrexate therapy are the same as for a folate deficiency (e.g., anemia and diarrhea). Methotrexate acting as a folate antagonist is also used to treat rheumatoid arthritis, psoriasis, asthma, alcoholic cirrhosis, and inflammatory bowel disease. When patients are given methotrexate, they need to follow a high-folate diet and/or take folic acid supplements because this reduces the toxic side effects of the drug. High supplemental doses generally have little or no influence on methotrexate's effectiveness.

Another key function of folate is the formation of neurotransmitters in the brain. Meeting folate needs can improve the depressed state in some cases of mental illness.

Although folate deficiency can be induced to treat cancer, folate deficiency may also cause concern with regard to cancer. Because folate aids in the transfer of methyl groups for DNA synthesis, it is hypothesized that even mild folate deficiency contributes to abnormal DNA integrity, which in turn affects certain cancer-protecting genes.[9] A daily intake of 400 µg (the RDA) is thought to be chemo-preventive.

About 10% of the North American population has a defect in one aspect of folate metabolism. They may need up to twice the RDA to compensate. Currently, testing for this defect is not routine in medical practice, but one day it may be.

Other Functions

THFA is important in amino acid metabolism, especially the interconversions of amino acids. It accepts one-carbon groups from various amino acids and is responsible for the glycine to serine reaction, the histidine to glutamatic acid reaction, and the homocysteine to methionine reaction.[1]

Folate in Foods

The biological availability of folate varies with the source of the vitamin. The best sources, from the standpoint of amount and availability, are liver, fortified breakfast cereals and other grain products, legumes, and dark green, leafy vegetables in general. Other, less rich sources of folate that contribute this vitamin to our diets include eggs, dried beans, and oranges.

Food processing and preparation can destroy 50 to 90% of the folate in food. Folate is extremely susceptible to destruction by heat, oxidation, and ultraviolet light. Consequently, it is important to eat fresh fruits and lightly cooked (or raw) vegetables on a regular basis. If vegetables must be cooked, this should be done quickly in a minimum amount of water—by steaming, stir-frying, or microwaving. Vitamin C in foods helps protect folate from oxidative destruction.

Food Sources of Folate

Food Item and Amount	*Folate (µg)*
Asparagus, 1 cup	263
Cooked spinach, 1 cup	262
Cooked lentils, ½ cup	179
Black-eyed peas, ½ cup	179
Romaine lettuce, 1½ cups	114
Great Grains cereal, ¾ cup	114
Tortilla, 1	89
Cooked turnips, ½ cup	85
Cooked broccoli, 1 cup	78
Sunflower seeds, ¼ cup	76
Fresh orange juice, 1 cup	75
Cooked beets, ½ cup	68
Kidney beans, ½ cup	65
Fried beef liver, 1 oz	62
Brewer's yeast, 1 tbsp	60

RDA adults, 400 µg

Folate Needs and Dietary Folate Equivalents

The RDA for folate for adults is 400 µg/day, as is the Daily Value used on food and supplement labels. This is based on the amount needed to maintain red blood cell folate, control blood homocysteine, and maintain normal blood folate concentrations.

The use of dietary folate equivalents (DFEs) instead of the actual amount of folate in a food has some important implications. Typically, many foods will be richer in folate than the Nutrition Facts label suggests since folate content is due primarily to synthetic folic acid added to the foods, such as in enriched grains and ready-to-eat breakfast cereals. This contributes substantially to the DFE calculation. Another implication is that food composition tables (such as the one in the back of this book) and nutrition analysis software programs (such as that supplied with this book) also underestimate the true folate contribution of a diet compared to folate needs because these have not been updated to DFE units.

Also considered was the intake necessary to prevent neural tube defects for women capable of becoming pregnant (see the next section on folate deficiency).[7]

Dietary folate equivalents (DFE) are the units used to express folate needs for all stages of life except childbearing years. (As covered in the next section, women of childbearing age should meet such recommendations with synthetic folic acid.) These units reflect the differences in absorption of food folate and synthetic folic acid. To estimate the amount of DFE requires some calculations. First, determine how much of a day's food intake comes from food folate and how much comes from synthetic folic acid added to foods. When in doubt, assume all folate in a diet is derived from food in that form, except that coming from ready-to-eat breakfast cereals and refined grain products. Also include in this second category any folic acid consumed as part of dietary supplements. To calculate the DFE for the diet, multiply total synthetic folic acid intake by 1.7 and add that value to the total food folate intake. The following is an example. The Daily Value for a serving of ready-to-eat breakfast cereal consumed is listed on the label as 50%, so the amount of "folate" is 200 μg per serving (Daily Value of 400 μg × 0.50). Since this folate is synthetic folic acid, the 200 μg is multiplied by 1.7, or 340 μg. Assume the diet also contains 300 μg of food folate. To obtain the total DFE intake for the day, add the 300 μg to the 340 μg, which equals 640 μg DFE, more than enough for a man or older woman.

Folate Deficiency

Folate deficiency can result from a low intake; inadequate absorption, which often is associated with alcoholism; increased requirement, most commonly occurring in pregnancy; compromised utilization, typically associated with vitamin B-12 deficiency; use of certain chemotherapy medications; and excessive excretion, linked to long-standing diarrhea.

Megaloblastic Anemia

As mentioned already, a deficiency of folate first affects cell types that are actively synthesizing DNA; such cells have a short life span and rapid turnover rate. Thus, one of the major folate-deficiency signs is changes in the early phases of red blood cell synthesis, as these cells turn over every 120 days. Without folate, the precursor cells in the bone marrow cannot divide normally to become mature red blood cells because they cannot form new DNA. The cells grow larger because there is continuous formation of RNA, leading to increased synthesis of protein and other cell components to make new cells. Hemoglobin synthesis also intensifies. However, when it is time for the cells to divide, they lack sufficient DNA for normal division. The cells thus remain in a large, immature form in the bone marrow, known as **megaloblasts** (Fig. 10-5). Unlike normal, mature red blood cells, megaloblasts retain their nuclei. Once these cells enter the bloodstream, they are called **macrocytes.** This results in a form of anemia called **megaloblastic** (or **macrocytic**) **anemia.**

Large, immature cells also appear along the entire length of the gastrointestinal tract during chronic folate deficiency. This occurs because these cells are replaced very frequently, which means that DNA for the new cells has to be produced rapidly. In a folate deficiency, cell division in the GI tract is impaired. This change contributes to decreased absorptive capacity of the GI tract and a persistent diarrhea. White blood cell synthesis also is disrupted by a folate deficiency because these cells are made in rapid bursts during immune challenges (i.e., infections). Thus, immune function can be diminished during a folate deficiency. This effect likely can occur with milder folate deficiency than is needed to produce anemia.[7]

megaloblast A large, nucleated, immature red blood cell in the bone marrow, which results from the inability of a precursor cell to divide when it normally should.

macrocyte Literally "large cell," such as a large red blood cell.

megaloblastic anemia An anemia characterized by large, nucleated, immature red blood cells in the bone marrow. This results from the inability of a precursor cell to divide when it normally should. A folate deficiency is often the cause.

macrocytic anemia Anemia characterized by the presence of abnormally large red blood cells in the bloodstream.

Neural Tube Defects

A maternal deficiency of folate and a genetic predisposition have been linked to the development of **neural tube defects** in the fetus (Fig. 10-6). These defects include spina

neural tube defect A defect in the formation of the neural tube occurring during early fetal development. This type of defect results in various nervous system disorders, such as spina bifida. Folate deficiency in the pregnant woman increases the risk that the fetus will develop this disorder.

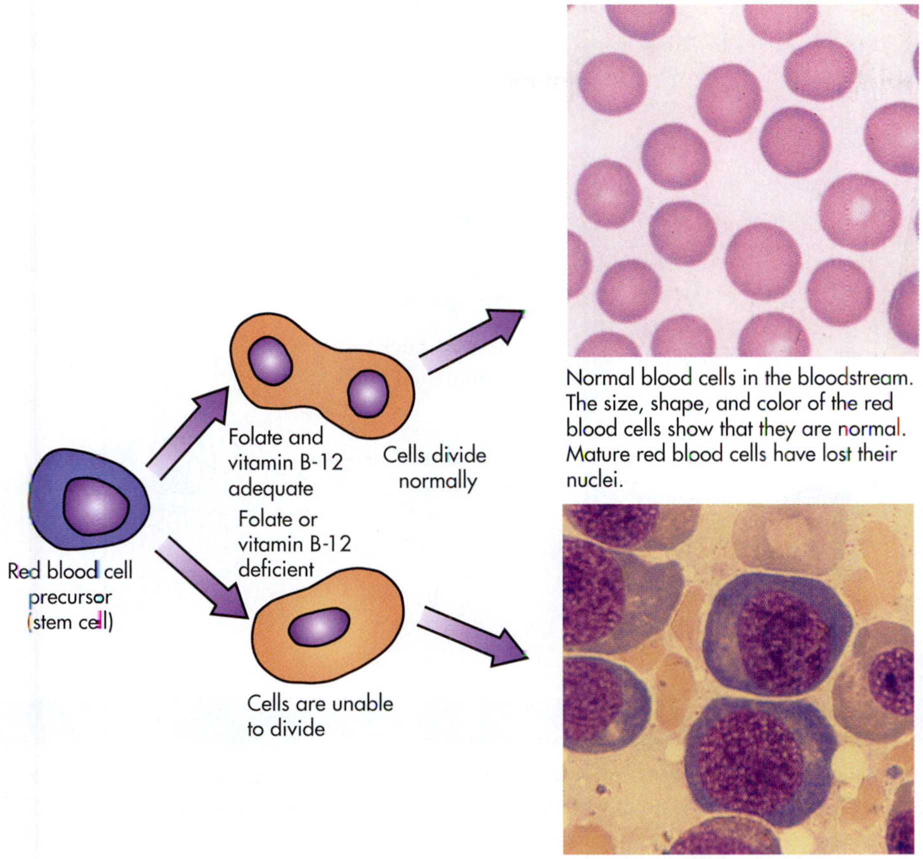

Normal blood cells in the bloodstream. The size, shape, and color of the red blood cells show that they are normal. Mature red blood cells have lost their nuclei.

Megaloblastic blood cells seen here in the bone marrow are arrested at an immature stage of development. They still have their nuclei and are slightly larger than normal red blood cells.

Figure 10-5 Megaloblastic anemia occurs when blood cells are unable to divide, leaving large, immature red blood cells. Either a folate or vitamin B-12 deficiency may cause this condition. Measurements of blood concentrations of both vitamins are taken to help determine the cause of the anemia.

bifida (spinal cord or spinal fluid bulge through the back) and anencephaly (absence of a brain). Approximately 2000 infants are so affected annually in the United States. Victims of spina bifida may exhibit paralysis, incontinence, hydrocephalus, and learning disabilities. Children born with anencephaly die shortly after birth. Adequate folate nutriture is crucial for all women of childbearing years, since neural tube closure begins 21 days after conception and is completed by day 28, a time when many women are not even aware that they are pregnant. Perhaps as many as 70% of these defects could be avoided by adequate folate status before conception (see Chapter 16 for details).[11] All research has been done with synthetic folic acid supplementation, and it appears that even women with varied diets may not consume adequate folic acid to prevent neural tube defects (400 μg/day) unless specific attention to synthetic folic acid sources, such as many ready-to-eat breakfast cereals, is given. Earlier it was noted that most grain products are now fortified with folic acid.

Because the metabolism and functions of folate and B-12 are linked, regular consumption of large amounts of folate can prevent the appearance of the primary early warning sign of vitamin B-12 deficiency—enlarged red blood cells.[7] To prevent such masking of vitamin B-12 deficiency, it is the goal of FDA to increase the folate intake of women of childbearing years through grain fortification without producing excessive intake by other groups (> 1 mg/day of folic acid). It is currently estimated that this fortification supplies adults in the United States with about 200 μg/day of folic acid.

Steps in Folate Deficiency

1. Decrease in blood folate concentration
2. Decrease in red cell folate
3. Defective DNA synthesis
4. Change in structure of certain white blood cells
5. Increase in blood concentration of homocysteine
6. Megaloblastic changes in bone marrow and other rapidly dividing cells
7. Increase in the size of circulating red blood cells
8. Megaloblastic (macrocytic) anemia

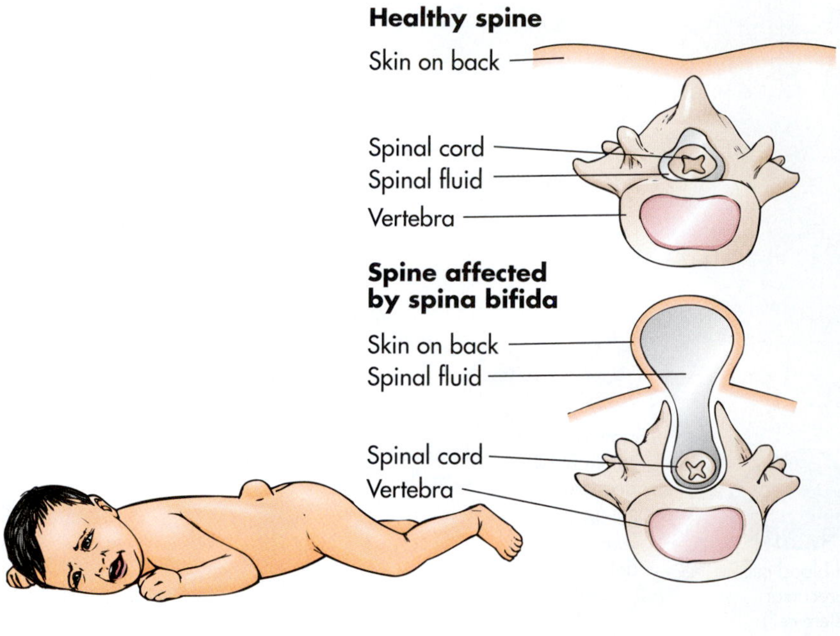

Figure 10-6 Neural tube defects result from a developmental failure affecting the spinal cord or brain in the embryo. Very early in fetal development, there is a ridge of neural-like tissue along the back of the embryo. As the fetus develops, this material differentiates into both the spinal cord and body nerves, at the lower end, and into the brain, at the upper end. At the same time, the bones that make up the back gradually surround the spinal cord on all sides. If any part of this sequence goes awry, many defects can appear. The worst is total lack of a brain (anencephaly). Much more common is spina bifida, in which the backbones do not form a complete ring to protect the spinal cord. Deficient folate status in the mother during the beginning of pregnancy increases the risk of neural tube defects. Women who have had a child with a neural tube defect are advised to consume 4 mg/day of folic acid, beginning at least one month before any future pregnancy. This must be done under strict physician supervision.

Case Scenario | Follow-up

Suzanne and Ted should remember that spina bifida is caused by a failure of the spinal cord to close during the first 28 days of pregnancy, a time when neither Ted nor Suzanne realized Suzanne was pregnant. The B-vitamin folate must be available at the time of conception to prevent spina bifida and other birth defects. One hopes that Suzanne's prepregnancy diet provided enough synthetic folic acid; if not, there is a reason to worry. The fact that a close relative of Suzanne's has already produced a child with this birth defect should have been a warning sign.

Other Folate Deficiency States

Folate deficiencies sometimes appear in pregnant women. They need extra folate to meet an increased rate of cell division and thus of DNA synthesis in their own bodies and in the developing fetus. Today, prenatal care often includes vitamin and mineral supplements enriched with folate to compensate for the extra needs associated with pregnancy.

Young women in general also often show low blood folate values. It is important for them to seek good sources of synthetic folic acid that they enjoy eating and then to eat those foods regularly, such as ready-to-eat cereals. The use of a balanced multivitamin and mineral supplement is another option (see the Nutrition Perspective in Chapter 9). Older adults are also at risk for folate deficiency. Finally, persons suffering from alcohol abuse or taking certain prescription drugs need to recognize that they may develop a folate deficiency.

Toxicity of Folate

FDA limits the amount of folic acid in nonprescription vitamin supplements for nonpregnant individuals to 400 μg when no statement of age is listed on the supplement label. When age-related doses are listed, there can be no more than 100 μg for infants, 300 μg for children, and 400 μg for adults. Prenatal supplements sold over-the-counter can contain 800 μg. FDA regulates the potency of folic acid supplements because of the ability of excessive amounts of folic acid to mask a vitamin B-12 deficiency. The Upper Level for synthetic folic acid is 1000 μg (1 mg), based on this observation.[7] However, this does not apply to folate in foods since absorption is limited.

Vitamin B-12

What we call vitamin B-12 includes the free vitamin (cyanocobalamin) and two active coenzymes—methylcobalamin and 5-deoxyadenosylcobalamin. This vitamin has a complex structure containing the mineral cobalt.[1]

All vitamin B-12 compounds are synthesized exclusively by bacteria, fungi, and algae. Animals such as cows and sheep obtain vitamin B-12 either from bacterial synthesis in the multiple compartments of their stomachs (rumen) or from the soil they ingest while eating and grazing. The only reliable source of the vitamin for humans is animal foods. Plants do not synthesize vitamin B-12. There is minor contamination of vegetable products by bacteria and soil. The process of fermentation also contributes a small amount of vitamin B-12 to a food.

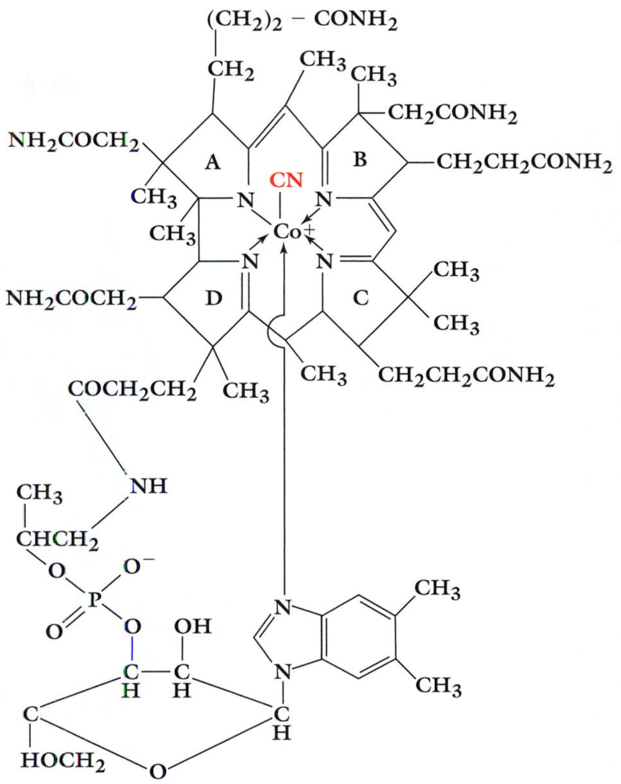

Vitamin B-12 (cyanocobalamin)

The cyanocobalamin form of vitamin B-12 is converted to the active coenzyme forms by replacement of the cyano group (red) with another group, such as a methyl group or a hydroxyl group.

Absorption, Transport, and Storage of Vitamin B-12

In the stomach, vitamin B-12 in food is released from proteins by the action of HCl and pepsin in gastric juice. The free B-12 binds to a protein, designated **R-protein,** that originates in the salivary glands in the mouth and is swallowed along with the food. The R-protein/vitamin B-12 complex travels to the small intestine, where it encounters pancreatic proteases (e.g., trypsin), which release the vitamin. Awaiting the free B-12 is **intrinsic factor,** a glycoprotein produced by the parietal cells in the stomach. The intrinsic factor/vitamin B-12 complex travels to the terminal portion of the small intestine, the ileum, where it attaches to special receptor cells on the brush border. Several hours later, cells within the ileum absorb vitamin B-12 and transfer it to a specific transport protein, transcobalamin II. This vitamin-protein complex enters the portal vein and is taken up by the liver, and eventually the bone marrow and red blood cells (Fig. 10-7).

It is assumed that 50% of dietary vitamin B-12 is absorbed by healthy adults with normal gastric function. Vitamin B-12 is continually secreted into the bile, and most of it is reabsorbed by enterohepatic circulation. Failure in any of the links found in the absorptive process reduces absorption to 2% or less of dietary vitamin B-12.[7]

Absorption of vitamin B-12 can be disrupted by numerous defects, including the following:

- Absence or defective synthesis of R-protein, pancreatic proteases, or intrinsic factor
- Defective binding of the intrinsic factor/vitamin B-12 complex to receptor cells in the ileum
- Absence (or surgical removal) of much or all of the ileum and stomach
- Bacterial overgrowth of the small intestine
- Tapeworm infestation
- Use of certain anti-ulcer medications that significantly reduce acid production by the parietal cells (e.g., omeprazole [Prilosec])
- Chronic malabsorption syndromes, as can be seen in AIDS

Three types of therapy are possible for patients diagnosed with a defect in vitamin B-12 absorption: monthly injections of vitamin B-12 to bypass the gastrointestinal tract, use of a vitamin B-12 nasal gel (nasal absorption does not require the intrinsic factor), and weekly ingestion of vitamin B-12 supplements in megadoses (300 times the RDA), which allow absorption by passive diffusion.[5] Most cases of vitamin B-12 deficiency among otherwise healthy people in North America result from a defect in vitamin B-12 absorption, rather than from inadequate intake.

About 50 to 90% of the body's total supply of vitamin B-12 is stored in the liver. Storage is so great that a single monthly injection of vitamin B-12 is sufficient to prevent

R-protein A protein produced by the salivary glands that enhances absorption of vitamin B-12, possibly by protecting the vitamin during its passage through the stomach.

intrinsic factor A substance present in gastric juice that enhances vitamin B-12 absorption.

In the 1920s, researchers found that a vitamin B-12 deficiency can be cured by consumption of massive amounts of liver or concentrated water extracts of liver. In this case, the deficiency was caused by an absorption defect. If enough of the vitamin is ingested, it can be absorbed by simple diffusion, thereby overcoming the defective R-protein/intrinsic factor system.

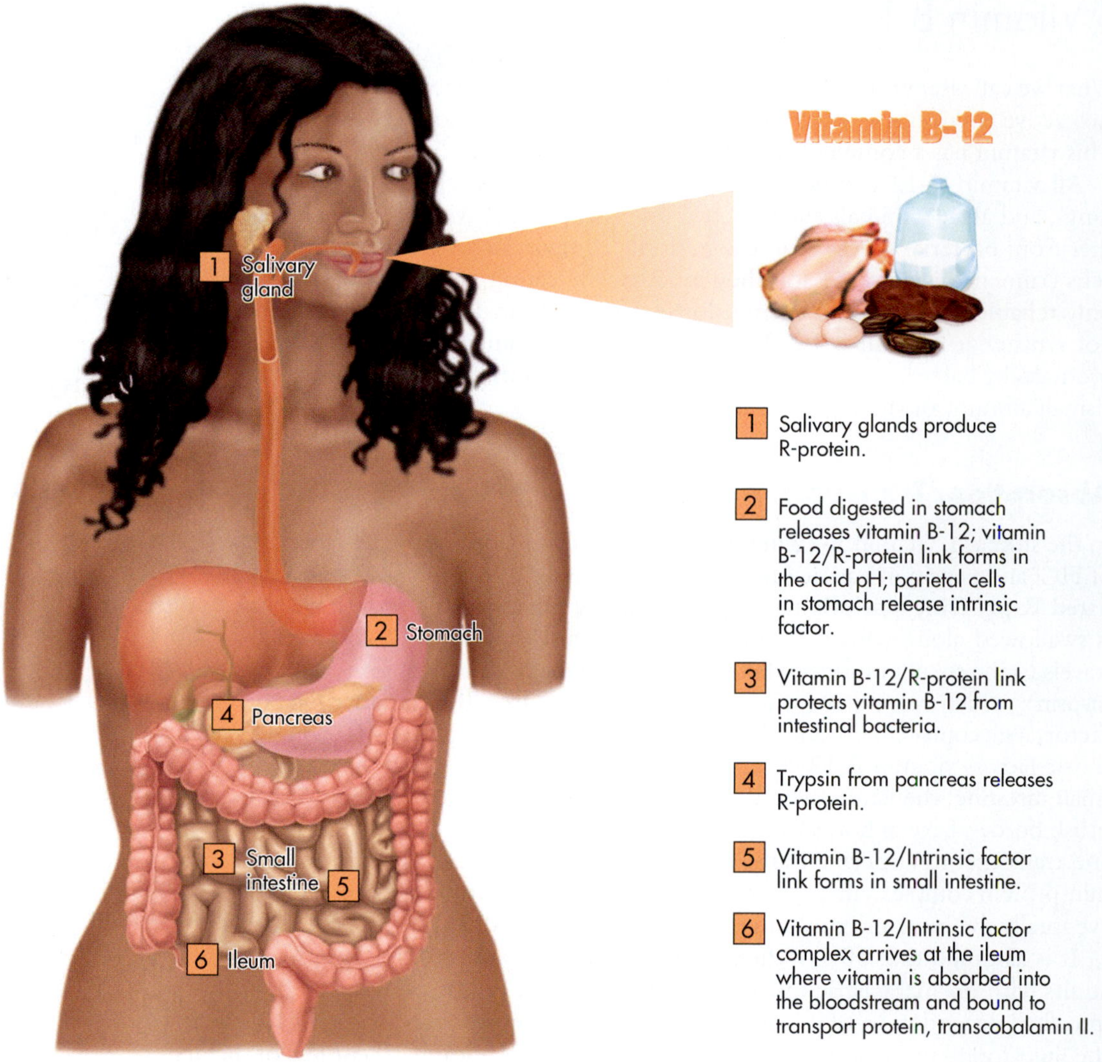
Vitamin B-12
1 Salivary gland
2 Stomach
4 Pancreas
3 Small intestine
5
6 Ileum
1 Salivary glands produce R-protein.
2 Food digested in stomach releases vitamin B-12; vitamin B-12/R-protein link forms in the acid pH; parietal cells in stomach release intrinsic factor.
3 Vitamin B-12/R-protein link protects vitamin B-12 from intestinal bacteria.
4 Trypsin from pancreas releases R-protein.
5 Vitamin B-12/Intrinsic factor link forms in small intestine.
6 Vitamin B-12/Intrinsic factor complex arrives at the ileum where vitamin is absorbed into the bloodstream and bound to transport protein, transcobalamin II.

Figure 10-7 Absorption of vitamin B-12. Many factors and sites in the gastrointestinal tract participate. Defects arising in the stomach or small intestine can interfere with vitamin B-12 absorption, in turn causing pernicious anemia.

a deficiency when absorption of dietary sources is hampered. In the body, little vitamin B-12 is lost—just the small amount that escapes enterohepatic circulation of the bile.

Functions of Vitamin B-12

mutase An enzyme that rearranges the functional groups on a molecule.

Vitamin B-12 is associated with coenzymes that move one carbon units. An example of an enzyme that uses a vitamin B-12 coenzyme is methylmalonyl CoA **mutase,** which requires the coenzyme 5-deoxyadenosyl cobalamin. The methylmalonyl CoA mutase requires vitamin B-12 to convert methylmalonyl CoA to succinyl CoA, an intermediate in the citric acid cycle. This reaction allows fatty acids with an odd number of carbons (most, but not all, fatty acids have an even number) to be oxidized for energy. Methionine synthase requires methylcobolamin as its coenzyme for the transfer of a methyl group from methyltetrahydrofolate to homocysteine to form methionine and tetrahydrofolate.

Vitamin B-12 coenzymes also end up helping recycle folate coenzymes. When folate coenzymes function, their chemical composition changes as various single carbon units are added. In a variety of chemical reactions vitamin B-12 is needed to put the folate coenzyme back in the original chemical structure that can resume function. Vitamin B-12 also plays some roles in the nervous system, some of which are not fully understood.

Vitamin B-12 in Foods

Sources of vitamin B-12 include animal products such as meat, poultry, seafood, and eggs. Especially rich sources of vitamin B-12 (μg/kcal) are organ meats (especially liver, kidneys, and heart). Another source of vitamin B-12 is dairy products.

Food Sources of Vitamin B-12

Food Item and Amount	*Vitamin B-12 (μg)*
Fried beef liver, 1 oz	31.7
Baked clams, 1 oz	15.7
Boiled oysters, 2	14.4
Brewer's yeast, 2 tbsp	3.0
Lobster, 3 oz	2.7
Pot roast, 3 oz	2.5
Plain yogurt, 1 cup	1.4
Corn Flakes cereal, ¾ cup	1.1
Shrimp, 3 oz	1.0
1% milk, 1 cup	0.9
Soy milk, 1 cup	0.8
Boiled egg, 1	0.6
Lean ham, 3 oz	0.6
Beef hot dog, 1	0.5
Ham lunch meat, 2 oz	0.4

RDA adults, 2.4 μg

Vitamin B-12 Needs

The RDA of vitamin B-12 for adults is 2.4 μg/day. It is based on maintaining enough vitamin B-12 in the body to adequately synthesize red blood cells. The Daily Value used on food and supplement labels is 6 μg. On average, adult men consume 3 times the RDA and women consume 2 times the RDA. This high intake provides the average meat-eating person with 2 to 3 years' storage of vitamin B-12 in the liver. For men and women 51 years and older, the RDA is also 2.4 μg of vitamin B-12 per day, but this population group is advised to select foods fortified with vitamin B-12 (e.g., ready-to-eat breakfast cereals) and/or to take a supplemental form. This is because absorption of foodborne vitamin B-12 is hampered by the typical fall in gastric acid output seen in aging, called **achlorhydria.**[7]

No adverse effects have been observed with excess vitamin B-12 intake from food or from supplements, so there is no Upper Level for this vitamin.

Vitamin B-12 Deficiency

Researches in midnineteenth-century England noted a form of anemia that causes death within 2 to 5 years of initial diagnosis. They called this disease **pernicious anemia** (*pernicious* literally means "leading to death"). We now know that this is caused by a genetic problem in the production of intrinsic factor which is needed for vitamin B-12 absorption. Clinically, this disease looks like a folate-deficiency anemia. This is because a vitamin B-12 deficiency impairs folate function.[5] For patients with either a folate or vitamin B-12 deficiency, many megaloblasts (macrocytes) are seen in the blood. As in folate deficiency, the cause of the anemia is an interference with normal synthesis of DNA.

A vitamin B-12 deficiency also produces nerve degeneration, which can be fatal. The neurological complications produce sensory disturbances in the legs, such as tingling and numbness (collectively referred to as **paresthesia**). These often are worse in the lower legs. Walking is difficult and "position sense" is seriously affected. Many mental problems exist as well, such as loss of concentration and memory, disorientation, and dementia. As the condition worsens, bowel and bladder control is lost. Visual disturbances are common. There also are numerous gastrointestinal problems, from sore tongue to constipation.

Infants who are breastfed by vegetarian or vegan mothers can develop vitamin B-12 deficiency, accompanied by anemia and long-term neurological problems, such as diminished brain growth, degeneration of the spinal cord, and poor intellectual development. The problems may have their origins during pregnancy if the mother is deficient in vitamin B-12.

Adult vegetarians can also become vitamin B-12 deficient, though if an adult becomes a vegetarian, vitamin B-12 stores in the liver can delay a severe deficiency for a long time (even years). Vegetarians have several options for obtaining vitamin B-12. If they are not strict vegetarians, they can eat eggs or dairy products. In addition, vegetarians can take a supplement that contains vitamin B-12 or eat food products fortified with vitamin B-12.

People with malabsorption syndromes of any kind have an increased need for vitamin B-12. These include postgastrectomy patients, postgastric bypass surgery patients, and

achlorhydria A decrease in stomach acid output primarily due to age associated loss of acid-producing gastric cells.

pernicious anemia The anemia that results from the inability to absorb sufficient vitamin B-12; it is associated with nerve degeneration, which can result in eventual paralysis and death.

paresthesia An abnormal spontaneous sensation such as of burning, prickling, and numbness.

Fish, seafood, and related products are good sources of vitamin B-12.

ileal resection patients, as well as patients with Crohn's disease or any disease involving the ileum. HIV-positive patients with chronic diarrhea may require oral or supplemental intravenous vitamin B-12. Several other medical conditions, such as reduced secretions of the pancreas (chronic pancreatic disease) and bacterial infections of the intestinal tract, require extra vitamin B-12 because of decreased bioavailability of the vitamin from food.

Older people may often have problems with absorbing vitamin B-12 due to reduced stomach production of hydrochloric acid, which frees vitamin B-12 from food proteins. This can lower vitamin B-12 absorption to the extent that it creates a marginal vitamin B-12 deficiency. This deficiency is not severe enough to produce anemia, but can cause neurological problems and elevated blood homocysteine.[5] The latter is due to impaired folate recycling. This degree of impaired vitamin B-12 absorption, unlike the case with pernicious anemia, can usually be overcome by a moderate increase of oral vitamin B-12 intake via supplements or fortified foods. Injections are not normally needed.

A Closer Look at Homocysteine Metabolism: Integrating Your Nutrition Knowledge

As noted earlier, a fourth B-vitamin—riboflavin—may also affect blood levels of homocysteine in some people. Low levels of FAD (the riboflavin cofactor) reduce folate's ability to donate a methyl ($-CH_3$) group.

Normally, the compound homocysteine mentioned numerous times in this and other chapters doesn't build up in the body to any large extent. It is just a temporary intermediate in the metabolism of sulfur-containing amino acids when methionine is broken down and cysteine is made.

How do cells prevent a buildup of homocysteine? Three B-vitamins plus choline (see the next section) are especially involved in eliminating homocysteine (Fig. 10-8).[1] One of the relevant B-vitamins is folate, which automatically brings vitamin B-12 into the picture, since their two functions are intertwined. The other B-vitamin involved is vitamin B-6, which is involved in a different homocysteine-related reaction than the one where folate comes into play. This shows how nutrients can work together for a common purpose.

Concept | Check

Folate is needed for cell division because it is essential for DNA synthesis. A folate deficiency results in macrocytic anemia, as well as diarrhea, inflammation of the tongue, and poor growth—all signs of inadequate cell division. Folate is found in fresh vegetables and organ meats. Folate deficiency is most commonly found in pregnant women, when needs are elevated, and in alcoholics, since alcohol interferes with absorption of folate. Vitamin B-12 is necessary for folate metabolism. Without dietary vitamin B-12, folate deficiency symptoms, such as macrocytic anemia, develop. In addition, vitamin B-12 is necessary for maintaining the nervous system; paralysis can develop from a vitamin B-12 deficiency. Vitamin B-12 is found only in animal foods; meat eaters generally have a 3- to 5-year supply stored in the liver. However, vitamin B-12 absorption may decline in older persons. In this case, a deficiency of vitamin B-12 is generally corrected by monthly injections of the vitamin.

Choline

For many years, choline was often included in supplements as a supposed B-vitamin. However, most nutrition experts claimed that choline was not a vitamin at all because the body makes enough of it to meet its needs in most stages of life. Recent research has contradicted some of this attitude, however. Apparently in some cases, the body's production of choline is not sufficient to cover requirements.[7] However, choline still is not considered a B-vitamin. Choline does not have a coenzyme function, and the amount of choline in the body is much greater than the amount of a typical B-vitamin.

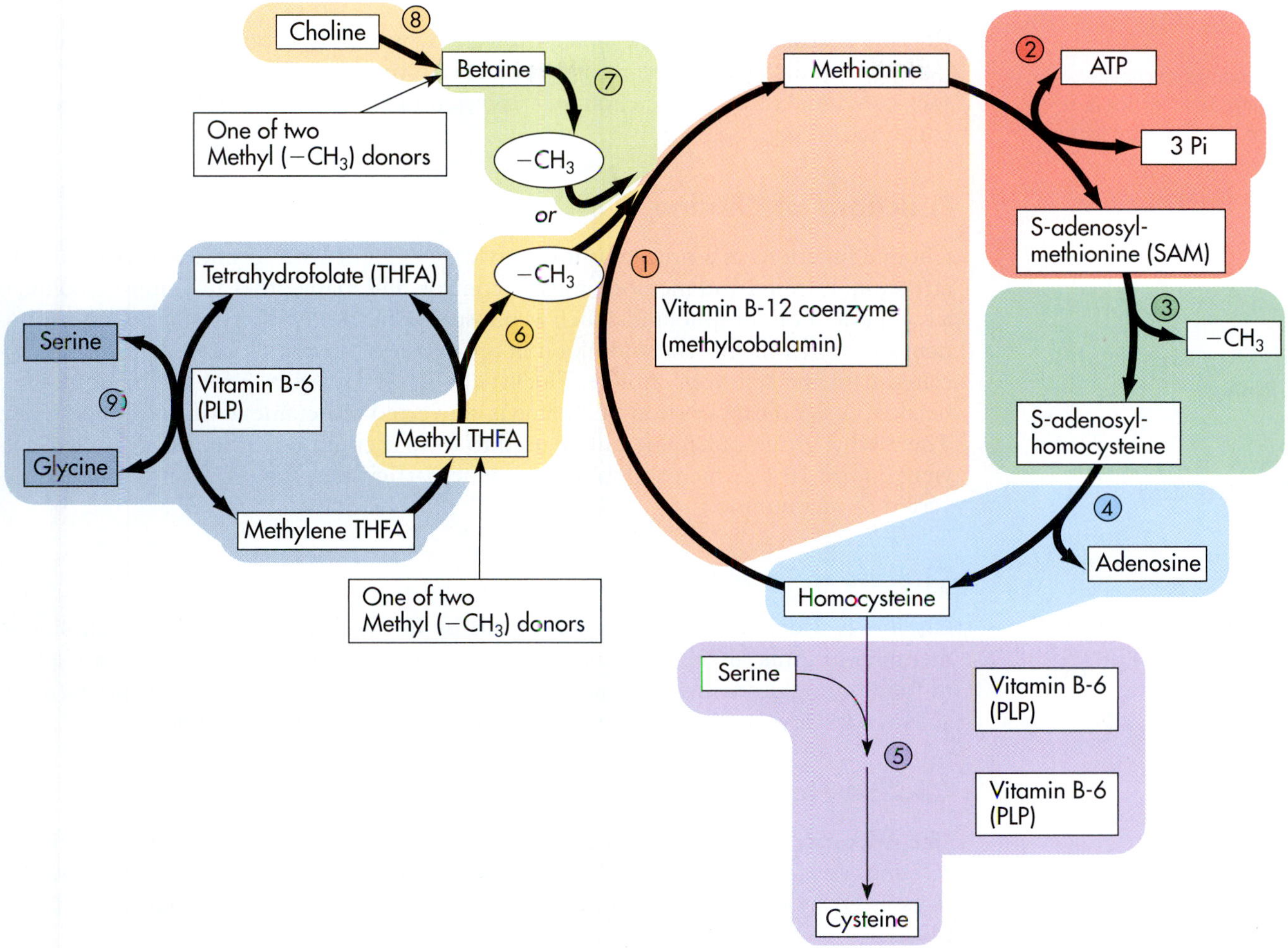

① With the aid of the vitamin B-12 coenzyme (methylcobalamin), the methyl group ($-CH_3$) is transferred from the folate coenzyme, methyl THFA, to homocysteine to form methionine. Another important function of this reaction is to make the resulting tetrahydrafolate coenzyme available to participate in DNA synthesis.

② Methionine can be converted to S-Adenosyl-methionine (SAM) with the addition of adenosine from ATP. The three phosphate groups are removed.

③ S-Adenosyl-methionine is converted to S-Adenosyl homocysteine by removal of the $-CH_3$, which is donated to a variety of methyl group acceptors.

④ S-Adenosyl homocysteine is converted back to homocysteine with the removal of adenosine.

Overall, this cycle, especially step ①, helps control the concentration of homocysteine in the blood.

⑤ With the aid of vitamin B-6 coenzyme PLP, homocysteine is used to make the nonessential amino acid cysteine. The nonessential amino acid serine contributes part of its carbon skeleton to homocysteine. This is another pathway that helps control blood homocysteine concentration.

⑥ Either methyl tetrahydrofolate or

⑦ Betaine is a donor of a methyl group to form methionine.

⑧ The betaine is derived from choline.

⑨ Note that the serine-glycine reaction is reversible in conjunction with THFA and methylene THFA. Here is another example of vitamin B-6 in action as PLP.

In summary, the coenzymes of vitamin B-12, folate, and vitamin B-6, along with choline, work together as a team to control the amount of homocysteine in the blood. The vitamin riboflavin also participates (not shown).

Figure 10-8 Detailed diagram of folate, vitamin B-12, vitamin B-6, and choline metabolism in relation to homocysteine metabolism.

Absorption, Metabolism, and Excretion of Choline

Choline is absorbed from the small intestine by way of transport proteins. Choline is taken up rapidly by the liver from the portal vein that drains the small intestine. All tissues contain choline. Some choline is excreted in the urine, but most of the excess is converted to **betaine.**

betaine An oxidation product of choline metabolism and a methyl (CH_3) donor in methionine metabolism.

Functions of Choline

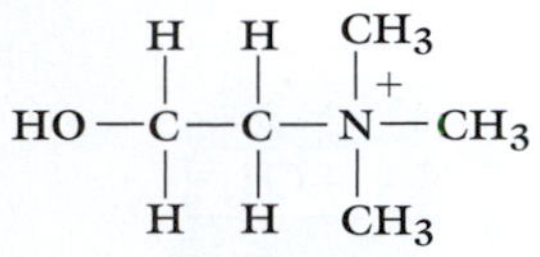
Choline

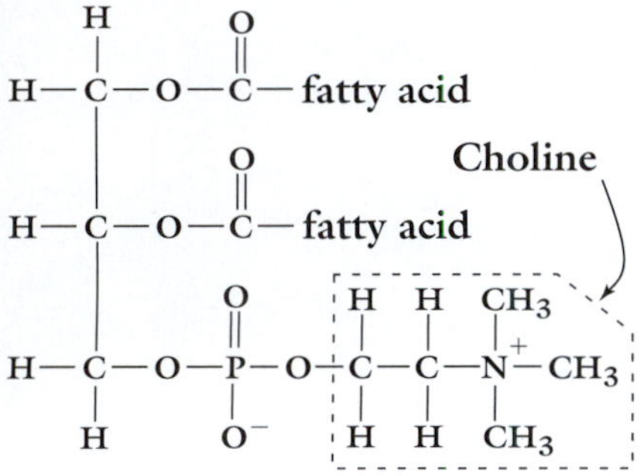

Lecithin

Choline forms part of the natural emulsifiers called *lecithins.*

Choline functions as a precursor for acetylcholine, a neurotransmitter associated with attention, learning and memory, muscle control, and many other functions. Choline is a component of phospholipids, such as phosphatidylcholine (lecithin), a major component of the cell membrane and blood lipoproteins. Liver export of VLDL is also associated with the action of choline. Finally, choline is a precursor for the methyl donor betaine. A significant portion of choline is converted to betaine in the liver and kidney. The methyl group of betaine can be used to form methionine from homocysteine. Review Figure 10-8, which shows how choline participates when homocysteine is converted to methionine.[1]

Choline in Foods

Choline is widely distributed in foods, mostly in the form of phosphatidylcholine in membranes. Milk, liver, eggs, and peanuts are rich sources. Lecithins often are added to food during processing, so this is yet another source. There is so much choline available in ordinary foods that it is unlikely that a dietary deficiency will develop.

Choline Needs

The Adequate Intake for choline for adult men is 550 mg/day; for adult women it is 425 mg/day. This is based on the intake of choline required to maintain liver function as assessed by measuring an enzyme (alanine aminotransferase) concentration in the blood.

Few data exist to assess whether a dietary supply is needed at all life stages. Although Adequate Intakes are set for choline, it may be that the choline requirement can be met by body synthesis at some or all stages of life. We also consume ample choline from food, at least 700 to 1000 mg/day.

Peanuts are a good source of choline. Body cells also produce choline.

Choline Deficiency

There has been only one published study examining the effect of inadequate dietary intake of choline in healthy humans. The study of male volunteers showed decreased choline stores and liver damage. When humans were fed choline-deficient total parental nutrition solutions, they developed fatty livers and liver damage. Based on these observations, plus laboratory animal studies, choline has been deemed essential, at least in some life stages and health conditions.

Choline Toxicity

Very high doses of choline have been associated with a fishy body odor, vomiting, salivation, sweating, low blood pressure (hypotension), and gastrointestinal effects. The fishy odor is due to the excretion of a choline metabolite. The Upper Level for adults is 3.5 g/day, based on development of a fishy body odor and low blood pressure.[7]

Vitamin C

Vitamin C, also known as ascorbic acid, is involved in many processes in the human body. Ascorbic acid is also needed by all other life forms, but all plants and most animals make ascorbic acid. So, ascorbic acid is a vitamin only for humans, plus a few other animals: nonhuman primates, guinea pigs, a few birds, fruit bats, and some fish.

The term *vitamin C* actually refers not only to ascorbic acid but also to its oxidized form dehydroascorbic acid. Both forms are found in the foods we eat.

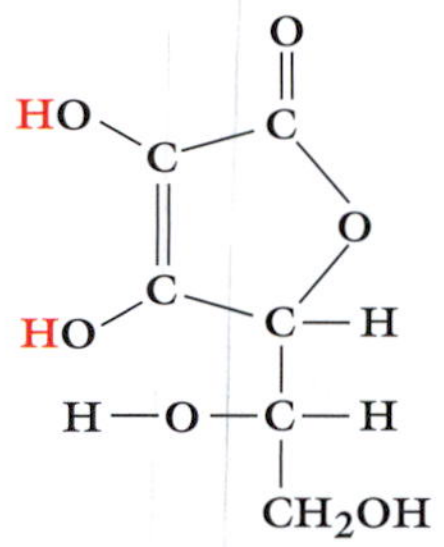

Ascorbic acid (reduced)

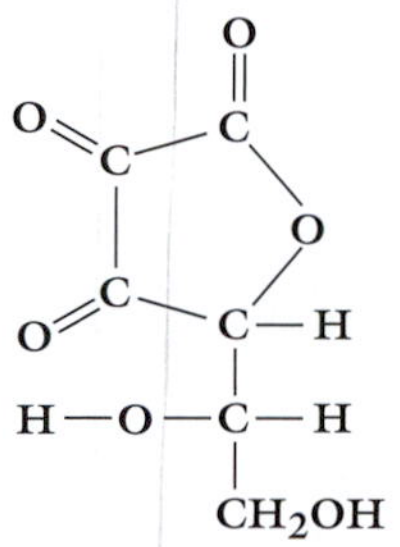

Dehydroascorbic acid (oxidized)

Vitamin C undergoes reversible oxidation and reduction by loss or addition of two hydrogens (red).

Absorption, Metabolism, Storage, and Excretion of Vitamin C

Absorption of vitamin C occurs in the small intestine by means of active transport (for ascorbic acid) and by facilitated diffusion (for dehydroascorbic acid). Efficiency of the absorptive mechanism decreases as intake increases. About 70 to 90% of vitamin C is absorbed at daily intakes between 30 and 180 mg, whereas absorption efficiency declines to about 50% or less with increasing doses above 1 g/day. Excretion by the kidneys increases as dietary intake increases.[17]

Within the cell and in blood, vitamin C exists predominately in the reduced form, ascorbic acid (ascorbate). The amount of vitamin C varies widely by tissue. High concentrations are found in the pituitary and adrenal glands, white blood cells, eyes, and brain. The lowest concentrations are in the blood and saliva. The total amount of vitamin C in the body varies over a wide range.[8]

Functions of Vitamin C

Vitamin C performs a variety of important cell functions. It does so primarily by acting as a nonspecific **reducing agent.** As mentioned in conjunction with riboflavin and niacin functions, a reducing agent is a substance that donates electrons and, in turn, becomes oxidized (loses electrons). Ascorbic acid donates electrons as part of hydrogen atoms; however, unlike the coenzyme function of riboflavin or niacin, ascorbic acid donates hydrogens in a way that the electrons of the atom go to different molecules than the rest of the hydrogen.[17] For example, vitamin C can donate electrons to metal ions, such as iron and copper. In the oxidized state, ferric iron (Fe^{3+}) can be reduced to ferrous ion (Fe^{2+}), and cupric ion (Cu^{2+}) to cuprous ion (Cu^{+}). The metals get the electrons while the rest of the hydrogen goes elsewhere (i.e., as H^{+}).

Some vitamin C actions are associated with enzymes, while others are not. Even when enzymes are involved, vitamin C is not considered a coenzyme in the same way B-vitamins are because the chemistry is different. For example, a riboflavin coenzyme can modify a compound, whereas a vitamin C may act on a metal in an enzyme.

reducing agent A compound capable of donating electrons (also hydrogen ions) to another compound.

Collagen Synthesis

Collagen is the fibrous protein that gives strength to **connective tissue.** Collagen fibers are critical to the structure of bone and blood vessels, and they are essential in wound healing.

A collagen molecule is like a three-stranded rope. It consists of three-polypeptide chains wound together to form a triple helix. To get the three strands in the right shape to form the triple helix, which gives a ropelike structure, vitamin C is needed. Vitamin C changes the structure of two amino acids, lysine and proline. These are converted to hydroxylysine and hydroxyproline.

These two amino acids are formed only in collagen and not in other proteins. Thus, they are not among the 20 "normal" amino acids in the genetic code. The role of vitamin C in the formation of these unusual amino acids is to interact with the enzymes involved in making the conversions (Fig. 10-9).[17] These enzymes use iron as part of the catalytic process. In this process, the iron is converted from Fe^{2+} to Fe^{3+}. For the enzymes to continue functioning, the iron must be recycled to Fe^{2+}. Vitamin C, as a reducing agent, can provide electrons for this purpose.

collagen The major protein of the material that holds together the various structures of the body.

connective tissue The material that holds together the various structures of the body. Tendons and cartilage are composed largely of connective tissue. Connective tissue also forms part of bone and the nonmuscular structures of arteries and veins.

Antioxidant Activity

In vitro (in a test tube), vitamin C can be an antioxidant by donating electrons to free radicals. Recall that a free radical has an unpaired electron. A vitamin C molecule can

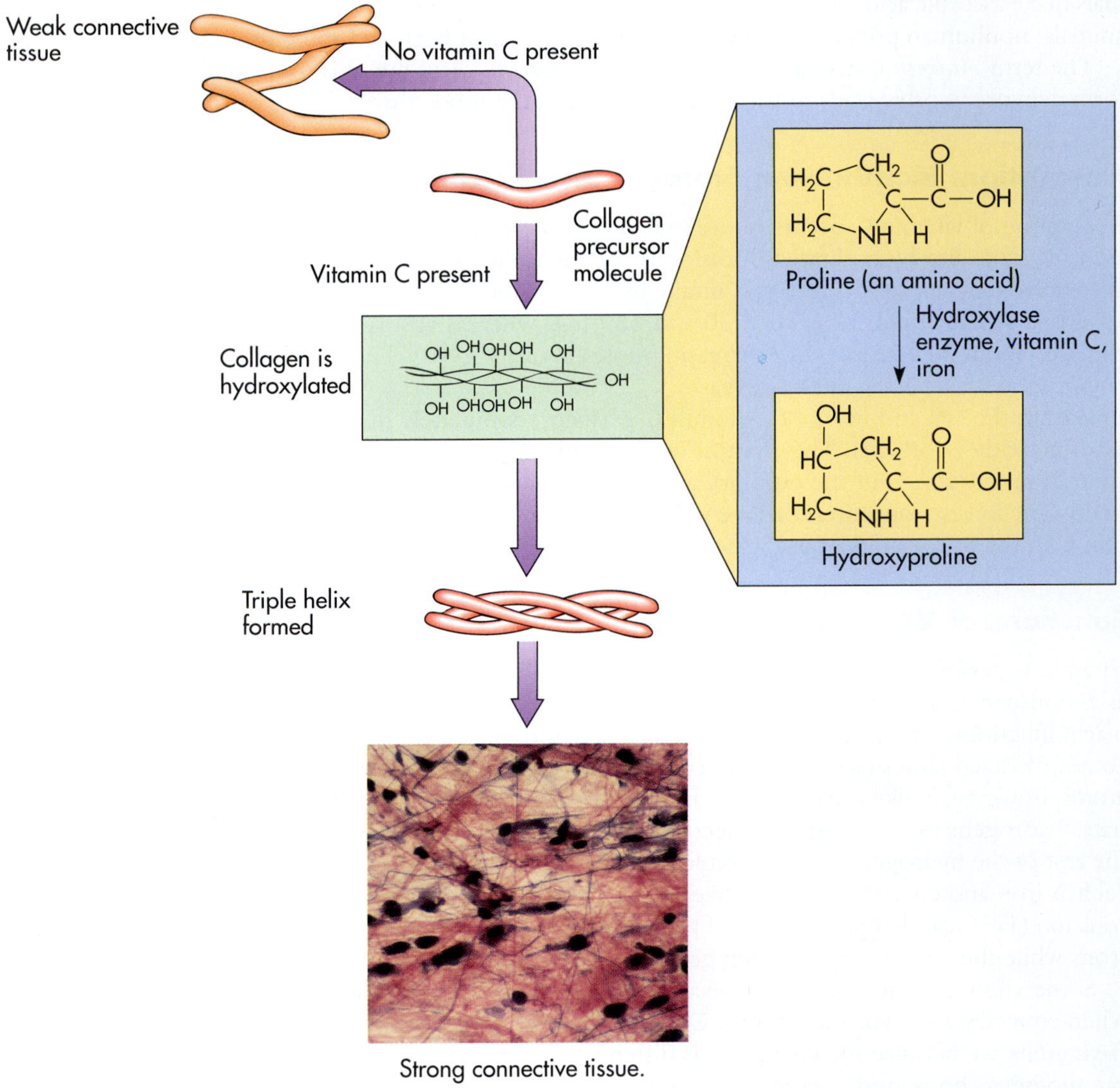

Figure 10-9 Vitamin C is needed for the addition of hydroxyl groups (-OH) to the amino acid proline in collagen molecules. Collagen is unique among body proteins because it contains large amounts of the amino acid hydroxyproline, which is necessary for the formation of stable collagen fibers.

donate electrons to free radicals so that they become stable. This has led to the proposition that vitamin C in the body's water-based fluids (i.e., blood) acts just like vitamin E does in lipid-rich environments. It has also been suggested that vitamin C can recycle vitamin E and make it function more effectively.

Although these vitamin C antioxidant actions work well in a test tube, does it do the same in humans? Despite what you may have read to the contrary, we don't actually know if vitamin C plays major or minor antioxidant roles in humans.[17] Research in this area is ongoing. So far, some data suggest that vitamin C does have some important in vivo antioxidant effects. However, not all the results have been that positive. In fact, some research suggested that vitamin C can increase oxidant stress (though this work's design has been given some criticism). This whole area should be more clear in the next few years.

Vitamin C is present in high concentrations in the eye possibly to protect against photolytically generated free radicals.[20] It is also present in high concentrations in white blood cells (e.g., neutrophils), possibly for protection against the free radicals produced during immune functions.[17]

Iron Absorption

Vitamin C added to meals modestly facilitates the intestinal absorption of nonheme iron (iron that is not in hemoglobin) due to the conversion of iron in the gastrointestinal tract to ferrous iron (Fe^{2+}). Vitamin C also counters the action of certain food components that inhibit iron absorption.

Synthesis of Other Vital Compounds

Carnitine is a transport compound that moves fatty acids from the cytoplasm into the mitochondria for energy production. Vitamin C participates in two separate steps in carnitine biosynthesis. The biosynthesis of the hormones and neurotransmitters norepinephrine and epinephrine depends on vitamin C as an electron donor. The conversion of the essential amino acid tryptophan to the neurotransmitter serotonin requires vitamin C. Vitamin C is necessary for the biosynthesis of thyroxine (the thyroid hormone) and many other nervous system components. Vitamin C is also involved in the biosynthesis of corticosteroids and aldosterone, the conversion of cholesterol to bile acids, and tyrosine (an amino acid) metabolism.[8]

Critical | Thinking

Carlos just returned from a local mall and is excited because he saw an advertisement claiming that vitamin C will cure just about everything, from colds to heart disease. How would you explain to him vitamin C's main functions in the human body?

Immune Function

White blood cells, part of the immune defenses of the body, contain the highest vitamin C concentration of all body constituents. As noted on the previous page, a high concentration of vitamin C in white blood cells may provide protection against the oxidative damage associated with cellular **respiration.** Free radicals generated during phagocytosis and **neutrophil activation,** though intended to kill bacteria or damaged tissue, can also kill the body's own immune cells. Vitamin C may reduce this self-destruction by this vitamin's antioxidant actions. Vitamin C may also have other roles in immune function. Note that supplemental vitamin C beyond body needs may not necessarily improve immune function.

respiration The intracellular oxidation of substances coupled with the production of ATP; may be anaerobic or aerobic.

neutrophil activation A type of white blood cell being prepared for immune response.

Vitamin C in Foods

All fruits and vegetables contain some vitamin C, but certain fruits and vegetables provide much more than others. Citrus fruits, potatoes, and green vegetables in general are good sources of vitamin C. Animal products and grains are generally not good sources. The Food Guide Pyramid guideline of at least 5 servings/day of combined fruits and vegetables provides ample vitamin C. The major contributors of vitamin C to North American diets are oranges and orange juice, grapefruit and grapefruit juice, tomatoes and tomato juice, fortified fruit drinks, tangerines, and potatoes. Vitamin C is easily lost in processing and cooking. Juices are good foods to fortify with vitamin C because their acidity reduces vitamin C destruction. Vitamin C is very unstable when in contact with heat, iron, copper, and oxygen.

Food Sources of Vitamin C

Food Item and Amount	*Vitamin C (mg)*
Orange, 1	98
Cooked brussels sprouts, 1 cup	97
Strawberries, 1 cup	94
Grapefruit juice, 1 cup	80
Red peppers, ¼ cup	71
Kiwi fruit, 1	57
Green pepper rings, 5	45
Tomato juice, 1 cup	45
Cooked broccoli, ½ cup	33
Kale, ½ cup	27
Raw cauliflower, ½ cup	23
Sweet potato, 1	17
Baked potato, 1 medium	16
Pineapple chunks, ½ cup	12
Cooked spinach, ½ cup	9

RDA adult men, 90 mg; adult women, 75 mg

Vitamin C Needs

The RDA for vitamin C for adult men is 90 mg/day; for adult women it is 75 mg/day.[8] Most of us consume this much and more. The RDA is based on near maximal vitamin C concentrations in neutrophils (a white blood cell) with minimal urinary excretion. Because smoking causes oxidative stress, the requirement for smokers increases by 35 mg/day. Smokers have a higher turnover of vitamin C probably because of its antioxidant activity. Vitamin C needs are also increased by oral contraceptive use (for reasons that are not clear). Vitamin C needs can be increased by burns or surgery that removes a lot of tissue. This is because of the need for a lot of collagen production to replace lost tissue. However, there is no agreed upon amount of extra vitamin C needed in the medical literature. The Daily Value for vitamin C used on food and supplement labels is 60 mg.

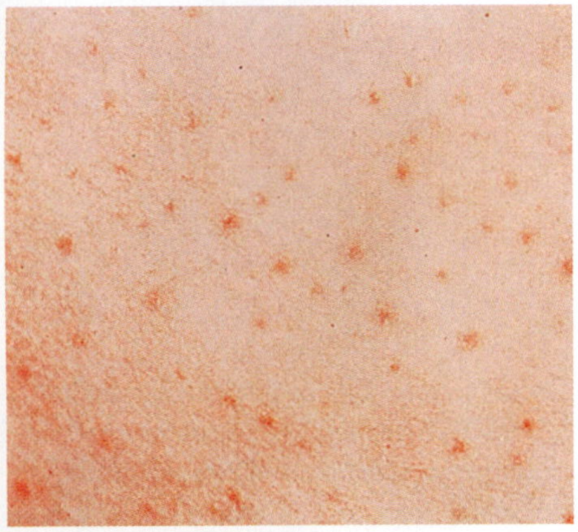

Figure 10-10 Pinpoint hemorrhages of the skin—an early symptom of scurvy. The spots on the skin are caused by slight bleeding into hair follicles. The person also will often show inadequate wound healing—all signs of defective collagen synthesis.

Vitamin C Deficiency

A deficiency of vitamin C prevents the normal synthesis of collagen, thus causing widespread and significant changes in connective tissues throughout the body. The first signs and symptoms of scurvy, the deficiency disease, appear after about 20 to 40 days on a vitamin C-free diet and include fatigue and pinpoint hemorrhages around hair follicles on the back of the arms and legs (Fig. 10-10). These hemorrhages are the most characteristic sign of scurvy. In addition, there is bleeding in the gums and joints, a classic sign of connective tissue failure. Other effects of scurvy include impaired wound healing, bone pain, fractures, and diarrhea. Psychological problems, such as depression, are common in advanced scurvy.[8]

Worldwide, scurvy is associated with poverty. It is especially common in infants who are fed boiled milk (all forms of milk are poor sources of vitamin C) and are not provided with a good food source of vitamin C or a supplement.

In North America, vitamin C deficiency is most likely to occur in alcoholics and those addicted to other drugs, as they often consume a nutrient-poor diet. Anyone who eats very few fruits and vegetables is also susceptible to vitamin C deficiency. Men in general are more at risk of vitamin C deficiency compared with women because they are less apt to consume vitamin supplements. Finally, people exposed to cigarette smoke generally have lower vitamin C status than nonsmokers.

Although the development of scurvy in an otherwise healthy child is rare, it is possible. A 5-year-old boy developed scurvy after eating nothing but Pop-Tarts, cheese pizza, biscuits, and water for 5 months. The boy, who was growing and maturing normally, started to limp; his gums became swollen; and small, purple spots began to appear on his skin. His baffled doctors finally diagnosed the boy as having scurvy and gave him vitamin C, and his condition began to improve within a week.

Vitamin C Intake Above the RDA

Some popular authors and speakers advocate consumption of vitamin C at amounts higher than the RDA. Surprisingly, there is not much research comparing different vitamin C intakes. Note that if vitamin C intake is above about 100 mg/day, much of the additional vitamin C is excreted in the urine. Some research also indicates that 200 mg/day is the most a person would need to maximize the health benefits of vitamin C intake.[17] Choosing several vitamin C-rich foods each day can boost intakes to 200 mg/day.

One aspect of high vitamin C intake that has drawn a lot of attention is its possible use for prevention or treatment of the common cold. This use is not focused on correcting vitamin C deficiency. Although such an intake may help with cold severity, probably by improving immune function, most of the attention has been on a high vitamin C intake by people with no deficiency. At these doses, the vitamin C could exert multiple actions, including actions which do not occur at more typical vitamin C intakes. The idea that high doses of vitamin C are useful for preventing and treating colds, and perhaps some other maladies, gained a lot of momentum about thirty years ago. At that time, high dose vitamin C supplementation was advocated strongly by Linus Pauling, a Nobel prize winner in chemistry. Although Dr. Pauling did not originate the idea, he gave it a lot of publicity. Since then, a number of studies have been done. A recent statistical analysis of many of these studies concluded that high dose vitamin C use (up to about 1000 mg/day) may have small effects on cold severity (not incidence) in some people.[6] This less-than-spectacular conclusion has led many physicians and registered dietitians not to recommend high dose vitamin C for prevention or treatment of colds.

Toxicity of Vitamin C

The principal adverse effects associated with a very high intake of vitamin C are gastrointestinal disturbances, including nausea, abdominal cramps, and diarrhea. A variety of other problems have been blamed on very high vitamin C intakes, but none have been proven in healthy people, such as kidney stone formation. The Upper Level for vitamin C is 2 g/day, based on diarrhea and gastrointestinal disturbances.[8]

Table 10-2 summarizes much of what is known about the B-vitamins, choline, and vitamin C.

Concept | Check

Only guinea pigs, monkeys, some birds and fish, and humans need dietary vitamin C. It is used mainly in the synthesis of collagen, a major connective tissue protein. A vitamin C deficiency causes scurvy, which is marked by many changes in the skin and gums, such as small hemorrhages, because of reduced collagen synthesis. Vitamin C also modestly improves iron absorption and is involved in the synthesis of certain hormones and neurotransmitters. Citrus fruits, green peppers, cauliflower, broccoli, and strawberries are good sources of vitamin C. As with folate, fresh or lightly cooked foods are the best sources, since loss of vitamin C in cooking can be high. At intakes greater than about 2 g/day, vitamin C can lead to diarrhea and other gastrointestinal upsets.

Vegetables such as green peppers are a good source of vitamin C, and fruits such as strawberries are another good source.

Vitamin-like Compounds

The various vitamin-like compounds—carnitine, inositol, taurine, and lipoic acid—are necessary to maintain normal metabolism in the body. They all can be synthesized by the body, but their biosynthesis often occurs at the expense of other nutrients, such as essential amino acids. The need for these compounds often increases during times of rapid tissue growth, as is the case with the preterm infant.

There is no concern that deficiencies of these vitamin-like compounds exist in the average healthy adult. But more research is needed to clarify whether deficiencies might arise in certain disease states and whether the compounds should be included in infant formulas and total parenteral nutrition solutions. Currently, manufacturers often add these vitamin-like compounds to infant formulas.

Carnitine

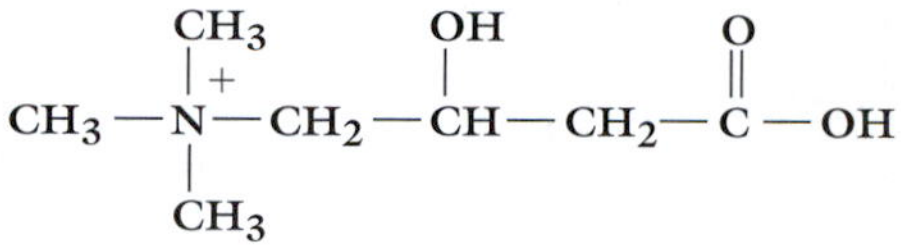

Carnitine

Carnitine is a relatively simple compound that can be synthesized in the liver from the amino acids lysine and methionine. Human needs for carnitine are met from both animal foods and biosynthesis. Adults and children who are severely malnourished or on total parenteral nutrition can have lower-than-normal concentrations of carnitine in their blood. An inadequate supply of protein (i.e., a lack of the amino acids needed for making carnitine) leads to abnormal fatty-acid metabolism. There is speculation that people with cirrhosis may need carnitine from the diet to offset inadequate liver production.

Within the cell, carnitine transports fatty acids from the cytosol into the mitochondria, where the fatty acids are then metabolized for energy. Carnitine also aids the mitochondria in removing excess organic acids, products of metabolic pathways.[1]

Meat and dairy products are the main sources of carnitine. We consume about 100 to 300 mg/day. Vegetarian diets are very low in carnitine because it is almost absent from plant foods. However, vegetarians show normal blood concentrations of carnitine. Consequently, it is doubtful that carnitine is necessary in the diets of healthy people. It may be considered a conditionally essential nutrient in times of recovery from disease, serious trauma, kidney dialysis, or preterm birth.

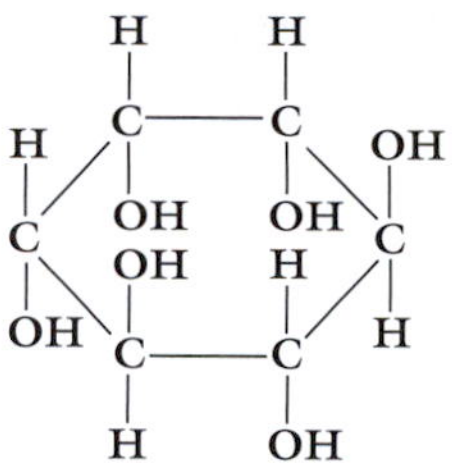

Myo-inositol

In addition, carnitine has displayed pharmaceutical usefulness in the removal of compounds that can build to toxic amounts in people with inborn errors of metabolism. Dosages approximately 10 times typical dietary intakes have also been shown to improve the condition of persons with progressive muscle disease and heart muscle deterioration. There have been some sales of carnitine supplements to promote weight loss or as an exercise aid; however, the research on these uses is still very limited.

Table 10-2 A Summary of Water-Soluble Vitamins

Vitamin	Major Functions	Deficiency Symptoms	People Most at Risk
Thiamin	Coenzyme in energy release	Beriberi: anorexia, weight loss, weakness, peripheral neuropathy; Wernicke-Korsakoff syndrome	Alcoholics and people living in poverty
Riboflavin	Coenzyme in numerous oxidation-reduction reactions, including those of energy release	Ariboflavinosis: inflammation of mouth and tongue, cracks at corner of mouth	People taking certain medications if no dairy products consumed
Niacin	Coenzyme in numerous oxidation-reduction reactions in energy metabolism, synthesis and breakdown of fatty acids	Pellagra: diarrhea, dermatitis, dementia (death)	Alcoholics and people living in poverty where corn is the dominant food
Pantothenic acid	Coenzyme involved in energy metabolism and fatty-acid synthesis	Weakness, fatigue, impaired muscle function, GI tract disturbances	None
Biotin	Cofactor for four carboxylases	Dermatitis, conjunctivitis hair loss, nervous system abnormalities	Alcoholics
Vitamin B-6	Coenzymes involved in amino acid metabolism, heme synthesis, lipid metabolism; homocysteine metabolism	Dermatitis, anemia, convulsion, depression, confusion	Alcoholics
Folate	Coenzyme involved in DNA synthesis, homocysteine metabolism	Megaloblastic (macrocytic) anemia; birth defects	Alcoholics, pregnant women, people on certain medications
Vitamin B-12	Coenzymes affecting folate metabolism, homocysteine metabolism	Megaloblastic (macrocytic) anemia, paresthesia, pernicious anemia	Older adults, vegans, HIV-positive patients, patients with malabsorption syndromes
Vitamin C	Collagen synthesis, some antioxidant capability, hormone and neurotransmitter synthesis	Scurvy: poor wound healing, pinpoint hemorrhages, bleeding gums	Alcoholics, individuals who eat few fruits and vegetables
Choline	Precursor for acetylcholine, phospholipids, and betaine; homocysteine metabolism	No natural deficiency	None

Inositol in supplement form is promoted as treatment for insomnia. There are a variety of causes for sleep disorders, but probably none are linked to an inositol deficiency.

Inositol

Of the nine possible isomers of inositol, only one—called myo-inositol—has nutritional implications for humans. The structure of inositol is related to that of glucose, from which it is synthesized in the body.

Much of the inositol in body cells occurs in phosphorylated forms, such as inositol triphosphate (IP_3), which is found free in the cell cytosol. Inositol is also incorporated into the phospholipids located in cell membranes. These inositol phospholipids are important precursors of the eicosanoids, which have numerous hormonelike actions (see Chapter 6). Under certain conditions (e.g., the binding of hormones), enzymes in the cell membrane act on the inositol phospholipids, releasing IP_3. This compound, in turn, mobilizes calcium ions (Ca^{2+}) from stores within cells.[1]

Both free inositol and inositol phospholipids are present in animal foods. Some plant foods (e.g., wheat bran) also contain inositol, mostly as part of phytic acid, a compound that binds minerals. The average North American diet provides about 1 g of inositol per day, and another 4 g/day or more are synthesized in the kidneys.

The metabolism of inositol is altered by several medical conditions. The hyperglycemia associated with diabetes inhibits inositol transport. Abnormal inositol metab-

Dietary Sources	RDA or Adequate Intake	Toxicity*
Pork and pork products, enriched and whole-grain cereals, nuts and seeds	Men: 1.2 mg/day; women: 1.1 mg/day	None recognized
Milk, mushrooms, spinach, liver, enriched grains	Men: 1.3 mg/day; women: 1.1 mg/day	None recognized
Meat, poultry, fish, enriched and whole-grain breads and cereals; also from tryptophan conversion to niacin	Men: 16 mg NE/day; women: 14 mg NE/day	Flushing of skin: Upper Level for adults is 35 mg/day from supplements, based on flushing of skin
Widely distributed in foods	Adequate Intake for adults: 5 mg/day	None recognized
Widely distributed in foods	Adequate Intake for adults: 30 µg/day	Unknown
Animal protein foods, spinach, potatoes, bananas, salmon, sunflower seeds	Adults 19 to 50: 1.3 mg/day; men over 50: 1.4 mg/day; women over 50: 1.3 mg/day	None from food but excess intake from supplements causes neuropathy, skin lesions; Upper Level is 100 mg/day, based on nerve destruction
Green vegetables, liver, enriched cereal products, legumes, oranges	400 µg/day of dietary folate equivalents (Note: dietary folate equivalents are not used for women in childbearing years; actual µg folic acid is used.)	None; Upper Level for adults set at 1000 µg/day for synthetic folate, exclusive of food folate, based on masking vitamin B-12 deficiency
Animal foods and fortified ready-to-eat breakfast cereals	Adults 19-50: 2.4 µg/day; adults 51 and older: same, but use of fortified foods or supplements is recommended	None recognized
Citrus fruits, strawberries, broccoli, greens	Men: 90 mg/day; women: 75 mg/day; + 35 mg/day for smokers	Diarrhea and other gastrointestinal problems; Upper Level is 2 g/day, based on development of diarrhea; can also alter some diagnostic tests
Widely distributed in foods, plus self-synthesis	Adequate Intake for Men: 550 mg/day; women: 425 mg/day	Upper Level is 3.5 g/day, based on development of fishy body odor and reduced blood pressure

*Toxicity arises only from supplement use.

olism is also noted in multiple sclerosis, kidney failure, and certain cancers. Overall, it appears that inositol is an essential nutrient only in certain medical conditions.

Taurine

Taurine is synthesized from the sulfur-containing amino acids methionine and cysteine. It is abundant in muscle, platelets, and nerve tissue. It is also attached to bile acids.[1] Although its mechanism of action is not well understood, taurine is involved in many vital functions. It is associated with photoreceptor activity in the eye, antioxidant activity in white blood cells, the protection of pulmonary tissue from oxidation, central nervous system function, platelet aggregation, cardiac contraction, insulin action, and cell differentiation and growth.

Taurine is found only in animal foods. North Americans consume about 40 to 400 mg/day. No clear cases of taurine deficiencies have been diagnosed in vegans, even though it is not found in plants, suggesting that synthesis by the body meets needs. Thus, it appears that healthy people need not worry about consuming taurine.

Taurine supplementation may be of benefit to children with cystic fibrosis. Some experience increased growth when treated with taurine, perhaps because of increased fat

One website states that many individuals are deficient in L-taurine. Since taurine is found in the central nervous system, the website claims it controls epileptic seizures, motor tics, and facial twitches. It is also promoted as preventing cataracts and certain forms of cardiovascular disease. Scientific evidence for these claims is lacking.

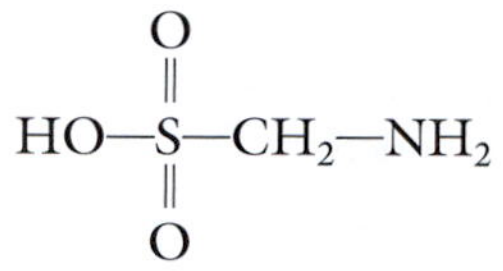

Taurine

absorption from the action of taurine as part of bile. Preterm infants supplemented with taurine may also exhibit improved fat absorption.

Some supplement manufacturers claim the body is unable to manufacture sufficient lipoic acid. They also claim that a deficiency of lipoic acid prevents antioxidants from working properly together. Research has yet to confirm such claims.

Lipoic Acid

Lipoic acid is used in reactions in which a carbon dioxide molecule is lost from a substrate, as when pyruvate is converted into acetyl-CoA. Lipoic acid also works with several antioxidants in the body.[1]

Even though lipoic acid serves such beneficial functions in the body, it is unnecessary to obtain it from outside sources. Rich dietary sources are meats, liver, and yeast.

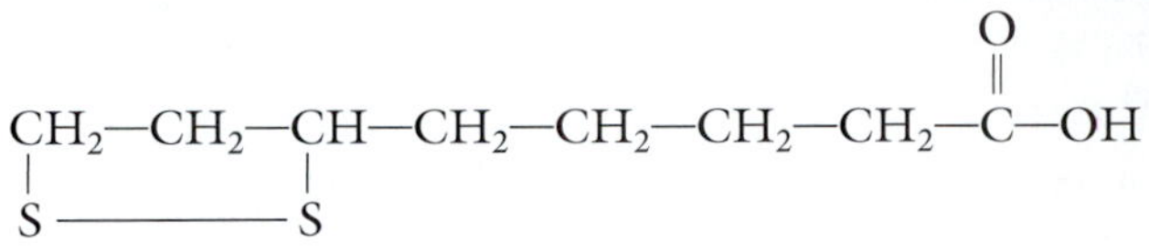

Lipoic acid

Concept | Check

A variety of vitamin-like compounds are found in the body. They can be synthesized by cells using common building blocks, such as amino acids and glucose. Sometimes in disease states synthesis may not meet body needs, and so dietary intake can be crucial. The needs for dietary carnitine and taurine in certain conditions (e.g., in preterm infants or in total parenteral nutrition) are current areas of research.

Summary

1. Thiamin in its functional form as TPP serves as a coenzyme in energy release. About the only North American population that could be deficient in thiamin are alcoholics. Pork, pork products, and enriched grains are reliable sources of thiamin.
2. Riboflavin in functional form, FAD and FMN, participates in a wide variety of oxidation-reduction reactions including those in numerous metabolic pathways that produce energy. A pure riboflavin deficiency is unlikely but could accompany other B-vitamin deficiencies. Dairy products and enriched grains are good dietary sources.
3. Niacin as NAD and NADP are coenzymes. NAD is important in oxidation-reduction reactions including reactions that yield energy. A deficiency of the vitamin produces the disease pellagra. Alcoholism can lead to a deficiency. Food sources of niacin are enriched cereal grains and protein foods. The body is able to synthesize the vitamin from the amino acid tryptophan. Megadoses of niacin produce a variety of toxic symptoms.
4. Pantothenic acid in coenzyme form (CoA) shuttles two carbon fragments from the metabolism of glucose, amino acids, fatty acids, and alcohol into the citric acid cycle during energy metabolism. A deficiency of pantothenic acid is unlikely, since it is widely distributed in foods.
5. Biotin functions as a cofactor in four carboxylases, enzymes that add carbon dioxide to a substance. Biotin is widely distributed in foods. No deficiency exists in healthy people. Intestinal bacteria also synthesize biotin.
6. Vitamin B-6 in coenzyme form (PLP) participates in amino acid metabolism, especially the synthesis of nonessential amino acids. It is essential in the synthesis of heme in hemoglobin and the formation of certain neurotransmitters. Anemia, convulsions, and decreased immune response are symptoms of a deficiency. Animal protein foods, a few fruits and vegetables, and whole-grain cereals are good sources of this vitamin. Toxic effects from excess consumption include nerve damage.
7. Folate in its many coenzyme forms (tetrahydrofolic acid) accepts one-carbon groups from various donors and donates one-carbon groups. The most notable job performed by folate is in DNA synthesis. A dietary lack of the vitamin produces megaloblastic anemia, may increase the risk of spina bifida, and may be one cause of cardiovascular disease (through the homocysteine link). Deficiency is common among alcoholics. Folate is found in green vegetables, legumes, liver, and fortified cereal grains. Folate is destroyed by high cooking temperatures.
8. Vitamin B-12 in coenzyme form moves one-carbon units. Because of its interaction with folate, a deficiency of vitamin B-12 results in the same type of megaloblastic anemia, as well as excess homocysteine in the blood. Defective absorption of vitamin B-12 is the cause of the deficiency disease pernicious anemia. In such cases, injection of the vitamin is necessary. Vitamin B-12 is found in animal foods but not in plant foods. Vegans need to look for foods fortified with the vitamin or take it as part of a multivitamin and mineral supplement.

9. Choline is a dietary component that is available from a wide variety of foods and is synthesized in the body. No natural deficiency of choline has been reported. The amino acid methionine, vitamin B-6, vitamin B-12, and folate, along with choline, are intricately involved in the metabolism of the amino acid homocysteine.

10. Vitamin C functions as a reducing agent in many processes, including the synthesis of collagen, a protein in connective tissue. A deficiency of vitamin C causes the disease scurvy. Fresh fruits and vegetables are reliable sources of this vitamin. Like folate, vitamin C is destroyed by heat. Among North Americans, alcoholics and individuals who don't eat many fruits or vegetables are most likely to develop a deficiency.

11. Carnitine, inositol, taurine, and lipoic acid, while participating in many important biochemical reactions in the body, are not true vitamins because they can be synthesized in the body from readily available precursors. In some medical circumstances, dietary intake may be needed to augment cellular production.

Study Questions

1. Define and explain the term *coenzyme*.
2. Which vitamins can be synthesized in the body, and how are they synthesized?
3. Explain why individual B-vitamin deficiencies are rare in North America. Which B-vitamins are added to cereal grains as part of the enrichment program?
4. Homocysteine is of some health concern today. Why?
5. Define Upper Level and explain why certain vitamins have this designation.
6. Some vitamins have an Adequate Intake designation rather than an RDA. Why?
7. Draw a map of the energy-transformation pathways in the cell and identify the biochemical reactions where B-vitamins participate in energy metabolism (Hint: review Fig. 10-2).
8. Name the vitamins that have been used as pharmacologic agents, and identify the medical conditions for which they are used as therapy.
9. Draw the Food Guide Pyramid and place the various B-vitamins and vitamin C into the food groups where they are most likely to be found.
10. Suppose you read in the newspaper or hear on TV news that a "new" vitamin has been discovered. What criteria will have to be met in order for this substance to be a true vitamin?

Annotated References

1. Berg JM and others: *Biochemistry.* 5th ed. New York: W.H. Freeman and Company, 2002.

   Excellent biochemistry textbook for studying the metabolic pathways in which vitamins participate. A detailed depiction of homocysteine metabolism is also presented.

2. Byers T and others: American Cancer Society guidelines on nutrition and physical activity for cancer prevention: Reducing the risk of cancer with healthy food choices and physical activity. *CA: Cancer Journal for Clinicians* 52:92, 2002.

   A diet low in red and processed meats and rich in fruits, vegetables, and whole grains is advocated as a strategy for reducing cancer risk. Regular physical activity is also important to add.

3. Chen H and others: Dietary patterns and adenocarcinoma of the esophagus and distal stomach. *American Journal of Clinical Nutrition* 75:137, 2002.

   A diet rich in fruits and vegetables may decrease the risk of upper GI tract cancers, whereas a diet rich in meats may increase such risk. The authors suggest following a diet high in fruits, vegetables, and whole grains to reduce the risk of upper GI tract cancers.

4. Cotunga N: Obesity, physical activity, and cancer risk. *Today's Dietitian,* p. 14, October 2002.

   Key factors for reducing cancer risk are maintaining a healthy body weight and performing regular physical activity. Avoiding weight gain in adulthood is especially important. If obesity and physical inactivity continue to escalate in our population, a rising number of cancer cases seems likely.

5. Dharmarajan TS, Norkus EP: Approaches to vitamin B_{12} deficiency: Early treatment may prevent devastating complications. *Postgraduate Medicine* 110(1):99, 2001.

   Vitamin B-12 deficiency is a more common problem than many physicians suspect, and it affects older adults in particular. If the disorder is not treated, severe nervous system complications can result. Effective screening and diagnostic procedures are currently available, as well as low-cost treatment if such a deficiency is found.

6. Douglas RM and others: Vitamin C for preventing and treating the common cold. *Cochrane Database Systems Reviews* 2:CD000980, 2000.

   The conclusion is made that supplemental vitamin C may have a modest effect on cold severity, but not incidence, in some people.

7. Food and Nutrition Board, Institute of Medicine: *Dietary Reference Intakes for thiamin, riboflavin, niacin, vitamin B-6, folate, vitamin B-12, pantothenic acid, biotin, and choline.* Washington, DC: National Academy Press, 1998.

   Explanation as to how nutrient recommendations were established for the B-vitamins and choline, with specific reference to establishing RDA and related standards. The functions of each of the B-vitamins and choline are explained.

8. Food and Nutrition Board, Institute of Medicine: *Dietary Reference Intakes for vitamin C, vitamin E, selenium, and carotenoids.* Washington, DC: National Academy Press, 2000.

   The functions of antioxidant nutrients; how RDA and related standards were determined. Deficiency and toxicity symptoms are explained.

9. Giovannucci E: Epidemiologic studies of folate and colorectal neoplasia: A review. *Journal of Nutrition* 132:2350S, 2002.

   An adequate folate intake may be important for reducing risk of colorectal cancer. Folate contributes to DNA stability, and so a lower cancer risk arising from DNA damage.

10. Go VLW and others: Diet, nutrition and cancer prevention: Where do we go from here? *Journal of Nutrition* 131:3121S, 2001.

    The article discusses the biological processes of carcinogen metabolism and cancer cell development. It is likely that a poor diet and unhealthy lifestyle lead to 30 to 40% of all cancers. Inadequate fruit and vegetable intake especially increases such risk.

11. Green NS: Folic acid supplementation and prevention of birth defects. *Journal of Nutrition* 132:2356S, 2002.

    If all women began pregnancy with adequate folate status, neural tube birth defects could be decreased by up to 70%. The current recommendation is for all women of childbearing age to consume 400 μg of synthetic folic acid daily. Women who have given birth to a child with a neural tube defect should consume 4000 µg (4 mg) of synthetic folic acid per day in anticipation of a pregnancy (or when such a possibility exists).

12. Harnack L and others: An evaluation of the Dietary Guidelines for Americans in relation to cancer occurrence. *American Journal of Clinical Nutrition* 76:889, 2002.

    Adherence to the cluster of nutrition- and lifestyle-related behaviors included in the Dietary Guidelines for Americans reduces cancer risk, especially regarding maintaining a healthy weight and performing regular physical activity. It is best to consider all the advice, rather than focusing on one specific guideline.

13. How you can lower your cancer risk. *Harvard Health Letter* 27(10):1, August 2002.

    Genetic background is an important risk factor for many forms of cancer, and in the future will likely play a large role in providing more specific dietary advice for cancer prevention. In the meantime, there is good evidence that staying lean and physically active, limiting energy dense foods, and including a variety of fruit and vegetables in a daily diet decreases cancer risk.

14. Lichtenstein P and others: Environmental and heritable factors in the causation of cancer—Analyses of cohorts of twins from Sweden, Denmark, and Finland. *The New England Journal of Medicine* 343:78, 2000.

    Inherited genetic factors make only a minor contribution to susceptibility to most types of cancers. Environmental factors, such as smoking, infections, and diet, play the principal role in causing cancer.

15. Liebmam B: Cancer: How to lower your risk. *Nutrition Action Health Letter* 29(8):1, October 2002.

    Diet and lifestyle habits associated with lower cancer risk include breastfeeding; maintaining a healthy body weight; consuming alcohol in moderation, if at all; adequate intake of fruits and vegetables; low intake of red meat; maintaining adequate folate status, especially if one consumes alcohol; and avoiding smoking. The article discusses specific forms of cancer and the unique diet and lifestyle factors associated with reduced risk of each form of cancer.

16. Mason JB: Folate in the prevention of cancer. *Nutrition & the M.D.*, p. 1, August 2001.

    Most experts in nutrition and the cancer prevention field feel that increasing folate intake to achieve a cancer-preventive effect is best accomplished by increasing consumption of foods that contain the vitamin, because these are likely to contain other cancer-preventive factors. However, as long as total intake of folic acid does not exceed approximately 1000 µg/day, there is little risk associated with synthetic folic acid supplementation.

17. Padayatty SJ and others: Vitamin C as an antioxidant: Evaluation of its role in disease prevention. *Journal of the American College of Nutrition* 22: 18, 2003.

    Vitamin C is a potent antioxidant in vitro, but such a role in vivo is still a research question. The benefits from vitamin C intake seen in human studies might arise more from the fact that it found in fruits and vegetables, which are rich in many antioxidants.

18. Savage PD: Molecular basis of human neoplasm. In Shils ME and others (eds.): *Modern nutrition in health and disease.* 9th ed. Baltimore, MD: Williams & Wilkins, 1999.

    This is a tutorial describing the crucial steps in changing the normal cell to a cancer cell. An analogy of the automobile gas pedal (oncogenes) and brake pedal (tumor suppressor genes) explains the progression of cell changes.

19. Talalay P, Fahey JW: Phytochemicals from cruciferous plants protect against cancer by modulating carcinogen metabolism. *Journal of Nutrition* 131:3027S, 2001.

    Cruciferous vegetables such as broccoli increase the activity of phase 2 enzymes in cells. These enzymes in turn exert a variety of protective mechanisms against cancer, such as participating in carcinogen excretion and providing antioxidant defense for the cell.

20. Valero MP and others: Vitamin C is associated with reduced risk of cataract in a Mediterranean population. *Journal of Nutrition* 132:1299, 2002.

    An adequate vitamin C intake is associated with reduced risk of cataracts. A diet rich in fruits and vegetables, such as oranges, is sufficient to maintain a vitamin C intake that can lower such risk.

Take | Action

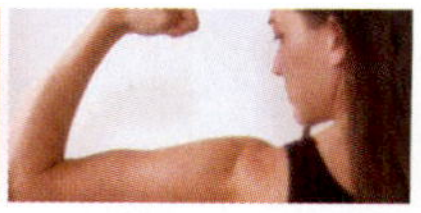

I. Spotting Fraudulent Claims on the Internet.

Using the World Wide Web, search for vitamins and vitamin-like substances that are sold over the Internet. Then write a report concerning any claims made on behalf of these products that you consider fraudulent or misleading. Are these websites really selling vitamins, or are they actually a cover for selling something else? Compare the price of the vitamins from these sites with the price you would pay at the local supermarket. Do any of these sites display any disclaimers or warnings about the products?

II. Spotting Fraudulent Claims in Popular Books for Sale at Health Food Stores and Book Stores.

Visit a health food store in order to examine the books that are for sale. How many books represent sound nutrition, and how many are mostly filled with nutrition quackery? Visit your campus book store. Identify the books (and authors) that represent sound nutrition and the ones that are mostly filled with nutrition quackery. Consult last Sunday's edition of the *New York Times* best-seller list. How many books represent sound nutrition, and how many are nutrition quackery? Write a report comparing these three sources of nutrition information.

Nutrition and Cancer

Cancer is currently the second leading cause of death for North American adults.[15] The good news is that new cancer cases and cancer deaths for all cancers (except lung cancer in women) have declined between 1990 and 1997 in the United States. The number of new cases per 100,000 persons declined an average of 0.8% each year between 1990 and 1997. The number of new cases each year peaked in 1992 and has been declining since. The decrease has been greater among men, who have a higher number of cases than women.

Lung, prostate, breast, and colorectal cancers account for slightly over half of all cancers in North America and are the leading cause of cancer death for every racial and ethnic group. Cases are declining for prostate cancer incidence and mortality. The incidence of breast cancer remains unchanged, but deaths have dropped since 1995. Overall deaths from lung cancer continue to decrease for men since 1990, but for women it is up. Colorectal cancer has been decreasing since 1985.

What Is Cancer?

Cancer is not a single disease but exists in at least 100 different forms (Fig. 10-11). Some of the factors that cause skin cancer may be different from those leading to breast cancer, and treatments for the different varieties of cancer vary with the type of cancer itself.[15] Cancer is essentially abnormal and uncontrollable cell division. If untreatable or not treated, it leads to death. Most cancers take the form of tumors, although not all tumors are cancerous. A tumor is spontaneous new tissue growth that serves no physiological purpose. Tumors can be **benign,** such as a wart that doesn't spread, or **malignant,** such as lung cancer that spreads to surrounding tissues and organs. A malignant **neoplasm** means the same thing as a malignant tumor.

Most cancers fall into one of three groups: **carcinomas** comprise 80 to 90% of all cancers; they develop from cells that cover the body. They affect secretory organs, such as the breast. **Sarcomas** are cancers of connective tissues, such as in bone. Leukemias and lymphomas form the third group. **Leukemias** are malignant neoplasms of the blood-forming tissues, the bone marrow. **Lymphomas** are various malignant tumors that are in the lymph nodes or lymphoid tissues.

Benign tumors are enclosed in a membrane that prevents them from spreading. They are dangerous only if they interfere with normal function. For instance, a benign brain tumor can cause illness and death if it blocks blood flow in the brain. Malignant tumors, on the other hand, are capable of invading surrounding structures, including blood vessels, the lymph system, and nerve tissue. They can **metastasize** to

benign Noncancerous; describes tumors that do not spread.

malignant Essentially, malicious; in reference to a tumor, the property of spreading locally and to distant sites.

neoplasm A new and abnormal growth of tissues, which may be benign or cancerous.

carcinoma An invasive malignant tumor derived from the epithelial tissues that cover the body.

sarcoma A malignant tumor arising from connective tissues.

leukemia A malignant neoplasm of blood-forming tissues, the bone marrow.

lymphoma A malignant tumor arising from lymph nodes or other lymph tissues.

metastasize Spreading disease from one part of the body to another, even to parts of the body that are remote from the site of the original tumor. Cancer cells can spread via blood vessels, the lymphatic system, or direct growth of the tumor.

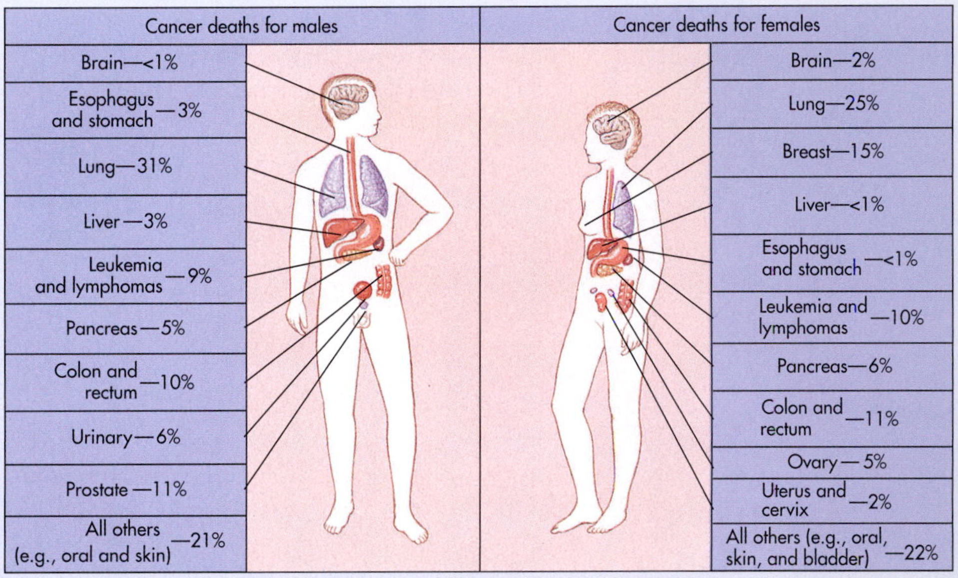

Figure 10-11 Cancer is actually many diseases. Numerous types of cells and organs are its target. Note that about one-third of all cancers arise from smoking.
Illustration by William Ober.

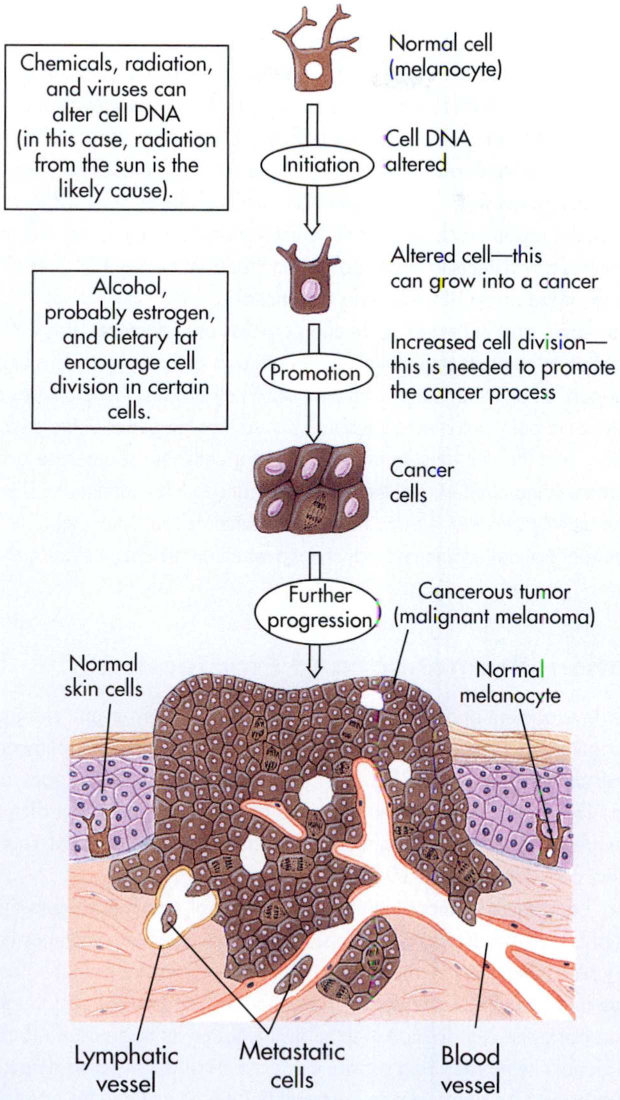

Figure 10-12 Progression from a normal skin cell to skin cancer through the initiation, promotion, and progression stages. The ball of cells is a developing tumor. As the mass of cells grows, it can invade surrounding tissues, eventually penetrating into both lymph and blood vessels. These vessels carry spreading (metastatic) cancer cells throughout the body, where they can form new cancer sites.
Illustration by William Ober.

distant sites via the blood or lymph, thereby producing invasive tumors in almost any part of the body (Fig. 10-12).

Because leukemia, a cancer found in white blood cells (leukocytes), does not produce a mass, it isn't classified as a tumor; however, it exhibits the fundamental property of rapid and inappropriate growth. It is still malignant and therefore represents a form of cancer.

Mechanisms of Carcinogenesis

Most cells exist in a homeostatic state; there is a balance between the turning-on and turning-off of cellular replication. Regulation of the cell cycle exists between the gene products that spur replication and gene products that deter replication.[18]

Oncogenes and Other Genes

Genes that produce products that cause a resting cell to divide are referred to as **protooncogenes,** and genes that produce products that prevent cells from dividing are known as **tumor suppressor genes.** Cancer often results from a lack of suppressor genes or too much action by the protooncogenes. The cancer gene, or **oncogene,** is the protooncogene out of control; it is making dozens or hundreds of copies of

protooncogenes Genes that cause a resting cell to divide.

tumor suppressor genes Genes that prevent cells from dividing.

oncogene A protooncogene out of control.

p53 A tumor-suppressor gene that can prevent inappropriate cell division.

telomeres Caps at the end of chromosomes.

telomerase An enzyme that maintains length and completeness of chromosomes.

cancer initiation The stage in the process of cancer development that begins with alterations in DNA, the genetic material in a cell. This may cause the cell to no longer respond to normal physiological controls.

cancer promotion The stage in the cancer process when cell division increases, in turn decreasing the time available for repair enzymes to act on altered DNA and encouraging cells with altered DNA to develop and grow.

cancer progression The final stage in the cancer process, during which the cancer cells proliferate, forming a mass large enough to significantly affect body functions.

genotoxic carcinogen A compound that directly alters DNA or is converted in cells to metabolites that alter DNA, thereby providing the potential for cancer to develop.

mutation A change in the chemistry of a gene, which is perpetuated in subsequent divisions of the cell in which it occurred; a change in the sequence of the DNA base pairs.

itself, and there are no mechanisms to overcome the process. In the final analysis, all cancer is genetic, in that defects in specific genes lead to the proliferative growth.[10]

The tumor suppressor genes are the braking mechanisms within a cell, preventing uncontrolled growth. When something goes wrong with these tumor suppressor genes, the oncogenes are free to promote rapid cell growth. One tumor suppressor gene, known as **p53,** can prevent the abnormal growth associated with tumors. Alteration in this gene has been discovered to cause cancers of the ovary, breast, lung, and colon.

There are repair mechanisms within a cell that constantly look for errors in DNA replication and make corrections. Sometimes the repair mechanisms fail, which results in an inherited defect for cancer, such as hereditary colon cancer. Early defects in DNA replication that aren't caught and repaired are likely to predispose the cell to even more errors, thus leading to cancer.

Other agents that play a part in the cell replication process are **telomeres,** caps at the ends of chromosomes. An enzyme called **telomerase** maintains their length and completeness. This enzyme is active when we are young, and tapers off as we age. Each time an adult cell divides, the telomeres of the daughter cells are slightly shorter. At some point, telomeres become so short that the genes at the ends of the chromosome can no longer function, and the cell dies. In malignant tumor cells, the telomerase activity increases, and the length of the telomere is maintained, resulting in a cell that can live indefinitely. There seems to be a difference in telomerase activity between normal tissue and cancer tissue. Much more is to be learned about conditions that promote abnormal telomerase activity and whether this enzyme can become a target in cancer therapy.

Cancer Initiation, Promotion, and Progression

Carcinogenesis, the development of cancer in a body, is a multiple-step event, starting with the exposure of a cell to a carcinogen, which triggers **cancer initiation.** Subsequently, it is followed by **cancer promotion** and finally **cancer progression** (review Fig. 10-12). Initiation can develop spontaneously or can be induced by agents known as **genotoxic carcinogens.** The affected cells can then dictate their own rate of division. Agents that are responsible for carcinogenesis include tobacco, alcohol, radiation, occupational toxins, infections, diet, and drugs. (Table 10-3.)

A mechanism that can prevent cancer initiation is a family of enzymes in cells that can detoxify and speed up excretion of cancer-producing chemicals. These enzymes are sometimes called "phase 2" enzymes. Some dietary phytochemicals increase the amount of these enzymes in the body.[19] The p53 gene, already identified as a tumor suppressor gene, is another way to prevent abnormal growth associated with tumors, as it can postpone cell division. This allows time for damage repair. Enzymes can travel up and down the DNA double helix, repairing broken components and correcting defects. About 99% of the time, the repair enzymes find the damage and correct it before the cell divides again and thus undergoes **mutation.**

The initiation stage of carcinogenesis, during which time DNA is altered, is relatively short. It could be minutes or days. The promotion state may last for months or years. During this period, the damage is "locked" into the genetic material in cells. Compounds that increase cell division are called promoters or epigenetic carcinogens. These are thought to promote cancer either by decreasing the time available for repair enzymes to act or by encouraging cells with altered DNA to develop and grow. Some putative promoters are estrogen, alcohol, and possibly a high intake of dietary fat. Bacterial infections in the stomach are also suspected agents. For example, infection with *Helicobacter pylori,* which cause ulcers, may ultimately promote stomach cancer.[15]

The final stage in carcinogenesis, cancer progression, begins with the appearance of cells that grow autonomously (out of control). During the progression phase, these malignant cells proliferate, invade surrounding tissue, and metastasize to other sites. Early in this stage, the immune system may find the altered cells and destroy them, or the cancer cells may be so defective that their own DNA limits their ability to grow, and they die. If nothing impedes cancer cell growth, one or more tumors eventually develop that are large enough to affect body functions, and the signs and symptoms of cancer appear (review Table 10-3).

Is Cancer Environmental or Hereditary?

Inherited mutations cannot account for the dramatic differences in cancer rates around the world. In poorer countries, cancers of the stomach, liver, mouth, esophagus, and uterus are most common,

Table 10-3 The Cancer Development Process

Cancer Initiation

Process: DNA alteration occurs in this relatively short phase (minutes to days).

Causes:

Radiation: e.g., sun overexposure

Cross-links double strands of DNA or breaks them into fragments

Chemicals: e.g., aflatoxin (mold from peanuts and cereal grains), benzo(a)pyrene (smoke from charbroiled meat fat). These agents are transformed to highly reactive cancer initiators by **cytochrome P450,** an enzyme system that alters foreign compounds in the body. These metabolites are then able to cause mutations in DNA, RNA, and proteins.

Biological agents: e.g., viruses

Promote uncontrolled growth of cells by inserting viral DNA or RNA into normal cells, which alters the cell's genes

Cancer Promotion

Process: DNA alterations are "locked" into the genetic material of cells over a period of months to more than 10 years.

Causes:

Long-term excess estrogen exposure

Excess alcohol

Excess dietary fat (controversial)

Bacterial infections: e.g., *Helicobacter pylori*

Cancer Progression

Process: Cells that can grow autonomously appear. These cells spread to surrounding tissue and other sites.

Causes:

Excess energy intake

Lack of early detection

Development of blood supply to the tumor

The tumor uses newly formed capillaries to grow and spread cancer cells to remote sites in the body.

Anything that increases the rate of cell division decreases the chance that the repair enzymes will find the altered part of the DNA in time to do their work. Once a cell multiplies and incorporates its newly altered DNA into its genetic instructions, the repair enzymes can no longer detect the changes in DNA.

cytochrome P450 A set of enzymes in cells that act on compounds foreign to the body. This action aids in their excretion, but also creates short-lived, highly reactive forms.

whereas, in affluent countries, cancers of the lung, colon-rectum, breast, and prostate predominate. Our best source of cancer information comes from studies of twins, the standard for distinguishing between genetics and environmental factors.[14] In a recently published study of 44,788 twins, the researchers concluded that inherited genetic factors make only a minor contribution to the susceptibility to most types of cancer. The environment has the principal role in causing sporadic cancer. For nearly all body sites, the twin of a person with cancer has only a moderate risk of developing cancer at the same site. The researchers found that risk factors in the environment shared by a family can include human papillomavirus infection for cervical cancer, smoking (passive and active) for lung cancer, diet for colon cancer, and *Helicobacter pylori* for stomach cancer. There were, however, heritable factors detected in this study for colorectal, breast, and prostate cancer. This was in agreement with other population-based studies.[13] For colorectal cancer, 35% could be explained by heritable factors; for breast cancer, 27%; and, for prostate cancer, 42%. In these cases, knowing your family history is very important. The impact of heredity on the other cancers was so small that inherited genetic factors accounted for only 1 to 15% of all the cancers.

Diet and Cancer

Oxidative damage to DNA is likely to cause mutations and can be enhanced by some dietary factors or reduced by enzymes such as those that incorporate the trace mineral selenium. There is evidence that intake of selenium above the RDA has an anticancer effect in humans, but there aren't enough data at this time to make a recommendation as to the extra amount needed.

Excessive energy intake in relation to need increases the risk of human cancer. Laboratory animal studies have shown that energy restriction during periods of rapid growth is protective against cancer. No doubt obesity increases the risk of cancers of the uterus, breast, kidney, and possibly the prostate, colon, and gallbladder. Excess body fat may affect sex hormone and insulin production, which increases cancer risk, or cancer cells may grow more easily when fuel is plentiful.[15]

However, no link has been found between a low-fat diet and the development of breast cancer, but excess body weight increases the risk. Perhaps certain fatty acids, such as monounsaturated and polyunsaturated fatty acids in fish and canola oil, are beneficial. More research is needed in the area of body fat and the amount and types of dietary fats consumed.

People who meet their vitamin C needs may have a lower risk of cancer of the oral cavity, esophagus, stomach, and breast. Whether this is due to vitamin C itself or because these people eat a lot of fruits and vegetables, which provide many other nutrients, is still unknown.

High intakes of vegetables and fruits have been associated with lower risks of many cancers. The constituents that are protective against cancer have not been identified, but evidence supports the B-vitamin folate as one of the factors.[9, 16] Studies of colorectal cancer show an inverse relationship between folate status and the rate of cancer. An inadequate intake of folate could also influence the risk of mutation.

High intake of meat and protein products has been associated with an increased risk of prostate cancer.[2, 3] This might be related to the saturated fat content of the food. In addition, meat cooked at high temperatures over an open flame, such as in charcoal broiling, produces polyaromatic hydrocarbons, one being benzo-[a]pyrene. In generating benzo-[a]pyrene, this cooking method produces a by-product, which binds to DNA and produces tumors, such as in the colon.

Excess alcohol consumption increases the risks of upper gastrointestinal tract cancers. Even moderate alcohol intake seems to increase the risk of cancers of the breast and colon.

Nitrosamines are carcinogenic. Nitrosamines are formed from nitrite, which exists in various foods and is produced endogenously from nitrate in vegetables. Nitrosamine compounds are found in cooked bacon, sausage, hot dogs, beer, cheese, and some nitrite-preserved foods.

Mycotoxins are toxins produced by fungi. Among the many examples is aflatoxin B_1, a component of many moldy foods, such as moldy grain and peanuts. It is classified as a human carcinogen and is thought to cause liver cancer. Drought conditions in Asian and African countries have resulted in the widespread contamination of foods by aflatoxins. Even in the United States, corn has been found with increased carcinogen levels from aflatoxin B_1 due to changing weather conditions, but grain elevator operators and FDA monitor grains for unsafe amounts. Current studies are focusing on various antioxidants that may protect us from environmental carcinogens, such as aflatoxins.

Cruciferous vegetables contain many cancer-preventing phytochemicals.

The National Academy of Sciences' 1980 review of *Diet, Nutrition, and Cancer* recommended a fat intake of no more than 30% of energy intake, primarily to reduce the incidence of cancer. More recent evidence raises questions about this recommendation. The association between fat intake and cancer rates has come from large international differences in rates of breast, colon, prostate, and endometrial cancer. These international differences are assumed to be due to the effect of animal fats, but the type of fat has remained controversial. Moreover, there are still more recent surveys that fail to find a correlation between fat intake and cancer. Certainly, there are wide gaps in the knowledge linking fat and cancer. A long-standing excess energy intake is likely a more important cause of cancer than fat per se.[15]

Another recent discovery resulting from attempts to find dietary solutions to the prevention of cancer suggests that calcium and vitamin D (or moderate sun exposure) may be part of the answer. Calcium intake is inversely related to cancer, especially colon cancer. It may be that calcium binds free fatty acid and bile acids in the colon, so that they are less likely to interact with certain types of intestinal cells, which in turn become cancer.[15]

The hormone form of vitamin D—1,25 $(OH)_2$ vitamin D—has been shown to inhibit the progression of human colorectal cells from cancerous polyps in vitro. Vitamin D also has been shown to inhibit rapid colon/rectal cell growth in patients with ulcerative colitis. These combined data suggest a chemopreventive action of vitamin D against colon neoplasms. This may be the beneficial effect of vitamin D-fortified dairy foods.[15]

Based on our current knowledge of diet and cancer risk, the following guidelines are about all that can be recommended at this time: Remain physically active, avoid obesity, engage in physical training that promotes the formation of lean muscle, consume an abundance of fruits, vegetables, and whole grains, consume plenty of low-fat and nonfat dairy products, avoid a high intake of red meat and animal fat, and avoid excessive use of alcohol (Tables 10-4 and 10-5).[2, 4, 12, 13]

Table 10-4 Some Food Constituents Suspected of Having a Role in Cancer

Constituent	Dietary Sources	Action
Possibly Protective*		
Vitamin A	Liver, fortified milk, fruits, vegetables	Encourages normal cell development and differentiation
Vitamin D	Fortified milk	Increases production of a protein that suppresses cell growth, such as in the colon
Vitamin E	Whole grains, vegetable oil, green, leafy vegetables	Antioxidant; prevents formation of nitrosamines
Vitamin C	Fruits, vegetables	Antioxidant (but degree of in vivo activity not currently known); can block conversion of nitrites and nitrates to potent carcinogens
Folate	Fruits, vegetables, whole grains	Encourages normal cell development; especially reduces the risk of colon cancer
Selenium	Meats, whole grains	Part of antioxidant system that inhibits tumor growth and kills early cancer cells in the promotion stage
Carotenoids, such as lycopene	Fruits, vegetables	Likely act as antioxidants; some of these possibly influence cell metabolism. Lycopene in particular may reduce the risk of prostate cancer
Indoles, phenols, and other plant substances	Vegetables†, especially cabbage, cauliflower, broccoli, brussels sprouts, garlic, onions, tea	May reduce carcinogen activation in the liver and other cells
Calcium	Milk products, green vegetables	Slows cell division in the colon, binds bile acids and free fatty acids, thus reducing colon cancer risk
Omega-3 fatty acids	Cold-water fish, such as salmon and tuna	May inhibit tumor growth; reduces prostate cancer risk
Soy products	Tofu, soy milk, tempeh	Phytic acid present possibly binds carcinogens in the intestinal tract; the genistein component possibly reduces growth and metastasis of malignant cells
Conjugated linoleic acid	Milk products, meats, fish	May inhibit tumor development and act as an antioxidant
Possibly Carcinogenic		
Excessive energy intake	All macronutrients can contribute	Excess fat mass; linked to increased synthesis of estrogen and other sex hormones, which in excess may themselves increase the risk for cancer; resulting excess insulin output from creation of an insulin-resistant state is also implicated
Total fat	Meats (especially red meat), high-fat milk and milk products, vegetable oils	The strongest evidence is for excessive saturated and polyunsaturated fat intake. Saturated fat is linked to an increased risk of prostate cancer
Alcohol	Beer, wine, liquor	Contributes to cancers of the throat, liver, bladder, breast, and colon (especially if the person does not consume enough folate); increased cell turnover and liver metabolism of carcinogens are the main mechanism
Nitrites, nitrates	Cured meats, especially ham, bacon, and sausages	Under very high temperatures will bind to amino acid derivatives to form nitrosamines, potent carcinogens
Multi-ring compounds: Aflatoxin	Formed when mold is present on peanuts and other grains	May alter DNA structure and inhibit its ability to properly respond to physiologic controls; aflatoxin linked to liver cancer
Benzo(a)pyrene	Charcoal-broiled foods, especially meats	Benzo(a)pyrene linked to stomach and colon cancer. To limit this risk, trim fat from meat before cooking, cut barbecuing time by partially cooking meat (such as in a microwave oven), and don't consume blackened parts

*Many of the actions listed for these possibly protective agents are speculative and have been verified only by experimental animal studies.

†Some are part of the family of cruciferous vegetables, which includes cabbage, Brussels sprouts, and broccoli.

Table 10-5 Example of a Diet Intended to Limit the Risk for Cancer—Low in Fat and High in Fruits and Vegetables and Provides Plenty of Calcium

Breakfast
6 oz orange juice
1 cup ready-to-eat whole-grain breakfast cereal
1 cup 1% fat milk
1 banana
1 slice whole-wheat toast, jelly, soft margarine
Hot tea

Lunch
Sandwich:
½ cup chicken salad served on ½ of a bagel or 1 slice of whole-wheat bread
Assorted raw vegetables: carrots, celery, broccoli, chopped lettuce
1 cup 1% fat milk
Fresh fruit in season: strawberries, melon, grapes, apple
2 fig cookies

Dinner
3 oz baked fish (e.g., cod, white fish, salmon)
Baked potato topped with shredded mozzarella cheese (⅓ cup)
Roasted corn on the cob, soft margarine
Fresh garden salad with "lite" Italian dressing
1 whole-wheat dinner roll
1 scoop lemon ice or orange sherbet
Hot tea

Snack
12-oz can diet cola
2 cups popcorn
¼ cup mixed nuts

Nutrient Breakdown:
2300 kcal
% energy from fat: 25%

Cancer Warning Signs

Remember also that, if a cancer is left untreated, it can spread quickly throughout the body. When this happens, it is much more likely to lead to death. Thus, early detection is critical. Aids to early detection include the following warning signs (acronym is CAUTION):

- A **c**hange in bowel or bladder habits
- **A** sore that does not heal
- **U**nusual bleeding or discharge
- A **t**hickening or lump in the breast or elsewhere
- **I**ndigestion or difficulty in swallowing
- An **o**bvious change in a wart or mole
- A **n**agging cough or hoarseness

There are still other ways to detect cancer early. Colonoscopy examinations for middle-age and older adults, PSA (prostate-specific antigen) tests for men over age 50, and Papanicolaou tests (Pap smears) and regular breast examinations (and mammograms starting about age 40 to 50) for women are recommended. Finally, to learn still more about cancer, review these sources of credible cancer information on the Internet:

www.cancer.org American Cancer Society
www.icic.nci.nih.gov CancerNet
www.cancer.med.upenn.edu Oncolink

chapter 11

Water and the Major Minerals

Chapter | Outline

Case | Scenario

Jana, a sophomore in high school, recently became a vegan. Her mother is concerned about her diet because she is not a vegan herself, and worries about Jana's health. One of her primary concerns is osteoporosis, particularly because she knows that 95% of bone growth occurs by ages 16 to 17. Jana needs an adequate source of calcium in her diet to aid with her rapid bone development. Jana also recently started smoking, and her only recreational activity is choir practice.

Jana's diet on a recent day consisted of the following items. For breakfast, she had oatmeal made with water, a banana, and a cup of fruit juice. At midmorning, she bought a snack cake from the vending machine. At lunch, she had vegetable pasta, bread with olive oil, a side salad, one ounce of mixed nuts, and a soft drink. For dinner, she had a soy burger along with mixed vegetables and rice. As an evening snack, she had some cookies and another soft drink.

What factors place Jana at risk for osteoporosis in the future? Suggest any necessary changes to her current diet.

Refresh | Your Memory

As you begin your study of water and the major minerals in Chapter 11, you may want to review:

- The Dietary Guidelines and Food Guide Pyramid (and related pyramids) in Chapter 2.
- The functions of vitamin D and vitamin K related to calcium and bone health in Chapter 9.
- The role of vitamin C in collagen synthesis in Chapter 10.
- Intracellular and extracellular fluid compartments in Appendix C.
- The muscular and skeletal systems in Appendix C.

Boost | Your Study

Check out the ***Perspectives in Nutrition: Online Learning Center*** **www.mhhe.com/wardlawpers6** *for quizzes, flash cards, activities, and web links designed to further help you learn about water and the major minerals.*

Chapter | Objectives

Chapter 11 is designed to allow you to:

1. Classify the minerals as major or trace minerals.
2. List conditions of the body, dietary factors, and other pertinent relationships that influence the absorption, retention, and availability of specific major minerals.
3. List and briefly explain the functions of water in the body, as well as typical sources of intakes and losses.
4. Discuss how body water balance is maintained by the mechanisms of thirst, absorption, and hormonal regulation.
5. List key functions of the major minerals.
6. Identify possible deficiency and toxicity symptoms associated with the major minerals.
7. List at least two food sources for each of the major minerals.
8. Describe the processes involving minerals that aid in maintaining bone health as well as those that aid in control of blood pressure.

Water—the most versatile medium for a variety of chemical reactions—constitutes the major portion of the human body. Without water, biological processes necessary to life would cease in a matter of days. We operate on about 2 quarts (2 L) of water daily and must replenish it regularly because the body does not store water per se.[9] We experience this constant demand for water as thirst. Many nutrients, including minerals, exist in the body dissolved in water. Because the functioning of minerals is related to the characteristics of water, water and its roles in the body are explored first in this chapter.

Many minerals, like water, are vital to health. They are key participants in body metabolism, muscle movement, body growth, and water balance, among other wide-ranging processes.[17] Some of the minerals found in our bodies—for example, vanadium and arsenic—may not be necessary to sustain human life. Nevertheless, we know that some mineral deficiencies can cause severe health problems.[7] For this reason, the study of minerals is critical to understanding human nutrition. This chapter focuses on the major minerals, such as calcium and magnesium; Chapter 12 focuses on the trace minerals, such as iron and zinc.

Water

To appreciate how minerals operate in the body, it helps to understand the nature and general chemical properties of water, as well as specific nutrient-related functions. Water is the largest component of the human body, making up 50 to 70% of the body's weight (about 10 gallons, or 40 liters).[17] Lean muscle tissue contains about 73% water. Adipose tissue is about 20% water. Thus, as fat content increases (and the percentage of lean tissue decreases) in the body, total body water decreases toward 50%.

Depending on how much fat has been stored, an adult can survive for about 8 weeks without eating food but only a few days without drinking water. In a desert environment, a person wouldn't survive for more than one day without water. This occurs not because water is more important than carbohydrate, fat, protein, vitamins, or minerals but, rather, because the body has no storage site for water.

Looking at a molecular level, water is highly polar, as the positive charges tend to be located near the hydrogens and the negative charges near the oxygen.

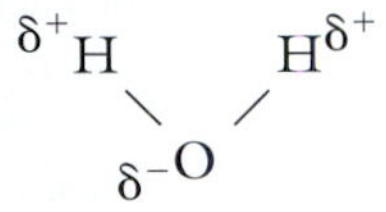

δ denotes partial charge

Because of this, water can dissolve most substances, and, in doing so, it enables minerals and other chemicals to undergo biological reactions in the body (see Appendix A for details).

Water in the Body—Intracellular and Extracellular Fluid

Water flows in and out of body cells through cell membranes. Water inside cells forms part of the **intracellular fluid**—fluid within the cells. When water is outside cells or in the bloodstream, it is part of the **extracellular fluid**—fluid outside cells (Figure 11-1). Extracellular fluid is further divided into **interstitial fluid**—water between cells—and **intravascular fluid**—water in the bloodstream and lymph. Interstitial fluid forms a transport link between tissue cells and the blood.

Because cell membranes are permeable to water, water shifts freely in and out of cells. For example, if blood volume decreases, water can move from the areas inside and around cells to the bloodstream to increase blood volume.

The body controls the amount of water in each compartment mainly by controlling the electrolyte concentrations in each compartment. In solution, electrolytes dissociate into charged particles called ions. Water is attracted to ions, such as sodium, potassium, chloride, phosphate, magnesium, and calcium. By controlling the movements of ions in

intracellular fluid Fluid contained within a cell represents about two-thirds of all body fluid.

extracellular fluid Fluid present outside the cells; it includes intravascular and interstitial fluids; represents about one-third of all body fluid.

interstitial fluid Fluid between cells.

intravascular fluid Fluid within the bloodstream (that is, in the arteries, veins, and capillaries and lymph vessels); represents about 25% of all body fluids.

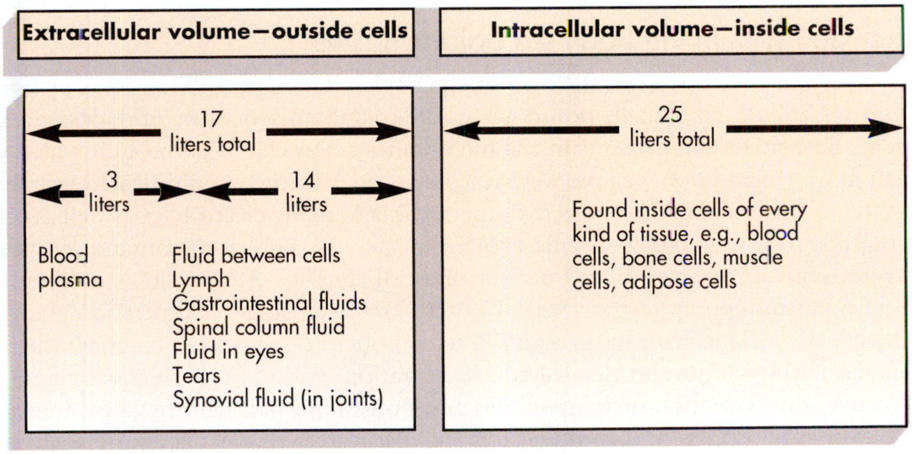

Figure 11-1 The fluid compartments in the body.

electrolytes Substances that break down into ions in water and, in turn, are able to conduct an electrical current. These include sodium, chloride, and potassium.

osmosis The passage of a solvent (water) through a semipermeable membrane from a less concentrated compartment to a more concentrated compartment.

osmotic pressure The exerted pressure needed to keep particles in a solution from drawing liquid toward them across a semipermeable membrane.

and out of the cellular compartments, the body maintains the appropriate amount of water in each compartment. Where ions go, water follows.[17]

Osmosis

Much of the movement of body water results from water's tendency to move across a semipermeable membrane so as to equalize the total particle concentration in the compartments on each side of the membrane. A semipermeable membrane is one through which water, but not particles, can pass. In the body, the particles are primarily **electrolytes** (such as sodium and potassium), and the membranes are cell membranes. This passage of water (or other solvent), called **osmosis,** results in the movement of water from a less concentrated to a more concentrated solution. The specific concentration is expressed as **osmolality,** representing the number of particles per kg of solvent.

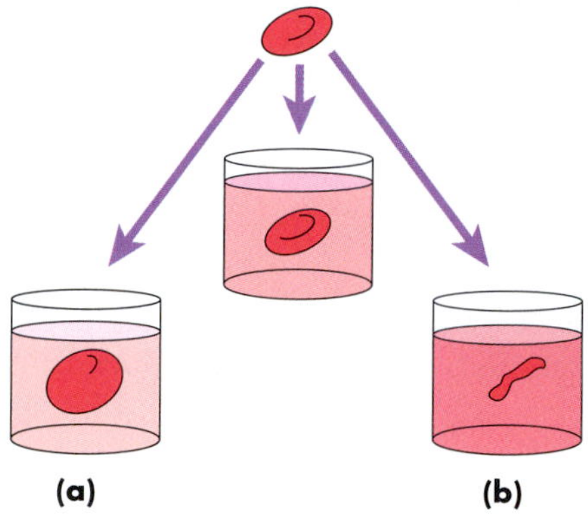

The effects of osmosis are easily demonstrated with red blood cells. (*a*) When the fluid surrounding the cells is made more dilute, water moves into the cells, causing them to expand. (*b*) Conversely, when the fluid is made more concentrated, water moves out of the cells, causing them to shrink.

Figure 11-2 A graphic representation of osmosis and osmotic pressure. *1.* An equal number of particles on each side allows equal amounts of water. *2.* Now additional particles are added to side B, but the particles cannot flow across the membrane. *3.* Water can flow across the membrane, so it flows to side B, causing the particle concentration on sides A and B to again become equal. *4.* If physical pressure (such as a pump) were to compress the fluid on side B to restore its original volume, the pressure would equal the osmotic pressure exerted by the added particles.

Figure 11-2 illustrates how osmosis works. When particles are added to the compartment on one side of a semipermeable membrane, this makes that compartment more concentrated than the other compartment. Since particles can't pass easily across the membrane, water moves by diffusion from the diluted compartment to the more concentrated compartment until their particle concentrations become identical. The term **osmotic pressure** refers to the amount of force needed to prevent dilution of the compartment containing the higher particle concentration. Examples of osmosis are sugar pulling fluid from strawberries, a salty salad dressing wilting lettuce, and red blood cells swelling or shrinking when put into solutions of different salt concentrations. Adding water—instead of particles—to a compartment dilutes its particle concentration, so the compartment tends to donate water by the action of osmosis to more concentrated compartments nearby. This happens when you drink water. Some water absorbed by the body moves from the bloodstream into body cells, which in turn equalizes the particle concentration in the cells with that in the various nearby body sites.

Water and Ions in the Body—a Balancing Act

The movement of water across the membrane, depicted in Figure 11-2 occurs by simple diffusion. Little of this actually occurs across cell membranes because of their high lipid content. Rather, certain proteins in cell membranes act as channels through which water can move. In addition, cell membranes possess an extremely sophisticated gatekeeping system, which makes them selectively permeable to many electrolytes as well as other compounds. For example, a specific protein located in the cell membrane can pump potassium ions into and sodium ions out of a cell (Fig. 11-3). Energy is used by this sodium-potassium pump to move each of these ions against its concentration gradient. By the use of such mechanisms in addition to osmotic processes, cells maintain their intracellular water volume and electrolyte concentrations within quite narrow ranges.

Positive ions (cations), such as sodium and potassium, pair with negative ions (anions), such as phosphate and chloride. Intracellular water volume depends primarily on

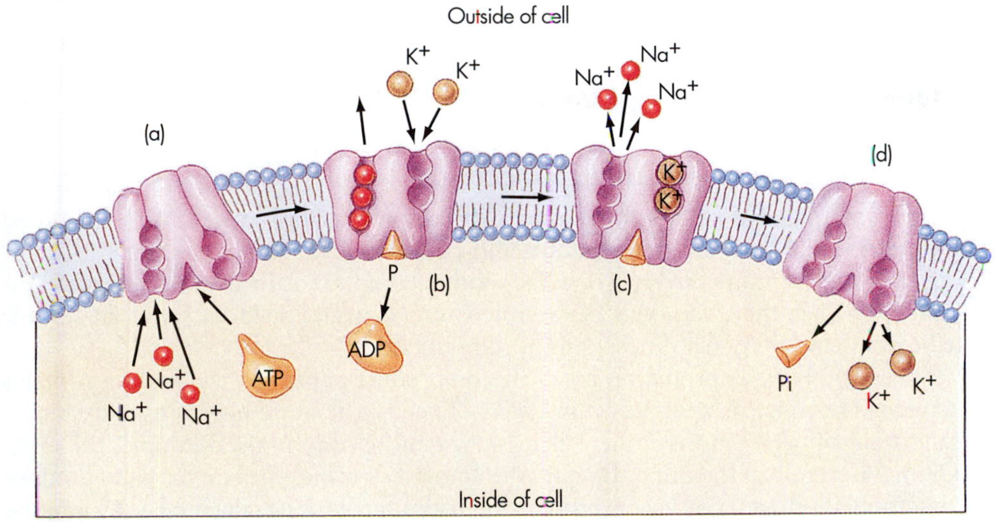

Figure 11-3 Schematic diagram of the sodium (Na^+) and potassium (K^+) pump cycle. (*a*) Three Na^+ ions bind from inside the cell. (*b*) The Na^+-K^+ pump is activated by ATP. (*c*) Activation causes a change of the protein form. This results in a decrease in the affinity of Na^+-binding sites and an increase in affinity of K^+-binding sites. The three Na^+ ions are then released to the outside of the cell. (*d*) Two K^+ ions occupy the K^+-binding sites, and the pump protein releases the phosphate donated from ATP and returns to its original conformation. The affinity of the K^+-binding sites decreases, and that of the Na^+ sites increases. The K^+ ions are released to the cell. The pump is now ready to bind three Na^+ ions, and the cycle starts again. This Na-K pump uses about 20 to 40% of the energy expended by the body at rest.
Illustration by William Ober.

the intracellular potassium and phosphate concentration. Extracellular water volume depends primarily on the extracellular sodium and chloride concentration.[19]

Besides balancing the ion concentrations between the inside and outside of cells, body cells must also balance ion charges. If a negative ion enters a cell, a positive ion must also enter the cell, or another negative electrolyte must leave it.

Functions of Water

Because of its unique chemical and physical characteristics, water plays several key roles in metabolic processes. Water functions in several ways in the body's chemical reactions: Because it is polar, it serves as a solvent for many chemical compounds, it provides a medium in which many chemical reactions occur, and it actively participates as a reactant or becomes a product in some reactions, such as in the citric acid cycle. It also is the transport medium of the body.

Water Contributes to Temperature Regulation

Water changes temperature slowly because it has a great ability to hold heat. It takes much more energy to heat water than it does to heat fat. Compare the time it takes to melt ice cubes with the time it takes to melt frozen butter in a microwave oven. Foods with high water content heat up and cool down slowly. Because water requires so much energy to change states—for example, from a liquid to a gas—it forms an ideal medium for removing heat from the body. Water has this high heat capacity **(specific heat)** because water molecules are strongly attracted to each other. In contrast, the molecules in fat are not strongly attracted to each other, and fats thus exhibit lower specific heat values than water.

specific heat The amount of heat required to raise the temperature of any substance 1°C compared with the heat required to raise the temperature of the same volume of water 1°C. Water has a high specific heat, meaning that a relatively large amount of heat is required to raise its temperature; therefore, it tends to resist large temperature fluctuations.

As the amount of heat energy contained within the body increases, water in the surrounding tissues absorbs any excess heat energy. The body then secretes fluids in the form of perspiration, which evaporates through skin pores. To evaporate water, heat energy is required, so, as perspiration evaporates, heat energy is taken from the skin, cooling it in the process. Each quart (liter) of perspiration evaporated represents approximately 600 kcal of energy lost from the skin and surrounding tissues. For this reason, fever increases one's need for energy.

Recall from Chapter 4 that about 60% of the chemical energy in food is turned directly into body heat. Only about 40% is converted to ATP energy, and almost all of that energy eventually leaves the body in the form of heat. If this heat could not be dissipated, the body temperature would rise enough to prevent enzyme systems from functioning efficiently. Perspiration is the primary way to prevent this rise in body temperature.

However, to cool efficiently, perspiration must be allowed to evaporate. If it simply rolls off the skin or soaks into clothing, perspiration doesn't cool us much. Evaporation of perspiration occurs readily when humidity is low. This is why humans feel more comfortable in hot, dry climates than in hot, humid climates.

Water Helps Remove Waste Products

Water is an important vehicle for ridding the body of waste products. Most unwanted substances in the body are water-soluble and can leave the body via the urine. In addition, liver metabolism converts some fat-soluble compounds into water-soluble compounds, so that they, too, can be excreted in the urine, such as some fat-soluble medications and potential cancer-causing substances.

A major body waste product is urea. This by-product of protein metabolism contains nitrogen. The more protein we eat in excess of needs, the more nitrogen we excrete—in the form of urea—in the urine. Likewise, the more sodium we consume, the more sodium we excrete in the urine. Overall, the amount of urine a person needs to produce is determined primarily by excess protein and sodium chloride (salt) intake. By limiting excess protein and salt intakes, it is possible to limit urine output—a useful practice, for example, in space flights. This type of diet is also used to treat some kidney diseases in which the ability to produce urine output is hampered.

A typical urine volume is about 1 to 2 liters (1 to 2 quarts) per day, depending mostly on the amount of fluid, protein, and sodium intake. Somewhat more urine output than that is fine, but less—especially less than 600 ml (2½ cups)—forces the kidneys to form a very concentrated urine. The heavy ion concentration increases the risk of kidney stone formation in susceptible people, especially among men. Kidney stones are simply minerals and other substances that have precipitated out of the urine and accumulated in kidney tissues.

Other Functions of Water

Water is incompressible, so it helps form the lubricants found in knees and other joints of the body. It is the basis for saliva, bile, and **amniotic fluid.** Amniotic fluid acts as an important shock absorber surrounding the growing fetus. Electrolyte concentrations vary in each fluid compartment to accommodate specific needs, such as maintenance of a specific range in pH.

amniotic fluid The fluid contained in a sac within the uterus. This surrounds and protects the fetus during its development.

Water in Foods

Water can be found in abundance in fruits and vegetables. Foods that are highest in water content include fruits and vegetables, particularly romaine lettuce, tomatoes, watercress, zucchini, asparagus, cantaloupe, grapefruit, and honeydew; orange juice; cottage cheese; tofu; water-packed tuna; and milk. Other sources that fall between 75 and 50% water are potatoes, corn, rice, hard-cooked eggs, bananas, beans, skinless chicken, part-skim mozzarella cheese, pasta, ice cream, baked salmon, and cod. The foods that are less than 35% water include breads, other cheeses, dry cereals, popcorn, and sugar.

Water Content of Various Foods

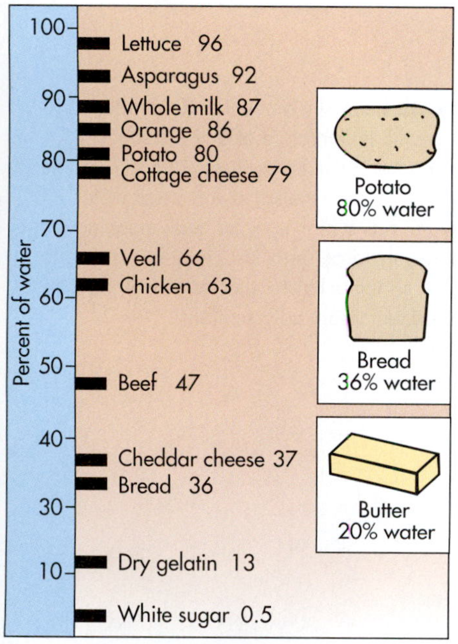

Water Needs

Adults need roughly 1 ml of water per kcal expended. This works out to about 8 cups of water and/or other fluids per day but our actual needs are being reexamined by the Food and Nutrition Board (see the website for this book or www.iom.edu/IOM/IOMHome.nsf/Pages/Food+and+Nutrition+Board for updates).[6] We consume about 1 liter (1 quart) of water a day in various liquids, such as fruit juice, coffee, tea, soft drinks, and water itself (Fig. 11-4). Foods supply another liter of fluid; many fruits, vegetables, and beverages are more than 80% water (Table 11-1). Water as a by-product of metabolism provides approximately 350 ml (1½ cups) of additional water. All these sources together yield a total of about 2.4 liters (10 cups) of water for a 2400-kcal diet, or about 1 ml per kcal expended.

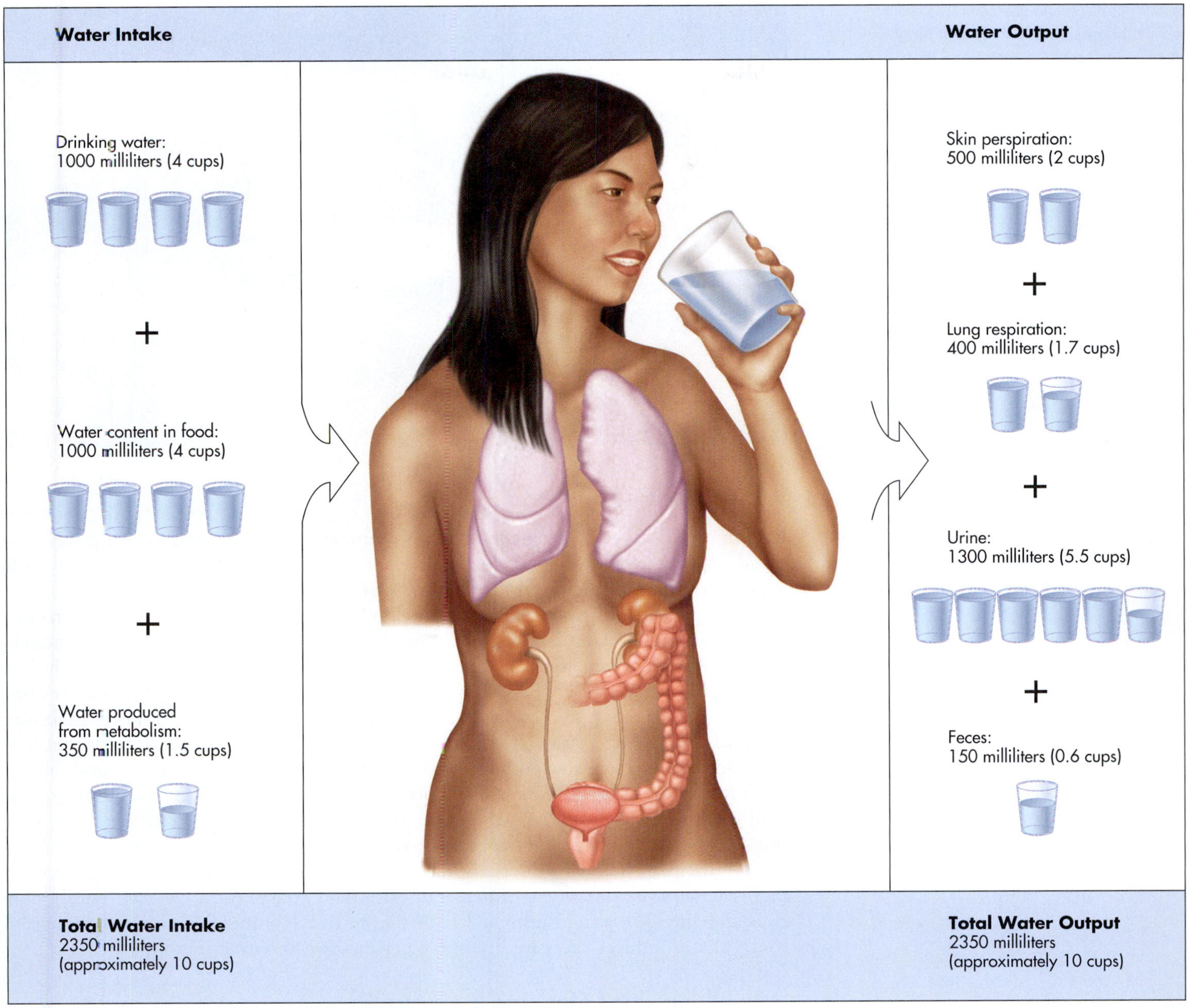

Figure 11-4 Water balance—intake versus output. We maintain body fluids at an optimum amount by adjusting water intake and output. Most water comes from the liquids we consume. Some comes from the moisture in more solid foods, and the remainder is produced during metabolism. Water output includes that lost via lungs, kidneys, skin, and feces.

Of the 2.4 liters of water needed, about 1.4 liters is used to produce urine. The rest, about 1 liter, compensates for typical water losses through the lungs (400 ml), feces (150 ml), and skin (500 ml for normal perspiration) (review Fig. 11-4). We are not normally aware of these **insensible water losses,** as opposed to losses we more easily notice, called **sensible water losses.** Urine output and heavy perspiration fall into this latter category. Note also that, when we consider the large amount of water used to facilitate gastrointestinal (GI) tract function, the loss of only 150 ml of water a day through the feces is remarkable. About 8000 ml of water enters the GI tract daily via secretions from the mouth, stomach, intestine, pancreas, and other organs. The diet supplies an additional 2000 ml or more. The kidneys also conserve water, reabsorbing about 97% of the water filtered from waste products.[17]

insensible water losses In this case, not perceived by the person, such as water lost with each breath.

sensible water losses Water losses we readily notice, such as urine output and heavy perspiration.

Regular intake of fluid is essential to replace daily fluid losses. A recent trend in North America is to carry this water and other fluids with us.

Water Deficiency

It is important to achieve an adequate water intake, either through drinking water or by adding water-rich foods to your diet. Dark yellow instead of pale urine is a typical sign of insufficient water intake, as is urine with a very strong odor.

If you don't drink enough water, your body generally lets you know by signaling thirst. Your brain is communicating the need to drink. This thirst mechanism is not always reliable, however, especially during athletic practices and events, in infancy, during illness, and in one's older years. For this reason, athletes should weigh themselves before and after training sessions to determine their rate of water loss and thus their water needs. Replacing at least 75% of this weight loss is advised, especially as weight loss approaches 2 to 3%. Three cups (¾ liter) of water are recommended per pound (about half a kilogram) of weight loss (see Chapter 14 for details on fluid use in athletics). Sick youngsters—especially those with fever, vomiting, diarrhea, and increased perspiration—and older persons often need to be reminded to drink plenty of fluids. As Chapter 17 discusses in further detail, infants easily become dehydrated. Long airplane flights are another situation that demands extra fluid intake: A traveler can lose about 6 cups (1.5 liters) of water during a 3-hour flight. The dehumidified air in an airplane is so dry that it induces excessive insensible perspiration and evaporation.

What If the Thirst Message Is Ignored?

Once the body registers an increase in blood concentration, it increases fluid conservation. The pituitary gland releases **antidiuretic hormone (ADH)** to force the kidneys to conserve water. The kidneys respond by reducing urine flow. At the same time, as fluid volume decreases in the bloodstream, blood pressure falls. This fall initiates a sequence of events beginning in the kidneys. Signaled by highly sensitive pressure receptors, the kidneys release an enzyme called **renin.** Renin, in turn, activates a circulating blood protein originally produced in the liver called angiotensinogen to form angiotensin I. Angiotensin I is converted to **angiotensin II,** which, among other effects, triggers the adrenal glands to release the hormone **aldosterone.** This hormone, in turn, signals the kidneys to retain more sodium and chloride, and, therefore, more water (Fig. 11-5). Remember that water always follows electrolytes. Thus, low blood pressure, through this roundabout measure using the kidneys, causes increased water conservation in the body.[17]

However, despite these mechanisms to conserve water, fluid is still constantly lost via the insensible routes—feces, skin, and lungs. Those losses must be replaced. In addition, there is a limit to how concentrated urine can become. Eventually, if fluid is not consumed, the body becomes dehydrated and suffers ill effects.

antidiuretic hormone (ADH) A hormone that is secreted by the pituitary gland and acts on the kidneys to cause a decrease in water excretion. It is also called arginine vasopressin (AVP).

renin An enzyme formed in the kidneys and released in response to low blood pressure; it acts on a blood protein to produce angiotensin I.

angiotensin II A compound, produced from angiotensin I, that increases blood vessel constriction and triggers production of the hormone aldosterone.

aldosterone A hormone produced in the adrenal glands that acts on the kidneys, causing them to retain sodium and, therefore, water.

Table 11-1 Water Content of a Typical Day's Food Intake

Meal	Fluid Oz
Breakfast	
8 fl oz orange juice	7.2
½ cup skim milk	3.6
½ cup strawberries	2.7
1 cup Cheerios	0.4
Midmorning Snack	
1 cup of water	8.0
1 banana	3.0
Lunch	
2 oz water-packed tuna	2.2
2 slices whole-wheat bread	0.9
1 large tomato	5.0
8 oz low-fat yogurt	6.8
1 cup water	8.0
1 kiwi fruit	2.6
Dinner	
2 oz baked skinless chicken	1.3
2 cups romaine lettuce	4.0
2 oz sliced red peppers	1.8
1 slice bread	1.0
1 baked potato	3.5
1 cup skim milk	7.0
1 tbsp oil-and-vinegar dressing	0.0
1 cup of tea	8.0
Total	77 fluid ounces (9.6 cups)

Alcohol inhibits the action of ADH. One reason people feel so weak the day after heavy drinking is that they are very dehydrated. Even though they may have consumed a lot of liquid in their drinks, they have lost even more liquid because alcohol has inhibited ADH. Caffeine also produces a diuretic effect on the body.

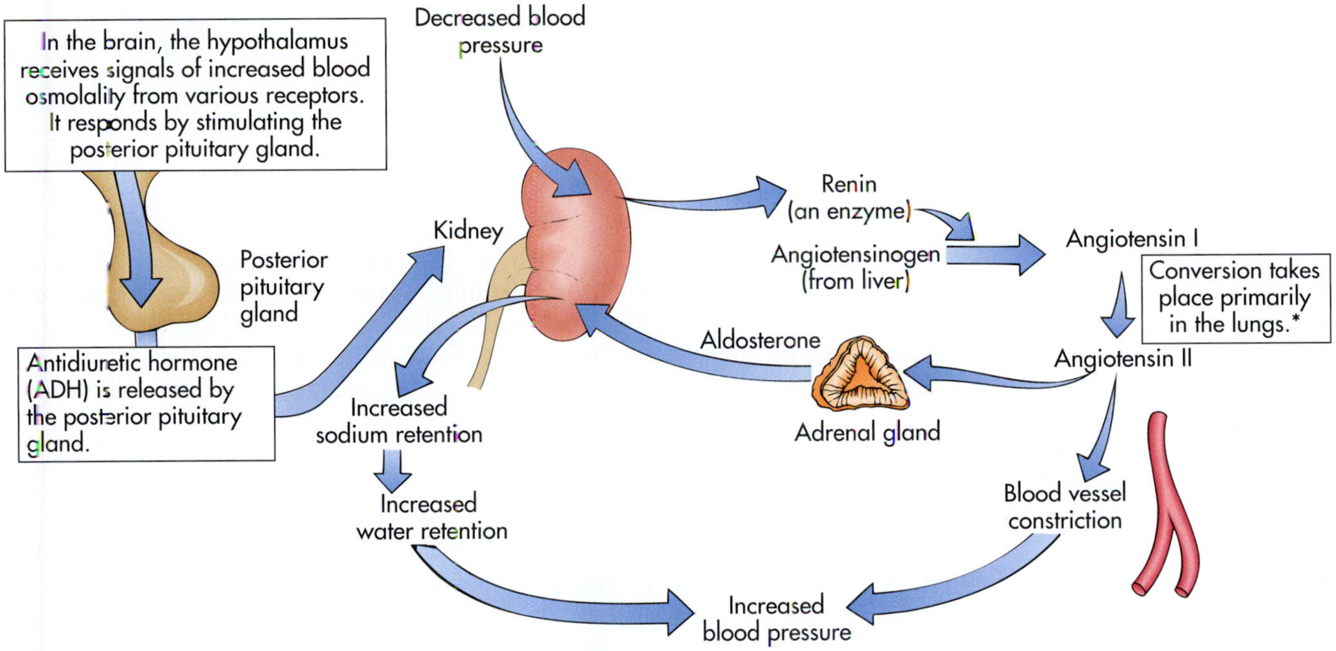

Figure 11-5 The renin-angiotensin system is one regulator of blood pressure. It functions with antidiuretic hormone to control blood pressure.
*The angiotensin-converting enzyme (ACE) inhibitors used to treat hypertension and other disorders act at this site (see the Nutrition Perspective for details).

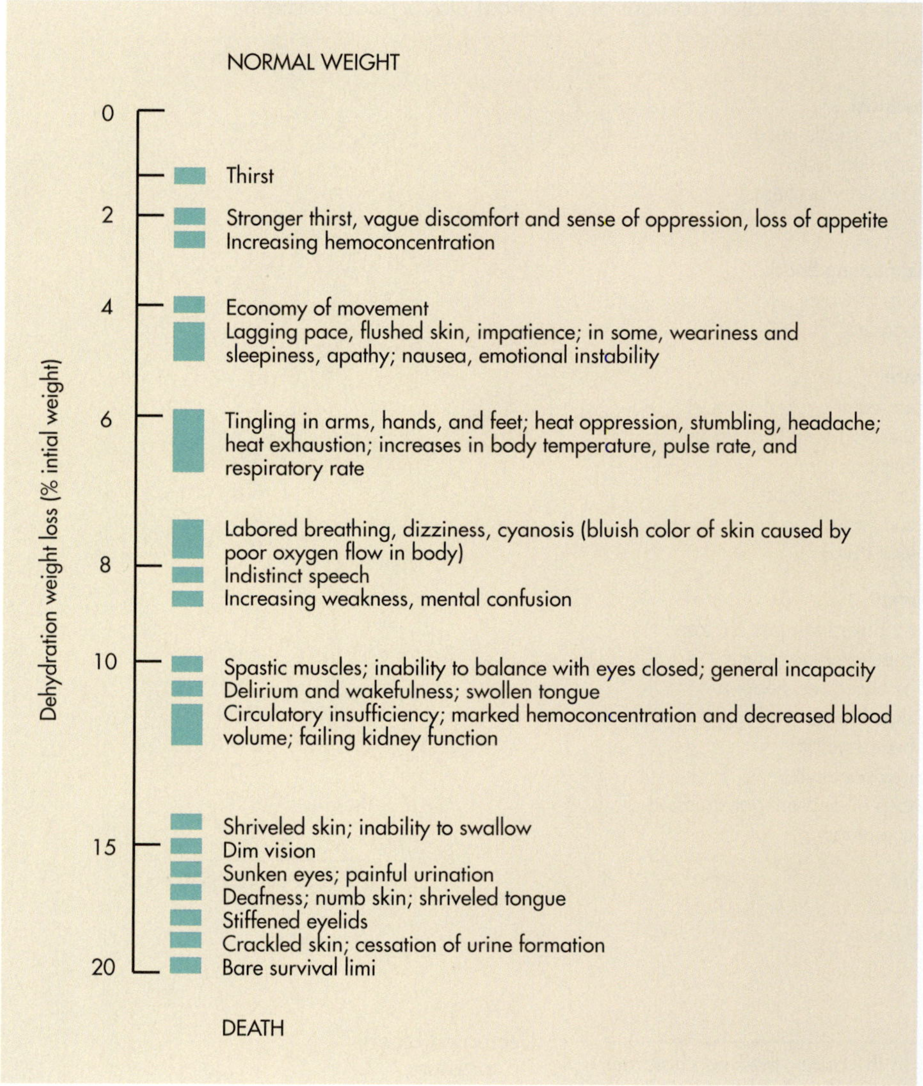

Figure 11-6 The effects of dehydration range from thirst to death, depending on the extent of body weight loss.

Critical | Thinking

Stacy has been working in the yard with her brother Tom. They have been busy mowing the lawn and pulling weeds since noon. Tom tells Stacy that he is feeling weak and has a headache. Stacy is concerned that her brother might be somewhat dehydrated. How can his symptoms be explained? How could Tom's risk of dehydration have been decreased?

As bottled water becomes more and more popular, the industry now generates more than $3 billion per year. In 1996, FDA instituted definitions for the various types of bottled water on the market; FDA also tests products for microbial and chemical content. For a list of manufacturers that meet federal guidelines, contact the International Bottled Water Association at 1-800-928-3711 or www.nsf.org. Some experts recommend that children not be given bottled water exclusively, as many brands do not contain an adequate fluoride supply to protect against dental caries. For adults, bottled water is typically an unnecessary expense, as it is often very similar to tap water. Chapter 19 reviews issues surrounding water safety in North America, such as possible bacterial and lead contamination.

By the time a person loses 1 to 2% of body weight in fluids, he or she will be thirsty. This loss of body weight contributes to fatigue, as well as impaired physiological and performance responses. At a 4% loss of body weight, muscles lose significant strength and endurance. By the time body weight is reduced by 10 to 12%, heat tolerance is decreased and weakness results. At a 20% reduction, coma and death may soon follow (Fig. 11-6).[10]

Water Toxicity

Too much water—whatever amount the kidneys are unable to excrete—can also lead to serious side effects. Water intoxication is most likely to occur if water intake is not accompanied by sufficient electrolytes. However, an excessive amount would have to approach many quarts (liters) each day. Very few people are at risk of drinking too much water, but problems do accompany some disease states and mental disorders. When excessive water overwhelms the kidneys' capacity to excrete it, headache, blurred vision, cramps, convulsions, and ultimately death may occur.

Concept | Check

Because the body cannot store water, we can survive only a few days without it. Water dissolves substances, serves as a medium for chemical reactions and as a lubricant, and aids in temperature regulation. Water accounts for 50 to 70% of body weight and distributes itself throughout the body: among lean and other tissues (in both intracellular and extracellular fluids) and in urine and other body fluids. Adults need about 1 ml of water or other fluids for each kcal expended. Thirst is the body's first sign of dehydration. If this thirst mechanism is faulty, as it may be during illness or vigorous exercise, hormonal mechanisms also help conserve water by reducing urine output. Excess fluid intake can be hazardous to a person's health.

Chapter 20 discusses the scarcity of clean water as a growing problem in many developing countries.

Minerals

Minerals are divided into major minerals and trace minerals, depending on the amount we need per day. Generally speaking, if we require 100 mg (1/50 of a teaspoon) or more per day of a mineral, it is considered a **major mineral;** otherwise, it is considered a **trace mineral.** Using these criteria, calcium and phosphorus are major minerals, and iron and zinc are trace minerals.

The functions and nutritional significance of the major minerals are discussed in this chapter, and the trace minerals in Chapter 12. But, before examining the properties of the individual major minerals, let's consider some topics relevant to all these minerals.

major mineral A mineral vital to health that is required in the diet in amounts greater than 100 mg/day.

trace mineral A mineral vital to health that is required in the diet in amounts less than 100 mg/day.

Absorption, Transport, and Excretion of Minerals

A significant factor determining the degree to which a mineral may be absorbed is the physiological need for that mineral at the time of consumption. Other factors are discussed in the following paragraphs.

Many minerals have similar molecular weights and charges (valences). Magnesium, calcium, iron, and copper can exist in the 2^+ valence state. Having similar size and the same charge causes some of these minerals to compete with each other for absorption mechanisms, thereby affecting each other's **bioavailability** and metabolism. Because of this, people should avoid taking individual mineral supplements unless a medical condition specifically warrants it. This is because an excess of one mineral influences the absorption and metabolism of other minerals. For example, the presence of a large amount of zinc in the diet decreases copper absorption.

bioavailability The degree to which the amount of an ingested nutrient is absorbed and is available to the body.

Some vitamins improve mineral absorption. Vitamin C can improve iron absorption when the two are consumed in the same meal. The vitamin D hormone 1,25 $(OH)_2$ vitamin D improves calcium, phosphorus, and magnesium absorption.[7]

Mineral bioavailability can be greatly influenced by nonmineral substances in the diet. Foods contain and supply us with many minerals, but the body varies in its capacity to absorb and use available minerals. Although minerals may be present in foods, they are not bioavailable unless the body can absorb them. The ability to absorb minerals from a diet depends on many factors. The amount of a mineral listed in a food composition table does not necessarily reflect the amount that can be actually absorbed.

Components of fiber, especially phytic acid (phytate) in wheat grain fiber, can limit the absorption of some minerals by chemically binding to them and preventing these from being released during digestion. As noted in Chapter 5, an intake greatly above the recommendation of 25 to 38 g/day of total fiber can cause problems with mineral status of the body. However, if grains are leavened with yeast, as they are in bread, enzymes produced by the yeast can break some of the chemical bonds between phytic acid and minerals. This in some cases reduces the effect of phytates on mineral absorption. The zinc deficiencies found among some Middle Eastern populations are attributed partly to

Spinach is often touted as a rich source of calcium, but little of the calcium present is bioavailable—that which is available to the body.

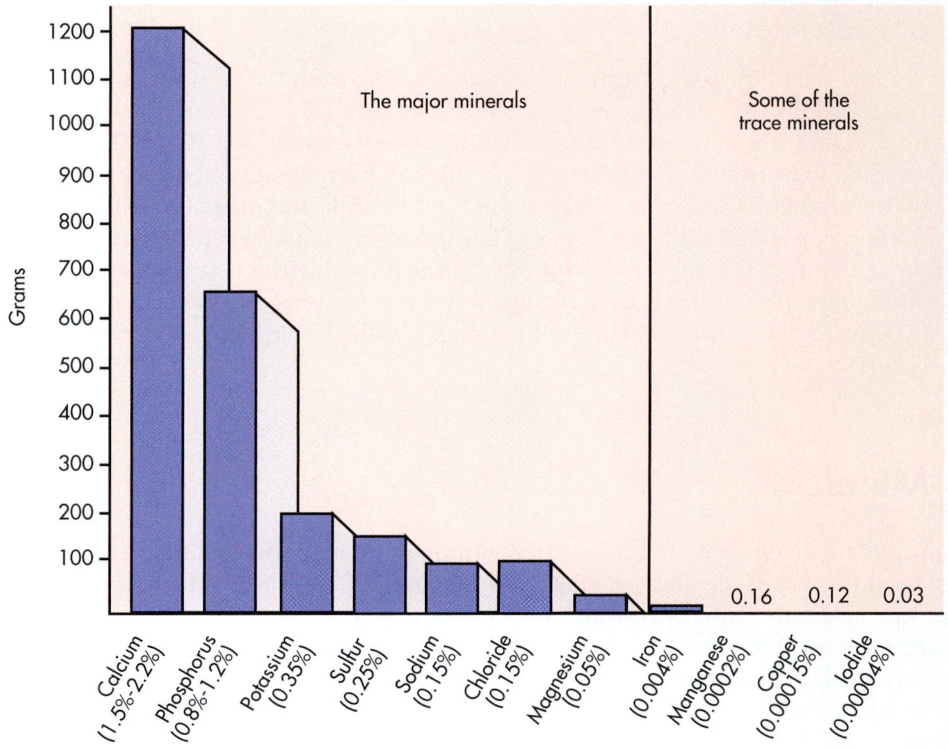

Figure 11-7 Approximate amounts of various minerals present in the average human body. The percent values in parentheses indicate the amounts as percentages of body weight. Other trace minerals of nutritional importance not listed include chromium, fluoride, molybdenum, selenium, and zinc.

their consumption of unleavened breads, resulting in low bioavailability of dietary zinc. This is discussed in detail in Chapter 12.

oxalic acid (oxalate) An organic acid that is found in spinach, rhubarb, and other leafy green vegetables and that can depress the absorption of certain minerals present in the food, such as calcium.

Oxalic acid (oxalate) is another substance in plants that binds minerals and makes them less available to the body. Spinach, for example, contains plenty of calcium, but only about 5% of it can be absorbed because of the vegetable's high concentration of oxalic acid. On average, about 25% of dietary calcium is absorbed by adults, with the highest percentage coming from dairy products.[7]

Once absorbed, minerals travel in the blood either in a free form or bound to proteins. For example, calcium ions can be found in the blood as such, as well as bound to the blood protein albumin. Many of the trace minerals have specific binding proteins, which transport them in the bloodstream. Trace minerals in their free form are often highly reactive and, so, would be toxic if not so bound. You will see, as well, in Chapter 12 that many trace minerals also are bound by specific cellular proteins once taken up by cells.

Mineral excretion takes place primarily through the urine. When kidney function fails, mineral intake must be controlled in order to avoid mineral toxicity, such as with phosphorus and magnesium. Some minerals are discharged through the bile into the intestinal tract and then excreted through the feces, such as copper.

Functions of Minerals

The metabolic roles of minerals and the amounts of them in the body vary considerably (Fig. 11-7). Some minerals, such as copper and selenium, function as cofactors, enabling enzymes to carry out a chemical reaction. Minerals also are components of many body compounds. For example, iron is a component of hemoglobin in red blood cells. Sodium, potassium, and calcium aid in the transmission of nerve impulses throughout the body.[17] Body growth and development also depend on certain minerals, such as calcium and phosphorus. Water balance requires sodium, potassium, calcium, and phosphorus. At all levels—cellular, tissue, organ, and whole body—minerals clearly play important roles in maintaining body functions.

Food Sources of Minerals

Minerals in the average North American's diet come from both plant and animal sources. For some minerals, animal sources are the food sources with the highest amounts and best bioavailability. For example, dairy products are rich sources of bioavailable calcium, while meat and related foods are rich sources of bioavailable iron and zinc. On the other hand, magnesium and manganese are minerals found more in plant-based foods than animal food products.

Generally the more refined a plant food—as in the case of white flour—the lower its mineral content. With regard to minerals, the enrichment process for grains adds only iron. The selenium, zinc, copper, and other minerals lost when grains are refined are not replaced. This is just one more reason to consume whole grains on a regular basis.

North Americans at Risk for Mineral Deficiencies

Typically, the major mineral at risk for being deficient in adult diets is calcium. Currently, most North Americans do not meet the recommended intake for calcium.[7] For trace minerals, iron and zinc are most likely to be deficient in diets; these minerals are discussed in Chapter 12.

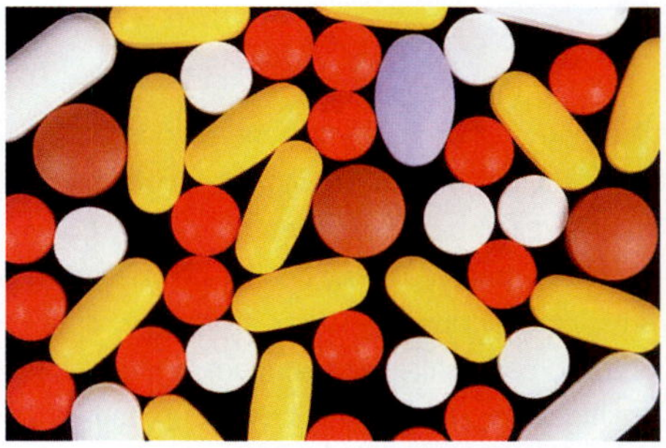

Mineral supplements pose a high risk for toxicity. Generally, mineral intake from a supplement should not exceed 100% of the Daily Value, unless otherwise specified by a physician.

Toxicity of Minerals

Excess mineral intake can lead to toxic results, especially with the trace minerals, such as iron and copper. This potential for toxicity is yet another reason to consider carefully the use of mineral supplements. Many trace minerals are quite toxic at doses not much above typical needs, which is approximated by the Daily Value on the food or supplement label. Thus, doses of mineral supplements should be examined carefully, especially if intake will exceed the Tolerable Upper Intake Level (Upper Level or UL). Such intakes should be taken only under a physician's supervision because toxicity and nutrient interactions are possible (see the inside cover of this text for Upper Levels for minerals).

Concept | Check

Minerals are vital to the functioning of many body processes. Their bioavailability depends on many factors, including a mineral's interaction with dietary fiber, vitamins, and other minerals. Both animal and plant sources help us meet our mineral needs. Taking large amounts of an individual mineral supplement can greatly diminish the absorption and metabolism of other minerals. In addition, some minerals are potentially toxic at intakes not much in excess of human needs. These are two good reasons to consider carefully any use of mineral supplements.

Sodium (Na)

Health professionals issuing dietary recommendations generally suggest North Americans limit intake of sodium.[11] Salt contributes almost all the sodium to our diets. Salt is 40% sodium and 60% chloride. North Americans currently consume twice or more of the amount of sodium typically recommended. Still, as reviewed in the Nutrition Perspective at the end of this chapter, salt intake is not the major cause of the epidemic of **hypertension** in North America (obesity and inactivity are more important).[12]

The importance of salt to human health has been recognized since antiquity. Salt was a commodity in the classical world. Indeed, the Latin word *salary* reflects the way a soldier's wages were paid.

hypertension A condition in which blood pressure remains persistently elevated. Obesity, inactivity, excess alcohol intake, and excess salt (sodium) intake all can contribute to the problem; also called high blood pressure.

Absorption, Transport, Storage, and Excretion of Sodium

The human body absorbs almost all sodium that is consumed. Sodium is easily absorbed from the stomach, small intestine, and colon. Some sodium in the bloodstream

To assess the sodium, potassium, chloride, magnesium, or phosphorus status of a person, blood concentrations can be measured. Other methods, often more sensitive ones, when appropriate, will be noted in this chapter.

is filtered by the kidneys, where the excess is excreted into the urine. The rest is returned to the blood to maintain an appropriate sodium concentration. Excretion of sodium is via the kidneys.[17] Some sodium is stored in the bones.

Functions of Sodium

Sodium is the major positive ion (cation) in extracellular fluid and a key factor in retaining body fluids. Sodium balance is regulated by the hormone aldosterone. Sodium also helps regulate the fluid balance of the body both within and outside the cells. The high blood levels of sodium contribute to its osmolality and, in turn, the regulation of fluid volume of the extracellular and intracellular compartments.[17]

As both potassium and sodium shift across the cell membrane, they create an electrical potential charge, which allows muscles to contract and nerve impulses to be conducted. Sodium also participates in the absorption of other nutrients (e.g., glucose and amino acids) in the small intestine.

Sodium in Foods

Many commercially prepared condiments, sauces, and seasonings are high in sodium. Examples include onion, celery, garlic, seasoned, and sea salts; baking powder; salad dressings; pickles; soy, steak, barbecue, chili, and Worcestershire sauces; meat tenderizer; baking soda; salt pork; brine; catsup; mustard; bouillon; monosodium glutamate (MSG); and relish.

About one-third to one-half the sodium we consume is added during cooking or at the table. Most of the rest is added during food manufacturing (Table 11-2). Many health authorities are calling for manufacturers to use less salt, so that our total sodium intakes fall. To some extent, this is taking place (e.g., low-sodium soups and crackers). Almost all foods naturally contain a little sodium; the higher amount found in milk (about 120 mg/cup) is one exception. The more home cooking a person does, the more control over sodium consumption that person has.

Major contributors of sodium in the adult diet are white bread and rolls, hot dogs and lunch meats, cheese, soups, and spaghetti with tomato sauce, partly because these foods are eaten so often. Other foods that generally are especially high in sodium include salted snack foods, french fries and potato chips, and sauces and gravies. (If we were to eat only unprocessed foods and add no salt, we would consume about 500 mg of sodium per day, or about ⅒ of current intakes.)[9] And, in cases where sodium intake must be very limited,

Cured meats are very high in sodium.

Table 11-2 Increase in Sodium Content of Foods During Processing*

Food Category	Sodium (mg)
Dairy Products	
Fruited yogurt, ¾ cup	107
2% milk, 1½ cups	182
Cheddar cheese, 1¾ oz	307
American cheese food, 2 oz	548
Meats	
Beef roast, 1 oz	17
Beef jerky, ⅔ oz	540
Pork loin, 1 oz	22
Bacon, 2 pieces	202
Ham, 1½ oz	564
Vegetables	
Fresh peas, 1 cup	5
Frozen peas, 1 cup	139
Frozen peas in cheese sauce, ⅔ cup	205
Canned peas, 1 cup	372
Grain Products	
Flour, ⅓ cup	1
Bread, 2 slices	286
Saltine crackers, 12	486

*All examples in a particular group contain the same amount of food energy.

even contributions from tap water (especially from softened water, which contains more sodium), as well as medicines that contain sodium, must be considered.

As discussed in Chapter 2, nutrition labels list a food's sodium content. In addition, various descriptive terms, such as sodium-free, salt-free, and low-sodium, may appear elsewhere on labels (review Table 2-11 in Chapter 2). When dietary sodium must be severely restricted, these labels are very helpful.

Food Sources of Sodium

Food Item and Amount	*Sodium Content (mg)*
Pepperoni pizza, 2 slices	2045
Slice ham, 1 oz	1215
Chicken noodle soup, canned, 1 cup	1106
V8 vegetable juice, 8 oz	620
Macaroni salad, ½ cup	561
Hard pretzels, 1 oz	486
Hamburger with bun, 1 each	474
Green beans, canned, ½ cup	390
Saltine crackers, 6 each	234
Cheddar cheese, 1 oz	176
Peanut butter, 2 tbsp	156
Nonfat milk, 1 cup	127
7 grain bread, 1 slice	126
Animal crackers, 1 oz	112
Grape juice, 1 cup	10

Adult minimum needs, 500 mg

Sodium Needs

The body needs only about 100 mg of sodium a day. The Food and Nutrition Board has set 500 mg/day as the current minimum requirement.[6] The needs for this and the other major minerals, potassium and chloride, is currently being reexamined. See the website for this book or the Food and Nutrition Board website at (www.iom.edu/IOM/IOMHome.nsf/Pages/Food+and+Nutrition+Board) for updates. The Daily Value for sodium used on food and supplement labels is 2400 mg. FDA established this value because it is consistent with the many government reports that encourage reduced sodium intakes. The American Heart Association also recently supported this recommendation. As noted earlier, typical sodium intakes of adults are generally two or more times this amount (4–7 g/day).

Sodium Deficiency

Only when weight loss from perspiration exceeds 2 to 3% of total body weight (or about 5 to 6 lb) should sodium losses be of concern. Even then, merely salting foods is sufficient to restore body sodium for most people. Endurance athletes, however, may need to consume sports drinks during competition to avoid depletion of sodium (see Chapter 14). Note also that, although perspiration tastes salty on the skin, sodium is not highly concentrated in perspiration. Rather, water evaporating from the skin leaves concentrated sodium behind. Perspiration contains about two-thirds the sodium concentration found in blood. Sodium depletion also can occur due to diarrhea or vomiting, especially in infants. There are electrolyte drinks designed to replace sodium in such cases (see Chapter 17).

How Much Sodium Do You Consume?

You can evaluate your sodium consumption habits by completing the questionnaire in Table 11-3. The more checks in the "often" or "regularly" column, the higher your dietary sodium intake. However, not all the habits in the table contribute the same amount of sodium. For example, many natural cheeses are relatively moderate in sodium, whereas processed cheeses and cottage cheese are much higher. You can choose to reduce your sodium intake by cutting back on those items for which you checked "often" or "regularly." You needn't suddenly eliminate foods from your diet. Rather, to moderate sodium intake, choose lower-sodium foods from each food group more often and balance high-sodium food choices with low-sodium ones.[11] It is also important to pay attention to the sodium values listed on food labels and to taste foods before adding salt. In addition, when eating out, avoiding foods commonly prepared with lots of sodium and asking to have sauces served on the side and then using only small amounts are two other ideas.

It is also a good idea to have your blood pressure checked regularly. If you have hypertension due to salt sensitivity (this is true in about half of all cases of hypertension), you should try to reduce your sodium intake as part of a comprehensive plan to treat this disease and see if this helps the problem.[8]

One way to control sodium intake is to use the salt shaker less.

Adapting to a Lower Sodium Intake

Should you be advised by a physician or simply choose to consume less sodium, you can eventually adapt to a low-sodium diet. At first, foods will taste quite flat, but eventually you will perceive more flavor as the tongue's salt receptors become more sensitive to the natural salt content of foods. By slowly reducing dietary salt and substituting garlic, oregano, lemon juice, and other herbs and spices, you can eventually become

Table 11-3 Questionnaire for Evaluating Your Sodium Habits with Respect to Typically Rich Sources

How Often Do You . . .	Rarely	Occasionally	Often	Regularly (Daily)
1. Eat cured or processed meats, such as ham, bacon, sausage, frankfurters, and other luncheon meats?	☐	☐	☐	☐
2. Choose canned or frozen vegetables with sauce?	☐	☐	☐	☐
3. Use commercially prepared meals, main dishes, or canned or dehydrated soups?	☐	☐	☐	☐
4. Eat cheese, especially processed cheese?	☐	☐	☐	☐
5. Eat salted nuts, popcorn, pretzels, corn chips, or potato chips?	☐	☐	☐	☐
6. Add salt to cooking water for vegetables, rice, or pasta?	☐	☐	☐	☐
7. Add salt, seasoning mixes, salad dressings, or condiments—such as soy sauce, steak sauce, catsup, and mustard—to foods during preparation or at the table?	☐	☐	☐	☐
8. Salt your food before tasting it?	☐	☐	☐	☐
9. Ignore labels for sodium content when buying foods?	☐	☐	☐	☐
10. When dining out, choose foods with sauces, or foods that are obviously salty?	☐	☐	☐	☐
The more checks you have in the last two columns, the higher your dietary sodium intake.				

Adapted from *USDA Home and Garden Bulletin* No. 232-6, April 1986.

accustomed to a diet containing less sodium. Many new cookbooks offer tested recipes for flavorful low-sodium foods. Except when baking breads with yeast, omitting salt from food preparation can still yield many excellent products.

Toxicity of Sodium

Most humans can adapt to an excess dietary sodium intake, although it can contribute to hypertension in some people. A sodium intake $>$ 2 g/day also increases calcium loss in the urine. This is especially a problem for people who consume much salt and little calcium (and too little potassium). Another health area where salt may be at fault is kidney stone formation. A high salt intake may contribute to stone formation in certain people, linked to the increased calcium excretion just described. A very high sodium intake also can be toxic, especially when the kidneys cannot excrete the excess in the urine. Sodium is also toxic when a high intake is accompanied by a lack of water.

Critical | Thinking

Mrs. Massa has recently seen and heard a lot about the amount of salt (sodium) in foods. She has been surprised by the number of articles that advise the public to decrease the amount of salt in their food. If sodium is such a bad thing, Mrs. Massa wonders, why do you need to have any at all? How would you explain this need for some sodium to her?

Concept | Check

Sodium is the major positive ion in the extracellular fluid. It is important for maintaining fluid balance and conducting nerve impulses. In the North American diet, sodium is provided predominantly through processed foods and salt added in cooking and at the table. The more foods prepared at home, the more control one has over sodium intake. For adults, minimum requirement is set at 500 mg/day. Many scientific groups suggest that, for all adults, sodium intake should be limited to about 2.4 g/day, but there is not universal support for this recommendation. An average adult consumes twice of this amount or more. Some North Americans are especially sensitive to dietary sodium and may develop hypertension as a result of high salt intakes. Sodium depletion is unlikely, since North American diets have abundant sources, and most sodium consumed is absorbed.

Potassium (K)

Like sodium, potassium is a primary electrolyte in body fluids. Unlike sodium, potassium is associated with lower, rather than higher, blood pressure values.

The DASH (Dietary Approaches to Stop Hypertension) study showed that when people ate 8 to 10 servings of fruits, vegetables, and nuts each day (along with low-fat dairy products)—all sources of potassium—their blood pressure went down. This trend was especially true for people who had hypertension (see the Nutrition Perspective).[15]

Absorption, Transport, and Excretion of Potassium

The body absorbs about 90% of the potassium consumed. As with sodium, potassium balance is achieved primarily through the kidney excretion or retention as it is carried by the bloodstream to this organ.[17]

Functions of Potassium

Potassium performs many of the same functions as sodium, such as fluid balance and nerve-impulse transmission. It also influences the contractility of smooth, skeletal, and cardiac muscle. Potassium is the major cation inside the cell. Intracellular fluids contain 95% of the potassium in the body.[14]

Potassium in Foods

Unlike sodium, potassium is not generally added to foods. Overall, fresh fruits and vegetables are good sources of potassium. Milk, whole grains, dried beans, and meats are also sources. Major contributors of potassium to the adult diet include milk, potatoes, coffee, tomatoes, and orange juice.

Food Sources of Potassium

Food Item and Amount	*Potassium (mg)*
Kidney beans, 1 cup	715
Winter squash, ¾ cup	670
Plain yogurt, 1 cup	570
Orange juice, 1 cup	495
Cantaloupe, 1 cup	495
Lima beans, ½ cup	480
Banana, 1 medium	470
Zucchini, 1 cup	450
Soybeans, ½ cup	440
Artichoke, 1 medium	425
Tomato juice, ¾ cup	400
Pinto beans, ½ cup	400
Baked potato, 1 small	385
Buttermilk, 1 cup	370
Sirloin steak, 3 oz	345

Adequate Intake, 2000 mg

Potassium Needs

The minimum requirement for potassium for adults is currently set at 2000 mg per day.[6] Typically, adults meet potassium needs by eating a wide variety of foods. North Americans average 2 to 3 g/day. The Daily Value for potassium used for food and supplement labels is 3500 mg. Information about a food's potassium content is required on the Nutrition Facts panel only if the food contains added potassium as a nutrient or if claims about this nutrient appear on the label. In all other cases, it is voluntary.

Potassium Deficiency

Low blood potassium is a life-threatening problem. Symptoms often include a loss of appetite, muscle cramps, confusion, constipation, and increased urinary calcium excretion. Eventually, the heart beats irregularly, decreasing its capacity to pump blood.[14]

Some diuretics used to treat hypertension deplete the body's potassium. People who take potassium-wasting diuretics need to monitor their potassium intakes carefully. A recent study showed an increase in risk of stroke in people on these medications who did not consume enough potassium. For these people, high-potassium foods—such as fruits, fruit juices, and vegetables—are good additions to the diet, and, if recommended by a physician, so are potassium chloride supplements.

A continual deficient food intake, as may be the case in alcoholism, can also result in potassium deficiency. This also can be true for people with anorexia nervosa and bulimia nervosa, whose diets are poor and whose bodies can be depleted of potassium because of vomiting (see Chapter 15). People on very low-calorie diets are also at risk, as well as athletes who exercise heavily. In this latter group, potassium depletion is often considered a cause of cramps, though this is not as common a cause of cramps as is dehydration. As covered in Chapters 13 and 14, all of these people should compensate for potentially low body potassium by consuming potassium-rich foods.

Bananas are a rich source of potassium.

Toxicity of Potassium

Potassium in supplement form is harmless if the kidneys function normally; however, taken in excessive amounts, it causes gastrointestinal upset. When the kidneys function poorly, potassium builds up in the blood. This inhibits heart function, causing slowed heartbeat. If untreated, it can be fatal, as the heart eventually stops beating.[17] Consequently, in cases of reduced kidney function, close control of potassium intake is critical.

Chloride (Cl)

Chlorine is an element, but humans need the chloride ion (Cl^-).

Absorption, Transport, and Excretion of Chloride

Chloride is almost completely absorbed in the small intestine and colon. As is the case with sodium and potassium, excretion of chloride occurs mainly through the kidneys.

Functions of Chloride

Chlorine is a poisonous gas. In our bodies, chloride—the anion form of chlorine—forms an important negative ion for the extracellular fluid. Chloride's negative charge balances the positive charges on sodium ions and is therefore of great importance in the maintenance of electrolyte balance. Chloride is a component of hydrochloric acid produced in the stomach and is used during immune responses as white blood cells attack foreign cells. Chloride aids in the transport of carbon dioxide from cells to the lungs, as well as the disposal of carbon dioxide by way of exhaled air.[14]

Chloride in Foods

Seaweed, olives, rye, lettuce, a few fruits, and some vegetables are naturally good sources of chloride. Chlorinated water is also a source. However, we consume most chloride as salt added to foods. Knowing a food's salt content, one can predict closely its chloride content; recall that salt is 60% chloride. Naturally occurring sodium or chloride won't significantly affect the prediction.

Chloride Needs

The minimum requirement for chloride for adults is currently set at 700 mg/day.[6] The Daily Value for chloride used on food and supplement labels is 3400 mg. Assuming that the average adult consumes at least 7.5 g of salt daily, that supplies 4.5 g (4500 mg) of chloride, an abundance of this ion.

Chloride Deficiency

A chloride deficiency is generally unlikely, however, because our dietary sodium chloride (salt) intake is so high. Frequent and lengthy bouts of vomiting—if coupled with a nutrient-poor diet—can cause a deficiency because stomach secretions contain much chloride.[14]

Toxicity of Chloride

Dietary chloride has been implicated in the blood pressure-raising ability of sodium chloride. Still, as one lowers sodium intake as part of hypertension therapy, chloride intake automatically falls as well. Large chloride intakes, above 15 g/day, may cause fluid retention.

Concept | Check

Potassium performs functions similar to those of sodium, except that it is the main positive ion (cation) found inside, not outside, cells. Potassium is vital to fluid balance and nerve transmission. A potassium deficiency—caused by an inadequate intake of potassium, persistent vomiting, or use of some diuretics—can lead to loss of appetite, muscle cramps, confusion, and heartbeat irregularities. Fruits and vegetables are generally good sources of potassium. Potassium intake can be toxic if a person's kidneys do not function properly. Chloride is the major negative ion (anion) of extracellular fluid. Chloride also functions in digestion as part of hydrochloric acid and in immune and nervous system responses. Deficiencies of chloride are highly unlikely because we eat so much sodium chloride (salt), the major source.

Calcium (Ca)

All cells need calcium, but more than 99% of the calcium in the body is used as a structural component of bones and teeth. This calcium represents 40% of all the minerals present in the body and equals about 2.5 lb (1200 g). As calcium circulates in the bloodstream, it supplies the calcium needs of body cells.[17]

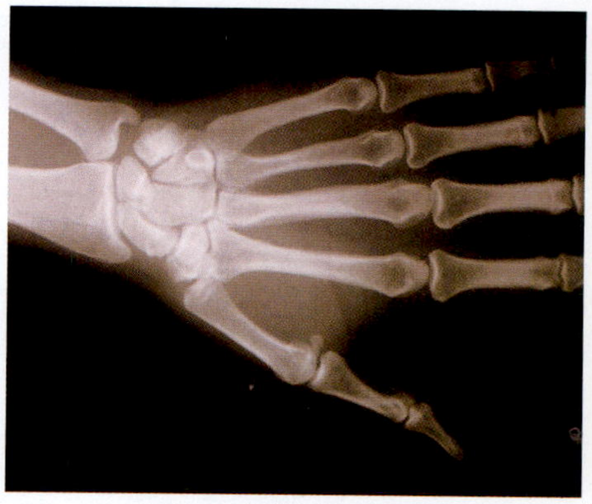

Ninety-nine percent of calcium in the body is in bones.

Absorption, Transport, Storage, and Excretion of Calcium

Unlike sodium, potassium, and chloride, the amount of calcium in the body greatly depends on the amount absorbed from the diet.

Absorption

Calcium absorption occurs primarily in the upper part of the small intestine because calcium requires a pH below 6 to stay in solution in an ionic state (Ca^{2+}). As the acidic stomach contents reach the small intestine, they are partially neutralized by bicarbonate released from the pancreas but are still slightly acidic. This provides a suitable environment for calcium absorption. In addition, calcium absorption within the upper small intestine depends on the active vitamin D hormone 1,25 $(OH)_2$ vitamin D. Because the intestinal contents become more alkaline as they pass down the gastrointestinal tract, calcium absorption decreases at the terminal end of the small intestine and colon, although some still occurs via passive diffusion.[7]

Humans absorb about 25% of the calcium in the foods eaten; however, when the body needs extra calcium—such as during infancy and pregnancy—absorption might reach as high as 60%. Young people tend to absorb calcium better than do older people, especially those older than 70. Postmenopausal women generally absorb the least calcium.[7]

Other factors that enhance the absorption of calcium include parathyroid hormone; dietary glucose and lactose; and normal intestinal motility (flow). Factors limiting calcium absorption include large amounts of phytic acid in fiber from wheat bran; excessive amounts of dietary phosphorus; polyphenols (tannins) in tea; a vitamin D deficiency; and diarrhea.

The tooth consists of a hard, yellowish tissue called dentin, which is covered with enamel in the crown and cementum in the root. When dentin and cementum are damaged, they can repair themselves. Damaged enamel cannot be naturally repaired because enamel is a secretion produced before the tooth erupts, and it does not have a blood supply like the other two tissues. To repair broken or damaged enamel requires the skills of a dentist. In contrast, bone is well supplied with blood vessels, so a fracture can be repaired (healed) by the body given time.

Transport, Storage, and Excretion

Each cell has a critical need for calcium, obtaining it from the bloodstream. This critical need is probably the reason humans have such excellent hormonal systems to control blood calcium. Normal blood calcium can be maintained despite an inadequate calcium intake, as much is stored in bones. (The bones, however, pay the price.) This makes blood calcium a poor measure of calcium status.

As discussed in Chapter 9, when blood calcium falls, the parathyroid gland releases parathyroid hormone. This hormone, working with 1,25 $(OH)_2$ vitamin D, increases the kidneys' retrieval of calcium before it is excreted in the urine (review Fig. 9-7 in Chapter 9). Parathyroid hormone also helps increase calcium absorption indirectly by increasing the synthesis of 1,25 $(OH)_2$ vitamin D. In addition, parathyroid hormone, often working in conjunction with 1,25 $(OH)_2$ vitamin D, causes increased calcium release from bones. In all these ways, then, parathyroid hormone increases blood calcium (Fig. 11-8).[17]

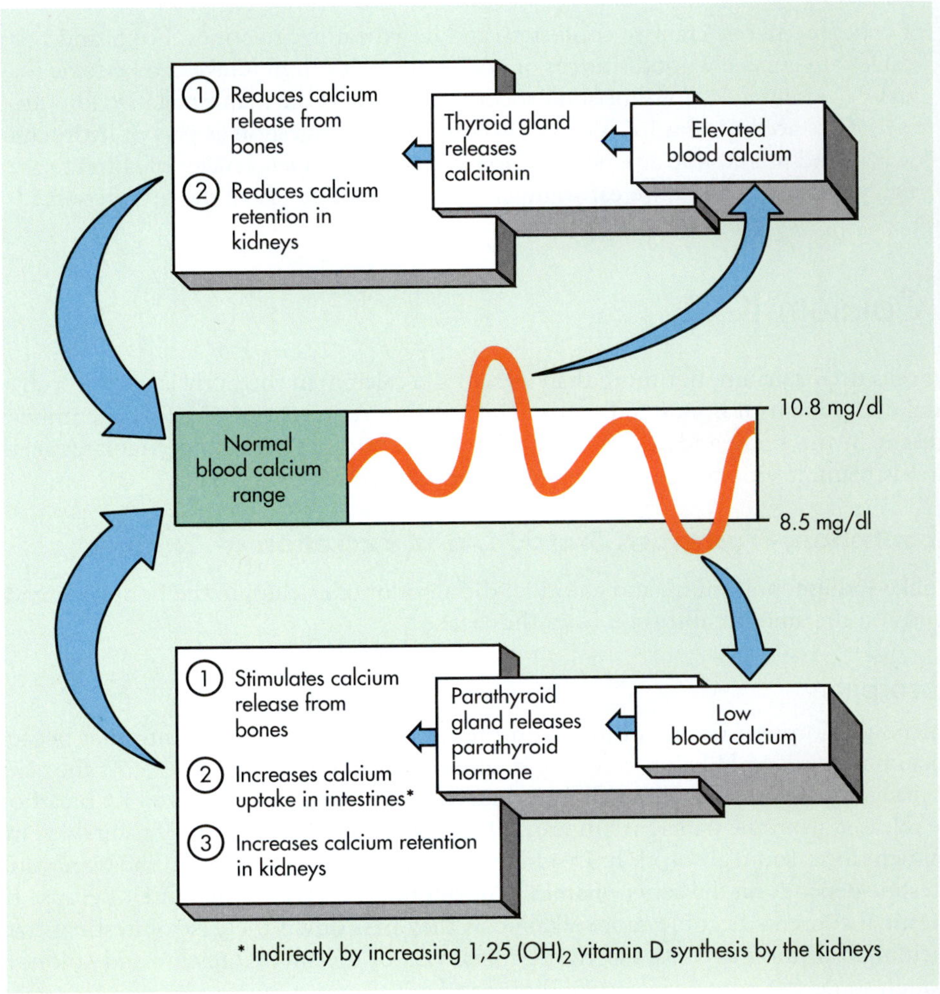

Figure 11-8 Regulation of blood parathyroid hormone (PTH) and calcitonin are key factors in controlling blood calcium. On a day-to-day basis, parathyroid hormone is the most important regulator. Recall from Figure 9-7 that the actions of parathyroid hormone also involve the active vitamin D hormone (1,25 $(OH)_2$ vitamin D) in various ways.

When blood calcium is too high, the release of parathyroid hormone falls. Then calcium loss from the kidneys increases. Synthesis of 1,25 $(OH)_2$ vitamin D also decreases; thus, calcium absorption decreases. In addition, the thyroid gland secretes the hormone calcitonin, which decreases calcium loss from bones. All these metabolic changes cause blood calcium to remain within the normal range.

Other routes for calcium loss include the skin and the feces losses that result from intestinal secretions into the intestinal lumen.

Functions of Calcium

Forming and maintaining bones are calcium's major roles in the body.

Bone Development and Maintenance

Despite its "dead" appearance, bone is very active metabolically. Bone contains two types of cells—**osteoblasts** and **osteoclasts**—which are integral to maintaining bones. Osteoblasts secrete a collagen protein matrix, which forms the support structure of bone. They mature to osteocytes and then secrete bone mineral, which causes bone mineralization. This mineral matures and eventually approaches the composition of $Ca_{10}(PO_4)_6OH_2$, called hydroxyapatite. In contrast, osteoclasts continually break down bone in areas where bone is not needed. Osteoclast activity is stimulated by parathyroid hormone, often in conjunction with 1,25 $(OH)_2$ vitamin D. These bone cells are very active when a diet is deficient in calcium; their action releases calcium from the bone so it can enter the blood. Remember, a supply of calcium is vital to all cells, not just to bone cells.[17]

osteoblasts Cells in bone that secrete mineral and bone matrix.

osteoclasts Bone cells that arise originally from a type of white blood cell. Osteoclasts secrete substances that lead to bone erosion. This erosion can set the stage for subsequent bone mineralization.

Table 11-4 Diet and Lifestyle Factors Associated with Bone Status and Related Action Plans to Implement for Bone Health[2, 5, 20]

Positive Diet and Lifestyle Factors	**Action Plans to Implement for Bone Health**
Adequate diet containing a sufficient amount of protein, calcium, phosphorus, magnesium, potassium, vitamin A, vitamin C, vitamin D, vitamin K, zinc, copper, fluoride, and manganese (and boron?)	Follow a diet plan such as the Food Guide Pyramid with special emphasis on adequate amounts of fruits and vegetables. Consider use of fortified foods (or supplements) to make up for specific nutrient shortfalls, such as vitamin D and calcium.
Healthy body weight	Be aware that low body weight (slender figure) increases the risk for low bone mass.
Normal menses	During childbearing years, seek medical advice if menses cease (such as in cases of anorexia nervosa or extreme athletic training). Women at menopause and beyond should consider use of current medical therapies to reduce bone loss linked to the fall in estrogen output.
Weight-bearing physical activity	Perform weight-bearing activity as this contributes to bone maintenance, whereas bed rest and a sedentary lifestyle lead to bone loss. Strength training is especially helpful to bone maintenance.
Negative Diet and Lifestyle Factors	**Action Plans to Implement**
Excessive intake of protein, phosphorus, sodium, caffeine, wheat bran, and alcohol	Moderate intake of these dietary constituents is recommended. Problems primarily arise if adequate calcium is not consumed. Excessive soft drink consumption is especially discouraged.
Smoking	Since smoking lowers estrogen output in women, smoking cessation is advised.
Use of certain medications, such as **corticosteroids**	Corticosteroid medications lead to bone loss, and so medical therapy to counteract the bone loss should be instituted if use is long term.

Bone turnover **(bone remodeling)** represents a cycle of bone breakdown by osteoclasts, followed by bone rebuilding by osteoblasts. In this way, bone is re-formed when necessary to respond to the physical demands placed on it. Before new bone can be built, the old bone in that area must be partially broken down.

During human growth, total osteoblast activity exceeds osteoclast activity, so we make more bone than we break down, with more bone being built in areas put under high stress. A right-handed tennis player, for example, builds more bone in that arm than in the left arm. In older years, osteoclast activity generally becomes more dominant. Most bone is built from infancy through the late adolescent years.[2] Small increases in **bone mass** continue between 20 and 30 years of age. Genes control up to 80% of the variation in the peak bone mass ultimately built.[5]

Bone loss begins in midadulthood and increases significantly at menopause in women. By age 65 to 70, the rate of bone loss falls to about the same rate as before menopause. In men, bone loss is slow and steady from around age 30. Overall, this bone loss in both genders progresses without signs or symptom. During their lifetimes, about one-third to one-half of all women go on to experience fractures associated with low bone mass. This is especially true of women who live beyond age 75. In addition, some women have much more bone than others. They probably built more bone when they were young, so they are able to endure greater bone loss without experiencing fractures. Actually, the reason for such variations in bone mass and fracture risk in women of any age still needs more research. However, researchers have identified numerous factors—including physical activity and body weight—associated with higher bone mass (Table 11-4). Even more factors are associated with low bone mass: slim figure; family history of hip fracture or osteoporosis; vitamin D receptor activity in the intestine; irregular menstruation; premature menopause; use of certain medications (such as corticosteroids); excess dietary protein and caffeine (which increase calcium loss in the urine); and prolonged bed rest.

Visual observation of the cross sections of a bone reveals two primary bone structural types in the body: **cortical** (also called compact) bone and **trabecular** (also called cancellous or spongy) bone. These in turn interact within each bone to form quite an engineering marvel of strength (Fig. 11-9).The entire outer surface of all bones is composed

corticosteroid A steroid hormone produced by the adrenal gland, an example of which is cortisol.

bone remodeling A process by which bone is first resorbed by osteoclasts and then re-formed by osteoblasts. This process allows the body to form bone where needed, such as in areas of high mechanical stress.

bone mass The total mineral substance (such as calcium or phosphorus) in a cross section of bone, generally expressed as grams per centimeter of length. In contrast, bone mineral density is the total mineral content of bone at a specific bone site divided by the width of the bone at that site, generally expressed as grams per cubic centimeter.

cortical bone Dense, compact bone that comprises the outer surface and shafts of bone; also called compact bone.

trabecular bone The spongy, inner matrix of bone, found primarily in the spine, pelvis, and ends of bones; also called cancellous bone.

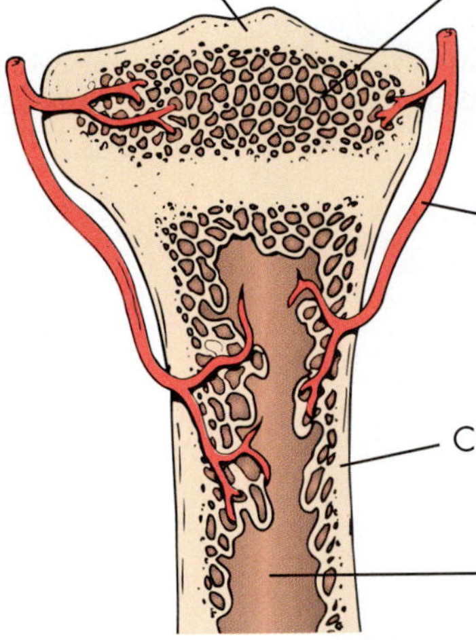

Figure 11-9 Cortical and trabecular bone. Cortical bone forms the shafts of bones and the outer mineral covering. Trabecular bone supports the outer shell of cortical bone in various bones of the body, as in the bone pictured.

of cortical bone, which is very dense. The shafts of long bones, such as those of the arm, are almost entirely cortical bone. Trabecular bone is found in the ends of the long bones, inside the spinal vertebrae, and inside the flat bones of the pelvis. Trabecular bone forms an internal scaffolding network for a bone. It supports the outer cortical shell of the bone, especially in heavily stressed areas, such as joints.

Bone strength especially depends on a person's bone mineral density (bone mass/bone width). The more densely packed the bone crystals, the stronger the bone structure. Another important element of bone strength is the trabecular bone support network inside a bone.

Blood Clotting

Calcium ions participate in several reactions in the cascade that leads to the formation of fibrin, the main protein component of a blood clot (review Fig. 9-10 in Chapter 9). For example, the conversion of prothrombin to thrombin requires the calcium ion.

Transmission of Nerve Impulses to Target Cells

When a nerve impulse reaches its target site—such as a muscle, other nerve cells, or a gland—the impulse is transmitted across the junction between the nerve and its target cells, called a **synapse.** In many nerves, the arrival of the impulse at the target site stimulates an influx of calcium ions into the nerve from the extracellular medium. The rise in intracellular calcium ions then triggers the release of neurotransmitters from synaptic vesicles, which are responsible for storing the neurotransmitter until needed. The released neurotransmitter then carries the impulse across the synapse to the target cells (Fig. 11-10).

synapse The space between the end of one nerve cell and the beginning of another nerve cell.

In an entirely different process, nerve impulses develop spontaneously if insufficient calcium is available, leading to what is called hypocalcemic **tetany.** This condition is characterized by muscle spasms, as the muscles receive continual nerve stimulation. Inadequate parathyroid hormone release or action is the typical cause of **hypocalcemia.**

tetany A body condition marked by sharp contraction of muscles and failure to relax afterward; usually caused by abnormal calcium metabolism.

hypocalcemia Low blood calcium, typically arising from inadequate parathyroid hormone release or action.

Muscle Contraction

The critical role of calcium in muscle contraction is most easily understood in the case of skeletal muscles. When a skeletal muscle is stimulated by a nerve impulse from the brain, calcium ions are released from intracellular stores within the muscle cells. The resulting increase in the concentration of calcium ions in a muscle cell is one factor, along with ATP, that permits the contractile proteins to slide along each other. This leads to muscle contraction. Then, to allow for subsequent relaxation, the calcium ions are returned to intracellular stores, and the contractile proteins slide apart (review Fig. C-4 in Appendix C).

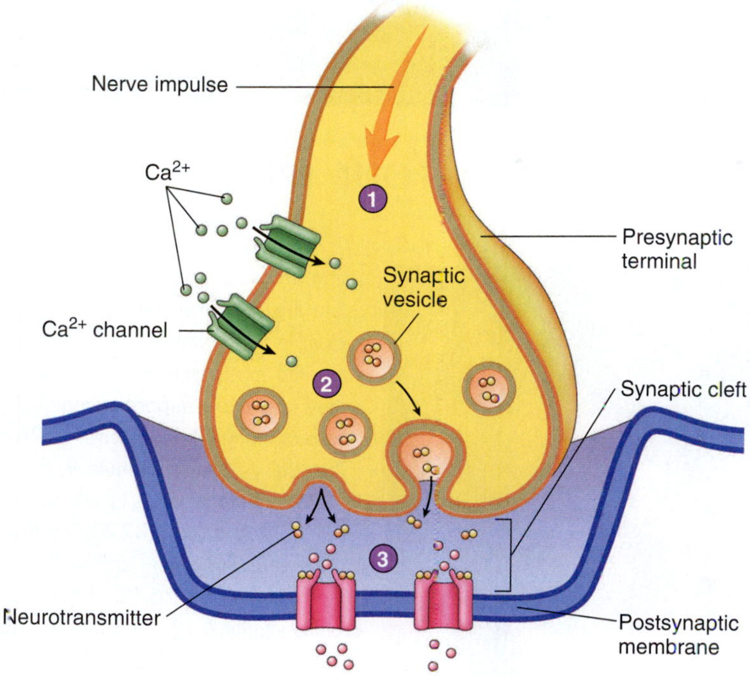
Nerve impulse
Ca^{2+}
1
Synaptic vesicle
Presynaptic terminal
Ca^{2+} channel
2
Synaptic cleft
3
Neurotransmitter
Postsynaptic membrane

Figure 11-10 The release of a neurotransmitter. (*1*) Nerve impulses, by opening Ca^{2+} channels, (*2*) stimulate the fusion of synaptic vesicles containing neurotransmitters with the cell membrane of the nerve terminals. (*3*) This leads to exocytosis and the release of a neurotransmitter. The neurotransmitters will bind to and stimulate the postsynaptic membrane of nearby cells.

Cell Metabolism

Calcium ions help regulate metabolism in the cell by participating in the **calmodulin** system. When calcium enters a cell (often because of hormone action) and binds to the protein calmodulin, the resulting protein-calcium complex can regulate the activity of various enzymes, including one that breaks down glycogen to many units of glucose 1-phosphate (Fig. 11-11). Dr. Gregory D. Miller discusses further roles of calcium and related health benefits in the Expert Opinion.

Calcium in Foods

Dairy products, such as milk and cheese, provide about 72% of the calcium in North American diets. The exception is cottage cheese, because most calcium is lost during production. White bread, rolls, crackers, and other foods made with milk products are secondary contributors. Leafy greens (such as spinach), broccoli, sardines, and canned salmon are also sources. However, much of the calcium in some leafy green vegetables, notably spinach, is not absorbed because of the presence of oxalic acid. This effect is not as significant, however, in kale, collard, turnip, and mustard greens. The calcium-fortified versions of orange juice, cranberry juice, and other beverages, as well as calcium-fortified cottage cheese, yogurt, breakfast cereals, breakfast bars, bread, chocolate candies, and snacks also provide much calcium. Another source of calcium is soybean curd (tofu), if it is made with calcium carbonate (check the label). Note that it is the bones in canned fish, such as salmon and sardines, that supply the calcium.

One reason the Food Guide Pyramid contains a milk, yogurt, and cheese group is to supply calcium to the diet. People who do not like milk can use products made with milk, such as chocolate milk, yogurt, cheese, and ice cream. All forms of milk, yogurt, and cheese allow about the same degree of calcium absorption. Information about calcium is mandatory on food labels.

Calcium Supplements

Calcium supplements can be used by people who don't like milk or who can't incorporate enough milk products or calcium-fortified foods into their diet. Calcium carbonate, the form found in calcium-containing antacids, has the highest concentration of calcium by weight (40%). Calcium citrate has 21% calcium, and calcium phosphate has

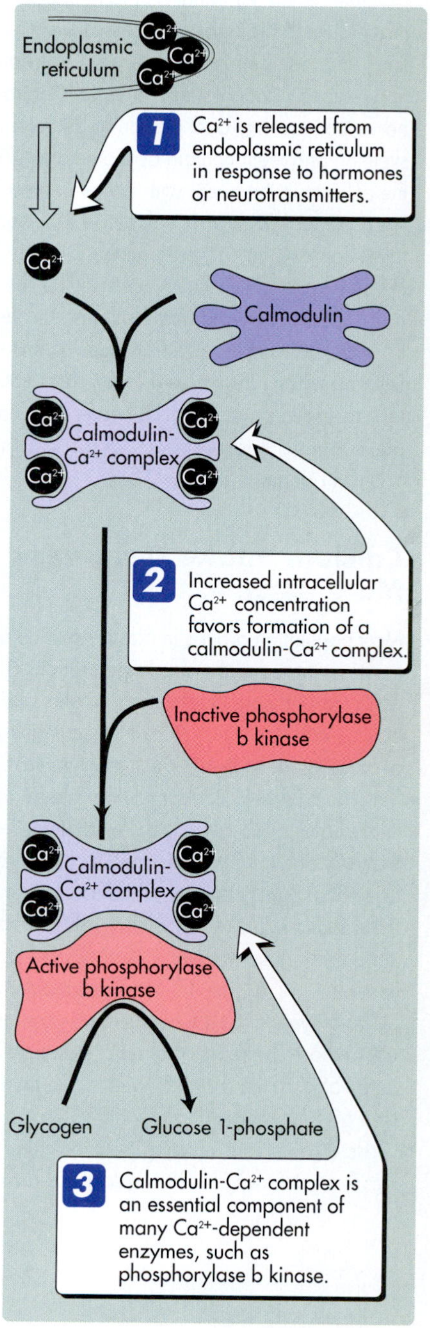
Endoplasmic reticulum
Ca^{2+}
1 Ca^{2+} is released from endoplasmic reticulum in response to hormones or neurotransmitters.
Calmodulin
Calmodulin-Ca^{2+} complex
2 Increased intracellular Ca^{2+} concentration favors formation of a calmodulin-Ca^{2+} complex.
Inactive phosphorylase b kinase
Active phosphorylase b kinase
Glycogen
Glucose 1-phosphate
3 Calmodulin-Ca^{2+} complex is an essential component of many Ca^{2+}-dependent enzymes, such as phosphorylase b kinase.

Figure 11-11 Calmodulin mediates many of the effects of intracellular calcium—in this case, the regulation of the breakdown of glycogen to many units of glucose 1-phosphate. Note that a kinase is an enzyme that adds a phosphorus group to another molecule.

Expert Opinion

The Many Benefits of Calcium in Your Diet

Gregory D. Miller, Ph.D., F.A.C.N.

Calcium is an essential nutrient important for many diverse biological processes such as structural support, cell adhesiveness, cell reproduction, blood coagulation, muscle contraction, nerve conduction, and glandular secretion. The skeleton and teeth contain approximately 99% of the calcium in the body, with the remaining 1% in extracellular space or in soft tissue. Adequate Intakes for calcium as part of the Dietary References Intakes (DRIs) have been set by the Food and Nutrition Board of the National Academy of Science: 500 mg for children ages 1 to 3 years, 800 mg for children ages 4 to 8 years, 1300 mg for adolescents ages 9 to 18 years, 1000 mg for adults ages 19 to 50 years, and 1200 mg for adults 51 years and older.

Milk is a rich as well as convenient source of calcium.

Calcium Intake Deserves More Attention

Most population groups in North America are not meeting these intake recommendations. This is particularly true of adolescent females and older adults. Males consume more calcium than females at all ages due to their higher energy intake. Data from the 1994–1996 Continuing Survey of Food Intakes by Individuals in the United States indicate that only about 12% of females 12 to 19 years of age and 32% of males of similar age are meeting the Adequate Intake for calcium. This survey also indicated that for women, only 16% of 20- to 29-year-olds, 11.5% of 40- to 49-year-olds, 5% of 50- to 59-year-olds, 4% of 60- to 69-year-olds and 4% of those 70 years or older are doing so. And only 15% of men 50 to 59 years of age, 13% of men 60 to 69 years of age, and 13% of those 70 years or older are meeting their calcium needs. This low intake of calcium is recognized as a major public health issue. In fact, the U.S. government's *Healthy People 2010* objective for the nation identifies low calcium intake as a priority nutrition problem.

The Reasons Behind the Calcium Shortfall

There are many factors that contribute to the low intake of calcium. One of the most important factors is the low intake of dairy foods. Milk and other dairy foods are the major source of calcium in our food supply, contributing 72% of the available calcium. It is difficult to meet calcium needs without dairy foods in the diet. The *Healthy People 2010* report states that "with current food selection practices, use of dairy products may constitute the difference between getting enough calcium in one's diet or not." Although dairy foods are the most important food source of calcium, they also make important contributions to the intake of many other nutrients. USDA data indicate that dairy foods contribute 9.3% of the energy, 19.4% of the protein, 12.6% of the fat, 4.6% of the carbohydrates, 32.4% of the phosphorus, 16.2% of the zinc, 15.8% of the magnesium, 1.8% of the iron, 26.1% of the riboflavin, 21.6% of the vitamin B-12, 15.3% of the vitamin A, 8.7% of the vitamin B-6, 6.2% of the folate, 4.7% of the thiamin, as well as other nutrients. Studies have demonstrated that dairy intake is a maker of better nutritional intake. This is why health professional organizations like the American Academy of Pediatrics, American Dietetic Association, American Medical Association, National Medical Association, National Institute of Child Health and Human Development, and many other health professional organizations recommend meeting calcium needs through foods, particularly dairy foods.

You need 3 to 4 servings of dairy foods a day to meet current recommendations for calcium intake. However, North Americans on average are consuming only about 1.5 servings of dairy a day. African Americans do worse, consuming only 1.1 servings of dairy a day. Studies also indicate that as people eat less from the Food Guide Pyramid food groups, they eat more from the tip. It is estimated that 27% of the energy consumed by adults is from energy-dense, nutrient-poor foods. As an example, carbonated soft drinks have displaced milk in the diet. In 1945 we consumed more than 4 times more milk than carbonated soft drinks, while in 1998 we con-

sumed 2⅓ times more carbonated soft drinks than milk. It has been observed that substitution for milk by soft drinks compromises calcium intake and may lead to adverse health effects.

Eating away from home appears to be a threat to meeting nutrient intake recommendations, such as calcium, as the calcium density of restaurant foods is lower than that for foods from home. Skipping meals may also limit nutrient intake. Studies have demonstrated that young children who skip breakfast consume less milk and compromise the nutrient quality of their diet. The misperception that dairy foods are fattening may result in reduced consumption, especially among adolescent girls. In addition, dairy consumption may be reduced due to lactose maldigestion, which can produce symptoms of intolerance when too much lactose is consumed. However, it has been demonstrated that lactose maldigestors can consume up to 1500 mg of calcium a day from dairy foods without experiencing symptoms of intolerance. To prevent symptoms of intolerance, select dairy foods that are low in lactose or lactose-free. One can drink milk with meals, consume yogurt with active cultures, or consume smaller servings over time to increase tolerance. Overall, the real and perceived barriers to consumption of dairy foods can be easily overcome with small eating behavior changes.

Why This Focus on Calcium?

Meeting calcium needs has been associated with reduced risk of osteoporosis, hypertension, colon/breast cancer, kidney stones, lead exposure, premenstrual syndrome (PMS), and obesity/overweight. More recent research data indicate that consumption of calcium from food sources, such as dairy foods, has a stronger and more consistent effect on some of these disease relationships than use of calcium supplements. This is likely due to the fact that other dairy nutrients (potassium, magnesium, phosphorus) probably have a modulating effect. Calcium-related disorders are the result of decreased calcium reserve, decreased food residue calcium in the intestinal chyme, or from adaptive hormonal mechanisms that work to maintain extracellular levels of calcium.

Recommendations for calcium intake have been set to provide maximal retention. Assuring the highest level of retention will build calcium reserves (the skeleton) to their genetic maximum during growth and minimize age-related losses. When calcium intake is low, inadequate amounts are deposited in the body's bone reserves. This increases the risk of osteoporosis. When calcium intake is at a level to supply maximum retention, only a minimal adaptive response will be required to insure extracellular levels. When intake is below the amount needed for maximum retention, adaptive hormonal responses will be activated to ensure extracellular calcium is maintained at adequate levels. It is when these hormonal (parathyroid hormone, 1,25 $(OH)_2$ vitamin D) systems are activated that they can have effects on organ and cell systems that increase the risk of hypertension, pre-eclampsia, PMS, polycystic ovary syndrome, and weight gain/obesity. For example, when calcium intake is low the levels of parathyroid hormone and 1,25 $(OH)_2$ vitamin D in circulation increase. These hormones affect smooth muscle cells that line the arteries, causing an increase in intracellular levels of free calcium, which signals the arteries to constrict, resulting in an elevation in blood pressure.

Another way calcium impacts disease risk is through its interaction with other dietary constituents in the intestinal lumen. Unabsorbed dietary calcium can bind certain food constituents that may be harmful and render them inactive. The risk of calcium oxalate kidney stones can be reduced with binding of the oxalate in the intestinal lumen by calcium, which prevents its absorption and subsequent clearance by the kidneys. Calcium may reduce colon cancer risk through the binding to free fatty acids and bile acids to neutralize their irritating effect on the colon. Calcium also competes with lead for absorption by the intestine. Thus, high residues of calcium in the intestinal chyme can reduce lead intoxication. Meeting calcium needs is important to ensure residual amounts are available to interact with potentially harmful constituents in the intestinal lumen.

Look to Foods First

Consuming calcium-rich foods is the preferred approach to achieving optimal intakes. Meeting calcium needs with foods can increase the intake of newly identified food components with potential health effects. Conjugated linoleic acid and sphingolipids found in milk fat have been observed to have anticancer effects. Consumption of calcium-fortified foods and supplements are options for those who cannot meet their needs from foods. However, their use does not correct the poor dietary pattern that is the underlying cause for low calcium intake in North America. Increasing calcium intake, through the consumption of dairy foods can be easily done and improves the overall nutrient quality of the diet.

Dr. Miller is Senior Vice President, Nutrition and Scientific Affairs, National Dairy Council and President of the American College of Nutrition (2001–2002). His considerable expertise in calcium nutrition is widely recognized.

Food Sources of Calcium

Food Item and Amount	*Calcium (mg)*
Parmesan cheese, 2 oz	780
Romano cheese, 2 oz	605
Swiss cheese, 2 oz	545
Plain yogurt, 1 cup	450
Fortified orange juice, 1 cup	350
Cheddar cheese, 1.5 oz	305
1% milk, 1 cup	300
Buttermilk, 1 cup	285
Spinach, 1 cup	250
Salmon, 3 oz	210
Total Raisin Bran cereal, ¾ cup	180
Sardines, 2 oz	170
Chocolate pudding, ½ cup	160
Tofu, ½ cup	140

Adequate Intake, adults, 1000 mg;
Adequate Intake, adults over 50, 1200 mg

Some calcium supplements are poorly digested, because they do not readily dissolve. To test for solubility, put a supplement in 6 oz of cider vinegar. Stir every 5 minutes. It should dissolve within 30 minutes.

Critical | Thinking

Manuela is a vegan. She stopped eating meat and dairy products when she was 12 years old and is now in her mid-twenties. She wants to start a family but is concerned about whether she can obtain enough calcium from her diet to ensure her baby's health. How can she consume enough calcium to meet her own and her baby's needs?

To estimate your calcium intake, use the rule of 300s. Give yourself 300 mg for calcium provided by a typical diet of moderate energy intake. Add to that another 300 mg for every 8 oz of milk or yogurt or 1.5 ounces of cheese you consume. If you eat a lot of tofu, almonds, or sardines or drink calcium-fortified beverages, use Table 11-5 or food composition tables to obtain a more accurate estimate of your calcium intake.

8% calcium by weight. Despite these consideration, calcium citrate may be a good choice for people prone to kidney stones. In contrast, calcium carbonate may elevate the risk of kidney stones in certain people, while the risk may be actually lowered by calcium citrate (as well as the calcium in dairy products). Other forms of calcium in supplements include calcium gluconate and calcium lactate.

Calcium carbonate is the most common supplement used. People with ample output of gastric acid should generally take this supplement between meals or at bedtime in doses of about 500 mg. This practice enhances absorption and limits its negative impact on absorption of other minerals, such as iron. People with low gastric acid production, such as older persons, should take the calcium carbonate supplement with meals, so that what little acid is produced during digestion can aid absorption. People with low gastric acid production also can use a supplement containing calcium citrate, which is acidic itself, between meals. The lower percentage of calcium in calcium citrate, however, requires using a greater number or size of pills or consuming it in a tablet form that is designed to be dissolved first in water.

Some calcium supplements pose a risk for lead toxicity. Currently, FDA has no standards for lead in food supplements, but in the future it does plan to regulate the lead content of supplements, including calcium. Until then, it is important to avoid bonemeal, the worst offender when it comes to lead. Tablet or liquid calcium supplements with the USP (United States Pharmacopeia) seal of approval are much less likely than others to contain high concentrations of lead or other contaminants.

Usually, taking 1000 mg of calcium daily in divided doses of 500 mg each in the form of calcium carbonate or calcium citrate is safe, but people using a supplement should notify their physician of the practice. Still, many people have difficulty adhering to a supplement regimen. In contrast, regular food habits can be integrated easily into a routine. In addition, it is difficult to consume an excess amount of calcium in foods. All this points to focusing first on improving diet when addressing calcium needs.

Calcium Needs

The Adequate Intake for calcium for adults ranges from 1000 to 1200 mg/day. For adolescents between the ages of 9 and 18, the Adequate Intake is set higher at 1300 mg/day to contribute to building a higher bone mass.[7] The Adequate Intake for adults is based on the amount of calcium needed each day to offset calcium losses in urine, feces and other routes. The Adequate Intake for young people includes an additional amount to allow for increases in bone mass during growth and development. The Daily Value for calcium used on food and supplement labels is 1000 mg.

In North America, average calcium intakes range from approximately 600 to 800 mg/day for women and 800 to 1000 mg/day for men. About 25% of women consume only about 300 mg/day. Thus, dietary intakes of calcium by many women, especially young women, are well below the Adequate Intake amount, whereas intakes by most men are roughly equivalent to it.

Calcium Deficiency

The most common calcium-related disease is osteoporosis, but calcium is not the only nutrient needed to maintain bone health (review Table 11-4). When experiencing low blood calcium, the body withdraws calcium from bone to preserve indispensable functions of calcium, such as those that keep the heart and muscles working. Still, this preservation may not be 100% effective in preserving all nonbone calcium functions. Along these lines, there is some evidence that a low calcium intake may increase blood pressure and the risk of certain cancers (by affecting cell turnover). Some recent research is indicating that low calcium intake is also associated with low bone mass in growing children.

Although it is assumed that calcium intake is a factor in most cases of bone loss, the exact contribution of calcium intake versus other factors is hard to quantify. Bone loss is not due to a calcium deficiency in the same way that scurvy is due to a vitamin C deficiency. In the latter case, low vitamin C intake is typically the only factor, whereas

Table 11-5 A Tool for Estimating Current Calcium Intake

For all of the following foods, write the number of servings eaten in a day. Total the number of servings in each category and then multiply the totals by the milligrams of calcium for each category. Finally, add the total milligrams to estimate calcium intake for that day.

Food	Serving Size	Number of Servings	Calcium (mg)	Total Calcium (mg)
Plain low-fat yogurt	1 cup	______		
Nonfat dry milk powder	½ cup	______		
	Total servings	______	× 400	= ______ mg
Canned sardines (with bones)	3 oz	______		
Fruit flavored yogurt	1 cup	______		
Skim or low-fat milk, buttermilk	1 cup	______		
Whole milk, chocolate milk	1 cup	______		
Parmesan cheese (grated)	¼ cup	______		
Swiss cheese	1 oz	______		
	Total servings	______	× 300	= ______ mg
Cheese (all other hard cheese)	1 oz	______		
Pancakes	3	______		
	Total servings	______	× 200	= ______ mg
Canned pink salmon	3 oz	______		
Tofu (processed with calcium)	4 oz	______		
	Total servings	______	× 150	= ______ mg
Collards or turnip greens, cooked	½ cup	______		
Ice cream or ice milk	½ cup	______		
Almonds	1 oz	______		
	Total servings	______	× 75	= ______ mg
Chard, cooked	½ cup	______		
Cottage cheese	½ cup	______		
Corn tortilla	1 med	______		
Orange	1 med	______		
	Total servings	______	× 50	= ______ mg
Kidney, lima, or navy beans, cooked	½ cup	______		
Broccoli	½ cup	______		
Carrot, raw	1 med	______		
Dates or raisins	¼ cup	______		
Egg	1 large	______		
Whole-wheat bread	1 slice	______		
Peanut butter	2 tbsp	______		
	Total servings	______	× 25	= ______ mg
Calcium-fortified orange juice	6 oz	______		
Calcium-fortified snack bars	1 each	______		
Calcium-fortified breakfast bars	½ bar	______		
	Total servings	______	× 200	= ______ mg
Calcium supplements	1 each	______	× 500	= ______ mg
			Total calcium intake	= ______ mg

Other calcium sources to consider include many breakfast cereals (100 to 250 mg per cup) and some multivitamin and mineral supplements (up to 500 mg per tablet).

Reprinted with permission from *Topics in Clinical Nutrition*, "Putting Calcium into Perspective for Your Clients," G. Wardlaw and N. Weese; 11:1, p. 29. © 1995 Aspen Publishers, Inc.

multiple factors likely contribute to most cases of bone loss. It is difficult to pinpoint the extent to which various factors contribute to bone health, because the disease can take decades to develop. So, studies have to look back at what happened over a long period of time, or look forward at what could happen.

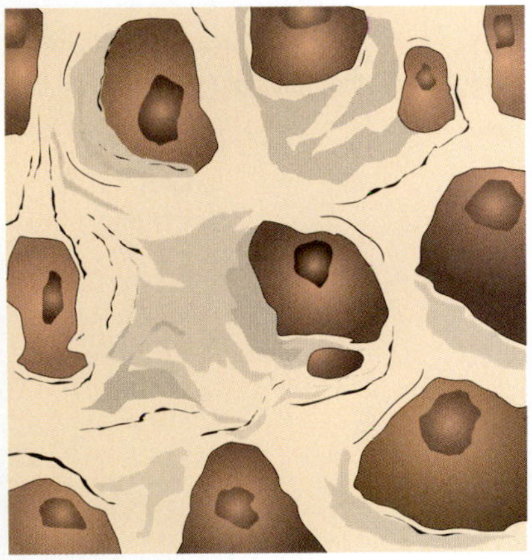

Normal bone

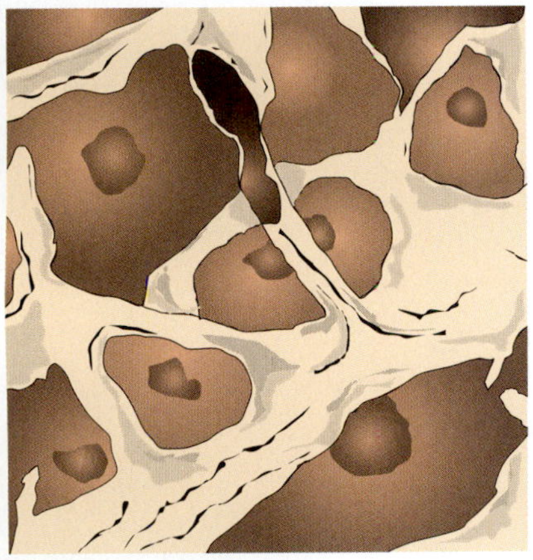

Osteoporotic bone

Figure 11-12 Normal and osteoporotic bone. Note in the lower picture how there is much less trabecular bone. It is especially critical for the horizontal trabeculae to extend continuously—without breaks—between the areas of vertical trabeculae. Any break in either the horizontal or more vertical trabecular beams weakens the support system of a bone and increases the risk for bone fracture. And, once these beams are broken, there is currently no way to rebuild them. This is why it is so important to limit bone loss as people age.

Failure to maintain adequate bone mass in the body throughout life first leads to a state of **osteopenia.** Osteopenia can be caused by the vitamin D deficiency disease osteomalacia, the use of certain medications, cancer, and other conditions. The diagnosis of osteoporosis generally is made when the bone loss becomes marked and/or a fracture occurs and there is no obvious cause, such as those just listed (Fig. 11-12). Typically both cortical and trabecular portions of the bone are affected, and particularly the trabecular portion. People who develop more bone by early adulthood can sustain greater age-related bone loss with less fracture risk than those with who have built less bone. Thus, osteoporosis is considered to be a "pediatric disease" with geriatric consequences.[2]

Osteoporosis currently leads to approximately 1.5 million fractures per year, resulting in over $14 billion in direct health-care costs. Many older women in North America show low values for bone mass, and therefore at risk for these fractures.[16]

As women mature, different strategies for preventing osteoporosis are needed, based on the risk factors present.[19] Young women should meet calcium, vitamin D, and other nutrient needs, as well as see a physician with any sign of irregular menstruation. In young women, regular menstruation is a main contributor to bone maintenance, as evidenced by low bone mass in some nonmenstruating female athletes and other women with irregular menstruation (e.g., those with anorexia nervosa). An active lifestyle that includes weight-bearing physical activity is also important (to build and maintain muscle mass). Greater muscle mass linked to physical activity is associated with greater bone mass, as muscle keeps tension on bone.[2] Still, physical activity cannot prevent the bone loss associated with irregular menstruation. Thus, female athletes with irregular menstruation should be closely monitored by a physician.

Smoking and excessive alcohol intake decrease bone mass at any age. Smoking lowers the estrogen concentration in the blood in women, increasing bone loss. Alcohol is toxic to bone cells, and alcoholism is probably a major undiagnosed and unrecognized cause of osteoporosis. Moderation in phosphorus, caffeine, sodium, and protein intake is also advised. These are especially problematic when insufficient calcium is consumed.[19]

At menopause, women should discuss approved osteoporosis-related therapies with a physician. They also need to accurately track their height. A decrease of more than 1½ inches from premenopausal values is a sign that significant bone loss is taking place (Fig. 11-13). Currently, there are four medical therapies that can be used to slow bone loss at menopause in women.[3] Some can even be used in men who develop low bone mass. The approved drugs are estrogen (various forms are available); bisphosphonates (alendronate [Fosamax] and risedronate [Actonel]); selective estrogen receptor modulators (SERMs) (raloxifene [Evista]); and calcitonin (nasal form is Miacalcin). Estrogen and SERMs blunt bone turnover by binding to receptors on bone; bisphosphonates blunt bone resorption by binding to bone mineral; and calcitonin inhibits osteoclast activity and, so, bone resorption. All these medications have side effects, so use needs to be tailored to a person's current health status. The latest thinking is that estrogen replacement is most useful for treating menopausal symptoms such as hot flashes, while the **bisphosphonates** are most useful for preventing bone loss.[3, 19] The recent trend to use bisphosphonates as the major form of medical therapy for osteoporosis rather than estrogen replacement stems from the observation that greater than 5 to 10 years of estrogen use increases the risk for breast and some other forms of cancer, such as in the ovaries. If a woman at menopause begins estrogen therapy to relieve related menopausal symptoms, experts suggest she should consider switching to another form of osteoporosis therapy as soon as possible.[18] FDA recently supported this recommendation. Any use of these medications also benefits from meeting calcium and vitamin D needs.[19]

Older men and women need to stay physically active—including some weight-bearing and resistance activities—and they should meet the Adequate Intake for calcium set for their particular age. This combination of physical activity and calcium intake is most likely to limit bone loss in some areas of the body, such as the hip. Older people also need to minimize the risk for falls, especially by limiting their use of medications and alcohol, which might disturb coordination, and they should take corrective measures if visual function is impaired. Hip protective garments are also available to

osteopenia Decreased bone mass caused by cancer, hyperthyroidism, or other reasons.

bisphosphonates Compounds primarily composed of carbon and phosphorus that bind to bone mineral and in turn reduce bone breakdown.

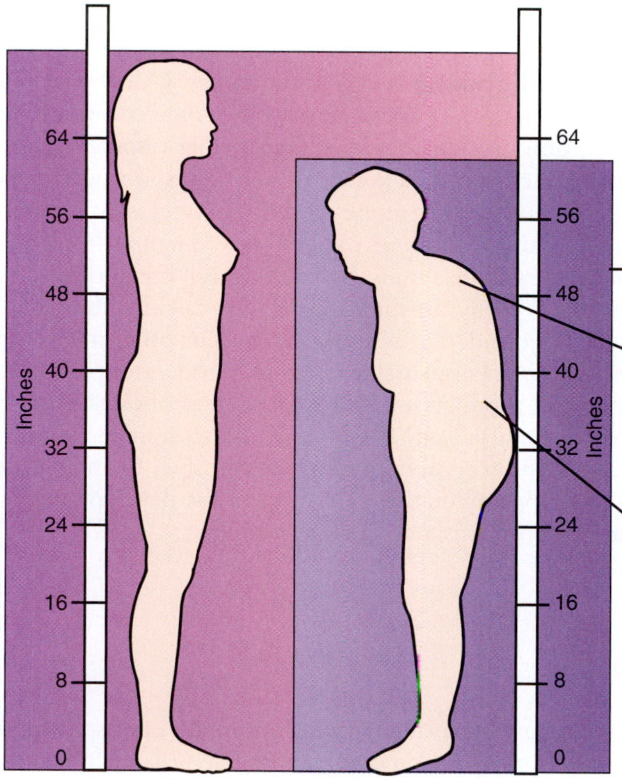

Figure 11-13 A loss of height and a distorted body shape are common signs of osteoporosis. Monitor your adult height changes to detect early osteoporosis. All women 65 years and older should be screened for this disease. Medicare covers the cost of the needed DEXA (dual energy X-ray absorptiometry) bone scan (see Fig. 13-10 in Chapter 13). It measures bone mass and bone density in the spine, hip, and total body, using a small amount of X-ray radiation. The ability of a bone to block the path of the radiation is used as a measure of bone mass and bone density at that bone site. Younger women are advised to have the same test at menopause if they have associated risk factors or if the results of the screening would help them decide what treatment plan is appropriate at menopause. A less accurate measure uses ultrasound evaluation of the foot.

reduce hip fracture risk. Regular sun exposure and the consumption of food sources of vitamin D are very important. Supplements of about 20 to 25 μg (800 to 1000 IU) are also appropriate (see Chapter 9).[13] To find out more about osteoporosis, check out the website of the National Osteoporosis Foundation (www.nof.org) or call 800-464-6700. Another helpful website is that of the National Dairy Council (www.nationaldairycouncil.org).

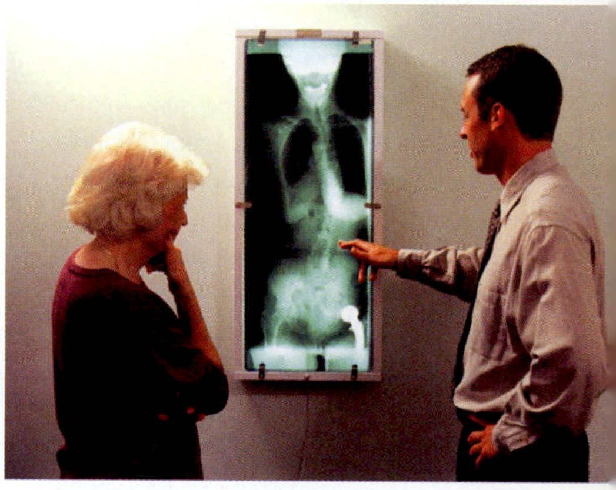

Fractures of the vertebrae in the spine are a typical result of osteoporosis in older women.

Toxicity of Calcium

Normally, the small intestine prevents excess calcium from being absorbed. If, at this level of control, the system breaks down, the calcium concentration in the blood may rise and lead to calcification of the kidneys and other organs, irritability, headache, kidney failure, kidney stones in some people, possibly prostate cancer, and decreased absorption of other minerals.[7] Ordinarily, calcium in food and usual doses of calcium supplements do not pose a health threat because it is present in relatively modest amounts. Calcium toxicity is reported to occur only among individuals using excessive amount of supplemental calcium. The Upper Level for calcium is 2500 mg/day, based on the risk of developing kidney stones.

Case Scenario | Follow-up

Jana is increasing her chances of developing osteoporosis later in life because of her current high-risk lifestyle. Many factors contributing to her potential risk include physical inactivity, smoking, and poor dietary intake of calcium and other important minerals. If Jana remains a vegan, she especially needs to find some reliable sources of calcium. These could include calcium-fortified juices, calcium-fortified bread and snack bars, and calcium-fortified chocolate candies. Tofu (made with calcium) is another potential source, as well as calcium-fortified soy milk. Meeting the Adequate Intake of 1300 mg/day for her age would not be that hard if she were to make a conscious effort to use these calcium-rich foods and/or find other rich sources.

Concept | Check

About 99% of calcium in the body is found in the bones. Calcium requires a slightly acid pH and the vitamin D hormone for efficient absorption. Factors that reduce calcium absorption include large amounts of fiber (especially wheat bran), decreased estrogen production, and a great excess of phosphorus in the diet. Blood calcium is regulated primarily by hormones and does not closely reflect daily intake. Aside from its critical role in bone, calcium also functions in blood clotting, muscle contraction, nerve-impulse transmission, and cell metabolism. A person can decrease risk for osteoporosis by consuming adequate calcium and vitamin D; weight-bearing exercise; considering bisphosphonates or other medications that decrease bone loss, if a postmenopausal female; and moderating sodium, alcohol, and caffeine intake. Dairy products are rich food sources of calcium. Certain calcium-fortified foods, such as some beverages, are rich sources as well. Supplemental forms, such as calcium carbonate, are well absorbed by most people. However, overzealous supplementation can result in the development of kidney stones and other health problems among some people.

Phosphorus (P)

Efficient absorption plus the wide availability in food makes phosphorus a much less important major mineral than calcium in diet planning.

People who have experienced weight loss and long-standing poor nutrient intake are at risk of low blood phosphorus and a related condition called refeeding syndrome. If these individuals are aggressively refed, such as in a hospital or in a famine relief setting (in the developing world), much of the small amount of phosphorus in the bloodstream shifts into cells in order to participate in essential metabolic pathways. This reduces phosphorus in the blood even further; it can cause blood phosphorus to be so low that respiratory failure and other critical health conditions may result. To avoid this problem, clinicians generally check blood phosphorus before feeding such a person, so as to correct a phosphorus deficiency if present. Under such circumstances, people then are gradually refed and blood phosphorus is monitored to make sure it remains within the normal range.

Absorption, Transport, and Excretion of Phosphorus

The body absorbs phosphorus quite efficiently, up to about 70% of dietary intake in adults. The active vitamin D hormone 1,25 $(OH)_2$ vitamin D enhances phosphorus absorption, as it does for calcium, but most absorption occurs by passive absorption based on the phosphorus concentration in the lumen of the small intestine and colon. Excretion of phosphorus is achieved via the kidneys. This is the primary mechanism by which blood phosphorus is regulated, which in turn makes phosphorus available to all cells. This mechanism differs from that of calcium, in which changes in absorption are a more significant factor.[7]

Functions of Phosphorus

Phosphorus plays many roles in the body. It is found in abundance in body tissues. Approximately 80% is found in bones and teeth in the form of calcium phosphate. The remainder of phosphate is found in every cell in the body and in the extracellular fluid, as PO_4^{2-}. Phosphorus is a component of many enzyme systems, adenosine triphosphate (ATP), DNA and RNA, and the phospholipids in cell membranes. It also participates in acid-base balance.[7]

Phosphorus in Foods

Milk, cheese, yogurt, bakery products, and meat provide most of the phosphorus in the adult diet. Cereals, bran, eggs, nuts, and fish are also sources. About 20 to 30% of dietary phosphorus comes from food additives, especially in baked goods, cheeses, processed meats, and many soft drinks (about 75 mg per 12-oz [⅓ liter] serving of soft drinks). Next time you have a soft drink, look for a listing of phosphoric acid on the label.

Phosphorus Needs

The RDA is 700 mg/day. Phosphorus needs are based on the amount that maintains an adequate blood concentration. Adults consume about 1000 to 1600 mg or more of phosphorus per day. Thus, a phosphorus deficiency is unlikely in healthy adults, especially because it is so efficiently absorbed. The Daily Value for phosphorus used on food and supplement labels is 1000 mg.

Phosphorus Deficiency

A chronic deficiency of phosphorus can contribute to bone loss, decreased growth, and poor tooth development. Symptoms of rickets may occur in phosphorus-deficient children. Furthermore, symptoms of a deficiency include anorexia, weight loss, weakness, irritability, stiff joints, and bone pain.[1] Marginal phosphorus status can be found in preterm infants, alcoholics, older people on nutrient-poor diets, people experiencing long-term bouts of diarrhea and weight loss, and people who use aluminum-containing antacids daily (in the small intestine, these bind phosphorus).

Toxicity of Phosphorus

Typical phosphorus intakes in and of themselves do not appear to be toxic for healthy adults, but large amounts can lead to problems in patients with certain kidney diseases. In this case, reduced excretion by the kidneys leads to high blood concentrations, which in turn can cause calcium-phosphorus precipitates to form in body tissues, as well as contribute to bone loss by inducing the release of parathyroid hormone (see Chapter 9 to review the relationship between blood phosphorus and parathyroid hormone).

A chronic imbalance in the calcium-to-phosphorus ratio in the diet, resulting from a high phosphorus intake coupled with a low calcium intake, can also contribute to bone loss. This situation most likely arises when calcium needs are not met, as can occur in adolescents and adults who regularly substitute soft drinks for milk or otherwise underconsume calcium. The Upper Level for phosphorus in adulthood is 3-4 g/day, based on the risk of developing impaired kidney function.[7]

Food Sources of Phosphorus

Food Item and Amount	*Phosphorus (mg)*
Plain yogurt, 1 cup	350
Swiss cheese, 2 oz	345
Almonds, ½ cup	340
Sunflower seeds, 1 oz	330
1% milk, 1 cup	235
Cheddar cheese, 1.5 oz	220
Salmon, 3 oz	220
Sirloin steak, 3 oz	210
Raisin Bran cereal, 1 cup	215
Chicken breast, 3 oz	180
Roasted turkey, 3 oz	180
Pot roast, 3 oz	170
Lean ham, 3 oz	165
American cheese, 1 slice	155
Egg, 1 hard-boiled	100

RDA adults, 700 mg

Meats are rich in phosphorus.

Magnesium (Mg)

Magnesium, like calcium, is a divalent cation. Because magnesium is found in chlorophyll, green leafy vegetables are rich sources.

Absorption, Transport, Storage, and Excretion of Magnesium

We normally absorb about 40 to 60% of the magnesium in our diets, but absorption efficiency can increase up to about 80% if intakes are low. Both passive and active absorption in the small intestine is used. The active vitamin D hormone 1,25 $(OH)_2$ vitamin D enhances magnesium absorption to a limited extent. The kidneys primarily regulate the blood concentration of magnesium and are able to reduce magnesium loss into the urine when blood magnesium is low. Some magnesium is stored in bones; a small amount is stored in other tissues, such as muscles.[7]

Functions of Magnesium

Magnesium has a vital role in a varying range of biochemical and physiological processes. Most enzymes that utilize ATP require magnesium (more than 300 enzymes total). Magnesium ions bind to ATP to form active ATP. One of the enzyme systems using magnesium pumps sodium out of cells and potassium into cells. This process seems especially sensitive to magnesium deficiency. Magnesium also contributes to DNA and RNA synthesis during cell proliferation. Its role in calcium metabolism contributes to bone structure. Magnesium is also important for nerve and heart function, as well as insulin release from the pancreas and ultimate insulin action on cells. Other possible benefits of magnesium include decreasing blood pressure by dilating arteries, and preventing heart rhythm abnormalities.[7]

Food Sources of Magnesium

Food Item and Amount	*Magnesium (mg)*
Spinach, 1 cup	157
Squash, 1 cup	105
Wheat germ, ¼ cup	90
Raisin Bran cereal, 1 cup	90
Navy beans, ½ cup	54
Peanut butter, 2 tablespoons	51
Black-eyed peas, ½ cup	46
Plain yogurt, 1 cup	43
Kidney beans, ½ cup	43
Sunflower seeds, ¼ cup	41
Broccoli, 1 cup	37
Banana, 1 medium	34
1% milk, 1 cup	34
Watermelon, 1 slice	32
Oatmeal, ½ cup	28
Whole-wheat bread, 1 slice	25

RDA, adult men = 400 mg
RDA, adult women = 310 mg

Magnesium in Foods

The richest sources of magnesium are plant products, such as whole grains (such as wheat bran), broccoli, squash, green leafy vegetables, beans, nuts, seeds, and chocolate. Animal products, such as milk and meats, supply some magnesium, although less than the foods just listed. Another source of magnesium is hard tap water, which contains a high mineral content (hard water also contains calcium). About 45% of dietary magnesium comes from vegetables, fruits, grains, and nuts, whereas about 30% comes from milk, meat, and eggs. Refined foods generally are low in magnesium.

Magnesium Needs

The RDA for magnesium is 400 mg/day for men 19 to 30 years of age and 310 mg/day for women 19 to 30 years of age. Magnesium needs increase slightly (an additional 10 mg/day) beyond this age for adult men and women. Magnesium needs are based on a daily intake that equals daily losses. The Daily Value for magnesium used on food and supplement labels is 400 mg.

Adult men consume an average of 325 mg/day, whereas women consume closer to 225 mg/day. Women particularly should find some good food sources of magnesium that they like and eat them regularly.[7]

Magnesium Deficiency

Animals deficient in magnesium become very irritable and, with severe deficiency, eventually suffer convulsions and often die. In humans a magnesium deficiency causes a rapid heartbeat, sometimes accompanied by weakness, muscle spasms, disorientation, nausea and vomiting, and seizures. These symptoms may be related to abnormal nerve cell function due to impairment of sodium and potassium pumping. Currently, an intravenous dose of magnesium is being investigated as part of the treatment during the early phases of a heart attack. A fall in blood calcium is also seen in magnesium deficiency, as well as resistance to 1,25 $(OH)_2$ vitamin D. It is possible that a chronically deficient intake of magnesium then may increase the risk of osteoporosis. Note that a magnesium deficiency develops very slowly because our bodies store it readily.[7]

Poor magnesium status is especially found among users of certain diuretics, which increase magnesium excretion in the urine. In addition, heavy perspiration for weeks in hot climates and bouts of long-standing diarrhea or vomiting cause significant magnesium loss. Alcoholism also increases the risk of a deficiency because dietary intake may be poor and because alcohol increases magnesium excretion in the urine. The disorientation and weakness associated with alcoholism closely resemble the behavior of people with low blood magnesium. People with diabetes and some other health problems may have high magnesium needs, which makes them vulnerable to marginal magnesium deficiency. The expression "marginal deficiency" should not be equated to mean of little importance. This deficiency, though not immediately producing classical signs of magnesium deficiency, could be serious in the long run. This marginal deficiency could aggravate the symptoms of a disease plus increase the risk of secondary complications (i.e., a heart attack in a diabetic person). Unfortunately, a lot of this is still speculative because diagnosis of a marginal magnesium deficiency is complex.

Nuts are a rich source of magnesium.

Toxicity of Magnesium

Magnesium toxicity does not occur in healthy people who eat typical foods. The Upper Level of 350 mg refers to supplement and other nonfood sources only, such as certain laxatives and antacids.[7] Resulting intakes above this amount can lead to diarrhea. Toxicity also can be seen in kidney failure because the kidneys primarily regulate blood magnesium. In this case, high blood magnesium leads to weakness, nausea, slowed breathing, eventual malaise, coma, and death. Older people in general are at particular risk of magnesium toxicity, as kidney function may be compromised.

Table 11-6 A Summary of the Major Minerals

Name	Major Functions	Deficiency Symptoms	People Most at Risk	RDA, Adequate Intake, or Minimum Requirement	Nutrient-Dense Dietary Sources	Results of Toxicity
Sodium	Functions as a major cation of the extracellular fluid; aids nerve impulse transmission; water balance.	Muscle cramps	People who severely restrict sodium to lower blood pressure (250–500 mg/day); excessive sweating	500 mg	Table salt, processed foods, condiments, sauces, soups, chips	Contributes to hypertension in susceptible individuals: leads to increased calcium loss in urine.
Potassium	Functions as a major cation of intracellular fluid; aids nerve impulse transmission; water balance.	Irregular heart beat, loss of appetite, muscle cramps	People who use potassium-wasting diuretics or have poor diets, as seen in poverty and alcoholism	2000 mg	Spinach, squash, bananas, orange juice, other vegetables and fruits, milk, meat, legumes, whole grains	Slowing of the heartbeat, as seen in kidney failure
Chloride	Functions as a major anion of the extracellular fluid; participates in acid production in stomach; aids nerve transmission; water balance.	Convulsions in infants	No one	750 mg	Table salt, some vegetables, processed foods	Linked to hypertension in susceptible people when combined with sodium
Calcium	Provides bone and tooth structure, blood clotting; aids nerve-impulse transmission; required for muscle contractions; contributes to cell permeability.	Increases the risk for osteoporosis.	Women, especially those who consume few dairy products	1000-1200 mg (age > 18 years) 1300 mg (age 9–18 years)	Dairy products, canned fish, leafy vegetables, tofu, fortified orange juice (and other fortified foods)	Intakes > 2.5 g/day (Upper Level) may cause kidney stones and other problems in susceptible people; poor mineral absorption in general.
Phosphorus	Required for bone and tooth strength; serves as part of various metabolic compounds; functions as major ion of intracellular fluid, acid-base balance.	Probably none; poor bone maintenance is a possibility.	Older people consuming very-nutrient-poor diets; possibly vegans and people with alcoholism	700 mg (age > 18 years) 1250 mg (age 9–18 years)	Dairy products, processed foods, fish, soft drinks, bakery products, meats	Impairs bone health in people with kidney failure; results in poor bone mineralization if calcium intakes are low. Upper Level is 3–4 g/day, based on the development of poor kidney function.
Magnesium	Provides bone strength; aids enzyme function; aids nerve and heart function.	Weakness, muscle pain, poor heart function	Women and patients on thiazide diuretics	Men: 400–420 mg Women: 310–320 mg	Wheat bran, green vegetables, nuts, chocolate, legumes	Causes diarrhea, as well as weakness in people with kidney failure. Upper Level of 350 mg/day refers to supplements only, based on the development of diarrhea.
Sulfur	Comprises part of vitamins and amino acids; aids drug detoxification; participates in acid-base balance.	None have been described.	No one, as long as protein needs are met	None	Protein foods	None are likely.

Protein-rich foods supply sulfur in the diet.

Sulfur (S)

The minerals discussed so far function in the body primarily in the form of charged ions. In contrast, much of the sulfur in the body occurs in nonionic forms as an integral component of organic compounds, such as the vitamins biotin and thiamin. Because the amino acids methionine and cysteine both contain sulfur, it also is present in proteins. Disulfide bridges form when the sulfur atoms in two cysteine residues bind to each other; these bridges stabilize the structure of many protein molecules (see Chapter 7). For example, this is necessary for the formation of collagen, the protein found in connective tissue, and for keratin, which is found in nails, skin, and hair. Ionic forms of sulfur, such as sulfate (SO_4^{2-}), participate in the acid-base balance in the body, are present in many substances found in the extracellular fluid, and play an important role in some drug-detoxifying pathways in the body.

We actually do not need to consume sulfur as such in our diets because proteins supply the sulfur we need. Sulfur compounds are also used to preserve foods (see Chapter 19).

Table 11-6 provides a summary of the major minerals.

Concept | Check

Magnesium is a mineral found mostly in plant foods. It is important for nerve and heart function and as an activator of many enzymes. Whole grains (bran portion), vegetables, nuts, seeds, milk, and meats are good food sources. Sulfur is incorporated into certain vitamins and amino acids. Its ability to bond with other sulfur atoms enables it to stabilize protein structure.

Summary

1. Water constitutes 50 to 70% of the human body. Its unique chemical properties enable it to dissolve substances as well as serve as a medium for chemical reactions, temperature regulation, and lubrication. Water also helps regulate the acid-base balance in the body. For adults, daily water needs are estimated at 1 ml/kcal expended.
2. Many minerals are vital for sustaining life. For humans, animal products are the most bioavailable sources of most minerals. Supplements of minerals exceeding the Daily Value, and especially the Upper Level, should be taken only under a physician's supervision because toxicity and nutrient interactions are a likely possibility.
3. Sodium, the major positive ion (cation) found outside cells, is vital in fluid balance and nerve impulse transmission. The North American diet provides abundant sodium through processed foods and table salt.
4. Potassium, the major positive ion (cation) found inside cells, has similar functions to those of sodium. Milk, fruits, and vegetables are good sources. Chloride is the major negative ion (anion) found outside cells. It is important in digestion as part of gastric hydrochloric acid and in immune and nerve functions. Table salt supplies most of the chloride in our diets.
5. Calcium forms a vital part of bone structure and is very important in blood clotting, muscle contraction, nerve transmission, and cell metabolism. Calcium absorption is enhanced by stomach acid and the active vitamin D hormone. Dairy products are rich calcium sources. Women are particularly at risk for not meeting calcium needs. They are also typically at risk of developing osteoporosis as they age. Numerous lifestyle and medical options help reduce this risk.
6. Phosphorus aids function of some enzymes and forms part of key metabolic compounds, cell membranes, and bone. It is efficiently absorbed, and deficiencies are rare. Typical food sources are dairy products, bakery products, and meats.
7. Magnesium is a mineral found mostly in plants. It is important for nerve and heart function and as an activator for many enzymes. Whole grains (bran portion), vegetables, nuts, seeds, milk, and meats are typical food sources. Sulfur is incorporated into certain vitamins and amino acids. Its ability to bond with other sulfur atoms enables it to stabilize protein structure.

Study Questions

1. Approximately how much water does one need each day to stay healthy? Identify at least two situations that increase the need for water. Then list three sources of water in the average person's diet.
2. Why are most minerals present in higher concentrations in animal foods than in plant foods?
3. How is water eliminated from the body? What physiological forces regulate this output?

4. What is the main physiological difference between teeth and bones?

5. Identify four factors that influence the bioavailability of minerals from food.

6. What is the relationship between sodium and water balance, and how is that relationship monitored as well as maintained in the body?

7. Within what physiological system do potassium, chloride, and calcium interact? What are the individual roles of these minerals in this system?

8. What might you tell a 12-year-old child about the importance of consuming sufficient calcium?

9. In terms of total amounts in the body, calcium and phosphorus are the first and second most abundant minerals, respectively. Name two ways in which phosphorus and calcium are alike and two ways in which they differ.

10. Describe the relationship between magnesium and the function/health of the heart.

Annotated References

1. Anderson JJB and others: Phosphorus. In Bowman BA, Russell RM (eds.): *Present knowledge in nutrition*. Washington, DC: ILSI Press, 2001.

   Phosphorus is one of the most plentiful elements on earth. Phosphorus is used in the body in all cellular processes, is a component of DNA and RNA, and provides structure and rigidity to the skeleton. Phosphorus is widespread in the food supply and is found in high-protein foods and in foods with phosphate additives, such as colas.

2. Anderson JJB: The important role of physical activity in skeletal development: How exercise may counter low calcium intake. *American Journal of Clinical Nutrition* 71:1384, 2000.

   A greater bone mass gained early in life is now considered a critical factor in protecting against osteoporotic fractures later in life. The critical years for skeletal growth and accumulation of bone mass are in the prepubertal and pubertal decades. These years are a particularly good time for regular physical activity, as it, along with adequate diet, increases bone mass.

3. Bare bones: How to keep yours strong. *Nutrition Action Healthletter*, p. 29, January/February 2002.

   This article provides a review of the current pharmacological treatments available for the treatment of osteoporosis. Low doses of estrogen are effective for treating menopausal symptoms and can safely be used by most women for 5 to 10 years following menopause. After 5 to 10 years, it is generally recommended that women with or at risk for osteoporosis switch to either a bisphosphonate or a selective estrogen receptor modulator (SERM).

4. Blood pressure perils. *Consumer Reports on Health*. Part 1 14(9):1, 2002, Part 2 14(10):6, 2002.

   Four key lifestyle factors to implement to prevent and treat hypertension are to maintain (or lose weight to attain) a healthy body weight; perform regular physical activity; follow a diet rich in low-fat dairy products, fruits, and vegetables; and moderate sodium intake.

5. Dawson-Hughes B: Osteoporosis. In Bowman BA, Russell RM (eds.): *Present knowledge in nutrition*. Washington, DC: ILSI Press, 2001.

   Heredity has a pronounced effect on the amount of bone one builds in youth. Also important are adequate calcium, vitamin D, and protein. Weight-bearing physical activity also contributes to a healthy skeleton.

6. Food and Nutrition Board, Commission on Life Sciences, National Research Council: *Recommended Dietary Allowances*, National Academy Press, 1989.

   Minimum requirements for water, sodium, potassium, and chloride are discussed. The Food and Nutrition Board will release new standards for water and some of the major minerals in the near future.

7. Food and Nutrition Board, Institute of Medicine: *Dietary Reference Intakes for calcium, phosphorus, magnesium, vitamin D, and fluoride*. Washington, DC: Standing Committee on the Scientific Evaluation of Dietary Reference Intakes National Academy Press, 1997.

   Dietary standards have recently been set for many major minerals. The rationale used to set RDA or Adequate Intakes and Upper Levels for these nutrients is discussed in detail.

8. Hooper L and others: Systematic review of long term effects of advice to reduce dietary salt in adults. *British Medical Journal* 325 (Sept 21):1, 2002.

   Advice to reduce salt intake is especially helpful for those on antihypertensive medications. Such advice to healthy people has less justification as the decline seen in blood pressure is small. Still, there appears to be no risk from implementing such advice.

9. Kaplan NM: The dietary guideline for sodium: Should we shake it up? No. *American Journal of Clinical Nutrition* 71:1020, 2000.

   The U.S. Dietary Guideline for sodium (2400 mg/day) may not be set low enough to prevent the development of hypertension in some people. In order to reduce sodium intake, certain interventions can be accomplished: promoting consumer label reading, targeting fast-food chains to offer alternative choices, and encouraging less salt added to processed foods.

10. Kleiner SM: Water: An essential but overlooked nutrient. *Journal of the American Dietetic Association* 99:200, 1999.

    Dehydration of as little as a 2% loss of body weight results in decreased physiological responses. New research indicates that fluid consumption in general and water consumption in particular can reduce the risk of kidney stones, certain cancers, obesity, and mitral valve prolapse. Adequate fluid intake is especially important for the overall health of older adults.

11. Loria CM and others: Choose and prepare foods with less salt: Dietary advice for all Americans. *Journal of Nutrition* 131:536S, 2001.

    Most North American adolescents and adults consume much more sodium than is recommended. Dietary advice to prepare foods with less salt is critical to reducing the number of cases of hypertension and its associated disease risks.

12. McCarron DA: The dietary guideline for sodium: Should we shake it up? Yes. *American Journal of Clinical Nutrition* 71:1013, 2000.

    Some experts have concluded that current sodium intakes in the majority of the North American population have only minimal effects on blood pressure. These experts feel that sodium restrictions are beneficial only to those in the older population group who have an established diagnosis of hypertension.

13. NIH Consensus Development Panel on Osteoporosis Prevention, Diagnosis, and Treatment: Osteoporosis prevention, diagnosis, and treatment. *Journal of the American Medical Association* 285:785, 2001.

    Optimal treatment of osteoporosis with any drug therapy also requires calcium and vitamin D intake meeting recommended levels. The preferred source of calcium is dietary. Calcium supplements need to be absorbable and should have United States Pharmacopeia designation.

14. Preuss H: Sodium, chloride, and potassium. In Bowman BA, Russell RM (eds.): *Present knowledge in nutrition*. Washington, DC: ILSI Press, 2001.

    Sodium and chloride are the primary extracellular electrolytes, and potassium is the primary intracellular cation. Sodium and chloride function in the body to regulate extracellular fluid volume. Potassium functions in the body in energy metabolism and membrane transport. While high intakes of sodium have been associated with increased risk of developing hypertension in salt-sensitive individuals, high intakes of potassium seem to be protective against hypertension.

15. Sacks F and others: Effects on blood pressure of reduced dietary sodium and the dietary

approaches to stop hypertension (DASH) diet. *New England Journal of Medicine* 344:3, 2001.

The DASH diet consists of generous amounts of fruits, vegetables, and low-fat dairy products and has been shown to be an effective diet for lowering blood pressure. Consuming a low-sodium diet in addition to following the DASH diet has been shown to reduce blood pressure even further in both individuals with and without hypertension.

16. Siris E and others: Identification and fracture outcomes of undiagnosed low bone mineral density in postmenopausal women: Results from the national osteoporosis risk assessment. *Journal of the American Medical Association* 286:2815, 2001.

Data from the recent National Osteoporosis Risk Assessment study indicate that osteopenia and osteoporosis are more common in women over the age of 50 in the United States than was previously thought. This study found that almost 40% of the women tested had osteopenia and over 7% had osteoporosis. Increased detection of these conditions is necessary to provide adequate treatment for this population.

17. Vander A and others: *Human physiology.* 8th ed. Boston: McGraw-Hill, 2001.

This is an excellent textbook to refer to for more information on the renin-angiotensin system and physiological mechanisms for maintaining water balance.

18. Vastag B: Hormone replacement therapy falls out of favor with expert committee. *Journal of the American Medical Association* 287:1923, 2002.

Hormone replacement therapy (HRT) has frequently been recommended to women for the prevention of heart disease, bone fractures, and depression. However, new findings from well-controlled clinical trials are calling into question the effectiveness of HRT for the prevention and/or treatment of these conditions. In addition, recent evidence seems to suggest that HRT may increase the risk for these and other serious conditions, including cancer. Therefore, many physicians are now being more cautious when it comes to prescribing HRT for long-term use.

19. What's best for your bones? *Consumer Reports on Health* 3(7):1, 2001 (July).

Many factors contribute to optimal bone health, including meeting calcium and vitamin D needs, regular strength training and aerobic physical activities that put stress on bones, not smoking, and drinking alcohol moderately if one drinks. Bisphosphonates currently are becoming the first choice of drug therapy for preventing or treating osteoporosis; newer versions need be taken only once per week.

20. Whelton PK and others: Primary prevention of hypertension. *Journal of the American Medical Association* 288:1882, 2002.

A healthy diet and active lifestyle should be implemented in adults to lessen or prevent rising blood pressure as one ages. Important goals are maintaining a healthy weight and eating many fruits and vegetables daily. Moderating salt and alcohol intake is also important.

Take | Action

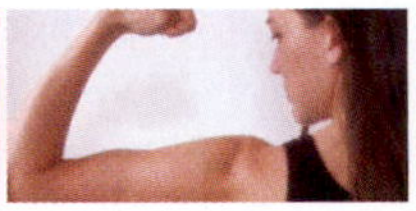

I. How Does Your Mineral Intake Measure Up?

To complete this activity, reexamine your nutritional assessment from Chapter 2. Compare your intake of selective minerals with the RDA or Adequate Intake (AI). Use your completed nutritional assessment to complete the following table. For each mineral, record your intake, the intake recommended, the percentage of that intake you consumed, and a +, −, or = to indicate an intake higher, lower, or equal to that intake.

Mineral	Intake	Needs	% of Needs	+/−/=
Calcium				
Phosphorus				
Sodium				
Potassium				
Chloride				
Magnesium				

Analysis

1. Which of your mineral intakes equaled or exceeded the RDA (or other standard set)? Do the nutrients for which you exceeded the desired amounts pose a likely risk for toxicity, based on the total amount consumed?

2. Which of your intakes were below the RDA (or other estimates of one's needs)?

3. What foods and cooking practices could be emphasized or deemphasized to modify your deficient intakes? Indicate for each food the specific amount of the missing nutrient(s) supplied.

Take | Action

II. Working for Denser Bones.

Osteoporosis and related low bone mass affect many adults in North America, especially older women. In fact, one-third of all women experience fractures because of this disease, amounting to about 1.5 million bone fractures per year.

This is a disease you can do something about. Some risk factors can't be changed, but others can. To what degree are you doing the things that can help prevent this debilitating disease? Answer yes or no to the following questions by placing an X in the appropriate blank.

	Yes	No
1. Do you average at least 10 to 20 minutes of sun exposure per day to at least your hands and face to get vitamin D, or do you drink vitamin D-fortified milk regularly?	______	______
2. Do you engage in weight-bearing physical activity (jogging, brisk walking, etc.) for at least 30 and preferably 60 minutes on most or all days of the week?	______	______
3. If you are a woman, do you experience regular menstruation?	______	______
4. Do you avoid smoking cigarettes?	______	______
5. Do you avoid regular consumption of large amounts (greater than one to two drinks per day) of alcohol?	______	______
6. Do you consume milk and other dairy products regularly or substitute other sources to meet at least the Adequate Intake for calcium for your age?	______	______
7. Do you regularly meet the Food Guide Pyramid recommendations for fruit and vegetable intake?	______	______
8. Do you moderate your intake of phosphorus, sodium, protein, and caffeine?	______	______

The more *yes* answers you have, the more you are actively preserving your bone density for the future. Also, remember that this is not just a consideration for women, because if men plan to live well into their 80s and 90s, they are also at risk for osteoporosis. In fact, about 14% of all spine fractures and 25% of all hip fractures linked to osteoporosis occur in men.

Minerals and Hypertension

More than 50 million North American adults have hypertension, as does one out of two of those over age 65. Blood pressure is expressed by two numbers. The higher number represents systolic blood pressure, which is the pressure in the arteries when the heart actively pumps blood. The second value is for diastolic blood pressure, which is the artery pressure when the heart is relaxed. Optimal systolic blood pressure is less than 120 mm of mercury (mm Hg). Optimal diastolic blood pressure is less than 80 mm Hg. A high diastolic pressure shows a strong relationship to various diseases (especially strokes and other cardiovascular diseases), as does a high systolic pressure.[20]

For adults, hypertension is defined as sustained systolic pressure exceeding 140 mm Hg or diastolic blood pressure exceeding 90 mm Hg (Table 11-7). Most cases of hypertension (about 95% of cases) have no clear-cut cause. It is described as primary, or essential, in nature (e.g., essential hypertension). Kidney disease, sleep-disordered breathing (sleep apnea), and other causes often lead to the other 5% of cases, known as secondary hypertension. African Americans are more likely than Caucasians to develop hypertension and to do so earlier in life. As a result, they also suffer more from hypertension-related diseases and, so, are particularly advised to have their blood pressure checked regularly and to have any evidence of hypertension treated aggressively.

Unless blood pressure is measured periodically, the development of hypertension is easily overlooked. Thus, it's described as a silent disorder, because it usually does not cause symptoms.[4] A physician usually does not treat hypertension with medication until the diastolic blood pressure measures at least 90 mm Hg and/or the systolic blood pressure reaches 140 mm Hg on three or more occasions.

Symptoms of Stroke

Individuals experiencing any of the following symptoms of stroke should seek immediate treatment. This is because physicians can administer drugs that can reduce the extent of the damage caused by most strokes (i.e., ischemic strokes). Currently about 700,000 North Americans suffer strokes each year.

- Sudden disturbances in sight, speech, and steadiness
- Sudden sleepiness or severe headache
- Sudden temporary blindness in one eye or other visual effects
- Sudden numbness, weakness, or paralysis of an arm, a leg, or an entire side of the body
- Sudden difficulty with speech or the ability to swallow
- Coma or convulsions

Why Control Blood Pressure?

Blood pressure needs to be controlled mainly to prevent cardiovascular disease, kidney disease, strokes and related declines in brain function, poor blood circulation in the legs, problems with vision, and sudden death. All these conditions are much more likely to be found in individuals with hypertension than in people with normal blood pressure. Smoking and elevated blood lipoproteins (LDL and VLDL) make these diseases even more likely. Individuals with hypertension need to be diagnosed and treated as soon as possible, as the condition generally progresses to a more serious stage over time and even resists therapy if it persists for years.[4]

Causes of Hypertension

Blood pressure usually increases as a person ages. Some increase is caused by atherosclerosis. As plaque builds up in the arteries, the arteries become less flexible and cannot expand. When vessels remain rigid, blood pressure remains high. Eventually, the plaque begins to choke off the blood supply to the kidneys, decreasing their ability to control blood volume and, in turn, blood pressure.

Table 11-7 Classification of Blood Pressure for Adults Age 18 Years and Older in Millimeters of Mercury (mm Hg)*

Category	Systolic		Diastolic
Optimal	< 120	and	< 80
Normal	< 130	and	< 85
High-normal†	130–139	or	85–89
Hypertension			
Stage 1	140–159	or	90–99
Stage 2	160–179	or	100–109
Stage 3	≥ 180	or	≥ 110

*Not taking high blood pressure drugs and not acutely ill

†People with diabetes or kidney or heart disease should be treated at this stage.

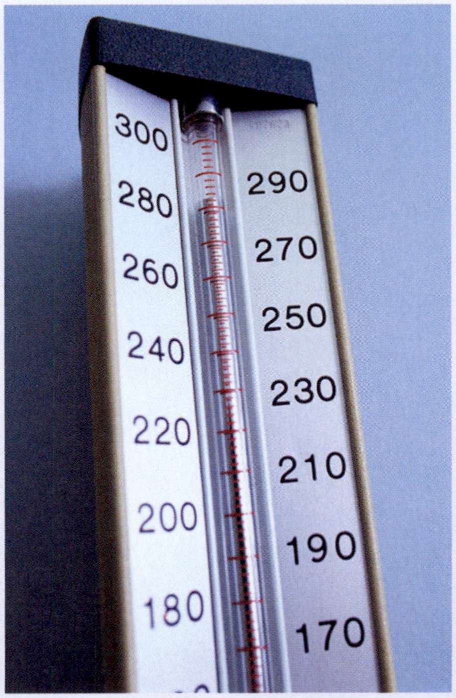

High blood pressure is harmful to many organs in the body. Maintenance of healthy systolic and diastolic blood pressure is a key to disease prevention throughout life.

Preliminary studies show a link between bone lead concentrations and increased risk of hypertension. More information is needed, but it is suspected that even small amounts of lead stored over decades may damage the kidneys and eventually result in hypertension. This is just one of the deleterious effects of lead exposure (see Chapter 19 for more information on lead).

The enzyme renin (secreted by the kidneys) and some hormonelike compounds affect blood pressure. Medications are available to reduce their effect on the renin-angiotensin system.[4]

Obesity is often associated with high blood pressure, especially in women. In fact, overweight people have six times greater risk of having hypertension than lean people. Overall, obesity is considered the number 1 lifestyle factor related to hypertension.[20] The increase in fat mass increases the need for blood circulation. The extra miles of associated blood vessels increases work by the heart and increase blood pressure. Elevated blood insulin concentration associated with insulin-resistant adipose cells is another reason for this link to obesity. Insulin increases sodium retention in the body and accelerates atherosclerosis. Additionally, an estimated 65% of people with diabetes also have hypertension.

A weight loss of as little as 10 to 15 pounds often can help treat hypertension. This, then, can decrease the need for hypertension drugs, which, by themselves may cause headache, impotence, reduced exercise tolerance, persistent cough, and other side effects. The sleep apnea linked to hypertension also typically improves with weight loss.

Inactivity also is associated with hypertension. It is considered the number 2 lifestyle factor related to hypertension.[20] If an obese person can engage in regular physical activity (at least five days per week for 30 to 45 minutes per session) and lose weight, blood pressure often returns to normal.[4]

Excess alcohol intake is responsible for about 10% of all cases of hypertension, especially in middle-aged males and among African Americans in general. It is considered the number 3 lifestyle factor related to hypertension.[20] When hypertension is caused by excessive alcohol intake, it is usually reversible. A sensible intake for people with hypertension is two or fewer drinks per day for men and one or no drinks per day for women and older adults. These are the same recommendations given to healthy adults. As discussed in Chapter 8, some studies suggest that such a moderate alcohol intake reduces the risk of ischemic stroke. These data, however, should not be used to encourage alcohol use in nonconsumers.

Salt and Blood Pressure

Excess salt intake tends to increase blood pressure, particularly in African Americans, older persons, obese persons, and people in general who are susceptible to developing a problem regulating sodium concentration in the body.[8] This last group is termed "sodium sensitive" because they are not good at excreting excess salt via the kidney. This excess salt retention has some tendency to increase blood pressure in these people. It is not clear whether the sodium ion or the chloride ion is most responsible for the effect. Still, as reviewed in this chapter, if one reduces sodium intake, chloride intake naturally falls; the opposite is also true. For the most part, when nutrition recommendations suggest consuming less sodium, that is equivalent to saying consume less salt. Since only some North Americans are very susceptible to increases in blood pressure from salt intake, it is likely only the number 4 lifestyle factor related to hypertension.[12] Thus, it is unfortunate that salt intake receives the major portion of public attention with regard to hypertension; obesity, inactivity, and alcohol abuse should be given much more attention. This is especially true for people who are not sodium sensitive. Again, about half the people with hypertension are not. However, many people with hypertension do not know whether they are not sodium sensitive, and testing for this sensitivity takes a lot of time and is not routinely done.

The latest dietary advice from the Dietary Guidelines for Americans and the American Heart Association suggests that adults consume no more than the Daily Value for sodium (2400 mg). Currently, North Americans consume daily, on average, almost double that amount (4 to 7 g). Both sets of recommendations note that there is no risk in reducing sodium intake to the Daily Value.

The exact mechanism whereby sodium increases blood pressure is not clear. Studies suggest that there is a genetically influenced ability that determines the ease at which the body can excrete sodium. In salt-sensitive individuals, the kidneys require a higher blood pressure in order to excrete sodium from the body, compared with salt-resistant people. This causes salt-sensitive individuals to retain more sodium. This sodium retention in the body then leads to fluid retention. Ultimately, the fluid retention leads to increased blood volume and, in turn, the increased blood pressure needed to maintain sodium excretion.

Physicians usually resort to a combination of antihypertensive medications, such as diuretics (to increase urine output) and moderate sodium restriction (3–4 g/day) as an initial form of therapy. This combination typically reduces blood volume and, therefore, is often effective in controlling blood pressure.

Other Minerals and Blood Pressure

Minerals such as calcium, potassium, and magnesium also deserve attention when it comes to prevention and treatment of hypertension.[20] People often register slightly lower blood pressures—especially the systolic component—when they consume at least the 1000 mg of calcium per day, as compared with one-third to one-half that amount. It is reasonable for a person with hypertension to experiment, in consultation with a physician, with increasing calcium intake to see if that produces the desired effect.[11] So far, FDA has found the evidence linking calcium to a decrease in blood pressure too inconsistent to approve a health claim regarding hypertension and calcium-containing products.

Potassium supplementation in the range of 2 to 4 g/day also has been shown to moderately decrease blood pressure in people currently consuming far below this amount. FDA recently approved the following health claim for potassium and a reduction in blood pressure: "Diets containing foods that are good sources of potassium and low in sodium may reduce the risk of high blood pressure and stroke." This health claim will be allowed on foods that contain at least 350 mg of potassium (10 percent of the Daily Value) and 140 mg or less of sodium. In addition, qualifying foods must have less than 3 g of fat, 1 g or less of saturated fat, and 20 mg or less of cholesterol. Some studies indicate that magnesium also is capable of lowering blood pressure at intakes of about twice the RDA.

Recent studies show that a diet rich in calcium, potassium, and magnesium and low in sodium can lead to a decrease in blood pressure within days of beginning a specific diet, especially among African Americans.[15] The response is even similar to that seen with commonly used medications. The diet, called the DASH diet, closely follows the Food Guide Pyramid, with a few modifications (Fig. 11-14). The DASH diet is seen as a total dietary approach to treating hypertension. It is not clear which of the many factors contributed by this diet are responsible for the fall in blood pressure. An additional attribute of the DASH diet is that the participants in the study also experienced a fall in blood homocysteine, which may contribute to a lower risk of cardiovascular disease and stroke, especially in some people. Other studies also show a reduction in stroke risk among people who consume a diet rich in fruits, vegetables, and vitamin C (recall that fruits and vegetables are rich sources of potassium). Overall, a diet rich in low-fat and nonfat dairy products, fruits, vegetables, whole grains, and some nuts can substantially reduce blood pressure and stroke risk in many people.[20] The current challenge is to find a way to convince North Americans to follow such a diet.

Regular intake of fruits and vegetables has been linked to a decreased risk of both hypertension and stroke.

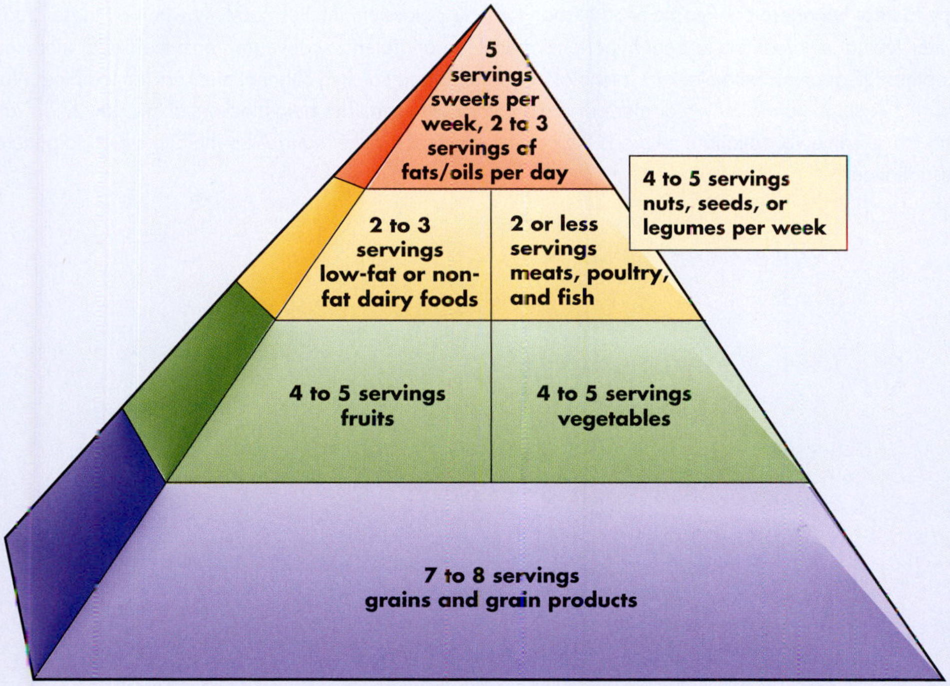

Figure 11-14 The Dietary Approaches to Stop Hypertension (DASH) diet was found to decrease systolic blood pressure by 5.5 mm Hg and diastolic blood pressure by 3.0 mm Hg more than the control diet. Overall, this diet provides approximately 18% of energy as protein, 55% as carbohydrate, and 27% as fat, with 6% from saturated fat. The diet contains more fruit and vegetable servings than the Food Guide Pyramid, contains less fat, and includes a serving of nuts. All DASH participants consumed no more than 3 g of sodium and one to two alcoholic drinks per week. Researchers estimate that if North Americans were to follow the DASH diet, there would be a 15% decrease in heart disease and 27% fewer strokes.

A DASH 2 diet trial tested three daily sodium intakes (3300 mg, 2400 mg, and 1500 mg). People showed a steady decline in blood pressure on the DASH diet as sodium intake declined.

Table 11-8 A Nutritional Plan to Minimize Hypertension and Stroke Risk*[20]

1. Follow the Food Guide Pyramid. Also consider going beyond this to include more fruit, vegetables, and some nuts (e.g., DASH diet), especially if one has hypertension.
2. Make sure to meet nutrient recommendations for calcium, potassium, and magnesium listed in this chapter.
3. Attain and maintain a healthy body weight.
4. Incorporate regular physical activity (at least five times per week for 60 minutes per session).
5. Consume alcoholic beverages in moderation, if at all (two drinks per day maximum for men and one drink per day maximum for women and older adults).
6. Consume moderate amounts of sodium (salt) and see if this helps. The Daily Value is a reasonable limit (2400 mg sodium or 6 g salt [1¼ tsp]). One might even try to lower intake to 1500 mg of sodium. This was shown to lower blood pressure even more than the DASH diet alone did in people with hypertension.
7. Don't smoke.
8. Maintain blood lipoproteins in the normal range (see Chapter 6).

*In addition, make sure to have blood pressure measured on a regular basis (i.e., yearly physical checkups).

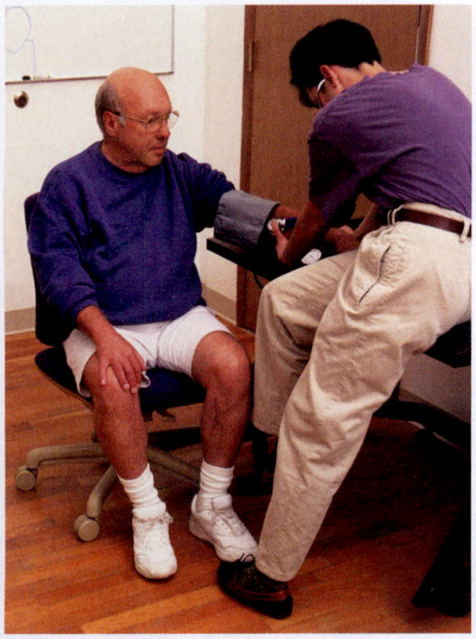

Older adults are particularly at risk of hypertension.

Prevention of Hypertension

Many of these and other risk factors for hypertension and stroke are controllable, and appropriate lifestyle changes can reduce a person's risk (Table 11-8). Experts typically recommend that those with hypertension in the high-normal and Stage 1 categories attempt to lower blood pressure through diet and lifestyle changes before resorting to blood pressure medications. Such a focus on diet and lifestyle is important because many people discontinue their blood pressure medications because of expense and side effects. Currently, physicians and registered dietitians have a long way to go in establishing good blood pressure control among people with hypertension.[4]

Medications to Treat Hypertension

Potassium-wasting diuretics, such as thiazides (chlorothiazide [Diuril]) are commonly used for drug therapy to treat hypertension. People need to monitor their potassium intakes carefully when on these drugs. Other typical medications to treat hypertension include angiotensin-converting enzyme (ACE) inhibitors (captopril [Capoten], beta-blockers (atenolol [Tenormin]), and calcium channel blockers (amlodipine [Norvasc]).[4] A combination of two or more drugs is commonly used. The beta-blockers act to slow heart rate and cause some vasodilation, whereas the calcium channel blockers and ACE inhibitors lead to general vasodilation.

chapter 12

Trace Minerals

Chapter | Outline

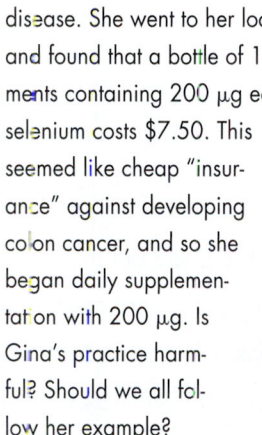

Case | Scenario

At a recent family gathering, Gina found out that she has a history of colon cancer in her family. In response, she did a lot of reading on the web about cancer and has come across a number of references to the potential importance of an intake of 200 µg/day of the trace mineral selenium in prevention of this disease. She went to her local supermarket and found that a bottle of 100 supplements containing 200 µg each of selenium costs $7.50. This seemed like cheap "insurance" against developing colon cancer, and so she began daily supplementation with 200 µg. Is Gina's practice harmful? Should we all follow her example?

Refresh | Your Memory

As you begin your study of trace minerals in Chapter 12, you may want to review:

- Digestion and absorption processes in Chapter 3.
- The process of oxidation and reduction and the electron transport chain in Chapter 4.
- Vitamins in Chapters 9 and 10.
- Calcium in Chapter 11.
- Chemistry terms such as valence and free radicals in Appendix A.
- Respiration, the muscular and skeletal systems, cell structure and function, immunity, and the endocrine system in Appendix C.

Boost | Your Study

Check out the ***Perspectives in Nutrition: Online Learning Center*** www.mhhe.com/wardlawpers6 *for quizzes, flash cards, activities, and web links designed to further help you learn about issues surrounding the trace minerals.*

Chapter | Objectives

Chapter 12 is designed to allow you to:

1. List conditions of the body, dietary factors, and other pertinent influences that determine the absorption, retention, and availability of specific trace minerals.
2. List key functions of the trace minerals.
3. Identify possible deficiency and toxicity symptoms associated with the trace minerals.
4. List at least two food sources for each of the trace minerals.

Trace minerals constitute less than 1% of all minerals in the body but their functions are absolutely essential for life.[11, 12] A trace mineral is defined as a mineral for which our daily nutritional need is less than 100 mg. Grouping them together this way, however, is too simplistic because the functions, mechanisms of absorption, transport in the body, and metabolism of the various trace minerals vary considerably. For example, the body carefully regulates the absorption and transport of iron and copper, but not selenium and iodide. This makes these latter trace minerals potentially toxic at intakes not much above our needs. The trace minerals are also very interactive; the abundance of one mineral in the diet and in the body can affect the absorption and metabolism of several other minerals.[8]

Information about trace minerals is one of the most rapidly expanding area of nutrition science. With the exception of iron and iodide, the importance of trace minerals to humans has been recognized only within the last 50 years. The chapter examines some of these new findings.

Trace Minerals—An Introduction

The terms *trace mineral* and *micromineral* are somewhat imprecise, since there are several definitions of these terms that have evolved over time. Originally, the terms were used to describe minerals that were not easily quantified by existing analytical methods, but today we have precise techniques for determining the concentration of tiny amounts of minerals in tissues and in foods. Thus, we will use the terms trace mineral and micromineral as related to "a daily nutritional need of less than 100 mg." These minerals are dietary essentials, in that they have specified biological functions, and a dietary deficiency produces physiological or structural abnormalities.

Discovering the importance of these trace minerals to humans has a fairly recent history, although the use of dietary iron to treat the effects of blood loss can be traced back to ancient civilizations. In 1961, scientists linked dwarfism in villagers in the Middle East to a zinc deficiency. Other researchers later recognized that an obscure form of heart disease in an isolated area of China was linked to a selenium deficiency. In the United States, deficiencies of some trace minerals were first observed in the late 1960s to early 1970s, when these nutrients were omitted in the preparation of synthetic formulas used in total parenteral nutrition. This "accident" also led to proof that some trace minerals were essential parts of a human diet. Because research on trace minerals in humans still has a long way to go, our current understanding of trace mineral metabolism relies heavily on the knowledge gained from studies with farm and laboratory animals.

Seafood, such as scallops, is a good source of many trace minerals.

Research on Trace Minerals

Not only are trace minerals needed in much smaller amounts than the macrominerals, the actual need for some trace minerals is also still debatable. In Table 1-3 in Chapter 1 nine essential trace minerals and some possible entries were listed. Demonstrating the essential nature of this latter group of nutrients is hampered by difficulty in measuring their amounts and by not knowing all of the functions that may be associated with the trace mineral. Before looking at each of the trace minerals, let's look at why research in this area is so complex.

Difficulties in Studying Trace Minerals

Determining trace mineral needs is difficult because the body requires only minute amounts, and highly sophisticated technology is needed to measure such small amounts in both food and body tissues. Rigorous protocols often are required to produce a deficiency in animals. (All animal research referred to in this discussion was conducted with farm and/or laboratory animals.) The animals may need to be raised in ultraclean environments and have their diets carefully formulated from individual essential nutrients to ensure that no trace mineral contamination occurs. Stainless steel and plastic cages may also be needed, so that the animals do not obtain any trace minerals, such as zinc, from chewing on the cages. Trace minerals must sometimes even be filtered from the air, and the water must be as free of trace minerals as possible. In addition, glassware used for chemical analysis may need to be rinsed repeatedly in acid to eliminate trace mineral contamination; sometimes only plastic bottles are appropriate.

Despite the difficulties encountered in experimentally producing most trace mineral deficiencies in laboratory animals, overt human deficiencies still occur.[9, 20] In addition, some evidence is available indicating that marginal dietary intakes of certain trace minerals (e.g., iron, zinc, copper, and chromium) also occur, leading to mild, undetected deficiencies in humans.[4, 6, 14] The lack of precise tests to pinpoint these deficiencies is one reason there is concern but not hard evidence. Most of these tests involve blood samples. However, for many trace minerals, the blood tests most commonly used don't respond well to small changes in trace mineral status. Moreover, the values for many of these blood tests are also influenced by factors not related to the trace mineral status.

ceruloplasmin A blue copper-containing protein in the blood that can remove an electron from Fe^{2+} (ferrous form) to yield Fe^{3+} (the ferric form). The Fe^{3+} form of iron can then bind with iron transport and storage proteins, such as transferrin.

For example, copper deficiency is often detected by the amount of copper, or the protein that contains most of the copper (called **ceruloplasmin**) in the blood. Based on work with laboratory rats, these values don't fall as readily during a mild copper deficiency as do some other copper-related parameters in various tissues. In addition, it is known from both laboratory rat and human studies that copper or ceruloplasmin readings in the blood are affected by factors such as inflammation, pregnancy, fluctuating estrogen levels, and oral contraceptive use. For reasons like this, diagnosing marginal trace mineral deficiencies can be seen as an art that only a few researchers have developed.

Another reason why marginal trace mineral deficiencies often go undetected is that the effects may be subtle and may involve interactions with other factors. For example, a marginal trace mineral deficiency might produce a change in cardiovascular health risk factors or immune function.[4] However, these changes are not obvious to the person affected. Even the person's physician might not recognize that these effects involve trace minerals since many other factors are also involved in cardiovascular health or immune function, such as a number of different trace minerals, plus other nutrient and nonnutrient factors. Therefore, it is important that research with trace minerals continues. In the meanwhile, you would do well to eat a balanced diet and pay attention to situations that may cause low trace mineral intake or lead to high trace mineral needs. Many of these situations are discussed in this chapter.

Nutrient Needs for Trace Minerals

The difficulty in measuring trace mineral nutrition in humans makes setting specific human needs problematic. Some trace minerals have only an Adequate Intake (AI), not a more precise RDA.

The primary method used to set trace mineral nutrient needs is the balance study. The same basic technique used for nitrogen balance studies works for trace minerals (review Chapter 7). Researchers try to determine the lowest trace mineral intake that compensates for all trace mineral losses from urine, feces, hair, skin, perspiration, menses, and so on. These studies are very expensive to perform. In addition, a balance study tells only the amount of dietary intake needed to maintain a specific pool of the trace mineral in the body, but this pool does not necessarily represent the amount needed to maintain all body functions or insure good health.

Another complication is that trace minerals interact with each other. For example, an overabundance of iron in the digestive tract can interfere with the absorption of other minerals, such as zinc. Thus, to set human dietary needs for zinc, nutrition scientists must estimate the amount of iron that will be consumed to predict how much zinc the body will actually absorb. Overall, quite a lot of scientific judgment must go into setting desired intakes for trace minerals.[11]

Trace Minerals in Foods

The trace mineral content of plant foods reflects the trace mineral concentration in the soil in which they were grown.

Trace minerals are found in both plant and animal foods. However, the bioavailability of trace minerals is an important issue to consider, especially when planning diets. Even if a food is high in a particular trace mineral, it will not supply much to the body unless the trace mineral is absorbed well. Many factors found in foods inhibit trace mineral absorption. Mineral absorption from some sources can amount to only 1 to 6% of the total present, with the lowest percentages typically seen in plant sources.

By eating a variety of foods, you can obtain nutrients derived from a variety of soils and, thus, maximize your chances of consuming adequate amounts of trace minerals. In addition, with regard to most trace minerals, it is best to consume as many minimally processed foods as possible. Generally, the more refined a food, the lower its content of trace minerals. For example, during the refining of whole wheat into white flour, much of the trace mineral content of iron, selenium, zinc, and copper is lost. The enrichment of white flour restores iron but not the other trace minerals.

Table 12-1 Factors That Affect Iron Absorption

Increase Absorption	Decrease Absorption
Gastric acid	Phytic acid (in dietary fiber)
Heme iron in food	Oxalic acid in leafy vegetables
High body demand for red blood cells (blood loss, high altitude, physical training, pregnancy)	Polyphenols in tea, as well as in coffee, red wine, and other foods
	Full body stores of iron
Low body stores of iron	Excess of other minerals (Zn, Mn, Ca)*
Meat protein factor (MPF)	Reduced gastric acid output
Vitamin C	Some antacids

*Especially when taken as supplements.

Iron (Fe)

Iron is found in every living cell; total body content is about 5 g (about 1 tsp). The importance of iron for the maintenance of health has been recognized for centuries. In 4000 B.C., the Persian physician Melampus gave iron supplements to sailors to compensate for the iron lost from bleeding during battles. Today, iron deficiency and iron deficiency anemia are common worldwide, affecting an estimated 1 billion or more people in developing and developed countries. In most developing nations, about two-thirds of all children and women of childbearing age experience iron deficiency.

Absorption, Transport, Storage, and Excretion of Iron

The body uses a variety of mechanisms to absorb iron and distribute it in the body.[20] This maximizes iron function and minimizes iron toxicity. Although this system doesn't work perfectly if body iron is very low or very high, it still works well most of the time. The body's handling of iron is affected by a number of factors, but the most influential factor is body iron stores. If stores are low, the small intestine becomes more efficient at iron absorption. Diet composition also plays a major role. Factors which affect iron absorption are summarized in Table 12-1.

Iron occurs in foods in various forms.[11] In meat, fish, and poultry, some of the iron is present as **hemoglobin** and **myoglobin,** which collectively are called **heme iron.** The rest of the iron present in these foods, as well as all of the iron in vegetables, grains, and supplements, is **nonheme iron.** Heme iron is absorbed more readily than nonheme iron, which is one reason meat products are an efficient way to obtain iron from foods. The amount of iron in meat is also higher than the amount naturally occurring in plant foods. (This discussion does not discount the value of iron in plant foods. Those sources also help meet iron needs.) Another reason that meat is advantageous is that it helps us absorb the nonheme iron from other foods, although the exact mechanisms aren't well understood. A meat protein factor (MPF) may explain part of this effect.

Organic acids, such as vitamin C, also increase nonheme iron absorption by adding an electron to Fe^{3+} (the ferric form), yielding Fe^{2+} (the ferrous form). Vitamin C then forms a complex, called a **chelate,** with Fe^{2+}, thereby enhancing absorption. For vegetarians, or those who limit intake of animal flesh, combining vitamin C–rich foods with plant foods containing iron is a useful strategy.

Ferrous iron (Fe^{2+}) is absorbed better than ferric iron (Fe^{3+}) because it crosses the mucous layer of the small intestine more readily to reach the brush border of intestinal absorptive cells. There, Fe^{2+} must then have an electron removed, oxidizing it to Fe^{3+},

hemoglobin The iron-containing protein in red blood cells that transports oxygen to the body tissues and some carbon dioxide away from the tissues. It is also responsible for the red color of blood.

myoglobin The iron-containing protein that controls the rate of diffusion of oxygen (O_2) from red blood cells to muscle cells.

heme iron Iron provided from animal tissues primarily as a component of hemoglobin and myoglobin. Approximately 40% of the iron in meat is heme iron; it is readily absorbed.

nonheme iron Iron provided from plant sources and elemental iron components of animal tissues. Nonheme iron is less efficiently absorbed than heme iron, and absorption is also more closely dependent on body needs.

chelates Complexes formed between metal ions and substances with polar groups, such as proteins. The polar groups form two or more attachments with the metal ions, forming a ringed structure. The metal ion is then firmly bound and sequestered.

before it enters the absorptive cells. At the cell membrane of the brush border, Fe^{3+} binds to a receptor protein, called membrane iron-binding protein, which finally transfers iron into the absorptive cell.

Critical | Thinking

Annie, Tom's friend, is taking a nutrition class at her university. She suggested that he consume some extra vitamin C-rich foods every day. Tom is confused by this advice, since his doctor told him to increase the amount of iron in his diet to help treat low blood iron, but not the amount of vitamin C. How can Annie explain her recommendation to him?

Although no iron absorption occurs in the stomach, gastric acid plays an important role in iron absorption by promoting the conversion of Fe^{3+} to Fe^{2+} and by solubilizing nonheme iron. The decreased production of gastric acid experienced by many older people can lower their iron absorption and ultimately body stores of iron. Once acted on by acid in the stomach, iron absorption then occurs primarily in the small intestine.

Heme iron follows a different absorptive process. It is likely absorbed directly into the absorptive cells after the globin (protein) fraction has been removed. Once inside the absorptive cells, the iron is released from the heme portion.

Several dietary factors interfere with our ability to absorb iron. Phytic acid and other factors in grain fibers and oxalic acid in vegetables can all bind iron, reducing its absorption. For this reason, spinach is not a good iron source, despite containing relatively high amounts of iron for a plant food. Polyphenols, such as tannins found in tea and related substances found in coffee, also reduce iron absorption. People trying to rebuild iron stores are advised to reduce coffee and tea consumption, particularly at meal times. Finally, several studies have shown that calcium interferes with dietary iron absorption, but the effect is mild at best. Still, experts on calcium and iron interactions recommend that individuals with high iron requirements avoid taking calcium supplements at meals that contain most of the dietary iron. They could also consider taking calcium supplements between meals or at bedtime to avoid this potential interaction.

As noted above, because iron is both essential and very toxic, the body has an elaborate system to try to place iron where it belongs and inhibit iron toxicity (a few highlights of this iron processing are noted in Figure 12-1).[20] First, cells of the small intestine make an iron-binding protein called **ferritin** in proportion to body iron stores. If stores are low, little ferritin is made. This condition elevates iron absorption since ferritin is a barrier to iron reaching the bloodstream. If iron stores are high, much ferritin is made, which binds iron as it enters these intestinal cells. Much of this iron is kept from ever entering the bloodstream because after just a few days, intestinal cells are sloughed off and excreted. Any iron bound to ferritin goes out with the cells. The process is termed a mucosal block, as it in effect is blocking iron absorption. This response of ferritin to an increase in iron stores can be fairly rapid.

ferritin A protein compound that serves as the storage form of iron in the blood and tissues.

The copper-containing blood protein ceruloplasmin removes an electron from Fe^{2+}, yielding Fe^{3+}, the form bound by transferrin. Thus, copper metabolism and iron metabolism are closely linked.

Once iron is absorbed from the small intestine, it can be stored in the liver. As with the intestine, ferritin is the primary iron-binder in the liver. Iron can be transported out of the liver to other body sites using a step that involves a copper enzyme mentioned

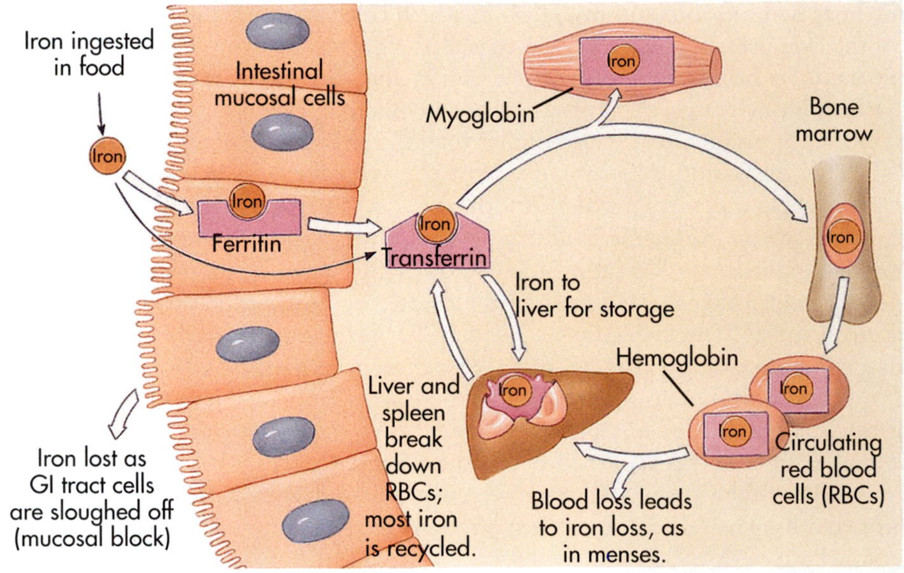

Figure 12-1 Iron absorption and distribution. Iron binds with a protein called apoferritin to form ferritin when stored in cells. If the intestinal absorptive cells are sloughed before iron is absorbed from them, the iron is not absorbed into the blood. This allows the body to control the absorption of iron. The mechanism for resisting absorption of excess iron, primarily that in the nonheme form, is termed a mucosal block.

earlier (ceruloplasmin). In the blood, iron is carried to these sites via a transport protein called **transferrin.** This protein then binds to receptors on cells, which take up the whole transferrin protein by a process called endocytosis, described in Chapter 3. The transferrin then finds its way to a cell organelle called the lysosome where acid releases the iron from transferrin. The released iron can then go to various iron molecules such as iron-containing enzymes, hemoglobin (if a red blood cell is being made), myoglobin (a protein which traps oxygen in tissues), and ferritin (which stores iron and helps prevent toxicity). In states of iron overload, another protein called **hemosiderin** is made to bind up as much iron as it can. This also helps reduce iron toxicity, but it does not prevent it. Overall, the main defense against iron toxicity is ferritin in the small intestine. If a lot of iron manages to get by this defense, then other mechanisms become an important consideration (see the section on iron toxicity).

transferrin A protein that transports iron in the blood.

hemosiderin An insoluble iron-protein compound in the liver. Hemosiderin stores iron when the amount of iron in the body exceeds the storage capacity of ferritin.

Much of the iron in the body is inserted into hemoglobin, which transports oxygen in red blood cells (Fig. 12-2). The iron in hemoglobin is what actually binds the oxygen. These red blood cells do eventually die, but most of the iron from hemoglobin is conserved by the body. The same is true for iron used for other purposes. Nonetheless, some iron is lost each day via the GI tract, urine, and skin. Women who are menstruating also lose iron as part of that blood loss.

Functions of Iron

Iron plays an important role in many parts of the body, including immune function, cognitive development, temperature regulation, energy metabolism, and work performance.[11]

Iron is a component of two proteins that are involved in the transport and metabolism of oxygen. In hemoglobin, iron is the oxygen carrier of the blood, which transports oxygen from the lungs to all tissues and assists in the transport of some carbon dioxide back to the lungs for expiration. When the oxygen-carrying capacity of the blood begins to decline, the kidneys produce the hormone **erythropoietin,** which targets the bone marrow to produce more red blood cells. As a red blood cell matures, its nucleus is expelled, along with DNA. Such a cell cannot replace itself. The red blood cell goes on to have a life span of about 120 days.

erythropoietin A hormone secreted mostly by the kidneys that enhances red blood cell synthesis and stimulates red blood cell release from bone marrow.

In myoglobin, iron provides oxygen to skeletal and heart muscle cells. Within the mitochondria, the electron transport chain uses iron as a component of cytochromes

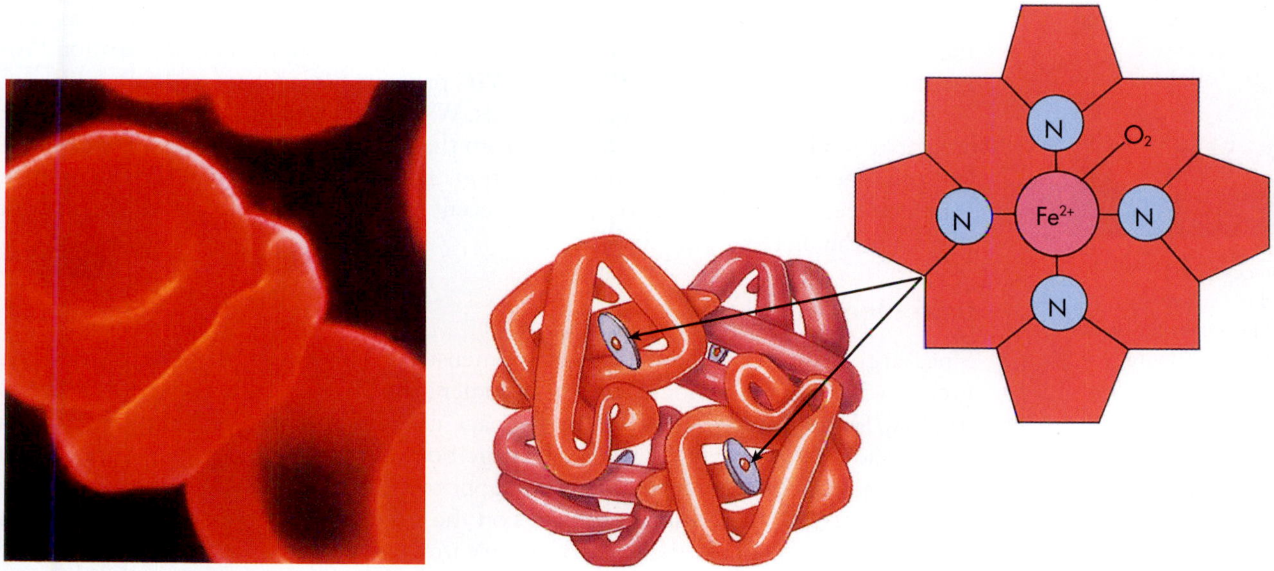

Figure 12-2 Most iron in the body is present in the hemoglobin molecules in the red blood cells. Iron gives hemoglobin the ability to carry oxygen.

Food Sources of Iron

Food Item and Amount, with Bioavailability (in parentheses)	*Iron (mg)*
Oat bran cereal, 1 cup	15.0 (low)
Baked clams, 3 oz	14.0 (high)
Spinach, 1 cup	6.4 (low)
Kidney beans, 1 cup	5.3 (low)
Pot roast, 4 oz	3.9 (high)
Sirloin steak, 4 oz	3.8 (high)
Fried beef liver, 2 oz	3.6 (high)
Shrimp, 3 oz	2.7 (high)
Braunschweiger sausage, 1 piece	2.7 (high)
Flour tortilla, 1	2.4 (low)
Garbanzo beans, ½ cup	2.4 (low)
Navy beans, ½ cup	2.3 (low)
Baked potato, 1	1.7 (low)
Artichoke, 1	1.6 (low)
Whole-wheat bread, 1 slice	1.0 (low)

RDA, adult men, 8 mg
RDA, adult women, 18 mg

Red meat is a major source of iron in the North American diet. As noted in Chapter 7, a moderate serving about two times a week or less is a typical recommendation for red meat intake.

that carry electrons from NADH + H^+ and $FADH_2$ to molecular oxygen. The first step in the citric acid cycle, the conversion of citrate to isocitrate, requires an iron-containing enzyme. The limitation of these three processes in iron deficiency helps explain why it leads to fatigue upon physical exertion. Iron found in cytochrome P450 in the endoplasmic reticulum contributes to many processes, such as alcohol metabolism, drug detoxification, and carcinogen excretion in the liver.

Iron in the peroxidase enzymes helps break down toxic oxygen species, such as hydrogen peroxide (H_2O_2). Peroxidase enzymes are found in white blood cells and platelets (clotting factors in the blood). Iron also functions as a cofactor for some other enzymes, including those involved in the synthesis of collagen, various neurotransmitters (e.g., dopamine, epinephrine, norepinephrine, and serotonin), and eicosanoids.

When iron functions in cytochromes of the electron transport chain and in iron-requiring enzymes, it can exist stably in two different valences (2^+ and 3^+). Within cytochromes and enzymes, iron will switch between these two valences, which catalyze the movement of electrons either along the electron transport chain, or, as part of an enzyme reaction. This feature of iron is very useful when the iron is confined within these systems, but this ability to readily change valences also makes iron very toxic if the iron roams free. In the latter case, iron can catalyze destructive reactions, including the formation of free radicals.

Iron in Foods

Because much of the iron in animal foods is heme iron, the most bioavailable form, meats are the richest sources of iron. The major iron sources in North American diets are animal foods, such as beef steaks, roasts, and hamburger. The next greatest sources are bakery products, including white breads, rolls, and crackers. Most of the iron in these products is elemental forms of iron added to refined flour as part of the enrichment process. For some cereal products, iron is added in higher amounts than used for enrichment. This makes the product a "fortified" product. About 5% of the iron added to grain products is absorbed. Overall, the North American diet contains about 5 to 7 mg of iron per 1000 kcal.[11] And as noted earlier, the bioavailability of the iron present in a meal depends on its form and the presence or absence of factors that influence absorption. The body's need for iron then ultimately determines how much iron actually is delivered to the body.[20]

A common cause of iron deficiency anemia in children is an overreliance on milk, a very poor source of iron, and too little meat in their diets. In the United States, a major contributor to decreasing rates of iron deficiency anemia in preschool children has been the use of iron-fortified formulas and cereals in the Special Supplemental Nutrition Program for Women, Infants, and Children (WIC program) (see Chapters 16 and 20).

Another source of iron is cooking utensils. When acidic foods, such as tomato sauce, are cooked in iron cookware, some iron from the pan is taken up by the food. Vegetarians can especially benefit from this interaction. The replacement of iron cookware with stainless steel and aluminum cookware in recent times likely has decreased the amount of iron in the diet.

Iron Needs

Since a great source of iron loss can be menstrual blood loss, the iron RDA varies greatly with age and gender. For adult women, the RDA is 18 mg/day, while it is 8 mg/day for adult men. The RDA for teenage girls, 15 mg/day, is slightly lower than that for adult women. The RDA for teenage boys, 11 mg/day, is slightly higher than that for adult men due to the need to support more lean tissue growth during the teenage years. All these values are based on the need to balance iron intake with iron losses. It is also assumed that 18% of dietary iron will be absorbed.[11] The Daily Value for iron used on food and supplement labels is 18 mg. The average daily intake for North American women is 12 mg, while among men it is about 17 mg.

Iron Deficiency

Iron deficiency is probably the most common micronutrient deficiency both worldwide and in North America. In severe iron deficiency, there is not enough iron to make all the hemoglobin needed. This results in iron deficiency anemia. Anemia represents any impairment in transporting oxygen in the blood, and iron deficiency anemia is the most common form of anemia. When this anemia occurs, evidence can be seen under a microscope in that the red blood cells appear small and show less color, resulting in a **microcytic, hypochromic** anemia[20] (Fig. 12-3). Iron deficiency anemia can be detected by a blood measurement called **hematocrit,** which is the percent of blood volume occupied by the red blood cells. Values below 34 to 37% suggest iron deficiency anemia. An even more accurate measure is blood hemoglobin. A value less than 10 to 11 g/dl also suggest iron deficiency anemia.

microcytic Describing red blood cells that are smaller than normal; literally, "small cell."

hypochromic Describing pale red blood cells lacking sufficient hemoglobin as a result of iron deficiency. Hypochromic cells have a reduced oxygen-carrying ability.

hematocrit The percentage of total blood volume occupied by red blood cells.

Anemia in any form impairs energy because aerobic respiration cannot occur without oxygen. Obvious signs of anemia include fatigue upon exertion and difficulties in mental concentration. However, aerobic respiration is also important to many unseen body processes, including those which contribute to organ system development during growth. Energy impairments due to iron deficiency anemia are also made worse by other effects of iron deficiency. Since iron functions in the electron transport chain and in the citric acid cycle, impairments in those functions impair aerobic respiration. In addition to effects on energy metabolism, iron deficiency also compromises immune function.

It is very important to note that some people can have a marginal iron deficiency that does not produce anemia.[6] In this state, aerobic respiration is still impaired to some extent. However, this occurs not due to anemia, but rather due to iron's other roles in aerobic respiration. In addition, immune function can be impaired.[4] Since marginal deficiency does not involve anemia, a hemoglobin or hematocrit measurement will not detect marginal iron deficiency. For this reason, if a physician or a registered dietitian is seeing a client that shows signs of low energy (such as fatigue upon exertion and concentration problems), a hemoglobin or hematocrit measurement should not be the sole means of ruling out an iron concern. Fortunately, unlike the cases for marginal deficiencies of some other trace minerals, many clinical laboratories can perform other tests for iron status. The most used method has been serum ferritin, but another blood measure, serum transferrin receptors, may soon become more widely used.

Many different groups are at risk for iron deficiency. In fact, it may be simpler to say who tends not to be at risk than list everyone at risk. One group that tends not to be at high risk are adult males who consume meat regularly. On the other hand, young adult women, as well as teenage girls, are often at risk for iron deficiency due to blood iron losses, plus lower average meat consumption than their male counterparts. Women with heavy menstrual blood losses are especially prone to iron deficiency. Pregnant women don't have to contend with menstrual blood losses, but iron is still a concern. During pregnancy, much of body's iron is used to expand the blood supply and for other physical changes. As a person reaches one's older years, iron can become a problem for both genders as food intake often falls. In addition, body iron absorption and distribution can become less efficient. At the opposite end of the age spectrum, just after birth, preterm infants (born before 37 weeks after conception) can have iron problems. During the first six months to one year of age, iron stores present at birth should be able to meet much of the infant's needs. Because these iron stores are built mostly during the last weeks of pregnancy, a preterm birth cuts short the extent of this iron storage time.

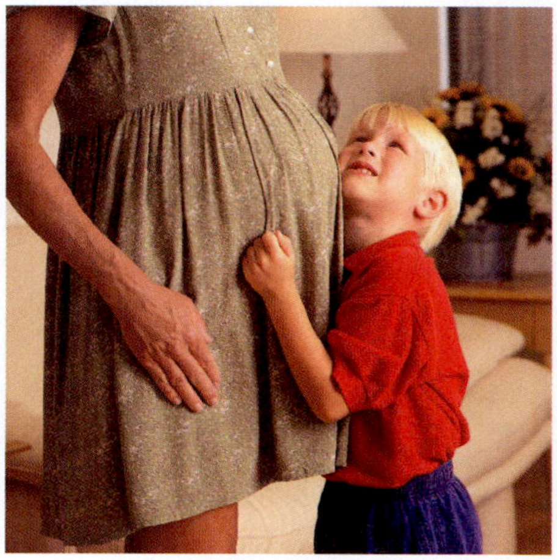

Pregnancy greatly increases iron needs, as does growth in childhood.

Two other groups of people prone to iron deficiency are children who are picky eaters (these children typically avoid iron-rich foods) and vegetarians. The latter group has a challenge to get enough iron because, as noted earlier, meat provides relatively well-absorbed dietary heme iron, plus meat promotes iron absorption from other foods. Moreover, the high oxalic acid content of many vegetarian diets can further depress iron absorption. On the other hand, vegetarian diets usually are rich in vitamin C. Such vegetarians should consume vitamin C–rich foods simultaneously with the few

(a)

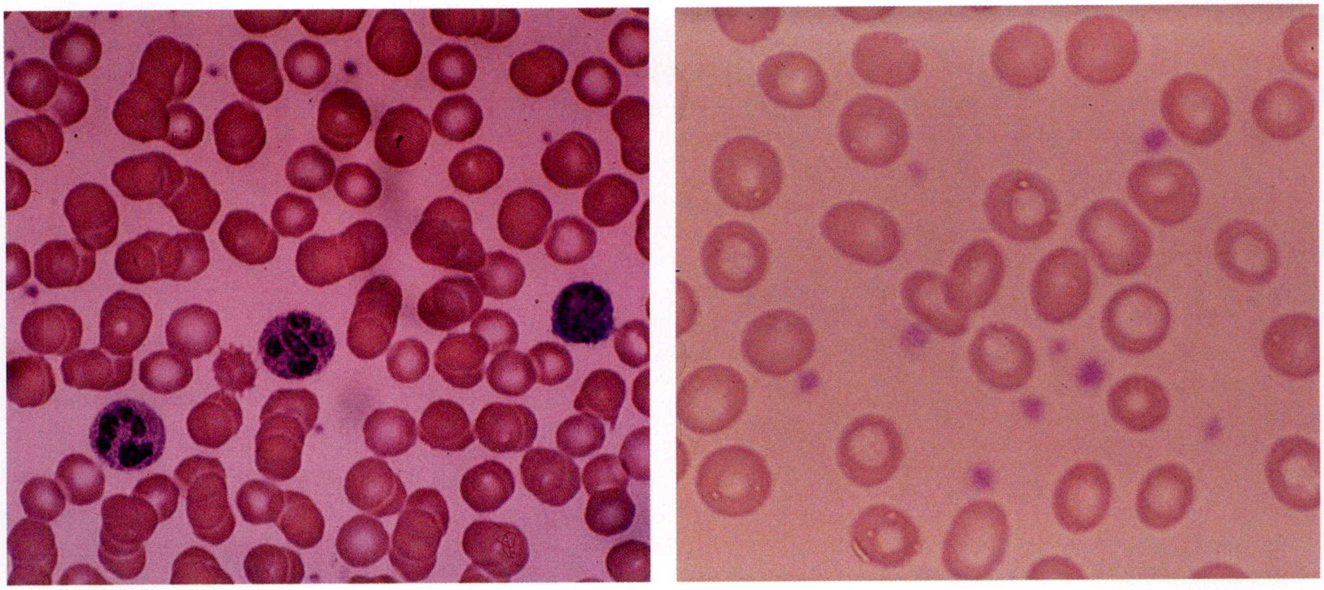

(b)

Figure 12-3 Iron deficiency anemia. (*a*) Normal cells—both cell size and color are normal. (*b*) Iron-deficient cells—both cell size and color are decreased. The loss of color stems from the lower amount of the pigment hemoglobin. The stages of iron depletion in the body progress from (1) low ferritin in the blood to (2) low transferrin saturation in the blood to (3) microcytic hypochromic anemia.

Consumption of dirt and similar nonfood substances may lead to iron deficiency anemia because these can bind much of the iron in the GI tract. The practice of eating nonfood items, termed *pica*, is discussed in Chapter 16. Blood loss caused by intestinal and bloodborne parasite infections is another common cause of anemia among poor populations, especially when people do not wear shoes. Parasites, such as hookworms, can easily penetrate the soles of the feet and legs and enter the bloodstream. Although hookworm disease has been largely eradicated through improved sanitation in North America and other industrialized areas of the world, it continues to plague more than one-fifth of the world's population, mostly in tropical regions.

hemochromatosis A disorder of iron metabolism characterized by increased absorption of iron, saturation of iron-binding proteins, and deposition of hemosiderin in the liver tissue.

Testing is available to determine the presence of the genes that are responsible for hemochromatosis. The cost is usually around $150.

nonanimal foods that contain appreciable amounts of iron. Consumption of a multivitamin and mineral supplement containing iron or an iron-fortified ready-to-eat breakfast cereal can be useful for vegetarians, even though this iron is not as well absorbed as heme iron. Adding milk to a vegetarian diet is not very helpful because milk is not a good iron source.

Finally, the donation of 1 pint (0.5 L) of blood represents a loss of 200 to 250 mg of iron. It generally takes several months to replace this iron. Most healthy people can donate blood two to four times a year without harmful consequences; generally, women need a longer interval between donations to rebuild their iron stores. As a precaution, blood banks first screen potential donors' blood for evidence of anemia.

Iron Toxicity

Although there is often concern surrounding iron deficiency, iron also poses a risk for toxicity. A single property of iron is responsible for some of both iron's function and iron's toxicity. As noted earlier, iron's ability to alternate between two valences (2^+ vs. 3^+) is functional when confined to cytochromes and enzymes, but is toxic when not. One reason for the toxicity is that changes in iron valences can catalyze the formation of free radicals, as mentioned earlier. Two prominent causes of iron toxicity are the genetic condition **hemochromatosis** and repeated blood transfusions.[3] The body has a mucosal block in place for protecting itself from oral iron, but in hemochromatosis this mucosal block works less efficiently. The iron introduced into the body through repeated blood transfusions also bypasses the protective system, and can result in dangerously high iron stores in the body.

Because of the body's protective system, it is generally not easy to produce severe toxicity due to oral iron consumption. One exception to this general rule involves the susceptibility of children to iron toxicity. Children are more vulnerable to oral iron poisoning than adults because their protective system cannot respond as rapidly as an adult's. The prime source of iron overload in children is the consumption of excess chewable iron-containing supplements.

Treatment of iron toxicity depends on the situation. For hemochromatosis, a normal treatment is periodic blood removal (the same removal process as when blood is donated to blood banks). Another approach that is used in some situations is administration of a drug that binds iron and enhances its excretion. More can be found on iron overload in the accompanying Expert Opinion by Dr. Barbara Bowman and Dr. Giuseppina Imperatore. Finally, besides overt toxicity, there is some (but conflicting) evidence that mild iron toxicity contributes to health problems, such as cardiovascular disease and arthritis.[17] More on this topic can be found in the Nutrition Perspective.

Concept | Check

Iron absorption depends mostly on its form and the body's need for it. Absorption is hindered by a mucosal block, but excess iron intake can override the system, leading to toxicity. Iron absorption increases in the presence of vitamin C and decreases in the presence of large amounts of oxalates and some components of grains, such as phytic acid. Iron is most important in synthesizing hemoglobin and myoglobin, in supporting immune function, and in energy metabolism. Iron deficiency can cause a form of anemia. It is particularly important for women of child-bearing age to consume adequate iron, primarily to replace that lost in menstrual blood. Sources include red meat, pork, liver, enriched grains and cereals, and oysters. Iron toxicity usually results from a genetic disorder called hemochromatosis. This disease causes the overabsorption and accumulation of iron, which can result in severe liver and heart damage.

Hemosiderosis is the storage of excess iron in the form of hemosiderin. This form of excess iron is not associated with the organ damage of hemochromatosis, as excess iron is stored in areas of normal storage. In hemochromatosis, the iron accumulates in body organs outside normal areas and causes organ deterioration, such as in the liver and heart.

Zinc (Zn)

Although zinc has been recognized as an essential nutrient in animals since the early 1900s, zinc deficiency was first recognized in humans in the early 1960s in Egypt and Iran. The deficiency was determined to be the cause of growth retardation and inadequate sexual development in humans. Curiously, the dietary zinc content was not that low. The key factor was that the customary diet contained almost exclusively unleavened bread and little animal protein. Unleavened bread is very high in phytic acid and other factors that decrease zinc bioavailability. Yeast fermentation in the preparation of bread dough reduces the effect of phytic acid by tenfold. In addition, parasite infestation and the practice of eating dirt also contributed to these cases of severe zinc deficiency observed in humans.

In North America, zinc deficiencies were first observed in the early 1970s in hospitalized patients receiving total parenteral nutrition. Originally, zinc was not added to the intravenous solutions, but the protein source in the solutions was based on milk protein or blood fibrin, which contain zinc. When the solutions were later changed to include mostly isolated amino acids as the protein source, zinc-deficiency symptoms quickly developed. This isolated amino acids source of protein is very low in zinc.

Minimal intakes of energy, protein, and zinc limit the growth of people worldwide.

Absorption, Transport, Storage, and Excretion of Zinc

Zinc is absorbed throughout the small intestine. Factors that affect the absorption of zinc include the body's need for zinc and the composition of the meal in which zinc is consumed.[5] The absorption and transport of zinc utilizes a two-step process. The first step is the uptake or membrane binding at the mucosal surface. The second step is the transport of zinc across the mucosal cell and the release into the bloodstream, but the process is not completely understood. After entering the blood, zinc binds to blood proteins, such as albumin, for transport to the liver. The liver releases zinc into general circulation bound to proteins, such as globulins.

When zinc is absorbed into intestinal cells, it induces the synthesis of **metallothionein**, a protein that binds zinc in much the same way that ferritin binds iron.

metallothionein A protein that binds and regulates the release of zinc and copper in intestinal and liver cells.

Expert Opinion

Iron Overload: Too Much of a Good Thing

Barbara A. Bowman, Ph.D., and Giuseppina Imperatore, M.D., Ph.D.

Nutritionists consider iron to be the gold standard of micronutrients, because we know more about the dietary intake, metabolism, and nutritional requirements of iron than any other trace element. Despite this extensive knowledge and the array of sophisticated techniques for evaluating iron nutrition, however, more than 1 billion people suffer from iron deficiency, which is the most prevalent micronutrient deficiency in the world.

Iron deficiency is also a significant health problem in the United States, especially in young children and women of childbearing age, particularly pregnant women. Iron deficiency is a special concern for women and children because one of its major consequences is anemia. Anemia, defined as a low concentration of hemoglobin in blood, leads to decreased work capacity in adults, developmental delays and behavioral disturbances in children, increased susceptibility to infection, and increased mortality in both children and adults. In the United States, about 3.3 million women of childbearing age and 240,000 children age 1 to 2 years have iron deficiency anemia, the most severe form of iron deficiency.

Iron overload lies at the opposite end of the spectrum of iron status. If untreated, iron overload disease, like iron deficiency, can lead to illness and even death. Let's examine iron overload in more detail.

Etiology of Iron Overload

What causes iron overload? The major cause of iron overload in the United States is hereditary hemochromatosis, a genetic condition that affects about one person out of every 200 to 500 in the United States. Iron overload can also occur in chronic liver disease due to alcohol abuse, viral infections, and chronic anemias requiring frequent blood transfusions (e.g., thalassemia). The specific genetic lesion in hereditary hemochromatosis was identified in 1996, and two major mutations have been identified. The fundamental defect involves the regulation of iron absorption. In hereditary hemochromatosis, iron absorption is excessive, and iron absorption is not reduced when iron status is normal. The human body does not have a mechanism for eliminating excess iron. Therefore, after many years of absorbing too much iron, excessive amounts of iron can accumulate in the body, leading to iron overload and tissue injury. If undetected and untreated for many years, iron levels can build up in the liver, heart, pancreas, joints, and pituitary gland and can eventually lead to liver disease, heart disease, diabetes, arthritis, and hypopituitarism with hypogonadism. People at a late stage of iron overload may have skin that turns bronze or gray. The diseases caused by iron overload usually appear by age 40 to 60, although some people are affected earlier and others never become ill. With early detection and treatment, organ damage can be prevented. However, without lifelong treatment, organ damage may be permanent and life-threatening.

Up to 1 million Americans, mostly people of European descent, have the mutation for hemochromatosis. However, far fewer actually develop iron overload. Some people have the mutation but never get iron overload. This is probably because clinical expression of iron overload depends on additional factors, including the severity of the metabolic defect, the amount and type of iron in the diet, other dietary factors that enhance or inhibit iron absorption, environmental factors, and blood loss (menstruation, for example).

Diagnosis and Treatment of Iron Overload

Early detection and lifelong treatment can prevent the complications of hemochromatosis. The major approach to diagnosis is a series of blood tests to measure the amount of iron in the blood, such as the extent to which transferrin is saturated with iron. The same blood tests are used during treatment to monitor the amount of iron in the body and the response to treatment. Genetic testing is

Homeostatic regulation of zinc absorption may partly be due to the synthesis of metallothionein, since it hinders the movement of zinc from intestinal cells. If zinc is not transferred to the blood from the intestinal cells within their short lifetime, it is sloughed off along with the cell and excreted. Thus, a mucosal block works against the overabsorption of zinc and iron, but much more so in the case of iron. If large doses of zinc are taken, they override the mucosal block. Luckily for overconsumers, zinc is also readily excreted via the pancreas into the intestinal tract and then leaves the body by the feces. It is also excreted in small amounts in urine and sweat.

Like iron absorption, zinc absorption is influenced by the types of food ingested. Absorption is more likely when animal protein sources are consumed, when the body's zinc needs are elevated, or when small amounts are consumed. The RDA for zinc is based on absorption of about 40% of intake.

also being studied. However, not everyone with the mutation develops iron overload. Because of concern about the need for privacy and possible discrimination in employment and insurance, genetic screening for hereditary hemochromatosis is not recommended. People who have been diagnosed with hereditary hemochromatosis should tell their family members and urge them to get tested, too.

Treatment of iron overload is straightforward, safe, and effective. After they have been diagnosed, people with iron overload have blood removed regularly, usually a unit or pint of blood, to remove the excess iron that has accumulated. The procedure, which is called phlebotomy, is exactly the same as when you donate blood. The frequency of phlebotomy depends on how much iron has built up. When iron overload is first diagnosed, phlebotomy may be needed every week or two. When accumulated iron has been reduced to a safe amount, phlebotomy may be needed only a few times a year, but it must be continued. Health care providers use blood testing to determine when phlebotomy treatment is needed.

People with hemochromatosis must be sure to follow their doctor's advice and get tested regularly to prevent complications from developing. For most, periodic phlebotomy will be needed for the rest of their lives. It is also important for people with hemochromatosis to avoid alcohol and raw shellfish, which can damage the liver.

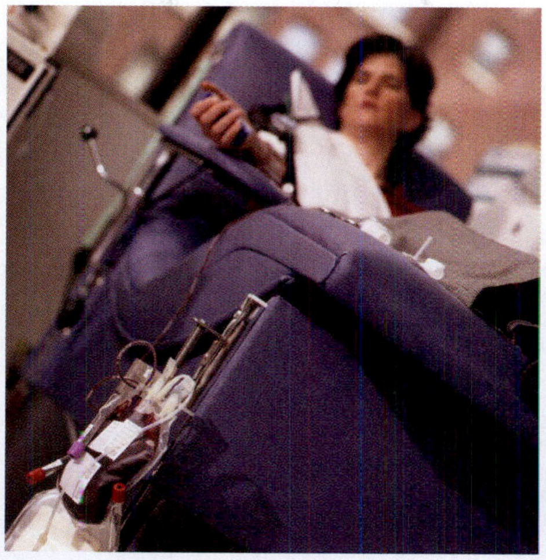

Regular donation of blood is the main intervention for treating iron overload in the body.

Dietary supplements that contain iron must not be used, and foods highly fortified with iron, should be avoided. The same advice may be given as well for vitamin C supplements. Most people with hereditary hemochromatosis are not aware that they have a predisposition to accumulating excessive amounts of iron. If such a person were to decide to use iron supplements to increase his or her energy or to combat fatigue, for example, iron accumulation and tissue damage could be accelerated and enhanced, increasing the risk of chronic disease. For this reason, iron supplements should not be used indiscriminately but should be used only when iron deficiency has been diagnosed by a health professional and iron therapy is prescribed.

As you can see, with iron more than perhaps any other nutrient, it is critical to meet daily requirements for the proper nutrient intake—not too little, not too much, but just the right amount. Different individuals have different needs. People who don't consume enough iron to meet their needs can develop iron deficiency and eventually anemia. On the other hand, for some people, consuming too much iron every day can lead to serious illness, including death. Hereditary hemochromatosis is one of the first examples of how a gene interacts with nutrition (iron intake) to affect risk of disease. As the public and health professionals become more aware of hereditary hemochromatosis, iron overload can be detected earlier, treated more effectively, and, ultimately, prevented.

Drs. Imperatore and Bowman are epidemiologists at the Centers for Disease Control and Prevention in Atlanta, GA. Dr. Imperatore is a genetic epidemiologist and Dr. Bowman is Chief of the Chronic Disease Nutrition Branch. Both are especially interested in the disease hemochromatosis.

Whereas inadequate dietary intake of zinc may be the cause of poor zinc status in some, inhibitors of zinc absorption are also a causative factor in depleted zinc status. As previously mentioned, phytic acid decreases zinc absorption, as do high intakes of calcium. Studies have found that up to a 50% decrease in zinc absorption occurs when calcium supplements are taken with a meal. For this reason, postmenopausal women and other groups who take calcium supplements may need to increase their zinc intake, as well as avoid use of calcium supplements at meals that are rich in zinc. Certain milk proteins also have been shown to have a negative effect on zinc absorption. Finally, zinc is known to compete with copper and iron for absorption. Although this competition can be harmful if excess zinc is routinely consumed, it can also be advantageous as part of the treatment of disease, such as Wilson's disease, in which there is limited copper excretion (this will be discussed further in a following section on zinc toxicity).

Critical | Thinking

As noted in the Nutrition Perspective, zinc lozenges have received much attention as a treatment for the common cold. You tell a classmate that you do not feel that the evidence is convincing enough to recommend this practice to the general public. Your friend would like to know what it would take to convince you that zinc is a reasonable treatment for the common cold.

Food Sources of Zinc

Food Item and Amount	*Zinc (mg)*
Steamed oysters, 6	49.9
Sirloin steak, 4 oz	7.4
Peanuts, 1 cup	4.8
Pot roast, 3 oz	4.6
Special K cereal, 1 cup	3.8
Wheat germ, ¼ cup	3.5
Lamb chops, 3 oz	2.7
Black-eyed peas, 1 cup	2.2
Plain yogurt, 1 cup	2.2
Lean ham, 3 oz	1.9
Swiss cheese, 1.5 oz	1.7
Ricotta cheese, ½ cup	1.7
Sunflower seeds, 1 oz	1.5
Cheddar cheese, 1.5 oz	1.3
Enriched white rice, ½ cup	1.1

RDA, adult male, 11 mg
RDA, adult female, 8 mg

Peanuts are a plant source of zinc.

Functions of Zinc

It is hard to name a body process or body structure that isn't affected either directly or indirectly by zinc. Some zinc functions involve enzymes where zinc is either part of the catalytic reaction or it stabilizes the enzyme structure. The exact number of known zinc-dependent enzymes depends on classification (i.e., two similar enzymes can be called two different enzymes or a single enzyme with different forms). Suffice it to say that over 50 (and as many as 200 or more) enzymes need zinc to function. These functions contribute to DNA and RNA synthesis, alcohol metabolism, protein metabolism and related growth and development of the body, antioxidant defenses (see the functions of copper for details), immune function, and acid/base balance in the body.[8] In addition to enzyme-related functions, zinc also stabilizes the structures of cell membrane proteins, certain hormones, and gene transcription factors (called zinc fingers). The cell membrane function has very broad effects because cell membrane stability influences receptors, which signal all types of actions in cells. If zinc function is impaired, some receptors become less active while others become more active. Therefore, some body functions become sluggish while others become overactive. Both of these effects can be seen in regard to immune responses. On one hand, an impairment in zinc function can limit the ability of the immune system to respond to challenges like a bacterial infection. On the other hand, impaired zinc function causes some immune cells to activate without a "good reason." This in turn produces harmful free radicals and oxidant stress.

Zinc in Foods

In general, protein-rich diets are also rich in zinc. North Americans get about 70% of their dietary zinc from animal foods. Lean meats—especially beef, other red meats, and shellfish—are among the best zinc sources. Plant sources of zinc, such as nuts, beans, and whole grains, can also deliver substantial amounts of zinc to body cells. Zinc is not part of the enrichment process, so refined flours are not a good source.

Zinc Needs

The RDA for zinc of 11 mg/day for adult males and 8 mg/day for adult females is based on replacing daily losses via feces, skin, and urine.[11] The Daily Value used on food and supplement labels for zinc is 15 mg. Average adult intakes in North America are 9 to 13 mg/day, with men showing the higher value.

One key issue in understanding zinc needs is body adaptation to different intakes. Some research suggests that people change their zinc absorption and excretion rates to allow them to get by on lower intakes than what is seen in people who eat relatively high amounts of zinc.

Zinc Deficiency

In a zinc deficiency, not all zinc functions decrease at the same rates. Some are impaired even in mild zinc deficiency, while others do not show a major impairment unless the deficiency becomes severe.[1] Cell membrane functions may be the most sensitive change to a mild zinc deficiency.[15] Still other zinc-requiring functions manage to use zinc so effectively that they operate fairly well even in a pronounced zinc deficiency. Thus, the symptoms of zinc deficiency depend a lot on its severity. The symptoms seem also to depend on what else is happening in the body at the same time, such that some zinc functions are affected mainly when zinc deficiency is combined with certain other factors (e.g., the presence of another disease or a period of rapid growth).

Linking poor health with zinc deficiency can be challenging. This is because zinc affects so many molecular processes and functions, either directly or indirectly. For example, severe zinc deficiency can affect bone growth. There are many possible reasons, including a number of zinc-dependent enzymes and hormones.

As noted at the beginning of the zinc section, severe deficiency in humans was first reported in areas of the Middle East. Symptoms included severely stunted growth, poor taste sensitivity, and impaired sexual maturation in the males (Fig. 12-4).

In certain parts of the world, where economics limit food choices, the effects of zinc deficiency can be clearly seen in children.[11] Symptoms include severe, even fatal diarrhea, poor growth, impaired vitamin A function, and high risk of pneumonia (presumably due to impaired immune function). In these same parts of the world, zinc deficiency in pregnant women may contribute to increased infant mortality and birth defects.

Besides dietary causes of severe zinc deficiency, this state can also be produced by a genetic condition where zinc absorption is impaired. This disease, acrodermatitis enteropathica, is recognizable by a skin condition that develops in infancy. The condition can be treated with supplemental zinc. Preterm infants can also show signs of zinc deficiency for the same general reason described for iron and preterm infants. However, the extent and significance of this state for zinc deficiency has not been well studied.

Marginal zinc deficiency may occur in many people, though there are still many questions to be answered. The classic example of documented marginal zinc deficiency involves a study done some time ago on a group of children in the Denver, Colorado area. The study reported that marginal zinc deficiency was responsible for impaired growth in a number of children. It is noteworthy that the marginal zinc deficiency seemed to be caused not by economic reasons, but rather due to poor food choices.

Many situations are suspected to produce marginal zinc deficiencies for various reasons. One reason can be moderately low intake, but other factors may include impaired zinc absorption, high zinc excretion, abnormal body distribution of zinc (e.g., one zinc protein absorbs high amounts of zinc), and high needs for certain zinc functions. However, in almost all of these situations, there is still uncertainty about how frequent the problem is and what symptoms result. One reason is that the symptoms may be produced by a combination of the zinc-related problem plus some other factor. This makes it challenging to tease out how much zinc status is actually involved. Another major issue has been the lack of a good test for marginal zinc deficiency. Most of the tests that are used either are not sensitive to small changes in zinc status, have readings that can be affected by factors other than zinc status, require specialized equipment or expertise, or all of the above. Despite these barriers, zinc researchers are slowly making progress on marginal zinc deficiencies. A few examples of groups that may be prone to marginal zinc deficiencies are Crohn's disease patients, people on kidney dialysis, diabetic individuals, older adults, sickle-cell anemia patients, alcoholics, and children with Down's syndrome. Vegetarians may also be vulnerable to marginal zinc status. However, there is some contention that vegetarians adapt to low intake by reducing zinc excretion while increasing zinc absorption.[13]

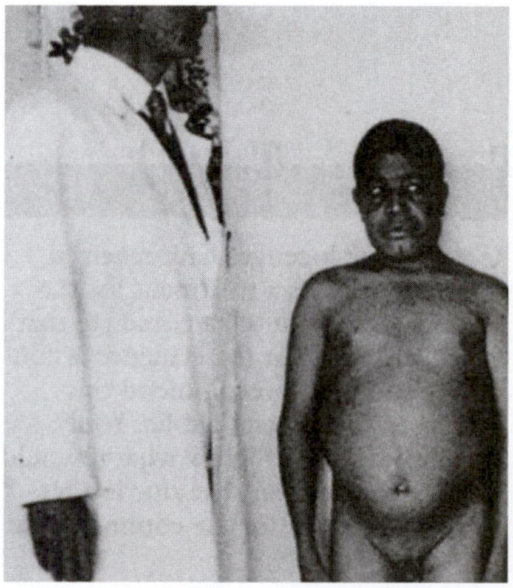

Figure 12-4 An example of zinc deficiency. An Egyptian farm boy, age 16 years and 49 inches tall, with dwarfism and inadequate sexual development associated with a zinc deficiency.

Toxicity of Zinc

The Upper Level set for zinc is 40 mg/day, based on the ability of zinc to interfere with copper status as measured by a fall in the activity of copper-containing enzymes. Zinc supplements at approximately 5 to 20 times the RDA can reduce HDL-cholesterol, perhaps by interfering with copper absorption. Again, this shows why mineral supplements should not be consumed in excess of the Upper Level unless under close scrutiny of a physician. Zinc intakes over 100 mg/day also result in diarrhea, cramps, nausea, vomiting, and depressed immune system function, especially if intake exceeds 2 g/day.

Copper (Cu)

Like iron, copper can catalyze certain reactions by alternating between two valences (Cu^{+} and Cu^{2+}). As with iron, this property is very useful when copper is harnessed within enzymes or other proteins, but dangerous when not. As with iron, specific chaperone proteins also distribute copper around the body. Copper enzymes perform a number of different functions and are quite impaired by severe copper deficiency. In addition, some research suggests that moderate copper deficiency may impair copper function enough to have subtle, but important, long-term effects on health.

Absorption, Transport, Storage, and Excretion of Copper

Copper is absorbed mostly in the small intestine, with a percent absorption that can vary widely (12 to 70%). The factors affecting copper absorption have not been studied as well as the factors affecting iron or zinc. However, one major factor in copper absorption can be zinc supplementation. High-dose zinc supplementation can impair copper absorption to the point of causing a severe copper deficiency.[10] This probably involves some competition between copper and zinc for a common intestinal receptor.

After intestinal absorption, copper moves rapidly into the liver and kidney, the main sites of storage. Following this initial distribution, copper transport is very controlled. Copper moves from the liver to other tissues tightly bound to the protein ceruloplasmin, which also has an enzyme function (see below). Ceruloplasmin releases copper to cells via a specific receptor. The copper then seems to bind to chaperone proteins.[10] There may be situations where copper is transported by other means, but the process just described is likely the most common pathway. Excess copper is excreted primarily in the bile. In a genetic disorder called Wilson's disease, this excretion is impaired, which can produce copper toxicity (see section on toxicity of copper).

Seafood is a good source of copper.

Functions of Copper

As noted above, copper functions in enzymes as a catalyst that alternates between two different valences. One of these enzymes, ceruloplasmin (and possibly some other copper enzymes) are needed to transport iron from the liver to various functional sites, including where iron is inserted into hemoglobin. Ceruloplasmin may also have an antioxidant function by inhibiting iron catalyzed formation of free radicals. An even better characterized antioxidant function for copper is its role in two of the three members of a family of enzymes known as **superoxide dismutase** (also called **SOD**). This family of enzymes eliminates one particular free radical known as superoxide ($O_2^{\cdot -}$). Copper is needed for function of the SOD enzyme found in the cytosol of cells (partners with zinc) and for another SOD enzyme found outside of cells (again partners with zinc). (A third SOD enzyme is found in mitochondria, but it contains only manganese.)

superoxide dismutase (SOD) An enzyme that can quench (deactivate) a superoxide negative free radical ($O_2^{\cdot -}$). This can contain the trace minerals copper, zinc, and manganese.

Copper is also part of a number of other enzymes. One of these enzymes is cytochrome C oxidase, which catalyzes the last step of the electron transport chain. In this step of the chain, oxygen enters and water leaves. This enzyme is one reason cyanide is so toxic. Cyanide binds to the copper in this enzyme, which in turn blocks aerobic respiration. Another copper enzyme forms norepinephrine, which is important both as a hormone and a neurotransmitter. Still another copper enzyme, lysyl oxidase, is very important in connective tissue formation. Lysyl oxidase cross-links the strands within two structural proteins that give tensile strength to connective tissues. Connective tissue comprises a large portion of structures such as blood vessels, lungs, skin, and the protein portion of bone. The two structural proteins that are cross-linked by lysyl oxidase are elastin and collagen. The latter is the same protein whose structure is affected by vitamin C (review Chapter 10). Vitamin C is needed to put collagen in the right shape for the three individual strands to curl around each other. Lysyl oxidase completes the process by "gluing" the strands together.

Copper is also essential to optimal immune function, though the exact reasons are still unclear. Possibly, copper antioxidant functions help protect immune cells, which are often under a lot of oxidant stress.

Copper in Foods

Good food sources of copper include liver, shellfish, nuts, seeds, soy products, avocados, and dark chocolate. Legumes, whole-grain products, and some drinking water are also important sources. Meat is not as good a source of copper as it is for iron or zinc. Nonetheless, if you consume a lot of meat, the copper can add up to an amount that covers at least part of your copper needs. In addition, meat may promote copper absorption from other foods, just as it does with iron. Cow's milk is not a good copper source. It should also be mentioned that unlike some trace minerals, copper is not typically added to ready-to-eat breakfast cereals in high amounts. This is because cereal fats can be oxidized by the copper complexes most often used for food fortification.

Food Sources of Copper

Food Item and Amount	*Copper (μg)*
Fried beef liver, 3 oz	3800
Power bar, 1	700
Walnuts, ½ cup	600
Kidney beans, 1 cup	500
Lobster, 3 oz	400
Molasses, 3 tbsp	300
Sunflower seeds, 2 tbsp	300
Shrimp, 3 oz	300
Raisin Bran cereal, 1 cup	300
Great Grains cereal, 1 cup	300
Semi-sweet chocolate, 1 oz	210
Black-eyed peas, ½ cup cooked	200
Wheat germ, ¼ cup	200
Milk chocolate, 1 oz	110
Whole-wheat bread, 1 slice	80

RDA for adults, 900 μg

Copper Needs

The adult RDA for copper is 900 μg for adults.[11] The Daily Value on food and supplement labels for copper is 2 mg. The average adult intake in North America is about 1 to 1.6 mg per day. Women generally consume the smaller amount.

Copper Deficiency

The most common cause of severe copper deficiency is high-dose zinc supplementation, which inhibits copper absorption. Prominent symptoms include iron deficiency-like anemia and a low count for one type of white blood cells. Some medical situations, such as recovery from burns or kidney dialysis, may also produce risk of copper deficiency. Preterm infants are also prone to copper deficiency during the first few days of life, and then again during the catch-up growth period of the first year. The reason for this is the same as noted for iron and zinc.

For a number of years, copper researchers have been interested in marginal copper deficiency.[5] Two concerns have spurred this interest. One, many health problems, especially when involving inflammation, such as rheumatoid arthritis, may raise copper needs. Two, the types of symptoms observed in experimental animals with copper deficiency (sometimes with just marginal deficiency) resemble common human health problems (elevated blood cholesterol, suboptimal immune function, and poor resistance to oxidant stress). More research will likely determine how much we should be concerned about marginal copper deficiency.

Toxicity of Copper

The Upper Level for copper is 10 mg/day, based on the risk of liver damage.[11] Generally, copper toxicity in humans is not very common because intakes are usually not very high and because our bodies can regulate copper storage through excretion via the bile. At single supplemental doses of 10 to 15 mg, though, copper provided in aqueous forms tends to cause vomiting.

An inherited copper-related disease called Wilson's disease results in the accumulation of copper in the liver, brain, kidneys, and cornea of the eye. People with this disease can't incorporate copper into ceruloplasmin and also have a decreased ability to excrete copper in the bile. Wilson's disease is present at birth but usually is not detected until later in childhood, adolescence, or young adulthood. The disease can be very difficult to diagnose, because up to 15% of patients have normal ceruloplasmin concentration, an indicator of copper status. Some of the wide range of symptoms includes liver, nervous system, and psychiatric disorders, as well as kidney abnormalities. If caught early, lifelong treatment with agents that bind copper, such as penicillamine, or use of high dosages of zinc to block copper absorption, can prevent tissue damage and reduce the mental degeneration commonly seen in Wilson's disease. Otherwise, these people die prematurely.

Concept | Check

As with iron absorption, zinc absorption is partly regulated by a mucosal block. Animal protein sources, increased body needs, and small intakes lead to increased

You have now seen that the absence of many nutrients from the diet can lead to anemia:

- Vitamin E deficiency can lead to hemolytic anemia (see Chapter 9).
- Vitamin K deficiency, especially coupled with use of certain antibiotics, can lead to blood loss and thus to hemorrhagic anemia (see Chapter 9).
- Vitamin B-6 deficiency can lead to microcytic anemia and sideroblastic anemia (see Chapter 10).
- Folate deficiency can lead to megaloblastic anemia (see Chapter 10).
- Vitamin B-12 malabsorption can lead to megaloblastic anemia (see Chapter 10).
- An iron deficiency can lead to microcytic hypochromic anemia.
- A copper deficiency can lead, although rarely, to a secondary iron deficiency anemia, as copper aids in iron metabolism.

zinc absorption. Zinc functions as a cofactor for many enzymes and is important for growth and development, and immune function. Beef, seafood, and whole grains are rich food sources of zinc. Copper functions mainly as part of enzymes and other compounds involved in iron metabolism, cross-linking of collagen, and neurotransmitter synthesis. A copper deficiency can result in a form of anemia and impaired immune function. Food sources of copper are liver, seafood, legumes, nuts, and whole grains.

Selenium (Se)

Selenium deficiency and toxicity have occurred in livestock where the soil is very high or very low in selenium. The same is true in humans, though the number of documented cases is fewer in humans. Selenium functions in certain enzymes. Selenium has drawn interest for its roles in antioxidant defense and thyroid hormone production, as well as possible applications in cancer prevention.

Absorption, Transport, Storage, and Excretion of Selenium

Selenium enters the body in many ionic forms. Most selenium in foods is bound to derivatives of the amino acids methionine and cysteine. Because these substances are readily absorbed, the bioavailability of selenium is considerably higher than that of iron and zinc. About 50 to 100% of dietary selenium intake is absorbed, and it is not affected by selenium nutritional status. Since no physiological mechanism appears to control selenium absorption, selenium has a definite potential for toxicity.

Not much is known about the transport of selenium. What is known is that selenium is made available for use when the particular amino acid it is bound to is catabolized. The selenium can then be incorporated into macromolecules, transported to various organs, or excreted. Homeostasis of selenium in the body is achieved through excretion, mainly via the urine and feces. Urinary excretion of selenium increases as dietary intake increases. Selenium is stored primarily bound to the amino acid methionine and as part of glutathione peroxide enzyme. Both are found throughout the body.

Functions of Selenium

Selenium is incorporated into certain enzymes as part of an amino acid known as selenocysteine.[18] Normally, the amino acid cysteine contains sulfur, but in selenocysteine, the sulfur is replaced by selenium. The best understood enzymatic function of selenium occurs as part of two enzymes, each named glutathione peroxidase (one is inside cells, the other is outside cells including in the serum portion of the blood). Glutathione peroxidase is part of the body's antioxidant defense network described in the vitamin E section of Chapter 9. Some of this network is shown in Figure 12-5. Glutathione peroxidase eliminates peroxides, including hydrogen peroxide. These peroxides occur in the body as a by-product of certain body reactions and can also arise in other ways. Peroxide accumulation is a concern because peroxides can easily form free radicals. Another antioxidant system that uses selenium is the newly described **thioredoxin** family of enzymes.

thioredoxin A family of three selenium-dependent enzymes that have an antioxidant and other roles in the body.

Selenium also functions in an enzyme that is part of the process that makes thyroid hormones. Thyroid hormones are very important in stimulating energy input to various body processes needed for growth or maintenance. There are a few other proteins in the body that have been found to contain selenium, but their function is not yet known.[16]

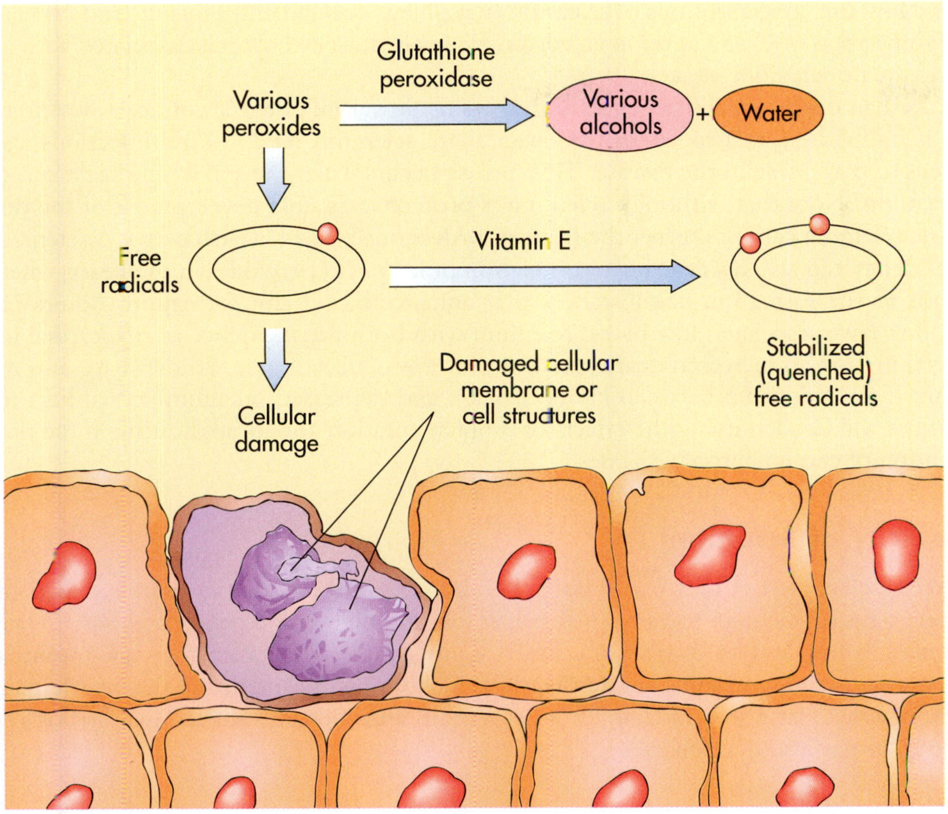

Figure 12-5 Selenium is part of the glutathione peroxidase system, which breaks down peroxides, such as H_2O_2 to water (H_2O), before they can form free radicals. This, in turn, spares some of the need for vitamin E, which is a major free radical scavenger.

Critical | Thinking

Tammy read an article about antioxidants and their role in preventing free radical damage to cells. When Tammy went to the drug store to take a closer look at such supplements, she saw that selenium was one of the antioxidants in the supplements. Why does selenium deserve consideration as an antioxidant?

Selenium in Foods

Animal products are good sources of selenium, though some are better than others. Grain products and nuts are also good sources. Whole-grain products generally have more selenium than white flour, though the latter can also provide a good deal of selenium. The exact amount of selenium in grain products depends on the selenium content of the soil in which the grains are grown.[7] For example, in the United States, pasta tends to be high in selenium because the durum wheat used tends to come from high-selenium soils in the Dakotas.

Food Sources of Selenium

Food Item and Amount	*Selenium (μg)*
Tuna, 3 oz	68
Lean ham, 3 oz	42
Clams, 3 oz	41
Salmon, 3 oz	40
Egg noodles, 1 cup	35
Sirloin steak, 3 oz	28
Chicken breast, 3 oz	20
Special K cereal, 1 cup	17
Oat bran cereal, 1 cup	14
Whole-wheat bread, 1 slice	10
Cooked oatmeal, ½ cup	10
White bread, 1 slice	9
Raisin Bran cereal, 1 cup	4

RDA for adults, 55 μg

Selenium Needs

The RDA for selenium is 55 μg/day for adult men and women.[12] This is based on the amount of selenium needed to maximize glutathione peroxidase activity in blood. In North America average intakes are about 105 μg/day from food. The Daily Value used on food and supplement labels for selenium is 70 μg. Some interesting, but controversial work has raised the possibility that higher selenium intakes (200 μg/day) may help prevent cancer (see the Nutrition Perspective).

Selenium Deficiency

The signs and symptoms of a selenium deficiency in animals and humans include muscle pain, muscle wasting, and cardiomyopathy, which is a form of heart disease resulting from heart muscle damage. These same signs and symptoms are noted when there is insufficient selenium in total parenteral nutrition solutions. Farm animals in areas

Pasta is generally a good source of selenium, as is any meat in the accompanying sauce.

with low soil concentrations of selenium (e.g., New Zealand and Finland) and humans in some areas of China develop characteristic heart muscle disorders associated with an inadequate selenium intake.

Keshan disease, a deficiency state that results in varying degrees of heart deterioration in children, is associated with inadequate selenium intake. Viral infections also seem to play a role in the disease. This disease occurs when the soil is almost devoid of selenium. Note that, although selenium is protective against development of the disease, selenium cannot correct the heart disorders once they have occurred. A selenium deficiency can also result in an accumulation of fatty acid peroxides in the heart, which leads to the formation of substances that enhance blood clot formation. Additional studies have associated low blood selenium with both the incidence of myocardial infarctions and an increased death rate from cardiovascular disease. Studies have also reported a relationship between kidney disease and depressed selenium status. Further studies will be identifying the effects of supplementation and its application in the prevention of certain chronic diseases.

Toxicity of Selenium

Excess selenium can be toxic. The Upper Level is 400 μg/day for adults, based on overt signs of selenium toxicity, such as hair loss and high blood concentrations.[12] Daily intakes as low as 1 to 3 mg can cause toxicity symptoms if taken for many months. These signs and symptoms besides hair loss, include a garlicky odor of the breath, nausea, diarrhea, fatigue, and changes in fingernails and toenails. Rashes and cirrhosis of the liver may also develop.

Case Scenario | Follow-up

Some research has raised the possibility that a moderately high dose of supplemental selenium, such as 200 μg/day, may reduce cancer risk, though the reason is not fully understood. Gina's supplement dose of 200 μg/day, plus a typical dietary intake of 105 μg/day is below the Upper Level of 400 μg/day. Therefore, her practice is probably safe. Whether it will be helpful or not awaits further research. Thus, widespread use of such a high dose of selenium is not currently recommended.

Iodide (I)

goiter An enlargement of the thyroid gland, which can be caused by a lack of iodide in the diet.

Iodine (I_2), present in food as iodide (I^-) and other nonelemental forms, was linked to the presence of an enlarged thyroid gland **(goiter)** during World War I. Men drafted from areas such as the Great Lakes region of the United States had a much higher rate of goiter than men from some other areas of the country. The soil in these areas is very low in iodide. During the 1920s, researchers in Ohio found that goiter can be prevented in children by feeding them low doses of iodide for an extended period. Following the lead of the Swiss, American companies began adding iodide to table salt. Use of iodized salt is the major method for correcting iodide deficiencies.

Iodine (I_2), which is quite poisonous, can be used in a water solution as a topical anti-infective agent. The iodide ion (I^-) is the form of this trace mineral that is an essential nutrient. The term *iodine* is sometimes used in nutrition instead of iodide; however, to avoid confusion with this poisonous form, the term *iodide* will be used exclusively in this textbook.

Today, many nations, such as Canada, require iodide fortification of salt. In the United States, salt can be purchased either fortified or plain. Check for this on the label of a package of salt next time you are in a grocery store. By law, the label on a salt container sold in the United States must clearly state if iodide is present or not. Some areas of Europe, such as northern Italy, have very low iodide concentrations in the soil but have yet to adopt the practice of fortifying salt with iodide. People in these areas, especially women, still suffer from goiter, as do people in areas of Latin America, the Indian subcontinent, Southeast Asia, and Africa. About 2 billion people worldwide are at risk of iodide deficiency, and approximately 800 million of these people have suffered the widespread effects of such a deficiency.

Absorption, Transport, Storage, and Excretion of Iodide

Iodide is efficiently absorbed along the gastrointestinal tract in its inorganic form, the most common form of dietary iodine. Iodide is also easily absorbed in other forms, such as the iodate (IO_3^-) form that is added to bread. After iodide is absorbed into the bloodstream, it is transported as free ions and bound to proteins, including thyroid-binding globulin and albumin. The transported iodide is then distributed throughout the body's extracellular compartments.

About three-quarters of the iodide found in the adult human body is located in the thyroid gland. The thyroid gland actively accumulates and traps iodide from the bloodstream to support thyroid hormone synthesis. The thyroid hormones thyroxine (T_4) and triiodothyronine (T_3) are synthesized from the amino acid tyrosine and iodide. If a person's iodide intake is insufficient, the thyroid gland enlarges as it attempts to take up more iodide from the blood. When iodide intake is low, the body is able to recycle it by removing iodide from the thyroid hormones in the liver and then releasing the iodide into the bloodstream for reabsorption by the thyroid gland.

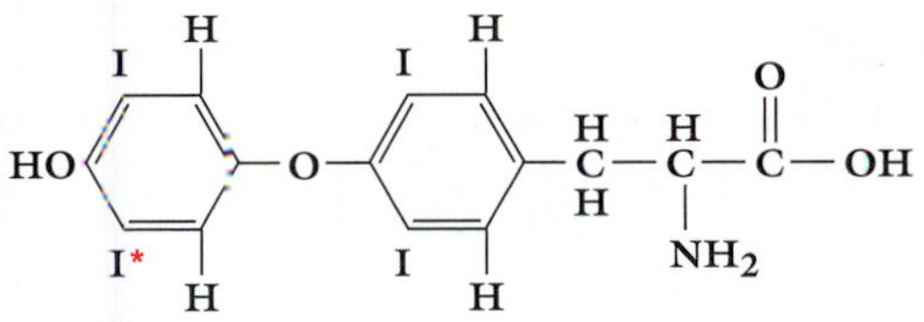

Structure of thyroxine (T_4). Note that triiodothyronine (T_3) lacks one iodide (I), indicated in this figure with a red asterisk.

The kidneys are the principal route for iodide excretion. The amount of iodide found in urine is an adequate measurement of the status of iodide intake, along with current blood concentration of iodide.

basal metabolism The minimal energy the body requires to support itself when resting and awake in a warm, quiet environment. It amounts to roughly 1 kcal/minute, or about 1400 kcal/day, the values are often referred to as basal metabolic rate.

goitrogens Substances in food and water that interfere with thyroid gland metabolism and thus may cause goiter if consumed in large amounts.

Functions of Iodide

The major function of iodide is the synthesis of the thyroid hormone thyroxine (T_4).[11] Almost all organs in the body are targets for T_4, but T_4 is actually considered a prehormone. Within the target cell, T_4 is converted to T_3, the active form of the hormone (Fig. 12-6). T_3 controls the rate of cell metabolism (called the **basal metabolism**).

T_3 stimulates mRNA and protein synthesis, which is especially important for development of the central nervous system. During periods of rapid growth (the first 6 months in utero), T_3 is essential to normal brain development. Under normal circumstances, T_3 also increases glucose utilization and protein synthesis.

Iodide in Foods

Saltwater fish, seafood, iodized salt, molasses, and some plants contain various forms of iodide, especially the leaves of plants grown near the sea. Sea salt found in health-food stores, however, is not a good source because the iodide is lost during processing. A half teaspoon (about 2 g) of iodide-fortified salt supplies the adult RDA for iodide. The actual amount of fortification in the United States is 76 µg of iodide per gram of salt.

The bioavailability of iodide in the diet is associated with the consumption of **goitrogens.** Large amounts of these substances are found in raw vegetables, such as turnips, cabbage, Brussels sprouts, cauliflower, broccoli, rutabagas, and cassava, as well as other plants and even waterborne sources. Goitrogens inhibit iodide metabolism by the thyroid gland and, in turn, inhibit thyroid hormone synthesis. However, goitrogens

Food Sources of Iodide

Food Item and Amount	*Iodide (µg)*
Table salt, ½ tsp	195
Plain yogurt, 1 cup	87
Buttermilk, 1 cup	60
1% fat milk, 1 cup	59
Luna bar, 1	38
Soy protein bar, 1	38
Egg, 1 large	35
1% cottage cheese, ½ cup	28
Mozzarella cheese, 1 oz	10

Adult RDA, 150 µg

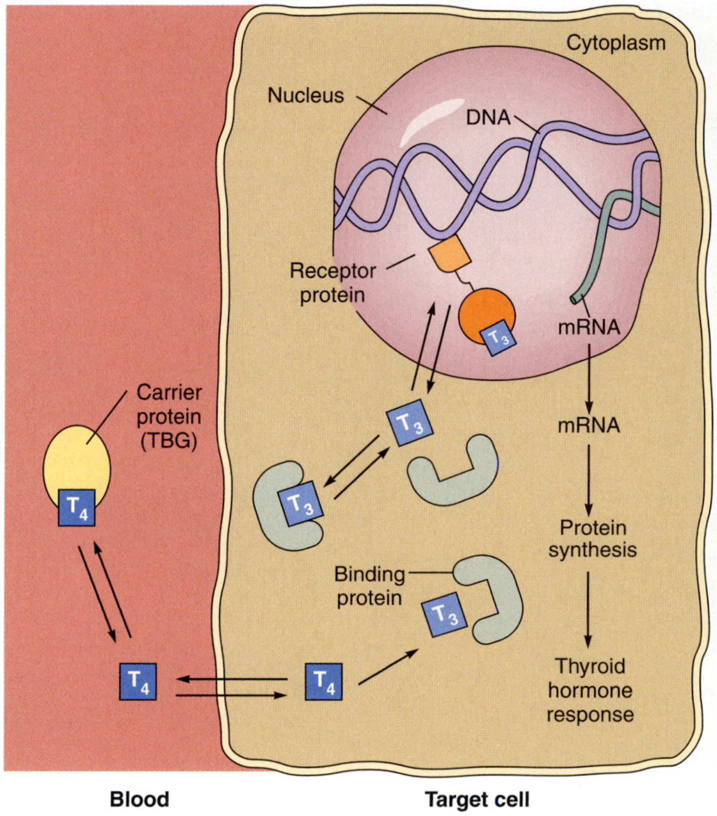

Figure 12-6 The mechanism of the action of thyroid hormones on the target cell. T_4 is carried by a thyroid-binding globulin in the blood. Upon release T_4 enters the target cell and is converted into T_3 in the cytoplasm. T_3 enters the nucleus and binds to its nuclear receptor. The hormone-receptor complex can then bind to a specific area of DNA to activate specific genes and produce the hormone response. T_4 binding can lead to the same response, but it is 10 times weaker than that of T_3.

are not that important in developed countries, since they are destroyed by cooking, and the foods they are found in do not play a central role in the customary diets. They are, however, important to consider in less-developed parts of the world.

Iodide Needs

The RDA for iodide for adults is 150 μg/day.[11] This amount of iodide is needed to maintain adequate iodide uptake and turnover by the thyroid gland. The Daily Value used on food and supplement labels for iodide is also 150 μg/day. Most North Americans consume much more iodide than the RDA. Consumption is estimated to be about 190 to 300 μg/day (not including the iodide contributed by the use of iodized salt at the table), with men consuming the higher amounts.

Such intakes of iodide are typical because it is used as a sterilizing agent in dairies and restaurants, as a dough conditioner in bakeries, in food colorants, and in iodized salt.

Iodide Deficiency

In an iodide deficiency, insufficient T_4 is produced. An adaptive response causes continual growth of the thyroid gland, eventually producing a greatly enlarged gland, or goiter. A fall in metabolic rate and an increase in blood cholesterol are two other symptoms of thyroid hormone deficiency.

Simple goiter is a painless condition, but if uncorrected it can lead to pressure on the trachea (windpipe), which may cause difficulty in breathing. In addition, other serious metabolic problems can result from low T_4 levels. Treatment with iodide can result in a slow reduction in the size of the thyroid gland, although surgical removal of part of the gland may be required in severe cases.

An iodide-deficient diet poses a major threat to pregnant women and the fetus, especially during the latter two-thirds of pregnancy.[9] Some of the harmful documented

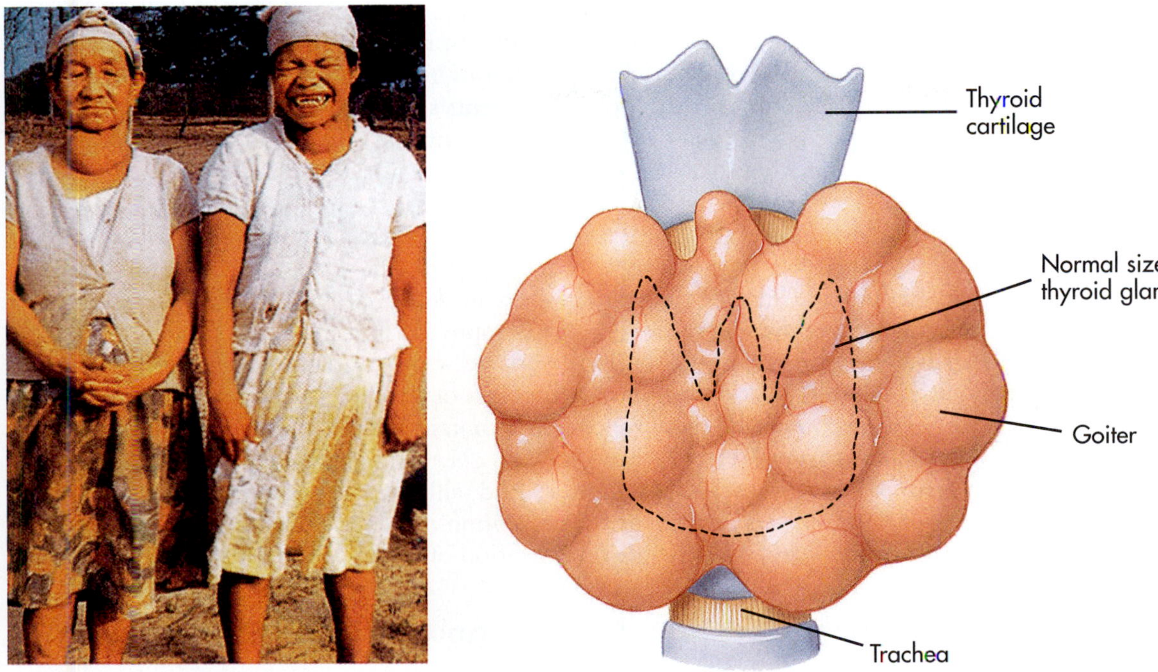

Figure 12-7 Goiter and cretinism in Bolivia. The mother on the left is goitrous but otherwise normal. The daughter is goitrous, mentally retarded, deaf, and mute. Both mother and daughter exhibit characteristics typical of iodide deficiency.
Illustration by William Ober.

effects include stillbirth, low birth weight, increased infant mortality, goiter, impaired mental function, and retarded development. Increasing the mother's intake of iodide prior to the fourth month of pregnancy, but preferably sooner, can prevent these abnormalities. The World Health Organization estimates that at least 50 million people in the world suffer from varying degrees of preventable brain damage due to the effects of iodide deficiency on fetal brain development. The resulting retardation of body growth and mental development is referred to as **cretinism.** Cretinism was common in certain areas of the United States before the program to fortify salt with iodide. Today, cretinism still appears in parts of Europe, Africa, Latin America, and Asia (Fig. 12-7). In these areas, iodinated vegetable oil given orally or by injection is being used in an attempt to decrease iodide deficiency, in addition to the fortification of salt with iodide. The eradication of iodide deficiency is a goal of many health-related and service organizations worldwide. Iodide deficiency is common and poses a major threat to public health in many countries.[9] As noted before, an estimated 2 billion people are at risk of iodide deficiency disease. Correction of the problem, though seemingly simple, is often hindered by political, economic, and cultural issues.

cretinism The stunting of body growth and mental development during fetal and later development that results from inadequate maternal intake of iodide during pregnancy.

Toxicity of Iodide

When very high amounts of iodide are consumed, thyroid hormone synthesis is inhibited, as in a deficiency. The Upper Level of 1.1 mg/day is based on such an effect.[11] This can appear in people who eat a lot of seaweed, which is rich in iodide.

Fluoride (F)

Fluoride may not be an essential nutrient per se because all basic body functions may proceed without it. However, fluoride does have some health-promoting attributes. Dentists in the early 1900s noticed a lower incidence of dental caries in the southwestern

mottling The discoloration or marking of the surfaces of teeth from exposure to excessive amounts of fluoride (also called enamel fluorosis).

United States, where the water naturally contained high concentrations of fluoride. Many people in these areas had small spots on the teeth, called **mottling** (or enamel fluorosis), due to deposits of fluoride; although discolored, these mottled teeth were virtually free of dental caries. After experiments showed that fluoride in the water does indeed decrease the rate of dental caries, the controlled fluoridation of water in parts of the United States began in 1945 (see Chapter 5 for a review of the development of dental caries).

Like chlorine, fluorine (F_2) is a poisonous gas. The fluoride ion (F^-) is the form of this trace mineral that contributes to human health.

People who have grown up drinking fluoridated water generally have 40 to 60% fewer dental caries than people who did not drink fluoridated water as children. Dentists can provide fluoride treatments, and schools can provide fluoride tablets, but it is much less expensive and more reliable to simply add fluoride to the community's drinking water. However, not all public or private water sources contain enough fluoride. When in doubt, contact your local water plant or have the water in your home analyzed for fluoride content. If the water doesn't contain the recommended amount—1 part per million parts of water (1 ppm, or 1 mg/L)—talk to your dentist about the best means for obtaining sufficient fluoride. And, although the most important clinical aspect of fluoride is its benefits in the prevention of dental caries, fluoride has also been shown to protect against the demineralization of other calcified tissues.[1]

Absorption, Transport, Storage, and Excretion of Fluoride

The absorption of fluoride occurs very rapidly. A significant proportion of dietary fluoride is absorbed in the stomach. Absorption continues to take place throughout the GI tract by passive diffusion. Overall, about 80 to 90% is absorbed. Fluoride is then transported throughout the body via the bloodstream in the ionic form.

Calcified tissue deposition and renal excretion are the two major mechanisms by which fluoride is removed from circulation. An estimated 50% of the fluoride absorbed each day is deposited in calcified tissues, bones and teeth. The amount of fluoride deposited depends on the stage of development of the bone, with the developing stages being the most significant. The major path for the excretion of fluoride from the body occurs via the urine.

Functions of Fluoride

Although an essential function has not been described for fluoride, it is still recognized as a trace mineral with the beneficial property of protecting against the demineralization of calcified tissues.[11] The action of fluoride on the erupted teeth of children and adults is due to its effects on the metabolism of bacteria in dental plaque. It also works to reduce dental caries by

fluorapatite A fluoride-containing, acid-resistant crystalline substance that is produced during bone and tooth development. Its presence in teeth helps prevent dental caries.

- Reducing the acid solubility of the enamel by forming **fluorapatite** crystals, rather than the typical hydroxyapatite crystals
- Promoting the remineralization of enamel lesions
- Increasing the deposition of minerals that retard the development of caries
- Reducing the net rate of transport of minerals from the enamel surface

The fluoride present in bones is constantly released into the blood, and more so if the bone fluoride content is high. This combines with daily fluoride exposure from fluoridated water (if available) and toothpaste (if used). Blood fluoride then contributes to fluoride in the saliva, which in turn bathes the teeth to provide daily fluoride protection. Overall, lifelong fluoride exposure on a daily basis is the most beneficial way to receive the dental caries-preventive function of fluoride.

Due to its ability to increase bone mass, high doses of fluoride (>20 mg/day) are being used experimentally in adults to treat severe osteoporosis, especially that seen in the spine. Fluoride has the means to stimulate osteoblasts (bone-forming cells) to increase the production of proteins that ultimately undergo rapid mineralization to form new bone. Such high fluoride dosages can cause significant side effects, such as stomach upset and bone pain. Ongoing research is attempting to establish an effective dose and duration of treatment. Sodium fluoride is an appealing treatment option for osteoporosis, due to its low cost and rapid response. A recent study reported that low-dose fluoride therapy increases spine bone mass and reduces vertebral fracture. The question remains as to how strong the treated bone actually will be in the long run.

Toothpaste with fluoride is a typical source of dietary fluoride.

Fluoride in Foods

In North America, the major source of dietary fluoride is drinking water. Typical fluoridated water contains about 0.2 mg/cup. Tea, seafood (especially marine fish that are consumed with their bones), and seaweed are among the richest dietary sources of fluoride. Estimating fluoride content in food can be difficult, since water sources can vary in amount. Toothpaste, mouth rinses, and fluoride treatments performed by dentists are other sources of fluoride.

Fluoride Needs

The Adequate Intake for fluoride is 3.1 mg/day for women and 3.8 mg/day for men.[11] For infants up to 6 months of age, the Adequate Intake is 0.01 mg/day and increases to 0.5 mg/day through age 1. For childhood and adolescence, the fluoride Adequate Intake ranges from 0.7 to 3.2 mg/day. This range of intake provides the benefits of resistance to dental caries without causing mottling of the teeth, which is the basis for setting the Adequate Intake.

Toxicity of Fluoride

Although life-threatening cases of acute fluoride toxicity are extremely rare, substantial amounts of fluoride in toothpastes, mouth rinses, or dietary supplements are found in most North American households and should be of special concern for parents with young children. The signs and symptoms of fluoride toxicity can develop very rapidly and include nausea, vomiting, diarrhea, abdominal pain, excessive salivation and tearing, pulmonary disturbances, cardiac insufficiency and weakness, convulsions, sensory disturbances, paralysis, and coma.

A fluoride intake greater than 6 mg/day can mottle teeth during their developmental stage. Children who swallow large amounts of fluoridated toothpaste as part of daily tooth care are at greatest risk. Limiting the amount used to "pea" size is the best way to prevent this problem.[1] When fluoride intakes reach 20 mg/day during tooth development, the tooth structure is weakened and can crumble. The same deterioration happens throughout the skeleton and is called **skeletal fluorosis.** With this in mind, the Upper Level set for children over 9 years of age and adults is 10 mg/day, based on the risk of skeletal fluorosis. Note that high fluoride intake in adults does not cause mottling of teeth.

skeletal fluorosis A condition caused by a greatly excessive fluoride intake that is characterized by weakened skeletal structure.

Concept | Check

Selenium is important for the activity of glutathione peroxidase, an enzyme that reduces the concentration of peroxides, thus lessening the free radical load in the body. In this way, selenium spares some of the need for vitamin E. A deficiency results in muscle and heart disorders. Organ meats, eggs, fish, and grains are good selenium sources; however, the selenium content in grains depends on the selenium concentration in the soil. A high selenium intake is potentially toxic. Iodide is vital in the synthesis of thyroid hormones. A prolonged insufficient intake will cause the thyroid gland to enlarge, resulting in goiter. Insufficient intake in pregnancy can lead to mental retardation in the offspring. The use of iodized salt has virtually eliminated this condition in North America. Fluoride incorporated into teeth during development makes them resistant to acid and bacterial attack, in turn reducing development of dental caries. Regular fluoride exposure also aids in the remineralization of teeth once decay begins. Most of us receive adequate amounts of fluoride from that added to drinking water and toothpaste. A high fluoride intake during tooth development can lead to spotted, or mottled, teeth.

Chromium (Cr)

Chromium is an essential trace mineral that is widely distributed in small amounts throughout the food supply. The importance of chromium in human diets has been recognized only in the past 40 years. Although not much is understood about this mineral, many studies suggest that chromium plays an important role in maintaining proper carbohydrate and lipid metabolism, which may help alleviate type 2 and certain other forms of diabetes in some individuals.

Absorption, Transport, Storage, and Excretion of Chromium

Only about 0.5 to 2% of chromium from food is absorbed. However, the bioavailability of chromium in humans is difficult to assess because the concentrations in human tissues are very low. Chromium is transported in the bloodstream primarily by the iron-binding protein transferrin, and it appears to be a bone-seeking trace mineral. Chromium accumulates as well in the spleen, liver, and kidneys. The excretion of chromium occurs via the feces.[19]

Functions of Chromium

Mushrooms are a good source of chromium.

The most studied function of chromium is the maintenance of glucose uptake into cells, but the actual mechanism is still under debate. One proposal is that chromium's ability to enhance insulin action occurs when a chromium-binding protein binds to insulin receptors and then boosts receptor activity.

Chromium in Foods

As previously mentioned, chromium is widely distributed in small quantities throughout the food supply. Specific data regarding the chromium content of various foods are scant, and most food composition tables do not include values for this trace mineral. Processed meats, organ meats (liver), whole-grain products, egg yolks, mushrooms, broccoli, nuts, some legumes (such as dried beans), and beer are the most reliable sources. Yeast is also a source. Generally speaking, whole grains and cereals contain higher concentrations of chromium than do fruits and vegetables. The amount of chromium in foods is closely tied to the local soil content of chromium. To provide yourself with an adequate chromium intake, regularly choose whole grains in preference to refined grains.

Chromium Needs

As discussed further in the Nutrition Perspective, chromium supplements have been touted to help with weight loss and exercise-induced increases in muscle mass. Most research, however, does not support this assertion.

The Adequate Intake for chromium is 35 μg/day for men and 25 μg/day for women.[11] This is based on the amount typically found in well-balanced diets. The average dietary intake for adults in North America generally meets the Adequate Intake standards. The Daily Value used on food and supplement labels for chromium is 120 μg.

Chromium Deficiency

A chromium deficiency is characterized by impaired glucose tolerance and elevated blood cholesterol and triglycerides. The mechanism by which chromium influences cholesterol metabolism is not known but may involve enzymes that control cholesterol synthesis. Chromium deficiency appears in people maintained on total parenteral nutrition not supplemented with chromium, as well as in children suffering from undernutrition. In addition, some adults may become chromium-deficient as they age, and this may contribute to the increased risk for the development of type 2 diabetes in older persons. A recent study observed that, when yeast chromium was fed to older persons, there was improvement in glucose tolerance. Since sensitive measures of chromium status are not available, marginal chromium deficiencies may go undetected.

Toxicity of Chromium

Chromium in foods has not shown any toxicity, so no Upper Level has been set. Chromium toxicity has been reported in people exposed to chromium in industrial settings and in painters using art supplies with a very high chromium content. Exposure to chromium occurs most frequently from workplace air or food or water from soil near chromium waste sites. Chromium poisoning damages the lungs and causes allergic responses in the skin. In addition, the most popular form of chromium in dietary supplements, chromium picolinate, appears to be absorbed in a fashion different from dietary chromium and can lead to the production of harmful free radicals.[19]

Manganese (Mn)

It is easy to confuse the mineral manganese (Mn) with magnesium (Mg). Their names are similar, and in a few metabolic pathways they can substitute for each other. Both of these minerals form bridges between ATP or ADP and enzymes. In some cases, these enzymes can use either magnesium or manganese, but in many other cases, magnesium seems to be the preferred mineral. On the other hand, there are some enzymes that prefer manganese. These include an enzyme involved in glucose production, and a family of enzymes which put together protein-carbohydrate complexes that are in the protein portion of bone.[14] Besides bridge-forming activities, manganese is an actual part of some enzymes, much like copper, zinc, and iron. Manganese-containing enzymes include mitochondrial superoxide dismutase. Manganese enzymes also work in the urea cycle and in carbohydrate metabolism.

Nuts are a good source of manganese.

Based on balance studies of intakes and losses, an Adequate Intake for manganese is set at 2.3 mg/day for adult men and 1.8 mg/day for adult women.[11] It has been generally assumed that almost everyone consumes plenty of manganese, but a few studies have raised the possibility that this may not always be true. Unfortunately, very little manganese research has been done in humans. The Daily Value used for manganese on food and supplement labels is 2 mg.

Foods that contain the most manganese include nuts, legumes, tea, and whole grains, but little is known about how well manganese is absorbed from various foods. Animal products generally contribute little manganese to the diet.

A concern has been raised for manganese toxicity due to some high-dose supplements. The Upper Level for manganese is 11 mg/day based on the development of nerve damage.[11]

Molybdenum (Mo)

Molybdenum is notable for its interactions with iron and copper. In particular, high intakes of molybdenum inhibit copper absorption.

Several enzymes—including **xanthine dehydrogenase** and a related form, xanthine oxidase—require molybdenum. The oxidase form of the enzyme is produced from the dehydrogenase form during tissue injury. No molybdenum deficiency has been observed in people consuming a normal diet, although deficiency signs and symptoms have appeared in people on total parenteral nutrition.[14] These symptoms include

xanthine dehydrogenase An enzyme containing molybdenum and iron, which functions in the formation of uric acid and the mobilization of iron from liver ferritin stores.

increased heart and respiration rates, night blindness, mental confusion, edema, weakness, and coma.

Good food sources of molybdenum include milk and milk products, beans, liver, whole grains, and nuts. The RDA for molybdenum is 45 μg/day for adults.[11] This is based on the amount needed to balance daily losses. The Daily Value used on food and supplement labels for molybdenum is 75 μg. Typical North American intakes are 75 to 110 μg/day, with the higher intakes seen in men. When laboratory animals consume high dosages of molybdenum, they develop evidence of toxicity, including anemia, weight loss, and decreased growth. The Upper Level of 2 mg/day is based on decreased growth and reproduction in laboratory animals.

See Table 12-2 to review the minerals discussed so far in this chapter.

Ultratrace Minerals

There are many elements of the periodic table that occur in microgram/gram amounts in body tissues (Table 12-3). Ultimately, some may be elevated to the status of essential nutrients, but at this time elements such as aluminum, cadmium, bromine, germanium, lead, lithium, rubidium, and tin have not been shown to have any beneficial effects in humans.[14] In fact, lead is a danger to young children, as evidenced by toxicity to those children living in older homes that have been contaminated with peeling lead-based paint (see Chapter 19 for more details on lead).

One possibility to consider is that many ultratrace minerals present in tissues are there by accident, and, although they don't provide any health benefits, neither do they represent a threat. Most of the current knowledge about the ultratrace elements has come from animal studies, which may suggest possible benefits for humans, but the evidence is tentative at best.

What follows is some material about five ultratrace minerals that may have a role in human nutrition. Since these minerals have not yet been declared as essential trace minerals, there are no RDAs or Adequate Intakes set. However, since these ultratrace minerals, like all minerals, can be toxic, in some cases an Upper Level has been established.

Fruits are a source of boron.

Boron (B)

Boron has long been known as an important growth factor for plants. In humans, boron may be involved in the metabolism of steroid (cholesterol-containing) hormones, such as the vitamin D hormone and the estrogens. There appears to be a close interrelation among boron, calcium, and magnesium, but more information is needed to understand how each mineral affects the absorption of the others. Several hypotheses suggest that boron acts as a regulator in cell membrane function, such as membrane stability, or acts as the regulator of the movement of cations and anions through the cell membrane. Sources of boron are peanuts, fruits (especially raisins), legumes, potatoes, vegetables, and wine. In a recent survey, coffee and milk, which are low in boron, were two major contributors of boron to the North American diet due to the high volume consumed. Adults consume about 0.75 to 1.35 mg/day. The Upper Level for boron is 20 mg/day, based on developmental abnormalities in laboratory animals.[11]

Nickel (N)

No biochemical function has been clearly defined for nickel for humans, but a variety of deficiency signs have been reported for farm animals and rats. Nickel may function as a cofactor in a variety of enzymes. It seems to be involved in the breakdown of the branched-chain amino acids and the odd-chain-length fatty acids. It also may be involved in the metabolism of vitamin B-12 and folic acid during the synthesis of methionine from homocysteine. It is found in chocolate, nuts, legumes, and grains. North Americans have an intake of 69 to 162 μg/day. The Upper Level is 1 mg/day, based on poor weight gain in laboratory animals.[11]

Table 12-2 A Summary of Key Trace Minerals

Mineral	Major Functions	Deficiency Symptoms	People Most at Risk	RDA or Adequate Intake	Good Dietary Sources	Results of Toxicity
Iron	Functional component of hemoglobin and other key compounds used in respiration; immune function; cognitive development	Fatigue upon exertion; small, pale red blood cells; low blood hemoglobin values, poor immune function	Infants, preschool children, women in childbearing years	Men: 8 mg Women: 18 mg	Meats, seafood, enriched breads, fortified cereals, molasses	Gastrointestinal upset; toxicity especially seen when children consume many iron pills; toxicity also seen in people with hemochromatosis; Upper Level is 45 mg/day, based on gastric irritation
Zinc	Required for many enzymes, stabilizes cell membranes and other body molecules	Skin rash, diarrhea, decreased appetite and sense of taste, hair loss, poor growth and development	Vegetarians, elderly people, people with alcoholism, malnourished populations	Men: 11 mg Women: 8 mg	Seafoods, meats, whole grains	Supplement use can reduce copper absorption; can cause diarrhea, cramps, depressed immune function; Upper Level is 40 mg/day, based on interaction with copper
Copper	Aids in iron metabolism; works in antioxidant enzymes, and those involved in connective tissue metabolism and hormone synthesis	Anemia, low white blood cell count, poor growth	Overzealous supplementation of zinc	900 µg	Liver, cocoa, beans, nuts, whole grains, shellfish	Excessive supplement use can cause vomiting; nervous system and liver disorders; Upper Level is 8–10 mg/day, based on liver damage
Selenium	Part of an antioxidant system	Muscle pain, muscle weakness, form of heart disease	Only known in one section of China	55 µg	Meats, eggs, fish, seafoods, whole grains	Excessive supplement use can cause nausea, vomiting, hair loss, weakness, liver disease; Upper Level is 400 mg/day, based on hair loss
Iodide	Component of thyroid hormones	Goiter; mental retardation, poor growth in infancy when mother is iodide deficient during pregnancy	Major problem in some parts of the world	150 µg	Iodized salt, white bread, saltwater fish, dairy products	Inhibition of function of the thyroid gland; Upper Level is 1.1 mg/day, based on decreased T_4 synthesis
Fluoride	Increases resistance of tooth enamel to dental caries	Although not a true deficiency symptom, dental caries is a risk	Areas where water is not fluoridated	Men: 3.8 mg Women: 3.1 mg	Fluoridated water, toothpaste, dental treatments, tea, seaweed	Stomach upset; mottling (staining) of teeth during development; bone deterioration; Upper Level is 10 mg/day, based on bone problems
Chromium	Enhances insulin action	High blood glucose after eating	People on intravenous nutrition, perhaps elderly people with type 2 diabetes	25–35 µg	Egg yolks, whole grains, pork, nuts, mushrooms	Caused by industrial contamination, not dietary excess; no Upper Level set
Manganese	Cofactor of some enzymes, such as those involved in carbohydrate metabolism	None in humans	Unknown	1.8–2.3 mg	Nuts, oats, beans, tea	Nervous system disorders; Upper Level is 11 mg/day, based on nerve damage
Molybdenum	Aids action of some enzymes	None in healthy humans	Unsupplemented total parenteral nutrition support	45 µg	Beans, grains, nuts	Poor growth in laboratory animals; Upper Level is 2 mg/day, based on poor growth in laboratory animals

Table 12-3 A Summary of Ultratrace Minerals for Which Human Needs Have Not Been Definitely Established[14]

Mineral	Proposed Functions	Estimates of Daily Human Needs	Dietary Sources
Boron	Cell membrane function (ion transport), steroid hormone metabolism	1–13 mg	Fruits, leafy vegetables, nuts, beans
Nickel	Amino acid and fatty acid metabolism	25–35 μg	Chocolate, nuts, beans, whole grains
Silicon	Bone formation	25–30 mg	Root vegetables, whole grains
Arsenic	Amino acid metabolism, DNA function	12–25 μg	Fish, grains, cereal products
Vanadium	Mimicry of insulin action	10 μg	Shellfish, mushrooms, black pepper

Deficiency symptoms have been produced mostly in experimental animals. Many trace minerals pose a high risk for toxicity. Any supplement use should not exceed the estimates of human needs listed in this table.

Silicon (Si)

Next to oxygen, silicon is the most abundant element in the earth's crust. If that surprises you, realize that quartz is made of silicon and sand is made of quartz. With all this silicon around, it is obvious that some should find its way into plants, animals, and humans. What is not so obvious is whether people actually need silicon. Studies with laboratory rats and chickens suggest that the answer may be yes. In these animals, silicon has shown some relationship to the formation of connective tissue, especially in the protein portion of bone.[14] There has been some speculative research on silicon and human bone structure, but nothing definitive is known. Silicon can be found in foods like high-fiber grain products and root vegetables, but knowledge about silicon absorption from foods is limited.

Beans are a good source of some ultratrace minerals.

Arsenic (As)

Arsenic is a potentially very toxic mineral, but it has also been used in small amounts over the centuries to treat a variety of medical conditions. It is seldom used today, as it has been replaced by more effective medications. Depending on the form of arsenic consumed, absorption varies from 20 to 90%. It is rapidly excreted in the urine and via the bile. Although not clearly defined, arsenic is probably biologically active in the metabolism of the amino acid methionine and methyl groups. Another possible role is in the regulation of gene expression to produce certain proteins. Also, arsenic seems to enhance DNA synthesis in white blood cells. For this reason arsenic is being used in some cancer chemotherapy regimens. North Americans consume about 30 μg/day. Fish, grains, and cereal products contribute the most arsenic to the diet.[11]

Vanadium (V)

Vanadium, both in vivo and in vitro, shows pharmacological activity that mimics the actions of insulin, preventing the symptoms of diabetes in diabetic rats; thus, vanadium may have a role in treating human diabetes. Clinical studies with the trace mineral in both type 1 and type 2 diabetes showed some improvement in glucose utilization. Type 2 diabetes patients displayed improved insulin sensitivity. Vanadium is poorly absorbed and is excreted in the urine and bile. Other than vanadium's possible pharmacologic properties in diabetes treatment, a defined biochemical function for humans has not been described. In laboratory animals, it also seems to stimulate the mineralization of bones and teeth and has a variety of in vitro actions. A vanadium deficiency has not been identified in humans. Human diets supply about 6 to 18 μg per day. Vanadium is found in shellfish, mushrooms, parsley, dill, and some prepared foods. The Upper Level is 1.8 mg/day, based on development of kidney toxicity.[11]

Concept | Check

Chromium may increase the action of the hormone insulin. The amount of chromium found in food depends on soil content. Whole grains, egg yolks, and meat are some of the better sources of chromium. Manganese is a component of bone and many enzymes, including those involved in glucose production. Since our need for it is low, deficiencies are rare. Good food sources of manganese are nuts, oats, tea, and beans. Molybdenum is a component of some enzymes. Deficiencies have appeared only with total parenteral nutrition. Beans, milk and milk products, grains, and nuts are sources of molybdenum. Boron contributes to ion transport across cell membranes, nickel contributes to amino acid metabolism, and silicon contributes to bone metabolism. The roles for some other trace minerals—including arsenic and vanadium—have not been fully established in humans. These minerals are required in such small amounts that diets including a variety of foods and containing some plant protein and whole grains most likely supply adequate amounts.

Summary

1. Six of the trace minerals (iron, zinc, copper, molybdenum, iodide, and selenium) have an RDA. An Adequate Intake has been set for three trace minerals (manganese, chromium, and fluoride).
2. Some trace minerals are difficult to detect in humans, and it is often hard to determine the exact amount of a trace mineral in food. Deficiencies were first observed in small, geographically isolated groups (e.g., selenium deficiency in an area of China) or people nourished exclusively by total parenteral nutrition that did not contain sufficient trace minerals.
3. Iron is a critical component of hemoglobin, myoglobin, and cytochromes. Iron acts as a cofactor for several enzyme systems. Two-thirds of the body's iron is found in hemoglobin in red blood cells, where its job is to transport oxygen from the lungs to the tissues. A prolonged low intake of iron can lead to decreased production of red blood cells and a lack of oxygen being delivered to the tissues. This condition is called iron deficiency anemia, which results in fatigue upon exertion and apathy, as well as decreased learning ability in children.
4. The absorption of iron depends on the body's need for the mineral and on the form of iron in food. The body cannot readily excrete excess iron, but the body has a mucosal block, which limits overabsorption. Heme iron from animal foods is better absorbed than nonheme iron obtained from plant sources. The best sources of dietary iron are animal protein, including beef and other dark meats, oysters, and liver.
5. Girls and women have a higher RDA for iron than men because of menstrual blood loss. Infants and children who live in poverty are often iron deficient because of little heme iron in the diet.
6. Iron toxicity occurs because of a genetic disorder called hemochromatosis, which causes the overabsorption of iron. A common form of poisoning also occurs among toddlers and young children who swallow a large number of iron pills. Death can occur.
7. Zinc functions as a cofactor for many enzyme systems, plus stabilizes membranes and other body molecules. Among the processes affected by zinc are growth, sexual development, immune function, and taste. A zinc deficiency can result in growth failure, loss of appetite, inadequate mental function, a persistent rash, and decreased immune function.
8. Like iron, the best dietary sources of zinc are found in animal foods. Need drives absorption. And like iron, there is a mucosal block in the intestinal cells, which regulates the amount of zinc that can be absorbed. Calcium and iron in supplement form can interfere with zinc absorption. The richest source of zinc is oysters. Other animal proteins are excellent sources. Plant sources are whole grains, peanuts, and legumes.
9. Copper aids in iron mobilization from body stores. Copper is responsible for the cross-linking in collagen formation and it acts as part of antioxidant enzymes. A copper deficiency can result in a secondary iron deficiency. Copper is found in liver, cocoa, legumes, and whole grains.
10. Selenium acts as a cofactor for the enzyme glutathionine peroxidase, which protects cells against destruction by hydrogen peroxide and free radicals. In some instances, selenium can replace some of the need for vitamin E. Human deficiency is rare in North America. The selenium content of the soil where a plant is grown greatly affects the selenium content of the plant food. In a few areas in China where the soil is selenium poor, the inhabitants experience selenium deficiency. Meat, eggs, fish, and shellfish are sources of selenium. Plant sources include grains and seeds.

11. Iodide forms part of the thyroid hormones, one being thyroxine T_4. Thyroid hormone controls the basal metabolic rate. A lack of dietary iodide causes an enlarged thyroid gland, known as goiter. The iodide content of the soil where a plant is grown greatly affects the iodide content of the plant food. Iodide deficiency at one time was common in areas around the Great Lakes in North America because the soil is iodide poor. Today, iodide deficiency in North America is virtually unknown because of the fortification of table salt with iodide, but deficiency is still a major problem in some parts of the world.

12. Fluoride exposure makes the tooth crystal resistant to dental caries, and fluoride in saliva aids in the remineralization of damaged tooth surfaces. Most North Americans receive fluoride from fluoridated drinking water and toothpaste.

13. Chromium contributes to the action of insulin. Chromium is found in meats and whole grains.

14. Manganese functions in several important enzyme systems. Deficiency is rare. Whole grains, legumes, tea, and nuts are food sources.

15. Molybdenum is found in several enzyme systems. Deficiency is rare. Molybdenum is found in plant foods such as legumes and whole grains.

16. Boron contributes to ion transport in cell membranes. Fruits, leafy vegetables, nuts, and beans are sources.

17. Nickel likely participates in amino acid metabolism. Nickel is found in nuts, beans, and whole grains.

18. Silicon is involved in bone formation. Root vegetables and whole grains are sources.

19. Arsenic likely participates in amino acid and DNA metabolism. Fish, grains and cereal products are sources.

20. Vanadium likely has insulin-like actions in the body. Shellfish and mushrooms are sources.

Study Questions

1. What is a balance study, and why is it only a limited tool in evaluating the need for trace minerals?

2. What is anemia? How does a deficiency of vitamins E, K, B-6, and B-12 and the trace minerals iron and copper cause anemia? Describe the signs and symptoms of such anemias.

3. Explain three key functions of iron in the human body.

4. What factors increase the absorption of dietary iron? How might an excess of zinc, manganese, and calcium inhibit iron absorption?

5. What are some tests used to measure iron status? What exactly do these tests measure?

6. Why does zinc affect so many body processes?

7. The fluoridation of drinking water began in the United States in 1945. Today, what percentage of the population consumes fluoridated water? How else do humans obtain fluoride?

8. Describe the chief function in the body of fluoride, copper, chromium, manganese, boron, nickel, and silicon.

9. Why are animal foods a better source of iron, zinc, and selenium than foods of plant origin?

10. Prior to the 1920s, why was goiter such a health problem for people living in the Great Lakes region of the United States? How was this deficiency disease eventually controlled?

Annotated References

1. ADA Reports: Position of the American Dietetic Association: The impact of fluoride on health. *Journal of the American Dietetic Association* 101:126, 2001.

   The American Dietetic Association reaffirms that fluoride is an important element for all mineralized tissues in the body. Appropriate fluoride intake is beneficial to bone and tooth health.

2. Age-Related Eye Disease Study Research Group: A randomized, placebo-controlled, clinical trial of high-dose supplementation with vitamins C and E and beta-carotene for age-related cataract and vision loss. *Arch Ophthalmol* 119:1439–1452, 2001.

   Megadose zinc supplements (80 mg/day of zinc oxide) combined with 2 mg/day of copper reduced progression of macular degeneration in people who showed evidence of the disease. The zinc supplements worked even better when provided in combination with 400 IU of vitamin E, 500 mg of vitamin C, and 15 mg of beta-carotene. The authors suggest that adults who have evidence of macular degeneration talk to their physicians about possibly following such a protocol.

3. Andrews NC: Disorders of iron metabolism. *The New England Journal of Medicine* 341:1986, 1999.

   Iron is able to accept and donate electrons, so it is capable of binding oxygen and participating in many enzyme systems. However, iron can damage tissues by causing the conversion of hydrogen peroxide to free radicals. Iron can't be readily excreted from the body; the cells that line the gastrointestinal tract act as a barrier to overabsorption.

4. Bhaskaram P: Immunobiology of mild micronutrient deficiencies. *British Journal of Nutrition* 85:S75, 2001.

   Mild deficiencies of a number of micronutrients, including iron and zinc, are discussed as having implications for immune function.

5. Bonham M and others: The immune system as a physiological indicator of marginal copper status? *British Journal of Nutrition* 87:393, 2002.

   Long-term marginal copper deficiency could compromise health, including effects on immune function. However, it is also contended that more research is needed in this area.

6. Brownlie T and others: Marginal iron deficiency without anemia impairs aerobic adaptation among previously untrained women. *American Journal of Clinical Nutrition* 75:734, 2002.

   Marginal iron deficiency can impair energy use even if no anemia exists. Active people must be careful to maintain iron status.

7. Combs GF: Selenium in global food systems. *British Journal of Nutrition* 85:517, 2001.

   Variations in selenium intake, which can be dependent on soil selenium, can have varying influences on health.

8. Dibley MJ: Zinc. In Bowman BA, Russell RM (eds.): *Present knowledge in nutrition.* 8th ed. Washington, DC: International Life Sciences Institute, 2001.

   Presentation of various subjects relevant to this mineral. Zinc is especially important to cells which have a high turnover, such as immune cells.

9. Dunn JT: Endemic goiter and cretinism: An update on iodine status. *Journal of Pediatric Endocrinology and Metabolism.* 14S:1469, 2001.

   Iodine deficiency is still a problem in parts of the world, but it is a correctable problem.

10. Failla ML and others: Copper. In Bowman BA, Russell RM (eds.): *Present knowledge in nutrition*. 8th ed. Washington, DC: International Life Sciences Institute, 2001.

Presentation of various subjects relevant to this mineral, including the diverse roles of copper in the body.

11. Food and Nutrition Board, Institute of Medicine: *Dietary Reference Intakes for vitamin A, vitamin K, arsenic, boron, chromium, copper, iodine, iron, manganese, molybdenum, nickel, silicon, vanadium, and zinc*. Washington, DC: Standing Committee on the Scientific Evaluation of Dietary Reference Intakes National Academy Press, 2001.

Dietary standards have been set for trace minerals. The rationale used to derive the RDA or Adequate Intakes, as well as the Upper Levels, are presented along with information on function, intake, and deficiency.

12. Food and Nutrition Board, Institute of Medicine: *Dietary Reference Intakes for vitamin C, vitamin E, selenium, and carotenoids*. Washington, DC: National Academy of Sciences, 2000.

The functions of antioxidant nutrients; how RDA and related standards were determined; and deficiency and toxicity symptoms are explained.

13. Hunt JR: Moving toward a plant-based diet: Are iron and zinc at risk? *Nutrition Reviews* 60:127, 2002.

Although plant-based diets would seem to present problems for iron and zinc nutrition, so far, adverse consequences have not been reported. A need in this area is to decide on the best methodology to study this issue.

14. Nielsen F: Ultratrace minerals. In Shils ME and others (eds.): *Modern nutrition in health and disease*. 9th ed. Baltimore: Williams & Wilkins, 1999.

At least 18 elements could be considered ultratrace minerals: aluminum, arsenic, boron, bromine, cadmium, chromium, fluoride, germanium, iodine, lead, lithium, molybdenum, nickel, rubidium, selenium, silicon, tin, and vanadium. The role of each in human and laboratory animal physiological systems is reviewed in this chapter.

15. O'Dell BL: Role of zinc in plasma membrane function. *Journal of Nutrition:* 1432S, 2000.

Based on laboratory animal studies, zinc effects on cell membrane structure may be the first system to be affected by progressing zinc deficiency.

16. Rayman MP: The importance of selenium to human health. *Lancet* 356:233, 2000.

Selenium is said to have both known and unknown functions. In some cases, moderately high selenium intakes may help prevent certain diseases, such as cancer.

17. Schumann K: Safety aspects of iron in food. *Annals of Nutrition & Metabolism* 45:91, 2001.

This article reviews the possible dangers of subtle iron toxicity. Although the limitations of current studies are noted, the article supports the recommendation of minimizing iron stores.

18. Sunde RA: Selenium. In Bowman BA, Russell RM (eds.): *Present knowledge in nutrition*. 8th ed. Washington, DC: International Life Sciences Institute, 2001.

Presentation of various subjects relevant to this mineral. Included is a discussion of thioredoxin, a recently described set of antioxidant enzymes that contain selenium.

19. Vincent J: The biochemistry of chromium. *Journal of Nutrition* 130:715, 2000.

Chromium has been known to be an essential micronutrient for mammals for four decades. However, the most popular form of chromium in dietary supplements, chromium picolinate, appears to be absorbed in a different fashion than dietary chromium and can lead to the production of harmful hydroxyl radicals.

20. Yip R: Iron. In Bowman BA, Russell RM (eds.): *Present knowledge in nutrition*. 8th ed. Washington, DC: International Life Sciences Institute, 2001.

Presentation of various subjects relevant to this mineral. The need for iron is the driving force behind absorption, especially for nonheme iron.

Take | Action

I. How Does Your Trace Mineral Intake Measure Up?

To complete this activity, you must reexamine the nutritional assessment you did for Chapter 2. Based on that analysis of your nutritional intake for 1 day, fill in the values for your intake, the RDA and the percentage of the RDA you consumed for each of the minerals listed in the following table. In the right-hand column, indicate whether your intake was higher than (+), lower than (−), or about equal to (=) the recommended intakes.

Mineral	Intake	RDA	% of RDA	+, −, =
Iron	____	________	________	____
Zinc	____	________	________	____
Selenium	____	________	________	____
Copper	____	________	________	____

Analysis

1. Which of your mineral intakes equaled or exceeded the RDA?

____

2. Which of your intakes were below this standard for your age and gender?

____

3. What foods or cooking practices could be emphasized or deemphasized to modify your dietary deficiencies?

____

____

____

____

____

____

II. Check Out Your Municipal Water Supply.

Healthy People 2010 set a goal that 75% of people in the United States will be served by community water systems that add sufficient fluoride. Today, only about 60% of Americans have access to naturally or artificially fluoridated water. Is your hometown (or college town) water supply fluoridated? To find the answer, check with your local water department. What amount of fluoride is added to drinking water, and how long has this procedure been in operation? You can also check with your family dentist, as he or she will know how much fluoride is added to the water in your hometown. If the water supply is not fluoridated, what procedures does your dentist recommend for obtaining sufficient fluoride?

Modern Mineral Status Research: Searching for Subtleties

At one time, most mineral nutritional status research centered on assigning striking symptoms to severe deficiencies or toxicities of a given mineral. This was done both with human subjects and with controlled studies in experimental animals. In the case of the human situations, the symptoms would be readily perceptible to the people with them, and often easily recognized by other people. Examples of such symptoms included skin lesions, stunted growth, visual impairment, and extreme fatigue. In addition to these physically apparent symptoms, some dramatic problems could be detected by blood tests. These problems included anemia, very low counts of white blood cell populations, high blood glucose, and very abnormal serum mineral concentrations. In each case, changing the intake of the relevant mineral could clearly prevent the symptoms, or even reverse them if the problem was not too far developed.

With time, the face of mineral nutritional status research has changed. Today much of this research is focusing on more subtle relationships between variations in mineral intake and health. This "searching for subtleties" can be challenging for the following reasons:

- Many studies involve deficiencies or toxicities that are not severe, but are "marginal" (which can be a difficult state to diagnose);
- Some studies don't even deal with deficiency or toxicity, but instead compare two very similar adequate states: a good status (basic functions are covered) and an optimal status (extra protection against certain health problems);
- Some consequences of varied intake of one mineral are affected by the intakes of other minerals, as well as intakes of vitamins and phytochemicals;
- The consequences under consideration are often a blend of the effects of mineral status plus nonnutritional factors, such as disease or prescription drug use;
- Many of the "big picture" health issues take years to develop or change (e.g., cancer).

The rest of this Nutrition Perspective briefly discusses some examples of research areas where one or more of these challenges are present. Each of these examples includes studies of supplements. The reason for this is that compared to studies of whole food interventions, supplement studies make it easier to isolate the effects of a given mineral. Even so, this approach does have a downside. Intake of foods allows a mineral to be consumed along with other nutrients and phytochemicals that may cooperate in a given effect. Nonetheless, supplement studies are often preferred for a cleaner interpretation.

Trace mineral supplements may be needed to study their effects in double-blind research trials, but foods should be the focus of your daily intake of these minerals.

Selenium and Cancer

Selenium and cancer research is a classic example of trying to distinguish adequate intake versus optimal intake. Some interesting research has suggested that a moderately high-dose supplement of selenium (i.e., 200 μg/day) may lower the risk of certain cancers, such as in the prostate gland. (A current trial using 200 μg/day, with megadose vitamin E supplementation [400 mg/day] as well, is testing that hypothesis in older men with enlarged prostate glands.) This selenium intake is well above what is expected to maximize plasma glutathione peroxidase activities in most individuals. Nonetheless, at higher intakes, selenium may function in additional pathways outside of glutathione peroxidase to signal certain metabolic processes to resist cancer development. Although it is not yet known that this actually happens, more research is justified.

Obviously, this work is not simple because cancer development, as discussed in the Nutrition Perspective in Chapter 10, can be influenced by many factors (some of which are unknown). Moreover, the disease can take years to develop. Due to this latter issue, some upcoming studies may assess short-term changes that have some predictive power for cancer risk. This is not unlike studying blood pressure or blood cholesterol to predict risk of cardiovascular diseases. Although not as ideal as examining actual disease incidence or severity, the "predictor" approach can sort out many issues before undertaking long and expensive studies.

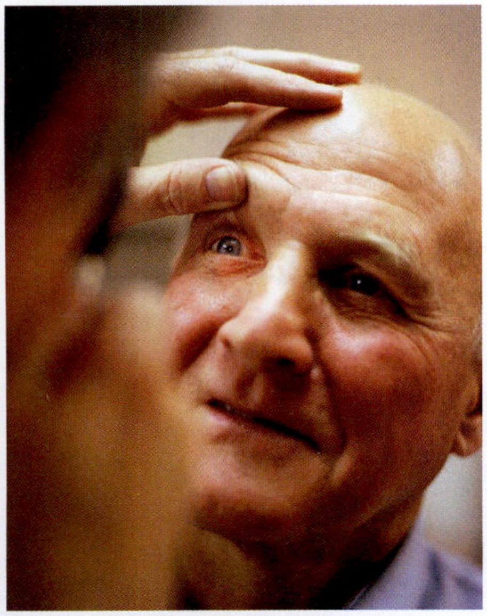

Various age-related eye disorders are common in older adults. An example is macular degeneration.

Zinc and Macular Degeneration

Macular degeneration is the leading cause of age-related blindness. A study sponsored by the National Eye Institute considered the role of zinc and other nutritional factors on this problem. The project was lengthy (average subject participation time of 6 years), and included a large number of subjects at different stages of macular degeneration. The subjects were given supplements of either zinc plus copper, a trio of organic antioxidants (vitamins E and C, plus high-dose beta-carotene, which would be acting mostly as a phytochemical), a combination of both supplements, or a placebo. In people who had already developed some macular degeneration, the combination supplement seemed to reduce the risk for more advanced macular degeneration. The same was true for zinc plus copper alone, though to a lesser degree.[2] Although these results were positive, it has been asked: could the risk-lowering tendencies have been even stronger? The answer may be yes. For one thing, the minerals could have been given in a more absorbable form (zinc and copper oxide were used, which are not considered extremely absorbable). In addition, more attention could have been paid to starting zinc status of the subjects. However, in fairness to the study designers, it should be noted that at the study initiation time, there was no universally accepted means of diagnosing marginal zinc status. Another concern is that the study could not tell if zinc had an effect on people in the very earliest stages of macular degeneration. The problem was that vision deterioration in those people was too slow and variable during the study period.

Despite the limitations of this study, the positive effect of zinc in some groups means that more attention should be given to zinc and macular degeneration. One difficulty in giving this attention is the expense and time required to do another study like the one sponsored by the National Eye Institute. Some progress in this area may have to rely on shorter, smaller studies. As with studies on selenium and cancer, some studies can measure indicators that may have predictive power for disease development.

Chromium: Body Mass Issues and Subtle Toxicities

Chromium affects insulin utilization, which in theory, can affect fat loss and lean body weight gain. Chromium intakes at RDA amounts prevent insulin function abnormalities associated with chromium deficiencies. However, it has been suggested that higher intakes will make insulin function even better in some people. Supposedly, this intake, especially when combined with exercise, could help people lose fat while gaining lean body mass. The most popular way to produce the higher chromium intake has been via supplementation with an organic complex called chromium picolinate. This complex is reported to have better absorption properties than inorganic chromium, which is absorbed very poorly.

A number of studies have not supported the idea that chromium picolinate supplementation can accelerate fat loss and lean body mass gain. Nonetheless, limited positive data, including some revised interpretations of the negative studies, has kept this idea alive. At present, there is still much skepticism, but the issue is still considered open. This whole area is not easy to consider due to the many variables that can affect such studies (e.g., the fitness level of the participants, the initial glucose handling abilities of the subjects, the amount and type of carbohydrates in the diet, the amount of energy consumed, the type and intensity of exercise performed).

Studies of chromium picolinate have recently taken another turn. Some researchers have suggested that this complex enters cells intact and produces hydroxyl radical, a powerful initiator of oxidant stress.[19] Critics of this accusation contend that such speculation is based mostly on observations in cultured cells under non-physiological conditions. One difficulty in evaluating this issue is that hydroxyl radicals are so short lived that they cannot be measured in living people or even in experimental animals. Even so, there are indirect ways to evaluate toxicity. Hopefully, such evaluations will be done. Meanwhile, a chromium-niacin complex has been touted as a more absorbable, less toxic supplement than chromium picolinate. Future research should be able to sort out these issues.

Osteoporosis: Role of Copper, Manganese, and Zinc

Each of the minerals copper, manganese, and zinc has a functional connection to bone health (see this chapter's sections on these minerals). In humans or experimental animals, severe deficiency of any one of these minerals is known to create bone problems. However, this is a different issue than asking: Can intake of these minerals play a major role in the osteoporosis that develops in many older women? Development of osteoporosis could be affected by many factors including calcium and vitamin D status, hormonal states, genetics, and exercise history. Therefore, analysis of copper, manganese, and zinc regarding osteoporosis must compare potential effects of these minerals to other factors that influence osteoporosis development. In addition, researchers have to consider the effects of the individual minerals compared to the combined effects of all three. Another issue is that osteoporosis can take decades to develop. Again, as with other diseases mentioned in this Nutrition Perspective, studies often have to look at markers that predict disease risk. One study did try a first look at this issue by looking at a supplement of copper, manganese, zinc, and calcium in postmenopausal women. There was some evidence that this supplement could reduce bone loss. Although this is an interesting study, it is a long way from showing that this trio of minerals can play a major role in osteoporosis prevention in a large number of people. Unfortunately, this study has not produced any major follow-up work as yet.

Subtle Iron Toxicity

There is no question that untreated, severe iron toxicity can produce major problems, even death. In contrast, there are questions about the contention that there are dangers associated with having iron stores near or slightly above minimal levels.[17] This idea has arisen for three reasons. One, in test tube settings, iron is very good at catalyzing free radical formation. Two, in some animal models for diseases, such as rheumatoid arthritis and cardiovascular disease, injury can be lessened by providing chemicals that bind iron. Three, groups of people with certain diseases show average blood ferritin levels that are higher than the average levels in control subjects. Recall that ferritin is an iron-binding protein whose levels rise in response to increasing iron stores.

Some researchers have taken an extreme position that everyone should minimize iron stores by donating blood regularly, eating only enough iron to barely prevent anemia, and for some people, taking drugs that deplete iron stores. In contrast, many nutrition researchers are not convinced that this is necessary. They point out that low iron stores, even without anemia, can impair immune function and reduce energy levels. They also point out that the studies linking high ferritin values to disease states may be deceiving. High ferritin values are caused not only by high iron stores, but also by most internal physiological stress states. Thus, the high ferritin values in disease could be a result of the stress of the disease, not an indication that high iron stores caused the disease. Some researchers take a middle ground. It is conceded that when iron comes loose from binding proteins such as ferritin and transferrin, free iron may generate free radicals. These radicals is turn could be involved in certain diseases. The proposed solution is not exhausting iron stores, but preventing the formation of free iron. One way this could be done is by consuming an adequate amount of antioxidants. In the test tube, certain free radicals release iron from its binding proteins, which then results in more free radical production. If the same thing happens in "real life," then consuming an adequate amount of antioxidants could slow the effects of free iron. Another approach could be maintaining good copper status since the copper protein ceruloplasmin can stimulate iron uptake by binding proteins. This dispute about subtle iron toxicity is far from over.

Zinc and Immune Function

There is no question that zinc is involved in immune function, but there are questions about some issues relating to zinc and immune function. One such question is: how much and in whom does marginal zinc deficiency compromise immune function? As noted in this chapter's section on zinc, a number of types of people may be prone to marginal zinc deficiency. Often, this state could involve high zinc requirements combined with a marginal zinc intake. Some studies have supported the idea that marginal zinc deficiency does affect immune function. For example, increased zinc intake has improved some aspects of immunocompetence in children with Down's syndrome. Note that this increased zinc intake does not cure Down's syndrome, but it did affect immune parameters.

Studies like this do tie marginal zinc deficiency to immune function impairments, but there are still a lot of issues remaining.[4] For example, there are many different components of immune function, and most studies of marginal zinc deficiency only examine one or two of these. In addition, most such studies used

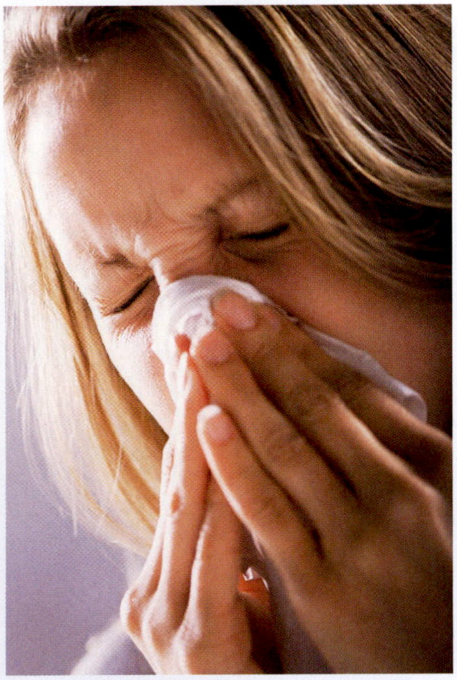

Many companies are singing the praises of zinc lozenges as a cold remedy. Adults can determine if the benefits outweigh the poor taste. Zinc expert Dr. Ananda Prasad recommends discontinuing use of zinc lozenges after 3 to 4 days unless they are showing evidence of effectiveness. Any use beyond a week or so also is potentially harmful.

blood tests rather than a "big picture" approach, such as number and duration of infections. In addition, for many types of people, the actual contribution of marginal zinc deficiency to poor immune function remains largely untested. Despite these study limitations (and all studies have limitations), the work done so far does support the idea that marginal zinc deficiency affects immune function.

Another gray area in the relationship between zinc and immune function is zinc lozenges to treat the common cold. It is still not known whether the lozenges are effective. Some studies using lozenges (containing 13 mg of zinc) every 2 hours as symptoms remain suggest the answer is yes, while others seem to say no. Part of the conflict may have to do with differences in methodology, subject selection, and control of other factors that affect cold incidence and severity. Another issue is how the zinc lozenges function. The simplest answer would be that the lozenges correct a marginal zinc deficiency and this improves immune function. However, this explanation may not be correct. Instead, zinc lozenges, whose doses typically exceed RDA levels, may elevate blood zinc to high levels that produce actions not seen for "normal" zinc function. An example of such actions could be blocking virus entry into cells. Another possibility could be an actual inhibition of some aspects of immune function. This inhibition may have antihistamine and anti-inflammatory effects that reduce cold symptoms. At the moment, there is no clear consensus as to whether zinc lozenges are a major help in fighting colds.

You can see that there is still much to be learned about trace minerals. Any use of megadoses described in this Nutrition Perspective should be supervised by a physician, but in some cases research may eventually establish such use to have positive health benefits.

chapter 13

Energy Balance and Weight Control

Chapter | Outline

Case | Scenario

Chris has a hectic schedule. During the day he works full-time at a mail-order warehouse filling orders in the stockroom. At night, three times a week he attends class at the local community college in pursuit of computer certification. On weekends he tries to squeeze in studying and time for his family and friends. He has little time to think about what he eats—convenience rules. Unfortunately, over the past few years Chris's weight has been climbing. Watching television a few nights ago, he saw an infomercial for a product that promises he can eat large portions of tasty foods but not gain weight. Famous celebrities support the claim that this product allows one to eat at will and not gain weight. He doesn't have a lot of spare money, but the claim that by taking this product he can eat whatever he wants and never gain weight is tempting. What do you think he should do? What advice can you offer Chris for evaluating weight-loss programs?

Refresh | Your Memory

As you begin your study of weight control in Chapter 13, you may want to review:

- The concept of energy density in Chapter 2.
- The causes and consequences of ketosis in Chapter 4.
- The carbohydrate, fat, and protein content of various foods in Chapters 5, 6, and 7.
- The long-term risks of high-protein diets in Chapter 7.

Boost | Your Study

Check out the ***Perspectives in Nutrition: Online Learning Center*** www.mhhe.com/wardlawpers6 *for quizzes, flash cards, activities, and web links designed to further help you learn about weight control.*

Chapter | Objectives

Chapter 13 is designed to allow you to:

1. Describe the uses of energy by the body and what constitutes energy balance.
2. Characterize the terms hunger, appetite, and satiety.
3. Outline the internal and external forces involved in satiety regulation.
4. Describe how to establish a healthy weight for a person and various ways to diagnose overweight and obesity.
5. Outline the risks to health posed by overweight and obesity.
6. List and discuss factors affecting energy balance in overweight and obesity with respect to nature and nurture, and describe the concept of set point with regard to body weight.
7. Describe why and how reduced energy intake, behavior modification, and increased physical activity fit into a weight-loss plan.
8. Outline the benefits and hazards of various weight-loss methods for severe obesity.
9. Describe possible reasons and treatments for underweight status.
10. Evaluate popular (fad) weight-reduction diets and determine which are unsafe, doomed to fail, or both.

Of people you see on the street in North America, one-fourth of the men and nearly half the women are struggling to control their weight. Still, despite all their efforts, the ranks of the obese here and worldwide are growing in epidemic proportions.[6] Recall from Chapter 1 that it is estimated that about 1 billion people in the world are overweight. This problem is increasing in North America, Brazil, China, India, Russia, the United Kingdom, and Germany. This excess weight increases the likelihood of many health problems, such as cardiovascular disease, cancer, hypertension, certain bone and joint disorders, and type 2 diabetes.

Currently, most weight-reduction efforts fizzle before bodies fall into a healthy weight range. Monotonous, ineffective, and confusing, typical popular (also called fad) diets even endanger some populations, such as children, teenagers, pregnant women, and people with various health disorders. Yet a more logical approach to weight loss is actually very straightforward: (1) Eat less; (2) increase physical activity; and (3) change problematic eating behaviors.[1]

Experts are calling for national commitments to address the growing weight problem in North America. They suspect that, without a major commitment to weight maintenance and effective new approaches to making the environment more favorable to maintaining healthy weight, the current trends will not be reversed.[9] This chapter discusses these recommendations to help you understand obesity's effects, causes, and potential treatments.

Energy Balance

This chapter on weight control starts with some good news and some bad news. The good news is that if you stay at a healthy body weight you can have a longer and healthier life. The bad news is that over 65% of all North American adults are overweight (about 40% of these people are obese [25% of the total population]), and there is a good chance that any of us can join those ranks if we don't pay attention to the prevention of significant adult weight gain.[6] Gaining more than 10 pounds or 2 inches in waist circumference should be a red flag that diet and lifestyle re-evaluation is in order. This preventive strategy is currently considered the most potent form of therapy for the problem of overweight in our society. Other strategies do exist; however, as you will see, they have not shown to be as successful as prevention of the problem in the first place.[3]

Positive and Negative Energy Balance

Many of us would benefit by paying more attention to an important concept—that of **energy balance.** This balance depends on energy input and energy output. These in turn influence energy stores, primarily, the amount of triglyceride in adipose tissue (Fig. 13-1). Energy balance can be thought of as an equation: energy consumed minus energy expended. You are in positive energy balance when energy consumed is greater than energy expended. The result of **positive energy balance** is the storage of the excess energy.

An example of when positive energy balance is necessary is during pregnancy because the surplus of energy supports the developing fetus. Infants and children also need to be in positive energy balance to grow. In non-pregnant and non-lactating adults, however, even a small positive energy balance causes creeping weight gain.

Negative energy balance results from an energy deficit. Energy consumed is less than energy expended. Weight loss occurs when a person is in a state of negative energy balance. In adulthood, however, the weight that is lost consists of a combination of lean and adipose tissue.

As noted in the overview, the maintenance of energy balance—energy intake matching energy output over the long run—substantially contributes to health and wellbeing in adults by minimizing the risk of developing many common health problems. As well, adulthood is often a time of creeping weight gain, which eventually turns into obesity if not checked. However, increasing age is not the primary reason for this weight gain; it is caused primarily by the pattern of excess food intake, coupled with limited physical activity.[18] Let's look in detail at the factors that affect the relationship between positive and negative energy balance.

energy balance The state in which energy intake, in the form of food and/or alcohol, matches the energy expended, primarily through basal metabolism and physical activity.

positive energy balance The state in which energy intake is greater than energy expended, generally resulting in weight gain.

negative energy balance The state in which energy intake is less than energy expended, resulting in weight loss.

Energy Intake

Energy needs are met by food intake, represented by the number of calories eaten each day. Determining the appropriate amount and type of food to match energy needs over the long run is a challenge for many of us. Our ability to consume food and use it efficiently is an evolutionary survival mechanism. However, given modern North American food supplies, many of us are now too successful in obtaining food energy. The refrigerator has essentially replaced the need to store body fat—food is always at hand. And given the wide availability of food in vending machines, drive-up windows, social gatherings, and fast-food (quick-service) restaurants—combined with the ubiquitous *super-sized* portions—it is no wonder that the average adult is 8 pounds heavier than just 10 years ago.[11] You might say "food hunts man" today, rather than man hunting food as in earlier times. In response "defensive eating" (i.e. making careful food choices) is important for many of us.

How much food energy is contained in a meal? A bomb calorimeter is used to determine the amount of energy in a food (Fig. 13-2). The process involves burning a

Today we demand food that is immediately available, tastes great, requires little or no preparation, and is served in generous quantities. Of all these characteristics, the generous quantities are the most troublesome for many of us. As noted in Chapter 1, in response consider sharing the meal with another person.

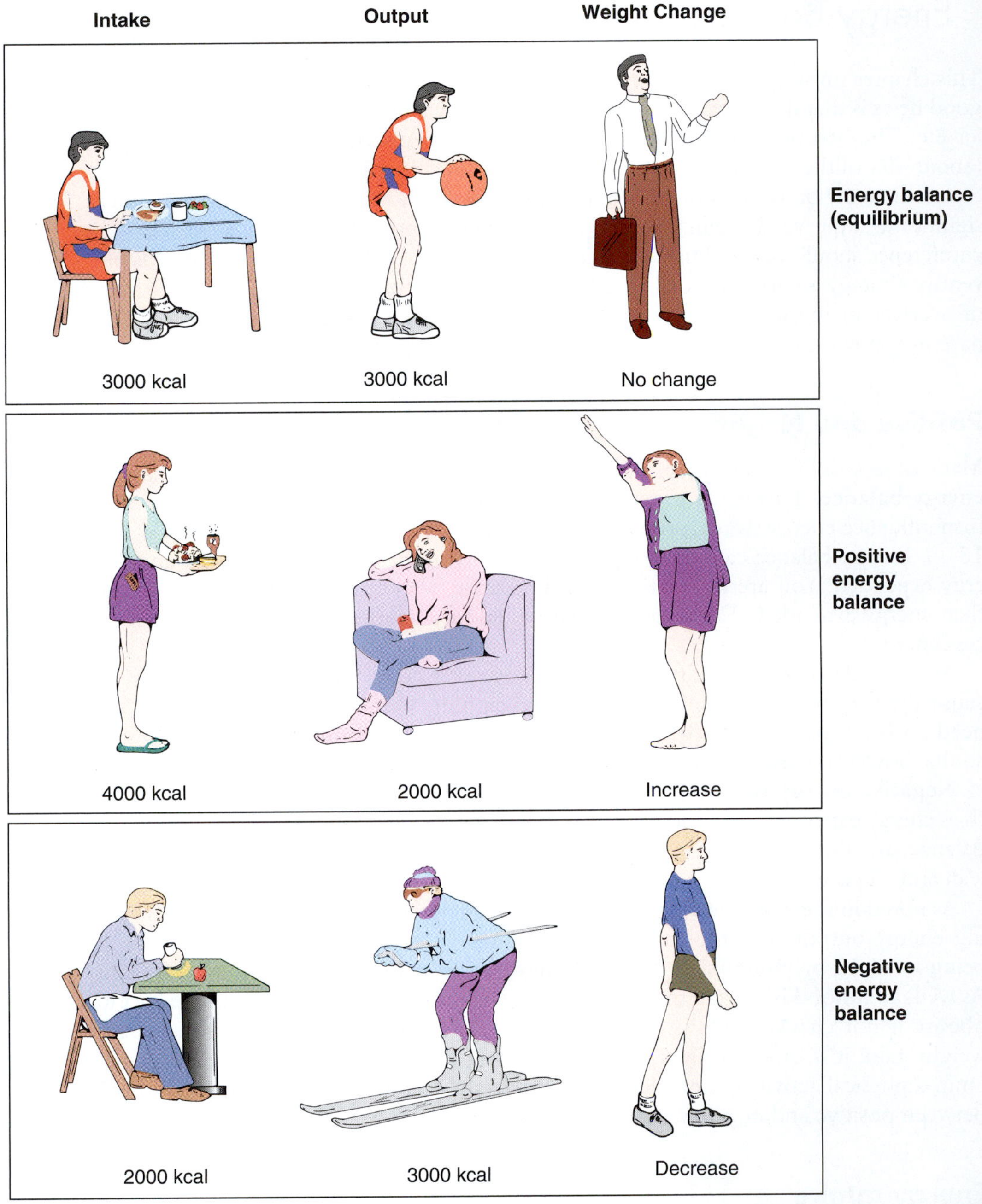

Figure 13-1 A model for energy balance—input vs. output. This figure depicts energy balance in practical terms.

Critical | Thinking

A 26-year-old classmate of yours has been thinking about the process of aging. One of the things she fears most as she gets older is gaining weight. How would you explain energy balance to her?

portion of food inside a chamber of the calorimeter that is surrounded by water. As the food burns, it gives off heat, which raises the temperature of the water surrounding the chamber. The increase in water temperature measured after the food has burned indicates the amount of energy in the food. One kcal is the amount of energy required to increase the temperature of 1 kg (about 2.2 lb) of water 1° Celsius.

The bomb calorimeter provides values for the amount of energy that can be derived from carbohydrate, fat, protein, and alcohol. Recall that carbohydrates yield about 4 kcal/g, proteins yield about 4 kcal/g, fats yield about 9 kcal/g, and alcohol yields 7 kcal/g. These energy figures have been adjusted for (1) digestibility and (2) substances in food, such as fibrous plant parts that burn in the bomb calorimeter but are unusable by the human body for energy needs. The figures are then rounded to whole numbers.

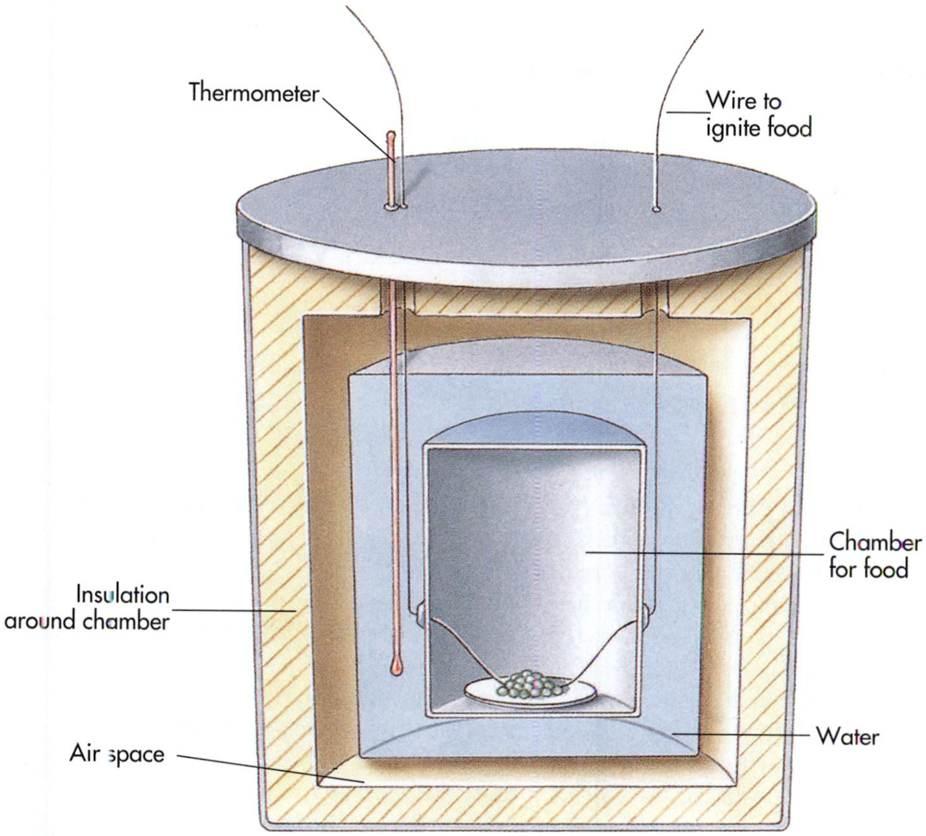

Figure 13-2 Cross section of a bomb calorimeter. To determine energy content, a dried portion of food is burned inside a chamber charged with oxygen and surrounded by water. As the food is burned, it gives off heat, which raises the temperature of the water surrounding the chamber. The amount of increase in water temperature indicates the number of kcal contained in the food. Recall that 1 kcal equals the amount of heat needed to raise the temperature of 1 kg of water 1°C. Illustration by William Ober.

Today, scientific journals often express energy intake and output in kjoules, rather than kcal (see Chapter 1).

Energy Use

So far, some factors concerning energy intake have been discussed. Now let's look at the other side of the relationship—energy output.

The body uses energy for three general purposes: basal metabolism, physical activity, and the thermic effect of food. Shivering in response to cold and fidgeting both demonstrate another minor form of energy turned into heat production, which can be lumped together under the term thermogenesis (Fig. 13-3).[7]

While a person is resting, the percentage of total energy use by various organs is about as follows:

Brain	19%
Skeletal muscle	18%
Liver	27%
Kidney	10%
Heart	7%
Other	19%

Basal Metabolism

As covered in Chapter 12, basal metabolism represents the minimum energy expended in a fasting state (12 hours or more) to keep a resting, awake body alive in a warm, quiet environment. When a person is sedentary, this requires about 60 to 70% of total energy use by the body. The processes involved include maintaining a heartbeat, respiration, temperature, and other functions. It does not include energy used for physical activity or food digestion. For an example of how basal metabolism contributes to energy needs, consider a 130-lb woman. Convert her weight, in pounds, into kilograms ($130 \div 2.2 = 59$ kg). Then, multiply 59 kg $\times$ 0.9 kcal/kg/hr $\times$ 24 hours = 1274 kcal needed for basal metabolism for an entire day. (The 0.9 kcal/kg/hr represents a rough estimate of her basal metabolic rate.) Note that basal metabolism varies 25 to 30% among individuals.

The amount of energy used for basal metabolism depends primarily on **lean body mass.** That is, basal metabolism is generally higher in people with greater amounts of lean body mass than in those with large proportions of fat mass. The participating tissues—such as muscle, liver, brain, and kidney—show high metabolic activity at rest and have high energy needs. Other influences that determine basal metabolism include the following:[14]

lean body mass Body weight minus fat storage weight equals lean body mass. This includes organs such as the brain, muscles, and liver, as well as blood and other body fluids.

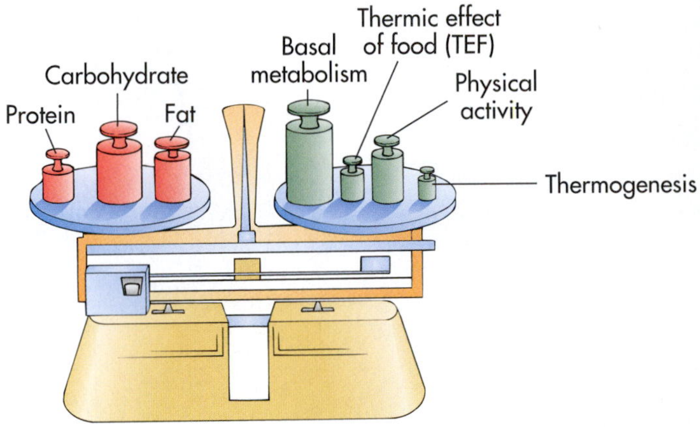

Figure 13-3 The components of energy intake and expenditure. This figure incorporates the major variables, discussed in the chapter, that influence energy balance. Note that alcohol is an additional source of energy for some of us, but is not depicted.
Illustration by William Ober.

When planning a smoking cessation program, a plan to limit weight gain should also be implemented. Smoking cessation is linked to an increased risk of weight gain and obesity. Any form of regular physical activity can be extremely beneficial in an attempt to keep weight in check. Various risk factors associated with smoking, however, make it essential that this population obtain approval from a physician before beginning an intensive exercise regimen.

- The amount of body surface (the greater the area, the greater the heat loss)
- Gender (males average higher energy use because of greater lean body mass)
- Body temperature (fever increases basal metabolism)
- Thyroid hormones (increase basal metabolism)
- Aspects of nervous system activity, such as norepinephrine release (increases basal metabolism)
- Age (basal metabolism rate falls as we age through adulthood)
- Nutritional state (eating less slows basal metabolism rate in the short term)
- Pregnancy (increases basal metabolism)
- Caffeine and tobacco use (increase basal metabolism)

A low energy intake decreases the basal metabolism by about 10 to 20%, or about 150 to 300 kcal/day. This makes losing weight difficult. In addition, the effects of aging make weight maintenance hard. Basal metabolism declines 1 to 2% each decade past age 30 as active cells slowly and steadily decrease.[7] However, because physical activity helps maintain lean body mass, remaining active as one ages helps maintain a high basal metabolism and, in turn, aids in weight control.[18]

Energy for Physical Activity

Physical activity increases energy expenditure above and beyond basal energy needs by as much as 25 to 40%. In choosing to be active or inactive, we determine much of our total energy expenditure for a day. Unlike basal metabolism, energy expenditure from physical activity varies widely among people.

Climbing stairs rather than riding the elevator, walking rather than driving to the store, and standing in a bus rather than sitting increase physical activity and, hence, energy use. People who fidget use more energy (an extra 100 to 800 kcal daily) than do those who readily relax.

The alarming rate of and recent increase in obesity in North America are caused in part by our inactivity.[19] We eat little more than people did at the turn of the twentieth century, but we are less active. Jobs demand less physical activity, and leisure time is usually spent slouched before a television or computer.

Studying leads to mental stress but puts little physical stress on the body. Hence, energy needs are only about 1.5 kcal/minute.

Thermic Effect of Food (TEF)

In addition to basal metabolism and physical activity, the body uses energy to digest, absorb, and further process food nutrients. Energy used for these tasks accounts for the **thermic effect of food (TEF).** The energy cost of this thermic effect is analogous to a sales tax. It is like being taxed about 5 to 10% for the total energy you eat. The charge covers the cost of processing that energy. To supply the body with 100 kcal for basal metabolism and physical activity, you must eat between 105 and 110 kcal. The

thermic effect of food (TEF) The increase in metabolism occurring during the digestion, absorption, and metabolism of energy-yielding nutrients. This represents 5 to 10% of energy consumed.

processes of digestion, absorption, and metabolism use the extra 5 to 10 kcal to modify the energy-yielding nutrients for use. Given a daily energy intake of 3000 kcal, the thermic effect of food uses 150 to 300 kcal ($3000 \times 0.05 = 150$; $3000 \times 0.1 = 300$). However, the total amount can vary somewhat among individuals.

The TEF value for a protein-rich meal (20 to 30%) is higher than for a carbohydrate-rich meal (5 to 10%) or fat-rich meal (0 to 5%). This is because it takes less energy to transfer absorbed fat into adipose stores or convert glucose into glycogen than to metabolize excess amino acids into fat (review Chapter 4). In addition, large meals show higher values for TEF than the same amount of food eaten over many hours. Some possible mechanisms for this phenomenon include changes in central nervous system activity, greater production and release of hormones (such as insulin) and enzymes, and the rate of absorption and storage of macronutrients.[14]

Other names for the thermic effect of food include *specific dynamic action* and *diet-induced thermogenesis.*

Thermogenesis

Thermogenesis, also called nonexercise activity thermogenesis (NEAT) or thermoregulation, represents the increase in nonvoluntary physical activity triggered by cold conditions or overeating. This activity includes shivering, fidgeting, maintenance of muscle tone, and maintenance of body posture when not lying down. Studies have shown that some people resist weight gain from overfeeding by inducing thermogenesis, whereas others are not able to do so to as great an extent. As well, some people show lower amounts of thermogenesis when exposed to cold conditions.

Overall, a sedentary person uses 70 to 80% of energy for a combination of basal metabolism and the thermic effect of food. The remainder is used mostly for physical activity; a small amount may be used for thermogenesis (Table 13-1).[7]

thermogenesis This term encompasses the ability of humans to regulate body temperature within narrow limits, especially as temperature falls below that which is comfortable, called thermoregulation. Increased shivering is part of this response. Also included in this general term is the increase in metabolism elicited by fidgeting, called spontaneous nonexercise activity. This also may be increased by overfeeding in some people. Other terms used to describe thermogenesis are adaptive thermogenesis and nonexercise activity thermogenesis (NEAT).

Concept | Check

Energy balance compares energy intake with energy output. Energy content of food is expressed in kcal and determined using a bomb calorimeter. This analysis yields the 4-9-4-7 estimates for carbohydrate, fat, protein, and alcohol.

The body uses this energy for four main purposes:

1. Basal metabolism represents the minimal amount of energy needed to maintain a body in a resting state. The rate of a person's basal metabolism depends greatly on the amount of lean body mass, the amount of body surface, and thyroid hormone concentrations in the bloodstream.
2. Physical activity expenditure represents energy use for total body cell metabolism above what is needed during rest (that is, basal metabolism).
3. The thermic effect of food represents the energy needed to digest, absorb, and process absorbed nutrients. This corresponds to 5 to 10% of total energy output.
4. Thermogenesis includes heat production in response to cold, overfeeding, and other stimuli. Increased shivering or fidgeting is generally seen.

In a sedentary person, 70 to 80% of energy is used for basal metabolism and the thermic effect of food; the remainder is used for physical activity and thermogenesis.

Brown adipose tissue is a specialized form of adipose tissue found in small amounts in infants. The brown appearance results from its rich blood flow. Brown adipose tissue contributes to thermogenesis by uncoupling the use of energy-yielding nutrients and the production of ATP (it contains a protein called uncoupling protein [UPC]). In brown adipose tissue more of the energy released from metabolism is simply lost as heat compared to other types of cells. The role of brown adipose tissue in adults is unknown, but adults have little brown adipose tissue anyway. One interesting finding regarding brown adipose tissue is that hibernating animals contain much of it. This allows them to create the heat needed to withstand a long winter.

Determination of Energy Use by the Body

The amount of energy a body uses can be measured by both direct and indirect calorimetry or can be simply estimated based on height, weight, degree of physical activity, and age.

Calculating Resting Energy Use Using Harris-Benedict Equation

We have estimated Carlos's total energy use. Let's calculate Carlos's resting energy expenditure using the appropriate **Harris-Benedict equation,** commonly used in clinical practice, and then compare it with the basal metabolism we determined for him:

Harris-Benedict Equation

66.5 + 13.8 (weight in kg) + 5 (height in cm) − 6.8 (age in years)

Carlos weighs 70 kg, is 175 cm tall, and is 25 years old. Therefore, Carlos's resting energy expenditure is as follows:

66.5 + 13.8 (70 kg) + 5 (175 cm) − 6.8 (25) = 1738 kcal/day

Resting energy use = 1738 kcal/day

Compare this with the estimate of basal metabolism of 1680 kcal/day we determined in Table 13-1. The values are not very different. Note also that the Harris-Benedict equation for women is 655.1 + 9.6 (weight in kg) + 1.9 (height in cm) − 4.7 (age in years).

In clinical practice the value for resting energy needs from the Harris-Benedict equation is then multiplied by predetermined factors to reflect a patient's degree of physical activity and illness, both of which raise energy needs above resting needs. The final value calculated gives an estimate of total energy needs.

Harris-Benedict equation An equation that predicts resting metabolic rate based on a person's weight, height, and age.

direct calorimetry A method of determining a body's energy use by measuring heat that emanates from the body, usually using an insulated chamber.

Table 13-1 Calculating Energy Use

The following examples illustrate how to estimate energy expenditure in a simple format. Thermogenesis is not included because of limited knowledge regarding its contribution to daily energy output. Carlos weighs 154 lb (70 kg), is 5 feet 9 inches tall (175 cm), is 25 years old, and is involved in moderate physical activity each day.

Basal Metabolism

Use the value 1 kcal/kg body weight/hour for *men*,
0.9 kcal/kg body weight/hour for *women*.

For Carlos:

1. Multiply his weight in kilograms by the appropriate value for men.
   70 kg × 1 kcal/kg/hr = 70 kcal/hr
2. Multiply kcal used in an hour by hours in a day.
   70 kcal/hr × 24 hr/day = 1680 kcal/day

Basal metabolism = 1680 kcal/day

Physical Activity

Select one of the following categories based on the amount of muscular activity performed in a day:
- Sedentary activity (mostly sitting): add 20 to 40% of basal metabolism
- Light activity (a clerk involved in a daily walking program): add 55 to 65% of basal metabolism
- Moderate activity (a teacher involved in daily vigorous exercise): add 70 to 75% of basal metabolism
- Heavy activity (a mail carrier who walks the route or an adult involved in a daily exercise program): add 80 to 100% or more of basal metabolism

If Carlos performs moderate activity,
Take 70% of his basal metabolism.
1680 kcal/day × 0.70 = 1176 kcal/day.

Physical activity = 1176 kcal/day

Thermic Effect of Food

A quick way to approximate this value is to take 10% of the sum of the basal metabolism and physical activity kcal. For Carlos,

1. 1680 kcal/day + 1176 kcal/day = 2856 kcal/day.
2. 2856 kcal/day × 0.10 = 286 kcal/day.

Thermic effect of food = 286 kcal/day

Total Energy Use

Now sum the energy contributions from each factor.

For Carlos,
1680 kcal/day + 1176 kcal/day + 286 kcal/day = 3142 kcal/day

Total energy use = 3142 kcal/day

Direct and Indirect Calorimetry

Direct calorimetry measures the amount of body heat released by a person. The subject is put into an insulated chamber, often the size of a small bedroom, and body heat released raises the temperature of a layer of water surrounding the chamber. A kcal, as you recall, is related to the amount of heat available to raise the temperature of the water. By measuring the water temperature in the direct calorimeter before and after the body releases heat, scientists can determine the energy expended. This method resembles the bomb calorimeter method for measuring the energy content in food.

Direct calorimetry works because almost all the energy used by the body eventually leaves as heat. However, few studies use direct calorimetry, mostly because of its expense and complexity.

For **indirect calorimetry,** instead of measuring heat output, the most commonly used method measures the amount of oxygen a person uses (Fig. 13-4). A predictable relationship exists between the body's use of energy and oxygen. For example, when metabolizing a mixed diet of carbohydrate, fat, and protein—a typical blend of nutrients—the human body needs 1 liter of oxygen to yield about 4.85 kcal of energy.

Instruments used to measure oxygen consumption for indirect calorimetry have great versatility. They can be mounted on carts and rolled up to a hospital bed or carried in backpacks while a person plays tennis or jogs. There are even new handheld instruments. Tables showing energy demands of exercises rely on information gained from indirect calorimetry studies.

Another approach to indirect calorimetry uses **stable isotopes** of oxygen and hydrogen.[7] In this method, a person consumes isotopically labeled water (^2H_2O and $H_2{}^{18}O$). A technician measures the ^2H_2O and the $H_2{}^{18}O$ later that arises in body fluids, such as urine. Using the difference between the decline in the amount of ^2H_2O compared to $H_2{}^{18}O$ over a week or so and some mathematical formulas, total carbon dioxide (CO_2) output per day can be estimated. This method works because ^2H diffuses throughout the body's water and the ^{18}O diffuses throughout both the body water and bicarbonate (HCO_3^-) stores. ^2H is then only eliminated from the body via water production, while the ^{18}O is eliminated both as water and carbon dioxide originally associated with bicarbonate. This ultimate estimate of CO_2 output is used to calculate energy expenditure, just as is done with oxygen use in indirect calorimetry. ^2H and ^{18}O are stable isotopes of hydrogen and oxygen (therefore, they are nonradioactive); special instruments can measure them in body fluids. This stable isotope method is quite accurate but also very expensive. It is the basis for setting energy needs for humans (see next section).

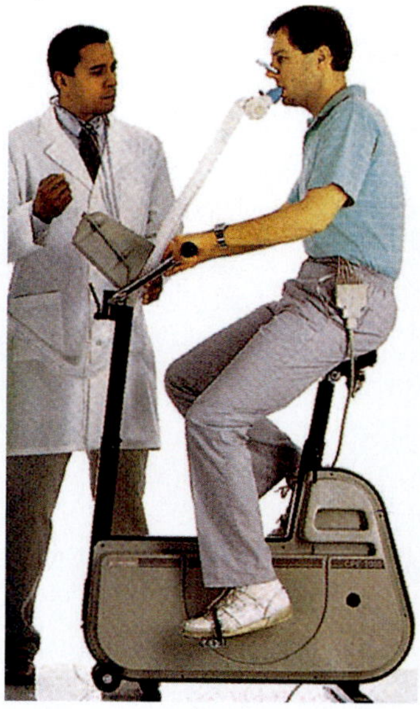

Figure 13-4 Indirect calorimetry. This method can be used to measure energy output during daily activities by monitoring oxygen uptake and carbon dioxide output.

indirect calorimetry A method to measure the energy use by the body by measuring oxygen uptake. Formulas are then used to convert this gas exchange value into energy use.

stable isotope An isotope is a specific form of a chemical element. It differs from atoms of other forms (isotopes) of the same element in the number of neutrons in its nucleus. *Stable* means that the isotope is not radioactive, in contrast to some other types of isotopes.

Estimates of Energy Needs

The Food and Nutrition Board has recently published a number of formulas to estimate energy needs, termed an Estimated Energy Requirement (EER).[7] Those for adults are listed below. Formulas for children, teenagers, pregnant women, and lactating women will be listed in Chapter 16 and Chapter 17.

Men 19 years and older

$$EER = 662 - (9.53 \times \text{Age [y]}) + PA \times (15.91 \times \text{Weight [kg]} + 539.6 \times \text{Height [m]})$$

Where PA is the physical activity estimate:

PA = 1.00 if the person is sedentary (typical daily activities only).
PA = 1.11 if the person is low active (e.g. the equivalent exercise output of walking 2 miles/day at 3–4 mph in addition to typical daily activities).
PA = 1.25 if the person is active (e.g. the equivalent exercise output of walking 7 miles/day at 3–4 mph in addition to typical daily activities).
PA = 1.48 if the person is very active (e.g. the equivalent exercise output of walking 17 miles/day at 3–4 mph in addition to typical daily activities).

Women 19 years and older

$$EER = 354 - (6.91 \times \text{Age [y]}) + PA \times (9.36 \times \text{Weight [kg]} + 726 \times \text{Height [m]})$$

PA = 1.00 if the person is sedentary.
PA = 1.12 if the person is low active.
PA = 1.27 if the person is active.
PA = 1.45 if the person is very active.

Consider Carlos in Table 13-1. Recall he was 25 years old, 5′9″ (175 cm), 154 lb (70 kg), and had an active lifestyle. His EER is: $662 - (9.53 \times 25) + 1.25 \times (15.91 \times 70 + 539.6 \times 1.75)$, which equals 2997 kcal, or about 3000 kcal. The estimate using the components of energy expenditure in Table 13-1 was 3142 kcal. Both estimates show close agreement.

Rough guidelines for energy needs found in the Food Guide Pyramid publication are as follows:

- Sedentary women and some older adults — 1600 kcal
- Children, teenage girls, active women, most men — 2200 kcal
- Teenage boys, active men, very active women — 2800 kcal
- Young children, pregnant and breastfeeding women — Check with a registered dietitian

These values then need to be fine-tuned based on personal characteristics and experiences, such as amount of physical activity performed.

A simple method of tracking your energy expenditure, and thus your energy needs, is to use the forms in Appendix G. Begin by taking an entire 24-hour period and listing all activities performed, including sleep. Record the number of minutes spent in each activity; the total should equal 1440 minutes (24 hours). Next record the energy cost for each activity in kcal/min following the directions in Appendix G. Multiply the energy cost by the minutes. This gives the energy expended for each activity. Total all the kcal values. This gives your estimated energy expenditure for the day.

Concept | Check

Energy use by the body can be measured by direct calorimetry as heat given off and by indirect calorimetry as oxygen used. A person's Estimated Energy Requirement can be estimated based on a one's characteristics: height, weight, age, and amount of physical activity. In addition, the Food Guide Pyramid publication provides rough guidelines for energy intake.

Why Am I Hungry?

Two drives influence our desire to eat and thus take in food energy, **hunger** and **appetite.** These differ dramatically (Fig. 13-5). Hunger, our primarily physical drive to eat, is controlled by internal body mechanisms. Organs, such as the liver and brain, interact with hormones, hormonelike **(neuroendocrine)** factors, the nervous system, and other aspects of body physiology to influence feeding behavior (Table 13-2).[14] For example, carbohydrate intake induces in the GI tract the release of the hormonelike compound glucagon-like peptide-1 (GLP-1). This then reduces further food intake.[6] Then as macronutrients in general are absorbed, the liver and surrounding organs communicate with the brain through the two **vagus nerves.** This changes subsequent food choices by sending information about the rate of digestion and energy metabolism from the GI tract and the liver to the brain.

Appetite, our primarily psychological drive to eat, is affected by external food choice mechanisms, such as seeing a tempting dessert. Fulfilling either or both drives by eating sufficient food normally brings a state of satiety, temporarily halting our desire to continue eating.

hunger The primarily physiological (internal) drive to find and eat food, mostly regulated by innate cues to eating.

appetite The primarily psychological (external) influences that encourage us to find and eat food, often in the absence of obvious hunger.

neuroendocrine Linked to the combined action of the endocrine glands and the nervous system. Examples include substances released from glands in response to nerve stimulation.

vagus nerves Nerves arising from the brain that branch off to other organs essential for control of speech, swallowing, and gastrointestinal function.

Hypothalamus: One Satiety Regulator

The **hypothalamus,** a portion of the brain, is the key integration site for the regulation of food intake. When stimulated, cells in the feeding centers of the hypothalamus signal us to eat. Then, as we eat, hunger decreases. Eventually, we stop eating as cells in the satiety centers of the hypothalamus are stimulated. Various cues to eat come from other groups of cells in the vicinity of the hypothalamus, macronutrients such as glucose in the

hypothalamus A region at the base of the brain that contains cells that play a role in the regulation of hunger, respiration, body temperature, and other body functions.

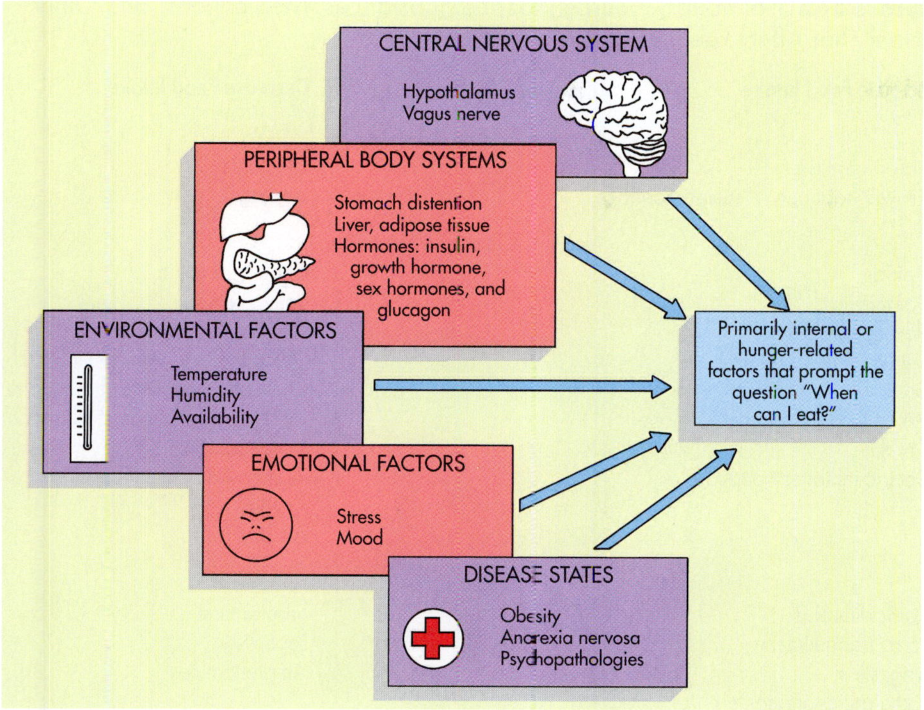

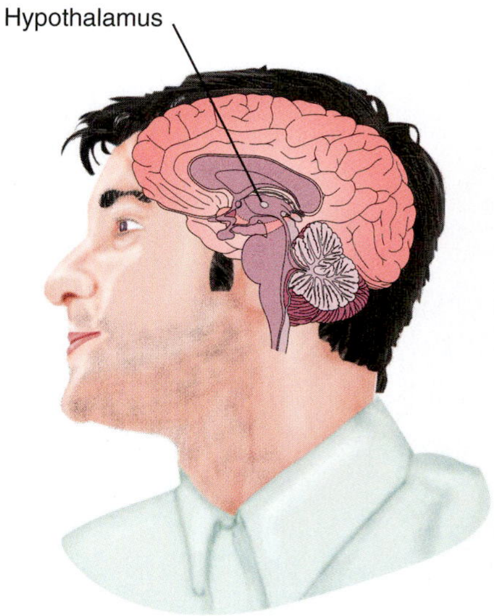

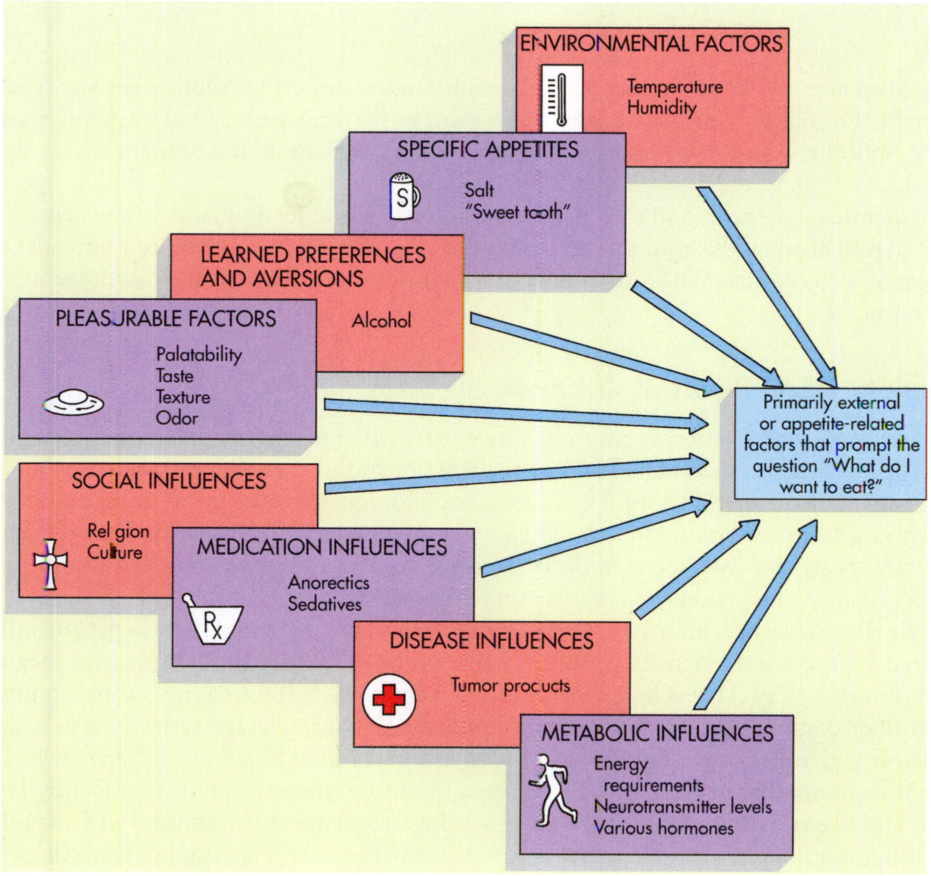

Figure 13-5 A model incorporating many factors that influence satiety. Note that there is some overlap between influences on hunger and appetite. Overall, feeding is regulated by a group of complex and interrelated processes.
Illustration by William Ober.

Table 13-2 Hormones, Neuroendocrine Substances, Medications, and Other Factors That Affect Feeding Behavior†[14, 18]

Increase Food Intake	Decrease Food Intake
Neurotransmitters	
Norepinephrine	Serotonin
Growth hormone releasing hormone	Dopamine
Neuropeptides and Hormones	
Opiods	Cholecystolcinin
Galanin	Enterostatin
Neuropeptide Y	Tumor necrosis factor
Agouti-related protein	Glucagon-like peptide-1 (GLP-1)
Orexin-A	Corticotropin releasing hormone
Melanin-concentrating hormone	Melanocyte-stimulating hormone
Ghrelin	Melanocortin
Gastric inhibitory peptide	Peptide 443-36
	Amylin
	Adipsin
Medications	
Corticosteroids	Sibutramine
Some tranquilizers	Leptin*
Progestins	Amphetamines
Some antidepressants	

†Some of these medications are also body hormones. Many of the neuropeptides are also found in the gastrointestinal tract (see Chapter 3).

*In conjunction with the hormone insulin when both are present in the brain.

sympathetic nervous system Part of the nervous system that regulates involuntary vital functions, including the activity of the heart muscle, smooth muscle, and adrenal glands.

bloodstream, various hormones and other substances, and **sympathetic nervous system** activity. Overall, as sympathetic nervous system activity decreases, food intake increases. The opposite is also true. Thus, many internal signals both inhibit and encourage food intake.

Chemicals, surgery, and some cancers can destroy the feeding and satiety centers in the hypothalamus. Without satiety-center activity, laboratory animals (and humans) eat their way to obesity. Without feeding-center activity, animals eat little and eventually lose weight.

Satiety Regulation at Other Body Sites

As just mentioned, satiety is controlled by a network of mechanisms spread throughout the body. Satiety is maintained first by the sensory stimulation that food elicits, coupled with the knowledge that a meal was eaten. Second, the effects of nutrient digestion, absorption, and metabolism are felt. The satiety and feeding centers in the hypothalamus communicate and interact with other decision points in the brain, small intestine, and liver. Overall, the process of satiety is very complex.

Dr. Barbara Rolls, an expert in this field, has found that satiety is also greatly influenced by the energy density of foods. Lower energy density foods show the greatest amount of satiety. This is linked to the total weight of such foods (i.e., water content) and fiber content. Other factors that influence satiety are dietary variety, particle size, viscosity, glycemic load, palatability, and visual clues such as size and shape. Still, Dr. Rolls suggests that in the long run our eyes might be the most important factor. Thus the practice of recognizing appropriate serving sizes of foods discussed in Chapter 2 and training oneself to expect that amount can help control energy intake in the long run. If a person has trouble controlling body weight, he or she should try to train the eye to expect less food by slowly decreasing serving sizes. Food intake will be reduced as one expects less food but still experiences satiety.[2]

Control of Feeding Through Body Composition

Feeding behavior also changes in response to body fat content. When body fat is surgically removed from animals, their food consumption increases. Based on work with genetic forms of obesity in animals, researchers have identified a group of substances that circulates in the blood and communicates the degree of body fatness to the central nervous system. The gene for one such substance in mice and humans has been isolated (called the ob gene). The product produced by the gene has been named **leptin.** Work with one strain of mice suggests that leptin partly decreases the activity of **neuropeptide Y** and other small proteins present in the brain (review Table 13-2). This then reduces food intake.[8] Some people exhibit leptin resistance, in that it doesn't readily bind to its receptors. This then leads to greater hunger than seen in people who don't have this problem. Only a few people have been found to be truly leptin deficient.

Theoretically, when adipose tissue stores are increasing, leptin (and/or related substances) causes satiety. Conversely, when adipose tissue stores are decreasing, not as much leptin (and/or related substances) is released into the bloodstream, and the desire to eat is enhanced. The main function of leptin is probably energy conservation during periods of inadequate food supply. Low leptin output leads to decreased thyroid gland activity and, thus, a fall in basal metabolism. Leptin-deficient animals also show decreased spontaneous activity, suggesting that they are conserving body energy. Experts suggest that leptin actually may be more important for lessening the effects of starvation than for preventing obesity. Thus, leptin is not there primarily to protect against obesity but, instead, to serve as a signal for inadequate energy intake.[8]

Studies using leptin to induce weight loss have shown that such administration is safe. It is a protein and therefore must be injected into the body. Interestingly, not all people treated with leptin have lost significant amounts of weight; some people have even gained weight during the therapy. At this time, we are a long way off from routine leptin use in the management of obesity, and there is even a question of whether the company that owns the patent for leptin will ever produce it for commercial use.

leptin A hormone (167 amino acids) made by adipose tissue that influences long-term regulation of fat mass. Leptin also influences reproductive functions, as well as other physiological processes, such as insulin release.

neuropeptide Y A small protein (36 amino acids) that increases food intake and reduces energy expenditure when injected into the brains of experimental animals.

Social customs, peers, and authority figures can influence the desire to eat. Concern about appearance when on a date can influence the food choices made. A woman concerned about looking "petite" in company may choose a smaller portion of food than when alone. We are also likely to eat more at a meal when with a large group of people than when with a few people or alone, or when someone else is "picking up the check."

Does Appetite Regulate What We Eat?

Various feeding and satiety messages from body cells do not single-handedly determine what we eat. Almost everyone has encountered a mouthwatering dessert and devoured it, even on a full stomach. We have an innate taste for sweet and acquire a taste for fat. Appetite can be affected by a variety of external forces, such as environmental and psychological factors, as well as social customs (review Fig. 13-5).

We often eat because food confronts us. It smells good, tastes good, and looks good. We might eat because it is the right time of day, we are celebrating, or we are trying to overcome the blues. Appetite may not be a biological process, but it does influence food intake After a meal, memories of pleasant tastes and feelings reinforce appetite. If stress or depression sends you to the refrigerator, you are mostly seeking comfort, not food energy.

Hormones That Affect Satiety

Endorphins, the body's natural opiod painkillers, and hormones, such as high amounts of cortisol, can prod us to eat. On the other hand, other hormones, hormonelike compounds, and still other chemical factors in the body can contribute to the feeling of satiety. With eating, blood concentrations of some digestive hormones, such as cholecystokinin (CCK), increase. This increase, also combined with **gastrointestinal distention,** helps shut off hunger. Note that the latter is suspected but not proven.[2]

Certain parts of the nervous system also contribute to satiety, in part linked to the release of the neurotransmitter histamine. Increased production of **serotonin,** another brain neurotransmitter, has also been linked to intake of various nutrients, especially carbohydrate. High serotonin concentrations in the brain can be calming, induce

endorphins Natural body tranquilizers that may be involved in the feeding response and function in pain reduction.

gastrointestinal distention Expansion of the wall of the stomach or intestines due to pressure caused by the presence of gases, food, drink, or other factors. This contributes to a feeling of satiety brought on by food intake.

serotonin A neurotransmitter synthesized from the amino acid tryptophan that appears to both decrease the desire to eat food and to induce sleep.

sleepiness, and reduce food intake. Medications that prolong serotonin action are used to treat certain eating disorders for this reason (see Chapter 15).

nutrient receptors Proposed sites in the small intestine that contribute signals to the brain that in turn elicit a feeling of satiety. These receptors are stimulated by nutrient exposure in the lumen of the small intestine

Following the likely influence of gastrointestinal distention, **nutrient receptors** in the small intestine are believed to take over in promoting satiety after a meal. This concept is supported by experiments in which an individual feels satiated when fats or carbohydrates are infused directly into his or her small intestine. This effect is not reported, however, when the same fats or carbohydrates are infused directly into the person's bloodstream.

Nutrients in the Blood That Affect Satiety

Accumulating evidence from both human and animal studies on the regulation of hunger suggests that an underlying hunger for food is never actually absent. After a meal, blood concentrations of macronutrients increase, the brain registers satiety, and hunger is temporarily relieved. Studies suggest that an apolipoprotein on the chylomicrons (apolipoprotein A-IV) also signals satiety to the brain as these appear in the blood after a meal.

Several hours after eating, when concentrations of macronutrients in the blood begin to fall, the body must start using energy found in body stores; hunger then returns. This is because satiety is no longer registered by the metabolism of ingested energy-yielding compounds. In other words, feeding signals begin to dominate again.

Satiety Cascade

Early → Late

- Sense hunger or see a tempting food
- ↓ Taste of food
- ↓ Knowing a meal was just eaten
- ↓ Likely influence of gastrointestinal distention, as well as receptors in the intestinal tract
- ↓ Influence of nutrient metabolism in liver and resulting communication with the brain

Hunger and Appetite in Perspective

Internal and external signals—driving hunger and appetite—generally operate simultaneously and combine into a momentary decision whether to reject or eat a food item. For example, visual and taste stimulation can cause something called *cephalic phase responses* by the body. Saliva flows and digestive hormones, ghrelin and insulin are released in response to seeing, smelling, and initially tasting food, such as a favorite hamburger. This readies the body for the meal. These internal forces are elicited by external cues, again showing the degree to which internal and external forces are intertwined.

The next time you pick up a candy bar or ask for second helpings, remember the physiological influences on eating behavior. Body cells (brain, stomach, intestine, liver, and other organs), hormones (such as insulin and ghrelin), neurological components (such as histamine and serotonin), and social customs all influence food intake. Where food is ample, appetite—not hunger—mostly triggers eating.[11] Keep track of what triggers your eating for a few days. Is it primarily hunger or appetite? Note as well that this system is not perfect; your body weight can increase (or decrease) over time if you are not careful to balance energy intake with energy output.

Concept | Check

Hunger is the primarily physiological or internal desire to find and eat food. Appeasing it creates satiety—no further desire to eat exists. Satiety is influenced by hunger-related (internal) forces in the brain, gastrointestinal tract, adipose tissue, liver, and other organs. Various hormones and neuroendocrine compounds participate. Food intake is also affected by appetite-related (external) forces such as social custom, time of day, palatability, and presence of others. North Americans probably respond more to external, appetite-related forces than to hunger-related ones in choosing when and what to eat.

Healthy weight is currently the preferred term to use for weight recommendations. Older terms, such as *ideal weight* and *desirable weight,* are no longer used in the medical literature. However, you still may hear these terms in clinical practice.

Estimation of a Healthy Weight

Numerous methods are used to set what body weight should be, typically called *healthy body weight*. Several tables exist, generally based on weight-for-height. These tables arise from studies of large population groups. When applied to a population, they provide good estimates of weight associated with health and longevity. These tables, however, do not necessarily refer directly to an individual's weight and health status.

Ideally, family history of weight-related disease and current health parameters should be considered when establishing a healthy weight for an individual, in addition to weight-for-height. Evidence of the following weight-related conditions is important:[19]

- Hypertension
- Elevated LDL-cholesterol
- Family history of obesity, cardiovascular disease, or certain forms of cancer (e.g., breast, colon)
- Pattern of fat distribution in the body
- Elevated blood glucose

On a more practical note, other questions can be pertinent: What is the least one has weighed as an adult for at least a year? What is the largest size clothing one would be happy with? What weight has one been able to maintain during previous diets without feeling constantly hungry? Overall, the individual, under a physician's guidance, should establish a "personal" healthy weight (or need for weight reduction) based on weight history, fat distribution patterns, family history of weight-related disease, and current health status. This assessment points out how well the person is tolerating any existing excess weight. Thus, current height/weight standards are only a rough guide. Furthermore, a healthy lifestyle may make a more important contribution to a person's health status than the number on the scale. Fit and overweight are not necessarily mutually exclusive, but still not often seen together in our society. And neither is thin synonymous with healthy if the person is also not physically active. This topic is discussed at greater length later in the chapter with regard to the appropriateness of a recommendation for weight loss.

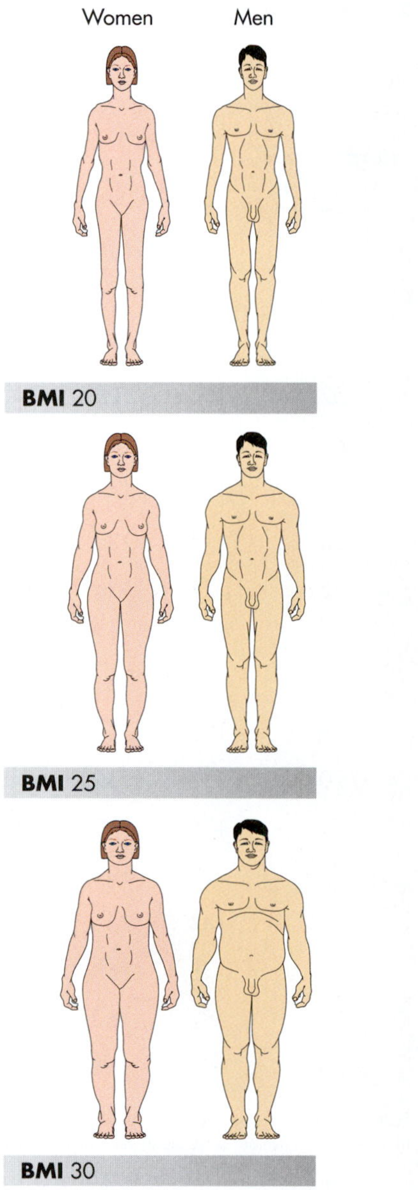

Estimates of body shapes at different BMI values.

Using Body Mass Index (BMI) to Set Healthy Weight

For the past 50 years, weight-for-height tables issued by the Metropolitan Life Insurance Company have been the typical way healthy weight was established. These tables considered gender and frame size, predicting the weight range at a specific height that was associated with the greatest longevity. The latest table (issued in 1983) and methods for determining frame size are in Appendix I.

Currently in the medical and nutrition literature there is almost exclusive use of **body mass index (BMI)** as a weight-for-height standard.[7] Still, you may see either in current medical practice. This chapter will focus on body mass index. Research has shown it is the weight-for-height standard that is most closely related to body fat content.

Body mass index is calculated as

$$\frac{\text{body weight (in kilograms)}}{\text{height}^2\text{ (in meters)}}$$

An alternate method for calculating BMI is

$$\frac{\text{weight (pounds)} \times 703.1}{\text{height}^2\text{ (inches)}}$$

body mass index (BMI) Weight (in kilograms) divided by height (in meters) squared; a value ≥ 25 indicates overweight and a value ≥ 30 indicates obesity. A BMI ≥ 25 increases risk for weight-related health disorders such as type 2 diabetes and cardiovascular disease. As a rough estimate, 1 BMI unit equals 6 to 7 pounds.

Table 13-3 lists BMI for various heights and weights. Health risks from excess weight may begin when the body mass index ≥ 25. A healthy weight-for-height is a BMI 18.5 to 24.9. What is your BMI? How much would your weight need to change to yield a BMI of 25? 30? These are general cut-off values for the presence of overweight and obesity, respectively.

The concept of body mass index is convenient to use because the values apply to both men and women (i.e., gender neutral). However, any body weight-for-height standard is actually a crude measure. Keep in mind, however, that a BMI of 25 to 29.9 is a marker of *overweight* (compared to a standard population) and not necessarily a marker of *overfat*. Many men have a BMI greater than 25 because of extra muscle tissue. Also, very

Table 13-3 Body Weight in Pounds According to Height and Body Mass Index (BMI)

	BMI (kg/m^2)													
	19	20	21	22	23	24	25	26	27	28	29	30	35	40
Height (Inches)	Body Weight (Pounds)													
58	91	96	100	105	110	115	119	124	129	134	138	143	167	191
59	94	99	104	109	114	119	124	128	133	138	143	148	173	198
60	97	102	107	112	118	123	128	133	138	143	148	153	179	204
61	100	106	111	116	122	127	132	137	143	148	153	158	185	211
62	104	109	115	120	126	131	136	142	147	153	158	164	191	218
63	107	113	118	124	130	135	141	146	152	158	163	169	197	225
64	110	116	122	128	134	140	145	151	157	163	169	174	204	232
65	114	120	126	132	138	144	150	156	162	168	174	180	210	240
66	118	124	130	136	142	148	155	161	167	173	179	186	216	247
67	121	127	134	140	146	153	159	166	172	178	185	191	223	255
68	125	131	138	144	151	158	164	171	177	184	190	197	230	262
69	128	135	142	149	155	162	169	176	182	189	196	203	236	270
70	132	139	146	153	160	167	174	181	188	195	202	207	243	278
71	136	143	150	157	165	172	179	186	193	200	208	215	250	286
72	140	147	154	162	169	177	184	191	199	206	213	221	258	294
73	144	151	159	166	174	182	189	197	204	212	219	227	265	302
74	148	155	163	171	179	186	194	202	210	218	225	233	272	311
75	152	160	168	176	184	192	200	208	216	224	232	240	279	319
76	156	164	172	180	189	197	205	213	221	230	238	246	287	328

Each entry gives the body weight in pounds for a person of a given height and BMI. Pounds have been rounded off. To use the table, find the appropriate height in the far left column. Move across the row to a weight. The number at the top of the column is the BMI for the height and weight.

short adults (under 5 feet tall) may have high BMIs that may not reflect overweight or fatness. For this reason, any weight-for-height measurement should be used only as a screening test for overweight or obesity.

Still, overfat and overweight conditions generally appear together. The focus is on body weight-for-height standards in clinical settings mainly because these are easier to measure than total body fat.

A shortcut method of estimating healthy body weight is the pounds per inch of height method. For women, allow 100 pounds for the first 5 feet, then add 5 pounds for every inch thereafter. To estimate a man's healthy body weight, allow 106 pounds for the first 5 feet and then add 6 pounds for each inch thereafter. The estimate of weight is then given a $\pm$ 10% range. Based on this system, a 6-foot-tall man should weigh about 178 $\pm$ 18 pounds (106 + [12 $\times$ 6 = 178]).

Even agreed upon weight standards for BMI are not for everyone. Adult BMI should not be applied to children, adolescents who are still growing, frail older people, pregnant and lactating women, and highly muscular individuals. Children and pregnant women have unique BMI standards (see Chapters 16 and 17).

Putting Healthy Weight into Perspective

One current school of thought is to let nature take its course with regard to body weight. According to this proposal, by trying to lose weight in order to fall within a specific (often unrealistic) height/weight range, people often regain their original

Table 13-4 Health Problems Associated with Excess Body Fat[6]

Health Problem	Partially Attributable To
Surgical risk	Increased anesthesia needs and greater risk of wound infections
Pulmonary disease and sleep disorders	Excess weight over lungs and pharynx
Type 2 diabetes	Enlarged adipose cells, which poorly bind insulin and poorly respond to the message insulin sends to the cell
Hypertension	Increased miles of blood vessels found in adipose tissue, increased blood volume, and increased resistance to blood flow
Cardiovascular disease (e.g., coronary heart disease and stroke)	Increases in LDL-cholesterol and triglyceride values, low HDL-cholesterol, and decreased physical activity. A greater risk for heart failure is also seen.
Bone and joint disorders (including gout)	Excess pressure put on knee, ankle, and hip joints
Gallstones	Increased cholesterol content of bile
Skin disorders	Trapping of moisture and microorganisms in tissue folds
Various cancers	Estrogen production by adipose cells; animal studies suggest excess energy intake encourages tumor development
Shorter stature (in some forms of obesity)	Earlier onset of puberty
Pregnancy risks	More difficult delivery, increased number of birth defects, and increased need for anesthesia
Reduced physical agility and increased risk of accidents and falls	Excess weight that impairs movement
Menstrual irregularities and infertility	Hormones produced by adipose cells, such as estrogen
Vision problems	Cataracts are more often present
Premature death	A variety of risk factors for disease, listed in this table

The greater the degree of obesity, the more likely and the more serious these health problems generally become. They are much more likely to appear in people who show an upper body fat distribution pattern and/or greater than twice healthy body weight.

weight plus more. In contrast, listening to the body for hunger cues, eating a healthy diet, and remaining physically active (not to be overlooked) eventually helps one maintain an appropriate height/weight value. This concept will be further addressed in the upcoming discussion on treatment for obesity. It is a cornerstone of the current "size acceptance" movement.[13] The clearest idea regarding a healthy weight is that it is personal. Weight has to be considered in terms of health, not simply fashion.

Concept | Check

Healthy body weight is generally determined in a clinical setting using a body mass index or another weight-for-height standard. The presence of existing weight-related disease should be considered in determining healthy body weight. Total health and a healthy lifestyle, not simply fashion, should be the major considerations when determining healthy weight.

Energy Imbalance

If energy intake exceeds expenditure over time, overweight and eventual obesity are likely results. Often, health problems eventually follow (Table 13-4). In this context, medical experts recommend that an individual's cutoff value for obesity should not be

Former U.S. Surgeon General Dr. C. Everett Koop is spearheading a campaign, called "Shape Up America!" to convince overweight people to lose weight and increase physical activity. According to Dr. Koop, obesity is the number two killer in the United States. What many North Americans don't understand, he explains, is how serious the problem of excess pounds is: Although many North Americans are aware that smoking is responsible for more than 400,000 deaths per year, they are not aware that obesity is responsible for about 300,000 deaths annually in the United States alone. Before long, obesity will surpass cigarette smoking as the leading cause of death in North America.

based primarily on body weight but, rather, on the total amount of fat in the body, the location of body fat, and the presence or absence of weight-related medical problems.

Estimating Body Fat Content and Diagnosing Obesity

Body fat can range from 2 to 70% of body weight. In this regard, men with over 24% body fat and women with over about 35% body fat are considered obese. Desirable amounts are about 8 to 24% body fat for men and 21 to 35% fat for women. Women need more body fat because some "sex-specific" fat is associated with reproductive functions. This fat is normal and factored into calculations.

underwater weighing A method of estimating total body fat by weighing the individual on a standard scale and then weighing him or her again submerged in water. The difference between the two weights is used to estimate total body fat.

Various methods are used to estimate body fat content. **Underwater weighing** is among the most accurate and works because adipose tissue is less dense than lean tissue; because fat floats, the more adipose tissue present, the less a person weighs when submerged. This procedure requires a trained technician and submersion (Fig. 13-6).

Air displacement (plethysmography) works to measure body volume. Once body volume is known, along with body weight, body density and in turn body fat can be calculated (using the same formula as in the caption for Fig. 13-6). A common instrument used is called the BodPod (Fig. 13-7).

Still other methods to estimate body fat include total-body electrical conductance when placed in an electromagnetic field (TOBEC).

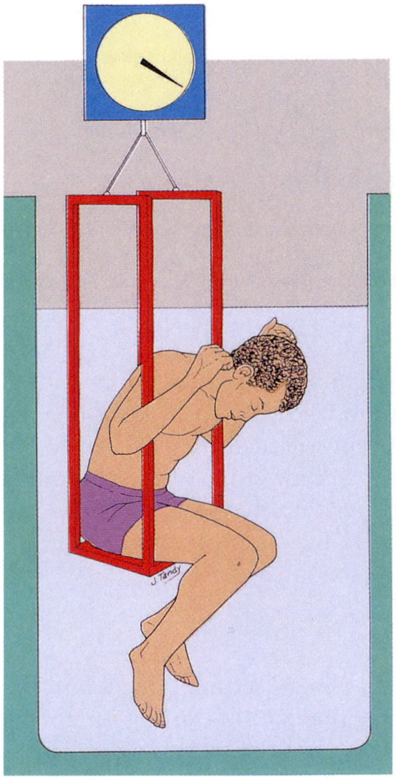

Figure 13-6 Underwater weighing. To get an accurate estimate of body fat, the subject exhales as much air as possible and then holds his or her breath and bends over at the waist. Once the subject is totally submerged, the underwater weight is recorded. For example, the loss of weight when submerged might yield a body density of 1.06 g/cm^3. This would be put into the formula such as: % body fat = (495 ÷ body density) − 450. The subject is 17% body fat based on use of this formula.

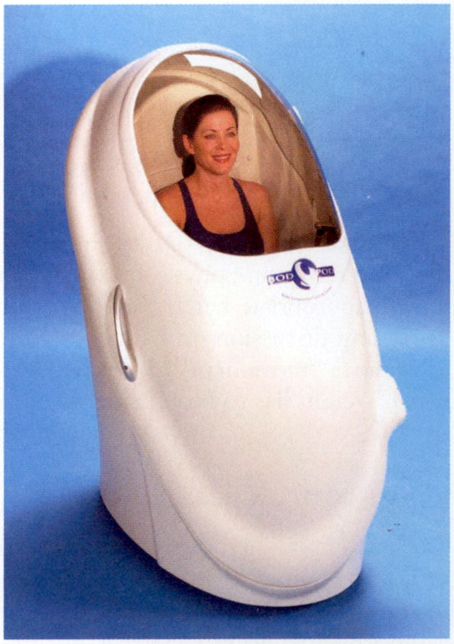

Figure 13-7 BodPod. This device is used to determine body fat in a similar way to that of underwater weighing. The difference is that instead of using loss of weight while submerged as a measure of body volume, the BodPod determines body volume based on the volume of displaced air, measured as a person sits in a sealed chamber.

Although there are some limits to its accuracy, skinfold thickness is the method most widely used to estimate total body fat. Clinicians use calipers to measure the fat layer directly under the skin at multiple sites (Fig. 13-8).

Clinicians have begun measuring total body fat using **bioelectrical impedance.** This technique sends a painless, low-energy electrical current to and from the body via wires and electrode patches. Researchers surmise that adipose tissue resists electrical flow more so than lean tissue. This is because adipose tissue has a lower electrolyte and water content than lean tissue, and so more adipose tissue proportionately means greater electrical resistance. Within a few minutes, bioelectrical impedance analyzers convert body electrical resistance into an approximate estimate of total body fat, as long as body hydration status is normal (Fig. 13-9).

bioelectrical impedance The method to estimate total body fat that uses a low-energy electrical current. The more fat storage a person has, the more impedance (resistance) to electrical flow will be exhibited.

Another method for estimating total body fat, infrared reactance, exposes the biceps to infrared light, assessing the interactions with the fat and protein in arm muscle. After only 2 seconds, this flashlight-size device can give an estimate.

A further advance in determining body fat is use of dual energy X-ray absorptiometry (DEXA). It is currently considered the most accurate way to determine body fat. This X-ray system allows the clinician to separate body weight into three components—fat, fat-free soft tissue, and bone mineral. The usual whole-body scan requires about 5 to 20 minutes and delivers a minimal radiation dose. Obesity, osteoporosis, and other aspects of nutritional health can be investigated using this method (Fig. 13-10).

BMI offers an alternative way to define obesity (Fig. 13-11). Recall it is the weight-for-height measure most closely associated with body fat content.

30–39.9	Obese	Increased health risk
> 40	Severely obese	Major health risk. Note that the number of North Americans falling into this category is increasing rapidly.

A planned treatment program should be implemented after BMI reaches 30.

(a) (b) (c) (d)

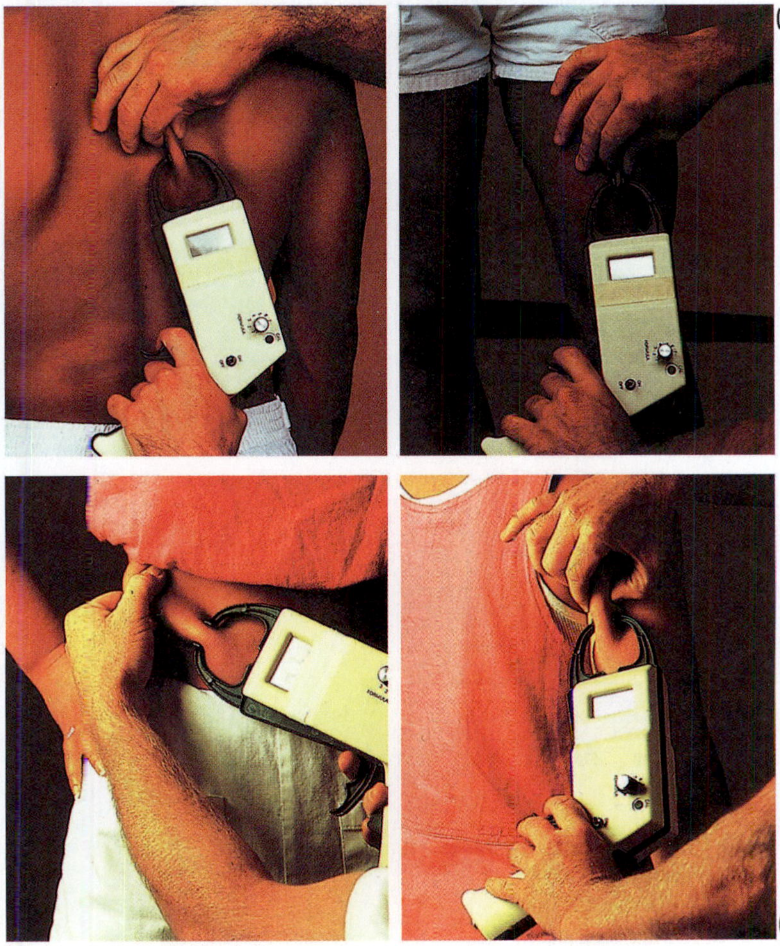

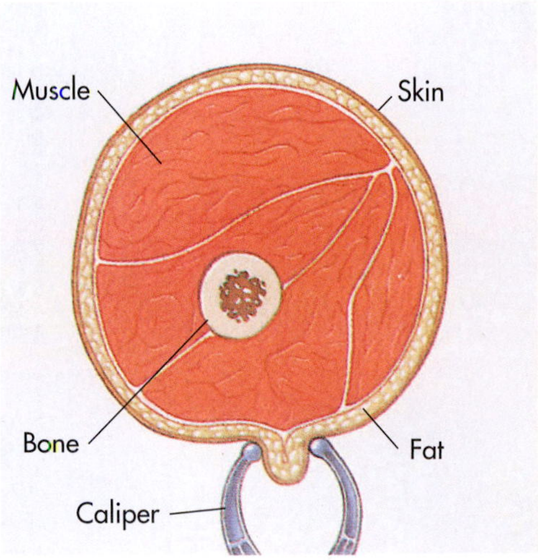

Figure 13-8 Skinfold measurements. The use of proper technique, calibrated equipment, and standards in multiple skinfold measurements can accurately predict body fat content in about 10 minutes. Commonly measured skinfolds for this method are (*a*) subscapular, (*b*) thigh, (*c*) suprailiac, and (*d*) triceps.

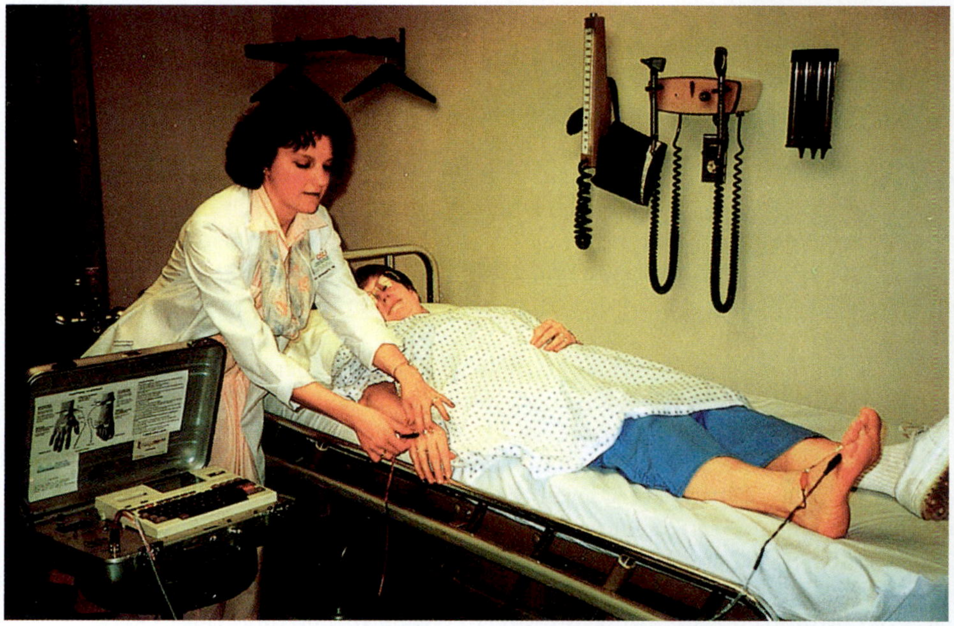

Figure 13-9 Bioelectrical impedance. This method can estimate total body fat in less than 5 minutes and is based on the principle that adipose tissue in the body resists the flow of applied low-energy electricity. The degree of resistance to the flow of electricity per increment of body height is used to estimate body fatness.

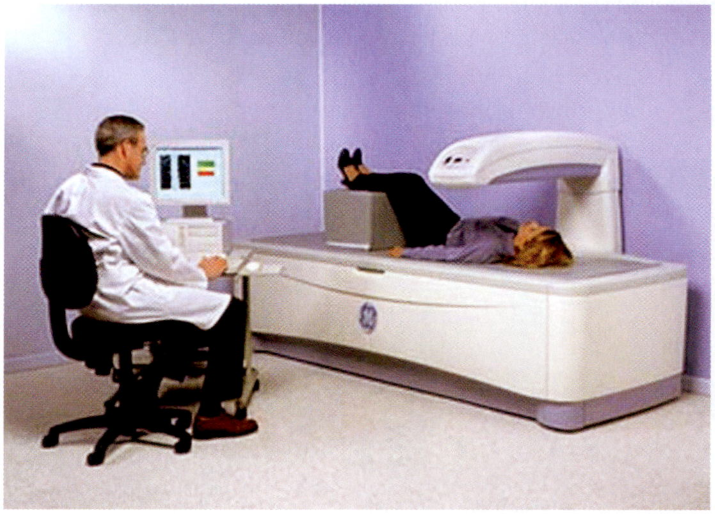

Figure 13-10 DEXA (dual energy X-ray absorptiometry scan). This method measures body fat by passing small doses of radiation through the body which a detector then quantifies as fat, lean tissue, or bone. The scanner arm moves from head to toe and in doing so can determine body fat as well as bone density. DEXA is currently considered the most accurate method for determining body fat. The radiation dose is minimal.

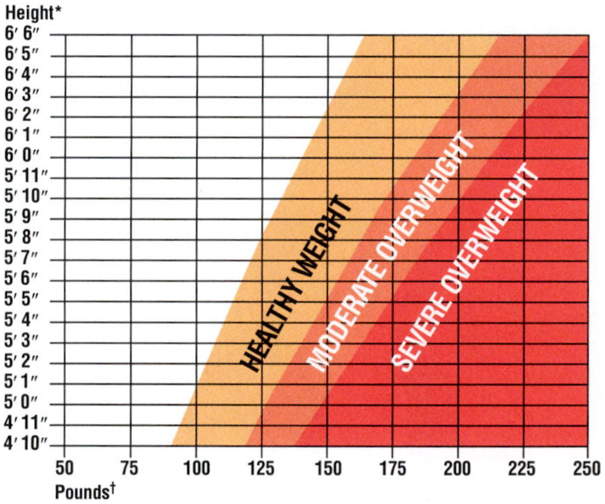

Figure 13-11 Height/weight table included as part of the latest Dietary Guidelines publication. The upper ends of the healthy weight ranges correspond to a body mass index of 25.

* Without shoes.

† Without clothes. The higher weights apply to people with more muscle and bone, such as many men.

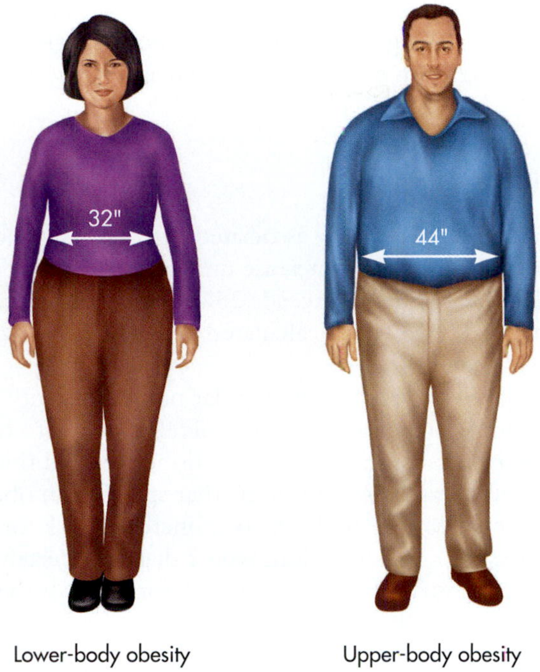

Figure 13-12 Body fat distribution, showing upper-body and lower-body obesity. The upper-body (android) form brings higher risks for ill health associated with obesity. The woman has a waist circumference of 32". The man has a waist circumference of 44". Thus, the man has upper-body obesity, but the woman does not, based on a cutoff of > 40 inches for men and > 35 inches for women.

Using Body Fat Distribution to Establish Obesity

Where we store fat, as well as how much, can predict health risks. Some people store fat in upper body areas. Others hold fat lower on the body. Excess fat in either place generally spells trouble, but each storage space also has its unique risks. Fat deposited in the lower body often resists being shed. However, **upper-body (android) obesity** is related to more cardiovascular disease, hypertension, and type 2 diabetes.[20] Whereas other adipose cells empty fat directly into general circulation, the contents of abdominal adipose cells go straight to the liver, by way of the portal vein, before being circulated to the muscles. This process likely interferes with the liver's ability to clear insulin and alters lipoprotein metabolism by the liver. Both changes spell trouble for the body.

upper-body (android) obesity The type of obesity in which fat is stored primarily in the abdominal area; defined as a waist circumference > 40 inches (102 cm) in men and > 35 inches (89 cm) in women; closely associated with a high risk for cardiovascular disease, hypertension, and type 2 diabetes.

High blood testosterone (a primarily male hormone) levels apparently encourage upper-body obesity, as does alcohol intake. This characteristic male pattern of fat storage appears in the "apple-on-a-stick" shape (large abdomen [pot belly] and small buttocks and thighs). This type of android-related risk is assessed by simply measuring the waist. A waist circumference more than 40 inches in men and more than 35 inches in women indicates such a shape (Fig. 13-12). If BMI is also ≥ 25, health risks are significantly increased.

Estrogen and progesterone (primarily female hormones) encourage lower-body fat storage and **lower-body (gynecoid or gynoid) obesity**—the typical female pattern. The small abdomen and much larger buttocks and thighs give a pearlike appearance. After menopause, blood estrogen falls, encouraging upper-body fat distribution.

lower-body (gynecoid, gynoid) obesity The type of obesity in which fat storage is primarily located in the buttocks and thigh area.

Using Age of Onset in the Evaluation of Obesity

Obesity can be classified as juvenile-onset or adult-onset. When obesity develops in infancy or childhood, numerous adipose cells develop, each with the ability to grow larger. (This is discussed further in Chapter 17, particularly in reference to weight control in childhood.) In adult obesity, fewer adipose cells are usually present, but these contain an excess amount of fat. Still, as obesity progresses in adulthood, adipose cells can increase in number again.

Juvenile-onset obesity presents a special concern because the greater number of adipose cells may increase the body's resistance to cutting down fat stores. Adipose cells have a long life span and apparently need to store some fat. If more adipose cells automatically require more fat storage, reducing total body fat becomes a tough task. Although the reasons are still puzzling, long-term obesity appears to make losing weight more difficult.

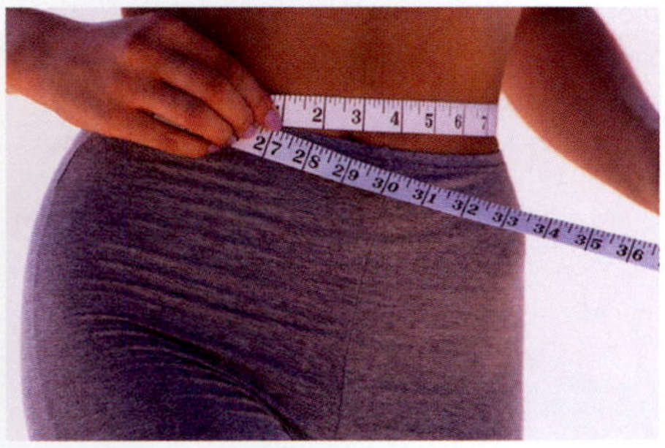

Waist circumference is an important measure of weight-related health risk.

Concept | Check

Overweight and obesity are typically associated with excessive body fat storage. Related health problems especially increase under the following conditions:

- A man's percentage of body fat exceeds 25%; a woman's exceeds about 35%.
- Body mass index (BMI) is ≥ 30 (calculated as weight in kilograms divided by height squared in meters).

However, if a healthy lifestyle including regular physical activity is being followed and no current health problems exist, these guidelines need to be re-evaluated.

Body fat storage can be estimated clinically using skinfold thickness or bioelectrical impedance. Fat storage distribution further specifies an obese state as either upper body or lower body. Obesity leads to an increased risk for cardiovascular disease, some types of cancer, hypertension, type 2 diabetes, certain bone and joint disorders, and some digestive disorders. The risk for some of these diseases are greater with upper-body fat storage.

Why Some People Are Obese—Nature Versus Nurture

Both genetic traits and psychological factors can increase the risk for obesity. These diverse influences spark controversies concerning which factor yields the greater influence.

How Does Nature Contribute to Obesity?

identical twins Two offspring who develop from a single ovum and sperm and consequently have the same genetic makeup.

Identical twins raised apart tend to show similar weight gain patterns, whether lean or obese. It appears that nurture—what we learn about eating habits and nutrition, which varies between twins who are raised apart—has less to do with obesity than genes do. In fact, research using twins suggests that genetic background accounts for up to 70% of weight differences between people. Twins even tend to accumulate fat in the same body sites. Our genes help determine rates of metabolism, fuel use, and differences in brain chemistry. All affect weight.

We also inherit specific body types, such as short and stocky, pencil-thin, or muscular. Some of us have short, stubby bones; short trunks; round heads; and wide chest and hips. Others of us are tall and slender with long, thin bones and narrow chests, hips, heads, and fingers. Still others exhibit a muscular build with large shoulders and arms and defined abdominal muscles.

Tall, thin people appear to have an inherently easier time maintaining healthy body weight. Basal metabolism increases as body surface increases. Tall people have more body surface (based on body weight comparisons) than short, stocky people. Therefore, taller people use more energy than do shorter ones, even when resting.

thrifty metabolism A metabolism that characteristically conserves more energy than normal, so that it increases the risk of weight gain and obesity.

Some rats and mice have a genetic predisposition to obesity. They inherit a **thrifty metabolism,** one that uses energy frugally. This enables them to store fat more readily than the typical animal. Some people probably inherit a thrifty metabolism as well. Farmers once bred cows and hogs based on their ability to acquire fat. Today, because we know that eating too much animal fat can increase the risk for cardiovascular disease, farmers breed leaner animals.

A thrifty human metabolism requires less energy to get through the day. In earlier times, when food supplies were scarce, a thrifty metabolism helped protect people against starvation. With today's general abundance of food, people operating in this low gear require a high-energy output and wise food choices to prevent obesity.[11] If you think your metabolism promotes weight gain, you may have inherited a thrifty metabolism.

A child with no obese parent has only a 10% chance of becoming obese. A child with one obese parent (common in our society) has a 40% risk, and one with two obese parents has an 80% risk. It can be argued that these probabilities are related, in part, to the eating behaviors a child learns. **Fraternal twins,** who are not genetically identical, vary less in weight than do two unrelated people. This pattern supports the theory that environment, or nurture, affects obesity. Still, the close association of body weights between identical twins strongly supports a genetic linkage. This varied evidence shows how complicated it is to separate nature from nurture when searching for the causes of obesity.

fraternal twins Offspring that develop from two separate ova and sperm and therefore have separate genetic identities, although they develop simultaneously in the mother.

Does the Body Have a Set Point for Weight?

The **set-point** theory of weight maintenance espouses the notion that weight is closely regulated by the body. It proposes that humans have a genetically predetermined body weight or body fat content, which the body attempts to defend. Some research suggests that the hypothalamus monitors the amount of body fat in humans and tries to keep that amount constant over time. This regulation of body fat content is referred to as a "set point." You have already seen in this chapter that the hormone *leptin* forms one communication link between adipose cells and the brain that allows for some weight regulation.

set point Often refers to the close regulation of body weight. It is not known what cells control this set point or how it actually functions in weight regulation. There is evidence, however, that mechanisms exist that help regulate weight.

In the major studies of humans cited to support the set-point theory, volunteers who lost weight through starvation later ate in a way to regain their original weight or a little more. In addition, studies in the 1960s using prisoners with no history of obesity found it was hard for some men to gain weight. This was supported by later studies (see the previous section on thermogenesis). Also, after an illness is resolved, a person generally gains lost weight.

Nature or nurture: What causes these twins to have similar body weights?

Sound physiological evidence also suggests that body weight tends to be regulated. If energy intake is reduced, the blood concentration of the thyroid hormones fall, and the metabolic rate slows. In addition, lower body weight decreases the energy cost of each future weight-bearing activity, and the total energy used by lean tissue falls because some of these tissues are also lost. Furthermore, the enzyme used by adipose and muscle cells to take up fat from the bloodstream (lipoprotein lipase) often increases its activity. Through these changes, the body resists further weight loss.[7]

If a person overeats, in the short run the metabolic rate tends to increase. This causes some resistance to weight gain. People often recognize the body's resistance to weight loss when dieting but do not think much about the resistance to weight gain after eating a big holiday meal. However, in the long run, resistance to weight gain is much less than resistance to weight loss.[14] When a person gains weight and stays at that weight for a while, the body tends to defend the new weight.

Arguments against the set-point theory cite the fact that, during pregnancy, women slowly increase body weight and fat. Also, an average person's weight does not remain constant throughout adulthood; it usually increases slowly, at least until old age. This means that a person must be able to shift his or her set point. It is also argued that, if an individual is placed in a different social, emotional, or physical environment, weight can become markedly higher or lower and is maintained. These arguments suggest that humans, rather than having a set point determined by genetics or number of adipose cells, actually settle into a particular stable weight based on an interaction between nature and nurture influences.[14]

In the final analysis, we must bear much of the responsibility for weight maintenance ourselves since set point is weaker in preventing weight gain than in preventing weight loss. The odds are against the likelihood that, even with a set point helping us, we can avoid creeping weight gain in adulthood without great attention to this tendency.[1]

Does Nurture Have a Role?

Genetic factors determine some differences in energy metabolism and explain certain weight-gain variations among people. However, environmental factors, such as high-fat diets and inactivity, can literally shape us as well. Consider that our gene pool hasn't changed much in the past 50 years, but the ranks of obese people have grown, and in what the U.S. Centers for Disease Control and Prevention describe as epidemic proportions in the last 10 years.[6]

Family members often have similar eating habits and choose similar foods. Even husbands and wives—who have no genetic link—may behave similarly toward food and eventually assume similar degrees of leanness or fatness. Therefore, the family that bonds at the local fast food restaurant can influence each other's eating habits and, ultimately, fatness.

Is poverty associated with obesity? Ironically, the answer is often yes. North Americans of lower socioeconomic status, especially females, are more likely to be obese than those in upper socioeconomic groups. Are cultural expectations or socioeconomic stress the cause of this?

Adult obesity in women is often rooted in childhood obesity. In addition, relative inactivity, periods of stress and boredom, as well as excess weight gain in pregnancy, contribute to female obesity. These patterns suggest both social and genetic links. Male obesity, however, is not strongly linked to childhood obesity and, instead, tends to appear after age 30. In part, marriage and a working life encourage a sedentary state for many men. This powerful and prevalent pattern suggests a primary role of nurture in obesity, with less genetic influence.

Infants who are fed formula, rather than breastmilk, may have a higher risk of overweight or obesity later in childhood. A pediatrician will keep track of a baby's weight gain and will see if this pattern continues as the child grows. If a child becomes obese by 5 years of age, immediate attention is necessary. Obesity in childhood is strongly related to obesity in adulthood.

Nature and Nurture Together

Overall, both nature and nurture influence the tendency toward obesity (Table 13-5). Consider the possibility that obesity is nurture allowing nature to express itself, like an accident waiting to happen. Some people begin life with a slower metabolism. Put these people in an inactive environment, feed them lots of food, and praise them for eating. Like any of us, they can be nurtured into gaining weight, which allows their natural

Does the difference in body fat between grandfathers and grandsons arise from nature, nurture, or both?

Table 13-5 What Encourages Excess Body Fat Stores and Obesity?

Factor	How Fat Storage Is Affected
Age	Excess body fat is more common in adults and middle-aged individuals.
Menopause	Increase in abdominal fat deposition is favored.
Gender	Females have more fat.
Insulin resistance	This often develops as obesity develops.
Positive energy balance	This is especially important if over a relatively long period.
Composition of diet	Excess energy intake from a high fat intake, generous alcohol intake, and preference for energy dense (sugary, fat-rich) foods are likely to contribute to obesity.
Physical activity	Low or decreasing amount of physical activity ("couch potato") affects energy balance and body fat stores.
Resting metabolic rate	A low value with respect to lean body mass is linked to weight gain.
Sympathetic nervous system	Low activity favors weight gain.
Thermic effect of food	This is low for some obesity cases.
Use of fat for energy	There can be limited fat release into the bloodstream.
Total fat mass	Leptin, produced by adipose tissue, affects food intake. Greater fat mass leads to greater leptin production.
Ratio of fat to lean tissue	A high ratio of fat mass to lean body mass is correlated with weight gain.
Fat uptake by adipose tissue	This is high in some obese individuals and remains high (perhaps even increases) with weight loss.
Blood cortisol value	Elevated values promote increased hunger and loss of lean body mass, in turn promoting fat gain.
Variety of social and behavioral factors	Obesity is associated with socioeconomic status; familial conditions; network of friends; busy lifestyles that discourage balanced meals; binge eating; easy availability of inexpensive, "supersized" high-fat food (such as in quick-service restaurants); pattern of leisure activities; television time; smoking cessation; excessive alcohol intake; and number of meals eaten away from home. These meals are often served in large portions and high in fat and energy content. Today, "food hunts man" to a great extent in Western societies.
Undetermined genetic characteristics	These affect energy balance, particularly via the energy expenditure components, the deposition of the energy surplus as adipose tissue or as lean tissue, and the relative proportion of fat and carbohydrate use by the body.
Race	In some ethnic groups, higher body weight may be more socially acceptable.
Certain medications	Food intake increases.
Childbearing	Women may not lose all weight gained in pregnancy, leading to creeping weight gain.
National region	Regional differences, such as high-fat diets and sedentary lifestyles in the Midwest and areas of the South, lead to different rates of obesity in different places.

Student life is often full of physical activity. This is not necessarily true for a person's later working life; hence, weight gain is a strong possibility.

tendency for obesity to blossom. The eventual location of fat storage is strongly influenced by genetics.

Still, genes do not control this destiny. With increased physical activity and decreased food consumption, even those with a genetic tendency toward obesity can maintain a healthy or "healthier" (i.e., somewhat lower) body weight.[1]

The importance of environment in the development of obesity is exhibited in the treatment of Prader-Willi syndrome. Children with this inherited disorder (1 in every 12,000 to 15,000 births) have an extreme appetite and become very obese if food availability is not carefully controlled. If such a child has become obese, however, further careful control of food availability (e.g., locking all kitchen cabinets and not allowing the child access to money) can lead to significant weight loss, often 100 pounds or more. This environmental therapy is effective, despite the fact that the children maintain their extreme appetite.

Concept | Check

Genetic background plays a role in obesity, influencing body shape, sites of fat deposition, and rate of basal metabolism. The role of nurture is evident in families, who tend to have similar eating habits, activity patterns, and degrees of fatness. Men tend to develop obesity after age 30, and women tend to have both childhood and adult roots for obesity; this suggests an especially important influence of nurture in men. Because both factors have an impact, it makes sense to assume that nurture serves as a catalyst for expressing or denying a genetic tendency toward obesity.

Treatment of Obesity

The total costs attributable to weight-related disease approaches $100 billion annually in the United States.

Obesity should be considered similar to any chronic disease. Treatment requires long-term lifestyle changes, rather than simply taking medicine for 2 weeks, as for a sore throat, or following a quick fix promoted by a popular (also called fad) diet book.[1, 10, 12] We often, however, view a "diet" as something one goes on temporarily, only to resume prior (typically poor) habits once satisfactory results have been achieved. It is for this reason that so many people regain lost weight. In place of this, healthy, active living with dietary modifications one can live with should be the emphasis for both obese and thin people. Let's explore why obesity must be regarded and treated in this way.

Some Basic Premises

As you begin to consider current treatment options for obesity, first focus on six important general principles concerning weight loss for adults. (Chapter 17 provides weight-loss strategies for children.)

Much of the Current Mania Surrounding Dieting Is Misdirected

People on diets often fall within a BMI of 18.5 to 25. Rather than worrying about weight loss, these individuals should be focusing on a healthy lifestyle that allows for weight maintenance. Incorporating necessary lifestyle changes and learning to accept one's particular body characteristics should be the overriding goal.

Actually, this dieting mania can be viewed as mostly a social problem, stemming from unrealistic weight expectations (especially for women) and lack of appreciation for the natural variety in body shape and weight. Not every woman can look like a Hollywood actress, nor can every man look like a Greek god, but all of us can strive for good health and, if physically possible, an active lifestyle.

Here are some practices that can stimulate metabolism while one is dieting:

- Perform physical activity regularly throughout the day. Find opportunities for increasing activity, such as quick walks, stair climbing, or calisthenics (crunches, push-ups, etc.).
- Fidget when sitting and standing.
- Eat breakfast, so that food intake is spread throughout the day. Each time food is consumed, metabolism increases.
- Avoid "crash" dieting. Slow weight loss is a better idea because it leads to a smaller decline in metabolism during a diet.

The Body Defends Itself Against Weight Change

As noted in the discussion on set point, the body makes numerous physiological adjustments during times of underfeeding or overfeeding that resist weight change. The compensation is most pronounced during times of underfeeding.

Weight Cycling Is a Common Phenomenon

Only about 5% of people who follow commercial diet programs actually lose weight and then remain close to that weight. Typically, one-third of the weight lost during dieting is regained within 1 year of the end of dietary restriction, and almost all weight lost is regained within 3 to 5 years. Some programs have higher success rates than 5%, as do some people who simply lose weight on their own without enrolling in any supervised plan. Overall, however, the statistics are grim. Currently, only the surgical approaches to obesity treatment show routine success in maintaining the weight loss in most people.[4]

Negative health consequences associated with this weight cycling are an increased risk for upper-body fat deposition, profound discouragement and erosion of self-esteem, and possibly a fall in HDL-cholesterol. Nevertheless, experts still encourage obese people to attempt weight loss, with a strong focus on maintaining that lower weight. Still, dieters need to be aware of the trap of today's crash diet, which too often leads to the next month's weight gain. Weight-loss programs that claim you can lose weight and keep it off without changing food intake or increasing physical activity are selling a fantasy. A weight-loss program should be considered successful only when the subjects involved in the process remain at or close to their lower weights.

Weight Gain in Adulthood Is All Too Common

In adulthood, weight gain is common, especially in those aged 25 to 44 years. Particular care should be practiced in these decades, although childhood and the adolescent years also deserve attention.[9] Adults should generate a goal of not gaining greater than about 10 to 16 pounds more than their weight was on reaching age 21. People who gain weight rapidly should closely monitor food intake and activity patterns to discover the causes and then moderate the increases or reverse the trend in appropriate ways.

Critical | Thinking

Hal has been dieting to lose weight for 2½ months. However, like many dieters, he has reached a plateau. Although he continues to restrict his energy intake, he's no longer losing weight. How would you explain to Hal the physical factors that fight weight loss?

Changes in Body Composition Deserve a Primary Focus in Weight Loss

Weight should be lost mostly from adipose tissue stores, not from muscle and other lean tissues. Rapid weight loss at the start of a diet program often represents fluid lost as a result of decreased salt intake and loss of glycogen from the liver and muscle. Substantial muscle tissue may be lost as well, and this is mostly (about 73%) water. People are fooled when they weigh themselves after starting a highly restrictive diet. They lose weight, but very little of it represents fat loss. Any loss of lean tissue means a decrease in basal metabolism and thus a decrease in overall energy expenditure.

Weight Loss in Perspective

All this shows the importance of preventing obesity. This concept has wide support because curing the disorder is very difficult. Public-health and political strategies to address the obesity epidemic must begin with weight maintenance for the adult population and increased physical activity. There is a particular need to focus on children and adolescents, in which excess weight and sedentary lifestyle may form the basis for a lifetime of weight-related illness and increased mortality.

Only the very motivated person should try to lose weight, and ideally this attempt should be preceded by a period of weight maintenance for about 6 months in order to begin the process of balancing energy intake with a degree of energy output that can be maintained.

Wishful Shrinking—Why Can't Quick Weight Loss Be Mostly Fat?

Rapid weight loss cannot consist mostly of fat loss because such a high energy deficit is needed to lose a large amount of adipose tissue. Adipose tissue, which is mostly fat, contains about 3500 kcal per pound. Fat loss, which includes adipose tissue plus supporting lean tissues, represents approximately 3300 kcal per pound (about 7.2 kcal/g).[7] To lose 1 to 2 pounds of adipose tissue per week, energy intake must be decreased by approximately 500 to 1000 kcal/day, with the addition of participating in 60 minutes of physical activity on most (or all) days of the week. Behavioral strategies to reinforce lifestyle changes are also effective for weight loss and later weight maintenance.[15] Diets that promise 10 to 15 lb of weight loss per week can't ensure that the weight loss is from adipose tissue stores alone. Producing an energy deficit sufficient to lose that amount of adipose tissue simply isn't practical. Lean tissue, rather than adipose tissue, accounts for the major part of the weight lost.

Weight-Control Objectives from *Healthy People 2010*

Increase by 40% the proportion of adults who are at a healthy weight (body mass index between 18.5 and 25).

Reduce by 50% the proportion of adults who are obese (body mass index of 30 or more).

Reduce by 50% the proportion of children and adolescents who are overweight or obese.

Expert Opinion

Why Is Weight Management so Difficult?

Sachiko T. St. Jeor, Ph.D., R.D.

Currently we are expecting a worldwide epidemic of obesity; approximately 65% of adults in the United States are overweight (body mass index, or BMI, $\geq 85^{th}$ percentile of 25.0 to 29.9 kg/m^2) or obese (BMI in the $\geq 95^{th}$ percentile or > 30.0 kg/m^2). This is a sad commentary on the history of weight gain over the years. Although North Americans are weight conscious, it appears that they are not successful in weight management overall.

Why is weight management so difficult? The first reason is that small weight gains over time go unnoticed. According to the statistics of two nationally representative surveys, the National Health and Nutrition Examination Survey II, or NHANES II (1976–1980), and NHANES III (1988–1994), it appears that the average weight gain over 10 years is approximately 8 lbs (3.6 kg), or approximately 1 lb/year. We would rarely notice a 1-lb weight gain over a year but hopefully would notice a 10- to 20-lb weight gain over a 10- to 20-year period. In addition, many of us would rather not notice a small weight gain over time and certainly would like to think that these small weight gains are temporary and will even out over time. Thus, new weight monitoring techniques may be of importance.

Second, little emphasis has been placed on weight maintenance or on the prevention of weight gain. This epidemic of obesity could have been partially halted if we did not gain so much weight and instead accept weight stability as our first goal. Since the conditions of overweight and obesity are associated with increased morbidity and mortality from at least five major diseases (hypertension, diabetes, dyslipidemia, cardiovascular disease, and stroke) as well as some types of cancers (endometrium, breast, prostate, and colon), the problem is of major significance. Our research group has defined weight maintenance as ±5 lb between any two points in time. This reflects about a 3% change in body weight. However, there has been no standard definition broadly accepted for weight maintenance, and individual fluctuations vary widely.

Using this practical definition, only 20% of a group of both normal and overweight males and females of all ages studied in my laboratory were weight maintainers over 4 years. Furthermore, more normal-weight individuals were weight maintainers (75%) than those who were overweight (25%). Older males, adults who experienced lower weight variability, and adults undergoing less dieting were also more successful at maintaining their weight. The weight maintainers tended to have better health profiles, were characterized by being more physically active, used more problem-solving and self-monitoring strategies, and had more "normalized" eating patterns, social support, and self-efficacy. These results point to the difficulty of implementing well-accepted strategies for weight management over the long term.

Third, we are a population with very unrealistic expectations. Weight maintenance is not a popular concept; instead, weight loss is always the goal. A fad diet is usually on the bestseller list, and losing large amounts of weight in short periods of time (10 lbs/10 days) is always attractive. Few individuals are really committed to putting in the long-term effort needed to lose weight gradually (1–3 lb/week) in a healthy manner, by making a conscious effort to decrease energy intake and increase physical activity daily. Furthermore, the amount of weight loss desired is always much higher than that which generally can be achieved and maintained in the longer term.

The fourth reason is that little emphasis is put on obesity prevention, and insurance reimbursement for weight-management counseling is very limited. Most individuals who seek professional

A typical fast-food hamburger in 1957 contained little more than 1 oz of cooked meat, compared with up to 6 oz today. A theater serving of popcorn was 3 cups in 1957, compared with 16 cups (medium-size popcorn) today.

What to Look for in a Sound Weight-Loss Diet

A dieter can try to devise a plan of action by seeking advice from a registered dietitian or other health professional, or by consulting current books. Either way, a sound weight-loss program should include three components: control of energy intake; increased energy expenditure through physical activity; and acknowledgment that a lifelong change in habits is required, not simply a short-term weight-loss period (Fig. 13-13). Focusing on just consuming less energy represents a difficult path to success. Adding regular physical activity and an appropriate psychological component contributes to success and later maintenance of the weight loss.[1] Dr. Sachiko St. Jeor discusses these concepts in greater detail in the Expert Opinion.

Specifically, any weight-loss plan should have the following characteristics:

1. The plan should meet nutritional needs, except for energy. To do that, it should follow the Food Guide Pyramid (or related pyramid), emphasizing a wide variety of

We are faced with many opportunities to overeat, in this case meat. It takes much perseverance to then eat sensibly.

counseling are those with medically related diseases. In contrast, the majority of the dieting population uses self-help methods (books, over-the-counter medications, supplements, clubs, etc.), which may work only temporarily. The most intelligent adults are also susceptible to diet fads, as they might be desperate to find quick and easy answers. Because the medical profession has put little emphasis on weight management, the burden of success and prevention lies on the individual and interested professionals. However, recent emphasis on obesity as a disease, its recognition as one of the leading health indicators in the Healthy People 2010 objectives, and emphasis on weight management is the major message of "aim for a healthy weight" is the 2000 Dietary Guidelines will certainly help put obesity and weight management on the national agenda as higher priorities in the future.

The last reason is that healthy lifestyles are difficult to maintain in our busy and demanding lives. We need to be more physically active. Ways to more easily incorporate increased activity need facilitation and motivation. Simultaneously, since tasty foods and social occasions increase our food consumption, strategies to balance our energy intake and output need more emphasis. Health reasons for weight management are less immediate but should be stressed and somehow rewarded. Time is of the essence in all regards.

In summary, there are many reasons that weight management is difficult. However, a winning strategy is to take small steps in balancing energy intake with output. Small, additive changes, even in 100 kcal increments, will make a difference in the long run. On the intake side, 100 kcal is not much and can be as little as a bite of food in less than 1 minute. On the expenditure side, calories burned take more effort. For example, a mile walked in approximately 15–20 minutes is approximately 100 kcal. Still, the resulting 200-kcal deficit in one day and 1400 kcal deficit in 1 week equates to approximately 0.5 lb/week fat loss and could result in a weight change of 26 lb/year. It takes time, education, awareness, motivation, and action for successful weight management. A good message is to start where you are and prevent weight gain—whether you currently are healthy-weight, overweight, or obese. Then, concentrate on small changes to implement additive weight losses over time. Initial targets of approximately 5 to 10% weight loss in the first 6 months is reasonable. Prevention of weight gain or regain is more difficult (concentrate on weight maintenance at ±5 lb or 3% of weight between any two points in time). Patience, realistic goals, and time without relapse will work. We can be successful at weight management if we place primary emphasis on weight maintenance, especially when weight loss is not possible.

Dr. St. Jeor is professor and director of the Nutrition Education and Research Program at the University of Nevada School of Medicine, Reno. She is internationally known for her research focusing on efforts to improve weight control and overall health in adults.

low-fat and high-fiber choices and adequate fluids (about 8 cups per day). Meeting calcium needs may also help; however, we need some double-blind, placebo-controlled research trials to actually prove this is important. Overall, this controlled eating should remain a satisfying and pleasurable experience.

2. Expect slow weight loss. This helps with later weight maintenance. A loss of 1 or so pounds of fat storage per week is desirable. Once about 10% of excess weight is lost, maintenance of that loss for about 6 months is recommended before more weight loss is attempted. That may seem like a disappointing prescription, but a more radical approach to weight loss is likely to produce a yo-yo episode. Then, careful evaluation should be made to determine whether further weight loss is needed, based on current health state.
3. The plan should allow adaptations to individual habits and tastes. The same plan does not work for everyone.

Liquids are getting more attention, since liquid calories do not stimulate satiety mechanisms to the same extent as solid foods. The advice from experts is to use beverages that have few or no calories and limit calorie-containing beverages.

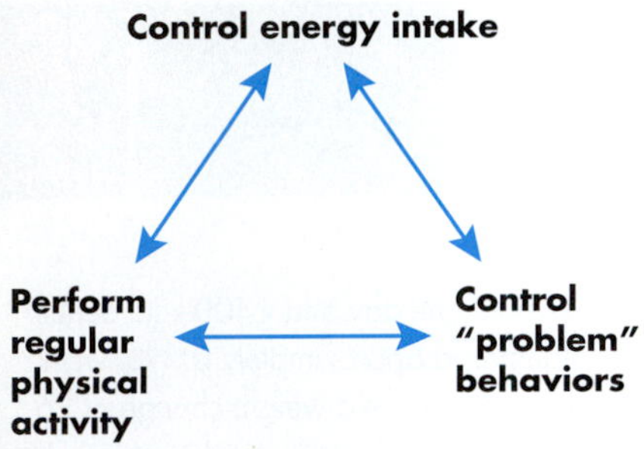

Figure 13-13 Weight-loss triad. The key to weight loss and maintenance can be thought of as a triangle in which the three corners consist of (1) controlling energy intake, (2) performing regular physical activity, and (3) controlling "problem" behaviors. The three corners of the triangle support each other in that without one corner the triangle becomes incomplete. In the same way, without one of the three keys to weight loss, weight loss and later maintenance become unlikely.[4]

When you read brochures or research reports about specific diet plans, ask not only whether the people lost weight but also whether they maintained much of that weight loss. If this did not happen, then the entire dieting program was in vain.

For more information on weight control, obesity, and nutrition, visit the Weight-Control Information Network (WIN) at www.niddk.nih.gov/health/nutrit/win.htm or call 800-WIN-8098. Complete guidelines for weight management are available at www.nhlbi.nih.gov/guidelines/index.htm. Other websites include www.caloriecontrol. org, www.weight.com, www.obesity.org, and www. cyberdiet.com.

4. The plan should minimize hunger and fatigue. To do this, it should contain at least 1200 to 1600 kcal per day. Otherwise, consuming sufficient vitamins and minerals, especially enough iron for young women, is difficult. In reality, however, 1000 kcal per day is generally regarded as the minimum energy intake because many dieters perform so little physical activity and therefore need very restricted energy allowances. If the eating plan calls for an energy intake below 1600 kcal per day, it should recommend the use of either fortified foods (ready-to-eat breakfast cereals, for example) or a balanced multivitamin and mineral supplement (review Chapter 9 for advice on nutrient supplement use).
5. The plan should contain common foods. There is no magical food that can speed weight loss (see the Nutrition Perspective). If a diet suggests that there is, whether ginseng, tofu, or garlic, advice should be sought elsewhere. Furthermore, if special foods were required, maintaining this practice indefinitely would be difficult.
6. The plan should fit into any social situation. The healthier lifestyle should allow attendance at parties, eating at restaurants, and participation in normal daily activities.
7. The plan should help change problem eating habits. It should promote reshaping food habits and lifestyle to make weight loss and then weight maintenance possible and, so, thwart weight regain. Eating at least three meals per day (including breakfast) and avoiding binge eating are two important considerations. Maintenance should be a key concern of any plan—the plan must have a lifetime focus. For example, a 150-lb person should reduce energy intake, increase physical activity, and start eating like a 130-lb person to become a 130-lb person. Moreover, once the weight is lost, the person can't go back to the habits of his or her 150-lb self. The program should also focus on changing obesity-promoting beliefs and rallying healthy social support.
8. The plan should improve overall health. It should emphasize regular physical activity, proper rest, stress reduction, and other health changes in lifestyle. All too often, people know how to diet, but they don't know how to live. They find it easier to count calories and follow a plan than to deal with underlying issues that encourage eating, such as stress.
9. The plan should insist that the person see a physician before starting if any of the following are true:
   - He or she has existing health problems, such as cardiovascular disease or hypertension.
   - He or she plans to lose weight as quickly as possible.
   - He or she is over 40 years of age for men or 50 years of age for women and plans to perform substantially increased physical activity (according to the latest Dietary Guidelines for Americans publication).

Concept | Check

Obesity is a chronic disease that necessitates lifelong treatment. Key points to consider when attempting to treat obesity include the following: (1) The primary focus should be on a healthy lifestyle that can be maintained; (2) the body resists weight loss; (3) typical weight-loss attempts often are followed by weight regain; (4) emphasis should be placed on preventing obesity, since curing this disorder is very difficult; (5) weight should be lost from adipose stores, not mostly from lean tissues. Appropriate weight-loss programs have the following characteristics in common: (1) They meet nutritional needs; (2) they can adjust to accommodate habits and tastes; (3) they emphasize readily obtainable foods; (4) they promote changing habits that discourage overeating; (5) they encourage regular physical activity; and (6) they help change obesity-promoting beliefs and rally healthy social support.

Control of Energy Intake—The Main Key to Weight Loss

A goal of losing 1 lb or so of stored fat per week may require limiting energy intake to 1200 kcal per day for women and 1500 kcal for men. The energy allowance could also be higher for very active people. Keep in mind that, in a very sedentary society, decreasing energy intake is vital because it is difficult to burn much energy without ample physical activity. With regard to consuming less energy, some experts suggest consuming less fat (especially saturated fat and trans fat), while others suggest consuming less carbohydrate, especially refined (high glycemic load) carbohydrate sources. Protein intakes in excess of what is typically needed by adults are also receiving attention. Using all these approaches simultaneously is also fine. Currently the low-fat, high-fiber approaches have been the most successful in long-term studies.[5, 10, 16] Finding what works for a single individual is a process of trial and error.

One way for a dieter to monitor energy intake at the start of a weight-loss program is reading labels. Label reading is important, because many foods are more energy dense than people suppose (Fig. 13-14). Another method is to write down food intake for 24 hours and then calculate energy intake from the food table in Appendix N or your diet analysis software, adjusting future food choices as needed. Because people often underestimate portion size when recording food intake, measuring cups can help.

Whatever the method chosen, it is unreasonable to think that measuring food and keeping records will continue for a lifetime. These methods are suggested as a temporary practice for people who need to get a handle on their portion sizes. Once the eyes and stomach are trained to know what constitutes a specific portion size, it will be possible to then "eyeball" appropriate meals.

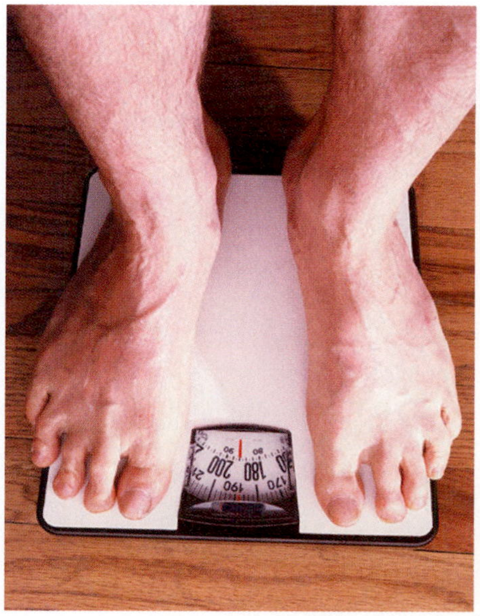

Slow, steady weight loss is one of the characteristics of a sound weight-loss plan.

Figure 13-14 Reading labels helps you choose foods with less energy. Which frozen dessert is the best choice for a person on a weight-loss diet? The % Daily Values are based on a 2000 kcal diet.

Table 13-6 Saving Kcal: Ideas to Help Get Started

Instead Of	Try	Number of kcal Saved
3 oz well-marbled meat (prime rib)	3 oz lean meat (eye of round)	140
½ chicken breast, batter-fried	½ chicken breast, broiled with lemon	175
½ cup beef stroganoff	3 oz lean roast beef (or use a fat-reduced recipe)	210
½ cup home-fried potatoes	1 medium baked potato	65
½ cup green bean-mushroom casserole	½ cup cooked green beans	50
½ cup potato salad	1 cup raw vegetable salad	140
½ cup pineapple chunks in heavy syrup	½ cup pineapple chunks canned in juice	25
2 tbsp bottled French dressing	2 tbsp low-calorie French dressing	150
⅐ 9-inch apple pie	1 baked apple	185
3 oatmeal-raisin cookies	1 oatmeal-raisin cookie	125
½ cup ice cream	½ cup ice milk	45
1 danish pastry	½ English muffin	150
1 cup sugar-coated corn flakes	1 cup plain corn flakes	60
1 cup whole milk	1 cup 1% low-fat milk	45
7-fluid-oz gin and tonic	6-fluid-oz wine cooler made with sparkling water	150
1-oz bag potato chips	1 cup plain popcorn	120
1/12 8-inch white layer cake with chocolate frosting	1/12 angel food cake, 10-inch tube	185
Regular beer	Light beer	40

Spot-reducing using diet and physical activity is not possible. "Problem" local fat deposits can be reduced in size, however, using suction lipectomy. Lipectomy means surgical removal of fat. A pencil-thin tube is inserted into an incision in the skin, and the fat tissue, such as that in the buttocks and thigh area, is suctioned. This procedure carries some risks, such as infection; lasting depressions in the skin; and blood clots, which can lead to kidney failure and sometimes death. The procedure is designed to help a person lose about 4 lb per treatment. Cost is about $1600 per site; total costs range as high as $2600–$9000.

Table 13-6 shows how to start reducing energy intake. As you should realize by now, it is best to consider healthy eating a lifestyle change, rather than simply a weight-loss plan.

Regular Physical Activity—A Second Key to Weight Loss and Especially Important for Later Weight Maintenance

Regular physical activity is very important for everyone, especially those who are trying to lose weight or maintain a lower body weight. Energy use is enhanced.[18] Therefore, it greatly complements a reduction in energy intake for weight loss (but does not substitute for it).[18] Many of us rarely do more than sit, stand, and sleep. Obviously, much more energy is used during physical activity than at rest. In addition, expending only 200 to 300 extra kcal per day above and beyond normal daily activity, while controlling energy intake, can lead to about a half pound of adipose tissue loss per week, or about 25 pounds of adipose tissue loss per year. Furthermore, physical activity often boosts overall self-esteem.

Adding any of the activities in Table 13-7 to one's lifestyle leads to more energy expenditure. Duration and regular performance, rather than intensity, are the keys to success with this approach to weight loss. One should search for activities that can be

Table 13-7 Approximate Energy Costs of Various Activities, and Those Projected for a 150-lb (68 kg) Person

Activity	Kcal per kg per Hour	Number of kcal per Hour	Activity	Kcal per kg per Hour	Number of kcal per Hour
Aerobics—heavy	8.0	544	Horseback trotting	5.1	346
Aerobics—light	3.0	204	Ice skating (10 MPH)	5.8	394
Aerobics—medium	5.0	340	Jogging—medium	9.0	612
Backpacking	9.0	612	Jogging—slow	7.0	476
Basketball—vigorous	10.0	680	Lying—at ease	1.3	89
Bicycling (5.5 MPH)	3.0	204	Racquetball—social	8.0	544
Bowling	3.9	265	Roller-skating	5.1	346
Calisthenics—heavy	8.0	544	Running or jogging (10 MPH)	13.2	897
Calisthenics—light	4.0	272	Skiing (10 MPH)	8.8	598
Canoeing (2.5 MPH)	3.3	224	Sleeping	1.2	80
Cleaning (female)	3.7	253	Swimming (.25 MPH)	4.4	299
Cleaning (male)	3.5	236	Tennis	6.1	414
Cooking	2.8	190	Volleyball	5.1	346
Cycling (13 MPH)	9.7	659	Walking (2.5 MPH)	3.0	204
Dressing/showering	1.6	106	Walking (3.75 MPH)	4.4	299
Driving	1.7	117	Water skiing	7.0	476
Eating (sitting)	1.4	93	Weight lifting—heavy	9.0	612
Food shopping	3.6	245	Weight lifting—light	4.0	272
Football—touch	7.0	476	Window cleaning	3.5	240
Golf	3.6	244	Writing (sitting)	1.7	118

The values in the table refer to total energy expenditure, including that needed to perform the physical activity, plus that needed for basal metabolism, the thermic effect of food, and nonexercise activity thermogenesis. Use your diet analysis software for your personal estimate.

Digiwalker is a device that monitors activity. It costs about $35.00. An often-stated goal for activity is to take at least 10,000 steps per day—typically we take half that many or less. Digiwalker tracks this activity.

continued over time. In this regard, walking vigorously 3 miles per day can be as helpful as aerobic dancing or jogging if it is maintained. Moreover, walking is less likely to lead to injuries. Some resistance exercises (weight training) should also be added to increase lean body mass and, in turn, fat use (see Chapter 14). Exercise also can build more muscle mass, which in turn increases overall metabolic rate. Exercise even helps maintain bone health during weight loss. Keep in mind that bone health sufferers most in those involved in weight-reduction programs that do not include an exercise component.

Opportunities in daily lives to expend energy have diminished: technology is systematically eliminating almost every reason to move our muscles.[11] The easiest way to increase physical activity is to make it part of a daily routine. To start, one could consider walking every day and then incorporating some regular stair climbing. A simple trick is to park the car farther from school, work, and the shopping mall, so that one must walk farther.

Physical activity complements any diet plan.

The motivation to lose weight and keep it off generally comes with a proverbial "flip of the switch," in which the desire to lose weight finally becomes more important than the desire to overeat.

Fruit is a great low-cal snack—high nutrient density and low energy density.

chain-breaking Breaking the link between two or more behaviors that encourage overeating, such as snacking while watching television.

stimulus control Altering the environment to minimize the stimuli for eating—for example, removing foods from sight and storing them in kitchen cabinets.

cognitive restructuring Changing one's frame of mind regarding eating—for example, instead of using a difficult day as an excuse to overeat, substituting other pleasures or rewards, such as a relaxing walk with a friend.

contingency management Forming a plan of action to respond to a situation in which overeating is likely, such as when snacks are within arm's reach at a party.

self-monitoring Tracking foods eaten and conditions affecting eating; actions are usually recorded in a diary, along with location, time, and state of mind. This is a tool to help people understand more about their eating habits.

relapse prevention A series of strategies used to help prevent and cope with weight-control lapses, such as recognizing high-risk situations and deciding beforehand on appropriate responses.

Behavior Modification—A Third Strategy for Weight Loss

Controlling energy intake, so important to weight loss, also means modifying *problem* behaviors. Only the dieter can decide what behaviors keep the person from reaching for the wrong foods at the wrong times for the wrong reasons.[15]

What events start (or stop) eating? What factors influence food choices? Psychologists often use terms such as **chain-breaking, stimulus control, cognitive restructuring, contingency management,** and **self-monitoring** when discussing behavior modification (Table 13-8). This terminology helps place the problem in perspective and organize the intervention strategy into manageable steps.

Chain-breaking separates behaviors that tend to occur together—for example, snacking on chips while watching television. Although these activities do not have to occur together, they often do. Dieters may need to break the chain reaction (see the Take Action at the end of this chapter for more details).

Stimulus control puts us in charge of temptations. Options include pushing tempting food to the back of the refrigerator, removing fat-laden snacks from the kitchen counter, and avoiding the path by the vending machines. Provide a positive stimulus by keeping low-fat snacks ready to satisfy hunger/appetite. Note that alcohol and foods offer quick, easy stress relief. We need to plan healthful alternatives.

Cognitive restructuring changes our frame of mind. For example, after a hard day, respond with a walk or satisfying talk with a friend instead of a binge. Replace eating reactions to stress with healthful, relaxing alternatives.

Decreeing some food off limits sets up an internal struggle to resist the urge to eat that food. This hopeless battle can keep us feeling deprived. We lose the fight. Managing food choices with the principle of moderation is best. If a favorite food becomes troublesome, place it off limits only temporarily, until it can be enjoyed in moderation.

Contingency management prepares us for potential pitfalls and high-risk situations. We might rehearse in advance some appropriate responses to pressure—such as food being passed at a party.

Did you keep a record of what you ate and what catalysts urged you to pick up the fork or put it down as suggested in Take Action in Chapter 1? If so, you already know one key tool in modifying behavior—self-monitoring. A self-monitoring record can reveal patterns—such as unconscious overeating—that may explain problem eating habits. This record can encourage new habits to counteract unwanted behaviors. Obesity experts note that this is the key behavioral tool to use in any weight-loss program.

Overall, it's important to *address specific* problems, such as snacking, compulsive eating, and mealtime overeating. Behavior modification principles end up as critical components of weight reduction and maintenance. Without behavior modification, it is difficult to make lifelong lifestyle changes needed to meet weight-control goals.

Relapse Prevention Is Important

A dieter can tolerate an occasional lapse but needs to plan for lapses. The key is not to overreact, but take charge immediately. Change responses such as "I ate that cookie; I'm a failure" to "I ate that cookie, but I did well to stop after only one!" An occasional cookie is fine; a pound of cookies in an afternoon deserves reconsideration. When dieters lapse from their diet plan, newly learned food habits should steer them back toward the plan. This should enable dieters to avoid the lapse-relapse-collapse trap. Without a strong behavioral program for **relapse prevention** in place, a lapse frequently turns into a relapse. Once a pattern of poor food choices begins, dieters may feel that they have failed and stray further from the plan. As the relapse lengthens, the diet plan collapses, and dieters fall short of their weight-loss goal. Even with a good behavioral plan, one may fail at a diet. Losing weight is difficult. Overall, maintenance of weight loss is fostered by the "3 *M*s": motivation, movement, and monitoring.

Table 13-8 Behavior Modification Principles for Weight Loss

Stimulus Control
Shopping 1. Shop for food after eating—buy nutritious foods. 2. Shop from a list; limit purchases of irresistible "problem" foods. Shopping the perimeter first helps. 3. Avoid ready-to-eat foods. 4. Put off food shopping until absolutely necessary.
Plans 1. Plan to limit food intake as needed. 2. Substitute periods of physical activity for snacking. 3. Eat meals and snacks at scheduled times; don't skip meals.
Activities 1. Store food out of sight, preferably in the freezer, to discourage impulsive eating. 2. Eat all food in the same place. 3. Keep serving dishes off the table, especially dishes of sauces and gravies. 4. Use smaller dishes and utensils.
Holidays and Parties 1. Drink fewer alcoholic beverages. 2. Plan eating behavior before parties. 3. Eat a low-calorie snack before parties. 4. Practice polite ways to decline food. 5. Don't get discouraged by an occasional setback.
Eating Behavior 1. Put fork down between mouthfuls. 2. Chew thoroughly before taking the next bite. 3. Leave some food on the plate. 4. Pause in the middle of the meal. 5. Do nothing else while eating (for example, reading, watching television).
Reward 1. Plan specific rewards for specific behavior (behavioral contracts). 2. Solicit help from family and friends and suggest how they can help you. Encourage family and friends to provide this help in the form of praise and material rewards. 3. Use self-monitoring records as basis for rewards.
Self-Monitoring 1. Note the time and place of eating. 2. List the type and amount of food eaten. 3. Record who is present and how you feel. 4. Use the diet diary to identify problem areas.
Cognitive Restructuring 1. Avoid setting unreasonable goals. 2. Think about progress, not shortcomings. 3. Avoid imperatives such as *always* and *never.* 4. Counter negative thoughts with positive restatements.
Portion Control 1. Make substitutions, such as a regular hamburger instead of a "quarter pounder" or cucumbers instead of croutons in salads. 2. Think small. Order half, and save the other half. Order the entrée and share it with another person. Order a cup of soup instead of a bowl or an appetizer in place of an entrée. 3. Use a doggie bag. Ask your server to put half the entrée in a doggie bag before bringing it to the table.
As we said at the start of the chapter, many of us need to become "defensive eaters." Know when to refuse food after satiety registers, and reduce portion sizes.

Plain popcorn (i.e., limited added fat) is a wise snack choice when eaten in a reasonable quantity.

Successful weight losers and maintainers from the National Weight Control Registry:[10]

- Eat a low-fat, high-carbohydrate diet (on average 25% of energy intake as fat).
- Eat breakfast almost every day.
- Self-monitor by weighing and keeping a food journal.
- Exercise for about 1 hour per day.
- Eat at restaurants only once or twice per week.

Critical | Thinking

With regard to readiness to lose weight, what would you say to a young woman who has just had a baby, needs to find a new job, and recently has gone back to school part-time?

Social Support Aids Behavioral Change

Healthy social support is helpful in weight control. Helping others understand how they can be supportive can make weight control easier. Family and friends can provide praise and encouragement. A registered dietitian or other weight-control professional can keep dieters accountable and help them learn from difficult situations. Long-term contact with a professional can be quite helpful for later weight maintenance.[1] Groups of individuals attempting to lose weight or maintain losses can provide empathetic support.

Concept | Check

Increasing physical activity in daily life should be part of any weight-loss plan. Daily activity, such as walking and stair climbing, is recommended. Behavior modification can improve conditions for losing weight. One behavioral area that requires change is habit chains that encourage overeating, such as snacking while watching television. Another tactic is to modify the environment to reduce temptation; for example, put foods into cupboards to keep them out of sight. In addition, rethinking attitudes about eating—for example, substituting pleasures other than food as a reward for coping with a stressful day—can be important for altering undesirable behavior. Advanced planning to prevent and deal with lapses is vital, as is rallying healthy social support. Finally, the careful observation and recording of eating habits can reveal subtle cues that lead to overeating. Overall, weight loss and maintenance are fostered by controlling energy intake, performing regular physical activity, and modifying problem behaviors.

Professional Help for Weight Loss

At a time when quick fixes for weight are not only expected but are, in fact, demanded, North Americans are willing to try almost anything to shed unwanted pounds. Operation Waistline is a program designed by the U.S. Federal Trade Commission to terminate fraudulent claims being made by the weight-loss and health-store industry with regard to diet products. The program is designed in hopes of putting an end to the $6 billion spent by people in the United States on counterfeit products.

The first professional to see for advice about a weight-loss program is the family physician.[12] Doctors are best equipped to assess overall health and the appropriateness of weight loss. The physician may then recommend a registered dietitian for a specific weight-loss plan and answers to diet-related questions. Registered dietitians are uniquely qualified to help design a weight-loss plan because they understand both food composition and the psychological importance of food.[1] Exercise physiologists can provide advice about programs to increase physical activity. The expense for such professional interventions is now tax deductible in the United States in some cases (see a tax advisor).

Many communities have a variety of weight-loss organizations. These include self-help groups, such as Take Off Pounds Sensibly and Weight Watchers. Other programs, such as Jenny Craig and Physicians' Weight Loss Center, are less desirable for the average dieter. Often, the employees are not registered dietitians or other appropriately trained health professionals. These programs also tend to be expensive because of their requirements for intense counseling or mandatory diet foods and supplements. In addition, the Federal Trade Commission has charged these and other commercial diet-program companies with misleading consumers through unsubstantiated weight-loss claims and deceptive testimonials.

Pharmacotherapy for Weight Loss

People who are candidates for pharmacotherapy for obesity include those with a BMI > 30 or a BMI > 27 with weight-related conditions, such as type 2 diabetes, cardiovascular disease, hypertension, or excess waist circumference; those with no contraindications to use of the medication; and those ready to undertake lifestyle change.[19] Success with pharmacotherapy has been shown only in those who modify their behavior and energy intake and increase their physical activity. Pharmacotherapy alone has not been found to be successful. In addition, if a person has not lost at least 4.4 pounds (2 kg) after 4 weeks, it is not likely that the person will benefit from further use of the medication.

Currently three main classes of medications are used.[19] An **amphetamine**-like medication (phenteramine [Fastin or Ionamin]) is available. This prolongs the activity of epinephrine and norepinephrine in the brain. This therapy is effective for some people in the short run but has not yet been proved effective in the long run. Most state medical boards currently limit use to 12 weeks unless the person is participating in a medical study using the product. The drug should not be used in pregnant or nursing women or those under 18 years of age.

Sibutramine (Meridia) is a second class of medication that has been approved by FDA for weight loss. It enhances both norepinephrine and serotonin activity in the brain by reducing reuptake of these neurotransmitters by the secreting neurons. The neurotransmitters then remain active in the brain for a longer period of time, and so prolong a sense of reduced hunger. The most common side effects are constipation, dry mouth, insomnia, and a mild increase in blood pressure in some people. Thus, sibutramine should be used with caution in people with a history of hypertension (or cardiovascular disease). Studies have shown that it is effective in helping some people who already eat healthy diets, but just eat too much. The main effect is to moderately reduce appetite to allow people to eat less. Sibutramine is safe and effective only when combined with a comprehensive weight-control program and when supervised by a physician.

The third class of medication approved by FDA for weight loss is orlistat (Xenical). This medication inhibits lipase action in the small intestine, reducing fat digestion by about 30% and in turn the subsequent absorption of dietary fat by one-third for about 2 hours when taken along with a meal containing fat. This malabsorbed fat simply is deposited in the feces. *Fat intake has to be controlled*, however, because large amounts of fat in the feces cause numerous side effects, such as gas, bloating, and oily discharge. Interestingly, orlistat use can actually remind the person to follow a fat-controlled diet, as the symptoms resulting from consuming a high-fat meal quickly develop. Orlistat costs about $1.00 per pill, and a pill is taken with each meal containing fat. One way to reduce the cost of orlistat use is to eat a very-low-fat breakfast (e.g., breakfast cereal, juice, and skim milk) and use the medication to inhibit fat absorption at lunch and dinner.

Since the malabsorbed fat carries fat-soluble vitamins into the feces, the person taking orlistat must take a multivitamin and mineral supplement at bedtime. In this way, any micronutrients not absorbed during the day can be replaced; fat malabsorption from the dinner meal will not greatly influence micronutrient absorption in the late evening.

Overall, in skilled hands, prescription medications can aid weight loss in some instances. However, they do not replace the need for reducing energy and fat intake, modifying problem behavior, and increasing physical activity, both during and after therapy. And, more times than not, any weight loss during drug treatment can be attributed mostly to the individual's hard work.[19]

Chapter 9 discussed the risks of self-diagnosis and self-treatment of disease with megadose vitamin and mineral supplements. An even bigger danger exists using herbal substances to foster weight loss. Chapter 18 will discuss herbal remedies in detail. For now, know that, despite widespread advertising, ephedrine (also known as ephedra or ma huang) and St. John's wort are neither effective nor safe treatments for weight loss. Ephedrine has been linked to numerous health problems and even deaths in recent years, especially if large doses are taken. St. John's wort should not be taken with any other antidepressants. Many experts advise staying away from any over-the-counter diet pills, and especially these herbal combinations.

amphetamine A group of medications that stimulate the central nervous system, and have other effects in the body. Abuse is linked to physical and psychological dependence.

The only two medications approved by FDA for long-term use are sibutramine (Meridia) and orlistat (Xenical).

Treatment of Severe Obesity

Severe (morbid) obesity—weighing at least 100 pounds over healthy body weight (or twice one's healthy body weight)—requires professional treatment. Because of the serious health problems related to severe obesity, drastic measures may be necessary. Such treatments are recommended only when traditional diets fail. Drastic weight-loss procedures are not without side effects, both physical and psychological, making careful physician monitoring a necessity.

Very-Low-Calorie Diets

If more traditional diet changes have failed, treating severe obesity with a **very-low-calorie diet (VLCD)** is possible, especially if the person has obesity-related diseases

very-low-calorie diet (VLCD) Known also as *protein-sparing modified fast* (PSMF), this diet allows a person 400 to 800 kcal per day, often in liquid form. Of this, 120 to 480 kcal is carbohydrate, whereas the rest is mostly high-biological-value protein.

that are not well controlled (e.g., hypertension, type 2 diabetes). Optifast is one such commercial program. Some researchers believe that people with body weight greater than 30% above their healthy weight are also appropriate candidates. The diet allows a person to consume 400 to 800 kcal/day, often in liquid form. (These diets were known earlier as protein-sparing modified fasts.) Of this amount, about 30 to 120 g (120 to 480 kcal) is carbohydrate. The rest is high-quality protein, which contributes about 70 to 100 g per day (280 to 400 kcal). This low carbohydrate intake often causes ketosis, which may decrease hunger. However, the main reasons for weight loss are the minimal energy allowed and the absence of food choice. About 3 to 4 lb can be lost per week; men tend to lose at a faster rate than women. When physical activity and resistance training augment this diet, a greater loss of adipose tissue occurs. Careful physician monitoring is crucial throughout this very restrictive form of diet therapy during weight loss, refeeding, and later maintenance. Major health risks include heart problems and gallstones.

Weight regain remains a nagging problem with this type of therapy, especially without a behavioral and physical activity component. If behavioral therapy and physical activity supplement a long-term support program, maintenance of the weight loss is more likely but still difficult. Any program under consideration should include a maintenance plan. Today, antiobesity medications also may be included in this phase of the program.

Gastroplasty

gastroplasty Surgery performed on the stomach to limit its volume to approximately 30 ml.

Gastroplasty, or stomach stapling, is the most common surgical procedure for treating severe obesity. The procedure works by reducing the stomach to about 30 ml (1 oz). Overeating of solid foods is consequently less likely, because rapid vomiting would result. The smaller stomach also promotes more rapid satiety. With the enforced food reduction, about 75% of people with severe obesity eventually lose 50% or more of excess body weight. The surgery's success at long-term loss maintenance often leads to dramatic health improvements, such as reduced blood pressure and elimination of type 2 diabetes. Risk of death from the surgery itself is about 1%.[4]

Gastroplasty Criteria
1. BMI should be > 40.
2. BMI between 36 and 40 is considered when there is a serious obesity-related health concern.
3. Obesity must be present for a minimum of 5 years, with several nonsurgical attempts to lose weight.
4. There should be no history of alcoholism or major psychiatric disorders.

Gastroplasty has disadvantages. The surgery is costly ($20,000 to $40,000 or more) and may not be covered by medical insurance. In addition, follow-up surgery is often needed after weight loss to correct stretched skin, which used to be filled with fat. Furthermore, months of difficult adjustments face the dieter who has chosen this drastic approach to weight loss. The elimination of simple carbohydrates (sugar) from the diet is necessary to avoid *dumping syndrome.* Dumping syndrome is characterized by severe diarrhea, which begins almost immediately following the ingestion of concentrated sugar, such as regular soft drinks, Jell-o, candy, cookies, and other high-sugar foods. Nutrient deficiencies are also possible if an appropriate diet and nutrient supplement plan is not followed.

Three gastroplasty approaches are common today. For the Roux-en-Y gastroplasty procedure, the small intestine is cut at the jejunum (Fig. 13-15). The distal portion of the jejunum is then relocated to the top portion of the stomach and sewed into place. A staple line is then created across the upper portion of the stomach, yielding a stomach pouch of about 30 ml, about the size of a golf ball. (In time it stretches to about 2 to 3 times that size.) Food now travels through the stomach pouch into this limb of small intestine, and eventually into the main flow of the small intestine. In the vertical-banded gastroplasty procedure, a vertical staple line is made to create a small stomach pouch (Fig. 13-15). The outlet for this pouch is surrounded by a band in order to control the diameter of the outlet. This eliminates the possibility that the outlet will eventually stretch and allow for greater food intake. Food travels through the stomach pouch into the main portion of the stomach. Either surgery is not reversed, even after the desired weight loss is attained. Thus, although successful for weight loss, gastroplasty still requires major, lifelong lifestyle changes. A final procedure uses a band placed around the upper portion of the stomach. It is then tightened to reduce stomach volume. The procedure was introduced in 2001. Little is known about its long-term success. On the other hand, many people had successful weight-loss outcomes with the other two procedures.

Concept | Check

Severely obese people who have failed to lose weight with conservative weight-loss strategies may consider other options. Their doctors may recommend undergoing surgery such as reducing the volume of the stomach to approximately 30 ml or following a very-low-calorie diet plan containing 400 to 800 kcal per day. Careful physician monitoring is crucial in both cases.

Treatment of Underweight

Underweight can be caused by a variety of factors, such as anorexia nervosa (see Chapter 15 for details), cancer, infectious disease (e.g., tuberculosis), digestive tract disorders (e.g., chronic inflammatory bowel disease), and excessive physical activity. Genetic background may also lead to a higher resting metabolic rate, a slight body frame, or both. Significant underweight is also associated with increased death rates, especially when combined with cigarette smoking. Health problems associated with underweight include the loss of menstrual function, low bone mass, complications with pregnancy and surgery, and slow recovery after illness. We frequently hear about the risks of obesity, but seldom of underweight. In our culture, being underweight is much more socially acceptable than being obese.

Sometimes being underweight requires medical intervention. A physician should be consulted first to rule out hormonal imbalances, depression, cancer, infectious disease, digestive tract disorders, excessive physical activity, and other hidden disease, such as the eating disorders anorexia nervosa and bulimia nervosa (see Chapter 15 for a detailed discussion of eating disorders).

The causes of underweight are not altogether different from the causes of obesity. Internal and external satiety-signal irregularities, the rate of metabolism, hereditary tendencies, and psychological traits can all contribute to underweight.

In growing children, the demand for energy to support physical activity and growth can cause underweight. During growth spurts in adolescence, active children may not take the time to consume enough energy to support their energy needs. Moreover, gaining weight can be a formidable task for an underweight person. More than 500 extra kcal per day may be required to gain weight, even at a slow pace, in part because of the increased expenditure of energy in nonexercise activity thermogenesis. In contrast to the weight loser, the weight gainer may need to increase portion sizes.

When underweight requires a specific intervention, one approach for treating adults is to gradually increase their consumption of energy-dense foods (foods that provide a great deal of energy in a small volume), especially those high in vegetable fat. Italian cheeses, nuts, and granola can be good energy sources with low saturated-fat content. Dried fruit and bananas are energy-dense fruit choices. If eaten at the end of a meal, they don't cause early satiety. Underweight people should replace such foods as diet soft drinks with good energy sources, such as fruit juices.

Encouraging a regular meal and snack schedule aids in weight gain and maintenance. Sometimes people who are underweight have experienced stress at work or have been too busy to eat. Making regular meals a priority may not only help them attain an appropriate weight but also help with digestive disorders, such as constipation, which are sometimes associated with irregular eating times.

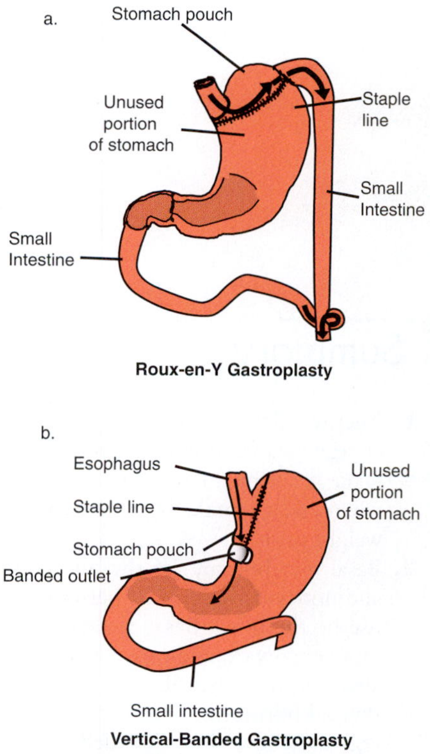

Figure 13-15 Two of the most common forms of gastroplasty for treatment of severe obesity. The Roux-en-Y procedure (*a*) is the most effective method, but is more technically demanding for the surgeon than the vertical-banded gastroplasty (*b*). In the latter the band prevents expansion of outlet for the stomach pouch.

underweight A body mass index below 18.5. The cutoff is less precise than for obesity because this condition has been less studied.

Excessively physically active people can reduce activity. If their weight remains low, they can add muscle mass through a resistance training (weight-lifting) program, but they must increase their energy intake to support that physical activity. Otherwise, weight gain will be hindered.

If these efforts fail to achieve the desired weight, they should at least prevent the health problems associated with being underweight. After achieving that, they may have to accept their lean frames.

Summary

1. Energy balance is energy intake minus energy output. Negative energy balance occurs when energy output surpasses energy intake, resulting in weight loss. Positive energy balance occurs when energy intake is greater than energy output. The result is weight gain.
2. Basal metabolism, the thermic effect of food, physical activity, and nonexercise activity thermogenesis account for total energy use by the body. Basal metabolism, which represents the minimum energy expenditure needed to keep the resting, awake body alive, is primarily affected by lean body mass, surface area, and thyroid hormone concentrations. Physical activity represents energy use above that expended at rest. The thermic effect of food represents the increase in metabolism to facilitate the digesting, absorbing, and processing of nutrients recently consumed. Thermogenesis is heat production caused by shivering when cold, fidgeting, and other responses. About 70 to 80% of energy use is accounted for by basal metabolism and the thermic effect of food in a primarily sedentary person.
3. Energy use by the body can be measured directly from heat output or indirectly from oxygen uptake, carbon dioxide output, or both. An Estimated Energy Requirement can be calculated using formulas based on various combinations of body height and weight with degree of physical activity and age.
4. Groups of cells in the hypothalamus and other regions in the brain affect hunger, the primarily internal desire to find and eat food. These cells monitor macronutrients and other substances in the blood and read low amounts as a signal to promote feeding.
5. A variety of external (appetite-related) forces, such as food availability, affect satiety. Hunger cues combine with appetite cues to promote feeding.
6. In North America, the major determinants of food intake are probably appetite-driven forces because food is so readily available. The physiological influences affecting food consumption are often suppressed or ignored.
7. A person of healthy weight shows good health and performs daily activities without weight-related problems. A body mass index (weight [in kilograms] $\div$ height^2 [in meters]) of 18.5 to 25 is one measure of healthy weight, although weight in excess of this value may not lead to ill health. This suggests that healthy weight is best determined in conjunction with a thorough health evaluation by a physician.
8. A body mass index of 25 to 29.9 represents overweight. Obesity is usually defined as total body fat percentage over 25% in men and about 35% in women, or a body mass index $\geq$ 30.
9. Fat distribution partially determines health risks from obesity. Upper-body fat-storage distribution (waist circumference $>$ 40 inches in men and $>$ 35 inches in women) suggests higher risks of hypertension, cardiovascular disease, and type 2 diabetes associated with obesity than does lower-body fat distribution.
10. Genetic factors influence the tendency toward obesity. Basal metabolism and body-fat distribution both have genetic links. How a person is raised (or nurtured) also influences the tendency toward obesity because family members often develop similar eating habits and activity patterns. Obesity can be viewed as nurture allowing nature to be expressed.
11. Those in search of a treatment for obesity should remember these five points: (1) A focus on healthy lifestyle rather than weight loss per se is more appropriate for many potential and current dieters; (2) the body resists weight loss; (3) the emphasis should be on preventing obesity because curing the disorder is very difficult; (4) weight loss should represent mostly a loss of fat storage and not primarily the loss of muscle and other lean tissues; and (5) rapid weight loss and quick regain can be especially harmful to emotional health.
12. A sound weight-loss program should meet the dieter's nutritional needs by emphasizing a wide variety of low energy, bulky foods (i.e., low energy density); adapts to the dieter's habits; consists of readily obtainable foods; strives to change poor eating habits; stresses regular physical activity; and stipulates the participation of a physician if weight is to be lost rapidly or if the person is over 40 (men) or 50 (women) years of age and plans to perform substantially greater physical activity than usual.
13. A pound of adipose tissue contains about 3500 kcal. A pound of adipose tissue lost or gained—the fat itself plus lean support tissue—represents approximately 3300 kcal. Thus, if energy output exceeds energy intake by about 500 kcal/day, a pound of adipose tissue can be lost per week.
14. Physical activity as part of a weight-loss program should be focused on duration rather than intensity. Ideally, vigorous activity for 60 minutes should be part of each day.
15. Behavior modification is a vital part of a weight-loss program because the dieter may have many habits that encourage overeating and thus discourage weight maintenance. Specific behavior-modification techniques, such as stimulus control and self-monitoring, can be used to help change problem behavior.
16. Medications to blunt appetite, such as phenteramine [Fastin] and sibutramine (Meridia), can aid weight-reduction strategies. Orlistat (Xenical) reduces fat absorption in a meal when taken with the meal. Use is reserved for those who are obese or have weight-related problems, and they must be administered under strict physician supervision.
17. The treatment of severe obesity may include surgery to reduce stomach volume to approximately 30 ml or very-low-calorie diets containing 400 to 800 kcal per day. Both these measures should

be reserved for people who have failed at more conservative approaches to weight loss. They require close medical supervision.

18. Underweight can be caused by a variety of factors, such as excessive physical activity and genetic background. Sometimes being underweight requires medical intervention. A physician should be consulted first to rule out ongoing disease. The underweight person may need to increase portion sizes and learn to like energy-dense foods. In addition, encouraging a regular meal and snack schedule aids in weight gain and maintenance.

Study Questions

1. After re-examining the internal and external forces associated with hunger, satiety, and food intake, propose two hypotheses for the development of obesity.
2. Knowing the four contributors to human energy expenditure, propose two hypotheses for the development of obesity, based on the classes of energy expenditure.
3. Define a healthy weight in a way that makes the most sense to you.
4. Describe a practical method to define obesity in a clinical setting.
5. What are the two most convincing pieces of evidence that both genetic and environmental factors play significant roles in the development of obesity?
6. What three health problems do obese people typically face? Describe a possible reason that each problem arises.
7. When searching for a sound weight-loss program, what three key characteristics would you look for?
8. Why is the claim for quick, effortless weight loss by any method always misleading?
9. Define the term *behavior modification.* Relate it to the terms *stimulus control, self-monitoring, chain-breaking, relapse prevention,* and *cognitive restructuring.* Give examples of each.
10. Why should the treatment of obesity be viewed as a lifelong commitment rather than just a short episode of weight loss?

Annotated References

1. ADA Reports: Position of the American Dietetic Association: Weight management. *Journal of the American Dietetic Association* 102:1145, 2002.

   Successful weight management to improve overall health for adults requires a lifelong commitment to healthful lifestyle behaviors, emphasizing sustainable and enjoyable eating practices and daily physical activity. Americans are increasing in body fat as they become more sedentary. Lifestyle modifications remain the hallmarks of effective treatment, but are difficult to initiate and sustain over the long term.

2. Bell EA, Rolls BJ: Regulation of energy intake: Factors contributing to obesity. In Bowman BA, Russell RM (eds.): *Present knowledge in nutrition.* Washington DC: ILSI Press, 2001.

   Factors such as the increased availability of energy dense foods, as well as the tendency to consume those foods in amounts exceeding energy needs, likely has contributed to the recent epidemic of obesity. Lowering the energy density of the diet by incorporating more fruits and vegetables, and consuming appropriate portion sizes, are two practices that can decrease energy intake.

3. Bren L: Losing weight: More than counting calories. *FDA Consumer,* p. 16, January-February 2002.

   Losing weight requires great commitment. Important lifestyle changes are eating less, regular physical activity, and behavior modification, but it is worth the effort as it can improve one's health.

4. Deitel M, Shikora SA: The development of the surgical treatment of morbid obesity. *Journal of the American College of Nutrition* 21(5):365, 2002.

   Conservative medical therapies in morbid obesity generally fail to sustain weight loss. Thus, surgical operations have evolved which are based primarily on gastric restriction. The surgery generally results in significant and lasting weight loss of about 50 percent of excess body weight, with improvements or resolution of most obesity-associated conditions.

5. Eisenstein J and others: High-protein weight-loss diets: Are they safe and do they work? A review of the experimental and epidemiologic data. *Nutrition Reviews* 60(7):189, 2002.

   Recommendations for increased consumption of protein are among the most common approaches of popular (fad) diets. Short-term studies do suggest that a high-protein diet results in a greater decrease in energy intake, and therefore greater weight and fat loss, than other diet approaches. In terms of safety, however, there is little information on the long-term negative health effects of high-protein diets, such as greater urinary calcium loss, development of kidney stones, and worsening of kidney disease, particularly in people with diabetes.

6. Flegal K and others: Prevalence and trends in obesity among adults, 1999–2000. *Journal of the American Medical Association* 288:1723, 2002.

   The prevalence of obesity has increased in recent years. Among women, obesity and overweight prevalences were highest among non-Hispanic black women: More than half of these women aged 40 years or older were obese (more than 80% were overweight). Overall, 65% of the U.S. population is now overweight, and of these people almost half are obese. The potential health benefits from a reduction in this overweight and obesity can pay great public health dividends.

7. Food and Nutrition Board: *Dietary reference intakes for energy, carbohydrate, fiber, fat, fatty acids, cholesterol, protein, and amino acids.* The National Academy Press, (Washington DC) 2002.

   This report provides the latest guidance for energy intakes. It also contains detailed descriptions of the components of energy use.

8. Friedman JM: The function of leptin in nutrition, weight, and physiology. *Nutrition Reviews* 60(10):S1, 2002.

   A key component of body systems that act to maintain relative constancy of weight is leptin. This is an adipose cell hormone that functions in a negative feedback loop regulating body weight. Weight loss among both lean and obese subjects results in decreased blood levels of leptin, which in turn lead to a state of positive energy balance through a number of physiologic responses. The opposite occurs when weight is gained. This biological effect must be considered as the causes of obesity are studied.

9. Hill JO and others: Obesity and the environment: Where do we go from here? *Science* 299:853, 2003.

   The obesity epidemic shows no signs of abating. There is an urgent need to push back against the environmental forces that are producing gradual weight gain in the population. A moderate decrease in energy intake and greater physical activity are advocated by the authors.

10. Kennedy ET and others: Popular diets: Correlation of health, nutrition, and obesity. *Journal*

of the American Dietetic Association 101:411, 2001.

For the most part, individuals successful at weight loss and later weight control restrict intake of certain types or classes of foods, eat all types of foods but in limited quantity, count calories, limit percentage of daily energy intake from fat, and participate in regular physical activity.

11. Liebman B: Defensive eating: Staying lean in a fattening world. *Nutrition Action Health Letter*, p. 1, December 2001.

    Food in North America is widely available and generally inexpensive, and the number of opportunities to eat has risen dramatically—drugstores, gas stations, and shopping malls to name a few. In response, one strategy for weight control is to fill your plate with salad greens and vegetables and use energy-dense foods as condiments. Also watch portion size—the bigger the portion, the more people eat.

12. Lyznicki JM and others: Obesity: Assessment and management in primary care. *American Family Physician* 63:2185, 2001.

    Basic treatment of overweight and obese patients requires a comprehensive approach involving diet and nutrition, regular physical activity, and behavioral change, with an emphasis on long-term weight management rather than short-term extreme weight reduction. The article discusses these interventions in detail.

13. Marcus J: Dietitians come in all sizes. *Today's Dietitian*, p. 26, October 1999.

    People who weigh more than current healthy BMI standards undergo unfair social hardships that erode self-esteem. Some health professionals are calling for size acceptance—less emphasis on body size and more emphasis on healthy eating and personal fitness.

14. Peter JC and others: Control of energy balance. In Stipanuk MH: *Physiological aspects of human nutrition*. Philadelphia, PA: W.B. Saunders, 2000.

    Set point with respect to body weight is more effective in preventing weight loss than weight gain. Throughout adult life a person may settle at a variety of "set-point" weights, rather than a single weight.

15. Poston WS, Foreyt JP: Successful management of the obese patient. *American Family Physician* 61:3615, 2000.

    Obesity is best thought of as a chronic disease requiring continuous care. Behavior modification provides an important part of the therapy.

16. Roberts SB and others: The influence of dietary composition on energy intake and body weight. *Journal of the American College of Nutrition* 21(2):140S, 2002.

    Both low fat and increased fiber interventions resulted in weight loss in men and women in this study. Combining the interventions was the most effective. Inducing more low GI load carbohydrates in place of high GI load carbohydrates also showed promise in helping people lose weight.

17. Travis JT: The hunger hormone? *Science News* 161:107, 2002.

    Ghrelin is one of the latest hormones found to regulate food intake. Using medications to block its action may someday lead to a more successful treatment for obesity.

18. Weinsier RL and others: Free-living activity energy expenditure in women successful and unsuccessful at maintaining a normal body weight. *American Journal of Clinical Nutrition* 75:499, 2002.

    Women most successful at avoiding weight gain had a higher degree of physical activity compared to women that gained weight over a year's time. The authors suggest that the general population should increase their daily physical activity to decrease the rising prevalence of obesity.

19. Yanovski SZ, Yanovski JA: Obesity. *The New England Journal of Medicine* 346:591, 2002.

    Excellent review on current management of obesity. Use of weight-loss medications is discussed; these can be helpful but do not replace attention to diet and physical activity.

20. Zhu SK: Waist circumference and obesity-associated risk factors among whites in the third National Health and Nutrition Examination Survey: clinical action thresholds. *American Journal of Clinical Nutrition* 76:743, 2002.

    Waist circumference is strongly linked to obesity-associated risks. Waist circumference is actually more closely linked to diabetes and cardiovascular disease than is body mass index.

Take | Action

I. A Close Look at Your Weight Status.

Determine the following two indices of your body status: body mass index and waist circumference.

Body Mass Index (BMI)

Record your weight in pounds: _____ lb
Divide your weight in pounds by 2.2 to determine your weight in kilograms (kg): _____ kg
Record your height in inches: _____ in
Divide your height in inches by 39.3 to determine your height in meters (m): _____ m
Calculate your BMI using the following formula:
$\text{BMI} = \text{weight (kg)}/\text{height}^2\ \text{(m)}$
$\text{BMI} =$ _____ kg/ _____ $\text{m}^2 =$ _____

Waist Circumference

Use a tape measure to measure the circumference of your waist (at the umbilicus with stomach muscles relaxed).
Circumference of waist (umbilicus) = _____ in

Interpretation

1. When BMI is greater than 25, health risks from obesity often begin. It is especially advisable to consider weight loss if your BMI exceeds 30. Does yours exceed 25 (or 30)?
   Yes _____ No _____
2. When a person has a BMI greater than 25 and a waist circumference of more than 40 inches in men or 35 inches in women, there is an increased risk of cardiovascular disease, hypertension, and type 2 diabetes. Does your circumference exceed the standard for your gender?
   Yes _____ No _____
3. Do you feel you need to pursue a program of weight loss?
   Yes _____ No _____

Application

From what you've learned in this chapter, what habits can you change in patterns of eating and physical activity to lose weight and help ensure maintenance of any loss?

II. An Action Plan to Change Weight Status.

Now that you have assessed your current weight status, do you feel that you would like to make some changes? Following is a step-by-step guide to behavioral change. This process can be useful even for those who are satisfied with their current weight, as it can be applied to changing exercise habits, self-esteem, and a variety of other behaviors (Fig. 13-16).

Becoming Aware of the Problem

By calculating your current weight status, you have already become aware of the problem, if one exists. From here, it is important to find out more information about the cause of the problem and whether it is worth working toward a change.

1. Look back at the food diary you completed in Chapter 1. What are some of the factors that most influence your eating habits? Do you eat due to stress, boredom, or depression? Is volume of food your problem, or do you eat mainly the wrong foods for you? Take some time to assess the root causes of your eating habits.

Take | Action

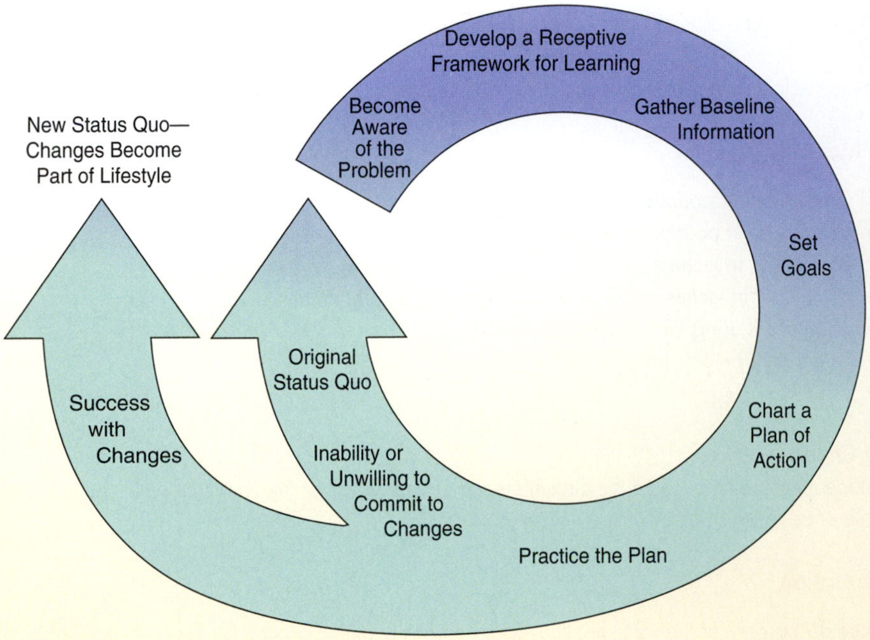

Figure 13-16 A model for behavioral change. It starts with awareness of the problem and ends with the incorporation of new behaviors intended to address the problem.

2. Once you have more information about your specific eating practices, you must decide if it is worth changing these practices. A benefits-and-costs analysis can be a useful tool in evaluating whether or not it is worth your effort to make life changes. Use the following example as a guide for listing benefits and costs pertinent to your own situation (Fig. 13-17).

Setting Goals

What can we accomplish, and how long will it take? Setting a realistic, achievable goal and allowing a reasonable amount of time to pursue it increase the likelihood of success.

1. Begin by determining the final outcome you would like to achieve. If you are trying to change your eating behaviors to be more healthy, list your reasons for doing so (e.g., overall health, weight loss, self-esteem).

   Overall goal:

   ____

   ____

   Reasons to pursue goal:

   ____

   ____

   ____

2. Now list several steps that will be necessary to achieve your goal. Keep in mind, however, that it is generally best to change only a few specific behaviors at first—walking briskly for 60 minutes five times a week, reducing fat intake, using more whole-grain products, and not eating after 7 P.M. Attempting small and perhaps easier dietary changes first reduces the scope of the problem and can increase the likelihood of success.

   Steps toward achieving goal:

   1. ____
   2. ____
   3. ____

BENEFITS AND COSTS ANALYSIS

1 Benefits of changing eating habits?
What do you expect to get, now or later, that you want? What do you get to avoid that would be unpleasant?
— *feel better physically and psychologically*
— *look better*
—
—
—
—

3 Costs involved in changing eating habits?
What do you have to do that you don't want to do? What do you have to stop doing that you would rather continue doing?
— *take time to plan meals and shop*
— *must give up some food volume*
—
—

2 Benefits of not changing eating habits?
What do you get to do that you enjoy doing? What do you avoid having to do?
— *no need for planning*
— *can eat without feeling guilty*
—
—
—
—

4 Costs of not changing eating habits?
What unpleasant or undesirable effects are you likely to experience now or in the future? What are you likely to lose?
— *creeping weight gain*
— *low self-esteem and poor health*
—
—
—

Figure 13-17 Benefits-and-costs analysis applied to increasing physical activity. This process helps put behavioral change into the context of total lifestyle.

Note that, if you are having trouble deciphering the steps needed to achieve your goal, health professionals are an excellent resource for aid in planning.

Measuring Commitment

Now that you have collected information and know what is required to reach your goal, you must ask yourself, "Can I do this?" Commitment is an essential component in the success of behavioral change. Be honest with yourself. Permanent change is not quick or easy. Once you have decided that you have the commitment required to see this through, continue on to the following sections.

Making It Official with a Contract

Drawing up a behavioral contract often adds incentive to follow through with a plan. The contract could list goal behaviors and objectives, milestones for measuring progress, and regular rewards for meeting the terms of the contract. After finishing a contract, you should sign it in the presence of some friends. This encourages commitment.

Initially, plans should reward positive behaviors, and then they should focus on positive results. Positive behaviors, such as regular physical activity, eventually lead to positive outcomes, such as increased stamina.

Fig. 13-18 is a sample contract for increasing physical activity. Keep in mind that this sample contract is only a suggestion; you can add your own ideas as well.

Psyching Yourself Up

Once your contract is in place, you need to psych yourself up. Discouragement from peers and your own temptations to stray from your plan need to be anticipated. Psyching yourself up can enable you to progress toward your goals in spite of others' attitudes and opinions. Almost everyone benefits from some assertiveness training when it comes to changing behaviors. The following are a few suggestions. Can you think of any others?

Take | Action

Figure 13-18 A behavioral contract. Completing such a contract can help generate commitment to behavioral change. What would your contract look like?

Name *Alan Young*

Goal

I agree to *ride my exercise bike*
(specify behavior)

under the following circumstances *for 30 minutes, 4 times per week*
(specify where, when, how much, etc.)
in the evening

Substitute behavior and/or reinforcement schedule *I will reinforce myself if I've achieved my goal after a month with a weekend off campus with my roommate.*

Environmental planning

In order to help me do this, I am going to (1) arrange my physical and social environment by *buying a new jogging suit at the local sporting goods store*

and (2) control my internal environment (thoughts, images) by *coordinating riding the bike with the first T.V. watching I do in the evening*

Reinforcements

Reinforcements provided by me daily or weekly (if contract is kept):
I will buy myself a new piece of clothing for off campus trip

Reinforcements provided by others daily or weekly (if contract is kept):
at the end of a month if I've completed my goal my parents will buy me a fitness club membership for winter.

Social support

Behavior change is more likely to take place when other people support you. During the quarter/semester please meet with the other person at least three times to discuss your progress.

The name of my "significant helper" is: *Mr. and Mrs. Young*

This contract should include:

1. Baseline data (one week)
2. Well-defined goal
3. Simple method for charting progress (diary, counter, charts, etc.)
4. Reinforcements (immediate and long-term)
5. Evaluation method (summary of experiences, success, and/or new learnings about self).

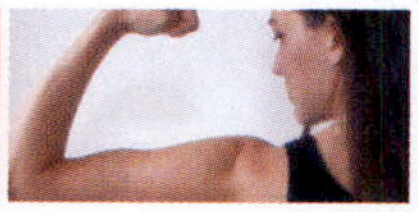

- No one's feelings should be hurt if you say, "No, thank you," firmly and repeatedly when others try to dissuade you from a plan. Rather, ask them—and yourself—why they want you to eat their way. Your needs are as important as anyone else's.
- You don't have to eat a lot to accommodate anyone—your mother, business clients, or the chef. For example, at a party with friends, you may feel you have to eat a lot to participate, but you don't. Another trap is ordering a lot just because someone else is paying for the meal.
- Learn ways to handle put-downs—inadvertent or conscious. An effective response can be to communicate feelings honestly, without hostility. Tell criticizers that they have annoyed or offended you, that you are working to change your habits and would really like understanding and support from them.

Practicing the Plan

Once you've set up a plan, the next step is to implement it. Start with a trial of at least 6 to 8 weeks. Thinking of a lifetime commitment can be overwhelming. Aim for a total duration of 6 months of new activities before giving up. We may have to persuade ourselves more than once of the value of continuing the program. The following are some suggestions to help keep a plan on track:

- *Focus on reducing, but not necessarily extinguishing, undesirable behaviors.* For example, it's usually unrealistic to say, "I'll never eat a certain food again." It's better to say, "I won't eat that *problem* food as regularly as before."
- *Monitor progress.* Note your progress in a diary and reward yourself according to your contract. While conquering some habits and seeing improvement, you may find yourself quite encouraged, even enthusiastic, about your plan of action. That can give you the impetus to move ahead with the program.
- *Control environments.* In the early phases of behavioral change, try to avoid problem situations, such as parties, coffee breaks, and favorite restaurants. Once new habits are firmly established, you can probably more successfully resist the temptations in these environments.

Re-evaluating and Preventing Relapse

After practicing a program for several weeks to months, it is important to reassess the original plan. In addition, you may now be able to pinpoint other problem areas for which you need to plan appropriately.

1. Begin by taking a close and critical look at your original plan. Does it actually lead to the goals you set? Are there any new steps toward your goal that you feel capable of adding to your contract? Do you need new reinforcements? It may even be necessary to make a new contract. For permanent change, it is worth this time of reassessment.
2. In practicing your plan over the past weeks or months, you have likely experienced relapses. What triggered these relapses? To prevent a total retreat to your old habits, it is important to set up a plan for such relapses. You can do this by identifying high-risk situations, rehearsing a response, and remembering your goals.

You may have noticed a behavior chain in some of your relapses. That is, the relapse may stem from a series of interconnected habitual activities. The way to break the chain is to first identify the activities, pinpoint the weak links, break those links, and substitute other behaviors. In Fig. 13-19 is a sample behavior chain and a substitute activities list. Consider compiling your own list based on your behavior chains.

Epilogue

If you have used the activities in this section, you are well on your way to permanent behavioral change. Recall that this exercise can be used for a variety of desired changes, including quitting smoking, increasing physical activity, and improving study habits. It is by no means an easy process, but the results can be well worth the effort. Overall, the keys to success are motivation (keeping the problem in the forefront of your mind), having a plan of action, securing the resources and skills needed for success, and looking for help from family, friends, or a group.

Take | Action

Figure 13-19 Identifying behavior chains. This is a good tool for understanding more about your habits and pinpointing ways to change unwanted habits. The earlier in the chain you substitute a nonfood link, the easier it is to intervene. Four types of behaviors can be substituted in an ongoing behavior chain.

1. Fun activities (taking a walk, reading a book)
2. Necessary activities (cleaning a room, balancing your checkbook)
3. Incompatible activities (taking a shower)
4. Urge-delaying activities (setting a kitchen timer for 20 minutes before allowing yourself to eat)

Using activities to interrupt behavior patterns that lead to inappropriate eating (or inactivity) can be a powerful means of changing eating habits.

ALTERNATIVE ACTIVITY SHEET

SUBSTITUTE ACTIVITIES

Pleasant activities
1. Singing/washing hair
2. Reading comics/biking
3. Sewing/calling a friend

Necessary activities
1. Ironing
2. Vacuuming
3. Straightening apartment

Situations when used
1. Wanted ice cream – delayed with bath
2. Wanted wheat thins – cleaned up apt.
3. Wanted snack – went for walk
4. Wanted cookies – did dishes first
5. Saw leftovers – went for bike ride
6. Tempted by cookies – set timer
7. Wanted snack – read comics

BEHAVIOR CHAIN

Identify the links in your eating response chain on the following diagram. Draw a line through the chain where it was interrupted. Add the link you substituted and the new chain of behavior this substitution started.

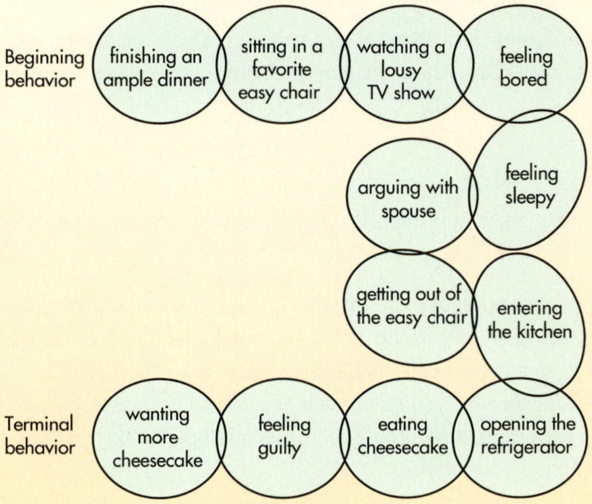

Popular Diets—Why All the Commotion?

Many overweight people try to help themselves by using the latest popular (also called fad) diet book. But, as you will see, most of these diets do not help, and some can actually harm those who follow them (Table 13-9).

Recently, weight-loss experts came together at the request of the USDA to evaluate weight-loss diets. They came to this conclusion: Forget these fads when it comes to dieting. Most of the popular diets are nutritionally inadequate and include certain foods that people would not normally choose to consume in large amounts. The experts stated that eating less of one's favorite foods and becoming more physically active can be much more effective when trying to implement a weight-loss diet.[10] People need a plan that they can live with in the long run so that weight control becomes permanent. The goal should be weight control over a lifetime, not immediate weight loss. Every popular diet leads to some immediate weight loss because daily intake is monitored—not necessarily because of certain imposed practices—and because monotonous food choices are typically part of the plan. Overall, a traditional moderate diet coupled with regular physical activity is adequate for weight loss.

You may wonder why popular diet books exist at all. Why doesn't the government put a stop to them? Many contain blatant misinformation. However, FDA concerns itself only when products are suspected of doing serious harm, as in the case of earlier forms of liquid protein diets. FDA is too busy and too underfunded to pursue every new diet plan. Ancient advice is still valid: "Let the buyer beware." Responsibility rests with the authors and publishers, who want to sell books and earn money and know there is little risk involved. Making outrageous claims sells more books than writing "eat less fat and walk more."

A practical example of the effectiveness of monotony contributing to weight loss is the experience of Jared Fogle. He primarily ate Subway sandwiches for 11 months and lost 245 pounds. He notes however that this is not a miracle diet—it takes a lot of hard work to lead to the success he experienced. There are also many other examples where diet monotony has led to weight loss.

How to Recognize a Dubious Popular Diet

The criteria for evaluating weight-loss programs with regard to their safety and effectiveness were discussed previously. In contrast, dubious popular diets typically share some different common characteristics:

1. They promote quick weight loss. As mentioned before, this loss primarily results from glycogen, sodium, and lean muscle mass depletion. All lead to a loss of body water.
2. They limit food selections and dictate specific rituals, such as eating only fruit for breakfast or cabbage soup every day.
3. They use testimonials from famous people and tie the diet to well-known cities, such as Beverly Hills and New York.
4. They bill themselves as cure-alls. These diets claim to work for everyone, whatever the type of obesity or the person's specific strengths and weaknesses.
5. They often recommend expensive supplements.
6. No attempts are made to change eating habits permanently. Dieters follow the diet until the desired weight is reached and then revert to old eating habits—they are told, for example, to eat rice for a month, lose weight, and then return to old habits.
7. They are generally critical of and skeptical about the scientific community. They suggest that physicians and registered dietitians do not really want people to lose weight. They encourage people to look outside the medical establishment for correct advice.

Probably the cruelest characteristic of these diets is that they essentially guarantee failure for the dieter. The diets are not designed for permanent weight loss. Habits are not changed, and the food selection is so limited that the person cannot follow the diet in the long run. Although dieters assume they have lost fat, they have actually lost mostly muscle and other lean tissue mass. As soon as they begin eating normally again, the lost tissue is replaced. In a matter of weeks, most of the lost weight is back. The dieter appears to have failed, when actually the diet has failed. This whole scenario can add more blame and guilt, challenging the self-worth of the dieter. If someone needs help losing weight, professional help is advised. It is unfortunate that current trends suggest people are spending more time and money on "quick fixes" rather than on such professional help.

Table 13-9 Summary of Popular Diet Approaches to Weight Control

Approach and Examples*		Characteristics and Possible Negative Health and Other Consequences
Moderate Calorie Restriction		
The Set-Point Diet Slim Chance in a Fat World Weight Watcher's Diet Mary Ellen's Help Yourself Diet Plan The Beyond Diet Staying Thin The Callaway Diet	Living Without Dieting Volumetrics Lose the Last 10 Pounds Dieting with the Dutchess Dieting for Dummies The Wedding Dress Diet Dr. Shapiro's Picture Perfect Diet	Usually 1000–1800 kcal per day, with moderate fat intake Reasonable balance of macronutrients Encourage exercise May use behavioral approach Acceptable if a multivitamin and mineral supplement is used and permission of family physician is granted
Macronutrient Restriction **Low or Restricted Carbohydrate**		
Dr. Atkins' Diet Revolution Calories Don't Count Miracle Diet for Fast Weight Loss Woman Doctor's Diet for Women The Doctor's Quick Weight Loss Diet The Complete Scarsdale Medical Diet Four Day Wonder Diet	Endocrine Control Diet Enter the Zone Protein Power The Five-Day Miracle Diet Healthy for Life Carbohydrate Addicts Diet Sugar Busters	Generally less than 100 g of carbohydrate per day Ketosis; reduced exercise capacity due to poor glycogen stores in the muscles; excessive animal fat intake
Low Fat		
The Rice Diet Report The Macrobiotic Diet (some versions) The Pritikin Diet Eat More, Weigh Less The 35+ Diet 20/30 Fat and Fiber Fat to Muscle Diet T-Factor Diet Fit or Fat Two Day Diet Complete Hip and Thigh Diet	The Maximum Metabolism Diet The Pasta Diet The McDougall Plan Ultrafit Diet Stop the Insanity G-Index Diet Outsmarting the Female Fat Cell Foods That Cause You to Lose Weight Lean Bodies Turn Off the Fat Genes	Less than 20% of energy from fat Limited (or elimination of) animal protein sources; also limited fats, nuts, seeds Little satiety; flatulence; possibly poor mineral absorption from excess dietary fiber; limited food choices sometimes leads to deprivation Not necessarily to be avoided, but certain aspects of many of the plans possibly unacceptable
Novelty Diets		
Dr. Abravenel's Body Type and Lifetime Nutrition Plan (or his other books) Dr. Berger's Immune Power Diet Fit for Life The Hilton Head Metabolism Diet The Beverly Hills Diet Dr. Debetz Champagne Diet Sun Sign Diet F-Plan Diet Fat Attack Plan Autohypnosis Diet The Ultrafit Diet The Princeton Diet The Diet Bible Eat to Succeed	The Underburner's Diet Eat to Win Two Day Diet Paris Diet Cabbage-Soup Diet Eat Great, Lose Weight Eat Smart Think Smart *Scent*sational Weight Loss Eat Right 4 Your Type The Greenwich Diet 3 Season Diet Metabolize God's Diet The Weigh Down Diet	Promotes certain nutrients, foods, or combinations of foods as having unique, magical, or previously undiscovered qualities Malnutrition; no change in habits leads to relapse; unrealistic food choices lead to possible bingeing
Very-Low-Calorie Diets (VLCDs)		
Optifast Cambridge Diet HMR	Ultrafast Thin So Fast	Less than 800 kcal per day Also known as protein-sparing modified fasts Must be under close physician scrutiny Organ tissue loss—especially from the heart; low blood potassium leads to heart failure; expense; kidney stones; gout; limited exercise tolerance
Formula Diets		
Optifast Genesis	Cambridge Diet Slimfast	Can help people who find it easier not to eat whole foods while dieting to lose weight Based on formulated or packaged products Tend to be very-low-calorie regimens; no change in habits, possibly leading to increased chance of relapse; expense; constipation

Table 13-9 Continued

Approach and Examples*	Characteristics and Possible Negative Health and Other Consequences
Premeasured Diets	
Jenny Craig Nutri/System	Most food supplied in premeasured servings to take much of the decision making out of the process of eating
	Expensive; may not allow for easy, sound eating later

*Diets may be listed in more than one category if multiple characteristics apply.

Types of Popular Diets

Low- or Restricted-Carbohydrate Approaches

This is the most common form of diet. The low-carbohydrate intake leads to less glycogen synthesis, and so less water in the body (about 3g of water are stored per gram of glycogen). As discussed in Chapter 4, a very-low-carbohydrate intake also forces the liver to produce needed glucose. The source of carbons for this glucose is mostly tissue proteins. Thus, a low-carbohydrate diet results in protein tissue loss (which is about 72% water), as well as urinary loss of essential ions, such as potassium. Since protein tissue is mostly water, the dieter loses weight very rapidly. When a normal diet is resumed, the protein tissue is rebuilt and the weight is regained.

Low-carbohydrate diets primarily work in the short run because they limit total food intake.[1] Consider a visit to a fast-food restaurant. You plan to order a hamburger, french fries, and a soft drink and pay a bit more for the *super-size* option. This will yield about 1500 kcal. If you were on a low-carbohydrate diet plan, you can't have the french fries or the soft drink, as they contain too much carbohydrate. You can have the hamburger, but you will have to discard the bun. This leaves a lunch containing about 240 kcal of mostly fat and protein. You will also soon tire of the limited food choices, and this will cause you to eat less.

In the short run, this low-carbohydrate gimmick can lead to weight loss. But this plan does not include the fruits, vegetables, and whole grains that nutrition experts point out are important components of a healthy diet.[3] Because of this the American Heart Association recently warned against following such a diet. Overall, the low-carbohydrate diet is not intended for long-term use.

Diet plans that use a low-carbohydrate approach are the Dr. Atkins' Diet Revolution, Dr. Stillman's Calories Don't Count Diet, the Scarsdale Diet, and the Four Day Wonder Diet. More moderate approaches are found in the various Zone diets (40% of energy intake as carbohydrate) and Sugar Busters diet. When you see a new diet advertisement, look first to see how much carbohydrate it contains. If breads, cereals, fruits, and vegetables are extremely limited, you are probably looking at a low- or restricted-carbohydrate diet.

In time, the very-low-carbohydrate, high-protein diets typically leave a person wanting more variety in meals, and so the diets are abandoned.

Low-Fat Approaches

The very-low-fat diet turns out to be a very-high-carbohydrate diet. These diets contain approximately 5% to 10% of energy intake as fat. The most notable is the Pritikin Diet and the Dr. Dean Ornish diet plans. This approach is not harmful for healthy adults, but it is extremely difficult to follow. People get bored with this type of diet very quickly because they can't eat many of their favorite foods. These dieters eat primarily grains, fruits, and vegetables, which most people cannot do for very long. Eventually, the person wants some foods higher in fat or protein. Thus, the dieter suffers a lapse, then a relapse, and probably a collapse. These diets are just too different from the typical North American diet for many adults to follow consistently, but may be acceptable for some people.

Novelty Diets

A variety of diets are built on gimmicks. Some novelty diets emphasize one food or food group and exclude almost all others. A rice diet was designed in the 1940s to lower blood pressure; now it has resurfaced as a weight-loss diet. The first phase consists of eating only rice and fruit until you can't stand them any longer. Another novelty diet is the egg diet, on which you eat all the eggs you want. On the Beverly Hills Diet, you eat mostly fruit.

The rationale behind these diets is that you can eat only eggs, fruit, or rice for just so long before becoming bored and, in theory, reducing your energy intake. However, chances are that you will abandon the diet entirely before losing much weight.

Since the 1960s, grapefruit has been touted for supposed unique ability to cause weight loss. No studies back up this claim. To add appeal to a grapefruit diet, proponents even suggest adding several "diet aids:" lecithin to help release fat from the tissues, vitamin B-6 to act as a diuretic, vinegar to provide potassium, and kelp to stimulate the thyroid gland.

The most bizarre of the novelty diets proposes that "food gets stuck in your body." Fit for Life, the Beverly Hills Diet, and Eat Great, Lose Weight are examples. The supposition is that food gets stuck in the intestine, putrefies, and creates toxins, which invade the blood and cause disease. This is utter nonsense. Nevertheless, the same idea has been promoted in health-food books since the 1800s. Today, Fit for Life suggests that meat eaten with potatoes is not digested and that fresh fruit should be consumed only before noon. These recommendations are absurd. They are gimmicks that appear controversial but are really designed to sell books.

Finally, some commercial schemes are used to sell diet books. Books describing the allergy approach to dieting, for instance, suggest that diseases, including obesity, are due to food allergies. Supposedly, once your food allergies are found and treated, you will no longer have the disease. However, no research supports the claim. In addition, see the Sun Sign Diet if you believe in astrology, the Champagne Diet if you need a drink, the Cabbage Soup Diet if you want to eat it every day, or the Body Type and Lifetime Nutrition Diet if you have a "dominant" gland.

Quackery Is Characteristic of Many Popular Diets

Many popular diets fall under the category of quackery—people taking advantage of others. They usually involve a product or service that costs a considerable amount of money. Often, those offering the product or service don't realize that they are promoting quackery, because they were victims themselves. For example, they tried the product and by pure coincidence it worked for them, so they wish to sell it to all their friends and relatives.

FDA recently announced that a weight-loss product sold over the Internet has been linked to six cases of liver failure. The product is called Lipokinetix and contains a form of thyroid hormone and other unsafe substances. This is another reason to avoid any weight-loss medicine or supplement that is not prescribed by a physician.

Recent examples of dubious recommendations in the field of weight loss are herbal laxative teas and chromium picolinate. These laxative teas, many of which have oriental-type labels, contain senna, which induces diarrhea. However, this diarrhea does not sufficiently reduce the absorption of calories from the diet. FDA is concerned that these teas may also result in serious injury or death linked to the diarrhea and related intestinal damage that is inducted. To date, these teas are linked to deaths of four young women.

Chromium picolinate, a nutritional supplement, has been touted as an aid for reducing body fat, increasing lean body mass, suppressing hunger, and increasing metabolic rate. However, chromium picolinate has not been approved for weight loss by FDA, nor has the agency seen any convincing data on the claims being made (see Chapter 12).

Numerous other gimmicks for weight loss have come and gone and are likely to resurface. If in the future an important aid for weight loss is discovered, you can feel confident that major journals, such as the *Journal of the American Dietetic Association,* the *Journal of the American Medical Association,* or *The New England Journal of Medicine,* will report it. You don't need to rely on paperback books or newspaper advertisements for information about weight loss.

Usually, quackery reduces only the bank account. Currently, $6 billion dollars per year are spent on such false hope in the United States alone. However, it can lead to life-threatening results. The rule of thumb on seeing a new diet aid on the market is that, if it sounds too good to be true, it is.

Case Scenario | Follow-up

As you have probably surmised, Chris will just be wasting his money if he buys the product seen in the infomercial. Unfortunately, regulation of the supplement industry currently is woefully lacking. In the future, if there is a meaningful breakthrough in weight loss and weight control, authorities such as the Surgeon General's Office or the National Institutes of Health will make North Americans aware of that fact. At this time, Chris would be better off simply paying more attention to what he is eating and trying to find time for daily physical activity.

chapter 14

Nutrition for Fitness and Sports

Chapter | Outline

Case | Scenario

Marcella has become hooked on fitness in the past year and is training for a 10K run coming up in 3 weeks. She has read a lot about sports nutrition, and especially about the importance of eating a high-carbohydrate diet while in training. She also has been struggling to keep her weight in a range that she feels contributes to better speed and endurance. Consequently, she is also trying to eat as little fat as possible. Unfortunately, over the past week her workouts in the afternoon have not met her expectations. Her run times are slower, and she shows signs of fatigue after just 20 minutes into her training program.

Her breakfast yesterday was a large bagel, a small amount of cream cheese, and orange juice. For lunch, she had a small salad with fat-free dressing, a large plate of pasta with tomato marinara sauce and broccoli, and a diet soft drink. For dinner, she had a small broiled chicken breast, a cup of rice, some carrots, and iced tea. Later, she snacked on fat-free pretzels.

What advice would you provide Marcella regarding her training diet? Note current strengths and weaknesses. Is her diet likely contributing to her recent fatigue during workouts?

Refresh | Your Memory

As you begin your study of nutrition for fitness and sports in Chapter 14, you may want to review:

- Metabolic pathways and the role of ATP in Chapter 4.
- The concept of glycemic load in Chapter 5.
- The various components of the macronutrient classes—carbohydrates, proteins, and lipids—in Chapters 5–7.
- The food sources of calcium in Chapter 11 and iron in Chapter 12.
- The components of the cell and functions of various organelles in Appendix C.

Boost | Your Study

Check out the ***Perspectives in Nutrition: Online Learning Center*** www.mhhe.com/wardlawpers6 *for quizzes, flash cards, activities, and web links designed to further help you learn about nutrition for fitness and sports.*

Chapter | Objectives

Chapter 14 is designed to allow you to:

1. List five positive health-related outcomes of a physically active lifestyle.
2. Design a fitness regimen that begins with no physical activity, moves to a first goal of at least 30 minutes of such activity on most (or all) days of the week, and then advances to more vigorous activity totaling 60 minutes per day.
3. Describe when and how glycogen, blood glucose, fat, and protein are used to meet energy needs during different types of physical activity.
4. Differentiate between anaerobic and aerobic use of glucose and identify advantages and disadvantages of each.
5. Show how muscles and related organs adapt to an increase in physical activity and describe how that physical activity is quantified (e.g., $VO_{2\,max}$).
6. Outline how to estimate an athlete's energy needs and discuss the general principles for meeting overall nutrient requirements in the training diet, focusing specifically on carbohydrate intake.
7. Examine the problems associated with rapid weight loss by dehydration and outline the importance of the use of water and/or sports drinks during exercise.
8. Show an understanding of the importance of maintaining a healthy status of various vitamins and minerals during training.
9. List several ergogenic aids and describe their effects on an athlete's performance.

Athletes invest a lot of time and effort in training. Because they often seek ways to enhance their diets to improve performance, athletes make easy targets for purveyors of nutrition misinformation. Still, most athletes don't want to miss out on any advantage, whether real or perceived, that might give them the winning edge.

Although good eating habits can't substitute for physical training and genetic endowment, proper diet choices are crucial for top-notch performance, contributing to endurance and helping speed the repair of injured tissues.[17]

In this chapter, you will also discover how physical fitness benefits the entire body; it is an essential ingredient in achieving maximal health. Experts might disagree on how much carbohydrate, protein, and fat we should consume, but there is no argument over the health benefits of regular physical activity.[19] It is even beneficial for overweight people who remain at that excess weight.[20]

Some people also are active simply because they enjoy it, whether they're swimming, playing basketball, walking briskly, or engaging in any of innumerable other activities. Let's now look further at nutrition as it relates to fitness and sports.

The Close Relationship Between Nutrition and Fitness

The ability to engage routinely in vigorous physical activity requires good health. The ability to perform also depends on a nutritious diet that supplies all the needed nutrients. Adequate carbohydrate intakes are especially important for endurance.[6]

Once muscles have nutrients available to them, what determines the type of fuel muscles will use? Athletes do to an extent, depending on how physically fit they are and how hard they perform. This physical fitness—defined as the ability to do moderate to vigorous activity without undue fatigue—especially affects fat use by the body. The greater one's fitness, the more fat used to supply energy needed for activity, and even more so if the activity lasts for 30 minutes or more.[20]

Beyond affecting fuel use, the benefits of regular physical activity include improvement in several aspects of heart function, less injury, better sleep habits, and improvement in body composition (less body fat, more muscle mass). Physical activity also can reduce stress and positively affect blood pressure, blood cholesterol, blood glucose regulation, and overall immune function. In addition, it aids in weight control, both by transiently raising resting energy expenditure and by increasing overall energy expenditure.[9, 10, 20] See Table 14-1 for a further look at the benefits of a physically active lifestyle.

Unfortunately, as noted in Chapter 13, many North American adults lead sedentary lives. Only about 15% of adults practice moderate to vigorous physical activity on a regular basis, and about half of all adults quit their exercise program within 3 months of onset. Does this discussion motivate you to assess your activity patterns and improve them as needed? Dr. Sheri A. Melton discusses how to plan your exercise program in the Expert Opinion.

Healthy People 2010 has set a number of specific objectives for adults related to physical activity:

- Reduce by 50% the proportion of adults engaging in no leisure-time physical activity (currently 40% of U.S. adults)
- Double the proportion of adults engaging regularly, preferably daily, in moderate physical activity for at least 30 minutes per day (currently 15% of U.S. adults)
- Increase by 30% the proportion of adults engaging in vigorous physical activity that promotes the development and maintenance of cardiorespiratory fitness 3 or more days per week for 20 or more minutes per occasion (currently 23% of U.S. adults)
- Increase by 50% the proportion of adults who perform physical activities that enhance and maintain muscular strength and endurance (currently 19% of U.S. adults)

Experts recommend that, to help yourself stay with an exercise program, you

- Start slowly
- Vary your activities; make it fun
- Include friends and others
- Set specific attainable goals and monitor progress
- Set aside a specific time each day for exercise; build it into your routine, but make it convenient
- Reward yourself for being successful in keeping up with your goals
- Don't worry about occasional setbacks; focus on the long-term benefits to your health

Concept | Check

Regular physical activity is a vital part of a healthy lifestyle, ideally constituting a total of at least 30 minutes on most (if not all) days of the week (60 minutes is even better), while also including some resistance activities. Physically active people show lower risks of cardiovascular disease such as coronary heart disease and stroke, hypertension, type 2 diabetes, obesity, and other common chronic diseases.

Applying Diet Principles to Physical Activity

Variety: Enjoy many different activities to exercise different muscles.

Balance: Different activities have different benefits, so balance your exercise pattern. For overall fitness, you need exercises that build cardiovascular endurance, muscular strength, and flexibility.

Moderation: Exercise to keep fit without overdoing it. You don't need a heavy workout to achieve fitness.

The Food and Nutrition Board recommends a total of 60 minutes of moderate physical activity per day.

One day in December, Joe Decker:
bicycled 100 miles,
ran 10 miles, hiked 10 miles,
power-walked 5 miles,
kayaked 6 miles,
skied on a NordicTrack 10 miles,
rowed 10 miles, swam 2 miles,
did 3000 abdominal crunches,
did 1100 jumping jacks,
did 1000 leg lifts, did 1100 push-ups.
And he lifted weights cumulatively totaling 278,540 pounds.
For his efforts (and pains), he earned a place in the *Guinness Book of Records:* the fittest man alive.

What is the best exercise? One you enjoy.

Table 14-1 Exercise Is Medicine—the Benefits of Regular, Moderate Physical Activity† [8, 10, 15, 20]

Cardiovascular health	Increases heart strength and overall cardiovascular function (including blood vessels), which decreases the chance of developing cardiovascular disease, such as coronary heart disease and strokes Reduces inflammation in the body (an emerging risk factor for cardiovascular disease), as shown by a decline in C-reactive protein Helps maintain healthy blood pressure Can increase HDL-cholesterol and lower LDL-cholesterol and triglycerides in the blood Aids in smoking-cessation programs
Obesity	Helps maintain lean tissue and promote loss of fat tissue (such as abdominal fat stores) Assists in better control of appetite and increases energy expenditure Helps prevent or reverse development of diseases associated with obesity, including type 2 diabetes, hypertension, and cardiovascular disease, even if one doesn't attain a more healthy weight
Muscular health	Contributes to building and maintaining muscle mass and muscle tone
Diabetes	Increases glucose uptake by muscle tissue cells independent of insulin action Contributes to energy balance, which decreases risk of type 2 diabetes and related complications
Osteoporosis	Helps strengthen bones and contributes to joint health
Infections	Reduces susceptibility to respiratory and other infections by enhancing various functions of the immune system
Cancer	Reduces risk of colon cancer and likely breast cancer
Gastrointestinal health	Improves peristaltic function in the small intestine and colonic mass movements Lessens risk for gallstones and related gallbladder disease
Fewer injuries (e.g., from falls)	Contributes to balance and agility, especially in older adulthood
Psychological health	Reduces depression, anxiety, and mental stress while enhancing a sense of well-being and self-image and improving sleep patterns. May also help treat chronic fatigue syndrome.

†For people who have been sedentary, most of these benefits can be seen with minimal physical exertion, such as with brisk walking (about 4 miles/hr) or household activities like vacuuming.

Energy Sources for Muscle Use

As you learned in Chapter 4, cells can't directly use the energy released from breaking down glucose or triglycerides. Rather, to utilize the chemical energy in foods, body cells must first convert the energy to a specific form, called adenosine triphosphate (ATP).

Adenosine Triphosphate (ATP)—Immediately Usable Energy

The partial breakdown of ATP by cells to yield ADP and Pi (the abbreviation for inorganic phosphate) releases usable energy for cell functions, including the muscle contractions required for locomotion. A resting muscle cell, however, contains just a small amount of ATP, enough to keep the muscle working maximally for about 2 to 4

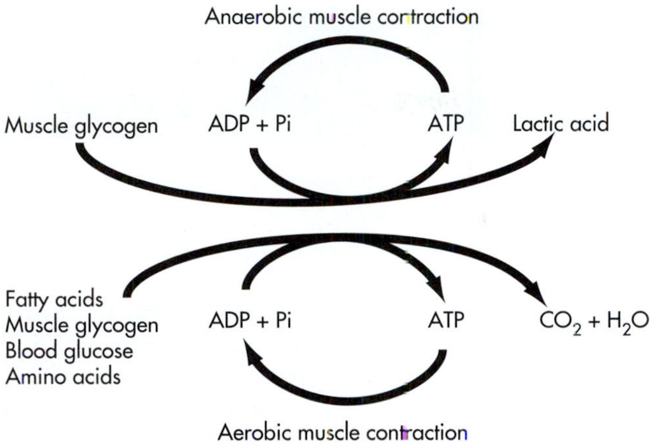

Figure 14-1 Energy sources for muscular activity. Different fuels are used for ATP synthesis. ATP can also be synthesized rapidly using phosphocreatine.

Table 14-2 Energy Sources Used by Resting and Working Muscle Cells

Source/System*	When in Use	Examples of an Exercise
ATP	At all times	All types
Phosphocreatine (PCr)	All exercise initially; short bursts of exercise thereafter	Shotput, jumping
Carbohydrate (anaerobic)	High-intensity exercise, especially lasting 30 seconds to 2 minutes	200-yard (20-meter) sprint
Carbohydrate (aerobic)	Exercise lasting 2 minutes to 3 hours or more; the higher the intensity (for example, running a 6-minute mile), the greater the use	Basketball, swimming, jogging
Fat (aerobic)	Exercise lasting more than a few minutes; greater amounts are used at lower exercise intensities	Long-distance running, long-distance cycling; much of the fuel used in a brisk walk is fat
Protein (aerobic)	Low quantity during all exercise; moderate quantity in endurance exercise, especially when carbohydrate fuel is lacking	Long-distance running

*At any given time, more than one system is operating.

Resistance activities complement more aerobic activities and regular stretching exercises, rounding out a total fitness plan.[20]

seconds. To produce more ATP for muscle contraction over extended periods, the body uses **phosphocreatine (PCr),** a high-energy compound that is formed and stored in the muscle cells from the amino acid derivative creatine (the amino acids glycine, arginine, and methionine participate in its synthesis). Dietary carbohydrates, fats, and proteins are also used as energy sources (Fig. 14-1). The breakdown of all of these compounds releases enough energy to make more ATP (Table 14-2).[18]

phosphocreatine (PCr) A high-energy compound that can be used to re-form ATP from ADP.

Phosphocreatine: The Initial Resupply of Muscle ATP

During periods of relaxation, muscles synthesize PCr from ATP and creatine and then store this in small amounts. As soon as ADP from the breakdown of ATP begins to accumulate in a contracting muscle, an enzyme is activated that transfers a high-energy Pi from PCr to ADP, thus reforming ATP (Fig. 14-2):

$$PCr + ADP \rightarrow ATP + Cr$$

If no other system for resupplying ATP were available, PCr could probably maintain maximal muscle contractions for about 10 seconds. However, since the energy released from the metabolism of glucose and fatty acids also begins to contribute ATP and thus

Strength-training athletes have begun to use creatine supplements (see the Nutrition Perspective at the end of this chapter for details).

Expert Opinion

Your Exercise Prescription

Sheri A. Melton, Ph.D.

The benefits of regular exercise, sometimes called "training effects," are well established. Most people can reap significant health benefits by participating in just a moderate amount of physical activity, even as little as 30 minutes on most (and preferably all) days in a week.

When developing a total exercise program, all components of fitness should be taken into consideration: cardiorespiratory (CR) endurance, muscular strength, muscular endurance, flexibility, and body composition (% body fat). However, the exercise prescription is usually developed specifically for the CR endurance component. CR endurance is defined as the ability of the heart, lungs, and circulatory system to supply oxygen to the working muscles during sustained physical activity. That is why this fitness component is also called aerobic capacity. Your exercise prescription should be tailor-made for you—depending on your current level of fitness, your activity preferences, and the goals you want to achieve.

A structured, formal exercise prescription has five distinct components: mode, frequency, intensity, duration, and progression. In order to gain a training effect and its accompanying cardiovascular benefits, the American College of Sports Medicine (ACSM) advises that each of these components meet certain criteria and thresholds.[4]

Mode

The mode of exercise is the type of exercise prescribed. It must be one that uses large muscle groups in a rhythmic fashion, such as running, walking, and cycling.

Duration

Duration is the amount of time spent in an exercise session. It should last 20 to 30 minutes, not counting time for warm-up and cooldown. Ideally, this should be continuous (without stopping) exercise, but an individual may have to participate in intermittent exercise at the start (sessions lasting 10 minutes several times a day), eventually working up to one continuous session.

Frequency

Frequency of exercise should be at least three times per week. Daily exercise reaps even more benefits.

Intensity

Intensity is the level of exertion that indicates the magnitude of energy expenditure required to sustain the activity. Health benefits are achieved with a moderate intensity of exercise. There are several methods of prescribing moderate-intensity exercise. One of the most popular, and simplest, methods is using a percentage of your age-predicted maximum heart rate. Subtract age from 220 (this is your age-predicted maximum heart rate); then multiply by 70% and 85%. The heart rate range that results is sometimes called the target zone. Beginner exercisers should stay close to the lower end of the range, so that a sufficient duration can be achieved.

Taking your pulse during the exercise session (count for 10 seconds and then multiply the result by 6) is recommended to ensure that you are in your target zone. Pulse meters are very popular, and they allow the exerciser immediate feedback without stopping to take the pulse. Another popular method for determining intensity is the Rating of Perceived Exertion scale (RPE). The original RPE scale is numbered 6 to 20; the revised rating scale is 0 to 10. Each number corresponds to a subjective feeling of exertion. For instance, in the revised scale, the number 0 is "nothing at all" (e.g., sitting at the table), and 10 is considered close to maximal effort, or very, very strong (e.g., sprinting at all out effort):

0	Nothing at all
0.5	Very, very weak
1	Very weak
2	Weak
3	Moderate
4	Somewhat strong
5	
6	Strong
7	
8	Very strong
9	
10	Very, very strong
*	Maximal

The goal is to aim for a range of 3 to 6 "moderate" through "somewhat strong." A good rule of thumb for knowing you are not exercising at a higher than moderate intensity is to try the talk test. The exerciser should be able to talk without getting breathless.

spares some PCr use, this results in PCr functioning as the major source of energy for all events lasting up to about 1 minute (review Table 14-2).[18]

The main advantage of PCr is that it can be activated instantly and can replenish ATP at rates fast enough to meet the energy demands of the fastest and most powerful sports events, including jumping, lifting, throwing, and sprinting actions. The disadvantage of PCr is that not enough is made and stored in the muscles to sustain a high rate of ATP resupply for more than a few minutes.

More exact methods for determining intensity may be used also, especially in the clinical setting. A maximum graded exercise test can be used to measure the true maximal physiological responses of heart rate, blood pressure, and oxygen consumption. The level attained is called functional capacity, and intensity is prescribed as a percentage of measured functional capacity.

Progression

The last component, progression, is how frequency, intensity, and duration of exercise are increased over a period of time. The first 3 to 6 weeks of your new exercise program is the initiation stage, which is the time it takes your body to adapt to the new behavior and routine. Generally, once the required duration is achieved, intensity is increased, so that work remains in the target zone. The next 5 or 6 months of training is the improvement stage, in which the intensity and possibly the duration of exercise are increased to a point of tapering off (and no appreciable gains are made in fitness). In this stage, intensity may be increased to the higher end of the target zone, depending on your goals. This plateau marks the beginning of your maintenance stage. Goals may be re-evaluated, but no changes need to be made to your exercise prescription in order to keep the gains that have already been accomplished.

A Word of Caution

Even though moderate exercise is considered safe for most individuals, it is recommended that all adults be screened prior to beginning an exercise program. Screening involves identifying risk factors that would compromise the safety of participation in exercise. It also identifies those who need to be medically evaluated prior to exercise. The ACSM uses the following risk factors in determining a person's risk: family history of heart disease, cigarette smoking, hypertension, high blood cholesterol, impaired fasting glucose (diabetes), obesity, and sedentary lifestyle. Younger individuals (males under 45 years old and females under 55 years) who are asymptomatic and have no more than one of these risk factors are considered at low risk. They may embark on a moderate or vigorous exercise program without a medical evaluation or an exercise test. Those at moderate risk are older individuals (males older than 44 and females older than 54) and anyone having at least two risk factors. (The current Dietary Guidelines for Americans use age 40 and 50 years, respectively, as cutoff points for the need for men and women to first seek a medical screening.) They may embark on a moderate exercise program without a medical evaluation or an exercise test prior to beginning a moderate exercise program, but both are recommended if embarking on a vigorous one.

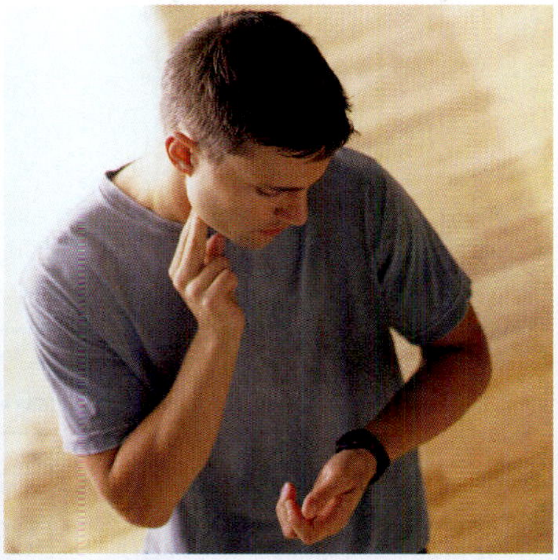

Checking one's pulse is one way to monitor exercise intensity.

A Final Note

Always start your exercise session with 5 to 10 minutes of a general warm-up, and a more specific warm-up for higher intensities. Be sure to round out your exercise program with daily stretching and some form of resistance (weight) training 2 to 3 days a week. Include a circuit of 8 to 10 exercises to condition major muscle groups of the upper body and lower body. Use an amount of weight that you can perform one (or more) set(s) of at least 8, but no more than 12, repetitions in proper form. If more than 12 repetitions are possible, increase the amount of weight (up to 15 is appropriate for older adults). Finally, an appropriate cooldown is necessary (about 5 to 10 minutes). Following these basic guidelines for an individualized exercise prescription will help you safely optimize your efforts in achieving your health, fitness, and wellness goals and improve your overall quality of life.

Dr. Melton is an assistant professor in the Kinesiology Department, School of Health Sciences, at West Chester University in West Chester, Pennsylvania. She is certified as an exercise specialist by the American College of Sports Medicine. Her experience encompasses cardiac and orthopedic rehabilitation and personal training.

Glucose: Major Fuel for Short-Term, High-Intensity and Medium-Term Exercise

Recall from Chapter 4 that glucose breaks down during glycolysis, producing the three-carbon compound pyruvic acid. Glycolysis does not require oxygen and yields a small amount of ATP. If oxygen is present, the pyruvic acid is metabolized further, yielding additional ATP.

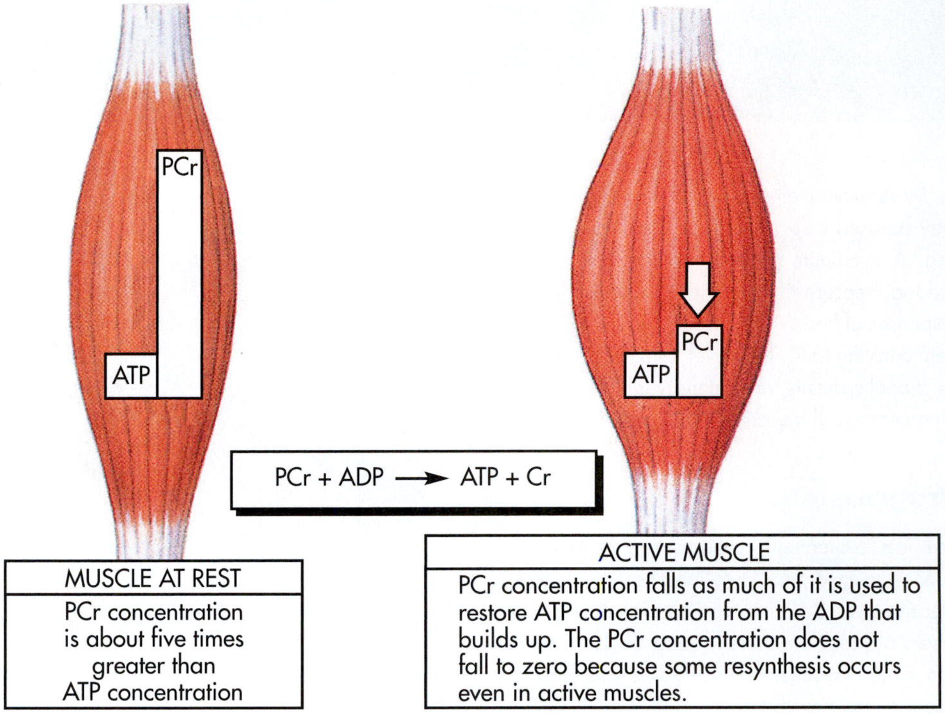
PCr
ATP
PCr
ATP
PCr + ADP → ATP + Cr
MUSCLE AT REST
PCr concentration is about five times greater than ATP concentration
ACTIVE MUSCLE
PCr concentration falls as much of it is used to restore ATP concentration from the ADP that builds up. The PCr concentration does not fall to zero because some resynthesis occurs even in active muscles.

Figure 14-2 Quick energy for muscle use includes a supply of phosphocreatine (PCr). This can rapidly replenish ATP stores as activity begins. Phosphocreatine can be almost depleted in maximally contracting human forearm muscles in less than 60 seconds. It takes 4 minutes of rest to replenish half the PCr and 7 minutes to replenish 95% of the PCr. Similarly, it takes about 7 minutes of rest to replenish 95% of the PCr depleted with repeated knee extensions against resistance.
Illustration by William Ober.

Anaerobic Pathway

Recall from Chapter 4 that, when acids lose a hydrogen ion, as typically happens at the pH of the body, they are given the ending *-ate*. Thus, pyruvic acid is called *pyruvate* and lactic acid is called *lactate* when in the context of body metabolism.

When the oxygen supply in muscle is limited (anaerobic state) or when the physical activity is intense (e.g., running 400 meters or swimming 100 meters), pyruvic acid resulting from glycolysis accumulates in the muscle and is converted to lactic acid (lactate). Since the breakdown of 1 glucose to 2 pyruvic acids yields 2 ATP, glycolysis can resupply some ATP depleted in muscle activity. Carbohydrate is the only fuel that can be used for this process. The advantage of the anaerobic pathway is that, other than PCr breakdown, it is the fastest way to resupply ATP in muscle.[18]

Glycolysis provides most of the energy for physical activity from about 30 seconds to 2 minutes after it has started. As you'll see shortly, fat utilization simply can't occur fast enough to meet the ATP demands of short-duration, high-intensity physical activity. If fat were the only available fuel, we would be unable to carry out physical activity more intense than a fast walk or jog.

The anaerobic pathway has three major disadvantages: (1) it can't sustain ATP production for long; (2) only about 5% of the energy available from glucose is released during glycolysis; and (3) the rapid accumulation of lactic acid from anaerobic glycolysis greatly increases the acidity of muscle cells. Because high acidity inhibits the activity of key enzymes in glycolysis, anaerobic ATP production soon slows and fatigue sets in. We learn by trial-and-error an exercise pace that controls muscle lactic acid concentrations from anaerobic glycolysis.

If the anaerobic glycolysis pathway uses glycogen as the starting material, 3 ATP are produced. This is because the first ATP-requiring step in glycolysis when starting with glucose is bypassed.

ATP → ADP + Pi
(glucose → glucose-6-phosphate).

Most of the lactic acid that accumulates in active muscle cells is eventually released into the bloodstream. The liver (and to some extent the kidneys) takes up some of the lactic acid from the blood and resynthesizes it into glucose, an energy-requiring process. This glucose then can re-enter the bloodstream, where it is available for cell uptake and breakdown. The heart can also use lactic acid directly for its energy needs, as can less active muscle cells situated near active ones.

Aerobic Pathway

If there is plenty of oxygen available in muscle (aerobic state) and the physical activity is of moderate to low intensity (e.g., jogging or distance swimming), the bulk of the

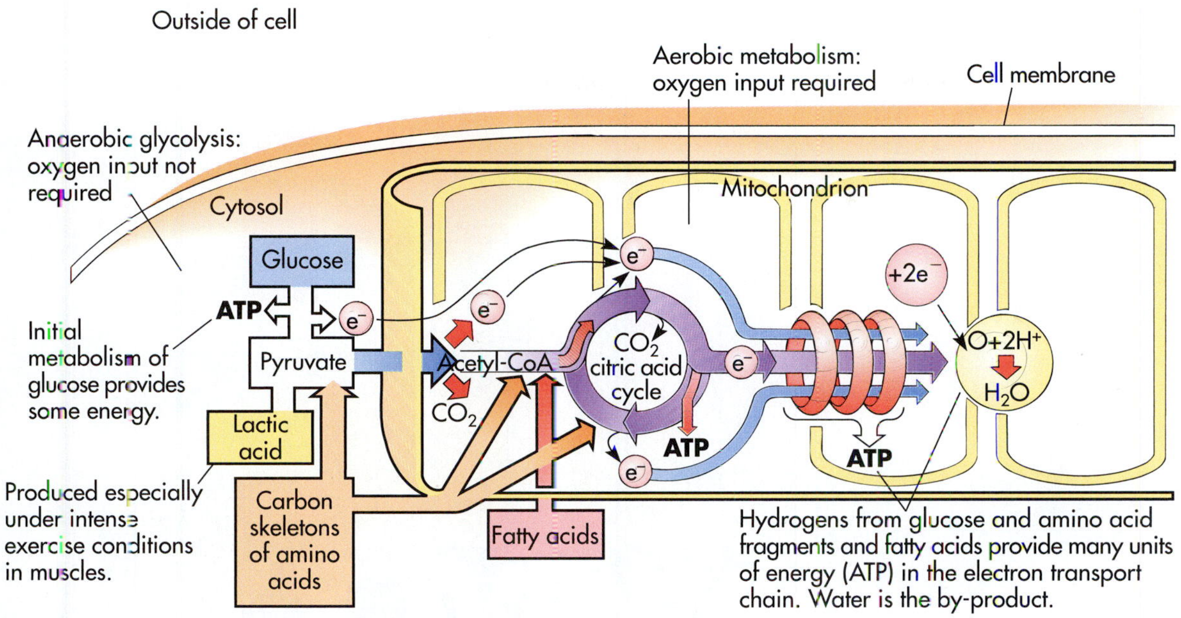

Figure 14-3 Metabolism of carbohydrate, fat, and protein supports ATP synthesis in a muscle cell. Carbohydrate metabolism occurs via both aerobic and anaerobic pathways, whereas fat and protein are metabolized for the most part via the aerobic pathway. Note that blood glucose is not an important source of energy during exercise for muscles, but it is important for the brain and certain other body cells. Any lactic acid produced in a muscle cell is eventually transported out of the muscle cell. It can then be used for energy by nearby muscle cells. In addition, heart tissue can use the lactic acid once it is transported from the muscle to the bloodstream. The lactic acid can also be transformed back to glucose by the liver (and to some extent the kidneys) once it is transported from the muscle to the bloodstream. Most of the ATP is produced as the hydrogen released from carbohydrate, fat, and protein metabolism combines with oxygen in the electron transport system to yield water. Recall from Chapters 10 through 12 that the B-vitamins and many minerals are key participants in these metabolic pathways.

pyruvic acid produced by glycolysis in the cytoplasm is shuttled to the mitochondria and further metabolized into carbon dioxide and water in a series of oxygen-requiring reactions. About 95% of the ATP produced from the complete metabolism of glucose is formed aerobically in mitochondria (Fig. 14-3).

Although the aerobic pathway supplies ATP more slowly than does the anaerobic pathway, it releases more energy. Furthermore, ATP production via the aerobic pathway can be sustained for hours. Accordingly, this pathway of glucose metabolism makes an important energy contribution to sports events lasting from about 2 minutes through 3 or more hours (Fig. 14-4).[17]

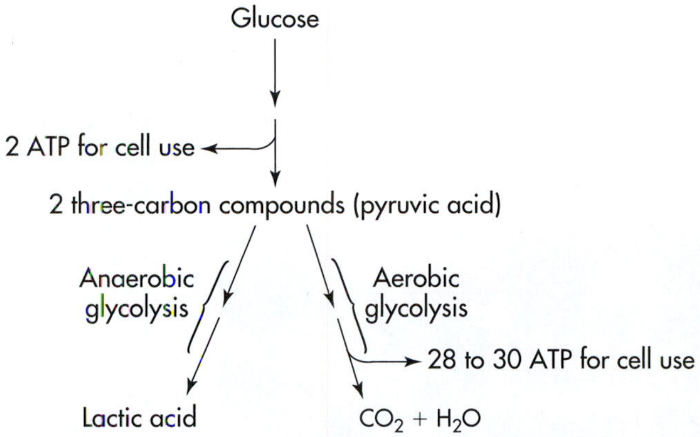

ATP yield from aerobic versus anaerobic glucose utilization.

Glycogen Versus Blood Glucose as Muscle Fuel

Glycogen is the temporary storage form of glucose in the liver (about 100 g) and muscles (about 300 g in sedentary people). It is broken down to a form of glucose, which in turn can be metabolized by both the anaerobic and aerobic pathways. Glycogen is, in fact, the primary source of glucose for ATP production in muscle cells during fairly intense activities that last for less than about 2 hours. In such activities, the depletion of glycogen in the liver leads to a fall in blood glucose, whereas the depletion of glycogen in the muscles contributes to fatigue. Once these glycogen stores are exhausted, an athlete can continue working at only about 50% of maximal capacity. Athletes call this point of glycogen depletion "hitting the wall," as

Figure 14-4 Rough estimates of fuel use during various forms of physical activity. With regard to the weight-lifting session, carbohydrate use could be somewhat greater if the session is intense and fast-paced.

VO_{2max} The maximum volume of oxygen that can be consumed per unit of time.

further exertion is hampered. Thus, when exertion meets or exceeds 70% of **$VO_{2\,max}$** for more than an hour or so, athletes (e.g., long-distance runners or cyclists) should consider increasing the amount of carbohydrate stored in muscles. Diets high in carbohydrate can be used to build up muscle glycogen stores—up to double the typical amounts—in advance of competition, thereby forestalling fatigue and improving endurance.[18] A later section on carbohydrate needs discusses how to plan such a diet.

As exercise duration increases beyond about 20 to 30 minutes, the maintenance of blood glucose becomes an increasingly important consideration. This can spare the use of muscle glycogen, saving it in the muscle for sudden bursts of effort that may be required, such as a sprint to the finish in a marathon race. Linked to the importance of maintaining a normal concentration of glucose in the bloodstream during prolonged exercise, carbohydrate intake of 0.7 g/kg/hour (about 30–60 g/hour) during strenuous endurance exercise, such as cycling that lasts about 1 hour or more, can help maintain adequate blood glucose concentrations. This, in turn, results in delay of fatigue.[3] A later section on sports drinks discusses this in more detail. This attention to carbohydrate intake also helps one tolerate vigorous training on a daily basis.

Bursts of muscle activity use a variety of energy sources, including PCr and ATP.

Without the maintenance of blood glucose in such endurance activities, there is a decline in mental function associated with low blood glucose (cyclists call this mental decline "bonking"). Note however that the fall in blood glucose is related to depletion of liver glycogen, not muscle glycogen.

Carbohydrate intake is not as important for the muscles in shorter events (e.g., one-half hour or so) because the muscles do not take up much blood glucose during short-term exercise, relying instead primarily on glycogen stores for carbohydrate fuel. This is because the action of insulin to increase glucose uptake by muscles is blunted by other hormones, such as epinephrine and glucagon, that increase initially during exercise.[17]

Concept | Check

ATP is the main form of energy that cells use. Carbohydrate metabolism to form ATP begins as glucose becomes available from the bloodstream or from glycogen breakdown. Carbohydrate feeding during exercise can also supply glucose. In a muscle cell, each glucose is broken down through a series of steps to yield either lactic acid or carbon dioxide (CO_2) plus water (H_2O). The breakdown of glucose to carbon dioxide and water is called the aerobic pathway because it requires oxygen. The conversion of glucose to lactate is called the anaerobic pathway because no oxygen is used. This latter process allows the cell to quickly re-form ATP and supports the demand for energy during intense physical activity, as does phosphocreatine (PCr). The aerobic pathway takes longer to supply ATP but provides more energy in the end. This pathway is used more for endurance activities.

Fat: The Main Fuel for Prolonged Low-Intensity Exercise

The majority of the stored energy in the body is found in the fatty acids of stored triglycerides. Most of this resides in adipose tissue depots; some is stored in the muscle itself. That stored in muscles is especially used as activity increases from a low to a moderate pace. When fat stores in various adipose tissue depots are broken down for energy, one triglyceride molecule first yields three fatty acids and one glycerol. The free fatty acids are then released into the bloodstream and travel to the muscles. Once fatty acids enter muscle cells, they combine with any of those released from intramuscular triglyceride storage. All these fatty acids then move into the mitochondria, using a shuttle system that uses carnitine. Then they are broken down into carbon dioxide and water, using in part the oxygen-requiring electron transport chain that yields much ATP. The rate at which muscles use fatty acids depends on a number of factors:[17]

- *The more trained a muscle, the greater its ability to use fat as a fuel.* After a period of aerobic training, muscle cells contain more and larger mitochondria. These and other changes enable muscle cells to produce more ATP via oxygen-requiring pathways, including the pathway used to burn fat for fuel (Table 14-3).
- *The more fatty acids that are released from adipose tissue stores into the bloodstream, the more fat will be used by the muscles.* Some athletes have attempted to raise their blood concentrations of fatty acids by consuming caffeinated beverages. Because this practice actually can increase fatty-acid release from the adipose tissue, it can be helpful to some athletes (see the Nutrition Perspective at the end of this chapter).
- *As exercise becomes increasingly prolonged, fat use predominates,* especially when exercise remains at a low or moderate (aerobic) rate. When energy is needed for long-duration exercise or physical labor, there is almost always plenty of fat that can be called on. In comparison, carbohydrate stores are quite limited.

The fatty acids can come from all over the body, not necessarily from depots near the active muscles. This is why spot reducing does not work. Exercise can tone the muscles underlying adipose tissue but does not preferentially use those stores. If this were not the case, we would all have lean cheeks and necks, because muscles in that vicinity are regularly used.

The other advantage of fat over other sources of energy is that it provides more "bang for the buck." That is, for a given weight of fuel, fat supplies more than twice as much energy as carbohydrate. The aerobic breakdown of a 6-carbon glucose molecule yields 30 to 32 ATP (ratio of about 5 ATP to 1 carbon), whereas a 16-carbon fatty acid molecule produces 108 ATP (ratio of about 6.8 ATP to 1 carbon).

However, carbohydrate is more efficient than fat in one very important way: the amount of ATP produced per unit of oxygen consumed. It takes 6 O_2 molecules to produce 30 to 32 ATP molecules during the aerobic breakdown of a molecule of glucose (ratio of about 5 ATP to 1 O_2), whereas 23 O_2 molecules are needed to produce 108 ATP molecules from a 16-carbon fatty acid (ratio of about 4.5 ATP to 1 O_2). Thus, in situations when an athlete's maximal performance would be limited by the activity of oxygen-requiring pathways (as in competitive endurance exercise), it is necessary that muscle cells also use carbohydrate as long as the carbohydrate supply, especially muscle glycogen, lasts.

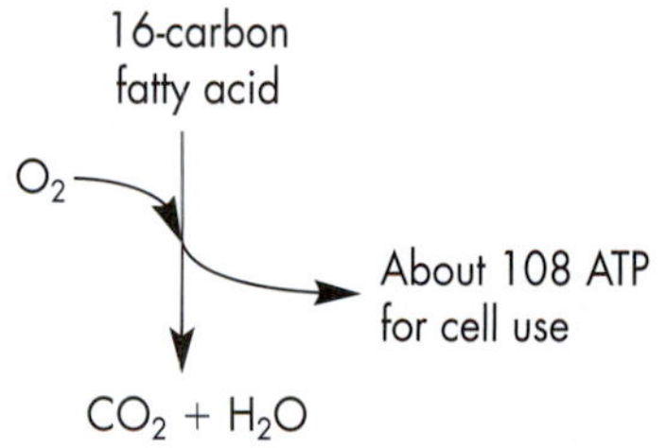

ATP yield from aerobic fatty acid utilization.

The energy to perform comes from carbohydrate, fat, and protein. The relative mix depends on the pace.

Table 14-3 Adaptations to Endurance Exercise in Skeletal Muscle

Changes	Advantage
Increased ability of muscle to store glycogen (high-carbohydrate diet increases this even further)	More glycogen fuel available for the final minutes of an event
Increased triglyceride storage in muscle	Conserves glycogen by allowing for increased fat use
Increased mitochondrial size and number	Conserves glycogen by allowing for increased fat use (even at high exercise outputs)
Increased myoglobin content	Increased oxygen delivery to muscles and increased ability to use fat for fuel

Overall, training allows an athlete to use fat for fuel more readily. This allows the athlete to conserve glycogen for when it is really needed—such as for a burst of speed at the end of a race.

During very lengthy activities, such as a triathlon, ultramarathon, manual labor in a foundry, or even work at a desk for 8 hours a day, fat supplies about 50 to 90% of the energy required. Overall, keep in mind that the only fuel we eat that can support intense (anaerobic) activity is carbohydrate; slow and steady (aerobic) activity uses all available energy sources: fat and carbohydrate, primarily.

Protein: A Minor Fuel Source, Primarily for Endurance Exercise

Although amino acids derived from protein are used to fuel muscles, their contribution is relatively small, compared with that of carbohydrate and fat. As a rough guide, only about 5% of the body's general energy needs, as well as the typical energy needs of exercising muscles, is supplied by the metabolism of amino acids.[3]

However, proteins can contribute significantly to energy needs in endurance exercise, perhaps as much as 10 to 15%, especially as glycogen stores in the muscle are exhausted. Most of the energy supplied from protein comes from metabolism of the branched-chain amino acids—leucine, isoleucine, and valine. Because a normal diet provides enough protein to supply this amount of fuel, protein supplements or amino acid supplements are not needed. Contrary to what many athletes believe, protein is used for fuel less in resistance types of exercise (e.g., weight lifting) than for endurance exercise (e.g., running) (review Fig. 14-4). The primary muscle fuels for the act of weight lifting are phosphocreatine (PCr) and carbohydrate. Despite this fact, high-protein products such as Pro-Complex, Amino Fuel 2000, High Voltage Protein Drink, and Instant Egg Protein are marketed in nearly every health-food and fitness store, specifically for weight lifters and bodybuilders. Note also that consuming high-carbohydrate, moderate-protein foods immediately after a weight-training workout enhances the anabolic effect of the activity, most likely by increasing the concentrations of insulin and growth hormone released into the blood.

Concept | Check

Fat is a key aerobic fuel for muscle cells, especially at low to moderate exercise intensities. Training enhances the ability to use fat for fuel, in turn conserving glycogen stores. At rest, muscles burn primarily fat for energy needs. On the other hand, little protein is used to fuel muscles. It supplies roughly 5% of energy needs under most conditions, and perhaps 10 to 15% of energy needs during endurance exercise when glycogen stores have essentially been exhausted.

The Body's Response to Physical Activity

We have discussed how muscle cells obtain the ATP energy needed to do work. Let's now focus on how muscles and related organs adapt to an increased workload.

Specialized Functions of Skeletal Muscle Fiber Types

The body actually contains three types of muscle tissue: skeletal muscle, the type involved in locomotion; smooth muscle, the type found in internal organs except the heart; and cardiac (heart) muscle. Skeletal muscle, our primary focus, is composed of three main types of muscle fiber, which exhibit distinct functional characteristics:[17]

- Type I (slow twitch—oxidative): Aerobic metabolism of fat primarily fuels type I fibers. These are also called red fibers because of their high myoglobin content.
- Type IIA (fast twitch—oxidative, glycolytic): Glycolysis using glucose (anaerobic) plus aerobic metabolism of both fat and glucose fuels type IIA fibers.
- Type IIB (fast twitch—glycolytic): Glycolysis using glucose (anaerobic) is the primary energy system for type IIB fibers. These are also called white fibers.

Prolonged low-intensity exercise, such as a slow jog, mainly involves use of type I muscle fibers, so the predominant fuel is fat. As exercise intensity increases, type IIA and type IIB fibers are gradually recruited; in turn the contribution of glucose as a fuel increases. Type IIA and type IIB fibers also are important for rapid movements, such as a jump shot in basketball.

The relative proportions of the three fiber types throughout the muscles of the body vary from person to person and are constant throughout each person's life. The individual differences in fiber-type distribution are partially responsible for producing elite marathon runners who could never compete at the same level as sprinters, or elite gymnasts who could never be competitive as long-distance swimmers. Although the proportion of muscle fiber types is largely determined by genetics, appropriate training can develop muscles within limits. For example, aerobic training enhances the capacity of type IIA muscle fibers to produce ATP and may bring about a relative change in size. Overall, great athletes are born, but their genetic potential then must be nurtured by training.[17]

Adaptation of Muscles and Body Physiology to Exercise

With training, muscle strength also becomes matched to the muscles' variable work demands. Muscles enlarge after being made to work repeatedly, a response called **hypertrophy.** Certain cells in the muscles gain bulk and improve their ability to work. Conversely, after several days without activity, muscles diminish in size and lose strength, a response called **atrophy.** Both hypertrophy and atrophy are forms of adaptation to the load applied. Thus, many marathon runners have well-developed leg muscles but little arm or chest muscle development.

hypertrophy An increase in tissue or organ size.

atrophy A wasting away of tissues or organs.

Beyond the effects on individual muscles describe earlier, repeated aerobic exercise also produces beneficial changes in the heart and blood vessels that are responsible for delivering oxygen to the mitochondria of the muscle cells. Because the body needs more oxygen during exercise, it responds to training by producing more red blood cells and expanding total blood volume. Training also leads to an increase in the number of capillaries in muscle tissue; as a result, oxygen can be delivered more easily to muscles. Finally, training causes the heart, a muscle itself, to strengthen. Then each contraction empties the heart's chamber more efficiently, so more blood is pumped with each beat. As exercise increases the efficiency of the heart, its rate of beating at rest and during submaximal exercise decreases.[17]

ATP (energy) needs dictate the amount of oxygen used by cells: 1.5 or 2.5 ATP molecules are produced from each molecule of oxygen.

Oxygen consumption indicates how hard a person is exercising. The more physically fit a person is, the more work the muscles and body can do, and the more oxygen the person can consume. A treadmill test commonly is used to determine a person's $VO_{2\,max}$, which is the maximum amount of oxygen that can be consumed in a unit of time

Critical | Thinking
Marty started going to the gym about 8 weeks ago. At first, he noticed that he began huffing and puffing about 7 minutes into his aerobic workout. Now, however, he can work out for about 25 minutes without tiring. What is a possible explanation for his ability to work out longer?

Typical VO_{2max} Values	*ml O_2/kg/min*
Sedentary elderly person	15
Typical middle-aged adult	35–45
Elite athlete	65–75

(ml/min). In this test, oxygen consumption is measured as the treadmill speed and/or grade is gradually increased until the subject becomes profoundly fatigued. The oxygen consumption measured right before total exhaustion is $VO_{2\ max}$. Most people can improve their $VO_{2\ max}$ by 15 to 20% or more with exercise training.

Because of individual differences in $VO_{2\ max}$, it is generally best to express exercise intensity as a percentage of $VO_{2\ max}$. The percentage of $VO_{2\ max}$ required for exercise of various intensity is as follows:

- Low intensity (e.g., fast walk)—30 to 50% of $VO_{2\ max}$
- Moderate intensity (e.g., fast jog)—50 to 65% of $VO_{2\ max}$
- High intensity (e.g., 3-hour marathon pace)—70 to 80% of $VO_{2\ max}$
- Very high intensity (e.g., sprints)—85 to 150% of $VO_{2\ max}$

In very-high-intensity activities, the ATP equivalent to the "extra" 50% above 100% of $VO_{2\ max}$ is produced anaerobically from PCr and glycolysis. In terms of fuel sources for muscle cells, fat use peaks at 45% of VO_{2max}. Carbohydrate use then becomes more important for meeting energy needs.

Exercise output is sometimes expressed in units called metabolic equivalents (METs). One MET is the expenditure of 1 kcal/kg/hr or, on average, 3.5 ml O_2/kg/min. This approximates resting energy expenditure. A brisk walk represents about 4.5 METs of energy expenditure. Exercise prescriptions given to people recovering from a heart attack are often given in MET units (see *ACSM Guidelines for Exercise Testing and Prescription* for details).[4]

Power Food: Dietary Advice for Athletes

Athletic training and genetic makeup are two very important determinants of athletic performance. A good diet won't substitute for either factor, but diet can further enhance and maximize an athlete's potential. More important, a poor diet can certainly harm performance.[3]

Energy Needs

Athletes need varying amounts of food energy, depending on each athlete's body size and current body composition and on the type of training or competition being considered. A small person may need only 1700 kcal daily to sustain normal daily activities without losing body weight; a large, muscular man may need 4000 kcal. These rough estimates can be viewed as starting points that need to be individualized by trial and error for each athlete.[3]

The energy needs required for sports training or competition has to be added to the basal energy needed just to carry on normal activities. Energy use averages 5 to 8 kcal/minute for moderate activity; again, this is just an estimate. For example, an hour of bowling requires little energy in addition to that required to sustain normal daily living. At the other extreme, a 12-hour endurance bicycle race over mountains can require an additional 4000 kcal/day. Therefore, some athletes may need as much as 7000 kcal or more daily just to maintain body weight while training, whereas others may need 1700 kcal or less. If an athlete experiences daily fatigue, the first consideration should be if he or she is consuming enough food. Up to 6 meals per day may be needed, including one before each workout.

Athletes often expend much energy. In such cases their resulting food intake should easily provide ample protein and other nutrients to support activity.

How can we know if an athlete is getting enough energy from food? Estimating daily intake from a food diary by the athlete is one way. Another step is to estimate the athlete's body fat percentage by measuring skinfold thicknesses, by using bioelectrical impedance, or by using the underwater weighing technique or DEXA scans (see Chapter 13). Body fat should be the typical amount found in athletes in the specific sport practiced. This corresponds to 5 to 18% for most male athletes and 17 to 28% for most female athletes.[17] Then one goes on to monitor body weight changes on a daily or weekly basis. If body weight starts to fall, food energy should be increased; if weight rises and it is because of increases in body fat, the athlete should eat less.

If the body composition test shows that an athlete has too much body fat, the athlete should lower energy intake by about 200 to 500 kcal/day, while maintaining a regular exercise program, until the desirable fat percentage is achieved. On the other hand, if an athlete needs to gain weight, increasing energy intake by 500 to 700 kcal/day will eventually lead to the needed weight gain.

Wrestlers, boxers, judoists, jockeys, and oarsmen often try to lose weight, so that they can be certified to compete in a lower weight class. This helps them gain a mechanical advantage over an opponent of smaller stature. They usually lose this weight before stepping on the scale for weight certification. Athletes can lose up to 22 pounds (10 kg) of body water in 1 day by sitting in a sauna, exercising in a plastic sweat suit, or taking diuretic drugs, which speed water loss from the kidneys. Losing as little as 2 to 3% of body weight by dehydration can adversely affect endurance performance. A pattern of repeated weight loss or gain of more than 5% of body weight by dehydration carries some risk of kidney malfunction and heat-related illness. Death is also a possibility.

To prevent such problems, the National Collegiate Athletic Association has begun requiring that a minimum safe weight and body fat percentage (e.g., 7%) be set by a physician or an athletic trainer for each wrestler at the start of the season and weigh-ins 1 to 2 hours before competition. Many states also have adopted this practice. If athletes, such as wrestlers, wish to compete in a lower-body-weight class and have enough extra fat stores, they should begin a gradual, sustained reduction in energy intake long before the competitive season starts. In so doing, the athlete attains a healthier body composition (less fat) while avoiding the potentially harmful and certainly misery-creating effects of severe dehydration. Athletes who have no extra body fat should not attempt to compete at a lower-body-weight class. Coaches and trainers should be aware of the decreased performance and serious side effects of severe dehydration.

Critical | Thinking

Joe is a wrestler who qualified for the 125-pound weight classification in his annual high school competition. After a few matches, Joe began to feel dizzy and faint. He was disqualified because he was unable to continue the match. Later, the coach found out that Joe had spent 2 hours in the sauna before weighing in, which had made him dehydrated. What are the consequences of dehydration? What can you suggest as an alternative way to lose weight?

Carbohydrate Needs

Anyone who regularly exercises vigorously for more than 1 hour per day on a regular basis needs to consume a diet that includes moderate to high amounts of carbohydrates.[6] The diet should include a variety of foods, such as recommended by the Food Guide Pyramid. Numerous servings of grains, starchy vegetables, and fruits provide enough carbohydrate to maintain adequate liver and muscle glycogen stores, especially for replacing glycogen losses from workouts on the previous day. Relatively low-carbohydrate diets, such as the *Zone Diet,* are not recommended for most athletes (recall that Chapter 13 discussed the Zone Diet. The carbohydrate content of this diet is only 40% of calories, rather than 50% or more that is typically recommended for athletes).

Carbohydrate intake should be at least 5 g/kg body weight. People engaged in aerobic training and endurance athletes (duration > 60 minutes per day) may need as much as 6 to 7 g/kg body weight. When duration approaches several hours per day, the carbohydrate recommendation increases to 8 to 10 g/kg body weight.[6] In other words, triathletes and marathoners should consider eating close to 500 to 600 g of carbohydrates daily, and even more if necessary, to (1) prevent chronic fatigue and (2) load the muscles and liver with glycogen. This is especially important when performing multiple training sessions in a day, such as swim practices, or heavy training on successive days, as in cross-country running. Depletion of carbohydrate ranks just behind depletion of fluid and electrolytes as a major cause of fatigue. Table 14-4 shows sample menus, based on the Food Guide Pyramid, for diets providing food energy ranging from 1500 to 5000 kcal/day. Table 14-5 lists the number of grams of carbohydrate in some representative foods in various food groupings.

So-called "energy" bars are becoming popular with athletes. A wide variety of bars is on the market, some with a mixture of protein, carbohydrate, and fat, whereas others are mostly protein. Choosing a bar with about 40 g of carbohydrate and no more than 10 g of protein, 4 g of fat, and 5 g of fiber is recommended. The bars are typically fortified with vitamins and minerals, often to 100% of the Daily Values. Overall these can be seen as a convenient, although somewhat expensive, source of nutrients. The need for a high-protein bar is especially questionable (see the Nutrition Perspective at the end of this chapter).

Note that one does not have to give up any specific food when planning a high-carbohydrate diet. The focus is to include more high-carbohydrate foods and moderation with concentrated fat sources. Sports nutritionists emphasize the difference between a high-carbohydrate meal and a high-carbohydrate/high-fat meal. Before endurance

Table 14-4 Sample Daily Menus Based on the Food Guide Pyramid That Provide Various Total Energy Intakes

1500 kcal Diet	2000 kcal Diet	3000 kcal Diet	4000 kcal Diet	5000 kcal Diet
Breakfast Fat-free milk, 1 cup Cheerios, ½ cup Bagel, ½ Cherry jam, 2 tsp Margarine, 1 tsp **Lunch** Chicken breast (roasted), 2 oz Figs, 1 Fat-free milk ½ cup Banana, 1 **Snack** Oatmeal-raisin cookie, 1 Low-fat fruit yogurt, 1 cup **Dinner** Spaghetti w/meatballs, 1 cup Romaine lettuce, 1 cup Italian dressing, 2 tsp Green beans, ½ cup Cranberry juice, 1½ cups ——— 18% protein (68 g) 64% carbohydrate (240 g) 19% fat (32 g)	**Breakfast** Fat-free milk, 1 cup Cheerios, 1 cup Bagel, ½ Cherry jam, 1 tbsp Margarine, 1 tsp **Lunch** Chicken breast (roasted), 2 oz Wheat bread, 2 slices Mayonnaise, 1 tsp Raisins, ¼ cup Cranberry juice, 1½ cups Banana, 1 **Snack** Oatmeal-raisin cookies, 3 Low-fat fruit yogurt, 1 cup **Dinner** Broiled beef sirloin, 3 oz Romaine lettuce, 1 cup Italian dressing, 2 tsp Green beans, 1 cup Fat-free milk, ½ cup ——— 17% protein (85 g) 63% carbohydrate (315 g) 20% fat (44 g)	**Breakfast** Fat-free milk, 1 cup Cheerios, 2 cups Bagel, 1 Cherry jam, 2 tsp Margarine, 1 tsp Oat bran muffins, 2 **Lunch** Chicken breast (roasted), 2 oz Wheat bread, 2 slices Provolone cheese, 1 oz Mayonnaise, 1 tsp Raisins, ⅓ cup Cranberry juice, 1½ cups Low-fat fruit yogurt, 1 cup **Snack** Banana, 1 Oatmeal-raisin cookies, 3 **Dinner** Broiled beef sirloin, 3 oz Romaine lettuce, 1 cup Garbanzo beans, 1 cup Italian dressing, 2 tsp Spinach pasta noodles, 1½ cups Margarine, 1 tsp Green beans, 1 cup Fat-free milk, ½ cup ——— 17% protein (128 g) 62% carbohydrate (465 g) 21% fat (70 g)	**Breakfast** Orange, 1 Cheerios, 2 cups Fat-free milk, 1 cup Bran muffins, 2 **Snack** Chopped dates, ¾ cup **Lunch** Romaine lettuce, 1 cup Garbanzo beans, 1 cup Grated carrots, ½ cup French dressing, 2 tbsp Macaroni and cheese, 3 cups Apple juice, 1 cup **Snack** Wheat bread, 2 slices Margarine, 1 tsp Jam, 2 tbsp **Dinner** Skinless turkey breast, 2 oz Mashed potatoes, 2 cups Peas and onions, 1 cup Banana, 1 Fat-free milk, 1 cup **Snack** Pasta, 1 cup cooked Margarine, 2 tsp Parmesan cheese, 2 tbsp Cranberry juice, 1 cup ——— 14% protein (140 g) 61% carbohydrate (610 g) 26% fat (116 g)	**Breakfast** Cheerios, 2 cups Bran muffins, 2 Orange, 1 Fat-reduced milk, 1 cup **Snack** Low-fat yogurt, 1 cup Chopped dates, 1 cup **Lunch** Apple juice, 1 cup Chicken enchilada, 1 Romaine lettuce, 1 cup Garbanzo beans, 1 cup Shredded carrots, ¾ cup Chopped celery, ½ cup Seasoned croutons, 1 oz French dressing, 2 tbsp Wheat bread, 2 slices Margarine, 1 tbsp **Snack** Banana, 1 Bagel, 1 Cream cheese, 1 tbsp **Dinner** Fat-reduced milk, 1 cup Beef sirloin, 5 oz Mashed potatoes, 2 cups Spinach pasta noodles, 1½ cups Grated parmesan cheese, 2 tbsp Green beans, 1 cup Oatmeal-raisin cookies, 3 **Snack** Cranberry juice, 2 cups Air-popped popcorn, 4 cups Raisins, ⅓ cup ——— 14% protein (175 g) 63% carbohydrate (813 g) 24% fat (136 g)

events, such as marathons or triathlons, some athletes seek to increase their carbohydrate reserves by eating potato chips, french fries, banana cream pie, and pastries. Although such foods contain carbohydrate, they also contain a lot of fat. Better high-carbohydrate food choices include pasta, rice, potatoes, bread, fruit and fruit juices, and many breakfast cereals (check the label for carbohydrate content). Sports drinks appropriate for carbohydrate loading, such as GatorLode and UltraFuel, can also help. Consuming a moderate amount of dietary fiber during the final day of training is a good precaution to reduce the chances of bloating and intestinal gas during the next day's event.

As a general rule, athletes should obtain 60% or more of their total energy needs from carbohydrate, rather than the 50% typical of most North American diets, espe-

Table 14-5 Grams of Carbohydrate Based on Serving Size of Typical Carbohydrate-Rich Foods

Starches—15 g Carbohydrate per Serving	
One Serving	
½–¾ cup dry breakfast cereal*	1 small baked potato
½ cup cooked breakfast cereal	½ bagel
½ cup cooked grits	½ English muffin
⅓ cup cooked rice	1 slice bread
½ cup cooked pasta	¾ oz pretzels
⅓ cup baked beans	6 saltine crackers
½ cup cooked corn	2 pancakes, 4 inches in diameter
½ cup cooked/dry beans	2 taco shells
Vegetables—5 g Carbohydrate per Serving	
One Serving	
½ cup cooked vegetables	
1 cup raw vegetables	
½ cup vegetable juice	
Examples: carrots, green beans, broccoli, cauliflower, onions, spinach, tomatoes, vegetable juice	
Fruits—15 g Carbohydrate per Serving	
One Serving	
½ cup canned fruit or berries	12 cherries or grapes
½ cup fruit juice	½ grapefruit
¼ cup dried fruit	1 nectarine
1 small apple	1 orange
4 apricots	1 peach
1 small banana	1¼ cups watermelon
Milk—12 g Carbohydrate per Serving	
One Serving	
1 cup milk	
¾ cup plain low-fat yogurt	
Sweets—15 g Carbohydrate per Serving	
One Serving	
2-inch square typical slice of cake	
2 small cookies	½ cup ice cream
3 ginger snaps	½ cup sherbet

Modified from *Exchange Lists for Meal Planning* by the American Diabetes Association and American Dietetic Association, 1995, Chicago, American Dietetic Association.

*Note that the carbohydrate content of dry cereal varies widely. Check the labels of the ones you choose and adjust serving size accordingly.

The athlete's plate should be covered two-thirds with grains and vegetables, and one-third with protein-rich sources.

cially if exercise duration is expected to exceed 2 hours and total energy intake is about 3000 kcal/day or less. Diets containing 4000 to 5000 kcal/day can be as low as 50% carbohydrate, as these will still provide sufficient carbohydrate (400–600 g/day). Fat should provide 20 to 35% of total energy needs. Protein then provides the rest of the total energy—about 15% of total needs.[3] This approach yields a training diet that is about two-thirds carbohydrate-rich foods and one-third protein-rich foods, with fat coming in as part of many of the food choices made.

For athletes who compete in continuous intense aerobic events lasting more than 60 to 90 minutes (or in shorter events repeated over a 24-hour period), undertaking a **carbohydrate-loading** regimen is often advantageous for maximizing muscle glycogen stores. (Note, however, that this duration applies to few athletes.) One possible regimen includes a gradual reduction, or "tapering," of exercise intensity and duration,

carbohydrate loading A process in which a very high carbohydrate intake is consumed for 6 days before an athletic event while tapering exercise duration in an attempt to increase muscle glycogen stores.

coupled with a gradual increase in dietary carbohydrate as a percentage of energy intake. The procedure can begin 6 days before competition, with the athlete completing a hard workout lasting about 60 minutes. Workouts for the next 4 days then last about 40, 40, 20, and 20 minutes, respectively, with exercise intensities being progressively reduced each day. On the final day before the competition, the athlete rests.

Appropriate Activities for Carbohydrate Loading

- Marathons
- Long-distance swimming
- Cross-country skiing
- 30-k runs
- Triathlons
- Tournament-play basketball
- Soccer
- Cycling time trials
- Long-distance canoe racing

The dietary carbohydrate on the first 3 days of this regimen contributes 45 to 50% of energy intake. The carbohydrate contribution increases to 70 to 80% (400–700 g/day depending on body weight) for the last 3 days before competition. This carbohydrate-loading technique usually increases muscle glycogen stores by 50 to 85% over typical conditions (that is, when dietary carbohydrate constitutes about 50% of the total energy intake). A typical carbohydrate-loading schedule looks like this:

Days Before Competition	6	5	4	3	2	1
Exercise time (minutes)	60	40	40	20	20	Rest
Carbohydrate (grams)	450	450	450	600	600	600

Total energy intake should decrease as exercise time decreases

A potential disadvantage of carbohydrate loading is that some water is incorporated in the muscles with the extra glycogen (about 3g/g of glycogen). Although it aids in maintaining hydration, in some individuals this additional water weight and related muscle stiffness are sufficient to detract from their sports performance, making carbohydrate loading inappropriate. Athletes considering carbohydrate loading should try it during training (and well before an important competition) to experience its effects on performance.[17] They can then determine whether it is worth the effort. Note also that carbohydrate feeding during exercise provides about the same advantage as carbohydrate loading. In fact, the trend is currently toward this second method coupled with a daily diet high in carbohydrate.

Inappropriate Activities for Carbohydrate Loading

- American football games
- 10-k or shorter runs
- Walking and hiking
- Most swimming events
- Single basketball games
- Weight lifting
- Most track and field events

Carbohydrate loading is safe for adolescents, but the activities for which this technique is useful, such as marathon runs, may not be. Adolescents should obtain the approval of their physician before participating in such a regimen.

Fat Needs

As just mentioned, a diet containing up to 35% of energy intake from fat is recommended for athletes. Rich sources of monounsaturated fat, such as canola oil, should be emphasized, and saturated and trans fat intake should be limited.

Protein Needs

Looking at protein intake more specifically, typical recommendations for athletes in the sports nutrition literature range from 1.2 to 1.4 g of protein per kg of body weight, considerably higher than the RDA of 0.8 g/kg body weight (Table 14-6). (Recall from Chapter 7 that the Food and Nutrition Board does not support this increase above the RDA.) Athletes engaged in endurance sports are typically encouraged to aim for the higher value, as protein supplies a greater percentage of the energy used (up to 15%) in these sports than in other athletic endeavors. Overall, the vast majority of athletes can meet protein needs without having to exceed twice the RDA. In addition, energy needs must be met or much of this protein will be diverted to fuel use.

High-protein products, which are often marketed to athletes, are unnecessary. The same holds true for high-protein bars, a current trend in marketing products to athletes.

For athletes beginning a weight-training program, some experts recommend up to 1.6 to 1.8 g of protein per kg of body weight.[11] That is up to approximately 2¼ times the RDA for protein. Certainly protein intake should not exceed 35% of energy intake, or 2 g/kg body weight, whichever is less. To date, the importance of excessive protein intakes during the initial phases of weight training has not been supported by sufficient research. In addition, protein intakes above this amount simply result in an increased use of amino acids for energy needs or glucose synthesis; no further increase in muscle protein synthesis is seen. Note also that energy needs for weight lifting itself are not the reason for the high protein recommendation, as the fuel used for this activity is

Table 14-6 Grams of Protein That Meet Recommendations for Individuals of Different Weights

Pounds	Kilograms	RDA (0.8 g/kg)	1.5 × RDA (1.2 g/kg)	2 × RDA (1.6 g/kg)
110	50	40	60	80
130	60	48	72	96
155	70	56	84	112
175	80	64	96	128
200	90	72	108	144
220	100	80	120	160

Compare these quantities with protein intake from the diets listed in Table 14-4. Note that diets supplying enough total energy for athletes yield plenty of protein, even for those who make no special attempt to consume high-protein foods.

Consuming excessive amounts of protein is not without its drawbacks. As noted in Chapter 7, it increases calcium loss in the urine. It also leads to increased urine production, possibly compromising body hydration. It also may lead to kidney stones in people with a history of such stones or other kidney problems. Finally, high-protein foods usually do not supply much carbohydrate, a key fuel source for athletes.

primarily PCr and carbohydrate. The extra protein, theoretically, is required for the synthesis of new tissue brought on by the loading effect of weight training. Once the desired muscle mass is achieved, protein intake need not exceed twice the RDA.

Any athlete not specifically on an energy-restricted diet can easily have a protein intake twice the RDA simply by eating a variety of foods (review Table 14-6). For example, a 123-lb (53-kg) woman can consume 82 g of her upper range of 85 g of protein (twice the RDA) by eating 4 oz of chicken (one chicken breast), 3 oz of beef (a small lean hamburger), and ½ cup of cooked beans and by drinking two glasses of milk during a single day. A 180-pound (77-kg) man needs to consume only 6 oz of chicken (a large chicken breast), ½ cup of cooked beans, a 6-oz can of tuna, and two glasses of milk a day to consume 122 g of his upper range of 123 g of protein (twice the RDA). And, for both athletes this does not even include the protein in the grains or vegetables they will also eat. In meeting their energy needs, many athletes consume even more protein. Thus, protein supplements are not needed despite marketing claims.[11]

Athletes who either feel they must significantly limit their energy intake or are vegetarians should specifically determine how much protein they eat. They should make sure to choose foods that provide overall at least 1.2 g of protein per kg of body weight.

Critical | Thinking

Some athletes believe that their diets should consist of 25% of energy intake from protein because they are body building and working out. Your neighbor is a high school baseball player. He has been listening to many professional athletes talk about diet, and he plans to begin consuming 25% of his energy intake from protein. How would you explain to him that this is too much protein?

Vitamin and Mineral Needs

Vitamin and mineral needs are the same or slightly higher for athletes, compared with those of sedentary adults. Still, because athletes usually have such high food-energy intakes, they tend to consume plenty of vitamins and minerals. An exception are athletes consuming energy-restricted diets (about 1200 kcal or less), such as seen with some female athletes participating in events in which maintaining a low body weight is crucial. They may not be meeting B-vitamin and other micronutrient needs. Vegetarian athletes are also a concern. In these cases, consuming fortified foods, such as ready-to-eat breakfast cereals, or a balanced multivitamin and mineral supplement is recommended.[13] Athletes' needs for vitamin E and vitamin C may be somewhat greater because of the antioxidant protection these nutrients provide; this effect could be especially important in the face of high oxygen use by muscles. Still, the use of megadoses of vitamin E and vitamin C requires more study and is not currently an accepted part of the dietary guidance for athletes. Experts first suggest following a diet containing foods rich in antioxidants, such as fruits, vegetables, whole grains, and vegetable oils.[1] This diet is rich in vitamin C (200 mg/day is a reasonable target for athletes) but still does not supply the amount of vitamin E currently used in studies of athletes (200 mg/day [about 400 IU/day]).[14] Adding this amount of vitamin E to a diet is generally safe; it provides no benefit to exercise performance but may offer some protection from exercise-induced muscle damage, especially for athletes competing at high altitudes.

Currently, however, the evidence regarding the importance of this practice is sketchy.[1] For other nutrients, if supplements are used, intakes below the Upper Level set for each is a safe guide, aside from iron. Men should generally not exceed the RDA for iron (see Chapter 12 on the risks of iron overload).

Iron Deficiency Impairs Performance

hemodilution A state in which blood volume increases more than red blood cell production. This leaves the blood appearing not to have enough red blood cells, but this is not the case. The total amount of red blood cells has not changed. Hemodilution is common in athletes and in pregnancy.

Many athletes, particularly females, can show results on blood tests that suggest the presence of iron deficiency anemia. In some cases, the anemia is real and needs to be treated with increased iron intake or iron supplements. In other cases, the anemia is a transient condition which occurs due to an accumulation of the fluid portion of the blood (an effect called **hemodilution**). Although the total amount of hemoglobin functioning in red blood cells hasn't changed, the red blood cells take up a lower percentage of the blood because the fluid portion has become more dilute. Therefore, a blood test gives the appearance of a lower red blood cell volume. By analogy, let's say that you took 8 oz of a soft drink and mixed it with 8 oz of water. If you drank all 16 oz of this diluted soft drink, you would still get the same amount of sugar as you would by drinking 8 oz of undiluted soft drink. However, if you drank just 2 oz of the diluted drink, you would consume less sugar than 2 oz of the undiluted soft drink. In the same way, a blood test of hemodiluted blood is like just drinking the 2 oz of diluted drink. In both cases, you are getting a diluted result, even though a total amount of "solid material" has not changed. Hemodilution in blood typically occurs with certain types of changes in an athlete's training. Normally, it is a temporary condition that goes away by itself.

In contrast to the hemodilution situation, some athletes, especially women, develop real anemia. One reason is simply that teenage and young adult females in general can be prone to anemia, whether they are athletes or not. As well, some athletic training seems to increase the risk of iron deficiency by increasing the amount of iron lost via sweat, urine, and the GI tract.

At some point, you may hear the expression "sports anemia." Unfortunately, not everyone uses this expression to mean the same thing. Some people apply this expression only to the transient, hemodilution state noted above, while others apply the expression to both transient and real anemia in athletes.

At one time in his career, long-distance runner Alberto Salazar experienced problems sleeping and performed poorly because of low iron intake and related iron deficiency anemia.

To see if iron deficiency is the cause of anemia in an athlete, iron supplements should be given for 1 month, and then the athlete should be retested to see if blood hemoglobin increases by at least 1 g/dl (review Chapter 12 for details on medicinal iron use). If so, the athlete was truly iron depleted, and the therapy was appropriate. A lesser or no response suggests that the problem may have been due merely to hemodilution.

Because iron deficiency can be caused by blood loss, it is important that physicians also investigate the cause of the deficiency. If caught early, some serious medical conditions can be treated or prevented. And, if blood iron is consistently low, the use of iron supplements by an athlete may be advisable. However, indiscriminate use of iron supplements is not advised because toxic effects are possible.

Some studies have suggested that iron deficiency without anemia may still have a negative effect on physical activity and performance. For this reason, athletes must be especially careful not to deplete iron stores.[5]

Calcium Intake Deserves Attention, Especially in Women

Athletes, especially women trying to lose weight by restricting their intake of dairy products, can have marginal or low dietary intakes of calcium. This practice compromises bone health. Of still greater concern are women athletes who have stopped menstruating because their arduous exercise training interferes with the normal secretion of the reproductive hormones. Disturbing reports show that female athletes who do not menstruate regularly have far less dense bones than both nonathletes and female athletes who menstruate regularly. Some of this bone loss is irreversible. This places them at increased risk for osteoporosis in later life, a risk that outweighs the benefit of weight-bearing exercise on bone mineral density. This is discussed further in Chapter

Heat index

Relative humidity (%)	70°	75°	80°	85°	90°	95°	100°	105°	110°
100	72°	80°	91°	108°					
90	71°	79°	88°	102°	122°				
80	71°	78°	86°	97°	113°	136°			
70	70°	77°	85°	93°	106°	124°	144°		
60	70°	76°	82°	90°	100°	114°	132°	149°	
50	69°	75°	81°	88°	96°	107°	120°	135°	150°
40	68°	74°	79°	86°	93°	101°	110°	123°	137°
30	67°	73°	78°	84°	90°	96°	104°	113°	123°
20	66°	72°	77°	82°	87°	93°	99°	105°	112°
10	65°	70°	75°	80°	85°	90°	95°	100°	105°
0	64°	69°	73°	78°	83°	87°	91°	95°	99°

Air temperature (°F)

Heat index	Heat disorders possible with prolonged exposure and/or physical activity
80° to 89°	Fatigue
90° to 104°	Sunstroke, heat cramps, and heat exhaustion
105° to 129°	Sunstroke, heat cramps, or heat exhaustion likely and heatstroke possible
130° or higher	Heatstroke/sunstroke highly likely

NOTE: Direct sunshine increases the heat index by up to 15°F.

Figure 14-5 Heat index chart, showing associated heat disorders.

15, with respect to the Female Athlete Triad, and in Chapter 11, where osteoporosis was reviewed in detail.

A woman runner who does not menstruate regularly may also have a higher risk for the development of a **stress fracture.** (Intakes below the Adequate Intake for calcium for one's age also increase the risk for stress fractures.) Female athletes whose menstrual cycles become irregular should consult a physician to ascertain the cause. Decreasing the amount of training or increasing energy intake and body weight often restores regular menstrual cycles. Extra calcium in the diet does not necessarily compensate for the effects of menstrual loss, but inadequate dietary calcium can make matters worse.

stress fracture A fracture that occurs from repeated jarring of a bone. Common sites include bones of the foot.

Fluid Needs

Water (fluid) needs for an average adult are about 1 ml/kcal expended. This is equivalent to about 8 cups of fluid per day. Athletes need this and generally even more water intake to maintain the body's ability to regulate internal temperature and to keep cool. Most energy released during metabolism appears immediately as heat. Furthermore, heat production in contracting muscles can rise 15 to 20 times above that of resting muscles. Unless this heat is quickly dissipated, heat exhaustion, heat cramps, and deadly heatstroke may ensue[16] (Fig. 14-5). In fact, typically three to five athletes die each year of heatstroke, primarily football players. In 2001, both college football players and a professional football player died in such a way.

Heat exhaustion occurs when heat stress causes loss of body fluid and then depletion of blood volume. As environmental temperature rises above 95°F (35°C), virtually all body heat is lost through the evaporation of sweat from the skin. Sweat rates during prolonged exercise range from 3 to 8 cups (750 to 2000 ml) per hour. However, as the

heat exhaustion The first stage of heat-related illness that occurs because of depletion of blood volume from fluid loss by the body. This increases body temperature and can lead to headache, dizziness, muscle weakness, and visual disturbances, among other effects.

Fluid intake during physical activity is important.

heat cramps A frequent complication of heat exhaustion. They usually occur in people who have experienced large sweat losses from exercising for several hours in a hot climate and have consumed a large volume of unsalted water. The cramps occur in skeletal muscles and consist of contractions for 1 to 3 minutes at a time.

heatstroke Heatstroke can occur when internal body temperature reaches 105°F. Sweating generally ceases if left untreated, and blood circulation is greatly reduced. Nervous system damage may ensue, and death is likely. Often the skin of individuals who suffer heatstroke is hot and dry.

humidity rises, especially when it rises above 75%, evaporation slows and sweating becomes inefficient. The result is rapid fatigue, increased work for the heart, and difficulty with prolonged exertion. Clearly, for athletes, the combination of heat and humidity can be as dangerous as extreme cold.

Increased body temperature associated with dehydration is most evident when the amount of water loss exceeds 3% of body weight. This dehydration then leads to a fall in endurance, strength, and overall performance. Wearing football equipment in hot weather can lead to a loss of 2% of body weight in 30 minutes. Marathon runners have been shown to lose 6 to 10% of body weight during a race.

Common symptoms of heat exhaustion include profuse sweating, headache, dizziness, nausea, vomiting, muscle weakness, visual disturbances, and flushing of the skin. A person with heat exhaustion should be taken to a cool environment immediately, and excess clothing should be removed. The body should be sponged with tap water. Fluid replacement, as tolerated, then should suffice to correct the problem.

Heat cramps are a frequent complication of heat exhaustion, but they may appear alone, without other symptoms of dehydration. They usually occur in individuals exercising for several hours in a hot climate who have large sweat losses and have consumed a large volume of unsalted water. It is important not to confuse heat cramps with other forms of muscle cramps, such as those caused by gastrointestinal upset. Heat cramps occur in skeletal muscles, including those of the abdomen and the extremities. They consist of a contraction for 1 to 3 minutes at a time. The cramp moves down the muscle and is associated with excruciating pain. The best way to prevent heat cramps is to exercise moderately at first in the heat and have both an adequate salt intake and fluid intake before engaging in long, strenuous exercise.

Heatstroke can occur when internal body temperature reaches 105°F or more. Related symptoms include nausea, confusion, irritability, poor coordination, seizures, and coma (in severe cases). Exertional heatstroke results from high blood flow to exercising muscles, which overloads the body's cooling capacity. Sweating generally ceases, and the body temperature may become dangerously high. If left untreated, circulatory collapse, central nervous system damage, and death are likely. The death rate is high, approximately 10%.

Many individuals who suffer heatstroke faint, and their skin becomes hot and dry. Ice packs or cold water is the usual recommended immediate treatment until medical help can be summoned. To decrease the risk of developing heatstroke, athletes should replace lost fluids, watch for rapid body-weight changes (2 to 3% or more of body weight), and avoid exercise under extremely hot, humid conditions.

Since dehydration during exercise leads to body-weight loss and sets the stage for heat exhaustion, heat cramps, and potentially fatal heatstroke, athletes must avoid becoming dehydrated. Fluid intake during exercise, when possible, should be adequate to minimize body-weight loss; this practice is a good idea even in the winter, when sweating can go unnoticed.[16]

The recommended goal is a loss of no more than 3% of body weight during exercise. Athletes should first calculate 2 to 3% of their body weight and then by trial and error determine how much fluid they must take in to avoid losing more than this amount of weight during exercise. This determination will be most accurate if an athlete is weighed before and after a typical workout. For every 1 lb (1/2 kg) lost, 3 cups (0.75 L) of water should be consumed during exercise or immediately afterward. Experts now recommend a total of 3 cups (0.75 L) of water per pound lost, rather than the previous recommendation of 2 cups per pound, as some of the fluid replacement will quickly be lost via increased sweating after exercise and increased urine output.[3] Much of this fluid replacement will have to take place after exercise since it is difficult to consume enough fluid during exercise to prevent weight loss. If weight change can't be monitored, urine color is another measure of hydration status. Urine color should be no more yellow than that of lemonade.

Thirst is not a reliable indicator of an athlete's need to replace fluid during exercise. An athlete who drinks only when thirsty is likely to take 48 hours to replenish fluid loss. After several days of training, an athlete relying on thirst as an indicator can build up a large enough fluid debt to impair performance. The following fluid replacement approach can meet athletes' fluid needs in most cases:

- Freely drink beverages (e.g., water, diluted fruit juice, sports drinks) during the 24-hour period before an event, even if not particularly thirsty.
- Drink 1½ to 2½ cups of fluid (400–600 ml) 2 to 3 hours before exercise. This allows time for both adequate hydration and excretion of excess fluid.
- During events lasting more than 30 minutes, consume about ½ to 1½ cup (150–350 ml) of fluid every 15 to 20 minutes as possible beginning at the start of the exercise. Consuming more than 1 quart (1 L) per hour can cause discomfort. On hot days, cold drinks are preferable to help cool the body. Again, the athlete should not wait until he or she feels thirsty. In many cases, athletes especially children and teenagers, need to be reminded to do this.
- After exercise, about 3 cups of fluid should be consumed for every pound lost, as just mentioned. It is also important that weight be restored before the next exercise period. Skipping fluids before or during events will almost certainly cause problems.

A question that often arises is whether to drink water or a sports-type carbohydrate-electrolyte drink (e.g., All Sport, Exceed Energy Drink, Gatorade, PowerAde, and Amino Force) during competition (Fig. 14-6). For sports that require less than 60 minutes of exertion or when total weight loss is less than 5 to 6 lb, the primary concern is replacing the water lost in sweat, because losses of carbohydrate stores and electrolytes (sodium, chloride, potassium, and other minerals) are not usually very great. Although electrolytes are lost in sweat, the quantities lost in exercise of brief to moderate duration can be easily replaced later by consuming normal foods, such as orange juice, potatoes, and tomato juice. Keep in mind that sweat is about 99% water and only 1% electrolytes and other substances.

Beyond 60 minutes of exertion, electrolyte (e.g., sodium and chloride) and carbohydrate replacement becomes increasingly important, especially in hot weather. Use of a sports drink then provides water for hydration, electrolytes both to enhance water and glucose absorption from the intestine and to help maintain blood volume, as well as carbohydrate to provide energy.[3]

Some experts prefer sports drinks over water for all athletes because sports drinks taste better than water. This may help the athlete drink more often—a clear advantage of this form of fluid replenishment. In addition, the carbohydrate in these drinks quickly replaces carbohydrate used during practice or competition, and the sodium present aids in glucose uptake in the small intestine. In addition, the sodium content stimulates thirst, so athletes drink more.

As mentioned before, optimum performance can be enhanced when carbohydrate is replaced throughout endurance exercise as opposed to replacement only near the end of exercise. For this reason, it may be beneficial for endurance athletes to begin carbohydrate replacement using sports drinks or another convenient source early (see Table 14-7 for some ideas).

Overall, the decision to use a sports drink hinges primarily on the duration of the activity. As the projected duration of continuous activity approaches 60 minutes or longer, the advantages of the use of a sports drink over plain water clearly emerge. However, athletes should first experiment with the suggested protocol during practice, instead of trying it for the first time during competition.

As an alternative to the use of sports drinks for providing a source of carbohydrate during prolonged physical activity, some athletes have begun to use carbohydrate gels (e.g., PowerGel, GU, and ClifShot) and so-called energy bars (e.g., PowerBar).[12] The amount to use can be calculated as follows. If one were to use 6 oz of a sports drink every 15 minutes, this would provide 13 g of carbohydrate, or a total of 52 g after 1 hour. One can use gels or energy bars in order to provide the same amount of carbohydrate (check the label for grams of carbohydrate per serving). Interestingly, one fig cookie also provides the 13 g carbohydrate dose (Gummy Bears work as well). Note that any use of these alternate carbohydrate sources must be accompanied by water

Figure 14-6 Sports drinks for fluid and electrolyte replacement typically contain a form of simple carbohydrate plus sodium and potassium. The various sugars in this product total 14 g per 1 cup (240 ml) serving. In percentage terms based on weight, the sugar content is about 6% ([14 g sugar/serving ÷ 240 g/serving] × 100 = 5.8%). Sports drinks typically contain 6 to 8% sugar. This provides ample glucose and other monosaccharides to aid in fueling working muscles, and it is well tolerated. Drinks with a sugar content above 10% may cause stomach distress.

Sports drinks containing glucose polymers (several glucose molecules chemically linked) and simple sugars (e.g., glucose, sucrose) have similar benefits for exercise if the carbohydrate concentration is between 6 and 10%. In addition, both types of sports drinks exit the stomach at similar times. Fructose is the exception, in that it takes longer to exit the stomach and may cause bloating or diarrhea.

Table 14-7 Convenient Pre-event Meals

Breakfast (about 500 kcal and 90 g of carbohydrate)
Cheerios, ¾ cup Reduced fat milk, 1 cup Blueberry muffin, 1 Orange, 1
Low-fat fruit yogurt, 1 cup Cracked wheat bread, 2 slices Apple juice, 4 oz Peanut butter (for bread), 1 tbsp
Whole-wheat toast, 1 slice Apple, 1 large Reduced fat milk, 1 cup Oatmeal, ½ cup Reduced fat milk, ½ cup
Lunch or Dinner (about 800 kcal and 150 g of carbohydrate)
Chili with beans, 8 oz Small baked potato with sour cream and chives Chocolate Frosty
Spaghetti noodles, 2 cups Spaghetti sauce, 1 cup Reduced fat milk, 1½ cups Green beans, 1 cup
Orange, 1 large Reduced fat milk, 1½ cups Chicken noodle soup, 1 cup Whole grain crackers, 12 Green beans, 1 cup Corn, 1 cup Vanilla wafers, 10

With regard to the timing of preactivity meals, the rule of thumb is to allow 4 hours for a big meal (about 1200 kcal), 3 hours for a moderate meal (about 800–900 kcal), 2 hours for a light meal (about 400–600 kcal), and an hour or less for a snack (about 300 kcal).

Alcohol and caffeine both have a dehydrating effect on the body, so fluids containing them should not be part of any hydration plan for exercise, especially before and after exercise.

consumption. In this way, the goal of fluid *and* carbohydrate replacement from the sports drink will be realized. Another thing to consider when using gels and energy bars is that they are relatively expensive.

It is also possible to drink too much water. Ultra-endurance athletes compete at relatively low exercise intensities for prolonged periods of time and therefore may not sweat as much as one might predict. Thus, water losses are not very high. In addition, some of these athletes have used one-half strength Coca-Cola as their fluid-replacement beverage, which is relatively low in sodium, and they drink this at every rest stop. This combination leads to fluid overload, low blood sodium, and low blood chloride. Drinking less fluid and choosing a sports drink containing sodium and chloride can help prevent this problem.[17]

Meals Before Endurance Events Should Emphasize Carbohydrate

A light meal supplying 300 to 1000 kcal should be eaten about 2 to 4 hours before an endurance event to top off muscle and liver glycogen stores, prevent hunger during the event, and provide extra fluid. The longer the period before an event, the larger the meal can be, as there will be more time available for digestion. A pre-event meal should consist primarily of carbohydrate, contain moderate amounts of fat ($<$ 25% of energy intake), relatively little fiber, and include a moderate amount of protein (review Table 14-7).[3] A pre-event meal eaten 1 to 2 hours before an event should be blended or liquid to promote rapid stomach emptying.

Good food choices for a pre-event meal include spaghetti, muffins, cracked wheat or rye bread, bananas, apples, oranges, pears, plums, nuts, and low-sugar breakfast cereals with reduced-fat or nonfat milk. Liquid meal-replacement formulas, such as Carnation Instant Breakfast, also can be used. Foods rich in fiber should be eaten the previous day to help empty the colon before an event, but they should not be eaten the night before or in the morning before the event. Foods to avoid are those that are fatty or fried, such as sausage, bacon, sauces, and gravies. A meal high in carbohydrate is quickly digested, promotes maintenance of blood glucose, and avoids the need to dip right away into glycogen stores.

The selection of carbohydrates for the pre-event meal (and postevent meal) based on their glycemic load is becoming increasingly popular among athletes (see Chapter 5 for a review of glycemic load and a table of values for specific foods). The rationale behind this practice is that the glycemic load of a carbohydrate is a major influence on the insulin response to that carbohydrate: high glycemic load carbohydrates generally cause high insulin responses, and low glycemic load carbohydrates result in lower insulin responses. You know, of course, that insulin is one of the hormones that regulates blood glucose.

An endurance athlete may wish to choose a low glycemic load food before an event in the attempt to achieve a moderate and sustained increase in blood glucose, which will lessen the insulin response (review Table 5-6). This decreased insulin response, in turn, may allow for greater access to the fatty acids from the adipose tissue as a fuel source, preserving glycogen stores for when they are needed late in the race.

In such a pre-event situation, there have been a number of studies that have examined the impact of the feeding of low glycemic load foods and high glycemic load foods 45 minutes to 1 hour prior to exercise. In general, these studies have shown a more favorable metabolic profile for endurance performance—lower blood insulin, higher blood free fatty acids, and more stable blood glucose—with low versus high glycemic load pre-event meals. However, not all these studies have shown improved endurance exercise performance with low glycemic load foods. Still, no detrimental effects have been observed, compared with higher glycemic load foods.

If an athlete feels a pre-event meal harms performance, eating a high carbohydrate diet the day and night before can help meet the same goal. Overall, athletes should experiment with various pre-event carbohydrate feedings to see whether their performance is adversely or positively affected.

Rule of Thumb for Approximate Pre-event Carbohydrate Intake (g)

Hours Before	*g/kg Body Weight (70 kg person)*
1	1 (70)
2	2 (140)
3	3 (210)
4	4 (280)

Carbohydrate Intake During Recovery from Prolonged Exercise

Carbohydrate-rich foods yielding 1.0 to 2 g of carbohydrate per kg body weight should be consumed within 2 hours after extended (endurance) exercise. The sooner this is begun the better, because immediately after exercise is when glycogen synthesis is greatest, as the muscles are very insulin-sensitive at this point. This process should then be repeated over the next 2-hour interval, with an overall goal of 400–600 g/24 hours. Athletes who are training hard can consume a simple sugar candy, sugared soft drink, fruit or fruit juice (e.g., cranapple juice), or a sports-type carbohydrate supplement right after training as they attempt to reload their muscles with glycogen. Later bread, mashed potatoes, and short grain rice can contribute additional carbohydrate. All these high glycemic load carbohydrates especially contribute to glycogen synthesis. Adding some rich protein sources is also recommended, with carbohydrate to protein ratio of about 3:1. For a 154-lb (70-kg) athlete, this corresponds to about 70 g carbohydrate and 25 g protein in each 2-hour interval (Table 14-8). In summary, the following are key factors for achieving the most rapid replenishment of muscle glycogen after exercise: (1) availability of adequate carbohydrate, (2) ingestion of carbohydrate as soon as possible after completion of exercise, (3) selection of high glycemic load carbohydrates, (4) combination of carbohydrate and protein foods, rather than either carbohydrate or protein alone.

Fluid and electrolyte (i.e., sodium and potassium) intake is also an essential component of an athlete's recovery diet. This helps replenish body fluids as quickly as possible. This is especially important if two workouts a day are followed and if the environment is hot and humid. If food and fluid intake is sufficient to restore weight loss, it generally will also supply enough electrolytes to meet needs during recovery from endurance activities.[3]

Table 14-8 Sample Postexercise Meals for Rapid Muscle Glycogen Replacement

Option 1 1 regular bagel 2 tbsp peanut butter, smooth 8 fl oz fat-free milk 1 medium banana 562 kcal, 77 g carbohydrate, 23 g protein, 18 g fat
Option 2 1 packet, Carnation Instant Breakfast 8 oz fat-free milk 1 medium banana 1 tbsp peanut butter Blend until smooth. 438 kcal, 70 g carbohydrate, 17 g protein, 10 g fat
Option 3 1.5 cans GatorPro (11 fl oz/can) 559 kcal, 89 g carbohydrate, 26 g protein, 11 g fat

For more information on sports medicine, visit **www.physsportsmed.com** on the Web. This home page of *The Physician and Sportsmedicine* journal details current issues in sports medicine, including injury prevention, nutrition, and exercise. Also helpful are the Web pages of the Gatorade Sports Science Institute (**www.gssiweb.com**), American College of Sports Medicine (**www.acsm.org**), Centers for Disease Control and Prevention (**www.cdc.gov/nccdphp/dnpa**), and the American Council on Exercise (**www.acefitness.org**).

Concept | Check

All athletes would do well to plan a diet following the Food Guide Pyramid. High-carbohydrate foods should be emphasized, and these should dominate in pre-event meals. Protein intake above twice the RDA is not needed in most cases. If nutrient supplements are used, dosages generally should not exceed the Upper Level set for each nutrient. Fluid should be consumed as liberally as possible before, during, and after an event. Carbohydrate and electrolytes in the fluid are especially helpful when exercise duration is expected to exceed 60 minutes to help delay fatigue and maintain electrolyte balance.

Case Scenario | Follow-up

Marcella is correct in following a high-carbohydrate diet. However, in her effort to minimize her fat intake, she is probably not consuming enough energy to support her training routine. Her diet is also low in protein, as well as calcium, potassium, and fiber. She has fallen into the bagel, pasta, and pretzel routine that sports nutritionists warn is not conducive to peak performance. Marcella would be smart to have a high-protein source at each meal. She could include milk with breakfast and possibly some low-fat yogurt or low-fat cheese at lunch. She should have a carbohydrate/protein snack before her workout, such as a half a sandwich and fruit and some water. The sandwich and fruit will help provide her with fuel to support her vigorous training. During her workouts, she could consume a sports drink to meet fluid needs and supply some carbohydrate, or she could consume water, along with a few fig cookies to provide the carbohydrate. In the evenings, she could substitute oil and vinegar dressing for the fat-free dressing on her salad and cheese and crackers for the pretzels to improve protein intake. Overall, it is important for Marcella to fuel her body before, during, and after workouts.

Summary

1. A gradual increase in regular physical activity is recommended for all healthy persons. A minimum plan includes at least a total of 30 minutes of physical activity on most (if not all) days of the week (60 minutes is even better). A more intense program should begin with warm-up exercises, to increase blood flow and warm the muscles, and end with cooldown exercises. Regular resistance activities and stretching add further benefits.
2. Human metabolic pathways extract chemical energy from food and transform it into ATP, the compound that provides energy for body functions.

3. In glycolysis, glucose is broken down (oxidized) into pyruvic acid, a three-carbon compound, yielding some ATP. The pyruvic acid is metabolized further via the aerobic pathway to form carbon dioxide (CO_2) and water (H_2O) or via the anaerobic pathway to form lactic acid.
4. At rest, muscle cells mainly use fat for fuel. For intense exercise of short duration, muscles mostly use phosphocreatine (PCr) for energy. During more sustained intense activity, muscle glycogen breaks down to lactic acid. For endurance exercise, both fat and carbohydrate are used as fuels; carbohydrate is used increasingly as activity intensifies. Little protein is used to fuel muscles.
5. $VO_{2\ max}$ is a measure of the maximum volume of oxygen one can consume per unit of time. Oxygen consumption is measured by exercising the subject at an increasing pace and workload until fatigue occurs. The amount of oxygen consumed right before total exhaustion is $VO_{2\ max}$. The value of $VO_{2\ max}$ varies among individuals but usually improves with exercise training.
6. Anyone who exercises regularly should consume a diet that meets energy needs and is moderate to high in carbohydrates and fluid.
7. Athletes should consume enough fluid to both minimize loss of body weight and ultimately restore preexercise weight. Sports drinks aid fluid, electrolyte, and carbohydrate replacement. Their use especially should be considered when continuous activity lasts beyond 60 minutes.
8. High glycemic load carbohydrates should be consumed by an athlete within 2 hours after a workout to begin restoration of muscle glycogen stores. Some protein in the meal is also helpful. The use of low glycemic load carbohydrates in the pre-event meal may help some endurance athletes.

Study Questions

1. How does greater physical fitness contribute to greater aerobic metabolism? Explain the process.
2. The store of ATP in muscle is rapidly depleted once contraction begins. For physical activity to continue, ATP must be resupplied immediately. Describe how this occurs after initiation of physical activity and at various times thereafter.
3. What is the difference between anaerobic and aerobic exercise? At what point is the switch made from mostly anaerobic to mostly aerobic fuel metabolism? Explain how aerobic metabolism is enhanced by a regular exercise routine.
4. What is glycogen? How does the body obtain it? How much can be stored? How long does it last during exercise?
5. Is fat from adipose tissue used as an energy source during exercise? If so, when?
6. What is the typical measure of physical fitness? Explain the physiological/biochemical bases for why this is an appropriate measure.
7. Physical activity can be classified into four types: low intensity; moderate intensity; prolonged high intensity (endurance); and brief maximal intensity (very high intensity). Compare and contrast the four types of exercise with respect to the percentage of $VO_{2\ max}$ used and the specific fuels used.
8. List five specific nutrients that athletes need and a nutrient-rich food source for each.
9. What advice would you give to your neighbor, who is planning to run a 50-kilometer (km) race, concerning fluid intake before and during the event?
10. One of your friends, who is a competitive athlete, asks your opinion about a nutritional supplement sold in a local sporting-goods store. She has read that such supplements, which contain vitamins, minerals, and amino acids, can help improve athletic performance. What would you tell her about the general effectiveness of such products?

Annotated References

1. Adams AK, Best TM: The role of antioxidants in exercise and disease prevention. *The Physician and Sportsmedicine* 30(5):37, 2002.

   The efficacy of antioxidant supplementation for preventing exercise-induced oxidative stress is still questionable. In fact, the inflammation and associated oxidative stress from exercise may be important in muscle healing. It is best to focus on an overall diet that contains five to seven servings of fruits and vegetables daily for providing antioxidant protection.

2. Ahrendt DM: Ergogenic aids: Counseling the athlete. *American Family Physician* 63:913, 2001.

   New products with ergogenic claims appear on the market almost daily. Most are classified as supplements, which means the contents of the product and the claims on the label have not been evaluated by FDA and therefore may not have any scientific basis. Supplying adequate fluid and energy intake, and carbohydrate and protein in the diet, and timing these to be used efficiently by the body will provide the most effective and safe results.

3. American College of Sports Medicine and others: Nutrition and Athletic Performance, *Medicine & Science in Sports & Exercise* 32:2130, 2000.

   The athlete who wants to optimize exercise performance needs to follow good nutrition and hydration practices, use supplements and ergogenic aids carefully, minimize severe weight-loss practices, and eat a variety of foods in adequate amounts. The various recommendations for carbohydrate, protein, fat, vitamins, minerals, and fluids in this chapter were taken from this article.

4. American College of Sports Medicine: *ACSM's guidelines for exercise testing and prescription.* 6th ed. Philadelphia: Lippincott, Williams & Wilkins, 2000.

   Detailed protocols are listed for exercise testing and exercise prescriptions by the American College of Sports Medicine. This is a reference for all health professionals in the practice of sports nutrition.

5. Beard J, Tobin B: Iron status and exercise. *American Journal of Clinical Nutrition* 72 (Suppl): 594S, 2000.

   Athletes most likely to develop iron deficiency anemia are female athletes in general, distance runners, and vegetarian athletes. These groups are advised to pay particular attention to maintaining adequate amounts of iron in their diets. They also may want to consider using low-dose iron supplements under medical supervision.

6. Coleman E: Carbohydrate requirements for exercise. *Today's Dietitian*, p. 15, March 2002.

   An intake of 6 to 7 g of carbohydrate per kg of body weight per day is sufficient when an athlete exercises hard for approximately one hour per day. An intake of 8 to 10 g of carbohydrate per kg of body weight per day is recommended when an athlete exercises hard for several hours or more per day.

7. Earnest CP: Dietary androgen supplements: Separating substance from hype. *The Physician and Sportsmedicine* 29(5):63, 2001.

   It is unfortunate that users of androgen supplements see these as a means of obtaining steroidlike results with fewer side effects. The current literature shows that androgens in prohormone supplements do not enhance performance, body composition, or various other parameters associated with good health.

8. Friedenreich CM, Orenstein MR: Physical activity and cancer prevention: etiologic evidence and biological mechanisms. *Journal of Nutrition* 132:3456S, 2002.

   There is good evidence to suggest that regular physical activity reduces the risk of colon cancer and breast cancer, and likely prostate cancer. Physical activity may also reduce the risk of cancer at several other sites.

9. Gilliant-Wimberly M and others: Effects of habitual physical activity on the resting metabolic rate and body composition of women aged 35 to 50 years. *Journal of the American Dietetic Association* 101:1181, 2001.

   Habitual physical activity increases resting metabolic rate in women and is associated with a lower body fat content. Registered dietitians and other health professionals should encourage life-long physical activity for adults of all ages.

10. Kesaniemi YA and others: Dose-response issues concerning physical activity and health: An evidence-based symposium. *Medicine & Science in Sports & Exercise* 33 (Suppl): S351, 2001.

    There is a clear relationship between physical activity and reduced risk of all-cause mortality, cardiovascular disease, and type 2 diabetes. Other health benefits may also accrue, but the relationship for these health outcomes is more difficult to determine given our current knowledge.

11. Lemon PWR: Beyond the Zone: Protein needs for active individuals, *Journal of the American College of Nutrition* 19:513S, 2000.

    Studies indicate that for physically active individuals daily protein intake needs could be as high as 1.6–1.8 g/kg (about twice the current RDA). Despite these increased protein needs, assuming energy intake is sufficient to match the additional expenditures of training and competition (which can be excessive), special protein supplementation is unnecessary for most who consume a varied diet containing protein-rich foods (meat, fish, eggs, and dairy products).

12. Ling N: Performance foods for active individuals: Sports drinks, energy bars and energy gels. *Today's Dietitian,* p. 26, March 2000.

    Sports drinks, energy bars, and energy gels are unnecessary for short workouts. If a preexercise meal or snack has been consumed, use need not begin until an hour into a workout. Bars and gels should be consumed with at least 8 ounces of water, but not with sports drinks. For high-intensity workouts, such as track running or swimming, an energy gel may be a better choice than an energy bar.

13. Manore MM: Effect of physical activity on thiamine, riboflavin, and vitamin B-6 requirements. *American Journal of Clinical Nutrition* 72(Suppl): 598S, 2000.

    Active individuals who restrict their energy intake or make poor dietary choices are at risk for poor B-vitamin status. However, the amount of these nutrients needed to cover losses or increased needs resulting from physical activity is small and can be met easily through wise food choices.

14. Sarubin A: *The health professionals' guide to popular dietary supplements.* Chicago: The American Dietetic Association, 2000.

    The author provides a detailed look at individual dietary supplements, including those used by athletes. One example is creatine, which may increase strength/power during short bouts of exercise.

15. Schmidt WD and others: Effects of long versus short bouts of exercise on fitness and weight loss in overweight females. *Journal of the American College of Nutrition* 20:494, 2001.

    Exercise accumulated in short bouts throughout the day is sufficient to contribute to fitness and weight loss.

16. Wexler R: Evaluation and treatment of heat-related illnesses. *American Family Physician* 65:2037, 2002.

    Both heat cramps and heat exhaustion can lead to weakness. These are typically treated with fluid and electrolyte replacement, as well as placing the person in a cool environment. On the other hand, heatstroke is a medical emergency that should be treated immediately with temperature-lowering techniques, such as immersion in an ice bath. Prevention of all three disorders is very important.

17. Williams MH: *Nutrition for health, fitness, & sport.* 6th ed. Boston: McGraw-Hill, 2002.

    Excellent textbook for reviewing nutrient needs of athletes, as well as learning more about ergogenic aids; also provides a detailed look at metabolism in exercise.

18. Wilmore JH: Physical energy: Fuel metabolism. *Nutrition Reviews* 59(1):S13, 2001.

    There are a number of systems the muscles use to provide ATP energy. These include phosphocreatine, anaerobic and aerobic glycolysis, and fatty acid oxidation. An adequate carbohydrate intake during prolonged strenuous activity is especially beneficial to delay fatigue associated with greater use of anaerobic glycolysis.

19. Wyatt HR, Hill JO: Let's get serious about promoting physical activity. *American Journal of Clinical Nutrition* 75:449, 2002.

    A general increase in physical activity is an important goal for both treating and combating obesity. The recommendation of 30 minutes of such activity on most (or all) days should be seen as a minimum; more time spent may provide even greater health benefits.

20. Your Exercise Rx. *Nutrition Action Health Letter* p. 1, December 2002.

    For most people brisk walking is the best exercise. Strength training is also an important part of maintaining overall health throughout life. The article provides much advice related to this topic.

Take | Action

I. Is Your Diet Measuring Up to the Numbers?

In this chapter, several key nutrients were discussed in relation to exercise performance. The following guidelines were mentioned, not only for athletes but for everyone maintaining generally good fitness.

- Eat a moderate to high amount of carbohydrates (generally 60% or more of total energy intake).
- Athletes should eat a minimum of 1.2 g of protein per kg of body weight.
- Consume the recommended standards of vitamins and minerals, making sure iron and calcium intakes are adequate (especially for women).
- Consume enough fluid, especially to approximately maintain weight during prolonged exercise or in hot conditions.

Review the results of the dietary assessment you completed in Chapter 2. Remember that you analyzed a 1-day food intake. Now answer the following questions, whether or not you consider yourself an athlete.

1. What percentage of your energy intake came from carbohydrate? Was your carbohydrate intake 60% or more of your total energy intake?

   ____

2. Did you eat at least 0.8 g of protein per kg of body weight? If you are an athlete, did you consume at least 1.2 g per kg of body weight? Did intake exceed 2 g per kg of body weight?

   ____

   ____

3. Did you consume your estimated needs of all vitamins and minerals, especially iron and calcium? Which ones were below the current nutrient standards?

   ____

   ____

4. For nutrients low in your diet, list one rich food source (see Chapters 9 through 12).

   ____

   ____

5. Did you consume sufficient fluid—about 8 cups for a good starting point?

   ____

   ____

6. What can you do to improve your dietary intake to aid general fitness and, if you are an athlete, to promote maximal performance in your chosen event(s)?

   ____

   ____

   ____

   ____

   ____

Take | Action

II. Evaluating Protein Intake—A Case Study.

Marcus is a college student who has been lifting weights at the student recreation center. The trainer at the center recommended a protein drink to help Marcus build muscle mass. Evaluate Marcus's current food intake and determine whether a protein drink is needed to supplement Marcus's diet.

1. The following is a tally of yesterday's intake.

Breakfast	Frosted Mini-Wheats cereal, 2 oz
	1% milk, 1½ cups
	Orange juice, chilled, 6 oz
	Glazed yeast doughnut, 1
	Brewed coffee, 1 cup
Lunch	Double hamburger with condiments, 1
	French fries, 30
	Cola, 12 oz
	Medium apple, 1
Dinner	Frozen lasagna w/meat, 2 pieces
	1% milk, 1 cup
	Looseleaf lettuce, chopped, 1 cup
	Creamy Italian salad dressing, 2 tsp
	Medium tomato, ½
	Whole carrot, raw, 1
Evening snack	Vanilla ice cream, 1 cup
	Hot fudge chocolate topping, 2 tsp
	Soft chocolate chip cookies, 2

Evaluate Marcus's diet—is he meeting the minimum recommendations of the Food Guide Pyramid? ________________

2. Marcus's weight has been stable at 70 kg (154 lb). Determine his protein needs based on the RDA (0.8 g per kg).
   a. Marcus's estimated protein RDA: ________________
   b. What are the maximum recommendations for protein intake for strength-training athletes (see p. 520)? ________________
   c. Apply the maximum recommendations to Marcus. ________________

3. An analysis of the total energy and protein content of Marcus's current diet is 3470 kcal, 125 g of protein (14% of total energy supplied by protein). This diet is representative of the food choices and amounts of food that Marcus chooses on a regular basis.
   a. What is the difference between Marcus's estimated protein needs as an athlete (from Part 2) and the amount of protein that his current diet provides? ________________
   b. Is his current protein intake inadequate, adequate, or excessive? ________________

4. Marcus takes his trainer's advice and goes to the supermarket to purchase a protein drink to add to his diet. Four products are available; they contain the following label information.

	Amino Fuel	Joe Weider's Sugar-Free 90% Plus Protein	Joe Weider's Dynamic Muscle Builder	Victory Super Mega Mass 2000
Serving size	3 tbsp	3 tbsp	3 tbsp	¼ scoop
Kcal	104	110	103	104
Protein (g)	15	24	10	5

The trainer recommends adding the supplement to Marcus's diet two times a day. Marcus chooses Joe Weider's Dynamic Muscle Builder.

a. How much protein would be added to Marcus's diet daily from two servings of the supplement alone (prior to mixing it with a beverage)?
b. Marcus mixes the powder with the milk he already consumes at breakfast and dinner. How much protein total would Marcus now consume in 1 day? (Add the protein amount from the nutrition analysis to the value from the previous question.)
c. What is the difference between Marcus's estimated protein needs as an athlete and this total value?

5. What is your conclusion—does Marcus need the protein supplement?

Answers to Calculations

2a. Marcus's estimated protein RDA: 70 kg × 0.8 g/kg = 56 g

2b. Maximum recommendation for protein intake for athletes = 1.6 to 1.8 g/kg (use the value of 1.8 for the calculation)

2c. Applied to Marcus: 1.8 × 70 = 126 g

3a. Difference between Marcus's estimated maximum protein needs if an athlete and the amount of protein provided by his current diet:
126 − 125 = 1 g protein

3b. Marcus's current diet is adequate

4a. Two servings of protein supplement alone = 20 g of protein

4b. Marcus's total protein consumption: 125 g + 20 g = 145 g protein

4c. Difference between Marcus's estimated maximum protein needs as an athlete and total value (from above): 145 g − 126 g = 19 g protein

Evaluating Ergogenic Aids to Enhance Athletic Performance

Attention to carbohydrate and fluid needs—along with meeting overall nutrient needs—is the most important ergogenic aid.

Diet manipulation to improve athletic performance is not a recent innovation. As long as 30 years ago, American football players were encouraged on hot practice days to "toughen up" for competition by liberally consuming salt tablets before and during practice and by not drinking water. Now it is widely recognized that this practice can be fatal. Today's athletes are as likely as their predecessors to experiment with artichoke hearts, bee pollen, dried adrenal glands from cattle, seaweed, freeze-dried liver flakes, gelatin, and ginseng. These are just some of the ineffective substances used by athletes in hopes of gaining an **ergogenic** (work-producing) edge.

Ergogenic aids are classified into five categories:

1. *Mechanical aids* are designed to increase energy efficiency—to provide a mechanical edge. Runners may use lightweight racing shoes in place of heavier ones to increase the economy of running.
2. *Psychological aids* are designed to enhance psychological processes during sport performance—to increase mental strength. Hypnosis, through posthypnotic suggestion, may help remove psychological barriers that can limit physiological performance.
3. *Physiological aids* are designed to augment natural physiological processes to increase physiological power. Some athletes use creatine supplements to increase creatine phosphate in muscles. One intent is to provide more energy for activities that use primarily creatine phosphate, such as weight lifting and sprinting.
4. *Pharmacological aids* are drugs designed to influence physiological or psychological processes to increase physical power or mental strength. Some athletes use androstenedione to boost testosterone levels with the intent of increasing muscle mass. (This practice, however, can lead to many side effects, as discussed later in this Nutrition Perspective.)
5. *Nutritional aids* are nutrients designed to influence physiological or psychological processes to increase physical power or mental strength. Sports drinks have been used to supply fluid, electrolytes, and glucose to offset that used (or lost) during prolonged physical activity.

ergogenic Work-producing. An ergogenic aid is a mechanical, nutritional, psychological, physiological, or pharmacological substance or treatment that is intended to directly improve exercise performance.

Of these five classes of ergogenic aids, the final three will be discussed. Based on what is known at this time, today's athletes can benefit from recent scientific evidence documenting the ergogenic properties of a few dietary substances. These ergogenic aids include sufficient water and electrolytes, lots of carbohydrates, and a balanced and varied diet consistent with the Food Guide Pyramid (or related pyramid). Protein and amino acid supplements are not among those aids because athletes can easily meet protein needs from foods, as Table 14-4 demonstrated. The use of nutrient supplements should be designed to meet a specific dietary shortcoming, such as an inadequate iron intake. These and other aids, which often have dubious benefits and may pose health risks, must be given close scrutiny before use. The risk-benefit ratio of any ergogenic aids especially needs to be examined.

As summarized in Table 14-9, no scientific evidence supports the effectiveness of many substances touted as performance-enhancing aids.[14] Many are useless; some are dangerous. Athletes should be skeptical of any substance until its ergogenic effect is scientifically verified. FDA has a limited ability to regulate these dietary supplements (review Chapter 1). As well, the manufacturing processes for dietary supplements are not as tightly regulated by FDA as they are for prescription drugs. Some may contain substances that will cause athletes to "test positive" for anabolic steroid use. This was shown to be the case in the 2002 Winter Olympics. Recent studies also have called into question the quality control associated with the manufacturing of dietary supplements. For example, a study looked at 16 brands of dehydroepiandrosterone (DHEA) purchased from health-food stores. As noted in Table 14-9, DHEA is a supplement that is claimed to increase muscle mass, decrease body fat, and increase blood testosterone. The study showed that only 7 of the 16 brands had a DHEA content within 90 to 110% of the stated label claim; 3 products had essentially no DHEA at all.

These results add yet another worry for the athlete. Not only must the athlete determine whether there is evidence that a dietary supplement is safe and effective (FDA does not regulate dietary supplements), but now must also question if the dietary supplement contains what it is supposed to contain.[2] To obtain information on independent laboratory tests on the quality of dietary supplements, the following website is helpful: www.consumerlab.com.

Table 14-9 An Evaluation of Ergogenic Aids Currently in the Limelight[2,14,17]

Substance/Practice	Alleged Benefit	Reality
Useful in Some Circumstances		
Creatine	Increase phosphocreatine (PCr) in muscles to keep ATP concentration high	Use of 20 g per day for 5 to 6 days and then a maintenance dose of 2 g per day may improve performance in those who undertake repeated bursts of activity, such as in sprinting and weight lifting. Some of the muscle weight gain noted with use results from water contained in muscles. Endurance athletes do not benefit from use. Little is known about the safety of long-term creatine use. Continual use of high doses has led to kidney damage in a few cases. Cost: $25–$65 per month.
Bicarbonate	Counter lactic acid buildup	Partially effective in some circumstances, such as wrestling, but induces nausea and diarrhea. The dose used is 300 mg/kg, given 1 to 3 hours before exercise. Cost: nil.
Caffeine	Increase use of fatty acids to fuel muscles, promote psychological effects	Drinking two to three 5-oz cups of coffee (equivalent to 3–9 mg of caffeine per kg of body weight) about 1 hour before events lasting about 5 minutes or longer is useful for some athletes; benefits are less apparent in those who have ample stores of glycogen, are highly trained, or habitually consume caffeine; intake of more than about 600 mg (6–8 cups of coffee) elicits a urine concentration illegal under Olympic rules (12 μg/ml). NCAA rules allow 15 μg/ml. A possible side effect is reduced body hydration. Cost: $0.08 per 300 mg.
Possibly Useful, Still Under Study		
Hydroxy-beta-methylbutyric acid (HMB)	Decrease protein catabolism, causing a net growth-promoting effect	Research in livestock and humans suggests that supplementation with HMB may increase muscle mass. Still, safety and effectiveness of long-term HMB use in humans is unknown. Cost: $100 per month.
Glutamine (an amino acid)	Enhance immune function, preserve lean body mass	Glutamine is the most abundant amino acid in plasma, and preservation of lean body mass levels fall in glycogen-depleted athletes. Overtrained athletes also have lower glutamine levels. Glutamine may be needed during metabolic stress and critical illness, and it is important for immunity. Some preliminary studies show decreased occurrence of upper respiratory tract infections in athletes with use. It also may promote muscle growth, but long-term studies are lacking. Protein foods are a rich source of glutamine. Cost: $10–$20 per month for 1 to 2 g per day.
Branched-chain amino acids (BCAA) (leucine, isoleucine, valine)	Important energy source, especially when carbohydrate stores are depleted. A high ratio of free tryptophan: BCAA in the brain increases serotonin in the brain, which depresses the central nervous system and causes fatigue.	Supplementation of BCAA (7–10 g/day) can increase BCAA in the blood when it has been lowered due to exercise, but there is no consistent evidence of improved performance. Carbohydrate feeding, by delaying use of BCAA as fuel, may negate the need for BCAA supplementation. Preliminary studies show that BCAA use increases muscle mass more than does carbohydrate supplementation alone in swimmers, but there are no studies regarding resistance training. Protein-rich foods are also rich in BCAA. Cost: $20 per month.
Useful in Some Circumstances, but Dangerous or Illegal		
Anabolic steroids	Increase muscle mass and strength	Although effective for increasing protein synthesis, are illegal in the United States unless prescribed by a physician; have numerous potential side effects, such as premature closure of growth plates in bones (thus possibly limiting the adult height of a teenage athlete), bloody cysts in the liver, increased risk of cardiovascular disease, increased blood pressure, and reproductive dysfunction. Possible psychological consequences include increased aggressiveness, drug dependence (addiction), withdrawal symptoms (such as depression), sleep disturbances, and mood swings (known as "roid rage"). Use of needles for injectable forms adds further health risk. Banned by the International Olympic Committee.
Growth hormone	Increase muscle mass	At critical ages may increase height; may also cause uncontrolled growth of the heart and other internal organs and even death; potentially dangerous; requires careful monitoring by a physician. Use of needles for injections adds further health risk. Banned by the International Olympic Committee.

(continues)

Table 14-9 Continued

Substance/Practice	Alleged Benefit	Reality
Insulin-like growth factor (IGF-1)	Increase muscle mass, enhance fat metabolism	Use can lead to enlargement of organs (as with growth hormone, as they have related functions in the body), back pain, headache, and difficulty breathing. Bovine colostrum is a new and expensive source of IGF-1. Use of needles for injections adds further health risk. Cost: $30 per month.
Blood doping	Red blood cells harvested previously from the athlete and then injected into the bloodstream, or alternately the athlete may use the hormone erythropoietin (Epogen) to increase red blood cell number in order to try to enhance aerobic capacity.	May offer aerobic benefit; very serious health consequences are possible, including thickening of the blood, which puts extra strain on the heart; is an illegal practice under Olympic guidelines.
Gamma hydroxybutyric acid (GHB)	Promoted as a steroid alternative for bodybuilding	FDA has never approved it for sale as a medical product; is illegal to produce or sell GHB in the United States. GHB-related symptoms include vomiting, dizziness, tremors, and seizures. Many victims have required hospitalization, and some have died. Clandestine laboratories produced virtually all of the chemical accounting for GHB abuse. FDA is working with the U.S. Attorney General's office to arrest, indict, and convict individuals responsible for the illegal operations.
Androstenedione	Increase muscle mass	Possibly converted to testosterone and estrogen but does not increase muscle mass. Its use is banned by the NFL, NCAA, and International Olympic Committee. Side effects are acne, fits of rage, baldness, development of breasts in men, stunted growth, lower HDL-cholesterol in the blood, and sterility. Cost: $30 per month.
Insulin	Promote muscle development and inhibit muscle breakdown	Use can lead to seizures, hypoglycemia, and resulting brain damage. The need for injection can lead to increased risk of hepatitis and other viral diseases. Overall, unsupervised use of this powerful hormone is fraught with danger to one's health.
Ephedrine	Increase stamina and exercise performance. When combined with caffeine, thought to decrease appetite and increase fat use.	No evidence that it enhances performance. Ephedrine (ephedra or ma juang in the herbal form) is currently under scrutiny by FDA due to more than 1000 reports of detrimental effects and at least 100 deaths. FDA is currently reviewing rules that would dictate amount of ephedrine allowed in each pill and taken within a 24-hour period, as well as a warning system on labels. Provisional advice is to consume no more than 25 mg per day for a total of 7 days, if at all. Ephedrine has caused heart attack, stroke, anxiety, seizure, and death. People who have hypertension, cardiovascular disease, diabetes, thyroid gland disorders, prostate gland enlargement, or nerve disease should not take ephedrine. Use is especially risky when combined with large quantities of caffeine (this is common). Recently banned for football players in the NFL. Cost: $0.08 per 25 mg.
Effectiveness not clearly demonstrated (or no benefit)		
Alcohol	Reduce fatigue, provide energy	Not a muscle fuel; actually impairs performance; abuse can lead to hypoglycemia and dehydration.
Medium chain triglyceride (MCT oil)	Excellent fuel for muscles; transfers directly from GI tract into bloodstream	Can provide a source of energy for muscles but provides no advantage over carbohydrate intake alone, and is very expensive. Doses over 25 to 30 g at one time lead to nausea and diarrhea, also it is not tolerated well by athletes. Cost: $50 per month.
Phosphate loading	Improve oxygen delivery to muscles	Not effective. A current trend is to combine phosphates with creatine when using the latter. Cost: $2 per month for phosphate supplement.
Inosine	Increase protein and ATP synthesis	Not effective. Cost: $18 per month.
Coenzyme Q-10	Increase energy metabolism	Sufficient amount is produced by the body for energy metabolism. May also lead to increased free radical damage in cells during exercise. Cost: $16 per month.

(continues)

Table 14-9 Continued

Substance/Practice	Alleged Benefit	Reality
Carnitine	Shuttle fatty acids into mitochondria of cells	Body cells produce enough; therefore, use is ineffective. Cost: $14 per month.
Chromium	Enhance insulin function	No benefit in performance. American College of Sports Medicine states that supplementation is unnecessary. Large doses can lead to kidney failure and possible damage to DNA in cells. Cost: $2 per month.
Conjugated linoleic acid (CLA)	Reduce body fat and increase lean mass	May be effective at doses of 3 to 7 g per day. Many supplements on the market are of poor quality. Cost: $30–$70 per month.
Ornithine, arginine (human growth hormone releasers)	Used to increase human growth hormone output for muscle growth	Studies with unrealistically high doses of these amino acids (over 10 g per day) given intravenously have been shown to increase human growth hormone. However, recent studies with more reasonable doses (2–4 g per day) as commercial dietary supplements have shown no effects on human growth hormone. In addition, the increase in human growth hormone (even if the amino acids were effective) would be of questionable value and may even be harmful (see the section in this table on growth hormone). Cost: $15 per month.
Amino acids not already mentioned	Increase bioavailability to promote protein synthesis and lessen the muscle loss that occurs during both strength and endurance exercise	Of no value; dietary protein intake is sufficient to meet amino acid needs.
Dehydroepiandrosterone (DHEA)	Increase production of testosterone and provide an anabolic steroid effect	Studies to date are inconclusive. Side effects are masculine traits in women, including hair loss and voice deepening. Men may develop irreversible breast development and prostate gland enlargement, possibly leading to prostate cancer. Recently banned by International Olympic Committee. Use is not recommended. Cost: $14–$52 per month.
Albuterol and clembuterol	Train harder as to increase muscle strength and mass	No immediate ergogenic effect on either power or endurance in humans.
Pyruvate	Increase energy available to muscles	No benefit with use in trained athletes. Cost: $125 per month.
Vanadyl sulfate (vanadium)	Has insulin-like effects on carbohydrate and amino acid metabolism; used to promote muscle growth and decrease body fat	Doses of 0.5 mg per kg per day for 12 weeks did not alter body composition in weight trainers (normal diet contains about 0.1–0.3 mg per day). Exceeding the Upper Level (1.8 mg per day) can lead to kidney toxicity. Cost: $20 per month.
Hydroxycitrate (HCA) (*Garcinia cambogia*)	HCA is a competitive inhibitor of an enzyme involved in the synthesis of fat from carbohydrate; used as a fat-burner.	Some poorly designed studies found body fat loss with HCA; however, the HCA was often given in combination with other herbs, vitamins, or minerals. A recent study with a more appropriate experimental design showed no impact of HCA (1500 mg per day), along with a 1200-kcal diet, on weight loss or body fat loss, compared to the diet alone. Cost: $30 per month.
Glycerol	Increase fluid retention in the body mass, enhancing body hydration	Limited research and small numbers of subjects used in studies provide conflicting evidence regarding the usefulness of glycerol in enhancing physical performance. Until more studies are completed, the claim that glycerol enhances sports performance is unsupported. Use of glycerol may produce headache and blurred vision, which could interfere with athletic performance. Cost: $30 per month.

(continues)

Table 14-9 Concluded

Substance/Practice	Alleged Benefit	Reality
Aspartates	May help reduce ammonia accumulation in muscles	Magnesium and/or potassium salts of aspartic acid have been used as potential aids to endurance performance. The small number of subjects used in current studies makes interpretation of the results difficult. To date, aspartate salts do not appear to reduce accumulation of ammonia in the blood. Until additional controlled trials with larger numbers of subjects are conducted, supplementation is not warranted. There appears to be no toxicity with the doses used in reported studies. Cost: $11 per month.
Ribose	Increase ATP synthesis	Although the monosaccharide ribose is part of the ATP molecule, no studies support the concept that increasing ribose intake increases ATP availability during physical activity. However, studies are underway with the product. Cost: $50 per month.

Even substances whose ergogenic effects have been supported by systematic scientific studies should be used with caution, as the testing conditions may not match those of the intended use.

The NCAA's Committee on Competitive Safeguards and Medical Aspects of Sports has developed lists of supplements that are permissible and nonpermissible for athletic departments to dispense. Following are key examples:

Permissible	**Nonpermissible**
Vitamins and minerals	Amino acids
"Energy" bars (if no more than 30% protein)	Creatine
Sports drinks	Glycerol
Meal replacement drinks such as Ensure Plus or Boost	HMB
	L-carnitine
	Protein powders

Finally, rather than waiting for a magic bullet to enhance performance, athletes are advised to concentrate their efforts on improving their training routines and sport techniques, while consuming well-balanced diets, as described in this chapter.[2]

chapter 15

Eating Disorders: Anorexia Nervosa, Bulimia Nervosa, Binge-Eating Disorder, and Other Conditions

Chapter | Outline

Case | Scenario

At age 16, Sarah suddenly became self-conscious about her body when the neighborhood children teased her about being overweight. She began exercising to an aerobics video for an hour each day and found that she had success in losing weight; this was just the beginning of her obsession to be thin. Next, Sarah turned to eating less food to lose even more weight and began eliminating certain foods from her diet, such as candy and meat. She increased her water and vegetable intake and chewed sugarless gum to curb her appetite. Once she began dieting, it was impossible for her to stop. She really enjoyed having a high degree of self-control over her body. She was literally obsessed with food and stared at others while they were eating a meal. She cooked large meals and then refused to eat all but a few bites. By the time Sarah was 19 years old and 5 feet 6 inches tall, her weight had dropped from 150 pounds to 85 pounds in 20 months. Her family was concerned about her weight status, demanding that she go to a physician for an evaluation. Sarah was not happy about this idea but believed that her family would stop pestering her if she just did this. Sarah did not think she had a problem; she truly thought she was still grotesquely overweight. She did notice, however, that she was intolerant of cold temperatures and had not menstruated in a year.

Does Sarah meet the qualifications to be diagnosed with an eating disorder? What types of therapy do you think the physician will suggest for Sarah? Where could she go for such therapy? What is the likelihood that she will fully recover from her condition?

Refresh | Your Memory

As you begin your study of eating disorders, such as anorexia nervosa and bulimia nervosa, in Chapter 15, you may want to review:

- The role of genetic risk in disease susceptibility in Chapter 1.
- The effects and treatment of osteoporosis in Chapter 11.
- The effects and treatment of iron deficiency anemia in Chapter 12.
- The distinction between hunger and appetite in Chapter 13.
- Calculation of BMI in Chapter 13.
- The effects of neurotransmitters on food intake in Chapter 13.

Boost | Your Study

Check out the ***Perspectives in Nutrition: Online Learning Center*** www.mhhe.com/wardlawpers6 *for quizzes, flash cards, activities, and web links designed to further help you learn about eating disorders.*

Chapter | Objectives

Chapter 15 is designed to allow you to:

1. Contrast health attitudes toward uses of food with behavior patterns that could lead to unhealthy uses of food.
2. Outline the causes of, effects of, typical persons affected by, and treatment for anorexia nervosa.
3. Outline the causes of, effects of, typical persons affected by, and treatment for bulimia nervosa.
4. Describe still other forms of eating disorders: binge-eating disorder, female athlete triad, and baryophobia.
5. Relate the presence of eating disorders to current social trends.
6. Describe methods to reduce the development of eating disorders, including the use of warning signs to identify early cases.

Although obesity is the most common eating disorder in our society, the eating disorders explored in this chapter involve much more severe distortions of the eating process. The eating disorders discussed here are serious and can develop into life-threatening conditions if left untreated. What's most alarming about these disorders—such as anorexia nervosa, bulimia nervosa, binge-eating disorder, and female athlete triad—is the increasing number of cases for many of these disorders reported each year.[1]

Some people are more receptive and vulnerable to these disorders than other people are—for genetic, psychological, and physical reasons.[5] And keep in mind that eating disorders are not restricted to any socioeconomic class or ethnicity. They can also strike at any age in both females and males.[2, 10] Let's examine the causes and treatments of these conditions in detail, because these eating disorders touch many of our lives.

From Ordered to Disordered Eating Habits

Eating—a completely instinctive behavior for animals—serves an extraordinary number of psychological, social, and cultural purposes for humans. Eating practices may take on religious meanings; signify bonds among family, cultural, and ethnic groups; and be a means to express hostility and affection, prestige, and class values. Similarly, providing, preparing, and distributing food may be a means of expressing love or hatred, or even power, in family relationships.

In our society, we are bombarded daily with images of the ideal body.[6] Dieting is promoted to achieve this ideal body—eternally young and acceptable to those around us. Television programs, billboard advertisements, magazine pictures, movies, and newspapers tell us that an ultra-slim body will bring happiness, love, and even success. This is despite the fact that much of society is becoming fatter. In response, some of us take this to the other extreme—the pathological pursuit of weight control or weight loss.

Not comparing media images with our own is hard. Not everyone can look like a fashion model. People who are overly susceptible to these messages, for genetic, psychological, and physical reasons, may be more likely than others to develop eating disorders in response.

Given the multiple functions associated with normal eating and the media bombardment about ideal body image, it is not surprising that some people progress from typical responses to hunger and satiety cues, to obsessive weight loss, and then to a full-blown eating disorder, often associated with unusual and strange rituals.

Progression from Ordered to Disordered Eating

Attention to hunger and satiety signals; limitation of energy intake to restore weight to a healthful level

↓

Some disordered eating habits begin as weight loss is attempted, such as very restricted eating

↓

Clinically evident eating disorder recognized

Food: More Than Just a Source of Nutrients

From birth, we link food with personal and emotional experiences. As infants, we associate milk with security and warmth, so the breast or bottle becomes a source of comfort as well as food. As noted in Chapter 1, even when older, most people continue to derive comfort and great pleasure from food. This is both a biological and a psychological phenomenon. Food can be a symbol of comfort, but eating can also stimulate the release of certain neurotransmitters (e.g., serotonin) and natural opioids (including endorphins), which produce a sense of calm and euphoria in the human body. Thus, in times of great stress some people turn to food for a druglike, calming effect.

Food is also used as a reward or a bribe. Haven't you heard or spoken something similar to the following comments?

You can have your dessert if you eat five more bites of your vegetables.
You can't play until you clean your plate.
I'll eat the broccoli if you let me watch TV.
If you love me, you'll eat what I fixed for dinner.

On the surface, using food as a reward or bribe seems harmless enough. Eventually, however, this practice encourages both caregivers and children to use food to achieve unstated goals. Food may then become much more than a source of nutrients. Regularly using food as a bargaining chip can contribute to abnormal eating patterns. Carried to the extreme, these patterns can lead to **disordered eating.**[3]

This disordered eating can be defined as mild and short-term changes in eating patterns that occur in relation to a stressful event, an illness, or even a desire to modify the diet for a variety of health and personal appearance reasons. The problem may be no more than a bad habit, a style of eating adapted from friends or family members, or an aspect of preparing for athletic competition. While disordered eating can lead to weight loss or weight gain and to certain nutritional problems, it rarely requires in-depth professional attention. If, however, disordered eating becomes sustained, distressing, or starts to interfere with everyday activities, it may require professional intervention.

disordered eating Mild and short-term changes in eating patterns that occur in relation to a stressful event, an illness, or a desire to modify one's diet for a variety of health and personal appearance reasons.

Overview of Anorexia Nervosa and Bulimia Nervosa

eating disorder Severe alterations in eating patterns linked to physiological changes. The alterations are associated with food restricting, binge eating, purging, and fluctuations in weight. They also involve a number of emotional and cognitive changes that affect the way a person perceives and experiences his or her body.

anorexia nervosa An eating disorder involving a psychological loss or denial of appetite and self-starvation, related in part to a distorted body image and to various social pressures commonly associated with puberty.

bulimia nervosa An eating disorder in which large quantities of food are eaten at one time (binge eating) and then purged from the body by vomiting, or misuse of laxatives, diuretics, or enemas. Alternate means to counteract the caloric excess use are fasting and excessive exercise. The use of nervosa refers to the person's disgust with one's body.

binge-eating disorder An eating disorder characterized by recurrent binge eating and feelings of loss of control over eating that has lasted at least 6 months. Binge episodes can be triggered by frustration, anger, depression, anxiety, permission to eat forbidden foods, and excessive hunger.

hypergymnasia Exercising more than is required for good physical fitness or maximal performance in a sport; excessive exercise.

Given the common practice of dieting in North America, it can sometimes be difficult to tell where disordered eating stops and an **eating disorder** begins. Indeed, many eating disorders get their start from a simple diet. Eating disorders then go on to involve physiological changes associated with food restricting, binge eating, purging, and fluctuations in weight. They also involve a number of emotional and cognitive changes that affect the way a person perceives and experiences his or her body, such as feelings of distress or extreme concern about body shape or weight (Fig. 15-1). Eating disorders are not due to a failure of will or behavior; rather, they are real, treatable medical illnesses in which certain maladaptive patterns of eating take on a life of their own.[13]

The main types of eating disorders are **anorexia nervosa** and **bulimia nervosa.** A third type, **binge-eating disorder,** has been recognized by the psychiatric community since 1994. Currently, scientists are researching whether binge-eating disorder should be included as a diagnosable disease alongside anorexia nervosa and bulimia nervosa. More than 5 million people in North America have one of these disorders; females outnumber males 5 to 1. Eating disorders frequently develop during adolescence or early adulthood (85% of the time), but some reports indicate their onset can occur during childhood or later in adulthood. Eating disorders frequently co-occur with other psychological disorders such as depression, substance abuse, and anxiety disorders. *People who suffer from eating disorders, especially anorexia nervosa and bulimia nervosa, can experience a wide range of physical health complications, including serious heart conditions and kidney failure, which may even lead to death.* Recognition of eating disorders as important and treatable diseases, therefore, is critical.[3]

Currently, up to 5% of women in North America develop some form of anorexia nervosa or bulimia nervosa in their lifetimes.[3] This section provides a brief description of the characteristics and diagnoses of these two disorders which primarily afflict those of college age and younger. Detailed discussion of these and related disorders, including treatment, then follows.

Anorexia nervosa is characterized by extreme weight loss, a distorted body image, and an irrational, almost morbid, fear of obesity and weight gain. Anorexic patients irrationally believe they are fat, even though others constantly comment on their thin physique. Some anorexics realize they are thin but are habitually haunted by certain areas of their bodies that they believe to be fat (such as thighs, buttocks, and stomach). The discrepancy between actual and perceived body shape is an important gauge of the severity of the disease.[18]

The term *anorexia* implies a loss of appetite; however, denying one's appetite more accurately describes the behavior of people with anorexia nervosa. By rough estimate, approximately 0.5% (1 in 200) adolescent girls in North America eventually develops anorexia nervosa. This high number may be due to the tendency for these females to blame themselves for the weight gain seen at that age. It happens less commonly among adult women and African American women. Men only account for approximately 10% of the cases of anorexia nervosa, partly because the ideal image conveyed for men is big and muscular. Among men, athletes are most prone to develop this (and other) eating disorders, especially those who participate in sports that require weight classes, such as boxers, wrestlers, and jockeys. Other activities that may foster eating disorders in men include swimming, dancing, and modeling.[16]

Bulimia nervosa (*bulimia* means "great [ox] hunger") is characterized by episodes of binge eating followed by attempts to purge the excess energy taken up by the body by vomiting or misuse of laxatives, diuretics, or enemas. Fasting and excessive exercise **(hypergymnasia)** also may be used to compensate for the caloric excess. People with this disorder may be difficult to identify because they keep their binge-purge behaviors secret, and their symptoms are not obvious. Up to 4% or more of adolescent and college-age women suffer from bulimia nervosa.[3] About 10% of the cases occur in men.

The *Diagnostic and Statistical Manual of Mental Disorders* lists specific criteria for diagnosing eating disorders (Table 15-1.).[3] People may exhibit some symptoms of an

Table 15-1 Diagnostic Criteria for Anorexia Nervosa and Bulimia Nervosa

Anorexia Nervosa

A. Refusal to maintain body weight at or above a minimally normal weight for age and height (e.g., weight loss leading to maintenance of body weight less than 85% of that expected; or failure to make expected weight gain during periods of growth, leading to body weight less than 85% of that expected)

B. Intense fear of gaining weight or becoming fat, even though underweight

C. Disturbance in the way in which one's body weight or shape is experienced, undue influence of body weight or shape on self-evaluation, or denial of the seriousness of the current low body weight

D. In postmenarcheal females, **amenorrhea**—i.e., the absence of at least three consecutive menstrual cycles. (A woman is considered to have amenorrhea if her periods occur only following hormone [e.g., estrogen] administration.)

Specify Type

Restricting type: During the current episode of anorexia nervosa, the person has not regularly engaged in binge-eating or purging behavior (such as self-induced vomiting and the misuse of laxatives, diuretics, or enemas).
Binge-eating/purging type: During the current episode of anorexia nervosa, the person has regularly engaged in binge-eating or purging behavior (such as self-induced vomiting and the misuse of laxatives, diuretics, or enemas).

Bulimia Nervosa

A. Recurrent episodes of binge eating. An episode of binge eating is characterized by both of the following:

1. Eating, in a discrete period of time (e.g., within any 2-hour period), an amount of food that is definitely larger than most people would eat during a similar period of time and under similar circumstances

2. A sense of lack of control over eating during the episode (e.g., a feeling that one cannot stop eating or control what or how much one is eating)

B. Recurrent inappropriate compensatory behavior to prevent weight gain, such as self-induced vomiting; misuse of laxatives, diuretics, enemas, or other medications; fasting; or excessive exercise

C. The binge eating and inappropriate compensatory behaviors both occur, on average, at least twice a week for 3 months.

D. Self-evaluation is unduly influenced by both body shape and weight.

E. The disturbance does not occur exclusively during episodes of anorexia nervosa.

Specify Type

Purging type: During the current episode of bulimia nervosa, the person has regularly engaged in self-induced vomiting or the misuse of laxatives, diuretics, or enemas.
Nonpurging type: During the current episode of bulimia nervosa, the person has used other inappropriate compensatory behaviors, such as fasting or excessive exercise, but has not regularly engaged in self-induced vomiting or the misuse of laxatives, diuretics, or enemas.

Eating Disorder Not Otherwise Specified (EDNOS)

This category is for disorders of eating that do not meet criteria for any specific eating disorder—for example:

1. For females, all of the criteria for anorexia nervosa are met except that the individual has regular menses.

2. All of the criteria for anorexia nervosa are met except that, despite significant weight loss, the individual's current weight is in the normal range.

3. All of the criteria for bulimia nervosa are met except that the binge eating and inappropriate compensatory mechanisms occur at a frequency of less than twice a week or for a duration of less than 3 months.

4. The regular use of inappropriate compensatory behavior by an individual of normal body weight after eating small amounts of food

5. Repeatedly chewing and spitting out, but not swallowing, large amounts of food

6. Binge-eating disorder (BED): Recurrent episodes of binge eating in the absence of the regular use of inappropriate compensatory behaviors characteristic of bulimia nervosa

This table will help you understand the characteristics of anorexia nervosa, bulimia nervosa, and binge-eating disorder. (Table 15-2 on page 544 provides more details on binge-eating disorder.) However, please do not attempt to diagnose these disorders in yourself or others. Instead, use this information to determine whether professional help is needed. Note also that for both anorexia nervosa and bulimia nervosa, all characteristics (A–D or A–E, respectively) must be present to make the diagnosis.

Figure 15-1 Self-image is an important part of adolescence. For people with eating disorders, the difference between the real and desired body images may be too difficult to accept. See the website www.4women.gov/bodyimage/index.htm.

Table 15-2 Research Criteria for Binge-Eating Disorder

A. Recurrent episodes of binge eating, an episode being characterized by both of the following:
1. Eating, in a discrete period of time (e.g., within any 2-hour period), an amount of food that is definitely larger than most people would eat during a similar period of time in similar circumstances
2. A sense of lack of control during the episodes (e.g., a feeling that one can't stop eating or control what or how much one is eating)
B. During most binge episodes, at least three of the following occur:
1. Eating much more rapidly than usual
2. Eating until feeling uncomfortably full
3. Eating large amounts of food when not feeling physically hungry
4. Eating alone because of being embarrassed by how much one is eating
5. Feeling disgusted with oneself, depressed, or very guilty after overeating
C. Marked distress regarding binge eating
D. The binge eating occurs, on average, at least 2 days a week for 6 months.
E. The behavior does not occur only during the course of bulimia nervosa or anorexia nervosa.

Reprinted by permission from the *Diagnostic and Statistical Manual of Mental Disorders*, Fourth Edition (Text Revision) (DSM-IV-TR). American Psychiatric Association, Washington DC, 2000.

eating disorder but not enough to enable a medical worker to diagnose the disease. These people may fall under the category Eating Disorders Not Otherwise Specified (EDNOS). One of the categories falling under EDNOS is binge-eating disorder (Table 15-2). And, as suggested in the diagnostic criteria, some people with anorexia nervosa will binge and purge (Fig. 15-2). In fact, about half of women diagnosed with anorexia nervosa will develop a binge and purge pattern. Despite this, their diagnosis is still anorexia nervosa. Bulimia nervosa is a separate condition with distinct criteria (review Table 15-1). Appreciating the differences between the disorders helps in understanding various approaches to prevention and treatment.

Table 15-3 lists some characteristics of people with anorexia nervosa and bulimia nervosa. Do you know someone who is at risk of these eating disorders? If so, suggest that the person seek a professional evaluation because, the sooner treatment begins, the better. However, do not try to diagnose eating disorders in your friends or family members. Only a professional can exclude other possible diseases and correctly evaluate the diagnostic criteria required to make a diagnosis of anorexia nervosa or bulimia nervosa. Once an eating disorder is diagnosed, immediate treatment is advisable. As a friend, the best you can do is to encourage an affected person to seek professional help. Note that such help is commonly available at student health centers and student guidance/counseling facilities on college campuses.

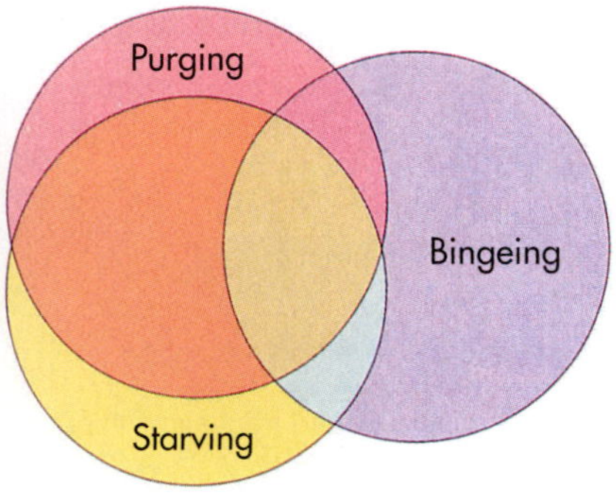

Figure 15-2 The overlap of eating disorders. A combination of binge eating, purging, and/or starving can be found in both anorexia nervosa and bulimia nervosa.

There are no simple causes of eating disorders, and there are no simple treatments. Stress may have an especially strong role in the development of eating disorders. An underlying commonality seems to be the lack of appropriate coping mechanisms as individuals begin to reach adolescence and young adulthood, coupled with dysfunctional family relationships.[14]

Is There a Genetic Connection to Eating Disorders?

A few research studies have investigated the possible link between genetic factors and the development of eating disorders. These studies have involved a comparison of identical twins with fraternal twins and the incidence of eating disorders. In general, these

Table 15-3 Typical Characteristics of Anorexic and Bulimic Persons[2]

Anorexia Nervosa	Bulimia Nervosa
• Rigid dieting causing dramatic weight loss, generally to less than 85% of what would be expected for one's age (or BMI of 17.5 or less)	• Secretive binge eating; generally not overeating in front of others
• False body perception—thinking "I'm too fat," even when extremely underweight; relentless pursuit of control	• Eating when depressed or under stress
• Rituals involving food, excessive exercise, and other aspects of life	• Bingeing on a large amount of food, followed by fasting, laxative or diuretic abuse, self-induced vomiting, or excessive exercise (at least twice a week for 3 months)
• Maintenance of rigid control in lifestyle; security found in control and order	• Shame, embarrassment, deceit, and depression; low self-esteem and guilt (especially after a binge)
• Feeling of panic after a small weight gain; intense fear of gaining weight	• Fluctuating weight resulting from alternate bingeing and fasting (±10 lb or 5 kg)
• Feelings of purity, power, and superiority through maintenance of strict discipline and self-denial	• Loss of control; fear of not being able to stop eating
• Preoccupation with food, its preparation, and observing another person eat	• Perfectionism, "people pleaser"; food as the only comfort/escape in an otherwise carefully controlled and regulated life
• Helplessness in the presence of food	• Erosion of teeth, swollen glands
• Lack of menstrual periods after what should be the age of puberty for at least 3 months	• Purchase of syrup of ipecac, a compound sold in pharmacies that induces vomiting
• Possible presence of bingeing and purging practices	

Those who exhibit only one or a few of these characteristics may be at risk but probably do not have either disorder. They should, however, reflect on their eating habits and related concerns and take appropriate action, such as seeking a careful evaluation by a physician.

Eating disorders are commonly seen in people who must maintain low body weight, such as ballet dancers.

studies have shown that identical twins have a higher likelihood of developing eating disorders than do fraternal twins.[3] This indicates that genetics may have a strong role in development of such disorders, since identical twins share the same DNA; however, these studies have not ruled out the impact of the environmental influences in eating disorder development. Identifying genes that cause eating disorders eventually could help in tailoring prevention efforts to those who are at risk, but affected individuals would still need the same counseling that is part of therapy today.

The Nutrition Perspective at the end of this chapter adds further insight into this topic, as it reviews some sociological aspects of these disorders. This helps you further understand how the disorders develop and why some people are more susceptible than others. As is true for many health problems, both nature and nurture play a role.

Anorexia Nervosa

Anorexia nervosa evolves from a dangerous mental state to an often life-threatening physical condition. People suffering from this disorder think they are fat and intensely fear obesity and weight gain. They lose much more weight than is healthful. Although food is entwined in this disease, it stems more from psychological conflict.

A person with anorexia nervosa may use the disorder to gain attention from the family, sometimes in hopes of holding the family together.

Depression is commonly found in conjunction with an eating disorder. In fact, a study done in the 1940s at the University of Minnesota found that depression and obsessional behaviors developed in the subjects during a 6-month period of restricted

Concern over appearance begins early in life; a focus on a healthful outlook with regard to body weight should also begin at this time.

energy intake. These abnormal behaviors did not reverse immediately after refeeding but, rather, took many weeks to return to normal (see Chapter 20 for details).

About 10% of people with anorexia eventually die from the disease—from suicide, heart ailments, and infections.[3] About one quarter of those with anorexia nervosa recover within 6 years, whereas the rest simply exist with the disease or go on to develop another form of eating disorder, such as bulimia nervosa. The longer someone suffers from this eating disorder, the poorer the chances for complete recovery. A young patient with a brief episode and a cooperative family has a better outlook than someone without these factors. Prompt and vigorous treatment with close follow-up improves the chances for success.

Anorexia nervosa may begin as a simple attempt to lose weight. A comment from a well-meaning friend, relative, or coach suggesting that the person seems to be gaining weight or is too fat may be all that is needed. The stress of having to maintain a certain weight to look attractive or competent on a job can also lead to disordered eating. Physical changes associated with puberty, the stress of leaving childhood, or the loss of a friend may serve as another trigger for extreme dieting. Leaving home for boarding school or college or starting a job can reinforce the desire to appear more "socially acceptable." Still, looking "good" does not necessarily help people deal with anger, depression, low self-esteem, or past experiences with sexual abuse. If these issues are behind the disorder and are not resolved as weight is lost, the individual may intensify efforts to lose weight "to look even better," rather than work through unresolved psychological concerns.

During adolescence, a period of turbulent sexual and social tensions, teenagers seek—and are often expected—to establish separate and independent lives. While declaring independence, they seek acceptance and support from peers and parents and react intensely to how they think others perceive them. At the same time, their bodies are changing, and much of the change is beyond their control. In response to the adolescent's or teenager's lack of control and coping mechanisms, dieting may start and then lead to a failure to gain appropriate weight-for-height. This may not be readily identified as a problem because the child has not actually lost any weight. Stunting (failure to grow in height) may also occur if inadequate energy is ingested during a period of growth. If anorexia develops before puberty, sexual maturation and menstruation may be delayed.

Teens with chronic illnesses, such as type 1 diabetes or asthma, are at even greater risk for disordered eating.[11] Any evidence of poor weight gain/maintenance or excessive exercise among these individuals needs to be investigated as possible disordered eating.

Extreme dieting is the most important predictor of an eating disorder.[15] (Adolescents expressing concern about their weight should be advised to focus on exercise, which does not appear to impart a risk for subsequent problems.) Once dieting begins, a person developing anorexia nervosa does not stop. The result is long periods of rigidly self-enforced semistarvation, practiced almost with a vengeance, in a relentless pursuit of control. For example, recently, a 19-year-old patient at the Ohio State University Hospitals was admitted on an emergency basis at a body weight of 60 pounds. She had lost 55 pounds in the previous 6 months and was at great risk of impending death. Upon interview, she said she started dieting and could not stop.

Anorexia nervosa may eventually lead to bingeing on large amounts of food in a short time, then purging. Purging occurs primarily through vomiting, but laxatives, diuretics, and enemas are also used. Thus, a person with anorexia nervosa may exist in a state of semistarvation or may alternate periods of starvation with periods of bingeing and purging.[2]

By severely restricting energy intake for long periods, adolescent girls and young adult women greatly compromise their nutritional status, impair their reproductive systems, and restrict growth.[18] The harm produced by milder, shorter periods of diet restriction is not clear. Evidence, however, suggests that even moderate diet restriction, if continued, contributes to the risks for various anemias, later pregnancy complications and low-birth-weight infants, and permanently reduced bone mass.

Profile of the Typical Person with Anorexia Nervosa

A person with anorexia nervosa refuses to eat enough food to maintain an acceptable weight. This refusal is the hallmark of the disease, whether or not other practices, such as binge-purge cycles, appear. The most typical anorexic person is a white female from the middle or upper socioeconomic class. Perhaps her mother also has distorted views of desirable body shape and acceptable food habits. The girl is often described by parents and teachers as responsible, meticulous, and obedient.

Figure 15-3 Stresses and changes are a common part of adolescence.

She is competitive and often obsessive.[8] Her parents set high standards for her. At home, she may not allow clutter in her bedroom. Physicians note that, after a physical examination, she may fold her examination gown very carefully and clean up the examination room before leaving. Even though such behavior may seem obvious, only a skilled professional can tell the difference between anorexia nervosa and other adolescent complaints, such as delayed puberty, fatigue, and depression.

A common thread underlying many—but not all—cases of anorexia nervosa is conflict within the family structure, typically manifested by an overbearing mother and an emotionally absent father. When family expectations are always too high—including those regarding body weight—resulting frustration leads to fighting. Overinvolvement, rigidity, overprotection, and denial are typical daily transactions of such families.

Often, the eating disorder allows an anorexic person to exercise control over an otherwise powerless existence (Fig. 15-3).[14] Losing weight may be the first independent success the person has had. People with anorexia evaluate their self-worth almost entirely in terms of self-control. Issues of control are central to the development of anorexia nervosa. Some sexually abused children develop anorexia nervosa, believing that if they control their appetite for food, sexual relations, and human contact, they will feel in control and competent and will eliminate shameful feelings. Moreover, food restriction, which arrests development and shuts down sexual impulses, may be a strategy to prevent future victimization and guilt feelings in such cases. Often anorexic persons feel hopeless about human relationships and socially isolated because of their dysfunctional families. They substitute the world of food, eating, and weight for the world of human relationships.

Parents may not consider a teenager mature enough to make decisions. If the teen disagrees and the situation is very tense, she may turn to purging or starving as a way to show her power: "You may try to control my life, but I can do anything I want with my body."

In the words of one young woman, "I couldn't get angry, because it would be like destroying someone else, like my mother. It felt like she would hate me forever, I got angry through anorexia nervosa. It was my last hope. It's my own body and this was my last-ditch effort."

Early Warning Signs

A person developing anorexia nervosa exhibits important warning signs. At first, dieting becomes the life focus. The person may think, "The only thing I am good at is dieting. I can't do anything else." This innocent beginning often leads to very abnormal self-perceptions and eating habits, such as cutting a pea in half before eating it. Other habits include hiding and storing food and or spreading food around a plate to make it look as if much has been eaten. An anorexic person may cook a large meal and watch others eat it while refusing to eat anything. Anorexics may also exercise compulsively to the point that it is obsessive and driven. It can interfere with life activities or occur at inappropriate times or settings—for example, doing squats while brushing teeth.

As the disorder progresses, the range of foods may narrow and be rigidly divided into safe and unsafe ones, with the list of safe foods becoming progressively shorter. For

Critical | Thinking

Jennifer is an attractive 13-year-old. However, she's very compulsive. Everything has to be perfect—her hair, her clothes, even her room. Since her body is beginning to mature, she's quite obsessed with having perfect physical features as well. Her parents are worried about her behavior. The school counselor told them to look for certain signs that could indicate an eating disorder. What might those signs be?

people developing anorexia nervosa, these practices say, "I am in control." These people may be hungry, but they deny it, driven by the belief that good things will happen by just becoming thin enough. It becomes a question of willpower.

Soon people with anorexia become irritable and hostile and begin to withdraw from family and friends. School performance generally crumbles. They refuse to eat out with family and friends, thinking, "I won't be able to have the foods I want to eat," or "I won't be able to throw up afterward."

Anorexic persons see themselves as rational and others as irrational. They also tend to be excessively critical of themselves and others. Nothing is good enough. Because it cannot be perfect, life appears meaningless and hopeless. A sense of joylessness colors everything.

As stress increases in the person's life, sleep disturbances and depression are common. Many of the psychological and physical problems associated with anorexia nervosa arise from insufficient energy intake, as well as deficiencies of nutrients, such as thiamin and vitamin B-6. For the latter reason, a multivitamin and mineral supplement is typically prescribed in therapy.[13] For a female, the combination of problems—coupled with lower and lower body weight and fat stores—causes menstrual periods to cease. This may be the first sign of the disease that a parent notices and represents the hallmark of the disease.

Ultimately, an anorexic person eats very little food; 300 to 600 kcal daily is not unusual. In place of food, the person may consume up to 20 cans of diet soft drinks and chew many pieces of sugarless gum each day.

Anorexia nervosa occurs much more frequently in young women than in young men.

Physical Effects of Anorexia Nervosa

Rooted in the emotional state of the victim, anorexia nervosa produces profound physical effects. The anorexic person often appears to be skin and bones. Body weight less than 85% of that expected is one clinical indicator of anorexia nervosa.[4] This percentage can be calculated using the Metropolitan Life Insurance tables (see Appendix I), but it is important to note that body build and weight history should also be used when estimating an appropriate weight. BMI is a more reliable indicator of the degree of malnourishment; generally, a BMI of 17.5 or less indicates a severe case (review Chapter 13 for more on BMI). For children under age 18, growth charts should be used to assess weight status (see Chapter 17).

This state of semistarvation disturbs many body systems, as it forces the body to conserve as much energy as possible (Fig. 15-4). This attempt to conserve energy results in most of the physical effects. Thus, many complications can be ended by returning to a healthy weight, provided the duration of the insult has not been too long. Following are predictable effects caused by hormonal responses to semistarvation:[2, 3, 18]

- Lowered body temperature and cold intolerance caused by loss of fat insulation
- Slower metabolic rate caused by decreased synthesis of the thyroid hormones
- Decreased heart rate as metabolism slows, leading to easy fatigue, fainting, and an overwhelming need for sleep. Other changes in heart function may also occur, including loss of heart tissue itself.
- Iron deficiency anemia from a deficient nutrient intake, which leads to further weakness
- Rough, dry, scaly, and cold skin from a deficient nutrient intake, iron deficiency anemia, and estrogen deficiency. The skin may also show multiple bruises because of the loss of protection from the fat layer normally present under the skin.
- Low white blood cell count caused by a deficient nutrient intake. This condition increases the risk of infection, one cause of death in people with anorexia nervosa.
- Abnormal feeling of fullness or bloating, which can last for several hours after eating
- Loss of hair caused by a deficient nutrient intake
- Appearance of lanugo—downy hairs on the body that trap air, reducing heat loss and in turn replacing some insulation lost with the fat layer

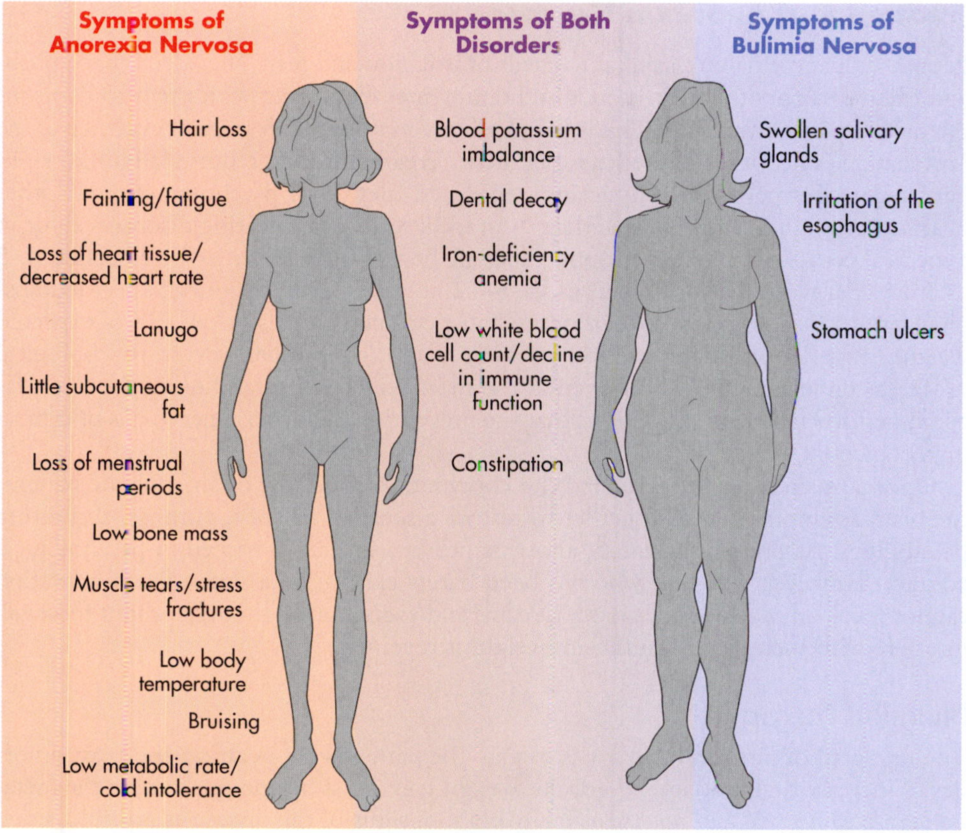

Figure 15-4 Signs and symptoms of eating disorders. A vast array of physical effects are associated with anorexia nervosa and bulimia nervosa. This figure contains many, but is not an exhaustive list of all potential consequences. These physical effects can also serve as warning signs that a problem exists. Professional evaluation is then indicated.

- Constipation from semistarvation and laxative abuse
- Low blood potassium caused by a deficient nutrient intake, loss of potassium from vomiting, and use of some types of diuretics. This increases the risk of heart rhythm disturbances, another leading cause of death in anorexic people.
- Loss of menstrual periods because of low body weight, low body fat content, and the stress of the disease. Accompanying hormonal changes cause a loss of bone mass and increase the risk of osteoporosis later in life.
- Changes in neurotransmitter function in the brain, which leads to depression
- Eventual loss of teeth caused by acid erosion if frequent vomiting occurs. Until vomiting ceases, one way to reduce this effect on teeth is to rinse the mouth with water right away and brush the teeth as soon as possible. Loss of teeth (along with low bone mass) can be lasting signs of the disease, even if the other physical and mental problems are resolved.
- Muscle tears and stress fractures in athletes because of decreased bone and muscle mass

A person with this disorder is psychologically and physically ill and needs help.

Erika Goodman, a former dancer with the Joffrey Ballet, is now in her fifties and is crippled from osteoporosis resulting from years of restricting food intake in order to maintain a low body weight. This led to irregular or absent menstrual periods for many years.

Concept | Check

Anorexia nervosa is an eating disorder characterized by semistarvation. It is found primarily—but not exclusively—in adolescent girls, starting at or around puberty. People with anorexia dwindle essentially to skin and bones but still believe they are fat. Semistarvation produces hormonal and other changes, which lower body temperature, slow the heart rate, decrease immune response, stop menstrual periods, and contribute to hair, muscle, and bone loss. It is a very serious disease, which often produces lifelong consequences and may be fatal.

Critical | Thinking

Jennifer continues her pursuit of the perfect thin body into her late teens. She ignores the advice of her parents and the counselor. As a 19-year-old entering college, she is finally beginning to realize that her anorexic behavior might have serious consequences. She has been fluctuating 15 to 20% below her healthy body weight and has been amenorrheic for a few years. She would like to marry someday and have a family. What might some of the health consequences be for a person such as Jennifer with anorexia nervosa?

Treatment of Anorexia Nervosa

People with anorexia often sink into shells of isolation and fear. They deny that a problem exists. Frequently, their friends and family members meet with them to confront the problem in a loving way. This is called an *intervention*. They present evidence of the problem and encourage immediate treatment. Treatment then requires a multidisciplinary team of experienced physicians, registered dietitians, psychologists, and other health professionals working together.[15] An ideal setting is an eating disorders clinic in a medical center. Outpatient therapy generally begins first. This may be extended to 3 to 5 days per week. Day hospitalization (6–12 hours) is another option, as is total hospitalization. This hospitalization is necessary once a person falls below 75% of expected weight, experiences acute medical problems, and/or exhibits severe psychological problems or suicidal risk.[2] Still, even in the most skilled hands and using the finest facilities, efforts may fail. This tells us that the prevention of anorexia nervosa is of utmost importance.

Once a medical team has gained the cooperation and trust of an anorexic patient, the team attempts to work together to restore a sense of balance, purpose, and future possibilities. As previously stated, anorexia nervosa is usually rooted in psychological conflict. However, a person who has been barely existing in a state of semistarvation cannot focus on much besides food. Dreams and even morbid thoughts about food will interfere with therapy until sufficient weight is regained.

Nutrition Therapy

The first goal of nutrition therapy is to gain the patient's cooperation and trust, in order to increase oral food intake. Ideally, weight gain must be enough to raise the metabolic rate to normal and reverse as many physical signs of the disease as possible. Food intake is designed first to minimize or stop any further weight loss. Then the focus shifts to restoring appropriate food habits. After this, the expectation can be switched to slow weight gain. A range of 2 to 3 pounds per week is appropriate. Tube feeding and/or total parenteral nutrition support is used only if immediate renourishment is required, as this can cause the patient to distrust medical staff.

Energy needs begin at 1000 to 1600 kcal/day, increasing this allocation in 100- to 200-kcal increments every few days as possible until an appropriate rate of weight gain is achieved. This appropriate weight is one in which normal menstruation is restored. An energy distribution of about 50 to 55% carbohydrate, 15 to 20% protein, and 25 to 30% fat is appropriate. This nutrition therapy may ultimately require an intake of 3500 kcal to attain a goal weight, as the increase in body metabolism associated with feeding needs to be accounted for.[18]

Patients need considerable reassurance during the refeeding process because of uncomfortable effects, such as bloating, increase in body heat, and increase in body fat. This is a frightening process because these changes can lead to the patient feeling out of control. Monitoring for rapid changes in electrolytes and minerals in the blood, especially potassium, phosphorus, and magnesium, is critically important during the process of incorporating more food into the diet.

In addition to helping patients reach and maintain adequate nutritional status, the registered dietitian on the medical team also provides accurate nutrition information throughout treatment, promotes a healthy attitude toward food, and helps the patient learn to eat based on natural hunger and satiety. Therapy with many anorexic persons can be frustrating for a dietitian because many of those affected are knowledgeable regarding the calorie and fat gram content of most food products. The focus should be on helping these patients identify healthy and adequate food choices that promote weight gain to achieve and maintain a clinically estimated goal weight (e.g., BMI of 20 or more).[1] The medical team also should assure patients that they will not be abandoned after gaining weight.

A young woman in a self-help group for those with anorexia nervosa explained her feelings to the other group members: "I have lost a specialness that I thought it gave me. I was different from everyone else. Now I know that I'm somebody who's overcome it, which not everybody does."

Because excessive energy expenditure prevents weight gain, professionals must work with anorexic patients to help them moderate their activity. At many treatment centers, patients are placed on moderate bed rest in the early stages of treatment to help promote weight gain.

Experienced professional help is the key. An anorexic patient may be on the verge of suicide and near starvation. In addition, anorexic people are often very clever and resistant. They may try to hide weight loss by wearing many layers of clothes, putting coins in their pockets or underwear, and drinking numerous glasses of water.

Psychological and Related Therapy

Once the physical problems of anorexic patients are addressed, the treatment focus shifts to the underlying emotional problems that led to excessive dieting and other symptoms of the disorder. To heal, these patients must reject the sense of accomplishment associated with an emaciated body and begin to accept themselves at an increased body weight. If therapists can discover reasons for the disorder, they can develop strategies for restoring normal weight and eating habits by resolving psychological conflicts. Education about the medical consequences of semistarvation is also helpful. A key aspect of psychological treatment is showing affected individuals how to regain control of some facets of their lives and cope with tough situations. As eating evolves into a normal routine, they then can turn to previously neglected activities.

Therapists may use **cognitive behavior therapy,** which involves helping the person confront and change irrational beliefs about body image, eating, relationships, and weight.[3] Underlying issues that may be the cause for the disease, such as sexual abuse, must be identified and addressed by the therapist. Interpersonal therapy is another psychological approach used in anorexia nervosa. Rather than focusing on the patient's eating habits and assumptions about weight and shape, interpersonal therapy formulates the problem in terms of the interpersonal context, usually in one or more of four areas: grief, interpersonal problems (e.g., difficulty forming or maintaining close relationships), interpersonal disputes (e.g., unresolved conflict regarding the expectations of significant others in the person's life), or role transitions (e.g., fear of independence due to lack of self-confidence). Treatment focuses on assisting the patient to change in one or more of these areas.

cognitive behavior therapy Psychological therapy in which the person's assumptions about dieting, body weight, and related issues are challenged. New ways of thinking are explored and then practiced by the person. In this way, the person can learn new ways to control disordered eating behaviors and related life stress.

Family therapy often is important in treating anorexia nervosa, especially for younger patients who still live with their families. It focuses on the role of the illness among family members, the reactions of individual family members, and ways in which their subconscious behavior might contribute to the abnormal eating patterns. Therapy includes all family members involved with the behavior problem. Frequently, a therapist finds family struggles at the heart of the problem. As the disorder resolves, patients must relate to family members in new ways to gain the attention previously tied to the disease. For example, the family may need to help the young person ease into adulthood and accept its responsibilities as well as its advantages.

Self-help groups for anorexic (and bulimic) people, as well as their families and friends, represent nonthreatening first steps into treatment. People can also attend to get a sense of whether they really do have an eating disorder.

Medications are generally not effective in treating the primary symptoms of anorexia nervosa.[20] Fluoxetine (Prozac) and other related antidepressant medications called selective serotonin reuptake inhibitors (SSRIs) may stabilize recovery in patients with anorexia who have attained 85% of their expected body weight. These work by prolonging serotonin activity in the brain, which in turn regulates mood and feelings of satiety. A variety of other types of pharmacologic agents may have some role in treating mood changes, anxiety, or psychotic symptoms associated with anorexia nervosa but have limited value in patients unless weight gain is also achieved. Food is the drug of choice for treating anorexic patients.

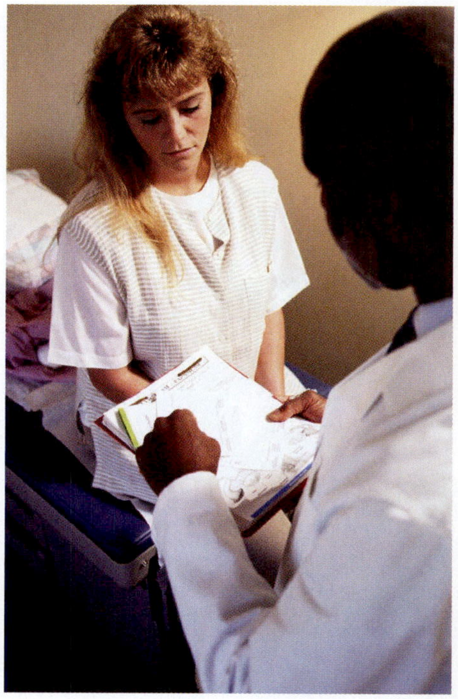
Early treatment for an eating disorder, such as anorexia nervosa, improves chances of success.

With professional help, many people with anorexia nervosa can lead normal lives. They then do not have to depend on unusual eating habits to cope with daily problems. Although they may not be totally cured, they do recover a sense of normality in their lives. No set answers or approaches exist because each case is different. Establishing a strong relationship with either a therapist or another supportive person is an especially important key to recovery. Once anorexic patients feel understood and accepted by another person, they can begin to build a sense of self and exercise some autonomy. Then they can progress to substituting healthy relationships with others for a relationship with food, emphasizing alternative coping mechanisms.

Case Scenario Follow-up

Sarah does have the characteristics to be diagnosed with anorexia nervosa because she refuses to maintain a healthy weight-for-height, is at a weight below 85% of that expected, has a distorted view of her appearance, and has had no menstrual periods for over 3 consecutive months.

Sarah would need to be hospitalized initially, due to her low BMI of 13.8. While in the hospital, her treatment would most likely consist of moderate bed rest to promote weight gain and an intake of 1000 to 1600 kcal initially, which is then increased by increments of about 100 to 200 kcal every few days until an acceptable rate of weight gain is achieved.

The goal is to achieve a body weight that is at least 90% of an expected weight for her age, such as a BMI of at least 19. This weight goal should also allow for resumption of menstrual periods. The physician would likely prescribe a multivitamin and mineral supplement, along with supplements of calcium as needed to make sure intake is in the range of 1200 to 1500 mg. This will correct vitamin and mineral deficiencies that exist, and the calcium will contribute to bone maintenance. A team of health professionals, most likely consisting of a physician, registered dietitian, and psychologist, would provide therapy. Sarah's cooperation would be the most important element for therapy to be successful. She needs to realize she has a problem and that she needs help, and she must be willing to accept the assistance these professionals are willing to offer. The team, especially the psychologist, may use cognitive behavior therapy to help Sarah improve her self-image.

Sarah's outlook for recovery is not good, unless she realizes she has a problem. Even if she is willing to accept the therapy and counseling, a relapse is likely to occur. Only about 50% of anorexia nervosa patients have been found to fully recover from the disease. Since Sarah's disordered eating habits have been in place for about 6 years, her problem is deep-rooted. The chances of recovery are greater if a vigorous treatment program is reinforced with close follow-up.

Singer Karen Carpenter's death from complications of anorexia nervosa in 1983 increased awareness of the serious nature of this disease. Currently, the average time for recovery from anorexia nervosa is 7 years; many insurance companies cover only a fraction of the estimated $150,000 cost of treatment.

Concept | Check

To relieve the semistarved condition of most anorexic patients, the initial treatment focuses on moderately increased food intake and slow weight gain. Once this is accomplished, psychotherapy can begin to uncover the causes of the disease and help patients develop the skills needed to return to a healthy life. Family therapy can be an important tool in treatment, whereas medications have a limited role.

Bulimia Nervosa

Bulimia nervosa involves episodes of binge eating followed by various means to purge the food. This eating disorder was first described in the medical literature in 1979 and classified as a clinical psychiatric disorder in 1980. It is most common among young adults of college age, although some high school students are also at risk. Susceptible people often have genetic factors and lifestyle patterns that predispose them to becoming overweight, and many try frequent weight-reduction diets as teenagers. Like people with anorexia nervosa, those with bulimia nervosa are usually female and successful. Unlike anorexics, however, they are usually at or slightly above a normal weight.[2] Females with bulimia nervosa are also more likely to be sexually active than those with anorexia nervosa.

Bingeing and purging (via vomiting) was evident in pre-Christian Roman times, but was practiced in a group setting. The eating disorder bulimia nervosa is generally practiced in private.

The person with bulimia nervosa may think of food constantly. In contrast to the anorexic person, who turns away from food when faced with problems, the bulimic person turns toward food in critical situations. Also, unlike those with anorexia nervosa, people with bulimia nervosa recognize their behavior as abnormal. These people often have very low self-esteem and are depressed. Approximately half of the people with bulimia nervosa have major depression. Lingering effects of child abuse may be one reason for these feelings. Many bulimic persons report that they have been sexually abused. The world sees their competence, while inside they feel out of control, ashamed, and frustrated.

Bulimic people tend to be impulsive, which may be expressed as stealing, increased sexual activity, drug and alcohol abuse, self-mutilation, or attempted suicide. Some experts have suggested that part of the problem may actually arise from an inability to control responses to impulse and desire. Some studies have demonstrated that bulimic people tend to come from disengaged families—ones that are loosely organized. Roles for family members are not clearly defined. Rules are very loose and a great deal of conflict exists. Anorexic people in comparison tend to have families so actively engaged that roles may be too well defined.[3]

Typical Behavior in Bulimia Nervosa

Many people with bulimic behavior are probably never diagnosed. The strict diagnostic criteria specify that, in order to be classified as having bulimia nervosa, a person must binge and purge at least twice a week for 3 months.[3] People with bulimia nervosa lead secret lives, hiding their abnormal eating habits. Moreover, it is impossible to recognize people with bulimia nervosa simply from their appearance. Because most diagnoses of bulimia nervosa are based on self-reports, current estimates of the number of cases are probably low. The disorder, especially in its milder forms, may be much more widespread than commonly thought.

Among sufferers of bulimia nervosa, bingeing often alternates with attempts to rigidly restrict food intake. Elaborate food rules are common, such as avoiding all sweets. Thus, eating just one cookie or donut may cause bulimic persons to feel they have broken a rule. Then the objectionable food must be eliminated. Usually, this leads to further overeating, partly because it is easier to regurgitate a large amount of food than a small amount. For intake to qualify as a binge, an atypically large amount of food must be consumed in a short time, and the person must exhibit a lack of control over this behavior.

Figure 15-5 The binge-purge cycle can lead to a sense of helplessness.

Binge-purge cycles may be practiced daily, weekly, or at longer intervals. A special time is often set aside. Most binge eating occurs at night, when other people are less likely to interrupt, and usually lasts from ½ to 2 hours. A binge can be triggered by a combination of hunger from recent dieting, stress, boredom, loneliness, and depression. It often follows a period of strict dieting and thus can be linked to intense hunger. The binge is not at all like normal eating; once begun, it seems to propel itself. The person not only loses control but generally doesn't even taste or enjoy the food that is eaten during a binge (Fig. 15-5). This separates the practice from simple overeating.

Most commonly, bulimic people consume cakes, cookies, ice cream, and similar high-carbohydrate convenience foods during binges because these foods can be purged relatively easily and comfortably by vomiting. In a single binge, foods supplying up to 3000 kcal or more may be eaten.[3] Purging follows in hopes that no weight will be gained. However, even when vomiting follows the binge, 33 to 75% of the food energy taken in is still absorbed, which causes some weight gain. When laxatives or enemas are used, about 90% of the energy is absorbed, as these act in the large intestine, beyond the point of most nutrient absorption. The common belief of bulimic persons that purging soon after bingeing will prevent excessive energy absorption and weight gain is clearly a misconception.

Early in the onset of bulimia nervosa, sufferers often induce vomiting by placing their fingers deep into the mouth. They may inadvertently bite down on these fingers. The resulting bite marks around the knuckles are a characteristic sign of this disorder.

Figure 15-6 Bulimia nervosa's vicious cycle of obsession.

Once the disease is established, however, a person can often vomit simply by contracting the abdominal muscles. Vomiting may also occur spontaneously.[3]

Another way bulimic people attempt to compensate for a binge is by engaging in excessive exercise to expend a large amount of energy. Some bulimic people try to estimate the amount of energy eaten in a binge and then exercise to counteract this energy intake. This practice, referred to as "debting," represents an effort to control their weight.

People with bulimia nervosa are not proud of their behavior. After a binge, they usually feel guilty and depressed. Over time, they experience low self-esteem and feel hopeless about their situation (Fig. 15-6). Compulsive lying, shoplifting to obtain food, and drug abuse can further intensify these feelings. Bulimic people caught in the act of bingeing by a friend or family member may order the intruder to "get out" and "go away." Sufferers gradually distance themselves from others, spending more and more time preoccupied by and engaging in bingeing and purging.

Excessive exercising can be one component of bulimia if it is used as a way to offset the energy intake from a binge. Exercise is considered excessive when it is done at inappropriate times or settings, or when a person does it despite injury or other medical complications.

Health Problems Stemming from Bulimia Nervosa

The vomiting that many bulimic sufferers induce is the most physically destructive method of purging. Indeed, the majority of health problems associated with bulimia nervosa arise from vomiting:[2, 7, 18]

- Repeated exposure of teeth to the acid in vomit causes demineralization, making the teeth painful and sensitive to heat, cold, and acids. Eventually, the teeth may severely decay, erode away from fillings, and finally fall out. Dental professionals are sometimes the first health professionals to notice signs of bulimia nervosa (Fig. 15-7). Until vomiting ceases, it is important to rinse the mouth with water after a vomiting episode, especially before brushing the teeth.
- Blood potassium can drop significantly with regular vomiting or the use of certain diuretics. This can disturb the heart's rhythm and even produce sudden death.
- Salivary glands may swell as a result of infection and irritation from persistent vomiting.
- Stomach ulcers and bleeding and tears in the esophagus develop in some cases.

- Constipation may result from frequent laxative use.
- Ipecac syrup, sometimes used to induce vomiting, is toxic to the heart, liver, and kidneys. It has caused accidental poisoning when taken repeatedly.

Overall, bulimia nervosa is a potentially debilitating disorder that can lead to death, usually from suicide, low blood potassium, or overwhelming infections.

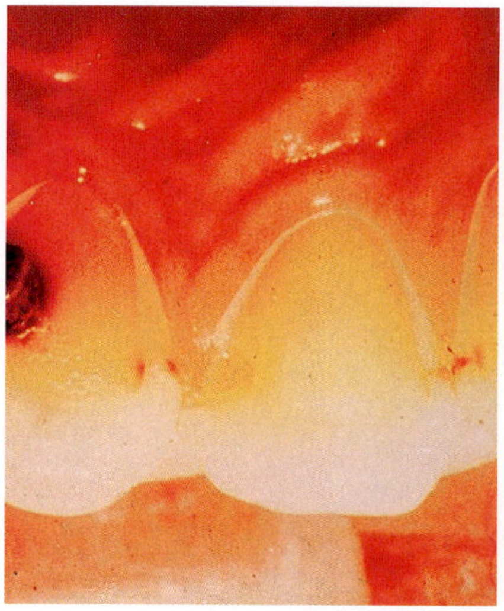

Figure 15-7 Excessive tooth decay is common in bulimic patients.

Concept | Check

Bulimia nervosa is characterized by episodes of binge eating followed by purging, usually by vomiting. Vomiting is very destructive to the body, often causing severe dental decay, stomach ulcers, irritation of the esophagus, and low blood potassium.

Treatment of Bulimia Nervosa

Therapy for bulimia nervosa, as for anorexia nervosa, requires a team of experienced clinicians.[19] These patients are less likely than those with anorexia to enter treatment in a state of semistarvation. However, if a bulimic patient has lost significant weight, this must be treated before psychological treatment begins. Although clinicians have yet to agree on the best therapy for bulimia nervosa, they generally agree that treatment should last at least 16 weeks. Hospitalization may be indicated in cases of extreme laxative abuse, regular vomiting, substance abuse, and depression, especially if physical harm is evident.

The first goal of treatment for bulimia nervosa is to decrease the amount of food consumed in a binge session in order to decrease the risk of esophageal tears from related purging by vomiting. A decrease in the frequency of this type of purging will also decrease damage to the teeth.

The primary aim of psychotherapy is to improve patients' self-acceptance and help them to be less concerned about body weight. Cognitive behavior therapy is generally used. Psychotherapy helps correct the all-or-none thinking typical of bulimic persons—"If I eat one cookie, I'm a failure and might as well binge." A patient may be asked to analyze the statement as a scientist would do when testing assumptions. In this way, patient and therapist together examine the validity of food and weight beliefs. The premise of this therapy is that, if abnormal attitudes and beliefs can be altered, normal eating will follow. In addition, the therapist guides the person in establishing food habits that will minimize bingeing: avoiding fasting, eating regular meals, and using alternative methods—other than eating—to cope with stressful situations. Group therapy is often useful to foster strong social support. One goal of therapy is to help bulimic persons accept as normal some depression and self-doubt.

Bulimia nervosa affects many college students. Counselors are aware of this and are available to help.

Although pharmacological agents should not be used as the sole treatment for bulimia nervosa, studies indicate that some medications may be beneficial in conjunction with other therapies. Fluoxetine (Prozac) is the only antidepressant that has been approved by FDA for use in the treatment of bulimia nervosa, but physicians also may prescribe other forms of both SSRI antidepressants and other psychiatric medications, such as imipramine (Tofranil) and lithium carbonate (Lithane).[20]

Nutritional counseling has two main goals: correcting misconceptions about food and re-establishing regular eating habits. Patients are given information about bulimia nervosa and its consequences. Avoiding binge foods and not constantly stepping on a scale may be recommended early in treatment. The primary goal, however, is to develop a normal eating pattern. To achieve this goal, some specialists encourage patients to develop daily meal plans and keep a food diary in which they record food intake, internal sensations of hunger, environmental factors that precipitate binges, and thoughts and feelings that accompany binge-purge cycles. Keeping a food diary not only is an accurate way to monitor food intake but also may help identify situations that seem to

The binge-purge cycle can create an initial state of euphoria in the person. Giving up this euphoria has been equated to giving up an addiction. Still, it is important to do so.

trigger binge episodes. With the help of a therapist, patients can develop alternative coping strategies.

In general, the focus is not on stopping bingeing and purging per se but on developing regular eating habits. Once this is achieved, the binge-purge cycle should start to break down. Patients are discouraged from following strict rules about healthy food choices, because this simply mimics the typical obsessive attitudes associated with bulimia nervosa. Rather, encouraging a mature perspective on nutrient intake—that is, regular consumption of moderate amounts of a variety of foods balanced among the food groups—helps patients overcome this disorder.[1]

Setting time limits for the completion of meals and snacks is important for people with eating disorders. Many bulimic persons eat very quickly, reflecting their difficulties with satiety. Suggesting that the patient put his or her utensil down after each bite is a behavioral technique that a therapist might try with a recovering bulimic person. (In comparison, many anorexic persons eat in an excessively slow manner—for example, taking 1 hour to eat a muffin cut into tiny, bite-size pieces.)

People with bulimia nervosa must recognize that it is a serious disorder that can have grave medical complications if not treated. Because relapse is likely, therapy should be long term. Note that those with bulimia nervosa need professional help because they can be very depressed and are at a high risk for suicide. About 50% of people with bulimia nervosa recover completely from the disorder. Others continue to struggle with it to varying degrees for the rest of their lives. This fact underscores the need for prevention because treatment is difficult.[12]

Concept | Check

Treatment of bulimia nervosa using nutrition counseling and psychotherapy attempts to restore normal eating habits, to help the person correct distorted beliefs about diet and lifestyle, and to find tools to cope with the stresses of life. Medications, such as fluoxetine (Prozac), can aid recovery when added to this regiment.

Eating Disorders Not Otherwise Specified (EDNOS)

As mentioned before, EDNOS is a broad category of eating disorders in which the individuals have partial syndromes that do not meet the strict criteria for the other more specific eating disorders. About 50% of people with eating disorders fall into this EDNOS category, especially adolescents.[3] Examples of disordered eating in this category include (1) a woman who meets all the criteria for anorexia nervosa but continues to sustain menses; (2) an individual who meets all the criteria for anorexia nervosa but, despite a significant weight loss, the individual's current weight is in the normal range (this could be a person who was once obese); (3) a person who meets all the criteria for bulimia nervosa except that binge eating occurs less than two times a week; (4) a person who meets all the criteria for bulimia nervosa but does not binge (this person might eat normal amounts of food but purges regularly out of fear of weight or fat gain); and (5) a person who repeatedly chews and spits out food but does not swallow it.

Treatment as outlined for anorexia nervosa or bulimia nervosa should be sought in such cases, depending on the specific symptoms exhibited.

Binge-Eating Disorder

EDNOS also includes binge-eating disorder as a sixth category. The typical characteristics for this disorder were listed in Table 15-2. Generally, it can be defined as binge-eating episodes not accompanied by purging (as typifies bulimia nervosa) at least two times per week for at least 6 months. Today health-care professionals recognize binge-eating disorder as a complex and potentially serious problem.[3]

Approximately 30 to 50% of subjects in organized weight-control programs have binge-eating disorder, whereas among the general North American population about 1 to 2% have this disorder. However, many more people in the general population are likely to have less severe forms of the disorder that do not meet the formal criteria for diagnosis. The number of cases of binge-eating disorder is far greater than that of either anorexia nervosa or bulimia nervosa. This disorder is also more common among the severely obese and those with a long history of frequent restrictive dieting, although obesity is not a criterion for having binge-eating disorder.

Development and Characteristics of Binge-Eating Disorder

Individuals with binge-eating disorder (about 40% of whom are males) often perceive themselves as hungry more often than normal. They usually started dieting at a young age, began bingeing during adolescence or in their early twenties, and did not succeed in commercial weight-control programs. Almost half of those with severe binge-eating disorder exhibit clinical depression.

Typical binge eaters isolate themselves and eat large quantities of a favorite food. Stressful events and feelings of depression or anxiety can trigger this behavior. Giving themselves permission to eat a forbidden food can also precipitate a binge. Other triggers include loneliness, anxiety, self-pity, depression, anger, rage, alienation, and frustration. They sometimes binge on whatever is easy to eat in large amounts—noodles, rice, bread, leftovers. Characteristically, however, binge eaters consume foods that carry the social stigma of "junk" or "bad" foods—ice cream, cookies, sweets, potato chips, and similar snack foods.

In general, people engage in binge eating to induce a sense of well-being and perhaps even numbness, usually in an attempt to avoid feeling and dealing with emotional pain and anxiety. They eat without regard to biological need and often in a recurrent, ritualized fashion. Some people with this disorder eat food continually over an extended period, called *grazing;* others cycle episodes of bingeing with normal eating.[3] For example, someone with a stressful or frustrating job might come home every night and graze until bedtime. Another person might eat normally most of the time but find comfort in consuming large quantities of food when an emotional setback occurs.

Spreading one's dietary intake into numerous, small meals (grazing) over a day does not pose a problem if overall energy intake remains appropriate.

Although people with anorexia nervosa and bulimia nervosa exhibit persistent preoccupation with body shape, weight, and thinness, binge eaters do not necessarily share these concerns. Thus, neither purging nor prolonged food restriction is characteristic of binge-eating disorder. Some physicians classify binge-eating disorder as an addiction to food, involving psychological dependence. The person becomes attached to the behavior itself and has a drive to continue it, senses only limited control over it, and needs to persist at it despite negative consequences. Food is used to reduce stress, produce feelings of power and well-being, avoid feelings of intimacy with others, and avoid life problems. Note that obesity and binge eating are not necessarily linked. Not all obese people are binge eaters, and, although obesity may result from trying to numb emotional pain with food, it is not necessarily an outcome.

Binge-eating disorder is most likely to develop in people who never learned to express and deal appropriately with their feelings. Rather than face their problems, they turn to food.[17] They continue to do the things that perpetuate the experiences of frustration, anger, and pain. For example, people who regularly become frustrated because they don't assert themselves when necessary may eat to forget their frustration rather than learn to deal with this inhibition and practice assertiveness. The frustration will continue because they never attack the basic problem. Binge eating makes them feel they cannot control the behavior pattern and therefore cannot control their lives. Worse, the binge eating usually increases feelings of guilt, embarrassment, and shame.

People with binge-eating disorder may come from families with alcoholism or may have suffered sexual abuse. Members of such dysfunctional families often do not know how to deal effectively with emotions. They cope by turning to substances. Family members learn to cover up dysfunctional patterns for the alcoholic person and to nurture him or her at the expense of each other and their own needs.

Often, people who practice binge eating have been shaped by families who do not address and express feelings in healthful ways. The parents nurture and comfort their children with food rather than engage in healthy exchanges of self-disclosure of feelings and potential solutions. Members of such families learn to eat in response to emotional needs and pain instead of hunger. Those who regularly practice binge eating may grow up nurturing others instead of themselves, avoiding their own feelings and taking little time for themselves. Not knowing how to satisfy their personal and emotional needs in more healthful ways, people in these families turn to food.

For some people, frequent dieting beginning in childhood or adolescence is a precursor to binge-eating disorder. During periods when little food is eaten, they get very hungry and obsessive about food. When allowed to eat more food, they feel driven to eat in a compulsive, uncontrolled way. The pattern of periods of strict dieting alternating with binge eating may continue over time.

Help for the Person with Binge-Eating Disorder

Binge-eating disorder is seen in both men and women.

Those with binge-eating disorder must learn to eat in response to hunger—a biological signal—rather than in response to emotional needs or external factors (such as the time of day or the simple presence of food). Counselors often direct binge eaters to record their perceptions of physical hunger throughout the day and at the beginning and end of every meal. These people must learn to respond to a prescribed amount of fullness at each meal. They should initially avoid weight-loss diets because feelings of food deprivation can lead to more disruptive emotions and a greater sense of unmet needs. Diets are likely to encourage more intense problems, such as extreme hunger.[17] Many people with binge-eating disorder may experience difficulty in identifying personal emotional needs and expressing emotions. Because this problem is a common predisposing factor in binge eating, communication issues should be addressed during treatment. Binge eaters often must be helped to recognize their own buried emotions in anxiety-producing situations, and then encouraged to share them with their therapist or therapy group. Learning simple but appropriate phrases to say to oneself can help stop bingeing when the desire is strong.

Self-help groups, such as Overeaters Anonymous, aim to help recovery from binge-eating disorder. The treatment philosophy parallels that of Alcoholics Anonymous. Overeaters Anonymous attempts to create an environment of encouragement and accountability to overcome this eating disorder. Dietary advice typically ranges from avoiding restraint in eating to limiting binge foods. Some experts feel that learning to eat all foods—but in moderation—is an effective goal for binge eaters. This practice can prevent the feelings of desperation and deprivation that come from limiting particular foods. Fluoxetine (Prozac) and related SSRI antidepressants, as well as other psychiatric medications, also have been found to help reduce binge eating in these individuals by decreasing depression.[20] Overall, people who have this disorder are usually unsuccessful in controlling it on their own. Professional help is advised.

Other Examples of Disordered Eating

female athlete triad A condition characterized by disordered eating, lack of menstrual periods, and osteoporosis.

baryophobia A disorder of young children and young adults characterized by stunted growth. It results from parental underfeeding in an attempt to prevent the development of obesity and heart disease.

In recent years, two other conditions—**female athlete triad** and **baryophobia**—have been recognized as requiring professional treatment. Although these disordered eating patterns share some characteristics with anorexia nervosa and bulimia nervosa, each has distinctive qualities.

Female Athlete Triad

Women participating in appearance-based and endurance sports are at risk of developing an eating disorder.[9] One study of college-age female athletes found that 15% of swimmers, 62% of gymnasts, and 32% of all varsity athletes exhibited disordered eating patterns. Estimates of eating disorders for college women not involved in competitive sports are much lower.

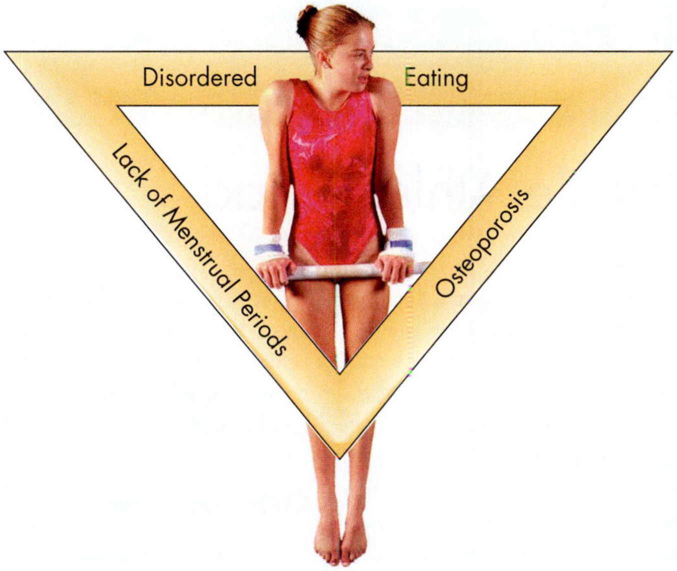

Figure 15-8 The female athlete triad occurs when the athlete has disordered eating, lack of menstrual periods, and osteoporosis. Stress fractures and recurrent fatigue also occur. This triad often is seen in appearance-related sports, such as gymnastics. Although not a specific DSM-IV category, long-term health is at risk. Thus, early treatment is most beneficial.

The tragic case of Christy Henrich illustrates why anyone at risk for the female athlete triad should seek professional help. As a young teenager, Christy weighed 95 pounds and was 4 feet 11 inches tall. She showed promise as a gymnast but was told that she was too fat to excel in gymnastics. Christy continued her training but often starved herself, some days consuming just an apple and frequently purging by vomiting. Her success in gymnastics continued, but at age 22 her weight had fallen to 52 pounds, and she died from the effects of long-term semistarvation.

In addition to disordered eating, college women athletes tend to experience irregular menstruation more frequently than other college women. Disordered eating, particularly food restriction and stress, can precipitate this, causing women to have less dense and weaker bones than normal because of lower estrogen concentrations in the blood. Some of these young women have bones equivalent to those of 50- to 60-year-olds, making them overly susceptible to bone and stress fractures during both sports and general activities. Much of the bone loss is irreversible.

The American College of Sports Medicine (ACSM) has named the syndrome female athlete triad because it consists of three parts: disordered eating, lack of menstrual periods, and osteoporosis (Fig. 15-8). The ACSM has issued a call to teachers, coaches, health professionals, and parents to educate female athletes about the triad and its health consequences.

Many coaches/trainers and even some health professionals wrongly believe that loss of menstrual periods is a normal consequence of a high level of physical activity. However, this loss of menstrual periods has negative consequences on the body, such as fragile bones, as just mentioned. Correcting menstrual irregularities by increasing caloric intake should help normalize hormone levels and increase bone mass. During therapy, a physician may prescribe a multivitamin and mineral supplement as well as calcium supplements as needed to maintain an intake of 1200 to 1500 mg. Dr. Jackie Berning discusses female athlete triad in more detail in the Expert Opinion.

Baryophobia

Some children and young adults who grow more slowly and have a shorter stature than normal may suffer from baryophobia (literally, "the fear of becoming heavy"). Inadequate growth in children usually results from disease—commonly, a hormonal or other metabolic abnormality. In the absence of a recognized disease in such children, the possibility of baryophobia, also called nutritional growth failure, should be investigated. This is not a specific psychiatric (DSM-IV) category, but can be serious nevertheless.

This disorder occurs when children are given the same low-fat, high-carbohydrate diet that adults follow. Adults do this in an attempt to prevent children from developing obesity or cardiovascular disease later in life. Today's parents and caregivers, themselves frequently harassed by weight problems, may be determined that the children in their care will avoid such ordeals. Although these caregivers are well intended, such severely restricted diets are detrimental to children because they don't supply enough

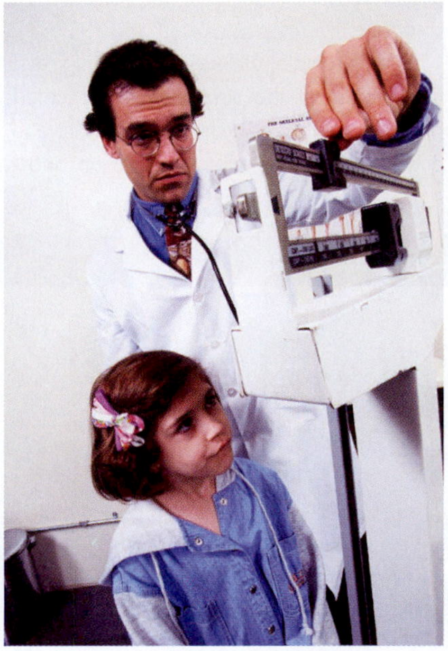

Gains in weight and height less than predicted for one's age can be a sign of baryophobia. If noted, this and other causes deserve further scrutiny.

Expert Opinion

A Closer Look at the Female Athlete Triad

Jackie Berning, Ph.D., R.D.

For the past 20 years participation in women's sports has surpassed all imagination. Today, women have many more opportunities to participate in high school and collegiate sports, as well as the potential to continue their athletic careers in the professional ranks. While these women derive significant health benefits from the physical training associated with sports they are also at risk for a syndrome of disordered eating, amenorrhea, and bone loss. This triad of disorders is known as "the female athlete triad."

Disordered Eating

Disordered eating is a medical term to include a broad spectrum of eating disorders. This can include anything from poor nutritional habits to the potentially lethal complications of anorexia nervosa and bulimia nervosa. In female athletes, depending on the sport studied, the prevalence of eating disorders ranges from 15 to 62%. Sports that emphasize leanness (such as endurance sports or aesthetic sports) are more likely to have a higher percentage of athletes with eating disorders.

Many female athletes with eating disorders may not meet the strict diagnostic criteria for anorexia nervosa or bulimia nervosa. Instead, they engage in regular energy restriction and fail to meet the energy demands for living and training. The motivation for this energy restriction is multifactorial. The most frequent factor is nutrition misinformation, which is the easiest to address. Dispelling myths and facts about training and diet or offering credible nutrition counseling can place the athlete "back on track." Unfortunately, the problem is often more complex than this. Female athletes in lean profile sports are under intensive pressure from coaches, peers, and judges about body weight and image. Unfortunately this intense pressure and any insensitive comment may play a key role in promoting disordered eating in these young athletes. In other cases, women with established eating disorders might choose a particular sport to participate in to help control her weight.

Amenorrhea

Most amenorrhea seen in female athletes is classified as secondary amenorrhea, since it results from the disease process rather than being a primary cause of the disease itself. Secondary amenorrhea is the loss of menstruation for three or more consecutive cycles in a female who has experienced the onset of menstruation. Between 1 to 44% of female athletes experience amenorrhea. Amenorrhea can be as high as 50% in elite runners and ballet dancers. The cause of the amenorrhea seems to be related to changes in the hypothalamus in the brain, but may be multifactorial. Potential factors include energy restriction, poor eating habits, disordered eating, energy imbalance, rapid weight loss, and increase in training.

Osteoporosis

This risk is related to less estrogen output, and so the athlete loses the protective effect of estrogen on bone. Athletic amenorrhea causes bone loss like that seen in menopause. Numerous studies have shown significant bone loss in amenorrheic athletes. Unfortunately, the bone that is lost is not replaced even if menstrual cycles are resumed. Because many of these young athletes are at a critical age of bone mass, many may never be able to reach their peak bone mass, and because 70% of bone mass is acquired during adolescence and early adulthood, these female athletes are at high risk for hip and spine fractures in later life stages. In addition, amenorrheic athletes are more prone to injury, especially stress fractures.

Identifying and Managing the Problem

Members of the sports medicine team, such as registered dietitians, must constantly beware of

energy to sustain an adequate growth rate. In young adults, low-energy diets may be self-imposed to avoid a perceived risk of obesity.

Because this disorder results largely from lack of appropriate nutrition information leading to poor food choices, nutritional counseling to caregivers and young adults is the most effective response. They need to be informed about the nutrient requirements and normal weight-gain patterns for the relevant age group. This counseling will show caregivers that including some sweets and medium-fat foods in a child's diet is appropriate (see Chapter 17). The diet can still minimize saturated fat and cholesterol intake, a more important focus in a diet designed to reduce the risk of cardiovascular disease. Supplying adequate carbohydrate, protein, fat, and other nutrients is the key to promoting growth in both height and weight during childhood and the young-adult years, and it can be done in a healthful manner.

Low body weight coupled with excessive exercise can lead to amenorrhea, and ultimately female athlete triad.

the symptoms and signs of female athlete triad. In the athletic culture, episodes of amenorrhea, weight loss, and injuries often may be attributed to some other cause other than the female athlete triad. For this reason, it is important for clinicians to obtain and maintain records of amenorrhea among female athletes. Each athlete with amenorrhea should be referred to a physician for ruling out other causes of the amenorrhea, such as pregnancy or thyroid disease. If an athlete appears to be excessively concerned about her weight or dieting, or if she is presenting with marked thinness, obsessive compulsion about training, fine lanugo hair, or erosion of tooth enamel, further investigation or confrontation about the eating disorder is recommended. Finally, any athlete presenting with a stress fracture should have a history obtained that includes a menstrual cycle history and baseline nutritional assessment.

The management of the athlete presenting with symptoms of the female athlete triad is best accomplished in a multidisciplinary approach including a physician, registered dietitian, psychologist, and athletic trainer. The primary goals of treatment are to control and manage the athlete's eating disorder, to restore normal hormone levels and to monitor and treat any injuries or other medical complications. Treatment strategies to reach these goals may include a slight reduction (10–20%) in the volume of training an athlete is participating in as well as a higher energy intake for a 2–5% increase in weight. It has been demonstrated that some amenorrheic athletes who gain weight either by cutting back on training or consuming more energy have a better chance of resuming normal menstrual activity. In addition to weight gain other factors need proper attention for normal menstruation, such as adequate sleep, management of stress, and nutritional intake. Most amenorrheic athletes fear weight gain and must be counseled that an increase in muscle weight could improve their stamina and performance. Calcium supplementation should be implemented in all athletes presenting with amenorrhea. Vegetarianism is another contributing factor to amenorrhea. Vegetarian athletes may be at risk for low energy, protein and micronutrient intakes because of elimination of food groups such as meat and dairy. Some researchers point out that along with the insufficient energy intake, inadequate amounts of protein may also play a role in the amenorrheic athlete.

Regardless of the cause of the amenorrhea in the female athlete a qualified nutrition professional can help improve the quality and quantity of the athlete's diet so that normal menstruation has a better chance of resuming. In addition to working individually with the athletes, the registered dietitian working with amenorrheic athletes should also work with the coach, athletic trainer, physician and strength and conditioning professional to provide amenorrheic athletes with the best possible environment for maximizing their performance as well as providing a normal, healthy functioning body.

Dr. Berning is a registered dietitian and assistant professor at the University of Colorado–Colorado Springs. She specializes in sports nutrition and consults for numerous professional sports teams in the United States. She works extensively with female athletes at the University of Colorado–Boulder and has been involved with counseling amenorrheic athletes for over 15 years. She has coauthored two books and numerous articles and chapters on sports nutrition.

Prevention of Eating Disorders

A key to developing and maintaining healthful eating behavior is to realize that some concern about diet, health, and weight is normal. It is also normal to experience variation in what we eat, how we feel, and even how much we weigh. For example, it is not abnormal to experience some minimal weight change (up to 2 to 3 pounds) throughout the day and even more over the course of a week. A large weight fluctuation or ongoing weight gain or weight loss is more likely to indicate that a problem is present. If you notice a large change in your diet, how you feel, or your body weight, it is a good idea to consult your personal physician. Treating physical and emotional problems early helps lead you to peace of mind and good health.

With a view to society as a whole, many people begin to form opinions about food, nutrition, health, weight, and body image prior to or during puberty. Parents, friends, and professionals working with young adults should help form positive habits and appropriate expectations, especially regarding body image.[10] To do this they should consider the following advice for preventing eating disorders:

- Discourage restrictive dieting, meal skipping, and fasting (except for religious reasons).
- Provide information about normal changes that occur during puberty.
- Correct misconceptions about nutrition, healthy body weight, and approaches to weight loss.
- Carefully phrase weight-related recommendations and comments and use them with caution.
- Don't overemphasize numbers on a scale. Instead, primarily promote healthful eating irrespective of body weight.
- Encourage normal expression of disruptive emotions.
- Encourage children to eat only when they're hungry.
- Teach the basics of proper nutrition and regular physical activity in school and at home.
- Provide adolescents with an appropriate, but not unlimited, degree of independence, choice, responsibility, and self-accountability for their actions.
- Increase self-acceptance and appreciation of the power and pleasure emerging from one's body.
- Enhance tolerance for diversity in body weight and shape, and personal food choices.
- Build respectful environments, supportive relationships.
- Encourage coaches to be sensitive to weight and body-image issues among athletes.
- Emphasize that thinness is not necessarily associated with better athletic performance.

Our society as a whole can benefit from a fresh focus on healthful food practices and a healthful outlook toward food and body weight.

Not only is treatment of eating disorders far more difficult than prevention, these disorders also have devastating effects on the entire family. For this reason, caregivers and health-care professionals alike must emphasize the importance of an overall healthful diet and moderation, as opposed to restriction and perfection.

Concept | Check

Food bingeing and grazing without purging are two behaviors characteristic of binge-eating disorder. Emotional disturbances are often at the root of this eating disorder. Treatment addresses deeper emotional issues and endorses avoiding food deprivation and restrictive diets, while restoring more normal eating behaviors. The female athlete triad consists of disordered eating, amenorrhea, and osteoporosis, and most commonly affects those in appearance-related and endurance sports. Parents, coaches, teachers, and health professionals need to initiate efforts to prevent and treat this problem. Baryophobia is a condition in which children are underfed by parents in an attempt to limit risk of future disease, such as obesity or cardiovascular disease. Growth failure—lack of expected weight and height gains—can result if nutrient intake is not increased to an appropriate amount.

Critical | Thinking

Tom, a high school teacher, is concerned about eating disorders. He wants to try to prevent young adults from falling into the discouraging traps of anorexia nervosa and bulimia nervosa. What are some of the topics and issues he should discuss with students in his health classes?

Books and Organizations to Help You Understand More About Eating Disorders

Along with the technical articles in the references, you can gain more insight into eating disorders from the following sources designed for the lay public:

Books

Andersen A, Cohn L, Holbrook T: *Making weight: Men's conflicts with food, weight, shape, and appearance.* Carlsbad, CA: Gurze Books, 2000.

Barnhill J, Taylor N: *If you think you have an eating disorder.* New York: Dell, 1998.
Berg FM: *Women afraid to eat. Breaking free in today's weight obsessed world.* Hettinger, ND: Healthy Weight Network, 2000.
Castle DJ, Phillips KA: *Disorders of body image.* Weightson, UK: Petersfied, 2002.
Costin C: *The eating disorder sourcebook.* Chicago: RGA, 1996.
Gilbert SD, Commeford MC: *The unofficial guide to managing eating disorders.* Foster City, CA: IDG, 2000.
Gordon RA: *Eating disorders: Anatomy of a social epidemic.* Malden, MA: Blackwell, 2000.
Nash JD: *Binge no more: Your guide to overcoming disordered eating.* Oakland, CA: New Harbinger, 1997.
Pipher M: *Hunger pains.* Holbrook, MA: Adams Publishing, 1995.
Robert-McComb JL: *Eating disorders in women and children: Stress management and prevention.* Boca Raton, FL: CRC Press, 2001.
Siegel M, Brisman J, Weinshel M: *Surviving an eating disorder. Strategies for families and friends.* New York: HarperCollins, 1998.
Woolsey MM: *Eating disorders: A clinical guide to counseling and treatment.* Chicago: American Dietetic Association, 2002.

Organizations and Self-Help Groups

Academy for Eating Disorders, 6728 McClean Village Dr., McLean, VA 22101; 703-556-9222; www.acadeatdis.org

American Anorexia Bulimia Association, 165 West 46th St., #1108, New York, NY 10036; 212-575-6200; www.aabainc.org

Eating Disorders Awareness and Prevention (EDAP), 603 Stewart St., Suite 803, Seattle, WA 98101; 206-382-3587 or 800 931-EDAP; www.nationaleatingdisorders.org

Harvard Eating Disorders Centers, 356 Boylston St., Boston, MA 02116; 617-236-7766; www.hedc.org

The National Eating Disorders Organization, 6655 South Yale Ave., Tulsa, OK 74136; 918-481-4044; www.laureate.com

The National Institute of Mental Health has recently published a concise review of eating disorders; www.nimh.nih.gov/publicat/eatingdisordersmenu.cfm

Summary

1. Anorexia nervosa is most common among high-achieving, perfectionist girls from families marked by conflict, high expectations, rigidity, and denial. The disorder usually starts with dieting in early puberty and proceeds to the near-total refusal to eat. Early warning signs include intense concern about weight gain and dieting, as well as abnormal food habits, such as cooking food that they won't allow themselves to eat.
2. Anorexic persons become irritable, hostile, overly critical, and joyless; they tend to withdraw from family and friends. Eventually, anorexia nervosa can lead to numerous physical effects, including a profound decrease in body weight and body fat, a fall in body temperature and heart rate, iron deficiency anemia, a low white blood cell count, hair loss, constipation, low blood potassium, and the loss of menstrual periods. Those with anorexia nervosa are physically very ill.
3. Treatment of anorexia nervosa includes increasing food intake to support slow weight gain. Psychological counseling attempts to help patients establish regular food habits and to find means of coping with the life stresses that led to the disorder. Hospitalization may be necessary, as well as use of certain medications.
4. Bulimia nervosa is characterized by secretive bingeing on large amounts of food at one sitting and then purging by vomiting or misuse of laxatives, diuretics, or enemas. Alternately fasting and excessive exercise may be used. Both men and women are at risk. Vomiting as a means of purging is especially destructive to the body; it can cause severe tooth decay, stomach ulcers, irritation of the esophagus, low blood potassium, and other problems. Bulimia nervosa poses a serious health problem and is associated with significant risk of suicide.
5. Treatment of bulimia nervosa includes psychological as well as nutritional counseling. During treatment, bulimic persons learn to accept themselves and to cope with problems in ways that do not involve food. Regular eating patterns are developed as these patients begin to plan meals in an informed, healthful manner. Certain medications can be a helpful addition to the regimen.
6. Binge-eating disorder, which is more widespread than either anorexia nervosa or bulimia nervosa, is most common among people with a history of frequent, unsuccessful dieting. Binge eaters typically either practice bingeing without purging or grazing (i.e., eating continually over extended periods). Thus, this condition

falls under the category Eating Disorders Not Otherwise Specified. Emotional disturbances are often at the root of this disordered form of eating. Treatment addresses deeper emotional issues, discourages food deprivation and restrictive diets, and helps restore normal eating behaviors. Certain medications may be a useful addition to this therapy.

7. The female athlete triad consists of disordered eating, loss of menstrual periods, and osteoporosis and is particularly common in appearance-related and endurance sports. If not corrected, this disorder eventually leads to decreased athletic performance and general health problems.

8. Baryophobia is a condition in which children are underfed by caregivers in an attempt to limit the risk of future disease, such as obesity or cardiovascular disease. Growth failure—in weight and height gains—can result if nutrient intake is not increased to appropriate amounts, and thus the condition is also called nutritional growth failure.

Study Questions

1. What are the typical characteristics of a person with anorexia nervosa? What may influence a person to begin rigid, self-imposed dietary patterns?

2. List the detrimental physical and psychological side effects of bulimia nervosa. Describe important goals of the psychological and nutrition therapy used to treat bulimic patients.

3. What is the current thinking concerning medication use for anorexia nervosa and bulimia nervosa?

4. Explain the role of excessive exercise in eating disorders.

5. How might parents significantly contribute to the development of an eating disorder? Suggest an attitude that a parent or an adult friend of yours displayed that may not have been conducive to developing a normal relationship to food.

6. Based on your knowledge of good nutrition and sound dietary habits, answer the following questions:

   a. How can repeated bingeing and purging lead to significant nutrient deficiencies?

   b. How can significant nutrient deficiencies contribute to major health problems in later life?

   c. A friend asks you, the nutrition expert, if it is okay to "cleanse" the body by eating only grapefruit for a week. What is your response?

7. How, in your opinion, has society contributed to the development of various forms of disordered eating? Provide an example.

8. How does binge-eating disorder differ from bulimia nervosa? Describe the factors that contribute to the development and treatment of binge-eating disorder.

9. List the three symptoms that constitute the female athlete triad. What is the major health risk associated with loss of menstrual periods in the female athlete?

10. Describe the common characteristics of a parent of a child with baryophobia (nutritional growth failure).

Annotated References

1. ADA Reports: Position of the American Dietetic Association: Nutrition intervention in the treatment of anorexia nervosa, bulimia nervosa, and Eating Disorders Not Otherwise Specified (EDNOS). *Journal of the American Dietetic Association* 101:810, 2001.

   Eating disorders are complex and serious illnesses, as described in detail in this article. To be effective in treating individuals who suffer from these illnesses, the expert interaction between professionals in many disciplines is required.

2. American Psychiatric Association: Practice guidelines for the treatment of patients with eating disorders (revision). *American Journal of Psychiatry* 157 (suppl): 4, 2000.

   People with eating disorders display a broad range of symptoms that occur along a continuum between those of anorexia nervosa and those of bulimia nervosa. The care of these people requires a comprehensive array of approaches to provide the best chance of treatment success.

3. American Psychiatric Association: *Diagnostic and statistical manual of mental disorders.* Fourth Edition (Text Revision) (DSM-IV-TR). Washington, DC: American Psychiatric Association, 2000.

   This manual contains the criteria used in diagnosing an eating disorder. The specific criteria for anorexia nervosa, bulimia nervosa, and binge-eating disorder are provided.

4. Becker AE and others: Eating disorders. *The New England Journal of Medicine* 340:1092, 1999.

   All facets of eating disorders, from detection to treatment, are reviewed. This is an excellent reference for more in-depth knowledge of eating disorders. All those with eating disorders should be evaluated and treated for medical complications of the disease at the same time psychotherapy and nutritional counseling are undertaken.

5. Chidley E: Eating disorders, nature or nurture? *Today's Dietitian*, p. 29, February 1999.

   Various studies have shown correlations between genetics and eating-disorder development. This new knowledge, however, is not going to change current therapy. We know that cognitive behavior therapy works for bulimia, and the fact that there are some genes that increase risk for developing the disease isn't going to change that practice.

6. Devlin MJ, Zhu AJ: Body image in the balance. *Journal of the American Medical Association* 286:2159, 2001.

   Dissatisfaction with body image is prevalent among North American men and women due, in part, to media influences. Body image distress is a problem in its own right and should be assessed with the care of a physician, registered dietitian, and psychologist.

7. Faine M, Mobley C: Case problem: Balancing nutrition advice with dental care in patients with anorexia and bulimia. *Journal of the American Dietetic Association* 99(10):1291, 1999.

   Extensive loss of tooth enamel is common in people with bulimia nervosa. The authors provide a detailed description of therapy for a patient who presented with an eating disorder and dental health problems.

8. Fairburn CG and others: Risk factors for anorexia nervosa: Three integrated case-control comparisons. *Archives of General Psychiatry* 56:468, 1999.

   Perfectionism and negative self-evaluation are common personality traits associated with eating disorders.

9. Hobart JA, Smucker DR: The female athlete triad. *American Family Physician* 61(11):3357, 2000.

The importance of the physician in detecting female athlete triad during a preparticipation sports physical exam is discussed. The author provides helpful hints in obtaining important information from the patient during the exam.

10. Hoerr SL and others: Risk for disordered eating relates to both gender and ethnicity for college students. *Journal of the American College of Nutrition* 21(4):307, 2002.

Both male and female college students of all races are at risk of eating disorders. Prevention is the key, especially by addressing body dissatisfaction.

11. Hoffman RP: Eating disorders in adolescents with type 1 diabetes. *Postgraduate Medicine* 109:67, 2001.

Adolescents, especially females, with type 1 diabetes have an increased risk of anorexia nervosa and bulimia nervosa, perhaps related to weight gain associated with strict glycemic control. Preventive treatments include decreasing dietary restraint and promoting healthful eating.

12. Keel PK: Long-term outcome of bulimia nervosa. *Archives of General Psychiatry* 56:63, 1999.

Long-term follow-up of bulimia nervosa patients has shown that about 30% continue to engage in binge eating or purging behaviors. The predictors of poor long-term outcome were longer duration of symptoms at the time of clinical presentation and a history of substance abuse.

13. Mehler PS: Diagnosis and care of patients with anorexia nervosa in primary care settings. *Annals of Internal Medicine* 134:1048, 2001.

Stress is an important cause of the loss of menstrual periods in anorexia nervosa. Thus reducing stress is an important goal of psychotherapy in this disorder.

14. Polivy J: Causes of eating disorders. *Annual Reviews of Psychology* 53:187, 2002.

Anorexia nervosa and bulimia nervosa have emerged as the predominant eating disorders in Western societies. These eating disorders may represent a way of coping with problems of identity and personal control. Still, there are many other contributing factors; none is sufficient to cause the problem.

15. Pritts SD, Susman J: Diagnosis of eating disorders in primary care. *American Family Physician* 67:297, 2003.

Excellent review of the diagnosis and stages of treatment of eating disorders. The many physical effects of the disorders are also highlighted.

16. Richards L: Body image and eating disorders: Not just women's issues. *Today's Dietitian,* p. 30, November 2001.

Men also are at risk of eating disorders. Treatment is often directed at a man's desire to be seen as athletic and should include other men in any group therapy.

17. Ruud J, Calhoun A: Nondiet approach to binge-eating disorder. *Today's Dietitian,* p. 30, March 2000.

This article includes two case studies that describe a nondiet approach to treating binge-eating disorder. This includes eating in response to hunger, normalizing feelings about food, and accepting one's size.

18. Walsh BT: Eating disorders. In Braunwald E and others (eds.): *Harrison's principles of internal medicine.* 15th ed. New York: McGraw-Hill, 2001.

Excellent review of the current knowledge in diagnosis and treatment of eating disorders. Highlighted is the need to provide up to 3000 to 4000 kcal/day during the treatment of people with anorexia nervosa.

19. Wells LA, Sadowski CA: Bulimia nervosa: Update and treatment recommendations. *Current Opinions in Pediatrics* 13:591, 2001.

Treatment of bulimia nervosa must be individualized and should include input from a variety of health professionals. Many patients respond well to the use of antidepressants and cognitive behavior therapy. Combining these two treatments seems to be a good strategy. Environmental and family issues also need to be addressed.

20. Zhu AJ, Walsh BT: Pharmacologic treatment of eating disorders. *Canadian Journal of Psychiatry* 47:225, 2002.

Medications have generally shown disappointing results in the treatment of anorexia nervosa. In contrast, numerous studies have demonstrated a clear role for antidepressants in the treatment of bulimia nervosa and possibly binge-eating disorder. There is also good efficacy for the combination of medication and psychotherapy in these latter two diseases.

Take | Action

I. Assessing Risk of Developing an Eating Disorder.

British investigators have developed a five-question screening tool called the SCOFF Questionnaire for recognizing eating disorders:†

1. Do you make yourself *Sick* because you feel full?
2. Do you lose *Control* over how much you eat?
3. Have you lost more than *One* stone (about 13 lb) recently?
4. Do you believe yourself to be *Fat* when others say you are thin?
5. Does *Food* dominate your life?

Two or more positive responses suggest an eating disorder.

1. After completing this questionnaire, do you feel that you might have an eating disorder or the potential to develop one?

   ____

   ____

2. Do you think some of your friends might have an eating disorder?

   ____

   ____

3. What counseling and education resources exist in your area or on your campus to help with a potential eating disorder?

   ____

   ____

4. If a friend has an eating disorder, what do you think is the best way to assist him or her in getting help?

   ____

   ____

†Morgan JF and others: The SCOFF Questionnaire, *British Medical Journal* 319:1467, 1999.

II. Helping Prevent Eating Disorders.

You have been asked to speak to a junior high school class about eating disorders. What are four major points that you would make to help prevent disordered eating in this population?

1. ____
2. ____
3. ____
4. ____

Here are points you may consider:

1. Extreme thinness is oversold in the media. Extremely low weight (i.e., BMI of less than 18.5, and even more so if less than 17.5) is generally not healthy.
2. Self-induced vomiting is dangerous. Damage to the teeth, stomach, and esophagus often results.
3. Loss of menstrual periods is a sign of illness. It is important to see a physician about this. Bone deterioration is a common result.
4. The treatment of eating disorders in early phases aids success. These diseases are difficult to treat once firmly established.

Nutrition | Perspective

Eating Disorders: A Sociological Perspective

One of the many criteria we use to evaluate ourselves is body image. We identify our bodies with our selves and judge them as we think others see us, knowing that our appearance affects their opinions of us.

Early in life, we develop images of "acceptable" and "unacceptable" body types. Of all the attributes that constitute attractiveness, many people view body weight as the most important, partly because we can control our weight somewhat. Fatness is the most dreaded deviation from our cultural ideals of body image, the one most derided and shunned, even among schoolchildren.

Females in particular are likely to diet because they feel strongly about what is acceptable in both size and weight. In general, though, most dieting women aren't technically obese. Rather, they diet to correct some perceived flaw or because they simply feel they should weigh less than they do now. Their impulse "to please" fosters this desire to look socially acceptable.

A recent survey in the magazine *Redbook* found that, of more than 3000 respondents, only 3% of the women were happy with their bodies. In contrast, 42% wanted to lose more than 50 pounds, 22% wanted to lose 20 to 50 pounds, 19% wanted to lose 10 to 20 pounds, and 11% wanted to lose 5 to 10 pounds.

Changing Times

The cultural ideal of the "full-bodied" woman did not survive into the twentieth century in Western society, although it is still in fashion in many nonindustrialized countries, where a large body is a sign of wealth. Over the course of the twentieth century, the ideal female body form in North America became progressively thinner. A thin waist with modest hips is now the overriding cultural "gold standard," at least as exemplified by models. Our passion for thinness may have its roots in the Victorian era, which specialized in denying "unpleasant" physical realities, such as appetite and sexual desire. Flappers of the 1920s cemented the twentieth century trend for thinness. Since 1922, the BMI values of Miss America winners has steadily decreased; during the last three decades, most winners had a BMI in the "underweight" range (less than 18.5).

Thinness as an Indicator of Competence

Unfortunately, many North Americans today view obesity as a failure of control, willpower, competence, and productivity. At stake are social acceptance and even access to scarce resources, such as good jobs and an attractive spouse. Whether we like it or not, in today's society our appearance says a lot about us, even though the way we were raised and our genetic background are beyond our control. Some people are simply much more likely to become obese than others. Implicit in our societal attitudes is the notion that those who can't control themselves enough to stay slim are unlikely to be good at supervising employees, organizing their work day, and shouldering heavy responsibilities. Clearly, fat is out. A prevailing myth is that thin people are more competent, energetic, and forceful than obese people.

Mixed Messages and Social Trends

Despite the pressure for thinness, our society is filled with mixed messages. Half the advertisements in women's magazines may describe diets or feature very thin models; the other half displays tasty foods. Movie and television stars are almost always perfect physical specimens. Nevertheless, television advertisements encourage us to visit our local quick-service restaurant. There you can buy a hamburger, french fries, and large soft drink, totaling approximately 1200 kcal or more—about the amount of energy our daily basal metabolism uses—without even leaving the car.

In the past several decades, divorce, alcohol abuse in families, child abuse, school- and work-related stress, socioeconomic changes, and crowded urban conditions have all increased. These changes in our family and social environments encourage children, adolescents, and adults alike to find a release from the pressure. Many find relief in food, which sets the stage for the development of an eating disorder.[15]

Internalizing the Thinness Ideal

Children's dolls often portray an extremely thin and distorted body shape.

Eating disorders are usually only a symptom of significant emotional trauma or psychological stress in a person's life. When psychiatrists are able to dig deeper, they find that eating disorders mask serious questions of self-worth, family struggles, and sometimes fears of puberty and the future.[3] The real illnesses are not the eating disorders—though they eventually contribute to poor health—but, rather, the way people feel about themselves. When people internalize the social value favoring thinness and can't meet that goal, their negative self-image is reinforced.

Researchers have linked this preference for a lean body type to the recent surge in eating disorders.[6] As the more full-figured woman was displaced by the ultrathin woman, the number of eating disorders increased, along with our society's preoccupation with obesity. The cultural pressures toward thinness seem to be stretching the physiological capabilities of many women (and men). For example, researchers surmise that the theoretical body fat content of the Barbie doll would not allow for menstruation. Given the natural variability in human basal metabolism and genetic makeup, as well as Americans' easy access to food and increasingly sedentary lifestyles, it is no surprise that some of us gain weight. People predisposed to eating disorders for either biological or emotional reasons may be nudged over the edge by these social changes.[5]

Glimmers of Hope

Because eating disorders stem in part from certain cultural values, changing these values might reduce the pressures predisposing some people to various types of disordered eating behavior. Feminists, for example, assert that true liberation means being free to find one's natural weight. Women who combine careers and motherhood are saying that they have more important things to worry about; some fashion leaders are tolerating more curves; exercise programs are encouraging regular brisk walking, rather than mostly jogging and working out. Writers, therapists, and some registered dietitians are working to help women accept their bodies, as noted in the "size acceptance" approach discussed in Chapter 13.

What is the difference between people who can accept themselves—even with a few more pounds than the glamorous people have—and those who chronically diet and feel dissatisfied? Perhaps it is the willingness to recognize that satisfaction comes from within, not from the mirror or the approval of others. The challenge facing many North Americans is achieving a healthy body weight without excessive dieting. This means adopting and maintaining sensible eating habits, a physically active lifestyle, and realistic and positive attitudes and emotions while practicing creative ways to handle stress.[1]

chapter 16

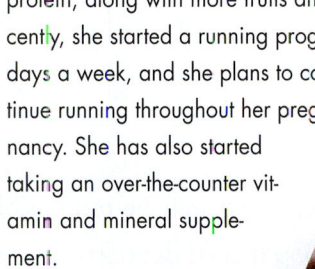

Pregnancy and Breastfeeding

Chapter | Outline

Case | Scenario

Tracey and her husband of 4 years have decided that they are ready to prepare for Tracey's first pregnancy. Tracey has been reading everything she can find on pregnancy because she knows that her prepregnancy health is important to the success of her pregnancy.

She just turned 25 and, so, is in the recommended childbearing age of 20 to 35 years. She knows to avoid alcohol, especially because she could become pregnant and not find that out right away. Alcohol is particularly toxic to the growing fetus in the first weeks of pregnancy. She is not a smoker, doesn't take any medications, and limits her coffee intake to 6 cups a day.

Based on her reading, she has decided to breastfeed her infant and has already checked out childbirth classes. She has modified her diet to include some extra protein, along with more fruits and vegetables. Recently, she started a running program 5 days a week, and she plans to continue running throughout her pregnancy. She has also started taking an over-the-counter vitamin and mineral supplement.

Tracey and her husband think that they have covered all the key areas of prepregnancy care. List a few positive attributes of her current practices you support. Can you identify some potential problems and what information they may have missed?

Refresh | Your Memory

As you begin your study of nutrition in pregnancy and breastfeeding in Chapter 16, you may want to review:

- Typical fortification in meal replacement bars in Chapter 1 and ready-to-eat breakfast cereals in Chapter 2.
- Causes and effects of ketosis in Chapter 4.
- The components of the macronutrient classes—carbohydrates, proteins, and lipids—in Chapters 5 to 7, especially omega-3 fatty aids.
- Alcohol content of various beverages in Chapter 8.
- The food sources of folate in Chapter 10, calcium in Chapter 11, and iron and zinc in Chapter 12.
- The calculation of body mass index in Chapter 13.
- Endocrine, reproductive, and immune systems in Appendix C.

Boost | Your Study

*Check out the **Perspectives in Nutrition: Online Learning Center** **www.mhhe.com/wardlawpers6** for quizzes, flash cards, activities, and web links designed to further help you learn about nutrition for pregnant and breastfeeding women.*

Chapter | Objectives

Chapter 16 is designed to allow you to:

1. List major physiological changes that occur in the body during pregnancy and how nutrient needs are altered.
2. List factors that predict a successful pregnancy outcome.
3. Specify the optimal weight gain during pregnancy for the normal adult woman.
4. Plan an adequate, balanced meal plan for a pregnant or lactating woman using the Food Guide Pyramid as a basis.
5. Identify the nutrients that may need to be supplemented during pregnancy and explain the reason for each.
6. Explain how some typical discomforts of pregnancy can be minimized by dietary changes.
7. Describe the physiological processes involved in breastfeeding, as well as some advantages of breastfeeding for both the infant and mother.
8. Describe the disease fetal alcohol syndrome and the related outcomes in an infant.

Pregnancy can be a very special time for a couple. Along with the responsibility of shaping a child's health and personality comes the prospective exhilaration of watching a child develop and grow. Those involved often feel an overriding desire to produce a healthy baby, which can pique new interest in nutrition and health information. They usually want to do everything possible to maximize their chances of having a robust, lively newborn.

Despite these possibilities, the infant mortality rate in North America is higher than that seen in many other industrialized nations. In Canada, about 6.1 of every 1000 infants per year die before their first birthday, while in the United States it is 6.9. Compare that to Sweden at roughly 3. In addition, in the United States, about 15 to 20% of pregnant women receive inadequate prenatal care in the early months of pregnancy. Teenage mothers are at the highest risk. These are alarming statistics for two countries that have such a high per capita expenditure for health care compared to many other countries in the world.

Producing a healthy baby is not just a matter of luck. True, some aspects of fetal and newborn health are beyond our control. Still, conscious decisions about social, health, and nutritional factors during pregnancy significantly affect the baby's health and future.[13, 15] Choosing to breastfeed the infant adds further benefits. Let's examine how eating well during pregnancy and breastfeeding can help a baby have a healthy start in life.

Planned Pregnancy

Pregnancy deserves planning because many practices or conditions of the mother that can harm the developing fetus are modifiable, such as the following:[4, 13, 15, 19]

- Alcohol consumption
- Use of certain medications, such as heavy use of aspirin
- Use of illegal drugs, such as cocaine and marijuana
- Job-related hazards and stresses
- Smoking
- Inadequate diet, such as too little iron, zinc, and too little synthetic folic acid intake
- Excess vitamin A intake and megadose use of other nutrient supplements
- Heavy caffeine use
- Lack of medical treatment with HIV-positive status or AIDS
- Poor control of ongoing diabetes or hypertension

Women need to pay attention to these risks in the months before conception. This precaution is necessary because women often do not suspect they are pregnant during the first few weeks after conception and may not seek medical attention until after the first 2 to 3 months.

Still, even without fanfare, the child-to-be grows and develops daily. For that reason, the health and nutrition habits of a woman who is trying to become pregnant—or has the potential to become pregnant—are particularly important. Although some aspects of fetal and newborn health are beyond control, a woman's conscious decisions about social, health, and nutritional factors affect her infant's health and future. Much research suggests that an adequate vitamin and mineral intake at least 8 weeks before conception and then during pregnancy can help prevent birth defects such as neural tube defects. This problem has been linked to folate deficiency (see Chapter 10). In addition, about 50% of pregnancies are unplanned. For these reasons, parents should be aware of the role nutrition plays in the development of a healthy infant both before and during pregnancy.[11]

Prenatal Growth and Development

For 8 weeks after conception, a human **embryo** develops from a fertilized **ovum** into a **fetus.** For about another 32 weeks, the fetus continues to develop. When its body finally matures, the infant is born. Until birth, the mother nourishes it via a **placenta,** an organ that forms in her uterus to accommodate the growth and development of the fetus (Fig. 16-1).

embryo In humans, the developing offspring in utero from about the beginning of the third week to the end of the eighth week after conception.

ovum The egg cell from which a fetus eventually develops if the egg is fertilized by a sperm cell.

fetus The developing life form from about the beginning of the ninth week after conception until birth.

placenta An organ that forms in pregnant women. Through this organ, oxygen and nutrients from the mother's blood are transferred to the fetus, and fetal wastes are removed. The placenta also releases hormones that maintain the pregnant state.

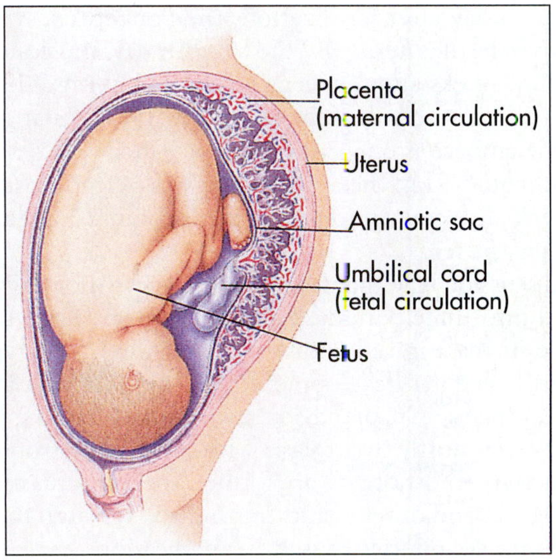

Figure 16-1 The fetus in relation to the placenta. The placenta is the organ through which nourishment flows to the fetus.
Illustration by William Ober.

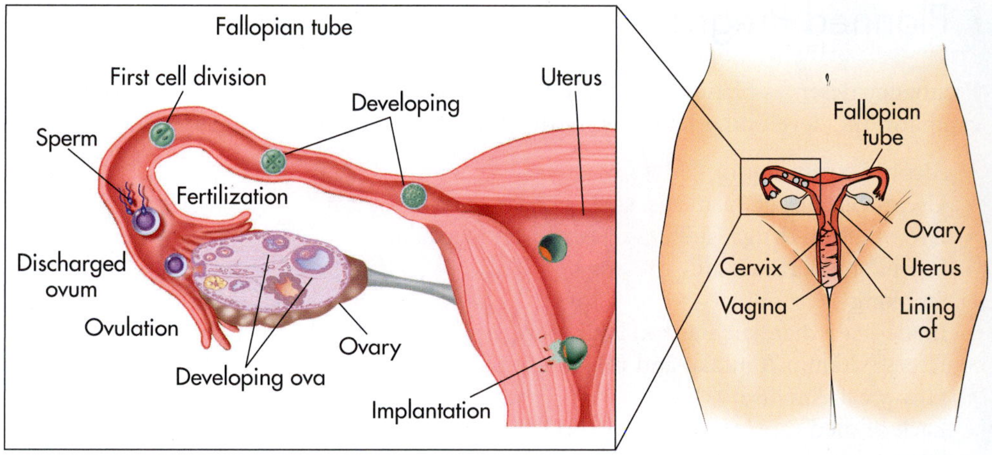

Figure 16-2 After ovulation, the discharged ovum first enters the abdominal cavity and then finds its way into the fallopian tube, where conception, or fertilization, takes place. Sperm cells "swim" up the fallopian tube toward the ovum. Fertilization most often occurs in the outer one-third of the fallopian tube. The ovum also takes an active role in the process of fertilization by attracting and "trapping" sperm with special receptor molecules on its surface. As soon as the head and neck of one spermatozoon enter the ovum (the tail drops off), complex mechanisms in the egg are activated to ensure that no more sperm enter. The 23 chromosomes from the sperm combine with the 23 chromosomes already in the ovum to make up the 46 chromosomes of the conceptus.

The role of the placenta is to exchange nutrients, oxygen and other gases, and waste products between the mother and the fetus. To do this, the placenta uses all of the absorption mechanisms employed by the GI tract (review Chapter 3). Even though the tissues of the placenta and the embryo are "interdigitated," the blood of the fetus and mother never mix. In fact, the fetal blood is separated from the maternal blood by just two layers of cells (5.5 μm). Fetal blood travels from the fetal heart to the placenta by way of two umbilical arteries and returns (nutrient-enriched and waste-free) to the fetus by means of one umbilical vein. In addition, the placenta also is a major site of hormone production during pregnancy. As the pregnancy continues, the placenta enlarges along with the fetus and usually weighs about 1.5 lb (0.7 kg) at delivery.

Early Growth—The First Trimester Is a Very Critical Time

The formation of the human organism begins when an egg and a sperm unite to form the **zygote** (Fig. 16-2). About 30 hours after the egg is fertilized, the zygote reproduces itself by dividing in half. The process of cell division then repeats many times. As the cluster of cells drifts down the fallopian tube to the woman's uterus, several kinds of cells emerge. The entire genetic code is passed to every cell, but each cell uses only a segment of the code to produce proteins. If this were not the case, there would be no different organs or body parts. For example, all cells carry genes which dictate hair color and eye color, but only the cells of the hair follicles and irises respond to that specific information.

zygote The fertilized ovum; the cell resulting from the union of an egg cell (ovum) and sperm until it divides.

On about the fourth day after fertilization, the **conceptus,** now about 64 to 128 cells and hollow, arrives in the uterus. By the seventh day, the conceptus implants into the uterine lining. Two weeks after conception the cell number has increased further, and the conceptus is now termed an embryo. By day 35 of gestation, the heart is beating, and, although the embryo is only 8 mm (about ⅜ inch) long, the eyes and so-called limb buds, which ultimately form the arms and legs, are clearly visible. From about the end of the eighth week after conception to its birth about 32 weeks later, the developing offspring is known as a fetus.

conceptus A generic term for any developmental stage derived from the fertilized ovum (zygote) until birth. The conceptus includes the extraembryonic membranes, as well as the embryo or fetus.

For purposes of discussion, the duration of pregnancy—normally, 38 to 42 weeks—is commonly divided into three periods, called **trimesters.** Growth begins in the first trimester with a rapid increase in cell number (hyperplasia). This type of growth dominates embryonic and later fetal development. The newly formed cells then begin to grow larger (hypertrophy; see Chapter 13 to review these terms). Further growth and development then involve mostly hyperplasia with some hypertrophy. By the end of 13 weeks—the first trimester—most organs are formed and the fetus can move (Fig. 16-3).

trimesters Three 13- to 14-week periods into which the normal pregnancy of 38 to 42 weeks is divided somewhat arbitrarily for purposes of discussion and analysis. Development of the offspring, however, is continuous throughout pregnancy, with no specific physiological markers demarcating the transition from one trimester to the next.

Nutritional deficiencies and other insults transmitted through the mother to the embryo or fetus—for example, injuries caused by medications and other drugs, high in-

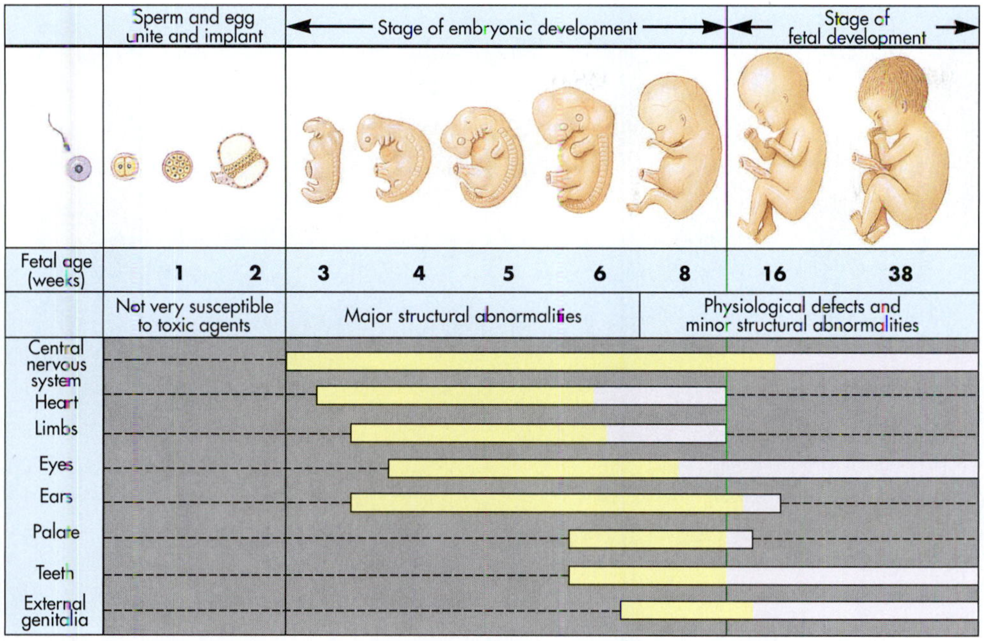

Figure 16-3 Vulnerable periods of fetal development. The most serious damage to the fetus from exposure to toxins is especially likely to occur during the first 13 weeks after conception (first trimester). The lighter bars indicate the time of greatest risk to the organ. As the chart shows, however, damage to vital parts of the body—including the eyes, brain, and genitals—can also occur during the last months of pregnancy.

Illustration by William Ober.

takes of vitamin A, radiation, or trauma—can alter or arrest the current phase of development (review Fig. 16-3).[1, 4, 15] The effects may last a lifetime. The most critical time for these problems to happen is during the first trimester. Most **spontaneous abortions**—premature terminations of pregnancy that occur naturally—happen at this time. Currently, about one-half or more of all pregnancies miscarry, often so early that a woman does not even realize she was pregnant. Early spontaneous abortions usually result from a genetic defect or fatal error in fetal development. Smoking, alcohol abuse, and illegal drug use also raise one's risk.

spontaneous abortion Cessation of pregnancy and expulsion of the embryo or nonviable fetus prior to 20 weeks gestation. This is the result of natural causes, such as a genetic defect or developmental problem; also called miscarriage.

A woman should avoid substances that may harm the developing fetus, especially during the first trimester. This holds true, as well, for the time when a woman is trying to become pregnant. As previously mentioned, she is unlikely to be aware of her pregnancy for at least a few weeks. In addition, the fetus develops so rapidly during the first trimester that, if an essential nutrient is not available, the fetus may be affected even before evidence of the deficiency appears in the mother.

For this reason, the quality of one's nutritional intake is more important than quantity during the first trimester. In other words, women should consume the same amount of food, but the foods should be more nutrient dense. Although some women lose their appetite and feel nauseated during the first trimester, they should be careful to meet nutrient needs as much as possible.[15]

Second Trimester

By the beginning of the second trimester, a fetus weighs about 1 oz. Arms, hands, fingers, legs, feet, and toes are fully formed. The fetus has ears and begins to form tooth sockets in its jawbone. Organs continue to grow and mature, and, with a stethoscope, physicians can detect the fetus's heartbeat. Most bones are distinctly evident through the body. Eventually, the fetus begins to look more like an infant. It may suck its thumb and kick strongly enough to be felt by the mother.

As shown in Figure 16-3, the fetus can now still be affected by exposure to toxins, but not to the degree seen in the first trimester. During the second trimester, the mother's breast weight increases by approximately 30% due to the deposition of 2 to 4 lb of fat for lactation. This stored fat serves as an energy reservoir for the extra energy needed to produce breast milk.

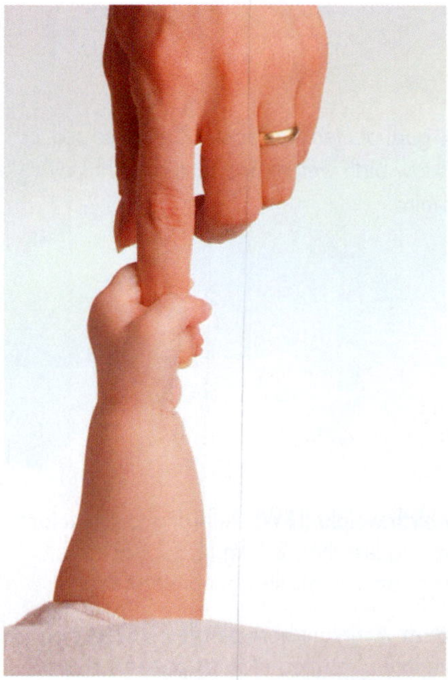

The time to begin thinking about prenatal nutrition is actually before becoming pregnant. This includes making sure synthetic folic acid intake is adequate (400 µg/day) and that any supplemental use of preformed vitamin A does not exceed 100% of the Daily Value (1000 µg RAE or 5000 IU).

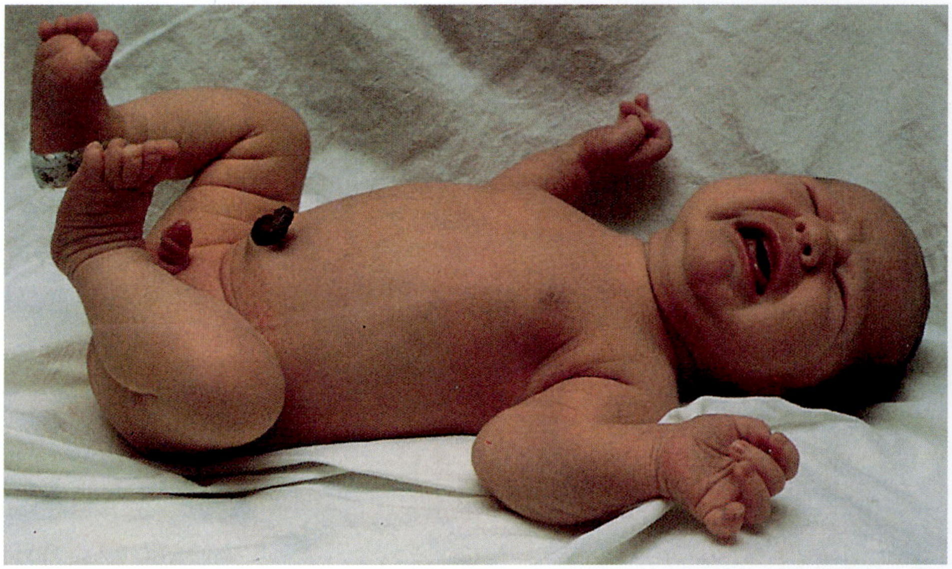

Figure 16-4 A healthy 1-week-old baby. At birth, a baby usually weighs about 7.5 lb and is 20 inches long.

Although a mother's decisions, practices, and precautions during pregnancy contribute to the health of her fetus, she cannot guarantee her fetus good health because some genetic and environmental factors are beyond her control. She and others involved in the pregnancy should not hold an unrealistic illusion of control.

Third Trimester

By the beginning of the third trimester, a fetus weighs about 2 to 3 lb. The third trimester is a crucial time for fetal growth. The fetus will double in length and will multiply its weight by five times. An infant that is born after about 26 weeks of **gestation** has a good chance of survival if it is cared for in a nursery for high-risk newborns. However, the infant will not contain the mineral (mainly iron and calcium) and fat stores normally accumulated during the last month of gestation. This and other medical problems, such as a poor ability to suck and swallow, complicate nutritional care for preterm infants. Note also that the fetus takes first priority with regard to iron, in that it will deplete the stores of the mother. If the mother is not meeting her iron needs, she can be severely depleted after delivery.[18]

gestation The period of intrauterine development of offspring, from conception to birth; in humans, gestation lasts for about 40 weeks after the woman's previous menstrual period.

At 9 months, the fetus usually weighs about 7 to 9 lb (3 to 4 kg) and is about 20 inches (50 cm) long (Fig. 16-4). A soft spot in the forehead indicates where the skull bones (fontanels) are growing together. The bones finally close by the time the baby is about 12 to 18 months of age.

A goal of *Healthy People 2010* is to reduce low birth weight and preterm births by one-third.

Definition of a Successful Pregnancy

To define a successful pregnancy, one common criterion is the protection of the mother's physical and emotional health, so that she can return to her prepregnancy health status. As for the infant, two widely accepted criteria are (1) a gestation period longer than 37 weeks and (2) a birth weight greater than 5.5 lb (2.5 kg). Sufficient lung development, which is likely to have occurred by 37 weeks' gestation, is critical to the survival of a newborn. The longer the gestation, the greater the ultimate birth weight and maturation state, and hence fewer medical problems are likely to occur.[1]

Low-birth-weight (LBW) infants are those weighing less than 5.5 lb (2.5 kg) at birth. Most commonly, LBW is associated with **preterm** birth. Full-term and preterm infants who weigh less than the expected weight for their duration of gestation, the result of insufficient growth, are described as **small for gestational age (SGA).** Thus, a full-term infant weighing less than 5.5 lb at birth is SGA but not preterm, whereas a preterm infant born at 30 weeks' gestation is probably LBW without SGA. Infants who are SGA are more likely than normal-weight infants to have medical complications, including problems with blood glucose control, temperature regulation, and growth and development in the early weeks after birth.

low birth weight (LBW) Referring to any infant weighing less than 2.5 kg (5.5 lb) at birth; most commonly results from preterm birth.

preterm An infant born before 37 weeks of gestation; also referred to as *premature.*

small for gestational age (SGA) Referring to infants who weigh less than the expected weight for their length of gestation. This corresponds to less than 2.5 kg (5.5 lb) in a full-term newborn. A preterm infant who is also SGA will most likely develop some medical complications.

The newborn's quality of life must also be considered in rating the success of a pregnancy. Overall, prospective parents should strive toward producing a baby who is born healthy, on time, and with the mental, physical, and physiological capabilities to take advantage of whatever life offers, while also protecting the mother's health.

Nutrition is one key to a successful pregnancy. Eating healthfully is vital during pregnancy to ensure the health of both the offspring and the mother. Fetal organs and body parts begin to develop very soon after conception. Again, the first trimester (13 weeks) is an especially critical period, when poor nutrition or drug use can result in birth defects.[11]

Studies from Britain suggest SGA infants are likely to develop diabetes, hypertension, and high blood cholesterol during later adult years. Reduced growth of the liver, the pancreas, and other organs during gestation is one possible reason. This increase in health risk is especially pronounced if the infants also fail to gain enough weight in the first year of life.[9]

Concept | Check

Adequate nutrition, especially meeting folate needs from a synthetic source starting 8 weeks before pregnancy begins, is vital both before and during pregnancy to help ensure the optimal health of both the mother and her offspring. Organs and body parts in the offspring begin to develop very soon after conception. The first trimester is a critical period when inadequate nutrient intake or alcohol and drug use can result in birth defects.

Infants born after 37 weeks of gestation who weigh more than 5.5 lb (2.5 kg) have the fewest medical problems at birth. To reduce infant and maternal medical problems or death, those involved with the pregnancy should take the steps necessary to allow the mother to carry the baby in her uterus for the entire 9 months and contribute to adequate growth. Good nutrition and health practices aid in this goal.

Critical | Thinking

Alexandra wants to have a baby. She has read that it is very important for the woman to be healthy during the pregnancy. However, Jane, her sister, tells her that, actually, before she becomes pregnant is the time to begin to assess her nutritional and health status. What additional information should Jane have given Alexandra?

Increased Nutrient Needs to Support Pregnancy

The first comprehensive scientific report about nutrition and pregnancy was issued in 1970 by the National Academy of Sciences and was updated in 1990. Both documents emphasized an increase (not restrictions) in nutritional requirements during pregnancy and the importance of individually assessing and counseling mothers-to-be.

Increased Energy Needs

An average pregnancy has an Estimated Energy Requirement approximately 350 to 450 kcal greater than prepregnancy needs during the second and third trimesters (the greater amount is needed in the third trimester). (Energy needs during the first trimester are essentially the same as for the nonpregnant woman.) An example of such an increase includes about six whole-wheat crackers, 1 oz cheese, and ½ cup of nonfat milk, or 1 cup of low-fat yogurt and an orange. Although she may "eat for two," the pregnant woman must not double her normal energy intake. She will want to seek the best-quality foods to ensure the best possible health for her child. Note that many vitamin and mineral needs are increased by up to 50% during pregnancy, whereas energy needs during the second and third trimesters represent only about a 20% increase, based on adding 400 kcal to an intake of 2000 kcal per day by nonpregnant women.[15]

Adequate energy intake is easy to achieve and can be assessed by appropriate weight gain throughout the pregnancy. However, to obtain the necessary vitamins and minerals without increasing her energy intake too much, a pregnant woman needs to pay attention to her nutrient intake.[1]

If a woman is active during pregnancy, she can add the extra energy she uses to the energy allowance for pregnancy. Her greater body weight requires more energy for activity. Women can continue most activities during pregnancy, except certain calisthenics, such as deep knee bends; scuba diving; downhill skiing; weight lifting; and contact sports (such as hockey). Walking, cycling, swimming, or light aerobics for 30 minutes or more on most, if not all, days of the week is generally advised. However, normally

Walking, cycling, swimming, and light aerobics are all suitable exercises during pregnancy.

During pregnancy, women in North America are more likely to gain excess weight and make poor food choices than to eat too little.

The American College of Obstetrics and Gynecology suggests the following guidelines for physical activity during pregnancy:

1. Do not allow heart rate to exceed 140 beats per minute.
2. Avoid exercising in hot, humid weather.
3. Discontinue exercise that causes discomfort or overheating.
4. Drink plenty of liquids to avoid dehydration and overheating.
5. After about the fourth month, don't exercise while lying on your back, as this decreases cardiac output.
6. Avoid an abrupt decrease in exertion. In other words, don't just stop and stand around after a hard workout; rather, continue exercising but at a slow pace, gradually reducing pulse rate.

Weight gain should be carefully monitored during pregnancy.

Table 16-1 Recommended Weight Gain in Pregnancy Based on Prepregnancy Body Mass Index (BMI)

	Total Weight Gain*	
BMI Category	**(lb)**	**(kg)**
Low (BMI < 19.8)	28–40	12.5–18
Normal (BMI 19.8 to 26)	25–35	11.5–16
High (BMI 26 to 29)	15–25	7–11.5
Obese (BMI > 29)	≤ 15	≤ 7

Reprinted with permission from *Nutrition During Pregnancy and Lactation*, Copyright 1992 by the National Academy of Sciences. Courtesy of the National Academy Press, Washington, DC.

*The listed values are for singleton pregnancies. Short women (< 62 inches) should strive for gains at the lower end of the ranges. For women of normal BMI who are carrying twins, the range is 35 to 45 pounds (16 to 20 kg). Adolescents within 2 years of menarche and African American women should strive for gains at the upper end of the ranges.

inactive women should not begin an intense exercise program during pregnancy. Because many women find that they are inactive during the later months, partly because of their increased size, an extra 350 to 450 kcal in their daily diet is usually enough.

Women with high-risk pregnancies, such as premature contractions of labor, may need to restrict their physical activity. To ensure optimal health for both herself and her infant, a pregnant woman should first consult her physician about physical activity and possible limitations.

Adequate weight gain for a mother is one of the best predictors of pregnancy outcome.[1] Her diet should allow for approximately 2 to 4 lb (0.9 to 1.8 kg) of weight gain during the first trimester and then a subsequent weight gain of 0.75 to 1 lb (0.3 to 0.5 kg) weekly during the second and third trimesters. Total weight gain goal for a woman of normal weight (based on BMI) (Table 16-1) averages about 25 to 35 lb (11.5 to 16 kg). Adolescents and African American women, who often have smaller babies, are strongly advised to aim for the greater amount. Women carrying twins should gain 35 to 45 lb, and those carrying triplets should gain 50 lb (23 kg).

For women with a low BMI, the goal increases to 28 to 40 lb (12.5 to 18 kg). The goal decreases to 15 to 25 lb (7 to 11.5 kg) for women at a high BMI, and 15 lb (7 kg) or less for an obese woman. Figure 16-5 shows why the typical recommendation begins at 25 lb.

A weight gain of between 25 and 35 lb for a woman starting at normal weight has repeatedly been shown to yield optimal health for both mother and fetus if gestation lasts at least 38 weeks. The weight gain should yield a birth weight of 7.5 lb (3.5 kg). Although some extra weight gain during pregnancy is usually not harmful, it can set the stage for creeping weight gain during the childbearing years if the mother does not return to about her prepregnancy weight.

Weight gain during pregnancy, especially in the teenage years, requires regular monitoring that approximately follows the pattern in Figure 16-5. Infant birth weights improve if the mother's weight gain meets the ranges previously mentioned. Keeping weekly records of a pregnant woman's weight gain helps assess how much to adjust her food intake. Weight gain is a key issue in prenatal care and a concern of many mothers. Inadequate weight gain can cause many problems. If a woman deviates from the desirable pattern, she should be warned of this and counseled on how to make the appropriate adjustment.[1]

For example, if a woman begins to gain too much weight during her pregnancy, she should not be encouraged to lose weight to get back on track. Even if a woman gains 35 lb in the first 7 months of pregnancy, she must still gain more during the last 2 months. She should simply slow the increase in weight to parallel the rise on the prenatal weight gain chart. In other words, the sources of the unnecessary food energy should be found and minimized. Alternately, if a woman has not gained the desired weight by a given

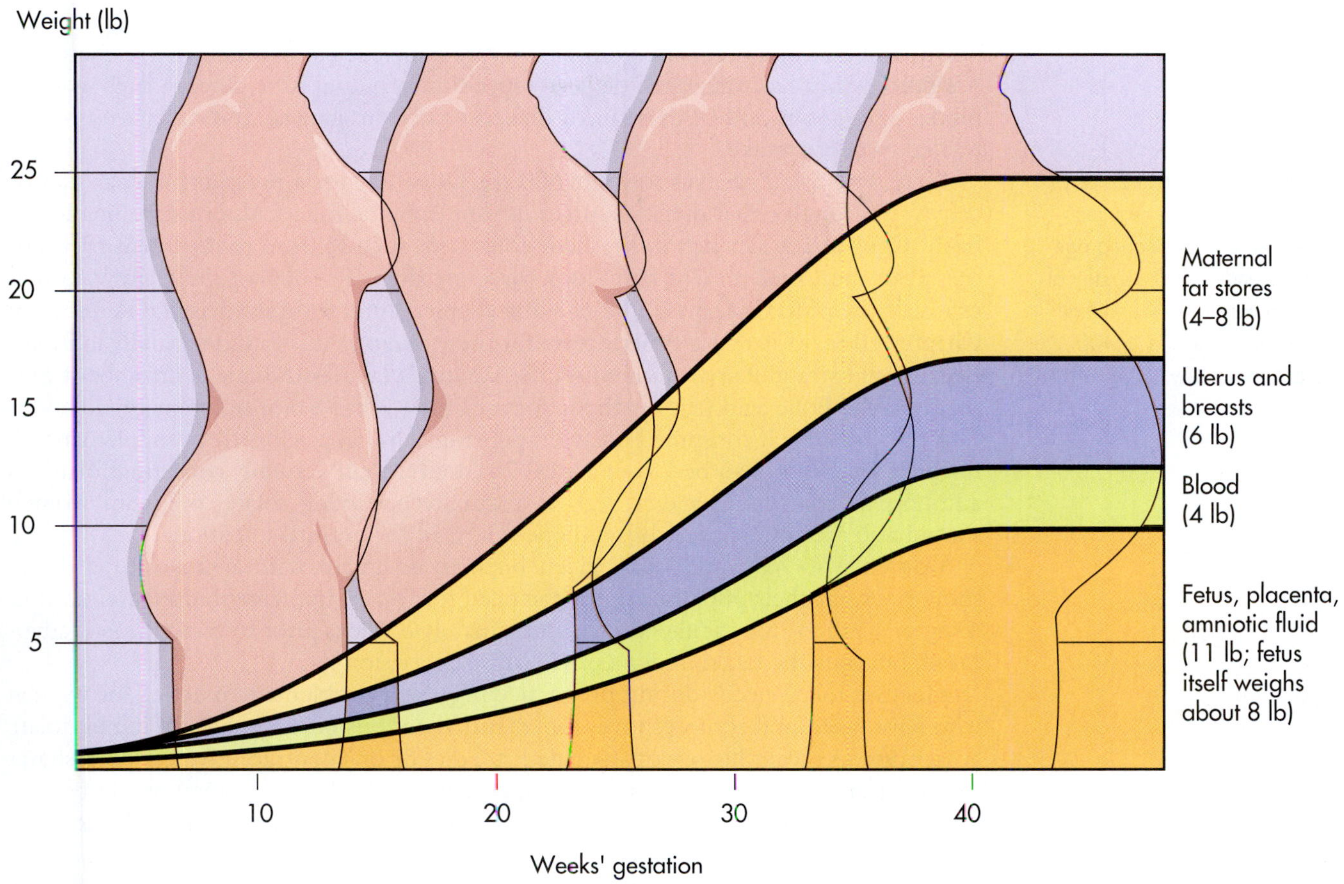

Figure 16-5 The components of weight gain in pregnancy. A weight gain of 25 to 35 pounds (lb) is recommended for most women. Note that the various components total about 25 pounds.

point in pregnancy, she shouldn't be encouraged to gain the needed weight rapidly. Instead, she should slowly gain a little more weight than the typical pattern to meet the goal by the end of the pregnancy. A registered dietitian can help stabilize her weight gain.

Increased Protein and Carbohydrate Needs

The RDA for protein increases by 25 g daily (or alternately to 1.1 g/kg body weight). A glass of milk alone contains 8 g. Many nonpregnant women already eat the recommended amount of protein per day and therefore don't need to increase protein intake. However, all women should check to make sure they are actually eating enough protein. The RDA for carbohydrate increases to 175 g daily. This amount prevents ketosis, which can harm the fetus (see later section on the effects of nutrition and other factors on pregnancy outcome). Most women already consume this amount and more.

Increased Vitamin Needs

Vitamin needs generally increase from prepregnancy RDAs/Adequate Intakes by up to 30% for the B-vitamins, except vitamin B-6 (45%) and folate (50%).

The extra amount of vitamin B-6 and other B-vitamins (except folate) needed in the diet is easily met via wise food choices, such as a serving of a typical ready-to-eat breakfast cereal and some animal protein. Folate needs, however, often merit specific diet planning. Because the synthesis of DNA requires folate, this nutrient is especially crucial during pregnancy. Ultimately, both fetal and maternal growth depend on an ample supply of folate. Red blood cell formation, which requires folate, increases during pregnancy. Serious megaloblastic anemia can result if folate intake is inadequate. The RDA

Healthy People 2010 has set a goal of increasing the number of pregnancies that begin with optimum folate status, to 80% from the current estimate of 21%, thus reducing the occurrence of neural tube defects.

for folate increases during pregnancy to 600 µg DFE/day. This is a critical goal in the nutritional care of a pregnant woman.[19] Folate deficiency at conception and thereafter has been associated with birth defects—specifically, neural tube defects, such as spina bifida. Still, about 30% of these birth defects arise from genetic and other reasons unrelated to folate intake.

Neural tube defects develop within 28 days after conception, and could be reduced by up to 70% if all women of childbearing age were to meet the recommended 400 µg/day of synthetic folic acid. A recent survey found that only 29% of women were consuming ≥ 400 µg of synthetic folic acid each day.

Increasing folate intakes to meet 600 µg DFE/day for a pregnant woman can be achieved through either dietary sources or supplemental folic acid, or a combination of both. Choosing a diet rich in synthetic folic acid, such as from ready-to-eat breakfast cereals or meal replacement bars (look for approximately 100% of the Daily Value), is especially helpful. Otherwise, the use of a supplemental form is advised.[1] Recall from Chapter 10 that folate is a generic term for the vitamin as it is found naturally in foods. Because of extra glutamates found on the vitamin's tail, food folate is only about 50% bioavailable. Folic acid (the synthetic form of folate) has a monoglutamate tail and is 100% bioavailable if consumed on an empty stomach. Folic acid—from supplements or fortified foods—is absorbed from a meal 70% better than naturally occurring folate. In addition to consuming a diet high in naturally occurring folate, pregnant women should also seek out sources of synthetic folic acid for optimal nutrition.

Women who have previously given birth to an infant with a neural tube defect should consult their physician about the need for folate supplementation; an intake of 4 mg of synthetic folic acid per day approximately 8 weeks prior to conception is advocated, but must be taken under a physician's supervision.

Meeting folate needs during pregnancy may be a problematic practice for women who have taken oral contraceptives for extended periods because this can inhibit folate absorption. A recent history of an inadequate diet or oral contraceptive use necessitates careful attention to folate intake during pregnancy. Ideally, the woman would begin a folate-rich diet (or take a supplement containing folic acid) approximately 8 weeks before conception.

Increased Mineral Needs

Mineral needs generally increase during pregnancy, especially the need for iodide and iron.

Pregnant women need extra iodide (total of 220 µg/day) for prevention of goiter. The extra iron (total of 27 mg/day) is needed to synthesize the greater amount of hemoglobin needed during pregnancy and to provide iron stores for the fetus.[18] Typical iodide intakes suffice if the woman uses iodized salt. However, women often need an iron supplement, especially if they do not consume iron-fortified foods, such as highly fortified breakfast cereals containing 90 to 100% of the Daily Value for iron (18 mg). Because iron supplements decrease appetite and can cause nausea and constipation, taking them between meals or just before going to bed is best. Milk, coffee, or tea should not be consumed with an iron supplement because these beverages have substances that interfere with iron absorption. Eating foods rich in vitamin C along with nonheme iron–containing foods helps increase iron absorption from those sources. Pregnant women who are not anemic may wait until the second trimester, when pregnancy-related nausea generally lessens, to start iron supplementation.

It is also important to meet zinc needs in pregnancy. The RDA for zinc increases to 11 mg/day, 35% higher than that for nonpregnant women. The protein foods in the diet of a healthy pregnant woman should supply this much zinc. In some cases a prenatal supplement containing zinc is also needed.[12]

Severe iron deficiency anemia in pregnancy, especially in the first half of pregnancy, may lead to preterm delivery, low birth weight, and increased risk for fetal death in the first weeks after birth.[18] As previously mentioned, infants take first priority when it comes to iron. This means that the fetus depletes the mother's iron stores during the third trimester. In other words, an inadequate iron intake may actually be more harmful to the mother than to the fetus.

Is There an Instinctive Drive During Pregnancy to Consume More Nutrients?

Extra needs for folate and iron are the most difficult for pregnant women to satisfy. These, then, should be the focus of diet planning for pregnant women. Before diet planning is discussed, however, one important misconception about pregnancy needs to be dispelled. You may have heard that mothers instinctively know what to eat and that their craving for pickles and ice cream is dictated by a natural desire to consume needed nutrients. Instead, these cravings, most common during the last two trimesters, are more likely related to hormonal changes in the mother, or just family traditions.

It remains an even greater mystery why some women crave nonfood items during pregnancy. The craving for and eating items such as starch, ice, chalk, burnt matchsticks, soap, plaster, and soil, especially noted during pregnancy, is called **pica.** This practice occurs more frequently among low-income women in North America and is sometimes associated with iron deficiency, even though the craved substances do not provide any iron. Pica also poses some health risks. Eating soil raises the risk of infections from parasites or lead toxicity and can cause anemia, as well as life-threatening blockages of the intestinal tract. The consumption of laundry starch, wall plaster, moth balls, and toilet air fresheners are also dangerous because they contain toxic compounds. Eating ice can break teeth. Overall, although women may have a natural instinct to consume the right foods in pregnancy, humans are so far removed from living by instinct that relying on our desires is risky. Nutrition counseling can focus food choices more reliably.[1]

pica The practice of eating nonfood items, such as dirt, laundry starch, or clay.

About one-third of pregnant women do not experience strong food cravings.

Food Plan for Pregnant Women

One approach to a diet that supports a successful pregnancy is based on the Food Guide Pyramid. It includes at least the following:

- Two servings from the milk, yogurt, and cheese group (three servings for teenagers, or substitute some calcium-fortified foods for some of the servings)
- Three servings from the meat, poultry, fish, dry beans, eggs, and nuts group
- Three servings from the vegetable group
- Two servings from the fruit group
- Six servings from the bread, cereal, rice, and pasta group

Specifically, the servings from the milk, yogurt, and cheese group could include low-fat or nonfat versions of milk, yogurt, and cheese. These foods supply extra protein and carbohydrate, as well as other nutrients. Servings from the meat, poultry, fish, dry beans, eggs, and nuts group include both animal and vegetable sources. Besides protein, these foods help provide the extra iron and zinc needed.

The vegetable and fruit group servings provide a variety of vitamins and minerals. One serving from this combination should be a good vitamin C source, and one serving should be a green vegetable or other rich source of folate. Selections from the bread, cereal, rice, and pasta group should focus on whole-grain and enriched foods. One serving of a ready-to-eat breakfast cereal significantly contributes to meeting many vitamin and mineral needs.

Table 16-2 illustrates one daily menu based on the basic diet plan shown. This daily menu supplies about 2000 kcal but still meets the extra nutrient needs associated with pregnancy. Women who need to consume more than this—and some do for various reasons—should add more servings from the fruit and vegetable groups and the bread, cereal, rice, and pasta group to the basic plan.

Recently FDA warned pregnant women to avoid swordfish, shark, king mackerel, and tile fish because of possible mercury contamination. Mercury can harm the nervous system of the fetus. Canned tuna is also a potential mercury source. It should be consumed not more than two times per week.

Use of Prenatal Vitamin and Mineral Supplements

Specially formulated supplements for pregnant women are prescribed routinely by most physicians. Some are sold over the counter, while others of these are dispensed by prescription because of their high folic acid content (1000 µg), which could pose problems for others, such as older people (review Chapter 10). This reliance on prenatal supplements may be common because it is easier for physicians to prescribe supplements than to discuss diet changes. Also, some pregnant women are simply unwilling to change their diets to meet their increased nutrient needs, or they simply expect (or

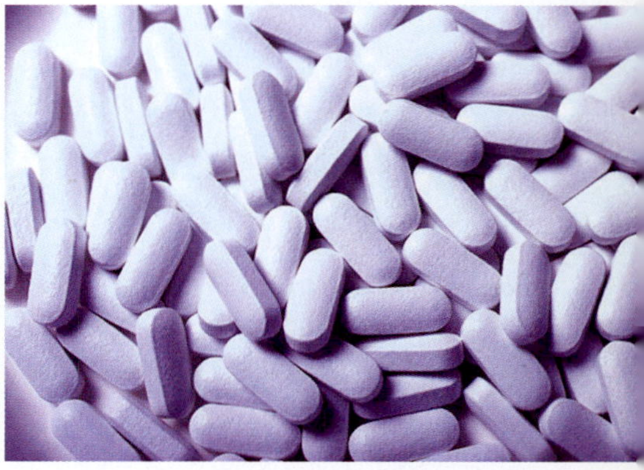

Pregnancy, in particular, is not a time to self-prescribe vitamin and mineral supplements. For example, although vitamin A is a routine component of prenatal vitamins, it is important to note that over four times the RDA has been shown to have toxic effects on the fetus.

A salad each day provides many nutrients for the prenatal diet.

Table 16-2 Sample 2000 kcal Daily Menu That Meets the Nutritional Needs of Most Pregnant and Breastfeeding Women

	Vitamin B-6	Folate	Iron	Zinc
Breakfast				
1½ cups Quaker Toasted Oatmeal Squares cereal	✓	✓	✓	✓
½ cup orange juice		✓		
¾ cup nonfat milk	✓			
Snack				
2 tbsp peanut butter	✓	✓	✓	✓
1 slice whole-wheat toast		✓	✓	✓
½ cup plain low-fat yogurt	✓			
½ cup strawberries				
Lunch				
1½ cups spinach salad with 1 tbsp oil and vinegar dressing		✓		
½ tomato				
1 slice whole-wheat toast		✓	✓	✓
1 oz provolone cheese	✓			
Snack				
4 whole-wheat crackers		✓	✓	✓
1 cup nonfat milk	✓			
Dinner				
3 oz lean hamburger, broiled (with condiments)	✓		✓	✓
½ cup baked beans	✓	✓	✓	✓
1 hamburger bun		✓	✓	
½ sliced tomato				
¾ cup cooked broccoli		✓		
1 tsp soft margarine				
Iced tea (milk if a teenager)				
Snack				
Nutri-Grain bar		✓	✓	✓

This diet meets nutrient needs for pregnancy and lactation. Lack of a check (✓) indicates a poor source of the nutrient. The vitamin- and mineral-fortified breakfast cereal used in this example makes an important contribution to meeting nutrient needs, such as for synthetic folic acid (400 µg per cup, which equals 680 DFE). If more food energy is needed, 1 cup of nonfat milk, 1 slice of whole-wheat bread, and 5 baby carrots would increase intake to 2200 kcal.

The breakdown of nutrients in a typical over-the-counter prenatal vitamin is 800 µg RAE (4000 IU) vitamin A, 100 mg vitamin C, 10 µg (400 IU) vitamin D, 5 mg (11 IU) vitamin E, 1.8 mg thiamin, 1.7 mg riboflavin, 18 mg niacin, 2.6 mg vitamin B-6, 800 µg folic acid, 4 µg vitamin B-12, 200 mg calcium, 27 mg iron, and 25 mg zinc. Prescription prenatal vitamins have 1000 µg folic acid (800 µg is the highest dose that can be sold over the counter).

demand) to be given a supplement. Prenatal supplements include the critical nutrients for pregnancy—that is, vitamin B-6, iron, zinc, and folate—and many others as well.

There is no evidence that use of such supplements causes significant health problems in pregnancy, aside perhaps from the combined amounts of supplementary and dietary vitamin A. During pregnancy, supplemental preformed vitamin A should not exceed 3000 µg RAE/day (15,000 IU/day). Toxicity of vitamin A is linked with **teratogenesis** (see Chapter 9). This occurs mainly during the first trimester. The primary instances when prenatal supplements may contribute to a successful pregnancy are with poor women, teenagers, those with a generally deficient diet, and women carrying multiple fetuses.[1]

teratogenic Tending to produce physical defects in a developing fetus.

Pregnant Vegetarians

Women who practice either lactoovovegetarianism or lactovegetarianism generally do not face special difficulties in meeting their nutritional needs during pregnancy. Like nonvegetarian women, they should be concerned primarily with meeting iron and folate needs, and, in addition, calcium and zinc needs.[1]

On the other hand, when a total vegetarian (vegan) becomes pregnant, she must carefully plan a diet that includes sufficient protein, vitamin D (or sufficient sun exposure), vitamin B-6, iron, calcium, and zinc and must have a supplemental source of vitamin B-12. The basic vegan diet listed in Chapter 7 should be modified to include more grains, beans, nuts, and seeds to supply the necessary extra amounts of some of these nutrients. Because iron and calcium are poorly absorbed from most plant foods, iron and calcium supplements are probably necessary.[17, 18] However, to avoid competition for absorption, they should not be taken together. The amounts provided by prenatal supplements should suffice to meet iron needs but not calcium needs (only 200 mg of calcium are contained in a typical prenatal supplement). The prenatal supplement also fulfills vitamin D needs if sufficient sun exposure does not take place.

Concept | Check

Energy needs increase by an average of about 350 to 450 kcal per day during the second and third trimesters of pregnancy. Weight gain should be slow and steady up to a total of 25 to 35 lb for a woman of healthy weight. Protein, vitamin, and mineral needs all increase during pregnancy. Vitamin B-6, folate, iron, iodide, and zinc are nutrients of particular concern. A pregnant woman's diet should be varied and generally include more milk products than a prepregnancy diet. A prenatal multivitamin and mineral supplement is commonly prescribed but may not be necessary, depending on one's diet and current health status. Taking too many supplements—especially vitamin A—can be hazardous to the fetus.

Effect of Nutritional Status on the Success of Pregnancy

Is this attention to nutrition worth the effort? Yes; evidence shows that the effort is justified. Extra nutrients and energy are used for fetal growth, as well as the changes in the mother's body to accommodate the fetus. Her uterus and breasts grow, the placenta develops, her total blood volume increases, the heart and kidneys work harder, and stores of body fat increase.

Although it is difficult to specify what degree of poor nutrition will affect each pregnancy, a daily diet containing only 1000 kcal has been shown to greatly restrict fetal growth and development. Increased maternal and infant death rates seen in famine-stricken areas of Africa supply further evidence (see Chapter 20).

Genetic background can explain very little of the observed differences in birth weight in North America. Both environmental factors and nutritional factors are more important. The worse the nutritional condition of the mother at the beginning of pregnancy, the more valuable a good prenatal diet and/or use of prenatal supplements are in improving the course and outcome of her pregnancy.

Obesity also increases pregnancy risks. These pregnancies require intense monitoring, and as well pose an increased risk for birth defects in the infant, primarily because of excess fetal growth.

During World War II, parts of Russia and much of Holland were blockaded. Food supplies were quickly exhausted. The resulting undernutrition greatly affected the birth weights of infants developing in the second or third trimester. Birth defects also occurred more commonly, and the number of new pregnancies fell. After the blockades were lifted, birth weights, subsequent infant health, and the numbers of new pregnancies quickly returned to prewar levels.

At the same time, researchers working in Boston noticed that an adequate protein intake is associated with a greater success of pregnancy. It appeared that the mother's diet—not only during pregnancy but also preceding conception—affects the health of both mother and infant. Studies in Toronto then showed that dietary supplements and nutritional counseling improved the health of the pregnant mother and produced a healthier baby. As health improved, complication rates also decreased. Researchers in

Great Britain took this one step further. They showed that height and social class are better predictors of pregnancy outcome than dietary intake during pregnancy. Supporting this is a study of middle-class African American women in Chicago. Even with nutritional supplements, their risk of having LBW infants still exceeded that of middle-class Whites, possibly reflecting the effects of poverty on previous generations. This finding suggests that long-term nutritional intake may be critical to pregnancy outcome.

Laboratory animal studies have supported the importance of diet during pregnancy. Food deprivation in pregnant laboratory animals led to smaller organ size in the offspring, affecting even the brain, which usually resists nutritional insults. In addition, placentas weighed less, and fewer healthy offspring survived the first weeks of life.

Effects of Other Factors on Pregnancy Outcome

In North America, about 11 of every 100,000 live births end in the mother's death. The infant mortality rate is even higher: for each 100,000 live births, about 600 to 700 infants die within the first year. The infant death rate among African Americans is more than double the rates among Whites and Hispanics in the United States. Based on the national statistics, the United States currently ranks 25th among industrialized nations in terms of maternal and infant death rates. Such grim and discomforting statistics can be attributed largely to the current number of teenage pregnancies in this country and to inadequate prenatal care, as well as marginal nutritional status among poor pregnant women.

Beyond the Nutrients

Many factors other than nutrition also affect the health of mother and fetus.[1, 5, 7, 11]

Low Socioeconomic Status

A constellation of characteristics that are typical of low socioeconomic status, such as poverty, inadequate health care, poor health practices, lack of education, and unmarried status, is associated with problems in pregnancy. Currently, in the United States about 31% of all births are to unwed mothers, many of whom are poor.

The risks of low birth weight and preterm delivery increase modestly, but progressively, with maternal age. Given close monitoring, however, a woman older than 35 has an excellent chance of producing a healthy infant. Most women in this age group exhibit typical pregnancy-related problems, which usually are manageable if under close medical supervision.

Closely Spaced Births

Siblings born in succession with less than a year between them are more likely to be born with low birth weights than are those further apart in age. In one study, the risks of low birth weight, preterm birth, or small size for gestational age were 30 to 40% higher for infants conceived less than 6 months following a birth compared to those conceived 18 to 23 months following a birth. This danger is especially prevalent among African American women.

Teenage Pregnancy

About half a million teenagers give birth in the United States each year, accounting for about 13% of all births. In Canada, the comparable statistics are about half that amount. Teenage pregnancy poses special health problems for both the mother and child. Young women continue maturing into physical adulthood for 5 years after **menarche.** Because the average age for menarche is 13 years in the United States, a woman younger than 18 years is not as physically ready to be pregnant as she will be later. However, by age 16 poor birth outcomes begin to decline.

menarche The onset of menstruation. Menarche usually occurs around age 13, 2 or 3 years after the first signs of puberty start to appear.

Pregnant teens frequently exhibit a variety of other risk factors that can complicate pregnancy and pose a risk to the fetus. For instance, teenagers are more likely than older women to be underweight at the beginning of pregnancy and to gain fewer than 16 lb during pregnancy. In addition, their bodies generally lack the maturity needed to safely carry a pregnancy. Sixteen percent of low-birth-weight infants are born to teenage mothers. This occurrence takes place even with adequate prenatal care. Furthermore, the specific needs of pregnant teenagers vary according to their own growth patterns, body build, and physical activity habits. Thus, it is difficult to estimate their nutrient needs. Overall, mothers who are between 25 and 34 have the best pregnancy outcomes.

Pregnant teenagers need close monitoring throughout pregnancy. Ideally, teenage pregnancy should be avoided.

Inadequate Prenatal Care

Inadequate, absent, or delayed prenatal care can allow maternal nutritional deficiencies to deprive a fetus of needed nutrients. Chronic diseases, such as hypertension or diabetes, increase the risk of fetal damage. Without prenatal care, a woman is three times more likely to give birth to an LBW baby—one who will be 40 times more likely to die during the first 4 weeks of life than a normal-birth-weight infant. (The ideal time to start prenatal care is before conception.) Still, about 20% of women in the United States receive no prenatal care in the first trimester—a critical time to change habits.

Lifestyle Factors

Smoking, alcohol consumption, use of some medications, and illegal drug use in pregnancy all lead to harmful effects. The Nutrition Perspective at the end of this chapter reviews one effect of alcohol—fetal alcohol syndrome. Smoking is linked to preterm birth and low birth weight and appears to increase the risk of birth defects, sudden infant death, and childhood cancer. Problem drugs include aspirin (when used heavily), hormone ointments, nose drops, rectal suppositories, weight-control pills, and medications prescribed for previous illnesses.

Marijuana is the most common drug used during the reproductive years. For pregnant women, marijuana use is very risky and potentially can result in reduced blood flow and oxygen to the uterus and placenta and poor fetal growth. Low birth weight and higher risk of premature delivery often are seen in infants whose mothers used marijuana during pregnancy.

Of the illegal drugs, cocaine has the most devastating consequences for the developing fetus. As cocaine use has become more common in recent years, the number of infants born to cocaine-using women has increased. Maternal use of cocaine during pregnancy has been linked to preterm birth, as well as to an undersized head and body and several other physical malformations in the newborn. Exposure of the fetus to cocaine appears to disrupt development of the brain and nervous system and may reduce interactive behaviors and responses to environmental stimuli in the infant.

Hospital-related costs of caring for low-birth-weight newborns total more than $2 billion per year in the United States, ranging from $20,000 to $200,000 per child. Compare this with an average hospital-related cost of $5800 for a normal delivery and an average of $800 for preventive prenatal care.

Prenatal Ketosis

Ketosis is not desirable for the growing fetus. Ketone bodies are thought to be poorly used by the fetal brain, implying possible slowing of fetal brain development. Researchers oppose crash diets or fasting for more than 12 hours during pregnancy. A pregnant woman can develop significant ketosis after only 20 hours of fasting. Eating at least 175 g of carbohydrate every day prevents such ketosis. Even nonpregnant women usually eat this amount and more.

Critical | Thinking

Hannah, a 16-year-old high school student, has just discovered that she is pregnant. At 5′3″ and 105 lbs. she is underweight and her typical diet lacks many essential nutrients. For breakfast, she will have coffee and a doughnut, if anything at all. She often skips lunch or eats chips from the vending machine. She then eats a well-rounded dinner with her family. What risks do you see in this situation for Hannah and her baby?

Caffeine Consumption

Research on the effects of caffeine consumption by pregnant women has produced some provocative findings. Caffeine decreases the absorption of iron and may reduce blood flow through the placenta, and studies have shown that the fetus is unable to detoxify caffeine. Studies using laboratory animals have shown that the risk of spontaneous abortion increases in the first trimester and early in the second trimester with heavy caffeine consumption (> 500 mg per day). About five cups of coffee per day contain this amount of caffeine (see Appendix J). In addition, as caffeine intake increases, so does the risk of delivering a low-birth-weight infant. Heavy caffeine use during pregnancy may also lead to caffeine withdrawal symptoms in the newborn. Finally, high caffeine intake often occurs in women who also smoke. In this case, it is the smoking that is the greater contributor to low birth weight.

Coffee intake should be limited to about three cups per day because the caffeine present can have deleterious effects on the fetus. In addition, caffeinated soft drinks and tea should also be limited.

Toxoplasmosis is another infection that causes birth defects, leading to about 3000 such cases per year in the United States. Pregnant women should limit exposure to the organism that causes toxoplasmosis by avoiding contact with cat feces (have someone else clean the cat's litter box or wear gloves), avoiding contact with kittens, bird feces, and garden soil (or wear garden gloves), and by not eating raw or undercooked meat.

Women with acquired immune deficiency syndrome (AIDS) may pass the virus that causes this disease to the fetus during pregnancy or the birth process. About one in three infected newborns will develop AIDS symptoms and die within just a few years. Studies show that these odds of mother-infant transmission can be cut significantly if the woman begins taking the drug azidothymidine (AZT) and other related AIDS medications by the fourteenth week of pregnancy. Thus, screening pregnant women for AIDS and treating those with AIDS using AZT are currently advocated by some experts.

Although more research is needed, it is advisable to limit caffeine intake. Drinking no more than three cups of coffee and no more than four cups of caffeinated soft drinks per day during pregnancy, or when pregnancy is possible, is advocated.[1] Limiting intake from tea, over-the-counter medicines containing caffeine, and chocolate is also important.

Aspartame Use

Phenylalanine, a component of aspartame (NutraSweet® and Equal®), causes concern for some pregnant women. High amounts of phenylalanine in maternal blood disrupt fetal brain development if the mother has a disease known as *phenylketonuria* (see Chapters 4, 5, and 7). If the mother does not have this condition, however, it is unlikely that the baby will be affected by aspartame use. Some experts still recommend caution with regard to aspartame, but total abstinence is hardly warranted, based on current knowledge.[1]

Listeria Infection

Infection by the bacterium *Listeria monocytogenes* causes mild flulike symptoms, such as fever, headache, and vomiting, about 7 to 30 days after exposure. However, pregnant women, newborn infants, and people with depressed immune function may suffer more severe symptoms, including spontaneous abortion and serious blood infections. In these high-risk people, 25% of infections may be fatal.

Because unpasteurized milk, soft cheeses made from raw milk (brie, camembert, feta, and blue cheeses), and raw cabbage can be sources of listeria organisms, it is especially important that pregnant women and other people at high risk avoid these products. Experts advise consuming only pasteurized milk products and cooking meat, poultry, and seafood thoroughly to kill this and other foodborne organisms. It is unsafe in pregnancy to eat any raw meats or other raw animal products. Chapter 19 covers foodborne illness, such as *Listeria* infections, in more detail.

Prenatal Care and Counseling

Education, an adequate diet, and early and consistent prenatal medical care maximize the chances of producing a healthy baby and avoiding the risks just covered, such as smoking, vitamin A supplements, medicines, illegal drugs, and alcohol use. If diabetes or hypertension is present or developing, it must be carefully controlled to minimize complications in the pregnancy.[5] X-ray exposure is also important to avoid.

Again, women should receive these examinations and counseling strategies before becoming pregnant. Certainly, they should begin early in pregnancy. Many potential problems that develop during pregnancy can be diagnosed and quickly treated medically.

Food habits cannot be predicted from income, education, or lifestyle. Although some women already have good dietary habits, most can benefit from nutritional advice. All should be reminded of habits that may harm the growing fetus, such as severe dieting or fasting. By focusing on appropriate prenatal care, nutrient intake, and proper health habits, as well as using common sense, parents give their fetus—and, later, their infant—the very best chance of thriving.[1]

Several U.S. government programs exist to reduce infant mortality by providing high-quality health care and foods. These are designed to alleviate the effects of poverty and insufficient education. An example of such a program is the Special Supplemental Nutrition Program for Women, Infants, and Children (WIC). This program offers health assessments and vouchers for foods that supply high-quality protein, calcium, iron, and vitamins A and C to pregnant women, infants, and children (to age 5 years) from low-income populations.

On the WIC program, participants' diets have improved markedly, as has the likelihood that these women will have healthy babies. This program is credited with decreasing the cases of iron deficiency anemia and LBW infants within the population it serves. Studies have estimated that every dollar spent on the prenatal component of WIC saves about $3 in public health expenditures for the care of LBW babies.

The WIC program is available in all areas of the United States and has a staff trained to help women have healthy babies. More than 7 million women, infants, and young children are currently enrolled in the program, but many eligible pregnant women are not participating in this program.

Attention to one's diet is especially important in pregnancy.

Case Scenario | Follow-up

From a dietary standpoint, Tracey is smart to take a close look at her protein intake because needs will increase slightly during pregnancy. More fruits and vegetables will provide some fiber to help prevent constipation, which is common in the later stages of pregnancy. These foods also supply folate, and her use of an over-the-counter vitamin and mineral supplement provides an ample amount of synthetic folic acid. Still, she should discuss this supplement use with her physician and would probably eventually benefit more from a prenatal supplement, as this will have more iron than over-the-counter multivitamin and mineral supplements. Her diet may not have enough calcium, so she should pay as much attention to consuming some extra calcium as she does for protein. Avoiding alcohol is a smart move.

Many experts would say that she is consuming too much caffeine and would be wise to cut down to three cups of coffee per day or less. Her exercise routine is probably too vigorous if she hasn't already been practicing regular running. Tracey should not begin a new exercise routine upon becoming pregnant unless it is at a moderate pace, such as brisk walking or stationary biking.

Concept | Check

Infants born after 37 weeks of gestation and weighing more than 5.5 lb (2.5 kg) have the fewest medical problems at birth. Individual mothers and whole societies can attempt to reduce infant and maternal death and medical problems by limiting the factors that increase the risk of having a preterm or small-for-gestational-age infant. Such contributing factors, besides an inadequate diet in general, include low socioeconomic status; closely spaced births; inadequate or absent prenatal care; cigarette smoking; alcohol consumption; illegal drug use, such as cocaine; teenage pregnancy; inadequate prenatal weight gain; heavy caffeine use; *Listeria* exposure; and prenatal ketosis. Adequate nutrition can reduce the risk of many medical problems in pregnancy.

A goal of *Healthy People 2010* is 100% abstinence from alcohol, cigarettes, and illicit drugs by pregnant women.

Physiological Changes That Can Cause Discomfort in Pregnancy

During pregnancy, the fetus's needs for oxygen, nutrients, and excretion increase the burden on the mother's lungs, heart, and kidneys. Although a mother's digestive and metabolic systems work very efficiently, some discomfort accompanies the changes her body undergoes to accommodate the fetus.

Heartburn, Constipation, and Hemorrhoids

Hormones (such as progesterone) produced by the placenta relax muscles in both the uterus and the intestinal tract. This often causes heartburn as stomach acid refluxes into the esophagus (see Chapter 3). When this occurs, the woman should avoid lying down after eating, eat less fat so that foods pass more quickly from the stomach into the small

Critical | Thinking

Sandy, who is 4 months pregnant, has been having heartburn after meals, constipation, and difficult bowel movements. As a nutrition student, you understand the digestive system and the role of nutrition in health. What remedies might you suggest to Sandy to relieve her problems?

intestine, and avoid spicy foods she can't tolerate. She should also consume liquids between meals to decrease the volume of food in the stomach, and thus related pressure that encourages reflux. Women with more severe cases may need antacids or related medications.

Constipation often results as the intestinal muscles relax during pregnancy. It is especially likely to develop late in pregnancy, as the fetus competes with the GI tract for space in the abdominal cavity. To offset these discomforts, a woman should perform regular exercise and consume more fluid, fiber, and dried fruits, such as prunes (dried plums). The Adequate Intake for fiber in pregnancy is 28 g, slightly more than for the nonpregnant woman. These practices can help prevent constipation and a problem that frequently accompanies it, hemorrhoids. Straining during elimination can lead to hemorrhoids, which are already more likely to occur during pregnancy because of other body changes. A reevaluation of the need and dose of iron supplementation also should be considered, as this practice is linked to constipation, especially intake > 120 mg/day.

Edema

Placental hormones cause various body tissues to retain fluid during pregnancy. Blood volume also greatly expands during pregnancy. The extra fluid normally causes some swelling (edema). There is no reason to restrict salt severely or use diuretics to limit mild edema. However, the edema may limit physical activity late in pregnancy and occasionally requires a woman to elevate her feet to control the symptoms. Overall, edema generally spells trouble only if hypertension and the appearance of extra protein in the urine accompany it (see later section on pregnancy-induced hypertension).

Morning Sickness

A few crackers between meals can help lessen morning sickness.

About 75% of pregnant women experience nausea during the early stages of pregnancy.[10] This nausea may be related to the increased sense of smell induced by pregnancy-related hormones circulating in the bloodstream. Although commonly called "morning sickness," pregnancy-related nausea may occur at any time and persist all day. It is often the first signal to a woman that she is pregnant. To help control mild nausea, pregnant women can try the following: avoiding nauseating foods, such as fried or greasy foods; cooking with windows open to dissipate nauseating smells; eating soda crackers or dry cereal before getting out of bed; avoiding large fluid intakes early in the morning; and eating smaller, more frequent meals. Because the iron in prenatal supplements triggers nausea in some women, changing the type of supplement used or postponing use until the second trimester may provide relief in some cases. If a woman thinks her prenatal supplement is related to morning sickness, she should discuss switching to another supplement with her physician.

Overall, whether it is broccoli, soda crackers, or lemonade, if a food sounds good to a pregnant woman with morning sickness, she should eat it and eat when she can, while also striving to follow her prenatal diet. Ginger (250 mg taken four times a day) also may help to relieve morning sickness. If she has a great deal of difficulty in following her diet, she should alert her physician to this and follow the advice given. Usually, nausea stops after the first trimester; however, in about 10 to 20% of cases, it can continue throughout the entire pregnancy. In cases of serious nausea, the preceding practices offer little relief. When appetite is severely reduced or vomiting persists, medical guidance is warranted. Hospitalization may be needed if the woman exhibits significant dehydration or weight loss. This is called hyperemesis gravidarum. Sometimes total parenteral nutrition is needed in these cases to support the health of the mother and the fetus until the problem remits.

Anemia

To supply fetal needs, the mother's blood volume expands to approximately 150% of normal. The number of red blood cells increases by only 20 to 30%, and this occurs more gradually. As a result a pregnant woman has a lower ratio of red blood cells to total blood volume in her system. This hemodilution is known as **physiological anemia.** It is a normal response to pregnancy, rather than the result of inadequate nutrient intake. If during pregnancy, however, iron stores and/or dietary iron intake are not sufficient to meet needs, any resulting iron deficiency anemia requires medical attention.[18]

physiological anemia The normal increase in blood volume in pregnancy that dilutes the concentration of red blood cells, resulting in anemia; also called *hemodilution*.

Gestational Diabetes

Hormones synthesized by the placenta (especially human placental lactogen) antagonize the action of insulin. This antagonism can precipitate **gestational diabetes,** often beginning in weeks 20 to 28, particularly in women who have a family history of diabetes or who are obese. In North America, gestational diabetes develops in about 4% of pregnancies; however, it increases to 7% in the Caucasian population. Today, pregnant women often are screened at 24 to 28 weeks for elevated blood glucose concentration 1 to 2 hours after consuming 100 g of glucose. If gestational diabetes is detected, a special diet distributing carbohydrate intake throughout the day needs to be implemented. Sometimes insulin injections are also needed. In addition, regular physical activity is helpful. Although gestational diabetes often disappears after the infant's birth, it is linked to the development of diabetes later in the mother's life, especially if she fails to maintain a healthy body weight. Proper control of both gestational diabetes (and any diabetes present in the mother before pregnancy) is extremely important. If not treated, the primary risk is that the fetus can grow quite large (fetal macrosomia). The fetus produces much insulin in an effort to compensate for the increase in blood glucose. This causes increased fetal growth. The pregnancy may require a cesarean section due to the size of the fetus. Other concerns are the potential need for early delivery, increased risk of birth trauma and malformations, and hypoglycemia in the infant at birth.

gestational diabetes A high blood glucose concentration that develops during pregnancy and returns to normal after birth; one cause is the placental production of hormones that antagonize the regulation of blood glucose by insulin.

Pregnancy-Induced Hypertension

Pregnancy-induced hypertension is a high-risk disorder and occurs in about 7 to 8% of pregnancies. In its mild forms, it is also known as *preeclampsia* and, in severe forms, as *eclampsia*. Early symptoms include a rise in blood pressure, excess protein in the urine, edema, changes in blood clotting, and nervous system disorders. Very severe effects, including convulsions, can occur in the second and third trimesters. If not controlled, eclampsia eventually damages the liver and kidneys, and mother and fetus both may die. The population most at risk for this disorder is women under age 17 or over age 35, and those who have had multiple-birth pregnancies. A family history of pregnancy-induced hypertension in the mother's or father's side of the family, diabetes, African American race, and a woman's first pregnancy also raise risk, as does a generally inadequate diet, such as too little calcium, zinc, and other nutrients.[16]

Pregnancy-induced hypertension resolves once the pregnancy ends, making delivery the most reliable treatment for the mother. However, since the problem often begins before the fetus is ready to be born, physicians in many cases must use treatments to prevent the worsening of the disorder. Bed rest and magnesium sulfate are currently the most effective treatment methods, although their effectiveness varies. Several other treatments, such as various antihypertensive medications, are under study.

pregnancy-induced hypertension A serious disorder that can include high blood pressure, kidney failure, convulsions, and even death of the mother and fetus. Although its exact cause is not known, an adequate diet (especially adequate calcium intake) and prenatal care may prevent or limit its severity. Mild cases are known as *preeclampsia;* more severe cases are called *eclampsia* (formerly called toxemia).

Concept | Check

Heartburn, constipation, hemorrhoids, nausea and vomiting, edema, anemia, and gestational diabetes are possible discomforts and complications of pregnancy. Changes in food habits can often ease these problems. Pregnancy-induced hypertension, with high blood pressure and kidney failure, can lead to severe complications or even death of both the mother and fetus if not treated.

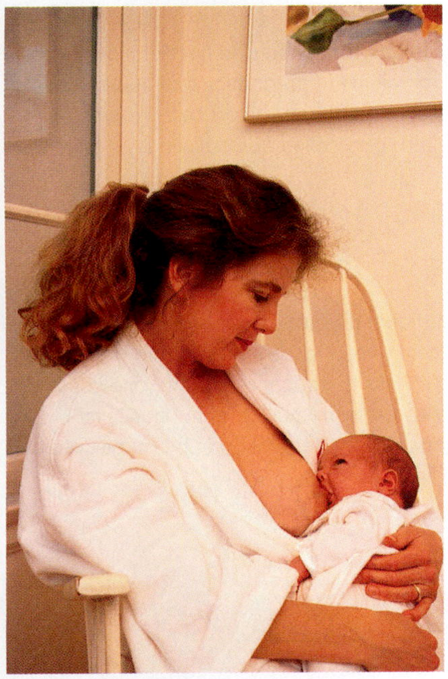

Breastfeeding is the preferred way to feed a young infant.

Breastfeeding

Before the 1900s, if a mother didn't breastfeed her infant, a substitute nursing mother (wet nurse) was hired to do it. Formula feeding was fraught with complications, primarily because people did not know the importance of sterilizing formulas against bacteria. Nor did people know much about the nutritional needs of infants. During the early 1900s, the technology of formulas based on cow's milk and methods of feeding improved. From the 1920s and especially in the 1940s, when women worked in armament factories during World War II, more and more babies were fed formula. Throughout the 1950s and early 1960s, interest in breastfeeding further waned. In the 1970s, breastfeeding enjoyed a resurgence, which has since leveled off.

Healthy People 2010 has set a goal of 75% of women breastfeeding their infants at time of hospital discharge, 50% breastfeeding for 6 months, and 25% still breastfeeding at 1 year. The American Dietetic Association and the American Academy of Pediatrics recommend breastfeeding exclusively for the first 6 months, with the continued combination of breastfeeding and infant foods until 1 year.[2] The World Health Organization goes beyond that to recommend breastfeeding for at least 2 years, supplemented with other foods. Surveys show that only about 70% of North American mothers now breastfeed their infants in the hospital, and at 4 and 6 months only 33% and 20%, respectively, are still breastfeeding their infants. Thus, many women are leaving the hospital breastfeeding, but there is a large dropoff, especially after 2 weeks.

Women who choose to breastfeed usually find it an enjoyable, special time in their lives and their relationship with their new infant. Bottle feeding with an infant formula is also safe for infants, as discussed in Chapter 17, but does not equal the benefits derived from human milk in all aspects. If a woman doesn't breastfeed her child, breast weight returns to normal very soon after birth.

Many of the benefits of breastfeeding can be found at www.4woman.gov./Breastfeeding/index.htm, sponsored by the U.S. Surgeon General.

Ability to Breastfeed

In most cases, problems encountered in breastfeeding are due to a lack of appropriate information, because almost all women are physically capable of breastfeeding their children (see later section on medical conditions precluding breastfeeding for exceptions). Anatomical problems in breasts, such as inverted nipples, can be corrected during pregnancy. Breast size is no indication of success in breastfeeding, and this generally increases during pregnancy. Most women notice a dramatic increase in the size and weight of their breasts by the third or fourth day of breastfeeding. If these changes don't occur, a woman needs to speak with her physician or a lactation consultant.[14]

Breastfed infants must be followed closely over the first days of life to ensure that the process is proceeding normally. Monitoring is especially important with a mother's first child, because the mother will be inexperienced with the process of breastfeeding. Nowadays, mothers and healthy infants are commonly discharged from the hospital 1 to 2 days after delivery, whereas 20 years ago they stayed in the hospital for 3 or 4 days or longer. One result of such rapid discharge is a decreased period of infant monitoring by health-care professionals. Incidents have been reported of infants developing dehydration and blood clots soon after hospital discharge when breastfeeding did not proceed smoothly. Careful monitoring in this first week by a physician or lactation consultant is advised.[20]

First-time mothers who plan to breastfeed should learn as much as they can about the process early in their pregnancy. Interested women should learn the proper technique, what problems to expect, and how to respond to them. Overall, breastfeeding is a learned skill, and mothers need knowledge to breastfeed safely, especially with the first child.

Production of Human Milk

lobules Saclike structures in the breast that store milk.

During pregnancy, cells in the breast form milk-producing **lobules** (Fig. 16-6). Hormones from the placenta stimulate these changes in the breast. After birth, the mother

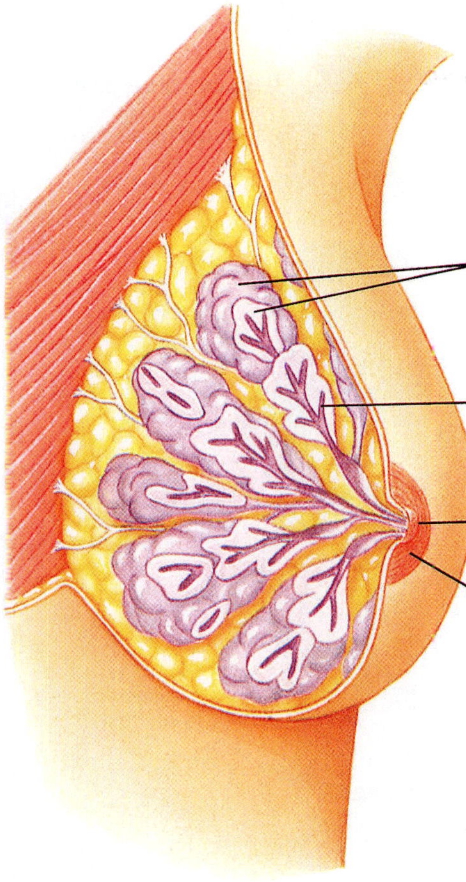

Figure 16-6 The anatomy of the breast. Many types of cells form a coordinated network to produce and secrete human milk.
Illustration by William Ober.

produces more **prolactin** hormone to maintain the changes in the breast and therefore the ability to produce milk. During pregnancy, breast weight increases by about 1 to 2 lb.

The hormone prolactin also stimulates the synthesis of milk. Suckling stimulates prolactin release from the pituitary gland. Milk synthesis then occurs as an infant nurses. The more the infant suckles, the more milk is produced. Milk production closely parallels infant demand. Because of this fact, even twins (and triplets) can be breastfed. Demand is the driving force for milk production.

Most protein found in human milk is synthesized by breast tissue. Some proteins also enter the milk directly from the mother's bloodstream. These proteins include immune factors and enzymes. Fats in human milk come from the mother's diet, and some are synthesized by breast tissue. The sugar galactose is synthesized in the breast, whereas glucose enters from the mother's bloodstream. Together, these sugars form lactose, the main carbohydrate in human milk.

prolactin A hormone secreted by the mother that stimulates the synthesis of milk.

Let-Down Reflex

An important brain-breast connection—commonly called the **let-down reflex**—is necessary for breastfeeding. The brain releases the hormone **oxytocin** to allow the breast tissues to let down (release) the milk from storage sites (Fig. 16-7). It then travels to the nipple area. A tingling sensation signals the let-down reflex shortly before milk flow begins. If the let-down reflex doesn't operate, little milk is available to the infant. The infant then gets frustrated, and this can frustrate the mother.

The let-down reflex is easily inhibited by nervous tension, a lack of confidence, and fatigue. Mothers should be especially aware of the link between tension and a weak let-down reflex. They need to find a relaxed environment where they can breastfeed.

let-down reflex A reflex stimulated by infant suckling that causes the release (ejection) of milk from milk ducts in the mother's breasts; also called milk ejection reflex.

oxytocin A hormone secreted by the posterior part of the pituitary gland. It causes contraction of the musclelike cells surrounding the ducts of the breasts and the smooth muscle of the uterus.

Figure 16-7 Let-down reflex. Suckling sets in motion the sequence of events that lead to milk let-down, the flow of milk into ducts of the breast.

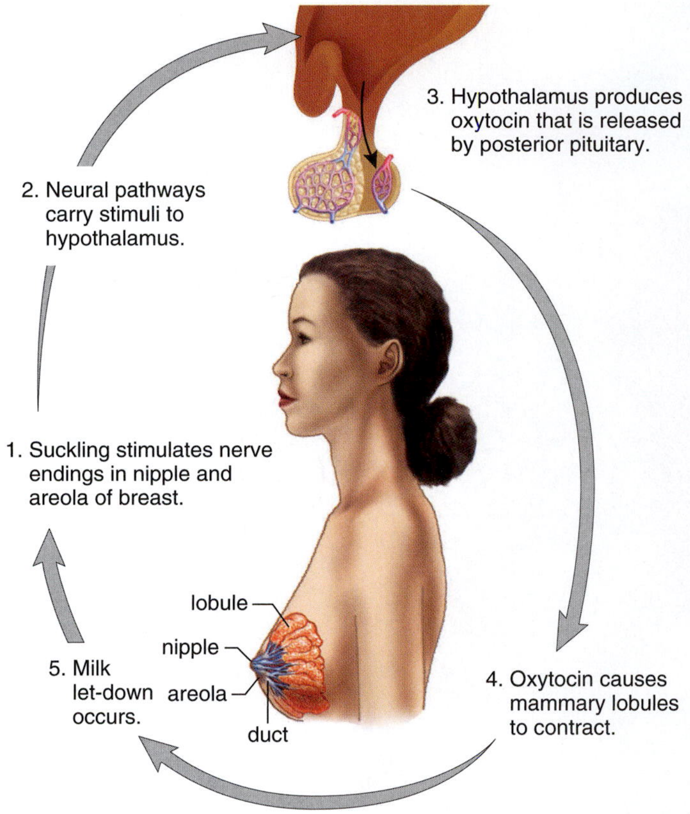

3. Hypothalamus produces oxytocin that is released by posterior pituitary.
2. Neural pathways carry stimuli to hypothalamus.
1. Suckling stimulates nerve endings in nipple and areola of breast.
lobule
nipple
5. Milk let-down occurs.
areola
duct
4. Oxytocin causes mammary lobules to contract.

After a few weeks, the let-down reflex becomes automatic. The mother's response can be triggered just by thinking about her infant or seeing or hearing another one. At first, however, the process can be a bit bewildering. Because she cannot measure the amount of milk the infant takes in, a mother may fear that she is not adequately nourishing the infant.

Disposable diapers can absorb so much urine that it is difficult to judge when they are wet. A strip of paper towel laid inside a disposable diaper makes a good wetness indicator. Or cloth diapers may be used for a day or two to assess whether nursing is supplying sufficient milk.

As a general rule, a well-nourished breastfed infant should (1) have six or more wet diapers per day after the second day of life, (2) show a normal weight gain, and (3) pass at least one or two stools per day that look like lumpy mustard. In addition, softening of the breast during the feeding helps indicate that enough milk is being consumed. Parents who sense their infant is not consuming enough milk should consult a physician immediately because dehydration can develop rapidly.

It generally takes 2 to 3 weeks to fully establish the feeding routine: Infant and mother both feel comfortable, the milk supply meets infant demand, and initial nipple soreness disappears. Establishing the breastfeeding routine requires patience, but the rewards are great. The adjustments are easier if supplemental formula feedings are not introduced until breastfeeding is well established, after at least 3 to 4 weeks. Then a supplemental bottle or two of infant formula per day is fine.

Parents need not be concerned that breastfed infants grow a bit more slowly in terms of body weight after about 3 months of age than formula-fed infants. In fact, several studies have shown that children who were breastfed are less likely to become obese, as most of this difference in infant weight is due to more body fat in the formula-fed infants.[8] Overall, the infant's physician is the best judge of whether the rate of growth of the breastfed infant is satisfactory.

Nutritional Qualities of Human Milk

Human milk is very different in composition from cow's milk. Unless altered, cow's milk should not be used in infant feeding until the infant is 12 months old because cow's milk is too high in minerals and protein and does not contain enough carbohydrate to meet infant needs. In addition, the major protein in cow's milk, casein, is harder for an infant to digest than the major proteins in human milk, lactalbumin and other whey proteins. Finally, certain compounds in human milk presently under study show other possible benefits for the infant.

Colostrum

The first fluid made by the human breast is **colostrum.** This thick, yellowish fluid may leak from the breast during late pregnancy and is produced in earnest for a few days to a week after birth. Colostrum contains antibodies and immune system cells, some of which pass unaltered through the immature GI tract of the infant into the bloodstream. The first few months of life are the only time when we can readily absorb whole proteins across the GI tract. These immune factors and cells protect the infant from some gastrointestinal diseases and other infectious disorders, compensating for the infant's own immature immune system during the first few months of life.

colostrum The first fluid secreted by the breast during late pregnancy and the first few days after birth. This thick fluid is rich in immune factors and protein.

Colostrum facilitates the passage of **meconium,** feces produced during fetal life. One component of colostrum, the ***Lactobacillus bifidus* factor,** encourages the growth of *Lactobacillus bifidus* bacteria. These bacteria limit the growth of potentially toxic bacteria in the intestine. Overall, breastfeeding promotes the intestinal health of the breastfed infant in this way.

meconium The first thick, mucuslike feces passed by the infant after birth.

***Lactobacillus bifidus* factor** A protective factor secreted in the colostrum that encourages growth of beneficial bacteria in the newborn's intestines.

Mature Milk

Human milk composition gradually changes until several days after delivery, when it achieves the normal composition of mature milk. Human milk looks very different from cow's milk. (Table 17-1 in the next chapter provides a direct comparison.) Human milk is thin and almost watery in appearance and often has a slightly bluish tinge. Its nutritional qualities are quite impressive.

Human milk's whey proteins form a soft, light curd in the infant's stomach, which eases digestion. Some human milk proteins bind iron, reducing the growth of iron-requiring bacteria. Many of these types of bacteria cause diarrhea. Still other proteins offer the important immune protection already noted.

The lipids in human breast milk are high in linoleic acid and cholesterol, which are needed for brain development. Breast milk also contains long-chain omega-3 fatty acids, such as docosahexaenoic acid (DHA). This polyunsaturated fatty acid is used for the synthesis of tissues in the brain and the rest of the central nervous system, and in the retina of the eye. Some evidence indicates that breastfed infants show greater visual acuity and better nervous system development than infants fed formulas lacking DHA.[3] Breastfeeding for at least 6 months is advocated to obtain this benefit.

For breastfeeding women, eating fish at least twice a week will help ensure that their infants receive important omega-3 fatty acids. It is important however to avoid those fish that are likely contaminated with mercury (listed on page 579; note that canned tuna intake need only be limited, rather than avoided altogether).

The World Health Organization recommends adding to infant formulas DHA (and arachadonic acid [AA] to balance the effects on the infant of the inclusion of DHA, such as on growth). Most European countries and some Asian countries do this. In the United States, manufacturers have been slow to add DHA and AA to infant formulas, although some now do. Safety has not been the concern; rather, nutrition experts have debated the expected benefits, especially for full-term infants. DHA and AA are more of a concern for preterm infants, who do not receive the normal amounts from their mothers when in utero because of a shortened gestational period. (DHA and AA also may have benefits in the maternal diet; some studies have shown that these fatty acids extend gestation, helping to reduce preterm births.)

Human milk changes in fat composition during each feeding. The consistency of milk released initially (fore milk) first resembles that of skim milk. It later has a greater fat proportion, similar to whole milk. Finally, the milk released after 10 to 20 minutes (hind milk) is essentially like cream. Babies need to nurse long enough (e.g., a total of 20 or more minutes) to get the energy in the rich hind milk to be satisfied between feedings and to grow well. The overall energy content of human milk is about the same as that of infant formulas (67 kcal/100 ml).

Human milk also allows for adequate hydration of the infant, provided the baby is exclusively breastfed. A question commonly asked is whether the infant needs additional water, if stressed by hot weather, diarrhea, vomiting, or fever. Providing up to 4 oz of water a day from a bottle to breastfed infants is fine. Note, however, that greater amounts of supplemental water can lead to brain disorders, low blood sodium, and other problems. Thus, extra water may be given, but only with a physician's guidance.

Food Plan for Women Who Breastfeed

Nutrient needs for a breastfeeding mother change to some extent from those of the pregnant woman (see the inside cover of this book). There is a decrease in folate and iron needs and an increase in the need for energy, vitamins A, E, and C, riboflavin, copper, chromium, iodide, manganese, selenium, and zinc. The diet for breastfeeding women can be the same as that for pregnant women, except teenagers generally should have about four servings from the milk, yogurt, and cheese group (review Table 16-2). As in pregnancy, a serving of a highly fortified ready-to-eat breakfast cereal is advised (or use of a typical multivitamin and mineral supplement) to meet extra nutrient needs. And as mentioned for pregnant women, women who are breastfeeding should consume fish at least twice a week (or 1 g/day of omega-3 fatty acids from a fish oil supplement) because the omega-3 fatty acids present in fish are thought to be important for brain development.

A reasonable approach for a breastfeeding woman is to eat a balanced diet that supplies at least 1800 kcal per day, has a moderate fat content, and includes a variety of dairy products, fruits, vegetables, and grains. The woman should drink fluids every time the infant nurses, because drinking to quench thirst encourages ample milk production (total of 8 to 12 cups/day). If a woman restricts her energy intake too severely, the quantity of milk also decreases. This is not a time to crash diet. More than two alcoholic drinks a day also decreases milk output, as does smoking. Finally, the same fish precautions for those likely to contain mercury given to pregnant women apply to the breastfeeding mother. Breastfeeding women also may want to avoid eating peanuts or peanut butter; several studies have shown that peanut allergens pass into breast milk, potentially increasing the infant's risk for peanut allergy.

Milk production requires approximately 800 kcal every day. The Estimated Energy Requirement during lactation is an extra 400 to 500 kcal daily above prepregnancy recommendations. The difference between energy needs and intake—about 300 kcal—should contribute to gradual loss of the extra body fat accumulated during pregnancy, especially if breastfeeding is continued for 6 months or more and the woman performs some physical activity. This shows how practical the link is between pregnancy and breastfeeding. Weight loss of 1 to 4 lb per month in the nursing mother is appropriate. Milk output decreases at significantly greater rates of weight loss, as occurs with severe dieting when energy intake is less than about 1500 kcal/day.

Most substances the mother ingests are secreted into her milk. For this reason, she should limit intake of or avoid all alcohol and caffeine and check all medications with a pediatrician. Some mothers believe that some foods, such as garlic and chocolate, flavor the breast milk and upset the infant. If a woman notices a connection between a food she eats and the infant's later fussiness, she could consider avoiding that food. However, she might experiment again with it later, as infants become fussy for other reasons. Some researchers, on the other hand, feel that the passage of flavors from the mother's diet into her milk affords an opportunity for the infant to learn about the flavor of the foods of its family long before solids are introduced. These researchers suspect that bottle-fed infants are missing significant sensory experiences that, until recent times in human history, were common to all infants.

Concept | Check

Recognition of the importance of breastfeeding has contributed to its greater popularity during the past 20 years. Almost all women have the ability to breastfeed. The hormone prolactin stimulates breast tissue to synthesize milk. Some components of human milk come directly from the mother's bloodstream. Infant suckling triggers a let-down reflex, which releases the milk. The more an infant nurses, the more milk is synthesized. The nutrient composition of human milk is very different from that of cow's milk and changes as the infant matures. The first fluid produced, colostrum, is rich in immune factors. The diet for breastfeeding is generally similar to that for pregnancy, except for additional fluids, as well as four servings from the milk, yogurt, and cheese group for teenage mothers in general.

Table 16-3 Advantages of Breastfeeding

Infant
• Bacteriologically safe
• Always fresh and ready to go
• Provides antibodies while infant's immune system is still immature, as well as substances that contribute to maturation of the immune system
• Contributes to maturation of gastrointestinal tract via *Lactobacillus bifidus* factor; decreases incidence of diarrhea and respiratory disease
• Reduces risk of food allergies and intolerances, as well as some other allergies
• Establishes habit of eating in moderation, thus decreasing possibility of obesity later in life by about 20%
• Contributes to proper development of jaws and teeth for better speech development
• Decreases ear infections
• May enhance nervous system development (by providing the fatty acid DHA) and eventual learning ability
• May reduce the risk of later developing hypertension
Mother
• Contributes to earlier recovery from pregnancy due to a quicker return of the uterus to the prepregnancy state
• Decreases the risk of ovarian and premenopausal breast cancer
• Potential for quicker return to prepregnancy weight.

Breastfeeding Today

As noted already, the vast majority of women are capable of breastfeeding and their infants benefit from it. The many benefits are listed in Table 16-3. Nonetheless, a woman's decision to breastfeed depends on a variety of factors, some of which may make breastfeeding impractical or undesirable for a woman. Mothers who don't want to breastfeed their infants should not feel compelled to do so. Breastfeeding provides distinct advantages, but none so great that a woman who decides to bottle-feed should feel she is significantly penalizing her infant.

Advantages of Breastfeeding

Human milk is tailored to meet infant nutrient needs for the first 4 to 6 months of life. The possible exceptions are the relative lack of fluoride, iron, and vitamin D. Infant supplements, used under the guidance of a pediatrician, can supply these and are often recommended. Some sun exposure also helps compensate for the gap in vitamin D intake compared to needs. Fluoride may be found in the household water supply. If it is not present in adequate amounts or the child is not receiving tap water, a fluoride supplement should be considered and a dentist consulted. Vitamin B-12 supplements are recommended for the breastfed infant whose mother is a complete vegetarian (vegan).

Fewer Infections Breastfeeding reduces the general risk of infections to the infant. This is partially because of the antibodies in human milk that an infant can use. Breastfed infants also have fewer ear infections (otitis media) because they do not sleep with a bottle in their mouths. Experts strongly discourage allowing infants to sleep with a bottle in their mouths. When that happens, milk pools there, backs up through the

Expert Opinion

Supporting Breastfeeding

Mary Ellen Rivero, M.S., R.D.

Health professionals play a key role in either encouraging or discouraging a woman's decision to breastfeed. Beginning in the 1940s, the practice of breastfeeding began a downward slide. At that time, North American society latched on to breast milk substitutes (fondly called "formula"), which fit into the medical and scientific model of the day. Formula was measurable for I/O (In and Out) logs, "clean" (because breast milk had not been scientifically analyzed yet), able to be force-fed or controlled as medical need dictated, and did not rely on mother's presence or her skills. In short, formulas were the perfect hospital food. Bottles enabled hospital staff to whisk babies away from mothers immediately after delivery so that they could be monitored, warmed, cleaned, tested, and injected with needed medications. Bottles could be propped in isolettes so that busy nurses could attend to their chores.

Keeping babies for hours or days before going to breast was not uncommon. Meanwhile, the mother's breasts languished in the room collecting dust—so to speak—until becoming engorged with mature milk, which came in on top of the unused colostrum. When mothers were allowed to breastfeed, they were given a laundry list of rules: wait until the milk "comes in" before breastfeeding, be older than 20 years, eat a "perfect" diet of bland foods, take extra vitamins, never be under stress, don't drink or smoke . . . basically, put your own life on hold for however long you expected to breastfeed. At times, mothers' milks were tested for cleanliness and nutrient content.

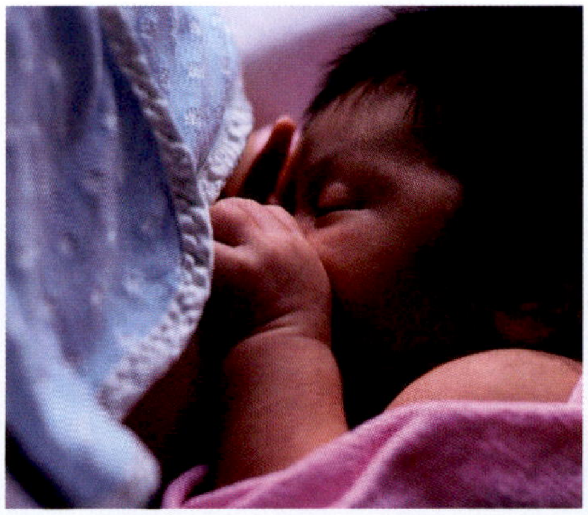

Breastfeeding is an art that is easily learned by most women. Many sources of information are available to help.

Surfaces of breasts were sterilized with alcohol wipes or washed repeatedly with soap and water before each breastfeeding. Feedings had to be timed and the breasts alternated. It is a wonder that our poor uneducated ancestors ever figured all of this out on their own!

Mothers were equally willing to abandon a natural system that preserved species since the development of mammals. Bottles were perceived as "freeing." Other people could feed the baby while mothers could get rest or go back to school or work. Also, a stigma attached to breasts as sex objects persisted in North American society. What once was acceptable behavior by Victorian women in black stockings on streetcars had now become "indecent exposure" in our sexually liberated society. All of these barriers added up to a self-fulfilling prophecy. Breastfeeding usually failed because it became so fraught with problems: engorgement, poor latch-on, sore nipples, and embarrassment. By losing practical tips that women handed down for generations, new mothers lacked the support and how-to information. By 1971, only 25% of infants born in the United States were breastfed at hospital discharge.

Today there is a large, compelling scientific body of knowledge to support breastfeeding as the preferred infant feeding. By 1999, the position of the American Academy of Pediatrics was to exclusively breastfeed (i.e., no water, formula, or solid foods) for an infant's first 6 months and to continue breastfeeding with complementary foods for at least a year. This policy mandates all health professionals to promote breastfeeding by providing sound advice and implementing policies that support, rather than interfere with, successful lactation. Telling a newly delivered mother to wait for the lactation consultant for help is unacceptable practice. Each of us in health care is responsible to educate and support breastfeeding, being well aware that there is a void where support systems once were. Breastfeeding is not a specialty; it is an integral part of maternal and infant care. Feeling that breastfeeding is good for mothers and babies is not good enough. We need to know how breasts work, how to teach women to breastfeed, what good breastfeeding looks like, and what weight gain pattern

Table 16-4 World Health Organization Baby Friendly Hospital Guidelines

Have a written breastfeeding policy that is routinely communicated to all health-care staff.
Train all health-care staff in skills necessary to implement this policy.
Inform all pregnant women about the benefits and management of breastfeeding.
Help mothers initiate breastfeeding within a half-hour of birth.
Show mothers how to breastfeed and how to maintain lactation even if they should be separated from their baby.
Give newborn infants no food or drink other than breastmilk, unless *medically* indicated.
Practice rooming-in: allow mothers and infants to remain together 24 hours a day.
Encourage breastfeeding on demand.
Give no artificial teats or pacifiers to breastfeeding infants.
Foster the establishment of breastfeeding support groups and refer mothers to them on discharge from the hospital or clinic.

is normal in breastfed babies. Currently, women are dependent on health professionals for the tips and advice that mothers and neighbors once provided. This situation is temporary until conventional wisdom is restored. There is a justice and an obligation that the systems responsible for the faltering of breastfeeding now take on the extra work to reverse the trend.

Wherever policies and education and breastfeeding promotion have been a priority, breastfeeding rates have increased dramatically. For example, the Special Supplemental Nutrition Program for Women, Infants, and Children (WIC) serves women who are least likely to breastfeed, but has enjoyed the greatest increase of breastfeeding rates after $23 per pregnant and breastfeeding woman was spent on support and promotion. In 2000, 57% of WIC infants were breastfed at hospital discharge; this is still 11% less than the national average, but the gap is closing through effective support. Hospitals that established Baby Friendly policies boast of 90% breastfeeding rates. Both of these programs take the strategy of educating all their staff in breastfeeding.

In addition, legislation is needed to protect women from attitudes that associate breastfeeding with lewd behavior and to enable them to return to work while lactating. Even today, breastfeeding women are arrested or asked to leave public places. Insurance companies need to be educated on the cost-benefits of breastfeeding so that they assume payment of lactation services and supplies. Model work policies need to be distributed to human resource agents to allow a working mother options that support breastfeeding her infant and/or pumping and storing her milk at work. Hospitals need Baby Friendly policies that outline strategies to make lactation a success, such as those recommended by the World Health Organization (Table 16-4). Practices that lead to lactation problems and failure include separating mothers and babies, delaying the first feeding past one hour after delivery, giving formula discharge packs, introducing bottles and pacifiers before one month of age, spacing and timing of feedings, uncorrected poor latch-on, and supplementing feedings. All of these increase infant illnesses and contribute to breast engorgement, sore nipples, and reduced milk supply.

Practices that increase the long-term success of breastfeeding include educating parents during pregnancy on breastfeeding, first feeding up to one hour after birth, minimal medication during labor, rooming-in (infant sleeps in same room as the mother), short and frequent feedings, evaluating and teaching good positioning and latch-on, and giving anticipatory guidance for the first week regarding feeding frequency and signs of good milk supply.

Gone are the days when the infant's first sign of urine output and the blood glucose were our major focus. We need education and policies that promote healthy babies and successful mothers.

Mary Ellen Rivero, M.S., R.D. is the Training Team Leader with the Office of Nutrition Services and Chronic Disease Prevention, Arizona Department of Health Services, Phoenix, Arizona.

throat, and eventually settles in the ears, creating a growth medium for bacteria. Infant ear infections are a common problem. By avoiding them, parents can decrease discomfort for the infant, avoid related trips to the doctor, and prevent possible hearing loss. Tooth decay from nighttime bottles is another likely consequence of sleeping with a bottle in the mouth (see Chapter 17).

Fewer Allergies and Intolerances Breastfeeding also reduces the chances of some allergies, especially in allergy-prone infants (see the Nutrition Perspective in Chapter 17). The key time to attain this benefit from breastfeeding is during the first 4 to 6 months of an infant's life. A longer commitment than 4 to 6 months is better, but the first few months are most critical. Breastfeeding for even just the first few weeks is beneficial. Another benefit of breastfeeding is that infants are better able to tolerate human milk than formulas. Formulas sometimes must be switched several times until caregivers find the best one for the infant.

Convenience and Cost Breastfeeding frees the mother from the time and expense involved in buying and preparing formula and washing bottles. Human milk is ready to go and sterile. This allows the mother to spend more time with her baby.

Barriers to Breastfeeding

Widespread misinformation, return to jobs, and social reticence all serve as barriers to breastfeeding.

Misinformation Probably the major barriers to breastfeeding are misinformation, such as the idea that one's breasts are too small, and lack of role models. One positive note has been the widespread increase in the availability of lactation consultants over the past several years. These consultants are a valuable resource for new mothers in the adjustment to breastfeeding. If a woman is interested in breastfeeding, she should also talk to women who have done it successfully. Experienced mothers can be an enormous help to the first-time mother. The first-time mother should find a friend she can call on for advice. In almost every community, a group called La Leche League offers classes in breastfeeding and advises women who have problems with it (800-LALECHE or www.lalecheleague.org). Other resources are www.breastfeeding.com and www.breastfeeding.org.

Frozen human milk should not be thawed in a microwave. The heat can destroy immune factors in the milk and create hot spots, which may scald the infant's tongue.

Return to an Outside Job Working outside the home can complicate plans to breastfeed. One possibility after a month or two of breastfeeding is for the mother to regularly express and save her own milk. She can use a breast pump or manually express milk into a sterile plastic bottle or nursing bag (used in a disposable bottle system). Saving human milk requires careful sanitation and rapid chilling. It can be stored in the refrigerator for 3 days and be frozen for 3 months. There is a knack to learning how to express milk, but the freedom can be worth it, because it allows others to feed the infant the mother's milk. A schedule of expressing milk and using supplemental formula feedings is most successful if begun after 1 to 2 months of exclusive breastfeeding. After 1 month or so, the baby is well adapted to breastfeeding and probably feels enough emotional security and other benefits from nursing to drink both ways.

Some women can juggle both a job and breastfeeding, but others find it too cumbersome and decide to formula-feed. A compromise—balancing some breastfeedings, perhaps early morning and night, with formula feedings during the day—is possible. However, too many supplemental formula feedings decrease milk production.

Social Concerns Another barrier for some women is embarrassment about nursing a child in public. Historically our society has stressed modesty and has discouraged public displays of breasts—even for as good a cause as nourishing babies. In the United States, no state or territory has a law prohibiting breastfeeding. However, indecent exposure (including the exposure of women's breasts) has long been a common law or statutory offense. During the 1990s, individual states, such as Florida and North Carolina, began to clarify the right to breastfeed and to decriminalize public breastfeeding. Since then, several other states have passed similar laws. Women who feel reticent should be reassured that they do have social support. The Expert Opinion by Mary Ellen Rivero "Supporting Breastfeeding" discusses this further.

Medical Conditions Precluding Breastfeeding Breastfeeding may be ruled out by certain medical conditions in either the infant or mother. For example, infants with the disease galactosemia can't break down galactose, the major sugar in breast milk. These infants do not grow well if breastfed and often suffer from vomiting and diarrhea. If left untreated, the infants ultimately develop liver disease, cataracts, and mental retardation. A special infant formula free of galactose must be used. Breastfeeding may also be detrimental to infants with phenylketonuria; the high concentration of phenylalanine in breast milk may overwhelm the impaired ability of these infants to metabolize this amino acid, leading to production of toxic products.

Mothers who take certain medications, which pass into the milk and adversely affect the nursing infant, may be advised to avoid breastfeeding. In addition, a woman in the United States and other developed countries who has a serious chronic disease (such as tuberculosis, AIDS, or HIV-positive status) or who is being treated with chemotherapy medications should not breastfeed. A final group can include immature mothers and those with psychiatric problems.

Breastfeeding mothers should get their physician's permission before embarking on a vigorous exercise program. Breastfeeding women must also take care to drink plenty of fluids before and after workouts and should avoid exercising when fatigued.

Environmental Contaminants in Human Milk

Some women wonder whether breastfeeding is safe for their infant. There is some legitimate concern over the levels of various environmental contaminants in human milk. However, the benefits from human milk are very well established and the risks from environmental contaminants are still largely theoretical. Thus, it is probably best to continue with what has been shown to work until sufficiently strong research data contradict it.

A few measures a woman could take to counteract some known contaminants are to (1) avoid freshwater fish from polluted waters, (2) carefully wash and peel fruits and vegetables, and (3) remove the fatty edges of meat, as this is where pesticides concentrate. In addition, a woman should not try to lose weight rapidly while nursing (more than ¾ to 1 lb per week) because contaminants stored in fat tissue might then enter her bloodstream and affect her milk. If a woman questions whether her milk is safe, especially if she has lived in an area known to have a high concentration of toxic wastes or environmental pollutants, she should consult her local health department.

Can a Preterm Infant Be Breastfed?

There is no clear-cut answer to whether a woman can breastfeed a preterm infant. In some cases, human milk is the most desirable form of nourishment, depending on weight and length of gestation. If so, it must usually be expressed from the breast and fed through a tube. This type of feeding demands great maternal dedication. Fortification of the milk with such nutrients as calcium, phosphorus, sodium, and protein is often necessary to match an infant's rapid growth. In other cases, special feeding problems may prevent the use of human milk or necessitate supplementing it with formula. Sometimes total parenteral nutrition support is the only option. Working as a team, the pediatrician, neonatal nurses, and registered dietitian must guide the parents in this decision.

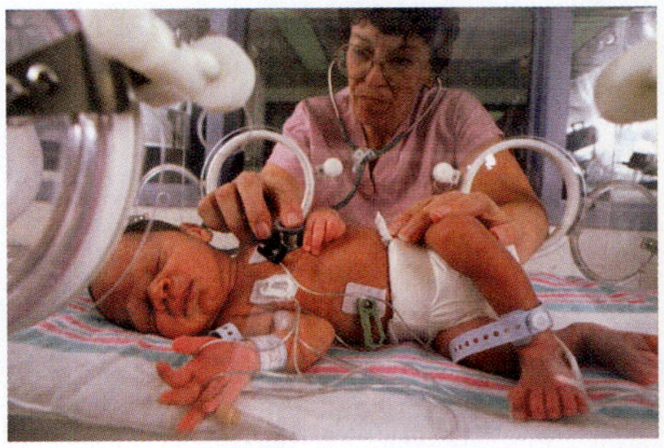

If human milk is used to feed the preterm infant, fortification of the milk with certain nutrients is often needed.

Concept | Check

Human milk supplies most of an infant's nutritional needs for the first 6 months, although supplementation with vitamin D, iron, and fluoride may be needed. Breastfeeding is often more convenient than formula feeding. Compared with formula-fed infants, breastfed infants have fewer intestinal, respiratory, and ear infections and are less susceptible to some allergies and food intolerances. Despite the advantages of breastfeeding, misinformation, a return to work, and social reticence may dissuade a mother from breastfeeding. A combination of breastfeeding and formula feeding is possible when a mother is regularly away from the infant and is not able to express and store her milk for later use. Breastfeeding is not desirable if a mother has certain diseases or must take medication potentially harmful to the infant. The preterm infant, depending on its condition, may benefit from consuming human milk.

Summary

1. Adequate nutrition is vital during pregnancy to ensure the well-being of both the infant and mother. Poor maternal nutrition and use of some medications, especially during the first trimester, can cause birth defects. Growth restriction and altered development can also occur if these insults happen later in pregnancy.
2. Infants born preterm (before 37 weeks gestation) usually have more medical problems at and following birth than normal infants.
3. A woman typically needs an additional 350 to 450 kcal per day during the second and third trimesters of pregnancy to meet her energy needs. A better measure of meeting energy needs is adequate weight gain. This should occur slowly, reaching a total of 25 to 35 lb in a woman of healthy weight.
4. Protein, carbohydrate, fiber, vitamin, and mineral needs increase during pregnancy. Extra servings from the milk, yogurt, and cheese group and the meat, poultry, fish, dry beans, eggs, and nuts group of the Food Guide Pyramid are recommended, as well as some whole-grain bread and cereal choices. Supplemental sources of folic acid and iron, in particular, may be needed. Folate nutriture especially should be adequate at the time of conception. Any supplement use needs to be guided by a physician, as an excess intake of vitamin A and other nutrients during pregnancy can have harmful effects on the fetus.
5. The factors that contribute to poor pregnancy outcome include inadequate health care in general and prenatal care in particular, teenage pregnancy, closely spaced births, smoking, alcohol consumption, illegal drug use (such as cocaine), insufficient carbohydrate intake (< 175 g/day), heavy caffeine use, and various infections, such as *Listeria* and AIDS.
6. Pregnancy-induced hypertension, gestational diabetes, heartburn, constipation, nausea, vomiting, edema, and anemia are all possible discomforts and complications of pregnancy. Nutrition therapy can help minimize some of these problems.
7. Almost all women are able to breastfeed their infants. The nutrient composition of human milk is very different from that of unaltered cow's milk and is much more desirable. Colostrum, the first fluid produced by the human breast, is very rich in immune factors. Mature milk is rich in whey proteins and in lactose.
8. For the infant, the advantages of breastfeeding over formula feeding are numerous, including fewer intestinal, respiratory, and ear infections and fewer allergies and food intolerances. Moreover, breastfeeding is also less expensive and possibly more convenient for the mother than formula feeding. However, an infant can be adequately nourished with formula if the mother chooses not to breastfeed. Breastfeeding is not desirable if the mother has certain diseases or must take medication potentially harmful to the infant. Likewise, breastfeeding is not advised for infants with certain medical conditions, including some preterm infants.

Study Questions

1. What historical evidence established the importance of nutrition in pregnancy outcome?
2. Provide three key pieces of advice for parents seeking to maximize their chances of having a healthy infant. Why did you identify those specific factors?
3. Outline current weight-gain recommendations for pregnancy. What is the basis for these recommendations?
4. How is the Food Guide Pyramid adapted to meet the increased nutrient needs of pregnancy?
5. Why does teenage pregnancy receive so much attention these days? At what age do you think pregnancy is ideal? Why?
6. Give three reasons a woman should give serious consideration to breastfeeding her infant.
7. Describe the physiological mechanisms that stimulate milk production and release. How can knowing about these help mothers breastfeed successfully?
8. What guidelines can a woman use to determine whether her breastfed infant is receiving sufficient nourishment?

9. How should the basic food plan suitable for pregnancy be modified during breastfeeding?

10. Where can new mothers go for help in establishing successful breastfeeding?

Annotated References

1. ADA Reports: Position of the American Dietetic Association: Nutrition and lifestyle for a healthy pregnancy outcome. *Journal of the American Dietetic Association* 102:1479, 2002.

   The key components of a healthy lifestyle during pregnancy include appropriate weight gain; consumption of a variety of foods; appropriate and timely vitamin and mineral intake; avoidance of alcohol, tobacco, and other harmful substances; and safe food handling. Vitamin and mineral supplementation is appropriate for some nutrients and situations.

2. American Dietetic Association: Position of the American Dietetic Association: Breaking the barriers to breastfeeding. *Journal of the American Dietetic Association* 101:1213, 2001.

   The American Dietetic Association joins rank with the American Academy of Pediatrics to promote exclusive breastfeeding for 6 months and breastfeeding with complementary foods for at least 12 months as the ideal feeding pattern for infants.

3. Auestad N and others: Growth and development in term infants fed long-chain polyunsaturated fatty acids: A double-masked, randomized, parallel, prospective, multivariate study. *Pediatrics* 108:372, 2001.

   Whether there are demonstrable benefits for including long-chain polyunsaturated fatty acids in infant formula continues to be debated, but considerable research has shown that these fatty acids may lead to greater visual acuity and slightly greater intelligence later in life.

4. Azais-Braesco V, Pscal G: Vitamin A in pregnancy: Requirements and safety limits. *American Journal of Clinical Nutrition* 71(Suppl):1325S, 2000.

   During pregnancy, the daily use of vitamin A supplements should not exceed 10,000 IU. To avoid toxicity, estimated dietary vitamin A should be considered, along with supervision by a physician before supplement use is initiated.

5. Brundage S: Preconception health care. *American Family Physician* 65:2507, 2002.

   Achieving optimal preconception health can help to reduce adverse pregnancy outcomes. It is recommended that women who are planning to become pregnant consume at least 400 μg of folic acid, get screened and, if necessary, treated for any infectious diseases, limit their exposure to environmental toxins, and optimize control of any chronic diseases. In addition, many experts recommend that women planning a pregnancy participate in regular moderate exercise, avoid both obesity and underweight, and avoid megadoses of vitamins A and D, as well as large amounts of caffeine.

6. Christensen D: Sobering work: Unraveling alcohol's effects on the developing brain. *Science News* 158:28, 2000.

   Studies report that about 4% of pregnant women drink the equivalent of a glass of wine a day. Total abstinence from alcohol is recommended during pregnancy.

7. Galtier-Dereure F and others: Obesity and pregnancy: Complications and cost. *American Journal of Clinical Nutrition* 71(Suppl):1242S, 2000.

   Maternal obesity and overweight increase the health risks for both mother and infant, such as gestational diabetes, hypertensive disorders, cesarean deliveries, and postoperative complications.

8. Gillman MW and others: Risk of overweight among adolescents who were breastfed as infants. *Journal of the American Medical Association* 285:2461, 2001.

   The prevalence of overweight among adolescents in the United States is high and continuing to increase. Breastfeeding promotion may be able to stall future rises in obesity because infants who are fed breast milk rather than infant formula have a lower risk of being overweight during older childhood and adolescence.

9. Godfrey KM, Barker DJP: Fetal nutrition and adult disease. *American Journal of Clinical Nutrition* 71(Suppl):1344S, 2000.

   Fetal undernutrition in middle and late pregnancy can lead to reduced fetal growth, especially in some organs, such as the liver and pancreas. This fetal undernutrition has been linked to disordered cholesterol metabolism and cardiovascular disease, insulin resistance, elevated blood pressure, and increased blood coagulation in adulthood.

10. Goodwin T: Managing nausea and vomiting of pregnancy. *Nutrition and the M.D.*, p. 1, June 2001.

    About 75% of pregnant women experience nausea and vomiting at some point during their pregnancy. The cause of this nausea and vomiting is unknown, but there are several proposed theories including excessive production of certain hormones. It is recommended that specific therapies for treating the nausea and vomiting, such as dietary changes, be initiated when symptoms begin to interfere with a woman's daily activities.

11. Hickey CA: Sociocultural and behavioral influences on weight gain during pregnancy. *American Journal of Clinical Nutrition* 71 (Suppl):1346S, 2000.

    During pregnancy, certain factors, such as socioeconomic status, age, education, and ethnicity, are associated with weight gain. Inadequate prenatal weight gain may be more amenable to treatment if these factors are considered when planning the course of therapy.

12. King JC: Determinants of maternal zinc status during pregnancy. *American Journal of Clinical Nutrition* 71(Suppl):1334S, 2000.

    Maternal zinc status can be reduced by alcohol abuse, high amounts of supplemental iron, and a cereal-based diet. Poor zinc status may limit fetal growth and cause serious birth defects. Supplemental zinc use may be prudent for pregnant women with any of these conditions.

13. Kurz KM, Galloway R: Improving iron status before childbearing. *Journal of Nutrition* 130:437S, 2000.

    Iron status early in pregnancy (reflecting prepregnancy iron status) appears to have a stronger influence on birth outcomes than does status later in pregnancy. This supports the importance of improving iron status before childbearing. The prevalence of anemia and requirements for iron are particularly high in the third trimester of pregnancy, suggesting the need to provide iron supplementation throughout pregnancy.

14. Lawrence RA: A 35-year-old woman experiencing difficulty with breastfeeding. *Journal of the American Medical Association* 285:73, 2001.

    This article provides much advice for successful breastfeeding. One key is careful follow-up immediately after birth. The American Academy of Pediatrics recommends an assessment 48 hours after discharge regarding the success of ongoing breastfeeding, at least by telephone, and visits to the office by the mother and infant within 7 days. It also is important to instill confidence in the mother regarding her ability to breastfeed her infant. She should also consume no less than 1800 kcal per day and include extra water and other fluids.

15. McGainty WJ and others: Maternal nutrition. In Shils ME and others (eds.): *Modern nutrition in health and disease.* 9th ed. Baltimore: Williams & Wilkins, 1999.

    Between 25 and 30% of all pregnant patients do not receive prenatal care prior to the second trimester. Ideally, improving diet and health habits should begin at least 8 weeks before conception. Thus, women should not wait until the first visit to their physician to begin improving their health habits as they anticipate becoming pregnant.

16. Pipkin FB: Risk factors for preeclampsia. *The New England Journal of Medicine* 344:926, 2001.

The high incidence of preeclampsia in many developing countries suggests that an inadequate diet may be a risk factor. The dietary inadequacies that have been proposed include calcium, zinc, vitamins C and E, and omega-3 fatty acids. Thus, recommendations for a sensibly balanced diet during pregnancy should be part of routine care.

17. Prentice A: Maternal calcium metabolism and bone mineral status. *American Journal of Clinical Nutrition* 71(Suppl):312S, 2000.

    There is an increase in demand for calcium by the fetus, particularly in the third trimester. Additionally, calcium absorption and urinary excretion of calcium are both higher during pregnancy. Mothers with a customarily low calcium intake likely benefit from higher calcium intakes during pregnancy.

18. Scholl TO, Reilly T: Anemia, iron and pregnancy outcome. *Journal of Nutrition* 130:443S, 2000.

    When maternal anemia is diagnosed before midpregnancy, it is associated with increased risk of preterm delivery. Maternal anemia detected during the later stages of pregnancy often reflects the expected (and necessary) expansion of maternal plasma volume. Thus, this anemia in the later stages of pregnancy is not associated with the same increased risk of preterm delivery.

19. Scholl TO, Johnson WG: Folic acid: Influence on the outcome of pregnancy. *American Journal of Clinical Nutrition* 71(Suppl):1295S, 2000.

    Poor dietary folate intake and low circulating concentrations of folate in pregnant women increase the risk of adverse birth outcomes. Supplementation studies likewise suggest that some women—most likely poor women—may benefit from receiving additional folic acid before, as well as during pregnancy.

20. Sinusas K, Gagliardi A: Initial management of breastfeeding. *American Family Physician* 64:981, 2001.

    Initiating breastfeeding and skin to skin contact as soon as possible after birth can help to ensure that both the mother and infant will be able to successfully maintain breastfeeding once they leave the hospital. Other factors that can help encourage continued breastfeeding include educating the mother about the benefits of breastfeeding, helping the mother to find a position that encourages the infant to achieve a proper latch-on, and delaying some standard nursery routines (such as weighing and measuring the infant) until after the mother and infant have had an hour of maternal-infant bonding time.

Take | Action

I. Targeting Nutrients Necessary for Pregnant Women.

This chapter mentioned that pregnant women may have difficulty meeting their increased needs for folate, vitamin B-6, iron, and zinc. List six foods rich in each of these nutrients next to the appropriate heading below. Refer to Chapters 9 through 12 if necessary.

Nutrient	Foods	Nutrient	Foods
Folate	____________	Iron	____________
	____________		____________
	____________		____________
	____________		____________
	____________		____________
	____________		____________
Vitamin B-6	____________	Zinc	____________
	____________		____________
	____________		____________
	____________		____________
	____________		____________
	____________		____________

1. Foods rich in more than one of these nutrients would be especially valuable for pregnant women. Write on the line below any foods you listed that are good sources of more than one of these critical nutrients.

   ____

2. The need for folate, vitamin B-6, iron, and zinc increases during pregnancy. For which of these nutrients can pregnant women usually obtain adequate intakes from dietary sources?

   ____

   Which of these nutrients are commonly taken in supplement form during pregnancy? Why might it be hard for pregnant women to meet their increased needs for these nutrients from food alone?

   ____

   ____

Take | Action

II. Putting Your Knowledge About Nutrition and Pregnancy to Work.

A college friend tells you that she is newly pregnant. You are aware that this friend usually likes to eat the following foods for her meals:

Breakfast
Skips this meal, or gets a granola bar
Coffee

Lunch
Sweetened yogurt
Bagel with cream cheese
Occasional piece of fruit
Regular caffeinated soda

Snack
Chocolate candy bar

Dinner
Pizza, macaroni and cheese, or eggs with toast
Seldom eats a salad or vegetable
Regular caffeinated soda

Snacks
Pretzels or chips
Regular caffeinated soda

1. Using your software, or Appendix N, evaluate your friend's diet for protein, carbohydrate, iron, vitamin B-6, folate, and zinc. How does her intake compare with the recommended amounts for pregnancy?

2. Now redesign her diet and make sure that her intake meets pregnancy needs for carbohydrates, protein, folate, vitamin B-6, and zinc. (Hint: Fortified foods, such as breakfast cereal, are generally nutrient-rich foods, which can more easily help meet one's needs.) Increase the iron content as well, but it still may be below the RDA for pregnancy.

Fetal Alcohol Syndrome

Although much is known about diagnosing and treating some learning problems in children, many causes remain elusive. One particular question haunts many mothers: Did something happen while I was pregnant that created a learning disability in my child? This question leads directly to the topic of alcohol use during pregnancy, since alcohol is the most common damaging substance to which fetuses are exposed.

Conclusive evidence shows that large amounts of alcohol harm the fetus, especially when associated with binge drinking (for a woman, consumption of four or more alcoholic drinks at one sitting). Binge drinking is especially perilous during the first 12 weeks of pregnancy, as this is when critical early developmental events take place in utero. Scientists don't know whether pregnant women must eliminate alcohol use entirely to avoid risk of damage to the fetus; however, until a safe level can be established, women are advised not to drink any alcohol during pregnancy or when there is a chance pregnancy might occur.

When a pregnant woman drinks more alcohol than she can metabolize, the excess reaches the embryo (and, at later stages, the fetus), which has no means of detoxifying it. Women with chronic alcoholism produce children with a recognizable pattern of malformations called **fetal alcohol syndrome (FAS).** A diagnosis of FAS is based mainly on poor fetal and infant growth, physical deformities (especially of facial features), and mental retardation (Fig. 16-8). The infant is frequently irritable and may develop hyperactivity and a short attention span. Limited hand-eye coordination is common. Defects in vision, hearing, and mental processing often develop over time.

fetal alcohol syndrome (FAS) A group of irreversible physical and mental abnormalities in the infant that result from the mother's consuming alcohol during pregnancy.

The range of abnormalities from alcohol exposure varies from the severe effects associated with FAS to reduced birth weight, behavioral effects, growth restriction, and hampered learning ability in infants born to women who report only social drinking. The latter condition, termed **fetal alcohol effects (FAE)**, is not marked by telltale facial abnormalities. For this reason, parents may not suspect the presence of subtle defects caused by alcohol, even when they exist. FAE can devastate learning potential.

fetal alcohol effects (FAE) Hyperactivity, attention deficit disorder, poor judgment, sleep disorders, and delayed learning as a result of being prenatally exposed to alcohol.

Up to 30 per 10,000 infants exhibiting FAS are born each year; the incidence of FAS also has increased since the late 1970s. Many more infants are born annually with FAE. About 4% of pregnant women report drinking the equivalent of at least a glass of wine a day.[6] A recent study showed it may even be as high as 15%. Alcohol use is, in fact, the leading cause of preventable birth defects and mental retardation in the United States and in the Western world as a whole.

Exactly how alcohol causes these defects is not known. One line of research suggests that alcohol, or products produced by the metabolism of alcohol (acetaldehyde), cause faulty migration of cells in the brain during early stages of development or block the action of certain neurotransmitters in the brain. In addition, inadequate nutrient intake, reduced nutrient and oxygen transfer across the placenta, cigarette smoking commonly linked to alcohol intake, drug use, and possibly other factors contribute to the overall result.

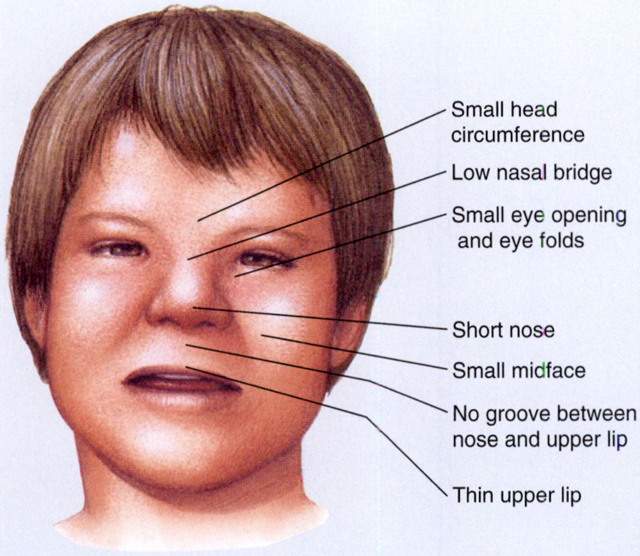

Figure 16-8 Fetal alcohol syndrome. Milder forms of alcohol-induced changes in the fetus and the infant are known as *fetal alcohol effects*. The facial features shown are typical of affected children. Additional abnormalities in the brain and other internal organs accompany fetal alcohol syndrome but are not immediately apparent from simply looking at the child.

Pregnant women should recognize that many cough syrups contain alcohol. Cases have been reported of infants with FAS born to mothers who consumed generous amounts of such cough syrups but no other alcoholic beverages.

Furthermore, it is not known how much alcohol it takes to produce these adverse effects. Again, for this reason, many authorities—including the U.S. Surgeon General and the American Medical Association—believe it is best that mothers-to-be avoid alcohol altogether. In other words, there is no safe drinking.

Abstinence is especially important during the first trimester, when key growth and development occur. Alcohol reaches the fetal blood at the same concentration as the mother's blood within 15 minutes of her drinking. However, the effect on the fetus may be up to 10 times greater. For example, just one bout of binge drinking can arrest and alter cell division during critical phases of fetal development. The fetus then may develop an irreversible defect.

Physical damage to the embryo (and later the fetus) results more from first-trimester drinking because the basic structures of tissues and organs develop during this period. Emotional and learning problems stem more from third-trimester drinking because this is when critical further development of the brain occurs. And, throughout the pregnancy, alcohol interferes with growth. Overall, mothers who drink at least one to two drinks a day throughout pregnancy are much more likely to have growth-restricted infants, and mothers who drink only in late pregnancy are more likely to give birth to preterm infants.

Because alcohol has the capacity to adversely affect each stage of fetal development, the earlier in pregnancy that drinking ceases, the greater the potential for improved outcome. The best course is to consider alcohol an indulgence that must be eliminated from the time of conception until after pregnancy. Currently about half of all women are drinking at the time of conception (i.e., before learning they are pregnant).

One step in the right direction is the mandated warnings about drinking during pregnancy that appear on all alcoholic beverage containers in the United States. As a further safeguard, the National Academy of Sciences recommends that health-care providers who encounter women abusing alcohol should consider either brief intervention therapy, instruction regarding the risks of drinking alcohol during pregnancy, or referral to an alcohol abuse treatment center, when appropriate. Recall that Chapter 8 contains a tool for asking about drinking habits, the CAGE Questionnaire.

Pregnancy lasts only 9 months. In contrast, parents may spend a lifetime caring, often at great expense (estimated at $1.5 to $2 million in the United States), for their offspring needlessly handicapped by FAS or FAE. Keep in mind that fetal alcohol syndrome is a completely preventable disease.

chapter 17

Nutrition from Infancy Through Adolescence

Chapter | Outline

Nutrition and Child Health—An Introduction

Infant Growth and Physiological Development
The Growing Infant • Effect of Undernutrition on Growth • Assessment of Infant Growth and Development • Brain Growth • Adipose Tissue Growth • Failure to Thrive • Infant Nutritional Needs • Formula Feeding for Infants • Development of Feeding Skills in Older Infants • Introduction of Solid Foods At About 6 Months of Age • Health Problems Related to Infant Nutrition

Case Scenario Follow-up

Preschool Children
How to Help a Child Choose Nutritious Foods • Childhood Feeding Problems • Do Children Need a Multivitamin and Mineral Supplement? • Nutritional Problems in Preschool Children • Modifications of Childhood Diets to Reduce Future Disease Risk • Vegetarianism in Childhood

School-Age Children
Breakfast, Fat Intake, and Snacks • Type 2 Diabetes • Obesity

Expert Opinion: Obesity and Type 2 Diabetes in Childhood: Lessons from the Pima Indians

The Teenage Years
Nutritional Problems and Concerns of Teens • A Closer Look at the Diets of Teenage Girls • Helping Teens Eat More Nutritious Foods • Overcoming the Teenage Mind-Set • Are Teenage Snacking Practices Harmful?

Take Action

Nutrition Perspective: Food Allergies and Intolerances

Case | Scenario

Damon is a 7-month-old boy who has been taken into a clinic for a routine checkup. On examination, he seemed thin and plotted on the growth chart at the 25th percentile for weight and the 50th percentile for length. His physician scheduled a follow-up appointment in 3 months. At the 10-month-visit, Damon appeared sluggish. He was again plotted on the growth chart and was now at the 5th percentile for weight but still at the 50th percentile for length.

A registered dietitian interviewed Damon's 16-year-old mother to collect dietary intakes. The 24-hour diet recall consisted of two bottles of formula, three bottles of Kool-Aid, and a hot dog. However, the mother was still in school, and at night she often left Damon with the neighbor, so that she could go out for a few hours. Thus, she was not aware of all that he ate, since much of her time was spent away from him.

What problems do you think are present in Damon's diet? What potential dangers await Damon if his health status continues along this current growth trend?

Refresh | Your Memory

As you begin your study of nutrition from infancy through adolescence in Chapter 17, you may want to review:

- The Food Guide Pyramid and Dietary Guidelines in Chapter 2.
- Diagnosis and treatment of type 2 diabetes in Chapter 5.
- Common sources of saturated fat and trans fat in Chapter 6.
- Vegetarianism in the Nutrition Perspective in Chapter 7.
- Rich sources of iron and zinc in Chapter 12.
- The concept of body mass index (BMI) and the treatment of obesity in Chapter 13.
- The benefits of regular physical activity in Chapter 14.
- Anorexia nervosa and other eating disorders in Chapter 15.

Boost | Your Study

Check out the ***Perspectives in Nutrition: Online Learning Center*** **www.mhhe.com/wardlawpers6** *for quizzes, flash cards, activities, and web links designed to further help you learn about nutrition for infants and adolescents.*

Chapter | Objectives

Chapter 17 is designed to allow you to:

1. Describe normal growth during infancy and childhood, and state why growth with regard to weight and height is an indicator of the adequacy of an infant's diet.
2. Identify the nutritional needs of infants and children.
3. Explain why infant formula is an acceptable substitute for human milk and why cow's milk is not.
4. Plan an adequate eating plan for an infant or child using food labels and the Food Guide Pyramid.
5. State why feeding an infant a high iron food at 6 months is recommended.
6. Explain the rationale for delaying feeding an infant solid foods until 4 to 6 months of age. Consider both nutrition and ongoing physical development in your answer.
7. Help parents overcome obstacles associated with children's eating habits.
8. Relate nutrient needs to growth rate in adolescence.
9. Explain some nutrition-related health issues facing children and teenagers today in North America.
10. Distinguish between food allergies and intolerances and provide recommendations for treating both.

As humans grow through early years into adulthood, our needs for energy and nutrients change. Infants need more energy, protein, vitamins, and minerals per pound of body weight than do adults to support their tremendous growth and development.[6] As growth tapers, children need and eat proportionately less.[1] The erratic eating behaviors of young children pose major challenges for parents and other caregivers. In turn, childhood becomes an important time to establish healthful habits, including those related to food choice and physical activity.

The family wields a subtle but important influence over the child. Thus, education designed to change children's eating behaviors must be directed simultaneously at the main caregivers. They usually determine what foods are purchased and how they are prepared. To help children adopt a lifelong healthy dietary intake, parents and caregivers should provide a variety of foods at home, limit fast food to a few times per week or less, and introduce new foods regularly. Maintaining a healthful eating (and physical activity) pattern should continue as children grow into teenagers.[8, 9] In exploring all these stages of life, this chapter looks at the key role nutrients play and how food choices should be tailored to meet one's changing needs.

Nutrition and Child Health—An Introduction

Current trends in nutrition and overall health among children and adolescents in North America have shown both positive and negative results. On a positive note, more children are receiving vaccinations than ever before, fewer teenagers are giving birth, and the poverty rate for children has fallen considerably. In contrast to this good news, the number of children and teenagers with obesity and type 2 diabetes is rising, and physical activity in general is on the decline as more time is spent sitting in front of computer screens and television sets.[3, 8] Low calcium intakes are also receiving much attention, as soft drinks have replaced much of the milk that children and teenagers used to consume on a daily basis.[9] In this chapter, we will look at these trends, especially their effects on nutrition and overall health in this age group.

Infant Growth and Physiological Development

During infancy, a child's attitudes toward foods and the whole eating process begin to take shape. If parents and other caregivers practice good nutrition and are flexible, they can lead an infant into lifelong healthful food habits. Such an infant has a good chance of both starting life with the nutrients needed to support brain and body growth spurts, and as well developing a willingness to try new foods. However, these physical and psychological advantages alone don't guarantee that a child will thrive.

Children also need specific attention focused on them; they need to grow in a stimulating environment, and they need a sense of security. For example, children hospitalized for growth failure gain weight more quickly when loving care accompanies needed nutrients.

The Growing Infant

All babies seem to do is eat and sleep. There's a good reason for this. An infant's birth weight doubles in the first 4 to 6 months and triples within the first year. Never again is growth so rapid.[6] Such rapid growth requires a lot of both nourishment and sleep. After the first year, growth is slower; it takes 5 more years to double the weight seen at 1 year. An infant also increases in length in the first year by 50% and then continues to gain height through the teen years. These gains are not necessarily continuous—spurts of growth alternate with plateaus. Height is essentially complete by age 19, although increases of several inches may occur in the early twenties, especially for boys (Fig. 17-1). Head size in proportion to total height shrinks from one-fourth to one-eighth during the climb from infancy to adulthood.

The human body needs a lot more food to support growth and development than it does to merely maintain its size once growth ceases. When nutrients are missing at critical phases of growth and development, growth slows and may even stop. From observations of Egyptian mummies, we see that infants were about the same size in 300 B.C. as they are today. However, adult mummies are much smaller than adults today. Furthermore, the suits of armor in museum collections of the Middle Ages typically would not fit modern adults. The average height of North American men in 1700 was approximately 5 feet 8 inches, whereas today it is approximately 5 feet 10 inches. This suggests that people of earlier times generally ate nutrient-poor diets, which did not support the growth we typically experience today.

In countries of the developing world today, about one-third of the children under 5 years of age are short and underweight for their ages. Poor nutrition—called *undernutrition*—is at the heart of the problem. This occurs to a lesser extent in North America. The undernourished children are simply smaller versions of nutritionally fit children. In poorer countries, when breastfeeding ceases, children are often fed a high-carbohydrate, low-protein diet. This diet supports some growth but does not allow children to attain their full genetic potential. To grow, children must consume adequate amounts of energy, protein, calcium, iron, zinc, and other nutrients.

Children benefit from the love and attention of adults.

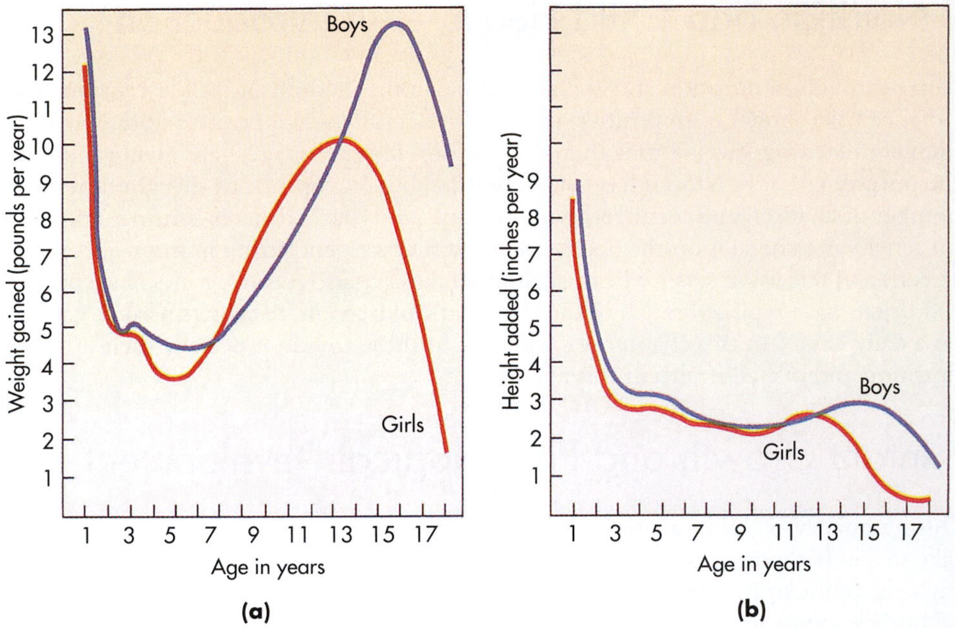

Figure 17-1 Growth rates. (*a*) Average gains in weight for girls and boys. (*b*) Average additions to height for girls and boys. The higher the line in any one year, the greater the amount of annual gain compared with that in other years. Large gains in weight occur in both infancy and puberty, whereas the very high length gain in infancy is never reached again. If graphs such as these were plotted in smaller time segments, they would appear as zigzag lines, rather than smooth lines, reflecting short, periodic spurts in growth in the course of each year.

Infant development follows a pattern in which body water falls from about 70% at birth to 60% at 1 year. The latter is also the proportion typical in adults. By age 1, a healthy infant's body nitrogen content (and thus protein content) has increased from 2% of body weight at birth to 3%, indicating that the infant has synthesized much new lean tissue.[6]

Effect of Undernutrition on Growth

As with the fetus in utero, the long-term effects of nutritional problems in infancy and childhood depend on the severity, timing, and duration of the nutritional insult to cell processes.

The single best indicator of a child's nutritional status is growth, particularly weight gain in the short run and length (height) in the long run. Mild zinc deficiencies in North American children have been linked to poor growth. Improving the diets of these children then leads to improved growth. Overall, eating a poor diet as an infant or a child hampers the cell division that occurs at that critical stage. Consuming an adequate diet later usually won't compensate for lost growth, as the hormonal and other conditions needed for growth will not likely be present. In addition, growth ceases in girls and boys when the skeleton reaches its final size. This happens as growth plates at the ends of the bones, called **epiphyses,** fuse. This begins around 14 years of age in girls and 15 years of age in boys. The final stages of this process end at about 19 years of age in girls and 20 years of age in boys. Furthermore, muscles can increase in diameter later in life but the growth is constrained by the length of the bone.

epiphyses Ends of long bones. The epiphyseal plate—sometimes referred to as the growth plate—is made of cartilage and allows growth of the bone to occur. During childhood, the cartilage cells multiply and absorb calcium, to develop into bone.

For these reasons, a 15-year-old Central American girl who is 4 feet 8 inches tall cannot attain the adult height of a typical North American girl simply by eating better. Girls experience their peak rate of growth before the onset of the menses. Once the time for growth ceases (in women, this is about 5 years after they start menstruating), a sufficient nutrient intake helps maintain health and weight but cannot make up for lost growth.

Assessment of Infant Growth and Development

Health professionals assess a child's increases in height and weight by comparing them with typical growth patterns recorded on charts (Fig. 17-2). The charts contain 7 to 9 percentile divisions, which represent 90 to 96% of children. A percentile represents the rank of the person among 100 peers matched for age and gender. If a young boy, for example, is at the 90th percentile height for age, he is shorter than 10 and taller than

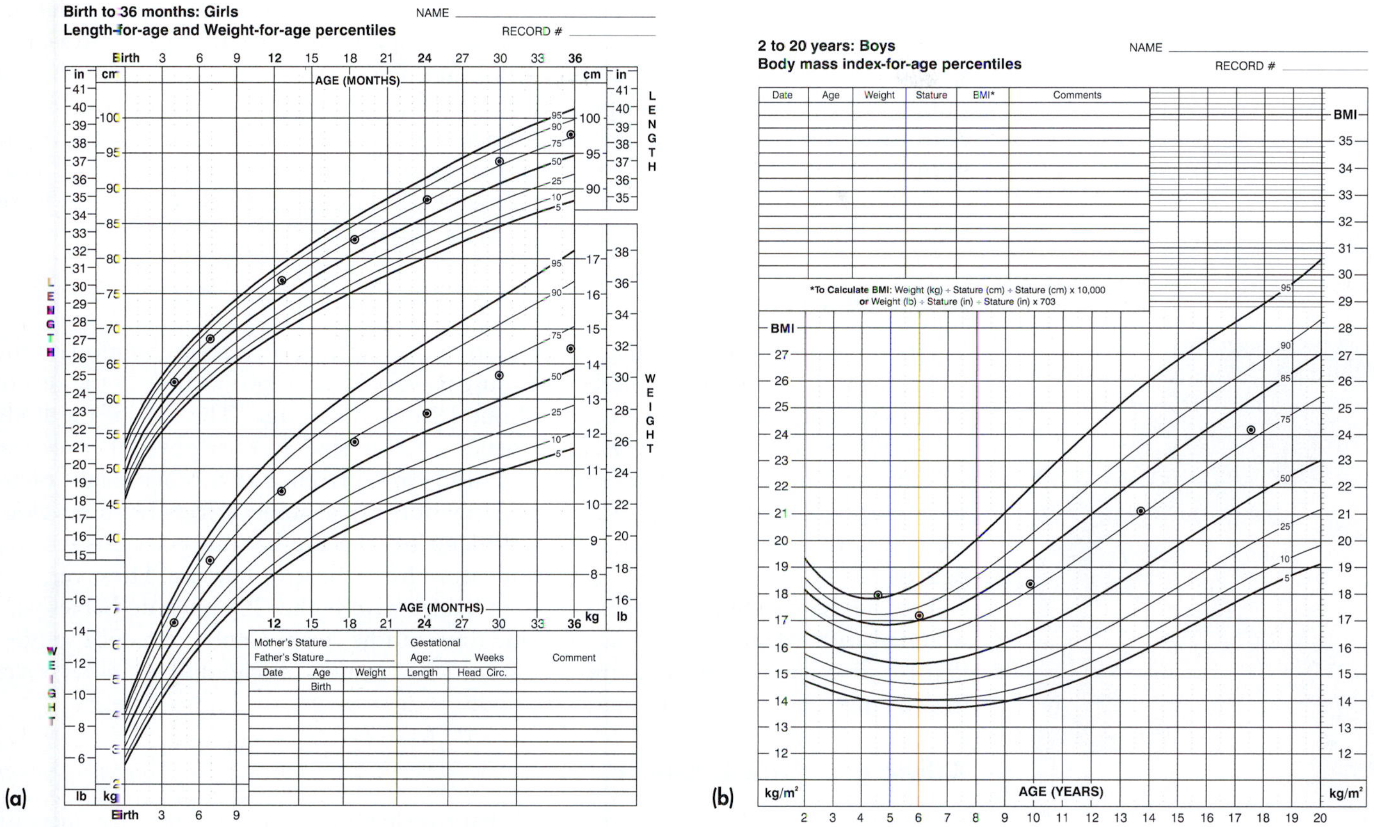

Figure 17-2 Growth charts for assessment of children in the growing years. The growth of a youngster is plotted to show how the charts are used in health-care settings. (*a*) Growth charts used to assess length (height) and weight in young girls. A certain weight and length (height) correspond to a percentile value, which is a ranking of the person among 100 peers. (*b*) Growth charts used to assess weight-for-height relationships in boys ages 2 to 20 years. Today these charts for older children and adolescents typically utilize BMI for the evaluation.

Source: Developed by the National Center for Health Statistics in collaboration with the National Center for Chronic Disease Prevention and Health Promotion (2000). www.cdc.gov/growthcharts. Revised November 21, 2000.

89. A child at the 50th percentile is considered average. Fifty children will be taller than this child; 49 will be shorter.

In May 2000, the Centers for Disease Control and Prevention (CDC) released updated growth charts, which are nationally representative. These growth charts replaced those developed in 1977 from small groups of children who were fed with infant formula. Individual growth charts are available for both males and females. For ages ranging from birth to 36 months, options for growth charts include weight-for-age, length-for-age, weight-for-length, and head circumference-for-age. For males and females who are 2 to 20 years old, growth charts are available to determine weight-for-age and height-for-age; however, the preferred growth chart for children and adolescents is body mass index (BMI)-for-age. For adults, BMI has fixed cutoff points (for example, a BMI of 25 for an adult is considered overweight). As Figure 17-2 shows, this is not true for children, for whom BMI is both gender- and age-specific.

Children under 2 to 3 years of age are measured with knees unflexed and while lying on their backs, so the term *length* is used rather than *height.*

Infants and children should have their growth assessed during regular health check-ups. It takes 1 to 3 years for an infant to establish his or her own genetic percentile. Once this figure is established, such as length (height) for age, the child's measurement should then track along that percentile. If the child's growth doesn't keep up with its length-for-age percentile, the physician needs to investigate whether a medical or nutritional problem is impeding the predicted growth. Inappropriate weight gain—too little or too much—should also be investigated.

Infants born preterm may catch up in growth in 2 to 3 years. This requires that the child jump up in the percentiles. If this occurs—especially in length-for-age—it is usually no cause for alarm. On the other hand, jumping percentiles in weight-for-height can be disturbing if the child approaches the 80th to 90th percentiles. A child at the 85th percentile or above for BMI is considered at risk for overweight. At or above the 95th percentile, the child is considered overweight. At the 95th percentile, the diagnosis of obesity can also be established if the physical exam of the child indicates he or she is truly overfat. This is generally the case at this percentile.

Brain Growth

Brain growth is faster in infancy than in any other stage of life.

The brain grows faster in infancy than at any other time of life. To accommodate the growth, an infant's head circumference must be very large in proportion to the rest of the body. The rapid growth stops at about 18 months of age. The rest of the body eventually grows to reach a typical proportion to head size. In early physical checkups, a health professional usually measures the head circumference as another means of assessing growth, especially brain growth. How nutritional status affects brain development and intelligence quotient (IQ) is difficult to measure because scientists haven't figured out how to separate the effects of nature from those of nurture. However, several studies have determined that breastfed babies have higher IQs than do babies who were fed with infant formula. At the same time, studies from Central America suggest that IQ after age 5 years relates more closely to the amount of schooling a child receives than to nutritional intake during childhood.

Adipose Tissue Growth

Since 1970, researchers have speculated that overfeeding during infancy may increase adipose tissue cell numbers. Today, we know that adipose cells can also increase as adulthood obesity develops (see Chapter 13). Still, if energy intake is limited during infancy to keep down the number of adipose cells, the growth of other organ systems may also be severely restricted. Special concern revolves around body growth and development, especially brain and nervous system development. In addition, most obese infants become normal-weight preschoolers without excessive diet restrictions. For these reasons, it's unwise to greatly restrict diet, and especially fat intake in infants. After the first 12 months, fat intake can range from 30 to 40% for ages 1 to 3 years, and 25 to 35% for older children (and teenagers).[5]

Failure to Thrive

Occasionally, an infant doesn't grow much in the first few months. Physical problems that may contribute to restricted growth range from poor oral cavity development, infections, and heart irregularities to constant diarrhea associated with intestinal problems. However, more than half the infants who fail to thrive have no apparent disease. Sometimes the cause is poor infant-parent interaction. This stems from misinformation, lack of a parent role model, or apathy about the child's welfare. In general, the problems arise from the parents' inexperience, rather than intentional negligence. In addition, many children who fail to thrive have inborn errors of metabolism that are very difficult to diagnose. For example, unusual enzyme deficiencies could lead to poor nutrient absorption and then malnutrition (see the Nutrition Perspective in Chapter 4). In all cases a physician should determine the actual cause.

Infants not only need cuddling; they also respond to voices and eye contact, especially at feeding times. New parents need to appreciate the importance of these practices to their infant's well-being. Some parents also may be overcommitted to maintaining a lean child in the hope of preventing future obesity, as discussed in Chapter 15. The result, even though the intention was good, can be failure to thrive.

When clinicians encounter an infant who is failing to thrive from a nutritional standpoint, they must first determine whether formula-fed infants are consuming enough energy (see section on formula feeding of infants for details). For a breastfed infant, the clinician needs to make sure that sufficient milk intake is possible (or taking place). As mentioned in Chapter 16, the child should be nursing about six to eight times a day for about 20 minutes a session and have six to eight wet diapers each day.

Children older than 2 years are less likely to experience failure to thrive because they can often get food for themselves. Younger children, for the most part, are limited to what caregivers provide.

Concept | Check

Growth occurs rapidly during infancy: Birth weight doubles in about 4 to 6 months and triples within the first year. Lean tissue increases, and the percentage of body water falls during the first year. Undernutrition in childhood can irreversibly inhibit growth and maturation, so that an individual never attains his or her full genetic potential for height. Infant and child growth is assessed by tracking body weight, length (height), and head circumference over time. Body mass index (BMI) is generally used to assess weight for height after 2 years of age. It is not desirable for infants to become obese, although no evidence strongly indicates that obese infants become obese adults. However, severe restriction of energy intake is not recommended for infants because it may slow the growth of organ systems. When infants do not grow properly, their failure to thrive may stem from physical disorders or inadequate care, including inappropriate feeding practices.

Infant Nutritional Needs

Infants' nutritional needs vary as they grow, and these differ from adult needs in both amount and proportion (Fig. 17-3).[6] Initially, human milk or infant formula (generally using heat-treated cow's milk as a base) supplies needed nutrients. Solid foods are not needed until around 6 months. Even after solid foods are added, the basis of an infant's diet for the first year is still human milk or infant formula. Because of the critical importance of adequate nutrition in infancy and the difficulties encountered in feeding some infants, more time is spent in this chapter on this developmental period than on the later periods of childhood.

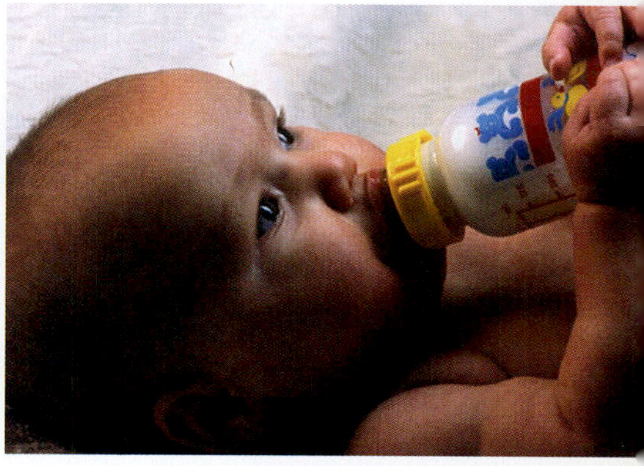

Infants who are formula-fed should remain on formula until 1 year of age. The formula should be iron-fortified to reduce the risk of developing iron deficiency anemia.

Energy

Estimated Energy Requirements (kcals) in infancy are (89 × weight of infant [kg]) + 75 from 0–3 months. From 4–6 months, such needs are (89 × weight of infant [kg]) + 44; 7–12 months, (89 × weight of infant [kg]) − 78.[5] At 6 months of age, this amounts to about 700 kcal daily. Based on body weight comparisons, this amounts to two to four times more energy than adults need. Infants need an easy way to get this amount of energy. Either human milk or infant formula is ideal for the first few months. Both are high in fat and supply about 650 kcal per quart of fluid (about 700 kcal per liter; Table 17-1). Later, human milk or infant formula, supplemented by solid foods, can provide even more energy.[6]

The infant's high energy needs are primarily driven by its rapid growth and high metabolic rate. The high metabolic rate is caused in part by the ratio of the infant's body surface to its weight. More body surface allows more heat loss from the skin; the body must use extra energy to replace that heat.

Carbohydrate Needs

Carbohydrate needs in infancy are 60 g/day at 0 to 6 months, and 95 g/day at 7 to 12 months. These needs are based on the typical intakes of breastfed infants, coming from both human milk and the eventual use of solid foods. Both carbohydrate goals are satisfied by usual intakes of infants on a proper diet.[5]

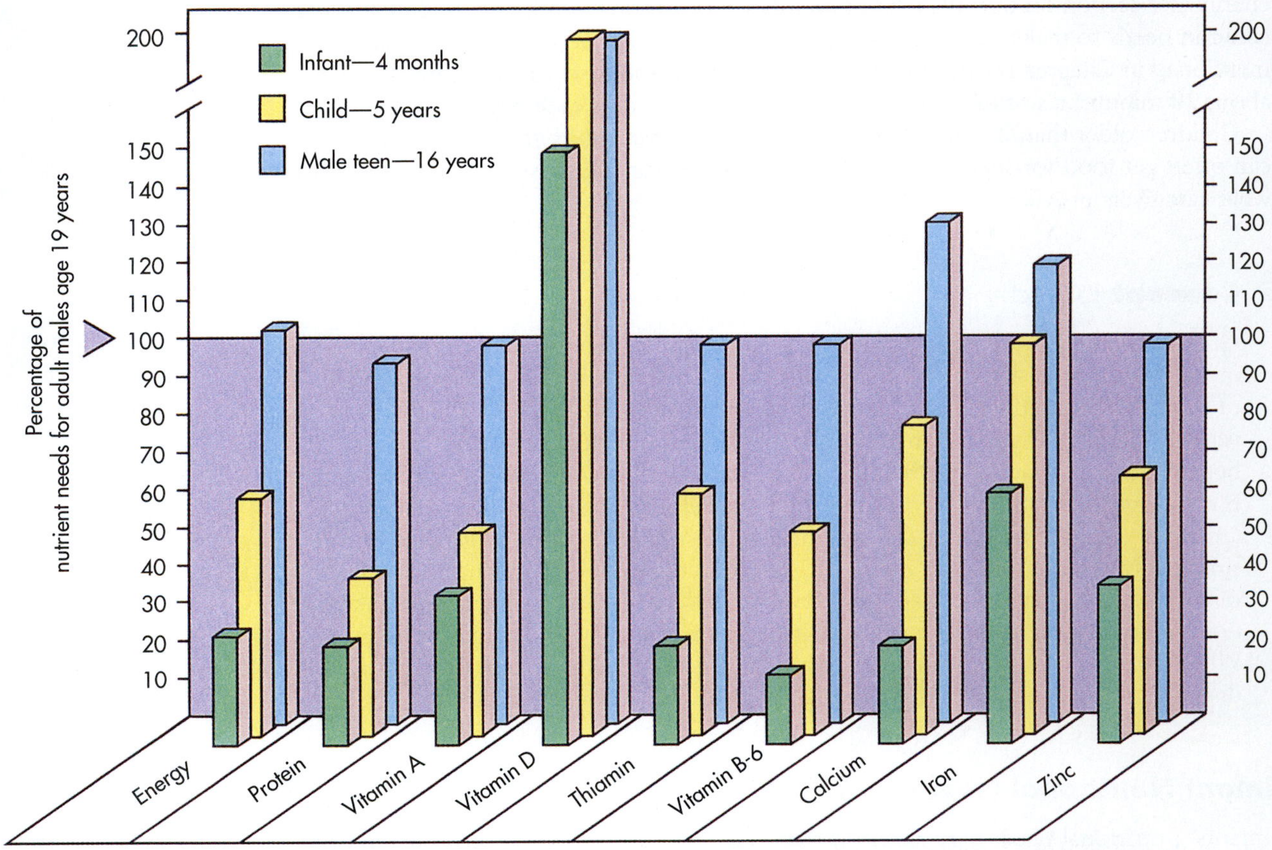

Figure 17-3 Nutrient needs for infants, children, and teenagers as percentages of those for adult males. Compared with adults, infants' relative energy needs are lower than are their needs for other nutrients, as illustrated by the different heights of the green bars. Thus, infants need to obtain relatively larger amounts of nutrients from a smaller intake of food than do adults. This is also true of young children (yellow bars), but to a lesser extent.

Protein

Daily protein needs in infancy are roughly 1.5 g/kg body weight/day, or 9.1 g/day for younger infants and 13.5 g/day for older infants.[5] These needs also are based on the typical intakes of breastfed infants for 0–6 months, and then on the needs for growth for older infants. About half of total protein intake should come from essential (indispensable) amino acids. As with carbohydrate, both goals again are satisfied by either human milk or infant formula. Protein intake should not greatly exceed this standard. Excess nitrogen and minerals supplied by high-protein diets would exceed the ability of an infant's kidneys to excrete the resulting metabolic waste products, thus putting much stress on overall kidney function.

In North America, infant protein deficiency is unlikely, except in cases of mistaken feeding practices, such as when an infant's formula is excessively diluted with water. Protein deficiency may also be induced by elimination diets used to detect food **allergies** (hypersensitivities). As foods are eliminated from the diet, infants may not be offered enough protein to compensate for the high-protein sources no longer present (see the Nutrition Perspective at the end of this chapter).

allergy A hypersensitive immune response that occurs when immune bodies produced by us react with a protein we sense as foreign (an antigen).

Fat

Infants need about 30 g of fat per day. The Adequate Intake ranges from 30 to 31 g. Essential fatty acids should make up about 15% of total fat intake (about 5 g/day). Both recommendations are again based on the typical intakes of breastfed infants from both

Table 17-1 Composition of Human and Cow's Milk and Infant Formulas per Liter (L)

Milk or Formula	Energy (kcal/L)	Protein (gram/L)	Fat (gram/L)	Carbohydrate (gram/L)	Minerals* (gram/L)
Milk					
Human milk	750	11	45	70	2
Cow's milk, whole	670	36	36	49	7
Cow's milk, skim	360	36	1	51	7
Casein/Whey-Based Formulas					
Similac	680	14	36	71	3
Enfamil	670	15	37	69	3
Carnation	670	16	34	73	3
Soybean Protein-Based Formulas					
ProSobee	670	20	35	67	4
Isomil	680	16	36	68	4
Predigested Protein					
Nutramigen	670	19	26	89	1
Alimentum	680	18	37	68	1
Transition Formulas/Beverages†					
Similac Toddler's Best	670	25	33	75	3
Enfamil Next Step	670	17	33	74	3
Carnation Follow-Up	670	17	27	88	3

*Calcium, phosphorus, and other minerals.

†For use after 6 months of age or later (see label).

human milk and the eventual introduction of solid foods.[5] Fats are an important part of the infant's diet because they are energy-dense and vital to the development of the nervous system. As a concentrated energy source, fat helps resolve the potential problem of the infant's high energy needs and small stomach capacity. Again, this is not an age to greatly restrict fat intake (Fig. 17-4).[6]

Arachidonic acid (AA) and docosahexaenoic acid (DHA) are two long-chain fatty acids that have a very important role in infant development. The nervous system, especially the brain and eyes, depend on these fatty acids for proper development. During the last trimester and the first few months of infancy, DHA and AA accumulate in the brain and retinas of the eyes. Infants who are breastfed are able to acquire these fatty acids, particularly so if their mothers are regularly eating fish. Until recently, no infant formulas sold in the United States included AA or DHA, but certain brands with both AA and DHA are now available.

Vitamins of Special Interest

As noted in Chapter 9, vitamin K is routinely given by injection to all infants at birth. Formula-fed infants receive the rest of the vitamins they need from the formula. Breastfed infants, especially dark-skinned ones (e.g., African Americans), likely require a vitamin D supplement if they are not exposed to much sunlight or if the mother has poor vitamin D status. (Recall that sunlight exposure on human skin activates the synthesis of vitamin D; review Chapter 9.) Breastfed infants whose mothers are total vegetarians (vegans) should receive a vitamin B-12 supplement. As well, infants who drink goat's milk need a dietary supplement of folic acid because this milk doesn't supply a sufficient amount of this essential nutrient. Goat's milk is also low in iron, vitamin C, and vitamin D, making it a poor choice for human infants.

Figure 17-4 The labels on infant foods in the United States, like those on adult foods, contain a Nutrition Facts panel. However, the information provided on infant food labels differs from that on adult food labels, especially with respect to total fat, saturated fat, and cholesterol intake (review Fig. 2-6 in Chapter 2 for a comparison).

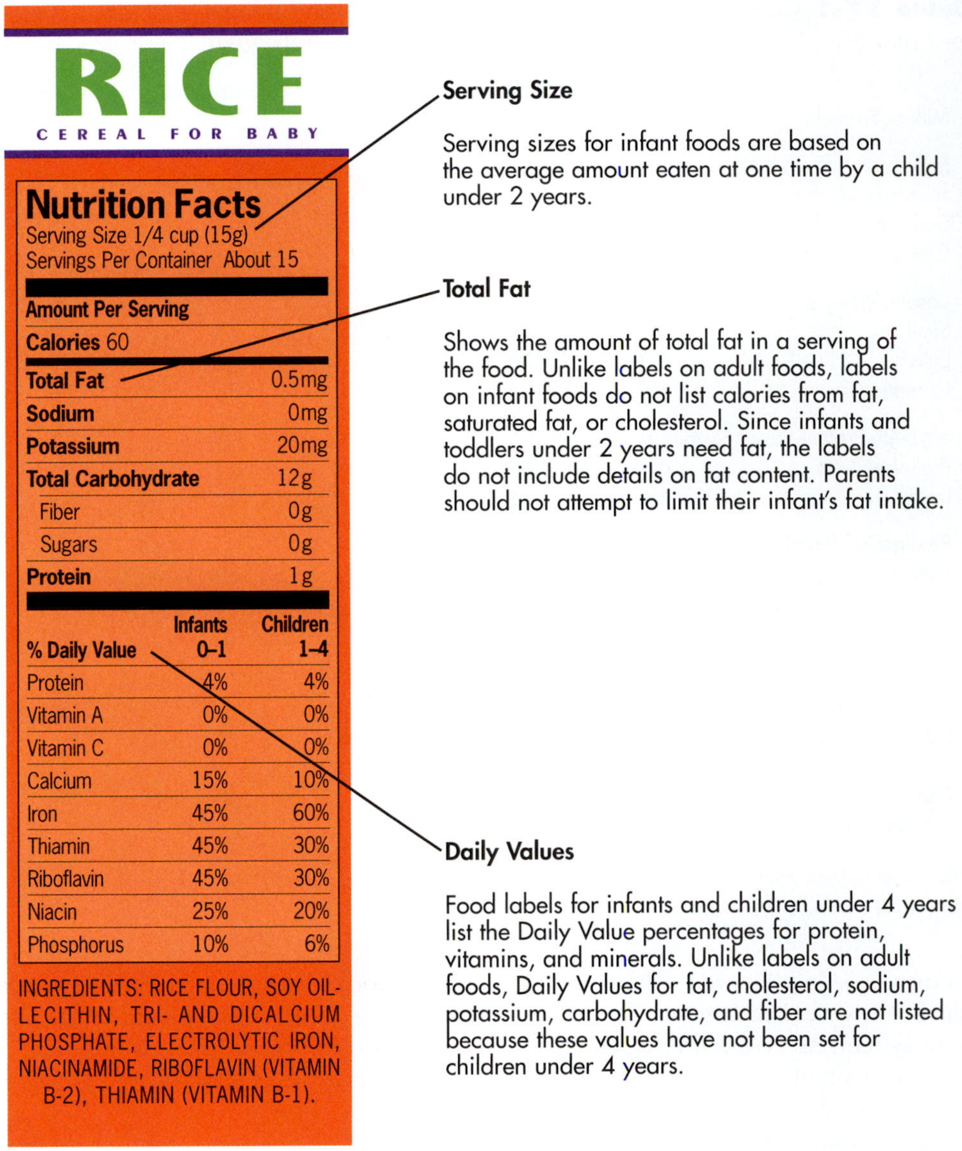

Critical | Thinking

Tatiana has been breastfeeding her baby exclusively since he was born 7 months ago. When she and her husband took the baby for his checkup, they were told that he was anemic. They were very surprised, since they thought that human milk contained all the nutrients the baby needed for the first year of life. How might you explain the baby's anemia?

Minerals of Special Interest

The iron stores with which children are born are generally depleted by the time birth weight doubles, in 4 to 6 months. If the mother was iron deficient during the pregnancy, these iron stores will be exhausted even sooner. The American Academy of Pediatrics recommends that, to maintain a desirable iron status, formula-fed infants should be given an iron-fortified formula from birth. These experts also discourage the use of low-iron infant formulas, which are sometimes prescribed to treat infants with various GI tract problems. Breastfed infants need solid foods to supply extra iron at about 6 months of age. The need for iron is a major consideration in deciding when to introduce solid foods.[4] Some physicians recommend liquid iron supplements from birth or by 1 month of age for breastfed infants if indicated by low blood values for hemoglobin or hematocrit.[7] Iron deficiency anemia can lead to poor cognitive development in infants.

Infants need adequate amounts of zinc and iodide to support growth. Human milk and infant formula adequately supply these needs when they supply enough energy to meet needs. In addition, clinicians recommend fluoride supplements to aid tooth development for breastfed infants after 6 months of age. The same holds true for formula-fed infants if the water supply used in home formula preparation—either tap or bottled water—doesn't contain fluoride. Note that formula manufacturers use fluoride-free water in formula preparation. Parents should consult their dentist for advice on meeting the infant's need for fluoride.[13]

Supplemental fluids should be limited to 4 oz per day unless the infant's physician prescribes a larger amount.

Water

An infant needs about 2 oz of water and other fluids combined per pound of body weight per day (about 150 ml/kg). Infants typically consume enough human milk or formula to supply this amount. In hot climates, however, supplemental water may be necessary. Furthermore, any conditions that lead to water loss—diarrhea, vomiting, fever, or too much sun—can call for supplemental water.

Infants are easily dehydrated, a condition that has serious effects if not remedied. Dehydration can result in rapidly decreasing kidney function, and the infant may then require hospitalization for rehydration. Special fluid-replacement formulas containing electrolytes such as sodium and potassium are available in supermarkets and pharmacies to treat dehydration. A physician should guide any use of these products.

Note that, in some stores, bottled water products marketed specifically for infants may be placed alongside infant formulas and electrolyte-replacement solutions. This placement may give parents and caregivers the mistaken impression that bottled water products are an appropriate feeding supplement or substitute for fluid replacement for infants; they are not and should not be used for such purposes. It is important to remember also that excessive fluid can also be harmful, especially to the brain.

Overall, it is best to limit supplemental fluids to about 4 oz (120 ml) per day, unless the physician thinks that a greater need exists because of disease or other conditions. In sum, extremes in fluid intake—either too little or too much—can lead to health problems.

Concept | Check

Most nutrient needs in the first 6 months are met by human milk or infant formula. Breastfed infants may need vitamin D and iron supplements; formula-fed infants and breastfed infants may need fluoride supplements after 6 months of age. Infants usually receive enough water from the human milk or formula they drink.

Formula Feeding for Infants

Breastfeeding was covered in detail in Chapter 16. Let's now focus on formula feeding. You'll recall that a major advantage of breastfeeding is the provision of immune protection to the infant. Overall, in areas of the world where high standards for water purity and cleanliness are common, formula feeding is a safe alternative for infants but may not be as beneficial as breastfeeding.

Formula Composition

Infants cannot tolerate cow's milk as such because of its high protein and mineral content. Cow's milk reflects the greater growth needs of calves. Thus, cow's milk must be altered to be safe for infant feeding. It is important to note that goat's milk, sweetened condensed milk, and evaporated milk also are inappropriate substances for infants. Altered forms of cow's milk, known as infant formulas, were first available commercially in 1931. Since 1980, they have been required to conform to strict federal guidelines for nutrient composition and quality. Formulas generally contain lactose and/or sucrose for carbohydrate, heat-treated **casein** and **whey** proteins from cow's milk, and vegetable oils for fat (review Table 17-1). Soy protein–based formulas are available for infants who can't tolerate lactose or the types of proteins found in cow's milk. If the soybean-based formula is not tolerated, the next step is to try a predigested

casein A protein found in milk that forms curds when exposed to acid and is difficult for infants to digest.

whey Proteins, such as lactalbumin, that are found in great amounts in human milk and are easy to digest.

(hydrolyzed) protein formula in which the proteins have been broken down into peptides and amino acids, such as Nutramigen or Alimentum. A variety of other specialized formulas also are available for specific medical conditions. In any case, it is important to use an iron-fortified formula unless a physician recommends otherwise.

Not even all formula-like products are designed for infant use. A 5-month-old girl was admitted to a hospital in Arkansas with symptoms of heart failure, rickets, inflamed blood vessels, and possible nerve damage after being fed Soy Moo (a soy beverage sold in health stores) since 3 days of age. The symptoms suggest severe vitamin deficiencies. Parents should consult a physician when choosing an appropriate infant formula.

Some transition formulas/beverages have been introduced for older infants and toddlers (review Table 17-1). Some of these products are intended for use after 6 months of age if the infant is consuming solid foods, whereas others are intended for use only by toddlers. These transition products are lower in fat than human milk or standard infant formulas; their iron content is higher than that of cow's milk, and their overall mineral content is generally more like that of human milk than cow's milk. According to the manufacturers, the advantages of these transition formulas/beverages over standard formulas for older infants and toddlers include reduced cost and better flavor. Parents should consult their physician with regard to the use of these products.

Formula Preparation

In the 1950s, it was common to prepare a day's supply of bottles and then sterilize them in boiling water for about 30 minutes. Today, bottles are often prepared one at a time. Some infant formulas even come in ready-to-feed form. These are poured into a clean bottle and fed immediately. Room-temperature formula is acceptable for many infants. Otherwise, to warm a bottle of formula, a caregiver can run hot water over it or place it briefly in a pan of simmering water. Note that infant formulas should not be heated in a microwave oven because hot spots may develop, which can burn the infant's mouth and esophagus.

Powdered and concentrated fluid formula preparations are more commonly used than ready-to-feed varieties. All utensils used in preparing formula from these preparations should be washed and thoroughly rinsed. Powdered or concentrated formulas are poured into a bottle, to which clean, cold water is added (following label directions) and then mixed. The formula is then warmed, if desired, and fed immediately to the infant. Hot water from the faucet should not be used to make formula, since it poses a risk for high lead content (see Chapter 19). Cold water poses much less risk.

Refrigerating diluted formula for 1 day is safe. However, formula left over from a feeding should be discarded because it will be contaminated by bacteria and enzymes in the infant's saliva. If well water is used, it should be boiled before making formula for at least the infant's first 3 months of life, and it should be analyzed for excessive concentration of naturally occurring nitrates, which can lead to a severe form of anemia. Note that, if nitrates are high in municipal water systems, consumers will be warned (such as in a local newspaper) not to use the water for making infant formula until the concentration falls to a safe amount. This problem with nitrates typically occurs in the summer, when these wash from fertilized farm fields into local rivers after heavy rains. Boiling tapwater is also advised by some groups, based on evidence that even municipal water may contain microorganisms that can harm the vulnerable, such as infants (see Chapter 19).

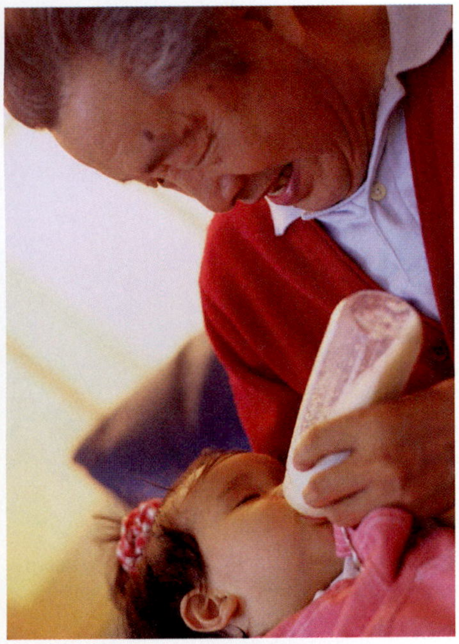

Careful attention during feeding allows the caregiver to notice the infant's signal as to when the feeding should cease.

Feeding Technique

Because infants swallow a lot of air along with either formula or human milk, it's important to burp an infant after either 10 minutes of feeding or 1 to 2 oz (30 to 60 ml) from a bottle and again at the end of feeding. Spitting up a bit of milk is normal at this time. Once fed, infants should be placed on their backs. Infants should not be placed on their stomachs because this sleeping position has been linked to sudden infant death syndrome (SIDS). The back to sleep campaign, started in 1994 in the United States, has reduced SIDS by 40%; however, plagiocephaly, otherwise known as flat-head syndrome, has increased as a result. Infant skulls are soft and can take on a different form. Flat-head syndrome can occur if an excessive amount of an infant's life is spent on his or her back, or against a highchair/car seat. In response to this concern the American Academy of Pediatrics has recommended periodic repositioning of an infant's head while asleep and allowing for time on his or her stomach while awake. In addition, some infants may need to wear specially fitted helmets to correct the shape of their head.

When the infant begins acting full, bottle-feeding should be stopped, even if some milk is left in the bottle. Common cues that signal that an infant has had enough include turning the head away, being inattentive, falling asleep, and becoming playful. Generally, the infant's appetite is a better guide than standardized recommendations concerning feeding amounts. Breastfeeding infants usually have had enough to eat after about 20 minutes. Although it's difficult to tell how much milk breastfed infants are getting, they also give signs when full. By carefully observing bottle-feeding or breastfeeding infants and responding to their cues appropriately, caregivers not only can be assured that the infants' energy needs are being met but also can foster a climate of trust and responsiveness.

Development of Feeding Skills in Older Infants

By 6 to 7 months the infant has learned to grab and transfer objects from one hand to the other (Table 17-2). At about this time, teeth begin to appear, and the infant begins to handle finger foods with some dexterity. Dry toast, sliced in strips, offers hours of enjoyment.

Table 17-2 Typical Progression of Infant Eating Skills and Solid-Food Introduction*

Age	Feeding Skills	Oral Motor Skills	Types of Food	Suggested Activities
Birth–4 months		Rooting reflex Suckling reflex Swallowing reflex Extrusion reflex	Human milk Infant formula	Breastfeed or bottle-feed
5 months	Is able to grasp objects voluntarily Is learning to reach mouth with hands	Disappearance of extrusion reflex		Possibly introduce thinned cereal if baby not satisfied by breastfeeding or bottle-feeding
6 months	Sits with balance while using hands	Transfers food from front of tongue to back	Infant cereal Strained fruit Strained vegetables Egg yolk (if no family history of egg allergy)	Prepare cereal with formula or human milk to a semiliquid texture Use spoon Feed from a dish Advance to ⅓–½ cup cereal before adding fruits or vegetables
7 months	Has improved grasp Can transfer objects from hand to hand	Mashes food with lateral movements of jaw Learns side-to-side, or "rotary," chewing Tooth eruption	Infant cereal Strained to junior texture of fruits, vegetables, and meats	Thicken cereal to lumpier texture Sit in high chair with feet supported Introduce cup
8–10 months	Holds bottle without help Drinks from cup Decreases fluid intake and increases solids Coordinates hand-to-mouth movement		Juices (small amounts) Soft, mashed, or minced table foods	Begin finger foods, such as toast or crackers Avoid adding salt, sugar, or fats to food Present soft foods in chunks ready for finger-feeding
10–12 months	Feeds self Holds cup without help	Improved ability to bite and chew	Soft, chopped table foods Whole egg and whole milk (at 1 year of age)	Provide meals in pattern similar to rest of family Use cup at meals

Adapted with permission from *Handbook of Pediatric Nutrition*, 2nd ed., Samour and Athens, p. 87. © 1999, Aspen Publishers, Inc.

*This time line is just an estimate, and individual infants may vary by several months from the ages given. A pediatrician should be consulted if caregivers are concerned about an infant's developmental progress. In general, there is no nutritional reason to begin introducing solid foods before 6 months of age.

By age 7 to 8 months infants can push food around on a plate and play with a drinking cup, can hold a bottle, and self-feed a cracker or piece of toast. In mastering these manipulations infants develop self-confidence and self-esteem. It's important that parents be patient and support these early feeding attempts, even though they appear inefficient.

At about 10 months of age, infants practice in earnest self-feeding finger foods and drinking from a cup. Feeding time is often very messy. Food is used as a means to explore the environment. By the first birthday, their bodies have developed sufficiently to accommodate crawling, probably walking, and self-feeding. Although attempts at feeding are still erratic, developing children take great pride in doing more things independently. As children drink from a cup more frequently, fewer bottle feedings and/or breastfeedings are necessary. The added mobility of walking should naturally lead to gradual weaning from the bottle or breast.

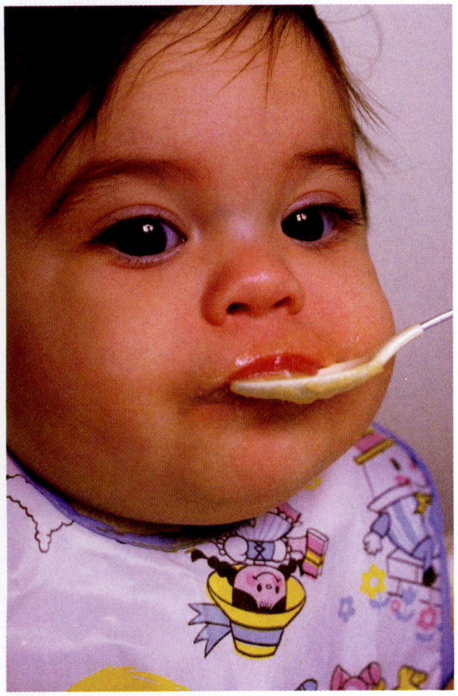

In the early stages of solid food introduction, these foods complement rather than replace human milk or infant formula in the diet.

Introduction of Solid Foods at About 6 Months of Age

The time to introduce solid foods into an infant's diet hinges on a few important factors:[4]

1. *Nutritional need.* Iron stores are exhausted by about 6 months of age. Either solid foods or iron supplements are then needed to supply iron if the child is breastfed or fed a formula not supplemented with iron. Iron, however, is not the only nutrient low in human milk and unfortified infant formulas. Vitamin D may also deserve attention, as previously mentioned. Still, before 6 months or so, it's generally unnecessary to add solid foods.
2. *Physiological capabilities.* Infants cannot readily digest starch before 3 months. As they age, their digestive capabilities increase. Kidney function likewise is quite limited until about 4 to 6 weeks of age. Until then, waste products from excessive amounts of dietary protein or minerals are difficult to excrete.
3. *Physical ability.* Three markers indicate that a child is ready for solid foods: (1) the disappearance of the extrusion reflex (thrusting the tongue forward and pushing food out of the mouth), (2) head and neck control, and (3) the ability to sit up with support. These usually occur around 4 to 6 months of age, but they vary with each infant.
4. *Allergy prevention.* An infant's intestinal tract can readily absorb whole proteins from birth until 4 to 5 months of age. Thus, early exposure to many types of proteins—particularly proteins in cow's milk and egg whites—may predispose a child to future allergies and other health problems because some types of these proteins may be absorbed intact. For this reason, it's best to minimize the number of different types of proteins in a child's diet, especially during the first 3 months.

With these considerations in mind—nutritional need, physiological and physical readiness, and allergy prevention—the American Academy of Pediatrics recommends that solid foods not be introduced until about 6 months of age and that infants receive no unaltered cow's milk before 1 year.

In general, a child starting solid foods should weigh at least 13 lb (6 kg) and should be drinking more than 32 oz (1 L) of formula daily or breastfeeding more than 8 to 10 times within 24 hours. This description generally applies to 6-month-old infants and to a few 4-month-old infants.

Parents may believe that the early addition of solid foods will help the infant sleep through the night. Actually, this achievement is a developmental milestone; the amount of food consumed by the infant is irrelevant.

Before 4 to 6 months, infants are not physically mature enough to consume much solid food. Attempts to push down solid foods have sometimes led to forcefeeding with a feeder (a giant syringe) or mixing infant cereal with milk and putting it in a bottle. Even if these are traditional alternatives in your family, there is no reason to carry on these practices. The inconvenience alone should make one consider whether all the effort is worth it. This practice is unnecessary nutritionally, tedious, and possibly dangerous for the infant because it increases the risk of allergies and choking or inhaling food when crying. Only occasionally does a rapidly growing infant—one who consumes more than 32 oz (1 L) of formula daily—really need solid foods at 4 months to meet high energy needs.

Solid Foods That Should Be Fed First

Before 6 months of age, the first solid foods should be iron-fortified cereals. A good idea is to offer foods after some breastfeeding or formula feeding, when the edge has been taken off the infant's hunger. This practice aids in early spoon-feeding. Rice cereal is the best cereal to begin with because it's least likely to cause allergies. After the age of 6 months, the first food is not such an important issue. Some pediatricians may recommend lean ground (strained) meats for more absorbable forms of iron. Although yogurt and cottage cheese are also well tolerated and their consistencies make them good candidates for early foods, they are not good sources of iron.

Start with teaspoon amounts of a single-ingredient food item, such as rice cereal, and increase the serving size gradually. Once the new food has been fed for about a week without ill effects, another food can be added to the infant's diet. At first, this can be another type of cereal or perhaps a cooked and strained (or mashed) vegetable, meat, fruit, or egg yolk. It is best to add vegetables before fruits. If fruits are offered first, the infant will prefer the sweet taste and may resist vegetables. Overall, build each feeding step on the previous step, making sure to add only a single ingredient each time.

Typical Solid Food Progression, Starting at 6 Months*

Week 1	Rice cereal
Week 2	Add strained carrots
Week 3	Add applesauce
Week 4	Add oat cereal
Week 5	Add cooked egg yolk
Week 6	Add strained chicken
Week 7	Add strained peas
Week 8	Add plums

*Extending the rice cereal step for a month or so is advised if solid food introduction begins at 4 months of age. Note also that, if at any point signs of allergy or intolerance develop, substitute another, similar food item.

Waiting about 7 days between new foods is important because it can take that long for evidence of an allergy or intolerance to develop. Symptoms to look for are diarrhea, vomiting, a rash, or wheezing. If one or more of these symptoms appear, the suspected problem food should be avoided for several weeks and then reintroduced in a small quantity. If the problem continues, a physician should be consulted.

It's important not to introduce mixed foods until each component of the mixed food has been given separately. Otherwise, if an allergy or intolerance develops, it will be difficult to identify the offending food. Note that many babies outgrow food sensitivities in childhood. Some foods that commonly cause an allergic response in infants are egg whites, chocolate, nuts, and cow's milk. It's best not to introduce these foods in infancy.[5]

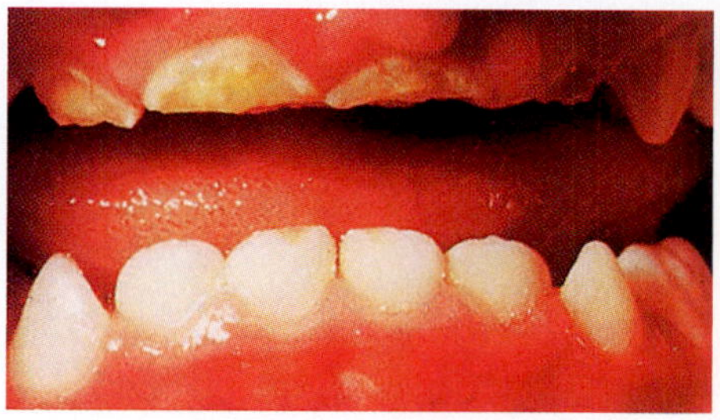

Figure 17-5 An extreme example of tooth decay caused by early childhood caries. This child was probably put to bed with a bottle. The upper teeth have decayed almost all the way to the gum line.

A variety of strained foods is available for infant feeding at the supermarket. Investigate these and other foods intended for infants the next time you're shopping. Single-food items are more desirable than mixed dinners and desserts, which are less nutrient-dense. Most brands have no added salt, but some fruit desserts contain a lot of added sugar.

As an alternative, plain foods from the table—vegetables, fruits, and meats (no seasoning added)—can be ground up in an inexpensive plastic baby food grinder/ mill. Another option is to purée a larger amount of food in a blender, freeze it in ice-cube portions, store in plastic bags, and defrost and warm as needed. Careful attention to cleanliness is necessary. Infant foods made at home should be ground before seasonings are added to please the rest of the family. The infant doesn't notice the difference if salt, sugar, or spices are omitted. It's best to introduce infants to a variety of foods, so that by the end of the first year the infant is consuming many foods—milk, meats, fruits, vegetables, and grains.

Around 6 months or so, juices can be offered in a sippy cup with a wide, flat bottom. Drinking from a cup helps prevent **early childhood caries** (Fig. 17-5). As an infant drinks continually from a bottle, the carbohydrate-rich fluid bathes the teeth, providing an ideal growth medium for bacteria. Bacteria on the teeth then make acids, which dissolve tooth enamel. Infants should never be put to bed with a bottle or placed in an infant seat with a bottle propped up. When children are allowed to do this, fluid (even milk) pools around the teeth, increasing the likelihood of dental caries. Again, infants need careful attention when being fed. Propping up a bottle does not constitute careful attention.

early childhood caries Tooth decay that results from formula or juice (and even human milk) bathing the teeth as the child sleeps with a bottle in his or her mouth. The upper teeth are mostly affected as the lower teeth are protected by the tongue; formerly called nursing bottle syndrome and baby bottle tooth decay.

Getting a baby out of the bedtime-bottle habit is difficult. Determined caregivers can either wince through a few nights of their baby's crying or slowly wean the baby away from the bottle with either a pacifier or water (for a week or so).

In the first attempts to introduce solid foods, just getting the food into the infant's mouth proves to be a challenge. The caregiver must proceed slowly. Initially, table

A Summary of Infant Feeding Recommendations

Breastfed Infants

- Breastfeed for 6 months or longer, if possible. Then introduce infant formula if and when breastfeeding declines or ceases. Breast milk can also be pumped and placed in a bottle for later use.
- Add iron-fortified cereal at about 6 months of age.
- Investigate the need for fluoride, iron, and vitamin D supplementation to prevent deficiencies.
- Provide a variety of basic, soft foods after 6 months of age, advancing to a varied diet.

Formula-Fed Infants

- Use infant formula for the first year of life, preferably an iron-fortified type.
- Add iron-fortified cereal at about 6 months of age.
- Investigate the need for a fluoride supplement if the water supply is not fluoridated.
- Provide a variety of basic, soft foods after 6 months, advancing to a varied diet.

Table 17-3 Sample Daily Menu for a 1-Year-Old Child*

Breakfast 1–2 tbsp applesauce ¼ cup Cheerios ½ cup whole milk	**Snack** ½ oz cheddar cheese 4 wheat crackers ½ cup whole milk
Snack ½ hard-cooked egg ½ slice wheat toast with ½ tsp margarine ½ cup orange juice	**Dinner** 1 oz hamburger (crumbled) 1–2 tbsp mashed potatoes with ½ tsp margarine 1–2 tbsp cooked carrots (cut in strips, not coins) ½ cup whole milk
Lunch 1 oz roasted chicken, minced 1–2 tbsp rice with ½ tsp margarine 1–2 tbsp cooked peas ½ cup whole milk	**Snack** ½ banana 2 oatmeal cookies (no raisins) ½ cup whole milk

Nutritional Analysis	
Total energy (kcal)	1100
% energy from	
Carbohydrate	40%
Protein	19%
Fat	41%

*This diet is just a start. A 1-year-old may need more or less food. In those cases, serving sizes should be adjusted. The milk can be fed by cup; some can be put into a bottle if the child has not been fully weaned from the bottle. The juice should be fed in a cup.

foods supplement—rather than replace—formula or human milk. Infants control the situation by signaling when they are hungry and when they have had enough to eat. Self-feeding skills require coordination and can develop only if the infant is allowed to practice and experiment. At 9 to 10 months, the infant's desire to explore, experience, and play with food can also hinder feeding. Presenting new foods for several consecutive days can aid in an infant's acceptance of that food.

Caregivers need to relax and take this phase of infant development in stride. Sloppy, friendly mealtimes actually make for good memories.

To ease efforts in feeding solid foods, consider the following tips:

- Use a baby-sized spoon; a small spoon with a long handle is best.
- Hold the infant comfortably on the lap, as for breastfeeding or bottle-feeding, but a little more upright to ease swallowing. When in this position, the infant expects food.
- Put a small dab of food on the spoon tip and gently place it on the infant's tongue.
- Convey a calm and casual approach to the infant, who needs time to get used to food.
- Expect the infant to take only two or three bites of the first meals. Anything more than that is real success.

By the end of the first year, finger-feeding becomes more efficient, drinking from a cup improves, and chewing is easier as more teeth erupt. Foods in the diet begin to resemble a balanced diet, such as a Food Guide Pyramid pattern (Table 17-3). Still, experimentation and unpredictability are to be expected.

What Not to Feed an Infant

Following are several foods and practices to avoid when feeding an infant:

- *Honey*. This product may contain spores of *Clostridium botulinum*. The spores can eventually develop into bacteria in the stomach and lead to a foodborne illness known as *botulism*. This can be fatal, including in children under 1 year old (see Chapter 19).

- *Very salty and very sweet foods.* Infants don't need a lot of sugar or salt added to their foods. They enjoy bland foods much more than do adults.
- *Excessive infant formula or human milk.* After 6 to 8 months, solid foods should play a greater role in satisfying an infant's increasing appetite. The main reason to switch is that solid foods contain considerably more bioavailable iron than do human milk and low-iron formulas. About 24 to 32 oz (¾ to 1 L) of human milk or formula daily is ideal after 6 months, with food supplying the rest of the infant's energy needs.
- *Foods that tend to cause choking.* These foods include hot dogs (unless finely cut into sticks, not coin shapes), candy, whole nuts, grapes, coarsely cut meats, raw carrots, popcorn, and peanut butter. Caregivers should not allow younger children to gobble snack foods during playtime and should supervise all meals.
- *Cow's milk, especially low-fat or nonfat cow's milk.* Beyond 2 years, children can drink fat-reduced, 1%, or nonfat milk, because by then they are consuming enough solid foods to supply energy and fat needs. Before that age, the amount of this milk needed for energy needs would supply too many minerals and in turn could overwhelm the kidneys' ability to excrete the excess. The lower fat intake might also harm nervous system development. The American Academy of Pediatrics strongly urges parents not to give children under age 2 fat-reduced, 1%, or nonfat milk.
- *Feeding excessive amounts of apple or pear juice.* The fructose and sorbitol contained in these juices can lead to diarrhea because they are slowly absorbed. Also, if fruit juice or related drink products are replacing formula or milk in the diet, the infant may not be receiving adequate amounts of calcium and other minerals that are essential for bone growth. In fact, studies have shown a link between excessive amounts of fruit juice and failure to thrive, GI tract complications, obesity, short stature, and poor dental heath. Thus, these substances should be used sparingly. Infants over the age of 6 months can usually safely consume up to 6 oz of juice in the course of a day, with no more than 2 to 4 oz at a time.[2]

Early feeding attempts should be encouraged, even though they're messy.

Egg whites also should not be fed to children before 1 year of age to help prevent the development of allergies.

Case Scenario | Follow-up

Damon's diet is inadequate for a 10-month-old infant because it lacks enough of the nutritious foods his growing body needs to support weight gain. These foods include iron-fortified cereal, puréed infant foods, and appropriate table foods. Damon should stay on the infant formula until 1 year of age and should not be given sugary drinks, nor should these drinks be fed by bottle if used. Damon needs a more energy-dense diet containing a healthful variety of solid foods to provide him with enough calories and essential nutrients to grow and develop.

Concept | Check

Infant formulas generally contain lactose or sucrose, heat-treated proteins from cow's milk, and vegetable oil. Formulas may or may not be fortified with iron. Sanitation is very important in preparing and storing formula. Solid foods should not be added to an infant's diet until the child is both ready for and needs solid food, usually at about 6 months of age. The first solid food can be iron-fortified infant cereals, with very gradual additions of other foods—one at a time each week. Some foods to avoid giving infants in the first year are honey, cow's milk (particularly fat-reduced, 1%, or nonfat milk), very salty or sweet foods, foods that may cause the child to choke, and excessive amounts of fruit juice or related products (e.g., fruit drinks).

Dietary Guidelines for Infant Feeding

In response to various controversies surrounding infant feeding, the American Academy of Pediatrics has issued a number of statements concerning infant diets. The following guidelines are based on these statements:

- *Build to a variety of foods.* For the first months of life, human milk is all an infant needs. When the infant is ready, start adding new foods, one at a time. During the first year, the goal is to teach an infant to enjoy a variety of nutritious foods. A lifetime of healthy eating habits begins with this important first step.
- *Pay attention to your infant's appetite to avoid overfeeding or underfeeding.* Feed infants when they are hungry. Never force an infant to finish an unwanted serving of food. Watch for signs that indicate hunger or fullness.
- *Infants need fat.* Although fat is the cause of many adult health problems, it's an essential source of energy for growing infants. Fat also helps the nervous system develop.
- *Choose fruits, vegetables, and grains, but don't overdo high-fiber foods.* Although many adults benefit from higher-fiber diets, they are not good for infants. They are bulky, filling, and often low in energy. The natural amounts of fiber and nutrients in fruits, vegetables, and grains are appropriate as part of a healthy infant diet.
- *Infants need sugars in moderation.* Sugars are an additional source of energy for active, rapidly growing infants. Foods such as human milk, fruits, and juices are natural sources of sugars and other nutrients as well. Foods that contain artificial sweeteners should be avoided; they don't provide the energy growing infants need.
- *Infants need sodium in moderation.* Sodium is a necessary mineral found naturally in almost all foods. As part of a healthy diet, infants need sodium for their bodies to work properly.
- *Choose foods containing iron, zinc, and calcium.* Infants need good sources of iron, zinc, and calcium for optimum growth in the first 2 years. These minerals are important for healthy blood, proper growth, and strong bones.

In essence, there is no evidence that very restrictive diets during infancy have positive effects, whereas their hazards are well documented.

Health Problems Related to Infant Nutrition

Parents, other caregivers, and clinicians should be alert for a variety of potential health problems related to infant nutrition, so that corrective action can be taken quickly. In some cases, such problems stem from inappropriate feeding practices and inadequate nutrient intakes, including the following:

- Diet providing insufficient iron
- Absence from the diet of an entire food group of the Food Guide Pyramid (or other related pyramid) as solid foods are introduced and become the main source of nutrients
- Drinking raw (unpasteurized) milk, which may be contaminated with bacteria or viruses
- Drinking goat's milk, which is low in folate, iron, vitamin C, and vitamin D; if used, it must be pasteurized and given in conjunction with a balanced multivitamin and mineral supplement
- Failure to begin drinking from a cup by 1 year of age
- Continuing to feed from a bottle past 18 months of age
- Intake of supplemental vitamins or minerals above 100% of the appropriate RDA or other nutrient standard
- Drinking large amounts of fruit juice after 6 months of age, especially as a substitute for infant formula or human milk. (Recall that fruit juice is not to be fed at all before 6 months of age.)

Now let's look more closely at five common infant health problems that cause concern for caregivers: colic, diarrhea, milk allergy, iron deficiency anemia, and gastroesophageal reflux. Parents and other caregivers usually need to consult with a physician in dealing with these conditions. The website of the American Academy of Pediatrics (www.aap.org) can also provide useful information.

Colic The first time an otherwise healthy, well-fed infant has a lengthy, unexplained crying spell, most parents panic. Repeated crying episodes, lasting 3 or more hours that don't respond to typical remedies—such as feeding, holding, or changing diapers—are characteristic of infants who develop **colic.** Colic affects about 10 to 30% of all infants, starting at about 2 to 6 weeks of age and lasting until about 3 months of age, so it is neither uncommon nor abnormal. Colicky infants typically cry during the late afternoon and early evening, and their nighttime sleeping is almost always disturbed by crying spells. In addition, these infants frequently pass gas rectally, clench their fists, draw up their legs, hold the body straight, and want to be held. The only good news is that colic usually goes away after a few months.

colic Sharp abdominal pain that generally occurs in otherwise healthy infants and is associated with periodic spells of inconsolable crying.

Colic generally occurs in the absence of any physical problem in the infant. It tends to be most common in "temperamental" infants—those who are more sensitive, more irritable, more intense, less adaptable, and less consolable than average for their age. In addition, a lack of harmonious interaction between parents and the infant may contribute to the problem. Some researchers have speculated that immature central nervous system mechanisms may cause colic.

Parents can do several things to help reduce excessive crying. For instance, many infants tend to become quiet and alert when held snugly to the shoulder. Parents should also check to see whether the infant is tired or bored or wants to suckle. Some infants can be calmed by rhythmic sounds or movement or with pacifiers.

Breastfeeding of colicky infants should continue. The breastfeeding mother's temporary decrease or cessation in consumption of dairy products, caffeine, chocolate, and vegetables such as broccoli and onions may help reduce colic in her infant. Formula-fed infants with severe colic are sometimes helped by changing from a standard formula to a soy-based or predigested protein formula (review Table 17-1). In addition, physicians may prescribe medication to calm colicky infants and reduce gas buildup.

Caring for an inconsolable, colicky infant is stressful and frustrating for parents. Most parents benefit from the counsel and support of other adults during this trying period, which may last for several months. Sharing with others who have been through similar experiences can help parents improve their tolerance of stress and ability to cope and can increase their confidence in their parenting abilities. Furthermore, to optimize their ability to be sensitive and responsive to their infant, parents need to be well rested and set aside some time for themselves.

Diarrhea Diarrhea in infants, characterized by numerous loose stools per day, results from various causes, including bacterial and viral infections. In the United States, about 500 infants die each year of simple dehydration resulting from diarrhea, and about 210,000 are hospitalized for this disorder. Typical symptoms include dry mouth or tongue, few or no tears when crying, no wet diapers for 3 hours or more, irritability and listlessness, and sunken eyes and cheeks. To prevent dehydration, infants with diarrhea should be given plenty of fluids, under the advice of a physician. Specialized electrolyte-replacement fluids, such as Pedialyte, may be recommended for one day or less. These contain glucose, sodium, potassium, chloride, and water.

Once diarrhea subsides, a bottle-fed infant may be switched to a soy-based, lactose-free formula for a few days. This allows time for the intestine to produce sufficient lactase enzyme to digest the large amount of lactose typically found in formulas. A breastfed infant should continue at the breast for the duration of the diarrhea. If solid foods are consumed, the physician may also prescribe a BRAT (bananas, rice, applesauce, toast) diet for short-term use; this is not a nutritionally adequate diet for long-term use.

Milk Allergy Cow's milk contains more than 40 proteins that can cause allergic reactions in infants. Although some of these proteins are inactivated by heating (scalding) milk, others are very heat stable. A true milk allergy develops in about 1 to 3% of formula-fed infants. Such infants may experience vomiting, diarrhea, blood in the stool, constipation, and other symptoms. If milk allergy is suspected, a formula-fed infant can be switched to a soy-based formula. In 20 to 50% of cases, however, the use of soy formula provides only temporary relief because the soy protein eventually triggers an allergic reaction in some infants. In such cases a predigested-protein formula is necessary (review Table 17-1). If the child is breastfeeding, the mother may experiment with eliminating cow's milk from her diet. Fortunately, milk allergies seldom last beyond 3 years of age.[14]

Iron Deficiency Anemia Iron deficiency anemia typically occurs in older infants (about 10 to 15% of 1- to 2-year-olds), especially those who consume few solid foods and whose diets are dominated by cow's milk, which both contains little iron and causes intestinal bleeding in young infants. Iron stores are then quickly depleted by the daily need to synthesize new red blood cells. The best way to prevent iron deficiency anemia is to feed an iron-fortified formula beginning at birth, if formula is used. Then start an infant on iron-fortified cereals and meats at about 6 months. Infant formula should also be limited to 16 to 25 oz (500 to 750 ml) daily at this age. If anemia does develop, medicinal iron is used under a physician's guidance.[7]

Gastroesophageal Reflux Many infants develop gastroesophageal reflux (GER), more commonly known as "spitting up," during their first year of life. In most cases, GER develops before 2 to 3 months of age and usually resolves on its own by the infant's first birthday. The problem arises because the lower esophageal sphincter may not close completely. This allows milk or solid food in the infant's stomach to move back up into the esophagus. The result can be a burning sensation, which causes the infant pain or discomfort. Or the infant might spit up the milk or food. In the majority of cases, GER poses no serious medical concerns. In very rare cases, surgery may be required to remedy the problem.

Feeding Preterm Infants

Preterm infants are fed either a specially designed formula or human milk. Total parenteral nutrition may also be required in the initial phase of hospitalization. As noted in Chapter 16, nutrients may be added to human milk to increase its protein, mineral, and energy content. Preterm infants must be fed immediately because their bodies store little fat or carbohydrate. The body composition of a full-term infant includes about 12% fat, whereas the composition of a very preterm infant can include as little as 2% fat.

Concept | Check

Colic is commonly associated with inconsolable crying. Switching to an infant formula made with soy or predigested proteins may reduce colic. It may also be helpful for breastfeeding mothers to decrease or avoid intake of dairy products, caffeine, chocolate, and certain vegetables, under a physician's guidance. Diarrhea requires additional fluids to prevent dehydration. Infants allergic to proteins in standard cow's milk formula can be switched to an infant formula containing soy protein or predigested protein. Introducing iron-containing solid foods at an appropriate time and avoiding the use of cow's milk during the first year can generally prevent iron deficiency anemia in infants. Any gastroesophageal reflux that develops typically resolves within the first year of life.

Preschool Children

The rapid growth rate that characterizes infancy tapers off quickly during the subsequent few years. The average annual weight gain is only 4.5 to 6.6 lb (2 to 3 kg), and the average annual height gain is only 3 to 4 in (7.5 to 10 cm) between the ages of 2 and 5 (review Fig. 17-1). As a toddler's growth rate tapers off, eating behavior changes. For example, the decreased growth rate leads to a decreased appetite, often called "picky eating," compared with infants.[1] Estimated Energy Requirements (kcals) are now $(89 \times \text{weight of child [kg]}) - 80$ for children 1–3 years. For older preschool children, see the formulas listed later for school-aged children.[5]

Because of the reduced appetite of preschool children, planning a diet that meets their nutrient needs poses a challenge to caregivers. Choosing nutrient-dense foods is particularly important with children who eat relatively little. This is a good time to emphasize some whole grains, fruits, and vegetables without increasing fat and simple sugar intake. A whole-grain ready-to-eat breakfast cereal with limited fat and sugar is an excellent choice.[15] There is no need to decrease fat or simple sugar intake severely, but fatty and sweet food choices should not overwhelm more nutritious ones.[1]

The preschool years are the best time for a child to start a healthful pattern of living and eating, focusing on regular physical activity and nutritious foods (Fig. 17-6). Parents and other caregivers are role models: If they eat a variety of foods, the children will eat a variety of foods. One possible policy is the one-bite rule: Within reason, children should take at least one bite or taste of the foods presented to them. For snacks, parents should select several possibilities of acceptable choices and allow children to choose one; responsibility for food choice ideally should start early.

Carbohydrate needs to supply energy for the central nervous system and prevent ketosis in childhood are 130 g/day, the same as for adults. The protein needs to allow for growth vary from 1.1 g/kg body weight/day (13 to 19 g/day) for children 1 to 3 years, to 0.95 g/kg body weight/day (34 to 52 g/day) for older children. No specific needs for total fat intake have been set, but the diet must contain at least 5 g/day of essential fatty acids (see the inside cover for details).[5] The general recommendation is that total fat intake gradually fall so as to fit into the adult range of 20 to 35% of total energy intake.

How to Help a Child Choose Nutritious Foods

One way adults can encourage young children to eat nutritious, well-balanced meals is to serve new foods and repeat exposure to them. If a child observes adults and older children eating and enjoying a food, there's a good chance that, most of the time, he or she will eventually accept it. The dinner hour is a good time for children to experience new foods and to develop their own food preferences. Preschool children especially

Figure 17-6 USDA has created a Food Guide Pyramid for children ages 2 through 6 years. The pyramid base recommends that young children consume six servings a day of grains such as bread, cereal, rice, and pasta; three servings of vegetables; and two servings each of fruit, milk, and meat. The pyramid is designed to be very child-friendly, showing foods children will recognize in appealing graphic format. It also emphasizes the importance of physical activity for good health by featuring many children playing actively around the pyramid to symbolize how eating and activity work hand-in-hand. The booklet accompanying this pyramid can be downloaded at www.usda.gov/cnpp.

Interest in food starts early in life.

tend to be wary of new foods. One reason is that they have more taste buds, and their taste buds are more sensitive than those of adults. In addition, they have a general distrust of unfamiliar foods. If adults can be patient and persevere, children will build good food habits. Above all, the dinner table should not become a battleground, and using one food as a bribe to eat another—for example, a piece of pie for peas—is strongly discouraged.

Perseverance with children is critical, because it takes effort and commitment to guide them into liking a variety of foods. Be ready for some surprises. Also, if left to their own devices, preschool children would find a few foods they like and eat them every day. However, by constantly being introduced to new foods, children at this age can expand their nutritional choices, develop an experimental approach, and learn to appreciate a variety of foods. It may take 10 to 15 exposures, but eventually children will accept most foods. A positive outlook by the caregivers helps a lot.

Children generally like certain foods—especially those with crisp textures and mild flavors—and familiar foods. Young children are especially sensitive to hot-temperature foods and tend to reject them.

Parents and other caregivers play a central role in teaching by example.[1] Children more readily learn good table manners alongside others who practice them. The harmony that comes from working at being polite creates a positive environment for learning good nutrition habits. Preschoolers eventually develop skill with spoons and forks and can even use dull knives (Table 17-4). However, it's still a good idea to serve some finger foods. A goal should be to make mealtime a happy, social time, sharing enjoyment of healthful foods. A regular family meal daily—whether breakfast, lunch, or dinner—is an appropriate setting for children to learn about healthful eating and to build good eating habits.

Childhood Feeding Problems

Tensions between parents, or between parents and children, especially during mealtime, often contribute to eating problems. Getting to the root of family problems and creating a more harmonious family atmosphere are important steps toward resolving many childhood feeding problems. In addition, many parents must be educated as to what to expect of a preschool child and what food-related goals to set (review Table 17-4). Let's consider some typical complaints and concerns of parents, the causes of the problems, and suggestions for correcting them.

Two-year-olds commonly prefer particular foods, but parents needn't worry about this. A child may switch from one specific food focus (often called a *jag*) to another with equal intensity (older infants may also act this way). If the caregiver continues to offer choices, the child will soon begin to eat a wider variety of foods again, and the specific food focus will disappear as suddenly as it appeared.

"My Child Won't Eat as Much or as Regularly as He Did as an Infant"

This behavior is typical of preschoolers, because their growth rate slows after infancy; thus, they don't need as much food. Parents often need reminding that a 3-year-old can't be expected to eat as voraciously as an infant or to eat adult-size portions. Table 17-5 shows a general food plan, based on the Food Guide Pyramid, that is appropriate for preschool and school-age children. Until about 5 years of age, serving sizes in the vegetable group, fruit group, and meat, poultry, fish, dry beans, eggs, and nuts group can be estimated as about 1 tablespoon per year of life. The same restriction does not apply to cereals or milk, but note that consuming too much milk can leave the diet short on iron.[7] Luckily, normal-weight children have a built-in feeding mechanism, which adjusts hunger to regulate food intake at each stage of growth. If a child is developing and growing normally and the caregiver is providing a variety of healthful foods, all can be confident the child isn't starving.[1] Caregivers should avoid nagging, forcing, and bribing. Overall, parents should focus on the specific food choices, while the child decides how much of each food to eat.

Appetite also varies with activity level and general health. An initial symptom of a sick child is poor appetite. Picky eating is also just another indication of a child's striving toward independence and his or her strong desire to establish routines. Asserting himself or herself about food preferences is a relatively easy way for the child to do this, and pickiness may be exacerbated if parents are too restrictive.[1]

Table 17-4 Observed Emotional Traits, Eating Behavior, and Food-Related Skills of Preschoolers

Age (years)	Emotional Traits	Eating Behavior	Food-Related Skills
1–2	• Fears new things • Sharing difficult • Requires constant supervision • Enjoys helping but can't be left alone • Curious • Often defiant • Eager for attention	• "Finicky" eater • Holds food in mouth without swallowing • May insist on eating the same food at meal after meal (called a food jag)	• Uses spoon with some skill (especially if hungry) • Can begin to tear, break, snap, and dip foods • Has good control of cup—lifts, drinks, sets it down, holds with one hand • Helps self-feed
3	• The "me too" age—wants to be included in everything • Responds well to options rather than demands • Sharing still difficult • Somewhat rigid about the "right" way to do things	• Eats most foods, except for certain vegetables • Dawdles over food when not hungry • Comments on how foods are served	• Uses spoon in semiadult fashion; may spear with fork • Medium hand muscle development • Feeds self independently, especially if hungry • Can pour milk and juice and serve individual portions from a serving dish if given instructions
4	• Shares well • Needs adult approval and attention—shows off • Understands; needs limits • Follows rules most of the time • Still rigid about the "right" way to do things	• Eating and talking get in the way—prefers to talk • Strong food likes and dislikes • Refuses to eat, to the point of tears	• Uses all eating utensils • Small-finger muscle development • Can wipe, wash, set table, and pour pre-measured ingredients • Can peel, spread, cut, roll, and mash foods; cracks eggs
5	• Helpful and cooperative with family chores and routines • Still somewhat rigid about the "right" way to do things • Very attached to parent, home, and family	• Likes familiar foods; prefers most vegetables raw • Latches on to food dislikes of family members and declares these as own	• Fine coordination in fingers and hands • Makes simple breakfast and lunch • Can measure, cut, grind, and grate with some supervision

Modified from M. Sigman-Grant, "Feeding Preschoolers: Balancing Nutritional and Developmental Needs," *Nutrition Today,* July/August 1992, p. 13. Used with permission.

Table 17-5 Food Plan for Preschool and School-Age Children Based on the Food Guide Pyramid

		Approximate Serving Size*			
Food Group	**No. of Servings**	**Age 1–2**	**Age 3–4**	**Age 5–6**	**Age 7–12**
Milk, yogurt (cups), and cheese (oz)	3	½–¾ cup or 1 oz	¾ cup or 1½ oz	1 cup or 2 oz	1 cup or 2 oz
Meat, poultry, fish, dry beans, eggs, and nuts	2 or more	1 oz or 1–2 tbsp	1½ oz or 3–4 tbsp	1½ oz or ½ cup	2 oz or ½ cup
Vegetables	3 or more	1–2 tbsp	3–4 tbsp	½ cup	½ cup
Fruit	2 or more	1–2 tbsp or ½ cup juice	3–4 tbsp or ½ cup juice	½ cup or ½ cup juice	½ cup or ½ cup juice
Bread, cereal, rice, and pasta	6 or more	½ slice or ½ cup	1 slice or ½ cup	1 slice or ¾ cup	1 slice or ¾ cup

*Use as a starting point. Increase serving size as energy yields dictate, but maintain variety in the diet by making sure all food groups are still appropriately represented.

Adapted from Food and Nutrition Service, U.S. Department of Agriculture. *Meal Pattern Requirements and Offer Versus Serve Manual,* FNS-265, 1990.

The foods that pose a risk for choking in infants also do so in young children.

Parents should also be reminded that food likes and dislikes change rapidly in childhood and are influenced by food temperature, appearance, texture, and taste. Sometimes children object to having foods mixed, as in stews and casseroles, even if they normally like the ingredients separately.

In addition, parents should recognize that this is an important age for children to explore the world around them. Even good eaters are sometimes more interested in exploring than eating. There's room for occasional indulgences, a skipped meal or two, or once in a while "less than ideal" choices. It's eating and lifestyle habits over the course of a month and lifetime that matter. Children master their eating when adults provide opportunities to learn, give support for exploration, and limit inappropriate behavior.

"My Child Is Always Snacking, Yet She Never Finishes Her Meal"

Children have small stomachs. Offering them six or so small meals succeeds better than limiting them to three meals each day. Sticking to three meals a day offers no special nutritional advantages; it's just a social custom. Snacking is fine, as long as good dental habits are practiced. When we eat isn't nearly as important as what we eat. If nutritious snacks are readily available, these are good to offer at midmorning or midafternoon when the child becomes hungry (Table 17-6). Fruits and vegetables (fresh, frozen, or juice) and whole-grain breads and crackers are good snack choices. Working parents should make sure their children are provided with nutritional snacks to tide them over until dinnertime.

When a child refuses to eat, it's best not to overreact. Doing so may give the child the idea that eating is a means of getting attention or manipulating a scene. Most children don't starve themselves to any point approaching physical harm. When children refuse to eat, have them sit at the table for a while; if they still aren't interested in eating, remove the food and wait until the next scheduled meal or snack.

"My Child Never Eats Vegetables"

Childhood is an ideal time to begin to enjoy healthful foods.

Children generally eat enough fruit but not an adequate amount of vegetables. Everyone dislikes certain foods. Again, the one-bite policy can be used, including for vegetable servings, and guidelines can be set to discourage fussing over unfamiliar foods. Children eventually learn that they can eat some of a food they don't particularly like without first gagging, choking, and yelling, "Oh, gross!" It takes time for a child to become enthusiastic about a new food; however, with continual exposure and a positive role model, chances are the child may even grow to like it.

Children cannot and should not be forced to eat. They need to develop independence and identities separate from their parents. As stated earlier, children have to choose for themselves—a practice that should be encouraged. No one food is an essential part of a diet. Hunger is still the best means for getting a child to eat. It may be effective to feed children vegetables at the start of a meal, when they are hungriest. Offer new foods with familiar ones. A platter of raw or lightly cooked carrots, broccoli, green and red peppers, cabbage, and mushrooms eaten as a snack with friends can do a lot to remedy a vegetable problem. A 4- or 5-year-old child can safely eat raw vegetables without fear of choking. Recall that children often are more sensitive than adults to strong flavors and odors. Nutritious dips "sell" vegetables to many children. Vegetables may acquire more appeal when children help prepare them. And, as with any food, it is important to remember that children have likes and dislikes, too.

Do Children Need a Multivitamin and Mineral Supplement?

Major scientific groups, such as the American Dietetic Association and the American Society for Clinical Nutrition, believe that multivitamin and mineral supplements are generally unnecessary for healthy children; it's better to emphasize good foods. Fortified ready-to-eat breakfast cereals with milk are especially helpful in closing any gap between current micronutrient intake and needs, such as for vitamin E, folate, and

Table 17-6 Ideas for Nutritious Snacks and Beverages

Snack	Serving Suggestion	Snack	Serving Suggestion	Snack	Serving Suggestion
Fresh raw vegetables	Serve with a dip of cottage cheese or yogurt blended with dried buttermilk dressing.	Ready-to-eat cereals	Use brands low in sugar and containing fiber; serve with raisins.	Parfait	Make with yogurt, fruit, and granola.
Celery	Spread with peanut butter and sprinkle on raisins, shredded carrots, or finely chopped nuts.	Pita bread	Place sliced meat, cheese, lettuce, and tomato in open pocket.	Gelatin	Add fruit or vegetable juice, vegetables, fruits, or cottage cheese
Bananas	Dip in sweetened yogurt or spread with peanut butter and roll in coconut, chopped nuts, or granola.	English muffins or pita bread	Top with spaghetti sauce, grated cheese, meats; broil or bake and cut in fourths.	Frozen fruit cubes	Freeze puréed applesauce or fruit juice into cubes.
Sliced apples or crackers	Serve with a dip of peanut butter, honey, nuts, raisins, and coconut.	Potato skins	Sprinkle with shredded cheese, broil, and top with yogurt and bacon bits.	Fruit fizz	Add club soda to juice instead of serving soft drinks.
Bagels	Spread with cream cheese or peanut butter and top with chopped bananas, crushed pineapple, or shredded carrots.	Canned chili with beans	Heat and top with onions, lettuce, and tomato; use as dip for Italian or French bread, biscuits, or corn-bread.	Fruit shake	Blend milk with fresh fruit (bananas, berries, or a peach) and a dash of cinnamon or nutmeg.
Quick bread or muffins	Make with carrots, zucchini, pumpkin, bananas, nuts, dates, raisins, lemons, squash, or berries.	Kabobs	Make with any combination of fruit, vegetables, and sliced or cubed cooked meat (remove toothpicks before serving).	Yogurt frost	Combine fruit juice and yogurt; add fresh fruit, if desired.
Flour tortillas	Spread with refried beans or canned chili with beans, sprinkle with grated cheese and broil; top with chili sauce.	Popcorn	Serve plain or make 3 quarts and sprinkle with ¼ cup grated cheese and ½ tsp garlic or onion salt.	Hot chocolate	Make hot chocolate or cocoa with milk chocolate and a dash of cinnamon.
				Seeds	Choose shelled sunflower seeds.
				Fish	Put tuna salad on crackers.
				Canned soup	Serve a cup of vegetable or minestrone; nice on a cold winter day.

vitamin D.[15] Two minerals of particular concern are iron and zinc. These may be lacking in children's diets because they consume such small portions of rich sources, such as animal protein foods. In addition, since the current Dietary Guidelines suggest that children over age 2 years follow a diet low in saturated fat and cholesterol, rich sources of iron and zinc may be lacking in their diets. To compensate, parents can search for a whole-grain breakfast cereal that the child likes that also has about 50% of the Daily Value for iron and 25% of the Daily Value for zinc. (This will supply sufficient amounts of both nutrients since the Daily Values are based on the higher needs of adults.) If that's not possible, especially for a child who is ill or has a very erratic food preference pattern or appetite, the child may benefit from a multivitamin and mineral supplement not exceeding 100% of Daily Values on the label, especially if these conditions persist.[11] Still, as mentioned many times in this textbook, such a practice does not substitute for an otherwise healthy diet, children included.

If current childhood feeding practices are to become more healthful, the focus should shift to the bottom half of the Food Guide Pyramid (or other pyramid shown in Chapter 2), including whole grains, fruits, and vegetables. Caregivers can model this behavior by ordering from the salad bar more often and ordering french fries less often at fast-food restaurants. Children do not need to be severely restricted but, rather, should modify food habits with small changes.[1] Some easy diet changes to begin with are bagels instead of doughnuts, nonfat frozen yogurt instead of ice cream, fat-reduced

Children who follow a totally vegetarian fare should also focus on protein and vitamin B-12 intake.

or 1% milk instead of whole milk, fruit instead of crackers and cheese for snacks, and air-popped popcorn instead of chips.

Nutritional Problems in Preschool Children

Chapter 5 noted that it's unlikely that the use of sugar is the cause of hyperactivity or antisocial behavior in most children.

Three nutrition-related problems found in preschool children are iron deficiency anemia, constipation, and dental caries. Proper diet can help correct or relieve these conditions.

Iron Deficiency Anemia

Childhood iron deficiency anemia is most likely to appear in children between the ages of 6 and 24 months.[7] It can lead to decreases in both stamina and learning ability because the oxygen supply to cells decreases.[9] Another effect is lowered resistance to disease. Fortunately, childhood anemia is less common today in North America, probably because of children's use of iron-fortified breakfast cereals. Also deserving of credit in the United States is the Special Supplemental Nutrition Program for Women, Infants, and Children (WIC), sponsored by the federal government. This program emphasizes the importance of iron-fortified formulas and cereals and distributes them—along with nutrition education—to low-income parents of infants and preschool children considered to be at nutritional risk.

The best way to prevent iron deficiency anemia in children is to regularly provide foods that are adequate sources of iron. Iron-fortified breakfast cereals and a few ounces of lean meat are convenient means of getting more iron into a child's diet. The high proportion of heme iron in many animal foods allows the iron to be more readily absorbed than is iron from plant foods. Consuming a vitamin C source along with the less readily absorbed iron in plants and supplements aids absorption.

Constipation

Constipation may be associated with another disease, yet some young children experience constipation that is unrelated to any medical condition. When presented with a constipated child, a physician first has to rule out a medical cause, such as intestinal blockage. And, although the most common gastrointestinal symptom that reflects intolerance to cow's milk is diarrhea, chronic constipation may also result. This possibility should be investigated by the physician. Treatment for constipation generally consists of first evacuating the bowels, generally with an enema. The promotion of regular bowel habits then follows, with laxative use as directed by the physician. Several months to years of supportive intervention may be required for effective treatment.

Excessive fruit juice and fruit drink use is another potential problem in preschool (and later adolescent) years. The American Academy of Pediatrics recommends no more than 4 to 6 oz per day for children 1 to 6 years (and 8 to 12 oz per day for ages 7 to 18 years).

Dietary interventions include eating more dietary fiber and drinking more fluids. Foods to emphasize for fiber are fruits, vegetables, whole-grain breads and cereals, and beans. The current daily fiber goal for children varies by age: 1–3 years, 19 g/day; 4–8 years, 25 g/day; 9–13 years, 31 g/day for boys and 25 g/day for girls. After age 13 years, typical adult recommendations are appropriate (see Chapter 5). Accompanying fluid recommendations are 5 cups per day for toddlers and about 8 cups per day for older children.

Dental Caries

A proper diet goes a long way in reducing the risk for dental caries in young children. Earlier it was mentioned that infants are prone to early childhood caries, which can lead to excessive tooth decay. The following tips can help reduce dental problems in children:

- Begin oral hygiene when teeth start to appear.
- Seek early pediatric dental care.
- Drink fluoridated water.
- Use small amounts of fluoridated toothpaste twice daily.
- Snack in moderation.

- Have a dentist apply tooth sealants if needed.
- Avoid sticky, high-sugar snacks, especially between meals.
- If toddlers or preschoolers are chewing gum, sugarless gum is the best choice, as this has been shown to reduce the incidence of dental caries.

Chapters 5 and 12 provide a fuller description of diet and dental health. If needed, these discussions will aid in putting this list of recommendations into perspective.

Modifications of Childhood Diets to Reduce Future Disease Risk

Earlier chapters covered the role of diet in development of cardiovascular disease and hypertension and the recommendations concerning diet to reduce the risk for these diseases. Parents sometimes wonder whether similar diet modifications are appropriate and beneficial during childhood.

Diets Designed to Limit Cardiovascular Disease for Children 2 Years of Age and Older

The development of atherosclerosis often begins in childhood. As a result, many experts recommend screening for blood cholesterol in children whose families have histories of early development of cardiovascular disease or high blood cholesterol and treating children found to have high blood cholesterol with appropriate diet and drug therapy, as discussed in Chapter 6.[19] With regard to diet, children in the United States currently derive about 33% of their energy from fat, with about 13% of energy from saturated fat. The Food and Nutrition Board recommends that fat intake range from 30 to 40% of energy intake for children 1 to 3 years, and 25 to 35% for children 4 to 18 years, so this fat intake is appropriate.[5] However, saturated fat, trans fat, and cholesterol intake should be minimized (no set limit). Thus, more work is needed in this regard. These recommendations are consistent with those of the National Cholesterol Education program in the United States, and as well those from the American Heart Association.[20] An emphasis on plant oils such as canola oil as a major source of fat in the diet helps meet the goals of reduced saturated fat, trans fat, and cholesterol intake. In general, it's unnecessary to discourage children from consuming nutrient-dense foods, such as milk and animal proteins, just because they contain some animal fat. The overriding message is moderation in these and other fat sources, while focusing on limiting saturated fat, trans fat, and cholesterol intake as possible.

Children benefit from opportunities to be physically active. This contributes to cardiovascular health. The current goal is 60 minutes of such activity each day, the same as for adults.

Salt-Restricted Diets

Scientific data neither confirm nor refute the notion that eating less salt (sodium) reduces the risk of future hypertension. Moderation in salt consumption does help build good health habits for the future—especially if the person later develops hypertension and needs to eat even less salt. If children become accustomed to less salt, they'll be less inclined to eat very salty foods as adults. This reduction in salt also contributes to better calcium retention in the body, as covered in Chapter 11. If a child with hypertension does not respond to diet and lifestyle therapy, typical antihypertensive medications may be used, but at lower doses than adults require.

Vegetarianism in Childhood

Vegetarian diets can pose several risks for young children. These include the possibility of developing iron deficiency anemia, a deficiency of vitamin B-12, and rickets. During the first few years of life, children also may not consume enough energy when following a bulky vegetarian diet. But these known pitfalls are easily avoided by informed diet planning (see the Nutrition Perspective in Chapter 7). Diets for children who eat totally vegetarian fare should focus on protein, vitamin B-12, iron, and zinc content, with additional emphasis on vitamin D (or regular sun exposure) and calcium. Some of these dietary inadequacies can be compensated for by increasing oils, nuts, seeds, ready-to-eat breakfast cereals, and fortified soy milk in the diet.

Concept | Check

The rapid growth rate of an infant's first year slows during the toddler and preschool years (ages 1 to 5). As a child's appetite decreases, adults need to serve nutrient-dense foods and allow the child to decide how much to eat. Sudden shifts in food preferences are to be expected. Snacking is fine if attention is given to the selection of healthful foods and good dental hygiene. A multivitamin and mineral supplement is usually not needed—a plan following the Food Guide Pyramid that includes a serving of fortified ready-to-eat breakfast cereal should meet nutrient needs, but such use is a reasonable practice, especially in some cases. Children need plenty of iron-rich food to prevent iron deficiency anemia, as well as zinc for growth. Adequate fiber and fluid help prevent constipation. Developing heart-healthy habits after the age of 2 years is advocated, but highly restrictive diets are not appropriate during childhood. Diets for children who eat totally vegetarian fare should focus on protein, vitamin D (or regular sun exposure), vitamin B-12, calcium, iron, and zinc content.

School-Age Children

In general, the nutritional concerns and goals applicable to school-age children are the same as those discussed in relation to preschoolers. The Food Guide Pyramid (or a related pyramid) continues to be a good basis for diet planning, with an emphasis on moderating fat intake and ensuring adequate iron, zinc, and calcium intake. The only difference is that serving size increases as energy needs increase (review Table 17-5). The Estimated Energy Requirements (kcals) are now $88.5 - (61.9 \times \text{Age [y]}) + (\text{PA} \times (26.7 \times \text{Weight [kg]} + 903 \times \text{Height [meters]}) + 20$ for boys 3 through 8 years. Recall from Chapter 13 that PA stands for physical activity. In this case, PA = 1.00 if the child is sedentary; PA = 1.13 if the child is low active; PA = 1.26 if the child is active; PA = 1.42 if the child is very active. For older boys the formula is the same except the last value (20) is replaced by the value 25.

For girls ages 3 through 8 years the formula is $135.3 - (30.8 \times \text{Age [y]}) + (\text{PA} \times (10.0 \times \text{Weight [kg]} + 934 \times \text{Height [meters]}) + 20$. In this case, PA = 1.00 if the child is sedentary; PA = 1.16 if the child is low active; PA = 1.31 if the child is active; PA = 1.56 if the child is very active. For older girls the formula is the same except again the last value (20) is replaced by the value 25. Now let's look at several other nutritional issues of particular concern during the school-age years.

Breakfast, Fat Intake, and Snacks

In a recent survey, 17% of children aged 10 years old said they skip breakfast.

Once children enter school, their eating patterns become more scheduled, and the consumption of regular meals—especially breakfast—becomes an important focus. A fortified ready-to-eat breakfast cereal is typically the greatest source of iron, vitamin A, and folic acid for children ages 2 to 18. Although there is controversy over the true benefit of breakfast for cognitive ability, children who eat breakfast likely meet their needs for vitamins and minerals compared to children not eating breakfast. To influence morning test performance, it currently appears that breakfast must be eaten within a few hours of a test; the rise in blood glucose is thought to change performance.

Critical | Thinking

Tim refuses to eat breakfast before school. He doesn't like cereal, toast, or any of the other usual breakfast foods. What can Tim's parents do to ensure that he eats nutritious foods before leaving for school?

Breakfast menus need not be limited to traditional fare. A little imagination can spark the interest of the most reluctant child. Instead of conventional breakfast foods, parents can offer leftovers from dinner—pizza, spaghetti, soups, yogurt topped with trail mix, chili with beans, or sandwiches, for starters.

There is general agreement that the diets of school-age children should include a variety of foods from each major group, not necessarily excluding any specific food because of its fat content.[1] Overemphasis on fat-reduced diets during childhood has been linked to an increase in eating disorders and encourages an inappropriate "good food, bad food" attitude.

Steering children toward healthful foods, in school and at home, is likely to be more successful if children are exposed to nutrition education. Since children spend much of their younger years in school, it is a great place to learn about positive, healthy eating habits. Such education can help children understand why eating a proper diet will make them feel more energetic, look better, and work more efficiently. One survey of U.S. schoolchildren highlighted the need for nutrition education. On the day of the survey, 40% of the children ate no vegetables, except for potatoes or tomato sauce; 20% ate no fruits; and 75% snacked at least twice. Some 36% of the students ate at least four different types of snack foods. Another study showed that only 2% of about 3300 children 2 to 19 years old had met their recommended servings from all five Food Guide Pyramid groups. Clearly, the diets of many school-age students can stand general improvement, particularly with regard to fruit, vegetable, whole grain, and dairy choices. Drinking minimal amounts of sugared soft drinks is also advised.

Nutrition education ideally begins in the home as parents and other caregivers provide a healthy, well-balanced diet.

Type 2 Diabetes

Type 2 diabetes is generally thought of as an adult condition. As reviewed in the Nutrition Perspective in Chapter 5, it frequently occurs in overweight people who are older than 40. However, recently physicians have noted an alarming increase in the frequency of the disease among children (and teenagers). This is primarily due to the rise in obesity in this age group, coupled with little physical activity. Up to 85% of children with the disease are overweight at diagnosis. Experts are currently calling for the screening of fasting blood glucose in at-risk children every 2 years, starting at age 10 or the onset of puberty.[12] Besides obesity and a sedentary lifestyle, other risk factors include having a first- or second-degree relative with the disease, or belonging to a non-White population. Appropriate diet and lifestyle intervention should be implemented, along with the use of medications when necessary (see Chapter 5). Dr. Arline D. Salbe discusses this in greater detail in the Expert Opinion.

Obesity

In the United States, about 25 to 30% of school-age children place above the 85th percentile for BMI and are considered at risk for or overweight, and the number of cases is currently increasing, especially in minority populations. Obesity is generally diagnosed when a child reaches the 95th percentile for BMI and a physical exam indicates the child is truly overfat. This usually is the case for a child who reaches this degree of BMI.[10] In the short run, ridicule, embarrassment, possibly depression, and short stature linked to early puberty are the main consequences of such obesity. In the long run, significant health problems associated with obesity, such as cardiovascular disease, type 2 diabetes, and hypertension, usually don't appear until adulthood. However, an increase in these health-related complications have been noted in children. Childhood obesity is a serious health threat, since about 40% of obese children (and about 80% of obese adolescents) become obese adults. Significant weight gain generally begins between ages 5 and 7, during puberty, or during the teenage years.

Regular physical activity is an important part of prevention and treatment of weight problems in childhood.

Current research points to many potential causes of childhood obesity. Recall the nature versus nurture discussion in Chapter 13. Some infants are born with lower metabolic rates; they use energy more efficiently and in turn can more easily save energy intake for fat storage. Studies also suggest, though, that this genetic link accounts for only one-third of individual differences in body weight.

Researchers believe that, although diet is still an important factor, inactivity is the key to the increase in childhood obesity.[18] Today's generation now glues itself to the TV for

Expert Opinion

Obesity and Type 2 Diabetes in Childhood: Lessons from the Pima Indians

Arline D. Salbe, Ph.D., R.D.

The prevalence of obesity among children and adolescents worldwide has reached epidemic levels and represents a significant public health problem. While malnutrition and food insecurity continue to be of great importance to child health in many parts of the developing world and in impoverished sectors of Western societies, pediatric obesity is increasing in industrialized societies as well as in countries undergoing rapid economic development.

The Third National Health and Nutrition Examination Survey (NHANES III), conducted from 1988 to 1994, found that 11% of children and adolescents 6 to 17 years old in the United States were overweight, defined as having a body mass index (BMI, kg/m^2) above the 95th percentile relative to sex- and age-specific national reference data. This represents almost a doubling of the prevalence rates reported in the previous NHANES II survey, which covered the period from 1974 to 1988. Initial results from the 1999 NHANES survey indicate that prevalence rates have increased even further, to 13% of children ages 6 to 11 years and 14% of adolescents ages 12 to 19 years. Moreover, it appears that the heaviest children in NHANES III were markedly heavier than in earlier surveys. These data suggest that despite the efforts of national health objectives such as *Healthy People 2010*, the prevalence of obesity in youth continues to rise.

Obesity in childhood and adolescence has been found to promote disease in three different ways. First, pediatric obesity has been associated with immediate adverse health effects, including problems with bones and joints, the GI tract, and the respiratory system. Recent reports also indicate a growing incidence of type 2 diabetes in overweight youth, especially minority youth. Secondly, obesity in childhood appears to track into adulthood, thereby predisposing these individuals to the adverse health outcomes attributed to adult obesity. Finally, adolescent obesity has been implicated as a cause of many adult-onset disorders, independent of adult weight, including an increased risk of cardiovascular disease, stroke, colorectal cancer, and type 2 diabetes.

What Can Research with Native Americans Tell Us

Nowhere is the trend in childhood obesity more apparent than in Native American communities where studies based on the same standards have found the overweight prevalence rates in children and adolescents to range from ~ 30 to 40%, much greater than in the overall population. Reports of elevated rates of childhood obesity can be found, for example, among Mohawk, Cree, and Pima Indian children, as well as children from other tribal affiliations.

Super-sized portions of foods served to children are contributing to the obesity and type 2 diabetes epidemics they are experiencing.

The Pima Indians of Arizona are particularly prone to the development of obesity and as a result, this Native American population has the highest reported prevalence of type 2 diabetes in the world: by the age of 35 years, half the population has diabetes. Several risk factors for the development of diabetes in Pima Indians have been identified, including fetal development in a diabetic pregnancy, elevated birth weight, infant feeding practices, childhood obesity, and genetic susceptibility.

an average of 24 hours a week; many children spend another 10 hours or so playing computer and video games. The American Academy of Pediatrics recommends a limit of 14 hours of TV and computer time per week. In addition, excessive snacking, overreliance on fast food restaurants, parental neglect, lack of safe areas to play, and high-fat/high-energy food choices also contribute to childhood obesity.[3]

The initial approach in treating an obese child is to assess how much physical activity he or she engages in. If a child spends much free time in sedentary activities (such as watching television or playing video games), more physical activities should be encouraged. Both the U.S. federal government and health professionals recommend 60 min-

The age of onset of diabetes in the Pima Indian population has decreased over time and as a result, the incidence of diabetes in women of childbearing age has increased. Maternal diabetes during pregnancy results in infants who are large for gestational age, which is a risk factor for developing obesity and diabetes later in life. However, regardless of birth weight, the fetus' diabetic environment carries an independent risk for obesity and diabetes in the offspring. This "cross-generational vicious cycle," whereby more women of childbearing age develop diabetes and have children who are, therefore, at greater risk of developing obesity and diabetes themselves, has substantially increased the prevalence of diabetes in Pima Indian children. Exposure to maternal diabetes during fetal development is associated with a tenfold increase in the risk of diabetes in childhood and is the single strongest predictor of type 2 diabetes in Pima Indian children.

Obesity in childhood carries an independent risk for the development of type 2 diabetes. In a population such as the Pima Indians who are predisposed to the disease, obesity is highly predictive of the development of the disease. In the absence of obesity, other metabolic predictors of type 2 diabetes, such as high levels of insulin in the bloodstream, don't predict the risk of type 2 diabetes very well. In the presence of obesity, however, each of the metabolic variables acts together, thereby increasing the likelihood of developing diabetes.

Among Pima Indians, parental diabetes status is a significant predictor of the development of diabetes in the offspring, at any age, and this is independent of weight status. After adjustment for age and obesity, diabetes incidence was found to be 2.3 times as high in subjects with one diabetic parent, and 3.9 times as high in those with two diabetic parents, compared to those with two nondiabetic parents. Moreover, diabetes prevalence varies with the degree of Indian heritage, suggesting that there is a genetic susceptibility to the disease. This genetic susceptibility has prompted the search for the genes responsible for type 2 diabetes. However, due to the multi-gene nature of the disease, identification of a specific genetic locus has thus far been unsuccessful, although several candidate genes have been tested.

Other Ethnic Groups at Particular Risk

Pima Indians are not the only population experiencing an increase in pediatric type 2 diabetes. The disease is appearing with greater frequency in many segments of the population, but most especially among minority youth. For example, 33% of all new cases of diabetes diagnosed in 10- to 19-year-old patients of a Cincinnati clinic in one year were type 2 diabetes; 69% of those cases occurred in children of African American descent. Among Mexican American children under 17 years of age in a California community, 31% of those with diabetes were reported to have type 2 diabetes. In all cases, obesity is the predominant predisposing factor. As a result, the American Diabetes Association recommends that an overweight child (body mass index or weight-for-height > 85th percentile), having two of the following additional risk factors, including: a history of type 2 diabetes in a first or second degree relative; American Indian, African American, Hispanic or Pacific Islander heritage; or signs of insulin resistance (including hypertension and abnormal blood lipid values), be tested for diabetes (fasting plasma glucose) starting at 10 years of age (or younger if puberty has already taken place) and continuing every two years after that.

The emerging epidemic of pediatric type 2 diabetes, especially among minorities, is likely to continue as long as the current epidemic of obesity continues. And because minority representation in the overall North American population is increasing, pediatric type 2 diabetes, and the complications thereof, promise to be a significant public health problem in the twenty-first century if this trend is not reversed.

Dr. Salbe is a Research Nutritionist for the National Institutes of Health, Phoenix, Arizona. She received her Ph.D. in nutrition from the University of California at Berkeley.

utes or more of moderate to intense physical activity per day for children and adolescents. An overall active lifestyle will help children not only to attain a healthy body weight but also to keep a similar body weight later in life. An increase in physical activity won't just happen; parents need to plan for it. Two good ideas are getting the family together for a brisk walk after dinner and finding an after-school sport the child enjoys.[17]

Moderation in energy intake is important, especially the limitation of high-fat and high-energy foods, such as sugared soft drinks and high-fat milk. The focus should be on more nutrient-dense foods and healthy snacks.[1]

Resorting to a weight-loss diet is usually not necessary. As a start, it's best to emphasize changing habits that allow for weight maintenance. Children have an advantage over adults in dealing with obesity; their bodies can use stored energy for growth. Thus, if weight gain can be moderated, increases in height and resulting lean body tissue may reduce the percentage of body weight accounted for as stored fat, yielding a more healthful weight-to-height ratio. This is one reason it's desirable to treat obesity in childhood. Further growth can contribute to success.

If a child is still obese after attaining ultimate adult height, a weight-loss regimen may be necessary. This is especially appropriate after the adolescent growth spurt. Weight loss should be gradual, perhaps ½ lb per week. If weight loss is necessary in younger children, the child should be watched closely to ensure that the rate of growth continues to be normal. The child's energy intake shouldn't be so low that gains in height diminish. In addition, medications may be prescribed under a physician's care to reduce fat absorption.

To get kids involved in exercise, new physical education classes have been introduced into schools. These classes provide lifelong fitness lessons in such activities as rock climbing, in-line skating, and recreational jogging. These classes help promote activity because they take the focus away from teams and competition, which often discourage and embarrass kids who lack athletic talent.

Obese children often need to find a new way to relate to foods, especially snack foods. An important family rule could be that children are allowed to eat only while sitting at the dining table or in the kitchen. This could stop endless hours of snacking in front of the television and make all family members more conscious of when they are eating. It also might be helpful to put portions of snack foods on plates, rather than allow snacking to go on indefinitely, as often happens when children eat directly from a full box of crackers or cookies.

A child's self-esteem is extremely fragile. Obesity itself often affects the child's psyche and mental outlook (e.g., depression). Humiliation doesn't work; it only makes the child feel worse. Support, admiration, and encouragement of the child's efforts at weight control are more effective and should be emphasized.

Finally, it is important to understand that not all children are designed to look like society's ideal. In other words, some children simply weigh more than others. A healthful lifestyle with plenty of physical activity and nutritious foods remains the key concern.[3, 18]

Concept | Check

The school-age child is advised to follow the Food Guide Pyramid (or a related pyramid), moderating choices high in fat and simple sugars. Breakfast is an important meal to refuel the body for a new school day and to help ensure fulfilling nutrient needs for the day. Attention to regular physical activity and healthy diet should help prevent/treat childhood obesity and build a desirable lifestyle pattern for later life.

The teenage years are noted for snacking. With reasonable food choices, teenagers can have healthful diets.

The Teenage Years

Most girls begin a rapid growth spurt between the ages of 10 and 13, and most boys experience rapid growth between the ages of 12 and 15. Nearly every organ in the body grows during these periods. Most noticeable are increases in height and weight and the development of secondary sexual characteristics. Girls usually begin menstruating (reach menarche) during this growth spurt, and they grow very little beyond 2 years after menarche. Early-maturing girls may begin their growth spurt as early as age 7 to 8, whereas early-maturing boys may begin growing by age 9 to 10.

During the growth spurt, girls gain about 10 in (25 cm) in height, and boys gain about 12 in (30 cm). Girls also tend to accumulate both lean and fat tissue, whereas boys tend to gain mostly lean tissue. This growth spurt provides about 50% of ultimate adult weight and about 15% of ultimate adult height (review Fig. 17-1).

As the growth spurt begins, teenagers begin to eat more. Estimated Energy Requirements are the same as previously listed for older children. If teens choose nutri-

Table 17-7 Food Plan for Teenagers Based on the Food Guide Pyramid*

Food Category	Minimum Number of Daily Servings†
Milk, yogurt, and cheese (preferably low fat or nonfat)	3
Meat, poultry, fish, dry beans, eggs, and nuts	2–3
Vegetables	3–5
Fruit	2–4
Bread, cereal, rice, and pasta (preferably whole grain; otherwise, enriched or fortified)	6–11
Fats, oils, and sweets	Use sparingly.

*Here we define "teenager" as a person who has some gain in height in the past year and is at least 12 years old. This food plan is applicable through age 18 years.

†Use same serving size as for adults (see Table 2-8 in Chapter 2).

A strictly vegetarian diet must be monitored for adequate energy, protein, iron, vitamin B-12, calcium, and vitamin D (the latter if sun exposure is not sufficient). These nutrients become particularly important in teenagers, as their diets are often already compromised.

tious food, they can take advantage of their increased hunger and easily satisfy their nutrient needs. As with older age groups, the Food Guide Pyramid can provide the basis for meeting these nutrient needs, with the major difference being three servings of milk and milk products (Table 17-7). Following such a plan will meet carbohydrate needs (130 g/day) and protein needs (0.85 g/kg body weight/day, or 52 g/day for males and 46 g/day for females).[5]

Nutritional Problems and Concerns of Teens

Anorexia nervosa and bulimia nervosa were covered in detail in Chapter 15. Other nutritional problems are more common during the teen years. A survey of high school students showed that only a little over 25% had eaten five servings of fruits and vegetables on the previous day, and they are consuming approximately 25% more sodium than recommended. Another concern is that many teenage girls stop drinking milk, so they may not consume enough calcium to allow for maximal mineralization of bones through their early twenties.[8] Many young women who don't consume enough calcium are likely to develop osteoporosis later, as discussed in Chapter 11.

Drinking soft drinks in place of milk causes many teenagers to have inadequate calcium intake. Over the last 20 years soft drinks have been replacing milk as a beverage for adolescents. This trend has been linked to decreased bone mass and increased bone fractures in this age group.

The Adequate Intake for calcium for both males and females between ages 9 and 18 years is 1300 mg per day, compared with 800 mg per day for younger children. Three servings per day from the milk, yogurt, and cheese group are recommended for all teenagers and young adults to meet calcium needs. Otherwise, alternative calcium sources need to be included.

A further concern is iron deficiency. Iron deficiency anemia sometimes appears in girls after they start menstruating (menarche) and in boys during their growth spurt. About 10% of teenagers have low iron stores or related anemia. Teens who strive to forge an identity by adopting dietary patterns unfamiliar to their families—vegetarianism, for example—may not know enough about the alternate diet pattern to keep from developing health problems, such as iron deficiency anemia. It's important that teenagers choose good food sources of iron, such as lean meats, whole grains, and enriched cereals. Teenage girls, particularly those with heavy menstrual flows, need to eat good sources of iron (or regularly consume an iron supplement). Iron deficiency anemia is a highly undesirable condition for a teen. It can produce increased fatigue and decreased ability to concentrate and learn. School and physical performance may suffer.

An active lifestyle coupled with a healthy diet should be part of the teen years.

Acne is a common teen concern—about 80% of teens experience it. Although it's popularly believed that eating nuts, chocolate, and pizza can make acne worse, scientific studies have failed to show a strong link between any dietary factor and acne. It is important to note that many acne medications contain analogs of vitamin A (e.g., 13-*cis* retinoic acid [Accutane]). Although these treatments can be quite effective, the close supervision by a physician is crucial, as these vitamin A analogs can be toxic. Vitamin A itself is no help in treating acne, and excess amounts of vitamin A or related analogs can cause birth defects. Thus, girls taking these vitamin A medications must not become pregnant.

A Closer Look at the Diets of Teenage Girls

Teenagers in general are apt to adopt fad diets, eat away from home or miss meals completely, and snack a lot. Teenage girls especially are very concerned with weight gain, appearance, and social acceptance. U.S. government statistics reveal that female students are significantly more likely to report currently trying to lose weight (44%) than male students (15%). Moreover, 27% of female students who considered themselves the right weight report they were currently trying to lose weight. It is important to inform teenage girls that weight gain in the form of increased body fat is to be expected in the adolescent growth spurt.

In an attempt to reach personal goals, teenage girls may eat dangerously little, select just a few items, and frequently skip meals altogether. If their limited food choices then consist of french fries, sugared soft drinks, and pastries, little room is left for foods that are good nutrient sources. Another common practice among teenage girls is having a fat phobia, focusing primarily on foods that are fat-free. However, many teens may not realize that some fat is essential for body functions, thus emphasizing the need for some fat in the diet. This concept is discussed in Chapter 6. The diets of teenage girls often lack adequate sources of folate, calcium, zinc, and vitamins A and C. The common use of diet pills and the increasing number of bulimia nervosa cases further add to these nutritional problems.

Alcoholism, a significant health problem that may have its roots in the teen years, is covered in detail in Chapter 8. Smoking—another habit that compromises health—also often begins in teen years. Some of this is in an attempt to control body weight—not an advisable method.

Helping Teens Eat More Nutritious Foods

Teenagers face a variety of challenges. They pursue their independence, experience identity crises, seek peer acceptance, and worry about physical appearance. All of these factors affect food choice. Advertisers take advantage of this by pushing a vast array of products—candy, gum, soft drinks, and snacks—at the teenage market. Potato chips and french fries make up more than one-third of the vegetable servings consumed by teens. Additionally, many schools offer french fries on a regular basis, and soft drink machines can be found in school hallways and cafeterias, in turn competing with the school lunch.[3]

Teens often don't think about the long-term benefits of good health. They have a hard time relating today's actions to tomorrow's health outcomes. Many teenagers tend to think they can just change habits later; there's no hurry.

Still, healthful teen food habits don't have to include giving up favorite foods. Small portions of fatty foods can complement larger portions of nonfat and low-fat dairy products, lean meats, vegetable proteins, fruits, vegetables, and whole-grain products. An example is a plain hamburger with a garden salad (minimize the amount of regular dressing or use a low-fat variety), small order of french fries or chili, and a medium diet soft drink or milk.

Clinicians who work with teenagers, including physicians, registered dietitians, and nurses, need to be prepared to discuss and deal with a variety of concerns: sports nutrition, eating disorders, use of steroids, and drug (and alcohol) abuse. Except for substance abuse, these topics usually are not a concern when working with older adult clients.

Overcoming the Teenage Mind-Set

One strategy for working with teenage boys is to stress the importance of nutrition and physical activity for physical development—especially muscular development—and for fitness, vigor, and health. With teenage girls, one approach is to help them understand how to choose nutrient-dense foods and activities that lead to better health while maintaining a healthy weight. For teenagers, it's more effective to focus on the benefits of healthful foods and regular physical activity they can reap right now than to talk about health hazards that may or may not happen later.[16]

Are Teenage Snacking Practices Harmful?

Teens often obtain one-fourth to one-third of all their energy and major nutrients from snacks. Unfortunately, studies have found just what you might expect—that teens snack mostly on potato and corn chips, cookies, candies, and ice cream. Key reasons for snacking include an opportunity to get out and socialize with friends, accessibility, hunger, and celebration of a special event. Teenagers can obtain many nutrients from snacking. Even fast food restaurants offer some good food choices. By choosing wisely and eating in moderation, teens can eat at fast food restaurants and still consume a very healthful diet. Snacks and fast food restaurants themselves are not the problem; poor food choices are.

Poor dietary habits and exercise formed during teenage years often continue into adulthood, giving rise to an increased risk of chronic diseases, such as cardiovascular disease, osteoporosis, and some types of cancer. Getting this message across to teenagers is an important and challenging task for parents and health professionals.[8]

One way to reduce energy intake in a restaurant is to choose diet soft drinks in place of regular soft drinks. This will greatly reduce sugar intake in the meal or snack, especially considering the large serving sizes typically offered.

Concept | Check

A second period of rapid growth occurs during the teen years. Girls generally start this growth spurt earlier than boys. The Food Guide Pyramid can guide meal planning. Common nutritional problems in these years arise from poor food choices and include inadequate calcium intake in girls, iron deficiency anemia, and sometimes excessive intake of total fat and saturated fat. Because changes occur so rapidly during these years, and in so many areas—psychological, social, and physical—it may be difficult to stress the importance of nutrition to teenagers. Moderation in fat and sugar intake are goals to consider when choosing snacks.

Summary

1. Growth is very rapid during infancy; birth weight doubles in 4 to 6 months, and length increases by 50% in the first year. An adequate diet, especially in terms of energy, as well as the nutrients protein and zinc, is essential to support normal growth. Undernutrition can cause irreversible changes in growth and development. Growth in infants and children can be assessed by measuring body weight, height (or length), and head circumference over time. Growth charts have recently been revised to include a more valid measurement for determining children's growth, body mass index (BMI).
2. Nutrient needs in the first 6 months can be met by human milk or iron-fortified infant formula. Supplementary vitamin D and iron may be needed in the first 6 months for breastfed infants, and many infants may need supplemental fluoride after 6 months of age.
3. Infant formulas generally contain lactose or sucrose, heat-treated proteins from cow's milk, and vegetable oil. These formulas may or may not be fortified with iron. Sanitation is very important when preparing and storing formula.
4. Most infants don't need solid foods before 6 months of age. Solid food should not be added to an infant's diet until the nutrients are needed, the GI tract can digest complex foods, the infant has the physical ability to control tongue thrusting, and the risk of developing food allergies has decreased.
5. The first solid food given should be iron-fortified infant cereals or ground meats. Other single foods can be added gradually, at the rate of about one each week. Some foods to avoid giving infants in the first year include honey, cow's milk (especially fat-reduced varieties), very salty or sweet foods, and foods that may cause choking.
6. Introducing iron-containing solid food at the appropriate time and not offering cow's milk until 1 year of age can generally prevent iron deficiency anemia in late infancy.
7. A slower growth rate in preschool years underlies the importance of children's eating nutrient-dense foods and reducing their food serving sizes. Choosing iron-rich foods, such as lean red meats, is important at this age. Portion sizes at meals of 1 tablespoon of each food for each year of life is a good rule of thumb for vegetables, fruits, and meats.
8. Preschoolers should be given some leeway in determining serving size and should be encouraged to try new foods. Highly restrictive diets designed to reduce the risk of cardiovascular disease or hypertension are not recommended for preschoolers or older children, unless prescribed by a physician.
9. Obese children and adolescents are more likely to become obese adults and, so, incur greater health risks. Parents can provide healthful food choices, and children should control portion sizes. When controlled early through diet and exercise interventions, a problem of obesity may correct itself as the child continues to grow in height.
10. During the adolescent growth spurt, both boys and girls have increased needs for iron and calcium. Inadequate calcium intake by teenage girls is a major concern because it can set the stage for the development of osteoporosis later in life. Teenagers generally should moderate their intake of high-fat and sugar-rich foods—especially snacks and fast food, which they often consume in abundance—and perform regular physical activity.

Study Questions

1. List two factors that limit "catch-up" growth in adulthood when a nutrient-deficient diet has been consumed throughout childhood.
2. Describe how you would assess whether an 8-month-old infant is consuming a healthful diet.
3. Outline three key factors that help determine when to introduce solid foods into an infant's diet.
4. A 3-month-old infant is taken to a clinic with failure to thrive. What are two possible explanations?
5. List three reasons why preschoolers are noted for "picky" eating. For each, describe an appropriate parent response.
6. What three factors are likely to contribute to obesity in a typical 10-year-old child?
7. Compare the guidelines for infant feeding summarized in the chapter with the Dietary Guidelines for Americans for children over 2 and adults discussed in Chapter 2. Which guidelines are similar? Do any contradict each other? If so, why?
8. Describe three pros and cons of snacking. What is the basic advice for healthful snacking from childhood through the teenage years?
9. Which two nutrients are of particular concern in planning diets for teenagers? Why does each deserve to be singled out?
10. List three nutrients of concern for a teenage vegetarian.

Annotated References

1. ADA Reports: Position of the American Dietetic Association: Dietary guidance for healthy children aged 2 to 11 years. *Journal of the American Dietetic Association* 99:93, 1999.

   Children older than 2 years of age should gradually adopt a diet by the age of 5 that reflects a lifelong healthy, nutrient-rich dietary pattern. The health status of U.S. children generally has improved over the past three decades; however, the number of children who are overweight has more than doubled.

2. American Academy of Pediatrics Committee on Nutrition: The use and misuse of fruit juice in pediatrics. *Pediatrics* 107:1210, 2001.

   The American Academy of Pediatrics suggests that no more than half of a child's recommended fruit servings come from fruit juice, with the remaining fruit servings coming from whole fruit. In addition, this committee recommends that only 100% fruit juice that has been pasteurized be provided to children. It is also recommended that fruit juice be consumed as part of a meal, and not be used throughout the day to pacify unhappy children.

3. Ebbeling C and others: Childhood obesity: Public health crisis, common sense cure. *The Lancet* 360:473, 2002.

   The prevalence of childhood obesity has increased both in North America and other parts of the world over the past few decades. Overweight and obese children face a greater risk for developing conditions such as type 2 diabetes, cardiovascular disease, and insulin resistance. Some common sense approaches for preventing and treating childhood obesity include greater physical education in the schools, building sidewalks and bike paths in the community, and limiting television viewing in the home.

4. Fomon SF: Feeding normal infants: Rationale for recommendations. *Journal of the American Dietetic Association* 101:1002, 2001.

   Breastfed infants should receive a daily supplement of iron and vitamin D, while formula-fed infants should receive iron-fortified formulas. Solid foods should not be introduced before 4 months of age. Iron-fortified cereals are the best solid foods to first introduce, but children with a strong family history of allergies may benefit from soft-cooked red meats as the first foods. Cow's milk should not be fed before 1 year of age.

5. Food and Nutrition Board: Dietary reference intakes for energy, carbohydrate, fiber, fat, fatty acids, cholesterol, protein, and amino acids. The National Academy Press, Washington, DC 2002.

   This report provides the latest guidance for macronutrient intakes. The many changes that have recently been made by the Board with regard to the macronutrient needs of infants and children are discussed in detail.

6. Heird WC: Nutritional requirements during infancy. In Bowman BA, Russel RM (eds.): *Present knowledge in nutrition.* Washington, DC: ILSI Press, 2001.

   This chapter provides a comprehensive review of dietary recommendations during infancy. Specific topics include macronutrient needs, use of human milk versus infant formula, eventual introduction of cow's milk, and the recent research on the benefits of intake of long-chain omega-3 fatty acids.

7. Kazal LA: Prevention of iron deficiency in infants and toddlers. *American Family Physician* 66:1217, 2002.

   Anemia is a possible problem during childhood. Anemia is most often caused by iron deficiency, and less often by deficiencies in folate and vitamin B-12. Screening for anemia in children occurs between ages 6 and 12 months for infants at high-risk for developing this disorder. Nutrition-related habits that increase risk are use of infant formula that is not fortified with iron, breastfeeding without iron supplementation, and excessive milk consumption in toddlers.

8. Kim SYS and others: Decline in physical activity in black and white girls during adolescence. *The New England Journal of Medicine* 347:707, 2002.

   Substantial declines in physical activity are common as girls reach the teenage years. This is especially seen in the late teens. Education to reverse this trend is important.

9. Lytle L: Nutritional issues for adolescents. *Journal of the American Dietetic Association* 102:S8, 2002.

   Data from large, population-based studies suggest that the typical adolescent's diet places them at increased risk for cardiovascular disease, cancer, osteoporosis, diabetes, and obesity in adulthood. The typical adolescent's diet contains too much total fat, saturated fat, sodium, and soft drinks, and not enough fruits, vegetables, fiber, and calcium.

10. Roberts S, Dallal G: The new childhood growth charts. *Nutrition Reviews* 59:31, 2001.

    The Centers for Disease Control and Prevention has published new childhood growth percentiles that are meant to replace the 1977 National Center for Health Statistics percentiles. The new percentile charts include more representative data for the birth to 3 years percentiles, and also include data on breastfed infants in addition to formula-fed infants. The previous growth charts were based on data from formula-fed infants only. In addition, the new growth charts include additional percentiles and extend to 20 years of age, as compared to the previous charts which only included percentiles for up to 18 years of age. Finally, the new growth charts also include body mass index values for children over 2 years of age.

11. Roberts SB, Heyman MB: Micronutrient shortfalls in young children's diets: Common, and owing to inadequate intakes both at home and at child care centers. *Nutrition Reviews* 58(1):27, 2000.

    Although not currently supported by The American Academy of Pediatrics, the routine use of a multivitamin and mineral supplement may be needed to help some young children in meeting their nutrient needs. This can be especially helpful for meeting iron and zinc needs, two nutrients that may be lacking in children's diets because they consume such small portions of rich sources, such as animal protein foods. In addition, since the current Dietary Guidelines for Americans suggest that children over age 2 years follow a diet low in saturated fat and cholesterol, rich sources of iron and zinc may be lacking in their diets. Fortified ready-to-eat breakfast cereals are a potential source of these nutrients.

12. Rocchini A: Childhood obesity and a diabetes epidemic. *The New England Journal of Medicine* 346:854, 2002.

Obesity has been named the most serious nutritional disorder affecting children in the United States. Over the past thirty years, rates of obesity have more than doubled in the United States, and there has been a similar increase in prevalence worldwide. Childhood obesity is a concern because it can lead to increased risk for cardiovascular disease, insulin resistance, and diabetes.

13. Sanchez O, Childers N: Anticipatory guidance in infant oral health: Rationale and recommendations. *American Family Physician* 61:115, 2000.

The American Academy of Pediatric Dentistry has recommended that infants go to the dentist for the first time within 6 months of the eruption of their first tooth, and no later than 12 months of age. More specifically, it is also recommended that soft-bristled tooth brushes be used with parental supervision, bottles should not be given to infants in bed, and that highly refined carbohydrate food intake should be limited.

14. Schardt D: Food allergies. *Nutrition Action Healthletter*, p. 10, April 2001.

Since there is no treatment or cure for food allergies, the only way to avoid allergic reactions is to avoid the offending foods. Allergies to peanuts, nuts, and seafood seldom disappear. Food intolerances on the other hand—except for those caused by sulfites—are not as serious a health problem.

15. Skinner JD and others: Longitudinal study of nutrient and food intakes of white preschool children aged 24 to 60 months. *Journal of the American Dietetic Association* 99:1514, 1999.

Diets of preschool-age children often lack adequate sources of zinc, folate, vitamin E, and vitamin D. Foods most commonly consumed by preschoolers include fruit drinks, carbonated beverages, fat-reduced milk, and french fries. Parents should encourage their children to eat more vegetables, zinc- and folate-fortified ready-to-eat breakfast cereals, lean red meats, seafood, vegetable oils, and fat-reduced milk.

16. Spear B: Adolescent growth and development. *Journal of the American Dietetic Association* 202:S23, 2002.

The changes in growth and development that occur during adolescence result in special nutrition needs. Due to the increased growth, adolescents have an increased need for certain nutrients, such as protein, calcium, and iron. Adolescence is also a time when lifestyle and food habits change, which in turn may place the adolescent at risk for sub-optimal nutrient intake.

17. St. Jeor S and others: Family-based interventions for the treatment of childhood obesity. *Journal of the American Dietetic Association* 102:640, 2002.

Family-based interventions are appropriate for treating childhood obesity because of the strong influences that family has in the eating habits and physical activity habits of a child. It is thought that positive changes in parental health behaviors will lead to similar positive changes in the child's health behaviors. Family-based interventions that encourage healthy eating and active lifestyles may help to prevent childhood obesity in the future.

18. Troiano R and others: Energy and fat intakes of children and adolescents in the United States: Data from the National Health and Nutrition Examination Surveys. *American Journal of Clinical Nutrition* 72:1343S, 2000.

Dietary data from the Third National Health and Nutrition Examination Survey were compared to earlier surveys to determine if there has been any change in consumption of energy and fat by 2- to 19-year-olds. Researchers found that there has not been an increase in energy intake among children and adolescents, leading to the conclusion that higher rates of overweight and obesity have more to do with declining physical activity participation than increased energy consumption.

19. Van Horn L: Primary prevention of cardiovascular disease starts in childhood. *Journal of the American Dietetic Association* 100:41, 2000.

Many of the problems in children's diets today are attributable to a lack of fruits, vegetables, and whole grains and to too many low-nutrient-dense foods, such as desserts, sweets, and snacks. These latter foods contribute excessive amounts of saturated fat, total fat, refined carbohydrate, and energy to the children's diets.

20. Williams CL and others: Cardiovascular health in childhood: A statement for health professionals. *Circulation* 106:143, 2002.

Recommendations from the American Heart Association regarding diets in childhood include emphasizing less than 10% of calories from saturated fat and less than 300 mg of cholesterol per day. The diet pattern should include 5 or more servings of fruits and vegetables, 6 to 11 servings of whole-grain and other grain foods, low-fat or nonfat milk, and other low-fat dairy products. Whole milk, however, is recommended for children 2 years of age or younger as they are weaned from breast milk or formula to cow's milk.

Take | Action

I. Getting Young Bill to Eat.

Bill is 3 years old, and his mother is worried about his eating habits. He absolutely refuses to eat vegetables, meat, and dinner in general. Some days he eats very little food. He wants to eat snacks most of the time. His mother wants him to eat a sit-down lunch and dinner to make sure he gets all the nutrients he needs. Mealtime is a battle because Bill says he isn't hungry, but his mother wants him to eat everything served on his plate. He drinks five or six glasses of whole milk per day because that is the one food he likes.

When his mother prepares dinner, she makes plenty of vegetables, boiling them until they are soft, hoping this will appeal to Bill. Bill's dad waits to eat his vegetables last, regularly telling the family that he eats them only because he has to. He also regularly complains about how dinner has been prepared. Bill saves his vegetables until last and usually gags when his mother orders him to eat them. Bill has been known to sit at the dinner table for an hour until the war of wills ends. Bill's mother serves casseroles and stews regularly because these are her best dishes. Bill likes to eat breakfast cereal, fruit, and cheese and regularly requests these foods for snacks. However, his mother tries to deny his requests, so that he will have an appetite for dinner. Bill's mother comes to you and asks you what she should do to get Bill to eat.

Analysis

1. List four mistakes Bill's parents are making that contribute to Bill's poor eating habits.

2. List four strategies they might try to promote good eating habits in Bill.

II. Evaluating a Teen Lunch.

The following are two typical teen lunches and nutritional information for each:

Meal 1	Meal 2
2 pieces cheese pizza	1 hamburger with condiments
1 milk chocolate candy bar	30 french fries
20 fl oz cola	20 fl oz cola

	Meal 1	Meal 2	Nutrient Needs for Teens
Energy (kcal)	990	1000	Males: 3000 Females: 2200
Protein	32	20	Males: 59 Females: 44
Vitamin C (mg)	5	18	Both genders: 45–75
Vitamin A (μg RAE)	300	10	Males: 900 Females: 700
Iron (mg)	3	4	Males: 11 Females: 15
Calcium (mg)	545	100	Both genders: 1300

1. Keeping in mind that meals should meet about one-third of nutrient needs, what are the shortcomings and excesses of these meals (i.e., given the nutritional information, compare these meals with one-third the RDA for protein, vitamin C, vitamin A, and iron and the Adequate Intake for calcium?

2. How would you change these meals to improve balance and to meet the nutrient needs above? (Hint: Use your software program or Appendix N.)

3. Reflect on your food choices as a teenager. Do you think your meal choices were balanced and varied? Why or why not? What could you have done to improve your nutritional habits at that time?

Food Allergies and Intolerances

Adverse reactions to foods—indicated by sneezing, coughing, nausea, vomiting, diarrhea, hives, and other rashes—are broadly classed as food allergies (also called *hypersensitivities*) or **food intolerances.** Allergies involve responses of the immune system designed to eliminate foreign proteins, called **allergens.**[14] The symptoms experienced by susceptible people, such as rapid increase in heart rate and shortness of breath, are the result of this battle. In contrast, the symptoms of food intolerances do not result from a true allergic reaction. Rather, food intolerances are caused by an individual's inability to digest certain food components or by the direct effect of a food component or contaminant on the body. Let's examine each process, first allergies and then intolerances, so you can learn how to reduce the risk of becoming a victim of the food you eat.

food intolerance An adverse reaction to food that does not involve an allergic reaction.

allergen A foreign protein, or antigen, that induces excess production of certain immune system antibodies; subsequent exposure to the same protein leads to allergic symptoms. Whereas all allergens are antigens, not all antigens are allergens.

Food Allergies: Symptoms and Mechanism

Allergic reactions to foods are common and occur more frequently in females than males. Food allergies occur most often during infancy and young adulthood. Experts estimate that up to about 2% of adults and up to about 8% of children are allergic to certain foods. Three types of reactions may occur after the ingestion of problem foods by susceptible people:

- *Classic*—itching, reddening skin, asthma, swelling, choking, and a runny nose
- *GI tract*—nausea, vomiting, diarrhea, intestinal gas, bloating, pain, constipation, and indigestion
- *General*—headache, skin reactions, tension and fatigue, tremors, and psychological problems

Any reaction that is milder than these distinct allergic ones is referred to as a **food sensitivity.**

food sensitivity A mild reaction to a substance in a food, which might be expressed as light itching or redness of the skin.

Allergic reactions vary not only in the body system affected but also in their duration, ranging from seconds to a few days. A generalized, all-systems reaction is called anaphylactic shock. This severe allergic response results in low blood pressure and respiratory and GI tract distress. It can be fatal. Overall, allergic reactions result in 30,000 emergency room visits and 150 to 200 deaths per year. A person who is extremely sensitive to a food may not be able to touch the food or even be in the same room where it is being cooked without responding to it. Although any food can trigger anaphylactic shock, the most common culprits are peanuts (actually a legume, not a nut), tree nuts (walnuts, pecans, etc.), shellfish, milk, eggs, soybeans, wheat, and fish. For a small number of people, avoiding foods such as peanuts or shellfish is a matter of life and death.

People with a history of serious allergic reactions should carry a self-administered form of epinephrine, such as EpiPen, to subside an episode of anaphylactic shock.

Almost all food allergies are caused by proteins in milk (also look for casein on the label), eggs (also look for albumin on the label), corn, tree nuts and peanuts, seafood, soy products, and wheat. Other foods frequently identified with adverse reactions include meat and meat products, fruits, and cheese.[14] These foods contain acidlike proteins, usually with a molecular weight between about 10,000 and 70,000, that stimulate the production of antibodies (specifically the **immunoglobulin** IgE) in susceptible people.

immunoglobulins Proteins found in the blood that are responsible for antibody-mediated immunity, and bind specifically to antigen. Also called *antibodies.* Immunoglobulins are produced by certain white blood cells in response to a foreign substance (antigen) in the bloodstream.

Testing for a Food Allergy

The diagnosis of a food allergy can often be a difficult task (Table 17-8). It requires the participation of a skilled physician. The first step in determining whether a food allergy is present is to record in detail a history of symptoms, time from ingestion to onset of symptoms, most recent reaction, quantity and nature of food needed to produce a reaction, and food suspected of causing a reaction. A family history of allergic diseases can also help, as allergic reactions tend to run in families. A physical examination may reveal evidence of an allergy, such as skin diseases and asthma. Various diagnostic tests can rule out other conditions.

Perhaps the best laboratory test for determining which compounds a person is allergic to is the RAST test. This test estimates the blood concentration of antibodies that bind certain foodborne antigens. Skin tests can also be used; a drop of antigen is placed under the skin where it has been scratched or punctured. If a person is allergic to the test antigen, a red eruption will develop.

Table 17-8 Assessment Strategies for Food Allergies

History	Includes description of symptoms, time between food ingestion and onset of symptoms, duration of symptoms, most recent allergic episode, quantity of food required to produce reaction, suspected foods, and allergic diseases in other family members
Physical examination	Look for signs of an allergic reaction (rash, itching, intestinal bloating, etc.).
Skin test	Place a sample of the suspected allergen under the skin and watch for an inflammatory reaction.
RAST test	Determine presence of IgE antibodies in blood that bind to antigens tested.
Elimination diet	Establish a diet lacking the suspected offending foods and stay on it for 1 to 2 weeks or until symptoms clear.
Food challenge	Add back small amounts of excluded foods, one at a time, as long as anaphylactic shock is not a possible consequence.

Eggs, wheat, milk, nuts, and seafood pose the greatest risk for food allergies in childhood.

The next step is to eliminate from the diet for 1 to 2 weeks all tested compounds that appear to cause allergic symptoms, plus all other foods suspected of causing an allergy based on the person's food history. The person generally starts out eating foods to which almost no one reacts, such as rice, vegetables, noncitrus fruits, and fresh meats and poultry. If symptoms are still present, the person can more severely restrict the diet or even use special formula diets that are hypoallergenic.

Once a diet is found that causes no symptoms, called an **elimination diet,** foods that are known not to trigger anaphylactic shock can be added back one at a time. Doses of ½ to 1 teaspoon (2.5 to 5 ml) are given at first. The amount is increased until the dose approximates usual intake. This should be done using a double-blind approach (see Chapter 1), especially when the reaction has a psychological component or when symptoms are vague or ill defined. Dried foods can be encapsulated and then given to the person. Any reintroduced food that causes significant symptoms to appear is identified as an allergen for the person.

elimination diet A restrictive diet that systematically tests foods that may cause an allergic response by first eliminating them for 1 to 2 weeks and then adding them back one at a time.

Treating Food Allergies

Once potential allergens are identified, the best treatment is to avoid them, especially for people with zero tolerance. Careful reading of food labels is essential for many allergic people and advisable for all. A major challenge for the clinician treating a person with a food allergy is to make sure that what remains in the diet can still provide essential nutrients. The small food intake of children permits less leeway in removing the offending foods that may contain numerous nutrients. A registered dietitian can help guide the diet-planning process to ensure that the remaining food choices still meet nutrient needs or to guide supplement use, if that is necessary.

If an allergy-prone woman is pregnant or breastfeeding, she should avoid offending foods—such as eggs, shellfish, and peanuts—because allergens can cross the placenta during pregnancy. Allergens are also secreted in her milk. She should work with her physician and registered dietitian to make sure she still consumes an adequate diet. In addition, when food allergies are common in the family, women are advised to breastfeed their infants exclusively for 6 months. Human milk contains factors that play a role in the maturation of the small intestine. Formula-fed infants, especially those on cow's milk–based formulas, have a greater risk for developing allergies. Breastfeeding, thus, should continue for as long as possible, preferably to 1 year.

The **prognosis** for food allergies that first appear before 3 years of age is good. About 80% of young children with food allergies outgrow them before 3 years.[14] Parents should be made aware of this and not assume the allergy will be long-lived. Food allergies diagnosed after 3 years of age, however, are often more long-lived, but not always. In these cases, about 33% of people outgrow their food allergies within 3 years. For others, the condition may be prolonged; some food allergies can last a lifetime, such as for peanuts, tree nuts, and shellfish. Periodic reintroduction of offending foods can be tried every 6 to 12 months or so to see whether the allergic reaction has decreased. If no symptoms appear, tolerance to the food has developed.

Critical | Thinking

Irene and Chris had a baby 11 months ago. At the last checkup, the doctor told them to start feeding the baby some new solid foods. After 5 days of eating a new food, the baby woke up with a runny nose and vomiting. The doctor told them to stop giving the baby that food. How can the doctor justify his recommendations?

prognosis A forecast of the course and end of a disease.

The American Academy of Allergy and Immunology has a 24-hour toll-free hot line (800-822-2762) to answer questions about food allergies and to help direct people to specialists who treat the problem. Free information on food allergies is available by writing to The Food Allergy Network, 4744 Holly Ave., Fairfax, VA 22030. The telephone number is 800-929-4040; the website is **www.foodallergy.org**.

Food Intolerances

Food intolerances are adverse reactions to food that do not involve allergic mechanisms. Generally, larger amounts of an offending food are required to produce the symptoms of an intolerance than to trigger allergic symptoms. Common causes of food intolerances include

- Constituents of certain foods (e.g., red wine, tomatoes, pineapples) that have a druglike activity, causing physiological effects such as changes in blood pressure
- Certain synthetic compounds added to foods, such as sulfites, food-coloring agents, and monosodium glutamate (MSG)
- Food contaminants, including antibiotics and other chemicals used in the production of livestock and crops, as well as insect parts not removed during processing
- Toxic contaminants resulting from the ingestion of improperly handled and prepared foods containing *Clostridium botulinum, Salmonella* bacteria, or other foodborne microbes (see Chapter 19)
- Deficiencies in digestive enzymes, such as lactase (see Chapter 5)

Almost everyone is sensitive to one or more of these causes of food intolerance, many of which produce GI tract symptoms.

Sulfites, which are added to foods and beverages as antioxidants, cause flushing, spasms of the airway, and a loss of blood pressure in susceptible people. Wine, dehydrated potatoes, dried fruits, gravy, soup mixes, and restaurant salad greens commonly contain sulfites. A reaction to MSG may include an increase in blood pressure, numbness, sweating, vomiting, headache, and facial pressure. MSG is commonly found in Chinese food and many processed foods (e.g., soups). A reaction to tartrazine, a food-coloring additive, includes spasm of the airway, itching, and reddening skin. Tyramine, a derivative of the amino acid tyrosine, is commonly found in "aged" foods, such as cheeses and red wines. This natural food constituent can cause high blood pressure in people taking monoamine-oxidase inhibitor medications, which may be prescribed for mental depression.

The basic treatment for food intolerances is to avoid specific offending components. However, total elimination often is not required because people generally are not as sensitive to compounds causing food intolerances as they are to allergens. For instance, a slight amount of sulfites in a glass of wine may be tolerable, whereas a large amount from a chef's salad may cause a reaction.

chapter 18

Nutrition During Adulthood

Chapter | Outline

Case | Scenario

Frances is a 78-year-old woman who suffers from macular degeneration, osteoporosis, and arthritis. Since her husband died 1 year ago, she has moved from their family house to a small one-bedroom apartment. Her eyesight is getting progressively worse, making it hard to go to the grocery store or even to cook for herself (for fear of burning herself). She is often lonely; her only son lives 1 hour away and works two jobs, but he visits her as often as he can. Frances has lost her appetite and, as a result, often skips meals throughout the week. She has resorted to eating mostly cold foods that are simple to prepare but, at the same time, she is seriously limiting diet variety. Frances is slowly losing weight as a result of her dietary changes and loss of appetite.

Her typical diet usually consists of a breakfast that may include one slice of wheat toast with margarine, honey, and cinnamon and one cup of hot tea. If she has lunch, she normally has ½ can of peaches, ½ of a turkey and cheese sandwich, and ½ glass of water. For dinner, she might have ½ of a tuna fish sandwich made with mayonnaise and one cup of iced tea. Occasionally, she includes one or two cookies at bedtime.

What services do you think are available that could help Frances improve her diet and possibly increase her appetite? What other convenience foods could be included in her diet to make it more healthful and more varied?

Refresh | Your Memory

As you begin your study of adult nutrition issues in Chapter 18, you may want to review:

- The effect of genetics on health in Chapter 1.
- Implications of the 1994 Dietary Supplement Health and Education Act in terms of what nutrients and related compounds can be sold today in the United States without FDA approval in Chapter 1.
- The various body systems in Chapter 3 and Appendix C.
- The sources of fiber in Chapter 5.
- Recommendations for alcohol intake in Chapter 8.
- The dietary sources of vitamin D, the various B-vitamins, and calcium in Chapters 9, 10, and 11, respectively.
- Definition of healthy body weight in Chapter 13.
- The benefits of regular physical activity in Chapter 14.

Boost | Your Study

Check out the ***Perspectives in Nutrition: Online Learning Center*** www.mhhe.com/wardlawpers6 *for quizzes, flash cards, activities, and web links designed to further help you learn about nutrient needs in adulthood.*

Chapter | Objectives

Chapter 18 is designed to allow you to:

1. Identify how the Dietary Guidelines for Americans relate to adult health.
2. List possible causes of aging.
3. Explain how aging affects nutritional status.
4. Discuss how nutrient needs change as individuals get older.
5. Make recommendations for dietary changes in the prevention and treatment of nutritional problems in older adults.
6. Describe community nutrition services for older persons.
7. List the potential benefits and risks associated with the use of various complementary and alternative medicine practices.

Eating is one of our great pleasures. Guided by common sense and moderation, eating well is also a means to good health. Most of us want a long, productive life, free of illness, yet many people from early middle age onward suffer cardiovascular disease, hypertension, type 2 diabetes, osteoporosis, and other chronic diseases. We can slow the development of, and in some cases even prevent, these diseases by pursuing a diet that works against them.[2] This action is most profitable if we begin early and continue throughout adulthood. We serve ourselves best—as individuals and as a nation—by striving to maintain vitality even in the later decades of life. This concept was first explored in Chapter 1 and is discussed again in this chapter, along with the special nutrition needs of older persons.

Keep in mind that present day-to-day health practices can significantly influence health during later life. Although genetics does play a role, as discussed in Chapter 1, many of the health problems that occur with age are not inevitable; they result from disease processes that influence physical health. Much can be learned from healthy older people whose attention to a healthy diet and daily physical activity—along with a little luck—keeps them active and vibrant well beyond typical retirement years.[4] Successful aging is the goal. Age quickly or slowly—it is partly your choice.

Nutrition and Adulthood—An Introduction

From a nutritional point of view, one's adult years are divided into four stages: 19 to 30, 31 to 50, 51 to 70, and beyond 70 years of age. The two intervals encompassing ages 19 to 50 can be seen as young adulthood; 51 to 70 then would be middle adulthood; and beyond 70 years of age would be older adulthood.

Nutritional needs change throughout these intervals. For example, calcium needs increase after age 50 for males and females. Vitamin B-12 needs also change after age 50, in that one should consume foods fortified with vitamin B-12 or take a multivitamin and mineral supplement containing vitamin B-12. Recall from Chapter 10 that this latter advice stems from the fact that about 10 to 30% of older people may malabsorb food-bound vitamin B-12 because of reduced acid production by the stomach. Vitamin D needs also change. Adults over age 70 need three times more vitamin D than they did when they were ages 19 to 50, and they need 50% more than they did during ages 51 to 70. In response to this increase in vitamin D needs for people over age 70, nutrition experts at Tufts University have suggested a modification of the Food Guide Pyramid to include a supplemental vitamin D source for this age group. Other such changes suggested by these experts for the Food Guide Pyramid will be mentioned in the section "Nutrient needs in middle and older adulthood."

Attention to healthy nutrition and overall lifestyle habits is important at all ages. In this chapter, we will look particularly at adult nutrition issues. Applying the principles of the Dietary Guidelines will be the focus of advice for adults ages 19 to 50 years. Then we will look at additional recommendations for adults 51 and older.

As we age, our nutrient needs change. For example, vitamin D needs are higher for older stages of adulthood than for younger stages or for childhood.

Besides having other long-lived family members, people who live to 100 years generally:

- Do not smoke, or drink heavily
- Gain little weight in adulthood
- Eat many fruits and vegetables
- Perform daily physical activity
- Challenge their minds
- Have a positive outlook
- Maintain close friendships
- Are (or were) married (especially true for men)

Compression of Morbidity

Although most of us wish for long life, we do not like the thought of failing health in old age. And rightly so! Rather than suffer the ravages of cardiovascular disease, obesity, diabetes, osteoporosis, and other chronic diseases from age 40 or 60 years until death, we should strive to be as free of disease as possible and enjoy vitality throughout even our last decade. **Life expectancy** is at a record high of about 77 years for the general population in North America today, although the span of healthy life is only about 65 years. Thus, an important focus here is not necessarily on living longer but on living healthier.

Striving to have the greatest number of healthy years and the fewest years of illness is often referred to as **compression of morbidity.**[2] In other words, a person tries to compress significant sickness related to aging into the last few years—or months—of life. An example of this concept is illustrated for cardiovascular disease in Figure 18-1. Of the three lines shown, the line on the top depicts rapid deterioration in health; symptoms of cardiovascular disease appear by about age 40, and death occurs at about age 60. In addition, between the ages of 40 and 60 years, symptoms of the disease, and therefore disability, are present.

A healthier lifestyle follows the middle line in Figure 18-1. Here, cardiovascular disease is postponed so that the first symptoms are not apparent until age 60; severe symptoms occur at age 80, with death following a few years later. The line on the bottom is ideal. Disease progresses so slowly that symptoms do not appear during a person's lifetime; therefore, the disease process never hampers activities.

Body cells age no matter what health practices we follow. However, to a considerable extent, you can choose how quickly you age throughout your adult years. In light of the many studies showing the ability even to reverse atherosclerosis, we can say that the rate at which you age is partly your choice.

Although there is little doubt of the benefits of a healthy lifestyle, scientists have also found a strong genetic component to longevity, as well as to certain diseases (review Chapter 1). Studies of families, and of twins in particular, provide some support for a genetic contribution to human longevity.[4]

life expectancy The average length of life for a given group of people (usually determined by the year one was born).

compression of morbidity The delay of the onset of disabilities caused by chronic disease.

Keep in mind that extending life without delaying onset of chronic disease prolongs suffering in many cases. In addition, the greater number of disabled years is a great cost to all North Americans. For these reasons, prolonging life without compressing the number of disabled years is called the "failure of success."

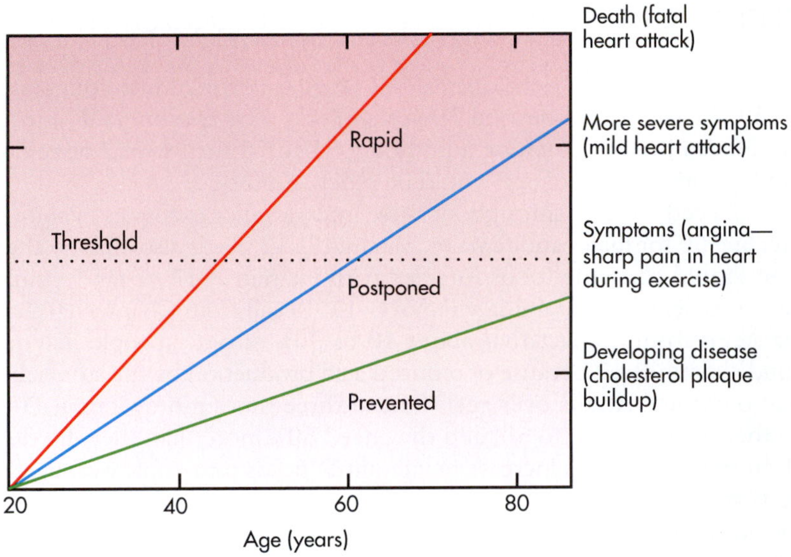

Figure 18-1 Compression of morbidity. The goal is to postpone illness until the final days of life. Cardiovascular disease is used as an example. The line on the top shows rapid deterioration in health status, in which symptoms of cardiovascular disease appear by about age 40 and death occurs at about age 60. In addition, between the ages of 40 and 60 years, symptoms of cardiovascular disease—and therefore disability—are present. A healthier lifestyle follows the middle line pattern. Here, cardiovascular disease is postponed, so that the first symptoms are not apparent until age 60; severe symptoms occur at age 80, with death following a few years later. The line on the bottom is the ideal: the disease progresses so slowly that symptoms do not appear during the lifetime; therefore, the disease process never hampers life's activities.

Still, many adults in North America today are doing what is within their control to achieve a healthy lifestyle, such as following a healthful diet and pursuing a regimen of regular physical activity. Coupled with avoidance of tobacco products, limitation of or other adaptation to stress, adequate sleep, adequate fluid intake, maintaining friendships and optimism; lifelong learning; keeping blood cholesterol, blood glucose, and blood pressure under control; and consultation with health-care professionals on a regular basis, these actions contribute to a healthful, long life. Overall, the key to maximizing health throughout life is to establish harmony between one's physical, mental, psychological, and social states (see Part I in Take Action at the end of this chapter).[14]

Diet for the Adult Years

One diet approach that optimizes long-term nutritional health emphasizes low-fat and nonfat dairy products, limited lean meats, some plant proteins such as nuts, a rich variety of fruits and vegetables, and generous amounts of whole-grain breads and cereals. The Food Guide Pyramid in Chapter 2 is one blueprint for this diet.

To further refine these food choices, recall also from Chapter 2 the latest Dietary Guidelines for Americans (Dietary Guidelines for short) issued by the USDA/DHHS. The U.S. Surgeon General, the American Heart Association, the American Dietetic Association, the American Medical Association, the National Cancer Institute, the National Academy of Sciences, and the World Health Organization have added recommendations to the framework of the Dietary Guidelines. Following is a summary of the advice provided by the Dietary Guidelines, with additional comments from various health-related organizations.

Many adults find that regular physical activity adds an important dimension to their lives.

Aim for Fitness

- *Aim for a healthy weight.* Use BMI to assess if you are at an acceptable weight for height. Measuring your waist circumference (just above your hip bones) is also a good way to determine your health risk (review Chapter 13 for more information on BMI and waist circumference). No matter what one's weight status is—healthy, overweight, or underweight—the number one goal is to first maintain that weight. Then, if weight gain or loss is needed, set a reasonable weight goal that can be met by following the Dietary Guidelines for diet and physical activity. Working closely with a registered dietitian can facilitate achieving that weight goal.

- *Be physically active each day.* Adults should strive to accumulate at least 30 minutes, and preferably 60 minutes, of moderate physical activity on most, if not all, days of the week because this works in many ways to keep the body healthy. Keep in mind that this does not have to come from continuous minutes of a workout; the minutes of physical activity can be tallied throughout the day. Daily activities such as walking up and down stairs at work, gardening, and washing a car can all be considered physical activity. Combining three types of physical activity—aerobic, strength training, and flexibility exercises—can assist in cardiovascular fitness, as well as building muscle strength and helping maintain bone mass. It is important to consult a physician prior to beginning an exercise program when one has a chronic health problem, such as cardiovascular disease, osteoporosis, hypertension, diabetes, or obesity. Men over age 40 and women over age 50—especially if one has cardiovascular disease, hypertension, or diabetes—should also consult a physician before starting an exercise regimen (review Chapter 14 for more details on exercise).

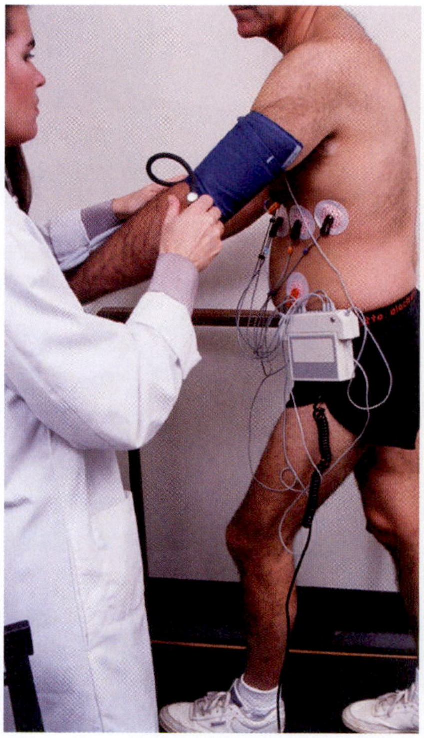

The Dietary Guidelines recommend that men over 40 and women over 50 years of age obtain physician approval before beginning a program of vigorous physical activity. This is especially important for people with evidence of cardiovascular disease, hypertension, or diabetes. The physician may suggest an exercise treadmill test be done to assess exercise tolerance.

Build a Healthy Base

- *Let the pyramid guide your food choices.* Make sure variety is part of the diet because no one food or food category can provide all the essential nutrients the body needs. Use the Food Guide Pyramid (or related pyramid) as a guide to choosing healthy foods to include in the diet, and then select from the range of the recommended number of servings per day from each group. Also, use the Food Guide Pyramid serving size guide as a reference for what constitutes a serving (review Chapter 2 for more details on Food Guide Pyramid serving sizes). Vegetarian diets can be consistent with the Dietary Guidelines, but special care is needed to meet nutrient needs (review Chapter 7 for details).

  Some younger adults especially benefit from a multivitamin and mineral supplement to meet specific nutrient needs. For example, women who could become pregnant are advised to consume foods fortified with folic acid or to take a supplement containing folic acid. This practice reduces the risk of some serious birth defects. People with little exposure to sunlight may need a supplemental source of vitamin D. Some people who seldom eat dairy products or other rich sources of calcium need a calcium supplement, and people who eat no animal foods should consider taking a supplement containing vitamin B-12. In addition, sometimes vitamins or minerals are prescribed for meeting nutrient needs for various medical purposes. For example, pregnant women or those with heavy menstrual periods may be advised to take an iron supplement. Still, supplements of some nutrients, such as vitamin A, can be harmful if taken in large amounts.

  Recall from Chapter 9 that medical and some nutrition experts go even further to recommend a balanced multivitamin and mineral supplement for all adults. Still, because foods contain many substances beyond vitamins and minerals that promote health, one should nevertheless use the Food Guide Pyramid (or related pyramid) as a starting point when planning a diet, rather than depending mostly on supplements to meet nutrient needs.
- *Choose a variety of grains daily, especially whole grains.* Include six or more servings of a combination of bread, cereals, rice, and pasta, many of which are whole-grain varieties. These food choices help meet the goal for younger adults of 25 g for women and 38 g for men of fiber per day. The current U.S. average for fiber intake is closer to 15 g/day. Whole grains are rich in vitamins, minerals, and fiber. Fiber adds bulk to the diet, which may lead to an earlier feeling of satiety; in addition, it decreases fecal transit time and improves regularity.
- *Choose a variety of fruits and vegetables daily.* Include five or more servings of vegetables and fruits daily. This recommendation enjoys the most overwhelming support of nutrition experts. Note that not many adults currently meet this goal, especially if potatoes are excluded from the vegetable category. Fruits and vegetables in combination with whole grains constitute a healthy diet because they are rich in the vitamins, minerals, and fiber that aid in preventing disease and maintaining health.

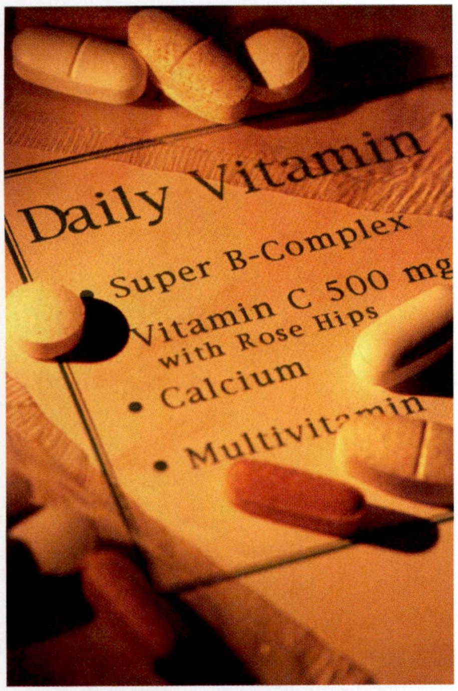

Nutrient supplements can complement, but should not substitute for a more comprehensive plan to maintain health as one ages.

- *Keep food safe to eat.* Wash hands thoroughly prior to and during cooking, especially when handling raw meats and eggs, to prevent cross-contamination. To prevent further cross-contamination, separate raw, cooked, and ready-to-eat foods while shopping, cooking, and storing food. Never thaw meats at room temperature; instead, thaw them in the refrigerator. To ensure you are cooking or reheating foods to a safe temperature, use a food thermometer. Keep cold foods cold and hot foods hot; do not leave cooked or refrigerated items at room temperature for more than 1 to 2 hours (see Chapter 19 for more details on food safety).

Choose Sensibly

- *Choose a diet that is low in saturated fat and cholesterol and moderate in total fat.* Be knowledgeable about the different kinds of fat—saturated, polyunsaturated, monounsaturated, trans fatty acids, and essential fatty acids. Saturated and trans fatty acids can raise blood cholesterol, whereas unsaturated fats generally have the opposite effect on blood cholesterol, and some of the long-chain fatty acids found in fatty fish offer additional protection against cardiovascular disease. Foods that are high in cholesterol (organ meats, egg yolks, and dairy fats) should be limited in the diet because they can also increase blood cholesterol if consumed in abundant amounts, especially in some people (review Chapter 6 for more details on cardiovascular disease and the different types of fats).
- *Choose beverages and foods to moderate your intake of sugars.* Keep added sugars in the diet to a minimum by limiting soft drinks (nondiet types), fruit drinks, and fruitades, as well as sweets, candies, and cookies. Limiting these products is important because they supply excess energy, which can promote weight gain, and they take the place of nutrient-dense foods, such as fruits and vegetables. An excess amount of added sugars in the diet also promotes dental caries. Some authorities recommend that simple sugars supply no more than 10% of total energy intake. North American adults currently consume about 16% of total energy intake as simple sugars (review Chapter 5 for more details on added sugars in the diet). Recall that a maximum of 25% of energy intake from added sugars has recently been set by the Food and Nutrition Board.
- *Choose and prepare foods with less salt.* Sodium and chloride found in salt are involved in regulating fluids in the body and blood pressure; limiting salt intake can reduce the risk of hypertension in some people. Certain individuals (e.g., overweight people and African Americans in general) are especially sensitive to salt causing a rise in blood pressure. Excess salt intake also increases the amount of calcium excreted in the urine. This can contribute to the development of osteoporosis if dietary calcium intake is inadequate.

  The recommended sodium intake is about 2400 mg/day (5000 mg/day of salt); the average American consumes 4000 to 7000 mg of sodium per day. To reduce sodium intake to the recommended 2400 mg/day would require a great change in food habits for many of us. It means not eating abundant amounts of processed (lunch) meats, salted snack foods, most canned and prepared soups, most types of cheese, and many tomato-based processed foods. Limiting the amount of salt used in cooking and avoiding adding it to food at the table also help reduce intake.
- *If you drink alcoholic beverages, do so in moderation.* A moderate alcohol intake by men over age 45 and women over age 55 is associated with a decreased risk of cardiovascular disease and ischemic stroke. Younger adults enjoy few, if any, benefits of moderate alcohol consumption. Moderation of alcohol intake consists of two or fewer drinks of 12 oz of beer, 5 oz of wine, or 1½ oz of distilled spirits (80 proof) per day. Women, and all adults over age 65, are advised to drink no more than one drink per day. Women are more sensitive than men to alcohol-related cirrhosis of the liver. Remember that alcohol adds excess energy to the diet and is low in or devoid of essential nutrients (review Chapter 8 for more details on alcohol).

Appendix D reviews diet planning guidelines issued by the Canadian government for Canadians. In addition, Chapter 1 discussed *Healthy People 2010*, a U.S. federal agenda aimed at disease prevention and health promotion.

Beyond these general recommendations, aim for the moderate use of salt-cured, smoked, and **nitrate**-cured foods because they are likely to increase the risk of certain

nitrate A nitrogen-containing compound used to cure meats. Its use contributes a pink color to meats and confers some resistance to bacterial growth.

forms of cancer (review Chapter 10). Obtain adequate fluoride to promote dental health and drink plenty of fluids. Finally, women of childbearing age need to eat iron-rich foods, primarily to avoid developing iron deficiency anemia.

This group of guidelines provides a good general focus for diet planning. The practices recommended can accommodate many cultural dietary patterns (review the Nutrition Perspective in Chapter 2). They are broad enough to allow adults to include all the foods one enjoys in an eating plan—one just may have to eat some foods less frequently than others or in smaller portions, depending on health needs and preferences. Moderation, rather than elimination, should be the overriding consideration.

Are Adults Following Current Dietary Recommendations?

In general, adults in North America, both young and old, are trying to follow many of the diet recommendations listed. Since the mid-1950s, they have consumed less saturated fat as more people substitute nonfat and low-fat milk for cream and whole milk. They eat more cheese, however, which is usually a concentrated form of saturated fat. Since 1963, they have eaten less butter, fewer eggs, less animal fat, and more vegetable fats and oils and fish. These changes generally follow the recommendations to reduce the intake of saturated fat and cholesterol and, instead, to emphasize unsaturated fat. Today, animal breeders are raising much leaner cattle and hogs than in 1950, which helps. Our demand for chicken, a relatively lean source of animal protein, has skyrocketed.

Other aspects of the average adult diet are more mixed. The latest nutrition survey of eating habits in the United States shows that the major contributors of energy to the adult diet are white bread, beef, milk, doughnuts, cakes and cookies, soft drinks, chicken, cheese, salad dressing, mayonnaise, margarine, and sugars/syrups/jams. If the trend in diets were truly toward decreasing sugar, saturated fat, and cholesterol intake and increasing fiber, many of these foods would not appear at the top of the list.

A list incorporating this book's suggestions for improvement would stress low-fat and nonfat milk and yogurt, whole-grain breads and cereals, limited amounts of lean meat, fish, peanuts and various tree nuts, beans, and vegetables and fruits.

The overriding consideration should be quality and length of life and the impact dietary changes might have on them. Adulthood is the key time to learn more about risk factors for chronic diseases and to do something about each one, where possible.[12]

Not all nutrition and health researchers agree with the blanket guidelines set by major health and science institutions, as noted in Chapter 2. Some scientists do not think that general recommendations for the public can be justified for sugar, salt, and cholesterol. Rather, they believe that these recommendations need to be individualized.

Concept | Check

Compression of morbidity, the delay of symptoms of and disabilities from chronic disease for as many years as possible, is a worthwhile goal. A basic plan to promote health and prevent disease includes eating a balanced, varied diet; performing regular physical activity; abstaining from smoking; limiting or abstaining from alcoholic beverages; and limiting or learning ways to deal with stress more effectively. More specific Dietary Guidelines for Americans direct people to eat a variety of foods; maintain healthy weight; choose a diet low in saturated fat, and cholesterol and moderate in total fat; choose a diet with plenty of vegetables, fruits, and grain products; use sugars only in moderation; use salt (sodium) only in moderation; and, if they drink alcohol, do so in moderation.

Critical | Thinking

The "fountain of youth" remains a mystery. Many people believe a source exists that can stop the aging process, allowing youth to remain. However, Neil, a history student, asserts that the fountain of youth is not a place or a particular thing but, rather, a combination of diet and lifestyle. How can he justify this claim?

Middle and Older Adulthood

How long do your family members generally live? Of those who died early in adulthood, can you pinpoint some causes? Do you plan to live longer than your parents did or will? How long will that be? Some basic statistics can help you predict this.

Life Span

life span The oldest age a person can potentially reach.

Life span refers to the maximal number of years humans live. As far as we know, this hasn't changed in recorded time. The longest human life documented to date is 122 years for a woman and 113 years for a man. One's genes play a key role in determining longevity, but environment is also important. Note also by comparison that the domestic dog has a life span of 20 years; a rat, 5 years.

Life Expectancy

Life expectancy is the number of years an average person born in a specific year, such as 2003, can expect to live. Currently, life expectancy in North America is about 73 years for men and about 80 years for women. Furthermore, if you survive to the age of 80, you can tack on another 7 to 10 years of life expectancy.

Worldwide, the highest average life expectancy is 82 years for women and 76 years for men in Japan, especially on the island of Okinawa. Researchers suggest that a diet based on rice, fish, vegetable protein sources, fruits, vegetables, tea, herbs for seasonings, and small amounts of meat, as well as a generally low energy intake (BMI remains ≈ 21), contributes to this record longevity.[2] Alcohol and salt intake is also minimal.

Life expectancy hasn't always been this long; for primitive humans, it was about 20 to 35 years. It increased to 40 years in Medieval England and increased to 49 years by the turn of the twentieth century. During the last 80 years, life expectancy for nearly all people has increased, mainly because of changes in the principal causes of death.

In the early 1900s, infectious diseases were the leading causes of death. Vaccines and antibiotics have tremendously lowered death from this cause. The decline in infant and childhood deaths, coupled with better diets and health care, has allowed more people to age first into maturity and then into older years. Now the principal causes of death in Western societies are related to cardiovascular diseases and cancer (Table 18-1).

Historically, the trend in the United States and other developed nations has been toward an ever older population. During Colonial times, half the U.S. population was over 16 years of age. By 1990, half were over 33. By 2050, half of the U.S. population could be over 43, and approximately 20% will be 65 years and older, twice as many as reach 65 today. This age—65 years—is arbitrarily listed as a dividing line for the beginning of later life because one can currently qualify for full Social Security benefits in the United States. The time at which old age occurs, however, varies for each person, according to health and independence.

Among the older population, the group constituting those aged 85+ years is the fastest growing segment. Between 1997 and 2050, the population aged 85+ years is expected to increase from 3.4 million to 19 million. This is the first time in history our society will need to accommodate such a large population of older people. The associated expense will be enormous if a large percentage need special care because of ill health.

Of all the people who have ever lived to age 65, more than half are now alive.

The Graying of North America

This "graying" of North America poses some problems. Today, although people older than age 65 account for 13% of the U.S. population, they account for more than 30% of all prescription medications used, 40% of acute care hospital stays, and 50% of the federal health budget. Hip fractures alone cost the nation about $12 billion per year. Of older persons, 85% have nutrition-related problems, such as cardiovascular disease, type 2 diabetes, hypertension, and osteoporosis.[1]

Postponing these chronic diseases for as long as possible will help control health-care costs. The more independent, healthy years people live, the better life can be for them and the less they burden the health-care system, which will increasingly have to scramble to accommodate a growing older population. Keep in mind that aging is not a disease. Furthermore, diseases that commonly accompany old age—osteoporosis and atherosclerosis, for example—are not an inevitable part of aging. Many can be prevented or managed. Some people do die of old age, not as a direct result of disease.

Table 18-1 Changes in Leading Causes of Death During the Twentieth Century in the United States

Chronic diseases, rather than infectious diseases, are now the major killers.

Rank	Cause of death	Percentage Mortality*
1900		
1	Pneumonia and influenza	12
2	Tuberculosis	11
3	Diarrhea and enteritis	8
4	Diseases of the heart	8
5	Cerebrovascular disease (stroke)	6
6	Nephritis	5
7	Accidents	4
8	Cancer	4
9	Diphtheria	2
10	Meningitis	2
Today		
1	Diseases of the heart	29
2	Cancer	22
3	Cerebrovascular disease (stroke)	7
4	Chronic obstructive pulmonary disease and allied conditions	5
5	Accidents and adverse effects	4
	Motor vehicle accidents	(2)
	All other accidents and adverse effects	(2)
6	Diabetes	3
7	Pneumonia and influenza	3
8	Alzheimer's disease	2
9	Kidney disease	2
10	Blood-borne infections	1

*Percentage of all deaths in that year.

A diet based on vegetables, fruits, pasta, and olive oil as a source of fat—and with a small amount of alcohol in the form of red wine—provides southern Italians with many healthy years of life. Their active lifestyle is an additional contributing factor.

What Actually Is Aging?

One view of aging describes it as a process of slow cell death, beginning soon after fertilization. When we are young, aging is not apparent because the major metabolic activities are geared toward growth and maturation. We produce plenty of active cells to meet physiological needs. During late adolescence and adulthood, the body's major task is to maintain cells. Inevitably, though, cells age and die. Eventually, as more cells die, the body can't adjust to meet all physiological demands. Body functioning begins to decline (Fig. 18-2). Still, organs usually retain enough **reserve capacity** that, for a long time, the body shows no outward disease. Although no symptoms appear, subclinical disease may develop, and, if the disease is allowed to progress unchecked, organ function and then body function eventually deteriorate noticeably.

reserve capacity The extent to which an organ can preserve essentially normal function despite decreasing cell number or cell activity.

The aging process is clearly illustrated by changes for many people in the function of the enzyme lactase. For some people, lactase activity in the small intestine slows during childhood. Generally, however, clear symptoms of the deficiency—gas and bloating after milk consumption—do not appear until adulthood. Although lactase output decreases in these cases, perhaps from birth, enough enzyme is present to digest the lactose consumed until adulthood.

Cells age probably because of automatic cellular changes and environmental influences. Even in the most supportive of environments, cell structure and function inevitably change. Eventually, cells lose their ability to regenerate the internal parts they need, and they die. This inevitable dying off of deteriorating cells is actually beneficial, as researchers have concluded it likely prevents diseases such as cancer.

Unfortunately, there are still consequences to this natural cell progression, because as more and more cells in an organ system die, organ function decreases. For example,

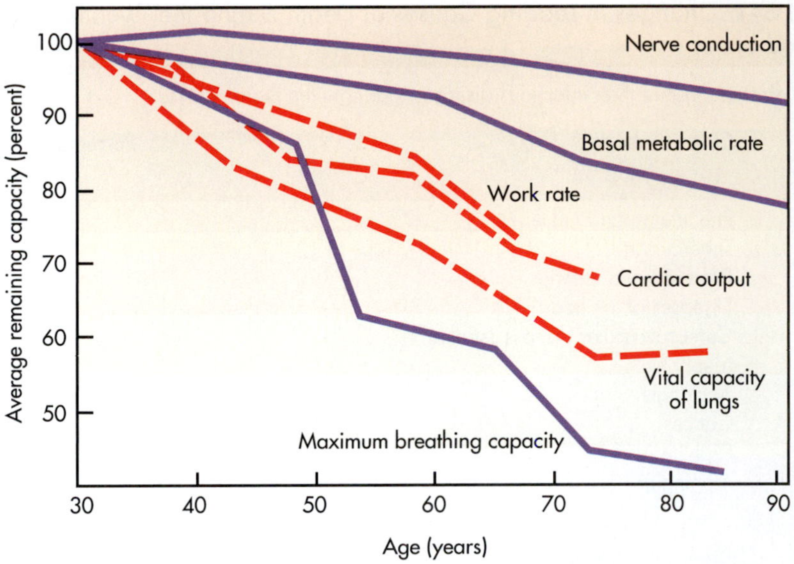

Figure 18-2 The declines in physiological function seen with aging. The decline in many body functions is seen primarily in sedentary people.

kidney nephrons The units of kidney cells that filter wastes from the bloodstream and deposit them into the urine.

kidney nephrons are continually lost as we age. In some people, this loss leads to eventual kidney failure, but most of us retain sufficient kidney function throughout life. Again, in aging, there is first a reduction in reserve capacity. Only after that is exhausted does actual organ function noticeably decrease.

Hypotheses About the Causes of Aging

The causes of this aging of the body are still a mystery. Most likely, aging results from an interaction of genetic background and the changes listed in Table 18-2. Even very healthy people have a shortened life expectancy if they are exposed to sufficient environmental stress, such as radiation and certain chemical agents like industrial solvents. Because cell aging and diseases such as cancer are aggravated by environmental factors, it makes good sense to avoid such risks as excessive sunlight exposure without sunscreen protection, and hazardous chemicals. You can obtain a free fact sheet on aging by going to the website for the National Institute on Aging at www.nih.gov/nia or by calling 800-222-2225.

Concept | Check

Although life span has not changed, life expectancy has increased dramatically over the past century. In many societies, this means an increasing proportion of the population is, and will be, over 65 years of age. Avoiding continually rising health-care costs and maximizing satisfaction with life require postponing and minimizing chronic illness. Aging begins early in life and probably results from both automatic cellular changes and environmental influences. Diet can play a role in slowing such processes.

Many older adults are healthy. The goal is to remain that way as long as possible.

Effects of Aging on Nutritional Health

Adults over age 50 vary more in health status among themselves than do persons in any other age group. This means that chronological age is not useful in predicting physical health status (physiological age). Among people aged 70 and over, some are totally independent, healthy people, whereas others are frail and require almost total care. To predict the nutritional problems of an older person, it is necessary to know the extent

Table 18-2 Current Hypotheses About the Causes of Aging[2, 4]

Errors occur in copying the genetic blueprint (DNA) Once sufficient errors in DNA copying accumulate, a cell can no longer synthesize the major proteins needed to function and it therefore dies.
Body proteins are oxidized and connective tissue stiffens Body proteins are oxidized by free radicals and related reactive oxygen species. This causes the proteins to cross-link with each other, reducing their function in the body. In addition, parallel protein strands found in connective tissue also cross-link to each other. The bonding decreases flexibility in key body components, altering organ function (e.g., joints and arteries stiffen).
Electron-seeking compounds damage cell parts Electron-seeking free radicals can break down cell membranes and proteins. One way to prevent some damage from these compounds is to consume adequate amounts of vitamins E and C, selenium, and carotenoids.
Hormone function changes The blood concentration of many hormones, such as DHEA and testosterone in men and estrogen in women, falls during the aging process. Replacement of these and other hormones is possible; research is ongoing (see the Nutrition Perspective).
Glycosylation of proteins Blood glucose, when chronically elevated, attaches to (glycates) various blood and body proteins. This decreases protein function and can encourage immune system attack on such altered proteins. Such problems are typical of people with poorly controlled diabetes.
The immune system loses some efficiency The immune system is most efficient during childhood and young adulthood, but with advancing age it is less able to recognize and counteract foreign substances, such as viruses, that enter the body. Nutrient deficiencies, particularly of protein, vitamin E, vitamin B-6, and zinc, also hamper immune function.
Autoimmunity develops Autoimmune reactions occur when white blood cells and other immune bodies fail to distinguish between substances normally present in the body and invading foreign proteins. White blood cells and other immune bodies then begin to attack body tissues in addition to foreign proteins. Many diseases, including some forms of arthritis, involve this autoimmune response.
Death is programmed into the cell Each human cell can divide only about 50 times. Once this number of divisions occurs, the cell automatically succumbs. This degradation occurs by design, probably as a way for the body to regulate cell number. One mechanism for this limitation is that DNA shortens in length with every cell division. Recall from Chapter 10 that cancer cells defeat this shortening process using the enzyme telomerase, in turn allowing for continued growth.
Excess energy intake speeds body breakdown Underfed animals, such as spiders, mice, and rats, live longer. Scientists have yet to pinpoint the exact mechanisms that allow for life extension in energy-restricted animals, but they speculate that modified glucose use, decreased free radical damage, changes in gene function, slower cell turnover, and a variety of other factors contribute to longer life. Researchers are currently studying rhesus monkeys that are on a 30% lower energy intake than typical rhesus monkeys. Although the energy-restricted monkeys have lower blood pressure, blood cholesterol and triglycerides, and higher HDL-cholesterol, the monkeys have the same appetite as typical monkeys, making them somewhat desperate for food. Their bone density is also reduced; and their reproductive ability is in question. Thus, the wisdom of lifelong energy restriction for humans is still an open question.

of physiological change caused by aging and whether the person shows early warning signs for long-term poor nutrition.[1] As you examine how aging affects body systems and how these changes contribute to nutritional health, note the suggested ways to lessen health risks (Table 18-3).

Decreased Appetite and Food Intake

Decreases in body weight are common in adults age 70 and older, who may not eat enough to meet energy needs. This phenomenon is a problem for older people in particular because it increases the risk of nutrition-related illness.

Many causes of inadequate food intake in older people are possible. Researchers suggest that biological origins, such as changes in neuroendocrine factors that influence feeding, account for some of this decline (review Chapter 13 for a list of these factors). When older men are underfed in experiments, they do not later increase food intake to compensate for reduced food consumption when given the opportunity. Changes in taste and smell may also be important, as are the effects of current medication use.[11] In

Critical | Thinking

Alexis has read several books supporting the idea that reducing one's typical energy intake by 30% can significantly extend one's life. Since she wants to do what is best for her two preschool children, she is thinking about adjusting her family's dietary habits to match this calorie restriction. What should you discuss with Alexis before she proceeds?

Table 18-3 A Summary of Typical Physiological Changes Experienced by Older Adults and Recommended Diet Lifestyle Responses

Change	Recommended Response
Decrease in appetite and food intake	Monitor weight and strive to eat enough to maintain healthy weight; consider liquid meal replacement products such as Boost and Ensure Plus® (liquid and bar form).
Decline in sense of taste and smell	Vary the diet and experiment with herbs and spices.
Loss of teeth	Work with a dentist to maximize chewing ability; modify food consistency as necessary; provide energy dense snacks.
Decreased sense of thirst	Consume about 8 cups of fluid each day, and watch for evidence of dehydration (e.g., minimal urine output or dark color).
Constipation	Consume enough fiber daily, choosing primarily fruits, vegetables, and whole grains; meet fluid needs (review Chapter 5).
Decline in lactase production	Limit milk serving size at each use; consume yogurt or cheese; use reduced-lactose or lactose-free products; seek other calcium sources (review Chapter 11 for ideas).
Iron-deficiency anemia	Include some lean meat and iron-fortified foods in the diet; ask physician to monitor blood iron status.
Decline in liver function	Consume alcohol in moderation, if at all; avoid excess vitamin A consumption.
Decline in insulin function	Maintain healthy body weight and perform regular physical activity.
Decline in kidney function	Modify protein and other nutrients in diet when advised by physician.
Decline in immune function	Meet nutrient needs, especially protein, vitamin E, vitamin B-6, and zinc, and perform regular physical activity.
Decline in lung function	Don't smoke tobacco products; perform regular physical activity.
Decline in vision	Consume fruits, vegetables, and whole grains regularly to gain the potential benefits of carotenoids, as well as vitamins C and E and the mineral zinc (wear sunglasses as well in sunny conditions and don't smoke).
Decrease in lean tissue	Meet nutrient needs (such as protein) and perform regular physical activity, including some resistance (strength-training) activity (review Chapter 14).
Increase in fat stores leading to obesity	Watch overeating; perform regular physical activity (review Chapter 13).
Decrease in cardiovascular function	Keep blood lipids and blood pressure within desirable range, using diet changes and medications when needed (review Chapters 6 and 11); stay physically active; remain in a healthy body weight range (review Chapter 13).
Decrease in bone mass	Meet nutrient needs, especially protein, calcium, and vitamin D (regular sun exposure helps meet needs for vitamin D), perform regular physical activity, and women should consider use of approved osteoporosis medications at menopause (review Chapter 11).
Decrease in mental function	Strive for lifelong learning; perform regular physical activity; obtain adequate sleep; follow a healthy dietary pattern.

The physiological changes associated with aging are the end products of natural processes and lifestyle practices. By adopting practices that minimize a decline in body function in the adult years, we invest in our future health. (The first Take Action activity outlines one comprehensive approach to healthful aging.)

Pharmaceutical companies have begun to market liquid meal-replacement formulas to older adults. Previously, these products were primarily used in hospitals and nursing homes. Many of these products have an unusual taste because of the vitamins and types of proteins that have been added. Older adults can decide if the convenience, cost, and taste make this a wise diet choice.

addition, social aspects play a role in reduced food intake. Many older people live alone, a circumstance that is associated with less food consumption.

To maintain health, older adults need to address the issue of declining weight. Significant weight loss in older people, sometimes termed the "dwindles," increases risk of death. It may also indicate ongoing illness and reduced tolerance to medication or simple withdrawal from life itself.[9] Even in apparently healthy older individuals, successful weight maintenance may require an increased conscious control over food intake, compared to younger individuals. Adding more spices to food may also stimulate food intake. Consuming energy-dense snacks, such as cheese, nuts, yogurt, oatmeal cookies, and bananas, between meals is also a strategy.[7] When assessing weight in older people, compare present weight with the previous year's weight.

Decline in Dental Health

About 30% or more older people in North America have lost all their teeth. Attention to dental hygiene and dental care throughout life greatly lessens this risk. Periodontal (gum) disease commonly causes tooth loss. Replacement dentures enable some to chew normally, but many older adults—especially men—have denture problems. Solving individual dietary needs requires identifying foods that need to be modified in consistency. When people have problems chewing, nutrient-dense snacks can help. Sometimes just allowing extra time for chewing and swallowing encourages more eating.[1]

Age is no reason not to continue whatever physical activity is possible. This contributes to many aspects of health, including that of the GI tract.

Reduced Thirst Sensation

Older adults often partially lose their sense of thirst and in turn don't drink enough fluids. They are then more likely to become dehydrated, a condition that leads to confusion and sometimes hospitalization. In addition, 25% of fluid comes from food. If older adults are not eating enough food, they increase the risk of becoming dehydrated. It is important for older people to consume enough fluids, and, if necessary, they should be monitored to ensure they do so.[12] About 8 cups of fluid daily is a good goal. This amount must be adjusted if diuretics are used or in certain other medical conditions, such as the presence of an **ostomy.** Some important signs of dehydration, other than confusion, include dry lips, sunken eyes, increased body temperature, decreased blood pressure, constipation, decreased urine output, and nausea.

ostomy A surgically created short circuit in intestinal flow where the end point usually opens from the abdominal cavity rather than the anus; for example, a colostomy.

Fall in Gastrointestinal Tract Function

The main intestinal problem for older people is constipation (review Chapter 3 for a review of this problem). To keep the intestinal tract performing efficiently, older people should meet fiber needs. The goal for adults over 50 years is 21 g for women and 30 g for men on a daily basis, unless a physician recommends otherwise. The regular consumption of nuts, fruits, vegetables, beans, and whole grains provides enough fiber. Fiber medications are generally unnecessary but may be used if overall energy intake does not allow for enough fiber intake. Older persons should also drink more fluid to move along masses that could form from high fiber intake. Physical activity likewise helps promote peristalsis. Because some medications can induce constipation, a physician should be consulted if constipation might be related to a medication. If mineral oil is taken as a laxative, it should always be used with caution—and not at mealtimes—because it binds fat-soluble vitamins and limits their absorption.

Lactase production frequently decreases with age. Chapter 5 listed several options for people with lactose malabsorption and intolerance.

The stomach slows its acid production as people age, as well as the synthesis of intrinsic factor. These changes can contribute to poor absorption of vitamin B-12 and eventually to pernicious anemia. Because of this, adults aged 51 years and older need to meet vitamin B-12 needs with foods or supplements fortified with synthetic vitamin B-12.

Reduced stomach acid production may also hamper iron absorption. Other conditions that affect the body's iron status in particular occur with the regular use of aspirin, which frequently causes blood loss in the stomach, and the use of antacids, which may bind iron. Ulcers and hemorrhoids can also cause blood loss. Careful attention to iron status is necessary in these cases.

Incontinence, the inability to control the muscle responsible for retaining urine, affects up to 20% of older adults living at home and about 75% of those in nursing homes. The embarrassment of having to wear adult diapers causes many to avoid fluids (resulting in dehydration and constipation) and to become socially isolated.

Changes in Liver, Gallbladder, and Pancreatic Function

With age, the liver functions less efficiently. When there is a history of significant alcohol consumption, fat buildup in the liver accounts for some decline. Alcohol abuse is a problem among a small but significant group of older individuals who may continue this pattern from earlier in life, or develop heavy drinking patterns and alcoholism later. Later development of this problem sometimes arises from the loneliness and social isolation of retirement or loss of a spouse. Alcohol-related sickness is high in older people, so the health consequences of this excess are considerable.[17] Also, older adults are more likely

The limit for alcohol intake for older adults is one drink per day.

to take medications affected by alcohol intake. If cirrhosis then ultimately develops, the liver functions even less efficiently (review Chapter 8). When its function significantly deteriorates, the liver cannot efficiently detoxify many substances. The possibility for vitamin A toxicity in turn increases.

The gallbladder also functions less efficiently as we age. Gallstones may dam up the bile in the gallbladder, causing it to pool and back up into the liver. Gallstones can also interfere with fat digestion by allowing less bile into the small intestine. Obesity is a prime risk factor for gallbladder disease. A low-fat diet or surgery to remove the organ may be necessary for treatment.

Although the digestive function of the pancreas may decline with age, the pancreas has a large reserve capacity. A sign of a failing pancreas is high blood glucose, which occurs under several conditions. Glucose may circulate in the bloodstream, instead of being taken up by cells, because the pancreas secretes less insulin or because cells resist insulin actions—especially muscle cells, and as well adipose cells in obese people with upper-body fat storage. Another cause can be insufficient chromium intake. Where appropriate, improved nutrient intake, regular physical activity, and weight loss (when needed) can improve insulin action and blood glucose regulation.

Decline in Kidney Function

Over time, the kidneys filter wastes more slowly as they lose nephrons (the functional filtration unit). The deterioration significantly decreases the kidneys' ability to excrete the products of protein breakdown, such as urea, and in turn typically requires a reduction in protein intake from habitual amounts to about the RDA or slightly below (0.6 g/kg body weight).

Reduced Immune Function

Chapter 9 noted that older adults should be cautious regarding use of megadose vitamin E supplements, especially during a respiratory infection. Such use can prolong these infections.

As previously mentioned, with age the immune system often operates less efficiently. Consuming adequate protein, the gamut of vitamins (especially enough vitamin E and vitamin B-6), and zinc helps maximize the health of the immune system. Recurrent sicknesses and poor wound healing are warning signs of a deficient diet, especially in protein and zinc. Eating too little food in general or too few animal proteins is usually the reason. Older people often eliminate meat from their diet because it's too hard to chew. A balanced vitamin and mineral supplement can help bridge gaps in vitamin and mineral intake. On the other hand, overnutrition appears to be equally harmful to the immune system. For example, obesity and excessive fat, iron, vitamin E, and zinc intake can suppress immune function.

Reduced Lung Function

Lung efficiency declines somewhat with age and is especially pronounced in older people who have smoked and continue to smoke tobacco products. Breathing becomes shallower, faster, and more difficult as the amount of active lung tissue decreases. Smoking often leads to emphysema and lung cancer. The decrease in lung efficiency contributes to a general downward spiral in body function; breathing difficulties limit physical activity and endurance and frequently discourage eating.

Besides not smoking, being physically active helps prevent lung problems. People need not lose their capacity to breathe deeply, as long as sufficient aerobic activity is part of their regular routine. Otherwise, merely walking can demand the exertion of a marathon pace.[16]

Reduced Hearing and Vision

Hearing and vision both decline in aging. Hearing impairment occurs mainly in members of industrial societies with urban traffic, aircraft noise, and loud music. Older people may avoid social contacts because they can't hear.

Declining eyesight, frequently caused by retinal degeneration, can affect a person's ability to get to a grocery store, locate the foods desired, read labels for nutritional content, and prepare the foods at home. Macular degeneration, one form of failing eyesight, has been associated with cigarette smoking—yet another reason to avoid the habit.

On a positive note, the regular consumption of foods rich in carotenoids—in particular, dark green, leafy vegetables, such as kale, collard greens, spinach, swiss chard, mustard greens, and romaine lettuce—may decrease the risk of developing this retinal degeneration. These vegetables are rich in lutein and zeaxanthin, two carotenoids found in the portion of the eye subject to damage from age-related changes. Adequate zinc intake is also important. The risk of developing cataracts of the eye is decreased by meeting vitamin C needs. Note that eventually such vision losses may make people afraid to socialize, be active, or take care of important routines of daily life, such as shopping.

A recent study discussed in Chapter 12 showed that megadose zinc supplements (80 mg/day of zinc oxide with 2 mg of copper oxide) reduced progression of macular degeneration in people who showed evidence of the disease. The zinc supplements worked even better when provided in combination with 400 IU of vitamin E, 500 mg of vitamin C, and 15 mg of beta-carotene. Adults who have evidence of macular degeneration and are considering implementing this protocol should talk to their physicians first because this can also lead to health problems.

Decrease in Lean Tissue

Some muscle cells shrink and others are lost as muscles age; some muscles lose their elasticity as they accumulate fat and collagen protein. Lifestyle greatly determines the rate of muscle mass deterioration. As you might predict, an active lifestyle tends to maintain muscle mass, whereas an inactive one encourages its loss.

The loss of muscle mass leads to a decrease in basal metabolism, muscle strength, and energy needs. Furthermore, less muscle mass leads to lower physical activity, which makes the prognosis for maintaining muscle mass even worse. Clearly, it is best to avoid this vicious cycle. Just when all seems lost, though, note that the benefits of exercise are quite striking, especially after the age of 50. Ideally, an active lifestyle should include some resistance activity (weight training) throughout life.

Physical activity increases muscle strength and mobility, improves balance, eases daily tasks that require some strength, improves sleep and balance, slows bone loss, and increases joint movement, thus reducing injuries. It also has a positive impact on one's mental outlook.[16] However, when older adults stop their strength-training program, gains in muscle strength are quickly lost.

After obtaining a physician's approval to get started, older people can seek out programs to begin strength and aerobic training at community recreation centers or the local YMCA or YWCA. Cardiac rehabilitation centers are another possibility. Most of these organizations have qualified trainers who can help set up a program. Dumbbells are inexpensive and thus ideal for engaging in strength training at home.

Older people benefit from both aerobic and strength-training exercises. Strength training especially helps reverse some of the decline in daily function associated with the muscle loss typically seen in older adulthood. Much of what we associate with old age is due to a lack of lifetime physical activity.

Increases in Fat Stores

As lean tissue decreases with age, the body often takes on more fat. Much of this results from overeating and minimal physical activity, although even athletic men gain some degree of midsection fat after the age of 50.

If obesity results, it can raise blood pressure and blood glucose and make walking and performing daily tasks more difficult. Although a small fat gain in adulthood may not compromise health, large gains are often problematic.

Reduced Cardiovascular Health

The heart often pumps blood less efficiently in older people, usually because of insufficient physical activity. Poor heart conditioning allows fatty and connective tissues to infiltrate the heart's muscular wall. However, this decline in **cardiac output** is not inevitable with aging and does not occur among older people who remain physically active. In fact, it is thought that the inactive lifestyles of nearly 60% of North American adults may contribute as much to the risk for cardiovascular disease as smoking a pack of cigarettes per day.

cardiac output The amount of blood pumped by the heart.

Heart attack and stroke, 2 of the 3 major causes of death in adults, are caused primarily by atherosclerosis and hypertension. As we age, atherosclerotic plaque accumulates in the arteries, reducing their elasticity, constricting blood flow, and consequently elevating blood pressure.

You already know the main way to limit the buildup of atherosclerotic plaque: Keep LDL-cholesterol and the total cholesterol/HDL-cholesterol ratio in the desirable range (review Chapter 6). New evidence shows that a diet very low in fat can cause some plaques to decrease in size. Other studies use diet and medications to lower blood cholesterol, which in turn reduces the amount of plaque in the arteries supplying the heart. This suggests that a heart-healthy diet is more important during middle to late adulthood than researchers previously thought. Consuming sufficient vitamin B-6, folate, and vitamin B-12 are also important to avoid elevated blood homocysteine, a probable risk factor for cardiovascular disease.

Much controversy surrounds the treatment for elevated LDL-cholesterol in people over the age of 70. If these people adhere to extremely restrictive diets limited in fat and energy to the point that they can't keep up their weight, or if their diets lack variety, they may become undernourished. This may be a worse predicament for them than having high LDL-cholesterol. Therefore, treating elevated LDL-cholesterol in an older person who has other illnesses, such as chronic lung disease and **dementia** (which are likely to shorten life as well as hamper its quality) is probably inappropriate. However, if a healthy 70-year-old who is likely to live another 10 to 15 years has both elevated LDL-cholesterol and evidence of cardiovascular disease, an eating and exercise plan is probably in order to reduce the chance of heart attack.

dementia General persistent loss or decrease in mental function.

Hypertension is heavily implicated in both stroke and heart attack in older adults. Blood pressure can be lowered in many people by restricting salt intake. A limit of 2400 mg of sodium per day helps many people with hypertension, but that is a difficult diet to plan and follow for older people who rely on convenience foods. Alternatively, a mild sodium restriction (not to exceed 4000 mg of sodium daily) may be effective for salt-sensitive people but is not so helpful by itself for those who have hypertension that is not salt sensitive; it does, however, aid the action of certain diuretics used to treat hypertension. (The Nutrition Perspective in Chapter 11 reviews the effects of other nutrients such as calcium and potassium and lifestyle interventions on blood pressure.)

We can do much to prevent heart attack and stroke just by eating a balanced diet, walking briskly and otherwise performing regular physical activity, controlling blood pressure, not smoking, and maintaining healthy weight. Regular physical activity and a diet rich in fruits and vegetables are also associated with fewer strokes as adults age, as is a moderate use of alcohol.

Decline in Bone Health

Chapter 11 discussed the decline in bone mass associated with aging. Recall that bone loss in women occurs primarily after menopause. Bone loss in men is slow and steady from middle age throughout later life. Use of bisphosphonate medications is one treatment to lessen bone loss in women, but other medication regimens are also effective (review Chapter 11). For adults in general over age 50, increasing calcium intake to 1200 mg/day (200 mg/day greater than the young adult Adequate Intake) is recommended. Meeting protein needs is also important, but easy to accomplish.

Some sun exposure greatly contributes to vitamin D needs in older people.

Maintaining adequate vitamin D nutriture is also critical, especially if the person experiences little sun exposure (10–15 μg/day [5–10 μg/day greater than the young adult Adequate Intake]). This corresponds to 400 to 600 IU/day. Note that the recommendation of 15 μg/day is for adults 70 years and older.

Many older people may suffer from hidden osteomalacia, a condition primarily caused by not enough sun exposure and therefore diminished vitamin D synthesis in the skin. When they can't get regular sun exposure—during the winter or when they are homebound—older people need a dietary (e.g., milk) or supplemental source of vitamin D.[18]

To these two measures, add not smoking and drinking alcohol moderately or not at all. In addition, underweight women are at especially high risk for developing osteoporosis. Performing weight-bearing activity, such as walking, can help preserve bone mass.[6]

Very severe osteoporosis limits the ability of older people to move about, shop, prepare food, and live normally. They eat less and as a result consume fewer nutrients. Older people should also work with their physician to develop a plan for limiting falls. Falls may be caused by the side effects of medication, lack of regular physical activity, gait and balance disorders, impaired vision, and environmental hazards. Protective hip padding can reduce the risk of fracture in individuals who tend to fall.

Other Factors That Influence Nutrient Needs in Aging

Medications and old age often go together. Medications can improve health and quality of life, but some of them also profoundly affect nutrient needs at all ages, including the later years (Table 18-4). Most older adults take prescription drugs; one-quarter of the elderly population regularly take multiple prescription drugs, called polypharmacy. Many drugs affect appetite or the absorption of nutrients. Often, people must take medications for long periods. They should make sure to work with their physician and pharmacist to coordinate all medications taken.[10] Pharmacists can advise when to take drugs—with or between meals—for maximum effectiveness.

Drug-related nutritional problems include (1) increased need for potassium when certain types of diuretics increase excretion from the body and (2) changes in appetite caused by antidepressant agents or certain antibiotics. Blood loss from the long-term use of aspirin or aspirin-like medications depletes iron reserves and can lead to anemia.

Grapefruit juice can increase or decrease the potency of some prescription medications, such as certain blood pressure medications, tranquillizers, antihistamines, blood cholesterol-lowering medications (statins), and others, such as a class of drugs used to treat HIV/AIDS. For this reason, a physician, registered dietitian, or pharmacist should be consulted before grapefruit juice is ingested by those on prescription medications.

Table 18-4 Potential Drug-Nutrient Interactions for Some Commonly Used Drugs

Drugs	Uses	Nutrients Affected	Potential Mechanism
Antacids (Maalox)	Reduce stomach acidity	Calcium, vitamin B-12, and iron	Decreased absorption due to altered gastrointestinal pH
Anticoagulants (Coumadin)	Prevent blood clots	Vitamin K	Interferes with utilization
Aspirin	Anti-inflammatory; reduces pain	Iron	Anemia from blood loss
Cathartics (laxatives)	Induce bowel movement	Calcium and potassium	Poor absorption
Cholestyramine	Reduces blood cholesterol	Vitamins A, D, E, and K	Poor absorption
Cimetidine (Tagamet)	Treats ulcers	Vitamin B-12	Poor absorption
Colchicine	Treats gout	Vitamin B-12, carotenoids, and magnesium	Decreased absorption due to damaged intestinal mucosa
Corticosteroids (prednisone)	Anti-inflammatory	Zinc Calcium	Poor absorption Poor utilization
Furosemide (Lasix)	Decreases blood pressure; potassium-wasting diuretic	Potassium and sodium	Increased loss
Hydrochlorothiazide	Decreases blood pressure; diuretic	Potassium and magnesium	Increased loss; decreased absorption
MAO inhibitors (Parnate)	Antidepressant	Tyramine (in aged foods)	High blood pressure caused by limited tyramine metabolism
Tricyclic antidepressants (Elavil)	Antidepressant	—	Weight gain from appetite stimulation

People who must take one or more medications for more than just a few weeks should closely watch their diets, eat nutrient-dense foods, and possibly take nutrient supplements to counteract the effects of certain medications. A physician should supervise this last practice, because some supplements can interfere with the function of certain medications. For example, vitamin K can reduce the activity of oral anticoagulants (review Chapter 9).

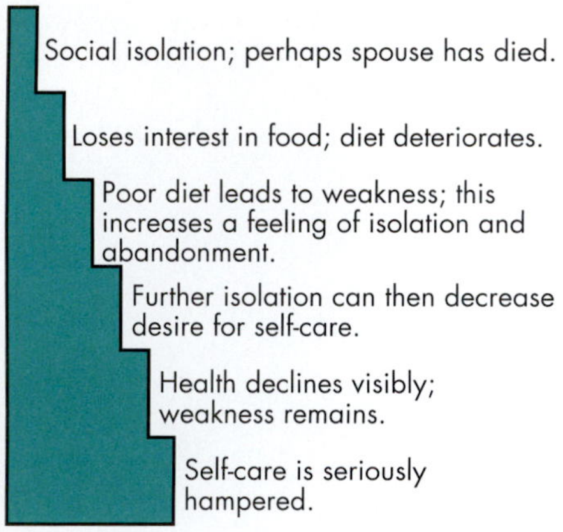
Social isolation; perhaps spouse has died.
Loses interest in food; diet deteriorates.
Poor diet leads to weakness; this increases a feeling of isolation and abandonment.
Further isolation can then decrease desire for self-care.
Health declines visibly; weakness remains.
Self-care is seriously hampered.

Figure 18-3 The decline of health often seen in older adults. This decline, illustrated by a set of stairs, needs to be prevented whenever possible.

Depression in Older Adults

Depression occurs in about 20% of nursing home residents. In contrast, it occurs in only 5 to 10% of older adults who reside outside of nursing homes. About 16% of persons who are 65 years old or older experience depression. This depression—combined with isolation and loneliness as family and friends die, move away, or become less mobile—frequently contributes to apathetic eating and weight loss. Depression can lead to a continual decline in which poor appetite produces weakness, which leads to even poorer appetite (Fig. 18-3). In older adults, the resulting poor nutritional state can produce further mental confusion and increased isolation and loneliness.

If depression is left untreated, it is estimated that 15% of the cases may be fatal (suicide). Depression also may be a sign of an underlying illness, which is another reason that early detection is important in older adults. Depression is often treatable, but medication alone will not help those who are experiencing major life changes, such as the death of a spouse. Adequate social support and possibly psychological intervention also are important.

Former President Jimmy Carter recommends that older adults stay connected to life to maximize health. This can include volunteering one's services and helping one's friends in their later years.

Alcoholism in Older Adults

Alcoholism is a problem in the older population.[17] Approximately two-thirds of these alcohol abusers turn to alcohol much earlier in life and simply continue the habit. About one-third begin the habit later in life, due to a variety of factors—more free time, social events centered around drinking, loneliness, or depression. Some of the symptoms of alcoholism in older persons include trembling hands, sleep problems, memory loss, and unsteady gait; these can be easily overlooked simply because they are common symptoms of old age in general.

Older adults become intoxicated on a smaller amount of alcohol than when younger because they metabolize alcohol more slowly and have lower amounts of body water in which to distribute the alcohol, compared to younger adults. Even small amounts of alcohol can react negatively with various medications that many older persons take. In addition to having adverse effects on the liver, drinking large amounts of alcohol increases the risk of hemorrhagic stroke and may worsen hypertension in older adults. Since drinking large amounts of alcohol produces adverse effects, both men and women over the age of 65 should limit alcohol consumption to no more than one drink per day. Recall from Chapter 8 that one drink per day is defined as 5 oz of wine, 12 oz of beer, or 1.5 oz shot of 80-proof liquor.

Aging is no reason to withdraw from life. Learning and practicing new skills throughout life contribute to overall health.

Alzheimer's Disease

The disease known as Alzheimer's often takes a terrible toll on the mental and eventual physical health of older people. It is now the eighth leading cause of death in North America. In general terms, Alzheimer's disease is best described as a progressive brain disorder marked by an inability to remember, reason, or understand what is going on.[5] Age is the primary risk factor. Scientists propose causes, including altered cell development and altered brain proteins, as well as hypertension, high blood cholesterol, high blood homocysteine, head trauma, certain apolipoprotein status (apolipoprotein E4), little education, and little mental stimulation. Four medications are approved for minimizing Alzheimer's symptoms (e.g., donepezil [Aricept]), but they show only limited benefits. Dietary concerns revolve around making sure the person eats enough food to maintain healthy weight and meet overall nutrient needs, as well as observation of the person's meals to make sure meal habits do not pose a health risk (e.g., holding food in one's mouth or forgetting how to swallow).[8] Warning signs of Alzheimer's disease are listed in the margin. Preventive measures for Alzheimer's disease focus on lifelong learning, regular physical activity, and meeting nutrient needs, especially vitamin B-6, folate, and vitamin B-12 (since high blood homocysteine is a risk factor). Experimental therapies currently in clinical trials include megadoses of vitamin E (from 200 mg/day [about 400 IU per day] to about 5 times that amount) and use of ibuprofen and related pain medications. To find out more about Alzheimer's disease, you can go to the website for the Alzheimer's Association at www.alz.org, or call 800-272-3900. You can also call the National Institute on Aging's Alzheimer's Disease Education and Referral Center at 800-428-4380.

Ten Warning Signs of Alzheimer's Disease

1. Recent memory loss that affects job performance
2. Difficulty performing familiar tasks
3. Problems with language
4. Disorientation to time and place
5. Faulty or decreased judgment
6. Problems with abstract thinking
7. Tendency to misplace things
8. Changes in mood or behavior
9. Changes in personality
10. Loss of initiative

Concept | Check

Nutritional problems common to aging adults relate to both the process of chronic diseases and the normal decrease in organ function that occurs with time. All these organ systems and functions can decrease as we age: appetite; sense of taste, smell, thirst, hearing, and sight; digestion and absorption; liver, gallbladder, pancreatic, kidney, lung, and heart function; and the immune system. In addition, bone mass and muscle mass gradually decrease, the latter largely because of a deficient diet and inactivity. Appropriate dietary changes and regular physical activity can often help reduce the impact of these results of aging.

Tufts University's Modified Food Pyramid for 70+ Adults

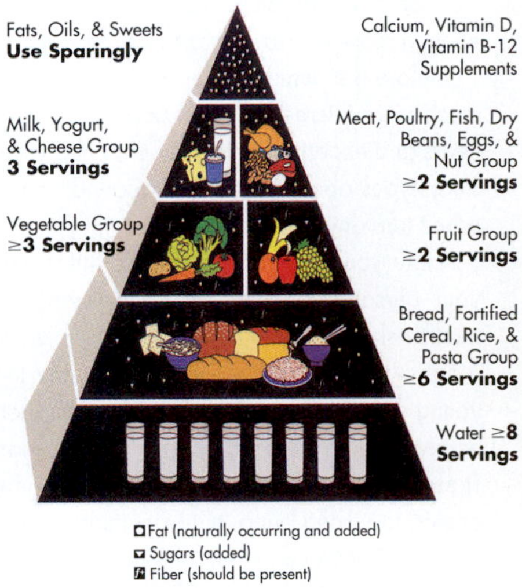

These symbols show fat, added sugars, and fiber in foods.

Nutrient Needs in Middle and Older Adulthood

The latest RDAs and related standards for nutrients and energy include separate categories for both men and women who are 51 to 70 years of age and those who are more than 70 years of age.

Macronutrient needs do not change from young adults' needs, but needs for some micronutrients do. In addition, because RDAs and related standards apply only to healthy people, many older people—for example, those who have ulcers or are heavy aspirin users—are not covered by these standards. Indeed, it is particularly tricky to develop nutrient standards that are valid for most older people because so many are ill and/or regularly take medications.

A well-planned diet that follows the Food Guide Pyramid can meet all nutrient needs for healthy older people consuming about 1600 to 1800 kcal, except for probably vitamin D, vitamin B-12, folate, and calcium. It would take at least three servings from the milk, yogurt, and cheese group to meet the need for calcium—a recommendation that most older people would find difficult to meet. Calcium-fortified foods can help when necessary (review Chapter 11 for details). Meeting the folate and vitamin B-12 standard also is aided by use of fortified foods, such as ready-to-eat breakfast cereals.

The use of a balanced multivitamin and mineral supplement is especially helpful for meeting vitamin D needs if the person has little sun exposure, but it should be low in or free of iron. Recall from Chapter 12 that men should not take a supplement containing iron unless they have evidence of iron deficiency anemia, as they consume enough iron and high iron intakes may have a pro-oxidant effect. This recommendation for avoiding supplemental iron now applies to women, as they experience minimal iron loss in the postmenopausal state.

Nutrition experts at Tufts University recently suggested a modification of the Food Guide Pyramid to include vitamin D, vitamin B-12, and calcium supplements for adults over 70 years of age. Other changes suggested were at least three servings from the milk, yogurt, and cheese group and at least eight servings of water (or other fluids). The use of a supplement to help meet vitamin D, vitamin B-12, and calcium needs is especially helpful for older people who require such a low energy intake that they are not able to consume enough food to supply these nutrients. Many nutrition experts go even further to recommend a balanced multivitamin and mineral supplement for all older adults.

Planning a Diet for People in Their Later Years

Recommended dietary practices would be to increase the diet's nutrient density and to make sure fiber intake is adequate. In addition, some protein should come from lean

Expert Opinion

Nutrition and Older Adults—Why Should You Care?

Nancy S. Wellman, Ph.D., R.D., F.A.D.A.

We all know people older than ourselves, yet whom we consider *old* depends a lot on our own age. Youngsters consider their *30-something* parents old. Almost everyone used to think anyone with gray hair or wrinkles or anyone who retired was old. Today, hair color, skin tone, or age 65 no longer defines *old*. In fact, many baby boomers and Xers have a goal to retire in their 40s or 50s—as soon as they can stockpile enough money for a comfortable lifestyle.

Before discounting older adults, just think how much more interesting you'll become as you add years and experiences to your own life. Although stereotypes about getting old abound, many just aren't true anymore.

How you age can be greatly influenced by your personal commitment to nutrition, fitness, health-risk reduction, and attitude. As a typical North American, your goal is probably to stay young as long as possible. To make it happen, it's essential to eat healthfully, stay active, manage stress, and think positively. Certainly, genetics counts, too. Long-living family members are a definite plus; however, even longevity isn't enough. We want a good quality of life in our later years.

We are the most death-denying nation on earth, and most of us will refuse to grow old gracefully. Inevitably, some of us *will* face similar health and nutrition problems if we live long enough. Let's look at some practical aspects of aging to determine why we should care about nutrition in older adults.

If it's too great a stretch to picture yourself in your 80s, in your 90s, or as a centenarian, think of some of the *oldest old* (those over 85) whom you know. They may be your great-grandparents, aunts, or neighbors, or they may be famous people. Many are living full, active, productive lives; others may not be as independent as they once were.

The following are some *likely* but not universal challenges as age and risk of malnutrition, frailty, and health problems increase. A lessened ability to taste, smell, chew, and digest food may interfere with getting all the nutrients we need. We might be too zealous in eliminating fat, salt, or sugar from our diets. If so, our food won't taste very good, and we may not bother to eat enough. The older we get, the harder it is to keep weight up. In fact, losing a lot of weight without wanting to is a warning sign that shouldn't be ignored. You'll find few among the *oldest old* at the opposite end of the weight spectrum. The overweight and obese have already paid the price with a shorter life span.

Staying active pays off in greater and longer independence and a good quality of life. If arthritis, osteoporosis, or other illnesses keep us from walking, we might not be able to grocery shop or cook or even feed ourselves—all crucial to good nutritional status.

Our sense of thirst may diminish or we may intentionally drink less to avoid accidents or trips to the bathroom because of fear of falling or painful walking. Dehydration may make us more confused, cause us to be constipated, or place us at greater risk of heat illness and death.

Some medicines we take might drastically decrease our appetites. The more medicines taken, the greater risk of nutrition-related side effects. Medications can radically change the way food tastes and cause constipation, diarrhea, dry mouth, nausea, drowsiness, and weakness.

If we haven't taken care of our teeth or dentures or have mouth problems, we may be excluding harder-to-chew, higher-protein foods, such as meats, or higher-fiber foods, such as fruits and vegetables. Our diets might be quite monotonous if we are forced to skimp on food to pay for heat, medicine, or rent. Monotonous diets shortchange us on energy intake and nutrients. Having less—or choosing to spend less—than $3 to $4 a day on food makes it hard to eat healthfully, yet that is the daily situation for one in six older North Americans.

If our memory isn't as sharp, we may forget if, what, and when we've eaten. Severe memory problems, whether labeled Alzheimer's, dementia, or senility may cause us to forget how to chew and swallow—even if a caregiver is helping us eat. If we live alone, we may not bother to fix a meal or to eat. The common tea and toast diet is not nutritious. Being with people daily improves our food intake and our morale. If we have recently lost a loved one, especially our spouse, it may be too painful to sit opposite the

meats to help meet protein needs, as well as vitamin B-6 and zinc needs, two nutrients of additional concern.[7]

Fluid needs are about 8 cups (about 2 L) per day. A high-fiber diet especially requires attention to fluid needs.

Great attention to food safety issues is also important for older adults. Chapter 19 provides much advice on this topic, such as avoiding raw and undercooked animal products.

Singles of all ages face logistical problems with food: Purchasing, preparing, storing, and using food with minimal waste is a challenging proposition. Economy packages of meats and vegetables are normally too large to be useful for a single person. Many singles live in small dwellings, some without kitchens and freezers. Creating a diet to accommodate a limited budget, restricted facilities, and a small appetite requires special attention. Following are some practical suggestions for diet planning for singles:

One's older years are often accompanied by admiration from those who are younger.

empty chair at the table. Among the one in four older adults who drinks too much alcohol, health problems usually worsen, and the energy supplied by alcohol is rarely replaced with nutritious foods.

Many of the challenges of nutrition and aging can be avoided. From a monetary perspective alone, the payoff is high. Reducing malnutrition in later years decreases costly health-care expenditures. Good nutritional status keeps us healthier and, should we become ill, we recover more quickly and have shorter hospital stays and fewer complications. Among the increasing numbers of frail, homebound older adults, 9 out of 10 are at considerable nutrition risk. Unless that risk is reduced, some will be admitted to hospitals again and again, others will be prematurely sent to nursing facilities, and others will die needlessly due to starvation or neglect.

Countries are rightfully measured by the care given their youngest and oldest. We, as individuals—citizens, or relatives—must assume some responsibility for those born decades before us. It is easy and very personally rewarding to make a difference in the life of an older person. The following are some suggestions:

- Use service learning opportunities in courses to volunteer with older adults. College students have repeatedly had inspirational experiences interacting with older persons in adult day centers and in assisted living and nursing facilities, as well as in the delivery of meals to the homebound.
- Take your oldest relative or neighbor out to eat and ask his or her opinions on current or historical events, the most significant experiences in his or her life, his or her feelings about himself or herself, and his or her joys and needs today.
- Drop off a bag of easy to prepare groceries or ready to eat food to an older person. Help relatives set up a weekly system of fresh, frozen, or canned convenience meals labeled "morning," "afternoon," or "evening" plus the day of the week.
- Make a friendly phone call, even long distance, near mealtime. This may be just the needed reminder to eat for someone you care about.
- Arrange for transportation to meals at senior centers or for home delivery of meals.
- Provide a small, simple (inexpensive) microwave oven plus some supervised practice time as a gift. Give food gifts and generally discourage gifts of clothing and other nonedibles by other people.
- Encourage or arrange a visit to a dentist who specializes in the care of the older adults.
- If an older relative, friend, or neighbor is hospitalized, be that person's advocate. See that the person's weight is measured regularly, question what and how much is eaten, find out which staff member is responsible for monitoring nutritional status, be company at mealtimes, and, if needed, feed the person at a comfortable pace and with dignity. See that the person will receive meals when he or she goes home or that someone is available to help fix meals.

Think positively! It's never too early or too late to eat smarter, get more active, and be healthier, adding not only years to your life but life to your later years.

Dr. Wellman, a past president of the American Dietetic Association, is a professor of dietetics and nutrition at Florida International University. There she directs the National Policy and Resource Center on Nutrition and Aging. She chairs the Nutrition Screening Initiative, a nationwide campaign to reduce nutrition risk in older adults.

- If one owns a freezer, cook large amounts, divide into portions, and freeze.
- Buy only what can be used before it spoils; small containers may be expensive, but letting food spoil is also costly.
- Ask the grocer to break open a family-sized package of wrapped meat or fresh vegetables and separate it into smaller units.
- Buy only several pieces of fruit—perhaps a ripe one, a medium-ripe one, and an unripe one—so that the fruit can be eaten over a period of several days.
- Keep a box of dry milk handy to add nutrients to recipes for baked foods and other foods for which this addition is acceptable.

Grocery shopping can become more difficult in one's older years. Often assistance from others is very helpful.

Nutritional deficiencies and protein-energy undernutrition have been identified among some aging populations, particularly those in nursing homes or long-term care facilities and those who are hospitalized. These nutritional problems increase the risk for many diseases, including bed sores (pressure ulcers), and compromise recovery from illness and surgery. Friends, relatives, and health-care personnel should look for poor nutrient intake in all older people, including those who live in nursing home settings. Family members have a unique opportunity to make sure nutrient needs are met by looking for weight maintenance based on regular, healthful meal patterns. If problems arise in instituting a healthful diet, registered dietitians can offer professional and personalized advice.

By the time we reach adulthood, our eating habits reflect regional tastes, social class, ethnic group, and life experiences. There is no generic food list for older people. Dr. Nancy Wellman discusses this in detail in the Expert Opinion.

Overall, good nutrition benefits older adults in many ways. Meeting nutrient needs delays the onset of some diseases; improves the management of some existing diseases; hastens recovery from many illnesses; can increase mental, physical, and social well-being; and often decreases the need for and length of hospitalization.[20] A variety of strategies can promote healthful eating in later life (Table 18-5). These should focus on presenting nutritious, tasty foods in a pleasant environment.

Obtaining enough food may be difficult for some older persons, especially if they are unable to drive and relatives do not live close enough to help with cooking or shopping. Older persons tend to see asking for help as a symbolic loss of independence. Pride, or fear of being victimized by those they hire, may stand in the way of much

To learn about meal programs for senior citizens in your area, call the Administration on Aging's Elder Care Locator, 800-677-1116. For general information on programs for older persons, visit the following websites:
National Institute on Aging
www.nih.gov/nia/
American Geriatrics Society
www.americangeriatrics.org/
and Administration on Aging
www.aoa.dhhs.gov/

Table 18-5 Guidelines for Healthful Eating in Later Years

- Eat regularly; small, frequent meals may be best. Use nutrient-dense foods as a basis for each menu.
- Find out which convenience foods and labor-saving devices can be of help.
- Try new foods, new seasonings, and new ways of preparing foods. Don't use just convenience foods and canned goods.
- Keep some easy-to-prepare foods on hand for times when you feel tired.
- Have a treat occasionally, perhaps an expensive cut of meat or a favorite fresh fruit.
- Eat in a well-lit or sunny area; serve meals attractively; use foods with different flavors, colors, shapes, textures, and smells.
- Arrange things so that food preparation and clean-up are easier.
- Eat with friends, relatives, or at a senior center when possible.
- Share cooking responsibilities with a neighbor.
- Use community resources for help in shopping and other daily care needs.
- Stay physically active.
- If possible, take a walk before eating to stimulate appetite.
- When necessary, chop, grind, or blend hard-to-chew foods. Softer, protein-rich foods can be substituted for meat when poor dental function limits normal food intake. Prepare soups, stews, cooked whole-grain cereals, and casseroles.
- If your feeding movements are limited, cut the food ahead of time, use utensils with deep sides or handles, and obtain more specialized utensils if needed.

needed help. In these cases, friends can be a big help. Special transportation arrangements may also be available through a local transit company or taxi service.

Many eligible older people are missing meals and are poorly nourished simply because they don't know of available programs to help them. Irregular meal patterns and weight loss, often caused by difficulties in preparing food, are warning signs that undernutrition may be developing. An effort should be made to identify poorly nourished people and inform them of community services.

Community Nutrition Services for Older Adults

Health-care advice and services for older people can come from clinics, private practitioners, hospitals, and health maintenance organizations. Home health-care agencies, adult day-care programs, adult overnight-care programs, and **hospice units** (for the terminally ill) can supply daily care.

hospice units A facility offering care that emphasizes comfort and dignity in death.

The Nutrition Screening Initiative's nutrition checklist for health-care workers, family members, and older persons can be used as a tool to increase health and nutrition awareness and to plan related education of older persons (Fig. 18-4). The Nutrition Screening Initiative incorporates the acronym "DETERMINE" (see margin). Overall, professionals in the just-mentioned organizations should try to identify older people whose health needs require extra attention.

DETERMINE:

- **D**isease
- **E**ating poorly
- **T**ooth loss or mouth pain
- **E**conomic hardship
- **R**educed social contact and interaction
- **M**ultiple medications
- **I**nvoluntary weight loss or gain
- **N**eed for assistance with self-care
- **E**lder at an advanced age

Nutrition programs for those age 60 and over offer congregate meal programs, which provide lunch at a central location, and home-delivered meals (often known as Meals on Wheels).[13] About 2.6 million Americans are served each year. Currently about half of the meals are offered through the home-delivered method.

The federal government sets specific standards for home-delivered meals and for those served in congregate feeding centers. The meals are designed to provide one-third of daily nutrient needs. The social aspect often improves appetite and general outlook.

Still, congregate-meal programs generally provide at most one meal a day and usually just 5 days a week. The problem with home-delivered meals is that the one or two meals delivered may not be eaten, and, if not eaten on delivery and left at room temperature, they may become unsafe to eat later. Thus, these programs can help older adults but probably don't meet all their nutritional needs.

In addition to congregate and home-delivered meals, federal commodity distribution is available in some areas of the United States to low-income older people. Food stamps can benefit older people who have low incomes (see Chapter 20 for details on these programs). Food cooperatives and a variety of clubs and social organizations provide additional aid.

Two other websites for organizations that focus on issues surrounding age are:
www.ilcusa.org
www.aging-institute.org

Case Scenario | Follow-up

Frances could contact a local government office that offers congregate meal programs at a central location. She could inquire about location and available transportation to the site. This would give her social contact with other older persons, which is probably an important element that is missing in her life. This could help alleviate her loneliness. She could also request Meals on Wheels (if available) to provide one hot meal a day if transportation isn't available. One hot meal a day that is prepared for her may be just what she needs to help stimulate her appetite. She could also have groceries delivered to her home if her budget could withstand the extra cost. Other convenience foods that could be included in her diet include milk, assorted nuts, peanut butter, breakfast cereals, canned chicken or deli meats, yogurt, sliced cheese, cottage cheese, calcium-fortified orange juice, canned or frozen fruits and vegetables, and some fresh fruits and vegetables that do not require preparation, such as prewashed lettuce and bananas. A further possibility is a liquid nutritional supplement, such as a can of Ensure®Plus, or a nutrition bar, such as an Ensure®Plus bar.

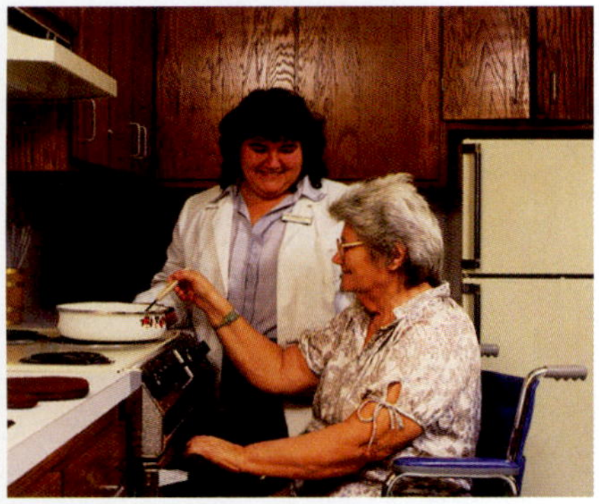

There are many resources in the community to help older adults maintain their nutritional health and overall independence.

Concept | Check

Specific nutrient requirements for older adults are only now being extensively studied. Diet plans should be modified for decreased physical abilities, the presence of drug-nutrient interactions, possible depression, and economic constraints. Particular attention should be paid to the opportunity for sun exposure and intake of the vitamins D, B-6, folate, and B-12, as well as the minerals calcium and zinc and dietary fiber. A nutrient-dense diet helps meet these needs. Carefully planned multivitamin and mineral supplement use can also help, especially after age 70. In the United States, many nutrition services—such as congregate and home-delivered meals—are available to help the aged population obtain a healthful diet.

A Nutrition Test for Older Adults

Here's a nutrition check for anyone over age 65. Circle the number of points for each statement that applies. Then compute the total and check it against the nutritional score.

1. The person has a chronic illness or current condition that has changed the kind or amount of food eaten. (2 points)
2. The person eats fewer than two full meals per day. (3 points)
3. The person eats few fruits, vegetables, or milk products. (2 points)
4. The person drinks 3 or more servings of beer, liquor, or wine almost every day. (2 points)
5. The person has tooth or mouth problems that make eating difficult. (2 points)
6. The person does not have enough money for food. (4 points)
7. The person eats alone most of the time. (1 point)
8. The person takes three or more different prescription or over-the-counter drugs each day. (1 point)
9. The person has unintentionally lost or gained 10 pounds within the last 6 months. (2 points)
10. The person cannot always shop, cook, or feed himself or herself. (2 points)

Nutritional score

0–2: Good. Recheck in 6 months.

3–5: Marginal. A local agency on aging has information about nutrition programs for the elderly. The National Association of Area Agencies on Aging can assist in finding help; call 800-677-1116. Recheck in 6 months.

6 or more: High risk. A doctor should review this test and suggest how to improve nutritional health.

Figure 18-4 A nutrition checklist for older adults.

Reprinted with permission by the Nutrition Screening Initiative, a project of the American Academy of Family Physicians, the American Dietetic Association, and the National Council on the Aging, Inc., and funded in part by a grant from Ross Products Division, Abbott Laboratories.

Summary

1. Compression of morbidity means delaying symptoms of and disabilities from chronic disease for as many years of life as possible. Good nutritional habits, especially following the Food Guide Pyramid and the Dietary Guidelines for Americans, play a role in this process.
2. Although scientists disagree as to the best diet recommendations for the general public, most agree on some general principles, including those of the Food Guide Pyramid and the Dietary Guidelines for Americans. Such authorities recommend that individuals eat a variety of foods; balance the food eaten with physical activity to maintain or improve weight; choose a diet with plenty of whole-grain products, vegetables, and fruits; choose a diet low in saturated fat and cholesterol; choose a diet moderate in sugars; choose a diet moderate in sodium (salt); and moderate or avoid alcoholic beverage intake. Regular physical activity is also important. In addition, recommendations to reduce cancer risk emphasize moderation in the use of cured and smoked meats.
3. Although maximum life span hasn't changed, life expectancy has increased dramatically over the past century. For many societies, this means that an increasing proportion of the population is over 65 years of age. As health-care costs rise, the goal of delaying disease becomes even more important for all of us.
4. Aging begins before birth. Cell aging probably results from automatic cellular changes and environmental influences, such as DNA damage. Add to this list damage caused by electron-seeking free radical compounds, high blood glucose, hormonal changes, alterations in the immune system, and excess energy intake as possible causes.
5. Nutritional problems of older adults are related to the presence of chronic diseases and to the normal decreases in organ function that occur with time. These include loss of teeth, lessened sensitivity to taste and smell, changes in gastrointestinal tract function, and deterioration in cardiovascular and bone health. Although disease affects nutritional state, the reverse is also true. Undernutrition adversely affects immune function, allowing for infection.
6. Diet plans for older adults should be based on a nutrient-dense approach and individualized for existing health problems, decreased physical abilities, presence of drug-nutrient interactions, possible depression, and economic constraints. Specific nutrients, such as protein, vitamin D, vitamin E, vitamin B-6, folate, vitamin B-12, zinc, and calcium, along with fiber, often deserve special attention in diet planning. A multivitamin and mineral supplement can be used to help meet needs, especially after age 70.
7. Health-care workers and family members should use available options for the procurement of food for the elderly, especially for those who are nutritionally compromised. Most communities have congregate or home-delivered meal systems, food stamps, and other provisions for those who qualify.

Study Questions

1. List four of the Dietary Guidelines for Americans and give an example of why each one may be difficult for the elderly to implement. What are some solutions to these barriers?
2. What is the difference between life span and life expectancy? As life expectancy increases, what consequence affects the entire population?
3. Name two hormones that decline with aging and the functions of each.
4. Describe two hypotheses proposed to explain the causes of aging, and note evidence for each in your daily life experiences.
5. List four organ systems that can decline in function in later years, along with a diet/lifestyle response to help cope with the decline.
6. Defend the recommendation for regular physical activity during late adulthood, including some resistance activity (weight training).
7. How might the nutritional needs of older people differ from those of younger people? How are their needs similar? Be specific.
8. What three resources in a community are widely available to aid older adults in maintaining nutritional health?
9. Describe some early warning signs of Alzheimer's disease and note two nutritional implications as this disease advances.
10. List four warning signs of undernutrition in older people that are part of the acronym DETERMINE. Briefly justify the inclusion of each.

Annotated References

1. ADA Reports: Position of the American Dietetic Association: Nutrition, aging, and the continuum of care. *Journal of the American Dietetic Association* 100:580, 2000.

   As the baby boomer population grows older, nutrition professionals need to focus more on developing successful interventions that will influence the proper nourishment of older adults, such as initiating nutrition screening of older adults and working with other health professionals to expand services to older persons. Multiple factors that influence nutritional status in older adults include medical problems, medications, housing, the availability of transportation, dental health, current diet modifications, and income.

2. Aging: Living to 100: What's the secret? *Harvard Health Letter* 27(3):1, 2002.

   Compression of morbidity is the goal in aging. Physical activity and a healthy diet are two keys, as shown by the lifestyle of the people on the island of Okinawa who typically are long-lived.

3. Barrett S, Herbert V: Alternative nutrition therapies. In Shils ME and others (eds.): *Modern nutrition in health and disease.* 9th ed. Baltimore MD: Williams & Wilkins, 1999.

   When someone feels better after using a product or procedure, it is natural to credit whatever was done. This can be misleading, however, because most ailments resolve spontaneously, and even those that persist can have symptoms that wax and wane. In addition, taking action for a problem often temporarily relieves symptoms via the placebo effect. People unaware of these facts often give undeserved credit to "alternative" methods of medical treatment.

4. Christensen D: Making sense of centenarians. *Science News* 159:156, 2001.

   The most important factors with regard to longevity can be found in a person's lifestyle: what foods they eat, how much they exercise, what social networks they have, and how well they handle stress. No more than 30% of the variation in life span between those individuals who live 100 years or more and those that do not is due to genetic differences.

5. Cummings JL, Cole G: Alzheimer disease. *Journal of the American Medical Association* 287:2335, 2002.

Alzheimer disease, the most common cause of dementia in older adults, is a progressive neurodegenerative disorder that gradually takes from the person cognitive function and eventually causes death. Several risk factors for Alzheimer disease have been identified in addition to age and female sex: the presence of the apolipoprotein E-4 on lipoproteins, head injury, elevated blood homocysteine, family history of Alzheimer disease or dementia, fewer years of formal education, lower income, and lower occupational status. Conversely, higher levels of education, moderate amounts of daily wine consumption, and regular fish intake have been associated with a lower risk.

6. Feskanich D and others: Walking and leisure-time activity and risk of hip fractures in postmenopausal women. *Journal of the American Medical Association* 288:2300, 2002.

   Moderate amounts of physical activity reduce the risk of hip fractures in older women. One effect of physical activity is maintenance of bone mass in the hip region.

7. Foote J and others: Older adults need guidance to meet nutritional recommendations. *Journal of the American College of Nutrition* 19:628, 2000.

   A recent cross-sectional study examined dietary habits of 1740 healthy adults between the ages of 51 and 85. In general, this group was found to consume higher than recommended amounts of protein and fat, and lower than recommended amounts of vitamin D, vitamin E, folate, and calcium. Nutrition professionals recommend that this group include more servings of nutrient-dense foods, especially fruits, vegetables, and low-fat dairy products.

8. How to protect your memory as you age. *Tufts University Health & Nutrition Letter,* p. 1, October 2001.

   Research has found that memory loss can be stopped, or at least slowed, by a variety of lifestyle changes. Recommended changes include following a diet high in the B-vitamins, as well as vitamins C, E, and beta-carotene, engaging in both physical and mental exercises, managing stress, and controlling other chronic conditions, such as hypertension and cardiovascular disease.

9. Huffmann G: Evaluating and treating unintentional weight loss in the elderly. *American Family Physician* 65:640, 2002.

   Unintentional weight loss in older adults can lead to a higher risk of infection, depression, and death. The causes of unintentional weight loss are numerous and varied, including medications, depression, alcoholism, swallowing disorders, dementia, and lack of money to spend on food. Treatment for unexplained weight loss is important.

10. Kaufman D and others: Recent patterns of medication use in the ambulatory adult population of the United States: The Slone Survey. *Journal of the American Medical Association* 287:337, 2002.

    A recent telephone survey of a random sample of 2590 individuals at least 18 years of age revealed that 81% had used at least one medication in the previous week, and 7% took 5 or more medications. In addition, 14% of the population mentioned taking herbal supplements in the previous week. Medical professionals are concerned that because North Americans are taking more medications and herbal supplements, the possibility of dangerous drug-drug and drug-herb interactions is increasing.

11. Mates R: The chemical senses and nutrition in aging: Challenging old assumptions. *Journal of the American Dietetic Association* 102:192, 2002.

    Nutrition and health professionals have long assumed that the aging process results in changes in taste and smell, and that these changes lead to decreased dietary intake. Now, some of these assumptions are being questioned. More recent research has demonstrated that changes in taste can occur from various health disorders, medications, oral hygiene practices, and chronic smoking, as opposed to simply being a result of aging. In addition, the practical significance of these changes is being challenged, as are the assumptions that age-related changes in sensory function increase the risk of foodborne illness and nutritional risk.

12. McBean LD and others: Healthy eating in later years. *Nutrition Today* 36(4):192, 2001.

    Older adults are a diverse, heterogeneous group with unique nutritional needs and health risks. Practical dietary and lifestyle advice tailored to this growing segment of the population can help them age successfully and ensure their quality of life. Healthful food choices, including high-quality, nutrient-dense foods, adequate hydration, and regular physical activity, are critical components of successful aging.

13. Millen B and others: The elderly nutrition program: An effective national framework for preventive nutrition interventions. *Journal of the American Dietetic Association* 102:234, 2002.

    The Elderly Nutrition Program (ENP) is the nation's oldest framework for providing both community and home-based nutrition and health-related services to older adults. ENP currently provides congregate meals to 7% of older adults, including 20% of the nation's poorest older individuals. This program continues to be both effective and efficient, and also serves as a model for other preventive nutrition intervention programs targeted to older populations.

14. Miller KE and others: The geriatric patient: A systematic approach to maintaining health. *American Family Physician* 61:1089, 2000.

    A nutritional health screening for older persons should consider whether an illness or a condition has made the person change the type or amount of food consumed. Other problems include eating fewer than two meals a day; consuming few fruits, vegetables, or milk products; consuming three or more alcoholic drinks a day; experiencing tooth loss; not having enough income to buy the food needed; eating alone most of the time; taking three or more different prescription drugs daily; losing or gaining 10 pounds in the past six months without particularly trying to do so; and not always being physically able to shop and feed oneself.

15. Missing from herbal supplements: Herbs. *Tufts University Health & Nutrition Letter,* p. 1, October 2001 (supplement issue).

    An independent organization that serves as a watchdog over the supplement industry has reported that supplement labels can often be misleading. This organization has found that in many cases, the advertised herb is not present in the quantities specified on the label, if it is present at all. They have also found that supplement manufacturers sometimes include additional, and sometimes dangerous, ingredients in their supplements that are not listed on the label.

16. Nied RJ, Franklin B: Promoting and prescribing exercise for the elderly. *American Family Physician* 66(3):419, 2002.

    Regular exercise provides many health benefits for older adults, including improvements in blood pressure, diabetes, lipid profile, osteoarthritis, osteoporosis, and cognitive function. Regular physical activity is also associated with decreased mortality and age-related morbidity in older adults. A recommended exercise prescription consists of three components: aerobic exercise, strength training, and balance and flexibility.

17. Rigler S: Alcoholism in the elderly. *American Family Physician* 661:1710, 2000.

    Alcoholism goes unrecognized in many older adults because its symptoms are easily confused with symptoms of old age. It is, however, a real problem, which needs to be properly diagnosed and treated.

18. Semba R and others: Vitamin D deficiency among older women with and without disability. *American Journal of Clinical Nutrition* 72:1529, 2000.

    Vitamin D is involved in calcium metabolism and maintenance of bone mass. Increasing age, African American race, low educational level, high body mass index, disability, and winter season are among the risk factors for a vitamin D deficiency. Vitamin D deficiency is of concern because it is associated with decreased bone mass and bone fractures.

19. Torpy J: Integrating complementary therapy into care. *Journal of the American Medical Association* 287:306, 2002.

    Complementary therapy, the integration of nontraditional therapies such as meditation or herbal therapies, can be combined with traditional western medicine. Caution must be exercised when initiating herbal preparations, however, because herbal products are not evaluated by FDA for safety or efficacy.

20. Tucker KL: Nutritional consequences of dietary patterns of the elderly. *Nutrition & the M.D.* 26(7):1, 2000.

    Although a multivitamin and mineral supplement can help protect older persons' nutritional status, there appears to be substantial benefit from healthy dietary patterns beyond that attained with such supplement use. A diet high in fruits, vegetables, low-fat dairy products, and whole grains can especially make important contributions to health maintenance and quality of life.

Take | Action

I. Am I Aging Healthfully?

Take Control of Your Aging by Dr. William B. Malarkey (Wooster Book Company, Wooster, OH, 1999) includes a plan that incorporates various diet and lifestyle factors that are associated with *healthful* aging. Indicate the degree to which you are following such a plan (or alternatively fill this out with a parent or another older relative in mind).

Physical: Do you eat a well-balanced diet, exercise on a regular basis, remain free of illness, abstain from smoking, not drink alcohol excessively, and experience refreshing sleep?

Intellectual: Are you analytical, do you read regularly, do you learn new things each day, do you engage your mental ability at work (or at school), and do you often reflect on your life?

Emotional: Are you at peace, do you like who you are, are you optimistic, and do you laugh and relax regularly?

Relational: Are you a good listener, do you feel supported by friends, do you attend social functions, do you talk with family members often, and do you feel close to coworkers (or fellow students)?

Spiritual: Do you appreciate nature, give to or serve others, meditate or seek religious worship, and feel life has meaning?

The more of these factors that you include in your life, the more well rounded is your plan for maintaining overall health. Any one of the five areas in which you are not achieving success should show you characteristics to work on in the future.

Take | Action

II. Helping Older Adults Eat Better.

During their lifetimes, most people usually eat meals with families or loved ones. As people reach their older ages, many of them are faced with living and eating alone. In a study of the diets of 4400 older North Americans, one man in every five living alone and over age 55 ate poorly. One of four women between the ages of 55 and 64 years followed a low-quality diet. These poor diets can contribute to deteriorating mental and physical health. Consider the following example of the living situation of an older adult.

Neal, a 70-year-old man, lives alone in a home in a local suburban area. His wife died 1 year ago. He doesn't have many friends; his wife was his primary confidante. His neighbors across the street and next door are friendly, and Neal used to help them with yard projects in his spare time. Neal's health has been good, but he has had trouble with his teeth recently. His diet has been poor, and in the past 3 months his physical and mental vigor have deteriorated. He has been slowly lapsing into a depression and, so, keeps the shades drawn and rarely leaves his house. Neal keeps very little food in the house because his wife did most of the cooking and shopping and he just isn't that interested in food.

If you were one of Neal's relatives and learned of Neal's situation, what six things could you do or suggest to help improve his nutritional status and mental outlook? Look back into the chapter to get some ideas.

1. ______________________________

2. ______________________________

3. ______________________________

4. ______________________________

5. ______________________________

6. ______________________________

Complementary and Alternative Medicine Practices

Consumer interest in complementary and alternative medicine (CAM) (also called complementary care and integrative medicine) is growing.[19] About 34% of people recently surveyed in the United States used alternative medical practices in the past year, and most of the associated expenses for these often expensive products and services (about $4 billion per year) were paid out-of-pocket. Interest in herbal supplements, however, is currently waning, likely because many people have tried them but have not experienced enough benefit to justify the cost. The majority of the consumers also did not discuss the practice with their primary care physician.

Given the phenomenal advances in medicine over the past decades, what brings people in such numbers and with such affinity to embrace alternative therapies? It may be that many people assume that natural substances are gentler forms of therapy, lacking the harsher side effects of some pharmacological medicines. People may also seek complementary medicine because standard medical treatments didn't work, standard medical treatments had too many adverse effects, they wanted to more actively participate in treatment, or they wanted to combat poor physician communication. The majority of alternative medicine consumers have illnesses for which conventional medicine cannot offer a cure, such as arthritis, terminal stages of AIDS, and stress-related conditions. These people will almost certainly benefit from the reassurance, hope, and relief that comes with being in a healing situation.

Some herbal products are effective for treating specific medical problems. Follow label instructions carefully, if used. Note potential side effects listed, as well as who should not use the product.

In many instances, self-prescription or healing rituals involve the participants' optimism, commitment, attention, and high expectations for improvement. The mind is a powerful component of a treatment situation, which is proven in many trials as a placebo effect in which a person takes a "sugar pill" but believes that he or she is being treated with a real medication and subsequently feels and reacts better.[3] It is likely that most alternative or natural treatments of the past probably have no intrinsic therapeutic value beyond the benefit of the placebo effect. And, besides the powerful placebo effect, there are many possible reasons that a traditional remedy may seem to work, such as the natural ups and downs of symptoms, the remission of disease, the possibility that the remedy contains the effective dose of a pharmaceutical medicine or is adulterated with medicines not listed on the label, and the denial of symptoms or misrepresentation of effectiveness by people who believe the remedy is effective.

In truth, little scientific evidence is available for physicians and health-care professionals to decipher the positive and negative aspects of natural therapies. Indeed, Western medicine is based on accurate scientific knowledge, which serves as a protective device to prevent harm. On the other hand, alternative therapies often involve **folk medicine** and weak scientific evidence (due to lack of large research trials). Still, health professionals should be aware of the scientific knowledge that does or does not exist on some alternative therapies, since clients will likely express interest in these therapies. Many clients wish physicians would take the time to explain (in simple terms) the nature of the problem; to acknowledge nutritional influences on health, rather than just recommend drugs and surgery as the only approaches for treating illness; to answer questions intelligently about dietary supplements; to be sensitive to mind-body interactions, and to respect questions about alternative practices.

folk medicine A medical treatment based on the beliefs, traditions, or customs of a particular society or ethnic/cultural group.

To date, few complementary and alternative therapies have been subjected to scientific scrutiny, and many of the practices are based on presumptions that are unconvincing at best, yet some of the therapies (e.g., acupuncture and chiropractic therapies) show promise in the treatment of certain conditions. The National Institutes of Health in the United States has created the following seven categories of complementary and alternative therapies:

1. Mind-body interventions: the use of the mind, such as hypnosis, meditation, biofeedback, and yoga, to enhance health. Integrative medicine teaches health-care providers to focus on the subtle yet complex interactions of mind, body, spirit, community, and environment. *Ayurveda* is a natural healing process from India, which includes eating healthful, fresh foods and taking medicinal herbs suited to one's particular mind-body type.
2. Bioelectrical magnetic therapies: the use of electrical currents or magnetic fields to promote healing, such as the use of electrical currents to help heal broken bones.
3. Alternative systems of medical practice: the use of medicine from another culture, such as Native American medicine and Chinese medicine (for example, acupuncture). Acupuncture likely works by stimulating sensory nerves leading to the spinal cord. This leads to a reduction in pain. Acupuncture also may

be effective for treating people who experience nausea and vomiting following surgery or chemotherapy, nausea that accompanies pregnancy, pain experienced after certain dental procedures, and recovery from a drug addiction. Typically, a course of treatments should end after 10 sessions if it is not showing benefit. FDA supports the use of acupuncture for such purposes. However, a qualified, certified practitioner must use sterile needles intended for single use and made from nonreactive materials.

4. Manual healing methods: the use of the hands to promote healing, such as chiropractic or osteopathic manipulation or massage. FDA recognizes the effectiveness of chiropractic care for the treatment of acute low back pain.
5. Pharmacologic and biologic treatments: the use of various substances to treat specific medical problems. This includes **chelation** therapy.
6. Herbal medicine: the use of plants as medicines to treat or prevent disease. By definition, an herb is any plant or part of a plant that is used primarily for medicinal purposes. This includes **aromatherapy.** Dosage forms include capsules, tablets, extracts or tinctures, powders, dried herbs, teas, creams, and ointments. FDA has established regulations that require the labels of such supplements to include name, quantity, dosage per day, and ingredient amounts.
7. Diet and nutrition: the use of foods, vitamins, and minerals to prevent illness and treat disease.

chelation The use of medicinal compounds, such as ethylenediaminetetraacetic acid (EDTA), to bind metals and other constituents in the blood.

aromatherapy The use of the vapors of essential oils extracted from flowers, leaves, stalks, fruits, and roots for therapeutic purposes.

The National Institutes of Health is also sponsoring sites around the United States to study complementary and alternative medicine practices. Thus we may know more about them in the future.

The following are a few practical tips on using complementary and alternative medicine practices:

- We often tend to believe what we hear or what close acquaintances tell us. This well-meaning advice does not substitute for scientific verification of safety and effectiveness when it comes to health practices.
- The U.S. federal government provides little regulation regarding nutrient supplements or remedies. "Let the buyer beware" is prudent advice to follow when using these products. Knowledgeable, professional guidance is needed.
- Fraudulent claims for diet- and health-related remedies have always been a part of our culture. It is important to scrutinize carefully the credentials and motives of anyone providing medical or health advice. Phony credentials and bogus practitioners are widespread.
- If it sounds too good to be true, it probably is. The medical community gains nothing by holding back effective cures from the public, despite what the alternative practitioners may say.[3]

Vitamin and Herbal Supplements Are Regulated Loosely by FDA

Another concern regarding use of herbal and related supplements is the actual content of the active ingredient(s) in the product. Recently, many of these products have been tested by independent laboratories and found to contain either less than or more than the stated label content (see the website www.consumerlabs.com for details).[15]

Unless FDA has evidence that a supplement is inherently dangerous or label makes illegal claims, FDA will not regulate it closely. FDA is, in fact, prevented from doing so by the Proxmire Amendment to the 1938 Food, Drug, and Cosmetic Act, along with follow-up legislation—the Dietary Supplement Health and Education Act (DSHEA), which was passed in 1994 (and reviewed in Chapter 1). FDA requires a standardized Supplement Facts label on herbs and other related supplements. These labels must list the ingredients, the percent of Daily Value if applicable, common name of the plant, the part of the plant that was used, how much is present in each pill, and a suggested daily dose (Fig. 18-5). It is permissible for the labels on such products to claim a benefit related to a classic nutrient-deficiency disease, describe how a nutrient affects human body structure or function (i.e., structure/function claim), and state that general well-being results from consumption of the ingredient(s). On the other hand, a supplement label cannot claim that a product treats, cures, or prevents a disease not completely related to a given nutrient deficiency. For example, an herbal product label can claim that it may help brain function, but not that it cures Alzheimer's disease. The latter would constitute a drug claim. Once in a while, a company will decide to market a supplement as a drug. In that case, the company has to go through the same FDA process mandated for any drug. However, most supplement companies prefer to avoid this whole process and keep their product labels in compliance with DSHEA.

Dietary Supplement Claims

Although structure/function claims do not have to be approved by FDA, manufacturers must have evidence that their marketing statements are truthful and not misleading. In addition, the labels of products

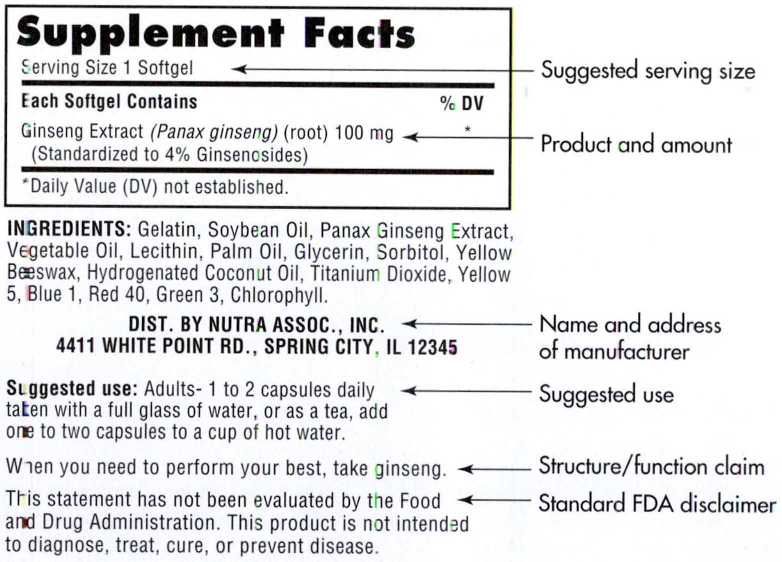

Figure 18-5 Supplement Facts label on an herbal product. Any nutrients or other food constituents would also be listed if contained in the product.

bearing such claims must prominently display in boldface type the following disclaimer: **"This statement has not been evaluated by the Food and Drug Administration. This product is not intended to diagnose, treat, cure, or prevent any disease."** Despite this statement, consumers may mistakenly assume FDA has carefully evaluated the products and related claims, as is done for approved health claims.

It is also noteworthy that FDA's requirement for "evidence" for a claim is not a very heavily enforced requirement. In many cases, the evidence used for a claim is vague or unsubstantiated, but FDA only ends up challenging a relatively low percent of these claims. For this reason, some other means are emerging for challenging such claims. Some involve government agencies other than FDA (e.g., the Federal Trade Commission [FTC]). In addition, the supplement industry itself is trying to develop means of self-policing their own industry. It will be interesting to see how much impact is produced via these efforts by government and industry groups. One of the biggest areas of concern is so-called "borrowed science." For example, let's say research on a garlic capsule from Company A shows that this product lowers blood pressure. Company B may also tout this research for their garlic product. However, their product can be prepared quite differently from that of Company A. How do we know that the research on the product of Company A applies to the product of Company B? We don't. This discourages many companies from sponsoring research on their products because their competitors will "borrow" their research (many people would call it stealing, not borrowing). Therefore, this is a big barrier to much needed research being conducted in the supplement area. How can "borrowed science" be stopped? Well, FDA can only investigate a limited number of cases, given its budget. Alternatively, lawsuits can be filed by an individual company against another company, but this is expensive and time consuming. Another possibility is the emerging government and industry approaches mentioned above, but we'll have to see how effective this will be.

Critical | Thinking

Jamila went to her local pharmacy yesterday to look for a product to help her stay awake while studying. On the shelves she found a dietary supplement claiming to be a Chinese herbal remedy for sleepiness and fatigue. She thought that since a pharmacy carried the product, it should be safe, and work as indicated on the label.

Is she correct in these assumptions? Are there specific risks associated with taking such herbal remedies?

A Closer Look at Herbal Therapy

Throughout history, healers have gone to the garden, forest, and sea to seek herbal remedies. Largely by trial and error, these healers have found the leaves and seeds of various herbs, roots, and barks to possess medicinal properties. As early as the second century B.C., the Egyptians used myrrh, cumin, peppermint, caraway, fennel, and clove oil for various ailments. In sixteenth-century Europe, physicians began experimenting with sarsaparilla, the dried root of the smilax plant, in an attempt to cure venereal disease. Later, the root was used to treat chronic rheumatism and skin disease. When late-nineteenth-century physicians abandoned a belief in its medicinal powers, sarsaparilla found new life as a syrup for soft drinks.

Some natural products may be harmless, others are potentially toxic, and still others may be effective for some problems but dangerous when taken in the wrong dose or by people with certain medical conditions (Table 18-6). Herb-drug interactions can be especially severe, such as increasing the risk of bleeding when one is taking anti-coagulant medications.[10] The National Cancer Institute is the world's leader in the search for medicinal compounds in plants. For example, the institute has tested extracts of more than

Table 18-6 Popular Herbal Remedies, Food Supplements, and Hormones

Herbal and Related Substances	Potential Effects	Side Effects	Who Should Avoid Them
Black cohosh	May reduce postmenopausal symptoms	Nausea, fall in blood pressure	Women taking estrogen, hypertension medications, or aspirin and related drugs
Chondroitin	Draws fluid to tissue and gives joints resistance and elasticity, which helps reduce the pain associated with osteoarthritis and improve mobility; research is encouraging for patients with osteoarthritis	None expected	Anyone taking an anticoagulant, such as vitamin E, warfarin, or aspirin
Coenzyme Q-10	Fat-soluble vitamin-like substance with antioxidant properties; healthy individuals have normal body amounts, although some people with chronic conditions have lower amounts in the body	Mild gastrointestinal distress	No specific persons are at risk
Echinacea	May stimulate the immune system and shorten the duration of flulike illnesses; studies show conflicting evidence	Nausea, skin irritation, allergic reactions	Anyone with an autoimmune disease or who has allergic reactions to daisies
Feverfew	May reduce the pain and frequency of migraines	Abdominal pain, mouth sores, skin rash	Anyone allergic to ragweed or taking anti-inflammatory drugs, such as aspirin
Garlic	May have antibiotic properties and slightly lower blood cholesterol and blood pressure	In large amounts, burning of the mouth, nausea, sweating, stomach irritation, lightheadedness, reduced blood clotting	Those taking anticoagulant medications, such as warfarin, for cardiovascular disease, or AIDS medicines
Ginger	May prevent motion sickness and nausea related to surgery and pregnancy	Gastrointestinal (GI) tract discomfort with high doses on an empty stomach	People with history of gallstones
Ginkgo biloba	May increase the circulation of blood in the body, especially to the brain and lower extremities; a few studies have shown increased ability to think, reason, and remember in older persons, but the evidence is very weak	GI upset, headache, irritability, reduced blood clotting	Anyone taking anti-inflammatory or anticoagulant medications, including vitamin E and aspirin; anyone who has had a stroke or is prone to them
Ginseng	May decrease weakness and fatigue and increase the body's resistance to stress; still, studies have not confirmed any benefit	Hypertension, asthma attacks, irregular heart beat, insomnia, headache, nervousness, GI upset, reduced blood clotting	Anyone taking anti-coagulant medications, such as warfarin; women on hormone replacement therapy; anyone with a chronic GI tract disease; anyone with diabetes
Glucosamine	May decrease joint inflammation and pain associated with osteoarthritis; research is underway for patients with osteoarthritis	GI discomfort, which may disappear after 2 weeks	May disrupt blood glucose regulation in people with diabetes
Kava kava	May alleviate mild anxiety and stress	GI complaints, headache, weakness, dizziness, pulmonary hypertension, allergic skin reactions, possible liver failure	Anyone with liver disease; those taking antidepressants, antipsychotics, barbiturates, and other sedatives, or those who use alcohol. Because of recent cases of liver failure, it is banned in some countries.
Ma huang (ephedra)	In combination with caffeine, stimulates the central nervous system and may increase metabolic rate (aiding in weight loss)	*Dangerous herb:* linked to over 100 deaths and 1200 reports of illness (hypertension, stroke, heart attack, seizure) in the United States	Generally, it is not regarded as safe for anyone to take more than 25 mg for longer than 7 days; people with cardiovascular disease should never take this herb
Milk thistle	May have a protective effect on the liver, which is thought to be due in part to its ability to prevent toxins from contaminating liver cell membranes	Diarrhea	No specific persons are at risk
Phytoestrogens: isoflavones from soy, lignans	May reduce postmenopausal symptoms and related bone loss and possibly reduce breast cancer risk	None expected with intakes less than 100 mg/day	Women who are taking estrogen or who have breast cancer
SAMe	S-adenosylmethionine is the active ingredient, may promote cartilage formation and decreases joint inflammation and pain associated with osteoarthritis; may also act as a mild antidepressant	Mild headaches, which last for short periods of time	Anyone with cardiovascular disease, obsessive compulsive disorder, manic-depression, or addictive tendencies

continues

Table 18-6 Concluded

Herbal and Related Substances	Potential Effects	Side Effects	Who Should Avoid Them
St. John's wort	Mild antidepressant effect that may work by inhibiting monoamine oxidase (an enzyme in the brain that destroys "feel-good" hormones, such as serotonin, epinephrine, and dopamine); scientific research is promising	Nausea, fatigue, dry mouth, dizziness, photosensitivity; increases metabolism and removal of many prescription drugs from the body	People taking prescription drugs to control depression, HIV, epilepsy, cardiovascular disease, asthma, and drugs that suppress the immune system to keep the body from rejecting a transplanted organ
Saw palmetto	May reduce symptoms of enlarged prostate gland (otherwise known as BPH or benign prostatic hyperplasia), by increasing urinary flow and easing urination; studies show moderate evidence of effectiveness	Generally uncommon; when taken in large doses: headache, GI upset	Those taking medication to treat enlarged prostate or BPH, anyone with a chronic GI tract disease
Valerian	May alleviate restlessness and other sleeping disorders that stem from nervous conditions	Headache, morning grogginess, irregular heart beat, GI upset (also has a disagreeable odor)	Anyone taking central nervous system depressants, such as sedatives; anyone who drinks alcohol
Hormones			
DHEA	Hormone that, when taken orally turns to estrogen and testosterone in the body; few, if any, benefits of supplementation are proven	Masculinization of women, acne, irritability, decreased HDL-cholesterol, possible prostate or breast cancer	Women, due to possible irreversible masculinization qualities
Growth hormone	Hormone that stimulates cell synthesis, such as muscle cells, and overall body growth in children. May be useful in adults who fail to make enough of the hormone.	**Carpal tunnel syndrome;** breast development in men; swollen ankles and legs, hypertension, diabetes, cancer	Only available by prescription; requires close physician scrutiny
Melatonin	Hormone that may help people fall asleep faster and reduce jet lag	Reduced ovulation in women, drowsiness, confusion, headache or morning grogginess	Anyone with cardiovascular disease, or anyone of childbearing age
Testosterone	Hormone that affects muscle mass and strength, and can reduce menopausal symptoms in women	Masculinization of women, decreased HDL-cholesterol, prostate gland enlargement in men (and possibly increased prostate cancer risk)	Only available by prescription; requires close physician scrutiny; risky in men showing prostate gland enlargement

Note that pregnant or breastfeeding women, children under 2 years old, anyone over the age of 65 years, and anyone with a chronic disease should never take supplements unless under the guidance of a physician.

30,000 plant species for activity against cancer. This work identified some anti-cancer compounds from flowering plants that have been approved for use in cancer patients. Other plant-derived compounds are currently being tested for safety and effectiveness in clinical trials but haven't yet been approved.

Traditional knowledge of the healing properties of plants provides leads for such scientists to explore. Any promising compounds they isolate are subjected to rigorous FDA-approved tests to determine safety, effectiveness, and side effects. This controlled testing provides a wealth of information far exceeding that available for most herbal remedies.

The German government publishes a manual that is the most authoritative reference for the use of popular herbal products *(Commission E Monographs)*. Unfortunately, little scientific data are available concerning the therapeutic value and safety of the 7000 or so herbs used in traditional medicine, which has been practiced and chronicled primarily by the Chinese. Proponents of Chinese herbal medicine suggest that its safety and efficacy have been well established during its 4000-year history. These individuals also point to the widespread use of herbal therapies in Europe. Still, numerous reports have documented significant health risks associated with the use of some herbal and alternative remedies, sometimes resulting in death. Studies especially implicate ephedra (herbal source is ma huang), germander, pokeroot, sassafras, mandrake, pennyroyal, comfrey, chaparral, yohimbe, lobelia, jin bu huan, kava kava, products containing stephanie and magnolia, senna, hai gen fen, paraguay tea, kombucha tea, tung shueh (Chinese black balls), and willow bark.

carpal tunnel syndrome A disease in which nerves that travel to the wrist are pinched as they pass through a narrow opening in a bone in the wrist.

Herbal products are part of Chinese culture. The best advice for the use of herbal products is to stick to one herb at a time and to consult your physician first about any such use. Note especially that the use of herbal mixtures is potentially very risky, as it is hard to predict how their various actions together will affect the body.

There is also a distinct risk that a traditional herbal product may be mislabeled, adulterated with prescription drugs or contaminants, or subject to extreme variations in potency. Chinese combination herbs should always be avoided, due to the reported cases of adverse health effects and adulteration.

A recent concern also has been raised with regard to patients who abruptly end alternative medicines at the start of hospital treatments or simply deny that they are involved in alternative therapy. Interactions between alternative therapies and pharmaceutical drugs can be drastic and include complications such as delirium, clotting abnormalities, and rapid heart beat, resulting in the need for intensive care. If these patients had disclosed their treatments, many of the complications could have been prevented. Experts recommend that, if time permits, patients stop taking herbal products for about a week before a scheduled surgery or otherwise take all original supplement containers to the hospital, so that the anesthesiologist can evaluate what was taken.

The following are questions that should be asked when evaluating a company's products. Still, what the label indicates as the active ingredient and the amount of the ingredient that a product claims to contain may or may not be valid, based on the recent analysis of many popular brands of herbal products.

- What forms of production control lab analysis are used to assure quality, quantity, and reproducibility of the ingredients in individual doses as labeled?
- Is the product labeled with Latin botanical names?
- Does the label have expiration dates and lot numbers, and if so what is the basis for the labeled expiration dates?
- Does the manufacturer offer a certificate of analysis for each product?
- Has the manufacturer been in business for at least 5 years and have national distribution of the product?

A rational approach to alternative therapy is to keep a diary of symptoms, follow only one therapy at a time, check with one's physician first before discontinuing a medication, and find out if the alternative practitioner has experience with the medical problem to be treated. Interested consumers might also see if they can enter a study of the agent or procedure in question. In addition, FDA advises anyone who experiences adverse side effects from an herbal remedy to contact a physician. Physicians are encouraged to report such adverse effects to FDA and state and local health departments and consumer protection agencies.

Overall, herbal products should be used with great caution and only in consultation with a person's primary physician. Otherwise, potential side effects may go undiagnosed, or dangerous herb-medicine interactions may develop.[19] Pregnant and nursing women, anyone with a chronic disease, and children under 2 years of age, especially, should not take herbal supplements unless their physicians consent to the practice and monitor them for potential complications.

Some herbalists claim that natural herbs cannot harm people. No evidence supports this claim. Indeed, if there's one thing experts agree on, it's this: An herb that has the ability to heal also has the ability, if misused, to harm. In addition, many conditions for which herbs are recommended (such as diabetes and arthritis) are not suitable for self-treatment. For a balanced discussion of herbal remedies, consult the following websites:

Alternative Medicine Foundation
www.amfoundation.org/
The NCCAM Complementary and Alternative Medicine (CAM) Citation Index (CI)
nccam.nih.gov/nccam/resources/cam-ci/
American Botanical Council
www.herbalgram.org/
Complementary and Alternative Medicine Program at Stanford (CAMPS)
scrdp.stanford.edu/camps.html
Center for Complementary and Alternative Medicine Research in Asthma, located at the University of California, Davis
www.camra.ucdavis.edu/
National Institutes of Health Office of Alternative Medicine
altmed.od.nih.gov/

chapter 19

Food Safety

Chapter | Outline

Case | Scenario

Aaron attended a gathering of his officemates on a warm July Saturday. The theme was international dining, and he and his wife were told to bring Argentine beef, a stewlike dish. They followed the recipe carefully, and it came out of the oven at 1 P.M. The couple kept the dish warm by wrapping the pan in a towel. They traveled in their car to the party and set the dish out on the buffet table at 3 P.M. Dinner was to be served at 4 P.M. However, the guests were enjoying themselves so much lounging around the host's pool and drinking ginger beer (also on the menu) that no one began to eat until 6 P.M. Aaron made sure he sampled the Argentine beef that he and his wife made, while his wife did not. He also had some salad, garlic bread, and a sweet dessert made with coconut.

The couple returned home at 11 P.M. and went to bed. About 2 A.M. Aaron knew something was wrong. He had severe abdominal pain and had to make a mad dash to the bathroom. For the next 3 hours he spent most of the time in the bathroom with severe diarrhea. By dawn, the diarrhea had subsided and he had started feeling better. After a few cups of tea and a light breakfast, he was feeling like himself by noon.

What type of foodborne illness did Aaron contract? What precautions for avoiding foodborne illness were ignored by Aaron and the rest of the people at the party? How could this scenario be rewritten, so that the party goers could substantially reduce their risk of foodborne illness?

Refresh | Your Memory

As you begin your study of food safety in Chapter 19, you may want to review:

- The disease phenylketonuria (PKU) in Chapters 4, 5, and 7.
- Alternative sweeteners in Chapter 5.
- Fat substitutes in Chapter 6.
- The causes of cancer in Chapter 10.

Boost | Your Study

Check out the ***Perspectives in Nutrition: Online Learning Center*** **www.mhhe.com/wardlawpers6** *for quizzes, flash cards, activities, and web links designed to further help you learn about issues surrounding food safety.*

Chapter | Objectives

Chapter 19 is designed to allow you to:

1. List some of the types of bacteria, fungi, viruses, and parasites found in food and their common sources.
2. Describe common means by which foods become contaminated.
3. State conditions that support growth of food microorganisms.
4. Describe the procedures that can be used to limit the risk of foodborne illness.
5. Compare and contrast how food-preservation methods, such as how pasteurization, canning, irradiation, and aseptic packaging, control the growth of microorganisms in food.
6. Describe the main reasons for using chemical additives in foods, the general classes of additives, and the functions of each class.
7. Identify toxic environmental contaminants in food, related complications of ingestion, and sources.
8. Understand the reasons behind pesticide use, the possible long-term health risks, and the safety limits set for their use.

At the turn of the twentieth century, conditions in Chicago's meat-packing industry were sickening. Moldy, spoiled meat was commonly doused with borax to cover up the smell, and glycerine was added to make it look fresh. By 1906, increasing public pressure forced the passage of the first Food and Drug Act in the United States. Federal inspection then safeguarded the public from worm-infested and diseased meat and generally improved food preparation standards.

Today, food safety warnings appear everywhere. Attention has turned to more contemporary food safety concerns, such as microbial and chemical contamination. On the one hand, we are told to eat more fruits, vegetables, fish, and poultry; on the other hand, we are warned that these foods may contain dangerous substances, so we still must ask, "How safe is our food?"

Scientists and health authorities agree that North Americans enjoy a relatively safe food supply, especially if foods are stored and prepared properly.[8] Over the past 90 or so years, tremendous progress has been made in food safety. Nonetheless, microorganisms and chemicals in foods still can pose a health risk.[12, 13] This chapter focuses on these food-related hazards—how real they are and how you can minimize their effect on your life. Note that you bear much responsibility for this—government agencies and industry can only do so much. Recall from Chapter 2 that one of the Dietary Guidelines for Americans is: Keep Food Safe to Eat.[18]

Setting the Stage

During the early stages of urbanization in North America, contaminated water and food—notably, milk—were responsible for many large outbreaks of typhoid fever, septic sore throat, scarlet fever, diphtheria, and other devastating human diseases. These experiences led to the development of processes for purifying water, treating sewage, and **pasteurizing** milk. Since that time, safe water and milk have become universally available in North America, with only occasional problems from either.

The greatest health risk from food today is contamination from the Norwalk **virus,** various **bacteria** (such as *Campylobacter jejuni*), and, to a lesser extent, from certain forms of other viruses, **fungi** and **parasites.** These microorganisms can all cause **foodborne illness.** For example, 1 child died and 50 others became ill from *Escherichia coli (E. coli)* bacteria, which was attributed to contaminated apple juice. In another case, 170 children became ill after their school lunch program served strawberries that had been contaminated with the hepatitis A virus.

Even though microbial contamination is the cause of most incidents of foodborne illness, North Americans seem more concerned about the health risks from chemicals in foods. Of consumers surveyed in a Gallup poll in the United States, about 75% said that pesticide contamination was a major concern to them. In the long run, this concern has some merit. On a day-to-day basis, however, food additives cause relatively few of the cases of foodborne illness in North America.[12]

Since microbial contamination of food is by far the more important issue for our day-to-day health, it will be discussed first. This chapter will then cover the use and safety of food additives and pesticides in foods.

pasteurizing The process of heating food products to kill pathogenic microorganisms.

virus The smallest known type of infectious agent, many of which cause disease in humans. They do not metabolize, grow, or move by themselves. They reproduce only with the aid of a living cellular host. A virus is essentially a piece of genetic material surrounded by a coat of protein.

bacteria Single-cell microorganisms; some produce poisonous substances, which cause illness in humans. They contain only one chromosome and lack many organelles found in human cells. Some can live without oxygen and survive by means of **spore** formation.

spores Dormant reproductive cells capable of turning into adult organisms without the help of another cell. Various bacteria and fungi form spores.

fungi Simple parasitic life forms, including molds, mildews, yeasts, and mushrooms. They live on dead or decaying organic matter. Fungi can grow as single cells, like yeast, or as a multicellular colony, as seen with molds.

parasite An organism that lives in or on another organism and derives nourishment from it.

foodborne illness Sickness caused by the ingestion of food containing toxic substances produced by microorganisms.

toxins Poisonous compounds produced by an organism that can cause disease.

Effects of Foodborne Illness

According to the U.S. Centers for Disease Control and Prevention, foodborne illness caused 76 million illnesses, 325,000 hospitalizations, and 5000 deaths in the United States in 1998.[8] Hospital costs are estimated at more than $3 billion per year, while the cost of lost productivity is $8 billion.

Some people are particularly susceptible to foodborne illness, including the following:[17]

- Infants and children
- Older adults
- Those with liver disease, diabetes, or HIV infection (and AIDS)
- Cancer patients
- Pregnant women
- People taking immunosuppressant agents

As you can see, foodborne illness has the greatest effect on the most vulnerable people in terms of health status. Some of these bouts of foodborne illness, coupled with the ongoing health conditions, are lengthy and lead to food allergies, seizures, blood poisoning (from **toxins** or microorganisms in the bloodstream), or other illnesses.

Because foodborne illness often results from the unsafe handling of food at home, we each bear some responsibility for preventing it.[11] Usually, you can't tell by taste, smell, or sight that a particular food contains harmful microorganisms, so you might not even be aware that food has caused your distress. In fact, your last case of diarrhea may have been caused by something you ate (Table 19-1).

Food contamination presents a unique risk to older adults for a variety of reasons. Poor eyesight and reduced senses of smell and taste may make it harder to spot spoiled food or dirty utensils. Aging and their typically reduced food intake can lead to a weakened immune system. Older adults face further risks because their stomachs may not produce enough acid, which destroys harmful bacteria, and because of poor blood circulation, which can prevent antibodies from reaching sites of infection.

Why Is Foodborne Illness So Common?

Foodborne illness is transported primarily by foods in which microorganisms can grow rapidly. These are foods that are moist, rich in protein, and have a neutral pH. Note that this describes many foods.

Table 19-1 Some Examples of Recent Cases of Foodborne Illness

Bacteria
• A previously healthy 5-month-old girl suddenly died at home from contact with a pet iguana infected with *Salmonella*. Unpasteurized juice products were recalled after 57 cases of *Salmonella* illness were reported in California and Colorado. Eight people became ill from *Salmonella* after consuming tiramisu, a dessert that contains raw eggs.
• Six persons were reported ill from a *Shigella* infection after eating chopped, uncooked parsley that was served on chicken sandwiches and in coleslaw. A cruise ship had to return to port when more than 600 people developed shigellosis and one person died.
• The first documented foodborne illness caused by *Listeria* organisms in North America occurred in commercially prepared coleslaw. Later, incidents that involved 48 deaths were associated with soft Mexican-style cheeses. A listeriosis outbreak associated with undercooked hot dogs and cold cuts resulted in more than 82 illnesses and 17 deaths in 19 U.S. states.
• The first community outbreak in the United States of *E. coli 0111:H8* sickened 58 teenagers at a cheerleading camp in Texas. Suspected sources of infection included the camp salad bar and a communal water barrel. One of the largest *E. coli* 0157:H7 outbreaks on record infected more than 1000 people in upstate New York at a county fair. The bacterium was found in infected well water. It killed a 79-year-old man and a 4-year-old girl, and it required 10 other children to undergo kidney dialysis. Six adults and a 2-year-old child were killed after an *E. coli* outbreak from contaminated drinking water in Canada. The bacteria entered the water supply from animal manure after flooding from a heavy storm. In northeastern Oklahoma, five children were infected with *E. coli* after consuming unpasteurized apple cider.
• A man in Arkansas developed botulism after eating stew that was cooked and then kept at room temperature for 3 days. He spent 49 days in the hospital—42 of them on mechanical ventilation. Another recent case involved a man who ate hard-boiled eggs that were left in a pickling solution at room temperature for 7 days.
• Since 1992, 17 people in Florida have died of *Vibrio vulnificus* infections after eating raw oysters.
• A teenage boy and his father experienced abdominal pain, vomiting, and diarrhea within 30 minutes of eating 4-day-old homemade pesto. The pesto had been reheated and left out a number of times during the 4-day period. It was apparently contaminated with *Bacillus cereus*. As a result the boy died of liver failure.
Viruses
• An estimated 6 million oysters from Louisiana were bathed with the Norwalk virus after ships with ill crewmembers dumped their sewage overboard. By the time the outbreak was recognized, an estimated 20,000 to 30,000 people had become ill. Another outbreak of the virus was attributed to an infected bakery worker, who stirred a vat full of buttercream frosting with his bare hand and arm. In Florida, 83 fraternity members caught the virus from the fraternity house ice machine. During the Gulf War, the Norwalk virus was one of the most common causes of gastroenteritis among U.S. troops.
Parasites
• A group attending a dinner banquet developed diarrhea after 3 to 9 days of eating green onions, which was the likely cause of the outbreak. Eight of 10 stool specimens obtained from the group with foodborne illness were positive for *Cryptosporidium*. Food workers at the restaurant reported they did not consistently wash green onions before using them to prepare food or serving them to patrons.
• Guatemalan raspberries have been associated with approximately 1000 cases of *Cyclospora* in the United States and Canada. Authorities speculate that contaminated water caused the outbreak. The United States has banned this source of the fruit until further precautions can be taken.
Risks from Seafood
• Four adults became ill with scombroid fish poisoning after eating tuna-spinach salad at a restaurant in Pennsylvania.
• An outbreak of ciguatera fish poisoning involved 17 crewmembers of a cargo ship that caught, cooked, and ate a barracuda in the Bahamas. All 17 men became ill with nausea, vomiting, abdominal cramps, and diarrhea within hours of eating the fish. Within 2 days, all of the men suffered from neurological symptoms, including muscle pain and weakness, dizziness, and numb or itchy feet, hands, and mouth.
• An outbreak of paralytic shellfish poisoning in Guatemala killed 26 people.

Information in this chapter primarily refers to statistics and laws that apply to the United States. Other people in North America face the same general food-safety risks described in the chapter, but the actual laws and agencies that oversee food safety differ. These laws and agencies (such as the Canadian Food Inspection Agency) are discussed in Appendix D.

The risk of contracting foodborne illness also is high because—in addition to problems from consumers' mishandling of food—recent trends have added new causes. First, there is greater consumer interest in eating foods of animal origin raw or undercooked. In addition, more people receive medication that suppresses their ability to combat foodborne infectious agents. Another factor is the continuing increase in the number of older adults in the population.

Furthermore, the food industry tries whenever possible to increase the shelf life of food products; however, a longer shelf life at room temperature allows more time for bacteria in foods to multiply. Some bacteria grow even at refrigeration temperatures.

Partially cooked—and some fully cooked—products pose a particular risk because refrigerated storage may only slow, not prevent, bacterial growth.[12]

The risk of illness from foodborne microorganisms increases as more of our foods are prepared in centralized kitchens outside the home. Supermarkets have become major food processors over the past decade and now offer a variety of prepared foods from specialty meat shops, salad bars, and bakeries. With the increasing number of two-income families, more people are looking for convenient, easy-to-prepare, nutritious foods. Supermarkets offer entrées that can be served immediately or reheated. The foods are usually prepared in central kitchens or processing plants and shipped to individual stores. If a food product is contaminated in the central kitchen or processing plant, patrons of stores over a wide area can suffer foodborne illness.

The centralization of food production by the food-processing industry also adds to the risk of foodborne illness. For example, a malfunction in an ice cream plant in 1994 resulted in 224,000 suspected cases of *Salmonella* bacterial infections, linked to the use of contaminated ice cream mix. In 1987, lettuce shredded in a Texas plant and then placed in large plastic bags was the cause of the largest *Shigella* bacterial outbreak ever reported in the United States. At least 347 people became ill. The nutrients released when the lettuce was shredded, coupled with the moist environment provided by the plastic bags, allowed growth and reproduction of the organism.

A survey showed that only 13% of U.S. restaurants implement the voluntary FDA Food Code for cooking temperatures for meat, eggs, fish, and poultry. It is no surprise, then, that in 1993 at least 4 people died and 700 became ill in Washington and surrounding western states after eating at a chain of fast-food restaurants. The source of the problem was undercooked hamburger contaminated with the bacterium *E. coli* 0157:H7. Overall, the growth of large-scale food production and distribution technologies has introduced new and different foodborne risks.

Still another cause of increased foodborne illness in North America is greater consumption of ready-to-eat foods imported from foreign countries. In the past, food imports were mostly raw products processed here under strict sanitation standards. Now, however, we import more processed foods—such as cheese from France and seafood from Asia—some of which are contaminated. Government authorities are currently examining inspection procedures for these imports.

The use of antibiotics in animal feeds is increasing the severity of cases of foodborne illness. This use encourages bacteria to develop resistant strains, those that can grow even if exposed to typical antibiotic medicines. This issue is currently receiving considerable attention.[9]

Finally, more cases of foodborne disease are reported now because scientists are more aware of the roles of various players in the process. In addition, physicians are more likely to suspect foodborne contaminants as a cause of illness. Every decade, the list of microorganisms suspected of causing foodborne illness lengthens (Table 19-2). Furthermore, we now know that food, besides serving as a good growth medium for some microorganisms, simply transmits many others as well. Seafood is receiving greater scrutiny and surveillance by FDA as a cause of foodborne illness. In addition, FDA is conducting a $500,000 campaign to educate consumers about the risks of eating raw oysters. For more information about these risks, contact FDA's Seafood Hotline at 1-800-FDA-4010.

Food contaminated in a central plant can go on to produce illness in people in surrounding states or even across the nation. In the case of juices, it is important that these are pasteurized to reduce the risk of foodborne illness.

When traveling to developing countries, it is recommended that you "boil it, peel it, or don't eat it." Ironically, up to 70% of our fruits and vegetables during certain seasons comes from these countries. In other words, you do not have to travel to acquire traveler's diarrhea. In response, we should carefully inspect and wash produce, as we would in a foreign country.

Food Preservation—Past, Present, and Future

For centuries, salt, sugar, smoke, fermentation, and drying have been used to preserve food. Ancient Romans used sulfites to disinfect wine containers and preserve wine. In the age of exploration, European adventurers traveling to the New World preserved their meat by salting it. Most preserving methods work on the principle of decreasing free water—that is, the amount of water not bound to other components in the food. Bacteria need abundant stores of water to grow; yeasts and molds can grow with less

A seafood hotline is also available through the American Seafood Institute. For free information on the purchase, preparation, and nutritional value of seafood products, call 1-800-328-3474 between 9 A.M. and 5 P.M. Eastern time on weekdays.

Table 19-2 Microorganisms and Related Factors That Cause Foodborne Illness (in Relative Order of Importance): Their Sources, Symptoms, and Prevention[2, 5, 12]

Microorganism	Sources	Symptoms	Prevention Methods
Bacteria			
Campylobacter jejuni	Found on poultry, beef, and lamb and can contaminate meat and milk. Chief food sources are raw poultry and meat and unpasteurized milk.	Onset: 2–5 days after eating, or longer Diarrhea, abdominal cramping, fever, and sometimes bloody stools. Lasts 2–7 days.	• Thorough cooking of foods • Sanitary food-handling practices • Avoidance of unpasteurized milk
Salmonella species	Found in raw meats, poultry, eggs, fish, sprouts, unpasteurized milk, and products made with these items. Multiplies rapidly at room temperature. The bacteria themselves are toxic.	Onset: 24–72 hours after eating Nausea, fever, headache, abdominal cramps, diarrhea, and vomiting Can be fatal in infants, the elderly, and the sick.	• Sanitary food-handling practices • Avoidance of any use of unpasteurized raw eggs or undercooked eggs • Thorough cooking of foods • Prompt and proper refrigeration of foods • Avoidance of cross-contamination
Shigella species	Transmitted via fecal-oral route and somewhat in food and water.	Onset: 1–3 days Abdominal cramps, diarrhea, fever, bloody stools	• Handwashing and sanitary food production
Escherichia coli (0157:H7 and other strains)	Undercooked beef, especially ground beef. Fruits, vegetables, sprouts, and yogurt are also possible sources.	Onset: 1–8 days Bloody diarrhea, abdominal cramps, kidney failure	• Thorough cooking, especially of beef • Avoidance of unpasteurized milk, untreated apple cider
Clostridium perfringens	Found throughout the environment. Generally found in meat and poultry dishes. Multiply rapidly in anaerobic conditions when foods are left for extended time at room temperature. The bacteria themselves are toxic.	Onset: 8–24 hours after eating (usually 12 hours) Abdominal pain and diarrhea Symptoms last a day or less, usually mild. Can be more serious in older or ill people.	• Sanitary handling of foods, especially meat and meat dishes, gravies, and leftovers • Thorough cooking and reheating of foods, especially leftovers • Prompt and proper refrigeration
Listeria monocytogenes	Found in soft cheeses made with unpasteurized milk and unpasteurized milk itself. Resists acid, heat, salt, and nitrate well.	Onset: 9–48 hours for early symptoms; 14–42 days for severe symptoms Fever, headache, vomiting, and sometimes more severe symptoms May be fatal.	• Thorough cooking of foods • Sanitary food-handling practices • Avoidance of unpasteurized milk
Staphylococcus aureus	Found in nasal passages and in cuts on skin. Toxin is produced when food contaminated by bacteria is left for extended time at room temperature. Meats, poultry, egg products, tuna, potato salad, macaroni salads, and cream-filled pastries pose greatest risk.	Onset: 2–6 hours after eating Diarrhea, vomiting, nausea, and abdominal cramps Mimics flu Lasts 24–36 hours Rarely fatal	• Sanitary food-handling practices • Prompt and proper refrigeration of foods • Covering cuts on skin
Clostridium botulinum	Found throughout the environment. However, bacteria produce toxin only in a low-acid, anaerobic environment, such as in canned green beans, mushrooms, spinach, olives, and beef. Honey may carry spores.	Onset: 12–72 hours after eating Neurotoxic symptoms include double vision, inability to swallow, speech difficulty, and progressive paralysis of the respiratory system. OBTAIN MEDICAL HELP IMMEDIATELY. BOTULISM CAN BE FATAL.	• Use proper methods for canning low-acid foods • Avoidance of commercial cans of low-acid foods that have leaky seals or are bent, bulging, or broken • Discard if toxin is suspected (off odors are a sign)
Yersinia enterocolitica	Found throughout the environment; carried in food, water, and feces. They multiply rapidly at both room and refrigerator temperatures. Generally found in raw vegetables, meats, water, and unpasteurized milk.	Onset: 2–3 days Fever, headache, nausea, diarrhea, and general malaise Mimics flu and appendicitis May cause gastroenteritis in children.	• Thorough cooking • Sanitizing of cutting instruments and cutting boards before preparing foods to be eaten raw • Avoidance of unpasteurized milk and untreated water

(continues)

Table 19-2 Continued

Microorganism	Sources	Symptoms	Prevention Methods
Vibrio parahaemolyticus	Raw seafood	Onset: 2–48 hours Watery diarrhea, abdominal cramps, nausea, vomiting	• Thorough cooking of seafood
Vibrio vulnificus	Raw seafood, especially raw oysters.	Onset: 1–7 days Diarrhea, fever, weakness, blood infection, death	• Thorough cooking of seafood
Vibrio cholerae	Human carriers, infected shellfish, contaminated water and food.	Onset: 2–3 days Vomiting, severe watery diarrhea, which can lead to dehydration and cardiovascular collapse; death	• Handwashing after using the bathroom
Bacillus anthracis	Contaminated food; undercooked meats from infected animals.	Onset: 15–72 hours Abdominal pain, vomiting of blood, severe diarrhea, and death in up to 60% of cases	• Avoid eating contaminated animals (anthrax is rare in North America). • Thorough cooking of food
Viruses			
Norwalk, human rota-virus	Found in the human intestinal tract and feces. Contamination occurs: (1) when sewage is used to enrich garden/farm soil (2) by direct hand-to-food contact during the preparation of meals (3) when shellfish are harvested from waters contaminated by sewage.	Onset: 1–2 days Severe diarrhea, nausea, and vomiting. Respiratory symptoms. Usually lasts 4–5 days but may last for weeks.	• Sanitary handling of foods • Use of pure drinking water • Adequate sewage disposal • Adequate cooking of foods
Hepatitis A virus	Fecal-oral route that contaminates food, beverages, or shellfish.	Onset: 15–50 days Anorexia, diarrhea, fever, jaundice, and fatigue. May cause liver damage and death. After recovery the person is immune to further infections.	• Sanitary handling of foods • Use of pure drinking water • Adequate sewage disposal • Thorough cooking of foods
Parasites			
Trichinella spiralis	Pork and wild game.	Onset: weeks to months Muscle weakness, fluid retention in face, fever, flulike symptoms	• Thorough cooking of pork and wild game
Anisakis	Raw fish.	Onset: 12 hours Stomach infection, severe stomach pain	• Thorough cooking of fish
Tapeworms	Raw beef, pork, and fish.	May cause abdominal discomfort, diarrhea	• Thorough cooking of all animal products • Avoidance of raw fish dishes, such as sushi
Cyclospora ccyetanensis	Carried to food via contaminated water; Guatemalan raspberries suspected in recent outbreaks.	Onset: 1–11 days Prolonged diarrhea, vomiting, muscle aches, fatigue	• Irradiation (not yet in practice)
Cryptosporidium	Contaminated water (especially fecal material). Large outbreaks have been caused by such contamination of municipal water in Milwaukee, Wisconsin, and Sydney, Australia.	Onset: 1–12 days Diarrhea, vomiting, fever	• Handwashing • Consume clean or treated water • Boil water if at high risk, such as one who is on immune suppression drugs or has AIDS

(continues)

Table 19-2 Concluded

Microorganism	Sources	Symptoms	Prevention Methods
Giardia lamblia	Contaminated water.	Onset: 3–25 days, usually about 7–10 days Diarrhea, abdominal cramps, nausea	• Consume clean or treated water • Wash raw fruits and vegetables • Handwashing
Toxoplasma gondii	Raw or undercooked meat, unwashed fruits and vegetables, cat feces.	Onset: 5–20 days Fever, headache, sore muscles, diarrhea (can be deadly to the fetus of pregnant women)	• Cook meats thoroughly • Wash raw fruits and vegetables • Wash hands after changing cat litter (avoid cat litter when pregnant)
Fungi A group of toxic compounds (mycotoxins) produced by molds, such as aflatoxin B-1	Found in foods that are relatively high in moisture. Chief food sources are beans and grains that have been stored in a moist place.	May cause liver and/or kidney disease	• Checking of foods for visible mold and discarding those that are contaminated • Proper storage of susceptible foods
Ciguatera	Large tropical fish, especially grouper, snapper, and barracuda that have consumed large amounts of dinoflagellate algae.	Onset: generally within 6 hours Diarrhea, abdominal pain, nausea, vomiting, and nerve disorders	• Avoid grouper, amberjack, and barracuda from Caribbean waters, especially larger fish
Paralytic Shellfish Poisoning	Shellfish that have consumed large amounts of dinoflagellate algae (i.e., red tide).	Onset: within 4 hours Respiratory difficulty	• Observe local precautions when harvesting shellfish
Scombroid Poisoning	Spoiled fish, especially tuna, mackerel, and mahi-mahi.	Onset: 1–180 minutes Facial flushing, burning sensation in the mouth, intestinal distress, and headache	• Avoid spoiled fish • Refrigerate fresh fish and use as soon as possible
Prions Proteins that help maintain nerve cells. These can turn into infectious prions, likely leading to diseases such as mad cow disease (bovine spongiform encephalopathy).	Cows, goats, and sheep harboring infectious prions. These are spread from one animal to another if certain by-products of the infected animal are used to feed other animals (this process is banned in the U.S.).	Dementia and psychosis, leading eventually to seizures, blindness, paralysis, and death, in about 2 to 30 years after infection. Once symptoms begin, death usually occurs within 1 year. At autopsy the person shows numerous holes in the brain.	• No case of mad cow disease has been confirmed in U.S. cattle, and FDA and USDA have banned imports of cows, goats, and sheep from Europe. The biggest risk is consumption of meat from these animals in Europe or Asia. Cooking does not destroy prions. There is a possibility that the prion also may be present in dietary supplements containing tissue from cows, especially brain tissue.

water, but some is still necessary. Adding sugar or salt decreases free water by binding to it. The process of drying drives off free water.

Decreasing the water content of some high-moisture foods, however, causes them to lose essential characteristics. To preserve such foods—cucumber pickles, sauerkraut, milk (yogurt), and wine—fermentation has been a traditional alternative. Selected bacteria or fungi are used to ferment or pickle foods. The fermenting bacteria and fungi make acids and alcohol, which minimize the growth of other microorganisms.

Today, we can add pasteurization, sterilization, refrigeration, freezing, **irradiation,** canning, and chemical preservatives to the list of food preservation techniques. An additional method of food preservation—**aseptic processing**—simultaneously sterilizes the food and package separately before the food enters the package. Liquid foods, such as fruit juices, are especially easy to process in this manner. With aseptic packaging, boxes of sterile milk and juices can remain on supermarket shelves, free of microbial growth, for many years.

Food irradiation is also a method used to treat food. It uses minimal doses of radiation in order to control pathogens such as *E. coli* 0157:H7 and *Salmonella*. Even

irradiation A process in which radiation energy is passed through foods, creating compounds (free radicals) within the food that destroy cell membranes, break down DNA, link proteins together, limit enzyme activity, and alter a variety of other proteins and cell functions that can lead to food spoilage. This process does not make the food radioactive.

aseptic processing A method by which food and container are simultaneously sterilized; it allows manufacturers to produce boxes of milk that can be stored at room temperature.

though FDA has permitted the irradiation of certain food products for more than a decade, the history of the technology goes back nearly a century, including scientific research, evaluation, and testing. The radiation used does not make the food radioactive. The rays essentially pass through the food, and no radioactive residues are left behind. However, the energy is strong enough to break chemical bonds, destroy cell walls and cell membranes, break down DNA, and link proteins together. Irradiation thereby controls the growth of insects, microorganisms, and parasites in foods.

FDA recently approved the use of irradiation for raw red meat to reduce the risk of *E. coli* and other infectious pathogens. Some supermarket chains are now doing so. Other additions to the approved list are shell eggs and seeds. Prior to this, the only animal products so treated were pork and chicken. Irradiation also extends the shelf life of spices, dry vegetable seasonings, meats in general, and fresh fruits and vegetables.

Irradiated food, except for dried seasonings, must be labeled with the international symbol, the Radura, and a statement that the product has been treated by irradiation. Foods treated this way are safe in the opinion of FDA and many other health authorities.[1] The process is as safe as using a microwave oven. Although the demand for irradiated foods has yet to get off the ground in the United States, other countries, including Canada, Japan, France, Italy, and Mexico, all use food irradiation technology widely. Certain consumer groups continually try to block its use in the United States, claiming that irradiation diminishes the nutritional value of food and that it can lead to the formation of harmful compounds. Similar claims were once made about pasteurization. Many experts speculate that consumers will eventually accept the process, just as they did with pasteurization during the late nineteenth century. Keep in mind also that, even when foods, especially meats, have been irradiated, it is still important to follow basic food-safety procedures, as later contamination in food preparation is possible.

This is the Radura, the international label denoting prior irradiation of the food product.

Foodborne Illness: When Undesirable Microorganisms Alter Foods

Many of the verifiable cases of foodborne illness are caused by specific toxin-producing bacteria. These microorganisms cause health problems either directly by invading the intestinal wall and producing an infection via a toxin contained in the microorganism (an *infection* caused by an endotoxin) or indirectly by producing a toxin that is secreted into the food, which later harms us (an *intoxication* caused by an exotoxin). The main way to tell an infectious route from an intoxication is time: If symptoms appear in 4 hours or less, it is an intoxication.[12]

Bacteria that cause foodborne illness include *Bacillus, Campylobacter, Clostridium, Escherichia, Listeria, Vibrio, Yersinia, Salmonella*, and *Staphylococcus.* Because each teaspoon of soil contains about 2 billion bacteria, we are constantly at risk for foodborne illness. Luckily, only a small number of all bacteria actually pose a threat. In addition, experts speculate that about 70% of cases of foodborne illness go undiagnosed because they result from viral causes, such as the Norwalk virus, and there is no easy way to test for many of these pathogens. To learn more about the latest on foodborne illness prevention, see the Expert Opinion by Dr. Lydia Medeiros.

The World Health Organization's Golden Rules for Safe Food Preparation

1. Choose foods processed for safety.
2. Cook food thoroughly.
3. Eat cooked foods immediately.
4. Store cooked foods carefully.
5. Reheat cooked foods thoroughly.
6. Avoid contact between raw and cooked foods.
7. Wash hands repeatedly.
8. Keep all kitchen surfaces meticulously clean.
9. Protect foods from insects, rodents, and other animals.
10. Use pure water.

General Rules for Preventing Foodborne Illness

You can greatly reduce the risk of foodborne illness by following some very important rules.[7, 11, 16, 17]

Purchasing Food

- When shopping, select frozen foods and perishable foods last, such as meat, poultry, or fish. Always have these products put in separate plastic bags, so that drippings don't contaminate other foods in the shopping cart. Then, don't let groceries sit in a warm car; this allows bacteria to grow. Get the perishable foods home and promptly refrigerate or freeze them.

A new website coordinating the U.S. government efforts on food safety is www.foodsafety.gov.

Expert Opinion

Food Safety—Why Should You Care?

Lydia Medeiros, Ph.D., R.D.

Why does every research journal article on food safety start out quoting statistics about how many illnesses, hospitalizations, and even deaths occur each year because of foodborne illness? It's so common that it's almost becoming a cliché. The reason is that the numbers are shocking. Just think, in a technologically advanced country such as the United States people die from illnesses that could be prevented by simply cooking food adequately or properly washing their hands. But, this is boring—these are things our mothers nagged us about when we were children. And who doesn't wash one's hands before handling food? Apparently, plenty of people don't, or if they do they aren't doing it properly. Why else are the statistics on foodborne illness so high?

Could it be that we confuse people with too many do's and don'ts—too many rules to follow. As a food safety educator I certainly am asking myself that question. When I began compiling a list of all the behaviors that people should practice to control the most common foodborne illness pathogens, I found almost 60 behaviors scattered among numerous references. After editing for vagueness, overlap, and redundancy, our research group asked nationally known experts in food safety to refine and associate each behavior to one of 13 pathogens known to cause the majority of foodborne illnesses.

We started to think in the language of the Hazard Analysis Critical Control Point (or HACCP) system where hazards are first identified and then control factors that, if practiced, will contain the contamination and growth of foodborne illness pathogens. Of the 29 remaining behaviors on our edited and refined list, we found that each could be organized under just 5 groupings that are control points, like in HACCP. These control factors are: Practice Personal Hygiene, Cook Foods Adequately, Avoid Cross-Contamination, Keep Foods at Safe Temperatures, and Avoid Foods from Unsafe Sources. These control factors can also serve as concise and easy-to-remember educational messages.

As I have applied our research findings to educational programs, I have found that two of the control factors fit well together, as do two others; the last one seems to stand separately. Practice Personal Hygiene and Avoid Cross-Contamination are similar because both involve human behaviors related to cleanliness, whether the hands, the body, or food preparation surfaces are at issue. The differences in the two control factors lie in the microbial pathogens that cause the foodborne illnesses. Practice Personal Hygiene, which focuses on hand cleanliness, is most applicable if the behaviors are practiced before food is touched and when the food is going to be served cold, such as salads. The pathogens controlled best by handwashing are Norwalk and Norwalk-like viruses, *Shigella* species, and foodborne sources of hepatitis A. Avoiding Cross-Contamination also concerns cleanliness, but the focus is on food preparation utensils, cookware, and food preparation surfaces. The Fight BAC! educational program of the United States Department of Agriculture is very similar in concept to the research findings of our group with the exception of how cleanliness is taught. Handwashing and food preparation surfaces are combined under the Fight BAC! concept of "CLEAN." We recommend separation of the concept into two control factors because the pathogens best controlled by cleaning and sanitizing food preparation surfaces are *Campylobacter jejuni*, *Salmonella* species, *Toxoplasma gondii*, *Yersinia enterocolitica*, and *Escherichia coli* 0157:H7. This is a very different list from the ones controlled by personal hygiene.

Cook Foods Adequately and Keep Food at Safe Temperatures also have similarities. Both factors focus on controlling temperature of food,

- Don't buy or use food from damaged containers that leak, bulge, or are severely dented or buy or use food from jars that are cracked or have loose or bulging lids. Don't taste or use food that has a foul odor or spurts liquid when the can is opened; the deadly *Clostridium botulinum* toxin may be present.
- Purchase only pasteurized milk, cheese, and juice (check the label). This is especially important for pregnant women because highly toxic bacteria and viruses that can harm the fetus thrive in unpasteurized foods.
- Purchase only the amount of produce needed for a week's time. The longer you keep fruits and vegetables, the more time is available for bacteria to grow.
- When purchasing precut produce, avoid those that look slimy, brownish, or dry; these are signs of improper holding temperatures.

Washing your hands before preparing food is the single best way to limit your risk for foodborne illness.

except Cook Foods Adequately is concerned about end-point temperatures of cooking and reheating, while Keep Food at Safe Temperatures advocates behaviors associated with holding and storage of cold or hot perishable foods. Foodborne illness pathogens that cause food infections, or illness symptoms due to ingestion of the pathogen itself, are controlled by heat destruction of the microorganisms. These are the same pathogens that are also controlled by avoiding cross-contamination. There are, therefore, two ways to control foodborne infections caused by microbial pathogens—controlling contamination of the food initially or by heating to an adequate temperature, which will result in the destruction of the pathogen. The pathogens best controlled by controlling holding and storage temperatures of foods are somewhat unique among foodborne illness pathogens. These are *Clostridium perfringens*, *Staphylococcus aureus*, and *Bacillus cereus*. Uniqueness of these pathogens comes from the fact that they either contain spores, which are not destroyed during heating, or they cause illness due to a toxin produced in a temperature-abused food. The toxin causes the illness.

The one remaining control factor is Avoid Foods from Unsafe Sources. These foods include raw eggs, unpasteurized milk or milk products made from raw milk, unpasteurized fruit juices, raw sprouts, and some types of pre-prepared foods served without heating (such as deli salads and hot dogs). For immune-compromised individuals like the elderly, pregnant women, or people with drug- or disease-induced immune suppression, consuming these foods can complicate existing conditions or, in extreme situations, cause death. There are certainly foodborne illness pathogens that are associated with these foods that have already been listed for the other control factors, such as *E. coli* 0157:H7 or *Salmonella* species. But for those pathogens, there are effective consumer behaviors that can be used to prevent illnesses in the home. However, for one pathogen—and especially for immune-compromised individuals—avoidance is the most prudent behavior. That pathogen is *Listeria monocytogenes*. (See the chapter for ways to minimize risk.)

With so much to remember about food safety, is there one single message that all people can remember that will control the majority of foodborne illnesses? If there were, that message would be either to practice personal hygiene or wash your hands before you eat or touch foods. For pathogens that cause the most severe illnesses or death, the public health concern clearly remains high; however, the numbers of cases are relatively few and susceptible groups can be targeted for special emphasis in educational programs.

Dr. Medeiros is an Associate Professor in the Department of Human Nutrition at The Ohio State University. She is an Extension Specialist in Food and Nutrition for Ohio State University, and has an active research program in food safety.

Preparing Food

- Thoroughly wash hands with hot, soapy water for 20 seconds before and after handling food. This practice is especially important when handling raw meat, fish, poultry, and eggs, and after using the bathroom, playing with pets, or changing diapers.
- Make sure counters, cutting boards, dishes, and other equipment are thoroughly cleaned and rinsed before use. Be especially careful to use hot, soapy water to wash surfaces and equipment that have come in contact with raw meat, fish, poultry, and eggs as soon as possible to remove *Salmonella* bacteria that may be present. In addition, wash or replace sponges and kitchen towels regularly.
- If possible, cut foods to be eaten raw on a clean cutting board reserved for that purpose. Then clean this cutting board using hot, soapy water. If the same board must

The 4 "F's" of food contamination are fingers, foods, feces, and flies. Handwashing before food preparation especially combats the fecal and finger routes.

Critical | Thinking
Jon wants to buy a cutting board for his new kitchen. He's been looking at all of the possibilities: plexiglass, plastic, and wood. How would you advise him, so that he can minimize the risk of any foodborne illness from his food preparation?

be used for both meat and other foods, cut any potentially contaminated items, such as meat, last. After cutting the meat, wash the cutting board thoroughly.

USDA recommends cutting boards with unmarred surfaces made of easy-to-clean, nonporous materials, such as plastic, marble, or glass. They must be free of seams and cracks. If you prefer a wooden board, make sure it is nonporous (e.g., maple and oak) and reserve it for a specific purpose; for example, set it aside for cutting raw meat and poultry. Then keep a separate wooden cutting board for chopping produce and slicing bread to prevent these products from picking up bacteria from raw meat. Note that many foods are served raw, so any bacteria clinging to them are not destroyed.

Furthermore, USDA recommends that all cutting boards be replaced when they become streaked with hard-to-clean grooves or cuts, which may harbor bacteria. In addition, cutting boards should be sanitized once a week in a solution of 3 teaspoons of chlorine bleach per quart of water. Flood the board with the solution, let it sit a few minutes, and then rise thoroughly.

- When thawing foods, do so in the refrigerator for 1 to 3 days, under cold running water, or in a microwave oven. Also, cook foods immediately after thawing under cold water or in the microwave. Never let frozen foods thaw unrefrigerated all day or night. Also, marinate food in the refrigerator.
- Avoid coughing or sneezing over foods, even when you're healthy. Cover cuts on hands with a sterile bandage. All this helps stop *Staphylococcus* from entering food.
- Carefully wash fresh fruit and vegetables under running water to remove dirt and bacteria clinging to the surface, using a vegetable brush if the skin is to be eaten. People have became ill from *Salmonella* that was introduced from melons used in making a fruit salad and from oranges used for freshly-squeezed orange juice. The bacteria were on the outside of the melons and oranges.
- Completely remove moldy portions of food, or don't eat the food. *When in doubt, throw the food out.* Mold growth is prevented by properly storing food at cold temperatures and using the food within a reasonable length of time.
- Use refrigerated ground meat and patties in 1 to 2 days and frozen meat and patties within 3 to 4 months.

In one of the largest recalls of meat products in U.S. history, an Arkansas-based processing plant voluntarily recalled 25 million pounds of hamburger suspected of contamination with *E. coli* 0157:H7.

Cooking Food

- Cook food thoroughly, using a thermometer to check internal temperatures and Table 19-3 as a guide for safe preparation. Cooking is by far the most reliable way to destroy foodborne bacteria, such as toxic strains of *E. coli,* whereas freezing only halts growth. FDA does not recommend that eggs be prepared sunny-side up or over-easy for consumption. Restaurants must now include an advisory on menus stating that an increased risk of foodborne illness is associated with eating undercooked eggs. As long as restaurants provide this warning on their menus, however, they are allowed to cook eggs to any temperature requested by the consumer. Still, a good general precaution is to eat no raw animal products. USDA answers questions about the safe use of animal products (800-535-4555, 10 A.M. to 4 P.M. weekdays, Eastern time).

  Seafood also poses a risk of foodborne illness. Properly cooked fish should flake easily and be opaque or dull and firm. If it's translucent or shiny, it's not done. Raw fish dishes, such as sushi, can be safe for most people to eat if they are made with very fresh fish that has been commercially frozen and then thawed. The freezing is important to eliminate potential health risks from parasites. FDA recommends that the fish be frozen to an internal temperature of −10°F for 7 days. If you choose to eat uncooked fish, purchase the fish from reputable establishments that have high standards for quality and sanitation. People at high risk for foodborne illness would be wise to avoid raw fish products (Fig. 19-1).
- Cook stuffing separately from poultry (or wash poultry thoroughly, stuff immediately before cooking, and then transfer the stuffing to a clean bowl immediately after cooking). Use a meat thermometer to make sure the stuffing reaches 165°F (74°C). Again, *Salmonella* is the major concern with poultry.

Current Safe Handling Instructions Issued by USDA for Labeling Meat and Poultry Products

This product was prepared from inspected and passed meat and/or poultry. Some food products may contain bacteria that could cause illness if the product is mishandled or cooked improperly. For your protection, follow these safe handling instructions.

Keep refrigerated or frozen.

Thaw in refrigerator or microwave.

Keep raw meat and poultry separate from other foods.

Wash working surfaces (including cutting boards), utensils, and hands after touching raw meat or poultry.

Cook thoroughly.

Keep hot foods hot. Refrigerate leftovers immediately or discard.

Table 19-3 Proper Cooking Temperatures for Foods

Food	Internal Temperature
Beef, Lamb, Veal	
Ground products	
Hamburger (prepared as patties, meatballs, etc.)	160°F (71°C)
Non-ground products	
Roasts and steaks	
Medium-rare	145°F (63°C)
Medium	160°F (71°C)
Well-done	170°F (77°C)
Poultry	
Ground chicken, turkey	165°F (74°C)
Whole chicken, turkey	180°F (82°C)
Boneless turkey roasts	170°F (77°C)
Poultry breast and roasts (white meat)	170°F (77°C)
Poultry thighs, wings, and drumstick (dark meat)	180°F (82°C)
Stuffing (cooked alone or in bird)	165°F (74°C)
Pork	
All cuts including ground products	
Medium	160°F (71°C)
Well-done	170°F (77°C)
Fresh, raw ham	160°F (71°C)
Fully cooked ham, to reheat	140°F (60°C)
Egg Dishes, Casseroles	**160°F (71°C)**
Leftovers, Reheated	**165°F (74°C)**

Figure 19-1 Sushi, like all raw fish or meat dishes, is a high-risk food. For maximum protection from foodborne illness, you should cook animal foods thoroughly before eating. If you choose to eat uncooked fish, purchase fish from reputable establishments that have high standards for quality and sanitation. People at high risk for foodborne illness would be wise to avoid these products.

- Once a food is cooked, consume it right away, or cool it to below 41°F (5°C) within 2 hours. If it is not to be eaten immediately, in hot weather (80°F and above) make sure this cooling is done within 1 hour. Do this by separating the food into as many shallow pans as needed to provide a large surface area. Be careful not to recontaminate cooked food by contact with raw meat or juices from hands, cutting boards, or dirty utensils or in other ways.
- Serve meat, poultry, and fish on a clean plate—never the same plate that was used to hold the raw product. For example, when grilling hamburgers, don't put cooked items on the same plate that was used to carry the raw product out to the grill.
- Cook food completely at a picnic site, with no partial cooking in advance.

Storing and Reheating Cooked Food

- Keep hot foods hot and cold foods cold. Hold food below 41°F (5°C) or above 140°F (60°C) (Fig. 19-2). Foodborne microorganisms thrive in more moderate temperatures (60° to 110°F [16° to 43°C]). Some microorganisms can even grow in the refrigerator. Again, don't leave cooked or refrigerated foods, such as meats and salads, at room temperature for more than 2 hours (or 1 hour in hot weather) because that gives microorganisms an opportunity to grow. Store dry food at 60°F to 70°F (16°C to 21°C).
- Reheat leftovers to 165°F (74°C); reheat gravy to a rolling boil to kill *Clostridium perfringens* bacteria, which may be present. Merely reheating to a good eating temperature isn't enough to kill sufficient bacteria.

To reduce the risk of bacteria surviving during microwave cooking,

- Cover food with glass or ceramic when possible to decrease evaporation and heat the surface.
- Stir and rotate food at least once or twice for even cooking. Then, allow microwaved food to stand, covered, after cooking is completed to help cook the exterior and equalize the temperature throughout.
- Use an oven temperature probe or a meat thermometer to check that food is done. Insert it at several spots.
- If thawing meat in the microwave, use the oven's defrost setting. Ice crystals in frozen foods are not heated well by the microwave oven and can create cold spots, which later cook more slowly.

Figure 19-2 The effects of temperature on microorganisms that cause foodborne illness.

Adapted from *Temperature Guide to Food Safety: Food and Home Notes*, No. 25, Washington, DC, June 20, 1977, USDA.

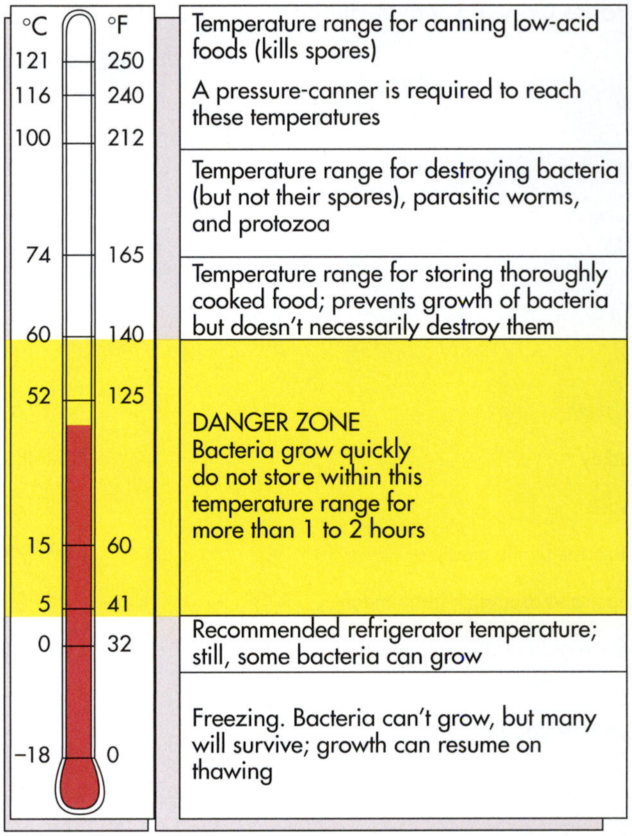
°C
°F
121
250
116
240
100
212
74
165
60
140
52
125
15
60
5
41
0
32
−18
0
Temperature range for canning low-acid foods (kills spores)
A pressure-canner is required to reach these temperatures
Temperature range for destroying bacteria (but not their spores), parasitic worms, and protozoa
Temperature range for storing thoroughly cooked food; prevents growth of bacteria but doesn't necessarily destroy them
DANGER ZONE
Bacteria grow quickly do not store within this temperature range for more than 1 to 2 hours
Recommended refrigerator temperature; still, some bacteria can grow
Freezing. Bacteria can't grow, but many will survive; growth can resume on thawing

- Store peeled or cut-up produce, such as melon balls, in the refrigerator.
- Make sure the refrigerator stays below 41°F (5°C). Using a refrigerator thermometer is the safest way to ensure foods are cold, rather than relying on how cold your cans of soda or cartons of milk feel.

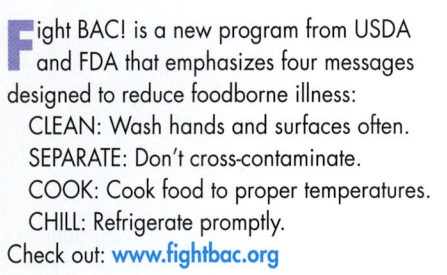

Fight BAC! is a new program from USDA and FDA that emphasizes four messages designed to reduce foodborne illness:

CLEAN: Wash hands and surfaces often.
SEPARATE: Don't cross-contaminate.
COOK: Cook food to proper temperatures.
CHILL: Refrigerate promptly.

Check out: www.fightbac.org

Food safety logo of USDA.

Microorganisms that cause foodborne illness commonly enter food through cross-contamination—from one source to another—and grow in temperatures favorable to them, as occurred at a large gathering where turkey franks were contaminated with bacteria. When the franks were later added to a salad, it too became contaminated, causing foodborne illness. Potential sources of cross-contamination are unsanitized work areas and dirty kitchen towels and sponges. It's essential to practice sanitary food-handling procedures when preparing any food.

As one final precaution, watch for safe food-handling techniques when you eat out. Check that foods in a salad bar are iced; custard and pudding pies are chilled; hot foods served on a hot food bar are, in fact, hot; and vending machines are checked regularly, especially those containing sandwiches and milk. Send back any meat, poultry, seafood, or fish that does not appear thoroughly cooked. Food stored and served in dormitory cafeterias should also be properly handled.

Concept | Check

Bacteria and the toxins they produce pose the greatest risk for foodborne illness. In the past, the addition to foods of sugar and salt, as well as smoking and drying, were used to prevent the growth of microorganisms. Today, we know that ensuring cleanliness, keeping hot foods hot and cold foods cold, and cooking foods thoroughly offer additional protection from foodborne illness. Commercial processes, such as pasteurization and irradiation, do the same. Treat all raw animal products, cooked food, and raw fruits and vegetables as potential sources of foodborne illness.

A Closer Look at the Primary Microorganisms That Cause Foodborne Illness

As previously mentioned, bacteria pose a significant risk for foodborne illness. Bacteria are extremely simple structures. They contain only one chromosome and lack mitochondria, endoplasmic reticulum, golgi body, and lysosomes. Many bacteria are enclosed in a carbohydrate-like capsule, which protects them and aids their adherence to tissues. Some bacteria can survive harsh environmental conditions through spore formation. In the spore state, bacteria can remain stable for months or years.

Certain bacteria can thrive in almost freezing temperatures, whereas others thrive in very high temperatures. The optimum temperature for most disease-causing bacteria is about 98°F (body temperature; 37°C). Bacteria living in the presence of oxygen are called *aerobes,* whereas those living in the absence of oxygen are called *anaerobes.* Those that prefer free oxygen but can live in its absence are called *facultative anaerobes.* Many bacteria produce toxins.

Finding the specific agent that has led to a foodborne illness requires some detective skills. Identifying the agent depends on knowing the food source, the incubation time for and types of symptoms, and the duration of the illness associated with an outbreak.[12] Let's look at the characteristics of the major contaminants individually. An informative website on the topic is www.ama-assn.org/foodborne.

Cook hamburgers to an internal temperature of 160°F (72°C). At this temperature they are brown throughout, the juices run clear, and the inside is hot.

Campylobacter jejuni (C. jejuni)

In recent years, *Campylobacter* has jumped to the top of the list as the number one cause of all domestic bacterial foodborne illnesses, resulting in up to 4 million human infections a year in the United States alone. The bacteria produce a toxin that destroys the mucosal surfaces of the small and large intestines.

Because *C. jejuni* is so difficult to detect in foods, an enormous number of cases of this foodborne illness probably go unreported in this country. Also, most infections are very sporadic and are not associated with a large outbreak, as are other foodborne infections, such as *E. coli* and *Salmonella.* In a study conducted by USDA, more than 90% of the poultry tested was positive for *Campylobacter.*

Symptoms of the illness are acute intestinal inflammation with fever, muscle pain, headache, and diarrhea. During the peak of the disease, 10 or more bowel movements per day are common, and stools are often bloody. Cases are associated with contaminated water, raw or inadequately cooked animal foods, including beef and unpasteurized milk. Poultry, especially chicken, is of most concern. Because this organism grows slowly, the onset of symptoms is delayed, occurring 2 to 5 days after ingesting the contaminated food; it may even take weeks. Older adults, children, and people with weakened immune systems are at particularly high risk.

Treatment uses antibiotic medication, with most people recovering in less than 1 week. Deaths are rare. However, the number of *Campylobacter* infections that are resistant to a class of antibiotics called fluoroquinolones have been on the rise. Antibiotic use in the U.S. poultry industry in fact is the main contributor to this antibiotic resistance. This creates a problem when physicians attempt to treat this foodborne illness, since those people infected with the resistant strains are more likely to have severe infections and bloody diarrhea and to be hospitalized. Also, the bacterium is recognized as a major contributing factor to Guillain-Barré syndrome, which is the most common cause of acute paralysis in both children and adults.

A goal of *Healthy People 2010* is to reduce the number of cases of foodborne illness from *Campylobacter, E. coli, Listeria,* and *Salmonella* by 50%.

Luckily, *Campylobacter* organisms are very sensitive to heat. This trait probably protects most people from infections. Prompt refrigeration, thorough cooking, avoidance of cross-contamination, thorough handwashing, and careful refrigeration of leftovers are important ways to prevent its growth.

Salmonella

There are 2000 strains of *Salmonella* bacteria, many of which cause foodborne illness. *Salmonella* can be killed by normal cooking. Nonetheless, they are responsible for many cases of foodborne illness, up to 23,000 per year in the United States alone, many of which go unreported. Related deaths average 33 per year.

Commonly found in animal and human feces, these bacteria enter food via infected water, contaminated cutting boards, contaminated meat products, cracked eggs, and actual bits of feces in food. Ingesting the live bacteria causes the problem. Recent outbreaks of salmonellosis have been traced back to alfalfa sprouts. It is thought that the seeds of these sprouts were contaminated by bird or rodent feces. According to FDA, children, older adults, and persons with weakened immune systems should not eat any raw sprouts, such as alfalfa, mung bean, clover, and radish. Feces from pet reptiles are also sources of *Salmonella* exposure. Infants and young children are at high risk for salmonellosis from indirect or direct contact with reptiles.

FDA warns us not to consume homemade ice cream, eggnog, and mayonnaise if made with unpasteurized, raw eggs because of the risk of *Salmonella* foodborne illness. Use instead eggs or egg products that have been pasteurized, which kills *Salmonella* bacteria.

Symptoms of *Salmonella* infections include nausea, fever, headache, abdominal cramps, diarrhea, and vomiting, which can develop in 24 to 72 hours. Bed rest and fluids are the only effective treatment, and recovery usually occurs within 2 to 3 days. Deaths are rare. *Salmonella* attacks occur most frequently from consuming eggs, chicken, meat, meat products, custard made with infected eggs, raw milk, and inadequately refrigerated and reheated leftovers. Unpasteurized orange juice and milk may also be contaminated with *Salmonella*.[7] Raw chicken is often contaminated, and undercooked food—including eggs—poses a particular risk. Recently a warning label has been added to egg cartons in an attempt to prevent the up to 66,000 illnesses and 40 deaths per year from eggs contaminated with *Salmonella* inside the shell. The new warning label provides instructions for safe handling to help prevent foodborne illness (see margin).[7]

SAFE HANDLING INSTRUCTIONS:
To prevent illness from bacteria: keep eggs refrigerated, cook eggs until yolks are firm, and cook foods containing eggs thoroughly.

Current safe handling instructions for eggs.

Most outbreaks of *Salmonella* infection can be traced to improper food handling. Picnics pose a special challenge, because food is frequently held for hours at a dangerously high temperature (between 41°F and 140°F or 5°C and 60°C). It takes only about 8 hours for *Salmonella* bacteria to multiply sufficiently to cause illness. Therefore, keep foods above 140°F (60°C) or below 41°F (5°C) to help prevent the growth of *Salmonella* bacteria.

Salmonella also poses a great risk for cross-contamination of foods. To avoid cross-contamination, keep produce, cooked foods, and ready-to-eat foods separate from uncooked meats and raw eggs. Thoroughly clean hands, cutting boards, counters, knives, and other utensils after handling uncooked foods, as well as in-between use.

Shigella sonnei (S. sonnei)

Foodborne illness caused by the *Shigella* bacterium is a common disease of youngsters in day-care centers, nurseries, and custodial institutions. The infection is transmitted by the fecal-oral route, primarily by way of the hands, as well as via food and water. The onset of symptoms usually occurs within 1 to 3 days of being infected. The symptoms include abdominal cramps, diarrhea, fever, and bloody stools. Some carriers of *Shigella* display no symptoms but represent a potential threat to all who come in contact with them. With as little as 10 organisms able to cause an infection, person-to-person transmission is easily accomplished where hygienic conditions are compromised.

Although reported infrequently, *Shigella* outbreaks have been associated with raw produce, including green onions, crisphead lettuce, and uncooked, raw parsley. Recent outbreaks have been traced back to raw, chopped parsley, which had been cut and stored at room temperature. To avoid contamination from parsley, food handlers should store chopped parsley for short times, keeping it refrigerated, and chop smaller batches. Handwashing and sanitary food production offer the best protection against *Shigella* infections.

Escherichia coli (E. coli)

Escherichia coli (E. coli) is commonly found in the intestinal tract of humans and other animals. Although there are hundreds of benign strains of the bacteria, 0157:H7 and 0111:H8 are especially virulent and cause severe illness. According to the U.S. Centers for Disease Control and Prevention, these *E. coli* bacteria, which are most commonly found in ground beef, kill about 60 people each year and cause illness in an estimated 73,000 more. They are quickly becoming a major threat for foodborne illness, with up to 4% of raw meat products in the United States possibly containing such bacteria. Recently 19 million pounds of ground beef patties were recalled due to possible *E. coli* 0157:47 contamination.

Children and older adults are most susceptible to the disease. The bacterium is transmitted primarily via contaminated ground beef and roast beef. In response, as previously mentioned, FDA has approved the irradiation of meat to reduce this risk. Although ground beef is the most common source of the *E. coli* bacteria, fruits, vegetables, and drinking water also can harbor the deadly pathogen. Unpasteurized milk, untreated apple cider, salad greens grown in cow manure, cantaloupe, dry-cured salami (because it is not cooked during processing), and many types of sprouts have also been implicated in *E. coli* infections. In one case, fresh apple juice was contaminated with *E. coli* because the apples used to produce the juice had fallen to the ground and had come into contact with animal feces. New methods for apple juice production are being researched; pasteurization is becoming routine.[7]

After an incubation period of 1 to 8 days, the disease normally lasts 4 to 10 days. The symptoms include severe abdominal cramps, bloody diarrhea, and hemolytic uremic syndrome, a condition that can lead to kidney failure. *E. coli* infection should be investigated as a possible cause in any case of bloody diarrhea.

Cooking with a meat thermometer and then avoiding recontamination are important ways to prevent this type of foodborne illness. Cider that is not pasteurized or that does not contain preservatives can be heated to a slow simmer until steam rises from the pan before serving or refrigerating to reduce risk.

Clostridium perfringens (C. perfringens)

The bacterium *Clostridium perfringens* lives throughout the environment, especially in soil, the intestines of farm animals and humans, and sewage. It is called the "cafeteria germ," because most foodborne outbreaks caused by this organism are associated with the food service industry or with events where large quantities of food are prepared and served. The symptoms of an infection resemble those of *Salmonella* cases, but the victim usually doesn't vomit. The symptoms occur within 8 to 24 hours of consuming enough live bacteria. Again, bed rest and fluids are the only effective treatment, and recovery usually occurs within a day or so.

C. perfringens thrives in an oxygen-free environment. It forms heat-resistant spores, which become bacteria at temperatures between 70°F and 120°F (21°C and 49°C), and at the same time produces a toxin. The bacteria then can quickly multiply to disease-causing numbers. Foods stored in deep refrigerator pans are especially fertile media for the growth of these bacteria because the centers are isolated from air and they stay warm.

C. perfringens organisms are often found in cooked beef, turkey, gravy, dressing, stews, and casseroles. The best way to prevent their growth is to maintain proper holding temperatures and divide large leftover portions into smaller ones. Be especially careful to cook meats completely and cool them rapidly in small containers. Thoroughly reheat leftover meat to 165°F (74°C) before serving. Always bring leftover gravy to a rolling boil. Refrigerate cold cuts and sliced meats below 41°F or 5°C, and serve them cold.

Critical | Thinking

Diana had a party at her house for her son's birthday. While cleaning up after the kids had gone home, she realized she had forgotten to put away the potato salad and coleslaw and decided to discard it. However, her husband, Tim, wanted her to just refrigerate it. "After all," he reasoned, "it was only left out for a couple of hours." Why was Diana right in wanting to throw away the leftover unrefrigerated food?

Listeria monocytogenes (L. monocytogenes)

Listeria monocytogenes is widely distributed in the environment and often enters food from contamination with animal or human feces. It is a very hardy microorganism, which resists heat, salt, and acidity much better than many other bacteria. This bacterium survives and even grows at refrigeration temperatures. Because pasteurization destroys *Listeria* organisms, reports of contaminated milk and cheese products suggest that contamination occurred following pasteurization, probably from the addition of unpasteurized milk. Listeriosis in the United States is estimated to kill 500 people a

In a recent period of 6 months, more than 45 million pounds of hot dogs, luncheon meats, and other ready-to-eat meat products were recalled due to contamination with potentially deadly *Listeria* bacteria.

A new tool in the battle against foodborne illness is HACCP, or Hazard Analysis and Critical Control Point. This was discussed in the Expert Opinion by Dr. Medeiros. As was noted, HACCP is a method of ensuring food safety. Rather than treating the cause after a foodborne illness outbreak has occurred, by applying the principles of HACCP, food handlers critically analyze how they approach food preparation and what conditions may exist that might allow pathogenic microorganisms to enter the food system. Once specific hazards and critical control points (where potential problems can occur) are identified, preventive measures can be used to reduce specific sources of contamination. Thus, the food handlers are using HACCP to stop a problem before it starts.

year and causes illness in 2000 more, which means that listeriosis kills 20% of the people it infects.

Listeria infections cause initial symptoms of fever, headache, and vomiting about 9 to 48 hours after exposure. However, newborn infants, pregnant women, and people with depressed immune function may suffer severe symptoms, including meningitis, spontaneous abortion, serious blood infections, and death. It is especially important that pregnant women and other people at high risk avoid products such as unpasteurized or expired milk, uncooked hot dogs, undercooked chicken, fresh paté or meat spreads (canned are fine), Mexican soft cheeses (e.g., queso fresco), and other soft cheeses such as feta, brie, Camembert, and blue-veined cheeses, all of which are suspected of being major sources of *Listeria* infection. USDA also warns pregnant women and other people at high risk to thoroughly cook all ready-to-eat meats, including hot dogs and cold cuts, until they are steaming.

Consuming only pasteurized milk products; cooking meat, poultry, and seafood thoroughly; keeping food refrigerated; and washing fresh produce thoroughly are ways to avoid *Listeria* infection.

Staphylococcus aureus (S. aureus)

The organism *Staphylococcus aureus (S. aureus)* produces toxins as it grows in food. Once ingested, the toxin causes nausea, vomiting, diarrhea, headache, and abdominal cramps. The symptoms usually develop within 2 to 6 hours of eating the contaminated food. People seldom die from the toxin, but they don't develop immunity against future attacks. And, as is true for almost all foodborne illnesses, continued unsafe food handling will result in repeated sickness. Bed rest and fluids are generally the only treatment needed. Recovery usually takes place within 2 to 3 days.

S. aureus bacteria live mainly in the nasal passages and skin sores. These microorganisms enter food when people sneeze and cough over food or handle food while they have open skin sores. Once present in significant numbers in a food, *S. aureus* can make enough toxin to cause human illness in about 4 hours if the food temperature stays near 100°F (38°C). The toxin is undetectable by flavor, odor, and appearance and can even withstand prolonged cooking.

Foods commonly associated with *S. aureus* intoxications are custard, ham, egg salad, cheese, seafood, cream-filled pastries, and milk. A frequent source is whipped cream left standing for hours at room temperature. Keeping these and other foods above 140°F (60°C) or below 41°F (5°C) prevents both the bacteria's growth and further toxin production. To limit the spread of this microorganism, it's important to work with clean hands, working surfaces, and utensils; to direct coughs and sneezes away from food; and to cover skin cuts on hands and arms when handling food.

Clostridium botulinum (C. botulinum)

The *Clostridium botulinum* bacterium can cause botulism, a foodborne illness that can be fatal. This microorganism comes from soil and may exist as a bacterium or spore in any food. As these bacteria multiply in food, they release a deadly toxin. The death rate for botulism receives much public attention; however, only a few cases are reported each year in North America. At one time, botulism was a serious problem in the canning industry, but now adequate heat processing and intact containers have virtually eliminated this danger from North American manufactured canned foods.

The symptoms of botulism appear within 12 to 72 hours of ingesting contaminated food. The toxin blocks acetylcholine release at neuromuscular junctions, causing vomiting, abdominal pain, double vision, dizziness, and acute respiratory failure. The prompt administration of the botulism antitoxin can help prevent the progression of paralysis and reduce the duration of the illness. Sometimes treatment requires intensive care, including mechanical ventilation. The combination of the antitoxin and supportive care has reduced mortality to less than 10%. If the person survives, recovery occurs within 10 days.

C. botulinum grows only in the absence of air, so it thrives primarily in canned food, especially improperly home-canned, low-acid foods, such as string beans, corn, mushrooms, beets, and asparagus. Recently, other foods with oxygen-deprived centers—such as potato salad, sautéed onions, stew, and chopped garlic—have also caused botulism. FDA now requires that chopped garlic in oil be acidified to protect against *C. botulinum*. Consumers should look for a commercially prepared product that contains phosphoric or citric acid. Cured meats also pose a risk for botulism; however, the nitrates and vitamin C used to preserve commercial products inhibit bacterial growth. Botulism has also occurred among Alaskan natives, who commonly consume uncooked, fermented fish.

Home-canned foods are the most common sources of botulism. Although the canning process may kill all bacteria and the heat may drive out all oxygen, spores of *C. botulinum* can still survive if the heating is insufficient. When the can or jar cools, the spores germinate into bacteria, which produce the toxin. Even foods that were previously thought to be safe due to their acidity, such as tomatoes, require greater care, as new varieties tend to have a higher pH. To ensure the safety of home-canned foods, it is crucial to follow the canning directions exactly. To be safe, always check all cans carefully, even those from commercial facilities. Look for holes, rust on the seams, and swollen sides or tops. Make sure the can sucks in air when opened to indicate the vacuum was maintained, and the liquid inside is clear, not milky or foul-smelling. If you see any signs of spoilage, return the can to the store or take it to the nearest public health department. Whatever you do, do not taste the food. One green bean can contain enough toxin to kill you. For questions on proper canning techniques, call the Ball Consumer Hotline at 1-800-240-3340.

Inspect cans for bulges and foul-smelling liquid before use to reduce risk for botulism.

Botulism also may develop in vivo (inside the living body). Infants between 2 and 9 months of age are at the highest risk because of low stomach acid production. About 250 cases are reported each year. Fortunately, the death rate is low, 1 to 2%. Adults with low stomach acid production are also at risk. Bacteria spores germinate in the stomach and produce the exotoxin. For this reason, honey should not be given to young infants because it can contain the spores of this *C. botulinum*.

Viruses

Viruses do not metabolize, grow, or move by themselves. Instead, they reproduce within a living host cell, and, thus, cannot grow in food once it is harvested or slaughtered. Viruses consist of a protein coat surrounding a nucleic acid core of either DNA or RNA. They have no cell wall. On entering a host cell, a virus takes over the cell's DNA replication processes and causes it to reproduce the virus's genetic material. Generally, the host cell dies in the process and bursts open, releasing new viruses into the surrounding medium. Many viruses cause disease in humans. And, because viruses cannot multiply in foods, they must enter in sufficient amounts through bits of feces that contaminate food.

First noted in Norwalk, Ohio, in 1968, the Norwalk virus is a little known but leading cause of stomach and intestinal distress caused by a virus. Norwalk viral infections usually cause nausea, vomiting, diarrhea, weakness, abdominal pain, loss of appetite, headache, and fever about 24 to 48 hours after exposure. The virus is found in water and foods, and shellfish and salads are most often implicated. Cooking destroys the virus. Norwalk viruses are probably responsible for about 30 to 40% of all cases of viral intestinal infection in adults, and, as noted in the introduction, are the leading cause of foodborne illness in general. The infection is typically found in nursing homes and hospitals, restaurants, cruise ships, and events with catered meals. The virus persists because it can survive chlorination and because a low amount of the virus can cause illness. The virus is of most concern for infants, young children, older adults, and people with chronic illnesses. There is no specific treatment.

Hepatitis A is a well-known form of foodborne illness caused by a virus, although this route accounts for only a small percentage of the total number of hepatitis A infections. As a foodborne agent it most often thrives because of unsanitary food handling

Recovery from hepatitis A generally occurs of its own accord in 3 to 6 months. This foodborne illness constitutes the only exception to the rule of immunity, as it is the only one in which those infected with the virus are then immune for the rest of their lives.

Rotaviruses are another important cause of diarrhea, mainly in children, leading to about 55,000 hospitalizations per year in the United States. Symptoms appear in 1 to 7 days. Day-care centers are common sites for infections. Thorough, regular handwashing is a necessary practice at these sites, particularly after diaper changing.

Grill pork to an internal temperature of 160°F (72°C) to eliminate the risk of trichinosis.

by carriers of the virus in restaurants. People have also contracted hepatitis A infections from eating raw or undercooked shellfish—clams, oysters, and mussels—harvested from waters contaminated with raw or improperly treated sewage. The virus that causes hepatitis A can endure notable heat, cold, and drying. Cooking foods at 212°F (100°C) for more than 5 minutes inactivates the virus, as does irradiation.

Symptoms of the infection include intestinal problems, weakness, fatigue, jaundice, and sometimes even the development of serious liver disease, requiring hospitalization. Because the symptoms of hepatitis A infection do not usually occur until about 15 to 50 days after eating contaminated food, the source is difficult to identify. It is diagnosed by detection of hepatitis A antibodies. About 30,000 cases are reported annually in the United States.

Raw clams and oysters are particularly risky foods because they are filter feeders, a process that concentrates viruses and toxins present in the water as it is filtered for food. Consumption of these raw shellfish results in the consumption of live viruses and bacteria, too. It is important to buy oysters and clams only from the most reliable sources. By law, shellfish offered for sale must come from licensed beds, but often they do not, so be careful when you either purchase these foods or harvest them yourself. Check with the local health department if you question the safety of waters in an area.

Proper handwashing by food service personnel is especially important in restaurants, day-care centers, hospitals, and other institutions to lessen hepatitis outbreaks. The chlorination of drinking water is a reliable means of destroying the virus.

Parasites

Parasites that enter the body through the intestinal tract include some single-celled protozoans, flukes, nematodes, roundworms, and tapeworms. Although not common in North America, the parasite most apt to be in the food supply is *Trichinella spiralis.* This tiny organism may be present in raw and undercooked pork and pork products, such as sausage. Trichinosis is rare today, probably because people realize that pork must be cooked thoroughly to kill the nematode worm that causes it and modern sanitary feeding practices have reduced *Trichinella* in hogs. About 20 cases of trichinosis per year are reported in the United States. However, other cases may be unreported. In addition to pork, bear meat and other raw meats are potential sources. It is seldom found in commercial meat.

Trichinosis begins with the consumption of meat containing the **larvae.** The larvae are released during digestion in the small intestine. Within 2 days, the larvae develop into adult nematodes. New larvae are then produced and move into the blood via the intestinal mucosa. The blood carries the larvae to muscle fibers, where they become resident.

larva An early developmental stage in the life history of some organisms, such as parasites.

In early stages, trichinosis is difficult to diagnose. The symptoms in mild cases develop over weeks to months and are usually thought to be flu. If enough larvae are present, muscle weakness, fever, and fluid retention in the face may eventually result. Thoroughly cooking meat, especially pork, destroys the larvae.

Fungi

mycotoxins Toxic compounds produced by molds, such as aflatoxin B-1, found on moldy grains.

Fungi are mostly multicellular organisms. Those of concern in food safety do not infect people, but some mushrooms are intrinsically toxic, and molds growing on foods may produce toxins called **mycotoxins.**[5] Fungi possess cell walls, a nucleus, and a nuclear membrane. They live on dead or decaying organic matter, living together with other organisms either in mutual advantage or as parasites. Fungi can grow as single cells, like yeasts, or as multicellular filamentous colonies, as with molds. They cannot synthesize their own food; rather, they digest their food outside their cell walls and absorb the simpler organic substances for use within the cell.

Most fungi are molds that consist of long, branched threads called *hyphae*. Hyphae form a tangled mass of filaments called *mycelium*. The mold often seen on bread consists of this mycelia.

Fungi require moisture to grow and can obtain water from the medium on which they live or from the atmosphere. When the atmosphere becomes dry, they can go into a resting state or form spores. They can live in a pH range of 2 to 9 and can grow in concentrated salt and sugar solutions. They thrive over a wide temperature range, even in the refrigerator. As spores, fungi can be scattered by the wind or carried by animals. When an airborne spore lands on an appropriate target, such as a ripe peach, the spore germinates and begins to grow, producing the typical mold observed on spoiled fruit.

The best-known mycotoxins are the aflatoxins, substances believed to cause liver cancer. Aflatoxin B-1 causes cancer in animals; thus, human exposure is regulated by FDA. The foods most often contaminated with aflatoxins are tree nuts (e.g., walnuts and pecans), peanuts, corn, wheat, and oil seeds, such as cottonseed. FDA considers aflatoxins unavoidable contaminants on foods and therefore has set practical limits for aflatoxins in food and animal feed. Aflatoxins are also present in certain water supply sources, such as pond and ditch water. Some people in China use this type of water for cooking, and they experience a high incidence of liver cancer.

Cooking and freezing halt fungal growth but do not eliminate mycotoxins already produced. Thus, moldy food should not be eaten, or at least not without discarding the moldy portion and much of the surrounding area. Again, when in doubt, throw the food out. Mold growth is prevented by properly storing perishable foods at cold temperatures and using them before evidence of mold growth appears.

Prions

Mad cow disease, or bovine spongiform encephalopathy, is likely caused by an infectious protein, called a prion, that kills by creating voids in the brain. The human condition, a variant of Creutzfeldt-Jakob disease, causes a form of dementia, which has killed about 100 people in Europe who apparently ate contaminated beef. Because of the recent evidence of mad cow disease in Europe, the U.S. government has worked diligently to make sure the cattle here are not exposed. The U.S. government has taken steps to ban beef from Europe since the late 1980s. As a precaution, however, FDA also has implemented a ban on the recycling of animal tissue from ruminant animals (e.g., cows, goats, sheep) for animal feed. These are suspected carriers of the prion.[2]

Concept | Check

Thoroughly cook all meat, poultry, and fish and other seafood to reduce the risk of foodborne illness from the Norwalk virus and the bacteria *Campylobacter* and *Salmonella*. In addition, always separate raw meats and poultry products from cooked foods. To prevent foodborne intoxication from *Staphylococcus* organisms, cover cuts on hands and avoid sneezing on foods. To avoid intoxication from *Clostridium perfringens,* rapidly cool leftover foods and thoroughly reheat them. To avoid intoxication from *Clostridium botulinum,* carefully examine canned foods. Overall, don't allow cooked food to stand for more than 1 to 2 hours at room temperature. For other causes of foodborne illness, precautions already mentioned generally apply as well. In addition, consume only pasteurized dairy products and wash all fruits and vegetables; and thoroughly wash your hands with soap and water before and after preparing food and after using the bathroom.

Case Scenario | Follow-up

Aaron likely contracted *Clostridium perfringens,* based on the fact that he had diarrhea but did not vomit, and the symptoms occurred about 8 hours after consuming the contaminated food. Spores of *Clostridium perfringens* are typically present in meat. Thorough cooking will kill any of the live bacteria present, but the product still may contain spores. These can later germinate if the product is kept in a warm setting for a few hours. The Argentine beef likely contained spores of *Clostridium perfringens,* and these germinated and produced a toxin as the product sat in the car and on the buffet table. Ideally, this product should have remained at room temperature for no longer than 1 hour, as the party took place in the summertime. Thus, soon after Aaron and his wife took it out of the oven, it should have been separated into a few smaller pans for speed cooling and then refrigerated. This is because they knew it was not going to be served within 1 hour. Before leaving, they could have recombined the dish into one clean pan. Once they arrived at the party, it should have been refrigerated again, and then thoroughly reheated when it was time to eat. Overall, it is risky to leave perishable items such as meat, fish, poultry, eggs, and dairy products at room temperature for more than 1 to 2 hours.

When buying food products, especially perishables, check the product date for safety. Four types of dates are commonly used. The pack date is the day the product was manufactured. The pull or sell date indicates the last date the product should be sold. It allows some time for storing food at home before eating. Check the expiration date of foods stored at home, because that is the last date the food can safely be consumed. Last, baked goods may have a freshness date, indicating that the product may safely be eaten for a short time after the date but may not taste the same.

Food Additives

By the time you see a food on the market shelf, it usually contains substances added to make it more palatable or to increase its nutrient content or shelf life. Manufacturers also add some substances to foods to make them easier to process. Other substances may have accidentally found their way into the foods you buy. All these extraneous substances are known as *additives,* and, although some may be beneficial, others may be harmful for some people, such as sulfites. All purposefully added substances must be evaluated by FDA.[6]

Why Are Food Additives Used?

Most additives are used to limit food spoilage. Food additives such as potassium sorbate are used to maintain the safety and acceptability of foods by retarding the growth of microorganisms implicated in foodborne illness.

Additives are also used to combat some enzymes that lead to undesirable changes in color and flavor in foods but don't cause anything as serious as foodborne illness. This second type of food spoilage occurs when enzymes in a food react to oxygen—for example, when apple and peach slices darken or turn rust color as they are exposed to air. Antioxidants are a type of preservative that slow the action of oxygen-requiring enzymes on food surfaces. These preservatives are not necessarily novel chemicals. They include vitamins E and C and a variety of sulfites.

Without the use of some food additives, it would be impossible to produce massive quantities of foods and safely distribute them nationwide or worldwide, as is now done. Despite consumer concerns about the safety of food additives, many have been extensively studied and proved safe when FDA guidelines for their use are followed.

Intentional Versus Incidental Food Additives

Food additives are classified into two types: **intentional food additives** (directly added to foods) and **incidental food additives** (indirectly added as contaminants). Both types of agents are regulated by FDA. Currently, more than 2800 substances are intentionally added to foods. As many as 10,000 other substances enter foods as contaminants. This includes substances that may reasonably be expected to enter food through surface contact with processing equipment or packaging materials.

intentional food additives Additives knowingly (directly) incorporated into food products by manufacturers.

incidental food additives Additives that appear in food products indirectly, from environmental contamination of food ingredients or during the manufacturing process.

The GRAS List

In 1958, all food additives used in the United States and considered safe at that time were put on a **generally recognized as safe (GRAS)** list. Congress established the GRAS list because it believed manufacturers did not need to prove the safety of substances that were already generally regarded as safe by knowledgeable scientists. Since that time, FDA has been responsible for proving that a substance does not belong on the GRAS list.

generally recognized as safe (GRAS) A list of food additives that in 1958 were considered safe for consumption. Manufacturers were allowed to continue to use these additives, without special clearance, when needed for food products. FDA bears responsibility for proving they are not safe but can remove unsafe products from the list.

Since 1958, some substances on the list have been reviewed. A few, such as cyclamates, failed the review process and were removed from the list. The additive red dye #3 was banned because it is linked to cancer. Many chemicals on the GRAS list have not yet been rigorously tested, primarily because of expense. These chemicals have received a low priority for testing, mostly because they have long histories of use without evidence of toxicity or because their chemical forms do not suggest they are potential health hazards.

Are Synthetic Compounds Always Harmful?

Nothing about a natural product makes it inherently safer than a synthetic product. Many synthetic products are simply laboratory copies of chemicals that also occur in nature (see the discussion in Chapter 20 on biotechnology for some examples). Moreover, although human endeavors contribute some toxins to foods, such as synthetic pesticides and industrial chemicals, nature's poisons are often even more potent and prevalent. Some cancer researchers suggest that we ingest at least 10,000 times more (by weight) natural toxins produced by plants than we do synthetic pesticide residues. This comparison doesn't make synthetic chemicals any less toxic, but it does lend perspective.

Consider vitamin E, which is often added to food to prevent rancidity of fats. This chemical is safe when used within certain limits. However, high doses have been associated with health problems, such as interfering with vitamin K activity in the body (review Chapter 9). Thus, even well-known chemicals we are comfortable using can be toxic in some circumstances and at some concentrations.

Some important definitions:

toxicology	The scientific study of harmful substances
safety	The relative certainty that a substance won't cause injury
hazard	The chance that injury will result from use of a substance
toxicity	The capacity of a substance to produce injury or illness at some dosage

Tests of Food Additives for Safety

Food additives are tested under FDA scrutiny for safety on at least two animal species, usually rats and mice. Scientists determine the highest dose of the additive that produces *no observable effects* in the animals. These doses are proportionately much higher than humans are ever exposed to. The maximum dosage is then divided by at least 100 to establish a margin of safety for human use. The rationale for reducing the **no-observable-effect level (NOEL)** by a 100-fold margin is that we assume humans are at least 10 times more sensitive to food additives than are laboratory animals and that any one person might be 10 times more sensitive than another. This very broad margin essentially ensures that the food additive in question will cause no harmful health effects in humans. In fact, many synthetic chemicals are probably less dangerous at these low doses than the natural compounds in foods, such as in apples or celery.

no-observable-effects level (NOEL) The highest dose of an additive that produces no deleterious health effects in animals.

Note that this 100-fold margin of safety is over 25 times that for vitamin A, when you compare the RDA with a potentially toxic dose for pregnant women.

One important exception applies to the schema for testing intentional food additives: If an additive is shown to cause cancer, even though only in very high doses, no margin of safety is allowed. The food additive cannot be used, because it would violate the **Delaney Clause** in the 1958 Food Additive Amendments. This clause prohibits intentionally adding to foods a compound that was introduced after 1958 and causes cancer. Evidence for cancer could come from either laboratory animal or human studies. Very few exceptions to this clause are allowed; the few are discussed in the following section on curing and pickling agents.

Incidental food additives are still another matter altogether. FDA cannot simply ban various industrial chemicals, pesticide residues, and mold toxins from foods, even though some of these contaminants can cause cancer. These products are not purposely added to foods. FDA sets an acceptable level for these substances. Basically, an incidental substance found in a food cannot contribute to more than one cancer case during the lifetimes of 1 million people. If a higher risk exists, the amount of the compound in a food must be reduced until the guideline is met.

Delaney Clause A clause to the 1958 Food Additives Amendment of the Pure Food and Drug Act in the United States that prevents the intentional (direct) addition to foods of a compound that has been shown to cause cancer in laboratory animals or humans.

Approval for a New Food Additive

Today, before a new food additive can be added to foods, FDA must approve its use. Besides rigorously testing an additive to establish its safety margins, manufacturers must give FDA information that (1) identifies the new additive, (2) gives its chemical composition,

Sugar, salt, corn syrup, and citric acid constitute 98% of all additives (by weight) used in food processing.

Table 19-4 Food Additive Categories

Anticaking agents Antimicrobial agents Antioxidants Color and adjuncts Conditioners Curing and pickling agents Dough strengtheners Drying agents Emulsifiers Enzymes Firming agents Flavor enhancers Flavoring agents	Flour treating agents Formulation aids: carriers, binders, fillers, plasticizers Fumigants Humectants Leavening Lubricants and release agents Nonnutritive sweeteners Nutritive sweeteners Oxidizing and reducing agents pH controllers	Processing aids: clarifying, clouding, catalyst, flocculants, filter aids, crystallization inhibitors Propellants Sequestrants Solvents and vehicles Stabilizers and thickeners Surface active agents Surface-finishing agents Synergists Texturizers

(3) states how it is manufactured, and (4) specifies the laboratory methods used to measure its presence in the food supply at the amount of intended use.

Manufacturers must also offer proof that the additive will accomplish its intended purpose in a food, that it is safe, and that it is to be used in no higher amount than needed. Additives cannot be used to hide defective food ingredients, such as rancid oils; to deceive customers; or to replace good manufacturing practices. A manufacturer must establish that the ingredient is necessary for producing a specific food product.

Common Food Additives

A list of food additive categories appears in Table 19-4. Some serve the general function of preservatives: acidic or alkaline agents, antioxidants, antimicrobial agents, curing and pickling agents, and **sequestrants.**[6] Let's look at some of the specific categories of additives to understand exactly why they are used and to learn more about the specific substances used.

sequestrants Compounds that bind free metal ions. By so doing, they reduce the ability of ions to cause rancidity in foods containing fat.

Acidic or Alkaline Agents

Acids, such as calcium lactate, have many uses in foods. As flavor-enhancing agents, they impart a tart taste to soft drinks, sherbets, and cheese spreads. As preservatives, they inhibit microbial growth. As antioxidants, they prevent discoloration and rancidity. They also adjust acid and base balance. Adding acids during food processing reduces the later risk of botulism from eating naturally low-acid vegetables, such as beets.

Alkaline products, such as sodium hydroxide, can alter the texture and flavor of foods, including chocolate. In processing, alkaline products are sometimes used to produce a milder flavor by neutralizing the acids produced during fermentation.

Soft drinks are typical sources of alternative sweeteners for many of us. Moderate use of these products generally poses no health risk for most people.

Alternative Sweeteners

Currently, saccharin (Sweet 'N Low®), sucralose (Splenda®), acesulfame potassium (Sunette®), and neotame are the only nonnutritive sweeteners used in foods. (Cyclamates is a nonnutritive sweetener available in Canada.) Because aspartame (Nutrasweet®) yields some energy, it is considered a nutritive sweetener. Recall from Chapter 5 that the moderate use of these alternative sweeteners is considered safe.

Anticaking Agents

By absorbing moisture, compounds such as calcium silicate, ammonium citrate, magnesium stearate, and silicon dioxide keep table salt, baking powder, powdered sugar, and other powdered food products free flowing. These chemicals prevent the caking and lumping that would make powdered or crystalline products hard to use.

Antimicrobial Agents

Sodium benzoate, sorbic acid, and calcium propionate are common preservatives. Sorbic acid is a potent inhibitor of molds and fungal growth. Calcium propionate, a natural part of some cheeses, inhibits mold growth.

Antioxidants

This type of food preservative helps delay food discoloration from oxygen exposure, such as occurs when potatoes are diced. It also helps keep fats from turning rancid. Two widely used antioxidants are BHA (butylated hydroxyanisole) and BHT (butylated hydroxytoluene). Alpha-tocopherol (vitamin E), which occurs naturally in nuts, whole grains, and oils, may be added to foods to keep them from becoming rancid. Ascorbic acid (vitamin C), which is another antioxidant, helps maintain the red color of luncheon meats and other cured foods, and it prevents the formation of cancer-promoting nitrosamines. (Vitamin C is also added to such foods as fruit drinks in order to increase the vitamin content; it is also used as a marketing tool for these products.)

Sulfites, a group of sulfur-based chemicals, are widely used as antioxidants in foods. Some people (1 in 100, according to FDA estimates) are extremely sensitive to sulfites and may have difficulty breathing, wheeze, and vomit, as well as develop hives, diarrhea, abdominal pain, cramps, and dizziness. As a result, FDA now limits the use of sulfites on raw fruits and vegetables—an action directed mainly at salad bars. FDA also requires manufacturers to declare the presence of sulfites on the labels of packaged foods containing at least 10 parts per million (ppm) of sulfites. Labels on wine bottles often contain a sulfite warning.

Colors

Color additives don't improve nutritional qualities, but they can make foods more visually appealing. Food colorings cannot be used to deceive consumers—for example, by covering blemishes, concealing any inferiority, or misleading people in any way. Although colorings are arguably unnecessary additives, manufacturers have satisfied FDA that color is "necessary" for the production of certain foods.

Controversy has surrounded the use of some food colors. Currently, the safety of using tartrazine (FD&C yellow No. 5) is disputed. It has caused allergic symptoms—such as hives, itching, and nasal discharge—in sensitive individuals, especially in people allergic to aspirin. Although few of us are sensitive to tartrazine, FDA requires manufacturers to list FD&C yellow No. 5 on labels of food products containing it. Some red dyes have also raised alarms, and some have been banned. Currently, FDA requires manufacturers to list all forms of synthetic colors on the labels of foods that contain them. Pigments extracted from plant sources are exempted from specific description.

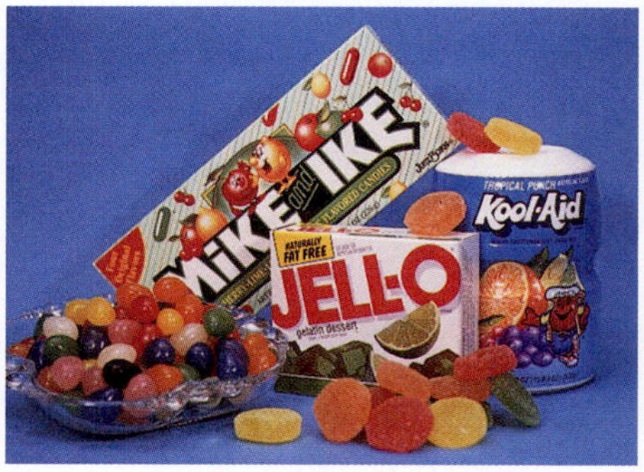

Color additives make some foods more desirable.

Curing and Pickling Agents

Nitrates and the related chemical group, nitrites, are used as preservatives, especially to prevent the growth of *Clostridium botulinum.* Sodium and potassium nitrates and nitrites are used to preserve meats such as bacon, ham, salami, and hot dogs. Nitrates and nitrites have been used for centuries, in conjunction with salt, to preserve meat. An added effect of nitrates is their reaction with pigments in meat to form a bright pink color. This gives ham, hot dogs, and other cured meats their characteristic appearance.

Nitrate and nitrite consumption from both cured foods and natural vegetables has been associated with the synthesis of nitrosamines in the stomach. Some nitrosamines are cancer-causing agents, particularly for the stomach and esophagus. The actual risk appears to be low, however, except for people who secrete little stomach acid (some older people, for example).

U.S. government agencies surmise that consumers take for granted a margin of microbial safety gained from nitrate and nitrite use in cured meats. People often serve these meats cold or at least underheated. Consequently, the government agencies have

You might wonder why, if nitrates and nitrites form chemical substances that can cause cancer, they aren't banned from use in meats by the Delaney Clause. In the United States, USDA regulates the use of chemicals in meats. The laws that govern USDA regulation of foods are different from those that govern FDA regulation. Because of this, the Delaney Clause does not apply to USDA actions. Currently, USDA sees no clear threat to public safety from the regulated use of nitrates and nitrites in meats, so no action has been taken. FDA also considers the risk of moderate use to be minimal.

Cured meats derive their pink color from nitrates and nitrites.

chosen not to ban nitrate or nitrite use in foods but, rather, to change manufacturing practices to lower amounts of preformed nitrosamines and suggest moderation in the use of these food products. Since 1975, there has been an 80% decrease in the amount of nitrites in cured meats.

The addition of vitamin C (sodium ascorbate) to cured meats, such as bacon, is one way to reduce the amount of nitrosamines formed in foods. This is a common manufacturing practice. Other antioxidants, such as sodium erythrobate, also inhibit the synthesis of nitrosamines.

Emulsifiers

By distributing and suspending fat in water, emulsifiers improve the uniformity, smoothness, and body of foods such as baked goods, ice cream, and candies. In mayonnaise, for example, egg yolks act as emulsifiers in suspending the acids, such as vinegar or lemon juice in the oil. Lecithin, derived from soybeans, acts as an emulsifier in chocolate and margarine. Monoglycerides and diglycerides are used as emulsifiers in cake mixes.

Fat Replacements

Fat replacements—such as Paselli SA2, Dur-Low, Oatrim, Sta-Slim 143 Stellar, and Z-trim—are being produced for commercial use. These carbohydrate-based products are an addition to other fat replacement products, such as Olean, discussed in Chapter 6.

Flavors and Flavoring Agents

Both naturally occurring and artificial agents can impart more flavor to foods. These agents include extracts from spices and herbs, as well as synthetic agents. You've probably recognized flavors of some spices and of liquid derivatives of onion, garlic, cloves, and peppermint in foods. To meet the demand of industry, manufacturers have developed synthetic flavors that not only taste like natural flavors but also have the advantage of stability. Often artificial flavors, such as butter and banana flavors, have the same chemical composition as the natural flavor.

Flavor Enhancers

Infants are more sensitive to MSG than adults, in part because infants have not yet developed a complete blood-brain barrier. This means they cannot fully exclude such substances as MSG from the brain.

Flavor enhancers are substances, such as monosodium glutamate (MSG), that help bring out the natural flavors of foods. Note that the glutamate portion is simply a nonessential amino acid. A small percentage of people are sensitive to the glutamate in MSG and, after exposure, experience flushing, chest pain, facial pressure, dizziness, sweating, rapid heart rate, nausea, vomiting, high blood pressure, and headache. MSG is often used in preparation of Chinese food. The onset of symptoms occurs about 10 to 20 minutes after ingestion and may last from 2 to 3 hours. People who find themselves sensitive to MSG should avoid it. It may be present alone (look for the word *glutamate*), as well as in any isolated protein source (caseinate, texturized vegetable protein, etc.), yeast extract, bouillon, soup stock, and seasonings. Tomatoes, mushrooms, and parmesan cheese are also sources of free glutamate. Fortunately, most of us find that moderate use of MSG or glutamate in foods poses no significant risk to our health.

Humectants

These chemicals—such as glycerol, propylene glycol, and sorbitol—are added to foods to help retain proper moisture, fresh flavor, and texture. They are often used in candies, shredded coconut, energy (sports) bars, and marshmallows.

Leavening Agents

Air and steam can be used to create a light texture in breads and cakes; however, carbon dioxide bubbles are much more reliable for this purpose. Common leavening agents that produce carbon dioxide gas include yeast, baking powder, and baking soda. Baking soda must react with acids to generate carbon dioxide. Baking powder can be used in either acid or alkaline conditions.

Maturing and Bleaching Agents

Such compounds as bromates, peroxides, and ammonium chloride hasten the natural aging and whitening processes of milled flour. This shortens the time needed for flour to become usable in baked products. Without these agents, freshly milled flour lacks the qualities necessary to make a stable, elastic dough and requires several months of aging to be useful in baking.

Nutrient Supplements

Vitamin and mineral supplements are added to foods to improve their nutritional quality. Sometimes they replace nutrients lost in processing, as occurs when enriching flour. Vitamin A is added to margarine and some forms of milk and yogurt. Vitamin D is added to some dairy products. Potassium iodide is added to salt, and calcium and folic acid are added to some flours, fruit juices, and other products. Ready-to-eat breakfast cereals often contain a variety of added nutrients.

Stabilizers and Thickeners

Stabilizers and thickeners impart a smooth texture and uniform color and flavor to candies, ice creams and other frozen desserts, chocolate milk, and artificially sweetened beverages. Commonly used substances are pectins, vegetable gums (such as guar gum and carrageenan), gelatins, and agars. They work by absorbing water. Without stabilizers and thickeners, ice crystals form in ice cream and other frozen desserts, and particles of chocolate separate from chocolate milk. Stabilizers are also used to prevent the evaporation and deterioration of flavorings used in cakes, puddings, and gelatin mixes.

If you are bewildered or concerned about all the additives creeping into your diet, you can easily avoid most of them by emphasizing unprocessed whole foods (Fig. 19-3). However, no evidence shows that this will necessarily make you healthier. It amounts to a personal decision. Do you have confidence that FDA and food manufacturers are adequately protecting your health and welfare, or do you want to take more personal control by minimizing your intake of compounds not naturally found in foods?

Sequestrants

Sequestrants include EDTA and citric acid. They bind many free chemical ions and, by doing so, help preserve food quality by reducing the ability of ions to cause rancidity in products containing fat.

(a) (b)

Figure 19-3 Depending on food choices, a diet can be either (*a*) essentially devoid of, or (*b*) high in food additives.

Critical | Thinking

Recognizing that Joseph is taking a nutrition class, his roommate asks him, "What is more risky: the bacteria that can be present in food or the additives listed on the label of my favorite snack cake?" How should Joseph respond? On what information should he base his conclusions?

Conclusion

In general, if you consume a variety of foods in moderation, the chances of food additives jeopardizing your health are minimal.[6] Pay attention to your body. If you suspect an intolerance or a sensitivity, consult your physician for further evaluation. Remember that, in the short run, you are more likely to suffer either from foodborne illness due to poor food-handling practices that allow bacteria to grow in food, or from the consumption of raw animal foods containing certain bacteria or viruses, than from consuming additives. Excess energy, saturated fat, cholesterol, salt, and other potential "problem" nutrients in our diets pose the greatest long-term risk.

Concept | Check

Food additives are used to reduce spoilage from microbial growth, oxygen, metals, and other compounds. Additives are also used to adjust pH, improve flavor and color, leaven, provide nutritional fortification, thicken, and emulsify food components. Additives are classified as intentional (direct), which are purposely added to foods, and incidental (indirect), which turn up in foods from environmental contamination or various manufacturing practices. The amount of an additive allowed in a food is limited to one-one-hundredth of the highest amount that has no observable effect when fed to animals. The Delaney Clause allows FDA to limit intentional addition of cancer-causing compounds to food under its jurisdiction. Also limited by law are the permissible amounts of carcinogens that incidentally enter foods.

Substances That Occur Naturally in Foods and Can Cause Illness

Foods contain a variety of naturally occurring substances that can cause illness. Here are some of the more important examples:[10]

Safrole—found in sassafras, mace, and nutmeg; causes cancer

Solanine—found in potato shoots and green spots on potato skins; inhibits the action of neurotransmitters

Mushroom toxins—found in some species of mushrooms such as aminita; can cause stomach upset, dizziness, hallucinations, and other neurological symptoms. The more lethal varieties can cause liver and kidney failure, coma, and even death. FDA regulates commercially grown and harvested mushrooms. These are cultivated in concrete buildings or caves. However, there are no systematic controls on individual gatherers harvesting wild species, except in Michigan and Illinois.

Avidin—found in raw egg whites; binds the vitamin biotin in a way that prevents its absorption, and so a biotin deficiency can develop

Thiaminase—found in raw fish, clams, and mussels; destroys the vitamin thiamin

Tetrodotoxin—found in puffer fish; causes respiratory paralysis

Oxalic acid—found in spinach, strawberries, sesame seeds, and other foods; binds calcium and iron in the foods, and so limits absorption of these minerals

Herbal teas—containing senna or comfrey; can cause diarrhea and liver damage

When hunting wild mushrooms, know what you are looking for. Many varieties contain deadly toxins.

People have coexisted for centuries with these naturally occurring substances and have learned to avoid some of them and limit intake of others. Today, they pose little health risk. Farmers know potatoes must be stored in the dark, so that solanine won't be synthesized. Furthermore, we've developed cooking and food-preparation methods to limit the potency of other substances, such as thiaminase. Spices are used in such small amounts that health risks don't result. Nevertheless, it's important to understand that some potentially harmful chemicals in foods occur naturally.

Environmental Contaminants in Foods

A variety of environmental contaminants can be found in foods. Table 19-5 in the Nutrition Perspective lists ways to limit pesticide residues in the diet. Aside from pesticide residues and products of fungal growth, though, other important contaminants deserve attention.

Lead

Ingesting lead can cause anemia, kidney disease, and damage to the nervous system, which can interfere with nerve impulse conduction. Because lead has a high atomic weight, it is a heavy metal. Many heavy metals are toxic at low doses.

Lead toxicity is a particular problem for children because it is associated with IQ deficits, behavior disorders, slowed growth, impaired hearing, and possibly hypertension and kidney disease later in life.[15] The precise mechanism by which lead affects the brain is not clear; however, because lead is chemically similar to calcium, it can disrupt brain mechanisms that depend on calcium. In addition, lead competes for absorption with iron, which means less oxygen could be carried to the brain. Despite the reduction of lead exposure in children over the past 20 years associated with the decline in leaded gasoline and lead solder used in homes and in the canning industry, approximately 1.7 million children have elevated blood lead. Nearly 900,000 of all children affected are under the age of 6, which is when the brain and central nervous system are most vulnerable. Medical costs for a child with lead intoxication average $2500 per treatment, and most children require two or more treatments.

An adequate calcium intake helps reduce risk of lead poisoning. Of course, milk is one rich source of calcium.

Exposed children who eat a high-fat diet low in calcium and low in iron absorb more lead than do those who eat a more healthful diet. For children with elevated lead levels, federal experts suggest nutritional and educational intervention, the location of the source of lead (and removal), and medical treatment.

Low-income African American children who reside disproportionately in inner cities are at an especially increased risk of harmful lead exposure because of the lead-based paint present on the interiors and exteriors of older buildings. As this paint flakes off walls or is abraded from window trim as windows are opened and closed, lead paint chips enter the environment and may be ingested. Regular home cleaning can be a particularly effective way of removing contaminated household dust for those who, unfortunately, are unable to move to lead-free housing.

Approximately 90 to 95% of adult lead exposures occur in the work environment. Occupations that are linked to high blood lead in workers include radiator repair, battery manufacture and recycling, smelting, and construction or remodeling involving lead-based paint.

Other sources of lead include brass fittings on water pumps used in wells, imported wine from areas where leaded gasoline is still used (especially Eastern Europe), and lead caps on wine bottles in general. Wiping the neck of the bottle with a towel limits this type of exposure. An additional risk is posed by acidic products, such as fruit juice, sauerkraut, and pickled vegetables stored in galvanized, tin, or other metal containers (except stainless steel). Acid can dissolve the metal, and any lead present can then leach into the food product. Foods packaged in ceramic jars from Mexico, some household candlewicks, and certain herbal remedies—such as Koo Soo pills, used to relieve menstrual cramping—have also been associated with lead poisoning. Because of this hazard, lead is no longer used on commercially produced dishes in the United States. However, there is no way to ensure the safety of homemade or imported pottery items, such as those from Mexico. Be sure not to use antiques or collectibles, including any made of leaded glass, for food or beverage storage.

Acrylamide is a potential neurotoxin and carcinogen found in deep-fried carbohydrate-rich foods. Acrylamide is a known carcinogen for laboratory animals; however, no studies have been conducted to determine the relationship between acrylamide ingestion and the development of cancer in humans. The average amount of acrylamide consumed by adults is about 70 μg/day. This is above the highest amount recommended in drinking water by the World Health Organization's Guideline Values for Drinking Water Quality, yet significantly below that which is associated with toxicity in laboratory animals. While researchers learn more about the relationship between acrylamide in the food supply and human health, you can act now to lower your intake of acrylamide by consuming fewer fried foods cooked at high temperatures for extended periods of time, such as french fries and potato chips.[13]

Lead can leach from solder joints into copper pipes, so it is important to let tap water run a minute or so before drinking it or cooking with it, especially first thing in the morning or when the water has been off for a few hours. Use only cold water for drinking, cooking, and preparing infant formula, as hot water causes greater leaching of lead from solder and pipes than cold water. Lead in drinking water makes up about 20% of the average person's total lead exposure. Laboratories certified by Environmental Protection Agency (EPA) can test drinking water for lead content for about $20 to $50. Softening drinking water is also not advised, because soft water can leach lead from pipes.

Some signs of lead poisoning include tiredness, irritability, muscle and joint pain, headaches, stomach aches and cramps, changes in behavior, and changes in school performance. If you suspect that someone you know has lead poisoning, contact your physician or the local health department. For more information, visit www.epa.gov/lead or call the National Lead Information Center and Clearinghouse at 1-800-424-LEAD.

Dioxin

Dioxin is a chemical that contains chlorine and benzene. It can be created by incinerating chlorine-based material, such as plastics, together with hydrocarbon-based material, such as paper. Dioxins are potent animal toxicants with the potential to produce adverse effects on reproduction and development, suppression of the immune system, and cancer.[4] Since dioxin causes cancer and other harmful effects in animals, even in small doses, it probably does so in humans as well, such as breast cancer. EPA characterizes most dioxins as likely human carcinogens. Besides trash-burning incinerators, other sources of dioxin are bottom-feeding fish from the Great Lakes—an area with a great deal of industrial activity and chemical production. Dioxin exposures also include small amounts from breathing air containing trace amounts of particles and in vapor form, from the inadvertent ingestion of soil containing dioxin, and from absorption through the skin contacting air, soil, or water containing small amounts.

For a typical person, dioxin exposure can also occur in the diet through the intake of animal fats. EPA presumes that most dioxin exposure that occurs through the diet is due to dioxin in the environment, which accumulates in the tissues of animals. This dioxin exposure from food is a problem primarily for people who frequently consume fish caught locally. People who eat commercial fish normally eat a variety, and even people who stick to one type of fish don't usually have a problem because fish in interstate commerce generally come from different waters, only a few of which may contain dioxin.

Mercury

FDA first limited mercury, another heavy metal, in foods in 1969, after 120 people in Japan became ill from eating fish contaminated with high amounts. Birth defects in the offspring of some of those people were also blamed on the mercury exposure. The fish most often contaminated is swordfish. Shark may also contain large amounts. Such large predatory fish that live for a long time can accumulate large amounts of mercury. Currently, these species are tested more frequently to ensure that the commercial supply is safe. FDA scientists responsible for seafood agree that these fish are safe for most people, provided they are eaten infrequently (no more than once a week). Since mercury is a neurotoxin, it slows fetal and child development and causes irreversible deficits in brain function. Therefore, pregnant women and women of childbearing age who may become pregnant are advised by FDA not to eat shark, swordfish, king mackerel, and tilefish. Note that other types of fish and seafood, especially smaller, younger varieties, generally contain little mercury.[7] Canned tuna consumption also should be limited to twice a week, though it is much lower in mercury than the other fish listed.

Urethane in Some Alcoholic Beverages

Urethane forms during the fermentation of alcoholic beverages. If the fermented product is heated, as in the production of sherry and bourbon, urethane concentration increases. Although urethane causes cancer in laboratory animals, it's unclear whether it causes cancer in humans. FDA research on urethane in food products is now a high priority. A prudent choice might be to limit the consumption of products such as fruit brandies and sake because these consistently show large amounts of urethane.

Polychlorinated Biphenyls (PCBs)

PCBs were widely used for years in a variety of industrial products; however, because they are linked to liver tumors and reproductive problems in animals, they are no longer produced. FDA has banned their use in machinery associated with food and animal feed since 1977 and has established limits for PCBs in susceptible foods and in paper used for food-packaging material. The most significant food source of PCB residues is fish, primarily freshwater fish, such as coho and chinook salmon from the Great Lakes, and bottom-feeding freshwater species from waters in other industrial areas, such as the Hudson River Valley in New York. Again, a key guideline for fish consumption is variety and moderation when local sources have the potential for contamination.

Genetic alteration of foods such as corn and soybeans has recently created concern, especially in Europe. FDA considers genetically altered products safe if approval for human use has been granted (see Chapter 20 for details).

Protection from Environmental Toxins in Foods

Environmental toxins that cause disease can be present in foods. To reduce exposure, find out which foods pose a risk. In addition, emphasize variety and moderation in food selection. The presence of mercury in swordfish or shark may concern you, but it's normally not a health risk unless your diet is dominated by these fish. The small amount of mercury in most swordfish or shark isn't harmful for most of us if we are exposed to it infrequently. Note also that tips provided in Table 19-6 in the Nutrition Perspective for reducing pesticide exposure also apply to reducing exposure to environmental contaminants.

Concept | Check

A general program to minimize exposure to environmental contaminants includes knowing which foods pose greater risks and consuming a wide variety of foods in moderation.

Summary

1. Bacteria and other microorganisms in food pose the greatest risk for foodborne illness. In the past, salt, sugar, smoke, fermentation, and drying were used to protect against foodborne illness. Today, careful cooking, pasteurization, and keeping hot foods hot and cold foods cold provide additional insurance.
2. Major causes of foodborne illness are the Norwalk virus and the bacteria *Campylobacter jejuni, Salmonella, Shigella, Staphylococcus aureus,* and *Clostridium perfringens.* In addition, such bacteria as *Clostridium botulinum, Listeria monocytogenes, Yersinia enterocolitica,* and *Escherichia coli* have been found to cause illness.
3. To protect against bacteria, cook susceptible foods thoroughly. In addition, cover cuts on the hands, do not sneeze or cough on foods, avoid contact between raw meat or poultry products and other food products, rapidly cool and thoroughly reheat leftovers, and use only pasteurized dairy products.
4. Cross-contamination commonly causes foodborne illness. It occurs particularly when bacteria on raw animal products contact foods that can support bacterial growth. Because of the risk of cross-contamination, no perishable food should be kept at room temperature for more than 1 to 2 hours (depending on the environmental temperature), especially if it may have come in contact with raw animal products.
5. Treatment for foodborne illness usually includes drinking lots of fluids, avoiding touching food while diarrhea is present, washing

hands thoroughly, and getting bed rest. Botulism, hepatitis A infections, and trichinosis are types of foodborne illness that require prompt medical attention.

6. Food additives are used primarily to extend shelf life by preventing microbial growth and the destruction of food components by oxygen, metals, and other substances. Food additives are classified as those intentionally added to foods and those that incidentally appear in foods. An intentional additive is limited to no more than one-one-hundredth of the greatest amount that causes no observed symptoms in animals. The Delaney Clause allows FDA to ban the use of any intentional food additive under its jurisdiction that causes cancer.

7. Antioxidants, such as BHA, BHT, vitamins E and C, and sulfites, prevent oxygen and enzyme destruction of food products. Emulsifiers suspend fat in water, improving the uniformity, smoothness, and body of foods such as ice cream. Common preservatives include sodium benzoate and sorbic acid, which prevent bacterial growth. Sequestrants bind metals and thus prevent spoilage of food from metal contamination.

8. Toxic substances occur naturally in a variety of foods, such as green potatoes, raw fish, mushrooms, raw soybeans, and raw egg whites. Cooking foods limits their toxic effects in some cases; others are best to avoid, such as toxic mushroom species and the green parts of potatoes.

9. A variety of environmental contaminants can be found in foods. It is helpful to know which foods pose risks and act accordingly to reduce exposure.

Study Questions

1. Identify three major classes of microorganisms that are responsible for foodborne illness.

2. Which kinds of foods are most likely to be involved in foodborne illness? Why are they targets for contamination?

3. What three trends in food purchasing and production have led to a greater number of cases of foodborne illness in recent years?

4. Why is thoroughly cooking food an important practice for reducing the risk of foodborne illness?

5. List four techniques other than thorough cooking that are important in preventing foodborne illness.

6. Define the term *food additive,* and give examples of four intentional food additives. What are their specific functions in foods? What is their relationship to the GRAS list?

7. Describe the federal process that governs the use of food additives, including the Delaney Clause.

8. Put into perspective the benefits and risks of using additives in food. Point out an easy way to reduce the consumption of food additives. Do you think this is worth the effort in terms of maintaining health? Why or why not?

9. Describe four recommendations for reducing the risk of toxicity from environmental contaminants.

10. Read the Nutrition Perspective before answering the following question: How do various federal agencies work together to maintain the safety of food?

Annotated References

1. ADA Reports: Position of the American Dietetic Association: Food irradiation. *Journal of the American Dietetic Association* 100:246, 2000.

   It is the position of ADA that food irradiation enhances the safety and quality of the food supply and helps protect consumers from foodborne illness. ADA encourages qualified professionals to work together to educate consumers about this additional food safety tool.

2. Bren L: Trying to keep mad cow disease out of U.S. herds. *FDA Consumer,* p. 12, March–April 2001.

   No cases of mad cow disease in humans has been identified in the United States. FDA and USDA are aggressively enforcing regulations to minimize the risk on the introduction of mad cow disease into U.S. herds.

3. Carpy SA and others: Health risk of low-dose pesticide mixtures: A review of the 1985-1998 literature on combination toxicology and health risk assessment. *Journal of Toxicology and Environmental Health. Part B, Critical Reviews* 3:1, 2000.

   Despite some exceptions, it has been demonstrated that interaction between various pesticide residues is not a common event at low levels of human exposure, such as those that may arise from food or drinking water. As a general rule, exposure to a mixture of pesticides at low doses of the individual constituents does not represent a potential source of concern to human health.

4. Dioxin more toxic than earlier estimates; spectrum of adverse effects found by EPA. *CNI Nutrition Week,* p. 4, June 30, 2000.

   Dioxins are potent animal toxicants with the potential to produce a broad spectrum of harmful effects in humans, including adverse effects on reproduction and development, suppression of the immune system, chloracne (a severe, acnelike condition), and cancer. EPA has characterized the most toxic dioxin, TCDD, as a human carcinogen. Other dioxins are classified as likely human carcinogens, based on the evidence of animal and human studies.

5. Etzel RA: Mycotoxins. *Journal of the American Medical Association* 287:425, 2002.

   Aflatoxins are one of the many toxic products produced by fungi. This and other mycotoxins may have developed to serve as a chemical defense against insects and grazing animals. Aflatoxins are common contaminants in peanuts, soybeans, and grains, especially in tropical areas of the world. Large amounts can cause acute toxic effects, while small amounts over time can cause liver cancer.

6. Food additives—what you need to know. *UC Berkeley Wellness Letter,* p. 4, June 2002.

   Food additives for the most part are a valuable part of our food supply in that they keep foods from spoiling, thus reducing food prices and also foodborne illness. The main problem with food additives is that the foods that have the most are heavily processed foods, high in saturated fat and sodium, and not very nutritious. The article goes on to describe current uses and risks of common food additives.

7. Formanek R: Highlights of FDA food safety efforts: Fruit juice, mercury in fish. *FDA Consumer,* p. 15, March-April 2001.

   Two of the latest food-related concerns of FDA are insuring that juice processors either pasteurize their juices or take other steps to reduce the risk of foodborne illness, and recommending pregnant women avoid fish known to typically contain mercury, such as shark, swordfish, king mackerel, and tile fish. Young children and breastfeeding women should also avoid these fish species. Safe handling instructions added to egg cartons are a further innovation to protect against foodborne illness.

8. Formanek R: Food for thought. *FDA Consumer,* p. 13, September–October 2001.

   North Americans enjoy one of the safest food supplies in the world. Despite this fact, diseases caused by food are responsible for an estimated 76 million cases of GI tract illnesses and 5000 deaths per year in the United States alone. Therefore, vigilance against foodborne illness should be an important consideration for everyone. The main consumer messages are: keep hands and cooking surfaces clean, cook food to proper temperatures, refrigerate food promptly, and separate food to avoid cross-contamination.

9. Gorbach SL: Antimicrobial use in animal feed—time to stop. *The New England Journal of Medicine* 345:1202, 2001.

   Antimicrobial agents are commonly given to food animals to treat or prevent infections, and in the absence of disease, in order to promote growth and enhance feed efficiency. Such antimicrobial agents should only be used when indicated in an individual infected animal, as current widespread use is leading to drug resistance in certain microorganisms.

10. Kline DA: Naturally occurring food contaminants. *Today's Dietitian,* p. 10, December 2001.

    A variety of naturally occurring toxins are present in our food supply. The mycotoxins from mold are common, as well as a variety of toxins present in mushrooms. The article discusses these and other naturally occurring toxins, and provides advice for minimizing such exposure.

11. Medeiros LC and others: Identification and classification of consumer food-handling behaviors for food safety education. *Journal of the American Dietetic Association* 101:1326, 2001.

    Foodborne illness is a major cause of economic burden, human suffering, and death in the United States. Each year more than 1 in 4 people in the United States become infected with some form of foodborne illness. Some new recommendations for preventing foodborne illness are heating lunch meat steaming hot to 165°F before eating if one is pregnant, immunocompromised, or of advanced age. Avoiding raw sprouts is also important.

12. Neill M: Foodborne illness and food safety. In Bowman BA, Russell RM (eds.): *Present knowledge in nutrition.* 8th ed. Washington, DC: ISLI Press, 2001.

    This is a detailed chapter on the various organisms that cause foodborne illness. The content supports the major points made in this chapter regarding such diseases.

13. Raloff J: Cooking up a carcinogen. *Science News* 162:120, 2002.

    Acrylamide forms to a variable degree during prolonged frying of high carbohydrate foods. This is another reason to limit fried snack and other foods, such as potato chips and french fries, but no reason to avoid these foods altogether.

14. *Residue monitoring 1999.* Washington, DC: Food and Drug Administration Pesticide Program, Food and Drug Administration, 1999.

    Based on FDA's Total Diet Study comprising 3500 different foods purchased from stores throughout the United States, only 0.8% of foods had pesticide residues exceeding EPA allowances. For imported products, 3.5% had pesticide residues exceeding EPA allowances. Otherwise, pesticide residues were either undetectable (about 60% of the time) or within allowable amounts for over 99% of domestic products and about 97% of imported products.

15. Rosen JF, Mushak P: Primary prevention of childhood lead poisoning—the only solution. *The New England Journal of Medicine* 344:1470, 2001.

    Lead poisoning can cause permanent brain damage even at low exposures. This then leads to reduced academic achievement and attention span. Medical therapies are available to reduce the lead burden in children, but it is much better to reduce exposure in the first place.

16. Safe food 2000 quiz. *Nutrition Action Healthletter,* p. 10, November 2000.

    About half of all foodborne illness cases occur because of practices in the home. This quiz challenges you to discover unsafe food practices in your daily life, such as whether it is safe to eat raw hot dogs.

17. Schardt D: Food poisoning's long shadow. *Nutrition Action Healthletter* 29(4):1, 2002.

    For some individuals foodborne illness can lead to life-long altering diseases, such as permanent effects on kidneys and the nervous system. The article discusses such potential problems and reviews the typical recommendations for preventing foodborne illness, such as cooking foods to recommended temperatures.

18. Woteki CE and others: Keep food safe to eat: Healthful food must be safe as well as nutritious. *Journal of Nutrition* 131:502S, 2001.

    Food safety education is a critical part of the overall strategy to reduce the incidence of foodborne illness. New technologies such as radiation are important risk management strategies. Inclusion of food safety in the Dietary Guidelines for Americans should go a long way toward ensuring that the public is aware of the importance of this issue.

Take | Action

I. Can You Spot the Improper Food Safety Practices?

In this chapter, you learned the following facts: (1) foodborne illness strikes about 76 million of us each year; (2) about 5000 deaths each year are caused by foodborne organisms.

Carefully preparing foods to prevent foodborne illness can minimize its occurrence for most of us. Read the following excerpt and find the food safety violations that could lead to illness.

A Local Health Department Inspector Gives the Following Account of His Visit to a Local Diner

As I walked through the kitchen of the Morningside Diner, I noticed that all food handlers washed their hands thoroughly with hot, soapy water before handling the food, especially after handling raw meat, fish, poultry, or eggs. Before preparing raw foods, they also thoroughly washed the cutting boards, dishes, and other equipment. As they used their cutting boards after cutting foods, they wiped them with a damp rag and used them again to cut more food.

When preparing fresh fruits and vegetables, they washed them but were careful to leave a little dirt on for fear of washing important nutrients from the outside. The cooks generally cooked meats to an internal temperature of 180°F (82°C). However, to preserve the flavor, pork was cooked to an internal temperature of 140°F (60°C). Some cooked foods to be served later were cooled to below 41°F (5°C) within 2 hours, and foods such as beef stew were cooled in shallow pans.

The diner served canned foods, even when the cans were dented. When leftovers were reheated, they were raised to an internal temperature of 150°F (66°C) and served immediately. Food handlers took great care to remove moldy portions of food. The cooks prepared stuffing separately from the poultry. The temperature of the refrigerators was approximately 45°F (7°C).

1. List the violations of food safety practices that could contribute to foodborne illness.

2. If you were writing a report describing ways to correct these practices, what would you say?

II. Take a Closer Look at Food Additives.

Evaluate a food label of a convenience food item either in the supermarket or one you have available.

1. Write out the list of ingredients.

2. Identify the ingredients that you think may be food additives.

3. Based on the information available in this chapter, what are the functions of these food additives?

4. How might this food product differ without these ingredients?

Nutrition | Perspective

Pesticides in Food

Pesticides used in food production produce both beneficial and unwanted effects. Most health authorities believe that the benefits greatly outweigh the risks. Pesticides help ensure a safe and adequate food supply and help make foods available at reasonable cost. However, sentiment is growing nationwide that pesticides pose avoidable health risks. Consumers have come to assume that synthetic is dangerous and organic is safe. Some researchers believe that this sentiment is grounded in fear and fueled by unbalanced reports.[3] Other researchers say concern about pesticides is valid and overdue.

Most concern about pesticide residues in food appropriately focuses on chronic rather than acute toxicity because the amounts of residue present, if any, are extremely small. These low concentrations found in foods are not known to produce adverse effects in the short term, although harm has been caused by the high amounts that occasionally result from accidents or misuse. For humans, pesticides pose a danger mainly in their cumulative effects, so their threats to health are difficult to determine. However, growing evidence, including the problems of the contamination of underground water supplies and destruction of wildlife habitats, indicates that North Americans would likely be better off if we could reduce our use of pesticides.

One of the problems with pesticides is that they create new pests because they destroy the spiders, wasps, and predatory beetles that naturally keep most plantfeeding insect populations in check. The brown plant hopper, which recently plagued Indonesian rice fields, was not a serious problem before heavy pesticide use began in the early 1970s. In the United States, such major pests as spider mites and the cotton bollworm were merely nuisances until pesticides decimated their predators.

What Is a Pesticide?

Federal law defines a pesticide as any substance or mixture of substances intended to prevent, destroy, repel, or mitigate any pest. The built-in toxic properties of pesticides lead to the possibility that other, nontarget organisms, including humans, might also be harmed. The term *pesticide* tends to be used as a generic reference to many types of products, including insecticides, **herbicides,** fungicides, and rodenticides. A pesticide product may be chemical or bacterial, natural or synthetic. For agriculture, EPA allows about 10,000 pesticide uses, involving some 300 active ingredients. About 1.2 billion pounds of pesticides are used each year in the United States, much of which is applied to agricultural crops.

herbicide A compound that reduces the growth and reproduction of plants.

Once a pesticide is applied, it can turn up in a number of unintended and unwanted places. It may be carried in the air and dust by wind currents, remain in soil attached to soil particles, be taken up by organisms in the soil, decompose to other compounds, be taken up by plant roots, enter groundwater, or invade aquatic habitats. Each is a route to the food chain; some are more direct than others.

Why Use Pesticides?

In the United States alone, pests destroy nearly $20 billion of food crops yearly, despite extensive pesticide use. The primary reason for using pesticides is economic—the use of agricultural chemicals increases production and lowers the cost of food, at least in the short run. Many farmers believe they would have a tough time staying in business without pesticides. Quick and direct, pesticides help protect farmers from ruinous losses caused by a sudden pest outbreak.

Consumer demands also have changed over the years. At one time, we wouldn't have thought twice about buying an apple with a worm hole; we simply took it home, cut out the wormy part, and ate the apple. Today, consumers find worm holes less acceptable, so farmers rely more and more on pesticides to produce cosmetically attractive fruits and vegetables. On the practical side, pesticides can protect against the rotting and decay of fresh fruits and vegetables. This is helpful because our food distribution system doesn't usually permit consumer purchase within hours of harvest. Also, food grown without pesticides can contain naturally occurring organisms that produce carcinogens at concentrations far above current standards for pesticide residues. For example, fungicides help prevent the carcinogen aflatoxin (caused by growth of a fungus) from forming on some crops. Thus, although some pesticides may do little more than improve the appearance of food products, others help keep some foods fresher and safer to eat.

Pesticide use poses a risk-versus-benefit question. Each side has points that deserve to be considered. Rural communities, where exposure is more direct, experience the greatest short-term risk.

Regulation of Pesticides

The responsibility for ensuring that residues of pesticides in foods are below amounts that pose a danger to health is shared by FDA, EPA, and the Food Safety and Inspection Service of USDA in the United

Table 19-5 U.S. Agencies Responsible for Monitoring the Food Supply

Agency Name	Responsibilities	Methods	How to Contact
United States Department of Agriculture (USDA)	• Enforces wholesomeness and quality standards for grains and produce (while in the field), meat, poultry, milk, and eggs	• Inspection • Grading • "Safe Handling Label"	www.usda.gov/fsis or www.nal.usda.gov/fnic/foodborne/foodborn.htm or call 1-800-535-4555
Bureau of Alcohol, Tobacco, and Firearms (ATF)	• Enforces laws on alcoholic beverages	• Inspection	www.atf.treas.gov
Environmental Protection Agency (EPA)	• Regulates pesticides • Establishes water quality standards	• Approval required for all U.S. pesticides • Sets pesticide residue limits in food	www.epa.gov
Food and Drug Administration (FDA)	• Ensures safety and wholesomeness of all foods in interstate commerce (except meat and poultry) • Regulates seafood • Controls product labels	• Inspection • Food sample studies • Sets standards for specific foods	www.fda.gov or call 1-800-FDA-4010
Centers for Disease Control and Prevention (CDC)	• Promotes food safety	• Responds to emergencies concerning foodborne illness • Surveys and studies environmental health problems • Directs/enforces quarantines • National programs for prevention and control of foodborne and other diseases	www.cdc.gov
The National Marine Fisheries Service or NOAA Fisheries	• Domestic and international conservation and management of living marine resources	• Voluntary seafood inspection program • Can use mark to show federal inspection	www.nmfs.noaa.gov
State and local governments	• Milk safety • Monitors food industry within their borders	• Inspection of food-related establishments	Government pages of telephone book

Fruits and vegetables grown without use of pesticides are available, and may bear an "organic" label (see Table 2-11 in Chapter 2 for rules regarding the use of the term "organic" on food labels). These products generally are more expensive than those grown using pesticides. Consumers need to decide if the potential benefits of the products are worth the extra cost.

States. Table 19-5 lists the roles of various food protection agencies. FDA is responsible for enforcing pesticide tolerances in all foods except meat, poultry, and certain egg products, which are monitored by USDA. A newly proposed pesticide is exhaustively tested, perhaps over 10 years or more, before it is approved for use. EPA must decide both that the pesticide causes no unreasonable adverse effects in people and the environment and that benefits of use outweigh the risks of using it. However, there is concern about older chemicals registered before 1970, when less stringent testing conditions were permitted. EPA is now asking chemical companies to retest the old compounds using more rigorous tests. Unfortunately, inadequate funding at EPA has hampered the review of older pesticides. The slow pace of this retesting has angered the critics of pesticide use. When weighing whether to approve or cancel a pesticide, EPA considers how much more it would cost farmers to use an alternative pesticide or process and whether cancellation would decrease productivity. After determining the dollar cost to farmers, EPA then looks at costs to processors and consumers. Once a pesticide is approved for use, it must follow the margin of safety provisions required of food additives (see the section on testing food additives for safety).

How Safe Are Pesticides?

Dangers from exposure to pesticides through food depend on how potent the chemical toxin is, how concentrated it is in the food, how much and how frequently it's eaten, and the consumer's resistance or susceptibility to the substance. Pesticide use is clearly associated with declining water quality. Accumulating information also links pesticide use to increased cancer rates in farm communities. For rural counties in the United States, the incidence of lymph, genital, brain, and digestive tract cancers increases with higher-than-average pesticide use. Respiratory cancer cases increase with greater insecticide use. In tests using laboratory animals, scientists have found that some of the chemicals present in pesticide residues cause birth defects, sterility, tumors, organ damage, and injury to the central nervous system. Some pesticides persist in the environment for years.

Still, some researchers argue that the cancer risk from minimal pesticide residues is hundreds of times less than the risk from eating such common foods as peanut butter, brown mustard, and basil. Plants manufacture their own toxic substances to defend themselves against insects, birds, and grazing animals (including humans). When plants are stressed or damaged, they produce even more of these toxins. Because of this, many foods contain naturally occurring chemicals considered toxic, and some are even carcinogenic. Other scientists argue that, if natural carcinogens are already in the food supply, then we should reduce the number of added carcinogens whenever possible. In other words, we should do what we can to decrease the problem.

The Risks of Pesticides to Children

Any discussion of pesticides and associated health risks must focus on children. They are not simply small adults in a biological sense. Children face a higher risk from pesticide exposure than do adults for several reasons:

1. Their exposure is greater; children eat more food in proportion to their body weight than do adults.
2. Children consume more foods that are potential sources of pesticide residues than do adults. For example, they drink more fruit juice.
3. Exposure at an early age carries a greater risk than does exposure later in life; residues can accumulate to toxic amounts over a longer period. Also, cancer has more time to develop.
4. Physiological susceptibility to the effects of carcinogens and neurotoxins in pesticides may be greater; the cells in children are dividing rapidly, and the enzyme systems that detoxify chemicals are not fully developed.

Rinsing fruits and vegetables under running water is advised to reduce pesticide exposure.

Previous to 1996, EPA did not consider these factors in risk calculations. However, the Food Quality Protection Act now requires EPA to look at age-related consumption data for the approval of new pesticides. Although children are at greater risk from pesticides, the magnitude of that risk and how best to calculate it are open to debate. Overall, experts stress the value of including fruits and vegetables in children's diets and caution parents not to change their children's diets to avoid certain foods. Carefully washing fruits and vegetables and consuming a wide variety are sufficient recommendations. Peeling fruits and vegetables is another option. A final general precaution is to keep children away from lawns, gardens, and flower beds that have recently been treated with pesticides and herbicides.

Tests of the Amounts of Pesticides in Foods

FDA tests thousands of raw products each year for pesticide residues. (A pesticide is considered illegal in this case if it is not approved for use on the crop in question or if the amount used exceeds the allowed tolerance.) A 1999 FDA study showed no residues in about 60% of samples. Less than 1% of domestic and about 3% of import samples had residues that were over tolerance. The findings for 1999 continue to support previous FDA studies over the past 10 years that pesticide residues in food are generally well below EPA tolerances, and they confirm the safety of the food supply relative to pesticide residues.[14]

Residues sometimes appear on the wrong crops or in excessive amounts because of contamination from nearby farms via wind or water. When a problem is identified, FDA takes steps to make sure it's corrected and that the tainted food in question never reaches the consumer. However, of 600 pesticides available on international markets, many are not even detected by any of FDA's multiresidue tests. This has raised concern by pesticide critics with regard to imported foods. Better tests, which detect single residues, are less frequently used because of cost.

Table 19-6 What You Can Do to Reduce Dietary Exposure to Pesticides

FDA's sampling and testing show that pesticide residues in foods do not pose a health hazard. Nevertheless, if you want to reduce dietary exposure to pesticides, follow this advice from the Environmental Protection Agency:

- Thoroughly rinse and scrub (with a brush if possible) fruits and vegetables. Peel them, if appropriate—although some nutrients will be peeled away.
- Remove the outer leaves of leafy vegetables, such as lettuce and cabbage.
- Trim fat from meat, poultry, and fish, remove skin (which contains most of the fat) from poultry and fish, and discard fats and oils in broths and pan drippings. Residues of some pesticides in feed concentrate in the animals' fat.
- When fishing, throw back the big fish—the little ones have had less time to take up and concentrate pesticides and other harmful residues. In addition, pay attention to any warnings by local authorities (and the fishing license) about the high risk for contamination in specific waters or species of fish.

Adapted from Food and Drug Administration: Safety first: Protecting America's food supply, *FDA Consumer*, p. 26, November 1988.

FDA's yearly evaluation of a "market basket" of typical foods shows that pesticide content is minimal in most foods.

Personal Action

We often take risks in our own lives, but we prefer to have a choice in the matter after weighing the pros and cons. For instance, we can choose not to immunize a child, but we do so with the understanding that the child might get sick. We can also choose to risk cancer from smoking or to avoid that risk, or we can drive recklessly. In regard to pesticides in food, however, someone else is deciding what is acceptable and what is not. Our only choice is whether to buy or avoid pesticide-containing foods. In reality, it's almost impossible to avoid pesticides entirely, because even organic produce often contains traces of pesticides, probably as the result of cross-contamination from nearby farms.

Short-term studies of the effects of pesticides on laboratory animals cannot pinpoint long-term cancer risks precisely. It should be clearly understood, however, that the presence of minute traces of an environmental chemical in a food doesn't mean that any adverse effect will result from eating that food.

FDA and other scientific organizations believe that the hazards are comparatively low and in the short run are less than the hazards of foodborne illness created in our own kitchens. We can't avoid pesticide risks entirely, but we can limit exposure by following the advice in Table 19-6.

We can also encourage farmers to use fewer pesticides to reduce exposure to our foods and water supplies, but we'll have to settle for produce that isn't perfect in appearance. Are you concerned enough about pesticides on food to change your shopping habits or take more political action?

chapter 20

Undernutrition Throughout the World

Chapter | Outline

Case | Scenario

Jamal traveled during summer break with his church group to the Philippines. During their stay, they were to help build shelters for people in the village in which a storm had destroyed most of the housing a few weeks before. Jamal noticed that many of the children in the village were short, much shorter than the children in his neighborhood. Mothers in the village stated that their children often had diarrhea and were ill. Jamal also noticed that the children were not as lively as he would expect.

A Filipino nurse at the local health clinic pointed out that these children generally did not have enough to eat and that health problems were rampant. She hoped that the recent storm would spur the Philippine government to send supplies to the village, particularly food and medicines.

Should Jamal have been surprised by widespread disease and general listlessness of the children in the Philippine village? What nutrients are likely to be deficient in the diets of these children, in turn contributing to their poor health status?

Refresh | Your Memory

As you begin your study of world hunger in Chapter 20, you may want to review:

- The health effects of protein-energy malnutrition in Chapter 7.
- The role of vitamin A and rich food sources in Chapter 9.
- The roles of iron, zinc and iodide, and rich food sources in Chapter 12.
- The advantage of breastfeeding to infants in Chapter 16.
- Methods to monitor the adequacy of growth in Chapter 17.

Boost | Your Study

Check out the ***Perspectives in Nutrition: Online Learning Center*** www.mhhe.com/wardlawpers6 *for quizzes, flash cards, activities, and web links designed to further help you learn about issues surrounding world hunger.*

Chapter | Objectives

Chapter 20 is designed to allow you to:

1. Define and characterize the terms *hunger, malnutrition,* and *undernutrition.*
2. Evaluate the consequences of undernutrition during critical periods in a person's life.
3. Examine undernutrition in the United States and highlight several programs established to combat this problem.
4. Examine undernutrition in the developing world and evaluate the major obstacles that hinder a solution.
5. Outline some possible solutions to undernutrition in the developing world.
6. List the worldwide effects of AIDS.
7. Consider how biotechnology may help solve the food shortage/distribution problem in the developing world.

The images are both vivid and heartrending. Emaciated children with enormous eyes and stomachs, too weak to cry, stare at us from news photos and television screens. Of the nearly 12 million children under 5 who die each year in developing countries, 55% of the deaths are attributable to undernutrition.

Today, nearly one in six people worldwide is chronically undernourished—too hungry to lead a productive, active life. Over the past 10 years, this problem has become even worse. Throughout the world, the problems of poverty and undernutrition are widespread and growing.

The majority (two-thirds) of undernourished people live in Asia. However, the largest increases in numbers of chronically hungry people currently occur in eastern Africa, particularly in Ethiopia, Sudan, Rwanda, Burundi, Sierra Leone, Kenya, Somalia, and Tanzania. South American countries such as Argentina and Brazil are also experiencing such problems. Their eyes haunt us.[9]

This chapter examines the problem of undernutrition and the conditions that create it, as well as some possible solutions. If we are to eradicate undernutrition, we all have to understand the problem and assume responsibility for supplying some answers. It is important to recognize that many political leaders and citizens worldwide contribute directly and indirectly to the economic and social destruction that spawns hunger.

World Hunger: A Continuing Plague

In November 1974, the United Nations World Food Conference proclaimed its bold objective "that within a decade no child will go to bed hungry, that no family will fear for its next day's bread, and that no human being's future and capacities will be stunted by malnutrition." Today, this promise remains unfulfilled: Uncertainty regarding from where one's next meal will come remains a daily experience for one in seven people in the developing world (840 million to 1.1 billion) and one in ten households in the United States.

The famines that occurred in Ethiopia in the 1980s elicited widespread public support for immediate aid to the victims. Still, far from ending, hunger remains frequently in the news. The past 3 years of extended drought have once again left many people in Ethiopia and other African countries without crops, livestock, and food. Civil wars and droughts in many parts of the world have brought millions of people to the brink of starvation. About two-thirds of these people live in Africa. Relief aid has been arriving but often with too little, too late. The deadly combination of political corruption, administrative ineptness, war, and poor weather has also led to increasing hunger in Bangladesh, Afghanistan, Haiti, the Philippines, Indonesia, Guinea, North Korea, and Cambodia.[9]

We must face the reality that the United Nations' members have yet to meet their pledge to elevate 3 billion people (half of the world's population) out of abject poverty (living on less than $2 per day). We also have to consider that 45% of the world's income currently goes to the 12% of the world's people who live in the rich industrial nations such as the United States and Canada.

Every year crises that develop worldwide put many people at risk of undernutrition.

World Hunger Today

Let's begin our look at the problem of world hunger today by first defining some key terms.

Hunger is the physiological state that results when not enough food is eaten to meet energy needs. It also describes an uneasiness, a discomfort, a weakness, or a pain caused by lack of food. If hunger is not relieved, the resulting medical and social costs of undernutrition are high—preterm births and mental retardation, inadequate growth and development in childhood, poor school performance, decreased work output in adulthood, and chronic disease (Table 20-1). Although malnutrition does occur in the United States, it is not due to extreme poverty over a large section of the population. Instead, there are usually specific causes such as an eating disorder, alcoholism, problems in nursing home settings, or homelessness. There is also some degree of moderate malnutrition in some of the poorer segments of U.S. society. Fortunately, there are resources such as food banks and food stamps that are available to many such people, though sometimes there are bureaucratic problems in getting these resources to the people that need them. In addition, there is also a problem known as **food insecurity** that is used to categorize individuals who have anxiety about running out of food or running out of money to buy more food. In 2000, over 10% of households in the United States reported that they experienced food insecurity. Of these, 3% reported that they experienced hunger at least one time during that year.[10] Food insecurity is also a problem in Canada.

food insecurity A condition of anxiety regarding running out of either food or money to buy more food.

According to UNICEF (United Nations Children's Fund), the United States ranks eleventh out of sixteen industrialized countries for child poverty. Fortunately, the United States does have food assistance programs for low-income families, and most children in the United States are shielded from hunger. In 2000, less than 1% of households with children reported that their children had been hungry at some point during that year.

Malnutrition is a condition of impaired development or function caused by either a long-term deficiency or an excess in energy and/or nutrient intake, the latter representing the state of overnutrition described in Chapter 2. When food supplies are low

Table 20-1 The Realities of Undernutrition

• Nearly one in six people worldwide is chronically undernourished—too hungry to lead a productive, active life. This includes one-third of the world's children.
• About 55,000 people die of hunger each day—two-thirds of them children.
• At least 250,000–500,000 children are permanently blinded each year simply from lack of vitamin A. About 100 million to 140 million children are deficient in vitamin A.
• Residents in developed countries spend more money on pet food, perfumes, and cosmetics than it would take to provide basic education, water and sanitation, health care, and nutrition for all those now deprived of it.
• About 50 million people worldwide have developed brain damage from maternal iodide deficiency; currently, 2 billion people are at risk for iodide deficiency.
• Every day the world produces enough food to provide about 2400 kcal for each person, generally meeting average energy needs. A daily intake less than 2100 kcal would not likely sustain an older child or adult, depending on workload.
• Poor women in developing countries face a 50 to 200-fold increased risk of death in pregnancy, compared with women in North America.
• In many developing countries, life expectancy of the population is one-half to two-thirds of that in North America.
• Almost half of the world's people earn less than $200 a year—many use 80 to 90% of that income to obtain food. About $2000 to $3000 of income each year is needed for a person to reach the life expectancy seen in North America.
• Of the 6.2 billion people on earth, about 1 billion drink contaminated water. In India alone, 300,000 children die each year from drinking polluted water.
• About 2 billion people in the world live without proper sanitation, such as reliable toilet facilities.
• About 1 billion people in the world have iron deficiency.
• Developing countries have 95% of the over 42 million AIDS cases worldwide.
• Developing countries bear 93% of the world's disease burden but expend only 11% of the world's health-care resources.

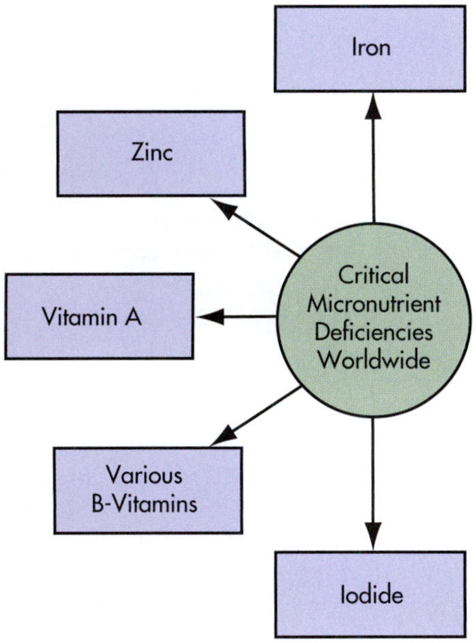

and the population is large, undernutrition is common, leading to nutritional deficiency diseases, such as goiter (from an iodide deficiency) and xerophthalmia (eye problems caused by poor vitamin A intake). However, when the food supply is ample or overabundant, incorrect food choices coupled with an excessive intake can lead to overnutrition-related chronic diseases, such as type 2 diabetes.

Undernutrition is the most common form of malnutrition among the poor in both developing and developed countries. Currently, about half of the 4 million African children under 5 years of age who die annually are undernourished. Undernutrition is also the primary cause of specific nutrient deficiencies that can result in muscle wasting, blindness, scurvy, pellagra, beriberi, anemia, rickets, goiter, and a host of other problems (Table 20-2).

The most critical micronutrients missing from diets worldwide are iron, vitamin A, and iodide, as well as zinc and various B-vitamins.[18] About 1 billion people, mostly in the developing world, are affected with iron deficiency. This impairs the cognitive development of children and likely is a permanent result if the iron deficiency is prolonged in early infancy. It is estimated that 50 million people worldwide show brain damage from preventable maternal iodide deficiency. Although severe vitamin A deficiency, which causes blindness, is on the decline, up to 250,000 to 500,000 preschool children are still affected by it each year. In addition, children who have measles have a much

Table 20-2 Effects of Nutrient-Deficiency Diseases That Commonly Accompany Undernutrition

Disease and Key Nutrient Involved	Typical Effects	Foods Rich in Deficient Nutrient	Where the Problem Currently Exists
Xerophthalmia Vitamin A	Blindness from chronic eye infections, restricted growth, dryness and keratinization of epithelial tissues	Liver, fortified milk, sweet potatoes, spinach, greens, carrots, cantaloupe, apricots	Asia, Africa
Rickets Vitamin D	Poorly calcified bones, bowed legs, other bone deformities	Fortified milk, fish oils, sun exposure	Asia, Africa, and other parts of the world where religious dress codes prevent women and children from receiving adequate sun exposure; older adults in developed nations
Beriberi Thiamin	Nerve degeneration, altered muscle coordination, cardiovascular problems	Sunflower seeds, pork, whole and enriched grains, dried beans	Areas of famine in Africa
Ariboflavinosis Riboflavin	Inflammation of tongue, mouth, face and oral cavity, nervous system disorders	Milk, mushrooms, spinach, liver, enriched grains	Areas of famine in Africa
Pellagra Niacin	Diarrhea, dermatitis, dementia	Mushrooms, bran, tuna, chicken, beef, peanuts, whole and enriched grains	Areas of famine in Africa, war-torn Eastern Europe
Scurvy Vitamin C	Delayed wound healing, internal bleeding, abnormal formation of bones and teeth	Citrus fruits, strawberries, broccoli	Areas of famine in Africa
Iron deficiency anemia Iron	Reduced work output, retarded growth, increased health risk in pregnancy	Meats, seafood, broccoli, peas, bran, whole-grain and enriched breads	Worldwide
Goiter Iodide	Enlarged thyroid gland in teenagers and adults, possible mental retardation, cretinism	Iodized salt, saltwater fish	South America, Eastern Europe, Africa

Often two or more nutrition-deficiency diseases are found in an undernourished person in the developing world. This separate discussion of nutrients just makes it easier to see the important role of each one.

greater chance of becoming vitamin A deficient. The United Nations Children's Fund reports that the lives of 1 million to 3 million children could be saved annually in the developing world if vitamin A supplements were provided a few times a year. The annual cost per child would be about 6 cents.

Of the 6.2 billion people in the world, about 2 billion may be affected by some form of micronutrient malnutrition and also experience episodes of food shortages. Death and disease from infections, particularly those causing acute and prolonged diarrhea or acute lower respiratory disease, increase dramatically when the infections are superimposed on a state of chronic undernutrition. Chronic undernutrition leaves many people in the developing world in a continual state of depressed immune function.[4] Diarrhea alone is the number one killer of children in developing countries, responsible for over 2 million deaths of children under 5 years of age.

Protein-energy malnutrition (PEM) is a form of undernutrition caused by an extremely deficient intake of energy or protein generally accompanied by an illness. The typically dramatic results of PEM—kwashiorkor and marasmus—were described in Chapter 7. This chapter focuses on the more subtle effects of a chronic lack of food.

Famine is not the same thing as chronic hunger. Although both result from poverty and a lack of food, famine is the extreme form of chronic hunger. Periods of famine are characterized by large-scale loss of life, social disruption, and economic chaos that slows food production. As a result of these extreme events, the affected community experiences a downward spiral characterized by human distress; sales of land, livestock, and other important farm assets; migration; division and impoverishment of the poorest families; crime; and the weakening of customary moral codes, as seen in Sudan and Rwanda. In the midst of all this, undernutrition rates soar; infectious diseases, such as cholera, spread; and many people die.

famine An extreme shortage of food, which leads to massive starvation in a population; often associated with crop failures, war, and political unrest.

Special efforts are needed to eradicate the fundamental causes of famine. Causes vary by region and decade, but the most common is crop failure. The most obvious reasons for crop failure are bad weather, war, and civil strife, or all three. War, in fact, deserves a special focus; this will be specifically addressed in a separate section on war and political/civil unrest.

More than 3 million people may have perished in the great famine of 1943 in Bengal, India. In 1974, another 1.5 million from that region starved in the country of Bangladesh. China suffered an almost unbelievable famine from 1959 to 1961—estimates of mortality range from 16 million to 64 million.

Critical Life Stages When Undernutrition Is Particularly Devastating

Prolonged undernutrition is detrimental to many aspects of human health (Fig. 20-1). It is particularly critical during some periods of growth and old age.

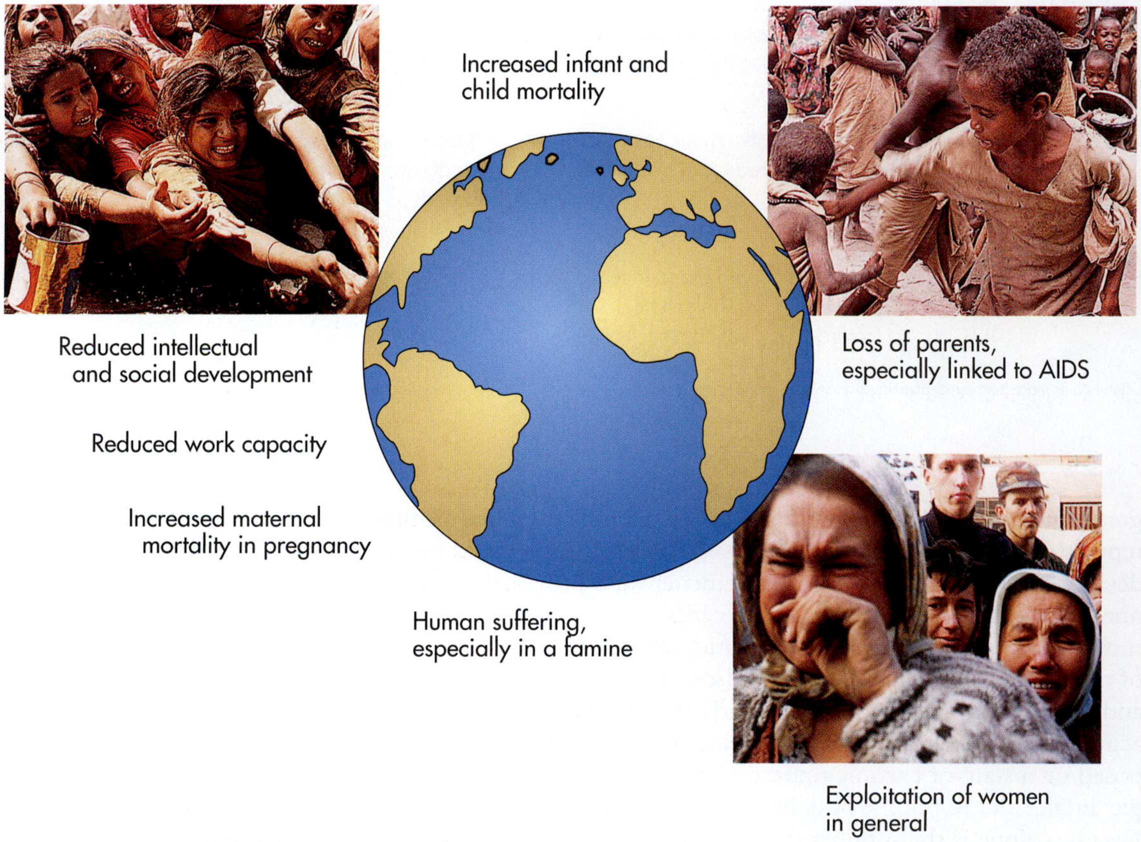

Figure 20-1 Undernutrition affects many aspects of human health and humanity in general.

Pregnancy

The period when undernutrition poses the greatest health risk is during pregnancy. Currently about 500,000 women worldwide die each year from complications of pregnancy and childbirth. A pregnant woman needs extra nutrients to meet both her own needs and those of her developing fetus. Nourishing the fetus may deplete stores of maternal nutrients. Maternal iron deficiency anemia is one possible consequence (see Chapter 16).

In Africa, women give birth, on average, to more than six live babies. Coupled with chronic undernutrition, these high birth rates create a 1 in 20 chance that a woman will die from pregnancy-related causes. In contrast, North American women face a risk of 1 death in about 8000 births from pregnancy-related causes. No other social indicator, including literacy, life expectancy, and infant mortality, betrays a wider gap between the developing and industrialized worlds.

The bounty of food we enjoy in North America relies on our rich agricultural resources. Many developing countries do not have such resources to employ.

Fetal and Infant Stages

The fetus faces major health risks from undernutrition during gestation. To support growth and development of the brain and other body tissues, a growing fetus requires a rich supply of protein, vitamins, and minerals. When these needs are not met, the infant is often born before 37 weeks of gestation, well before the 40 weeks of gestation that is considered ideal. The consequences of preterm birth include reduced lung function and a weakened immune system. These conditions not only compromise health but also increase the likelihood of premature death. Long-term problems in growth and development can result if the infant survives. In extreme cases, low-birth-weight babies (about 5.5 pounds [2.5 kg] or less) face 5 to 10 times the normal risk of dying before the age of 1 year, primarily because of reduced lung development as noted in Chapter 16. When low birth weight is accompanied by other physical abnormalities, medical intervention can cost $200,000 or more. These costs can only be met in developed countries.

Worldwide, more than 30 billion infants are born each year with low birth weight. In the United States, low birth weight accounts for more than half of all infant deaths and 75% of deaths of babies younger than 1 month old. Currently, about 7% of infants born in the United States have low birth weights. The comparable Canadian statistic is 6%.

The percentage of infants born with low birth weight in the United States has been increasing steadily during the past 20 years. One reason is that more twins, triplets, and higher-order multiple births are being born because of improvements in medicine and fertility research. Rates of low birth weight also vary by race. For example, about 13% of babies born to African American women have low birth weights. Among Hispanics in the United States, infants of Mexican origin have the lowest rate of low birth weight (6%), while infants of Puerto Rican heritage have the highest (9%). Among Asian subgroups, low-birth-weight rates range from 5% for infants of Chinese heritage to nearly 9% for Filipino infants.

Childhood

Early childhood, when growth is rapid, is another period when undernutrition is extremely risky. The central nervous system—including the brain—is particularly vulnerable because of rapid growth from conception through early childhood. After the preschool years, brain growth and development slow dramatically until maturity, when they cease. Nutritional deprivation, especially in early infancy, can lead to permanent brain impairment.[12] If more is not done, it is projected that ongoing undernutrition could leave more than 1 billion children with mental impairment by 2020.

In general, poor children experience more nutritional deprivation and overall illness and are more severely affected than other children.[20] Stunted growth is an obvious effect, seen in about one-third of children under 5 years of age worldwide. In addition, iron deficiency anemia is much more common among low-income children than children from less deprived families. This deficiency can lead to fatigue upon exertion, reduced stamina,

Minimal intakes of protein and zinc limit the growth of children worldwide. About 30% of children in developing countries show evidence of growth failure.

stunted growth, impaired motor development, and learning problems. Undernutrition in childhood can also weaken resistance to infection because immune function decreases when such nutrients as protein, vitamin A, and zinc are very low in a diet. Clearly, undernutrition and illness have a cyclical relationship. Not only does undernutrition cause illness, but illness worsens undernutrition, particularly by diarrhea and infectious diseases. For this reason, many children in developing countries are dying from the combination of malnutrition and infection. Conversely, when missing nutrients such as zinc are restored to children's diets, improvements in health can be obvious.[2]

Later Years

Older adults are also at risk for undernutrition. They often require nutrient-dense foods, in amounts depending on their state of health and degree of physical activity. Because many of them have fixed incomes and incur significant medical costs, food often becomes a low-priority item. In addition, older adults are often unable to take care of all their own needs, are sometimes isolated, and may be depressed—all important factors that influence food intake (see Chapter 18).[14]

General Effects of Semistarvation

In the initial stages, the results of undernutrition from semistarvation are often so mild that physical symptoms are absent and blood tests do not usually detect the slight metabolic changes. Even in the absence of clinical symptoms, however, undernourishment may affect reproductive capacity, resistance to and recovery from disease, physical activity and work output, and lead to fatigue and behavior problems. Recall from Chapter 2 that, as tissues continue to be depleted of nutrients, blood tests eventually detect biochemical changes, such as a drop in blood hemoglobin concentration. Physical symptoms, such as body weakness, appear with further depletion. Finally, the full-blown symptoms of the predominating deficiency are recognizable, such as when edema accompanies a protein deficiency.

In general, when a few people in a population develop a severe deficiency, this represents only the tip of the iceberg. Typically, a much greater number have milder degrees of undernutrition. These deficiencies should not, therefore, be dismissed as trivial, especially in the developing world. It is becoming clear that combined deficiencies of specific vitamins and the minerals iron and zinc can seriously reduce work performance, even when they don't cause obvious physical symptoms.

Hunger reduces energy and strength; it diminishes concentration. Hunger impairs a child's ability to learn. Hunger hurts businesses when workers are more concerned about their next meal than the task at hand. Hunger among older adults makes chronic health conditions worse and can cause others. Hunger is patient, quiet, and persistent, and its effects can be widespread.

This resulting state of ill health, in turn, diminishes the ability of individuals, communities, and even whole countries to perform at peak levels of physical and mental capacity, creating a dearth in human resources (Fig. 20-2). For example, in the 1940s, a group of researchers led by Dr. Ansel Keys maintained 32 previously healthy men on a diet averaging about 1600 kcal daily for 6 months. During this time, the men lost an average of 24% of their body weight. After about 3 months, the participants complained of fatigue, muscle soreness, irritability, and hunger pains. They exhibited a lack of ambition and self-discipline and poor concentration. They were often moody and depressed. They became less able to laugh heartily, sneeze, and tolerate heat. Heart rate and muscle tone also decreased. When the men were permitted to eat normally again, the desire for more food and a feeling of fatigue continued, even after 12 weeks of rehabilitation. Full recovery required about 8 months.

The effects of undernutrition in poor countries are probably even greater than this research indicated because the participants in this study had adequate vitamin and mineral intakes. In addition, the inhabitants of poorer countries must contend with recurrent infections, poor sanitary conditions, extreme weather conditions, and regular exposure to extremely infectious diseases. They require greater amounts of certain nutrients—especially iron—to combat rampant parasite and other infections. Deficiencies in both iron and zinc can lead to reduced immune function and thereby increase the risk of diseases such as diarrhea, pneumonia, and dysentery.

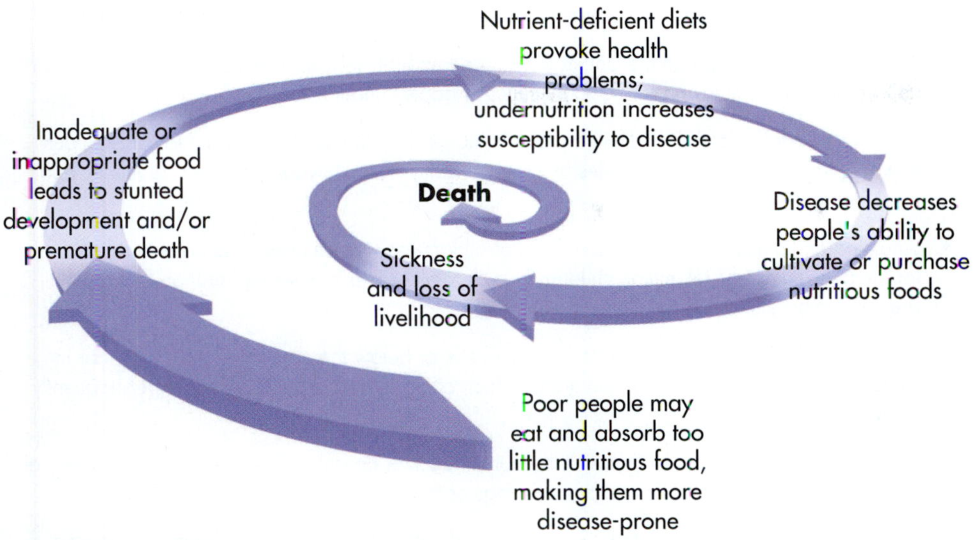

Figure 20-2 The downward spiral of poverty and illness can ultimately end in death (based on World Food Program graphic).

Case Scenario | Follow-up

Jamal should not be surprised that the children in the village were often sick and listless. Protein, vitamin A, iron, iodide, and zinc deficiencies contribute to poor growth and depressed immune function. One or more of these deficiencies is likely present in many children in the village. The diets of these children may also be marginal in energy content, further contributing to poor growth and overall health. We know from many nutrition intervention studies that the provision of more food energy, protein, vitamin A, iron, iodide, and zinc—along with other micronutrients—can reverse some of this disease pattern and improve health. Still, we know that many children throughout the world exist in a stunted and immune-depressed state associated with their chronically deficient diets.

Concept | Check

Hunger is the uneasiness and pain that results when insufficient food is eaten to meet energy needs. Food insecurity is anxiety about running out of food or money to buy more food. Chronic hunger leads to undernutrition, which can cause growth failure in children and weakness in adults. Risk of infection increases, and nutrient-deficiency diseases result. The primary cause of undernutrition is poverty. The critical periods for undernutrition occur during pregnancy, infancy, childhood, and old age. Chronic undernutrition causes decreased work performance and motivation and compromises immune function. The adverse effects in pregnancy and infancy are quite dramatic, as evidenced by mortality rates much higher than those of healthy populations. Irreversible developmental damage in surviving children is also common.

Undernutrition in the United States

About 33 million (12%) of people in the United States live at or below the poverty level, currently estimated at about $18,104 annually for a family of four (Table 20-3). These poor include about 16% of all children; children, in fact, comprise about 37% of the poor.

Currently, 8% of Caucasians are poor, 24% of African Americans are poor, and 23% of Hispanics are poor. Many Native Americans are also poor, as are 11% of Asian Americans. (Many Native Americans in Canada also live in poverty.)

Undernutrition in North America is a much more subtle problem than in developing countries. To the untrained eye, undernourished children may just seem skinny, when, in fact, their growth is being stunted by insufficient nutrients. More likely, though, children from food-insecure households are prone to be overweight. This may be the result of considerable reliance on convenience foods that provide mostly fat and sugar. Also, food-insecure families may buy candies and snack foods as treats when expensive toys and clothing aren't affordable.

Table 20-3 The Realities of Poverty and Undernutrition in the United States

- About 7% of infants born in the United States are low birth weight. This accounts for more than half of all infant deaths and for 75% of deaths of babies under 1 month of age.
- The infant mortality rate in the United States is higher than that of 26 other industrialized countries. Teenage pregnancy contributes to infant mortality because young mothers frequently don't meet their nutrient needs.
- Single-parent families constitute about 25% of all families with children. The poverty rate (40%) for the approximately 19 million children in such families is five times higher than that for children in two-parent families.
- About 33 million people in the United States live at or below the poverty level. These poor include about 16% of all children; children, in fact, comprise 37% of the poor. Hunger frequently accompanies poverty.
- A family of four in the United States at the bottom 20% of households has an average income of $17,196. Contrast that to the average earnings of the top 20% of households: $79,375.
- In the United States, an estimated 12 million people, or 6.5% of all adults, have experienced homelessness sometime during their lives. An episode of homelessness nearly always lasts for at least 1 week and often for a month or more.
- The Food Stamp program for low-income people provides each household with $170 per month. About 1 person in 16 currently participates in this program.
- Second Harvest, the largest U.S. food bank, estimates that more than 23 million people, or more than 1 person in 10, rely on food depositories and soup kitchens to feed themselves and their families. Most of these people, the organization reports, are workers who have lost their jobs.
- Food thrown out in U.S. cafeterias, supermarkets, and restaurants could feed 49 million people per year.

The poor often face difficult choices: whether to buy groceries for the family or pay this month's rent; whether to have dental work done or pay the current utility bill; whether to replace clothes the children have outgrown or pay for transportation to apply for a job. Food is one of the few flexible items in a poor person's budget. Rents are fixed, utility costs aren't negotiable, the price of medical care and prescription drugs can't be bargained down, and bus drivers won't accept less than the going rate to transport riders. A person can always eat less, however. The short-term consequences may be less dramatic than having the utilities shut off. The long-term cumulative effects, however, are disturbing.

Helping the Hungry in the United States: A Historical Perspective

Until the twentieth century, individuals and a wide variety of charitable, often church-related organizations, provided most of the help to poor, undernourished people in the United States. Few early efforts distributed direct cash payments to poor people because these were thought to reduce recipients' motivation to improve their circumstances or change behavior, such as excessive drinking, that contributed to their poverty. Beginning in the early 1900s, the involvement of local, county, and state governments in providing assistance to the poor has steadily increased.[13]

Critical | Thinking

While studying early childhood development, Nakia was surprised to learn that some children in the United States are undernourished. What evidence might Nakia observe in children that would suggest undernourishment?

Depression Era to the Mid-1970s

The Great Depression of the 1930s marked a decisive change. Studies at the time documented both undernutrition and the existence of widespread pellagra (niacin deficiency) and rickets (vitamin D deficiency). In response, the federal government sponsored soup kitchens and other programs that distributed food commodities throughout the country. During World War II, a large percentage of the men rejected for the draft for physical

Table 20-4 Some Current Federally Subsidized Programs That Supply Food for People in the United States

Program	Eligibility	Description
Food Stamps	Low income	Electronic Benefit Transfer (debit) cards are given to purchase food at grocery stores; the amount is based on size of household and income.
Emergency Food System	Low income	Food stamps are issued on 24-hour notice for 1 month while eligibility for further use of the program can be investigated.
Commodity Supplemental Food Program	Certain low-income populations, such as pregnant women, children until the age of 6 years, and seniors	USDA surplus foods are distributed by county agencies; not found in all states.
Special Supplemental Nutrition Program for Women, Infants, and Children (WIC)	Low-income pregnant/lactating women, infants, and children less than 5 years old at nutritional risk	Coupons are given to purchase milk, cheese, fruit juice, cereal, infant formula, and other specific food items at grocery stores.
School Lunch	Low income	Free or reduced-price lunch is distributed by the school; meal follows USDA pattern based on the Food Guide Pyramid; cost for the child depends on family income. For students who do not participate in the lunch program, special milk program may be available.
School Breakfast	Low income	Free or reduced-price breakfast is distributed by the school; meal follows USDA pattern; cost for the child depends on family income.
Child and Adult Care Food Program	Child enrolled in organized child-care program and seniors in adult care programs; income guidelines are the same as those for the School Lunch program	Reimbursement is given for meals supplied to children at the site; meals must follow USDA guidelines based on the Food Guide Pyramid.
Congregate Meals for the Elderly	Age 60 or over (no income guidelines)	Free noon meal is furnished at a site; meal follows specific pattern based on one-third of nutrient needs.
Home-Delivered Meals	Age 60 or over, homebound	Noon meal is delivered at no cost or for a donation at least 5 days a week. Sometimes other meals for later consumption are delivered at the same time; often referred to as "Meals on Wheels."
Summer Food Service Program	Residence in a low-income neighborhood or participation in a program	Free, nutritious meals and snacks are given to a group of children in a low-income area at a central site, such as a school or a community center during long school vacations.

reasons were found to have been undernourished 10 to 12 years earlier, during the Depression era. This practical demonstration of the long-term detrimental effects of childhood undernutrition led the U.S. Congress to enact legislation setting up the School Lunch program in 1946.

In the 1950s, it was assumed that all people in the United States had enough to eat. Nevertheless, occasional reports of undernutrition surfaced, mostly among the truly destitute: migrant workers, Native Americans, African Americans in the South, unemployed minorities in general, and some older people.

After observing extensive hunger and poverty during his presidential campaign in the 1960s, John F. Kennedy revitalized the Food Stamp program, which actually had begun two decades earlier, and expanded commodity distribution programs. Today the Food Stamp program for low-income people allows recipients to use a debit card to purchase food and seeds—but not tobacco, cleaning items, alcoholic beverages, and nonedible products—at stores authorized to accept them. Each participating household receives about $170 per month, on average. Currently about 20 million people in the United States participate in this program (Table 20-4).

The presence of undernutrition in the United States raises a broad question for the society at large: Where can people in such situations turn when their own resources fail? The responsibility for helping those in need could lie with federal, state, and local governments; religious groups; charitable organizations; and, in many cases, with the individuals themselves. All can be part of the solution.

The U.S. Congress established the school breakfast program in 1965 as politicians became aware of the number of children coming to school hungry. School breakfast and lunch programs still enable low-income students—8.4 million for breakfast and 27 million for lunch—to receive meals free or at reduced cost if certain income guidelines are met (under $22,945 to $32,653, respectively, for annual income of a family of four). In the same year, the U.S. Congress funded group noontime (called *congregate*) meals and home-delivered meals for all citizens over 60 years of age, regardless of income. Both remain active programs, serving about 1 million meals each day, but they still do not reach all who need help. In addition, in 1972 the Special Supplemental Nutrition Program for Women, Infants, and Children (WIC) was authorized. This program provides food vouchers and nutrition education to low-income pregnant and lactating women and their young children. Today, it serves about 7.6 million people.

Political and social awareness of hunger and undernutrition in the late 1960s was spurred by the book *Hunger USA* and a resulting television documentary, *Hunger in America,* first shown in May 1968. The film graphically demonstrated that hunger exists in all areas and ethnic groups in the United States. The response was dramatic. Between 1969 and 1971, some already large federal food programs were expanded and others were created. For example, the Food Stamp program served only 2 million people in 1968, but by 1971 it was serving 11 million. The School Lunch program, which served only 2 million poor children before 1970, was serving 8 million children by 1971. Soon after, the School Breakfast program, a pilot program for children living in impoverished areas, became available nationally. And, as just mentioned, in 1972 the Special Supplemental Nutrition Program for Women, Infants, and Children (WIC) began.

One goal of *Healthy People 2010* is to increase food security among U.S. households from the current 88 to 94%.

Sometimes, severe undernutrition due to involuntary hunger does occur in the United States. More often, though, Americans experience periodic episodes of hunger and food insecurity.[10] Dr. David H. Holben discusses food security and insecurity in more detail in the Expert Opinion. Although the safety net provided by food assistance programs is strong, it is also porous; unemployment, medical and housing expenses, and even occasional holiday shopping can cause a household to be hungry or food insecure.

Privately funded programs have stepped in to take an important role in augmenting state and federal efforts to combat hunger and related food insecurity in the United States. There are currently more than 150,000 charitable food providers (such as food banks and food pantries) helping to cope with this problem. About 2.4% of U.S. households rely on food pantries, and a recent survey found that slightly more than two of every three people requesting such emergency food assistance were members of families—children and their parents.

Socioeconomic Factors Related to Undernutrition

In the United States today, persistent hunger and food insecurity are largely associated with two interrelated conditions: poverty and homelessness. Thus, the economic, social, and political changes that lead to an increase in the number of poor or homeless people also tend to intensify the problem of undernutrition.

Poverty

The availability of cooking facilities affects nutrient intake among the poor. Without cooking facilities, people may buy expensive foods that require no preparation. These are typically processed snack foods, which provide food energy but are often lacking in nutrients.

Although highly trained people are quite competitive in the increasingly global economy, there is a glut of unskilled manual labor available throughout the world. Many families suffer hardships when layoffs occur seasonally or because of changes in the economy. Furthermore, many jobs available to low-income adults are in the service sector, such as fast-food restaurants or department stores. When one or both parents have one of these low-paying jobs—even full-time—their families may still be at or below the poverty level. Note that parents in most poor families do work; nearly two in three families contain at least one worker.

Another primary factor contributing to poverty has been the dramatic increase in the number of single-parent families in the United States, the result of high rates of divorce and out-of-wedlock births. Currently, single-parent families constitute about 4 million. The poverty rate (40%) for the approximately 19 million children in single-parent families is five times higher than the rate for those in two-parent families.

Some observers believe that many publicly funded assistance programs have actually provided an incentive for poor, single women to have more children: The more children they have, the more welfare and other assistance benefits they receive. The new welfare reform laws have addressed this issue by requiring able-bodied adults to get jobs, limiting future direct support to 5 years in a lifetime. It is up to each state to determine how to implement this work requirement and establish exceptions, for such situations as disability, short-term downturns in the economy, or other overwhelming hardships.

Many politicians and political writers point out that we need greater wisdom in our approach to illegitimacy and single parenthood. Some suggest improving child care, teaching parenting skills, and expanding job opportunities. To a great extent, states are doing this as they help people end their dependence on welfare payments. Nationwide, the number of people on welfare rolls has fallen 60% since 1992, but recently has stabilized, and even increased slightly in some states. People remaining on welfare typically have numerous barriers to overcome if they are to support themselves and family members. There is also concern that the incomes of many people leaving welfare are still too low to meet needs because most of the jobs they find pay minimum wage.

Homelessness

The economics of poverty and undernutrition have changed in one additional important way. Homelessness is much more evident now than in 1980. Families with children currently account for about 43% of the homeless. An estimated 12 million people, or 6.5% of all adults, in the United States have experienced homelessness sometime during their lives. Episodes of homelessness nearly always last for at least 1 week and often for a month or more. The estimated risk of homelessness rises to about 1 in 7 in the adult population in the United States when it includes people who have moved into someone else's residence during periods when they had nowhere else to live.

Homeless children suffer higher rates of many medical problems than do other children, some of which include:

- Upper respiratory tract infections
- Scabies and lice
- Tooth decay
- Ear and skin infections
- Diaper rash
- Eye infections
- Developmental delays
- Trauma-related injuries

Although many citizens of the United States in general are enjoying continuing prosperity, the economic status of many of the working poor has declined because affordable housing is harder and harder for them to find. Due to the nation's rising prosperity, higher-income tenants have bid up the prices of the apartments in some cities beyond the financial resources of the poorer tenants. The U.S. government considers housing costs, which include rent and utilities, to be affordable if they consume no more than 30% of a family's income. A recent U.S. government report stated that 1 in 8 low-income families pay more than half their incomes for housing or live in dilapidated units. These families, although not homeless, are likely to experience undernutrition without direct food assistance. Moreover, the continuing changes in the economic circumstances they face could force such poor families into actual homelessness, at least temporarily.

Other important causes of homelessness include the widespread release of mentally ill patients from mental institutions in the 1980s, unemployment, substance abuse, and personal crises. The abuse of alcohol and crack cocaine is another notable cause. Up to 85% of all homeless people in large cities in the United States abuse alcohol or drugs or have a mental illness. Most people with such problems are unable to find and hold employment; without support from family or friends, they and their dependents will probably become homeless.

Food pantries and soup kitchens are important sources of nutrients for a growing number of people in the United States.

Possible Solutions to Hunger in the United States

Few would argue the need to support the physically and mentally handicapped, as well as the multitude of poor children, in the United States. The debate begins when able-bodied adults are receiving public aid. Many of these people have extenuating circumstances or have dug such a deep hole for themselves financially that it is difficult to get

Expert Opinion

Food Security and Insecurity

David H. Holben, Ph.D., R.D.

Hunger. Take a minute and think about the last time that you had to skip a meal when you really did not want to. Have you ever wondered if people in the United States are actually hungry? Do some adults in the United States worry about not having enough money to buy food for their children? Well, hunger in the United States really exists. While severe forms of hunger are not as prevalent in America as they are in developing countries, less severe forms of food insecurity and hunger are a cause for concern.

Food Security—What Is It?

Food security means that all people at all times have access to enough food for an active, healthy life—they have nutritionally adequate, safe foods readily available and do not have to resort to emergency food supplies, like food banks, and/or begging, stealing, or scavenging for food. On the other hand, a household with food insecurity has limited access/availability of food or a limited/uncertain ability to acquire food in socially acceptable ways.

In the United States, a set of 18 questions known as the Food Security Core Survey Module is used to measure the food security status of households. The 18 questions basically relate to assessing if there is sufficient food in a household. The items include asking about: (1) anxiety related to food running out in a household before getting money to buy more; (2) household members being able or not able to eat balanced meals that include a variety of foods; (3) skimping on food and skipping meals by household members due to a lack of food and money; and (4) household member weight loss due to not having enough money to buy food.

1. We worried whether our food would run out before we got money to buy more.
2. The food that we bought just didn't last, and we didn't have money to get more.
3. We couldn't afford to eat balanced meals.
4. We relied on only a few kinds of low-cost food to feed our children because we were running out of money to buy food.
5. We couldn't feed our children a balanced meal, because we couldn't afford that.
6. Our children were not eating enough because we just couldn't afford enough food.
7. In the last 12 months, did you or other adults in your household ever cut the size of your meals or skip meals because there wasn't enough money for food?
8. How often did this happen?
9. In the last 12 months, did you ever eat less than you felt you should because there wasn't enough money for food?
10. In the last 12 months, were you ever hungry but didn't eat because you couldn't afford enough food?
11. In the last 12 months, did you lose weight because you didn't have enough money for food?
12. In the last 12 months, did you or other adults in your household ever not eat for a whole day because there wasn't enough money for food?
13. How often did this happen?
14. In the last 12 months, did you ever cut the size of your children's meals because there wasn't enough money for food?
15. In the last 12 months, were the children ever hungry but you just couldn't afford more food?
16. In the last 12 months, did your children ever skip a meal because there wasn't enough money for food?
17. How often did this happen?
18. In the last 12 months, did your children ever not eat for a whole day because there wasn't enough money for food?

These questions are included in the Current Population Survey conducted by the Census Bureau and other large surveys with a nutrition component. Based upon responses to the questions, household food security status is determined. Basically, *food secure* households show no or minimal evidence of food insecurity. Households that are *food insecure without hunger* have members concerned about adequacy of the household food supply and household food management, including reduced quality of food and increased unusual coping patterns; however, little or no reduction in members' food intake is reported. In households categorized as *food insecure with "moderate" hunger,* food intake for adults has been reduced to an extent that implies that adults have repeatedly experienced the physical sensa-

out. It is also true that the United States has enough money and food to feed every citizen. The question is, can government programs provide a permanent solution to poverty?

Private emergency-food network systems are also important, as noted earlier, but are not sufficient to meet all food needs in the United States. Furthermore, most of the donated items are limited in nutritional value. By necessity, processed and canned grocery items predominate, rather than protein-rich foods and perishable items, such as fresh produce and milk.

Food insecure people are part of the North American landscape. A "safety net" of programs exists, but it is "porous."

tion of hunger; however, children have not usually experienced these reductions. In *food insecure with "severe" hunger* households, households with children have reduced their children's food intake to an extent indicating that the children have experienced hunger, and adults in the household have experienced extensive reductions in food intake.

Is There Really Food Insecurity in the United States?

Several research reports have been published that discuss the food security status of American households and its consequences. According to the most recent reports, about 10% of households in the United States were food insecure in 2000. In the United States, food insecurity is evident when families have limited resources, lack access to food (due to limited resources, lack of transportation, living in remote areas, or limited access to food stores), depend on food assistance programs, skip meals, substitute nutritious foods with less expensive alternatives, and seek assistance from soup kitchens and food pantries. Typically, households with an income below the poverty line, especially those located in a central city or rural area, experience greater levels of food insecurity than other households.

Suboptimal quality of life and health may result from having experienced food insecurity. In fact, studies have been published that support that food insecurity negatively affects the nutritional quality of the diet, increasing chronic disease risk. For example, individuals may experience physical impairments, like illness or fatigue, due to insufficient food. Psychological issues may also arise, including stress at home. Finally, families may have to modify their eating patterns and customs or even turn to distorted means of acquiring food (begging, stealing) when they experience food insecurity.

What Is Being Done to Improve Food Security in the United States?

Healthy People 2010 includes the objective of decreasing the prevalence of food insecurity in the United States. Several federal and nonfederal programs address a variety of aspects of food security, including: (1) Child and Adult Care Food Program; (2) a variety of food distribution programs like the Food Assistance in Disaster Situations and Food Distribution Program on Indian Reservations; (3) Food Stamp Program; (4) National School Lunch, School Breakfast, Summer Food Service, and Special Milk Programs; (5) Special Supplemental Nutrition Program for Women, Infants, and Children (WIC); (6) WIC and Senior Farmers' Market Nutrition programs; and (7) emergency food providers like food pantries and soup kitchens.

What Can I Do to Help Improve the Food Security Status of the United States?

First, learn more about food security. A great website that can be used to learn about this issue is the food security briefing room, www.ers.usda.gov/briefing/foodsecurity. Getting involved in your community and learning about resources available to households to improve food security, including the federally funded and other nonfederal programs, is another one of the first steps in helping to solve this critical problem. Try volunteering at a soup kitchen or food pantry or get involved in food recovery efforts (gleaning) in your area. In addition, you can get involved by encouraging your local, state, and national representatives to fund food assistance, education, and other programs that help to improve food insecurity.

Dr. Holben is an Associate Professor in the Department of Human and Consumer Sciences at Ohio University in Athens, Ohio. His major research interest is in food security issues.

Still, a long-term solution to the problem of hunger in the United States can't be achieved by the government or private agencies alone. Change also requires a cultural shift emphasizing the responsibility of all citizens to provide as best they can for themselves, their families, and the less fortunate around them. Many in the United States consider an increase in individual responsibility as a critical goal. Government programs can't easily fix poverty and the resulting hunger that stem from irresponsible individual behavior. Government programs can, however, help reduce or prevent the poverty that results largely from lack of education or opportunity.

Clearly, the victims of poverty don't deserve all the blame. The poor confront substantial difficulties: substandard education and training, poor communication skills, lack of reliable and safe child care, inability to relocate, little employment experience, and no economic reserves to fall back on during crises. Even with a strong desire for a better life, people may get discouraged and apathetic in the face of apparently insurmountable obstacles. Moreover, many of the poor are unable to meet the demands of a modern, dynamic society—in particular, older adults, sick and disabled people, and young single mothers with children. Regardless of how repugnant government assistance appears to some people, it will probably always be necessary to some extent.

Because long-term undernutrition—especially among children—has both individual and societal consequences, everyone in the United States is affected by this problem, either directly or indirectly. The next few years are likely to bring further changes in both government and private assistance programs, demanding new initiatives. As the welfare system is reformed and government programs are redesigned, it is likely that some will suffer. The hope is that these new approaches will lead to long-term progress and the eventual relief of poverty and hunger.

Concept | Check

Federal programs in the United States designed to reduce hunger and undernutrition began in the 1930s, during the Great Depression. In response to reports of widespread poverty and hunger during the 1960s, the U.S. Congress established several food assistance programs and substantially increased funding for already existing programs. Largely as a result of these federal programs, undernutrition had decreased substantially by the mid-1970s. The presence of poverty, homelessness, and undernutrition is influenced by economic, cultural, and individual factors, as well as government policies. The serious questions about the long-term effectiveness of many government assistance programs are causing major changes in their administration, funding mechanisms, and program design. All citizens can help reduce the problem of undernutrition.

Undernutrition in the Developing World

Undernutrition in the developing world is also tied to poverty, and any true solution must address this problem. However, these countries have a multitude of problems so complex and interrelated that they cannot be treated separately. Programs that have proved immensely helpful in the United States (and throughout the rest of North America) are only a starting point in this context. The following major obstacles challenge those seeking a solution:

- Extreme imbalances in the food/population ratio in different regions of a country
- War and political/civil unrest
- The rapid depletion of natural resources
- Cultural attitudes toward certain foods
- The disease AIDS, especially in sub-Saharan Africa and Asia
- High external debt
- Poor **infrastructure,** especially poor housing, sanitation and storage facilities, education, communications, and transportation systems

infrastructure The basic framework of a system of organization. For a society, this includes roads, bridges, telephones, and other basic technologies.

Each problem deserves individual consideration (Fig. 20-3).[9]

Food/Population Ratio

Whether the earth can yield enough food for all people has been a long-standing question. As early as 1798, English clergyman and political economist, Thomas Malthus,

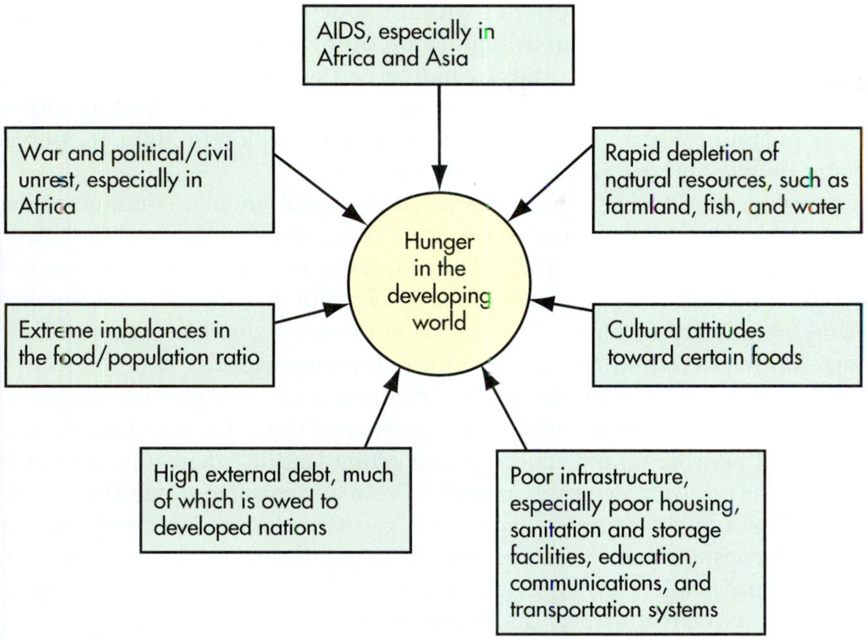

Figure 20-3 Many factors contribute to undernutrition in the developing world. Any solutions to the problem must take these factors into consideration.

proposed a rather pessimistic view of our prospects. He said that given the passion between the genders (which he felt should be discouraged), the population would always increase in **geometric ratio**—2, 4, 8, 16, 32, and so on. Meanwhile, at best, the food supply would increase only **arithmetically**—2, 4, 6, 8, 10, and so on. This prediction means that while the food/population ratio might begin at 2/2, eventually population will grow to 32 while food supplies will only increase to feed 10.

geometric ratio A series of numbers wherein the division of each number by the one to the left of it yields the same answer.

arithmetic ratio A series of numbers wherein the difference between each number is the same.

Malthus's proposals became the object of intense controversy in England and elsewhere, often meeting vigorous opposition. Eminent British scientists pointed out that scientific advances in agriculture would greatly increase food production. In fact, that has proved true. Nevertheless, the aptly named population explosion has undermined this progress. Overall population growth has not slowed significantly through natural checks, disease, or recent human interventions, such as birth control. In the year 1800, 1 billion people inhabited the earth. By the year 2000, this number skyrocketed to more than 6 billion. By 2050, the United Nations estimates that the world population could reach 8 to 12 billion. (The recent spread of AIDS throughout the world has put into question these future population estimates dropping the estimate to 7 to 9 billion.)

Currently, population growth exceeds economic growth in much of the developing world, and poverty is increasing. Because efforts to speed up economic development have failed, the only remaining way to improve the situation may be to slow down the growth of population, as Malthus recommended. If we want to ensure a decent life for a widening segment of humanity, the growth in the earth's most vulnerable populations should slow. According to the World Bank, the world's population increases by 1 billion people every 12 years, mostly in cities and in seacoast and river-basin areas, where the environment is most under stress. By 2050, the world may have 1 billion or more people than it does today—most of them in countries where the average person earns less than $2 a day. Currently in Africa's poorest countries, nearly 65% of people live on less than $1 per day. Unless a catastrophe occurs, more than 9 of 10 infants in the next generation will be born in the poorest parts of the world.

Poor infrastructure, including inadequate housing and sanitation facilities, aggravate the problem of hunger in the developing world.

Of the 6.2 billion people in the world, more than three-quarters live in countries in the developing world, and more than half live in Asia. A recent United Nations report on worldwide hunger revealed that almost two-thirds of the world's undernourished live in Asia and the Pacific Rim. The world's food supplies also are not distributed equally among consumers. Gross disparities exist between developed and developing countries, among the rich and poor within countries, and even within families.

Food supply and population trends within the developing world also vary greatly. Japan is facing a large decrease in its population over the next 50 years unless the birth rate increases from the average of 1.4 children per family to at least 2. On the other hand, the population in Africa will have more than doubled, constituting 19% of the world's population. When the world's population hit 6 billion in 2000, it doubled the number of people on earth in less than 40 years.

Economists estimate that world food production will, in fact, continue to increase more rapidly than world population in the near future, allowing the food/population ratio to increase through the year 2020. This will come at a high cost, however, in terms of the water, fertilizer, and pesticides needed to allow for this production. Overall, in the short run, the primary problem appears to be not food production *but* distribution and use, especially in poverty-stricken areas of the developing nations.

Eventually, though, food production will begin to lag behind population growth. We are currently drifting in that direction. Most good farmland in the world is already in use, and because of poor farming practices or competing land-use demands, the number of farmable acres worldwide decreases annually. For many reasons, sustainable world food output—an amount that doesn't deplete the earth's resources—is now running well behind food consumption. This discrepancy suggests that food production in less-developed countries will barely keep up with population growth and will soon lag behind.

Due to its exponential nature (discussed earlier), reproduction is said to be the ultimate driving force behind consumption. Although efforts on the supply side of the food/population ratio are essential, many experts still emphasize the need to reduce the demand side. They argue that the survival of our civilization depends on limiting reproduction.

In the 1960s, South Korean families averaged six children each. Through economic policies and family planning programs, this number has been decreased to two. Other countries, such as Indonesia and Thailand, prove that industrialization is not a necessary prerequisite to population control but, rather, family planning programs can lead to less births and economic progress.

Since history has been recorded, maximizing reproduction has been a measure of biological success. Because disease and difficult living conditions often claimed young lives, couples produced many offspring in an attempt to ensure the longevity of the family. These conditions still exist in countries in the developing world, where children also provide the primary means of support to their parents in old age. More children also means more helpers to farm, hunt, and prepare food. In India, a rigid class structure, which leaves many people destitute, encourages large families. Traditionally, poorer people bear more children, contrary to what one might predict. Now poor people in developing nations are being asked to reverse their attitude toward having children.

As one brake on population expansion, birth control programs have been effective in developed countries but relatively ineffective in developing countries—those that could really profit from them. Family planning and contraceptive use has increased to 60% of women today, up from 10% of women in 1969. If the United Nations, voluntary organizations, and governments had not started promoting family planning and contraceptive use, the population today may be as high as 7 or 8 billion. However, women (and men) in many countries are still lacking adequate access to contraceptives. Organizations such as Population Services International are trying to keep distribution costs low and make the products available to as many people as possible by subsidizing condoms and oral contraceptives to areas such as Bangladesh. Unless people are given the option of controlling their fertility, severe environmental and health problems loom in the near future throughout large parts of the world.

Still, experience with family planning programs in developing countries and historical changes in birth rates in many industrialized countries suggest an important conclusion: Generally, only when people have enough to eat and are financially secure do they feel safe that having fewer children will still result in enough surviving sons and/or daughters to provide for their care in later years. Increasing per capita income and improving education, especially for women in developing nations, are currently considered to be the most likely long-term solutions to excessive population growth. In the last few years this effort has led to a decline in family size in Brazil, Egypt, India, and Mexico. A major concern is whether there are enough resources worldwide to raise per capita income and provide enough education to slow population growth.

In addition to economics, other obstacles to family planning programs are ancient cultural, religious, and traditional beliefs. In sub-Saharan Africa, childlessness signifies the end of a line of descent, and women who don't have children are often perceived as evil. The Yoruba believe, for example, that a childless woman made a pact with evil spirits before her own birth to kill her children and, devoid of descendants, will return to join these evil spirits in some otherworldly sphere. These women fear being rendered functionally infertile by the death of all their children almost as much as they fear bearing none. Thus, female sterilization and even contraception have not been successful. Even women with four or five children fear, not unreasonably, that all their children may suddenly die. Also, Muslim religious practices typically promote a large, abundant family as a sign of prosperity and health.

By taking on the challenges of lack of education, economic insecurity, and population growth, the developing world can begin to escape the expensive trap of humanitarian intervention and crisis management for peoples in need. Otherwise, it is possible that Malthus's gloomy prediction may soon become a fact.

Breastfeeding contributes to infant survival because it helps space births farther apart. If no supplemental nourishment is given, breastfeeding an infant decreases ovulation—and therefore, the likelihood of fertilization—for an average of about 6 months, although breastfeeding is not a completely reliable form of birth control. When childbirths are more widely spaced, mother and infant are healthier and fewer total births occur. Women who do not breastfeed generally begin to ovulate within a month or so after giving birth.

Concept | Check

Currently, world food production is sufficient to meet the energy needs of the world's population. Despite adequate food resources, however, undernutrition exists because of poverty, politics, and unequal distribution. In addition, projected population growth may soon overwhelm food production. Most scientists and world leaders recommend limiting population growth, especially in developing countries where birth rates are high.

War and Political/Civil Unrest

The recent Millennium Summit of the United Nations pledged to "spare no effort to free our peoples from the scourge of war." Against that background stands the reality that worldwide military spending has doubled over the past 20 years. In the twentieth century, deadly weapons of war took an enormous toll on civilians living in poor, politically vulnerable, war-torn nations. Although Africa has been ravaged by economic decay and famines for years, military spending in Africa more than doubled in the 1970s and held firm through the 1990s. Currently, less than one-half of 1% of the world's yearly production of goods and services is devoted to economic development assistance, whereas approximately 6% goes to military expenditures.

Civil disruptions and wars are setting back the progress of the poor and contributing to massive undernutrition. All but two of the major conflicts in 2000 took place in the developing world. War-related famine affects at least 20 million people in southern and northeastern Africa. The border war between Ethiopia and neighboring Eritrea has had a tremendous negative impact on food resources. A World Bank official stated that the food shortage in Ethiopia is a problem that will persist until political changes are made. Currently, 12.4 million people in Ethiopia, Eritrea, Djibouti, Kenya, Somalia, and Zimbabwe are at risk for food shortages. Other conflicts continue between Congo and the Republic of Congo, as well as in Angola, where millions have been left to starve. Most of these people are without shelter, clothing, food, or any means of obtaining them. Worldwide, this problem is projected to worsen over the next 15 years.

Homes and infrastructure are often damaged during times of war and political unrest.

Even when food is available, political divisions may impede distribution to the point that undernutrition will plague many people for years to come. Especially during emergencies, programs designed to help the poor have been undermined by poor administration, corruption, and political influence. During such political chaos, relief agencies are often caught between warring factions and those they are trying to help. This was the case in Zaire, where Rwandan refugee camps fell under the control of a militant group. The rebels controlled the food coming in the camps and would not allow relief agencies to do their work.

During the 1960s and 1970s, the problem of undernutrition in developing countries was perceived as a technical one: how to produce enough food for the growing world population. The problem is now seen as largely political: how to achieve cooperation among and within nations, so that gains in food production and infrastructure are not wiped out by war. Only a combination of approaches—finding technical solutions to help with the problems of chronic hunger and poverty together with resolving political crises that push developing nations into a state of acute hunger and chaos—will help.

Rapid Depletion of Natural Resources

As we quickly deplete the earth's resources, population control grows increasingly critical. The productive capacity of agriculture is approaching its limits in many areas worldwide. Environmentally unsustainable farming methods undermine food production, especially in developing countries.

green revolution This refers to increases in crop yields that accompany the introduction of new agricultural technologies in less-developed countries, beginning in the 1960s. The key technologies were high-yielding, disease-resistant strains of rice, wheat, and corn; greater use of fertilizer and water; and improved cultivation practices.

The term **green revolution** describes a phenomenon that began in the 1960s when crop yields rose dramatically in some countries, such as the Philippines, India, and Mexico (countries in Africa did not benefit because climates were not compatible with the crops used). The increased use of fertilizers, irrigation, and the development of superior crops through careful plant breeding made this boost in agricultural production possible. Many of the technologies associated with the green revolution have now achieved most of their potential. For example, rice yields have not increased significantly since the release of superior varieties in 1966.

Future gains in productivity may be much harder to accomplish because of the need to farm less productive soils. Until the introduction of another superior strain of rice or other grain, developing countries will not benefit greatly from recent, more modest breakthroughs in biotechnology (see the Nutrition Perspective on use of biotechnology). Actually, the green revolution was never intended to solve the world's food problems, according to Dr. Norman Borlaug, its chief architect. It was just a stopgap measure until world leaders could control population growth.

ecosystem A community in nature that includes plants, animals, and their environment.

cash crop A crop grown specifically for export, so that goods from other countries can be purchased. Cultivation of cash crops diverts agricultural resources necessary to feed a country's own citizens. Examples of cash crops are coffee, tea, cocoa, and bananas.

Areas of the world that remain uncultivated or ungrazed are mostly unsuited to farming: rocky, steep, infertile, too dry, too wet, or inaccessible. Much of this land is nonetheless invaluable for the crucial **ecosystem** benefits it provides, such as a depository for a wide variety of plants. This is particularly true for humid tropical areas, such as the Amazon basin rain forests.

In Africa, an area of land twice the size of New Jersey is turned into unproductive desert each year because of soil erosion. The erosion results from overgrazing by livestock, destructive farming techniques, and burning of mature rain forests. Also, the cultivation of many **cash crops** in African countries damages the land, draining the soil of vital nutrients. Then, when the land has been used up, farmers move on to other areas, leaving behind desolate land vulnerable to soil erosion. In the short run, farmers can overplow and overpump water with impressive results, but in the long run they use up natural resources on which long-term productivity depends. Soil erosion is also a problem in North America. New farming techniques, such as "no till" planting, where plowing is kept to a minimum, are helping to minimize this problem.

Nearly all irrigation water available worldwide is currently being used, and groundwater supplies are becoming depleted at rapid rates in many regions. The eventual water shortage this will create is projected to increase war and civil unrest in arid areas of the world, such as Northern Africa and the Middle East. China, which has more than 20% of the world's irrigated land, is also plagued with a growing scarcity of fresh water. In the future billions of people will face ongoing water shortages.[17]

The prospects of obtaining substantially more food from the oceans are also poor. In recent years, the amount of fish caught worldwide has leveled off at about 80 million metric tons a year. Fish was once considered the poor person's protein. But, without actual farming of fish, which is becoming more common worldwide, this is unlikely to be true again.

Clearly, we can exploit the earth's resources only so far—world population probably cannot continue to expand as it does today without the potential for serious famine and death. The Food and Agriculture Organization (FAO) of the United Nations works on this principle: "The fight to ensure that all people have enough nutritious food to eat is worthy of our greatest efforts, but it must be fought with the full recognition that it cannot be won unless agricultural, fishery, and forestry production returns to the earth as much as—or more than—it takes." This statement highlights the need for immediate action to protect the earth's already deteriorated environment from further destruction, if food production is to keep up with the expanding population.

Cultural Attitudes Toward Certain Foods

Culture affects food use, just as it does family size. In India, for example, the Hindu reverence for cattle has worsened some already significant nutrition problems. These sacred cows consume food rather than provide it; the wandering cows also damage vegetation that could otherwise feed humans. Although the cows provide milk, no attempt is made to improve milk production through selective breeding practices. In certain areas of India, a child may not be fed milk curds because of a superstitious belief that they inhibit growth. Bananas may not be fed because they supposedly cause convulsions. These are obstacles, but not barriers, to good nutrition. Given adequate food resources, a healthful diet allowing for individual food taboos and prejudices is possible.

In North America, many people shun potential foods such as horse meat, insects, and algae.

Inadequate Shelter and Sanitation

When people die from undernutrition in developing countries, other influences, such as inadequate shelter and sanitation, almost always contribute. Poor sanitation raises the risk of infection, as does undernutrition. Together these represent a lethal combination (Fig. 20-4). For example, the 1994 plague, which killed almost 5000 people and sparked the panicked exodus of another half a million in Surat, in northwest India, was linked mainly to unsanitary housing conditions.

In Brazil, migrants displaced by multinational land developers have flooded from the north and northeast into Rio de Janeiro and São Paulo, attracted by the prospect of jobs. There they have built shantytowns next to apartment towers and affluent suburbs, but the jobs do not materialize, and urban poverty simply replaces rural impoverishment.

Inadequate and deteriorating shelters threaten the lives of more than 500 million people today. Many of the 15 million annual deaths of children—half of them under 5 years old—in developing countries could be prevented by improving the standards of environmental hygiene. Urban populations of some developing countries are currently growing at an annual rate of 5 to 7%. Such a skewed population distribution will result in more poverty. The current urban explosion is the result of both high birth rates and continuing migration of people to the cities from the countryside. People go to the cities to find employment and resources the countryside can no longer provide. Worldwide, 38% of people lived in urban areas in 1975. The figure is now about 50%, and is expected to reach 70% by 2050. Nine of the 10 largest cities 20 years from now will be in poor countries. Currently 12 of the 15 most polluted cities are in Asia alone.

In developing countries, the poor make up most of the urban population, and their needs for housing and community services often outstrip available governmental resources. Most of these urban poor live in overcrowded, self-made shelters, which lack a safe and adequate water supply and are only partially served by public utilities. The shantytowns and ghettos of the developing world are often worse than the rural areas the people left behind. Because the urban poor need cash to purchase food, they often subsist on diets that are even more meager than the homegrown rural fare. Making matters worse, haphazard shelters often lack facilities to protect food from spoilage or the ravages of insects and rodents. The inability to protect food supplies in some developing countries leads to the loss of as much as 40% of all perishable foods.

Inadequate sanitation facilities and the consumption of contaminated water cause the majority of all diseases, yet people in developing countries (about 1 billion people) often lack access to a safe water supply.

The shift from rural to urban life takes its greatest toll on infants and children. Infants are often weaned early from the breast, partly because the mother must find employment and partly because she may be influenced by the images of sophisticated,

Figure 20-4 Nutritional status and overall food supply combine with a variety of environmental factors to influence the risk of infection and the ultimate outcome.

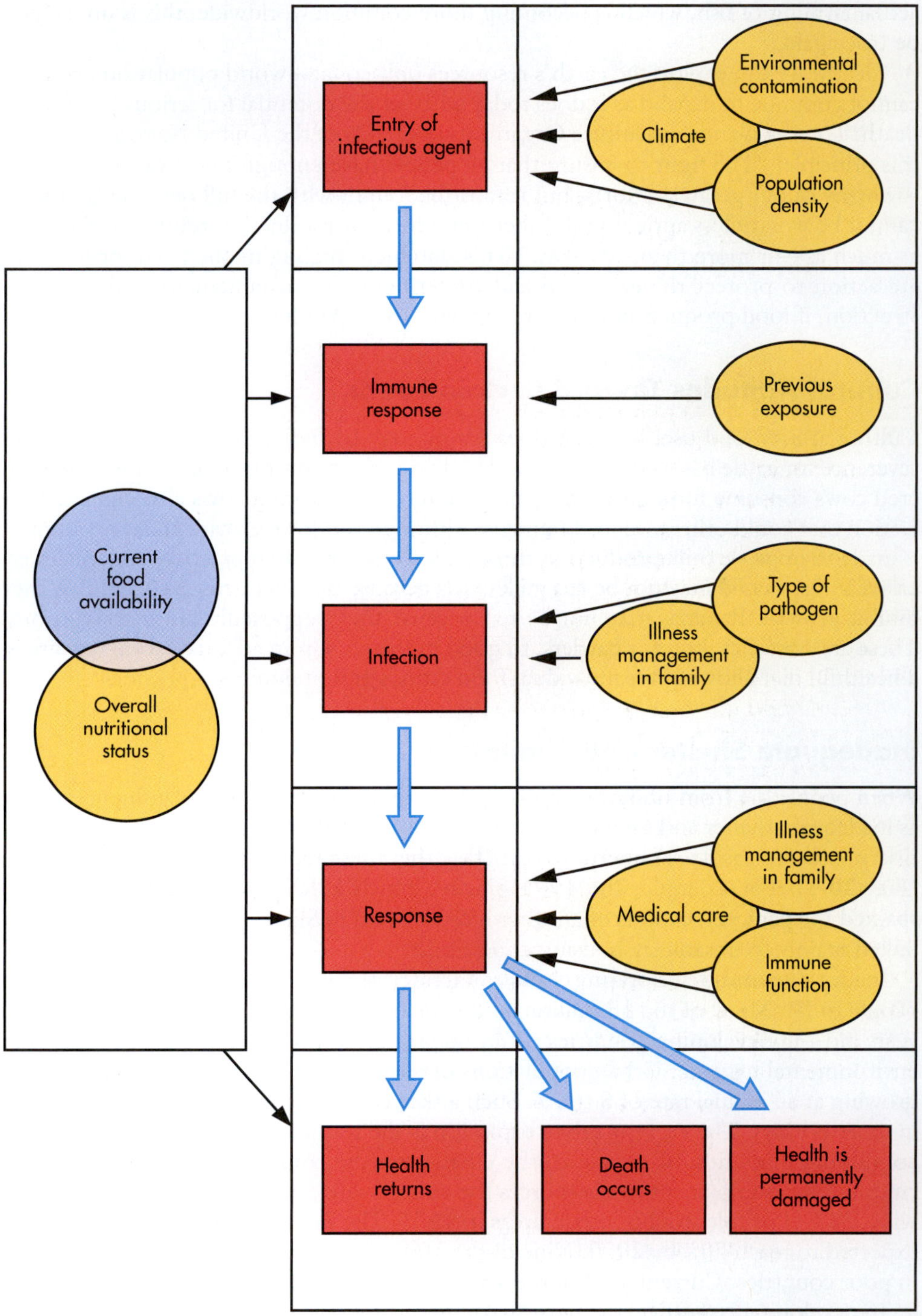

formula-using women promoted in advertisements. Unfortunately, because infant formulas are relatively expensive, poor parents may overdilute the mixture or use too little to meet the baby's needs. Because the water supply may not be safe, the prepared formula is also likely to be contaminated with bacteria. Human milk, in contrast, is generally much more hygienic, readily available, and nutritious. It also provides infants with immunity to some ailments. Promoting breastfeeding when it is safe for a mother to breastfeed her baby is important (see the discussion of AIDS in the next section).

Overall, the single most effective health advantage for people, wherever they live, is a safe and convenient water supply. Inadequate sanitation and the consumption of contaminated water cause 75% of all diseases and more than one-third of all deaths in developing countries. The World Health Organization (WHO) estimates that 1 billion people, about one-sixth of all people, have an unsafe and inadequate water supply. In addition, up to 90% of the diseases seen in developing countries may be attributed to contaminated water.

Poor sanitation, another example of inadequate infrastructure in the developing world, also creates a critical public health problem. Human feces, rotting garbage, and associated insect and rodent infestations are commonly seen in urban areas of the developing world. Potent sources of disease organisms—human urine and feces—are two of the most dangerous substances people encounter in routine daily living. The inability to dispose of the massive numbers of dead people (and dead animals) resulting from civil wars causes additional sanitation problems. In some developing countries, diarrheal diseases account for as many as one-third of all deaths in children under 5 years of age. WHO estimates that even with improvements in housing, 2 billion people in the world still lack proper sanitation facilities.

High External Debt

Since the 1970s many developing countries have become trapped in the cycle of borrowing repeatedly from foreign countries and international banks. Servicing these external debts, which now total about $2.5 trillion, has brought several countries to the verge of economic collapse. About $6 billion is owed to the United States. The external debt of Latin America represents 45% of the region's gross regional output of goods and services.

Many African nations also carry large debt burdens—currently, $350 billion. Recent drops in prices for raw commodities they export, higher prices for imported oil, and embezzlement of funds by high-ranking political officials make this problem even worse. Although the African debts are much smaller in absolute terms than those of Brazil, Argentina, and Mexico, for example, the actual burden is greater when national incomes and export earnings are considered. Nearly half the money African nations earn from exports goes to paying off the continent's multibillion-dollar debt. As a result, African nations have had to impose cuts in domestic programs, which can cause widespread undernutrition in many of these poor nations, in part because these countries still need to import—and pay for—machinery, concrete, trucks, and consumer goods. To make up the difference between export income and import expenses, countries have been forced to borrow billions of dollars from international banks.

Concept | Check

War and civil strife, along with a decline in the world's natural resources, contribute to the difficulty of ending undernutrition in many developing countries. In addition, inadequate housing conditions, impure water, and inadequate sanitation worldwide increase the risk for infection and disease. Infection then combines with undernutrition to compromise further the health of impoverished people. Finally, many developing countries are burdened by extremely high external debts, which severely limit their ability to implement programs to reduce undernutrition.

The Impact of AIDS

Currently, more than 42 million people around the world are infected with the **human immunodeficiency virus (HIV)** or have gone on to develop **acquired immune deficiency syndrome (AIDS)** from the infection. The male to female ratio is about 1:1. About 20 million people worldwide have died from AIDS. In comparison, about 25 million people succumbed to the Black Death in the fourteenth century. In 2002, 5 million people were newly infected with HIV and 3.1 million people died of the disease.

human immunodeficiency virus (HIV) The virus that leads to acquired immune deficiency syndrome.

acquired immunodeficiency syndrome (AIDS) A disorder in which a virus (human immunodeficiency virus [HIV]) infects specific types of immune system cells. This leaves the person with reduced immune function and in turn defenseless against numerous infectious agents; typically contributes to the person's death.

In the United States, it is estimated that about 900,000 people are infected with HIV, many of whom are unaware of their infections. This means that as many as 1 of every 280 people in the United States may be infected. About 450,000 people in the United States have died from the disease, about 25,000 in 2000 alone. Each year about 50,000 new cases also appear. Minority populations account for more cases than do Caucasians in the United States, based on their percentage of the population. Stopping the spread of this disease is imperative for the United States, especially in minority communities. People at risk are urged to seek testing.

An individual can be infected with HIV through contact with bodily fluids including blood, semen, vaginal secretions, and human milk. Thus the virus can be transmitted through sexual contact, through blood-to-blood contact, as well as from a mother to an infant during pregnancy, delivery, or during breastfeeding. The virus has a very limited ability to exist outside the body.

Once infected with HIV, the individual is said to be HIV-positive. If untreated, the viral disease progresses over the next few years, and the individual develops symptoms such as diarrhea, lung disease, weight loss, and a form of cancer. Once the individual has developed these symptoms, they are said to have AIDS. Without treatment, an individual will likely die from AIDS within 4 to 5 years.

In Africa, particularly sub-Saharan countries, HIV is rampant throughout the entire population, with this region containing nearly 70% of the world's HIV-positive people.[6] In most areas of sub-Saharan Africa, AIDS is reducing life expectancy by one-half, especially if the person also has tuberculosis. As noted in the chapter, world population projections for the next 50 years may have to be reduced to account for the impact of AIDS in Africa and in Asia. In many countries, AIDS also is creating orphans, an estimated 3.7 million worldwide (660,000 in South Africa alone).

Experts have blamed sexual promiscuity and prostitution in some African societies, as well as sexual practices that can make it easier for the virus to enter a woman's bloodstream, for the rapid spread of the disease in that area of the world. Many people in Africa engage in unprotected sex because they can't afford condoms, or because women cannot get their male partners to use them. Overall, 75 to 85% of all cases of HIV have been spread through sexual contact, homosexual as well as heterosexual. Intravenous drug use, via shared needles, accounts for a large number of the rest of the cases, along with sloppy blood donation practices.

The latest AIDS drugs can significantly slow the progression of the disease (no AIDS vaccine to prevent the disease is currently available). However, there are many barriers to the use of these drugs in the developing world.[5] The newest drug therapies require patients to take at least three different drugs and about 14 pills each day. And just a few missed doses can significantly reduce the effectiveness of the drugs and result in faster disease progression. Another barrier to the use of these drugs in developing countries is economic. A typical drug regimen can cost approximately $14,000 per year, not including any unforeseen hospital stays. Certain drug companies and governments are working to lower the cost of AIDS drugs to developing nations. Still, in many cases, the expense will remain out of reach to many who need the drugs. It has been suggested that developed nations step in and cover most of the costs. The United Nations is spearheading an effort to raise the $8 to $10 billion needed to fight the disease. The United States recently pledged $1.3 billion toward the effort, and Bill Gates of Microsoft fame has pledged $100 million from his private foundation.

On a more individual scale, can eating a balanced diet prevent HIV or stave off AIDS? The answer is no. Consuming a balanced diet, however, helps lessen the impact of infections but does not cure the disease or make it less deadly, while poor nutritional status contributes to quicker onset of symptoms such as body wasting and fever. This ultimately leads to a quicker demise. Overall, AIDS patients should consider maintaining nutritional status an integral part of their treatment regimen.[1]

The main hope for addressing the problem of AIDS in the developing world is prevention of new cases—safer sex, use of clean needles, and other behavior-linked approaches. The devastating effects of AIDS on our civilization have been very rapid when measured by earth's scale of time, and the true costs to society—other than the cost of human lives—have yet to emerge. The very nature of the disease is likely to wreak significant human devastation worldwide.[7] This is partly because its primary route of transmission is a basic human behavior—sexual activity. A recent study warns us that 57 countries risk major HIV outbreaks. Reported HIV cases are increasing rapidly in Africa, Southeast Asia, China, the Caribbean, and Russia (and much of the rest of Eastern Europe).

Behind the mind-boggling statistics on AIDS are less obvious costs to businesses, families, schools and universities, and society in general. For example, worker productivity will plummet because AIDS victims produce less and demand more, especially as they waste away in the latter stages of the disease. Business productivity drops even further when relatives take time away from work and school to care for family members afflicted with AIDS. Furthermore, AIDS demands a considerable amount of family income. Hard-pressed families, who have to devote much of their income to doctors and medicines, have little left for living expenses. Other family members must struggle to keep up with daily duties because they must care for orphans left behind in the disease's wake.

Breastfeeding becomes an issue for mothers who test HIV-positive. Research shows that babies have a 10% chance of getting the virus from their HIV-infected human milk if they breastfeed for 2 years. Many experts recommend the avoidance of breastfeeding as an intervention to prevent the transmission of the virus from mother to infant. However, in many situations, nutritionally adequate human milk substitutes are not available, especially in an environment where infectious diseases and undernutrition are the primary causes of death during infancy. In these instances, feeding with infant formulas can increase a child's risk of illness and death. In the end, the choice must lie with the mother and her health-care advisors, based on current circumstances.[16] Some African countries are now supplying infant formulas if an HIV-positive mother chooses to use this option. To learn more about this and other facets of AIDS, check out the website www.unaids.org.

A particularly sad development of AIDS in Africa is the number of AIDS orphans, children whose parents have both died of AIDS. The United Nations has estimated that there will be 20 million AIDS orphans in Africa by the year 2010.

Concept | Check

Currently, there are more than 42 million people around the world infected with the human immunodeficiency virus (HIV) or who have gone on to develop acquired immune deficiency syndrome (AIDS) from the infection. The virus can be transmitted through sexual contact, through blood-to-blood contact, as well as from a mother to a baby during pregnancy, delivery, and likely during breastfeeding. Without treatment, an individual once infected will likely die from AIDS within 4 to 5 years. The main hope currently for addressing the problem of AIDS in the developing world is prevention of new cases.

Reducing Undernutrition in the Developing World

As you have probably guessed, greatly reducing undernutrition in the developing world will be complicated and will take considerable time to accomplish. Today, it is a common practice for the more affluent nations to supply famine areas with direct food aid. However highly publicized and praised at the time, direct food aid is not a long-term solution. Although it reduces the number of deaths from famine, it can also reduce incentives for local production by driving down local prices. In addition, the affected countries may have little or no means of transporting the food to those who need it most. Furthermore, the donated foods may receive little cultural acceptance.

In the short run, there is no choice—aid must be given because people are starving. Still, improving the infrastructure for poor people, especially rural people, needs to be the long-term focus. This long-term approach is necessary because the most significant factor affecting the undernutrition of people in impoverished areas of the world is their reliance on outside sources for basic needs. Their dependence makes them constantly vulnerable.

Three basic approaches are suggested by the World Bank to counteract micronutrient deficiencies: increase diversity of the food supply; fortify specific foods with nutrients; and provide nutrient supplementation for individuals when necessary.

Women are receiving more attention as efforts to improve the health and welfare of the world's people evolve.

Development Tailored to Local Conditions Is Important

Recall that, in the past 40 years, world food supplies have grown faster than the population. Thus, the increase in undernutrition during this period is caused by an increase in the number of people cut off from their share of this supply. Millions of farmers are losing access to resources they need to be self-reliant. In response, careful, small-scale regional development is one option. There is a growing realization that rural people who own no land will flock to the overcrowded cities unless economic opportunities can be created as part of a plan for sustainable development.

For the most part, the solution lies in helping people meet their own needs and directing them to resources and employment opportunities, rather than simply giving them resources. Experience has shown that credit—along with training, food storage facilities, and marketing—allows rural people to participate in their own development so as to benefit their families and communities.

One U.S. program that has helped improve conditions in the developing nations is the Peace Corps, which provides education, distributes food and medical supplies, and builds structures for local use. The aim of the Peace Corps is to improve the infrastructure and education of developing countries and thereby help create independent, self-sustaining economies around the world.

Impoverished women are a special concern. In addition to working longer hours than do men, they grow most of the food for family consumption and make up three-fourths of the labor force in the informal sector and an increasing proportion in the formal economy. Economic opportunities for women and education regarding family planning must be augmented. Of the 3 billion people in the world living on less than $2 a day, 70% are women. Moreover, among the developing world's 900 million illiterate people, women outnumber men 2 to 1. Thus, an important means of propelling nations out of poverty is to end the cycle of female neglect.

Suitable technologies for processing, preserving, marketing, and distributing nutritious local staples also need to be encouraged, so that small farmers can flourish. Education on how to use these foods to create healthful diets, such as preparing vitamin A-rich vegetables, adds further benefit. Supplementing indigenous foods with nutrients that are in short supply, such as iron, various B-vitamins, zinc, and iodide, also deserves consideration.[12] One current program involves adding iron to sugar in various parts of the world. In addition, advances in water purification need to be employed.

Promoting extensive landownership may also be one part of the solution. Increasing the availability of food is one of the many advantages. If food resources are concentrated among a minority of people, as often happens with unequal landownership, food won't be equally distributed unless efficient transportation systems are in place. Inequitable distribution then proves a very difficult problem to resolve.

Raising the economic status of impoverished people by employing them is as important as expanding the food supply. If an increase in food supply is achieved without an accompanying rise in employment, there may be no long-term change in the number of undernourished people. Although food prices may fall with increased mechanization, use of fertilizers, and other modern technologies, it needs to be kept in mind that these advances can also displace people from jobs.

A shipment of high-technology tractors, for example, might put local laborers out of work. From this perspective, it is of little consequence that jobs are technologically primitive by Western standards. As mentioned before, increasing both per capita income and education is necessary. That effort must include employment. Making full use of the human resources available in the developing world itself is more essential than ever.

Critical | Thinking

Stan has read about various relief efforts to help undernourished people in developing countries, especially the emergency food aid programs for famine-ravaged areas. Many of these efforts appear to be only temporary, and he wonders what long-range approaches might help alleviate the problem of undernutrition. What suggestions would you give Stan about possible long-term solutions for undernutrition in developing countries?

Some Concluding Thoughts

Clearly, the developing world will have to rely largely on its own resources to finance development. For decades, countries in Africa could count on the Cold War as an economic resource. The United States and the former Soviet Union opposed each other through African proxies, pouring in money to prop up pro-Western or pro-Communist governments. Now the big powers' priorities have turned inward.

Today, the economic loss from undernutrition is staggering, and the amount of human pain and suffering is incalculable. With all the international relief efforts and assistance from governments and private organizations combined, we are still failing in our battle against undernutrition.

Currently, some experts are concerned about the "marginalization" of problems in the developing world, fearing rich nations might dismiss war, disease, and famine as a way of life for poorer nations. In a recent survey, people in the United States identified world famine as less of a concern than violence, drugs, and inflation. (Currently, U.S. food aid stands at $2.4 billion.) Ultimately, however, the depletion of world resources, the massive debt incurred by poorer countries, the threat of danger to more prosperous countries nearby, and the toll taken in human lives do affect the overall world economy and well-being.

Life is not necessarily fair, but the aim of civilization should be to make it more so. The world has both the food and the technical expertise to end hunger. What is lacking is the political will to do so.

There is no doubt that food aid is important in reducing death from famine, but it isn't a long-term solution.

With regard to the world food supply, the current generation of young adults and the next will not likely have to face the absolute limits. Instead, they will have to make difficult choices if the outlook for future generations is to improve.

Concept | Check

Overall, one important solution to reducing undernutrition in the developing world lies in providing sufficient employment, so that people can purchase the food their families need or provide access to land and other food production resources. Development programs must be sensitive to regional conditions to ensure that the new technologies introduced don't intensify existing problems for the poorest people.

Summary

1. Poverty is commonly linked to chronic or periodic undernutrition. Malnutrition can occur when the food supply is either scarce or abundant. The resulting deficiency conditions and degenerative diseases contribute to poor health.
2. Undernutrition is the most common form of malnutrition in developing countries. It results from inadequate intake, absorption, or use of nutrients or food energy. Many deficiency conditions consequently appear, and infectious diseases thrive because the immune system cannot function properly.
3. The greatest risk of undernutrition occurs during critical periods of growth and development: gestation, infancy, and childhood. Low birth weight is a leading cause of infant deaths worldwide. Many developmental problems are caused by nutritional deprivation during critical periods of brain growth. People in their later years are also at greater risk.
4. Undernutrition diminishes both physical and mental capabilities. In poor countries, this is worsened by recurrent infections, unsanitary conditions, extreme weather, inadequate shelter, and exposure to diseases.
5. In the United States, famine has been nonexistent since the 1930s, but food insecurity and undernutrition remain problems. Soup kitchens, food stamps, school lunch and breakfast programs, and the Special Supplemental Nutrition Program for Women, Infants, and Children (WIC) have focused on improving the nutritional health of poor and at-risk people. When adequately funded, these programs have proved effective in reducing undernutrition. The need to reduce out-of-wedlock pregnancies remains a national priority because single parents and their children are much more likely to live in poverty.
6. Multiple factors contribute to the problem of undernutrition in the developing world. In densely populated countries, food resources, as well as the means for distributing food, may be inadequate. Farming methods often encourage erosion, which deprives the soil of valuable nutrients and thereby hampers future efforts to grow food. Limited water availability limits food production. Naturally occurring devastation from droughts, excessive rainfall, fire, crop infestation, and human causes—such as urbanization, war and civil unrest, debt, and poor sanitation—all contribute to the major problem of undernutrition, as does AIDS.
7. Proposed solutions to world undernutrition must include consideration of the interaction of multiple factors, many of which are thoroughly embedded in cultural traditions. Family planning efforts, for example, may not succeed until life expectancy increases. Through education, efforts should be made to upgrade farming methods, improve crops, limit pregnancies, encourage breastfeeding when it is safe to do so, and improve sanitation and hygiene. Direct food aid is only a short-term solution. In what may appear to be a step backward, many experts recommend more sustainable subsistence-level farming. Small-scale industrial development is another way to create meaningful employment and purchasing power for vast numbers of the rural poor.

Study Questions

1. Describe the difference between malnutrition and undernutrition.
2. Describe in a short paragraph any evidence of undernutrition that you saw while you were growing up, such as on television. What are/were the likely roots of these problems?
3. What do you believe are the major factors contributing to undernutrition in wealthy nations, such as the United States? What are some solutions to this problem?
4. What three points would you make to a group of seventh-grade girls concerning the economic perils of teenage pregnancy and parenting?
5. Personal responsibility is a common theme in political circles. How does this relate to the problem of undernutrition in the United States? Does it apply to all causes of the problem?
6. Outline how war and civil unrest in developing countries have worsened problems of chronic hunger over the past few years.
7. How important is population control in addressing the problem of world hunger now and in the future? Support your answer with three main points.
8. Why is solving the problem of undernutrition a key factor in the development of the full potential of developing countries? What basic nutrients are keys to the health of these people?
9. Discuss how infrastructure could influence the causes and solutions of chronic hunger in a developing nation.
10. Name three nutrients that are often lacking in the diets of undernourished people. What effects can be expected with each deficiency?

Annotated References

1. ADA Reports: Position of the American Dietetic Association and Dietitians of Canada: Nutrition intervention in the care of persons with human immunodeficiency virus infection. *Journal of the American Dietetic Association* 100:708, 2000.

   Malnutrition, various forms of tissue wasting, fat accumulation, and risk of additional chronic disease have become central issues in health-care plans for patients living with HIV. Efforts to optimize nutritional status, including nutrition therapy and nutrition-related education, should be components of the total health care provided to people infected with the HIV virus.

2. Brown K and others: Effects of supplemental zinc on the growth and serum zinc concentrations of prepubertal children: A meta-analysis of randomized controlled trials. *American Journal of Clinical Nutrition* 75:1062, 2002.

   Zinc supplementation in children who have a zinc deficiency leads to increases in height and weight (especially from greater muscle mass). Correcting such deficiencies worldwide is important.

3. Brown K: Seeds of concern. *Scientific American*, p. 51, April 2001.

   Advocates of genetically modified crops argue that use of these crops reduces dependence on pesticides, since the plants are engineered to resist insects and pests. Critics of these genetically modified crops worry that these engineered plants will disrupt delicate ecosystems by harming innocent creatures and encouraging the development of "super-weeds." In addition, these critics question whether using genetically modified crops will actually result in a significant decrease in reliance on pesticides. This article discusses these controversies in detail.

4. Brundtland GH: Nutrition and infection: Malnutrition and mortality in public health. *Nutrition Reviews* 58(II):S1, 2000.

   The combination of malnutrition and infectious disease is deadly. These conditions arise from poverty and keep people in poverty—not just for one generation, but for many generations. Many infections are preventable. For example, when vitamin A is introduced as part of measles management, the fatality rate can be reduced by more than 50%.

5. Bullers A: Living with AIDS—20 years later. *FDA Consumer*, p. 29, November-December 2001.

   Scientific understanding of HIV/AIDS has increased dramatically since AIDS was first reported in 1981, leading to new and more effective drug therapies. Still, as the future of AIDS patients in North America is looking brighter, advocates are demanding that these new therapies and treatments be made more widely available to AIDS patients in the developing world.

6. Cock K, Janssen R: An unequal epidemic in an unequal world. *Journal of the American Medical Association* 288:236, 2002.

   The impact of HIV/AIDS is quite different in industrialized and developing nations. In general, in industrialized countries, the introduction of highly effective medical therapy has led to dramatic increases in life expectancy and quality of life in those infected with HIV. However, HIV/AIDS is still a major problem in developing countries. For example, 77% of worldwide AIDS deaths, and 68% of new HIV infections, occur in sub-Saharan Africa.

7. Ezzell C: Care for a dying continent. *Scientific American*, p. 96, May 2000.

   AIDS is destined to alter history in Africa—and, in fact, the world—to a degree not seen in humanity's past since the Black Death. It is estimated that between 20 and 25% of the population in Zimbabwe carries the virus, and an estimated 10 million children are destined to become orphaned on the continent of Africa due to the AIDS epidemic. The AIDS drugs available to many in the developed world—which cost upward of $14,000 per person per year—are unthinkable for the majority of people in Africa.

8. Falk M and others: Food biotechnology: Benefits and concerns. *Journal of Nutrition* 132:1384, 2002.

   There are both benefits and potential risks associated with the use of genetically modified crops. Thus far, the producers of these crops have mostly benefited. Consumers may benefit in the future from plants with enhanced yields and an extended shelf life. There is some worry that environmental damage, as well as harm to the consumer, may result from use of these such crops.

9. Food and Agriculture Organization: *The state of food insecurity in the world: 2000.* Rome, Italy: Food and Agriculture Organization of the United Nations, 2000.

   Countries with the highest numbers and greatest depth of hunger include 18 countries in Africa, as well as Afghanistan, Bangladesh, Haiti, the Democratic People's Republic of Korea, Republic of Korea, and Mongolia. These countries face difficult problems in feeding their people due to instability and conflict, poor governance, erratic weather, poverty, agricultural failure, population pressure, and fragile ecosystems.

10. Hampl J, Hall R: Dietetic approaches to U.S. hunger and food insecurity. *Journal of the American Dietetic Association* 102:919, 2002.

    Both hunger and food insecurity are realities for many individuals and families in the United States. There is encouraging news that the prevalence of both hunger and food insecurity has decreased in recent years. However, there is still much to be done to ensure that people in the United States are able to obtain adequate food for themselves and their families.

11. Harlander S: The evolution of modern agriculture and its future with biotechnology. *Journal of the American College of Nutrition* 21(3):161S, 2002.

Farmers have been genetically modifying plants for thousands of years by crossing commercially available crops with their wild relatives. Newer techniques for genetically modifying crops include radiation and genetic engineering. Crops created with the newest forms of biotechnology have only been made available to the consumer within the past few years, but already these crops are having an enormous impact on modern agriculture, specifically by reducing pesticide use in some crops.

12. Kapil U, Bhavna A: Adverse effects of poor micronutrient status during childhood and adolescence. *Nutrition Reviews* 60(5):S84, 2002.

Vitamin A, iron, and iodide are important for the development of normal cognitive functions, immunity, work capacity, and reproductive health. Yet deficiencies of these micronutrients are widespread across India and other areas of the developing world. Children are especially at risk for suffering the consequences of these micronutrient deficiencies.

13. Kennedy E, Cooney E: Development of child nutrition programs in the United States. *Journal of Nutrition* 131:431S, 2001.

Anti-hunger groups, university-based researchers, health and nutrition officials, government agencies, and religious groups have all played a role in the development of national child nutrition programs. Successful programs in the United States include the Special Supplemental Nutrition Program for Women, Infants, and Children (WIC), the School Breakfast Program, the School Lunch Program, the Summer Food Service Program, the Child and Adult Care Food Program, and the Food Stamps Program. It is important that the United States maintains this national nutrition "safety net."

14. Lee JS, Frongillo EA: Nutritional and health consequences are associated with food insecurity among U.S. elderly persons. *Journal of Nutrition* 131:1503, 2001.

Older persons experiencing food insecurity have poorer dietary intakes than those who are food secure. With an increasing aging population, making sure that every older person has enough food to eat to meet his or her nutritional needs is an important way to help older adults enjoy healthy, active, and successful aging. Food insecurity among older adults is also considered ethically unacceptable.

15. Mackey M: The application of biotechnology to nutrition: An overview. *Journal of the American College of Nutrition* 21(3):157S, 2002.

Improving global food availability and enhancing the nutritional composition of these foods are just two ways that crop biotechnology is being used to improve worldwide human nutrition. While some have worried that much of the developing world will never receive the benefits of crop biotechnology, this technology is currently being used to help improve locally grown crops in certain areas of Africa, Southeast Asia, and Latin America. There is hope that improved crop biotechnology will eventually allow even the small-scale farmer to harvest more crops in an environmentally safe manner.

16. Mbori-Ngacha D and others: Morbidity and mortality in breastfed and formula-fed infants of HIV-1-infected women. *Journal of the American Medical Association* 286(19):2413, 2001.

There is controversy as to whether HIV-positive women in the developing world should breastfeed or formula-feed their infants. Some worry that the risk of infection and/or death is greater when breast milk is withheld from infants, while others feel that the risk of HIV transmission from mother to infant is too high to justify breastfeeding. In general, however, with appropriate resources, education, and access to safe water, formula feeding is a safe alternative to breastfeeding infants in the developing world for mothers infected with HIV.

17. Perkins S: Crisis on tap? Pollution and burgeoning populations stress Earth's water resources. *Science News* 162:42, 2002 (July).

Approximately one-third of the world's population lives in areas of water scarcity. Included in this estimate are 450 million people who live in areas of severe water stress. Currently, aquifers are used in addition to precipitation to supply enough water to meet existing demands. Unfortunately, aquifers are considered a nonrenewable resource, and thus the world needs to focus on conservation efforts so that water demands may be met in the future.

18. Ramakrishnan U: Prevalence of micronutrient malnutrition worldwide. *Nutrition Reviews* 60(5):S46, 2002.

There are many reasons for the widespread micronutrient deficiencies that are seen in the developing world, including inadequate dietary intake, poor diet quality, low nutrient bioavailability, and the presence of infections. While vitamin A, iron, and iodide have long been recognized as common micronutrient deficiencies in the developing world, research has been slow to address the prevalence and consequences of other micronutrient deficiencies, such as zinc and folate.

19. Thompson L: Are bioengineered foods safe? *FDA Consumer,* p. 18, January/February 2000.

There is no evidence that bioengineered foods pose any human health concerns or that they are in any way less safe than crops produced through traditional breeding. No matter how a new crop is created—using traditional methods or biotechnology tools—breeders must conduct field testing for several seasons to make sure the crops are safe for widespread use.

20. UNICEF: *The state of the world's children 2001.* New York: United Nations Children's Fund, 2001.

Most brain development happens before a child reaches 3 years old. Long before many adults even realize what is happening, the brain cells of a new infant proliferate, synapses develop, and the patterns of a lifetime are established. In these early years, children develop their abilities to think and speak, learn and reason, and lay the foundation for their values and social behavior as adults.

Take | Action

I. Fighting World Undernutrition on a Personal Level.

If you want to do something about world and domestic undernutrition, consider the following activities. It is a noble act to try to make a difference, even if you make just one small step. As with any change in behavior, don't try to do too many things at once. Try one or two activities that represent your commitment to solving this problem.

1. Volunteer at a local soup kitchen or homeless shelter for a limited period of time (1 month, for example). What insights did you gain?
2. Coordinate the efforts of a campus organization to donate some money to a voluntary agency that does antihunger work, such as the following:

Bread for the World 802 Rhode Island Ave., NE Washington, DC 20018	Oxfam America 115 Broadway Boston, MA 02116	Save the Children Foundation P.O. Box 970 Westport, CT 06881	Earth Save Foundation 1509 Suite B1 Seabright Ave. Santa Cruz, CA 95062
Catholic Relief Services 209 W. Fayette St. Baltimore, MD 21201	CARE 660 First Ave. New York, NY 10016	Second Harvest 116 Michigan Ave., Suite #4 Chicago, IL 60603	

3. Take a contribution for the ongoing offering of nonperishable foods at your church, or mosque, or synagogue, or other place of worship near you. If your church doesn't have this offering, start one.
4. Get on a food recovery program's mailing list and read its newsletters for information on upcoming fund-raisers and programs to become involved.
5. Participate in food drives organized by local grocery stores through contributing food or services. Food-drive organizers may need volunteers to transport the donations from the store to a food pantry.
6. Point, click, and fight hunger. Internet users can find information on hunger at several sites, including the following:
   - Someone somewhere dies of hunger every 3.6 seconds. You can help stop the clock: go to **www.thehungersite.com** and click on Donate Free Food to send a meal to a needy someone. This site is affiliated with the UN World Food Program, which tracks the number of clicks and then sends a bill to one of its corporate or nonprofit sponsors.
   - HungerWeb, at Brown University, offers information on hunger research, programs, mailing lists, education, and advocacy, as well as an overview of the Alan Shawn Feinstein World Hunger Program at Brown. This site contains web links to Internet sites run by the UN, U.S. AID, and the World Bank. **www.brown.edu/Departments/World_Hunger_Program/**
   - The Food and Agriculture Organization of the United Nations has worked to alleviate poverty and hunger by promoting agricultural development, improved nutrition, and the pursuit of food security. This website will keep you up-to-date on recent issues and provides an extensive list of publications related to food security: **www.fao.org**
   - America's Second Harvest, the largest domestic hunger-relief organization, shows you how to help online and has information about the latest updates. **www.secondharvest.org**
   - Bread for the World is a nationwide Christian citizens' movement seeking justice for the world's hungry people by lobbying our nation's decision makers. **www.bread.org**
   - CARE is one of the world's largest private international relief and development organizations, with the goal of saving lives, building opportunity, and bringing hope to people in need. **www.care.org**

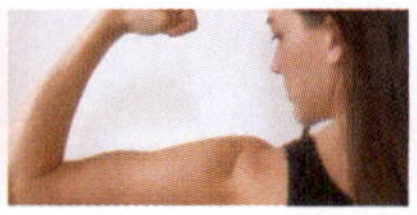

II. Joining the Battle Against Undernutrition.

Imagine that you recently spent your summer vacation in a developing country and saw evidence of undernutrition and hunger. Then imagine that you are now asking a large corporation to support your efforts to ease hunger and suffering in this area. Develop a two-paragraph statement outlining why addressing hunger issues in this area is important. Include how you think a large corporation could assist you in your efforts.

The Role of Biotechnology in Expanding Worldwide Food Availability

biotechnology A collection of processes that involve the use of biological systems for altering and, ideally, improving the characteristics of plants, animals, and other forms of life.

The ability of humans to manipulate nature has enabled us to improve the production and yield of many important foods. Traditional **biotechnology** is almost as old as agriculture. The first farmer to improve his stock by selectively breeding the best bull with the best cows was implementing biotechnology in a simple sense. The first baker to use yeast to make bread rise took similar advantage of biotechnology.

By the 1930s, biotechnology made possible the selective breeding of better plant hybrids: As a result, corn production in the United States quickly doubled. Through similar methods, agricultural wheat was crossed with wild grasses to confer more desirable properties, such as greater yield, increased resistance to mildew and bacterial diseases, and tolerance to salt or adverse climatic conditions.

Another type of biotechnology uses hormones rather than breeding. In the last decade, Canadian salmon have been treated with a hormone that allows them to mature three times faster than normal—without changing the fish in any other way. In general terms, biotechnology can be understood as the use of living things—plants, animals, bacteria—to manufacture products.

The New Biotechnology

genetic engineering Manipulation of the genetic makeup of any organism with recombinant DNA technology.

recombinant DNA technology A test tube technology that rearranges DNA sequences in an organism by cutting and rejoining DNA molecules with a series of enzymes.

genetically modified organism (GMO) Any organism created by genetic engineering.

transgenic Organism that contains genes originally present in another organism.

The new biotechnology used in agriculture includes several methods that directly modify products. It differs from traditional methods because it directly changes some of the genetic material (DNA) of organisms to improve characteristics. Crossbreeding plants or animals is no longer the only tool. Development of the new process, called **genetic engineering,** began in the 1970s. The field now features a wide range of cell and subcell techniques for the synthesis and placement of genetic material in organisms (Fig. 20-5). This process of **recombinant DNA technology** allows access to a wider gene pool, and it permits faster and more accurate production of new and more useful microbial, plant, and animal species.[11] Traditional breeding has had inconsistent results; biotechnology is more precise and provides more options of genetic material to utilize. Scientists select the traits they want and genetically engineer or introduce the gene that produces the desired trait into plants or animals, (now called a **genetically modified organism [GMO]** or **transgenic**). It is important to note, however, the genetic engineering doesn't replace conventional breeding practices; both work together.

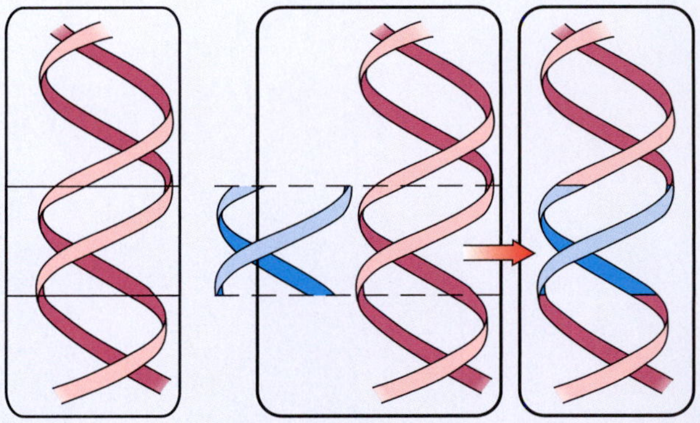
DNA of corn plant.
Gene from bacteria (Bt gene) that produces a protein toxic to the European corn borer.
Bt gene inserted into DNA of corn plant. Now the corn plant makes the Bt toxin and, so, is resistant to the European corn borer.

Figure 20-5 Biotechnology involves various techniques for transferring foreign DNA into an organism. In this diagram, a sample of DNA is cleaved out of a larger DNA fragment and inserted into the DNA of a host cell. Thus, the host cell contains new genetic information, with the potential of providing the cell with new capabilities. For corn, this means resistance to the European corn borer. The corn plant is now referred to as a genetically modified organism (GMO). In other applications, bacteria can be engineered to produce the human form of the hormone insulin and another hormone that increases milk production in cows.
Rollins Graphics

Already, genetic engineering at the agricultural level has allowed us to make use of new types of seeds, growth hormones, and microbial inoculants to stop pests and frost damage. Biotechnology is also used to develop drought-tolerant crops, as well as to detect *Listeria* and other microorganisms that cause foodborne illness. Scientists are engineering plants that grow without pesticides and new forms of potatoes that can last without preservatives. In addition, biotechnology can allow scientists to create fruits and grains with greater amounts of beta-carotene and vitamins E and C. Researchers are also examining ways to modify the fatty-acid makeup of vegetable oils. Because cautious use is the order of the day, these early benefits of the new biotechnology will strike us as only subtly different. The ultimate benefits, however, could be substantial if foods eaten by indigenous people can be so enhanced.[15]

Few consumers in the United States realize that currently about one-quarter of all corn and half of all soybeans produced in the United States have been genetically engineered in such a way to resist certain insects, in the case of corn, and to reduce pesticide use, in the case of soybeans. Some papaya plants have been genetically engineered to resist a certain virus. Corn is genetically altered by inserting a gene from the bacterium *Bacillus thuringiensis,* usually referred to as the Bt gene, in the corn DNA. The gene then allows the corn plant to make a protein that is lethal to certain caterpillars that destroy the plant. (Organic farmers even use the Bt bacteria to dust plants in order to destroy pests. This use, however, does not change the DNA of the plant.) The Bt protein in the corn, which is present in the plant in very low concentrations, has no effect on humans, as it is digested along with the other proteins in corn. FDA is confident that these currently approved varieties of genetically engineered foods are safe to consume. (The controversy over use of StarLink corn in 2000 arose because this GMO corn variety was not approved for human consumption. It found its way, however, into some corn products, such as taco shells.) Foods are not currently required to state the amount of GMO content, but some manufacturers have put GMO-free labels on their products. A recent study showed that even these foods typically have GMO content. FDA does not feel labeling of GMO products is needed because these pose no health risk.[19] The biggest debate in the United States surrounds the potential hazards to the environment from introducing genes from one species to another. There is also a question regarding the actual reduction in pesticide use that accompanies the cultivation of some of these products; it may not be as great as was originally predicted.[3]

Public response to use of the new biotechnology has been mixed. Even the scientific community has mixed feelings about this new technology, with supporters as convinced about the benefits as opponents are of the risks.[8] Although the use of genetically modified organisms may reduce the need for environmentally harmful activities, such as spraying crops with insecticides, critics point out that seeds produced with natural insecticides will lead to rapid insect resistance because the insecticides are continuously being emitted. When farmers use insecticides, they use them sparingly and only when needed, in part so the insects do not become resistant.

Although the risks may appear to be momentarily negligible, they may be cumulative and therefore dangerous in the long run. In addition, will allergens, such as those found in peanuts, eggs, milk, wheat, and shellfish, be added to genetically engineered foods that previously did not contain them? Evidence that this can happen has been seen in soybeans. Note, however, that FDA carefully examines all products developed using this technology and will enforce labeling of potential allergens that may be newly present in a biotech food.

The public has long been opposed to processes perceived as harmful to the environment, such as producing unnatural products. Because food reserves are high in the United States, Canada, and Europe, some question the need to increase food production. Skepticism surrounds unnatural products, as exemplified by western Europe's ban of a growth hormone previously used in beef production. Citizens believed the increase in meat supply was not worth the perceived risks associated with the product. Both scientists and concerned consumer groups are currently studying other potentially beneficial applications of the new biotechnology. Bovine somatotropin (BST), a hormone produced by cattle, has been known since the 1930s to maintain high milk production when injected into dairy cattle. Today an identical BST (Posilac) produced through genetic engineering can be used to greatly increase milk yield. Because it is a protein, any BST in the milk produced would be digested and therefore inactivated. People even produce their own form of somatotropin, but its structure differs considerably from that of BST. Because cows produce BST naturally, it has always been present in their milk. Treating the animals with the proposed higher levels of BST won't increase the concentration of hormone occurring naturally in the milk, nor will it alter the milk's nutrient composition.

Fish have been genetically engineered to grow four times faster than native varieties. The final adult size is the same, however.

Both traditional plant breeding and biotechnology have produced high-yielding plant varieties.

GMO products are widely distributed in our food supply. In fact, 70% of processed foods contain at least one GMO ingredient. So it is not surprising that when Gerber Products Co. tried to introduce a line of GMO-free baby foods, they found that they could not produce products from raw materials currently available.

Critical | Thinking

Bobbie is in a debate class and has been assigned to argue the biotechnologist's side of genetic engineering. Help her come up with a list of arguments in favor of biotechnology. What would the list look like if Bobbie were on the opposing side?

Soybeans are a common GMO food in the marketplace.

The European Economic Community is very skeptical regarding the use of genetic engineering in foods. This may be because citizens of these countries feel they cannot rely on their governments to ensure food safety, given the problem with mad cow disease in Britain. In contrast, U.S. citizens show great confidence in FDA oversight of food safety. Activism is also much more prevalent in Europe than in the United States. In addition, Europeans feel that the benefits of using GMO varieties are gained mostly by U.S. farmers and U.S. companies, not the Europeans themselves. Currently, it is illegal to import genetically engineered foods, such as products made from genetically engineered corn or soybeans, into Europe. (The same is true for Japan.)

Sweet potatoes have been genetically engineered to resist a virus common in Africa. Yields are increased when these GMO sweet potatoes are grown.

While FDA is still evaluating the safety of BST with respect to animals and the environment, the agency has determined that milk from treated animals is safe for human consumption. Currently about 1 in 10 dairy farms uses the product. Some critics question whether the increased milk production will stress the health of the cows, leading farmers to use more antibiotics. The public already appears to oppose BST, and the European Economic Community has banned its use.

Opponents to BST call for labeling of milk from treated cows. The biotech industry opposes labeling the milk because studies show no harmful effects from milk of BST-treated cows. FDA has not required such labeling, but such foods using genetic engineering cannot carry an "organic" label.

Again, with a surplus of milk in North America and Europe, garnering public support will be difficult. Furthermore, dairy farmers in Wisconsin and other dairy-producing regions generally oppose the introduction of the hormone, because they fear negative consumer reaction will lower milk consumption. The industry is also concerned that a sharp increase in milk output will adversely affect prices and thereby harm thousands of small dairy farms facing an already precarious economic situation.

Role of the New Biotechnology in the Developing World

Whether genetically engineered applications will help to significantly reduce undernutrition in the developing world remains to be seen. Unless price cuts accompany the increased production, only landowners and suppliers of biotechnology will enjoy the benefits. This point deserves emphasis: The person who can't afford to buy enough food today will still face that same predicament in the future.

As with most innovations, the more successful farmers, often those with larger farms, will adopt the new biotechnology first. Because of this, the present trend in the form of fewer and larger farms will continue in the developing world, a trend that undermines the solution of the most pressing undernutrition issues there. Furthermore, biotechnology does not promise dramatic increases in the production of most grains and cassava, the primary food resources in the world.

Perhaps the most promising potential of genetically engineered foods is the idea of plant breeding for micronutrients. The dilemma of micronutrient undernutrition may be decreased in developing countries if farmers have access to seeds and related plant materials that produce more of these nutrients.[15] Greater yields for indigenous plants, such as tomatoes that tolerate high amounts of salinity in the soil, is another hopeful outcome. Still, for the developing world, the focus needs to be on providing people with resources to produce and purchase their own food, not on simply growing more food. Biotechnology is a useful tool against the complex scourge of world undernutrition, but it's no panacea. Improved crops produced by this technology will likely be able to contribute to the battle, together with political and other efforts.

appendixes

appendix a

Chemistry: A Tool for Understanding Nutrition

You have already completed at least one basic high school and/or college course in chemistry; consequently, this appendix serves only to review key chemistry principles that arise in the study of nutrition. The study of human nutrition requires a basic awareness of and familiarity with general chemistry, organic chemistry, and biochemistry. This appendix provides fundamental concepts regarding atoms, molecules, chemical bonds, pH, organic compounds, and biochemical structures. An understanding of basic chemistry may make the study of nutrition easier and more interesting. It helps connect nutrient characteristics with the structural and chemical attributes of the individual components of food.

One concept to keep in mind is that the physical and chemical properties of almost anything are intimately related to its structure, whether atoms, molecules, or organisms (Table A-1). A basic knowledge of chemical structures can help you visualize important fundamental concepts in nutrition.

Properties of Matter and Mass

All living and nonliving things are composed of matter. Matter exists in three states, which are solid, liquid, or gas. An example of a solid is ice, a liquid is water, and a gas is steam. Two characteristics of matter are (1) it has mass and (2) it occupies space (volume). Mass is related to the amount of force it takes to move an object—it takes less force to move a paper clip than a pencil; therefore, the clip has less mass. Volume is related to the amount of space an object occupies—a pint of water occupies less space than a gallon; therefore, a pint has a smaller volume. Both of these properties depend on how much of the substance there is.

Another property of matter is density. Density is defined as the mass of an object divided by its volume:

$$\text{Density} = \frac{\text{Mass}}{\text{Volume}}$$

Density is independent of how much matter is available. The density of water in a lake is the same as in a cup. Density is commonly expressed in units of grams per cubic centimeter (g/cm^3). Table A-2 lists the densities of several common substances.

You can use density to compare objects. Using the density of pure water as a comparison ($1.0\ g/cm^3$), lean body tissue has a density of about $1.1\ g/cm^3$. The density of body fat in comparison is about $0.9\ g/cm^3$. Substances that are less dense than water are buoyant (they tend to float), whereas substances that are more dense than water sink. The next time you are at the swimming pool, note the density of men and women. Women tend to have more body fat, so they float; men are generally more muscular (have more lean tissue), so they tend to sink deeper in the water. This physical property is used to determine the amount of body fat stored in a person (see Chapter 13).

Table A-1 Periodic Table of the Elements

Key: 1 / H / 1.00794 — Atomic Number / Symbol / Atomic Mass (Atomic Weight)

Main-Group Elements (groups 1–2 and 13–18); Transitional Metals (groups 3–12)

Period	1 IA	2 IIA	3 IIIB	4 IVB	5 VB	6 VIB	7 VIIB	8	9 VIIB	10	11 IB	12 IIB	13 IIIA	14 IVA	15 VA	16 VIA	17 VIIA	18 VIIIA
1	1 H 1.00794																	2 He 4.002602
2	2 Li 6.941	3 Be 9.012182											5 B 10.811	6 C 12.011	7 N 14.00674	8 O 15.9994	9 F 18.998403	10 Ne 20.1797
3	11 Na 22.989768	12 Mg 24.3050											13 Al 26.981539	14 Si 28.0855	15 P 30.973762	16 S 32.066	17 Cl 35.4527	18 Ar 39.948
4	19 K 39.0983	20 Ca 40.078	21 Sc 44.955910	22 Ti 47.88	23 V 50.9415	24 Cr 51.9961	25 Mn 54.93805	26 Fe 55.847	27 Co 58.93320	28 Ni 58.69	29 Cu 63.546	30 Zn 65.39	31 Ga 69.723	32 Ge 72.61	33 As 74.92159	34 Se 78.96	35 Br 79.904	36 Kr 83.80
5	37 Rb 85.4678	38 Sr 87.62	39 Y 88.90585	40 Zr 91.224	41 Nb 92.90638	42 Mo 95.94	43 Tc (98)	44 Ru 101.07	45 Rh 102.90550	46 Pd 106.42	47 Ag 107.8682	48 Cd 112.411	49 In 114.82	50 Sn 118.710	51 Sb 121.75	52 Te 127.60	53 I 126.90447	54 Xe 131.29
6	55 Cs 132.90543	56 Ba 137.327	57 La* 138.9055	72 Hf 178.49	73 Ta 180.9479	74 W 183.85	75 Re 186.207	76 Os 190.2	77 Ir 192.22	78 Pt 195.08	79 Au 196.96654	80 Hg 200.59	81 Tl 204.3833	82 Pb 207.2	83 Bi 208.98037	84 Po (209)	85 At (210)	86 Rn (222)
7	87 Fr (223)	88 Ra (226)	89 Ac** (227)	104 Unq (261)	105 Unp (262)	106 Unh (263)	107 Uns (262)	108 Uno (265)	109 Une (267)									

Inner-transitional Metals

*Lanthanides	58 Ce 140.115	59 Pr 140.90765	60 Nd 144.24	61 Pm (145)	62 Sm 150.36	63 Eu 151.965	64 Gd 157.25	65 Tb 158.92534	66 Dy 162.50	67 Ho 164.93032	68 Er 167.266	69 Tm 168.93421	70 Yb 173.04	71 Lu 174.967
**Actinides	90 Th 232.0381	91 Pa (231)	92 U 238.0289	93 Np (237)	94 Pu (244)	95 Am (243)	96 Cm (247)	97 Bk (247)	98 Cf (251)	99 Es (252)	100 Fm (257)	101 Md (258)	102 No (259)	103 Lr (262)

Table A-1 concluded

Key to Abbreviations

Name	Symbol	Name	Symbol	Name	Symbol	Name	Symbol
Actinium	Ac	Europium	Eu	Molybdenum	Mo	Samarium	Sm
Aluminum	Al	Fermium	Fm	Neodymium	Nd	Scandium	Sc
Americium	Am	Fluorine	F	Neon	Ne	Selenium	Se
Antimony	Sb	Francium	Fr	Neptunium	Np	Silicon	Si
Argon	Ar	Gadolinium	Gd	Nickel	Ni	Silver	Ag
Arsenic	As	Gallium	Ga	Niobium	Nb	Sodium	Na
Astatine	At	Germanium	Ge	Nitrogen	N	Strontium	Sr
Barium	Ba	Gold	Au	Nobelium	No	Sulfur	S
Berkelium	Bk	Hafnium	Hf	Osmium	Os	Tantalum	Ta
Beryllium	Be	Hahnium	Ha	Oxygen	O	Technetium	Tc
Bismuth	Bi	Helium	He	Palladium	Pd	Tellurium	Te
Boron	B	Holmium	Ho	Phosphorus	P	Terbium	Tb
Bromine	Br	Hydrogen	H	Platinum	Pt	Thallium	Tl
Cadmium	Cd	Indium	In	Plutonium	Pu	Thorium	Th
Calcium	Ca	Iodine	I	Polonium	Po	Thulium	Tm
Californium	Cf	Iridium	Ir	Potassium	K	Tin	Sn
Carbon	C	Iron	Fe	Praseodymium	Pr	Titanium	Ti
Cerium	Ce	Krypton	Kr	Promethium	Pm	Tungsten	W
Cesium	Cs	Lanthanum	La	Protactinium	Pa	Uranium	U
Chlorine	Cl	Lawrencium	Lw	Radium	Ra	Vanadium	V
Chromium	Cr	Lead	Pb	Radon	Rn	Xenon	Xe
Cobalt	Co	Lithium	Li	Rhenium	Re	Ytterbium	Yb
Copper	Cu	Lutetium	Lu	Rhodium	Rh	Yttrium	Y
Curium	Cm	Magnesium	Lw	Rubidium	Rb	Zinc	Zn
Dysprosium	Dy	Manganese	Mg	Ruthenium	Ru	Zirconium	Zr
Einsteinium	Es	Mendelevium	Mm	Rutherfordium	Rf		
Erbium	Er	Mercury	Md				

Table A-2 Densities of Some Selected Substances

Example	Density	State
Oxygen	1.31	Gas g/l
Olive oil	0.92	Liquids g/ml (g/cm^3)
Water	1.00	
Sucrose	1.59	Solids g/cm^3
Salt	2.16	

Extensive and Intensive Properties

Properties of matter are divided into two categories: extensive and intensive. Extensive properties of matter depend on the amount of matter. Intensive properties are independent of the size of the sample. The boiling point and freezing point of a substance are intensive properties. No matter how much or how little water you have, it still boils at 100°C (**Celsius**) at one atmosphere of pressure. Intensive properties are much more useful than extensive properties, since they represent qualities associated with a particular substance.

Celsius A centigrade measure of temperature. For conversion: (degrees in Fahrenheit −32) $\times$ 5/9 = C°; (degrees in Celsius $\times$ 9/5) + 32 = F°.

Mass and volume of a sample are extensive properties. Energy is also an extensive property. Energy is defined as the ability to do work or to transfer heat. There are many forms of energy that can be converted into other forms of energy. For example, a potato plant obtains its energy from the sun in the form of solar energy, and it converts this energy into chemical energy stored in the chemical bonds of starch. Electrical energy can be converted into heat energy in order to bake a potato. Once eaten, the chemical energy in the baked potato can be converted to ATP energy to power muscle tissue. This muscle energy can be used to prepare the soil and plant more potatoes. This sequence of events is an example of the law of conservation of energy, "that energy can be converted from one form to another but it can't be created or destroyed."

Temperature is a measure of the degree of "hotness" of a material, whereas heat is a form of energy that can be transferred between two objects of different temperature. When heat energy is added to something, its temperature rises. It takes significantly more energy to boil water than to heat an empty teakettle. Therefore, different forms of matter respond differently to heat.

The specific heat of a substance is the quantity of heat energy required to change the temperature of 1 g of that substance by 1°C. Extrapolating from the definition of a calorie (the amount of heat to raise the temperature of 1 gram of water 1°C), the specific heat of water is 1 cal $g^{-1}°C^{-1}$. (The specific heat of water is 1.000) The specific heat of alcohol is 0.587 cal $g^{-1}°C^{-1}$; it takes only a little over half a calorie to increase the temperature of 1 gram of alcohol by 1°C.

Every substance has a characteristic set of intensive properties divided into two classes: physical and chemical properties. Physical properties can be determined without altering the chemical composition of the substance. Ice melts at 1°C. Sugar melts at 186°C. Melting and boiling points are common examples of physical properties.

Chemical properties, such as whether the compound is an acid or a base, determine the changes that a substance undergoes in **chemical reactions.** Other substances affect the chemical properties of a substance. A chemical change or reaction is a process whereby the composition of one or more substances is changed. What actually takes place is affected by the chemical properties of the participants. For example, given the right conditions, exposing glucose to oxygen causes it to break down to carbon dioxide and water.

chemical reaction An interaction between two chemicals that changes both participants.

$$\underset{\text{Glucose}}{C_6H_{12}O_6} + \underset{\text{Oxygen}}{6O_2} \rightarrow \underset{\text{Carbon dioxide}}{6CO_2} + \underset{\text{Water}}{6H_2O}$$

Units

The SI units *(Systeme International d'Unités)* used for scientific measurements designate a specific metric unit. The units used most frequently in nutrition are mass (kilogram), length (meter), temperature, and amount of substance. Prefixes indicate decimal fractions or multiples of the various units. For example, *kilo* means 1×10^3 and 1 *milli* is 1×10^{-3}.

The temperature scale commonly used in scientific studies is the Celsius scale. On this scale, water freezes at 0°Celsius (32°Fahrenheit). Water boils at 100°C (212°F). Normal body temperature is 37.0°C (98.6°F). For English-metric conversions for length, weight, temperature, and volume (amount) see Appendix L.

Calories and Joules

Energy is measured in calories or joules. A calorie is the amount of energy required to raise the temperature of 1 gram of water 1 degree C. The SI unit of energy is the joule (J). A mass of 1 g moving at a velocity of 1 m/s possesses the energy equivalent of 1 J. A joule is not a large amount of energy, so kilojoules (kJ) are widely used in nutrition chemistry, biology, and biochemistry. In terms of the joule, 1 calorie = 4.184J. Note that the energy content of foods is expressed as kilocalories (kcal), the amount of energy needed to raise the temperature of 1 kilogram of water 1°C. This corresponds to 4.184 kJ.

Scientific Notation

In science, very large and very small numbers frequently must be used, but they are awkward because large numbers have a long string of trailing zeros and small numbers have a long string of leading zeros. A more convenient way to express these numbers is to use the power of 10, or scientific notation.

In scientific notation, a number is expressed as a product of a coefficient multiplied by a power of 10. The coefficient is a number equal to or greater than 1 but less than 10. The power of 10 is the exponent. In other words:

$$a \times 10^b$$

where a is the coefficient and b is the exponent.

$$6.02217 \times 10^{23} = 602{,}217{,}000{,}000{,}000{,}000{,}000{,}000$$

$$2.99161 \times 10^{-23} = 0.0000000000000000000000299161$$

In the previous examples, the positive exponent for the number indicates that the number is very large, while the negative exponent indicates a very small number.

To change a number greater than 1 into scientific notation, move the decimal point to the left until the number is greater than 1 but less than 10. This is the coefficient. The number of places that the decimal is moved becomes the exponent of 10. To change a number less than 1 into scientific notation, move the decimal point to the right until the number is greater than 1 but less than 10. This is the coefficient. The number of places that the decimal is moved is again the exponent of 10, but this time it is given a negative sign in front of it.

Atoms

atom Smallest combining unit of an element.

The smallest unit of matter that can undergo a chemical change is called an **atom.** An element is composed of atoms of only one kind. For example, the element carbon is composed of just carbon atoms. There are more than 100 different elements.

Atomic Structure

The center of the atom is for the most part a nucleus containing two (subatomic) particles: **protons,** which carry a positive charge, and **neutrons,** with no charge. Usually the mass of the proton equals the mass of the neutron. Adding the number of protons and neutrons together equals the atomic mass of the atom. An atom of carbon containing 6 protons and 6 neutrons has an atomic mass of 12. The atomic mass of nitrogen is 14 and the atomic mass of oxygen is 16.

The atomic number is equal to the number of protons in the nucleus. What are the atomic numbers of hydrogen, carbon, nitrogen, and oxygen?

Surrounding the nucleus of the atom are negatively charged subatomic particles called **electrons.** The nucleus is actually surrounded by an electron cloud. Electrons have about 2000 times less mass than the mass of protons or neutrons. Thus, all the mass of an atom essentially is located within the nucleus. The structure of an atom can therefore be pictured as a very tiny, highly dense nuclear core surrounded by a cloud of electrons. The number of electrons in an atom equals the number of protons, so the net charge is zero.

Electrons surrounding the nucleus have a somewhat peculiar, nonintuitive (contrary to what would be expected) behavior. For instance, it's impossible to know precisely where any given electron is located at any given moment. It is only possible to define a volume of space where the electron is most likely to be found. This volume has a specific distribution of electron density in space and is called an orbital. An orbital is a volume of space. Each orbital has its own characteristic energy and shape. Different orbitals have different energies.

Orbitals of similar energy are grouped together into energy levels. The energy levels are assigned coordinate numbers—1, 2, 3, etc.—which increase as one moves away from the nucleus. Energy level 1 contains only one orbital, an s orbital. This orbital can hold a maximum of two electrons. Energy level 2 contains an s orbital and a p orbital; the s orbital can contain up to 2 electrons, and the p orbital up to 6. Energy level 3 contains an s orbital, a p orbital and a d orbital. As before, the s orbital and p orbital can hold up to 2 and 6 electrons respectively, while the d orbital can contain as many as 10. Thus each energy level can hold a maximum of 2, 8, 18, or 32 electrons, depending on the number of orbitals, and any energy level can hold less than the maximum number of electrons.

Atoms tend to exist in the lowest possible energy state. Thus electrons tend to occupy orbitals at low energy levels before filling orbitals at higher energy levels. The first energy level outside the nucleus has room for just two electrons. When that is full, the next energy level away from the nucleus is available for electrons, and there is room for 8 electrons. For example, hydrogen has one electron in energy level 1. Carbon has 2 electrons in energy level 1 and 4 in energy level 2. In energy level 3, there is room for 8 electrons. Sulfur, with an atomic number of 16, has 2 electrons in the first energy level, 8 in the second, and 6 in the third (Table A-3).

proton The part of an atom that is positively charged.

neutron The part of an atom that has no charge.

electron A part of an atom that is negatively charged. Electrons orbit the nucleus.

Hydrogen has an atomic mass of 1 because it has 1 proton and no neutrons.

Table A-3 Atoms Commonly Present in Organic Molecules

Atom	Symbol	Atomic Number	Atomic Mass	Energy Level 1	Energy Level 2	Energy Level 3	Number of Chemical Bonds to Attain Electron Stability
Hydrogen	H	1	1	1	0	0	1
Carbon	C	6	12	2	4	0	4
Nitrogen	N	7	14	2	5	0	3
Oxygen	O	8	16	2	6	0	2
Sulfur	S	16	32	2	8	6	2

Only the electrons in the outermost energy level (if it is incomplete) can participate in chemical reactions to form chemical bonds. The outermost electrons of an atom are known as its valence electrons.

An atom tends to bond with other atoms that will fill its outermost energy level and produce a number of valence electrons equal to the noble gas which is the farthest to the right in its row in the periodic table (e.g., helium and argon). For instance, a hydrogen atom, with only a single electron, will react with other atoms that provide another electron and fill the energy level with two electrons, the same number of electrons as in the noble gas helium.

Isotopes and Atomic Weight

isotope An alternate form of a chemical element. It differs from other atoms of the same element in the number of neutrons in its nucleus.

All the atoms of an element have the same number of protons in the nucleus, but the number of neutrons in the nuclei of elements such as carbon, nitrogen, and oxygen may vary. All elements have such varieties, called **isotopes,** that differ from each other only in the number of neutrons and, in turn atomic mass. Hydrogen atoms have only one proton, but isotopic forms can have one or two neutrons. Some isotopes are radioactive, but most are not. Tritium, a radioactive isotope of hydrogen, has one proton and two neutrons. Carbon nuclei can contain five, six, seven, or eight neutrons.

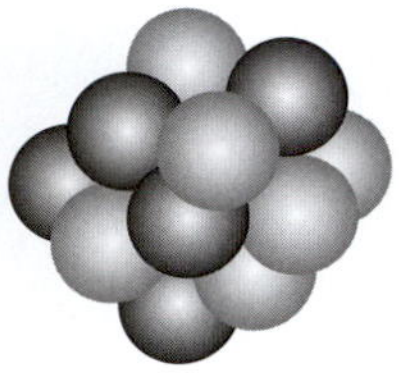

^{12}Carbon
6 Protons
6 Neutrons
6 Electrons

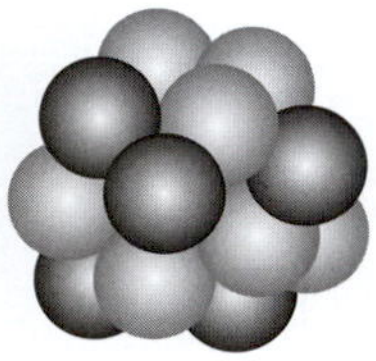

^{13}Carbon
6 Protons
7 Neutrons
6 Electrons

^{14}Carbon
6 Protons
8 Neutrons
6 Electrons

Isotopes are distinguished by adding the number of protons and neutrons together and writing the resultant sum as a superscript to the left of the symbol for the element. For example, a carbon nuclei with six protons and six neutrons is written as ^{12}C. The isotope containing seven neutrons is labeled ^{13}C, and the isotope containing eight neutrons is labeled ^{14}C. Note that, because all these atoms have six protons, they are all carbon atoms. However, because they possess different numbers of neutrons, they represent isotopes of carbon. All isotopes of an element behave the same way chemically.

Atomic weight actually considers this fact that an element is a mixture of isotopes. If all carbon were ^{12}C, the atomic weight would be the same as its atomic mass, 12. But, since some carbon exists as ^{13}C and ^{14}C, the atomic weight is slightly higher, 12.011. The atomic weight is based on the relative abundance of each isotope.

Although the ordinary chemical behavior of different isotopes of the same element is virtually identical, the radiochemical behavior is sometimes different. Isotopes exhibit such differences in physical behavior because they decay (break down) to more stable isotopes by giving off nuclear particles of ionizing radiation. Certain unstable isotopes (radioisotopes) are in an obvious process of decay. Every element has at least one such radioisotope. These radioisotopes have a physical half-life, which is the time required for 50% of its atoms to decay to a more stable state. Isotopes such as ^{32}P (phosphorus) emit radiation that can be measured by instruments such as Geiger counters and scintillation counters. The isotope ^{14}C decays more rapidly than other isotopes of carbon.

Other isotopes are not radioactive but still can be traced in bodily fluids or tissues using other types of instruments. Examples include ^{13}C and ^{15}N; these are called stable isotopes, since they decay very slowly and do not emit radiation.

Isotope "markers," such as ^{32}P and ^{13}C, have a practical use, as they can be used to trace nutrients as they follow various chemical pathways in the body. For example, researchers can "mark" a glucose molecule with a radioactive carbon atom (^{14}C). This allows the researchers to see where the carbons of glucose are distributed in the body, and it helps indicate what chemical transformations glucose undergoes when metabolized. Such studies have demonstrated that glucose can become part of the lipid stored in adipose cells, or form CO_2 (detected as $^{14}CO_2$) that is exhaled. Isotope techniques are widely used in nutrition research.

Atomic and Molar Mass

Dalton is another term used to indicate atomic mass, such as for proteins, DNA, and RNA. One Dalton is equivalent to one amu.

Atoms are very small. One ^{12}C atom has a mass of 1.993×10^{-23}g. The units used to quantify atomic mass are called atomic mass units (amu). The carbon amu is calculated for carbon by dividing the mass of that atom by 1.6605×10^{-24}, which is essentially the mass of one proton or neutron. Performing this division on ^{12}C, the mass of such an atom is 12 amu as ^{12}C. The amu for each element is listed in the bottom portion of each entry in the periodic table. These are based on comparing their mass to that of ^{12}C.

You are familiar with counting units, such as the number of sticks in a package of chewing gum. In chemistry, the unit of dealing with atoms, ions (an electrically charged atom), and molecules (a combination of atoms) is the mole. A mole is defined as the amount of matter that contains as many objects (things) as the number of atoms in 12 g of ^{12}C. The number of atoms in 12 g of ^{12}C is

$$12 \text{ g } ^{12}\text{C} \times \frac{1 \text{ atom}}{1.993 \times 10^{-23}\text{g } ^{12}\text{C}} = 6.023 \times 10^{23} \text{ atoms}$$

It is not their weight but the *number* of molecules that determines the physiological effect of a substance. Therefore, the number of "objects" in a mole is 6.02×10^{23}, which is called Avogadro's number. This concept of g per mole can be extended directly. A mole (mol) of any substance contains Avogadro's number of that substance:

$$1 \text{ mol } ^{12}\text{C atoms} = 6.02 \times 10^{23}\ ^{12}\text{C atoms}$$

$$1 \text{ mol of water molecules} = 6.02 \times 10^{23} \text{ H}_2\text{O molecules}$$

$$1 \text{ mol NO}_3^- \text{ ions} = 6.02 \times 10^{23} \text{ NO}_3^- \text{ ions}$$

In order to relate the number of units of matter to mass, as measured by instruments, the individual mass of each unit of matter is needed. The mass of the atom is expressed as atomic weight. The molecular weight of an individual molecule is the sum of the atomic weights of its constituent atoms. The molar mass of a substance is the mass, in g, of a mole of the substance.

A single ^{12}C atom has a mass of 12 amu, but a single ^{24}Mg is twice as massive, 24 amu. Because a mole always has the same number of particles, a mole of Mg is twice as massive as a mole of ^{12}C atoms. A mole of carbon weighs 12 g; a mole of Mg weighs 24 g. The same number that refers to the mass of a single atom of an element (in amu) also represents the mass (in g) of 1 mol of atoms of that element. For example, one ^{12}C atom weighs 12 amu. One mol ^{12}C weighs 12 g. One ^{24}Mg atom weighs 24 amu, and 1 mol ^{24}Mg weighs 24 g.

The mass in g of 1 mole of a substance is called its molar mass. The molar mass (in g) of any substance is always numerically equal to its formula weight (in amu). For example, one H_2O molecule weighs 18.0 amu, and 1 mol of H_2O weighs 18.0 g. One NaCl molecule weighs 58.5 amu, and 1 mol of NaCl weighs 58.5 g.

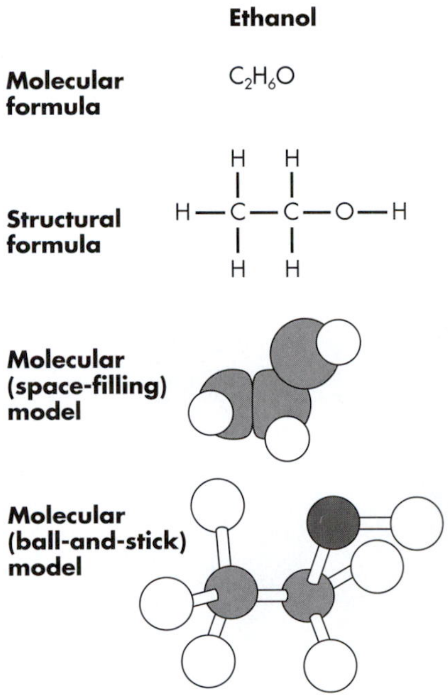

Figure A-1 Examples of the molecular and structural formulas and the molecular models of ethanol. The space-filling type of model gives a more realistic feeling of the space occupied by the atoms. On the other hand, the ball-and-stick type shows the bonds and bond angles more clearly.

Molecules, Covalent Bonds, Hydrogen Bonds, Ions and Ionic Compounds

Molecules

Molecules are formed through the interaction of the electrons, between two or more atoms in the outermost orbitals (valence electrons). When electrons are shared, chemical **bonds** are formed. The term **compound** refers to molecules composed of more than one element. Water is a compound. Each molecule (or compound) possesses its own properties, such as color, taste, and density.

The number of chemical bonds that an atom can form typically depends on the number of electrons needed to complete the outermost orbital. Hydrogen can form just one chemical bond because it has room for just one electron in its orbital of two electrons, in turn yielding a noble gas electron configuration. Carbon can form four chemical bonds, nitrogen three, and oxygen two (review Table A-3).

A molecular formula gives the elemental composition of a molecule or compound. This consists of the symbols of the atoms in the molecule, plus a subscript denoting the number of each type of atom.

molecule A group of atoms chemically linked together—that is, tightly connected by attractive forces (see also compound).

bond A sharing of electrons, charges, or attractions linking two atoms.

compound A group of different types of atoms bonded together in definite proportion (see also molecule). Not all chemical compounds exist as molecules. Some compounds are made up of ions attracted to each other, such as Na^+Cl^- (table salt).

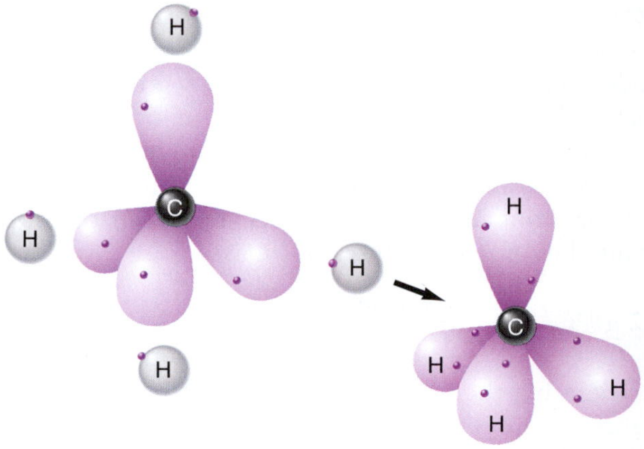

In each of the four bonds, one electron of the carbon is shared with the electron of a hydrogen atom in a single, sausage-shaped molecular orbital encompassing the two nuclei. Methane is the simplest organic molecule. Even the largest organic molecules are held together by strong covalent bonds like these.

A structural formula shows how the atoms are arranged with respect to each other. As an extension, molecular and ball-and-stick models approximate the shape of the molecule (Fig. A-1).

When molecules combine with each other, atoms do not increase or decrease in number. Atoms present in starting materials must be present in the products. For example, compare the number of oxygen atoms in glucose and the oxygen itself to the number in the products of the reaction (18 vs. 18). This example also illustrates the process of conservation of mass.

$$C_6H_{12}O_6 + 6\ O_2 \rightarrow 6\ CO_2 + 6\ H_2O$$

Covalent Bonds

covalent bond A union of two atoms formed by the sharing of electrons.

When atoms share their valence electrons, a **covalent bond** is formed. The electrons shared between atoms are bonding electrons; these represent the adhesive that holds the atoms together in molecular form.

When two identical atoms share electrons, such as in the formation of hydrogen gas (H_2) or oxygen gas (O_2), the covalent bond is very strong because the electrons are shared equally. This equal distribution between the atoms makes the molecule nonpolar. Consider the simple compound methane (CH_4). Hydrogen has one valence electron and its outermost (only) orbital can hold a maximum of two electrons. Carbon has four electrons in its outermost energy level or valence shell, and that shell can hold a maximum of eight electrons. Both carbon and hydrogen fill their valence shells to the maximum by sharing electrons with each other. Notice that each hydrogen in methane contains two electrons and that the carbon atom ends up with eight electrons. A good way to look at this is that the hydrogen atoms share one pair of electrons, whereas the carbon atoms share four pairs of electrons.

Guidelines that govern the formation of covalent bonds are as follows:

1. The valence shell of each element must have room to accommodate additional electrons.
2. Second-row nonmetallic elements of the periodic table (e.g., carbon, nitrogen, and oxygen) and hydrogen typically fill their outermost energy levels by sharing the necessary number of electrons with another element.
3. Third-row nonmetals and those beyond this point in the periodic table (e.g., phosphorus and sulfur) frequently attain stability by giving up electrons in the outermost energy level, rather than adding them. Phosphorus, for example, typically makes five

bonds to attain stability instead of the three that are needed to have the electron configuration of the noble gas argon (18 electrons).

A single covalent bond forms when two atoms share one electron pair. A double covalent bond forms when two atoms share two electron pairs.

When electrons spend approximately equal time around each atom nucleus, the bond is called a nonpolar covalent bond. These are the strongest covalent bonds. If the two nuclei are not equally attractive to electrons, their atoms can form a polar covalent bond in which the electrons spend more time orbiting the more attractive nucleus. For example, when hydrogen bonds with oxygen, the electrons are more attracted to the oxygen nucleus and orbit that nucleus more than they do the hydrogen nucleus. Electrons carry a negative charge. This makes the oxygen region of the molecule slightly negative and the hydrogen region slightly positive. The Greek letter delta (δ) is used to symbolize a charge less than that of one electron or proton. A slightly negative region of a molecule is shown as δ^- and a slightly positive region is shown as δ^+. A molecule such as this is called a dipole because it has two charged ends. Water is a good example. The oxygen atom pulls electrons from the two hydrogen atoms toward its side of the water molecule, so that the oxygen side is more negatively charged than the hydrogen side of the molecule. Water, the most abundant molecule in the body, serves as a good solvent because it is polar.

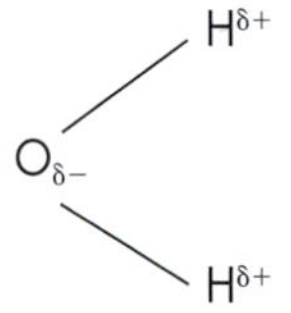

δ denotes partial charge

When two different atoms form a covalent bond, the bonding electrons are never shared equally. Consider again the H–O bond in water. It is unreasonable to expect that the hydrogen nucleus (containing one proton) and the oxygen nucleus (containing eight protons) have identical forces of attraction for the shared electron pair. In addition, other factors come into play, such as how many energy levels each atom has, how many electrons are in each, and the distance the shared electrons are from each nucleus. All of these factors lead to an unequal sharing of electrons in a covalent bond between different atoms.

The ability of an atom in a molecule to attract electrons is called electronegativity. Elements toward the top right corner of the periodic table have the highest electronegativity, and those toward the bottom left have the lowest (electronegativity generally increases from left to right in a row of the periodic table, and decreases going down a column; the difference in the electronegativities of bonded atoms can be used to determine the polarity of a bond). Metals have low electronegativity, whereas nonmetals have relatively high electronegativity. Oxygen and nitrogen have the highest electronegativities of the elements typically found in compounds important to nutrition. The electronegativity values of atoms determine the type of chemical bond formed. If the electronegativity values are not very different, a covalent bond is formed. If the electronegativity of two bonding atoms differs greatly, electron transfer occurs to yield an ionic bond, as in Na^+Cl^- (see the following section on ions and ionic compounds).

Polar molecules are weakly attracted both to ions and to other polar molecules. The positive end of the molecule can align itself with an anion or with the negative end of another molecule. These attractive forces, called, respectively, ion-dipole and dipole-dipole forces, are much weaker than covalent bonds individually, but, when there are many of them, they make a significant contribution to the total energy of a collection of molecules. Water, for instance, has a much higher boiling point than expected because the molecules are held together by such forces.

Hydrogen Bonds

Water, and most other molecules containing an O—H or N—H bond, exhibit a particularly strong interaction called hydrogen bonding (Fig. A-2). In this case, the hydrogen atom of one molecule is attracted to a nonbonded electron pair (called a lone pair) of a highly electronegative atom on a neighboring molecule, such as oxygen. Water molecules are attracted to each other by hydrogen bonds. This attraction is responsible for many of the biologically important properties of water. Hydrogen bonds, such as those found in large proteins and DNA, help to hold the molecule together. These

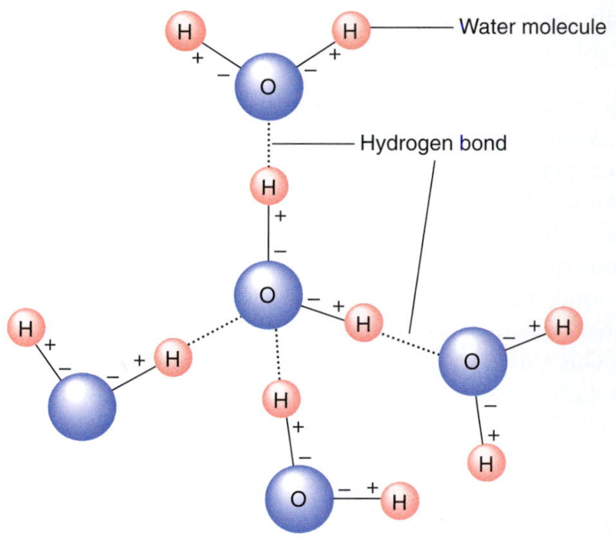

Figure A-2 Hydrogen bonds between water molecules. The oxygen atoms of water molecules are weakly joined together by the attraction of the electronegative oxygen for the positively charged hydrogen. These weak bonds are called hydrogen bonds.

molecules fold or twist into three-dimensional shapes due in part to the action of hydrogen bonds. Hydrogen bonds are usually symbolized by a dotted line between the atoms: —C—O · · · H—N—. Hydrogen bonds are the weakest of all chemical bonds. There will be much more about chemical bonds in the chapters on carbohydrate (Chapter 5), lipids (Chapter 6), and proteins (Chapter 7).

Ions and Ionic Compounds

ionic bond A union between two atoms formed by an attraction of a positive ion to a negative ion, as seen in table salt (NA^+Cl^-).

Atoms that have an equal number of positively charged protons and negatively charged electrons are electrically neutral. Atoms or molecules that have positive or negative charges are called ions. **Ionic bonds** result when one or more valence electrons from one atom are completely transferred to another atom or molecule. Elements that have one to three valence electrons have a tendency to give up electrons, and those with four to seven valence electrons have a tendency to accept electrons. The electrons are not shared. In both cases the elements are giving up or taking on electrons to achieve the electron configuration of the closest noble gas. Take the case of sodium chloride. One atom loses electrons, so that its number of electrons becomes smaller than its number of protons; thus, it becomes positively charged as Na^+ in sodium chloride. Now sodium has the same number of electrons as neon. The other atom gains electrons, so its number of electrons is greater than its number of protons, so it becomes negatively charged as Cl^- in sodium chloride. Now chloride has the same number of electrons as argon.

Positively charged ions are called cations; they move toward the negative pole in an electric field. An atom with more electrons than protons is negatively charged and is known as an anion; it moves to the positive pole. NaCl is an example of an ionic compound. Note the name change that occurs when an element gains an electron to become a negative ion; the suffix becomes *–ide*.

These charged atoms, where electron(s) have been added or removed, are collectively known as ions. Sodium (Na^+), potassium (K^+), and calcium (Ca^{2+}) are found in the body as cations. Chloride (Cl^-) is a common anion in the body. See Table A-4 for a more complete list of common ions found in the body.

Ionic bonds are weaker than polar covalent bonds. Ionic compounds easily separate when dissolved in water. Table salt (NaCl) is obvious when poured out of the salt shaker, but when the salt is stirred into a cup of water it disappears. It *dissociates.* The polar water's negative side (oxygen) is attracted to the Na^+, and the positive side (hydrogen) is attracted to Cl^-.

Water molecules that surround the ions, in turn, attract other water molecules to form hydration spheres around each ion. This mechanism makes ions or molecules soluble in water. Many organic molecules also dissolve in water. However, in this case, the

Table A-4 Important Ions in the Human Body

Common Ions	Symbol	Some Functions
Calcium	Ca^{2+}	Component of bones and teeth, necessary for blood clotting, muscle contraction, and nerve transmission
Sodium	Na^{+}	Helps maintain membrane potentials (electrical charge differences across a membrane) and water balance
Potassium	K^{+}	Helps maintain membrane potentials
Hydrogen	H^{+}	Helps maintain acid-base balance
Hydroxide	OH^{-}	Helps maintain acid-base balance
Chloride	Cl^{-}	Helps maintain acid-base balance
Bicarbonate	HCO_3^{-}	Helps maintain acid-base balance
Ammonium	NH_4^{+}	Helps maintain acid-base balance
Phosphate	PO_4^{3-}	Component of bones and teeth, involved in energy exchange and acid-base balance
Iron	Fe^{2+}	Necessary for red blood cell formation and function
Magnesium	Mg^{2+}	Necessary for enzyme function
Iodide	I^{-}	Part of the thyroid hormones
Fluoride	F^{-}	Strengthens bones and teeth

covalent bonds holding the molecule together remain intact. These molecules are called hydrophilic. Molecules that are composed of nonpolar covalent bonds, such as fats, are called hydrophobic. They don't carry a charge, so they are insoluble in water.

Salts

Salts are substances composed of cations and anions. Table salt is NaCl. The Na^+ and Cl^- are attracted to each other by electrostatic force, and the resulting ionic compound is known chemically as sodium chloride. Salts are formed by the interaction of acids and bases in a neutralization reaction. Water is also formed in such a reaction. In this type of reaction, hydrogen ions of an acid are replaced by the positive ions of a base, and a salt forms. For example, when hydrochloric acid reacts with sodium hydroxide, table salt is produced:

HCl	+	NaOH	→	NaCl	+	H_2O
Hydrochloric acid		Sodium hydroxide		Salt		Water

(Neutralization reaction)

The formula for salts can be misleading. For example, NaCl suggests that table salt exists as a discrete entity containing one sodium ion and one chloride ion. An inspection of the chemical structure of table salt shows that it is actually a three-dimensional stack of layers—much like having a ream of paper with all the pages glued together (Fig. A-3).

Salts separate to form positively and negatively charged ions when dissolved in water. Substances that dissolve in water and conduct electricity are called electrolytes. A solute that produces ions in solution forms an electrolytic solution that conducts an electrical current. A salt solution is a good conductor of electricity. (A sugar solution does not conduct electricity because it doesn't form ions.) Sodium (Na^+), potassium (K^+), calcium (Ca^{2+}), and chloride (Cl^-), magnesium (Mg^{2+}), phosphate (PO_4^{3-}), and bicarbonate (HCO_3^-) are various electrolytes commonly found in the body.

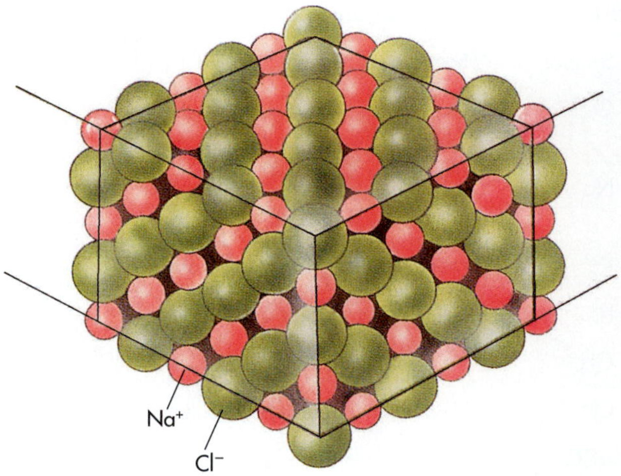

Figure A-3 Molecules of sodium chloride (table salt) in typical cube-shape formation.

Acids, Bases, and the pH Scales

We all have a pretty good idea of what acids and bases are. We know that lemon juice is acid and drain cleaners are strong bases.

Water molecules of two hydrogens and one oxygen are held together by polar covalent bonds. Although these are strong bonds, a *small* proportion of them break, releasing a hydrogen ion and a hydroxide ion. The hydrogen ion (a proton) is transferred to another oxygen in a water molecule, forming a *hydronium ion*. This means that a pair of water molecules can act as an acid and a base, since water self-ionizes, forming hydronium ions and hydroxide ions.

$$\underset{\text{Water}}{2H_2O} \longleftrightarrow \underset{\text{Hydronium ion}}{H_3O^+} + \underset{\text{Hydroxide ion}}{OH^-}$$

For simplicity, ionized water will be represented by H^+ and OH^-.

The ionization of water molecules produces equal amounts of hydronium and hydroxide ions, which are both equal to a 10^{-7} molar concentration. At this concentration of ionization, water is considered neutral.

A solution that has a higher concentration of H^+ is said to be acidic, and one that is lower is basic or alkaline. An acid is defined as a substance that can ionize and release protons (H^+) into solution. It is a proton donor.

Because a hydrogen atom without its electron is a proton (H^+), any substance that releases protons (hydrogen ions) when in water is an acid. For example, hydrogen chloride (HCl) forms hydrogen and chloride ions (H^+ and Cl^-) in solution and therefore is an acid.

$$HCl \rightarrow H^+ + Cl^-$$

Figure A-4 lists several common acids and bases. A base is a negatively charged ion or a molecule that ionizes to produce an anion. This then can combine with a proton (H^+), removing it from solution. This base is a proton acceptor. Any substance that can accept hydrogen ions while in water is a base.

Many bases can function as proton acceptors by releasing hydroxide ions (OH^-) when dissolved in water. Most strong bases release OH^- into solution. The OH^- combines with H^+ to form water.

$$\underset{\text{Sodium hydroxide}}{NaOH} \rightarrow \underset{\text{Sodium ion}}{Na^+} + \underset{\text{Hydroxide ion}}{OH^-}$$

The hydroxide ions are proton acceptors as they go on to combine with hydrogen ions to form water:

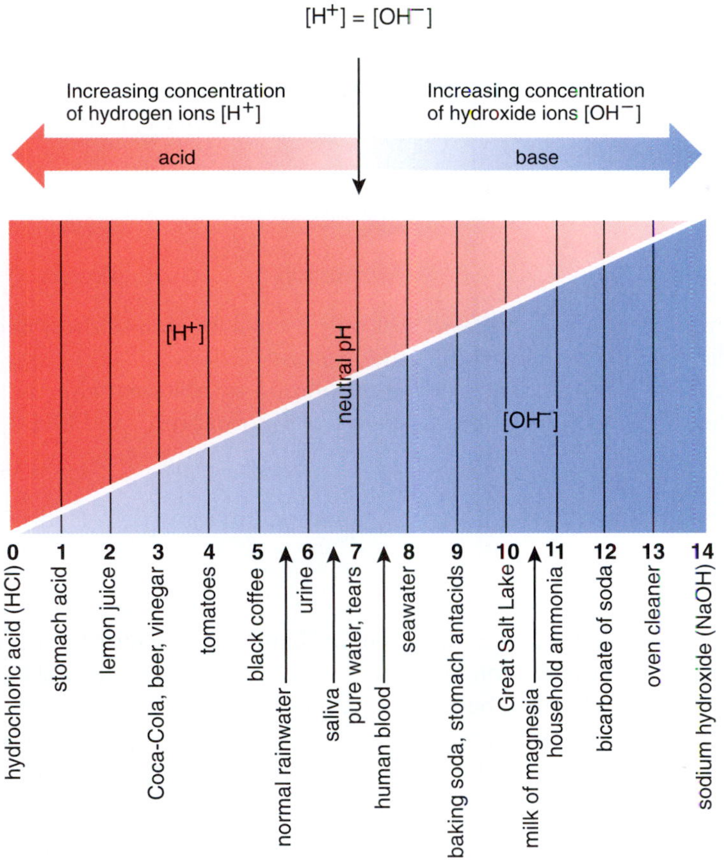

Figure A-4 pH scale. The diagonal line indicates the proportionate number of hydrogen ions to hydroxide ions. Any pH value above 7 is basic, while any pH value below 7 is acidic.

OH^-	+	H^+	→	H_2O
Hydroxide ion		Hydrogen ion		Water

pH

Acidity is expressed in terms of pH, a measure of the molarity (the ratio of solute per liter of solution) of H^+. Molarity is expressed by square brackets, so the molarity of H^+ is symbolized as $[H^+]$. pH is defined as the negative logarithm of the hydrogen ion molarity (concentration), or $pH = -\log [H^+]$. The pH unit is the H^+ concentration of a solution. Pure water has a neutral pH because it contains equal amounts of hydrogen (hydronium) and hydroxyl ions. The pH scale runs from 0 to 14 (see Fig. A-4).

Since pH is a negative logarithmic scale, a solution with a pH of 4 has a 10 times greater **acidic pH** as one with a pH of 5, and 100 times more acidic than one with a pH of 6. This may be confusing because it is inversely related to the hydrogen ion concentration: A solution with a high hydrogen ion concentration has a low pH number. A solution with a low hydrogen concentration has a high pH number. Acid solutions have a pH of less than 7. Basic, or **alkaline pH,** solutions have a pH greater than 7.

acidic pH A pH less than 7. Lemon juice has an acidic pH.

alkaline pH A pH greater than 7. Baking soda in water yields an alkaline pH.

A slight disruption of pH can seriously disturb normal physiological functions, so it is important the body be able to control pH. Blood normally has a pH range from 7.35 to 7.45. Any deviations from this range can cause dizziness, fainting, coma, paralysis, or death.

Acids and bases are classified as strong or weak. Strong acids and strong bases dissociate completely when dissolved in water. Consequently, they release all of their hydrogen ions or hydroxide ions when dissolved. In general, the more completely an acid or a base dissociates, the stronger it is. Hydrochloric acid, for example, is a strong acid because it completely dissociates in water.

Weak acids only partially dissociate in water. Consequently, they release only some of their acidic hydrogens. For example, when acetic acid ($CH_3C(=O)—OH$, the principal component of vinegar) dissolves in water, the acetic acid only partially dissociates.

$$\underset{\text{Acetic acid}}{CH_3\overset{O}{\overset{\|}{C}}—OH} \longleftrightarrow \underset{\text{Acetate ion}}{CH_3\overset{O}{\overset{\|}{C}}—O^-} + \underset{\text{Proton}}{H^+}$$

The equilibrium lies far to the left, so that only a small fraction of the acetic acid in the vinegar is dissociated into acetate ions and protons.

Most weak bases release hydroxide into solution by reacting with the water itself. For example, ammonia (NH_3) reacts with water to form NH_4^+ and OH^-.

$$\underset{\text{Ammonia}}{NH_3} + \underset{\text{Water}}{H_2O} \longleftrightarrow \underset{\text{Ammonium ion}}{NH_4^+} + \underset{\text{Hydroxide ion}}{OH^-}$$

Buffers

Many of the biochemical reactions that occur in living tissues require tight control of pH. To prevent changes in the H^+ concentration in the body, and to control the pH, a system of buffers is maintained. These buffers are ions and molecules that stabilize the pH of a solution. In the blood (plasma), the pH is maintained by the carbonic acid–bicarbonate buffer system. The acid is formed by the combination of water and carbon dioxide. Carbonic acid separates into bicarbonate ion (HCO_3^-) and the hydrogen ion (H^+).

$$\underset{\text{Bicarbonate}}{HCO_3^-} + \underset{\text{Hydrogen ion}}{H^+} \longleftrightarrow \underset{\text{Carbonic acid}}{H_2CO_3} \longleftrightarrow \underset{\text{Water}}{H_2O} + \underset{\text{Carbon dioxide}}{CO_2}$$

The reaction can go either way. The direction depends on the concentration of ions on either side of the arrows. For example, if an acid were released into the blood plasma (more H^+ in solution), the reaction would be driven to the right. The carbon dioxide produced could then be exhaled via the lungs. Acids that are present in the plasma come from cellular activities, but, despite the increase in H^+ ions by these activities, the blood plasma pH hardly changes; it is essentially constant. The buffer, bicarbonate, accomplishes this. It is constantly formed to maintain normal pH. The kidneys also play a role by absorbing or releasing H^+ or HCO_3^-, depending on the acid-base balance in the person. In fact, much of the excess acid leaves the body via the urine (urine has an acid pH). Thus, the kidneys and lungs keep this buffering system functioning and, in turn, are key to acid-base balance in the body.

Free Radicals

You are aware that atoms tend to share electron pairs when forming chemical bonds, and there is a tendency to share enough electrons to completely fill the valence shell so as to form a noble gas configuration. A consequence is that atoms or elements are rarely found with unpaired electrons. But, when a molecule with an extra electron does arise, it is called a free radical. An example is the superoxide anion. Oxygen is composed of two oxygen atoms (O_2); if an electron is added, it becomes superoxide, or $O_2^{\bullet -}$. The dot signifies an unpaired electron.

Superoxide and other free radicals are reactive, primarily because they contain an unpaired electron. Free radicals seek an electron by attacking and removing electrons from other compounds, such as at the location where hydrogens are attached to carbon. This not only damages the other molecule but transforms it into a free radical.

$$R^{\bullet} + —CH_2 \rightarrow RH^{+}—CH^{-\bullet}$$

Free radicals are also formed when a covalent bond breaks and each atom or molecule fragment recovers the electron originally used to make the bond. In this case, energy—usually in the form of sunlight, ultraviolet radiation, or heat—is used to break the bond.

$$A—B + \text{energy} \rightarrow A^{\bullet} + B^{\bullet}$$

Because free radicals are reactive, they can generate thousands of other free radicals within minutes in a chain-reaction process. The reactivity of free radicals sometimes produces detrimental effects in living systems. For instance, the development of cardiovascular disease and some types of cancer, such as skin and lung cancer, is probably promoted by free radicals. However, some normal physiological functions in the body involve free radical formation; for example, free radicals are used by various white blood cells to kill invading bacteria.

The body has a number of mechanisms, such as antioxidants, for neutralizing free radicals. These are substances that react with and neutralize free radical forms of oxygen and nitrogen. The enzyme superoxide dismutase (SOD) converts superoxide into oxygen and hydrogen peroxide. One form of SOD contains the minerals copper and zinc, whereas another form contains manganese. Other antioxidants obtained from the diet are vitamin E and vitamin C.

Some substances are used extensively in the food industry to trap free radicals or prevent their formation. This allows for increased storage time of food by decreasing chemical breakdown. These substances are part of a class of food additives called preservatives (see Chapter 19). Vitamin E added to cooking oils protects C=C bonds by trapping free radicals.

Organic Chemistry

Organic compounds contain carbon in combination with other elements, such as hydrogen, oxygen, and nitrogen. Carbon compounds are associated with living things, but why carbon? It is because carbon forms very stable covalent bonds, such as single, double, and even triple bonds. Carbon also forms these bonds with many other atoms. Carbon atoms can even form rings and chains by bonding to other carbons. Variation in the length of the chains, and their atomic configurations, allows the formation of a wide variety of molecules. Organic molecules generally contain hydrogen to form the hydrocarbon chains and rings.

Cyclic and Chain Compounds

Cyclic organic compounds are common forms of hydrocarbons. Note the diagram of butyric acid (a chain) in the margin and compare that to the structure of glucose, which is a ring. Even though the two compounds are only carbon, oxygen, and hydrogen, each conveys a very different property. Some ring structures are referred to as aromatic compounds.

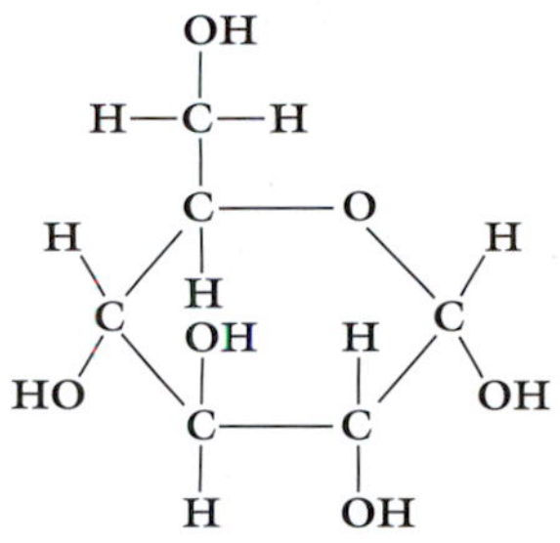

Glucose

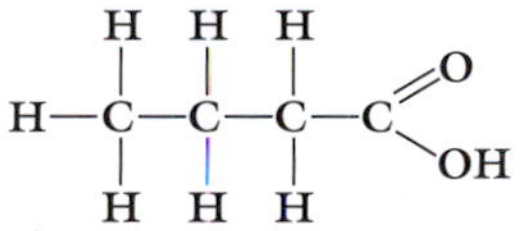

Butyric acid

Hydrocarbons as chains or rings provide the backbone of many groups of compounds that make up important organic nutrients. Other groups are attached to these backbones. They usually contain atoms of oxygen, nitrogen, phosphorus, and sulfur. The functional or reactive groups provide the unique chemical properties of organic molecules. Classes of organic molecules are known by their functional groups.

Several important organic compounds contain a functional group called a carbonyl group (C=O). The carbonyl group is the parent compound for ketones, aldehydes, and many related groups. Table A-5 has a list of all these compounds that are important to nutrition.

Ketones are organic compounds in which the carbonyl group occurs at the interior of a carbon chain and therefore flanked by carbon atoms. Body fat that is breaking

Table A-5 Typical Chemical Groups Found in Nutrients

Functional Group	Name	Typically Found In	Example
$-OH$	Hydroxide	Alcohols	CH_3-OH
$-C(H)=O$	Aldehyde	Sugars	$CH_3C(H)=O$
$C-C(C)=O$	Ketone	Ketones	$CH_3C(CH_3)=O$
$-C(OH)=O$	Carboxyl	Acids	$CH_3C(OH)=O$
$-S-S-$	Disulfide	Proteins	$-CH_2-S-S-CH_2-$
$-C(-)=O$	Carbonyl	Aldehydes, ketones, carboxylic acids, amides	$(CH_3)_2C=O$
$-C(-)(-)-NH_2$	Amine	Proteins	CH_3-NH_2
$-C(NH_2)=O$	Amide	Vitamins	$-CH_2C(NH_2)=O$
$^-O-P(O-)(O-)=O$	Phosphate	High-energy compounds	$-CH_2-O-P(O-)(O-CH_2-)=O$
$-C(O-C)=O$	Ester	Triglycerides	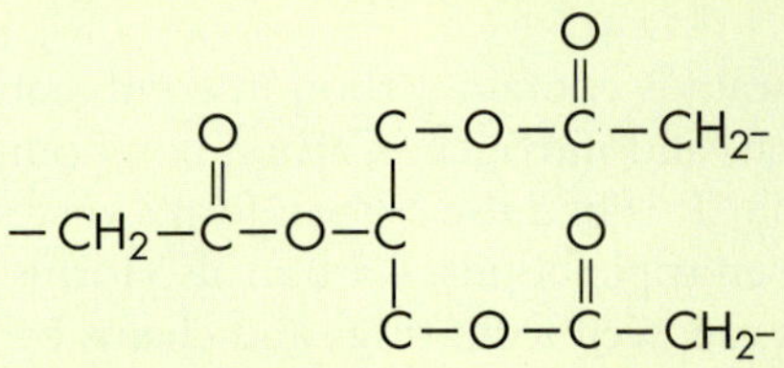
$-O-C(=O)-CH_2-$	Acyl	Triglycerides	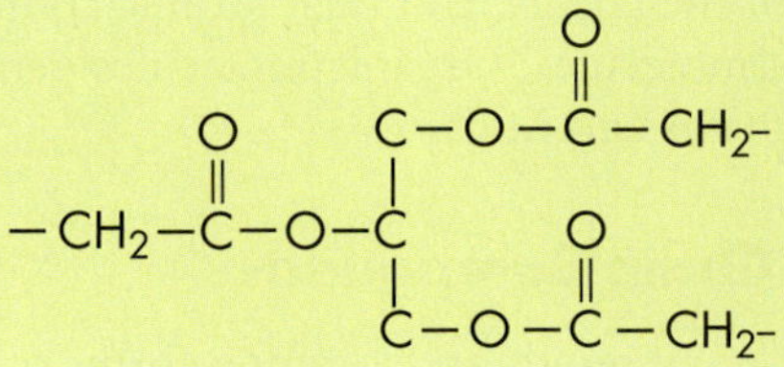

down at a rapid rate produces ketones ($C-C(=O)-C$), some of which are removed from the body by way of the urine (review Chapter 4).

Aldehydes ($-C(=O)-H$) are organic compounds that contain a carbonyl group to which at least one hydrogen atom is attached. This active group is found in one important form of vitamin A. As an aldehyde, it plays a central role in vision.

Many of the most common substances, both in foods and in the body, contain carboxylic acids. A carboxylic acid ($-C(=O)-OH$) contains the carbonyl group with an OH group attached. These acids are widely distributed in tissues and natural products. Vinegar contains acetic acid. Citrus fruits contain citric acid, and vitamin C is ascorbic acid.

The carboxyl group is an acid because it can donate a H^+ (proton) to a solution. A very common acid formed in muscle cells is known as lactic acid. When lactic acid ionizes, it releases the H^+ and becomes lactate. Since both forms of the acid (ionized and nonionized) are in solution, the proportion depends on the pH of the solution. The terms *lactic acid* and *lactate* are both correct.

An alcohol has the carbon-oxygen bond, but the O is also bonded to a single hydrogen. This leaves only a single bond between the carbon and oxygen, forming an —OH or hydroxide group (ROH).

An ester $\left(R{-}\overset{\overset{\displaystyle O}{\|}}{C}{-}O{-}C\right)$ is an organic compound that has an O-C group attached to a carbonyl group. An ester is the product of a reaction between a carboxylic acid and an alcohol. The formation of lipids called triglycerides involves the formation of ester bonds.

The carbonyl portion of a compound such as an ester is called an acyl group. Thus, removal of the hydroxyl group (OH) from an organic acid forms an acyl group.

Two sulfur atoms (S—S), each attached to a carbon, produce a disulfide group. This group is important to the structural characteristics of certain proteins.

A single carbon with an amine (also called amino) group attached (—NH_2) is a component of all amino acids.

Isomerism

Molecules that have identical chemical formulas but different structures are called **isomers.** A simple example of this is two compounds with the formula C_2H_6O.

CH_3CH_2OH	CH_3OCH_3
Ethanol	Methyl ether

isomers Different chemical structures for compounds that share the same chemical formula.

Both of these compounds can be harmful. However, there are intake levels where ethanol produces no toxic symptoms (i.e., the amount in a small glass of wine), but these same amounts of methyl ether would cause very toxic effects. This illustrates an important point about isomers: Since they have different structures, they can have different *chemical* properties.

The difference in properties between two isomers can be great (as in the preceding example) or very subtle, but the differences are there and are detectable. There are different types of isomerism but only two of the common types will be briefly reviewed in this section: structural isomers and stereoisomers.

Pentane $CH_3{-}CH_2{-}CH_2{-}CH_2{-}CH_3$

Neopentane $CH_3{-}CH_2{-}\underset{\displaystyle CH_3}{\underset{|}{C}H}{-}CH_3$

Isopentane $CH_3{-}\overset{\displaystyle CH_3}{\overset{|}{\underset{\displaystyle CH_3}{\underset{|}{C}}}}{-}CH_3$

Structural Isomers

Isomers in which the number and kinds of bonds differ are called structural isomers. Molecules containing chains of carbon atoms typically have many structural isomers. Any variation in the way the chain is branched gives rise to a new isomer. For example, pentane (C_5H_{12}) has three isomers, as shown in the margin.

Stereoisomers

Stereoisomers are another example of organic chemistry that is important to understanding nutrition. Stereoisomers have the same number and types of chemical bonds, but with different spatial arrangements (different configurations in space). Molecules containing double bonds illustrate this. Because there is no freedom to rotate around a C=C bond, molecules containing such bonds frequently exhibit stereoisomerism. For example, hydrogens or various chemical compounds can be located on the same side of the bond (***cis* isomer**) or on opposite sides of the double bond (***trans* isomer**).

Consider oleic acid and its isomer elaidic acid (Fig. A-5*a*). Oleic acid is a *cis* isomer, or the form found naturally in food. With food-processing technology, such as

***cis* isomer** An isomer form seen in compounds with double bonds, such as fatty acids, in which the hydrogens on both ends of the double bond lie on the same side of the plane of that bond.

***trans* isomer** Compound where the hydrogens lie opposite each other across a carbon-carbon double bond.

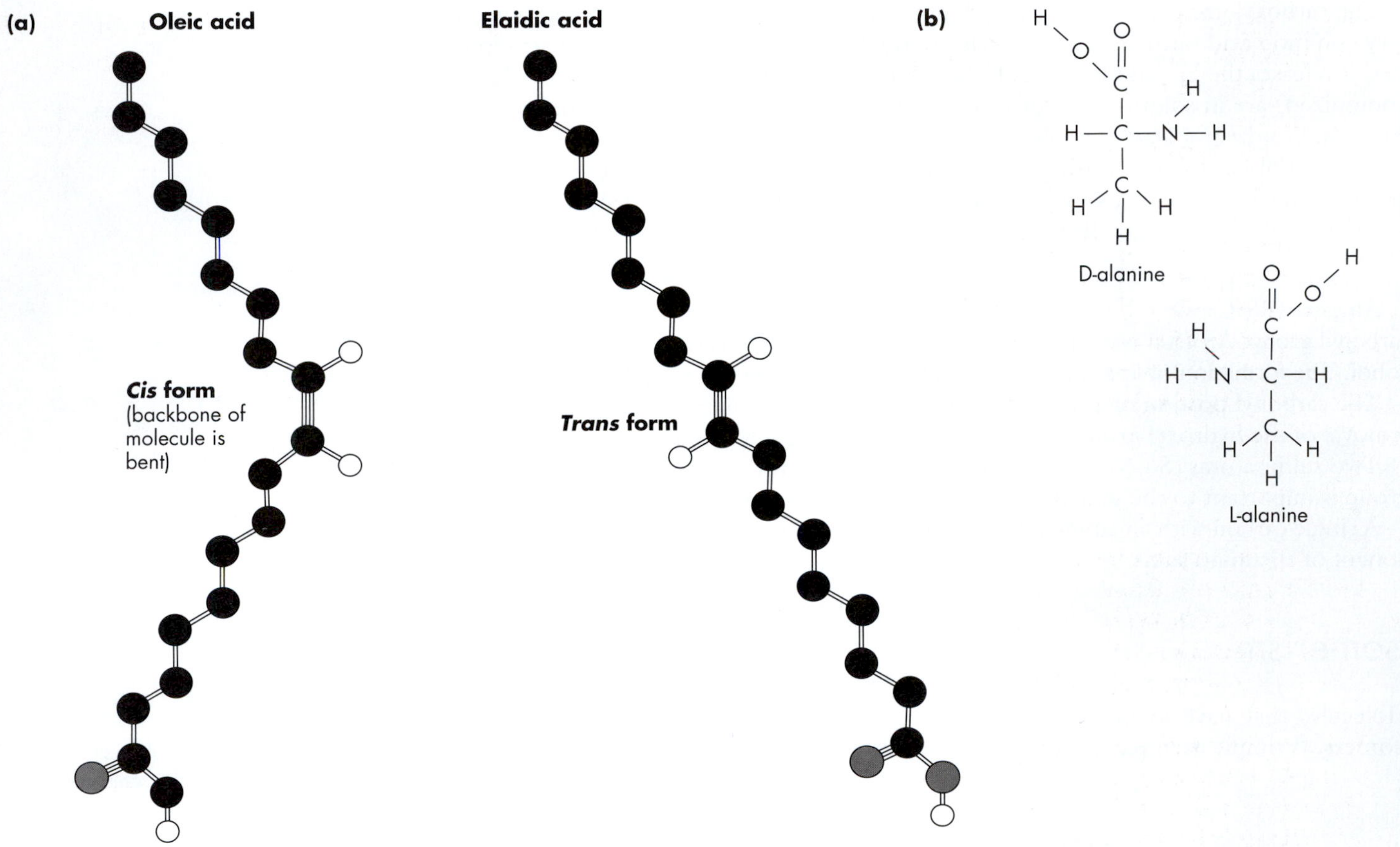

Figure A-5 (*a*) *Cis* and *trans* isomers of fatty acids. *Cis* forms are the most common forms in unprocessed foods. (*b*) Optical isomers of alanine—an amino acid. The L isomer is the most commonly found amino acid in nature.

hydrogenation, some *cis* bonds of fatty acids are converted to *trans* bonds. When vegetable oils are converted to vegetable fats, such as in margarine or shortening, some of the *trans* isomers are formed. The *trans* isomer elaidic acid is not the natural form. Isomers of these types (i.e., *cis* and *trans*) are called geometric isomers. Generous intakes of *trans* isomers of fatty acids are associated with an increased risk of cardiovascular disease (see Chapter 6).

Describing each stereoisomerism depends on which way the functional groups are arranged with respect to each other. If there are two isomers, *D* stands for dextro or right-handed, and *L* stands for levo or left-handed, such as alanine in D-alanine and L-alanine (Fig. A-5*b*). Stereoisomers that can't be superimposed on their mirror images are called optical isomers. Optical isomers can be identified from each other by their reaction to polarized light. One solution of an isomer that rotates the plane of polarized light to the right is dextrorotary. And the solution of its optical isomer rotates the plane of light to the left and, so, is levorotary.

The difference between two stereoisomers is "fit." This is important since the molecule has to fit an enzyme in order to make the chemical reaction proceed. For example, human enzymes use only L-amino acids (building blocks of protein) and D-sugars to build compounds. D-amino acids and L-sugars just won't function as such in the body. It is rather like trying to wear the left-hand glove on the right hand and do anything that requires manual skill.

A carbon atom with four different atoms or groups of atoms attached is described as being chiral (also called asymmetric). A molecule with one chiral carbon can have two stereoisomers, such as alanine (see above). When two or more (n) chiral carbons are present, there can be 2^n stereoisomers. Some stereoisomers are mirror images of each other, while others are not.

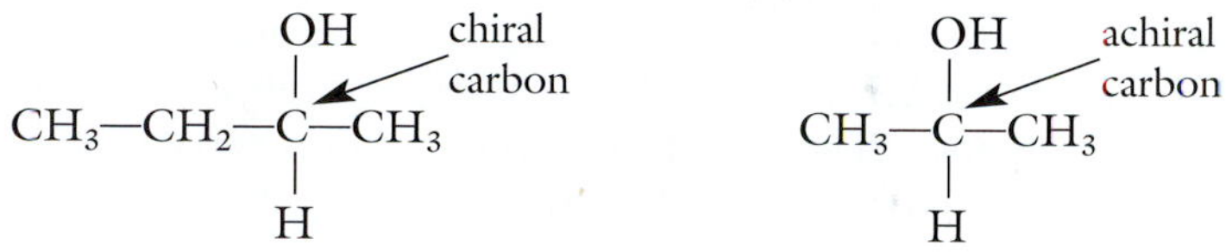

In all living organisms, many molecules are chiral.

When compounds have more than one chiral center, the "RS" system of naming is used, rather than the D and L system. Every chiral carbon is either R or S, based on specific rules.

This RS terminology is important to understanding vitamin E chemistry. It is now known that vitamin E as alpha-tocopherol has three chiral centers, and so has eight different stereoisomers (2^3). They are all found in synthetic preparations. The three chiral centers are identified as 2, 4, and 8 as related to the position on the tail of the molecule (see Chapter 9). The RRR isomer (i.e., R form at each of the 3 chiral centers on the phytal tail) is the natural form. A transfer protein in the liver only recognizes the R form of the chiral center at the 2 position. Of all the eight combinations of R and S in the phytal tail of synthetic vitamin E, the only biologically active ones are RRR, RSR, RSS, RRS, as they all have the R form in the 2 position.

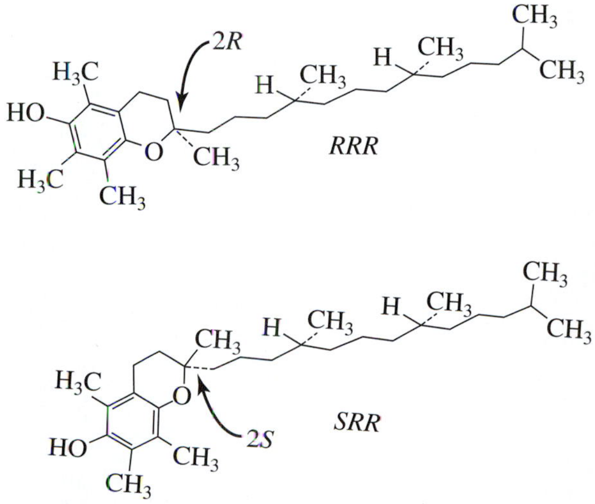

RRR and SRR isomers of vitamin E. Of the two, only the RRR isomer contributes to vitamin E needs.

Biochemistry

The study of the chemistry or molecular basis of life and the reactions, structures, and composition of living materials is known as biochemistry. Biochemical reactions are possible because of enzymes. Living organisms convert the energy they extract from food into energy for growth, maintenance, and reproduction. Energy can be stored for future use. The energy in the food is converted and used in the form of chemical energy contained in adenosine triphosphate (ATP). The fact that living organisms can self-replicate depends on deoxyribonucleic acid (DNA) and the genetic code. All forms of life store and transmit genetic information in the form of DNA.

Composition of Living Organisms

Approximately 98.5% of the body's weight is composed of the elements oxygen, carbon, hydrogen, nitrogen, calcium, and phosphorus. Elements such as iron, zinc, and copper are present in trace amounts in the body, but that doesn't mean they are unimportant. For instance, iron combines with a blood protein to form hemoglobin, an oxygen carrier. Hemoglobin transports oxygen from the lungs to the tissues and assists in returning carbon dioxide from the tissues to the lungs for removal.

Water is the most abundant chemical in the body, making up to about 70% of human tissue. Other important classes of compounds in the body are the proteins, carbohydrates, lipids, and nucleic acids.

Biochemical Reactions

All the biochemical reactions that occur in the body are described as metabolism. The intermediate compounds in metabolism are termed *metabolites*. Metabolic reactions that build (synthesize) complex molecules are described as anabolic. An example is the synthesis of protein from amino acids. The reactions that break down (degrade) larger molecules into smaller ones are described as catabolic. An example is starch breaking down to glucose molecules.

Carbohydrates

Carbohydrates are aldehydes with hydroxyl groups and ketones, containing carbon, hydrogen, and oxygen with the general formula CH_2O. (There are twice as many hydrogen atoms as carbon and oxygen atoms.) The suffix *-ose* indicates a sugar. *Hexose* refers to a 6-carbon monosaccharide. There are three structural isomers of hexose: galactose, glucose, and fructose. All have the same formula, $C_6H_{12}O_6$, but the arrangement of their individual atoms differs in small ways.

The simplest carbohydrates are monosaccharides. When two monosaccharides are chemically bonded, they form a disaccharide, or double sugar. The table sugar sucrose is an example of a disaccharide, formed from glucose and fructose.

Polysaccharides are many monosaccharides joined by covalent bonds. Plant starch and cellulose are examples of polysaccharides. Some starches have thousands of glucose subunits. In animals, carbohydrate is stored as an animal starch called glycogen, found in liver and muscle tissue.

Di- and *poly*saccharides are assembled by a condensation reaction. Water is a by-product of the reaction. Hydrolysis, or the splitting by the addition of water, digests di- and polysaccharides to smaller sugar units (see the later section entitled Important Chemical Reactions Related to the Study of Nutrition for details).

Lipids

Lipids are a class of nonpolar compounds that are grouped according to solubility in organic solvents. They don't readily dissolve in water because most are nonpolar or hydrophobic.

Simple lipids include fatty acids and steroids. The lipid cholesterol serves as the precursor (parent) for the steroid hormones, such as testosterone, estrogen, and progesterone. Complex lipids include triglycerides (often referred to as *triacylglycerols*), which are esters of glycerol and fatty acids. Phospholipids are composed of glycerol, phosphoric acid, and long-chain fatty acids; sphingolipids are composed of sphingosine, phosphoric acid, long-chain fatty acids and choline; and glycosphingolipids are composed of sphingosine, fatty acids, and carbohydrates.

Triglycerides represent fuel found in food and stored in adipose tissues. Phospholipids are part polar and part nonpolar, which allows them to interact with water and function as emulsifiers. Sphingophospholipids make up the material surrounding nerves. Glycosphingolipids are structural material for brain and nerve tissue. These complex lipids can be hydrolyzed to yield fatty acids.

Prostaglandins are a special type of fatty acid produced by almost all organs in the body and have specific regulatory functions. They are all derived from certain (dietary essential) fatty acids.

Proteins

Proteins are polymers of amino acids. Twenty of the amino acids are incorporated into the great variety of body proteins. Although the amino acids contain an amine (amino) group (NH_2) and a carboxylic acid group ($-\overset{\overset{\displaystyle O}{\|}}{C}-OH$), each has a distinctive structure (Fig. A-6). Proteins typically contain many atoms, such as carbon, nitrogen, sulfur, hydrogen, and oxygen.

The genetic information found in DNA in the nucleus of the cell is the code book for constructing a protein. The sequence of amino acids in a protein follows the DNA code for synthesizing the protein. This protein can be made over and over again because of the code carried in the person's genes.

Nucleic Acids (DNA and RNA)

Nucleic acids include DNA (deoxyribonucleic acid), RNA (ribonucleic acid), and the subunits from which they are formed, called nucleotides. The nucleotide is made of

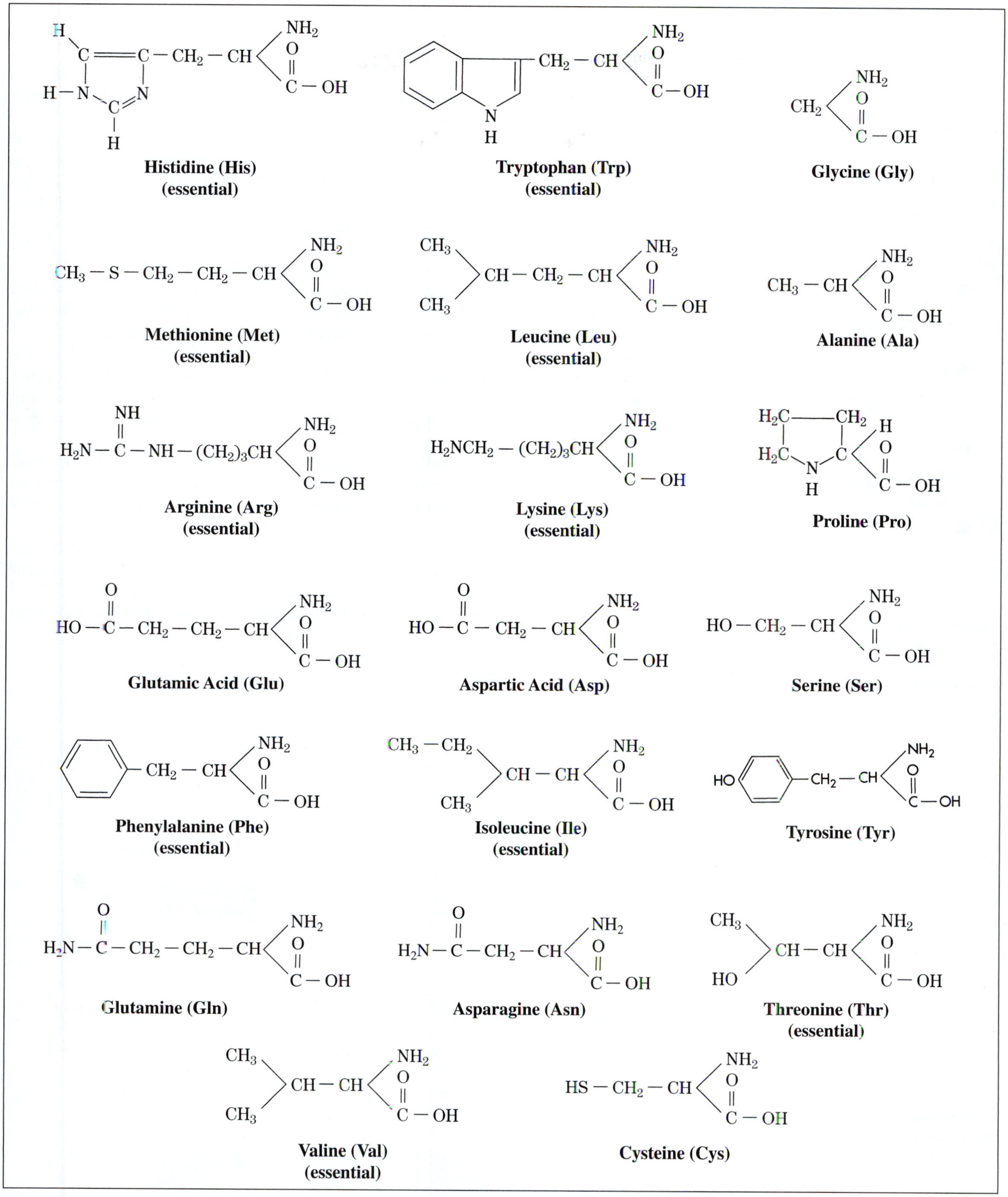

Figure A-6 The 20 common amino acids in foods.

three components: a 5-carbon pentose sugar, a phosphate group, and a nitrogenous base (Fig. A-7). There are two kinds of nitrogenous base: purines (double ring) and pyrimidines (single ring).

The sugar contained in RNA is ribose. The pyrimidine bases in ribonucleic acids are uracil and cytosine, and the purine bases are guanine and adenine. RNA is a single polynucleotide strand, not a double strand, like DNA.

DNA found in the nucleus of the cell is the basis of the genetic code. The sugar in DNA deoxyribose can be covalently bonded to the purine bases adenine and guanine and to the pyrimidines bases: cytosine and thymine (Fig. A-8). These are the four types of nucleotides that can produce the long chain that makes up a single strand of DNA. The DNA is a sugar phosphate chain made up of two strands that twist around each other to form a helix. The bases project into the center of the structure, forming a staircase structure. The two strands are held together by hydrogen bonds (Fig. A-9).

In DNA there is always an equal number of purine and pyrimidine bases. And there is a relationship called complementary base pairing—adenine pairs only with thymine, and guanine pairs only with cytosine. (In RNA adenine pairs with uracil.)

Although there are only four bases, the number of sequences of bases is endless. The total human genome consists of billions of base pairs making up about 35,000 genes. The applications of this knowledge can lead to genetic screening for breast cancer and, in the future, are likely to help produce drugs to treat obesity and inborn errors of metabolism.

During replication, the helix uncoils and separates, so that each chain or strand serves as a template for the synthesis of its complementary chain. This is known as cell division. Each daughter chain has one strand of the original molecule and one new strand.

RNA, another nucleic acid, takes its instructions from DNA. There are three types of RNA: ribosomal RNA, transfer RNA, and messenger RNA. Ribosomal RNA forms part of the structure of ribosomes in the cell; this is where proteins are synthesized. Messenger RNA contains the code for the synthesis of a specific protein transcribed

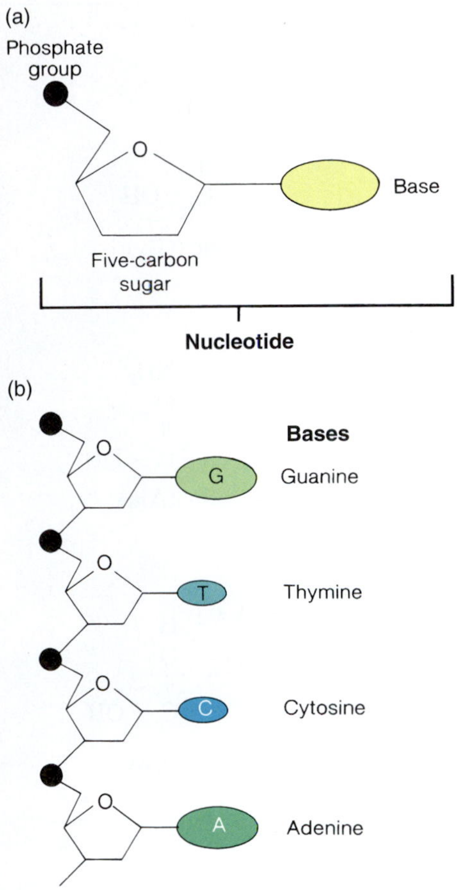

Figure A-7 (*a*) The general structure of a nucleotide. (*b*) A polymer of nucleotides, or polynucleotide, is formed by sugar-phosphate bonds between nucleotides.

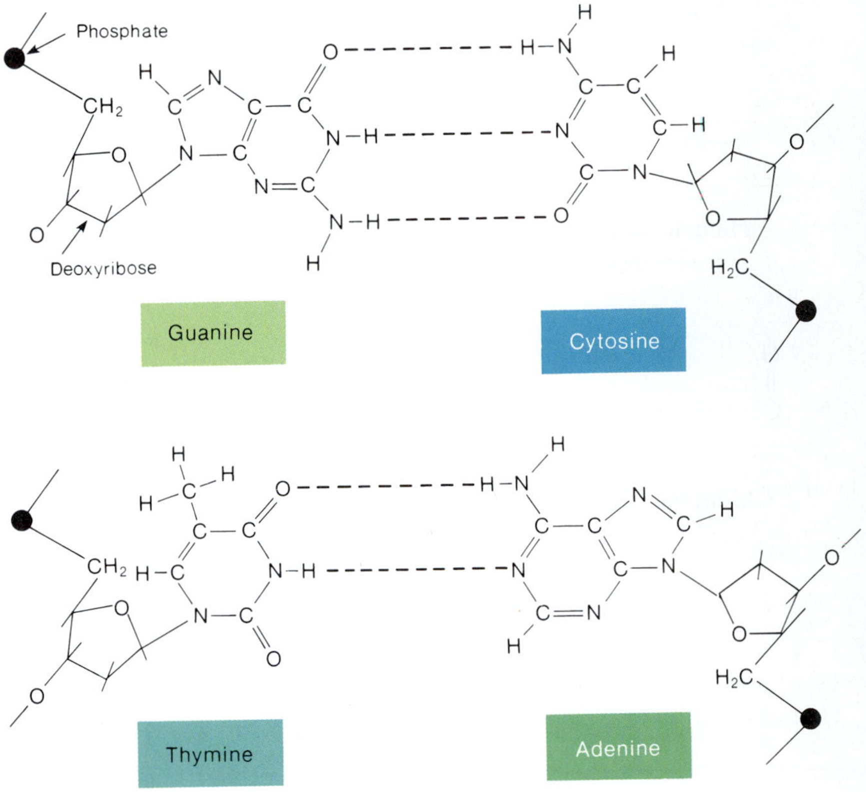

Figure A-8 The four nitrogenous bases in deoxyribonucleic acid (DNA). Notice that hydrogen bonds can form between guanine and cytosine and between thymine and adenine.

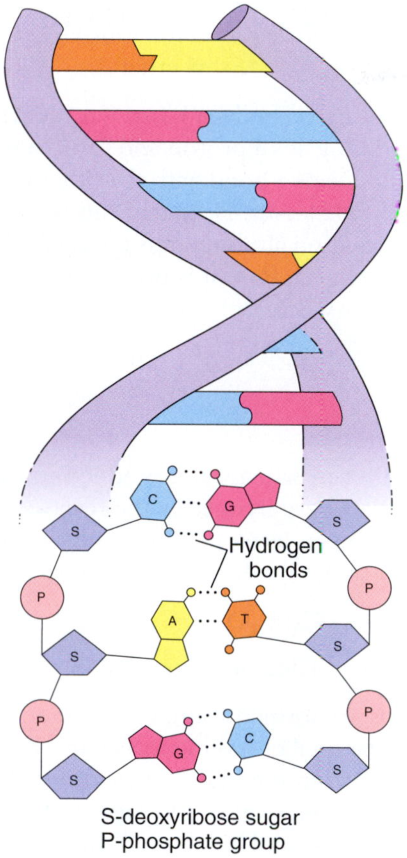

Figure A-9 The double-helix structure of DNA. The two strands are held together by hydrogen bonds between complementary bases in each strand.

from DNA. Transfer RNA decodes the genetic message in RNA and assembles the amino acids for the protein assembly line (see Chapter 7 for details). The process is called translation.

Important Chemical Reactions Related to the Study of Nutrition

One of the most important properties of chemical compounds is the type of reactions they undergo. Chemical reactions are responsible for vision, thinking, movement, and everything else that occurs in the human body.

In a chemical reaction, a compound or set of compounds (the reactants) is converted into another compound or set of compounds (the products), accompanied by the absorption or release of energy, which is typically heat in biological processes. In effect, the reactants reshuffle their atoms to form products. Clearly, then, no atoms lose their identity during a chemical reaction, and no atoms are gained, lost, or converted to another kind of atom during the course of chemical activity.

Chemists have grouped reactions according to their similarities in chemical behavior. Some of these reactions are performed over and over within each cell. Following is a brief overview of some important reaction types.

Condensation Reactions

A condensation reaction occurs when two molecules join together to form a larger molecule and water is released. The two-reactant molecules typically contain hydroxyl groups, meaning that there are two OH groups. A simple example is the condensation of ethanol to make ethyl ether and water.

$$CH_3CH_2OH + CH_3CH_2OH \rightarrow CH_3CH_2\text{—}O\text{—}CH_2CH_3 + H_2O$$

Ethanol Ethanol Ethyl ether Water

Although this reaction does not occur in the body, it illustrates the essential features of condensation reactions. One OH group gains a proton and forms a water molecule. The other OH group loses a proton and forms a bond with the other molecule—in exactly the same place that the water molecule leaves. Note that this is an overall description of what happens, not how it happens. And although it is typical for both molecules to contain an OH group in a condensation reaction, it is not a requirement for the reaction. A condensation reaction can occur where only one of the reactants contains an OH group.

Hydrolysis Reactions

Hydrolysis reactions are reactions that occur when water is added to a compound. In biological systems, hydrolysis reactions are very frequently the reverse of condensation reactions. That is, water is added to a large molecule, which results in the formation of two smaller molecules. This can be illustrated by the hydrolysis of lactose.

$$C_{12}H_{22}O_{11} + H_2O \rightarrow C_6H_{12}O_6 + C_6H_{12}O_6$$

Lactose Water Glucose Galactose

Many important compounds in cells are formed using condensation reactions, and the breakdown of many compounds into smaller fragments occurs via hydrolysis reactions. For instance, hydrolysis of foodstuffs in the intestine yields smaller compounds, which the body can absorb, such as the breakdown of the sugar lactose in milk by the action of the enzyme lactase to form glucose and galactose. The reverse occurs when the human mammary gland makes lactose. Also, when the carbohydrate glucose is converted to glycogen for storage, or to fat for muscle fuel, the synthetic processes use condensation reactions.

Oxidation and Reduction Reactions

Oxidation-reduction (redox) reactions are important in nutrition science because they release energy from food during oxidation and synthesize carbohydrates, fatty acids, and other organic compounds during reduction. An oxidation reaction takes place with a simultaneous reduction reaction. Redox reactions follow three rules:

1. No oxidation reaction takes place without something being reduced, and no reduction takes place without something being oxidized.
2. In inorganic chemistry, oxidation is the loss of electrons, and in organic chemistry oxidation is the loss of hydrogen (or gain of oxygen).
3. In inorganic chemistry reduction is the gain in electrons, and in organic chemistry reduction is the gain of hydrogen (or loss of oxygen).

A simple redox reaction involving iron is as follows:

$$Fe^{3+} + e^- \longleftrightarrow Fe^{2+}$$

A biochemical redox reaction involving the coenzyme form of riboflavin occurs as follows:

$$\text{FAD} \underset{-2H}{\overset{+2H}{\longleftrightarrow}} \text{FADH}_2$$

Chapters 4, 10, and 12 provide more information about coenzymes, cofactors, and oxidation-reduction reactions.

Energy and Enzymatic Reactions

Enzymes are large proteins with varying amino acid composition that behave as organic **catalysts.** They are highly specific. Enzymes help a reaction to proceed by lowering the "energy of activation," so that the reaction can go faster (Fig. A-10). Enzymes lower this energy barrier between the reactants and the products. Some of the enzyme reactions that occur in the cell require coenzymes (vitamins) at the active site to make the reaction go, whereas many others don't. Fortunately, an enzyme isn't consumed by the reaction, so it can be used over and over.

catalyst A compound that speeds reaction rates but is not altered by the reaction.

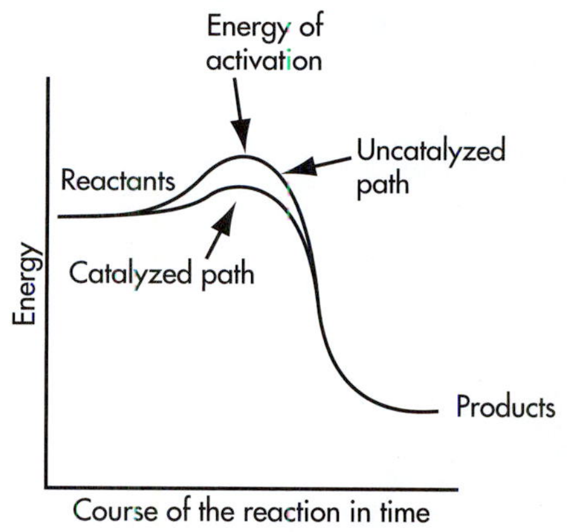

Figure A-10 Enzymes and other catalysts accelerate chemical reactions by reducing the energy barrier to the reaction. Reactants molecules free in solution can react only if they meet in just the right orientation and with enough energy. An enzyme holds its substrate molecules in the right orientation to react and exerts forces on them that cause chemical bonds to break and form. In this way, an enzyme lowers the energy barrier that substrates must pass and, so, increases their reaction rates.

Common Chemical Structures

Most compounds in the body are composed of carbon, hydrogen, and oxygen, with carbon often being the predominant atom. Some commonly encountered combinations of atoms, called functional groups, have been given specific names because they appear in many molecules. You need to be familiar with them, for they are the most important features in many of our nutrients. The important ones were listed in Table A-5. You will be using these names and studying these structures throughout this course.

The Drawing of Chemical Structures

Chemists have developed a shorthand notation for writing chemical formulas, called skeletal structures. In skeletal structures, neither carbon atoms nor the hydrogens bonded to the carbon atoms are expressly shown. What are shown are the bonds between the carbon atoms and the position of all atoms other than carbon and hydrogen. Keep in mind that there are carbon atoms at the apices of every angle in the structure (with the appropriate number of hydrogens attached to the carbon) and at the terminal end of the sticks. By way of illustration, look at a skeletal structure of propane ($CH_3CH_2CH_3$).

The advantage of using skeletal structures is that it allows for a clear representation of complex molecules without cluttering up the picture. This notation will be used throughout the text. It is handy when large structures, such as fatty acids, have to be represented.

Propane — Skeletal structure of propane

appendix b

Detailed Depictions of Glycolysis, Citric Acid Cycle, and Electron Transport Chain

The following illustrations are provided to help you better visualize the changes in chemical structures throughout the metabolic processes described. These figures reflect greater scientific detail than the more simplified versions in Chapter 4.

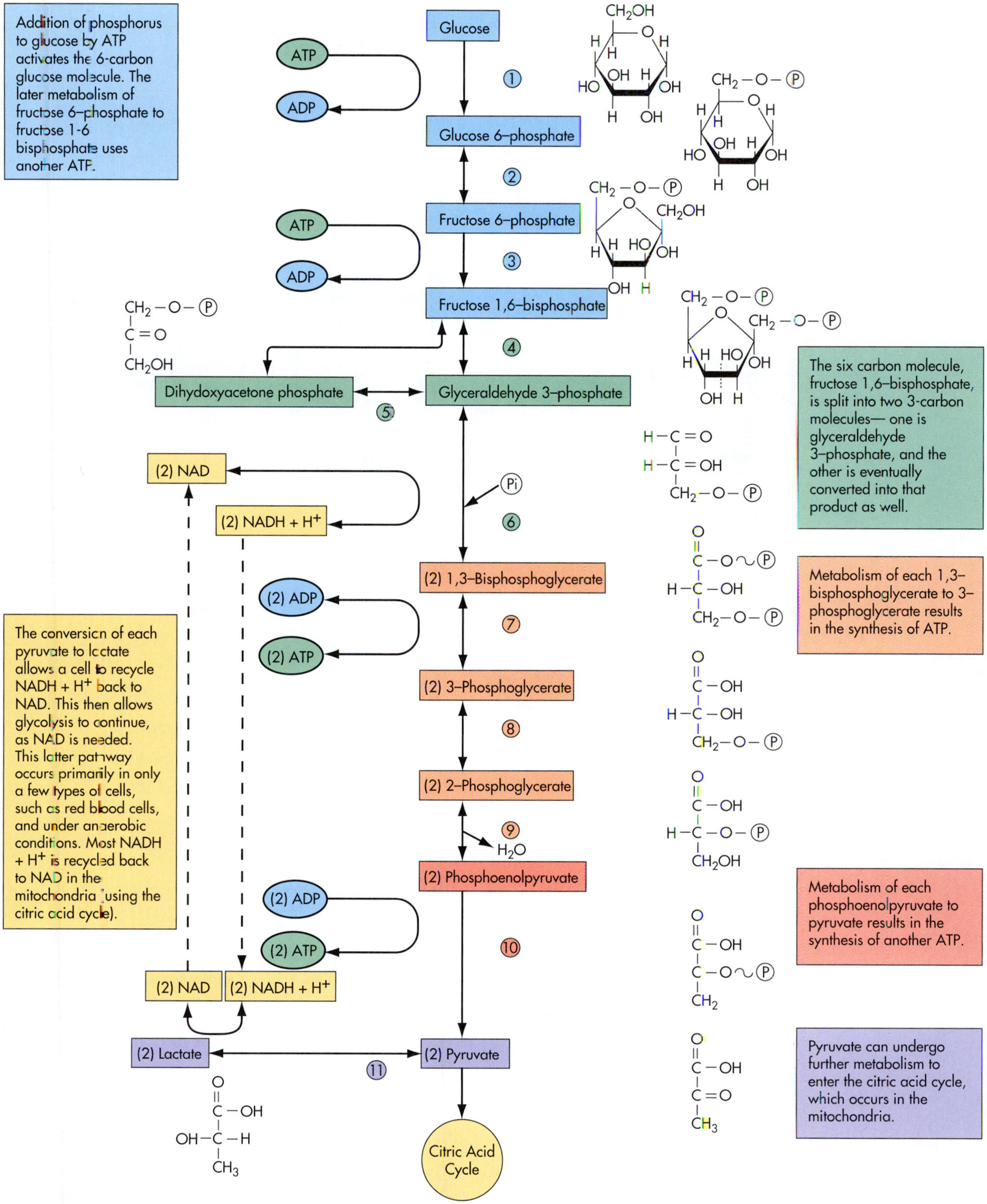

Addition of phosphorus to glucose by ATP activates the 6-carbon glucose molecule. The later metabolism of fructose 6-phosphate to fructose 1-6 bisphosphate uses another ATP.
Glucose
ATP
ADP
1
Glucose 6-phosphate
2
Fructose 6-phosphate
ATP
ADP
3
Fructose 1,6-bisphosphate
4
Dihydoxyacetone phosphate
Glyceraldehyde 3-phosphate
5
The six carbon molecule, fructose 1,6-bisphosphate, is split into two 3-carbon molecules— one is glyceraldehyde 3-phosphate, and the other is eventually converted into that product as well.
(2) NAD
(2) NADH + H+
Pi
6
(2) 1,3-Bisphosphoglycerate
Metabolism of each 1,3-bisphosphoglycerate to 3-phosphoglycerate results in the synthesis of ATP.
(2) ADP
(2) ATP
7
(2) 3-Phosphoglycerate
8
(2) 2-Phosphoglycerate
9
H2O
(2) Phosphoenolpyruvate
The conversion of each pyruvate to lactate allows a cell to recycle NADH + H+ back to NAD. This then allows glycolysis to continue, as NAD is needed. This latter pathway occurs primarily in only a few types of cells, such as red blood cells, and under anaerobic conditions. Most NADH + H+ is recycled back to NAD in the mitochondria (using the citric acid cycle).
(2) ADP
(2) ATP
10
Metabolism of each phosphoenolpyruvate to pyruvate results in the synthesis of another ATP.
(2) NAD
(2) NADH + H+
(2) Lactate
11
(2) Pyruvate
Citric Acid Cycle
Pyruvate can undergo further metabolism to enter the citric acid cycle, which occurs in the mitochondria.

Figure B-1 Detailed depiction of the individual chemical reactions that comprise glycolysis—glucose to pyruvate. Glycolysis takes place in the cytosol of the cell. The enzymes in the cytosol that participate at each step are (1) hexokinase, (2) phosphohexose isomerase, (3) phosphofructokinase, (4) aldolase, (5) phosphotriose isomerase, (6) glyceraldehyde-3-phosphate dehydrogenase, (7) phosphoglycerate kinase, (8) phosphoglycerate mutase, (9) enolase, (10) pyruvate kinase, and sometimes (11) lactate dehydrogenase. Pi represents a phosphate group. See also Figure 4–5.

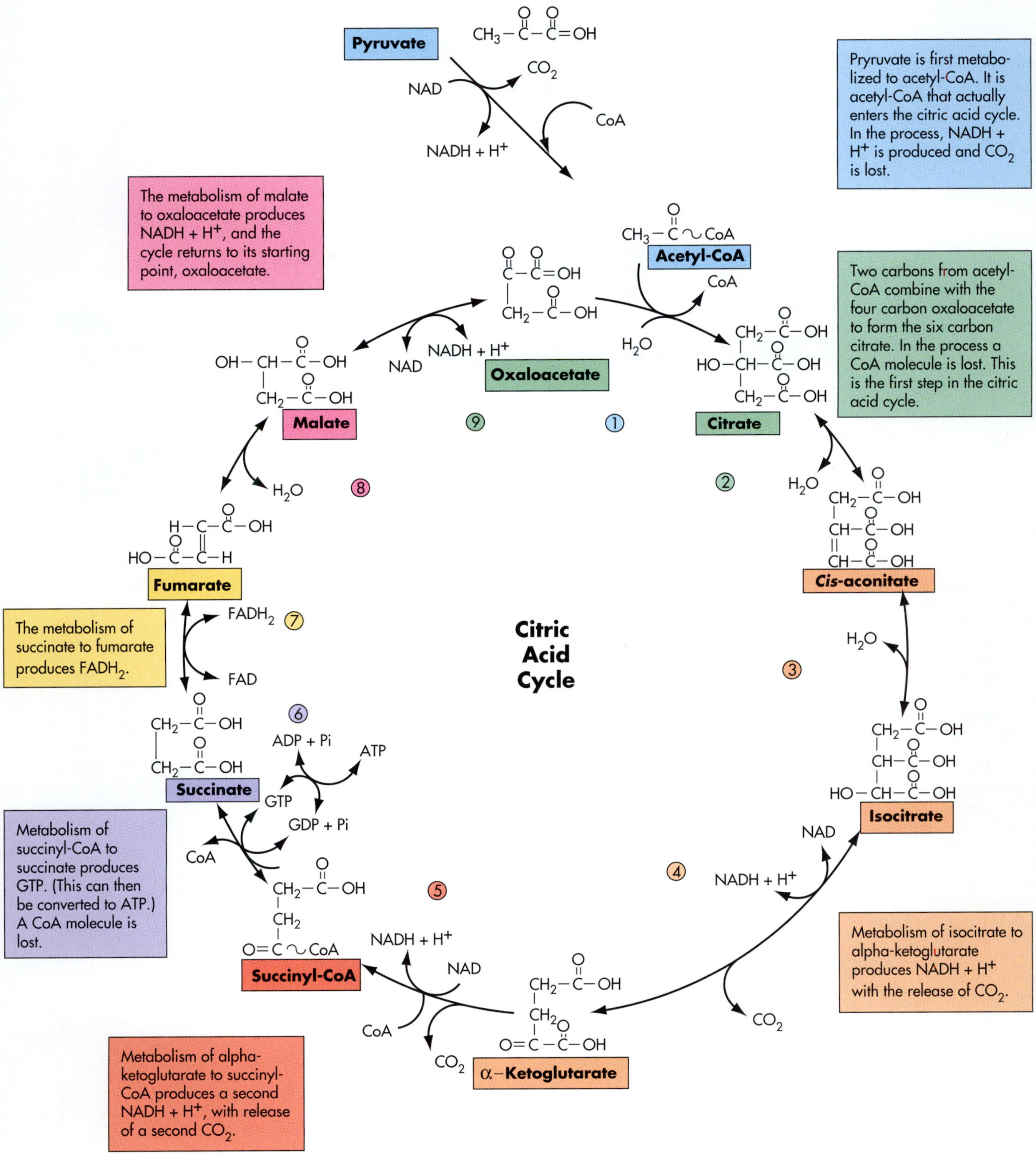
Pyruvate
NAD
CO_2
NADH + H^+
CoA
Pryruvate is first metabolized to acetyl-CoA. It is acetyl-CoA that actually enters the citric acid cycle. In the process, NADH + H^+ is produced and CO_2 is lost.
Acetyl-CoA
The metabolism of malate to oxaloacetate produces NADH + H^+, and the cycle returns to its starting point, oxaloacetate.
Oxaloacetate
H_2O
Two carbons from acetyl-CoA combine with the four carbon oxaloacetate to form the six carbon citrate. In the process a CoA molecule is lost. This is the first step in the citric acid cycle.
Citrate
Malate
Cis-aconitate
Fumarate
Citric Acid Cycle
The metabolism of succinate to fumarate produces $FADH_2$.
$FADH_2$
FAD
Succinate
ADP + Pi
ATP
GTP
GDP + Pi
Isocitrate
Metabolism of succinyl-CoA to succinate produces GTP. (This can then be converted to ATP.) A CoA molecule is lost.
Succinyl-CoA
Metabolism of isocitrate to alpha-ketoglutarate produces NADH + H^+ with the release of CO_2.
α−Ketoglutarate
Metabolism of alpha-ketoglutarate to succinyl-CoA produces a second NADH + H^+, with release of a second CO_2.

Figure B-2 Detailed depiction of conversion of pyruvate to acetyl-CoA and the individual chemical reactions of the citric acid cycle. Conversion of pyruvate to acetyl-CoA uses an enzyme complex that includes pyruvate dehydrogenase. The enzymes used in the citric acid cycle are (1) citrate synthase, (2) aconitase, (3) aconitase, (4) isocitrate dehydrogenase, (5) alpha-ketoglutarate dehydrogenase, (6) succinate thiokinase, (7) succinate dehydrogenase, (8) fumarase, and (9) malate dehydrogenase. CoA stands for coenzyme A, which is made from the vitamin pantothenic acid (see Chapter 10 for the chemical structure). Note that the CO2 molecules lost during one turn of the citric acid cycle are not those from the carbons donated by acetyl-CoA. Instead, the carbons are broken off of the portion of the citrate molecule derived from oxaloacetate. See also Figure 4–7.

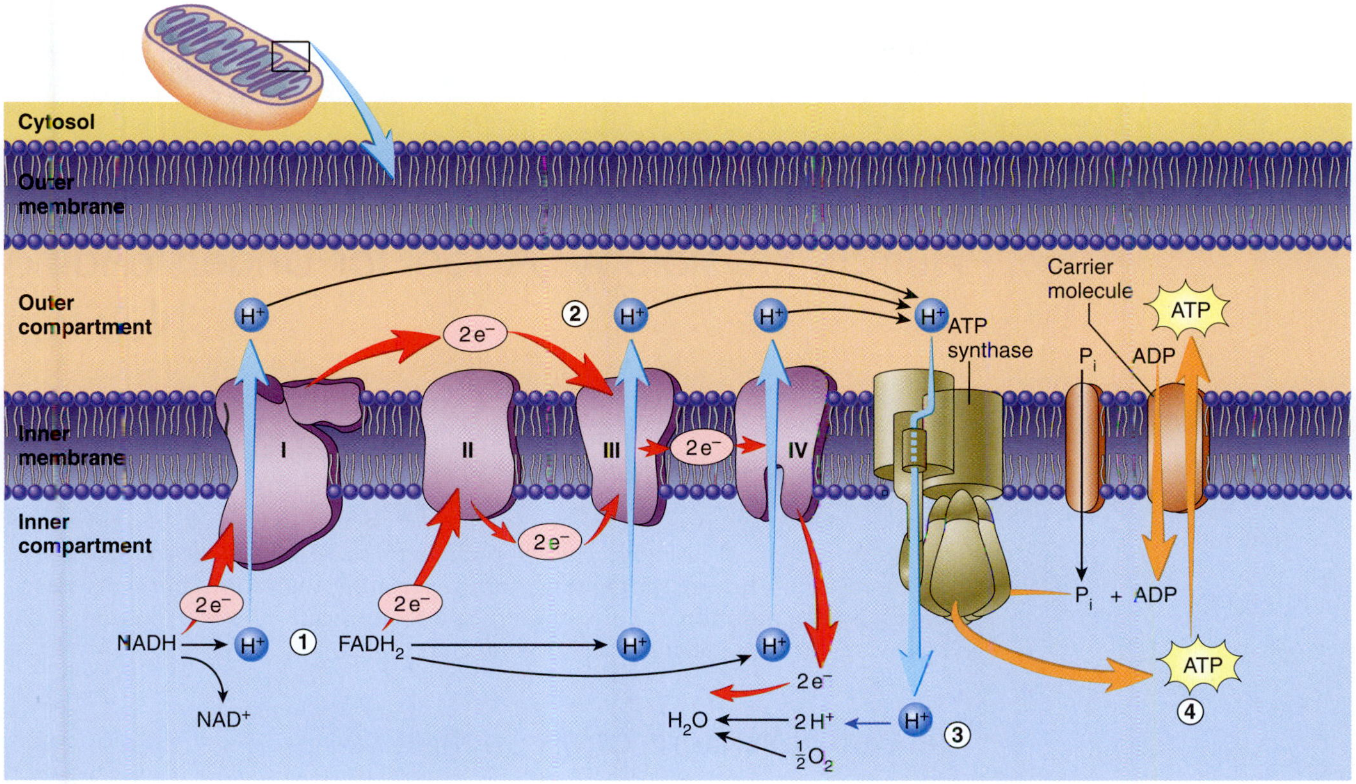

1. NADH or $FADH_2$ transfer their electrons to the electron-transport chain.

2. As the electrons move through the electron-transport chain, some of their energy is used to pump hydrogen ions into the outer compartment, resulting in a higher concentration of hydrogen ions in the outer than in the inner compartment.

3. The hydrogen ions diffuse back into the inner compartment through special channels (ATP synthase) that couple the hydrogen ion movement with the production of ATP. The electrons, hydrogen ions, and oxygen combine to form water.

4. ATP is transported out of the inner compartment by a carrier molecule that exchanges ATP for ADP. A different carrier molecule moves phosphate into the inner compartment.

Figure B-3 Detailed depiction of the electron-transport chain. $NADH+H^+$ and $FADH_2$ transfer their hydrogen ions and electrons to electron carriers located on the inner mitochondrial membrane. The electrons and hydrogen ions combine with oxygen to form water (H_2O). The energy yielded by the entire process is used to generate ATP. Each $NADH+H^+$ in the mitochondria releases enough energy to form the equivalent of 2.5 ATP, while each $FADH_2$ releases enough energy to form the equivalent of 1.5 ATP.

appendix c

Human Physiology: A Tool for Understanding Nutrition

Our task in this appendix is to explore the various systems in the body beyond that of the digestive system, focusing specifically on how these systems relate to the study of human nutrition. This will set the stage for investigating the various nutrients associated with human nutrition. Before we can begin that process, however, it is important to review the processes taking place in a human cell.

The Cell: Structure and Function

The cell is the basic structural and functional unit of life. Living organisms are made of many different kinds of cells specialized to perform particular functions, and all cells are derived from preexisting cells. In the human body, the 100 trillion or so cells all have certain basic characteristics that are alike. All cells have compartments, particles, or filaments that perform specialized functions; these structures are called organelles. There are at least 15 different organelles, but this section discusses only eight. The numbers preceding the names of the cell structures correspond to the structures illustrated in Figure C-1.

1. Cell (Plasma) Membrane

There is an outside and inside to every cell, as defined by the cell (plasma) membrane. This membrane holds in the cellular contents and regulates the direction and flow of substances into and out of the cell. Cell-to-cell communication also occurs by way of this membrane. Some cells can even penetrate another cell membrane and so invade that cell.

The cell membrane is a lipid bilayer (or double membrane) of **phospholipids** with their water-soluble (polar) heads facing into the interior of the cell and out to the exterior of the cell. The water-insoluble (nonpolar) tails are tucked into the interior of the cell membrane (Chapter 6 reviews phospholipids in detail and Appendix A reviews the concept of polar and nonpolar compounds).

phospholipid Any of a class of fat-related substances that contain phosphorus, fatty acids, and a nitrogen-containing base. The phospholipids are an essential part of every cell.

Cholesterol is a fat-soluble component of the membrane, so it is embedded within the bilayer. Together with phospholipids, cholesterol keeps the membrane fluid.

There are also various proteins embedded in the membrane. Proteins provide structural support, act as transport vehicles, and function as enzymes that affect chemical processes within the membrane. Some proteins are open channels that allow water-soluble substances to pass into and out of the cell. Proteins on the outside surface of the membrane act as receptors, snagging essential substances the cell needs and drawing them into the cell. Other proteins act as gates, opening and closing to control the flow of various particles into and out of the cell.

glycocalyx A hairlike projection on the extracellular surface of the plasma membrane; it consists of short, branched carbohydrate chains.

In addition to the lipid and protein, the membrane also contains carbohydrates that mark the exterior of the cell, called the **glycocalyx.** These carbohydrates are combined

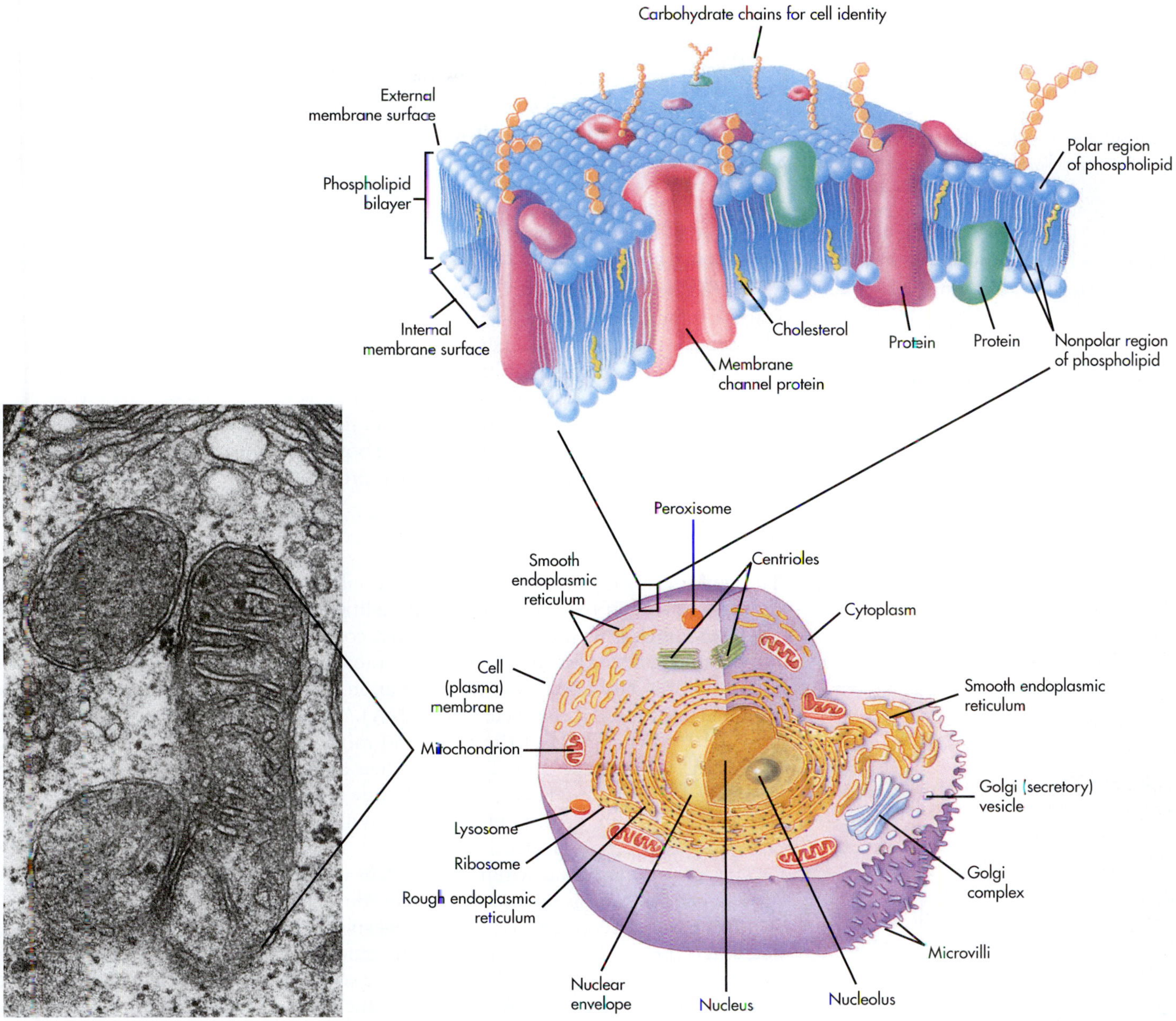

Figure C-1 An animal cell. Almost all human cells contain these various organelles. Shown in greater detail are mitochondria and the cell membrane. Note: Not all cells have microvilli. The nuclear envelope encloses the nucleus. The centrioles participate in cell division.

either with proteins or fats and provide a delivery service for sending messages to the cell's organelles. The structures also provide distinct identification for a cell. In addition, they detect invaders and initiate defensive actions. In sum, these carbohydrates provide tags that are important to cellular identity and interaction.

Organelles

Included within the cell membrane are **organelles.** They carry out vital roles in cell functions. Some structures allow the cell to replicate itself, others provide energy, and others destroy the cell when it is worn out. Still other organelles produce and secrete products destined for other cells.

organelles Compartments, particles, or filaments that perform specialized functions within a cell.

2. Cytoplasm

cytoplasm The fluid and organelles (except the nucleus) in a cell.

cytosol The water-based phase of the cytoplasm, with its dissolved substances; excludes the organelles such as mitochondria.

The **cytoplasm** is the fluid material and organelles within the cell, not including the nucleus. (The **cytosol** is the fluid surrounding the organelles.) A small amount of ATP energy for use by the cell can be produced by chemical reactions that occur in the cytoplasm. This contributes to our survival, as it is the key process in red blood cell energy metabolism; it is called anaerobic metabolism because it doesn't require oxygen.

3. Mitochondria

mitochondria The main sites of energy production in a cell. They also contain the pathway for oxidizing fat for fuel, among other metabolic pathways.

carbon skeleton An amino acid after the amino group has been removed.

Mitochondria are sometimes called "power plants," or the powerhouse of the cell. These organelles are capable of converting the energy in our energy-yielding nutrients (carbohydrate, protein, and fat) to a form that cells can use, again ATP. This is an aerobic process that uses the oxygen we inhale, and water, enzymes, and other compounds (see Chapter 4 for details). With the exception of red blood cells, all cells contain mitochondria; only the size, shape, and numbers vary.

The biochemical pathways that operate in the mitochondria are also capable of synthesizing cell components, such as the **carbon skeletons** needed to produce amino acids. These will eventually become cellular protein.

4. Cell Nucleus

cell nucleus An organelle bound by its own double membrane and containing chromosomes, the genetic information for cell protein synthesis and cell replication.

chromosome A single, large DNA molecule and its associated proteins containing many genes; stores and transmits genetic information.

ribonucleic acid (RNA) The single-stranded nucleic acid involved in the transcription of genetic information and translation of that information into protein structure.

ribosomes Cytoplasmic particles that mediate the linking together of amino acids to form proteins; attached to endoplasmic reticulum as bound ribosomes, or suspended in cytoplasm as free ribosomes.

nucleoli, nucleolus Center for production of ribosomes within the cell nucleus.

The **cell nucleus** is surrounded by its own double membrane. The nucleus controls actions that occur in the cell, using the hereditary material known as deoxyribonucleic acid (DNA). DNA is the "code book" that contains directions for making substances the cell needs. It consists of genes on **chromosomes.** This "code book" remains in the nucleus of the cell, but conveys its information to other cell organelles by way of a similar molecule called **ribonucleic acid (RNA).** The RNA has the responsibility of *transcribing* the information of the DNA and moving out through pores in the nuclear membrane to the cytoplasm. The RNA then carries the code to protein-synthesizing sites called **ribosomes.** There, the RNA code is *translated* into a specific protein (see Chapter 7 for details on protein synthesis). With the exception of the red blood cell, all cells have one or more nuclei.

The **nucleoli** are areas within the nucleus of the cell containing a combination of protein and RNA. This is where RNA is produced for export to the cytoplasm.

DNA has the secondary task of cell replication. DNA is a double-stranded molecule, and when the cell begins to divide, each strand is separated and an identical copy of each is made. Thus, each new DNA molecule contains one new strand of DNA and one strand from the original DNA. In this way, the genetic code is preserved from one cell generation to the next. The mitochondria contain their own DNA, so they reproduce themselves independent of action in the nucleus.

The transport of proteins, vitamins, and other material from the cytoplasm to the nucleus also occurs through pores in the nuclear membrane as just mentioned. These small molecules serve a variety of functions, including the activation (or inactivation) of certain parts of the DNA.

5. Endoplasmic Reticulum (ER)

endoplasmic reticulum (ER) An organelle in the cytoplasm composed of a network of canals running through the cytoplasm. Rough ER contains ribosomes. Smooth ER contains no ribosomes.

The outer membrane of the cell nucleus is continuous with a network of tubes called the **endoplasmic reticulum (ER).** The ER is found in two types: rough and smooth. The rough endoplasmic reticulum has ribosomes bound to it, whereas the smooth does not. As noted earlier, ribosomes are the sites where proteins are synthesized. Many of these proteins play a central role in human nutrition. The smooth ER is involved in lipid synthesis, detoxification of toxic substances, and calcium storage and release in the cell.

6. Golgi Complex

The **Golgi complex** is a packaging site for proteins and lipids that are used in the cytoplasm or exported from the cell. The Golgi complex consists of sacs within the cytoplasm in which products of the rough endoplasmic reticulum are received, processed, separated according to function and destination, and "packaged" in **secretory vesicles** for secretion by the cell.

Golgi complex The cell organelle near the nucleus that processes newly synthesized protein for secretion or distribution to other organelles.

secretory vesicles Membrane-bound vesicles produced by the Golgi apparatus; contain proteins and other compounds to be secreted by the cell.

7. Lysosomes

Lysosomes are the cell's digestive system. They are sacs that contain enzymes for the digestion of foreign material. Sometimes known as "suicide bags," they are responsible for digesting worn-out or damaged cells. They carry out **apoptosis,** or programmed cell death, which occurs naturally or is associated with illness or infections. Certain cells that are associated with immunity contain many lysosomes (see the later section on the immune system).

lysosome A cell organelle that contains digestive enzymes for use inside the cell for turnover of cell parts.

apoptosis A process that occurs over time in which enzymes in a cell set off a series of events that disable numerous cell functions, eventually leading to cell death.

8. Peroxisomes

Peroxisomes contain enzymes that detoxify harmful chemicals. **Hydrogen peroxide** (H_2O_2) is formed as a result of such enzyme action. Peroxisomes contain a protective enzyme called *catalase,* which prevents excessive accumulation of hydrogen peroxide in the cell, which would be very damaging. Peroxisomes also play a minor role in metabolizing one possible source of energy for cells—alcohol.

peroxisome A cell organelle that destroys toxic products within the cell.

hydrogen peroxide Chemically, H_2O_2.

Now let's look at the body systems. Keep in mind these depend on the cell functions just discussed.

Integumentary System

The first system to examine is the one we are most familiar with, the **integumentary** system, which is made up of dissimilar elements, such as the skin, hair, various glands, and nails. The largest organ in the body, the skin, consists of two principal layers, the **epidermis** and the **dermis** (Fig. C-2). The epidermis is the layer of skin composed largely of dead cells, which are used for protection from environmental pathogens, toxins, injury, and water. We don't want to absorb water through the skin, nor do we want water to readily escape the body.

integumentary Having to do with the skin, hair, glands, and nails, the largest organ in the body.

epidermis The outermost layer of the skin, composed of epithelial layers.

dermis The second, or deep, layer of the skin, under the epidermis.

The dermis is a deeper and thicker layer of skin, with an extensive network of blood vessels, sweat glands, oil-secreting glands, nerve endings, and hair follicles. When people are confined to bed for long periods of time, **decubitus ulcers,** also called bed sores, may develop due to restricted blood flow to the dermis. This lack of blood causes cells to die and open wounds to develop—a potentially life-threatening situation. Adequate protein, vitamin A, vitamin C, and zinc intake may help prevent this problem.

decubitus ulcers Chronic ulcers that appear in pressure areas of the skin over a body prominence. These develop when people are confined to bed or immobilized (i.e., bedsores).

The appearance of the skin, hair, and nails is clinically important, because it can indicate nutritional deficiencies. For instance, hot, dry skin is an obvious sign of dehydration due to inadequate water intake. (Other signs and symptoms of nutrient deficiencies, as manifested by the skin, are described in Chapters 5, 6, 7, 9, 10, 11, and 12 as the functions of individual nutrients are explained.)

The skin plays a vital role in temperature regulation. Heat produced by the body's metabolic processes, especially the processes that occur in muscle, must be removed before cells are damaged. Heat is removed from the body through the skin. And, when we are cold, we warm ourselves by shivering, as muscle contractions generate heat.

An important nutrient, vitamin D, can be obtained from our diet, but the skin can also make it from a cholesterol derivative located in the skin. There is more detail about this process in Chapter 9.

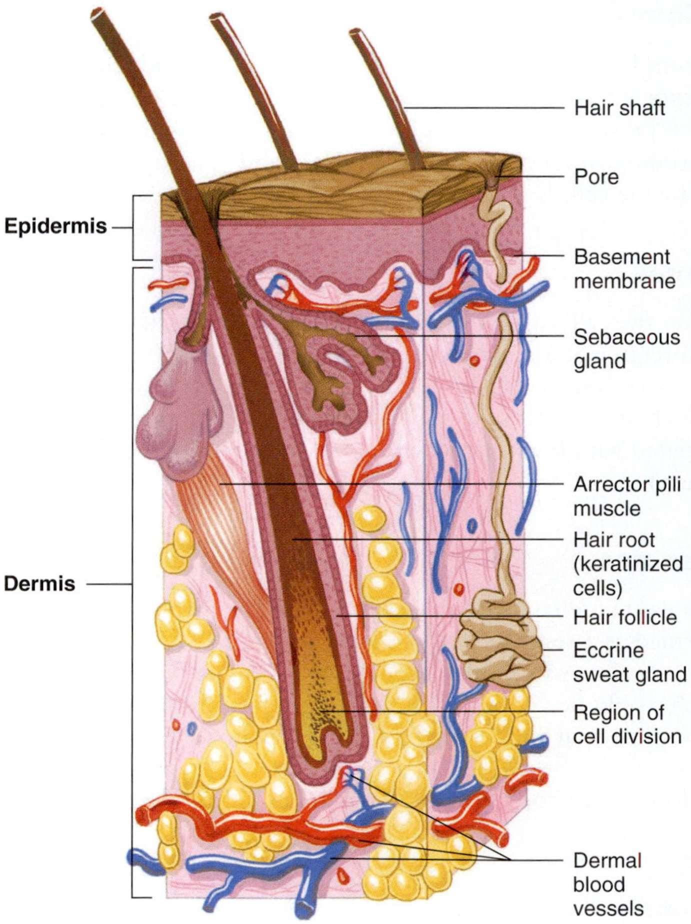

Figure C-2 Cross-section of the skin. This is the major organ of the integumentary system.

The sweat glands produce perspiration, or sweat, which helps evaporate fluids to cool the body and excrete certain wastes. Mammary glands within the breasts are modified sweat glands designed to secrete milk to feed a newborn.

Skeletal System

Approximately 206 bones make up the skeletal system; this is the rigid framework to which the soft tissues and organs of the body are attached. Each bone is an organ that participates in the overall functioning of the skeleton. Bones that make up the skull and vertebral column protect the brain and spinal cord from injury. Likewise, the rib cage protects the heart, lungs, liver, and spleen from external damage. Bones have attachment sites to most skeletal muscles, ligaments, and tendons. (Bones attached to muscles allow body movement when muscles contract.) Blood cell formation, known as **hematopoiesis,** takes place within the marrow of some bones. Bones also are a storehouse for minerals such as calcium, phosphorus, magnesium, sodium, and fluoride. Rather than being considered dried, dead tissues, bones are metabolically active and constantly adapting to a changing environment.

Long bones, such as those found in the arms and legs, consist of two types of body tissue: cortical and trabecular (Fig. C-3). **Cortical bone** is hard and dense. It forms a protective shell on the exterior of the bone. **Trabecular bone** is found within the cortical bone at the ends of long bones and in the vertebrae. The shaft of the long bones is a cylinder of cortical bone surrounding a central cavity containing the marrow (review Chapter 11).

At the end of the long bone is the **epiphysis,** consisting of trabecular bone covered by cortical bone. The epiphysis is strong and allows for the attachment of tendons and

hematopoiesis The production of blood cells.

cortical Tightly packed bone that is superficial to spongy bone, also called dense bone.

trabecular bone Bone tissue with a latticelike structure, also called spongy or cancellous bone.

epiphysis The end of a long bone. The epiphyseal plate—sometimes referred to as the growth plate—is made of cartilage and allows growth of the bone to occur. During childhood, the cartilage cells multiply and absorb calcium, to develop into bone.

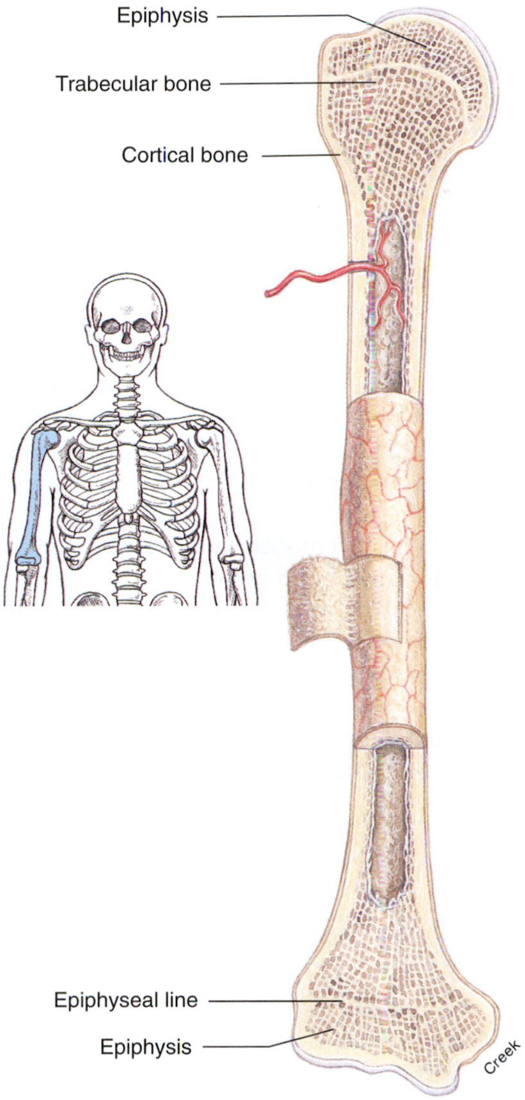

Figure C-3 Diagram of a long bone. The epiphysis, consisting of trabecular bone, is surrounded by a layer of cortical bone. The epiphyseal line indicates that the bone has completed growth. The production of blood cells occurs in the porous chambers of trabecular bone. The collagen material, the structural material of bone, is observed by the open flap. The skeletal system provides a reserve of calcium and phosphorus for day-to-day needs when dietary intake is inadequate.

ligaments. Red bone marrow is made of trabecular bone and is the source of red blood cells, as well as white blood cells and platelets. In children, just behind the epiphysis is the **epiphyseal plate.** This area of bone is responsible for linear growth. When linear growth is complete, an **epiphyseal line** replaces the plate.

Bones are constructed from several types of cells under the influence of a variety of growth factors. These factors stimulate the formation of **collagen,** a type of flexible protein matrix, which forms the basic shape of bone. Minerals—principally, calcium and phosphorus—are embedded in the matrix, which give the bone strength. **Hydroxyapatite,** the name of the calcium phosphorus salt deposited in the protein matrix, constitutes about 85% of minerals in bone and makes it possible for the bone to resist compression and bending.

Calcification (also called ossification) of bone varies from bone to bone, but most bones mature (are ossified) by ages 17 to 25. However, some bones, such as the sternum (breast bone), may not complete growth until age 30-plus.

Bone is constantly **remodeled** throughout life. Formation and **resorption** of bone occur due to the continual activity of **osteoblasts** and **osteoclasts.** Osteoblasts are bone-building cells and osteoclasts are bone resorbing cells. In the first 20 or so years of life, bone formation is greater than resorption. By age 50 or 60, resorption is greater than deposition and bone diseases are likely to occur. Exercise promotes deposition, whereas a lack of exercise results in bone loss.

epiphyseal plate A cartilage-like layer in the long bone. It functions in linear growth.

epiphyseal line When bone growth is complete, a line replaces the plate.

collagen The major protein of the material that holds together the various structures of the body.

hydroxyapatite A compound, composed primarily of calcium and phosphate, that is deposited into the bone protein matrix to give bone strength and rigidity ($Ca_{10}[PO_4]_6OH_2$).

remodeling The constant building and breakdown of bone throughout life.

resorption The loss of a substance by physiologic or pathologic means.

osteoblasts Cells in bone that secrete mineral and bone matrix (e.g., collagen).

osteoclasts Bone cells that arise originally from a type of white blood cell. Osteoclasts secrete substances that lead to bone erosion. This erosion can set the stage for subsequent bone remineralization.

Bone deposition (ossification) and bone resorption (dissolution) also maintain homeostasis of calcium and phosphorus in the blood. Three hormones control the process: the vitamin D hormone ($1,25(OH)_2$ vitamin D or calcitriol), calcitonin, and parathyroid hormone (PTH).

There are other hormones involved in bone maintenance, such as growth hormone; thyroid hormones; sex hormones, especially estrogen; and adrenocorticoid hormones. In addition, vitamins A, K, and C perform important jobs in bone metabolism. There is more about bones in the chapters covering vitamins, minerals, and exercise, in Chapters 9, 10, 11, and 14.

Muscular System

The functions of the muscular system are to provide movement and to generate body heat. Most of the energy released during physical exercise is in the form of heat. Muscle cells called **muscle fibers** respond when stimulated by motor **neurons** (nerve cells). A muscle cell converts the chemical energy in ATP into the mechanical energy of muscle contraction.

There are three types of muscle tissue: **smooth, cardiac,** and **skeletal.** Smooth muscle fibers have a single nucleus and function in involuntary movements within internal organs. Cardiac muscle fiber is **striated** (striped) with a single nucleus. The stripes in muscle fibers are caused by the arrangement of alternating dark and light contractile proteins (**myosin** and **actin**). This type of muscle performs the involuntary rhythmic contractions of the heart. Skeletal muscle, also containing striated muscle fibers, has several nuclei and is involved in voluntary movements. Skeletal muscle is attached to bone by **tendons.** (Note that Chapter 14 also discusses some specific muscle fiber types.)

neuron The structural and functional unit of the nervous system, consisting of cell body, dendrites, and axon.

smooth muscle Muscle tissue under involuntary control; found in the GI tract, artery walls, respiratory passages, the urinary tract, and the reproductive tract.

cardiac muscle Muscle tissue that makes up the walls of the heart; produces rhythmical involuntary contractions.

skeletal muscle Muscle tissue responsible for voluntary body movements.

myosin A thick filament protein that connects with actin to cause a muscle contraction.

actin A protein in muscle fiber that, together with myosin, is responsible for contraction.

tendon Dense connective tissue that attaches a muscle to a bone.

Skeletal Muscle

Skeletal muscle fibers are actually long cells with the same organelles as found in other cells. However, unlike most other cells, skeletal muscle cells possess an excellent supply of fuel in the form of glycogen, the body's storage form of the sugar glucose.

Skeletal muscles contract when stimulated by motor neurons. Motor neurons can stimulate several muscle fibers simultaneously. A single muscle fiber is not a very efficient machine. The activation of numerous muscle fibers by multiple motor neurons results in increased muscle strength as the number of fibers stimulated by neurons increases.

Muscle Contraction

As previously mentioned, within muscle fibers are the dark and light stripes called striations. Each muscle cell, when viewed in the electron microscope, contains subunits called **myofibrils.** The myofibrils are the source of the light and dark bands or stripes. The importance of these structures is the presence of unique proteins, actin and myosin. The functioning structure of the myofibril is the **sarcomere,** the contracting unit.

myofibrils A bundle of contractile fibers within a muscle cell.

sarcomere A portion of a muscle fiber that is considered the functional unit of a myofibril.

When a muscle fiber is stimulated by a neuron to contract, one of the first events to occur is the release of large amounts of calcium from storage in the smooth endoplasmic reticulum (also called sarcoplasmic reticulum). This is the "on" switch. The presence of calcium allows the two main proteins, myosin and actin, to get ready to slide into each other and set the **power stroke** in motion. Of course, all this action requires energy to carry out the muscle contraction. Here is where ATP plays the key role (Fig. C-4).

power stroke Movement of the thick filament alongside the thin filament, causing the muscle contraction.

Another ATP is needed to release the actin from the myosin. This is the end of the contraction. As the muscle moves to the "off" position, the calcium is transported back to storage, the muscle fiber relaxes, and it gets ready for another contraction.

The reason that muscle action occurs at all is due to the essential nutrient calcium. When the muscle is relaxed, there is very little calcium in the cytoplasm of the muscle cell because calcium is in storage. However, when the muscle is ready to go to work, as directed by the motor neuron, calcium is moved out of storage, which sets the stage for

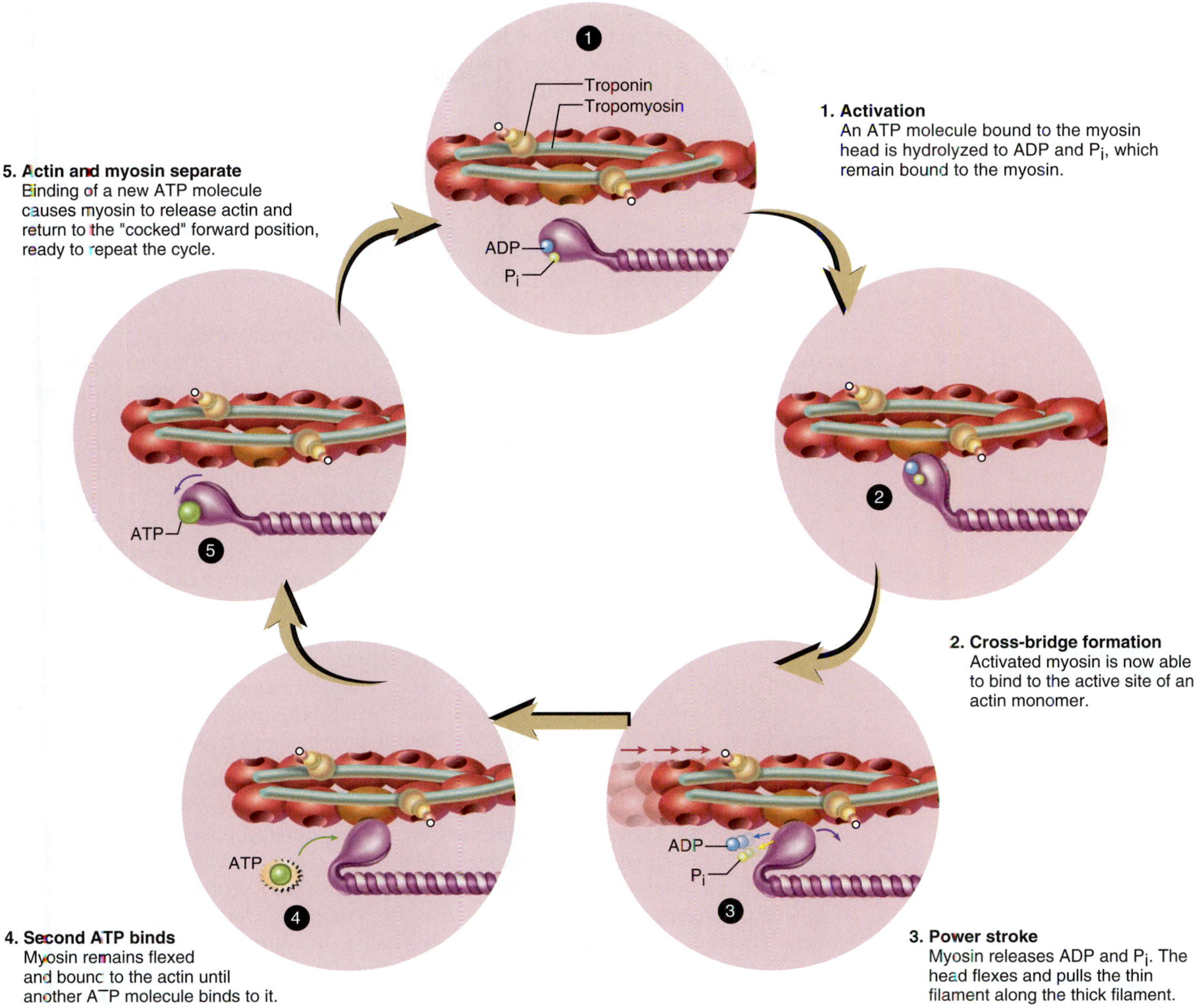

Troponin
Tropomyosin
ADP
P_i
1. Activation
An ATP molecule bound to the myosin head is hydrolyzed to ADP and P_i, which remain bound to the myosin.
2. Cross-bridge formation
Activated myosin is now able to bind to the active site of an actin monomer.
3. Power stroke
Myosin releases ADP and P_i. The head flexes and pulls the thin filament along the thick filament.
ADP
P_i
4. Second ATP binds
Myosin remains flexed and bound to the actin until another A~P molecule binds to it.
ATP
5. Actin and myosin separate
Binding of a new ATP molecule causes myosin to release actin and return to the "cocked" forward position, ready to repeat the cycle.
ATP

Figure C-4 Muscle contraction. In Step 1, or activation, an ATP is bound to the myosin head (purple) and is split into ADP and P_i. Troponin and tropomyosin are proteins that participate in this process. During Step 2, the activated myosin can now bind to the actin (the red beads). In Step 3, the myosin head releases the ADP and P_i. The head flexes and pulls the thin filament along the thick filament. This is the *power stroke*. In Step 4, the myosin remains bound to the actin until another ATP binds to the myosin. The new ATP causes the myosin to release the actin, so that it can get ready for another cycle, Step 5. Actin and myosin separate. This leads to muscle relaxation. The white dot in this figure is calcium, a nutrient required for muscle action.

the power stroke. And, when the contraction ends, the calcium is released and goes back into storage.

Cardiac and Smooth Muscle

Cardiac muscle and smooth muscle, although similar in many ways to skeletal muscle in their use of calcium as an off/on switch, operate under involuntary control.

In cardiac muscle, the stimulation occurs automatically by a group of muscle cells. These cells initiate the heartbeat and set the heart rate under control of the brain and the influence of certain hormones.

Smooth muscles are found in the lungs, blood vessels, GI tract, and other internal organs. In the GI tract, they produce important contractions in peristalsis (see Chapter 3 for details). A unique feature of smooth muscle is its ability to stretch. By the end of pregnancy, the smooth muscle in the uterus can be stretched up to eight times its prepregnant length.

Circulatory System

The circulatory system is made up of two separate systems: the cardiovascular system and the lymphatic system. The cardiovascular system consists of the heart and blood vessels. The lymphatic system consists of lymphatic vessels, lymph, and a number of lymph tissues.

One organ vital to our existence is the heart, a four-chambered pump that keeps blood continuously circulating around the body. It takes about 1 minute for blood to leave the heart, circulate to all tissues in the body, and return to the heart. When we are exercising strenuously, the blood can circulate at a rate of six times per minute.

The cells that make up the tissues of the body need a constant supply of water, oxygen, and nutrients. In addition, the body needs ATP energy, which in turn comes from the breakdown of energy nutrients within the cells. The blood carries oxygen from the lungs to all organs in the body. The blood also carries nutrients from the digestive tract to all tissues and to storage sites when nutrients are not immediately needed for energy, growth, or repair. Waste materials produced by cells must be removed by way of the skin, lungs, kidneys, and digestive tract. This, too, is a function of the cardiovascular system. The delivery of hormones to their target cells, the maintenance of a constant body temperature, and the distribution of white blood cells to protect against invading pathogens are all performed by the blood and circulatory systems without our ever being aware of any specific action. The circulatory system has chemical means to prevent excessive loss of blood from damaged vessels. It uses the clotting process (see Chapter 9).

Blood Constituents

Red blood cells, known as **erythrocytes,** are carriers of oxygen to all tissues and play a role in the return of carbon dioxide to the lungs. The white blood cells, known as **leukocytes,** function as part of the immune system. They protect the body from invading pathogens. The blood is able to clot because of platelets and other clotting factors. The liquid part of blood is known as **plasma.** In contrast, **serum** is the fluid that results after the blood is first allowed to clot before being centrifuged; this will not contain the blood-clotting factors.

Heart Structure

The heart has two sides, left and right. The right side is closest to your right arm; likewise, the left side is closest to your left arm. The upper part of the heart has left and right **atria,** which empty simultaneously into the lower part of the heart, the left and right **ventricles.**

Blood travels in blood vessels from the left side of the heart, through the **aorta** to major **arteries.** Arteries become smaller and smaller until they are so tiny they are classified as **arterioles.** The blood flows from the arterioles into microscopic, weblike structures called **capillaries.** Capillaries are just one cell layer thick and have pores, which allow oxygen, water, and other nutrients to leave the blood for surrounding cells and which allow waste and other products of cellular metabolism to enter the blood. There are few cells in the body that aren't close to a capillary. Larger blood vessels are not porous, so blood cannot escape these vessels. Only in the capillaries can the blood discharge and recover substances associated with nearby cells.

As the blood exits the capillaries, it flows into tiny **venules,** which enlarge and become **veins,** returning the blood to the right side of the heart. The route from the left side of the heart to the capillaries and then back to the right side of the heart is called the **systemic circuit** of blood (Figs. C-5 and C-6).

erythrocyte A mature red blood cell. It has no nucleus and a life span of about 120 days; contains hemoglobin, which transports oxygen and carbon dioxide.

leukocyte A white blood cell.

plasma The fluid, extracellular portion of the circulating blood. This includes the blood serum plus all blood-clotting factors.

serum The portion of the blood fluid remaining after (1) the blood is allowed to clot and (2) the red and white blood cells and other solid matter are removed by centrifugation.

atria The two upper chambers of the heart, which receive venous blood.

ventricles The two lower chambers of the heart, which contain blood to be pumped from the heart.

aorta The major blood vessel of the body leaving from the left ventricle.

artery A blood vessel that carries blood away from the heart.

capillary A microscopic blood vessel that connects an arteriole and a venule; the functional unit of the circulatory system.

vein A blood vessel that conveys blood to the heart.

systemic circuit The part of the circulatory system concerned with the flow of blood from the left ventricle to the body and back to the right atrium.

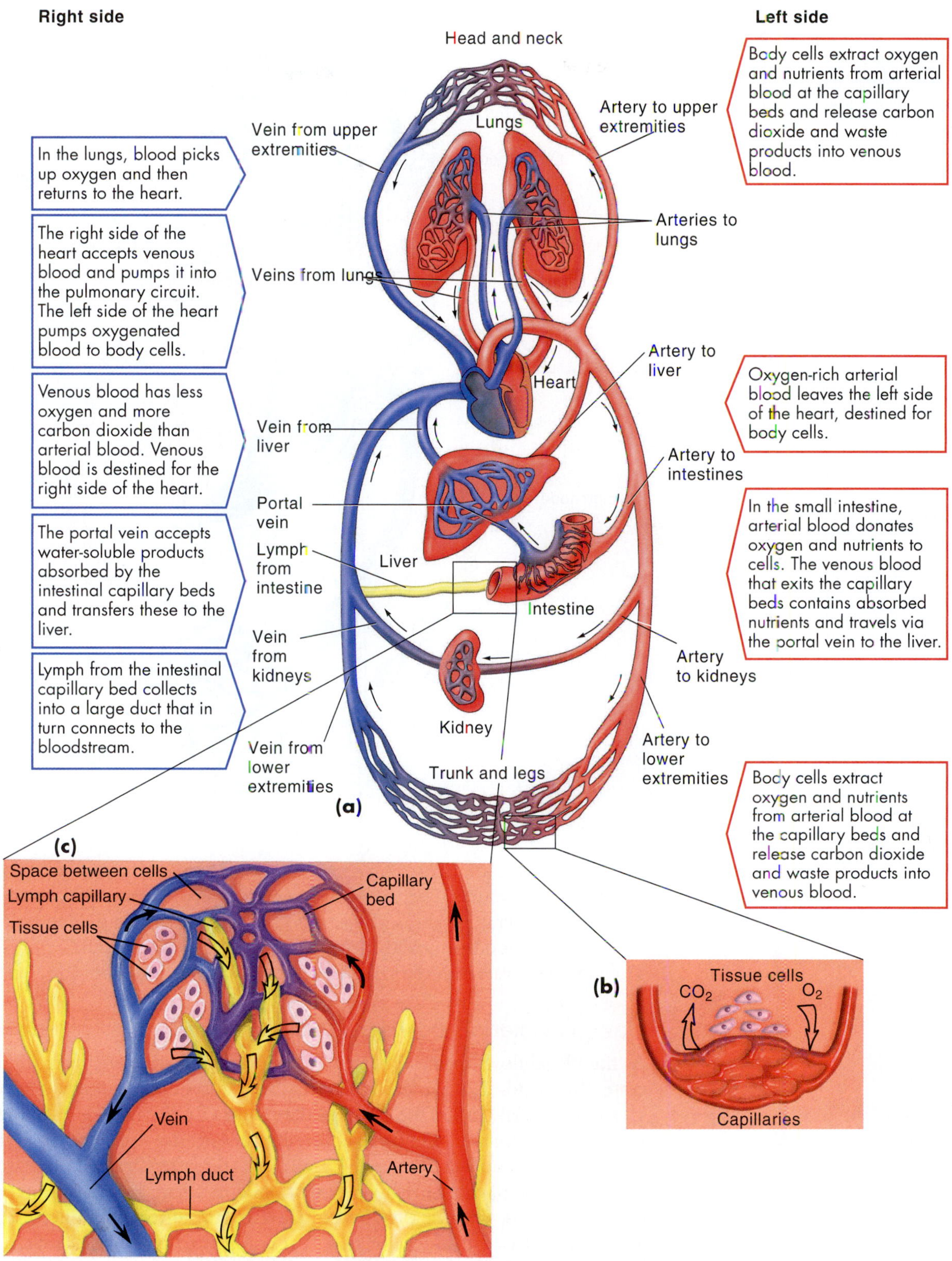
Right side
Left side
Head and neck
Lungs
Vein from upper extremities
Artery to upper extremities
Arteries to lungs
Veins from lungs
Heart
Artery to liver
Vein from liver
Artery to intestines
Portal vein
Lymph from intestine
Liver
Intestine
Vein from kidneys
Artery to kidneys
Kidney
Vein from lower extremities
Artery to lower extremities
Trunk and legs
(a)
In the lungs, blood picks up oxygen and then returns to the heart.
The right side of the heart accepts venous blood and pumps it into the pulmonary circuit. The left side of the heart pumps oxygenated blood to body cells.
Venous blood has less oxygen and more carbon dioxide than arterial blood. Venous blood is destined for the right side of the heart.
The portal vein accepts water-soluble products absorbed by the intestinal capillary beds and transfers these to the liver.
Lymph from the intestinal capillary bed collects into a large duct that in turn connects to the bloodstream.
Body cells extract oxygen and nutrients from arterial blood at the capillary beds and release carbon dioxide and waste products into venous blood.
Oxygen-rich arterial blood leaves the left side of the heart, destined for body cells.
In the small intestine, arterial blood donates oxygen and nutrients to cells. The venous blood that exits the capillary beds contains absorbed nutrients and travels via the portal vein to the liver.
Body cells extract oxygen and nutrients from arterial blood at the capillary beds and release carbon dioxide and waste products into venous blood.
(c)
Space between cells
Lymph capillary
Tissue cells
Capillary bed
Vein
Lymph duct
Artery
(b)
Tissue cells
CO_2
O_2
Capillaries

Figure C-5 Blood circulation throughout the body. (*a*) This represents the route blood takes through the two circuits that begin and end at the heart. The red color indicates blood that is richer in oxygen; blue is for blood carrying more carbon dioxide. (*b*) Oxygen and nutrients are exchanged for carbon dioxide and waste products in the capillaries, the points at which the arteries and veins merge. The bottom box (*c*) shows a close-up of a capillary bed in the small intestine, including the location of the lymphatic vessels. This second set of circulatory vessels—part of the lymphatic system—picks up fluid that builds up between cells and large particles, such as some fats. Notice that lymphatic capillaries are blind-ended. They are, however, highly permeable, so that substances can drain into the lymphatic system. All this becomes lymph, which travels through further lymph vessels to reach the bloodstream. Lymph vessels in the intestine are also called lacteals. Hold this book up to your chest in order to have this figure reflect the orientation of your heart.

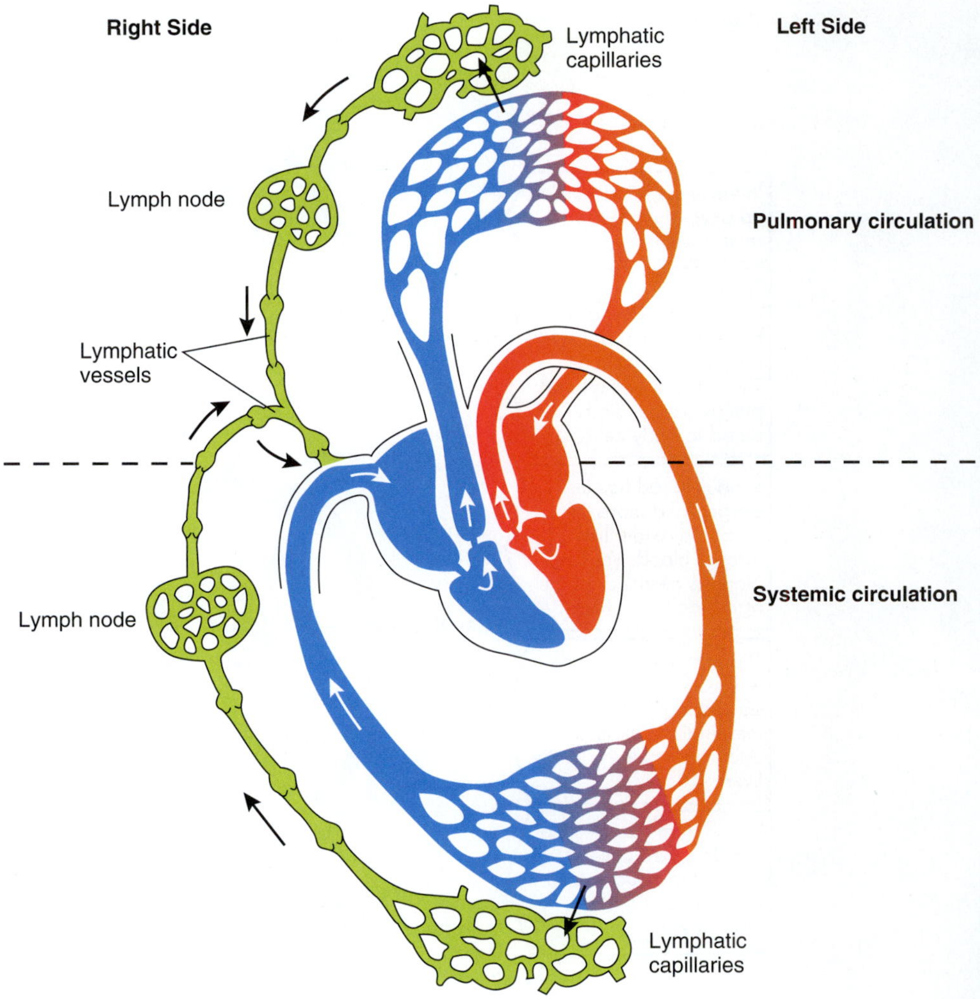

Figure C-6 Lymph. As lymph moves through the lymphatic system, it encounters lymph nodes, containing immune cells, which destroy invading pathogens. Lymph also carries dietary fat and fat-soluble nutrients from the digestive tract to the vascular system.

The flow of blood through the circulatory system is measured by pressure in millimeters of mercury. The average arterial (artery) pressure is about 100 mm Hg, whereas the average venous pressure is only 2 mm Hg. To guarantee return flow back to the heart, blood is moved through the veins by the contraction of skeletal muscles. There are also valves in the veins that prevent a backflow of blood.

Flow of Materials Between Capillaries and Cells

As the blood flows from the arterioles into the capillaries, the hydrostatic pressure generated by the force of the heart's contraction causes fluid to flow into spaces around the surrounding cells, called the **extracellular fluid (ECF)** (Fig. C-7). Some of this fluid returns to the capillaries and some enters another nearby vessel called a **lymphatic vessel.**

extracellular fluid (ECF) Fluid present outside the cells; this includes intravascular and interstitial fluids.

lymphatic vessel A vessel that carries lymph.

Oxygen and nutrients leave the capillaries and enter the ECF and are then delivered to cells by one of the mechanisms mentioned in Chapter 3: diffusion, active transport, and pinocytosis. Cellular products plus waste substances are collected in the ECF and are either released to the capillaries that connect to the venules or channeled into the lymph vessels. Oxygen travels to the cell by diffusing from the blood into the extracellular fluid and then in through the cell membrane. Carbon dioxide exits the cell and goes to the blood in the same way. This is one of two important gas exchange activities in the body and is often referred to as internal respiration.

The right atrium of the heart receives dark red venous blood from the body, which is then pumped into the right ventricle. The right ventricle pumps blood through the pulmonary arteries to the capillaries in the lungs. The lungs then return the freshly

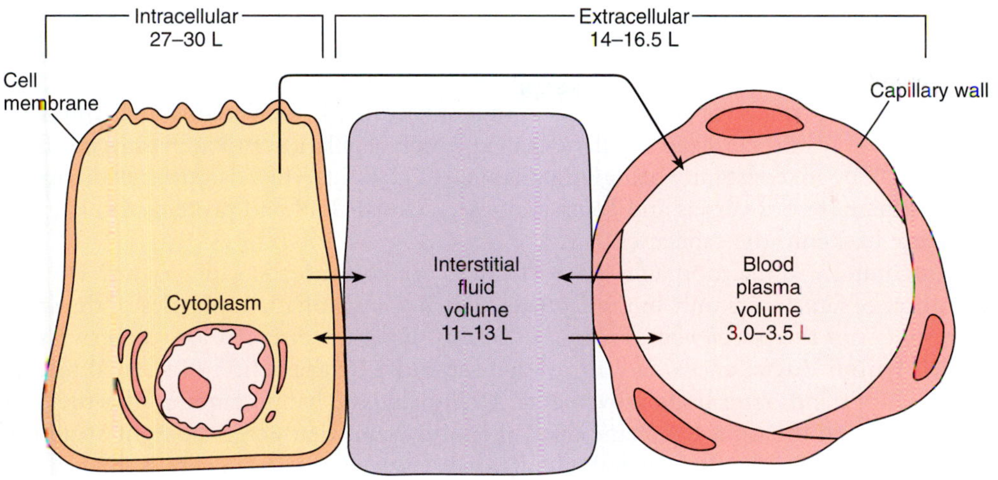

Figure C-7 Distribution of body fluids. The intracellular compartment contains fluid in the cell, which is free to move into the extracellular compartment. The extracellular compartment contains the fluid between the cell and the capillary, called the interstitial fluid. The extracellular fluid also includes the fluid within blood and lymph vessels. This figure shows the fluid (plasma) from the blood moving freely between cells and capillaries through the interstitial fluid.

oxygenated blood to the left atrium of the heart via the pulmonary veins. This route is known as **pulmonary circulation.**

As the blood moves through the pulmonary capillaries, carbon dioxide is released for expiration, and the inhaled oxygen is taken up by the blood. This is the other site for gas exchange in the body, often referred to as external respiration. The oxygenated blood (now a bright red) in the atrium is pumped to the left ventricle. From the left ventricle, the blood is pumped out again through the aorta to the systemic circuit.

pulmonary circulation The system of blood vessels from the right ventricle of the heart to the lungs and back to the left atrium of the heart.

Other Circulatory Systems

One specific capillary bed does not send blood back to the heart but, rather, directs it toward the liver. This is the **portal system** of the GI tract, composed of veins draining blood from the capillaries in the intestine and stomach. These veins empty into a large **portal vein,** which acts as a direct pipeline to the liver. (The brain also has a portal system.)

The heart also has it own circulatory system. Coronary vessels supply blood to meet cardiac needs. These arteries are particularly susceptible to damage by deposits of cholesterol and other lipids in the artery wall. This accumulation of cholesterol can lead to coronary heart disease. There is more about this disease in Chapter 6.

portal system A general term that describes veins in the GI tract that convey blood from capillaries in the intestines and portions of the stomach to the liver.

portal vein A large vein that ultimately distributes blood from the stomach and intestines to the liver.

Lymphatic System

The lymphatic system is closely related to the immune system in that both provide us with defense against pathogenic invaders. As the lymphatic system collects fluid from tissues, it picks up microorganisms as well. The fluid passes through many **lymph nodes** as it makes its way back to the bloodstream. In the nodes is an abundant collection of white blood cells ready to detect pathogens in the lymph fluid and quickly destroy them. The lymphatic system consists of lymph vessels, lymph fluid, lymph nodes, and lymphatic tissue, with its population of immune cells.

The interstitial or extracellular fluid (fluid surrounding the cell) contains many components that are too large to pass through holes in the capillaries, so they are blocked from returning directly to the bloodstream. Therefore, they take an indirect route back to general circulation, via the lymphatic system (review Fig. C-6).

Lymph also serves as the passageway by which fat-soluble nutrients are absorbed from the gastrointestinal tract and carried into the bloodstream. Lymph also contains bacteria, viruses, cellular trash, and cancer cells on their way to invade some distant site. Lymph generates immune cells, called **lymphocytes,** which combat these invaders (see next section on the immune system).

lymph node A small structure located along the course of the lymph vessels.

lymphocyte A class of white blood cells involved in the immune system, generally comprising about 25% of all white blood cells. There are several types of lymphocytes with diverse functions, including antibody production, allergic reactions, graft rejections, tumor control, and regulation of the immune system.

At the terminal end of the capillaries, the fluid released from the capillaries into the venules is less than the amount of fluid entering the capillaries from the arterioles. The missing 15% of fluid represents the extracellular fluid that is returned to the vascular system via the lymphatic system. This fluid is subsequently delivered to the lymphatic system by way of specialized capillaries called lymph capillaries. Blood plasma and fluid in the tissues are constantly being interchanged. The fluid, which is now called **lymph,** enters these porous vessels and consists of extracellular fluid and proteins too large to squeeze back into the capillaries.

lymph The clear, plasmalike fluid that flows through lymph vessels.

In addition to microorganisms, the lymph contains absorbed dietary fat. The absorption of fats occurs only in the **lacteals,** which are lymphatic capillaries of the small intestine, not the portal vein. From the lacteals, lymph is directed into larger vessels, called **lymph ducts,** and is moved toward the heart by the action of skeletal muscle contractions and other body movements. Eventually, the lymph empties into the thoracic duct and the right lymphatic duct, then into veins that enter the right atrium of the heart, and finally into general circulation (review Fig. C-6). There is further discussion of transport of lipid substances in the lymph system in Chapter 6.

lacteal A small lymphatic duct within a villus of the small intestine.

lymph duct A large lymphatic vessel, which empties lymph into the circulatory system.

As the lymph makes its way back to the heart, it encounters clusters of lymph nodes containing phagocytic cells, lymphocytes, and mobile **macrophages,** which help destroy invading pathogens and filter the lymph. **T lymphocytes** and **B lymphocytes** are found in these nodes and are major players in immunity (see the section Immune System). When you are ill and seek medical attention, do you ever wonder why your physician checks the lymph glands in your neck for swelling? Swelling means the lymph nodes are in combat against an invading pathogen.

macrophage Any large mononuclear phagocytic cell that is found in the tissues and is derived from a monocyte in the blood. Besides functioning as important phagocytes, macrophages secrete numerous cytokines and act as antigen-presenting cells.

T lymphocyte A type of white blood cell that recognizes intracellular antigens (e.g., viral antigens in infected cells), fragments of which move to the cell surface. T lymphocytes originate in the bone marrow but must mature in the thymus gland.

B lymphocyte A type of white blood cell that recognizes antigens (e.g., bacteria) present in extracellular sites in the body and is responsible for antibody-mediated immunity. B lymphocytes originate and mature in the bone marrow and are released into the blood and lymph.

The spleen, thymus gland, and tonsils are considered lymphoid organs. The spleen contains phagocytes, which filter out foreign substances and destroy worn-out red blood cells. The thymus gland is important in immunity during childhood. Tonsils protect against invaders that are inhaled or eaten.

Immune System

The cells that carry out immune functions are known collectively as the immune system. Unlike other systems in the body, they do not exist as anatomically connected organs, but rather as separate collections of cells throughout the body. They provide defense against invading pathogens—microorganisms, or substances capable of producing disease. They discriminate "self" from "nonself." They are very sensitive indicators of the body's nutritional status. The most numerous of the immune system cells are the leukocytes.

Our body constantly wages war against disease-producing microorganisms such as bacteria, viruses, fungi, and parasites; or substances capable of producing disease such as toxins from snake venom; or allergens, which trigger allergic reactions via **antigen** release; or cancer cells (Fig. C-8). The most common invaders are bacteria, which are one-cell organisms with a cell wall in addition to a plasma membrane and viruses, which are nucleic acids surrounded by a protein coat. Viruses can't multiply by themselves because they lack ribosomes for protein synthesis, so they survive by taking over a cell and instructing the host to produce the proteins and energy they need for survival.

antigen Any foreign substance, generally large in size, that induces a state of sensitivity and/or resistance to microbes or toxic substances after a lag period; substance that stimulates a specific aspect of the immune system.

Leukocytes and Macrophages

Leukocytes, also known as white blood cells, are produced in the bone marrow and may undergo further development in tissues outside the marrow. They travel via the blood and enter into tissues where they function. They are classified by their structure and the affinity for certain types of dye. For example, the monocyte has a single, horseshoe-shaped nucleus. Another type of immune cell takes up the red dye eosin, and so is called an eosinophil. There are five general types of leukocytes, which are listed in Table C-1, along with a brief description of their functions.

Macrophages are found in almost all tissues of the body. They are derived from one kind of leukocyte, the monocyte. When a monocyte leaves the blood and enters into a tissue it is transformed into a macrophage. At birth, the baby is already supplied with

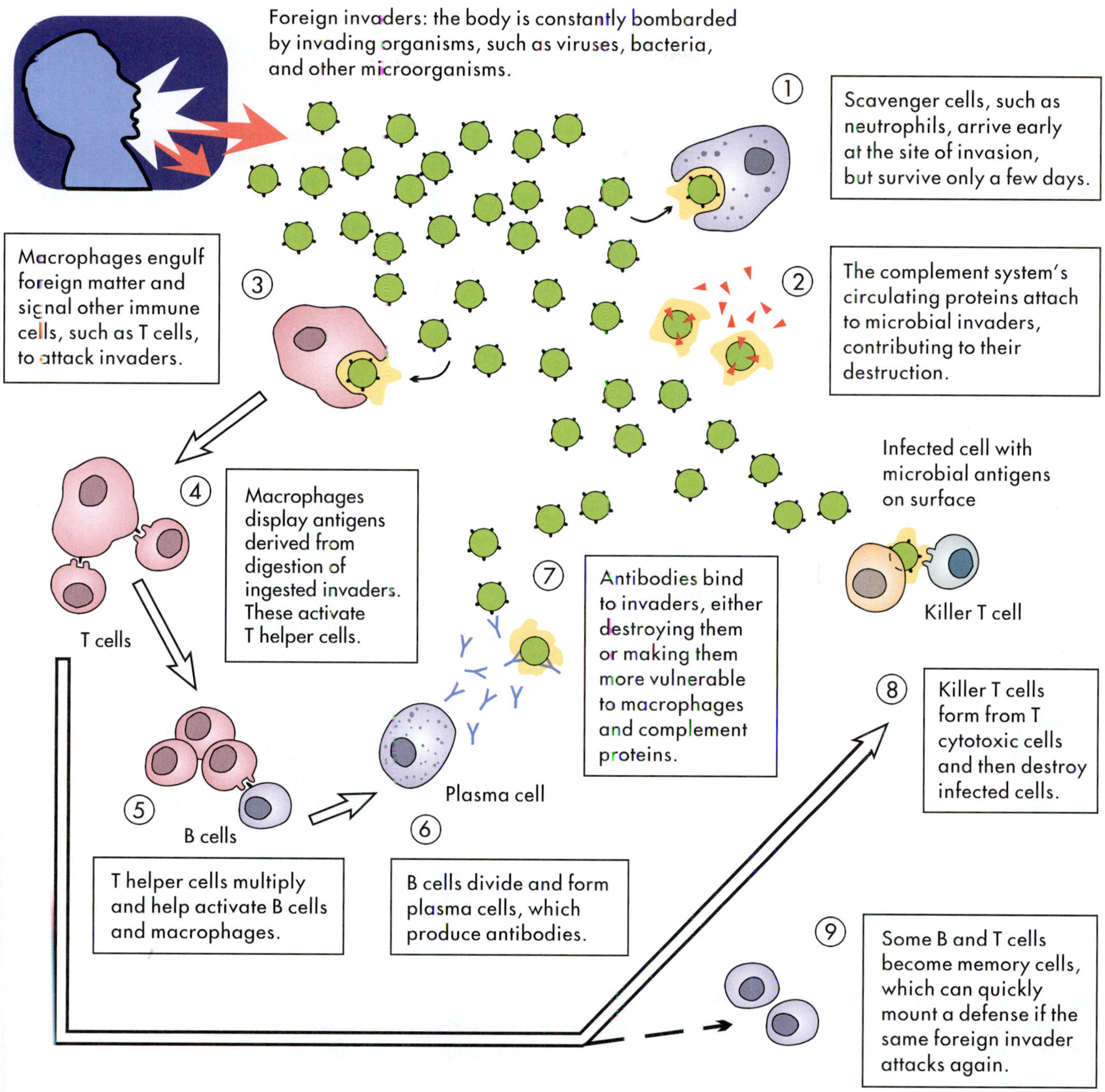

Foreign invaders: the body is constantly bombarded by invading organisms, such as viruses, bacteria, and other microorganisms.
1
Scavenger cells, such as neutrophils, arrive early at the site of invasion, but survive only a few days.
2
The complement system's circulating proteins attach to microbial invaders, contributing to their destruction.
3
Macrophages engulf foreign matter and signal other immune cells, such as T cells, to attack invaders.
4
Macrophages display antigens derived from digestion of ingested invaders. These activate T helper cells.
T cells
5
B cells
T helper cells multiply and help activate B cells and macrophages.
6
Plasma cell
B cells divide and form plasma cells, which produce antibodies.
7
Antibodies bind to invaders, either destroying them or making them more vulnerable to macrophages and complement proteins.
Infected cell with microbial antigens on surface
Killer T cell
8
Killer T cells form from T cytotoxic cells and then destroy infected cells.
9
Some B and T cells become memory cells, which can quickly mount a defense if the same foreign invader attacks again.

Figure C-8 Biological warfare. The body commands a wide assortment of defenders to reduce the danger of infection and help guard against repeat microbial infections. The ultimate target of all immune response is an antigen, commonly a foreign protein from a bacterium or other microbe.

macrophages, which continue to develop throughout life. They are strategically located throughout the body to phagocytize foreign material.

Mast cells are produced in the bone marrow and found in almost all tissues and organs. They release histamine and the other chemicals that are involved in inflammation.

Another participant in the immune system is **cytokines,** a complicated group of protein messengers that are produced by various cells throughout the body. They regulate the host cells' function and growth and are involved in nonspecific and specific immunity.

There are two types of immunity, nonspecific or natural immunity and specific or acquired immunity. The nonspecific immunity protects against foreign invaders without

mast cell Tissue cell that releases histamine and other chemicals involved in inflammation.

cytokine A protein secreted by a cell that functions to regulate the activity of neighboring cells.

Table C-1 Types and Functions of Leukocytes

Leukocyte	Function
Neutrophil	Phagocytizes bacteria. Forms highly toxic compounds, which destroy bacteria.
Eosinophil	Phagocytizes antigen-antibody complex, allergy-causing antigens, inflammatory chemicals. Attacks parasites, such as worms.
Basophil	Secretes histamine, a vasodilator, thus increasing blood flow to tissues. Secretes heparin, which prevents blood clotting.
Lymphocytes	Natural killer cells attack cells infected with viruses or that have turned cancerous. B lymphocytes present antigens and activate other cells of the immune system. Can become plasma cells that secrete antibodies. Serve as memory cells in humoral immunity. T lymphocytes destroy foreign cells, regulate the immune response, and serve as memory cells in cellular immunity.
Monocytes	Differentiate into numerous types of macrophages. Macrophages phagocytize pathogens, dead neutrophils, and debris of dead cells. They present antigens and activate other cells of the immune system.

having to recognize the specific appearance of the invaders, whereas specific immunity is acquired.

Nonspecific Immunity

Nonspecific immunity is an array of mechanisms that are present at birth and do not require any activation. They are barriers such as the skin and the **mucous membranes** of the gastrointestinal tract, reproductive system, urinary tract, and respiratory tract. The **mucus** produced by these tissues traps invaders. Internally, other forms of nonspecific immunity include phagocytic cells, which can swallow bacteria and other harmful substances and ultimately destroy them. Acid produced by the stomach (HCl) can destroy ingested pathogens. Inflammation is a local response to infection or injury. The purpose is to destroy or inactivate foreign invaders and begin the process of repair. Fever is also an internal defense mechanism. It seems to aid in the recovery process by reducing the amount of iron in the blood, which in turn reduces bacterial activity. Fever also seems to be associated with an increase in **interferons.** Viral infections are subject to short-term control by this group of proteins released by infected cells. Interferons are receiving a lot of attention today as potent weapons against cancers, hepatitis C, and other diseases.

nonspecific immunity Defenses that stop the invasion of pathogens. Requires no previous encounter with a pathogen.

mucous membranes Also called mucosae, line passageways open to the exterior environment.

mucus A thick fluid secreted by glands throughout the body. It contains a compound that has both carbohydrate and protein parts. It acts as a lubricant and means of protection for cells.

interferons A group of proteins released by virus-infected cells that bind to other cells, stimulating synthesis of antiviral proteins that in turn inhibit viral multiplication.

Specific Immunity

Specific immunity involving the lymphocytes is directed at specific molecules. When nonspecific immunological defenses fail to halt an invasion by pathogens or toxins produced by them, another mechanism comes into action. It is based on the action of antibodies, lymphocytes, and other cells of the immune system. This is known as **antibody-mediated immunity,** or humoral immunity.

Recall that antigens are molecules that are generally large in size and foreign to the body. A given molecule can have a number of antigenic determinant sites that stimulate the production of various antibodies. When we successfully fight off an invader, chemicals called **antibodies** have been in action. Antibodies are highly specific proteins produced by B lymphocytes in response to antigens. Antigens are detected as dangerous intruders. They are detected because the immune system can identify molecules that are "self"—they belong to *me* personally—from "nonself" molecules. (Recall that one role of the carbohydrates found on the cell membrane is to identify "self.")

The lymphocytes that produce antibodies, designated B lymphocytes, are produced in the bone marrow. These B lymphocytes wage war against bacterial infections, as well as some viral infections and even a few parasites. B lymphocytes (or B-cells) and antibodies, also known as **immunoglobulins,** come in five major classifications. These bind

specific immunity The function of lymphocytes directed at specific antigens.

antibody-mediated immunity Specific immunity provided by B lymphocytes; also known as humoral immunity.

antibodies Blood proteins that inactivate foreign proteins found in the body. This helps to prevent and control infections.

immunoglobulins Proteins found in the blood that bind to specific antigens; also called antibodies. The five major classes of immunoglobulins play different roles in antibody-mediated immunity.

to the antigen on the invader, and begin a process of attack. This antibody-antigen interaction soon produces **plasma cells,** which results in the production of more antibody proteins to continue the attack. A person can produce as many different antibodies as there are exposures to specific antigens. It is estimated that there are 100 million trillion antibody molecules per person, representing a few million species of antigens.

plasma cells A form of B lymphocytes that produce about 2000 antibodies per second.

Memory cells are then produced by B-cells and provide active immunity. Once you have been exposed to an antigen, you develop active immunity. Obviously, this is the basis of vaccinations; an inactivated pathogen is injected and the body develops immunity to that pathogen.

memory cells B lymphocytes that remain after an infection to convey long-lasting or permanent immunity.

The blood also contains a group of proteins called **complement** proteins. Complement proteins are released into the area of infection and attach to the target pathogen to be destroyed. It is not the antibody-antigen combination that causes the destruction of the pathogenic invader, but this combination of antibody-antigen does identify them, so that they can be attacked by nonspecific immune processes, such as the complement proteins. Complement attaches to the pathogenic invader and drills holes in its membrane, thus leading to its destruction. (The hole in the wall allows water to flow into the cell and causes it to burst.)

complement A series of blood proteins that participate in a complex reaction cascade following stimulation by an antigen-antibody complex on the surface of a bacterial cell. Various activated complement proteins can enhance phagocytosis, contribute to inflammation, and destroy bacteria.

T lymphocytes (T cells) directly attack and destroy specific cells, which are identified by specific antigens on the cell surface. T lymphocytes (or T-cells) produce **cell-mediated immunity** because they actually are in contact with the enemy cell. T cells must be first activated in the thymus gland.

cell-mediated immunity T lymphocytes do not secrete antibodies; they come in actual contact with the invading cells in order to destroy them.

The actual T lymphocytes that are killers are known as **cytotoxic T cells.** They recognize the infected cell and attach themselves through a CD8 receptor. There are also **helper T cells.** They attach to an infected cell through the CD4 receptor. They promote phagocytic activity. Together the cytotoxic and helper T cells bind to the infected cell and lead to the cell's destruction. You may have heard of CD4 cells because they are markers for AIDS. When the disease progresses, the CD4 count decreases as the virus attacks T helper cells (and macrophages).

cytotoxic T cells Type of T cells that interact with the infected host cell through special receptor sites on the T cell surface.

helper T cells Type of T cells that interact with macrophages and secrete substances to signal an invading pathogen. Stimulates B lymphocytes to proliferate.

Most of the information concerning the relationship of nutrition to immunity comes from studies in poor countries of the developing world, where children die of infectious diseases secondary to malnutrition. Protein-energy malnutrition deficiencies of vitamins and minerals, and an inadequate intake of certain fatty acids seriously alter immune function. There is more information about how individual nutrients make it possible to support an immune response in Chapters 9 through 12.

Allergies are types of immune responses. One type of allergic response is almost *immediate.* The symptoms are produced by B lymphocytes exposed to an allergen, as demonstrated by a runny nose, red eyes, and itchy skin (dermatitis). The culprit is **histamine,** an altered form of the common amino acid histidine. This type of immune response can be treated by antihistamine drugs. Allergies are further discussed with eicosanoids in Chapter 6 and adolescent nutrition in Chapter 17.

histamine A breakdown product of the amino acid histidine that stimulates acid secretion by the stomach and has other effects on the body, such as contraction of smooth muscles, increased nasal secretions, relaxation of blood vessels, and changes in constriction of airways. It appears to decrease hunger and food intake.

Delayed hypersensitivity, an abnormal T cell response, can occur as late as 72 hours after exposure. The best known example of this type of immune response is contact dermatitis caused by coming in contact with poison ivy, poison oak, or poison sumac.

A final type of immunity we will cover is known as autoimmunity. Here the immune system fails to recognize "self," thinking a normal cell is an **antigen.** The immune system then goes on the attack by activating T lymphocytes and the production of antibodies by B lymphocytes, which kills the cell. In other words, the defense mechanisms are confused and attack the body rather than invaders. There are at least 40 autoimmune diseases. Some well-known examples include rheumatoid arthritis, type 1 diabetes, and multiple sclerosis.

antigen Any substance that induces a state of sensitivity and/or resistance to microbes or toxic substances after a lag period; substance that stimulates a specific aspect of the immune system.

Respiratory System

In order to produce sufficient energy to meet body needs, there must be oxygen present to help convert food energy into ATP. When oxygen is supplied to the tissues, carbon

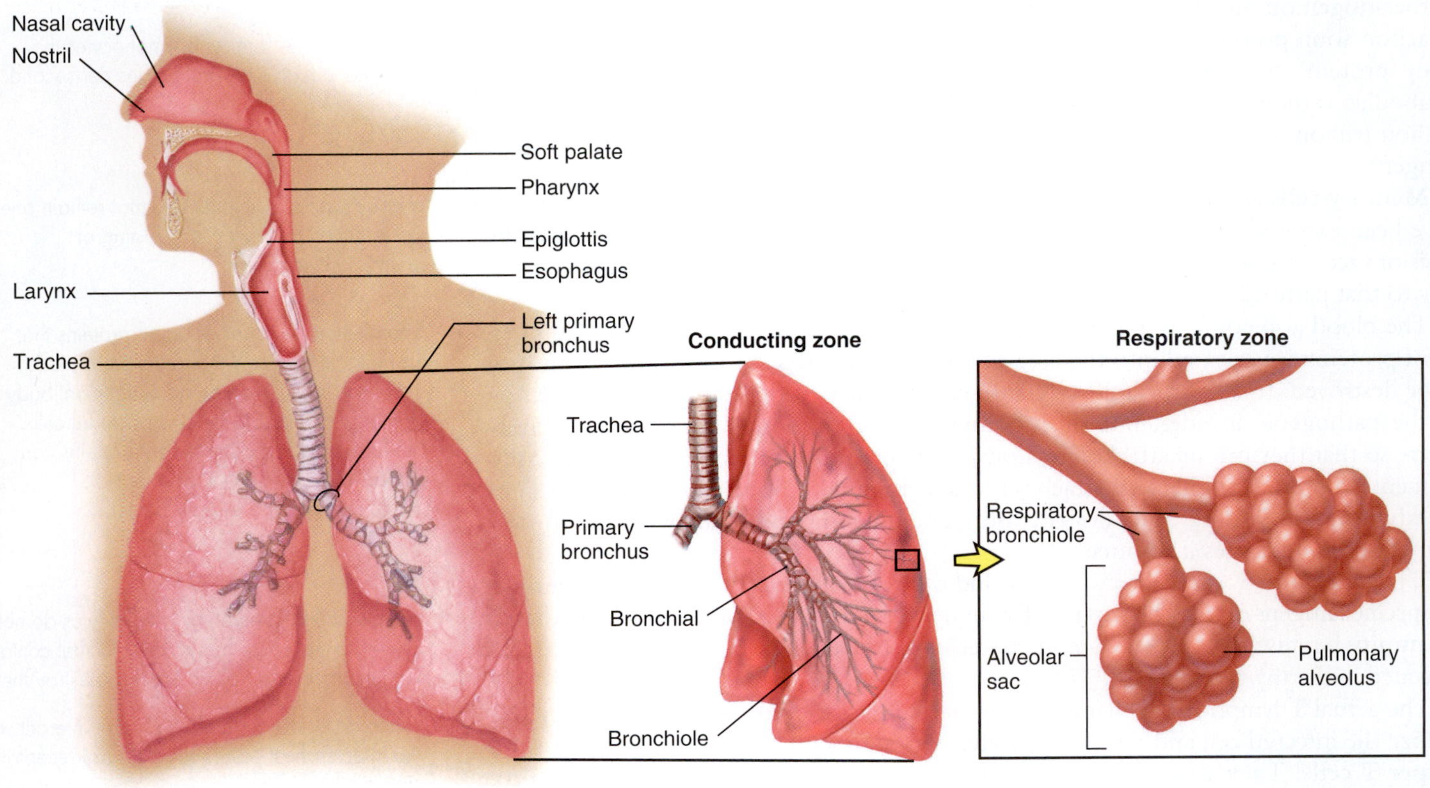

Figure C-9 Anatomy of the respiratory system. Air is conducted through the nose and mouth to the lungs. Once air is conducted into bronchioles, gas exchange occurs in the alveoli.

dioxide is produced and removed from the body by the combined actions of the cardiovascular and respiratory systems.

The organs of the respiratory system are the nose, pharynx, larynx, trachea, bronchi, and lungs. *Respiration* refers to breathing and to the exchange of gases between the blood and other tissues. The respiratory tract features the **alveoli** (plural) in the lungs. These are tiny structures where one form of gas exchange takes place, described previously as external respiration (Fig. C-9). The **alveolus** (singular), the basic functional unit of respiration, allows oxygen to be recovered from inhaled air and loads it onto red blood cells for transport to target tissues throughout the body. Simultaneously, carbon dioxide in the blood is released into the lungs and ultimately exhaled into the air.

Air reaches the lungs from the nasal cavity and the mouth by first passing through the **pharynx** to the **larynx.** The larynx is open to the trachea during breathing but closes during swallowing. The **trachea** is a tube that connects the larynx to the **bronchial tree.** The bronchial tree is located in the lungs and looks like a tree with branches. The branches on this tree get smaller and smaller the farther out they go from the tree trunk (the trachea) into lung tissue until finally they turn into **bronchioles,** the location of the pulmonary alveoli.

The distance across the alveoli is two cells thick; one cell for the alveoli plus one cell for the pulmonary capillaries. Gas exchange allows CO_2 and O_2 to diffuse easily between the blood and lungs. There is an estimated 300 million alveoli in the lungs, providing a tremendous surface area for the diffusion of gasses.

Another aspect of respiration is the discharge of water through the lungs. This is obvious on a cold day when the breath we exhale turns to ice crystals, and we can see vapor forming around the mouth and nose. Of course, such water loss is much more extensive during hot, humid weather when the body continues to remove heat from the body via the lungs.

alveoli, alveolus The basic functional units of the lungs.

pharynx The organ of the digestive tract and respiratory tract located at the back of the oral and nasal cavities.

larynx The structure located between the pharynx and trachea that contains the vocal cords.

trachea The airway leading from the larynx to the bronchi.

bronchial tree The bronchi and the branches that stem out to bronchioles.

bronchioles The smallest division of the bronchi.

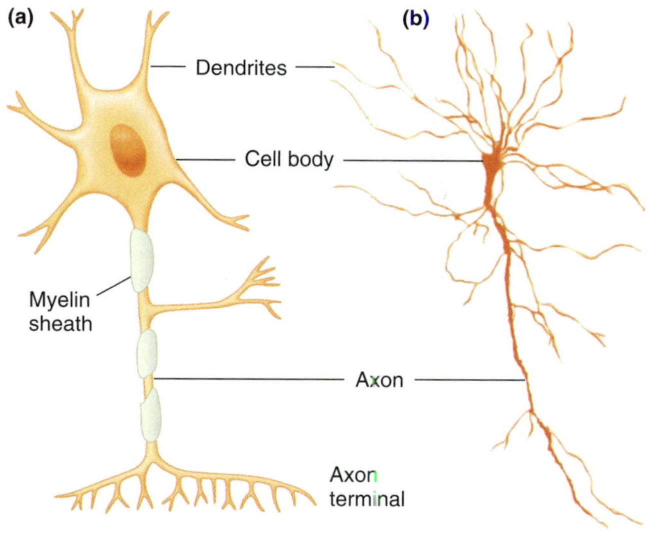

Figure C-10 (*a*) An illustration of a neuron or nerve cell, showing the cell body with dendrites and the axon. The axon releases the neurotransmitters. (*b*) How a neuron looks under a light microscope.

Nervous System

The next system, the nervous system, is a regulatory system controlling a variety of body functions. The nervous system can detect changes occurring in various organs and take corrective action when needed to maintain the constancy of the internal environment, **homeostasis.** The nervous system regulates activities that change almost instantly, such as muscle contractions and perception of danger.

The nervous system consists of the **central nervous system (CNS)** and the **peripheral nervous system (PNS).** The central nervous system contains the brain and spinal cord. The peripheral nervous system, with its nerves coming from the central nervous system, branch out to all organs of the body.

The basic structural and functional unit of the nervous system is the **neuron**—a cell that responds to electrical and chemical signals, conducts electrical impulses, and releases chemical regulators (Fig. C-10). Neurons allow us to perceive what is occurring in our environment, engage in learning, store vital information in memory, and control the body's voluntary actions. Incoming information to the body depends on sensory receptors, such as visual, auditory, smell, and tactile receptors.

Neurons can't produce new cells, although some can regenerate parts of their structures. Loss of nerve tissue causes loss of important functions. A spinal cord injury is likely to cause permanent paralysis.

Neuroglia (glial cells) protect neurons and aid in their function. They are far more abundant than neurons. For example, one group of neuroglia wraps nerves in a protective myelin sheath, a job associated with vitamin B-12 (review Fig. C-10). This acts like an insulating material, isolating one nerve conduction pathway from the others. Another group of neuroglia phagocytize pathogens and dispose of cellular debris in the CNS.

Each neuron contains a cell body with a nucleus and rough endoplasmic reticulum, **dendrites,** and an **axon.** Information (electrical or chemical stimuli) enters the cell through the dendrites and/or the cell body, and the output of electrical impulses leave by way of the axon.

By now, you may be wondering about the term *nerve*. A **nerve** is a bundle of axons located outside the CNS. Nerves contain axons of both sensory and motor neurons.

Axons end close to, or may be in physical contact with, the next neuron. In most cases, however, the electrical signal is converted to a chemical signal at the end of the axon as a chemical called a **neurotransmitter.** This is released into the gap (Fig. C-11). The transmission from neuron to neuron or from neuron to muscle cell is by way of these neurotransmitters. The space between one neuron and the next is known as a **synapse.** Neurotransmitters that bridge the gap are derived from common nutrients

homeostasis A series of adjustments that prevent change in the internal environment in the body.

central nervous system (CNS) Consists of the brain and spinal cord.

peripheral nervous system (PNS) The nerves of the central nervous system that lie outside the brain and spinal cord.

neuron The structural and functional unit of the nervous system. Consists of cell body, dendrites, and axon.

neuroglia (glial cells) Specialized support cells of the central nervous system.

neurotransmitter A compound made by a nerve cell that allows for communication between it and other cells.

synapse The space between the axon of one neuron and the dendrite of another neuron.

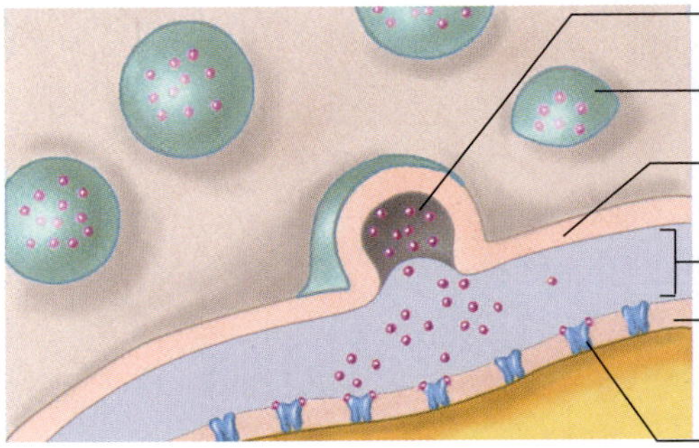

Figure C-11 Transmission of the message from one neuron to another neuron or other cell relies on neurotransmitters. Vesicles containing neurotransmitters fuse with the membrane of the neuron and the neurotransmitter is released into the synapse. The neurotransmitter then binds to the receptors on the nearby neuron (or cell). In this way, the message is sent from one neuron to another, or to the cell that ultimately performs the action directed by the message.

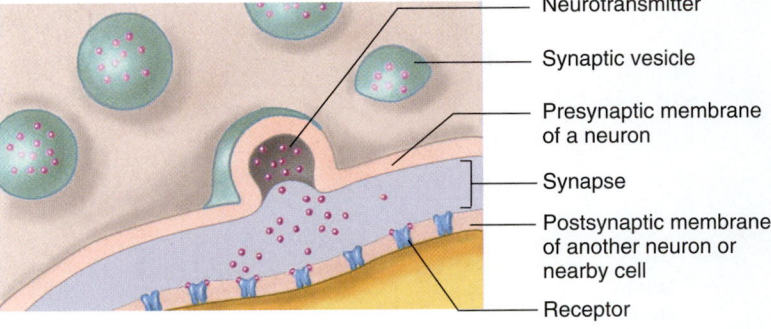

found in foods (review Chapter 11 for more details). There are a variety of neurotransmitters—**dopamine, norepinephrine, acetylcholine,** and **serotonin,** just to identify a few.

The body's fight or flight mechanism—the ability to survive a threat—depends on the **adrenergic** effect provided by andrenergic neurons secreting **epinephrine** and norepinephrine. The adrenergic effect stimulates the heart to beat faster, constricts blood vessels to raise blood pressure, increases breathing, and promotes the breakdown of glycogen in the liver. This is essential to survival, since it makes it possible to provide plenty of glucose, our basic muscle fuel, instantly, when there is an emergency and muscles need to respond quickly. **Cholinergic** effects usually produce the opposite response of adrenergic effects.

It is important to recognize that the brain has a tremendous metabolic rate, requiring a constant supply of blood, which accounts for 20% of the total cardiac output. This translates into 750 ml of blood per minute being pumped through the brain, yielding a steady supply of oxygen and glucose. Any interruption in the supply of these two molecules is life-threatening. The brain also generates waste materials, which are promptly removed by this high blood flow rate.

All the various structures that make up the nervous system are related to one's nutritional status. For example, most of the axons of the CNS and PNS are covered by a substance previously mentioned, myelin. Vitamin B-12 plays a key role in the formation of myelin. The transmission of information through the nervous system depends on nutrients obtained from the diet: calcium, sodium, and potassium. The sodium ion (Na^+) (mostly extracellular) and the potassium ion (K^+) (mostly intracellular) located on either side of the axon membrane exchange places as they flow through ion channels in response to electrical stimulation. This is how an electrical signal is transmitted. They are later pumped back to their previous location.

Other nutrients required for the nervous system are various amino acids. One amino acid we obtain from dietary protein, tryptophan, is converted to serotonin by neurons. This neurotransmitter has a variety of behavioral effects. Varying the amount of dietary tryptophan controls the amount of serotonin produced by neurons. The amino acid tyrosine can be converted to dopamine and norepinephrine.

The calcium ion (Ca^{2+}) plays a central role in nervous system control. Calcium allows the release of neurotransmitters from the axon of a neuron. As we have seen, the neurotransmitter carries the signal to the next neuron as it jumps the synapse. Fortunately, a calcium-deficient diet will never have a major effect on nerve transmission; the body can always find enough calcium to keep the nervous system functioning. There are, however, rare instances when a deficiency of calcium causes tetany. (More about tetany appears in Chapter 11.)

Certainly, the most important nutrient for continued efficient brain function is carbohydrate in the form of glucose. Should the diet fail to deliver enough carbohydrate that can form glucose, the body will synthesize it in sufficient amounts to provide for the needs of the brain. Alternately, the brain will learn to use an alternative fuel called ketone bodies, but this is not healthy for the body over the long term (review Chapter 4).

dopamine A neurotransmitter in the CNS.

norepinephrine A neurotransmitter released from nerve endings, and a hormone produced by the adrenal gland in times of stress.

epinephrine A hormone produced by the adrenal gland in times of stress. It may also have neurotransmitter functions, such as in the brain.

acetylcholine A neurotransmitter released from nerve endings.

serotonin A neurotransmitter synthesized from the amino acid tryptophan that appears to both decrease the desire to eat carbohydrates and induce sleep.

adrenergic Relating to the actions of epinephrine and norepinephrine.

cholinergic Relating to the actions of acetylcholine.

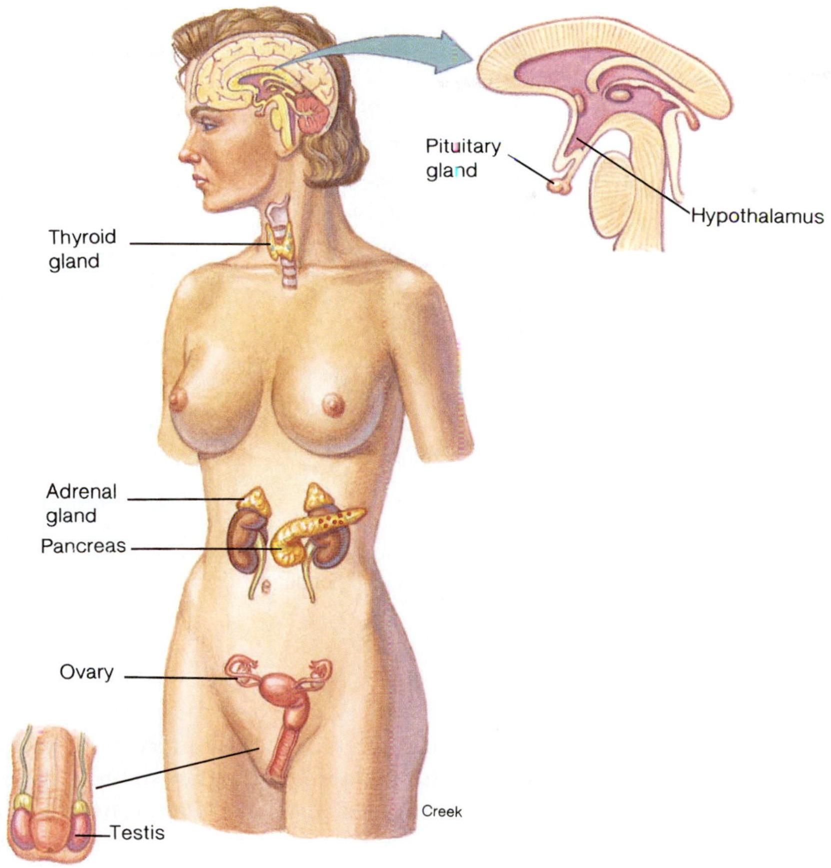

Figure C-12 The major endocrine glands. Note the location of some of the endocrine glands. These glands secrete a variety of hormones.

It should also be noted that the gastrointestinal tract has its own separate nervous system. The sight or smell of food, or one's emotions, can signal muscle cells and glands to prepare the way for food and turn on digestive processes (Chapter 3 has more details).

Endocrine System and Hormones

Endocrine glands secrete regulatory substances, hormones, into the blood for distribution to target tissues or organs. The endocrine gland that secretes a hormone is responding to the need to restore homeostasis. The following section is by no means a complete exploration of all the body's hormones, but it concentrates on those that affect nutrition (Fig. C-12).

Hormones control metabolic functions, such as appetite, and the transport of substances through cell membranes. Others control growth, and still others are responsible for sex and reproduction. Of all these hormones, some are described as "local," in that they function in the immediate vicinity of their production. There are also many interrelationships between hormones and the nervous system. For example, the adrenal gland and the pituitary gland respond to neural stimuli.

Some hormones from the pituitary gland control the secretion of other endocrine glands. And, as mentioned in the previous section, a substance such as norepinephrine secreted as a neurotransmitter, can act as a hormone.

Chemical Classification of Hormones

General hormones are classified according to chemical categories: **steroids, glycoproteins, polypeptides,** and **amines.**

Steroid hormones are lipid substances synthesized from cholesterol (Table C-2). The glycoproteins are long chains of amino acids (100 or more) bound to carbohydrate (Table C-3). Follicle-stimulating hormone (FSH), luteinizing hormone (LH), -

steroids A group of hormones and related compounds that are derivatives of cholesterol.

glycoprotein A protein containing a carbohydrate group.

polypeptide From a few to about 100 amino acids bonded together.

amines Can refer to hormones made of one or a few amino acids.

Table C-2 Steroid Hormones

Hormone	Gland	Target	Effect	Role in Nutrition
Testosterone	Testes, adrenal glands	Reproductive organs	Reproduction, secondary sexual development	Muscle growth
Estrogens, progesterone	Ovaries, adrenal glands	Reproductive organs	Reproduction, secondary sexual characteristics	Maintenance of bone
Cortisol	Adrenal glands	Liver	Glucocorticoid activity	Metabolism of protein, carbohydrate, fat
Aldosterone	Adrenal glands	Kidney	Mineral-corticoid activity	Electrolyte balance

Table C-3 Glycoprotein Hormones

Hormone	Gland	Target	Effect	Role in Nutrition
FSH, LH, TSH	Pituitary gland	Variety of organs	Stimulation of target organ to produce its own hormone	None directly

tropic hormone A hormone that stimulates the secretion of another secreting gland.

thyroid-stimulating hormone (TSH), and several other pituitary hormones are such hormones and are referred to as **tropic hormones** because they stimulate the secretion of another hormone and usually stimulate the growth of the associated gland. For example, TSH stimulates the production of the thyroid hormone. Another group of hormones are polypeptide chains made of fewer than 100 amino acids per chain (Table C-4). Amines are hormones synthesized from the amino acids tyrosine and tryptophan (Table C-5).

There are also special hormones that regulate the digestive tract. These are discussed in Chapter 3.

Interesting Features of Hormones

The steroid and thyroid hormones can be taken in pill form, since they are not digested in the GI tract; thus, they can be absorbed into the body in their active state. All the other hormones are deactivated when taken by mouth because their biological activity is destroyed by digestive enzymes. That is why the hormone insulin must be taken by injection to bypass the digestive tract.

Some hormones must undergo chemical changes before they can function. For example, vitamin D synthesized in the skin and/or obtained from food is converted to an active hormone by the kidneys and liver.

In most cases, a single gland secretes a single hormone, but, in a few cases, a gland secretes more than one hormone. Sometimes a hormone is produced by more than one gland.

Neural and Endocrine Regulation

Whether a chemical is acting as a hormone or a neurotransmitter, the target cell must have a receptor protein to combine with it. This causes a change in the target cell (Chapter 3 provides a fuller discussion of this concept). This also means that there must be a mechanism to turn off the action. Hormones are subject to control by an off switch. For example, when the blood glucose concentration has been returned to normal by the action of the hormone insulin, insulin production is turned off. If it were not, the person would experience decreasing glucose concentrations until such time as the concentration dropped so low the person would go into shock and die.

Table C-4 Polypeptide Hormones

Hormone	Gland	Target	Effect	Role in Nutrition
Antidiuretic hormone	Pituitary gland	Kidney	Water retention, vasoconstriction	Maintenance of proper blood volume
Prolactin (tropic hormone)	Pituitary gland	Mammary gland	Milk production; in males, indirect enhancement of testosterone secretions	Nourishment of newborn
Oxytocin	Pituitary gland	Uterus and mammary glands	Contraction of uterus, mammary secretions	Milk production
Insulin	Pancreas	Fat and muscle cells	Decreased blood glucose concentration	Storage of glucose as glycogen, increased fat storage, increased amino acid uptake by cells
Glucagon	Pancreas	Liver	Increased blood glucose concentration	Release of glucose from liver stores, increased fat mobilization
ACTH (adrenocorticotropic hormone)	Pituitary gland	Adrenal glands	Secretion of glucocorticoids	Secretion of adrenal cortical hormones
Growth hormone (tropic hormone)	Pituitary gland	Most cells	Promotion of amino acid uptake by cells	Promotion of protein synthesis and growth, increased fat utilization for energy
Parathyroid hormone	Parathyroid glands	Intestinal tract, kidneys	Increased blood calcium concentration	Release of calcium from bone into blood
Calcitonin	Thyroid gland	Bone	Inhibition of breakdown of bone, stimulation of calcium excretion by kidneys	Reduced blood calcium concentration
Leptin	No gland, just adipose tissue	Hypothalamus	Targeting of satiety center	Decreased appetite

Table C-5 Amine Hormones

Hormone	Gland	Target	Effect	Role in Nutrition
Epinephrine, norepinephrine*	Adrenal glands	Heart, blood vessels, brain, lungs	Increased metabolic rate	Release of glucose into the blood, fat mobilization
Thyroid hormones	Thyroid gland	Most organs	Increased oxygen consumption, growth, brain development, development of CNS in fetus	Protein synthesis, increased metabolic rate
Melatonin	Pineal gland	Specific neurons	Maintenance of body (circadian) rhythms, sleep	Scavenging of atoms and molecules that are highly reactive and dangerous

*Norepinephrine also functions as a neurotransmitter, depending on location in the body. Epinephrine is suspected of doing the same, such as in the brain.

Urinary System

The urinary system is composed of two kidneys located on the back of the abdominal wall, one on each side of the vertebral column (Fig. C-13). Each is connected to the urinary bladder by a **ureter.** The bladder is emptied by way of the **urethra.**

ureter A tube that transports urine from the kidney to the urinary bladder.

urethra The tube that transports urine from the urinary bladder to the outside of the body.

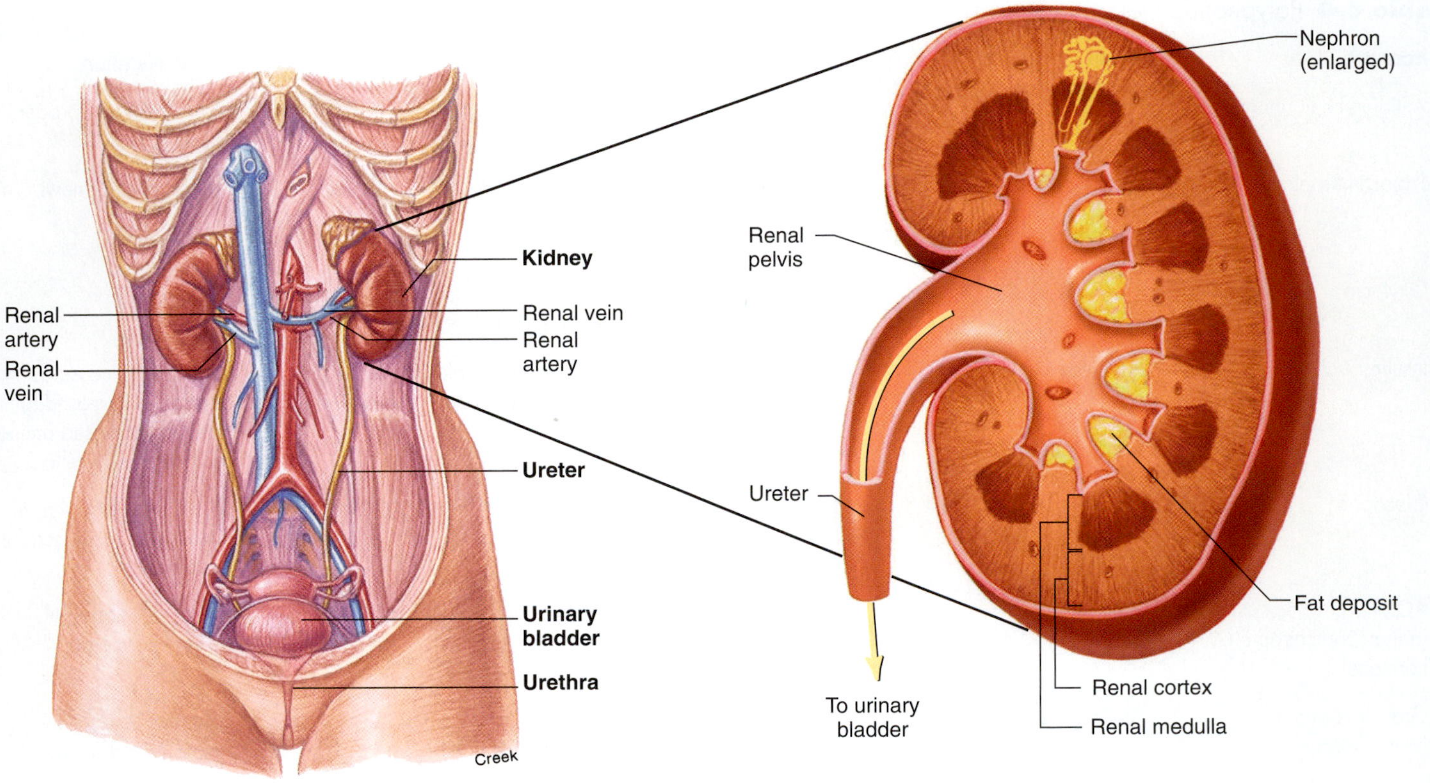

Figure C-13 Organs of the urinary system. (*a*) The kidneys, bean-shaped organs located on either side of the spinal column, filter waste from the blood, which is then stored in the bladder as urine. The kidneys are connected to the urinary bladder by ureters. The urinary system of the female is shown. The male's urinary system is the same, except that the urethra extends through the penis. (*b*) A cross section of the kidney. The outer section of the kidney is the cortex, the inner section is the medulla. The functional unit of the kidney, the nephron, loops through the cortex and medulla, and the fluid that flows through these tiny structures is separated so that the waste is removed from the blood into collecting ducts and drains into the renal pelvis. Thus the urine exits by way of the ureter to the bladder. The remaining fluid is returned to the circulatory system to maintain the normal composition of the blood.

Each bean-shaped kidney has an outer section called the cortex and an inner section called the medulla. The medulla is composed of cone-shaped pyramid structures, which empty waste materials into a funnel-shaped tube ending in the ureter. Ureters carry urine from the kidneys to the bladder for temporary storage. Blood flows through the kidneys at a rate of about 120 ml/minute.

Kidney Functions

The kidneys regulate the composition of the blood (plasma) and the interstitial fluid, known together as the extracellular fluid. This regulation is accomplished by filtering the blood and forming urine, which is basically the filtrate. As a result of kidney action and the formation of urine, the volume of blood plasma is controlled, and blood pressure is maintained. The kidneys remove metabolic waste and foreign chemicals from the blood, and they maintain a certain concentration of electrolytes such as Na^+, K^+, and HCO_3^- (bicarbonate) in the plasma. Together with the lungs, the kidneys maintain the pH of the blood. The kidneys constantly monitor the composition of the blood and produce hormones to maintain homeostasis. For example, the kidneys produce the hormone **erythropoietin,** which is responsible for the synthesis of red blood cells. The kidneys convert a form of vitamin D into its active hormone form. During times of fasting, the kidneys can produce glucose from amino acids.

erythropoietin A hormone secreted mostly by the kidneys that enhances red blood cell synthesis and stimulates red blood cell release from bone marrow.

Kidney Structure

Each kidney is enclosed in a fatty, fibrous sack, which protects it from external physical damage. Examined microscopically, the functional unit of the kidney, the **nephron,** is disclosed. Nephrons extend through the renal cortex and the renal medulla. There are more than 1 million nephrons per kidney. The nephron consists of small tubules allied with small blood vessels. The tiny capillary filtration unit, the **glomerulus,** is held in a small capsule (Bowman's capsule). The glomerulus filters large amounts of fluid from the blood, removing the dissolved waste and excess fluid to form urine, which leaves by way of the tubules. The remaining fluid is returned to the blood.

nephron The functional unit of the kidney.

glomerulus The capillaries in the kidney that filter waste products from the blood.

This ingenious mechanism constantly adjusts the composition of the blood. In doing so the essential components are recovered and returned to general circulation, waste products and excess water are removed, and unneeded nutrients (ones where storage compartments are full or there are no storage facilities) are flushed away by the urine.

Reproductive System

Reproduction is a fundamental property of all living things. We die, but our genes live on in our progeny. In humans, both ova and sperm, called gametes (sex cells), contain 23 chromosomes. The fertilized egg contains 46 chromosomes (23 from each parent) and is programmed to produce a new human. At conception, the instructions for the developing embryo are all present. Through the actions of the female reproductive organs, supported by hormonal secretions, a human is produced about 40 weeks after conception, providing that essential nutrients are present and no genetic defects are encountered. The most precarious time during pregnancy is during the development of the embryo (the first 13 weeks), when a woman is least likely to know she is pregnant.

The male reproductive organs consist of the scrotum (containing the testes), the penis, the urethra, the seminal vesicles, and the prostate. The female reproductive organs consist of the ovaries, uterus, and vagina (review Fig. C-12).

In addition to reproduction, the sex hormones stimulate bone growth and the closure of the epiphyseal plate, thus causing the cessation of bone growth. Estrogens protect against bone loss. The sex hormone testosterone stimulates protein synthesis, such as muscle growth and bone growth.

Puberty, or the onset of adult sex life, takes place during early adolescence. **Menarche,** the term used to describe the onset of menstruation, occurs usually between the ages of 11 and 16 in females. In the male, sexual maturation occurs somewhat later and is initiated by hormonal secretions from the brain.

menarche The onset of menstruation. Menarche usually occurs around age 13, 2 or 3 years after the first signs of puberty start to appear.

The female reproductive system is discussed in Chapter 15 in more detail.

appendix d

Dietary Advice for Canadians

Recommended Nutrient Intake (RNI) The Canadian version of RDA published in 1990.

The information in this appendix includes advice on dietary patterns, as well as regulations that apply to food labeling. Previous **RNIs** for nutrients have been replaced by the Dietary Reference Intakes (DRIs) that apply to Canadian and U.S. citizens. These are listed on the inside cover. Both Canadian and American scientists worked on the various DRI committees, coming up with a set of harmonized Dietary Reference Intakes for both countries.

Summary of the Nutrition Recommendations for Canadians

Excellent World Wide Web resources for Canadians are Health Canada (www.hc-sc.gc.ca), Dietitians of Canada (www.dietitians.ca), and the National Institute of Nutrition (www.nin.ca).

The latest Nutrition Recommendations of the Scientific Review Committee of the Office of Nutrition Policy and Promotion suggest that the Canadian diet should supply:

- essential nutrients in the amounts specified in the updated Recommended Nutrient Intakes (RNIs);
- sufficient energy to maintain a healthy weight when balanced with physical activity (energy intakes for adults should not be lower than 1800 kilocalories in order to meet RNIs);
- no more than 30% of energy as fat and no more than 10% of energy as saturated fat;
- at least 55% energy as carbohydrates;
- less sodium than is now used;
- no more than 5% of energy as alcohol, or 2 drinks per day (whichever is less), with no alcohol during pregnancy;
- no more caffeine than the equivalent of four regular cups of coffee per day; and
- water containing no less than 1 mg/litre of fluoride.

In essence, suggested actions toward healthful eating as listed in Canada's Guidelines for Healthy Eating include the following:

- Enjoy a VARIETY of foods.
- Emphasize cereals, breads, other grain products, vegetables, and fruit.
- Choose lower-fat dairy products, leaner meats, and foods prepared with little or no fat.
- Achieve and maintain a healthful body weight by enjoying regular physical activity and healthy eating.
- Limit salt, alcohol, and caffeine.

The *Canadian Food Guide* is a guide to help Canadians make wise food choices (Fig. D-1). The rainbow side of the Food Guide places foods into four groups: grain products; vegetables and fruit; milk products; and meat and meat alternatives. The rainbow

Healthy Canada

Health and Welfare Canada — Santé et Bien-être social Canada

CANADA'S

Food Guide

TO HEALTHY EATING

Enjoy a variety of foods from each group every day.

Choose lower-fat foods more often.

Grain Products
Choose whole-grain and enriched products more often.

Vegetables & Fruit
Choose dark green and orange vegetables and orange fruit more often.

Milk Products
Choose lower-fat milk products more often.

Meat & Alternatives
Choose leaner meats, poultry and fish, as well as dried peas, beans, and lentils more often.

Canada

Figure D-1 Canadian Food Guide to Healthy Eating.

CANADA'S
Food Guide
TO HEALTHY EATING
FOR PEOPLE FOUR YEARS AND OVER

Different People Need Different Amounts of Food

The amount of food you need every day from the four food groups and other foods depends on your age, body size, activity level, whether you are male or female and if you are pregnant or breastfeeding. That's why the Food Guide gives a lower and higher number of servings for each food group. For example, young children can choose the lower number of servings, while male teenagers can go to the higher number. Most other people can choose servings somewhere in between.

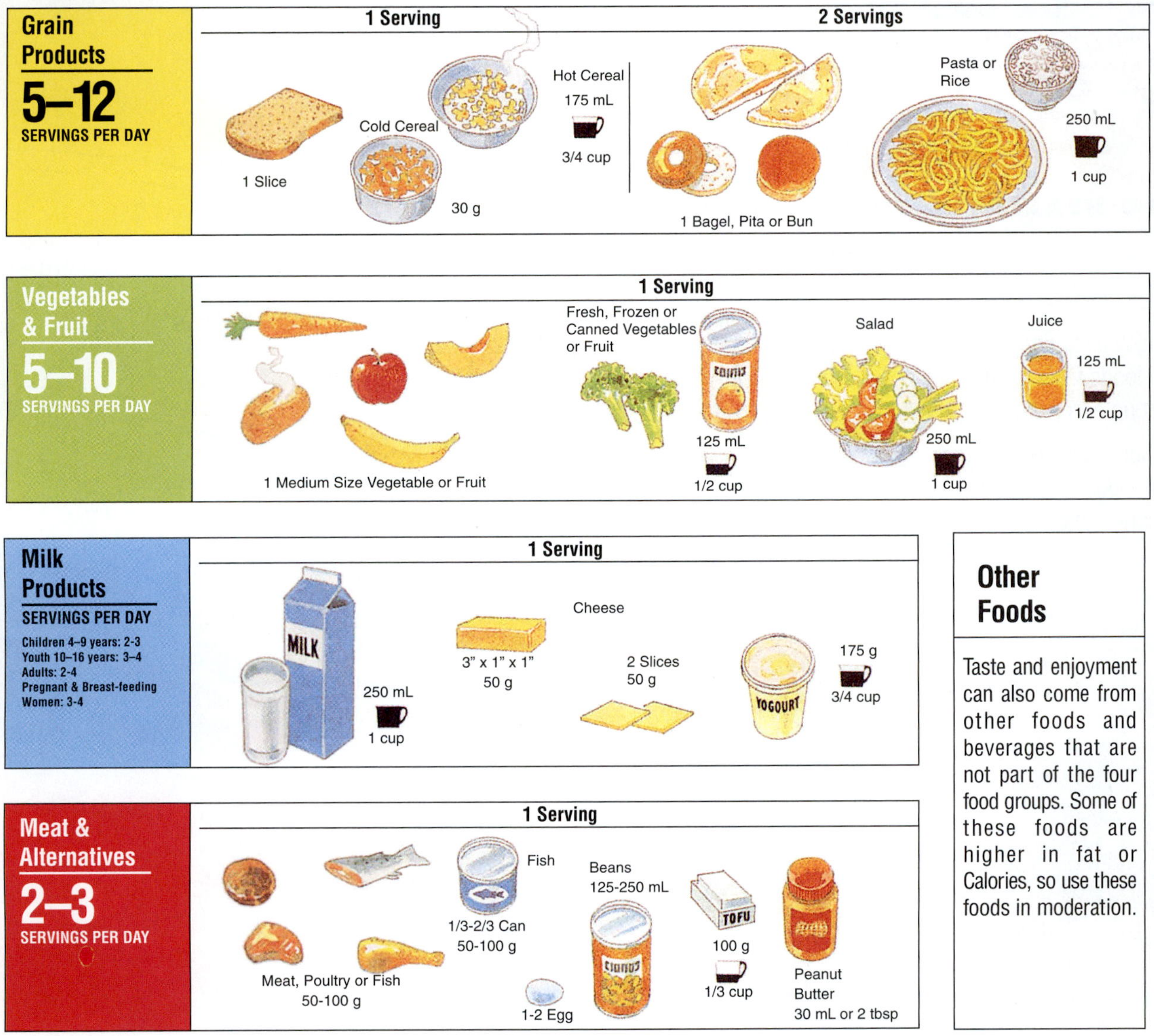

Enjoy eating well, being active, and feeling good about yourself. That's VITALIT®

ISBN 0-662-19648-1

Figure D-1 concluded.

includes information about the types of foods to choose from each food group for healthy eating.

The bar side of the Food Guide helps Canadians decide how much they need from each group every day. The guide gives a range for the number of servings for each food group, since different people need different amounts of food. The Food Guide also shows serving sizes for different foods.

The bar side of the Food Guide also tells how other foods that are not part of the four food groups can have a role in healthy eating. Since some of these "other foods" are higher in fat or calories, the Food Guide recommends using these foods in moderation.

Nutrition Labels

The current Canadian Nutrition Label is shown below. Consumers will soon start to see more information about the nutritional value of most prepackaged food under new labeling requirements that were published on January 1, 2003. The new regulations require most food labels to carry a mandatory *Nutrition Facts* table listing Calories and 13 key nutrients.

HOW TO READ THE ORIGINAL CANADIAN NUTRITION LABEL

Nutrition information is expressed per **suggested serving**. The serving size will vary according to food type and brand. Consider this fact when comparing foods.

Gives the calorie content (Cal)

Indicates the quantity of naturally occurring and added sugars as well as dietary fibre

Indicates the level of sodium from salt and all other sources

Vitamins and minerals are expressed as a percentage of the highest recommended amount

millilitres: 5 mL = 1 teaspoon

kilojoules: metric unit of energy 1 Cal = 4.18kJ

grams: 28 g = 1 ounce

LASAGNA
Nutrition Information
per 275 g serving
(1 cup/250 mL)

Energy	275	Cal
	1140	kJ
Protein	19	g
Fat	7	g
Polyunsaturates	0.8	g
Monounsaturates	1.9	g
Saturates	2.5	g
Cholesterol	46	mg
Carbohydrate	34	g
Starch	29	g
Sugars	5	g
Dietary Fibre	0.2	g
Sodium	850	mg
Potassium	675	mg

Percentage of Recommended Daily Intake

Thiamine	20%
Riboflavin	19%
Niacin	18%
Calcium	12%
Iron	28%

The New Canadian Nutrition Label

As noted on page A-59, new regulations published on January 1, 2003 make nutrition labelling mandatory on most food labels using a new format. The regulations also update requirements for nutrient content claims and permit, for the first time in Canada, diet-related health claims for foods.

How to Read the New Canadian Nutrition Label

The Regulations provide for the optional declaration of the number of Calories both from fat and from saturates plus *trans*. Recommendations on the % of Calories from fat apply to the total diet rather than to an individual food. Therefore, inclusion of the % of Calories from fat in the Nutrition Facts table may be confusing and is not permitted.

The Nutrition Facts table provides information on saturated and *trans* fatty acids which have been shown to raise serum cholesterol levels. The declaration of the other groups of fatty acids, mono-unsaturates, omega-3 and omega-6 polyunsaturates, is optional unless claims are made, in which case all three must be declared.

Potassium is not included as a mandatory nutrient of the Nutrition Facts table because it is not considered to be a nutrient of general public health importance. The declaration of potassium, however, is mandatory when a claim is made for the sodium or salt content of a food which contains an added potassium salt.

Nutrition Facts
Per 1 cup (264g)

Amount	**% Daily Value**
Calories 260	
Fat 13g	**20**%
Saturated Fat 3g + Trans Fat 2g	**25**%
Cholesterol 30mg	
Sodium 660mg	**28**%
Carbohydrate 31g	**10**%
Fibre 0g	**0**%
Sugars 5g	
Protein 5g	
Vitamin A 4%	Vitamin C 2%
Calcium 15%	Iron 4%

Daily Value is a comparison standard comprised of
(*a*) vitamin or mineral amounts referred to in the definition of a recommended daily intake for that vitamin or mineral
(*b*) nutrient amounts referred to in the definition of reference standard for that nutrient

Serving size is stipulated for various foods.

The amount of vitamins and minerals is expressed as a percentage of the Daily Value per serving of stated size.

There is also a new Canadian Nutrition Label for children under two years of age.

Nutrition Facts
Per 1 jar (126 mL)

	Amount
Calories	110
Fat	0g
Sodium	10 mg
Carbohydrate	27g
Fibre	4g
Sugars	18g
Protein	0g

% Daily Value

Vitamin A	6%	Vitamin C	45%
Calcium	2%	Iron	2%

Recommended Daily Intakes and Reference Standards

Below are the **Recommended Daily Intakes** and **Reference Standards** used on Nutrition Labels for persons 2 years of age and older.*†‡

Dietary Constituent	Amount		
Fat	**65 g**	Vitamin B_6	1.8 mg
The sum of saturated fatty acids and *trans* fatty acids	**20 g**	Folacin	220 µg
Cholesterol	**300 mg**	Vitamin B_{12}	2 µg
Carbohydrate	**300 g**	Pantothenic acid or pantothenate	7 mg
Fibre	**25 g**	Vitamin K	**80 mg**
Sodium	**2400 mg**	Biotin	**30 µg**
Chloride	**3400 µg**	Calcium	1100 mg
Potassium	**3500 mg**	Phosphorus	1100 mg
Vitamin A	1000 RE	Magnesium	250 mg
Vitamin D	5 µg	Iron	14 mg
Vitamin E	10 mg	Zinc	9 mg
Vitamin C	60 mg	Iodide	160 µg
Thiamin, thiamine or vitamin B_1	1.3 mg	Selenium	**50 µg**
Riboflavin or vitamin B_2	1.6 mg	Copper	**2 mg**
Niacin	23 NE	Manganese	**2 mg**
		Chromium	**120 µg**
		Molybdenum	**75 µg**

*RE = retinol equivalents
†NE = niacin equivalents
‡Together these constitute the Daily Values used on the new Canadian Nutrition Label. Reference Standards are bolded.

Approved Nutrient Content Claims

Below is a sample of approved nutrient content claims for food labels (for the complete list of regulations see the website http://canadagazette.gc.ca/partII/2003/20030101/html/sor11-e.html).

Energy

- *Free of energy:* The food provides less than 5 Calories or 21 kilojoules per reference amount and serving of stated size.
- *Low in energy:* The food provides 40 Calories or 167 kilojoules or less per reference amount and serving of stated size.
- *Reduced in energy:* The food is processed, formulated, reformulated or otherwise modified so that it provides at least 25% less energy per reference amount of a similar food.
- *Lower in energy:* The food provides at least 25% less energy per reference amount of a similar food.
- *Source of energy:* The food provides at least 100 Calories or 420 kilojoules per reference amount and serving of stated size.
- *More energy:* The food provides at least 25% more energy, totalling at least 100 more Calories or 420 more kilojoules per reference amount of a similar food.

Protein

- *Low in protein:* The food contains no more than 1 g of protein per 100 g of the food.
- *Source of protein:* The food has a protein rating of 20 or more, as determined by official method FO-1, *Determination of Protein Rating,* October 15, 1981, (*a*) per reasonable daily intake; or (*b*) per 30 g combined with 125 mL of milk, if the food is a breakfast cereal.
- *Excellent source of protein:* The food has a protein rating of 40 or more, as determined by official method FO-1, *Determination of Protein Rating,* October 15, 1981, (*a*) per reasonable daily intake; or (*b*) per 30 g combined with 125 mL of milk, if the food is a breakfast cereal.
- *More protein:* The food (*a*) has a protein rating of 20 or more, as determined by official method FO-1, *Determination of Protein Rating,* October 15, 1981, (i) per reasonable daily intake, or (ii) per 30 g combined with 125 mL of milk, if the food is a breakfast cereal; and (*b*) contains at least 25% more protein, totalling at least 7 g more, per reasonable daily intake compared to the reference food of the same food group or the similar reference food.

Fat

- *Free of fat:* The food contains less than 0.5 g of fat per reference amount and serving of stated size.
- *Low in fat:* The food contains 3 g or less of fat per reference amount and serving of stated size and, if the reference amount is 30 g or 30 mL or less, per 50 g.
- *Reduced in fat:* The food is processed, formulated, reformulated or otherwise modified so that it contains at least 25% less fat than the reference amount of a similar food.
- *Lower in fat:* The food contains at least 25% less fat per reference amount of the food, than the reference amount of the reference food of the same food group.
- *100% fat-free:* The food (*a*) contains less than 0.5 g of fat per 100 g; (*b*) contains no added fat.
- *No added fat:* (1) The food contains no added fats or oils set out in Division 9, or added butter or ghee, or ingredients that contain added fats or oils, or butter or ghee.
- *Free of saturated fatty acids:* The food contains less than 0.2 g saturated fatty acids and less than 0.2 g *trans* fatty acids per reference amount and serving of stated size.
- *Low in saturated fatty acids:* (1) The food contains 2 g or less of saturated fatty acids and *trans* fatty acids combined per reference amount and serving of stated size. (2) The food provides 15% or less energy from the sum of saturated fatty acids and *trans* fatty acids.
- *Reduced in saturated fatty acids:* The food is processed, formulated, reformulated or otherwise modified, without increasing the content of *trans* fatty acids, so that it contains at least 25% less saturated fatty acids per reference amount of the food than the reference amount of the similar reference food.
- *Lower in saturated fatty acids:* The food contains at least 25% less saturated fatty acids and the content of *trans* fatty acids is not higher per reference amount of the food, than the reference amount of the reference food of the same food group.
- *Free of* trans *fatty acids:* The food contains less than 0.2 g of *trans* fatty acids per reference amount and serving of stated size.
- *Reduced in* trans *fatty acids:* The food is processed, formulated, reformulated or otherwise modified, without increasing the content of saturated fatty acids, so that it contains at least 25% less *trans* fatty acids per reference amount of the food than the reference amount of the similar reference food.
- *Lower in* trans *fatty acids:* The food contains at least 25% less *trans* fatty acids and the content of saturated fatty acids is not higher per reference amount of the food compared to the reference amount of a smiilar food.
- *Source of omega-3 polyunsaturated fatty acids:* The food contains 0.3 g or more of omega-3 polyunsaturated fatty acids per reference amount and serving of stated size.
- *Source of omega-6 polyunsaturated fatty acids:* The food contains 2 g or more of omega-6 polyunsaturated fatty acids per reference amount and serving of stated size.

Cholesterol

- *Free of cholesterol:* The food contains less than 2 mg of cholesterol per reference amount and serving of stated size.
- *Low in cholesterol:* The food contains 20 mg or less of cholesterol per reference amount and serving of stated size (if the reference amount is 30 g or 30 mL or less, per 50 g.)
- *Reduced in cholesterol:* The food is processed, formulated, reformulated or otherwise modified so that it contains at least 25% less cholesterol per reference amount of a similar food.
- *Lower in cholesterol:* The food contains at least 25% less cholesterol per reference amount of a similar food.

Sodium or Salt

- *Free of sodium or salt:* The food contains less than 5 mg of sodium per reference amount and serving of stated size.
- *Low in sodium or salt:* The food contains 140 mg or less of sodium per reference amount and serving of stated size.
- *Reduced in sodium or salt:* (1) The food is processed, formulated, reformulated or otherwise modified so that it contains at least 25% less sodium per reference amount of a similar food.
- *Lower in sodium or salt:* The food contains at least 25% less sodium per reference amount of the food.
- *No added sodium or salt:* The food contains no added salt, other sodium salts, or ingredients that contain sodium that functionally substitute for added salt.
- *Lightly salted:* The food contains at least 50% less added sodium than the sodium added to a similar reference food.

Sugars

- *Free of sugars:* The food contains less than 0.5 mg of sugars per reference amount and serving of stated size.
- *Reduced in sugars:* The food is processed, formulated, reformulated or otherwise modified so that it contains at least 25% less, sugars, totalling at least 5 g less, per reference amount of the food.
- *Lower in sugars:* The food contains at least 25% less sugars, totalling at least 5 g less, per reference amount of the food.
- *No added sugars:* (1) The food contains no added sugars, no ingredients containing added sugars or ingredients that contain sugars

that functionally substitute for added sugars.

Fibre

- *Source of fibre:* (1) The food contains 2 g or more (*a*) of fibre per reference amount and serving of stated size, if no fibre or fibre source is identified in the statement or claim; or (*b*) of each identified fibre or fibre from an identified fibre source per reference amount and serving of stated size, if a fibre or fibre source is identified in the statement or claim.
- *High source of fibre:* The food contains 4 g or more (*a*) of fibre per reference amount and serving of stated size, if no fibre or fibre source is identified in the statement or claim; or (*b*) of each identified fibre or fibre from an identified fibre source per reference amount and serving of stated size, if a fibre or fibre source is identified in the statement or claim.
- *Very high source of fibre:* The food contains 6 g or more (*a*) of fibre per reference amount and serving of stated size, if no fibre or fibre source is identified in the statement or claim; or (*b*) of each identified fibre or fibre from an identified fibre source per reference amount and serving of stated size, if a fibre or fibre source is identified in the statement or claim.
- *More fibre:* The food contains at least 25% more fibre, totalling at least 1 g more, if no fibre or fibre source is identified in the statement or claim, or at least 25% more of an identified fibre or fibre from an identified fibre source, totalling at least 1 g more, if a fibre or fibre source is identified in the statement or claim compared to reference amount of a similar food

Light and Lean

- *Light in energy or fat:* The food meets the conditions set out for the subject "reduced in energy" or "reduced in fat."
- *Lean:* The food (*a*) is meat or poultry that has not been ground, a marine or fresh water animal or a product of any of these; and (*b*) contains 10% or less fat.
- *Extra lean:* The food (*a*) is meat or poultry that has not been ground, a marine or fresh water animal or a product of any of these; and (*b*) contains 7.5% or less fat.

Approved Health Claims for Nutrition Labels

If a manufacturer follows specific guidelines addressing both the nutrients noted in the claim as well as guidelines pertaining to other nutrients in a food, the following health claims can be made.

- A healthy diet containing foods high in potassium and low in sodium may reduce the risk of high blood pressure, a risk factor for stroke and heart disease.
- A healthy diet with adequate calcium and vitamin D, and regular physical activity, help to achieve strong bones and may reduce the risk of osteoporosis.
- A healthy diet low in saturated and trans fats may reduce the risk of heart disease.
- A healthy diet rich in a variety of vegetables and fruit may help reduce the risk of some types of cancer.
- Foods very low in starch and fermentable sugars can make the following health claims:
  - Won't cause cavities;
  - does not promote tooth decay;
  - does not promote dental caries; or is
  - non-cariogenic.

appendix e

The Exchange System: A Helpful Menu-Planning Tool

The Exchange System

The **Exchange System** is a valuable tool for roughly estimating the energy, protein, carbohydrate, and fat content of a food or meal. This tool organizes many details of the nutrient composition of foods into a manageable framework. By using the Exchange System, you can plan daily menus to fall roughly within specific percentages of macronutrients without having to look up or memorize the nutrient values of numerous foods, so the time you spend now becoming familiar with the Exchange System will pay dividends in the future.

Exchange System A system for classifying foods into numerous lists based on the foods' macronutrient composition and establishing serving sizes, so that one serving of each food on a list contains the same amount of carbohydrate, protein, fat, and energy content.

In the Exchange System, individual foods are placed into three broad groups: carbohydrate, meat and meat substitutes, and fat. Within these groups are lists that contain foods of similar macronutrient composition: various types of milk, fruit, vegetables, starch, other carbohydrates, meat and meat substitutes, and fat. These lists are designed so that, when the proper serving size is observed, each food on a list provides about the same amount of carbohydrate, protein, fat, and energy. This equality allows the exchange of foods on each list, hence the term *Exchange System.*

The Exchange System was originally developed for planning diabetic diets. Diabetes is easier to control if the person's diet has about the same composition day after day. If a certain number of **exchanges** from each of the various lists is eaten each day, that regularity is easier to achieve. However, because the Exchange System provides a quick way to estimate the energy, carbohydrate, protein, and fat content in any food or meal, it is a valuable menu-planning tool.

exchange The serving size of a food on a specific exchange list.

Becoming Familiar with the Exchange System

To use the Exchange System, you must know which foods are on each list and the serving sizes for each food.

Table E-1 gives the serving sizes for foods on each exchange list, as well as the carbohydrate, protein, fat, and energy content per exchange. Note that the meat and milk lists are divided into subclasses, which vary in fat content and, hence, in the amount of energy they provide. Foods on the meat and fat lists contain essentially no carbohydrate; those on the fruit and fat lists lack appreciable amounts of protein; and those on the vegetable, fruit, and other carbohydrates lists contain essentially no fat. You need to study Table E-1 and Figure E-1 to become familiar with the exchange lists, the sizes of the exchanges (that is, serving sizes) on each list, and the amounts of carbohydrate, protein, fat, and energy per exchange.

Before you can turn a group of exchanges into a daily meal plan, you must be aware of which foods are on each exchange list (Figure E-1). The entire U.S. Exchange System is presented in Appendix F, which you should consult frequently while exploring the system to discover its various peculiarities. For example, the starch list includes not

Table E-1 Nutrient Composition of Exchange System Lists (1995 Edition)

Groups/Lists	Household Measures*	Carbohydrate (g)	Protein (g)	Fat (g)	Energy (kcal)
Carbohydrate Group					
Starch	1 slice, ¾ cup raw, or ½ cup cooked	15	3	1 or less†	80
Fruit	1 small/medium piece	15	—	—	60
Milk	1 cup				
Nonfat/very low-fat		12	8	0–3†	90
Low-fat		12	8	5	120
Whole		12	8	8	150
Other carbohydrates	Varies	15	Varies	Varies	Varies
Vegetables	1 cup raw or ½ cup cooked	5	2	—	25
Meat and Meat Substitutes Group	1 oz				
Very lean		—	7	0–1	35
Lean		—	7	3	55
Medium-fat		—	7	5	75
High-fat		—	7	8	100
Fat Group	1 tsp	—	—	5	45

*Just an estimate; see exchange lists for actual amounts.

†Calculated as 1 g for purposes of energy contribution.

Starch exchange choices

Meat and meat substitutes exchange choices

Vegetable exchange choices

Fruit exchange choices

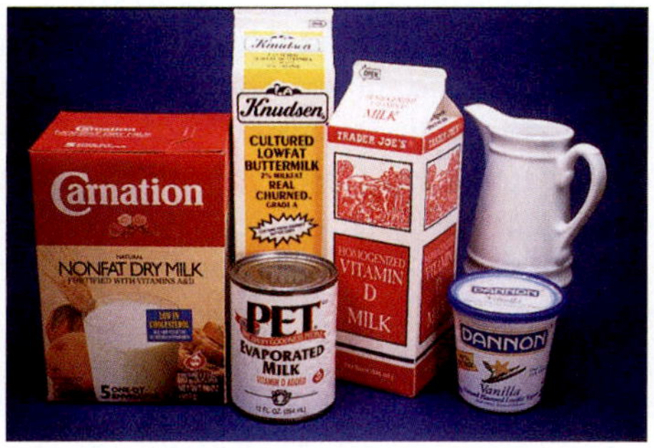

Milk exchange choices

Fat exchange choices

Figure E-1 Foods arranged according to the Exchange System lists.

Table E-2 Possible Exchange Patterns That Yield 55% of Energy as Carbohydrate, 30% as Fat, and 15% as Protein for Energy Intakes Greater Than 2000 kcal

kcal/Day Exchange List	1200*	1600*	2000	2400	2800	3200	3600
Milk (low-fat)	2	2	2	2	2	2	2
Vegetable	3	3	3	4	4	4	4
Fruit	3	4	5	6	8	9	9
Starch	5	8	11	13	15	18	21
Meat (lean)	4	4	4	5	6	7	8
Fat	2	4	6	8	10	11	13

This is just one set of options. More meat could be included if less milk were used, for example.

*Energy intakes of 1200 and 1600 kcal contain 20% of energy as protein and 50% energy as carbohydrate to allow for greater flexibility in diet planning.

only bread, dry cereal, cooked cereal, rice, and pasta, but also baked beans, corn on the cob, and potatoes. These foods are not identical to those composing the bread, cereal, rice, and pasta group in the Food Guide Pyramid. The Exchange System is not concerned with the origin of a food, whether animal or vegetable. It is primarily concerned with the macronutrients carbohydrate, protein, and fat in each food on a specific list. For example, the carbohydrate composition of potatoes resembles that of bread more than that of broccoli, although potatoes are vegetables. In addition, several foods on the meat and meat substitutes list are not meats. The list of other carbohydrates includes jam, angel food cake, fat-free frozen yogurt, and foods such as frosted cake that count as both other carbohydrate exchanges and fat exchanges. Bacon appears in the fat list, rather than the high-fat meat category.

Free foods (essentially calorie-free) include bouillon, diet soda, coffee, tea, dill pickles, and vinegar, as well as herbs and spices. Most vegetables, such as cabbage, celery, mushrooms, lettuce, and zucchini, also can be considered free foods; their minimal energy contribution need not count in the calculations when they are eaten in moderation (1 to 2 servings per meal or snack).

Using the Exchange System to Develop Daily Menus

Now let's use the Exchange System to plan a 1-day menu. Let's target an energy content of 2000 kcal, with 55% derived from carbohydrates (1100 kcal), 15% from protein (300 kcal), and 30% from fat (600 kcal). This can be translated into 2 low-fat milk exchanges, 3 vegetable exchanges, 5 fruit exchanges, 11 starch exchanges, 4 lean meat exchanges, and 6 fat exchanges (Table E-2). Note that this is only one of many possible combinations; the Exchange System offers great flexibility.

Table E-3 arbitrarily separates these exchanges into breakfast, lunch, dinner, and a snack. Breakfast includes 1 low-fat milk exchange, 2 fruit exchanges, 2 starch exchanges, and 1 fat exchange. This total corresponds to ¾ cup of a ready-to-eat breakfast cereal, 1 cup of reduced-fat milk, 1 slice of bread with 1 tsp margarine, and 1 cup of orange juice.

Lunch consists of 2 fat exchanges, 4 starch exchanges, 1 vegetable exchange, 1 low-fat milk exchange, and 2 fruit exchanges. This translates into one slice of bacon with 1 teaspoon mayonnaise on two slices of bread, with tomato—in other words, a bacon and tomato sandwich. You can also add lettuce to the sandwich. This can be considered a free vegetable choice. Add to this meal a 9-inch banana (1 exchange = 1 small banana), 1 cup of reduced-fat milk, and 6 graham crackers (2½ inches by 2½ inches). Later add a snack of ¾ oz of pretzels for another starch exchange.

Table E-3 Sample 1-Day 2000 kcal Menu Based on the Exchange System Plan*

Breakfast	
1 low-fat milk exchange	1 cup reduced-fat milk (some on cereal)
2 fruit exchanges	1 cup orange juice
2 starch exchanges	¾ cup ready-to-eat breakfast cereal, 1 piece whole-wheat toast
1 fat exchange	1 tsp soft margarine on toast
Lunch	
4 starch exchanges	2 slices whole-wheat bread, 6 graham crackers (2½ inches by 2½ inches)
2 fat exchanges	1 slice bacon, 1 tsp mayonnaise
1 vegetable exchange	1 sliced tomato
2 fruit exchanges	1 banana (9 inches)
1 low-fat milk exchange	1 cup reduced-fat milk
Snack	
1 starch exchange	¾ oz pretzels
Dinner	
4 lean meat exchanges	4 oz lean steak (well trimmed)
2 starch exchanges	1 medium baked potato
1 fat exchange	1 tsp soft margarine
2 vegetable exchanges	1 cup cooked broccoli
1 fruit exchange	1 kiwi fruit
	Coffee (if desired)
Snack	
2 starch exchanges	1 bagel
2 fat exchanges	2 tbsp regular cream cheese

*The target plan was a 2000 kcal energy intake, with 55% from carbohydrate, 15% from protein, and 30% from fat. Computer analysis indicates that this menu yielded 2040 kcal, with 53% from carbohydrate, 16% from protein, and 31% from fat—in close agreement with the targeted goals.

Dinner consists of 4 lean meat exchanges, 1 fruit exchange, 2 vegetable exchanges, 1 fat exchange, and 2 starch exchanges. This total corresponds to a 4-oz broiled steak (meat only, no bone), 1 medium baked potato (1 exchange = 1 small baked potato) with 1 tsp of margarine, 1 cup of broccoli, and 1 kiwi fruit. Coffee (if desired) is not counted, since it contains no appreciable energy.

Finally, we have a snack containing 2 starch exchanges and 2 fat exchanges. This translates into 1 bagel with 2 tbsp of regular cream cheese.

This 1-day menu is only one of many that are possible with the exchange lists. Apple juice could replace the orange juice; two apples could be exchanged for the banana. The choices are endless. Notice that an exchange diet is much easier to plan if you use individual foods, as was done here; however, the Exchange System tables list some combination foods to help you (see Appendix F). Using combination foods, such as pizza or lasagna, however, makes it more difficult to calculate the number of exchanges in a serving. For instance, lasagna typically has meat exchanges, vegetable exchanges, and starch exchanges. With practice, you will be able to tackle such complex foods (Fig. E-2). For now, using individual foods makes learning the Exchange System much easier. Finally, you might want to prove to yourself that the food choices listed in Table E-3 really meet the exchange plan. This demonstration will give you practice turning exchanges into actual food servings.

Exchange List	Total Exchanges to Be Consumed Daily	Exchanges Consumed at Each Meal		
		Breakfast	Lunch	Dinner
MILK				
VEGETABLE				
FRUIT				
STARCH				
MEAT AND SUBSTITUTES				
FAT				

Figure E-2 Record the Exchange System pattern you have chosen in the left-hand column. Then distribute the exchanges throughout the day, noting the food to be used and the serving size.

appendix f

Exchange System Lists

Milk Exchange List

Skim and Very Low-Fat Milk

(12 g carbohydrate, 8 g protein, 0–3 g fat, 90 kcal)

1 cup	skim or nonfat milk (½% and 1%)
⅓ cup	powdered (nonfat dry, before adding liquid)
½ cup	canned, evaporated skim milk
1 cup	buttermilk made from nonfat or low-fat milk
¾ cup	yogurt made from nonfat milk (plain, unflavored)
1 cup	nonfat or low-fat fruit-flavored yogurt sweetened with aspartame or nonnutritive sweetener

Low-Fat Milk

(12 g carbohydrate, 8 g protein, 5 g fat, 120 kcal)

1 cup	2% milk
¾ cup	plain low-fat yogurt (added milk solids)
1 cup	sweet acidophilus milk

Whole Milk

(12 g carbohydrate, 8 g protein, 8 g fat, 150 kcal)

1 cup	whole milk
½ cup	evaporated whole milk
1 cup	goat's milk
1 cup	kefir

Vegetable Exchange List

(5 g carbohydrate, 2 g protein, 0 g fat, 25 kcal)
1 vegetable exchange equals:

½ cup cooked vegetables or vegetable juice
1 cup raw vegetables

artichoke
artichoke hearts
asparagus
beans (green, wax, Italian)
bean sprouts
beets
broccoli
brussels sprouts
cabbage
carrots
cauliflower
celery
cucumber
eggplant
green onions or scallions
greens (e.g., collard)
kohlrabi
leeks
mixed vegetables (without corn, peas, or pasta)
mushrooms
okra
onions
pea pods
peppers (all varieties)
radishes
salad greens
sauerkraut
spinach
squash (summer)
tomato (fresh, canned, sauce)
tomato/vegetable juice
turnips
water chestnuts
watercress
zucchini

The exchange lists are the basis of a meal planning system designed by a committee of the American Diabetes Association and the American Dietetic Association. While designed primarily for people with diabetes and others who must follow special diets, the exchange lists are based on principles of good nutrition that apply to everyone.

Fruit Exchange List

Fruit

(15 g carbohydrate, 0 g protein, 0 g fat, 60 kcal)
1 fruit exchange equals:

1	apple (small)
4 rings	apple, dried
½ cup	applesauce (unsweetened)
4	apricots, fresh
8 halves	apricots, dried
1	banana (small)
¾ cup	blackberries
¾ cup	blueberries
⅓ melon	cantaloupe (small)
1 cup cubes	cantaloupe
12	cherries (3 oz)
½ cup	cherries, canned
3	dates
2	figs, fresh (3½ oz)
1½	figs, dried
½ cup	fruit cocktail
½	grapefruit
¾ cup	grapefruit sections
17	grapes (small)
1 slice	honeydew melon (or 1 cup cubes)
1	kiwi
¾ cup	mandarin orange sections
½	mango (or ½ cup cubes)
1	nectarine (small)
1	orange (small)
½	papaya (or 1 cup cubes)
1	peach, fresh (medium)
½ cup	peaches, canned
½	pear, fresh
½ cup	pear, canned
¾ cup	pineapple, fresh
½ cup	pineapple, canned
2	plums (small)
½ cup	plums, canned
3	prunes, dried
2 tbsp	raisins
1 cup	raspberries
1¼ cup	strawberries (raw, whole)
2	tangerines
1 slice	watermelon (or 1¼ cups cubes)

Fruit Juice

½ cup	apple juice/cider
⅓ cup	cranberry juice cocktail
1 cup	cranberry juice cocktail, reduced-calorie
⅓ cup	fruit juice blends, 100% juice
⅓ cup	grape juice
½ cup	grapefruit juice
½ cup	orange juice
½ cup	pineapple juice
⅓ cup	prune juice

Starch Exchange List

(15 g carbohydrate, 3 g protein, 0–1 g fat, 80 kcal)
1 starch exchange equals:

Bread

½ (1 oz)	bagel
2 slices (1½ oz)	bread, reduced-calorie
1 slice (1 oz)	bread, white, whole-wheat, pumpernickel, or rye
2 (⅔ oz)	bread sticks, crisp, 4 inches long × 3½ inches
½	English muffin
½ (1 oz)	hot dog or hamburger bun
½	pita, 6 inches across
1 slice (1 oz)	raisin bread, unfrosted
1 (1 oz)	roll, plain (small)
1	tortilla, corn, 6 inches across
1	tortilla, flour, 7–8 inches across
1	waffle, 4½ inches square, reduced-fat

Cereals and Grains

½ cup	bran cereal
½ cup	bulgur
½ cup	cereal
¾ cup	cereal, unsweetened, ready-to-eat
3 tbsp	cornmeal (dry)
⅓ cup	couscous
3 tbsp	flour (dry)
¼ cup	granola, low-fat
¼ cup	Grape-Nuts
½ cup	grits
½ cup	kasha
¼ cup	millet
¼ cup	muesli
½ cup	oats
½ cup	pasta
1½ cups	puffed cereal
½ cup	rice milk
⅓ cup	rice, white or brown
½ cup	Shredded Wheat
½ cup	sugar-frosted cereal
3 tbsp	wheat germ

Starchy Vegetables

⅓ cup	baked beans
½ cup	corn
1 (5 oz)	corn on the cob (medium)
1 cup	mixed vegetables with corn, peas, or pasta
½ cup	peas, green
½ cup	plantain

(continued)

1 (3 oz)	potato, baked or boiled (small)
½ cup	potato, mashed
1 cup	squash, winter (acorn, butternut)
½ cup	yam, sweet potato, plain

Crackers and Snacks

8	animal crackers
3	graham crackers, 2½-inch square
¾ oz	matzoh
4 slices	melba toast
24	oyster crackers
3 cups	popcorn (popped, no fat added or low-fat microwave)
¾ oz	pretzels
2	rice cakes, 4 inches across
6	saltine-type crackers
15–20 (¾ oz)	snack chips, fat-free (tortilla, potato)
2–5 (¾ oz)	whole-wheat crackers, no fat added

Dried Beans, Peas, and Lentils

(counts as 1 starch exchange plus 1 very lean meat exchange)

½ cup	beans and peas (garbanzo, pinto, kidney, white, split, black-eyed)
⅔ cup	lima beans
½ cup	lentils
3 tbsp	miso

Starchy Foods Prepared with Fat

(counts as 1 starch exchange plus 1 fat exchange)

1	biscuit, 2½ inches across
½ cup	chow mein noodles
1 (2 oz)	corn bread, 2-inch cube
6	crackers, round butter type
1 cup	croutons
16–25 (3 oz)	french-fried potatoes
¼ cup	granola
1 (1½ oz)	muffin (small)
2	pancakes, 4 inches across
3 cups	popcorn, microwave
3	sandwich crackers, cheese or peanut butter filling
⅓ cup	stuffing, bread (prepared)
2	taco shells, 6 inches across
1	waffle, 4½-inch square
4–6 (1 oz)	whole-wheat crackers, fat added

Other Carbohydrates Exchange List

One exchange equals 15 g carbohydrate, or 1 starch, or 1 fruit, or 1 milk.

Exchanges per Serving

⅟₁₂th cake	angel food cake, unfrosted	2 carbohydrates
2-inch square	brownie, unfrosted (small)	1 carbohydrate, 1 fat
2-inch square	cake, unfrosted	1 carbohydrate, 1 fat
2-inch square	cake, frosted	2 carbohydrates, 1 fat
2	cookies, fat-free (small)	1 carbohydrate
2	cookies or sandwich cookies with creme filling (small)	1 carbohydrate, 1 fat
¼ cup	cranberry sauce, jellied	1½ carbohydrates
1	cupcake, frosted (small)	2 carbohydrates, 1 fat
1 (1½ oz)	doughnut, plain cake (medium)	1½ carbohydrates, 2 fats
3¾ inches across (2 oz)	doughnuts, glazed	2 carbohydrates, 2 fats
1 bar (3 oz)	fruit juice bars, frozen, 100% juice	1 carbohydrate
1 roll (¾ oz)	fruit snacks, chewy (puréed fruit concentrate)	1 carbohydrate
1 tbsp	honey	1 carbohydrate
1 tbsp	sugar	1 carbohydrate
1 tbsp	fruit spread, 100% fruit	1 carbohydrate
½ cup	gelatin, regular	1 carbohydrate
3	gingersnaps	1 carbohydrate
1 bar	granola bar	1 carbohydrate, 1 fat
1 bar	granola bar, fat-free	2 carbohydrates

(continued)

⅓ cup	hummus	1 carbohydrate, 1 fat
½ cup	ice cream	1 carbohydrate, 2 fats
½ cup	ice cream, light	1 carbohydrate, 1 fat
½ cup	ice cream, fat-free, no sugar added	1 carbohydrate
1 tbsp	jam or jelly, regular	1 carbohydrate
1 cup	milk, chocolate, whole	2 carbohydrates, 1 fat
⅙ pie	pie, fruit, 2 crusts	3 carbohydrates, 2 fats
⅛ pie	pie, pumpkin or custard	1 carbohydrate, 2 fats
12–18 (1 oz)	potato chips	1 carbohydrate, 2 fats
½ cup	pudding, regular (made with low-fat milk)	2 carbohydrates
½ cup	pudding, sugar-free (made with low-fat milk)	1 carbohydrate
¼ cup	salad dressing, fat-free	1 carbohydrate
½ cup	sherbet, sorbet	2 carbohydrates
½ cup	spaghetti or pasta sauce, canned	1 carbohydrate, 1 fat
1 (2½ oz)	sweet roll or Danish	2½ carbohydrates, 2 fats
2 tbsp	syrup, light	1 carbohydrate
1 tbsp	syrup, regular	1 carbohydrate
6–12 (1 oz)	tortilla chips	1 carbohydrate, 2 fats
5	vanilla wafers	1 carbohydrate, 1 fat
⅓ cup	yogurt, frozen, low-fat or fat-free	1 carbohydrate, 0–1 fat
½ cup	yogurt, frozen, fat-free, no sugar added	1 carbohydrate
1 cup	yogurt, low-fat, with fruit	3 carbohydrates, 0–1 fat

Meat and Meat Substitutes Exchange List

Very Lean Meat and Substitutes List

(0 g carbohydrate, 7 g protein, 0–1 g fat, and 35 kcal)
One very lean meat exchange equals:

	Poultry
1 oz	chicken or turkey (white meat, no skin), Cornish hen (no skin)
	Fish
1 oz	fresh or frozen cod, flounder, haddock, halibut, trout; tuna, fresh or canned in water
	Shellfish
1 oz	clams, crab, lobster, scallops, shrimp, imitation shellfish
	Game
1 oz	duck or pheasant (no skin), venison, buffalo, ostrich
	Cheese with 1 g or less fat per oz
¼ cup	nonfat or low-fat cottage cheese
1 oz	fat-free cheese
	Other
1 oz	processed sandwich meats with 1 g or less fat per oz, such as deli thin, shaved meats, chipped beef, turkey, ham
2	egg whites
¼ cup	egg substitute, plain
1 oz	hot dogs with 1 g or less fat per oz
1 oz	kidney (high in cholesterol)
1 oz	sausage with 1 g or less fat per oz

Counts as one very lean meat and one starch exchange:

½ cup	dried beans, peas, lentils (cooked)

Lean Meat and Substitutes List

(0 g carbohydrate, 7 g protein, 3 g fat, and 55 kcal)
One lean meat exchange equals:

	Beef
1 oz	USDA Select or Choice grades of lean beef trimmed of fat, such as round, sirloin, and flank steak; tenderloin; roast (rib, chuck, rump); steak (T-bone, porterhouse, cubed), ground round
	Pork
1 oz	lean pork, such as fresh ham; canned, cured, or boiled ham; Canadian bacon; tenderloin, center loin chop
	Lamb
1 oz	roast, chop, leg

(continued)

	Veal
1 oz	lean chop, roast
	Poultry
1 oz	chicken, turkey (dark meat, no skin), chicken white meat (with skin), domestic duck or goose (well drained of fat, no skin)
	Fish
1 oz	herring (uncreamed or smoked)
6	oysters (medium)
1 oz	salmon (fresh or canned), catfish
2	sardines (canned, medium)
1 oz	tuna (canned in oil, drained)
	Game
1 oz	goose (no skin), rabbit
	Cheese
¼ cup	4.5%–fat cottage cheese
2 tbsp	grated Parmesan
1 oz	cheeses with 3 g or less fat per oz
	Other
1½ oz	hot dogs with 3 g or less fat per oz
1 oz	processed sandwich meat with 3 g or less fat per oz, such as turkey pastrami or kielbasa
1 oz	liver, heart (high in cholesterol)

Medium-Fat Meat and Substitutes List

(0 g carbohydrate, 7 g protein, 5 g fat, and 75 kcal)
One medium-fat meat exchange equals:

	Beef
1 oz	most beef products (ground beef, meatloaf, corned beef, short ribs, prime grades of meat trimmed of fat, such as prime rib)
	Pork
1 oz	top loin, chop, Boston butt, cutlet
	Lamb
1 oz	rib roast, ground
	Veal
1 oz	cutlet (ground or cubed, unbreaded)
	Poultry
1 oz	chicken dark meat (with skin), ground turkey or ground chicken, fried chicken (with skin)
	Fish
1 oz	any fried fish product
	Cheese (with 5 g or less fat per oz)
1 oz	feta
1 oz	mozzarella
¼ cup (2 oz)	ricotta
	Other
1	egg (high in cholesterol, limit to 3 per week)
1 oz	sausage with 5 g or less fat per oz
1 cup	soy milk
¼ cup	tempeh
4 oz or ½ cup	tofu

High-Fat Meat and Substitutes List

(0 g carbohydrate, 7 g protein, 8 g fat, and 100 kcal)
One high-fat meat exchange equals:

	Pork
1 oz	spareribs, ground pork, pork sausage
	Cheese
1 oz	all regular cheeses, such as American, cheddar, Monterey Jack, Swiss
	Other
1 oz	processed sandwich meats with 8 g or less fat per oz, such as bologna, pimento loaf, salami
1 oz	sausage, such as bratwurst, Italian, knockwurst, Polish, smoked
1 (10 per pound)	hot dog (turkey or chicken)
3 slices (20 slices per pound)	bacon

Counts as one high-fat meat plus one fat exchange:

1 (10 per pound)	hot dog (beef, pork, or combination)
2 tbsp	peanut butter (contains unsaturated fat)

Fat Exchange List

Monosaturated Fats List

(5 g fat and 45 kcal)
One exchange equals:

⅛ (1 oz)	avocado (medium)
1 tsp	oil (canola, olive, peanut)
	olives:
8	ripe, black (large)
10	green, stuffed (large)

(continued)

6 nuts	almonds, cashews
6 nuts	mixed (50% peanuts)
10 nuts	peanuts
4 halves	pecans
2 tsp	peanut butter, smooth or crunchy
1 tbsp	sesame seeds
2 tsp	tahini paste

Polyunsaturated Fats List

(5 g fat and 45 kcal)
One exchange equals:

	margarine:
1 tsp	stick, tub, or squeeze
1 tbsp	lower-fat (30 to 50% vegetable oil)
	mayonnaise:
1 tsp	regular
1 tbsp	reduced-fat
4 halves	nuts, walnuts, English
1 tsp	oil (corn, safflower, soybean)
	salad dressing:
1 tbsp	regular
2 tbsp	reduced-fat
	Miracle Whip Salad Dressing®:
2 tsp	regular
1 tbsp	reduced-fat
1 tbsp	seeds: pumpkin, sunflower

Saturated Fats List

(5 g fat and 45 kcal)
One exchange equals:

1 slice (20 slices per pound)	bacon, cooked
1 tsp	bacon, grease
	butter:
1 tsp	stick
2 tsp	whipped
1 tbsp	reduced-fat
2 tbsp	chitterlings, boiled (½ oz)
2 tbsp	coconut, sweetened, shredded
2 tbsp	cream, half and half
	cream cheese:
1 tbsp (½ oz)	regular
2 tbsp (1 oz)	reduced-fat
1 tsp	fatback, salt pork,* shortening, or lard
	sour cream:
2 tbsp	regular
3 tbsp	reduced-fat

Free Foods List

A *free food* is any food or drink that contains less than 20 kcal or less than 5 g of carbohydrate per serving. Foods with a serving size listed should be limited to three servings per day. Foods listed without a serving size can be eaten as often as you like.

Fat-Free or Reduced-Fat Foods

1 tbsp	cream cheese, fat-free
1 tbsp	creamers, nondairy, liquid
2 tsp	creamers, nondairy, powdered
1 tbsp	mayonnaise, fat-free
1 tsp	mayonnaise, reduced-fat
4 tbsp	margarine, fat-free
1 tsp	margarine, reduced-fat
1 tbsp	Miracle Whip®, nonfat
1 tsp	Miracle Whip®, reduced-fat nonstick cooking spray
1 tbsp	salad dressing, fat-free
2 tbsp	salad dressing, fat-free, Italian
¼ cup	salsa
1 tbsp	sour cream, fat-free, reduced-fat
2 tbsp	whipped topping, regular or light

Sugar-Free or Low-Sugar Foods

1 candy	candy, hard, sugar-free
	gelatin dessert, sugar-free
	gelatin, unflavored
	gum, sugar-free

(continued)

*Use a piece 1 in × 1 in × ¼ in if you plan to eat the fatback cooked with vegetables. Use a piece 2 in × 1 in × ½ in when eating only the vegetables with the fatback removed.

2 tsp	jam or jelly, low-sugar, or light sugar substitutes[†]	2 tbsp	syrup, sugar-free

Drinks

	bouillon, broth, consommé		coffee
	bouillon or broth, low-sodium		diet soft drinks, sugar-free
	carbonated or mineral water		drink mixes, sugar-free
	club soda		tea
1 tbsp	cocoa powder, unsweetened		tonic water, sugar-free

Condiments

1 tbsp	catsup	1½	pickles, dill (large)
	horseradish		soy sauce, regular or light
	lemon juice	1 tbsp	taco sauce
	lime juice		vinegar
	mustard		

Seasonings

flavoring extracts
garlic
herbs, fresh or dried
pimento
spices
Tabasco® or hot pepper sauce
wine, used in cooking
worcestershire sauce

Combination Foods List

	Entrées	**Exchanges per Serving**
1 cup (8 oz)	tuna noodle casserole, lasagna, spaghetti with meatballs, chili with beans, macaroni and cheese	2 carbohydrates, 2 medium-fat meats
2 cups (16 oz)	chow mein (without noodles or rice)	1 carbohydrate, 2 lean meats
¼ of 10 inch (5 oz)	pizza, cheese, thin crust	2 carbohydrates, 2 medium-fat meats, 1 fat
¼ of 10 inch (5 oz)	pizza, meat topping, thin crust	2 carbohydrates, 2 medium-fat meats, 2 fats
1 (7 oz)	pot pie	2 carbohydrates, 1 medium-fat meat, 4 fats
	Frozen Entrées	
1 (11 oz)	salisbury steak with gravy, mashed potato	2 carbohydrates, 3 medium-fat meats, 3-4 fats
1 (11 oz)	turkey with gravy, mashed potato, dressing	2 carbohydrates, 2 medium-fat meats, 2 fats
1 (8 oz)	entrée with less than 300 kcal	2 carbohydrates, 3 lean meats
	Soups	
1 cup	bean	1 carbohydrate, 1 very lean meat
1 cup (8 oz)	cream (made with water)	1 carbohydrate, 1 fat
½ cup (4 oz)	split pea (made with water)	1 carbohydrate
1 cup (8 oz)	tomato (made with water)	1 carbohydrate
1 cup (8 oz)	vegetable beef, chicken noodle, or other broth-type	1 carbohydrate

[†]Sugar substitutes, alternatives, or replacements that are approved by the Food and Drug Administration (FDA) are safe to use. Common brand names include:

Equal® (aspartame)
Sprinkle Sweet® (saccharin)
Sweet One® (acesulfame-K)
Sweet-10® (saccharin)
Sugar Twin® (saccharin)
Sweet 'N Low® (saccharin)
Splenda® (sucralose)

Fast (Quick-Service) Foods

	Exchanges per Serving	
2	burritos with beef	4 carbohydrates, 2 medium-fat meats, 2 fats
6	chicken nuggets	1 carbohydrate, 2 medium-fat meats, 1 fat
1 each	chicken breast and wing, breaded and fried	1 carbohydrate, 4 medium-fat meats, 2 fats
1	fish sandwich/tartar sauce	3 carbohydrates, 1 medium-fat meat, 3 fats
20–25	french fries, thin	2 carbohydrates, 2 fats
1	hamburger (regular)	2 carbohydrates, 2 medium-fat meats
1	hamburger (large)	2 carbohydrates, 3 medium-fat meats, 1 fat
1	hot dog with bun	1 carbohydrate, 1 high-fat meat, 1 fat
1	individual pan pizza	5 carbohydrates, 3 medium-fat meats, 3 fats
1	soft-serve cone (medium)	2 carbohydrates, 1 fat
1 sub (6 inches)	submarine sandwich	3 carbohydrates, 1 vegetable, 2 medium-fat meats, 1 fat
1 (6 oz)	taco, hard shell	2 carbohydrates, 2 medium-fat meats, 2 fats
1 (3 oz)	taco, soft shell	1 carbohydrate, 1 medium-fat meat, 1 fat

appendix g

Dietary Intake and Energy Expenditure Assessment

Although it may seem overwhelming at first, it is actually very easy to track the foods you eat. One tip is to record foods and beverages consumed as soon as possible after the actual time of consumption.

I. Fill in the food record form that follows. This appendix contains a blank copy (see the completed example in Table G-1). Then, to estimate the nutrient values of the foods you are eating, consult food labels and the food composition table in this book (Appendix N), or use the nutrition software package available with this book. If these resources do not have the serving size you need, adjust the value. If you drink ½ cup of orange juice, for example, but a table has values only for 1 cup, halve all values before you record them. Then, consider pooling all the same food to save time; if you drink a cup of 1% milk three times throughout the day, enter your milk consumption only once as 3 cups. As you record your intake for use on the nutrient analysis form that follows, consider the following tips:

- Measure and record the amounts of foods eaten in portion sizes of cups, teaspoons, tablespoons, ounces, slices, or inches (or convert metric units to these units).
- Record brand names of all food products, such as "Quick Quaker Oats."
- Measure and record all those little extras, such as gravies, salad dressings, taco sauces, pickles, jelly, sugar, catsup, and margarine.
- For beverages
  —List the type of milk, such as whole, skim, 1%, evaporated, chocolate, or reconstituted dry.
  —Indicate whether fruit juice is fresh, frozen, or canned.
  —Indicate type for other beverages, such as fruit drink, fruit-flavored drink, Kool-Aid, and hot chocolate made with water or milk.
- For fruits
  —Indicate whether fresh, frozen, dried, or canned.
  —If whole, record number eaten and size with approximate measurements (such as 1 apple—3 in. in diameter).
  —Indicate whether processed in water, light syrup, or heavy syrup.
- For vegetables
  —Indicate whether fresh, frozen, dried, or canned.
  —Record as portion of cup, teaspoon, or tablespoon, or as pieces (such as carrot sticks—4 in. long, ½ in. thick).
  —Record preparation method.
- For cereals
  —Record cooked cereals in portions of tablespoon or cup (a level measurement after cooking).
  —Record dry cereal in level portions of tablespoon or cup.

—If margarine, milk, sugar, fruit, or something else is added, measure and record amount and type.

- For breads
  —Indicate whether whole wheat, rye, white, and so on.
  —Measure and record number and size of portion (biscuit—2 in. across, 1 in. thick; slice of homemade rye bread—3 in. by 4 in., ¼ in. thick).
  —Sandwiches: list *all* ingredients (lettuce, mayonnaise, tomato, and so on).
- For meat, fish, poultry, and cheese
  —Give size (length, width, thickness) in inches or weight in ounces after cooking for meat, fish, and poultry (such as cooked hamburger patty—3 in. across, ½ in. thick).
  —Give size (length, width, thickness) in inches or weight in ounces for cheese.
  —Record measurements only for the cooked, edible part—without bone or fat that is left on the plate.
  —Describe how meat, poultry, or fish was prepared.
- For eggs
  —Record as soft or hard cooked, fried, scrambled, poached, or omelet.
  —If milk, butter, or drippings are used, specify kinds and amount.
- For desserts
  —List commercial brand or "homemade" or "bakery" under brand.
  —Purchased candies, cookies, and cakes: specify kind and size.
  —Measure and record portion size of cakes, pies, and cookies by specifying thickness, diameter, and width or length, depending on the item.

Time	Minutes Spent Eating	M or S*	H† (0–3)	Activity While Eating	Place of Eating	Food and Quantity	Others Present	Reason for Choice

*M or S: Meal or snack

†H: Degree of hunger (0 = none; 3 = maximum)

Table G-1 One Day's Food Record—This Activity Can Help You Understand More About Your Food Habits

Time	Minutes Spent Eating	M or S*	H† (0–3)	Activity While Eating	Place of Eating	Food and Quantity	Others Present	Reason for Choice
7:10 A.M.	15	M	2	Standing, fixing lunch	Kitchen	orange juice, 1 cup Crispix, 1 cup 2% milk, ½ cup Sugar, 2 tsp Black coffee	—	Health Habit Health Taste Habit
10:00 A.M.	4	S	1	Sitting, taking notes	Classroom	Diet cola, 12 oz	Class	Weight control
12:15 P.M.	40	M	2	Sitting, talking	Student union	Chicken sandwich with lettuce and mayonnaise (3 oz chicken, 2 slices of bread, 2 tsp mayonnaise) Pear, 1 2% milk, 1 cup	Friends	Taste Health Health
2:30 P.M.	10	S	1	Sitting, studying	Library	Regular cola, 12 oz	Friend	Hunger
6:30 P.M.	35	M	3	Sitting, talking	Kitchen	Pork chop, 1 Baked potato, 1 Margarine, 2 tbsp Lettuce and tomato salad Ranch dressing, 2 tbsp Peas, ½ cup Whole milk, 1 cup Cherry pie, 1 piece	Boyfriend	Convenience Health Taste Health Taste Health Habit Taste
9:10 P.M.	10	S	2	Sitting, studying	Living room	Apple, 1 Glass mineral water, 1	—	Weight control Weight control

*M or S: Meal or snack

†H: Degree of hunger (0 = none; 3 = maximum)

II. Now complete the nutrient analysis form as shown, using your food record. A blank copy of this form is printed on three pages ahead for your use. Note that the diet analysis software available with this book will create such a table for you if you simply enter all food eaten.

Nutrient Analysis Form (Sample)

Name	Quantity	kcal	Protein (g)	Carbohydrates (g)	Fiber (g)	Total fat (g)	Monounsaturated fat (g)	Polyunsaturated fat (g)	Saturated fat (g)	Cholesterol (g)	Calcium (mg)	Iron (mg)
Egg bagel, 3.5-in. diameter	1 ea.	180	7.45	34.7	0.748	1.00	0.286	0.400	0.171	44.0	20.0	2.10
Jelly	1 tbsp	49.0	0.018	12.7	—	0.018	0.005	0.005	0.005	—	2.00	0.120
Orange juice, prepared fresh or frozen	1½ cup	165	2.52	40.2	1.49	0.210	0.037	0.045	0.025	—	33.0	0.411
Cheeseburger, McDonald's	2 ea.	636	30.2	57.0	0.460	32.0	12.2	2.18	13.3	80.0	338	5.68
French fries, McDonald's	1 order	220	3.00	26.1	4.19	11.5	4.37	0.570	4.61	8.57	9.10	0.605
Cola beverage, regular	1½ cup	151	—	38.5	—	—	—	—	—	—	9.00	0.120
Pork loin chop, broiled, lean	4 oz	261	36.2	—	—	11.9	5.35	1.43	4.09	112	5.67	1.04
Baked potato with skin	1 ea.	220	4.65	51.0	3.90	0.200	0.004	0.087	0.052	—	20.0	2.75
Peas, frozen, cooked	½ cup	63.0	4.12	11.4	3.61	0.220	0.019	0.103	0.039	—	19.0	1.25
Margarine, regular or soft, 80% fat	20 g	143	0.160	0.100	—	16.1	5.70	6.92	2.76	—	5.29	—
Iceberg lettuce, chopped	2 cup	14.6	1.13	2.34	1.68	0.212	0.008	0.112	0.028	—	21.2	0.560
French dressing	2 oz	300	0.318	3.63	0.431	32.0	14.2	12.4	4.94	—	7.10	0.227
2% low-fat milk	1 cup	121	8.12	11.7	—	4.78	1.35	0.170	2.92	22.0	297	0.120
Graham crackers	2 ea.	60.0	1.04	10.8	1.40	1.46	0.600	0.400	0.400	—	6.00	0.367
Totals		2584	99.0	300	17.9	112	44.1	24.8	33.4	266	792	15.4
RDA or related nutrient standard*		2900	58		—						1000	8
% of nutrient needs		89	170		—						79	193

Abbreviations: g = grams, mg = milligrams, μg = micrograms

*Values from inside cover. The values listed are for a male age 19 years. Note that number of kcal is just a rough estimate. It is better to base energy needs on actual energy output.

†In RAE units. Table values generally are in RE units today since the food values have not been updated to reflect the latest vitamin A standards. RAE equal RE for foods with preformed vitamin A, such as for the pork chop, but RAE are only about half the RE listed for foods with provitamin A carotenoids, such as for the peas (see Chapter 9 for details).

‡Amounts refer to actual folate content, rather than dietary folate equivalents (DFE). This difference is important to consider if the food contains added synthetic folic acid as part of enrichment or fortification. Any such folic acid is absorbed about twice as much as the folate present naturally in foods. So the total contribution of folate in the food in comparison to human needs will be greater than if all the folate was naturally in the food product. Nutrient analysis tables have yet to be updated to reflect the dietary folate equivalents of products (see Chapter 10 for more details).

Nutrient Analysis Form (Sample) cont'd

Magnesium (mg)	Phosphorus (mg)	Potassium (mg)	Sodium (mg)	Zinc (mg)	Vitamin A (RE)	Vitamin C (mg)	Vitamin E (mg)	Thiamin (mg)	Riboflavin (mg)	Niacin (mg)	Vitamin B-6 (mg)	Folate (μg)	Vitamin B-12 (μg)
18.0	61.0	65.0	300	0.612	7.00	—	1.80	2.58	0.197	2.40	0.030	16.3	0.065
0.720	1.00	16.0	4.00	—	0.200	0.710	0.016	0.002	0.005	0.036	0.005	2.00	—
36.0	60.0	711	3.00	0.192	28.5	145	0.714	0.300	0.060	0.750	0.165	163	
45.8	410	314	1460	5.20	134	4.10	0.560	0.600	0.480	8.66	0.230	42.0	1.82
26.7	101	564	109	0.320	5.00	12.5	0.203	0.122	0.020	2.26	0.218	19.0	0.027
3.00	46.0	4.00	15.0	0.049	—	—	—	—	—	—	—	—	—
34.0	277	476	88.2	2.54	3.15	0.454	0.405	1.30	0.350	6.28	0.535	6.77	0.839
55.0	115	844	16.0	0.650	—	26.1	0.100	0.216	0.067	3.32	0.701	22.2	—
23.0	72.0	134	70.0	0.750	53.4	7.90	0.400	0.226	0.140	1.18	0.090	46.9	—
0.467	4.06	7.54	216	0.041	199	0.028	2.19	0.002	0.006	0.004	0.002	0.211	0.017
10.1	22.4	177	10.1	0.246	37.0	4.36	0.120	0.052	0.034	0.210	0.044	62.8	—
5.81	3.63	7.03	666	0.045	0.023	—	15.9	—	—	—	0.006	—	—
33.0	232	377	122	0.963	140	2.32	0.080	0.095	0.403	0.210	0.105	12.0	0.888
6.00	20.0	36.0	86.0	0.113	—	—	—	0.020	0.030	0.600	0.011	1.80	—
298	1425	3732	3165	11.7	607	204	22.5	5.52	1.79	25.9	2.14	395	3.65
400	700	2000	500	11	900†	90	15	1.2	1.3	16	1.3	400‡	2.4
75	204	187	633	106	67	226	150	450	138	162	160	99	152

Nutrient Analysis Form

Name	Quantity	kcal	Protein (g)	Carbohydrates (g)	Fiber (g)	Total fat (g)	Monounsaturated fat (g)	Polyunsaturated fat (g)	Saturated fat (g)	Cholesterol (g)	Calcium (mg)	Iron (mg)
Totals												
RDA or related nutrient standard*												
% of nutrient needs												

*Values from inside cover. Note that number of kcals is just a rough estimate. It is better to base energy needs on actual energy output.

†Use RAE values, even though food table is based on RE units.

‡Use DFE values, even though the food is based on total folate content, irrespective of natural or synthetic source.

Nutrient Analysis Form cont'd

Magnesium (mg)	Phosphorus (mg)	Potassium (mg)	Sodium (mg)	Zinc (mg)	Vitamin A (RE)	Vitamin C (mg)	Vitamin E (mg)	Thiamin (mg)	Riboflavin (mg)	Niacin (mg)	Vitamin B-6 (mg)	Folate (μg)	Vitamin B-12 (μg)
					†							‡	

III. Complete the following table as you summarize your dietary intake.

Percentage of kcal from Protein, Fat, Carbohydrate, and Alcohol

Intake

Protein (P):	____ g/day × 4 kcal/g	=	(P) ____ kcal/day
Fat (F):	____ g/day × 9 kcal/g	=	(F) ____ kcal/day
Carbohydrate (C):	____ g/day × 4 kcal/g	=	(C) ____ kcal/day
Alcohol (A):			(A) ____ kcal/day*
	Total kcal (T)/day	=	(T) ____ kcal/day

Percentage of kcal from protein:

$$\frac{(P)}{(T)} \times 100 = \_\_\_\_ \%$$

Percentage of kcal from fat:

$$\frac{(F)}{(T)} \times 100 = \_\_\_\_ \%$$

Percentage of kcal from carbohydrate:

$$\frac{(C)}{(T)} \times 100 = \_\_\_\_ \%$$

Percentage of kcal from alcohol:

$$\frac{(A)}{(T)} \times 100 = \_\_\_\_ \%$$

NOTE: The four percentages can total 99, 100, or 101, depending on the way in which figures were rounded off earlier.

*To calculate how many kcal in a beverage are from alcohol, look up the beverage in Appendix N. Determine how many kcal are from carbohydrate (multiply carbohydrate grams times 4), fat (fat grams times 9), and protein (protein grams times 4). The remaining kcal are from alcohol.

IV. Use the table on the following page to again record your food intake for one day, placing each food item in the correct category of the Food Guide Pyramid, with the correct number of servings (see Table 2-8 in Chapter 2). Note that a food such as toast with margarine contributes to two categories—namely, to the bread, cereal, rice, and pasta group and to the fats, oils, and sweets group. You can expect that many food choices will contribute to more than one group. Indicate the number of servings from the Food Guide Pyramid that each food yields.

Indicate the Number of Servings from the Food Guide Pyramid That Each Food Yields

Food or Beverage	Amount Eaten	Milk, Yogurt, and Cheese	Meat, Poultry, Fish, Dry Beans, Eggs, and Nuts	Fruits	Vegetables	Bread, Cereal, Rice, and Pasta	Fats, Oils, and Sweets
Group totals							
Recommended servings							In moderation
Shortages in numbers of servings							

V. Evaluation. Are there weaknesses suggested in your nutrient intake that correspond to missing servings in the Food Guide Pyramid? Consider replacing the missing servings to improve your nutrient intake.

VI. For the same day you keep your food record, also keep a 24-hour record of your activities. Include sleeping, sitting, and walking, as well as the obvious forms of exercise. Calculate your energy expenditure for these activities using Table 13-7 in Chapter 13 or the software available with this book. Try to substitute a similar activity if your particular activity is not listed. Calculate the total kcal you used for the day (total for column 3). Following is an example of an activity record. A blank form follows for your use. Ask your professor whether you are to turn in the form or the activity printout from the software.

Weight (kg)*: 70 kg

		Energy Cost		
Activity	Time (Minutes): Convert to Hours	Column 1 kcal/kg/hr (from Table 13-7)	Column 2 (Column 1 × Time)	Column 3 (Column 2 × Weight in kg)
Brisk walking	(60 min) 1 hr	4.4	(× 1) = 4.4	(× 70) = 308

*lb/2.2

Weight (kg)*:

		Energy Cost		
Activity	Time (Minutes): Convert to Hours	Column 1 kcal/kg/hr (from Table 13-7)	Column 2 (Column 1 × Time)	Column 3 (Column 2 × Weight in kg)

Total kcal used (from adding all of column 3)

*lb/2.2

appendix h

Fatty Acids, Including Omega-3 Fatty Acids, in Foods

Chain Length, Number, and Site of Double Bonds for Common Fatty Acids

Common Name of Fatty Acid	Number of Carbon Atoms and Number and Site of Double Bond(s), Counting from Methyl End ($-CH_3$) if Appropriate
Saturated Fatty Acids (No Double Bonds)	
Formic	1
Acetic	2
Propionic	3
Butyric	4
Valeric	5
Caproic	6
Caprylic	8
Capric	10
Lauric	12
Myristic	14
Palmitic	16
Stearic	18
Unsaturated Fatty Acids	
Oleic	18:1 (9-10) ω-9
Linoleic	18:2 (6-7, 9-10) ω-6
Alpha-linolenic	18:3 (3-4, 6-7, 9-10) ω-3
Arachidonic	20:4 (6-7, 9-10, 12-13, 15-16) ω-6
Eicosapentaenoic	20:5 (3-4, 6-7, 9-10, 12-13, 15-16) ω-3
Docosahexaenoic	22:6 (3-4, 6-7, 9-10, 12-13, 15-16, 18-19) ω-3

Fatty Acid Composition of Selected Foods*

	Fatty Acid†									
	Saturated									
Food Item	<C12:0	C12:0	14:0	C16:0	C18:0	C18:1 ω-9	C18:2 ω-6	C18:3 ω-3	C20:5 ω-3	C22:6 ω-3
Fats and Oils		Lauric Acid	Myristic Acid	Palmitic Acid	Stearic Acid	Oleic Acid	Linoleic Acid	Alpha-Linolenic Acid	EPA‡	DHA‡
Beef tallow	—	0.90	3.70	24.9	18.9	36.0	3.1	0.60	—	—
Butter	7.0	2.20	8.10	21.3	9.8	20.4	1.8	1.20	—	—
Cocoa butter	—	—	0.10	25.4	33.2	32.6	2.8	0.10	—	—
Corn oil	—	—	—	11.0	2.0	25.0	58.0	0.70	—	—
Cottonseed oil	—	—	0.80	22.7	2.3	17.0	51.5	0.20	—	—
Lard	0.1	0.20	1.30	23	15.2	40.9	9.7	1.10	—	—
Olive oil	—	—	—	11.0	2.5	72.5	7.5	0.60	—	—
Palm kernel oil	7	47.00	16.40	8.1	2.8	11.4	1.6	—	—	—
Palm oil	—	0.10	1.00	43.5	4.3	36.6	9.1	0.20	—	—
Safflower oil	—	—	—	4.2	1.9	14.4	74.6	—	—	—
Shortenings	0.2	0.10	1.60	23.0	15.2	41.0	9.7	1.10	—	—
Margarine, stick	—	—	0.20	9.7	6.0	36.0	24.3	1.10	—	—
Margarine, tub	—	—	0.100	8.7	5.0	37.3	24.6	1.10	—	—
Canola oil	—	—	—	4.0	1.8	56.0	20.3	9.30	—	—
Soybean oil	—	—	—	14.0	4.0	29.0	45.0	3.00	—	—
Coconut oil	14.0	45.00	17.00	8.2	3.0	6.0	1.8	—	—	—
Peanut oil	—	—	0.100	9.5	2.2	44.8	32.0	—	—	—
Cod liver oil	—	—	3.6	10.6	2.8	20.6	0.9	0.9	6.9	11.0
Menhaden oil	—	—	8.0	15.1	3.8	14.6	2.2	1.5	13.2	4.9
Meat, Fish, and Poultry										
Beef, lean only, uncooked	—	0.04	0.50	4.0	2.1	6.5	0.4	0.16	—	—
Chicken, white meat, cooked	—	0.03	0.01	2.1	0.7	3.5	2.1	0.10	0.01	0.05
Salmon, coho, cooked	—	—	0.18	0.8	0.3	1.7	0.2	0.40	0.40	1.40
Tuna, light, canned in water	—	—	0.02	0.2	0.1	0.1	—	0.02	0.05	0.20
Nuts and Seeds										
Walnuts	—	—	—	4.4	1.6	8.8	38	9	—	—
Flaxseeds	—	—	—	1.8	1.4	6.9	4.3	18.1	—	—

From USDA Nutrient Database for Standard Reference, Release 13.

*Only major fatty acids are presented.

†All values represent grams per 100 g edible portion.

‡EPA eicosapentaenoic acid } fish oil fatty acids
DHA docosahexaenoic acid }

appendix i

The 1983 Metropolitan Life Insurance Company Height-Weight Table and Determination of Frame Size

1983 Metropolitan Life Insurance Company Height-Weight Table*†

Women					Men				
Height		Frame			Height		Frame		
Ft.	In.	Small	Medium	Large	Ft.	In.	Small	Medium	Large
4	10	102–111	109–121	118–131	5	2	128–134	131–141	138–150
4	11	103–113	111–123	120–134	5	3	130–136	133–143	140–153
5	0	104–115	113–126	122–137	5	4	132–138	135–145	142–156
5	1	106–118	115–129	125–140	5	5	134–140	137–148	144–160
5	2	108–121	118–132	128–143	5	6	136–142	139–151	146–164
5	3	111–124	121–135	131–147	5	7	138–145	142–154	149–168
5	4	114–127	124–138	134–151	5	8	140–148	145–157	152–172
5	5	117–130	127–141	137–155	5	9	142–151	148–160	155–176
5	6	120–133	130–144	140–159	5	10	144–154	151–163	158–180
5	7	123–136	133–147	143–163	5	11	146–157	154–166	161–184
5	8	126–139	136–150	146–167	6	0	149–160	157–170	164–188
5	9	129–142	139–153	149–170	6	1	152–164	160–174	168–192
5	10	132–145	142–156	152–173	6	2	155–168	164–178	172–197
5	11	135–148	145–159	155–176	6	3	158–172	167–182	176–202
6	0	138–151	148–162	158–179	6	4	162–176	171–187	181–207

*Based on a weight-height mortality study conducted by the Society of Actuaries and the Association of Life Insurance Medical Directors of America, Metropolitan Life Insurance Medical Directors of America, Metropolitan Life Insurance Company, revised 1983.

†Weights at ages 25 to 59 based on lowest mortality. Height includes 1-in. heel. Weight for women includes 3 lb for indoor clothing. Weight for men includes 5 lb for indoor clothing.

Using the Metropolitan Life Insurance Table to Estimate Healthy Weight

The Metropolitan Life Insurance table is a common method for estimating healthy weight. The table lists for any height the weight that is associated with a maximum life span. The table does not tell the healthiest weight for a living person; it simply lists the weight associated with longevity.

There are many criticisms of this table. These stem from the inclusion of some people and the exclusion of others. For example, only policyholders of life insurance are included. In addition, smokers are included, but anyone over the age of 60 is excluded. Weight is only measured at the time of purchase of insurance, and there is no follow-up. All of these factors contribute to the fact that this table is to be used only as a rough screening tool; not meeting the exact recommendations should not be cause for alarm.

To diagnose overweight or obesity using the table, calculate the percentage of the Metropolitan Life Insurance table weight. Use the midpoint of a weight range for a specific height.

$$\frac{(\text{Current wt.} - \text{wt. from table})}{\text{Weight from table}} \times 100$$

Example:

$$\frac{140 - 120}{120} \times 100 = 17\% \text{ over standard}$$

Overweight can be defined as weighing at least 10% more than the weight listed on the table. Obesity weighs in at 20% more than that listed on the table. Moreover, this measure of obesity comes in degrees. Whereas mild obesity carries little health risk, severe obesity raises overall health risk twelvefold.

Degrees of Obesity

% Over Healthy Body Weight	Form of Obesity
20–40%	Mild
41–99%	Moderate
100%+	Severe

Determining Frame Size

Method 1

Height is recorded without shoes.

Wrist circumference is measured just beyond the bony (styloid) process at the wrist joint on the right arm, using a tape measure.

The following formula is used:

$$r = \frac{\text{Height (cm)}}{\text{Wrist circumference (cm)}}$$

Frame size can be determined as follows:†

Males	Females
$r > 10.4$ small	$r > 11$ small
$r = 9.6$–10.4 medium	$r = 10.1$–11 medium
$r < 9.6$ large	$r < 10.1$ large

†From Grant JP: *Handbook of total parenteral nutrition*. Philadelphia: WB Saunders, 1980.

Method 2

The patient's right arm is extended forward, perpendicular to the body, with the arm bent so the angle at the elbow forms 90 degrees, with the fingers pointing up and the palm turned away from the body. The greatest breadth across the elbow joint is measured with a sliding caliper along the axis of the upper arm, on the two prominent bones on either side of the elbow. This is recorded as the elbow breadth. The following tables give elbow breadth measurements for medium-framed men and women of various heights. Measurements lower than those listed indicate a small frame size; higher measurements indicate a large frame size.‡

Men		Women	
Height in 1″ Heels	Elbow Breadth	Height in 1″ Heels	Elbow Breadth
5′2″–5′3″	2½–2⅞″	4′10″–4′11″	2¼–2½″
5′4″–5′7″	2⅝–2⅞″	5′0″–5′3″	2¼–2½″
5′8″–5′11″	2¾–3″	5′4″–5′7″	2⅜–2⅝″
6′0″–6′3″	2¾–3¼″	5′8″–5′11″	2⅜–2⅝″
6′4″ and over	2⅞–3¼″	6′0″ and over	2½–2¾″

‡From Metropolitan Life Insurance Co., 1983.

appendix j

Caffeine Content of Foods

Beverages	Milligrams
Carbonated Beverages*	
Cherry Coke, Coca-Cola—12 fl oz (370 g)	46
Cherry cola, Slice—12 fl oz (360 g)	48
Cherry RC—12 fl oz (360 g)	12
Coca-Cola—12 fl oz (370 g)	46
Coca-Cola Classic—12 fl oz (369 g)	46
Cola, RC—12 fl oz (360 g)	18
Mello Yello—12 fl oz (372 g)	52
Mr. Pibb—12 fl oz (369 g)	40
Mountain Dew—12 fl oz (360 g)	54
Dr. Pepper-type soda—12 fl oz (368 g)	41
Pepsi Cola—12 fl oz (360 g)	38
Carbonated Beverages, Low-Calorie*	
Diet Cherry Coke, Coca-Cola—12 fl oz (354 g)	46
Diet cherry cola, Slice—12 fl oz (360 g)	41
Diet Coke, Coca-Cola—12 fl oz (354 g)	46
Diet cola, aspartame-sweetened—12 fl oz (355 g)	50
Diet Pepsi—12 fl oz (360 g)	36
Diet RC—12 fl oz (360 g)	48
Coffee	
Brewed—6 fl oz (177 g)	103
Instant powder—1 tsp (1.8 g)	57
Decaffeinated—1 rounded tsp (1.8 g)	2
With chicory—1 tsp (1.8 g)	37
Prepared from instant powder—6 fl oz & 1 tsp powder (179 g)	57
Amaretto, General Foods—6 fl oz & 11.5 g powder (189 g)	60
Amaretto, sugar-free, General Foods—6 fl oz water & 7.7 g powder (185 g)	60
Decaffeinated—6 fl oz water & 1 tsp powder (179 g)	2
Francais, General Foods—6 fl oz water & 11.5 g powder (189 g)	53
Francais, sugar-free, General Foods—6 fl oz water & 7.7 g powder (185 g)	59
Irish creme, General Foods—6 fl oz water & 12.8 g powder (190 g)	53
Irish creme, sugar free, General Foods—6 fl oz water & 7.1 g powder (185 g)	48
Irish mocha mint, General Foods—6 fl oz water & 11.5 g powder (189 g)	27
Irish mocha mint, sugar-free, General Foods—6 fl oz water & 6.4 g powder (189 g)	25
Orange cappuccino, General Foods—6 fl oz water & 14 g powder (191 g)	73
Orange cappuccino, sugar-free, General Foods—6 fl oz water & 6.7 g powder (184 g)	71
Suisse mocha, General Foods—6 fl oz water & 11.5 g powder (189 g)	41
Suisse mocha, sugar-free, General Foods—6 fl oz water & 6.4 g powder (184 g)	40
Vienna, General Foods—6 fl oz water & 14 g powder (191 g)	56
Vienna, sugar-free, General Foods—6 fl oz water & 6.7 g powder (184 g)	55
with chicory—6 fl oz water & 1 tsp powder (179 g)	38
Tea, Hot/Iced	
Brewed 3 min—6 fl oz water (178 g)	36
Instant powder—1 tsp (0.7 g)	31
With lemon flavor—1 rounded tsp (1.4 g)	25
With sugar & lemon flavor—3 tsp (23 g)	29
With sodium saccharin & lemon flavor—2 tsp (1.6 g)	36
Prepared from instant powder	
1 tsp powder in 8 fl oz water (237 g)	31
Crystal Light—8 fl oz (238 g)	11
With lemon flavor—1 tsp powder in 8 fl oz water (238 g)	26
With sugar & lemon flavor—3 tsp powder in 8 fl oz water (259 g)	29
With sodium, saccharin & lemon flavor—2 tsp powder in 8 fl oz water (238 g)	36
Candy	
Chocolate	
German sweet, Bakers—1 oz square (28 g)	8
Semi-sweet, Bakers—1 oz square (28 g)	13
Chocolate chips	
Bakers—¼ cup (43 g)	12
German sweet, Bakers—¼ cup (43 g)	15
Semi-sweet, Bakers—¼ cup (43 g)	14
Desserts	
Frozen Desserts	
Pudding pops, Jell-O	
Chocolate—1 pop (47 g)	2
Chocolate caramel swirl—1 pop (47 g)	1
Chocolate fudge—1 pop (47 g)	3
Chocolate vanilla swirl—1 pop (47 g)	2
Chocolate with chocolate coating—1 pop (49 g)	3
Double chocolate swirl pop (47 g)	2
Milk chocolate—1 pop (47 g)	2
Pies	
Chocolate mousse, from mix, Jell-O—1/8 pie (95 g)	6
Puddings, from Instant Mix	
Chocolate	
Jell-O—½ cup (150 g)	5
Sugar-free, D-Zerta—½ cup (130 g)	4

(continued)

Sugar-free, Jell-O—½ cup (133 g)	4
Chocolate fudge	
Jell-O—½ cup (150 g)	8
Chocolate fudge mousse, Jell-O—½ cup (86 g)	12
Chocolate mousse, Jell-O—½ cup (86 g)	9
Chocolate tapioca, Jell-O—½ cup (147 g)	8
Milk chocolate, Jell-O—½ cup (150 g)	5
Milk Beverages	
Chocolate flavor mix in whole milk—2–3 tsp powder in 8 fl oz milk (266 g)	8
Chocolate malted milk flavor powder	
In whole milk—3 tsp powder in 8 fl oz milk (265 g)	8
With added nutrients in whole milk—4–5 tsp powder in 8 fl oz milk (265 g)	5
Chocolate syrup in whole milk—2 tbsp syrup in 8 fl oz milk (282 g)	6
Cocoa/hot chocolate, prepared with water from mix —3–4 tsp powder in 6 fl oz water (206 g)	4
Milk Beverage Mixes	
Chocolate flavor mix, powder—2–3 tsp (22 g)	8
Chocolate malted milk flavor mix, powder—3/4 oz (3 tsp) (21 g)	8
Chocolate malted milk flavor mix with added nutrients, powder—3/4 oz (4–5 tsp) (21 g)	6
Chocolate syrup—2 tbsp (1 fl oz) (38 g)	5
Cocoa mix powder—1 oz pkt (3–4 tsp) (28 g)	5
Miscellaneous	
Baking chocolate, unsweetened, Bakers—1 oz (28 g)	25

Abbreviations: g for grams

*Caffeine-free carbonated beverages and most noncarbonated beverages contain no caffeine.

Data from Pennington JAT, *Bowes and Church's food values of portions commonly consumed*, ed. 17, 1998, JB Lippincott. Reprinted with permission.

appendix k

Sources of Nutrition Information

Consider the following reliable sources of food and nutrition information:

Journals That Regularly Cover Nutrition Topics

*American Family Physician**
American Journal of Clinical Nutrition
American Journal of Epidemiology
American Journal of Medicine
American Journal of Nursing
American Journal of Obstetrics and Gynecology
American Journal of Physiology
American Journal of Public Health
American Scientist
Annals of Internal Medicine
Annual Reviews of Medicine
Annual Reviews of Nutrition
Archives of Disease in Childhood
Archives of Internal Medicine
British Journal of Nutrition
BMJ (British Medical Journal)
Cancer
Cancer Research
Circulation
Diabetes
Diabetes Care
Disease-a-Month
FASEB Journal
*FDA Consumer**
Food Chemical Toxicology
Food Engineering
Gastroenterology
Geriatrics
Gut
Human Nutrition: Applied Nutrition
Human Nutrition: Clinical Nutrition
*Journal of the American College of Nutrition**
*Journal of the American Dietetic Association**
Journal of the American Geriatric Society
JAMA (Journal of the American Medical Association)
Journal of Applied Physiology
*Journal of the Canadian Dietetic Association**
Journal of Clinical Investigation
Journal of Food Service
Journal of Food Technology
JNCI (Journal of the National Cancer Institute)
Journal of Nutrition
*Journal of Nutritional Education**
Journal of Nutrition for the Elderly
Journal of Nutrition Research
Journal of Pediatrics
Lancet
Mayo Clinic Proceedings
Medicine and Science in Sports and Exercise
Nature
The New England Journal of Medicine
Nutrition
Nutrition Reviews
*Nutrition Today**
Pediatrics
The Physician and Sports Medicine
*Postgraduate Medicine**
Proceedings of the Nutrition Society
Science
*Science News**
*Scientific American**

The majority of these journals are available in college and university libraries or in a specialty library on campus, such as one designated for health services or home economics. As indicated, a few journals will be filed under their abbreviations, rather than the first word in their full name. A reference librarian can help you locate any of these sources. The asterisked (*) journals are ones you may find especially interesting and useful because of the number of nutrition articles presented each month or the less technical nature of the presentation.

Magazines for the Consumer That Cover Nutrition Topics

American Health for Women
Better Homes and Gardens
Good Housekeeping
Health
Parents
Self

Textbooks and Other Sources for Advanced Study of Nutrition Topics

Brody T: *Nutritional biochemistry.* 2nd ed. San Diego: Academic Press, 1999.
Groff JL, Gropper SS: *Advanced human nutrition and metabolism.* St. Paul, MN: West, 2000.
International Life Sciences Institute: *Present knowledge in nutrition.* 8th ed. Washington DC: The Nutrition Foundation, 2001.
Mahan LK, Escott-Stump S: *Krause's food, nutrition, and diet therapy.* 10th ed. Philadelphia: W.B. Saunders, 2000.
Murray RK and others: *Harper's biochemistry.* 25th ed. Norwalk, CT: Appleton & Lange, 2000.
Schils ME, Olson JA, Shike M, Ross AC: *Modern nutrition in health and disease.* 9th ed. Philadelphia: Lea & Febiger, 1999.
Stipanuk MH: *Biochemical and physiological aspects of human nutrition.* Philadelphia: W.B. Saunders, 2000.

Newsletters That Cover Nutrition Issues on a Regular Basis

American Institute for Cancer Research
(AICR) Washington, DC 20069
www.icr.ac.uk/

Dairy Council Digest
National Dairy Council
10255 West Higgins Road, Suite 900
Rosemont, IL 60018
(inexpensive)
www.nationaldairycouncil.org

Dietetic Currents
Ross Laboratories
Director of Professional Services
625 Cleveland Ave.
Columbus, OH 43216
(free)
www.ross.com

Egg Nutrition Center
1819 H St. N.W., No. 510
Washington, DC 20009
(free)
www.enc-online.org/

Environmental Nutrition
52 Riverside Dr.
New York, NY 10024
www.eatright.org

Food and Nutrition News
National Cattlemen's Beef Association
444 Michigan Ave.
Chicago, IL 60611
(free)
www.beef.org

Harvard Medical School Health Letter
Department of Continuing Education
25 Shattuck St.
Boston, MA 02115
www.hms.harvard.edu/news/index.html

Mayo Clinic Health Letter
P.O. Box 53889
Boulder, CO 80322-3889
mayohealth.org

National Council Against Health Fraud Newsletter (NCAHF)
P.O. Box 1276
Loma Linda, CA 92354
www.ncahf.org/

Nutrition Action Healthletter
1875 Connecticut Ave.
Washington, DC 20009-5728
www.cspinet.org

Nutrition Forum
George Stickley Co.
210 Washington Square
Philadelphia, PA 19106
www.quackwatch.com

Nutrition Research Newsletter
P.O. Box 700
Pallisades, NY 10964
www.biz-lib.com/ZTINR.html

Soy Connection
United Soybean Board
16305 Swingley Ridge Drive
Suite 110
Chesterfield, MO 63017
(free)
smartsoy.ag.uiuc.edu/usb/speced.html/

Tufts University Diet & Nutrition Letter
P.O. Box 10948
Des Moines, IA 50940
www.healthletter.tufts.edu/

University of California at Berkeley Wellness Letter
P.O. Box 420148
Palm Coast, FL 32142
magazines.enews.com/magazines/vcbw

Professional Organizations with a Commitment to Nutrition Issues

American Academy of Pediatrics
P.O. Box 1034
Evanston, IL 60204
www.aap.org

American Cancer Society
90 Park Ave.
New York, NY 10016
www.cancer.org

American College of Sports Medicine
P.O. Box 1440
Indianapolis, IN 46204
www.acsm.org

American Dental Association
211 E. Chicago Ave.
Chicago, IL 60611
www.ada.org

American Diabetes Association
2 Park Ave.
New York, NY 10016
www.diabetes.org

American Dietetic Association
120 S. Riverside Plaza
Suite 2000
Chicago, IL 60606
www.eatright.org

American Geriatrics Society
770 Lexington Ave.
Suite 400
New York, NY 10021
www.americangeriatrics.org

American Heart Association
7272 Greenville Ave.
Dallas, TX 75231
www.americanheart.org

American Home Economics Association
2010 Massachusetts Ave. N.W.
Washington, DC 20036
www.orst.edu

(continued)

American Medical Association
Nutrition Information Section
535 N. Dearborn St.
Chicago, IL 60610
www.ama-assn.org/

American Public Health Association
1015 Fifteenth St. N.W.
Washington, DC 20005
www.apha.org

American Society for Clinical Nutrition
9650 Rockville Pike
Bethesda, MD 20014
www.faseb.org/ajcn

American Society for Nutritional Sciences
9650 Rockville Pike
Bethesda, MD 20014
www.asns.org

The Canadian Diabetes Association
15 Toronto St.
Suite 1001
Toronto, Ontario M5C 2E3 Canada
www.diabetes.ca

The Canadian Dietetic Association
480 University Ave.
Suite 601
Toronto, Ontario M5G 1V2 Canada
www.dietitians.ca

The Canadian Society for Nutritional Sciences
Department of Foods and Nutrition
University of Manitoba
Winnipeg, Manitoba, R3T 2N2 Canada
www.hc-sc.gc.ca

Environmental Working Group (EWG)
1718 Connecticut Ave., NW Suite 600
Washington, DC 20009
www.ewg.org

Food and Nutrition Board
National Research Council
National Academy of Sciences
2101 Constitution Ave. N.W.
Washington, DC 20418
www.nas.edu

Institute of Food Technologies
221 N. LaSalle St.
Chicago, IL 60601
www.ift.org

National Council on the Aging
1828 L St. N.W.
Washington, DC 20036
www.ncoa.org

National Institute of Nutrition
1335 Carling Ave.
Suite 210
Ottawa, Ontario K1Z OL2 Canada
www.nin.ca/En/home.html

National Osteoporosis Foundation
1150 Seventeenth St. N.W., Suite 500
Washington, DC 20036
www.nof.org

Society for Nutrition Education
2001 Killebrew Dr., Suite 340
Minneapolis, MN 55425
www.sne.org

Professional or Lay Organizations Concerned with Nutrition Issues

Bread for the World Institute
1100 Wayne Ave.
Silver Spring, MD 20910
www.bread.org

California Council Against Health Fraud, Inc.
P.O. Box 1276
Loma Linda, CA 92354
www.ncahf.org

Children's Foundation
1420 New York Ave. N.W.
Suite 800
Washington, DC 20005
www.childrenfoundation.com

Food Research and Action Center (FRAC)
1875 Connecticut Ave. N.W. #540
Washington, DC 20009
www.frac.org

Institute for Food and Development Policy
1885 Mission St.
San Francisco, CA 94103
www.foodfirst.org

La Leche League International, Inc.
9616 Minneapolis Ave.
Franklin Park, IL 60131
www.lalecheleague.org

March of Dimes Birth Defects Foundation
(National Headquarters)
1275 Mamaroneck Ave.
White Plains, NY 10605
www.modimes.org

National WIC Association (NWA, formerly the National Association of WIC Directors)
2001 S Street, NW, Suite 580
Washington, DC 20009
www.nwica.org

Overeaters Anonymous (OA)
2190 190th St.
Torrance, CA 90504
www.overeatersanonymous.org

Oxfam America
115 Broadway
Boston, MA 02116
www.oxfamamerica.org

Local Resources for Advice on Nutrition Issues

Registered dietitians (RDs or in Canada also RDNs) in health care, city, county, or state agencies, as well as in private practice
Cooperative extension agents in county extension offices
Nutrition faculty affiliated with departments of food and nutrition, home economics, and dietetics

Government Agencies Concerned with Nutrition Issues or That Distribute Nutrition Information

United States
The Consumer Information Center
Department 609K
Pueblo, CO 81009
www.pueblo.gsa.gov

Food and Drug Administration (FDA)
5600 Fishers Lane
Rockville, MD 20852
www.fda.gov

Food and Nutrition Information and Education Resources Center
National Library of Congress
Beltsville, MD 20705
www.nal.usda.gov

Human Nutrition Research Division
Agricultural Research Center
Beltsville, MD 20705
www.usda.gov

National Center for Health Statistics
3700 East-West
Hyattsville, MD 20782
www.cdc.gov/nchs

National Heart, Lung, and Blood Institute
9000 Rockville Pike, Building 31, Room 4A21
Bethesda, MD 20892
www.nhlbi nih.gov

National Institute on Aging
Information Office
Building 31, Room 5C35
Bethesda, MD 20205
www.nih.gov/nia/

Office of Cancer Communications
National Cancer Institute
Building 31, Room 10A18
90 Rockville Pike
Bethesda, MD 20205
www.nci.nih.gov

USDA, Agricultural Research Service
6505 Belcrest Rd., Room 344
Hyattsville, MD 20782
www.usda.gov

USDA, Food Safety & Inspection Service
Room 1180 South, 14th and Independence Ave. S.W.
Washington, DC 20250
www.usda.gov

U.S. Government Printing Office
The Superintendent of Documents
Washington, DC 20402
www.gpo.gov/

Canada
Canadian Food Inspection Agency
59 Camelot Dr.
Nepean, Ontario K1A OY9
www.inspection.gc.ca/

Health and Welfare Canada
Canadian Government Publishing Center
Minister of Supply and Services
Ottawa, Ontario K1A 0S9
www.hc-sc.gc.ca

Nutrition Programs
446 Jeanne Mance Building
Tunney's Pasture
Ottawa, Ontario K1A 1B4
www.hc-sc.gc.ca

Nutrition Services
P.O. Box 488
Halifax, Nova Scotia B3J 3R8
www.fns.usda.gov

United Nations
Food and Agriculture Organization (FAO)
North American Regional Office
1001 22nd St. N.W.
Washington, DC 20437
or
Via della Terma di Caracella
0100 Rome, Italy
www.fao.org

World Health Organization (WHO)
1211 Geneva 27
Switzerland
www.who.org

Trade Organizations and Companies That Distribute Nutrition Information

American Institute of Baking
P.O. Box 1148
Manhattan, KS 66502
www.aibonline.org

American Meat Institute
P.O. Box 3556
Washington, DC 20007
www.meatami.com

Beech-Nut Nutrition Corporation
Booth 1414
Checkerboard Square
St. Louis, MO 63164
www.beech-nut.com/index.htm

Best Foods
Consumer Service Department
Division of CPC International
International Plaza
Englewood Cliffs, NJ 07632
www.bestfoods.com

Campbell Soup Co.
Food Service Products Division
Campbell Plaza
Camden, NJ 08103
www.campbellsoups.com

The Dannon Company, Inc.
120 White Plains Rd.
Tarrytown, NY 10591-5536
www.dannon.com

Del Monte Foods
One Market Plaza
San Francisco, CA 94105
www.delmonte-international.com

General Mills
P.O. Box 1113
Minneapolis, MN 55440
www.generalmills.com

Gerber Products Co.
445 State St.
Fremont, MI 49413
www.gerber.com

H.J. Heinz
Consumer Relations
P.O. Box 57
Pittsburgh, PA 15230
www.heinzbaby.com

Idaho Potato Commission
P.O. Box 1968
Boise, ID 83701
www.idahopotatoes.com

Kellogg Company
Department of Home Economics Services
Battle Creek, MI 49016
www.kellog.com

(continued)

Kraft General Foods
Three Lakes Dr.
Northfield, IL 60093
www.kraftfoods.com

Mead Johnson Nutritionals
2404 Pennsylvania Ave.
Evansville, IN 47721
www.meadjohnson.com

National Dairy Council
10255 W. Higgins Rd.
Rosemont, IL 60018-4233
www.natdairycoun.org

The NutraSweet Kelco Company
1751 Lake Cook Rd.
Deerfield, IL 60015
www.nutrasweetkelco.com/default.htm

Pillsbury Company
1177 Pillsbury Building
608 Second Ave. S.
Minneapolis, MN 55402
www.pillsbury.com

Ross Laboratories
Director of Professional Services
625 Cleveland Ave.
Columbus, OH 43216
www.ross.com

Sunkist Growers, Inc.
14130 Riverside Dr.
Sherman Oaks, CA 91423
www.sunkist.com/index.html

Vitamin Nutrition Information Service (VNIS)
Hoffmann-LaRoche
340 Kingsland Ave.
Nutley, NJ 07110
www.rocheusa.com

appendix I

English-Metric Conversions, and Metric and Household Units

Metric-English Conversions

Length

English (USA)	= Metric
inch (in)	= 2.54 cm, 25.4 mm
foot (ft)	= 0.30 m, 30.48 cm
yard (yd)	= 0.91 m, 91.4 cm
mile (statute) (5280 ft)	= 1.61 km, 1609 m
mile (nautical) (6077 ft, 1.15 statute mi)	= 1.85 km, 1850 m

Metric	= English (USA)
millimeter (mm)	= 0.039 in (thickness of a dime)
centimeter (cm)	= 0.39 in
meter (m)	= 3.28 ft, 39.37 in
kilometer (km)	= 0.62 mi, 1091 yd, 3273 ft

Weight

English (USA)	= Metric
grain	= 64.80 mg
ounce (oz)	= 28.35 g
pound (lb)	= 453.60 g, 0.45 kg
ton (short—2000 lb)	= 0.91 metric ton (907 kg)

Metric	= English (USA)
milligram (mg)	= 0.002 grain (0.000035 oz)
gram (g)	= 0.04 oz (1/28 of an oz)
kilogram (kg)	= 35.27 oz, 2.20 lb
metric ton (1000 kg)	= 1.10 tons

Volume

English (USA)	= Metric
cubic inch	= 16.39 cc
cubic foot	= 0.03 m^3
cubic yard	= 0.765 m^3
teaspoon (tsp)	= 5 ml
tablespoon (tbsp)	= 15 ml
fluid ounce	= 0.03 liter (30 ml)*
cup (c)	= 237 ml
pint (pt)	= 0.47 liter
quart (qt)	= 0.95 liter
gallon (gal)	= 3.79 liters

Metric	= English (USA)
milliliter (ml)	= 0.03 oz
liter (L)	= 2.12 pt
liter	= 1.06 qt
liter	= 0.27 gal

1 liter ÷ 1000 = 1 milliliter or 1 cubic centimeter (10^{-3} liter)

1 liter ÷ 1,000,000 = 1 microliter (10^{-6} liter)

*Note: 1 ml = 1 cc

Additional Metric and Other Units Commonly Used in Nutrition

Unit/Abbreviation	Other Equivalent Measure
milligram/mg	1/1000 of a gram
microgram/µg	1/1,000,000 of a gram
deciliter/dl	1/10 of a liter (about ½ cup)
milliliter/ml	1/1000 of a liter (5 ml is about 1 tsp)
International Unit/IU	Crude measure of vitamin activity generally based on growth rate seen in animals

Fahrenheit-Celsius Temperature Conversion Scale

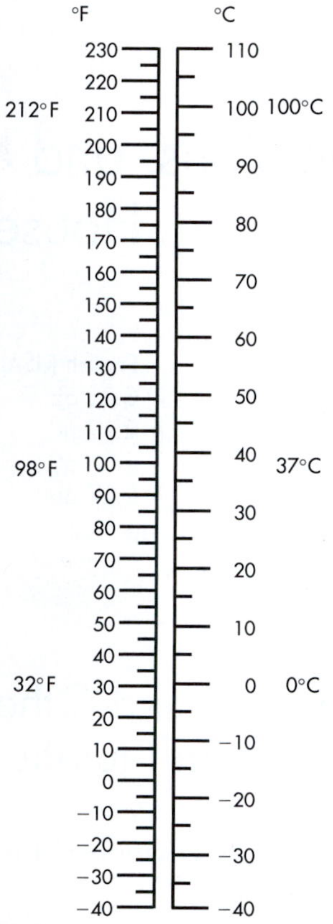

To convert temperature scales:
Fahrenheit to Celsius $°C = (°F - 32) \times \frac{5}{9}$
Celsius to Fahrenheit $°F = 9/5\ (°C) + 32$

Household Units

3 teaspoons	= 1 tablespoon
4 tablespoons	= ¼ cup
5⅓ tablespoons	= ⅓ cup
8 tablespoons	= ½ cup
10⅔ tablespoons	= ⅔ cup
16 tablespoons	= 1 cup
1 tablespoon	= ½ fluid ounce
1 cup	= 8 fluid ounces
1 cup	= ½ pint
2 cups	= 1 pint
4 cups	= 1 quart
2 pints	= 1 quart
4 quarts	= 1 gallon

appendix m

Estimated Average Requirements for Nutrients

Estimated Average Energy Requirements set by the Food and Nutrition Board, Institute of Medicine, National Academies

Life Stage Group	CHO (g/d)	PROT (g/kg/d)	Vitamin A (μg/d)	Vitamin C (mg/d)	Vitamin E (mg/d)	Thiamin (mg/d)	Riboflavin (mg/d)	Niacin (mg/d)	Vitamin B-6 (mg/d)
Children									
1–3 y	100	0.88	210	13	5	.4	.4	5	.4
4–8 y	100	0.76	275	22	6	.5	.5	6	.5
Males									
9–13 y	100	0.76	445	39	9	.7	.8	9	.8
14–18 y	100	0.73	630	63	12	1.0	1.1	12	1.1
19–30 y	100	0.66	625	75	12	1.0	1.1	12	1.1
31–50 y	100	0.66	625	75	12	1.0	1.1	12	1.1
51–70 y	100	0.66	625	75	12	1.0	1.1	12	1.4
> 70 y	100	0.66	625	75	12	1.0	1.1	12	1.4
Females									
9–13 y	100	0.76	420	39	9	.7	.8	9	.8
14–18 y	100	0.71	485	56	12	.9	.9	11	1.0
19–30 y	100	0.66	500	60	12	.9	.9	11	1.1
31–50 y	100	0.66	500	60	12	.9	.9	11	1.1
51–70 y	100	0.66	500	60	12	.9	.9	11	1.3
> 70 y	100	0.66	500	60	12	.9	.9	11	1.3
Pregnancy									
≤ 18 y	135	0.88	530	66	12	1.2	1.2	14	1.6
19–30 y	135	0.88	550	70	12	1.2	1.2	14	1.6
31–50 y	135	0.88	550	70	12	1.2	1.2	14	1.6
Lactation									
≤ 18 y	160	1.05	880	96	16	1.2	1.3	13	1.7
19–30 y	160	1.05	900	100	16	1.2	1.3	13	1.7
31–50 y	160	1.05	900	100	16	1.2	1.3	13	1.7

NOTE: This information taken from the various DRI reports (see www.nap.edu).

Folate (μg/d)	Vitamin B-12 (μg/d)	Copper (μg/d)	Iodine (μg/d)	Iron (mg/d)	Magnesium (mg/d)	Molybdenum (μg/d)	Phosphorus (mg/d)	Selenium (μg/d)	Zinc (mg/d)
120	.7	260	65	3.0	65	13	380	17	2.2
160	1.0	340	65	4.1	110	17	405	23	4
250	1.5	540	73	5.9	200	26	1055	35	7
330	2.0	685	95	7.7	340	33	1055	45	8.5
320	2.0	700	95	6	330	34	580	45	9.4
320	2.0	700	95	6	350	34	580	45	9.4
320	2.0	700	95	6	350	34	580	45	9.4
320	2.0	700	95	6	350	34	580	45	9.4
250	1.5	540	73	5.7	200	26	1055	35	7
330	2.0	685	95	7.9	300	33	1055	45	7.5
320	2.0	700	95	8.1	255	34	580	45	6.8
320	2.0	700	95	8.1	265	34	580	45	6.8
320	2.0	700	95	5	265	34	580	45	6.8
320	2.0	700	95	5	265	34	580	45	6.8
520	2.2	785	160	23	355	40	1055	49	10.5
520	2.2	800	160	22	290	40	580	49	9.5
520	2.2	800	160	22	300	40	580	49	9.5
450	2.4	985	209	7	300	50	1055	59	11.6
450	2.4	1000	209	6.5	255	50	580	59	10.4
450	2.4	1000	209	6.5	265	50	580	59	10.4

appendix n

Food Composition Table

The following table of nutrient values of foods represents a small portion of the database found in the NutritionCalc Plus diet analysis program available from McGraw-Hill. The nutrient data in the software and in this appendix comes from the ESHA Research database. Some nutrient or food component values for some foods are not included in the database because no *accurate* data values exist. The nutrient or component may in fact be present in the food, but insufficient laboratory analyses have been performed to establish an accurate value. These are indicated by a – (dash) in the appropriate nutrient columns.

Name-brand foods often have missing values because manufacturers are only required to analyze for nutrients that must appear on Nutrition Facts labels and only to the level of accuracy required by the nutrition labeling regulations. All missing nutrient or food component values are clearly marked in the table. You are encouraged to refer to the Nutrition Analysis website (**www.mhhe.com/nutritionanalysis**) for links to nutrient data sites provided by food manufacturers and restaurants not found in Appendix N.

The following is a list of abbreviations used in the Food Composition Table:

Abbreviation Key

Unit/Amt = Unit Amount
Wt (g) = Weight in grams
Energy (Kcal) = kilocalories
Prot (g) = Protein
Carb (g) = Carbohydrate
Fiber (g) = Dietary fiber
Fat (g) = Total fat
Sat (g) = Saturated fat
Mono (g) = Monounsaturated fat
Poly (g) = Polyunsaturated fat
Chol (mg) = Cholesterol
Vit A (RE) = Vitamin A
Thia (mg) = Thiamin
Ribo (mg) = Riboflavin
Niac (mg NE) = Niacin
Vit B-6 (mg) = Vitamin B-6

Note: g = gram
mg = milligram
µg = microgram
mg AT = milligrams of alpha-tocopheral
mg NE = milligrams of Niacin Equivalents

Vit B-12 (µg) = Vitamin B-12
Fol (µg) = Folate
Vit C (mg) = Vitamin C
Vit D (IU) = Vitamin D
Vit E (mg AT) = Vitamin E
Cal (mg) = Calcium
Iron (mg) = Iron
Magn (mg) = Magnesium
Phos (mg) = Phosphorus
Pota (mg) = Potassium
Sodi (mg) = Sodium
Zinc (mg) = Zinc
Wat (%) = Water
Alco (g) = Alcohol
Caff (g) = Caffeine

PAGE KEY: A-108 Beverage and Beverage Mixes A-112 Other Beverages A-112 Beverages, Alcoholic A-114 Candies and Confections, Gum A-114 Cereals, Breakfast Type A-118 Cheese and Cheese Substitutes A-120 Dairy Products and Substitutes A-122 Desserts A-128 Dessert Toppings A-128 Eggs, Substitutes, and Egg Dishes A-130 Ethnic Foods A-130 Fast Foods/Restaurants A-140 Fats, Oils, Margarines, Shortenings, and Substitutes A-142 Fish, Seafood, and Shellfish A-142 Food Additives A-142 Fruit, Vegetable, and Blended Juices A-144 Fruits A-146 Grains, Flours, and Fractions A-148 Grain Products, Prepared and Baked Goods

Code	Food Name	Unit/ Amt	Wt (g)	Energy (Kcal)	Prot (g)	Carb (g)	Fiber (g)	Fat (g)	Sat (g)	Mono (g)	Poly (g)	Chol (mg)	Vit A (RE)
BEVERAGE AND BEVERAGE MIXES													
Carbonated Drinks													
4794	Lemonade, cnd, Country Time	1 cup	247	90	0	23	0	0	0.0	0.0	0.0	—	0
20055	Soda, 7 Up	1 cup	240	100	0	26	0	0	0.0	0.0	0.0	0	0
4814	Soda, 7 Up, cherry	1 cup	246	100	0	26	0	0	0.0	0.0	0.0	—	0
20006	Soda, club	1 cup	237	0	0	0	0	0	0.0	0.0	0.0	0	0
20149	Soda, Coca Cola, cherry, can/btl	1 cup	250	104	0	28	0	0	0.0	0.0	0.0	0	0
20515	Soda, Coca Cola, cherry, diet, w/asp, can/btl	1 cup	240	1	0	0	0	0	0.0	0.0	0.0	0	0
20513	Soda, Coca Cola, classic, caff free, can/btl	1 cup	249	97	0	27	0	0	0.0	0.0	0.0	0	0
20148	Soda, Coca Cola, classic, can/btl	1 cup	249	97	0	27	0	0	0.0	0.0	0.0	0	0
20147	Soda, Coca Cola/Coke, can/btl	1 cup	246	103	0	27	0	0	0.0	0.0	0.0	0	0
20150	Soda, Coke, diet, can/btl	1 cup	240	1	0	0	0	0	0.0	0.0	0.0	0	0
20005	Soda, cola	1 cup	248	102	0	26	0	0	0.0	0.0	0.0	0	0
443	Soda, cola, caff free, 12 fl oz can	1 ea	372	153	0	39	0	0	0.0	0.0	0.0	0	0
20685	Soda, cola, diet, caff free, w/asp, 12 fl oz can	1 ea	355	4	0	0	0	0	0.0	0.0	0.0	0	0
20030	Soda, cola, diet, w/asp	1 cup	237	2	0	0	0	0	0.0	0.0	0.0	0	0
20843	Soda, cola, w/hi caff	12 fl-oz	370	152	0	38	0	0	0.0	0.0	0.0	0	0
20028	Soda, cream	1 cup	247	126	0	33	0	0	0.0	0.0	0.0	0	0
4796	Soda, Dr Pepper	1 cup	246	100	0	27	0	0	0.0	0.0	0.0	—	0
4798	Soda, Dr Pepper, caff free	1 cup	246	100	0	27	0	0	0.0	0.0	0.0	—	0
4797	Soda, Dr Pepper, diet	1 cup	246	0	0	0	0	0	0.0	0.0	0.0	—	0
4799	Soda, Dr Pepper, diet, caff free	1 cup	246	0	0	0	0	0	0.0	0.0	0.0	—	0
20536	Soda, Fresca, w/asp, can/btl	1 cup	240	3	0	0	0	0	0.0	0.0	0.0	0	0
20008	Soda, ginger ale	1 cup	244	83	0	21	0	0	0.0	0.0	0.0	0	0
4813	Soda, ginger ale, diet, Schweppes	1 cup	247	0	0	0	0	0	0.0	0.0	0.0	—	0
20692	Soda, grape, Welch's	1 cup	248	130	0	34	0	0	0.0	0.0	0.0	—	0
20159	Soda, Mello Yello, can/btl	1 cup	251	119	0	32	0	0	0.0	0.0	0.0	0	0
20535	Soda, Mello Yello, diet, w/asp, can/btl	1 cup	240	3	0	0	0	0	0.0	0.0	0.0	—	0
20271	Soda, Mountain Dew	1 cup	240	113	0	31	0	0	0.0	0.0	0.0	0	0
20407	Soda, Mountain Dew, caff free	1 cup	360	170	0	46	0	0	0.0	0.0	0.0	0	0
20272	Soda, Mountain Dew, diet	1 cup	240	0	0	0	0	0	0.0	0.0	0.0	0	0
20273	Soda, Mountain Dew, diet, caff free	1 cup	240	0	0	0	0	0	0.0	0.0	0.0	0	0
20161	Soda, Mr Pibb, can/btl	1 cup	249	97	0	26	0	0	0.0	0.0	0.0	0	0
20537	Soda, Mr Pibb, diet, w/asp, can/btl	1 cup	240	1	0	0	0	0	0.0	0.0	0.0	—	0
20029	Soda, orange	1 cup	248	119	0	31	0	0	0.0	0.0	0.0	0	0
20166	Soda, Pepsi	1 cup	240	100	0	27	0	0	0.0	0.0	0.0	0	0
20268	Soda, Pepsi, caff free	1 cup	240	100	0	27	0	0	0.0	0.0	0.0	0	0
20167	Soda, Pepsi, diet	1 cup	240	0	0	0	0	0	0.0	0.0	0.0	0	0
20269	Soda, Pepsi, diet, caff free	1 cup	240	0	0	0	0	0	0.0	0.0	0.0	0	0
20435	Soda, Pepsi, H20! All	1 cup	240	100	0	27	0	0	0.0	0.0	0.0	—	0
20270	Soda, Pepsi, wild cherry	1 cup	240	107	0	29	0	0	0.0	0.0	0.0	0	0
20009	Soda, root beer	1 cup	246	101	0	26	0	0	0.0	0.0	0.0	0	0
4785	Soda, root beer, A & W	1 cup	247	120	0	31	0	0	0.0	0.0	0.0	—	0
4786	Soda, root beer, diet, A & W	1 cup	247	0	0	0	0	0	0.0	0.0	0.0	—	0
20454	Soda, root beer, diet, w/nutrasweet	1 cup	240	0	0	0	0	0	0.0	0.0	0.0	0	—
20163	Soda, Sprite, can/btl	1 cup	249	96	0	26	0	0	0.0	0.0	0.0	0	0
20164	Soda, Sprite, diet, w/asp, can/btl	1 cup	240	3	0	0	0	0	0.0	0.0	0.0	0	0

PAGE KEY: A-154 Granola Bars, Cereal Bars, Diet Bars, Scones, and Tarts A-154 Meals and Dishes A-160 Meats A-164 Nuts, Seeds, and Products A-166 Poultry A-166 Salad Dressings, Dips, and Mayonnaise A-170 Salads A-170 Sandwiches A-172 Sauces and Gravies A-174 Snack Foods—Chips, Pretzels, Popcorn A-178 Soups, Stews and Chilis A-184 Spices, Flavors, and Seasonings A-184 Sports Bars and Drinks A-186 Supplemental Foods and Formulas A-186 Sweeteners and Sweet Substitutes A-188 Vegetables and Legumes A-200 Weight Loss Bars & Drinks A-200 Miscellaneous

Thia (mg)	Ribo (mg)	Niac (mg NE)	Vit B6 (mg)	Vit B12 (µg)	Fol (µg)	Vit C (mg)	Vit D (IU)	Vit E (mg AT)	Cal (mg)	Iron (mg)	Magn (mg)	Phos (mg)	Pota (mg)	Sodi (mg)	Zinc (mg)	Wat (%)	Alco (g)	Caff (g)
–	–	–	–	–	–	0.0	–	–	–	–	–	–	–	90	–	91	0.00	0.00
–	–	–	–	0.00	–	0.0	–	–	–	–	–	45	–	50	–	89	0.00	0.00
–	–	–	–	–	–	0.0	–	–	–	–	–	–	–	50	–	89	0.00	0.00
0.00	0.00	0.00	0.00	0.00	0.0	0.0	0.0	0.0	12	0.01	2.4	0	5	50	0.2	100	0.00	0.00
0.00	0.00	0.00	0.00	0.00	0.0	0.0	0.0	0.0	7	0.07	2.5	37	0	4	0.0	89	0.00	31.00
–	–	–	–	–	–	0.0	–	–	0	0.00	–	18	12	4	–	100	0.00	31.00
–	–	–	–	–	–	0.0	–	–	0	0.00	–	41	0	9	–	89	0.00	0.00
0.00	0.00	0.00	0.00	0.00	0.0	0.0	0.0	0.0	9	0.09	3.0	41	0	9	0.0	91	0.00	31.00
0.00	0.00	0.00	0.00	0.00	0.0	0.0	0.0	0.0	7	0.07	2.5	36	2	5	0.0	89	0.00	30.67
0.01	0.05	0.00	0.00	0.00	0.0	0.0	0.0	0.0	10	0.07	2.4	18	12	4	0.2	100	0.00	31.00
0.00	0.00	0.00	0.00	0.00	0.0	0.0	0.0	0.0	7	0.07	2.5	30	2	10	0.0	89	0.00	24.79
0.00	0.00	0.00	0.00	0.00	0.0	0.0	–	0.0	11	0.10	3.7	45	4	15	0.0	89	0.00	0.00
0.01	0.07	0.00	0.00	0.00	0.0	0.0	–	0.0	14	0.10	3.6	32	0	21	0.3	100	0.00	0.00
0.00	0.05	0.00	0.00	0.00	0.0	0.0	0.0	0.0	9	0.07	2.4	21	0	14	0.2	100	0.00	33.15
0.00	0.00	0.00	0.00	0.00	0.0	0.0	–	0.0	11	0.10	3.7	44	4	15	0.0	89	0.00	99.90
0.00	0.00	0.00	0.00	0.00	0.0	0.0	0.0	0.0	12	0.11	2.5	0	2	30	0.2	87	0.00	0.00
–	–	–	–	–	–	0.0	–	–	–	–	–	–	–	35	–	89	0.00	27.20
–	–	–	–	–	–	0.0	–	–	–	–	–	–	–	35	–	89	0.00	0.00
–	–	–	–	–	–	0.0	–	–	–	–	–	–	–	35	–	100	0.00	27.20
–	–	–	–	–	–	0.0	–	–	–	–	–	–	–	35	–	100	0.00	0.00
–	–	–	–	–	–	0.0	–	–	0	0.00	–	–	55	1	–	100	0.00	0.00
0.00	0.00	0.00	0.00	0.00	0.0	0.0	0.0	0.0	7	0.43	2.4	0	2	17	0.1	91	0.00	0.00
–	–	–	–	–	–	0.0	–	–	–	–	–	–	–	60	–	100	0.00	0.00
–	–	–	–	–	–	0.0	–	–	–	–	–	–	–	40	–	86	0.00	
0.00	0.00	0.05	0.00	0.00	0.0	0.0	0.0	0.0	5	0.18	2.5	0	22	9	0.1	87	0.00	35.00
–	–	–	–	–	–	0.0	–	–	0	0.00	–	–	35	–	–	100	0.00	35.00
–	–	–	–	0.00	–	0.0	–	–	0	0.00	–	0	–	47	–	87	0.00	36.66
–	–	–	–	0.00	–	0.0	–	–	0	0.00	–	0	–	70	–	87	0.00	0.00
–	–	–	–	0.00	–	0.0	–	–	0	0.00	–	0	–	23	–	97	0.00	36.66
–	–	–	–	0.00	–	0.0	–	–	0	0.00	–	0	–	23	–	97	0.00	0.00
0.00	0.00	0.00	0.00	0.00	0.0	0.0	0.0	0.0	7	0.07	2.5	29	14	7	0.0	90	0.00	27.00
–	–	–	–	–	–	0.0	–	–	0	0.00	–	29	20	2	–	100	0.00	27.00
0.00	0.00	0.00	0.00	0.00	0.0	0.0	0.0	0.0	12	0.15	2.5	2	5	30	0.2	88	0.00	0.00
–	–	–	–	0.00	–	0.0	–	–	0	0.00	–	35	–	23	–	88	0.00	24.67
–	–	–	–	0.00	–	0.0	–	–	0	0.00	–	35	–	23	–	86	0.00	0.00
–	–	–	–	0.00	–	0.0	–	–	0	0.00	–	27	5	23	–	100	0.00	24.00
–	–	–	–	0.00	–	0.0	–	–	0	0.00	–	27	–	23	–	100	0.00	0.00
–	–	–	–	0.00	–	0.0	–	–	0	0.00	–	0	–	23	–	86	0.00	0.00
–	–	–	–	0.00	–	0.0	–	–	0	0.00	–	35	–	23	–	86	0.00	25.32
0.00	0.00	0.00	0.00	0.00	0.0	0.0	0.0	0.0	12	0.11	2.5	0	2	32	0.2	89	0.00	0.00
–	–	–	–	–	–	0.0	–	–	–	–	–	–	–	30	–	87	0.00	0.00
–	–	–	–	–	–	0.0	–	–	–	–	–	–	–	45	–	100	0.00	0.00
–	–	–	–	0.00	–	–	–	–	–	–	–	–	–	30	–	100	0.00	0.00
0.00	0.00	0.05	0.00	0.00	0.0	0.0	0.0	0.0	5	0.17	2.5	0	0	23	0.1	89	0.00	0.00
0.00	0.00	0.00	0.00	0.00	0.0	0.0	0.0	0.0	10	0.10	–	0	67	0	0.1	100	0.00	0.00

PAGE KEY: A-108 Beverage and Beverage Mixes A-112 Other Beverages A-112 Beverages, Alcoholic A-114 Candies and Confections, Gum A-114 Cereals, Breakfast Type A-118 Cheese and Cheese Substitutes A-120 Dairy Products and Substitutes A-122 Desserts A-128 Dessert Toppings A-128 Eggs, Substitutes, and Egg Dishes A-130 Ethnic Foods A-130 Fast Foods/Restaurants A-140 Fats, Oils, Margarines, Shortenings, and Substitutes A-142 Fish, Seafood, and Shellfish A-142 Food Additives A-142 Fruit, Vegetable, and Blended Juices A-144 Fruits A-146 Grains, Flours, and Fractions A-148 Grain Products, Prepared and Baked Goods

Code	Food Name	Unit/ Amt	Wt (g)	Energy (Kcal)	Prot (g)	Carb (g)	Fiber (g)	Fat (g)	Sat (g)	Mono (g)	Poly (g)	Chol (mg)	Vit A (RE)
4815	Soda, Squirt	1 cup	246	100	0	27	0	0	0.0	0.0	0.0	–	0
20315	Soda, Squirt, diet	1 cup	246	0	0	0	0	0	0.0	0.0	0.0	–	0
4816	Soda, Squirt, ruby red	1 cup	246	120	0	31	0	0	0.0	0.0	0.0	–	0
20517	Soda, Surge, can/btl	1 cup	251	116	0	31	0	0	0.0	0.0	0.0	–	0
20165	Soda, Tab, w/sacc & asp, can/btl	1 cup	240	1	0	0	0	0	0.0	0.0	0.0	0	0
Coffee and Substitutes													
20494	Cappuccino, w/lowfat milk, double, tall	1.5 cup	244	110	8	11	0	4	2.5	–	–	15	80
20607	Cappuccino, w/whole milk, double, tall	1.5 cup	244	140	7	11	0	7	4.5	–	–	30	60
20048	Coffee Substitute, cereal grain, prep w/water f/pwd	1 cup	240	12	0	2	0	0	0.0	0.0	0.1	0	0
20065	Coffee, brewed, decaf	1 cup	240	5	0	1	0	0	0.0	0.0	0.0	0	0
20012	Coffee, brewed, prep w/tap water	1 cup	237	5	0	1	0	0	0.0	0.0	0.0	0	0
20225	Coffee, Cafe Francais, inst, prep f/dry	8 fl-oz	249	60	1	7	0	4	1.0	–	–	0	0
20228	Coffee, French Vanilla Cafe, inst, prep f/dry	8 fl-oz	250	60	1	10	0	2	0.5	–	–	0	0
20402	Coffee, French Vanilla, sugar/fat free, dry, svg	1 ea	7	25	0	5	0	0	0.1	–	–	0	0
20023	Coffee, reg, inst, prep w/water	1 cup	238	5	0	1	0	0	0.0	0.0	0.0	0	0
20439	Espresso, prep f/restaurant	1 cup	237	21	0	4	0	0	0.2	0.0	0.2	0	0
20659	Latte, iced, w/lowfat milk, tall	1.5 cup	392	90	7	10	0	3	2.0	–	–	15	60
20666	Latte, w/lowfat milk, decaf, tall	1.5 cup	366	170	12	17	0	6	4.0	–	–	25	100
20669	Latte, w/whole milk, decaf, tall	1.5 cup	366	210	11	17	0	11	7.0	–	–	45	80
20671	Latte, w/whole milk, tall	1.5 cup	366	210	11	17	0	11	7.0	–	–	45	80
Dairy Mixed Drinks and Mixes													
34	Chocolate Malt, prep w/milk f/dry mix	1 cup	265	236	9	30	0	9	5.3	2.4	0.4	34	3
44	Drink, carob, prep f/dry mix w/milk	1 cup	256	195	8	23	1	8	5.1	2.4	0.3	33	69
4298	Drink, chocolate, fat free, rtd, Nesquick	1 cup	254	160	8	31	1	0	0.0	0.0	0.0	0	100
39	Drink, chocolate, prep f/dry mix w/milk	1 cup	266	226	9	31	1	9	5.5	2.6	0.3	32	69
41	Drink, strawberry, prep f/dry mix w/milk	1 cup	266	234	8	33	0	8	5.1	2.4	0.3	32	69
48	Hot Chocolate, prep f/dry mix w/water	1 cup	275	137	4	30	3	2	0.9	0.5	0.0	3	–
151	Hot Chocolate, rducd cal, w/asp, prep f/dry w/water	1 cup	272	84	7	14	1	1	0.5	0.1	0.0	3	98
63088	Hot Chocolate, w/marshmallows, Swiss Miss, pkt	1 ea	16	60	2	10	1	1	0.0	–	–	0	0
4156	Instant Breakfast, chocolate malt, prep f/dry w/skm mlk	9 fl-oz	280	220	12	39	1	2	1.0	–	–	6	450
4158	Instant Breakfast, French vanilla, prep f/dry w/skm mlk	9 fl-oz	281	220	12	39	0	1	0.4	–	–	6	450
176	Malted Milk, milk, inst, prep w/2% milk	1 cup	264	210	11	27	0	7	4.0	–	–	25	100
300	Smoothie, strawberry banana	1 ea	312	367	3	68	2	7	3.0	–	–	23	70
Juice and Fruit Flavored Drinks													
20004	Drink, breakfast, orange, prep f/pwd	1 cup	248	117	0	29	0	0	0.0	0.0	0.0	0	191
20316	Drink, Crystal Light, lemon lime, low cal, prep f/mix	8 fl-oz	239	5	0	0	0	0	0.0	0.0	0.0	0	0
20081	Drink, fruit, low cal	1 cup	240	43	0	11	0	0	0.0	0.0	0.0	0	2
20296	Drink, Kool Aid, black cherry, prep w/sug	8 fl-oz	246	100	0	25	0	0	0.0	0.0	0.0	0	0
20385	Drink, Kool Aid, cherry, swtnd, prep	8 fl-oz	254	60	0	16	0	0	0.0	0.0	0.0	0	0
20297	Drink, Kool Aid, cherry, unswtnd, prep w/sug	8 fl-oz	246	100	0	25	0	0	0.0	0.0	0.0	0	0
20045	Drink, lemonade, prep f/pwd	1 cup	266	112	0	29	0	0	0.0	0.0	0.0	0	0
20070	Drink, orange, cnd	1 cup	248	126	0	32	0	0	0.0	0.0	0.0	0	5
20744	Drink, Snapple, raspberry peach	8 fl-oz	252	120	0	29	–	0	0.0	0.0	0.0	0	–
20804	Drink, Tang, orange, prep f/dry mix	8 fl-oz	241	90	0	23	0	0	0.0	0.0	0.0	0	100
20024	Fruit Punch, cnd	1 cup	248	117	0	30	0	0	0.0	0.0	0.0	0	5
20035	Fruit Punch, prep f/fzn conc w/water	1 cup	247	114	0	29	0	0	0.0	0.0	0.0	0	5
20568	Juice Drink, Hi-C, berry fruit punch, box	1 ea	251	120	0	34	0	0	0.0	0.0	0.0	0	0
20816	Lemonade, Country Time, cranberry raspberry, prep	8 fl-oz	241	90	0	21	0	0	0.0	0.0	0.0	0	0
20389	Lemonade, Kool Aid, swtnd, prep f/dry mix	8 fl-oz	255	70	0	17	0	0	0.0	0.0	0.0	0	0

PAGE KEY: A-154 Granola Bars, Cereal Bars, Diet Bars, Scones, and Tarts A-154 Meals and Dishes A-160 Meats A-164 Nuts, Seeds, and Products A-166 Poultry A-166 Salad Dressings, Dips, and Mayonnaise A-170 Salads A-170 Sandwiches A-172 Sauces and Gravies A-174 Snack Foods—Chips, Pretzels, Popcorn A-178 Soups, Stews and Chilis A-184 Spices, Flavors, and Seasonings A-184 Sports Bars and Drinks A-186 Supplemental Foods and Formulas A-186 Sweeteners and Sweet Substitutes A-188 Vegetables and Legumes A-200 Weight Loss Bars & Drinks A-200 Miscellaneous

Thia (mg)	Ribo (mg)	Niac (mg NE)	Vit B6 (mg)	Vit B12 (µg)	Fol (µg)	Vit C (mg)	Vit D (IU)	Vit E (mg AT)	Cal (mg)	Iron (mg)	Magn (mg)	Phos (mg)	Pota (mg)	Sodi (mg)	Zinc (mg)	Wat (%)	Alco (g)	Caff (g)
–	–	–	–	–	–	0.0	–	–	–	–	–	–	–	15	–	89	0.00	0.00
–	–	–	–	–	–	0.0	–	–	–	–	–	–	–	15	–	100	0.00	0.00
–	–	–	–	–	–	0.0	–	–	–	–	–	–	–	15	–	87	0.00	35.29
–	–	–	–	–	–	0.0	–	–	0	0.00	–	–	35	3	–	88	0.00	35.00
0.00	0.00	–	0.00	0.00	0.0	0.0	0.0	0.0	8	0.07	–	30	12	4	–	100	0.00	31.00
–	–	–	–	–	–	2.4	–	–	250	0.00	–	–	–	110	–	–	0.00	180.00
–	–	–	–	–	–	2.4	–	–	250	0.00	–	–	–	105	–	–	0.00	180.00
0.01	0.00	0.51	0.02	0.00	0.0	0.0	0.0	0.0	7	0.14	9.6	17	58	10	0.1	99	0.00	0.00
0.00	0.00	0.52	0.00	0.00	0.2	0.0	0.0	0.0	5	0.11	12.0	2	130	5	0.0	99	0.00	2.40
0.00	0.00	0.52	0.00	0.00	0.0	0.0	0.0	0.0	5	0.11	11.8	2	128	5	0.0	99	0.00	137.46
–	–	–	–	0.00	–	0.0	–	–	0	0.00	–	40	130	95	–	95	0.00	
–	–	–	–	0.00	–	0.0	–	–	0	0.00	–	20	80	55	–	94	0.00	
–	–	–	–	–	–	0.0	–	–	4	0.05	–	16	72	65	–	3	0.00	
0.00	0.00	0.67	0.00	0.00	0.0	0.0	0.0	0.0	7	0.11	9.5	7	86	7	0.1	99	0.00	76.29
0.00	0.41	12.34	0.00	0.00	2.4	0.5	0.0	0.0	5	0.31	189.6	17	273	33	0.1	98	0.00	502.44
–	–	–	–	–	–	1.2	–	–	250	0.00	–	–	–	100	–	–	0.00	90.00
–	–	–	–	–	–	3.6	–	–	400	0.00	–	–	–	170	–	–	0.00	4.00
–	–	–	–	–	–	3.6	–	–	400	0.00	–	–	–	170	–	–	0.00	4.00
–	–	–	–	–	–	3.6	–	–	400	0.00	–	–	–	170	–	–	0.00	90.00
0.12	0.43	0.62	0.14	0.89	15.9	2.7	97.5	0.3	305	0.61	47.7	265	501	172	1.1	81	0.00	7.94
0.09	0.38	0.30	0.11	0.87	12.8	2.3	0.0	0.1	292	0.67	33.3	228	369	133	0.9	84	0.00	0.00
–	0.34	–	–	–	–	0.0	100.0	–	250	0.00	–	–	410	140	–	84	0.00	5.00
0.10	0.43	0.31	0.10	0.87	13.3	2.4	160.4	0.2	301	0.80	53.2	255	497	165	1.3	81	0.00	7.98
0.09	0.41	0.21	0.10	0.87	13.3	2.4	106.4	0.3	293	0.20	31.9	229	370	128	0.9	81	0.00	0.00
0.03	0.20	0.21	0.03	0.49	0.0	0.5	0.0	0.1	129	0.46	33.0	118	269	198	0.6	86	0.00	5.48
0.02	0.55	0.36	0.02	0.68	10.9	0.3	0.0	0.0	256	2.20	62.6	242	639	228	1.1	91	0.00	5.44
–	–	–	–	–	–	0.0	–	–	300	0.00	–	–	–	180	–	10	0.00	
0.37	0.43	5.00	0.50	1.50	100.0	30.0	100.0	6.8	500	4.50	100.0	250	–	264	3.8	–	0.00	
0.37	0.43	5.00	0.50	1.50	100.0	30.0	100.0	6.8	500	4.50	100.0	250	–	216	3.8	–	0.00	
–	–	–	–	–	–	2.4	–	–	35	0.00	–	–	510	205	–	81	0.00	
–	–	–	–	–	–	13.2	–	–	190	1.25	–	–	–	136	–	–	0.00	0.00
0.00	0.21	2.53	0.25	0.00	0.0	76.1	0.0	2.6	122	0.05	2.5	55	60	10	0.1	87	0.00	0.00
–	–	–	–	0.00	–	6.0	–	–	0	0.00	–	0	5	0	–	100	0.00	0.00
0.01	0.05	0.05	0.00	0.00	4.8	77.5	0.0	0.0	17	0.64	4.8	5	50	50	0.3	95	0.00	0.00
–	–	–	–	0.00	–	6.0	–	–	0	0.00	–	0	0	15	–	90	0.00	0.00
–	–	–	–	0.00	–	6.0	–	–	0	0.00	–	0	0	0	–	94	0.00	0.00
–	–	–	–	0.00	–	6.0	–	–	0	0.00	–	0	0	5	–	90	0.00	0.00
0.00	0.00	0.00	0.00	0.00	0.0	34.0	0.0	0.0	29	0.05	2.7	3	3	19	0.1	89	0.00	0.00
0.00	0.00	0.07	0.01	0.00	5.0	84.6	0.0	0.0	15	0.68	5.0	2	45	40	0.2	87	0.00	0.00
–	–	–	–	–	–	0.0	–	–	–	–	–	–	–	10	–	88	0.00	0.00
–	0.17	0.50	0.20	–	–	60.0	–	2.7	80	0.00	–	40	50	0	–	–	0.00	0.00
0.05	0.05	0.05	0.00	0.00	2.5	73.4	–	0.0	20	0.51	5.0	2	62	55	0.3	88	0.00	0.00
0.01	0.02	0.05	0.00	0.00	2.5	108.5	0.0	0.0	10	0.21	4.9	2	32	10	0.1	88	0.00	0.00
–	–	–	–	0.00	–	100.0	–	–	–	–	–	–	–	30	–	86	0.00	0.00
–	–	–	–	–	–	0.0	–	–	0	0.00	–	0	0	0	–	–	0.00	0.00
–	–	–	–	0.00	–	6.0	–	–	0	0.00	–	0	0	0	–	93	0.00	0.00

PAGE KEY: A-108 Beverage and Beverage Mixes A-112 Other Beverages A-112 Beverages, Alcoholic A-114 Candies and Confections, Gum A-114 Cereals, Breakfast Type A-118 Cheese and Cheese Substitutes A-120 Dairy Products and Substitutes A-122 Desserts A-128 Dessert Toppings A-128 Eggs, Substitutes, and Egg Dishes A-130 Ethnic Foods A-130 Fast Foods/Restaurants A-140 Fats, Oils, Margarines, Shortenings, and Substitutes A-142 Fish, Seafood, and Shellfish A-142 Food Additives A-142 Fruit, Vegetable, and Blended Juices A-144 Fruits A-146 Grains, Flours, and Fractions A-148 Grain Products, Prepared and Baked Goods

Code	Food Name	Unit/ Amt	Wt (g)	Energy (Kcal)	Prot (g)	Carb (g)	Fiber (g)	Fat (g)	Sat (g)	Mono (g)	Poly (g)	Chol (mg)	Vit A (RE)
20047	Lemonade, low cal, w/asp, prep f/pwd w/water	1 cup	237	5	0	1	0	0	0.0	0.0	0.0	0	0
20046	Lemonade, prep f/pwd w/water	1 cup	264	103	0	27	0	0	0.0	0.0	0.0	0	0
20000	Lemonade, white, prep f/fzn conc w/water	1 cup	248	99	0	26	0	0	0.0	0.0	0.0	0	5
20002	Limeade, prep f/fzn conc w/water	1 cup	247	101	0	27	0	0	0.0	0.0	0.0	0	0
OTHER BEVERAGES													
Teas													
20869	Tea, black, classic, brewed	1 cup	237	0	0	0	0	0	0.0	0.0	0.0	0	0
20872	Tea, black, classic, decaf, brewed	1 cup	237	0	0	0	0	0	0.0	0.0	0.0	0	0
20868	Tea, black, English breakfast, brewed	1 cup	237	0	0	0	0	0	0.0	0.0	0.0	0	0
20888	Tea, black, organic, brewed	1 cup	237	0	0	0	0	0	0.0	0.0	0.0	0	0
20866	Tea, black, Total Antioxidant, brewed	1 cup	237	0	0	0	0	0	0.0	0.0	0.0	0	125
20014	Tea, brewed w/tap water	1 cup	237	2	0	1	0	0	0.0	0.0	0.0	0	0
20883	Tea, chai, original, brewed w/water only	1 cup	237	0	0	0	0	0	0.0	0.0	0.0	0	0
20349	Tea, Crystal Light, iced, decaf, low cal, dry 1/8 tub	0.5 tsp	1	5	0	0	0	0	0.0	0.0	0.0	0	0
20324	Tea, Crystal Light, iced, raspberry, low calt, rtd	8 fl-oz	241	5	0	0	0	0	0.0	0.0	0.0	0	0
20875	Tea, green, decaf, brewed	1 cup	237	0	0	0	0	0	0.0	0.0	0.0	0	0
20909	Tea, herbal, caffeine free, brewed	1 cup	237	0	0	0	0	0	0.0	0.0	0.0	0	0
20905	Tea, herbal, Cinnamon Apple Spice, brewed	1 cup	237	0	0	0	0	0	0.0	0.0	0.0	0	0
20538	Tea, Nestea, Cool Drink, can/btl	1 cup	248	82	0	22	0	0	0.0	0.0	0.0	0	0
20539	Tea, Nestea, Cool Drink, diet, can/btl	1 cup	240	1	0	0	0	0	0.0	0.0	0.0	0	0
30454	Tea, Nestea, iced, lemon & sugar, dry mix	2 Tbs	19	80	0	19	0	0	0.0	0.0	0.0	0	0
Water													
20051	Water, btld	1 cup	237	0	0	0	0	0	0.0	0.0	0.0	0	0
20041	Water, municipal	1 cup	237	0	0	0	0	0	0.0	0.0	0.0	0	0
20010	Water, tonic	1 cup	244	83	0	21	0	0	0.0	0.0	0.0	0	0
20121	Water, tonic, diet, can	1 cup	237	1	0	0	0	0	0.0	0.0	0.0	0	0
BEVERAGES, ALCOHOLIC													
22500	Beer, can/btl, 12fl oz	1 ea	356	146	1	13	1	0	0.0	0.0	0.0	0	0
22512	Beer, light, can/btl, 12 fl oz	1 ea	354	99	1	5	0	0	0.0	0.0	0.0	0	0
22826	Beer, non alcoholic, O'douls, malt beverage	1 ea	361	70	1	15	–	0	0.0	0.0	0.0	0	–
22671	Bourbon, 80 proof	1 fl-oz	28	64	0	0	0	0	0.0	0.0	0.0	0	0
22513	Brandy, 80 proof	1 fl-oz	28	64	0	0	0	0	0.0	0.0	0.0	0	0
22514	Gin, 80 proof	1 fl-oz	28	64	0	0	0	0	0.0	0.0	0.0	0	0
22547	Liqueur, Amaretto, 1 shot	1 ea	30	106	0	13	0	0	0.0	0.0	0.0	0	0
22551	Liqueur, Kahlua, 1 shot	1 ea	30	106	0	13	0	0	0.0	0.0	0.0	0	0
34057	Mixed Drink, Bloody Mary, prep f/rec	1 ea	209	46	1	7	1	0	0.0	–	–	0	58
22538	Mixed Drink, Daiquiri, cnd, 6.8 fl oz can	1 ea	207	259	0	33	0	0	0.0	0.0	0.0	0	0
34058	Mixed Drink, Gin & Tonic, prep f/rec	1 ea	232	160	0	8	0	0	0.0	0.0	0.0	0	0
22556	Mixed Drink, High Ball	1 ea	160	105	0	0	0	0	0.0	0.0	0.0	0	0
22557	Mixed Drink, Margarita	1 ea	77	170	0	11	0	0	0.0	0.0	0.0	0	0
22561	Mixed Drink, Pina Colada	1 ea	141	245	1	32	0	3	2.3	0.1	0.0	0	0
22593	Rum, 80 proof	1 fl-oz	28	64	0	0	0	0	0.0	0.0	0.0	0	0
22515	Tequila, 80 proof	1 fl-oz	28	64	0	0	0	0	0.0	0.0	0.0	0	0
22594	Vodka, 80 proof	1 fl-oz	28	64	0	0	0	0	0.0	0.0	0.0	0	0
22670	Whiskey, 80 proof	1 fl-oz	28	64	0	0	0	0	0.0	0.0	0.0	0	0
22577	Wine, all table types	6 fl-oz	177	124	0	2	0	0	0.0	0.0	0.0	0	0
22608	Wine, cooking, red	1 fl-oz	30	20	0	3	0	0	0.0	0.0	0.0	0	0
22609	Wine, cooking, white, Fleischmann's	1 fl-oz	30	20	0	3	0	0	0.0	0.0	0.0	0	0
22681	Wine, cooler	12 fl-oz	340	170	0	20	0	0	0.0	0.0	0.0	0	0

PAGE KEY: A-154 Granola Bars, Cereal Bars, Diet Bars, Scones, and Tarts A-154 Meals and Dishes A-160 Meats A-164 Nuts, Seeds, and Products A-166 Poultry A-166 Salad Dressings, Dips, and Mayonnaise A-170 Salads A-170 Sandwiches A-172 Sauces and Gravies A-174 Snack Foods—Chips, Pretzels, Popcorn A-178 Soups, Stews and Chilis A-184 Spices, Flavors, and Seasonings A-184 Sports Bars and Drinks A-186 Supplemental Foods and Formulas A-186 Sweeteners and Sweet Substitutes A-188 Vegetables and Legumes A-200 Weight Loss Bars & Drinks A-200 Miscellaneous

Thia (mg)	Ribo (mg)	Niac (mg NE)	Vit B6 (mg)	Vit B12 (µg)	Fol (µg)	Vit C (mg)	Vit D (IU)	Vit E (mg AT)	Cal (mg)	Iron (mg)	Magn (mg)	Phos (mg)	Pota (mg)	Sodi (mg)	Zinc (mg)	Wat (%)	Alco (g)	Caff (g)
0.00	0.00	0.00	0.00	0.00	0.0	5.9	0.0	0.0	50	0.09	2.4	24	0	7	0.1	99	0.00	0.00
0.00	0.00	0.02	0.00	0.00	2.6	8.4	0.0	0.0	71	0.15	2.6	34	34	13	0.1	90	0.00	0.00
0.00	0.05	0.03	0.00	0.00	5.0	9.7	0.0	0.0	7	0.40	5.0	5	37	7	0.1	89	0.00	0.00
0.00	0.00	0.05	0.00	0.00	2.5	6.7	0.0	0.0	7	0.07	2.5	2	32	5	0.0	89	0.00	0.00
–	–	–	–	–	–	0.0	–	–	0	0.00	–	–	–	0	–	100	0.00	60.00
–	–	–	–	–	–	0.0	–	–	0	0.00	–	–	–	0	–	100	0.00	5.00
–	–	–	–	–	–	0.0	–	–	0	0.00	–	–	40	0	–	100	0.00	60.00
–	–	–	–	–	–	0.0	–	–	0	0.00	–	–	45	0	–	100	0.00	65.00
–	–	–	–	–	–	15.0	–	5.0	0	0.00	–	–	–	0	–	100	0.00	
0.00	0.02	0.00	0.00	0.00	11.8	0.0	0.0	0.0	0	0.05	7.1	2	88	7	0.0	100	0.00	47.36
–	–	–	–	–	–	0.0	–	–	0	0.00	–	–	–	0	–	100	0.00	30.00
–	–	–	–	0.00	–	6.0	–	–	0	0.00	–	–	20	0	–	4	0.00	
–	–	–	–	–	–	0.0	–	–	0	0.00	–	0	35	40	–	–	0.00	0.00
–	–	–	–	–	–	0.0	–	–	0	0.00	–	–	25	0	–	100	0.00	5.00
–	–	–	–	–	–	0.0	–	–	0	0.00	–	–	20	0	–	100	0.00	0.00
–	–	–	–	–	–	0.0	–	–	0	0.00	–	–	25	0	–	100	0.00	0.00
–	–	–	–	–	–	0.0	–	–	0	0.00	–	73	38	33	–	91	0.00	11.00
–	–	–	–	–	–	0.0	–	–	0	0.00	–	69	26	27	–	100	0.00	7.00
–	–	–	–	–	–	0.0	–	–	0	0.00	–	–	30	0	–	0	0.00	10.00
0.00	0.00	0.00	0.00	0.00	0.0	0.0	0.0	0.0	2	0.01	2.4	0	0	2	0.0	100	0.00	0.00
0.00	0.00	0.00	0.00	0.00	0.0	0.0	0.0	0.0	5	0.01	2.4	0	0	7	0.1	100	0.00	0.00
0.00	0.00	0.00	0.00	0.00	0.0	0.0	0.0	0.0	2	0.01	0.0	0	0	10	0.2	91	0.00	0.00
0.00	0.00	0.00	0.00	0.00	0.0	0.0	0.0	0.0	9	0.09	2.4	26	5	38	0.1	100	0.00	0.00
0.01	0.09	1.61	0.18	0.07	21.4	0.0	0.0	0.0	18	0.10	21.4	43	89	18	0.1	92	12.82	0.00
0.02	0.10	1.38	0.11	0.03	14.2	0.0	0.0	0.0	18	0.14	17.7	42	64	11	0.1	95	11.32	0.00
–	0.10	2.58	–	0.00	–	0.0	–	–	17	–	24.5	165	139	9	0.0	96	1.10	0.00
0.00	0.00	0.00	0.00	0.00	0.0	0.0	0.0	0.0	0	0.00	0.0	1	1	0	0.0	67	9.28	0.00
0.00	0.00	0.00	0.00	0.00	0.0	0.0	0.0	0.0	0	0.00	0.0	1	1	0	0.0	67	9.28	0.00
0.00	0.00	0.00	0.00	0.00	0.0	0.0	0.0	0.0	0	0.00	0.0	1	1	0	0.0	67	9.28	0.00
0.00	0.00	0.01	0.00	0.00	0.0	0.0	0.0	0.0	0	0.01	0.5	1	4	2	0.0	30	7.73	0.00
0.00	0.00	0.01	0.00	0.00	0.0	0.0	0.0	0.0	0	0.01	0.5	1	4	2	0.0	30	7.73	0.00
0.00	0.00	0.03	0.00	0.00	2.4	23.6	0.0	0.0	19	1.07	2.2	4	52	558	0.0	94	1.38	0.00
0.00	0.00	0.02	0.00	0.00	2.1	2.7	0.0	0.0	0	0.01	2.1	4	23	83	0.1	75	19.90	0.00
0.00	0.00	0.00	0.00	0.00	0.0	0.0	0.0	0.0	3	0.03	0.9	2	1	7	0.1	88	18.56	0.00
0.00	0.00	0.00	0.00	0.00	0.0	0.0	0.0	0.0	6	0.02	1.2	2	3	25	0.1	90	15.09	0.00
0.00	0.00	0.03	0.00	0.00	1.2	1.0	0.0	0.0	2	0.05	1.4	4	15	4	0.0	62	18.50	0.00
0.03	0.02	0.17	0.05	0.00	16.5	6.9	0.0	0.1	11	0.27	10.6	10	100	9	0.2	65	13.89	0.00
0.00	0.00	0.00	0.00	0.00	0.0	0.0	0.0	0.0	0	0.02	0.0	1	1	0	0.0	67	9.28	0.00
0.00	0.00	0.00	0.00	0.00	0.0	0.0	0.0	0.0	0	0.00	0.0	1	1	0	0.0	67	9.28	0.00
0.00	0.00	0.00	0.00	0.00	0.0	0.0	0.0	0.0	0	0.00	0.0	1	0	0	0.0	67	9.28	0.00
0.00	0.00	0.00	0.00	0.00	0.0	0.0	0.0	0.0	0	0.00	0.0	1	1	0	0.0	67	9.28	0.00
0.00	0.02	0.12	0.03	0.01	1.8	0.0	0.0	0.0	14	0.73	17.7	25	158	14	0.1	89	16.45	0.00
0.30	0.30	0.30	–	0.00	–	0.3	–	–	2	0.30	–	4	24	180	–	88	3.59	0.00
0.15	0.15	0.15	–	0.00	–	0.2	–	–	2	0.15	–	4	26	180	–	88	3.59	0.00
0.01	0.01	0.15	0.03	0.00	4.0	6.1	0.0	0.0	19	0.92	17.9	22	153	29	0.2	90	13.22	0.00

PAGE KEY: A-108 Beverage and Beverage Mixes A-112 Other Beverages A-112 Beverages, Alcoholic A-114 Candies and Confections, Gum A-114 Cereals, Breakfast Type A-118 Cheese and Cheese Substitutes A-120 Dairy Products and Substitutes A-122 Desserts A-128 Dessert Toppings A-128 Eggs, Substitutes, and Egg Dishes A-130 Ethnic Foods A-130 Fast Foods/Restaurants A-140 Fats, Oils, Margarines, Shortenings, and Substitutes A-142 Fish, Seafood, and Shellfish A-142 Food Additives A-142 Fruit, Vegetable, and Blended Juices A-144 Fruits A-146 Grains, Flours, and Fractions A-148 Grain Products, Prepared and Baked Goods

Code	Food Name	Unit/ Amt	Wt (g)	Energy (Kcal)	Prot (g)	Carb (g)	Fiber (g)	Fat (g)	Sat (g)	Mono (g)	Poly (g)	Chol (mg)	Vit A (RE)
CANDIES AND CONFECTIONS, GUM													
23017	Baking Chips, milk chocolate	1.5 oz	43	218	3	25	1	13	7.9	4.2	0.5	9	20
90704	Candy Bar, 3 Musketeers, .8oz bar	1 ea	23	94	1	17	0	3	1.5	1.0	0.1	2	6
90678	Candy Bar, Baby Ruth, 1.2oz bar	1 ea	34	164	3	22	1	7	4.0	2.1	1.1	1	0
90653	Candy Bar, Butterfinger, 1.6oz bar	1 ea	45	218	6	30	1	8	4.7	2.5	1.3	0	0
23060	Candy Bar, Kit Kat, 1.5oz bar	1 ea	43	220	3	27	1	12	7.4	2.0	0.2	4	9
23016	Candy Bar, milk chocolate, 1.55oz bar	1 ea	44	225	3	26	1	13	8.1	4.4	0.5	10	21
90686	Candy Bar, Milky Way, .8oz bar	1 ea	23	96	1	16	0	4	1.8	1.4	0.1	3	7
23133	Candy Bar, Nestle Crunch, 1.4 oz bar	1 ea	40	207	2	26	1	10	6.0	3.4	0.3	5	5
23040	Candy Bar, Snickers, 2oz bar	1 ea	57	272	5	34	1	14	5.1	4.2	1.7	7	22
23146	Candy Bar, Symphony, milk chocolate, 1.5oz bar	1 ea	43	226	4	25	1	13	7.8	3.4	0.3	10	19
90705	Candy Bar, Twix, caramel, 2.06oz two bar pkg	1 ea	58	291	3	38	1	14	5.2	3.2	5.2	4	6
91074	Candy, candy corn, prep f/rec	10 pce	11	40	0	10	0	0	0.0	0.0	0.0	0	0
23308	Candy, caramels	5 pce	41	170	2	32	0	3	1.0	–	–	2	0
23518	Candy, Crystal Dark, maltballs, chocolate	9 pce	40	190	2	25	2	11	6.5	–	–	0	4
23030	Candy, gummy bears	10 pce	22	85	0	22	0	0	0.0	0.0	0.0	0	0
23031	Candy, hard, all flvrs	1 pce	6	24	0	6	0	0	0.0	0.0	0.0	0	0
23074	Candy, hard, dietetic/low cal	1 pce	3	11	0	3	0	0	0.0	0.0	0.0	0	0
23033	Candy, jellybeans, sml	10 pce	11	40	0	10	0	0	0.0	0.0	0.0	0	0
23063	Candy, Kisses, milk chocolate	6 pce	28	145	2	17	1	9	5.2	2.8	0.3	6	16
52155	Candy, licorice, red, vines/ropes	4 pce	40	140	1	34	0	0	0.0	0.0	0.0	0	0
90690	Candy, M & M's, milk chocolate peanut, 1.67oz pkg	1 ea	47	244	4	29	2	12	4.9	5.2	2.0	4	12
90691	Candy, M & M's, plain chocolate, 1.48oz box	1 ea	42	206	2	30	1	9	5.5	2.8	0.3	6	8
23081	Candy, peanut brittle, prep f/rec	1.5 oz	43	204	3	30	1	8	2.0	3.6	2.0	5	19
23021	Candy, peanuts, milk chocolate cvrd	1.5 oz	43	221	6	21	2	14	6.2	5.5	1.8	4	0
23088	Candy, peanuts, yogurt cvrd	1.5 oz	43	230	6	18	2	16	6.9	4.8	3.1	0	0
90803	Candy, pralines, prep f/rec	1 pce	40	174	1	22	1	10	2.7	–	–	10	36
23214	Candy, Raisinets, chocolate cvrd raisins, 1.58oz pkg	1 ea	45	185	2	32	2	7	3.3	2.7	0.9	2	3
23089	Candy, raisins, yogurt cvrd	1.5 oz	43	167	2	31	1	5	4.3	0.1	0.1	0	0
23043	Candy, Reese's peanut butter cups, 1.6oz double pkg	1 ea	45	234	5	25	2	14	4.9	5.3	2.5	3	7
23436	Candy, Reese's Pieces, 1.6oz pkg	1 ea	45	225	6	27	1	11	7.4	2.0	0.9	0	0
90698	Candy, Rolo, caramels in milk chocolate, 1.74oz roll	1 ea	49	234	3	34	0	10	7.1	1.9	0.2	6	4
23485	Candy, Skittles, original bite size candies, 2.17 oz pkg	1 ea	62	249	0	56	0	3	0.5	1.8	0.1	0	0
23144	Candy, Starburst, fruit chews	1 pce	5	20	0	4	0	0	0.1	0.2	0.2	0	0
91507	Candy, Twizzlers, cherry bits	27 pce	40	139	1	32	0	1	0.2	0.8	0.1	0	0
23084	Candy, Whoppers, chocolate malted milk balls	10 ea	29	144	2	18	1	8	4.6	2.5	0.2	6	3
90660	Candy, York peppermint patty, sml, .5oz	1 ea	14	54	0	11	0	1	0.6	0.1	0.0	0	0
11594	Fruit Leather, Fruit Roll Up, berry, w/vit C	2 ea	28	104	0	24	–	1	0.3	0.5	0.0	–	–
91256	Fudge, plain	1.5 oz	43	188	0	27	0	9	6.0	–	–	11	10
23007	Marshmallows	1 ea	7	23	0	6	0	0	0.0	0.0	0.0	0	–
23008	Marshmallows, miniature	1.5 oz	43	135	1	35	0	0	0.0	0.0	0.0	0	–
CEREALS, BREAKFAST TYPE													
Cereals, Cooked and Dry													
40078	Cereal, Cream Of Rice, ckd w/water w/o salt	1 cup	244	127	2	28	0	0	0.1	0.1	0.1	0	0
38156	Cereal, Cream Of Rye, ckd	1 cup	251	109	2	24	4	0	0.0	0.0	0.2	0	0
40162	Cereal, Cream Of Wheat, mix 'n eat, apple, dry, pkt	1 ea	35	132	2	29	1	0	0.1	0.1	0.2	0	375
40160	Cereal, Cream Of Wheat, prep f/inst w/water w/o salt	1 cup	241	154	4	32	3	0	0.1	0.1	0.3	0	0
38497	Cereal, farina, Crmy Wheat, enrich, prp w/wtr w/salt	1 cup	233	119	4	26	1	0	0.0	0.1	0.0	0	0

Thia (mg)	Ribo (mg)	Niac (mg NE)	Vit B6 (mg)	Vit B12 (µg)	Fol (µg)	Vit C (mg)	Vit D (IU)	Vit E (mg AT)	Cal (mg)	Iron (mg)	Magn (mg)	Phos (mg)	Pota (mg)	Sodi (mg)	Zinc (mg)	Wat (%)	Alco (g)	Caff (g)
0.02	0.12	0.14	0.01	0.17	3.4	0.2	70.2	0.5	81	0.58	25.5	92	164	35	0.6	1	0.00	11.06
0.00	0.02	0.05	0.00	0.03	0.0	0.1	9.1	0.1	19	0.17	6.6	21	30	44	0.1	6	0.00	2.49
0.02	0.02	0.93	0.01	0.01	10.5	0.0	0.0	0.6	14	0.07	27.2	51	135	77	0.4	5	0.00	1.36
0.03	0.02	1.12	0.02	0.00	12.2	0.0	0.0	0.7	12	0.34	35.8	59	173	90	0.5	2	0.00	1.80
0.01	0.07	0.09	0.00	0.09	1.3	0.6	0.0	0.1	57	0.36	1.3	48	123	28	0.0	1	0.00	8.51
0.02	0.12	0.14	0.01	0.17	3.5	0.2	72.5	0.5	84	0.61	26.4	95	169	36	0.6	1	0.00	11.43
0.00	0.05	0.07	0.00	0.07	2.3	0.2	0.4	0.1	29	0.17	7.7	33	55	54	0.2	6	0.00	1.80
0.12	0.21	1.57	0.15	0.15	31.4	0.1	0.0	0.4	67	0.20	23.0	80	137	53	0.6	1	0.00	9.52
0.05	0.09	0.89	0.02	0.09	15.9	0.3	0.2	0.8	53	0.43	27.8	86	147	151	0.6	5	0.00	5.67
0.03	0.15	0.14	0.01	0.17	—	0.9	0.0	0.1	107	0.38	23.4	88	186	43	0.5	1	0.00	28.06
0.10	0.14	0.77	0.01	0.12	21.6	0.2	0.0	2.0	53	0.46	14.0	64	104	113	0.4	4	0.00	1.75
0.00	0.00	0.00	0.00	0.00	0.0	0.0	0.0	0.0	0	0.00	0.0	0	0	2	0.0	7	0.00	0.00
—	—	—	—	—	—	0.0	—	—	80	0.00	—	—	120	110	—	8	0.00	0.00
—	—	—	—	—	—	0.0	—	—	34	4.00	—	—	—	100	—	2	0.00	
0.00	0.00	0.00	0.00	0.00	0.0	0.0	0.0	0.0	1	0.09	0.2	0	1	10	0.0	1	0.00	0.00
0.00	0.00	0.00	0.00	0.00	0.0	0.0	0.0	0.0	0	0.01	0.2	0	0	2	0.0	1	0.00	0.00
0.00	0.00	0.00	0.00	0.00	0.0	0.0	0.0	0.0	0	0.00	0.0	0	0	0	0.0	1	0.00	0.00
0.00	0.00	0.00	0.00	0.00	0.0	0.0	0.0	0.0	0	0.11	0.2	0	4	3	0.0	6	0.00	0.00
0.01	0.09	0.09	0.00	0.10	2.3	0.1	—	0.4	54	0.38	17.0	61	109	23	0.4	1	0.00	6.96
—	—	—	—	—	—	0.0	—	—	0	0.00	—	—	—	20	—	12	0.00	0.00
0.05	0.07	1.94	0.03	0.07	18.0	0.2	0.5	1.2	48	0.54	36.0	110	164	23	1.1	2	0.00	5.21
0.00	0.05	0.05	0.00	0.07	1.3	0.2	0.4	0.2	44	0.46	10.9	40	70	26	0.3	2	0.00	7.55
0.05	0.01	1.12	0.02	0.00	19.6	0.0	1.3	1.2	11	0.52	17.9	46	71	195	0.4	2	0.00	0.00
0.05	0.07	1.80	0.09	0.10	3.4	0.0	43.4	1.1	44	0.56	40.0	90	213	17	0.8	2	0.00	9.35
0.14	0.09	2.48	0.07	0.18	49.9	0.1	—	2.3	64	0.93	35.0	113	202	24	0.8	4	0.00	0.00
0.05	0.02	0.11	0.01	0.02	2.5	0.2	4.8	0.4	20	0.34	13.4	33	67	40	0.4	17	—	0.00
0.03	0.10	0.18	0.05	0.09	2.2	0.1	42.6	0.5	48	0.52	20.2	65	230	16	0.4	6	0.00	11.19
0.05	0.07	0.33	0.07	0.12	3.9	0.9	—	0.6	48	0.56	10.3	55	236	19	0.2	10	0.00	0.00
0.07	0.05	2.03	0.05	0.11	22.7	0.1	1.0	0.1	35	0.55	28.1	73	156	142	0.6	1	0.00	8.15
0.07	0.10	2.75	0.05	0.05	24.9	0.0	1.0	0.4	31	0.21	39.9	94	163	88	0.5	1	0.00	0.00
0.00	0.05	0.01	0.00	0.10	0.0	0.4	40.7	0.0	72	0.20	0.0	35	93	93	0.0	5	0.00	2.47
0.00	0.00	0.00	0.00	0.00	0.0	41.2	0.0	0.2	0	0.00	0.6	1	3	10	0.0	4	0.00	0.00
0.00	0.00	0.00	0.00	0.00	0.0	2.6	0.0	0.1	0	0.00	0.1	0	0	3	0.0	7	0.00	0.00
—	—	—	—	—	—	0.0	—	0.0	3	0.10	—	10	15	78	—	15	0.00	
0.01	0.07	0.12	0.01	0.10	2.6	0.1	—	0.4	50	0.21	14.2	56	99	42	0.3	2	0.00	6.67
0.00	0.00	0.11	0.00	0.00	—	0.0	0.0	0.0	2	0.12	8.9	0	16	4	0.1	9	0.00	1.41
—	—	—	—	—	—	33.6	—	—	—	—	—	—	—	89	—	10	0.00	0.00
—	—	—	—	—	—	0.0	—	—	0	0.18	—	—	—	42	—	—	0.00	0.00
0.00	0.00	0.00	0.00	0.00	0.1	0.0	0.0	0.0	0	0.01	0.1	1	0	3	0.0	16	0.00	0.00
0.00	0.00	0.02	0.00	0.00	0.4	0.0	0.0	0.0	1	0.10	0.9	3	2	20	0.0	16	0.00	0.00
0.00	0.00	0.98	0.07	0.00	7.3	0.0	0.0	0.0	7	0.49	7.3	41	49	2	0.4	88	0.00	0.00
0.07	0.02	0.20	0.05	0.00	4.6	0.0	0.0	0.2	11	0.52	22.9	55	66	7	0.6	89	0.00	0.00
0.38	0.25	4.98	0.50	0.00	99.8	0.0	0.0	0.1	40	8.10	9.2	20	55	241	0.2	8	0.00	0.00
0.23	0.00	1.69	0.02	0.00	149.4	0.0	0.0	0.0	60	12.05	14.5	43	48	7	0.4	84	0.00	0.00
0.15	0.10	1.80	0.01	0.00	53.6	0.0	0.0	0.0	9	11.00	7.0	30	33	128	0.2	87	0.00	0.00

PAGE KEY: A-108 Beverage and Beverage Mixes A-112 Other Beverages A-112 Beverages, Alcoholic A-114 Candies and Confections, Gum A-114 Cereals, Breakfast Type A-118 Cheese and Cheese Substitutes A-120 Dairy Products and Substitutes A-122 Desserts A-128 Dessert Toppings A-128 Eggs, Substitutes, and Egg Dishes A-130 Ethnic Foods A-130 Fast Foods/Restaurants A-140 Fats, Oils, Margarines, Shortenings, and Substitutes A-142 Fish, Seafood, and Shellfish A-142 Food Additives A-142 Fruit, Vegetable, and Blended Juices A-144 Fruits A-146 Grains, Flours, and Fractions A-148 Grain Products, Prepared and Baked Goods

Code	Food Name	Unit/ Amt	Wt (g)	Energy (Kcal)	Prot (g)	Carb (g)	Fiber (g)	Fat (g)	Sat (g)	Mono (g)	Poly (g)	Chol (mg)	Vit A (RE)
40014	Cereal, hot, Malt-O-Meal, pln/choc, ckd w/wtr w/o salt	1 cup	240	122	4	26	1	0	0.1	0.1	0.0	0	0
40138	Cereal, hot, multigrain, ckd	1 cup	246	202	7	40	4	2	0.3	0.5	1.1	0	116
38501	Cereal, hot, oat bran, prep w/water w/o salt	1 cup	219	94	4	16	4	2	0.4	0.7	0.8	0	4
40141	Cereal, hot, oat, reg, dry, General Mills	0.5 cup	40	148	6	27	4	3	0.5	0.9	0.7	0	–
40073	Cereal, hot, oatmeal, app cinn inst prep w/water f/pkt	1 ea	149	125	3	26	3	1	0.3	0.5	0.6	0	305
60923	Cereal, hot, oatmeal, fruit & cream, inst, dry pkt	1 ea	35	135	3	26	2	3	0.5	0.8	0.6	0	210
40468	Cereal, hot, oatmeal, inst, dry, Quaker	0.5 cup	40	149	5	25	4	3	0.4	0.9	0.9	0	194
40075	Cereal, hot, oatmeal, map & brwn sug, inst, prep f/pkt	1 ea	155	153	4	31	3	2	0.4	0.6	0.7	0	302
40072	Cereal, hot, oatmeal, plain, inst, fort, prep w/water f/pkt	1 ea	177	104	4	18	3	2	0.3	0.6	0.7	0	453
40002	Cereal, hot, whole wheat, natural, ckd w/water w/o salt	1 cup	242	150	5	33	4	1	0.1	0.1	0.5	0	0
40089	Grits, corn, inst, plain, prep w/water f/pkt	1 ea	137	89	2	21	1	0	0.0	0.0	0.1	0	0
40154	Grits, corn, inst, w/imit ham bits, dry, pkt	1 ea	28	95	3	21	1	1	0.1	0.1	0.1	0	0
Cereals, Ready To Eat													
54234	Cereal, 100% Bran, rte, dry	0.33 cup	29	83	4	23	8	1	0.1	–	–	0	150
40063	Cereal, 100% Natural, oat & honey, rte, dry	0.5 cup	48	218	5	32	4	9	4.0	2.1	0.9	1	1
40095	Cereal, All-Bran, rte, dry	0.5 cup	30	78	4	22	10	1	0.2	0.2	0.6	0	158
40394	Cereal, Basic 4, rte, dry	1 cup	55	202	4	42	3	3	0.4	1.0	1.1	0	118
40279	Cereal, Blueberry Morning, rte, dry	1.25 cup	55	211	4	43	2	2	0.3	–	–	0	150
40033	Cereal, Cap'N Crunch, crunchberries, rte, dry	0.75 cup	26	104	1	22	1	1	0.4	0.3	0.2	0	4
40032	Cereal, Cap'N Crunch, rte, dry	0.75 cup	27	108	1	23	1	2	0.4	0.3	0.2	0	4
40297	Cereal, Cheerios	1 cup	30	111	3	22	3	2	0.4	0.6	0.2	0	150
40051	Cereal, Cheerios, honey nut, rte, dry	1 cup	30	112	3	24	2	1	0.2	0.4	0.5	0	150
54235	Cereal, Cheerios, multigrain, rte, dry	1 cup	30	108	2	24	3	1	0.3	0.5	0.3	0	142
40323	Cereal, Chex, bran, rte, dry	1 cup	49	156	5	39	8	1	0.2	0.3	0.7	0	11
40325	Cereal, Chex, corn, rte, dry	1 cup	30	112	2	26	1	0	0.1	0.1	0.1	0	150
60924	Cereal, Chex, multi-bran, rte, dry	1 cup	49	166	3	41	6	1	0.2	0.3	0.5	0	134
40333	Cereal, Chex, rice, rte, dry	1.25 cup	31	117	2	27	0	0	0.1	0.1	0.1	0	155
40335	Cereal, Chex, wheat, rte, dry	1 cup	30	104	3	24	3	1	0.1	0.1	0.2	0	90
60938	Cereal, Cinnamon Crunch, rte, dry, bagged	1 oz	28	113	1	24	1	2	0.4	0.3	0.2	0	156
40102	Cereal, Cocoa Krispies, rte, dry	0.75 cup	31	118	1	27	1	1	0.5	0.3	0.2	0	153
40324	Cereal, Cookie Crisp, rte, dry	1 cup	30	117	1	26	0	1	0.2	0.4	0.2	0	150
40195	Cereal, corn flakes, rte, dry	1 cup	28	101	2	24	1	0	0.1	0.1	0.1	0	150
40206	Cereal, Corn Pops, rte, dry	1 cup	31	118	1	28	0	0	0.1	0.1	0.1	0	150
40205	Cereal, Cracklin' Oat Bran, rte, dry	0.75 cup	55	225	5	39	6	8	2.3	4.6	1.2	0	252
4354	Cereal, Cranberry Almond Crunch, rte, dry	1 cup	55	220	4	44	3	3	0.0	–	–	0	150
40104	Cereal, Crispix, rte, dry	1 cup	29	109	2	25	0	0	0.1	0.1	0.1	0	150
40130	Cereal, Fiber One, rte, dry	0.5 cup	30	59	2	24	14	1	0.1	0.1	0.4	0	0
40218	Cereal, Froot Loops, rte, dry	1 cup	30	118	1	26	1	1	0.6	0.3	0.4	0	145
40217	Cereal, Frosted Flakes, rte, dry	0.75 cup	31	114	1	28	1	0	0.1	0.0	0.1	0	160
40043	Cereal, Frosted Mini Wheats, rte, dry	1 cup	51	173	5	41	5	1	0.2	0.1	0.5	0	0
40493	Cereal, Fruit & Fibre, date raisin nut, rte, dry	1 cup	57	193	5	43	8	3	0.4	0.5	1.5	0	722
40266	Cereal, Fruity Pebbles, rte, dry	0.75 cup	27	108	1	24	0	1	0.2	0.5	0.3	0	150
40299	Cereal, Golden Grahams, rte, dry	0.75 cup	30	112	2	25	1	1	0.2	0.4	0.4	0	150
40009	Cereal, granola, 100% Nat, honey raisin oats, rte, dry	0.5 cup	51	225	5	34	3	9	3.6	3.8	1.1	1	1
40045	Cereal, granola, 100% Nat, w/raisins, low fat, rte, dry	0.66 cup	55	213	5	44	3	3	0.8	1.3	0.6	1	2
40277	Cereal, Grape Nuts, rte, dry	0.5 cup	58	208	6	47	5	1	0.2	0.2	0.7	0	150
60969	Cereal, Harmony, rte, dry	1 oz	28	103	3	22	1	1	0.1	–	–	0	77
40293	Cereal, Honey Bunches Of Oats, almond, rte, dry	0.75 cup	31	126	2	24	1	3	0.3	–	–	0	150

PAGE KEY: A-154 Granola Bars, Cereal Bars, Diet Bars, Scones, and Tarts A-154 Meals and Dishes A-160 Meats A-164 Nuts, Seeds, and Products A-166 Poultry A-166 Salad Dressings, Dips, and Mayonnaise A-170 Salads A-170 Sandwiches A-172 Sauces and Gravies A-174 Snack Foods—Chips, Pretzels, Popcorn A-178 Soups, Stews and Chilis A-184 Spices, Flavors, and Seasonings A-184 Sports Bars and Drinks A-186 Supplemental Foods and Formulas A-186 Sweeteners and Sweet Substitutes A-188 Vegetables and Legumes A-200 Weight Loss Bars & Drinks A-200 Miscellaneous

Thia (mg)	Ribo (mg)	Niac (mg NE)	Vit B6 (mg)	Vit B12 (µg)	Fol (µg)	Vit C (mg)	Vit D (IU)	Vit E (mg AT)	Cal (mg)	Iron (mg)	Magn (mg)	Phos (mg)	Pota (mg)	Sodi (mg)	Zinc (mg)	Wat (%)	Alco (g)	Caff (g)
0.47	0.23	5.76	0.01	0.00	4.8	0.0	0.0	0.0	5	9.60	4.8	24	31	2	0.2	88	0.00	2.40
0.38	0.46	4.42	0.46	0.00	17.2	0.0	0.0	3.4	69	5.40	66.4	184	138	2	0.9	79	0.00	0.00
0.25	0.07	0.20	0.02	0.00	11.0	0.0	0.0	0.1	24	2.11	65.7	182	151	7	1.2	89	0.00	0.00
0.15	0.05	0.37	–	–	–	–	–	–	22	1.86	–	–	153	1	–	12	0.00	0.00
0.30	0.34	4.07	0.40	0.00	93.9	0.3	0.0	0.1	104	3.89	29.8	113	106	121	0.7	79	0.00	0.00
0.31	0.36	4.19	0.41	0.00	84.0	0.1	–	0.1	106	4.00	27.6	105	97	169	0.6	6	0.00	
0.68	0.34	5.67	0.74	–	190.8	0.0	–	0.3	239	11.76	54.4	198	146	317	1.2	10	0.00	0.00
0.30	0.34	4.03	0.40	0.00	80.6	0.0	0.0	0.2	105	3.85	38.8	132	112	234	0.9	75	0.00	0.00
0.52	0.28	5.46	0.74	0.00	97.3	0.0	0.0	0.2	163	6.30	42.5	133	99	285	0.9	86	0.00	0.00
0.17	0.11	2.15	0.18	0.00	26.6	0.0	0.0	0.5	17	1.50	53.2	167	172	0	1.2	84	0.00	0.00
0.15	0.07	1.37	0.05	0.00	46.6	0.0	0.0	0.0	8	8.18	11.0	29	38	289	0.2	82	0.00	0.00
0.17	0.20	2.33	0.05	0.05	46.5	0.0	0.0	0.0	15	8.10	14.0	37	50	493	0.2	7	0.00	0.00
0.37	0.43	5.00	0.50	0.00	100.0	0.0	0.0	–	22	8.10	80.6	236	275	121	3.7	3	0.00	
0.15	0.12	0.95	0.09	0.11	17.3	0.2	0.0	1.7	57	1.24	53.3	165	238	23	1.1	2	0.00	0.00
0.36	0.41	4.80	1.79	6.00	393.0	6.0	51.0	0.6	99	4.80	114.0	339	339	77	1.8	3	0.00	0.00
0.30	0.34	3.90	0.38	1.14	78.7	0.0	31.4	0.7	196	3.51	40.2	232	155	316	3.0	7	0.00	0.00
0.37	0.41	5.00	0.50	1.50	100.1	0.0	40.2	–	15	1.79	23.6	70	91	266	0.9	7	0.00	0.00
0.40	0.46	5.48	0.55	0.00	404.6	0.0	0.0	0.2	5	4.94	14.6	44	54	182	4.1	2	0.00	0.00
0.43	0.47	5.71	0.56	0.00	420.1	0.0	0.0	0.2	4	5.15	15.1	45	54	202	4.3	2	0.00	0.00
0.37	0.43	5.01	0.50	1.50	200.1	6.0	39.9	0.2	100	8.10	39.9	100	96	273	3.8	3	0.00	0.00
0.37	0.43	5.01	0.50	1.50	200.1	6.0	39.9	0.3	100	4.50	32.1	100	92	269	3.8	2	0.00	0.00
1.41	1.61	18.95	1.89	5.67	378.9	14.1	37.8	19.1	95	17.04	27.9	98	88	201	14.2	3	0.00	0.00
0.63	0.25	8.61	0.87	2.59	173.0	26.0	0.0	0.6	29	13.98	69.1	173	216	345	6.5	2	0.00	0.00
0.37	0.43	5.01	0.50	1.50	200.1	6.0	0.0	0.1	100	9.00	8.4	22	25	288	3.8	2	0.00	0.00
0.33	0.37	4.46	0.44	1.32	356.2	5.4	35.8	0.2	89	14.44	53.4	178	190	322	3.3	2	0.00	0.00
0.38	0.43	5.17	0.51	1.54	206.8	6.2	41.2	0.0	103	9.30	9.3	35	30	292	3.9	3	0.00	0.00
0.23	0.25	3.00	0.30	0.89	240.0	3.6	24.0	0.4	60	8.69	24.0	90	113	267	2.4	2	0.00	0.00
0.38	0.43	5.19	0.51	0.00	396.9	6.2	0.0	0.2	9	4.67	17.6	54	57	220	3.9	2	0.00	
0.37	0.43	4.96	0.50	1.51	102.0	15.0	40.3	0.1	5	4.65	11.8	30	50	190	1.5	3	0.00	0.62
0.37	0.43	5.01	0.50	1.50	99.9	6.0	39.9	0.1	100	4.50	8.4	40	27	178	3.8	2	0.00	0.60
0.36	0.43	5.01	0.50	1.50	102.2	6.2	42.6	0.0	2	8.39	3.1	14	25	203	0.1	3	0.00	0.00
0.37	0.43	4.98	0.50	1.51	102.0	6.0	50.2	0.0	5	1.91	2.2	10	26	120	1.5	3	0.00	0.00
0.41	0.47	5.67	0.56	1.71	112.8	16.8	45.0	0.4	23	2.03	67.7	179	248	157	1.7	3	0.00	0.00
0.37	0.43	5.00	0.50	1.50	100.0	0.0	40.0	–	0	1.79	24.0	100	110	200	1.5	5	0.00	0.00
0.37	0.43	5.21	0.49	1.50	200.1	5.8	40.0	0.1	6	8.11	7.2	26	38	210	1.4	3	0.00	0.00
0.37	0.43	5.01	0.50	1.50	99.9	6.0	0.0	0.1	100	4.50	60.0	150	232	129	3.8	4	0.00	0.00
0.36	0.38	4.67	0.47	1.40	93.9	14.1	37.5	0.1	23	4.23	8.7	19	33	141	1.4	3	0.00	0.00
0.37	0.46	5.01	0.50	1.54	103.5	6.2	40.0	0.0	2	0.99	2.5	11	23	148	0.1	3	0.00	0.00
0.37	0.41	5.00	0.50	1.50	100.0	0.0	0.0	0.5	16	14.78	60.2	150	173	5	1.6	6	0.00	0.00
0.75	0.85	10.02	1.00	3.00	200.5	0.0	100.0	1.3	30	10.10	80.7	220	334	269	3.0	9	0.00	0.00
0.37	0.41	5.00	0.50	1.50	99.9	0.0	40.0	–	1	1.79	5.1	16	30	158	1.5	3	0.00	0.00
0.37	0.43	5.01	0.50	1.50	99.9	6.0	39.9	0.2	350	4.50	8.1	200	50	268	3.8	3	0.00	0.00
0.12	0.11	0.80	0.07	0.10	14.1	0.4	0.0	0.5	59	1.24	48.9	152	250	19	1.0	4	0.00	0.00
0.15	0.05	1.00	0.07	0.00	12.9	0.4	0.0	0.3	33	1.42	43.6	130	189	145	1.0	4	0.00	0.00
0.37	0.41	5.00	0.50	1.50	99.8	0.0	40.0	–	20	16.20	58.0	139	178	354	1.2	4	0.00	0.00
0.76	0.43	5.15	0.51	2.15	206.1	15.6	20.7	15.6	309	4.65	12.5	52	47	183	3.9	3	0.00	
0.37	0.41	5.00	0.50	1.50	100.1	0.0	40.0	–	11	8.10	21.4	60	70	187	0.3	3	0.00	0.00

PAGE KEY: A-108 Beverage and Beverage Mixes A-112 Other Beverages A-112 Beverages, Alcoholic A-114 Candies and Confections, Gum A-114 Cereals, Breakfast Type A-118 Cheese and Cheese Substitutes A-120 Dairy Products and Substitutes A-122 Desserts A-128 Dessert Toppings A-128 Eggs, Substitutes, and Egg Dishes A-130 Ethnic Foods A-130 Fast Foods/Restaurants A-140 Fats, Oils, Margarines, Shortenings, and Substitutes A-142 Fish, Seafood, and Shellfish A-142 Food Additives A-142 Fruit, Vegetable, and Blended Juices A-144 Fruits A-146 Grains, Flours, and Fractions A-148 Grain Products, Prepared and Baked Goods

Code	Food Name	Unit/ Amt	Wt (g)	Energy (Kcal)	Prot (g)	Carb (g)	Fiber (g)	Fat (g)	Sat (g)	Mono (g)	Poly (g)	Chol (mg)	Vit A (RE)
40264	Cereal, Honeycomb, rte, dry	1.33 cup	29	115	2	26	1	1	0.2	0.2	0.3	0	150
40134	Cereal, Just Right	1 cup	43	160	3	36	2	1	0.1	0.2	0.8	0	294
60957	Cereal, Kashi Go Lean, Crunch, rte, dry	1 oz	28	107	5	19	4	2	0.1	0.9	0.6	0	1
40054	Cereal, King Vitaman, rte, dry	1.5 cup	31	120	2	26	1	1	0.2	0.2	0.3	0	310
40010	Cereal, Kix, rte, dry	1.33 cup	30	113	2	26	1	1	0.2	0.2	0.2	0	159
40011	Cereal, Life, plain, rte, dry	0.75 cup	32	120	3	25	2	1	0.3	0.5	0.5	0	1
40300	Cereal, Lucky Charms, rte, dry	1 cup	30	114	2	25	2	1	0.2	0.3	0.3	0	150
40112	Cereal, Nut & Honey Crunch, rte, dry	1.25 cup	55	223	4	46	1	2	0.5	1.2	0.8	0	226
40348	Cereal, Oatmeal Crisp, w/almonds, rte, dry	1 cup	55	218	6	42	4	5	0.6	2.4	1.2	0	0
40302	Cereal, Oatmeal Raisin Crisp, rte, dry	1 cup	55	204	5	45	4	2	0.4	0.7	0.6	0	0
60950	Cereal, puffed rice, rte, dry	1 oz	28	117	2	25	0	0	0.1	0.1	0.2	0	–
60952	Cereal, Raisin Bran Crunch, rte, dry	1 cup	53	188	3	45	4	1	0.2	0.4	0.4	0	108
40260	Cereal, raisin bran, rte, dry	1 cup	59	187	5	46	8	1	0.2	0.2	0.7	0	150
40343	Cereal, Reese's Peanut Butter Puffs, rte, dry	0.75 cup	30	128	2	23	0	3	0.6	1.2	0.9	0	150
40210	Cereal, Rice Krispies, rte, dry	1.25 cup	33	128	2	29	0	0	0.1	0.1	0.2	0	153
40286	Cereal, Shredded Wheat, biscuits, rte, dry	2 ea	46	156	5	38	5	1	0.1	–	–	0	0
60956	Cereal, Smart Start, w/soy protein, rte, dry	1 oz	28	104	5	21	2	1	0.2	–	–	0	77
40211	Cereal, Special K, rte, dry	1 cup	31	117	7	22	1	0	0.1	0.1	0.2	0	230
40307	Cereal, Wheaties, rte, dry	1 cup	30	107	3	24	3	1	0.2	0.3	0.4	0	150
	CHEESE AND CHEESE SUBSTITUTES												
	Natural Cheeses												
1532	Cheese, asiago	1 oz	28	102	7	1	0	8	5.1	–	–	25	51
47855	Cheese, blue, 1″ cube	1 ea	17	61	4	0	0	5	3.2	1.3	0.1	13	35
47857	Cheese, brick, 1″ cube	1 ea	17	64	4	0	0	5	3.2	1.5	0.1	16	52
47859	Cheese, brie, 1″ cube	1 ea	17	57	4	0	0	5	3.0	1.4	0.1	17	31
47861	Cheese, camembert, 1″ cube	1 ea	17	51	3	0	0	4	2.6	1.2	0.1	12	43
47791	Cheese, cheddar & monterey jack, marbled	1 oz	28	110	7	1	0	9	6.0	–	–	30	60
47863	Cheese, cheddar, 1″ cube	1 ea	17	69	4	0	0	6	3.6	1.6	0.2	18	47
1551	Cheese, cheddar, fat free, 1″ cube	1 ea	28	40	8	1	0	0	0.0	0.0	0.0	3	60
47955	Cheese, cheddar, light, 50% rducd fat, sliced	1 pce	28	70	8	1	0	4	3.0	–	–	15	60
47939	Cheese, cheddar, low fat, 1″ cube	1 ea	17	30	4	0	0	1	0.8	0.4	0.0	4	11
1008	Cheese, cheddar, shredded	0.25 cup	28	114	7	0	0	9	6.0	2.7	0.3	30	79
47864	Cheese, cheddar, slice, 1 oz	1 ea	28	114	7	0	0	9	6.0	2.7	0.3	30	79
47953	Cheese, colby jack, 1″ cube	1 ea	28	110	7	1	0	9	5.0	–	–	30	60
47865	Cheese, colby, 1″ cube	1 ea	17	68	4	0	0	6	3.5	1.6	0.2	16	47
47940	Cheese, colby, low fat, 1″ cube	1 ea	17	30	4	0	0	1	0.8	0.4	0.0	4	11
47871	Cheese, feta, 1″ cube	1 ea	17	45	2	1	0	4	2.5	0.8	0.1	15	22
47873	Cheese, fontina, 1″ cube	1 ea	15	58	4	0	0	5	2.9	1.3	0.2	17	44
1080	Cheese, goat, soft	1 oz	28	76	5	0	0	6	4.1	1.4	0.1	13	80
1054	Cheese, gouda	1 oz	28	101	7	1	0	8	5.0	2.2	0.2	32	49
47878	Cheese, gruyere, 1″ cube	1 ea	15	62	4	0	0	5	2.8	1.5	0.3	16	45
47884	Cheese, monterey jack, 1″ cube	1 ea	17	64	4	0	0	5	3.3	1.5	0.2	15	39
1633	Cheese, mozzarella, fat & lactose free, 1″ cube	1 ea	28	40	8	1	0	0	0.0	0.0	0.0	3	60
1553	Cheese, mozzarella, fat free, 1″ cube	1 ea	28	40	8	1	0	0	0.0	0.0	0.0	3	60
13352	Cheese, mozzarella, low moist, 50% less fat	1 oz	28	70	8	1	0	3	2.0	–	–	10	60
47889	Cheese, mozzarella, low moist, part skm, 1″ cube	1 ea	18	49	5	1	0	3	1.9	0.9	0.1	10	34
1019	Cheese, mozzarella, low moist, part skm, shredded	0.25 cup	28	79	8	1	0	5	3.1	1.4	0.1	15	54
47890	Cheese, mozzarella, low moist, part skm, slice, 1oz	1 ea	28	79	8	1	0	5	3.1	1.4	0.1	15	54
1075	Cheese, parmesan, grated	1 Tbs	5	23	2	0	0	2	1.0	0.4	0.0	4	7

PAGE KEY: A-154 Granola Bars, Cereal Bars, Diet Bars, Scones, and Tarts A-154 Meals and Dishes A-160 Meats A-164 Nuts, Seeds, and Products A-166 Poultry A-166 Salad Dressings, Dips, and Mayonnaise A-170 Salads A-170 Sandwiches A-172 Sauces and Gravies A-174 Snack Foods—Chips, Pretzels, Popcorn A-178 Soups, Stews and Chilis A-184 Spices, Flavors, and Seasonings A-184 Sports Bars and Drinks A-186 Supplemental Foods and Formulas A-186 Sweeteners and Sweet Substitutes A-188 Vegetables and Legumes A-200 Weight Loss Bars & Drinks A-200 Miscellaneous

Thia (mg)	Ribo (mg)	Niac (mg NE)	Vit B6 (mg)	Vit B12 (μg)	Fol (μg)	Vit C (mg)	Vit D (IU)	Vit E (mg AT)	Cal (mg)	Iron (mg)	Magn (mg)	Phos (mg)	Pota (mg)	Sodi (mg)	Zinc (mg)	Wat (%)	Alco (g)	Caff (g)
0.37	0.43	5.00	0.50	1.50	100.0	0.0	40.0	—	5	2.70	10.7	27	35	215	1.5	2	0.00	0.00
0.30	0.34	3.91	0.38	1.15	80.0	0.0	—	1.8	11	12.68	26.7	83	95	264	0.7	3	0.00	0.00
0.01	0.00	0.09	0.00	—	0.6	0.0	—	0.8	25	0.99	23.5	60	160	109	0.3	4	0.00	
0.38	0.43	5.15	0.50	1.54	413.2	12.4	41.3	2.1	4	8.98	26.0	79	86	260	3.9	2	0.00	0.00
0.37	0.43	5.01	0.50	1.50	200.1	6.3	42.3	0.1	150	8.10	8.1	40	35	267	3.8	2	0.00	0.00
0.40	0.46	5.50	0.55	0.00	416.0	0.0	0.0	0.2	112	8.94	30.7	133	91	164	4.1	4	0.00	0.00
0.37	0.43	5.01	0.50	1.50	200.1	6.0	39.9	0.1	100	4.50	15.9	60	57	203	3.8	2	0.00	0.00
0.37	0.43	5.01	0.50	0.00	110.0	15.0	50.0	0.1	6	4.51	5.0	36	60	370	0.4	2	0.00	0.00
0.37	0.41	5.01	0.50	1.49	100.1	6.1	0.0	3.1	20	4.51	60.0	150	184	236	3.7	2	0.00	0.00
0.37	0.41	5.01	0.50	1.49	100.1	6.1	0.0	1.4	20	4.51	40.2	100	200	216	3.8	6	0.00	0.00
—	—	—	—	—	—	—	—	—	3	0.25	13.3	45	43	0	0.5	2	0.00	
0.37	0.41	5.30	0.47	1.53	100.7	0.7	39.7	—	19	4.50	46.6	137	213	209	1.6	5	0.00	
0.37	0.41	5.00	0.50	1.50	99.7	0.0	40.1	—	27	10.80	88.5	208	357	360	2.2	9	0.00	0.00
0.37	0.43	5.01	0.50	1.50	99.9	6.0	39.9	0.6	100	4.50	15.9	20	42	166	3.8	3	0.00	0.00
0.37	0.46	5.05	0.50	1.49	104.0	6.4	40.9	0.0	5	1.82	13.2	46	44	319	0.5	3	0.00	0.00
0.11	0.05	2.55	0.18	0.00	19.8	0.0	0.0	—	20	1.44	54.3	168	196	3	1.3	4	0.00	0.00
0.79	0.87	10.31	1.04	3.11	207.0	7.7	24.1	10.5	31	9.35	30.9	77	211	134	7.7	4	0.00	
0.52	0.58	7.13	1.98	6.05	399.9	21.0	50.0	7.1	9	8.36	19.2	68	61	224	0.9	3	0.00	0.00
0.75	0.85	9.98	1.00	3.00	200.1	6.0	39.9	0.4	0	8.10	32.1	100	111	218	7.5	3	0.00	0.00
—	—	—	—	—	—	0.0	—	—	213	0.18	—	—	—	346	—	40	0.00	0.00
0.00	0.07	0.18	0.02	0.20	6.2	0.0	1.6	0.1	91	0.05	4.0	67	44	241	0.5	42	0.00	0.00
0.00	0.05	0.01	0.00	0.21	3.4	0.0	1.8	0.1	116	0.07	4.1	78	23	96	0.4	41	0.00	0.00
0.00	0.09	0.05	0.03	0.28	11.1	0.0	1.4	0.1	31	0.09	3.4	32	26	107	0.4	48	0.00	0.00
0.00	0.07	0.10	0.03	0.21	10.5	0.0	2.0	0.1	66	0.05	3.4	59	32	143	0.4	52	0.00	0.00
—	0.10	—	—	—	—	0.0	—	—	200	0.00	—	150	20	190	0.9	36	0.00	0.00
0.00	0.05	0.00	0.00	0.14	3.1	0.0	2.0	0.1	123	0.11	4.8	87	17	106	0.5	37	0.00	0.00
—	—	—	—	—	—	—	—	—	400	—	—	—	—	220	—	63	0.00	0.00
—	—	—	—	—	—	0.0	—	—	200	0.00	—	—	—	170	—	51	0.00	0.00
0.00	0.03	0.00	0.00	0.07	1.9	0.0	0.0	0.0	72	0.07	2.8	84	11	106	0.3	63	0.00	0.00
0.00	0.10	0.01	0.01	0.23	5.1	0.0	3.4	0.1	204	0.18	7.9	145	28	175	0.9	37	0.00	0.00
0.00	0.10	0.01	0.01	0.23	5.1	0.0	3.4	0.1	204	0.18	7.9	145	28	176	0.9	37	0.00	0.00
—	—	—	—	—	—	0.0	—	—	200	0.00	—	—	—	170	—	35	0.00	0.00
0.00	0.05	0.01	0.00	0.14	3.1	0.0	1.6	0.1	118	0.12	4.5	79	22	104	0.5	38	0.00	0.00
0.00	0.03	0.00	0.00	0.07	1.9	0.0	0.0	0.0	72	0.07	2.8	84	11	106	0.3	63	0.00	0.00
0.02	0.14	0.17	0.07	0.28	5.4	0.0	3.4	0.0	84	0.10	3.2	57	11	190	0.5	55	0.00	0.00
0.00	0.02	0.01	0.00	0.25	0.9	0.0	1.4	0.1	82	0.02	2.1	52	10	120	0.5	38	0.00	0.00
0.01	0.10	0.11	0.07	0.05	3.4	0.0	1.8	0.1	40	0.54	4.5	73	7	104	0.3	61	0.00	0.00
0.00	0.09	0.01	0.01	0.43	6.0	0.0	2.7	0.1	198	0.07	8.2	155	34	232	1.1	41	0.00	0.00
0.00	0.03	0.01	0.00	0.23	1.5	0.0	1.5	0.1	152	0.02	5.4	91	12	50	0.6	33	0.00	0.00
0.00	0.07	0.01	0.00	0.14	3.1	0.0	1.6	0.1	128	0.11	4.6	76	14	92	0.5	41	0.00	0.00
—	—	—	—	—	—	—	—	—	400	—	—	—	—	220	—	63	0.00	0.00
—	—	—	—	—	—	—	—	—	400	—	—	—	—	220	—	63	0.00	0.00
—	—	—	—	—	—	0.0	—	—	250	0.00	—	—	—	200	—	53	0.00	0.00
0.00	0.05	0.01	0.00	0.15	1.8	0.0	0.9	0.1	129	0.03	4.6	92	17	93	0.6	49	0.00	0.00
0.00	0.10	0.02	0.01	0.25	2.8	0.0	1.5	0.1	207	0.07	7.3	148	27	149	0.9	49	0.00	0.00
0.00	0.10	0.02	0.01	0.25	2.8	0.0	1.5	0.1	207	0.07	7.4	149	27	150	0.9	49	0.00	0.00
0.00	0.01	0.01	0.00	0.07	0.4	0.0	1.4	0.0	69	0.05	2.5	40	5	93	0.2	18	0.00	0.00

PAGE KEY: A-108 Beverage and Beverage Mixes A-112 Other Beverages A-112 Beverages, Alcoholic A-114 Candies and Confections, Gum A-114 Cereals, Breakfast Type A-118 Cheese and Cheese Substitutes A-120 Dairy Products and Substitutes A-122 Desserts A-128 Dessert Toppings A-128 Eggs, Substitutes, and Egg Dishes A-130 Ethnic Foods A-130 Fast Foods/Restaurants A-140 Fats, Oils, Margarines, Shortenings, and Substitutes A-142 Fish, Seafood, and Shellfish A-142 Food Additives A-142 Fruit, Vegetable, and Blended Juices A-144 Fruits A-146 Grains, Flours, and Fractions A-148 Grain Products, Prepared and Baked Goods

Code	Food Name	Unit/ Amt	Wt (g)	Energy (Kcal)	Prot (g)	Carb (g)	Fiber (g)	Fat (g)	Sat (g)	Mono (g)	Poly (g)	Chol (mg)	Vit A (RE)
1103	Cheese, parmesan, low sod	1 Tbs	6	28	3	0	0	2	1.2	0.5	0.0	5	11
1112	Cheese, parmesan, shredded	1 Tbs	5	21	2	0	0	1	0.9	0.4	0.0	4	7
1510	Cheese, pepper jack, 1″ cube	1 ea	28	110	7	1	0	9	5.0	–	–	30	60
47900	Cheese, provolone, slice, 1oz ea	1 ea	28	100	7	1	0	8	4.8	2.1	0.2	20	67
1024	Cheese, ricotta, part skm	0.5 cup	124	171	14	6	0	10	6.1	2.9	0.3	38	140
1064	Cheese, ricotta, whole milk	0.5 cup	124	216	14	4	0	16	10.3	4.5	0.5	63	157
1065	Cheese, romano, 5oz pkg	1 ea	142	549	45	5	0	38	24.3	11.1	0.8	147	167
4357	Cheese, string, mozzarella, low moist, part skim	1 pce	28	80	7	0	0	6	4.0	–	–	20	40
47908	Cheese, Swiss, 1″ cube	1 ea	15	56	4	1	0	4	2.7	1.1	0.1	14	36
1428	Cheese, Swiss, 25% less fat, 53% less salt	1 oz	28	90	8	1	0	6	4.0	–	–	20	60
1772	Cheese, Swiss, baby	1 oz	28	110	8	1	0	8	6.0	–	–	25	80
1552	Cheese, Swiss, fat free, 1″ cube	1 ea	28	40	8	1	0	0	0.0	0.0	0.0	3	60
1508	Cottage Cheese	0.5 cup	114	100	13	4	0	4	3.0	–	–	15	60
1047	Cottage Cheese, 1% fat	0.5 cup	113	81	14	3	0	1	0.7	0.3	0.0	5	12
1014	Cottage Cheese, 2% fat	0.5 cup	113	102	16	4	0	2	1.4	0.6	0.1	9	24
1049	Cottage Cheese, creamed, w/fruit	0.5 cup	113	140	11	15	0	4	2.4	1.1	0.1	12	42
47848	Cottage Cheese, fat free	0.5 cup	124	80	13	6	0	0	0.0	0.0	0.0	5	40
1015	Cream Cheese	1 Tbs	14	51	1	0	0	5	3.2	1.4	0.2	16	56
1452	Cream Cheese, fat free	2 Tbs	29	28	4	2	0	0	0.3	0.1	0.0	2	81
1098	Cream Cheese, low fat	1 Tbs	15	35	2	1	0	3	1.7	0.7	0.1	8	33
47973	Cream Cheese, strawberry	1.25 oz	35	110	2	4	0	10	6.0	–	–	35	60
Process Cheese and Cheese Substitutes													
1072	Cheese Food, American	1 pce	21	70	4	2	0	5	3.3	1.5	0.2	14	47
1784	Cheese Loaf, American	1 oz	28	110	5	1	0	9	6.0	–	–	30	60
13349	Cheese Sauce, Cheez Whiz	2 Tbs	33	91	4	3	0	7	4.3	–	–	25	43
1272	Cheese Spread, Velveeta	2 oz	57	172	9	6	0	12	8.2	–	–	45	126
1456	Cheese, American	0.25 cup	28	106	6	0	0	9	5.6	2.5	0.3	27	82
1000	Cheese, American, slice .75oz	1 pce	21	80	5	0	0	7	4.2	1.9	0.2	20	62
DAIRY PRODUCTS AND SUBSTITUTES													
Creams and Substitutes													
500	Cream, half & half	1 Tbs	15	20	0	1	0	2	1.1	0.5	0.1	6	16
502	Cream, whipping, heavy	2 Tbs	30	103	1	1	0	11	6.9	3.2	0.4	41	124
511	Cream, whipping, light	2 Tbs	30	87	1	1	0	9	5.8	2.7	0.3	33	88
54262	Creamer, non-dairy	1 Tbs	17	20	0	2	0	1	0.0	0.5	0.0	0	0
54250	Creamer, non-dairy, low fat	1 Tbs	17	10	0	1	0	0	–	–	–	0	0
54315	Creamer, soy milk, plain, Silk	1 Tbs	15	15	0	1	0	1	0.0	–	–	0	0
504	Sour Cream, cultured	2 Tbs	29	62	1	1	0	6	3.8	1.7	0.2	13	56
550	Sour Cream, fat free	2 Tbs	32	29	2	5	0	0	0.3	–	–	3	43
505	Sour Cream, imitation, cultured	2 Tbs	29	60	1	2	0	6	5.1	0.2	0.0	0	0
54232	Sour Cream, rducd fat	2 Tbs	31	47	1	2	0	4	2.4	–	–	16	65
Milks and Non-Dairy Milks													
7	Buttermilk, low fat, cultured	1 cup	245	98	8	12	0	2	1.3	0.6	0.1	10	22
17	Eggnog	1 cup	254	343	10	34	0	19	11.3	5.7	0.9	150	236
81	Milk Substitute, fluid, w/hydrog veg oil	1 cup	244	149	4	15	0	8	1.9	4.9	1.2	0	0
54	Milk, 1%, low lactose	1 cup	246	103	8	12	0	3	1.6	0.8	0.1	10	145
4	Milk, 1%, w/add vit A	1 cup	244	102	8	12	0	3	1.6	0.7	0.1	10	146
214	Milk, 1%, w/add vit A & D	1 cup	249	110	9	13	0	2	1.5	1.0	–	15	100
220	Milk, 2%, acidophilus, w/add vit A & D	1 cup	245	110	9	13	0	2	1.5	–	–	15	100

PAGE KEY: A-154 Granola Bars, Cereal Bars, Diet Bars, Scones, and Tarts A-154 Meals and Dishes A-160 Meats A-164 Nuts, Seeds, and Products A-166 Poultry A-166 Salad Dressings, Dips, and Mayonnaise A-170 Salads A-170 Sandwiches A-172 Sauces and Gravies A-174 Snack Foods—Chips, Pretzels, Popcorn A-178 Soups, Stews and Chilis A-184 Spices, Flavors, and Seasonings A-184 Sports Bars and Drinks A-186 Supplemental Foods and Formulas A-186 Sweeteners and Sweet Substitutes A-188 Vegetables and Legumes A-200 Weight Loss Bars & Drinks A-200 Miscellaneous

Thia (mg)	Ribo (mg)	Niac (mg NE)	Vit B6 (mg)	Vit B12 (µg)	Fol (µg)	Vit C (mg)	Vit D (IU)	Vit E (mg AT)	Cal (mg)	Iron (mg)	Magn (mg)	Phos (mg)	Pota (mg)	Sodi (mg)	Zinc (mg)	Wat (%)	Alco (g)	Caff (g)
0.00	0.01	0.01	0.00	0.09	0.5	0.0	0.6	0.1	86	0.05	3.2	50	7	4	0.2	22	0.00	0.00
0.00	0.01	0.00	0.00	0.07	0.4	0.0	1.4	0.0	63	0.03	2.5	37	5	85	0.2	25	0.00	0.00
–	–	–	–	–	–	0.0	–	–	200	0.00	–	–	–	170	–	35	0.00	0.00
0.00	0.09	0.03	0.01	0.40	2.8	0.0	2.3	0.1	214	0.15	7.9	141	39	248	0.9	41	0.00	0.00
0.02	0.23	0.10	0.01	0.36	16.1	0.0	2.9	0.3	337	0.55	18.6	227	155	155	1.7	74	0.00	0.00
0.01	0.23	0.12	0.05	0.41	14.9	0.0	4.9	0.4	257	0.46	13.6	196	130	104	1.4	72	0.00	0.00
0.05	0.51	0.10	0.11	1.59	9.9	0.0	11.5	1.0	1508	1.09	58.1	1077	122	1701	3.7	31	0.00	0.00
–	–	–	–	–	–	0.0	–	–	150	0.00	–	150	35	240	–	50	0.00	0.00
0.00	0.05	0.00	0.00	0.25	0.9	0.0	6.6	0.1	144	0.02	5.4	91	17	39	0.6	37	0.00	0.00
–	–	–	–	–	–	0.0	–	–	250	0.00	–	–	–	35	–	43	0.00	0.00
–	–	–	–	–	–	0.0	–	–	250	0.00	–	–	–	75	–	35	0.00	0.00
–	–	–	–	–	–	–	–	–	400	–	–	–	–	220	–	63	0.00	0.00
–	–	–	–	–	–	0.0	–	–	100	0.00	–	–	–	400	–	79	0.00	0.00
0.01	0.18	0.14	0.07	0.70	13.6	0.0	0.4	0.1	69	0.15	5.7	151	97	459	0.4	82	0.00	0.00
0.02	0.20	0.15	0.09	0.80	14.7	0.0	–	0.1	78	0.18	6.8	171	108	459	0.5	79	0.00	0.00
0.01	0.15	0.10	0.05	0.55	11.3	0.0	1.1	0.1	54	0.11	4.5	119	76	458	0.3	72	0.00	0.00
–	0.25	–	–	0.47	–	0.0	–	–	80	0.00	–	150	150	440	–	83	0.00	0.00
0.00	0.02	0.00	0.00	0.05	1.9	0.0	1.0	0.1	12	0.17	0.9	15	17	43	0.1	54	0.00	0.00
0.00	0.05	0.05	0.00	0.15	10.7	0.0	0.0	0.0	54	0.05	4.1	126	47	158	0.3	76	0.00	0.00
0.00	0.03	0.01	0.00	0.09	2.7	0.0	0.8	0.1	17	0.25	1.2	22	25	44	0.1	64	0.00	0.00
–	–	–	–	–	–	1.2	–	–	20	0.00	–	–	–	105	–	51	0.00	0.00
0.00	0.09	0.02	0.02	0.23	1.5	0.0	6.0	0.2	122	0.18	6.6	98	59	253	0.6	43	0.00	0.00
–	–	–	–	–	–	0.0	–	–	200	0.00	–	–	–	430	–	42	0.00	0.00
–	0.07	–	–	–	–	0.1	–	–	118	0.05	–	266	79	541	0.5	52	0.00	0.00
–	0.20	–	–	–	–	0.1	–	–	264	0.10	–	489	190	850	1.0	46	0.00	0.00
0.00	0.10	0.01	0.01	0.20	2.3	0.0	2.4	0.1	174	0.10	6.2	210	46	404	0.8	39	0.00	0.00
0.00	0.07	0.00	0.01	0.15	1.7	0.0	1.8	0.1	131	0.07	4.7	158	34	304	0.6	39	0.00	0.00
0.00	0.01	0.00	0.00	0.05	0.5	0.1	2.4	0.0	16	0.00	1.5	14	20	6	0.1	81	0.00	0.00
0.00	0.02	0.00	0.00	0.05	1.2	0.2	15.5	0.2	19	0.00	2.1	18	22	11	0.1	58	0.00	0.00
0.00	0.03	0.00	0.00	0.05	1.2	0.2	2.2	0.2	21	0.00	2.1	18	29	10	0.1	64	0.00	0.00
–	–	–	–	–	–	0.0	–	–	0	0.00	–	–	25	0	–	–	0.00	0.00
–	–	–	–	–	–	0.0	–	–	0	0.00	–	–	25	5	–	–	0.00	0.00
–	–	–	–	–	–	0.0	–	–	0	0.00	–	–	–	5	–	–	0.00	0.00
0.00	0.03	0.01	0.00	0.09	3.2	0.3	1.7	0.2	33	0.01	3.2	24	41	15	0.1	71	0.00	0.00
0.00	0.07	–	–	0.11	–	0.4	–	–	45	0.01	–	37	70	23	–	78	0.00	0.00
0.00	0.00	0.00	0.00	0.00	0.0	0.0	0.0	0.0	1	0.10	1.7	13	46	29	0.3	71	0.00	0.00
–	–	–	–	–	–	0.3	–	–	50	0.01	–	34	65	18	–	76	0.00	0.00
0.07	0.37	0.14	0.07	0.54	12.2	2.5	4.9	0.1	284	0.11	27.0	218	370	257	1.0	90	0.00	0.00
0.09	0.47	0.27	0.12	1.13	2.5	3.8	43.4	0.6	330	0.50	48.3	277	419	137	1.2	74	0.00	0.00
0.02	0.20	0.00	0.00	0.00	0.0	0.0	–	2.6	81	0.94	14.6	181	278	190	2.9	88	0.00	0.00
0.10	0.40	0.20	0.10	0.91	12.5	2.4	98.4	0.1	303	0.11	34.0	237	384	124	1.0	90	0.00	0.00
0.10	0.40	0.20	0.10	0.89	12.2	2.4	97.6	0.1	300	0.11	34.2	234	381	124	1.0	90	0.00	0.00
–	–	–	–	–	–	1.2	100.0	–	300	0.00	–	–	–	130	–	89	0.00	0.00
–	–	–	–	–	–	0.0	100.0	–	30	0.00	–	–	–	130	–	89	0.00	0.00

PAGE KEY: A-108 Beverage and Beverage Mixes A-112 Other Beverages A-112 Beverages, Alcoholic A-114 Candies and Confections, Gum A-114 Cereals, Breakfast Type A-118 Cheese and Cheese Substitutes A-120 Dairy Products and Substitutes A-122 Desserts A-128 Dessert Toppings A-128 Eggs, Substitutes, and Egg Dishes A-130 Ethnic Foods A-130 Fast Foods/Restaurants A-140 Fats, Oils, Margarines, Shortenings, and Substitutes A-142 Fish, Seafood, and Shellfish A-142 Food Additives A-142 Fruit, Vegetable, and Blended Juices A-144 Fruits A-146 Grains, Flours, and Fractions A-148 Grain Products, Prepared and Baked Goods

Code	Food Name	Unit/ Amt	Wt (g)	Energy (Kcal)	Prot (g)	Carb (g)	Fiber (g)	Fat (g)	Sat (g)	Mono (g)	Poly (g)	Chol (mg)	Vit A (RE)
2	Milk, 2%, w/add vit A	1 cup	244	122	8	12	0	5	2.9	1.4	0.2	20	139
218	Milk, 2%, w/add vit A & D	1 cup	245	130	8	13	0	5	3.0	–	–	20	100
18	Milk, chocolate, 2%, cmrcl	1 cup	250	180	8	26	1	5	3.1	1.5	0.2	18	142
59	Milk, chocolate, skim	1 cup	250	144	9	27	1	1	0.7	0.3	0.0	4	142
187	Milk, cond, low fat, swtnd	1 cup	312	934	24	182	–	12	7.6	2.6	0.3	49	160
11	Milk, cond, swtnd, cnd	2 Tbs	38	123	3	21	0	3	2.1	0.9	0.1	13	31
173	Milk, evaporated	2 Tbs	32	40	2	3	0	2	1.5	0.4	0.1	10	0
80	Milk, evaporated, 2%	2 Tbs	32	29	2	4	0	1	0.4	0.2	0.0	3	41
165	Milk, evaporated, nonfat/skim	2 Tbs	32	25	2	4	0	0	0.0	0.0	0.0	0	20
23	Milk, goat	1 cup	244	168	9	11	0	10	6.5	2.7	0.4	27	137
22	Milk, human breast	1 cup	246	172	3	17	0	11	4.9	4.1	1.2	34	157
19	Milk, low fat, chocolate, cmrcl	1 cup	250	158	8	26	1	2	1.5	0.8	0.1	8	150
6	Milk, skim, w/add vit A	1 cup	245	86	8	12	0	0	0.3	0.1	0.0	5	149
1	Milk, whole, 3.25%	1 cup	244	149	8	11	0	8	5.1	2.4	0.3	34	78
20440	Rice Milk, Rice Dream, cnd	1 cup	245	120	0	25	0	2	0.2	1.3	0.3	0	–
20033	Soy Milk	1 cup	245	81	7	4	3	5	0.5	0.8	2.0	0	10
20920	Soy Milk, Silk, chocolate	1 cup	250	140	5	23	0	4	0.0	–	–	0	100
Yogurt													
2834	Yogurt, blueberry, fruit on the bottom	1 ea	227	220	9	41	1	2	1.0	–	–	10	0
2426	Yogurt, custard, Yoplait	6 oz	170	190	7	32	0	4	2.6	1.1	0.1	15	20
2449	Yogurt, French vanilla, nonfat	1 cup	227	130	8	24	0	0	0.0	0.0	0.0	5	200
2001	Yogurt, fruit, low fat	1 cup	245	250	11	47	0	3	1.7	0.7	0.1	10	29
2425	Yogurt, fruit, Yoplait	6 oz	170	190	8	32	0	3	1.9	0.8	0.1	10	17
2000	Yogurt, plain, low fat	1 cup	245	154	13	17	0	4	2.5	1.0	0.1	15	39
2012	Yogurt, plain, skim	1 cup	245	137	14	19	0	0	0.3	0.1	0.0	5	5
2013	Yogurt, plain, whole milk	1 cup	245	149	9	11	0	8	5.1	2.2	0.2	32	76
71587	Yogurt, soy, vanilla, 6oz ctn, Silk	1 ea	170	120	4	23	1	2	0.0	–	–	0	10
2015	Yogurt, vanilla, low fat	1 cup	245	208	12	34	0	3	2.0	0.8	0.1	12	34
DESSERTS													
Brownies and Bars													
47100	Bar, apple cinnamon, fruit & oatmeal	1 ea	37	136	2	26	1	3	0.4	1.0	0.2	0	261
47587	Bar, lemon, prep f/dry mix	1 ea	57	250	3	46	0	6	1.5	2.5	0.5	50	20
23171	Bar, Rice Krispie (marshmallow & Rice Krispies)	1 ea	28	107	1	20	0	3	0.6	1.3	0.8	0	85
62904	Brownie, cmrcl prep, large	1 ea	56	227	3	36	1	9	2.4	5.0	1.3	10	12
47019	Brownie, prep f/rec, 2" square	1 ea	24	112	1	12	1	7	1.8	2.6	2.3	18	46
Cakes													
46004	Cake, angel food, 9" whl or 1/12 pce	1 pce	28	73	2	16	0	0	0.0	0.0	0.1	0	0
46002	Cake, Boston cream pie, 9" whl or 1/6 pce	1 pce	92	232	2	39	1	8	2.2	4.2	0.9	34	22
71607	Cake, carrot, Mrs. Smith's, pce	1 pce	172	730	6	81	2	43	10.0	–	–	70	–
46403	Cake, chocolate chocolate, prep w/oil & eggs f/dry mix	1 pce	44	200	3	26	1	10	2.5	3.0	3.5	25	0
46250	Cake, chocolate, fat & cholest free, Entenmann's	1 pce	85	210	3	51	2	0	0.0	0.0	0.0	0	0
71629	Cake, coconut, whl or 1/26 pce	1 pce	76	310	3	39	0	16	6.0	–	–	35	–
46005	Cake, coffee, cinnamon, prep, 1/8 pce	1 pce	56	178	3	30	1	5	1.0	2.2	1.8	27	23
46249	Cake, coffee, fat & cholest free, Entenmann's	1 pce	54	130	2	29	2	0	0.0	0.0	0.0	0	0
46387	Cake, devils food, prep w/oil & eggs	1 pce	44	210	3	25	0	10	3.0	3.0	3.5	25	0
42721	Cake, Ding Dongs, w/cream filling, Hostess	1 ea	80	368	3	45	2	19	11.0	4.0	1.2	14	–
45562	Cake, funnel	1 pce	90	278	7	29	1	14	2.7	4.4	6.3	63	58
46409	Cake, German chocolate, prep w/oil & eggs f/dry mix	1 pce	44	200	3	26	0	10	2.5	3.0	3.0	25	0
46000	Cake, gingerbread, prep f/rec, 1/9 of 8" square	1 pce	74	263	3	36	1	12	3.1	5.3	3.1	24	10

PAGE KEY: A-154 Granola Bars, Cereal Bars, Diet Bars, Scones, and Tarts A-154 Meals and Dishes A-160 Meats A-164 Nuts, Seeds, and Products A-166 Poultry A-166 Salad Dressings, Dips, and Mayonnaise A-170 Salads A-170 Sandwiches A-172 Sauces and Gravies A-174 Snack Foods—Chips, Pretzels, Popcorn A-178 Soups, Stews and Chilis A-184 Spices, Flavors, and Seasonings A-184 Sports Bars and Drinks A-186 Supplemental Foods and Formulas A-186 Sweeteners and Sweet Substitutes A-188 Vegetables and Legumes A-200 Weight Loss Bars & Drinks A-200 Miscellaneous

Thia (mg)	Ribo (mg)	Niac (mg NE)	Vit B6 (mg)	Vit B12 (µg)	Fol (µg)	Vit C (mg)	Vit D (IU)	Vit E (mg AT)	Cal (mg)	Iron (mg)	Magn (mg)	Phos (mg)	Pota (mg)	Sodi (mg)	Zinc (mg)	Wat (%)	Alco (g)	Caff (g)
0.10	0.40	0.20	0.10	0.87	12.2	2.4	97.6	0.2	298	0.11	34.2	232	376	122	1.0	89	0.00	0.00
—	—	—	—	—	—	1.2	100.0	—	250	0.00	—	—	—	125	—	89	0.00	0.00
0.09	0.40	0.31	0.10	0.85	12.5	2.2	100.0	0.1	285	0.60	32.5	255	422	150	1.0	84	0.00	5.00
0.09	0.34	0.28	0.10	0.87	13.6	2.3	100.0	0.1	292	0.68	45.5	265	486	121	1.2	85	0.00	7.50
0.21	1.22	0.52	—	—	—	3.1	—	—	856	0.34	73.2	682	1126	312	2.9	28	0.00	0.00
0.02	0.15	0.07	0.01	0.17	4.2	1.0	1.8	0.1	109	0.07	9.9	97	142	49	0.4	27	0.00	0.00
0.00	0.10	0.05	0.01	0.05	2.5	0.0	25.0	0.0	80	0.00	7.6	60	95	30	0.2	76	0.00	0.00
0.00	0.10	0.05	0.01	0.07	2.7	0.4	—	0.0	90	0.09	8.4	60	103	36	0.3	78	0.00	0.00
—	0.10	—	—	—	—	0.0	23.9	—	80	0.00	—	60	110	40	—	80	0.00	0.00
0.11	0.34	0.68	0.10	0.17	2.4	3.2	29.3	0.2	327	0.11	34.2	271	498	122	0.7	87	0.00	0.00
0.02	0.09	0.43	0.02	0.11	12.3	12.3	9.8	2.2	79	0.07	7.4	34	125	42	0.4	88	0.00	0.00
0.09	0.40	0.31	0.10	0.85	12.5	2.2	100.0	0.1	288	0.60	32.5	258	425	152	1.0	84	0.00	5.00
0.09	0.34	0.21	0.10	0.93	12.2	2.5	98.0	0.1	301	0.10	27.0	247	407	127	1.0	91	0.00	0.00
0.09	0.40	0.20	0.10	0.87	12.2	2.2	97.6	0.2	290	0.11	31.7	227	371	120	0.9	88	0.00	0.00
0.07	0.00	1.90	0.03	0.00	90.6	1.2	0.0	1.8	20	0.20	9.8	34	69	86	0.2	89	0.00	0.00
0.38	0.17	0.36	0.10	0.00	4.9	0.0	0.0	0.0	10	1.41	46.5	120	345	29	0.6	93	0.00	0.00
—	0.50	—	—	3.00	24.0	0.0	120.0	—	300	1.44	—	—	350	75	0.6	87	0.00	
—	—	—	—	—	—	0.0	—	—	300	0.00	—	—	440	210	—	76	0.00	0.00
0.05	0.25	—	0.07	0.36	—	1.0	—	—	200	0.25	—	150	290	95	0.6	—	0.00	0.00
—	—	—	—	—	—	12.0	80.0	—	250	0.00	—	—	—	115	—	85	0.00	0.00
0.09	0.43	0.23	0.10	1.14	22.1	1.7	2.7	0.1	372	0.17	36.8	292	478	142	1.8	74	0.00	0.00
0.09	0.34	—	0.07	0.36	—	0.3	—	—	250	0.15	—	200	350	105	0.6	—	0.00	0.00
0.10	0.51	0.28	0.11	1.37	27.0	2.0	3.9	0.1	448	0.20	41.7	353	573	172	2.2	85	0.00	0.00
0.11	0.56	0.30	0.12	1.49	29.4	2.2	3.9	0.0	488	0.21	46.5	385	625	189	2.4	85	0.00	0.00
0.07	0.34	0.18	0.07	0.91	17.1	1.2	3.9	0.2	296	0.11	29.4	233	380	113	1.4	88	0.00	0.00
—	—	—	—	—	—	0.0	—	—	500	0.72	—	—	—	20	—	83	0.00	0.00
0.10	0.49	0.25	0.10	1.29	27.0	2.0	3.9	0.1	419	0.17	39.2	331	537	162	2.0	79	0.00	0.00
0.23	0.49	5.80	0.57	0.00	116.1	0.2	0.0	0.0	10	0.46	8.2	34	49	85	0.2	15	0.00	0.00
0.09	0.02	0.80	—	—	—	0.0	—	—	0	0.72	—	—	35	150	—	—	0.00	0.00
0.10	0.10	1.30	0.12	0.00	27.5	3.9	0.0	0.4	2	0.50	4.2	12	12	123	0.1	13	0.00	0.00
0.14	0.11	0.95	0.01	0.03	11.8	0.0	2.3	1.2	16	1.25	17.4	57	83	175	0.4	14	0.00	1.12
0.02	0.05	0.23	0.01	0.03	7.0	0.1	1.9	0.7	14	0.43	12.7	32	42	82	0.2	13	0.00	
0.02	0.14	0.25	0.00	0.01	9.9	0.0	0.0	0.0	40	0.15	3.4	9	26	212	0.0	33	0.00	0.00
0.37	0.25	0.18	0.01	0.15	13.8	0.2	22.5	1.0	21	0.34	5.5	45	36	132	0.1	45	0.00	0.00
—	—	—	—	—	—	—	—	—	—	—	—	—	—	520	—	23	0.00	0.00
0.09	0.07	0.40	—	—	—	0.0	—	—	20	1.08	—	—	1	280	—	—	0.00	
—	—	—	—	—	—	0.0	—	—	20	1.44	—	—	210	270	—	—	0.00	
—	—	—	—	—	—	—	—	—	—	—	—	—	—	260	—	22	0.00	0.00
0.09	0.10	0.85	0.02	0.07	26.9	0.1	17.2	0.9	76	0.80	10.1	120	63	236	0.3	30	0.00	0.00
—	—	—	—	—	—	0.0	—	—	20	0.36	—	—	75	110	—	—	0.00	0.00
0.09	0.10	0.40	—	—	—	0.0	—	—	20	1.08	—	—	170	270	—	14	0.00	
—	—	—	—	—	—	—	—	—	3	1.84	—	—	—	241	—	12	0.00	
0.23	0.31	1.86	0.05	0.23	13.6	0.4	—	2.4	128	1.86	17.7	137	155	117	0.6	42	0.00	0.00
0.09	0.07	0.40	—	—	—	0.0	—	—	20	1.08	—	—	105	260	—	11	0.00	
0.14	0.11	1.28	0.14	0.03	24.4	0.1	2.7	1.8	53	2.13	51.8	40	325	242	0.3	28	0.00	0.00

PAGE KEY: A-108 Beverage and Beverage Mixes A-112 Other Beverages A-112 Beverages, Alcoholic A-114 Candies and Confections, Gum A-114 Cereals, Breakfast Type A-118 Cheese and Cheese Substitutes A-120 Dairy Products and Substitutes A-122 Desserts A-128 Dessert Toppings A-128 Eggs, Substitutes, and Egg Dishes A-130 Ethnic Foods A-130 Fast Foods/Restaurants A-140 Fats, Oils, Margarines, Shortenings, and Substitutes A-142 Fish, Seafood, and Shellfish A-142 Food Additives A-142 Fruit, Vegetable, and Blended Juices A-144 Fruits A-146 Grains, Flours, and Fractions A-148 Grain Products, Prepared and Baked Goods

Code	Food Name	Unit/ Amt	Wt (g)	Energy (Kcal)	Prot (g)	Carb (g)	Fiber (g)	Fat (g)	Sat (g)	Mono (g)	Poly (g)	Chol (mg)	Vit A (RE)
46406	Cake, lemon, prep w/oil & eggs f/dry mix	1 pce	44	200	2	26	0	10	2.5	3.0	3.0	25	0
46070	Cake, pineapple upside down, prep f/rec, 1/9th of 8″ sq	1 pce	115	367	4	58	1	14	3.4	6.0	3.8	25	75
71261	Cake, pound, w/butter, cmrcl prep, 1/10th pce	1 pce	30	116	2	15	0	6	3.5	1.8	0.3	66	47
46008	Cake, snack, sponge, w/cream filling	1 ea	42	155	1	27	0	5	1.1	1.7	1.4	7	2
46007	Cake, white, w/chocolate icing, f/recipe, 1/12 piece	1 pce	100	428	2	75	1	14	7.2	–	–	21	56
46003	Cake, white, w/coconut frosting, prep f/rec, 1/12 of 9″	1 pce	112	399	5	71	1	12	4.4	4.1	2.4	1	12
46085	Cake, white, w/o frosting, prep f/rec, 9″ or 1/12 pce	1 pce	74	264	4	42	1	9	2.4	3.9	2.3	1	13
46455	Cake, yellow, prep f/ mix, Krusteaz, pce	1 pce	55	150	2	27	0	4	1.0	2.5	0.0	0	0
46012	Cake, yellow, w/chocolate icing, cmrcl prep, 1/8 of 18oz	1 pce	64	243	2	35	1	11	3.0	6.1	1.4	35	21
62352	Cheesecake, cherry	1 ea	113	330	6	27	1	22	13.0	–	–	100	300
49004	Cheesecake, cmrcl prep, 1/6 of 17oz	1 pce	80	257	4	20	0	18	7.9	6.9	1.3	44	118
46011	Cupcake, chocolate, w/frosting & cream filling	1 ea	50	188	2	30	0	7	1.4	2.8	2.6	8	2
46426	Cupcake, chocolate, w/frosting, low fat	1 ea	43	131	2	29	2	2	0.5	0.8	0.2	0	0
Cookies													
47747	Biscotti, almond	1 ea	27	120	1	17	1	5	2.0	–	–	25	0
90633	Cookie, animal cracker, 2oz box	1 ea	57	253	4	42	1	8	2.0	4.3	1.1	0	0
47005	Cookie, butter, enrich, cmrcl prep	5 ea	25	117	2	17	0	5	2.8	1.4	0.2	29	42
47036	Cookie, chocolate chip, bkd f/refrig dough, med, 2¼″	1 ea	12	59	1	8	0	3	0.9	1.4	0.3	3	2
47031	Cookie, choc chip, enrich, high fat, cmrcl, med 2.25″	1 ea	10	48	1	7	0	2	0.7	1.2	0.2	0	–
47032	Cookie, chocolate chip, lower fat, cmrcl prep	1 ea	10	45	1	7	0	2	0.4	0.6	0.5	0	–
47001	Cookie, chocolate chip, soft, cmrcl prep	1 ea	15	69	1	9	0	4	1.1	2.0	0.5	0	–
47006	Cookie, chocolate sandwich, creme filled	4 ea	40	189	2	28	1	8	1.5	3.4	2.9	0	–
47164	Cookie, chocolate sandwich, low fat, Snackwell's	3 ea	33	135	2	26	1	3	0.8	1.0	0.2	0	0
50962	Cookie, chocolate, fudge stripes	3 ea	32	159	2	21	1	8	5.1	–	–	2	5
47045	Cookie, gingersnap	1 ea	7	29	0	5	0	1	0.2	0.4	0.1	0	–
47737	Cookie, Girl Scout, lemon drop	3 ea	33	160	2	20	0	8	2.0	–	–	0	0
47734	Cookie, Girl Scout, Samoas	2 ea	28	160	2	17	2	9	6.0	–	–	0	0
47739	Cookie, Girl Scout, thin mints	4 ea	28	140	1	18	1	8	2.0	–	–	0	0
47077	Cookie, granola	1 ea	13	60	1	9	1	2	1.6	0.2	0.2	0	0
47537	Cookie, molasses, iced, home style	1 ea	28	114	1	20	0	4	1.1	1.1	0.5	0	0
47161	Cookie, newton, fig, Nabisco	1 ea	16	60	1	10	1	2	0.5	0.5	0.0	0	–
47496	Cookie, oatmeal raisin, home style	1 ea	26	107	1	17	1	4	0.8	1.3	0.3	3	1
90640	Cookie, oatmeal, cmrcl prep, big, 3½″ to 4″ diameter	1 ea	25	112	2	17	1	5	1.1	2.5	0.6	0	0
47180	Cookie, Oreo chocolate sandwich, Nabisco	3 ea	33	160	2	23	1	7	1.5	3.0	0.5	0	–
50948	Cookie, peanut butter	2 ea	28	134	2	16	1	7	1.5	–	–	0	0
47551	Cookie, pecan ice box, home style	1 ea	24	120	1	15	0	6	1.4	2.6	0.5	6	2
47007	Cookie, shortbread, plain, cmrcl prep, 1⅝″ square	4 ea	32	161	2	21	1	8	2.0	4.3	1.0	6	4
47069	Cookie, sugar wafer, creme filled, lrg, 3½″ x 1 x ½″	1 ea	9	46	0	6	0	2	0.3	0.9	0.8	0	0
47064	Cookie, sugar, cmrcl prep	1 ea	15	72	1	10	0	3	0.8	1.8	0.4	8	4
49065	Cookie, vanilla wafer, golden, art flvr	8 ea	31	147	2	22	–	6	1.1	3.5	0.5	–	–
62909	Cookie, vanilla wafer, lower fat, sml	1 ea	3	13	0	2	0	0	0.1	0.2	0.1	2	0
Doughnuts													
45777	Churro	1 ea	26	116	1	12	0	7	2.0	4.1	0.9	2	6
45658	Doughnut, cake, plain	1 ea	41	180	3	19	1	11	2.0	–	–	15	0
45524	Doughnut, cake, w/chocolate icing, med, 3″ diameter	1 ea	43	204	2	21	1	13	3.5	7.5	1.6	26	5
45563	Doughnut, creme filled, 3½″ oval	1 ea	85	307	5	26	1	21	4.6	10.3	2.6	20	17
45626	Doughnut, eclair, chocolate, Entenmann's	1 ea	102	250	3	44	0	9	2.0	–	–	70	20
71341	Doughnut, glazed, enrich, extra lrg, 5″ diameter	1 ea	122	492	8	54	1	28	7.1	15.7	3.5	7	5
45507	Doughnut, jelly filled, 3½″ oval	1 ea	85	289	5	33	1	16	4.1	8.7	2.0	22	14

PAGE KEY: A-154 Granola Bars, Cereal Bars, Diet Bars, Scones, and Tarts A-154 Meals and Dishes A-160 Meats A-164 Nuts, Seeds, and Products A-166 Poultry A-166 Salad Dressings, Dips, and Mayonnaise A-170 Salads A-170 Sandwiches A-172 Sauces and Gravies A-174 Snack Foods—Chips, Pretzels, Popcorn A-178 Soups, Stews and Chilis A-184 Spices, Flavors, and Seasonings A-184 Sports Bars and Drinks A-186 Supplemental Foods and Formulas A-186 Sweeteners and Sweet Substitutes A-188 Vegetables and Legumes A-200 Weight Loss Bars & Drinks A-200 Miscellaneous

Thia (mg)	Ribo (mg)	Niac (mg NE)	Vit B6 (mg)	Vit B12 (μg)	Fol (μg)	Vit C (mg)	Vit D (IU)	Vit E (mg AT)	Cal (mg)	Iron (mg)	Magn (mg)	Phos (mg)	Pota (mg)	Sodi (mg)	Zinc (mg)	Wat (%)	Alco (g)	Caff (g)
0.09	0.07	0.40	—	—	—	0.0	—	—	0	0.36	—	—	35	260	—	14	0.00	0.00
0.18	0.18	1.37	0.03	0.09	29.9	1.4	9.2	1.5	138	1.70	14.9	94	129	367	0.4	32	0.00	0.00
0.03	0.07	0.38	0.00	0.07	12.3	0.0	7.1	0.2	10	0.40	3.3	41	36	119	0.1	25	0.00	0.00
0.07	0.05	0.51	0.00	0.05	12.3	0.0	0.9	0.9	19	0.55	3.4	79	37	155	0.1	20	0.00	0.00
0.12	0.10	1.12	0.00	0.03	30.4	0.0	4.3	0.5	43	0.93	19.4	148	80	356	0.3	6	—	
0.14	0.20	1.19	0.02	0.07	24.6	0.1	0.7	0.8	101	1.29	13.4	78	111	318	0.4	21	0.00	0.00
0.14	0.13	1.12	0.01	0.05	23.7	0.1	8.0	0.7	96	1.12	8.9	69	70	242	0.2	23	0.00	0.00
—	—	—	—	—	—	0.0	—	—	12	0.54	—	90	45	240	—	39	0.00	0.00
0.07	0.10	0.80	0.01	0.10	14.1	0.0	10.2	1.5	24	1.33	19.2	103	114	216	0.4	22	0.00	5.46
—	—	—	—	—	—	1.2	—	—	60	1.08	—	—	—	250	—	51	0.00	0.00
0.01	0.15	0.15	0.03	0.14	14.4	0.3	—	1.3	41	0.50	8.8	74	72	166	0.4	46	0.00	0.00
0.10	0.15	1.21	0.00	0.02	14.5	0.0	0.0	1.7	36	1.67	20.5	46	61	212	0.3	20	0.00	1.50
0.01	0.05	0.31	0.00	0.00	6.5	0.0	0.0	0.8	15	0.66	10.8	79	96	178	0.2	23	0.00	0.86
—	—	—	—	—	—	0.0	—	—	0	0.36	—	—	—	45	—	12	0.00	0.00
0.20	0.18	1.97	0.00	0.02	48.2	0.0	0.0	1.0	24	1.55	10.2	65	57	223	0.4	4	0.00	0.00
0.09	0.07	0.80	0.00	0.09	9.8	0.0	3.0	0.1	7	0.56	3.0	26	28	88	0.1	5	0.00	0.00
0.01	0.01	0.23	0.00	0.00	5.3	0.0	2.9	0.2	3	0.30	3.2	9	24	28	0.1	3	0.00	1.41
0.01	0.02	0.27	0.00	0.00	4.2	0.0	0.0	0.3	2	0.28	3.1	11	14	32	0.1	4	0.00	1.10
0.02	0.02	0.28	0.02	0.00	7.0	0.0	0.0	0.2	2	0.31	2.8	8	12	38	0.1	4	0.00	0.69
0.01	0.02	0.23	0.01	0.00	5.9	0.0	3.8	0.4	2	0.36	5.2	8	14	49	0.1	12	0.00	1.04
0.02	0.07	0.82	0.00	0.00	17.2	0.0	1.9	1.4	10	1.54	18.0	39	70	242	0.3	2	0.00	5.19
0.03	0.05	0.74	0.00	0.00	—	0.0	—	—	18	0.87	15.7	67	53	253	0.2	4	0.00	
—	—	—	—	—	—	0.0	—	—	14	0.61	—	—	—	128	—	—	0.00	
0.00	0.01	0.23	0.00	0.00	5.0	0.0	0.0	0.1	5	0.44	3.4	6	24	46	0.0	5	0.00	0.00
—	—	—	—	—	—	0.0	—	—	0	0.72	—	—	—	150	—	8	0.00	0.00
—	—	—	—	—	—	2.4	—	—	0	0.72	—	—	—	45	—	—	0.00	0.00
—	—	—	—	—	—	0.0	—	—	200	—	—	—	—	80	—	3	0.00	0.00
0.07	0.02	0.23	0.05	0.00	10.5	0.1	—	0.0	9	0.37	13.1	46	47	43	0.2	3	0.00	0.00
0.07	0.05	0.74	—	—	—	0.0	—	—	7	1.16	—	—	21	130	—	11	0.00	0.00
—	—	—	—	—	—	—	—	—	—	0.36	—	—	40	60	—	—	0.00	0.00
0.07	0.03	0.44	—	—	—	0.0	—	—	8	0.58	—	—	60	98	—	11	0.00	0.00
0.07	0.05	0.56	0.01	0.00	11.2	0.1	0.0	0.6	9	0.63	8.2	34	36	96	0.2	6	0.00	0.00
—	—	—	—	—	—	—	—	—	—	0.72	—	—	60	220	—	—	0.00	
0.05	0.05	1.20	—	—	17.4	0.0	—	—	10	0.62	—	—	—	114	—	8	0.00	0.00
0.07	0.05	0.56	—	—	17.3	0.0	—	—	4	0.49	—	—	17	75	—	6	0.00	0.00
0.10	0.10	1.07	0.02	0.02	18.9	0.0	2.0	1.0	11	0.87	5.4	35	32	146	0.2	4	0.00	0.00
0.00	0.01	0.21	0.00	0.00	3.9	0.0	0.0	0.4	2	0.18	1.0	5	5	13	0.0	1	0.00	0.00
0.02	0.02	0.40	0.00	0.02	6.8	0.0	0.6	0.4	3	0.31	1.8	12	9	54	0.1	5	0.00	0.00
0.05	0.02	0.46	—	—	13.0	0.0	—	—	11	0.74	—	—	—	120	—	4	0.00	0.00
0.00	0.00	0.09	0.00	0.00	1.5	0.0	0.1	0.0	1	0.07	0.4	3	3	9	0.0	5	0.00	0.00
0.03	0.02	0.37	0.00	0.00	1.2	0.0	—	1.0	2	0.33	1.7	8	8	7	0.1	23	0.00	0.00
—	—	—	—	—	—	0.0	—	—	20	0.72	—	—	—	210	—	—	0.00	0.00
0.05	0.05	0.56	0.01	0.10	12.5	0.1	0.0	1.8	15	1.05	17.2	87	84	184	0.3	14	0.00	0.86
0.28	0.12	1.90	0.05	0.11	54.4	0.0	0.0	2.3	21	1.55	17.0	65	68	263	0.7	38	0.00	0.00
—	—	—	—	—	—	0.0	—	—	100	0.36	—	—	105	220	—	44	0.00	
0.43	0.25	3.48	0.07	0.10	52.5	0.1	10.0	3.7	52	2.49	26.8	113	132	417	0.9	25	0.00	0.00
0.27	0.11	1.82	0.09	0.18	52.7	0.0	1.3	2.1	21	1.50	17.0	72	67	249	0.6	36	0.00	0.00

PAGE KEY: A-108 Beverage and Beverage Mixes A-112 Other Beverages A-112 Beverages, Alcoholic A-114 Candies and Confections, Gum A-114 Cereals, Breakfast Type A-118 Cheese and Cheese Substitutes A-120 Dairy Products and Substitutes A-122 Desserts A-128 Dessert Toppings A-128 Eggs, Substitutes, and Egg Dishes A-130 Ethnic Foods A-130 Fast Foods/Restaurants A-140 Fats, Oils, Margarines, Shortenings, and Substitutes A-142 Fish, Seafood, and Shellfish A-142 Food Additives A-142 Fruit, Vegetable, and Blended Juices A-144 Fruits A-146 Grains, Flours, and Fractions A-148 Grain Products, Prepared and Baked Goods

Code	Food Name	Unit/ Amt	Wt (g)	Energy (Kcal)	Prot (g)	Carb (g)	Fiber (g)	Fat (g)	Sat (g)	Mono (g)	Poly (g)	Chol (mg)	Vit A (RE)
45519	Doughnut, raised, Bismarck, custard filled, w/icing	1 ea	70	245	3	37	0	10	2.6	5.5	1.2	4	7
Frozen Desserts													
496	Frozen Dessert, Rice Dream Supreme, pralines 'n dream	0.5 cup	92	180	1	24	1	9	1.0	–	–	0	20
1777	Frozen Dessert, Rice Dream, mint chocolate chip	0.5 cup	92	170	1	26	1	8	1.5	–	–	0	20
2045	Frozen Yogurt Cone, chocolate, sml	1 ea	78	168	4	24	1	7	4.2	2.3	0.4	1	37
70401	Frozen Yogurt, all flvrs, nonfat	0.5 cup	76	80	3	18	–	0	0.0	0.0	0.0	0	–
71819	Frozen Yogurt, chocolate, nonfat, w/art swtnr	1 cup	186	199	8	37	4	1	0.9	0.4	0.1	7	2
2035	Frozen Yogurt, chocolate, soft serve	0.5 cup	72	115	3	18	2	4	2.6	1.3	0.2	4	32
70341	Frozen Yogurt, fruit, Yoplait	0.5 cup	73	120	3	21	0	3	1.6	0.8	0.1	7	18
625	Frozen Yogurt, vanilla, Haagen Dazs	0.5 cup	93	140	6	29	0	0	0.0	0.0	0.0	3	0
2064	Frozen Yogurt, vanilla, soft serve	0.5 cup	72	114	3	17	0	4	2.5	1.1	0.2	1	42
2089	Ice Cream Bar, cookie sandwich	1 ea	59	144	3	22	1	6	3.2	1.7	0.4	20	53
2030	Ice Cream Bar, Fudgesicle	1 ea	73	104	3	18	1	3	2.1	1.0	0.1	10	33
71818	Ice Cream Bar, vanilla, choc coated, light, no sugar add	4 oz	113	243	7	29	2	11	6.3	3.1	1.5	11	78
11485	Ice Cream Bar, vanilla, chocolate coated, Klondike	1 ea	148	488	6	36	–	36	19.4	–	–	40	49
52152	Ice Cream Bar, vanilla, dark choc coated, Eskimo Pie	1 ea	50	166	2	12	–	12	7.2	–	–	14	–
2113	Ice Cream Cone, chocolate	1 ea	78	173	3	25	1	7	4.4	2.2	0.4	18	62
2092	Ice Cream Cone, chocolate dipped	1 ea	78	187	3	24	1	10	5.7	2.9	0.5	29	77
2029	Ice Cream Cone, Drumstick, Nestle Foods	1 ea	60	159	3	18	1	9	4.4	3.1	1.0	21	55
2093	Ice Cream Cone, vanilla	1 ea	78	166	3	21	0	8	5.0	2.4	0.4	32	86
71778	Ice Cream Sandwich	1 ea	70	190	3	28	0	8	4.0	–	–	20	40
2216	Ice Cream, chocolate chip cookie dough, Ben & Jerry's	0.5 cup	105	300	5	34	0	16	10.0	–	–	65	150
2391	Ice Cream, chocolate chip mint, Haagen Dazs	0.5 cup	102	300	5	25	1	20	11.0	–	–	95	100
2905	Ice Cream, chocolate chunk, low fat, Healthy Choice	0.5 cup	71	120	3	21	2	2	1.0	–	–	5	40
2050	Ice Cream, chocolate	0.5 cup	66	143	3	19	1	7	4.5	2.1	0.3	22	77
2008	Ice Cream, French vanilla, soft serve	0.5 cup	86	185	4	19	0	11	6.4	3.0	0.4	78	125
2004	Ice Cream, vanilla	0.5 cup	66	133	2	16	0	7	4.5	2.1	0.3	29	80
71507	Ice Cream, vanilla, fat free, Breyers	0.5 cup	67	90	3	19	1	0	0.0	0.0	0.0	0	60
2009	Ice Cream, vanilla, light, 50% less fat	0.5 cup	66	92	3	15	0	3	1.7	0.8	0.1	9	46
71128	Milk Shake, chocolate, fast food, med, 16 fl oz	1 ea	333	423	11	68	3	12	7.7	3.6	0.5	43	80
199	Milk Shake, vanilla, thick	1 cup	227	254	9	40	0	7	4.3	2.0	0.3	27	66
2011	Sherbet, orange	0.5 cup	74	102	1	22	0	1	0.9	0.4	0.1	4	11
23051	Slushy	1 cup	193	247	1	63	0	0	0.0	0.0	0.0	0	0
23114	Snow Cone	1 ea	190	243	1	62	0	0	0.0	0.0	0.0	0	0
2066	Sorbet, citrus fruit	0.5 cup	100	92	0	23	0	0	0.0	0.0	0.0	0	27
2032	Sundae, hot fudge	1 ea	158	284	6	48	0	9	5.0	2.3	0.8	21	62
Fruit Desserts													
49003	Cobbler, apple, f/recipe, 3"x3" pce	1 pce	104	199	2	35	2	6	1.2	–	–	1	61
49023	Crisp, cherry	1 cup	246	704	6	113	3	27	4.7	12.3	8.6	2	250
49057	Strudel, apple, Entenmann's	1 pce	110	310	3	44	2	14	3.5	–	–	0	0
Pastries and Sweet Rolls													
42465	Buns, cinnamon, Entenmann's	1 ea	61	220	4	31	0	10	6.0	–	–	55	60
42363	Buns, honey	1 ea	65	270	3	35	1	13	3.0	–	–	0	0
45572	Danish, cheese	1 ea	71	266	6	26	1	16	4.8	8.0	1.8	11	31
71316	Danish, raspberry, enrich, lrg, 7" diameter	1 ea	142	527	8	68	3	26	6.9	14.2	3.4	162	31
45549	Dumpling, apple	1 ea	190	672	7	85	3	35	6.9	15.2	10.7	0	8
45590	Fruit Burrito, apple, lrg	1 ea	155	484	5	73	–	20	9.6	7.2	2.2	8	87
45763	Pastry, apple cinnamon, frosted, low fat, Pop Tarts	1 ea	52	191	2	40	1	3	0.6	1.5	0.8	0	100

PAGE KEY: A-154 Granola Bars, Cereal Bars, Diet Bars, Scones, and Tarts A-154 Meals and Dishes A-160 Meats A-164 Nuts, Seeds, and Products A-166 Poultry A-166 Salad Dressings, Dips, and Mayonnaise A-170 Salads A-170 Sandwiches A-172 Sauces and Gravies A-174 Snack Foods—Chips, Pretzels, Popcorn A-178 Soups, Stews and Chilis A-184 Spices, Flavors, and Seasonings A-184 Sports Bars and Drinks A-186 Supplemental Foods and Formulas A-186 Sweeteners and Sweet Substitutes A-188 Vegetables and Legumes A-200 Weight Loss Bars & Drinks A-200 Miscellaneous

Thia (mg)	Ribo (mg)	Niac (mg NE)	Vit B6 (mg)	Vit B12 (μg)	Fol (μg)	Vit C (mg)	Vit D (IU)	Vit E (mg AT)	Cal (mg)	Iron (mg)	Magn (mg)	Phos (mg)	Pota (mg)	Sodi (mg)	Zinc (mg)	Wat (%)	Alco (g)	Caff (g)
0.15	0.10	1.19	0.02	0.07	9.6	0.1	—	1.2	31	0.86	10.7	49	61	161	0.4	28	0.00	0.00
—	—	—	—	—	—	1.2	—	—	20	0.72	—	—	—	95	—	—	0.00	0.00
—	—	—	—	—	—	1.2	—	—	20	0.72	—	—	—	95	—	—	0.00	
0.07	0.18	0.68	0.05	0.18	4.7	0.5	—	0.2	99	0.97	30.8	116	197	84	0.6	53	0.00	
—	—	—	—	—	—	—	—	—	100	—	—	—	120	40	—	72	0.00	0.00
0.07	0.33	0.37	0.07	0.91	22.3	1.3	—	0.1	296	0.07	74.4	240	631	151	0.9	74	0.00	5.57
0.02	0.15	0.21	0.05	0.20	7.9	0.2	1.2	0.1	106	0.89	19.4	100	188	71	0.4	64	0.00	2.16
0.03	0.12	—	0.07	—	—	0.7	—	—	107	0.21	—	—	—	53	—	63	0.00	0.00
—	—	—	—	—	—	0.0	—	—	200	0.00	—	—	—	45	—	62	0.00	0.00
0.02	0.15	0.20	0.05	0.20	4.3	0.6	1.2	0.0	103	0.21	10.1	93	152	63	0.3	65	0.00	0.00
0.02	0.11	0.18	0.02	0.18	4.8	0.3	2.4	0.1	60	0.28	12.7	64	122	36	0.4	48	0.00	
0.03	0.20	0.12	0.05	0.46	5.1	0.6	6.0	0.0	101	0.51	24.4	98	221	60	0.5	66	0.00	2.90
0.07	0.31	0.15	0.07	0.43	4.5	0.0	—	0.1	252	0.33	31.8	196	346	118	0.9	56	0.00	6.80
—	—	—	—	—	—	—	—	—	212	—	—	—	—	108	—	47	0.00	
—	—	—	—	—	—	—	—	—	60	—	—	—	—	34	—	46	0.00	
0.03	0.12	0.36	0.02	0.27	4.3	0.4	6.2	0.3	88	0.49	17.3	83	168	46	0.4	54	0.00	2.33
0.03	0.18	0.34	0.03	0.25	3.8	0.4	3.7	0.2	88	0.46	18.2	83	161	61	0.6	52	0.00	2.33
0.03	0.14	0.87	0.03	0.18	8.3	0.3	4.8	0.4	66	0.40	21.2	82	145	44	0.7	48	0.00	3.59
0.03	0.18	0.28	0.03	0.28	3.9	0.4	3.7	0.1	95	0.23	11.5	82	151	65	0.5	58	0.00	0.00
—	—	—	—	—	—	0.0	0.0	—	40	0.72	—	—	—	170	—	43	0.00	
—	—	—	—	—	—	0.0	—	—	100	1.08	—	—	—	95	—	47	0.00	
—	—	—	—	—	—	0.0	—	—	100	1.08	—	—	—	65	—	50	0.00	
—	—	—	—	—	—	0.0	—	—	100	0.72	—	—	—	45	—	62	0.00	
0.02	0.12	0.15	0.03	0.18	10.6	0.5	10.6	0.2	72	0.61	19.1	71	164	50	0.4	56	0.00	1.98
0.03	0.15	0.07	0.03	0.43	7.7	0.7	7.5	0.3	113	0.18	10.3	100	152	52	0.4	60	0.00	0.00
0.02	0.15	0.07	0.02	0.25	2.6	0.4	3.0	0.1	84	0.05	9.2	69	131	53	0.5	61	0.00	0.00
—	—	—	—	—	—	0.0	—	—	100	0.00	—	—	—	65	—	—	0.00	0.00
0.03	0.17	0.05	0.03	0.43	4.0	0.5	1.5	0.0	92	0.07	9.9	72	139	56	0.3	68	0.00	0.00
0.18	0.81	0.54	0.17	1.12	13.3	1.3	53.2	0.2	376	1.02	56.6	339	666	323	1.4	72	0.00	9.97
0.07	0.43	0.33	0.10	1.17	15.9	0.0	90.7	0.2	331	0.23	27.2	261	415	215	0.9	74	0.00	0.00
0.01	0.05	0.03	0.01	0.14	3.7	2.3	0.0	0.1	40	0.10	5.9	30	71	34	0.4	66	0.00	0.00
0.00	0.00	0.00	0.00	0.00	0.0	1.9	0.0	0.0	4	0.31	1.9	2	6	42	0.0	67	0.00	0.00
0.00	0.00	0.00	0.00	0.00	0.0	1.9	0.0	0.0	4	0.30	1.9	2	6	42	0.0	67	0.00	0.00
0.00	0.02	0.15	0.01	0.00	22.0	25.7	0.0	0.1	9	0.46	8.0	13	100	8	0.0	76	0.00	0.00
0.05	0.30	1.07	0.12	0.64	9.5	2.4	19.0	0.7	207	0.57	33.2	228	395	182	0.9	60	0.00	1.58
0.09	0.07	0.76	0.03	0.03	11.2	0.3	4.0	0.9	66	0.87	6.4	47	86	345	0.2	57	0.00	0.00
0.20	0.25	1.98	0.14	0.14	16.1	2.7	—	4.3	153	3.50	19.7	323	219	836	0.4	40	0.00	0.00
—	—	—	—	—	—	0.0	—	—	0	0.36	—	—	75	230	—	44	0.00	
—	—	—	—	—	—	0.0	—	—	60	0.72	—	—	85	190	—	25	0.00	0.00
—	—	—	—	—	—	0.0	—	—	0	0.36	—	—	—	160	—	20	0.00	0.00
0.12	0.18	1.41	0.02	0.11	42.6	0.1	0.4	1.8	25	1.13	10.6	77	70	320	0.5	31	0.00	0.00
0.37	0.31	2.82	0.05	0.12	46.9	5.5	0.0	3.5	65	2.50	21.3	126	118	503	0.8	27	0.00	0.00
0.40	0.30	3.53	0.05	0.00	11.2	1.6	—	4.5	13	3.11	16.6	76	130	10	0.5	33	0.00	0.00
0.36	0.37	3.89	0.15	1.07	51.1	1.5	—	—	33	2.25	15.5	31	219	443	0.8	36	0.00	0.00
0.15	0.15	1.98	0.20	0.00	52.0	0.0	—	0.0	6	1.82	4.7	21	28	206	0.2	12	0.00	0.00

PAGE KEY: A-108 Beverage and Beverage Mixes A-112 Other Beverages A-112 Beverages, Alcoholic A-114 Candies and Confections, Gum A-114 Cereals, Breakfast Type A-118 Cheese and Cheese Substitutes A-120 Dairy Products and Substitutes A-122 Desserts A-128 Dessert Toppings A-128 Eggs, Substitutes, and Egg Dishes A-130 Ethnic Foods A-130 Fast Foods/Restaurants A-140 Fats, Oils, Margarines, Shortenings, and Substitutes A-142 Fish, Seafood, and Shellfish A-142 Food Additives A-142 Fruit, Vegetable, and Blended Juices A-144 Fruits A-146 Grains, Flours, and Fractions A-148 Grain Products, Prepared and Baked Goods

Code	Food Name	Unit/ Amt	Wt (g)	Energy (Kcal)	Prot (g)	Carb (g)	Fiber (g)	Fat (g)	Sat (g)	Mono (g)	Poly (g)	Chol (mg)	Vit A (RE)
45766	Pastry, strawberry, low fat, Pop Tarts	1 ea	52	192	2	40	1	3	0.6	1.6	0.7	0	100
42365	Sweet Roll, cinnamon	1 ea	64	250	4	33	2	12	2.5	6.0	1.0	15	0
45788	Turnover, apple, fzn, rtb	1 ea	89	284	4	31	2	16	4.0	8.6	0.8	–	–
Pies													
48004	Pie, apple, cmrcl prep, w/enrich flour, 8″ whl or ⅙ pce	1 pce	117	277	2	40	2	13	4.4	5.1	2.6	0	35
48024	Pie, banana cream, prep f/rec, 9″ whl or ⅛ pce	1 pce	144	387	6	47	1	20	5.4	8.2	4.7	73	102
48025	Pie, blueberry, cmrcl prep, 8″ whl or ⅙ pce	1 pce	117	271	2	41	1	12	2.0	5.0	4.1	0	41
48005	Pie, cherry, cmrcl prep, 8″ whl or ⅙ pce	1 pce	117	304	2	47	1	13	3.0	6.8	2.4	0	64
48031	Pie, chocolate cream, cmrcl prep, 8″ whl or ⅙ pce	1 pce	113	344	3	38	2	22	5.6	12.6	2.7	6	0
48035	Pie, coconut cream, cmrcl prep, 7″ whl or ⅙ pce	1 pce	64	191	1	24	1	11	4.5	4.6	1.0	0	17
71646	Pie, key lime, w/o topping, Mrs. Smith's, pce	1 pce	113	420	6	55	–	20	12.0	–	–	20	40
48008	Pie, lemon meringue, cmrcl prep, 8″ whl or ⅙ pce	1 pce	113	303	2	53	1	10	2.0	3.0	4.1	51	60
48040	Pie, peach, 8″ whl or ⅙ pce	1 pce	117	261	2	38	1	12	1.8	5.0	4.4	0	12
48000	Pie, pumpkin, cmrcl prep, 8″ whl or ⅙ pce	1 pce	109	229	4	30	3	10	1.9	4.4	3.4	22	407
Puddings, Custards, and Pie Fillings													
2622	Custard, egg, prep f/dry mix w/2% milk	0.5 cup	133	148	5	23	0	4	1.8	1.1	0.3	64	82
2624	Custard, flan, prep f/dry mix w/2% milk	0.5 cup	133	137	4	25	0	2	1.4	0.6	0.1	9	70
2628	Pudding, banana, inst, prep f/dry mix w/2% milk	0.5 cup	147	154	4	29	0	2	1.4	0.7	0.2	9	68
2807	Pudding, chocolate fudge, Healthy Choice, snack cup	1 ea	99	110	3	21	0	2	0.5	–	–	0	0
4388	Pudding, chocolate, inst, fat free, prep w/skm mlk	0.5 cup	151	140	5	31	1	0	0.0	0.0	0.0	5	40
2604	Pudding, chocolate, prep f/dry mix w/whole milk	0.5 cup	142	158	5	26	1	5	3.0	1.4	0.2	17	40
2651	Pudding, rice, rte, 5oz can	1 ea	142	231	3	31	0	11	1.7	4.6	4.0	1	35
2653	Pudding, tapioca, prep f/dry mix w/2% milk	0.5 cup	141	148	4	28	0	2	1.4	0.6	0.1	8	68
4385	Pudding, vanilla, inst, fat free, prep w/skm mlk	0.5 cup	148	140	4	29	0	0	0.0	0.0	0.0	5	40
2777	Pudding, vanilla, inst, prep w/2% milk	0.5 cup	147	150	4	29	0	2	1.5	–	–	10	40
DESSERT TOPPINGS													
46037	Frosting, chocolate, creamy, 16oz can	1.328 oz	38	149	0	24	0	7	2.1	3.4	0.8	0	–
46330	Frosting, lemon creme, rte	2 Tbs	35	150	0	24	0	6	1.5	–	–	0	0
46009	Frosting, vanilla, creamy, rte, 16oz pkg	1.328 oz	38	158	0	26	0	6	1.8	3.3	0.9	0	0
23069	Topping, butterscotch	2 Tbs	41	103	1	27	0	0	0.0	0.0	0.0	0	11
23070	Topping, caramel	2 Tbs	41	103	1	27	0	0	0.0	0.0	0.0	0	11
23014	Topping, chocolate fudge	2 Tbs	38	133	2	24	1	3	1.5	1.5	0.1	1	2
23071	Topping, marshmallow cream, 7oz jar	1 ea	198	639	2	157	0	1	0.1	0.2	0.1	0	–
23164	Topping, strawberry	2 Tbs	42	108	0	28	0	0	0.0	0.0	0.0	0	1
510	Topping, whipped cream, pressurized	2 Tbs	8	19	0	1	0	2	1.0	0.5	0.1	6	16
326	Topping, whipped, fat free, Cool Whip	2 Tbs	9	15	0	3	0	0	0.0	0.0	0.0	0	0
565	Topping, whipped, light, Cool Whip	2 Tbs	9	20	0	2	0	1	1.0	0.0	0.0	0	0
564	Topping, whipped, non-dairy, Cool Whip	2 Tbs	9	25	0	2	0	2	1.5	0.0	0.0	0	0
EGGS, SUBSTITUTES, AND EGG DISHES													
19581	Egg Substitute, Egg Beaters, new	0.25 cup	61	30	6	1	0	0	0.0	0.0	0.0	0	60
19507	Egg Whites, raw	0.25 cup	61	30	6	1	0	0	0.0	0.0	0.0	0	0
19572	Egg Yolks, raw, fzn	2 oz	57	172	9	1	0	15	4.4	5.5	2.1	610	240
19510	Eggs, hard bld, lrg	1 ea	50	78	6	1	0	5	1.6	2.0	0.7	212	84
19509	Eggs, whole, lrg, fried	1 ea	46	92	6	1	0	7	1.9	2.7	1.3	211	114
19504	Eggs, whole, raw, med	1 ea	44	66	5	1	0	4	1.4	1.7	0.6	187	84
19535	Omelette, one egg w/cheese & ham	1 ea	78	156	11	2	0	11	4.5	4.4	1.4	198	133
19536	Omelette, w/onions peprs tom & mushrooms, Spanish	1 ea	145	178	8	6	1	14	3.4	5.9	3.0	220	211

PAGE KEY: A-154 Granola Bars, Cereal Bars, Diet Bars, Scones, and Tarts A-154 Meals and Dishes A-160 Meats A-164 Nuts, Seeds, and Products A-166 Poultry A-166 Salad Dressings, Dips, and Mayonnaise A-170 Salads A-170 Sandwiches A-172 Sauces and Gravies A-174 Snack Foods—Chips, Pretzels, Popcorn A-178 Soups, Stews and Chilis A-184 Spices, Flavors, and Seasonings A-184 Sports Bars and Drinks A-186 Supplemental Foods and Formulas A-186 Sweeteners and Sweet Substitutes A-188 Vegetables and Legumes A-200 Weight Loss Bars & Drinks A-200 Miscellaneous

Thia (mg)	Ribo (mg)	Niac (mg NE)	Vit B6 (mg)	Vit B12 (µg)	Fol (µg)	Vit C (mg)	Vit D (IU)	Vit E (mg AT)	Cal (mg)	Iron (mg)	Magn (mg)	Phos (mg)	Pota (mg)	Sodi (mg)	Zinc (mg)	Wat (%)	Alco (g)	Caff (g)
0.15	0.15	1.98	0.20	0.00	52.0	0.0	—	0.0	6	1.82	4.7	23	30	222	0.2	12	0.00	0.00
0.21	0.10	1.60	—	—	—	0.0	—	—	40	1.44	—	—	—	220	—	22	0.00	0.00
—	—	—	—	—	—	0.0	—	—	—	1.22	—	—	—	176	—	42	0.00	0.00
0.02	0.02	0.31	0.03	0.00	25.7	3.7	0.0	0.1	13	0.52	8.2	28	76	311	0.2	52	0.00	0.00
0.20	0.30	1.51	0.18	0.36	38.9	2.3	—	2.1	108	1.50	23.0	132	238	346	0.7	48	0.00	0.00
0.00	0.03	0.34	0.03	0.00	25.7	3.2	0.0	2.3	9	0.34	5.8	27	58	380	0.2	52	0.00	0.00
0.02	0.02	0.23	0.05	0.00	25.7	1.1	0.0	1.8	14	0.56	9.4	34	95	288	0.2	46	0.00	0.00
0.03	0.11	0.76	0.01	0.00	14.7	0.0	45.2	3.1	41	1.21	23.7	77	144	154	0.3	44	0.00	0.00
0.02	0.05	0.12	0.03	0.07	4.5	0.0	—	1.2	19	0.50	12.8	54	42	163	0.3	43	0.00	0.00
—	—	—	—	—	—	0.0	—	—	150	0.72	—	—	—	200	—	—	0.00	0.00
0.07	0.23	0.73	0.02	0.18	14.7	3.6	9.1	2.5	63	0.68	17.0	119	101	165	0.6	42	0.00	0.00
0.07	0.03	0.23	0.02	0.00	28.1	1.1	0.0	2.4	9	0.57	7.0	26	146	316	0.1	54	0.00	0.00
0.05	0.17	0.20	0.05	0.28	21.8	1.1	19.3	1.9	65	0.86	16.4	77	168	307	0.5	58	0.00	0.00
0.07	0.28	0.17	0.09	0.60	12.0	1.1	1.1	0.3	193	0.46	25.3	184	298	118	0.7	75	0.00	0.00
0.03	0.20	0.10	0.05	0.34	5.3	0.9	47.8	0.1	150	0.07	16.0	114	217	150	0.5	76	0.00	0.00
0.05	0.20	0.10	0.05	0.43	5.9	1.2	48.8	0.1	150	0.09	17.6	318	193	435	0.5	75	0.00	0.00
—	—	—	—	—	—	0.0	—	—	100	0.72	—	—	—	125	—	73	0.00	
—	—	—	—	—	—	0.0	—	—	150	0.72	—	350	280	410	—	75	0.00	0.00
0.03	0.25	0.15	0.05	0.34	5.7	1.0	49.0	0.1	158	0.50	21.3	132	231	146	0.6	74	0.00	2.83
0.02	0.10	0.23	0.03	0.30	4.3	0.7	0.0	2.0	74	0.43	11.3	96	85	120	0.7	68	0.00	0.00
0.03	0.20	0.10	0.05	0.34	5.6	1.0	48.5	0.1	148	0.07	16.9	116	188	171	0.5	75	0.00	0.00
—	—	—	—	—	—	0.0	—	—	150	0.00	—	300	200	410	—	78	0.00	
—	—	—	—	—	—	0.0	—	—	150	0.00	—	300	190	410	—	75	0.00	0.00
0.00	0.00	0.03	0.00	0.00	0.4	0.0	0.0	0.9	3	0.52	7.9	30	74	69	0.1	17	0.00	0.75
—	—	—	—	—	—	0.0	—	—	0	0.00	—	—	—	75	—	13	0.00	0.00
0.00	0.00	0.00	0.00	0.00	0.0	0.0	0.0	1.8	1	0.03	0.4	15	14	67	0.0	13	0.00	0.00
0.00	0.03	0.01	0.00	0.03	0.8	0.1	0.0	0.0	22	0.07	2.9	19	34	143	0.1	32	0.00	0.00
0.00	0.03	0.01	0.00	0.03	0.8	0.1	0.0	0.0	22	0.07	2.9	19	34	143	0.1	32	0.00	0.00
0.01	0.07	0.10	0.01	0.07	1.5	0.1	0.0	1.1	31	0.49	19.4	51	138	131	0.3	22	0.00	2.27
0.00	0.00	0.15	0.00	0.00	2.0	0.0	0.0	0.0	6	0.43	4.0	16	10	97	0.1	20	0.00	0.00
0.00	0.00	0.10	0.00	0.00	0.9	10.6	0.0	0.1	10	0.40	1.7	6	31	9	0.2	33	0.00	0.00
0.00	0.00	0.00	0.00	0.01	0.2	0.0	0.5	0.0	8	0.00	0.8	7	11	10	0.0	61	0.00	0.00
—	—	—	—	—	—	0.0	—	—	0	0.00	—	0	0	5	—	66	0.00	0.00
—	—	—	—	—	—	0.0	—	—	0	0.00	—	0	0	0	—	66	0.00	0.00
—	—	—	—	—	—	0.0	—	—	0	0.00	—	0	0	0	—	61	0.00	0.00
—	0.85	—	0.07	0.60	32.0	0.0	16.0	0.8	20	1.08	—	—	85	125	0.6	—	0.00	0.00
0.00	0.27	0.05	0.00	0.11	1.8	0.0	0.0	0.0	4	0.01	6.7	8	87	100	0.0	88	0.00	0.00
0.09	0.28	0.02	0.20	1.02	65.8	0.0	53.3	1.4	78	1.88	5.1	236	67	38	1.6	56	0.00	0.00
0.02	0.25	0.02	0.05	0.56	22.0	0.0	26.0	0.5	25	0.60	5.0	86	63	62	0.5	75	0.00	0.00
0.02	0.23	0.03	0.07	0.41	17.5	0.0	26.0	0.8	25	0.72	5.1	89	61	162	0.5	69	0.00	0.00
0.02	0.21	0.02	0.05	0.43	20.7	0.0	22.9	0.5	22	0.62	4.4	78	53	55	0.5	75	0.00	0.00
0.10	0.31	0.60	0.11	0.61	17.0	0.1	—	0.8	113	0.81	12.4	179	145	372	1.2	67	0.00	0.00
0.07	0.36	0.81	0.17	0.50	29.7	19.0	—	2.0	60	1.15	16.2	142	269	170	0.8	80	0.00	0.00

PAGE KEY: A-108 Beverage and Beverage Mixes A-112 Other Beverages A-112 Beverages, Alcoholic A-114 Candies and Confections, Gum A-114 Cereals, Breakfast Type A-118 Cheese and Cheese Substitutes A-120 Dairy Products and Substitutes A-122 Desserts A-128 Dessert Toppings A-128 Eggs, Substitutes, and Egg Dishes A-130 Ethnic Foods A-130 Fast Foods/Restaurants A-140 Fats, Oils, Margarines, Shortenings, and Substitutes A-142 Fish, Seafood, and Shellfish A-142 Food Additives A-142 Fruit, Vegetable, and Blended Juices A-144 Fruits A-146 Grains, Flours, and Fractions A-148 Grain Products, Prepared and Baked Goods

Code	Food Name	Unit/ Amt	Wt (g)	Energy (Kcal)	Prot (g)	Carb (g)	Fiber (g)	Fat (g)	Sat (g)	Mono (g)	Poly (g)	Chol (mg)	Vit A (RE)
ETHNIC FOODS													
Oriental Foods													
1989	Dish, fish curry, Thai, f/recipe, svg	1 ea	188	256	17	11	2	17	11.2	–	–	32	140
1990	Dish, fried rice, Thai, f/recipe, svg	1 ea	314	402	7	62	3	14	2.0	–	–	35	49
2994	Dish, spicy Thai noodles, Thai, f/recipe, svg	1 ea	310	626	34	65	3	26	4.4	–	–	212	111
7503	Miso	1 cup	275	566	32	77	15	17	2.4	3.7	9.4	0	22
FAST FOODS/RESTAURANTS													
Generic Fast Food													
56601	Biscuit, w/egg & bacon	1 ea	150	458	17	29	1	31	8.0	13.4	7.5	352	57
56602	Biscuit, w/egg & ham	1 ea	192	442	20	30	1	27	5.9	11.0	7.7	300	253
66029	Biscuit, w/egg cheese & bacon	1 ea	144	477	16	33	0	31	11.4	14.2	3.5	261	192
66016	Cheeseburger, double, plain	1 ea	155	457	28	22	–	28	13.0	11.0	1.9	110	99
56654	Cheeseburger, double, w/condiments & veg	1 ea	228	650	30	53	–	35	12.8	12.6	6.4	93	84
56648	Cheeseburger, lrg, plain	1 ea	185	609	30	47	–	33	14.8	12.7	2.4	96	185
66015	Cheeseburger, reg, w/condiments & veg	1 ea	154	359	18	28	–	20	9.2	7.2	1.5	52	91
15065	Chicken, pieces, brd, fried	1 pce	18	53	3	3	0	3	0.8	1.8	0.8	10	0
5461	Cole Slaw, fast food	0.75 cup	99	147	1	13	2	11	1.6	2.4	6.4	5	50
6175	Corn, cob, w/butter	1 ea	146	155	4	32	–	3	1.6	1.0	0.6	6	51
56606	Croissant, w/egg & cheese	1 ea	127	368	13	24	–	25	14.1	7.5	1.4	216	282
56608	Croissant, w/egg cheese & ham	1 ea	152	474	19	24	–	34	17.5	11.4	2.4	213	132
66031	English Muffin, w/cheese & sausage	1 ea	115	393	15	29	1	24	9.9	10.1	2.7	59	98
66032	English Muffin, w/egg cheese & Canadian bacon	1 ea	146	308	18	28	2	13	5.0	5.0	1.7	250	188
42353	French Toast, w/butter	2 pce	135	356	10	36	0	19	7.7	7.1	2.4	116	138
56662	Hamburger, double, lrg, w/condiment & veg	1 ea	226	540	34	40	–	27	10.5	10.3	2.8	122	9
66009	Hamburger, double, reg, plain	1 ea	176	544	30	43	–	28	10.4	12.1	2.3	99	0
66007	Hamburger, reg, plain	1 ea	90	274	12	31	–	12	4.1	5.5	0.9	35	0
56658	Hamburger, reg, w/condiment	1 ea	106	272	12	34	2	10	3.6	3.4	1.0	30	8
66004	Hot Dog, plain, w/bun	1 ea	98	242	10	18	–	15	5.1	6.9	1.7	44	0
56667	Hot Dog, w/chili & bun	1 ea	114	296	14	31	–	13	4.9	6.6	1.2	51	7
2031	Ice Milk Cone, vanilla, soft serve	1 ea	103	164	4	24	0	6	3.5	1.8	0.4	28	53
56639	Nachos, w/cheese	7 pce	113	346	9	36	–	19	7.8	8.0	2.2	18	154
56641	Nachos, w/cheese beans beef & peppers	7 pce	225	502	17	49	–	27	11.0	9.7	5.0	18	488
6176	Onion Rings, breaded, fried, svg	8.5 pce	83	276	4	31	–	16	7.0	6.7	0.7	14	2
45122	Pancakes, w/butter & syrup	2 ea	232	520	8	91	1	14	5.9	5.3	2.0	58	81
5463	Potatoes, hash browns	0.5 cup	72	151	2	16	–	9	4.3	3.9	0.5	9	3
6185	Potatoes, mashed	0.333 cup	80	66	2	13	–	1	0.4	0.3	0.2	2	10
6173	Salad, potato	0.333 cup	95	108	1	13	–	6	1.0	1.6	2.9	57	28
56623	Salad, tossed, w/o dressing	1.5 cup	207	33	3	7	–	0	0.0	0.0	0.1	0	236
2033	Sundae, strawberry	1 ea	153	268	6	45	0	8	3.7	2.7	1.0	21	60
Arby's													
6428	Potatoes, baked, deluxe, svg	1 ea	361	650	20	67	6	34	20.0	10.4	3.6	90	104
8986	Potatoes, french fries, curly, med	1 ea	128	400	5	50	4	19	4.5	12.4	2.5	0	0
8997	Salad, caesar	1 ea	223	90	7	8	3	4	2.5	–	–	10	–
8998	Salad, caesar, chicken, grilled	1 ea	338	230	33	8	3	8	3.5	–	–	80	–
52074	Salad, garden	1 ea	349	70	4	14	6	1	0.0	–	–	0	518
69045	Sandwich, beef, Arby Q	1 ea	186	360	16	40	2	14	4.0	6.5	3.5	70	–
8988	Sandwich, beef, melt w/cheddar	1 ea	150	320	16	36	2	14	6.0	–	–	45	–
69055	Sandwich, beef, philly & swiss cheese	1 ea	311	670	36	46	4	40	16.0	16.3	7.7	75	–
69043	Sandwich, French dip	1 ea	285	410	28	43	2	16	9.0	–	–	45	–

PAGE KEY: A-154 Granola Bars, Cereal Bars, Diet Bars, Scones, and Tarts A-154 Meals and Dishes A-160 Meats A-164 Nuts, Seeds, and Products A-166 Poultry A-166 Salad Dressings, Dips, and Mayonnaise A-170 Salads A-170 Sandwiches A-172 Sauces and Gravies A-174 Snack Foods—Chips, Pretzels, Popcorn A-178 Soups, Stews and Chilis A-184 Spices, Flavors, and Seasonings A-184 Sports Bars and Drinks A-186 Supplemental Foods and Formulas A-186 Sweeteners and Sweet Substitutes A-188 Vegetables and Legumes A-200 Weight Loss Bars & Drinks A-200 Miscellaneous

Thia (mg)	Ribo (mg)	Niac (mg NE)	Vit B6 (mg)	Vit B12 (µg)	Fol (µg)	Vit C (mg)	Vit D (IU)	Vit E (mg AT)	Cal (mg)	Iron (mg)	Magn (mg)	Phos (mg)	Pota (mg)	Sodi (mg)	Zinc (mg)	Wat (%)	Alco (g)	Caff (g)
0.14	0.12	1.87	0.43	12.09	24.6	24.1	0.0	1.8	49	4.26	80.3	260	501	206	1.3	75	0.00	0.00
0.09	0.12	1.17	0.21	0.09	34.1	42.9	4.3	2.8	35	1.44	42.7	117	279	708	1.2	73	—	0.00
0.25	0.31	9.47	0.55	1.08	90.3	20.4	77.5	2.0	73	4.76	95.0	308	623	1660	2.3	58	0.00	0.00
0.27	0.68	2.36	0.58	0.00	90.8	0.0	0.0	0.0	182	7.53	115.5	421	451	10029	9.1	41	0.00	0.00
0.14	0.23	2.40	0.14	1.02	60.0	2.7	—	2.1	189	3.74	24.0	238	250	999	1.6	47	0.00	0.00
0.67	0.60	2.00	0.27	1.19	65.3	0.0	—	2.2	221	4.55	30.7	317	319	1382	2.2	55	0.00	0.00
0.30	0.43	2.29	0.10	1.04	53.3	1.6	—	1.4	164	2.54	20.2	459	230	1260	1.5	41	0.00	0.00
0.25	0.37	6.01	0.25	2.30	68.2	0.0	—	1.2	232	3.41	32.5	374	308	636	5.0	42	0.00	0.00
0.56	0.43	8.34	0.27	2.06	91.2	2.7	—	2.0	169	4.71	36.5	349	390	921	4.1	47	0.00	0.00
0.47	0.56	11.17	0.28	2.52	74.0	0.0	22.2	—	91	5.46	38.9	422	644	1589	5.6	39	0.00	0.00
0.31	0.23	6.38	0.15	1.23	64.7	2.3	—	1.3	182	2.65	26.2	216	229	976	2.6	55	0.00	0.00
0.01	0.02	1.25	0.05	0.05	5.1	0.0	2.1	0.2	2	0.15	4.1	48	51	86	0.2	47	0.00	0.00
0.03	0.02	0.07	0.10	0.18	38.6	8.3	—	4.0	34	0.72	8.9	36	177	267	0.2	74	0.00	0.00
0.25	0.10	2.18	0.31	0.00	43.8	6.9	—	—	4	0.87	40.9	108	359	29	0.9	72	0.00	0.00
0.18	0.37	1.50	0.10	0.76	47.0	0.1	—	—	244	2.20	21.6	348	174	551	1.8	45	0.00	0.00
0.51	0.30	3.19	0.23	1.00	45.6	11.4	—	—	144	2.13	25.8	336	272	1081	2.2	51	0.00	0.00
0.69	0.25	4.13	0.15	0.68	66.7	1.3	—	0.5	168	2.25	24.1	186	215	1036	1.7	38	0.00	0.00
0.52	0.47	3.54	0.15	0.72	73.0	1.9	46.7	0.9	161	2.59	24.8	288	212	777	1.7	57	0.00	0.00
0.57	0.50	3.92	0.05	0.36	72.9	0.1	—	—	73	1.88	16.2	146	177	513	0.6	51	0.00	0.00
0.36	0.37	7.57	0.54	4.07	76.8	1.1	—	—	102	5.84	49.7	314	570	791	5.7	54	0.00	0.00
0.33	0.37	8.25	0.31	2.92	77.4	0.0	28.2	1.3	86	4.55	37.0	234	363	554	5.7	41	0.00	0.00
0.33	0.27	3.72	0.05	0.88	53.1	0.0	10.8	0.5	63	2.40	18.9	103	145	387	2.0	38	0.00	0.00
0.28	0.23	3.91	0.11	1.09	51.9	2.2	—	0.4	126	2.71	23.3	114	251	534	2.2	45	0.00	0.00
0.23	0.27	3.65	0.05	0.50	48.0	0.1	—	0.3	24	2.30	12.7	97	143	670	2.0	54	0.00	0.00
0.21	0.40	3.74	0.05	0.30	73.0	2.7	—	—	19	3.27	10.3	192	166	480	0.8	48	0.00	0.00
0.05	0.25	0.31	0.05	0.20	12.4	1.1	8.2	0.4	153	0.15	15.4	139	169	92	0.6	65	0.00	0.00
0.18	0.37	1.53	0.20	0.81	10.2	1.2	—	—	272	1.27	55.4	276	172	816	1.8	40	0.00	0.00
0.20	0.61	2.95	0.36	0.89	33.8	4.3	—	—	340	2.45	85.5	342	398	1588	3.2	56	0.00	0.00
0.07	0.10	0.92	0.05	0.11	54.8	0.6	—	0.3	73	0.85	15.8	86	129	430	0.3	37	0.00	0.00
0.38	0.56	3.39	0.11	0.23	51.0	3.5	—	1.4	128	2.61	48.7	476	251	1104	1.0	50	0.00	0.00
0.07	0.00	1.07	0.17	0.00	7.9	5.5	—	0.1	7	0.47	15.8	69	267	290	0.2	60	0.00	0.00
0.07	0.03	0.95	0.18	0.03	6.4	0.3	—	—	17	0.37	14.4	44	235	182	0.3	79	0.00	0.00
0.07	0.10	0.25	0.14	0.10	23.8	1.0	—	—	13	0.68	7.6	53	256	312	0.2	79	0.00	0.00
0.05	0.10	1.13	0.17	0.00	76.6	48.0	—	—	27	1.29	22.8	81	356	54	0.4	96	0.00	0.00
0.05	0.28	0.89	0.07	0.63	18.4	2.0	18.4	0.8	161	0.31	24.5	155	271	92	0.7	61	0.00	0.00
0.09	0.14	3.10	—	0.00	—	36.0	—	—	100	3.59	—	—	1576	750	—	66	0.00	0.00
0.07	0.09	2.57	—	0.00	—	15.5	—	—	0	1.86	—	—	934	993	0.8	41	0.00	0.00
—	—	—	—	—	—	42.0	—	—	200	1.79	—	—	—	170	—	91	0.00	0.00
—	—	—	—	—	—	42.0	—	—	200	1.79	—	—	—	920	—	85	0.00	0.00
0.17	0.20	1.26	—	—	—	42.0	—	—	80	1.44	—	—	635	45	0.9	94	0.00	0.00
0.25	0.37	9.00	—	—	—	4.8	—	—	80	3.59	—	—	456	1530	—	60	0.00	0.00
—	—	—	—	—	—	0.0	—	—	80	2.70	—	—	—	850	—	54	0.00	0.00
0.44	0.72	13.89	—	—	—	9.0	—	—	300	2.70	—	—	646	1850	5.9	60	0.00	0.00
0.36	0.87	15.55	—	—	—	1.2	—	—	80	4.50	—	—	679	1200	—	69	0.00	0.00

PAGE KEY: A-108 Beverage and Beverage Mixes A-112 Other Beverages A-112 Beverages, Alcoholic A-114 Candies and Confections, Gum A-114 Cereals, Breakfast Type A-118 Cheese and Cheese Substitutes A-120 Dairy Products and Substitutes A-122 Desserts A-128 Dessert Toppings A-128 Eggs, Substitutes, and Egg Dishes A-130 Ethnic Foods A-130 Fast Foods/Restaurants A-140 Fats, Oils, Margarines, Shortenings, and Substitutes A-142 Fish, Seafood, and Shellfish A-142 Food Additives A-142 Fruit, Vegetable, and Blended Juices A-144 Fruits A-146 Grains, Flours, and Fractions A-148 Grain Products, Prepared and Baked Goods

Code	Food Name	Unit/ Amt	Wt (g)	Energy (Kcal)	Prot (g)	Carb (g)	Fiber (g)	Fat (g)	Sat (g)	Mono (g)	Poly (g)	Chol (mg)	Vit A (RE)
Boston Market													
7393	Beans, baked, bbq	0.75 cup	201	270	8	48	12	5	2.0	–	–	0	80
15247	Chicken, ½, w/skin	1 ea	277	590	70	4	0	33	10.0	–	–	290	0
57529	Dish, macaroni & cheese	0.75 cup	192	280	13	32	1	11	6.0	–	–	30	60
57530	Dish, pot pie, chicken, original	1 ea	425	780	32	61	4	46	13.0	–	–	135	450
7390	Potatoes, mashed, homestyle	0.66 cup	161	190	3	24	1	9	6.0	–	–	25	60
52110	Salad, pasta, tortellini	0.75 cup	159	380	14	29	2	24	4.5	–	–	90	40
69084	Sandwich, ham & turkey, club, w/o cheese & sauce	1 ea	266	430	29	64	4	6	2.0	–	–	55	40
69080	Sandwich, ham, w/cheese & sauce	1 ea	337	750	38	72	5	34	12.0	–	–	100	150
Burger King													
56355	Cheeseburger, Whopper	1 ea	303	780	34	55	4	47	17.0	–	–	105	150
57000	Cheeseburger, Whopper Jr	1 ea	180	460	21	33	2	27	10.0	–	–	60	80
9087	Chicken, Tenders, 4 pce svg	1 ea	62	170	11	10	0	9	3.0	–	–	25	0
56354	Hamburger, Whopper	1 ea	278	680	29	53	4	39	12.0	–	–	80	100
56999	Hamburger, Whopper Jr	1 ea	167	410	18	32	2	23	7.0	–	–	50	40
2129	Milk Shake, vanilla, med	1 ea	397	440	12	79	2	8	5.0	–	–	25	60
9041	Onion Rings, lrg	1 ea	137	480	7	60	5	23	6.0	–	–	0	0
9065	Potatoes, french fries, salted, lrg	1 ea	160	500	6	63	5	25	7.0	–	–	0	0
56362	Sandwich, Big Fish	1 ea	263	710	24	67	4	38	14.0	–	–	50	20
9057	Sandwich, chicken tenders	1 ea	148	450	14	37	2	27	5.0	–	–	30	40
Carl's Junior													
91433	Burrito, breakfast	1 ea	185	480	27	26	2	30	13.0	–	–	465	150
91402	Hamburger, Carl's Famous Star	1 ea	254	580	25	49	2	32	9.0	–	–	70	60
91420	Potatoes, baked, w/broccoli & cheese, Great Stuff	1 ea	411	530	11	74	7	21	4.5	–	–	15	300
91414	Potatoes, french fries, svg	1 ea	92	290	5	37	3	14	3.0	–	–	0	0
91424	Salad, chicken, charbroiled, Salad To Go	1 ea	350	200	25	12	3	7	3.5	–	–	75	1200
Chick-Fil-A													
15263	Chicken, nuggets, 8 pce svg	1 ea	113	260	26	12	1	12	2.5	–	–	70	0
15262	Chicken, strips, Chick-N-Strips, 4 pce svg	1 ea	108	250	25	12	0	11	2.5	–	–	70	0
52135	Salad, Chick-N-Strips	1 ea	315	340	30	19	3	16	5.0	–	–	85	600
69152	Sandwich, chicken	1 ea	170	410	28	38	1	16	3.5	–	–	60	40
69183	Wrap, chicken caesar, Cool Wrap	1 ea	227	460	38	51	3	11	6.0	–	–	85	150
69182	Wrap, chicken, spicy	1 ea	225	390	31	51	3	7	3.5	–	–	70	40
Chili's Grill&Bar													
4823	Dish, pasta, veg, svg, Guiltless Grill	0.5 ea	326	351	18	53	3	7	2.1	–	–	64	319
Dairy Queen													
71694	Cake, ice cream, layered, ⅛ of 8" round	1 pce	147	330	6	49	0	12	6.0	–	–	15	80
2135	Ice Cream Bar, Dilly, chocolate	1 ea	85	210	3	21	0	13	7.0	–	–	10	60
2222	Ice Cream Cone, chocolate, med	1 ea	198	340	8	53	0	11	7.0	–	–	30	150
2136	Ice Cream Cone, dipped, med	1 ea	220	490	8	59	1	24	13.0	–	–	30	150
2143	Ice Cream Cone, vanilla, med	1 ea	213	355	9	57	0	10	6.5	–	–	32	161
2133	Ice Cream Dessert, Buster Bar	1 ea	149	450	10	41	2	28	12.0	–	–	15	80
2134	Ice Cream Sandwich	1 ea	85	200	4	31	1	6	3.0	–	–	10	40
2370	Ice Cream, Blizzard, chocolate chip cookie dough, med	1 ea	439	950	17	143	2	36	19.0	–	–	75	350
2227	Ice Cream, Blizzard, strawberry, med	1 ea	383	570	12	95	1	16	11.0	–	–	50	300
2365	Ice Cream, Lemon Freez'r	0.5 cup	92	80	0	20	0	0	0.0	0.0	0.0	0	0
Dennys													
56329	Breakfast, All American Slam, w/o bread	1 ea	425	1028	48	24	2	87	21.0	–	–	724	720
25238	Breakfast, Country Slam	1 ea	510	1000	41	61	1	66	21.0	–	–	467	300

Thia (mg)	Ribo (mg)	Niac (mg NE)	Vit B6 (mg)	Vit B12 (µg)	Fol (µg)	Vit C (mg)	Vit D (IU)	Vit E (mg AT)	Cal (mg)	Iron (mg)	Magn (mg)	Phos (mg)	Pota (mg)	Sodi (mg)	Zinc (mg)	Wat (%)	Alco (g)	Caff (g)
–	–	–	–	0.00	–	6.0	–	–	100	3.59	–	–	–	540	–	68	0.00	0.00
–	–	–	–	–	–	0.0	–	–	0	2.70	–	–	–	1010	–	61	0.00	0.00
–	–	–	–	–	–	0.0	–	–	300	1.44	–	–	–	830	–	70	0.00	0.00
–	–	–	–	–	–	3.6	–	–	40	3.59	–	–	–	1480	–	66	0.00	0.00
–	–	–	–	0.00	–	6.0	–	–	60	0.36	–	–	–	570	–	77	0.00	0.00
–	–	–	–	–	–	9.0	–	–	60	0.72	–	–	–	530	–	57	0.00	0.00
–	–	–	–	–	–	9.0	–	–	80	2.70	–	–	–	1330	–	62	0.00	0.00
–	–	–	–	–	–	30.0	–	–	150	2.70	–	–	–	1730	–	57	0.00	0.00
–	–	–	–	–	–	9.0	–	–	250	5.40	–	–	–	1390	–	–	0.00	0.00
–	–	–	–	–	–	4.8	–	–	150	3.59	–	–	–	740	–	54	0.00	0.00
–	–	–	–	–	–	0.0	–	–	0	0.36	–	–	–	420	–	49	0.00	0.00
–	–	–	–	–	–	9.0	–	–	100	5.40	–	–	–	940	–	–	0.00	0.00
–	–	–	–	–	–	4.8	–	–	80	3.59	–	–	–	520	–	55	0.00	0.00
–	–	–	–	–	–	6.0	–	–	400	0.00	–	–	–	340	–	–	0.00	0.00
–	–	–	–	–	–	0.0	–	–	150	0.00	–	–	–	690	–	–	0.00	0.00
–	–	–	–	–	–	12.0	–	–	20	1.08	–	–	–	940	–	39	0.00	0.00
–	–	–	–	–	–	0.0	–	–	80	3.59	–	–	–	1200	–	49	0.00	0.00
–	–	–	–	–	–	3.6	–	–	60	1.79	–	–	–	680	–	–	0.00	0.00
–	–	–	–	–	–	0.0	–	–	350	2.70	–	–	–	750	–	–	0.00	0.00
–	–	–	–	–	–	6.0	–	–	100	4.50	–	–	–	910	–	–	0.00	0.00
–	–	–	–	–	–	60.0	–	–	150	3.59	–	–	–	950	–	–	0.00	0.00
–	–	–	–	–	–	21.0	–	–	0	1.08	–	–	–	170	–	36	0.00	0.00
–	–	–	–	–	–	27.0	–	–	200	1.79	–	–	–	440	–	–	0.00	0.00
–	–	–	–	–	–	0.0	–	–	40	1.08	–	–	–	1090	–	54	0.00	0.00
–	–	–	–	–	–	0.0	–	–	40	1.08	–	–	–	570	–	54	0.00	0.00
–	–	–	–	–	–	6.0	–	–	150	1.08	–	–	–	680	–	–	0.00	0.00
–	–	–	–	–	–	0.0	–	–	100	2.70	–	–	–	1300	–	–	0.00	0.00
–	–	–	–	–	–	0.0	–	–	400	3.59	–	–	–	1540	–	–	0.00	0.00
–	–	–	–	–	–	4.8	–	–	200	3.59	–	–	–	1150	–	–	0.00	0.00
–	–	–	–	–	–	3.6	–	–	126	3.60	–	–	–	392	–	75	0.00	0.00
–	–	–	–	–	–	0.0	–	–	200	1.44	–	–	–	350	–	–	0.00	0.00
–	–	–	–	–	–	0.0	–	–	100	0.36	–	–	–	75	–	55	0.00	
–	–	–	–	–	–	1.2	–	–	250	1.79	–	–	–	160	–	63	0.00	
–	–	–	–	–	–	2.4	–	–	250	1.79	–	–	–	190	–	58	0.00	
–	–	–	–	–	–	2.6	–	–	269	1.94	–	–	–	172	–	64	0.00	0.00
–	–	–	–	–	–	0.0	–	–	150	1.08	–	–	–	280	–	47	0.00	
–	–	–	–	–	–	0.0	–	–	80	1.08	–	–	–	140	–	51	0.00	
–	–	–	–	–	–	1.2	–	–	450	2.70	–	–	–	660	–	55	0.00	
0.15	0.68	–	–	–	–	9.0	–	–	450	1.79	–	350	700	260	–	68	0.00	0.00
–	–	–	–	–	–	0.0	–	–	0	0.00	–	–	–	10	–	78	0.00	0.00
–	–	–	–	–	–	6.6	–	–	500	3.42	–	–	–	1924	–	–	0.00	0.00
–	–	–	–	–	–	0.0	–	–	70	4.13	–	–	–	2727	–	–	0.00	0.00

PAGE KEY: A-108 Beverage and Beverage Mixes A-112 Other Beverages A-112 Beverages, Alcoholic A-114 Candies and Confections, Gum A-114 Cereals, Breakfast Type A-118 Cheese and Cheese Substitutes A-120 Dairy Products and Substitutes A-122 Desserts A-128 Dessert Toppings A-128 Eggs, Substitutes, and Egg Dishes A-130 Ethnic Foods A-130 Fast Foods/Restaurants A-140 Fats, Oils, Margarines, Shortenings, and Substitutes A-142 Fish, Seafood, and Shellfish A-142 Food Additives A-142 Fruit, Vegetable, and Blended Juices A-144 Fruits A-146 Grains, Flours, and Fractions A-148 Grain Products, Prepared and Baked Goods

Code	Food Name	Unit/ Amt	Wt (g)	Energy (Kcal)	Prot (g)	Carb (g)	Fiber (g)	Fat (g)	Sat (g)	Mono (g)	Poly (g)	Chol (mg)	Vit A (RE)
25242	Breakfast, meat lover's skillet	1 ea	482	1344	59	34	3	108	37.0	–	–	673	680
25249	Chicken, buffalo wings	1 ea	35	71	8	0	0	4	1.4	–	–	42	15
25250	Quesadilla, chicken	1 ea	454	827	50	43	2	55	23.0	–	–	181	630
Dominos Pizza													
91362	Pizza, America's Favorite Feast, hand tossed, 12"	2 pce	205	508	22	57	4	22	9.2	–	–	49	138
56386	Pizza, cheese, hand tossed, 12"	2 pce	159	375	15	55	3	11	4.8	–	–	23	131
91360	Pizza, Hawaiian Feast, hand tossed, 12"	2 pce	204	450	21	58	3	16	7.2	–	–	41	173
91361	Pizza, Pepperoni Feast, hand tossed, 12"	2 pce	196	534	24	56	3	25	10.9	–	–	57	175
Dunkin' Donuts													
49125	Doughnut, eclair	1 ea	90	290	4	42	1	12	3.0	–	–	0	0
44614	Muffin, banana nut	1 ea	95	340	6	53	2	12	3.0	–	–	35	0
El Pollo Loco													
15936	Burrito, chicken, classic	1 ea	312	580	31	66	9	22	7.0	–	–	108	330
1656	Salad, tostada	1 ea	397	304	29	28	4	11	3.0	–	–	57	190
7198	Taco, al carbon	1 ea	85	164	13	14	1	6	2.0	–	–	68	60
7204	Taco, chicken, soft	1 ea	128	238	17	15	0	12	4.0	–	–	74	120
Hardees													
9280	Cheeseburger	1 ea	124	313	16	26	1	14	7.0	–	–	40	–
56412	Hamburger	1 ea	110	265	14	26	1	10	4.0	–	–	35	–
9283	Potatoes, french fries, Crispy Curls, lrg svg	1 ea	147	520	7	62	0	28	5.0	–	–	0	–
56419	Sandwich, roast beef, big	1 ea	165	411	24	27	2	23	9.4	–	–	68	–
In-N-Out Burgers													
81111	Hamburger, w/mustard & ketchup	1 ea	243	310	16	41	3	10	4.0	–	–	35	150
81119	Potatoes, french fries	1 ea	125	400	7	54	2	18	5.0	–	–	0	0
Jack in the Box													
56434	Cheeseburger	1 ea	116	300	14	31	2	13	6.0	5.0	2.0	40	40
57014	Dish, chicken, teriyaki, bowl	1 ea	502	670	26	128	3	4	1.0	–	–	15	1300
56445	Dish, egg roll, sml, 3pce svg	1 ea	170	440	15	40	4	24	6.0	14.9	3.1	30	150
56436	Hamburger, Jumbo Jack	1 ea	271	550	27	43	2	30	10.0	12.4	7.6	75	100
2163	Milk Shake, chocolate, med	1 ea	332	630	11	85	1	27	16.0	–	–	85	150
56446	Onion Rings, svg	1 ea	120	450	7	50	3	25	5.0	18.9	1.1	0	40
62550	Potatoes, french fries, curly, chili cheese, svg	1 ea	230	650	14	60	4	41	12.0	–	–	25	150
56448	Salad, side	1 ea	86	50	2	3	1	3	1.5	1.5	0.0	10	75
56377	Taco	1 ea	90	170	7	12	2	10	3.5	–	–	15	60
Kentucky Fried Chicken													
15169	Chicken, breast, extra crispy	1 ea	168	470	39	17	1	28	8.0	16.7	3.3	160	20
15163	Chicken, breast, original rec	1 ea	153	400	29	16	1	24	6.0	14.4	3.6	135	20
50997	Chicken, popcorn style, lrg	1 ea	170	620	30	36	0	40	10.0	–	–	73	0
81092	Chicken, strips, Colonel's Crispy	3 ea	115	300	26	18	1	16	4.0	–	–	56	20
15171	Chicken, thigh, extra crispy	1 ea	118	380	21	14	1	27	7.0	15.8	4.2	118	20
56451	Cole Slaw, svg	1 ea	142	232	2	26	3	14	2.0	3.5	7.0	8	90
6152	Corn, cob	1 ea	162	150	5	35	2	2	0.0	0.6	0.9	0	10
56443	Sandwich, chicken, supreme	1 ea	305	830	33	66	3	49	7.0	–	–	65	100
Long John Silvers													
56477	Cornbread, hush puppies, svg	1 ea	23	60	1	9	–	2	0.0	–	–	–	–
57003	Dinner, fish, w/lemon crumb	1 ea	471	730	31	89	–	29	6.0	–	–	60	–
56461	Fish, batter dipped, reg	1 pce	92	230	12	16	–	13	4.0	–	–	30	–
19108	Shrimp, battered	1 pce	14	45	2	3	–	2	1.0	–	–	15	–
91386	Shrimp, popcorn, svg	1 ea	113	320	15	33	–	15	2.5	–	–	85	–

PAGE KEY: A-154 Granola Bars, Cereal Bars, Diet Bars, Scones, and Tarts A-154 Meals and Dishes A-160 Meats A-164 Nuts, Seeds, and Products A-166 Poultry A-166 Salad Dressings, Dips, and Mayonnaise A-170 Salads A-170 Sandwiches A-172 Sauces and Gravies A-174 Snack Foods—Chips, Pretzels, Popcorn A-178 Soups, Stews and Chilis A-184 Spices, Flavors, and Seasonings A-184 Sports Bars and Drinks A-186 Supplemental Foods and Formulas A-186 Sweeteners and Sweet Substitutes A-188 Vegetables and Legumes A-200 Weight Loss Bars & Drinks A-200 Miscellaneous

Thia (mg)	Ribo (mg)	Niac (mg NE)	Vit B6 (mg)	Vit B12 (µg)	Fol (µg)	Vit C (mg)	Vit D (IU)	Vit E (mg AT)	Cal (mg)	Iron (mg)	Magn (mg)	Phos (mg)	Pota (mg)	Sodi (mg)	Zinc (mg)	Wat (%)	Alco (g)	Caff (g)
–	–	–	–	–	–	9.6	–	–	380	5.21	–	–	–	3063	–	–	0.00	0.00
–	–	–	–	–	–	2.4	–	–	16	1.29	–	–	–	462	–	65	0.00	0.00
–	–	–	–	–	–	54.0	–	–	640	1.79	–	–	–	1982	–	–	0.00	0.00
–	–	–	–	–	–	0.7	–	–	202	3.70	–	–	–	12	–	48	0.00	0.00
–	–	–	–	–	–	0.0	–	–	187	2.99	–	–	–	776	–	47	0.00	0.00
–	–	–	–	–	–	1.9	–	–	274	3.29	–	–	–	1102	–	51	0.00	0.00
–	–	–	–	–	–	0.1	–	–	279	3.40	–	–	–	1349	–	44	0.00	0.00
–	–	–	–	–	–	1.2	–	–	0	0.72	–	–	–	280	–	34	0.00	0.00
–	–	–	–	–	–	1.2	–	–	40	1.79	–	–	–	210	–	24	0.00	0.00
–	–	–	–	–	–	25.8	–	–	400	4.86	–	–	–	1596	–	60	0.00	0.00
–	–	–	–	–	–	22.8	–	–	180	3.24	–	–	–	1175	–	–	0.00	0.00
–	–	–	–	–	–	1.8	–	–	50	1.44	–	–	–	21	–	61	0.00	0.00
–	–	–	–	–	–	10.2	–	–	181	1.62	–	–	–	631	–	–	0.00	0.00
–	–	–	–	–	–	–	–	–	–	–	–	–	–	895	–	–	0.00	0.00
–	–	–	–	–	–	–	–	–	–	–	–	–	–	663	–	50	0.00	0.00
–	–	–	–	–	–	–	–	–	–	–	–	–	–	1450	–	–	0.00	0.00
–	–	–	–	–	–	–	–	–	–	–	–	–	–	1128	–	–	0.00	0.00
–	–	–	–	–	–	15.0	–	–	40	3.59	–	–	–	720	–	–	0.00	0.00
–	–	–	–	–	–	0.0	–	–	20	1.79	–	–	–	245	–	–	0.00	0.00
0.23	0.23	3.16	–	–	–	0.0	–	–	150	3.59	–	–	180	840	–	48	0.00	0.00
–	–	–	–	–	–	24.0	–	–	100	4.50	–	–	620	1730	–	68	0.00	0.00
0.60	0.33	6.17	–	–	–	12.0	–	–	80	4.50	–	–	500	1020	–	53	0.00	0.00
0.43	0.34	2.09	–	–	–	9.0	–	–	150	4.50	–	–	490	880	–	62	0.00	0.00
–	–	–	–	–	–	0.0	–	–	350	0.36	–	–	720	330	–	62	0.00	
0.34	0.20	3.02	–	0.00	–	18.0	–	–	40	2.70	–	–	150	780	–	30	0.00	0.00
–	–	–	–	–	–	0.0	–	–	150	2.70	–	–	810	1760	–	49	0.00	0.00
0.05	0.07	–	–	–	–	0.0	–	–	80	0.72	–	–	160	75	–	90	0.00	0.00
0.07	0.20	1.14	0.15	0.55	–	0.2	–	–	100	1.08	40.4	168	235	390	1.4	66	0.00	0.00
–	–	–	–	–	–	1.2	–	–	20	1.08	–	–	–	874	–	48	0.00	0.00
–	–	–	–	–	–	1.2	–	–	40	1.08	–	–	–	1116	–	53	0.00	0.00
–	–	–	–	–	–	0.0	–	–	20	0.72	–	–	–	1046	–	36	0.00	0.00
–	–	–	–	–	–	1.2	–	–	20	1.08	–	–	–	1165	–	47	0.00	0.00
–	–	–	–	–	–	1.2	–	–	20	1.08	–	–	–	625	–	45	0.00	0.00
–	–	–	–	–	–	34.3	–	–	30	0.36	–	–	–	285	–	70	0.00	0.00
–	–	–	–	–	–	3.6	–	–	20	0.36	–	–	–	20	–	73	0.00	0.00
0.49	0.40	13.68	–	–	–	9.0	–	–	200	3.59	–	–	250	2140	–	49	0.00	0.00
–	–	–	–	–	–	–	–	–	–	–	–	–	–	25	–	43	0.00	0.00
–	–	–	–	–	–	–	–	–	–	–	–	–	–	1720	–	–	0.00	0.00
–	–	–	–	–	–	–	–	–	–	–	–	–	–	700	–	53	0.00	0.00
–	–	–	–	–	–	–	–	–	–	–	–	–	–	125	–	46	0.00	0.00
–	–	–	–	–	–	–	–	–	–	–	–	–	–	1440	–	–	0.00	0.00

PAGE KEY: A-108 Beverage and Beverage Mixes A-112 Other Beverages A-112 Beverages, Alcoholic A-114 Candies and Confections, Gum A-114 Cereals, Breakfast Type A-118 Cheese and Cheese Substitutes A-120 Dairy Products and Substitutes A-122 Desserts A-128 Dessert Toppings A-128 Eggs, Substitutes, and Egg Dishes A-130 Ethnic Foods A-130 Fast Foods/Restaurants A-140 Fats, Oils, Margarines, Shortenings, and Substitutes A-142 Fish, Seafood, and Shellfish A-142 Food Additives A-142 Fruit, Vegetable, and Blended Juices A-144 Fruits A-146 Grains, Flours, and Fractions A-148 Grain Products, Prepared and Baked Goods

Code	Food Name	Unit/ Amt	Wt (g)	Energy (Kcal)	Prot (g)	Carb (g)	Fiber (g)	Fat (g)	Sat (g)	Mono (g)	Poly (g)	Chol (mg)	Vit A (RE)
McDonalds													
69003	Biscuit, sausage	1 ea	112	410	10	30	1	28	8.0	–	–	35	2
56675	Burrito, sausage, breakfast	1 ea	113	290	13	24	2	16	6.0	–	–	170	100
69009	Cheeseburger	1 ea	121	330	15	36	2	14	6.0	–	–	45	60
69012	Cheeseburger, Quarter Pounder	1 ea	200	530	28	38	2	30	13.0	–	–	95	100
15174	Chicken, nuggets, McNuggets, 4 pce svg	1 ea	72	190	10	13	1	11	2.5	–	–	35	0
42337	Danish, cheese	1 ea	105	400	7	45	2	21	5.0	–	–	40	60
69008	Hamburger	1 ea	107	280	12	35	2	10	4.0	–	–	30	22
69010	Hamburger, Big Mac	1 ea	216	590	24	47	3	34	11.0	–	–	85	60
69011	Hamburger, Quarter Pounder	1 ea	172	430	23	37	2	21	8.0	–	–	70	20
69006	McMuffin, sausage	1 ea	112	360	13	26	1	23	8.0	–	–	45	40
2168	Milk Shake, strawberry, sml	1 ea	294	360	11	60	0	9	6.0	–	–	40	60
4713	Nuts, sundae style, svg	1 ea	7	35	2	2	1	3	0.0	–	–	0	0
48136	Pie, apple, svg	1 ea	77	260	3	34	1	13	3.5	–	–	0	–
6421	Potatoes, french fries, lrg svg	1 ea	176	540	8	68	6	26	4.5	–	–	0	0
5462	Potatoes, french fries, med svg	1 ea	147	450	6	57	5	22	4.0	–	–	0	0
6155	Potatoes, hash browns, svg	1 ea	53	130	1	14	1	8	1.5	–	–	0	0
56479	Salad, garden, shaker	1 ea	149	100	7	4	2	6	3.0	–	–	75	150
81097	Sandwich, chicken, crisp deluxe	1 ea	234	550	23	54	2	27	4.5	–	–	50	60
81098	Sandwich, chicken, grilled, McGrill	1 ea	229	450	26	46	2	18	3.0	–	–	60	60
49141	Sandwich, ham, egg & cheese, bagel	1 ea	218	550	26	58	2	23	8.0	–	–	255	150
49142	Sndwch, Omlt, Spanish (saus, egg & cheese), bagel	1 ea	258	690	27	60	3	38	14.0	–	–	275	150
Olive Garden													
4836	Breadsticks	1 ea	50	140	5	26	–	2	0.0	–	–	0	–
4831	Dinner, capellini pomodoro	1 ea	588	550	16	84	–	17	2.5	–	–	5	–
4833	Dinner, linguini alla marinara	0.5 ea	368	225	7	40	–	4	0.8	–	–	0	–
4834	Dinner, shrimp primavera	1 ea	535	603	44	84	–	13	2.0	–	–	275	–
4829	Dish, linguini alla marinara	1 ea	302	280	8	48	–	6	1.0	–	–	0	–
Pizza Hut													
56489	Pizza, cheese, hand tossed, med, 12″	1 pce	106	240	12	28	2	10	5.0	–	–	10	150
831	Pizza, cheese, The Big New Yorker, lrg, 16″	1 pce	174	380	19	41	7	17	9.0	–	–	20	200
57816	Pizza, cheese, The Insider, med, 12″	1 pce	141	370	17	41	3	16	8.0	–	–	30	200
56485	Pizza, cheese, thin 'n crispy, med, 12″	1 pce	85	200	10	22	2	9	5.0	–	–	10	150
57383	Pizza, Meat Lover's, pan, med, 12″	1 pce	133	360	14	29	3	21	7.0	–	–	30	100
57381	Pizza, Pepperoni Lover's, pan, med, 12″	1 pce	122	330	14	29	2	18	7.0	–	–	20	150
57812	Pizza, Pepperoni Lover's, stuffed crust, med, 12″	1 pce	192	525	26	46	3	26	12.5	–	–	40	130
56493	Pizza, pepperoni, personal pan PHI	1 ea	257	620	26	70	5	28	11.0	–	–	30	250
56486	Pizza, pepperoni, thin 'n crispy, med, 12″	1 pce	81	190	9	21	2	9	4.0	–	–	15	100
57379	Pizza, Veggie Lover's, hand tossed, med, 12″	1 pce	126	220	9	29	2	8	3.0	–	–	5	100
57382	Pizza, Veggie Lovers, pan, med, 12″	1 pce	130	270	10	30	3	12	4.0	–	–	5	100
Subway													
47657	Cookie, peanut butter	1 ea	48	220	3	26	1	12	2.5	–	–	0	0
47660	Cookie, sugar	1 ea	48	230	2	28	0	12	3.0	–	–	20	0
52128	Salad, BLT	1 ea	276	140	7	10	2	8	3.0	–	–	16	273
52122	Salad, tuna	1 ea	331	356	12	10	1	30	5.0	–	–	36	278
52125	Salad, turkey, breast & ham	1 ea	316	109	11	11	1	3	1.0	–	–	24	273
69135	Sandwich, bacon, lettuce & tomato, on white, 6″	1 ea	191	311	14	38	3	10	3.0	–	–	16	120
69120	Sandwich, beef, steak & cheese, on wheat, 6″	1 ea	264	398	30	47	3	10	6.0	–	–	70	176

PAGE KEY: A-154 Granola Bars, Cereal Bars, Diet Bars, Scones, and Tarts A-154 Meals and Dishes A-160 Meats A-164 Nuts, Seeds, and Products A-166 Poultry A-166 Salad Dressings, Dips, and Mayonnaise A-170 Salads A-170 Sandwiches A-172 Sauces and Gravies A-174 Snack Foods—Chips, Pretzels, Popcorn A-178 Soups, Stews and Chilis A-184 Spices, Flavors, and Seasonings A-184 Sports Bars and Drinks A-186 Supplemental Foods and Formulas A-186 Sweeteners and Sweet Substitutes A-188 Vegetables and Legumes A-200 Weight Loss Bars & Drinks A-200 Miscellaneous

Thia (mg)	Ribc (mg)	Niac (mg NE)	Vit B6 (mg)	Vit B12 (µg)	Fol (µg)	Vit C (mg)	Vit D (IU)	Vit E (mg AT)	Cal (mg)	Iron (mg)	Magn (mg)	Phos (mg)	Pota (mg)	Sodi (mg)	Zinc (mg)	Wat (%)	Alco (g)	Caff (g)
0.44	0.28	3.69	0.10	0.40	4.7	0.0	–	1.0	40	2.38	14.4	388	195	930	1.0	36	0.00	0.00
–	–	–	–	–	–	12.0	–	–	150	2.70	–	–	–	680	–	52	0.00	0.00
0.31	0.31	3.77	0.15	1.19	23.5	2.4	0.0	0.5	250	2.70	27.0	176	279	830	2.6	44	0.00	0.00
0.38	0.43	6.82	0.27	2.91	33.4	2.4	0.0	0.8	350	4.50	–	–	–	1310	–	50	0.00	0.00
0.07	0.10	4.92	0.20	0.20	–	0.0	7.7	0.9	9	0.70	16.4	191	202	360	0.7	51	0.00	0.00
0.30	0.25	2.00	–	–	–	0.3	–	–	80	1.44	–	0	111	400	–	29	0.00	0.00
0.31	0.25	3.76	0.14	1.02	20.6	2.4	0.0	0.2	200	2.70	23.6	111	258	590	2.2	45	0.00	0.00
0.49	0.43	6.07	0.25	2.25	49.3	3.6	0.0	1.0	300	4.50	45.5	267	455	1090	4.8	50	0.00	0.00
0.38	0.33	6.82	0.25	2.58	27.5	2.4	0.0	0.4	200	4.50	33.7	208	408	840	4.7	52	0.00	0.00
0.56	0.27	3.75	0.14	0.50	15.7	0.0	–	0.7	200	1.79	21.7	156	191	740	1.5	42	0.00	0.00
0.11	0.50	0.40	0.10	–	–	6.0	25.4	–	350	0.72	–	329	542	180	–	72	0.00	0.00
0.02	0.00	0.82	0.01	0.00	8.9	0.0	0.0	0.5	3	0.14	10.7	22	40	48	0.2	3	0.00	0.00
0.18	0.10	1.41	0.02	0.00	8.3	24.0	–	1.4	20	1.08	6.5	35	63	200	0.2	34	0.00	0.00
0.14	–	5.01	0.62	0.00	66.2	21.0	–	2.1	20	1.44	68.5	227	1213	350	0.8	40	0.00	0.00
0.11	0.00	4.19	0.52	0.00	55.3	18.0	–	1.8	20	1.08	57.2	190	1013	290	0.7	40	0.00	0.00
0.07	0.01	0.89	0.07	0.00	8.3	2.4	0.0	0.6	7	0.36	11.0	51	212	330	0.2	55	0.00	0.00
–	–	–	–	–	–	15.0	–	–	150	1.08	–	–	–	120	–	88	0.00	0.00
–	–	–	–	–	–	6.0	–	–	200	3.59	–	–	–	1180	–	54	0.00	0.00
–	–	–	–	–	–	6.0	–	–	200	3.59	–	–	–	970	–	59	0.00	0.00
–	–	–	–	–	–	0.0	–	–	200	4.50	–	–	–	1490	–	50	0.00	0.00
–	–	–	–	–	–	15.0	–	–	250	4.50	–	–	–	1570	–	51	0.00	0.00
–	–	–	–	–	–	–	–	–	–	–	–	–	–	270	–	36	0.00	0.00
–	–	–	–	–	–	–	–	–	–	–	–	–	–	1090	–	–	0.00	0.00
–	–	–	–	–	–	–	–	–	–	–	–	–	–	385	–	–	0.00	0.00
–	–	–	–	–	–	–	–	–	–	–	–	–	–	1220	–	–	0.00	0.00
–	–	–	–	–	–	–	–	–	–	–	–	–	–	510	–	–	0.00	0.00
–	–	–	–	–	–	2.4	–	–	200	1.44	–	–	–	650	–	51	0.00	0.00
–	–	–	–	–	–	0.0	–	–	350	1.79	–	–	–	1140	–	54	0.00	0.00
–	–	–	–	–	–	3.6	–	–	150	1.79	–	–	–	890	–	–	0.00	0.00
–	–	–	–	–	–	2.4	–	–	200	1.44	–	–	–	590	–	49	0.00	0.00
–	–	–	–	–	–	2.4	–	–	150	1.79	–	–	–	840	–	50	0.00	0.00
–	–	–	–	–	–	2.4	–	–	200	1.79	–	–	–	760	–	48	0.00	0.00
–	–	–	–	–	–	0.0	–	–	370	2.51	–	–	–	1413	–	–	0.00	0.00
–	–	–	–	–	–	6.0	–	–	300	4.50	–	–	–	1430	–	49	0.00	0.00
–	–	–	–	–	–	2.4	–	–	100	1.44	–	–	–	610	–	50	0.00	0.00
–	–	–	–	–	–	9.0	–	–	100	1.79	–	–	–	580	–	61	0.00	0.00
–	–	–	–	–	–	12.0	–	–	100	1.79	–	–	–	510	–	58	0.00	0.00
–	–	–	–	–	–	0.0	–	–	16	1.00	–	–	–	180	–	13	0.00	0.00
–	–	–	–	–	–	0.0	–	–	0	0.72	–	–	–	180	–	11	0.00	0.00
–	–	–	–	–	–	32.0	–	–	24	1.00	–	–	–	672	–	91	0.00	0.00
–	–	–	–	–	–	32.0	–	–	29	2.00	–	–	–	601	–	84	0.00	0.00
–	–	–	–	–	–	32.0	–	–	27	2.00	–	–	–	1076	–	92	0.00	0.00
–	–	–	–	–	–	15.0	–	–	27	3.00	–	–	–	945	–	67	0.00	0.00
–	–	–	–	–	–	18.0	–	–	95	5.00	–	–	–	1117	–	67	0.00	0.00

PAGE KEY: A-108 Beverage and Beverage Mixes A-112 Other Beverages A-112 Beverages, Alcoholic A-114 Candies and Confections, Gum A-114 Cereals, Breakfast Type A-118 Cheese and Cheese Substitutes A-120 Dairy Products and Substitutes A-122 Desserts A-128 Dessert Toppings A-128 Eggs, Substitutes, and Egg Dishes A-130 Ethnic Foods A-130 Fast Foods/Restaurants A-140 Fats, Oils, Margarines, Shortenings, and Substitutes A-142 Fish, Seafood, and Shellfish A-142 Food Additives A-142 Fruit, Vegetable, and Blended Juices A-144 Fruits A-146 Grains, Flours, and Fractions A-148 Grain Products, Prepared and Baked Goods

Code	Food Name	Unit/ Amt	Wt (g)	Energy (Kcal)	Prot (g)	Carb (g)	Fiber (g)	Fat (g)	Sat (g)	Mono (g)	Poly (g)	Chol (mg)	Vit A (RE)
69126	Sandwich, chicken breast, rstd, on wheat, 6″	1 ea	253	348	27	47	3	6	1.0	–	–	48	123
69118	Sandwich, club, on wheat, 6″	1 ea	253	312	21	46	3	5	1.0	–	–	26	120
69113	Sandwich, cold cut trio, on white, 6″	1 ea	246	362	19	39	3	13	4.0	–	–	64	130
69116	Sandwich, ham, on wheat, 6″	1 ea	239	302	19	45	3	5	1.0	–	–	28	120
69140	Sandwich, Italian BMT, on wheat, 6″	1 ea	253	460	21	45	3	22	7.0	–	–	56	151
69130	Sandwich, meatball, on wheat, 6″	1 ea	267	419	19	51	3	16	6.0	–	–	33	142
69121	Sandwich, roast beef, on white, 6″	1 ea	232	288	19	39	3	5	1.0	–	–	20	120
69105	Sandwich, seafood & crab, deli style	1 ea	178	298	12	37	2	11	2.0	–	–	17	113
69142	Sandwich, tuna, on wheat, 6″	1 ea	253	542	19	44	3	32	5.0	–	–	36	126
69137	Sandwich, turkey breast & ham, on white, on 6″	1 ea	232	280	18	39	3	5	1.0	–	–	24	120
69110	Sandwich, veggie delite, on wheat, 6″	1 ea	182	237	9	44	3	3	0.0	–	–	0	120
Taco Bell													
56519	Burrito, bean, w/red sauce	1 ea	198	380	13	55	13	12	4.0	–	–	10	450
56690	Burrito, beef, big supreme	1 ea	298	520	24	54	11	23	10.0	–	–	55	600
57678	Burrito, chicken, grilled	1 ea	202	400	19	50	3	14	4.0	–	–	40	700
56522	Burrito, supreme	1 ea	255	440	17	51	10	19	8.0	–	–	35	500
45585	Churro, cinnamon twists, svg	1 ea	28	140	1	19	0	6	0.0	–	–	0	40
38561	Dish, rice, Mexican, svg	1 ea	135	190	5	23	1	9	3.5	–	–	15	1000
57663	Gordita, beef, fiesta	1 ea	139	290	13	29	4	13	4.5	–	–	25	100
57665	Gordita, beef, supreme	1 ea	139	291	13	27	4	15	6.4	–	–	32	91
56615	Gordita, chicken	1 ea	255	500	22	44	3	26	6.0	–	–	55	150
56534	Nachos, bellgrande, svg	1 ea	312	770	21	84	17	39	11.0	–	–	35	150
56533	Nachos, svg	1 ea	99	320	5	34	3	18	4.0	–	–	5	60
56531	Pizza, Mexican	1 ea	220	570	21	42	8	35	10.0	–	–	45	400
7972	Potatoes, hash browns, nuggets, svg	1 ea	99	280	2	29	1	18	5.0	–	–	0	0
57688	Quesadilla, breakfast, w/bacon	1 ea	170	450	19	33	2	27	11.0	–	–	290	450
57685	Quesadilla, cheese	1 ea	120	350	16	32	2	18	9.0	–	–	50	80
57689	Quesadilla, chicken	5 tsp	163	163	10	13	1	8	4.0	–	–	30	40
57674	Salad, taco, w/salsa, w/o shell	1 ea	468	420	24	32	15	22	11.0	–	–	60	1600
56524	Taco	1 ea	78	180	9	12	3	10	4.0	–	–	25	100
56692	Taco, supreme	1 ea	113	220	10	14	3	14	7.0	–	–	35	150
56528	Tostada	1 ea	177	300	10	31	12	15	5.0	–	–	15	500
57682	Wrap, chicken fajita	1 ea	220	460	19	51	3	20	5.0	–	–	45	300
57690	Wrap, fajita veggie	1 ea	227	420	10	53	3	19	5.0	–	–	20	350
57691	Wrap, veggie supreme, fajita	1 ea	255	470	11	55	3	22	7.0	–	–	30	350
Taco Johns													
7486	Beans, refried, svg	1 ea	262	301	17	39	–	8	1.5	–	–	8	–
57576	Burrito, bean	1 ea	170	340	15	45	–	11	3.0	–	–	15	27
57577	Burrito, beef	1 ea	170	415	22	39	–	19	6.4	–	–	43	27
57578	Burrito, combination	1 ea	170	378	18	46	–	13	5.6	–	–	30	0
57579	Burrito, super	1 ea	241	424	20	45	–	19	6.7	–	–	35	45
49127	Churro	1 ea	42	147	2	17	–	8	1.8	–	–	4	0
57581	Dish, fajita, chicken, softshell	1 ea	120	216	13	20	–	8	3.1	–	–	33	13
2479	Ice Cream Dessert, Choco Taco	1 ea	99	320	3	38	–	17	11.0	–	–	20	–
57590	Mexi Rolls, w/nacho cheese	1 ea	276	813	30	77	–	43	10.5	–	–	46	24
57593	Nachos, svg	1 ea	99	294	2	31	–	17	3.8	–	–	6	18
7487	Potatoes, oles, svg	1 ea	157	442	3	45	–	28	6.6	–	–	–	2
57596	Taco Burger	1 ea	142	275	14	29	–	11	4.3	–	–	26	8
57602	Taco, bravo	1 ea	170	332	15	38	–	14	4.4	–	–	22	8

PAGE KEY: A-154 Granola Bars, Cereal Bars, Diet Bars, Scones, and Tarts A-154 Meals and Dishes A-160 Meats A-164 Nuts, Seeds, and Products A-166 Poultry A-166 Salad Dressings, Dips, and Mayonnaise A-170 Salads A-170 Sandwiches A-172 Sauces and Gravies A-174 Snack Foods—Chips, Pretzels, Popcorn A-178 Soups, Stews and Chilis A-184 Spices, Flavors, and Seasonings A-184 Sports Bars and Drinks A-186 Supplemental Foods and Formulas A-186 Sweeteners and Sweet Substitutes A-188 Vegetables and Legumes A-200 Weight Loss Bars & Drinks A-200 Miscellaneous

Thia (mg)	Ribo (mg)	Niac (mg NE)	Vit B6 (mg)	Vit B12 (µg)	Fol (µg)	Vit C (mg)	Vit D (IU)	Vit E (mg AT)	Cal (mg)	Iron (mg)	Magn (mg)	Phos (mg)	Pota (mg)	Sodi (mg)	Zinc (mg)	Wat (%)	Alco (g)	Caff (g)
—	—	—	—	—	—	15.0	—	—	42	3.00	—	—	—	978	—	68	0.00	0.00
—	—	—	—	—	—	15.0	—	—	35	4.00	—	—	—	1352	—	71	0.00	0.00
—	—	—	—	—	—	16.0	—	—	49	4.00	—	—	—	1401	—	71	0.00	0.00
—	—	—	—	—	—	15.0	—	—	35	3.00	—	—	—	1319	—	71	0.00	0.00
—	—	—	—	—	—	15.0	—	—	50	4.00	—	—	—	1664	—	64	0.00	0.00
—	—	—	—	—	—	16.0	—	—	39	4.00	—	—	—	1046	—	67	0.00	0.00
—	—	—	—	—	—	15.0	—	—	25	4.00	—	—	—	928	—	72	0.00	0.00
—	—	—	—	—	—	14.0	—	—	24	3.00	—	—	—	544	—	66	0.00	0.00
—	—	—	—	—	—	15.0	—	—	38	3.00	—	—	—	886	—	62	0.00	0.00
—	—	—	—	—	—	15.0	—	—	29	3.00	—	—	—	1350	—	73	0.00	0.00
—	—	—	—	—	—	15.0	—	—	32	3.00	—	—	—	593	—	69	0.00	0.00
0.03	2.01	1.98	0.31	—	—	0.0	—	—	150	2.70	—	—	495	1100	—	58	0.00	0.00
—	—	—	—	—	—	4.8	—	—	150	2.70	—	—	—	1520	—	64	0.00	0.00
—	—	—	—	—	—	2.4	—	—	150	1.44	—	—	—	1250	—	57	0.00	0.00
0.40	2.09	2.89	0.34	—	—	4.8	—	—	150	9.00	49.7	—	422	1230	—	64	0.00	0.00
0.07	0.02	0.56	0.02	—	—	0.0	—	—	0	0.36	—	—	22	190	—	6	0.00	0.00
—	—	—	—	—	—	1.2	—	—	150	1.44	—	—	—	760	—	71	0.00	0.00
—	—	—	—	—	—	0.0	—	—	150	1.79	—	—	—	680	—	62	0.00	0.00
—	—	—	—	—	—	3.3	—	—	136	1.63	—	—	—	572	—	58	0.00	0.00
—	—	—	—	—	—	15.0	—	—	150	2.70	—	—	—	1160	—	63	0.00	0.00
0.10	0.37	2.35	—	—	—	3.6	—	—	200	3.59	—	—	733	1310	—	52	0.00	0.00
0.15	0.15	0.63	0.18	—	9.2	0.0	—	—	100	0.72	—	—	149	570	1.6	40	0.00	0.00
0.31	0.33	2.92	1.10	—	59.0	4.8	—	—	250	3.59	79.0	—	403	1040	5.3	53	0.00	0.00
—	—	—	—	0.00	—	0.0	—	—	0	1.08	—	—	—	570	—	49	0.00	0.00
—	—	—	—	—	—	0.0	—	—	300	2.70	—	—	—	1200	—	51	0.00	0.00
—	—	—	—	—	—	0.0	—	—	450	1.79	—	—	—	860	—	42	0.00	0.00
—	—	—	—	—	—	1.0	—	—	179	0.72	—	—	—	413	—	80	0.00	0.00
—	—	—	—	—	—	21.0	—	—	250	4.50	—	—	—	1520	—	82	0.00	0.00
0.05	0.14	1.20	0.11	—	—	0.0	—	—	80	1.08	—	—	159	330	—	58	0.00	0.00
—	—	—	—	—	—	0.0	—	—	100	1.08	—	—	—	350	—	65	0.00	0.00
0.05	0.18	0.70	0.28	—	—	1.2	—	—	150	1.79	—	—	455	650	—	67	0.00	0.00
—	—	—	—	—	—	3.6	—	—	150	1.44	—	—	—	1170	—	57	0.00	0.00
—	—	—	—	—	—	3.6	—	—	150	1.44	—	—	—	980	—	63	0.00	0.00
—	—	—	—	—	—	6.0	—	—	150	1.44	—	—	—	990	—	65	0.00	0.00
—	—	—	—	—	—	—	—	—	136	3.96	—	—	—	955	—	75	0.00	0.00
—	—	—	—	—	—	0.7	—	—	260	6.28	—	—	—	654	—	56	0.00	0.00
—	—	—	—	—	—	0.9	—	—	250	5.98	—	—	—	703	—	51	0.00	0.00
—	—	—	—	—	—	1.5	—	—	155	2.85	—	—	—	659	—	52	0.00	0.00
—	—	—	—	—	—	8.8	—	—	298	6.84	—	—	—	736	—	64	0.00	0.00
—	—	—	—	—	—	0.2	—	—	14	3.92	—	—	—	160	—	35	0.00	0.00
—	—	—	—	—	—	5.1	—	—	110	1.52	—	—	—	1083	—	64	0.00	0.00
—	—	—	—	—	—	—	—	—	—	—	—	—	—	100	—	41	0.00	
—	—	—	—	—	—	1.1	—	—	288	3.56	—	—	—	1201	—	45	0.00	0.00
—	—	—	—	—	—	—	—	—	—	—	—	—	—	447	—	50	0.00	0.00
—	—	—	—	0.00	—	1.3	—	—	17	1.91	—	—	—	385	—	51	0.00	0.00
—	—	—	—	—	—	4.0	—	—	141	2.46	—	—	—	566	—	61	0.00	0.00
—	—	—	—	—	—	4.9	—	—	127	2.50	—	—	—	654	—	61	0.00	0.00

PAGE KEY: A-108 Beverage and Beverage Mixes A-112 Other Beverages A-112 Beverages, Alcoholic A-114 Candies and Confections, Gum A-114 Cereals, Breakfast Type A-118 Cheese and Cheese Substitutes A-120 Dairy Products and Substitutes A-122 Desserts A-128 Dessert Toppings A-128 Eggs, Substitutes, and Egg Dishes A-130 Ethnic Foods A-130 Fast Foods/Restaurants A-140 Fats, Oils, Margarines, Shortenings, and Substitutes A-142 Fish, Seafood, and Shellfish A-142 Food Additives A-142 Fruit, Vegetable, and Blended Juices A-144 Fruits A-146 Grains, Flours, and Fractions A-148 Grain Products, Prepared and Baked Goods

Code	Food Name	Unit/ Amt	Wt (g)	Energy (Kcal)	Prot (g)	Carb (g)	Fiber (g)	Fat (g)	Sat (g)	Mono (g)	Poly (g)	Chol (mg)	Vit A (RE)
57601	Taco, soft shell	1 ea	128	278	14	32	–	11	4.2	–	–	22	8
Taco Time													
56540	Burrito, bean, crispy	1 ea	164	427	15	53	9	18	5.0	–	–	12	26
1698	Burrito, chicken, Big Juan	1 ea	361	620	34	69	12	24	11.0	–	–	65	200
56543	Burrito, meat, soft	1 ea	193	491	31	48	12	21	8.0	–	–	56	99
56617	Burrito, taco meat, Big Juan	1 ea	361	640	34	71	15	25	12.0	–	–	60	200
56620	Burrito, veggie	1 ea	321	491	21	70	10	16	6.0	–	–	24	–
56550	Cheeseburger, taco	1 ea	215	633	31	48	7	36	10.0	–	–	66	115
1701	Chimichanga, chicken	1 ea	365	711	31	57	9	40	16.0	–	–	89	–
45587	Empanada, cherry	1 ea	114	250	5	37	–	9	–	–	–	0	18
56674	Taco, fish	1 ea	231	470	19	32	2	29	8.0	–	–	60	–
56548	Tostada, w/meat	1 ea	219	447	35	33	12	21	9.0	–	–	61	87
56903	Wrap, big island	1 ea	572	804	24	125	5	23	7.0	–	–	52	–
56941	Wrap, Thai, spicy	1 ea	479	802	26	105	5	30	9.0	–	–	52	–
Wendy's													
56570	Cheeseburger, jr	1 ea	129	310	17	34	2	12	5.0	–	–	45	60
15176	Chicken, nuggets, 5 pce svg	1 ea	75	220	11	13	0	14	3.0	–	–	35	0
50637	Chili, lrg, 12oz svg	1 ea	340	300	25	31	7	9	3.5	–	–	50	200
2177	Frosty, dairy dessert, med	1 ea	298	440	11	73	0	11	7.0	–	–	50	200
56574	Hamburger, Big Bacon Classic	1 ea	282	570	34	46	3	29	12.0	–	–	100	150
6167	Potatoes, baked, plain	1 ea	284	310	7	72	7	0	0.0	0.0	0.0	0	0
71596	Salad, spring mix, w/o dressing	1 ea	315	180	11	12	5	11	6.0	–	–	30	1700
69059	Sandwich, chicken, grilled	1 ea	188	300	24	36	2	7	1.5	–	–	55	40
FATS, OILS, MARGARINES, SHORTENINGS, AND SUBSTITUTES													
Fats and Oils, Animal													
8000	Butter, salted	1 Tbs	14	100	0	0	0	11	7.1	3.3	0.4	31	106
8001	Butter, salted, pat	1 ea	5	36	0	0	0	4	2.5	1.2	0.2	11	38
90208	Butter, salted, stick	1 Tbs	14	100	0	0	0	11	7.1	3.3	0.4	31	106
8142	Butter, salted, whipped	1 Tbs	9	68	0	0	0	8	4.8	2.2	0.3	21	71
8107	Fat, lard	1 Tbs	13	115	0	0	0	13	5.0	5.8	1.4	12	0
Fats and Oils, Vegetable													
8084	Oil, canola	1 Tbs	14	124	0	0	0	14	1.0	8.2	4.1	0	0
8037	Oil, coconut	1 Tbs	14	117	0	0	0	14	11.8	0.8	0.2	0	0
8009	Oil, corn, salad or cooking	1 Tbs	14	120	0	0	0	14	1.7	3.3	8.0	0	0
8081	Oil, cottonseed, salad or cooking	1 Tbs	14	120	0	0	0	14	3.5	2.4	7.1	0	0
8008	Oil, olive, salad or cooking	1 Tbs	14	119	0	0	0	14	1.8	9.9	1.1	0	0
8082	Oil, palm	1 Tbs	14	120	0	0	0	14	6.7	5.0	1.3	0	0
8027	Oil, sesame, salad or cooking	1 Tbs	14	120	0	0	0	14	1.9	5.4	5.7	0	0
90965	Oil, veg, pure, Crisco	1 Tbs	14	120	0	0	0	14	1.5	6.0	6.0	0	0
Margarines and Spreads													
671	Garlic, spread, rtu	1 Tbs	15	100	0	2	–	10	–	–	–	–	–
90233	Margarine, hard, unspecified oil, w/o add salt, stick	1 tsp	5	34	0	0	0	4	0.7	1.7	1.2	0	38
8131	Margarine, rducd cal	1 Tbs	14	49	0	0	0	6	1.1	2.2	2.0	0	154
609	Margarine, soft, fat free, promise	1 Tbs	14	5	0	0	0	0	0.0	0.0	0.0	0	100
8605	Margarine, soft, tub, Parkay	1 Tbs	14	100	0	0	0	11	2.0	–	–	0	100
44409	Margarine, spread, fat free, bottle	1 Tbs	15	7	0	1	0	0	0.1	0.1	0.2	0	–
Shortenings													
8007	Shortening, household, hydrog soybean & cttnsd oil	1 Tbs	13	113	0	0	0	13	3.2	5.7	3.3	0	0
8267	Shortening, household, lard & veg oil	1 Tbs	13	115	0	0	0	13	5.2	5.7	1.4	7	0

PAGE KEY: A-154 Granola Bars, Cereal Bars, Diet Bars, Scones, and Tarts A-154 Meals and Dishes A-160 Meats A-164 Nuts, Seeds, and Products A-166 Poultry A-166 Salad Dressings, Dips, and Mayonnaise A-170 Salads A-170 Sandwiches A-172 Sauces and Gravies A-174 Snack Foods—Chips, Pretzels, Popcorn A-178 Soups, Stews and Chilis A-184 Spices, Flavors, and Seasonings A-184 Sports Bars and Drinks A-186 Supplemental Foods and Formulas A-186 Sweeteners and Sweet Substitutes A-188 Vegetables and Legumes A-200 Weight Loss Bars & Drinks A-200 Miscellaneous

Thia (mg)	Ribo (mg)	Niac (mg NE)	Vit B6 (mg)	Vit B12 (µg)	Fol (µg)	Vit C (mg)	Vit D (IU)	Vit E (mg AT)	Cal (mg)	Iron (mg)	Magn (mg)	Phos (mg)	Pota (mg)	Sodi (mg)	Zinc (mg)	Wat (%)	Alco (g)	Caff (g)
–	–	–	–	–	–	4.3	–	–	169	1.35	–	–	–	556	–	55	0.00	0.00
0.36	0.21	2.21	0.38	–	14.3	–	–	–	158	4.40	–	238	383	453	2.2	47	0.00	0.00
–	–	–	–	–	–	21.0	–	–	350	6.30	–	–	–	1230	–	64	0.00	0.00
0.25	0.38	5.30	0.43	–	83.4	4.6	–	–	209	5.30	–	309	609	1197	4.6	47	0.00	0.00
–	–	–	–	–	–	–	–	–	400	7.19	–	–	–	1120	–	–	0.00	0.00
–	–	–	–	–	–	–	–	–	–	–	–	–	–	643	–	66	0.00	0.00
0.43	0.41	4.59	0.28	–	77.4	3.7	–	–	283	4.59	–	336	520	1291	3.7	45	0.00	0.00
–	–	–	–	–	–	–	–	–	–	–	–	–	–	1291	–	–	0.00	0.00
0.15	0.20	2.01	49.56	–	24.3	3.0	–	–	64	2.01	–	53	161	46	0.0	55	0.00	0.00
–	–	–	–	–	–	–	–	–	–	–	–	–	–	660	–	–	0.00	0.00
0.40	0.31	4.13	0.56	–	58.9	2.1	–	–	285	6.19	–	432	646	834	5.2	59	0.00	0.00
–	–	–	–	–	–	–	–	–	–	–	–	–	–	1987	–	–	0.00	0.00
–	–	–	–	–	–	–	–	–	–	–	–	–	–	1907	–	–	0.00	0.00
–	–	–	–	–	–	3.6	–	–	150	3.59	–	–	230	820	–	49	0.00	0.00
–	–	–	–	–	–	1.2	–	–	20	0.72	–	–	190	480	–	48	0.00	0.00
–	–	–	–	–	–	3.6	–	–	150	3.59	–	–	700	1310	–	–	0.00	0.00
–	–	–	–	–	–	0.0	–	–	400	1.44	–	–	770	260	–	68	0.00	
–	–	–	–	–	–	15.0	–	–	200	5.40	–	–	580	1460	–	61	0.00	0.00
–	–	–	–	–	–	36.0	–	–	20	3.59	–	–	1190	25	–	–	0.00	0.00
–	–	–	–	–	–	30.0	–	–	300	1.79	–	–	620	230	–	89	0.00	0.00
–	–	–	–	–	–	9.0	–	–	80	2.70	–	–	430	740	–	64	0.00	0.00
0.00	0.00	0.00	0.00	0.01	0.4	0.0	7.8	0.2	3	0.01	0.3	3	4	116	0.0	16	0.00	0.00
0.00	0.00	0.00	0.00	0.00	0.2	0.0	2.8	0.1	1	0.00	0.1	1	1	41	0.0	16	0.00	0.00
0.00	0.00	0.00	0.00	0.01	0.4	0.0	7.8	0.2	3	0.01	0.3	3	4	116	0.0	16	0.00	0.00
0.00	0.00	0.00	0.00	0.00	0.3	0.0	5.3	0.1	2	0.01	0.2	2	2	78	0.0	16	0.00	0.00
0.00	0.00	0.00	0.00	0.00	0.0	0.0	–	0.2	0	0.00	0.0	0	0	0	0.0	0	0.00	0.00
0.00	0.00	0.00	0.00	0.00	0.0	0.0	0.0	2.9	0	0.00	0.0	0	0	0	0.0	0	0.00	0.00
0.00	0.00	0.00	0.00	0.00	0.0	0.0	0.0	0.0	0	0.00	0.0	0	0	0	0.0	0	0.00	0.00
0.00	0.00	0.00	0.00	0.00	0.0	0.0	0.0	2.9	0	0.00	0.0	0	0	0	0.0	0	0.00	0.00
0.00	0.00	0.00	0.00	0.00	0.0	0.0	0.0	5.2	0	0.00	0.0	0	0	0	0.0	0	0.00	0.00
0.00	0.00	0.00	0.00	0.00	0.0	0.0	0.0	1.7	0	0.05	0.0	0	0	0	0.0	0	0.00	0.00
0.00	0.00	0.00	0.00	0.00	0.0	0.0	0.0	3.0	0	0.00	0.0	0	0	0	0.0	0	0.00	0.00
0.00	0.00	0.00	0.00	0.00	0.0	0.0	0.0	0.6	0	0.00	0.0	0	0	0	0.0	0	0.00	0.00
–	–	–	–	–	–	0.0	–	3.0	0	0.00	–	–	–	0	–	0	0.00	0.00
–	–	–	–	0.00	–	–	–	–	–	–	–	–	–	190	–	–	0.00	0.00
0.00	0.00	0.00	0.00	0.00	0.0	0.0	0.0	0.6	1	0.00	0.1	1	1	0	0.0	18	0.00	0.00
0.00	0.00	0.00	0.00	0.00	0.1	0.0	0.0	0.3	3	0.00	0.2	2	4	136	0.0	58	0.00	0.00
–	–	–	–	–	–	0.0	–	–	0	0.00	–	–	–	90	–	–	0.00	0.00
–	–	–	–	–	–	0.0	–	–	0	0.00	–	–	10	105	–	–	0.00	0.00
0.15	0.00	0.00	0.00	0.00	0.0	0.0	–	0.1	1	0.02	0.9	6	32	128	0.0	89	0.00	
0.00	0.00	0.00	0.00	0.00	0.0	0.0	0.0	1.1	0	0.00	0.0	0	0	0	0.0	0	0.00	0.00
0.00	0.00	0.00	0.00	0.00	0.0	0.0	–	0.2	0	0.00	0.0	0	0	0	0.0	0	0.00	0.00

Code	Food Name	Unit/ Amt	Wt (g)	Energy (Kcal)	Prot (g)	Carb (g)	Fiber (g)	Fat (g)	Sat (g)	Mono (g)	Poly (g)	Chol (mg)	Vit A (RE)
FISH, SEAFOOD, AND SHELLFISH													
19041	Abalone, fried, mixed species	3 oz	85	161	17	9	0	6	1.4	2.3	1.4	80	2
71707	Calamari, fried, mixed species	3 oz	85	149	15	7	0	6	1.6	2.3	1.8	221	9
19110	Clams, brd, fried	0.75 cup	115	451	13	39	–	26	6.6	11.4	6.8	87	37
19036	Crab, Alaska king, leg, stmd	1 ea	134	130	26	0	0	2	0.2	0.2	0.7	71	12
19054	Crab, king, leg, bkd/brld	3 oz	85	117	16	0	0	5	1.0	2.2	1.7	80	41
17002	Fish Sticks, heated f/fzn	1 ea	28	76	4	7	0	3	0.9	1.4	0.9	31	9
17088	Fish, catfish, channel, fillet, brd, fried	1 ea	87	199	16	7	1	12	2.9	4.9	2.9	70	7
17037	Fish, cod, Atlantic, fillet, bkd/brld	1 ea	180	189	41	0	0	2	0.3	0.2	0.5	99	25
71757	Fish, flounder, fillet, brd/floured, fried	3 oz	85	189	17	7	0	10	2.1	4.1	2.9	59	16
71748	Fish, mahi mahi, fillet, bkd/brld	1 ea	159	173	38	0	0	1	0.4	0.2	0.3	149	99
17121	Fish, orange roughy, fillet, bkd/brld"	3 oz	85	76	16	0	0	1	0.0	0.5	0.0	22	20
17003	Fish, portions, heated f/fzn, 4" x 2" x ½"	1 ea	57	155	9	14	0	7	1.8	2.9	1.8	64	18
17170	Fish, salmon, chum, fillet, bkd/brld	0.5 ea	154	237	40	0	0	7	1.7	3.0	1.8	146	52
17171	Fish, salmon, pink, fillet, bkd/brld	3 oz	85	127	22	0	0	4	0.6	1.0	1.5	57	35
17296	Fish, sardines, in oil, drained, 3.75oz can	3 oz	85	177	21	0	0	10	1.3	3.3	4.4	121	57
17068	Fish, sole, fillet, bkd/brld	3 oz	85	100	21	0	0	1	0.3	0.2	0.5	58	9
17218	Fish, trout, fillet, raw, mixed species	1 ea	79	117	16	0	0	5	0.9	2.6	1.2	46	13
17025	Fish, tuna, light, cnd in oil, drained	3 g	3	6	1	0	0	0	0.0	0.1	0.1	1	1
17027	Fish, tuna, light, cnd in water, drained	3 oz	85	99	22	0	0	1	0.2	0.1	0.3	26	14
19084	Lobster, spiny, stmd, mixed species	1 ea	163	233	43	5	0	3	0.5	0.6	1.2	147	10
19090	Oysters, eastern, bkd/brld, farmed, med	6 ea	59	47	4	4	0	1	0.4	0.1	0.4	22	11
19402	Salad, crab, made w/imit crab	1 cup	208	299	18	28	1	12	1.8	3.2	6.6	74	43
19146	Scallops, ckd, sml	14 ea	84	120	22	2	0	1	0.0	–	–	55	0
19401	Shrimp, cocktail	1 cup	230	218	28	21	5	3	0.5	0.4	1.0	196	72
70702	Shrimp, popcorn, breaded, fzn, Van de Kamp's	20 ea	112	270	11	28	1	13	2.0	5.0	2.0	35	0
19428	Shrimp, scampi	1 cup	136	311	26	1	0	22	12.9	6.1	1.6	247	206
FOOD ADDITIVES													
Bases and Preps													
50705	Prep, au jus	100 g	100	95	17	6	–	0	0.1	0.1	0.0	1	–
54032	Prep, consomme, chckn style w/o msg veget dry mix	1 cup	246	522	21	76	–	15	2.0	–	–	1	–
Colors, Flavors, and Aromas													
26290	Flavor, vanillin	1 tsp	5	22	0	5	0	0	0.0	0.0	0.0	0	–
Gums, Fibers, Starches, Pectins, Emulsifiers													
27021	Pectin, unswtnd, dry, 1.75oz pkg	1 ea	50	161	0	45	4	0	0.0	0.0	0.0	0	0
30000	Starch, corn	1 Tbs	8	30	0	7	0	0	0.0	0.0	0.0	0	0
Ingredient Sweeteners													
8654	Fat Replacer, Fruitrim, liquid, GMO free, w/o MSG	1 cup	335	1030	3	254	0	1	–	–	–	–	7
63196	Sweetener, saccharin	1 oz	28	103	0	27	0	0	0.0	0.0	0.0	0	0
Nutritional Additives													
32088	Multi Vitamin & Mineral, Centrum	1 ea	2	1	0	1	–	0	0.0	0.0	0.0	–	1100
52192	Multi Vitamin & Minrl, Daily One Caps, w/iron, capsule	1 ea	2	0	0	0	0	0	0.0	0.0	0.0	–	1000
52200	Multi Vitamin & Minrl, One A Day, womn's form, tablet	1 ea	2	0	0	0	0	0	0.0	0.0	0.0	–	1000
7517	Protein, soy, isolate	1 oz	28	96	23	2	2	1	0.1	0.2	0.5	0	0
FRUIT, VEGETABLE, AND BLENDED JUICES													
4085	Juice, apple cider	1 cup	227	120	0	30	0	0	0.0	0.0	0.0	0	0
3008	Juice, apple, unswtnd, cnd/btld	1 cup	248	117	0	29	0	0	0.0	0.0	0.1	0	0
3010	Juice, apple, unswtnd, prep f/fzn conc w/water	1 cup	239	112	0	28	0	0	0.0	0.0	0.1	0	0

PAGE KEY: A-154 Granola Bars, Cereal Bars, Diet Bars, Scones, and Tarts A-154 Meals and Dishes A-160 Meats A-164 Nuts, Seeds, and Products A-166 Poultry A-166 Salad Dressings, Dips, and Mayonnaise A-170 Salads A-170 Sandwiches A-172 Sauces and Gravies A-174 Snack Foods—Chips, Pretzels, Popcorn A-178 Soups, Stews and Chilis A-184 Spices, Flavors, and Seasonings A-184 Sports Bars and Drinks A-186 Supplemental Foods and Formulas A-186 Sweeteners and Sweet Substitutes A-188 Vegetables and Legumes A-200 Weight Loss Bars & Drinks A-200 Miscellaneous

Thia (mg)	Riba (mg)	Niac (mg NE)	Vit B6 (mg)	Vit B12 (µg)	Fol (µg)	Vit C (mg)	Vit D (IU)	Vit E (mg AT)	Cal (mg)	Iron (mg)	Magn (mg)	Phos (mg)	Pota (mg)	Sodi (mg)	Zinc (mg)	Wat (%)	Alco (g)	Caff (g)
0.18	0.10	1.62	0.12	0.58	11.9	1.5	3.4	5.1	31	3.23	47.6	185	242	503	0.8	60	0.00	0.00
0.05	0.38	2.21	0.05	1.04	11.9	3.6	3.4	1.6	33	0.86	32.3	213	237	260	1.5	65	0.00	0.00
0.20	0.25	2.85	0.02	1.10	42.5	0.0	—	—	21	3.04	31.0	238	266	834	1.6	29	0.00	0.00
0.07	0.07	1.79	0.23	15.40	68.3	10.2	2.7	1.2	79	1.01	84.4	375	351	1436	10.2	78	0.00	0.00
0.07	0.03	2.64	0.14	5.84	40.7	2.7	3.4	1.4	85	0.73	26.6	166	262	270	3.4	74	0.00	0.00
0.03	0.05	0.60	0.01	0.50	12.6	0.0	1.7	0.4	6	0.20	7.0	51	73	163	0.2	46	0.00	0.00
0.05	0.11	1.99	0.17	1.64	26.1	0.0	435.0	1.1	38	1.24	23.5	188	296	244	0.7	59	0.00	0.00
0.15	0.14	4.51	0.50	1.88	14.4	1.8	101.5	0.5	25	0.87	75.6	248	439	140	1.0	76	0.00	0.00
0.11	0.11	2.98	0.17	1.15	9.1	1.1	57.5	2.3	41	0.95	30.5	174	324	157	0.5	59	0.00	0.00
0.03	0.14	11.81	0.73	1.10	9.5	0.0	70.0	0.6	30	2.30	60.4	291	847	180	0.9	71	0.00	0.00
0.10	0.15	3.10	0.28	1.96	6.8	0.0	—	0.5	32	0.20	32.3	218	327	69	0.8	69	0.00	0.00
0.07	0.10	1.21	0.02	1.02	25.6	0.0	3.4	0.8	11	0.41	14.2	103	149	332	0.4	46	0.00	0.00
0.14	0.34	13.13	0.70	5.32	7.7	0.0	—	2.6	22	1.09	43.1	559	847	99	0.9	68	0.00	0.00
0.17	0.05	7.25	0.20	2.94	4.3	0.0	—	1.1	14	0.83	28.1	251	352	73	0.6	70	0.00	0.00
0.07	0.18	4.46	0.14	7.59	10.2	0.0	231.3	0.3	325	2.48	33.2	417	338	430	1.1	60	0.00	0.00
0.07	0.10	1.85	0.20	2.13	7.7	0.0	51.0	1.6	15	0.28	49.3	246	293	89	0.5	73	0.00	0.00
0.28	0.25	3.55	0.15	6.15	10.3	0.4	—	0.2	34	1.19	17.4	194	285	41	0.5	71	0.00	0.00
0.00	0.00	0.37	0.00	0.07	0.1	0.0	7.1	0.0	0	0.03	0.9	9	6	11	0.0	60	0.00	0.00
0.02	0.05	11.28	0.30	2.53	3.4	0.0	136.1	0.5	9	1.29	23.0	139	202	287	0.7	75	0.00	0.00
0.00	0.09	7.98	0.28	6.59	1.6	3.4	—	3.3	103	2.29	83.1	373	339	370	11.9	67	0.00	0.00
0.07	0.02	1.05	0.03	14.34	14.2	3.5	—	0.5	33	4.57	19.5	68	90	96	26.6	82	0.00	0.00
0.05	0.20	3.09	0.28	2.82	14.6	2.5	—	1.7	75	0.75	66.6	222	430	748	0.6	70	0.00	0.00
—	—	—	—	—	—	0.0	—	—	20	0.36	—	—	280	260	—	68	0.00	0.00
0.10	0.10	4.30	0.25	1.26	47.7	25.7	147.2	3.5	91	3.76	59.4	307	576	1129	1.6	75	0.00	0.00
—	—	—	—	—	—	0.0	—	—	40	1.44	—	—	—	610	—	52	0.00	0.00
0.02	0.05	3.07	0.11	1.27	2.7	2.6	—	1.4	72	3.08	46.1	265	240	392	1.4	62	0.00	0.00
—	—	—	—	—	—	—	—	—	—	—	—	—	1430	5910	—	—	0.00	0.00
—	—	—	—	—	—	—	—	—	—	—	—	—	492	46494	—	—	0.00	0.00
—	—	—	—	0.00	—	—	—	—	0	0.00	0.0	0	0	0	—	0	0.00	0.00
0.00	0.02	0.00	0.00	0.00	0.5	0.0	0.0	0.0	3	1.34	0.5	1	3	99	0.2	9	0.00	0.00
0.00	0.00	0.00	0.00	0.00	0.0	0.0	0.0	0.0	0	0.03	0.2	1	0	1	0.0	8	0.00	0.00
0.07	0.07	3.54	—	—	—	17.7	—	—	90	2.38	—	132	796	130	—	22	0.00	0.00
0.00	0.00	0.00	0.00	0.00	0.0	0.0	—	0.0	0	0.00	0.0	0	1276	113	0.0	0	0.00	0.00
1.50	1.70	20.00	2.00	6.00	400.0	60.0	400.0	13.6	162	18.00	100.0	109	80	—	15.0	—	0.00	0.00
25.00	25.00	100.00	25.00	100.00	400.0	150.0	400.0	67.1	25	10.00	7.2	—	5	—	15.0	—	0.00	0.00
1.50	1.70	20.00	2.00	6.00	400.0	60.0	400.0	13.6	450	27.00	—	—	—	—	15.0	—	0.00	0.00
0.05	0.02	0.40	0.02	0.00	49.9	0.0	0.0	0.0	50	4.11	11.1	220	23	285	1.1	5	0.00	0.00
—	—	—	—	—	—	0.0	—	—	0	0.00	—	—	—	25	—	—	0.00	0.00
0.05	0.03	0.25	0.07	0.00	0.0	2.2	0.0	0.0	17	0.92	7.4	17	295	7	0.1	88	0.00	0.00
0.00	0.03	0.09	0.07	0.00	0.0	1.4	0.0	0.0	14	0.62	12.0	17	301	17	0.1	88	0.00	0.00

PAGE KEY: A-108 Beverage and Beverage Mixes A-112 Other Beverages A-112 Beverages, Alcoholic A-114 Candies and Confections, Gum A-114 Cereals, Breakfast Type A-118 Cheese and Cheese Substitutes A-120 Dairy Products and Substitutes A-122 Desserts A-128 Dessert Toppings A-128 Eggs, Substitutes, and Egg Dishes A-130 Ethnic Foods A-130 Fast Foods/Restaurants A-140 Fats, Oils, Margarines, Shortenings, and Substitutes A-142 Fish, Seafood, and Shellfish A-142 Food Additives A-142 Fruit, Vegetable, and Blended Juices A-144 Fruits A-146 Grains, Flours, and Fractions A-148 Grain Products, Prepared and Baked Goods

Code	Food Name	Unit/ Amt	Wt (g)	Energy (Kcal)	Prot (g)	Carb (g)	Fiber (g)	Fat (g)	Sat (g)	Mono (g)	Poly (g)	Chol (mg)	Vit A (RE)
5226	Juice, carrot, cnd	1 cup	236	94	2	22	2	0	0.1	0.0	0.2	0	2582
3963	Juice, citrus punch, rtd	1 cup	247	140	0	36	0	0	0.0	0.0	0.0	0	0
20042	Juice, clam & tomato, cnd, 5.5oz can	1 ea	166	80	1	18	0	0	0.1	0.0	0.0	0	37
3983	Juice, cranberry apple, rtd	1 cup	247	120	0	30	0	0	0.0	0.0	0.0	0	0
3042	Juice, cranberry cocktail	1 cup	253	144	0	36	0	0	0.0	0.0	0.1	0	1
3964	Juice, fruit punch, rtd	1 cup	247	130	0	32	0	0	0.0	0.0	0.0	0	0
3064	Juice, grape, swtnd, w/add vit C, prep f/fzn w/water	1 cup	250	128	0	32	0	0	0.1	0.0	0.1	0	2
3455	Juice, grapefruit, pink, fresh	1 cup	247	96	1	23	0	0	0.0	0.0	0.1	0	109
3053	Juice, grapefruit, unswtnd, prep f/fzn w/water	1 cup	247	101	1	24	0	0	0.0	0.0	0.1	0	2
3304	Juice, guava nectar	1 cup	250	149	0	38	2	0	0.1	0.0	0.1	0	21
3303	Juice, mango nectar	1 cup	250	146	1	38	2	0	0.1	0.1	0.0	0	292
3898	Juice, orange blend, 100%, can/btl, Minute Maid	1 cup	252	124	0	32	0	0	0.0	0.0	0.0	–	0
3092	Juice, orange, chilled, includes f/conc	1 cup	249	110	2	25	0	1	0.1	0.1	0.2	0	20
3478	Juice, orange, homestyle, rtd, Season's Best	1 cup	247	110	1	27	0	0	0.0	0.0	0.0	0	0
28096	Juice, orange, rtd, Pure Premium	1 cup	247	110	1	26	0	0	0.0	0.0	0.0	0	0
3480	Juice, orange, w/calc, rtd, Season's Best	1 cup	247	110	1	27	0	0	0.0	0.0	0.0	0	0
3201	Juice, passion fruit, yellow, fresh	1 cup	247	148	2	36	0	0	0.0	0.1	0.3	0	598
3119	Juice, pineapple, prep f/fzn conc w/water	1 cup	250	130	1	32	0	0	0.0	0.0	0.0	0	5
3465	Juice, prune, 100%, 68558, prep f/conc	4 oz	113	90	0	23	–	0	0.0	0.0	0.0	0	–
4000	Juice, raspberry, country, fzn, conc	62.64 g	63	140	1	34	0	0	0.0	0.0	0.0	0	0
5188	Juice, tomato, w/add salt, cnd	1 cup	243	41	2	10	1	0	0.0	0.0	0.1	0	136
3905	Juice, tropical carrot, Splash	1 cup	246	120	0	30	0	0	0.0	0.0	0.0	0	500
20080	Juice, vegetable cocktail, cnd	1 cup	242	46	2	11	2	0	0.0	0.0	0.1	0	286
FRUITS													
3001	Apples, fresh, lrg, 3¼″ diameter	1 ea	212	125	0	32	6	1	0.1	0.0	0.2	0	13
3003	Apples, fresh, peeled, med, 2¾″ diameter	1 ea	128	73	0	19	2	0	0.1	0.0	0.1	0	5
3147	Applesauce, swtnd, w/o salt, cnd	1 cup	255	194	0	51	3	0	0.1	0.0	0.1	0	5
3657	Apricots, fresh, sliced	1 cup	165	79	2	18	4	1	0.0	0.3	0.1	0	432
3399	Apricots, sulfured, dehyd, unckd	1 cup	119	381	6	99	14	1	0.1	0.3	0.1	0	1507
3018	Avocado, avg, fresh, cubed	1 cup	150	242	3	11	8	23	3.7	14.4	2.9	0	93
3307	Banana, chips	3 oz	85	441	2	50	7	29	24.6	1.7	0.5	0	7
71081	Banana, fresh, extra lrg, 9″ or longer	1 ea	152	140	2	36	4	1	0.3	0.1	0.1	0	12
3024	Blackberries, fresh	1 cup	144	75	1	18	8	1	0.0	0.1	0.3	0	23
3029	Blueberries, fresh	1 cup	145	81	1	20	4	1	0.0	0.1	0.2	0	14
3031	Blueberries, unswtnd, fzn	1 cup	155	79	1	19	4	1	0.1	0.1	0.4	0	12
3403	Cherries, red, sour, in heavy syrup, cnd, not drained	0.5 cup	128	116	1	30	1	0	0.0	0.0	0.0	0	92
3037	Cherries, sweet, fresh	1 cup	145	104	2	24	3	1	0.3	0.4	0.4	0	32
3673	Cranberries, fresh, chpd	1 cup	110	54	0	14	5	0	0.0	0.0	0.1	0	4
3487	Cranberries, swtnd, dried, Craisins	0.33 cup	40	130	0	33	2	0	0.0	0.0	0.0	0	0
3040	Cranberry Sauce, swtnd, cnd	1 cup	277	418	1	108	3	0	0.0	0.1	0.2	0	6
3043	Dates, fresh, pitted	1 cup	178	490	4	131	13	1	0.3	0.3	0.1	0	11
3162	Figs, dried, unckd	1 ea	19	48	1	12	2	0	0.0	0.0	0.1	0	3
3411	Fruit Cocktail, in extra light syrup, cnd, not drained	0.5 cup	123	55	0	14	1	0	0.0	0.0	0.0	0	30
3164	Fruit Cocktail, in juice, cnd, not drained	1 cup	237	109	1	28	2	0	0.0	0.0	0.0	0	71
3817	Grapefruit, pink, fresh, sections	1 cup	230	69	1	18	3	0	0.0	0.0	0.1	0	60
3054	Grapes, thompson seedless, fresh	1 cup	160	114	1	28	2	1	0.3	0.0	0.3	0	13
3634	Guava, fresh	1 cup	165	84	1	20	9	1	0.3	0.1	0.4	0	132
3249	Java Plum, fresh	3 ea	9	5	0	1	0	0	–	–	–	0	0
3065	Kiwi, fresh, w/o skin, med	1 ea	76	46	1	11	3	0	0.0	0.0	0.2	0	14

PAGE KEY: A-154 Granola Bars, Cereal Bars, Diet Bars, Scones, and Tarts A-154 Meals and Dishes A-160 Meats A-164 Nuts, Seeds, and Products A-166 Poultry A-166 Salad Dressings, Dips, and Mayonnaise A-170 Salads A-170 Sandwiches A-172 Sauces and Gravies A-174 Snack Foods—Chips, Pretzels, Popcorn A-178 Soups, Stews and Chilis A-184 Spices, Flavors, and Seasonings A-184 Sports Bars and Drinks A-186 Supplemental Foods and Formulas A-186 Sweeteners and Sweet Substitutes A-188 Vegetables and Legumes A-200 Weight Loss Bars & Drinks A-200 Miscellaneous

Thia (mg)	Ribo (mg)	Niac (mg NE)	Vit B6 (mg)	Vit B12 (µg)	Fol (µg)	Vit C (mg)	Vit D (IU)	Vit E (mg AT)	Cal (mg)	Iron (mg)	Magn (mg)	Phos (mg)	Pota (mg)	Sodi (mg)	Zinc (mg)	Wat (%)	Alco (g)	Caff (g)
0.21	0.12	0.91	0.50	0.00	9.4	20.1	0.0	0.0	57	1.09	33.0	99	689	68	0.4	89	0.00	0.00
0.00	–	0.00	0.00	–	0.0	0.0	–	0.0	0	0.00	–	–	0	15	–	–	0.00	0.00
0.07	0.05	0.31	0.14	50.83	26.6	6.8	0.0	0.8	20	1.00	36.5	130	149	601	1.8	87	0.00	0.00
0.00	–	0.00	0.00	–	0.0	60.0	–	0.0	0	0.00	–	–	200	35	–	88	0.00	0.00
0.01	0.01	0.09	0.05	0.00	0.0	89.5	0.0	0.0	8	0.37	5.1	5	46	5	0.2	86	0.00	0.00
0.00	–	0.00	0.00	–	0.0	0.0	–	0.0	0	0.00	–	–	0	15	–	87	0.00	0.00
0.03	0.05	0.31	0.10	0.00	2.5	59.8	0.0	0.1	10	0.25	10.0	10	52	5	0.1	87	0.00	0.00
0.10	0.05	0.49	0.10	0.00	24.7	93.9	0.0	0.6	22	0.49	29.6	37	400	2	0.1	90	0.00	0.00
0.10	0.05	0.54	0.10	0.00	9.9	83.2	0.0	0.1	20	0.34	27.2	35	336	2	0.1	89	0.00	0.00
0.01	0.01	0.38	0.05	0.00	2.5	46.5	0.0	0.4	11	0.15	5.4	10	93	7	0.1	84	0.00	0.00
0.05	0.05	0.52	0.11	0.00	7.0	19.4	0.0	1.1	12	0.15	10.3	11	141	6	0.1	84	0.00	0.00
–	–	–	–	0.00	–	60.0	–	–	0	0.00	–	–	434	33	–	87	0.00	0.00
0.28	0.05	0.69	0.12	0.00	44.8	81.9	0.0	0.5	25	0.41	27.4	27	473	2	0.1	88	0.00	0.00
0.15	–	0.80	0.11	–	60.0	60.0	–	0.0	20	0.00	–	–	430	15	–	89	0.00	0.00
0.15	–	0.80	0.11	–	60.0	30.0	–	0.0	20	0.00	–	–	450	0	0.0	89	0.00	0.00
0.00	–	0.00	0.00	–	40.0	78.0	–	0.0	300	0.00	–	–	430	15	–	89	0.00	0.00
0.00	0.25	5.53	0.15	0.00	19.8	45.0	0.0	0.1	10	0.88	42.0	62	687	15	0.1	84	0.00	0.00
0.17	0.05	0.50	0.18	0.00	27.5	30.0	0.0	0.0	28	0.75	22.5	20	340	2	0.3	86	0.00	0.00
–	–	–	–	0.00	–	60.0	–	–	–	–	–	–	290	0	–	80	0.00	0.00
0.00	–	0.00	0.00	–	0.0	60.0	–	0.0	20	0.72	–	–	220	30	–	–	0.00	0.00
0.10	0.07	1.63	0.27	0.00	48.6	44.5	0.0	2.2	22	1.40	26.7	46	535	877	0.3	94	0.00	0.00
–	–	–	–	0.00	–	60.0	–	–	0	0.00	–	–	–	20	–	87	0.00	0.00
0.10	0.07	1.75	0.34	0.00	50.8	67.0	0.0	0.8	27	1.01	26.6	41	467	653	0.5	94	0.00	0.00
0.03	0.02	0.15	0.10	0.00	6.4	12.1	0.0	0.7	15	0.37	10.6	15	244	0	0.1	84	0.00	0.00
0.01	0.00	0.11	0.05	0.00	0.0	5.1	0.0	0.1	5	0.09	3.8	9	145	0	0.1	84	0.00	0.00
0.02	0.07	0.47	0.07	0.00	2.5	4.3	0.0	0.0	10	0.88	7.6	18	156	8	0.1	80	0.00	0.00
0.05	0.07	0.99	0.09	0.00	14.8	16.5	0.0	1.5	23	0.88	13.2	31	488	2	0.4	86	0.00	0.00
0.05	0.18	4.26	0.62	0.00	4.8	11.3	0.0	3.0	73	7.51	75.0	187	2202	15	1.2	8	0.00	0.00
0.15	0.18	2.88	0.41	0.00	93.0	11.9	0.0	2.0	16	1.52	58.5	62	898	15	0.6	74	0.00	0.00
0.07	0.00	0.60	0.21	0.00	11.9	5.4	0.0	4.6	15	1.05	64.6	48	456	5	0.6	4	0.00	0.00
0.07	0.15	0.81	0.87	0.00	28.9	13.8	0.0	0.4	9	0.46	44.1	30	602	2	0.2	74	0.00	0.00
0.03	0.05	0.57	0.07	0.00	49.0	30.2	0.0	1.0	46	0.81	28.8	30	282	0	0.4	86	0.00	0.00
0.07	0.07	0.51	0.05	0.00	8.7	18.9	0.0	1.5	9	0.25	7.2	14	129	9	0.2	85	0.00	0.00
0.05	0.05	0.81	0.09	0.00	10.8	3.9	0.0	1.5	12	0.28	7.8	17	84	2	0.1	87	0.00	0.00
0.01	0.05	0.21	0.05	0.00	10.2	2.6	0.0	0.2	13	1.65	7.7	13	119	9	0.1	76	0.00	0.00
0.07	0.09	0.57	0.05	0.00	5.8	10.2	0.0	0.2	22	0.56	16.0	28	325	0	0.1	81	0.00	0.00
0.02	0.01	0.10	0.07	0.00	2.2	14.9	0.0	0.1	8	0.21	5.5	10	78	1	0.1	87	0.00	0.00
0.00	0.03	0.00	–	0.00	–	0.0	–	–	0	0.20	3.3	5	16	0	0.0	17	0.00	0.00
0.03	0.05	0.28	0.03	0.00	2.8	5.5	0.0	0.3	11	0.61	8.3	17	72	80	0.1	61	0.00	0.00
0.15	0.18	3.92	0.34	0.00	23.1	0.0	0.0	0.2	57	2.04	62.3	71	1161	5	0.5	22	0.00	0.00
0.00	0.01	0.12	0.03	0.00	1.5	0.2	0.0	0.0	27	0.41	11.2	13	135	2	0.1	28	0.00	0.00
0.03	0.00	0.62	0.05	0.00	3.7	3.7	0.0	0.4	10	0.37	7.4	15	128	5	0.1	88	0.00	0.00
0.02	0.03	0.95	0.11	0.00	7.1	6.4	0.0	0.5	19	0.50	16.6	33	225	9	0.2	87	0.00	0.00
0.07	0.05	0.43	0.10	0.00	27.6	87.6	0.0	0.6	25	0.28	18.4	21	297	0	0.2	91	0.00	0.00
0.15	0.09	0.47	0.18	0.00	6.4	17.3	0.0	1.1	18	0.41	9.6	21	296	3	0.1	81	0.00	0.00
0.07	0.07	1.98	0.23	0.00	23.1	302.8	0.0	1.8	33	0.50	16.5	41	469	5	0.4	86	0.00	0.00
0.00	0.00	0.01	0.00	0.00	–	1.3	0.0	–	2	0.01	1.4	2	7	1	0.0	83	0.00	0.00
0.01	0.03	0.37	0.07	0.00	28.9	74.5	0.0	0.9	20	0.31	22.8	30	252	4	0.1	83	0.00	0.00

PAGE KEY: A-108 Beverage and Beverage Mixes A-112 Other Beverages A-112 Beverages, Alcoholic A-114 Candies and Confections, Gum A-114 Cereals, Breakfast Type A-118 Cheese and Cheese Substitutes A-120 Dairy Products and Substitutes A-122 Desserts A-128 Dessert Toppings A-128 Eggs, Substitutes, and Egg Dishes A-130 Ethnic Foods A-130 Fast Foods/Restaurants A-140 Fats, Oils, Margarines, Shortenings, and Substitutes A-142 Fish, Seafood, and Shellfish A-142 Food Additives A-142 Fruit, Vegetable, and Blended Juices A-144 Fruits A-146 Grains, Flours, and Fractions A-148 Grain Products, Prepared and Baked Goods

Code	Food Name	Unit/ Amt	Wt (g)	Energy (Kcal)	Prot (g)	Carb (g)	Fiber (g)	Fat (g)	Sat (g)	Mono (g)	Poly (g)	Chol (mg)	Vit A (RE)
3252	Kumquats, fresh	1 ea	19	12	0	3	1	0	0.0	0.0	0.0	0	6
3071	Limes, peeled, fresh, 2 diameter	1 ea	67	20	0	7	2	0	0.0	0.0	0.0	0	1
71774	Mandarin Oranges, in light syrup, cnd	1 cup	252	154	1	41	2	0	0.0	0.0	0.1	0	212
3221	Mango, fresh, whole	1 ea	207	135	1	35	4	1	0.1	0.2	0.1	0	807
3075	Melon, cantaloupe/musk, fresh, cubes	1 cup	160	56	1	13	1	0	0.1	0.0	0.2	0	515
3080	Melon, honeydew, fresh, diced	1 cup	170	60	1	16	1	0	0.0	0.0	0.1	0	7
71104	Mix Fruit, pch chry grpe & berry, swtnd, thawed, 10oz	1 ea	284	278	4	69	5	1	0.1	0.1	0.2	0	91
3168	Mixed Fruit, prunes apricots & pears, dried, 11oz pkg	1 ea	312	758	8	200	24	2	0.1	0.7	0.3	0	761
3215	Nectarines, fresh, 2½″ diameter	1 ea	136	67	1	16	2	1	0.1	0.2	0.3	0	101
3230	Oranges, Florida, fresh, 2 11/16″ diameter	1 ea	151	69	1	17	4	0	0.0	0.1	0.1	0	30
3085	Oranges, fresh, lrg, 3 1/16″ diameter	1 ea	184	86	2	22	4	0	0.0	0.0	0.0	0	37
3172	Papaya, fresh, cubes	1 cup	140	55	1	14	3	0	0.1	0.1	0.0	0	39
3199	Passion Fruit, purple, fresh	1 ea	18	17	0	4	2	0	0.0	0.0	0.1	0	13
3725	Peaches, fresh, lrg, 2¾″ diameter, w/o skin	1 ea	157	68	1	17	3	0	0.0	0.1	0.1	0	85
3099	Peaches, halves, in heavy syrup, cnd, not drained	1 ea	98	73	0	20	1	0	0.0	0.0	0.0	0	33
3272	Pears, fresh, asian	1 ea	122	51	1	13	4	0	0.0	0.1	0.1	0	0
3103	Pears, fresh, bartlett, med	1 ea	166	98	1	25	4	1	0.0	0.1	0.2	0	3
3432	Pears, halves, in extra light syrup, cnd, not drained	1 cup	247	116	1	30	4	0	0.0	0.1	0.1	0	0
3108	Pears, halves, in heavy syrup, cnd, not drained	1 ea	76	56	0	15	1	0	0.0	0.0	0.0	0	0
3194	Persimmon, native, fresh	1 ea	25	32	0	8	0	0	—	—	—	0	—
71114	Pineapple, chunks, in juice, cnd, not drained	1 cup	249	149	1	39	2	0	0.0	0.0	0.1	0	10
3116	Pineapple, crushed, in heavy syrup, cnd, not drained	1 cup	254	198	1	51	2	0	0.0	0.0	0.1	0	5
3183	Pineapple, crushed, in juice, cnd, not drained	1 cup	249	149	1	39	2	0	0.0	0.0	0.1	0	10
3112	Pineapple, fresh	1 ea	472	231	2	58	6	2	0.2	0.2	0.7	0	9
71115	Pineapple, tidbits, in juice, cnd, not drained	1 cup	249	149	1	39	2	0	0.0	0.0	0.1	0	10
3745	Plantain, fresh, med	1 ea	179	218	2	57	4	1	0.3	0.1	0.1	0	200
3121	Plums, fresh, 2⅛″ diameter	1 ea	66	36	1	9	1	0	0.0	0.3	0.1	0	21
3197	Pomegranate, fresh, 3⅜″ diameter	1 ea	154	105	1	26	1	0	0.1	0.1	0.1	0	0
3126	Prunes, dried	10 ea	84	201	2	53	6	0	0.0	0.3	0.1	0	166
3129	Raisins, seedless, packed	1 cup	165	495	5	131	7	1	0.2	0.0	0.2	0	1
3765	Raisins, seedless, small box, 1.5 oz ea	1 ea	43	129	1	34	2	0	0.1	0.0	0.1	0	0
3131	Raspberries, red, fresh	1 cup	123	60	1	14	8	1	0.0	0.1	0.4	0	17
3209	Rhubarb, fresh, diced	1 cup	122	26	1	6	2	0	0.1	0.0	0.1	0	12
3781	Strawberries, fresh, lrg	1 ea	18	5	0	1	0	0	0.0	0.0	0.0	0	0
3134	Strawberries, fresh, whole	1 cup	144	43	1	10	3	1	0.0	0.1	0.3	0	3
3137	Strawberries, fzn, unswtnd	1 cup	149	52	1	14	3	0	0.0	0.0	0.1	0	6
3087	Tangelo, fresh, 2⅜″ diameter	1 ea	96	45	1	11	2	0	0.0	0.0	0.0	0	19
3717	Tangerines, fresh, lrg, 2½″ diameter	1 ea	98	43	1	11	2	0	0.0	0.0	0.0	0	90
3143	Watermelon, fresh, slice, 1/16″ melon	1 pce	286	92	2	21	1	1	0.1	0.3	0.4	0	103
	GRAINS, FLOURS, AND FRACTIONS												
38003	Barley, pearled, ckd	1 cup	157	193	4	44	6	1	0.1	0.1	0.3	0	1
38078	Bran, oat, ckd	1 cup	219	88	7	25	6	2	0.4	0.6	0.7	0	0
38072	Buckwheat	1 cup	170	583	23	122	17	6	1.3	1.8	1.8	0	0
38252	Corn, white, dry	1 cup	166	606	16	123	16	8	1.1	2.1	3.6	0	0
38279	Corn, yellow, dry	0.5 cup	83	303	8	62	11	4	0.6	1.0	1.8	0	38
19615	Egg Substitute, Egg Replacer, wheat free, low prot, dry	1.5 tsp	4	15	0	4	0	0	0.0	0.0	0.0	0	24
38030	Flour, all purpose, white, bleached, enrich	1 cup	125	455	13	95	3	1	0.2	0.1	0.5	0	0
38033	Flour, all purpose, white, self rising, enrich	1 cup	125	442	12	93	3	1	0.2	0.1	0.5	0	0
38548	Flour, barley	1 cup	148	511	16	110	15	2	0.5	0.3	1.1	0	0

PAGE KEY: A-154 Granola Bars, Cereal Bars, Diet Bars, Scones, and Tarts A-154 Meals and Dishes A-160 Meats A-164 Nuts, Seeds, and Products A-166 Poultry A-166 Salad Dressings, Dips, and Mayonnaise A-170 Salads A-170 Sandwiches A-172 Sauces and Gravies A-174 Snack Foods—Chips, Pretzels, Popcorn A-178 Soups, Stews and Chilis A-184 Spices, Flavors, and Seasonings A-184 Sports Bars and Drinks A-186 Supplemental Foods and Formulas A-186 Sweeteners and Sweet Substitutes A-188 Vegetables and Legumes A-200 Weight Loss Bars & Drinks A-200 Miscellaneous

Thia (mg)	Ribo (mg)	Niac (mg NE)	Vit B6 (mg)	Vit B12 (µg)	Fol (µg)	Vit C (mg)	Vit D (IU)	Vit E (mg AT)	Cal (mg)	Iron (mg)	Magn (mg)	Phos (mg)	Pota (mg)	Sodi (mg)	Zinc (mg)	Wat (%)	Alco (g)	Caff (g)
0.01	0.01	0.09	0.00	0.00	3.0	7.1	0.0	0.0	8	0.07	2.5	4	37	1	0.0	82	0.00	0.00
0.01	0.00	0.12	0.02	0.00	5.4	19.5	0.0	0.2	22	0.40	4.0	12	68	1	0.1	88	0.00	0.00
0.12	0.10	1.12	0.10	0.00	12.6	49.9	0.0	0.9	18	0.93	20.2	25	197	15	0.6	83	0.00	0.00
0.11	0.11	1.21	0.28	0.00	29.0	57.3	0.0	2.3	21	0.27	18.6	23	323	4	0.1	82	0.00	0.00
0.05	0.02	0.92	0.18	0.00	27.2	67.5	0.0	0.2	18	0.34	17.6	27	494	14	0.3	90	0.00	0.00
0.12	0.02	1.01	0.10	0.00	10.2	42.2	0.0	0.3	10	0.11	11.9	17	461	17	0.1	90	0.00	0.00
0.05	0.10	1.12	0.07	0.00	22.7	212.6	0.0	1.7	20	0.79	17.0	34	371	9	0.1	74	0.00	0.00
0.14	0.49	6.01	0.50	0.00	12.5	11.9	0.0	2.0	119	8.44	121.6	240	2482	56	1.6	31	0.00	0.00
0.01	0.05	1.35	0.02	0.00	5.4	7.3	0.0	1.2	7	0.20	10.9	22	288	0	0.1	86	0.00	0.00
0.15	0.05	0.60	0.07	0.00	25.7	67.9	0.0	0.4	65	0.14	15.1	18	255	0	0.1	87	0.00	0.00
0.15	0.07	0.51	0.10	0.00	55.2	97.9	0.0	0.4	74	0.18	18.4	26	333	0	0.1	87	0.00	0.00
0.03	0.03	0.46	0.02	0.00	53.2	86.5	0.0	1.6	34	0.14	14.0	7	360	4	0.1	89	0.00	0.00
0.00	0.01	0.27	0.01	0.00	2.5	5.4	0.0	0.2	2	0.28	5.2	12	63	5	0.0	73	0.00	0.00
0.02	0.05	1.54	0.02	0.00	4.7	10.4	0.0	1.1	8	0.17	11.0	19	309	0	0.2	88	0.00	0.00
0.00	0.01	0.60	0.01	0.00	2.9	2.7	0.0	0.9	3	0.25	4.9	11	90	6	0.1	79	0.00	0.00
0.00	0.00	0.27	0.02	0.00	9.8	4.6	0.0	0.6	5	0.00	9.8	13	148	0	0.0	88	0.00	0.00
0.02	0.07	0.17	0.02	0.00	11.6	6.6	0.0	0.8	18	0.40	10.0	18	208	0	0.2	84	0.00	0.00
0.01	0.05	0.99	0.02	0.00	2.5	4.9	0.0	0.2	17	0.49	12.4	17	111	5	0.2	87	0.00	0.00
0.00	0.01	0.18	0.00	0.00	0.8	0.8	0.0	0.4	4	0.17	3.0	5	49	4	0.1	80	0.00	0.00
—	—	—	—	0.00	2.0	16.5	0.0	0.2	7	0.62	—	6	78	0	—	64	0.00	0.00
0.23	0.05	0.70	0.18	0.00	12.4	23.7	0.0	0.2	35	0.69	34.9	15	304	2	0.2	84	0.00	0.00
0.23	0.05	0.73	0.18	0.00	12.7	18.8	0.0	0.3	36	0.97	40.6	18	264	3	0.3	79	0.00	0.00
0.23	0.05	0.70	0.18	0.00	12.4	23.7	0.0	0.2	35	0.69	34.9	15	304	2	0.2	84	0.00	0.00
0.43	0.17	1.98	0.40	0.00	51.9	72.7	0.0	0.5	33	1.75	66.1	33	533	5	0.4	86	0.00	0.00
0.23	0.05	0.70	0.18	0.00	12.4	23.7	0.0	0.2	35	0.69	34.9	15	304	2	0.2	84	0.00	0.00
0.09	0.10	1.23	0.54	0.00	39.4	32.9	0.0	0.5	5	1.07	66.2	61	893	7	0.3	65	0.00	0.00
0.02	0.05	0.33	0.05	0.00	1.3	6.3	0.0	0.4	3	0.07	4.6	7	114	0	0.1	85	0.00	0.00
0.05	0.05	0.46	0.15	0.00	9.2	9.4	0.0	0.8	5	0.46	4.6	12	399	5	0.2	81	0.00	0.00
0.07	0.14	1.64	0.21	0.00	3.4	2.8	0.0	1.2	43	2.07	37.8	66	626	3	0.4	32	0.00	0.00
0.25	0.15	1.35	0.40	0.00	4.9	5.4	0.0	1.2	81	3.43	54.5	160	1239	20	0.4	15	0.00	0.00
0.07	0.03	0.34	0.10	0.00	1.3	1.4	0.0	0.3	21	0.88	14.2	42	323	5	0.1	15	0.00	0.00
0.03	0.10	1.11	0.07	0.00	32.0	30.8	0.0	0.6	27	0.69	22.1	15	187	0	0.6	87	0.00	0.00
0.01	0.03	0.37	0.02	0.00	8.5	9.8	0.0	0.2	105	0.27	14.6	17	351	5	0.1	94	0.00	0.00
0.00	0.00	0.03	0.00	0.00	3.2	10.2	0.0	0.0	3	0.07	1.8	3	30	0	0.0	92	0.00	0.00
0.02	0.10	0.33	0.07	0.00	25.9	81.6	0.0	0.2	20	0.55	14.4	27	239	1	0.2	92	0.00	0.00
0.02	0.05	0.68	0.03	0.00	25.3	61.4	0.0	0.4	24	1.12	16.4	19	221	3	0.2	90	0.00	0.00
0.07	0.03	0.27	0.05	0.00	28.8	51.1	0.0	0.2	38	0.10	9.6	13	174	0	0.1	87	0.00	0.00
0.10	0.01	0.15	0.07	0.00	19.6	30.2	0.0	0.2	14	0.10	11.8	10	154	1	0.2	88	0.00	0.00
0.23	0.05	0.56	0.40	0.00	5.7	27.5	0.0	0.4	23	0.49	31.5	26	332	6	0.2	92	0.00	0.00
0.12	0.10	3.24	0.18	0.00	25.1	0.0	0.0	0.1	17	2.08	34.5	85	146	5	1.3	69	0.00	0.00
0.34	0.07	0.31	0.05	0.00	13.1	0.0	0.0	0.5	22	1.92	87.6	261	201	2	1.2	84	0.00	0.00
0.17	0.72	11.93	0.36	0.00	51.0	0.0	0.0	1.8	31	3.74	392.7	590	782	2	4.1	10	0.00	0.00
0.63	0.33	6.01	1.02	0.00	46.5	0.0	0.0	1.7	12	4.50	210.8	349	476	58	3.7	10	0.00	0.00
0.31	0.17	3.00	0.51	0.00	15.8	0.0	0.0	0.6	6	2.25	105.4	174	238	29	1.8	10	0.00	0.00
0.00	0.00	0.00	0.00	0.00	—	0.0	0.0	0.0	128	0.01	—	0	1	7	—	—	0.00	0.00
0.98	0.62	7.38	0.05	0.00	242.5	0.0	0.0	0.2	19	5.80	27.5	135	134	2	0.9	12	0.00	0.00
0.83	0.51	7.28	0.05	0.00	245.0	0.0	0.0	0.1	422	5.84	23.8	744	155	1588	0.8	11	0.00	0.00
0.55	0.17	9.27	0.58	0.00	11.8	0.0	—	—	47	3.97	142.1	438	457	6	3.0	12	0.00	0.00

PAGE KEY: A-108 Beverage and Beverage Mixes A-112 Other Beverages A-112 Beverages, Alcoholic A-114 Candies and Confections, Gum A-114 Cereals, Breakfast Type A-118 Cheese and Cheese Substitutes A-120 Dairy Products and Substitutes A-122 Desserts A-128 Dessert Toppings A-128 Eggs, Substitutes, and Egg Dishes A-130 Ethnic Foods A-130 Fast Foods/Restaurants A-140 Fats, Oils, Margarines, Shortenings, and Substitutes A-142 Fish, Seafood, and Shellfish A-142 Food Additives A-142 Fruit, Vegetable, and Blended Juices A-144 Fruits A-146 Grains, Flours, and Fractions A-148 Grain Products, Prepared and Baked Goods

Code	Food Name	Unit/ Amt	Wt (g)	Energy (Kcal)	Prot (g)	Carb (g)	Fiber (g)	Fat (g)	Sat (g)	Mono (g)	Poly (g)	Chol (mg)	Vit A (RE)
367	Flour, bleached, self rising, enrich	0.25 cup	32	110	3	23	1	0	0.0	–	–	0	0
38277	Flour, bread, white, enrich	1 cup	137	495	16	99	3	2	0.3	0.2	1.0	0	0
38451	Flour, buckwheat	0.25 cup	30	100	4	21	3	1	0.0	–	–	0	0
46086	Flour, cake, white, enrich, unsftd	1 cup	137	496	11	107	2	1	0.2	0.1	0.5	0	0
38005	Flour, corn, masa, enrich	1 cup	114	416	11	87	11	4	0.6	1.1	2.0	0	0
38363	Flour, enrich	1 cup	125	450	13	94	4	1	0.4	0.3	0.6	0	–
38569	Flour, harina, preparada para tortillas, dry	0.33 cup	40	163	4	27	1	4	1.3	2.0	0.7	0	0
38445	Flour, oat	0.33 cup	30	120	5	20	4	2	0.0	–	–	0	0
38056	Flour, rye, med	1 cup	102	361	10	79	15	2	0.2	0.2	0.8	0	0
7514	Flour, soy, defatted, stirred	1 cup	100	329	47	38	18	1	0.1	0.2	0.5	0	4
38123	Flour, wheat, durum	1 cup	167	569	22	116	20	5	–	–	–	0	–
38032	Flour, whole wheat	1 cup	120	407	16	87	15	2	0.4	0.3	0.9	0	0
38455	Grits, corn, white, dry	0.25 cup	38	140	3	30	1	0	0.0	0.0	0.0	0	0
38006	Grits, corn, yellow, reg/quick, enrich, dry	1 cup	156	579	14	124	2	2	0.2	0.5	0.8	0	69
38080	Oats	1 cup	156	607	26	103	17	11	1.9	3.4	4.0	0	0
38289	Rice, wild, dry	1 cup	160	571	24	120	10	2	0.2	0.3	1.1	0	3
38034	Tapioca, pearl, dry	1 cup	152	544	0	135	1	0	0.0	0.0	0.0	0	0
38027	Wheat, bulgur, dry	1 cup	140	479	17	106	26	2	0.3	0.2	0.8	0	0
38090	Wheat, durum, grain	1 cup	192	651	26	137	24	5	0.9	0.7	1.9	0	0
60939	Wheat, germ, reg, Kretschmer	2 Tbs	13	48	4	6	2	1	0.2	0.2	0.8	0	2
38026	Wheat, germ, tstd	1 cup	113	432	33	56	15	12	2.1	1.7	7.5	0	0
GRAIN PRODUCTS, PREPARED AND BAKED GOODS													
Bagels													
71168	Bagel, cinnamon raisin, 3″	1 ea	57	156	6	31	1	1	0.2	0.1	0.4	0	5
71165	Bagel, egg, 3″	1 ea	57	158	6	30	1	1	0.2	0.2	0.4	14	19
71174	Bagel, oat bran, 3″	1 ea	57	145	6	30	2	1	0.1	0.1	0.3	0	0
71142	Bagel, onion, enrich	1 ea	57	157	6	30	1	1	0.1	0.1	0.4	0	0
71141	Bagel, plain, enrich	1 ea	57	157	6	30	1	1	0.1	0.1	0.4	0	0
71143	Bagel, poppy seed, enrich	1 ea	57	157	6	30	1	1	0.1	0.1	0.4	0	0
62743	Bagel, whole grain	1 ea	85	170	6	37	6	2	0.0	–	–	0	0
Biscuits													
42001	Biscuits, buttermilk, homemade, 2½″	1 ea	60	212	4	27	1	10	2.6	4.2	2.5	2	14
71190	Biscuits, plain, prep f/dry mix	1 oz	28	95	2	14	1	3	0.8	1.2	1.2	1	8
Breads and Rolls													
71024	Bread Crumbs, white, soft, enrich	1 cup	45	120	4	22	1	2	0.2	0.3	0.9	0	0
71021	Bread, 7 grain, slice	1 pce	26	65	3	12	2	1	0.2	0.4	0.2	0	0
71200	Bread, banana, loaf, individual size	1 ea	57	186	2	31	1	6	1.3	2.6	1.8	25	66
42086	Bread, cheese	1 pce	26	71	2	12	1	1	0.5	0.5	0.2	2	4
42471	Bread, cinnamon, Pepperidge Farms	1 pce	28	80	3	14	2	2	0.5	1.5	0.0	0	0
42042	Bread, cracked wheat, slice, reg	1 pce	25	65	2	12	1	1	0.2	0.5	0.2	0	0
49143	Bread, French, crusty loaf, refrig dough, svg	1 ea	62	154	6	29	–	2	0.5	0.6	0.3	–	–
71218	Bread, fry, Navajo Indian, 10½″ diameter	1 ea	160	526	11	85	3	15	3.7	6.4	4.1	0	0
49144	Bread, garlic, crusty Italian, svg	1 ea	50	186	4	21	–	10	2.4	3.9	1.8	6	–
42076	Bread, oat bran, rducd cal, slice	1 pce	23	46	2	9	3	1	0.1	0.2	0.4	0	–
42080	Bread, pita, wheat, lrg, 6½″ diameter	1 ea	64	170	6	35	5	2	0.3	0.2	0.7	0	0
42007	Bread, pita, white, enrich, lrg, 6½″ diameter	1 ea	60	165	5	33	1	1	0.1	0.1	0.3	0	0
42180	Bread, potato	1 pce	26	69	2	13	1	1	0.2	0.4	0.2	0	0
71231	Bread, pumpernickel, slice, 5″ x 4″ x ⅜″	1 ea	32	80	3	15	2	1	0.1	0.3	0.4	0	0
62800	Bread, seven grain herb	1 pce	34	70	4	16	4	1	0.0	–	–	0	0

PAGE KEY: A-154 Granola Bars, Cereal Bars, Diet Bars, Scones, and Tarts A-154 Meals and Dishes A-160 Meats A-164 Nuts, Seeds, and Products A-166 Poultry A-166 Salad Dressings, Dips, and Mayonnaise A-170 Salads A-170 Sandwiches A-172 Sauces and Gravies A-174 Snack Foods—Chips, Pretzels, Popcorn A-178 Soups Stews and Chilis A-184 Spices, Flavors, and Seasonings A-184 Sports Bars and Drinks A-186 Supplemental Foods and Formulas A-186 Sweeteners and Sweet Substitutes A-188 Vegetables and Legumes A-200 Weight Loss Bars & Drinks A-200 Miscellaneous

Thia (mg)	Ribo (mg)	Niac (mg NE)	Vit B6 (mg)	Vit B12 (µg)	Fol (µg)	Vit C (mg)	Vit D (IU)	Vit E (mg AT)	Cal (mg)	Iron (mg)	Magn (mg)	Phos (mg)	Pota (mg)	Sodi (mg)	Zinc (mg)	Wat (%)	Alco (g)	Caff (g)
0.23	0.14	1.60	—	—	40.0	0.0	—	—	80	1.44	—	—	—	380	—	13	0.00	0.00
1.11	0.69	10.35	0.05	0.00	250.7	0.0	0.0	1.0	21	6.03	34.2	133	137	3	1.2	13	0.00	0.00
0.15	0.07	2.00	—	—	—	0.0	—	—	0	1.08	—	—	175	0	—	11	0.00	0.00
1.22	0.58	9.30	0.05	0.00	254.8	0.0	0.0	0.0	19	10.02	21.9	116	144	3	0.8	13	0.00	0.00
1.62	0.86	11.22	0.41	0.00	213.2	0.0	0.0	0.3	161	8.22	125.4	254	340	6	2.0	9	0.00	0.00
0.75	0.50	6.61	—	—	192.5	—	—	—	20	5.50	—	—	119	2	—	—	0.00	0.00
0.30	0.18	2.28	0.01	0.00	52.6	0.0	0.0	0.1	64	1.98	5.4	117	52	399	0.2	10	0.00	0.00
0.21	—	—	—	—	—	0.0	—	—	20	1.44	—	—	100	0	—	8	0.00	0.00
0.28	0.11	1.75	0.27	0.00	19.4	0.0	0.0	1.4	24	2.16	76.5	211	347	3	2.0	10	0.00	0.00
0.69	0.25	2.60	0.56	0.00	305.0	0.0	0.0	0.2	241	9.23	290.0	674	2384	20	2.5	7	0.00	0.00
1.10	0.18	6.55	—	0.00	—	0.0	0.0	—	58	7.76	—	620	—	3	—	10	0.00	0.00
0.54	0.25	7.63	0.40	0.00	52.8	0.0	0.0	1.5	41	4.65	165.6	415	486	6	3.5	10	0.00	0.00
0.05	—	0.40	—	—	—	0.0	—	—	0	0.36	—	—	30	0	—	10	0.00	0.00
1.00	0.58	7.73	0.23	0.00	291.7	0.0	0.0	0.4	3	6.09	42.1	114	214	2	0.6	10	0.00	0.00
1.19	0.21	1.50	0.18	0.00	87.4	0.0	0.0	1.1	84	7.36	276.1	816	669	3	6.2	8	0.00	0.00
0.18	0.41	10.77	0.62	0.00	152.0	0.0	0.0	1.2	34	3.14	283.2	693	683	11	9.5	8	0.00	0.00
0.00	0.00	0.00	0.00	0.00	6.1	0.0	0.0	0.0	30	2.40	1.5	11	17	2	0.2	11	0.00	0.00
0.31	0.15	7.15	0.47	0.00	37.8	0.0	0.0	0.2	49	3.44	229.6	420	574	24	2.7	9	0.00	0.00
0.80	0.23	12.93	0.80	0.00	82.6	0.0	0.0	2.8	65	6.76	276.5	975	828	4	8.0	11	0.00	0.00
0.25	0.10	0.73	0.07	0.02	87.0	0.8	0.0	4.6	6	1.08	40.7	147	143	1	2.1	5	0.00	
1.88	0.93	6.32	1.11	0.00	397.8	6.8	0.0	20.5	51	10.27	361.6	1295	1070	5	18.8	6	0.00	0.00
0.21	0.15	1.75	0.03	0.00	51.3	0.4	0.0	0.1	11	2.17	16.0	57	84	184	0.6	32	0.00	0.00
0.31	0.12	1.96	0.05	0.09	50.2	0.3	2.2	0.1	7	2.26	14.2	48	39	288	0.4	33	0.00	0.00
0.18	0.18	1.69	0.01	0.00	46.2	0.1	0.0	0.1	7	1.75	17.7	63	66	289	0.5	33	0.00	0.00
0.31	0.18	2.59	0.02	0.00	50.2	0.0	0.0	0.0	42	2.02	16.5	55	58	304	0.5	33	0.00	0.00
0.31	0.18	2.59	0.02	0.00	50.2	0.0	0.0	0.0	42	2.02	16.5	55	58	304	0.5	33	0.00	0.00
0.31	0.18	2.59	0.02	0.00	50.2	0.0	0.0	0.0	42	2.02	16.5	55	58	304	0.5	33	0.00	0.00
0.44	0.50	8.00	0.60	1.79	—	0.0	—	—	200	1.08	120.0	—	—	200	4.5	45	0.00	0.00
0.20	0.18	1.76	0.01	0.05	36.6	0.1	12.0	0.8	141	1.74	10.8	98	73	348	0.3	29	0.00	0.00
0.10	0.10	0.86	0.01	0.05	14.7	0.1	3.1	0.1	52	0.57	7.1	133	53	271	0.2	29	0.00	0.00
0.20	0.15	1.78	0.02	0.00	42.8	0.0	3.8	0.2	49	1.36	10.8	42	54	242	0.3	37	0.00	0.00
0.10	0.09	1.12	0.09	0.01	20.8	0.1	0.0	0.2	24	0.89	13.8	46	53	127	0.3	38	0.00	0.00
0.10	0.10	0.81	0.09	0.05	18.8	1.0	3.3	1.0	12	0.80	8.0	33	76	172	0.2	29	0.00	0.00
0.11	0.09	0.98	0.01	0.00	8.6	0.0	2.1	0.1	36	0.75	6.3	30	31	141	0.2	37	0.00	0.00
0.09	0.07	0.80	—	—	—	0.0	—	—	0	0.72	—	—	—	115	—	28	0.00	0.00
0.09	0.05	0.92	0.07	0.00	15.2	0.0	0.0	0.1	11	0.69	13.0	38	44	134	0.3	36	0.00	0.00
—	—	—	—	—	—	—	—	—	—	1.48	—	—	—	389	—	40	0.00	0.00
0.68	0.49	5.82	0.03	0.00	118.4	0.0	—	1.2	373	5.76	25.6	251	118	1112	0.8	26	0.00	0.00
—	—	—	—	—	—	—	—	—	—	1.17	—	—	—	200	—	29	0.00	0.00
0.07	0.05	0.87	0.01	0.00	15.2	0.0	0.0	0.1	13	0.72	12.7	32	23	81	0.2	46	0.00	0.00
0.21	0.05	1.82	0.17	0.00	22.4	0.0	0.0	0.6	10	1.96	44.2	115	109	340	1.0	31	0.00	0.00
0.36	0.20	2.77	0.01	0.00	57.0	0.0	0.0	0.0	52	1.57	15.6	58	72	322	0.5	32	0.00	0.00
0.11	0.09	1.02	0.01	0.00	8.8	0.0	—	0.1	28	0.79	6.2	24	31	140	0.2	37	0.00	0.00
0.10	0.10	0.99	0.03	0.00	25.6	0.0	0.9	0.1	22	0.92	17.3	57	67	215	0.5	38	0.00	0.00
0.15	0.17	2.00	0.30	0.89	60.0	0.0	—	—	100	0.89	60.0	—	—	70	1.5	36	0.00	0.00

PAGE KEY: A-108 Beverage and Beverage Mixes A-112 Other Beverages A-112 Beverages, Alcoholic A-114 Candies and Confections, Gum A-114 Cereals, Breakfast Type A-118 Cheese and Cheese Substitutes A-120 Dairy Products and Substitutes A-122 Desserts A-128 Dessert Toppings A-128 Eggs, Substitutes, and Egg Dishes A-130 Ethnic Foods A-130 Fast Foods/Restaurants A-140 Fats, Oils, Margarines, Shortenings, and Substitutes A-142 Fish, Seafood, and Shellfish A-142 Food Additives A-142 Fruit, Vegetable, and Blended Juices A-144 Fruits A-146 Grains, Flours, and Fractions A-148 Grain Products, Prepared and Baked Goods

Code	Food Name	Unit/ Amt	Wt (g)	Energy (Kcal)	Prot (g)	Carb (g)	Fiber (g)	Fat (g)	Sat (g)	Mono (g)	Poly (g)	Chol (mg)	Vit A (RE)
42075	Bread, sourdough, slice, med, tstd	1 pce	59	176	6	33	2	2	0.4	0.8	0.4	0	0
42036	Bread, sticks, plain, 7⅝" x ⅝"	1 ea	10	41	1	7	0	1	0.1	0.4	0.4	0	0
42012	Bread, wheat, slice	1 pce	25	65	2	12	1	1	0.2	0.4	0.2	0	0
42084	Bread, white, rducd cal, slice	1 pce	23	48	2	10	2	1	0.1	0.2	0.1	0	0
71242	Bread, white, soft, enrich, slice	1 ea	25	67	2	12	1	1	0.1	0.2	0.5	0	0
71020	Bread, whole grain, slice	1 pce	26	65	3	12	2	1	0.2	0.4	0.2	0	0
42020	Buns, hamburger	1 ea	43	123	4	22	1	2	0.5	0.4	1.1	0	0
42021	Buns, hot dog/frankfurter	1 ea	43	123	4	22	1	2	0.5	0.4	1.1	0	0
49012	Cornbread, hush puppies, prep f/rec	1 ea	22	74	2	10	1	3	0.5	0.7	1.6	10	12
42115	Cornbread, prep f/dry mix, pce	1 ea	60	188	4	29	1	6	1.6	3.1	0.7	37	28
42015	Croissant, butter, med	1 ea	57	231	5	26	1	12	6.6	3.1	0.6	38	107
43512	Matzoh Balls	3 ea	42	58	2	7	0	2	0.5	0.8	0.5	44	20
42261	Pizza Crust, all ready, refrig dough	0.2 ea	57	150	5	27	1	2	0.0	–	–	0	0
42454	Pretzels, soft, original	1 ea	138	391	12	83	3	1	0.0	–	–	0	0
42255	Rolls, crescent, refrig dough	1 ea	28	110	2	11	0	6	1.5	–	–	0	0
42018	Rolls, dinner, brown & serve, browned	1 ea	28	84	2	14	1	2	0.5	1.0	0.3	0	0
42161	Rolls, French	1 ea	38	105	3	19	1	2	0.4	0.7	0.3	0	0
42022	Rolls, hard, 3½" diameter	1 ea	57	167	6	30	1	2	0.3	0.6	1.0	0	0
71361	Rolls, hoagie, whole wheat, lrg	1 ea	135	359	12	69	10	6	1.1	1.6	2.9	0	0
42185	Rolls, Mexican, bolillo	1 ea	117	307	10	61	2	2	0.5	0.2	0.6	1	4
42034	Rolls, submarine/hoagie/sandwich	1 ea	135	386	11	68	4	7	1.6	3.4	1.2	0	0
42734	Rolls, wheat, dinner, refrig dough	1 ea	40	110	4	18	1	2	0.0	–	–	0	0
Bread Crumbs, Croutons, Breading Mixes & Batters													
42004	Bread Crumbs, plain, grated, dry	1 cup	108	427	14	78	3	6	1.3	2.6	1.2	0	–
26557	Coating & Glaze, chicken, bbq, ⅛ dry pkt, svg	1 ea	12	45	0	9	0	1	0.0	–	–	0	40
43550	Cracker Meal	1 cup	115	440	11	93	3	2	0.3	0.2	0.8	0	0
42424	Croutons, Italian, zesty, homestyle, Pepperidge Farms	9 pce	7	35	1	4	0	2	0.5	0.5	0.0	2	0
Crackers													
71273	Crackers, cheese, 1 square	10 ea	10	50	1	6	0	3	0.9	1.2	0.2	1	3
71276	Crackers, cheese, gold fish	10 ea	6	30	1	3	0	2	0.6	0.7	0.1	1	2
11717	Crackers, club style, original	4 ea	14	69	1	9	0	3	0.6	–	–	0	0
43574	Crackers, garden veg, snack type, Frookie	13 ea	30	130	3	19	2	4	0.0	0.0	4.0	0	0
43502	Crackers, graham, plain, 2½" square	2 ea	14	59	1	11	0	1	0.2	0.6	0.5	0	0
43509	Crackers, melba toast, plain, pce, 3¾" x 1¾" x ⅛"	1 pce	5	20	1	4	0	0	0.0	0.0	0.1	0	0
43507	Crackers, oyster	1 ea	1	4	0	1	0	0	0.0	0.1	0.0	0	0
43546	Crackers, peanut butter filled, sandwich type	1 ea	7	34	1	4	0	2	0.4	0.9	0.3	0	0
71280	Crackers, rye, wafer	1 ea	10	37	1	8	2	0	0.0	0.0	0.1	0	0
43506	Crackers, saltines	4 ea	12	52	1	9	0	1	0.4	0.8	0.2	0	0
43553	Crackers, saltines, low sod	1 ea	3	13	0	2	0	0	0.1	0.2	0.1	0	0
71288	Crackers, soda	4 ea	12	52	1	9	0	1	0.4	0.8	0.2	0	0
70963	Crackers, svg, Ritz	1 ea	16	79	1	10	0	4	0.6	2.8	0.3	0	0
43584	Crackers, triscuit	7 ea	31	150	3	21	3	6	1.0	2.0	0.5	0	–
43581	Crackers, wheat thins, original	16 ea	29	136	2	20	1	6	0.9	2.0	0.4	0	0
43508	Crackers, whole wheat	2 ea	8	35	1	5	1	1	0.3	0.5	0.5	0	0
Muffins													
42149	English Muffin, mixed grain	1 ea	66	155	6	31	2	1	0.2	0.5	0.4	0	0
71034	English Muffin, sourdough, enrich	1 ea	57	134	4	26	2	1	0.1	0.2	0.5	0	0
42153	English Muffin, wheat	1 ea	57	127	5	26	3	1	0.2	0.2	0.5	0	–

PAGE KEY: A-154 Granola Bars, Cereal Bars, Diet Bars, Scones, and Tarts A-154 Meals and Dishes A-160 Meats A-164 Nuts, Seeds, and Products A-166 Poultry A-166 Salad Dressings, Dips, and Mayonnaise A-170 Salads A-170 Sandwiches A-172 Sauces and Gravies A-174 Snack Foods—Chips, Pretzels, Popcorn A-178 Soups, Stews and Chilis A-184 Spices, Flavors, and Seasonings A-184 Sports Bars and Drinks A-186 Supplemental Foods and Formulas A-186 Sweeteners and Sweet Substitutes A-188 Vegetables and Legumes A-200 Weight Loss Bars & Drinks A-200 Miscellaneous

Thia (mg)	Ribo (mg)	Niac (mg NE)	Vit B6 (mg)	Vit B12 (µg)	Fol (µg)	Vit C (mg)	Vit D (IU)	Vit E (mg AT)	Cal (mg)	Iron (mg)	Magn (mg)	Phos (mg)	Pota (mg)	Sodi (mg)	Zinc (mg)	Wat (%)	Alco (g)	Caff (g)
0.27	0.18	2.74	0.01	0.00	47.8	0.0	0.0	0.2	48	1.62	17.7	67	72	390	0.6	29	0.00	0.00
0.05	0.05	0.52	0.00	0.00	12.2	0.0	0.0	0.1	2	0.43	3.2	12	12	66	0.1	6	0.00	0.00
0.10	0.07	1.02	0.01	0.00	19.2	0.0	0.0	0.1	26	0.82	11.5	38	50	132	0.3	37	0.00	0.00
0.09	0.07	0.83	0.00	0.05	21.9	0.1	1.8	0.0	22	0.73	5.3	28	17	104	0.3	43	0.00	0.00
0.11	0.09	0.99	0.01	0.00	23.8	0.0	2.1	0.1	27	0.75	6.0	24	30	134	0.2	37	0.00	0.00
0.10	0.09	1.12	0.09	0.01	20.8	0.1	0.0	0.2	24	0.89	13.8	46	53	127	0.3	38	0.00	0.00
0.20	0.12	1.69	0.01	0.02	40.9	0.0	0.0	0.7	60	1.36	8.6	38	61	241	0.3	34	0.00	0.00
0.20	0.12	1.69	0.01	0.02	40.9	0.0	0.0	0.7	60	1.36	8.6	38	61	241	0.3	34	0.00	0.00
0.07	0.07	0.61	0.01	0.03	16.3	0.0	–	0.5	61	0.67	5.3	42	32	147	0.1	29	0.00	0.00
0.15	0.15	1.23	0.05	0.10	33.0	0.1	12.0	0.7	44	1.13	12.0	226	77	467	0.4	32	0.00	0.00
0.21	0.14	1.25	0.02	0.09	35.3	0.1	3.3	0.2	21	1.15	9.1	60	67	424	0.4	23	0.00	0.00
0.02	0.07	0.31	0.01	0.09	4.5	0.0	–	0.3	6	0.43	3.3	26	22	13	0.2	72	0.00	0.00
–	–	–	–	–	–	0.0	–	–	0	1.44	–	–	–	380	–	38	0.00	0.00
–	–	–	–	–	–	0.0	–	–	34	2.69	–	–	–	1035	–	–	0.00	0.00
–	–	–	–	–	–	0.0	–	–	0	0.72	–	–	–	220	–	29	0.00	0.00
0.14	0.09	1.12	0.01	0.01	26.6	0.0	4.5	0.2	33	0.87	6.4	32	37	146	0.2	32	0.00	0.00
0.20	0.10	1.64	0.00	0.00	36.1	0.0	0.0	0.2	35	1.02	7.6	32	43	231	0.3	35	0.00	0.00
0.27	0.18	2.42	0.01	0.00	54.1	0.0	0.8	0.2	54	1.87	15.4	57	62	310	0.5	31	0.00	0.00
0.33	0.20	4.96	0.25	0.00	40.5	0.0	2.0	1.8	143	3.26	114.8	302	367	645	2.7	33	0.00	0.00
0.69	0.46	6.59	0.03	0.00	41.1	0.0	0.3	0.1	14	3.80	22.1	90	98	7	0.8	37	0.00	0.00
0.64	0.41	5.30	0.05	0.02	36.5	0.0	0.0	0.6	188	4.28	27.0	119	190	756	0.8	34	0.00	0.00
–	–	–	–	–	–	0.0	–	–	0	1.08	–	–	–	270	–	38	0.00	0.00
0.82	0.46	7.40	0.10	0.01	117.7	0.0	15.4	0.6	245	6.61	49.7	159	239	931	1.3	6	0.00	0.00
–	–	–	–	0.00	–	0.0	–	–	0	0.00	–	0	35	410	–	13	0.00	0.00
0.80	0.54	6.55	0.03	0.00	132.2	0.0	0.0	0.1	26	5.34	27.6	120	132	32	0.8	8	0.00	0.00
0.02	0.00	0.00	–	–	–	0.0	–	–	40	0.00	–	–	–	65	–	–	0.00	0.00
0.05	0.03	0.46	0.05	0.05	8.0	0.0	0.4	0.3	15	0.47	3.6	22	14	100	0.1	3	0.00	0.00
0.02	0.02	0.28	0.02	0.02	4.8	0.0	0.2	0.2	9	0.28	2.2	13	9	60	0.1	3	0.00	0.00
0.05	0.05	0.56	–	–	10.8	0.0	–	–	8	0.10	–	–	–	170	–	3	0.00	0.00
–	–	–	–	–	–	0.0	–	–	0	1.44	–	–	–	380	–	10	0.00	0.00
0.02	0.03	0.57	0.00	0.00	8.4	0.0	0.0	0.3	3	0.51	4.2	15	19	85	0.1	4	0.00	0.00
0.01	0.00	0.20	0.00	0.00	6.2	0.0	0.0	0.0	5	0.18	3.0	10	10	41	0.1	5	0.00	0.00
0.00	0.00	0.05	0.00	0.00	1.2	0.0	0.0	0.0	1	0.05	0.3	1	1	13	0.0	4	0.00	0.00
0.02	0.01	0.40	0.00	0.00	5.9	0.0	0.0	0.3	7	0.20	3.7	17	16	66	0.1	3	0.00	0.00
0.01	0.00	0.10	0.01	0.00	4.7	0.0	0.0	0.1	3	0.23	7.8	27	32	26	0.2	6	0.00	0.00
0.07	0.05	0.62	0.00	0.00	14.9	0.0	0.0	0.2	14	0.64	3.2	13	15	156	0.1	4	0.00	0.00
0.01	0.00	0.15	0.00	0.00	3.7	0.0	0.0	0.0	4	0.15	0.8	3	22	19	0.0	4	0.00	0.00
0.07	0.05	0.62	0.00	0.00	14.9	0.0	0.0	0.2	14	0.64	3.2	13	15	156	0.1	4	0.00	0.00
0.03	0.05	0.61	0.00	0.00	9.6	0.0	–	–	24	0.64	3.2	48	15	124	0.2	3	0.00	0.00
–	–	–	–	–	–	–	–	–	–	1.44	–	–	95	160	–	4	0.00	0.00
0.09	0.09	1.15	0.02	–	12.2	0.0	–	–	23	1.07	15.1	60	56	168	–	2	0.00	0.00
0.01	0.00	0.36	0.00	0.00	2.2	0.0	0.0	0.1	4	0.25	7.9	24	24	53	0.2	3	0.00	0.00
0.28	0.20	2.35	0.02	0.00	52.8	0.0	0.0	0.2	129	1.99	27.1	53	103	275	0.9	40	0.00	0.00
0.25	0.15	2.21	0.01	0.01	42.2	0.0	0.0	0.1	30	1.41	12.0	76	75	264	0.4	42	0.00	0.00
0.25	0.17	1.90	0.05	0.00	31.4	0.0	0.0	0.3	101	1.63	21.1	61	106	218	0.6	42	0.00	0.00

PAGE KEY: A-108 Beverage and Beverage Mixes A-112 Other Beverages A-112 Beverages, Alcoholic A-114 Candies and Confections, Gum A-114 Cereals, Breakfast Type A-118 Cheese and Cheese Substitutes A-120 Dairy Products and Substitutes A-122 Desserts A-128 Dessert Toppings A-128 Eggs, Substitutes, and Egg Dishes A-130 Ethnic Foods A-130 Fast Foods/Restaurants A-140 Fats, Oils, Margarines, Shortenings, and Substitutes A-142 Fish, Seafood, and Shellfish A-142 Food Additives A-142 Fruit, Vegetable, and Blended Juices A-144 Fruits A-146 Grains, Flours, and Fractions A-148 Grain Products, Prepared and Baked Goods

Code	Food Name	Unit/ Amt	Wt (g)	Energy (Kcal)	Prot (g)	Carb (g)	Fiber (g)	Fat (g)	Sat (g)	Mono (g)	Poly (g)	Chol (mg)	Vit A (RE)
44658	Muffin, apple cinnamon, low fat, prep f/dry mix, 2oz	1 ea	57	140	2	31	1	1	0.0	0.9	0.1	0	0
44665	Muffin, banana nut, prep f/dry mix, 2oz ea	1 ea	57	190	3	29	1	7	1.5	3.0	2.0	5	0
44631	Muffin, basic, low fat, dry mix	100 g	100	377	6	81	2	3	1.1	1.6	0.3	1	0
44516	Muffin, blueberry	1 ea	57	158	3	27	1	4	0.8	1.1	1.4	17	5
44530	Muffin, chocolate chip	1 ea	58	188	4	27	1	7	2.4	2.9	1.6	23	21
44521	Muffin, cornmeal	1 ea	57	174	3	29	2	5	0.8	1.2	1.8	15	21
44529	Muffin, cranberry nut, 2⅝" diameter	1 ea	58	161	3	28	2	4	0.7	1.4	1.2	17	5
44541	Muffin, oat bran, dry mix	100 g	100	433	7	71	4	14	3.7	5.2	1.4	10	–
28145	Muffin, raisin bran	1 ea	71	150	5	32	4	2	0.0	–	–	0	0
44531	Muffin, whole wheat	1 ea	47	140	4	20	2	6	1.3	2.3	1.6	20	18
Pancakes, French Toast, and Waffles													
45032	Crepe, fruit filled	1 ea	78	145	4	21	1	6	1.4	2.4	1.3	60	75
42156	French Toast, homemade w/2% milk	1 pce	65	149	5	16	1	7	1.8	2.9	1.7	75	84
42155	French Toast, rth, fzn	1 pce	59	126	4	19	1	4	0.9	1.2	0.7	48	32
45023	Pancakes, blueberry, prep f/rec, 4	1 ea	38	84	2	11	0	3	0.8	0.9	1.6	21	20
45192	Pancakes, buttermilk	1.5 oz	43	99	3	16	0	3	0.6	1.3	0.9	5	73
353	Pancakes, buttermilk, mini, microwave, fzn, svg	1 ea	54	116	4	22	–	2	0.2	0.7	0.3	–	600
45115	Pancakes, plain, prep f/complete dry mix, 6"	1 ea	77	149	4	28	1	2	0.4	0.7	0.6	9	8
5263	Pancakes, potato, homemade	1 ea	76	207	5	22	2	12	2.3	3.5	5.0	73	11
7819	Pancakes, potato, mix	3 Tbs	24	80	2	18	2	1	0.5	–	–	0	0
45151	Pancakes, swedish, 7", prep f/dry mix	2 ea	80	150	6	20	0	6	3.0	2.0	1.0	125	39
45098	Waffles, apple cinnamon, fzn	2 ea	70	200	5	30	2	7	1.5	4.5	1.0	20	200
45153	Waffles, belgian, 7", prep f/dry mix	1 ea	113	370	10	59	2	10	2.0	5.0	3.0	0	0
45093	Waffles, buttermilk, fzn, Eggo	2 ea	70	190	5	28	2	7	1.5	4.5	1.0	20	200
45003	Waffles, plain, prep f/rec, round, 7" diameter	1 ea	75	218	6	25	1	11	2.1	2.6	5.1	52	50
Pasta													
38390	Pasta, cellophane noodles, dry	0.5 cup	20	70	0	17	–	0	0.0	0.0	0.0	–	–
38346	Pasta, chow mein noodles	100 g	100	499	16	61	7	22	4.6	–	–	0	0
38047	Pasta, egg noodles, enrich, ckd	1 cup	160	213	8	40	2	2	0.5	0.7	0.7	53	10
38160	Pasta, egg noodles, spinach, enrich, ckd	1 cup	160	211	8	39	4	3	0.6	0.8	0.6	53	22
91204	Pasta, elbow, casserole, enrich, dry, all brands	1 oz	28	103	4	21	1	0	0.1	–	–	0	0
91182	Pasta, fettuccine noodles, enrich, dry, all brands	1 oz	28	103	4	21	1	0	0.1	–	–	0	0
38159	Pasta, homemade, prep w/egg, ckd	2 oz	57	74	3	13	2	1	0.2	0.3	0.3	23	10
91211	Pasta, lasagna, enrich, dry, all brands	1 oz	28	103	4	21	1	0	0.1	–	–	0	0
66124	Pasta, lasagna, wheat free, low prot, dry	2 oz	57	194	0	48	0	0	0.0	–	–	0	–
91296	Pasta, linguine noodles, enrich, dry, all brands	1 oz	28	103	4	21	1	0	0.1	–	–	0	0
38102	Pasta, macaroni noodles, enrich, ckd	1 cup	140	197	7	40	2	1	0.1	0.1	0.4	0	0
91206	Pasta, mostaccioli rigati, enrich, dry, all brands	1 oz	28	103	4	21	1	0	0.1	–	–	0	0
38391	Pasta, noodles, Chinese, dry	0.5 cup	45	150	5	34	6	1	0.0	–	–	–	–
38092	Pasta, noodles, fresh refrigerated, ckd	2 oz	57	74	3	14	1	1	0.1	0.1	0.2	19	3
91197	Pasta, penne rigate, enrich, dry, all brands	1 oz	28	103	4	21	1	0	0.1	–	–	0	0
38067	Pasta, ramen noodles, ckd	1 cup	227	154	3	20	1	7	1.7	1.2	3.3	0	2
57412	Pasta, ravioli, cheese, square, preckd, Bernardi	9 pce	146	292	15	39	1	8	4.8	–	–	63	–
57419	Pasta, ravioli, florentine, round, jumbo, preckd, Bernardi	1 cup	214	370	21	53	3	10	6.0	–	–	60	150
38551	Pasta, rice noodle, ckd	1 cup	176	192	2	44	2	0	0.0	0.0	0.0	0	0
91193	Pasta, rotini noodles, enrich, dry, all brands	1 oz	28	103	4	21	1	0	0.1	–	–	0	0
91327	Pasta, shells, jumbo, enrich, dry, all brands	1 oz	28	103	4	21	1	0	0.1	–	–	0	0
38121	Pasta, spaghetti noodles, enrich, ckd w/add salt	1 cup	140	197	7	40	2	1	0.1	0.1	0.4	0	0
38118	Pasta, spaghetti noodles, enrich, ckd w/o add salt	1 cup	140	197	7	40	2	1	0.1	0.1	0.4	0	0

PAGE KEY: A-154 Granola Bars, Cereal Bars, Diet Bars, Scones, and Tarts A-154 Meals and Dishes A-160 Meats A-164 Nuts, Seeds, and Products A-166 Poultry A-166 Salad Dressings, Dips, and Mayonnaise A-170 Salads A-170 Sandwiches A-172 Sauces and Gravies A-174 Snack Foods—Chips, Pretzels, Popcorn A-178 Soups, Stews and Chilis A-184 Spices, Flavors, and Seasonings A-184 Sports Bars and Drinks A-186 Supplemental Foods and Formulas A-186 Sweeteners and Sweet Substitutes A-188 Vegetables and Legumes A-200 Weight Loss Bars & Drinks A-200 Miscellaneous

Thia (mg)	Ribo (mg)	Niac (mg NE)	Vit B6 (mg)	Vit B12 (μg)	Fol (μg)	Vit C (mg)	Vit D (IU)	Vit E (mg AT)	Cal (mg)	Iron (mg)	Magn (mg)	Phos (mg)	Pota (mg)	Sodi (mg)	Zinc (mg)	Wat (%)	Alco (g)	Caff (g)
–	–	–	–	–	–	0.0	–	–	59	0.46	–	140	40	320	–	39	0.00	0.00
–	–	–	–	–	–	0.0	–	–	30	0.62	–	110	70	370	–	30	0.00	0.00
–	–	–	–	–	–	0.0	–	–	183	0.93	–	452	97	934	–	8	0.00	0.00
0.07	0.07	0.62	0.00	0.33	25.6	0.6	9.1	0.6	32	0.92	9.1	112	70	255	0.3	38	0.00	0.00
0.17	0.18	1.37	0.02	0.09	7.5	0.2	18.6	0.7	91	1.51	16.1	87	92	117	0.4	32	0.00	0.69
0.15	0.18	1.15	0.05	0.05	35.3	0.0	11.4	1.0	42	1.60	18.2	162	39	297	0.3	33	0.00	0.00
0.07	0.07	0.63	0.00	0.34	9.3	0.6	11.6	0.6	33	0.93	9.3	114	71	259	0.3	38	0.00	0.00
0.25	0.18	1.99	–	–	–	–	–	–	35	2.79	–	–	144	672	–	7	0.00	0.00
0.15	0.17	2.00	0.20	0.89	40.0	0.0	–	–	100	2.70	80.0	–	–	155	2.2	42	0.00	0.00
0.07	0.09	1.17	0.07	0.07	8.5	0.1	9.4	0.9	102	0.99	31.3	123	119	140	0.7	34	0.00	0.00
0.07	0.15	0.60	0.03	0.18	9.2	4.1	15.6	1.0	38	0.67	7.9	59	89	72	0.3	61	0.00	0.00
0.12	0.20	1.05	0.05	0.20	27.9	0.2	7.5	0.7	65	1.09	11.0	76	87	311	0.4	55	0.00	0.00
0.15	0.21	1.61	0.28	0.99	30.7	0.2	3.8	0.4	63	1.29	10.0	82	79	292	0.5	53	0.00	0.00
0.07	0.10	0.57	0.01	0.07	13.7	0.8	9.1	0.4	78	0.64	6.1	57	52	157	0.2	53	0.00	0.00
0.10	0.11	1.47	0.15	0.43	22.1	0.6	–	0.0	15	1.32	7.7	145	44	225	0.3	47	0.00	
–	–	–	–	–	–	–	–	–	–	1.46	–	–	–	290	–	48	0.00	0.00
0.15	0.17	1.32	0.07	0.15	28.5	0.2	39.0	0.7	97	1.20	15.4	257	135	484	0.3	53	0.00	0.00
0.10	0.12	1.62	0.28	0.14	17.5	16.7	8.7	1.5	18	1.19	25.1	84	597	386	0.6	47	0.00	0.00
–	–	–	–	0.00	–	2.4	–	–	0	0.36	–	–	–	500	–	10	0.00	0.00
–	–	–	–	–	–	0.0	–	–	27	1.09	–	80	100	210	–	59	0.00	0.00
0.30	0.34	4.00	0.40	1.20	30.0	0.0	–	–	100	3.59	–	200	90	400	–	37	0.00	0.00
–	–	–	–	–	–	0.0	–	–	49	2.50	–	590	220	1360	–	28	0.00	0.00
0.30	0.34	4.00	0.40	1.20	40.0	0.0	–	–	100	3.59	–	200	80	420	–	40	0.00	0.00
0.20	0.25	1.54	0.03	0.18	34.5	0.3	23.5	1.7	191	1.73	14.2	142	119	383	0.5	42	0.00	0.00
–	–	–	–	–	–	–	–	–	–	–	–	–	–	0	–	13	0.00	0.00
–	–	–	–	–	–	0.0	–	–	24	1.62	–	–	–	747	–	–	0.00	0.00
0.30	0.12	2.38	0.05	0.14	102.4	0.0	6.5	0.1	19	2.53	30.4	110	45	11	1.0	69	0.00	0.00
0.38	0.20	2.35	0.18	0.21	102.4	0.0	0.0	0.1	30	1.74	38.4	91	59	19	1.0	69	0.00	0.00
0.23	0.12	1.51	–	–	60.7	0.0	–	–	5	0.91	15.2	40	41	1	0.3	10	0.00	0.00
0.23	0.12	1.51	–	–	60.7	0.0	–	–	5	0.91	15.2	40	41	1	0.3	10	0.00	0.00
0.10	0.10	0.70	0.01	0.05	24.4	0.0	0.0	0.1	6	0.66	7.9	29	12	47	0.2	69	0.00	0.00
0.23	0.12	1.51	–	–	60.7	0.0	–	–	5	0.91	15.2	40	41	1	0.3	10	0.00	0.00
–	–	–	–	–	–	0.5	–	–	3	0.68	–	–	52	–	–	14	0.00	0.00
0.23	0.12	1.51	–	–	60.7	0.0	–	–	5	0.91	15.2	40	41	1	0.3	10	0.00	0.00
0.28	0.14	2.33	0.05	0.00	107.8	0.0	0.0	0.2	10	1.96	25.2	76	43	1	0.7	66	0.00	0.00
0.23	0.12	1.51	–	–	60.7	0.0	–	–	5	0.91	15.2	40	41	1	0.3	10	0.00	0.00
–	–	–	–	–	–	–	–	–	20	1.79	–	–	–	0	–	9	0.00	0.00
0.11	0.09	0.56	0.01	0.07	36.3	0.0	0.0	0.1	3	0.64	10.2	36	14	3	0.3	69	0.00	0.00
0.23	0.12	1.51	–	–	60.7	0.0	–	–	5	0.91	15.2	40	41	1	0.3	10	0.00	0.00
0.01	0.00	0.25	0.00	0.00	3.2	0.0	0.0	2.3	13	0.38	10.4	24	49	802	0.2	86	0.00	0.00
–	–	–	–	–	–	–	–	–	115	0.79	–	–	–	285	–	56	0.00	0.00
–	–	–	–	–	–	0.0	–	–	200	2.70	–	–	–	440	–	–	0.00	0.00
0.02	0.00	0.12	0.00	0.00	5.3	0.0	–	–	7	0.25	5.3	35	7	33	0.4	74	0.00	0.00
0.23	0.12	1.51	–	–	60.7	0.0	–	–	5	0.91	15.2	40	41	1	0.3	10	0.00	0.00
0.23	0.12	1.51	–	–	60.7	0.0	–	–	5	0.91	15.2	40	41	1	0.3	10	0.00	0.00
0.28	0.14	2.33	0.05	0.00	107.8	0.0	0.0	0.2	10	1.96	25.2	76	43	140	0.7	66	0.00	0.00
0.28	0.14	2.33	0.05	0.00	107.8	0.0	0.0	0.2	10	1.96	25.2	76	43	1	0.7	66	0.00	0.00

PAGE KEY: A-108 Beverage and Beverage Mixes A-112 Other Beverages A-112 Beverages, Alcoholic A-114 Candies and Confections, Gum A-114 Cereals, Breakfast Type A-118 Cheese and Cheese Substitutes A-120 Dairy Products and Substitutes A-122 Desserts A-128 Dessert Toppings A-128 Eggs, Substitutes, and Egg Dishes A-130 Ethnic Foods A-130 Fast Foods/Restaurants A-140 Fats, Oils, Margarines, Shortenings, and Substitutes A-142 Fish, Seafood, and Shellfish A-142 Food Additives A-142 Fruit, Vegetable, and Blended Juices A-144 Fruits A-146 Grains, Flours, and Fractions A-148 Grain Products, Prepared and Baked Goods

Code	Food Name	Unit/ Amt	Wt (g)	Energy (Kcal)	Prot (g)	Carb (g)	Fiber (g)	Fat (g)	Sat (g)	Mono (g)	Poly (g)	Chol (mg)	Vit A (RE)
38066	Pasta, spaghetti noodles, spinach, ckd	1 cup	140	182	6	37	5	1	0.1	0.1	0.4	0	22
38060	Pasta, spaghetti noodles, whole wheat, ckd	1 cup	140	174	7	37	6	1	0.1	0.1	0.3	0	0
38407	Pasta, udon noodles, Japanese, ckd	100 g	100	101	2	20	0	0	–	–	–	–	0
91299	Pasta, vermicelli, enrich, dry, all brands	1 oz	28	103	4	21	1	0	0.1	–	–	0	0
91198	Pasta, ziti, enrich, dry, all brands	1 oz	28	103	4	21	1	0	0.1	–	–	0	0
Rice													
90200	Pasta, noodles, mung bean, dehyd	1 cup	140	491	0	121	1	0	0.0	0.0	0.0	0	0
38341	Rice, basmati, brown, Calif, organic, dry	0.25 cup	46	158	4	34	2	2	0.4	0.5	0.6	0	0
38010	Rice, brown, long grain, ckd	1 cup	195	216	5	45	4	2	0.4	0.6	0.6	0	0
38082	Rice, brown, med grain, ckd	0.5 cup	98	109	2	23	2	1	0.2	0.3	0.3	0	0
38013	Rice, white, long grain, ckd	1 cup	158	205	4	45	1	0	0.1	0.1	0.1	0	0
38157	Rice, white, short grain, ckd	1 cup	186	242	4	53	2	0	0.1	0.1	0.1	0	0
38021	Rice, wild, ckd	1 cup	164	166	7	35	3	1	0.1	0.1	0.3	0	0
Stuffing and Mixes													
38491	Baking Mix, dry, Bisquick	0.33 cup	40	162	3	24	1	6	1.6	2.5	0.5	0	0
28059	Baking Mix, rducd fat, Bisquick	0.33 cup	40	150	3	28	0	2	0.5	–	–	0	–
38387	Cornmeal Mix, yellow, dry, Aunt Jemima	3 Tbs	25	83	2	19	1	0	0.1	0.1	0.3	0	14
42037	Stuffing, bread, prep f/dry mix	0.5 cup	100	178	3	22	3	9	1.7	3.8	2.6	0	82
57604	Stuffing, mushroom & onion, prep f/dry mix w/marg	0.5 cup	103	180	4	20	1	9	1.5	–	–	0	60
Tortillas and Taco/Tostada Shells													
90644	Taco Shells, bkd, lrg, 6½″ diameter	1 ea	21	98	2	13	2	5	0.7	1.9	1.8	0	0
42449	Taco Shells, soft, Old El Paso	2 ea	50	160	3	26	0	4	1.0	1.8	1.8	0	0
42023	Tortilla, corn, med, 6″ diameter	1 ea	26	58	1	12	1	1	0.1	0.2	0.3	0	0
42025	Tortilla, flour, 10″ diameter	1 ea	72	234	6	40	2	5	1.3	2.7	0.8	0	0
42079	Tortilla, whole wheat	1 ea	35	73	3	20	2	0	0.1	0.1	0.2	0	0
GRANOLA BARS, CEREAL BARS, DIET BARS, SCONES, AND TARTS													
23219	Bar, cereal, apple cinnamon	1 ea	37	136	2	27	1	3	0.6	1.9	0.3	0	225
53227	Bar, cereal, mixed berry	1 ea	37	137	2	27	1	3	0.6	1.9	0.4	0	150
44221	Bar, chocolate chip, whole grain	1 ea	37	162	2	25	1	6	3.5	1.9	0.3	50	6
23100	Bar, granola, almond, hard	1 ea	24	117	2	15	1	6	3.0	1.8	0.9	0	1
47591	Bar, granola, cinnamon, Nature Valley	2 ea	42	195	3	29	2	7	0.8	4.7	1.6	0	–
23095	Bar, granola, peanut butter, chocolate coated, soft	1 ea	37	187	4	20	1	11	6.2	2.4	0.7	4	2
23059	Bar, granola, plain, hard	1 ea	24	115	2	16	1	5	0.6	1.1	3.0	0	4
42071	Scones	1 ea	42	150	4	19	1	6	2.0	2.6	1.3	49	69
49074	Tart, cherry, sweet red, healthy, fat free, Health Valley	1 ea	52	150	3	35	3	0	0.0	0.0	0.0	0	20
MEALS AND DISHES													
Canned Meals and Dishes													
7037	Beans, baked, homemade	1 cup	253	382	14	54	14	13	4.9	5.4	1.9	13	0
91532	Beans, baked, vegetarian, cnd, Bush's Best	0.5 cup	130	130	5	24	6	0	0.0	0.0	0.0	0	160
50987	Beans, baked, w/pork, cnd, B&M	0.5 cup	131	180	8	33	7	2	0.5	–	–	3	0
91057	Dish, chicken, sweet & sour, w/veg & fruit, cnd	1 ea	254	165	6	32	–	2	–	–	–	23	0
57660	Dish, pasta, w/meatballs, in tomato sauce, cnd	100 g	100	103	4	12	3	4	1.6	1.7	0.2	8	38
7004	Pork & Beans, in tomato sauce, cnd	1 cup	253	248	13	49	12	3	1.0	1.1	0.3	18	30
Dry and Prepared Pasta and Pasta/Rice Dishes													
57074	Dish, macaroni & cheese, original, deluxe, prep f/mix	1 cup	175	320	14	44	1	10	6.0	–	–	25	100
Dry and Prepared Rice/Grain Dishes													
56131	Dish, rice, Spanish	1 cup	243	216	5	42	3	4	0.6	1.5	1.4	0	115
38645	Falafel, dry, Near East	0.25 cup	34	102	10	18	5	1	0.2	0.3	0.5	0	6

PAGE KEY: A-154 Granola Bars, Cereal Bars, Diet Bars, Scones, and Tarts A-154 Meals and Dishes A-160 Meats A-164 Nuts, Seeds, and Products A-166 Poultry A-166 Salad Dressings, Dips, and Mayonnaise A-170 Salads A-170 Sandwiches A-172 Sauces and Gravies A-174 Snack Foods—Chips, Pretzels, Popcorn A-178 Soups, Stews and Chilis A-184 Spices, Flavors, and Seasonings A-184 Sports Bars and Drinks A-186 Supplemental Foods and Formulas A-186 Sweeteners and Sweet Substitutes A-188 Vegetables and Legumes A-200 Weight Loss Bars & Drinks A-200 Miscellaneous

Thia (mg)	Ribo (mg)	Niac (mg NE)	Vit B6 (mg)	Vit B12 (µg)	Fol (µg)	Vit C (mg)	Vit D (IU)	Vit E (mg AT)	Cal (mg)	Iron (mg)	Magn (mg)	Phos (mg)	Pota (mg)	Sodi (mg)	Zinc (mg)	Wat (%)	Alco (g)	Caff (g)
0.14	0.14	2.14	0.12	0.00	16.8	0.0	0.0	0.0	42	1.46	86.8	151	81	20	1.5	68	0.00	0.00
0.15	0.05	0.99	0.10	0.00	7.0	0.0	0.0	0.1	21	1.48	42.0	125	62	4	1.1	67	0.00	0.00
0.01	0.00	0.10	–	–	–	0.0	–	–	7	0.20	–	18	6	45	–	76	0.00	0.00
0.23	0.12	1.51	–	–	60.7	0.0	–	–	5	0.91	15.2	40	41	1	0.3	10	0.00	0.00
0.23	0.12	1.51	–	–	60.7	0.0	–	–	5	0.91	15.2	40	41	1	0.3	10	0.00	0.00
0.20	0.00	0.28	0.07	0.00	2.8	0.0	0.0	0.2	35	3.03	4.2	45	14	14	0.6	13	0.00	0.00
–	–	–	–	–	–	0.4	–	–	4	0.69	–	–	–	3	–	13	0.00	0.00
0.18	0.05	2.98	0.28	0.00	7.8	0.0	0.0	0.4	20	0.81	83.8	162	84	10	1.2	73	0.00	0.00
0.10	0.00	1.29	0.15	0.00	3.9	0.0	0.0	0.3	10	0.51	42.9	75	77	1	0.6	73	0.00	0.00
0.25	0.01	2.32	0.15	0.00	91.6	0.0	0.0	0.1	16	1.89	19.0	68	55	2	0.8	68	0.00	0.00
0.31	0.02	2.77	0.10	0.00	109.7	0.0	0.0	0.1	2	2.72	14.9	61	48	0	0.7	69	0.00	0.00
0.09	0.14	2.10	0.21	0.00	42.6	0.0	0.0	0.4	5	0.98	52.5	134	166	5	2.2	74	0.00	0.00
0.20	0.15	1.67	–	–	–	0.0	–	–	60	1.39	–	–	50	499	–	16	0.00	0.00
0.15	0.10	1.60	–	–	–	–	–	–	40	1.44	–	–	30	460	–	–	0.00	0.00
0.25	0.15	2.08	0.05	0.00	97.2	0.0	0.0	0.0	75	1.67	7.9	140	47	319	0.2	10	0.00	0.00
0.14	0.10	1.48	0.03	0.00	101.0	0.0	0.0	1.4	32	1.09	12.0	42	74	543	0.3	65	0.00	0.00
0.09	0.07	0.80	–	–	16.0	0.0	–	–	20	1.08	–	40	85	480	–	66	0.00	0.00
0.05	0.00	0.28	0.05	0.00	22.0	0.0	0.0	0.8	34	0.51	22.0	52	38	77	0.3	6	0.00	0.00
–	–	–	–	–	–	0.0	–	–	80	1.79	–	–	–	350	–	31	0.00	0.00
0.02	0.01	0.38	0.05	0.00	29.6	0.0	0.0	0.0	46	0.36	16.9	82	40	42	0.2	44	0.00	0.00
0.37	0.20	2.56	0.03	0.00	88.6	0.0	0.0	0.7	90	2.38	18.7	89	94	344	0.5	27	0.00	0.00
0.10	0.01	0.85	0.07	0.00	8.4	0.0	0.0	0.4	10	0.73	25.5	82	82	171	0.5	31	0.00	0.00
0.37	0.40	4.98	0.51	0.00	40.0	0.0	0.0	0.0	15	1.79	10.0	38	73	110	1.5	14	0.00	0.00
0.37	0.40	4.98	0.51	0.00	40.0	0.0	–	0.0	14	1.80	9.6	36	70	110	1.5	14	0.00	0.00
0.05	0.07	0.56	0.03	0.05	4.8	17.2	0.0	4.0	290	3.39	25.9	77	103	104	0.5	5	0.00	
0.07	0.01	0.14	0.00	0.00	2.8	0.0	0.0	0.4	8	0.58	19.1	54	64	60	0.4	3	0.00	0.00
0.07	0.01	–	–	–	–	–	–	–	19	0.67	–	–	104	123	–	4	0.00	0.00
0.03	0.07	1.21	0.03	0.00	9.2	0.2	0.0	0.5	40	0.52	24.6	83	124	71	0.5	3	0.00	2.20
0.05	0.02	0.38	0.01	0.00	5.6	0.2	0.0	0.3	15	0.72	23.8	68	82	72	0.5	4	0.00	0.00
0.15	0.15	1.21	0.02	0.10	7.9	0.1	6.7	0.7	80	1.32	7.1	74	49	171	0.3	27	0.00	0.00
–	–	–	–	–	–	1.2	–	–	0	0.72	–	–	–	30	–	26	0.00	0.00
0.34	0.11	1.02	0.23	0.00	121.4	2.8	0.0	1.3	154	5.03	108.8	276	906	1068	1.8	65	0.00	0.00
–	–	–	–	–	–	0.0	–	–	40	0.54	–	–	–	–	–	–	0.00	0.00
–	–	–	–	–	–	0.0	–	–	60	2.70	–	–	–	430	–	65	0.00	0.00
–	–	–	–	–	–	30.2	–	–	–	–	–	–	–	564	–	84	0.00	0.00
0.07	0.05	1.32	0.07	0.23	25.0	3.0	–	0.5	11	0.93	14.0	46	165	418	0.7	78	0.00	0.00
0.12	0.11	1.25	0.17	0.00	58.2	7.8	0.0	1.4	142	8.30	88.5	296	759	1113	14.8	73	0.00	0.00
0.37	0.25	3.00	–	–	60.0	0.0	–	–	200	1.79	40.0	450	190	730	–	60	0.00	0.00
0.23	0.07	2.99	0.31	0.00	20.2	37.3	–	1.4	77	2.42	39.3	90	537	295	0.9	78	0.00	0.00
0.23	0.27	1.77	–	–	–	0.5	–	–	48	2.67	–	224	374	559	–	7	0.00	0.00

PAGE KEY: A-108 Beverage and Beverage Mixes A-112 Other Beverages A-112 Beverages, Alcoholic A-114 Candies and Confections, Gum A-114 Cereals, Breakfast Type A-118 Cheese and Cheese Substitutes A-120 Dairy Products and Substitutes A-122 Desserts A-128 Dessert Toppings A-128 Eggs, Substitutes, and Egg Dishes A-130 Ethnic Foods A-130 Fast Foods/Restaurants A-140 Fats, Oils, Margarines, Shortenings, and Substitutes A-142 Fish, Seafood, and Shellfish A-142 Food Additives A-142 Fruit, Vegetable, and Blended Juices A-144 Fruits A-146 Grains, Flours, and Fractions A-148 Grain Products, Prepared and Baked Goods

Code	Food Name	Unit/Amt	Wt (g)	Energy (Kcal)	Prot (g)	Carb (g)	Fiber (g)	Fat (g)	Sat (g)	Mono (g)	Poly (g)	Chol (mg)	Vit A (RE)
Frozen/Refrigerated Breakfasts													
56991	Bagel Bites, eggs bacon cheddar	4 pce	88	200	10	24	2	8	3.5	–	–	10	60
70753	Burrito, breakfast w/scrambled eggs, Great Starts	1 ea	99	200	8	25	2	8	3.0	–	–	60	20
70830	Eggs, scrambled, low fat, Great Starts	1 ea	170	240	12	18	2	13	3.0	–	–	40	225
70129	Eggs, scrambled, w/sausage & hashbrowns, fzn	1 ea	177	419	16	19	1	32	9.2	11.8	7.9	257	102
70157	French Toast, w/sausage, fzn	1 ea	184	432	22	34	1	23	7.4	9.8	3.0	251	83
70158	Pancakes, w/sausage, fzn	1 ea	170	477	15	47	1	25	6.9	10.9	5.2	90	128
Frozen/Refrigerated Dinners													
4125	Dinner, beef, cntry fried steak, w/potatoes, hmestyle fzn	1 ea	454	560	22	61	7	25	10.0	–	–	50	1100
70333	Dinner, beef, pepper steak, fzn	1 ea	283	94	5	19	4	0	0.0	–	–	0	60
11118	Dinner, beef, pot roast, fzn, Healthy Choice	1 ea	312	300	20	41	8	6	2.0	–	–	40	250
70001	Dinner, beef, sirloin, chpd, w/mash potato gravy veg fzn	1 ea	347	551	27	47	6	29	13.5	10.5	2.2	141	164
16247	Dinner, chicken, white meat, fried, ckd f/fzn	1 ea	248	480	18	40	2	28	11.0	–	–	100	0
70766	Dinner, meatloaf, Swanson	1 ea	468	640	24	65	6	31	14.0	–	–	45	60
11071	Dinner, steak, salisbury, Swanson	1 ea	461	610	34	46	10	33	17.0	–	–	80	150
56938	Lunchables, bologna, w/American cheese, pkg	1 ea	128	450	18	19	0	34	15.0	–	–	85	60
Frozen/Refrigerated Dishes													
70962	Burrito, beef & chse, w/grn chili, Marquez Primera, fzn	1 ea	142	324	15	40	–	12	3.8	3.4	2.7	27	0
56668	Corn Dog	1 ea	175	460	17	56	–	19	5.2	9.1	3.5	79	61
4101	Dish, broccoli, au gratin, fzn	4 oz	113	100	5	8	2	5	2.0	–	–	10	40
16167	Dish, chicken & noodles, casserole, Swanson	1 ea	284	300	18	36	2	9	3.0	–	–	50	20
1722	Dish, chicken, teriyaki, w/rice, bwl, fzn, Healthy Choice	1 ea	269	270	17	41	4	4	1.0	–	–	30	400
83009	Dish, egg roll, pork, restaurant, ckd, La Choy	1 ea	170	220	5	24	2	11	2.5	–	–	10	60
4301	Dish, enchilada, beef, fzn, Ortega	1 ea	266	360	12	49	5	13	5.0	–	–	25	200
4310	Dish, fajitas, steak, skillet, fzn, Ortega	2 oz	57	35	4	3	1	1	0.5	–	–	5	60
70749	Dish, fish & chips, Swanson	1 ea	156	350	16	38	4	15	4.5	–	–	30	40
70734	Dish, pot pie, beef, Swanson	1 ea	198	415	11	41	2	23	9.0	–	–	25	150
16163	Dish, pot pie, chicken, Swanson	1 ea	198	410	10	43	2	22	9.0	–	–	25	200
16915	Dish, pot pie, turkey, Swanson	1 ea	198	400	10	42	3	21	8.0	–	–	25	100
42739	Nachos, stuffed w/nacho cheese, fzn, Totino's	6 ea	87	220	7	26	1	10	3.5	–	–	15	0
83024	Perogies, potato cheese, ckd f/fzn	6 ea	130	230	7	42	3	3	1.0	–	–	10	0
Frozen/Refrigerated Dinners/Dishes—Vegetarian													
83094	Burrito, bean & rice, w/cheddar, organic, fzn	1 ea	170	280	10	43	6	8	2.5	0.0	0.0	10	60
7762	Corn Dog, vegetarian, fzn	1 ea	71	159	8	22	1	4	0.5	1.2	2.5	0	0
7556	Dish, pot pie, vegetarian	1 ea	227	510	14	41	5	32	8.6	12.4	9.6	20	785
57514	Dish, quiche, spinach, vegetarian	2 oz	57	136	4	7	0	10	4.8	3.5	1.4	63	165
Homemade and Generic Meals and Dishes													
66025	Burrito, bean	2 ea	217	447	14	71	8	13	6.9	4.7	1.2	4	35
56629	Burrito, bean & cheese	2 ea	186	378	15	55	–	12	6.8	2.5	1.8	28	154
66024	Burrito, beef	2 ea	220	524	27	59	2	21	10.5	7.4	0.9	64	26
56634	Chimichanga, beef	1 ea	174	425	20	43	2	20	8.5	8.1	1.1	9	14
56635	Chimichanga, beef & cheese	1 ea	183	443	20	39	–	23	11.2	9.4	0.7	51	137
11013	Curry, beef	1 cup	236	436	27	13	3	31	7.0	14.5	7.4	69	367
56156	Dish, beef & noodles, w/gravy	1 cup	249	302	31	21	1	9	3.5	3.8	0.6	91	4
56168	Dish, beef & rice, w/soy sauce	1 cup	244	345	22	23	1	18	6.5	6.7	2.7	69	3
56197	Dish, chicken & noodles, w/cheese sauce	1 cup	224	330	25	32	1	11	4.5	3.5	1.8	95	54
56200	Dish, chicken & noodles, w/tomato sauce	1 cup	224	291	20	31	2	9	2.1	3.8	2.5	74	143
15904	Dish, chicken, cacciatore	1 cup	244	459	42	13	2	26	6.3	9.7	7.2	128	132
56112	Dish, chili rellenos	1 ea	143	365	17	8	1	30	12.5	9.0	6.7	168	250

PAGE KEY: A-154 Granola Bars, Cereal Bars, Diet Bars, Scones, and Tarts A-154 Meals and Dishes A-160 Meats A-164 Nuts, Seeds, and Products A-166 Poultry A-166 Salad Dressings, Dips, and Mayonnaise A-170 Salads A-170 Sandwiches A-172 Sauces and Gravies A-174 Snack Foods—Chips, Pretzels, Popcorn A-178 Soups, Stews and Chilis A-184 Spices, Flavors, and Seasonings A-184 Sports Bars and Drinks A-186 Supplemental Foods and Formulas A-186 Sweeteners and Sweet Substitutes A-188 Vegetables and Legumes A-200 Weight Loss Bars & Drinks A-200 Miscellaneous

Thia (mg)	Ribo (mg)	Niac (mg NE)	Vit B6 (mg)	Vit B12 (µg)	Fol (µg)	Vit C (mg)	Vit D (IU)	Vit E (mg AT)	Cal (mg)	Iron (mg)	Magn (mg)	Phos (mg)	Pota (mg)	Sodi (mg)	Zinc (mg)	Wat (%)	Alco (g)	Caff (g)
–	–	–	–	–	–	1.2	–	–	60	1.08	–	–	105	610	–	–	0.00	0.00
–	–	–	–	–	–	2.4	–	–	80	1.44	–	–	–	510	–	57	0.00	0.00
–	–	–	–	–	–	4.8	–	–	40	0.72	–	–	–	620	–	73	0.00	0.00
0.36	0.40	2.96	0.27	1.09	23.2	4.1	–	2.3	60	2.04	23.9	216	463	843	1.7	61	0.00	0.00
0.62	0.60	4.21	0.27	1.55	37.4	1.2	–	0.8	148	2.85	30.6	263	373	1068	2.2	55	0.00	0.00
0.57	0.43	3.99	0.18	1.03	16.4	1.1	–	1.9	89	2.55	22.9	188	294	1197	1.6	46	0.00	0.00
–	–	–	–	–	–	3.6	–	–	200	2.70	–	–	910	1750	–	76	0.00	0.00
–	–	–	–	–	–	12.7	–	–	5	6.28	–	–	–	2468	–	91	0.00	0.00
–	–	–	–	–	–	18.0	–	–	20	1.79	–	–	–	600	–	78	0.00	0.00
0.43	0.38	5.71	0.67	2.38	73.8	22.8	–	0.9	52	4.15	73.8	328	812	1982	5.0	68	0.00	0.00
–	–	–	–	–	–	2.4	–	–	40	1.44	–	–	–	1100	–	64	0.00	0.00
–	–	–	–	–	–	18.0	–	–	150	5.40	–	–	–	1870	–	73	0.00	0.00
–	–	–	–	–	–	4.8	–	–	200	5.40	–	–	–	1620	–	74	0.00	0.00
–	–	–	–	–	–	0.0	–	–	300	2.70	–	–	–	1620	–	–	0.00	0.00
–	–	–	–	–	–	–	–	–	125	2.84	–	–	–	768	–	51	0.00	0.00
0.28	0.69	4.15	0.09	0.43	103.2	0.0	–	0.7	102	6.17	17.5	166	262	973	1.3	47	0.00	0.00
–	–	–	–	–	–	18.0	–	–	150	0.36	–	–	220	370	–	83	0.00	0.00
–	–	–	–	–	–	0.0	–	–	200	3.59	–	–	–	940	–	76	0.00	0.00
–	–	–	–	–	–	12.0	–	–	20	1.08	–	–	–	570	–	76	0.00	0.00
–	–	–	–	–	–	0.0	–	–	20	1.08	–	–	–	390	–	–	0.00	0.00
–	–	–	–	–	–	9.0	–	–	150	1.79	–	–	–	1460	–	–	0.00	0.00
–	–	–	–	–	–	6.0	–	–	0	0.36	–	–	–	190	–	–	0.00	0.00
–	–	–	–	–	–	1.2	–	–	150	1.44	–	–	–	930	–	54	0.00	0.00
–	–	–	–	–	–	0.0	–	–	20	1.79	–	–	–	740	–	61	0.00	0.00
–	–	–	–	–	–	1.2	–	–	20	1.79	–	–	–	780	–	60	0.00	0.00
–	–	–	–	–	–	2.4	–	–	20	1.79	–	–	–	700	–	62	0.00	0.00
–	–	–	–	–	–	0.0	–	–	80	0.72	–	–	–	710	–	49	0.00	0.00
–	–	–	–	–	–	1.2	–	–	0	1.79	–	–	–	480	–	–	0.00	0.00
–	–	–	–	–	–	4.8	–	–	100	2.70	–	–	–	540	–	63	0.00	0.00
0.10	0.05	0.00	–	–	–	0.0	–	–	12	0.64	–	113	66	527	0.2	49	0.00	0.00
0.81	0.43	5.17	0.40	1.00	57.8	9.9	8.2	4.2	68	2.96	32.4	263	378	486	1.1	60	0.00	0.00
0.07	0.15	0.44	0.05	0.15	22.5	2.1	–	0.7	98	0.87	16.1	84	110	44	0.5	61	0.00	0.00
0.62	0.61	4.05	0.30	1.09	86.8	2.0	0.0	1.7	113	4.51	86.8	98	653	985	1.5	53	0.00	0.00
0.21	0.70	3.56	0.23	0.88	74.4	1.7	–	–	214	2.26	80.0	180	497	1166	1.6	54	0.00	0.00
0.23	0.92	6.44	0.31	1.96	129.8	1.1	–	1.1	84	6.09	81.4	174	739	1492	4.7	50	0.00	0.00
0.49	0.63	5.78	0.28	1.50	83.5	4.7	–	–	63	4.53	62.6	124	586	910	5.0	51	0.00	0.00
0.37	0.86	4.67	0.21	1.29	91.5	2.7	–	–	238	3.83	60.4	187	203	957	3.4	53	0.00	0.00
0.18	0.34	5.42	0.47	3.04	20.3	24.6	–	5.9	44	4.23	59.0	292	978	802	6.1	68	0.00	0.00
0.23	0.28	5.23	0.37	2.82	15.1	0.0	–	0.2	18	4.01	38.3	291	453	606	5.3	73	0.00	0.00
0.15	0.20	5.86	0.28	2.18	19.1	3.0	–	0.9	46	3.16	29.8	191	399	874	4.6	73	0.00	0.00
0.23	0.36	4.88	0.21	0.56	14.0	0.9	–	0.3	215	2.25	46.1	299	321	581	2.0	69	0.00	0.00
0.27	0.23	5.73	0.31	0.20	16.5	11.8	–	2.1	34	2.90	47.2	177	478	658	1.9	72	0.00	0.00
0.18	0.31	13.98	0.72	0.43	16.5	14.8	29.3	3.0	61	3.02	56.1	305	690	247	3.1	66	0.44	0.00
0.07	0.40	0.93	0.25	0.46	29.4	112.9	–	4.7	398	1.67	36.2	307	386	522	2.1	59	0.00	0.00

PAGE KEY: A-108 Beverage and Beverage Mixes A-112 Other Beverages A-112 Beverages, Alcoholic A-114 Candies and Confections, Gum A-114 Cereals, Breakfast Type A-118 Cheese and Cheese Substitutes A-120 Dairy Products and Substitutes A-122 Desserts A-128 Dessert Toppings A-128 Eggs, Substitutes, and Egg Dishes A-130 Ethnic Foods A-130 Fast Foods/Restaurants A-140 Fats, Oils, Margarines, Shortenings, and Substitutes A-142 Fish, Seafood, and Shellfish A-142 Food Additives A-142 Fruit, Vegetable, and Blended Juices A-144 Fruits A-146 Grains, Flours, and Fractions A-148 Grain Products, Prepared and Baked Goods

Code	Food Name	Unit/ Amt	Wt (g)	Energy (Kcal)	Prot (g)	Carb (g)	Fiber (g)	Fat (g)	Sat (g)	Mono (g)	Poly (g)	Chol (mg)	Vit A (RE)
56243	Dish, chop suey, beef, w/o noodles	1 cup	220	271	22	12	3	15	3.7	6.5	3.5	50	116
56234	Dish, chop suey, pork, w/noodles	1 cup	220	448	22	31	4	27	4.8	7.7	12.8	48	19
57517	Dish, creole, shrimp, w/rice	1 cup	243	310	27	28	1	9	1.8	3.8	2.8	181	133
56287	Dish, egg foo young, chicken	1 ea	86	121	8	4	1	8	1.9	2.8	2.3	167	87
56132	Dish, egg foo yung	1 ea	86	113	6	3	1	8	2.0	3.4	2.1	185	86
56126	Dish, egg roll, shrimp	1 ea	64	104	4	10	1	6	1.2	2.7	1.4	40	17
56124	Dish, fajitas, beef	1 ea	223	399	23	36	3	18	5.5	7.6	3.5	45	43
56123	Dish, fajitas, chicken	1 ea	223	363	20	44	5	12	2.3	5.5	3.1	39	65
56181	Dish, ham & potatoes, w/cheese sauce	1 cup	249	385	26	20	2	22	9.8	8.6	2.4	80	103
56108	Dish, lasagna, w/meat, prep f/rec	1 pce	245	392	23	40	3	16	8.0	5.2	0.8	58	158
56071	Dish, lasagna, w/o meat, prep f/rec	1 pce	218	306	16	40	3	10	5.6	2.5	0.6	32	157
56082	Dish, macaroni & cheese, prep w/margarine, f/rec	1 cup	200	302	15	28	1	15	9.0	–	–	45	163
56310	Dish, macaroni & cheese, w/beef, Hamburger Helper	1 cup	243	340	28	22	1	15	7.7	5.1	0.7	92	70
56235	Dish, pork & rice, sweet & sour	1 cup	244	270	13	40	1	6	1.6	2.4	1.7	28	23
56100	Dish, spaghetti, w/meatballs, f/rec	1 cup	248	362	18	28	3	18	4.8	–	–	65	92
11003	Dish, steak, salisbury, w/gravy	1 ea	129	219	16	7	0	14	5.5	5.9	0.6	60	5
11022	Dish, steak, swiss	1 ea	170	177	20	7	1	8	1.9	2.8	2.0	49	207
11008	Dish, stroganoff, beef	1 cup	256	408	26	16	1	27	10.6	7.9	6.3	85	99
56158	Dish, stroganoff, beef, w/noodles	1 cup	256	344	20	23	2	19	7.4	5.6	4.5	74	71
56089	Dish, tuna noodle casserole, f/rec	1 cup	202	238	17	25	1	7	1.9	–	–	41	13
56242	Gumbo, w/rice, New Orleans type	1 cup	244	193	14	17	2	8	1.6	2.6	2.7	40	63
56150	Hash, beef	1 cup	190	312	21	21	2	16	4.9	5.7	3.3	57	0
13093	Hot Dog, chicken, plain, w/bun	1 ea	85	235	9	24	1	11	3.0	5.0	2.2	45	17
56130	Pasta, tortellini, meat	1 cup	190	373	25	33	1	15	5.4	5.7	2.1	240	134
56122	Quesadilla	1 ea	54	183	6	18	1	10	3.5	3.4	2.2	13	41
19400	Shrimp, sweet & sour	1 cup	176	481	12	46	1	30	3.8	9.1	15.5	71	48
56244	Sukiyaki	1 cup	162	172	19	7	1	8	2.9	3.1	0.7	148	256
56315	Sushi, w/egg, rolled in seaweed, w/o veg & fish	1 cup	166	202	9	22	0	8	2.2	3.2	1.6	224	145
56313	Sushi, w/veg & fish	1 cup	166	232	9	47	2	1	0.2	0.2	0.2	11	136
56314	Sushi, w/veg, rolled in seaweed	1 cup	166	194	4	43	1	0	0.1	0.1	0.1	0	66
56642	Taco, lrg	1 ea	263	568	32	41	–	32	17.5	10.1	1.5	87	213
91464	Tamale, w/beef & sauce	2 ea	190	310	6	26	4	23	10.0	–	–	20	–
56645	Tostada, beef & cheese	1 ea	163	315	19	23	–	16	10.4	3.3	1.0	41	83
Pizza													
56995	Bagel Bites, cheese & pepperoni	4 pce	88	210	11	24	3	8	3.0	–	–	15	80
90774	Pizza, Canadian bacon, original, 12″ or ¼ pce, Jack's	1 pce	124	280	16	31	2	10	5.0	–	–	30	100
81019	Pizza, cheese, for one, microwv, fzn, Totino's	1 ea	104	240	10	26	1	11	3.5	–	–	15	0
56788	Pizza, deluxe, ¼″ ea, fzn, Celeste	1 pce	158	378	16	29	3	22	7.0	7.0	2.0	20	190
90772	Pizza, hamburger, original, 12″ or ¼ pce, Jack's	1 pce	125	300	16	28	2	14	7.0	–	–	35	100
57259	Pizza, hamburger, Pizza Rolls Pizza Snacks, fzn, svg	1 ea	85	231	9	26	–	10	3.0	6.8	0.0	–	0
70940	Pizza, peproni & saus, w/Italian style pastry crust fzn	1 ea	447	1319	46	126	–	70	20.9	28.4	9.1	72	0
56735	Pizza, pepperoni, french bread, Lean Cuisine	1 ea	149	300	15	43	3	8	3.5	3.0	1.0	25	40
90789	Pizza, sausage, Italian, 8″ or ⅓ pce, Di Giorno	1 pce	124	300	15	33	2	12	6.0	–	–	25	100
90771	Pizza, sausage, original, 12″ or ¼ pce, Jack's	1 pce	123	300	15	28	2	14	7.0	–	–	30	100
91605	Pizza, soy cheeze, organic, fzn, ⅓ of whole, Amy's	1 pce	123	290	12	37	2	11	1.0	–	–	0	40
91614	Pizza, spinach & feta, snack bites, organic, fzn, Amy's	6 pce	85	170	7	24	2	6	3.0	–	–	15	500
1907	Pizza, sun dried tomato, french bread, fzn, Lean Cuisine	1 ea	170	350	17	50	5	9	6.0	2.0	0.5	20	80
81075	Pizza, supreme, french bread, fzn, Healthy Choice	1 ea	180	330	21	51	6	5	1.5	–	–	20	40
57216	Pizza, vegetable, light, 12″ or ⅕ pce, Tombstone	1 pce	131	240	14	31	3	7	2.5	–	–	10	150

PAGE KEY: A-154 Granola Bars, Cereal Bars, Diet Bars, Scones, and Tarts A-154 Meals and Dishes A-160 Meats A-164 Nuts, Seeds, and Products A-166 Poultry A-166 Salad Dressings, Dips, and Mayonnaise A-170 Salads A-170 Sandwiches A-172 Sauces and Gravies A-174 Snack Foods—Chips, Pretzels, Popcorn A-178 Soups, Stews and Chilis A-184 Spices, Flavors, and Seasonings A-184 Sports Bars and Drinks A-186 Supplemental Foods and Formulas A-186 Sweeteners and Sweet Substitutes A-188 Vegetables and Legumes A-200 Weight Loss Bars & Drinks A-200 Miscellaneous

Thia (mg)	Ribo (mg)	Niac (mg NE)	Vit B6 (mg)	Vit B12 (μg)	Fol (μg)	Vit C (mg)	Vit D (IU)	Vit E (mg AT)	Cal (mg)	Iron (mg)	Magn (mg)	Phos (mg)	Pota (mg)	Sodi (mg)	Zinc (mg)	Wat (%)	Alco (g)	Caff (g)
0.18	0.25	4.19	0.40	1.96	42.0	23.4	–	2.0	38	2.91	41.5	238	556	924	3.5	75	0.00	0.00
0.77	0.43	6.23	0.41	0.41	41.8	20.2	–	2.7	45	3.29	52.8	249	489	848	2.6	62	0.00	0.00
0.28	0.10	4.76	0.21	1.17	12.2	16.9	–	2.3	104	4.38	63.6	300	439	370	1.7	72	0.00	0.00
0.05	0.23	0.88	0.11	0.34	22.3	3.1	–	1.1	27	0.81	11.4	96	136	132	0.8	76	0.00	0.00
0.03	0.25	0.43	0.09	0.37	29.5	4.8	–	1.2	31	1.03	11.6	93	117	317	0.7	77	0.00	0.00
0.07	0.10	0.89	0.05	0.11	10.0	2.3	–	0.9	17	0.89	9.8	47	100	293	0.3	69	0.00	0.00
0.38	0.30	5.40	0.37	2.05	23.0	26.8	–	1.7	84	3.75	37.6	238	479	316	3.5	65	0.00	0.00
0.43	0.33	6.11	0.37	0.10	41.8	36.8	–	1.7	101	3.31	48.2	188	534	343	1.6	65	0.00	0.00
0.52	0.43	5.13	0.49	0.77	14.9	6.3	–	0.8	258	1.36	47.8	420	688	1266	3.2	70	0.00	0.00
0.23	0.34	4.19	0.25	0.98	19.8	14.5	–	1.2	270	3.06	50.4	299	460	391	3.3	67	0.00	0.00
0.23	0.28	2.50	0.17	0.17	17.2	14.4	–	1.1	265	2.34	44.3	248	373	365	1.8	69	0.00	0.00
0.25	0.34	1.46	0.10	0.50	69.2	1.5	42.7	0.7	273	0.79	40.8	235	210	525	1.4	70	0.00	0.00
0.20	0.30	3.96	0.25	1.96	15.7	0.0	–	0.3	188	3.36	36.4	335	348	736	4.6	71	0.00	0.00
0.52	0.15	3.80	0.37	0.25	9.9	14.4	–	0.8	28	1.99	34.6	142	311	618	1.5	75	0.00	0.00
0.25	0.30	4.38	0.28	0.94	67.7	16.3	16.9	2.5	92	3.32	43.7	173	479	1133	3.4	71	–	0.00
0.07	0.23	3.46	0.11	1.16	8.4	0.8	10.3	0.2	32	2.07	18.9	137	292	438	3.6	70	0.00	0.00
0.11	0.20	3.75	0.28	1.89	12.1	8.7	20.4	1.0	27	2.39	31.3	203	496	142	3.1	78	0.00	0.00
0.18	0.38	4.51	0.28	2.60	20.2	1.8	–	2.4	92	3.64	40.4	308	556	677	4.9	72	0.00	0.00
0.20	0.31	3.81	0.20	1.83	17.1	1.3	–	1.6	70	3.26	37.2	244	394	468	3.7	75	0.00	0.00
0.18	0.15	7.80	0.20	1.52	55.3	0.7	77.3	1.1	34	2.29	30.7	156	182	686	1.2	75	0.00	0.00
0.20	0.15	4.51	0.20	2.41	45.6	13.5	–	1.4	71	2.60	40.1	152	446	542	15.2	83	0.00	0.00
0.15	0.20	3.74	0.49	1.79	16.5	7.1	–	1.2	19	2.46	36.4	204	587	470	5.0	69	0.00	0.00
0.18	0.15	2.71	0.15	0.10	16.9	0.0	–	0.1	83	2.01	12.9	82	76	819	0.8	45	0.00	0.00
0.46	0.56	4.48	0.21	0.89	29.1	0.0	–	1.1	178	3.11	28.1	290	231	437	2.2	61	0.00	0.00
0.12	0.14	1.09	0.03	0.05	5.8	14.7	–	1.0	132	1.21	13.4	107	77	230	0.6	35	0.00	0.00
0.05	0.10	2.86	0.21	0.46	9.7	9.2	112.6	6.8	45	2.48	42.3	154	362	2019	0.9	46	0.00	0.00
0.12	0.40	3.10	0.36	1.51	60.8	4.5	–	0.7	62	3.23	46.7	204	463	675	3.6	78	0.00	0.00
0.12	0.30	1.44	0.14	0.46	30.2	2.0	–	0.9	45	1.74	19.4	140	136	562	1.0	75	0.27	0.00
0.28	0.07	2.96	0.15	0.34	15.3	4.0	–	0.6	25	2.32	26.7	109	218	93	0.8	65	0.07	0.00
0.20	0.03	1.99	0.15	0.00	10.7	2.5	–	0.1	22	1.64	21.5	64	106	5	0.7	71	0.07	0.00
0.23	0.68	4.94	0.37	1.60	105.2	3.4	–	2.9	339	3.71	107.8	313	729	1233	6.0	58	0.00	0.00
–	–	–	–	–	–	1.8	–	–	40	1.08	–	–	–	870	–	–	0.00	0.00
0.10	0.55	3.15	0.23	1.16	75.0	2.6	–	–	217	2.86	63.6	179	572	896	3.7	62	0.00	0.00
–	–	–	–	–	–	9.0	–	–	100	1.44	–	–	150	650	–	–	0.00	0.00
–	–	–	–	–	–	0.0	–	–	250	1.08	–	–	270	620	–	53	0.00	0.00
–	–	–	–	–	–	0.0	–	–	200	1.79	–	–	–	540	–	53	0.00	0.00
0.20	0.55	2.65	0.17	2.00	57.0	0.0	–	3.0	267	1.85	38.0	357	352	903	3.0	55	0.00	0.00
–	–	–	–	–	–	0.0	–	–	250	1.44	–	–	270	580	–	53	0.00	0.00
0.00	–	–	–	–	–	–	–	–	–	–	–	–	–	417	–	44	0.00	0.00
–	–	–	–	–	–	–	–	–	514	9.56	–	–	–	2186	–	44	0.00	0.00
–	–	–	–	–	–	1.2	–	–	100	1.79	–	–	410	590	–	55	0.00	0.00
–	–	–	–	–	–	0.0	–	–	200	1.08	–	–	240	830	–	51	0.00	0.00
–	–	–	–	–	–	0.0	–	–	250	1.44	–	–	290	580	–	51	0.00	0.00
–	–	–	–	–	–	2.4	–	–	20	1.79	–	–	–	590	–	49	0.00	0.00
–	–	–	–	–	–	3.6	–	–	150	2.70	–	–	–	430	–	–	0.00	0.00
–	–	–	–	–	–	2.4	–	–	350	1.79	–	–	600	500	–	54	0.00	0.00
–	–	–	–	–	–	0.0	–	–	200	3.59	–	–	–	580	–	57	0.00	0.00
–	–	–	–	–	–	2.4	–	–	200	1.08	–	–	310	500	–	60	0.00	0.00

PAGE KEY: A-108 Beverage and Beverage Mixes A-112 Other Beverages A-112 Beverages, Alcoholic A-114 Candies and Confections, Gum A-114 Cereals, Breakfast Type A-118 Cheese and Cheese Substitutes A-120 Dairy Products and Substitutes A-122 Desserts A-128 Dessert Toppings A-128 Eggs, Substitutes, and Egg Dishes A-130 Ethnic Foods A-130 Fast Foods/Restaurants A-140 Fats, Oils, Margarines, Shortenings, and Substitutes A-142 Fish, Seafood, and Shellfish A-142 Food Additives A-142 Fruit, Vegetable, and Blended Juices A-144 Fruits A-146 Grains, Flours, and Fractions A-148 Grain Products, Prepared and Baked Goods

Code	Food Name	Unit/ Amt	Wt (g)	Energy (Kcal)	Prot (g)	Carb (g)	Fiber (g)	Fat (g)	Sat (g)	Mono (g)	Poly (g)	Chol (mg)	Vit A (RE)
MEATS													
Beef													
10265	Beef, average of all cuts, ckd, 0" trim	3 oz	85	232	23	0	0	15	5.8	6.3	0.5	74	0
10093	Beef, average of all cuts, ckd, ¼" trim	3 oz	85	259	22	0	0	18	7.3	7.8	0.7	75	0
10820	Beef, average of all cuts, ckd, ⅛" trim	3 oz	85	247	22	0	0	17	6.6	7.2	0.6	74	0
10095	Beef, average of all cuts, ckd, choice, ¼" trim	3 oz	85	274	22	0	0	20	8.0	8.6	0.7	75	0
10822	Beef, average of all cuts, ckd, choice, ⅛" trim	3 oz	85	256	22	0	0	18	7.0	7.6	0.6	74	0
10493	Beef, average of all cuts, ckd, prime, ½" trim	3 oz	85	344	20	0	0	29	11.9	12.9	1.1	78	0
10267	Beef, average of all cuts, ckd, select, 0" trim	3 oz	85	222	23	0	0	14	5.3	5.8	0.5	73	0
11239	Beef, bottom round roast, rstd, choice, ¼" trim	3 oz	85	221	22	0	0	14	5.2	6.1	0.5	68	0
10485	Beef, brisket, corned, cured, raw	4 oz	85	168	12	0	0	13	4.0	6.1	0.5	46	0
10118	Beef, chuck arm pot roast, brsd, ¼" trim	3 oz	85	282	23	0	0	20	8.0	8.7	0.8	84	0
10840	Beef, chuck blade roast, brsd, ⅛" trim	3 oz	85	290	23	0	0	21	8.5	9.2	0.8	88	0
58100	Beef, chuck tender steak, raw, ¼" trim	4 oz	113	128	22	0	0	4	1.4	1.9	0.4	62	0
58075	Beef, chuck top blade, lean, raw, ¼" trim	4 oz	113	154	22	0	0	7	2.3	3.2	0.3	67	0
10740	Beef, cube steak	1 ea	91	251	15	2	0	20	8.1	8.7	0.8	64	17
10031	Beef, ground, hamburger patty, bkd, well done, 18% fat	1 ea	88	257	26	0	0	16	6.3	7.1	0.6	87	0
10466	Beef, ground, hamburger patty, brld f/fzn, 20% fat	3 oz	85	240	21	0	0	17	6.6	7.3	0.6	80	0
58112	Beef, ground, hamburger patty, brld, 10% fat	3 oz	85	185	22	0	0	10	4.0	4.3	0.3	72	0
58117	Beef, ground, hamburger patty, brld, 15% fat	3 oz	85	213	22	0	0	13	5.2	5.8	0.4	77	0
58107	Beef, ground, hamburger patty, brld, 5% fat	3 oz	85	145	22	0	0	6	2.4	2.3	0.3	65	0
10032	Beef, ground, hamburger patty, brld, well done, 18% fat	1 ea	85	238	24	0	0	15	5.9	6.6	0.6	86	0
58118	Beef, ground, hamburger patty, pan brld, 15% fat	3 oz	85	197	21	0	0	12	4.7	5.2	0.3	73	0
58120	Beef, ground, hamburger, bkd, 15% fat	3 oz	85	204	22	0	0	12	4.8	5.3	0.3	77	0
10722	Beef, ground, hamburger, blrd, well done, 16% fat	3 oz	85	225	24	0	0	13	5.3	5.9	0.5	84	0
10453	Beef, ground, raw, 17% fat	4 oz	113	265	21	0	0	19	7.7	8.4	0.8	78	0
10051	Beef, jerky, lrg pce	1 ea	20	81	7	2	0	5	2.1	2.2	0.2	10	0
11019	Beef, meatballs	4 ea	112	240	19	7	0	14	5.1	6.3	0.7	93	21
10738	Beef, pepper steak	1 ea	91	267	14	2	0	22	9.4	8.6	0.8	61	29
10791	Beef, porterhouse steak, brld, ¼" trim	3 oz	85	280	19	0	0	22	8.6	9.8	0.8	61	0
10227	Beef, porterhouse steak, raw, choice, ¼" trim	4 oz	113	284	21	0	0	22	8.5	9.9	0.8	77	0
10959	Beef, rib pot roast, brld, choice, ¼" trim	3 oz	85	312	18	0	0	26	10.6	11.1	1.0	69	0
10965	Beef, rib pot roast, brld, select, ¼" trim	3 oz	85	276	18	0	0	22	8.9	9.3	0.8	68	0
10980	Beef, rib pot roast, lean, rstd, prime, ¼" trim	3 oz	85	241	23	0	0	16	6.7	6.9	0.5	69	0
10953	Beef, rib steak, brld, select, ¼" trim	3 oz	85	273	20	0	0	21	8.4	8.9	0.7	71	0
10997	Beef, rib steak, lean, brld, select, ¼" trim	3 oz	85	176	24	0	0	8	3.3	3.5	0.2	68	0
10190	Beef, round roast, lean, brld, select, ¼" trim	3 oz	85	146	25	0	0	4	1.6	1.9	0.2	66	0
10058	Beef, round tip roast, lean, rstd, ¼" trim	3 oz	85	157	24	0	0	6	2.0	2.3	0.2	69	0
11144	Beef, round tip roast, rstd, ¼" trim	3 oz	85	199	23	0	0	11	4.3	4.7	0.4	70	0
11148	Beef, round tip roast, rstd, select, ¼" trim	3 oz	85	191	23	0	0	10	3.9	4.3	0.4	70	0
57891	Beef, sndwch steak, formed & thin sliced, raw, 14oz pkg	1 ea	397	1226	65	0	0	107	45.8	43.8	1.9	282	0
10624	Beef, short ribs, brsd, choice, ¼" trim	3 oz	85	401	18	0	0	36	15.1	16.1	1.3	80	0
10046	Beef, short ribs, w/bbq sauce, med svg	2 ea	132	503	22	5	0	43	18.1	19.3	1.8	95	31
11199	Beef, sirloin strip steak, brld, ¼" trim	3 oz	85	244	22	0	0	17	6.7	7.1	0.6	67	0
10064	Beef, sirloin strip steak, lean, brld, ¼" trim	3 oz	85	176	24	0	0	8	3.1	3.2	0.3	65	0
10049	Beef, stew meat, ckd	0.75 cup	105	322	29	0	0	22	8.5	9.4	0.8	106	0
10805	Beef, T-bone steak, brld, ¼" trim	3 oz	85	260	20	0	0	19	7.6	8.6	0.7	55	0

PAGE KEY: A-154 Granola Bars, Cereal Bars, Diet Bars, Scones, and Tarts A-154 Meals and Dishes A-160 Meats A-164 Nuts, Seeds, and Products A-166 Poultry A-166 Salad Dressings, Dips, and Mayonnaise A-170 Salads A-170 Sandwiches A-172 Sauces and Gravies A-174 Snack Foods—Chips, Pretzels, Popcorn A-178 Soups, Stews and Chilis A-184 Spices, Flavors, and Seasonings A-184 Sports Bars and Drinks A-186 Supplemental Foods and Formulas A-186 Sweeteners and Sweet Substitutes A-188 Vegetables and Legumes A-200 Weight Loss Bars & Drinks A-200 Miscellaneous

Thia (mg)	Ribo (mg)	Niac (mg NE)	Vit B6 (mg)	Vit B12 (μg)	Fol (μg)	Vit C (mg)	Vit D (IU)	Vit E (mg AT)	Cal (mg)	Iron (mg)	Magn (mg)	Phos (mg)	Pota (mg)	Sodi (mg)	Zinc (mg)	Wat (%)	Alco (g)	Caff (g)
0.07	0.18	3.13	0.28	2.13	6.0	0.0	10.2	0.2	8	2.31	19.6	179	275	53	5.2	54	0.00	0.00
0.07	0.18	3.09	0.28	2.07	6.0	0.0	10.2	0.2	9	2.23	18.7	173	266	53	5.0	51	0.00	0.00
0.07	0.18	3.16	0.28	2.09	6.0	0.0	—	0.2	8	2.27	19.6	177	271	54	5.1	53	0.00	0.00
0.07	0.18	3.03	0.27	2.04	6.0	0.0	10.2	0.1	9	2.19	18.7	169	260	52	4.9	50	0.00	0.00
0.07	0.18	3.15	0.28	2.08	6.0	0.0	—	0.2	8	2.25	19.6	175	270	53	5.0	52	0.00	0.00
0.05	0.17	2.76	0.25	1.96	6.0	0.0	10.2	0.2	9	2.07	16.2	152	229	48	4.3	43	0.00	0.00
0.07	0.18	3.14	0.28	2.14	6.0	0.0	10.2	0.1	8	2.33	19.6	180	276	54	5.2	55	0.00	0.00
0.07	0.18	3.19	0.28	2.18	9.4	0.0	10.2	0.2	5	2.43	21.3	185	302	54	3.6	55	0.00	0.00
0.03	0.12	3.10	0.25	1.50	4.3	23.0	10.2	0.1	6	1.44	11.9	100	253	1035	2.4	67	0.00	0.00
0.05	0.20	2.70	0.23	2.50	7.7	0.0	10.2	0.2	9	2.65	16.2	187	209	51	5.8	48	0.00	0.00
0.05	0.20	2.06	0.21	1.95	4.3	0.0	—	0.2	11	2.66	16.2	172	198	55	7.2	48	0.00	0.00
0.12	0.20	3.77	0.44	3.52	7.9	0.0	—	0.1	7	2.76	23.8	227	439	85	5.2	74	0.00	0.00
0.12	0.21	3.82	0.44	3.56	7.9	0.0	—	0.1	6	2.49	23.8	204	375	68	7.1	73	0.00	0.00
0.10	0.17	4.40	0.23	1.97	19.0	8.0	—	—	17	1.89	—	129	337	53	5.3	58	0.00	0.00
0.05	0.20	4.80	0.23	1.99	10.6	0.0	10.6	0.2	11	2.33	18.5	144	252	62	5.7	51	0.00	0.00
0.03	0.17	4.48	0.21	2.09	7.7	0.0	10.2	0.2	9	1.78	17.0	134	250	65	4.6	55	0.00	0.00
0.03	0.15	4.80	0.34	2.18	6.8	0.0	—	0.4	11	2.29	18.7	172	283	58	5.4	61	0.00	0.00
0.03	0.15	4.57	0.31	2.25	7.7	0.0	—	0.4	15	2.21	17.9	168	270	61	5.4	58	0.00	0.00
0.03	0.15	5.05	0.34	2.09	6.0	0.0	—	0.3	6	2.41	18.7	175	296	55	5.5	66	0.00	0.00
0.05	0.20	5.07	0.25	2.30	9.4	0.0	10.2	0.2	10	2.07	20.4	155	297	76	5.3	53	0.00	0.00
0.03	0.15	4.90	0.31	2.39	6.8	0.0	—	0.4	17	2.27	18.7	179	297	67	5.3	61	0.00	0.00
0.02	0.15	4.19	0.28	2.11	5.1	0.0	—	0.4	15	2.32	17.0	158	243	54	5.5	59	0.00	0.00
0.05	0.27	4.98	0.27	2.18	9.4	0.0	10.2	0.2	8	2.35	21.3	162	314	70	5.5	54	0.00	0.00
0.07	0.28	5.13	0.28	2.33	9.1	0.0	13.6	0.2	8	2.21	22.7	160	322	75	4.7	63	0.00	0.00
0.02	0.02	0.34	0.03	0.20	26.5	0.0	2.4	0.1	4	1.07	10.1	81	118	438	1.6	23	0.00	0.00
0.07	0.28	4.17	0.15	1.72	12.4	0.6	—	0.1	45	2.10	23.3	167	306	138	3.8	62	0.00	0.00
0.00	0.15	4.09	0.21	1.79	20.0	0.0	—	—	19	1.89	—	122	346	155	5.1	56	0.00	0.00
0.07	0.18	3.26	0.28	1.78	6.0	0.0	—	0.2	7	2.27	17.0	151	217	53	3.5	50	0.00	0.00
0.10	0.18	4.03	0.43	3.07	6.8	0.0	13.6	0.1	7	2.22	21.5	193	287	60	3.8	61	0.00	0.00
0.05	0.14	2.29	0.20	2.40	5.1	0.0	10.2	0.2	9	1.80	15.3	150	253	54	4.1	46	0.00	0.00
0.05	0.14	2.35	0.20	2.46	5.1	0.0	10.2	0.2	9	1.86	16.2	155	262	54	4.3	50	0.00	0.00
0.07	0.18	3.77	0.21	2.22	7.7	0.0	10.2	0.2	7	2.40	21.3	178	304	62	6.3	54	0.00	0.00
0.07	0.15	3.42	0.28	2.47	6.0	0.0	10.2	0.2	11	1.87	18.7	150	279	53	4.8	49	0.00	0.00
0.09	0.18	4.07	0.34	2.81	6.8	0.0	10.2	0.1	11	2.19	23.0	177	335	59	5.9	59	0.00	0.00
0.09	0.18	3.63	0.34	2.70	8.5	0.0	10.2	0.1	4	2.29	23.8	218	360	54	4.0	62	0.00	0.00
0.09	0.23	3.18	0.34	2.46	6.8	0.0	—	0.1	4	2.50	23.0	206	328	55	6.0	65	0.00	0.00
0.07	0.20	2.99	0.31	2.34	6.0	0.0	10.2	0.1	5	2.33	21.3	191	305	54	5.5	60	0.00	0.00
0.07	0.20	3.00	0.31	2.35	6.8	0.0	10.2	0.1	5	2.35	21.3	193	308	54	5.6	61	0.00	0.00
0.15	0.61	18.19	0.98	10.76	27.8	0.0	—	0.8	48	7.38	63.5	528	925	270	14.4	56	0.00	0.00
0.03	0.12	2.08	0.18	2.23	4.3	0.0	10.2	0.2	10	1.96	12.8	138	191	43	4.2	36	0.00	0.00
0.05	0.15	2.79	0.25	2.65	6.4	2.5	15.8	0.7	19	2.66	21.6	171	289	345	5.0	46	0.00	0.00
0.07	0.15	4.00	0.31	1.64	6.0	0.0	10.2	0.0	8	1.89	19.6	165	297	54	3.9	53	0.00	0.00
0.07	0.17	4.53	0.36	1.70	6.8	0.0	—	0.1	7	2.09	23.0	185	337	58	4.4	60	0.00	0.00
0.07	0.25	3.10	0.30	2.58	7.3	0.0	12.6	0.2	11	3.27	21.6	231	265	66	7.9	50	0.00	0.00
0.07	0.18	3.36	0.28	1.80	6.0	0.0	—	0.2	6	2.63	18.7	157	240	57	3.7	52	0.00	0.00

PAGE KEY: A-108 Beverage and Beverage Mixes A-112 Other Beverages A-112 Beverages, Alcoholic A-114 Candies and Confections, Gum A-114 Cereals, Breakfast Type A-118 Cheese and Cheese Substitutes A-120 Dairy Products and Substitutes A-122 Desserts A-128 Dessert Toppings A-128 Eggs, Substitutes, and Egg Dishes A-130 Ethnic Foods A-130 Fast Foods/Restaurants A-140 Fats, Oils, Margarines, Shortenings, and Substitutes A-142 Fish, Seafood, and Shellfish A-142 Food Additives A-142 Fruit, Vegetable, and Blended Juices A-144 Fruits A-146 Grains, Flours, and Fractions A-148 Grain Products, Prepared and Baked Goods

Code	Food Name	Unit/ Amt	Wt (g)	Energy (Kcal)	Prot (g)	Carb (g)	Fiber (g)	Fat (g)	Sat (g)	Mono (g)	Poly (g)	Chol (mg)	Vit A (RE)
10814	Beef, T-bone steak, lean, brld, choice, 0" trim	3 oz	85	168	22	0	0	8	2.8	4.0	0.3	48	0
11278	Beef, tenderloin, filet mignon, brld, 0" trim	3 oz	85	200	23	0	0	11	4.3	4.4	0.4	72	0
11193	Beef, tenderloin, filet mignon, lean, brld, select ¼" trim	3 oz	85	169	24	0	0	7	2.8	2.8	0.3	71	0
10942	Beef, tenderloin, filet mignon, rstd, prime, ⅛" trim	3 oz	85	292	20	0	0	23	9.0	9.4	0.9	75	0
10912	Beef, top round steak, brld, choice, ⅛" trim	3 oz	85	184	26	0	0	8	3.0	3.3	0.3	72	0
11266	Beef, top round steak, brsd, ¼" trim	3 oz	85	211	29	0	0	10	3.7	4.0	0.4	77	0
11169	Beef, top round steak, lean, brld, choice, ¼" trim	3 oz	85	161	27	0	0	5	1.7	1.9	0.2	71	0
11217	Beef, top sirloin steak, fried, choice, ¼" trim	3 oz	85	277	24	0	0	19	7.6	8.2	1.5	83	0
11224	Beef, top sirloin steak, lean, brld, select, ¼" trim	3 oz	85	158	26	0	0	5	2.0	2.2	0.2	76	0
10132	Beef, whole rib, brld, ¼" trim	3 oz	85	291	19	0	0	23	9.5	9.9	0.9	70	0
10142	Beef, whole rib, lean, brld, ¼" trim	3 oz	85	190	22	0	0	10	4.2	4.3	0.4	65	0
Game Meats													
40569	Deer, tenderloin, lean, brld	3 oz	85	127	25	0	0	2	1.0	0.5	0.1	75	0
14033	Venison, jerky	3 pce	42	143	14	6	0	6	2.5	2.7	0.8	57	0
Lamb													
13604	Lamb, average of all cuts, ckd, choice, ¼" trim	3 oz	85	250	21	0	0	18	7.5	7.5	1.3	82	0
13524	Lamb, ground, brld, 20% fat	3 oz	85	241	21	0	0	17	6.9	7.1	1.2	82	0
Lunchmeats and Sausages													
13010	Hot Dog, beef & pork, 10 pack, 5"x¾" diameter	1 ea	45	135	5	1	0	12	4.8	6.2	1.2	22	8
58027	Hot Dog, beef, ckd	1 ea	52	170	6	2	0	15	5.9	7.4	0.6	29	0
57964	Hot Dog, beef, cocktail franks	5 ea	57	180	7	1	0	16	7.0	–	–	40	0
13250	Hot Dog, beef, fat free	1 ea	50	39	7	3	0	0	0.1	0.1	0.0	15	0
13272	Hot Dog, beef, light	1 ea	57	110	6	2	0	8	3.6	4.3	0.6	28	0
13260	Hot Dog, chicken	1 ea	45	116	6	3	0	9	2.5	3.8	1.8	45	18
13012	Hot Dog, turkey	1 ea	45	102	6	1	0	8	2.7	2.5	2.2	48	0
13034	Lunchmeat Spread, ham salad	1 Tbs	15	32	1	2	0	2	0.8	1.1	0.4	6	0
13000	Lunchmeat, beef, thin slice	5 pce	21	37	6	1	0	1	0.3	0.4	0.0	9	0
13177	Lunchmeat, bologna, beef, svg	1 pce	28	88	3	1	0	8	3.6	4.2	0.3	18	0
13251	Lunchmeat, bologna, fat free, svg	1 pce	28	22	4	2	0	0	0.1	0.1	0.0	7	0
13152	Lunchmeat, chicken, white, oven rstd, svg	1 pce	28	36	5	1	0	2	0.4	0.7	0.3	17	0
13306	Lunchmeat, corned beef, chpd pressed & ckd, pkg	1 ea	71	101	14	1	0	5	2.0	2.6	0.2	46	–
11810	Lunchmeat, ham, brown sugar cured, Hearty Deli	3 pce	58	70	10	3	0	2	0.5	–	–	30	0
13169	Lunchmeat, ham, honey flvr, slice	3 pce	63	70	11	2	0	2	0.7	1.1	0.2	28	0
13338	Lunchmeat, ham, smkd, sliced, pkg	1 ea	71	116	13	1	0	7	2.2	3.6	0.8	39	–
13114	Lunchmeat, turkey breast, oven rstd, fat free, slice	1 pce	28	24	4	1	0	0	0.1	0.1	0.0	9	0
13146	Lunchmeat, turkey ham, square, svg	1 ea	28	32	5	0	0	1	0.3	0.3	0.2	19	0
58013	Pastrami, beef, 98% fat free, slices	6 pce	57	54	11	1	0	1	0.0	0.3	0.0	27	0
13101	Pastrami, beef, cured, slice, 1oz	1 ea	28	99	5	1	0	8	3.0	4.1	0.3	26	0
13023	Salami, beef, ckd, slice, 4"x⅛, 10/8oz pkg	1 pce	23	84	4	0	0	7	2.0	2.2	0.2	16	0
58014	Salami, Italian, pork	3 oz	85	361	18	1	0	31	11.1	15.5	3.1	68	0
13182	Sausage, beef, smokies	1 ea	43	127	5	1	0	11	4.8	5.5	0.4	27	0
13066	Sausage, brnschwger, liver pork 2.5 diameter ¼" slice	1 pce	18	65	2	1	0	6	2.0	2.7	0.7	28	760
11854	Sausage, breakfast, Whol-E-Smokes, link	2 ea	47	120	6	2	0	10	3.5	–	–	25	0
58003	Sausage, polish, beef & chicken, hot	5 pce	55	142	10	2	0	11	4.4	5.3	0.4	36	0
13185	Sausage, pork, link, ckd	2 ea	48	165	8	0	0	15	5.1	7.1	1.8	37	0
13309	Sausage, pork/turkey, patty, Healthy Choice	2 ea	45	50	7	3	0	2	0.5	–	–	15	0
13184	Sausage, smokies, links	1 ea	43	130	5	1	0	12	4.0	5.7	1.2	27	0

PAGE KEY: A-154 Granola Bars, Cereal Bars, Diet Bars, Scones, and Tarts A-154 Meals and Dishes A-160 Meats A-164 Nuts, Seeds, and Products A-166 Poultry A-166 Salad Dressings, Dips, and Mayonnaise A-170 Salads A-170 Sandwiches A-172 Sauces and Gravies A-174 Snack Foods—Chips, Pretzels, Popcorn A-178 Soups, Stews and Chilis A-184 Spices, Flavors, and Seasonings A-184 Sports Bars and Drinks A-186 Supplemental Foods and Formulas A-186 Sweeteners and Sweet Substitutes A-188 Vegetables and Legumes A-200 Weight Loss Bars & Drinks A-200 Miscellaneous

Thia (mg)	Ribo (mg)	Niac (mg NE)	Vit B6 (mg)	Vit B12 (µg)	Fol (µg)	Vit C (mg)	Vit D (IU)	Vit E (mg AT)	Cal (mg)	Iron (mg)	Magn (mg)	Phos (mg)	Pota (mg)	Sodi (mg)	Zinc (mg)	Wat (%)	Alco (g)	Caff (g)
0.09	0.20	3.94	0.33	1.92	6.8	0.0	—	0.1	3	3.10	22.1	183	278	60	4.3	62	0.00	0.00
0.10	0.25	3.21	0.36	2.13	6.0	0.0	10.2	0.1	6	2.92	24.7	194	341	53	4.5	58	0.00	0.00
0.10	0.25	3.32	0.37	2.19	6.0	0.0	10.2	0.1	6	3.03	25.5	202	356	54	4.8	61	0.00	0.00
0.07	0.23	2.55	0.28	2.15	6.0	0.0	—	0.2	7	2.65	19.6	173	286	47	3.7	48	0.00	0.00
0.09	0.21	4.92	0.46	2.06	10.2	0.0	—	0.1	5	2.35	25.5	202	361	51	4.5	59	0.00	0.00
0.05	0.20	3.06	0.23	2.21	7.7	0.0	10.2	0.1	4	2.65	20.4	180	268	38	3.6	54	0.00	0.00
0.10	0.23	5.13	0.47	2.10	10.2	0.0	10.2	0.1	5	2.45	26.4	209	376	52	4.7	61	0.00	0.00
0.10	0.23	3.19	0.37	2.78	7.7	0.0	10.2	0.2	10	2.82	23.8	195	337	60	4.6	48	0.00	0.00
0.10	0.25	3.64	0.37	2.42	8.5	0.0	10.2	0.1	9	2.85	27.2	208	343	56	5.5	63	0.00	0.00
0.07	0.14	2.75	0.23	2.44	5.1	0.0	10.2	0.2	10	1.85	17.0	151	265	54	4.4	48	0.00	0.00
0.07	0.17	3.26	0.27	2.81	6.0	0.0	10.2	0.1	9	2.19	21.3	181	324	60	5.6	58	0.00	0.00
0.21	0.47	7.46	0.51	3.07	7.7	0.0	—	0.5	4	3.60	28.1	254	369	48	3.4	67	0.00	0.00
0.07	0.28	2.97	0.10	2.74	2.4	0.0	5.0	0.2	4	2.11	12.2	107	158	1230	1.3	27	0.00	0.00
0.09	0.20	5.65	0.10	2.17	15.3	0.0	—	0.1	14	1.60	19.6	160	264	61	3.8	54	0.00	0.00
0.09	0.20	5.69	0.11	2.22	16.2	0.0	10.2	0.2	19	1.51	20.4	171	288	69	4.0	55	0.00	0.00
0.09	0.05	1.19	0.05	0.57	1.8	1.0	16.2	0.1	10	0.51	4.5	39	75	504	0.8	56	0.00	0.00
0.01	0.07	1.22	0.05	0.86	3.6	—	—	0.1	6	0.81	7.3	89	76	600	1.2	52	0.00	0.00
—	—	—	—	—	—	0.0	—	—	0	0.72	—	—	—	450	—	55	0.00	0.00
—	—	—	—	—	—	0.0	—	—	10	0.98	9.5	64	234	464	1.2	78	0.00	0.00
—	—	—	—	—	—	0.0	—	—	12	0.88	10.3	93	229	615	1.2	67	0.00	0.00
0.02	0.05	1.38	0.14	0.10	1.8	0.0	0.0	0.1	43	0.89	4.5	48	38	616	0.5	58	0.00	0.00
0.01	0.07	1.86	0.10	0.12	3.6	0.0	6.0	0.3	48	0.82	6.3	60	81	642	1.4	63	0.00	0.00
0.07	0.01	0.31	0.01	0.10	0.2	0.0	0.8	0.3	1	0.09	1.5	18	22	137	0.2	63	0.00	0.00
0.01	0.03	1.11	0.07	0.54	2.3	0.0	2.5	0.0	2	0.56	4.0	35	90	302	0.8	58	0.00	0.00
0.00	0.02	0.68	0.05	0.40	3.6	0.0	9.0	—	3	0.37	3.9	31	47	330	0.6	54	0.00	0.00
—	—	—	—	—	—	0.0	—	—	4	0.25	6.2	43	44	274	0.3	78	0.00	0.00
—	—	—	—	—	—	0.0	—	—	5	0.43	6.7	69	85	335	0.3	72	0.00	0.00
0.05	0.17	2.98	—	—	—	—	—	—	12	1.70	—	—	250	953	—	69	0.00	0.00
—	—	—	—	—	—	0.0	—	—	0	0.36	—	—	—	480	—	71	0.00	0.00
—	—	—	—	—	—	0.0	—	—	6	0.85	19.5	163	177	786	1.3	73	0.00	0.00
0.52	0.25	3.67	—	—	—	—	—	—	11	1.44	—	—	241	981	—	67	0.00	0.00
—	—	—	—	—	—	0.0	—	—	3	0.31	7.6	65	57	334	0.2	76	0.00	0.00
—	—	—	—	—	—	0.0	—	—	1	0.36	6.2	82	81	316	0.7	73	0.00	0.00
0.05	0.10	2.89	0.10	1.00	4.0	19.7	—	0.1	5	1.58	10.3	86	130	576	2.4	74	0.00	0.00
0.02	0.05	1.44	0.05	0.50	2.0	0.0	—	0.1	3	0.54	5.1	43	65	348	1.2	47	0.00	0.00
0.01	0.03	0.74	0.03	0.69	0.5	0.0	11.0	0.0	3	0.43	3.2	26	64	382	0.5	44	0.00	0.00
0.79	0.28	4.76	0.46	2.38	1.7	0.0	—	0.2	9	1.28	18.7	195	289	1607	3.6	35	0.00	0.00
—	—	—	—	—	4.7	0.0	—	—	5	0.75	6.5	99	74	416	1.3	56	0.00	0.00
0.03	0.27	1.50	0.05	3.61	7.9	0.0	8.6	0.1	2	1.67	2.0	30	36	206	0.5	48	0.00	0.00
—	—	—	—	—	—	0.0	—	—	20	0.36	—	—	—	440	—	59	0.00	0.00
0.28	0.07	1.88	0.10	0.54	1.1	0.0	24.2	0.0	7	0.47	7.7	75	130	847	1.1	55	0.00	0.00
—	—	—	—	—	—	0.0	—	—	8	0.82	8.6	76	114	401	1.2	50	0.00	0.00
—	—	—	—	—	—	0.0	—	—	0	0.00	—	—	—	300	—	71	0.00	0.00
—	—	—	—	—	—	0.0	—	—	4	0.50	7.3	103	77	433	0.9	56	0.00	0.00

PAGE KEY: A-108 Beverage and Beverage Mixes A-112 Other Beverages A-112 Beverages, Alcoholic A-114 Candies and Confections, Gum A-114 Cereals, Breakfast Type A-118 Cheese and Cheese Substitutes A-120 Dairy Products and Substitutes A-122 Desserts A-128 Dessert Toppings A-128 Eggs, Substitutes, and Egg Dishes A-130 Ethnic Foods A-130 Fast Foods/Restaurants A-140 Fats, Oils, Margarines, Shortenings, and Substitutes A-142 Fish, Seafood, and Shellfish A-142 Food Additives A-142 Fruit, Vegetable, and Blended Juices A-144 Fruits A-146 Grains, Flours, and Fractions A-148 Grain Products, Prepared and Baked Goods

Code	Food Name	Unit/ Amt	Wt (g)	Energy (Kcal)	Prot (g)	Carb (g)	Fiber (g)	Fat (g)	Sat (g)	Mono (g)	Poly (g)	Chol (mg)	Vit A (RE)
Pork and Ham													
27096	Bacon Bits, Oscar Mayer	1 Tbs	7	24	3	0	0	1	0.5	0.7	0.2	5	0
12000	Bacon, brld/pan fried/rstd, med slice	3 pce	19	109	6	0	0	9	3.3	4.5	1.1	16	0
12244	Bacon, low sod, ckd, Oscar Mayer	2 pce	12	56	4	1	0	4	1.6	2.1	0.5	12	0
28143	Canadian Bacon, svg	1 ea	56	68	9	1	—	3	1.0	1.4	0.3	27	0
12240	Pork, average of retail cuts, loin & shoulder blade, ckd	3 oz	85	214	24	0	0	13	4.5	5.6	1.0	73	2
12040	Pork, chop, blade loin, lean, pan fried	3 oz	85	205	21	0	0	13	4.4	5.3	1.7	70	2
12213	Pork, cured, ham, center slice, country style, lean, raw	3 oz	85	166	24	0	0	7	2.4	3.2	0.8	60	0
12099	Pork, ground, ckd	3 oz	85	253	22	0	0	18	6.6	7.9	1.6	80	2
12124	Pork, ham, w/bbq sauce	1 cup	263	473	52	8	1	24	8.3	11.1	2.7	148	51
12010	Pork, ribs, spareribs, brsd	3 oz	85	338	25	0	0	26	9.5	11.5	2.3	103	3
12125	Pork, ribs, w/bbq sauce	1 ea	68	122	14	2	0	6	2.2	2.9	0.7	38	13
12022	Pork, roast, blade loin, rstd	3 oz	85	275	20	0	0	21	7.8	9.0	1.8	79	3
12065	Pork, roast, top loin, lean, rstd	3 oz	85	165	26	0	0	6	2.2	2.9	0.4	66	2
12900	Pork, sweet & sour	1 cup	226	231	15	25	2	8	2.1	3.2	2.3	39	31
Veal													
11552	Veal, avg of all cuts, lean, ckd	3 oz	85	167	27	0	0	6	1.6	2.0	0.5	100	0
11530	Veal, ground, brld, 8% fat	3 oz	85	146	21	0	0	6	2.6	2.4	0.5	88	0
11518	Veal, loin chop, lean, brsd	3 oz	85	192	29	0	0	8	2.2	2.8	0.7	106	0
Variety Meats and By-Products													
10010	Beef, liver, fried	3 oz	85	185	23	7	0	7	2.3	1.4	1.5	410	9064
15105	Chicken, broiler/fryer, giblets, chpd, fried	1 cup	145	402	47	6	0	20	5.5	6.4	4.9	647	5194
13258	Pate, liver, unspecified, cnd	1 Tbs	13	41	2	0	0	4	1.2	1.6	0.4	33	129
Meat Substitutes, Soy Tofu and Vegetable													
7509	Bacon Substitute, vegetarian, strips	3 ea	15	46	2	1	0	4	0.7	1.1	2.3	0	1
91055	Burger Substitute, vegetarian, fzn	1 ea	85	91	14	8	4	1	0.1	0.3	0.2	0	0
8817	Burger Substitute, vegetarian, Gardenburger, vegan	1 ea	71	140	11	23	4	0	—	—	—	0	2
7547	Chicken Substitute, vegetarian	2 ea	60	132	10	4	3	8	1.3	2.0	4.4	0	0
7560	Meatloaf Substitute, vegetarian, slice	1 ea	71	142	15	6	3	6	1.0	1.6	3.3	0	0
7519	Tofu, dried, fzn	1 pce	17	82	8	2	1	5	0.7	1.1	2.9	0	9
7540	Tofu, extra firm, silken, slice	1 pce	84	46	6	2	0	2	0.3	0.3	0.9	0	0
7542	Tofu, firm, silken, slice	1 pce	84	52	6	2	0	2	0.3	0.5	1.2	0	0
91240	Tofu, rducd fat, water pack, block or ⅕ pce, Silk	1 pce	91	90	10	4	2	4	0.0	—	—	0	0
7541	Tofu, soft, silken, slice	1 pce	84	46	4	2	0	2	0.3	0.4	1.3	0	0
NUTS, SEEDS, AND PRODUCTS													
4574	Coconut, dried, flaked, swtnd, pkg	1 cup	74	351	2	35	3	24	21.1	1.0	0.3	0	0
4508	Coconut, fresh, 2" x 2" x ½"	1 pce	45	159	1	7	4	15	13.4	0.6	0.2	0	0
4500	Nuts, almonds	1 cup	142	821	30	28	17	72	5.5	45.7	17.3	0	3
4519	Nuts, cashews, dry rstd, salted	1 cup	137	786	21	45	4	63	12.5	37.4	10.7	0	0
4621	Nuts, cashews, dry rstd, unsalted	1 cup	137	786	21	45	4	63	12.5	37.4	10.7	0	0
4646	Nuts, chestnuts, Chinese, ckd	2 oz	57	87	2	19	1	0	0.1	0.2	0.1	0	8
4644	Nuts, chestnuts, Chinese, raw	2 oz	57	127	2	28	1	1	0.1	0.3	0.2	0	11
4514	Nuts, filberts/hazelnuts, chpd	1 cup	115	722	17	19	11	70	5.1	52.5	9.1	0	5
51070	Nuts, macadamia, dry rstd, salted	11 ea	28	203	2	4	2	22	3.4	16.8	0.4	0	0
4595	Nuts, mixed, w/o peanuts, oil rstd, salted	1 cup	144	886	22	32	8	81	13.1	47.7	16.5	0	3
4594	Nuts, mixed, w/o peanuts, oil rstd, unsalted	1 cup	144	886	22	32	8	81	13.1	47.7	16.5	0	3
4592	Nuts, mixed, w/peanuts, dry rstd, salted	1 cup	137	814	24	35	12	70	9.5	43.0	14.8	0	3
4591	Nuts, mixed, w/peanuts, dry rstd, unsalted	1 cup	137	814	24	35	12	70	9.5	43.0	14.8	0	3
4753	Nuts, peanuts, ckd w/salt, shelled	33 ea	28	89	4	6	2	6	0.9	3.1	1.9	0	0
4763	Nuts, peanuts, oil rstd, salted	1 ea	1	5	0	0	0	0	0.1	0.2	0.1	0	0

PAGE KEY: A-154 Granola Bars, Cereal Bars, Diet Bars, Scones, and Tarts A-154 Meals and Dishes A-160 Meats A-164 Nuts, Seeds, and Products A-166 Poultry A-166 Salad Dressings, Dips, and Mayonnaise A-170 Salads A-170 Sandwiches A-172 Sauces and Gravies A-174 Snack Foods—Chips, Pretzels, Popcorn A-178 Soups, Stews and Chilis A-184 Spices, Flavors, and Seasonings A-184 Sports Bars and Drinks A-186 Supplemental Foods and Formulas A-186 Sweeteners and Sweet Substitutes A-188 Vegetables and Legumes A-200 Weight Loss Bars & Drinks A-200 Miscellaneous

Thia (mg)	Ribo (mg)	Niac (mg NE)	Vit B6 (mg)	Vit B12 (µg)	Fol (µg)	Vit C (mg)	Vit D (IU)	Vit E (mg AT)	Cal (mg)	Iron (mg)	Magn (mg)	Phos (mg)	Pota (mg)	Sodi (mg)	Zinc (mg)	Wat (%)	Alco (g)	Caff (g)
–	–	–	–	–	–	0.0	–	–	2	0.20	4.6	43	39	224	0.3	35	0.00	0.00
0.12	0.05	1.38	0.05	0.33	0.9	0.0	2.3	0.1	2	0.31	4.6	64	92	303	0.6	13	0.00	0.00
–	–	–	–	–	–	0.0	–	–	2	0.20	5.9	58	185	175	0.4	22	0.00	0.00
–	–	–	–	–	–	0.8	–	–	3	0.50	10.6	–	156	569	1.0	73	0.00	0.00
0.72	0.28	4.21	0.34	0.62	5.1	0.3	10.2	0.2	20	0.83	20.4	193	308	48	2.2	57	0.00	0.00
0.62	0.30	3.77	0.34	0.81	3.4	0.7	10.2	0.2	19	0.91	22.1	188	310	66	3.3	59	0.00	0.00
0.47	0.20	3.29	0.36	0.75	4.3	0.0	10.2	0.2	9	0.93	21.3	270	434	2292	2.4	56	0.00	0.00
0.60	0.18	3.57	0.33	0.46	5.1	0.6	10.2	0.2	19	1.10	20.4	192	308	62	2.7	53	0.00	0.00
1.65	0.62	11.11	0.81	1.46	11.4	4.3	–	1.2	44	2.98	54.6	502	846	1949	5.5	65	0.00	0.00
0.34	0.31	4.65	0.30	0.92	3.4	0.0	10.2	0.2	40	1.57	20.4	222	272	79	3.9	40	0.00	0.00
0.43	0.15	2.88	0.20	0.37	3.0	1.1	–	0.3	11	0.76	14.1	130	219	504	1.4	65	0.00	0.00
0.44	0.25	3.59	0.31	0.62	3.4	0.2	10.2	0.3	29	0.93	17.0	179	277	26	2.8	51	0.00	0.00
0.54	0.27	4.55	0.34	0.46	7.7	0.3	10.2	0.3	4	0.89	21.3	188	301	38	2.0	62	0.00	0.00
0.55	0.20	3.63	0.40	0.34	10.3	19.6	27.1	1.1	28	1.44	34.4	149	386	839	1.5	77	0.00	0.00
0.05	0.28	7.15	0.28	1.39	13.6	0.0	10.2	0.4	20	0.99	23.8	213	287	76	4.3	60	0.00	0.00
0.05	0.23	6.82	0.33	1.08	9.4	0.0	10.2	0.1	14	0.83	20.4	185	287	71	3.3	67	0.00	0.00
0.03	0.28	8.55	0.23	1.12	12.8	0.0	10.2	0.4	27	0.93	23.0	202	253	71	3.5	57	0.00	0.00
0.18	3.51	12.27	1.22	95.08	187.1	19.6	10.2	0.5	9	5.34	19.6	392	310	90	4.6	56	0.00	0.00
0.14	2.21	15.93	0.87	19.29	549.5	12.6	17.4	3.6	26	14.96	36.2	415	479	164	9.1	48	0.00	0.00
0.00	0.07	0.43	0.00	0.41	7.8	0.3	–	–	9	0.70	1.7	26	18	91	0.4	54	0.00	0.00
0.66	0.07	1.12	0.07	0.00	6.3	0.0	0.0	1.0	3	0.36	2.9	10	26	220	0.1	49	0.00	0.00
0.25	0.55	4.11	0.20	0.00	245.7	0.0	–	0.0	87	2.90	16.1	181	434	382	0.7	71	0.00	0.00
0.03	0.20	4.90	0.25	0.00	5.9	0.6	2.9	0.5	18	1.00	24.7	53	181	250	0.6	50	0.00	0.00
0.66	0.23	3.18	0.41	1.25	45.6	0.0	–	1.6	21	0.77	10.2	201	198	474	0.4	59	0.00	0.00
0.63	0.43	7.09	0.85	1.70	55.4	0.0	–	1.2	21	1.49	12.8	244	128	390	1.3	58	0.00	0.00
0.07	0.05	0.20	0.05	0.00	15.6	0.1	0.0	0.0	62	1.64	10.0	82	3	1	0.8	6	0.00	0.00
0.07	0.02	0.20	0.00	0.00	–	0.0	–	0.1	26	1.00	22.7	84	129	53	0.5	88	0.00	0.00
0.07	0.02	0.20	0.00	0.00	–	0.0	–	0.2	27	0.87	22.7	76	163	30	0.5	87	0.00	0.00
–	–	–	–	–	–	0.0	–	–	40	1.44	–	–	–	5	–	79	0.00	0.00
0.07	0.02	0.25	0.00	0.00	–	0.0	–	0.2	26	0.68	24.4	52	151	4	0.4	89	0.00	0.00
0.01	0.00	0.21	0.18	0.00	5.9	0.0	0.0	0.5	10	1.33	35.5	74	234	189	1.3	16	0.00	0.00
0.02	0.00	0.23	0.01	0.00	11.7	1.5	0.0	0.3	6	1.09	14.4	51	160	9	0.5	47	0.00	0.00
0.34	1.14	5.57	0.18	0.00	41.2	0.0	0.0	37.2	352	6.11	390.5	673	1034	1	4.8	5	0.00	0.00
0.27	0.27	1.91	0.34	0.00	94.5	0.0	0.0	0.8	62	8.22	356.2	671	774	877	7.7	2	0.00	0.00
0.27	0.27	1.91	0.34	0.00	94.5	0.0	0.0	0.8	62	8.22	356.2	671	774	22	7.7	2	0.00	0.00
0.05	0.07	0.31	0.15	0.00	26.1	14.0	0.0	0.2	7	0.55	32.9	37	174	1	0.3	62	0.00	0.00
0.09	0.10	0.44	0.23	0.00	38.6	20.4	0.0	0.3	10	0.80	47.6	54	253	2	0.5	44	0.00	0.00
0.74	0.12	2.06	0.64	0.00	129.9	7.2	0.0	17.5	131	5.40	187.4	334	782	0	2.8	5	0.00	0.00
0.20	0.01	0.63	0.10	0.00	2.8	0.2	–	0.2	20	0.75	33.5	56	103	75	0.4	2	0.00	0.00
0.73	0.69	2.82	0.25	0.00	80.6	0.7	0.0	8.6	153	3.70	361.4	647	783	1008	6.7	3	0.00	0.00
0.73	0.69	2.82	0.25	0.00	80.6	0.7	0.0	8.6	153	3.70	361.4	647	783	16	6.7	3	0.00	0.00
0.27	0.27	6.44	0.40	0.00	68.5	0.5	0.0	8.2	96	5.07	308.2	596	818	917	5.2	2	0.00	0.00
0.27	0.27	6.44	0.40	0.00	68.5	0.5	0.0	8.2	96	5.07	308.2	596	818	16	5.2	2	0.00	0.00
0.07	0.01	1.47	0.03	0.00	21.0	0.0	0.0	0.9	15	0.28	28.6	55	50	210	0.5	42	0.00	0.00
0.00	0.00	0.12	0.00	0.00	1.1	0.0	0.0	0.1	1	0.01	1.7	5	6	4	0.1	2	0.00	0.00

PAGE KEY: A-108 Beverage and Beverage Mixes A-112 Other Beverages A-112 Beverages, Alcoholic A-114 Candies and Confections, Gum A-114 Cereals, Breakfast Type A-118 Cheese and Cheese Substitutes A-120 Dairy Products and Substitutes A-122 Desserts A-128 Dessert Toppings A-128 Eggs, Substitutes, and Egg Dishes A-130 Ethnic Foods A-130 Fast Foods/Restaurants A-140 Fats, Oils, Margarines, Shortenings, and Substitutes A-142 Fish, Seafood, and Shellfish A-142 Food Additives A-142 Fruit, Vegetable, and Blended Juices A-144 Fruits A-146 Grains, Flours, and Fractions A-148 Grain Products, Prepared and Baked Goods

Code	Food Name	Unit/ Amt	Wt (g)	Energy (Kcal)	Prot (g)	Carb (g)	Fiber (g)	Fat (g)	Sat (g)	Mono (g)	Poly (g)	Chol (mg)	Vit A (RE)
4542	Nuts, peanuts, oil rstd, unsalted, chpd	1 cup	133	773	35	25	9	66	9.1	32.5	20.7	0	0
4699	Nuts, peanuts, Spanish, oil rstd, salted	0.5 cup	74	426	21	13	7	36	5.6	16.2	12.5	0	0
4517	Nuts, peanuts, Spanish, raw	1 cup	146	832	38	23	14	72	11.2	32.6	25.1	0	0
4578	Nuts, pecans, halves	1 cup	108	746	10	15	10	78	6.7	44.1	23.3	0	9
4586	Nuts, pecans, oil rstd, salted	1 cup	110	786	10	14	–	83	8.0	45.1	25.9	0	11
4764	Nuts, pine, pignolia, dried	1 cup	136	770	33	19	6	69	10.6	25.9	29.0	0	3
4540	Nuts, pistachio, dry rstd, salted	47 ea	28	161	6	8	3	13	1.6	6.9	3.9	0	15
4520	Nuts, pistachio, raw	1 cup	128	713	26	36	13	57	7.0	29.8	17.2	0	72
63261	Nuts, soy, wheat free	1 oz	28	137	11	8	3	6	1.0	–	–	1	1
4525	Nuts, walnuts, black, dried, chpd	1 cup	125	772	30	12	8	74	4.2	18.8	43.8	0	5
62938	Peanut Butter, creamy, rducd fat, Jif	2 Tbs	36	190	8	15	2	12	2.5	–	–	0	0
4627	Peanut Butter, creamy, w/salt	2 Tbs	32	190	8	6	2	16	3.3	7.8	4.4	0	0
62937	Peanut Butter, crunchy, extra, Jif	2 Tbs	32	190	8	7	2	16	3.0	–	–	0	0
4747	Peanut Butter, rducd fat	1 Tbs	16	81	4	5	1	5	1.0	2.8	1.6	0	–
4625	Seeds, pumpkin & squash, kernels, rstd, salted	1 cup	227	1185	75	30	9	96	18.1	29.7	43.6	0	86
4676	Seeds, safflower, kernels, dried	1 oz	28	147	5	10	2	11	1.0	1.4	8.0	0	2
4545	Seeds, sunflower, kernels, dried	1 cup	144	821	33	27	15	71	7.5	13.6	47.1	0	9
4708	Seeds, sunflower, kernels, tstd, salted	1 cup	134	829	23	28	15	76	8.0	14.5	50.3	0	0
POULTRY													
Chicken—BBQ, Breaded, Fried, Glazed, Grilled, Raw													
81186	Chicken, breast, oven rstd, fat free, sliced	2 pce	42	33	7	1	0	0	0.1	0.1	0.0	15	0
81147	Chicken, breast, w/o skin	3 oz	85	151	15	0	–	10	3.3	4.6	2.1	54	–
15004	Chicken, broiler/fryer, breast, w/o skin, rstd	3 oz	85	140	26	0	0	3	0.9	1.1	0.7	72	5
15003	Chicken, broiler/fryer, breast, w/skin, flour fried	3 oz	85	189	27	1	0	8	2.1	3.0	1.7	76	13
15001	Chicken, broiler/fryer, breast, w/skin, rstd	3 oz	85	168	25	0	0	7	1.9	2.6	1.4	71	24
15218	Chicken, broiler/fryer, dark meat, w/o skin, rstd	3 oz	85	174	23	0	0	8	2.3	3.0	1.9	79	19
15113	Chicken, broiler/fryer, dark meat, w/skin, batter fried	3 oz	85	253	19	8	0	16	4.2	6.4	3.8	76	26
15080	Chicken, broiler/fryer, dark meat, w/skin, rstd	3 oz	85	215	22	0	0	13	3.7	5.3	3.0	77	51
15010	Chicken, broiler/fryer, thigh, w/skin, rstd	3 oz	85	210	21	0	0	13	3.7	5.2	2.9	79	43
15059	Chicken, broiler/fryer, wing, w/o skin, rstd	3 oz	85	173	26	0	0	7	1.9	2.2	1.5	72	15
15034	Chicken, broiler/fryer, wing, w/skin, batter fried	3 oz	85	276	17	9	0	19	5.0	7.6	4.3	67	29
15029	Chicken, broiler/fryer, wing, w/skin, flour fried	3 oz	85	273	22	2	0	19	5.2	7.6	4.2	69	32
15002	Chicken, broiler/fryer, wing, w/skin, rstd	3 oz	85	247	23	0	0	17	4.6	6.5	3.5	71	40
15913	Chicken, drumstick, w/mushroom soup sauce	1 ea	68	99	11	2	0	5	1.3	1.4	1.6	33	8
15252	Chicken, ground, mechanically, prep, svg, 4oz	1 ea	64	103	13	1	0	5	1.4	–	–	43	17
15243	Chicken, nuggets	4 pce	73	207	12	11	0	13	4.0	6.2	1.6	44	22
15947	Chicken, tenders, ckd f/fzn, Banquet	3 pce	89	250	12	15	1	15	3.5	–	–	40	0
Turkey													
13125	Bacon, turkey, svg	1 ea	14	35	2	0	0	3	0.7	1.1	0.7	13	0
16086	Turkey, avg, breast, w/skin, rstd	3 oz	85	161	24	0	0	6	1.8	2.1	1.5	63	0
16028	Turkey, avg, dark meat, w/skin, rstd	3 oz	85	188	23	0	0	10	3.0	3.1	2.6	76	0
16027	Turkey, avg, light meat, w/skin, rstd	3 oz	85	168	24	0	0	7	2.0	2.4	1.7	65	0
16000	Turkey, avg, w/o skin, rstd	3 oz	85	145	25	0	0	4	1.4	0.9	1.2	65	0
Duck, Emu, Ostrich and Other													
15069	Cornish Game Hen, rstd	3 oz	85	221	19	0	0	15	4.3	6.8	3.1	111	27
16294	Duck, domesticated, whole, rstd, chpd	1 cup	140	472	27	0	0	40	13.5	18.1	5.1	118	88
SALAD DRESSINGS, DIPS, AND MAYONNAISE													
Dips													
27132	Dip, avocado	2 Tbs	32	60	1	4	0	4	3.0	–	–	0	0
11802	Dip, bean, black, Old El Oaso	2 Tbs	30	25	1	5	1	0	0.0	0.0	0.0	0	0

Thia (mg)	Ribo (mg)	Niac (mg NE)	Vit B6 (mg)	Vit B12 (µg)	Fol (µg)	Vit C (mg)	Vit D (IU)	Vit E (mg AT)	Cal (mg)	Iron (mg)	Magn (mg)	Phos (mg)	Pota (mg)	Sodi (mg)	Zinc (mg)	Wat (%)	Alco (g)	Caff (g)
0.34	0.14	18.98	0.34	0.00	167.6	0.0	0.0	9.9	117	2.43	246.1	688	907	8	8.8	2	0.00	0.00
0.23	0.05	10.97	0.18	0.00	92.6	0.0	0.0	7.4	74	1.67	123.5	284	570	318	1.5	2	0.00	0.00
0.99	0.20	23.25	0.50	0.00	350.4	0.0	0.0	10.8	155	5.71	274.5	566	1086	32	3.1	6	0.00	0.00
0.70	0.14	1.25	0.23	0.00	23.8	1.2	0.0	4.4	76	2.73	130.7	299	443	0	4.9	4	0.00	0.00
0.51	0.11	1.32	0.20	0.00	16.5	0.8	0.0	5.7	74	2.72	133.1	289	431	432	4.9	1	0.00	0.00
1.10	0.25	4.86	0.15	0.00	77.5	2.6	0.0	4.8	35	12.51	316.9	691	815	5	5.8	7	0.00	0.00
0.23	0.03	0.40	0.47	0.00	14.2	0.7	0.0	1.2	31	1.19	34.0	137	295	115	0.7	2	0.00	0.00
1.11	0.20	1.65	2.18	0.00	65.3	6.4	0.0	5.9	137	5.30	154.9	627	1312	1	2.8	4	0.00	0.00
–	–	–	–	–	–	0.0	–	–	60	1.80	–	–	–	11	–	3	0.00	0.00
0.07	0.15	0.58	0.73	0.00	38.8	2.1	0.0	5.9	76	3.90	251.2	641	654	2	4.2	5	0.00	0.00
–	–	5.00	0.11	0.00	24.0	0.0	–	–	0	0.72	60.0	–	–	250	0.9	2	0.00	0.00
0.02	0.02	4.28	0.15	0.00	23.7	0.0	0.0	3.2	12	0.58	50.9	118	214	149	0.9	1	0.00	0.00
–	0.02	4.00	–	0.00	–	0.0	–	2.0	0	0.72	–	–	–	130	–	1	0.00	0.00
–	–	2.07	–	0.00	–	–	–	–	6	0.31	–	59	115	89	–	3	0.00	0.00
0.47	0.72	3.95	0.20	0.00	129.4	4.1	0.0	2.3	98	33.90	1212.2	2660	1830	1305	16.9	7	0.00	0.00
0.33	0.11	0.64	0.33	0.00	45.4	0.0	0.0	4.2	22	1.38	100.1	183	195	1	1.4	6	0.00	0.00
3.29	0.36	6.48	1.11	0.00	326.9	2.0	0.0	72.4	167	9.75	509.8	1015	992	4	7.3	5	0.00	0.00
0.43	0.37	5.63	1.08	0.00	318.9	1.9	0.0	67.4	76	9.13	172.9	1552	658	821	7.1	1	0.00	0.00
0.00	0.00	1.44	0.05	0.03	0.4	0.0	–	0.0	3	0.12	3.8	25	28	457	0.1	77	0.00	0.00
–	–	–	–	–	–	–	–	–	–	–	–	–	–	4	–	70	0.00	0.00
0.05	0.10	11.65	0.50	0.28	3.4	0.0	10.2	0.2	13	0.87	24.7	194	218	63	0.9	65	0.00	0.00
0.07	0.10	11.68	0.49	0.28	5.1	0.0	10.2	0.5	14	1.00	25.5	198	220	65	0.9	57	0.00	0.00
0.05	0.10	10.81	0.47	0.27	3.4	0.0	10.2	0.2	12	0.91	23.0	182	208	60	0.9	62	0.00	0.00
0.05	0.18	5.57	0.31	0.27	6.8	0.0	10.2	0.2	13	1.12	19.6	152	204	79	2.4	63	0.00	0.00
0.10	0.18	4.76	0.20	0.23	15.3	0.0	10.2	1.0	18	1.22	17.0	123	157	251	1.8	49	0.00	0.00
0.05	0.18	5.40	0.25	0.25	6.0	0.0	10.2	0.5	13	1.15	18.7	143	187	74	2.1	59	0.00	0.00
0.05	0.18	5.40	0.25	0.25	6.0	0.0	10.2	0.2	10	1.13	18.7	148	189	71	2.0	59	0.00	0.00
0.03	0.10	6.21	0.50	0.28	3.4	0.0	10.2	0.2	14	0.99	17.9	141	179	78	1.8	63	0.00	0.00
0.09	0.12	4.48	0.25	0.20	15.3	0.0	10.2	0.9	17	1.10	13.6	103	117	272	1.2	46	0.00	0.00
0.05	0.11	5.69	0.34	0.23	5.1	0.0	10.2	0.5	13	1.05	16.2	128	151	65	1.5	49	0.00	0.00
0.03	0.10	5.65	0.36	0.25	2.6	0.0	10.2	0.2	13	1.08	16.2	128	156	70	1.5	55	0.00	0.00
0.02	0.09	3.50	0.18	0.15	3.2	0.3	–	0.4	19	0.55	10.8	85	114	216	0.9	73	0.00	0.00
–	–	–	–	–	–	1.4	–	–	8	0.40	–	–	–	103	–	66	0.00	0.00
0.07	0.10	4.90	0.23	0.21	8.0	0.3	8.8	1.4	12	0.91	14.6	146	180	388	0.8	49	0.00	0.00
0.23	0.09	6.80	–	–	–	1.2	–	–	0	0.72	–	257	342	480	–	52	0.00	0.00
–	–	–	–	–	1.1	0.0	–	–	6	0.20	2.7	28	29	170	0.4	59	0.00	0.00
0.05	0.10	5.40	0.40	0.31	5.1	0.0	10.2	0.2	18	1.19	23.0	179	245	54	1.7	63	0.00	0.00
0.05	0.20	3.00	0.27	0.31	7.7	0.0	10.2	0.5	28	1.92	19.6	167	233	65	3.5	60	0.00	0.00
0.05	0.10	5.34	0.40	0.30	5.1	0.0	10.2	0.1	18	1.20	22.1	177	242	54	1.7	63	0.00	0.00
0.05	0.15	4.63	0.38	0.31	6.0	0.0	10.2	0.3	21	1.50	22.1	181	253	60	2.6	65	0.00	0.00
0.05	0.17	5.01	0.25	0.23	1.7	0.4	10.2	0.2	11	0.76	15.3	124	208	54	1.3	59	0.00	0.00
0.23	0.37	6.75	0.25	0.41	8.4	0.0	–	1.0	15	3.77	22.4	218	286	83	2.6	52	0.00	0.00
–	–	–	–	–	–	0.0	–	–	0	0.00	–	0	25	240	–	71	0.00	0.00
–	–	–	–	–	–	0.0	–	–	0	0.36	–	–	–	280	–	76	0.00	0.00

PAGE KEY: A-108 Beverage and Beverage Mixes A-112 Other Beverages A-112 Beverages, Alcoholic A-114 Candies and Confections, Gum A-114 Cereals, Breakfast Type A-118 Cheese and Cheese Substitutes A-120 Dairy Products and Substitutes A-122 Desserts A-128 Dessert Toppings A-128 Eggs, Substitutes, and Egg Dishes A-130 Ethnic Foods A-130 Fast Foods/Restaurants A-140 Fats, Oils, Margarines, Shortenings, and Substitutes A-142 Fish, Seafood, and Shellfish A-142 Food Additives A-142 Fruit, Vegetable, and Blended Juices A-144 Fruits A-146 Grains, Flours, and Fractions A-148 Grain Products, Prepared and Baked Goods

Code	Food Name	Unit/ Amt	Wt (g)	Energy (Kcal)	Prot (g)	Carb (g)	Fiber (g)	Fat (g)	Sat (g)	Mono (g)	Poly (g)	Chol (mg)	Vit A (RE)
53557	Dip, cheddar cheese, mild	2 Tbs	34	60	1	3	0	4	1.5	—	—	5	0
27125	Dip, cheese 'n salsa, med, Old El Paso	2 Tbs	29	40	1	3	0	3	1.0	—	—	3	0
44416	Dip, clam	2 Tbs	28	50	1	1	0	5	3.0	—	—	15	40
53554	Dip, French onion	2 Tbs	33	60	1	4	0	5	3.0	—	—	15	20
8773	Dip, hummus, dry mix	2 Tbs	16	60	3	9	2	2	0.0	—	—	0	0
27137	Dip, jalapeno	2 Tbs	31	60	1	3	0	4	3.0	—	—	0	0
27138	Dip, ranch	2 Tbs	31	60	1	3	0	4	3.0	—	—	0	0
90861	Dip, salsa con queso, med/mild	2 Tbs	34	45	1	5	1	2	0.5	—	—	5	20
90086	Dip, salsa, fat free	2 Tbs	32	20	1	3	0	0	0.0	0.0	0.0	5	0
8136	Dip, sour cream, w/onion soup mix	1 cup	243	536	9	20	2	48	29.5	14.2	1.9	100	437
27143	Dip, spinach, Marie's	2 Tbs	28	140	0	3	0	14	2.0	—	—	10	80
44414	Dip, Veggie	2 Tbs	28	50	1	2	0	5	3.0	—	—	15	60
4012	Guacamole	1 ea	50	52	0	5	0	3	0.0	—	—	0	30
Mayonnaise													
8069	Mayonnaise, fat free	1 Tbs	16	11	0	2	0	0	0.1	—	—	2	3
8032	Mayonnaise, imit, soybean	1 Tbs	15	35	0	2	0	3	0.5	0.7	1.6	4	0
8231	Mayonnaise, imit, soybean, no cholest	1 Tbs	14	68	0	2	0	7	1.1	1.5	3.9	0	0
4070	Mayonnaise, light, Smart Balance	1 Tbs	15	50	0	2	—	5	0.0	2.5	1.5	5	0
8148	Mayonnaise, low cal, low sod	1 Tbs	14	32	0	2	0	3	0.5	0.6	1.5	3	1
Salad Dressings-Lower Calorie/Fat/Sodium/Cholest		—	—	—	—	—	—	—	—	—	—	—	—
90831	Salad Dressing, caesar Italian, fat free	2 Tbs	33	25	1	4	0	0	0.0	0.0	0.0	0	0
8138	Salad Dressing, caesar, low cal	1 Tbs	15	16	0	3	0	1	0.1	0.2	0.4	0	0
8499	Salad Dressing, French, fat free	2 Tbs	35	45	0	11	1	0	0.0	0.0	0.0	0	100
285	Salad Dressing, Italian, creamy, Benecol	2 Tbs	29	100	0	3	0	10	2.0	—	—	0	0
8475	Salad Dressing, Miracle Whip, fat free	1 Tbs	16	13	0	2	0	0	0.1	—	—	1	2
8502	Salad Dressing, Miracle Whip, light	1 Tbs	16	37	0	2	0	3	0.5	—	—	4	1
8122	Salad Dressing, Miracle Whip, low cal	1 Tbs	14	36	0	3	0	3	0.4	0.6	1.5	4	9
287	Salad Dressing, ranch	2 Tbs	29	130	0	3	0	13	2.0	—	—	0	0
8493	Salad Dressing, ranch, fat free	2 Tbs	35	48	0	11	0	0	0.1	—	—	0	1
8427	Salad Dressing, ranch, light	2 Tbs	30	100	0	5	0	8	1.5	—	—	5	0
90827	Salad Dressing, raspberry vinaigrette, fat free	2 Tbs	34	30	0	7	0	0	0.0	0.0	0.0	0	0
8562	Salad Dressing, red wine vinegar & oil, rducd fat, ⅓ less	2 Tbs	31	45	0	3	0	4	0.0	—	—	0	0
27212	Salad Dressing, vinegar, balsamic	2 Tbs	34	35	0	8	0	0	0.0	0.0	0.0	0	0
8765	Salad Dressing, zesty herb, fat free, prep f/dry mix	2 Tbs	31	10	0	2	0	0	0.0	0.0	0.0	0	0
Salad Dressings-Regular													
51087	Salad Dressing, blue cheese	1.5 oz	43	170	1	3	0	17	3.0	—	—	25	0
90838	Salad Dressing, caesar Italian	2 Tbs	31	100	1	2	0	10	1.5	—	—	0	0
8570	Salad Dressing, catalina	2 Tbs	32	120	0	7	0	10	1.5	—	—	0	100
8569	Salad Dressing, French, creamy	2 Tbs	32	160	0	5	0	15	2.5	—	—	0	250
90834	Salad Dressing, herb vinaigrette	2 Tbs	30	140	0	1	0	15	2.0	—	—	0	0
8579	Salad Dressing, honey dijon	2 Tbs	31	110	0	6	0	10	1.5	—	—	0	0
8612	Salad Dressing, Italian, zesty	2 Tbs	31	109	0	2	0	11	1.2	—	—	0	2
8479	Salad Dressing, Miracle Whip	1 Tbs	15	70	0	2	0	7	1.0	—	—	5	0
8594	Salad Dressing, ranch	2 Tbs	30	160	0	2	0	17	2.5	—	—	5	0
8595	Salad Dressing, red wine vinegar & oil	2 Tbs	30	90	0	2	0	9	1.0	—	—	0	0
51088	Salad Dressing, thousand island	1.5 oz	43	190	0	6	0	18	3.0	—	—	15	0
8429	Salad Dressing, vinaigrette, olive oil	2 Tbs	30	60	0	4	0	5	0.5	—	—	0	0

PAGE KEY: A-154 Granola Bars, Cereal Bars, Diet Bars, Scones, and Tarts A-154 Meals and Dishes A-160 Meats A-164 Nuts, Seeds, and Products A-166 Poultry A-166 Salad Dressings, Dips, and Mayonnaise A-170 Salads A-170 Sandwiches A-172 Sauces and Gravies A-174 Snack Foods—Chips, Pretzels, Popcorn A-178 Soups, Stews and Chilis A-184 Spices, Flavors, and Seasonings A-184 Sports Bars and Drinks A-186 Supplemental Foods and Formulas A-186 Sweeteners and Sweet Substitutes A-188 Vegetables and Legumes A-200 Weight Loss Bars & Drinks A-200 Miscellaneous

Thia (mg)	Ribo (mg)	Niac (mg NE)	Vit B6 (mg)	Vit B12 (µg)	Fol (µg)	Vit C (mg)	Vit D (IU)	Vit E (mg AT)	Cal (mg)	Iron (mg)	Magn (mg)	Phos (mg)	Pota (mg)	Sodi (mg)	Zinc (mg)	Wat (%)	Alco (g)	Caff (g)
–	–	–	–	–	–	0.0	–	–	60	0.00	–	–	–	330	–	73	0.00	0.00
–	–	–	–	–	–	0.0	–	–	20	0.00	–	–	–	300	–	72	0.00	0.00
–	–	–	–	–	–	0.0	–	–	20	0.00	–	–	–	120	–	70	0.00	0.00
–	–	–	–	–	–	0.0	–	–	0	0.00	–	–	–	230	–	69	0.00	0.00
–	–	–	–	–	–	0.0	–	–	20	1.08	–	–	–	220	–	11	0.00	0.00
–	–	–	–	–	–	0.0	–	–	0	0.00	–	0	25	260	–	69	0.00	0.00
–	–	–	–	–	–	0.0	–	–	0	0.00	–	–	20	210	–	68	0.00	0.00
–	–	–	–	–	–	0.0	–	–	20	0.00	–	–	–	270	–	–	0.00	0.00
–	–	–	–	–	–	0.0	–	–	60	0.00	–	100	85	240	–	–	0.00	0.00
0.12	0.44	1.12	0.05	0.67	27.3	2.4	13.4	1.5	288	0.41	37.3	252	449	1821	0.7	66	0.00	0.00
–	–	–	–	–	–	0.0	–	–	0	0.36	–	–	–	200	–	–	0.00	0.00
–	–	–	–	–	–	0.0	–	–	20	0.00	–	–	–	125	–	70	0.00	0.00
–	–	–	–	–	–	4.2	–	–	40	0.73	–	–	–	282	–	83	0.00	0.00
–	–	–	–	–	–	0.0	–	0.5	1	0.01	–	4	8	120	–	82	0.00	0.00
0.00	0.00	0.00	0.00	0.00	0.0	0.0	0.0	1.0	0	0.00	0.0	0	2	75	0.0	63	0.00	0.00
0.00	0.00	0.00	0.00	0.00	0.0	0.0	–	1.3	0	0.00	0.0	0	1	50	0.0	35	0.00	0.00
–	–	–	–	–	–	–	–	0.6	–	–	–	–	–	125	–	51	0.00	0.00
0.00	0.00	0.00	0.00	0.00	0.3	0.0	–	0.5	0	0.00	0.0	0	1	15	0.0	63	0.00	0.00
—	—	—	—	—	—	—	—	—	—	—	—	—	—	—	—	—	—	
–	–	–	–	–	–	0.0	–	–	20	0.00	–	80	50	480	–	83	0.00	0.00
0.00	0.00	0.00	0.00	0.00	0.3	0.0	0.0	0.1	4	0.02	0.3	3	4	162	0.0	73	0.00	0.00
–	–	–	–	–	–	0.0	–	–	0	0.00	–	0	25	300	–	68	0.00	0.00
–	–	–	–	–	–	0.0	–	–	0	0.00	–	–	–	170	–	52	0.00	0.00
–	–	–	–	–	–	0.0	–	0.0	1	0.01	–	1	8	126	–	79	0.00	0.00
–	–	–	–	–	–	0.0	–	0.1	1	0.02	–	2	4	131	–	63	0.00	0.00
0.00	0.00	0.00	0.00	0.02	0.8	0.0	–	0.6	2	0.02	0.3	4	1	99	0.0	54	0.00	0.00
–	–	–	–	–	–	0.0	–	–	0	0.00	–	–	–	250	–	43	0.00	0.00
–	–	–	–	–	–	0.0	–	–	9	0.01	–	28	31	354	–	64	0.00	0.00
–	–	–	–	–	–	0.0	–	–	0	0.00	–	–	–	240	–	56	0.00	0.00
–	–	–	–	–	–	0.0	–	–	0	0.00	–	0	15	320	–	78	0.00	0.00
–	–	–	–	–	–	0.0	–	–	0	0.00	–	0	10	320	–	76	0.00	0.00
–	–	–	–	–	–	0.0	–	–	0	0.00	–	–	15	460	–	76	0.00	0.00
–	–	–	–	–	–	0.0	–	–	0	0.00	–	0	70	260	–	92	0.00	0.00
–	–	–	–	–	–	0.0	–	–	20	0.00	–	–	–	330	–	47	0.00	0.00
–	–	–	–	–	–	0.0	–	–	20	0.00	–	20	25	480	–	56	0.00	0.00
–	–	–	–	–	–	0.0	–	–	0	0.00	–	0	35	390	–	46	0.00	0.00
–	–	–	–	–	–	0.0	–	–	0	0.00	–	0	20	270	–	37	0.00	0.00
–	–	–	–	–	–	0.0	–	–	0	0.00	–	0	10	250	–	46	0.00	0.00
–	–	–	–	–	–	0.0	–	–	0	0.00	–	0	35	210	–	48	0.00	0.00
–	–	–	–	–	–	0.2	–	–	1	0.05	–	4	9	505	–	53	0.00	0.00
–	–	–	–	–	–	0.0	–	0.0	0	0.00	–	0	0	95	–	34	0.00	0.00
–	–	–	–	–	–	0.0	–	–	0	0.00	–	0	20	260	–	36	0.00	0.00
–	–	–	–	–	–	0.0	–	–	0	0.00	–	0	10	500	–	62	0.00	0.00
–	–	–	–	–	–	0.0	–	–	0	0.00	–	–	–	430	–	41	0.00	0.00
–	–	–	–	–	–	0.0	–	–	0	0.00	–	–	–	250	–	69	0.00	0.00

PAGE KEY: A-108 Beverage and Beverage Mixes A-112 Other Beverages A-112 Beverages, Alcoholic A-114 Candies and Confections, Gum A-114 Cereals, Breakfast Type A-118 Cheese and Cheese Substitutes A-120 Dairy Products and Substitutes A-122 Desserts A-128 Dessert Toppings A-128 Eggs, Substitutes, and Egg Dishes A-130 Ethnic Foods A-130 Fast Foods/Restaurants A-140 Fats, Oils, Margarines, Shortenings, and Substitutes A-142 Fish, Seafood, and Shellfish A-142 Food Additives A-142 Fruit, Vegetable, and Blended Juices A-144 Fruits A-146 Grains, Flours, and Fractions A-148 Grain Products, Prepared and Baked Goods

Code	Food Name	Unit/ Amt	Wt (g)	Energy (Kcal)	Prot (g)	Carb (g)	Fiber (g)	Fat (g)	Sat (g)	Mono (g)	Poly (g)	Chol (mg)	Vit A (RE)
SALADS													
57482	Cole Slaw, homemade	0.5 cup	60	41	1	7	1	2	0.2	0.4	0.8	5	39
7827	Salad, bean, deli style, cnd	0.5 cup	127	80	4	20	4	0	0.0	0.0	0.0	0	100
57510	Salad, bean, three, f/rec	1 cup	270	215	9	45	12	1	0.0	–	–	0	26
56628	Salad, chef, w/turkey ham & cheese, w/o dressing	1.5 cup	326	267	26	5	–	16	8.2	5.2	1.4	140	183
52061	Salad, chicken	0.5 cup	100	250	10	9	2	20	4.0	–	–	55	20
56253	Salad, crab	1 cup	208	282	27	11	1	14	2.0	3.5	7.1	142	37
3246	Salad, fruit, in light syrup, cnd, not drained	0.5 cup	126	73	0	19	1	0	0.0	0.0	0.0	0	53
52029	Salad, macaroni, elbow, classic	0.66 cup	140	260	4	33	2	12	2.0	–	–	10	–
52094	Salad, pasta, garden primavera, prep f/dry	0.75 cup	142	240	8	35	2	8	1.5	–	–	5	60
4839	Salad, pasta, Greek, w/feta cheese	0.66 cup	140	200	6	27	3	8	2.0	–	–	5	–
52038	Salad, pasta, w/vegetables	0.66 cup	140	200	5	34	2	5	1.0	–	–	0	0
56005	Salad, potato, homemade	1 cup	250	358	7	28	3	20	3.6	6.2	9.3	170	88
52065	Salad, seafood	0.5 cup	100	230	6	14	8	17	2.5	–	–	20	0
5537	Salad, spinach, w/o dressing	1 cup	74	108	5	11	2	5	1.4	2.2	0.7	77	176
56643	Salad, taco	1.5 cup	198	279	13	24	–	15	6.8	5.2	1.7	44	93
5677	Salad, tossed green	0.75 cup	104	19	1	4	2	0	0.0	–	–	0	189
56624	Salad, tossed, w/cheese & egg, w/o dressing	1.5 cup	217	102	9	5	–	6	3.0	1.8	0.5	98	135
56007	Salad, tuna	1 cup	205	383	33	19	0	19	3.2	5.9	8.5	27	53
56006	Salad, waldorf, f/rec	1 cup	137	411	4	12	3	41	4.3	–	–	21	38
SANDWICHES													
56647	Cheeseburger, reg, w/condiments	1 ea	113	295	16	27	–	14	6.3	5.3	1.1	37	97
56022	Sandwich, avocado & cheese, on part whole wheat	1 ea	201	402	14	30	6	27	7.8	–	–	29	127
56260	Sandwich, bbq beef, w/bun	1 ea	186	358	18	36	2	15	5.0	6.6	1.4	46	73
56276	Sandwich, bbq pork, w/bun	1 ea	186	322	23	34	2	10	2.8	4.4	1.4	51	70
70917	Sandwich, beef & cheddar, Hot Pocket, fzn	1 ea	142	403	16	39	–	20	8.8	6.7	1.2	53	0
56020	Sandwich, beef & swiss, on rye	1 ea	156	427	28	22	6	26	9.5	–	–	83	82
10047	Sandwich, beef steak	1 ea	41	105	10	0	0	7	2.6	2.9	0.3	33	0
56265	Sandwich, beef, corned	1 ea	130	268	19	25	2	10	3.7	4.0	0.8	46	3
56011	Sandwich, BLT, bcn, lett & tomato, on part whole wheat	1 ea	124	313	11	26	3	19	4.6	–	–	22	32
56009	Sandwich, BLT, bacon, lettuce & tomato, on soft white	1 ea	124	318	10	29	2	18	4.1	–	–	20	29
56281	Sandwich, bologna	1 ea	83	256	7	26	1	13	4.1	6.3	2.1	16	37
56013	Sandwich, cheese, grilled, on soft white	1 ea	119	399	17	30	1	23	11.9	–	–	53	198
56017	Sandwich, chicken salad, on soft white	1 ea	110	365	10	31	2	22	2.7	–	–	30	23
56018	Sandwich, chicken salad, on whole wheat	1 ea	123	398	13	31	5	26	3.4	–	–	34	27
56278	Sandwich, chicken, bbq	1 ea	119	251	21	27	1	6	1.6	2.4	1.4	50	20
56657	Sandwich, egg & cheese	1 ea	146	340	16	26	–	19	6.6	8.3	2.6	291	201
56027	Sandwich, egg salad, on part whole wheat	1 ea	116	379	10	27	2	26	4.3	–	–	167	81
57518	Sandwich, fajita beef, w/cheese, on pita bread	1 ea	207	292	19	28	2	11	4.4	3.2	2.7	39	95
66011	Sandwich, fish, w/cheese & tartar sauce	1 ea	183	523	21	48	0	29	8.1	8.9	9.4	68	130
66010	Sandwich, fish, w/tartar sauce	1 ea	158	431	17	41	0	23	5.2	7.7	8.2	55	33
56268	Sandwich, French dip, w/au jus	1 ea	193	363	25	34	2	13	4.7	5.8	0.9	54	0
56272	Sandwich, gyro (pita bread w/beef & lamb)	1 ea	105	170	12	21	1	4	1.5	1.4	0.4	34	11
57780	Sandwich, ham & cheddar, Lean Pocket	1 ea	128	280	13	42	2	7	3.0	–	–	30	0
56664	Sandwich, ham & cheese	1 ea	146	352	21	33	–	15	6.4	6.7	1.4	58	96
70920	Sandwich, ham & cheese, Hot Pocket, fzn	1 ea	128	340	15	38	–	14	5.8	4.4	1.5	50	0
56665	Sandwich, ham egg & cheese	1 ea	143	347	19	31	–	16	7.4	5.7	1.7	246	167
56064	Sandwich, ham salad, on soft white	1 ea	131	360	10	37	1	19	4.2	–	–	29	8

PAGE KEY: A-154 Granola Bars, Cereal Bars, Diet Bars, Scones, and Tarts A-154 Meals and Dishes A-160 Meats A-164 Nuts, Seeds, and Products A-166 Poultry A-166 Salad Dressings, Dips, and Mayonnaise A-170 Salads A-170 Sandwiches A-172 Sauces and Gravies A-174 Snack Foods—Chips, Pretzels, Popcorn A-178 Soups, Stews and Chilis A-184 Spices, Flavors, and Seasonings A-184 Sports Bars and Drinks A-186 Supplemental Foods and Formulas A-186 Sweeteners and Sweet Substitutes A-188 Vegetables and Legumes A-200 Weight Loss Bars & Drinks A-200 Miscellaneous

Thia (mg)	Ribo (mg)	Niac (mg NE)	Vit B6 (mg)	Vit B12 (μg)	Fol (μg)	Vit C (mg)	Vit D (IU)	Vit E (mg AT)	Cal (mg)	Iron (mg)	Magn (mg)	Phos (mg)	Pota (mg)	Sodi (mg)	Zinc (mg)	Wat (%)	Alco (g)	Caff (g)
0.03	0.03	0.15	0.07	0.00	16.2	19.6	–	0.1	27	0.34	6.0	19	109	14	0.1	82	0.00	0.00
–	–	–	–	–	–	1.2	–	–	40	0.72	–	–	190	670	–	81	0.00	0.00
0.18	0.20	0.93	0.07	0.00	115.7	5.6	0.0	0.3	32	1.22	64.2	170	154	555	1.2	78	0.00	0.00
0.38	0.38	5.96	0.41	0.85	101.1	16.3	–	–	235	1.96	48.9	401	401	743	3.1	82	0.00	0.00
–	–	–	–	–	–	1.2	–	–	40	0.36	–	–	–	600	–	–	0.00	0.00
0.15	0.09	4.50	0.28	9.76	79.4	6.9	–	2.8	157	1.45	48.6	292	536	700	5.7	74	0.00	0.00
0.01	0.02	0.46	0.03	0.00	3.8	3.2	0.0	0.8	9	0.37	6.3	11	103	8	0.1	84	0.00	0.00
–	–	–	–	–	–	–	–	–	–	–	–	–	–	740	–	–	0.00	0.00
0.21	0.10	1.20	–	–	40.0	3.6	–	–	60	1.08	–	100	190	710	–	63	0.00	0.00
–	–	–	–	–	–	–	–	–	–	–	–	–	–	780	–	–	0.00	0.00
–	–	–	–	–	–	1.2	–	–	4	1.79	–	–	–	410	–	–	0.00	0.00
0.18	0.15	2.22	0.34	0.00	17.5	25.0	20.8	4.7	48	1.62	37.5	130	635	1322	0.8	76	0.00	0.00
–	–	–	–	–	–	0.0	–	–	20	0.36	–	–	–	770	–	–	0.00	0.00
0.12	0.28	1.66	0.10	0.20	59.9	6.7	0.0	0.9	46	1.46	27.1	83	242	227	0.6	70	0.00	0.00
0.10	0.36	2.46	0.21	0.62	83.2	3.6	–	–	192	2.27	51.5	143	416	762	2.7	72	0.00	0.00
0.07	0.07	0.54	0.07	0.00	75.3	18.1	0.0	0.6	35	0.98	19.2	31	287	19	0.3	94	0.00	0.00
0.09	0.17	0.98	0.10	0.30	84.6	9.8	–	–	100	0.67	23.9	132	371	119	1.0	90	0.00	0.00
0.05	0.14	13.72	0.17	2.46	16.4	4.5	264.4	1.9	35	2.04	39.0	365	365	824	1.1	63	0.00	0.00
0.09	0.05	0.54	0.36	0.09	33.7	5.4	0.0	8.6	44	0.97	37.1	89	258	235	0.7	58	0.00	0.00
0.25	0.23	3.72	0.10	0.93	54.2	1.9	–	0.5	111	2.43	20.3	176	223	616	2.1	48	0.00	0.00
0.30	0.37	3.46	0.31	0.25	84.7	12.3	2.5	3.2	272	5.96	56.3	224	576	454	1.6	63	0.00	0.00
0.28	0.27	5.73	0.23	1.51	21.8	5.8	–	1.3	92	3.63	35.5	149	368	1008	3.2	61	0.00	0.00
0.75	0.37	5.65	0.34	0.44	19.7	5.7	–	1.3	94	2.89	39.2	198	426	948	2.2	62	0.00	0.00
–	–	–	–	–	–	–	–	–	337	2.93	–	–	–	906	–	44	0.00	0.00
0.20	0.33	2.75	0.18	1.73	31.8	0.2	15.9	2.6	267	3.02	28.0	269	232	1470	3.6	47	0.00	0.00
0.01	0.10	1.92	0.10	0.81	3.7	0.0	4.9	0.1	3	0.97	8.6	66	128	29	2.2	58	0.00	0.00
0.23	0.25	3.23	0.10	0.87	21.6	2.0	–	0.3	67	2.67	20.3	110	186	1177	2.2	57	0.00	0.00
0.37	0.20	3.67	0.18	0.36	53.1	6.5	2.3	2.6	61	2.22	32.3	152	288	624	1.2	53	0.00	0.00
0.40	0.25	3.69	0.15	0.34	66.3	6.0	6.8	2.3	68	2.20	22.0	123	239	631	1.0	52	0.00	0.00
0.28	0.20	2.73	0.07	0.37	18.7	0.0	–	0.8	60	1.96	15.4	74	112	598	0.9	41	0.00	0.00
0.28	0.40	2.36	0.07	0.40	60.4	0.0	9.7	1.0	407	2.00	26.5	470	162	1155	2.0	37	0.00	0.00
0.30	0.23	4.07	0.27	0.14	62.8	0.5	7.2	5.5	76	2.20	20.1	100	146	481	0.8	41	0.00	0.00
0.25	0.18	4.46	0.37	0.15	38.8	0.6	8.0	6.6	59	2.59	63.1	201	251	527	1.8	41	0.00	0.00
0.28	0.28	7.25	0.30	0.18	21.2	0.9	–	0.4	66	2.32	28.4	159	217	422	1.5	54	0.00	0.00
0.25	0.56	2.06	0.12	1.13	97.8	1.5	–	–	225	2.98	21.9	302	188	804	1.6	56	0.00	0.00
0.25	0.34	2.30	0.23	0.46	60.5	0.0	21.4	4.7	81	2.39	29.4	152	165	481	1.0	44	0.00	0.00
0.34	0.30	4.15	0.41	1.65	36.9	33.4	–	1.5	182	2.53	38.5	252	464	778	2.7	70	0.00	0.00
0.46	0.41	4.23	0.10	1.08	91.5	2.7	36.6	1.8	185	3.50	36.6	311	353	939	1.2	45	0.00	0.00
0.33	0.21	3.40	0.10	1.07	85.3	2.8	–	0.9	84	2.60	33.2	212	340	615	1.0	47	0.00	0.00
0.37	0.37	5.92	0.21	2.02	24.9	0.0	–	0.4	104	4.19	31.7	212	380	616	5.1	61	0.00	0.00
0.23	0.20	3.14	0.12	0.89	17.8	3.8	–	0.3	46	1.85	20.9	116	209	272	2.3	64	0.00	0.00
–	–	–	–	–	–	0.0	–	–	200	2.70	–	–	–	600	–	50	0.00	0.00
0.31	0.47	2.69	0.20	0.54	75.9	2.8	–	0.3	130	3.24	16.1	152	291	771	1.4	51	0.00	0.00
–	–	–	–	–	–	–	–	–	251	2.60	–	–	–	666	–	45	0.00	0.00
0.43	0.56	4.19	0.15	1.23	75.8	2.7	–	0.6	212	3.09	25.7	346	210	1005	2.0	51	0.00	0.00
0.55	0.28	3.68	0.18	0.50	59.0	0.0	8.4	3.3	72	2.24	20.7	132	166	932	1.1	47	0.00	0.00

PAGE KEY: A-108 Beverage and Beverage Mixes A-112 Other Beverages A-112 Beverages, Alcoholic A-114 Candies and Confections, Gum A-114 Cereals, Breakfast Type A-118 Cheese and Cheese Substitutes A-120 Dairy Products and Substitutes A-122 Desserts A-128 Dessert Toppings A-128 Eggs, Substitutes, and Egg Dishes A-130 Ethnic Foods A-130 Fast Foods/Restaurants A-140 Fats, Oils, Margarines, Shortenings, and Substitutes A-142 Fish, Seafood, and Shellfish A-142 Food Additives A-142 Fruit, Vegetable, and Blended Juices A-144 Fruits A-146 Grains, Flours, and Fractions A-148 Grain Products, Prepared and Baked Goods

Code	Food Name	Unit/ Amt	Wt (g)	Energy (Kcal)	Prot (g)	Carb (g)	Fiber (g)	Fat (g)	Sat (g)	Mono (g)	Poly (g)	Chol (mg)	Vit A (RE)
56032	Sandwich, ham, on rye	1 ea	150	344	22	29	4	15	3.1	–	–	49	8
56029	Sandwich, ham, on soft white	1 ea	157	365	24	30	2	16	3.3	–	–	54	8
56267	Sandwich, pastrami	1 ea	134	331	14	27	2	18	6.2	8.7	1.0	51	3
56042	Sandwich, peanut butter & jam, on part whole wheat	1 ea	101	339	12	45	6	15	3.0	–	–	0	0
56040	Sandwich, peanut butter & jam, on soft white	1 ea	101	348	11	47	3	14	2.7	–	–	1	0
70919	Sandwich, pepperoni pizza, Hot Pocket, fzn	1 ea	128	367	14	39	–	18	6.6	6.3	2.0	41	90
70905	Sandwich, philly beef steak, fzn, Healthy Choice	1 ea	173	310	17	50	3	5	1.5	–	–	20	0
56987	Sandwich, pizza, pepperoni, pocket, fzn	1 ea	170	510	19	50	4	26	7.0	–	–	35	150
81195	Sandwich, pizza, veg, w/soy cheese, fzn, Amy's	1 ea	128	260	9	39	6	8	0.5	–	–	0	80
56277	Sandwich, pork	1 ea	136	324	26	32	1	9	2.9	4.1	1.0	62	1
56266	Sandwich, reuben	1 ea	181	464	21	30	3	29	9.9	9.7	6.7	82	94
56044	Sandwich, roast beef, on soft white	1 ea	156	404	29	34	1	16	2.9	–	–	43	11
56286	Sandwich, salami	1 ea	82	234	8	25	1	11	3.4	5.2	1.9	19	35
56261	Sandwich, sloppy joe, w/bun	1 ea	186	358	18	36	2	15	5.0	6.6	1.4	46	73
56670	Sandwich, steak	1 ea	204	459	30	52	–	14	3.8	5.3	3.3	73	39
56671	Sandwich, submarine, w/cold cuts	1 ea	228	456	22	51	2	19	6.8	8.2	2.3	36	82
56672	Sandwich, submarine, w/roast beef	1 ea	216	410	29	44	–	13	7.1	1.8	2.6	73	50
56048	Sandwich, tuna salad, on soft white	1 ea	122	326	13	35	1	14	1.9	–	–	13	21
56106	Sandwich, turkey ham, on wheat	1 ea	156	347	21	25	2	18	3.6	–	–	57	12
56052	Sandwich, turkey, on soft white	1 ea	156	346	24	29	1	14	1.9	–	–	43	11
56054	Sandwich, turkey, on wheat	1 ea	156	337	25	25	2	15	2.1	–	–	45	12
SAUCES AND GRAVIES													
Gravies													
53034	Gravy, au jus, cnd	1 cup	238	38	3	6	0	0	0.2	0.2	0.0	0	0
53006	Gravy, beef, homemade	0.5 cup	135	107	3	7	1	8	1.9	3.4	2.0	3	150
53398	Gravy, biscuit, country style, prep f/dry mix	1 ea	5	25	0	3	0	2	0.0	1.0	0.0	0	0
50939	Gravy, brown, homestyle, savory, cnd	0.25 cup	60	25	1	3	–	1	0.3	0.3	0.0	2	–
53575	Gravy, chicken	0.25 cup	60	50	1	4	0	3	0.5	–	–	5	0
53022	Gravy, chicken, cnd	1 cup	238	188	5	13	1	14	3.4	6.1	3.6	5	264
53565	Gravy, chicken, fat free	0.25 cup	60	15	1	3	0	0	0.0	0.0	0.0	5	20
53191	Gravy, country sausage, rts	0.25 cup	62	96	3	4	0	8	2.0	2.9	2.2	13	0
53026	Gravy, mushroom, cnd	1 cup	238	119	3	13	1	6	1.0	2.8	2.4	0	0
53499	Gravy, southern, dry mix, tbsp	1 Tbs	10	48	0	6	0	3	0.6	0.3	1.2	0	5
53578	Gravy, turkey	0.25 cup	61	30	1	3	0	2	0.0	–	–	5	0
53203	Gravy, turkey, dry mix, tbsp	1 Tbs	8	29	1	6	0	0	0.1	0.1	0.1	1	0
Sauces													
53591	Marinade, cooking sauce, mequite	1 Tbs	17	10	0	3	0	0	0.0	0.0	0.0	0	0
53615	Marinade, teriyaki sauce	1 Tbs	18	15	1	2	0	0	0.0	0.0	0.0	0	0
53431	Sauce, alfredo	0.5 cup	126	180	6	10	1	13	9.0	–	–	35	40
53000	Sauce, barbecue	1 cup	250	188	4	32	3	4	0.7	1.9	1.7	0	215
53392	Sauce, basil pesto	0.25 cup	62	320	7	2	1	31	6.0	–	–	15	100
53100	Sauce, black bean	1 cup	275	258	7	28	4	12	2.2	5.5	4.0	0	19
53015	Sauce, cheese, f/rec	0.5 cup	101	222	10	9	0	17	7.9	–	–	37	148
53198	Sauce, cheese, jalapeno, rts	0.25 cup	63	81	2	8	0	5	1.8	1.7	0.8	6	14
53577	Sauce, cheese, nacho	0.25 cup	62	100	1	7	1	7	2.0	–	–	5	20
1441	Sauce, cheese, prep f/rec	1 cup	243	479	25	13	0	36	19.5	11.5	3.4	92	411
9108	Sauce, Chili	2 Tbs	34	35	0	8	–	0	0.0	0.0	0.0	0	–
53355	Sauce, creole, rts	0.25 cup	62	25	1	4	–	1	0.1	0.2	0.3	0	47
53016	Sauce, curry, f/rec	0.5 cup	115	74	3	3	0	6	1.0	–	–	0	49

PAGE KEY: A-154 Granola Bars, Cereal Bars, Diet Bars, Scones, and Tarts A-154 Meals and Dishes A-160 Meats A-164 Nuts, Seeds, and Products A-166 Poultry A-166 Salad Dressings, Dips, and Mayonnaise A-170 Salads A-170 Sandwiches A-172 Sauces and Gravies A-174 Snack Foods—Chips, Pretzels, Popcorn A-178 Soups, Stews and Chilis A-184 Spices, Flavors, and Seasonings A-184 Sports Bars and Drinks A-186 Supplemental Foods and Formulas A-186 Sweeteners and Sweet Substitutes A-188 Vegetables and Legumes A-200 Weight Loss Bars & Drinks A-200 Miscellaneous

Thia (mg)	Ribo (mg)	Niac (mg NE)	Vit B6 (mg)	Vit B12 (µg)	Fol (µg)	Vit C (mg)	Vit D (IU)	Vit E (mg AT)	Cal (mg)	Iron (mg)	Magn (mg)	Phos (mg)	Pota (mg)	Sodi (mg)	Zinc (mg)	Wat (%)	Alco (g)	Caff (g)
0.82	0.41	6.40	0.37	0.55	53.8	0.4	20.3	2.4	54	2.88	40.1	273	389	1241	2.8	52	0.00	0.00
0.89	0.43	6.82	0.38	0.61	59.8	0.1	25.1	2.5	76	3.09	32.1	270	384	1237	2.6	52	0.00	0.00
0.28	0.27	4.76	0.12	0.97	21.2	2.0	–	0.3	68	2.64	23.1	135	243	1335	2.7	53	0.00	0.00
0.21	0.15	5.42	0.21	0.00	52.9	1.8	4.8	2.9	54	2.41	88.0	221	320	418	1.8	27	0.00	0.00
0.28	0.23	5.44	0.15	0.01	79.0	1.7	4.9	2.6	76	2.28	51.8	143	240	429	1.1	27	0.00	0.00
–	–	–	–	–	–	–	–	–	280	3.16	–	–	–	676	–	43	0.00	0.00
–	–	–	–	–	–	0.0	–	–	200	2.70	–	–	–	600	–	57	0.00	0.00
–	–	–	–	–	–	0.0	–	–	250	4.50	–	–	320	1040	–	43	0.00	0.00
–	–	–	–	–	–	6.0	–	–	20	2.70	–	–	–	520	–	–	0.00	0.00
0.91	0.46	6.25	0.34	0.55	26.4	0.2	–	0.4	85	2.75	34.1	229	343	392	2.5	49	0.00	0.00
0.23	0.34	3.45	0.21	1.34	37.2	4.1	–	0.8	299	2.92	38.7	291	261	1348	4.0	53	0.00	0.00
0.34	0.36	6.76	0.40	2.21	66.5	0.0	15.1	3.4	76	4.11	30.2	200	434	1601	3.7	46	0.00	0.00
0.30	0.28	2.96	0.09	1.07	17.2	0.0	–	0.7	58	2.25	16.1	80	117	612	0.9	44	0.00	0.00
0.28	0.27	5.73	0.23	1.51	21.8	5.8	–	1.3	92	3.63	35.5	149	368	1008	3.2	61	0.00	0.00
0.40	0.37	7.30	0.37	1.57	89.8	5.5	–	–	92	5.15	49.0	298	524	798	4.5	51	0.00	0.00
1.00	0.80	5.48	0.14	1.09	86.6	12.3	–	–	189	2.50	68.4	287	394	1651	2.6	58	0.00	0.00
0.40	0.40	5.96	0.31	1.80	71.3	5.6	–	–	41	2.80	67.0	192	330	845	4.4	59	0.00	0.00
0.30	0.23	5.88	0.12	0.66	62.5	1.1	72.0	2.8	76	2.40	24.5	152	168	588	0.7	46	0.00	0.00
0.25	0.36	5.17	0.34	0.23	45.8	0.1	12.5	1.2	69	4.23	39.3	250	395	1266	3.1	56	0.00	0.00
0.31	0.28	9.27	0.41	1.74	60.3	0.0	15.0	3.3	72	2.18	30.9	250	306	1586	1.3	54	0.00	0.00
0.25	0.23	9.56	0.44	1.83	45.0	0.0	10.7	3.5	64	2.16	42.0	286	357	1632	1.6	55	0.00	0.00
0.05	0.14	2.15	0.01	0.23	4.8	2.4	0.0	0.0	10	1.42	4.8	72	193	119	2.4	94	0.00	0.00
0.01	0.05	0.60	0.00	0.14	2.7	0.0	1.0	0.2	27	0.62	2.7	39	147	779	1.1	85	0.00	0.00
0.00	0.00	0.00	–	–	–	0.0	–	–	0	0.00	–	–	15	80	–	–	0.00	0.00
–	–	–	–	–	–	–	–	–	–	–	–	–	–	352	–	90	0.00	0.00
–	–	–	–	–	–	0.0	–	–	0	0.00	–	–	–	270	–	85	0.00	0.00
0.03	0.10	1.04	0.01	0.23	4.8	0.0	2.4	0.4	48	1.12	4.8	69	259	1373	1.9	85	0.00	0.00
–	–	–	–	–	–	0.0	–	–	0	0.00	–	–	–	320	–	92	0.00	0.00
0.10	0.03	0.64	0.03	0.20	0.6	0.1	–	0.2	4	0.34	3.1	25	48	236	0.3	75	0.00	0.00
0.07	0.15	1.60	0.05	0.00	28.6	0.0	0.8	0.2	17	1.57	4.8	36	252	1357	1.7	89	0.00	0.00
0.00	0.00	0.00	0.00	0.01	0.3	0.1	–	0.4	8	0.05	1.4	7	14	290	0.0	4	0.00	0.00
–	–	–	–	–	–	0.0	–	–	0	0.00	–	–	–	310	–	89	0.00	0.00
0.01	0.07	0.27	0.01	0.05	12.7	0.0	–	0.0	10	0.10	4.6	29	57	271	0.1	5	0.00	0.00
–	–	–	–	–	–	1.8	–	–	0	0.00	–	–	25	400	–	79	0.00	0.00
–	–	–	–	–	–	0.0	–	–	0	0.00	–	–	–	610	–	78	0.00	0.00
–	–	–	–	–	–	0.0	–	–	150	0.00	–	–	–	500	–	76	0.00	0.00
0.07	0.05	2.25	0.18	0.00	10.0	17.5	0.0	2.8	48	2.25	45.0	50	435	2038	0.5	81	0.00	0.00
0.00	0.07	0.00	–	–	8.0	0.0	–	–	250	0.36	–	150	100	530	–	34	0.00	0.00
0.15	0.10	0.93	0.12	0.01	69.2	4.7	0.0	1.5	63	1.63	43.5	103	375	1722	0.8	80	1.50	0.00
0.07	0.23	0.50	0.05	0.43	18.1	0.6	26.8	1.0	269	0.56	17.4	204	127	542	1.1	63	0.00	0.00
0.00	0.03	0.03	0.00	0.05	1.9	0.5	–	0.3	54	0.11	3.8	52	16	571	0.3	74	0.00	0.00
–	–	–	–	–	–	0.0	–	–	40	0.36	–	–	–	540	–	73	0.00	0.00
0.10	0.58	0.50	0.10	0.85	24.3	1.5	–	0.6	756	0.85	46.2	556	345	1198	3.1	67	0.00	0.00
–	–	–	–	–	–	1.8	–	–	0	0.00	–	–	–	370	–	72	0.00	0.00
0.02	[illegible]	0.52	0.07	0.00	8.7	0.0	–	0.6	35	0.31	8.7	17	187	339	0.1	89	0.00	0.00
0.02	0.05	1.64	0.01	0.10	5.4	0.1	0.0	0.8	9	0.50	3.1	38	103	392	0.1	89	0.00	0.00

PAGE KEY: A-108 Beverage and Beverage Mixes A-112 Other Beverages A-112 Beverages, Alcoholic A-114 Candies and Confections, Gum A-114 Cereals, Breakfast Type A-118 Cheese and Cheese Substitutes A-120 Dairy Products and Substitutes A-122 Desserts A-128 Dessert Toppings A-128 Eggs, Substitutes, and Egg Dishes A-130 Ethnic Foods A-130 Fast Foods/Restaurants A-140 Fats, Oils, Margarines, Shortenings, and Substitutes A-142 Fish, Seafood, and Shellfish A-142 Food Additives A-142 Fruit, Vegetable, and Blended Juices A-144 Fruits A-146 Grains, Flours, and Fractions A-148 Grain Products, Prepared and Baked Goods

Code	Food Name	Unit/ Amt	Wt (g)	Energy (Kcal)	Prot (g)	Carb (g)	Fiber (g)	Fat (g)	Sat (g)	Mono (g)	Poly (g)	Chol (mg)	Vit A (RE)
53139	Sauce, enchilada	1 Tbs	16	6	0	1	0	0	0.0	0.0	0.1	0	–
53103	Sauce, enchilada, green	1 cup	250	187	4	13	4	14	8.1	3.9	1.2	43	156
53104	Sauce, fish/bagoong	1 cup	272	95	14	10	0	0	0.0	0.0	0.0	0	2
27162	Sauce, lemon, rts, tbsp	2 Tbs	32	43	0	10	0	0	0.0	0.1	0.1	0	0
53432	Sauce, marinara	0.5 cup	127	120	2	20	2	4	1.0	–	–	0	50
7563	Sauce, miso/ae	1 cup	248	389	13	73	6	7	1.0	1.5	3.8	0	10
53125	Sauce, mole poblano, prep f/rec	1 cup	242	398	9	31	10	27	8.0	11.7	6.9	2	–
90263	Sauce, mushroom, dehyd, svg, makes 1 cup prep	1 ea	23	79	3	12	0	2	0.3	0.9	0.8	0	0
7435	Sauce, pasta, cabernet marinara, organic	0.5 cup	126	49	2	10	3	0	0.0	–	–	0	75
7431	Sauce, pasta, Italian herb, organic	0.5 cup	126	68	2	14	2	0	–	–	–	0	65
53273	Sauce, pasta, marinara, cnd, Progresso	0.5 cup	123	80	2	8	2	4	0.5	1.5	2.5	3	50
53275	Sauce, pasta, meat flvr, cnd, Progresso	0.5 cup	124	100	4	12	3	4	1.0	1.8	1.8	5	60
53650	Sauce, pasta, old world, smooth, traditional, jar Ragu	0.5 cup	125	80	2	12	3	3	0.4	0.5	1.3	0	65
91148	Sauce, pasta, tomato, sun dried, Di Capri	1 oz	28	18	1	2	–	1	0.2	0.3	0.4	0	15
53629	Sauce, pasta, traditional, cnd, Healthy Choice	0.5 cup	126	50	2	11	2	0	0.0	0.0	0.0	0	30
433	Sauce, pasta, w/rstd garlic, cnd, Healthy Choice	0.5 cup	126	50	2	11	3	0	0.0	0.0	0.0	0	10
53281	Sauce, pasta, white clam, cnd, can, Progresso	0.5 cup	124	140	7	5	0	10	1.5	5.5	3.0	15	40
53470	Sauce, pepper/hot, rts	1 tsp	5	1	0	0	0	0	0.0	0.0	0.0	0	1
53133	Sauce, pesto	1 cup	232	781	18	15	4	72	12.2	–	–	42	1117
53277	Sauce, pizza, cnd	0.25 cup	61	20	1	4	1	0	0.0	0.0	0.0	0	30
53215	Sauce, pizza, original, Contadina	0.25 cup	63	30	1	6	1	0	0.0	0.0	0.0	0	30
53071	Sauce, plum	2 Tbs	30	60	0	13	0	0	0.0	0.0	0.0	0	0
53425	Sauce, sloppy joe, cnd	0.25 cup	73	50	2	11	2	0	0.0	0.0	0.0	0	150
53280	Sauce, spaghetti, cnd, Progresso	0.5 cup	124	100	3	12	2	4	1.0	1.5	2.0	3	50
53334	Sauce, spaghetti, extra chunky, zesty basil	0.5 cup	130	110	2	22	3	2	0.5	–	–	0	150
53539	Sauce, spaghetti, low sod	1 cup	250	272	4	40	8	12	1.6	8.3	1.3	0	308
53343	Sauce, spaghetti, tomato & basil	0.5 cup	130	110	2	19	3	3	0.5	–	–	0	125
53341	Sauce, spaghetti, w/mushrooms	0.5 cup	130	150	2	23	3	5	1.5	–	–	0	125
53008	Sauce, spaghetti/marinara	1 cup	250	142	4	21	4	5	0.7	2.2	1.8	0	95
53447	Sauce, stir fry, Hunan, China Bowl	0.25 cup	59	110	0	13	–	6	–	–	–	–	–
53620	Sauce, stir fry, Kikkoman	1 Tbs	17	15	1	3	0	0	0.0	0.0	0.0	0	0
53265	Sauce, stir fry, Mandarin, La Choy	100 g	100	56	2	12	1	0	0.0	–	–	0	16
53260	Sauce, stir fry, teriyaki, Kikkoman	100 g	100	80	2	18	1	0	0.0	–	–	0	18
53621	Sauce, sweet & sour, Kikkoman	2 Tbs	34	35	0	9	0	0	0.0	0.0	0.0	0	0
8983	Sauce, tartar	2 Tbs	28	139	0	1	0	15	2.7	0.7	2.3	11	6
53415	Sauce, tartar, fat free	2 Tbs	32	25	0	5	0	0	0.0	0.0	0.0	0	0
53122	Sauce, tartar, low cal	1 Tbs	14	31	0	2	0	3	0.4	0.6	1.4	3	1
53618	Sauce, teriyaki, baste/glaze, Kikkoman	2 Tbs	36	50	1	11	0	0	0.0	0.0	0.0	0	0
9115	Sauce, tomato, cnd	0.25 cup	62	15	0	4	1	0	0.0	0.0	0.0	0	–
7291	Tomato Paste, w/add salt, cnd, 6oz can	1 ea	170	139	6	33	7	1	0.1	0.1	0.4	0	415
9162	Tomato Puree, cnd	0.25 cup	63	25	2	6	2	0	0.0	0.0	0.0	0	–
53712	Tomato Sauce, cnd	0.25 cup	61	20	1	4	0	0	0.0	0.0	0.0	0	20
7232	Tomato Sauce, low sod, cnd	1 cup	245	74	3	18	4	0	0.1	0.1	0.2	0	240
7422	Tomato Sauce, organic, cnd	0.25 cup	62	20	1	5	1	0	–	–	–	0	69
6294	Tomato Sauce, thick & zesty, cnd, Contadina	0.25 cup	62	20	1	3	1	0	0.0	0.0	0.0	0	40
SNACK FOODS-CHIPS, PRETZELS, POPCORN													
60920	Banana, chips, dried	1 oz	28	150	0	20	1	8	7.0	–	–	–	10
44328	Cheese Puffs, cheddar, svg	1 ea	30	180	3	13	2	13	3.0	–	–	5	0

Thia (mg)	Ribo (mg)	Niac (mg NE)	Vit B6 (mg)	Vit B12 (µg)	Fol (µg)	Vit C (mg)	Vit D (IU)	Vit E (mg AT)	Cal (mg)	Iron (mg)	Magn (mg)	Phos (mg)	Pota (mg)	Sodi (mg)	Zinc (mg)	Wat (%)	Alco (g)	Caff (g)
0.00	0.00	0.00	0.00	–	–	0.0	–	–	2	0.05	–	3	21	71	–	90	0.00	0.00
0.09	0.15	2.92	0.18	0.14	13.3	23.1	0.0	0.9	77	1.17	41.4	118	540	30	0.6	87	0.00	0.00
0.02	0.15	6.28	1.08	1.30	138.7	1.4	–	0.0	117	2.11	476.0	19	783	20998	0.5	–	0.00	0.00
0.00	0.00	0.00	0.00	0.00	0.3	2.8	–	0.0	1	0.11	0.6	1	6	3	0.0	67	0.00	0.00
–	–	–	–	0.00	–	1.2	–	–	0	0.72	–	–	–	480	–	79	0.00	0.00
0.10	0.28	0.95	0.23	0.00	36.7	0.0	0.0	0.0	77	3.23	52.8	173	208	4062	3.7	57	0.00	0.00
0.05	0.00	3.98	0.61	0.11	67.9	0.0	0.0	3.5	58	4.48	77.6	199	791	325	1.1	72	0.00	0.00
0.01	0.10	1.03	0.01	0.00	6.1	0.0	2.7	0.0	2	0.23	4.1	30	98	1414	0.2	4	0.00	0.00
–	–	–	–	0.00	–	4.1	–	–	64	0.74	–	–	–	315	–	89	0.00	0.00
–	–	–	–	0.00	–	19.5	–	–	28	1.25	–	–	–	287	–	85	0.00	0.00
–	–	–	–	0.00	–	0.0	–	–	20	0.72	–	–	–	480	–	86	0.00	0.00
–	–	–	–	–	–	0.0	–	–	40	1.08	–	–	–	610	–	83	0.00	0.00
–	–	–	–	–	–	–	–	–	–	1.01	–	–	–	756	–	84	0.00	0.00
0.00	0.00	0.38	–	–	–	2.2	–	–	14	0.23	5.5	11	103	100	0.0	87	0.00	0.00
–	–	–	–	–	–	6.0	–	–	40	1.08	–	–	–	390	–	87	0.00	0.00
–	–	–	–	–	–	6.0	–	–	20	0.36	–	–	–	390	–	–	0.00	0.00
–	–	–	–	–	–	1.2	–	–	20	1.44	–	–	–	510	–	79	0.00	0.00
0.00	0.00	0.00	0.00	0.00	0.3	3.5	–	–	0	0.01	0.2	1	7	124	0.0	90	0.00	0.00
–	–	–	–	–	–	1.2	–	–	675	4.63	–	–	–	1489	–	52	0.00	0.00
–	–	–	–	–	–	4.8	–	–	0	0.72	–	–	–	170	–	91	0.00	0.00
–	–	–	–	–	–	6.0	–	–	20	0.36	–	–	–	340	–	88	0.00	0.00
–	–	–	–	–	–	0.0	–	–	0	0.00	–	–	–	190	–	55	0.00	0.00
–	–	–	–	–	–	0.0	–	–	0	0.72	–	–	–	420	–	80	0.00	0.00
–	–	–	–	–	–	2.4	–	–	20	1.08	–	–	–	620	–	82	0.00	0.00
–	–	–	–	0.00	–	9.0	–	–	60	0.36	–	–	–	510	–	78	0.00	0.00
0.15	0.15	3.75	0.87	0.00	52.5	28.0	–	3.8	70	1.62	60.0	90	960	75	0.5	75	0.00	0.00
–	–	–	–	0.00	–	21.0	–	–	40	1.08	–	–	–	420	–	79	0.00	0.00
–	–	–	–	0.00	–	15.0	–	–	40	1.08	–	–	–	670	–	75	0.00	0.00
0.14	0.10	2.66	0.28	0.00	25.0	20.0	0.0	3.1	55	1.79	42.5	80	738	1030	0.4	87	0.00	0.00
–	–	–	–	–	–	–	–	–	–	–	–	–	–	550	–	63	0.00	0.00
–	–	–	–	–	–	0.0	–	–	0	0.00	–	–	–	530	–	73	0.00	0.00
–	–	–	–	–	–	4.7	–	–	1	3.50	–	–	–	670	–	84	0.00	0.00
–	–	–	–	–	–	5.7	–	–	1	12.39	–	–	–	879	–	77	0.00	0.00
–	–	–	–	–	–	0.0	–	–	0	0.00	–	–	–	190	–	73	0.00	0.00
–	–	–	–	–	–	0.7	–	–	6	0.14	–	–	38	153	–	39	0.00	0.00
–	–	–	–	–	–	0.0	–	–	0	0.00	–	0	20	200	–	84	0.00	0.00
0.00	0.00	0.00	0.00	0.00	0.1	0.1	–	0.8	1	0.05	0.3	1	4	82	0.0	63	0.00	0.00
–	–	–	–	–	–	0.0	–	–	0	0.00	–	–	–	810	–	64	0.00	0.00
–	–	–	–	–	–	4.8	–	–	0	0.00	–	–	–	380	–	92	0.00	0.00
0.25	0.31	5.48	0.64	0.00	37.4	72.1	0.0	7.3	60	3.29	86.8	134	1594	1344	1.4	74	0.00	0.00
–	–	–	–	–	–	12.0	–	–	0	0.00	–	–	–	25	–	88	0.00	0.00
–	–	–	–	–	–	4.8	–	–	0	0.36	–	–	–	340	–	91	0.00	0.00
0.17	0.15	2.81	0.38	0.00	22.1	32.1	–	3.4	34	1.88	46.5	78	909	27	0.6	89	0.00	0.00
–	–	–	–	0.00	–	0.8	–	–	13	0.62	–	–	–	192	–	88	0.00	0.00
–	–	–	–	–	–	4.8	–	–	0	0.72	–	–	–	340	–	91	0.00	0.00
–	–	–	–	–	–	–	–	–	–	0.36	–	–	–	–	–	–	0.00	0.00
–	–	–	–	–	–	0.0	–	–	40	0.36	–	–	–	270	–	2	0.00	0.00

PAGE KEY: A-108 Beverage and Beverage Mixes A-112 Other Beverages A-112 Beverages, Alcoholic A-114 Candies and Confections, Gum A-114 Cereals, Breakfast Type A-118 Cheese and Cheese Substitutes A-120 Dairy Products and Substitutes A-122 Desserts A-128 Dessert Toppings A-128 Eggs, Substitutes, and Egg Dishes A-130 Ethnic Foods A-130 Fast Foods/Restaurants A-140 Fats, Oils, Margarines, Shortenings, and Substitutes A-142 Fish, Seafood, and Shellfish A-142 Food Additives A-142 Fruit, Vegetable, and Blended Juices A-144 Fruits A-146 Grains, Flours, and Fractions A-148 Grain Products, Prepared and Baked Goods

Code	Food Name	Unit/ Amt	Wt (g)	Energy (Kcal)	Prot (g)	Carb (g)	Fiber (g)	Fat (g)	Sat (g)	Mono (g)	Poly (g)	Chol (mg)	Vit A (RE)
44248	Cheetos, cheese puffs	29 pce	28	158	2	15	1	10	2.5	2.7	3.1	0	0
44245	Cheetos, cheese puffs, crunchy	21 pce	28	158	2	15	1	10	2.5	2.7	3.1	0	0
44061	Chips, bagel	5 pce	70	298	6	52	4	7	1.3	2.1	3.4	0	0
44279	Chips, corn, bbq	29 pce	28	148	2	16	1	9	1.0	2.5	5.4	0	4
44278	Chips, corn, original	32 pce	28	158	2	15	1	10	1.0	2.5	6.4	0	0
44232	Chips, potato, bbq, KC Masterpiece	15 pce	28	158	2	15	1	10	3.0	1.9	5.0	0	0
4029	Chips, potato, bkd, Ruffles	9 pce	28	130	2	24	1	3	0.0	–	–	0	0
44240	Chips, potato, cheddar & sour cream, Ruffles	13 pce	28	158	2	14	1	10	3.0	1.9	5.0	0	0
43703	Chips, potato, classic, Lay's	20 pce	28	150	2	15	1	10	3.0	–	–	0	0
4025	Chips, potato, deli style, original, Lay's	17 pce	28	150	1	16	1	10	3.0	–	–	0	0
8856	Chips, potato, fat free, Wow	20 pce	28	75	2	18	1	0	0.0	0.0	0.0	0	0
53673	Chips, potato, original, fat free, Wow	17 pce	28	75	2	17	1	0	0.0	0.0	0.0	0	0
44230	Chips, potato, original, Lay's	18 pce	28	148	2	15	1	10	3.0	1.9	5.0	0	0
8857	Chips, potato, sour cream & chive, fat free, Wow	19 pce	28	80	2	17	1	0	0.0	0.0	0.0	0	0
44238	Chips, potato, unsalted, Lay's	19 pce	28	158	2	16	1	10	3.0	–	–	0	0
44121	Chips, pretzel, Mr. Phipps	1 ea	32	130	3	24	1	3	0.5	1.0	0.0	0	–
44234	Chips, sour cream & onion, Lay's	22 pce	28	148	2	15	1	9	2.5	1.7	4.7	0	0
44257	Chips, Sun, French onion	10 pce	28	140	2	18	2	7	1.0	–	–	0	0
44256	Chips, Sun, original	11 pce	28	140	2	19	2	6	0.5	–	–	0	0
44125	Chips, Tortilla Crisps, nacho cheese, Mr. Phipps	11 pce	28	128	2	22	–	4	–	–	–	–	–
42515	Chips, Tortilla Crisps, salsa	36 pce	30	130	3	18	3	7	1.0	–	–	2	0
44224	Chips, tortilla, Doritos, cooler ranch	15 pce	28	138	2	18	1	7	1.5	1.9	2.2	0	0
53701	Chips, tortilla, Doritos, flamin' hot	11 pce	28	140	2	17	1	7	1.5	3.0	2.5	0	0
44225	Chips, tortilla, Doritos, nacho cheesier	15 pce	28	138	2	17	1	7	1.5	1.9	2.2	0	0
4039	Chips, tortilla, Doritos, salsa verde	12 pce	28	150	2	19	1	7	1.5	3.0	2.5	0	0
44227	Chips, tortilla, Doritos, taco	12 pce	28	140	2	18	1	7	1.5	–	–	0	0
44298	Chips, tortilla, yellow corn, Guiltless Gourmet	18 pce	28	110	3	22	2	2	0.0	–	–	0	0
44031	Corn Nuts, plain	2 oz	57	249	5	42	4	8	1.4	4.1	1.8	0	0
23404	Fruit Leather, roll, lrg	1 ea	21	74	0	18	1	1	0.1	0.3	0.1	0	3
23086	Fruit Leather, roll, sml	1 ea	14	49	0	12	1	0	0.1	0.2	0.1	0	2
8877	Nuts, soy, salted	5 pce	28	120	12	9	5	4	1.0	–	–	0	0
62808	Nuts, soy, unsalted	5 pce	28	120	12	9	5	4	1.0	–	–	0	0
11719	Party Mix, w/cheese crackers	0.5 cup	30	138	4	19	1	5	1.1	–	–	0	0
44022	Popcorn Cake	1 ea	10	38	1	8	0	0	0.0	0.1	0.1	0	1
44012	Popcorn, air popped	1 cup	8	31	1	6	1	0	0.0	0.1	0.2	0	2
53709	Popcorn, butter flvr	3 cup	30	160	2	15	3	12	1.5	–	–	0	450
44014	Popcorn, caramel coated, w/o peanuts	1 oz	28	122	1	22	1	4	1.0	0.8	1.3	1	3
44038	Popcorn, cheese flvrd	1 cup	11	58	1	6	1	4	0.7	1.1	1.7	1	5
4018	Popcorn, Cracker Jacks, caramel, fat free	0.75 cup	28	110	1	26	1	0	0.0	0.0	0.0	0	0
43701	Popcorn, Cracker Jacks, original	0.5 cup	28	120	2	23	1	2	0.0	–	–	0	0
44065	Popcorn, microwv	1 ea	87	435	8	50	9	24	4.3	7.1	11.7	0	13
44072	Popcorn, white, air popped	1 cup	8	31	1	6	1	0	0.0	0.1	0.2	0	0
44073	Popcorn, white, oil popped	1 cup	11	55	1	6	1	3	0.5	0.9	1.5	0	0
44039	Pork Skins, bbq flvr	0.5 oz	14	76	8	0	–	5	1.6	2.1	0.5	16	13
44015	Pretzels, hard, salted	10 pce	60	229	5	48	2	2	0.5	0.8	0.7	0	0
44271	Pretzels, rods, Rold Gold	3 pce	28	109	3	22	1	1	0.0	0.2	0.4	0	0
42093	Pretzels, soft	1 ea	55	190	5	38	1	2	0.4	0.6	0.5	2	0
44120	Pretzels, sticks, very thin, pkg, Mr. Salty	1 ea	32	120	3	25	1	0	–	–	–	0	–

PAGE KEY: A-154 Granola Bars, Cereal Bars, Diet Bars, Scones, and Tarts A-154 Meals and Dishes A-160 Meats A-164 Nuts, Seeds, and Products A-166 Poultry A-166 Salad Dressings, Dips, and Mayonnaise A-170 Salads A-170 Sandwiches A-172 Sauces and Gravies A-174 Snack Foods—Chips, Pretzels, Popcorn A-178 Soups, Stews and Chilis A-184 Spices, Flavors, and Seasonings A-184 Sports Bars and Drinks A-186 Supplemental Foods and Formulas A-186 Sweeteners and Sweet Substitutes A-188 Vegetables and Legumes A-200 Weight Loss Bars & Drinks A-200 Miscellaneous

Thia (mg)	Ribo (mg)	Niac (mg NE)	Vit B6 (mg)	Vit B12 (μg)	Fol (μg)	Vit C (mg)	Vit D (IU)	Vit E (mg AT)	Cal (mg)	Iron (mg)	Magn (mg)	Phos (mg)	Pota (mg)	Sodi (mg)	Zinc (mg)	Wat (%)	Alco (g)	Caff (g)
0.10	0.05	0.72	–	–	–	0.0	–	–	22	0.58	–	15	20	365	0.0	2	0.00	0.00
0.10	0.05	0.74	–	–	–	0.0	–	–	17	0.60	–	20	20	286	0.0	2	0.00	0.00
0.12	0.11	1.62	0.15	0.00	46.0	0.0	–	1.7	9	1.38	39.2	145	167	419	0.9	3	0.00	0.00
0.00	0.03	0.33	–	–	–	0.0	–	–	44	0.37	–	54	54	286	0.0	2	0.00	0.00
0.00	0.03	0.33	–	–	–	0.0	–	–	44	0.37	–	54	54	104	0.0	1	0.00	0.00
0.03	0.05	1.19	–	0.00	–	5.9	–	–	10	0.44	–	44	489	198	0.4	2	0.00	0.00
–	–	–	–	–	–	3.6	–	–	40	0.00	–	–	–	200	–	–	0.00	0.00
0.03	0.05	1.09	–	0.00	–	5.9	–	–	0	0.44	–	44	489	188	0.4	3	0.00	0.00
–	–	–	–	–	–	6.0	–	–	0	0.00	–	–	–	180	–	1	0.00	0.00
–	–	–	–	–	–	6.0	–	–	0	0.00	–	–	–	180	–	1	0.00	0.00
0.01	0.03	0.27	–	–	–	6.0	–	–	0	0.36	–	44	76	200	0.4	26	0.00	0.00
–	–	–	–	–	–	6.0	–	–	0	0.36	–	–	–	200	–	29	0.00	0.00
0.05	0.03	1.09	–	0.00	–	5.9	–	–	6	0.44	–	44	489	178	0.4	2	0.00	0.00
–	–	–	–	–	–	6.0	–	–	20	0.36	–	–	–	230	–	29	0.00	0.00
–	–	–	–	0.00	–	5.9	–	–	0	0.00	–	–	–	15	–	1	0.00	0.00
–	–	–	–	–	–	–	–	–	60	0.14	–	–	30	760	–	–	0.00	0.00
0.03	0.05	1.48	–	0.00	–	5.9	–	–	66	0.44	–	44	489	178	0.4	3	0.00	0.00
–	–	–	–	–	–	0.0	–	–	0	0.36	–	–	–	160	–	2	0.00	0.00
0.05	0.15	0.50	–	–	–	0.0	–	–	0	0.36	–	70	75	115	0.0	2	0.00	0.00
–	–	–	–	–	–	–	–	–	–	–	–	–	–	138	–	–	0.00	0.00
0.11	0.07	1.20	–	–	–	–	–	–	40	0.72	–	–	–	350	–	4	0.00	0.00
0.02	0.02	0.49	–	–	–	0.0	–	–	40	0.41	–	64	69	168	0.0	2	0.00	0.00
0.02	0.00	0.40	–	–	–	0.0	–	–	20	0.00	–	19	38	210	0.2	6	0.00	0.00
0.02	0.02	0.40	–	–	–	0.0	–	–	43	0.41	–	59	64	188	0.0	3	0.00	0.00
0.02	0.00	0.43	–	–	–	0.0	–	–	20	0.00	–	18	38	210	0.2	–	0.00	0.00
–	–	–	–	–	–	0.0	–	–	40	0.00	–	–	–	170	–	1	0.00	0.00
–	–	–	–	–	–	0.0	–	–	60	0.36	–	–	–	160	–	3	0.00	
0.01	0.07	0.95	0.12	0.00	0.0	0.0	0.0	0.6	5	0.94	64.1	156	158	311	1.0	1	0.00	0.00
0.00	0.00	0.01	0.05	0.00	1.7	1.3	0.0	0.1	7	0.20	4.2	7	62	13	0.0	11	0.00	0.00
0.00	0.00	0.00	0.03	0.00	1.1	0.9	0.0	0.0	4	0.14	2.8	4	41	9	0.0	11	0.00	0.00
–	–	–	–	–	–	0.0	–	–	60	1.08	–	–	–	150	–	–	0.00	0.00
–	–	–	–	–	–	0.0	–	–	60	1.08	–	–	–	10	–	–	0.00	0.00
–	–	–	–	–	–	0.0	–	–	36	1.37	–	–	–	273	–	3	0.00	0.00
0.00	0.01	0.60	0.01	0.00	1.8	0.0	0.0	0.0	1	0.18	15.9	28	33	29	0.4	5	0.00	0.00
0.01	0.01	0.15	0.01	0.00	1.8	0.0	0.0	0.0	1	0.20	10.5	24	24	0	0.3	4	0.00	0.00
–	–	–	–	–	–	0.0	–	–	0	0.72	–	–	–	330	–	3	0.00	0.00
0.01	0.01	0.62	0.00	0.00	0.6	0.0	0.0	0.3	12	0.49	9.9	24	31	58	0.2	3	0.00	0.00
0.00	0.02	0.15	0.02	0.05	1.2	0.1	0.0	0.0	12	0.25	10.0	40	29	98	0.2	2	0.00	0.00
–	–	–	–	–	–	0.0	–	–	0	0.36	–	–	–	70	–	2	0.00	0.00
–	–	–	–	–	–	0.0	–	–	0	0.00	–	–	–	70	–	2	0.00	0.00
0.11	0.11	1.35	0.18	0.00	14.8	0.3	–	0.1	9	2.42	94.0	218	196	769	2.3	3	0.00	0.00
0.01	0.01	0.15	0.01	0.00	1.8	0.0	0.0	0.0	1	0.20	10.5	24	24	0	0.3	4	0.00	0.00
0.00	0.00	0.17	0.01	0.00	1.9	0.0	0.0	0.0	1	0.31	11.9	28	25	97	0.3	3	0.00	0.00
0.00	0.05	0.47	0.01	0.01	4.4	0.2	0.0	–	6	0.15	0.0	31	26	378	0.1	2	0.00	0.00
0.28	0.37	3.15	0.07	0.00	102.6	0.0	0.0	0.1	22	2.58	21.0	68	88	1029	0.5	3	0.00	0.00
0.17	0.10	1.37	–	–	–	0.0	–	–	6	1.09	–	–	30	365	0.2	3	0.00	0.00
0.23	0.15	2.34	0.00	0.00	7.7	0.0	0.0	0.0	13	2.16	11.6	43	48	772	0.5	15	0.00	0.00
–	–	–	–	–	–	–	–	–	–	0.36	–	–	30	900	–	–	0.00	0.00

PAGE KEY: A-108 Beverage and Beverage Mixes A-112 Other Beverages A-112 Beverages, Alcoholic A-114 Candies and Confections, Gum A-114 Cereals, Breakfast Type A-118 Cheese and Cheese Substitutes A-120 Dairy Products and Substitutes A-122 Desserts A-128 Dessert Toppings A-128 Eggs, Substitutes, and Egg Dishes A-130 Ethnic Foods A-130 Fast Foods/Restaurants A-140 Fats, Oils, Margarines, Shortenings, and Substitutes A-142 Fish, Seafood, and Shellfish A-142 Food Additives A-142 Fruit, Vegetable, and Blended Juices A-144 Fruits A-146 Grains, Flours, and Fractions A-148 Grain Products, Prepared and Baked Goods

Code	Food Name	Unit/ Amt	Wt (g)	Energy (Kcal)	Prot (g)	Carb (g)	Fiber (g)	Fat (g)	Sat (g)	Mono (g)	Poly (g)	Chol (mg)	Vit A (RE)
44067	Pretzels, yogurt cvrd	2 ea	8	38	1	6	0	1	1.1	0.1	0.1	0	0
44082	Rice Cake, brown rice & multigrain, unsalted	1 ea	9	35	1	7	0	0	0.1	0.1	0.1	0	0
60918	Rice Cake, buttery caramel, no sod	1 ea	21	80	2	18	1	0	–	–	–	0	–
44157	Rice Cake, cheddar cheese, crispy, mini	1 ea	2	8	0	1	0	0	0.0	0.2	0.0	0	0
44159	Rice Cake, peanut butter	1 ea	15	61	1	12	0	1	0.2	0.2	0.1	0	0
44016	Rice Cake, plain	1 ea	9	35	1	7	0	0	0.1	0.1	0.1	0	0
60903	Rice Cake, salted	1 ea	18	71	1	15	0	0	0.1	0.2	0.2	–	0
44219	Rice Krispies Treats, square	1 ea	22	91	1	18	0	2	0.3	0.6	1.1	0	71
44032	Snack Mix, Chex	1 cup	42	181	5	28	2	7	2.3	3.9	1.1	0	6
57097	Snacks, cheese n' pretzels, pkg	1 ea	29	100	4	11	1	5	3.0	–	–	15	40
8879	Snacks, Soy Crisps, bbq	25 pce	28	110	8	17	2	2	0.0	–	–	0	20
62810	Snacks, Soy Crisps, creamy ranch	25 pce	28	100	7	14	2	2	0.0	–	–	0	20
44058	Trail Mix, regular	1 cup	150	693	21	67	8	44	8.3	18.8	14.5	0	3
44060	Trail Mix, tropical	1 cup	140	570	9	92	9	24	11.9	3.5	7.2	0	6
SOUPS, STEWS AND CHILIS													
Canned/Frozen/Prepared Soups, Stews and Chilis													
50312	Chili, con carne	1 cup	253	256	25	22	4	8	3.4	3.4	0.5	134	167
57658	Chili, con carne, w/beans, cnd, svg	1 ea	222	255	20	24	8	8	2.1	2.2	1.4	24	89
57132	Chili, con carne, w/o beans, cnd	1 cup	253	380	19	22	5	24	9.0	–	–	–	250
7760	Chili, vegetarian, cnd	1 cup	230	176	16	26	13	1	0.2	0.2	0.5	1	47
7796	Chili, vegetarian, low fat	1 cup	230	165	18	21	11	1	0.2	0.2	0.5	0	47
50065	Soup, bean, w/ham, chnky, rts, cnd, 19.25oz can	1 ea	546	518	28	61	25	19	7.5	8.6	2.1	49	884
90299	Soup, beef ndle, prep f/cnd w/water, 10.75oz can	1 ea	593	202	12	22	2	7	2.8	3.0	1.2	12	154
90296	Soup, black bean, prep f/cnd w/water, cmrcl, 11oz can	1 ea	600	282	14	48	11	4	1.0	1.3	1.1	0	120
50259	Soup, broccoli cheese, 73467, prep	1 cup	248	364	9	13	–	31	–	–	–	–	–
50418	Soup, chicken & wild rice, prep f/cnd	1 cup	239	93	6	12	–	2	0.6	1.0	0.5	14	263
90303	Soup, chicken bouillon/broth, prep f/cnd w/water, can	1 ea	593	95	12	2	0	3	0.9	1.4	0.7	0	0
47395	Soup, chicken corn chowder, chunky, rts, cnd, svg	1 ea	240	238	7	18	2	15	4.2	3.0	4.6	26	552
50080	Soup, chicken mushroom, prep f/cnd w/water, cmrcl	1 cup	244	132	4	9	0	9	2.4	4.0	2.3	10	112
50982	Soup, chicken noodle, chunky, rts, cnd, svg	1 ea	243	114	8	14	–	3	0.8	1.2	0.6	24	262
50085	Soup, chicken rice, chunky, rts, cnd	1 cup	240	127	12	13	1	3	1.0	1.4	0.7	12	586
50020	Soup, chicken rice, prep f/cnd w/water, cmrcl	1 cup	241	60	4	7	1	2	0.5	0.9	0.4	7	67
50089	Soup, chicken vegetable, chunky, rts, cnd, 19oz can	1 ea	539	372	28	42	0	11	3.2	4.8	2.3	38	1347
90309	Soup, chicken veg, prep f/cnd w/water 10.5oz can	1 ea	586	182	9	21	2	7	2.1	3.1	1.5	23	645
50899	Soup, chicken, w/pasta, rts, cnd, Healthy Choice	1 cup	246	110	6	19	3	2	0.5	–	–	5	200
50007	Soup, chili beef, prep f/cnd w/water, cmrcl	1 cup	250	170	7	21	10	7	3.4	2.8	0.3	12	150
50262	Soup, clam chowder, Boston style, prep w/whole milk	1 cup	248	175	10	16	–	7	–	–	–	–	29
50093	Soup, clam chowder, Manhattan style, chunky, rts, cnd	1 cup	240	134	7	19	3	3	2.1	1.0	0.1	14	334
50195	Soup, clam chwder, New England prep f/cnd w/water	1 cup	244	95	5	12	1	3	0.4	1.2	1.1	5	–
50764	Soup, clam chowder, New Eng, 98%fat free, rts, cnd	1 cup	245	120	4	18	1	3	1.0	–	–	10	20
50704	Soup, clam chowder, prep	100 g	100	365	8	65	–	8	3.8	2.3	1.9	4	–
50271	Soup, corn chowder, old fash, 64763, prep w/milk	1 cup	248	175	7	19	–	7	–	–	–	–	29
1792	Soup, corn, sweet, creamy, organic	1 cup	243	100	5	15	1	3	0.5	–	–	0	20
50057	Soup, cream of asparagus, prep f/cnd w/milk, cmrcl	1 cup	248	161	6	16	1	8	3.3	2.1	2.2	22	84
50736	Soup, cream of broccoli, 98%fat free, cond, cnd	0.5 cup	126	80	2	12	1	3	1.0	–	–	5	40
50402	Soup, cream of broccoli, rts, cnd	1 cup	244	88	2	13	2	3	0.7	0.9	0.6	5	59
50807	Soup, cream of cauliflower, restaurant style, cond, fzn	0.5 cup	124	150	4	12	3	10	5.0	–	–	20	150
50737	Soup, cream of celery, 98%fat free, cond, cnd	0.5 cup	124	70	2	9	1	3	1.0	–	–	5	20

PAGE KEY: A-154 Granola Bars, Cereal Bars, Diet Bars, Scones, and Tarts A-154 Meals and Dishes A-160 Meats A-164 Nuts, Seeds, and Products A-166 Poultry A-166 Salad Dressings, Dips, and Mayonnaise A-170 Salads A-170 Sandwiches A-172 Sauces and Gravies A-174 Snack Foods—Chips, Pretzels, Popcorn A-178 Soups, Stews and Chilis A-184 Spices, Flavors, and Seasonings A-184 Sports Bars and Drinks A-186 Supplemental Foods and Formulas A-186 Sweeteners and Sweet Substitutes A-188 Vegetables and Legumes A-200 Weight Loss Bars & Drinks A-200 Miscellaneous

Thia (mg)	Ribo (mg)	Niac (mg NE)	Vit B6 (mg)	Vit B12 (μg)	Fol (μg)	Vit C (mg)	Vit D (IU)	Vit E (mg AT)	Cal (mg)	Iron (mg)	Magn (mg)	Phos (mg)	Pota (mg)	Sodi (mg)	Zinc (mg)	Wat (%)	Alco (g)	Caff (g)
0.00	0.03	0.23	0.00	0.02	4.0	0.0	–	0.1	10	0.18	1.9	12	18	72	0.1	3	0.00	0.00
0.00	0.01	0.58	0.00	0.00	1.8	0.0	0.0	0.0	2	0.18	12.3	33	26	0	0.2	6	0.00	0.00
–	–	–	–	–	–	–	–	–	–	–	–	–	75	0	–	–	0.00	0.00
0.00	0.00	0.01	0.00	0.00	0.2	0.0	0.0	0.1	0	0.00	0.2	1	1	23	0.0	3	0.00	0.00
0.05	0.00	0.69	0.05	0.00	1.9	0.0	0.0	0.1	3	0.17	14.6	34	28	61	0.2	3	0.00	0.00
0.03	0.00	0.58	0.05	0.00	1.8	0.0	0.0	0.0	1	0.12	14.2	33	25	14	2.0	3	0.00	0.00
–	–	–	–	–	–	0.0	–	–	5	0.15	–	–	63	54	–	5	0.00	0.00
0.28	0.30	3.57	0.20	0.00	24.0	0.0	0.0	0.0	1	0.28	2.9	9	9	77	0.1	6	0.00	0.00
0.66	0.20	7.15	0.66	5.26	21.2	20.2	0.0	0.1	15	10.50	26.8	79	114	432	0.9	4	0.00	0.00
–	–	–	–	–	–	0.0	–	–	60	0.00	–	150	50	410	–	–	0.00	0.00
–	–	–	–	–	–	1.2	–	–	80	1.79	–	–	–	160	–	–	0.00	0.00
–	–	–	–	–	–	1.2	–	–	100	1.79	–	–	–	330	–	–	0.00	0.00
0.68	0.30	7.07	0.44	0.00	106.5	2.1	–	5.3	117	4.57	237.0	518	1028	344	4.8	9	0.00	0.00
0.62	0.15	2.06	0.46	0.00	58.8	10.6	–	3.1	80	3.70	134.4	260	993	14	1.6	9	0.00	0.00
0.12	1.13	2.48	0.33	1.13	45.5	1.5	–	1.6	68	5.19	45.5	197	691	1007	3.6	77	0.00	0.00
0.15	0.15	2.06	0.18	0.57	57.7	0.9	–	0.3	67	3.30	55.5	193	608	1032	2.4	74	0.00	0.00
–	–	–	–	–	–	4.8	–	–	40	3.59	–	–	–	1340	–	73	0.00	0.00
0.00	0.15	0.00	–	0.00	–	0.0	–	–	40	3.68	–	237	645	1144	0.6	79	0.00	0.00
0.63	0.20	0.00	0.30	0.00	–	0.0	–	–	37	2.46	–	285	491	869	1.4	79	0.00	0.00
0.33	0.33	3.81	0.27	0.15	65.5	9.8	2.2	0.3	175	7.26	103.7	322	955	2183	2.4	79	0.00	0.00
0.17	0.14	2.58	0.09	0.46	47.4	0.6	2.4	0.0	36	2.67	11.9	113	243	2313	3.7	92	0.00	0.00
0.18	0.12	1.29	0.23	0.05	60.0	1.8	0.0	0.2	108	5.21	102.0	258	666	2910	3.4	87	0.00	0.00
–	0.50	–	–	–	–	–	–	–	219	–	–	–	204	1225	–	78	0.00	0.00
–	–	–	–	–	–	0.0	–	–	–	–	–	–	–	784	–	90	0.00	0.00
0.01	0.17	8.14	0.05	0.58	11.9	0.0	0.0	0.1	24	1.25	5.9	178	510	1886	0.6	96	0.00	0.00
–	–	–	–	–	–	–	–	–	–	–	–	–	–	718	–	82	0.00	0.00
0.01	0.10	1.62	0.05	0.05	0.0	0.0	1.0	1.2	29	0.87	9.8	27	154	942	1.0	90	0.00	0.00
–	–	–	–	–	–	–	–	–	–	1.19	–	–	–	875	–	89	0.00	0.00
0.01	0.10	4.09	0.05	0.31	4.8	3.8	1.0	0.1	34	1.87	9.6	72	108	888	1.0	87	0.00	0.00
0.01	0.01	1.12	0.01	0.14	0.0	0.2	1.0	0.1	17	0.75	0.0	22	101	815	0.3	94	0.00	0.00
0.09	0.37	7.38	0.21	0.54	26.9	12.4	2.2	0.2	59	3.28	21.5	237	824	2397	4.8	83	0.00	0.00
0.10	0.12	2.99	0.11	0.28	11.7	2.3	2.4	0.2	41	2.10	17.6	100	375	2297	0.9	93	0.00	0.00
–	–	–	–	–	–	1.2	–	–	40	0.72	–	–	–	480	–	88	0.00	0.00
0.05	0.07	1.07	0.15	0.31	17.5	4.0	1.0	0.2	42	2.11	30.0	148	525	1035	1.4	85	0.00	0.00
0.21	0.37	1.16	–	–	–	–	–	–	146	1.04	–	–	379	919	–	86	0.00	0.00
0.05	0.05	1.85	0.25	7.92	9.6	12.2	1.0	0.1	67	2.64	19.2	84	384	1001	1.7	86	0.00	0.00
0.01	0.03	0.95	0.07	8.00	4.9	2.0	–	0.1	44	1.49	7.3	54	146	915	0.8	91	0.00	0.00
–	–	–	–	–	–	0.0	–	–	20	0.72	–	–	–	850	–	89	0.00	0.00
–	–	–	–	–	–	–	–	–	–	–	–	–	450	3670	–	–	0.00	0.00
0.21	1.24	–	–	–	–	–	–	–	146	1.57	–	–	306	889	–	86	0.00	0.00
–	–	–	–	–	–	0.0	–	–	0	0.36	–	–	–	340	–	–	0.00	0.00
0.10	0.28	0.87	0.05	0.50	29.8	4.0	–	0.8	174	0.87	19.8	154	360	1042	0.9	86	0.00	0.00
–	–	–	–	–	–	6.0	–	–	20	0.36	–	–	–	720	–	85	0.00	0.00
0.02	0.05	0.31	0.07	0.00	29.3	5.9	5.9	0.4	41	1.22	14.6	39	161	578	0.3	92	0.27	0.00
–	–	–	–	–	–	9.0	–	–	100	0.36	–	–	–	980	–	78	0.00	0.00
–	–	–	–	–	–	0.0	–	–	40	0.36	–	–	–	850	–	87	0.00	0.00

PAGE KEY: A-108 Beverage and Beverage Mixes A-112 Other Beverages A-112 Beverages, Alcoholic A-114 Candies and Confections, Gum A-114 Cereals, Breakfast Type A-118 Cheese and Cheese Substitutes A-120 Dairy Products and Substitutes A-122 Desserts A-128 Dessert Toppings A-128 Eggs, Substitutes, and Egg Dishes A-130 Ethnic Foods A-130 Fast Foods/Restaurants A-140 Fats, Oils, Margarines, Shortenings, and Substitutes A-142 Fish, Seafood, and Shellfish A-142 Food Additives A-142 Fruit, Vegetable, and Blended Juices A-144 Fruits A-146 Grains, Flours, and Fractions A-148 Grain Products, Prepared and Baked Goods

Code	Food Name	Unit/ Amt	Wt (g)	Energy (Kcal)	Prot (g)	Carb (g)	Fiber (g)	Fat (g)	Sat (g)	Mono (g)	Poly (g)	Chol (mg)	Vit A (RE)
50016	Soup, cream of celery, prep f/cnd w/water, cmrcl	1 cup	244	90	2	9	1	6	1.4	1.3	2.5	15	63
50738	Soup, cream of chicken, 98%fat free, cond, cnd	0.5 cup	124	80	3	9	0	3	1.0	—	—	10	80
50006	Soup, cream of chicken, prep f/cnd w/milk, cmrcl	1 cup	248	191	7	15	0	11	4.6	4.5	1.6	27	186
50573	Soup, cream of chicken, rts, cnd	1 cup	245	210	3	8	2	18	6.0	—	—	15	0
50184	Soup, cream of mushroom, low sod, prep w/water	1 cup	244	129	2	9	0	9	2.5	1.7	4.2	2	0
50011	Soup, cream of mushroom, prep f/cnd w/milk, cmrcl	1 cup	248	203	6	15	0	14	5.1	3.0	4.6	20	45
50049	Soup, cream of mushroom, prep f/cnd w/water, cmrcl	1 cup	244	129	2	9	0	9	2.4	1.7	4.2	2	0
50574	Soup, cream of mushroom, rts, cnd	1 cup	245	170	3	9	3	13	4.0	—	—	15	0
50194	Soup, cream of onion, prep f/cnd w/milk, cmrcl	1 cup	248	186	7	18	1	9	4.0	3.3	1.6	32	69
50026	Soup, cream of potato, prep w/milk	1 cup	248	149	6	17	0	6	3.8	1.7	0.6	22	67
50676	Soup, cream of shrimp, cond, cnd	1 cup	251	181	6	16	1	10	6.5	3.0	0.4	33	85
50128	Soup, cream of shrimp, prep f/cnd w/water, cmrcl	1 cup	244	90	3	8	0	5	3.2	1.5	0.2	17	39
91621	Soup, cream of tomato, rts, cnd, Amy's	1 cup	206	100	2	17	4	2	1.5	—	—	10	200
50103	Soup, gazpacho, rts, cnd	1 cup	244	46	7	4	0	0	0.0	0.0	0.1	0	259
50999	Soup, gumbo, zesty, rts, cnd, Healthy Choice	1 cup	244	100	6	15	3	2	1.0	—	—	10	40
91625	Soup, lentil vegetable, organic, rts, cnd, Amy's	1 cup	206	150	8	23	9	4	0.5	—	—	0	350
50430	Soup, lentil, prep f/cnd, Progresso	1 cup	241	140	9	22	7	2	0.0	1.0	1.0	0	150
50858	Soup, matzo ball, inst, microwv	1 cup	14	40	1	9	1	2	0.5	—	—	14	0
50107	Soup, minestrone, chunky, rts, cnd	1 cup	240	127	5	21	6	3	1.5	0.9	0.3	5	437
50356	Soup, minestrone, Italian, real, fat free, cnd, Health Valle	1 cup	240	80	8	21	11	0	0.0	0.0	0.0	0	2000
50009	Soup, minestrone, prep f/cnd w/water, cmrcl	1 cup	241	82	4	11	1	3	0.6	0.7	1.1	2	236
50757	Soup, mushroom & rice, country style, rts, cnd	1 cup	245	80	3	16	2	0	0.0	—	—	0	500
1791	Soup, mushroom, portobello, creamy	1 cup	243	80	4	10	2	3	0.0	—	—	0	0
50022	Soup, onion, prep f/cnd w/water, cmrcl	1 cup	241	58	4	8	1	2	0.3	0.7	0.7	0	0
50624	Soup, pasta fagioli, fat free, cnd, Health Valley	1 cup	240	80	6	17	4	0	0.0	0.0	0.0	0	400
50752	Soup, pasta, penne, zesty, rts, cnd, Healthy Request	1 cup	245	90	4	17	2	0	0.0	—	—	5	450
50768	Soup, pasta, w/garden veg, in glass, rts, cnd	1 cup	245	110	4	21	2	0	0.5	0.0	0.0	5	700
50286	Soup, pea, green, prep w/water	6 oz	170	80	4	12	—	1	—	—	—	—	—
90289	Soup, pea, green, prep f/cnd w/milk, 11.25oz can	1 ea	616	579	31	78	7	17	9.7	5.3	1.3	43	185
50920	Soup, pea, split, w/ham & bacon, cond, cnd, svg	1 ea	135	189	12	29	4	3	0.9	1.2	0.6	4	40
50390	Soup, penne, in chicken broth, hearty, prep, Progresso	1 cup	238	80	4	14	1	1	0.0	0.0	1.0	0	150
50122	Soup, pepper pot, prep f/cnd w/water, cmrcl	1 cup	241	104	6	9	0	5	2.0	2.0	0.4	10	87
50996	Soup, potato ham cheese, prep f/cnd, Progresso	1 cup	245	170	6	21	1	7	2.0	—	—	10	0
51092	Soup, potato leek, creamy, organic	1 cup	245	90	3	14	2	2	0.0	—	—	0	0
42741	Soup, tomato basil, prep f/cnd, Progresso	1 cup	250	100	2	19	1	2	0.0	0.5	1.5	0	50
50134	Soup, tomato bisque, prep f/cnd w/milk, cmrcl	1 cup	251	198	6	29	1	7	3.1	1.9	1.2	23	103
50137	Soup, tomato rice, prep f/cnd w/water, cmrcl	1 cup	247	119	2	22	1	3	0.5	0.6	1.4	2	74
50360	Soup, tomato vegetable, fat free, cnd, Health Valley	1 cup	240	80	6	17	5	0	0.0	0.0	0.0	0	2000
50504	Soup, tomato, cond, cnd	0.5 cup	124	80	2	18	2	0	0.0	0.0	0.0	0	50
50566	Soup, tomato, w/veg & pasta, rts, cnd, Healthy Request	1 cup	245	120	4	22	3	2	0.5	—	—	5	900
50143	Soup, turkey vegetable, prep f/cnd w/water, cmrcl	1 cup	241	72	3	9	0	3	0.9	1.3	0.7	2	246
50567	Soup, turkey, w/veg & wild rice, rts, cnd, Hlthy Request	1 cup	245	120	7	17	2	2	1.0	—	—	15	1200
91628	Soup, vegetable broth, fat free, rts, Amy's	1 cup	198	35	1	8	1	0	0.0	0.0	0.0	0	300
50359	Soup, vegetable, 5 bean, fat free, cnd, Healthy Valley	1 cup	240	140	10	32	13	0	0.0	0.0	0.0	0	2000
50508	Soup, vegetable, cond, cnd	0.5 cup	126	90	3	16	2	1	0.5	—	—	5	600
50409	Soup, vegetable, rts, cnd	1 cup	238	81	4	13	1	1	0.3	0.4	0.3	5	639
50181	Soup, won ton	1 cup	241	182	14	14	1	7	2.3	3.0	1.0	53	99
50316	Stew, beef, cnd	1 cup	252	192	15	19	3	6	2.3	2.5	0.3	33	310

PAGE KEY: A-154 Granola Bars, Cereal Bars, Diet Bars, Scones, and Tarts A-154 Meals and Dishes A-160 Meats A-164 Nuts, Seeds, and Products A-166 Poultry A-166 Salad Dressings, Dips, and Mayonnaise A-170 Salads A-170 Sandwiches A-172 Sauces and Gravies A-174 Snack Foods—Chips, Pretzels, Popcorn A-178 Soups, Stews and Chilis A-184 Spices, Flavors, and Seasonings A-184 Sports Bars and Drinks A-186 Supplemental Foods and Formulas A-186 Sweeteners and Sweet Substitutes A-188 Vegetables and Legumes A-200 Weight Loss Bars & Drinks A-200 Miscellaneous

Thia (mg)	Ribo (mg)	Niac (mg NE)	Vit B6 (mg)	Vit B12 (μg)	Fol (μg)	Vit C (mg)	Vit D (IU)	Vit E (mg AT)	Cal (mg)	Iron (mg)	Magn (mg)	Phos (mg)	Pota (mg)	Sodi (mg)	Zinc (mg)	Wat (%)	Alco (g)	Caff (g)
0.02	0.05	0.33	0.00	0.23	2.4	0.2	5.5	0.9	39	0.62	7.3	37	122	949	0.1	92	0.00	0.00
–	–	–	–	–	–	0.0	–	–	20	0.00	–	–	–	910	–	86	0.00	0.00
0.07	0.25	0.92	0.07	0.55	7.4	1.2	49.1	0.2	181	0.67	17.4	151	273	1047	0.7	85	0.00	0.00
–	–	–	–	–	–	2.4	–	–	20	0.72	–	–	–	1170	–	87	0.00	0.00
0.05	0.10	0.73	0.01	0.05	4.9	1.0	–	1.2	46	0.50	4.9	49	100	49	0.6	90	0.00	0.00
0.07	0.28	0.91	0.05	0.50	9.9	2.2	49.1	1.3	179	0.60	19.8	156	270	918	0.6	85	0.00	0.00
0.05	0.09	0.72	0.00	0.05	4.9	1.0	–	1.2	46	0.50	4.9	49	100	881	0.6	90	0.00	0.00
–	–	–	–	–	–	0.0	–	–	0	0.00	–	–	–	970	–	89	0.00	0.00
0.10	0.27	0.61	0.07	0.50	22.3	2.5	–	0.1	179	0.68	22.3	154	310	1004	0.6	84	0.00	0.00
0.07	0.23	0.63	0.09	0.50	9.9	1.2	49.1	0.1	166	0.55	17.4	161	322	1061	0.7	87	0.00	0.00
0.03	0.05	0.85	0.07	1.17	7.5	0.0	23.9	1.7	35	1.04	17.6	65	118	1953	1.5	85	0.00	0.00
0.01	0.02	0.43	0.05	0.58	4.9	0.0	–	0.8	17	0.54	9.8	32	59	976	0.8	92	0.00	0.00
–	–	–	–	–	–	12.0	–	–	–	1.44	–	–	–	690	–	–	0.00	0.00
0.05	0.01	0.93	0.15	0.00	9.8	7.1	0.0	0.5	24	0.98	7.3	37	224	739	0.2	94	0.00	0.00
–	–	–	–	–	–	3.6	–	–	40	0.72	–	–	–	480	–	88	0.00	0.00
–	–	–	–	–	–	12.0	–	–	60	2.70	–	–	–	680	–	81	0.00	0.00
–	–	–	–	–	–	0.0	–	–	40	3.59	–	–	–	750	–	85	0.00	0.00
–	–	–	–	–	–	0.0	–	–	40	0.00	–	–	–	800	–	13	0.00	0.00
0.05	0.11	1.17	0.23	0.00	52.8	4.8	0.0	0.7	60	1.77	14.4	110	612	864	1.4	87	0.00	0.00
–	–	–	–	–	–	4.8	–	–	40	3.59	–	–	–	210	–	88	0.00	0.00
0.05	0.03	0.93	0.10	0.00	36.2	1.2	0.0	0.1	34	0.92	7.2	55	313	911	0.7	91	0.00	0.00
–	–	–	–	–	–	2.4	–	–	40	0.36	–	–	–	820	–	91	0.00	0.00
–	–	–	–	–	–	0.0	–	–	20	0.72	–	–	–	310	–	–	0.00	0.00
0.02	0.01	0.60	0.05	0.00	14.5	1.2	0.0	0.3	27	0.67	2.4	12	67	1053	0.6	93	0.00	0.00
–	–	–	–	–	–	15.0	–	–	40	0.18	–	–	–	250	–	90	0.00	0.00
–	–	–	–	–	–	60.0	–	–	40	0.72	–	–	–	470	–	90	0.00	0.00
–	–	–	–	–	–	2.4	–	–	60	1.08	–	–	–	720	–	88	0.00	0.00
–	–	4.00	–	–	–	–	–	–	–	0.72	–	–	140	560	–	89	0.00	0.00
0.37	0.64	3.25	0.25	1.04	18.5	6.8	118.9	0.4	419	4.86	135.5	579	912	2353	4.3	78	0.00	0.00
–	–	–	–	–	–	–	–	–	–	2.15	–	–	–	984	–	65	0.00	0.00
–	–	–	–	–	–	0.0	–	–	0	0.72	–	–	–	1020	–	91	0.00	0.00
0.05	0.05	1.22	0.05	0.17	9.6	1.4	0.0	0.1	24	0.88	4.8	41	152	971	1.2	90	0.00	0.00
–	–	–	–	–	–	2.4	–	–	60	0.36	–	–	–	860	–	85	0.00	0.00
–	–	–	–	–	–	0.0	–	–	20	1.79	–	–	–	380	–	–	0.00	0.00
–	–	–	–	–	–	12.0	–	–	0	1.08	–	–	–	790	–	90	0.00	0.00
0.10	0.27	1.25	0.14	0.43	22.6	7.0	49.2	1.0	186	0.87	25.1	173	605	1109	0.6	82	0.00	0.00
0.05	0.05	1.04	0.07	0.00	14.8	14.8	0.0	0.8	22	0.79	4.9	35	331	815	0.5	88	0.00	0.00
0.10	0.07	2.25	0.14	–	0.4	9.0	–	–	40	5.40	–	–	608	240	–	90	0.00	0.00
–	–	–	–	–	–	2.4	–	–	20	0.72	–	–	–	730	–	82	0.00	0.00
–	–	–	–	–	–	4.8	–	–	60	1.08	–	–	–	480	–	87	0.00	0.00
0.02	0.03	1.00	0.05	0.17	4.8	0.0	1.0	0.1	17	0.76	4.8	41	176	906	0.6	93	0.00	0.00
–	–	–	–	–	–	2.4	–	–	40	0.72	–	–	–	480	–	87	0.00	0.00
–	–	–	–	–	–	6.0	–	–	40	0.72	–	–	–	680	–	–	0.00	0.00
–	–	–	–	–	–	12.0	–	–	80	5.40	–	–	–	250	–	82	0.00	0.00
–	–	–	–	–	–	1.2	–	–	20	0.72	–	–	–	820	–	82	0.00	0.00
0.07	0.07	1.83	0.07	0.07	28.6	1.4	–	0.1	31	1.51	21.4	74	290	466	0.4	91	0.00	0.00
0.40	0.25	4.59	0.20	0.40	18.8	3.4	–	0.4	31	1.75	20.6	153	316	543	1.1	84	0.00	0.00
0.18	0.25	3.09	0.30	0.55	–	2.5	–	0.6	63	1.59	35.3	159	388	1187	2.5	83	0.00	0.00

PAGE KEY: A-108 Beverage and Beverage Mixes A-112 Other Beverages A-112 Beverages, Alcoholic A-114 Candies and Confections, Gum A-114 Cereals, Breakfast Type A-118 Cheese and Cheese Substitutes A-120 Dairy Products and Substitutes A-122 Desserts A-128 Dessert Toppings A-128 Eggs, Substitutes, and Egg Dishes A-130 Ethnic Foods A-130 Fast Foods/Restaurants A-140 Fats, Oils, Margarines, Shortenings, and Substitutes A-142 Fish, Seafood, and Shellfish A-142 Food Additives A-142 Fruit, Vegetable, and Blended Juices A-144 Fruits A-146 Grains, Flours, and Fractions A-148 Grain Products, Prepared and Baked Goods

Code	Food Name	Unit/ Amt	Wt (g)	Energy (Kcal)	Prot (g)	Carb (g)	Fiber (g)	Fat (g)	Sat (g)	Mono (g)	Poly (g)	Chol (mg)	Vit A (RE)
70857	Stew, beef, old fash, homestyle	1 cup	249	220	18	20	6	7	3.0	–	–	40	350
70787	Stew, chicken	1 cup	245	180	11	17	2	8	3.0	–	–	35	700
50024	Stew, oyster, prep f/cnd w/milk, cmrcl	1 cup	245	135	6	10	0	8	5.0	2.1	0.3	32	59
7559	Stew, vegetarian	1 ea	270	324	46	19	3	8	1.3	2.0	4.2	0	0
Dry and Prepared Soups and Chilis													
91229	Chili, three bean, hearty, dry mix, Soup Starter	1 oz	28	101	5	19	5	1	0.1	0.1	0.3	0	30
56842	Soup, beans & rice, red, homestyle, in a cup, dry	1 ea	53	166	10	35	10	1	0.2	0.2	0.7	0	2
50192	Soup, beef bouillon/broth, cube	1 ea	4	6	1	1	0	0	0.1	0.1	0.0	0	1
50032	Soup, beef bouillon/broth, prep f/pwd w/water	1 cup	244	20	1	2	0	1	0.3	0.3	0.0	0	1
91219	Soup, beef flvr bouillon/broth, sodfree, inst, dry	1 oz	28	86	3	16	0	1	0.5	0.6	0.0	1	1
90244	Soup, beef noodle, dehyd, svg, makes 1 cup prep	1 ea	14	47	3	7	0	1	0.3	0.4	0.2	2	1
50928	Soup, beefy onion, dry mix	1 ea	8	25	1	5	0	1	0.1	–	–	0	0
50155	Soup, cauliflower, prep f/dehyd w/water	1 cup	256	69	3	11	0	2	0.3	0.7	0.6	0	–
50193	Soup, chicken bouillon/broth, cube	1 ea	5	10	1	1	0	0	0.1	0.1	0.1	1	3
50611	Soup, chicken bouillon/broth, dry	1 ea	6	20	0	3	0	1	0.0	–	–	0	0
50935	Soup, chicken bouillon/broth, fat free, dry, svg	1 ea	6	18	1	3	0	0	0.0	–	–	0	0
50930	Soup, chicken noodle, dry mix, svg	1 ea	20	77	3	11	0	2	0.6	–	–	15	5
50161	Soup, chicken rice, prep f/dehyd w/water	1 cup	240	58	2	9	1	1	0.3	0.6	0.4	2	0
50619	Soup, chicken, supreme, hearty, dry mix	1 ea	21	90	1	14	1	4	1.4	–	–	1	5
50164	Soup, clam chwdr, New Eng, dehyd, makes 1 cup prep	1 ea	13	53	2	7	1	2	0.3	0.9	0.7	0	1
50166	Soup, consomme, w/gelatin, prep f/dehyd w/water	1 cup	249	17	2	2	0	0	0.0	0.0	0.0	0	–
50346	Soup, corn & potato chowder, creamy, in a cup, dry	1 ea	47	170	7	34	2	1	0.0	–	–	0	200
50149	Soup, cream of asparagus, prep f/dehyd w/water	1 cup	251	58	2	9	0	2	0.1	0.8	0.7	0	25
50157	Soup, cream of celery, prep f/dehyd w/water	1 cup	254	64	3	10	0	2	0.3	0.7	0.6	0	25
50036	Soup, cream of chicken, prep f/dehyd w/water	1 cup	261	107	2	13	0	5	3.4	1.2	0.4	3	123
91556	Soup, cream of mushroom, mix, wheat free	25 g	25	106	1	13	0	5	1.4	3.7	0.2	0	0
50857	Soup, matzo ball, prep f/dry mix	1 cup	242	110	3	13	3	5	2.0	–	–	35	250
50170	Soup, minestrone, prep f/dehyd w/water	1 cup	254	79	4	12	1	2	0.8	0.7	0.1	3	30
49181	Soup, navy bean, in a cup, dry	1 ea	43	160	8	30	9	1	0.0	0.0	0.0	0	126
56833	Soup, noodle, Cantonese, in a cup, dry	1 ea	26	97	4	19	1	1	0.0	0.0	0.0	0	41
49179	Soup, noodle, Thai, spicy, in a cup, dry	1 ea	36	128	4	25	1	3	0.0	0.0	0.0	0	4
50526	Soup, onion, dry mix	1 Tbs	7	20	0	5	0	0	0.0	0.0	0.0	0	0
56835	Soup, pasta, Mediterranean, homestyle, in a cup, dry	1 ea	53	207	9	33	2	4	2.6	1.6	0.2	11	14
12227	Soup, pea, split, w/carrots, low fat, organic, inst, dry	2 oz	57	219	14	38	10	1	0.0	–	–	0	86
50777	Soup, ramen noodle, bkd, chicken flvr, dry	0.5 ea	40	140	4	30	1	1	0.0	–	–	0	0
50697	Soup, ramen noodle, chicken flvr, dry Of Noodles	1 ea	64	296	6	37	–	14	6.3	–	–	–	80
50785	Soup, ramen noodle, fried, pork flvr, dry	0.5 ea	40	170	4	26	1	6	4.0	–	–	0	0
50790	Soup, ramen noodle, fried, shrimp flvr, dry	0.5 ea	40	170	3	26	1	6	4.0	–	–	0	0
50609	Soup, vegetable, harvest, hearty, dry	1 ea	23	90	1	17	2	2	0.5	–	–	0	60
Homemade/Generic Soups and Chilis													
56114	Chili, con carne, w/beans & pork	1 cup	254	274	24	27	7	8	2.5	3.5	1.4	51	121
54188	Soup, beef, stock, f/rec	1 cup	237	43	4	3	0	1	0.3	–	–	0	62
50210	Soup, bird's nest, chicken ham noodle	1 cup	244	112	14	6	0	3	0.8	1.1	0.5	27	2
50651	Soup, cheese, cond, cnd, cmrcl	1 cup	257	311	11	21	2	21	13.3	5.9	0.6	59	216
56206	Soup, chicken & rice, w/mushroom	1 cup	248	455	28	35	1	22	4.9	8.7	6.7	66	160
50213	Soup, crab/seafood, bisque/soup, prep w/milk	1 cup	248	236	20	12	0	12	3.4	4.7	2.7	85	145
50189	Soup, cream of broccoli	1 cup	237	206	9	17	2	12	4.0	5.1	2.5	15	258
50190	Soup, egg drop	1 cup	244	73	8	1	0	4	1.1	1.5	0.6	103	41
50689	Soup, fish broth/stock, homemade	1 cup	233	40	5	0	0	2	0.5	0.5	0.3	2	0
50211	Soup, fish chowder	1 cup	244	194	24	12	1	5	2.4	1.9	0.6	56	63

PAGE KEY: A-154 Granola Bars, Cereal Bars, Diet Bars, Scones, and Tarts A-154 Meals and Dishes A-160 Meats A-164 Nuts, Seeds, and Products A-166 Poultry A-166 Salad Dressings, Dips, and Mayonnaise A-170 Salads A-170 Sandwiches A-172 Sauces and Gravies A-174 Snack Foods—Chips, Pretzels, Popcorn A-178 Soups, Stews and Chilis A-184 Spices, Flavors, and Seasonings A-184 Sports Bars and Drinks A-186 Supplemental Foods and Formulas A-186 Sweeteners and Sweet Substitutes A-188 Vegetables and Legumes A-200 Weight Loss Bars & Drinks A-200 Miscellaneous

Thia (mg)	Ribo (mg)	Niac (mg NE)	Vit B6 (mg)	Vit B12 (µg)	Fol (µg)	Vit C (mg)	Vit D (IU)	Vit E (mg AT)	Cal (mg)	Iron (mg)	Magn (mg)	Phos (mg)	Pota (mg)	Sodi (mg)	Zinc (mg)	Wat (%)	Alco (g)	Caff (g)
–	–	–	–	–	–	2.4	–	–	40	1.79	–	–	–	950	–	81	0.00	0.00
–	–	–	–	–	–	2.4	–	–	40	1.08	–	–	–	1110	–	84	0.00	0.00
0.07	0.23	0.34	0.05	2.61	9.8	4.4	137.9	0.5	167	1.04	19.6	162	235	1041	10.3	89	0.00	0.00
1.88	1.62	32.40	2.97	5.94	278.1	0.0	–	1.3	84	3.50	342.9	594	324	1080	3.0	70	0.00	0.00
0.09	0.03	0.64	–	–	–	2.4	–	–	54	1.67	29.8	92	349	655	0.5	6	0.00	0.00
0.18	0.10	1.14	0.07	0.00	27.7	2.4	0.0	0.1	90	3.00	17.9	201	587	590	0.3	6	0.00	0.00
0.00	0.00	0.11	0.00	0.03	1.2	0.0	–	0.0	2	0.07	1.8	8	15	864	0.0	3	0.00	0.00
0.00	0.01	0.36	0.00	0.00	0.0	0.0	0.0	0.0	10	0.01	7.3	24	37	1362	0.1	97	0.00	0.00
0.05	0.00	0.09	–	–	–	0.3	–	–	17	0.14	3.8	13	3473	22	0.1	3	0.00	0.00
0.14	0.07	0.79	0.03	0.00	17.3	0.6	1.0	0.0	7	0.37	10.8	45	93	1194	0.1	5	0.00	0.00
0.00	0.01	0.11	–	–	0.0	0.7	–	–	11	0.11	–	–	–	607	–	4	0.00	0.00
0.07	0.07	0.50	0.02	0.18	2.6	2.6	0.0	–	10	0.50	2.6	51	105	843	0.3	93	0.00	0.00
0.00	0.01	0.18	0.00	0.00	1.5	0.0	0.0	0.0	9	0.09	2.7	9	18	1152	0.0	2	0.00	0.00
–	–	–	–	–	–	0.0	–	–	0	0.00	–	–	–	580	–	24	0.00	0.00
0.00	0.00	0.17	–	–	0.0	0.0	–	–	2	0.09	–	–	–	442	–	4	0.00	0.00
0.23	0.07	1.62	–	–	0.0	0.1	–	–	10	0.68	–	–	–	690	–	4	0.00	0.00
0.00	0.00	0.34	0.01	0.07	0.0	0.0	0.9	0.0	7	0.00	0.0	10	10	931	0.1	94	0.00	0.00
0.05	0.05	0.60	–	–	0.0	0.1	–	–	23	0.18	–	–	–	635	–	4	0.00	0.00
0.00	0.09	0.46	0.03	4.90	1.9	1.1	0.6	0.1	42	0.70	3.8	55	114	414	0.4	4	0.00	0.00
0.00	0.01	0.56	0.01	0.11	5.0	0.0	0.0	0.0	7	0.11	7.5	40	57	3299	0.0	95	0.00	0.00
–	–	–	–	–	–	18.0	–	–	150	2.70	–	–	–	580	–	9	0.00	0.00
0.05	0.05	0.50	0.00	0.02	7.5	0.8	0.1	–	23	0.50	2.5	30	133	800	0.7	94	0.00	0.00
0.02	0.05	0.30	0.00	0.05	2.5	0.3	0.2	0.3	36	0.50	5.1	33	109	838	0.1	93	0.00	0.00
0.10	0.20	2.60	0.05	0.25	5.2	0.5	1.0	0.1	76	0.25	5.2	97	214	1185	1.6	91	0.00	0.00
0.00	0.00	0.00	0.00	0.00	0.1	0.0	0.6	0.1	4	0.05	0.5	42	92	900	0.0	–	0.00	0.00
–	–	–	–	–	–	2.4	–	–	0	1.08	–	–	–	710	–	89	0.00	0.00
0.07	0.05	1.01	0.10	0.00	35.5	1.0	0.0	0.1	38	1.01	7.6	61	340	1026	0.8	92	0.00	0.00
0.00	0.00	0.95	0.00	0.00	0.3	8.4	0.0	0.0	15	2.07	2.5	5	66	554	0.1	8	0.00	0.00
0.00	0.00	1.15	0.00	0.00	0.2	13.1	0.0	0.0	19	1.05	9.8	7	68	362	0.0	8	0.00	0.00
0.00	0.00	1.60	0.00	0.00	0.2	5.6	0.0	0.0	19	1.26	1.3	3	69	521	0.0	8	0.00	0.00
–	–	–	–	–	–	0.0	–	–	0	0.00	–	–	–	530	–	4	0.00	0.00
–	–	–	–	–	–	2.5	–	–	93	1.25	–	–	240	636	–	8	0.00	0.00
–	–	–	–	–	–	1.7	–	–	48	2.40	–	–	–	476	–	5	0.00	0.00
–	–	–	–	–	–	0.0	–	–	0	1.44	–	–	–	720	–	8	0.00	0.00
–	–	–	–	–	–	–	–	–	–	2.18	–	–	–	1434	–	6	0.00	0.00
–	–	–	–	–	–	0.0	–	–	0	1.08	–	–	–	850	–	6	0.00	0.00
–	–	–	–	–	–	0.0	–	–	0	1.08	–	–	–	740	–	4	0.00	0.00
–	–	–	–	–	–	4.8	–	–	0	0.00	–	–	–	450	–	13	0.00	0.00
0.68	0.34	4.71	0.43	0.43	42.9	21.4	–	1.8	65	2.83	57.0	261	793	892	2.4	75	0.00	0.00
0.00	0.05	2.43	0.01	0.18	3.5	14.8	0.0	0.0	17	0.63	1.8	53	152	88	0.2	95	0.00	0.00
0.10	0.11	5.17	0.17	0.31	5.3	0.0	–	0.2	14	0.85	10.5	125	246	747	0.9	90	0.00	0.00
0.02	0.27	0.80	0.05	0.00	7.7	0.0	6.8	0.4	285	1.49	7.7	272	308	1920	1.3	77	0.00	0.00
0.21	0.18	12.57	0.40	0.31	6.6	1.4	–	2.8	61	2.65	41.0	274	395	1170	1.6	64	0.00	0.00
0.15	0.28	2.90	0.20	5.78	46.7	4.6	–	2.0	253	1.03	46.4	299	490	585	3.7	81	0.00	0.00
0.12	0.40	0.85	0.15	0.37	40.2	48.2	–	2.4	256	0.91	41.1	222	481	204	1.0	83	0.00	0.00
0.01	0.18	3.02	0.05	0.49	15.1	0.0	–	0.3	21	0.75	4.6	108	220	729	0.5	94	0.00	0.00
0.07	0.18	2.75	0.09	1.61	46.6	0.2	–	3.0	7	0.01	16.3	130	336	363	0.1	97	0.00	0.00
0.17	0.25	2.88	0.36	1.25	16.3	7.3	–	0.4	148	0.70	49.1	298	711	180	1.1	83	0.00	0.00

PAGE KEY: A-108 Beverage and Beverage Mixes A-112 Other Beverages A-112 Beverages, Alcoholic A-114 Candies and Confections, Gum A-114 Cereals, Breakfast Type A-118 Cheese and Cheese Substitutes A-120 Dairy Products and Substitutes A-122 Desserts A-128 Dessert Toppings A-128 Eggs, Substitutes, and Egg Dishes A-130 Ethnic Foods A-130 Fast Foods/Restaurants A-140 Fats, Oils, Margarines, Shortenings, and Substitutes A-142 Fish, Seafood, and Shellfish A-142 Food Additives A-142 Fruit, Vegetable, and Blended Juices A-144 Fruits A-146 Grains, Flours, and Fractions A-148 Grain Products, Prepared and Baked Goods

Code	Food Name	Unit/ Amt	Wt (g)	Energy (Kcal)	Prot (g)	Carb (g)	Fiber (g)	Fat (g)	Sat (g)	Mono (g)	Poly (g)	Chol (mg)	Vit A (RE)
50182	Soup, hot & sour, Chinese	1 cup	244	162	15	5	1	8	2.7	3.4	1.2	34	2
414	Soup, menudo, Mexican beef soup	661.801 g	662	319	37	17	3	11	5.0	3.4	0.7	227	58
1749	Soup, seafood chowder	1 cup	244	194	24	12	1	5	2.4	1.9	0.6	56	63
50217	Soup, shrimp, gumbo	1 cup	244	170	10	19	3	7	1.3	3.0	2.0	51	159
50709	Soup, vegetable bouillon/broth	1 cup	235	16	2	2	0	0	–	–	–	0	1
50205	Stew, seafood, w/potatoes & veg, tomato base sauce	1 cup	252	177	21	15	2	4	1.1	1.4	0.7	97	431
SPICES, FLAVORS, AND SEASONINGS													
26046	Basil, fresh, leaves	5 ea	2	1	0	0	0	0	0.0	0.0	0.0	0	10
26108	Chervil, dried	1 tsp	1	1	0	0	0	0	0.0	0.0	0.0	0	4
26002	Chili Powder	1 tsp	3	8	0	1	1	0	0.1	0.1	0.2	0	91
26004	Curry Powder	1 tsp	2	6	0	1	1	0	0.0	0.1	0.1	0	2
669	Garlic Salt	0.25 tsp	1	0	0	0	0	0	0.0	0.0	0.0	–	–
26026	Nutmeg, ground	1 tsp	2	12	0	1	0	1	0.6	0.1	0.0	0	0
26175	Onion Salt, gl	1 tsp	6	3	0	1	0	0	–	–	–	0	0
5113	Onion, flakes, dehyd	0.25 cup	14	49	1	12	1	0	0.0	0.0	0.0	0	0
26310	Oregano, fresh	1 tsp	2	1	0	0	–	0	–	–	–	–	3
26016	Pepper, black	1 tsp	2	5	0	1	1	0	0.0	0.0	0.0	0	0
26037	Pepper, white	1 tsp	2	7	0	2	1	0	0.0	0.0	0.0	0	0
26015	Poppy Seeds	1 tsp	3	15	1	1	0	1	0.1	0.2	0.9	0	0
26627	Rosemary, fresh	1 tsp	1	1	0	0	0	0	0.0	0.0	0.0	0	2
26111	Saffron	1 tsp	1	2	0	0	0	0	0.0	0.0	0.0	0	0
26090	Salt Substitute	0.25 tsp	1	0	0	0	–	0	0.0	0.0	0.0	–	–
90622	Salt Substitute, Mrs. Dash, original blend	0.25 tsp	1	0	0	0	0	0	0.0	0.0	0.0	0	0
26291	Salt, table, iodized	0.25 tsp	2	0	0	0	0	0	0.0	0.0	0.0	0	–
26123	Salt, table, non-iodized	0.25 tsp	2	0	0	0	0	0	0.0	0.0	0.0	0	–
26634	Seasoning, ground, Puerto Rican	1 tsp	4	3	0	0	0	0	0.0	0.1	0.1	0	2
26028	Seasoning, poultry	1 tsp	2	5	0	1	0	0	0.0	0.0	0.0	0	4
26633	Seasoning, sofrito, Puerto Rican	1 tsp	4	9	0	0	0	1	0.3	0.4	0.1	1	1
26321	Seasoning, taco salad, dry mix	1 tsp	4	15	0	3	–	0	0.0	0.0	0.0	–	–
26032	Tarragon, ground	1 tsp	2	5	0	1	0	0	0.0	0.0	0.1	0	7
664	Tenderizer, original, sodfree, unseasoned, Adolph's	0.5 tsp	1	2	0	0	–	0	0.0	0.0	0.0	–	–
663	Tenderizer, original, w/o msg, unseasoned, Adolph's	0.25 tsp	1	0	0	0	0	0	0.0	0.0	0.0	–	–
26624	Vanilla, extract	1 Tbs	13	37	0	2	0	0	0.0	0.0	0.0	0	0
SPORTS BARS AND DRINKS													
62275	Bar, energy, apple cinnamon, PowerBar	1 ea	65	230	10	45	3	2	0.5	1.5	0.5	0	0
43711	Bar, energy, chai tea, Luna Bar	1 ea	48	175	10	26	2	4	2.7	–	–	0	993
62709	Bar, energy, chocolate chip, Clif Bar	1 ea	68	238	10	42	5	4	0.9	–	–	0	278
62724	Bar, energy, chocolate, Balance Bar	1 ea	50	200	14	22	1	6	3.5	–	–	3	500
62720	Bar, energy, cookie dough, Ironman	1 ea	57	230	16	25	0	7	1.5	–	–	0	500
63015	Bar, energy, fresh wild berry, Results for Women	1 ea	55	190	11	28	4	6	2.0	–	–	0	250
62723	Bar, energy, granola, Ironman	1 ea	57	230	16	23	1	8	1.5	–	–	10	500
63026	Bar, energy, Muscle Drive, power oats spice	1 ea	80	280	33	27	1	6	5.0	–	–	15	350
4320	Bar, energy, Myoplex Carb Sense, blueberry	1 ea	70	240	28	25	4	6	3.5	–	–	5	300
62205	Bar, energy, peanut butter, Tiger's Milk	1 ea	35	140	6	18	1	5	1.0	–	–	0	150
62831	Bar, energy, Prot Plus, choc fudge brownie, PowerBar	1 ea	78	290	24	38	4	5	4.0	–	–	5	0
43708	Bar, energy, s'mores, Luna Bar	1 ea	48	178	10	26	2	4	3.0	–	–	0	754
62719	Bar, energy, yogurt berry, Ironman	1 ea	57	230	16	24	0	8	3.0	–	–	10	500
62833	Carbohydrate Gel, chocolate, pkt, PowerBar	1 ea	41	120	0	28	0	2	1.0	–	–	0	0
1954	Drink, Anabolic Activator III, chocolate, pwd, scoop	2 ea	57	180	26	15	1	2	1.0	–	–	15	500

PAGE KEY: A-154 Granola Bars, Cereal Bars, Diet Bars, Scones, and Tarts A-154 Meals and Dishes A-160 Meats A-164 Nuts, Seeds, and Products A-166 Poultry A-166 Salad Dressings, Dips, and Mayonnaise A-170 Salads A-170 Sandwiches A-172 Sauces and Gravies A-174 Snack Foods—Chips, Pretzels, Popcorn A-178 Soups, Stews and Chilis A-184 Spices, Flavors, and Seasonings A-184 Sports Bars and Drinks A-186 Supplemental Foods and Formulas A-186 Sweeteners and Sweet Substitutes A-188 Vegetables and Legumes A-200 Weight Loss Bars & Drinks A-200 Miscellaneous

Thia (mg)	Ribo (mg)	Niac (mg NE)	Vit B6 (mg)	Vit B12 (µg)	Fol (µg)	Vit C (mg)	Vit D (IU)	Vit E (mg AT)	Cal (mg)	Iron (mg)	Magn (mg)	Phos (mg)	Pota (mg)	Sodi (mg)	Zinc (mg)	Wat (%)	Alco (g)	Caff (g)
0.27	0.25	5.00	0.20	0.41	12.7	0.7	–	0.1	29	1.89	28.8	188	384	1011	1.5	87	0.91	0.00
0.02	0.46	0.37	0.18	2.75	9.8	7.9	0.0	0.4	45	5.67	43.0	235	754	905	7.1	90	0.00	0.00
0.17	0.25	2.88	0.36	1.25	16.3	7.3	–	0.4	148	0.70	49.1	298	711	180	1.1	83	0.00	0.00
0.18	0.10	2.53	0.18	0.30	59.1	25.1	–	1.9	104	2.25	51.4	126	515	343	0.9	85	0.00	0.00
0.00	0.01	0.54	0.01	0.11	3.8	0.0	–	0.0	7	0.11	7.0	38	54	3114	0.0	95	0.00	0.00
0.18	0.20	3.56	0.34	24.25	35.2	29.9	–	1.7	80	9.36	44.8	226	817	521	1.9	83	0.00	0.00
0.00	0.00	0.01	0.00	0.00	1.6	0.5	0.0	0.0	4	0.07	2.0	2	12	0	0.0	91	0.00	0.00
0.00	0.00	0.02	0.00	0.00	1.6	0.3	0.0	0.0	8	0.18	0.8	3	28	0	0.1	7	0.00	0.00
0.00	0.01	0.20	0.10	0.00	2.6	1.7	0.0	0.0	7	0.37	4.4	8	50	26	0.1	8	0.00	0.00
0.00	0.00	0.07	0.01	0.00	3.1	0.2	0.0	0.0	10	0.58	5.1	7	31	1	0.1	10	0.00	0.00
–	–	–	–	0.00	–	–	–	–	–	–	–	–	–	240	–	11	0.00	0.00
0.00	0.00	0.02	0.00	0.00	1.7	0.1	0.0	0.1	4	0.07	4.0	5	8	0	0.0	6	0.00	0.00
0.00	0.00	0.00	0.00	0.00	1.1	0.1	0.0	0.0	5	0.02	2.5	3	8	1812	0.0	1	0.00	0.00
0.07	0.00	0.14	0.21	0.00	23.2	10.5	0.0	0.2	36	0.21	12.9	42	227	3	0.3	4	0.00	0.00
0.00	–	–	–	0.00	–	0.9	0.0	–	6	–	1.1	1	7	0	0.0	82	0.00	0.00
0.00	0.00	0.01	0.00	0.00	0.2	0.4	0.0	0.0	9	0.61	4.1	4	26	1	0.0	11	0.00	0.00
0.00	0.00	0.00	0.00	0.00	0.2	0.5	0.0	0.1	6	0.34	2.2	4	2	0	0.0	11	0.00	0.00
0.01	0.00	0.02	0.00	0.00	1.6	0.1	0.0	0.1	41	0.25	9.3	24	20	1	0.3	7	0.00	0.00
0.00	0.00	0.00	0.00	0.00	0.8	0.2	–	0.0	2	0.05	0.6	0	5	0	0.0	68	0.00	0.00
0.00	0.00	0.00	0.00	0.00	0.7	0.6	0.0	0.0	1	0.07	1.8	2	12	1	0.0	12	0.00	0.00
–	–	–	–	0.00	–	–	–	–	7	–	0.0	5	604	0	–	0	0.00	0.00
–	–	–	–	0.00	–	0.0	–	–	0	0.00	–	–	–	0	–	–	0.00	0.00
–	–	–	–	0.00	–	–	–	–	–	–	–	–	–	590	–	0	–	0.00
–	–	–	–	0.00	–	–	–	–	–	–	–	–	–	590	–	0	–	0.00
0.00	0.00	0.01	0.00	0.00	0.6	1.4	–	0.1	0	0.01	0.4	1	7	0	0.0	87	0.00	0.00
0.00	0.00	0.03	0.01	0.00	2.1	0.2	0.0	0.0	15	0.52	3.4	3	10	0	0.0	9	0.00	0.00
0.00	0.00	0.05	0.00	0.00	0.5	0.8	–	0.0	1	0.01	0.6	4	10	32	0.0	61	0.00	0.00
–	–	–	–	0.00	–	–	–	–	–	–	–	–	–	200	–	5	0.00	0.00
0.00	0.01	0.14	0.03	0.00	4.4	0.8	0.0	0.0	18	0.51	5.6	5	48	1	0.1	8	0.00	0.00
–	–	–	–	0.00	–	–	–	–	–	–	–	–	–	0	–	–	0.00	0.00
–	–	–	–	0.00	–	–	–	–	–	–	–	–	–	420	–	–	0.00	0.00
0.00	0.00	0.05	0.00	0.00	0.0	0.0	–	0.0	1	0.01	1.6	1	19	1	0.0	53	4.46	0.00
1.50	1.70	20.00	2.00	6.00	400.0	60.0	–	18.4	300	6.30	140.0	350	110	90	5.2	10	0.00	0.00
1.72	1.69	19.89	2.41	5.90	415.8	59.2	–	18.2	450	8.03	11.0	418	108	144	5.4	15	0.00	0.00
0.34	0.28	3.49	0.38	0.98	85.6	66.1	–	20.3	265	5.21	95.5	286	206	76	3.5	15	0.00	
0.60	0.50	9.00	0.60	1.20	80.0	60.0	80.0	13.6	100	3.59	40.0	100	180	230	3.0	15	0.00	
0.75	0.85	10.00	1.00	3.00	200.0	30.0	200.0	9.2	250	9.00	200.0	250	100	220	7.5	14	0.00	0.00
0.44	0.50	5.00	0.50	1.50	120.0	21.0	–	4.1	300	6.30	40.0	250	170	150	5.2	16	0.00	0.00
0.75	0.85	10.00	1.00	3.00	200.0	30.0	200.0	9.2	150	9.00	200.0	200	290	105	7.5	15	0.00	0.00
0.15	0.17	2.00	0.69	2.09	40.0	21.0	40.0	4.5	200	1.79	40.0	40	80	110	1.5	17	0.00	0.00
0.44	0.50	6.00	0.60	2.40	120.0	18.0	120.0	4.1	300	5.40	40.0	200	95	140	4.5	14	0.00	0.00
1.26	0.60	3.00	0.60	1.50	–	6.0	60.0	–	300	2.70	100.0	100	–	75	–	14	0.00	0.00
1.50	1.70	20.00	2.00	6.00	400.0	60.0	–	18.3	300	6.30	140.0	350	–	150	5.2	13	0.00	
1.32	1.27	15.14	1.84	4.48	321.6	45.0	–	13.8	347	6.75	11.3	343	126	183	4.3	14	0.00	0.00
0.75	0.85	10.00	1.00	3.00	200.0	30.0	200.0	9.2	250	9.00	200.0	200	140	130	7.5	14	0.00	0.00
–	–	–	–	–	–	9.0	–	2.8	0	0.00	–	–	40	50	–	–	0.00	25.00
0.75	0.85	–	1.00	3.00	200.0	30.0	200.0	9.2	250	4.50	100.0	250	490	240	3.8	–	0.00	

PAGE KEY: A-108 Beverage and Beverage Mixes A-112 Other Beverages A-112 Beverages, Alcoholic A-114 Candies and Confections, Gum A-114 Cereals, Breakfast Type A-118 Cheese and Cheese Substitutes A-120 Dairy Products and Substitutes A-122 Desserts A-128 Dessert Toppings A-128 Eggs, Substitutes, and Egg Dishes A-130 Ethnic Foods A-130 Fast Foods/Restaurants A-140 Fats, Oils, Margarines, Shortenings, and Substitutes A-142 Fish, Seafood, and Shellfish A-142 Food Additives A-142 Fruit, Vegetable, and Blended Juices A-144 Fruits A-146 Grains, Flours, and Fractions A-148 Grain Products, Prepared and Baked Goods

Code	Food Name	Unit/ Amt	Wt (g)	Energy (Kcal)	Prot (g)	Carb (g)	Fiber (g)	Fat (g)	Sat (g)	Mono (g)	Poly (g)	Chol (mg)	Vit A (RE)
63036	Drink, carbohydrate, Carbo Max, pwd	0.5 cup	57	220	0	57	–	0	0.0	0.0	0.0	0	–
1950	Drink, creatine, effervescent, orange, pwd	0.78 oz	22	50	0	12	–	0	0.0	0.0	0.0	–	150
1974	Drink, protein, egg, 100%, inst, chocolate, pwd, scoop	1 ea	29	100	22	4	1	0	0.0	0.0	0.0	0	–
63030	Drink, protein, Max Pro, whey, all flvrs, pwd	2 Tbs	24	80	20	1	0	1	–	–	–	18	0
1964	Drink, protein, muscle build mix, nat, choc pwd scoop	2 ea	70	270	54	7	–	2	1.5	–	–	75	500
63006	Drink, protein, Simply Protein, whey, choc, pwd, scoop	2 ea	28	115	20	4	1	2	1.0	–	–	45	0
62995	Drink, supplement, Myoplex Pro, vanilla, rtd	0.33 ea	250	110	15	8	2	2	0.5	–	–	13	168
63012	Shake, supplement, milk chocolate, rtd	1 ea	250	140	15	15	2	3	0.0	–	–	0	400
20421	Sports Drink, All Sport, fruit punch, rtd	1.5 cup	360	80	0	22	0	0	0.0	0.0	0.0	0	0
20422	Sports Drink, All Sport, lemon lime, rtd	1.5 cup	360	70	0	20	0	0	0.0	0.0	0.0	0	0
20641	Sports Drink, Gatorade, Citrus Cooler, btld	1 cup	241	60	0	15	0	0	0.0	0.0	0.0	0	0
20646	Sports Drink, Gatorade, lemon lime, btld	1 cup	241	60	0	15	0	0	0.0	0.0	0.0	0	0
20650	Sports Drink, Gatorade, strawberry kiwi, btld	1 cup	241	60	0	15	0	0	0.0	0.0	0.0	0	0
SUPPLEMENTAL FOODS AND FORMULAS													
Medical Nutritionals													
62851	Bar, supplement, Boost, chocolate crunch	1 ea	44	190	4	29	1	7	3.5	–	–	5	150
4346	Bar, supplement, Ensure, honey graham crunch	1 ea	35	130	6	21	2	3	1.0	1.5	0.5	5	150
62852	Drink, supp, Boost Hi Protein, prep f/pwd w/skm mlk	8 fl-oz	299	290	21	48	0	1	0.5	–	–	14	358
62796	Drink, supplement, Boost Plus, vanilla, rtu	8 fl-oz	260	360	14	45	1	14	1.5	–	–	10	250
4343	Drink, supplement, Ensure Plus, rtu, coffee	8 fl-oz	260	360	13	50	0	11	1.0	6.3	3.8	5	250
62324	Drink, supplement, Ensure, hi prot, rtu, choc royale	8 fl-oz	253	230	12	31	0	6	0.6	3.0	2.0	5	250
62222	Instant Breakfast, vanilla, dry mix	0.25 cup	34	130	8	24	0	0	0.0	–	–	–	300
62108	Instant Breakfast, vanilla, rducd cal, dry mix	2.5 Tbs	19	70	7	10	0	0	0.0	0.0	0.0	–	300
62348	Pudding, supplement, Ensure, butterscotch, snack cup	1 ea	113	170	4	27	1	5	1.0	3.0	1.0	5	100
Soy Nutritionals													
62934	Bar, soy milk, vegetarian	1 ea	41	140	7	23	–	2	1.5	–	–	0	–
62792	Bar, soy, cafe mocha	1 ea	62	220	14	34	1	4	2.5	–	–	0	250
SWEETENERS AND SWEET SUBSTITUTES													
Jams and Jellies													
23000	Fruit Butter, apple	1 Tbs	18	31	0	8	0	0	0.0	0.0	0.0	0	2
90974	Fruit Spread, apricot, 100% fruit	1 Tbs	19	40	0	10	0	0	0.0	0.0	0.0	0	0
90976	Fruit Spread, blueberry, 100% fruit	1 Tbs	19	40	0	10	0	0	0.0	0.0	0.0	0	0
90979	Fruit Spread, strawberry, 100% fruit	1 Tbs	19	40	0	10	0	0	0.0	0.0	0.0	0	0
23054	Jam	1 Tbs	20	56	0	14	0	0	0.0	0.0	0.0	0	0
23239	Jam, grape, pkt	1 ea	12	30	0	7	0	0	0.0	0.0	0.0	0	0
23167	Jam, rducd sug	1 Tbs	20	36	0	9	0	0	0.0	0.0	0.1	0	0
23003	Jelly	1 Tbs	19	54	0	13	0	0	0.0	0.0	0.0	0	0
23293	Jelly, grape, concord	1 Tbs	20	50	0	13	0	0	0.0	0.0	0.0	0	0
90881	Jelly, mixed fruit	1 Tbs	20	50	0	13	0	0	0.0	0.0	0.0	0	0
23165	Jelly, rducd sug, all flvrs	1 Tbs	19	34	0	9	0	0	0.0	0.0	0.0	0	0
23294	Jelly, strawberry	1 Tbs	20	50	0	13	0	0	0.0	0.0	0.0	0	0
23295	Marmalade, orange	1 Tbs	20	50	0	13	0	0	0.0	0.0	0.0	0	0
3869	Preserves, green papaya, Puerto Rico	100 g	100	308	1	79	2	0	0.0	0.0	0.0	0	1
23296	Preserves, peach	1 Tbs	20	50	0	13	0	0	0.0	0.0	0.0	0	0
90900	Preserves, raspberry, red, low sugar	1 Tbs	17	25	0	6	0	0	0.0	0.0	0.0	0	0
23297	Preserves, red raspberry	1 Tbs	20	50	0	13	0	0	0.0	0.0	0.0	0	0
23301	Preserves, strawberry	1 Tbs	20	50	0	13	0	0	0.0	0.0	0.0	0	0
Sugars, Sugar Substitutes, and Syrups													
25310	Honey, dark	1 Tbs	21	64	0	17	0	0	0.0	0.0	0.0	0	0

PAGE KEY: A-154 Granola Bars, Cereal Bars, Diet Bars, Scones, and Tarts A-154 Meals and Dishes A-160 Meats A-164 Nuts, Seeds, and Products A-166 Poultry A-166 Salad Dressings, Dips, and Mayonnaise A-170 Salads A-170 Sandwiches A-172 Sauces and Gravies A-174 Snack Foods—Chips, Pretzels, Popcorn A-178 Soups, Stews and Chilis A-184 Spices, Flavors, and Seasonings A-184 Sports Bars and Drinks A-186 Supplemental Foods and Formulas A-186 Sweeteners and Sweet Substitutes A-188 Vegetables and Legumes A-200 Weight Loss Bars & Drinks A-200 Miscellaneous

Thia (mg)	Ribo (mg)	Niac (mg NE)	Vit B6 (mg)	Vit B12 (µg)	Fol (µg)	Vit C (mg)	Vit D (IU)	Vit E (mg AT)	Cal (mg)	Iron (mg)	Magn (mg)	Phos (mg)	Pota (mg)	Sodi (mg)	Zinc (mg)	Wat (%)	Alco (g)	Caff (g)
–	–	–	–	–	–	–	–	–	–	–	–	–	–	0	–	0	0.00	0.00
–	–	–	–	–	–	60.0	–	–	200	–	–	–	700	135	–	–	0.00	0.00
–	–	–	–	–	–	–	–	–	20	0.60	23.0	50	390	340	–	–	0.00	
–	–	–	–	–	–	0.0	–	–	284	0.00	–	–	500	25	–	–	0.00	
–	0.85	10.00	1.00	7.50	200.0	30.0	200.0	10.1	243	0.63	–	–	200	420	–	–	0.00	
–	–	–	–	–	–	–	0.0	–	160	0.40	–	–	200	60	–	7	0.00	
0.25	0.33	3.32	0.33	1.33	120.0	15.0	66.7	4.5	116	–	59.3	141	167	177	2.5	89	0.00	0.00
0.60	0.68	8.00	0.80	2.40	300.0	21.0	–	10.2	300	1.79	100.0	300	460	210	6.0	86	0.00	
–	–	–	–	0.00	–	0.0	–	–	0	0.00	–	10	55	55	–	94	0.00	0.00
–	–	–	–	0.00	–	0.0	–	–	0	0.00	–	37	55	55	–	94	0.00	0.00
0.00	0.00	0.00	0.00	0.00	0.0	0.0	0.0	0.0	0	0.11	2.4	22	26	96	0.0	94	0.00	0.00
0.00	0.00	0.00	0.00	0.00	0.0	0.0	0.0	0.0	0	0.11	2.4	22	26	96	0.0	94	0.00	0.00
0.00	0.00	0.00	0.00	0.00	0.0	0.0	0.0	0.0	0	0.11	2.4	22	26	96	0.0	94	0.00	0.00
0.23	0.23	3.00	0.30	0.89	60.0	9.0	60.0	2.0	150	1.08	60.0	150	105	90	2.3	7	0.00	
0.23	0.25	3.00	0.30	0.89	60.0	21.0	60.0	2.7	250	2.70	60.0	200	200	115	2.3	–	0.00	0.00
0.49	0.54	7.00	0.64	1.92	146.0	22.0	133.0	4.6	590	6.09	133.0	500	970	320	5.0	74	0.00	0.00
0.37	0.43	5.00	0.69	2.09	140.0	60.0	150.0	13.6	330	4.50	105.0	310	380	170	4.5	72	0.00	0.00
0.37	0.43	5.00	0.50	1.50	100.0	30.0	100.0	3.4	200	4.50	100.0	200	440	240	3.8	69	0.00	
0.37	0.43	5.00	0.50	1.50	100.0	30.0	100.0	5.4	300	4.50	100.0	250	500	290	5.7	80	0.00	0.00
0.15	0.60	6.00	0.60	1.50	140.0	21.0	–	–	200	6.30	60.0	350	260	100	0.9	2	0.00	0.00
0.15	0.60	6.00	6.00	0.60	140.0	21.0	–	–	200	6.30	6.0	350	320	100	0.9	5	0.00	0.00
0.23	0.25	3.00	0.30	1.20	60.0	9.0	40.0	2.7	100	2.70	40.0	100	180	135	3.0	68	0.00	0.00
–	–	–	–	–	–	–	–	–	400	–	–	250	25	140	–	20	0.00	0.00
0.37	0.43	5.00	0.50	1.50	100.0	15.0	100.0	13.6	250	4.50	100.0	250	250	150	3.8	14	0.00	
0.00	0.00	0.01	0.00	0.00	0.2	0.1	0.0	0.0	3	0.05	0.9	2	16	1	0.0	56	0.00	0.00
–	–	–	–	–	–	0.0	–	–	0	0.00	–	–	–	0	–	–	0.00	0.00
–	–	–	–	–	–	0.0	–	–	0	0.00	–	–	–	0	–	–	0.00	0.00
–	–	–	–	–	–	0.0	–	–	0	0.00	–	–	–	0	–	–	0.00	0.00
0.00	0.00	0.00	0.00	0.00	6.6	1.8	0.0	0.0	4	0.10	0.8	2	15	6	0.0	30	0.00	0.00
–	–	–	–	–	–	0.0	–	–	0	0.00	–	–	–	0	–	41	0.00	0.00
0.00	0.01	0.05	0.02	0.00	1.7	7.6	–	0.0	6	0.23	5.0	8	102	5	0.0	52	0.00	0.00
0.00	0.00	0.00	0.00	0.00	0.2	0.2	0.0	0.0	2	0.03	1.1	1	12	5	0.0	29	0.00	0.00
–	–	–	–	–	–	0.0	–	–	0	0.00	–	–	–	0	–	35	0.00	0.00
–	–	–	–	–	–	0.0	–	–	0	0.00	–	–	–	0	–	35	0.00	0.00
0.00	0.00	0.02	0.00	0.00	0.2	0.0	–	0.0	1	0.02	1.1	1	13	0	0.0	53	0.00	0.00
–	–	–	–	–	–	0.0	–	–	0	0.00	–	–	–	0	–	35	0.00	0.00
–	–	–	–	–	–	0.0	–	–	0	0.00	–	–	–	0	–	35	0.00	0.00
0.01	0.03	0.27	0.01	0.00	6.7	26.2	–	0.0	50	0.67	14.7	24	246	14	0.1	19	0.00	0.00
–	–	–	–	–	–	0.0	–	–	0	0.00	–	–	–	0	–	35	0.00	0.00
–	–	–	–	–	–	0.0	–	–	0	0.00	–	–	–	0	–	–	0.00	0.00
–	–	–	–	–	–	0.0	–	–	0	0.00	–	–	–	0	–	35	0.00	0.00
–	–	–	–	–	–	0.0	–	–	0	0.00	–	–	–	0	–	35	0.00	0.00
0.00	0.05	0.05	0.00	0.00	2.1	0.1	0.0	0.0	1	0.05	0.4	1	10	1	0.0	17	0.00	0.00

PAGE KEY: A-108 Beverage and Beverage Mixes A-112 Other Beverages A-112 Beverages, Alcoholic A-114 Candies and Confections, Gum A-114 Cereals, Breakfast Type A-118 Cheese and Cheese Substitutes A-120 Dairy Products and Substitutes A-122 Desserts A-128 Dessert Toppings A-128 Eggs, Substitutes, and Egg Dishes A-130 Ethnic Foods A-130 Fast Foods/Restaurants A-140 Fats, Oils, Margarines, Shortenings, and Substitutes A-142 Fish, Seafood, and Shellfish A-142 Food Additives A-142 Fruit, Vegetable, and Blended Juices A-144 Fruits A-146 Grains, Flours, and Fractions A-148 Grain Products, Prepared and Baked Goods

Code	Food Name	Unit/ Amt	Wt (g)	Energy (Kcal)	Prot (g)	Carb (g)	Fiber (g)	Fat (g)	Sat (g)	Mono (g)	Poly (g)	Chol (mg)	Vit A (RE)
25309	Honey, light	1 Tbs	21	64	0	17	0	0	0.0	0.0	0.0	0	0
25003	Molasses	1 cup	328	872	0	226	0	0	0.1	0.1	0.2	0	0
25121	Molasses, light, Brer Rabbit	1 Tbs	21	60	0	15	0	0	0.0	0.0	0.0	0	–
25038	Sugar Substitute, Equal, pkt	1 ea	1	4	0	1	0	0	0.0	0.0	0.0	0	0
25041	Sugar Substitute, saccharin	1 ea	0	0	0	0	0	0	0.0	0.0	0.0	0	0
25208	Sugar Substitute, Sweet 'N Low, granular	1 ea	1	4	0	1	0	0	0.0	0.0	0.0	0	0
25005	Sugar, brown, packed	1 cup	220	827	0	214	0	0	0.0	0.0	0.0	0	0
25040	Sugar, brown, Twin	1 tsp	0	1	0	0	0	0	0.0	0.0	0.0	0	0
25235	Sugar, cane, organic, unrefined	1 Tbs	4	16	0	4	0	0	0.0	0.0	0.0	0	0
25009	Sugar, confectioners/powdered, unsftd	1 cup	120	467	0	119	0	0	0.0	0.0	0.1	0	0
25071	Sugar, raw, washed, turbinado, natural	1 cup	195	733	0	190	0	0	0.0	0.0	0.0	0	0
25006	Sugar, white, granulated	1 cup	200	774	0	200	0	0	0.0	0.0	0.0	0	0
25007	Sugar, white, granulated, pkt	1 ea	6	23	0	6	0	0	0.0	0.0	0.0	0	0
25042	Sweetener, fructose	1 ea	3	11	0	3	0	0	0.0	0.0	0.0	0	0
31180	Sweetener, sucralose, Splenda, gran, consumer use only	0.5 cup	12	48	0	12	0	0	0.0	0.0	0.0	0	0
91268	Syrup, blueberry, fruit swtnd	1 Tbs	15	30	0	8	0	0	0.0	0.0	0.0	0	0
23437	Syrup, chocolate	2 Tbs	39	102	1	24	1	0	0.3	0.1	0.0	0	–
25010	Syrup, corn, dark	1 cup	328	925	0	251	0	0	0.0	0.0	0.0	0	0
25000	Syrup, corn, light	1 cup	328	925	0	251	0	0	0.0	0.0	0.0	0	0
25066	Syrup, grenadine	1 cup	320	854	0	229	0	0	0.0	0.0	0.1	0	1
25002	Syrup, maple	1 Tbs	20	52	0	13	0	0	0.0	0.0	0.0	0	0
25153	Syrup, maple, butter, light	0.25 cup	57	100	0	24	0	0	0.0	0.0	0.0	0	0
23042	Syrup, pancake	1 Tbs	20	57	0	15	0	0	0.0	0.0	0.0	0	0
23172	Syrup, pancake, rducd cal	1 Tbs	15	25	0	7	0	0	0.0	0.0	0.0	0	0
3298	Syrup, raspberry	1 Tbs	20	52	0	13	0	0	0.0	0.0	0.0	0	–
VEGETABLES AND LEGUMES													
Raw Vegetables													
5010	Alfalfa Sprouts, raw	0.5 cup	16	5	1	1	0	0	0.0	0.0	0.1	0	3
6709	Artichokes, globe/French, med, raw	1 ea	128	60	4	13	7	0	0.0	0.0	0.1	0	23
6033	Arugula, chpd, raw	0.5 cup	10	2	0	0	0	0	0.0	0.0	0.0	0	24
5002	Asparagus, spears, raw, med, 5¼" to 7" long	1 ea	16	4	0	1	0	0	0.0	0.0	0.0	0	9
5230	Bamboo Shoots, slices, raw	1 cup	151	41	4	8	3	0	0.1	0.0	0.2	0	3
5020	Bean Sprouts, mung, mature, raw	1 cup	104	31	3	6	2	0	0.0	0.0	0.1	0	2
5573	Beets, raw, slices	0.5 cup	68	29	1	7	2	0	0.0	0.0	0.0	0	3
6928	Bhaji, leaves, raw	1 cup	28	6	1	1	0	0	0.0	0.0	0.0	0	82
90179	Bindi, raw	0.5 cup	50	16	1	4	2	0	0.0	0.0	0.0	0	33
5406	Borage, raw, 1" pces	1 cup	89	19	2	3	1	1	0.2	0.2	0.1	0	374
90412	Broccoli, bunch, raw	1 ea	608	170	18	32	18	2	0.3	0.1	1.0	0	936
5556	Broccoli, florets, raw	1 cup	71	20	2	4	2	0	0.0	0.0	0.1	0	213
6757	Broccoli, raw	1 cup	71	20	2	4	2	0	0.0	0.0	0.1	0	109
6771	Cabbage, bok choy/pak choi, leaf, raw	1 ea	14	2	0	0	0	0	0.0	0.0	0.0	0	42
5608	Cabbage, pickled, Japanese, raw	1 cup	150	32	2	7	5	0	0.0	0.0	0.1	0	28
6764	Cabbage, raw, chpd	1 cup	89	22	1	5	2	0	0.0	0.0	0.1	0	12
6766	Cabbage, red, raw, chpd	1 cup	89	24	1	5	2	0	0.0	0.0	0.1	0	4
6443	Cabbage, yu choy sum	1 cup	85	20	2	3	0	0	0.0	0.0	0.0	0	850
7262	Cactus, nopales, slices, raw	1 cup	86	14	1	3	2	0	0.0	0.0	0.0	0	36
7320	Carrots, 7" x 1¼", raw	1 ea	78	35	1	8	2	0	0.0	0.0	0.0	0	1350
90605	Carrots, baby, raw, lrg	1 ea	15	6	0	1	0	0	0.0	0.0	0.0	0	225
6772	Carrots, raw, chpd	1 cup	128	55	1	13	4	0	0.0	0.0	0.1	0	3599

PAGE KEY: A-154 Granola Bars, Cereal Bars, Diet Bars, Scones, and Tarts A-154 Meals and Dishes A-160 Meats A-164 Nuts, Seeds, and Products A-166 Poultry A-166 Salad Dressings, Dips, and Mayonnaise A-170 Salads A-170 Sandwiches A-172 Sauces and Gravies A-174 Snack Foods—Chips, Pretzels, Popcorn A-178 Soups, Stews and Chilis A-184 Spices, Flavors, and Seasonings A-184 Sports Bars and Drinks A-186 Supplemental Foods and Formulas A-186 Sweeteners and Sweet Substitutes A-188 Vegetables and Legumes A-200 Weight Loss Bars & Drinks A-200 Miscellaneous

Thia (mg)	Ribo (mg)	Niac (mg NE)	Vit B6 (mg)	Vit B12 (µg)	Fol (µg)	Vit C (mg)	Vit D (IU)	Vit E (mg AT)	Cal (mg)	Iron (mg)	Magn (mg)	Phos (mg)	Pota (mg)	Sodi (mg)	Zinc (mg)	Wat (%)	Alco (g)	Caff (g)
0.00	0.05	0.05	0.00	0.00	2.1	0.1	0.0	0.0	1	0.05	0.4	1	10	1	0.0	17	0.00	0.00
0.12	0.00	3.04	2.20	0.00	0.0	0.0	0.0	0.0	672	15.47	793.8	102	4802	121	1.0	26	0.00	0.00
—	—	—	—	—	—	—	—	—	60	1.44	—	—	340	10	—	—	0.00	0.00
0.00	0.00	0.00	0.00	0.00	0.0	0.0	—	0.0	0	0.00	0.0	0	0	0	0.0	12	0.00	0.00
0.00	0.00	0.00	0.00	0.00	0.0	0.0	0.0	0.0	0	0.00	0.0	0	1	0	0.0	0	0.00	0.00
—	—	—	—	—	—	0.0	—	—	0	0.00	—	—	—	0	—	—	0.00	0.00
0.01	0.01	0.18	0.05	0.00	2.2	0.0	0.0	0.0	187	4.19	63.8	48	761	86	0.4	2	0.00	0.00
0.00	0.00	0.00	0.00	0.00	0.0	0.0	0.0	0.0	4	0.00	0.0	0	0	2	0.0	0	0.00	0.00
—	—	—	—	—	—	0.0	—	—	1	0.25	—	—	—	0	—	1	0.00	0.00
0.00	0.00	0.00	0.00	0.00	0.0	0.0	0.0	0.0	1	0.07	0.0	2	2	1	0.0	0	0.00	0.00
0.01	0.00	0.15	0.05	0.00	2.0	0.0	0.0	0.0	166	3.72	56.6	43	675	76	0.4	2	0.00	0.00
0.00	0.03	0.00	0.00	0.00	0.0	0.0	0.0	0.0	2	0.11	0.0	4	4	2	0.1	0	0.00	0.00
0.00	0.00	0.00	0.00	0.00	0.0	0.0	0.0	0.0	0	0.00	0.0	0	0	0	0.0	0	0.00	0.00
0.00	0.00	0.00	0.00	0.00	0.0	0.0	0.0	0.0	0	0.00	0.0	0	0	0	0.0	0	0.00	0.00
—	—	—	—	—	—	0.0	—	—	0	0.00	—	—	—	0	—	—	0.00	0.00
—	—	—	—	—	—	0.0	—	—	30	0.72	—	—	—	2	—	47	0.00	0.00
—	—	—	—	—	—	—	—	—	6	0.57	—	—	—	19	—	34	0.00	
0.03	0.02	0.07	0.02	0.00	0.0	0.0	0.0	0.0	59	1.21	26.2	36	144	508	0.1	23	0.00	0.00
0.03	0.02	0.07	0.02	0.00	0.0	0.0	0.0	0.0	10	0.15	6.6	7	13	397	0.1	23	0.00	0.00
0.01	0.05	0.09	0.02	0.00	2.9	9.1	0.0	0.0	22	0.54	10.9	17	96	153	0.1	27	0.00	0.00
0.00	0.00	0.00	0.00	0.00	0.0	0.0	0.0	0.0	13	0.23	2.8	0	41	2	0.8	32	0.00	0.00
—	—	—	—	—	—	0.0	—	—	0	0.00	—	—	—	180	—	57	0.00	0.00
0.00	0.00	0.00	0.00	0.00	0.0	0.0	0.0	0.0	0	0.01	0.4	2	0	17	0.0	24	0.00	0.00
0.00	0.00	0.00	0.00	0.00	0.0	0.0	0.0	0.0	0	0.00	0.0	6	0	30	0.0	55	0.00	0.00
0.00	0.00	0.02	0.00	0.00	—	3.2	0.0	—	3	0.38	1.4	3	18	0	—	31	0.00	0.00
0.00	0.01	0.07	0.00	0.00	5.9	1.4	0.0	0.0	5	0.15	4.5	12	13	1	0.2	91	0.00	0.00
0.09	0.07	1.34	0.15	0.00	87.0	15.0	0.0	0.2	56	1.63	76.8	115	474	120	0.6	85	0.00	0.00
0.00	0.00	0.02	0.00	0.00	9.7	1.5	0.0	0.0	16	0.15	4.7	5	37	3	0.0	92	0.00	0.00
0.01	0.01	0.18	0.01	0.00	20.5	2.1	0.0	0.3	3	0.14	2.9	9	44	0	0.1	92	0.00	0.00
0.23	0.10	0.91	0.36	0.00	10.6	6.0	0.0	1.5	20	0.75	4.5	89	805	6	1.7	91	0.00	0.00
0.09	0.12	0.77	0.09	0.00	63.4	13.7	0.0	0.0	14	0.94	21.8	56	155	6	0.4	90	0.00	0.00
0.01	0.02	0.23	0.05	0.00	74.1	3.3	0.0	0.2	11	0.54	15.6	27	221	53	0.2	88	0.00	0.00
0.00	0.03	0.18	0.05	0.00	23.8	12.1	0.0	0.2	60	0.64	15.4	14	171	6	0.3	92	0.00	0.00
0.10	0.02	0.50	0.10	0.00	44.0	10.6	0.0	0.3	40	0.40	28.5	32	152	4	0.3	90	0.00	0.00
0.05	0.12	0.80	0.07	0.00	11.6	31.1	0.0	—	83	2.94	46.3	47	418	71	0.2	93	0.00	0.00
0.40	0.72	3.88	0.97	0.00	431.7	566.7	0.0	10.1	292	5.34	152.0	401	1976	164	2.4	91	0.00	0.00
0.05	0.07	0.44	0.10	0.00	50.4	66.2	0.0	1.2	34	0.62	17.8	47	231	19	0.3	91	0.00	0.00
0.05	0.07	0.44	0.10	0.00	50.4	66.2	0.0	1.2	34	0.62	17.8	47	231	19	0.3	91	0.00	0.00
0.00	0.00	0.07	0.02	0.00	9.2	6.3	0.0	0.0	15	0.10	2.7	5	35	9	0.0	95	0.00	0.00
0.00	0.05	0.27	0.15	0.00	63.0	1.0	0.0	0.2	72	0.74	18.0	64	1280	416	0.3	91	0.00	0.00
0.03	0.03	0.27	0.09	0.00	38.3	28.7	0.0	0.1	42	0.52	13.3	20	219	16	0.2	92	0.00	0.00
0.03	0.02	0.27	0.18	0.00	18.7	50.7	0.0	0.1	45	0.43	13.3	37	183	10	0.2	92	0.00	0.00
—	—	—	—	0.00	—	108.0	—	—	200	1.44	—	—	—	20	—	93	0.00	0.00
0.00	0.03	0.44	0.05	0.00	2.6	11.5	—	0.0	140	0.57	49.9	15	274	19	0.2	94	0.00	0.00
—	—	—	—	0.00	—	6.0	—	—	20	0.00	—	—	280	40	—	88	0.00	0.00
0.00	0.00	0.12	0.00	0.00	5.0	1.3	0.0	0.1	3	0.11	1.8	6	42	5	0.0	90	0.00	0.00
0.11	0.07	1.19	0.18	0.00	17.9	11.9	0.0	0.6	35	0.63	19.2	56	413	45	0.3	88	0.00	0.00

PAGE KEY: A-108 Beverage and Beverage Mixes A-112 Other Beverages A-112 Beverages, Alcoholic A-114 Candies and Confections, Gum A-114 Cereals, Breakfast Type A-118 Cheese and Cheese Substitutes A-120 Dairy Products and Substitutes A-122 Desserts A-128 Dessert Toppings A-128 Eggs, Substitutes, and Egg Dishes A-130 Ethnic Foods A-130 Fast Foods/Restaurants A-140 Fats, Oils, Margarines, Shortenings, and Substitutes A-142 Fish, Seafood, and Shellfish A-142 Food Additives A-142 Fruit, Vegetable, and Blended Juices A-144 Fruits A-146 Grains, Flours, and Fractions A-148 Grain Products, Prepared and Baked Goods

Code	Food Name	Unit/ Amt	Wt (g)	Energy (Kcal)	Prot (g)	Carb (g)	Fiber (g)	Fat (g)	Sat (g)	Mono (g)	Poly (g)	Chol (mg)	Vit A (RE)
90425	Carrots, raw, med	1 ea	61	26	1	6	2	0	0.0	0.0	0.0	0	1715
5356	Cassava, raw	1 cup	206	330	3	78	4	1	0.2	0.2	0.1	0	4
5050	Cauliflower, florets, raw	1 ea	13	3	0	1	0	0	0.0	0.0	0.0	0	0
5049	Cauliflower, raw	0.5 cup	50	12	1	3	1	0	0.0	0.0	0.0	0	1
5054	Celery, raw, diced	0.5 cup	60	10	0	2	1	0	0.0	0.0	0.0	0	8
5055	Celery, stalk, med, 7.5"–8" long, raw	1 ea	40	6	0	1	1	0	0.0	0.0	0.0	0	6
90433	Celery, strips, 4" long, raw	1 cup	124	20	1	5	2	0	0.0	0.0	0.1	0	17
5399	Chili Peppers, green, hot, raw, whole	0.5 cup	75	30	2	7	1	0	0.0	0.0	0.1	0	58
7931	Chili Peppers, jalapeno, raw	1 ea	14	4	0	1	0	0	0.0	0.0	0.0	0	3
5359	Chives, raw	1 Tbs	3	1	0	0	0	0	0.0	0.0	0.0	0	13
5060	Collards, chpd, raw	1 cup	36	11	1	2	1	0	0.0	0.0	0.1	0	138
5380	Corn, yellow, sweet, cob, ckd w/o salt, drained	1 ea	77	83	3	19	2	1	0.2	0.3	0.5	0	17
5372	Cress, garden, raw	0.5 cup	25	8	1	1	0	0	0.0	0.1	0.1	0	232
7920	Cucumber, w/o skin, raw, med	1 ea	201	24	1	5	1	0	0.1	0.0	0.1	0	16
9176	Curly Endive, raw, chpd	1 cup	50	8	1	2	2	0	0.0	0.0	0.0	0	103
5241	Dandelion Greens, raw	1 cup	55	25	1	5	2	0	0.1	0.0	0.2	0	770
5371	Eggplant, raw, cubes	1 cup	82	21	1	5	2	0	0.0	0.0	0.1	0	7
5202	Endive, raw, chpd	1 cup	50	8	1	2	2	0	0.0	0.0	0.0	0	103
9177	Escarole, raw, chpd	1 cup	50	8	1	2	2	0	0.0	0.0	0.0	0	103
5450	Fennel, bulb, raw, slices	1 cup	87	27	1	6	3	0	—	—	—	0	12
26005	Garlic, cloves, raw	4 ea	12	18	1	4	0	0	0.0	0.0	0.0	0	0
7081	Hummus, homemade	1 cup	246	421	12	50	13	21	3.1	8.7	7.8	0	5
5077	Jerusalem Artichoke, raw	1 cup	150	114	3	26	2	0	0.0	0.0	0.0	0	3
5419	Jute, corchorus olitorius, raw	0.5 cup	14	5	1	1	0	0	0.0	0.0	0.0	0	78
5208	Kale, raw, chpd	1 cup	67	34	2	7	1	0	0.1	0.0	0.2	0	596
5078	Kohlrabi, raw	0.5 cup	68	18	1	4	2	0	0.0	0.0	0.0	0	3
5205	Leeks, bulb & lower leaf, raw, chpd	1 cup	89	54	1	13	2	0	0.0	0.0	0.1	0	9
7317	Lettuce, iceberg, med, raw FDA	0.17 ea	89	15	1	3	1	0	0.0	0.0	0.0	0	20
5083	Lettuce, iceberg/crisphead, raw, chpd	1 cup	55	7	1	1	1	0	0.0	0.0	0.1	0	19
90448	Lettuce, iceberg/crisphead, raw, head, sml	1 ea	324	39	3	7	5	1	0.1	0.0	0.3	0	110
5087	Lettuce, looseleaf, raw, leaf	1 pce	10	2	0	0	0	0	0.0	0.0	0.0	0	19
440	Mushrooms, brown, raw	1 ea	14	3	0	1	0	0	0.0	0.0	0.0	0	0
5440	Mushrooms, enoki, med, raw	1 ea	3	1	0	0	0	0	0.0	0.0	0.0	0	0
51067	Mushrooms, portabella, raw	1 oz	28	7	1	1	0	0	0.0	0.0	0.0	0	0
5090	Mushrooms, raw, pces/slices	0.5 cup	35	9	1	1	0	0	0.0	0.0	0.0	0	0
5207	Mustard Greens, raw, chpd	1 cup	56	15	2	3	2	0	0.0	0.1	0.0	0	297
5098	Okra, ckd w/o salt, drained, pods	8 ea	85	27	2	6	2	0	0.0	0.0	0.0	0	49
5775	Okra, raw	0.5 cup	50	16	1	4	2	0	0.0	0.0	0.0	0	33
5114	Onion, green/spring, tops & bulb, raw, chpd	0.5 cup	50	16	1	4	1	0	0.0	0.0	0.0	0	19
7809	Onion, red, raw, lrg, slice, ¼" thick	1 pce	38	14	0	3	1	0	0.0	0.0	0.0	0	0
5104	Onion, white, raw, med, whole, 2½" diameter	1 ea	110	42	1	9	2	0	0.0	0.0	0.1	0	0
90470	Onion, yellow, raw, rings	10 pce	60	23	1	5	1	0	0.0	0.0	0.0	0	0
5298	Pea Sprouts, raw	1 cup	120	154	11	34	5	1	0.1	0.1	0.4	0	19
6844	Peppers, bell, green, sweet, raw, sliced	0.5 cup	46	12	0	3	1	0	0.0	0.0	0.0	0	29
7326	Peppers, bell, raw	1 ea	148	30	1	7	2	0	0.0	0.0	0.0	0	40
9300	Peppers, bell, yellow, sweet, raw, med	1 ea	119	32	1	8	1	0	0.0	0.0	0.1	0	29
7333	Radishes, raw FDA	7 ea	85	15	1	3	0	0	0.0	0.0	0.0	0	0
7214	Rutabaga, raw, cubes	0.5 cup	70	25	1	6	2	0	0.0	0.0	0.1	0	41

PAGE KEY: A-154 Granola Bars, Cereal Bars, Diet Bars, Scones, and Tarts A-154 Meals and Dishes A-160 Meats A-164 Nuts, Seeds, and Products A-166 Poultry A-166 Salad Dressings, Dips, and Mayonnaise A-170 Salads A-170 Sandwiches A-172 Sauces and Gravies A-174 Snack Foods—Chips, Pretzels, Popcorn A-178 Soups, Stews and Chilis A-184 Spices, Flavors, and Seasonings A-184 Sports Bars and Drinks A-186 Supplemental Foods and Formulas A-186 Sweeteners and Sweet Substitutes A-188 Vegetables and Legumes A-200 Weight Loss Bars & Drinks A-200 Miscellaneous

Thia (mg)	Ribo (mg)	Niac (mg NE)	Vit B6 (mg)	Vit B12 (μg)	Fol (μg)	Vit C (mg)	Vit D (IU)	Vit E (mg AT)	Cal (mg)	Iron (mg)	Magn (mg)	Phos (mg)	Pota (mg)	Sodi (mg)	Zinc (mg)	Wat (%)	Alco (g)	Caff (g)
0.05	0.03	0.56	0.09	0.00	8.5	5.7	0.0	0.3	16	0.31	9.2	27	197	21	0.1	88	0.00	0.00
0.18	0.10	1.75	0.18	0.00	55.6	42.4	0.0	0.4	33	0.56	43.3	56	558	29	0.7	60	0.00	0.00
0.00	0.00	0.07	0.02	0.00	7.4	6.0	0.0	0.0	3	0.05	1.9	6	39	4	0.0	92	0.00	0.00
0.02	0.02	0.25	0.10	0.00	28.5	23.2	0.0	0.0	11	0.21	7.5	22	152	15	0.1	92	0.00	0.00
0.02	0.02	0.18	0.05	0.00	16.8	4.2	0.0	0.2	24	0.23	6.6	15	172	52	0.1	95	0.00	0.00
0.01	0.01	0.12	0.02	0.00	11.2	2.8	0.0	0.1	16	0.15	4.4	10	115	35	0.1	95	0.00	0.00
0.05	0.05	0.40	0.10	0.00	34.7	8.7	0.0	0.4	50	0.50	13.6	31	356	108	0.2	95	0.00	0.00
0.07	0.07	0.70	0.20	0.00	17.2	181.9	0.0	0.5	14	0.89	18.8	34	255	5	0.2	88	0.00	0.00
0.01	0.00	0.15	0.07	0.00	6.6	6.2	—	0.1	1	0.10	2.7	4	30	0	0.0	92	0.00	0.00
0.00	0.00	0.01	0.00	0.00	3.1	1.7	0.0	0.0	3	0.05	1.3	2	9	0	0.0	91	0.00	0.00
0.01	0.05	0.27	0.05	0.00	59.8	12.7	0.0	0.8	52	0.07	3.2	4	61	7	0.0	91	0.00	0.00
0.17	0.05	1.24	0.05	0.00	35.4	4.8	0.0	0.1	2	0.46	24.6	79	192	13	0.4	70	0.00	0.00
0.01	0.05	0.25	0.05	0.00	20.0	17.2	0.0	0.2	20	0.31	9.5	19	152	4	0.1	89	0.00	0.00
0.03	0.01	0.20	0.14	0.00	28.1	5.6	—	0.2	28	0.31	24.1	42	297	4	0.3	96	0.00	0.00
0.03	0.03	0.20	0.00	0.00	71.0	3.2	0.0	0.2	26	0.40	7.5	14	157	11	0.4	94	0.00	0.00
0.10	0.14	0.43	0.14	0.00	14.9	19.2	0.0	1.4	103	1.71	19.8	36	218	42	0.2	86	0.00	0.00
0.03	0.02	0.49	0.07	0.00	15.6	1.4	0.0	0.0	6	0.21	11.5	18	178	2	0.1	92	0.00	0.00
0.03	0.03	0.20	0.00	0.00	71.0	3.2	0.0	0.2	26	0.40	7.5	14	157	11	0.4	94	0.00	0.00
0.03	0.03	0.20	0.00	0.00	71.0	3.2	0.0	0.2	26	0.40	7.5	14	157	11	0.4	94	0.00	0.00
0.00	0.02	0.56	0.03	0.00	23.5	10.4	0.0	—	43	0.63	14.8	44	360	45	0.2	90	0.00	0.00
0.01	0.00	0.07	0.15	0.00	0.4	3.7	0.0	0.0	22	0.20	3.0	18	48	2	0.1	59	0.00	0.00
0.23	0.12	1.00	0.98	0.00	145.1	19.4	0.0	2.5	123	3.85	71.3	276	428	600	2.7	65	0.00	0.00
0.30	0.09	1.95	0.11	0.00	19.5	6.0	0.0	0.3	21	5.09	25.5	117	644	6	0.2	78	0.00	0.00
0.01	0.07	0.18	0.07	0.00	17.2	5.2	0.0	—	29	0.67	9.0	12	78	1	0.1	88	0.00	0.00
0.07	0.09	0.67	0.18	0.00	19.4	80.4	0.0	0.5	90	1.13	22.8	38	299	29	0.3	84	0.00	0.00
0.02	0.00	0.27	0.10	0.00	10.8	41.9	0.0	0.3	16	0.27	12.8	31	236	14	0.0	91	0.00	0.00
0.05	0.02	0.36	0.20	0.00	57.0	10.7	0.0	0.8	53	1.87	24.9	31	160	18	0.1	83	0.00	0.00
—	—	—	—	0.00	—	3.6	—	—	20	0.36	—	—	120	10	—	95	0.00	0.00
0.02	0.01	0.10	0.01	0.00	30.8	2.1	0.0	0.2	10	0.28	5.0	11	87	5	0.1	96	0.00	0.00
0.15	0.10	0.61	0.12	0.00	181.4	12.6	0.0	0.9	62	1.62	29.2	65	512	29	0.7	96	0.00	0.00
0.00	0.00	0.03	0.00	0.00	5.0	1.8	0.0	0.0	7	0.14	1.1	2	26	1	0.0	94	0.00	0.00
0.00	0.07	0.52	0.01	0.00	2.0	0.0	—	0.0	3	0.05	1.3	17	63	1	0.2	92	0.00	0.00
0.00	0.00	0.10	0.00	0.00	0.9	0.4	2.3	0.0	0	0.02	0.5	3	11	0	0.0	89	0.00	0.00
0.01	0.14	1.27	0.02	0.00	6.2	0.0	—	0.0	2	0.17	3.1	37	137	2	0.2	91	0.00	0.00
0.02	0.15	1.40	0.03	0.00	4.2	0.8	26.6	0.0	2	0.36	3.5	36	130	1	0.3	92	0.00	0.00
0.03	0.05	0.44	0.10	0.00	104.7	39.2	0.0	1.1	58	0.81	17.9	24	198	14	0.1	91	0.00	0.00
0.10	0.05	0.74	0.15	0.00	39.1	13.9	0.0	0.6	54	0.37	48.5	48	274	4	0.5	90	0.00	0.00
0.10	0.02	0.50	0.10	0.00	44.0	10.6	0.0	0.3	40	0.40	28.5	32	152	4	0.3	90	0.00	0.00
0.02	0.03	0.25	0.02	0.00	32.0	9.4	0.0	0.1	36	0.74	10.0	18	138	8	0.2	90	0.00	0.00
0.01	0.00	0.05	0.03	0.00	7.2	2.4	0.0	0.1	8	0.07	3.8	13	60	1	0.1	90	0.00	0.00
0.05	0.01	0.15	0.12	0.00	20.9	7.0	0.0	0.3	22	0.23	11.0	36	173	3	0.2	90	0.00	0.00
0.02	0.00	0.09	0.07	0.00	11.4	3.8	0.0	0.2	12	0.12	6.0	20	94	2	0.1	90	0.00	0.00
0.27	0.18	3.71	0.31	0.00	172.8	12.5	0.0	0.0	43	2.71	67.2	198	457	24	1.3	62	0.00	0.00
0.02	0.00	0.23	0.10	0.00	10.1	41.1	0.0	0.3	4	0.20	4.6	9	81	1	0.1	92	0.00	0.00
—	—	—	—	0.00	—	114.0	—	—	20	0.36	—	—	270	0	—	94	0.00	0.00
0.02	0.02	1.05	0.20	0.00	30.9	218.4	0.0	0.8	13	0.55	14.3	29	252	2	0.2	92	0.00	0.00
—	—	—	—	0.00	—	18.0	—	—	20	0.00	—	—	230	25	—	95	0.00	0.00
0.05	0.02	0.49	0.07	0.00	14.7	17.5	0.0	0.2	33	0.36	16.1	41	236	14	0.2	90	0.00	0.00

PAGE KEY: A-108 Beverage and Beverage Mixes A-112 Other Beverages A-112 Beverages, Alcoholic A-114 Candies and Confections, Gum A-114 Cereals, Breakfast Type A-118 Cheese and Cheese Substitutes A-120 Dairy Products and Substitutes A-122 Desserts A-128 Dessert Toppings A-128 Eggs, Substitutes, and Egg Dishes A-130 Ethnic Foods A-130 Fast Foods/Restaurants A-140 Fats, Oils, Margarines, Shortenings, and Substitutes A-142 Fish, Seafood, and Shellfish A-142 Food Additives A-142 Fruit, Vegetable, and Blended Juices A-144 Fruits A-146 Grains, Flours, and Fractions A-148 Grain Products, Prepared and Baked Goods

Code	Food Name	Unit/ Amt	Wt (g)	Energy (Kcal)	Prot (g)	Carb (g)	Fiber (g)	Fat (g)	Sat (g)	Mono (g)	Poly (g)	Chol (mg)	Vit A (RE)
5253	Seaweed, agar, raw	0.5 cup	40	10	0	3	0	0	0.0	0.0	0.0	0	0
5427	Shallots, chpd, raw	1 Tbs	10	7	0	2	0	0	0.0	0.0	0.0	0	12
5458	Soybean Sprouts, mature, raw	1 cup	70	85	9	7	1	5	0.7	1.1	2.6	0	1
6863	Spinach, raw, leaf	1 ea	10	2	0	0	0	0	0.0	0.0	0.0	0	67
5800	Squash, acorn, raw, cubes	0.5 cup	70	28	1	7	1	0	0.0	0.0	0.0	0	24
5801	Squash, butternut, raw, cubes	0.5 cup	120	54	1	14	4	0	0.0	0.0	0.1	0	936
5804	Squash, spaghetti, raw, cubes	0.5 cup	50	16	0	3	1	0	0.1	0.0	0.1	0	3
90537	Squash, summer, all types, raw, med	1 ea	196	39	2	9	4	0	0.1	0.0	0.2	0	39
90604	Squash, zucchini, baby, med, raw	1 ea	11	2	0	0	0	0	0.0	0.0	0.0	0	6
5251	Succotash, ckd w/o salt, drained	0.5 cup	96	110	5	23	4	1	0.1	0.1	0.4	0	29
5058	Swiss Chard, leaf, raw	1 ea	48	9	1	2	1	0	0.0	0.0	0.0	0	158
5444	Tomatillo, raw, chpd/diced	0.5 cup	66	21	1	4	1	1	0.1	0.1	0.3	0	8
90530	Tomatoes, cherry, raw	1 ea	17	4	0	1	0	0	0.0	0.0	0.0	0	11
5173	Tomatoes, red, raw, med slices, ¼"	2 pce	40	8	0	2	0	0	0.0	0.0	0.1	0	25
5169	Tomatoes, red, raw, med, 2⅗" diameter	0.5 ea	74	16	1	3	1	0	0.0	0.0	0.1	0	46
6492	Tomatoes, roma, raw, raw	1 ea	62	13	1	3	1	0	0.0	0.0	0.1	0	38
5547	Turnip Greens, chpd, raw	1 cup	55	15	1	3	2	0	0.0	0.0	0.1	0	418
5184	Turnips, ckd w/o salt, drained, mashed	0.5 cup	115	24	1	6	2	0	0.0	0.0	0.0	0	0
6898	Waterchestnuts, Chinese/Matai, raw	4 ea	36	35	1	9	1	0	0.0	0.0	0.0	0	0
5222	Watercress, raw, chpd	1 cup	34	4	1	0	0	0	0.0	0.0	0.0	0	160
5306	Yams, raw, cubes	0.5 cup	75	88	1	21	3	0	0.0	0.0	0.1	0	0
Cooked Vegetables													
5192	Artichokes, globe/French, ckd f/fzn w/o salt, drained	1 cup	168	76	5	15	8	1	0.2	0.0	0.4	0	27
6936	Artichokes, globe/French, hearts, ckd w/salt, drained	0.5 cup	84	42	3	9	5	0	0.0	0.0	0.1	0	15
6939	Asparagus, ckd f/fzn w/salt, drained	1 cup	180	50	5	9	3	1	0.2	0.0	0.3	0	148
5249	Bamboo Shoots, slices, ckd w/o salt, drained	1 cup	120	14	2	2	1	0	0.1	0.0	0.1	0	0
5725	Bean Sprouts, kidney, mature, ckd w/o salt, drained	1 cup	129	43	6	6	2	1	0.1	0.1	0.4	0	0
5848	Bean Sprouts, kidney, mature, ckd w/salt, drained	1 cup	124	41	6	6	2	1	0.1	0.1	0.4	0	0
5022	Beets, ckd, drained, sliced	0.5 cup	85	37	1	8	2	0	0.0	0.0	0.1	0	3
5679	Broccoflower, stmd	1 cup	156	50	5	10	5	0	0.1	0.0	0.2	0	11
6644	Broccoli & Cauliflower	0.5 cup	91	22	2	5	2	0	0.1	–	–	0	41
5028	Broccoli, chpd, ckd w/o salt, drained	0.5 cup	78	22	2	4	2	0	0.0	0.0	0.1	0	108
5457	Broccoli, ckd w/cream sauce	0.5 cup	114	87	4	8	2	5	1.3	2.0	1.4	3	154
6091	Broccoli, ckd w/salt, drained, chpd	0.5 cup	78	22	2	4	2	0	0.0	0.0	0.1	0	108
5234	Broccoli, spears, ckd f/fzn w/o salt, drained	0.5 cup	92	26	3	5	3	0	0.0	0.0	0.1	0	175
5871	Brussels Sprouts, ckd f/fzn w/salt, drained	1 cup	155	65	6	13	6	1	0.1	0.0	0.3	0	90
5237	Cabbage, bok choy/pak choi, ckd w/o salt, drained	1 cup	170	20	3	3	3	0	0.0	0.0	0.1	0	435
5878	Cabbage, ckd w/salt, drained, shredded	0.5 cup	75	16	1	3	2	0	0.0	0.0	0.1	0	10
5238	Cabbage, red, ckd w/o salt, drained, shredded	0.5 cup	75	16	1	3	2	0	0.0	0.0	0.1	0	2
5889	Carrots, ckd f/fzn w/salt, drained, slices	0.5 cup	73	26	1	6	3	0	0.0	0.0	0.0	0	1292
5633	Carrots, glazed, ckd	1 cup	161	217	2	28	5	12	2.3	5.6	3.3	0	3543
5656	Carrots, stir fried	1 cup	156	67	2	16	5	0	0.0	0.0	0.1	0	3955
5625	Cassava, yuca blanca, pieces, ckd	1 cup	137	221	2	53	2	0	0.1	0.1	0.1	0	2
5539	Cauliflower, batter dipped, fried	5 pce	130	264	6	17	2	20	4.4	5.0	9.4	14	39
5890	Cauliflower, florets, ckd w/salt, drained	3 ea	54	12	1	2	1	0	0.0	0.0	0.1	0	1
56722	Cauliflower, w/cheese sauce	0.5 cup	123	64	4	7	2	3	1.5	0.8	0.5	7	362
5894	Celery, ckd w/salt, drained, diced	0.5 cup	75	14	1	3	1	0	0.0	0.0	0.1	0	10
5659	Celery, stmd	1 cup	150	24	1	5	3	0	0.1	0.0	0.1	0	19

PAGE KEY: A-154 Granola Bars, Cereal Bars, Diet Bars, Scones, and Tarts A-154 Meals and Dishes A-160 Meats A-164 Nuts, Seeds, and Products A-166 Poultry A-166 Salad Dressings, Dips, and Mayonnaise A-170 Salads A-170 Sandwiches A-172 Sauces and Gravies A-174 Snack Foods—Chips, Pretzels, Popcorn A-178 Soups, Stews and Chilis A-184 Spices, Flavors, and Seasonings A-184 Sports Bars and Drinks A-186 Supplemental Foods and Formulas A-186 Sweeteners and Sweet Substitutes A-188 Vegetables and Legumes A-200 Weight Loss Bars & Drinks A-200 Miscellaneous

Thia (mg)	Ribo (mg)	Niac (mg NE)	Vit B6 (mg)	Vit B12 (µg)	Fol (µg)	Vit C (mg)	Vit D (IU)	Vit E (mg AT)	Cal (mg)	Iron (mg)	Magn (mg)	Phos (mg)	Pota (mg)	Sodi (mg)	Zinc (mg)	Wat (%)	Alco (g)	Caff (g)
0.00	0.00	0.01	0.00	0.00	34.0	0.0	0.0	0.3	22	0.74	26.8	2	90	4	0.2	91	0.00	0.00
0.00	0.00	0.01	0.02	0.00	3.4	0.8	0.0	0.0	4	0.11	2.1	6	33	1	0.0	80	0.00	0.00
0.23	0.07	0.80	0.11	0.00	120.4	10.7	0.0	0.0	47	1.47	50.4	115	339	10	0.8	69	0.00	0.00
0.00	0.01	0.07	0.01	0.00	19.4	2.8	0.0	0.2	10	0.27	7.9	5	56	8	0.1	92	0.00	0.00
0.10	0.00	0.49	0.10	0.00	11.9	7.7	0.0	0.1	23	0.49	22.4	25	243	2	0.1	88	0.00	0.00
0.11	0.01	1.44	0.18	0.00	32.4	25.2	0.0	0.2	58	0.83	40.8	40	422	5	0.2	86	0.00	0.00
0.01	0.00	0.47	0.05	0.00	6.1	1.1	0.0	0.1	12	0.15	6.1	6	55	9	0.1	92	0.00	0.00
0.12	0.07	1.08	0.20	0.00	51.0	29.0	0.0	0.2	39	0.89	45.1	69	382	4	0.5	94	0.00	0.00
0.00	0.00	0.07	0.01	0.00	2.2	3.8	0.0	0.0	2	0.09	3.6	10	50	0	0.1	93	0.00	0.00
0.15	0.09	1.26	0.10	0.00	31.7	7.9	0.0	0.3	16	1.46	50.9	112	394	16	0.6	68	0.00	0.00
0.01	0.03	0.18	0.05	0.00	6.7	14.4	0.0	0.9	24	0.86	38.9	22	182	102	0.2	93	0.00	0.00
0.02	0.01	1.22	0.03	0.00	4.6	7.7	0.0	0.3	5	0.40	13.2	26	177	1	0.1	92	0.00	0.00
0.00	0.00	0.10	0.00	0.00	2.5	3.2	0.0	0.1	1	0.07	1.9	4	38	2	0.0	94	0.00	0.00
0.01	0.01	0.25	0.02	0.00	6.0	7.6	0.0	0.2	2	0.18	4.4	10	89	4	0.0	94	0.00	0.00
0.03	0.03	0.46	0.05	0.00	11.2	14.2	0.0	0.3	4	0.34	8.2	18	165	7	0.1	94	0.00	0.00
0.03	0.02	0.38	0.05	0.00	9.3	11.8	0.0	0.2	3	0.28	6.8	15	138	6	0.1	94	0.00	0.00
0.03	0.05	0.33	0.14	0.00	106.7	33.0	0.0	1.6	104	0.61	17.1	23	163	22	0.1	91	0.00	0.00
0.02	0.02	0.34	0.07	0.00	10.3	13.3	0.0	0.0	25	0.25	9.2	22	155	58	0.2	94	0.00	0.00
0.05	0.07	0.36	0.11	0.00	5.8	1.4	0.0	0.4	4	0.01	7.9	23	210	5	0.2	73	0.00	0.00
0.02	0.03	0.07	0.03	0.00	3.1	14.6	0.0	0.3	41	0.07	7.1	20	112	14	0.0	95	0.00	0.00
0.07	0.01	0.40	0.21	0.00	17.2	12.8	0.0	0.1	13	0.40	15.8	41	612	7	0.2	70	0.00	0.00
0.10	0.27	1.53	0.15	0.00	199.9	8.4	0.0	0.3	35	0.93	52.1	102	444	89	0.6	86	0.00	0.00
0.05	0.05	0.83	0.09	0.00	42.8	8.4	0.0	0.2	38	1.08	50.4	72	297	278	0.4	84	0.00	0.00
0.11	0.18	1.87	0.03	0.00	243.0	43.9	0.0	2.2	41	1.14	23.4	99	392	432	1.0	91	0.00	0.00
0.01	0.05	0.36	0.11	0.00	2.4	0.0	0.0	0.8	14	0.28	3.6	24	640	5	0.6	96	0.00	0.00
0.46	0.34	3.90	0.11	0.00	60.6	45.9	0.0	0.0	25	1.14	29.7	49	250	9	0.6	89	0.00	0.00
0.44	0.34	3.75	0.11	0.00	58.3	44.1	0.0	0.0	24	1.10	28.5	47	241	301	0.5	89	0.00	0.00
0.01	0.02	0.28	0.05	0.00	68.0	3.1	0.0	0.3	14	0.67	19.6	32	259	65	0.3	87	0.00	0.00
0.10	0.15	1.19	0.28	0.00	75.6	98.1	0.0	0.5	50	1.09	31.2	100	502	36	0.8	90	0.00	0.00
—	—	—	—	0.00	—	—	54.7	—	29	0.44	—	—	—	22	—	92	0.00	0.00
0.03	0.09	0.44	0.10	0.00	39.0	58.2	0.0	1.3	36	0.66	18.7	46	228	20	0.3	91	0.00	0.00
0.07	0.14	0.50	0.10	0.12	22.7	27.6	15.5	1.3	89	0.56	20.0	83	194	180	0.4	84	0.00	0.00
0.03	0.09	0.44	0.10	0.00	39.0	58.2	0.0	1.3	36	0.66	18.7	46	228	204	0.3	91	0.00	0.00
0.05	0.07	0.41	0.11	0.00	27.6	36.9	0.0	0.9	47	0.56	18.4	51	166	22	0.3	91	0.00	0.00
0.15	0.18	0.82	0.44	0.00	156.5	70.8	0.0	0.9	37	1.14	37.2	84	504	401	0.6	87	0.00	0.00
0.05	0.10	0.73	0.28	0.00	69.7	44.2	0.0	0.2	158	1.76	18.7	49	631	58	0.3	96	0.00	0.00
0.03	0.03	0.20	0.07	0.00	15.0	15.1	0.0	0.1	23	0.12	6.0	11	73	191	0.1	94	0.00	0.00
0.02	0.00	0.15	0.10	0.00	9.8	25.8	0.0	0.1	28	0.25	8.2	22	105	6	0.1	94	0.00	0.00
0.01	0.02	0.31	0.09	0.00	8.0	2.0	0.0	0.3	20	0.34	7.3	19	115	215	0.2	90	0.00	0.00
0.05	0.07	0.72	0.34	0.00	18.7	3.1	7.9	2.3	59	1.13	22.6	48	371	232	0.4	73	0.00	0.00
0.14	0.09	1.37	0.21	0.00	20.7	11.6	0.0	0.7	42	0.77	23.4	69	504	55	0.3	88	0.00	0.00
0.10	0.05	1.05	0.10	0.00	24.3	18.5	10.1	0.3	21	0.34	27.6	34	338	18	0.4	59	0.00	0.00
0.15	0.21	1.57	0.17	0.14	35.3	29.4	13.0	3.5	111	1.44	18.3	198	257	240	0.7	66	0.00	0.00
0.01	0.02	0.21	0.09	0.00	23.8	23.9	0.0	0.0	9	0.18	4.9	17	77	131	0.1	93	0.00	0.00
0.05	0.14	0.37	0.10	0.25	35.4	33.7	—	—	90	0.41	14.8	102	205	382	—	87	0.00	0.00
0.02	0.03	0.23	0.05	0.00	16.5	4.6	0.0	0.3	32	0.31	9.0	19	213	245	0.1	94	0.00	0.00
0.20	0.05	0.46	0.11	0.00	35.8	9.0	0.0	0.5	60	0.60	16.5	38	432	130	0.2	95	0.00	0.00

PAGE KEY: A-108 Beverage and Beverage Mixes A-112 Other Beverages A-112 Beverages, Alcoholic A-114 Candies and Confections, Gum A-114 Cereals, Breakfast Type A-118 Cheese and Cheese Substitutes A-120 Dairy Products and Substitutes A-122 Desserts A-128 Dessert Toppings A-128 Eggs, Substitutes, and Egg Dishes A-130 Ethnic Foods A-130 Fast Foods/Restaurants A-140 Fats, Oils, Margarines, Shortenings, and Substitutes A-142 Fish, Seafood, and Shellfish A-142 Food Additives A-142 Fruit, Vegetable, and Blended Juices A-144 Fruits A-146 Grains, Flours, and Fractions A-148 Grain Products, Prepared and Baked Goods

Code	Food Name	Unit/ Amt	Wt (g)	Energy (Kcal)	Prot (g)	Carb (g)	Fiber (g)	Fat (g)	Sat (g)	Mono (g)	Poly (g)	Chol (mg)	Vit A (RE)
6016	Corn, white, sweet, kernels, ckd w/salt, drained	0.5 cup	82	89	3	21	2	1	0.2	0.3	0.5	0	0
6964	Corn, yellow, swt kernels ckd f/fzn cob w/salt drned	0.5 cup	82	76	3	18	2	1	0.1	0.2	0.3	0	18
5900	Corn, yellow, sweet, kernels, ckd w/salt, drained	0.5 cup	82	89	3	21	2	1	0.2	0.3	0.5	0	18
5642	Eggplant, batter dipped, fried	1 pce	50	75	1	6	1	5	1.1	2.3	1.7	8	4
5640	Hominy, ckd	1 cup	165	119	2	24	4	1	0.2	0.4	0.7	0	0
5187	Mixed Vegetables, ckd f/fzn w/o salt, drained	1 cup	182	107	5	24	8	0	0.1	0.0	0.1	0	779
5514	Mushrooms, batter dipped, fried	5 ea	70	156	2	11	1	12	1.5	3.6	6.0	2	6
5092	Mushrooms, ckd w/o salt, drained	0.5 cup	78	21	2	4	2	0	0.0	0.0	0.1	0	0
5924	Mushrooms, ckd w/salt, drained, pces	0.5 cup	78	21	2	4	2	0	0.0	0.0	0.1	0	0
5658	Mushrooms, stir fried w/o oil	1 cup	156	39	3	7	2	1	0.1	0.0	0.3	0	0
5643	Mushrooms, stuffed	2 ea	48	138	5	13	1	7	2.2	3.1	1.6	6	50
5927	Mustard Greens, ckd w/salt, drained, chpd	0.5 cup	70	10	2	1	1	0	0.0	0.1	0.0	0	213
5644	Okra, batter dipped, fried	1 cup	92	175	2	14	2	13	1.7	3.1	7.1	2	39
90171	Okra, ckd w/o add salt f/fzn, drained, slices	0.5 cup	92	26	2	5	3	0	0.1	0.0	0.1	0	48
70623	Onion Rings	6 ea	88	222	3	27	–	12	1.9	4.1	5.1	0	9
5933	Onion, chpd, ckd f/fzn w/salt, drained, chpd/dices	0.5 cup	105	29	1	7	2	0	0.0	0.0	0.0	0	4
5530	Onion, pearl, ckd, diced	1 cup	185	81	3	19	3	0	0.1	0.0	0.1	0	0
7811	Onion, red, ckd w/o salt, drained, chpd	0.5 cup	105	46	1	11	1	0	0.0	0.0	0.1	0	0
5108	Onion, white, ckd w/o salt, drained, chpd	0.5 cup	105	46	1	11	1	0	0.0	0.0	0.1	0	0
7812	Onion, yellow, ckd w/o salt, drained, chpd	0.5 cup	105	46	1	11	1	0	0.0	0.0	0.1	0	0
5522	Palm Hearts, ckd	1 cup	146	150	4	39	2	0	0.1	0.0	0.1	0	9
6849	Peppers, bell, grn, swt, ckd w/o salt drained strips cup	0.5 cup	68	19	1	5	1	0	0.0	0.0	0.1	0	40
5278	Peppers, bell, red, sweet, ckd w/o salt, drained, chpd	0.5 cup	68	19	1	5	1	0	0.0	0.0	0.1	0	256
5963	Pumpkin, ckd w/salt, drained, mashed	0.5 cup	122	24	1	6	1	0	0.0	0.0	0.0	0	132
5974	Spinach, chpd/leaf, ckd f/fzn w/salt	0.5 cup	95	27	3	5	3	0	0.0	0.0	0.1	0	739
5148	Spinach, ckd f/fzn w/o add salt, drained	0.5 cup	95	27	3	5	3	0	0.0	0.0	0.1	0	739
5972	Spinach, ckd w/salt, drained	0.5 cup	90	21	3	3	2	0	0.0	0.0	0.1	0	738
5975	Squash, summer, all types, ckd w/salt, drained	0.5 cup	90	18	1	4	1	0	0.1	0.0	0.1	0	25
5303	Squash, winter, all types, bkd w/o salt, cubes	0.5 cup	102	40	1	9	3	1	0.1	0.0	0.3	0	365
6206	Vegetables, Japanese style	0.5 cup	127	78	2	8	2	5	2.3	–	–	12	96
5168	Yams, ckd/bkd w/o salt, cubes	0.5 cup	68	79	1	19	3	0	0.0	0.0	0.0	0	0
Frozen, Dehydrated, and Dried Vegetables													
5723	Artichokes, globe/French, fzn, 9oz pkg	1 ea	255	97	7	20	10	1	0.3	0.0	0.5	0	41
5361	Asparagus, spears, fzn	4 pce	58	14	2	2	1	0	0.0	0.0	0.1	0	55
6584	Broccoli Cauliflower Carrots, fzn	1 cup	97	30	2	5	3	0	0.0	0.0	0.0	0	200
6758	Broccoli, chpd, fzn	1 cup	156	41	4	7	5	0	0.1	0.0	0.2	0	321
6551	Broccoli, florets, select, fzn	1.33 cup	83	25	2	4	2	0	0.0	0.0	0.0	0	50
56915	Broccoli, w/cheese flvd sauce, fzn	1 cup	168	113	4	15	–	4	0.8	1.7	0.4	–	454
6351	Brussels Sprouts, baby, w/butter sauce, fzn	0.66 cup	104	60	3	9	4	2	1.5	0.0	0.0	3	40
6583	Carrots, baby, cut, fzn	0.66 cup	85	20	0	5	2	0	0.0	0.0	0.0	0	400
5741	Cauliflower, fzn, unprep, 1 pces	0.5 cup	66	16	1	3	2	0	0.0	0.0	0.1	0	3
6382	Corn, cob, extra sweet, fzn	1 ea	125	120	4	22	3	2	0.0	–	–	0	20
6392	Corn, niblets, fzn	0.66 cup	96	80	3	17	3	0	0.0	–	–	0	0
6391	Mixed Vegetables, fzn	0.66 cup	88	50	2	10	3	0	0.0	0.0	0.0	0	150
9274	Poi, dehyrated	1 oz	28	91	0	21	2	1	0.0	–	–	0	0
5596	Spinach, chpd/leaf, fzn, unprep	0.5 cup	78	19	2	3	2	0	0.0	0.0	0.1	0	605
47390	Vegetables, alfredo, w/cream sauce, fzn	0.75 cup	109	80	4	9	3	3	1.5	–	–	5	400
Canned Vegetables													
7850	Artichokes, hearts, quartered, marinated, cnd	2 pce	28	20	0	2	1	2	0.0	–	–	0	0

Thia (mg)	Ribo (mg)	Niac (mg NE)	Vit B6 (mg)	Vit B12 (µg)	Fol (µg)	Vit C (mg)	Vit D (IU)	Vit E (mg AT)	Cal (mg)	Iron (mg)	Magn (mg)	Phos (mg)	Pota (mg)	Sodi (mg)	Zinc (mg)	Wat (%)	Alco (g)	Caff (g)
0.18	0.05	1.32	0.05	0.00	37.7	5.1	0.0	0.1	2	0.50	26.2	84	204	207	0.4	70	0.00	0.00
0.14	0.05	1.24	0.18	0.00	25.4	3.9	0.0	0.1	2	0.50	23.8	62	206	197	0.5	73	0.00	0.00
0.18	0.05	1.32	0.05	0.00	37.7	5.1	0.0	0.1	2	0.50	26.2	84	204	207	0.4	70	0.00	0.00
0.05	0.03	0.46	0.03	0.02	7.4	0.6	–	0.8	14	0.34	7.6	23	106	15	0.1	74	0.00	0.00
0.00	0.00	0.05	0.00	0.00	1.6	0.0	0.0	0.1	16	1.01	26.4	58	15	346	1.7	83	0.00	0.00
0.12	0.21	1.54	0.12	0.00	34.6	5.8	0.0	0.7	46	1.49	40.0	93	308	64	0.9	83	0.00	0.00
0.10	0.25	2.25	0.03	0.02	8.3	1.2	–	2.3	15	1.22	6.8	119	154	112	0.4	63	0.00	0.00
0.05	0.23	3.48	0.07	0.00	14.0	3.1	59.3	0.1	5	1.36	9.4	68	278	2	0.7	91	0.00	0.00
0.05	0.23	3.48	0.07	0.00	14.0	3.1	59.3	0.1	5	1.36	9.4	68	278	186	0.7	91	0.00	0.00
0.14	0.66	6.13	0.14	0.00	26.5	4.7	0.0	0.2	8	1.92	15.6	162	577	6	1.1	92	0.00	0.00
0.15	0.25	2.64	0.07	0.10	11.0	2.8	25.0	0.8	100	1.49	14.3	107	209	298	0.7	43	0.07	0.00
0.02	0.03	0.30	0.07	0.00	51.1	17.7	0.0	1.2	52	0.49	10.5	29	141	176	0.1	94	0.00	0.00
0.18	0.14	1.44	0.11	0.03	38.1	10.3	11.0	3.0	61	1.25	35.8	122	190	122	0.5	67	0.00	0.00
0.09	0.10	0.72	0.03	0.00	134.3	11.2	0.0	0.6	88	0.62	46.9	42	215	3	0.6	91	0.00	0.00
0.07	0.03	1.05	–	0.00	–	4.2	–	–	18	0.82	–	–	161	200	–	52	0.00	0.00
0.01	0.02	0.15	0.07	0.00	13.6	2.7	0.0	0.1	17	0.31	6.3	20	113	260	0.1	92	0.00	0.00
0.07	0.03	0.31	0.23	0.00	27.8	9.6	0.0	0.2	41	0.43	20.4	65	307	6	0.4	88	0.00	0.00
0.03	0.01	0.17	0.14	0.00	15.7	5.5	0.0	0.1	23	0.25	11.5	37	174	3	0.2	88	0.00	0.00
0.03	0.01	0.17	0.14	0.00	15.7	5.5	0.0	0.1	23	0.25	11.5	37	174	3	0.2	88	0.00	0.00
0.03	0.01	0.17	0.14	0.00	15.7	5.5	0.0	0.1	23	0.25	11.5	37	174	3	0.2	88	0.00	0.00
0.07	0.25	1.25	1.05	0.00	29.8	9.9	0.0	0.7	26	2.47	14.6	204	2637	20	5.4	70	0.00	0.00
0.03	0.01	0.31	0.15	0.00	10.8	50.2	0.0	0.5	6	0.31	6.8	12	112	1	0.1	92	0.00	0.00
0.03	0.01	0.31	0.15	0.00	10.9	116.3	0.0	0.5	6	0.31	6.8	12	113	1	0.1	92	0.00	0.00
0.03	0.10	0.50	0.05	0.00	11.0	5.8	0.0	1.3	18	0.69	11.0	37	282	290	0.3	94	0.00	0.00
0.05	0.15	0.40	0.14	0.00	102.6	11.7	0.0	0.9	139	1.44	65.5	46	283	306	0.7	90	0.00	0.00
0.05	0.15	0.40	0.14	0.00	102.6	11.7	0.0	0.9	139	1.44	65.5	46	283	82	0.7	90	0.00	0.00
0.09	0.20	0.43	0.21	0.00	131.4	8.8	0.0	0.9	122	3.21	78.3	50	419	275	0.7	91	0.00	0.00
0.03	0.03	0.46	0.05	0.00	18.0	4.9	0.0	0.1	24	0.31	21.6	35	173	213	0.4	94	0.00	0.00
0.09	0.01	0.72	0.07	0.00	28.7	9.8	0.0	0.1	14	0.34	8.2	20	448	1	0.3	89	0.00	0.00
0.05	0.09	0.37	0.10	0.00	35.4	44.4	–	–	40	0.69	21.6	50	179	320	–	88	0.00	0.00
0.05	0.01	0.37	0.15	0.00	10.9	8.2	0.0	0.1	10	0.34	12.2	33	456	5	0.1	70	0.00	0.00
0.15	0.36	2.19	0.20	0.00	321.5	13.5	0.0	0.4	48	1.27	68.9	148	633	120	0.8	89	0.00	0.00
0.07	0.07	0.69	0.05	0.00	110.8	18.4	0.0	1.2	14	0.41	8.1	37	147	5	0.3	92	0.00	0.00
–	–	–	–	0.00	–	24.0	–	–	20	0.36	–	–	–	125	–	92	0.00	0.00
0.07	0.15	0.73	0.20	0.00	104.5	88.0	0.0	2.4	87	1.25	28.1	78	331	37	0.7	91	0.00	0.00
–	–	–	–	–	–	36.0	–	–	0	0.00	–	–	–	20	–	92	0.00	0.00
–	–	–	–	–	–	59.5	–	–	91	1.08	–	–	–	806	–	84	0.00	0.00
–	–	–	–	0.00	–	42.0	–	–	20	0.36	–	–	–	270	–	86	0.00	0.00
–	–	–	–	0.00	–	0.0	–	–	20	0.00	–	–	–	70	–	94	0.00	0.00
0.02	0.05	0.28	0.07	0.00	42.2	32.2	0.0	0.0	15	0.36	7.9	23	127	16	0.1	93	0.00	0.00
–	–	–	–	–	–	3.6	–	–	0	0.72	–	–	–	0	–	79	0.00	0.00
–	–	–	–	0.00	–	1.2	–	–	0	0.36	–	–	–	60	–	78	0.00	0.00
–	–	–	–	0.00	–	4.8	–	–	0	0.72	–	–	–	125	–	86	0.00	0.00
–	–	–	–	–	–	0.0	–	–	0	2.73	–	–	–	20	–	–	–	
0.07	0.11	0.34	0.10	0.00	93.6	19.0	0.0	0.7	87	1.60	45.2	32	252	58	0.3	92	0.00	0.00
–	–	–	–	–	–	18.0	–	–	80	0.72	–	–	–	450	–	84	0.00	0.00
–	–	–	–	0.00	–	–	6.0	–	0	0.00	–	–	55	80	–	85	0.00	0.00

PAGE KEY: A-108 Beverage and Beverage Mixes A-112 Other Beverages A-112 Beverages, Alcoholic A-114 Candies and Confections, Gum A-114 Cereals, Breakfast Type A-118 Cheese and Cheese Substitutes A-120 Dairy Products and Substitutes A-122 Desserts A-128 Dessert Toppings A-128 Eggs, Substitutes, and Egg Dishes A-130 Ethnic Foods A-130 Fast Foods/Restaurants A-140 Fats, Oils, Margarines, Shortenings, and Substitutes A-142 Fish, Seafood, and Shellfish A-142 Food Additives A-142 Fruit, Vegetable, and Blended Juices A-144 Fruits A-146 Grains, Flours, and Fractions A-148 Grain Products, Prepared and Baked Goods

Code	Food Name	Unit/ Amt	Wt (g)	Energy (Kcal)	Prot (g)	Carb (g)	Fiber (g)	Fat (g)	Sat (g)	Mono (g)	Poly (g)	Chol (mg)	Vit A (RE)
5007	Asparagus, cnd, drained, 5" long	1 pce	18	3	0	0	0	0	0.0	0.0	0.1	0	10
5401	Bamboo Shoots, slices, cnd, drained	1 cup	131	25	2	4	2	1	0.1	0.0	0.2	0	1
5310	Beets, pickled, cnd, not drained, slices	1 cup	227	148	2	37	6	0	0.0	0.0	0.1	0	5
5534	Cabbage, red, sweet & sour	1 cup	150	220	1	57	1	0	0.0	0.0	0.1	0	2
51030	Carrots, slices, cnd	0.5 cup	123	35	0	8	3	0	0.0	0.0	0.0	0	1500
5607	Cauliflower, pickled	1 ea	27	12	0	3	1	0	0.0	0.0	0.0	0	11
6419	Chili Peppers, green, w/tomatoes	0.25 cup	58	10	0	2	0	0	0.0	0.0	0.0	0	10
51058	Corn, gold & white, whole kernel, supersweet, cnd	0.5 cup	125	80	2	18	2	1	0.0	–	–	0	0
51031	Corn, golden, cream style, cnd	0.5 cup	125	90	2	20	2	1	0.0	–	–	0	0
6613	Corn, niblets, 50 % less salt, cnd	0.33 cup	77	60	2	14	1	0	0.0	0.0	0.0	0	0
6268	Corn, niblets, cnd	0.33 cup	77	70	2	15	2	0	0.0	0.0	0.0	0	0
5564	Corn, white, sweet, cream style, cnd	1 cup	256	184	4	46	3	1	0.2	0.3	0.5	0	0
7855	Corn, whole kernel, cnd	0.5 cup	125	90	2	14	2	1	0.0	–	–	0	0
5610	Cucumber, kim chee	1 cup	150	32	2	7	2	0	0.0	0.0	0.1	0	50
5611	Eggplant, pickled	1 cup	136	46	1	10	3	1	0.2	0.1	0.4	0	7
7840	Hominy, white, cnd	0.5 cup	122	65	2	18	3	0	0.0	–	–	0	0
5470	Hominy, yellow, cnd	1 cup	160	115	2	23	4	1	0.2	0.4	0.6	0	19
6462	Mixed Vegetables, Chinese style, cnd	100 g	100	12	1	2	2	0	0.0	–	–	0	1
51044	Mixed Vegetables, cnd	0.5 cup	124	40	2	8	2	0	0.0	0.0	0.0	0	225
90453	Mushrooms, cnd, drained, can	1 ea	132	32	2	7	3	0	0.0	0.0	0.1	0	0
5094	Mushrooms, cnd, drained, pces/slices	0.5 cup	78	19	1	4	2	0	0.0	0.0	0.1	0	0
5613	Mushrooms, pickled	10 ea	120	28	2	6	1	0	0.1	0.0	0.2	0	0
7844	Olives, black, extra lrg, pitted, cnd	3 ea	14	25	0	1	0	2	0.0	–	–	0	0
7847	Olives, green, queen, cnd	2 ea	13	20	0	1	0	2	0.0	1.5	0.5	0	0
5227	Pimentos, cnd	1 Tbs	12	3	0	1	0	0	0.0	0.0	0.0	0	32
6298	Pumpkin, solid pack, cnd	0.5 cup	117	40	2	9	5	0	0.0	–	–	0	1750
90508	Sauerkraut, cnd, drained	0.5 cup	71	13	1	3	2	0	0.0	0.0	0.0	0	1
5595	Spinach, cnd, not drained	0.5 cup	117	22	2	3	2	0	0.1	0.0	0.2	0	753
5600	Succotash, w/cream style corn, cnd	0.5 cup	133	102	4	23	4	1	0.1	0.1	0.3	0	19
51002	Tomatoes, crushed, Italian recipe, cnd	0.5 cup	125	45	2	9	1	0	0.0	0.0	0.0	0	75
6292	Tomatoes, crushed, recipe ready, cnd	0.25 cup	61	20	1	4	1	0	0.0	0.0	0.0	0	20
51005	Tomatoes, dices, cnd	0.5 cup	126	25	1	6	2	0	0.0	0.0	0.0	0	50
7425	Tomatoes, dices, organic, cnd	0.5 cup	127	25	1	4	1	0	0.0	0.0	0.0	0	48
51009	Tomatoes, dices, w/green pepper & onion, cnd	0.5 cup	126	40	1	9	2	0	0.0	0.0	0.0	0	50
6394	Tomatoes, halves	1 oz	28	5	0	1	1	0	0.0	0.0	0.0	0	0
7423	Tomatoes, peeled, ground, organic, cnd	0.5 cup	130	24	2	4	2	0	0.0	0.0	0.0	0	86
5476	Tomatoes, puree, w/add salt, cnd	1 cup	250	100	4	24	5	0	0.1	0.1	0.2	0	320
5474	Tomatoes, red, stwd, cnd, not drained	0.5 cup	128	36	1	9	1	0	0.0	0.0	0.1	0	69
6992	Tomatoes, red, whole, cnd, w/o add salt, can	1 ea	190	36	2	8	2	0	0.0	0.0	0.1	0	114
9169	Tomatoes, stwd, cnd	0.5 cup	121	35	1	8	1	0	0.0	0.0	0.0	0	–
51021	Tomatoes, stwd, Mexican recipe, cnd	0.5 cup	126	35	1	9	2	0	0.0	0.0	0.0	0	50
7885	Tomatoes, stwd, w/o salt, cnd	0.5 cup	123	35	1	7	2	0	0.0	0.0	0.0	0	50
7896	Tomatoes, whole, peeled, cnd	0.5 cup	121	25	1	4	1	0	0.0	0.0	0.0	0	50
6254	Vegetables, garden medley, cnd	0.5 cup	121	40	1	9	2	0	0.0	0.0	0.0	0	200
6460	Waterchestnuts, slices, cnd	100 g	100	50	1	12	5	0	0.0	–	–	0	0
7877	Yams, candied, old fash, cnd	0.5 cup	141	170	2	46	4	0	0.0	0.0	0.0	0	200
Legumes													
9308	Beans, baked, w/tom sauce, veget, organic, rts, cnd	0.5 cup	130	120	5	24	6	0	0.0	–	–	0	60
7165	Beans, bbq	0.5 cup	100	160	6	32	6	2	0.5	–	–	–	–

PAGE KEY: A-154 Granola Bars, Cereal Bars, Diet Bars, Scones, and Tarts A-154 Meals and Dishes A-160 Meats A-164 Nuts, Seeds, and Products A-166 Poultry A-166 Salad Dressings, Dips, and Mayonnaise A-170 Salads A-170 Sandwiches A-172 Sauces and Gravies A-174 Snack Foods—Chips, Pretzels, Popcorn A-178 Soups, Stews and Chilis A-184 Spices, Flavors, and Seasonings A-184 Sports Bars and Drinks A-186 Supplemental Foods and Formulas A-186 Sweeteners and Sweet Substitutes A-188 Vegetables and Legumes A-200 Weight Loss Bars & Drinks A-200 Miscellaneous

Thia (mg)	Ribc (mg)	Niac (mg NE)	Vit B6 (mg)	Vit B12 (µg)	Fol (µg)	Vit C (mg)	Vit D (IU)	Vit E (mg AT)	Cal (mg)	Iron (mg)	Magn (mg)	Phos (mg)	Pota (mg)	Sodi (mg)	Zinc (mg)	Wat (%)	Alco (g)	Caff (g)
0.00	0.01	0.17	0.01	0.00	17.3	3.3	0.0	0.1	3	0.33	1.8	8	31	52	0.1	94	0.00	0.00
0.02	0.02	0.18	0.18	0.00	3.9	1.4	0.0	0.5	10	0.41	5.2	33	105	9	0.9	94	0.00	0.00
0.01	0.10	0.56	0.10	0.00	61.3	5.2	0.0	0.3	25	0.93	34.0	39	336	599	0.6	82	0.00	0.00
0.02	0.01	0.23	0.12	0.00	12.1	30.9	0.0	0.1	73	1.28	36.3	35	318	27	0.2	60	0.00	0.00
–	–	–	–	–	–	3.6	–	–	20	0.36	–	–	–	300	–	93	0.00	0.00
0.00	0.00	0.09	0.03	0.00	6.9	8.7	0.0	0.0	6	0.11	3.6	9	56	5	0.1	88	0.00	0.00
–	–	–	–	0.00	–	2.4	–	–	20	0.00	–	–	–	300	–	95	0.00	0.00
–	–	–	–	–	–	3.6	–	–	0	0.36	–	–	–	360	–	82	0.00	0.00
–	–	–	–	–	–	2.4	–	–	0	0.36	–	–	–	360	–	81	0.00	0.00
–	–	–	–	–	–	2.4	–	–	0	0.00	–	–	–	115	–	78	0.00	0.00
–	–	–	–	–	–	2.4	–	–	0	0.00	–	–	–	230	–	77	0.00	0.00
0.05	0.14	2.46	0.15	0.00	115.2	11.8	0.0	0.2	8	0.97	43.5	131	343	730	1.4	79	0.00	0.00
–	–	–	–	0.00	–	2.4	–	–	0	0.36	–	–	0	340	–	85	0.00	0.00
0.03	0.03	0.68	0.15	0.00	34.5	5.2	0.0	0.2	14	7.23	12.0	20	176	1532	0.8	91	0.00	0.00
0.07	0.10	0.89	0.18	0.00	27.2	0.0	0.0	0.0	34	1.04	8.2	12	16	2277	0.3	87	0.00	0.00
–	–	–	–	0.00	–	2.4	–	–	0	0.36	–	–	5	530	–	82	0.00	0.00
0.00	0.00	0.05	0.00	0.00	1.6	0.0	0.0	0.2	16	0.99	25.6	56	14	336	1.7	83	0.00	0.00
–	–	–	–	0.00	–	7.3	–	–	12	0.14	–	–	–	52	–	95	0.00	0.00
–	–	–	–	–	–	2.4	–	–	20	0.72	–	–	–	360	–	91	0.00	0.00
0.10	0.02	2.08	0.07	0.00	15.8	0.0	52.6	0.2	14	1.03	19.7	87	170	559	0.9	91	0.00	0.00
0.07	0.01	1.24	0.05	0.00	9.4	0.0	31.2	0.1	9	0.62	11.7	51	101	332	0.6	91	0.00	0.00
0.07	0.41	3.63	0.09	0.00	14.2	2.7	48.0	0.1	6	1.28	12.5	98	357	4	0.7	92	0.00	0.00
–	–	–	–	0.00	–	0.0	–	–	0	0.00	–	–	0	110	–	73	0.00	0.00
–	–	–	–	0.00	–	0.0	–	–	0	0.00	–	–	0	220	–	72	0.00	0.00
0.00	0.00	0.07	0.02	0.00	0.7	10.2	0.0	0.1	1	0.20	0.7	2	19	2	0.0	93	0.00	0.00
–	–	–	–	0.00	–	0.0	–	–	20	0.72	–	–	–	5	–	90	0.00	0.00
0.00	0.01	0.10	0.09	0.00	17.0	10.4	0.0	0.1	21	1.03	9.2	14	121	469	0.1	93	0.00	0.00
0.01	0.11	0.31	0.09	0.00	67.9	15.8	0.0	1.3	97	1.85	65.5	37	269	373	0.5	93	0.00	0.00
0.03	0.09	0.81	0.17	0.00	58.5	8.5	0.0	0.3	15	0.73	1.3	78	243	326	0.6	78	0.00	0.00
–	–	–	–	–	–	9.0	–	–	0	0.72	–	–	–	390	–	90	0.00	0.00
–	–	–	–	–	–	6.0	–	–	20	0.36	–	–	–	150	–	91	0.00	0.00
–	–	–	–	–	–	9.0	–	–	20	0.36	–	–	–	160	–	93	0.00	0.00
–	–	–	–	0.00	–	15.2	–	–	8	0.81	–	–	–	368	–	95	0.00	0.00
–	–	–	–	–	–	9.0	–	–	20	0.36	–	–	–	480	–	91	0.00	0.00
0.00	0.00	0.07	0.01	0.00	0.6	0.0	–	–	16	0.10	2.4	10	46	320	0.0	93	0.00	0.00
–	–	–	–	0.00	–	18.3	–	–	17	1.20	–	–	–	191	–	94	0.00	0.00
0.18	0.14	4.28	0.37	0.00	27.5	26.0	0.0	6.3	42	3.09	60.0	100	1065	998	0.6	87	0.00	0.00
0.05	0.03	0.91	0.01	0.00	6.4	14.5	0.0	0.5	42	0.93	15.3	26	303	282	0.2	91	0.00	0.00
0.09	0.05	1.39	0.17	0.00	15.2	27.0	0.0	0.7	57	1.03	22.8	36	431	19	0.3	94	0.00	0.00
–	–	–	–	–	–	15.0	–	–	60	1.08	–	–	–	390	–	92	0.00	0.00
–	–	–	–	–	–	9.0	–	–	20	0.36	–	–	–	400	–	91	0.00	0.00
–	–	–	–	0.00	–	12.0	–	–	40	1.44	–	–	150	15	–	93	0.00	0.00
–	–	–	–	0.00	–	12.0	–	–	20	0.72	–	–	200	220	–	95	0.00	0.00
–	–	–	–	–	–	0.0	–	–	0	0.72	–	–	–	360	–	91	0.00	0.00
–	–	–	–	0.00	–	0.0	–	–	3	0.27	–	–	–	12	–	86	0.00	0.00
–	–	–	–	0.00	–	4.8	–	–	20	1.08	–	–	210	360	–	65	0.00	0.00
–	–	–	–	–	–	2.4	–	–	40	2.70	–	–	–	480	–	76	0.00	0.00
–	–	–	–	–	–	–	–	–	–	–	–	–	–	640	–	–	0.00	0.00

PAGE KEY: A-108 Beverage and Beverage Mixes A-112 Other Beverages A-112 Beverages, Alcoholic A-114 Candies and Confections, Gum A-114 Cereals, Breakfast Type A-118 Cheese and Cheese Substitutes A-120 Dairy Products and Substitutes A-122 Desserts A-128 Dessert Toppings A-128 Eggs, Substitutes, and Egg Dishes A-130 Ethnic Foods A-130 Fast Foods/Restaurants A-140 Fats, Oils, Margarines, Shortenings, and Substitutes A-142 Fish, Seafood, and Shellfish A-142 Food Additives A-142 Fruit, Vegetable, and Blended Juices A-144 Fruits A-146 Grains, Flours, and Fractions A-148 Grain Products, Prepared and Baked Goods

Code	Food Name	Unit/ Amt	Wt (g)	Energy (Kcal)	Prot (g)	Carb (g)	Fiber (g)	Fat (g)	Sat (g)	Mono (g)	Poly (g)	Chol (mg)	Vit A (RE)
9262	Beans, black, cnd, Bush's Best	0.5 cup	130	100	7	20	7	0	0.0	—	—	0	0
5115	Beans, blackeyed/cowpeas ckd f/fzn w/o salt drained	1 cup	170	224	14	40	11	1	0.3	0.1	0.5	0	14
7823	Beans, butter, cnd	0.5 cup	124	70	6	18	5	0	0.0	0.0	0.0	0	0
7088	Beans, chickpea/garbanzo, mature, cnd	0.5 cup	120	143	6	27	5	1	0.1	0.3	0.6	0	2
7000	Beans, chickpea/garbanzo, mature, dry	1 cup	200	728	39	121	35	12	1.3	2.7	5.4	0	12
7055	Beans, fava/broad, mature, cnd, not drained	0.5 cup	128	91	7	16	5	0	0.0	0.1	0.1	0	3
56638	Beans, frijoles, w/cheese, fast food	1 cup	167	225	11	29	—	8	4.1	2.6	0.7	37	55
51056	Beans, golden, wax, cut, cnd	0.5 cup	121	20	1	4	2	0	0.0	0.0	0.0	0	0
7131	Beans, great northern, mature, cnd	1 cup	262	299	19	55	13	1	0.3	0.0	0.4	0	0
6219	Beans, green, cut	0.5 cup	83	25	1	6	2	0	0.0	—	—	0	44
5733	Beans, green, snap, all types, fzn	0.5 cup	62	20	1	5	2	0	0.0	0.0	0.1	0	30
5013	Beans, green, snap, ckd f/fzn w/o salt, drained	1 cup	135	38	2	9	4	0	0.1	0.0	0.1	0	54
5015	Beans, green, snap, cnd, drained	1 cup	135	27	2	6	3	0	0.0	0.0	0.1	0	46
51042	Beans, Italian, cut, cnd	0.5 cup	121	30	1	6	3	0	0.0	0.0	0.0	0	20
7087	Beans, kidney, all types, mature, cnd	0.5 cup	128	104	7	19	4	0	0.1	0.0	0.2	0	0
5850	Beans, lima, baby, immature, ckd f/fzn w/salt, drained	0.5 cup	90	94	6	18	5	0	0.1	0.0	0.1	0	14
7022	Beans, navy, mature, ckd f/dry w/o salt	1 cup	182	258	16	48	12	1	0.3	0.1	0.4	0	0
7160	Beans, refried, cnd, Ortega	0.5 cup	136	120	6	22	5	2	0.0	—	—	0	20
5858	Beans, yellow, snap, all types, fzn	0.5 cup	62	20	1	5	2	0	0.0	0.0	0.1	0	7
9181	Jicama, raw, chpd	1 cup	130	49	1	11	6	0	0.0	0.0	0.1	0	3
7005	Lentils, dry	1 cup	192	649	54	110	59	2	0.3	0.3	0.9	0	8
5282	Peas & Carrots, fzn	0.5 cup	70	37	2	8	2	0	0.1	0.0	0.2	0	665
5939	Peas, green, ckd f/fzn w/salt, drained	0.5 cup	80	62	4	11	4	0	0.0	0.0	0.1	0	53
5119	Peas, green, cnd, drained	0.5 cup	85	59	4	11	3	0	0.1	0.0	0.1	0	65
5280	Peas, green, fzn	0.5 cup	72	55	4	10	3	0	0.0	0.0	0.1	0	52
5116	Peas, green, raw	1 cup	145	117	8	21	7	1	0.1	0.1	0.3	0	93
5122	Peas, snow/edible pod, ckd w/o salt, drained	1 cup	160	67	5	11	4	0	0.1	0.0	0.2	0	22
90026	Peas, split, ckd f/dry w/salt	1 cup	196	231	16	41	16	1	0.1	0.2	0.3	0	1
51047	Peas, sweet, cnd	0.5 cup	125	60	3	13	4	0	0.0	0.0	0.0	0	30
6364	Peas, sweet, fzn	0.66 cup	94	60	4	12	4	0	0.0	0.0	0.0	0	30
90028	Soybeans, mature, ckd f/dry w/salt	1.25 cup	215	372	36	21	13	19	2.8	4.3	10.9	0	2
7014	Soybeans, mature, dry	1 cup	186	774	68	56	17	37	5.4	8.2	20.9	0	4
Potatoes													
56754	Dish, potatoes, au gratin, side, fzn, svg	1 ea	130	130	4	15	1	6	2.5	—	—	15	0
5275	Potatoes, au gratin, prep f/recipe w/margarine	1 cup	245	323	12	28	4	19	8.6	6.3	2.6	37	167
70612	Potatoes, baked, twice, w/butter	1 ea	143	204	4	27	4	9	3.1	3.1	0.5	0	86
5336	Potatoes, baked, w/o salt, lrg, 3" to 4¼"	1 ea	299	278	7	63	7	0	0.1	0.0	0.2	0	6
5691	Potatoes, french fries, battered, shoestring, fzn	3 oz	85	170	4	17	1	10	2.5	—	—	0	0
5332	Potatoes, french fries, cottage cut, hted f/fzn w/o salt	10 ea	50	109	2	17	2	4	1.9	1.7	0.3	0	0
90736	Potatoes, french fries, fried in veg oil, med svg	1 ea	134	458	6	53	5	25	5.2	14.3	4.2	0	0
6171	Potatoes, french fries, svg	1 ea	97	301	2	38	5	15	—	—	—	—	0
6401	Potatoes, hash browns, country style	1 cup	75	60	2	13	1	0	0.0	0.0	0.0	0	0
5273	Potatoes, hash browns, homemade	1 cup	78	163	2	17	2	11	4.2	4.8	1.2	0	0
5140	Potatoes, hash browns, plain, prep f/fzn	1 cup	78	170	2	22	2	9	3.5	4.0	1.0	0	0
5138	Potatoes, mashed, flake, prep f/dry w/milk & marg	0.5 cup	105	119	2	16	2	6	1.5	2.4	1.6	4	52
56453	Potatoes, mashed, w/gravy, svg	1 ea	136	120	1	17	2	6	1.0	3.6	1.4	1	20
5569	Potatoes, mashed, w/whole milk & butter	0.5 cup	105	111	2	18	2	4	2.9	1.2	0.2	13	40
7316	Potatoes, med, raw FDA	1 ea	148	100	4	26	3	0	0.0	0.0	0.0	0	0

PAGE KEY: A-154 Granola Bars, Cereal Bars, Diet Bars, Scones, and Tarts A-154 Meals and Dishes A-160 Meats A-164 Nuts, Seeds, and Products A-166 Poultry A-166 Salad Dressings, Dips, and Mayonnaise A-170 Salads A-170 Sandwiches A-172 Sauces and Gravies A-174 Snack Foods—Chips, Pretzels, Popcorn A-178 Soups, Stews and Chilis A-184 Spices, Flavors, and Seasonings A-184 Sports Bars and Drinks A-186 Supplemental Foods and Formulas A-186 Sweeteners and Sweet Substitutes A-188 Vegetables and Legumes A-200 Weight Loss Bars & Drinks A-200 Miscellaneous

Thia (mg)	Ribo (mg)	Niac (mg NE)	Vit B6 (mg)	Vit B12 (µg)	Fol (µg)	Vit C (mg)	Vit D (IU)	Vit E (mg AT)	Cal (mg)	Iron (mg)	Magn (mg)	Phos (mg)	Pota (mg)	Sodi (mg)	Zinc (mg)	Wat (%)	Alco (g)	Caff (g)
–	–	–	–	–	–	0.0	–	–	40	1.79	–	–	–	460	–	–	0.00	0.00
0.43	0.10	1.24	0.15	0.00	239.7	4.4	0.0	0.7	39	3.59	85.0	207	638	8	2.4	66	0.00	0.00
–	–	–	–	–	–	2.4	–	–	40	1.79	–	–	470	440	–	79	0.00	0.00
0.02	0.03	0.17	0.56	0.00	80.4	4.6	0.0	0.2	38	1.62	34.8	108	206	359	1.3	70	0.00	0.00
0.94	0.41	3.07	1.07	0.00	1114.0	8.0	0.0	1.6	210	12.47	230.0	732	1750	48	6.9	12	0.00	0.00
0.02	0.05	1.23	0.05	0.00	42.2	2.3	0.0	0.1	33	1.27	41.0	101	310	580	0.8	80	0.00	0.00
0.12	0.33	1.49	0.20	0.68	111.9	1.5	–	–	189	2.24	85.2	175	605	882	1.7	69	0.00	0.00
–	–	–	–	–	–	3.6	–	–	20	0.36	–	–	–	360	–	95	0.00	0.00
0.37	0.15	1.21	0.28	0.00	212.2	3.4	0.0	0.7	139	4.11	133.6	356	920	10	1.7	70	0.00	0.00
0.03	0.07	0.02	0.03	0.00	10.8	8.9	–	–	35	0.70	16.6	22	128	3	–	91	0.00	0.00
0.05	0.05	0.31	0.02	0.00	9.3	8.0	0.0	0.3	26	0.52	13.6	20	115	2	0.2	90	0.00	0.00
0.05	0.11	0.51	0.07	0.00	31.1	5.5	0.0	0.2	66	1.19	32.4	42	170	12	0.6	91	0.00	0.00
0.01	0.07	0.27	0.05	0.00	43.2	6.5	0.0	0.2	35	1.22	17.6	26	147	354	0.4	93	0.00	0.00
–	–	–	–	–	–	2.4	–	–	20	0.72	–	–	–	390	–	94	0.00	0.00
0.14	0.09	0.63	0.09	0.00	62.7	1.5	0.0	0.3	35	1.57	39.7	134	329	444	0.7	78	0.00	0.00
0.05	0.05	0.68	0.10	0.00	14.4	5.2	0.0	0.6	25	1.75	50.4	101	370	238	0.5	72	0.00	0.00
0.37	0.10	0.97	0.30	0.00	254.8	1.6	0.0	0.7	127	4.51	107.4	286	670	2	1.9	63	0.00	0.00
–	–	–	–	0.00	–	2.4	–	–	40	2.51	–	–	–	560	–	77	0.00	0.00
0.05	0.05	0.31	0.02	0.00	9.3	8.0	0.0	0.1	26	0.52	13.6	20	115	2	0.2	90	0.00	0.00
0.02	0.03	0.25	0.05	0.00	15.6	26.3	0.0	0.6	16	0.77	15.6	23	195	5	0.2	90	0.00	0.00
0.91	0.46	5.03	1.02	0.00	831.4	11.9	0.0	0.6	98	17.31	205.4	872	1738	19	6.9	11	0.00	0.00
0.12	0.05	0.99	0.07	0.00	25.2	7.8	0.0	0.2	19	0.75	12.6	42	136	55	0.4	84	0.00	0.00
0.23	0.07	1.17	0.09	0.00	47.2	7.9	0.0	0.1	19	1.25	23.2	72	134	258	0.8	80	0.00	0.00
0.10	0.07	0.62	0.05	0.00	37.4	8.2	0.0	0.3	17	0.81	14.5	57	147	214	0.6	82	0.00	0.00
0.18	0.07	1.23	0.09	0.00	38.2	13.0	0.0	0.1	16	1.10	18.0	58	107	81	0.6	80	0.00	0.00
0.38	0.18	3.02	0.25	0.00	94.2	58.0	0.0	0.6	36	2.13	47.9	157	354	7	1.8	79	0.00	0.00
0.20	0.11	0.86	0.23	0.00	46.4	76.6	0.0	0.6	67	3.15	41.6	88	384	6	0.6	89	0.00	0.00
0.37	0.10	1.74	0.09	0.00	127.4	0.8	0.0	0.8	27	2.52	70.6	194	710	466	2.0	69	0.00	0.00
–	–	–	–	–	–	9.0	–	–	20	1.44	–	–	–	390	–	86	0.00	0.00
–	–	–	–	0.00	–	6.0	–	–	0	1.08	–	–	–	200	–	82	0.00	0.00
0.33	0.61	0.86	0.50	0.00	116.1	3.7	0.0	4.2	219	11.05	184.9	527	1107	510	2.5	63	0.00	0.00
1.62	1.62	3.01	0.69	0.00	697.5	11.2	0.0	1.6	515	29.20	520.8	1309	3342	4	9.1	9	0.00	0.00
0.00	0.10	0.68	–	0.00	–	2.4	–	–	100	0.00	–	–	250	590	–	80	0.00	0.00
0.15	0.28	2.43	0.43	0.00	27.0	24.3	36.5	1.3	292	1.57	49.0	277	970	1061	1.7	74	0.00	0.00
0.09	0.10	3.03	–	0.00	–	21.4	–	–	57	1.02	–	–	601	357	–	70	0.00	0.00
0.18	0.14	4.21	0.93	0.00	83.7	28.7	0.0	0.1	45	3.23	83.7	209	1599	30	1.1	75	0.00	0.00
–	–	–	–	–	–	3.6	–	–	0	0.36	–	–	–	190	–	63	0.00	0.00
0.05	0.01	1.21	0.11	0.00	8.5	4.8	0.0	0.1	5	0.75	11.0	32	240	22	0.2	53	0.00	0.00
0.10	0.05	3.81	0.47	0.00	50.9	15.5	–	1.6	19	1.04	52.3	173	923	265	0.6	35	0.00	0.00
–	–	–	–	0.00	–	–	–	–	–	–	–	–	–	193	–	42	0.00	0.00
–	–	–	–	0.00	–	3.6	–	–	0	0.00	–	–	240	10	–	–	0.00	0.00
0.05	0.01	1.55	0.21	0.00	6.2	4.4	0.0	0.1	6	0.62	15.6	33	250	19	0.2	62	0.00	0.00
0.09	0.01	1.88	0.10	0.00	5.5	4.9	0.0	0.1	12	1.17	13.3	56	340	27	0.2	56	0.00	0.00
0.11	0.05	0.69	0.00	0.00	7.3	10.2	8.4	0.7	51	0.23	18.9	59	245	349	0.2	76	0.00	0.00
–	–	–	–	–	–	1.2	–	–	20	0.36	–	–	–	440	–	82	0.00	0.00
0.09	0.03	1.12	0.23	0.00	8.4	6.4	8.4	0.3	27	0.27	18.9	48	303	310	0.3	76	0.00	0.00
–	–	–	–	0.00	–	27.0	–	–	20	1.08	–	–	720	0	–	79	0.00	0.00

PAGE KEY: A-108 Beverage and Beverage Mixes A-112 Other Beverages A-112 Beverages, Alcoholic A-114 Candies and Confections, Gum A-114 Cereals, Breakfast Type A-118 Cheese and Cheese Substitutes A-120 Dairy Products and Substitutes A-122 Desserts A-128 Dessert Toppings A-128 Eggs, Substitutes, and Egg Dishes A-130 Ethnic Foods A-130 Fast Foods/Restaurants A-140 Fats, Oils, Margarines, Shortenings, and Substitutes A-142 Fish, Seafood, and Shellfish A-142 Food Additives A-142 Fruit, Vegetable, and Blended Juices A-144 Fruits A-146 Grains, Flours, and Fractions A-148 Grain Products, Prepared and Baked Goods

Code	Food Name	Unit/ Amt	Wt (g)	Energy (Kcal)	Prot (g)	Carb (g)	Fiber (g)	Fat (g)	Sat (g)	Mono (g)	Poly (g)	Chol (mg)	Vit A (RE)
5957	Potatoes, microwv in skin, peeled, w/salt	0.5 cup	78	78	2	18	1	0	0.0	0.0	0.0	0	0
5269	Potatoes, o'brien, ckd f/fzn	0.5 cup	97	198	2	21	2	13	3.2	5.6	3.4	0	17
5954	Potatoes, peeled, ckd w/salt	0.5 cup	78	67	1	16	2	0	0.0	0.0	0.0	0	0
9244	Potatoes, russet, w/skin, baked, med 2¼"-3¼" diameter	1 ea	173	168	5	37	4	0	0.1	0.0	0.1	0	3
5271	Potatoes, scall, prep f/dry w/whole milk & butter, svg	1 ea	137	127	3	17	2	6	3.6	1.7	0.3	15	51
5339	Potatoes, skin, bkd w/o salt	1 ea	58	115	2	27	5	0	0.0	0.0	0.0	0	0
5950	Potatoes, skin, bkd w/salt	1 ea	58	115	2	27	5	0	0.0	0.0	0.0	0	0
6924	Potatoes, sweet, bkd in skin, w/salt	0.5 cup	100	103	2	24	3	0	0.0	0.0	0.0	0	2182
5166	Potatoes, sweet, candied, homemade, 2½" x 2" ea	1 pce	105	144	1	29	3	3	1.4	0.7	0.2	8	439
5555	Potatoes, sweet, in syrup, cnd, drained	1 cup	196	212	3	50	6	1	0.1	0.0	0.3	0	1403
70598	Potatoes, tater tots	0.5 cup	62	107	1	16	1	6	1.1	1.8	0.0	0	0
7906	Potatoes, wedges, commodity, fzn	100 g	100	123	3	26	2	2	0.6	1.5	0.1	0	0
5163	Yams, orange, mashed f/cnd	1 cup	256	259	5	59	4	1	0.1	0.0	0.2	0	3871
WEIGHT LOSS BARS & DRINKS													
Weight Loss Bars													
62736	Bar, diet, Figurines, vanilla	2 ea	43	220	4	25	0	11	2.5	–	–	3	200
62876	Bar, diet, hi prot, chocolate raspberry	1 ea	70	260	31	11	1	5	3.5	–	–	0	–
62643	Bar, diet, Slim Fast Ultra, rich chewy caramel	1 ea	28	120	0	22	2	4	2.5	–	–	5	150
62861	Bar, diet, Slim Fast, honey peanut, meal on the go	1 ea	56	220	8	34	2	5	3.5	–	–	5	350
Weight Loss Drinks													
1922	Drink, diet, Pro Lite, natural, chocolate, pwd, scoop	1 ea	50	190	15	30	–	2	0.5	–	–	20	350
62650	Drink, diet, Slim Fast Ultra, milk choc, milk base rtd can	1 ea	350	220	10	40	5	3	1.0	1.5	0.5	5	350
62649	Drink, diet, Slim Fast Ultra, straw crm, milk base rtd can	1 ea	350	220	10	40	5	2	0.5	1.5	0.5	5	350
62647	Drink, diet, Slim Fast Ultra, vanilla, milk base, rtd can	1 ea	350	220	10	40	5	3	0.5	1.5	0.5	5	350
63025	Shake, weight management, vanilla, rtd	1 ea	250	90	15	3	1	2	0.0	–	–	15	150
MISCELLANEOUS													
Baking Chips, Chocolates, Coatings, and Cocoas													
23119	Baking Chips, butterscotch, confectioner's coating candy	1 cup	170	916	4	114	–	49	41.0	3.9	0.7	0	0
23012	Baking Chips, chocolate, semi sweet	10 pce	5	23	0	3	0	1	0.8	0.5	0.0	0	0
23423	Baking Chips, M & M's, milk chocolate, mini bits	1 Tbs	14	71	1	10	0	3	2.1	1.1	0.1	2	6
23443	Baking Chips, milk chocolate	1 Tbs	15	81	1	9	0	4	2.6	0.9	0.1	3	7
4153	Baking Chips, Nestle Crunch, pieces	1.5 Tbs	15	80	1	10	0	4	2.0	–	–	0	0
23446	Baking Chips, Reese's peanut butter	1 Tbs	15	79	3	7	1	4	3.6	0.4	0.2	0	–
23500	Baking Chips, vegan carob, grain swtnd	31 pce	15	70	0	11	0	3	3.0	–	–	0	0
44068	Baking Chips, yogurt	1 oz	28	149	3	16	1	8	2.1	4.7	1.0	1	3
4356	Baking Chocolate, bar, bittersweet	0.5 pce	14	70	1	7	1	6	3.0	–	–	0	0
23329	Baking Chocolate, bar, German, sweet	2 pce	13	60	1	8	0	4	2.0	–	–	0	0
23401	Baking Chocolate, bar, semi sweet	0.5 pce	14	70	1	8	1	4	2.5	–	–	0	0
28063	Baking Chocolate, bar, unswtnd	0.5 pce	14	70	2	4	2	7	4.5	–	–	0	0
4355	Baking Chocolate, bar, white	0.5 pce	14	80	1	8	0	4	3.0	–	–	5	0
28200	Cocoa Powder, unswntd	1 cup	86	197	17	47	29	12	6.9	3.9	0.4	0	2
Baking Ingredients													
28006	Baking Powder, low sod	1 tsp	5	5	0	2	0	0	0.0	0.0	0.0	0	0
28003	Baking Soda	1 tsp	5	0	0	0	0	0	0.0	0.0	0.0	0	0
3977	Pineapple, slices, natural glace	1 pce	63	180	0	46	0	0	0.0	0.0	0.0	0	0
28000	Yeast, baker's, dry active	1 tsp	4	12	2	2	1	0	0.0	0.1	0.0	0	0
Condiments													
27050	Bacon Bits, Bac O Bits	1 Tbs	6	25	2	2	–	1	–	–	–	0	–
9149	Catsup	1 cup	240	250	4	65	3	1	0.1	0.1	0.4	0	245

PAGE KEY: A-154 Granola Bars, Cereal Bars, Diet Bars, Scones, and Tarts A-154 Meals and Dishes A-160 Meats A-164 Nuts, Seeds, and Products A-166 Poultry A-166 Salad Dressings, Dips, and Mayonnaise A-170 Salads A-170 Sandwiches A-172 Sauces and Gravies A-174 Snack Foods—Chips, Pretzels, Popcorn A-178 Soups, Stews and Chilis A-184 Spices, Flavors, and Seasonings A-184 Sports Bars and Drinks A-186 Supplemental Foods and Formulas A-186 Sweeteners and Sweet Substitutes A-188 Vegetables and Legumes A-200 Weight Loss Bars & Drinks A-200 Miscellaneous

Thia (mg)	Ribo (mg)	Niac (mg NE)	Vit B6 (mg)	Vit B12 (µg)	Fol (µg)	Vit C (mg)	Vit D (IU)	Vit E (mg AT)	Cal (mg)	Iron (mg)	Magn (mg)	Phos (mg)	Pota (mg)	Sodi (mg)	Zinc (mg)	Wat (%)	Alco (g)	Caff (g)
0.10	0.07	1.26	0.25	0.00	9.4	11.8	0.0	0.0	4	0.31	19.5	85	321	190	0.3	74	0.00	0.00
0.05	0.12	1.39	0.37	0.00	11.6	10.1	0.0	0.2	19	0.93	33.0	90	459	42	0.5	62	0.00	0.00
0.07	0.00	1.01	0.20	0.00	7.0	5.8	0.0	0.0	6	0.23	15.6	31	256	188	0.2	77	0.00	0.00
0.11	0.07	2.32	0.61	0.00	19.0	22.3	—	0.1	31	1.85	51.9	123	952	14	0.6	74	0.00	
0.02	0.07	1.40	0.05	0.00	13.7	4.5	16.4	0.2	49	0.51	19.2	77	278	467	0.3	79	0.00	0.00
0.07	0.05	1.77	0.36	0.00	12.8	7.8	0.0	0.0	20	4.07	24.9	59	332	12	0.3	47	0.00	0.00
0.07	0.05	1.77	0.36	0.00	12.8	7.8	0.0	0.0	20	4.07	24.9	59	332	149	0.3	47	0.00	0.00
0.07	0.12	0.60	0.23	0.00	23.0	24.6	0.0	0.3	28	0.44	20.0	55	348	246	0.3	73	0.00	0.00
0.01	0.03	0.40	0.03	0.00	11.5	7.0	0.0	4.0	27	1.19	11.5	27	198	74	0.2	67	0.00	0.00
0.05	0.07	0.67	0.11	0.00	15.7	21.2	0.0	0.5	33	1.86	23.5	49	378	76	0.3	72	0.00	0.00
0.03	0.00	1.04	0.14	0.00	—	0.7	—	—	0	0.00	—	—	162	251	—	61	0.00	0.00
0.10	0.03	1.53	0.34	0.00	—	11.2	—	—	15	0.69	19.0	87	394	49	0.4	68	0.00	0.00
0.07	0.23	2.44	0.60	0.00	28.2	13.3	0.0	0.7	77	3.40	61.4	133	538	192	0.5	74	0.00	0.00
0.30	0.17	5.00	0.40	0.89	100.0	15.0	16.0	3.4	150	4.50	80.0	100	190	115	3.0	4	0.00	0.00
—	—	—	—	0.60	—	—	—	—	200	1.08	—	200	—	130	—	—	0.00	
0.21	0.25	3.00	0.30	0.89	60.0	9.0	60.0	2.0	250	2.70	—	100	—	65	—	7	0.00	0.00
0.21	0.60	7.00	0.69	2.09	60.0	21.0	140.0	4.8	300	2.70	140.0	250	170	160	2.2	8	0.00	0.00
0.52	0.60	7.00	0.69	2.09	140.0	21.0	140.0	7.1	275	1.79	134.0	266	210	220	4.0	—	0.00	
0.51	0.60	7.00	0.69	2.09	120.0	60.0	140.0	13.6	400	2.70	140.0	400	600	220	2.2	83	0.00	
0.51	0.60	7.00	0.69	2.09	120.0	60.0	140.0	13.6	400	2.70	140.0	400	600	220	2.2	84	0.00	0.00
0.51	0.60	7.00	0.69	2.09	120.0	60.0	140.0	13.6	400	2.70	140.0	400	600	220	2.2	84	0.00	0.00
0.30	0.34	—	0.40	1.50	120.0	—	—	4.1	100	0.00	80.0	150	170	170	3.0	91	0.00	0.00
0.14	0.00	0.11	0.02	0.17	1.7	0.2	—	3.8	58	0.14	8.5	54	318	151	0.2	1	0.00	0.00
0.00	0.00	0.01	0.00	0.00	0.1	0.0	4.3	0.1	2	0.15	5.4	6	17	1	0.1	1	0.00	2.93
0.00	0.02	0.02	0.00	0.03	0.7	0.1	0.0	0.1	16	0.17	6.5	24	42	10	0.2	2	0.00	2.50
—	—	—	—	—	—	0.1	—	—	26	0.23	—	—	62	10	—	2	0.00	
—	—	—	—	—	—	0.0	—	—	0	0.00	—	—	—	25	—	2	0.00	
—	—	—	—	—	—	—	—	—	19	0.18	—	—	87	32	—	3	0.00	
—	—	—	—	—	—	0.0	—	—	1	0.00	—	—	—	5	—	4	0.00	
0.11	0.11	1.01	0.01	0.07	5.0	0.1	—	1.2	37	0.88	7.4	47	64	14	0.3	5	0.00	0.00
—	—	—	—	—	—	0.0	—	—	0	0.36	—	40	75	0	—	—	0.00	
—	—	—	—	—	—	0.0	—	—	0	0.36	—	20	50	0	—	2	0.00	
—	—	—	—	—	—	0.0	—	—	0	0.72	—	40	70	0	—	3	0.00	
—	—	—	—	—	—	0.0	—	—	0	1.44	—	60	140	0	—	5	0.00	
—	—	—	—	—	—	0.0	—	—	20	0.00	—	20	45	15	—	—	0.00	
0.07	0.20	1.87	0.10	0.00	27.5	0.0	0.0	0.3	110	11.92	429.1	631	1311	18	5.9	3	0.00	197.80
0.00	0.00	0.00	0.00	0.00	0.0	0.0	0.0	0.0	217	0.40	1.5	343	505	4	0.0	6	0.00	0.00
0.00	0.00	0.00	0.00	0.00	0.0	0.0	0.0	0.0	0	0.00	0.0	0	0	1259	0.0	0	0.00	0.00
—	—	—	—	0.00	—	0.0	—	—	0	0.00	—	—	5	40	—	27	0.00	0.00
0.09	0.21	1.59	0.05	0.00	93.6	0.0	0.0	0.0	3	0.66	3.9	52	80	2	0.3	8	0.00	0.00
0.51	0.01	0.10	—	—	—	—	—	—	13	0.40	—	—	164	103	—	11	0.00	0.00
0.20	0.18	3.27	0.41	0.00	36.0	36.2	0.0	3.5	46	1.67	52.8	94	1154	2846	0.6	67	0.00	0.00

PAGE KEY: A-108 Beverage and Beverage Mixes A-112 Other Beverages A-112 Beverages, Alcoholic A-114 Candies and Confections, Gum A-114 Cereals, Breakfast Type A-118 Cheese and Cheese Substitutes A-120 Dairy Products and Substitutes A-122 Desserts A-128 Dessert Toppings A-128 Eggs, Substitutes, and Egg Dishes A-130 Ethnic Foods A-130 Fast Foods/Restaurants A-140 Fats, Oils, Margarines, Shortenings, and Substitutes A-142 Fish, Seafood, and Shellfish A-142 Food Additives A-142 Fruit, Vegetable, and Blended Juices A-144 Fruits A-146 Grains, Flours, and Fractions A-148 Grain Products, Prepared and Baked Goods

Code	Food Name	Unit/ Amt	Wt (g)	Energy (Kcal)	Prot (g)	Carb (g)	Fiber (g)	Fat (g)	Sat (g)	Mono (g)	Poly (g)	Chol (mg)	Vit A (RE)
90602	Catsup, low sod, pkt	1 ea	6	6	0	2	0	0	0.0	0.0	0.0	0	6
27036	Chutney	1 Tbs	17	26	0	7	0	0	0.0	0.0	0.0	0	11
27004	Horseradish, prep, tsp	1 tsp	5	2	0	1	0	0	0.0	0.0	0.0	0	–
27000	Ketchup	1 Tbs	15	16	0	4	0	0	0.0	0.0	0.0	0	15
27058	Mustard, dijon, Grey Poupon	0.5 cup	125	151	8	13	1	11	0.5	3.9	3.0	0	12
26435	Mustard, honey	1 tsp	6	12	0	2	0	0	0.0	0.0	0.0	0	0
435	Mustard, yellow, prep	1 tsp	5	3	0	0	0	0	0.0	0.1	0.0	0	1
27169	Olives, black, jumbo, cnd	1 ea	8	7	0	0	0	1	0.1	0.4	0.0	0	3
27042	Olives, green, stuffed	10 ea	40	41	1	1	0	4	0.6	3.2	0.4	0	25
27192	Pickles, bread & butter, chips, original	28 g	28	25	0	6	0	0	0.0	0.0	0.0	0	0
90583	Pickles, dill, chpd/diced	1 cup	143	26	1	6	2	0	0.1	0.0	0.1	0	46
27013	Pickles, dill, slices	10 ea	70	13	0	3	1	0	0.0	0.0	0.1	0	22
27031	Pickles, sweet, low sod, slices	10 pce	60	70	0	19	1	0	0.0	0.0	0.1	0	7
90585	Pickles, sweet, slices	1 ea	7	8	0	2	0	0	0.0	0.0	0.0	0	1
27049	Pickles, tsukemono, Japanese	1 cup	135	29	2	6	4	0	0.1	0.0	0.1	0	13
27104	Pickles, whole	0.5 ea	28	4	0	0	0	0	0.0	0.0	0.0	0	0
27052	Relish, pickle, sweet	1 cup	245	318	1	86	3	1	0.1	0.5	0.3	0	39
27048	Relish, vegetable	1 cup	140	50	1	12	1	0	0.0	0.1	0.1	0	37
51011	Sauce, cocktail, seafood	0.25 cup	78	100	1	24	0	0	0.0	0.0	0.0	0	100
52149	Sauce, hot, jalapeno	1 ea	14	5	0	1	0	0	0.0	0.0	0.0	0	0
53525	Sauce, soy, f/hydrolyzed veg prot	1 Tbs	18	7	0	1	0	0	0.0	0.0	0.0	0	0
53471	Sauce, tabasco, rts	1 tsp	5	1	0	0	0	0	0.0	0.0	0.0	0	8
91056	Sauce, taco, green, med	1 Tbs	15	5	0	1	0	0	–	–	–	0	1
27161	Sauce, teriyaki, rts	1 Tbs	16	21	0	4	0	1	0.1	0.2	0.3	0	0
53099	Sauce, worcestershire	1 cup	272	182	0	45	0	0	0.0	0.0	0.0	0	30
27092	Spread, pimento/pimiento	2 Tbs	30	90	2	3	1	8	2.0	–	–	10	20
27061	Vinegar, apple cider, 50 grain	1 Tbs	15	1	0	0	0	0	–	–	–	0	0
27130	Vinegar, balsamic, 60 grain	1 Tbs	15	10	0	2	0	0	–	–	–	0	0
27007	Vinegar, cider	1 Tbs	15	2	0	1	0	0	0.0	0.0	0.0	0	0
27202	Vinegar, distilled, white	1 Tbs	15	0	0	0	0	0	0.0	0.0	0.0	0	0
27204	Vinegar, red wine	1 Tbs	16	0	0	0	0	0	0.0	0.0	0.0	0	0
27033	Vinegar, rice, white	1 Tbs	15	0	0	0	0	0	0.0	0.0	0.0	0	0
Salsas													
4016	Salsa, con queso, low fat, Tostitos	70 g	70	80	2	8	2	3	2.0	–	–	10	0
53642	Salsa, green chili, mild	2 Tbs	30	8	0	1	0	0	–	–	–	–	14
53638	Salsa, green, jalapena	2 Tbs	30	10	0	1	0	0	–	–	–	0	9
53645	Salsa, picante, med	2 Tbs	30	8	0	1	0	0	–	–	–	0	14
53639	Salsa, thick 'n chunky, hot	2 Tbs	30	9	0	1	0	0	–	–	–	0	16

PAGE KEY: A-154 Granola Bars, Cereal Bars, Diet Bars, Scones, and Tarts A-154 Meals and Dishes A-160 Meats A-164 Nuts, Seeds, and Products A-166 Poultry A-166 Salad Dressings, Dips, and Mayonnaise A-170 Salads A-170 Sandwiches A-172 Sauces and Gravies A-174 Snack Foods—Chips, Pretzels, Popcorn A-178 Soups Stews and Chilis A-184 Spices, Flavors, and Seasonings A-184 Sports Bars and Drinks A-186 Supplemental Foods and Formulas A-186 Sweeteners and Sweet Substitutes A-188 Vegetables and Legumes A-200 Weight Loss Bars & Drinks A-200 Miscellaneous

Thia (mg)	Ribo (mg)	Niac (mg NE)	Vit B6 (mg)	Vit B12 (µg)	Fol (µg)	Vit C (mg)	Vit D (IU)	Vit E (mg AT)	Cal (mg)	Iron (mg)	Magn (mg)	Phos (mg)	Pota (mg)	Sodi (mg)	Zinc (mg)	Wat (%)	Alco (g)	Caff (g)
0.00	0.00	0.07	0.00	0.00	0.9	0.9	0.0	0.1	1	0.03	1.3	2	29	1	0.0	67	0.00	0.00
0.00	0.00	0.12	0.01	0.00	2.2	3.9	–	0.1	5	0.18	4.7	7	70	3	0.0	58	0.00	0.00
0.00	0.00	0.01	0.00	0.00	2.9	1.2	0.0	0.0	3	0.01	1.4	2	12	16	0.0	85	0.00	0.00
0.00	0.00	0.20	0.02	0.00	2.2	2.3	0.0	0.2	3	0.10	3.3	6	72	178	0.0	67	0.00	0.00
0.17	0.11	2.55	0.10	0.00	0.0	1.0	–	–	170	3.25	–	273	222	3030	1.9	70	0.00	0.00
–	–	–	–	–	–	0.1	–	–	3	0.09	–	–	8	42	–	44	0.00	0.00
0.00	0.00	0.01	0.00	0.00	0.4	0.1	–	0.1	4	0.09	1.9	4	8	56	0.0	82	0.00	0.00
0.00	0.00	0.00	0.00	0.00	0.0	0.1	0.0	0.2	8	0.28	0.3	0	1	75	0.0	84	0.00	0.00
0.00	0.00	0.03	0.01	0.00	1.4	4.8	0.0	1.1	21	0.63	7.9	7	28	826	0.1	80	0.00	0.00
–	–	–	–	–	–	0.0	–	–	0	0.00	–	–	–	170	–	76	0.00	0.00
0.01	0.03	0.09	0.01	0.00	1.4	2.7	0.0	0.2	13	0.75	15.7	30	166	1833	0.2	92	0.00	0.00
0.00	0.01	0.03	0.00	0.00	0.7	1.3	0.0	0.1	6	0.37	7.7	15	81	897	0.1	92	0.00	0.00
0.00	0.01	0.10	0.00	0.00	0.6	0.7	0.0	0.1	2	0.34	2.4	7	19	11	0.0	65	0.00	0.00
0.00	0.00	0.00	0.00	0.00	0.1	0.1	0.0	0.0	0	0.03	0.3	1	2	66	0.0	65	0.00	0.00
0.00	0.05	0.33	0.14	0.00	34.4	0.5	0.0	0.1	51	0.49	13.5	50	801	720	0.3	91	0.00	0.00
0.00	0.00	0.05	0.00	–	1.1	1.0	–	–	21	0.10	2.8	15	33	327	0.0	94	0.00	0.00
0.00	0.07	0.56	0.03	0.00	2.5	2.5	–	0.1	7	2.13	12.2	34	61	1987	0.3	62	0.00	0.00
0.05	0.03	0.43	0.07	0.00	18.4	11.2	0.0	0.2	24	0.58	18.1	32	247	12	0.2	90	0.00	0.00
–	–	–	–	–	–	2.4	–	–	0	0.00	–	–	–	910	–	–	0.00	0.00
–	–	–	–	–	–	0.0	–	–	0	0.00	–	–	–	109	–	92	0.00	0.00
0.00	0.01	0.50	0.02	0.00	2.3	0.0	–	0.0	1	0.27	1.1	17	27	1024	0.1	76	0.00	0.00
0.00	0.00	0.00	0.00	0.00	0.0	0.2	–	–	1	0.05	0.6	1	6	30	0.0	95	0.00	0.00
–	–	–	–	–	–	0.7	–	–	1	0.00	–	–	–	96	–	91	0.00	0.00
0.00	0.00	0.09	0.00	0.00	0.5	0.0	–	0.0	1	0.09	1.3	3	8	159	0.0	69	0.00	0.00
0.18	0.34	1.89	0.00	0.00	0.0	35.4	0.0	0.0	291	14.42	35.4	163	2176	2666	0.5	70	0.00	0.00
–	–	–	–	–	–	0.0	–	–	60	0.00	–	–	–	290	–	–	0.00	0.00
–	–	–	–	–	–	0.1	–	–	1	0.09	–	–	–	3	–	99	0.00	0.00
–	–	–	–	–	–	0.1	–	–	5	0.11	–	–	12	4	–	84	0.00	0.00
0.00	0.00	0.00	0.00	0.00	0.0	0.0	0.0	0.0	1	0.09	3.3	1	15	0	0.0	94	0.00	0.00
–	–	–	–	–	–	0.0	–	–	0	0.00	–	–	0	0	–	100	0.00	0.00
–	–	–	–	–	–	0.0	–	–	0	0.00	–	–	0	0	–	100	0.00	0.00
–	–	–	–	–	–	0.0	–	–	0	0.00	–	–	–	0	–	95	0.00	0.00
–	–	–	–	–	–	0.0	–	–	40	0.00	–	–	–	560	–	80	0.00	0.00
–	–	–	–	–	–	4.1	–	–	5	0.28	–	–	–	175	–	92	0.00	0.00
–	–	–	–	–	–	3.6	–	–	5	0.11	–	–	–	181	–	91	0.00	0.00
–	–	–	–	–	–	2.5	–	–	4	0.01	–	–	–	150	–	92	0.00	0.00
–	–	–	–	–	–	1.6	–	–	3	0.01	–	–	–	133	–	92	0.00	0.00

Answers to Critical Thinking Questions

Chapter 1

1. Supplements purchased in a store can provide vitamins and minerals. However, that is all they provide. Foods, on the other hand, supply not only vitamins and minerals but also carbohydrates, proteins, fats, and fiber. These provide energy and bulk for a healthy digestive system. The phytochemicals present are another bonus (see Chapter 2 for details). In addition, it is possible to overdose on certain vitamins and minerals when supplements are used.
2. A diet consisting primarily of foods derived from animal sources contains mostly proteins and fats, with a high percentage of fats as saturated fats. Saturated fats lead to a rise in blood cholesterol in many people. High blood cholesterol is linked to increased risk of cardiovascular disease. A diet high in saturated fat is also related to increased risk of prostate cancer in men.

   Fruits and vegetables are rich in fiber, which helps decrease blood cholesterol and increases the rate of muscle contractions in the gastrointestinal tract. Fruits and vegetables, for the most part, contain low amounts of fat, if any, and are low in calories, thus helping maintain healthy body weight.

   Early humans lived only 30 years or so. Today our life expectancy is more than double that. History can give us clues to improve our diets, but only actual studies—such as double-blind research—can establish the actual advantages of any diet. Subjects could be placed on one of the two diets and followed for a number of years. Tests such as blood pressure, blood cholesterol, and body weight would show how the diets affect overall health.
3. Unfortunately for Wesley, he is at high risk for developing alcoholism. He should carefully consider the consequences of alcohol use. Wesley may choose to avoid alcohol completely or consume it in moderation only. It may be helpful for him to recognize the signs of alcohol abuse to prevent any problems before they begin.

Chapter 2

1. Increasing one's fruit and vegetable intake can be easy; it just takes planning.
   - Search for fast-food restaurants with a salad bar.
   - Buy a variety of fruits and vegetables at the grocery store.
   - Include a fruit and/or vegetable at every meal.
   - Carry snacks, such as an apple, a banana, or carrots, with you so that, when you get hungry, you can avoid grabbing a candy bar.
   - Buy canned fruits and vegetables. These are convenient, and, because they are canned immediately after harvest, they retain their vitamins and minerals.
   - In the refrigerator, keep a bowl of fresh vegetables handy for snacks.
   - Mostly choose 100% fruit and vegetable juices.
2. Since the typical North American diet consists of many foods high in saturated fat and cholesterol, and low in fiber, Athe should assess her diet with respect to these components. She should list all of the foods she eats, preferably for a whole week, and estimate how much saturated fat, cholesterol, and fiber she consumes. She could use Appendix N in this textbook or the accompanying software. She then should change her eating habits to obtain recommended amounts of saturated fat and cholesterol, and fiber. Most likely, Athe will need to decrease saturated fat and probably cholesterol intake, as well as increase fiber intake.
3. Physical activity would be a healthful addition to the Food Guide Pyramid. We would recommend "Include 60 minutes of activity every day, and some strength training and stretching every other day." With regards to alcohol use, Chapter 8 notes it does have some health benefits. We would say "Possibly consume alcohol on a moderate basis, but talk to your physician first, since for some people any alcohol use is hazardous to health."

Chapter 3

1. The cells lining the small intestine undergo a rapid turnover, every 2 to 5 days. If new cells are not produced because cancer therapy has blocked cell production, new intestinal cells to replace those that have died will not appear. The intestine will then lose much of its absorptive capacity, and nutrients that remain in the intestinal lumen unabsorbed will cause diarrhea as they attract fluid into the intestinal lumen. The intestine will also not be able to absorb much water, which also contributes to diarrhea.
2. The small intestine is the most important absorption site in the digestive system because of its large surface area. Since much of the young girl's small intestine was removed, many of the nutrients she consumes are escaping absorption. It is likely that only a highly refined diet or intravenous total parenteral nutrition therapy will succeed in keeping her adequately nourished.
3. Digestive enzymes work efficiently no matter what combination of food is eaten. For this reason, there is no benefit to eating only certain foods at certain times of the day. If any weight is lost this way, it is because Joci is controlling the amount of energy she is consuming. Laxatives and enemas are usually not necessary. Ordinary constipation can be remedied by increasing

the fiber content of the diet, drinking adequate amounts of water, and engaging in regular physical activity. Defecating soon after the urge is also helpful. Furthermore, continued use of potent laxatives is not only expensive but may lead to dependency because they can damage the body's natural ability of the bowel to function.

Chapter 4

1. Mitochondria are the sites for cellular ATP synthesis—the powerhouses of the cell. Aerobic metabolism also takes place in the mitochondria. Wherever there is a need for the production of large amounts of ATP, such as in muscle cells, mitochondria will be found in greater numbers. The greater the need for energy, the greater the number of mitochondria.
2. The liver produces many compounds for export into the blood and eventual use by other organs. This synthesis requires much input of hydrogen, and the coenzyme NADPH + H^+ typically provides the hydrogen needed.
3. Body fat is gained when energy consumption exceeds energy expenditure. This is true whether the energy (calories) comes from carbohydrate, protein, or fat. A great excess of carbohydrate intake can promote fat synthesis. If eaten in excess, the same is true of protein. Unless Stephanie learns to control the amount of energy she consumes, she will continue to gain fat even though she is on a "fat-free diet." Furthermore, this lack of fat can be harmful because fat provides essential fatty acids to the body and performs a variety of other needed functions.

Chapter 5

1. Diet pills, even over-the-counter ones, are expensive. The psyllium in Celia's diet pills is a fiber that produces bulk, which helps make the dieter feel satiated. However, instead of buying expensive pills that make her feel full so that she will not each as much, Celia should simply change her eating habits to include more fruits and vegetables. Not only do they contain fiber, but they also supply vitamins and minerals. Beans, whole grains, oats, fruits, and vegetables all contain ample fiber and are great low-energy sources of nutrients.
2. A key recommendation is to receive regular examinations by a physician to find colon cancer early if and when it occurs. A diet rich in vegetables may prevent the disease, as well as regular exercise. Meeting calcium, selenium, and folate needs is also important. Things to limit or avoid are obesity, smoking, saturated fat, and red meat, especially processed meats. These are just some of the possible recommendations.
3. Foods that remain in the mouth, usually caught between the teeth, are a source of food that bacteria can metabolize. As a byproduct of this metabolism, bacteria produce acids, which can decay tooth enamel, causing caries. Chewing sugar-free gum after meals decreases the risk of caries because chewing stimulates the secretion of saliva, which helps dislodge foods that remain in the mouth. Sugar-free gums also contain sugar substitutes, which bacteria can't metabolize. In addition, saliva has a higher pH than the acids produced by bacterial metabolism. This helps neutralize the acids.

Chapter 6

1. The general term *fats* refers to lipids in foods without reference to their structure. Only dietary fats with a high proportion of saturated fatty acids (or trans fatty acids) have been associated with an increased risk of cardiovascular disease. In the body, fat (primarily in the form of triglycerides) has many beneficial functions. Triglycerides form the main energy stores in the body and can release fatty acids, which serve as fuel for many cells, such as those in muscles at rest and during light activity. Stored fat insulates the body and protects vital organs. Absorption of fat-soluble vitamins from the intestine is aided by their association with dietary fats. In addition, the two essential fatty acids, linoleic acid and alpha-linolenic acid, are not synthesized by the body and must be in the diet to maintain health. Thus, some fat is needed in the diet; moderation of intake, not elimination, is the goal.
2. Added fats are not the only sources of fat in the diet. To consume a low-fat diet, one must also be aware of common sources of hidden fat in the diet. So-called hidden fat can often be found in crackers, cheeses, whole milk, cookies, pastries, french fries, sauces, and meats. Refer to the Nutrition Facts label (when available) to determine the fat content of a specific food. Another effective way of reducing fat intake is to consume moderate portion sizes of foods that have a high fat content.
3. The amount of cholesterol carried in HDL (high-density lipoprotein) also indicates the risk of cardiovascular disease. If one's HDL is greater than 60 mg/dl, the risk of cardiovascular disease is low. If it's less than 40 mg/dl, the risk is high. The ratio of total serum cholesterol to HDL-cholesterol is also a good indicator of one's risk. If the ratio exceeds 4 to 1, the risk is high. Since Juan's total cholesterol was 210 mg/dl and HDL-cholesterol was 65 mg/dl, the ratio was 3.2 to 1 (210 mg/dl ÷ 65 mg/dl), which means he has a low risk for developing cardiovascular disease. LDL-cholesterol, which is 125 mg/dl, is also not elevated (LDL = total cholesterol − HDL − (triglycerides ÷ 5); 210 mg/dl − 65 mg/dl − [100 mg/dl ÷ 5] = 125 mg/dl).

Chapter 7

1. PKU is the abbreviation for the disease *phenylketonuria*. The liver of a person with phenylketonuria cannot readily convert phenylalanine, an essential amino acid, to tyrosine, a nonessential amino acid. Insufficient enzyme action causes this defect.

   The inability to metabolize excess phenylalanine to tyrosine leads to the formation of abnormal products that arise from alternative metabolic pathways; these products can cause mental retardation. Thus, it is vital to determine which infants have PKU, since the amount of phenylalanine in their diets must be monitored. However, because it is an essential amino acid, some phenylalanine must be consumed. Since phenylalanine cannot be sufficiently metabolized to tyrosine, the latter must now be considered an essential amino acid for people with PKU.
2. Protein synthesis is a complex process by which a specific sequence and number of amino acids determine the primary structure of a protein. If a given amino acid is not present during protein synthesis, production will stop. In other words, protein is an all-or-none process: All of the amino acids necessary to make the protein must be available, or the protein will not be made at all. A mixed diet of plant products will likely contain enough of all nine essential amino acids, so the all-or-none principle won't typically be an issue in diet planning, even in vegetarianism.
3. Much of the nitrogen that is part of amino acids is converted into urea in the liver as part of amino acid metabolism. This urea is excreted by the kidneys. Samantha's mother shows evidence of kidney problems. Overall, Samantha's mother is consuming more protein than her kidney function can tolerate. Lowering protein in her diet would help.

Chapter 8

1. Many risks and diseases correlate with behaviors often combined with alcohol abuse. Unplanned sexual activity can lead to the contraction of STDs and other diseases, feelings of guilt, unplanned pregnancy, and

toxicity to a fetus. If property is damaged, others can be harmed, and the persons responsible must deal with the legal and financial consequences. Both cigarettes and excessive alcohol can lead to cancer. When alcohol is used, the liver and other gastrointestinal tract organs can be harmed. The addition of smoking can compound poor health by increasing the risk of oral cancer.

2. Typical signs of alcohol abuse in teenagers are withdrawal from family activities, poor (failing) school performance, and increased colds and other general ills. The person may also make references to suicide.
3. There is no one simple answer to the problems of campus binge drinking, but there are a number of actions you plan to take to combat the epidemic. As president of your university, you may publicize that 41% of all academic problems stem from alcohol abuse, and 28% of the students who are dropping out of the school are doing so in part because of alcohol-related course failures. You may want the students to know binge drinking has caused many injuries and even deaths on campus, and you may publicize the names of the victims and the circumstances under which they were hospitalized or died: circumstances such as car accidents, murder, suicide, rape, alcohol poisoning, and personal injures. Faculty and student leaders may be asked to schedule regular campuswide seminars for students to help them take charge of staying sober. Alcohol-free dorms may be the rule, and alcohol-free social events on campus may be considered a high priority. Alcohol counseling may be made available on a confidential basis through the student health center and local social service organizations. AA may be invited to campus to speak about its programs and institute a campus chapter.

Chapter 9

1. Many vitamins, such as the water-soluble ones, can often be excreted when taken in excess; however, the fat-soluble vitamins are not as readily excreted. Vitamin A in particular can accumulate in large amounts, causing toxic effects. These effects can occur at just 2 to 4 times or more than the Daily Values with regular usage of such excess quantities. Excessive intakes of some water-soluble vitamins can also be toxic, such as vitamin B-6.
2. Some cereal manufacturers add beta-carotene to their products to reduce the risk of vitamin A toxicity. This is because the body converts beta-carotene to vitamin A only if it is needed. Once the body has enough vitamin A, the remainder stays in the beta-carotene form, which is nontoxic. Some supplement manufacturers are also using this principle by supplying some vitamin A content as beta-carotene.
3. A possible explanation for the lack of clot dissolution in Tim's leg is that he has been consuming many foods rich in vitamin K, such as dark green leafy vegetables, soybean oil, and members of the cabbage family. Vitamin K is also produced by the intestinal bacteria. This vitamin assists in clot formation and is antagonistic to oral anticoagulant medications. If the vitamin K is not reduced in Tim's diet, the anticoagulant therapy won't be very effective.

Chapter 10

1. People with alcoholism usually have unbalanced diets, which can impair absorption of vitamins and minerals from the GI tract. An associated problem is poor metabolism. The B-vitamins are essential for metabolism: gluconeogenesis, lipogenesis, lipolysis, and overall carbohydrate metabolism. Alcohol consumption decreases the absorption of many B-vitamins, such as thiamin, riboflavin, niacin, and folate. All of these vitamins are important in maintaining proper metabolic and nervous system function.
2. Of course niacin will cure the disease, as pellagra results from a niacin deficiency. Protein foods contain the amino acid tryptophan, some more than others. This amino acid can be converted into niacin in the body, thereby supplying the body with the vitamin, and so cure the disease.
3. Humans must obtain vitamin C from foods because the body cannot synthesize it. A major function of this vitamin is to promote the formation of collagen, an important protein found in connective tissue. Collagen is an integral component of bone, skin, and blood vessels. Thus, a low intake of vitamin C will impair wound healing. Deficiency can also lead to scurvy, whose symptoms include bleeding gums and pinpoint hemorrhages on the skin.

   Vitamin C has antioxidant capabilities. It may work with vitamin E against free radicals and may help "reactivate" vitamin E so that it can continue to function. Vitamin C also enhances iron absorption, assists in carnitine production, and synthesizes norepinephrine, a neurotransmitter.

   Finally, vitamin C is essential for lymphocytic activity within the immune system. Since it assists in the production of lymphocytes, maintaining appropriate vitamin C intake gives the body the building blocks it needs to fight off infections. However, vitamin C does not *cure* the common cold or cardiovascular disease.

Chapter 11

1. When doing physical work, such as mowing the lawn, one perspires. The degree of perspiration varies among people and depends on the time of day. Muscle strength and endurance decline significantly when there is a 3% loss of body weight. Symptoms such as thirst may indicate a 2% loss of body weight caused by dehydration. With greater water loss, a headache and dizziness may develop. Even further water loss may induce a coma.

   Any person who anticipates significant loss of body water through perspiration would benefit from hydrating before the activity, just as in preparation for an athletic event. Doing so will minimize dehydration. Drinking fluids during such exertion is also helpful.
2. Almost all foods contain sodium. Most of the sodium in our diets is added during food processing, during cooking, and at mealtimes. The American Heart Association recommends that all people limit their sodium intake to no more than 2.4 g/day. Still, sodium is essential to maintenance of normal fluid balance throughout the body and to normal nerve impulse conduction. If sodium intake is inadequate, neuromuscular symptoms will appear, including muscle weakness, headache, irritability, and confusion.
3. Calcium is needed for normal bone growth and development. Bones serve as reservoirs of calcium for blood calcium homeostasis. Regulation of blood calcium may necessitate the resorption of bone mineral deposits for the release of calcium from bone. Thus, bone mineralization is vital before and during adolescence, when the greatest amount of bone development occurs. Manuela is already an adult, but she can still consume calcium in amounts sufficient to decrease the need for bone demineralization.

   Some of the richest sources of calcium are milk and sardines, which Manuela, a vegan, will not eat. As an alternative, she should become aware of which vegetables contain calcium, but most are poor sources. She should also choose calcium-fortified foods, such as some brands of orange juice. However, if she cannot meet her calcium needs by modifying her diet, based on a nutrient analysis of her current intake, calcium supplements are advised.

Chapter 12

1. Vitamin C is important not only for collagen synthesis but also for treating iron

deficiency anemia, since it enhances iron absorption in the GI tract. Vitamin C increases absorption of nonheme iron by donating an electron to the ferric form (Fe^{3+}) of iron to create the ferrous form (Fe^{2+}) of iron, which is absorbed better, and then chelating it as well.

2. For zinc to be considered a reasonable treatment for the common cold, we need more definitive studies. Research results are quite mixed at this time. Further studies should include a greater number of participants, and determination of the presence of a cold should be standardized. Finally, researchers should ensure that the placebo lozenge has the same flavor as the zinc lozenge. In this way, positive or negative results will not be attributed to the good or poor flavor of the lozenges. Overall, more convincing evidence is necessary for zinc lozenges to be considered a scientifically proven cold treatment.
3. The mineral selenium is a cofactor for the activity of the enzyme glutathione peroxidase. This enzyme participates in a system that metabolizes peroxides into less toxic alcohol derivatives and water. Peroxides tend to become free radicals, which in turn can attack and break down cell membranes, causing cell damage. Selenium is considered to be important in protecting heart cells and other cells against oxidative damage. In addition, because it reduces the amount of free radical damage to cells, selenium may be important in protecting against cancer. The antioxidant enzyme thioredoxin also utilizes selenium.

Chapter 13

1. Energy intake must equal energy output for body weight to remain the same. Weight increases when energy intake is more than output. Since basal metabolism decreases as we age, either energy intake or energy output must be modified to maintain the same weight.

   Energy balance can be attained in this case by increasing physical activity, a facet of life that tends to decrease with aging. Taking up a sport, jogging, or even parking the car farther away from a building to increase walking distance are all good strategies. People tend to become less active and therefore expend less energy without reducing food intake as they age. By increasing physical activity, energy balance and desirable weight can be maintained.
2. Although Hal has seen a steady decrease in his weight for the duration of his diet thus far, his body has built-in mechanisms that tend to fight weight loss. One of those factors is his basal metabolism. This tends to decrease to conserve energy as the number of calories in the diet decreases. Also, lipoprotein lipase activity increases in the body, which increases lipid uptake into adipose cells. The increased activity of this enzyme allows the body to take up fats more efficiently from the blood after the dieting has stopped.

   Thus, the body resists weight loss by physiological means; however, it may finally surrender to persistent dieting, and Hal will continue to lose weight as long as he continues to diet.
3. For a weight-loss plan to be successful, the person must be mentally prepared for the time and commitment involved. Weight loss requires a certain amount of time for planning meals, purchasing more healthy foods, and devising a plan for when temptations arise. This woman obviously has her hands full with other obligations at this time. Because of her busy schedule, it would be difficult to follow a restricted eating plan. Weight-loss failure can be discouraging. It would be wise for this woman to wait until her schedule lightens up a bit and, instead, focus now on weight maintenance.

Chapter 14

1. Marty has enhanced his cardiovascular fitness, a laudable goal. In addition, after a period of training, muscle cells worked on a regular basis will make more mitochondria. Since mitochondria are the sites of aerobic metabolism, this means that more ATP can be generated. ATP is a necessary component for muscle action.
2. Many wrestlers and other athletes lose weight quickly by losing large amounts of water, usually by sweating. By doing so, an athlete can compete in a lower weight class and thus gain an advantage over an opponent. However, losing weight this way can significantly impede performance. Over time, repeated dehydration episodes can lead to serious complications, such as kidney failure. Athletes also risk developing heat stress during the event.

   The loss of water before a competition is the quick method of losing weight. But, if an athlete is serious about his or her sport, a gradual change in diet to create the best possible weight/muscle composition should be the goal.
3. A person's appropriate dietary intake of protein should be determined using the RDA for protein: 0.8 g/kg body weight. Athletes could increase their protein intake to 1.2 to 2 g/kg body weight to supply the amount of protein needed for muscle growth and development, but clear evidence for the benefits of such an intake is lacking. Overall, about 15% of energy intake as protein is often recommended, and no more than 35% of energy intake. About 50 to 60% of energy intake should be supplied by carbohydrates, leaving up to 30% of energy intake to be supplied by fat. A high carbohydrate intake is necessary to supply glucose for glycogen synthesis; glycogen is the storage form of glucose in muscles.

Chapter 15

1. Signs that indicate an eating disorder include the following:
   a. Refusal to eat much food
   b. Obsession with being and looking thin
   c. Obsession with counting calories
   d. Not wanting to eat with others (e.g., refusing to go to a restaurant)
   e. Continually criticizing one's looks and comparing oneself to others, especially slender people
   f. Being convinced that one is fat
2. In addition to the detrimental social aspects of anorexia nervosa, such as alienation from others, there are serious physical consequences. Nutritional deficiencies may develop that can cause an imbalance of the sex hormones. Jennifer has already stopped menstruating, compromising her fertility. The disease may also prevent her from gaining enough weight to support the developing fetus if she were to become pregnant later. Starvation leads to a loss of lean body tissue, such as muscle. The heart rate decreases as metabolism slows, which causes the person to become easily tired, increasing the need for sleep. Since tissue is lost from the heart muscle as well as from the rest of the body, heart function may also be impaired. Another potential problem is anemia caused by inadequate nutrient intake.
3. One of the most important topics Tom should discuss is proper nutrition. Using the concepts of adequacy, balance, and moderation, he can teach students about their diets. He could also present case studies of real people who have anorexia nervosa and bulimia nervosa, so that his students can see firsthand the outcome of these diseases. Tom should also focus on increasing awareness of the challenges facing these young adults. The prepuberty and teenage years are a time of self-evaluation and criticism. It is important for Tom to help his students feel good from within by emphasizing the importance of self-worth, regardless of one's physical appearance. Finally, Tom can teach his students how to

cope with difficult situations by showing them how to alleviate stress in positive and constructive ways.

Chapter 16

1. Many changes occur in a woman during pregnancy. Her uterus and breasts grow, and her total blood volume increases. The placenta develops, the heart and kidneys work harder, stores of body fat increase, and, toward the latter part of the pregnancy, mammary glands prepare to produce milk. The nutrients needed to support these changes are listed below:
   a. Increased energy, about 400 more kcal/day is necessary, especially during the second and third trimesters. This amount should allow adequate weight gain (25 to 35 lb for a woman who begins pregnancy at a healthy weight).
   b. Protein needs are also increased, by about 25 g/day. She likely eats enough protein to meet her needs already. This extra protein should help support adequate growth.
   c. Carbohydrate intake should be at least 175 g/day, partly to prevent ketosis.
   d. Vitamin D should be increased to 10 µg/day by either increasing sunlight exposure or increasing vitamin D–fortified milk consumption. This amount will support fetal bone growth.
   e. Folate intake should increase to 600 µg DFE/day to support red blood cell formation and DNA synthesis.
   f. Iron intake should increase to about 27 mg/day. This will support hemoglobin synthesis.
   g. Calcium is needed to promote mineralization of fetal bones and teeth. Calcium intake should meet 1000 mg/day.
   h. Zinc is important for growth and development. Intake should increase to 11 mg/day to support this.

   These nutrients should be obtained mostly from foods. However, prenatal supplements can aid in supplying these nutrients to the pregnant woman, especially in circumstances that may prevent her from adequately consuming sufficient nutrients from foods.
2. Since Hannah is below a healthy body weight, she needs to consume additional energy to nourish her fetus as well as to nourish her own growing body. Her food selections should emphasize fortified whole grains, fruits, vegetables, and calcium sources. She also needs a good source of protein at each meal to build body tissues. It would be beneficial for her to visit her physician regularly throughout the pregnancy.
3. As the pregnancy advances, the uterus continues to grow to accommodate the growing fetus. As it does, it presses against the stomach as well as the intestines. Also, hormones produced in increased amounts during pregnancy relax muscles. This explains why heartburn may occur; the lower esophageal (cardiac) sphincter relaxes somewhat, allowing some foods and acid to regurgitate back into the esophagus—hence the heartburn. It is recommended that smaller quantities of foods be ingested and that the woman not recline after eating. Since hormones relax muscles, the rate of peristalsis may also decrease and constipation may develop. It would be wise to gradually increase the amount of fiber in Sandy's diet to improve her digestive system's peristaltic activity.

Chapter 17

1. Human milk is low in iron. Although it provides many essential nutrients to the baby, it doesn't meet all of a baby's needs after about 6 months, since iron stores are depleted by this time. This iron deficiency leads to a form of *anemia*. To prevent such iron deficiency anemia in infants, it is wise to begin feeding them iron-fortified cereal between 4 and 6 months of age. In addition, to prevent anemia, some pediatricians recommend giving iron supplements to breastfed infants beginning shortly after birth.
2. Typical breakfast foods include cereal, eggs, toast, and pancakes, but any food can be a breakfast, lunch, or dinner food as long as it is nutrient dense. If Tim doesn't like the traditional breakfast foods but enjoys a sandwich, macaroni and cheese, or yogurt, his parents can offer them. These nutritious foods are no more beneficial at lunchtime than they are at 7 A.M.

   The depletion of carbohydrate stores that occurs during the night can cause children to be lethargic and inattentive in the morning. Eating early in the morning replenishes carbohydrate stores. Many experts believe that the nutrients consumed stimulate attention in children, allowing them to perform better in school.
3. It usually takes a few days for signs of a food allergy to develop. Common allergic symptoms are diarrhea, vomiting, runny nose, wheezing, and swelling. An infection could produce the same symptoms but is usually accompanied by a fever. If Irene and Chris's baby is indeed having an allergic reaction, ceasing to feed the food to the baby should cause the symptoms to disappear. If they do disappear, it is likely that the food caused the allergy. The food can probably be reintroduced later, since babies outgrow most food allergies. Fortunately, the baby did not have the most generalized and severe kind of allergic reaction, an often fatal condition called *anaphylactic shock*.

Chapter 18

1. Science has established a considerable link between nutrition (diet) and health. For example, very-low-fat diets have been shown to reverse atherosclerosis, and weight loss can improve type 2 diabetes in some people by reducing body fat. Although body cells will age no matter what health practices are followed, morbidity can be decreased through diet and lifestyle. A consistently healthful diet and a regimen of regular physical activity have proven effective in maintaining a healthful body: Muscles are firmer, bone fractures are less likely, and the person looks and feels better. The secret to enjoying "youth" throughout life is to establish a healthful physical, mental, and social framework.
2. Though it is true that a 30% energy restriction in laboratory animals increases life expectancy, it is too soon to know the full implications of such a restriction in humans. As well, appetite does not appear to decrease even in laboratory animals who have been restricted for most of their lives, and maintenance of reproductive function is still in question. Most humans would be unwilling to restrict themselves to this degree, and such restriction may not be appropriate in humans. Certainly, childhood is a highly inappropriate time to restrict energy intake, since this is the major time for growth and development. Alexis would do more harm than good by implementing such a plan with her family.
3. The 1994 DSHEA law allows companies to market herbal products without prior approval by FDA as long as they make vague structure/function claims. Jamila has to rely on the truthfulness of the manufacturer of the herbal product concerning any possible health benefits from use. Ideally, Jamila should make sure that any use of herbal products follow four specific guidelines:
   a. Follow label directions carefully and start with a low dose.
   b. Increase the dose gradually as needed, watching for potential side effects. These potential side effects should be listed on the label.
   c. Do not use products that contain mixtures of herbal substances. Many of these products have been especially linked to health problems with use.
   d. Talk to her physician about any such use.

Chapter 19

1. USDA recommends cutting boards with unmarred surfaces made from nonporous materials. These include Plexiglass™, plastic, and marble, which are easy to clean. Grooves or cuts on surfaces provide a "home" where bacteria can thrive. If Jon wants to buy a wooden cutting board, he should plan to clean it using hot, soapy water every time he cuts something. He should also try not to use the same board for both meats and vegetables or fruits. If he must use it for everything, he should cut the vegetables first, wash the board in hot, soapy water, and then cut the meats. Jon should also sanitize any board once a week in a solution of chlorine bleach and water to minimize any bacterial growth.
2. Bacteria thrive at room temperature, especially between 41° and 140°F. Some bacteria cause foodborne illness by releasing endotoxins and some by producing exotoxins. Cooling by refrigeration slows down bacterial growth, but it does not stop it or destroy toxins already produced. Foods left at room temperature for 2 hours, or even 1 hour in hot weather, provide microorganisms with the opportunity to grow. Refrigeration after that time is too late. Diana is correct in wanting to discard the food.
3. Viruses, bacteria, and other microorganisms in foods cause more than 96% of all food-related illness. Only a small minority of people are susceptible to the health effects of food additives, such as sulfites. USDA states that most foodborne illnesses arise from poor food-handling practices by consumers. Thus, Joseph is at more risk from how he stores and prepares food rather than the food additives in the snack cakes he eats on occasion.

Chapter 20

1. Undernourished children (and adults) often show apathy, muscular weakness, and decreased physical activity and work capability. Since undernutrition decreases resistance to disease, undernourished children are likely to have more frequent infections and to recover more slowly from illness than are well-fed children.
2. Where extreme food shortages exist, there is no choice but to supply hungry people with food—they are starving and dying. However, reliance on outside help is not a long-range solution. Rather, developing countries need to develop their economies and infrastructures, so that people are able to produce or buy sufficient amounts of nutritious food to meet their needs. Appropriate development includes many aspects: education, control of population growth (if indicated), availability of machinery and other agricultural tools, and nonfarm employment opportunities. Small farms and businesses should be encouraged. As the overall economy expands, more people will be able to afford nutritious food.
3. For every supporter of biotechnology, there is an equally convinced opponent. The first list here is in support of biotechnology, and the second is in opposition of it.

   Probiotechnology
   - Improved quality of product
   - Increased resistance to certain pests, such as the European corn borer
   - Improved crop yield
   - Faster, more accurate production of improved crop varieties
   - Elimination of certain pests
   - Increased tolerance to droughts
   - Decreased incidence of foodborne illness
   - Decreased need for pesticides and preservatives
   - Improved nutrient content of foods

   Antibiotechnology
   - Potential insect resistance to insecticides that have been genetically engineered into plants
   - Possible addition of allergens to these "new" foods
   - Unnecessary because we have an adequate food supply
   - Unnatural and may harm the environment

   There are other arguments on both sides of this issue, and it will likely be quite some time before all the questions about biotechnology are answered.

Glossary

Medical Terminology to Aid in the Study of Nutrition

Term Meaning

a- Without, from
aden-, adeno- Gland
-algia Pain
aliment Food
-amine Containing nitrogen
andr-, andro- Man or male
apo-, ap- Detached
arteri-, arterio- Artery
arthr-, arthro- Joint
-ase Enzyme
-blast Immature form, embryonic
brady- Slow
buli- Ox
canc-, carcino- Malignancy
cardi-, cardio- Heart
centi- Divided into 100 parts
chol-, chole-, cholo- Bile, gall
cholecyst- Gallbladder
chondr-, chondri-, chondro- Cartilage
chrom-, chromo- Color, colored
-clast Something that breaks
col-, coli-, colo- Colon
cyano-, cyan- Blue
cyt-, cyto- Cell
derm-, dermato- Skin
dextr-, dextro- Right, on or toward the right
duoden-, duodeno- Duodenum
dys- Difficult, painful
ect-, ecto- Without, outside, external
-ectomy Excision of
-ein A protein
em- Blood
-emia In blood
encephal-, encephalo- Brain
endo-, ento-, end-, ent- Within
enter-, entero- Intestine
erythr-, erythro- Red
esophag-, esophago- Esophagus
eu- Well, easy, good
gastr-, gastro-, gastri- Stomach
gen- To become or produce
gloss-, glosso- Tongue
glyco-, glyc- Sugar
gynec-, gyn-, gyne- Women or female (especially female reproductive organs)
hem-, hemat- Blood
hepat-, hepato- Liver
hexa-, hex- Six
histo-, hist- Tissue
homeo-, homoeo-, homoio- Sameness, similarity
hydr-, hydro- Water
hyper- Excessive, above, beyond
hypo-, hyp- Under, beneath, deficient
hyster-, hystero- Uterus
idio- One's own, peculiar to, separate, distinct
ile-, ileo- Ileum
inter- Between, among
intra- Within, during, between layers of
-itis Inflammation of
jejun-, jejuno- Jejunum
kilo- One thousand
lact-, lacti-, lacto- Milk
leuc-, leuk- White, colorless
lev-, levo- Left, toward the left
lip-, lipo- Fat, lipid
litho-, lith- Stone
lymph-, lympho- Waterlike
lysis Destruction
mal- Bad, badly
malac-, malaco- Soft, a condition of abnormal softness
mega-, meg- Large, great
meta- After, later; change, exchange
metallo- Containing metal
micro- Divided into 1 million parts
milli- Divided into 1000 parts
mono- One
morph-, morpho- Form, shape
my-, myo- Muscle
myel-, myelo- Marrow, spinal cord
nas-, naso- Nose, nasal
necr-, necro- Dead
nephr-, nephro- Kidney
neur-, neuro- Nerve
-oid Formed like, resembling
-ol Alcohol
olig-, oligo- Few, scant
-oma Tumor
ophthalmo-, ophthalm- Eye, eyeball
-orex Mouth
-orexis Desire, appetite
-ose Sugar, carbohydrate
-osis Action, process, result, usually abnormal or diseased
ost-, osteo-, oste- Bone
ot- Ear
ovari-, ovario- Ovary
ovo-, ovi Eggs
pan- All
pancreat-, pancreato- Pancreas
para- Beside
parieto- Wall of a cavity, parietal bone
patho-, path- Disease
ped- Child, foot
-penia Without, lack of
-phobia Fear of
-plasm, -plasma Formative, formed, cell or tissue substance
pneum-, pneumo-, pneumono- Lung
-poiesis Production, format
poly- Many, much
post- After
pre- Before
prot-, proto- First
pseud-, pseudo- False
pulmo-, pulmon-, pulmono- Lung
pyel-, pyelo- Pelvis
pyr- Fever, fire
rect-, recto- Rectum
reni-, reno- Kidney
rhin-, rhino- Nose
-rrhagia Rupture, excessive fluid discharge
-rrhea Flow, discharge
sate To fill
scler-, sclero- Hard, hardness
-scopy Viewing
seb-, sebi-, sebo- Hard fat sebum, sebaceous glands
semi- Half
-soma, somat-, somato- Body
-stasia, -stasis Slowing or stopping of
stenosis Narrowing of
stomat-, stomato- Mouth, stoma
-stomy Surgical opening

sub- Under, below
super- Over, above
tachy- Swift, fast
thi-, thio- Containing sulfur
thromb-, thrombo- Blood clot
tox-, toxi-, toxo- Poison
trache-, tracheo- Trachea
-trophy Growth or mutation
ure-, urea-, ureo- Urine
uter-, utero- Uterus
vas-, vaso- Blood vessel
ven-, veni-, veno- Vein
vita- Life
xer-, xero- Dry

Glossary Terms

absorption The process by which substances are taken up from the GI tract and enter the bloodstream or the lymph.

absorptive cells A class of cells, also called *enterocytes*, that line the villi. These villi are fingerlike projections in the small intestine that participate in nutrient absorption.

Acceptable Macronutrient Distribution Range (AMDR) Range of intake for a specific macronutrient that is associated with a reduced risk of chronic diseases while providing for recommended intakes of essential nutrients. AMDR are set for carbohydrate, protein, and fat (various forms); each is intended to provide guidance in dietary planning.

acesulfame K (ay-SUL-fame) An alternative sweetener that yields no energy to the body; it is 200 times sweeter than sucrose.

acetic acid (a-SEE-tic) A two-compound fatty acid that is used in the synthesis of lipids.

$$CH_3{-}\overset{\overset{\displaystyle O}{\|}}{C}{-}OH$$

acetylcholine (a-SEE-toe-coal-ene) A neurotransmitter from nerve endings.

achlorhydria (ay-clor-HIGH-dre-ah) A decrease in stomach acid primarily due to age associated loss of acid-producing gastric cells.

acidic pH A pH less than 7. Lemon juice has an acidic pH.

acquired immunodeficiency syndrome (AIDS) A disorder in which a virus (human immunodeficiency virus [HIV]) infects specific types of immune system cells. This leaves the person with reduced immune function and, in turn, defenseless against numerous infectious agents; typically contributes to the person's death.

actin (AK-tin) A protein in muscle fiber that, together with myosin, is responsible for contraction.

active absorption transport Absorption using a carrier and expending ATP energy. In this way, the absorptive cell absorbs nutrients, such as glucose, when a high concentration of the nutrient is already present in the absorptive cells.

acute alcohol intoxication A temporary deterioration in mental function, accompanied by muscular incoordination and partial paralysis as a result of drinking alcoholic beverages too rapidly.

adenosine diphosphate (ADP) (ah-DEN-o-scene di-FOS-fate) A breakdown product of ATP. ADP is synthesized into ATP using energy from foodstuffs and a phosphate group (abbreviated Pi).

adenosine triphosphate (ATP) (ah-DEN-o-scene tri-FOS-fate) The main energy currency for cells. ATP energy is used to promote ion pumping, enzyme activity, and muscular contraction.

Adequate Intake (AI) Recommendations for nutrient intake when not enough information is available to establish an RDA. AIs are based on observed or experimentally determined estimates of the average nutrient intake that appears to maintain a defined nutritional state (e.g., bone health) in a specific population. Used when no RDA can be set.

adipose tissue (ad-i-POSE) A group of fat-storing cells.

ad libitum (ad-LIB-itum) At one's desire or pleasure.

adrenergic (ADD-ren-er-gic) Relating to actions of epinephrine and norepinephrine.

aerobic (air-ROW-bic) Requiring oxygen.

alcohol Ethyl alcohol (CH_3CH_2OH).

alcohol abuse Severe alcohol-related problems, such as a person's inability to fulfill major obligations, use in hazardous situations (e.g., when driving), related legal problems, or use despite social and interpersonal difficulties.

alcohol dehydrogenase (dee-high-DRO-jen-ase) The enzyme used in alcohol (ethanol) metabolism; the major enzyme used in the liver when alcohol is in low concentration.

alcohol dependence Repeated alcohol-related difficulties, such as a person's inability to control use, spending a great deal of time associated with alcohol use, continued use of alcohol despite physical or psychological consequences, persistent desire or unsuccessful efforts to cut down or control alcohol use, and withdrawal symptoms. Tolerance is also seen.

aldosterone (al-DOS-ter-own) A hormone produced by the adrenal glands that acts on the kidneys to cause sodium reabsorption and, in turn, water conservation.

alkaline pH A pH greater than 7. Baking soda in water yields an alkaline pH.

allergen A foreign protein, or antigen, that induces excess production of certain immune system antibodies; subsequent exposure to the same protein leads to allergic symptoms. Whereas all allergens are antigens, not all antigens are allergens.

allergy A hypersensitive immune response that occurs when antibodies produced by the body react with a protein foreign to the body (antigen).

alpha (α) bond A type of chemical bond that can be broken by human intestinal enzymes in digestion; drawn as C⌞O⌟C.

alpha-linolenic acid (AL-fah-lin-oh-LE-nik) An essential omega-3 fatty acid with 18 carbons and 3 double bonds (C18:3, omega-3).

alpha-tocopherol (to-ca-FUR-all) The most potent form of vitamin E in terms of antioxidant function in humans.

alveoli (al-VE-o-lye) Basic functional units of the lungs.

amenorrhea (A-men-or-ee-a) The absence of three or more consecutive menstrual cycles; the absence of menses in a female.

amines Can refer to hormones made of one or a few amino acids.

amino acid (ah-MEE-noh) The building block for proteins containing a central carbon atom with a nitrogen atom and other atoms attached.

amniotic fluid (am-nee-OTT-ik) Fluid contained in a sac within the uterus. This fluid surrounds and protects the fetus during development.

amphetamine (am-FET-ah-mean) A group of medications that stimulate the central nervous system, among other effects. Abuse is linked to physical and psychological dependence.

amylase (AM-uh-lace) Starch-digesting enzyme from the salivary glands or pancreas.

amylopectin (AM-uh-low-pek-tin) A digestible branched-chain type of starch composed of multiple glucose units.

amylose (AM-uh-los) A digestible straight-chain type of starch made of multiple glucose units.

anabolic/anabolism (an-AH-bol-iz-um) Building compounds.

anaerobic (AN-ah-ROW-bic) Not requiring oxygen.

analog (AN-a-log) A chemical compound that differs slightly from another, usually natural, compound. Analogs generally contain extra or altered chemical groups and may have similar or opposite metabolic effects compared with the native compound.

anal sphincters A group of two sphincters (inner and outer) that help control expulsion of feces from the body.

anaphylactic shock (an-ah-fih-LAK-tic) A severe allergic response that results in lowered blood pressure and respiratory and gastrointestinal distress. This can be fatal.

androgenic (AN-dro-jenic) A general term for hormones that stimulate development in male sex organs—for example, testosterone.

android obesity (AN-droyd) The type of obesity in which fat is stored primarily in the abdominal area; defined as a waist circumference greater than 40 inches (102 centimeters) in men and greater than 35 inches (89 centimeters) in women; closely associated with a high risk for cardiovascular disease, hypertension, and type 2 diabetes.

anemia (ah-NEM-ee-a) Generally refers to a decreased oxygen-carrying capacity of the blood. This can be caused by many factors, such as iron deficiency or blood loss.

anergy (AN-er-jee) Lack of an immune response to foreign compounds entering the body.

angiotensin I (an-jee-oh-TEN-sin) An intermediary compound produced during the body's attempt to conserve water and sodium; it is converted in the lungs to angiotensin II.

angiotensin II A compound produced from angiotensin I, which increases blood vessel constriction and triggers production of the hormone aldosterone.

animal model Study of disease in laboratory animals that duplicates human disease. This can be used to understand more about human disease.

anorexia nervosa (an-oh-REX-ee-uh ner-VOH-sah) An eating disorder involving a psychological loss or denial of appetite and self-starvation, related in part to a distorted body image and to various social pressures commonly associated with puberty.

anthropometry (an-throw-PO-meh-tree) Pertaining to the measurement of body weight and the lengths, circumferences, and thicknesses of parts of the body.

antibody (AN-tih-bod-ee) Blood protein that inactivates foreign proteins found in the body. This helps prevent and control infections.

antibody-mediated immunity Immunity provided by B lymphocytes. Also known as humoral immunity.

antidiuretic hormone (ADH) (an-tie-dye-u-RET-ik) A hormone secreted by the pituitary gland that acts on the kidney to cause a decrease in water excretion. It is also called arginine vasopressin (AVP).

antigen (AN-ti-jen) Any foreign substance, generally large in size, that induces a state of sensitivity and/or resistance to microbes or toxic substances after a lag period; substance that stimulates a specific aspect of the immune system.

antioxidant (an-tie-OX-ih-dant) Generally a compound that stops the damaging effects of reactive substances seeking an electron (i.e., oxidizing agent). This prevents the breakdown of substances in food or the body, particularly lipids. An antioxidant is able to donate electrons to electron-seeking compounds. This in turn reduces electron capture and, thus, breakdown of unsaturated fatty acids and other cell (and food) components by oxidizing agents. Some compounds have antioxidant capabilities (i.e., stop oxidation) but are not electron donors per se.

anus (A-nus) Last portion of the GI tract; serves as an outlet for that organ.

aorta (a-ORT-ah) The major arterial vessel of the body leaving from the left ventricle.

apoferritin (ape-oh-FERR-ih-tin) A protein in the intestinal cell that binds with the ferric form of iron (Fe^{3+}) to form ferritin.

apolipoprotein (ape-oh-LIP-oh-pro-teen) A protein attached to the surface of a lipoprotein or embedded in its outer shell. Apolipoproteins can help enzymes function, act as a lipid-transfer protein, or assist in the binding of a lipoprotein to a cell-surface receptor.

apoptosis (ah-pop-TOE-sis) A process that occurs over time in which enzymes in a cell sets off a series of events that disable numerous cell functions, eventually leading to cell death.

appetite The primarily psychological (external) influences that encourage us to find and eat food, often in the absence of obvious hunger.

arachidonic acid (ar-a-kih-DON-ik) An omega-6 fatty acid with 20 carbon atoms and 4 carbon-carbon double bonds (C20:4, omega-6).

areola (ah-REE-oh-lah) The circular dark area of skin surrounding the nipple of the breast.

ariboflavinosis (ah-rih-bo-flay-vih-NOH-sis) A condition resulting from a lack of riboflavin. The *a* means "without," and the *osis* stands for "a condition of."

arithmetic ratio A series of numbers wherein the difference between each number is the same.

aromatherapy The use of the vapors of essential oils extracted from flowers, leaves, stalks, fruits, and roots for therapeutic purposes.

arrhythmias (ah-RITH-me-ahs) Abnormal heart rhythms which may be too slow, too early, too rapid, or irregular.

arteriole (ar-TEAR-e-ol) A tiny artery branch.

artery A blood vessel that carries blood away from the heart.

arthritis Inflammation at a point where bones join together. The disease has many possible causes.

atria/atrium (A-tree-um) Either of the two upper chambers of the heart that receive venous blood.

atrophy (AT-row-fee) A wasting away of tissue or organs.

aseptic processing (ah-SEP-tik) A method by which food and containers are simultaneously sterilized; it allows manufacturers to produce boxes of milk that can be stored at room temperature. Variations of this process are also known as *ultrahigh temperature (UHT)* packaging.

aspartame (AH-spar-tame) An alternative sweetener made of two amino acids and methanol; it is about 200 times sweeter than sucrose.

atherosclerosis (ath-e-roh-scle-ROH-sis) A buildup of fatty material (plaque) in the arteries, including those surrounding the heart.

atom Smallest combining unit of an element.

autodigestion Literally, "self-digestion." The stomach limits autodigestion by covering itself with a thick layer of mucus and producing enzymes and acid only when needed for digestion of foodstuff.

autoimmune Immune reactions against normal body cells; self against self.

avidin (AV-ih-din) A protein found in raw egg whites that can bind biotin and inhibit its absorption; cooking destroys avidin.

axon The part of a nerve cell that conducts impulses away from the main body of the cell.

bacteria Single-cell microorganisms, some of which produce poisonous substances that cause illness in humans. They contain only one chromosome and lack many of the organelles found in human cells. Some can live without oxygen and survive harsh conditions by means of spore formation.

baryophobia (bear-ee-oh-FO-bee-ah) A disorder of young children and young adults characterized by stunted growth. It results from parental underfeeding in an attempt to prevent development of obesity and cardiovascular disease.

basal metabolism The minimal energy the body requires to support itself in a fasting state when resting and awake in a warm, quiet environment. It amounts to roughly 1 kcal per kilogram per hour for men and 0.9 kcal per kilogram per hour for women; these values are often referred to as basal metabolic rate (BMR).

benign Noncancerous; tumors that do not spread.

beriberi (BEAR-ee-BEAR-ee) The thiamin deficiency disorder characterized by muscle weakness, loss of appetite, nerve degeneration, and sometimes edema.

beta (β) bond A type of bond that cannot be broken by human intestinal enzymes during digestion when it is part of a long chain of glucose molecules; drawn as C⌒O‿C.

betaine (bee-TAINE) A product of choline metabolism and a methyl ($—CH_3$) donor in methionine metabolism.

beta oxidation The breakdown of a fatty acid into numerous acetyl-CoA molecules.

BHA Butylated hydroxyanisole, a synthetic antioxidant added to food.

BHT Butylated hydroxytoluene, a synthetic antioxidant added to food.

bile A liver secretion that is stored in the gallbladder and released through the common bile duct into the duodenum. It is essential for the absorption of fat.

bile acids Emulsifiers synthesized by the liver and released by the gallbladder during digestion.

binge-eating disorder An eating disorder characterized by recurrent binge eating and feelings of loss of control over eating. Binge episodes can be triggered by frustration, anger, depression, anxiety, permission to eat forbidden foods, and excessive hunger.

bioavailability The degree to which the amount of an ingested nutrient is absorbed and is available to the body.

biochemical lesion An indication of reduced biochemical function (e.g., low concentrations of nutrient by-products or enzyme activities in the blood or urine) resulting from a nutritional deficiency.

bioelectrical impedance A method to estimate total body fat that uses a low-energy electrical current. The more fat storage a person has, the more impedance (resistance) to electrical flow will be exhibited.

biological value (BV) A measure of how efficiently food protein, once absorbed from the gastrointestinal tract, can be turned into body tissues.

biotechnology A collection of processes that involve the use of advanced scientific techniques to alter and, ideally, improve characteristics of animals, plants, and other forms of life.

bisphosphonates (bis-FOS-foh-nates) Compounds primarily composed of carbon and phosphorus that bind to bone mineral and in turn reduce bone breakdown.

bleaching process The process by which light depletes the rhodopsin concentration in the eye. This fall in rhodopsin concentration allows the eye to become adapted to bright light.

blood doping A technique by which an athlete's red blood cell count is increased. Blood is taken from the athlete, and the red blood cells are concentrated and then later reinjected into the athlete. Alternately, a hormone may be injected to increase red blood cell synthesis (erythropoetin [Epogen]).

B lymphocyte (LIM-fo-site) White blood cells processed by liver and spleen tissues that are responsible for antibody production. They are responsible for recognition of foreign substances (such as bacteria) in extracellular sites in the body.

body mass index (BMI) Weight (in kilograms) divided by height (in meters) squared. A normal value is 18.5 to 24.9. A value of 25 or greater indicates a risk for body weight-related health disorders, such as type 2 diabetes and cardiovascular disease, especially when it is 30 or greater. 1 BMI unit equals 6–7 pounds.

bolus (BOWL-us) A mass of food that is swallowed.

bomb calorimeter (kal-oh-RIM-eh-ter) An instrument used to determine the energy content of a food.

bond A sharing of electrons, charges, or attractions linking two atoms.

bone mass Total mineral substance (such as calcium or phosphorus) in a cross section of bone, generally expressed as grams per centimeter of length.

bone mineral density Total mineral content of bone at a specific bone site divided by the width of the bone at that site, generally expressed as grams per cubic centimeter.

bone remodeling A process by which bone is first resorbed by osteoclast cells and then reformed by osteoblast cells. This process allows the body to form bone where needed, such as in areas of high mechanical stress.

bronchial tree (BRON-key-al) The bronchi and the branches that stem out to bronchioles.

bronchioles Smallest division of the bronchi.

brown adipose tissue (ADD-ih-pose) A specialized form of adipose tissue that produces large amounts of heat by metabolizing energy-yielding nutrients without synthesizing much useful energy for the body. The unused energy is released as heat.

buffers Compounds that cause a solution to resist changes in acid-base balance.

bulimia nervosa (boo-LEEM-ee-uh) An eating disorder in which large quantities of food are eaten at one time (binge eating) and then purged from the body by vomiting, or misuse of laxatives, diuretics, or enemas. Alternate means to counteract the caloric excess are fasting and excessive exercise.

calcitonin (kal-sih-TONE-in) A thyroid gland hormone that inhibits bone resorption.

calcitriol (kal-sih-TRIH-ol) The name sometimes given to the active hormone form of vitamin D [1,25$(OH)_2$ vitamin D] that contains a derivative of cholesterol as part of its structure.

calmodulin (kal-MOD-ju-lyn) A cell protein that binds calcium ions. The resulting calmodulin-Ca^{2+} complex influences the activity of some enzymes in the cell.

cancer A condition characterized by uncontrolled growth of abnormal body cells.

cancer initiation The step in the process of cancer development that begins with alterations in DNA, the genetic material in a cell. This may cause the cell to no longer respond to normal physiological controls.

cancer progression The final stage in the cancer process, during which the cancer cells proliferate, forming a mass large enough to significantly affect body functions.

cancer promotion The stage in the cancer process when cell division increases, in turn decreasing the time available for repair enzymes to act on altered DNA, and encouraging cells with altered DNA to develop and grow. Anything that increases the rate of cell division decreases the chance that the repair enzymes will find the altered part of the DNA in time to do their work.

capillary (KAP-ill-air-ee) Microscopic blood vessel that connects the smallest arteries and veins; site of nutrient, oxygen, and waste exchange between body cells and the blood.

capillary bed Minute vessels one cell thick that create a junction between arterial and venous circulation. Gas and nutrient exchange occurs here between body cells and the bloodstream.

carbohydrate (kar-bow-HIGH-drate) A compound containing carbon, hydrogen, and oxygen atoms; most are known as *sugars, starches,* and *fibers.*

carbohydrate counting Diet method that assigns a certain number of carbohydrate grams to each meal and snack. Insulin is matched to carbohydrate intake, and carbohydrate grams can come from several combinations of exchanges.

carbohydrate loading A process in which a very high carbohydrate intake is consumed for 6 days before an athletic event while tapering exercise duration in an attempt to increase muscle glycogen stores.

carbon skeleton Amino acid after the amino group has been removed.

carcinogenic Describes a compound with the potential to cause cancer.

carcinoma Invasive malignant tumor derived from epithelial tissues that cover the body.

cardiac muscle Muscle that makes up the walls of the heart; produces rhythmical involuntary contractions.

cardiac output (CARD-ee-ack) The amount of blood pumped by the heart.

cardiomyopathy Primary heart-muscle disease of unknown origin.

cardiovascular disease A disease characterized by the deposition of fatty material in the blood vessels that serve the heart, often called hardening of the arteries. These deposits restrict blood flow through the heart, which in turn can lead to heart damage and death. Also termed *coronary heart disease* (CHD), as the vessels of the heart are the primary site of disease. The term cardiovascular disease (CVD) is typically used, since in addition to the heart, the arteries that serve the rest of the body can experience the same deterioration.

cardiovascular system The body system consisting of the heart, blood vessels, and blood. This system transports nutrients, waste products, gases, and hormones throughout the body and plays an important role in immune responses and regulation of body temperature.

cariogenic (CARE-ee-oh-jen-ik) Literally "caries producing;" a substance often carbohydrate-rich (such as caramel), that promotes dental caries.

carnitine (CAR-nih-teen) A compound used to shuttle fatty acids from the cytoplasm of the cell into mitochondria.

carotenoids (kah-ROT-en-oyds) Pigment materials in fruits and vegetables that range in color from yellow to orange to red; three yield vitamin A activity in humans and thus are called provitamin A. Many have antioxidant properties as well. One example is beta-carotene.

carpal tunnel syndrome (CAR-pull) (SIN-drom) A disease in which nerves that travel to the wrist are pinched as they pass through a narrow opening in a bone in the wrist.

cartilage Connective tissue, usually part of the skeleton, that is composed of cells in a flexible network.

case-control study Individuals who have the condition in question, such as lung cancer, are compared with individuals who do not have the condition.

casein (KAY-seen) Protein found in milk that forms curds when exposed to acid and is difficult for infants to digest.

cash crop A crop grown specifically for export, so that goods from other countries can be purchased. Cultivation of cash crops diverts agricultural resources necessary to feed a country's own citizens. Examples are coffee, tea, cocoa, and bananas.

catabolic/catabolism (cat-ah-BOL-ik) Breaking down compounds.

catalase An enzyme that breaks down hydrogen peroxide (H_2O_2) to water. It is also an alternative enzyme pathway in alcohol metabolism; alcohol is broken down in conjunction with the breakdown of hydrogen peroxide.

catalyst (CAT-ul-ist) A compound that speeds reaction rates but is not altered by the reaction.

cecum (SEE-come) The first portion of the large intestine, which connects to the ileum.

celiac disease (SEE-lee-ak) An immunological or allergic reaction to the protein gluten in certain cereals, such as wheat and rye. The effect is to destroy the intestinal enterocytes, resulting in a much reduced surface area due to flattening of the villi. Elimination of wheat, rye, and certain other grains from the diet typically restores the intestinal surface.

cell A minute structure; the living basis of plant and animal organization. In animals it is bounded by a cell membrane. Cells contain both genetic material and systems for synthesizing energy-yielding compounds. Cells have the ability to take up compounds from and excrete compounds into their surroundings.

cell differentiation The process of transforming an unspecialized cell into a specialized cell.

cell-mediated immunity A process in which white blood cells come in actual contact with the invading cells in order to destroy them.

cell nucleus Organelle bound by its own double membrane and containing chromosomes, the genetic information for cell protein synthesis and cell replication.

cellulose (SELL-you-lows) A straight-chain polysaccharide of glucose molecules that is undigestible because of the presence of beta bonds; part of insoluble fiber.

Celsius A centigrade measure of temperature. For conversion: (degrees in Fahrenheit $-$ 32) $\times$ 5/9 = °C; (degrees in Celsius $\times$ 9/5) + 32 = °F.

central nervous system (CNS) Consists of the brain and spinal cord.

cerebrovascular accident (CVA) (se-REE-bro-VAS-cue-lar) Death of part of the brain tissue due typically to a blood clot; also called *stroke*.

ceruloplasmin (se-RUE-low-PLAS-min) A blue, copper-containing protein component in the blood that can remove an electron from Fe^{2+} (the ferrous form) to yield Fe^{3+} (the ferric form). The Fe^{3+} form of iron can then bind with transport and storage proteins, such as transferrin.

chain-breaking Breaking the link between two or more actions that encourage overeating such as snacking while watching television.

chelates (KEY-lates) Complexes formed between metal ions and substances with charged groups, such as proteins. The charged groups on the substance form two or more attachments with the metal ions, forming a ring structure. The metal ion is then firmly attached.

chelation (key-LAY-shun) The use of medicinal compounds, such as ethylenediaminetetraacetic acid (EDTA), to bind metals and other constituents in the blood.

chemical reaction An interaction between two chemicals that changes both participants.

chemical score A ratio comparing the essential amino acid content of the protein in a food with the essential amino acid content in a reference protein. The lowest amino acid ratio calculated for any essential amino acid is the chemical score.

chief cell Gastric gland cell that secretes pepsinogen, precursor of pepsin.

cholecystokinin (CCK) (ko-la-sis-toe-KY-nin) A hormone that stimulates enzyme release from the pancreas, bile release from the gallbladder, and hunger regulation.

cholesterol (ko-LES-te-rol) A waxy lipid found in all body cells. It has a structure containing multiple chemical rings that is found only in foods that contain animal products.

cholinergic (coal-in-NER-jic) Relating to actions of acetylcholine.

chromosome A single large DNA molecule and its associated proteins containing many genes; stores and transmits genetic information.

chronic (KRON-ik) Long-standing, developing over time. When referring to disease, this term indicates that the disease progress, once developed, is slow and tends to remain; a good example is cardiovascular disease.

chylomicron (kye-lo-MY-kron) Lipoprotein made of dietary fats that are surrounded by a shell of cholesterol, phospholipids, and protein. Chylomicrons are formed in the absorptive cells (enterocytes) in the small intestine after fat absorption and travel through the lymphatic system to the bloodstream.

chyme (KIME) A mixture of stomach secretions and partially digested food.

cirrhosis (see-ROH-sis) A loss of functioning liver cells, which are replaced by nonfunctioning connective tissue. Any substance that poisons liver cells can lead to cirrhosis. The most common cause is chronic, excessive alcohol intake.

***cis* isomer (sis EYE-so-mer)** An isomer form seen in compounds with double bonds, such as fatty acids, in which the hydrogens on both ends of the double bond lie on the same side of the plane of that bond.

citric acid cycle A pathway that breaks down acetyl-CoA, yielding carbon dioxide, $FADH_2$, NADH + H^+, and GTP. The pathway can also be used to synthesize compounds.

clinical lesion A sign seen on physical examination or a symptom perceived by the patient resulting from a nutritional deficiency.

clinical symptoms Generally, a change in health status noted by the individual (such as stomach pain) or noticed by a clinician during physical examination (the latter is technically called a clinical sign).

***Clostridium botulinum* (klo-STRID-ee-um BOT-you-LY-num)** A bacterium that can cause a fatal type of foodborne illness.

coenzyme An organic compound that combines with an inactive protein (apoenzyme) to form a catalytically active enzyme. In this manner, coenzymes aid in enzyme function.

cofactor An organic or inorganic substance that interacts with a specific region on an enzyme and is necessary for the enzyme's activity.

cognitive behavior therapy Psychological therapy in which the person's assumptions about dieting, body weight, and related issues are challenged. New ways of thinking are explored and then practiced by the person. In this way, the person can learn new ways to control disordered eating behaviors and related life stress.

cognitive restructuring Changing one's frame of mind regarding eating—for example, instead of using a difficult day as an excuse to overeat, substituting other pleasures for rewards, such as a relaxing walk with a friend.

colic (KOL-ik) Periodic, inconsolable crying in a healthy young infant associated with sharp abdominal pain.

colipase (co-LIE-pace) A protein the pancreas secretes that changes the shape of pancreatic lipase, facilitating its action.

collagen (KOL-ah-jen) The major protein of the material that holds together the various structures of the body.

colostrum (ko-LAHS-trum) The first fluid secreted by the breast during late pregnancy and the first few days after birth. This thick fluid is rich in immune factors and protein.

comorbid A disease process that accompanies another disease. For example, if hypertension develops as obesity is established, hypertension is said to be a comorbid condition accompanying the obesity.

complement A series of blood proteins that participate in a complex reaction cascade following stimulation by an antigen-antibody complex on the surface of a bacterial cell. Various activated complement proteins can enhance phagocytosis, contribute to inflammation, and destroy bacteria.

complementary proteins Two food protein sources that make up for each other's inadequate supply of specific essential amino acids; together they yield a sufficient amount of all nine and so provide high-quality (complete) protein for the diet.

complete proteins Proteins that contain ample amounts of all nine essential amino acids.

compound A group of different types of atoms bonded together in definite proportion (see also molecule). Not all chemical compounds exist as molecules. Some compounds are made up of ions attracted to each other, such as Na^+Cl^- (table salt).

compression of morbidity The goal of delaying the onset of disabilities caused by chronic disease until the very end of life.

concentration gradient Gradation in concentration that occurs between two regions having different concentrations.

conceptus (kon-SEP-tus) A generic term for any developmental stage derived from the fertilized ovum (zygote) until birth. The conceptus includes the extraembryonic membranes, as well as the embryo or fetus.

congenital (con-JEN-i-tal) A term that means "present at birth." Thus, a congenital abnormality is a defect that has been present since birth. These defects may be inherited from the parents, may occur as a result of damage or infection while in the uterus, or may occur at the time of birth.

conjugase (KON-ju-gase) Enzyme systems in the intestine that enhance folate absorption; they remove glutamate molecules from polyglutamate forms of folate.

conjunctiva (kon-junk-TEA-vah) Mucous membrane covering the anterior surface of the eyeball and the posterior surface of the eyelids.

connective tissue Protein tissue that holds different structures in the body together. Some structures are made up of connective tissue—notably, tendons and cartilage. Connective tissue also forms part of bone and the nonmuscular structures of arteries and veins.

constipation A condition in which bowel movements are infrequent.

contingency management Forming a plan of action to respond to a situation in which overeating is likely, such as when snacks are within arm's reach at a party.

control group Participants in an experiment who are not given the treatment being tested.

cortical bone (KORT-ih-kal) Tightly packed bone; also called compact or dense bone.

corticosteroid (kor-ti-ko-STARE-oyd) A steroid produced by the adrenal gland, an example of which is cortisol.

cortisol (KORT-ih-sol) A hormone made by the adrenal glands that, among other functions, stimulates the production of glucose from amino acids and increases the desire to eat.

covalent bond (ko-VAY-lent) A union of two atoms formed by the sharing of electrons.

creatinine (cree-A-tin-in) Nitrogenous waste product of the compound creatine found in muscles.

cretinism (KREET-in-ism) The stunting of body growth and poor mental development in the offspring that results from inadequate maternal intake of iodide during pregnancy.

Crohn's disease An inflammatory disease of the gastrointestinal tract, but generally more pronounced in the terminal ileum. A family history is a major risk factor. The disease limits the absorptive capacity of the small intestine.

crude fiber Outdated term for what remains of fiber after extended acid and alkaline treatment. This consists primarily of cellulose and lignins.

cryptosporidiosis (krip-toe-spore-id-ee-O-sis) An intestinal disease, characterized by diarrhea, that originates from a protozoan parasite of the genus *Cryptosporidium*.

cyclamate (sigh-cla-MATE) An alternative sweetener that yields no energy to the body; it is 30 times sweeter than sucrose.

cyclooxygenase (sigh-cl-OXY-jen-ase) An oxygenase enzyme used to synthesize prostaglandins, thromboxanes, and other eicosanoids.

cystic fibrosis (SIS-tik figh-BRO-sis) A disease that often leads to overproduction of mucus. Mucus can invade the pancreas, decreasing enzyme output. The lack of lipase enzyme output then contributes to severe fat malabsorption.

cytochrome (SITE-o-krome) Electron-transfer compound that participates in the electron transport chain.

cytokine (SITE-o-kine) A protein secreted by a cell that regulates the activity of neighboring cells.

cytoplasm (SITE-o-plas-um) The semifluid part of the cell between the cell membrane and the nucleus; it also does not include membrane-bound organelles. The cytoplasm contains many enzymes and structural proteins.

cytosol The water-based phase of the cytoplasm; excludes organelles such as mitochondria.

cytotoxic T cell (cite-o-TOX-ik) Type of T cell that interacts with the infected host cell through special receptor sites on the T cell surface.

cytotoxic test (cite-o-TOX-ik) An unreliable test to define food allergies that involves mixing white blood cells with food proteins.

Daily Reference Values (DRVs) Nutrient-intake standards established for carbohydrate, protein, and fiber, as well as some other dietary components lacking an RDA or a related nutrient standard, including total fat, saturated fat, and cholesterol. The DRVs for cholesterol, sodium, and potassium are constant; those for other nutrients increase as energy intake increases. The DRVs constitute part of the Daily Values used in food labeling.

Daily Values A set of standard nutrient-intake values developed by FDA and used as a reference for expressing nutrient content on nutrition labels. Note that Canadians have a separate set of Daily Values on nutrition labels.

dark adaptation The process by which the rhodopsin concentration in the eye increases in dark conditions, allowing improved vision in the dark.

deamination (dee-am-ih-NA-shun) The removal of an amino group from an amino acid.

decarboxylation (dee-car-box-ih-LAY-shun) The action of removing one molecule of carbon dioxide from a carboxylic acid.

decubitus ulcers (dee-CUBE-ih-tus) Chronic ulcers that appear in pressure areas of the skin over a body prominent in patients confined to bed or immobilized (i.e., bedsores).

Delaney Clause A clause to the 1958 Food Additives Amendment of the Pure Food and Drug Act in the United States that prevents the intentional (direct) addition to foods of a compound that has been shown to cause cancer in laboratory animals or humans.

dementia (de-MEN-sha) General persistent loss or decrease in mental function.

denature (dee-NAY-ture) Alteration of a protein's three-dimensional structure, usually because of treatment by heat, enzymes, acid or alkaline solutions, or agitation.

dendrite (DEN-dright) A relatively short, highly branched nerve cell process that carries electrical activity to the main body of the nerve cell.

dental caries (KARE-ees) Erosions in the surface of a tooth caused by acids made by bacteria as they metabolize sugars.

deoxyribonucleic acid (DNA) The site of hereditary information in cells; DNA directs the synthesis of cell proteins.

depolarization Reversal of membrane potential, which triggers generation of the nerve impulse in nerve cells.

dermatitis (dur-ma-TIE-tis) Inflammation of the skin.

dermis (DUR-miss) The second, or deep, layer of the skin under the epidermis.

DEXA bone scan Method to measure bone density that uses small amounts of X ray radiation. The ability of a bone to block the path of the radiation is used as a measure of bone density at that bone site. DEXA stands for dual energy X ray absorptiometry.

dextrin (DECK-strin) Partial breakdown product of starch that contains few to many glucose molecules. These appear when starch is being digested into many units of maltose by salivary and pancreatic amylase.

diabetes (DYE-uh-BEET-eez) A disease characterized by high blood glucose, resulting from either insufficient or no release of the hormone insulin by the pancreas or the general inability of insulin to act on certain body cells, such as muscle cells. The two major forms are type 1 (requires daily insulin therapy) and type 2 (may or may not require insulin therapy).

diastolic blood pressure (dye-ah-STOL-ik) The pressure in the arterial blood vessels when the heart is between beats.

dietary fiber Substances found naturally in plant foods that are not digested by the processes that take place in the stomach or small intestine. These add bulk to feces.

Dietary Guidelines for Americans General goals for nutrient intake and diet composition set by USDA and the Department of Health and Human Services (DHHS).

Dietary Reference Intakes (DRIs) The overarching frameworks for nutrient recommendations made by the Food and Nutrition Board, a part of the National Academy of Science. These include RDAs.

dietitian See *Registered Dietitian.*

diffusion The net movement of molecules or ions from regions of higher to regions of lower concentration.

digestibility (dye-JES-tih-bil-i-tee) The proportion of food substances eaten that can be broken down in the intestinal tract for absorption into the body.

digestion The process by which large ingested molecules are mechanically and chemically broken down to produce smaller forms that can be absorbed across the wall of the GI tract.

digestive system The body system consisting of the gastrointestinal tract and accessory structures such as the liver, gallbladder, and pancreas. This system performs the mechanical and chemical processes of digestion, absorption of nutrients, and elimination of wastes.

dihomo-gama-linolenic acid (die-homo-gama-lin-oh-lenik) An omega-6 fatty acid with 20 carbons and 4 double bonds; the precursor to some eicosanoids.

direct calorimetry (kal-oh-RIM-eh-tree) A method of determining a body's energy use by measuring heat that emanates from the body, usually using an insulated chamber.

disaccharides (dye-SACK-uh-rides) Class of sugars formed by the chemical bonding of two monosaccharides.

disordered eating Mild and short-term changes in eating patterns that occur in relation to a stressful event, an illness, or desire to modify one's diet for a variety of health and personal appearance reasons.

distillation (dis-te-LAY-shun) A physical method used to separate liquids based on their boiling points.

diuretic (dye-u-RET-ik) A substance that, when ingested, increases the flow of urine.

diverticula (DYE-ver-TIK-you-luh) Pouches that protrude through the exterior wall of the large intestine.

diverticulitis (DYE-ver-tik-you-LITE-us) An inflammation of the diverticula caused by acids produced by bacterial metabolism inside the diverticula.

diverticulosis (DYE-ver-tik-you-LOW-sus) The condition of having many diverticula in the large intestine.

docosahexaenoic acid (DHA) (DOE-co-sa-hex-ee-no-ik) An omega-3 fatty acid with 22 carbons and 6 carbon-carbon double bonds (C22:6, omega-3). It is present in large amounts in fatty fish and is synthesized slowly in the body from alpha-linolenic acid. DHA is especially present in the retina of the eye.

dopamine (DOE-pah-mean) A type of neurotransmitter in the central nervous system that leads to feelings of euphoria, among other functions; it is also used to form norepinephrine, another neurotransmitter molecule.

double-blind study An experiment in which the participants and researchers are unaware of the participant's assignment (test or placebo) or the outcome of the study until it is completed. An independent third party holds the code and the data until the study is completed.

duodenum (doo-oh-DEE-num, or doo-ODD-num) First portion of the small intestine. Leads from pyloric sphincter to the jejunum.

dyslipidemia (DIS-lip-ah-DEEM-E-ah) Generally refers to a state in which various blood lipids such as LDL-cholesterol and triglycerides are greatly elevated, and in the case of HDL-cholesterol, greatly decreased.

early childhood caries Tooth decay that results from formula or juice (and even human milk) bathing the teeth as the child sleeps with a bottle in his or her mouth. The upper teeth are mostly affected, as the lower teeth are protected by the tongue; formerly called *nursing bottle syndrome.*

eating disorder Severe alterations in eating patterns linked to physiological changes. The alterations are associated with food restricting, binge eating, purging, and fluctuations in weight. They also involve a number of emotional and cognitive changes that affect the way a person perceives and experiences his or her body.

ecosystem A "community" in nature that includes plants, animals, and the environment.

edema (uh-DEE-muh) The buildup of excess fluid in extracellular spaces.

eicosanoids (eye-KOH-san-oyds) Hormonelike compounds synthesized from polyunsaturated fatty acids, such as arachidonic acid. Within this class of compounds are prostaglandins, thromboxanes, and leukotrienes.

eicosapentaenoic acid (EPA) (eye-KOH-sah-pen-tah-ee-NO-ik) An omega-3 fatty acid with 20 carbons and 5 carbon-carbon double bonds (C20:5, omega-3). It is present in large amounts in fatty fish and is synthesized slowly in the body from alpha-linolenic acid.

electrolytes (ih-LEK-tro-lites) Compounds that separate into ions in water and, in turn, are able to conduct an electrical current. These include sodium, chloride, and potassium.

electron A part of an atom that is negatively charged. Electrons orbit the nucleus.

electron transport chain A series of reactions using oxygen to convert NADH + H^+ and $FADH_2$ molecules to free NAD^+ and FAD molecules by the donation of electrons and hydrogen ions, yielding water and ATP.

elements Substances that cannot be separated into simpler substances by chemical processes. Common elements in nutrition include carbon, oxygen, hydrogen, nitrogen, calcium, phosphorus, and iron.

elimination diet A restrictive diet that systematically tests foods that may cause an allergic response by first eliminating them for 1 to 2 weeks and then adding them back, one at a time.

embryo (EM-bree-oh) In humans, the developing in utero offspring from about the beginning of the third and lasting to the end of the eighth week after conception.

emulsifier (ee-MULL-sih-fire) A compound that can suspend fat in water by isolating individual fat droplets using a shell of water molecules or other substances to prevent the fat from coalescing.

endocrine gland (EN-doh-krin) A hormone-producing gland.

endocrine system (EN-doh-krin) The body system consisting of the various glands and the hormones these glands secrete. This system has major regulatory functions in the body, such as in reproduction and cell metabolism.

endocytosis (phagocytosis/pinocytosis) Forms of active absorption in which the absorptive cell forms an indentation in its membrane and particles (phagocytosis) or fluids (pinocytosis) entering the indentation are then engulfed by the cell.

endometrium (en-doh-ME-tree-um) The membrane that lines the inside of the uterus. It increases in thickness during the menstrual cycle until ovulation occurs. The surface layers are shed during menstruation if conception does not take place.

endoplasmic reticulum (ER) (en-doh-PLAZ-mik re-TIK-u-lum) An organelle in the cytoplasm composed of a network of canals running through the cystoplasm. Rough ER contains ribosomes. Smooth ER does not contain ribosomes.

endorphins (en-DOR-fins) Natural body tranquilizers that may be involved in the feeding response.

endothelial cells (en-doh-THEE-lee-al) A layer of flat cells lining the blood and lymphatic vessels and the chambers of the heart.

energy balance A state in which energy intake, in the form of food and/or alcohol, matches the energy expended, primarily through basal metabolism and physical activity.

energy density A state determined by comparing the energy (kcal) content of a food to its weight of the food. An energy-dense food is high in calories but weighs very little (e.g., many fried foods), whereas a food low in energy density has few calories but weighs a lot, such as an orange.

enriched A term generally meaning that the vitamins thiamin, niacin, riboflavin, and folate and the mineral iron have been added to a grain product to improve nutritional quality.

enterocytes (en-TER-oh-sites) Epithelial cells, which are highly specialized for digestion and absorption, that line the intestinal villi.

enterohepatic circulation (EN-ter-oh-heh-PAT-ik) Recycling of compounds between the small intestine and the liver over and over again, as happens with certain bile constituents.

enzyme (EN-zime) A compound that speeds the rate of a chemical process, but is not altered by the process. Almost all enzymes are proteins (some are made of nucleic acids).

epidemiology (ep-uh-dee-me-OLL-uh-gee) The study of how disease patterns vary between different population groups, such as the cases of stomach cancer in Japan compared with that in Germany.

epidermis (ep-ih-DUR-miss) The outermost layer of the skin, composed of epithelial layers.

epigenetic carcinogens (promoters) (ep-ih-je-NET-ik car-SIN-oh-jens) Compounds that increase cell division and thereby increase the chance that a cell with altered DNA will develop into cancer.

epiglottis (ep-ih-GLOT-iss) Flap that folds down over the trachea during swallowing.

epinephrine (ep-ih-NEF-rin) A hormone also known as *adrenaline;* it is released by the adrenal gland (located on each kidney) at times of stress. It acts to increase glycogen breakdown in the liver, among other functions. May also act as a neurotransmitter, such as in the brain.

epiphyseal line (ep-ih-FEES-ee-al) When bone growth is complete, a line replaces the plate.

epiphyseal plate A cartilage-like layer in the long bone. It functions in linear growth.

epiphyses (e-PIF-ih-seas) Ends of long bones. The epiphyseal plate—sometimes referred to as the growth plate—is made of cartilage and allows growth of the bone to occur. During childhood, the cartilage cells multiply and absorb calcium, to develop into bone.

epithelial cells (ep-ih-THEE-lee-ul) The surface cells that line the outside of the body and all external passages within it.

epithelial tissue The covering in internal and external surfaces of the body, including the lining of vessels and other small cavities. It consists of epithelial cells joined by a small amount of cementing material.

equilibrium (ee-kwih-LIB-ree-um) In nutrition, a state in which nutrient intake equals nutrient losses. Thus, the body maintains a stable condition.

ergogenic (ur-go-JEN-ic) Work-producing. An ergogenic acid is a mechanical, nutritional, psychological, pharmacological, or physiological substance or treatment that is intended to directly improve exercise performance.

erythrocyte (eh-RITH-row-site) Mature red blood cell that has no nucleus and a life span of about 120 days; it contains hemoglobin, which transports oxygen and carbon dioxide.

erythropoietin (eh-REE-throw-POY-eh-tin) A hormone secreted mostly by the kidneys that enhances red blood cell synthesis and stimulates red blood cell release from bone marrow.

esophagus (eh-SOF-ah-gus) A tube in the GI tract that connects the pharynx with the stomach.

essential fatty acids Fatty acids that must be supplied by the diet to maintain health. Currently only linoleic acid and alpha-linolenic acid are classified as essential fatty acids.

essential (indispensable) amino acids Amino acids that cannot be synthesized by humans in sufficient amounts and therefore must be included in the diet; there are nine essential amino acids. These are also called indispensable amino acids.

essential nutrient In nutritional terms, a substance that, when left out of a diet, leads to signs of poor health. The body either can't produce this nutrient or can't produce it fast enough to meet its needs. Then, if added back to a diet before permanent damage occurs, the affected aspects of health are restored.

esterification (e-ster-ih-fih-KAY-shun) With regard to fats, the process of attaching fatty acids to a glycerol molecule, creating an ester bond and releasing water. Removing a fatty acid is called deesterification; reattaching a fatty acid is called reesterification.

Estimated Average Requirement (EAR) An amount of nutrient intake that is estimated to meet the needs of 50% of the individuals in a specific age and gender group.

Estimated Energy Requirement (EER) Estimate of average energy needs for various ages and genders; these are set by the Food and Nutrition Board of the National Academy of Sciences.

eustachian tubes (you-STAY-shun) Thin tubes connected to the middle ear that open into the throat.

exchange The serving size of a food on a specific exchange list.

Exchange System A system for classifying foods into numerous lists based on their macronutrient composition and establishing serving sizes, so that one serving of each food on a list contains the same amount of carbohydrate, protein, fat, and energy content.

exocrine gland (EK-so-krin) A cluster of epithelial cells specialized for secretion. They have ducts that lead to an epithelial surface.

exocytosis (ek-so-sigh-TOE-sis) The process of cellular secretion in which the secretory products are contained within a membrane-enclosed vesicle. The vesicle fuses with the cell membrane and is open to the extracellular environment.

experiment A test made to examine the validity of a hypothesis.

extracellular fluid (ECF) Fluid present outside the cells; represents one-third of all body fluid.

extracellular space The space outside cells.

facilitated diffusion The carrier-mediated transport of molecules through the cell membrane along the direction of their concentration gradients. It does not require the expenditure of energy.

failure to thrive Inadequate gains in height and weight in infancy, often due to an inadequate food intake.

famine An extreme shortage of food that leads to massive starvation in a population; often associated with crop failures, war, and political strife.

fasting hypoglycemia (HIGH-po-gligh-SEE-me-ah) Low blood glucose that follows after about a day of fasting.

fat-soluble vitamins Vitamins that dissolve in such substances as ether and benzene, but not readily in water. These vitamins are A, D, E, and K.

fatty acid Major part of most lipids; composed of a chain of carbons flanked by hydrogen with an acid group $(-\overset{\text{O}}{\overset{\|}{\text{C}}}-\text{OH})$ at one end and a methyl group $(-CH_3)$ at the other.

feces (FEE-seas) Substances discharged from the bowel during defecation, consisting of the undigested residue of food, dead GI tract cells, mucus, bacteria, and other waste material. Another term for feces is *stool.*

feeding center A group of cells in the hypothalamus that, when stimulated, causes hunger.

female athlete triad A condition characterized by disordered eating, lack of menstrual periods, and osteoporosis.

fermentation The conversion, without the use of oxygen, of carbohydrates to alcohols, acids, and carbon dioxide.

fetal alcohol effect (FAE) (FEET-al) Hyperactivity, attention deficit disorder, poor judgment, sleep disorders, and delayed learning as a result of being prenatally exposed to alcohol.

fetal alcohol syndrome (FAS) A group of irreversible physical and mental abnormalities in the infant that result from the mother's consuming alcohol during pregnancy.

fetus (FEET-us) The developing life form from about the beginning of the ninth week after conception until birth.

flavin adenine dinucleotide (FAD) A compound that readily accepts and donates electrons and hydrogen ions; formed from the vitamin riboflavin.

fluoroapatite (fleur-oh-APP-uh-tite) A tooth crystal containing fluoride ions. Presence of this crystal makes the tooth relatively acid resistant.

folk medicine A medical treatment based on the beliefs, traditions, or customs of a particular society or ethnic/cultural group.

follicular hyperkeratosis (fo-LICK-you-lar high-per-ker-ah-TOE-sis) A condition in which keratin, a protein, accumulates around hair follicles. This skin change occurs in a vitamin A deficiency.

foodborne illness Sickness caused by the ingestion of food containing toxic substances produced by microorganisms.

food diary A written record of sequential food intake for a period of time. Details associated with the food intake are often recorded as well.

food insecurity A condition of anxiety regarding running out of either food or money to buy more food.

food intolerance An adverse reaction to food that does not involve an allergic reaction.

food sensitivity A mild reaction to a substance in a food that might be expressed as slight itching or redness of the skin.

fore milk The first breast milk delivered in the breastfeeding session.

fortified A term generally meaning that vitamins, minerals, or both have been added to a food product in excess of what was originally found in the product.

fraternal twins Offspring that develop from two separate ova and sperm and therefore have separate genetic identities, although they develop simultaneously in the mother.

free radicals Short-lived form of compounds that exist with an unpaired electron, causing it to seek an electron from another compound. Free radicals can be very destructive to electron-dense components, such as the DNA and cell membranes.

free water The water not bound to the compounds in a food. This is available for microbial use.

fructose (FROOK-tose) A monosaccharide with six carbons that form a five-membered or six-membered ring with oxygen in the ring; found in fruits and honey.

fruitarian (froot-AIR-ee-un) A person who eats primarily fruits, nuts, honey, and vegetable oils.

functional fiber Fiber added to foods that has shown to provide health benefits.

functional foods Foods that provide health benefits beyond those supplied by the traditional nutrients they contain. For example, a tomato contains the phytochemical lycopene, so it can be called a functional food.

fungi Simple parasitic life forms, including molds, mildews, yeasts, and mushrooms. They live on dead or decaying organic matter. Fungi can grow as single cells, like yeast, or as multicellular colonies, as seen with molds.

galactose (gah-LAK-tos) A six-carbon monosaccharide that forms a six-membered ring with oxygen in the ring; closely related to glucose.

galactosemia (gah-LAK-toh-SEE-mee-ah) A rare genetic disease characterized by the buildup of the single sugar galactose in the bloodstream, resulting from the inability of the liver to metabolize it. If present at birth and left untreated, this disease causes severe mental retardation and cataracts in the infant.

gallbladder The organ attached to the underside of the liver and in which bile is stored and secreted.

gastric inhibitory peptide (GIP) (GAS-trik in-HIB-ih-tor-ee PEP-tide) A hormone that slows gastric motility and stimulates insulin release from the pancreas.

gastrin (GAS-trin) A hormone that stimulates enzyme and acid secretion in the stomach.

gastroesophageal reflux disease (GERD) (gas-troh-eh-SOF-ah-jee-al) Disease that results from stomach acid backing up into the esophagus. The acid irritates the lining of the esophagus, causing pain.

gastrointestinal distention (gas-troh-in-TEST-in-al) Expansion of the wall of the stomach or intestines due to pressure caused by the presence of gases, food, drink, or other factors. This contributes to a feeling of satiety brought on by food intake.

gastrointestinal (GI) tract The main sites in the body used for digestion and absorption of nutrients. It consists of the mouth, esophagus, stomach, small intestine, large intestine, rectum, and anus.

gastroplasty (GAS-troh-plas-tee) Surgery performed on the stomach to limit its volume to approximately 30 milliliters.

gene expression (JEAN) Use of information on a gene via transcription and translation leading to production of a protein. Thought to be a major determinant of cellular differentiation.

generally recognized as safe (GRAS) A list of food additives that in 1958 were considered safe for consumption. Manufacturers were allowed to continue to use these additives, without special clearance, when needed for food products. FDA bears responsibility for proving they are not safe but can remove unsafe products from the list.

genes (JEANs) The hereditary material on chromosomes. Genes provide the blueprint for the production of cell proteins. The nucleus of the cell contains about 30,000 genes.

genetic engineering Alteration of genetic material in plants or animals with the intent of improving growth, disease resistance, or other characteristics.

genetically modified organism (GMO) Any organism created by genetic engineering.

genotoxic carcinogen (initiator) (JEH-no-TOK-sik car-SIN-oh-jen) A compound that directly alters DNA or is converted in cells to metabolites that alter DNA, thereby providing the potential for cancer to develop.

geometric ratio A series of numbers wherein the division of each number by the one to the left of it yields the same answer.

gestation (jes-TAY-shun) The period of intrauterine development of offspring, from conception to birth; in humans, gestation lasts for about 37 to 41 weeks after the woman's last menstrual period.

gestational diabetes (jes-TAY-shun-al) Elevated blood glucose that develops during pregnancy and returns to normal after birth; one cause is placental production of hormones that interfere with the regulation of blood glucose by insulin.

glomerulus (glo-MER-you-lus) The capillaries in the kidney that filter waste products from the blood.

glucagon (GLOO-kuh-gon) A hormone made by the pancreas that stimulates the breakdown of glycogen in the liver into glucose; this increases blood glucose. Glucagon also performs other functions.

gluconeogenesis (gloo-ko-nee-oh-JEN-uh-sis) The production of new glucose molecules by metabolic pathways in the cell. Amino acids derived from protein usually provide the carbons for this glucose.

glucose (GLOO-kos) A six-carbon monosaccharide that forms a six-membered ring with oxygen in the ring; found as such in blood, and in table sugar bound to fructose; also known as *dextrose*, it is one of the simple sugars.

glucose polymer A carbohydrate source used in some sports drinks that consists of a few glucose molecules bonded together.

glutathione (gloo-tah-THIGH-on) A reducing agent. It can remove toxic peroxides that form in the cell during aerobic metabolism.

glutathione peroxidase (gloo-tah-THIGH-on per-OX-ih-dase) A selenium-containing enzyme that can destroy peroxides. It acts in conjunction with vitamin E to reduce free radical damage to cells.

glycemic index (GI) (gli-SEA-mik) The blood glucose response of a given food, compared to a standard (typically, glucose or white bread). Glycemic index of a food is influenced by starch structure, fiber content, food processing, physical structure, and macronutrients in the meal, such as fat.

glycerol (GLIS-er-ol) A three-carbon alcohol used to form triglycerides.

glycocalyx (gli-ko-KAL-iks) Hairlike projections on the extracellular surface of the plasma membrane of cells; consists of short, branched carbohydrate chains.

glycogen (GLI-ko-jen) A carbohydrate made of multiple units of glucose with a highly branched structure; sometimes known as *animal starch*. It is the storage form of glucose in humans and is synthesized (and stored) in the liver and muscles.

glycolipid (gli-ko-LIP-id) A lipid (fat) containing a carbohydrate group.

glycolysis (gli-KOL-ih-sis) The metabolic pathway that converts glucose into two molecules of pyruvic acid, with the net gain of two ATP and two NADH + H^+.

glycoprotein (gli-ko-PRO-teen) A protein containing a carbohydrate group.

glycosylation (gli-COS-ih-lay-shun) The process by which glucose attaches to (glycates) other compounds, such as proteins.

goiter (GOY-ter) An enlargement of the thyroid gland that can be caused by a lack of iodide in the diet.

goitrogens (GOY-troh-jens) Substances in food and water that interfere with thyroid gland metabolism and thus may cause goiter if consumed in large amounts.

Golgi complex (GOAL-jee) The cell organelle near the nucleus that processes newly synthesized protein for secretion or distribution to other organelles.

gout Joint inflammation caused by accumulation of a body compound called uric acid. Obesity is a risk factor for developing gout.

green revolution Increases in crop yields accompanying the introduction of new agricultural technologies in less developed countries, beginning in the 1960s. The key technologies were high-yielding, disease-resistant strains of rice, wheat, and corn; greater use of fertilizer and water; and improved cultivation practices.

growth hormone A pituitary hormone that stimulates body growth and release of fat from storage; it also has other effects.

gums Fiber consisting of chains of galactose, glucuronic acid, and other monosaccharides; characteristically found in exudates from plant stems.

gynecoid obesity (GI-nih-coyd) Obesity in which fat storage is located primarily in the buttocks and thigh area.

H_2 blockers Medications, such as cimetidine (Tagamet), that block the stimulation of stomach acid production caused by histamine.

Harris-Benedict equation An equation that predicts resting metabolic rate based on a person's weight, height, and age.

heart attack Rapid fall in heart function caused by reduced blood flow through the heart's blood vessels. Often part of the heart dies in the process. It is technically called a *myocardial infarction*.

heartburn A pain emanating from the esophagus, caused by stomach acid backing up into the esophagus and irritating the esophageal tissue.

heart disease See *cardiovascular disease.*

heat cramps Heat cramps are a frequent complication of heat exhaustion. They usually occur in individuals exercising for several hours in a hot climate who have experienced large sweat losses and have consumed a large volume of water. The cramps occur in skeletal muscles and consist of contractions for 1 to 3 minutes at a time.

heat exhaustion The first stage of heat-related illness that occurs because of depletion of blood volume from fluid loss by the body. This increases body temperature and can lead to headaches, dizziness, muscle weakness, and visual disturbances, among other effects.

heatstroke Heatstroke can occur when internal body temperature reaches 105°F. Sweating generally ceases if left untreated, and blood circulation is greatly reduced. Nervous system damage may ensue and death is likely. Often in individuals who suffer heatstroke the skin is hot and dry.

helper T cell Type of T cell that interacts with macrophages and secretes substances to signal an invading pathogen. Stimulates B lymphocytes to proliferate.

hematocrit (hee-MAT-oh-krit) The percentage of total blood volume made up of red blood cells.

hematopoiesis (heem-oh-po-EE-sis) Production of blood cells. Also called hemopoiesis.

heme iron (HEEM) Iron provided from animal tissues as hemoglobin and myoglobin. Approximately 40% of the iron in meat is heme iron; it is readily absorbed.

hemicellulose (hem-ih-SELL-you-los) A fiber containing xylose, galactose, glucose, and other monosaccharides bonded together.

hemochromatosis (heem-oh-krom-ah-TOE-sis) A disorder of iron metabolism characterized by increased iron absorption, saturation of iron-binding proteins, and deposition in the liver and heart tissue. This deposition eventually poisons the cells in those organs

hemoglobin (HEEM-oh-glow-bin) The iron-containing part of the red blood cell that carries oxygen to the cells and some carbon dioxide away from the cells. It is also responsible for the red color of blood.

hemolysis (hee-MOL-ih-sis) Destruction of red blood cells caused by the breakdown of the red blood cell membranes. This causes the cell contents to leak into the fluid portion (plasma) of the blood.

hemorrhage (hem-OR-ij) An escape of blood from blood vessels.

hemorrhagic stroke (hem-oh-RAJ-ik) Damage to part of the brain resulting from rupture of a blood vessel and subsequent bleeding within or over the internal surface of the brain.

hemorrhoid (HEM-or-oid) A pronounced swelling in a large vein, particularly veins found in the anal region.

hemosiderin (heem-oh-SID-er-in) An insoluble iron-protein compound found in the liver. Hemosiderin stores iron when the amount of iron in the body exceeds the storage capacity of ferritin.

hepatic portal system (vein) (he-PAT-ik) The vein in the GI tract that conveys blood from capillaries in the intestines and portions of the stomach to capillaries in the liver. Also simply referred to as portal vein.

hepatic vein (he-PAT-ik) The vein that drains the liver.

herbicide (ERB-ih-side) A compound that reduces the growth and reproduction of plants.

hexose (HEK-sos) A general term describing a carbohydrate containing 6 carbon atoms.

high-density lipoprotein (HDL) The lipoprotein that picks up cholesterol from dying cells and other sources and transfers it to the other lipoproteins in the bloodstream, as well as directly to the liver. A low blood HDL value increases the risk for cardiovascular disease.

high-fructose corn syrup A corn syrup that has been manufactured to contain between 40 and 90% fructose.

high-quality (complete) proteins Dietary proteins that contain ample amounts of all nine essential amino acids.

hind milk (HYND) The milk secreted at the end of a breastfeeding session; it is higher in fat than fore milk.

histamine (HISS-tuh-meen) A breakdown product of the amino acid histidine that stimulates acid secretion by the stomach and has other effects on the body, such as contraction of smooth muscles, increased nasal secretions, relaxation of blood vessels, and changes in constriction of airways. It appears to decrease hunger and food intake.

homeostasis (home-ee-oh-STAY-sis) A series of adjustments that act to prevent change in the internal environment in the body.

homocysteine (homo-CYS-ti-ene) An amino acid not used in protein synthesis, but instead arises during metabolism of the amino acid methionine. Homocysteine is likely toxic to many cells, such as those that line blood vessels.

hormone A compound secreted into the bloodstream by one type of cell that acts to control the function of another type of cell. For example, certain cells in the pancreas produce insulin, which in turn acts on muscle and other types of cells. Protein forms, such as insulin or leptin, must be injected if used as therapy since they would be digested and broken down if taken orally.

hospice units (HAHS-pis) A facility offering care that emphasizes comfort and dignity in death.

human immunodeficiency virus (HIV) The virus that leads to acquired immune deficiency syndrome (AIDS).

hunger The primarily physiological (internal) drive to find and eat food, mostly regulated by innate cues to eating.

hydrogen peroxide Chemically, H_2O_2.

hydrogenation (high-dro-jen-AY-shun) Addition of hydrogen to a carbon-carbon double bond, producing a single bond. Because hydrogenation of unsaturated fatty acids in a vegetable oil increases its hardness, this process is used to convert liquid oils into more solid fats, which are used in making margarine and shortening. *Trans* fatty acids are a by-product of hydrogenation of vegetable oils.

hydrolysis (high-DROL-ih-sis) A chemical reaction in which a compound is broken down by the addition of water. One product receives a hydrogen ion (H^+), while the other product receives a hydroxyl ion (OH^-). Hydrolytic enzymes break down compounds using water in the manner just described.

hydrophilic (high-dro-FILL-ik) Attracts water; literally means "water loving."

hydrophobic (high-dro-FO-bik) Repels water; literally means "water fearing."

hydroxyapatite (high-drox-ee-APP-uh-tite) A compound, composed primarily of calcium and phosphate, that is deposited into the bone protein matrix to give bone strength and rigidity ($Ca_{10}[PO_4]_6OH_2$).

hyperactivity A poorly defined term generally used to label inattention, irritability, and excessively active behavior in children. Technically referred to as attention deficit hyperactive disorder.

hypercalcemia (high-per-kal-SEE-mee-ah) A high concentration of calcium in the bloodstream. This can lead to loss of appetite, calcium deposits in organs, and other health problems.

hypercarotenemia (high-per-car-oh-teh-NEEM-ee-ah) High amounts of carotenoids in the bloodstream, usually caused by consuming a diet high in carrots or squash or by taking beta-carotene supplements.

hyperglycemia (HIGH-per-gligh-SEE-me-uh) High blood glucose, above 125 milligrams per 100 milliliters (dl) of blood.

hypergymnasia (high-per-jim-NAY-zee-ah) Exercising more than is required for physical fitness or maximum performance in a sport; excessive exercise.

hyperlipidemia (high-per-lip-ih-DEE-me-ah) The presence of an abnormally large amount of lipids in the circulating blood.

hyperplasia (high-per-PLAY-zee-uh) An increase in cell number.

hypertension (high-per-TEN-shun) A condition in which blood pressure remains persistently elevated. Obesity, inactivity, excess alcohol intake, and excess salt intake all can contribute to the problem.

hypertrophy (high-PURR-tro-fee) An increase in tissue or organ size.

hypervitaminosis A (HIGH-per-vi-tah-mi-NO-sis) A condition resulting from intake of excessive amounts of vitamin A.

hypocalcemia (HIGH-po-kal-SEE-me-ah) Low blood calcium, typically arising from inadequate parathyroid hormone release or action.

hypochromic (high-po-KROM-ik) Describing pale red blood cells lacking sufficient hemoglobin as a result of iron deficiency. Hypochromic cells have a reduced oxygen-carrying ability.

hypoglycemia (HIGH-po-gligh-SEE-me-uh) Low blood glucose, below 40 to 50 milligrams per 100 milliliters (dl) of blood.

hypothalamus (high-po-THALL-uh-mus) A region at the base of the brain that contains cells that play a role in the regulation of hunger, respiration, body temperature, and other body functions.

hypothesis (high-POTH-eh-sis) An "educated guess" by a scientist to explain a phenomenon.

hysterectomy (hiss-te-RECK-toe-mee) Surgical removal of the uterus.

identical twins Two offspring that develop from a single ovum and sperm and, consequently, have the same genetic makeup.

ileocecal sphincter (ill-ee-oh-SEE-kal SFINK-ter) Ring of smooth muscle between the end of the small intestine and the large intestine.

ileum (ILL-ee-um) Terminal portion of the small intestine.

immune system The body system consisting of white blood cells, lymph glands and vessels, and various other body tissues. The immune system provides defense against foreign invaders, primarily due to the production of various types of white blood cells.

immunoglobulins (em-you-no-GLOB-you-lins) Proteins found in the blood that bind to specific antigens, also called antibodies. The five major classes of immunoglobins play different roles in antibody-related immunity.

incidence The number of new cases of a disease in a defined population over a specific period of time, such as 1 year.

incidental food additives Additives that appear in food products indirectly, from environmental contamination of food ingredients or during the manufacturing process.

incomplete (lower-quality) protein Food protein that lacks ample amount of one or more of the essential amino acids needed to support human protein needs.

indirect calorimetry (kal-oh-RIM-eh-tree) A method to measure the energy use by the body by measuring oxygen uptake. Formulas are then used to convert this gas exchange value into energy use.

infancy Earliest stage of childhood—from birth to 1 year of age.

infectious disease (in-FEK-shus) Any disease caused by an invasion of the body by microorganisms, such as bacteria, fungi, or viruses.

infrastructure (IN-fra-struck-sure) The basic framework of a system or organization. For society, this includes roads, bridges, telephones, and other basic technologies.

inorganic (in-or-GAN-ik) Any substance lacking carbon atoms bonded to hydrogen atoms in the chemical structure.

insensible In a physiological context, not perceived by the person, such as water lost with each breath.

insoluble fibers Fibers that mostly do not dissolve in water and are not generally metabolized by bacteria in the large intestine. These include cellulose, some hemicelluloses, and lignins. More formally called *poorly fermented fibers*.

insulin (IN-su-lynn) A hormone produced by the beta cells of the pancreas. Among other processes, insulin increases the synthesis of glycogen in the liver and the movement of glucose from the bloodstream into body cells.

integumentary system (in-teg-you-MEN-tah-ree) A system consisting of the skin, hair, nails, and sweat glands. This system protects the body, regulates temperature, prevents water loss, and produces a substance that converts to vitamin D.

intentional food additive Additives knowingly (directly) incorporated into food products by manufacturers.

interferons (in-ter-FEAR-ons) A group of proteins released by virus-infected cells that bind to other cells, stimulating synthesis of antiviral proteins, which in turn inhibit viral multiplication.

intermediate A chemical compound formed in one of many steps in a metabolic pathway. For example, pyruvate is an intermediate in the glycolysis pathway.

international unit (IU) A crude measure of vitamin activity, often based on the growth rate of animals. Today these units have generally been replaced by precise measurement of actual quantities in milligrams or micrograms.

interstitial fluid (in-ter-STISH-al) Fluid between cells.

intracellular (in-tra-SELL-you-lar) Within a cell.

intracellular fluid Fluid contained within a cell; represents about two-thirds of all body fluid.

intravascular fluid (in-tra-VAS-kyu-lar) Fluid within the bloodstream (i.e., in the arteries, veins, capillaries, and lymph vessels); represents about 25% of all body fluids.

intrinsic factor (in-TRIN-zik) A substance present in gastric juice that enhances vitamin B-12 absorption.

in utero (in-YOU-ter-oh) "In the uterus," or during pregnancy.

in vitro (in-VEE-troh) Refers to experiments performed outside the body, such as in a test tube—literally, *in glass*.

in vivo (in-VEE-vo) Within the living body.

ion (EYE-on) An atom with an unequal number of electrons and protons. Negative ions have more electrons than protons; positive ions have more protons than electrons.

ionic bond (eye-ON-ik) A union between two atoms formed by an attraction of a positive ion to a negative ion, as seen in table salt (NA^+Cl^-).

irradiation (ir-RAY-dee-AY-shun) A process in which radiation energy is applied to foods, creating compounds (free radicals) within the food that destroy cell membranes, break down DNA, link proteins together, limit enzyme activity, and alter a variety of other proteins and cell functions that would otherwise lead to food spoilage. This process does not make the food radioactive.

ischemia (ih-SKI-mee-ah) Lack of blood flow due to mechanical obstruction of the blood supply, mainly from arterial narrowing.

ischemic stroke (ih-SKI-mik) A stroke caused by the absence of blood flow to a part of the brain.

isomers (EYE-so-mers) Different chemical structures for compounds that share the same chemical formula.

isotope (EYE-so-towp) An alternate form of a chemical element. It differs from other atoms of the same element in the number of neutrons in its nucleus.

jaundice (JOHN-diss) A yellow staining of the skin and sclera (white of the eye) resulting from a buildup of bile pigments in the bloodstream. Liver or gallbladder disease is often the cause.

jejunum (je-JOO-num) The first half of the small intestine (minus the first 12 in., which is the duodenum).

ketogenic (kee-toe-JEN-ik) A name often given to diets that lead to the abundant production of ketone bodies by the liver. This can be caused by a low carbohydrate intake.

ketone bodies (KEE-tone) Incomplete breakdown products of fat, containing three or four carbons.

ketosis (kee-TOE-sis) The condition of having a high concentration of ketone bodies and related breakdown products in the bloodstream and tissues.

kidney nephrons (NEF-rons) Units of kidney cells that filter wastes from the bloodstream and deposit them in the urine.

kilocalorie (kill-oh-KAL-oh-ree) (kcal) The heat energy needed to raise the temperature of 1000 grams (1 L) of water 1 degree Celsius; also written as Calories, with a capital *C*.

kilojoule (KIL-oh-jool) (kJ) A measure of work. A mass of one kilogram moving at a velocity of 1 m/sec possesses the energy of 1 kJ. One kcal equals 4.18 kJ.

kwashiorkor (kwash-ee-OR-core) A disease occurring primarily in young children who have an existing disease and who consume a marginal amount of energy and minimal amounts of protein in relation to needs. The child suffers from infections and exhibits edema, poor growth, weakness, and an increased susceptibility to further illness.

lactase An enzyme made by cells of the intestinal wall; this enzyme digests lactose into glucose and galactose.

lacteal (LACK-tee-al) A small lymphatic duct associated within a villus of the small intestine.

lactic acid (LAK-tik) A three-carbon acid formed during anaerobic cell metabolism; a partial breakdown product of glucose; also called *lactate*.

***lactobacillus bifidus* factor (lak-toe-bah-SIL-us BIFF-id-us)** A protective factor secreted in the colostrum that encourages growth of beneficial bacteria in the newborn's intestines.

lacto-ovo-pesco vegetarian (lak-toe-o-vo-pes-co-vej-eh-TEAR-ree-an) A person who consumes only plant products, dairy products, eggs, and fish.

lactoovovegetarian (lak-toe-o-vo-vej-eh-TEAR-ree-an) A person who consumes only plant products, dairy products, and eggs.

lactose (LAK-tose) Glucose bonded to another sugar galactose.

lactose intolerance A condition where noticeable symptoms such as abdominal gas and bloating appear as a result of severe lactose maldigestion.

lactose maldigestion (primary and secondary) Primary lactose maldigestion occurs when lactase production declines for no apparent reason. Secondary lactose maldigestion occurs when a specific cause, such as long-standing diarrhea, results in a decline in lactase production. Severe cases resulting in profound clinical symptoms are also called *lactose intolerance*.

lactovegetarian (lak-toe-vej-eh-TEAR-ree-an) A person who consumes only plant products and dairy products.

lanugo (lah-NEW-go) Downlike hair that appears after a person has lost much body fat through semistarvation. The hair stands erect and traps air, acting as insulation for the body to compensate for the relative lack of body fat, which usually functions as insulation. Fetuses also have lanugo.

larva (LAR-va) An early developmental stage in the life history of some microorganisms, such as parasites.

larynx (LAYR-ingks) Structure located between the pharynx and trachea that contains the vocal cords; also called *voice box*.

laxative A medication or other substance that stimulates evacuation of the intestinal tract.

lean body mass The part of the human body that is free of all but essential body fat; calculated as body weight minus fat storage weight. This includes organs such as the brain, muscles, and liver, as well as blood and other body fluids.

lecithins (LESS-uh-thins) A group of phospholipids containing two fatty acids, a phosphate group, and a choline molecule. Lecithins are a group of compounds, since they can differ based on the types of fatty acids found on each lecithin molecule.

leptin (LEP-tin) A hormone made by adipose tissue in proportion to total fat mass in the body that influences long-term regulation of fat mass. Leptin also influences reproductive functions, as well as other body processes, such as release of the hormone insulin.

"let-down reflex" A reflex stimulated by infant suckling that causes the release (ejection) of milk from milk ducts in the mother's breasts, also called *milk ejection reflex*.

leukemia (loo-KEY-mee-ah) A malignant neoplasm of blood-forming tissues, the bone marrow.

leukocyte (LOO-ko-site) A white blood cell.

leukotriene (LT) (loo-ko-TRY-een) An important mediator of many diseases involving inflammatory or hypersensitivity reactions, such as asthma; it is derived from fatty acids.

life expectancy The average length of life for a given group of people born in a certain year, such as this year.

life span The potential oldest age to which a person can reach.

lignans A phytochemical class that acts as a phytoestrogen in the body. Food sources are whole grains and flax seeds.

lignins (LIG-nins) Insoluble fiber made up of a multiringed alcohol (noncarbohydrate) structure.

limiting amino acid The essential amino acid in the lowest concentration in a food or diet relative to body needs.

linoleic acid (lin-oh-LEE-ik) An essential omega-6 fatty acid with 18 carbon and 2 double bonds (C18:2, omega-6).

lipase (LYE-pase) Fat-digesting enzyme; lipase is produced by the stomach, salivary glands, and the pancreas.

lipid (LIP-id) A compound composed of much carbon and hydrogen, little oxygen, and sometimes other elements. Lipids dissolve in ether or benzene, but not water, and include fats, oils, and cholesterol.

lipid peroxidation (per-OX-ih-day-shun) A process initiated by an environmental component that induces the formation of an organic free radical, R•. In the formation of a fatty acid of this type, first a carbon-carbon double bond is broken. The resulting breakdown products react with oxygen to form peroxides (a) or free radicals (b):

a.
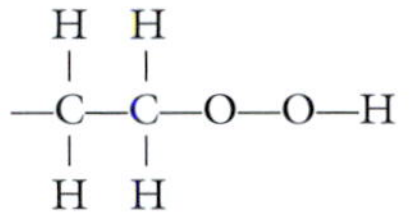

b.
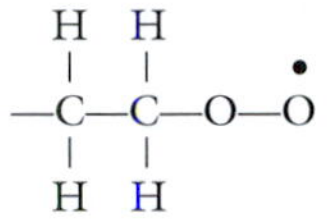

lipogenesis (lye-poh-JEN-eh-sis) The building of fatty acids using derivatives of acetyl-CoA.

lipogenic (lye-poh-JEN-ik) Creating lipid. The liver is the major organ with lipogenic potential in the human body.

lipolysis (lye-POL-ih-sis) The breakdown of triglycerides to glycerol and fatty acids.

lipoprotein (ly-poh-PRO-teen) A compound found in the bloodstream containing a core of lipids with a shell composed of protein, phospholipid, and cholesterol.

lipoprotein lipase (lye-poh-PRO-teen LYE-pase) An enzyme attached to the outside of endothelial cells that line the capillaries in the blood vessels; it breaks down triglycerides into free fatty acids and glycerol.

lipoxin (LX) (lih-POX-in) Eicosanoids made by white blood cells that are involved in the immune system and allergic responses.

lipoxygenase (lih-POX-ih-jen-ace) An oxygenase enzyme used to synthesize leukotrienes and lipoxins, two types of eicosanoids.

liter (LEE-ter) (L) A measure of volume in the metric system. One liter equals 0.96 quarts.

liver Largest organ in the body, located in the abdominal cavity below the diaphragm; performs many vital functions that maintain balance in blood composition.

lobules (LOB-you-els) Saclike structures in the breast that store milk.

long-chain fatty acids Fatty acids that contain 12 or more carbons.

low birth weight (LBW) Referring to any infant weighing less than 5.5 pounds (2.5 kilograms) at birth; most commonly results from preterm birth.

low-density lipoprotein (LDL) The lipoprotein in the blood containing primarily cholesterol; elevated LDL-cholesterol is strongly linked to cardiovascular disease risk.

lower-body obesity The type of obesity, also called *gynoid*, in which fat storage is primarily located in the buttocks and thigh area.

lower esophageal sphincter (en-sof-ah-GEE-al SFINK-ter) A circular muscle that constricts the opening of the esophagus to the stomach.

lower-quality (incomplete) proteins Dietary proteins that are low in or lack one or more essential amino acids.

lumen (LOO-men) The inside cavity of a tube, such as the GI tract or a blood vessel.

lymph (limf) A clear, plasmalike fluid that flows through lymph vessels.

lymphatic system (lim-FAT-ick) System of vessels that can accept fluid surrounding cells and large particles, such as products of fat absorption. This lymph fluid eventually passes into the bloodstream via the lymphatic system.

lymphatic vessel (lim-FAT-ick) Vessel that carries lymph.

lymph duct A large lymphatic vessel that empties lymph into the circulatory system.

lymph node A small tissue located along the course of the lymph vessels.

lymphocyte (LIM-fo-site) A class of white blood cells involved in the immune system, generally composing about 25% of all white blood cells. There are several types of lymphocytes with diverse functions, including antibody production, allergic reactions, graft rejections, tumor control, and regulation of the immune system.

lymphoma (lim-FO-ma) A malignant tumor arising from lymph nodes or other lymph tissues.

lysosome (LYE-so-som) A cell organelle that contains digestive enzymes for use inside the cell for turnover of cell parts.

lysozyme (LYE-so-zime) A set of enzyme substances produced by a variety of cells; it can destroy bacteria by rupturing cell membranes.

macrocyte (MACK-ro-site) Literally "large cell," such as a large red blood cell.

macrocytic anemia (mack-ro-SIT-ik ah-NEM-ee-a) Anemia characterized by the presence of abnormally large red blood cells in the bloodstream. A typical cause is folate or vitamin B-12 deficiency.

macrophage (MACK-ro-faj) Any large mononuclear phagocytic cell that is found in the tissues and is derived from a monocyte in the blood. Besides functioning as important phagocytes, macrophages secrete numerous cytokines and act as antigen-presenting cells.

macular degeneration A painless condition leading to disruption of the central part of the retina and, in turn, blurred vision.

major mineral A mineral vital to health that is required in the diet in amounts greater than 100 milligrams per day.

malignant (ma-LIG-nant) Essentially, to do anything malicious. In reference to a tumor, the property of spreading locally and to distant sites.

malnutrition Failing health that results from long-standing dietary practices that do not coincide with nutritional needs.

malonyl-CoA (MAL-o-kneel) A chemical intermediate in fatty-acid synthesis. The vitamin biotin participates in its synthesis.

maltase (MALL-tase) An enzyme made by cells of the intestinal wall; this enzyme digests maltose to two glucose molecules.

maltose (MALL-tos) Glucose bonded to glucose.

marasmus (ma-RAZ-mus) A disease that results from consuming a minimal amount of protein and energy; one of the diseases classed as protein-energy malnutrition. Victims have little or no fat stores, little muscle mass, and poor strength. Death from infection is common.

mass movement A peristaltic wave that simultaneously coordinates contraction over a large area of the large intestine. Mass movements propel material from one portion of the large intestine to another and from the large intestine into the rectum.

mast cell Tissue cell that releases histamine and other chemicals involved in inflammation.

meconium (me-KO-nee-um) The first thick, mucuslike stool passed by the infant after birth.

medium-chain fatty acid A fatty acid that contains 6 to 10 carbons.

megadose Generally an intake of a nutrient in excess of 10 times human need.

megaloblast (MEG-ah-low-blast) A large, nucleated, immature red blood cell in the bone marrow that results from the inability of a precursor cell to divide when it normally should.

megaloblastic anemia (MEG-ah-low-BLAST-ik) A form of anemia characterized by enlarged, immature red blood cells. A folate deficiency is often the cause.

menarche (men-AR-kee) The onset of menstruation. Menarche usually occurs around age 13, 2 or 3 years after the first signs of puberty start to appear.

menopause (MEN-oh-paws) The cessation of menses in women, usually beginning at about 50 years of age.

mesomorph (MEZ-oh-morf) A body type associated with average bone size, trunk size, and finger length.

metabolic syndrome A condition in which the person has insulin resistance, hypertension, increased blood triglycerides, and decreased HDL-cholesterol. This condition is usually accompanied by obesity, lack of physical activity, and a diet high in refined carbohydrates. Also called *Syndrome X.*

metabolism (meh-TAB-oh-lizm) Chemical processes in the body that provide energy in useful forms and sustain vital activities.

metallothionein (meh-TAL-oh-THIGH-oh-neen) A protein that binds and regulates the release of zinc and copper in intestinal and liver cells.

metastasize (ma-TAS-tah-size) The spreading of disease from one part of the body to another, even to parts of the body that are remote from the site of original tumor. Cancer cells can spread via blood vessels, the lymphatic system, or direct growth of the tumor.

meter A measure of length in the metric system. One meter equals 39.4 inches.

micelles (my-SELLS) Water-soluble spherical structures formed by lecithin and bile acids, in which the hydrophobic parts of the molecules face inward and the hydrophilic parts face outward. Lipids enclosed within micelles do not separate out into an oily layer, as they normally do when mixed with water.

microcytic (my-kro-SIT-ik) Literally means "small cell." Microcytic red blood cells are smaller than normal.

microcytic hypochromic anemia An anemia exhibiting small, pale red blood cells lacking sufficient hemoglobin and thus having reduced oxygen-carrying ability. It is often caused by an iron deficiency.

microfractures Small fractures, undetectable by X rays or other bone scans, that may develop constantly in bones.

microsomal ethanol oxidizing system (my-kro-SO-mol) An alternative pathway for alcohol metabolism when alcohol is in high concentration in the liver; uses rather than yields energy for the body, in contrast to alcohol dehydrogenase activity.

microvilli (my-kro-VIL-eye) Microscopic, hairlike projections of cell membranes of certain epithelial cells.

minerals Elements used in the body to promote chemical reactions and to form body structures.

miscarriage Nonelective termination of pregnancy that occurs before the fetus can survive; typically called *spontaneous abortion.*

mitochondria (my-toe-KON-dree-ah) The main sites of energy production in a cell. They also contain the pathway for oxidizing fat for fuel, among other metabolic pathways.

modified food starch A product consisting of chemically linked starch molecules that are more stable than normal, unmodified starches.

molecule A group of atoms chemically linked together—that is, tightly connected by attractive forces (see also *compound*).

monoamine (MON-oh-ah-MEAN) A molecule containing one amide group.

monoglyceride (mon-oh-GLIS-er-ide) A breakdown product of a triglyceride consisting of one fatty acid bonded to a glycerol backbone. A diglyceride contains 2 fatty acids bonded to glycerol.

monosaccharide (mon-oh-SACK-uh-ride) A simple sugar, such as glucose, that is not broken down further during digestion.

monounsaturated fatty acid (mon-oh-un-SAT-ur-ated) A fatty acid containing one carbon-carbon double bond.

morbidity A disease condition or state; illness.

mortality This represents a population's death rate. The term *morbidity* refers to the amount of sickness present.

motility Generally, the ability to move spontaneously. It also refers to movement of food through the GI tract.

mottling (MOT-ling) The discoloration or marking of the surface of teeth from fluorosis.

mucilages (MYOU-sih-laj) Fiber consisting of chains of galactose, mannose, and other monosaccharides; characteristically found in seaweed.

mucopolysaccharide (MYOO-ko-POL-ee-SAK-ah-ride) Substance containing protein and carbohydrate parts; found in bone and other organs.

mucosa (MYOO-co-sa) Mucous membrane consisting of cells and supporting connective tissue. In the digestive tract, there is also a layer of smooth muscle supporting the mucosa. Mucosa lines cavities that open to the outside of the body, such as the stomach and intestine, and generally contains glands that secrete mucus.

mucous membranes (MYOO-cuss) Also called *mucosae,* these line passageways open to the exterior environment.

mucus (MYOO-cuss) A thick fluid secreted by glands throughout the body. It contains a compound that has both carbohydrate and protein parts. It acts as a lubricant and means of protection for cells.

muscle fiber Component of a muscle cell.

muscle tissue A type of tissue adapted to contract.

muscular system The system consisting of smooth, cardiac, and skeletal muscle. This system produces body movement, maintains posture, and produces body heat.

mutagen (MYOO-tah-jen) Any agent that promotes a mutation (e.g., radioactive substances, X rays, or certain chemicals).

mutagenicity An agent that can induce or increase the frequency of mutation in an organism.

mutase (MYOO-tace) An enzyme that rearranges the functional groups on a molecule.

mutation (myoo-TAY-shun) A change in the chemistry of a gene that remains in subsequent divisions of the cell in which it occurred; a change in the sequence of the DNA.

mycotoxin (MY-ko-tok-sin) A group of toxic compounds produced by molds, such as aflatoxin B-1 found on moldy grains.

myelin sheath (MY-eh-lyn) A combined lipid and protein structure (lipoprotein) that covers nerve fibers.

myocardial depression Decreased activity of the heart muscle.

myocardial infarction (MY-oh-CARD-ee-ahl in-FARK-shun) Death of part of the heart muscle.

myofibrils (my-oh-FIB-rils) A bundle of contractile fibers within a muscle cell.

myoglobin (my-oh-GLOW-bin) The iron-containing protein that controls the rate of diffusion of oxygen (O_2) from red blood cells into the muscle cells.

myosin (MY-oh-sin) A thick filament protein that connects with actin to cause a muscle contraction.

negative energy balance The state in which energy intake is less than energy expended, resulting in weight loss.

negative nitrogen balance The state in which nitrogen losses from the body exceed intake, as in cases of starvation.

neoplasm (KNEE-oh-plaz-em) New and abnormal growth of tissues, which may be benign or cancerous.

neotame A general purpose nonnutritive sweetener that is approximately 7000 to 13,000 times sweeter than table sugar. It has a chemical structure similar to aspartame. Neotame is heat stable and can be used as a tabletop sweetener as well as in cooking applications. It is not broken down to its amino acid components in the body after consumption.

nephron (NEF-ron) The functional unit of the kidney.

nerve A bundle of nerve cells outside the central nervous system.

nervous system The body system consisting of the brain, spinal cord, nerves, and sensory receptors. This system detects sensations and controls physiological and intellectual functions and movement.

nervous tissue Tissues composed of highly branched, elongated cells that transport nerve impulses from one part of the body to another.

neural tube defect A defect in the formation of the neural tube occurring during early fetal development. These are seen in about 2500 infants per year in the United States. This type of defect results in various nervous system disorders, such as spina bifida. Folate deficiency in a pregnant woman increases the risk of the fetus's developing this disorder.

neuroglia (nyoo-row-GLEE-ah) (glial cells) Specialized support cells of the central nervous system.

neuroendocrine (nyoo-row-EN-do-krin) Substances or functions linked to combined action of both endocrine glands and the nervous system. Examples include substances released from glands in response to nerve stimulation.

neuron (NYOUR-on) The structural and functional unit of the nervous system. Consists of a cell body, dendrites, and axons.

neuromuscular junction (nyoo-row-MUS-kyo-lar) A chemical synapse between a motor neuron and a muscle fiber.

neuropeptide Y (nyoo-row-PEP-tide) A chemical substance made in the hypothalamus that stimulates food intake. The hormone leptin inhibits neuropeptide Y production.

neurotransmitter (nyoo-row-TRANS-mit-er) A compound made by a nerve cell that allows for communication between it and other cells.

neutron (NEW-tron) The part of an atom that has no charge.

neutrophil (NEW-tro-fil) A type of phagocytic white blood cell, normally constituting about 60 to 70% of the white blood cell count. Forms highly toxic compounds, which destroy bacteria.

nicotinamide adenine dinucleotide (NAD) A compound that readily accepts and donates electrons and hydrogen ions; made from the vitamin niacin.

night blindness A vitamin A deficiency condition in which the retina in the eye cannot adjust to low amounts of light.

nitrate (NI-trait) A nitrogen-containing compound used to cure meats. Its use contributes a pink color to meats and confers some resistance to bacterial growth.

nitrosamine (ni-TROH-sa-mean) A carcinogen formed from nitrates and breakdown products of amino acids; can lead to stomach cancer.

nonessential (dispensable) amino acids Amino acids that can be synthesized by a healthy body in sufficient amounts; there are 11 nonessential amino acids. These are also called *dispensable amino acids.*

nonheme iron (non-HEEM) Iron provided from plant sources and animal tissues other than hemoglobin and myoglobin. Nonheme iron is less efficiently absorbed than heme iron, as absorption is also more closely dependent on body needs.

nonpolar A neutral compound; no positive or negative poles present.

nonspecific immunity Defenses that stop the invasion of pathogens. Requires no previous encounter with a pathogen.

no-observable-effect level (NOEL) The highest dose of an additive that produces no deleterious health effects in animals.

norepinephrine (nor-ep-ih-NEF-rin) A neurotransmitter released from nerve endings and a hormone produced by the adrenal gland. It is released in times of stress and is involved in hunger regulation, blood glucose regulation, and other body processes.

nuclear receptor A site on the DNA in a cell where compounds (such as hormones) bind. Cells that contain DNA receptors for a specific compound are affected by that compound.

nucleoli, nucleolus (NEW-klee-o-lie) Center for production of ribosomes within the cell nucleus.

nucleus (NEW-klee-us) In chemistry, the core of an atom; it contains protons and neutrons.

nutrient Chemical substance in food that contributes to health, many of which are essential parts of a diet. Nutrients nourish us by providing energy, materials for building body parts, and factors to regulate necessary chemical processes in the body.

nutrient density The ratio calculated by dividing a food's contribution to the needs for a nutrient by its contribution to energy needs. When its contribution to nutrient needs exceeds its energy contribution, the food is considered to have a favorable nutrient density.

nutrient receptors Proposed sites in the small intestine that contribute signals to the brain that in turn elicit a feeling of satiety. These receptors are stimulated by nutrient exposure in the lumen of the small intestine.

nutrition The Council on Food and Nutrition of the American Medical Association defines nutrition as "the science of food; the nutrients and the substances therein; their action, interaction, and balance in relation to health and disease; and the process by which the organism (i.e., body) ingests, digests, absorbs, transports, utilizes, and excretes food substances."

nutritional status The nutritional health of a person as determined by anthropometric measures (height, weight, circumferences, and so on), biochemical measures of nutrients or their by-products in blood and urine, a clinical (physical) examination, a dietary analysis, and a review of economic status; also called *nutritional state.*

nutritionist A person who advises about nutrition and/or works in the field of food and nutrition. In many states in the United States, a person does not need formal training to use this title. Some states reserve this title for registered dietitians.

nutrition label A label containing "Nutrition Facts" that must be included on most foods. It depicts nutrient content in comparison to the Daily Values set by FDA. Canada has a separate set of nutrition labels.

obesity (oh-BEES-ih-tee) A condition characterized by excess body fat, typically defined in clinical settings as body mass index (BMI) of 30 or more.

oleic acid (oh-LAY-ik) An omega-9 fatty acid with 18 carbons and one double bond (C18:1, omega-9).

olfactory (ol-FAK-toe-ree) Sense of smell.

olfactory cells Cells in the nasal region that discriminate numerous chemical molecules and transmit that information to the brain. This information represents one of the components of flavor.

oligosaccharides (ol-ih-go-SAK-ah-rides) Carbohydrates containing 2 to 10 monosaccharide units.

omega-3 (ω-3) fatty acid Unsaturated fatty acid with the first double bond on the third carbon atom from the methyl end ($-CH_3$).

omega-6 (ω-6) fatty acid Unsaturated fatty acid with the first double bond on the sixth carbon atom from the methyl end ($-CH_3$).

omnivore (AHM-nih-voor) A person who consumes foods from both plant and animal sources.

oncogene (AHN-ko-jeen) Gene that codes for a protein that in turn leads to cellular growth and development.

oncotic force (ahn-KAH-tik) The osmotic potential exerted by blood proteins in the bloodstream.

opportunistic infection An infection that arises primarily in people who are already ill because of another disease.

organ A group of tissues designed to perform a specific function—for example, the heart. It contains muscle tissue, nerve tissue, and so on.

organelles (OAR-gan-ells) A compartment, particle, or filament that performs specialized functions within a cell.

organic Any substance that contains carbon atoms bonded to hydrogen atoms in the chemical structure.

organism A living thing. The human body is an organism consisting of many organs, which act in a coordinated manner to support life.

osmolality (oz-mo-LAL-ih-tee) A measure of the total concentration of a solution; the number of particles of solute per kilogram of solvent.

osmosis (oz-MO-sis) The passage of a solvent such as water through a semipermeable membrane from a less concentrated solution to a more concentrated compartment.

osmotic pressure The exerted pressure needed to keep particles in a solution from drawing liquid toward them across a semipermeable membrane.

osteoblast (OS-tee-oh-blast) Cells in bone that secrete mineral and bone matrix.

osteocalcin (OS-tee-oh-KAL-sin) A protein produced in bone that is thought to bind calcium; synthesis of osteocalcin is aided by vitamin K.

osteoclasts (OS-tee-oh-klasts) Bone cells that arise originally from a type of white blood cell. Osteoclasts secrete substances that lead to bone erosion. This erosion can set the stage for subsequent bone remineralization.

osteomalacia (OS-tee-oh-mal-AY-shuh) Softening of the bones that occurs in adults as the result of poor bone mineralization linked to inadequate vitamin D status.

osteopenia (os-tee-oh-PEE-nee-ah) Decreased bone mass caused by cancer, hyperthyroidism, or other reasons.

osteoporosis (os-tee-oh-po-ROH-sis) Decreased bone mass wherein no outward causes can be found. This bone loss is related to the effects of aging, poor diet, and hormonal effects of menopause in women.

ostomy (OS-toe-me) A surgically created short circuit in intestinal flow where the end point usually opens from the abdominal cavity rather than the anus—for example, a colostomy.

overnutrition A state in which nutritional intake greatly exceeds the body's needs.

ovum (OH-vum) The egg cell from which a fetus eventually develops if the egg is fertilized by a sperm cell.

oxalic acid (oxalate) An organic acid found in spinach, rhubarb, and other leafy green vegetables that can depress the absorption of certain minerals present in the food, such as calcium.

oxidation (ox-ih-DAY-shun) Loss of an electron by an atom or a molecule; in metabolism, often associated with a gain of oxygen or loss of hydrogen. Oxidation (loss of an electron) and reduction (gain of an electron) take place simultaneously in metabolism, because an electron that is lost by one atom is accepted by another.

oxidize (OX-ih-dize) In the most basic sense, this means a chemical substance has either lost an electron or gained an oxygen. This change typically alters the shape and/or function of the substance. An oxidizing agent then is a substance capable of capturing an electron from another source. That source is then "oxidized" when it loses the electron.

oxidizing agent In one sense, a substance capable of capturing an electron from another compound. A compound is "oxidized" when it loses an electron.

oxygenase (OK-si-jen-ace) Enzyme that incorporates oxygen directly into a molecule.

oxytocin (ok-si-TO-sin) A hormone secreted by the posterior part of the pituitary gland. It causes contraction of the musclelike cells surrounding the ducts of the breasts and the smooth muscle of the uterus.

p53 gene A tumor suppressant gene that can prevent inappropriate cell division.

palatable (PAL-it-ah-bull) Pleasing to taste.

pancreas (pan-KREE-us) Endocrine organ, located near the stomach, that secretes digestive enzymes into the small intestine and produces hormones, notably insulin.

parasite An organism that lives in or on another organism and derives nourishment from it.

parasthesia (para-STEE-zya) An abnormal spontaneous sensation, such as of burning, prickling, and numbness.

parathyroid hormone (PTH) A hormone made by the parathyroid glands that increases synthesis of the vitamin D hormone and aids calcium release from bone and calcium uptake by the kidneys, among other functions.

parietal cell Gastric gland cell that secretes hydrochloric acid and intrinsic factor.

passive absorption (transport) Absorption that uses no energy. It requires permeability for the substance through the wall of the small intestine and a concentration gradient higher in the lumen of the intestine than in the absorptive cell. The higher concentration of the substance in the lumen of the intestine in comparison with that in the absorptive cells promotes the absorption of the nutrient.

pasteurizing (PAS-tur-i-zing) Heating food products rapidly to kill pathogenic microorganisms.

pathway A metabolic progression of individual steps from starting materials to ending products, such as $C_6H_{12}O_6$ (glucose) + O_2 yielding CO_2 + H_2O.

pectins (PEK-tin) Fiber containing chains of galacturonic acid and other monosaccharides; characteristically found between plant cell walls.

peer-reviewed journal A journal that publishes research only after two or three scientists who were not part of the study agree the study was well conducted and the results are fairly represented. Thus, the research has been approved by peers of the research team.

pellagra (peh-LAHG-rah) A disease characterized by inflammation of the skin, diarrhea, and eventual mental incapacity; results from an insufficient amount of the vitamin niacin in the diet.

pepsin (PEP-sin) A protein-digesting enzyme produced by the stomach.

peptide A few amino acids chemically bonded together; often two to four.

peptide bond A chemical bond formed between amino acids in a protein. The acid group $\left(\begin{matrix}\mathrm{O}\\ \|\\ -\mathrm{C}-\mathrm{OH}_2\end{matrix}\right)$ from one amino acid reacts with the amino group ($-NH_2$) of another amino acid to form the peptide bond $\left(\begin{matrix}\mathrm{O}\\ \|\\ -\mathrm{C}-\mathrm{NH}-\end{matrix}\right)$. Water ($H_2O$) is a by-product of the reaction.

percentile Classification of a measurement of a unit into divisions of 100 units.

peripheral nervous system (PNS) (peh-RIF-er-al) The nerves of the nervous system that lie outside the brain and spinal cord.

peripheral neuropathy (peh-RIF-er-al nyoo-ROP-ah-thee) Impaired sensory, motor, and reflex actions affecting arms and legs, and causing calf muscle tenderness and difficulty in rising from a squatting position.

peristalsis (per-ih-STALL-sis) A coordinated muscular contraction that is used to propel food down the gastrointestinal tract.

pernicious anemia The anemia that results from the inability to absorb sufficient vitamin B-12; it is associated with nerve degeneration, which can result in eventual paralysis and death.

peroxisome (per-OK-si-som) Cell organelle that destroys toxic products within the cell.

peroxyl radical (per-OK-syl) Compounds containing O-O are peroxides. The radical has one unpaired electron designated $ROO^{\bullet}$.

pesticide A general term for an agent that can destroy bacteria, fungi, insects, rodents, or other pests.

pH A measure of relative acidity or alkalinity of a solution. The pH scale is 0–14. A pH below 7 is acidic; a pH above 7 is alkaline.

phagocytic cells (fag-oh-SIT-ick) Cells that engulf substances; these cells include neutrophils and macrophages.

phagocytosis (FAG-oh-sigh-TOW-sis) A form of active absorption in which the absorptive cell forms an indentation, and particles or fluids entering the indentation are then engulfed by the cell.

pharynx (FAIR-ingks) The organ of the digestive tract and respiratory tract located at the back of the oral and nasal cavities.

phenylalanine (fen-ihl-AL-ah-neen) An essential (indispensable) amino acid.

phenylketonuria (PKU) (fen-ihl-kee-toh-NEW-ree-ah) A disease caused by a defect in the ability of the liver to metabolize the amino acid phenylalanine into the amino acid tyrosine. Toxic by-products of phenylalanine can then build up in the body and lead to mental retardation.

phosphocreatine (PCr) (fos-fo-CREE-a-tin) A high-energy compound that can be used to re-form ATP. It is used primarily during bursts of activity, such as lifting and jumping.

phospholipase (fos-fo-LY-pase) Enzyme that splits a fatty acid from a cell membrane phospholipid.

phospholipid Any of a class of fat-related substances that contain phosphorus, fatty acids, and a nitrogen-containing component. The phospholipids are an essential part of every cell.

photoisomerization (foto-eye-SOM-er-eye-zay-shun) Molecular isomerization of a compound by the energy of light.

photon (FO-ton) A unit of light intensity at the retina, having the brightness of one candle.

photosynthesis (foto-SIN-tha-sis) The process by which plants use solar energy from the sun to produce energy-yielding compounds, such as glucose.

phylloquinone (fil-oh-KWIN-own) A form of vitamin K that comes from plants; also called *vitamin K_1*.

physiological anemia The normal increase in blood volume in pregnancy that dilutes the concentration of red blood cells, resulting in anemia; also called *hemodilution*.

phytic acid (phytate) (FY-tick, FY-tate) A constituent of plant fibers that binds positive ions to its multiple phosphate groups.

phytobezoar (fy-tow-BEE-zor) A pellet of fiber characteristically found in the stomach.

phytochemical A chemical found in plants. Some phytochemicals may contribute to a reduced risk of cancer or cardiovascular disease in people who consume them regularly.

pica (PIE-kah) The practice of eating nonfood items, such as dirt, laundry starch, or clay.

pinocytosis (pee-no-sigh-TOE-sis) Formation of a vesicle that brings molecules into a cell; also called cell drinking.

placebo (plah-SEE-bo) A fake medicine used to disguise the roles of participants in an experiment; if fake surgery is performed, that is called a *sham operation*.

placenta (plah-SEN-tah) An organ that forms in pregnant women. Through this organ, oxygen and nutrients from the mother's blood are transferred to the fetus and fetal wastes are removed. The placenta also releases hormones that maintain the pregnant state.

plaque (PLACK) A cholesterol-rich substance deposited in the blood vessels; it contains various white blood cells, smooth muscle cells, various proteins, cholesterol and other lipids, and eventually calcium.

plasma The fluid, extracellular portion of the blood that results when blood is centrifuged but is not allowed to clot beforehand. This includes the blood serum plus all blood-clotting factors.

plasma cells Mature B lymphocytes; these can produce 2000 antibodies per second.

polar A compound with distinct positive and negative charges (poles) on it. These charges act like poles on a magnet.

polyglutamate form of folate (POL-ee-GLOO-tah-mate) Folate with more than one glutamate molecule attached.

polyneuropathy (POL-ee-nyoo-ROP-ah-thee) A disease process involving a number of peripheral nerves.

polypeptide (POL-ee-PEP-tide) A group of amino acids bonded together; from a few to a thousand or more.

polysaccharide (POL-ee-SACK-uh-ride) Large carbohydrates containing from 10 to 1000 or more glucose units; also known as *complex carbohydrates*.

polyunsaturated fatty acid A fatty acid containing two or more carbon-carbon double bonds.

pool The amount of a nutrient found within the body that can be easily mobilized when needed.

portal system A general term that describes a process which utilizes veins to convey blood from capillaries in the intestines and portions of the stomach to the liver.

portal vein A large vein that ultimately distributes blood from the stomach and intestines to the liver. Also called hepatic portal vein to distinguish it from a portal vein found in the brain.

positive energy balance State in which energy intake is greater than energy expended, generally resulting in weight gain.

positive nitrogen balance A state in which nitrogen intake exceeds related losses. This causes a net gain of nitrogen in the body, such as when tissue protein is gained during growth.

post-translational Occurring or formed after protein synthesis is completed by the ribosomes.

power stroke Movement of the thick filament alongside the thin filament in a muscle cell, causing muscle contraction.

prebiotic A substance that stimulates bacterial growth in the large intestines.

precursor A compound that comes before; to precede.

preeclampsia (pre-ee-KLAMP-see-ah) Part of the disease pregnancy-induced hypertension. This serious disorder can include high blood pressure, kidney failure, convulsions, and even death of the mother and fetus. Mild cases are known as preeclampsia: more severe cases are called eclampsia or, more correctly, toxemia.

pregnancy-induced hypertension A serious disorder that can include high blood pressure, kidney failure, convulsions, and even death of the mother and fetus. Although its exact cause is not known, meeting nutrient needs and obtaining prenatal care may prevent or limit its severity. Mild cases are known as *preeclampsia;* more severe cases are called *eclampsia* (or more correctly *toxemia*).

premenstrual syndrome A disorder (also referred to as *PMS*) found in some women a few days before the onset of menses and characterized by depression, anxiety, headache, bloating, and mood swings. Severe cases are currently termed *premenstrual dysphoric disorder (PDD)*.

preservatives Compounds that extend the shelf life of foods by inhibiting microbial growth or minimizing the destructive effect of oxygen and metals.

preterm An infant born before 37 weeks of gestation; also referred to as *premature*.

prevalence The number of people at any one time who have a specific disease, such as obesity or cancer.

previtamin D_3 Precursor of one form of vitamin D. Produced as a result of sunlight opening a ring on 7-dehydrocholesterol.

primary disease A disease process that is not simply caused by another disease process.

primary prevention The attempt to prevent a disease from developing in the first place—for example, following a diet low in saturated fat and cholesterol in an attempt to prevent cardiovascular disease.

primary structure of a protein The order of amino acids in the protein molecule.

probiotic (PRO-bye-ah-tic) A product that contains specific types of bacteria. Use is intended to colonize the large intestine with the specific bacteria in the product. An example is yogurt.

progestins (pro-JES-tins) Hormones, including progesterone, that are necessary for maintaining pregnancy and lactation.

prognosis (prog-NO-sis) A forecast of the course and end of a disease.

prohormone Precursor of a hormone.

prolactin (pro-LACK-tin) A hormone secreted by the mother that stimulates the synthesis of milk.

prospective Research that follows individuals during a current course of treatment. This is in contrast to retrospective research, which examines the past habits of individuals.

prostacyclin (PGI) (prost-tah-SIGH-klin) Eicosanoid made by the blood vessel walls that is a potent inhibitor of blood clotting, (PGI_2).

prostaglandin (PG) (pros-tah-GLAN-din) One of several potent hormonelike compounds made of polyunsaturated fatty acids that produce diverse effects in the body.

prostanoids (PROS-ta-noid) The group of prostaglandins, prostacyclins, and thromboxanes produced from 20 carbon (C:20) fatty acids. Not as inclusive a term as is eicosanoids, since leukotrienes and lipoxins are not included.

prostate gland (PROS-tait) A solid, chestnut-shaped organ surrounding the first part of the urethra in the male. The prostate gland is situated immediately under the bladder and in front of the rectum. The prostate gland secretes substances into the semen as the fluid passes through ducts leading from the seminal vesicles into the urethra.

protein Food and body components made of amino acids; proteins contain carbon, hydrogen, oxygen, nitrogen, and sometimes other atoms, in a specific configuration. Proteins contain the form of nitrogen most easily used by the human body.

protein-efficiency ratio (PER) A measure of protein quality in a food, determined by the ability of a protein to support the growth of a young animal.

protein-energy malnutrition (PEM) A condition resulting from regularly consuming insufficient amounts of energy and protein. The deficiency eventually results in body wasting of primarily lean tissue and an increased susceptibility to infection.

protein kinase (ky-nace) C An enzyme that adds a phosphorus to many proteins that control cell growth and development.

protein quality A measure of the ability of a food protein to support body growth and maintenance.

prothrombin (pro-THROM-bin) One of the numerous proteins that participate in the formation of blood clots. Conversion of its precursor protein to the active blood-clotting factor in the liver requires vitamin K.

proton (PRO-ton) The part of an atom that is positively charged.

protooncogenes (pro-toe-ON-ko-jeans) Genes that code for proteins that in turn cause a resting cell to divide.

psyllium (SIL-ee-um) A mostly soluble type of dietary fiber found in the seeds of the plantain plant.

pulmonary circulation (pulmonary circuit) The system of blood vessels from the right side of the heart to the lungs and back to the left side of the heart.

pyloric sphincter (pi-LOR-ik SFINK-ter) Ring of smooth muscle between the stomach and the small intestine.

pyruvic acid A three-carbon compound formed during glucose metabolism; also called *pyruvate.*

racemase Enzymes that catalyze reactions involving structural rearrangement of a molecule (e.g., conversion of D-alanine isomer to L-alanine isomer).

radiation Literally, energy that is emitted from a center in all directions. Various forms of radiation energy include X rays and ultraviolet rays from the sun.

raffinose (RAF-ih-nos) An indigestible oligosaccharide made of three monosaccharides (galactose-glucose-fructose).

rancid (RAN-sid) Containing products of decomposed fatty acids; they yield unpleasant flavors and odors.

reactive hypoglycemia (HIGH-po-gligh-SEE-mee-uh) Low blood glucose that may follow a meal high in simple sugars, with corresponding symptoms of irritability, headache, nervousness, sweating, and confusion; actually called *postprandial hypoglycemia.*

reactive oxygen species (ROS) Several oxygen derivatives produced during the formation of ATP and other ways. Formed constantly in the human body and shown to kill bacteria and inactivate proteins, they are also implicated in a number of diseases. They have been linked to inflammatory processes.

receptive framework for learning The process by which a person opens up to learning more about a problem; it usually involves seeking more information about the issue from books and people. In the case of seeking behavior changes, it involves examining background experience to evaluate whether a behavior change is feasible.

receptor (ri-SEP-ter) A site in a cell at which compounds (such as hormones) bind. Cells that contain receptors for a specific compound are partially controlled by that compound.

receptor pathway for cholesterol uptake A process by which LDL particles (cholesterol-containing) are bound by cell receptors and incorporated into the cell.

recombinant DNA (re-KOM-bih-nant) A molecule composed of the DNA of two different species spliced together, such as a combination of bacterial and human DNA used to produce unique bacteria that now can synthesize human proteins.

Recommended Dietary Allowances (RDAs) Recommended intakes of nutrients that meet the needs of nearly all (97 to 98%) healthy individuals of similar age and gender. These are established by the Food and Nutrition Board of the National Academy of Sciences.

Recommended Nutrient Intake (RNI) The Canadian version of RDA published in 1990.

rectum Terminal portion of the large intestine.

redox agents (RE-doks) Chemicals that can readily undergo both oxidation (loss of an electron) and reduction (gain of an electron).

reducing agent A compound capable of donating electrons (also hydrogen ions) to another compound.

reduction In chemical terms, the gain of an electron by an atom; takes place simultaneously with oxidation (loss of an electron by an atom) in metabolism because an electron that is lost by one atom is accepted by another. In metabolism, reduction is often associated with the gain of hydrogen.

Reference Daily Intake (RDI) Nutrient-intake standards set by FDA based on the 1968 RDA standards for various vitamins and minerals. RDIs have been set for four categories of people: infants, toddlers, people over 4 years of age, and pregnant or lactating women. Generally the highest RDA value in each category is used as the RDI. The RDIs constitute part of the Daily Values used in food labeling.

registered dietitian (RD) (dye-eh-TISH-shun) A person who has completed a baccalaureate degree program approved by The American Dietetic Association, performed at least 900 hours of supervised professional practice, and passed a registration examination.

reinforcement A reaction by others in response to a person's behavior. Positive reinforcement entails encouragement; negative reinforcement entails criticism or penalty.

relapse prevention A series of strategies used to help prevent and cope with weight-control lapses, such as recognizing high-risk situations and deciding beforehand on appropriate responses.

remodeling The constant building and breakdown of bone throughout life.

renin (REN-in) An enzyme formed in the kidney and released in response to low blood pressure; it acts on a blood protein to produce angiotensin I.

reproductive system The system consisting of the gonads, accessory structures, and genitals of males and females. This system performs the process of reproduction and influences sexual functions and behaviors.

requirement The amount of a nutrient required by one person to maintain health. This varies between individuals. We do not know our individual requirements for each nutrient.

reserve capacity The extent to which an organ can preserve essentially normal function despite decreasing cell number or cell activity.

resorption The loss of a substance by physiologic or pathologic means.

respiration The utilization of oxygen; in the human organism, the inhalation of oxygen and the exhalation of carbon dioxide; in cells, the oxidation (electron removal) of food molecules, particularly in the citric acid cycle, to obtain energy.

respiratory system The body system consisting of the lungs and various associated organs such as the nose and various conducting tubes. This system transports oxygen from outside air to the lungs, and allows carbon dioxide to be expelled from the body. Oxygen and carbon dioxide are exchanged with the blood in the lungs. It also regulates acid-base balance in the body.

restraint A feeling that occurs as a result of restricted food intake, often associated with the belief that there are good and bad foods.

retinoids (RET-ih-noyds) A collective term for the biologically active forms of vitamin A, including retinol, retinal, and retinoic acid.

reverse transport of cholesterol The process by which cholesterol is picked up by HDL particles and transferred to the liver or to other lipoproteins that can dispose of it in the liver.

rhodopsin (row-DOP-sin) Photoreceptor in the rod cells composed of 11-*cis* retinal and opsin.

ribonucleic acid (RNA) (RI-bow-new-CLAY-ik) Single-stranded nucleic acid involved in the transcription of genetic information and translation of that information into protein structure.

ribose (RIGH-bos) A 5-carbon sugar found in genetic material—specifically, RNA.

ribosomes (RI-bow-soms) Cytoplasmic particles that mediate the linking together of amino acids to form proteins; attached to endoplasmic reticulum as bound ribosomes, or suspended in cytoplasm as free ribosomes.

rickets (RIK-its) A disease characterized by soft, unmineralized bones caused by limited calcium deposition during growth. This deficiency disease arises in infants and children with a poor vitamin D status.

risk factor A term used frequently when discussing diseases and factors contributing to their development. A risk factor is an aspect of our lives—such as heredity, lifestyle choices (e.g., smoking), or nutritional habits—that make us more likely to develop a disease.

rough endoplasmic reticulum Portion of the endoplasmic reticulum that contains ribosomes. This is the site of protein synthesis in a cell.

R-protein A protein produced by the salivary glands that enhances absorption of vitamin B-12, possibly protecting the vitamin during its passage through the stomach.

RXR, RAR Abbreviation for retinoid X receptor and retinoic acid receptor. These subfamilies of retinoid receptors interact with retinoic acid and bind to specific sites on DNA. This allows for gene expression.

saccharin (SACK-ah-rin) An alternate sweetener that yields no energy to the body; it is 300 times sweeter than sucrose.

saliva (sah-LIGH-vah) A watery fluid, produced by the salivary glands in the mouth, that contains lubricants, enzymes, and other substances.

salivary amylase (SAL-ih-var-ee AM-ih-lace) Starch-digesting enzyme produced by salivary glands.

salt Generally refers to a compound of sodium and chloride in a 40 60 ratio.

sarcoma (sar-KO-mah) A malignant tumor arising from connective tissues.

satiety (suh-TIE-uh-tee) State in which there is no longer a desire to eat; a feeling of satisfaction.

saturated fatty acid A fatty acid containing no carbon-carbon double bonds.

scavenger pathway for cholesterol uptake A process by which LDL particles (cholesterol-containing) are taken up by scavenger cells embedded in the blood vessels.

scurvy (SKER-vee) The deficiency disease that results after a few weeks to months of consuming a diet that lacks vitamin C; pinpoint sites of bleeding on the skin are an early sign.

secondary deficiency A deficiency caused not by lack of the nutrient in question but by lack of a substance or process that is needed for that nutrient to function.

secondary disease A disease process that develops as a result of another disease.

secondary prevention Interventions to prevent further development of a disease so as to reduce the risk of further damage to health; for example, smoking cessation for a person who has already suffered a heart attack.

secretin (SEE-kreh-tin) A hormone that causes bicarbonate ion release from the pancreas.

secretory vesicles (see-KRE-tor-ee VES-ih-kels) Membrane-bound vesicles produced by the Golgi apparatus; contain proteins and other compounds to be secreted by the cell.

segmentation Contractions of the circular muscles in the intestines that lead to a dividing and mixing of the intestinal contents. This action aids digestion and absorption of nutrients.

self-monitoring A process of tracking a behavior and conditions affecting that behavior; actions are usually recorded in a diary, along with location, time, and state of mind. This can be a tool to help people understand more about their eating habits.

self-talk The internal dialogue that we carry on in our heads as we sort out beliefs, feelings, attitudes, and events happening in our lives.

semiessential amino acids Amino acids that, when consumed, spare the need to use an essential amino acid for their synthesis. Tyrosine in the diet, for example, spares the need to use phenylalanine for tyrosine synthesis.

sensible water losses Water losses we readily notice, such as urine output and heavy perspiration.

sequestrants (see-KWES-trants) Compounds that bind free metal ions. By so doing, they reduce the ability of ions to cause rancidity in foods containing fat.

serotonin (ser-oh-TONE-in) A neurotransmitter synthesized from the amino acid tryptophan that appears to decrease the desire to consume carbohydrates and to induce sleep.

serum (SEER-um) The portion of the blood fluid remaining after (1) the blood is allowed to clot and (2) the red and white blood cells and other solid matter are removed by centrifugation.

set point Often refers to the close regulation of body weight. It is not known what cells control this set point or how it actually functions in weight regulation. There is evidence, however, that mechanisms exist that help regulate weight.

sexually transmitted disease (STD) A contagious disease usually acquired by sexual intercourse or genital contact. Common examples include AIDS, gonorrhea, and syphilis. Also called *venereal disease.*

short-chain fatty acids Fatty acids that contain fewer than six carbon atoms.

sickle-cell disease (sickle-cell anemia) An anemia that results from a malformation of the red blood cell because of an incorrect primary structure in part of its hemoglobin protein chains. The disease can lead to episodes of severe bone and joint pain, abdominal pain, headache, convulsions, paralysis, and even death.

sideroblastic anemia An anemia characterized by altered red blood cells in the bone marrow that have a ring of iron just inside the cell membrane. This anemia can be corrected by providing extra vitamin B-6 in some cases.

sign A change in health status that is apparent on physical examination.

simple sugar Term used to describe the group of typical sugars in our diets: glucose, fructose, and sucrose.

skeletal fluorosis (flo-ROW-sis) A condition caused by a greatly excessive fluoride intake, characterized by weakened skeletal structure.

skeletal muscle Muscle responsible for voluntary body movements.

skeletal system The system consisting of the bones, associated cartilage, and joints. This system supports the body, allows for body movement, produces blood cells, and stores minerals.

slough (SLUF) To shed or cast off.

small for gestational age (SGA) (jes-TAY-shun-al) Referring to infants who weigh less than the expected weight for their length of gestation. This corresponds to less than 5.5 pounds (2.5 kilograms) in a full-term newborn. A preterm infant who is also SGA will most likely develop some medical complications.

smooth endoplasmic reticulum Portion of the endoplasmic reticulum that does not contain ribosomes. This is the site of lipid synthesis in a cell.

smooth muscle Muscle under involuntary control; found in GI tract, artery walls, respiratory passages, urinary tract, and reproductive tract.

sodium bicarbonate (SO-dee-um bi-KAR-bow-nait) An alkaline substance made basically of sodium and carbon dioxide ($NaHCO_3$).

soft palate (PAL-it) The fleshy posterior portion of the roof of the mouth.

soluble fibers (SOL-you-bull) Fibers that either dissolve or swell in water and are metabolized (fermented) by bacteria in the large intestine. These include pectins, gums, and mucilages. More formally called *viscous fibers.*

solvent A substance that other substances dissolve in.

sorbitol (SOR-bih-tol) An alcohol derivative of glucose.

specific heat Heat required to raise the temperature of 1 g of a substance 1°C. Water has a high specific heat, meaning that a relatively large amount of heat is required to raise its temperature; therefore, it tends to resist large temperature fluctuations.

specific immunity Function of white blood cells directed at specific antigens.

sphincter (SFINK-ter) A muscular valve that controls flow of foodstuff in the GI tract.

spontaneous abortion Cessation of pregnancy and expulsion of the embryo or nonviable fetus prior to 20 weeks gestation. This can be as the result of natural causes, such as a genetic defect or developmental problem; also called *miscarriage.*

spores Dormant reproductive cells capable of forming into adult organisms without the help of another cell. Various fungi and bacteria form spores.

sports anemia (ah-NEE-me-ah) A decrease in the blood's ability to carry oxygen, found in athletes, which may be caused by iron loss through perspiration and feces or increased blood volume.

stable isotope An isotope is a specific form of a chemical element. It differs from atoms of other forms (isotopes) of the same element in the number of neutrons in its nucleus. "Stable" means that the isotope is not radioactive, in contrast to some other types of isotopes.

stachyose (STACK-ee-os) An indigestible oligosaccharide made of four monosaccharides (galactose-galactose-glucose-fructose).

starch A carbohydrate made of multiple units of glucose attached together in a form the body can digest; also known as *complex carbohydrate.*

stem cell Cell that, in an adult body, divides continuously and forms a supply of cells for differentiation.

stenosis (ste-NO-sis) Narrowing or stricture of a duct or canal.

steroids (STARE-oyds) A group of hormones and related compounds that are derivatives of cholesterol.

sterol (STARE-ol) A compound containing a multiring (steroid) structure and a hydroxyl group (–OH).

stimulus control Altering the environment to minimize the stimuli for eating—for example, removing foods from sight and storing them in kitchen cabinets.

stress fracture A fracture that occurs from repeated jarring of a bone. Common sites include bones of the foot.

striated muscle Muscles showing a striped pattern when viewed under the microscope. These stripes are due to presence and specific organization of the contractile proteins actin and myosin.

stroke The loss of body function that results from a blood clot or other change in the brain that affects blood flow. This in turn causes the death of brain tissue. Also called a *cerebrovascular accident.*

subclinical Disease or disorder that is present but not severe enough to produce signs and symptoms that can be detected or diagnosed.

submucosal layer (sub-myoo-KO-sal) A layer of blood and lymph vessels along with nerve fibers and connective tissue that stretch the whole length of the GI tract.

sucralose (SOO-kra-los) An alternative sweetener that has chlorines in place of three hydroxyl (–OH) groups on sucrose. It is 600 times sweeter than sucrose.

sucrase An enzyme made by cells of the intestinal wall; this enzyme digests sucrose to glucose and galactose.

sucrose (SOO-kros) Fructose bonded to another sugar glucose; table sugar.

sugar Simple carbohydrate form with a chemical composition $(CH_2O)_n$. Most sugars form ringed structures when in solution.

superoxide dismutase (soo-per-OX-ide DISS-myoo-tase) An enzyme that can quench (deactivate) a superoxide negative free radical ($O2^{\bullet -}$). This can contain the minerals manganese, copper, or zinc.

sympathetic nervous system Part of the nervous system that regulates involuntary vital functions, including the activity of the heart, smooth muscles, and adrenal glands. The sympathetic nervous system specifically accelerates heart rate, constricts blood vessels, and raises blood pressure. The parasympathetic nervous system slows heart rate, increases intestinal peristalsis and gland activity, and relaxes sphincters.

symptom A change in health status noted by the person with the problem, such as a stomach pain.

synapse (SIN-aps) The space between the beginning of one nerve cell and the beginning of another nerve cell.

system A collection of organs that work together to perform an overall function.

systemic circulation (system circuit) The part of the circulatory system concerned with the flow of blood from the left ventricle to the body and back to the right atrium.

systolic blood pressure (sis-TOL-lik) The pressure in the arterial blood vessels associated with the pumping of blood from the heart.

telomerase (teh-LO-mer-ace) Enzyme that maintains length and completeness of chromosomes.

telomeres (TELL-oh-meers) Caps at the end of chromosomes.

tendon (TEN-don) Dense connective tissue that attaches a muscle to a bone.

teratogenic (ter-A-toe-jen-ic) Tending to produce physical defects in a developing fetus (literally means "monster producing").

tertiary structure of a protein (TER-she-air-ee) The three-dimensional structure of a protein, formed by interactions of amino acids placed far apart in the primary structure.

tetany (TET-ah-nee) A state marked by sharp contraction of muscles with failure to relax afterward; usually caused by abnormal calcium metabolism.

theory An explanation for a phenomenon that has numerous lines of evidence to support it.

thermic effect of food (TEF) The increase in metabolism that occurs during the digestion, absorption, and metabolism of energy-yielding nutrients. This represents 5 to 10% of energy consumed.

thermogenesis The ability of humans to regulate body temperature within narrow limits, especially as temperature falls below that which is comfortable. Increased shivering is part of this response. Also included in this general term is the increase in metabolism elicited by overfeeding, often linked to increased fidgeting. Other terms used to describe thermogenesis are thermoregulation, adaptive thermogenesis, and nonexercise activity thermogenesis (NEAT).

thioredoxin (THIGH-o-re-dock-sin) An antioxidant enzyme in cells that utilizes the mineral selenium.

thrifty metabolism A metabolism that characteristically conserves more energy than normal, such that it increases risk of weight gain and obesity.

thromboxane (TX) (throm-BOK-sane) A stimulant of blood clotting made in the blood from polyunsaturated fatty acids.

thyroid hormone Hormone produced by the thyroid gland that increases the rate of overall metabolism in the body.

thyroid-stimulating hormone (TSH) The hormone that regulates the uptake of iodide by the thyroid gland and release of thyroid hormone. TSH is secreted in response to a low concentration of circulating thyroid hormone (thyroxine).

tissue (TISH-you) Collection of cells adapted to perform a specific function.

T lymphocyte (tee-LYMF-oh-site) A type of white blood cell that recognizes intracellular antigens (e.g., viral antigens in infected cells), fragments of which move to the cell surface. T cells originate in the bone marrow but must mature in the thymus gland.

tocopherols (tuh-KOFF-er-alls) A group of four structurally similar compounds that have vitamin E activity. The RRR, RSR, RRS, and RSS isomer forms of alpha form (listed as "d" on a label) is the most potent form.

tocotrienols (toe-co-TRY-en-ols) A group of four compounds with the same basic chemical structure as the tocopherols but containing slightly altered side chains. They exhibit much less vitamin E activity than the corresponding tocopherols.

Tolerable Upper Intake Level (UL) Maximum chronic daily intake of a nutrient that is unlikely to cause adverse health effects in almost all people in a population. This number applies to a chronic daily use.

total fiber Combination of dietary fiber and functional fiber in a food. Also just called *fiber.*

total parenteral nutrition The intravenous provision of all necessary nutrients, including the most basic forms of protein, carbohydrates, lipids, vitamins, minerals, and electrolytes.

toxic Poisonous; caused by a poison.

toxicity The capacity of a substance to produce injury or illness at some dosage.

toxin Poisonous compounds produced by an organism that can cause disease.

trabecular bone (trah-BEK-you-lar) Bone tissue found inside the bone with a lattice-like structure; also called *spongy* or *cancellous* bone.

trace mineral A mineral vital to health that is required in the diet in amounts less than 100 milligrams per day.

trachea (TRAY-key-ah) The airway leading from the larynx to the bronchi.

transamination (trans-am-ih-NAY-shun) The transfer of an amino group from an amino acid to a carbon skeleton to form a new amino acid.

***trans* fatty acids** A form of an unsaturated fatty acid, usually a monounsaturated one when found in food, in which the hydrogens on both carbons forming that double bond lie on opposite sides of that bond. Stick margarine, shortenings, and deep-fat fried foods in general are rich sources.

transferrin (trans-FER-in) A blood protein that transports iron in the blood.

transgenic Organism that contains genes originally present in another different organism.

***trans* isomers** Compound where the hydrogens lie opposite each other across a carbon-carbon double bond.

transketolase (trans-KEY-toe-lace) An enzyme whose functional component is TPP (thiamin pyrophosphate); converts glucose to pentose sugars.

triglyceride (try-GLISS-uh-ride) The major form of lipid in the body and in food. It is composed of three fatty acids bonded to glycerol, an alcohol.

trimesters Three 13- to 14-week periods into which the normal pregnancy of about 37 to 41 weeks is divided somewhat arbitrarily for purposes of discussion and analysis. Development of the offspring, however, is continuous throughout pregnancy, with no specific physiological markers demarcating the transition from one trimester to the next.

tropic hormone (TROW-pic) Hormone that stimulates the secretion of another secreting gland.

trypsin (TRIP-sin) A protein-digesting enzyme secreted by the pancreas to act in the small intestine.

tumor Mass of cells; may be cancerous (malignant) or noncancerous (benign).

tumor suppressor genes Genes that prevent cells from dividing.

type 1 diabetes A form of diabetes that is prone to ketosis and requires insulin therapy.

type 2 diabetes A form of diabetes in which ketosis is not commonly seen. Insulin therapy can be used but often is not required. This form of the disease is often associated with obesity.

ulcer (UL-sir) Erosion of the tissue lining, usually in the stomach (gastric ulcer) or the upper small intestine (duodenal ulcer). These are generally referred to as *peptic ulcers.*

umami (you-MA-mee) A brothy, meaty, savory flavor in some foods. Monosodium glutamate enhances this flavor when added to foods.

undernutrition Failing health that results from a long-standing dietary intake that does not meet nutritional needs.

underwater weighing A method of estimating total body fat by weighing the individual on a standard scale and then weighing him or her again submerged in water. The difference between the two weights is used to estimate total body fat.

underweight A body mass index below 18.5. The cutoff is less precise than for obesity because this condition has been studied less.

unsaturated fatty acid A fatty acid with one or more carbon-carbon double bonds in its chemical structure.

upper-body obesity The type of obesity, also called android, in which fat is stored primarily in the abdominal area; defined as a waist circumference greater than 40 inches in men and greater than 35 inches in women; closely associated with a high risk of cardiovascular disease, hypertension, and type 2 diabetes.

urea (yoo-REE-ah) Nitrogenous waste product of protein metabolism; major source of nitrogen in the urine, chemically $NH_2\text{–}\overset{\overset{\displaystyle O}{\|}}{C}\text{–}NH_2$.

ureter (YOUR-ih-ter) Tube that transports urine from the kidney to the urinary bladder.

urethra (yoo-REE-thra) Tube that transports urine from the urinary bladder to the outside of the body.

urinary system The body system consisting of the kidneys, urinary bladder, and the ducts that carry urine. This system removes waste products from the circulatory system and regulates blood acid-base balance, overall chemical balance, and water balance in the body.

vagus nerves (VAY-guss) Nerves arising from the brain that branch off to other organs and are essential for control of speech, swallowing, and gastrointestinal function.

vegan (VEE-gun) A person who eats only plant foods.

vegetarian A person who avoids eating animal products to a varying degree, ranging from consuming no animal products to simply not consuming four-footed animal products.

vein A blood vessel that conveys blood to the heart.

ventricle (VEN-tri-kel) Either of the two lower chambers of the heart that contain blood to be pumped from the heart. The term is also used to describe the four interconnecting cavities in the brain.

venule (VEN-yool) A tiny vessel that carries blood from the capillary to a vein.

very-low-calorie diet (VLCD) Known also as *protein-sparing modified fast (PSMF)*, this diet allows a person 400 to 800 kcal per day, often in liquid form. Of this, 120 to 480 kcals are carbohydrate; the rest is mostly high-quality protein.

very-low-density lipoprotein (VLDL) The lipoprotein created in the liver that carries both the cholesterol and lipids taken up from the bloodstream by the liver, as well as newly synthesized by the liver.

villi (VIL-eye) Fingerlike protrusions into the small intestine that participate in digestion and absorption of foodstuff.

virus (VI-rus) The smallest known type of infectious agent, many of which cause disease in humans. Viruses do not metabolize, grow, or move by themselves. They reproduce by the aid of a living cellular host. Viruses are essentially a piece of genetic material surrounded by a coat of protein.

visual cycle A chemical process in the eye that participates in vision. Forms of vitamin A participate in the process.

vitamins Compounds needed in very small amounts in the diet to help regulate and support chemical reactions in the body.

VO_{2max} Maximum volume of oxygen that can be consumed per unit of time.

water The universal solvent of life; chemically, H_2O. The body is composed of about 60% water. Water (fluid) needs are about 8 cups per day; needs are greater if one exercises heavily.

water-soluble vitamins Vitamins that dissolve in water. These vitamins are the B-vitamins and vitamin C.

Wernicke-Korsakoff syndrome Thiamin-deficiency disease caused by excessive alcohol consumption. Symptoms include eye problems, difficulty walking, and deranged mental functions.

whey (WAY) Proteins, such as lactalbumin, that are found in great amounts in human milk and are easy to digest.

white blood cells One of the formed elements of the circulating blood system; also called *leukocytes.* Five types of leukocytes are lymphocytes, monocytes, neutrophils, basophils, and eosinophils. White blood cells are able to squeeze through intracellular spaces and migrate. Leukocytes phagocytize bacteria, fungi, and viruses, as well as detoxify proteins that may result from allergic reactions, cellular injury, and other immune system cells.

whole grains Grains containing the entire seed of the plant, including the bran, germ, and endosperm (starchy interior). Examples are whole wheat and brown rice.

xanthine dehydrogenase (ZAN-thin de-HY-droj-eh-nase) An enzyme containing molybdenum and iron, which functions in the formation of uric acid and the mobilization of iron from liver ferritin stores.

xenobiotic (ZEE-no-bye-OT-ic) Compound that is foreign to the body. The principal classes are drugs, chemical carcinogens, and environmental substances such as pesticides.

xerophthalmia (zer-op-THAL-mee-uh) A condition marked by dryness of the cornea and eye membranes that results from vitamin A deficiency and can lead to blindness. The specific cause is a lack of mucus production by the eye, which then leaves it more vulnerable to surface dirt and bacterial infections.

xylitol (ZIGH-lih-tol) An alcohol derivative of a 5-carbon monosaccharide, called xylose.

zygote (ZIGH-goat) The fertilized ovum; the cell resulting from union of an egg cell (ovum) and sperm until it divides.

zymogen (ZY-mow-gin) An inactive form of an enzyme that requires the removal of a minor part of the chemical structure for it to work. The zymogen is converted into an active enzyme at the appropriate time, such as when released into the stomach or small intestine.

Credits

PHOTO

Chapter 1

Opener: © PhotoDisc website; **p. 3:** © PhotoDisc website; **p. 4:** © Corbis/Vol. 30; **p. 6 (top):** Wheat Foods Council; **(middle):** National Sunflower Association; **(bottom):** National Fisheries Institute; **p. 8:** Corbis/CB011688; **p. 9:** Ken Halfmann/Photographix; **Fig 1-2(both):** © PhotoDisc website; **p. 12:** MHHE Image Library; **p. 14:** Gordon Wardlaw; **Fig 1-4(top):** © Corbis/Vol. 115; **(bottom):** Ohio State University Extension; **p. 16:** Ohio State University; **p. 17:** © PhotoDisc website; **p. 18:** Greg Kidd & Joanne Scott; **p. 21:** © Corbis/Medical Matters; **p. 22:** USDA; **p. 24:** Ohio State University Extension; **p. 31:** © Digital Art/Corbis; **p. 34:** © Corbis/Vol. 40

Chapter 2

Opener: © Corbis/Small Office Life; **p. 37:** USA Rice Federation; **p. 38:** Reproduced with permission. © Culinary Hearts Kitchen, 1982; **p. 39:** Quaker® Oats; **p. 41:** © PhotoDisc/Vol. 67; **Fig 2-2(a):** © Corbis/Vol. 76; **(b):** © PhotoDisc/Vol. 29, **(c):** © PhotoDisc website. **(d):** © Corbis/Vol. 102; **(e):** © Corbis/Vol. 81; **p. 49:** Corbis/CB039031; **p. 52:** © PhotoDisc/Vol. 25; **Fig 2-5(golf):** © Corbis/Vol. 127; **(tennis):** © PhotoDisc/Object Series 25; **(yo-yo):** © Corbis website; **(mouse):** © Corbis/Vol. 127; **(baseball):** © PhotoDisc/Object Series 25; **(fist):** © PhotoDisc/Object Series 02; **p. 57:** Corbis/AFB0017; **p. 59:** © PhotoDisc/Object Series 49; **p. 62:** © PhotoDisc/Vol. 17; **p. 65:** Ohio State University Extension/Malcolm W. Emmons; **p. 67(top):** © PhotoDisc/Vol. 25; **(bottom):** © Corbis/Modern Cuisine; **p. 68:** Greg Kidd & Joanne Scott; **p. 73:** © Joanne Scott; **p. 75:** Gordon Wardlaw; **p. 76:** National Cattlemen's Beef Assoc.; **p. 77:** William Wardlaw; **p. 78:** Corbis/OFI0014

Chapter 3

Opener: © PhotoDisc website; **p. 97:** © PhotoDisc/Vol. 83; **p. 99:** © Corbis/Eat Natural; **p. 104:** Gordon Wardlaw

Chapter 4

Opener: © Getty Images/Eyewire; **p. 110:** Corbis/CB036366; **p. 111:** The Ohio State University Communications Photo Service; **p. 117:** National Pork Producers Council; **p. 120:** Corbis/Active Lifestyles; **p. 127:** © PhotoDisc website; **p. 130:** Corbis/CB031652; **p. 135:** MHHE Image Library; **p. 136:** © Corbis/Food is Fun

Chapter 5

Opener: © Getty Images/Eyewire; **p. 139:** © Object Series 49/PhotoDisc; **p. 142:** Beano® is a registered trademark of AkPharma, Inc.; **p. 143:** Gred Kidd & Joanne Scott; **p. 146:** © The Ohio State University Communications Photo Service, Jodi Miller; **p. 151:** PhotoDisc/Vol. 4; **p. 153:** Quaker® Oats; **p. 154:** Courtesy of Wheat Foods Council; **p. 158:** Courtesy of The Sugar Association, Inc., Washington, D.C.; **p. 159:** © The Ohio State University Communications Photo Service; **p. 162:** © Vol. 49/PhotoDisc; **p. 163:** Greg Kidd & Joanne Scott; **p. 166:** © PhotoDisc website; **p. 171:** Corbis/RLM0049; **p. 175:** © Vol. 70/PhotoDisc

Chapter 6

Opener: PhotoDisc/Vol. 66; **p. 181:** Greg Kidd & Joanne Scott; **p. 185:** Corbis/Modern Cuisine; **p. 186:** The Ohio State University Communications Photo Service; **p. 197:** © Vol. 20/PhotoDisc; **p. 199(top):** © Saffola Quality Foods, Inc.; **p. 99(bottom):** Corbis FOD0010; **p. 206:** © Mark Kempf; **p. 207:** © Vol. 48/PhotoDisc; **p. 208:** © William Wardlaw; **Fig 6-14(both):** Ed Reschke; **p. 218:** © American Egg Board; **p. 220:** Courtesy of Avacado Commission

Chapter 7

Opener: © PhotoDisc/Vol. 38; **p. 225:** Courtesy of Florida Tomato Committee; **p. 228:** © Greg Kidd & Joanne Scott; **p. 229:** © PhotoDisc/Vol. 20; **Fig 7-5(both):** Bill Loncore/SPL/Photo Researchers, Inc.; **p. 243:** © The Ohio State University Communications Photo Service; **p. 245:** Courtesy of Walnut Marketing Board; **Fig 7-11(left):** © Kevin Fleming/Corbis; **(right):** © Peter Turnley/Corbis; **p. 250:** © PhotoDisc website; **p. 257:** © Gordon Wardlaw

Chapter 8

Opener: © PhotoDisc/Vol. 66; **p. 261(top):** © Greg Kidd & Joanne Scott; **(bottom):** © PhotoDisc/Vol. 7; **p. 262:** © Corbis website; **p. 265:** © Corbis website; **p. 266(top):** © PhotoDisc/Vol. 20; **(bottom):** © PhotoDisc/Vol. 48; **p. 268:** © James Mulligan; **p. 271:** © PhotoDisc/Vol. 25; **p. 272:** © Corbis/Vol. 94; **p. 273:** © Corbis website; **p. 275:** © PhotoDisc/Vol. 94; **p. 277:** © PhotoDisc website; **p. 283:** © Corbis website

Chapter 9

Opener: © PhotoDisc/Vol. 94; **p. 287:** Reproduced with permission. © Culinary Hearts Kitchen, 1982 © American Heart Association; **p. 289 & 295:** © Greg Kidd & Joanne Scott; **p. 296:** © Corbis/Around the House People; **p. 298:** *A Colour Atlas and Text of Nutritional Disorders* by Dr. Donald D. McLaren/Mosby-Wolfe Europe Ltd.; **p. 302:** Corbis Travel & Romance Vol. 82/TRO0015; **Fig 9-8:** *A Colour Atlas and Text of Nutritional Disorders* by Dr. Donald D. McLaren/Mosby-Wolfe Europe Ltd.; **p. 305:** © Greg Kidd & Joanne Scott; **p. 307:** Bill Longcore/SPL/Photo Researchers; **p. 309:**

© Greg Kidd & Joanne Scott; **Fig 9-12:** © Greg Kidd & Joanne Scott; **p. 312:** © Corbis/Vol. 83; **p. 319:** © The Ohio State University Communications Photo Service, Jodi Miller; **p. 320:** © Vol. 67/PhotoDisc

Chapter 10

Opener: © PhotoDisc/Vol. 79; **p. 329:** © Corbis/Vol. 609; **p. 330:** Courtesy of National Pork Producers Council; **p. 333(top):** Corbis Food Perspectives Vol. 130/FPE0087; **Fig 10-3:** *A Colour Atlas and Text of Nutritional Disorders* by Dr. Donald D. McLaren/Mosby-Wolfe Europe Ltd.; **p.335(top):** Corbis Modern Cuisine Vol. 43/MCU0062; **Fig 10-4:** *A Colour Atlas and Text of Nutritional Disorders* by Dr. Donald D. McLaren/Mosby-Wolfe Europe Ltd.; **p. 337:** Mark Kempf; **p. 341(top):** Corbis Food Perspectives Vol. 130/FPE0061; **p. 341(bottom):** © Greg Kidd & Joanne Scott; **Fig 10-5(top):** Michael Abbey/Photo Researchers; **(bottom):** Biophoto Associates/SPL/Photo Researchers; **p. 349:** Corbis Vol. 30/FOD0028; **p. 352:** Corbis/CB035896; **Fig 10-9, 10-10:** *A Colour Atlas and Text of Nutritional Disorders* by Dr. Donald D. McLaren/Mosby-Wolfe Europe Ltd.; **p. 357(top):** Ohio State University; **p. 357(bottom):** California Strawberry Commission; **p. 368:** Greg Kidd & Joanne Scott

Chapter 11

Opener: © Getty Images/Digital Vision; **p. 378:** © PhotoDisc; **p. 381, 383–385:** MHHE Image Library; **p. 387:** © Vol. 83/Corbis; **p. 389:** MHHE Image Library; **p. 394:** © PhotoDisc/Vol. 12; **p. 399:** © Vol. 40/PhotoDisc; **p. 401:** Corbis Modern Cuisine/MCU0020; **p. 402:** Corbis/CB012177; **p. 404:** © Corbis website; **p. 409:** © PhotoDisc; **p. 411:** MHHE Image Library; **p. 412:** © PhotoDisc/Vol. 40

Chapter 12

Opener: © PhotoDisc/Vol. 70; **p. 415:** Florida Tomato Committee; **p. 416:** Ohio State University Extension/Malcolm W. Emmons; **p. 421:** © Corbis/Vol. 92; **Fig 12-3(both):** SPL/Photo Researchers; **p. 423:** Ohio State University Extension; **p. 425:** © PhotoDisc/Vol. 59; **p. 426:** © Corbis/Vol. #130; **p. 427:** Dr. Amanda S. Prasad; **p. 428:** Courtesy Fishery Products Internationals, Danver, MA; **p. 432:** © Corbis/Vol. 43; **p. 437:** Corbis Medical Objects/OMD0093; **p. 438:** Corbis/CB035895; **p. 439:** Gordon Wardlaw; **p. 440 & 442:** MHHE Image Library; **p. 447:** © PhotoDisc/Vol. 48; **p. 448:** © Corbis/R-F website; **p. 450:** © Getty Images/Eyewire/Vol. 46

Chapter 13

Opener: © Corbis/R-F website; **p. 453:** © Vol. 130/Corbis; **p. 456:** © PhotoDisc website; **p. 459:** Medical Graphics, Inc.; **p. 468:** Courtesy BodPod®; **Fig 13-8(all):** Diana Linsley/Linsley Photographics; **Fig 13-9:** Dr. M. Rosita Schiller; **Fig 13-10:** DEXA; **p. 472:** © Corbis website; **p. 473:** © Signature Series 79/PhotoDisc; **p. 474:** © The Ohio State University Communications Photo Service, Jodi Miller; **p. 475:** © The Ohio State University Communications Photo Service; **p. 479:** © PhotoDisc/Vol. 20; **p. 481:** © PhotoDisc; **p. 483:** © Vol. 180/Corbis; **p. 484:** Courtesy of California Strawberry Commission; **p. 485:** Ohio State University Extension; **p. 501:** © PhotoDisc website

Chapter 14

Opener: PhotoDisc Volume Series 67 Fitness/Well-Being/SP005586; **p. 506(top):** © Vol. 45/PhotoDisc; **p. 506(bottom):** © Vol. 164/Corbis; **p. 509:** © PhotoDisc/Vol. 67; **p. 512:** PhotoDisc/Sports Metaphors; **p. 514:** © Vol. 20/Corbis; **p. 516:** © James Mulligan; **p. 519:** Shore Grilled Shrimp® Courtesy of Fishery Products International, Danvers, MA; **p. 520:** © Gordon Wardlaw; **p. 524:** © Vol. 103/Corbis; **p. 534:** © Vol. 20/Corbis

Chapter 15

Opener: PhotoDisc Volume Series 67 Fitness/Well-Being/MD002552; **15-1:** © Corbis/R-F website; **p. 545:** © Vol. 75/Corbis; **p. 546:** © Getty Images/Eyewire; **15-3:** © David Frazier Photo Library; **p. 548:** © PhotoDisc website; **p. 551:** © PhotoDisc website; **Fig 15-5:** © James Mulligan; **p. 554:** © PhotoDisc website; **Fig 15-7:** © Paul Casamassimo, DDS, MS; **p. 555(bottom):** © Vol. 83/PhotoDisc; **p. 558:** © PhotoDisc website; **Fig 15-8:** Corbis #CSP067; **p. 559(bottom):** © PhotoDisc website; **p. 561:** © Getty Images/Eyewire; **p. 568:** © Gordon Wardlaw

Chapter 16

Opener: © PhotoDisc website; **p. 573:** © Corbis/Children & Teens; **p. 574:** © Gordon Wardlaw, photographer Greg Wolff; **p. 575:** © Gordon Wardlaw; **p. 576:** © Vol. 15/PhotoDisc; **p. 579, 580:** © Corbis website; **p. 583:** Corbis/CB037568; **p. 584:** Corbis Food & Ingredients Vol. 83/OFI0024; **p. 585:** © Joanne Scott; **p. 586:** © Vol. 83/Corbis; **p. 588:** © Corbis website; **p. 591:** © PhotoDisc/Vol. 192; **p. 594:** PhotoDisc Volume Series 61 Babies, Kids, Teens/LS019029; **p. 597:** © Corbis/Vol. 52

Chapter 17

Opener: © Getty Images/Eyewire; **p. 607(top):** © Vol. 180/Corbis; **p. 607(bottom):** © Joanne Scott; **p. 610:** © PhotoDisc; **p. 611:** © Vol. 135/Corbis; **p. 615:** © Vol. 9/Corbis; **p. 616:** © Vol. 58/PhotoDisc; **p. 618:** © Vol. 26/Corbis; **Fig. 17-5:** © Paul Casamassimo, DDS, MS; **p. 621:** © Gordon Wardlaw; **p. 626:** © Joanne Scott; **p. 628:** USDA, photograph by Ken Hammond; **p. 631:** © Vol. 124/Corbis; **p. 633(top):** © Vol. 124/Corbis; **p. 633(bottom):** © Vol. 24/PhotoDisc; **p. 634:** © Corbis/R-F website; **p. 636:** © Vol. 19/Corbis; **p. 637:** © Vol. 51/PhotoDisc; **p. 639:** © PhotoDisc website; **p. 645:** © Greg Kidd & Joanne Scott

Chapter 18

Opener: © PhotoDisc website; **p. 649:** © Vol. 141/Corbis; **p. 650:** © David Craddock; **p. 651:** PhotoDisc; **p. 652:** © Vol. 83/PhotoDisc; **p. 654:** © Corbis/R-F website; **p. 655:** © Vol. 36/Corbis; **p. 656:** © Corbis/R-F website; **p. 659:** Corbis Senior Living Vol. 81/SLI0015; **p. 660:** © PhotoDisc/Vol. 48; **p. 661:** © Vol. 81/Corbis; **p. 662:** © Corbis/R-F website; **p. 664:** © Vol. 81/Corbis; **p. 667:** © PhotoDisc/Vol. 58; **p. 668:** © Getty Images/Digital Vision; **p. 675:** © Gordon Wardlaw; **p. 680:** © Gordon Wardlaw

Chapter 19

Opener: © PhotoDisc website; **p. 685:** © Vol. 12/Corbis; **p. 691:** © Gordon Wardlaw; **Fig 19-1:** © Vol. 48/PhotoDisc; **p. 694:** USDA; **p. 695:** © The Ohio State University Communications Photo Service; **p. 699:** © Corbis/R-F website; **p. 700:** National Pork Producers Council; **p. 704:** © Vol. 83/Corbis; **p. 705:** © Greg Kidd & Joanne Scott; **p. 706:** © Object Series 36/PhotoDisc; **Fig 19-3 (both):** © Gordon Wardlaw; **p. 708:** © The Ohio State University Communications Photo Service; **p. 709:** © Corbis/R-F website; **p. 715:** © The Ohio State University Communications Photo Service, Lloyd Lemmermann; **p. 716:** © PhotoDisc website; **p. 717:** © Vol. 130/Corbis; **p. 718:** © Object Series Vol. 49/PhotoDisc

Chapter 20

Opener: © PhotoDisc website; **p. 721:** © Corbis website; **Fig 20-1 (all):** AP / Wide World Photo; **p. 725(top, middle):** © The Ohio State University Communications Photo Service; **p. 725(bottom):** Corbis/CB002280; **p. 731:** © PhotoDisc website; **p. 733:** USDA photo by Peter Manzelli; **p. 735 & 737:** © The McGraw-Hill Companies, Inc./Barry Barker, photographer; **p. 739:** © Corbis website; **p. 743:** © Vol. 25/Corbis; **p. 744:** © The Ohio State University Communications Photo Service; **p. 745:** © PhotoDisc website; **p. 751:** © The Ohio State University Communications Photo Service, Ken Chamberlain; **p. 752(top):** © The Ohio State University Communications Photo Service, Jodi Miller; **p. 752(bottom):** © Vol. 12/PhotoDisc

Appendices

Fig C-1: K.G. Murti/Visuals Unlimited; **Fig E-1 (all):** Greg Kidd & Joanne Scott

Index

B

C

D

E

G

H

J

K

L

M

P

Q

R

S

T

U

V

Dietary Reference Intakes (DRIs): Tolerable Upper Intake Levels (UL[a]) , Vitamins

Food and Nutrition Board, Institute of Medicine, National Academies

Life Stage Group	Vitamin A (µg/d)[b]	Vitamin C (mg/d)	Vitamin D (µg/d)	Vitamin E (mg/d)[c,d]	Vitamin K	Thiamin	Riboflavin	Niacin (mg/d)[d]	Vitamin B_6 (mg/d)	Folate (µg/d)[d]	Vitamin B_{12}	Pantothenic Acid	Biotin	Choline (g/d)	Carotenoids[e]
Infants															
0–6 mo	600	ND[f]	25	ND	ND	ND	ND	ND	ND	ND	ND	ND	ND	ND	ND
7–12 mo	600	ND	25	ND	ND	ND	ND	ND	ND	ND	ND	ND	ND	ND	ND
Children															
1–3 y	600	400	50	200	ND	ND	ND	10	30	300	ND	ND	ND	1.0	ND
4–8 y	900	650	50	300	ND	ND	ND	15	40	400	ND	ND	ND	1.0	ND
Males, Females															
9–13 y	1,700	1,200	50	600	ND	ND	ND	20	60	600	ND	ND	ND	2.0	ND
14–18 y	2,800	1,800	50	800	ND	ND	ND	30	80	800	ND	ND	ND	3.0	ND
19–70 y	3,000	2,000	50	1,000	ND	ND	ND	35	100	1,000	ND	ND	ND	3.5	ND
> 70 y	3,000	2,000	50	1,000	ND	ND	ND	35	100	1,000	ND	ND	ND	3.5	ND
Pregnancy															
≤18 y	2,800	1,800	50	800	ND	ND	ND	30	80	800	ND	ND	ND	3.0	ND
19–50 y	3,000	2,000	50	1,000	ND	ND	ND	35	100	1,000	ND	ND	ND	3.5	ND
Lactation															
≤18 y	2,800	1,800	50	800	ND	ND	ND	30	80	800	ND	ND	ND	3.0	ND
19–50 y	3,000	2,000	50	1,000	ND	ND	ND	35	100	1,000	ND	ND	ND	3.5	ND

[a]UL = The maximum level of daily nutrient intake that is likely to pose no risk of adverse effects. Unless otherwise specified, the UL represents total intake from food, water, and supplements. Due to lack of suitable data, ULs could not be established for vitamin K, thiamin, riboflavin, vitamin B_{12}, pantothenic acid, biotin, or carotenoids. In the absence of ULs, extra caution may be warranted in consuming levels above recommended intakes.

[b]As preformed vitamin A only.

[c]As α-tocopherol; applies to any form of supplemental α-tocopherol.

[d]The ULs for vitamin E, niacin, and folate apply to synthetic forms obtained from supplements, fortified foods, or a combination of the two.

[e]β-Carotene supplements are advised only to serve as a provitamin A source for individuals at risk of vitamin A deficiency.

[f]ND = Not determinable due to lack of data of adverse effects in this age group and concern with regard to lack of ability to handle excess amounts. Source of intake should be from food only to prevent high levels of intake.

SOURCES: Dietary Reference Intakes for Calcium, Phosphorus, Magnesium, Vitamin D, and Fluoride (1997); Dietary Reference Intakes for Thiamin, Riboflavin, Niacin, Vitamin B_6, Folate, Vitamin B_{12}, Pantothenic Acid, Biotin, and Choline (1998); Dietary Reference Intakes for Vitamin C, Vitamin E, Selenium, and Carotenoids (2000); and Dietary Reference Intakes for Vitamin A, Vitamin K, Arsenic, Boron, Chromium, Copper, Iodine, Iron, Manganese, Molybdenum, Nickel, Silicon, Vanadium, and Zinc (2001). These reports may be accessed via www.nap.edu.

Estimated minimum sodium, chloride, and potassium requirements for healthy persons[a]

Age	Weight (kg)[a]	Sodium (mg)[a,b]	Chloride (mg)[a,b]	Potassium (mg)[c]
Months				
0–5	4.5	120	180	500
6–11	8.9	200	300	700
Years				
1	11	225	350	1000
2–5	16	300	500	1400
6–9	25	400	600	1600
10–18	50	500	750	2000
>18[d]	70	500	750	2000

mg = milligram; kg = kilogram (2.2 pounds)

[a]No allowance has been included for large, prolonged losses from the skin through sweat.

[b]There is no evidence that higher intakes confer any additional health benefit.

[c]Desirable intakes of potassium may considerably exceed these values (~3500 mg for adults).

[d]No allowance has been included for growth. Values given for people under 18 years of age assume a growth rate corresponding to the 50th percentile reported by the National Center for Health Statistics and averaged for males and females.

Reprinted with permission from *Recommended Daily Allowances,* 10th edition. Copyright 1989 by the National Academy of Sciences. Courtesy of the National Academy Press, Washington, D.C.

Acceptable Macronutrient Distribution Ranges

	Range (percent of energy)		
Macronutrient	**Children, 1–3 y**	**Children, 4–18 y**	**Adults**
Fat	30–40	25–35	20–35
n-6 polyunsaturated fats (linoleic acid)	5–10	5–10	5–10
n-3 polyunsaturated fats[a] (α-linoleic acid)	0.6–1.2	0.6–1.2	0.6–1.2
Carbohydrate	45–65	45–65	45–65
Protein	5–20	10–30	10–35

[a]Approximately 10% of the total can come from longer-chain *n*-3 fatty acids.

SOURCE: *Dietary Reference Intakes for Energy, Carbohydrate, Fiber, Fat, Fatty Acids, Cholesterol, Protein, and Amino Acids* (2002). The report may be accessed via www.nar.edu.

W